Weiss Ratings' Investment Research Guide to Exchange-Traded Funds

Weiss Ratings' Investment Research Guide to Exchange-Traded Funds

Winter 2018-19

GREY HOUSE PUBLISHING

Weiss Ratings
4400 Northcorp Parkway
Palm Beach Gardens, FL 33410
561-627-3300

Independent. Unbiased. Accurate. Trusted.

Published by Grey House Publishing, Inc., located at 4919 Route 22, Amenia, NY 12501; telephone 518-789-8700. Grey House Publishing neither guarantees the accuracy of the data contained herein nor assumes any responsibility for errors, omissions or discrepancies. Grey House Publishing accepts no payment for listing; inclusion in the publication of any organization, agency, institution, publication, service or individual does not imply endorsement of the publisher.

Edition #7, Winter 2018-19

ISBN: 978-1-64265-175-1

Contents

Terms and Conditions

Date of Data Analyzed: December 31, 2018

Welcome to Weiss Ratings' Investment Research Guide to Exchange-Traded Funds

With investing such a complex subject and the enormous popularity of exchange-traded funds as a simple way to enter the markets it is no surprise that consumers need assistance. It is a complex subject and consumers want unbiased, independent guidance in helping them find a path to investing that is focused on their needs.

This is where Weiss Ratings comes in. We take all the data and process it, daily, to ensure that you receive not only the most up-to-date rating possible but also data that you may not easily find elsewhere. We publish this data in guides, and on our website so that you can feel empowered to make decisions about your investing future. Our focus is on balance and our ratings reflect this. No matter how strong a return has been if the level of risk taken is too high, in our opinion, then the overall rating will be reduced.

Weiss Ratings' Mission Statement

Weiss Ratings' mission is to empower consumers, professionals, and institutions with high quality advisory information for selecting or monitoring a financial services company or financial investment.

In doing so, Weiss Ratings will adhere to the highest ethical standards by maintaining our independent, unbiased outlook and approach for our customers.

Why rely on Weiss Ratings?

Weiss Ratings are fundamentally incomparable to nearly all other ratings available in America today. Here's why ...

Complete Independence

We are America's only 100% independent rating agency covering stocks, ETFs, mutual funds, insurance companies, banks, and credit unions; and our independence is grounded in a very critical difference in the way we do business: Unlike most other rating agencies,

- we never accept compensation from any company for its rating;
- we never allow companies to influence our analysis or conclusions (although they are always free to provide us with supplemental data that's not publicly available);
- we reserve the right to publish our ratings based exclusively on publicly available data;
- we never suppress publication of our ratings at a company's request; and
- we are always dedicated to providing our analysis and opinions with complete objectivity.

Dedication to End Users -- Investors and Consumers

Other rating agencies derive most of their revenues from the very same companies that they cover.

In contrast, our primary source of revenues is the end user – investors seeking the best combination of risk and reward, plus consumers seeking the best deals with the most safety.

Unmatched Accuracy and Performance

Our independence and objectivity help explain why the U.S. Government Accountability Office (GAO) concluded that Weiss was first in warning consumers about future insurance company failures three times more often than our closest competitor (A.M. Best) and why, in comparison to S&P or Moody's, there was no contest.

It's the reason why The New York Times wrote "Weiss was the first to warn of dangers and say so unambiguously."

And it's also why The Wall Street Journal was able to report that the Weiss Stock Ratings outperformed all Wall Street investment banks, brokers and independent research organizations in a third-party study of stock ratings.

Broader Coverage

While other rating agencies focus mostly on larger companies that can afford to pay them large fees, Weiss Ratings covers all companies, large or small, as long as they report sufficient data for us to analyze. This allows us to provide far broader coverage, including nearly all U.S.-traded stocks, ETFs and mutual funds plus nearly all U.S. banks, credit unions and insurance companies.

Overall ...

Weiss Ratings gives you more accuracy, more choices, and better wealth-building potential – all with stronger risk protection and safety.

How to Use This Guide

The purpose of the *Weiss Ratings' Investment Research Guide to Exchange-Traded Funds* is to provide investors with a reliable source of investment ratings and analyses on a timely basis. We realize that past performance is an important factor to consider when making the decision to purchase shares in an exchange-traded fund. The ratings and analyses in this Guide can make that evaluation easier when you are considering Exchange-Traded funds. The rating for a particular fund indicates our opinion regarding that fund's past risk-adjusted performance.

When evaluating a specific exchange-traded fund, we recommend you follow these steps:

Step 1 Confirm the fund name and ticker symbol. To ensure you evaluate the correct exchange-traded fund, verify the fund's exact name and ticker symbol as it was given to you in its prospectus or appears on your account statement. Many funds have similar names, so you want to make sure the fund you look up is really the one you are interested in evaluating.

Step 2 Check the fund's Investment Rating. Turn to Section I, the *Weiss Ratings' Investment Research Guide to Exchange-Traded Funds*, and locate the fund you are evaluating. This section contains all Exchange-Traded funds analyzed by Weiss Ratings, including those that did not receive an Investment Rating. All funds are listed in alphabetical order by the name of the fund with the ticker symbol following the name for additional verification. Once you have located your specific fund, the fourth column after the ticker symbol under the Ratings header shows its overall Investment Rating. Turn to *About Weiss Investment Ratings* for information about what this rating means.

Step 3 Analyze the supporting data. In addition to the Weiss Exchange-Traded Fund Rating are some of the various measures we have used in rating the fund. Refer to the Section I introduction to see what each of these factors measures. In most cases, lower rated funds will have a low reward rating and/or a low risk rating (i.e., high volatility). Bear in mind, however, that the Weiss Exchange-Traded Fund Rating is the result of a complex proprietary computer-generated analysis which cannot be reproduced using only the data provided here.

Step 4 When looking to identify an exchange-traded fund that achieves your specific investing goals, we recommend the following:

- **Check the detailed analysis of the BUY rated Exchange-Traded Funds.** If your priority is to invest in only highest rated funds, then this list if for you. Here you will find full analysis of each ETF on the BUY list.

- **Check the detailed analysis of all rated funds with assets over $50 million.** If your priority is the size of an Exchange-Traded Funds, then this list is where you need to look. This list includes detailed analysis of all rated funds with over $50 million in assets.

- **Check the listing of the Largest funds.** If your priority is to stick with large funds because you believe that the size of the fund matters then these funds should be looked at. In this listing of the 100 largest funds you can also be assured that the Weiss Exchange-Traded Fund Rating is just as important as for the smallest fund.

- **Check the listing of the Best One-Year Return BUY Rated Funds.** If you are looking to invest in funds that can provide you with highest total returns over a one-year period, then look at this list. Here you will find all BUY rated funds that are in the top 10% when it comes to providing highest one-year total returns.

- **Check the listing of the Best Low Expense Exchange-Traded Funds.** If your priority is to find an Exchange-Traded Fund that charges the lowest fee, then this list is worth looking at. Here you will find highly rated funds with lowest expense ratios.

- **Check out the Top-Rated Funds by Fund Type.** If you are looking to invest in a particular type of exchange-traded fund turn to our listing of "Buy" rated Exchange-Traded Funds by Fund Type. There you will find the top exchange-traded funds with the highest performance rating in each category.

Step 5 Refer back to Section I. Once you have identified a particular fund that interests you, refer back to Section I, the Index of Exchange-Traded Funds, for a more thorough analysis.

Step 6 Always remember:

- **Read our warnings and cautions.** In order to use Weiss Investment Ratings most effectively, we strongly recommend you consult the Important Warnings and Cautions. These are more than just "standard disclaimers." They are very important factors you should be aware of before using this guide.

- **Stay up to date.** Periodically review the latest Weiss Exchange-Traded Fund Ratings for the funds that you own to make sure they are still in line with your investment goals and level of risk tolerance. You can find more detailed information and receive automated updates on ratings through www.weissratings.com

Data Source: Weiss Ratings
                Morningstar, Inc.

Date of data analyzed: December 31, 2018

About Weiss Investment Ratings

Weiss Investment Ratings of stocks, ETFs and mutual funds are in the same realm as "buy," "sell" and "hold" ratings. They are designed to help investors make more informed decisions with the goal of maximizing gains and minimizing risk. Safety is also an important consideration. The higher the rating, the more likely the investment will be profitable. But when using our investment ratings, you should always remember that, by definition, all investments involve some element of risk.

A   Strong Buy
B   Buy
C   Hold or Avoid
D   Sell
E   Strong Sell

Our **Overall Rating** is measured on a scale from A to E based on each fund's risk and performance. The funds are analyzed using the latest daily data available and the quarterly filings with the SEC. Weiss takes thousands of pieces of fund data and, based on its own model, balances reward against the amount of risk to assign a rating. The results provide a simple and understandable opinion as to whether we think the fund is a BUY, SELL, or HOLD.

Our **Reward Rating** is based on the total return over a period of up to five years, including net asset value and price growth. The total return figure is stated net of the expenses and fees charged by the fund. Based on proprietary modeling the individual components of the risk and reward ratings are calculated and weighted and the final rating is generated.

Our **Risk Rating** includes the risk ratings of component stocks where applicable and also includes the financial stability of the fund, turnover where applicable, together with the level of volatility as measured by the fund's daily returns over a period of up to five years.   Funds with greater stability are considered less risky and receive a higher risk rating. Funds with greater volatility are considered riskier, and will receive a lower risk rating. In addition to considering the fund's volatility, the risk rating also considers an assessment of the valuation and quality of a fund's holdings.

In order to help guarantee our objectivity, we reserve the right to publish ratings expressing our opinion of an investment reward and risk based exclusively on publicly available data and our own proprietary standards for safety. But when using our investment ratings, you should always remember that, by definition, all investments involve some element of risk.

Current Weiss Ratings Distribution
of Exchange-Traded Funds

as of December 31, 2018

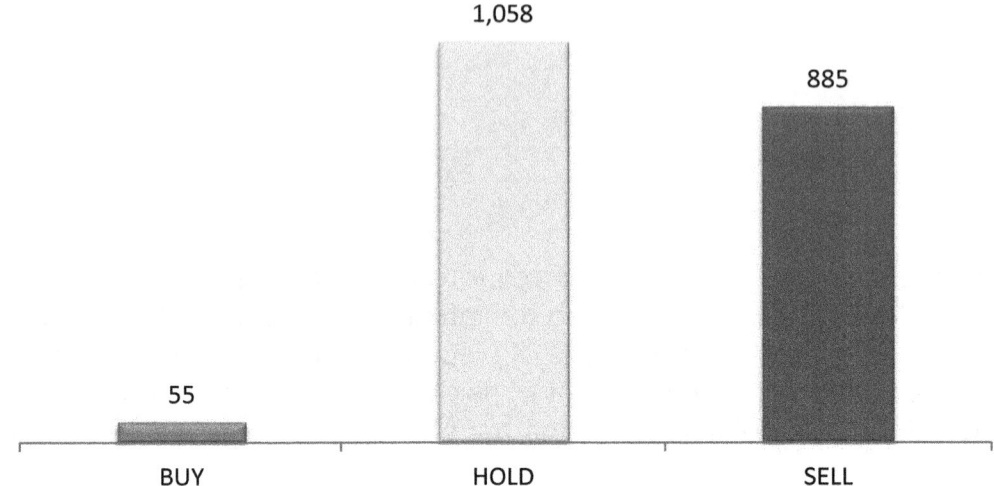

What Our Ratings Mean

Weiss Mutual Funds, Closed-End Funds, and Exchange Traded Funds Ratings represent a completely independent, unbiased opinion of funds—now, and in the future. The funds are analyzed using the latest daily data available and the quarterly filings with the SEC. Weiss takes thousands of pieces of fund data and, based on its own model, balances reward against the amount of risk to assign a rating. The results provide a simple and understandable opinion as to whether we think the fund is a BUY, SELL, or HOLD.

In order to help guarantee our objectivity, we reserve the right to publish ratings expressing our opinion of an investment reward and risk based exclusively on publicly available data and our own proprietary standards for safety. But when using our investment ratings, you should always remember that, by definition, all investments involve some element of risk.

Strong Buy

A   **Excellent.** The fund has an excellent track record for maximizing performance while minimizing risk, thus delivering the best possible combination of total return on investment and reduced volatility. It has made the most of the recent economic environment to maximize risk-adjusted returns compared to other exchange-traded funds. Although even the best funds can decline in a down market, our "A" rating can generally be considered the equivalent of a "Strong Buy".

Buy

B   **Good.** The fund has a good track record for balancing performance with risk. Compared to other exchange-traded funds, it has achieved above-average returns given the level of risk in its underlying investments. Although even good funds can decline in a down market, our "B" rating is considered the equivalent of a "Buy".

Hold or Avoid

C   **Fair.** In the trade-off between performance and risk, the fund has a track record which is about average. It is neither significantly better nor significantly worse than most other funds. With some funds in this category, the total return may be better than average, but this can be misleading if the higher return was achieved with higher than average risk. With other funds, the risk may be lower than average, but the returns are also lower. Although funds can be driven higher or lower by general market trends, our "C" rating can generally be considered the equivalent of a "Hold" or "Avoid."

Sell

D   **Weak.** The fund has underperformed the universe of other funds given the level of risk in its underlying investments, resulting in a weak risk-adjusted performance. Thus, its investment strategy and/or management has not been attuned to capitalize on the recent economic environment. Even weak funds can rise in an up market. However, our "D" rating can generally be considered equivalent to a "Sell."

Strong Sell

E   **Very Weak.** The fund has significantly underperformed most other funds given the level of risk in its underlying investments, resulting in a very weak risk-adjusted performance. Thus, its investment strategy and/or management has done just the opposite of what was needed to maximize returns in the recent economic environment. Even some of the weakest funds can rise in certain market conditions. However, our "E" rating can generally be considered the equivalent of a "Strong Sell."

+   The plus sign is an indication that the fund is in the upper third of the letter grade.

-   The minus sign is an indication that the fund is in the lower third of the letter grade.

U   Unrated. The fund is unrated because it is too new to make a reliable assessment of its risk-adjusted performance. Typically, a fund must be established for at least one year before it is eligible to receive a Weiss Investment Rating.

Important Warnings & Cautions

1. A rating alone cannot tell the whole story. Please read the explanatory information contained here, in the section introductions and in the appendix. It is provided in order to give you an understanding of our rating methodology as well as to paint a more complete picture of an exchange-traded fund's strengths and weaknesses.

2. Investment ratings shown in this directory were current as of the publication date. In the meantime, the rating may have been updated based on more recent data. Weiss Ratings offers a notification service for ratings changes on companies that you specify. For more information visit www.weissratings.com.

3. When deciding to invest in or sell holdings in a specific exchange-traded fund, your decision must be based on a wide variety of factors in addition to the Weiss Exchange-Traded Fund Rating. These include any charges you may incur from switching funds, to what degree it meets your long-term planning needs, and what other choices are available to you. Weiss Ratings recommends that you should always consult an independent financial advisor over your investment decisions.

4. Weiss Exchange-Traded Fund Ratings represent our opinion of an exchange-traded fund's past risk adjusted performance. As such, a high rating means we feel that the exchange-traded fund has at least achieved above-average returns at the same time as it has balanced risk and returns. A high rating is not a guarantee that a fund will continue to perform well, nor is a low rating a prediction of continued weak performance. Any references to "Buy", "Hold", or "Sell" correlate with our opinion of a particular fund and Weiss Exchange-Traded Fund Ratings are not deemed to be a recommendation concerning the purchase or sale of any exchange-traded fund.

5. All funds that have the same Weiss Investment Rating should be considered to be essentially equal from a risk/reward perspective. This is true regardless of any differences in the underlying numbers which might appear to indicate greater strengths.

6. Our rating standards are more consumer-oriented than those used by other rating agencies. We make more conservative assumptions about the amortization of loads and other fees as we attempt to identify those funds that have historically provided superior returns with only little or moderate risk.

7. We are an independent rating agency and do not depend on the cooperation of the managers operating the exchange-traded funds we rate. Our data is obtained from a data aggregator. Data is input daily, as available, into our proprietary models where a complex series of algorithms provide us with ratings based on quantitative analysis. We do not grant exchange-traded fund managers the right to stop or influence publication of the ratings. This policy stems from the fact that this Guide is designed for the information of the consumer.

The Retirement Tug-of-War: Spending Today vs. Saving for the Future

Tony Sagami
Friday, September 14, 2018

I get it. It's a lot more fun to spend money than to save it. I often find myself daydreaming about a convertible sports car, a lake house, business-class airline seats and five-star hotels.

But unless you're born into big money, you need to find a comfortable balance between enjoying life (spending) today and preparing for retirement (saving).

Don't get me wrong. I live a comfortable life, but it's not a luxurious one. I can afford a Mercedes, but I drive a Toyota. I can afford a Rolex, but I wear a Seiko instead. And I do a lot of shopping at Costco and Walmart instead of Whole Foods and Nordstrom.

I turn 62 in another week, but I plan on working for at least another 10 to 15 years. Not because I have to — I've already socked away a small mountain of money in my pension plan and a tax-deferred annuity — but because I really, really enjoy what I do.

Study after study shows that most Americans are enjoying life, too — although perhaps a little too much — today at the expense of saving for tomorrow.

Amount Saved for Retirement	% of Workers	% of Retirees
Less than $1,000	24%	21%
$1,000 to $9,999	14%	8%
$10,000 to $24,999	9%	6%
$25,000 to $49,999	8%	3%
$50,000 to $99,999	10%	7%
$100,000 to $249,999	15%	16%
$250,000 or more	20%	38%

Data source: 2017 Retirement Confidence Survey

A new study from MagnifyMoney found that the average American has only saved $11,700 between bank accounts and retirement savings accounts.

And that's just the average. A shocking 21% of retirees have less than $1,000 saved for retirement, according to the Employee Benefit Research Institute's 2017 Retirement Confidence Survey. And 38% have less than $50,000.

Clearly, millions of Americans are counting on Social Security to provide the bulk of their retirement income.

That's a terrible strategy!

The average Social Security retirement benefit is just $1,413 a month, or about $17,000 per year. So much for that dream retirement, right?

And even if you qualify for the maximum benefit at full retirement age, the most you can receive is $2,788 per month, or about $33,000 for the year.

Compounding the lack of savings is our increasing life expectancy. According to the Social Security Administration, "About one out of every four 65-year-olds today will live past age 90, and one out of 10 will live past age 95."

Wow! If you retire at 65, you could very well be spending 30 years — or longer — in retirement. That's great news ... except for the cost of funding such a lengthy retirement.

And don't forget: A 65-year-old couple retiring today can expect to spend an average of $280,000 out of pocket on healthcare expenses over the course of their retirement, according to Fidelity Investments.

That's probably why 9 million people age 65-plus are still working. That's twice the number of working seniors in 2000.

It's also why 76% of baby boomers say they are not confident that they had enough saved for retirement, according to the Insured Retirement Institute. Some 68% also wished they'd saved more, and 67% wished they had started saving earlier.

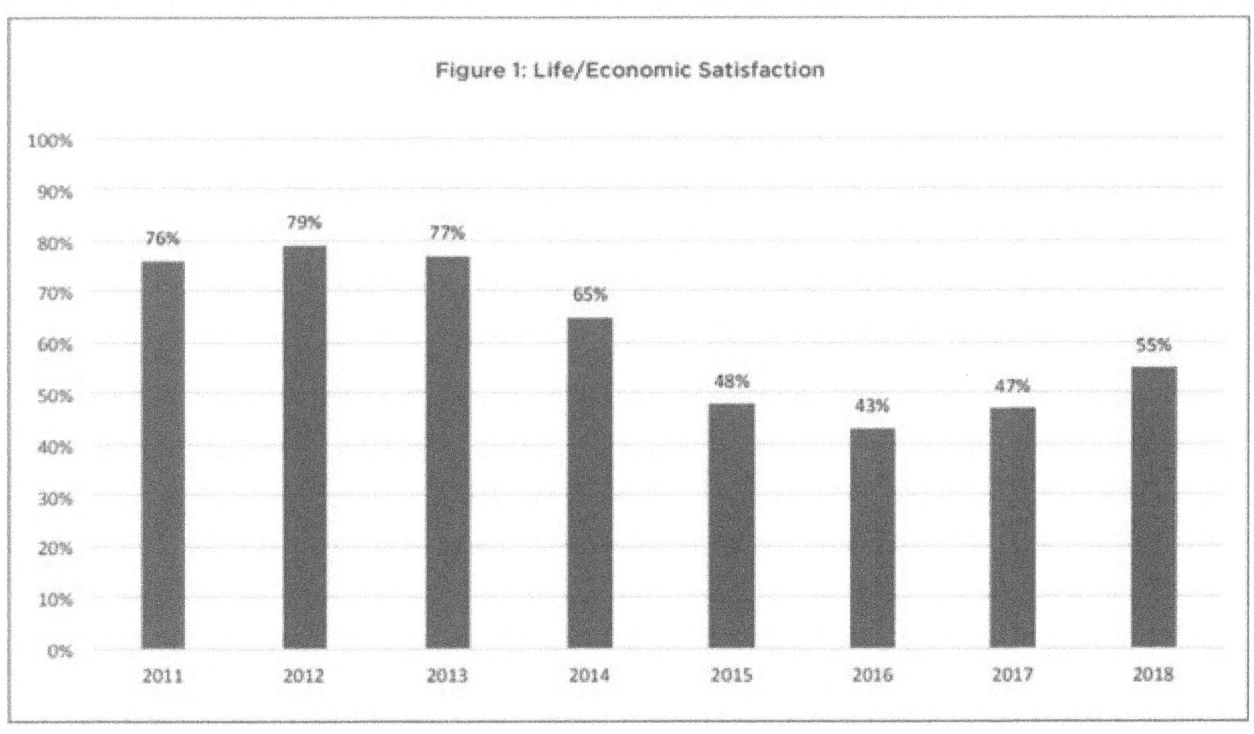

The percentage of baby boomers who report life/economic satisfaction is about the same as the percentage with retirement savings. Source: Insured Retirement Institute.

My point is that most of the people reading this column today need to take a hard look at their attitudes about how much they can afford to enjoy life today at the expense of saving for tomorrow. And then take it one step further to get more growth out of the dollars that you are saving for retirement.

In fact, I think that the surest way to build an insufficient nest egg is to invest too conservatively. Conservative investments can be just as dangerous as overly aggressive ones for retirees, thanks to the erosive effects of inflation and longer life expectancies.

I recommend a basket of high-growth stocks that have both strong fundamentals (high Weiss Safety Ratings) and strong momentum (high Weiss Performance Ratings). That is exactly what we do with the Weiss Ultimate Portfolio, which has regularly beaten the pants off the S&P 500 … and has done so with less volatility.

The odds are that both you and I are going to spend a very long time in our "golden years." And I believe the Weiss Ultimate Portfolio is an effective strategy to build a prosperous, secure retirement.

Best wishes,
Tony Sagami

Tony Sagami is one of the early pioneers in the application of technical and quantitative analysis to mutual funds and stocks. His four decades of investing experience serve him well here at Weiss Ratings, where he writes and edits founder Martin D. Weiss Ph.D.'s Weiss Ultimate Portfolio stock and ETF trading service.

How to Build Your Nest Egg Amid America's Retirement Crisis

Tony Sagami
Friday, August 17, 2018

Egad. How did I get so old?

In one more month, I turn 62 years old. And if I were so inclined, I could start collecting a monthly Social Security check.

Of course, I am still productive and expect to work for another couple decades, so I don't need a Social Security check.

Yes, I enjoy what I do so much that I hope to keep at it until my 80s — but I do wonder whether Social Security will still be around when I hit that age.

According to the 2018 annual Social Security report, the people running the Social Security fund estimate that it will run out of money by 2034. Zilch! Nada! Zero!

My guess is that our politicians will figure out some way to kick the can down the road for another couple decades with some combination of means testing, higher payroll taxes and raising the retirement age. But the sad truth is that it's not wise to rely on Social Security as the primary source of your retirement income.

The days of enjoying a monthly retirement pension check are long gone. Unless you have a government job, you are unlikely to receive a traditional retirement pension.

They've been replaced by 401(k)s and profit-sharing plans, which means that YOU have to take personal responsibility for your financial well-being.

I am sad to say that the early results show many Americans are doing a lousy job of it! The median retiree household has a mere $60,600 in savings, and a disturbing 25% of households only have $3,260 of savings.

The New York Times

'Too Little Too Late': Bankruptcy Booms Among Older Americans

Sadly, that lack of a financial cushion is pushing a growing number of retirees to the brink of poverty.

Get this: The rate of people 65 and older filing for bankruptcy is three times what it was in 1991. Seniors now account for the largest share of bankruptcy filings in the U.S.

- There were 3.6 bankruptcy filers per 1,000 people 65 to 74; in 1991, there were 1.2 per thousand.

- 2% of filers are now 65 or older, up from 2.1% in 1991.

Many Americans (three out of five) cited large medical expenses, while three-quarters cited too large of a debt load, for their financial woes.

Bankruptcy filings per 1,000 people, by age

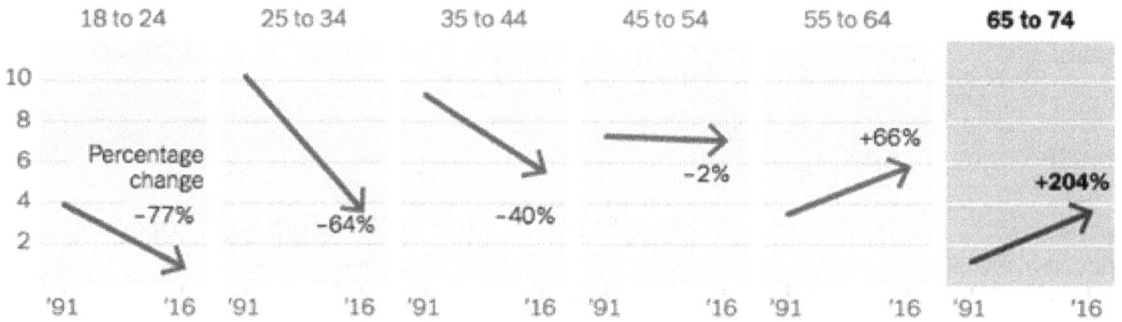

Source: The Federal Reserve's survey of consumer finances, via the Consumer Bankruptcy Project

The solution is simple: Save more and avoid debt. Yet that is a lot easier said than done — even though the cost of not doing so is — as the above graphic shows — just too dehumanizing to consider.

Your first step should be to shovel as much money as possible into a retirement plan.

- You can sock away as much as $18,500 a year into a 401(k), but as much as $24,500 if you are over 50 years old.

- For individual IRAs, the numbers are $5,500 and $6,500 for 50-plus workers.

Hint: If you're self-employed, you can put away as much as $61,000 a year into a "solo" 401(k).

As far as debt, you need to pay off as much as you can, as fast as you can. Perhaps that means fewer restaurant meals, more stay-at-home vacations, or keeping your car until you drive it into the ground.

Lastly, like me, you should consider delaying retirement. A lot of Americans are choosing to "downshift" into retirement by working longer than they had planned or by working part-time.

A survey from Bankrate found that 70% of Americans plan to "work as long as possible." Their rationale?

70% of Americans plan to work as long as possible

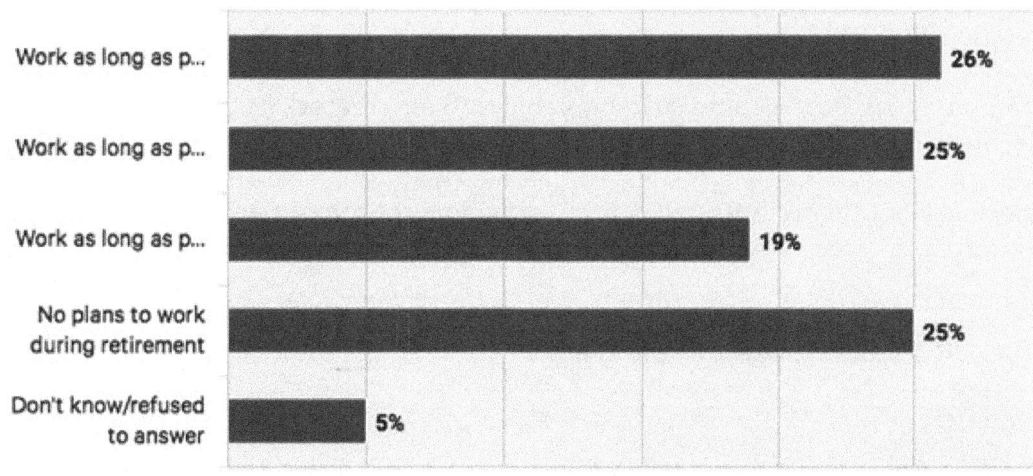

Source: Bankrate Money Pulse Survey, Aug. 18-21, 2016.

* 26% because they like the work

* 25% because they need the money

* 19% because they like the work and need the money

Delaying retirement doesn't just mean more wages; it also increases the size of your Social Security check.

If you wait until you're 67 years old to collect, you'll get 108% of the monthly benefit because you delayed getting benefits for 12 months.

If you wait until age 70, you'll get 132% of the monthly benefit because you delayed getting benefits for 48 months.

Moreover, a larger Social Security check will also help you spend less of your savings each year. And that will make your nest egg last even longer.

Best wishes,

Tony Sagami

Tony Sagami is one of the early pioneers in the application of technical and quantitative analysis to mutual funds and stocks. His four decades of investing experience serve him well here at Weiss Ratings, where he writes and edits founder Martin D. Weiss Ph.D.'s Weiss Ultimate Portfolio stock and ETF trading service.

Why Roth IRAs are One of the Best Wealth-building Vehicles Around

Tony Sagami
Friday, November 02, 2018

Roth IRAs are one of the best wealth-building vehicles ever created, but I make too much money to be eligible to open one. Darn!

What's so special about them? A Roth IRA is an individual retirement account similar to traditional IRAs in that it offers tax-free growth. But there is no tax whatsoever on withdrawals after you reach age 59 1/2.

That's right — ZERO federal taxes on your gains.

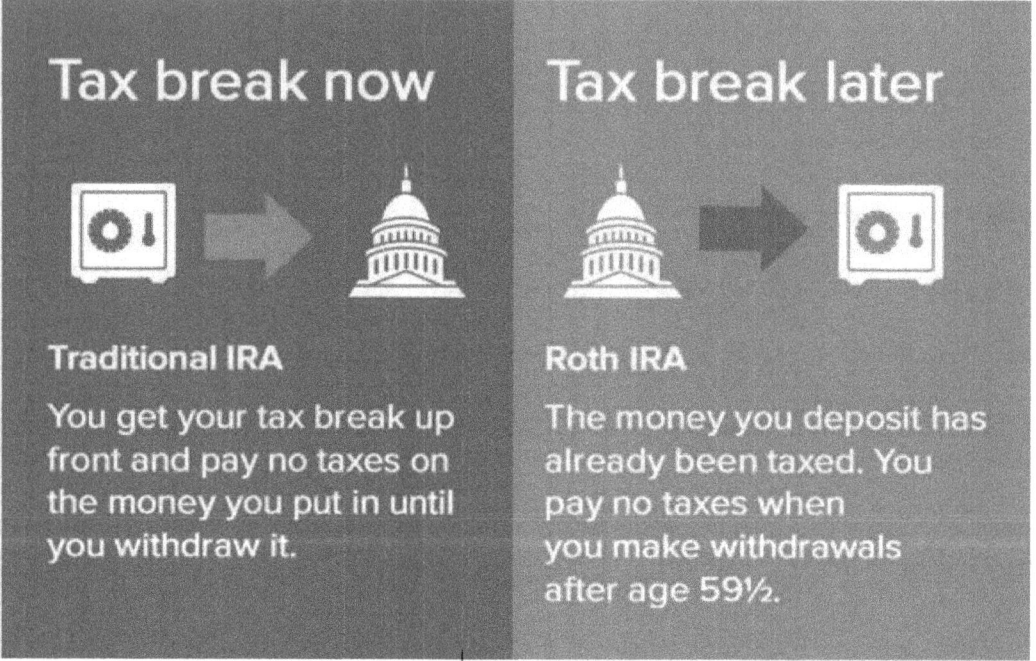

The only caveat is that you do not get to deduct your Roth IRA contribution like you do with traditional IRAs. Roth IRA contributions are made with after-tax money.

The result is that a Roth IRA will generate a 100% tax-free retirement income. That's right — even if you accumulate millions of dollars, you won't pay a penny of income tax on your Roth IRA dollars.

One of my dearest friends, a medical research doctor, has invested $100,000 of his Roth IRA in shares of a young biotechnology company that he thinks has a great shot at developing a cure for cancer.

He thinks its shares will go up 100-fold … or more. If he's right, this would turn his $100,000 into $10 million or more. All tax-free!

That's the power of Roth IRAs!

My friend is certainly optimistic, but the Roth IRA math is very compelling …

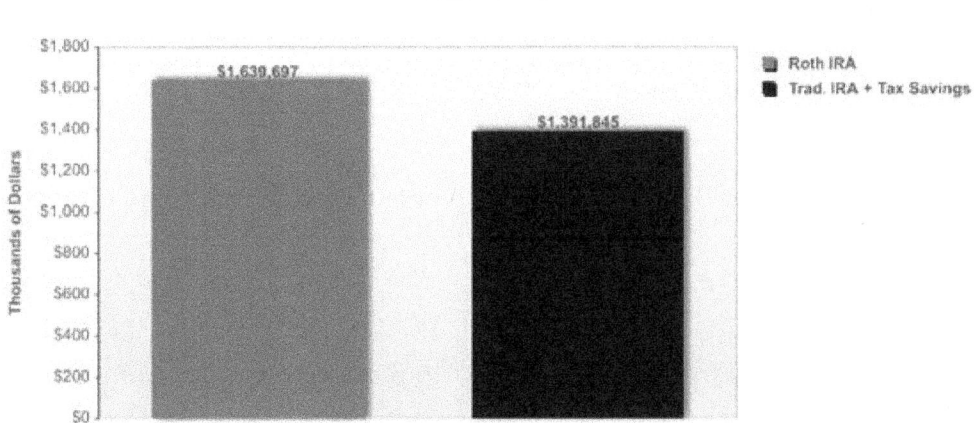

A Roth IRA may be worth $247,852 more than a Traditional IRA.

Totals At Retirement

A 30-year old today who contributes $5,500 a year until age 65 — assuming a 10% annual return — will accumulate approximately $250,000 more with a Roth IRA than a traditional IRA, even after including the tax savings.

And the difference is even greater once you start to draw upon those dollars in retirement …

- If you withdraw $100,000 from your Roth IRA … you pocket $100,000 because there are no taxes.

- If you withdraw $100,000 from your traditional IRA … you'll only pocket $70,000 (assuming a 30% tax bracket).

And you have to ask yourself, do you trust the numbskulls in Congress not to raise taxes in the future? With our runaway spending and our $21 trillion national debt, I think there is no question that tax rates will be going substantially higher.

That makes Roth IRAs even more attractive.

On top of that …

No Required Minimum Distribution: With traditional IRAs as well as 401(k)s, you must start to withdraw some of your dollars — and pay income tax — whether you need the money or not. There is no RMD with Roth IRAs. Plus, you can leave the money to compound without taxes for the rest of your life.

No age limit: I am 62 years old and I plan on working for many more years. However, the cutoff to fund traditional IRAs is 70 1/2. But there is no age limit for Roth IRAs as long as you have earned income.

Tax-free to beneficiaries: With traditional IRAs, somebody — either you or your heirs — will pay income tax on every dollar in it. With Roth IRAs, every penny goes to your heirs without a penny of income taxes. I like that!

In fact, Roth IRAs are so good that there are limits to how much you can contribute each year. Currently, the maximum you can contribute to a Roth IRA is $5,500 if you are under 50 years of age. That increases to $6,500 if you are over 50.

Moreover, there are limits on how much money you can make. In 2018, for single filers, eligibility starts to phase out at $120,000. It disappears above $135,000 of annual income. For married filing jointly, the phase-out range is $189,000 to $199,000.

Therein lies the problem for anybody fortunate enough to make a six-figure income. Many of the successful investors I talk to would love to contribute but think they can't because they make too much.

Wrong!

There is a sneaky backdoor way to open a Roth IRA, no matter how much money you make.

How?

What you do is contribute to a traditional IRA and then convert it to a Roth. You'd need to pay taxes on both (a) the contribution and (b) any growth on the dollars in the traditional IRA. But if you make the conversion shortly thereafter, you'll probably have no gains or very few gains.

Currently, anyone can convert a traditional IRA to a Roth IRA regardless of how much they make — and they can roll as much money as they want from an existing traditional IRA into a Roth IRA.

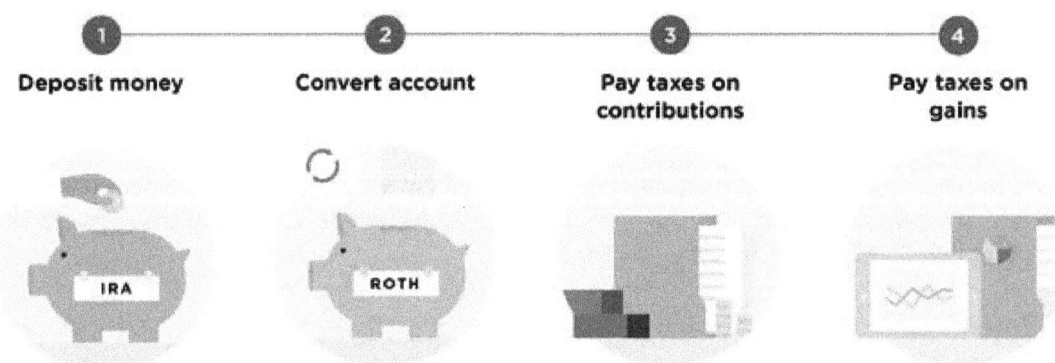

There are several ways you can shoot yourself in the foot if the conversion is not done correctly, though. So please talk to your tax adviser before making any moves.

The benefits, however, of Roth IRAs are so compelling that you should jump through whatever hoops are necessary to fund the greatest wealth-building tool ever created.

Best wishes,
Tony Sagami

Tony Sagami is one of the early pioneers in the application of technical and quantitative analysis to mutual funds and stocks. His four decades of investing experience serve him well here at Weiss Ratings, where he writes and edits founder Martin D. Weiss Ph.D.'s Weiss Ultimate Portfolio stock and ETF trading service.

Mutual Funds vs. Exchange-Traded Funds... Which is Right For You?

Both ETF's and Mutual Funds give you an inexpensive and easy way to diversify your investments and allow you to gain access to different asset classes with a single purchase. Ultimately, you'll need to consider a variety of factors including your tax strategy, the amount of money available to invest, and your overall investment strategy in order to determine which option is right for you.

Mutual Funds

Pros

- Mutual Funds are typically actively managed compared to ETF's which are typically tracking an index. Some of the better fund managers can regularly beat an index, although they will mostly have higher fees associated with them.
- Bigger Universe: There are over 28,000 Mutual Funds vs. less than 2,000 ETF's. You'll have more choices if you choose mutual funds, though the gap is narrowing every year.

Cons

- Mutual funds can only be purchased or sold at the end of the trading day after the market closes and their price is based on Net Asset Value (NAV), the value of fund assets minus liabilities divided by the number of shares.
- Mutual Fund holders can only see the holding of the Funds on a semi-annual basis.
- They are more tax prone- because the buying and selling within the fund by the Portfolio Manager creates more taxable events.
- Higher Minimum Investments

Stock Mutual Funds vs. Bond Mutual Funds

- Primarily, investors purchase stock mutual funds for appreciation or growth from within the companies inside the mutual fund itself. Conversely, bond mutual funds are primarily targeted for income reasons, since the entities inside a bond mutual fund give off income in the form of a coupon payment. Bonds and stocks frequently have an inverse relationship in market cycles, bonds will do well in down markets and stocks will do well in bull markets. For this reason, and for other diversification principles, it's important to have both bond and stock mutual funds in a long term retirement portfolio.
- It's important to note that there are exceptions to this rule, some stocks funds will give off an income in the form of dividend payments and many bond funds seek appreciation as well as income.
- There are risks associated with both bond and stock mutual funds. The risks in stock funds are primarily "market risk" meaning if the overall market is trending lower many stock funds will follow. The risks associated with bond funds are mostly associated with interest rates. In an environment with interest rates rising bond prices will follow and vice versa.

Exchange-Traded Funds (ETFs)

Pros

- ETFs offer much more flexibility. ETFs trade like stocks. They are priced on what Investors believe is Fair Market Value and you can buy and sell shares throughout the day.
- ETFs offer much more transparency, which means that investors can typically see the fund's holdings on a daily basis
- ETFs are more tax efficient than Mutual Funds. Because they are based off an index, there are fewer taxable events. Keep in mind, however, that capital gains and dividends are taxed the same as a Mutual Fund.
- ETFs have a lower expense ratio. In 2016, the average was .23 vs .82 of actively managed funds according to the Investment Company Institute.
- ETFs typically require lower minimum investments. Most of the time you can buy just a single share of the fund.
- You are typically paying a commission on buying and selling an exchange-traded fund. You'll pay a front or back end load when you purchase regular Mutual Funds.

Cons

- Some ETFs have limited choices in their asset class. Mutual Funds typically have more options.
- Given that an ETF trades like a stock, every purchase or sale requires paying a commission.

Section I:
Index of Exchange-Traded Funds

Investment Ratings and analysis of all rated and unrated Exchange-Traded Funds. Funds are listed in alphabetical order.

Section I: Contents

This section contains Weiss Investment Ratings, key rating factors, and summary financial data for over 2,200 Exchange-Traded funds. Funds are listed in alphabetical order.

Left Pages

Fund Name
Describes the fund's assets, regions of investments and investment strategies. Many funds have similar names, so you want to make sure the fund you look up is really the one you are interested in evaluating.

MARKET

Ticker Symbol
An arrangement of characters (usually letters) representing a particular security listed on an exchange or otherwise traded publicly. When a company issues securities to the public marketplace, it selects an available ticker symbol for its securities which investors use to place trade orders. Every listed security has a unique ticker symbol, facilitating the vast array of trade orders that flow through the financial markets every day.

Traded On (Exchange)
The stock exchange on which the fund is listed. The core function of a stock exchange is to ensure fair and orderly trading, as well as efficient dissemination of price information. Exchanges such as: NYSE (New York Stock Exchange), AMEX (American Stock Exchange), NNM (NASDAQ National Market), and NASQ (NASDAQ Small Cap) give companies, governments and other groups a platform to sell securities to the investing public. NASDAQ is abbreviated as NAS.

RATINGS

Overall Rating
The Weiss rating measured on a scale from A to E based on each fund's risk and performance. See the preceding section, "What Our Ratings Mean," for an explanation of each letter grade rating.

Reward Rating

This is based on the total return over a period of up to five years, including net asset value and price growth. The total return figure is stated net of the expenses and fees charged by the fund.   Based on proprietary modeling the individual components of the risk and reward ratings are calculated and weighted and the final rating is generated.

Risk Rating

This is includes the risk ratings of component stocks where applicable and also includes the financial stability of the fund, turnover where applicable, together with the level of volatility as measured by the fund's daily returns over a period of up to five years. Funds with greater stability are considered less risky and receive a higher risk rating. Funds with greater volatility are considered riskier, and will receive a lower risk rating. In addition to considering the fund's volatility, the risk rating also considers an assessment of the valuation and quality of a fund's holdings.

Recent Upgrade/Downgrade

An "Up" or "Down" indicates that the Weiss Exchange-Traded Fund rating has changed since the publication of the last print edition. If a fund has had a rating change since September 30, 2018, the change is identified with an "Up" or "Down."

PRICE

Price

The price at which the fund is traded on a regular trading day. Prices in this guide are listed as of December 31, 2018.

52-Week High

The highest price that a fund has achieved during the previous 52 weeks.

52-Week Low

The lowest price that a fund has achieved during the previous 52 weeks.

Open to New Investors

Indicates whether the fund accepts investments from those who are not existing investors. A "Y" in this column identifies that the fund accepts new investors. No data in this column indicates that the fund is closed to new investors. The fund may be closed to new investors because the fund's asset base is getting too large to effectively execute its investing style. Although, the fund may be closed, in most cases, existing investors are able to add to their holdings.

CATEGORY & OBJECTIVE

Category

Identifies funds according to their actual investment styles as measured by their portfolio holdings. This categorization allows investors to spread their money around in a mix of funds with a variety of risk and return characteristics.

Prospectus Objective

Gives a general idea of a fund's overall investment approach and goals.

Right Pages

RETURNS & PERFORMANCE

3-Month Total Return

The rate of return on an investment over three months that includes interest, capital gains, dividends and distributions realized.

6-Month Total Return

The rate of return on an investment over six months that includes interest, capital gains, dividends and distributions realized.

1-Year Total Return

The rate of return on an investment over one year that includes interest, capital gains, dividends and distributions realized.

3-Year Total Return

The rate of return on an investment over three years that includes interest, capital gains, dividends and distributions realized.

5-Year Total Return

The rate of return on an investment over five years that includes interest, capital gains, dividends and distributions realized.

Dividend Yield (TTM)

Trailing twelve months dividends paid out relative to the share price. Expressed as a percentage and measures how much cash flow an investor is getting for each invested dollar. **Trailing Twelve Months (TTM)** is a representation of a fund's financial performance over the most recent 12 months. TTM uses the latest available financial data from a company's interim, quarterly or annual reports.

Expense Ratio

A measure of what it costs an investment company to operate an exchange-traded fund. An expense ratio is determined through an annual calculation, where a fund's operating expenses are divided by the average dollar value of its assets under management. Operating expenses may include money spent on administration and management of the fund, advertising, etc. An expense ratio of 1 percent per annum means that each year 1 percent of the fund's total assets will be used to cover expenses.

3-Year Standard Deviation

A statistical measurement of dispersion about an average, which depicts how widely the returns varied over the past three years. Investors use the standard deviation of historical performance to try to predict the range of returns that are most likely for a given fund. When a fund has a high standard deviation, the predicted range of performance is wide, implying greater volatility. Standard deviation is most appropriate for measuring risk if it is for a fund that is an investor's only holding. The figure cannot be combined for more than one fund because the standard deviation for a portfolio of multiple funds is a function of not only the individual standard deviations, but also of the degree of correlation among the funds' returns. If a fund's returns follow a normal distribution, then approximately 68 percent of the time they will fall within one standard deviation of the mean return for the fund, and 95 percent of the time within two standard deviations.

Effective Duration

Effective duration for all long fixed income positions in a portfolio. This value gives a better estimation of how the price of bonds with embedded options, which are common in many exchange-traded funds, will change as a result of changes in interest rates. Effective duration takes into account expected mortgage prepayment or the likelihood that embedded options will be exercised if a fund holds futures, other derivative securities, or other funds as assets, the aggregate effective duration should include the weighted impact of those exposures.

ASSETS

NAV (Net Asset Value)

A fund's price per share. The value is calculated by dividing the total value of all the securities in the portfolio, less any liabilities, by the number of fund shares outstanding.

Total Assets (MIL)

The total of all assets listed on the institution's balance sheet. This figure primarily consists of loans, investments, and fixed assets. Total Assets are displayed in millions.

ASSET ALLOCATION & TURNOVER

Asset Allocation

Indicates the percentage of assets in each category. Used as an investment strategy that attempts to balance risk versus reward by adjusting the percentage of each asset in an investment portfolio according to the investor's risk tolerance, goals and investment time frame. Allocation percentages may not add up to 100%. Negative values reflect short positions.

%Cash

The percentage of the fund's assets invested in short-term obligations, usually less than 90 days, that provide a return in the form of interest payments. This type of investment generally offers a low return compared to other investments but has a low risk level.

%Stocks

The percentage of the fund's assets invested in stock.

%Bonds

The percentage of the fund's assets invested in bonds. A bond is an unsecured debt security issued by companies, municipalities, states and sovereign governments to raise funds. When a company issues a bond it borrows money from the bondholder to boost the business, in exchange the bondholder receives the principal amount back plus the interest on the determined maturity date.

%Other

The percentage of the fund's assets invested in other financial instruments.

Turnover Ratio

The percentage of an exchange-traded fund or other investment vehicle's holdings that have been replaced with other holdings in a given year. Generally, low turnover ratio is favorable, because high turnover equates to higher brokerage transaction fees, which reduce fund returns.

VALUATION

Premium/Discount 1-Year Average

The annual average premium or discount of the market price to the NAV (Net Asset Value), expressed as a percentage of the NAV. This value provides a year-by-year picture a fund's trading status. A negative number indicates that, on average, the fund's shares sold at a discount to NAV, and a positive number indicates the shares sold at a premium. If the number shown is –10.00, for example, the shares sold at an average 10% discount to NAV during the listed time-period.

Inception Date

The date on which the fund began its operations. The commencement date indicates when a fund began investing in the market. Many investors prefer funds with longer operating histories. Funds with longer histories have longer track records and can thereby provide investors with a more long-standing picture of their performance.

Fund Name	Ticker Symbol	Traded On	Overall Rating	Reward Rating	Risk Rating	Recent Up/ Downgrade	Price as of 12/31/2018	52-Week High	52-Week Low	Open to New Investors	Category & (Prospectus Objective)
			MARKET	**RATINGS**			**PRICE**				**CATEGORY & OBJECTIVE**
AAM S&P 500 High Dividend Value ETF	SPDV	NYSE Arca	D+	C-	D+		23.64	28.19	22.63	Y	US Equity Large Cap Value (Growth & Inc)
AAM S&P Emerging Markets High Dividend Value ETF	EEMD	NYSE Arca	D	D	D		21.37	28.41	21.10	Y	Global Emerg Mkts Equity (Div Emerg Mkts)
Aberdeen Standard Bloomberg All Commod Longer Dated Strat	BCD	NYSE Arca	D	D	D	Down	23.16	27.53	23.14	Y	Commodities Broad Basket (Growth & Inc)
● Aberdeen Standard Bloomberg All Commod Strat K-1 Free ETF	BCI	NYSE Arca	D+	D	C		21.50	25.57	21.50	Y	Commodities Broad Basket (Growth & Inc)
Aberdeen Standard Bloomberg Energy Commod Longer Dated Str	BEF	NYSE Arca	D+	D+	D+	Down	22.04	31.18	21.77	Y	Commodities Specified (Natl Res)
★ Aberdeen Standard Physical Palladium Shares ETF	PALL	NYSE Arca	B-	B+	C-	Up	119.05	123.65	80.32	Y	Commodities Specified (Prec Metals)
● Aberdeen Standard Physical Platinum Shares ETF	PPLT	NYSE Arca	D	D	D		75.24	96.81	72.98	Y	Commodities Specified (Prec Metals)
● Aberdeen Standard Physical Prec Metals Basket Shares ETF	GLTR	NYSE Arca	D+	D	D+		63.16	67.81	56.51	Y	Commodities Specified (Prec Metals)
● Aberdeen Standard Physical Silver Shares ETF	SIVR	NYSE Arca	D	D-	D	Down	15.04	17.12	13.61	Y	Commodities Specified (Prec Metals)
● Aberdeen Standard Physical Swiss Gold Shares ETF	SGOL	NYSE Arca	D+	D	C-	Down	123.68	131.40	113.37	Y	Commodities Specified (Prec Metals)
AdvisorShares Cornerstone Small Cap ETF	SCAP	NYSE Arca	D+	C-	D	Down	31.98	41.18	30.08	Y	US Equity Small Cap (Small Company)
● AdvisorShares Dorsey Wright ADR ETF	AADR	NYSE Arca	C	C	D+		40.07	63.31	38.43	Y	Global Equity Large Cap (Growth)
AdvisorShares Dorsey Wright Micro-Cap ETF	DWMC	NYSE Arca	U	U	U		18.53	26.02	18.04	Y	US Equity Small Cap (Growth)
AdvisorShares Dorsey Wright Short ETF	DWSH	NYSE Arca	U	U	U		30.57	32.72	24.33	Y	Multialternative (Growth)
● AdvisorShares DoubleLine Value Equity ETF	DBLV	NYSE Arca	C-	C	D+		58.54	75.63	56.67	Y	US Equity Mid Cap (Growth)
★ AdvisorShares Focused Equity ETF	CWS	NYSE Arca	B-	B	C		28.70	34.55	28.19	Y	US Equity Large Cap Blend (Growth)
AdvisorShares Madrona Domestic ETF	FWDD	NYSE Arca	C-	C-	D+		45.24	56.82	43.17	Y	US Equity Large Cap Blend (Growth)
AdvisorShares Madrona Global Bond ETF	FWDB	NYSE Arca	D+	D+	D+	Down	24.20	27.29	24.07	Y	Global Fixed Income (Growth)
AdvisorShares Madrona International ETF	FWDI	NYSE Arca	C-	C	D+		23.55	33.10	23.02	Y	Global Equity Large Cap (Growth)
AdvisorShares New Tech and Media ETF	FNG	NYSE Arca	C	C+	D+	Down	15.57	23.34	14.55	Y	Technology Sector Equity (Growth & Inc)
● AdvisorShares Newfleet Multi-Sector Income ETF	MINC	NYSE Arca	C-	C-	C-		47.33	48.44	47.16	Y	US Fixed Income (Income)
AdvisorShares Pacific Asset Enhanced Floating Rate ETF	FLRT	NYSE Arca	D+	C-	D	Down	46.96	49.92	46.79	Y	US Fixed Income (Income)
● AdvisorShares Ranger Equity Bear ETF	HDGE	NYSE Arca	D+	D	D+		8.43	8.97	7.24	Y	Alternative Misc (Growth)
● AdvisorShares Sage Core Reserves ETF	HOLD	NYSE Arca	C-	C	D+		99.11	99.59	99.04	Y	US Fixed Income (Income)
AdvisorShares STAR Global Buy-Write ETF	VEGA	NYSE Arca	C-	C-	D+	Down	28.67	32.34	27.65	Y	Long/Short Equity (Income)
AdvisorShares Vice ETF	ACT	NAS CM	C+	B	C-		21.40	27.29	21.03	Y	Consumer Goods & Svcs (Growth)
Affinity World Leaders Equity ETF	WLDR	BATS	U	U	U		20.10	27.38	19.39	Y	Global Equity Large Cap (Growth & Inc)
AGFiQ Hedged Dividend Income Fund	DIVA	NYSE Arca	C	C	D+	Up	23.07	24.99	23.01	Y	Long/Short Equity (Growth)
AGFiQ U.S. Market Neutral Anti-Beta Fund	BTAL	NYSE Arca	C	C	C-	Up	22.11	22.30	18.35	Y	Market Neutral (Growth & Inc)
AGFiQ U.S. Market Neutral Momentum Fund	MOM	NYSE Arca	D+	D+	D+		24.72	30.48	23.71	Y	Market Neutral (Growth & Inc)
AGFiQ U.S. Market Neutral Size Fund	SIZ	NYSE Arca	D-	D	E		18.67	20.44	18.61	Y	Market Neutral (Growth & Inc)
AGFiQ U.S. Market Neutral Value Fund	CHEP	NYSE Arca	D	D	D		21.47	26.71	21.47	Y	Market Neutral (Growth & Inc)
● AI Powered Equity ETF	AIEQ	NYSE Arca	D+	D+	D+		21.82	29.89	20.35	Y	US Equity Large Cap Blend (Growth & Inc)
Alerian Energy Infrastructure ETF	ENFR	NYSE Arca	C	C+	D+	Down	18.14	24.04	17.34	Y	Energy Sector Equity (Natl Res)
● Alerian MLP ETF	AMLP	NYSE Arca	C	B-	D		8.73	11.83	8.32	Y	Energy Sector Equity (Natl Res)
● Alpha Architect International Quantitative Momentum ETF	IMOM	BATS	D	D+	D	Down	23.20	32.78	22.43	Y	Global Equity Large Cap (Growth)
● Alpha Architect International Quantitative Value ETF	IVAL	BATS	D+	D+	D+	Down	24.98	34.94	24.27	Y	Global Equity Large Cap (Growth)
● Alpha Architect U.S. Quantitative Momentum ETF	QMOM	BATS	C-	C	D+	Down	25.23	34.22	23.31	Y	US Equity Mid Cap (Growth)
● Alpha Architect U.S. Quantitative Value ETF	QVAL	BATS	C	C	C-		25.04	33.41	23.89	Y	US Equity Mid Cap (Growth)
● Alpha Architect Value Momentum Trend ETF	VMOT	BATS	D	D	D	Down	24.26	31.26	23.44	Y	Long/Short Equity (Growth & Inc)
AlphaClone Alternative Alpha ETF	ALFA	BATS	C	C	C-		42.29	51.31	39.63	Y	US Equity Mid Cap (Growth)
AlphaMark Actively Managed Small Cap ETF	SMCP	NAS CM	C	C+	D+		20.84	27.84	19.79	Y	US Equity Small Cap (Small Company)
ALPS Clean Energy ETF	ACES	BATS	U	U	U		22.71	26.90	21.36	Y	Energy Sector Equity (Growth & Inc)
ALPS Disruptive Technologies ETF	DTEC	BATS	D	D	D		23.88	30.17	22.47	Y	Technology Sector Equity (Growth)
ALPS Emerging Sector Dividend Dogs ETF	EDOG	NYSE Arca	D+	D+	D+		20.18	27.23	19.82	Y	Global Emerg Mkts Equity (Div Emerg Mkts)
● ALPS Equal Sector Weight ETF	EQL	NYSE Arca	C-	C-	D+	Down	63.85	73.70	60.34	Y	US Equity Large Cap Blend (Growth)
● ALPS International Sector Dividend Dogs ETF	IDOG	NYSE Arca	D+	D+	C-	Down	23.82	30.21	23.10	Y	Global Equity Large Cap (Growth)
● ALPS Medical Breakthroughs ETF	SBIO	NYSE Arca	C-	C-	D+	Down	28.14	39.37	25.86	Y	Healthcare Sector Equity (Health)
● ALPS Sector Dividend Dogs ETF	SDOG	NYSE Arca	C	C	C	Down	39.13	49.24	37.25	Y	US Equity Large Cap Value (Income)
ALPS Sprott Junior Gold Miners ETF	SGDJ	NYSE Arca	D	D	D	Down	24.99	34.58	21.48	Y	Prec Metals (Prec Metals)
American Century Diversified Corporate Bond ETF	KORP	NYSE Arca	U	U	U		48.10	50.14	47.83	Y	US Fixed Income (Govt Bond - Gen)
American Century Diversified Municipal Bond ETF	TAXF	NYSE Arca	U	U	U		49.99	49.99	49.47	Y	US Muni Fixed Inc (Muni Bond - Natl)

★ Expanded analysis of this fund is included in Section II: Analysis of All BUY Rated Funds. ● Expanded analysis of this fund is included in Section III: Analysis of All Rated Funds with Assets over $50 million.

3-Month Total Return	6-Month Total Return	1-Year Total Return	3-Year Total Return	5-Year Total Return	Dividend Yield (TTM)	Expense Ratio	3-Yr Std Deviation	Effective Duration	NAV	Total Assets (MIL)	%Cash	%Stocks	%Bonds	%Other	Turnover Ratio	Premium/Discount 1-Year Avg	Inception Date
-13.35	-9.45	-6.65			2.72	0.29			23.66	19.9	0	100	0	0		0.30	Nov-17
-4.73	-6.45	-14.56			4.65	0.49			21.33	2.2	0	100	0	0		0.29	Nov-17
-11.33	-11.88	-11.20			0.07	0.29			23.10	3.6	70	0	14	16		-0.15	Mar-17
-11.80	-12.47	-8.12			5.28	0.25			21.38	174.3	30	20	50	0		0.01	Mar-17
-29.00	-24.95	-13.71			7.02	0.39			21.86	3.7	0	15	85	0		-0.02	Mar-17
19.76	33.81	18.88	126.76	72.37	0	0.6	30.01		119.66	159.9	0	0	0	100		-0.40	Jan-10
-2.96	-5.64	-14.86	-10.57	-43.26	0	0.6	19.18		75.22	492.2	0	0	0	100		0.02	Jan-10
7.90	3.12	-2.48	20.78	-4.37	0	0.6	13.79		63.03	337.0	0	0	0	100		0.09	Oct-10
6.20	-3.36	-8.57	10.89	-21.87	0	0.3	19.28		15.03	322.5	0	0	0	100	4	0.16	Jul-09
7.67	2.53	-1.51	19.27	4.62	0	0.39	12.62		123.61	798.6	0	0	0	100	11	0.17	Sep-09
-19.94	-17.21	-6.34	31.18	35.13	0.09	0.9	14.87		31.82	4.9	1	99	0	0		0.13	Jun-12
-25.37	-24.00	-31.18	6.74	10.49	0.97	0.88	15.44		40.18	142.9	0	100	0	0		0.00	Jul-10
-22.39						0.99			18.85	3.2	1	99	0	0		0.15	Jul-18
20.98						0.99			30.50	10.0	160	-78	18	0		0.08	Jul-18
-14.41	-11.73	-15.78	12.91	27.79	0.7	0.9	11.14		59.26	76.5	6	94	0	0		0.01	Oct-11
-14.63	-9.33	-7.38			0.27	0.68			28.68	14.7	0	99	0	1		0.37	Sep-16
-17.49	-13.89	-14.20	12.86	21.52	0.36	1.25	11.52		45.50	29.8	3	97	0	0		0.28	Jun-11
-3.16	-2.32	-3.15	9.93	13.67	3.71	1.41	3.39	3.77	24.20	17.9	4	2	68	0		-0.05	Jun-11
-15.56	-19.93	-22.49	4.88	-9.94	1.44	1.25	12.43		23.58	11.7	2	98	0	0		0.21	Jun-11
-30.59	-27.56	-27.15			0	0.86			15.61	28.3	3	97	0	0		0.00	Jul-17
-0.27	0.50	0.53	6.19	9.81	2.79	0.75	0.88	1.59	47.37	128.4	6	0	94	0		-0.13	Mar-13
-3.94	-1.91	-0.66	9.81		3.79	1.14	2.7	0.57	46.94	29.0	32	0	82	-14		0.23	Feb-15
13.30	8.21	7.11	-21.58	-33.98	0	2.72	13.96		8.43	130.0	144	-89	45	0	245	-0.01	Jan-11
0.32	0.96	1.75	4.38		1.87	0.35	0.34	0.41	99.09	67.0	8	0	91	0		0.00	Jan-14
-10.08	-6.90	-6.35	12.16	16.51	0	2.06	6.17	4.76	28.74	15.4	8	76	14	0		0.23	Sep-12
-18.40	-14.62	-16.28				0.75			21.52	13.4	0	100	0	0		0.22	Dec-17
-15.51	-11.89					0.47			20.32	5.6	0	99	0	0		1.74	Jan-18
-1.36	1.07	-0.07	18.41		6.52	0.75	5.52		23.09	2.4	50	50	0	0	141	0.49	Jan-15
9.52	10.34	15.05	6.59	14.82	0	0.76	11.97		21.98	22.3	94	6	0	0	273	0.05	Sep-11
-2.24	-0.23	2.68	-11.28	-4.27	0	1.88	10.03		24.62	4.8	104	-4	0	0	402	-0.14	Sep-11
-4.74	-7.92	-7.43	-12.51	-26.62	0	1.71	6.69		18.73	1.9	105	-5	0	0	105	-0.03	Sep-11
-3.20	-6.62	-14.48	-9.04	-20.08	0	1.12	8.79		21.87	1.1	104	-4	0	0	152	-0.26	Sep-11
-18.74	-14.72	-7.28			0.45	0.75			21.87	176.7	4	96	0	0		0.03	Oct-17
-18.35	-15.51	-18.31	15.96	-18.07	2.88	0.65	15.87		18.21	41.7	2	98	0	0	37	0.12	Oct-13
-18.00	-10.04	-12.71	-6.97	-27.75	8.49	0.85	17.65		8.75	8,702	0	100	0	0	23	-0.08	Aug-10
-18.23	-18.00	-22.13	-6.40		1.06	0.79			23.31	57.3	0	100	0	0	119	0.39	Dec-15
-17.11	-15.87	-21.62	11.38		3.14	0.79	13.92		25.18	89.8	0	100	0	0	30	0.16	Dec-14
-25.02	-18.36	-11.03	8.12		0	0.79			25.30	66.1	0	100	0	0	91	0.31	Dec-15
-18.06	-18.13	-16.55	18.28		1.18	0.79	14.84		25.18	102.8	0	100	0	0	46	0.14	Oct-14
-16.25	-14.97	-15.69			1.27	0.79			24.23	101.8	77	23	0	0	44	0.00	May-17
-16.21	-10.06	-0.44	13.77	13.21	0	0.69	12.47		42.52	21.0	0	100	0	0	371	-0.02	May-12
-20.47	-20.89	-19.61	-4.59		0	0.92	14.65		20.88	23.7	2	98	0	0	41	-0.34	Apr-15
-10.89						0.65			22.68	16.3	0	100	0	0		0.57	Jun-18
-18.11	-12.98	-3.28				0.5			24.06	48.5	0	100	0	0		0.41	Dec-17
-2.22	-1.58	-15.82	15.83		3.98	0.6	15.48		20.33	35.2	1	99	0	0	42	-0.33	Mar-14
-12.00	-6.91	-6.00	25.72	39.74	2.07	0.48	8.64		63.90	154.7	0	100	0	0	5	0.06	Jul-09
-9.92	-9.18	-13.08	13.65	0.18	4.33	0.5	10.96		23.96	285.3	1	99	0	0	37	0.03	Jun-13
-24.23	-22.59	-11.19	-6.84		1.73	0.5	30.4		28.23	223.4	0	100	0	0	43	0.11	Dec-14
-14.23	-10.04	-11.29	22.32	36.10	3.58	0.4	10.59		39.14	2,167	0	100	0	0	48	0.00	Jun-12
3.37	-14.16	-25.66	31.19		0.22	0.57	41.04		24.88	36.8	0	100	0	0	74	-0.03	Mar-15
-0.30	0.71					0.45		3.82	47.94	31.3	1	0	99	0	38	0.23	Jan-18
0.50						0.29		6.13	49.90	12.4	0	0	100	0		0.08	Sep-18

Fund Name	Ticker Symbol	Traded On	Overall Rating	Reward Rating	Risk Rating	Recent Up/Downgrade	Price as of 12/31/2018	52-Week High	52-Week Low	Open to New Investors	Category & (Prospectus Objective)
American Century Quality Diversified International ETF	QINT	NYSE Arca	U	U	U		34.32	41.33	33.21	Y	Global Equity Large Cap (Foreign Stock)
American Century STOXX U.S. Quality Value ETF	VALQ	NYSE Arca	U	U	U		35.53	41.84	33.85	Y	US Equity Large Cap Value (Growth & Inc)
American Century U.S. Quality Growth ETF	QGRO	NYSE Arca	U	U	U		33.44	40.35	31.21	Y	US Equity Large Cap Growth (Growth)
● American Customer Satisfaction ETF	ACSI	BATS	C-	C-	C-		28.86	34.38	27.89	Y	US Equity Large Cap Blend (Growth & Inc)
American Energy Independence ETF	USAI	NYSE Arca	C	C+	D		20.48	27.72	19.53	Y	Energy Sector Equity (Natl Res)
Amplify Advanced Battery Metals and Materials ETF	BATT	NYSE Arca	U	U	U		11.61	19.79	11.31	Y	Natural Resources (Growth & Inc)
Amplify EASI Tactical Growth ETF	EASI	NYSE Arca	U	U	U		23.97	26.31	23.15	Y	Aggressive Allocation (Growth)
● Amplify Online Retail ETF	IBUY	NAS CM	C	C+	C-	Down	40.09	54.51	37.41	Y	Consumer Goods & Svcs (Growth & Inc)
Amplify Transformational Data Sharing ETF	BLOK	NYSE Arca	U	U	U		14.77	21.31	14.46	Y	Technology Sector Equity (Technology)
★ Amplify YieldShares CWP Dividend & Option Income ETF	DIVO	BATS	B-	B	C	Down	26.72	30.53	25.34	Y	Long/Short Equity (Growth & Inc)
Anfield Capital Diversified Alternatives ETF	DALT	BATS	D+	D+	C-		8.94	10.55	8.53	Y	Multialternative (Growth & Inc)
Anfield Universal Fixed Income ETF	AFIF	BATS	U	U	U		9.91	10.08	9.88	Y	US Fixed Income (Income)
★ Aptus Behavioral Momentum ETF	BEMO	BATS	B-	B	C	Down	28.25	37.07	28.17	Y	US Equity Large Cap Blend (Growth & Inc)
Aptus Defined Risk ETF	DRSK	BATS	U	U	U		24.96	25.94	24.82	Y	Long/Short Equity (Growth & Inc)
● Aptus Fortified Value ETF	FTVA	BATS	D+	C-	D		23.66	29.57	23.23	Y	Long/Short Equity (Growth & Inc)
● ARK Genomic Revolution Multi-Sector ETF	ARKG	NYSE Arca	D+	D+	D		23.98	34.45	22.36	Y	Healthcare Sector Equity (Unaligned)
● ARK Industrial Innovation ETF	ARKQ	NYSE Arca	C	C+	D+		29.49	37.37	28.79	Y	Technology Sector Equity (Unaligned)
● ARK Innovation ETF	ARKK	NYSE Arca	C-	C	D+	Down	37.19	49.70	35.34	Y	Technology Sector Equity (Unaligned)
ARK Israeli Innovation ETF Hedged	IZRL	BATS	D+	D+	D+		18.56	22.32	18.16	Y	Equity Misc (Technology)
● ARK Web x.0 ETF	ARKW	NYSE Arca	C	C+	C-	Down	42.42	59.90	42.01	Y	Technology Sector Equity (Technology)
Arrow Dogs of the World ETF	DOGS	NYSE Arca	U	U	U		46.07	52.60	45.74	Y	Global Equity Large Cap (Growth)
● Arrow Dow Jones Global Yield ETF	GYLD	NYSE Arca	D+	D+	C-	Down	15.07	18.96	14.88	Y	Moderate Allocation (Growth & Inc)
Arrow DWA Country Rotation ETF			D	D	D		24.78	32.93	24.72	Y	Global Equity Large Cap (Growth)
Arrow DWA Tactical ETF	DWAT	NAS CM	C-	C-	D+	Down	9.89	12.84	9.89	Y	Moderate Allocation (Growth)
Arrow QVM Equity Factor ETF	QVM	NYSE Arca	C-	C	D		24.09	30.15	23.08	Y	US Equity Large Cap Value (Growth)
● Arrow Reserve Capital Management ETF	ARCM	BATS	D	D+	D		99.65	100.76	99.63	Y	US Fixed Income (Growth & Inc)
Barclays ETN+ FI Enhanced Europe 50 ETN Series B	FLEU	NYSE Arca	D	D	D	Down	108.55	179.71	100.85	Y	Global Equity Large Cap (Growth & Inc)
Barclays ETN+ FI Enhanced Europe 50 ETN Series C	FFEU	NYSE Arca	U	U	U		74.08	105.40	68.81	Y	Europe Equity Large Cap (Growth)
Barclays ETN+ FI Enhanced Global High Yield ETN B	FIYY	NYSE Arca	U	U	U		84.66	104.72	77.47	Y	Global Equity Large Cap (Equity-Income)
Barclays ETN+ S&P VEQTOR™ ETN	VQT	NYSE Arca	D+	C-	D		154.44	181.89	152.88	Y	Long/Short Equity (Growth)
● Barclays ETN+ Select MLP ETN	ATMP	NYSE Arca	C-	D+	C-	Up	17.73	22.74	16.98	Y	Energy Sector Equity (Growth)
● Barclays ETN+ Shiller Capet ETN	CAPE	NYSE Arca	C-	C	D+	Down	112.41	133.10	106.83	Y	US Equity Large Cap Value (Growth)
Barclays Inverse US Treasury Aggregate ETN	TAPR	NAS CM	C-	C-	D+	Down	23.51	32.37	21.97	Y	Trading Tools (Growth & Inc)
Barclays Return on Disability ETN	RODI	NYSE Arca	D	C-	E+	Down	70.00	70.00	70.00	Y	US Equity Large Cap Blend (Growth & Inc)
Barclays Women in Leadership ETN	WIL	NYSE Arca	D+	C-	D		59.20	70.23	55.92	Y	US Equity Large Cap Blend (Equity-Income)
● Barron's 400 ETF	BFOR	NYSE Arca	C-	C-	D+	Down	35.48	46.14	33.40	Y	US Equity Mid Cap (Equity-Income)
Bernstein Global Research Fund	BRGL	BATS	D	D	D		22.37	28.14	21.47	Y	Global Equity Large Cap (Growth & Inc)
Bernstein U.S. Research Fund	BERN	BATS	D	D+	D		24.35	30.05	22.98	Y	US Equity Large Cap Blend (Growth & Inc)
● Bitcoin Investment Trust	GBTC	OTC BB	D+	C-	D+	Down	3.97	25.69	3.84	Y	Trading Tools (Growth & Inc)
● BlueStar Israel Technology ETF	ITEQ	NYSE Arca	C	C+	C-		31.43	36.72	29.60	Y	Technology Sector Equity (Technology)
BMO Elkhorn DWA MLP Select™ Index Exchange Traded Notes	BMLP	NAS CM	D	D+	E+		46.70	53.24	43.29	Y	Energy Sector Equity (Growth & Inc)
Brand Value ETF	BVAL	NYSE Arca	C-	C-	D+		14.14	16.68	13.71	Y	US Equity Large Cap Value (Growth & Inc)
Brandes Value NextShares	BVNSC	NAS CM	U	U	U		9.13	100.04	8.73	Y	US Equity Large Cap Value (Growth)
Breakwave Dry Bulk Shipping ETF	BDRY	NYSE Arca	U	U	U		18.38	25.58	14.66	Y	Equity Misc (Growth)
BUZZ US Sentiment Leaders ETF	BUZ	NYSE Arca	C	C	D+		31.28	39.00	29.08	Y	US Equity Large Cap Growth (Growth & Inc)
Calvert Ultra-Short Duration Income NextShares	CRUSC	NAS CM	U	U	U		9.95	100.02	9.94	Y	US Fixed Income (Growth & Inc)
● Cambria Core Equity ETF	CCOR	NYSE Arca	C-	C-	C-		26.58	26.61	24.37	Y	Long/Short Equity (Growth & Inc)
Cambria Emerging Shareholder Yield ETF	EYLD	BATS	D+	D+	D+		27.82	38.25	27.48	Y	Global Emerg Mkts Equity (Div Emerg Mkts)
Cambria Foreign Shareholder Yield ETF	FYLD	BATS	D+	D+	C-	Down	21.51	27.81	21.10	Y	Global Eq Mid/Small Cap (Foreign Stock)
● Cambria Global Asset Allocation ETF	GAA	BATS	D+	D+	D+	Down	24.80	28.52	24.59	Y	Cautious Allocation (Asset Allocation)
● Cambria Global Momentum ETF	GMOM	BATS	D+	D+	C-	Down	24.31	29.35	24.26	Y	Moderate Allocation (Growth & Inc)
● Cambria Global Value ETF	GVAL	BATS	C-	C-	C-		21.00	28.37	20.97	Y	Global Eq Mid/Small Cap (Div Emerg Mkts)

★ Expanded analysis of this fund is included in Section II: Analysis of All BUY Rated Funds. ● Expanded analysis of this fund is included in Section III: Analysis of All Rated Funds with Assets over $50 million.

				TOTAL RETURNS & PERFORMANCE					ASSETS		ASSET ALLOCATION & TURNOVER					VALUATION	
3-Month Total Return	6-Month Total Return	1-Year Total Return	3-Year Total Return	5-Year Total Return	Dividend Yield (TTM)	Expense Ratio	3-Yr Std Deviation	Effective Duration	NAV	Total Assets (MIL)	%Cash	%Stocks	%Bonds	%Other	Turnover Ratio	Premium/ Discount 1-Year Avg	Inception Date
-16.32						0.39			34.36	12.7	1	99	0	0		-0.91	Sep-18
-12.97	-7.73					0.29			35.66	11.9	0	100	0	0	77	0.18	Jan-18
-16.39						0.29			33.57	10.1	0	100	0	0		-0.59	Sep-18
-13.16	-8.34	-4.41			1.12	0.66			28.98	56.9	0	100	0	0	72	0.18	Oct-16
-19.63	-17.21	-17.25				0.75			20.54	9.3	0	100	0	0		0.61	Dec-17
-24.08	-32.34					0.72			11.66	6.5	0	100	0	0		0.18	Jun-18
-6.71	0.00					0.75		2.98	23.95	13.1	6	0	94	0		0.08	Jun-18
-22.09	-21.87	-1.56			0	0.65			40.19	361.2	0	100	0	0	11	0.09	Apr-16
-26.07	-22.25					0.7			14.88	122.2	0	100	0	0		-0.06	Jan-18
-9.46	-2.43	-2.47			5.6	0.49			26.85	16.1	8	92	0	0		0.20	Dec-16
-12.82	-9.41	-9.22			3.28	2.41			8.97	35.3	2	81	9	0		0.16	Sep-17
-0.59						1			9.91	51.3	8	0	94	-3		-0.13	Sep-18
-23.09	-16.53	-5.88			0.31	0.79			28.26	75.9	0	100	0	0	124	0.08	Jun-16
1.69						0.78		3.30	24.88	55.8	4	6	90	0		0.12	Aug-18
-17.53	-14.33	-12.13			0.12	0.79			23.73	83.6	0	100	0	0		0.14	Oct-17
-25.58	-18.20	-0.55	17.41		0.65	0.75	29.31		24.04	324.9	0	100	0	0	80	0.15	Oct-14
-19.10	-14.92	-10.16	54.82		0.07	0.75	19.43		29.52	176.6	0	100	0	0	57	0.11	Sep-14
-21.36	-18.20	0.56	84.74		0.11	0.75	23.78		37.18	1,315	0	100	0	0	89	0.07	Oct-14
-14.27	-9.14	-7.88				0.49			18.68	21.7	0	100	0	0	40	-0.27	Dec-17
-25.91	-23.14	-6.34	90.59		0.7	0.75	20.21		42.45	504.3	0	99	0	1	68	0.06	Sep-14
-6.41	-2.80	-5.38				1.64			46.28	5.0	0	100	0	0		0.61	Jan-18
-10.27	-8.65	-9.35	9.24	-14.98	7.49	0.75	11.55		15.42	63.7	0	58	41	1	90	-1.25	May-12
-11.55	-9.25	-15.20				1.34			24.97	17.3	0	100	0	0		0.34	Dec-17
-20.41	-14.83	-13.28	5.90		0.41	1.7	9.86		9.92	5.5	8	86	2	4	125	-0.21	Oct-14
-14.93	-11.27	-9.87	15.91		2.77	0.65	11.05		24.27	4.1	0	100	0	0	127	0.10	Feb-15
0.19	0.72	1.57			1.63	0.42			99.72	71.1	23	0	77	0	66	-0.05	Mar-17
-23.65	-21.77	-32.30			0	0.76				22.1						-0.56	Nov-16
-23.15	-23.00					1.05				674.4						0.00	Mar-18
-19.26	-10.77					0.93				1,540						-0.10	Mar-18
-10.71	-4.91	-1.69	12.37	6.11	0	0.95	8.54			21.6						0.10	Aug-10
-16.22	-10.20	-10.85	12.06	-17.40	6.04	0.95	17.47			407.8						0.08	Mar-13
-15.75	-6.93	-3.40	38.61	66.95	0	0.45	10.32			119.7						0.23	Oct-12
-17.37	-6.78	11.27	-26.06		0	0.43	36.66			19.7						0.05	Jul-14
-14.40	-8.33	-7.17	27.97		0	0.45	10.56			38.8						-7.96	Sep-14
-15.08	-10.55	-12.02	14.55		0	0.45	8.69			36.9						0.04	Jul-14
-19.91	-17.25	-13.43	20.88	23.65	0.61	0.66	13.01		35.52	165.7	1	99	0	0	84	0.17	Jun-13
-15.97	-13.07	-13.13			0.15	0.65			22.38	4.9	0	99	0	0	195	0.67	Oct-17
-17.62	-11.77	-7.56			0.2	0.5			24.62	7.0	0	100	0	0	132	-0.09	Oct-17
-43.01	-42.55	-74.61	732.52	344.57	0	2	91.94		3.72	826.3	-55	0	0	155		42.55	Sep-13
-11.78	-8.32	-0.17	32.29		0.51	0.75	13.59		31.46	54.1	1	99	0	0	11	0.25	Nov-15
6.46	21.38	15.13			6.48	0.85				49.9						-0.26	Dec-16
-11.15	-5.75	-8.08			0.8	0.65			14.21	6.4	0	100	0	0	86	0.51	Jun-17
-10.30	-5.59					0.4			9.13	3.0	11	87	0	0	8	0.00	Feb-18
-17.61	-14.00					3.5			18.56	2.5	27	0	2	71		0.25	Mar-18
-18.88	-12.29	-0.73			0.41	0.75			31.44	10.5	0	100	0	0	260	0.04	Apr-16
0.07	0.72	1.64				0.38			9.95	10.0						0.00	Jan-18
5.34	10.20	4.86			1.98	1.21			26.63	80.7	3	97	0	0	8	-0.08	May-17
-6.62	-6.93	-11.69			3.38	0.65			27.77	16.3	3	97	0	0	26	0.66	Jul-16
-12.62	-11.08	-13.65	18.15	1.66	3.44	0.59	11.04		21.59	26.6	2	98	0	0	44	0.12	Dec-13
-6.22	-5.02	-6.84	16.60		2.6	0.33	5.88	6.73	24.85	61.7	9	42	45	4	30	0.06	Dec-14
-7.84	-6.31	-8.72	14.81		1.4	1.07	7.6	4.54	24.45	108.3	15	37	44	3	50	0.18	Nov-14
-8.70	-7.60	-13.46	29.40		2.42	0.68	14.46		21.12	142.5	3	97	0	0	14	-0.06	Mar-14

Fund Name	Ticker Symbol	Traded On	Overall Rating	Reward Rating	Risk Rating	Recent Up/ Downgrade	Price as of 12/31/2018	52-Week High	52-Week Low	Open to New Investors	Category & (Prospectus Objective)
● Cambria Shareholder Yield ETF	SYLD	BATS	C-	C	C-	Down	32.47	40.83	30.75	Y	US Equity Mid Cap (Growth & Inc)
Cambria Sovereign Bond ETF	SOVB	BATS	D	D+	D	Down	24.63	29.12	23.98	Y	Emerging Mkts Fixed Inc (Corp Bond-High Yld)
Cambria Tail Risk ETF	TAIL	BATS	D	D	D		22.87	24.70	19.82	Y	Alternative Misc (Growth & Inc)
Cambria Value and Momentum ETF	VAMO	BATS	C+	B-	C	Up	21.90	26.79	21.58	Y	Long/Short Equity (Growth & Inc)
Causeway Global Value NextShares	CGVIC	NAS CM	U	U	U		8.42	100.10	8.10	Y	Global Equity Large Cap (World Stock)
Causeway International Value NextShares	CIVEC	NAS CM	U	U	U		8.00	100.12	7.78	Y	Global Equity Large Cap (Foreign Stock)
CBOE Vest S&P 500 Div Aristocrats Target Income Ind ETF	KNG	BATS	U	U	U		38.19	43.77	36.81	Y	US Equity Large Cap Blend (Growth & Inc)
Change Finance U.S. Large Cap Fossil Fuel Free ETF	CHGX	NYSE Arca	D+	D+	D+		17.65	20.70	16.84	Y	US Equity Large Cap Blend (Growth & Inc)
Citigroup ETNs - VelocityShares Daily 4X Long AUD vs. USD	UAUD	NYSE Arca	D	D	D-		17.83	32.65	17.70	Y	Currency (Growth & Inc)
Citigroup ETNs - VelocityShares Daily 4X Long CHF vs. USD	UCHF	NYSE Arca	D	D	D-		22.38	32.08	20.81	Y	Currency (Growth & Inc)
Citigroup ETNs - VelocityShares Daily 4X Long EUR vs. USD	UEUR	NYSE Arca	D	D	D-		19.80	31.62	18.64	Y	Currency (Growth & Inc)
Citigroup ETNs - VelocityShares Daily 4X Long GBP vs. USD	UGBP	NYSE Arca	D	D	D-		18.85	32.17	17.45	Y	Currency (Growth & Inc)
Citigroup ETNs - VelocityShares Daily 4X Long JPY vs. USD	UJPY	NYSE Arca	D	D	D-		25.54	33.04	22.12	Y	Currency (Growth & Inc)
Citigroup ETNs - VelocityShares Daily 4X Long USD vs. AUD	DAUD	NYSE Arca	D	D	D		31.06	31.33	18.85	Y	Currency (Growth & Inc)
Citigroup ETNs - VelocityShares Daily 4X Long USD vs. CHF	DCHF	NYSE Arca	D	D+	E+		25.85	28.19	19.08	Y	Currency (Growth & Inc)
Citigroup ETNs - VelocityShares Daily 4X Long USD vs. EUR	DEUR	NYSE Arca	D+	D+	D+		29.08	31.06	19.66	Y	Currency (Growth & Inc)
Citigroup ETNs - VelocityShares Daily 4X Long USD vs. GBP	DGBP	NYSE Arca	D	D+	D		29.61	32.06	18.65	Y	Currency (Growth & Inc)
Citigroup ETNs - VelocityShares Daily 4X Long USD vs. JPY	DJPY	NYSE Arca	D	D+	D		23.04	26.45	18.50	Y	Currency (Growth & Inc)
Claymore CEF GS Connect ETN	GCE	NYSE Arca	D+	D+	D+	Down	13.01	17.09	12.49	Y	Moderate Allocation (Asset Allocation)
● ClearBridge All Cap Growth ETF	CACG	NAS CM	C-	C-	C-	Down	26.73	31.81	25.40	Y	US Equity Large Cap Growth (Growth)
ClearBridge Dividend Strategy ESG ETF	YLDE	NAS CM	C-	C	D		25.52	29.55	25.52	Y	US Equity Large Cap Value (Growth & Inc)
ClearBridge Large Cap Growth ESG ETF	LRGE	NAS CM	C	C	C-		28.64	34.23	27.10	Y	US Equity Large Cap Growth (Growth)
● ClearShares OCIO ETF	OCIO	NYSE Arca	D	D+	D		23.99	27.77	23.78	Y	Moderate Allocation (Growth & Inc)
ClearShares Ultra-Short Maturity ETF	OPER	NYSE Arca	U	U	U		100.02	103.07	100.00	Y	US Fixed Income (Income)
● Cohen & Steers Global Realty Majors ETF	GRI	NYSE Arca	C-	C	D+	Down	41.11	45.22	40.34	Y	Real Estate Sector Equity (Real Estate)
Columbia Beyond BRICs ETF	BBRC	NYSE Arca	D+	D+	D+	Down	15.71	20.39	15.38	Y	Global Emerg Mkts Equity (Foreign Stock)
● Columbia Diversified Fixed Income Allocation ETF	DIAL	NYSE Arca	D	D	C-		18.87	20.01	18.78	Y	US Fixed Income (Growth & Inc)
Columbia EM Core ex-China ETF	XCEM	NYSE Arca	C-	C-	D+		23.77	30.22	23.14	Y	Global Emerg Mkts Equity (Div Emerg Mkts)
Columbia EM Quality Dividend ETF	HILO	NYSE Arca	D+	C-	D+	Down	13.27	16.94	13.04	Y	Global Emerg Mkts Equity (Div Emerg Mkts)
● Columbia Emerging Markets Consumer ETF	ECON	NYSE Arca	D	D	D	Down	20.37	29.85	19.79	Y	Global Emerg Mkts Equity (Unaligned)
● Columbia India Consumer ETF	INCO	NYSE Arca	D+	D+	D+	Down	44.20	51.04	37.36	Y	India Equity (Unaligned)
Columbia India Infrastructure ETF	INXX	NYSE Arca	D+	D+	D		11.91	16.60	10.68	Y	India Equity (Foreign Stock)
Columbia India Small Cap ETF	SCIN	NYSE Arca	D	D	D	Down	14.92	24.92	13.04	Y	India Equity (Foreign Stock)
Columbia Sustainable Global Equity Income ETF	ESGW	NYSE Arca	D+	C-	D		23.35	32.13	22.36	Y	Global Equity Large Cap (Growth & Inc)
Columbia Sustainable International Equity Income ETF	ESGN	NYSE Arca	D+	D+	C-		23.40	32.19	22.75	Y	Global Equity Large Cap (Growth & Inc)
Columbia Sustainable U.S. Equity Income ETF	ESGS	NYSE Arca	D+	C-	D		24.15	31.48	22.87	Y	US Equity Large Cap Value (Growth & Inc)
Communication Services Select Sector SPDR® Fund	XLC	NYSE Arca	U	U	U		41.28	51.81	38.97	Y	Communications Sector Equity (Comm)
★ Consumer Discretionary Select Sector SPDR® Fund	XLY	NYSE Arca	B-	B	C	Down	99.01	117.79	91.98	Y	Consumer Goods & Svcs (Unaligned)
● Consumer Staples Select Sector SPDR® Fund	XLP	NYSE Arca	C+	B	C		50.78	58.71	48.73	Y	Consumer Goods & Svcs (Unaligned)
Credit Suisse FI Enhanc Europe 50 Exchange Traded Notes (E	FEUL	NYSE Arca	U	U	U		70.80	101.24	66.15	Y	Europe Equity Large Cap (Growth & Inc)
● Credit Suisse FI Large Cap Growth Enhanced ETN	FLGE	NYSE Arca	C-	C	D+	Down	189.34	300.04	167.09	Y	US Equity Large Cap Growth (Growth)
● Credit Suisse S&P MLP Index ETN	MLPO	NYSE Arca	D-	D	E		13.92	16.57	13.92	Y	Energy Sector Equity (Growth & Inc)
Credit Suisse X-Links Crude Oil Shares Covered Call ETNs	USOI	NAS CM	D+	D+	D+	Down	19.15	30.61	18.45	Y	Commodities Specified (Natl Res)
Credit Suisse X-Links Gold Shares Covered Call ETN	GLDI	NAS CM	D+	D	C-		8.52	9.29	7.99	Y	Commodities Specified (Income)
Credit Suisse X-Links Month Pay 2xLev Alerian MLP Ind ETN	AMJL	NYSE Arca	D	D	D		16.74	26.41	13.57	Y	Trading Tools (Growth & Inc)
● Credit Suisse X-Links Monthly Pay 2xLev Mortg REIT ETN	REML	NYSE Arca	C-	C-	C-	Up	22.51	30.60	20.77	Y	Trading Tools (Real Estate)
Credit Suisse X-Links Multi-Asset High Income ETN	MLTI	NYSE Arca	D	D+	D		27.00	29.12	27.00	Y	Moderate Allocation (Income)
Credit Suisse X-Links Silver Shares Covered Call ETN	SLVO	NAS CM	D	D-	D		6.90	8.18	6.40	Y	Commodities Specified (Income)
CSOP FTSE China A50 ETF	AFTY	NYSE Arca	D+	C-	D+		13.11	20.49	13.05	Y	Greater China Equity (Pacific Stock)
CSOP MSCI China A International Hedged ETF	CNHX	NYSE Arca	D-	D	E	Down	22.13	31.99	22.01	Y	Greater China Equity (Pacific Stock)
● C-Tracks Exchange-Traded Notes Based on the Miller/Howard	MLPC	NYSE Arca	D	D	D+		12.05	16.87	11.82	Y	Energy Sector Equity (Growth)
● C-Tracks Exchange-Traded Notes Miller/Howard Strat Div Rei	DIVC	NYSE Arca	D	C-	E+	Down	30.76	37.34	29.19	Y	US Equity Large Cap Value (Income)

★ Expanded analysis of this fund is included in Section II: Analysis of All BUY Rated Funds. ● Expanded analysis of this fund is included in Section III: Analysis of All Rated Funds with Assets over $50 million.

3-Month Total Return	6-Month Total Return	1-Year Total Return	3-Year Total Return	5-Year Total Return	Dividend Yield (TTM)	Expense Ratio	3-Yr Std Deviation	Effective Duration	NAV	Total Assets (MIL)	%Cash	%Stocks	%Bonds	%Other	Turnover Ratio	Premium/ Discount 1-Year Avg	Inception Date
-17.12	-13.11	-13.36	19.56	31.15	2.12	0.59	11.68		32.48	120.3	1	99	0	0	16	0.12	May-13
2.66	0.51	-6.90			3.36	0.59			24.64	18.7	3	0	97	0	25	0.24	Feb-16
14.90	8.09	2.33			1.65	0.59			22.76	21.6	0	8	91	0	56	0.04	Apr-17
-11.23	-14.02	-11.55	-2.98		0.79	0.65	9.57		22.09	32.2	55	45	0	0	93	0.00	Sep-15
-15.49	-9.84					1.05			8.42	5.0	3	97	0	0	21	0.00	Apr-18
-14.98	-13.00					1.05			8.00	4.4	2	98	0	0	12	0.00	Apr-18
-9.69	-2.48					0.75			38.41	20.0	0	100	0	0		0.13	Mar-18
-12.70	-6.47	-4.12			0.28	0.49			17.71	4.0	0	100	0	0	70	0.23	Oct-17
-10.70	-17.55	-36.70				1.5			17.87	3.0						1.27	Dec-17
-3.71	-2.62	-15.66				1.5			22.23	3.4						1.71	Dec-17
-8.37	-11.54	-26.64				1.5			19.71	2.6						-0.67	Dec-17
-10.70	-13.71	-27.37				1.5			19.06	2.9						-0.11	Dec-17
11.73	-2.63	-1.82				1.5			25.18	3.6						0.56	Dec-17
8.84	14.68	40.56				1.5			31.02	4.2						0.64	Dec-17
2.68	-0.48	10.32				1.5			26.03	4.4						0.44	Dec-17
7.76	9.31	26.07				1.5			29.22	2.9						0.26	Dec-17
9.28	10.08	23.46				1.5			29.26	4.7						-0.55	Dec-17
-11.23	0.87	-3.76				1.5			23.38	4.0						0.10	Dec-17
-17.90	-18.31	-22.07	1.66	-1.75	0	0.95	10.98			7.5					0	0.00	Dec-07
-14.17	-9.71	-2.92			0.23	0.53			26.82	81.4	2	98	0	0	15	0.17	May-17
-10.48	-4.70	-5.04			1.68	0.6			25.94	4.3	7	93	0	0	5	0.25	May-17
-14.43	-7.43	-0.18			0.34	0.59			28.86	6.4	3	97	0	0	7	0.09	May-17
-9.21	-6.48	-7.52			0.87	0.67		4.24	24.03	108.4	13	65	22	0	31	0.34	Jun-17
0.51						0.3			100.02	25.2	100	0	0	0		0.00	Jul-18
-3.71	-3.83	-4.84	7.56	24.87	4.15	0.55	10.65		41.48	55.2	0	99	0	1	10	-0.10	May-08
-6.59	-3.07	-10.34	20.27	-7.98	2.92	0.6	12.78		15.85	49.4	0	99	0	1	34	-0.86	Aug-12
-0.16	1.02	-1.53			3.65	0.28			18.91	91.5	8	0	92	0		-0.11	Oct-17
-5.46	-1.35	-10.07	41.53		2.29	0.35	15.26		23.71	8.7	0	99	0	1	37	0.02	Sep-15
-7.38	-3.94	-13.37	25.15	-10.41	3.39	0.6	13.45		13.43	6.2	0	100	0	0	91	-0.57	Aug-11
-7.46	-14.93	-26.72	-2.44	-19.55	0.46	0.59	15.5		20.46	332.2	0	100	0	0	27	-0.28	Sep-10
7.24	-3.06	-11.56	36.28	98.18	0.06	0.76	19.79		44.12	137.5	0	100	0	0	28	-0.11	Aug-11
2.06	-2.83	-23.54	17.64	19.63	0.83	0.76	22.38		11.96	31.7	0	99	0	1	54	-0.27	Aug-10
4.84	-11.07	-36.42	-3.33	31.73	1.12	0.77	28.65		14.94	16.3	0	99	0	1	107	-0.01	Jul-10
-14.60	-11.28	-13.05			3.01	0.4			23.47	7.0	1	99	0	0	66	0.08	Jun-16
-12.84	-10.04	-15.41			3.48	0.45			23.56	5.3	1	99	0	1	87	0.04	Jun-16
-15.78	-12.07	-11.40			2.4	0.35			24.20	4.3	1	99	0	0	55	0.52	Jun-16
-15.15	-16.69					0.13			41.26	3,109	0	100	0	0	7	0.02	Jun-18
-14.98	-8.93	1.66	32.14	59.04	1.19	0.13	12.2		98.99	13,593	0	100	0	0	23	0.01	Dec-98
-4.88	0.73	-8.01	9.04	34.98	2.66	0.13	9.91		50.78	10,300	0	100	0	0	12	-0.02	Dec-98
-23.09	-20.83					1				25.0						-0.14	May-18
-37.20	-26.78	-16.81	52.43		0	0.85	21.96			1,985						0.37	Jun-14
-9.88	-3.34	-13.99	-33.78		5.58	0.95	21.05			50.8						-0.05	Dec-14
-36.88	-32.30	-22.65			11.35	0.85				4.2						-0.18	Apr-17
6.93	3.13	-0.93	8.77	-1.38	5.48	0.65	9.62			38.1						-0.18	Jan-13
-23.31	-9.71	-31.26			17.47	0.85				14.1						1.64	May-16
-9.79	-7.74	-7.56			21.18	0.5				61.4						0.70	Jul-16
-2.25	-2.62	-2.46			4.53	0.84				7.0						-0.24	Sep-15
4.99	-3.86	-7.92	0.22	-31.94	6.62	0.65	15.77			27.4						-0.20	Apr-13
-12.53	-8.78	-24.14	0.54		8.29	0.7	20.82		13.14	9.9	0	100	0	0	20	0.46	Mar-15
-11.41	-9.56	-22.62	-21.54		0	0.79	19.08		22.39	1.2	0	100	0	0	16	-0.99	Oct-15
-19.32	-15.47	-18.00	-9.38	-40.41	5.09	0.95	18.01		12.05	94.4						0.00	Sep-13
-15.48	-15.48	-12.12	23.16		0	0.7	13.85		30.76	136.7						0.00	Sep-14

Fund Name	Ticker Symbol	Traded On	Overall Rating	Reward Rating	Risk Rating	Recent Up/ Downgrade	Price as of 12/31/2018	52-Week High	52-Week Low	Open to New Investors	Category & (Prospectus Objective)
Cushing® 30 MLP Index ETN	PPLN	NYSE Arca	D	D	D	Down	14.96	21.31	14.47	Y	Energy Sector Equity (Income)
CWA Income ETF	CWAI	BATS	D	D	D		24.19	25.67	23.93	Y	Cautious Allocation (Growth & Inc)
● Davis Select Financial ETF	DFNL	NAS CM	C+	B-	C	Down	20.50	25.51	20.12	Y	Financials Sector Equity (Financial)
Davis Select International ETF	DINT	NAS CM	U	U	U		15.08	20.49	14.59	Y	Global Equity Large Cap (Growth)
● Davis Select U.S. Equity ETF	DUSA	NAS CM	C+	B-	C	Down	20.02	25.81	19.43	Y	US Equity Large Cap Blend (Growth)
● Davis Select Worldwide ETF	DWLD	NAS CM	D+	C-	D	Down	19.55	28.88	19.39	Y	Global Equity Large Cap (World Stock)
DB Agriculture Double Long ETN	DAG	NYSE Arca	D-	D-	D-		2.16	3.13	2.07	Y	Trading Tools (Natl Res)
DB Agriculture Double Short ETN	AGATF	NYSE Arca	C-	C	E	Down	24.46	32.50	24.46	Y	Trading Tools (Natl Res)
DB Agriculture Long ETN	AGF	NYSE Arca	D	D	D		9.68	12.50	7.20	Y	Commodities Specified (Natl Res)
DB Agriculture Short ETN	ADZ	NYSE Arca	C-	C	E+	Down	37.00	37.00	21.13	Y	Trading Tools (Natl Res)
DB Base Metals Double Long ETN	BDD	NYSE Arca	D+	C-	D	Down	6.89	10.99	6.52	Y	Trading Tools (Natl Res)
DB Base Metals Double Short ETN	BOM	NYSE Arca	D	D+	E		8.91	12.41	6.00	Y	Trading Tools (Natl Res)
DB Base Metals Long ETN	BDG	NYSE Arca	U	U	U		16.29	16.29	11.84	Y	Commodities Industrial Metals (Natl Res)
DB Base Metals Short ETN	BOS	NYSE Arca	D	D+	E		20.69	22.02	15.12	Y	Trading Tools (Natl Res)
DB Commodity Double Long ETN	DYY	NYSE Arca	C-	C-	D+	Up	2.02	3.80	1.83	Y	Trading Tools (Natl Res)
DB Commodity Double Short ETN	DEE	NYSE Arca	D	D	E		55.00	77.00	55.00	Y	Trading Tools (Natl Res)
DB Commodity Long ETN	DPU	NYSE Arca	C	C-	C		9.15			Y	Commodities Broad Basket (Natl Res)
DB Commodity Short ETN	DDP	NYSE Arca	D	D	E		45.93	61.00	37.66	Y	Trading Tools (Natl Res)
DB Crude Oil Double Short ETN	DTO	NYSE Arca	D	D-	D		100.97	107.47	46.18	Y	Trading Tools (Natl Res)
DB Crude Oil Long ETN	OLO	NYSE Arca	C-	C-	D+	Down	4.38	7.14	4.23	Y	Commodities Specified (Natl Res)
DB Crude Oil Short ETN	SZO	NYSE Arca	D	D	E		82.67	82.81	44.71	Y	Trading Tools (Natl Res)
● DB Gold Double Long ETN	DGP	NYSE Arca	D	D	D	Down	23.12	27.04	19.73	Y	Trading Tools (Prec Metals)
DB Gold Double Short ETN	DZZ	NYSE Arca	C-	D+	D+	Up	5.80	6.75	4.93	Y	Trading Tools (Prec Metals)
DB Gold Short ETN	DGZ	NYSE Arca	C-	D+	D+		14.28	15.60	13.07	Y	Trading Tools (Prec Metals)
● Deep Value ETF	DVP	NYSE Arca	C	B	D		30.07	37.21	28.82	Y	US Equity Mid Cap (Growth & Inc)
Defiance Future Tech ETF	AUGR	NYSE Arca	U	U	U		19.66	25.73	18.77	Y	Technology Sector Equity (Growth & Inc)
Defiance Quantum ETF	QTUM	NYSE Arca	U	U	U		20.00	24.88	18.83	Y	Technology Sector Equity (Technology)
● DeltaShares S&P 400 Managed Risk ETF	DMRM	NYSE Arca	D	D+	D	Down	48.28	56.91	47.01	Y	US Equity Mid Cap (Growth)
● DeltaShares S&P 500 Managed Risk ETF	DMRL	NYSE Arca	D+	D+	D+		51.10	58.34	49.51	Y	US Equity Large Cap Blend (Growth)
DeltaShares S&P 600 Managed Risk ETF	DMRS	NYSE Arca	D	D+	D	Down	50.41	61.38	48.97	Y	US Equity Small Cap (Small Company)
● DeltaShares S&P International Managed Risk ETF	DMRI	NYSE Arca	D	D	D	Down	45.41	56.64	44.43	Y	Global Equity Large Cap (Foreign Stock)
Deutsche Bank FI Enhanced Global High Yield ETN	FIEG	NYSE Arca	D+	C-	D		155.50	204.00	106.78	Y	Global Equity Large Cap (Growth & Inc)
Diamond Hill Valuation-Weighted 500 ETF	DHVW	NYSE Arca	C-	C	D+	Down	28.60	34.79	27.65	Y	US Equity Large Cap Blend (Growth)
● Direxion All Cap Insider Sentiment Shares	KNOW	NYSE Arca	C-	C	C-	Down	33.66	43.61	32.19	Y	US Equity Mid Cap (Balanced)
● Direxion Auspice Broad Commodity Strategy ETF	COM	NYSE Arca	D+	D+	D+		23.98	26.10	23.78	Y	Commodities Broad Basket (Growth & Inc)
Direxion Daily 20+ Year Treasury Bear 1X Shares	TYBS	NYSE Arca	D+	D+	D	Down	20.28	22.00	19.92	Y	Trading Tools (Govt Bond - Treasury)
● Direxion Daily 20+ Year Treasury Bear 3X Shares	TMV	NYSE Arca	C-	D+	D+	Up	18.23	23.66	17.63	Y	Trading Tools (Govt Bond - Treasury)
● Direxion Daily 20+ Year Treasury Bull 3X Shares	TMF	NYSE Arca	D	D	D		19.37	22.11	15.21	Y	Trading Tools (Govt Bond - Treasury)
Direxion Daily 7-10 Year Treasury Bear 1X Shares	TYNS	NYSE Arca	D+	C-	E+	Down	28.11	29.47	28.11	Y	Trading Tools (Govt Bond - Treasury)
Direxion Daily 7-10 Year Treasury Bear 3X Shares	TYO	NYSE Arca	C-	D+	D+		13.82	15.99	13.82	Y	Trading Tools (Govt Bond - Treasury)
Direxion Daily 7-10 Year Treasury Bull 3X Shares	TYD	NYSE Arca	D	D	D		43.70	43.96	37.70	Y	Trading Tools (Govt Bond - Treasury)
● Direxion Daily Aerospace & Defense Bull 3X Shares Direxion	DFEN	NYSE Arca	C	C	C		29.66	63.35	24.66	Y	Trading Tools (Unaligned)
● Direxion Daily CSI 300 China A Share Bear 1X Shares	CHAD	NYSE Arca	C-	D+	C-	Up	39.78	41.12	27.72	Y	Trading Tools (Foreign Stock)
● Direxion Daily CSI 300 China A Share Bull 2X Shares	CHAU	NYSE Arca	D	D-	D	Down	14.44	37.42	14.17	Y	Trading Tools (Growth)
● Direxion Daily CSI China Internet Bull 2X Shares	CWEB	NYSE Arca	D	D	D	Down	18.70	68.87	18.29	Y	Trading Tools (Technology)
Direxion Daily Energy Bear 3X Shares	ERY	NYSE Arca	D	D	D		64.99	80.39	29.65	Y	Trading Tools (Natl Res)
● Direxion Daily Energy Bull 3X Shares	ERX	NYSE Arca	D	D	D	Down	15.15	43.69	12.78	Y	Trading Tools (Natl Res)
Direxion Daily EURO STOXX 50 (R) Bull 3X Shares Direxion D	EUXL	NYSE Arca	D	D-	D		13.08	33.18	11.90	Y	Trading Tools (Europe Stock)
● Direxion Daily Financial Bear 3X Shares	FAZ	NYSE Arca	D	D-	D	Up	13.57	16.62	8.88	Y	Trading Tools (Financial)
● Direxion Daily Financial Bull 3X Shares	FAS	NYSE Arca	C	C	C-		44.77	81.71	37.55	Y	Trading Tools (Financial)
● Direxion Daily FTSE China Bear 3X Shares	YANG	NYSE Arca	D	D-	D		66.67	77.18	36.30	Y	Trading Tools (Pacific Stock)
● Direxion Daily FTSE China Bull 3X Shares	YINN	NYSE Arca	D+	D+	D+	Down	17.39	53.80	16.54	Y	Trading Tools (Pacific Stock)

★ Expanded analysis of this fund is included in Section II: Analysis of All BUY Rated Funds. ● Expanded analysis of this fund is included in Section III: Analysis of All Rated Funds with Assets over $50 million.

			TOTAL RETURNS & PERFORMANCE						ASSETS		ASSET ALLOCATION & TURNOVER					VALUATION	
3-Month Total Return	6-Month Total Return	1-Year Total Return	3-Year Total Return	5-Year Total Return	Dividend Yield (TTM)	Expense Ratio	3-Yr Std Deviation	Effective Duration	NAV	Total Assets (MIL)	%Cash	%Stocks	%Bonds	%Other	Turnover Ratio	Premium/ Discount 1-Year Avg	Inception Date
-22.09	-17.49	-24.83			0	0.95			15.01	5.1						0.33	Jun-17
-1.63	-0.14	-2.61			2.81	0.75			24.24	8.6	4	20	77	0	6	-0.04	Mar-17
-13.73	-10.34	-10.79			0.41	0.65			20.64	156.7	0	100	0	0	13	0.25	Jan-17
-16.23	-20.08					0.75			15.09	65.3	0	98	0	0		0.39	Mar-18
-18.78	-14.57	-11.57			0.33	0.65			20.03	139.3	0	100	0	0	6	0.33	Jan-17
-20.08	-21.85	-22.09			0.08	0.65			19.60	226.0	0	100	0	0	14	0.20	Jan-17
0.28	0.22	-22.36	-32.56	-69.73	0	0.75	25.25			5.3					0	-0.30	Apr-08
0.16	0.16	23.38	24.82	88.77	0	0.75	25.31			0.37					0	-19.67	Apr-08
0.37	0.60	-10.48	-15.31	-41.00	0	0.75	12.61			0.90					0	-3.56	Apr-08
0.31	0.56	12.55	14.78	46.60	0	0.75	12.67			0.26					0	-0.93	Apr-08
-13.94	-20.06	-36.44	63.20	-19.30	0	0.75	29.65			1.8					0	0.66	Jun-08
15.13	22.84	51.24	-52.74	-21.35	0	0.75	29.79			0.75					0	-4.25	Jun-08
3.68	12.99	11.74	-14.25	-23.44	0	0.75	14.43			0.38					0	-0.10	Jun-08
7.71	11.65	24.63	-28.27	-6.26	0	0.75	14.94			0.66					0	-1.62	Jun-08
-42.19	-32.93	-24.15	-0.65	-75.58	0	0.75	27.8			1.1					0	12.47	Apr-08
60.57	45.78	24.33	-14.95	156.50	0	0.75	29.97			0.29					0	9.25	Apr-08
-22.84	-16.72	-10.95	3.05	-47.08	0	0.75	13.89			0.18					0	-8.54	Apr-08
28.02	22.24	13.52	-4.50	70.77	0	0.75	15			0.49					0	0.36	Apr-08
128.38	97.20	19.60	-35.35	189.45	0	0.75	57.32			28.2					0	1.94	Jun-08
-38.64	-30.41	-16.57	-6.02	-68.12	0	0.75	25.15			4.8					0	-0.71	Jun-08
55.43	45.16	15.01	-9.67	113.63	0	0.75	28.66			1.2					0	-1.21	Jun-08
14.59	3.93	-8.29	26.87	-7.93	0	0.75	25.54			77.5					0	0.02	Feb-08
-12.86	-3.72	8.99	-34.41	-24.61	0	0.75	25.63			21.0					0	-0.07	Feb-08
-6.35	-1.35	5.35	-16.39	-9.27	0	0.75	12.84			10.9					0	0.05	Feb-08
-12.88	-11.76	-5.48	50.09		2.47	0.59	15.26		30.20	190.4	0	100	0	0	126	0.12	Sep-14
-22.25						0.4			19.62	2.2	0	100	0	0		-0.20	Jul-18
-18.63						0.65			19.96	3.3	0	100	0	0		-0.07	Sep-18
-12.65	-10.16	-9.18			1.22	0.45			48.30	106.2	1	65	34	0	6	0.35	Jul-17
-11.51	-4.72	-4.16			1.19	0.35			51.23	405.8	3	66	31	0	2	0.34	Jul-17
-13.82	-12.01	-5.91			0.72	0.45			50.35	43.1	1	60	39	0	21	0.35	Jul-17
-11.56	-9.22	-13.30			2.68	0.5			44.94	207.9	2	92	7	0	3	1.00	Jul-17
-15.89	-8.39	-14.88	32.06	29.48	0	0.1	14.64			7.2						-5.72	Oct-13
-14.67	-8.66	-6.19	30.42	48.66	1.56	0.1	9.88		28.75	24.4	0	100	0	0	32	0.09	Dec-11
-17.22	-15.53	-14.78	13.41	38.40	4.25	0.59	10.36		33.77	188.3	0	100	0	0	932	0.03	Dec-11
-5.81	-2.56	-1.91			0.64	0.7			23.97	52.3	92	0	0	8	0	0.06	Mar-17
-4.29	-0.20	3.59	-8.65	-31.79	0.9	0.48	9.85		20.36	5.5	103	0	0	-3	0	0.04	Mar-11
-13.58	-3.08	5.67	-33.51	-75.01	0.25	1.02	29.71		18.43	346.0	124	0	-2	-22	0	0.08	Apr-09
13.84	0.33	-12.06	4.40	83.30	1.67	1.11	28.99	17.03	19.22	90.5	38	0	62	0	66	-0.10	Apr-09
-3.59	-2.19	0.56	-4.47	-17.18	0.87	0.48	4.78		28.15	1.5	102	0	-2	0	0	-0.06	Mar-11
-10.46	-7.40	-0.85	-16.93	-46.38	0.15	1.07	14.26		13.84	20.4	110	0	-5	-5	0	-0.13	Apr-09
11.28	7.47	-0.70	4.70	35.88	0.82	1.09	13.96	7.41	43.25	5.8	36	0	69	-5	134	0.04	Apr-09
-52.65	-33.45	-32.70			2.13	0.97			29.67	56.4	31	69	0	0	7	0.05	May-17
11.58	9.01	28.76	-4.94		0.52	0.85	20.29		39.81	93.0	109	-9	0	0	0	-0.03	Jun-15
-24.83	-25.98	-51.17	-37.29		0.38	1.04	41.16		14.41	83.8	93	7	0	0	1,747	0.04	Apr-15
-40.40	-60.96	-62.79			0.77	1.36			18.78	56.5	89	11	0	0	0	-0.07	Nov-16
109.56	86.62	43.71	-55.76	-35.53	0.35	1.07	55.25		64.63	32.4	102	-2	0	0	0	-0.04	Nov-08
-60.89	-57.97	-55.83	-33.79	-82.69	2.55	1.1	55.91		15.15	365.4	37	63	0	0	59	0.02	Nov-08
-36.83	-38.03	-48.99			2.49	1.18			13.15	2.3	48	52	0	0	70	0.26	Jul-17
39.91	24.25	16.26	-66.83	-84.13	0.35	1.1	33.08		13.56	135.0	114	-14	0	0	0	-0.05	Nov-08
-36.04	-29.22	-33.59	55.90	100.55	0.89	1.02	36.88		44.80	1,708	29	71	0	0	4	0.02	Nov-08
18.14	4.82	12.95	-73.01	-87.24	0.3	1.09	52.32		66.66	85.7	108	-8	0	0	0	0.09	Dec-09
-27.69	-26.61	-48.50	0.22	-40.79	2.4	1.34	56.74		17.42	325.6	46	54	0	0	112	-0.05	Dec-09

Fund Name	Ticker Symbol	Traded On	Overall Rating	Reward Rating	Risk Rating	Recent Up/ Downgrade	Price as of 12/31/2018	52-Week High	52-Week Low	Open to New Investors	Category & (Prospectus Objective)
			MARKET					**PRICE**			**CATEGORY & OBJECTIVE**
Direxion Daily FTSE Europe Bull 3X Shares	EURL	NYSE Arca	D	D+	D	Down	20.00	46.84	18.27	Y	Trading Tools (Europe Stock)
● Direxion Daily Gold Miners Index Bear 3X Shares	DUST	NYSE Arca	D+	D	D	Up	22.86	46.37	19.61	Y	Trading Tools (Prec Metals)
● Direxion Daily Gold Miners Index Bull 3X Shares	NUGT	NYSE Arca	E+	E+	D-	Down	17.50	36.98	11.14	Y	Trading Tools (Prec Metals)
● Direxion Daily Healthcare Bull 3X Shares	CURE	NYSE Arca	C	C	C		47.59	67.75	39.11	Y	Trading Tools (Health)
Direxion Daily High Yield Bear 2X Shares	HYDD	NYSE Arca	C-	D+	D+	Up	20.05	20.91	17.65	Y	Trading Tools (Corp Bond-High Yld)
Direxion Daily Homebuilders & Supplies Bull 3X Shares	NAIL	NYSE Arca	C-	C	D+	Down	23.96	109.00	20.86	Y	Trading Tools (Unaligned)
Direxion Daily Industrials Bull 3X Shares Direxion Daily I	DUSL	NYSE Arca	D	D	D	Down	19.51	43.97	16.62	Y	Trading Tools (Unaligned)
Direxion Daily Japan Bull 3X Shares	JPNL	NYSE Arca	D+	D+	D+	Down	42.50	96.48	38.77	Y	Trading Tools (Foreign Stock)
● Direxion Daily Junior Gold Miners Index Bear 3X Shares	JDST	NYSE Arca	D	D	D	Up	50.27	89.22	43.66	Y	Trading Tools (Prec Metals)
● Direxion Daily Junior Gold Miners Index Bull 3X Shares	JNUG	NYSE Arca	E+	E+	D-	Down	9.21	19.96	6.23	Y	Trading Tools (Prec Metals)
Direxion Daily Latin America Bull 3X Shares	LBJ	NYSE Arca	D+	C-	D+	Up	19.31	48.95	17.05	Y	Trading Tools (Foreign Stock)
Direxion Daily Mid Cap Bear 3X Shares	MIDZ	NYSE Arca	D	D-	D	Up	17.57	21.19	10.06	Y	Trading Tools (Growth)
● Direxion Daily Mid Cap Bull 3X Shares	MIDU	NYSE Arca	C-	C	C-	Down	28.04	55.59	23.80	Y	Trading Tools (Growth)
● Direxion Daily MSCI Brazil Bull 3X Shares	BRZU	NYSE Arca	D+	C-	D	Up	24.97	63.39	14.42	Y	Trading Tools (Foreign Stock)
Direxion Daily MSCI Developed Markets Bear 3X Shares	DPK	NYSE Arca	C-	D	D+	Up	18.17	20.08	10.15	Y	Trading Tools (Foreign Stock)
Direxion Daily MSCI Developed Markets Bull 3X Shares	DZK	NYSE Arca	D	D+	D	Down	45.80	100.42	42.05	Y	Trading Tools (Foreign Stock)
● Direxion Daily MSCI Emerging Markets Bear 3X Shares	EDZ	NYSE Arca	D+	D	D	Up	59.74	70.95	33.35	Y	Trading Tools (Div Emerg Mkts)
● Direxion Daily MSCI Emerging Markets Bull 3X Shares	EDC	NYSE Arca	D+	C-	D	Down	62.79	168.60	57.53	Y	Trading Tools (Div Emerg Mkts)
Direxion Daily MSCI European Financials Bull 2X Shares	EUFL	NYSE Arca	D	D+	D		23.90	55.50	22.78	Y	Trading Tools (Financial)
● Direxion Daily MSCI India Bull 3x Shares	INDL	NYSE Arca	D+	D+	D		66.96	119.33	46.97	Y	Trading Tools (Foreign Stock)
Direxion Daily MSCI Mexico Bull 3X Shares Direxion Daily M	MEXX	NYSE Arca	D-	D-	D	Down	9.60	26.87	7.44	Y	Trading Tools (Foreign Stock)
Direxion Daily MSCI Real Estate Bear 3X Shares	DRV	NYSE Arca	D	D-	D		10.95	15.50	8.33	Y	Trading Tools (Real Estate)
Direxion Daily MSCI Real Estate Bull 3X Shares	DRN	NYSE Arca	C-	C-	C-		16.65	24.07	14.85	Y	Trading Tools (Real Estate)
Direxion Daily Natural Gas Related Bear 3X Shares	GASX	NYSE Arca	D+	D	D	Up	53.14	68.64	15.63		Trading Tools (Natl Res)
Direxion Daily Natural Gas Related Bull 3X Shares	GASL	NYSE Arca	D-	D-	D	Down	5.13	31.28	4.29	Y	Trading Tools (Natl Res)
Direxion Daily Pharmaceutical & Medical Bull 3X Shares ETF	PILL	NYSE Arca	D+	C-	D		21.29	38.03	17.94	Y	Trading Tools (Growth & Inc)
Direxion Daily Regional Banks Bear 3X Shares	WDRW	NYSE Arca	D	D	D		47.67	56.36	19.86	Y	Trading Tools (Financial)
Direxion Daily Regional Banks Bull 3X Shares	DPST	NYSE Arca	D+	C-	D+	Down	31.08	94.50	26.92	Y	Trading Tools (Financial)
Direxion Daily Retail Bull 3X Shares	RETL	NYSE Arca	D+	D+	D	Down	23.17	51.92	19.42	Y	Trading Tools (Unaligned)
Direxion Daily Robotics, Artificial Intelligence & Automat	UBOT	NYSE Arca	U	U	U		7.05	23.72	6.09	Y	Trading Tools (Technology)
Direxion Daily Russia Bear 3X Shares	RUSS	NYSE Arca	D	E+	D	Up	20.46	24.37	14.47	Y	Trading Tools (Foreign Stock)
● Direxion Daily Russia Bull 3X Shares	RUSL	NYSE Arca	D+	D+	D+		29.81	73.38	28.52	Y	Trading Tools (Foreign Stock)
Direxion Daily S&P 500® Bear 1X Shares	SPDN	NYSE Arca	D+	D	D+	Up	31.84	34.17	27.53	Y	Trading Tools (Growth)
● Direxion Daily S&P 500® Bear 3X Shares	SPXS	NYSE Arca	D	D-	D-	Up	30.79	38.16	21.06	Y	Trading Tools (Growth)
Direxion Daily S&P 500® Bull 2X Shares	SPUU	NYSE Arca	C-	C	D+	Down	40.58	59.00	36.67	Y	Trading Tools (Growth)
● Direxion Daily S&P Biotech Bear 3X Shares	LABD	NYSE Arca	D	E+	D	Up	42.78	59.28	21.65	Y	Trading Tools (Technology)
● Direxion Daily S&P Biotech Bull 3X Shares	LABU	NYSE Arca	D	D	D	Down	32.86	114.79	25.21	Y	Trading Tools (Technology)
Direxion Daily S&P Oil & Gas Exp. & Prod. Bear 3X Shares	DRIP	NYSE Arca	D	D-	D		17.59	25.44	4.94	Y	Trading Tools (Natl Res)
● Direxion Daily S&P Oil & Gas Exp. & Prod. Bull 3X Shares	GUSH	NYSE Arca	D	D	D	Down	7.80	45.19	6.21	Y	Trading Tools (Natl Res)
● Direxion Daily S&P500® Bull 3X Shares	SPXL	NYSE Arca	C	C	C	Down	32.90	55.38	27.54	Y	Trading Tools (Growth)
● Direxion Daily Semiconductor Bear 3X Shares	SOXS	NYSE Arca	D	E+	D-	Up	13.19	16.99	8.89	Y	Trading Tools (Technology)
● Direxion Daily Semiconductor Bull 3X Shares	SOXL	NYSE Arca	C	C	D+	Down	83.32	201.20	67.00	Y	Trading Tools (Technology)
● Direxion Daily Small Cap Bear 3X Shares	TZA	NYSE Arca	D	D-	D	Up	15.22	18.62	7.85	Y	Trading Tools (Small Company)
Direxion Daily Small Cap Bull 2X Shares	SMLL	NYSE Arca	D+	C	D	Down	35.70	63.35	32.10	Y	Trading Tools (Small Company)
● Direxion Daily Small Cap Bull 3X Shares	TNA	NYSE Arca	C-	C	D+	Down	42.09	96.51	35.43	Y	Trading Tools (Small Company)
Direxion Daily South Korea Bull 3X Shares	KORU	NYSE Arca	D+	D+	D	Down	24.76	72.85	22.44	Y	Trading Tools (Pacific Stock)
Direxion Daily Technology Bear 3X Shares	TECS	NYSE Arca	D-	E+	D-		27.66	36.50	17.85	Y	Trading Tools (Technology)
● Direxion Daily Technology Bull 3X Shares	TECL	NYSE Arca	C	C	C-	Down	85.00	171.14	68.96	Y	Trading Tools (Technology)
Direxion Daily Total Bond Market Bear 1X Shares	SAGG	NYSE Arca	D+	C-	E+	Down	31.58	32.50	31.12	Y	Trading Tools (Govt Bond - Treasury)
Direxion Daily Transportation Bull 3X Shares	TPOR	NYSE Arca	C+	B	C	Up	18.85	42.06	16.14	Y	Trading Tools (Utility)
Direxion Daily Utilities Bull 3X Shares	UTSL	NYSE Arca	D+	D	C-	Up	26.50	32.81	20.02	Y	Trading Tools (Utility)
● Direxion NASDAQ-100® Equal Weighted Index Shares	QQQE	NYSE Arca	C	C	C-		40.56	47.92	38.25	Y	US Equity Large Cap Growth (Growth)

★ Expanded analysis of this fund is included in Section II: Analysis of All BUY Rated Funds. ● Expanded analysis of this fund is included in Section III: Analysis of All Rated Funds with Assets over $50 million.

3-Month Total Return	6-Month Total Return	1-Year Total Return	3-Year Total Return	5-Year Total Return	Dividend Yield (TTM)	Expense Ratio	3-Yr Std Deviation	Effective Duration	NAV	Total Assets (MIL)	%Cash	%Stocks	%Bonds	%Other	Turnover Ratio	Premium/Discount 1-Year Avg	Inception Date
-37.00	-36.14	-46.33	-15.57		2.76	1.06	37.53		20.03	42.7	51	48	0	0	0	0.00	Jan-14
-41.18	-7.77	-2.92	-97.20	-98.95	0.18	1.08	95.37		22.95	115.3	153	-3	0	-50	0	-0.01	Dec-10
34.91	-26.40	-44.78	-10.01	-92.02	0.49	1.2	123.28		17.45	1,067	80	28	0	-8	234	0.17	Dec-10
-29.36	4.31	2.91	43.82	178.47	0.42	1.09	38.02		47.62	187.1	19	81	0	0	23	-0.03	Jun-11
11.17	4.29	8.04			0.57	0.89			20.00	3.8	101	0	0	-1	0	-0.09	Jun-16
-42.63	-56.30	-73.87	-12.89		0.07	1.12	56.17		24.07	40.4	53	47	0	0	164	0.15	Aug-15
-48.53	-31.93	-44.90			1.23	1.08			19.86	5.8					111	0.51	May-17
-43.01	-33.08	-44.90	-6.00	-19.14	0.25	1.21	31.67		42.54	13.8	53	47	0	0	0	-0.02	Jun-13
-35.78	-3.17	-1.45	-99.14	-99.89	0.24	1.1	101.32		50.40	62.7	135	0	0	-35	0	-0.14	Oct-13
23.89	-30.47	-48.22	-25.84	-96.95	0	1.18	144.57		9.20	583.1	107	24	0	-31	245	0.13	Oct-13
-11.06	4.37	-39.16	64.01	-77.40	1.03	1.23	80.52		19.32	11.1	48	55	0	-3	58	0.01	Dec-09
62.61	49.97	29.73	-61.15	-75.98	0.13	1.09	35.02		17.53	4.0	122	-22	0	0	0	-0.37	Jan-09
-45.26	-41.54	-38.94	41.71	48.29	0.24	1.08	35.88		28.12	64.5	38	62	0	0	130	0.02	Jan-09
35.55	44.63	-37.21	121.03	-87.40	1.46	1.29	108.08		25.03	352.1	21	79	0	0	42	-0.03	Apr-13
46.81	36.15	47.98	-41.03	-44.88	0.36	1.1	31		18.13	5.2	101	-1	0	0	0	-0.10	Dec-08
-36.15	-32.79	-43.42	-5.31	-36.49	2.18	1.12	32.36		45.99	19.4	58	42	0	0	87	-0.05	Dec-08
17.32	13.43	32.61	-74.43	-69.97	0.29	1.12	42.16		59.80	87.1	113	-13	0	0	0	0.00	Dec-08
-26.10	-28.78	-49.96	37.09	-44.90	1.12	1.26	47.58		62.73	228.9	48	52	0	0	38	0.04	Dec-08
-28.43	-29.21	-45.04			16.9	1.09			24.02	8.4					190	0.95	Jul-16
3.30	-6.37	-33.91	26.83	23.51	0.46	1.36	55.16		67.54	102.1	39	61	0	0	15	-0.10	Mar-10
-53.01	-36.94	-52.19			6.14	1.12			9.57	10.7	67	33	0	0	647	0.02	May-17
14.67	11.66	4.97	-43.81	-82.90	0.38	1.09	36.03		10.95	18.5	119	-19	0	0	0	0.06	Jul-09
-20.67	-20.90	-25.02	-8.48	82.45	2.69	1.08	38.98		16.67	44.6	10	90	0	0	113	-0.02	Jul-09
197.30	192.76	125.70	-75.35		0.27	1.08			52.77	4.1	102	-2	0	-1	0	-0.06	Dec-15
-76.17	-77.71	-79.73	-91.69	-99.96	0	1.06	90.02		5.14	30.8	71	29	0	0	48	0.00	Jul-10
-38.63	-25.94	-19.57			0.35	1.12			21.54	4.7	21	68	11	0		0.74	Nov-17
77.68	98.66	53.81	-74.66		0.36	1.07	54.13		47.23	3.0	147	-47	0	0	0	-0.74	Aug-15
-52.39	-59.18	-56.21	-0.87		1.13	1.16	63.06		31.37	35.3	14	86	0	0	184	0.05	Aug-15
-50.18	-44.16	-35.02	-36.17	20.04	0.72	1.12	43.05		23.26	27.5	32	68	0	0	659	0.07	Jul-10
-64.45	-59.72					1.22			7.06	5.2	54	51	-5	0		0.27	Apr-18
27.36	6.03	-10.30	-88.99	-90.77	0.32	1.13	51.01		20.46	21.3	106	-6	0	0	0	0.01	May-11
-31.73	-28.31	-40.05	36.15	-91.80	3.56	1.28	56.94		29.82	136.3	56	44	0	0	65	0.04	May-11
15.70	8.22	5.34			1.16	0.56			31.86	13.1	102	-2	0	0	0	-0.08	Jun-16
46.52	18.34	3.39	-63.19	-81.30	0.32	1.1	26.22		30.92	257.3	104	-4	0	0	7	-0.03	Nov-08
-27.25	-16.15	-13.56	51.31		1.68	0.67	19.06		41.13	6.7	1	99	0	0	363	0.10	May-14
66.66	64.62	-7.45	-86.25		0.47	1.11	111.28		42.50	53.6	117	-17	0	0	0	-0.04	May-15
-62.76	-66.28	-57.27	-60.71		0.22	1.08	86.13		33.03	677.5	96	4	0	0	642	0.02	May-15
233.37	182.03	49.10	-83.13		0.38	1.07	90.91		17.54	42.0	114	-14	0	0	0	-0.11	May-15
-80.87	-78.99	-73.46	-75.74		0.06	1.15	97.89		7.79	156.4	67	33	0	0	350	0.11	May-15
-39.74	-25.99	-24.86	66.11	116.39	0.52	1.04	29.08		32.86	1,124	23	77	0	0	99	0.04	Nov-08
36.67	17.72	-19.62	-93.39	-98.23	0.36	1.11	52.4		13.16	62.2	108	0	-8	0	0	-0.02	Mar-10
-46.29	-41.69	-38.94	229.33	412.13	0.86	1.02	59.26		83.40	616.1	36	64	0	0	17	0.00	Mar-10
73.87	66.89	24.79	-65.79	-77.40	0.42	1.1	43.15		15.20	264.1	105	-5	0	0	0	-0.06	Nov-08
-36.62	-35.33	-25.77	33.59		6.13	0.72	29.33		35.90	3.1	5	95	0	0	109	0.64	Jul-14
-50.77	-49.78	-39.94	32.41	9.74	0.19	1.1	44.13		42.19	949.9	40	60	0	0	185	-0.02	Nov-08
-36.87	-34.48	-59.94	15.43	-54.02	2.12	1.28	56.2		24.75	25.2	59	41	0	0	88	0.07	Apr-13
53.83	16.93	-19.51	-82.08	-93.35	0.53	1.1	34.52		27.69	31.7	118	-18	0	0	0	-0.05	Dec-08
-49.94	-38.03	-24.04	133.94	272.89	0.44	1.09	41.3		84.92	626.7	28	74	-2	0	0	0.01	Dec-08
-0.92	-0.13	2.80	-2.66	-10.41	0.9	0.5	2.92		31.63	3.2	80	0	-1	21	0	0.02	Mar-11
-51.40	-37.91	-44.46			9.86	1.02			18.92	11.3	32	68	0	0	0	0.18	May-17
0.83	1.82	-1.24			1.78	1.09			26.59	3.1	39	61	0	0	86	0.13	May-17
-13.73	-9.71	-4.92	28.76	57.59	0.7	0.35	11.94		40.69	187.7	0	100	0	0	31	0.07	Mar-12

Fund Name	Ticker Symbol	Traded On	Overall Rating	Reward Rating	Risk Rating	Recent Up/Downgrade	Price as of 12/31/2018	52-Week High	52-Week Low	Open to New Investors	Category & (Prospectus Objective)
● Direxion Zacks MLP High Income Index Shares	ZMLP	NYSE Arca	C	B-	D		11.85	17.82	11.78	Y	Energy Sector Equity (Income)
Eaton Vance Floating-Rate NextShares	EVFTC	NAS CM	D+	D	D+		9.57	100.05	9.56	Y	US Fixed Income (Income)
Eaton Vance Global Income Builder NextShares™	EVGBC	NAS CM	D+	C-	D	Down	8.87	100.02	8.62	Y	Moderate Allocation (Income)
Eaton Vance Oaktree Diversified Credit NextShares	OKDCC	NAS CM	D+	D	C-		9.63	100.10	9.62	Y	Global Fixed Income (Growth & Inc)
Eaton Vance Stock NextShares™	EVSTC	NAS CM	C-	C	D	Down	11.67	100.02	10.97	Y	US Equity Large Cap Blend (Growth)
Eaton Vance TABS 5-to-15 Year Ladder Muni Bond NextShares™	EVLMC	NAS CM	C-	D+	C-		10.00	99.97	9.78	Y	US Muni Fixed Inc (Muni Bond - Natl)
ELEMENTS Dogs of the Dow - Dow Jones High Yld Select 10 To	DOD	NYSE Arca	C	B	D+		22.74	28.58	21.22	Y	US Equity Large Cap Value (Growth)
ELEMENTS Linked to SPECTRUM Large Cap U.S. Sector Momentum	EEH	NYSE Arca	D+	C-	D		18.23	23.75	17.94	Y	US Equity Large Cap Blend (Growth)
ELEMENTS - MLCX Biofuels Ind (Exchange Series) - Total Ret	FUE	NYSE Arca	D-	D-	E	Down	6.34	8.10	5.58	Y	Commodities Specified (Natl Res)
ELEMENTS Linked to the MLCX Grains Index - Total Return	GRU	NYSE Arca	D	D	D		3.26	3.88	3.20	Y	Commodities Specified (Natl Res)
ELEMENTS - Morningstar Wide Moat Focus Total Ret Ind	WMW	NYSE Arca	C	C	D+		29.87	33.66	28.39	Y	US Equity Large Cap Blend (Growth)
● ELEMENTS - Rogers Intl Commod Ind - Agriculture Total Ret	RJA	NYSE Arca	D	D	D		5.60	6.44	5.59	Y	Commodities Specified (Natl Res)
ELEMENTS - Rogers Intl Commodity Ind - Energy Total Ret	RJN	NYSE Arca	C-	C-	C-		2.46	3.61	2.45	Y	Commodities Specified (Natl Res)
ELEMENTS - Rogers Intl Commodity Ind - Metals Total Ret	RJZ	NYSE Arca	D+	D+	D+	Down	7.73	9.14	7.45	Y	Commodities Specified (Natl Res)
● ELEMENTS - Rogers Intl Commodity Ind - Total Ret	RJI	NYSE Arca	C-	C-	C	Down	4.89	5.88	4.87	Y	Commodities Broad Basket (Natl Res)
● EMQQ The Emerging Markets Internet & Ecommerce ETF	EMQQ	NYSE Arca	C-	C	D	Down	26.71	43.50	26.22	Y	Global Emerg Mkts Equity (Div Emerg Mkts)
● Energy Select Sector SPDR® Fund	XLE	NYSE Arca	C	B-	C-	Down	57.35	78.91	53.84	Y	Energy Sector Equity (Natl Res)
Equbot AI Powered International Equity ETF	AIIQ	NYSE Arca	U	U	U		20.95	25.45	20.05	Y	Global Equity Large Cap (Technology)
EquityCompass Risk Manager ETF	ERM	NYSE Arca	D+	D+	D+		19.93	23.74	18.96	Y	US Equity Large Cap Blend (Growth)
● EquityCompass Tactical Risk Manager ETF	TERM	NYSE Arca	D+	D+	D+		20.06	23.80	19.01	Y	US Equity Large Cap Blend (Growth)
● ERShares Entrepreneur 30 ETF	ENTR	NYSE Arca	C+	B	C-		14.01	18.84	13.02	Y	US Equity Large Cap Growth (Growth & Inc)
ETF Industry Exposure & Financial Services ETF	TETF	NYSE Arca	C+	B	C	Down	16.07	21.53	15.14	Y	Financials Sector Equity (Growth & Inc)
● ETFMG Alternative Harvest ETF	MJ	NYSE Arca	C	C-	C	Up	24.94	43.01	23.66	Y	Misc (Unaligned)
ETFMG Drone Economy Strategy ETF	IFLY	NYSE Arca	C-	C-	D+	Down	29.35	39.50	28.19	Y	Global Eq Mid/Small Cap (Growth & Inc)
● ETFMG Prime Cyber Security ETF	HACK	NYSE Arca	C	C	C		33.70	40.58	30.95	Y	Technology Sector Equity (Growth)
ETFMG Prime Junior Silver ETF	SILJ	NYSE Arca	D+	C-	D	Down	8.04	12.30	7.49	Y	Prec Metals (Prec Metals)
★ ETFMG Prime Mobile Payments ETF	IPAY	NYSE Arca	B-	B	C+	Up	34.95	43.27	32.45	Y	Equity Misc (Growth & Inc)
● ETFMG Video Game Tech ETF	GAMR	NYSE Arca	D+	D+	C-	Down	38.90	54.26	37.44	Y	Technology Sector Equity (Technology)
Ethereum Classic Investment Trust	ETCG	OTC BB	D-	D-	D	Down	6.65	59.99	5.05	Y	Trading Tools (Growth & Inc)
Etho Climate Leadership U.S. ETF	ETHO	NYSE Arca	C-	C-	D+	Down	32.01	38.09	30.11	Y	US Equity Mid Cap (Growth & Inc)
ETRACS 2xMonthly Pay Leveraged Preferred Stock Index ETN	PFFL	NYSE Arca	U	U	U		21.84	25.11	20.90	Y	Trading Tools (Growth)
EventShares U.S. Policy Alpha ETF	PLCY	BATS	D	D	D+		19.00	23.25	18.32	Y	Long/Short Equity (Growth & Inc)
● Fidelity® Corporate Bond ETF	FCOR	NYSE Arca	D+	D+	D+	Down	47.65	50.94	46.30	Y	US Fixed Income (Corp Bond - Gen)
● Fidelity® Dividend ETF for Rising Rates	FDRR	NYSE Arca	C	C	C+	Up	28.68	32.73	27.18	Y	US Equity Large Cap Value (Growth & Inc)
● Fidelity® High Dividend ETF	FDVV	NYSE Arca	C	C	C-		27.28	31.10	26.00	Y	US Equity Large Cap Value (Growth & Inc)
Fidelity® High Yield Factor ETF	FDHY	NYSE Arca	U	U	U		48.00	50.63	47.35	Y	US Fixed Income (Corp Bond-High Yld)
Fidelity® International High Dividend ETF	FIDI	NYSE Arca	U	U	U		19.55	25.55	18.75	Y	Global Equity Large Cap (Equity-Income)
Fidelity® International Value Factor ETF	FIVA	NYSE Arca	U	U	U		19.87	25.59	19.24	Y	Global Equity Large Cap (Growth & Inc)
● Fidelity® Limited Term Bond ETF	FLTB	NYSE Arca	C-	C-	C-		49.39	50.11	49.01	Y	US Fixed Income (Income)
Fidelity® Low Duration Bond Factor ETF	FLDR	NYSE Arca	U	U	U		49.80	50.57	49.79	Y	US Fixed Income (Growth & Inc)
● Fidelity® Low Volatility Factor ETF	FDLO	NYSE Arca	C	C	C-	Up	30.01	33.98	28.31	Y	US Equity Large Cap Blend (Growth & Inc)
● Fidelity® Momentum Factor ETF	FDMO	NYSE Arca	C	C	C-		29.65	35.53	27.72	Y	US Equity Large Cap Growth (Growth & Inc)
● Fidelity® MSCI Communication Services Index ETF	FCOM	NYSE Arca	C+	B	C-	Up	28.49	31.90	26.75	Y	Communications Sector Equity (Comm)
● Fidelity® MSCI Consumer Discretionary Index ETF	FDIS	NYSE Arca	C	C+	C	Down	38.32	45.63	35.51	Y	Consumer Goods & Svcs (Unaligned)
● Fidelity® MSCI Consumer Staples Index ETF	FSTA	NYSE Arca	C+	B	C	Up	30.50	35.42	29.30	Y	Consumer Goods & Svcs (Unaligned)
● Fidelity® MSCI Energy Index ETF	FENY	NYSE Arca	C	C	C-	Down	15.62	22.04	14.63	Y	Energy Sector Equity (Natl Res)
● Fidelity® MSCI Financials Index ETF	FNCL	NYSE Arca	C	C	C+	Down	34.56	43.73	32.43	Y	Financials Sector Equity (Financial)
● Fidelity® MSCI Health Care Index ETF	FHLC	NYSE Arca	C+	C+	C		41.32	46.93	38.79	Y	Healthcare Sector Equity (Health)
● Fidelity® MSCI Industrials Index ETF	FIDU	NYSE Arca	C	C	C	Down	32.76	41.16	30.66	Y	Industrials Sector Equity (Unaligned)
● Fidelity® MSCI Information Technology Index ETF	FTEC	NYSE Arca	C+	C+	C+	Down	49.24	60.66	45.74	Y	Technology Sector Equity (Technology)
● Fidelity® MSCI Materials Index ETF	FMAT	NYSE Arca	C	C	C-	Down	28.39	37.07	26.67	Y	Natural Resources (Natl Res)
● Fidelity® MSCI Real Estate Index ETF	FREL	NYSE Arca	C	C	C+	Down	22.39	25.35	21.52	Y	Real Estate Sector Equity (Real Estate)

★ Expanded analysis of this fund is included in Section II: Analysis of All BUY Rated Funds.   ● Expanded analysis of this fund is included in Section III: Analysis of All Rated Funds with Assets over $50 million.

3-Month Total Return	6-Month Total Return	1-Year Total Return	3-Year Total Return	5-Year Total Return	Dividend Yield (TTM)	Expense Ratio	3-Yr Std Deviation	Effective Duration	NAV	Total Assets (MIL)	%Cash	%Stocks	%Bonds	%Other	Turnover Ratio	Premium/ Discount 1-Year Avg	Inception Date
-21.58	-14.11	-16.81	-8.15		8.61	0.65	21.66		11.90	53.0	0	100	0	0	86	0.03	Jan-14
-2.55	-0.62	1.73			3.87	0.73		0.21	9.57	5.3	8	1	91	0		0.04	Nov-17
-10.81	-7.18	-8.20			11.43	0.91			8.87	6.2	2	57	37	1	143	0.00	Mar-16
-2.89	-0.92	-0.15			4.19	0.9			9.63	49.8	11	0	80	2		0.12	Nov-17
-16.19	-10.24	-8.00	-37.85		0.22	0.65			11.67	6.1	0	100	0	0	101	0.00	Feb-16
1.80	1.62	0.50			2.13	0.35		5.40	10.00	6.9	3	0	97	0	35	0.00	Mar-16
-6.11	3.53	-9.99	46.83	65.91	0	0.75	13.99			49.2					0	0.00	Nov-07
-0.30	-12.84	-8.35	14.59	30.41	0	0.75	13.34			4.0					0	-0.07	Aug-07
5.66	2.06	-9.42	-14.32	-36.40	0	0.75	12.78			1.1					0	0.00	Feb-08
-0.60	-0.75	-1.91	-20.38	-43.25	0	0.75	17.27			4.4					0	0.01	Feb-08
-11.99	-5.85	-1.61	44.65	50.33	0	0.75	13.58			31.9					0	0.00	Oct-07
-2.09	-4.41	-6.50	-10.52	-29.78	0	0.75	9.62			114.2					0	0.00	Oct-07
-30.96	-24.56	-11.76	8.11	-64.53	0	0.75	25.99			20.3					0	-0.01	Oct-07
-1.53	-6.88	-13.66	18.98	-12.68	0	0.75	12.5			12.1					0	0.00	Oct-07
-14.38	-12.85	-9.62	6.31	-40.19	0	0.75	11.23			375.5					0	0.00	Oct-07
-15.54	-26.50	-29.21	14.80		0.47	0.86	21.14		26.89	317.8	0	100	0	0	33	-0.04	Nov-14
-24.68	-22.08	-18.10	3.72	-25.55	2.96	0.13	18.54		57.33	15,447	0	100	0	0	8	0.03	Dec-98
-13.17	-9.49					0.79			20.96	3.5	1	99	0	0		0.12	Jun-18
-13.97	-8.24	-8.21			1.37	0.65			20.01	31.5	0	100	0	0	121	0.33	Apr-17
-13.92	-8.20	-8.15			1.34	0.65			20.10	61.9	0	100	0	0	120	0.31	Apr-17
-19.57	-14.63	-1.66			0.08	0.49			14.04	71.0	1	99	0	0	32	0.23	Nov-17
-15.22	-18.67	-14.56			0.59	0.64			16.14	7.3	0	100	0	0	48	0.33	Apr-17
-38.51	-15.66	-23.00	27.67		0.69	0.75			24.87	650.7	0	100	0	0	97	0.02	Dec-15
-24.15	-15.64	-17.94			0.39	0.79			29.54	42.0	0	100	0	0	42	0.20	Mar-16
-14.24	-9.24	7.06	32.19		0.01	0.64	16.29		33.85	1,561	0	100	0	0	41	-0.01	Nov-14
-6.24	-23.59	-28.45	62.08	-10.54	0	0.72	54.08		8.01	39.8	0	100	0	0	36	-0.15	Nov-12
-17.99	-9.31	1.33	44.41		0.02	0.8	13.84		35.02	419.8	0	100	0	0	16	0.09	Jul-15
-17.36	-19.15	-16.89			1.43	0.82			39.19	107.8	1	99	0	0	42	0.04	Mar-16
-54.35	-69.04	-81.80			0	3			4.90	22.7						51.87	Apr-17
-14.01	-9.09	-4.51	34.07		0.82	0.47	11.3		32.04	37.2	1	99	0	0	19	0.22	Nov-15
-11.42						0.85			21.86	22.6						0.13	Sep-18
-16.86	-10.86	-10.34			0.34	0.85			19.05	19.2	16	84	0	0	214	0.27	Oct-17
-0.75	0.41	-2.92	10.64		3.62	0.36	4.12	6.72	47.57	54.3	3	0	96	0	81	0.00	Oct-14
-10.71	-3.77	-3.23			3.03	0.29			28.75	416.8	0	100	0	0		0.13	Sep-16
-10.06	-4.60	-0.93			3.82	0.29			27.33	239.0	0	100	0	0		0.17	Sep-16
-4.30	-1.48					0.45			47.51	14.7	3	0	97	0		0.45	Jun-18
-11.32	-9.19					0.39			19.49	22.8	0	100	0	0		0.50	Jan-18
-12.09	-9.99					0.39			19.89	12.6	0	100	0	0	65	0.33	Jan-18
0.80	1.38	0.87	5.09		2.49	0.36	1.35	2.57	49.29	120.0	1	0	98	0	113	0.04	Oct-14
0.07	0.68					0.15		0.92	49.75	21.2	8	0	90	0		0.11	Jun-18
-10.16	-2.27	0.53			1.57	0.29			30.15	92.3	1	99	0	0		0.12	Sep-16
-16.01	-9.04	-3.71			1.03	0.29			29.71	102.7	0	100	0	0		0.15	Sep-16
-9.21	1.12	-5.44	20.64	32.54	2.71	0.08	12.05		28.43	248.6	1	99	0	0	38	0.14	Oct-13
-15.27	-9.91	-0.73	29.94	51.11	0.99	0.08	11.77		38.32	724.2	0	100	0	0	5	0.07	Oct-13
-5.41	-0.27	-8.29	9.26	33.63	2.63	0.08	9.6		30.52	535.7	0	100	0	0	24	0.05	Oct-13
-27.00	-24.19	-19.95	-0.78	-31.09	2.78	0.08	19.24		15.61	487.8	0	100	0	0	5	0.03	Oct-13
-13.82	-11.47	-13.36	29.65	46.84	1.95	0.08	14.46		34.54	1,278	0	100	0	0	5	0.03	Oct-13
-10.88	1.12	5.52	25.80	68.65	1.26	0.08	13.18		41.31	1,661	0	100	0	0	8	0.05	Oct-13
-18.54	-10.95	-13.81	26.98	30.33	1.65	0.08	13.24		32.74	409.6	0	100	0	0	5	0.02	Oct-13
-17.85	-11.06	-0.17	55.70	93.22	0.99	0.08	14.2		49.33	2,225	0	100	0	0	4	0.02	Oct-13
-15.58	-14.57	-17.40	23.82	17.56	1.92	0.08	14.67		28.37	181.3	0	100	0	0	10	0.00	Oct-13
-5.52	-5.45	-4.49	12.40		5.19	0.08	11.81		22.37	690.7	0	100	0	0	8	0.02	Feb-15

Fund Name	Ticker Symbol	Traded On	Overall Rating	Reward Rating	Risk Rating	Recent Up/ Downgrade	Price as of 12/31/2018	52-Week High	52-Week Low	Open to New Investors	Category & (Prospectus Objective)
★ Fidelity® MSCI Utilities Index ETF	FUTY	NYSE Arca	B-	B-	C+		34.88	37.49	31.11	Y	Utilities Sector Equity (Utility)
● Fidelity® NASDAQ Composite Index® Tracking Stock Fund	ONEQ	NAS CM	C	C	C-	Down	259.96	318.63	243.03	Y	US Equity Large Cap Growth (Growth)
● Fidelity® Quality Factor ETF	FQAL	NYSE Arca	C	C	C-	Up	29.92	34.96	28.26	Y	US Equity Large Cap Blend (Growth & Inc)
● Fidelity® Total Bond ETF	FBND	NYSE Arca	C-	D+	C-		48.53	50.25	47.95	Y	US Fixed Income (Income)
● Fidelity® Value Factor ETF	FVAL	NYSE Arca	C	C	C-	Up	29.71	35.44	28.19	Y	US Equity Large Cap Value (Growth & Inc)
Fieldstone Merlin Dynamic Large Cap Growth ETF	FMDG	NYSE Arca	C+	B	C-	Down	23.24	31.46	23.08	Y	US Equity Large Cap Growth (Growth)
Fieldstone UVA Unconstrained Medium-Term Fixed Income ETF	FFIU	NYSE Arca	D	D	D+		24.02	24.89	23.30	Y	US Fixed Income (Income)
● Financial Select Sector SPDR® Fund	XLF	NYSE Arca	C+	C	C+	Down	23.82	30.17	22.31	Y	Financials Sector Equity (Financial)
First Trust Alternative Absolute Return Strategy ETF	FAAR	NAS CM	D	D	C-	Down	26.50	30.18	26.40	Y	Commodities Broad Basket (Growth & Inc)
First Trust Asia Pacific Ex-Japan AlphaDEX® Fund	FPA	NAS CM	D+	D+	D+	Down	27.22	38.07	26.70	Y	Asia ex-Japan Equity (Pacific Stock)
First Trust Australia AlphaDEX® Fund	FAUS	NYSE Arca	D	D+	E+	Down	27.53	34.24	26.66	Y	Equity Misc (Foreign Stock)
● First Trust BICK Index Fund	BICK	NAS CM	C-	C-	C-		24.75	33.60	23.64	Y	Global Emerg Mkts Equity (Foreign Stock)
● First Trust Brazil AlphaDEX® Fund	FBZ	NAS CM	C	C	C-	Up	13.24	17.59	10.52	Y	Latin America Equity (Foreign Stock)
● First Trust BuyWrite Income ETF	FTHI	NAS CM	C-	C	D+	Down	20.17	23.95	19.24	Y	Long/Short Equity (Income)
First Trust California Municipal High Income ETF	FCAL	NAS CM	D+	D+	D+	Up	50.21	51.58	49.04	Y	US Muni Fixed Inc (Muni Bond - Natl)
First Trust Canada AlphaDEX® Fund	FCAN	NAS CM	D	D	D+	Down	20.14	27.34	19.57	Y	Equity Misc (Foreign Stock)
● First Trust Capital Strength ETF	FTCS	NAS CM	C	C	C+	Down	48.28	55.82	45.20	Y	US Equity Large Cap Blend (Growth)
First Trust CEF Income Opportunity ETF	FCEF	NAS CM	D+	C-	D+	Down	18.89	22.56	18.07	Y	Moderate Allocation (Income)
First Trust China AlphaDEX® Fund	FCA	NAS CM	C-	C-	D+		23.62	34.60	23.08	Y	Greater China Equity (Pacific Stock)
● First Trust Chindia ETF	FNI	NYSE Arca	C	C+	D+		30.86	43.90	29.74	Y	Equity Misc (Pacific Stock)
● First Trust Cloud Computing ETF	SKYY	NAS CM	C+	B	C-	Down	48.47	56.87	45.20	Y	Technology Sector Equity (Technology)
● First Trust Consumer Discretionary AlphaDEX® Fund	FXD	NYSE Arca	C	C	C+		36.85	45.22	34.86	Y	Consumer Goods & Svcs (Unaligned)
● First Trust Consumer Staples AlphaDEX® Fund	FXG	NYSE Arca	C+	B	C-	Up	42.20	51.44	40.68	Y	Consumer Goods & Svcs (Unaligned)
First Trust Developed International Equity Select ETF	RNDM	NAS CM	D	D	D+	Down	45.09	55.12	44.31	Y	Global Equity Large Cap (Equity-Income)
● First Trust Developed Markets Ex-US AlphaDEX® Fund	FDT	NAS CM	D+	D+	C-	Down	49.02	67.08	47.63	Y	Global Equity Large Cap (Foreign Stock)
First Trust Developed Mkts ex-US Small Cap AlphaDEX® Fund	FDTS	NAS CM	D+	D+	D+	Down	33.32	48.13	32.03	Y	Global Eq Mid/Small Cap (Foreign Stock)
First Trust Dorsey Wright DALI 1 ETF	DALI	NAS CM	U	U	U		16.93	21.47	16.00	Y	Aggressive Allocation (Growth & Inc)
● First Trust Dorsey Wright Dynamic Focus 5 ETF	FVC	NAS CM	C-	C-	C	Down	23.42	29.60	21.74	Y	US Equity Mid Cap (Growth & Inc)
● First Trust Dorsey Wright Focus 5 ETF	FV	NAS CM	C-	C-	C	Down	25.25	31.75	23.41	Y	US Equity Mid Cap (Growth & Inc)
● First Trust Dorsey Wright International Focus 5 ETF	IFV	NAS CM	D+	D+	D+	Down	17.42	24.22	16.87	Y	Global Equity Large Cap (Growth & Inc)
First Trust Dorsey Wright Momentum & Dividend ETF	DDIV	NAS CM	C	C	C-	Down	20.69	25.90	19.63	Y	US Equity Mid Cap (World Stock)
First Trust Dorsey Wright Momentum & Low Volatility ETF	DVOL	NAS CM	U	U	U		17.98	20.20	17.33	Y	US Equity Large Cap Blend (Growth & Inc)
First Trust Dorsey Wright Momentum & Value ETF	DVLU	NAS CM	U	U	U		14.93	19.95	14.57	Y	US Equity Large Cap Value (Growth & Inc)
First Trust Dorsey Wright People's Portfolio ETF	DWPP	NAS CM	C-	C-	D+	Down	25.86	30.79	24.51	Y	Long/Short Equity (Growth & Inc)
★ First Trust Dow 30 Equal Weight ETF	EDOW	NYSE Arca	B-	B	C	Up	21.31	23.87	20.09	Y	US Equity Large Cap Value (Growth & Inc)
● First Trust Dow Jones Global Select Dividend Index Fund	FGD	NYSE Arca	D+	D+	C-	Down	21.86	28.07	21.06	Y	Global Equity Large Cap (World Stock)
● First Trust Dow Jones Internet Index Fund	FDN	NYSE Arca	C+	B	C-	Down	116.66	147.65	107.21	Y	Technology Sector Equity (Technology)
● First Trust Dow Jones Select MicroCap Index Fund	FDM	NYSE Arca	C-	C-	C-	Down	40.58	53.18	38.71	Y	US Equity Small Cap (Growth)
● First Trust Emerging Markets AlphaDEX® Fund	FEM	NAS CM	C-	C-	C	Down	22.83	31.30	22.37	Y	Global Emerg Mkts Equity (Div Emerg Mkts)
First Trust Emerging Markets Equity Select ETF	RNEM	NAS CM	D	D	D		48.06	59.22	45.46	Y	Global Emerg Mkts Equity (Equity-Income)
● First Trust Emerging Markets Local Currency Bond ETF	FEMB	NAS CM	D+	D+	D+		37.02	43.95	35.67	Y	Emerging Mkts Fixed Inc (Div Emerg Mkts)
● First Trust Emerging Markets Small Cap AlphaDEX® Fund	FEMS	NAS CM	C-	C-	D+	Down	32.19	47.41	31.64	Y	Global Emerg Mkts Equity (Div Emerg Mkts)
● First Trust Energy AlphaDEX® Fund	FXN	NYSE Arca	C	C	D+		11.51	18.18	10.71	Y	Energy Sector Equity (Natl Res)
● First Trust Enhanced Short Maturity ETF	FTSM	NAS CM	C	C	C+		59.85	60.10	59.79	Y	US Fixed Income (Income)
● First Trust Europe AlphaDEX® Fund	FEP	NAS CM	D+	D+	C-	Down	30.98	42.36	30.01	Y	Europe Equity Large Cap (Foreign Stock)
● First Trust Eurozone AlphaDEX® ETF	FEUZ	NAS CM	D+	D+	D+	Down	34.17	48.11	33.28	Y	Europe Equity Large Cap (Income)
● First Trust Financials AlphaDEX® Fund	FXO	NYSE Arca	C	C-	C+	Down	27.01	32.91	25.49	Y	Financials Sector Equity (Financial)
First Trust FTSE EPRA/NAREIT Dev Mkts Real Estate Ind Fund	FFR	NYSE Arca	C-	C-	D+	Down	41.87	46.47	40.92	Y	Real Estate Sector Equity (Real Estate)
● First Trust Germany AlphaDEX® Fund	FGM	NAS CM	D+	D+	D+	Down	37.68	55.25	36.33	Y	Europe Equity Large Cap (Europe Stock)
First Trust Global Engineering and Construction ETF	FLM	NYSE Arca	D+	D+	D+	Down	45.93	63.84	43.71	Y	Industrials Sector Equity (Unaligned)
● First Trust Global Tactical Commodity Strategy Fund	FTGC	NAS CM	D	D	D+	Down	17.93	21.79	17.93	Y	Commodities Broad Basket (Growth & Inc)
● First Trust Global Wind Energy ETF	FAN	NYSE Arca	C-	C-	C-		11.46	14.07	11.09	Y	Utilities Sector Equity (Natl Res)

★ Expanded analysis of this fund is included in Section II: Analysis of All BUY Rated Funds. ● Expanded analysis of this fund is included in Section III: Analysis of All Rated Funds with Assets over $50 million.

			TOTAL RETURNS & PERFORMANCE						ASSETS		ASSET ALLOCATION & TURNOVER					VALUATION	
3-Month Total Return	6-Month Total Return	1-Year Total Return	3-Year Total Return	5-Year Total Return	Dividend Yield (TTM)	Expense Ratio	3-Yr Std Deviation	Effective Duration	NAV	Total Assets (MIL)	%Cash	%Stocks	%Bonds	%Other	Turnover Ratio	Premium/ Discount 1-Year Avg	Inception Date
1.14	2.56	4.40	37.72	66.31	3.02	0.08	11.59		34.86	488.8	0	100	0	0	6	0.02	Oct-13
-17.13	-11.15	-3.06	36.43	67.09	0.93	0.21	12.44		259.98	1,699	12	88	0	0	12	0.07	Sep-03
-13.10	-6.53	-3.72			1.55	0.29			30.05	120.3	0	100	0	0		0.08	Sep-16
0.56	0.86	-0.66	10.24		2.89	0.36	3	5.75	48.35	453.4	7	0	93	0	91	0.22	Oct-14
-14.06	-7.83	-7.07			1.72	0.29			29.88	102.1	0	100	0	0		0.14	Sep-16
-22.20	-19.38	-18.20			0	0.8				6.7	1	99	0	0		0.66	Aug-17
-0.41	0.41	-0.44			2.53	0.46			24.05	44.6	10	0	79	7		0.01	Aug-17
-13.38	-9.92	-13.08	29.98	47.11	1.77	0.13	14.88		23.82	29,463	0	100	0	0	3	0.00	Dec-98
-7.74	-7.73	-9.23			3.16	0.95			26.48	18.6	80	0	3	17	0	0.36	May-16
-11.82	-13.29	-20.71	8.14	13.82	4.27	0.8	14.89		27.65	32.8	0	100	0	0	94	-0.25	Apr-11
-14.17	-13.30	-15.46	18.29	15.57	5.4	0.8	13.24		27.57	1.4	0	100	0	0	75	0.24	Feb-12
-5.46	-7.66	-15.89	35.36	7.54	1.34	0.64	16.14		24.78	163.2	0	100	0	0	65	0.19	Apr-10
20.50	21.70	-1.12	99.55	-2.87	6.67	0.8	32.34		13.37	153.7	2	98	0	0	159	-0.09	Apr-11
-11.57	-8.88	-9.10	16.21	26.96	4.35	0.85	8.03		20.28	61.2	2	98	0	0	239	0.16	Jan-14
1.04	1.22	1.09			3.01	0.5		6.65	49.98	22.3	5	0	95	0	91	0.33	Jun-17
-20.07	-21.02	-21.93	-2.13	-39.80	1.08	0.8	15.84		20.38	6.5	0	100	0	0	85	0.28	Feb-12
-12.50	-4.98	-4.09	31.70	54.53	1.02	0.61	8.7		48.28	1,364	0	100	0	0	85	0.03	Jul-06
-13.36	-10.17	-9.60			5.43	2.78		2.96	18.95	41.1	-2	46	51	-3	15	0.02	Sep-16
-13.26	-16.46	-17.86	23.67	16.23	3.58	0.8	20.78		23.81	7.7	-1	101	0	0	69	0.33	Apr-11
-9.63	-19.02	-20.71	14.31	16.64	2.72	0.6	16.67		30.93	152.5	0	100	0	0	35	0.03	May-07
-14.63	-10.41	5.62	62.60	84.94	0.29	0.6	13.21		48.25	1,766	0	100	0	0	7	0.04	Jul-11
-14.26	-12.28	-11.43	11.49	19.71	0.96	0.64	11.49		36.89	365.6	0	100	0	0	93	0.01	May-07
-9.22	-8.10	-11.43	-0.01	28.45	2.2	0.64	9.26		42.20	352.8	0	100	0	0	100	-0.02	May-07
-9.65	-6.64	-11.43			2.03	0.65			45.24	23.6	0	100	0	0	21	0.24	Jun-17
-16.98	-15.88	-19.52	11.30	5.32	2.57	0.8	12.59		49.24	1,072	0	99	0	0	104	0.05	Apr-11
-19.18	-17.72	-24.00	6.59	0.97	2.15	0.8	13.86		33.54	10.9	0	99	0	1	111	-0.19	Feb-12
-18.75	-15.21					0.92			17.03	50.0	0	100	0	0		0.09	May-18
-17.84	-14.89	-8.05			0.59	0.89			23.55	551.4	0	100	0	0	42	0.02	Mar-16
-17.84	-14.90	-8.06	9.78		0.58	0.89	13.29		25.31	2,446	0	100	0	0	44	-0.03	Mar-14
-13.68	-14.80	-20.25	1.50		2.27	1.06	14.21		17.46	598.0	0	100	0	0	0	-0.12	Jul-14
-16.58	-14.09	-15.97	11.73		2.68	0.6	9.33		20.74	32.9	0	100	0	0	297	0.11	Mar-14
-8.98						0.6			18.05	13.8	0	100	0	0	0	0.27	Sep-18
-20.14						0.6			15.43	12.5	0	100	0	0	0	0.42	Sep-18
-14.19	-9.54	-8.27	12.24	21.70	1.06	0.6	9.11		25.96	38.8	0	100	0	0	30	0.27	Aug-12
-9.34	-0.24	-0.89			1.78	0.5			21.43	51.6	0	100	0	0	20	0.30	Aug-17
-11.21	-8.04	-12.40	15.20	2.71	4.8	0.58	9.34		21.89	459.6	0	99	0	1	31	0.07	Nov-07
-17.02	-16.47	6.22	56.30	94.93	0	0.53	15.62		116.65	7,706	0	100	0	0	22	0.01	Jun-06
-18.90	-20.13	-12.69	28.26	32.93	1	0.6	15.66		40.76	142.1	0	100	0	0	55	0.20	Sep-05
-9.28	-10.20	-15.44	36.63	6.77	3.99	0.8	16.28		22.80	453.4	0	100	0	0	101	-0.03	Apr-11
-2.67	-1.55	-9.64			2.04	0.75			47.66	4.9	0	100	0	0	111	0.38	Jun-17
2.32	1.07	-7.22	12.57		6.28	0.85	10.53	4.88	37.02	57.1	2	0	98	0	16	-0.18	Nov-14
-9.94	-13.84	-21.47	30.71	7.61	3.6	0.8	17.37		32.45	171.3	0	100	0	0	113	-0.27	Feb-12
-34.83	-30.14	-24.64	-13.84	-51.09	1.07	0.63	26.2		11.53	280.2	0	100	0	0	55	0.03	May-07
0.30	0.92	1.85	4.58		2.06	0.35	0.16	0.28	59.83	3,496	37	0	62	0	56	0.01	Aug-14
-18.59	-17.31	-18.66	11.60	4.15	2.84	0.8	14.07		31.11	694.4	0	99	0	1	100	0.02	Apr-11
-17.88	-17.56	-19.82	15.07		2.25	0.8	14.82		34.43	66.9	0	100	0	0	77	0.10	Oct-14
-14.34	-12.73	-11.65	23.10	35.42	2.05	0.63	11.97		27.01	1,052	0	100	0	0	80	-0.01	May-07
-4.95	-4.98	-5.15	9.56	24.86	3.72	0.6	10.37		41.95	45.0	0	99	0	1	9	-0.25	Aug-07
-19.45	-17.87	-25.41	9.09	-1.72	2.03	0.8	15.65		37.57	165.6	0	100	0	0	82	-0.07	Feb-12
-18.28	-15.35	-21.05	9.94	-2.38	2.13	0.7	13.69		46.21	12.5	0	100	0	0	16	0.13	Oct-08
-9.96	-11.39	-12.98	-10.04	-38.60	1.39	0.95	7.54		17.92	193.9	78	0	10	13	0	-0.02	Oct-13
-6.65	-7.44	-11.12	13.06	19.51	2.06	0.6	14.84		11.51	71.6	0	100	0	0	22	-0.11	Jun-08

Fund Name	Ticker Symbol	Traded On	Overall Rating	Reward Rating	Risk Rating	Recent Up/ Downgrade	Price as of 12/31/2018	52-Week High	52-Week Low	Open to New Investors	Category & (Prospectus Objective)
● First Trust Health Care AlphaDEX® Fund	FXH	NYSE Arca	C	C	C+		68.87	84.88	64.01	Y	Healthcare Sector Equity (Health)
First Trust Hedged BuyWrite Income ETF	FTLB	NAS CM	C-	C	D+	Down	20.20	23.64	19.51	Y	Long/Short Equity (Income)
First Trust Hong Kong AlphaDEX® Fund	FHK	NAS CM	D	D+	D	Down	33.30	46.25	32.03	Y	Greater China Equity (Pacific Stock)
● First Trust Horizon Managed Volatility Developed Intl ETF	HDMV	NYSE Arca	D+	D+	D+		30.87	36.34	29.97	Y	Global Equity Large Cap (Growth)
● First Trust Horizon Managed Volatility Domestic ETF	HUSV	NYSE Arca	C	C	C-	Up	22.22	24.28	21.11	Y	US Equity Large Cap Blend (Growth)
First Trust India NIFTY 50 Equal Weight ETF	NFTY	NAS CM	D	D+	D	Down	35.32	39.68	31.35	Y	India Equity (Growth)
● First Trust Industrials/Producer Durables AlphaDEX® Fund	FXR	NYSE Arca	C	C	C+	Down	34.09	43.14	32.01	Y	Industrials Sector Equity (Unaligned)
First Trust Indxx Global Agriculture ETF	FTAG	NAS CM	D+	D+	D	Down	22.24	29.98	21.29	Y	Commodities Specified (Unaligned)
First Trust Indxx Global Natural Resources Income ETF	FTRI	NAS CM	C-	C	D+	Down	10.92	13.25	10.60	Y	Natural Resources (Natl Res)
First Trust Indxx Innovative Transaction & Process ETF	LEGR	NAS CM	U	U	U		25.53	30.70	24.47	Y	Technology Sector Equity (Growth & Inc)
● First Trust Institutional Pref Securities & Income ETF	FPEI	NYSE Arca	D	D	C-	Down	18.24	20.23	18.05	Y	US Fixed Income (Growth & Inc)
First Trust International IPO ETF	FPXI	NAS CM	D+	D+	D+	Down	30.30	39.87	29.75	Y	Global Equity Large Cap (World Stock)
First Trust IPOX Europe Equity Opportunities ETF	FPXE	NAS CM	U	U	U		16.58	19.49	16.44	Y	Europe Equity Large Cap (Europe Stock)
● First Trust Japan AlphaDEX® Fund	FJP	NAS CM	D+	D+	C-	Down	48.09	63.21	46.52	Y	Japan Equity (Pacific Stock)
● First Trust Large Cap Core AlphaDEX® Fund	FEX	NAS CM	C	C-	C+		52.12	63.04	48.95	Y	US Equity Large Cap Blend (Growth)
● First Trust Large Cap Growth AlphaDEX® Fund	FTC	NAS CM	C	C-	C+	Down	57.32	70.61	53.12	Y	US Equity Large Cap Growth (Growth)
First Trust Large Cap US Equity Select ETF	RNLC	NAS CM	D+	D+	D+		19.41	23.16	18.51	Y	US Equity Large Cap Blend (Equity-Income)
● First Trust Large Cap Value AlphaDEX® Fund	FTA	NAS CM	C-	C-	C-	Down	46.23	57.69	43.92	Y	US Equity Large Cap Value (Growth)
First Trust Latin America AlphaDEX® Fund	FLN	NAS CM	C-	C-	D+		18.16	23.18	17.35	Y	Latin America Equity (Foreign Stock)
● First Trust Long/Short Equity ETF	FTLS	NYSE Arca	C	C	C-		37.09	41.72	35.84	Y	Long/Short Equity (Growth)
● First Trust Low Duration Opportunities ETF	LMBS	NAS CM	C	C	C+		51.05	51.74	50.81	Y	US Fixed Income (Govt Bond - Mortgage)
First Trust Lunt U.S. Factor Rotation ETF	FCTR	BATS	U	U	U		17.59	20.88	16.74	Y	US Equity Large Cap Blend (Growth)
● First Trust Managed Municipal ETF	FMB	NAS CM	C-	C	C-	Down	52.62	53.59	51.54	Y	US Muni Fixed Inc (Growth & Inc)
● First Trust Materials AlphaDEX® Fund	FXZ	NYSE Arca	C	C	C-		33.52	46.42	31.50	Y	Natural Resources (Unaligned)
● First Trust Mega Cap AlphaDEX® Fund	FMK	NAS CM	C	C	C-		32.03	37.47	30.39	Y	US Equity Large Cap Blend (Growth)
● First Trust Mid Cap Core AlphaDEX® Fund	FNX	NAS CM	C-	C-	C-	Down	57.82	73.03	54.08	Y	US Equity Mid Cap (Growth)
● First Trust Mid Cap Growth AlphaDEX® Fund	FNY	NAS CM	C-	C	C-	Down	36.22	47.12	33.42	Y	US Equity Mid Cap (Growth)
First Trust Mid Cap US Equity Select ETF	RNMC	NAS CM	D+	D+	D+		18.64	23.12	17.65	Y	US Equity Mid Cap (Equity-Income)
● First Trust Mid Cap Value AlphaDEX® Fund	FNK	NAS CM	C-	C-	D+	Down	30.45	37.84	29.15	Y	US Equity Small Cap (Growth)
● First Trust Morningstar Dividend Leaders Index Fund	FDL	NYSE Arca	C	C	C	Down	27.24	31.14	25.99	Y	US Equity Large Cap Value (Growth & Inc)
First Trust Morningstar Managed Futures Strategy Fund	FMF	NYSE Arca	D+	D+	D+		45.67	50.71	45.65	Y	Alternative Misc (Growth & Inc)
● First Trust Multi Cap Growth AlphaDEX® Fund	FAD	NAS CM	C-	C-	C-	Down	61.30	77.58	56.57	Y	US Equity Mid Cap (Growth)
● First Trust Multi Cap Value AlphaDEX® Fund	FAB	NAS CM	C-	C-	D+	Down	47.81	59.21	45.89	Y	US Equity Mid Cap (Growth)
● First Trust Multi-Asset Diversified Income Index Fund	MDIV	NAS CM	C	C-	C+		16.83	19.42	16.21	Y	Moderate Allocation (Income)
First Trust Municipal CEF Income Opportunity ETF	MCEF	NAS CM	D+	D	C-	Up	17.23	18.84	17.01	Y	US Muni Fixed Inc (Income)
First Trust Municipal High Income ETF	FMHI	NAS CM	D+	D+	D+		49.99	50.77	49.43	Y	US Muni Fixed Inc (Muni Bond - Natl)
First Trust Nasdaq Artificial Intelligence & Robotics ETF	ROBT	NAS CM	U	U	U		25.72	32.78	24.55	Y	Technology Sector Equity (Technology)
★ First Trust Nasdaq Bank ETF	FTXO	NAS CM	B-	B	C	Down	22.26	32.18	21.01	Y	Financials Sector Equity (Financial)
● First Trust NASDAQ Cybersecurity ETF	CIBR	NAS CM	C	C+	C-	Down	23.42	28.89	21.94	Y	Technology Sector Equity (Technology)
★ First Trust Nasdaq Food & Beverage ETF	FTXG	NAS CM	B-	B	C		18.04	21.28	17.50	Y	Consumer Goods & Svcs (Unaligned)
First Trust NASDAQ Global Auto Index Fund	CARZ	NAS CM	D+	D+	D	Down	31.35	44.89	30.82	Y	Consumer Goods & Svcs (Unaligned)
First Trust Nasdaq Oil & Gas ETF	FTXN	NAS CM	C+	B	D+		16.40	26.00	15.61	Y	Energy Sector Equity (Natl Res)
First Trust Nasdaq Pharmaceuticals ETF	FTXH	NAS CM	C	C+	D+		19.21	23.90	18.25	Y	Healthcare Sector Equity (Health)
★ First Trust Nasdaq Retail ETF	FTXD	NAS CM	B-	B	C		20.84	24.94	19.60	Y	Consumer Goods & Svcs (Unaligned)
First Trust Nasdaq Semiconductor ETF	FTXL	NAS CM	C+	B	C-	Down	25.75	35.68	23.92	Y	Technology Sector Equity (Technology)
First Trust NASDAQ Smartphone Index Fund	FONE	NAS CM	C-	C-	D+		42.72	55.21	41.69	Y	Technology Sector Equity (Technology)
● First Trust NASDAQ Technology Dividend Index Fund	TDIV	NAS CM	C+	B	C	Down	33.16	38.63	31.20	Y	Technology Sector Equity (Technology)
★ First Trust Nasdaq Transportation ETF	FTXR	NAS CM	B-	B	C		21.64	27.50	21.05	Y	Industrials Sector Equity (Unaligned)
● First Trust NASDAQ® ABA Community Bank Index Fund	QABA	NAS CM	C-	C-	C-	Down	43.08	58.34	41.05	Y	Financials Sector Equity (Financial)
● First Trust NASDAQ® Clean Edge® Green Energy Index Fund	QCLN	NAS CM	C	C+	D+		17.62	21.55	16.31	Y	Technology Sector Equity (Technology)
First Trust NASDAQ® Clean Edge® Smart Grid Infrastr Ind Fu	GRID	NAS CM	C-	C-	D+	Down	39.03	53.53	37.28	Y	Equity Misc (Utility)
● First Trust NASDAQ-100 Equal Weighted Index Fund	QQEW	NAS CM	C-	C	C-	Down	54.60	64.28	51.19	Y	US Equity Large Cap Growth (Growth)

★Expanded analysis of this fund is included in Section II: Analysis of All BUY Rated Funds. ● Expanded analysis of this fund is included in Section III: Analysis of All Rated Funds with Assets over $50 million.

3-Month Total Return	6-Month Total Return	1-Year Total Return	3-Year Total Return	5-Year Total Return	Dividend Yield (TTM)	Expense Ratio	3-Yr Std Deviation	Effective Duration	NAV	Total Assets (MIL)	%Cash	%Stocks	%Bonds	%Other	Turnover Ratio	Premium/Discount 1-Year Avg	Inception Date
-18.50	-7.69	-1.26	13.99	43.28	0	0.63	14.41		68.89	2,353	0	100	0	0	112	0.04	May-07
-10.27	-8.09	-8.98	12.54	19.59	3.01	0.85	7.52		20.33	12.1	3	97	0	0	219	0.25	Jan-14
-3.65	-11.65	-17.91	16.05	6.60	7.42	0.8	16.61		34.16	3.6	0	100	0	0	76	-0.43	Feb-12
-7.40	-3.23	-7.69			2.64	0.8			30.81	60.7	0	100	0	0	133	0.43	Aug-16
-7.12	-1.54	-2.10			1.17	0.7			22.21	159.5	0	100	0	0	157	0.09	Aug-16
2.36	-2.03	-2.77	31.43	24.72	1.55	0.8	13.83		35.36	3.5	1	99	0	0	64	0.12	Feb-12
-18.85	-12.54	-15.02	33.71	25.14	0.71	0.62	15.79		34.11	465.1	0	100	0	0	101	0.01	May-07
-13.82	-12.90	-18.99	9.06	-61.49	1.49	0.7	14.68		22.39	4.5	0	100	0	0	30	0.30	Mar-10
-13.86	-9.79	-8.98	24.97	-43.31	3.97	0.7	13.29		10.91	8.1	0	100	0	0	50	-0.17	Mar-10
-15.35	-9.99					0.65			25.58	47.0	0	100	0	0	53	0.30	Jan-18
-4.26	-2.09	-5.37			5.55	0.85		3.49	18.00	95.3	3	0	57	0	13	0.16	Aug-17
-12.62	-10.96	-12.31	18.04		1.75	0.7	15.45		30.61	24.1	0	100	0	0	83	0.13	Nov-14
-14.61						0.7			16.82	1.7	0	99	0	1		0.26	Oct-18
-15.04	-10.24	-17.67	7.35	12.09	1.61	0.8	12.35		48.55	163.1	0	100	0	0	101	0.00	Apr-11
-16.17	-11.63	-9.81	25.05	35.03	1.11	0.61	10.38		52.13	1,394	0	100	0	0	90	0.02	May-07
-18.68	-13.33	-5.98	20.69	44.07	0.32	0.61	11.54		57.26	910.6	0	100	0	0	148	0.09	May-07
-14.19	-9.34	-8.35			1.43	0.6			19.51	19.6	0	100	0	0	11	0.09	Jun-17
-13.96	-10.61	-13.58	26.84	26.17	1.86	0.61	11.11		46.21	1,158	0	100	0	0	72	0.03	May-07
-0.29	5.77	-7.42	59.48	-4.75	9.08	0.8	24.63		18.33	17.5	0	100	0	0	187	-0.22	Apr-11
-8.18	-4.60	-4.79	16.03		0.62	1.48	7.41		37.04	156.9	42	58	0	0	176	0.11	Sep-14
0.59	0.84	1.24	10.08		2.69	0.68	1.16	2.45	50.97	1,905	18	0	82	0	190	0.12	Nov-14
-14.48						0.65			17.67	31.2	0	100	0	0		0.07	Jul-18
1.27	1.06	0.88	9.92		2.59	0.5	3.57	6.23	52.54	460.9	2	0	98	0	85	0.11	May-14
-18.82	-18.99	-22.55	23.73	10.44	1.15	0.64	15.81		33.54	167.6	0	100	0	0	84	0.01	May-07
-13.70	-7.14	-2.80	27.09	38.12	1.11	0.7	10.28		32.14	19.6	0	100	0	0	128	0.23	May-11
-18.16	-14.88	-11.11	24.07	20.36	0.88	0.62	12.78		57.83	847.1	0	100	0	0		0.04	May-07
-20.79	-16.52	-7.35	26.63	31.35	0.11	0.7	13.13		36.24	233.6	0	100	0	0	153	0.10	Apr-11
-15.38	-13.22	-11.92			1.31	0.6			18.72	12.7	0	100	0	0	40	0.46	Jun-17
-15.96	-14.38	-14.47	20.38	10.39	1.55	0.7	13.62		30.47	53.9	0	100	0	0		0.04	Apr-11
-7.79	-2.45	-5.86	27.20	47.56	3.39	0.45	8.14		27.24	1,513	0	100	0	0	43	0.01	Mar-06
-8.53	-4.66	-3.15	-5.61	-8.42	0.87	0.95	5.01		45.38	14.4	80	16	3	0	0	0.27	Aug-13
-19.90	-15.16	-6.22	24.91	38.09	0.18	0.69	12.4		61.15	187.8	0	100	0	0	142	0.22	May-07
-15.48	-13.35	-13.97	23.54	16.63	1.66	0.71	12.41		47.94	87.1	0	100	0	0	81	0.19	May-07
-7.74	-5.20	-5.75	10.62	10.45	6.44	0.79	7.24	2.68	16.84	626.6	0	60	22	0	84	-0.03	Aug-12
-0.77	-1.93	-4.28			3.75	2.11		5.21	17.27	8.6	-6	0	108	-3	11	0.05	Sep-16
0.53	1.00	2.03			3.43	0.55		6.00	49.86	32.2	1	0	99	0	74	0.17	Nov-17
-19.59	-11.74					0.65			25.79	34.4	1	99	0	0	67	0.31	Feb-18
-18.17	-20.50	-21.57			1.58	0.6			22.28	222.6	0	100	0	0	39	0.02	Sep-16
-16.47	-11.96	1.91	33.71		0.07	0.6	14.93		23.44	737.0	0	100	0	0	56	0.15	Jul-15
-6.36	-7.60	-12.38			1.35	0.6			18.05	1.00	0	100	0	0	76	-0.03	Sep-16
-13.03	-13.92	-23.41	-7.08	-11.47	2.71	0.7	15.63		31.47	16.9	0	100	0	0	16	0.07	May-11
-34.50	-31.45	-20.21			1.54	0.6			16.50	19.8	0	100	0	0	92	0.42	Sep-16
-17.35	-10.73	-8.35			0.63	0.6			19.34	4.4	0	100	0	0	70	0.20	Sep-16
-14.32	-7.72	-2.06			0.85	0.6			20.86	9.1	0	100	0	0	126	0.29	Sep-16
-14.94	-19.13	-13.51			0.57	0.6			25.87	22.9	0	100	0	0	59	0.20	Sep-16
-12.73	-10.64	-16.81	23.18	36.89	2.18	0.7	11.81		43.01	13.8	0	100	0	0	80	-0.07	Feb-11
-12.97	-5.36	-3.04	41.44	53.64	2.41	0.5	12.25		33.16	888.2	0	100	0	0	27	0.07	Aug-12
-14.52	-11.05	-15.00			1.32	0.6			21.65	2.5	0	100	0	0	78	0.03	Sep-16
-17.44	-21.10	-16.17	15.98	28.53	1.42	0.6	19.15		43.16	314.9	0	100	0	0	14	0.04	Jun-09
-10.86	-9.12	-12.23	13.18	2.66	0.66	0.6	13.54		17.63	91.6	0	100	0	0	32	0.07	Feb-07
-17.79	-19.36	-22.30	24.25	14.84	1.37	0.7	14.1		39.18	29.8	0	100	0	0	60	0.16	Nov-09
-13.80	-9.85	-5.16	27.88	55.71	0.48	0.6	11.96		54.61	518.8	0	100	0	0	26	0.06	Apr-06

Fund Name	Ticker Symbol	Traded On	Overall Rating	Reward Rating	Risk Rating	Recent Up/Downgrade	Price as of 12/31/2018	52-Week High	52-Week Low	Open to New Investors	Category & (Prospectus Objective)
● First Trust NASDAQ-100 Ex-Technology Sector Index Fund	QQXT	NAS CM	C-	C	D+	Down	45.66	53.38	43.14	Y	US Equity Large Cap Growth (Growth)
● First Trust NASDAQ-100-Technology Sector Index Fund	QTEC	NAS CM	C	C+	C	Down	68.06	82.65	63.38	Y	Technology Sector Equity (Technology)
● First Trust Natural Gas ETF	FCG	NYSE Arca	C-	C	D		14.70	24.49	13.59	Y	Energy Sector Equity (Natl Res)
● First Trust North American Energy Infrastructure Fund	EMLP	NYSE Arca	C	C	C+		21.45	24.98	20.55	Y	Energy Sector Equity (Utility)
● First Trust NYSE Arca Biotechnology Index Fund	FBT	NYSE Arca	C	C	D+		124.20	159.14	114.50	Y	Healthcare Sector Equity (Health)
● First Trust Preferred Securities and Income ETF	FPE	NYSE Arca	C	D+	C+		17.95	20.07	17.82	Y	US Fixed Income (Income)
● First Trust RBA American Industrial Renaissance™ ETF	AIRR	NAS CM	C+	B-	C-	Down	21.69	28.50	20.46	Y	Industrials Sector Equity (Growth & Inc)
● First Trust Rising Dividend Achievers ETF	RDVY	NAS CM	C	C	C+	Down	26.51	31.91	24.76	Y	US Equity Large Cap Value (Income)
First Trust RiverFront Dynamic Asia Pacific ETF	RFAP	NAS CM	D+	D+	D+	Down	47.54	64.57	46.26	Y	Asia Equity (Growth)
● First Trust RiverFront Dynamic Developed International ETF	RFDI	NAS CM	D+	D+	C-	Down	51.24	68.93	49.45	Y	Global Equity Large Cap (Growth)
● First Trust RiverFront Dynamic Emerging Markets ETF	RFEM	NAS CM	D+	D+	D		55.99	79.03	54.25	Y	Global Emerg Mkts Equity (Div Emerg Mkts)
● First Trust RiverFront Dynamic Europe ETF	RFEU	NAS CM	D+	D+	C-	Down	52.61	70.57	50.49	Y	Europe Equity Large Cap (Growth)
First Trust S&P International Dividend Aristocrats ETF	FID	NAS CM	D+	C-	D+	Down	15.81	19.55	15.33	Y	Moderate Allocation (Multi-Asset Global)
● First Trust S&P REIT Index Fund	FRI	NYSE Arca	C	C	C-		21.62	24.29	20.31	Y	Real Estate Sector Equity (Real Estate)
● First Trust Senior Loan Fund	FTSL	NAS CM	C	C-	C+		45.52	48.38	45.42	Y	US Fixed Income (Income)
● First Trust Small Cap Core AlphaDEX® Fund	FYX	NAS CM	C-	C-	C-		54.15	70.34	50.98	Y	US Equity Small Cap (Small Company)
● First Trust Small Cap Growth AlphaDEX® Fund	FYC	NAS CM	C-	C	C-	Down	40.12	53.13	37.33	Y	US Equity Small Cap (Small Company)
First Trust Small Cap US Equity Select ETF	RNSC	NAS CM	D+	D+	D+		18.60	23.66	17.89	Y	US Equity Small Cap (Equity-Income)
● First Trust Small Cap Value AlphaDEX® Fund	FYT	NAS CM	C-	C-	C-	Down	30.95	40.19	29.75	Y	US Equity Small Cap (Small Company)
First Trust SMID Cap Rising Dividend Achievers ETF	SDVY	NAS CM	D	D	D		17.55	21.96	16.85	Y	US Equity Mid Cap (Growth & Inc)
First Trust South Korea AlphaDEX® Fund	FKO	NAS CM	D	D+	D	Down	22.55	31.53	21.65	Y	Equity Misc (Pacific Stock)
● First Trust SSI Strategic Convertible Securities ETF	FCVT	NAS CM	C-	C-	C-	Down	27.52	31.05	26.47	Y	Convertibles (Convertible Bond)
● First Trust STOXX® European Select Dividend Index Fund	FDD	NYSE Arca	C-	D+	C	Down	11.94	14.77	11.69	Y	Europe Equity Large Cap (Europe Stock)
● First Trust Strategic Income ETF	FDIV	NAS CM	C-	C-	C-	Down	46.26	52.01	45.32	Y	Cautious Allocation (Income)
● First Trust Switzerland AlphaDEX® Fund	FSZ	NAS CM	D+	D+	C-	Down	43.84	56.69	42.24	Y	Europe Equity Large Cap (Europe Stock)
● First Trust Tactical High Yield ETF	HYLS	NAS CM	C	C-	C+		44.85	48.97	44.51	Y	US Fixed Income (Corp Bond-High Yld)
● First Trust TCW Opportunistic Fixed Income ETF	FIXD	NAS CM	D+	D	C-		49.34	50.75	48.40	Y	US Fixed Income (Growth & Inc)
First Trust TCW Unconstrained Plus Bond ETF	UCON	NYSE Arca	U	U	U		24.90	25.26	24.78	Y	Fixed Income Misc (Multisector Bond)
● First Trust Technology AlphaDEX® Fund	FXL	NYSE Arca	C	C	C+	Down	52.55	64.60	48.15	Y	Technology Sector Equity (Technology)
First Trust Total US Market AlphaDEX ETF	TUSA	NAS CM	C-	C-	D+	Down	29.37	36.45	28.10	Y	US Equity Mid Cap (Growth)
First Trust Trust Heitman Global Prime Real Estate ETF	PRME	NYSE Arca	D+	C-	D	Down	17.94	21.64	17.64	Y	Real Estate Sector Equity (Real Estate)
First Trust United Kingdom AlphaDEX® Fund	FKU	NAS CM	D	D	D	Down	32.01	43.39	31.21	Y	Equity Misc (Europe Stock)
First Trust US Equity Dividend Select ETF	RNDV	NAS CM	D+	D+	D+		19.41	23.04	18.70	Y	US Equity Large Cap Value (Equity-Income)
● First Trust US Equity Opportunities ETF	FPX	NYSE Arca	C	C	C		62.06	75.93	57.83	Y	US Equity Large Cap Growth (Growth)
★ First Trust Utilities AlphaDEX® Fund	FXU	NYSE Arca	B	B+	C+	Up	26.78	28.86	23.56	Y	Utilities Sector Equity (Utility)
First Trust Value Line® 100 Exchange-Traded Fund	FVL	NYSE Arca	D+	D+	D+	Down	18.79	25.04	17.84	Y	US Equity Mid Cap (Growth)
● First Trust Value Line® Dividend Index Fund	FVD	NYSE Arca	C	C	C+	Down	29.08	32.16	27.80	Y	US Equity Large Cap Value (Growth & Inc)
● First Trust Water ETF	FIW	NYSE Arca	C+	B	C	Down	43.91	51.62	41.46	Y	Industrials Sector Equity (Natl Res)
FLAG-Forensic Accounting Long-Short ETF	FLAG	NYSE Arca	C-	C	D+	Down	36.67	44.98	34.88	Y	US Equity Large Cap Value (Growth & Inc)
FlexShares Core Select Bond Fund	BNDC	NYSE Arca	D	D	D+		23.99	25.05	23.61	Y	US Fixed Income (Multisector Bond)
● FlexShares Credit-Scored US Corporate Bond Index Fund	SKOR	NAS CM	C-	D+	C-	Up	48.85	50.89	48.38	Y	US Fixed Income (Convertible Bond)
FlexShares Credit-Scored US Long Corporate Bond Index Fund	LKOR	NAS CM	D+	D+	C-		48.59	54.82	47.27	Y	US Fixed Income (Corp Bond - Gen)
FlexShares Curr Hedg Morningstar DM ex-US Factor Tilt Ind	TLDH	NYSE Arca	D+	D+	D+	Down	24.59	30.04	23.84	Y	Global Equity Large Cap (Foreign Stock)
FlexShares Curr Hedg Morningstar EM Factor Tilt Ind Fund	TLEH	NYSE Arca	D+	D+	D+	Down	26.03	33.14	25.64	Y	Global Emerg Mkts Equity (Div Emerg Mkts)
● FlexShares Disciplined Duration MBS Index Fund	MBSD	NAS CM	D+	D	C-	Up	22.90	23.69	22.69	Y	US Fixed Income (Income)
● FlexShares Global Quality Real Estate Index Fund	GQRE	NYSE Arca	D+	C-	D+	Down	55.51	63.88	53.78	Y	Real Estate Sector Equity (Real Estate)
● FlexShares iBoxx 3-Year Target Duration TIPS Index Fund	TDTT	NYSE Arca	C-	D+	C	Down	23.82	24.41	23.71	Y	US Fixed Income (Govt Bond - Treasury)
● FlexShares iBoxx 5-Year Target Duration TIPS Index Fund	TDTF	NYSE Arca	C-	D	C	Down	24.12	24.95	23.80	Y	US Fixed Income (Govt Bond - Treasury)
● FlexShares Intl Quality Dividend Defensive Ind Fund	IQDE	NYSE Arca	C-	C-	C-		20.47	26.98	19.98	Y	Global Equity Large Cap (World Stock)
● FlexShares Intl Quality Dividend Dynamic Ind Fund	IQDY	NYSE Arca	D+	C-	D+	Down	21.72	30.65	21.17	Y	Global Equity Large Cap (World Stock)
● FlexShares International Quality Dividend Index Fund	IQDF	NYSE Arca	D+	C-	D+	Down	21.04	28.63	20.28	Y	Global Equity Large Cap (World Stock)
● FlexShares Morningstar Dev Mkts ex-US Factor Tilt Ind Fund	TLTD	NYSE Arca	D+	D+	C-	Down	55.51	73.66	53.42	Y	Global Equity Large Cap (Foreign Stock)

★Expanded analysis of this fund is included in Section II: Analysis of All BUY Rated Funds. ● Expanded analysis of this fund is included in Section III: Analysis of All Rated Funds with Assets over $50 million.

									ASSETS		ASSET ALLOCATION & TURNOVER					VALUATION	
3-Month Total Return	6-Month Total Return	1-Year Total Return	3-Year Total Return	5-Year Total Return	Dividend Yield (TTM)	Expense Ratio	3-Yr Std Deviation	Effective Duration	NAV	Total Assets (MIL)	%Cash	%Stocks	%Bonds	%Other	Turnover Ratio	Premium/ Discount 1-Year Avg	Inception Date
-13.66	-8.67	-5.58	11.26	34.42	0.26	0.6	11.74		45.66	85.6	0	100	0	0	25	0.15	Feb-07
-14.08	-11.99	-4.71	64.56	102.57	0.83	0.58	15.04		67.97	2,240	0	100	0	0	21	0.03	Apr-06
-35.10	-35.65	-34.76	-30.96	-83.64	1.08	0.6	31.79		14.69	114.0	0	100	0	0	53	0.00	May-07
-8.13	-5.69	-8.52	19.86	10.83	3.98	0.95	10.41		21.44	2,233	9	91	0	0	24	0.02	Jun-12
-21.08	-12.15	-0.20	9.90	80.05	0	0.56	25.71		124.25	2,779	0	100	0	0	36	0.03	Jun-06
-4.22	-2.71	-4.68	13.00	33.12	5.94	0.85	4.02	4.06	17.98	3,282	0	0	39	0	13	0.01	Feb-13
-20.98	-18.59	-20.45	32.63		0.3	0.7	18.98		21.73	152.4	0	100	0	0	35	0.05	Mar-14
-15.51	-10.55	-9.72	34.84	46.00	1.32	0.5	11.51		26.53	697.7	0	100	0	0	40	0.09	Jan-14
-14.76	-12.30	-18.41			2.45	0.83			48.22	44.6	0	100	0	0	131	0.01	Apr-16
-16.13	-12.66	-17.60			2.64	0.83			51.60	456.7	0	99	0	0	106	0.08	Apr-16
-9.37	-13.41	-18.07			2.14	0.95			56.34	105.8	0	100	0	0	87	0.07	Jun-16
-16.93	-12.87	-17.27			2.78	0.83			52.68	85.2	0	99	0	1	110	0.08	Apr-16
-7.37	-6.70	-11.63	13.66	-1.41	4.45	0.6	10.01		15.70	11.6	0	100	0	0	196	-0.01	Aug-13
-5.31	-4.68	-4.23	7.36	41.85	2.88	0.48	12.82		21.63	112.2	0	100	0	0	7	-0.06	May-07
-3.66	-2.05	-0.83	9.23	11.65	4.18	0.88	2.04	0.47	45.73	1,895	7	0	93	1	110	0.12	May-13
-19.73	-17.13	-10.27	26.01	16.28	0.85	0.66	15.42		54.33	626.3	0	100	0	0	111	0.05	May-07
-21.85	-17.81	-5.60	32.47	32.61	0.15	0.7	15.84		40.16	404.4	0	100	0	0	162	0.13	Apr-11
-16.60	-16.03	-10.67			1.97	0.6			18.73	5.3	0	100	0	0	49	0.57	Jun-17
-18.56	-18.47	-14.53	19.41	3.23	1.4	0.76	16.04		31.08	60.7	0	100	0	0	110	0.07	Apr-11
-15.66	-14.02	-13.81			1.17	0.6			17.72	4.0	0	100	0	0	72	0.55	Nov-17
-11.44	-8.03	-20.98	4.06	-12.85	1.48	0.8	18.19		22.67	2.3	0	100	0	0	77	-0.30	Apr-11
-9.27	-6.10	-1.54	19.44		2.29	0.95	7.55	1.97	27.65	204.4	2	4	0	2	56	0.24	Nov-15
-7.84	-7.35	-8.80	11.24	7.41	4.69	0.6	10.55		11.98	384.0	0	100	0	0	35	-0.04	Aug-07
-4.50	-2.10	-4.05	14.12		5.35	0.88	4.66	3.10	46.35	82.3	3	46	44	0	119	0.03	Aug-14
-13.78	-11.76	-15.12	16.03	16.81	2.21	0.8	11.59		43.89	174.8	0	100	0	0	50	-0.09	Feb-12
-4.30	-1.69	-1.79	13.11	15.68	5.76	1.1	2.94	2.78	45.07	1,306	-5	0	105	0	75	-0.07	Feb-12
1.72	2.01	0.69			3.08	0.55		6.19	49.37	355.1	4	0	96	0	358	0.03	Feb-17
-0.13	1.04					0.75		2.21	24.94	134.7	3	0	96	0	70	0.07	Jun-18
-16.69	-7.64	2.57	60.77	80.91	0.12	0.63	16.08		52.52	1,942	0	100	0	0	115	0.03	May-07
-17.91	-14.20	-10.13	23.99	19.25	0.94	0.7	11.63		29.22	14.8	1	99	0	0	112	0.28	Dec-06
-7.34	-7.59	-6.90	3.61		6.34	0.95	9.82		18.14	2.0	0	100	0	0	104	0.52	Nov-15
-15.14	-17.30	-16.12	-11.75	-11.76	4.77	0.8	15.27		32.11	8.4	1	98	0	2	98	0.06	Feb-12
-12.14	-6.69	-6.48			3.42	0.5			19.48	5.4	0	100	0	0	37	0.24	Jun-17
-15.90	-13.25	-8.23	24.32	42.16	0.74	0.59	11.8		62.07	1,067	0	100	0	0	31	0.04	Apr-06
-1.89	3.65	5.59	30.61	53.40	3.04	0.63	10.38		26.80	390.5	0	100	0	0		0.01	May-07
-18.25	-17.72	-18.83	-2.50	5.14	0.58	0.7	13.63		18.82	42.9	0	100	0	0	466	0.10	Jun-03
-7.21	-2.67	-3.45	30.27	52.93	2.2	0.7	7.56		29.07	4,678	0	100	0	0	50	0.03	Aug-03
-12.86	-8.42	-8.88	49.68	35.48	0.62	0.56	13.03		43.96	319.8	0	100	0	0	24	0.08	May-07
-12.43	-10.60	-11.94	27.00	34.55	1.27	1.61	11.24		36.85	14.4	0	100	0	0	71	0.20	Jan-13
0.56	0.90	-1.54			2.86	0.35		5.97	23.99	40.4	3	0	97	0		0.01	Nov-16
0.68	1.46	-0.82	5.98		2.86	0.22	2.53	4.65	48.81	75.1	0	0	99	0		0.05	Nov-14
-1.42	-0.07	-7.91	13.03		4.28	0.22	7.51	13.49	48.39	26.2	1	0	99	0		0.14	Sep-15
-13.70	-10.44	-12.88	12.21		4.14	0.44	9.77		24.60	8.6	2	98	0	0		0.06	Nov-15
-7.16	-7.40	-13.41	18.31		3.06	0.64	10.72		26.03	4.7	2	98	0	0		-0.10	Nov-15
1.17	1.08	0.07	2.09		3.2	0.2	1.67	4.38	22.92	71.9	3	0	97	0		0.07	Sep-14
-8.21	-8.75	-9.06	7.23	29.86	3.14	0.45	10.47		55.36	282.2	3	96	0	1		0.02	Nov-13
-0.09	-0.39	0.12	3.58	1.74	2.79	0.18	1.51		23.82	1,592	0	0	100	0		-0.02	Sep-11
0.13	-0.92	-0.87	5.33	4.64	2.93	0.18	2.77		24.09	833.5	0	0	100	0		0.00	Sep-11
-10.31	-8.91	-16.12	8.69	-4.55	5.91	0.47	10.7		20.38	73.3	1	99	0	0		0.02	Apr-13
-12.88	-12.83	-19.03	10.83	-2.41	5.46	0.47	12.16		21.88	59.0	1	99	0	0		0.23	Apr-13
-11.43	-10.19	-16.94	10.61	-3.59	5.71	0.47	11.11		21.10	756.0	0	99	0	0		-0.08	Apr-13
-14.04	-12.45	-17.24	9.84	2.63	3.59	0.39	11.56		55.62	962.7	2	98	0	0		0.01	Sep-12

Fund Name	Ticker Symbol	Traded On	Overall Rating	Reward Rating	Risk Rating	Recent Up/Downgrade	Price as of 12/31/2018	52-Week High	52-Week Low	Open to New Investors	Category & (Prospectus Objective)
● FlexShares Morningstar Emerg Mkts Factor Tilt Ind Fund	TLTE	NYSE Arca	C-	C-	C-		47.98	65.31	46.27	Y	Global Emerg Mkts Equity (Div Emerg Mkts)
● FlexShares Morningstar Global Upstream Natl Res Ind Fund	GUNR	NYSE Arca	C	C	C+		29.28	35.42	28.13	Y	Natural Resources (Natl Res)
● FlexShares Morningstar US Market Factors Tilt Index Fund	TILT	BATS	C-	C-	C-	Down	100.12	121.21	94.13	Y	US Equity Large Cap Blend (Growth)
● FlexShares Quality Dividend Defensive Index Fund	QDEF	NYSE Arca	C	C	C-		39.54	47.54	37.31	Y	US Equity Large Cap Value (Income)
FlexShares Quality Dividend Dynamic Index Fund	QDYN	NYSE Arca	C-	C	D	Down	38.64	47.20	36.30	Y	US Equity Large Cap Value (Income)
● FlexShares Quality Dividend Index Fund	QDF	NYSE Arca	C	C	C+	Down	39.81	48.07	37.39	Y	US Equity Large Cap Value (Income)
● FlexShares Ready Access Variable Income Fund	RAVI	NYSE Arca	C-	C	C-		75.03	75.62	74.89	Y	US Fixed Income (Income)
FlexShares Real Assets Allocation Index Fund	ASET	NAS CM	D+	D+	D+	Down	25.32	29.32	24.97	Y	Global Equity Large Cap (Asset Allocation)
● FlexShares STOXX Global Broad Infrastructure Index Fund	NFRA	NYSE Arca	C-	C-	C-	Down	43.69	49.97	42.10	Y	Infrastructure Sector Equity (Utility)
FlexShares STOXX Global ESG Impact Index Fund	ESGG	NAS CM	C-	C	D+		85.32	101.95	80.43	Y	Global Equity Large Cap (Growth & Inc)
FlexShares STOXX US ESG Impact Index Fund	ESG	BATS	C-	C	D+		59.38	69.52	56.27	Y	US Equity Large Cap Blend (Growth & Inc)
● FlexShares US Quality Large Cap Index Fund	QLC	NAS CM	C	C	C-		30.13	36.18	28.41	Y	US Equity Large Cap Value (Growth)
FlexShares® High Yield Value-Scored Bond Index Fund	HYGV	NYSE Arca	U	U	U		45.46	50.44	44.70	Y	US Fixed Income (Corp Bond-High Yld)
● FormulaFolios Hedged Growth ETF	FFHG	BATS	D+	D+	D+		26.00	30.27	24.91	Y	Long/Short Equity (Growth)
FormulaFolios Smart Growth ETF	FFSG	BATS	D	D	D		23.06	27.43	21.78	Y	US Equity Large Cap Blend (Growth)
FormulaFolios Tactical Growth ETF	FFTG	BATS	D	D	D		21.93	26.51	21.11	Y	Moderate Allocation (Growth)
● FormulaFolios Tactical Income ETF	FFTI	BATS	D	D	C-	Down	23.12	25.02	22.89	Y	US Fixed Income (Multisector Bond)
Franklin FTSE Asia ex Japan ETF	FLAX	NYSE Arca	U	U	U		19.75	24.70	19.23	Y	Asia ex-Japan Equity (Foreign Stock)
Franklin FTSE Australia ETF	FLAU	NYSE Arca	D	D	D		22.07	27.14	21.16	Y	Equity Misc (Foreign Stock)
Franklin FTSE Brazil ETF	FLBR	NYSE Arca	D	D+	D		23.67	29.48	19.14	Y	Latin America Equity (Foreign Stock)
Franklin FTSE Canada ETF	FLCA	NYSE Arca	D+	C-	D		21.08	26.24	20.45	Y	Equity Misc (Foreign Stock)
Franklin FTSE China ETF	FLCH	NYSE Arca	D	D	D		20.28	29.49	19.79	Y	Greater China Equity (Foreign Stock)
● Franklin FTSE Europe ETF	FLEE	NYSE Arca	D	D	D		20.95	27.21	20.33	Y	Europe Equity Large Cap (Foreign Stock)
Franklin FTSE Europe Hedged ETF	FLEH	NYSE Arca	D	D	D		20.32	25.84	19.90	Y	Europe Equity Large Cap (Foreign Stock)
Franklin FTSE France ETF	FLFR	NYSE Arca	D	D	D		21.57	27.15	20.80	Y	Global Equity Large Cap (Foreign Stock)
Franklin FTSE Germany ETF	FLGR	NYSE Arca	D	D	D		19.50	27.31	18.78	Y	Global Equity Large Cap (Foreign Stock)
Franklin FTSE Hong Kong ETF	FLHK	NYSE Arca	D	D	D		23.21	27.96	22.05	Y	Greater China Equity (Foreign Stock)
Franklin FTSE India ETF	FLIN	NYSE Arca	U	U	U		22.14	24.32	19.56	Y	India Equity (Foreign Stock)
Franklin FTSE Italy ETF	FLIY	NYSE Arca	D	D	D		20.28	27.91	19.63	Y	Equity Misc (Foreign Stock)
● Franklin FTSE Japan ETF	FLJP	NYSE Arca	D	D	D		22.50	28.53	21.71	Y	Japan Equity (Foreign Stock)
Franklin FTSE Japan Hedged ETF	FLJH	NYSE Arca	D	D	D		21.22	27.72	20.49	Y	Japan Equity (Foreign Stock)
Franklin FTSE Mexico ETF	FLMX	NYSE Arca	D	D	D		20.89	27.10	19.55	Y	Global Equity Large Cap (Foreign Stock)
Franklin FTSE Russia ETF	FLRU	NYSE Arca	U	U	U		20.80	25.74	20.51	Y	Equity Misc (Foreign Stock)
Franklin FTSE South Korea ETF	FLKR	NYSE Arca	D	D	D		20.36	27.67	19.95	Y	Equity Misc (Foreign Stock)
Franklin FTSE Switzerland ETF	FLSW	NYSE Arca	U	U	U		21.34	24.27	20.61	Y	Equity Misc (Foreign Stock)
Franklin FTSE Taiwan ETF	FLTW	NYSE Arca	D	D	D		22.77	27.31	22.31	Y	Greater China Equity (Foreign Stock)
Franklin FTSE United Kingdom ETF	FLGB	NYSE Arca	D	D	D		21.54	27.38	21.00	Y	Global Equity Large Cap (Foreign Stock)
Franklin Liberty High Yield Corporate ETF	FLHY	BATS	U	U	U		23.82	25.47	23.70	Y	US Fixed Income (Corp Bond-High Yld)
Franklin Liberty Intermediate Municipal Opportunities ETF	FLMI	NYSE Arca	D-	D	E	Down	24.44	25.00	24.05	Y	US Muni Fixed Inc (Muni Bond - Natl)
Franklin Liberty International Aggregate Bond ETF	FLIA	BATS	U	U	U		24.23	25.18	23.82	Y	Global Fixed Income (Growth & Inc)
Franklin Liberty International Opportunities ETF	FLIO	NYSE Arca	D	D	D		24.15	31.52	23.46	Y	Global Equity Large Cap (Foreign Stock)
Franklin Liberty Investment Grade Corporate ETF	FLCO	NYSE Arca	D	D+	D		23.13	24.78	22.86	Y	US Fixed Income (Corp Bond - Gen)
Franklin Liberty Municipal Bond ETF	FLMB	NYSE Arca	D	D	D		24.52	25.08	23.77	Y	US Muni Fixed Inc (Muni Bond - Natl)
Franklin Liberty Senior Loan ETF	FLBL	BATS	U	U	U		24.27	25.36	24.26	Y	US Fixed Income (Income)
● Franklin Liberty Short Duration U.S. Government ETF	FTSD	NYSE Arca	C-	C-	C-		94.78	95.86	94.18	Y	US Fixed Income (Growth)
Franklin Liberty U.S. Low Volatility ETF	FLLV	NYSE Arca	C-	C	D+	Up	29.22	33.23	27.74	Y	US Equity Large Cap Blend (Growth)
● Franklin LibertyQ Emerging Markets ETF	FLQE	NYSE Arca	D+	D+	C-	Down	28.22	35.46	27.64	Y	Global Emerg Mkts Equity (Growth & Inc)
Franklin LibertyQ Global Dividend ETF	FLQD	NYSE Arca	C-	C-	D+		25.61	30.47	24.68	Y	Global Equity Large Cap (Growth & Inc)
Franklin LibertyQ Global Equity ETF	FLQG	NYSE Arca	D+	C-	D		27.41	32.51	26.42	Y	Global Equity Large Cap (Growth & Inc)
Franklin LibertyQ International Equity Hedged ETF	FLQH	NYSE Arca	D+	D+	D+		22.39	25.91	21.67	Y	Global Equity Large Cap (Growth & Inc)
● Franklin LibertyQ U.S. Equity ETF	FLQL	BATS	C-	D+	C-		27.62	31.54	26.18	Y	US Equity Large Cap Blend (Growth & Inc)
Franklin LibertyQ U.S. Mid Cap Equity ETF	FLQM	BATS	D+	D+	D+		26.28	30.49	24.95	Y	US Equity Mid Cap (Growth & Inc)

★ Expanded analysis of this fund is included in Section II: Analysis of All BUY Rated Funds. ● Expanded analysis of this fund is included in Section III: Analysis of All Rated Funds with Assets over $50 million.

		TOTAL RETURNS & PERFORMANCE							ASSETS		ASSET ALLOCATION & TURNOVER					VALUATION	
3-Month Total Return	6-Month Total Return	1-Year Total Return	3-Year Total Return	5-Year Total Return	Dividend Yield (TTM)	Expense Ratio	3-Yr Std Deviation	Effective Duration	NAV	Total Assets (MIL)	%Cash	%Stocks	%Bonds	%Other	Turnover Ratio	Premium/ Discount 1-Year Avg	Inception Date
-7.25	-8.21	-16.12	24.37	5.94	3.18	0.59	14.86		48.38	508.2	1	99	0	0		-0.18	Sep-12
-12.79	-10.70	-9.21	40.77	-1.58	2.78	0.46	14.39		29.36	5,333	1	99	0	0		0.06	Sep-11
-15.55	-11.05	-8.51	26.10	35.71	1.76	0.25	10.76		100.18	1,406	2	98	0	0		0.08	Sep-11
-15.05	-9.95	-7.96	24.19	40.58	2.72	0.37	8.56		39.47	334.1	2	98	0	0		0.13	Dec-12
-14.24	-9.43	-9.78	25.95	33.80	2.77	0.37	10.94		38.65	45.2	1	99	0	0		0.05	Dec-12
-15.43	-10.56	-9.13	24.72	38.37	2.73	0.37	9.52		39.78	1,771	1	99	0	0		0.04	Dec-12
0.23	0.95	1.82	4.38	5.55	2.04	0.25	0.31	0.48	75.09	290.1	19	0	78	0		0.01	Oct-12
-7.50	-6.04	-8.37	12.89		1.97	0.57	9		25.48	14.3	2	98	0	0		0.32	Nov-15
-5.90	-2.90	-7.92	15.93	19.08	3.02	0.47	8.65		43.67	802.1	1	99	0	0		-0.07	Oct-13
-13.93	-8.20	-8.49			1.84	0.42			85.05	78.3	2	98	0	0		0.55	Jul-16
-13.49	-6.49	-3.56			1.65	0.32			59.62	32.9	2	98	0	0		0.43	Jul-16
-15.00	-9.59	-7.51	22.70		1.53	0.32	9.88		30.28	64.0	1	99	0	0		0.33	Sep-15
-6.22						0.37			45.49	38.2	1	0	99	0		0.04	Jul-18
-11.74	-7.56	-5.41			0.58	1.16			26.01	72.7	-10	110	0	0	138	0.15	Jun-17
-13.87	-10.84	-9.29			1.43	0.7			22.93	43.1	0	100	0	0	0	0.18	Oct-17
-10.99	-9.47	-12.44			1.62	1.04			21.99	45.0	1	99	0	0	56	0.12	Oct-17
-2.82	-1.36	-3.76			3.6	1.05		2.45	23.15	201.5	3	0	91	0	48	0.11	Jun-17
-8.35	-9.59					0.19			19.72	16.5	0	99	0	0	1	0.74	Feb-18
-9.66	-11.12	-12.24			2.18	0.09			22.08	7.0	0	100	0	0	2	-0.16	Nov-17
16.00	20.61	-0.87			1.9	0.19			23.75	19.7	0	89	0	0	5	0.07	Nov-17
-14.89	-12.92	-15.79			0.87	0.09			21.05	3.5	0	100	0	0	1	0.44	Nov-17
-10.10	-16.96	-18.27			0.46	0.19			20.50	35.3	0	100	0	0	3	0.24	Nov-17
-12.75	-12.14	-14.80			2.54	0.09			20.96	71.1	1	98	0	0	1	0.14	Nov-17
-10.72	-9.02	-8.23			1.67	0.09			20.32	33.0	1	98	0	0	5	0.82	Nov-17
-15.00	-12.46	-12.10			2.5	0.09			21.54	2.3	0	99	0	1	2	0.57	Nov-17
-15.81	-16.03	-22.07			2.91	0.09			19.32	4.1	0	100	0	0	2	0.59	Nov-17
-6.14	-7.62	-10.18			1.96	0.09			23.22	17.6	0	100	0	0	1	0.49	Nov-17
2.05	-1.09					0.19			22.01	6.6	0	99	0	0	2	0.38	Feb-18
-11.54	-15.60	-17.09			2.74	0.09			20.17	9.5	0	100	0	0	3	-0.24	Nov-17
-14.27	-11.38	-13.10			0.51	0.09			22.66	250.8	0	100	0	0	1	0.17	Nov-17
-17.02	-11.46	-13.95			0.1	0.09			21.35	45.1	1	99	0	0	2	-0.25	Nov-17
-19.25	-11.22	-13.69			1.07	0.19			20.85	3.1	0	100	0	0	10	0.33	Nov-17
-9.78	-5.55					0.19			20.75	11.2	0	100	0	0	8	-0.40	Feb-18
-12.13	-11.65	-20.33			1.27	0.09			20.45	19.0	0	100	0	0	4	-0.08	Nov-17
-9.30	-3.60					0.09			21.14	2.2	0	100	0	0	3	0.19	Feb-18
-13.80	-6.93	-8.92			0	0.19			22.78	14.0	0	100	0	0	4	-0.41	Nov-17
-11.98	-13.81	-14.65			2.78	0.09			21.61	13.7	1	99	0	0	2	-0.10	Nov-17
-4.52	-1.88					0.4			23.71	9.8	0	0	99	0		0.07	May-18
1.16	1.12	0.38			2.38	0.3			24.39	7.2	1	0	99	0	17	0.35	Aug-17
0.12	-0.52					0.35			24.19	4.8	0	0	100	0		0.30	May-18
-13.20	-12.04	-16.16			2.49	0.6			24.18	10.3	1	98	0	0	34	0.49	Jan-17
-0.67	0.34	-3.06			3.88	0.35			23.11	17.1	4	0	95	0	63	0.06	Oct-16
2.67	1.96	0.21			2.72	0.3			24.47	7.2	2	0	98	0	5	0.54	Aug-17
-2.95	-1.40					0.45			24.19	57.3	14	0	87	0		0.36	May-18
0.66	0.93	1.19	3.02	3.99	2.62	0.25	0.43		94.37	184.0	2	0	98	0	103	0.05	Nov-13
-9.93	-2.76	-0.40			1.35	0.5			29.34	13.0	0	100	0	0	66	0.02	Sep-16
-5.73	-3.75	-11.72			2.98	0.55			28.16	281.7	1	99	0	0	33	-0.18	Jun-16
-7.60	-3.42	-7.94			3.24	0.45			25.73	16.6	0	100	0	0	43	-0.04	Jun-16
-10.34	-5.61	-7.13			2.65	0.35			27.56	17.9	0	100	0	0	35	0.16	Jun-16
-8.37	-5.45	-6.17			1.35	0.4			22.40	7.3	1	99	0	0	33	-0.05	Jun-16
-11.03	-4.25	-1.97			1.58	0.25			27.69	413.5	0	100	0	0	21	0.24	Apr-17
-12.28	-6.38	-3.57			1.42	0.3			26.36	7.3	0	100	0	0	36	-0.03	Apr-17

Fund Name	Ticker Symbol	Traded On	Overall Rating	Reward Rating	Risk Rating	Recent Up/Downgrade	Price as of 12/31/2018	52-Week High	52-Week Low	Open to New Investors	Category & (Prospectus Objective)
Franklin LibertyQ U.S. Small Cap Equity ETF	FLQS	BATS	D+	D+	D+		25.05	30.65	23.78	Y	US Equity Small Cap (Small Company)
Gabelli Food of All Nations NextShares	FOANC	NAS CM	C-	C-	C-	Down	9.12	100.04	8.96	Y	Consumer Goods & Svcs (Unaligned)
Gabelli Media Mogul NextShares	MOGLC	NAS CM	C	C	D+		9.87	100.04	9.46	Y	Communications Sector Equity (Unaligned)
Gabelli Pet Parents'™ NextShares™	PETZC	NAS CM	U	U	U		9.02	100.04	8.62	Y	Equity Misc (Growth)
Gabelli RBI NextShares	GRBIC	NAS CM	U	U	U		7.87	100.05	7.43	Y	Infrastructure Sector Equity (Growth)
Global X Adaptive U.S. Factor ETF	AUSF	NYSE Arca	U	U	U		22.03	25.36	21.22	Y	US Equity Large Cap Blend (Growth)
Global X Autonomous & Electric Vehicles ETF	DRIV	NAS CM	U	U	U		11.66	15.71	11.45	Y	Global Equity Large Cap (Unaligned)
● Global X Conscious Companies ETF	KRMA	NAS CM	C-	C-	D+	Up	18.33	21.46	17.71	Y	US Equity Large Cap Blend (Growth & Inc)
● Global X Copper Miners ETF	COPX	NYSE Arca	D+	C-	D	Down	18.31	29.10	18.14	Y	Natural Resources (Natl Res)
Global X Fertilizers/Potash ETF	SOIL	NYSE Arca	C-	C-	D+		8.87	10.97	8.64	Y	Natural Resources (Unaligned)
● Global X FinTech ETF	FINX	NAS CM	C+	B-	C		22.09	29.31	20.71	Y	Technology Sector Equity (Technology)
Global X Founder-Run Companies ETF	BOSS	BATS	D	D+	D	Down	16.34	20.94	15.57	Y	US Equity Mid Cap (Growth & Inc)
Global X FTSE Nordic Region ETF	GXF	NYSE Arca	D+	C-	D+	Down	19.63	24.43	19.24	Y	Equity Misc (Europe Stock)
Global X FTSE Southeast Asia ETF	ASEA	NYSE Arca	C-	C	D+		15.24	18.30	14.66	Y	Asia ex-Japan Equity (Foreign Stock)
Global X Future Analytics Tech ETF	AIQ	NAS CM	U	U	U		12.86	16.04	12.25	Y	Technology Sector Equity (Technology)
Global X Gold Explorers ETF	GOEX	NYSE Arca	D	D+	D	Down	19.85	24.09	17.60	Y	Prec Metals (Prec Metals)
● Global X Guru™ Index ETF	GURU	NYSE Arca	C-	C	D+	Down	27.60	32.92	26.14	Y	US Equity Large Cap Growth (Income)
Global X Health & Wellness Thematic ETF	BFIT	NAS CM	C-	C	D+	Down	17.60	19.90	16.50	Y	Global Eq Mid/Small Cap (Health)
● Global X Internet of Things ETF	SNSR	NAS CM	C	C	C-		16.14	21.29	15.40	Y	Technology Sector Equity (Technology)
● Global X Lithium & Battery Tech ETF	LIT	NYSE Arca	C	C	C-		26.98	41.08	26.49	Y	Natural Resources (Unaligned)
Global X Longevity Thematic ETF	LNGR	NAS CM	C-	C	D+	Down	18.97	22.60	18.13	Y	Healthcare Sector Equity (Unaligned)
Global X Millennials Thematic ETF	MILN	NAS CM	C	C	C-		19.67	23.73	18.58	Y	US Equity Large Cap Growth (Growth & Inc)
● Global X MLP & Energy Infrastructure ETF	MLPX	NYSE Arca	C	B-	D+		10.93	14.60	10.40	Y	Energy Sector Equity (Growth & Inc)
● Global X MLP ETF	MLPA	NYSE Arca	C	B-	D		7.67	10.80	7.33	Y	Energy Sector Equity (Utility)
● Global X MSCI Argentina ETF	ARGT	NYSE Arca	C-	C	D	Down	23.47	38.39	21.88	Y	Equity Misc (Foreign Stock)
● Global X MSCI Colombia ETF	GXG	NYSE Arca	D+	D+	D	Down	7.79	11.47	7.75	Y	Equity Misc (Foreign Stock)
● Global X MSCI Greece ETF	GREK	NYSE Arca	D	D	D	Down	6.90	11.49	6.79	Y	Europe Equity Mid/Small Cap (Foreign Stock)
Global X MSCI Nigeria ETF	NGE	NYSE Arca	D	D	D		16.37	26.85	16.37	Y	Equity Misc (Foreign Stock)
● Global X MSCI Norway ETF	NORW	NYSE Arca	C	C	C+	Down	11.54	15.42	11.43	Y	Equity Misc (Europe Stock)
Global X MSCI Pakistan ETF	PAK	NYSE Arca	D-	D-	D	Down	8.07	13.75	8.03	Y	Equity Misc (Foreign Stock)
Global X MSCI Portugal ETF	PGAL	NYSE Arca	D+	D+	C-	Down	10.08	13.17	9.88	Y	Equity Misc (Foreign Stock)
Global X MSCI SuperDividend® EAFE ETF	EFAS	NAS CM	D	D	D+	Down	15.08	19.06	14.94	Y	Global Equity Large Cap (Equity-Income)
Global X MSCI SuperDividend® Emerging Markets ETF	SDEM	NYSE Arca	D+	D+	D+		12.70	17.90	12.56	Y	Global Emerg Mkts Equity (Div Emerg Mkts)
Global X Next Emerging & Frontier ETF	EMFM	NYSE Arca	D+	C-	D+	Down	19.67	26.16	19.55	Y	Global Emerg Mkts Equity (Foreign Stock)
● Global X Robotics & Artificial Intelligence ETF	BOTZ	NAS CM	D+	D+	D+	Down	16.74	27.38	16.06	Y	Equity Misc (Technology)
● Global X S&P 500® Catholic Values ETF	CATH	NAS CM	C-	C	C-	Down	30.40	36.43	29.28	Y	US Equity Large Cap Blend (Growth & Inc)
Global X S&P 500® Quality Dividend ETF	QDIV	BATS	U	U	U		21.65	26.14	21.03	Y	US Equity Large Cap Value (Equity-Income)
Global X Scientific Beta Asia ex-Japan ETF	SCIX	NYSE Arca	D+	D+	D+		21.93	27.08	21.93	Y	Asia ex-Japan Equity (Pacific Stock)
Global X Scientific Beta Europe ETF	SCID	NYSE Arca	D+	D+	D+	Down	21.98	29.68	21.85	Y	Europe Equity Large Cap (Europe Stock)
Global X Scientific Beta Japan ETF	SCIJ	NYSE Arca	D+	D+	D+		25.83	33.72	25.52	Y	Japan Equity (Pacific Stock)
● Global X Scientific Beta US ETF	SCIU	NYSE Arca	C-	C-	C-	Down	27.92	33.43	27.01	Y	US Equity Large Cap Blend (Growth)
● Global X Silver Miners ETF	SIL	NYSE Arca	D	D+	D	Down	25.02	33.93	22.47	Y	Prec Metals (Prec Metals)
● Global X Social Media ETF	SOCL	NAS CM	C-	C	C-	Down	27.55	38.73	26.60	Y	Technology Sector Equity (Technology)
Global X SuperDividend® Alternatives ETF	ALTY	NAS CM	C-	C-	D+		13.29	15.57	12.93	Y	Aggressive Allocation (Growth & Inc)
● Global X SuperDividend® REIT ETF	SRET	NAS CM	C+	B	C	Down	13.57	15.83	13.25	Y	Real Estate Sector Equity (Real Estate)
● Global X SuperDividend™ ETF	SDIV	NYSE Arca	C-	C-	C	Down	17.10	22.55	16.68	Y	Global Eq Mid/Small Cap (Equity-Income)
● Global X SuperDividend™ U.S. ETF	DIV	NYSE Arca	C	C	C-		22.41	25.60	21.69	Y	US Equity Mid Cap (Income)
● Global X SuperIncome™ Preferred ETF	SPFF	NYSE Arca	D+	D+	C-	Down	11.03	12.33	10.92	Y	US Fixed Income (Equity-Income)
Global X TargetIncome™ 5 ETF	TFIV	BATS	U	U	U		22.80	25.23	22.54	Y	Allocation Misc (Income)
Global X TargetIncome™ Plus 2 ETF	TFLT	BATS	U	U	U		22.95	25.22	22.74	Y	Allocation Misc (Income)
● Global X U.S. Infrastructure Development ETF	PAVE	BATS	C	C	C-		13.46	17.72	12.79	Y	Infrastructure Sector Equity (Utility)
● Global X U.S. Preferred ETF	PFFD	BATS	D+	D	C		22.54	24.88	22.14	Y	US Fixed Income (Growth & Inc)

★Expanded analysis of this fund is included in Section II: Analysis of All BUY Rated Funds. ● Expanded analysis of this fund is included in Section III: Analysis of All Rated Funds with Assets over $50 million.

3-Month Total Return	6-Month Total Return	1-Year Total Return	3-Year Total Return	5-Year Total Return	Dividend Yield (TTM)	Expense Ratio	3-Yr Std Deviation	Effective Duration	NAV	Total Assets (MIL)	%Cash	%Stocks	%Bonds	%Other	Turnover Ratio	Premium/ Discount 1-Year Avg	Inception Date
-14.71	-13.09	-4.57			1.07	0.35			25.10	9.8	0	100	0	0	24	0.18	Apr-17
-10.30	-9.61	-14.02			0.84	0.9			9.16	1.8	5	95	0	0	16	0.03	Feb-17
-13.46	-9.73	-8.89			0	0.9			9.83	5.4	3	96	0	0	19	0.03	Dec-16
-12.51	-10.42					0.9			9.02	1.2	7	93	0	0	59	0.00	Jun-18
-20.02	-19.28					0.9			7.87	1.1	14	86	0	0	7	0.00	Feb-18
-10.68						0.27			22.09	102.4	-1	101	0	0		0.17	Aug-18
-20.75	-18.78					0.68			11.72	15.2	0	100	0	0		0.08	Apr-18
-12.13	-5.99	-3.17			1.14	0.43			18.38	56.5	0	100	0	0	42	0.24	Jul-16
-17.07	-23.12	-32.41	59.61	-30.12	2.17	0.65	36.41		18.45	68.1	0	100	0	0	44	-0.10	Apr-10
-17.98	-13.43	-15.57	2.14	-14.01	0.77	0.69	15.23		8.89	13.1	0	100	0	0	24	-0.33	May-11
-22.53	-14.92	1.38			0.01	0.68			22.16	327.7	0	100	0	0	12	0.08	Sep-16
-18.91	-15.40	-3.52			0.21	0.65			16.38	4.7	0	100	0	0		0.45	Feb-17
-10.91	-5.44	-10.48	1.55	-3.31	3.95	0.55	12.26		19.64	24.3	-3	103	0	0	7	-0.19	Aug-09
-6.19	-0.64	-9.15	29.86	9.53	1.7	0.65	12.28		15.28	18.3	0	100	0	0	8	0.16	Feb-11
-17.92	-13.96					0.68			13.00	42.0	0	100	0	0		0.04	May-18
6.95	-9.83	-14.10	71.93	40.14	0	0.66	48.51		19.98	31.6	0	100	0	0	84	-0.19	Nov-10
-15.48	-12.94	-7.35	19.05	9.72	0.52	0.75	11.1		27.45	56.8	0	100	0	0	95	0.19	Jun-12
-10.45	-6.48	5.85			0.77	0.5			17.40	10.2	0	100	0	0	17	0.50	May-16
-18.80	-15.49	-16.44			0.6	0.68			16.19	83.0	0	100	0	0	25	0.09	Sep-16
-17.96	-16.01	-29.84	41.59	10.96	4.01	0.75	17.76		27.17	738.5	0	100	0	0	68	-0.29	Jul-10
-14.99	-7.84	-1.51			0.42	0.5			19.03	16.5	0	100	0	0	10	0.26	May-16
-15.95	-11.29	3.06			0.22	0.5			19.73	31.3	0	100	0	0	21	0.17	May-16
-18.83	-14.70	-15.31	9.83	-17.09	5.36	0.45	18.96		10.93	540.4	0	100	0	0	40	-0.34	Aug-13
-19.83	-11.93	-15.47	-6.32	-31.83	8.98	0.46	18.17		7.68	830.3	0	100	0	0	35	0.08	Apr-12
-11.58	-11.48	-33.38	32.13	23.61	0.68	0.59	20.51		23.58	91.8	0	100	0	0	24	-0.08	Mar-11
-19.10	-22.87	-19.26	12.15	-51.55	2.14	0.61	20.64		7.87	82.2	0	99	0	0	41	0.06	Feb-09
-16.24	-23.34	-31.56	-10.58	-66.46	2.92	0.59	28.56		6.96	255.0	0	100	0	0	22	-0.15	Dec-11
-1.72	-17.89	-16.55	-35.20	-67.92	2.44	0.88	31.03		17.01	38.7	0	100	0	0	21	-0.85	Apr-13
-20.86	-14.95	-8.38	31.53	-14.46	2.89	0.5	15.23		11.54	109.5	0	100	0	0	10	-0.27	Nov-10
-21.08	-24.75	-30.35	-27.64		4.26	0.87	16.67		7.97	37.4	0	100	0	0	66	0.01	Apr-15
-12.63	-16.16	-11.45	11.97	-22.44	3.32	0.58	17.13		10.10	28.9	0	100	0	0	25	-0.57	Nov-13
-9.17	-7.60	-11.07			6.86	0.55			15.08	4.8	0	100	0	0	45	0.37	Nov-16
-5.83	-6.61	-17.14	22.13		6.92	0.66	16.96		12.73	12.5	0	100	0	0	122	0.20	Mar-15
-6.13	-4.68	-16.21	22.11	-8.80	2	0.56	14.47		19.70	13.4	0	100	0	0	8	-0.33	Nov-13
-25.66	-21.89	-27.79			0.01	0.68			16.87	1,726	0	100	0	0	15	-0.09	Sep-16
-14.26	-7.65	-5.09			1.19	0.29			30.57	163.1	0	100	0	0	6	0.18	Apr-16
-12.85						0.35			22.25	2.5	0	100	0	0		-0.42	Jul-18
-7.70	-7.07	-10.38	19.70		4.72	0.38	11.7		22.02	3.5	0	100	0	0	53	0.15	May-15
-14.08	-12.53	-16.27	7.41		5.79	0.38	12.62		22.03	6.1	0	100	0	0	27	0.18	May-15
-13.13	-9.02	-15.28	13.08		4.78	0.39	10.69		26.10	7.1	0	100	0	0	18	0.29	May-15
-13.83	-9.26	-7.35	21.92		1.44	0.19	8.71		27.91	118.3	0	100	0	0	28	0.21	May-15
3.73	-12.01	-23.60	39.19	-22.62	0.03	0.65	41.54		24.98	311.3	0	100	0	0	24	-0.03	Apr-10
-12.82	-22.66	-16.04	41.20	33.15	1.67	0.65	17.59		27.74	135.0	0	100	0	0	41	-0.14	Nov-11
-9.72	-6.43	-5.80	22.10		7.96	2.84	8.89	6.52	13.30	16.7	0	78	21	0	35	0.16	Jul-15
-7.28	-6.62	-5.14	38.25		8.86	0.55	10.96		13.59	130.1	0	100	0	0	55	0.20	Mar-15
-13.26	-13.69	-15.36	6.82	3.35	8.1	0.58	10.53		17.20	914.1	0	100	0	0	67	0.00	Jun-11
-9.38	-7.29	-6.66	13.41	19.19	6.38	0.45	6.66		22.37	418.3	0	100	0	0	53	0.04	Mar-13
-4.52	-3.86	-2.62	3.31	7.47	7.47	0.58	4.59		11.06	179.8	0	0	0	0	45	-0.02	Jul-12
-6.82						0.77			22.81	2.4	1	34	46	1		0.04	Jul-18
-6.68						0.78			22.96	2.4	1	24	56	1		0.56	Jul-18
-20.98	-16.42	-18.62			0.32	0.47			13.50	140.9	0	100	0	0		0.15	Mar-17
-4.97	-5.49	-4.41			6.16	0.23			22.46	188.3	0	1	0	3	4	0.24	Sep-17

Fund Name	Ticker Symbol	Traded On	Overall Rating	Reward Rating	Risk Rating	Recent Up/ Downgrade	Price as of 12/31/2018	52-Week High	52-Week Low	Open to New Investors	Category & (Prospectus Objective)
● Global X Uranium ETF	URA	NYSE Arca	D	D	D	Down	11.67	15.83	11.30	Y	Natural Resources (Unaligned)
Global X YieldCo Index ETF	YLCO	NAS CM	C	C	C-		11.23	12.67	11.12	Y	Global Eq Mid/Small Cap (Growth & Inc)
Global X/JPMorgan Efficiente Index ETF	EFFE	NYSE Arca	D+	C-	D	Down	24.59	27.58	24.59	Y	Moderate Allocation (Growth & Inc)
Global X/JPMorgan US Sector Rotator Index ETF	SCTO	NYSE Arca	D+	C-	D	Down	22.99	28.03	22.22	Y	Aggressive Allocation (Growth & Inc)
Goldman Sachs Access High Yield Corporate Bond ETF	GHYB	NYSE Arca	D+	D+	D+		45.98	50.04	45.28	Y	US Fixed Income (Corp Bond-High Yld)
Goldman Sachs Access Inflation Protected USD Bond ETF	GTIP	BATS	U	U	U		49.48	49.69	49.05	Y	US Fixed Income (Income)
● Goldman Sachs Access Investment Grade Corporate Bond ETF	GIGB	NYSE Arca	D	D	C-	Down	47.27	50.22	46.80	Y	Canada Fixed Income (Corp Bond - Gen)
● Goldman Sachs Access Treasury 0-1 Year ETF	GBIL	NYSE Arca	C	C-	C+	Up	100.05	100.23	99.95	Y	US Fixed Income (Govt Bond - Treasury)
● Goldman Sachs ActiveBeta® Emerging Markets Equity ETF	GEM	NYSE Arca	C-	C-	C	Down	30.12	39.44	28.94	Y	Global Emerg Mkts Equity (Div Emerg Mkts)
Goldman Sachs ActiveBeta® Europe Equity ETF	GSEU	NYSE Arca	D+	D+	C-	Down	26.38	33.92	25.60	Y	Europe Equity Large Cap (Europe Stock)
● Goldman Sachs ActiveBeta® International Equity ETF	GSIE	NYSE Arca	C-	D+	C	Down	25.36	31.92	24.56	Y	Global Equity Large Cap (Foreign Stock)
Goldman Sachs ActiveBeta® Japan Equity ETF	GSJY	NYSE Arca	C-	C-	D+		28.82	36.01	27.89	Y	Japan Equity (Pacific Stock)
● Goldman Sachs ActiveBeta® U.S. Large Cap Equity ETF	GSLC	NYSE Arca	C	C	C+	Down	50.29	59.25	47.19	Y	US Equity Large Cap Blend (Growth)
● Goldman Sachs ActiveBeta® U.S. Small Cap Equity ETF	GSSC	NYSE Arca	D+	D+	C-		38.88	49.50	36.76	Y	US Equity Small Cap (Growth)
● Goldman Sachs Equal Weight U.S. Large Cap Equity ETF	GSEW	BATS	D+	D+	C-		39.39	46.90	37.41	Y	US Equity Large Cap Blend (Growth & Inc)
● Goldman Sachs Hedge Industry VIP ETF	GVIP	NYSE Arca	C-	C-	C-	Down	49.13	58.76	46.00	Y	US Equity Large Cap Blend (Growth & Inc)
Goldman Sachs JUST U.S. Large Cap Equity ETF	JUST	NYSE Arca	U	U	U		35.93	42.53	33.79	Y	US Equity Large Cap Blend (Growth & Inc)
● GraniteShares Bloomberg Commod Broad Strategy No K-1 ETF	COMB	NYSE Arca	D+	D	C-		22.97	27.33	22.97	Y	Commodities Broad Basket (Growth & Inc)
● GraniteShares Gold Trust	BAR	NYSE Arca	D	D	D+		127.88	135.42	117.19	Y	Commodities Specified (Prec Metals)
GraniteShares HIPS US High Income ETF	HIPS	NYSE Arca	C-	C	D+	Down	14.90	18.12	14.45	Y	Aggressive Allocation (Income)
GraniteShares Platinum Trust	PLTM	NYSE Arca	U	U	U		79.08	100.39	76.50	Y	Commodities Specified (Growth & Inc)
GraniteShares S&P GSCI Commodity Broad Strategy No K-1 ETF	COMG	NYSE Arca	D+	D+	D+	Up	19.45	31.88	19.37	Y	Commodities Broad Basket (Growth & Inc)
● GS Connect S&P GSCI Enhanced Commodity Total Return ETN	GSC	NYSE Arca	D+	C-	D		19.30	30.97	17.93	Y	Commodities Broad Basket (Natl Res)
Hartford Global Impact NextShares Fund	HFGIC	NAS CM	D	D	D		17.29	100.11	16.60	Y	Global Eq Mid/Small Cap (Growth)
● Hartford Multifactor Developed Markets (ex-US) ETF	RODM	NYSE Arca	C	D+	C+		25.80	30.81	25.02	Y	Global Equity Large Cap (Foreign Stock)
● Hartford Multifactor Emerging Markets ETF	ROAM	NYSE Arca	C-	C-	C-		22.06	28.10	21.30	Y	Global Emerg Mkts Equity (Div Emerg Mkts)
Hartford Multifactor Global Small Cap ETF	ROGS	NYSE Arca	C-	C-	D+	Down	26.93	33.41	25.82	Y	Global Eq Mid/Small Cap (Small Company)
Hartford Multifactor Low Volatility Intl Equity ETF	LVIN	BATS	D	D	D		24.49	28.87	23.92	Y	Global Equity Large Cap (Growth & Inc)
Hartford Multifactor Low Volatility US Equity ETF	LVUS	BATS	D+	D+	D+	Up	25.34	29.55	24.10	Y	US Equity Large Cap Blend (Growth & Inc)
Hartford Multifactor REIT ETF	RORE	NYSE Arca	C-	C	D		13.75	16.07	13.29	Y	Real Estate Sector Equity (Real Estate)
● Hartford Multifactor US Equity ETF	ROUS	NYSE Arca	C-	C-	C-	Down	27.80	33.64	26.23	Y	US Equity Large Cap Blend (Growth)
● Hartford Municipal Opportunities ETF	HMOP	NYSE Arca	D	D+	D		39.89	40.34	39.08	Y	US Muni Fixed Inc (Growth & Inc)
Hartford Schroders Tax-Aware Bond ETF	HTAB	NYSE Arca	U	U	U		20.00	20.15	19.64	Y	US Muni Fixed Inc (Growth & Inc)
Hartford Short Duration ETF	HSRT	BATS	U	U	U		39.60	40.34	39.56	Y	US Fixed Income (Growth & Inc)
● Hartford Total Return Bond ETF	HTRB	NYSE Arca	D+	D	C		38.78	40.06	38.34	Y	US Fixed Income (Income)
★ Health Care Select Sector SPDR® Fund	XLV	NYSE Arca	B-	B	C+		86.51	95.87	79.55	Y	Healthcare Sector Equity (Health)
● High Yield ETF	HYLD	NYSE Arca	C-	C-	C-	Down	33.66	37.18	33.66	Y	US Fixed Income (Income)
● Highland/iBoxx Senior Loan ETF	SNLN	NAS CM	C	C-	C+		17.18	18.40	17.10	Y	US Fixed Income (Income)
● Hull Tactical US ETF	HTUS	NYSE Arca	C-	C-	D+		22.43	28.43	20.79	Y	Long/Short Equity (Growth)
Impact Shares NAACP Minority Empowerment ETF	NACP	NYSE Arca	U	U	U		18.04	20.83	17.06	Y	US Equity Large Cap Blend (Growth & Inc)
Impact Shares Sustainable Dev Goals Global Equity ETF	SDGA	NYSE Arca	U	U	U		18.30	19.93	17.53	Y	Global Equity Large Cap (Growth)
Impact Shares YWCA Women's Empowerment ETF	WOMN	NYSE Arca	U	U	U		17.60	20.48	16.65	Y	US Equity Large Cap Blend (Growth & Inc)
● Industrial Select Sector SPDR® Fund	XLI	NYSE Arca	C	C	C+	Down	64.41	80.66	60.34	Y	Industrials Sector Equity (Unaligned)
● InfraCap MLP ETF	AMZA	NYSE Arca	C	C+	D+		5.02	9.04	4.76	Y	Energy Sector Equity (Growth & Inc)
InfraCap REIT Preferred ETF	PFFR	NYSE Arca	D	D	D+	Down	22.16	25.43	21.65	Y	US Fixed Income (Real Estate)
Innovation Shares NextGen Protocol ETF	KOIN	NYSE Arca	U	U	U		21.86	27.04	20.71	Y	Technology Sector Equity (Unaligned)
Innovation Shares NextGen Vehicles and Technology ETF	EKAR	NYSE Arca	U	U	U		18.85	26.50	18.17	Y	Technology Sector Equity (Technology)
● Innovator IBD® 50 ETF	FFTY	NYSE	C	C+	C	Down	27.62	38.44	25.43	Y	US Equity Mid Cap (Growth)
Innovator IBD® Breakout Opportunities ETF	BOUT	NYSE Arca	U	U	U		17.39	25.00	16.35	Y	US Equity Large Cap Blend (Growth)
Innovator IBD® ETF Leaders ETF	LDRS	NYSE Arca	D	D	D		21.38	27.19	20.54	Y	Aggressive Allocation (Convertible Bond)
Innovator Loup Frontier Tech ETF	LOUP	NYSE Arca	U	U	U		20.31	26.76	19.08	Y	Technology Sector Equity (Technology)
● Innovator Lunt Low Vol/High Beta Tactical ETF	LVHB	BATS	C-	C-	D+		29.60	34.33	28.29	Y	US Equity Large Cap Blend (Growth & Inc)

★ Expanded analysis of this fund is included in Section II: Analysis of All BUY Rated Funds. ● Expanded analysis of this fund is included in Section III: Analysis of All Rated Funds with Assets over $50 million.

3-Month Total Return	6-Month Total Return	1-Year Total Return	3-Year Total Return	5-Year Total Return	Dividend Yield (TTM)	Expense Ratio	3-Yr Std Deviation	Effective Duration	NAV	Total Assets (MIL)	%Cash	%Stocks	%Bonds	%Other	Turnover Ratio	Premium/ Discount 1-Year Avg	Inception Date
-12.31	-7.72	-20.51	-7.92	-54.69	2.43	0.69	33.15		11.82	314.4	-1	101	0	0	12	-0.12	Nov-10
-4.40	-1.73	-5.46	22.39		5.17	0.65	12.3		11.32	15.1	0	97	0	3	26	-0.47	May-15
-6.03	-4.45	-4.23	19.54		2.66	0.86	6.77	2.26	24.66	3.9	2	40	58	0	233	0.23	Oct-14
-14.79	-10.65	-10.51	8.08		1.46	0.83	7.82	1.88	23.13	3.9	2	40	57	0	816	-0.25	Oct-14
-4.46	-2.11	-2.26			5.75	0.34			46.06	47.4	2	0	98	0	69	-0.20	Sep-17
0.06						0.12			49.44	4.9						-0.06	Oct-18
-0.65	0.35	-3.12			3.26	0.14			47.26	353.9	1	0	99	0	22	-0.05	Jun-17
0.37	0.84	1.58			1.51	0.12			100.03	2,745	44	0	56	0		0.02	Sep-16
-6.98	-7.33	-13.51	28.38		2.29	0.45	14.25		30.24	1,610	0	100	0	0	28	0.03	Sep-15
-13.40	-12.63	-13.98			3.47	0.25			26.41	36.1	0	100	0	0	23	0.26	Mar-16
-13.06	-11.16	-12.92	11.32		2.57	0.25	10.69		25.42	1,091	0	100	0	0	16	0.25	Nov-15
-12.70	-9.79	-10.51			1.94	0.25			29.08	25.4	0	100	0	0	23	0.08	Mar-16
-14.10	-7.57	-4.01	27.75		1.67	0.09	9.35		50.26	4,067	0	100	0	0	16	0.04	Sep-15
-17.67	-16.17	-8.71			1.21	0.2			38.89	50.5	0	100	0	0	27	0.23	Jun-17
-13.97	-9.08	-7.28			1.64	0.09			39.58	76.7	0	100	0	0	34	0.16	Sep-17
-15.36	-10.68	-6.66			0.26	0.45			49.17	109.1	0	100	0	0	1	0.06	Nov-16
-14.97	-7.95					0.2			35.94	212.9	0	100	0	0	2	0.01	Jun-18
-10.74	-9.77	-11.80			0.21	0.25			22.87	50.9	79	0	4	16		0.06	May-17
7.71	2.61	-1.33			0	0.17			127.83	298.8	0	0	0	100		0.18	Aug-17
-13.78	-9.92	-8.90	18.19		7.84	1.3	12.13		14.99	6.6	-1	94	7	0	33	-0.01	Jan-15
-2.93	-5.60					0.5			79.02	3.6	0	0	0	100		0.02	Jan-18
-23.06	-21.25	-13.93			0.17	0.35				7.8	83	0	0	17		0.18	May-17
-35.10	-32.89	-25.35	-10.75	-62.06	0	1.25	18.09			98.3					0	0.00	Jul-07
-10.89	-9.61	-10.21				0.71			17.29	5.6	0	100	0	0		0.00	Dec-17
-10.21	-7.10	-9.73	17.18		2.32	0.29	9.81		25.77	1,165	2	98	0	0	47	0.21	Feb-15
-2.94	0.23	-11.61	22.62		2.07	0.49	13.84		22.17	61.7	1	98	0	0	25	0.01	Feb-15
-12.95	-12.41	-11.89	25.66		2.49	0.39	10.8		26.98	20.6	1	99	0	0	41	0.28	Mar-15
-9.08	-6.29	-9.45			2.29	0.29			24.49	5.2	0	100	0	0	35	0.32	May-17
-10.84	-4.74	-2.87			1.87	0.22			25.42	5.6	0	100	0	0	26	0.32	May-17
-8.29	-8.72	-7.19			4.27	0.45			13.79	27.3	0	99	0	0	35	-0.04	Oct-16
-15.00	-10.44	-8.97	24.27		1.54	0.19	10.25		27.84	204.1	0	100	0	0	36	0.31	Feb-15
1.71	1.61	1.44				0.29			39.84	102.7	7	0	93	0	37	0.14	Dec-17
1.60	1.29					0.39			19.98	20.8	6	0	94	0	60	-0.08	Apr-18
-0.24	0.71					0.29			39.59	105.5	21	0	77	0	1	0.04	May-18
0.45	0.98	-0.79			2.47	0.29			38.72	445.0	16	0	82	0	46	0.23	Sep-17
-9.19	4.11	6.29	25.69	68.07	1.38	0.13	12.5		86.43	19,897	1	99	0	0	5	0.12	Dec-98
-5.68	-3.90	-0.29	26.95	-3.36	7.83	1.25	5.69		33.93	172.3	6	0	94	0		-0.21	Nov-10
-4.77	-2.85	-1.11	9.16	7.47	4.72	0.55	2.62		17.16	487.0	8	1	91	0	126	0.01	Nov-12
-8.89	-6.02	-5.95	13.45		0.6	0.96	5.41		22.88	62.9	37	63	0	0	1,827	-0.09	Jun-15
-12.21						0.76			18.13	2.1	3	97	0	0		0.00	Jul-18
-7.17						0.76			18.33	2.0	14	86	0	0		-0.13	Sep-18
-12.34						0.76			17.70	2.0	3	97	0	0		0.37	Aug-18
-18.00	-9.21	-13.09	29.07	36.47	1.92	0.13	13.16		64.43	11,901	1	99	0	0	6	0.01	Dec-98
-29.20	-22.83	-25.19	-12.92		8.98	1.93	25.11		5.10	506.6	-45	144	0	1	104	0.19	Oct-14
-7.60	-8.26	-8.71			6.36	0.45			22.23	21.9	2	1	0	0		-0.04	Feb-17
-17.49	-9.59					0.65			21.96	10.3	1	99	0	0		-0.33	Jan-18
-18.37	-18.68					0.65			18.81	1.0	1	99	0	0		0.11	Feb-18
-27.31	-22.28	-16.62	24.91		0.18	0.8	18.13		27.65	432.1	0	100	0	0		0.02	Apr-15
-28.61						0.8			17.45	10.9	0	100	0	0		0.29	Sep-18
-14.66	-14.46	-15.41				1.11			21.48	34.0	1	99	0	0		-0.03	Dec-17
-23.08						0.7			20.34	12.7	0	100	0	0		0.13	Jul-18
-5.74	-1.88	-7.58			1.07	0.49			29.69	141.2	0	100	0	0	667	0.04	Oct-16

Fund Name	Ticker Symbol	Traded On	Overall Rating	Reward Rating	Risk Rating	Recent Up/ Downgrade	Price as of 12/31/2018	52-Week High	52-Week Low	Open to New Investors	Category & (Prospectus Objective)
Innovator S&P 500 Buffer ETF – July	BJUL	BATS	U	U	U		23.45	25.93	22.50	Y	Long/Short Equity (Growth)
Innovator S&P 500 Buffer ETF - October	BOCT	BATS	U	U	U		22.07	24.70	21.34	Y	Long/Short Equity (Growth)
Innovator S&P 500 Power Buffer ETF — July	PJUL	BATS	U	U	U		23.98	25.69	23.30	Y	Long/Short Equity (Growth)
Innovator S&P 500 Power Buffer ETF - October	POCT	BATS	U	U	U		22.84	24.74	22.21	Y	Long/Short Equity (Growth)
Innovator S&P 500 Ultra Buffer ETF — July	UJUL	BATS	U	U	U		23.76	25.64	23.62	Y	Long/Short Equity (Growth)
Innovator S&P 500 Ultra Buffer ETF - October	UOCT	BATS	U	U	U		23.03	24.62	22.72	Y	Long/Short Equity (Growth)
Innovator S&P Investment Grade Preferred ETF	EPRF	BATS	D+	D	D+	Down	21.35	24.03	20.89	Y	US Fixed Income (Corp Bond - High Quality)
InsightShares LGBT Employment Equality ETF	PRID	NYSE Arca	U	U	U		23.12	27.22	21.72	Y	US Equity Large Cap Blend (Growth & Inc)
InsightShares Patriotic Employers ETF	HONR	NYSE Arca	U	U	U		21.51	25.36	20.44	Y	US Equity Large Cap Value (Growth & Inc)
Inspire 100 ETF	BIBL	NYSE Arca	C-	C-	D+		23.79	28.39	22.55	Y	US Equity Large Cap Blend (Growth & Inc)
● Inspire Corporate Bond Impact ETF	IBD	NYSE Arca	D	D	D+	Down	24.42	25.43	24.16	Y	US Fixed Income (Corp Bond - Gen)
● Inspire Global Hope ETF	BLES	NYSE Arca	D	D	D+	Down	24.24	30.44	23.44	Y	Global Equity Large Cap (Growth)
● Inspire Small/Mid Cap Impact ETF	ISMD	NYSE Arca	D+	D+	C-		22.84	30.11	21.59	Y	US Equity Mid Cap (Growth)
● Invesco 1-30 Laddered Treasury ETF	PLW	NAS CM	D+	D	C-		31.99	32.79	30.35	Y	US Fixed Income (Govt Bond - Treasury)
Invesco Active U.S. Real Estate Fund	PSR	NYSE Arca	C	C	C-		76.33	84.67	73.39	Y	Real Estate Sector Equity (Real Estate)
★ Invesco Aerospace & Defense ETF	PPA	NYSE Arca	B-	B	C+	Down	49.45	61.91	46.46	Y	Industrials Sector Equity (Unaligned)
Invesco Balanced Multi-Asset Allocation ETF	PSMB	BATS	D+	D+	D+		12.52	13.94	12.21	Y	Moderate Allocation (Asset Allocation)
Invesco BLDRS Asia 50 ADR Index Fund	ADRA	NAS CM	C	B-	D+	Down	28.53	37.70	27.87	Y	Asia Equity (Pacific Stock)
Invesco BLDRS Developed Markets 100 ADR Index Fund	ADRD	NAS CM	C-	C	C-	Down	19.59	25.20	18.89	Y	Global Equity Large Cap (Foreign Stock)
● Invesco BLDRS Emerging Markets 50 ADR Index Fund	ADRE	NAS CM	C	B-	D+	Down	36.07	48.87	34.99	Y	Global Emerg Mkts Equity (Div Emerg Mkts)
Invesco BLDRS Europe Select ADR Index Fund	ADRU	NAS CM	C-	C	D+	Down	18.99	24.56	18.42	Y	Europe Equity Large Cap (Europe Stock)
● Invesco BRIC ETF	EEB	NYSE Arca	C-	C-	D+	Down	32.09	41.99	31.24	Y	Global Emerg Mkts Equity (Growth)
Invesco BulletShares (R) 2021 USD Emerg Mkts Debt ETF	BSAE	NYSE Arca	U	U	U		24.94	25.06	24.85	Y	Emerging Mkts Fixed Inc (Div Emerg Mkts)
Invesco BulletShares (R) 2022 USD Emerg Mkts Debt ETF	BSBE	NYSE Arca	U	U	U		24.92	25.03	24.76	Y	Emerging Mkts Fixed Inc (Div Emerg Mkts)
Invesco BulletShares (R) 2023 USD Emerg Mkts Debt ETF	BSCE	NYSE Arca	U	U	U		24.78	24.91	24.61	Y	Emerging Mkts Fixed Inc (Div Emerg Mkts)
Invesco BulletShares (R) 2024 Emerging Markets Debt ETF	BSDE	NYSE Arca	U	U	U		24.67	24.84	24.61	Y	Emerging Mkts Fixed Inc (Div Emerg Mkts)
● Invesco BulletShares 2018 Corporate Bond ETF	BSCI	NYSE Arca	C	C	C+		21.14	21.19	21.09	Y	US Fixed Income (Corp Bond - Gen)
● Invesco BulletShares 2018 High Yield Corporate Bond ETF	BSJI	NYSE Arca	C	C	C+		25.09	25.18	24.86	Y	US Fixed Income (Corp Bond-High Yld)
● Invesco BulletShares 2019 Corporate Bond ETF	BSCJ	NYSE Arca	C	C	C+		21.06	21.11	20.94	Y	US Fixed Income (Corp Bond - Gen)
● Invesco BulletShares 2019 High Yield Corporate Bond ETF	BSJJ	NYSE Arca	C	C	C+		23.64	24.51	23.46	Y	US Fixed Income (Corp Bond-High Yld)
● Invesco BulletShares 2020 Corporate Bond ETF	BSCK	NYSE Arca	C	C	C+		21.07	21.29	20.97	Y	US Fixed Income (Corp Bond - Gen)
● Invesco BulletShares 2020 High Yield Corporate Bond ETF	BSJK	NYSE Arca	C	C	C+	Down	23.43	24.69	23.23	Y	US Fixed Income (Corp Bond-High Yld)
● Invesco BulletShares 2021 Corporate Bond ETF	BSCL	NYSE Arca	C	C-	C+		20.75	21.13	20.62	Y	US Fixed Income (Corp Bond - Gen)
● Invesco BulletShares 2021 High Yield Corporate Bond ETF	BSJL	NYSE Arca	C	C	C+		23.66	25.08	23.39	Y	US Fixed Income (Corp Bond-High Yld)
● Invesco BulletShares 2022 Corporate Bond ETF	BSCM	NYSE Arca	C	C-	C+		20.61	21.17	20.47	Y	US Fixed Income (Corp Bond - Gen)
● Invesco BulletShares 2022 High Yield Corporate Bond ETF	BSJM	NYSE Arca	C	C	C+		23.21	25.14	22.88	Y	US Fixed Income (Corp Bond-High Yld)
● Invesco BulletShares 2023 Corporate Bond ETF	BSCN	NYSE Arca	C	C-	C+	Up	20.17	20.83	20.00	Y	US Fixed Income (Corp Bond - Gen)
● Invesco BulletShares 2023 High Yield Corporate Bond ETF	BSJN	NYSE Arca	C-	C-	C-	Down	24.63	26.67	24.23	Y	US Fixed Income (Corp Bond-High Yld)
● Invesco BulletShares 2024 Corporate Bond ETF	BSCO	NYSE Arca	C-	C-	C-		19.97	20.89	19.77	Y	US Fixed Income (Corp Bond - Gen)
● Invesco BulletShares 2024 High Yield Corporate Bond ETF	BSJO	NYSE Arca	D+	D+	D+	Down	23.41	25.83	23.03	Y	US Fixed Income (Corp Bond-High Yld)
● Invesco BulletShares 2025 Corporate Bond ETF	BSCP	NYSE Arca	C-	D+	C-		19.66	20.70	19.40	Y	US Fixed Income (Corp Bond - Gen)
Invesco BulletShares 2025 High Yield Corporate Bond ETF	BSJP	NYSE Arca	D+	D+	D+		22.44	25.20	21.97	Y	US Fixed Income (Corp Bond-High Yld)
● Invesco BulletShares 2026 Corporate Bond ETF	BSCQ	NYSE Arca	D+	D+	C-		18.61	19.70	18.38	Y	US Fixed Income (Corp Bond - Gen)
Invesco BulletShares 2026 High Yield Corporate Bond ETF	BSJQ	NYSE Arca	U	U	U		23.50	25.32	23.02	Y	US Fixed Income (Corp Bond-High Yld)
Invesco BulletShares 2027 Corporate Bond ETF	BSCR	NYSE Arca	D	D	C-		18.84	20.00	18.58	Y	US Fixed Income (Corp Bond - Gen)
Invesco BulletShares 2028 Corporate Bond ETF	BSCS	NYSE Arca	U	U	U		19.69	20.17	19.39	Y	US Fixed Income (Income)
● Invesco BuyBack Achievers ETF	PKW	NAS CM	C	C	C		52.17	63.28	49.25	Y	US Equity Large Cap Blend (Unaligned)
● Invesco California AMT-Free Municipal Bond ETF	PWZ	NYSE Arca	C	C-	C+		25.80	26.38	25.05	Y	US Muni Fixed Inc (Muni Bond - Single State)
Invesco Canadian Energy Income ETF	ENY	NYSE Arca	D+	D+	D	Down	5.82	8.75	5.57	Y	Energy Sector Equity (Natl Res)
● Invesco CEF Income Composite ETF	PCEF	NYSE Arca	C	D+	C+		20.23	24.17	19.45	Y	Cautious Allocation (Income)
● Invesco CEF Income Composite ETF	YAO	NYSE Arca	D+	C-	D+	Down	27.61	39.91	27.23	Y	Greater China Equity (Pacific Stock)
Invesco China Real Estate ETF	TAO	NYSE Arca	C-	C-	C-	Down	24.35	33.34	23.45	Y	Greater China Equity (Real Estate)

★ Expanded analysis of this fund is included in Section II: Analysis of All BUY Rated Funds. ● Expanded analysis of this fund is included in Section III: Analysis of All Rated Funds with Assets over $50 million.

			TOTAL RETURNS & PERFORMANCE						ASSETS		ASSET ALLOCATION & TURNOVER					VALUATION	
3-Month Total Return	6-Month Total Return	1-Year Total Return	3-Year Total Return	5-Year Total Return	Dividend Yield (TTM)	Expense Ratio	3-Yr Std Deviation	Effective Duration	NAV	Total Assets (MIL)	%Cash	%Stocks	%Bonds	%Other	Turnover Ratio	Premium/ Discount 1-Year Avg	Inception Date
-8.67						0.79			23.47	3.7						0.02	Aug-18
-9.83						0.79			22.24	21.3	5	95	0	0		0.43	Sep-18
-6.50						0.79			23.95	4.4	3	97	0	0		0.39	Aug-18
-6.58						0.79			22.91	13.1	4	96	0	0		0.42	Sep-18
-6.82						0.79			23.85	5.0	1	99	0	0		0.15	Aug-18
-6.71						0.79			22.97	32.9	2	98	0	0		0.49	Sep-18
-5.42	-7.16	-5.99			5.59	0.47			21.43	15.2	0	0	0	0		-0.07	May-16
-14.82	-7.70					0.65				28.2	0	100	0	0		0.12	Jan-18
-13.38	-8.33					0.65				27.8	0	100	0	0		0.32	Jan-18
-15.31	-9.41	-7.36			1.66	0.35			23.81	39.1	0	100	0	0		0.22	Oct-17
0.78	1.37	-0.23			2.17	0.61			24.35	58.0	3	0	97	0		0.48	Jul-17
-13.35	-11.31	-12.74			1.85	0.61			24.31	87.8	0	100	0	0		0.66	Feb-17
-20.60	-18.89	-10.56			0.79	0.61			22.94	50.8	0	100	0	0		0.14	Feb-17
3.83	1.93	-0.37	5.28	20.93	2.22	0.25	5.93	10.64	31.94	134.4	3	0	97	0		-0.04	Oct-07
-4.71	-4.67	-4.59	11.94	49.24	1.72	0.35	11.66		76.16	29.1	0	100	0	0	134	-0.04	Nov-08
-19.45	-9.86	-7.35	43.58	68.74	0.56	0.6	13.63		49.50	906.1	0	100	0	0	7	0.03	Oct-05
-7.61	-4.86	-4.41			2.61	0.39		6.99	12.52	2.7	1	60	39	0	6	0.32	Feb-17
-12.26	-12.31	-15.42	12.24	7.76	2.41	0.3	13.25		28.40	18.2	0	100	0	0		0.34	Nov-02
-11.83	-10.20	-13.54	4.40	-5.40	3.48	0.27	10.82		19.66	46.1	0	100	0	0	3	-0.14	Nov-02
-10.72	-10.14	-14.00	31.06	7.64	1.97	0.18	16.57		36.20	129.3	0	100	0	0	10	0.02	Nov-02
-11.78	-10.61	-13.55	4.16	-6.23	3.53	0.3	11.24		19.11	13.2	0	100	0	0	2	0.08	Nov-02
-9.68	-11.48	-14.35	35.50	0.67	1.81	0.64	16.44			63.2	0	100	0	0	39	-0.02	Sep-06
1.08						0.29			24.92	9.9	1	0	99	0		0.13	Oct-18
1.17						0.29			24.92	9.9	1	0	99	0		0.14	Oct-18
0.55						0.29			24.77	9.8	0	0	100	0		0.17	Oct-18
0.36						0.29			24.69	9.8	1	0	99	0		0.67	Oct-18
0.49	1.07	1.89	6.02	10.48	1.85	0.1	0.76	0.17		625.7	100	0	0	0	0	-0.08	Mar-12
0.28	1.08	2.43	17.85	14.38	2.97	0.42	2.54	0.32		509.8	96	0	4	0	0	-0.15	Apr-12
0.48	1.26	1.71	6.77	12.73	2	0.1	1.33	0.73	21.01	1,242	21	0	79	0	3	0.16	Mar-12
-1.06	0.50	1.55	19.26	15.74	4.41	0.42	3.36	0.73	23.70	1,149	8	0	92	0	25	-0.02	Sep-13
0.68	1.44	1.14	7.67	15.16	2.28	0.1	1.91	1.64	21.02	1,408	0	0	100	0	1	0.25	Mar-12
-2.15	-0.27	0.46	20.32	16.63	5.05	0.42	3.78	1.48	23.46	966.1	2	0	98	0	27	-0.02	Sep-13
0.74	1.53	0.66	9.02	17.98	2.58	0.1	2.52	2.51	20.69	1,118	0	0	100	0	3	0.23	Jul-13
-2.92	-0.70	0.01	20.74		5.07	0.42	3.51	2.07	23.71	513.5	3	0	97	0	14	-0.07	Sep-14
0.73	1.54	0.03	9.97	19.17	2.81	0.1	3.09	3.37	20.56	895.3	0	0	100	0	0	0.24	Jul-13
-4.03	-1.69	-1.38	20.31		5.66	0.42	3.7	2.52	23.29	290.3	2	0	98	0	17	-0.06	Sep-14
0.75	1.71	-0.35	10.80		3	0.1	3.22	4.15	20.13	452.5	0	0	100	0	0	0.22	Sep-14
-4.64	-1.97	-1.35	17.39		5.18	0.42	3.5	3.13	24.63	129.7	1	0	98	0	6	-0.07	Oct-15
0.52	1.63	-1.06	10.69		3.36	0.1	3.62	4.98	19.93	323.5	0	0	100	0	2	0.29	Sep-14
-4.51	-1.55	-3.19			5.37	0.42		3.83	23.40	55.5	0	0	100	0	8	0.19	Sep-16
0.23	1.30	-1.90	9.20		3.43	0.1	3.94	5.72	19.59	137.1	1	0	99	0	1	0.19	Oct-15
-7.32	-4.06	-5.42			5.82	0.42		4.53		25.5	0	0	100	0	9	0.11	Sep-17
0.33	1.31	-2.38			3.5	0.1		6.50	18.55	57.9	0	0	100	0	0	0.18	Sep-16
-4.80						0.42		5.22	23.43	4.9	2	0	98	0	0	-0.08	Aug-18
0.15	1.19	-2.89			3.44	0.1		7.08	18.78	36.3	0	0	100	0	0	0.20	Sep-17
-0.40						0.1		7.59	19.66	5.8	2	0	98	0	0	0.18	Aug-18
-13.80	-7.81	-10.42	19.05	28.46	0.99	0.63	10.79		52.20	1,510	0	100	0	0	66	0.03	Dec-06
1.49	0.78	0.39	7.99	28.25	2.58	0.28	4.09	8.14	25.76	300.6	0	0	100	0		-0.05	Oct-07
-28.46	-27.66	-29.86	-6.42	-54.42	4.42	0.66	18.16			14.0	0	100	0	0	28	-0.29	Jul-07
-9.73	-7.84	-8.89	18.68	22.81	7.81	2.07	6.91		20.20	681.0	-1	27	67	-2		0.11	Feb-10
-12.91	-18.36	-19.90	16.81	15.14	2.33	0.7	18.04		28.05	681.0	0	100	0	0	10	-0.26	Oct-09
-0.90	-7.29	-8.42	41.90	53.36	6.15	0.7	20		24.48	40.5	0	100	0	0	20	-0.31	Dec-07

Fund Name	Ticker Symbol	Traded On	Overall Rating	Reward Rating	Risk Rating	Recent Up/ Downgrade	Price as of 12/31/2018	52-Week High	52-Week Low	Open to New Investors	Category & (Prospectus Objective)
● Invesco China Small Cap ETF	HAO	NYSE Arca	D+	D+	D+	Down	22.73	33.19	22.03	Y	Greater China Equity (Pacific Stock)
● Invesco China Technology ETF	CQQQ	NYSE Arca	D+	C-	D	Down	39.37	66.86	38.20	Y	Greater China Equity (Technology)
● Invesco Chinese Yuan Dim Sum Bond ETF	DSUM	NYSE Arca	D+	D+	C-	Down	21.62	24.65	21.23	Y	Emerging Mkts Fixed Inc (Worldwide Bond)
● Invesco Cleantech™ ETF	PZD	NYSE Arca	C-	C-	D+	Down	36.80	45.28	35.15	Y	Industrials Sector Equity (Technology)
Invesco Conservative Multi-Asset Allocation ETF	PSMC	BATS	D	D+	D		12.16	12.95	11.98	Y	Cautious Allocation (Asset Allocation)
Invesco Corporate Income Defensive ETF	IHYD	NYSE Arca	U	U	U		24.47	25.05	24.29	Y	US Fixed Income (Corp Bond-High Yld)
Invesco Corporate Income Value ETF	IHYV	NYSE Arca	U	U	U		23.43	25.09	23.12	Y	US Fixed Income (Corp Bond-High Yld)
● Invesco CurrencyShares® Australian Dollar Trust	FXA	NYSE Arca	D+	D	C-		70.45	81.14	70.31	Y	Currency (Worldwide Bond)
● Invesco CurrencyShares® British Pound Sterling Trust	FXB	NYSE Arca	D	D	D+	Down	123.65	139.18	121.25	Y	Currency (Worldwide Bond)
● Invesco CurrencyShares® Canadian Dollar Trust	FXC	NYSE Arca	D+	D+	C-		72.29	80.39	72.20	Y	Currency (Worldwide Bond)
Invesco CurrencyShares® Chinese Renminbi Trust	FXCH	NYSE Arca	D-	D	E	Down	71.12	78.35	70.05	Y	Currency (Growth & Inc)
● Invesco CurrencyShares® Euro Currency Trust	FXE	NYSE Arca	C-	D+	C	Down	109.48	120.47	107.47	Y	Currency (Worldwide Bond)
● Invesco CurrencyShares® Japanese Yen Trust	FXY	NYSE Arca	D+	D	C-		87.11	91.52	83.60	Y	Currency (Worldwide Bond)
Invesco CurrencyShares® Singapore Dollar Trust	FXSG	NYSE Arca	D+	C-	D	Up	71.85	75.87	70.63	Y	Currency (Growth & Inc)
Invesco CurrencyShares® Swedish Krona Trust	FXS	NYSE Arca	D	D	D+		105.65	121.32	102.32	Y	Currency (Worldwide Bond)
● Invesco CurrencyShares® Swiss Franc Trust	FXF	NYSE Arca	D	D	C-		94.88	102.20	92.44	Y	Currency (Worldwide Bond)
● Invesco DB Agriculture Fund	DBA	NYSE Arca	D	D	D		16.94	19.63	16.85	Y	Commodities Specified (Natl Res)
● Invesco DB Base Metals Fund	DBB	NYSE Arca	C-	C-	C-	Down	15.39	19.89	15.39	Y	Commodities Specified (Prec Metals)
● Invesco DB Commodity Index Tracking Fund	DBC	NYSE Arca	C	C-	C		14.49	18.54	14.39	Y	Commodities Broad Basket (Natl Res)
● Invesco DB Energy Fund	DBE	NYSE Arca	C	C-	C		12.44	18.74	12.16	Y	Commodities Specified (Natl Res)
Invesco DB G10 Currency Harvest Fund	DBV	NYSE Arca	C-	C-	D+		23.53	24.99	21.39	Y	Currency (Growth & Inc)
● Invesco DB Gold Fund	DGL	NYSE Arca	D+	D	D+		39.54	43.10	36.93	Y	Commodities Specified (Prec Metals)
● Invesco DB Oil Fund	DBO	NYSE Arca	C-	C-	C-	Down	8.47	14.02	8.12	Y	Commodities Specified (Natl Res)
● Invesco DB Precious Metals Fund	DBP	NYSE Arca	D	D	D+	Down	36.37	40.07	34.00	Y	Commodities Specified (Prec Metals)
Invesco DB Silver Fund	DBS	NYSE Arca	D	D-	D		22.98	27.00	21.18	Y	Commodities Specified (Prec Metals)
Invesco DB US Dollar Index Bearish Fund	UDN	NYSE Arca	D+	D	C-	Down	20.99	23.24	20.79	Y	Currency (Worldwide Bond)
● Invesco DB US Dollar Index Bullish Fund	UUP	NYSE Arca	C	C	C+	Up	25.45	26.04	23.13	Y	Currency (Growth & Inc)
● Invesco Defensive Equity ETF	DEF	NYSE Arca	C	C	C-		44.04	50.42	41.71	Y	US Equity Large Cap Blend (Growth)
● Invesco Dividend Achievers™ ETF	PFM	NAS CM	C	C	C-		24.70	28.02	23.52	Y	US Equity Large Cap Value (Equity-Income)
Invesco Dow Jones Industrial Average Dividend ETF	DJD	NYSE Arca	C+	B	C	Down	33.28	36.68	31.25	Y	US Equity Large Cap Value (Growth & Inc)
● Invesco DWA Basic Materials Momentum ETF	PYZ	NAS CM	C	C	D+	Down	52.93	75.00	50.28	Y	Natural Resources (Unaligned)
● Invesco DWA Consumer Cyclicals Momentum ETF	PEZ	NAS CM	C+	B	C-	Down	46.67	60.10	43.46	Y	Consumer Goods & Svcs (Unaligned)
★ Invesco DWA Consumer Staples Momentum ETF	PSL	NAS CM	B-	B	C	Down	65.21	73.71	62.43	Y	Consumer Goods & Svcs (Unaligned)
● Invesco DWA Developed Markets Momentum ETF	PIZ	NAS CM	D+	D+	D+	Down	22.97	29.67	22.12		Global Equity Large Cap (Foreign Stock)
● Invesco DWA Emerging Markets Momentum ETF	PIE	NAS CM	D+	D+	D+	Down	15.56	22.21	15.34		Global Emerg Mkts Equity (Div Emerg Mkts)
● Invesco DWA Energy Momentum ETF	PXI	NAS CM	C	B-	D+		28.39	46.27	26.03	Y	Energy Sector Equity (Natl Res)
Invesco DWA Financial Momentum ETF	PFI	NAS CM	C	C	C-	Down	28.59	37.13	27.13	Y	Financials Sector Equity (Financial)
● Invesco DWA Healthcare Momentum ETF	PTH	NAS CM	C	C	C-		71.18	98.76	64.96	Y	Healthcare Sector Equity (Health)
● Invesco DWA Industrials Momentum ETF	PRN	NAS CM	C	C	C-	Down	50.95	66.35	47.61	Y	Industrials Sector Equity (Unaligned)
Invesco DWA Momentum & Low Volatility Rotation ETF	DWLV	NAS CM	C-	C-	D+	Up	27.52	34.27	26.41	Y	US Equity Mid Cap (Growth & Inc)
● Invesco DWA Momentum ETF	PDP	NAS CM	C	C	C+	Down	48.47	60.08	45.29	Y	US Equity Mid Cap (Growth)
Invesco DWA NASDAQ Momentum ETF	DWAQ	NAS CM	C-	C	D+	Down	87.96	118.73	80.71	Y	US Equity Mid Cap (Growth)
● Invesco DWA SmallCap Momentum ETF	DWAS	NAS CM	C-	C-	C-	Down	43.50	59.39	40.08	Y	US Equity Small Cap (Small Company)
Invesco DWA Tactical Multi-Asset Income ETF	DWIN	NAS CM	D+	D	C-		23.87	27.22	23.61	Y	Cautious Allocation (Multi-Asset Global)
● Invesco DWA Tactical Sector Rotation ETF	DWTR	NAS CM	C-	C-	C-	Down	24.59	32.22	22.70	Y	US Equity Mid Cap (Growth & Inc)
● Invesco DWA Technology Momentum ETF	PTF	NAS CM	C	C	C-	Down	52.67	68.61	48.33	Y	Technology Sector Equity (Technology)
★ Invesco DWA Utilities Momentum ETF	PUI	NAS CM	B	B	C+	Up	28.96	31.29	24.57	Y	Utilities Sector Equity (Utility)
● Invesco Dynamic Biotechnology & Genome ETF	PBE	NYSE Arca	C	C+	D+		47.07	60.27	43.44	Y	Healthcare Sector Equity (Health)
● Invesco Dynamic Building & Construction ETF	PKB	NYSE Arca	C+	B	C-	Down	23.78	36.11	22.38	Y	Industrials Sector Equity (Unaligned)
● Invesco Dynamic Energy Exploration & Production ETF	PXE	NYSE Arca	C+	B	C-	Up	17.37	28.22	15.89	Y	Energy Sector Equity (Natl Res)
★ Invesco Dynamic Food & Beverage ETF	PBJ	NYSE Arca	B-	B	C		29.67	34.92	28.60	Y	Consumer Goods & Svcs (Unaligned)
● Invesco Dynamic Large Cap Growth ETF	PWB	NYSE Arca	C	C+	C	Down	41.47	48.53	38.42	Y	US Equity Large Cap Growth (Growth)

★Expanded analysis of this fund is included in Section II: Analysis of All BUY Rated Funds. ●Expanded analysis of this fund is included in Section III: Analysis of All Rated Funds with Assets over $50 million.

3-Month Total Return	6-Month Total Return	1-Year Total Return	3-Year Total Return	5-Year Total Return	Dividend Yield (TTM)	Expense Ratio	3-Yr Std Deviation	Effective Duration	NAV	Total Assets (MIL)	%Cash	%Stocks	%Bonds	%Other	Turnover Ratio	Premium/ Discount 1-Year Avg	Inception Date
-16.74	-25.37	-25.07	-2.05	-3.64	4.12	0.75	18.14			66.2	0	100	0	0	34	-0.54	Jan-08
-17.19	-29.13	-34.40	13.14	21.01	1.96	0.7	21.4			483.0	0	100	0	0	21	0.03	Dec-09
0.86	-2.34	-3.12	6.30	2.63	4.17	0.45	5.42	1.80	21.86	70.4	6	0	94	0	60	-0.49	Sep-11
-14.32	-11.55	-12.34	28.87	21.49	0.55	0.67	13.17		36.89	158.6	0	100	0	0	17	0.34	Oct-06
-3.32	-1.63	-1.98			3.47	0.37		5.53	12.16	1.2	1	20	70	0	4	0.17	Feb-17
-1.40						0.23		2.92	24.48	12.4	0	0	100	0		-0.13	Jul-18
-4.81						0.23		4.43	23.43	12.1	1	0	99	0		0.03	Jul-18
-2.63	-3.56	-9.13	-0.58	-16.48	0.99	0.4	9.35		70.45	113.4	100	0	0	0	0	-0.19	Jun-06
-2.34	-3.01	-6.04	-14.39	-24.31	0	0.4	9.21		123.54	142.5	100	0	0	0	0	-0.09	Jun-06
-5.23	-3.16	-7.88	1.55	-22.31	0.31	0.4	8.03		72.26	152.4	100	0	0	0	0	-0.10	Jun-06
0.00	-2.88	-5.49	-5.23	-13.11	0	0.4	4.91		71.22	3.5	100	0	0	0		0.08	Sep-11
-1.78	-1.90	-5.56	2.73	-19.79	0	0.4	7		109.25	272.2	100	0	0	0		-0.05	Dec-05
3.39	0.69	2.16	8.04	-6.35	0	0.4	10.3		87.03	147.5	100	0	0	0	0	0.01	Feb-07
0.33	0.75	-1.76	3.72	-8.37	0.17	0.4	5.06		72.19	3.6	100	0	0	0		-0.19	Feb-13
-0.11	0.64	-9.18	-9.40	-31.81	0	0.4	9.74		105.60	15.5	100	0	0	0	0	0.06	Jun-06
-1.20	0.19	-2.28	-1.93	-14.12	0	0.4	7.4		94.60	182.8	100	0	0	0	0	-0.07	Jun-06
0.61	-2.88	-8.74	-17.15	-29.47	0	0.85	8.98		16.94	581.6	33	0	17	50		-0.04	Jan-07
-8.18	-11.19	-20.37	30.03	-7.98	0	0.75	14.8		15.44	169.7	38	0	18	44	0	-0.06	Jan-07
-20.04	-15.44	-12.02	9.59	-42.87	0	0.85	13.2		14.44	2,020	35	0	15	45	0	-0.06	Feb-06
-32.42	-25.10	-14.06	12.44	-56.99	0	0.75	21.96		12.33	166.3	37	0	13	50		-0.10	Jan-07
-1.86	-1.77	0.67	2.24	-6.31	0.08	0.75	5.03		23.52	24.6	77	0	23	0	0	-0.15	Sep-06
5.64	0.78	-5.04	13.76	-2.16	0.11	0.75	12.78		39.42	99.5	47	0	3	0	0	0.01	Jan-07
-39.50	-31.42	-17.88	-7.58	-69.72	0	0.75	25.1		8.38	287.9	37	0	12	51		-0.17	Jan-07
5.82	0.11	-6.17	12.57	-7.24	0.13	0.75	13.79		36.29	111.5	59	0	31	10		-0.03	Jan-07
4.94	-6.32	-12.08	5.31	-28.42	0.07	0.75	20.87		23.05	17.1	50	0	0	50		-0.26	Jan-07
-2.34	-2.65	-6.46	-1.97	-22.49	0.11	0.75	6.27		20.98	29.4	181	-105	23	0		0.00	Feb-07
0.69	2.05	6.29	-0.54	18.54	0.09	0.75	6.34		25.48	535.1	38	50	12	0		-0.03	Feb-07
-10.84	-3.85	-3.73	33.14	43.45	1.55	0.6	8.62		44.00	192.8	0	100	0	0	136	0.10	Dec-06
-10.12	-2.42	-4.40	28.61	38.44	2.08	0.55	8.32		24.71	324.1	0	100	0	0	5	0.11	Sep-05
-8.03	0.76	0.11	42.43		2.3	0.07			33.17	45.4	0	100	0	0		0.30	Dec-15
-22.04	-20.50	-23.31	12.96	10.18	0.99	0.6	18.18		53.48	81.4	0	100	0	0	75	0.16	Oct-06
-20.83	-14.26	-6.30	8.10	16.02	0.34	0.6	14.35		46.82	66.4	0	100	0	0	185	0.20	Oct-06
-8.03	-6.89	1.51	18.93	56.25	0.46	0.6	6.89		65.44	184.1	0	100	0	0	80	0.09	Oct-06
-16.17	-14.71	-16.17	0.80	-6.03	1.36	0.81	12.64		23.03	204.6	0	100	0	0	98	0.05	Dec-07
-11.36	-20.34	-21.24	10.02	-7.24	3.02	0.9	13.4		15.67	180.0	-1	101	0	0	174	-0.17	Dec-07
-35.99	-32.33	-27.34	-12.83	-45.99	0.93	0.6	28.36		28.51	62.3	0	100	0	0	95	0.10	Oct-06
-15.22	-16.58	-16.66	-2.23	5.03	1.25	0.6	12.06		28.67	30.8	0	100	0	0	105	0.18	Oct-06
-26.44	-19.29	-0.86	29.61	50.80	0	0.6	25.82		71.48	275.0	0	100	0	0	130	0.11	Oct-06
-19.80	-14.19	-15.54	16.94	9.80	0.17	0.6	13.77		51.22	102.2	0	100	0	0	106	0.18	Oct-06
-15.76	-13.56	-9.32			1.09	0.68			27.66	24.4	0	100	0	0		0.16	Jul-16
-18.27	-12.64	-5.88	18.62	34.74	0.08	0.63	11.92		48.49	1,500	0	100	0	0	68	0.01	Mar-07
-23.01	-20.52	-13.46	19.62	27.94	0.11	0.6	15.57		88.34	39.4	0	100	0	0	80	0.11	May-03
-22.47	-20.06	-10.18	16.84	11.09	0.2	0.6	17.6		43.66	338.9	0	100	0	0		0.08	Jul-12
-2.27	-2.98	-5.77			5.14	0.58		5.56	23.86	45.8	2	0	77	0		-0.06	Mar-16
-21.07	-16.28	-12.61	-0.50		0.28	0.75	13.62		24.70	64.6	0	100	0	0		-0.22	Oct-15
-18.56	-12.96	0.98	33.87	50.94	0.07	0.6	18.1		52.94	125.0	0	100	0	0	107	0.09	Oct-06
1.57	4.92	6.10	41.06	60.02	2.27	0.6	12.27		28.91	69.8	0	100	0	0	41	0.04	Oct-05
-19.58	-14.69	0.23	-5.53	31.43	0	0.59	24.96		47.29	294.1	0	100	0	0	141	0.05	Jun-05
-19.37	-21.73	-30.87	1.25	7.81	0.4	0.58	17.8		23.83	148.6	0	100	0	0	143	-0.05	Oct-05
-36.87	-34.34	-23.16	-12.02	-42.03	1.07	0.65	30.39		17.40	72.8	0	100	0	0	87	0.06	Oct-05
-7.27	-8.89	-10.77	-4.01	20.34	0.99	0.63	8.76		29.80	74.3	0	100	0	0	147	0.03	Jun-05
-14.19	-7.46	1.06	35.80	66.13	0.67	0.57	9.93		41.49	672.4	0	100	0	0	119	0.07	Mar-05

Fund Name	Ticker Symbol	Traded On	Overall Rating	Reward Rating	Risk Rating	Recent Up/ Downgrade	Price as of 12/31/2018	52-Week High	52-Week Low	Open to New Investors	Category & (Prospectus Objective)
● Invesco Dynamic Large Cap Value ETF	PWV	NYSE Arca	C	C	C		32.63	40.51	30.83	Y	US Equity Large Cap Value (Growth)
● Invesco Dynamic Leisure and Entertainment ETF	PEJ	NYSE Arca	C+	B	C-	Down	39.80	48.32	38.07	Y	Consumer Goods & Svcs (Unaligned)
● Invesco Dynamic Market ETF	PWC	NYSE Arca	C	C	C-	Down	88.02	106.71	83.08	Y	US Equity Mid Cap (Growth)
● Invesco Dynamic Media ETF	PBS	NYSE Arca	C+	B	C-		28.42	33.68	26.83	Y	Consumer Goods & Svcs (Comm)
● Invesco Dynamic Networking ETF	PXQ	NYSE Arca	C	B-	D+	Down	48.37	58.89	45.28	Y	Technology Sector Equity (Technology)
Invesco Dynamic Oil & Gas Services ETF	PXJ	NYSE Arca	D+	C	D	Down	5.70	10.67	5.44	Y	Energy Sector Equity (Natl Res)
● Invesco Dynamic Pharmaceuticals ETF	PJP	NYSE Arca	C	B-	D+		62.35	74.14	58.29	Y	Healthcare Sector Equity (Health)
Invesco Dynamic Retail ETF	PMR	NYSE Arca	C+	B	C-	Down	33.73	43.06	31.76	Y	Consumer Goods & Svcs (Unaligned)
● Invesco Dynamic Semiconductors ETF	PSI	NYSE Arca	C+	B	C-	Down	44.31	57.52	41.12	Y	Technology Sector Equity (Technology)
● Invesco Dynamic Software ETF	PSJ	NYSE Arca	C	C+	C-	Down	73.90	88.71	63.50	Y	Technology Sector Equity (Technology)
Invesco Emerging Markets Debt Defensive ETF	IEMD	NYSE Arca	U	U	U		24.96	24.99	24.83	Y	Emerging Mkts Fixed Inc (Div Emerg Mkts)
Invesco Emerging Markets Debt Value ETF	IEMV	NYSE Arca	U	U	U		24.75	24.84	24.47	Y	Emerging Mkts Fixed Inc (Income)
Invesco Emerging Markets Infrastructure ETF	PXR	NYSE Arca	D+	C-	D+		31.28	40.76	30.62		Global Emerg Mkts Equity (Utility)
● Invesco Emerging Markets Sovereign Debt ETF	PCY	NYSE Arca	C-	D	C		26.42	29.71	25.56	Y	Emerging Mkts Fixed Inc (Worldwide Bond)
● Invesco Financial Preferred ETF	PGF	NYSE Arca	C	C-	C+	Down	17.36	18.87	17.04	Y	US Fixed Income (Financial)
● Invesco Frontier Markets ETF	FRN	NYSE Arca	C-	C-	D+		12.18	16.52	12.00	Y	Global Emerg Mkts Equity (Div Emerg Mkts)
● Invesco FTSE International Low Beta Equal Weight ETF	IDLB	NAS CM	D+	D+	D+	Down	25.83	31.82	25.28		Global Equity Large Cap (Growth & Inc)
Invesco FTSE RAFI Asia Pacific ex-Japan ETF	PAF	NYSE Arca	D+	C-	D		47.95	62.65	47.16		Asia ex-Japan Equity (Pacific Stock)
● Invesco FTSE RAFI Developed Markets ex-U.S. ETF	PXF	NYSE Arca	C-	D+	C-	Down	37.52	48.66	36.29		Global Equity Large Cap (Foreign Stock)
● Invesco FTSE RAFI Developed Markets ex-U.S. Small-Mid ETF	PDN	NYSE Arca	C-	D+	C-		27.56	36.59	26.23		Global Eq Mid/Small Cap (Foreign Stock)
● Invesco FTSE RAFI Emerging Markets ETF	PXH	NYSE Arca	C	C-	C		19.77	25.30	19.25		Global Emerg Mkts Equity (Div Emerg Mkts)
● Invesco FTSE RAFI US 1000 ETF	PRF	NYSE Arca	C	C	C+	Down	101.57	120.82	95.78	Y	US Equity Large Cap Value (Growth)
● Invesco FTSE RAFI US 1500 Small-Mid ETF	PRFZ	NAS CM	C-	C-	C-	Down	113.66	146.04	107.24	Y	US Equity Small Cap (Growth)
● Invesco Fundamental High Yield® Corporate Bond ETF	PHB	NYSE Arca	C	C	C+		17.67	19.03	17.49	Y	US Fixed Income (Corp Bond-High Yld)
● Invesco Fundamental Investment Grade Corporate Bond ETF	PFIG	NYSE Arca	C-	D+	C-		24.65	25.58	24.40	Y	US Fixed Income (Corp Bond - High Quality)
Invesco Global Agriculture ETF	PAGG	NAS CM	C-	C	D+		23.66	28.86	23.06		Natural Resources (Natl Res)
● Invesco Global Clean Energy ETF	PBD	NYSE Arca	D+	D+	D+	Down	10.42	13.74	9.75		Equity Misc (Natl Res)
Invesco Global Gold and Precious Metals ETF	PSAU	NAS CM	D+	D+	D		17.42	20.89	14.45		Prec Metals (Prec Metals)
● Invesco Global Listed Private Equity ETF	PSP	NYSE Arca	C-	D+	C-	Down	10.01	13.52	9.72	Y	Financials Sector Equity (Growth)
● Invesco Global Short Term High Yield Bond ETF	PGHY	NYSE Arca	C	C	C-		22.70	24.03	22.65	Y	Global Fixed Income (Worldwide Bond)
● Invesco Global Water ETF	PIO	NAS CM	C-	C	C-	Down	23.08	27.15	22.13		Equity Misc (Natl Res)
● Invesco Golden Dragon China ETF	PGJ	NAS CM	C	B-	D	Down	31.53	50.87	30.95	Y	Greater China Equity (Pacific Stock)
Invesco Growth Multi-Asset Allocation ETF	PSMG	BATS	D+	D+	D+		12.80	14.47	12.35	Y	Aggressive Allocation (Asset Allocation)
● Invesco High Yield Equity Dividend Achievers™ ETF	PEY	NAS CM	C	C	C+		15.84	18.61	15.14	Y	US Equity Mid Cap (Growth & Inc)
● Invesco India ETF	PIN	NYSE Arca	D+	D+	C-	Down	24.17	27.85	21.45	Y	India Equity (Foreign Stock)
● Invesco Insider Sentiment ETF	NFO	NYSE Arca	C-	C	D+	Down	56.52	67.06	53.28	Y	US Equity Mid Cap (Growth)
● Invesco International BuyBack Achievers™ ETF	IPKW	NAS CM	D+	D+	D+	Down	28.81	40.11	28.19	Y	Global Equity Large Cap (Growth)
● Invesco International Corporate Bond ETF	PICB	NYSE Arca	D+	D+	C-	Down	25.18	28.56	24.84	Y	Global Fixed Income (Worldwide Bond)
● Invesco International Dividend Achievers ETF	PID	NAS CM	C	C-	C		14.13	17.36	13.74	Y	Global Equity Large Cap (Foreign Stock)
Invesco Investment Grade Defensive ETF	IIGD	NYSE Arca	U	U	U		25.05	25.15	24.88	Y	US Fixed Income (Corp Bond - Gen)
Invesco Investment Grade Value ETF	IIGV	NYSE Arca	U	U	U		24.79	25.18	24.57	Y	US Fixed Income (Corp Bond - Gen)
★ Invesco KBW Bank ETF	KBWB	NAS CM	B-	B	C	Down	43.98	60.11	41.50		Financials Sector Equity (Financial)
● Invesco KBW High Dividend Yield Financial ETF	KBWD	NAS CM	C	B-	C-		19.84	23.79	18.90		Financials Sector Equity (Financial)
● Invesco KBW Premium Yield Equity REIT ETF	KBWY	NAS CM	C	B-	D+		26.95	36.70	26.11		Real Estate Sector Equity (Real Estate)
★ Invesco KBW Property & Casualty Insurance ETF	KBWP	NAS CM	B-	B	C		56.62	64.80	53.39		Financials Sector Equity (Growth)
● Invesco KBW Regional Banking ETF	KBWR	NAS CM	C-	C	C-	Down	44.80	61.82	42.37		Financials Sector Equity (Financial)
Invesco LadderRite 0-5 Year Corporate Bond ETF	LDRI	NAS CM	C-	C	D+		24.57	24.88	24.08	Y	US Fixed Income (Corp Bond - Gen)
Invesco Moderately Conservative Multi-Asset Allocation ETF	PSMM	BATS	D+	D+	C-	Up	12.37	13.41	12.11	Y	Cautious Allocation (Asset Allocation)
Invesco MSCI Emerging Markets Equal Country Weight ETF	EWEM	NYSE Arca	D+	C-	D+	Down	29.60	37.78	29.08	Y	Global Emerg Mkts Equity (Growth)
● Invesco MSCI Global Timber ETF	CUT	NYSE Arca	D+	C-	D+	Down	24.06	34.52	23.21	Y	Natural Resources (Natl Res)
Invesco Multi-Factor Core Fixed Income ETF	IMFC	NYSE Arca	U	U	U		25.15	25.15	24.68	Y	US Fixed Income (Multisector Bond)
Invesco Multi-Factor Core Plus fixed Income ETF	IMFP	NYSE Arca	U	U	U		24.92	25.12	24.70	Y	US Fixed Income (Multisector Bond)

★ Expanded analysis of this fund is included in Section II: Analysis of All BUY Rated Funds. ● Expanded analysis of this fund is included in Section III: Analysis of All Rated Funds with Assets over $50 million.

			TOTAL RETURNS & PERFORMANCE						ASSETS		ASSET ALLOCATION & TURNOVER					VALUATION	
3-Month Total Return	6-Month Total Return	1-Year Total Return	3-Year Total Return	5-Year Total Return	Dividend Yield (TTM)	Expense Ratio	3-Yr Std Deviation	Effective Duration	NAV	Total Assets (MIL)	%Cash	%Stocks	%Bonds	%Other	Turnover Ratio	Premium/ Discount 1-Year Avg	Inception Date
-12.25	-7.40	-13.93	19.50	27.87	2.14	0.56	9.68		32.65	1,263	0	100	0	0	128	0.03	Mar-05
-14.04	-13.82	-8.93	10.77	20.78	0.54	0.63	13		39.86	126.9	0	100	0	0	177	0.15	Jun-05
-16.49	-12.10	-5.84	27.01	37.65	1.94	0.6	11.15		88.15	160.3	0	100	0	0	215	0.07	May-03
-12.54	-12.41	2.33	15.30	10.11	0.63	0.63	12.6		28.47	60.1	0	100	0	0	150	0.04	Jun-05
-14.82	-8.37	6.36	43.98	57.16	0.46	0.63	15.48		48.44	70.6	0	100	0	0	79	0.16	Jun-05
-43.95	-39.67	-39.75	-49.26	-76.14	3.2	0.63	29.96		5.72	20.0	0	100	0	0	91	-0.04	Oct-05
-13.32	-7.05	-1.69	-8.46	30.21	0.61	0.57	17.1		62.40	542.1	0	100	0	0	98	-0.04	Jun-05
-16.50	-13.48	-7.82	-5.60	1.69	1.19	0.63	15.25		33.77	11.0	1	99	0	0	131	0.30	Oct-05
-15.94	-15.39	-11.19	79.64	144.15	0.55	0.61	21.86		44.46	185.2	0	100	0	0	65	0.04	Jun-05
-13.99	-4.18	16.63	75.07	105.31	0	0.63	15.78		73.98	266.4	0	100	0	0	145	0.11	Jun-05
0.96						0.29		2.63	24.93	24.8	0	0	100	0		0.06	Jul-18
1.10						0.29		5.13	24.70	36.7	0	0	100	0		-0.06	Jul-18
-11.07	-4.83	-14.79	20.75	-9.84	2.87	0.75	18.44		31.58	17.9	0	100	0	0	39	-0.20	Oct-08
-1.12	1.92	-6.14	11.94	24.65	4.87	0.5	6.87	9.31	26.38	3,687	0	0	100	0	30	-0.20	Oct-07
-2.50	-3.50	-2.71	8.92	35.62	5.66	0.63	4.45		17.38	1,409	0	0	0	1	5	-0.02	Dec-06
-6.44	-9.95	-16.06	24.94	-13.64	4.07	0.7	13.42		12.24	53.4	0	100	0	0	98	-0.03	Jun-08
-11.52	-9.76	-12.55	13.39		3.14	0.45	10.55		25.90	111.8	0	100	0	0	39	0.06	Nov-15
-9.22	-7.86	-14.65	26.19	4.97	5.07	0.49	14.4		48.57	20.2	0	100	0	0	17	-0.23	Jun-07
-12.72	-10.39	-15.12	12.79	0.69	3.51	0.45	11.87		37.51	1,303	0	99	0	0	13	0.04	Jun-07
-14.89	-14.26	-17.71	13.22	11.96	3.19	0.49	11.49		27.66	292.6	0	100	0	0	19	0.25	Sep-07
-5.61	-1.40	-8.12	52.93	12.42	3.47	0.5	18.06		19.83	1,197	0	100	0	0	24	0.14	Sep-07
-14.13	-8.76	-8.56	24.22	35.43	1.99	0.39	9.66		101.56	5,117	0	100	0	0	9	0.00	Dec-05
-18.78	-18.10	-11.39	25.62	23.76	1.22	0.39	13.68		113.68	1,962	0	100	0	0	26	0.03	Sep-06
-3.50	-1.36	-2.37	15.73	14.77	4.26	0.5	3.86	3.55	17.72	875.4	0	0	100	0		-0.23	Nov-07
0.75	1.54	-0.59	6.98	12.74	2.86	0.22	2.54	4.56	24.64	118.4	1	0	99	0		0.15	Sep-11
-12.49	-8.66	-10.55	10.09	-10.89	1.4	0.77	10.28		24.19	19.4	0	100	0	0	45	-0.28	Sep-08
-11.67	-9.83	-19.02	-3.29	-6.42	1.87	0.75	13.29		10.48	50.0	0	95	0	5	40	-0.02	Jun-07
13.64	-4.45	-11.25	51.51	-1.38	2.08	0.75	35.6		17.40	22.9	0	100	0	0	11	0.23	Sep-08
-18.70	-14.22	-14.91	16.29	13.41	9.54	2.03	13.91		10.04	213.2	12	76	0	12	44	-0.02	Oct-06
-1.00	0.09	0.61	17.55	18.65	5.4	0.35	2.44	1.25	22.82	211.6	7	0	92	1	38	-0.14	Jun-13
-9.75	-5.94	-9.37	15.38	8.58	1.81	0.75	11.48		23.19	171.9	0	100	0	0	34	-0.12	Jun-07
-17.61	-31.02	-29.15	0.45	10.13	2.05	0.7	20.24		31.62	182.4	0	100	0	0	25	-0.12	Dec-04
-9.56	-6.29	-5.23			2.28	0.36		7.59	12.78	2.7	0	80	19	0	6	0.39	Feb-17
-10.49	-7.96	-7.35	32.42	59.88	3.95	0.54	9.72		15.85	745.0	0	100	0	0	38	-0.01	Dec-04
1.07	-0.66	-8.09	26.16	44.69	0	0.79	17.72		24.08	216.2	1	99	0	0	27	-0.07	Mar-08
-13.95	-11.07	-7.35	27.38	29.86	1.46	0.6	10.49		56.63	69.1	0	100	0	0		0.18	Sep-06
-14.93	-17.43	-20.97	18.00		2.33	0.55	13.2		28.98	238.6	0	100	0	0	118	0.04	Feb-14
-2.57	-2.72	-7.39	5.28	-5.49	1.72	0.5	7.87	7.23	25.14	117.2	0	0	100	0	14	-0.14	Jun-10
-9.81	-6.35	-11.08	16.34	-6.95	3.78	0.55	12.21		14.17	737.7	0	100	0	0	55	-0.04	Sep-05
0.99						0.13		3.41	25.03	6.2	1	0	99	0		0.20	Jul-18
0.21						0.13		6.04	24.77	6.1	2	0	98	0		0.39	Jul-18
-17.72	-17.18	-17.95	24.12	35.44	1.93	0.35	19.88		44.12	864.7	0	100	0	0		0.03	Nov-11
-10.84	-11.34	-8.77	23.15	19.70	8.57	2.4	13.48		19.81	303.5	0	100	0	0		0.06	Dec-10
-17.47	-21.33	-18.04	9.98	25.08	7.58	0.35	16.03		26.97	371.8	0	100	0	0		0.03	Dec-10
-8.79	-2.99	-2.24	26.85	61.23	2.3	0.35	10.28		56.92	64.0	0	100	0	0		0.19	Dec-10
-17.84	-21.37	-17.77	15.44	24.31	2.06	0.35	20.21		44.89	124.7	0	100	0	0		0.27	Nov-11
0.62	1.43	1.02	4.74		2.17	0.22	1.18	2.22	24.57	12.2	6	0	94	0		-0.17	Sep-14
-5.53	-3.35	-3.38			3.12	0.38		5.90	12.36	2.6	1	40	53	0	5	0.21	Feb-17
-5.81	-5.00	-12.24	25.01	-0.38	2.79	0.7	13.73		29.69	12.2	0	100	0	0	23	-0.15	Dec-10
-21.91	-22.40	-21.10	9.67	5.36	1.83	0.55	14.99		24.20	165.0	0	100	0	0	10	-0.07	Nov-07
1.92						0.12		5.34	25.14	24.8	1	0	99	0		0.03	Jul-18
0.87						0.16		5.32	24.90	49.4	1	0	99	0		-0.02	Jul-18

Fund Name	Ticker Symbol	Traded On	Overall Rating	Reward Rating	Risk Rating	Recent Up/ Downgrade	Price as of 12/31/2018	52-Week High	52-Week Low	Open to New Investors	Category & (Prospectus Objective)
Invesco Multi-Factor Large Cap ETF	GMFL	NYSE Arca	D+	C-	D		24.02	28.81	22.68	Y	US Equity Large Cap Blend (Growth)
Invesco Multi-Strategy Alternative ETF	LALT	NAS CM	D+	D+	D+	Up	21.68	25.26	20.15	Y	Multialternative (Growth)
● Invesco NASDAQ Internet ETF	PNQI	NAS CM	C+	B	C-	Down	109.83	146.88	102.97	Y	Technology Sector Equity (Technology)
● Invesco National AMT-Free Municipal Bond ETF	PZA	NYSE Arca	C	C-	C+		24.98	25.81	24.38	Y	US Muni Fixed Inc (Muni Bond - Natl)
● Invesco New York AMT-Free Municipal Bond ETF	PZT	NYSE Arca	C-	D+	C-	Down	23.80	24.66	23.24	Y	US Muni Fixed Inc (Muni Bond - Single State)
● Invesco Optimum Yield Div Commod Strategy No K-1 ETF	PDBC	NAS CM	C-	C-	C	Down	15.07	19.39	14.98	Y	Commodities Broad Basket (Growth)
● Invesco Preferred ETF	PGX	NYSE Arca	C-	D+	C	Down	13.47	14.86	13.18	Y	US Fixed Income (Growth & Inc)
Invesco PureBeta 0-5 Yr US TIPS ETF	PBTP	BATS	D	D+	D		24.38	24.90	24.30	Y	US Fixed Income (Income)
Invesco PureBeta FTSE Developed ex-North America ETF	PBDM	BATS	D-	D	E		21.33	27.90	21.02	Y	Global Equity Large Cap (Foreign Stock)
Invesco PureBeta FTSE Emerging Markets ETF	PBEE	BATS	D-	D	E		21.80	28.84	21.37	Y	Global Emerg Mkts Equity (Div Emerg Mkts)
Invesco PureBeta MSCI USA ETF	PBUS	BATS	D+	D+	D		24.77	29.30	23.49	Y	US Equity Large Cap Blend (Growth & Inc)
Invesco PureBeta MSCI USA Small Cap ETF	PBSM	BATS	D	D+	E		22.96	30.17	22.37	Y	US Equity Small Cap (Small Company)
Invesco PureBeta US Aggregate Bond ETF	PBND	BATS	D	D	D		24.22	24.90	23.65	Y	US Fixed Income (Growth & Inc)
★ Invesco QQQ Trust	QQQ	NAS CM	B-	C+	B	Down	154.26	186.74	143.50	Y	US Equity Large Cap Growth (Growth)
● Invesco Raymond James SB-1 Equity ETF	RYJ	NYSE Arca	C-	C-	D+	Down	36.50	49.48	34.27	Y	US Equity Mid Cap (Growth)
● Invesco Russell 1000 Enhanced Equal Weight ETF	USEQ	BATS	D+	D+	D+		23.97	29.05	22.78	Y	US Equity Large Cap Value (Growth & Inc)
● Invesco Russell 1000 Equal Weight ETF	EQAL	NYSE Arca	C-	C-	C-	Down	27.90	33.62	26.31		US Equity Mid Cap (Growth)
● Invesco Russell 1000 Low Beta Equal Weight ETF	USLB	NAS CM	C-	C-	D+	Down	28.02	33.45	27.11		US Equity Mid Cap (Growth & Inc)
Invesco Russell 2000 Equal Weight ETF	EQWS	NYSE Arca	D+	C-	D	Down	36.56	48.01	34.82	Y	US Equity Small Cap (Growth)
● Invesco Russell 2000 Pure Growth ETF	PXSG	NYSE Arca	C-	C	C-	Down	30.85	40.72	28.65	Y	US Equity Small Cap (Growth)
● Invesco Russell 2000 Pure Value ETF	PXSV	NYSE Arca	C-	C-	D+	Down	26.39	33.59	25.28	Y	US Equity Small Cap (Growth)
Invesco Russell MidCap Equal Weight ETF	EQWM	NYSE Arca	D+	C-	D	Down	42.77	51.66	40.08	Y	US Equity Mid Cap (Growth)
● Invesco Russell MidCap Pure Growth ETF	PXMG	NYSE Arca	C	C	C-	Down	44.97	55.63	41.61	Y	US Equity Mid Cap (Growth)
● Invesco Russell MidCap Pure Value ETF	PXMV	NYSE Arca	C-	C-	D+	Down	27.55	32.21	26.32	Y	US Equity Mid Cap (Growth)
● Invesco Russell Top 200 Equal Weight ETF	EQWL	NYSE Arca	C-	C	D+	Down	48.64	56.84	45.99	Y	US Equity Large Cap Blend (Growth)
● Invesco Russell Top 200 Pure Growth ETF	PXLG	NYSE Arca	C	C+	C	Down	45.78	54.72	42.07	Y	US Equity Large Cap Growth (Growth)
● Invesco Russell Top 200 Pure Value ETF	PXLV	NYSE Arca	C	C	C-		34.20	40.69	32.62	Y	US Equity Large Cap Value (Growth)
Invesco S&P 100® Equal Weight ETF	OEW	NYSE Arca	D+	C-	D		29.69	35.19	28.20	Y	US Equity Large Cap Blend (Growth & Inc)
● Invesco S&P 500 BuyWrite ETF	PBP	NYSE Arca	C	C	C+	Down	19.75	22.88	19.12	Y	Long/Short Equity (Growth)
Invesco S&P 500 Minimum Variance ETF	SPMV	BATS	D	D+	E+		24.95	29.48	24.28	Y	US Equity Large Cap Blend (Growth & Inc)
Invesco S&P 500 Value With Momentum ETF	SPVM	BATS	D	D+	D	Down	24.46	30.41	23.24	Y	US Equity Large Cap Value (Growth & Inc)
Invesco S&P 500® Downside Hedged ETF	PHDG	NYSE Arca	C-	C-	D+		26.24	30.25	26.17	Y	Long/Short Equity (Growth & Inc)
Invesco S&P 500® Enhanced Value ETF	SPVU	NYSE Arca	C	C	D+		30.75	37.33	29.09		US Equity Large Cap Value (Growth)
● Invesco S&P 500® Equal Weight Consumer Discretionary ETF	RCD	NYSE Arca	C-	C	D+	Down	89.86	108.34	84.82	Y	Consumer Goods & Svcs (Unaligned)
● Invesco S&P 500® Equal Weight Consumer Staples ETF	RHS	NYSE Arca	C+	B	C	Up	116.48	137.38	112.22	Y	Consumer Goods & Svcs (Unaligned)
● Invesco S&P 500® Equal Weight Energy ETF	RYE	NYSE Arca	C	C+	D+		43.14	64.61	40.29	Y	Energy Sector Equity (Natl Res)
● Invesco S&P 500® Equal Weight ETF	RSP	NYSE Arca	C	C-	C+	Down	91.40	108.58	86.19	Y	US Equity Large Cap Blend (Growth)
● Invesco S&P 500® Equal Weight Financials ETF	RYF	NYSE Arca	C-	C	C-	Down	36.35	47.31	34.13	Y	Financials Sector Equity (Financial)
● Invesco S&P 500® Equal Weight Health Care ETF	RYH	NYSE Arca	C	C	C-		177.53	206.09	165.92	Y	Healthcare Sector Equity (Health)
● Invesco S&P 500® Equal Weight Industrials ETF	RGI	NYSE Arca	C	C	C-		103.29	129.25	96.98	Y	Industrials Sector Equity (Unaligned)
● Invesco S&P 500® Equal Weight Materials ETF	RTM	NYSE Arca	C+	B	C-		94.52	118.23	88.78	Y	Natural Resources (Unaligned)
● Invesco S&P 500® Equal Weight Real Estate ETF	EWRE	NYSE Arca	C+	B-	C-	Up	25.86	28.69	24.88	Y	Real Estate Sector Equity (Real Estate)
● Invesco S&P 500® Equal Weight Technology ETF	RYT	NYSE Arca	C	C	C+	Down	140.83	170.41	131.48	Y	Technology Sector Equity (Technology)
★ Invesco S&P 500® Equal Weight Utilities ETF	RYU	NYSE Arca	B-	B	C	Up	88.76	95.55	77.51	Y	Utilities Sector Equity (Utility)
● Invesco S&P 500® ex-Rate Sensitive Low Volatility ETF	XRLV	NYSE Arca	C	C	C-		32.31	36.81	30.55		US Equity Large Cap Blend (Growth)
● Invesco S&P 500® High Beta ETF	SPHB	NYSE Arca	C-	C	C-	Down	35.29	45.93	32.76		US Equity Large Cap Blend (Growth)
● Invesco S&P 500® High Dividend Low Volatility ETF	SPHD	NYSE Arca	C	C	C+	Down	38.20	43.25	36.52		US Equity Large Cap Value (Income)
★ Invesco S&P 500® Low Volatility ETF	SPLV	NYSE Arca	B	C	A	Up	46.65	50.45	44.55		US Equity Large Cap Value (Growth)
Invesco S&P 500® Momentum ETF	SPMO	NYSE Arca	C	C+	C	Down	33.76	40.89	31.20		US Equity Large Cap Growth (Growth)
● Invesco S&P 500® Pure Growth ETF	RPG	NYSE Arca	C	C	C+	Down	99.65	121.33	93.15	Y	US Equity Large Cap Growth (Growth)
● Invesco S&P 500® Pure Value ETF	RPV	NYSE Arca	C	C	C+		56.86	71.10	53.85	Y	US Equity Large Cap Value (Growth)
● Invesco S&P 500® Quality ETF	SPHQ	NYSE Arca	C+	C	C+	Down	27.81	32.91	25.94	Y	US Equity Large Cap Blend (Growth)

★ Expanded analysis of this fund is included in Section II: Analysis of All BUY Rated Funds. ● Expanded analysis of this fund is included in Section III: Analysis of All Rated Funds with Assets over $50 million.

		TOTAL RETURNS & PERFORMANCE							ASSETS		ASSET ALLOCATION & TURNOVER					VALUATION	
3-Month Total Return	6-Month Total Return	1-Year Total Return	3-Year Total Return	5-Year Total Return	Dividend Yield (TTM)	Expense Ratio	3-Yr Std Deviation	Effective Duration	NAV	Total Assets (MIL)	%Cash	%Stocks	%Bonds	%Other	Turnover Ratio	Premium/ Discount 1-Year Avg	Inception Date
-13.95	-10.24	-9.38			1.51	0.25			24.12	1.3	2	98	0	0		-0.06	Jun-17
-0.59	-2.48	1.26	-1.35		0.44	0.98	3.36		21.61	6.6	419	1	-320	0	169	-0.43	May-14
-17.98	-21.79	-5.02	37.12	61.04	0.02	0.6	16.2		109.84	519.5	0	100	0	0	20	0.04	Jun-08
1.57	0.88	0.22	8.20	28.50	3.22	0.28	3.7	8.04	25.02	1,520	0	0	100	0		-0.11	Oct-07
1.59	0.89	0.23	7.19	27.32	2.96	0.28	3.62	7.44	23.92	60.3	0	0	100	0		-0.21	Oct-07
-20.64	-16.07	-13.19	8.53		4.22	0.59	13.46		15.02	2,099	71	0	29	0		-0.06	Nov-14
-3.82	-4.93	-4.24	7.39	33.81	5.98	0.51	4.81		13.49	4,605	0	0	0	1		0.01	Jan-08
-0.25	-0.17	0.48			2.75	0.07		2.42	24.36	2.4	3	0	97	0	0	0.05	Sep-17
-12.69	-10.32	-14.47			3.09	0.07			21.52	2.3	0	100	0	0	2	1.10	Sep-17
-6.28	-6.44	-13.76			2.87	0.14			21.83	2.3	0	100	0	0	1	0.77	Sep-17
-14.22	-7.75	-4.79			1.79	0.04			24.87	2.8	0	100	0	0		0.40	Sep-17
-20.91	-18.76	-13.27			1.35	0.06			22.90	2.7	0	100	0	0		0.64	Sep-17
1.55	1.57	-0.31			2.79	0.05		6.04	24.19	23.8	0	0	100	0		-0.08	Sep-17
-16.95	-9.64	-0.14	41.79	85.01	0.78	0.2	13.13		154.14	65,965	0	100	0	0		0.06	Mar-99
-24.93	-22.70	-16.59	12.85	10.81	0	0.75	14.13			173.8	0	100	0	0	82	0.13	May-06
-14.20	-10.63	-10.19			1.55	0.29			24.07	141.2	0	100	0	0		0.23	Jul-17
-15.25	-11.24	-8.90	23.89		1.49	0.2	10.67		27.92	451.7	0	100	0	0		0.08	Dec-14
-13.18	-9.81	-7.37	20.54		1.7	0.35	8.61		28.32	156.3	0	100	0	0		0.20	Nov-15
-20.86	-20.55	-14.17	18.96	17.95	1.16	0.25	15.53		36.67	21.0	0	100	0	0	40	0.33	Dec-06
-20.84	-15.92	-2.88	28.45	34.72	0.5	0.39	16.22		30.93	78.6	0	100	0	0	43	0.16	Mar-05
-16.89	-16.92	-11.81	23.29	18.25	2.29	0.39	16.06		26.42	70.0	0	100	0	0	56	0.11	Mar-05
-15.99	-12.39	-9.72	21.87	28.29	1.41	0.25	11.25		42.52	23.7	0	100	0	0	28	0.13	Dec-06
-16.46	-8.13	6.81	52.28	59.39	0.06	0.39	15.67		45.15	253.3	0	100	0	0	29	0.16	Mar-05
-10.61	-9.47	-9.66	19.61	24.46	2.6	0.39	10.68		27.56	50.7	0	100	0	0	52	-0.04	Mar-05
-12.85	-7.40	-5.67	32.72	48.74	1.88	0.25	9.37		48.74	61.7	0	100	0	0	32	0.16	Dec-06
-16.00	-9.72	1.80	37.60	69.42	0.73	0.39	12.27		45.76	248.9	0	100	0	0	19	0.10	Jun-11
-11.90	-7.81	-8.59	29.07	35.16	2.68	0.39	9.58		34.19	100.7	0	100	0	0	25	0.22	Jun-11
-13.41	-6.88	-6.89			1.74	0.4			29.93	3.3	0	100	0	0		0.02	Jun-16
-11.05	-6.78	-5.26	12.84	23.56	1.2	0.49	5.78		19.80	331.3	0	100	0	0	16	0.08	Dec-07
-13.88	-7.90	-7.02			2.62	0.1			25.06	1.4	0	100	0	0		0.03	Jul-17
-14.85	-10.20	-12.30			1.81	0.15			24.57	2.8	1	99	0	0		0.53	Apr-17
-10.92	-5.02	-2.38	12.62	7.06	1.85	0.39	8.46		26.31	25.1	14	86	0	0	54	0.03	Dec-12
-12.33	-7.53	-9.26	29.39		3.18	0.13	12.47		30.78	22.6	0	100	0	0		0.51	Oct-15
-14.59	-11.96	-8.48	10.87	19.90	1.37	0.4	11.7		89.92	90.3	0	100	0	0		0.13	Nov-06
-8.32	-4.74	-10.72	6.69	42.31	2.05	0.4	9.86		116.47	534.0	0	100	0	0		0.02	Nov-06
-30.93	-28.85	-24.45	-2.78	-41.00	1.8	0.4	24.37		43.18	210.8	0	100	0	0		0.03	Nov-06
-13.92	-9.31	-7.76	24.98	38.84	1.74	0.2	9.95		91.39	14,754	0	100	0	0		-0.01	Apr-03
-15.00	-13.55	-15.62	26.53	43.31	1.74	0.4	14.38		36.36	348.3	0	100	0	0		0.04	Nov-06
-13.71	-2.87	-0.33	17.46	64.98	0.45	0.4	13.21		177.68	739.5	1	99	0	0		0.13	Nov-06
-17.75	-9.22	-12.98	30.07	35.19	1.08	0.4	13.79		103.40	217.4	1	99	0	0		0.04	Nov-06
-13.02	-10.85	-14.52	30.33	28.02	1.48	0.4	14.6		94.60	134.8	0	100	0	0		0.02	Nov-06
-4.18	-3.81	-4.12	8.39		2.84	0.4	12.53		25.88	17.0	0	100	0	0		-0.03	Aug-15
-15.91	-11.39	-0.57	57.38	93.16	0.88	0.4	13.38		140.89	1,518	0	100	0	0		0.00	Nov-06
2.16	5.08	6.95	34.57	65.37	3.08	0.4	10.85		88.83	268.8	0	100	0	0		-0.03	Nov-06
-10.44	-3.69	-2.83	33.30		1.52	0.25	9.02		32.33	141.5	0	100	0	0		0.09	Apr-15
-21.29	-17.52	-15.43	25.60	23.49	1.67	0.25	18.05		35.29	113.9	0	100	0	0		0.01	May-11
-6.88	-4.53	-6.12	28.51	62.02	3.97	0.3	8.96		38.18	2,682	0	100	0	0		0.01	Oct-12
-5.11	-0.69	0.03	28.92	57.22	1.99	0.25	8.02		46.64	8,398	0	100	0	0		0.02	May-11
-16.94	-8.77	-0.14	34.64		0.75	0.13	11.04		33.79	39.0	0	100	0	0		0.06	Oct-15
-17.03	-13.38	-4.58	25.16	45.85	0.38	0.35	11.93		99.58	2,293	0	100	0	0		0.01	Mar-06
-16.74	-12.30	-12.26	22.54	26.16	1.94	0.35	12.14		56.82	932.6	0	100	0	0		0.02	Mar-06
-15.05	-6.66	-6.98	26.50	49.31	1.75	0.15	8.86		27.80	1,326	0	100	0	0	60	-0.01	Dec-05

Fund Name	Ticker Symbol	Traded On	Overall Rating	Reward Rating	Risk Rating	Recent Up/ Downgrade	Price as of 12/31/2018	52-Week High	52-Week Low	Open to New Investors	Category & (Prospectus Objective)
● Invesco S&P 500® Top 50 ETF	XLG	NYSE Arca	C	C+	C	Down	179.82	210.70	167.99	Y	US Equity Large Cap Blend (Growth)
● Invesco S&P Emerging Markets Low Volatility ETF	EELV	NYSE Arca	C-	C-	C-		22.75	27.55	22.50		Global Emerg Mkts Equity (Div Emerg Mkts)
Invesco S&P Emerging Markets Momentum ETF	EEMO	NYSE Arca	D+	C-	D+	Down	14.97	22.50	14.82		Global Emerg Mkts Equity (Div Emerg Mkts)
Invesco S&P Global Dividend Opportunities Index ETF	LVL	NYSE Arca	C-	C	D+	Down	10.27	11.79	9.93	Y	Global Equity Large Cap (World Stock)
● Invesco S&P Global Water Index ETF	CGW	NYSE Arca	C-	C-	C-	Down	31.14	36.40	29.76	Y	Equity Misc (Natl Res)
● Invesco S&P High Income Infrastructure ETF	GHII	NYSE Arca	C-	C-	D+	Down	23.48	28.46	22.90	Y	Infrastructure Sector Equity (Equity-Income)
Invesco S&P Intl Dev High Div Low Vol ETF	IDHD	BATS	D	D	D+		25.72	30.80	25.19	Y	Global Equity Large Cap (World Stock)
● Invesco S&P International Developed Low Volatility ETF	IDLV	NYSE Arca	C	D+	C+		29.84	35.29	29.12		Global Equity Large Cap (Foreign Stock)
Invesco S&P International Developed Momentum ETF	IDMO	NYSE Arca	D+	D+	D		22.79	30.35	21.95		Global Equity Large Cap (Growth)
Invesco S&P International Developed Quality ETF	IDHQ	NYSE Arca	D+	D+	D+	Down	20.45	25.45	19.90		Global Equity Large Cap (Foreign Stock)
● Invesco S&P MidCap 400® Equal Weight ETF	EWMC	NYSE Arca	C-	C-	D+	Down	55.57	69.54	52.58	Y	US Equity Mid Cap (Growth)
● Invesco S&P MidCap 400® Pure Growth ETF	RFG	NYSE Arca	C-	C	D+	Down	131.71	169.49	124.17	Y	US Equity Mid Cap (Growth)
● Invesco S&P MidCap 400® Pure Value ETF	RFV	NYSE Arca	C-	C	D+	Down	56.16	73.79	53.74	Y	US Equity Small Cap (Growth)
● Invesco S&P MidCap Low Volatility ETF	XMLV	NYSE Arca	C	C	C+	Down	44.39	49.42	42.36	Y	US Equity Mid Cap (Income)
Invesco S&P SmallCap 600® Equal Weight ETF	EWSC	NYSE Arca	C-	C-	D+	Down	47.89	63.36	45.30	Y	US Equity Small Cap (Growth)
● Invesco S&P SmallCap 600® Pure Growth ETF	RZG	NYSE Arca	C-	C	D+	Down	104.15	139.81	98.06	Y	US Equity Small Cap (Small Company)
● Invesco S&P SmallCap 600® Pure Value ETF	RZV	NYSE Arca	C-	C-	C-	Down	57.79	81.41	55.11	Y	US Equity Small Cap (Small Company)
● Invesco S&P SmallCap Consumer Discretionary ETF	PSCD	NAS CM	C-	C	D+	Down	54.78	71.63	51.80		Consumer Goods & Svcs (Unaligned)
● Invesco S&P SmallCap Consumer Staples ETF	PSCC	NAS CM	C+	B-	C	Down	69.15	85.94	66.72		Consumer Goods & Svcs (Unaligned)
Invesco S&P SmallCap Energy ETF	PSCE	NAS CM	D+	C-	D	Down	8.77	18.54	8.14		Energy Sector Equity (Natl Res)
● Invesco S&P SmallCap Financials ETF	PSCF	NAS CM	C-	C	D+	Down	47.94	60.46	46.25		Financials Sector Equity (Financial)
● Invesco S&P SmallCap Health Care ETF	PSCH	NAS CM	C	C+	C-	Down	107.53	144.96	98.52		Healthcare Sector Equity (Health)
Invesco S&P SmallCap High Dividend Low Volatility ETF	XSHD	BATS	C-	C-	D+		22.07	26.95	21.23	Y	US Equity Small Cap (Small Company)
● Invesco S&P SmallCap Industrials ETF	PSCI	NAS CM	C-	C	D+	Down	55.67	75.51	52.49		Industrials Sector Equity (Unaligned)
● Invesco S&P SmallCap Information Technology ETF	PSCT	NAS CM	C-	C-	C-	Down	69.02	89.71	64.05		Technology Sector Equity (Technology)
● Invesco S&P SmallCap Low Volatility ETF	XSLV	NYSE Arca	C	C-	C+	Down	42.64	51.11	40.81		US Equity Small Cap (Income)
Invesco S&P SmallCap Materials ETF	PSCM	NAS CM	C+	B-	C-	Down	39.74	56.96	37.59		Natural Resources (Unaligned)
Invesco S&P SmallCap Quality ETF	XSHQ	BATS	C-	C-	C-	Up	25.08	31.74	23.57	Y	US Equity Small Cap (Small Company)
● Invesco S&P SmallCap Utilities & Communication Services ET	PSCU	NAS CM	C+	B-	C-		49.20	58.10	46.95		Utilities Sector Equity (Utility)
● Invesco S&P Spin-Off ETF	CSD	NYSE Arca	C	B-	C-		42.36	56.49	39.90	Y	US Equity Mid Cap (Growth)
● Invesco Senior Loan ETF	BKLN	NYSE Arca	C	C-	B	Down	21.78	23.27	21.59	Y	US Fixed Income (Income)
● Invesco Shipping ETF	SEA	NYSE Arca	D	D	D		8.22	12.33	8.05	Y	Industrials Sector Equity (Unaligned)
● Invesco Solar ETF	TAN	NYSE Arca	D+	D+	D		18.55	26.93	17.70	Y	Technology Sector Equity (Natl Res)
Invesco Strategic Developed ex-US ETF	ISDX	NAS CM	U	U	U		22.25	25.90	22.25	Y	Global Equity Large Cap (Growth)
Invesco Strategic Developed ex-US Small Company ETF	ISDS	NAS CM	U	U	U		21.05	25.72	20.49	Y	Global Eq Mid/Small Cap (Small Company)
Invesco Strategic Emerging Markets ETF	ISEM	NAS CM	U	U	U		23.33	26.54	23.33	Y	Global Emerg Mkts Equity (Div Emerg Mkts)
Invesco Strategic US ETF	IUS	NAS CM	U	U	U		21.82	25.50	21.82	Y	US Equity Large Cap Blend (Growth)
Invesco Strategic US Small Company ETF	IUSS	NAS CM	U	U	U		20.11	25.24	19.40	Y	US Equity Small Cap (Small Company)
● Invesco Taxable Municipal Bond ETF	BAB	NYSE Arca	C	C-	C+		29.69	30.69	28.54	Y	US Fixed Income (Muni Bond - Natl)
Invesco Total Return Bond ETF	GTO	NYSE Arca	C-	C-	D+		50.03	52.81	50.00	Y	US Fixed Income (Corp Bond - Gen)
● Invesco Treasury Collateral ETF	CLTL	NYSE Arca	D+	D+	C-	Up	105.44	106.48	105.29	Y	US Fixed Income (Govt Bond - Treasury)
Invesco U.S. Large Cap Optimized Volatility ETF	OVLC	NYSE Arca	D	C	E+	Down	27.99	32.48	26.76	Y	US Equity Large Cap Blend (Growth)
● Invesco Ultra Short Duration ETF	GSY	NYSE Arca	C	C	C+		50.07	50.34	50.04	Y	US Fixed Income (Income)
● Invesco Variable Rate Investment Grade ETF	VRIG	NAS CM	C	C-	C+	Up	24.63	25.26	24.60	Y	US Fixed Income (Income)
● Invesco Variable Rate Preferred ETF	VRP	NYSE Arca	C	D+	C+		22.82	25.70	22.45	Y	US Fixed Income (Growth & Inc)
● Invesco VRDO Tax-Free Weekly ETF	PVI	NYSE Arca	C-	C-	D+		24.93	25.00	24.83	Y	US Muni Fixed Inc (Muni Bond - Natl)
★ Invesco Water Resources ETF	PHO	NAS CM	B-	B	C		28.21	32.43	26.56	Y	Industrials Sector Equity (Utility)
● Invesco WilderHill Clean Energy ETF	PBW	NYSE Arca	C	C+	D+		21.39	26.92	20.12	Y	Technology Sector Equity (Natl Res)
Invesco WilderHill Progressive Energy ETF	PUW	NYSE Arca	C-	C	D+	Down	21.40	28.11	20.38	Y	Equity Misc (Utility)
Invesco Wilshire Micro-Cap ETF	WMCR	NYSE Arca	C-	C-	D+	Down	27.82	38.40	26.59	Y	US Equity Small Cap (Growth)
Invesco Wilshire US REIT ETF	WREI	NYSE Arca	C	C	D		42.89	49.01	41.27	Y	Real Estate Sector Equity (Real Estate)
Invesco Zacks International Multi-Asset Income ETF	HGI	NYSE Arca	D	D+	D	Down	14.07	18.58	13.56	Y	Global Equity Large Cap (Foreign Stock)

★Expanded analysis of this fund is included in Section II: Analysis of All BUY Rated Funds. ● Expanded analysis of this fund is included in Section III: Analysis of All Rated Funds with Assets over $50 million.

		TOTAL RETURNS & PERFORMANCE							ASSETS		ASSET ALLOCATION & TURNOVER					VALUATION	
3-Month Total Return	6-Month Total Return	1-Year Total Return	3-Year Total Return	5-Year Total Return	Dividend Yield (TTM)	Expense Ratio	3-Yr Std Deviation	Effective Duration	NAV	Total Assets (MIL)	%Cash	%Stocks	%Bonds	%Other	Turnover Ratio	Premium/ Discount 1-Year Avg	Inception Date
-14.03	-6.17	-3.48	31.90	53.18	1.79	0.2	9.29		179.73	792.9	0	100	0	0		0.09	May-05
-6.79	-1.35	-5.70	22.97	-3.20	4.3	0.29	12.11		22.77	267.6	0	100	0	0	81	-0.08	Jan-12
-19.17	-20.48	-25.74	13.61	-16.42	0.78	0.31	16.76		15.07	11.5	0	100	0	0	111	-0.16	Feb-12
-6.04	-2.75	-6.21	32.20	-1.18	3.36	0.64	10.72		10.29	31.5	0	100	0	0	66	-0.29	Jun-07
-8.57	-4.52	-10.01	21.64	24.05	1.81	0.61	10.41		31.23	552.1	0	100	0	0	13	-0.04	May-07
-10.24	-10.13	-11.20	27.30		5.34	0.45	10.85			55.8	0	100	0	0	45	0.11	Feb-15
-5.51	-4.31	-7.19			5.19	0.3			25.48	8.0	0	100	0	0	72	1.18	Nov-16
-6.83	-4.86	-7.91	15.95	13.19	4.17	0.25	9.05		29.89	567.2	0	100	0	0	69	-0.09	Jan-12
-16.06	-12.24	-16.57	6.79	-12.03	2.74	0.26	16.15		22.88	2.4	0	100	0	0	134	-0.04	Feb-12
-12.06	-9.75	-12.73	8.42	14.19	2.52	0.29	10.42		20.44	35.4	0	100	0	0	49	0.92	Jun-07
-17.32	-15.53	-12.26	21.92	27.16	1.37	0.4	12.57		55.72	101.6	0	100	0	0		-0.08	Dec-10
-19.12	-18.09	-13.76	8.11	10.40	0.7	0.35	12.56		131.89	573.4	0	100	0	0		0.20	Mar-06
-20.32	-18.81	-17.95	23.24	19.11	1.26	0.35	16.67		56.59	102.4	0	100	0	0		0.06	Mar-06
-7.10	-4.44	-0.19	38.10	72.01	2.3	0.25	8.86		44.38	1,747	0	100	0	0		0.01	Feb-13
-19.68	-19.08	-10.55	23.05	11.16	1.13	0.4	16.39		48.10	38.6	0	100	0	0		0.09	Dec-10
-20.74	-18.42	-7.74	31.15	34.22	0.42	0.35	16.69		104.25	295.7	0	100	0	0		0.10	Mar-06
-23.26	-25.03	-19.52	8.75	-2.25	1.59	0.35	19.59		57.81	155.6	0	100	0	0		0.05	Mar-06
-18.27	-15.96	-8.21	24.29	18.42	1.11	0.29	15.64		55.02	82.8	0	100	0	0		0.28	Apr-10
-15.05	-13.02	-6.20	31.97	49.44	0.98	0.29	13.3		69.39	108.2	0	100	0	0		0.21	Apr-10
-45.79	-47.26	-42.98	-42.73	-80.79	0.22	0.29	37.96		8.77	38.5	0	100	0	0		-0.01	Apr-10
-13.08	-14.18	-8.81	28.51	38.85	2.58	0.29	15.45		48.11	167.6	0	100	0	0		0.10	Apr-10
-21.96	-16.83	9.69	50.33	100.77	0	0.29	18.55		107.89	1,170	0	100	0	0		0.16	Apr-10
-12.76	-13.40	-7.73			4.92	0.3			22.13	9.9	0	100	0	0		0.13	Nov-16
-22.02	-17.82	-12.39	32.50	28.08	0.66	0.29	17.88		56.02	114.7	0	100	0	0		0.05	Apr-10
-16.59	-17.05	-9.13	33.53	57.41	0.51	0.29	15.05		69.20	386.1	0	100	0	0		0.06	Apr-10
-11.35	-10.91	-5.33	35.14	53.89	2.17	0.25	12.05		42.64	1,400	0	100	0	0		0.03	Feb-13
-26.17	-24.15	-22.32	31.31	-2.68	1.05	0.29	22.14		40.01	23.2	0	100	0	0		0.06	Apr-10
-15.84	-14.16	-6.07			1.01	0.29			25.09	29.7	0	100	0	0		0.30	Apr-17
-13.03	-7.88	-4.46	33.42	66.46	2.96	0.29	12.21		49.27	75.7	0	100	0	0		0.15	Apr-10
-21.70	-21.10	-17.83	13.79	1.40	0.65	0.64	12.64		42.37	176.2	0	100	0	0		0.06	Dec-06
-3.92	-1.94	-0.55	10.88	8.46	4.04	0.65	2.61		21.97	6,124	6	0	92	0	74	-0.10	Mar-11
-19.96	-17.73	-26.90	-24.84	-49.76	5.24	0.65	17.72		8.26	57.0	0	100	0	0		-0.09	Jun-10
-10.48	-20.50	-25.76	-35.01	-41.53	2.12	0.7	24.64			278.9	0	100	0	0	54	-0.21	Apr-08
-12.41						0.23			22.37	2.4	0	100	0	0		-0.42	Sep-18
-15.64						0.35			21.41	2.3	0	100	0	0		-1.13	Sep-18
-10.10						0.35			23.70	2.5	0	100	0	0		-0.43	Sep-18
-13.10						0.19			21.92	2.4	0	100	0	0		-1.31	Sep-18
-18.24						0.23			20.06	2.3	0	100	0	0		-0.96	Sep-18
2.30	1.48	0.63	14.62	33.83	4.26	0.28	4.26	8.09	29.51	833.2	0	0	100	0		-0.32	Nov-09
-1.74	-1.48	-1.71			3.35	0.52			50.13	40.7	2	0	95	0	219	-0.02	Feb-16
0.58	1.05	1.80			2.13	0.08			105.44	518.0	51	0	49	0		0.02	Jan-17
-10.63	-6.49	-3.71			2.45	0.3			28.12	1.6	0	100	0	0	114	0.12	May-16
0.39	1.03	2.16	5.99	7.92	2.62	0.25	0.25		50.07	1,806	37	0	62	0	56	0.00	Feb-08
-0.68	0.13	1.03			2.79	0.3			24.71	448.1	1	0	97	0	23	0.07	Sep-16
-6.25	-5.14	-5.69	10.49		4.97	0.5	4.82		23.05	1,662	1	0	63	0		-0.12	May-14
0.33	0.60	1.10	1.89	1.61	1.06	0.25	0.14		24.93	61.1	1	0	99	0	0	-0.07	Nov-07
-10.71	-6.49	-6.26	31.87	10.59	0.34	0.62	11.32		28.24	813.5	0	100	0	0	23	0.00	Dec-05
-13.38	-13.84	-13.71	-4.39	-25.97	1.47	0.7	16.12		21.41	108.8	0	100	0	0	43	0.05	Mar-05
-17.17	-16.45	-19.37	13.61	-29.29	0.64	0.7	16.91		21.51	15.9	0	100	0	0	24	0.14	Oct-06
-22.67	-23.11	-15.51	17.11	16.48	2.08	0.85	14.96		28.26	26.2	0	100	0	0		1.10	Sep-06
-6.89	-6.55	-5.84	4.27	42.41	3.14	0.32	12.65			14.3	0	100	0	0	10	-1.92	Mar-10
-13.79	-12.66	-16.19	9.54	-8.67	4.37	0.98	11.55	4.92	14.15	9.0	1	90	10	-2	99	-0.51	Jul-07

Fund Name	Ticker Symbol	Traded On	Overall Rating	Reward Rating	Risk Rating	Recent Up/ Downgrade	Price as of 12/31/2018	52-Week High	52-Week Low	Open to New Investors	Category & (Prospectus Objective)
Invesco Zacks Micro Cap ETF	PZI	NYSE Arca	D	D+	D	Down	15.96	20.88	15.36	Y	US Equity Small Cap (Growth)
● Invesco Zacks Mid-Cap ETF	CZA	NYSE Arca	C	C	C-		58.98	69.62	56.31	Y	US Equity Mid Cap (Growth)
● Invesco Zacks Multi-Asset Income ETF	CVY	NYSE Arca	C-	C-	C-	Down	19.22	23.39	18.31	Y	Aggressive Allocation (Multi-Asset Global)
iPath® Asian & Gulf Currency Revaluation ETN	PGD	NYSE Arca	D	C-	E+		40.10	50.00	40.00	Y	Currency (Worldwide Bond)
iPath® Bloomberg Agriculture Subindex Total Return(SM) ETN	JJATF	OTC BB	D	D-	D		26.44	32.99	25.90	Y	Commodities Specified (Natl Res)
iPath® Bloomberg Aluminum Subindex Total Return(SM) ETN	JJUFF	NYSE Arca	D	D+	E	Down	20.10	20.10	17.02	Y	Commodities Specified (Natl Res)
iPath® Bloomberg Cocoa Subindex Total Return(SM) ETN	NIB	NYSE Arca	D	D	D		28.09	35.55	22.83	Y	Commodities Specified (Natl Res)
● iPath® Bloomberg Coffee Subindex Total Return(SM) ETN	JJOFF	OTC BB	D-	D-	D		10.71	16.31	10.35	Y	Commodities Specified (Natl Res)
● iPath® Bloomberg Commodity Index Total Return(SM) ETN	DJP	NYSE Arca	D+	D	C-	Down	21.22	25.68	21.22	Y	Commodities Broad Basket (Natl Res)
iPath® Bloomberg Copper Subindex Total Return(SM) ETN	JJCTF	OTC BB	D+	C-	D+	Down	28.72	37.54	28.32	Y	Commodities Specified (Natl Res)
iPath® Bloomberg Cotton Subindex Total Return(SM) ETN	BALTF	OTC BB	D+	C-	D	Down	47.70	63.65	47.70	Y	Commodities Specified (Natl Res)
iPath® Bloomberg Energy Subindex Total Return(SM) ETN	JJETF	NYSE Arca	D	C-	E		6.54	6.92	5.76	Y	Commodities Specified (Natl Res)
● iPath® Bloomberg Grains Subindex Total Return(SM) ETN	JJGTF	OTC BB	D	D	D		22.48	27.81	21.90	Y	Commodities Specified (Natl Res)
iPath® Bloomberg Industrial Metals SubInd Total Ret(SM) ET	JJMTF	NYSE Arca	D	C-	E		29.55	30.93	28.17	Y	Commodities Specified (Natl Res)
iPath® Bloomberg Lead Subindex Total Return(SM) ETN	LD	NYSE Arca	D	D	E		43.11	62.00	43.11	Y	Commodities Specified (Natl Res)
iPath® Bloomberg Livestock Subindex Total Return(SM) ETN	COWTF	NYSE Arca	D	D+	E	Up	23.08	24.10	20.09	Y	Commodities Specified (Natl Res)
iPath® Bloomberg Natural Gas Subindex Total Return(SM) ETN			D	D	D	Up	0.02	0.30	0.00	Y	Commodities Energy (Natl Res)
iPath® Bloomberg Nickel Subindex Total Return(SM) ETN	JJNTF	OTC BB	D+	C-	D+	Down	12.35	19.49	12.35	Y	Commodities Specified (Natl Res)
iPath® Bloomberg Platinum Subindex Total Return(SM) ETN	PGMFF	NYSE Arca	D-	D	E		18.68	20.88	18.41	Y	Commodities Specified (Prec Metals)
iPath® Bloomberg Precious Metals SubInd Total Ret(SM) ETN	JJPFF	NYSE Arca	D-	D	E	Down	59.06	60.17	57.81	Y	Commodities Specified (Prec Metals)
iPath® Bloomberg Softs Subindex Total Return(SM) ETN	JJSSF	NYSE Arca	D-	D	E	Up	28.21	32.54	28.21	Y	Commodities Specified (Natl Res)
iPath® Bloomberg Sugar Subindex Total Return(SM) ETN	SGGFF	OTC BB	D	D	D	Up	21.65	31.37	18.80	Y	Commodities Specified (Natl Res)
iPath® Bloomberg Tin Subindex Total Return(SM) ETN	JJTFF	NYSE Arca	D	D	E+		48.42	50.60	45.85	Y	Commodities Specified (Natl Res)
iPath® CBOE S&P 500 BuyWrite Index(SM) ETN	BWVTF	NYSE Arca	D	C-	E+	Down	77.50	79.74	74.65	Y	US Equity Large Cap Blend (Growth)
iPath® EUR/USD Exchange Rate ETN	EROTF	NYSE Arca	D	D+	E		45.01	47.15	42.09	Y	Currency (Worldwide Bond)
iPath® GBP/USD Exchange Rate ETN	GBBEF	OTC BB	D	D	E		28.65	37.50	28.32	Y	Currency (Worldwide Bond)
iPath® GEMS Asia 8 ETN	AYTEF	NYSE Arca	D	D+	E		42.16	44.96	40.57	Y	Currency (Worldwide Bond)
iPath® GEMS Index ETN	JEMTF	NYSE Arca	D	D	E		29.20	29.49	29.20	Y	Currency (Worldwide Bond)
★ iPath® Global Carbon ETN	GRNTF	NYSE Arca	B-	A+	E	Down	17.90	18.23	9.49	Y	Commodities Specified (Natl Res)
iPath® Inverse S&P 500 VIX Short-Term Futures™ ETN	XXVFF	NYSE Arca	D+	C-	E+	Up	37.00	38.53	36.44	Y	Alternative Misc (Growth)
iPath® JPY/USD Exchange Rate ETN	JYNFF	NYSE Arca	D	D	E		52.02	62.32	47.55	Y	Currency (Worldwide Bond)
iPath® Long Enhanced MSCI EAFE® Index ETN	MFLAF	NYSE Arca	D	D+	E		194.36	194.36	162.00	Y	Trading Tools (Foreign Stock)
iPath® Long Enhanced MSCI Emerging Markets Index ETN	EMLBF	NYSE Arca	D	C-	E		80.80	119.99	80.80	Y	Trading Tools (Foreign Stock)
iPath® Long Extended Russell 1000® TR Index ETN	ROLAF	NYSE Arca	D	C	E+	Down	228.79	314.07	228.79	Y	Trading Tools (Growth & Inc)
iPath® Long Extended Russell 2000® TR Index ETN	RTLAF	NYSE Arca	D	C	E+	Down	209.90	209.90	201.05	Y	Trading Tools (Small Company)
iPath® Long Extended S&P 500® TR Index ETN	SFLAF	NYSE Arca	D	C	E+	Down	245.01	245.01	214.83	Y	Trading Tools (Growth & Inc)
● iPath® MSCI India Index(SM) ETN	INPTF	OTC BB	D+	D+	D+	Down	80.92	93.40	69.81	Y	India Equity (Foreign Stock)
iPath® Optimized Currency Carry ETN	ICITF	NYSE Arca	D	C	E+		37.90	37.90	36.05	Y	Currency (Worldwide Bond)
● iPath® Pure Beta Broad Commodity ETN	BCM	NYSE Arca	D+	C-	D+		25.77	31.40	25.68	Y	Commodities Broad Basket (Natl Res)
iPath® Pure Beta Crude Oil ETN	OLEM	NYSE Arca	D+	C-	D	Down	14.48	23.25	13.93	Y	Commodities Specified (Natl Res)
iPath® S&P 500 Dynamic VIX ETN	XVZ	NYSE Arca	D	D	D	Up	20.73	22.94	17.40	Y	Alternative Misc (Growth)
iPath® S&P 500 VIX Mid-Term Futures™ ETN	VXZ	NYSE Arca	D	D-	D	Up	22.20	22.77	16.50	Y	Alternative Misc (Growth)
● iPath® S&P 500 VIX Short-Term Futures™ ETN	VXX	NYSE Arca	D-	E+	D	Up	46.88	55.24	25.84	Y	Alternative Misc (Growth)
● iPath® S&P GSCI® Crude Oil Total Return Index ETN	OILNF	NYSE Arca	D	D+	E	Down	9.26	9.49	6.43	Y	Commodities Specified (Natl Res)
iPath® S&P GSCI® Total Return Index ETN	GSP	NYSE Arca	C-	C-	C-		12.97	18.31	12.78	Y	Commodities Broad Basket (Natl Res)
iPath® S&P MLP ETN	IMLP	NYSE Arca	D+	D+	D+		14.74	19.89	14.10	Y	Energy Sector Equity (Income)
iPath® Series B Bloomberg Agriculture SubInd Total Ret ETN	JJA	NYSE Arca	U	U	U		44.86	54.51	43.84	Y	Commodities Specified (Growth & Inc)
iPath® Series B Bloomberg Aluminum SubInd Total Ret ETN	JJU	NYSE Arca	U	U	U		42.99	58.39	42.90	Y	Commodities Specified (Growth & Inc)
iPath® Series B Bloomberg Coffee Subindex Total Return ETN	JO	NYSE Arca	U	U	U		37.45	49.96	36.40	Y	Commodities Broad Basket (Growth & Inc)
iPath® Series B Bloomberg Copper Subindex Total Return ETN	JJC	NYSE Arca	U	U	U		40.65	51.27	39.94	Y	Commodities Specified (Growth & Inc)
iPath® Series B Bloomberg Cotton Subindex Total Return ETN	BAL	NYSE Arca	U	U	U		44.16	57.64	44.16	Y	Commodities Specified (Growth & Inc)
iPath® Series B Bloomberg Energy Subindex Total Return ETN	JJE	NYSE Arca	U	U	U		42.13	57.32	42.13	Y	Commodities Specified (Growth & Inc)

★ Expanded analysis of this fund is included in Section II: Analysis of All BUY Rated Funds.   ● Expanded analysis of this fund is included in Section III: Analysis of All Rated Funds with Assets over $50 million.

3-Month Total Return	6-Month Total Return	1-Year Total Return	3-Year Total Return	5-Year Total Return	Dividend Yield (TTM)	Expense Ratio	3-Yr Std Deviation	Effective Duration	NAV	Total Assets (MIL)	%Cash	%Stocks	%Bonds	%Other	Turnover Ratio	Premium/ Discount 1-Year Avg	Inception Date
-19.24	-21.14	-15.57	12.08	5.06	1.73	1.13	13.5		16.11	18.3	1	99	0	1	127	-0.16	Aug-05
-12.51	-7.80	-8.75	28.56	38.25	1.1	0.68	10.29		58.98	249.9	0	100	0	0		0.06	Apr-07
-12.31	-10.48	-10.42	20.24	-1.13	4.24	0.88	9.17	3.86	19.25	263.1	0	81	9	-1		-0.09	Sep-06
-0.11	1.76	3.32	0.72	-0.52	0.67	0.89	1.82			0.45						-1.91	Feb-08
-0.96	-2.75	-12.27	-22.51	-42.71	0	0.75	14.65			7.4					0	-0.14	Oct-07
-13.35	-13.29	-19.22	18.52	-15.10	0	0.75	20.03			2.0					0	5.99	Jun-08
22.25	-6.57	21.71	-32.72	-22.31	0	0.75	31.41			24.6					0	-0.15	Jun-08
-4.96	-17.29	-32.41	-46.44	-50.86	0	0.75	26.95			70.9					0	-0.40	Jun-08
-11.29	-10.18	-12.51	-0.30	-41.73	0	0.75	10.32			820.1					0	-0.04	Jun-06
-4.45	-10.45	-22.09	19.08	-29.39	0	0.75	21.2			30.4					0	-0.11	Oct-07
-7.63	-15.21	-8.67	13.53	-10.24	0	0.75	21.6			5.8					0	0.10	Jun-08
-31.38	-23.61	-13.86	-3.13	-69.80	0	0.75	25.42			0.72					0	-5.15	Oct-07
-0.42	0.98	-6.54	-24.93	-47.31	0	0.75	18.15			50.8					0	0.00	Oct-07
-9.31	-14.89	-21.31	25.41	-18.78	0	0.75	18.45			5.9					0	5.95	Oct-07
2.40	-13.78	-17.19	13.19	-14.27	0	0.75	24.85			0.49					0	4.64	Jun-08
-0.54	4.58	-2.65	-3.77	-14.98	0	0.75	19.45			8.4					0	-0.01	Oct-07
320.00	200.59	1.13	-78.17	-92.72	0	0.75	147.78			1.1					0	-52.15	Oct-07
-16.20	-29.59	-18.88	17.45	-32.89	0	0.75	33.67			7.2					0	-0.04	Oct-07
-4.76	-2.85	-17.87	-15.94	-48.40	0	0.75	22.18			3.3					0	7.33	Jun-08
7.91	1.41	-5.78	14.28	-8.33	0	0.75	15.35			2.7					0	6.22	Jun-08
0.10	-9.02	-24.57	-28.81	-44.10	0	0.75	21.79			0.81					0	4.03	Jun-08
8.60	1.13	-27.72	-35.63	-59.50	0	0.75	32.04			31.4					0	0.05	Jun-08
3.57	-0.13	-0.37	44.52	-9.14	0	0.75	14.47			1.1					0	3.91	Jun-08
-12.55	-8.18	-6.55	12.49	23.70	0	0.75	6.1			5.5					0	-2.76	May-07
-1.56	-2.02	-5.97	2.20	-21.16	0	0.4	7.3			1.5					0	3.48	May-07
-2.90	-3.56	-6.55	-15.02	-25.00	0	0.4	9.67			2.4					0	-3.88	May-07
1.41	0.20	-2.36	5.89	-1.25	2.06	0.89	4.41			0.61					0	2.73	Apr-08
1.91	-0.55	-7.39	5.94	-10.51	5.86	0.89	7.79			0.32	-97	0	0	197		6.21	Feb-08
15.58	67.22	225.95	221.73	445.54	0	0.75	62.25			10.4					0	-12.64	Jun-08
0.29	0.58	0.94	0.88	-0.14	0	0.89	0.24			0.18						-2.66	Jul-10
3.24	-0.01	1.40	7.02	-8.08	0	0.4	10.77			0.21					0	2.14	May-07
-21.18	-18.28	-24.59	7.01	-5.84	0	0.8	18.91			0.44						-4.20	Nov-10
-16.18	-17.44	-29.97	69.83	3.76	0	0.8	37.72			0.53						-32.27	Nov-10
-20.73	-12.83	-9.68	40.15	71.04	0	0.5	14.33			1.2						-19.98	Nov-10
-28.82	-27.72	-19.34	33.00	30.51	0	0.5	23.82			1.5						-15.63	Nov-10
-20.18	-11.84	-8.84	41.44	75.47	0	0.35	13.91			0.66						-19.80	Nov-10
1.86	0.30	-9.04	25.09	43.97	0	0.89	19.86			122.2					0	-1.32	Dec-06
-1.41	-1.07	1.92	-1.11	-3.84	0	0.65	4.72			0.62					0	-7.24	Jan-09
-14.13	-12.55	-11.92	9.00	-34.72	0	0.6	11.09			51.3						-0.11	Apr-11
-38.80	-32.15	-19.67	-4.17	-66.00	0	0.75	26.36			2.1						0.61	Apr-11
10.56	10.62	-7.33	-17.90	-37.40	0	0.95	11.08			8.4						-0.56	Aug-11
31.47	17.31	27.75	-49.33	-64.34	0	0.89	25.67			44.8					0	0.09	Jan-09
84.82	32.62	73.51	-84.69	-92.83	0	0.89	55.06			833.2					0	0.15	Jan-09
-49.54	-46.00	-28.64	-17.93	-79.61	0	0.75	39.05			228.9					0	6.95	Aug-06
-28.48	-24.38	-17.02	-0.77	-60.31	0	0.75	18.73			33.3					0	-0.07	Jun-06
-21.02	-15.99	-15.48	-2.67	-34.08	5.53	0.8	18.69			33.0						0.28	Jan-13
-0.76	-2.26					0.45				7.0						-0.28	Jan-18
-12.07	-11.96					0.45				4.6						0.74	Jan-18
-3.90	-14.15					0.45				53.8						-0.15	Jan-18
-3.94	-9.37					0.45				14.3						-0.30	Jan-18
-7.01	-14.09					0.45				6.9						0.06	Jan-18
-25.71	-18.88					0.45				4.5						-1.14	Jan-18

Fund Name	Ticker Symbol	Traded On	Overall Rating	Reward Rating	Risk Rating	Recent Up/ Downgrade	Price as of 12/31/2018	52-Week High	52-Week Low	Open to New Investors	Category & (Prospectus Objective)
iPath® Series B Bloomberg Grains Subindex Total Return ETN	JJG	NYSE Arca	U	U	U		46.90	56.35	45.59	Y	Commodities Specified (Growth & Inc)
iPath® Ser B Bloomberg Industrial Metals SubInd Total Ret	JJM	NYSE Arca	U	U	U		41.15	53.12	41.15	Y	Commodities Specified (Growth & Inc)
iPath® Series B Bloomberg Livestock SubInd Total Ret ETN	COW	NYSE Arca	U	U	U		48.82	50.40	44.03	Y	Commodities Specified (Growth & Inc)
iPath® Ser B Bloomberg Natural Gas SubInd Total RetSM ETN	GAZ	NYSE Arca	D	D+	D	Up	41.06	63.89	36.95	Y	Commodities Specified (Natl Res)
iPath® Series B Bloomberg Nickel Subindex Total Return ETN	JJN	NYSE Arca	U	U	U		42.71	64.11	42.71	Y	Commodities Specified (Growth & Inc)
iPath® Series B Bloomberg Platinum SubInd Total Ret ETN	PGM	NYSE Arca	U	U	U		39.31	49.80	38.30	Y	Commodities Specified (Growth & Inc)
iPath® Ser B Bloomberg Prec Metals SubInd Total Ret ETN	JJP	NYSE Arca	U	U	U		46.74	51.58	43.13	Y	Commodities Specified (Growth & Inc)
iPath® Series B Bloomberg Softs Subindex Total Return ETN	JJS	NYSE Arca	U	U	U		40.70	50.10	39.84	Y	Commodities Broad Basket (Growth & Inc)
iPath® Series B Bloomberg Sugar Subindex Total Return ETN	SGG	NYSE Arca	U	U	U		41.46	51.63	37.02	Y	Commodities Specified (Growth & Inc)
iPath® Series B Bloomberg Tin Subindex Total Return ETN	JJT	NYSE Arca	U	U	U		48.72	53.26	45.53	Y	Commodities Specified (Growth & Inc)
iPath® Series B S&P 500® VIX Mid-Term Futures™ ETN	VXZB	BATS	U	U	U		22.29	23.08	16.72	Y	Alternative Misc (Growth & Inc)
iPath® Series B S&P 500® VIX Short-Term Futures™ ETN	VXXB	BATS	U	U	U		46.99	55.18	26.20	Y	Alternative Misc (Growth & Inc)
● iPath® Series B S&P GSCI® Crude Oil Total Return Index ETN	OIL	NYSE Arca	D+	D+	D	Down	47.46	79.07	45.57	Y	Commodities Specified (Natl Res)
● iPath® US Treasury 10-year Bear ETN	DTYS	NAS CM	C	C	D+	Down	19.29	25.60	18.25	Y	Trading Tools (Govt Bond - Treasury)
iPath® US Treasury 10-year Bull ETN	DTYL	NAS CM	D-	D	E		76.00	77.11	72.11	Y	Trading Tools (Govt Bond - Treasury)
iPath® US Treasury 2-year Bear ETN	DTUS	NAS CM	C	C+	D	Down	37.25	42.67	35.02	Y	Trading Tools (Govt Bond - Treasury)
iPath® US Treasury 2-year Bull ETN	DTUL	NAS CM	D-	D-	E		55.03	60.50	54.73	Y	Trading Tools (Govt Bond - Treasury)
iPath® US Treasury 5-year Bear ETN	DFVS	NAS CM	C	C	D+		34.22	39.50	31.58	Y	Trading Tools (Govt Bond - Treasury)
iPath® US Treasury 5-year Bull ETN	DFVL	NAS CM	D-	D	E		60.34	65.48	60.34	Y	Trading Tools (Govt Bond - Treasury)
iPath® US Treasury Flattener ETN	FLAT	NAS CM	C-	C	E+		66.29	66.42	61.72	Y	Trading Tools (Govt Bond - Treasury)
iPath® US Treasury Long Bond Bear ETN	DLBS	NAS CM	C	C-	D+		17.90	23.79	16.34	Y	Trading Tools (Govt Bond - Treasury)
iPath® US Treasury Long Bond Bull ETN	DLBL	NAS CM	D-	D	E	Down	75.08	77.88	75.08	Y	Trading Tools (Govt Bond - Treasury)
iPath® US Treasury Steepener ETN	STPP	NAS CM	D	D	D+		29.61	32.92	28.91	Y	Trading Tools (Govt Bond - Treasury)
IQ 50 Percent Hedged FTSE Europe ETF	HFXE	NYSE Arca	D	D+	D	Down	17.07	21.29	16.85	Y	Europe Equity Large Cap (Europe Stock)
● IQ 50 Percent Hedged FTSE International ETF	HFXI	NYSE Arca	C-	D+	C	Down	18.17	22.78	17.88	Y	Global Equity Large Cap (World Stock)
IQ 50 Percent Hedged FTSE Japan ETF	HFXJ	NYSE Arca	D+	C-	D	Down	18.69	23.96	18.21	Y	Japan Equity (Pacific Stock)
● IQ Chaikin U.S. Large Cap ETF	CLRG	NAS CM	D+	D+	D		21.33	27.28	20.41	Y	US Equity Large Cap Blend (Growth & Inc)
● IQ Chaikin U.S. Small Cap ETF	CSML	NAS CM	D	D	D	Down	22.32	29.80	21.19	Y	US Equity Small Cap (Small Company)
● IQ Enhanced Core Bond U.S. ETF	AGGE	NYSE Arca	D+	D	C-	Up	18.61	19.57	18.31	Y	US Fixed Income (Income)
● IQ Enhanced Core Plus Bond U.S. ETF	AGGP	NYSE Arca	D+	D+	C-		18.91	19.99	18.74	Y	US Fixed Income (Income)
IQ Global Agribusiness Small Cap ETF	CROP	NYSE Arca	D+	C-	D+		30.17	35.99	29.00	Y	Consumer Goods & Svcs (Unaligned)
● IQ Global Resources ETF	GRES	NYSE Arca	C-	D+	C-		25.23	29.23	25.05	Y	Natural Resources (World Stock)
IQ Hedge Event-Driven Tracker ETF	QED	NYSE Arca	D+	C-	D	Down	19.56	21.62	19.51	Y	Market Neutral (Growth & Inc)
IQ Hedge Long/Short Tracker ETF	QLS	NYSE Arca	D	C-	E+	Down	19.57	22.97	19.56	Y	Long/Short Equity (Growth & Inc)
IQ Hedge Macro Tracker ETF	MCRO	NYSE Arca	D	D+	D	Down	24.96	27.20	24.91	Y	Cautious Allocation (Growth)
IQ Hedge Market Neutral Tracker ETF	QMN	NYSE Arca	D+	C-	D+	Down	25.18	25.98	24.98	Y	Market Neutral (Growth & Inc)
● IQ Hedge Multi-Strategy Tracker ETF	QAI	NYSE Arca	C-	D+	C	Down	28.88	31.25	28.81	Y	Multialternative (Growth)
IQ Leaders GTAA Tracker ETF	QGTA	NYSE Arca	D+	C-	D	Down	21.95	25.44	21.58	Y	Moderate Allocation (Growth & Inc)
IQ MacKay Shields Municipal Insured ETF	MMIN	NYSE Arca	D	D+	D		25.02	27.08	24.32	Y	US Muni Fixed Inc (Muni Bond - Natl)
IQ MacKay Shields Municipal Intermediate ETF	MMIT	NYSE Arca	D	D+	D		25.06	25.09	24.44	Y	US Muni Fixed Inc (Muni Bond - Natl)
● IQ Merger Arbitrage ETF	MNA	NYSE Arca	C+	C+	C	Up	31.71	32.06	30.32	Y	Market Neutral (Growth)
● IQ Real Return ETF	CPI	NYSE Arca	D+	C-	D+	Down	26.61	28.08	26.47	Y	Moderate Allocation (Growth & Inc)
● IQ S&P High Yield Low Volatility Bond ETF	HYLV	NYSE Arca	D	D	D+	Down	23.28	25.37	23.07	Y	US Fixed Income (Corp Bond-High Yld)
● IQ U.S. Real Estate Small Cap ETF	ROOF	NYSE Arca	C-	C	D+	Down	21.93	27.39	21.70	Y	Real Estate Sector Equity (Real Estate)
● iShares 0-5 Year High Yield Corporate Bond ETF	SHYG	NYSE Arca	C	C	C+	Down	44.55	47.44	43.90	Y	US Fixed Income (Corp Bond-High Yld)
● iShares 0-5 Year Investment Grade Corporate Bond ETF	SLQD	NAS CM	C	C	C+		49.53	50.26	49.20	Y	US Fixed Income (Corp Bond - Gen)
● iShares 0-5 Year TIPS Bond ETF	STIP	NYSE Arca	C	C-	C+		98.02	100.14	97.69	Y	US Fixed Income (Govt Bond - Treasury)
iShares 10+ Year Investment Grade Corporate Bond ETF	LLQD	BATS	D	D	D		45.34	51.25	44.23	Y	US Fixed Income (Corp Bond - Gen)
● iShares 10-20 Year Treasury Bond ETF	TLH	NYSE Arca	D	D	C-	Down	133.51	136.01	125.72	Y	US Fixed Income (Govt Bond - Treasury)
● iShares 1-3 Year International Treasury Bond ETF	ISHG	NAS CM	D+	D+	D+		79.76	87.66	78.94	Y	Global Fixed Income (Worldwide Bond)
● iShares 1-3 Year Treasury Bond ETF	SHY	NAS CM	C	C-	C+	Up	83.62	83.85	82.85	Y	US Fixed Income (Govt Bond - Treasury)
● iShares 20+ Year Treasury Bond ETF	TLT	NAS CM	D+	D	C-	Down	121.51	126.86	112.00	Y	US Fixed Income (Govt Bond - Treasury)

★ Expanded analysis of this fund is included in Section II: Analysis of All BUY Rated Funds. ● Expanded analysis of this fund is included in Section III: Analysis of All Rated Funds with Assets over $50 million.

3-Month Total Return	6-Month Total Return	1-Year Total Return	3-Year Total Return	5-Year Total Return	Dividend Yield (TTM)	Expense Ratio	3-Yr Std Deviation	Effective Duration	NAV	Total Assets (MIL)	%Cash	%Stocks	%Bonds	%Other	Turnover Ratio	Premium/ Discount 1-Year Avg	Inception Date
-0.29	1.00					0.45				18.7						0.19	Jan-18
-8.36	-13.44					0.45				4.2						0.70	Jan-18
-0.42	4.27					0.45				7.7						0.48	Jan-18
7.16	15.54	9.76			0	0.45				6.0						-0.07	Mar-17
-14.24	-26.54					0.45				5.2						0.91	Jan-18
-4.08	-2.34					0.45				3.5						1.25	Jan-18
7.25	1.42					0.45				4.4						0.04	Jan-18
0.17	-7.76					0.45				4.2						0.36	Jan-18
7.20	1.09					0.45				25.6						-0.16	Jan-18
3.37	0.01					0.45				4.0						0.07	Jan-18
31.47	17.31					0.89				11.9						-1.57	Jan-18
84.82	32.62					0.89				127.7						0.85	Jan-18
-39.82	-36.42	-21.00			0	0.75				76.2						0.15	Nov-16
-17.65	-10.93	8.89	-2.75	-38.96	0	0.75	39.49			61.9						0.32	Aug-10
6.43	4.16	-0.82	1.29	17.76	0	0.75	8.29			4.7						0.30	Aug-10
-8.84	-3.99	7.61	13.36	-4.24	0	0.75	13.49			5.3						-0.16	Aug-10
7.37	3.94	-2.70	-6.38	0.87	0	0.75	7.03			4.6						1.63	Aug-10
-11.64	-6.91	6.68	4.36	-20.33	0	0.75	21.22			4.3						-0.04	Jul-11
8.01	5.02	-1.74	-0.77	13.92	0	0.75	9.17			4.3						2.68	Jul-11
1.18	1.79	2.37	8.41	18.42	0	0.75	5.11			4.6						-0.89	Aug-10
-16.46	-6.62	11.87	-15.05	-50.09	0	0.75	35.31			18.8						0.15	Aug-10
5.33	2.52	-1.20	4.94	28.27	0	0.75	7.51			0.56						0.17	Aug-10
-1.37	-1.67	-1.63	-14.02	-28.36	0	0.75	9.97			4.4						0.66	Aug-10
-11.83	-9.65	-11.89	9.68		2.94	0.3	10.19		17.12	10.0	0	100	0	0		0.00	Jul-15
-13.57	-10.52	-13.26	9.24		3.14	0.2	9.91		18.25	422.5	0	100	0	0		0.22	Jul-15
-15.72	-9.80	-13.86	6.35		2.2	0.3	12.14		18.94	32.3	0	100	0	0		0.03	Jul-15
-17.39	-12.45	-13.10				0.25			21.48	432.2	0	100	0	0		0.14	Dec-17
-19.45	-22.15	-19.51			0.76	0.35			22.36	443.0	0	100	0	0		0.05	May-17
1.23	0.97	-2.57			2.82	0.3		4.46	18.60	58.0	1	0	99	0		-0.02	May-16
-0.21	0.53	-2.31			3.3	0.38		3.77	18.93	178.1	1	0	99	0		-0.03	May-16
-3.14	-5.97	-12.35	10.62	17.31	0.99	0.76	9.98		30.34	11.0	0	100	0	0		0.14	Mar-11
-6.51	-6.63	-10.23	22.29	-6.45	0	0.78	9.82		25.39	188.7	0	90	0	10		-0.02	Oct-09
-5.43	-3.63	-1.92	12.01		2.22	1.11	4.07	3.19	19.56	3.2	2	8	71	1		0.11	Mar-15
-7.71	-6.00	-6.22	11.04		0.39	1.04	5.22	6.61	19.58	4.3	6	56	28	2		0.08	Mar-15
-3.88	-3.28	-5.10	4.00	-1.56	0	0.99	3.67	2.64	24.98	6.5	31	36	28	3		-0.03	Jun-09
-2.71	-1.92	-2.14	2.47	1.76	0	1.01	1.78	2.96	25.19	14.0	27	12	58	2		0.03	Oct-12
-4.06	-2.89	-3.21	3.55	3.73	0	0.79	3.38	2.96	28.92	1,194	27	25	43	3		0.03	Mar-09
-8.24	-5.58	-7.15	14.32		2.56	0.4	6.93	5.55	22.00	43.9	2	49	38	5		0.11	Sep-15
1.94	2.02	1.58			2.94	0.3			24.97	16.1	11	0	89	0		0.35	Oct-17
1.97	2.02	1.98			2.55	0.31			24.99	29.7	6	0	94	0		-0.24	Oct-17
-0.01	3.08	2.08	13.33	20.83	0	0.78	3.34		31.68	757.7	7	80	11	3		0.22	Nov-09
-3.81	-2.60	-1.78	2.93	5.14	1.07	0.44	2.07		26.62	59.1	41	19	39	1		0.06	Oct-09
-3.39	-0.96	-3.38			4.31	0.4			23.29	85.7	0	0	99	1		0.11	Feb-17
-12.50	-13.59	-11.19	8.04	21.35	5.81	0.7	13.99		21.94	76.8	0	99	0	0		0.02	Jun-11
-3.30	-1.07	0.43	18.88	15.02	5.53	0.3	3.04	2.43	44.54	2,849	2	0	98	0	35	0.19	Oct-13
0.73	1.43	1.15	5.53	8.16	2.38	0.06	1.16	2.26	49.48	1,392	5	0	95	0	20	0.12	Oct-13
-0.32	-0.17	0.49	4.10	2.67	2.69	0.06	1.23	2.57	97.99	2,296	1	0	99	0	27	0.03	Dec-10
-2.00	-0.46	-7.76			4.53	0.06		13.18	45.17	8.9	3	0	97	0	2	0.22	Sep-17
4.52	2.58	-0.10	4.89	21.56	2.21	0.15	5.9	10.54	132.92	668.4	0	0	100	0	27	0.01	Jan-07
-0.18	-1.10	-3.67	4.69	-13.69	0.49	0.35	6.48	1.84	79.69	76.1	1	0	99	0	48	-0.02	Jan-09
1.28	1.48	1.45	2.49	3.42	1.62	0.15	0.76	1.88	83.60	17,171	0	0	100	0	85	0.02	Jul-02
4.74	1.10	-2.07	8.11	35.42	2.75	0.15	9.58	17.03	121.01	7,782	0	0	100	0	25	-0.08	Jul-02

Fund Name	Ticker Symbol	Traded On	Overall Rating	Reward Rating	Risk Rating	Recent Up/ Downgrade	Price as of 12/31/2018	52-Week High	52-Week Low	Open to New Investors	Category & (Prospectus Objective)
● iShares 3-7 Year Treasury Bond ETF	IEI	NAS CM	C-	D	C	Up	121.40	122.16	118.21	Y	US Fixed Income (Govt Bond - Treasury)
iShares 5-10 Year Investment Grade Corporate Bond ETF	MLQD	BATS	D	D	D	Down	47.17	49.41	45.70	Y	US Fixed Income (Corp Bond - Gen)
● iShares 7-10 Year Treasury Bond ETF	IEF	NAS CM	D+	D	C		104.20	105.57	99.72	Y	US Fixed Income (Govt Bond - Treasury)
● iShares Aaa - A Rated Corporate Bond ETF	QLTA	NYSE Arca	D+	D+	C-	Down	50.08	52.84	49.32	Y	US Fixed Income (Corp Bond - High Quality)
iShares Adaptive Currency Hedged MSCI EAFE ETF	DEFA	BATS	D+	D+	D+	Down	24.58	30.45	24.15	Y	Global Equity Large Cap (Foreign Stock)
iShares Adaptive Currency Hedged MSCI Eurozone ETF	DEZU	BATS	D	D+	E	Down	24.07	30.64	23.50	Y	Europe Equity Large Cap (Foreign Stock)
iShares Adaptive Currency Hedged MSCI Japan ETF	DEWJ	BATS	D	D+	E+	Down	24.77	31.33	24.27	Y	Japan Equity (Pacific Stock)
● iShares Agency Bond ETF	AGZ	NYSE Arca	C-	C-	C-	Up	112.13	113.09	109.93	Y	US Fixed Income (Govt Bond - Gen)
● iShares Asia 50 ETF	AIA	NAS CM	C-	C-	C-	Down	55.30	72.96	53.63	Y	Asia ex-Japan Equity (Pacific Stock)
iShares Asia/Pacific Dividend ETF	DVYA	NYSE Arca	D+	C-	D+	Down	40.31	51.42	39.35	Y	Asia Equity (Pacific Stock)
iShares Bloomberg Roll Select Broad Commodity ETF	CMDY	NYSE Arca	U	U	U		43.95	52.86	43.95	Y	Commodities Broad Basket (Growth & Inc)
● iShares Broad USD High Yield Corporate Bond ETF	USHY	BATS	D+	D	C-		45.84	50.30	45.07	Y	US Fixed Income (Corp Bond-High Yld)
● iShares Broad USD Investment Grade Corporate Bond ETF	USIG	NAS CM	D-	E+	D-	Down	52.95	112.03	52.37	Y	US Fixed Income (Income)
● iShares California Muni Bond ETF	CMF	NYSE Arca	C	C-	C+		58.45	59.30	56.95	Y	US Muni Fixed Inc (Muni Bond - Single State)
● iShares China Large-Cap ETF	FXI	NYSE Arca	C-	C-	C	Down	39.08	54.00	38.26	Y	Greater China Equity (Pacific Stock)
● iShares CMBS ETF	CMBS	NYSE Arca	C-	D+	C-	Up	50.28	51.27	49.03	Y	US Fixed Income (Growth)
★ iShares Cohen & Steers REIT ETF	ICF	BATS	B-	B	C		95.70	106.05	88.56	Y	Real Estate Sector Equity (Real Estate)
● iShares Commodities Select Strategy ETF	COMT	NAS CM	C	C-	C+		30.49	40.38	29.85	Y	Commodities Broad Basket (Growth & Inc)
● iShares Convertible Bond ETF	ICVT	BATS	C-	C-	C-	Down	52.52	60.12	50.03	Y	Convertibles (Convertible Bond)
● iShares Core 10+ Year USD Bond ETF	ILTB	NYSE Arca	D+	D	C-	Down	59.02	64.77	57.00	Y	US Fixed Income (Growth)
● iShares Core 1-5 Year USD Bond ETF	ISTB	NAS CM	C	C-	C+		49.06	49.83	48.64	Y	US Fixed Income (Multisector Bond)
● iShares Core 5-10 Year USD Bond ETF	IMTB	NYSE Arca	D	D	D+	Down	48.00	49.71	46.97	Y	US Fixed Income (Income)
● iShares Core Aggressive Allocation ETF	AOA	NYSE Arca	C	C-	C+		48.55	56.92	47.04	Y	Aggressive Allocation (Asset Allocation)
● iShares Core Conservative Allocation ETF	AOK	NYSE Arca	C	C-	C+		32.72	35.24	32.37	Y	Cautious Allocation (Asset Allocation)
● iShares Core Dividend Growth ETF	DGRO	NYSE Arca	C	C	C+	Down	33.18	37.86	31.18	Y	US Equity Large Cap Value (Equity-Income)
● iShares Core Growth Allocation ETF	AOR	NYSE Arca	C	C-	C+		41.31	46.74	40.34	Y	Moderate Allocation (Asset Allocation)
★ iShares Core High Dividend ETF	HDV	NYSE Arca	B-	B	C	Up	84.38	94.20	80.00	Y	US Equity Large Cap Value (Equity-Income)
● iShares Core International Aggregate Bond ETF	IAGG	BATS	C-	C	C-		52.21	52.91	51.58	Y	Global Fixed Income (Worldwide Bond)
● iShares Core Moderate Allocation ETF	AOM	NYSE Arca	C	C-	C+		35.68	39.00	35.24	Y	Cautious Allocation (Asset Allocation)
● iShares Core MSCI EAFE ETF	IEFA	BATS	C-	D+	C	Down	55.00	70.84	53.06	Y	Global Equity Large Cap (Growth & Inc)
● iShares Core MSCI Emerging Markets ETF	IEMG	NYSE Arca	C-	C-	C-	Down	47.15	62.69	45.85	Y	Global Emerg Mkts Equity (Div Emerg Mkts)
● iShares Core MSCI Europe ETF	IEUR	NYSE Arca	D+	D+	C-	Down	41.33	53.89	40.03	Y	Europe Equity Large Cap (Europe Stock)
● iShares Core MSCI International Developed Markets ETF	IDEV	NYSE Arca	D	D	D+	Down	48.85	62.47	47.08	Y	Global Equity Large Cap (Foreign Stock)
● iShares Core MSCI Pacific ETF	IPAC	NYSE Arca	D+	D+	C-	Down	50.62	63.85	49.08	Y	Asia Equity (Pacific Stock)
● iShares Core MSCI Total International Stock ETF	IXUS	NAS CM	C-	D+	C	Down	52.53	67.91	50.85	Y	Global Equity Large Cap (Foreign Stock)
● iShares Core S&P 500 ETF	IVV	NYSE Arca	C+	C	B	Down	251.61	295.76	236.09	Y	US Equity Large Cap Blend (Growth)
● iShares Core S&P Mid-Cap ETF	IJH	NYSE Arca	C	C-	C+	Down	166.06	204.98	156.48	Y	US Equity Mid Cap (Growth)
● iShares Core S&P Small-Cap ETF	IJR	NYSE Arca	C	C-	B-	Down	69.32	90.31	65.14	Y	US Equity Small Cap (Small Company)
● iShares Core S&P Total U.S. Stock Market ETF	ITOT	NYSE Arca	C	C	C+	Down	56.76	67.36	53.25	Y	US Equity Large Cap Blend (Growth)
● iShares Core S&P U.S. Growth ETF	IUSG	NAS CM	C	C	C+	Down	52.70	62.28	49.22	Y	US Equity Large Cap Growth (Growth)
● iShares Core S&P U.S. Value ETF	IUSV	NAS CM	C	C	C+	Down	49.09	58.63	46.36	Y	US Equity Large Cap Value (Growth)
● iShares Core Total USD Bond Market ETF	IUSB	NAS CM	C	D+	C+	Up	49.25	50.87	48.37	Y	US Fixed Income (Corp Bond - Gen)
● iShares Core U.S. Aggregate Bond ETF	AGG	NYSE Arca	C	D+	C+		106.49	109.33	104.01	Y	US Fixed Income (Corp Bond - Gen)
● iShares Core U.S. REIT ETF	USRT	NYSE Arca	C	C	C+		44.85	51.10	43.17	Y	Real Estate Sector Equity (Real Estate)
iShares Currency Hedged JPX-Nikkei 400 ETF	HJPX	NYSE Arca	D	C-	E+	Down	25.27	32.09	24.76	Y	Japan Equity (Growth)
iShares Currency Hedged MSCI ACWI ex U.S. ETF	HAWX	NYSE Arca	D+	D+	D+	Down	23.68	27.98	23.30	Y	Global Equity Large Cap (Growth & Inc)
iShares Currency Hedged MSCI Australia ETF	HAUD	NYSE Arca	D	C-	E+	Down	22.00	25.31	21.93	Y	Equity Misc (Foreign Stock)
iShares Currency Hedged MSCI Canada ETF	HEWC	NYSE Arca	C-	C-	C-	Down	22.79	27.27	22.32	Y	Equity Misc (Foreign Stock)
● iShares Currency Hedged MSCI EAFE ETF	HEFA	BATS	C	C-	C+	Down	25.81	30.85	25.29	Y	Global Equity Large Cap (Foreign Stock)
iShares Currency Hedged MSCI EAFE Small-Cap ETF	HSCZ	NYSE Arca	C-	D+	C-	Down	25.21	32.36	24.63	Y	Global Eq Mid/Small Cap (Small Company)
● iShares Currency Hedged MSCI Emerging Markets ETF	HEEM	BATS	C-	C-	C	Down	23.03	28.95	22.75	Y	Global Emerg Mkts Equity (Div Emerg Mkts)
● iShares Currency Hedged MSCI Eurozone ETF	HEZU	NYSE Arca	C-	D+	C	Down	25.94	31.54	25.39	Y	Europe Equity Large Cap (Europe Stock)

★Expanded analysis of this fund is included in Section II: Analysis of All BUY Rated Funds. ● Expanded analysis of this fund is included in Section III: Analysis of All Rated Funds with Assets over $50 million.

		TOTAL RETURNS & PERFORMANCE							ASSETS		ASSET ALLOCATION & TURNOVER					VALUATION	
3-Month Total Return	6-Month Total Return	1-Year Total Return	3-Year Total Return	5-Year Total Return	Dividend Yield (TTM)	Expense Ratio	3-Yr Std Deviation	Effective Duration	NAV	Total Assets (MIL)	%Cash	%Stocks	%Bonds	%Other	Turnover Ratio	Premium/ Discount 1-Year Avg	Inception Date
2.71	2.48	1.35	3.80	8.85	1.9	0.15	2.64	4.47	121.36	7,799	0	0	100	0	66	0.02	Jan-07
0.43	1.54	-1.58			3.34	0.06		6.20	47.05	9.3	0	0	99	0	1	0.16	Sep-17
3.87	3.01	0.82	4.34	15.40	2.2	0.15	4.63	7.41	104.02	9,265	0	0	100	0	46	0.00	Jul-02
0.45	1.15	-2.29	7.41	15.26	3.05	0.15	3.38	6.83	50.00	138.5	1	0	98	0	16	0.05	Feb-12
-12.90	-9.90	-11.55	19.43		3.19	0.34			24.58	8.1	1	99	0	0	8	-0.01	Jan-16
-12.56	-11.21	-12.30	19.70		3.1	0.52			24.08	2.6	0	100	0	0	7	0.20	Jan-16
-18.57	-12.19	-15.63	14.60		1.56	0.49			24.77	4.2	0	100	0	0	5	-0.45	Jan-16
1.96	1.87	1.33	4.54	9.34	2.05	0.2	1.82	3.94	111.88	454.1	0	0	100	0	78	0.03	Nov-08
-9.96	-9.68	-13.94	38.10	30.58	1.9	0.5	15.5		55.43	936.8	0	100	0	0	16	-0.06	Nov-07
-6.50	-6.35	-15.01	19.29	-3.83	5.89	0.49	13.43		40.37	32.1	1	99	0	0	21	-0.33	Feb-12
-10.48	-9.92					0.28			43.63	39.9	100	0	0	0		0.38	Apr-18
-4.90	-2.08	-2.54			5.86	0.22		4.06	45.56	254.1	2	0	98	0	0	0.39	Oct-17
-0.03	0.69	-51.20	-45.45	-42.00	3.37	0.06	3.55	6.77	52.81	2,229	3	0	97	0	11	0.03	Jan-07
1.34	0.84	0.68	5.34	19.70	2.16	0.25	3.42	6.28	58.22	1,032	0	0	100	0	32	0.14	Oct-07
-7.07	-7.67	-12.40	19.84	18.28	3.6	0.74	18.37		39.47	5,837	0	100	0	0	18	0.01	Oct-04
1.74	2.17	0.59	6.83	11.21	2.74	0.25	2.77	5.04	50.14	317.2	0	1	99	0	19	0.17	Feb-12
-2.94	-2.18	-2.45	7.05	52.09	3.09	0.34	12.62		95.71	2,021	0	100	0	0	12	-0.03	Jan-01
-15.01	-11.84	-6.59	26.48		5.81	0.48	12.72		30.48	601.6	67	32	1	0	44	0.02	Oct-14
-10.48	-7.55	-1.85	26.13		1.97	0.2	8.6	1.63	52.05	301.9	1	1	0	0	14	0.10	Jun-15
0.71	0.40	-4.99	13.47	29.74	4.19	0.06	6.95	13.94	58.86	195.0	0	0	99	0	11	0.05	Dec-09
1.11	1.59	1.18	5.76	7.78	2.43	0.06	1.26	2.70	49.03	2,255	2	0	97	0	124	0.09	Oct-12
1.45	1.84	0.06			2.8	0.06		5.75	47.82	56.8	8	0	92	0	504	0.22	Nov-16
-10.45	-6.93	-7.76	19.16	25.08	1.98	0.25	7.82	5.97	48.56	882.4	1	80	19	0	40	0.04	Nov-08
-3.65	-2.10	-3.31	11.42	14.50	2.3	0.25	3.8	5.97	32.74	466.6	3	31	66	0	41	0.07	Nov-08
-10.22	-2.31	-2.24	38.42		2.21	0.08	8.95		33.16	5,128	0	100	0	0	24	0.06	Jun-14
-7.62	-4.86	-5.83	16.38	22.29	2.08	0.25	6.13	5.97	41.25	1,151	2	60	37	0	44	0.05	Nov-08
-6.58	1.27	-2.92	27.41	43.02	3.42	0.08	8		84.33	6,672	0	100	0	0	46	0.00	Mar-11
1.92	1.54	2.92	10.76		1.6	0.09	2.62	7.29	52.03	919.0	0	0	100	0	20	0.13	Nov-15
-4.69	-2.72	-3.85	13.48	17.13	2.18	0.25	4.51	5.97	35.69	999.7	3	40	57	0	40	0.06	Nov-08
-12.91	-10.78	-14.20	9.94	5.19	3.2	0.08	11.21		55.05	54,938	1	99	0	0	2	-0.01	Oct-12
-7.19	-7.72	-14.69	28.32	8.29	2.87	0.14	14.58		47.21	49,953	0	100	0	0	6	0.07	Oct-12
-13.33	-11.70	-15.24	7.07		4.03	0.1	12.22		41.27	2,929	1	99	0	0	3	-0.06	Jun-14
-13.06	-10.91	-14.31			2.45	0.05			48.84	1,108	1	99	0	0	6	-0.04	Mar-17
-11.95	-9.14	-12.37	15.26		3.4	0.1	11.12		50.95	852.9	1	99	0	0	5	-0.01	Jun-14
-11.83	-10.33	-14.55	14.53	4.91	2.99	0.1	11.34		52.49	12,421	1	99	0	0	2	0.08	Oct-12
-13.95	-7.27	-4.54	30.09	49.78	1.82	0.04	9.4		251.40	162,725	0	100	0	0	4	0.03	May-00
-16.65	-14.22	-11.14	24.54	33.50	1.54	0.07	11.85		166.03	47,620	0	100	0	0	10	0.00	May-00
-18.92	-16.30	-12.23	25.67	30.14	1.31	0.07	14.71		69.35	42,979	0	100	0	0	12	0.01	May-00
-14.54	-8.64	-5.36	29.16	47.37	1.76	0.03	9.8		56.69	15,845	0	100	0	0	8	0.02	Jan-04
-15.13	-7.85	-0.79	35.23	59.55	1.2	0.04	10.73		52.64	5,462	0	100	0	0	24	0.05	Jul-00
-12.60	-7.30	-9.08	23.79	33.53	2.24	0.04	9.84		49.09	4,864	0	100	0	0	27	0.02	Jul-00
1.17	1.49	-0.37	7.57		2.85	0.06	2.65	5.72	49.14	2,445	4	0	96	0	264	0.11	Jun-14
1.69	1.71	-0.04	6.12	13.07	2.57	0.05	2.72	5.91	106.27	53,588	3	0	96	0	252	0.02	Sep-03
-5.83	-4.95	-4.55	8.49	44.41	5.2	0.08	12.39		44.86	784.5	0	100	0	0	8	0.02	May-07
-19.45	-12.00	-16.54	1.30		1.62	0.48	15.3		25.22	2.9	1	99	0	0	11	-0.12	Sep-15
-11.41	-8.65	-9.98	14.64		2.65	0.35	8.38		23.74	30.4	0	100	0	0	10	0.20	Jun-15
-10.21	-9.79	-5.85	14.70		4.58	0.52	9.15		22.15	1.1	1	99	0	0	12	-0.53	Jun-15
-12.00	-12.21	-10.79	16.81		2.27	0.52	7.6		22.80	37.9	-2	102	0	0	10	-0.03	Jun-15
-12.53	-9.01	-9.69	12.30		3.16	0.35	8.98		25.82	3,180	1	99	0	0	12	0.00	Jan-14
-16.84	-14.79	-14.73	13.96		2.57	0.43	10.06		25.28	24.4	1	99	0	0	10	0.18	Jun-15
-9.24	-8.54	-12.30	21.24		2.45	0.69	11.1		23.08	287.8	0	100	0	0	7	0.02	Sep-14
-12.76	-11.39	-10.68	8.90		3.2	0.52	11.37		25.96	1,443	0	100	0	0	11	0.01	Jul-14

Fund Name	Ticker Symbol	Traded On	Overall Rating	Reward Rating	Risk Rating	Recent Up/ Downgrade	Price as of 12/31/2018	52-Week High	52-Week Low	Open to New Investors	Category & (Prospectus Objective)
● iShares Currency Hedged MSCI Germany ETF	HEWG	NAS CM	D+	D+	C-	Down	23.75	30.33	22.95	Y	Equity Misc (Foreign Stock)
iShares Currency Hedged MSCI Italy ETF	HEWI	NYSE Arca	D	C-	D	Down	14.37	19.09	14.28	Y	Equity Misc (Foreign Stock)
● iShares Currency Hedged MSCI Japan ETF	HEWJ	NYSE Arca	C	C-	C+		28.09	35.21	27.38	Y	Japan Equity (Pacific Stock)
iShares Currency Hedged MSCI Mexico ETF	HEWW	NYSE Arca	D	D	D		16.26	20.77	16.11	Y	Equity Misc (Foreign Stock)
iShares Currency Hedged MSCI South Korea ETF	HEWY	NYSE Arca	C-	C-	C-	Up	24.12	31.88	24.12	Y	Equity Misc (Foreign Stock)
iShares Currency Hedged MSCI Spain ETF	HEWP	NYSE Arca	D+	D+	D+	Down	19.50	23.67	19.49	Y	Equity Misc (Foreign Stock)
iShares Currency Hedged MSCI Switzerland ETF	HEWL	NYSE Arca	D+	C-	D		24.01	27.79	23.30	Y	Equity Misc (Foreign Stock)
iShares Currency Hedged MSCI United Kingdom ETF	HEWU	NYSE Arca	C-	C-	D+	Down	21.32	25.42	21.25	Y	Equity Misc (Foreign Stock)
● iShares Dow Jones U.S. ETF	IYY	NYSE Arca	C	C	C-		124.45	147.06	116.74	Y	US Equity Large Cap Blend (Growth)
iShares Edge High Yield Defensive Bond ETF	HYDB	BATS	D+	D+	D+	Up	46.31	51.18	45.60	Y	US Fixed Income (Corp Bond-High Yld)
● iShares Edge Investment Grade Enhanced Bond ETF	IGEB	BATS	D	D	C-		47.39	50.40	46.87	Y	US Fixed Income (Corp Bond - Gen)
● iShares Edge MSCI Intl Momentum Factor ETF	IMTM	NYSE Arca	C-	D+	C-	Down	25.60	32.95	24.83	Y	Global Equity Large Cap (World Stock)
● iShares Edge MSCI Intl Quality Factor ETF	IQLT	NYSE Arca	D+	D+	C-	Down	25.81	31.34	24.90	Y	Global Equity Large Cap (World Stock)
iShares Edge MSCI Intl Size Factor ETF	ISZE	NYSE Arca	D	D+	E	Down	23.72	29.64	22.98	Y	Global Equity Large Cap (Growth)
● iShares Edge MSCI Intl Value Factor ETF	IVLU	NYSE Arca	D+	D+	C-	Down	21.87	28.41	21.28	Y	Global Equity Large Cap (Foreign Stock)
● iShares Edge MSCI Min Vol Asia ex Japan ETF	AXJV	NYSE Arca	D+	D+	D+	Down	33.31	38.95	32.70	Y	Asia ex-Japan Equity (Pacific Stock)
● iShares Edge MSCI Min Vol EAFE ETF	EFAV	BATS	C	C-	C		66.66	76.47	65.01	Y	Global Equity Large Cap (Foreign Stock)
● iShares Edge MSCI Min Vol Emerging Markets ETF	EEMV	BATS	C	D+	C+		55.87	65.47	53.54	Y	Global Emerg Mkts Equity (Div Emerg Mkts)
iShares Edge MSCI Min Vol Europe ETF	EUMV	NYSE Arca	D+	D+	D+	Down	22.93	26.59	22.37	Y	Europe Equity Large Cap (Growth)
● iShares Edge MSCI Min Vol Global ETF	ACWV	BATS	C	C	C+		81.26	88.19	78.32	Y	Global Equity Large Cap (World Stock)
iShares Edge MSCI Min Vol Japan ETF	JPMV	NYSE Arca	C-	C-	D+		62.99	72.32	61.00	Y	Japan Equity (Pacific Stock)
★ iShares Edge MSCI Min Vol USA ETF	USMV	BATS	B	C	A	Up	52.40	57.58	49.77	Y	US Equity Large Cap Blend (Growth)
● iShares Edge MSCI Min Vol USA Small-Cap ETF	SMMV	BATS	C-	C-	C-		29.05	33.12	27.66	Y	US Equity Small Cap (Small Company)
● iShares Edge MSCI Multifactor Emerging Markets ETF	EMGF	BATS	D+	D+	D+	Down	38.73	53.84	38.00	Y	Global Emerg Mkts Equity (Div Emerg Mkts)
● iShares Edge MSCI Multifactor Global ETF	ACWF	NYSE Arca	C-	C-	C-	Down	25.97	33.19	24.98	Y	Global Equity Large Cap (Growth & Inc)
● iShares Edge MSCI Multifactor Intl ETF	INTF	NYSE Arca	C-	D+	C	Down	23.71	31.08	22.95	Y	Global Equity Large Cap (Growth & Inc)
● iShares Edge MSCI Multifactor Intl Small-Cap ETF	ISCF	NYSE Arca	D+	D+	C-	Down	25.87	34.65	24.74	Y	Global Eq Mid/Small Cap (Small Company)
● iShares Edge MSCI Multifactor USA ETF	LRGF	NYSE Arca	C	C	C+	Down	27.86	34.13	26.57	Y	US Equity Large Cap Value (Growth & Inc)
● iShares Edge MSCI Multifactor USA Small-Cap ETF	SMLF	NYSE Arca	C-	C-	C-	Down	35.82	44.87	33.54	Y	US Equity Small Cap (Small Company)
● iShares Edge MSCI USA Momentum Factor ETF	MTUM	BATS	C+	C+	C+	Down	100.23	119.62	92.80	Y	US Equity Large Cap Growth (Growth)
● iShares Edge MSCI USA Quality Factor ETF	QUAL	BATS	C	C	C+	Down	76.76	91.26	71.91	Y	US Equity Large Cap Blend (Growth)
● iShares Edge MSCI USA Size Factor ETF	SIZE	NYSE Arca	C-	C-	C-	Down	76.63	89.69	72.15	Y	US Equity Large Cap Blend (Growth)
● iShares Edge MSCI USA Value Factor ETF	VLUE	BATS	C	C	C	Down	72.57	89.39	68.64	Y	US Equity Large Cap Value (Growth)
● iShares Edge U.S. Fixed Income Balanced Risk ETF	FIBR	BATS	D+	C-	D+	Down	95.77	100.17	94.77	Y	Fixed Income Misc (Income)
● iShares Emerging Markets Dividend ETF	DVYE	NYSE Arca	C	C-	C+	Up	37.43	46.10	36.59	Y	Global Emerg Mkts Equity (Div Emerg Mkts)
● iShares Emerging Markets High Yield Bond ETF	EMHY	BATS	C-	C-	C-	Up	44.37	50.46	44.09	Y	Emerging Mkts Fixed Inc (Corp Bond-High Yld)
iShares Emerging Markets Infrastructure ETF	EMIF	NAS CM	D	D	D+	Down	27.68	35.07	26.69	Y	Global Emerg Mkts Equity (Utility)
iShares ESG 1-5 Year USD Corporate Bond ETF	SUSB	NAS CM	D+	D	C-		24.45	24.96	24.33	Y	US Fixed Income (Corp Bond - Gen)
● iShares ESG MSCI EM ETF	ESGE	NAS CM	D+	D+	D		30.67	40.80	29.80	Y	Global Emerg Mkts Equity (Div Emerg Mkts)
iShares ESG USD Corporate Bond ETF	SUSC	NAS CM	D	D	D+	Down	23.87	25.46	23.63	Y	US Fixed Income (Corp Bond - Gen)
iShares Europe Developed Real Estate ETF	IFEU	NAS CM	D+	C-	D+	Down	34.44	42.61	34.29	Y	Real Estate Sector Equity (Real Estate)
● iShares Europe ETF	IEV	NYSE Arca	D+	D+	C-	Down	39.12	50.71	37.89	Y	Europe Equity Large Cap (Europe Stock)
iShares Evolved U.S. Consumer Staples ETF	IECS	BATS	U	U	U		23.02	26.04	22.54	Y	Consumer Goods & Svcs (Unaligned)
iShares Evolved U.S. Discretionary Spending ETF	IEDI	BATS	U	U	U		24.40	28.65	22.91	Y	Consumer Goods & Svcs (Unaligned)
iShares Evolved U.S. Financials ETF	IEFN	BATS	U	U	U		20.37	25.48	19.24	Y	Financials Sector Equity (Financial)
iShares Evolved U.S. Healthcare Staples ETF	IEHS	BATS	U	U	U		26.17	29.89	24.00	Y	Healthcare Sector Equity (Health)
iShares Evolved U.S. Innovative Healthcare ETF	IEIH	BATS	U	U	U		23.56	27.41	22.22	Y	Healthcare Sector Equity (Health)
iShares Evolved U.S. Media and Entertainment ETF	IEME	BATS	U	U	U		23.04	27.91	21.99	Y	Communications Sector Equity (Unaligned)
iShares Evolved U.S. Technology ETF	IETC	BATS	U	U	U		23.04	28.40	21.55	Y	Technology Sector Equity (Technology)
● iShares Expanded Tech Sector ETF	IGM	NYSE Arca	C	C+	C	Down	171.71	210.69	159.35	Y	Technology Sector Equity (Technology)
● iShares Expanded Tech-Software Sector ETF	IGV	BATS	C+	B-	C	Down	173.53	205.52	154.57	Y	Technology Sector Equity (Technology)
● iShares Exponential Technologies ETF	XT	NAS CM	C	C	C+	Down	33.26	39.12	31.56	Y	Equity Misc (Technology)

★ Expanded analysis of this fund is included in Section II: Analysis of All BUY Rated Funds. ● Expanded analysis of this fund is included in Section III: Analysis of All Rated Funds with Assets over $50 million.

	TOTAL RETURNS & PERFORMANCE								ASSETS		ASSET ALLOCATION & TURNOVER					VALUATION	
3-Month Total Return	6-Month Total Return	1-Year Total Return	3-Year Total Return	5-Year Total Return	Dividend Yield (TTM)	Expense Ratio	3-Yr Std Deviation	Effective Duration	NAV	Total Assets (MIL)	%Cash	%Stocks	%Bonds	%Other	Turnover Ratio	Premium/ Discount 1-Year Avg	Inception Date
-13.46	-12.33	-15.17	4.80		2.88	0.53	12.72		23.77	271.8	1	99	0	0	11	-0.01	Jan-14
-11.17	-13.65	-12.21	-2.89		3.71	0.49	18.11		14.39	2.3	0	100	0	0	11	0.06	Jun-15
-19.01	-11.04	-15.28	1.96		1.48	0.49	15.6		28.02	1,060	1	99	0	0	9	0.03	Jan-14
-16.35	-13.00	-18.25	-12.11		3.24	0.53	12.03		16.26	0.82	0	100	0	0	23	0.16	Jun-15
-12.92	-10.98	-16.97	19.08		3.42	0.61	12.34		24.24	30.1	0	100	0	0	11	-0.57	Jun-15
-8.00	-8.87	-10.32	5.03		3.43	0.52	15.74		19.53	15.8	0	100	0	0	11	0.03	Jun-15
-8.49	-2.35	-5.60	15.24		2.28	0.52	8.96		24.00	5.3	1	99	0	0	14	0.00	Jun-15
-11.33	-11.09	-9.70	19.20		4.67	0.49	9.37		21.36	17.1	1	99	0	0	17	0.10	Jun-15
-14.27	-8.09	-5.22	28.73	45.87	1.64	0.2	9.64		124.41	1,193	0	100	0	0	4	0.00	Jun-00
-5.07	-2.33	-2.87			6.12	0.35		4.26	46.13	16.7	2	0	98	0	36	0.46	Jul-17
-0.14	1.03	-3.06			3.69	0.18		6.86	47.14	67.9	1	0	98	0	36	0.30	Jul-17
-15.24	-11.41	-13.96	8.61		2.18	0.3	11.04		25.68	147.1	1	99	0	0	131	0.10	Jan-15
-11.94	-8.37	-10.86	11.27		2.45	0.3	10.5		25.80	114.0	0	99	0	0	21	0.15	Jan-15
-11.86	-9.68	-12.84	12.98		3.13	0.3	10.16		23.85	5.1	0	99	0	0	13	0.18	Jun-15
-12.42	-9.87	-14.71	8.26		3.32	0.3	11.88		21.94	277.4	1	99	0	0	16	0.15	Jun-15
-5.71	-3.53	-6.20	21.47		3.48	0.35	10.46		33.54	12.0	0	100	0	0	38	-0.08	Jun-14
-7.11	-4.27	-5.80	12.38	26.77	2.66	0.2	8.68		66.60	9,033	1	99	0	0	23	-0.03	Oct-11
-4.44	-2.06	-6.07	23.06	9.08	2.63	0.25	11		55.73	4,733	1	99	0	0	22	-0.09	Oct-11
-8.80	-5.93	-7.83	5.52		3.2	0.25	10.28		22.81	23.8	1	99	0	0	26	-0.14	Jun-14
-6.46	-0.79	-1.34	25.57	43.80	2.04	0.2	7.71		81.21	3,599	1	99	0	0	23	-0.05	Oct-11
-7.16	-4.75	-5.59	16.40		1.42	0.3	8.91		63.09	19.8	1	99	0	0	23	0.09	Jun-14
-7.51	-0.53	1.35	33.24	63.54	1.81	0.15	7.79		52.39	19,373	0	100	0	0	22	-0.02	Oct-11
-9.98	-6.08	1.48			1.45	0.2			29.00	58.3	0	100	0	0	47	0.16	Sep-16
-8.39	-13.38	-18.64	24.77		2.47	0.45			39.03	268.6	0	100	0	0	39	0.14	Dec-15
-14.87	-12.32	-13.38	18.03		1.98	0.35	10.44		25.97	65.4	0	99	0	0	46	0.64	Apr-15
-14.52	-11.89	-15.66	7.85		3.5	0.3	11.46		23.77	1,017	1	99	0	1	39	0.02	Apr-15
-16.50	-15.77	-18.18	11.47		2.43	0.4	12.55		25.92	67.2	1	98	0	1	44	0.53	Apr-15
-16.84	-12.27	-10.96	22.41		1.69	0.2	9.98		27.83	1,213	0	100	0	0	46	-0.07	Apr-15
-16.65	-14.71	-8.16	26.05		1.05	0.3	13.09		35.75	181.5	0	100	0	0	46	0.06	Apr-15
-15.97	-8.60	-1.76	41.78	77.11	1.09	0.15	11.14		100.06	9,501	0	100	0	0	104	0.02	Apr-13
-15.02	-7.31	-5.77	25.78	48.20	1.78	0.15	9.2		76.65	6,872	0	100	0	0	41	0.00	Jul-13
-12.47	-7.79	-6.58	25.84	46.23	1.97	0.15	8.91		76.57	235.3	0	100	0	0	17	0.09	Apr-13
-17.15	-11.33	-11.18	25.31	35.73	2.26	0.15	10.8		72.47	4,165	0	100	0	0	18	0.02	Apr-13
-0.48	0.70	-1.01	8.25		3.25	0.25	2.33	5.30	95.45	119.4	-11	0	110	0	683	0.10	Feb-15
-3.18	-0.91	-5.41	43.01	-1.01	5.62	0.49	14.05		37.48	521.2	1	99	0	0	55	-0.16	Feb-12
-0.36	1.52	-5.10	18.67	23.27	5.27	0.5	6.63	5.29	44.30	390.1	1	0	99	0	25	0.15	Apr-12
-1.27	0.51	-12.99	10.27	-6.81	3.54	0.75	13.9		27.86	29.5	0	100	0	0	21	-0.16	Jun-09
0.78	1.49	0.83			2.54	0.12		2.75	24.42	48.6	0	0	99	0	30	0.35	Jul-17
-6.27	-5.96	-14.31			2.17	0.25			30.88	436.6	0	99	0	0	45	0.33	Jun-16
-0.14	0.71	-2.78			3.34	0.18		7.05	23.77	18.8	0	0	99	0	17	0.47	Jul-17
-10.07	-11.15	-12.96	2.33	18.47	4.67	0.48	14.62		34.41	34.5	1	94	0	5	12	-0.02	Nov-07
-12.71	-10.90	-15.01	5.69	-4.05	3.3	0.6	12.02		39.15	2,118	1	99	0	0	3	-0.20	Jul-00
-5.67	-2.27					0.18			23.09	3.9	1	99	0	0		-0.23	Mar-18
-13.00	-5.02					0.18			24.53	5.4	1	99	0	0		0.27	Mar-18
-15.54	-13.20					0.18			20.46	4.7	2	98	0	0		-0.09	Mar-18
-11.22	0.69					0.18			26.30	5.9	3	97	0	0		0.14	Mar-18
-12.59	-2.50					0.18			23.66	5.2	1	99	0	0		0.20	Mar-18
-15.71	-13.54					0.18			23.13	5.2	0	100	0	0		0.19	Mar-18
-17.59	-10.19					0.18			23.11	5.1	1	99	0	0		-0.10	Mar-18
-17.85	-11.50	2.53	58.91	99.52	0.51	0.47	14.47		172.02	1,461	0	100	0	0	6	0.03	Mar-01
-15.02	-6.52	12.43	69.21	114.83	0.03	0.47	15.18		173.45	1,922	0	100	0	0	12	0.02	Jul-01
-13.78	-7.44	-4.67	38.96		1.08	0.47	12.11		33.32	2,345	0	100	0	0	19	0.03	Mar-15

Fund Name	Ticker Symbol	Traded On	Overall Rating	Reward Rating	Risk Rating	Recent Up/ Downgrade	Price as of 12/31/2018	52-Week High	52-Week Low	Open to New Investors	Category & (Prospectus Objective)
● iShares Fallen Angels USD Bond ETF	FALN	NAS CM	C-	C-	C-		24.40	27.77	24.12	Y	US Fixed Income (Corp Bond-High Yld)
● iShares Floating Rate Bond ETF	FLOT	BATS	C	C	C+		50.36	51.06	50.22	Y	US Fixed Income (Worldwide Bond)
● iShares Global 100 ETF	IOO	NYSE Arca	C	C	C+	Down	42.40	49.46	40.41	Y	Global Equity Large Cap (World Stock)
● iShares Global Clean Energy ETF	ICLN	NAS CM	C-	C-	C-		8.26	10.02	7.91	Y	Utilities Sector Equity (Natl Res)
● iShares Global Comm Services ETF	IXP	NYSE Arca	C	C	C-	Up	50.18	62.51	48.09	Y	Communications Sector Equity (Comm)
● iShares Global Consumer Discretionary ETF	RXI	NYSE Arca	C	C	C-	Down	100.89	120.77	94.89	Y	Consumer Goods & Svcs (Unaligned)
● iShares Global Consumer Staples ETF	KXI	NYSE Arca	C-	C-	C-		45.97	54.53	44.53	Y	Consumer Goods & Svcs (Unaligned)
● iShares Global Energy ETF	IXC	NYSE Arca	C	C	C	Down	29.35	39.39	27.97	Y	Energy Sector Equity (Natl Res)
● iShares Global Financials ETF	IXG	NYSE Arca	C	C-	C		56.87	75.99	54.20	Y	Financials Sector Equity (Financial)
● iShares Global Healthcare ETF	IXJ	NYSE Arca	C	C	C		56.65	63.41	53.92	Y	Healthcare Sector Equity (Health)
● iShares Global Industrials ETF	EXI	NYSE Arca	C-	C-	C-	Down	77.92	99.02	73.93	Y	Industrials Sector Equity (World Stock)
● iShares Global Infrastructure ETF	IGF	NAS CM	C	C-	C		39.38	46.35	38.21	Y	Infrastructure Sector Equity (Utility)
● iShares Global Materials ETF	MXI	NYSE Arca	D+	C-	D+	Down	57.37	75.12	54.93	Y	Natural Resources (Natl Res)
● iShares Global REIT ETF	REET	NYSE Arca	C	C	C+		23.42	26.45	22.86	Y	Real Estate Sector Equity (Real Estate)
● iShares Global Tech ETF	IXN	NYSE Arca	C+	C+	C+	Down	144.03	177.45	134.75	Y	Technology Sector Equity (Technology)
● iShares Global Timber & Forestry ETF	WOOD	NAS CM	C-	C	D+	Down	57.13	83.76	55.24	Y	Natural Resources (Natl Res)
● iShares Global Utilities ETF	JXI	NYSE Arca	C	C	C		49.10	52.26	45.53	Y	Utilities Sector Equity (Utility)
● iShares GNMA Bond ETF	GNMA	NAS CM	D+	D	C-		48.70	49.52	47.32	Y	US Fixed Income (Govt Bond - Mortgage)
iShares Gold Strategy ETF	IAUF	BATS	U	U	U		48.93	50.11	45.51	Y	Commodities Specified (Growth & Inc)
● iShares Gold Trust	IAU	NYSE Arca	D+	D+	C-	Down	12.29	13.05	11.26	Y	Commodities Specified (Prec Metals)
● iShares Government/Credit Bond ETF	GBF	NYSE Arca	D+	D	D+		110.44	113.94	108.16	Y	US Fixed Income (Income)
● iShares iBonds Dec 2019 Term Corporate ETF	IBDK	NYSE Arca	C	C	C+		24.80	24.87	24.71	Y	US Fixed Income (Corp Bond - Gen)
● iShares iBonds Dec 2020 Term Corporate ETF	IBDL	NYSE Arca	C	C	C+		24.98	25.33	24.92	Y	US Fixed Income (Corp Bond - Gen)
● iShares iBonds Dec 2021 Term Corporate ETF	IBDM	NYSE Arca	C	C-	C+		24.36	24.80	24.16	Y	US Fixed Income (Corp Bond - Gen)
● iShares iBonds Dec 2021 Term Muni Bond ETF	IBMJ	NYSE Arca	C-	C-	C-	Up	25.45	25.54	25.19	Y	US Muni Fixed Inc (Muni Bond - Natl)
● iShares iBonds Dec 2022 Term Corporate ETF	IBDN	NYSE Arca	C	C-	C+	Up	24.17	24.98	24.10	Y	US Fixed Income (Corp Bond - Gen)
● iShares iBonds Dec 2022 Term Muni Bond ETF	IBMK	NYSE Arca	C-	C-	C-	Up	25.62	25.76	25.21	Y	US Muni Fixed Inc (Muni Bond - Natl)
● iShares iBonds Dec 2023 Term Corporate ETF	IBDO	NYSE Arca	C-	C-	C-		24.19	25.07	23.99	Y	US Fixed Income (Corp Bond - Gen)
● iShares iBonds Dec 2023 Term Muni Bond ETF	IBML	BATS	D+	D	C-		25.11	25.27	24.60	Y	US Muni Fixed Inc (Muni Bond - Natl)
● iShares iBonds Dec 2024 Term Corporate ETF	IBDP	NYSE Arca	C-	C-	C-		23.90	25.05	23.69	Y	US Fixed Income (Corp Bond - Gen)
iShares iBonds Dec 2024 Term Muni Bond ETF	IBMM	BATS	U	U	U		25.46	25.47	24.83	Y	US Muni Fixed Inc (Growth & Inc)
● iShares iBonds Dec 2025 Term Corporate ETF	IBDQ	NYSE Arca	C-	D+	C-		23.60	25.03	23.51	Y	US Fixed Income (Corp Bond - Gen)
● iShares iBonds Dec 2026 Term Corporate ETF	IBDR	NYSE Arca	D+	D+	C-		23.03	24.54	22.85	Y	US Fixed Income (Corp Bond - Gen)
● iShares iBonds Dec 2027 Term Corporate ETF	IBDS	NYSE Arca	D	D	C-	Down	23.39	24.94	23.05	Y	US Fixed Income (Corp Bond - Gen)
iShares iBonds Dec 2028 Term Corporate ETF	IBDT	NYSE Arca	U	U	U		24.94	25.22	24.64	Y	US Fixed Income (Corp Bond - Gen)
● iShares iBonds Mar 2020 Term Corporate ETF	IBDC	NYSE Arca	C	C	C-		25.94	26.08	25.83	Y	US Fixed Income (Corp Bond - Gen)
● iShares iBonds Mar 2020 Term Corporate ex-Financials ETF	IBCD	NYSE Arca	C-	C	D+		24.39	24.52	24.26	Y	US Fixed Income (Corp Bond - High Quality)
● iShares iBonds Mar 2023 Term Corporate ETF	IBDD	NYSE Arca	D+	C-	D+	Down	25.60	26.46	25.36	Y	US Fixed Income (Corp Bond - Gen)
iShares iBonds Mar 2023 Term Corporate ex-Financials ETF	IBCE	NYSE Arca	D+	C-	D+		23.56	24.27	23.34	Y	US Fixed Income (Corp Bond - High Quality)
● iShares iBonds Sep 2019 Term Muni Bond ETF	IBMH	NYSE Arca	C-	C-	C-		25.39	25.43	25.27	Y	US Muni Fixed Inc (Muni Bond - Natl)
● iShares iBonds Sep 2020 Term Muni Bond ETF	IBMI	NYSE Arca	C-	C-	C-		25.37	25.42	25.17	Y	US Muni Fixed Inc (Muni Bond - Natl)
● iShares iBoxx $ High Yield Corporate Bond ETF	HYG	NYSE Arca	C+	C-	A-	Down	81.10	87.97	79.63	Y	US Fixed Income (Corp Bond-High Yld)
iShares iBoxx $ High Yield ex Oil & Gas Corporate Bond ETF	HYXE	NAS CM	D+	C-	D	Up	48.02	51.38	47.38	Y	US Fixed Income (Corp Bond-High Yld)
● iShares iBoxx $ Investment Grade Corporate Bond ETF	LQD	NYSE Arca	C	D+	C+		112.82	121.56	111.35	Y	US Fixed Income (Corp Bond - Gen)
● iShares India 50 ETF	INDY	NAS CM	C-	D+	C	Down	35.32	39.29	31.33	Y	India Equity (Foreign Stock)
iShares Inflation Hedged Corporate Bond ETF	LQDI	BATS	U	U	U		23.89	25.34	23.75	Y	US Fixed Income (Corp Bond - Gen)
● iShares Interest Rate Hedged Corporate Bond ETF	LQDH	NYSE Arca	C-	C-	C-	Down	90.67	98.72	90.67	Y	US Fixed Income (Growth & Inc)
iShares Interest Rate Hedged Emerging Markets Bond ETF	EMBH	NYSE Arca	C-	C-	D+		24.24	26.95	24.21	Y	Emerging Mkts Fixed Inc (Growth & Inc)
● iShares Interest Rate Hedged High Yield Bond ETF	HYGH	NYSE Arca	C-	C-	C-	Down	84.77	92.71	84.42	Y	US Fixed Income (Corp Bond-High Yld)
iShares Interest Rate Hedged Long-Term Corporate Bond ETF	IGBH	NYSE Arca	C-	C-	C-		23.94	27.41	23.91	Y	US Fixed Income (Growth & Inc)
● iShares Intermediate Government/Credit Bond ETF	GVI	BATS	C	D+	C+	Up	108.22	109.76	106.45	Y	US Fixed Income (Income)
● iShares Intermediate-Term Corporate Bond ETF	IGIB	NAS CM	D-	E+	D-	Down	52.42	109.21	52.01	Y	US Fixed Income (Growth & Inc)

★ Expanded analysis of this fund is included in Section II: Analysis of All BUY Rated Funds. ● Expanded analysis of this fund is included in Section III: Analysis of All Rated Funds with Assets over $50 million.

3-Month Total Return	6-Month Total Return	1-Year Total Return	3-Year Total Return	5-Year Total Return	Dividend Yield (TTM)	Expense Ratio	3-Yr Std Deviation	Effective Duration	NAV	Total Assets (MIL)	%Cash	%Stocks	%Bonds	%Other	Turnover Ratio	Premium/Discount 1-Year Avg	Inception Date
-5.96	-3.58	-4.36			5.55	0.25		5.92	24.47	65.7	0	0	98	0	31	0.13	Jun-16
-0.21	0.51	1.56	5.01	5.45	2.18	0.2	0.33	0.15	50.42	12,404	6	0	92	0	21	0.08	Jun-11
-12.64	-6.07	-6.19	25.88	26.47	2.26	0.4	9.28		42.49	1,922	1	99	0	0	8	-0.07	Dec-00
-2.06	-4.19	-8.61	-7.46	-8.64	2.38	0.47	16.98		8.27	165.5	1	99	0	0	29	0.13	Jun-08
-11.66	-4.77	-13.54	-2.88	-3.86	4.26	0.47	10.57		50.33	235.1	0	100	0	0	3	-0.06	Nov-01
-15.35	-10.98	-6.19	18.39	29.77	1.52	0.47	11.79		100.91	218.0	0	100	0	0	6	-0.04	Sep-06
-6.99	-3.79	-10.59	6.35	20.46	2.45	0.47	9.11		46.08	630.7	0	100	0	0	5	-0.05	Sep-06
-21.61	-18.69	-14.59	15.31	-20.58	3.16	0.47	16.32		29.43	1,531	1	99	0	0	4	-0.06	Nov-01
-12.69	-10.03	-15.97	16.43	15.13	2.85	0.47	13.86		57.02	539.1	0	99	0	0	4	-0.01	Nov-01
-9.98	1.21	2.24	15.43	43.85	1.36	0.47	11.61		56.69	1,782	1	99	0	0	4	-0.03	Nov-01
-16.45	-10.12	-14.31	20.91	20.25	1.94	0.47	11.41		77.91	205.7	1	99	0	0	6	-0.03	Sep-06
-5.45	-6.59	-10.19	19.46	17.93	3.13	0.47	9.78		39.31	2,636	0	100	0	0	11	-0.04	Dec-07
-14.08	-12.37	-15.79	34.73	3.39	2.2	0.47	15.25		57.52	223.5	0	100	0	0	8	-0.03	Sep-06
-5.03	-4.81	-4.89	8.64		5.33	0.14	10.77		23.50	1,337	0	99	0	1	7	0.03	Jul-14
-17.62	-12.15	-5.13	51.83	82.93	0.87	0.47	13.82		144.24	2,516	0	100	0	0	5	0.05	Nov-01
-22.95	-25.04	-17.56	25.45	18.92	1.51	0.47	16.43		57.23	312.7	1	99	0	0	31	-0.06	Jun-08
1.21	1.36	2.02	24.16	33.90	3.3	0.47	10.97		49.07	170.7	1	99	0	0	4	0.00	Sep-06
1.93	1.89	0.68	3.75	11.05	2.41	0.15	1.94	5.26	48.68	105.5	14	0	85	1	917	-0.07	Feb-12
7.57	2.95					0.25			48.83	4.7	76	0	0	24		0.20	Jun-18
7.69	2.58	-1.37	19.79	5.30	0	0.25	12.62		12.28	10,635	0	0	0	100	0	0.13	Jan-05
1.49	1.48	-0.60	6.07	12.29	2.67	0.2	3.05	6.20	110.29	103.4	1	0	99	0	17	-0.01	Jan-07
0.54	1.28	1.82	7.07		2	0.1	1.22	0.60	24.74	719.4	23	0	77	0	7	0.16	Mar-15
0.68	1.42	1.17	7.70		2.28	0.1	1.79	1.54	24.97	856.3	2	0	98	0	4	0.18	Dec-14
0.82	1.57	0.81	8.55		2.54	0.1	2.32	2.42	24.30	857.8	0	0	99	0	3	0.22	Mar-15
1.02	0.86	1.35	3.46		1.31	0.18	2.72	2.51	25.42	239.3	0	0	100	0	0	0.08	Sep-15
0.73	1.49	0.08	9.68		2.79	0.1	2.82	3.31	24.22	570.1	1	0	99	0	7	0.22	Mar-15
1.29	1.07	1.25	4.16		1.5	0.18	3.28	3.38	25.58	239.1	0	0	100	0	1	0.10	Sep-15
0.79	1.69	-0.20	10.55		3.04	0.1	3.1	4.09	24.17	490.0	1	0	99	0	8	0.20	Mar-15
1.64	1.34	1.20			1.58	0.18		4.15	25.05	121.8	0	0	100	0	0	0.16	Apr-17
0.51	1.59	-1.08	10.69		3.29	0.1	3.44	4.90	23.88	308.5	1	0	99	0	8	0.30	Mar-15
2.19	1.94					0.18		4.98	25.40	30.2	0	0	100	0		0.13	Mar-18
0.34	1.38	-1.69	10.27		3.44	0.1	3.71	5.67	23.68	331.9	1	0	99	0	5	0.20	Mar-15
0.38	1.29	-2.30			3.46	0.1		6.44	23.04	152.2	1	0	99	0	6	0.21	Sep-16
0.17	1.13	-2.74			3.67	0.1		7.14	23.26	137.4	1	0	99	0	2	0.28	Sep-17
0.36						0.1		7.63	24.79	38.2	1	0	99	0		0.54	Sep-18
0.57	1.31	1.60	7.38	14.20	2.14	0.1	1.4	0.90	25.89	126.9	3	0	97	0	7	0.11	Jul-13
0.56	1.26	1.50	6.42	12.86	1.88	0.1	1.42	0.92	24.37	85.3	4	0	96	0	11	0.11	Apr-13
0.72	1.55	-0.09	9.69	19.83	3.01	0.1	2.96	3.59	25.57	59.8	0	0	100	0	12	0.02	Jul-13
0.98	1.69	0.04	8.22	18.84	2.81	0.1	2.96	3.60	23.56	44.5	1	0	99	0	10	0.00	Apr-13
0.48	0.55	1.33	2.78		1.03	0.18	1.32	0.68	25.37	289.2	0	0	100	0	0	0.04	Feb-14
0.75	0.61	1.35	2.95		1.19	0.18	2.03	1.62	25.35	315.0	0	0	100	0	0	0.08	Aug-14
-4.58	-1.76	-1.93	18.52	14.18	5.34	0.49	4.16	3.78	80.90	14,220	1	0	99	0	17	0.15	Apr-07
-3.69	-0.70	-0.66			5.96	0.5		3.70	47.77	9.8	2	0	98	0	18	0.14	Jun-16
-0.51	0.67	-3.75	9.29	17.37	3.6	0.15	4.51	8.27	112.69	29,908	0	0	99	0	10	0.04	Jul-02
3.30	1.43	-4.48	30.19	54.62	0.37	0.92	18.08		35.29	783.3	0	100	0	0	14	-0.15	Nov-09
-4.41	-3.37					0.2		8.38	23.82	9.6	4	0	95	0		-0.14	May-18
-3.96	-1.71	-2.07	9.37		3.07	0.24	4.12	0.12	90.86	211.3	-22	0	121	0	0	0.05	May-14
-4.98	-1.92	-4.81	13.86		4.22	0.48	5.42	-0.07	24.26	13.6	-18	0	118	0	2	0.17	Jul-15
-7.12	-3.70	-1.83	18.10		5.57	0.54	4.38	0.23	84.83	396.6	-2	0	102	0	0	0.01	May-14
-5.71	-2.39	-3.34	13.39		3.73	0.16	6.57	-0.16	23.97	50.0	-32	0	132	0	6	0.10	Jul-15
1.63	1.84	0.70	4.61	8.60	2.15	0.2	2.01	3.86	108.15	1,961	1	0	99	0	19	0.02	Jan-07
0.38	1.03	-50.25	-46.78	-44.34	3.13	0.06	2.28	6.13	52.49	5,513	1	0	98	0	21	0.01	Jan-07

Fund Name	Ticker Symbol	Traded On	Overall Rating	Reward Rating	Risk Rating	Recent Up/Downgrade	Price as of 12/31/2018	52-Week High	52-Week Low	Open to New Investors	Category & (Prospectus Objective)
● iShares International Developed Property ETF	WPS	NYSE Arca	D+	D+	C-	Down	34.48	41.74	34.00	Y	Real Estate Sector Equity (Real Estate)
● iShares International Developed Real Estate ETF	IFGL	NAS CM	C	C-	C		27.03	31.71	26.69	Y	Real Estate Sector Equity (Real Estate)
● iShares International Dividend Growth ETF	IGRO	BATS	D+	D+	D+	Down	49.24	61.72	48.08	Y	Global Equity Large Cap (Equity-Income)
● iShares International High Yield Bond ETF	HYXU	BATS	D+	D+	C-	Down	48.30	56.93	47.72	Y	Global Fixed Income (Corp Bond-High Yld)
● iShares International Preferred Stock ETF	IPFF	BATS	D+	D+	C-	Down	15.11	19.76	14.47	Y	US Fixed Income (Growth & Inc)
● iShares International Select Dividend ETF	IDV	BATS	C	D+	C+		28.71	35.88	27.96	Y	Global Equity Large Cap (Foreign Stock)
● iShares International Treasury Bond ETF	IGOV	NAS CM	D+	D+	C-	Down	48.47	52.07	47.13	Y	Global Fixed Income (Worldwide Bond)
● iShares J.P. Morgan EM Corporate Bond ETF	CEMB	BATS	D+	C-	D+	Down	47.47	51.40	47.04	Y	Emerging Mkts Fixed Inc (Income)
● iShares J.P. Morgan EM Local Currency Bond ETF	LEMB	NYSE Arca	D+	D	D+	Down	43.08	50.76	41.58	Y	Emerging Mkts Fixed Inc (Worldwide Bond)
● iShares J.P. Morgan USD Emerging Markets Bond ETF	EMB	NAS CM	C-	D+	C	Down	103.91	116.72	102.36	Y	Emerging Mkts Fixed Inc (Div Emerg Mkts)
● iShares JPX-Nikkei 400 ETF	JPXN	NYSE Arca	D+	D+	D+	Down	54.48	70.06	52.64	Y	Japan Equity (Pacific Stock)
● iShares Latin America 40 ETF	ILF	NYSE Arca	C	C	C		30.82	39.50	28.72	Y	Latin America Equity (Growth)
● iShares Long-Term Corporate Bond ETF	IGLB	NYSE Arca	D+	D+	C-	Down	56.30	63.20	55.17	Y	US Fixed Income (Growth & Inc)
● iShares MBS ETF	MBB	NAS CM	C-	D+	C+		104.65	106.59	101.79	Y	US Fixed Income (Govt Bond - Mortgage)
● iShares Micro-Cap ETF	IWC	NYSE Arca	C-	C-	C-	Down	82.45	109.91	77.77	Y	US Equity Small Cap (Growth)
● iShares Morningstar Large-Cap ETF	JKD	NYSE Arca	C	C	C-		142.53	169.91	133.93	Y	US Equity Large Cap Blend (Growth)
● iShares Morningstar Large-Cap Growth ETF	JKE	NYSE Arca	C	C	C	Down	158.53	186.55	147.58	Y	US Equity Large Cap Growth (Growth)
● iShares Morningstar Large-Cap Value ETF	JKF	NYSE Arca	C	C	C-		96.33	112.57	91.27	Y	US Equity Large Cap Value (Growth)
● iShares Morningstar Mid-Cap ETF	JKG	NYSE Arca	C-	C	D+	Down	161.64	194.75	152.72	Y	US Equity Mid Cap (Growth)
● iShares Morningstar Mid-Cap Growth ETF	JKH	NYSE Arca	C-	C	D+	Down	194.39	237.43	180.97	Y	US Equity Mid Cap (Growth)
● iShares Morningstar Mid-Cap Value ETF	JKI	NAS CM	C-	C	D+	Down	138.81	168.36	132.21	Y	US Equity Mid Cap (Growth)
● iShares Morningstar Multi-Asset Income ETF	IYLD	BATS	C-	D+	C-	Down	23.28	25.94	23.02	Y	Cautious Allocation (Multi-Asset Global)
● iShares Morningstar Small-Cap ETF	JKJ	NYSE Arca	C-	C-	D+	Down	147.86	186.23	139.81	Y	US Equity Small Cap (Small Company)
● iShares Morningstar Small-Cap Growth ETF	JKK	NYSE Arca	C-	C-	D+	Down	166.47	215.87	154.61	Y	US Equity Small Cap (Small Company)
● iShares Morningstar Small-Cap Value ETF	JKL	NYSE Arca	C-	C-	D+	Down	123.17	158.92	117.04	Y	US Equity Small Cap (Small Company)
★ iShares Mortgage Real Estate Capped ETF	REM	BATS	B-	B	C		39.94	45.65	38.44	Y	Real Estate Sector Equity (Real Estate)
● iShares MSCI ACWI ETF	ACWI	NAS CM	C	C-	C+	Down	64.16	77.54	61.18	Y	Global Equity Large Cap (World Stock)
● iShares MSCI ACWI ex U.S. ETF	ACWX	NAS CM	C-	D+	C	Down	41.96	53.74	40.69	Y	Global Equity Large Cap (Foreign Stock)
● iShares MSCI ACWI Low Carbon Target ETF	CRBN	NYSE Arca	C-	C-	C-	Down	103.02	125.90	99.00	Y	Global Equity Large Cap (World Stock)
● iShares MSCI All Country Asia ex Japan ETF	AAXJ	NAS CM	C-	C-	C-	Down	63.53	83.50	61.12	Y	Asia ex-Japan Equity (Pacific Stock)
● iShares MSCI All Peru ETF	EPU	NYSE Arca	C-	C	C-	Down	35.50	44.95	34.49	Y	Equity Misc (Foreign Stock)
iShares MSCI Argentina and Global Exposure ETF	AGT	BATS	C-	C	D	Down	20.12	32.91	18.45	Y	Equity Misc (Foreign Stock)
● iShares MSCI Australia ETF	EWA	NYSE Arca	C-	C-	C	Down	19.25	24.11	18.42	Y	Australia & New Zealand Equity (Pacific Stock)
● iShares MSCI Austria Capped ETF	EWO	NYSE Arca	C-	C-	C-	Down	18.36	27.26	17.50	Y	Europe Equity Mid/Small Cap (Europe Stock)
iShares MSCI Belgium Capped ETF	EWK	NYSE Arca	D+	D+	D+	Down	16.34	23.00	16.01	Y	Equity Misc (Europe Stock)
● iShares MSCI Brazil Capped ETF	EWZ	NYSE Arca	C	C	C-	Up	38.20	47.33	30.72	Y	Latin America Equity (Foreign Stock)
● iShares MSCI Brazil Small-Cap ETF	EWZS	NAS CM	C-	C	D+		14.43	18.06	11.01	Y	Latin America Equity (Foreign Stock)
● iShares MSCI BRIC ETF	BKF	NYSE Arca	C-	C-	C-		37.51	50.87	36.50	Y	Global Emerg Mkts Equity (Foreign Stock)
● iShares MSCI Canada ETF	EWC	NYSE Arca	C	C	C	Down	23.96	30.42	23.10	Y	Canadian Equity Large Cap (Foreign Stock)
● iShares MSCI Chile Capped ETF	ECH	BATS	C-	C-	C-	Down	41.41	56.17	40.69	Y	Equity Misc (Foreign Stock)
● iShares MSCI China A ETF	CNYA	BATS	D	D	D	Down	22.68	35.66	22.52	Y	Greater China Equity (Pacific Stock)
● iShares MSCI China ETF	MCHI	NAS CM	C-	C-	D+	Down	52.62	76.72	51.05	Y	Greater China Equity (Pacific Stock)
iShares MSCI China Small-Cap ETF	ECNS	NYSE Arca	D+	D+	D	Down	39.10	56.12	37.83	Y	Greater China Equity (Pacific Stock)
iShares MSCI Colombia ETF	ICOL	NYSE Arca	D	D+	D	Down	11.16	16.44	10.81	Y	Equity Misc (Foreign Stock)
iShares MSCI Denmark ETF	EDEN	BATS	D+	D+	D+	Down	56.81	71.02	55.52	Y	Equity Misc (Europe Stock)
● iShares MSCI EAFE ESG Optimized ETF	ESGD	NAS CM	D+	D+	C-	Down	57.38	72.49	55.20	Y	Global Equity Large Cap (Growth & Inc)
● iShares MSCI EAFE ETF	EFA	NYSE Arca	C-	D+	C	Down	58.78	75.25	56.89	Y	Global Equity Large Cap (Foreign Stock)
● iShares MSCI EAFE Growth ETF	EFG	BATS	C-	D+	C	Down	69.07	85.74	66.77	Y	Global Equity Large Cap (Foreign Stock)
● iShares MSCI EAFE Small-Cap ETF	SCZ	NAS CM	C-	D+	C-	Down	51.82	69.19	49.58	Y	Global Eq Mid/Small Cap (Small Company)
● iShares MSCI EAFE Value ETF	EFV	BATS	D+	D+	C-	Down	45.22	59.57	43.66	Y	Global Equity Large Cap (Foreign Stock)
● iShares MSCI Emerging Markets Asia ETF	EEMA	NAS CM	C-	C-	C-		60.85	81.27	58.61	Y	Asia ex-Japan Equity (Pacific Stock)
● iShares MSCI Emerging Markets ETF	EEM	NYSE Arca	C-	C-	C-	Down	39.06	52.08	38.00	Y	Global Emerg Mkts Equity (Div Emerg Mkts)

★Expanded analysis of this fund is included in Section II: Analysis of All BUY Rated Funds. ● Expanded analysis of this fund is included in Section III: Analysis of All Rated Funds with Assets over $50 million.

			TOTAL RETURNS & PERFORMANCE						ASSETS		ASSET ALLOCATION & TURNOVER					VALUATION	
3-Month Total Return	6-Month Total Return	1-Year Total Return	3-Year Total Return	5-Year Total Return	Dividend Yield (TTM)	Expense Ratio	3-Yr Std Deviation	Effective Duration	NAV	Total Assets (MIL)	%Cash	%Stocks	%Bonds	%Other	Turnover Ratio	Premium/ Discount 1-Year Avg	Inception Date
-4.68	-6.44	-8.89	12.74	15.36	4.96	0.48	10.66		34.61	129.2	1	97	0	2	11	-0.22	Jul-07
-4.85	-5.54	-6.68	13.07	11.11	5.69	0.48	10.97		26.96	463.1	1	97	0	2	8	-0.20	Nov-07
-12.00	-8.53	-13.11			3	0.22			49.10	59.4	1	99	0	0	42	0.51	May-16
-4.84	-3.05	-8.03	14.82	-4.19	0	0.4	8.98	3.96	48.01	64.6	0	0	100	0	49	0.14	Apr-12
-14.21	-11.16	-16.03	6.39	-21.11	4.53	0.55	14.74		15.18	52.5	1	0	0	4	15	-0.62	Nov-11
-10.56	-7.04	-10.49	15.28	-2.32	5.22	0.5	10.93		28.76	4,157	1	99	0	0	24	-0.18	Jun-07
1.00	-1.03	-2.68	9.29	-0.71	0.04	0.35	7.26	8.31	48.35	822.8	2	0	98	0	9	0.01	Jan-09
-0.25	0.85	-2.82	16.30	18.63	4.49	0.5	4.28	4.93	47.34	71.1	1	0	98	0	62	0.17	Apr-12
3.26	1.08	-7.64	11.00	-6.00	0	0.3	10.72	4.73	42.96	404.3	1	0	99	0	97	0.19	Oct-11
-1.56	0.73	-5.67	13.50	21.62	4.77	0.4	6	7.04	103.17	14,972	0	0	100	0	26	0.16	Dec-07
-14.37	-10.08	-13.94	8.93	14.15	1.66	0.48	10.9		55.03	116.2	1	99	0	0	8	0.00	Oct-01
-0.63	7.26	-6.71	54.90	-5.95	2.55	0.48	25.68		30.86	1,156	0	100	0	0	16	0.05	Oct-01
-1.44	-0.66	-7.17	14.34	25.82	4.62	0.06	6.93	12.90	56.08	562.8	1	0	99	0	12	-0.02	Dec-09
2.10	2.04	0.81	4.52	12.38	2.56	0.09	2.11	5.43	104.60	11,639	5	0	95	0	745	0.03	Mar-07
-21.01	-22.34	-13.07	18.10	16.10	1.11	0.6	16.01		82.37	920.7	0	100	0	0	22	0.03	Aug-05
-15.30	-6.66	-8.39	27.05	46.79	1.9	0.2	8.97		142.58	926.5	0	100	0	0	46	0.02	Jun-04
-14.91	-8.91	2.08	35.43	66.00	0.73	0.25	11.76		158.44	1,065	0	100	0	0	48	0.14	Jun-04
-9.93	-3.56	-6.10	27.80	37.05	2.54	0.25	9.06		96.31	410.5	0	100	0	0	24	0.10	Jun-04
-14.02	-10.99	-11.41	18.78	35.15	1.62	0.25	10.73		161.81	706.7	0	100	0	0	50	0.06	Jun-04
-16.84	-11.16	-3.38	28.71	39.65	0.34	0.3	12.66		194.56	320.8	0	100	0	0	43	0.12	Jun-04
-13.20	-11.47	-10.76	25.46	35.52	2.16	0.3	10.38		139.05	445.5	0	100	0	0	45	0.07	Jun-04
-3.92	-1.95	-4.75	15.94	21.63	5.12	0.59	5.02	5.40	23.25	294.5	1	35	59	0	64	0.01	Apr-12
-16.48	-16.73	-13.80	20.22	22.95	1.4	0.25	12.93		148.04	235.6	0	100	0	0	56	0.05	Jun-04
-20.36	-16.23	-5.79	27.35	30.31	0.42	0.3	15.12		166.99	188.3	0	100	0	0	51	0.27	Jun-04
-18.55	-17.81	-16.79	14.95	15.15	2.11	0.3	14.54		123.36	397.5	0	100	0	0	54	0.11	Jun-04
-5.62	-4.16	-2.95	40.34	48.51	10.11	0.48	10.27		39.96	1,236	0	100	0	0	31	-0.02	May-07
-12.92	-8.59	-9.21	22.17	24.79	2.11	0.32	9.65		64.19	9,456	1	99	0	0	4	-0.04	Mar-08
-11.44	-9.60	-14.08	13.85	3.09	2.84	0.32	11.24		41.96	3,538	1	99	0	0	6	-0.14	Mar-08
-12.76	-8.46	-9.38	20.66		2.26	0.2	9.68		103.66	524.0	1	99	0	0	18	0.01	Dec-14
-8.70	-9.69	-14.81	25.48	17.56	2.47	0.69	14.63		63.65	3,892	0	100	0	0	13	-0.15	Aug-08
-3.86	-8.87	-12.18	84.91	16.53	3.2	0.62	21.89		35.49	144.7	0	100	0	0	11	-0.17	Jun-09
-10.39	-10.39	-32.64			2.45	0.59			20.20	20.6	0	100	0	0	42	-0.12	Apr-17
-9.41	-10.02	-12.31	16.41	0.44	4.79	0.47	13.93		19.25	1,195	1	99	0	0	3	-0.17	Mar-96
-19.20	-17.07	-23.19	25.44	5.17	3.31	0.47	17.05		18.32	105.2	1	99	0	0	19	-0.25	Mar-96
-14.46	-15.77	-20.35	-3.04	11.91	3.51	0.47	13.38		16.37	46.8	0	98	0	2	13	-0.29	Mar-96
15.79	22.04	-1.78	96.23	-1.49	2.4	0.59	34.48		38.32	7,355	0	100	0	0	30	-0.03	Jul-00
26.52	20.12	-7.17	131.21	-13.08	4.91	0.59	35.47		14.36	66.4	1	99	0	0	67	-0.08	Sep-10
-4.96	-9.01	-13.57	35.45	12.91	1.87	0.67	16.89		37.81	186.6	0	100	0	0	22	-0.29	Nov-07
-16.03	-14.29	-17.21	19.36	-8.40	2.23	0.47	12.32		24.00	2,677	0	100	0	0	3	-0.03	Mar-96
-8.80	-8.80	-19.13	35.81	-2.86	2.25	0.59	20.82		41.58	432.8	0	100	0	0	54	-0.13	Nov-07
-11.20	-11.74	-26.26			1.31	0.65			22.61	56.5	0	100	0	0	154	1.24	Jun-16
-10.56	-17.58	-19.18	24.16	22.42	2.04	0.59	18.88		52.96	3,793	0	100	0	0	14	0.07	Mar-11
-10.74	-19.17	-18.16	-1.53	3.18	3.85	0.59	16.8		39.43	19.2	-1	101	0	0	63	-0.35	Sep-10
-17.91	-23.18	-20.11	13.13	-50.74	1.86	0.61	20.65		11.34	22.9	0	100	0	0	26	0.51	Jun-13
-12.48	-10.83	-14.87	5.43	36.09	2.54	0.53	13.88		56.50	43.9	1	99	0	0	13	-0.11	Jan-12
-12.61	-10.03	-13.62			2.88	0.2			57.19	450.4	1	99	0	0	24	0.17	Jun-16
-12.43	-10.12	-13.82	8.70	2.28	3.35	0.31	11.06		58.91	64,666	1	99	0	0	4	-0.15	Aug-01
-13.41	-10.83	-13.01	8.04	6.87	1.83	0.4	11.15		69.02	3,619	1	99	0	0	22	-0.07	Aug-05
-15.82	-15.12	-17.64	11.77	15.89	2.71	0.39	12.37		51.79	9,071	1	99	0	0	8	-0.06	Dec-07
-11.46	-9.50	-14.87	8.20	-3.91	4.58	0.38	11.91		45.23	5,652	1	99	0	0	22	-0.06	Aug-05
-9.13	-10.27	-15.53	26.58	18.93	2.11	0.5	14.85		60.97	434.8	0	100	0	0	33	-0.14	Feb-12
-7.43	-7.79	-14.98	28.17	5.35	2.41	0.67	14.77		39.17	29,838	0	100	0	0	16	-0.02	Apr-03

Fund Name	Ticker Symbol	Traded On	Overall Rating	Reward Rating	Risk Rating	Recent Up/Downgrade	Price as of 12/31/2018	52-Week High	52-Week Low	Open to New Investors	Category & (Prospectus Objective)
iShares MSCI Emerging Markets ex China ETF	EMXC	NAS CM	D	D	D		45.74	58.41	44.67	Y	Global Emerg Mkts Equity (Div Emerg Mkts)
● iShares MSCI Emerging Markets Small-Cap ETF	EEMS	NYSE Arca	D+	D+	D+	Down	41.81	57.26	39.95	Y	Global Emerg Mkts Equity (Div Emerg Mkts)
● iShares MSCI Europe Financials ETF	EUFN	NAS CM	D+	D+	D	Down	16.95	25.83	16.38	Y	Financials Sector Equity (Financial)
● iShares MSCI Europe Small-Cap ETF	IEUS	NAS CM	D+	D+	C-	Down	44.93	62.07	43.21	Y	Europe Equity Large Cap (Small Company)
● iShares MSCI Eurozone ETF	EZU	BATS	D+	D+	D+	Down	35.06	47.11	33.85	Y	Europe Equity Large Cap (Europe Stock)
iShares MSCI Finland ETF	EFNL	BATS	C-	C-	C-	Down	35.55	44.30	34.19	Y	Equity Misc (Europe Stock)
● iShares MSCI France ETF	EWQ	NYSE Arca	C-	C-	C-	Down	26.52	33.73	25.56	Y	Europe Equity Large Cap (Europe Stock)
● iShares MSCI Frontier 100 ETF	FM	NYSE Arca	D+	C-	D+	Down	26.15	36.15	26.01	Y	Global Emerg Mkts Equity (Div Emerg Mkts)
● iShares MSCI Germany ETF	EWG	NYSE Arca	D+	C-	D+	Down	25.35	35.65	24.44	Y	Europe Equity Large Cap (Europe Stock)
iShares MSCI Germany Small-Cap ETF	EWGS	BATS	D+	D+	D+	Down	48.19	70.20	46.49	Y	Equity Misc (Europe Stock)
iShares MSCI Global Agriculture Producers ETF	VEGI	NYSE Arca	C	C	D+		25.99	31.00	24.90	Y	Natural Resources (Unaligned)
iShares MSCI Global Energy Producers ETF	FILL	NYSE Arca	C	C	C-		18.49	24.37	17.48	Y	Energy Sector Equity (Natl Res)
● iShares MSCI Global Gold Miners ETF	RING	NAS CM	D	D+	D	Down	16.22	20.18	13.59	Y	Prec Metals (Prec Metals)
iShares MSCI Global Impact ETF	SDG	NAS CM	D+	D+	D+	Down	53.00	62.47	51.40	Y	Global Equity Large Cap (Growth & Inc)
● iShares MSCI Global Metals & Mining Producers ETF	PICK	BATS	C	C-	C		26.98	37.82	26.26	Y	Prec Metals (Prec Metals)
iShares MSCI Global Silver Miners ETF	SLVP	BATS	D+	C-	D	Down	8.34	11.31	7.32	Y	Prec Metals (Prec Metals)
● iShares MSCI Hong Kong ETF	EWH	NYSE Arca	C-	D+	C	Down	22.57	26.90	21.26	Y	Greater China Equity (Pacific Stock)
● iShares MSCI India ETF	INDA	BATS	C-	D+	C-	Down	33.34	38.06	29.30	Y	India Equity (Pacific Stock)
● iShares MSCI India Small-Cap ETF	SMIN	BATS	D+	D+	D	Down	38.57	55.07	33.38	Y	India Equity (Small Company)
● iShares MSCI Indonesia ETF	EIDO	NYSE Arca	D+	D+	D+		24.82	30.56	20.88	Y	Asia ex-Japan Equity (Pacific Stock)
● iShares MSCI Ireland ETF	EIRL	NYSE Arca	D+	D+	D+	Down	37.01	50.05	36.16	Y	Equity Misc (Europe Stock)
● iShares MSCI Israel Capped ETF	EIS	NYSE Arca	C-	C	C-		48.42	58.28	46.52	Y	Equity Misc (Foreign Stock)
● iShares MSCI Italy Capped ETF	EWI	NYSE Arca	D+	D+	D	Down	24.21	34.44	23.28	Y	Europe Equity Large Cap (Europe Stock)
● iShares MSCI Japan ETF	EWJ	NYSE Arca	C	D+	C+		50.69	64.67	49.12	Y	Japan Equity (Pacific Stock)
● iShares MSCI Japan Small-Cap ETF	SCJ	NYSE Arca	C-	D+	C-	Down	65.23	85.22	61.80	Y	Japan Equity (Pacific Stock)
● iShares MSCI KLD 400 Social ETF	DSI	NYSE Arca	C	C	C-		93.00	107.67	87.24	Y	US Equity Large Cap Blend (Growth)
● iShares MSCI Kokusai ETF	TOK	NYSE Arca	C-	C-	D+	Down	58.10	69.65	55.44	Y	Global Equity Large Cap (World Stock)
● iShares MSCI Malaysia ETF	EWM	NYSE Arca	C-	C-	D+	Down	29.77	36.47	28.48	Y	Asia ex-Japan Equity (Pacific Stock)
● iShares MSCI Mexico Capped ETF	EWW	NYSE Arca	D	D	D		41.18	54.16	37.76	Y	Mexico Equity (Foreign Stock)
● iShares MSCI Netherlands ETF	EWN	NYSE Arca	C-	C-	C-	Down	26.30	34.04	25.35	Y	Europe Equity Large Cap (Europe Stock)
● iShares MSCI New Zealand ETF	ENZL	NAS CM	C-	C-	C-	Down	46.02	50.80	43.93	Y	Australia & New Zealand Equity (Pacific Stock)
iShares MSCI Norway ETF	ENOR	BATS	C-	C	C-	Down	23.06	29.70	22.37	Y	Equity Misc (Europe Stock)
● iShares MSCI Pacific ex Japan ETF	EPP	NYSE Arca	C-	D+	C	Down	40.70	50.31	39.46	Y	Asia ex-Japan Equity (Pacific Stock)
● iShares MSCI Philippines ETF	EPHE	NYSE Arca	D	D	D		31.88	40.18	28.20	Y	Asia ex-Japan Equity (Pacific Stock)
● iShares MSCI Poland ETF	EPOL	NYSE Arca	C-	C-	C-	Up	23.03	30.00	21.09	Y	Europe Equity Mid/Small Cap (Europe Stock)
● iShares MSCI Qatar ETF	QAT	NAS CM	C	C	C-	Up	18.49	19.56	15.43	Y	Equity Misc (Foreign Stock)
● iShares MSCI Russia Capped ETF	ERUS	NYSE Arca	C+	C+	C+	Up	30.80	39.23	30.59	Y	Equity Misc (Foreign Stock)
● iShares MSCI Saudi Arabia ETF	KSA	NYSE Arca	C-	C-	C-	Down	28.89	31.96	26.00	Y	Equity Misc (Growth)
● iShares MSCI Singapore Capped ETF	EWS	NYSE Arca	C-	C-	C	Down	22.10	28.19	21.71	Y	Asia ex-Japan Equity (Pacific Stock)
● iShares MSCI South Africa ETF	EZA	NYSE Arca	D	D+	D	Down	50.45	75.98	47.13	Y	Equity Misc (Foreign Stock)
● iShares MSCI South Korea Capped ETF	EWY	NYSE Arca	D+	C-	D+	Down	58.86	79.04	56.85	Y	Korea Equity (Pacific Stock)
● iShares MSCI Spain Capped ETF	EWP	NYSE Arca	D+	C-	D+	Down	26.82	36.24	26.26	Y	Europe Equity Large Cap (Europe Stock)
● iShares MSCI Sweden Capped ETF	EWD	NYSE Arca	C-	C-	C-	Down	28.24	36.58	26.79	Y	Europe Equity Large Cap (Europe Stock)
● iShares MSCI Switzerland Capped ETF	EWL	NYSE Arca	C	D+	C+		31.52	37.74	30.43	Y	Europe Equity Large Cap (Europe Stock)
● iShares MSCI Taiwan Capped ETF	EWT	NYSE Arca	C-	D+	C	Down	31.62	39.32	30.86	Y	Greater China Equity (Pacific Stock)
● iShares MSCI Thailand Capped ETF	THD	NYSE Arca	C	C	C+		82.81	101.73	81.53	Y	Thailand Equity (Pacific Stock)
● iShares MSCI Turkey ETF	TUR	NAS CM	D-	D-	D	Down	24.57	46.66	19.07	Y	Equity Misc (Foreign Stock)
iShares MSCI UAE ETF	UAE	NAS CM	D	D	D+	Down	13.70	18.08	13.40	Y	Equity Misc (Foreign Stock)
● iShares MSCI United Kingdom ETF	EWU	NYSE Arca	C-	D+	C-	Down	29.35	37.88	28.56	Y	UK Equity Large Cap (Europe Stock)
iShares MSCI United Kingdom Small-Cap ETF	EWUS	BATS	D+	D+	D	Down	33.77	45.85	32.68	Y	Equity Misc (Europe Stock)
● iShares MSCI USA Equal Weighted ETF	EUSA	NYSE Arca	C-	C-	C-	Down	49.79	59.92	47.02	Y	US Equity Large Cap Blend (Growth)
● iShares MSCI USA ESG Optimized ETF	ESGU	NAS CM	C-	D+	C-		54.93	64.63	51.48	Y	US Equity Large Cap Blend (Growth & Inc)

★ Expanded analysis of this fund is included in Section II: Analysis of All BUY Rated Funds.   ● Expanded analysis of this fund is included in Section III: Analysis of All Rated Funds with Assets over $50 million.

		TOTAL RETURNS & PERFORMANCE							ASSETS		ASSET ALLOCATION & TURNOVER					VALUATION	
3-Month Total Return	6-Month Total Return	1-Year Total Return	3-Year Total Return	5-Year Total Return	Dividend Yield (TTM)	Expense Ratio	3-Yr Std Deviation	Effective Duration	NAV	Total Assets (MIL)	%Cash	%Stocks	%Bonds	%Other	Turnover Ratio	Premium/ Discount 1-Year Avg	Inception Date
-5.82	-2.73	-12.73			1.8	0.49			45.67	9.4	0	99	0	0	9	0.36	Jul-17
-6.76	-9.94	-18.19	11.54	2.73	3.38	0.67	14.12		42.04	230.7	0	100	0	0	39	-0.19	Aug-11
-14.53	-13.76	-23.18	-5.36	-17.17	5.32	0.48	18.89		16.99	977.3	1	99	0	1	3	-0.22	Jan-10
-17.99	-17.84	-19.82	6.52	14.48	3.11	0.4	14.72		45.12	193.2	0	99	0	1	15	-0.04	Nov-07
-14.22	-13.19	-16.97	7.58	-3.15	3.28	0.47	14.06		35.07	7,570	0	100	0	0	5	-0.19	Jul-00
-14.24	-12.07	-7.47	17.02	17.43	4.21	0.53	13.01		35.33	28.7	1	99	0	0	11	-0.19	Jan-12
-15.08	-11.51	-12.68	18.09	6.20	2.65	0.47	13.21		26.60	588.1	0	100	0	0	4	-0.13	Mar-96
-5.12	-6.12	-17.45	14.15	0.56	4.34	0.81	12.31		26.49	492.8	0	100	0	0	35	-0.40	Sep-12
-16.04	-15.19	-22.29	1.57	-10.95	3.1	0.47	15.06		25.17	2,421	1	99	0	0	6	-0.14	Mar-96
-19.61	-18.57	-23.09	22.71	30.51	2.42	0.59	16.77		48.03	44.7	0	100	0	0	14	-0.29	Jan-12
-10.94	-6.05	-9.06	24.64	6.59	1.73	0.39	9.43		26.21	29.8	0	100	0	0	25	0.00	Jan-12
-21.69	-17.14	-11.64	23.14	-17.83	3.1	0.39	16.68		18.52	45.5	1	99	0	0	5	0.36	Jan-12
13.12	-6.75	-13.57	53.05	-6.63	0.8	0.39	38.81		16.19	175.2	0	100	0	0	4	-0.10	Jan-12
-7.60	-4.40	-7.55			2.74	0.49			53.05	39.4	0	100	0	0	36	0.35	Apr-16
-14.26	-13.46	-18.50	75.63	-15.48	3.34	0.39	26.59		27.05	304.3	0	100	0	0	14	-0.04	Jan-12
1.92	-16.74	-22.28	54.79	-14.83	1.18	0.39	44.56		8.32	44.6	1	99	0	0	19	0.07	Jan-12
-4.68	-5.54	-8.26	26.56	30.51	4.78	0.48	15.02		22.72	2,271	0	100	0	0	7	-0.21	Mar-96
2.45	1.33	-7.44	23.23	41.90	0.94	0.68	18.1		33.16	4,699	0	100	0	0	10	-0.13	Feb-12
6.34	-7.38	-25.43	20.13	91.53	2.92	0.75	23.77		38.73	255.1	2	97	0	1	49	-0.05	Feb-12
8.47	9.90	-10.57	23.72	19.67	1.92	0.62	16.42		24.89	483.8	0	100	0	0	7	-0.15	May-10
-16.57	-19.57	-20.98	-5.47	14.67	1.97	0.49	14.07		37.24	57.4	2	96	0	2	20	0.19	May-10
-13.01	-6.29	-4.98	3.05	9.66	1.92	0.59	13.24		48.54	127.5	0	100	0	0	6	-0.05	Mar-08
-11.14	-14.29	-17.51	-3.99	-9.96	3.93	0.47	21.01		24.15	167.1	0	100	0	0	10	-0.12	Mar-96
-14.13	-9.49	-13.17	9.38	14.29	1.55	0.47	11.07		51.20	16,799	1	99	0	0	4	-0.07	Mar-96
-14.72	-13.26	-16.35	17.83	33.95	1.32	0.47	11.57		65.82	326.4	1	99	0	0	9	-0.15	Dec-07
-12.81	-7.42	-3.80	28.39	44.66	1.42	0.25	10.02		92.98	1,238	0	100	0	0	11	0.02	Nov-06
-13.48	-8.64	-8.11	21.92	27.22	2.67	0.25	9.52		58.37	147.0	1	99	0	0	6	-0.27	Dec-07
-5.72	-1.96	-6.27	12.08	-20.23	7.09	0.47	14.65		29.92	559.9	0	100	0	0	63	-0.16	Mar-96
-19.61	-8.88	-14.93	-12.63	-32.71	2.68	0.47	22.32		41.20	1,048	0	100	0	0	7	0.05	Mar-96
-12.35	-12.21	-14.99	17.83	13.75	2.41	0.47	12.88		26.42	140.1	0	100	0	0	14	-0.13	Mar-96
-3.69	-1.42	-0.22	37.23	53.12	3.59	0.49	16.16		46.15	146.7	0	100	0	0	14	-0.26	Sep-10
-20.92	-15.05	-8.53	31.29	-13.96	2.72	0.53	15.2		23.09	35.3	0	100	0	0	13	-0.16	Jan-12
-7.57	-7.82	-10.68	20.29	8.67	4.89	0.48	13.25		40.85	2,161	1	99	0	0	6	-0.18	Oct-01
6.26	5.07	-17.44	-5.38	6.06	0.47	0.62	16.53		31.90	139.8	0	100	0	0	8	-0.07	Sep-10
-2.27	8.51	-14.30	34.44	-12.65	1.92	0.63	22.84		22.99	260.7	0	100	0	0	7	-0.23	May-10
5.87	13.45	22.57	9.50		3.9	0.62	19.91		18.59	54.8	-1	101	0	0	58	0.84	Apr-14
-8.45	-4.31	-3.66	54.98	-11.81	3.25	0.59	19.96		30.96	524.0	0	100	0	0	32	-0.29	Nov-10
-2.57	-4.60	15.29	32.43		2.17	0.74	18.37		28.87	205.7	0	100	0	0	20	0.79	Sep-15
-6.68	-3.83	-11.00	20.40	1.67	4.93	0.49	15.61		22.21	526.9	0	100	0	0	26	0.01	Mar-96
-3.14	-8.00	-24.58	19.16	-7.69	2.81	0.62	23.64		50.97	467.1	0	99	0	1	15	-0.03	Feb-03
-12.36	-9.53	-20.30	23.28	1.29	3.6	0.62	18.12		58.86	3,838	0	100	0	0	18	-0.03	May-00
-7.45	-8.71	-15.07	5.48	-15.39	3.69	0.49	18.69		26.96	991.5	0	100	0	0	21	-0.22	Mar-96
-13.90	-6.72	-13.22	7.14	-4.50	6.12	0.49	13.78		28.17	240.2	2	98	0	0	5	-0.19	Mar-96
-9.86	-3.09	-9.77	7.91	7.58	2.44	0.49	10.96		31.35	903.2	1	99	0	0	9	-0.22	Mar-96
-13.76	-8.46	-9.59	33.13	26.98	3.06	0.62	13.76		31.74	3,480	0	100	0	0	12	-0.24	Jun-00
-12.46	0.26	-8.76	50.13	39.72	2.5	0.62	14.41		82.24	499.6	0	100	0	0	10	0.09	Mar-08
3.80	-17.64	-41.41	-26.14	-40.92	3.96	0.62	32.69		24.68	549.9	0	100	0	0	7	0.15	Mar-08
-8.36	-6.66	-12.48	1.08		5.54	0.62	14.1		14.02	37.7	7	93	0	0	33	0.05	Apr-14
-11.73	-11.96	-14.60	3.29	-10.52	4.75	0.49	11.38		29.48	1,798	1	99	0	0	5	-0.14	Mar-96
-18.07	-19.49	-20.46	-6.73	-5.73	3.7	0.59	16.43		33.89	47.3	1	98	0	2	20	-0.45	Jan-12
-14.74	-10.43	-8.23	24.67	38.04	1.72	0.15	10.37		50.00	217.7	0	100	0	0	23	0.05	May-10
-14.06	-7.31	-4.13			1.42	0.15			54.78	112.1	0	100	0	0	28	0.29	Dec-16

Fund Name	Ticker Symbol	Traded On	Overall Rating	Reward Rating	Risk Rating	Recent Up/Downgrade	Price as of 12/31/2018	52-Week High	52-Week Low	Open to New Investors	Category & (Prospectus Objective)
● iShares MSCI USA ESG Select ETF	SUSA	NYSE Arca	C	C	C		103.14	120.97	96.94	Y	US Equity Large Cap Blend (Growth)
iShares MSCI USA Small-Cap ESG Optimized ETF	ESML	BATS	U	U	U		22.66	28.82	21.37	Y	US Equity Small Cap (Growth & Inc)
● iShares MSCI World ETF	URTH	NYSE Arca	C	C-	C+		78.87	94.07	75.04	Y	Global Equity Large Cap (World Stock)
● iShares Nasdaq Biotechnology ETF	IBB	NAS CM	C	C	C-		96.43	122.19	89.61	Y	Healthcare Sector Equity (Technology)
● iShares National Muni Bond ETF	MUB	NYSE Arca	C	C-	C+		109.04	110.74	106.42	Y	US Muni Fixed Inc (Muni Bond - Natl)
● iShares New York Muni Bond ETF	NYF	NYSE Arca	C-	C-	C-	Down	54.77	55.78	53.49	Y	US Muni Fixed Inc (Muni Bond - Single State)
● iShares North American Natural Resources ETF	IGE	BATS	C-	C-	C-	Down	27.18	38.04	25.63	Y	Natural Resources (Natl Res)
● iShares North American Tech-Multimedia Networking ETF	IGN	NYSE Arca	C	B-	D+		47.25	56.34	44.15	Y	Technology Sector Equity (Technology)
★ iShares PHLX Semiconductor ETF	SOXX	NAS CM	B-	B	C-	Down	156.91	196.31	145.00	Y	Technology Sector Equity (Technology)
● iShares Residential Real Estate Capped ETF	REZ	NYSE Arca	C+	B	C		62.34	68.12	53.95	Y	Real Estate Sector Equity (Real Estate)
iShares Robotics and Artificial Intelligence ETF	IRBO	NYSE Arca	U	U	U		20.17	25.46	19.24	Y	Technology Sector Equity (Technology)
● iShares Russell 1000 ETF	IWB	NYSE Arca	C	C	C+	Down	138.69	163.43	129.86	Y	US Equity Large Cap Blend (Growth)
● iShares Russell 1000 Growth ETF	IWF	NYSE Arca	C	C	C+	Down	130.91	156.36	121.77	Y	US Equity Large Cap Growth (Growth)
iShares Russell 1000 Pure U.S. Revenue ETF	AMCA	NAS CM	D+	D+	D+		24.75	28.97	23.45	Y	US Equity Large Cap Blend (Growth & Inc)
● iShares Russell 1000 Value ETF	IWD	NYSE Arca	C+	C	B		111.05	131.54	104.79	Y	US Equity Large Cap Value (Growth)
● iShares Russell 2000 ETF	IWM	NYSE Arca	C	C-	B-	Down	133.90	173.02	125.88	Y	US Equity Small Cap (Small Company)
● iShares Russell 2000 Growth ETF	IWO	NYSE Arca	C	C-	C+	Down	168.00	220.33	156.33	Y	US Equity Small Cap (Growth)
● iShares Russell 2000 Value ETF	IWN	NYSE Arca	C	C-	C+	Down	107.54	137.10	102.04	Y	US Equity Small Cap (Growth)
iShares Russell 2500 ETF	SMMD	BATS	D+	D+	C-		38.21	48.83	36.00	Y	US Equity Small Cap (Growth & Inc)
● iShares Russell 3000 ETF	IWV	NYSE Arca	C	C	C+	Down	146.92	174.15	137.69	Y	US Equity Large Cap Blend (Growth)
● iShares Russell Mid-Cap ETF	IWR	NYSE Arca	E+	E	D	Down	46.48	224.09	43.70	Y	US Equity Mid Cap (Growth)
● iShares Russell Mid-Cap Growth ETF	IWP	NYSE Arca	C	C-	C+	Down	113.71	137.48	106.03	Y	US Equity Mid Cap (Growth)
● iShares Russell Mid-Cap Value ETF	IWS	NYSE Arca	C	C-	C+	Down	76.35	92.83	72.26	Y	US Equity Mid Cap (Growth)
● iShares Russell Top 200 ETF	IWL	NYSE Arca	C	C	C-		58.39	68.21	54.65	Y	US Equity Large Cap Blend (Growth)
● iShares Russell Top 200 Growth ETF	IWY	NYSE Arca	C	C+	C	Down	71.75	85.82	66.58	Y	US Equity Large Cap Growth (Growth)
● iShares Russell Top 200 Value ETF	IWX	NYSE Arca	C	C	C-		47.80	55.81	44.99	Y	US Equity Large Cap Value (Growth)
● iShares S&P 100 ETF	OEF	NYSE Arca	C	C	C+	Down	111.53	130.65	104.34	Y	US Equity Large Cap Blend (Growth)
● iShares S&P 500 Growth ETF	IVW	NYSE Arca	C	C	C+	Down	150.67	177.72	140.58	Y	US Equity Large Cap Growth (Growth)
● iShares S&P 500 Value ETF	IVE	NYSE Arca	C	C	C+	Down	101.14	121.11	95.36	Y	US Equity Large Cap Value (Growth)
● iShares S&P GSCI Commodity-Indexed Trust	GSG	NYSE Arca	C-	C-	C	Down	14.02	18.72	13.86	Y	Commodities Broad Basket (Unaligned)
● iShares S&P Mid-Cap 400 Growth ETF	IJK	NYSE Arca	C	C-	C+	Down	191.23	237.87	179.90	Y	US Equity Mid Cap (Growth)
● iShares S&P Mid-Cap 400 Value ETF	IJJ	NYSE Arca	C	C-	C+		138.34	170.48	130.36	Y	US Equity Mid Cap (Growth)
● iShares S&P Small-Cap 600 Growth ETF	IJT	NAS CM	C	C	C+	Down	161.33	209.07	151.48	Y	US Equity Small Cap (Small Company)
● iShares S&P Small-Cap 600 Value ETF	IJS	NYSE Arca	C	C-	C+	Down	131.85	173.25	124.11	Y	US Equity Small Cap (Small Company)
● iShares Select Dividend ETF	DVY	NAS CM	C	C	C+	Down	89.31	102.32	85.20	Y	US Equity Large Cap Value (Equity-Income)
● iShares Short Maturity Bond ETF	NEAR	BATS	C	C	C+		49.85	50.24	49.82	Y	US Fixed Income (Income)
● iShares Short Maturity Municipal Bond ETF	MEAR	BATS	C-	C-	C-		49.94	50.03	49.66	Y	US Muni Fixed Inc (Muni Bond - Natl)
● iShares Short Treasury Bond ETF	SHV	NAS CM	C	C-	C+		110.30	110.47	110.20	Y	US Fixed Income (Govt Bond - Treasury)
● iShares Short-Term Corporate Bond ETF	IGSB	NAS CM	E+	E+	D-	Down	51.64	104.54	51.35	Y	US Fixed Income (Growth & Inc)
● iShares Short-Term National Muni Bond ETF	SUB	NYSE Arca	C	C-	C	Up	105.40	105.40	104.30	Y	US Muni Fixed Inc (Muni Bond - Natl)
● iShares Silver Trust	SLV	NYSE Arca	D	D-	D	Down	14.52	16.56	13.15	Y	Commodities Specified (Prec Metals)
● iShares TIPS Bond ETF	TIP	NYSE Arca	C-	D	C	Down	109.51	114.08	108.28	Y	US Fixed Income (Govt Bond - Treasury)
★ iShares Transportation Average ETF	IYT	BATS	B	B+	C		165.01	208.48	155.39	Y	Industrials Sector Equity (Unaligned)
● iShares Treasury Floating Rate Bond ETF	TFLO	NYSE Arca	C	C-	C+	Up	50.27	50.35	50.15	Y	US Fixed Income (Govt Bond - Treasury)
★ iShares U.S. Aerospace & Defense ETF	ITA	BATS	B-	B	C+	Down	172.86	217.63	162.03	Y	Industrials Sector Equity (Growth)
● iShares U.S. Basic Materials ETF	IYM	NYSE Arca	C	C	C-	Down	83.96	108.05	78.95	Y	Natural Resources (Natl Res)
★ iShares U.S. Broker-Dealers & Securities Exchanges ETF	IAI	BATS	B-	B	C		56.03	70.28	52.67	Y	Financials Sector Equity (Financial)
● iShares U.S. Consumer Goods ETF	IYK	NYSE Arca	C	C	C-		106.44	130.64	102.26	Y	Consumer Goods & Svcs (Unaligned)
● iShares U.S. Consumer Services ETF	IYC	NYSE Arca	C	C+	C	Down	180.90	211.88	168.12	Y	Consumer Goods & Svcs (Unaligned)
iShares U.S. Dividend and Buyback ETF	DIVB	BATS	D+	D+	D+		23.66	28.07	22.41	Y	US Equity Large Cap Blend (Growth & Inc)
● iShares U.S. Energy ETF	IYE	NYSE Arca	C	C	C-	Down	31.16	43.43	29.27	Y	Energy Sector Equity (Natl Res)
★ iShares U.S. Financial Services ETF	IYG	NYSE Arca	B-	B	C+	Down	112.27	141.49	105.05	Y	Financials Sector Equity (Financial)

★ Expanded analysis of this fund is included in Section II: Analysis of All BUY Rated Funds. ● Expanded analysis of this fund is included in Section III: Analysis of All Rated Funds with Assets over $50 million.

		TOTAL RETURNS & PERFORMANCE							ASSETS		ASSET ALLOCATION & TURNOVER					VALUATION	
3-Month Total Return	6-Month Total Return	1-Year Total Return	3-Year Total Return	5-Year Total Return	Dividend Yield (TTM)	Expense Ratio	3-Yr Std Deviation	Effective Duration	NAV	Total Assets (MIL)	%Cash	%Stocks	%Bonds	%Other	Turnover Ratio	Premium/ Discount 1-Year Avg	Inception Date
-13.68	-7.75	-5.56	29.87	44.62	1.51	0.25	9.94		103.16	862.2	0	100	0	0	13	0.09	Jan-05
-18.02	-15.73					0.17			22.72	10.3	0	100	0	0	15	0.33	Apr-18
-13.58	-8.72	-8.44	20.95	26.09	2.18	0.24	9.41		78.82	551.0	1	99	0	0	3	0.03	Jan-12
-19.94	-12.54	-9.13	-13.58	29.19	0.29	0.47	23.08		96.83	8,353	0	100	0	0	26	0.01	Feb-01
1.60	1.27	0.86	5.57	18.10	2.45	0.07	3.21	6.16	108.73	10,565	1	0	99	0	10	0.06	Sep-07
1.58	1.12	0.56	5.09	17.85	2.48	0.25	3.11	6.16	54.55	316.7	0	0	100	0	31	0.21	Oct-07
-24.60	-24.06	-21.44	2.94	-30.22	2.15	0.47	18.51		27.20	812.4	0	100	0	0	7	0.02	Oct-01
-12.49	-10.09	-0.93	31.28	51.59	0.67	0.47	14.17		47.40	53.8	0	100	0	0	23	0.12	Jul-01
-15.31	-11.93	-6.47	81.00	130.26	1.26	0.47	19.04		156.88	1,288	0	100	0	0	20	-0.01	Jul-01
1.18	1.38	4.09	11.63	67.81	3.35	0.48	13.98		62.39	334.6	0	100	0	0	19	0.01	May-07
-19.64	-14.99					0.47			20.11	13.2	0	100	0	0		0.15	Jun-18
-14.07	-7.75	-4.90	29.33	47.45	1.76	0.15	9.57		138.54	17,407	1	99	0	0	4	0.00	May-00
-16.13	-8.78	-1.69	36.58	62.57	1.13	0.2	11.01		130.78	41,688	0	100	0	0	13	-0.01	May-00
-11.86	-6.49	-6.55			1.92	0.15			24.82	11.1	0	100	0	0	4	0.25	Aug-17
-12.01	-6.77	-8.39	21.70	32.34	2.28	0.2	9.31		110.94	39,099	0	100	0	0	15	0.01	May-00
-19.08	-17.95	-11.02	23.80	24.30	1.3	0.19	14.59		134.01	45,632	0	100	0	0	16	-0.01	May-00
-20.43	-18.11	-9.33	23.55	29.06	0.69	0.24	15.35		168.12	9,405	0	100	0	0	26	0.00	Jul-00
-17.67	-17.82	-12.93	23.46	18.88	1.91	0.24	14.53		107.57	9,645	0	100	0	0	23	0.00	Jul-00
-17.76	-15.01	-10.00			1.41	0.15			38.24	19.6	0	100	0	0	5	0.47	Jul-17
-14.44	-8.56	-5.39	28.79	45.21	1.67	0.2	9.79		146.82	8,603	0	100	0	0	4	0.00	May-00
-15.04	-77.81	-77.28	-69.46	-66.37	1.8	0.2	10.62		46.46	17,592	0	100	0	0	10	0.01	Jul-01
-15.60	-10.10	-4.94	27.28	41.60	0.94	0.25	11.76		113.63	8,871	0	100	0	0	24	0.00	Jul-01
-14.70	-12.07	-12.36	18.63	29.12	2.28	0.25	10.45		76.34	11,177	0	100	0	0	20	0.00	Jul-01
-13.69	-6.35	-3.20	32.09	52.60	1.68	0.15	9.36		58.34	202.6	0	100	0	0	5	0.10	Sep-09
-16.20	-8.26	-0.76	39.45	70.62	1.22	0.2	10.99		71.62	1,237	0	100	0	0	11	0.05	Sep-09
-10.70	-4.07	-6.40	23.21	33.85	2.22	0.2	9.09		47.71	394.5	0	100	0	0	13	0.21	Sep-09
-13.94	-6.24	-4.05	29.87	49.74	1.85	0.2	9.41		111.47	4,772	0	100	0	0	4	0.02	Oct-00
-15.00	-7.39	-0.17	35.53	63.70	1.18	0.18	10.52		150.56	21,444	0	100	0	0	21	0.01	May-00
-12.42	-6.95	-9.09	22.69	33.14	2.37	0.18	9.55		101.11	15,475	0	100	0	0	23	0.01	May-00
-24.33	-20.64	-14.27	-1.54	-56.51	0	0.75	15.63		13.99	1,246	100	0	0	0	0	-0.09	Jul-06
-16.99	-14.69	-10.53	22.59	34.04	1.09	0.25	11.58		191.20	7,586	0	100	0	0	40	0.00	Jul-00
-16.38	-13.82	-12.07	24.34	29.65	1.77	0.25	12.62		138.26	5,873	0	100	0	0	37	0.00	Jul-00
-18.46	-15.05	-4.28	33.79	42.44	0.79	0.25	14.88		161.56	6,151	0	100	0	0	47	0.00	Jul-00
-19.52	-19.25	-12.79	27.37	27.29	1.54	0.25	14.94		131.84	6,063	0	100	0	0	39	0.00	Jul-00
-9.95	-7.04	-6.30	30.82	47.25	3.31	0.39	7.49		89.29	17,115	0	100	0	0	28	0.01	Nov-03
0.20	0.85	1.71	4.75	6.27	2.11	0.25	0.2	0.48	49.87	5,644	13	0	87	0	56	0.04	Sep-13
0.39	0.66	1.44	3.03		1.31	0.25	0.49	0.57	49.88	137.2	7	0	93	0	163	0.00	Mar-15
0.57	1.02	1.74	2.84	2.84	1.47	0.15	0.19	0.39	110.29	17,317	44	0	56	0	47	0.02	Jan-07
0.73	1.33	-49.33	-47.70	-46.95	2.23	0.06	0.84	2.70	51.67	10,220	1	0	98	0	46	0.01	Jan-07
0.94	0.91	1.56	2.44	3.69	1.25	0.07	1.12	2.00	105.05	1,798	5	0	95	0	21	0.07	Nov-08
6.15	-3.48	-8.76	10.21	-22.66	0	0.5	19.28		14.52	4,577	0	0	0	100		0.15	Apr-06
-0.34	-1.46	-1.43	6.07	8.03	3	0.2	3.13	7.29	109.46	21,829	0	0	100	0	32	0.00	Dec-03
-19.31	-11.76	-12.82	26.54	31.81	1.08	0.43	16.49		164.99	732.1	0	100	0	0	5	-0.01	Oct-03
0.50	0.97	1.82	3.22		1.63	0.15	0.19	0.01	50.24	397.6	19	0	81	0	68	0.06	Feb-14
-20.18	-9.87	-7.15	51.10	72.68	1.06	0.43	14.06		172.98	5,339	0	100	0	0	14	0.01	May-06
-15.09	-14.15	-16.49	24.73	12.01	1.61	0.43	14.71		84.01	453.3	0	100	0	0	6	0.01	Jun-00
-9.67	-12.38	-9.29	42.19	56.17	1.43	0.43	17.92		56.08	251.5	0	100	0	0	13	0.02	May-06
-9.94	-8.45	-13.72	5.42	24.28	2.46	0.43	8.28		106.51	507.1	0	100	0	0	7	0.03	Jun-00
-14.09	-6.36	1.79	28.78	55.95	0.81	0.43	11.55		180.89	888.0	0	100	0	0	10	0.03	Jun-00
-13.19	-6.14	-6.45			2.01	0.25			23.79	9.3	0	100	0	0	14	0.32	Nov-17
-26.21	-23.43	-19.20	-0.49	-30.06	2.63	0.43	18.72		31.17	874.7	1	99	0	0	6	0.02	Jun-00
-15.50	-13.08	-12.44	30.59	43.84	1.48	0.43	16.77		112.32	1,683	0	100	0	0	4	0.03	Jun-00

		MARKET		RATINGS				PRICE				CATEGORY & OBJECTIVE
Fund Name	Ticker Symbol	Traded On	Overall Rating	Reward Rating	Risk Rating	Recent Up/ Downgrade	Price as of 12/31/2018	52-Week High	52-Week Low	Open to New Investors	Category & (Prospectus Objective)
● iShares U.S. Financials ETF	IYF	NYSE Arca	C	C	C+	Down	106.37	126.31	100.04	Y	Financials Sector Equity (Financial)
● iShares U.S. Healthcare ETF	IYH	NYSE Arca	C+	C+	C	Up	180.81	204.02	168.20	Y	Healthcare Sector Equity (Health)
★ iShares U.S. Healthcare Providers ETF	IHF	NYSE Arca	B	B	C+		165.19	201.83	155.72	Y	Healthcare Sector Equity (Health)
● iShares U.S. Home Construction ETF	ITB	BATS	C	B-	D+	Down	30.04	46.25	28.55	Y	Consumer Goods & Svcs (Real Estate)
● iShares U.S. Industrials ETF	IYJ	BATS	C	C	C+		128.53	159.01	120.07	Y	Industrials Sector Equity (Unaligned)
iShares U.S. Infrastructure ETF	IFRA	BATS	U	U	U		22.97	27.86	22.00	Y	Infrastructure Sector Equity (Utility)
● iShares U.S. Insurance ETF	IAK	NYSE Arca	C	C	C-	Down	57.72	69.88	54.51	Y	Financials Sector Equity (Financial)
★ iShares U.S. Medical Devices ETF	IHI	NYSE Arca	B-	B	C		199.81	227.72	172.67	Y	Healthcare Sector Equity (Health)
● iShares U.S. Oil & Gas Exploration & Production ETF	IEO	BATS	C+	B	C-	Up	51.63	78.42	47.66	Y	Energy Sector Equity (Natl Res)
● iShares U.S. Oil Equipment & Services ETF	IEZ	NYSE Arca	D+	C	D	Down	20.42	40.37	19.30	Y	Energy Sector Equity (Natl Res)
● iShares U.S. Pharmaceuticals ETF	IHE	NYSE Arca	C	C+	C-		140.77	169.55	132.01	Y	Healthcare Sector Equity (Health)
● iShares U.S. Preferred Stock ETF	PFF	NAS CM	C-	D+	C	Down	34.23	38.19	33.41	Y	US Fixed Income (Growth & Inc)
● iShares U.S. Real Estate ETF	IYR	NYSE Arca	C+	C	B		74.94	83.29	71.79	Y	Real Estate Sector Equity (Real Estate)
★ iShares U.S. Regional Banks ETF	IAT	NYSE Arca	B-	B	C	Down	39.84	54.54	37.63	Y	Financials Sector Equity (Financial)
★ iShares U.S. Technology ETF	IYW	NYSE Arca	B-	B	C	Down	159.93	195.97	148.42	Y	Technology Sector Equity (Technology)
● iShares U.S. Telecommunications ETF	IYZ	BATS	C+	B	C-	Up	26.35	30.08	24.71	Y	Communications Sector Equity (Comm)
● iShares U.S. Treasury Bond ETF	GOVT	BATS	C-	D	C		24.65	25.08	24.07	Y	US Fixed Income (Govt Bond - Treasury)
★ iShares U.S. Utilities ETF	IDU	NYSE Arca	B-	B-	C+		134.22	144.20	119.94	Y	Utilities Sector Equity (Utility)
● iShares Ultra Short-Term Bond ETF	ICSH	BATS	C	C	C+		50.08	50.21	50.00	Y	US Fixed Income (Income)
● iShares US & Intl High Yield Corp Bond ETF	GHYG	BATS	C-	C-	C-	Down	46.03	51.59	45.07	Y	Global Fixed Income (Corp Bond-High Yld)
iShares Yield Optimized Bond ETF	BYLD	NYSE Arca	C-	C-	C-		23.63	25.02	23.53	Y	US Fixed Income (Income)
Ivy Focused Energy NextShares	IVENC	NAS CM	C	C+	D		12.04	100.02	11.16	Y	Energy Sector Equity (Unaligned)
★ Ivy Focused Growth NextShares™	IVFGC	NAS CM	B	B+	C+		26.09	100.02	24.17	Y	US Equity Large Cap Growth (Growth)
Ivy Focused Value NextShares™	IVFVC	NAS CM	C+	B	C-	Down	19.00	100.02	17.78	Y	US Equity Large Cap Value (Growth & Inc)
James Purpose Based Investment ETF	JPBI	BATS	D	D	D		19.51	26.80	18.41	Y	US Equity Large Cap Blend (Growth)
Janus Henderson Mortgage-Backed Securities ETF	JMBS	NYSE Arca	U	U	U		50.38	50.38	49.20	Y	US Fixed Income (Convertible Bond)
● Janus Henderson Short Duration Income ETF	VNLA	NYSE Arca	C	D+	C+		49.00	50.23	49.00	Y	US Fixed Income (Multisector Bond)
Janus Henderson Small Cap Growth Alpha ETF	JSML	NAS CM	C-	C	D+	Down	35.55	46.54	33.68	Y	US Equity Small Cap (Growth)
● Janus Henderson Small/Mid Cap Growth Alpha ETF	JSMD	NAS CM	C-	C	D+	Down	36.81	47.33	34.41	Y	US Equity Mid Cap (Growth)
John Hancock Multifactor Consumer Discretionary ETF	JHMC	NYSE Arca	C-	C	D+	Down	28.06	33.40	26.49	Y	Consumer Goods & Svcs (Growth & Inc)
John Hancock Multifactor Consumer Staples ETF	JHMS	NYSE Arca	C+	B-	C-	Up	24.55	28.69	23.55	Y	Consumer Goods & Svcs (Unaligned)
● John Hancock Multifactor Developed International ETF	JHMD	NYSE Arca	D	D	D+	Down	25.52	32.49	24.81	Y	Global Equity Large Cap (Foreign Stock)
John Hancock Multifactor Emerging Markets ETF	JHEM	NYSE Arca	U	U	U		23.22	25.13	22.41	Y	Global Emerg Mkts Equity (Div Emerg Mkts)
John Hancock Multifactor Energy ETF	JHME	NYSE Arca	C-	C	D+	Down	22.82	33.64	21.30	Y	Energy Sector Equity (Unaligned)
● John Hancock Multifactor Financials ETF	JHMF	NYSE Arca	C-	C	D+	Down	31.31	39.60	29.33	Y	Financials Sector Equity (Financial)
● John Hancock Multifactor Health Care ETF	JHMH	NYSE Arca	C	C	C		31.54	36.25	29.55	Y	Healthcare Sector Equity (Health)
John Hancock Multifactor Industrials ETF	JHMI	NYSE Arca	D+	C-	D	Down	30.29	37.81	28.59	Y	Industrials Sector Equity (Unaligned)
● John Hancock Multifactor Large Cap ETF	JHML	NYSE Arca	C-	C-	C-	Down	32.05	37.87	30.10	Y	US Equity Large Cap Blend (Growth)
John Hancock Multifactor Materials ETF	JHMA	NYSE Arca	C	B-	C-	Down	28.43	37.85	26.95	Y	Natural Resources (Growth & Inc)
● John Hancock Multifactor Mid Cap ETF	JHMM	NYSE Arca	C	C-	C+		30.44	36.91	28.59	Y	US Equity Mid Cap (Growth)
● John Hancock Multifactor Small Cap ETF	JHSC	NYSE Arca	D	D	D		22.62	28.48	21.34	Y	US Equity Small Cap (Small Company)
● John Hancock Multifactor Technology ETF	JHMT	NYSE Arca	C	C	D+		39.34	48.42	36.84	Y	Technology Sector Equity (Technology)
● John Hancock Multifactor Utilities ETF	JHMU	NYSE Arca	C+	C+	C		28.36	30.63	25.00	Y	Utilities Sector Equity (Utility)
● JPMorgan Alerian MLP Index ETN	AMJ	NYSE Arca	D+	D+	C-		22.32	30.57	21.22	Y	Energy Sector Equity (Unaligned)
JPMorgan BetaBuilders Canada ETF	BBCA	BATS	U	U	U		20.66	25.10	19.94	Y	Canadian Equity Large Cap (Growth)
JPMorgan BetaBuilders Developed Asia ex-Japan ETF	BBAX	BATS	U	U	U		22.76	25.59	22.06	Y	Asia ex-Japan Equity (Growth)
JPMorgan BetaBuilders Europe ETF	BBEU	BATS	U	U	U		21.36	25.24	20.77	Y	Europe Equity Large Cap (Europe Stock)
JPMorgan BetaBuilders Japan ETF	BBJP	BATS	U	U	U		21.12	25.13	20.43	Y	Japan Equity (Pacific Stock)
JPMorgan BetaBuilders MSCI U.S. REIT ETF	BBRE	BATS	U	U	U		71.99	82.65	69.49	Y	Real Estate Sector Equity (Real Estate)
● JPMorgan Disciplined High Yield ETF	JPHY	BATS	C-	C-	C-		47.64	51.62	47.14	Y	US Fixed Income (Corp Bond-High Yld)
● JPMorgan Diversified Alternative ETF	JPHF	NYSE Arca	D	D	C-		24.00	26.55	23.72	Y	Multialternative (Asset Allocation)
● JPMorgan Diversified Return Emerging Markets Equity ETF	JPEM	NYSE Arca	C-	C-	C-		50.84	64.42	49.44	Y	Global Emerg Mkts Equity (Div Emerg Mkts)

★ Expanded analysis of this fund is included in Section II: Analysis of All BUY Rated Funds. ● Expanded analysis of this fund is included in Section III: Analysis of All Rated Funds with Assets over $50 million.

			TOTAL RETURNS & PERFORMANCE							ASSETS		ASSET ALLOCATION & TURNOVER					VALUATION	
3-Month Total Return	6-Month Total Return	1-Year Total Return	3-Year Total Return	5-Year Total Return	Dividend Yield (TTM)	Expense Ratio	3-Yr Std Deviation	Effective Duration	NAV	Total Assets (MIL)	%Cash	%Stocks	%Bonds	%Other	Turnover Ratio	Premium/ Discount 1-Year Avg	Inception Date
-11.93	-8.73	-9.25	26.72	44.16	1.7	0.43	12.07		106.38	1,815	0	100	0	0	6	0.01	May-00
-10.98	1.72	5.02	24.84	65.86	1.03	0.43	12.83		180.79	2,540	0	100	0	0	7	0.02	Jun-00
-14.25	-2.95	9.60	38.77	85.89	0.2	0.43	12.95		165.15	1,210	0	100	0	0	20	0.09	May-06
-14.64	-21.07	-30.96	12.05	23.15	0.49	0.43	18.63		29.99	859.6	0	100	0	0	18	0.04	May-06
-17.85	-10.09	-11.59	30.36	36.38	1.24	0.43	12.46		128.56	941.6	0	100	0	0	7	0.01	Jun-00
-13.50	-13.39					0.4			23.03	3.8	0	100	0	0		0.48	Apr-18
-11.59	-5.09	-11.05	20.12	34.02	2.13	0.43	12.32		57.97	104.0	0	100	0	0	12	0.06	May-06
-12.11	-0.50	15.46	65.06	122.04	0.23	0.43	13.98		199.77	3,074	0	100	0	0	15	0.03	May-06
-32.60	-28.70	-19.36	1.16	-33.07	1.12	0.43	25.96		51.66	389.4	0	100	0	0	17	0.00	May-06
-43.23	-42.21	-42.48	-39.61	-65.57	1.42	0.43	29.75		20.40	190.9	0	100	0	0	25	0.02	May-06
-14.88	-6.68	-7.67	-9.80	27.34	1.13	0.43	15.16		140.74	417.6	0	100	0	0	23	0.06	May-06
-5.34	-6.13	-4.77	4.45	23.96	5.79	0.46	4.45	4.61	34.26	14,578	1	0	0	0	22	-0.01	Mar-07
-5.11	-5.03	-4.28	12.00	44.12	3.73	0.43	11.71		74.91	3,568	0	100	0	0	13	0.03	Jun-00
-17.54	-18.50	-17.38	20.70	32.11	1.87	0.43	18.71		39.86	691.3	0	100	0	0	4	-0.01	May-06
-17.60	-11.10	-0.96	53.78	90.48	0.82	0.43	14.71		159.77	3,734	0	100	0	0	15	0.01	May-00
-11.07	-4.19	-8.54	-1.24	-0.25	2.89	0.43	13.1		26.34	421.2	0	100	0	0	86	-0.02	May-00
2.68	1.99	0.74	3.90	9.91	1.95	0.15	3.19	5.79	24.78	6,794	0	0	100	0	47	0.01	Feb-12
1.01	2.27	3.91	35.55	64.15	2.53	0.43	11.73		134.18	795.7	0	100	0	0	5	0.00	Jun-00
0.57	1.26	2.26	5.06	5.70	2.01	0.08	0.27	0.39	50.05	689.4	63	0	36	0	11	0.05	Dec-13
-4.77	-2.21	-3.67	18.44	10.12	5.59	0.4	4.88	3.84	46.00	208.4	1	0	99	0	22	0.26	Apr-12
-1.05	0.13	-1.85	8.40		3.86	0.25	2.54	5.42	23.64	33.1	2	0	98	0	27	0.01	Apr-14
-37.93	-34.91	-34.98			1.34	0.95			12.04	6.5	1	99	0	0	44	0.00	Oct-16
-15.03	-7.37	5.18			0.23	0.78			26.09	12.8	2	98	0	0	25	0.00	Oct-16
-10.93	-6.43	-4.94			1.85	0.78			19.00	10.4	0	100	0	0	66	0.01	Oct-16
-20.85	-19.98	-21.39				0.65				4.5	0	99	0	1		0.23	Dec-17
3.34						0.35			50.38	37.4	17	0	83	0		0.09	Sep-18
0.08	0.85	1.57			2.43	0.35			49.05	805.9	10	3	85	0	44	0.10	Nov-16
-19.62	-11.88	-1.34			0.58	0.35			35.78	26.4	0	100	0	0	117	0.23	Feb-16
-18.52	-12.45	-3.82			0.34	0.35			36.97	50.4	0	100	0	0	76	0.21	Feb-16
-14.08	-10.65	-6.33	16.93		1.02	0.4	10.89		28.18	39.1	6	94	0	0	9	0.04	Sep-15
-6.52	-1.95	-8.47			1.67	0.5			24.57	26.7	0	100	0	0	14	0.07	Mar-16
-12.62	-10.22	-13.92			2.66	0.45			25.61	94.1	3	97	0	0	15	0.23	Dec-16
-7.04						0.55			23.22	289.5	1	98	0	1		-0.54	Sep-18
-30.08	-27.94	-21.01			2.01	0.5			22.87	27.0	1	99	0	0	16	0.42	Mar-16
-14.85	-12.41	-13.15	26.26		1.24	0.5	14.61		31.35	57.5	1	99	0	0	8	0.08	Sep-15
-12.45	-1.23	2.50	22.87		0.68	0.5	13.03		31.55	63.0	1	99	0	0	11	0.14	Sep-15
-16.96	-9.36	-11.57			0.98	0.5			30.44	24.6	2	98	0	0	3	0.27	Mar-16
-14.05	-8.32	-6.33	27.94		1.44	0.35	9.59		32.02	769.9	2	98	0	0	5	0.05	Sep-15
-15.84	-15.77	-19.18			1.44	0.5			28.47	19.4	0	100	0	0	10	0.04	Mar-16
-15.43	-11.80	-9.62	23.73		0.93	0.45	10.86		30.44	720.5	3	97	0	0	11	0.10	Sep-15
-17.83	-15.64	-12.12			0.55	0.5			22.63	336.1	7	93	0	0	17	0.20	Nov-17
-16.44	-12.36	-2.75	52.13		0.65	0.5	14.1		39.54	63.3	2	98	0	0	7	0.09	Sep-15
1.23	2.80	5.46			2.21	0.5			28.34	56.1	0	100	0	0	12	0.14	Mar-16
-17.14	-12.24	-13.19	-5.90	-33.78	7.61	0.85	18.13			2,925					0	-0.31	Apr-09
-15.63						0.19			20.73	2,220	1	99	0	0		0.20	Aug-18
-7.06						0.19			22.74	682.5	1	99	0	0		0.29	Aug-18
-12.45	-10.87					0.09			21.35	1,428	0	99	0	0		0.58	Jun-18
-14.53	-9.72					0.19			21.17	2,806	1	99	0	0		0.16	Jun-18
-5.81	-5.25					0.11			72.16	113.1	1	99	0	0		-0.26	Jun-18
-3.98	-1.01	-2.53			4.91	0.4		4.20	47.30	140.3	2	0	97	0	23	0.42	Sep-16
-3.60	-3.76	-7.82			0	0.85			24.04	209.2	35	66	0	0	107	0.15	Sep-16
-6.24	-3.95	-10.55	30.58		4.7	0.47	13.27		50.58	235.5	1	99	0	0	60	0.40	Jan-15

Fund Name	Ticker Symbol	Traded On	Overall Rating	Reward Rating	Risk Rating	Recent Up/ Downgrade	Price as of 12/31/2018	52-Week High	52-Week Low	Open to New Investors	Category & (Prospectus Objective)
JPMorgan Diversified Return Europe Currency Hedged ETF	JPEH	NYSE Arca	D+	D+	D+	Down	24.59	29.66	24.03	Y	Europe Equity Large Cap (Growth & Inc)
● JPMorgan Diversified Return Europe Equity ETF	JPEU	NYSE Arca	D+	D+	D+	Down	50.70	64.29	49.14	Y	Europe Equity Large Cap (Europe Stock)
● JPMorgan Diversified Return Global Equity ETF	JPGE	NYSE Arca	C-	D+	C-	Down	54.39	65.59	52.65	Y	Global Equity Large Cap (Growth & Inc)
JPMorgan Diversified Return Intl Currency Hedged ETF	JPIH	NYSE Arca	D	D+	D	Down	26.14	30.83	25.46	Y	Global Equity Large Cap (Foreign Stock)
● JPMorgan Diversified Return International Equity ETF	JPIN	NYSE Arca	C-	D+	C	Down	50.89	63.18	49.33	Y	Global Equity Large Cap (Growth & Inc)
● JPMorgan Diversified Return U.S. Equity ETF	JPUS	NYSE Arca	C-	C-	C-	Down	64.87	75.64	61.37	Y	US Equity Large Cap Blend (Growth & Inc)
● JPMorgan Diversified Return U.S. Mid Cap Equity ETF	JPME	NYSE Arca	C-	C-	C-	Down	57.11	68.32	54.16	Y	US Equity Mid Cap (Growth)
● JPMorgan Diversified Return U.S. Small Cap Equity ETF	JPSE	NYSE Arca	D+	D+	C-	Down	26.84	33.30	25.38	Y	US Equity Small Cap (Small Company)
JPMorgan Event Driven ETF	JPED	NYSE Arca	D	D	D		23.38	26.55	22.61	Y	Long/Short Equity (Growth & Inc)
● JPMorgan Global Bond Opportunities ETF	JPGB	BATS	D+	D	C-		47.31	51.54	47.26	Y	US Fixed Income (Multi-Asset Global)
JPMorgan Long/Short ETF	JPLS	NYSE Arca	U	U	U		22.63	24.82	22.10	Y	Long/Short Equity (Growth & Inc)
● JPMorgan Managed Futures Strategy ETF	JPMF	NYSE Arca	D	D	D+		23.41	25.34	23.03	Y	Alternative Misc (Growth & Inc)
JPMorgan U.S. Dividend ETF	JDIV	NYSE Arca	D	D	D+		23.29	26.85	22.29	Y	US Equity Large Cap Value (Growth & Inc)
JPMorgan U.S. Minimum Volatility ETF	JMIN	NYSE Arca	D	D	D+		24.85	27.70	23.72	Y	US Equity Large Cap Blend (Growth & Inc)
JPMorgan U.S. Momentum Factor ETF	JMOM	NYSE Arca	D	D+	D		23.99	28.75	22.40	Y	US Equity Large Cap Growth (Growth & Inc)
JPMorgan U.S. Quality Factor ETF	JQUA	NYSE Arca	D+	D+	C-		24.80	28.56	23.43	Y	US Equity Large Cap Blend (Growth & Inc)
JPMorgan U.S. Value Factor ETF	JVAL	NYSE Arca	D+	D+	D+		23.21	27.44	21.96	Y	US Equity Large Cap Value (Growth & Inc)
● JPMorgan Ultra-Short Income ETF	JPST	BATS	C	D+	C+	Up	50.13	50.27	50.02	Y	US Fixed Income (Growth & Inc)
JPMorgan USD Emerging Markets Sovereign Bond ETF	JPMB	NYSE Arca	U	U	U		45.69	50.14	44.79	Y	Emerging Mkts Fixed Inc (Div Emerg Mkts)
● Knowledge Leaders Developed World ETF	KLDW	NYSE Arca	C-	C-	C-	Down	29.05	35.72	27.85	Y	Global Equity Large Cap (Growth & Inc)
● KraneShares Bosera MSCI China A ETF	KBA	NYSE Arca	D	D	D		24.46	39.22	24.29	Y	Greater China Equity (Pacific Stock)
KraneShares CCBS China Corp High Yield Bond USD Ind ETF	KCCB	NYSE Arca	U	U	U		39.35	40.04	39.17	Y	Emerging Mkts Fixed Inc (Corp Bond-High Yld)
KraneShares CICC China Leaders 100 Index ETF	KFYP	NYSE Arca	D	C-	D	Down	21.73	37.41	21.62	Y	Greater China Equity (Growth & Inc)
● KraneShares CSI China Internet ETF	KWEB	NYSE Arca	C-	C	D	Down	37.50	68.34	37.50	Y	Greater China Equity (Pacific Stock)
KraneShares E Fund China Commercial Paper ETF	KCNY	NYSE Arca	D+	C-	D+	Down	33.42	37.60	33.42	Y	Emerging Mkts Fixed Inc (Foreign Stock)
KraneShares Electric Vehicles & Future Mobility Ind ETF	KARS	NYSE Arca	U	U	U		17.82	25.45	17.45	Y	Industrials Sector Equity (Unaligned)
KraneShares Emerging Markets Healthcare Index ETF	KMED	NYSE Arca	U	U	U		20.34	25.04	20.11	Y	Global Emerg Mkts Equity (Health)
KraneShares FTSE Emerg Mkts Consumer Technology Ind ETF	KEMQ	NYSE Arca	D	D+	D-		19.01	28.97	18.43	Y	Global Emerg Mkts Equity (Growth & Inc)
KraneShares MSCI All China Health Care Index ETF	KURE	NYSE Arca	U	U	U		17.25	30.41	17.20	Y	Greater China Equity (Health)
KraneShares MSCI All China Index ETF	KALL	NYSE Arca	D	D+	D	Down	20.91	29.85	20.88	Y	Global Emerg Mkts Equity (Div Emerg Mkts)
KraneShares MSCI China Environment Index ETF	KGRN	NYSE Arca	D	D	D-		17.52	27.22	16.98	Y	Greater China Equity (Pacific Stock)
KraneShares MSCI One Belt One Road Index ETF	OBOR	NYSE Arca	D	D	D		21.63	28.13	21.33	Y	Infrastructure Sector Equity (Growth & Inc)
LeaderSharesTM AlphaFactor® US Core Equity ETF	LSAF	NYSE Arca	U	U	U		21.15	23.57	19.87	Y	US Equity Large Cap Blend (Growth)
Legg Mason Developed ex-US Diversified Core ETF	DDBI	NAS CM	D	D+	D	Down	25.04	31.47	24.40	Y	Global Equity Large Cap (Foreign Stock)
Legg Mason Emerging Markets Diversified Core ETF	EDBI	NAS CM	D	D+	D	Down	26.99	35.60	26.99	Y	Global Emerg Mkts Equity (Div Emerg Mkts)
Legg Mason Emerg Mkts Low Volatility High Dividend ETF	LVHE	BATS	D	D+	D	Down	25.76	30.55	25.38	Y	Global Emerg Mkts Equity (Div Emerg Mkts)
Legg Mason Global Infrastructure ETF	INFR	NAS CM	D	D	D+	Down	26.37	29.90	25.73	Y	Infrastructure Sector Equity (Unaligned)
Legg Mason International Low Volatility High Dividend ETF	LVHI	BATS	D+	D+	D+		24.14	28.92	24.04	Y	Global Equity Large Cap (Growth & Inc)
● Legg Mason Low Volatility High Dividend ETF	LVHD	NAS CM	C	C	C		28.68	31.98	27.85	Y	US Equity Large Cap Value (Income)
Legg Mason Small-Cap Quality Value ETF	SQLV	NAS CM	D+	D+	D+		24.10	30.84	23.02	Y	US Equity Small Cap (Small Company)
Legg Mason US Diversified Core ETF	UDBI	NAS CM	D	C-	E+	Down	26.02	33.77	26.02	Y	US Equity Large Cap Blend (Income)
LHA Market State Tactical U.S. Equity ETF	MSUS	BATS	U	U	U		22.07	26.45	21.12	Y	Long/Short Equity (Growth & Inc)
Loncar Cancer Immunotherapy ETF	CNCR	NAS CM	D+	C-	D	Up	18.87	31.97	17.21	Y	Healthcare Sector Equity (Health)
Loncar China BioPharma ETF	CHNA	NAS CM	U	U	U		19.18	25.75	18.70	Y	Greater China Equity (Health)
● Main Sector Rotation ETF	SECT	BATS	D+	D+	D+		24.31	29.53	23.31	Y	US Equity Large Cap Blend (Growth & Inc)
Market Vectors® Chinese Renminbi/USD ETN	CNY	NYSE Arca	D	D+	D	Down	43.18	49.16	42.10	Y	Currency (Worldwide Bond)
Market Vectors® Double Long Euro ETN	URR	NYSE Arca	D	D	E	Down	17.27	21.49	13.16	Y	Trading Tools (Worldwide Bond)
Market Vectors® Double Short Euro ETN	DRR	NYSE Arca	D+	D+	D	Up	56.22	58.80	44.20	Y	Trading Tools (Worldwide Bond)
Market Vectors® Indian Rupee/USD ETN	INR	NYSE Arca	D	D+	D		40.87	45.30	36.99	Y	Currency (Worldwide Bond)
● Materials Select Sector SPDR® Fund	XLB	NYSE Arca	C	B-	C-	Down	50.52	64.09	47.34	Y	Natural Resources (Natl Res)
Metaurus U.S. Equity Cumulative Dividends Fund-Series 2027	IDIV	NYSE Arca	U	U	U		11.33	14.39	11.33	Y	US Equity Large Cap Blend (Equity-Income)
Metaurus U.S. Equity Ex-Dividend Fund-Series 2027	XDIV	NYSE Arca	U	U	U		49.63	58.83	46.12	Y	US Equity Large Cap Blend (Growth)

★ Expanded analysis of this fund is included in Section II: Analysis of All BUY Rated Funds.   ● Expanded analysis of this fund is included in Section III: Analysis of All Rated Funds with Assets over $50 million.

3-Month Total Return	6-Month Total Return	1-Year Total Return	3-Year Total Return	5-Year Total Return	Dividend Yield (TTM)	Expense Ratio	3-Yr Std Deviation	Effective Duration	NAV	Total Assets (MIL)	%Cash	%Stocks	%Bonds	%Other	Turnover Ratio	Premium/Discount 1-Year Avg	Inception Date
-13.22	-11.44	-9.45			2.98	0.38			24.61	28.6	0	100	0	0	12	0.11	Apr-16
-12.80	-11.55	-13.55	7.74		5.67	0.38			50.67	68.7	0	100	0	0	18	0.27	Dec-15
-10.76	-7.72	-10.33	18.01		3.42	0.38	9.16		54.49	207.6	1	99	0	0	26	0.11	Jun-14
-11.69	-7.52	-8.75			2.3	0.38			26.26	31.6	1	99	0	0	5	-0.79	Apr-16
-11.52	-8.97	-12.50	10.59		4.3	0.38	10.34		51.07	1,410	0	100	0	0	29	0.20	Nov-14
-12.37	-7.55	-6.02	27.03		2.61	0.19	8.5		64.88	578.4	1	99	0	0	27	0.09	Sep-15
-13.90	-10.51	-8.42			2.31	0.24			57.35	133.5	1	99	0	0	31	0.14	May-16
-16.09	-14.45	-8.13			1.42	0.29			26.89	108.8	0	100	0	0		0.14	Nov-16
-7.90	-6.62	-3.83			0.05	0.85			23.28	26.8	22	62	17	0		0.45	Nov-17
-4.52	-2.79	-4.41			3.37	0.55		3.06	47.34	181.5	7	0	90	0		0.16	Apr-17
0.35	1.62					0.69			22.52	23.3	27	64	9	0		0.50	Jan-18
-2.38	-2.91	-5.70				0.59			23.42	50.6	91	9	0	0		0.53	Dec-17
-9.77	-6.37	-6.33			3.36	0.12			23.36	27.1	0	100	0	0		0.35	Nov-17
-8.02	-1.75	-0.89			1.95	0.12			24.93	31.1	1	99	0	0		0.09	Nov-17
-15.88	-10.19	-5.04			1.22	0.12			24.00	29.0	1	100	0	0		0.18	Nov-17
-11.64	-4.69	-1.90			1.76	0.12			24.91	38.0	0	100	0	0		-0.09	Nov-17
-13.11	-7.85	-8.58			2.27	0.12			23.22	29.8	1	99	0	0		0.71	Nov-17
0.49	1.20	2.19			1.99	0.18		0.51	50.09	4,362	26	0	73	0		0.06	May-17
-1.07	1.51					0.39		6.76	45.40	53.8	1	0	99	0		0.48	Jan-18
-15.19	-11.64	-11.43	20.98		0.72	0.75	10.3		29.26	148.0	1	99	0	0	10	0.31	Jul-15
-12.01	-12.74	-26.76	-24.04		0.69	0.6	21		24.58	309.8	1	99	0	0	52	0.21	Mar-14
-0.29						0.69			39.14	11.7	6	0	75	0		0.86	Jun-18
-17.13	-22.07	-23.88	12.27	11.90	0.86	0.71	18.46		22.11	2.7	1	99	0	0	105	-1.06	Jul-13
-19.93	-34.50	-33.51	3.11	20.69	0.78	0.7	23.26		37.67	1,773	1	99	0	0	29	0.12	Jul-13
1.06	-1.17	-0.92	3.99		2.87	0.62	4.65		33.53	11.8	24	0	76	0	717	-0.14	Dec-14
-17.05	-17.77					0.7			17.90	30.7	0	100	0	0	18	0.71	Jan-18
-17.08						0.79			20.42	5.4						0.20	Aug-18
-12.08	-20.67	-24.79			0	0.79			19.14	26.3	1	99	0	0	3	0.03	Oct-17
-21.50	-35.17					0.82			17.42	43.0	1	99	0	0		0.79	Jan-18
-11.00	-13.26	-20.70	8.14		1.46	0.72	15.71		20.80	2.2	2	98	0	0	3	0.79	Feb-15
-8.07	-16.70	-29.57			0	0.78			17.65	5.9	0	100	0	0	36	0.68	Oct-17
-6.08	-2.02	-12.12			0.12	0.8			21.78	20.1	-2	101	0	1	1	0.23	Sep-17
-15.29						0.75			21.16	51.8	0	100	0	0		0.49	Oct-18
-11.62	-9.37	-11.68	9.84		1.68	0.4			25.01	11.0	0	100	0	0	29	0.76	Dec-15
-6.40	-6.02	-15.86	19.67		2.52	0.5			27.05	14.3	0	100	0	0	30	0.07	Dec-15
-7.42	-1.63	-3.42			4.63	0.51			25.33	6.3	1	99	0	0	27	1.43	Nov-16
-3.58	-4.87	-7.18			3.77	0.4			26.38	30.1	0	100	0	0	45	-0.09	Dec-16
-10.36	-6.89	-9.70			5.08	0.4			24.04	49.2	2	98	0	0	41	-0.31	Jul-16
-5.14	-1.55	-5.17	28.03		3.47	0.27			28.76	605.8	0	100	0	0	44	0.01	Dec-15
-17.22	-17.55	-9.14			0.4	0.6			24.33	6.9	0	100	0	0	80	0.30	Jul-17
-17.22	-12.53	-10.75	19.78		1.56	0.3			26.76	3.3	1	99	0	0	24	0.86	Dec-15
-15.57	-11.12					1.25			22.01	6.7	3	97	0	0		-0.03	Apr-18
-23.39	-22.20	-20.26	-32.68		1.63	0.79	32.55		18.92	45.2	0	100	0	0	78	0.09	Oct-15
-17.80						0.79			18.89	2.2	0	100	0	0		0.35	Aug-18
-15.25	-11.59	-9.30			0.94	0.78			24.40	405.7	0	100	0	0	12	0.25	Sep-17
1.10	-2.14	-2.41	4.94	1.65	0	0.55	5.02			7.6					0	-0.07	Mar-08
-3.72	-5.65	-14.15	-1.37	-42.63	0	0.65	15.14			1.4					0	-1.78	May-08
4.24	6.29	16.07	-3.78	48.98	0	0.65	14.6			12.6					0	-0.62	May-08
7.61	0.06	-3.11	11.15	16.83	0	0.55	6.72			0.95					0	-0.61	Mar-08
-13.07	-11.55	-14.77	23.21	20.84	1.98	0.13	14.07		50.53	4,035	0	100	0	0	17	0.00	Dec-98
-11.39	-9.54					0.58			11.32	5.0	2	55	43	0		0.70	Feb-18
-15.18	-7.92					0.29			49.98	13.8	4	49	47	0		0.02	Feb-18

Fund Name	Ticker Symbol	Traded On	Overall Rating	Reward Rating	Risk Rating	Recent Up/ Downgrade	Price as of 12/31/2018	52-Week High	52-Week Low	Open to New Investors	Category & (Prospectus Objective)
MicroSectors™ FANG+™ Index -2X Inverse Leveraged ETN	FNGZ	NYSE Arca	U	U	U		67.19	77.98	47.91	Y	Trading Tools (Technology)
MicroSectors™ FANG+™ Index 2X Leveraged ETN	FNGO	NYSE Arca	U	U	U		30.54	54.22	26.94	Y	Trading Tools (Technology)
MicroSectors™ FANG+™ Index -3X Inverse Leveraged ETN	FNGD	NYSE Arca	U	U	U		40.12	51.89	23.52	Y	Trading Tools (Growth & Inc)
MicroSectors™ FANG+™ Index 3X Leveraged ETN	FNGU	NYSE Arca	U	U	U		27.53	72.15	22.61	Y	Trading Tools (Growth & Inc)
MicroSectors™ FANG+™ Index Inverse ETN	GNAF	NYSE Arca	U	U	U		59.37	63.69	48.89	Y	Trading Tools (Technology)
Motley Fool 100 Index ETF	TMFC	BATS	U	U	U		18.64	22.24	17.54	Y	US Equity Large Cap Growth (Growth & Inc)
Nationwide Maximum Diversification Emerg Mkts Core Eq ETF	MXDE	NYSE Arca	U	U	U		20.97	25.66	20.64	Y	Global Emerg Mkts Equity (Div Emerg Mkts)
● Nationwide Maximum Diversification U.S. Core Equity ETF	MXDU	NYSE Arca	D+	D+	D+		24.80	29.79	23.92	Y	US Equity Large Cap Blend (Growth)
● Nationwide Risk-Based International Equity ETF	RBIN	NYSE Arca	D	D	D		22.76	27.45	22.56	Y	Global Equity Large Cap (Foreign Stock)
● Nationwide Risk-Based U.S. Equity ETF	RBUS	NYSE Arca	D	D+	D		24.41	28.05	23.93	Y	US Equity Large Cap Blend (Growth)
Natixis Loomis Sayles Short Duration Income ETF	LSST	NYSE Arca	D+	D	D+		24.60	25.06	24.54	Y	US Fixed Income (Corp Bond - Gen)
Natixis Seeyond International Minimum Volatility ETF	MVIN	NYSE Arca	D+	D+	D+		39.33	47.10	38.46	Y	Global Equity Large Cap (Growth)
NuShares Enhanced Yield 1-5 Year U.S. Aggregate Bond ETF	NUSA	NYSE Arca	D	D	D		24.32	24.78	24.12	Y	US Fixed Income (Income)
● NuShares Enhanced Yield U.S. Aggregate Bond ETF	NUAG	NYSE Arca	D+	D+	D+		23.18	24.46	22.81	Y	US Fixed Income (Corp Bond - Gen)
NuShares ESG Emerging Markets Equity ETF	NUEM	BATS	D	D	D		23.87	32.04	23.23	Y	Global Emerg Mkts Equity (Div Emerg Mkts)
NuShares ESG International Developed Markets Equity ETF	NUDM	BATS	D	D	D		22.38	28.60	22.18	Y	Global Equity Large Cap (World Stock)
● NuShares ESG Large-Cap Growth ETF	NULG	BATS	C-	C	C-	Down	30.09	37.47	29.07	Y	US Equity Large Cap Growth (Growth)
● NuShares ESG Large-Cap Value ETF	NULV	BATS	C-	C-	C-		26.15	30.90	25.77	Y	US Equity Large Cap Value (Growth)
● NuShares ESG Mid-Cap Growth ETF	NUMG	BATS	D+	C-	D+	Down	26.22	34.48	25.81	Y	US Equity Mid Cap (Growth)
NuShares ESG Mid-Cap Value ETF	NUMV	BATS	D+	C-	D+	Down	23.84	29.65	23.64	Y	US Equity Mid Cap (Growth)
● NuShares ESG Small-Cap ETF	NUSC	BATS	D+	D+	C-	Down	24.74	32.42	24.25	Y	US Equity Small Cap (Small Company)
NuShares ESG U.S. Aggregate Bond ETF	NUBD	NYSE Arca	D	D	D+		24.26	24.94	23.73	Y	US Fixed Income (Growth & Inc)
★ NuShares Short-Term REIT ETF	NURE	BATS	B-	B	C		24.99	28.09	23.69	Y	Real Estate Sector Equity (Real Estate)
NYSE® Pickens Oil Response™ ETF	BOON	NYSE Arca	U	U	U		19.07	27.76	17.88	Y	Energy Sector Equity (Natl Res)
Oppenheimer Emerging Markets Revenue ETF	REEM	BATS	D	D	D		23.62	30.65	23.37	Y	Global Emerg Mkts Equity (Div Emerg Mkts)
Oppenheimer Emerging Markets Ultra Dividend Revenue ETF	REDV	NYSE Arca	U	U	U		22.57	24.00	22.30	Y	Global Emerg Mkts Equity (Div Emerg Mkts)
Oppenheimer ESG Revenue ETF	ESGL	NYSE Arca	D+	C-	D+	Down	27.77	33.08	26.60	Y	US Equity Large Cap Value (Growth & Inc)
Oppenheimer Global ESG Revenue ETF	ESGF	NYSE Arca	D	D	D		26.38	33.48	25.72	Y	Global Equity Large Cap (Growth & Inc)
Oppenheimer Global Revenue ETF	RGLB	BATS	D	D	D+		23.74	30.09	22.97	Y	Global Equity Large Cap (Growth & Inc)
Oppenheimer International Revenue ETF	REFA	BATS	D	D	D		22.83	29.82	22.51	Y	Global Equity Large Cap (Growth & Inc)
Oppenheimer International Ultra Dividend Revenue ETF	RIDV	NYSE Arca	U	U	U		21.65	25.50	21.35	Y	Global Equity Large Cap (Foreign Stock)
● Oppenheimer Russell 1000 Dynamic Multifactor ETF	OMFL	BATS	C-	C-	C-		25.10	29.21	23.84	Y	US Equity Large Cap Blend (Growth)
Oppenheimer Russell 1000 Low Volatility Factor ETF	OVOL	BATS	D	D+	E+		24.50	27.27	23.37	Y	US Equity Large Cap Blend (Growth & Inc)
Oppenheimer Russell 1000 Momentum Factor ETF	OMOM	BATS	D	D+	D		23.99	28.99	22.70	Y	US Equity Large Cap Growth (Growth & Inc)
Oppenheimer Russell 1000 Quality Factor ETF	OQAL	BATS	D	D+	E+		24.49	28.89	23.22	Y	US Equity Large Cap Blend (Growth & Inc)
Oppenheimer Russell 1000 Size Factor ETF	OSIZ	BATS	D-	D	E		23.36	28.48	22.28	Y	US Equity Large Cap Blend (Growth & Inc)
Oppenheimer Russell 1000 Value Factor ETF	OVLU	BATS	D	D+	E+		23.51	27.51	22.51	Y	US Equity Large Cap Value (Growth & Inc)
Oppenheimer Russell 1000 Yield Factor ETF	OYLD	BATS	D	D+	D		23.69	26.61	22.83	Y	US Equity Large Cap Blend (Growth & Inc)
Oppenheimer Russell 2000 Dynamic Multifactor ETF	OMFS	BATS	D	D	D		23.20	28.76	22.06	Y	US Equity Small Cap (Growth)
● Oppenheimer S&P 500 Revenue ETF	RWL	NYSE Arca	C	C	C-		46.54	55.26	44.16	Y	US Equity Large Cap Value (Growth)
● Oppenheimer S&P Financials Revenue ETF	RWW	NYSE Arca	C	C	C-	Down	57.71	74.08	54.38	Y	Financials Sector Equity (Financial)
● Oppenheimer S&P MidCap 400 Revenue ETF	RWK	NYSE Arca	C-	C-	C-	Down	51.25	65.07	48.52	Y	US Equity Mid Cap (Growth)
● Oppenheimer S&P SmallCap 600 Revenue ETF	RWJ	NYSE Arca	C-	C-	C-	Down	57.31	78.89	54.53	Y	US Equity Small Cap (Small Company)
● Oppenheimer S&P Ultra Dividend Revenue ETF	RDIV	NYSE Arca	C	C	C	Down	33.48	39.77	32.38	Y	US Equity Large Cap Value (Growth)
Opus Small Cap Value Plus ETF	OSCV	NYSE Arca	U	U	U		21.64	26.10	20.79	Y	US Equity Small Cap (Growth)
O'Shares FTSE Europe Quality Dividend ETF	OEUR	NYSE Arca	D+	D+	D+	Down	21.72	26.77	21.31	Y	Europe Equity Large Cap (Europe Stock)
● O'Shares FTSE Russell Small Cap Quality Dividend ETF	OUSM	NYSE Arca	C-	D+	C-		23.61	29.15	22.48	Y	US Equity Small Cap (Small Company)
● O'Shares FTSE U.S. Quality Dividend ETF	OUSA	NYSE Arca	C	C	C+		30.02	33.39	28.55	Y	US Equity Large Cap Value (Growth)
O'Shares Global Internet Giants ETF	OGIG	NYSE Arca	U	U	U		19.07	25.97	17.77	Y	Technology Sector Equity (Growth & Inc)
Pacer Benchmark Data & Infrastructure Real Estate SCTR ETF	SRVR	NYSE Arca	U	U	U		23.34	27.08	22.35	Y	Real Estate Sector Equity (Growth & Inc)
Pacer Benchmark Industrial Real Estate SCTR ETF	INDS	NYSE Arca	U	U	U		23.99	26.20	23.10	Y	Real Estate Sector Equity (Real Estate)
Pacer Benchmark Retail Real Estate SCTR ETF	RTL	NYSE Arca	U	U	U		24.81	28.56	23.88	Y	Real Estate Sector Equity (Growth & Inc)

★ Expanded analysis of this fund is included in Section II: Analysis of All BUY Rated Funds. ● Expanded analysis of this fund is included in Section III: Analysis of All Rated Funds with Assets over $50 million.

				TOTAL RETURNS & PERFORMANCE						ASSETS		ASSET ALLOCATION & TURNOVER					VALUATION	
3-Month Total Return	6-Month Total Return	1-Year Total Return	3-Year Total Return	5-Year Total Return	Dividend Yield (TTM)	Expense Ratio	3-Yr Std Deviation	Effective Duration	NAV	Total Assets (MIL)	%Cash	%Stocks	%Bonds	%Other	Turnover Ratio	Premium/ Discount 1-Year Avg	Inception Date
38.01						0.95			66.56	57.8						6.68	Aug-18
-39.12						0.95			30.81	37.6						-5.11	Aug-18
51.93						0.95			40.24	33.4						-0.03	Jan-18
-55.61						0.95			27.60	83.9						0.12	Jan-18
20.05						0.95			59.10	54.7						2.48	Aug-18
-15.39	-7.24					0.5			18.69	144.3	0	100	0	0	10	0.10	Jan-18
-7.70	-9.70					0.64			21.05	26.0	0	100	0	0		0.41	Mar-18
-14.19	-10.09	-4.37			0.41	0.34			24.86	102.9	0	100	0	0		0.09	Sep-17
-12.33	-10.04	-11.91			0.43	0.42			22.80	112.8	0	100	0	0		0.27	Sep-17
-10.13	-5.45	-3.94			0.4	0.3			24.44	112.7	1	99	0	0		0.21	Sep-17
0.38	1.20	0.97				0.38		1.89	24.62	27.1	3	0	96	0	0	0.19	Dec-17
-8.47	-6.56	-7.08			3.36	0.55			39.43	21.3	2	98	0	0	93	0.46	Oct-16
0.92	1.39	0.86			3.04	0.2		2.81	24.28	29.0	1	0	99	0	37	0.17	Mar-17
0.25	0.61	-1.86			3.93	0.2		6.29	23.19	71.2	1	0	99	0	123	0.03	Sep-16
-8.81	-8.72	-18.43			0.71	0.45			23.80	39.9	0	100	0	0	13	0.47	Jun-17
-14.52	-11.64	-16.70			0.49	0.4			22.36	48.8	0	100	0	0	9	0.34	Jun-17
-17.48	-9.94	-0.15			0.27	0.35			30.06	61.6	0	100	0	0	30	0.12	Dec-16
-12.03	-6.66	-6.48			0.9	0.35			26.25	52.2	0	100	0	0	33	0.10	Dec-16
-18.89	-11.35	-5.40			0.13	0.4			26.30	50.9	0	100	0	0	53	0.40	Dec-16
-15.29	-13.62	-13.66			0.69	0.4			23.91	48.7	0	100	0	0	46	0.15	Dec-16
-18.34	-16.66	-10.23			0.64	0.4			24.80	84.0	0	100	0	0	36	0.10	Dec-16
1.57	1.47	-0.26			2.85	0.2		5.84	24.22	47.8	1	0	98	0	17	0.02	Sep-17
-6.90	-6.76	-2.09			3.21	0.35			25.05	32.9	0	100	0	0	20	-0.40	Dec-16
-26.78	-25.21					0.85			19.16	4.6	0	100	0	0		0.13	Feb-18
-6.14	-2.94	-11.90			3.25	0.46			23.59	12.1	1	99	0	0		0.50	Jul-17
-3.70						0.46			22.46	2.3	1	99	0	0		0.47	Aug-18
-13.37	-7.15	-7.83			2.1	0.4			27.91	23.4	1	99	0	0		0.28	Oct-16
-13.12	-8.83	-12.81			2.27	0.45			26.42	22.8	0	99	0	0		0.35	Oct-16
-12.43	-8.27	-12.08			2.32	0.43			23.73	12.8	1	99	0	0		0.33	Jul-17
-13.11	-10.20	-14.60			2.68	0.42			22.95	12.2	1	99	0	0		0.30	Jul-17
-11.97						0.42			21.57	2.3	0	100	0	0		1.01	Aug-18
-13.02	-4.95	-2.30			1.05	0.29			25.09	253.8	0	100	0	0		0.14	Nov-17
-10.85	-2.93	-2.62			1.8	0.19			24.61	5.4	0	100	0	0		-0.25	Nov-17
-16.37	-9.52	-4.56			1.28	0.19			24.09	5.3	0	100	0	0		0.35	Nov-17
-14.38	-7.93	-2.87			1.32	0.19			24.60	5.4	0	100	0	0		0.42	Nov-17
-15.73	-12.10	-8.55			1.32	0.19			23.45	5.3	0	100	0	0		-0.38	Nov-17
-12.66	-7.93	-8.25			1.78	0.19			23.61	5.3	0	100	0	0		0.04	Nov-17
-9.26	-3.64	-5.05			2.64	0.19			23.79	5.2	0	100	0	0		-0.57	Nov-17
-15.65	-14.03	-8.42			1.18	0.39			23.24	12.0	0	100	0	0		0.41	Nov-17
-13.89	-7.35	-7.57	24.35	39.25	1.69	0.39	9.89		46.51	1,032	1	99	0	0		0.08	Feb-08
-14.07	-9.70	-14.71	25.86	36.46	1.36	0.45	14.9		57.76	52.2	0	100	0	0		0.55	Nov-08
-17.47	-15.48	-14.49	17.33	21.01	1.01	0.39	13.21		51.27	362.1	0	100	0	0		0.04	Feb-08
-22.10	-21.37	-16.87	14.10	11.16	1.07	0.39	16.93		57.44	474.9	0	100	0	0		-0.01	Feb-08
-12.85	-9.91	-4.47	36.82	57.67	4.17	0.39	10.86		33.53	1,213	0	100	0	0		0.04	Sep-13
-14.43						0.79			21.61	20.4	0	100	0	0		0.19	Jul-18
-9.36	-6.90	-11.77	3.43		3.97	0.48	10.91		21.83	28.6	1	98	0	1		-0.38	Aug-15
-15.31	-12.06	-10.29			2.08	0.48			23.67	128.9	0	100	0	0		0.05	Dec-16
-8.36	-0.92	-3.43	28.81		2.9	0.48	8.1		30.00	600.8	0	100	0	0		0.00	Jul-15
-18.22	-20.84					0.48			19.17	49.1	0	100	0	0		-0.07	Jun-18
-9.07	-9.10					0.6			23.42	5.1	0	100	0	0		0.07	May-18
-2.88	-4.55					0.6			24.03	2.6	0	100	0	0		0.02	May-18
-6.33	-4.54					0.6			24.85	2.7	1	99	0	0		-0.12	May-18

Fund Name	Ticker Symbol	Traded On	Overall Rating	Reward Rating	Risk Rating	Recent Up/ Downgrade	Price as of 12/31/2018	52-Week High	52-Week Low	Open to New Investors	Category & (Prospectus Objective)
Pacer CFRA-Stovall Equal Weight Seasonal Rotation ETF	SZNE	NYSE Arca	U	U	U		23.17	26.38	21.90	Y	US Equity Large Cap Blend (Growth & Inc)
Pacer Developed Markets International Cash Cows 100 ETF	ICOW	BATS	D	D	D	Down	24.05	30.94	23.28	Y	Global Equity Large Cap (Growth & Inc)
● Pacer Global Cash Cows Dividend ETF	GCOW	BATS	C-	C-	C-	Down	27.92	33.33	26.95	Y	Global Equity Large Cap (Growth & Inc)
Pacer Military Times Best Employers ETF	VETS	NAS CM	U	U	U		23.81	28.04	23.81	Y	US Equity Large Cap Blend (Growth & Inc)
● Pacer Trendpilot™ 100 ETF	PTNQ	BATS	C	C+	C	Down	32.68	36.30	29.80	Y	US Equity Large Cap Growth (Growth)
● Pacer Trendpilot™ European Index ETF	PTEU	BATS	D+	D+	D+	Down	25.05	33.20	25.05	Y	Europe Equity Large Cap (Growth & Inc)
● Pacer Trendpilot™ US Large Cap ETF	PTLC	BATS	C	C-	C+	Down	28.77	31.65	27.65	Y	US Equity Large Cap Blend (Growth)
● Pacer Trendpilot™ US Mid Cap ETF	PTMC	BATS	C-	C-	C-	Down	30.84	33.83	29.35	Y	US Equity Mid Cap (Growth)
● Pacer US Cash Cows 100 ETF	COWZ	BATS	C-	C-	C-		25.70	31.30	24.24	Y	US Equity Large Cap Blend (Growth & Inc)
Pacer US Export Leaders ETF	PEXL	NYSE Arca	U	U	U		20.80	25.67	19.60	Y	US Equity Large Cap Blend (Growth)
Pacer US Small Cap Cash Cows 100 ETF	CALF	BATS	D+	D+	D+		23.18	30.25	21.63	Y	US Equity Small Cap (Small Company)
● Pacer WealthShield ETF	PWS	BATS	D+	D+	D+		24.14	27.20	23.18	Y	Moderate Allocation (Growth & Inc)
Perth Mint Physical Gold ETF	AAAU	NYSE Arca	U	U	U		12.82	12.82	11.74	Y	Commodities Specified (Prec Metals)
PGIM Active High Yield Bond ETF	PHYL	NYSE Arca	U	U	U		38.02	40.39	37.63	Y	US Fixed Income (Corp Bond-High Yld)
PGIM Ultra Short Bond ETF	PULS	NYSE Arca	U	U	U		49.92	50.15	49.89	Y	US Fixed Income (Growth & Inc)
● PIMCO 0-5 Year High Yield Corp Bond Ind ETF	HYS	NYSE Arca	C	C-	C+	Down	95.12	101.41	94.14	Y	US Fixed Income (Corp Bond-High Yld)
● PIMCO 1-3 Year U.S. Treasury Index Exchange-Traded Fund	TUZ	NYSE Arca	C-	C-	D+	Up	50.15	50.29	49.70	Y	US Fixed Income (Govt Bond - Treasury)
● PIMCO 1-5 Year U.S. TIPS Index Exchange-Traded Fund	STPZ	NYSE Arca	C-	C-	C-		50.84	51.99	50.72	Y	US Fixed Income (Govt Bond - Treasury)
● PIMCO 15+ Year U.S. TIPS Index Exchange-Traded Fund	LTPZ	NYSE Arca	D+	D	C-	Down	62.39	69.23	60.38	Y	US Fixed Income (Govt Bond - Treasury)
● PIMCO 25+ Year Zero Coupon U.S. Treasury Ind ETF	ZROZ	NYSE Arca	D+	D	D+	Down	112.49	121.42	100.48	Y	US Fixed Income (Govt Bond - Treasury)
● PIMCO Active Bond Exchange-Traded Fund	BOND	NYSE Arca	C	D+	C+	Up	102.77	106.05	100.83	Y	US Fixed Income (Income)
● PIMCO Broad U.S. TIPS Index Exchange-Traded Fund	TIPZ	NYSE Arca	D+	D	D+	Down	56.03	58.23	55.39	Y	US Fixed Income (Govt Bond - Treasury)
● PIMCO Enhanced Low Duration Active Exchange-Traded Fund	LDUR	NYSE Arca	C	C	C-		98.76	100.40	98.71	Y	US Fixed Income (Income)
● PIMCO Enhanced Short Maturity Active Exchange-Traded Fund	MINT	NYSE Arca	C	C	C+		100.95	101.71	100.95	Y	US Fixed Income (Income)
● PIMCO Intermediate Muni Bond Active ETF	MUNI	NYSE Arca	C-	C-	C-	Down	52.82	53.65	51.81	Y	US Muni Fixed Inc (Muni Bond - Natl)
● PIMCO Investment Grade Corp Bond Ind ETF	CORP	NYSE Arca	C-	D+	C-		99.05	105.67	97.96	Y	US Fixed Income (Corp Bond - High Quality)
● PIMCO RAFI Dynamic Multi-Factor Emerg Mkts Equity ETF	MFEM	NYSE Arca	D	D	D		22.10	28.32	21.67	Y	Global Emerg Mkts Equity (Div Emerg Mkts)
PIMCO RAFI Dynamic Multi-Factor International Equity ETF	MFDX	NYSE Arca	D	D	D	Down	22.34	28.41	21.85	Y	Global Equity Large Cap (Growth & Inc)
● PIMCO RAFI Dynamic Multi-Factor U.S. Equity ETF	MFUS	NYSE Arca	D+	D+	D+		25.21	30.12	24.14	Y	US Equity Large Cap Blend (Growth & Inc)
● PIMCO Short Term Muni Bond Active ETF	SMMU	NYSE Arca	C-	C-	D+		49.83	50.19	49.50	Y	US Muni Fixed Inc (Muni Bond - Natl)
Point Bridge GOP Stock Tracker ETF	MAGA	BATS	D+	D+	D+		23.29	29.77	22.04	Y	US Equity Large Cap Blend (Growth & Inc)
PortfolioPlus Developed Markets ETF	PPDM	NYSE Arca	U	U	U		19.79	25.60	18.91	Y	Trading Tools (Growth)
PortfolioPlus Emerging Markets ETF	PPEM	NYSE Arca	U	U	U		18.83	25.90	18.73	Y	Trading Tools (Div Emerg Mkts)
● PortfolioPlus S&P 500® ETF	PPLC	NYSE Arca	C-	C	D+	Down	32.66	40.60	30.45	Y	Trading Tools (Growth)
PortfolioPlus S&P® Mid Cap ETF	PPMC	NYSE Arca	U	U	U		21.22	27.86	20.00	Y	Trading Tools (Growth)
PortfolioPlus S&P® Small Cap ETF	PPSC	NYSE Arca	D+	C-	D	Down	30.67	43.60	28.77	Y	Trading Tools (Small Company)
PPTY – U.S. Diversified Real Estate ETF	PPTY	NYSE Arca	U	U	U		25.83	29.00	24.89	Y	Real Estate Sector Equity (Real Estate)
Premise Capital Frontier Advantage Div Tactical ETF	TCTL	BATS	D+	D+	D+	Down	28.63	31.53	28.53	Y	Flexible Allocation (Growth & Inc)
● Principal Active Global Dividend Income ETF	GDVD	BATS	D+	D+	D+	Down	24.25	29.52	23.59	Y	Global Equity Large Cap (Growth & Inc)
Principal Contrarian Value Index ETF	PVAL	NAS CM	D	D	D		22.19	27.50	22.19	Y	US Equity Large Cap Value (Growth & Inc)
● Principal EDGE Active Income ETF	YLD	NYSE Arca	C-	C-	D+		37.93	41.70	37.44	Y	Cautious Allocation (Income)
Principal Healthcare Innovators Index ETF	BTEC	NAS CM	D+	C-	D+	Down	27.60	38.06	25.07	Y	Healthcare Sector Equity (Health)
Principal International Multi-Factor Index ETF	PXUS	NAS CM	D	D	E		98.95	106.29	98.95	Y	Global Equity Large Cap (Growth & Inc)
Principal Investment Grade Corporate Active ETF	IG	NYSE Arca	U	U	U		24.10	24.99	23.97	Y	US Fixed Income (Corp Bond - Gen)
Principal Millennials Index ETF	GENY	NAS CM	C-	C	D+		31.18	39.30	30.03	Y	Global Equity Large Cap (Growth & Inc)
Principal Price Setters Index ETF	PSET	NAS CM	C-	C	D+	Down	31.05	35.55	30.51	Y	US Equity Large Cap Growth (Growth & Inc)
Principal Shareholder Yield Index ETF	PY	NAS CM	C-	C-	D+	Down	27.67	34.81	27.03	Y	US Equity Mid Cap (Growth & Inc)
● Principal Spectrum Preferred Securities Active ETF	PREF	BATS	D	D	D+		90.07	100.79	89.81	Y	US Fixed Income (Equity-Income)
Principal Sustainable Momentum Index ETF	PMOM	NAS CM	D	D	D		24.17	30.52	23.01	Y	US Equity Large Cap Blend (Growth & Inc)
● Principal U.S. Mega-Cap Multi-Factor Index ETF	USMC	NAS CM	C-	C	C-		25.11	28.47	23.78	Y	US Equity Large Cap Blend (Growth & Inc)
● Principal U.S. Small-Cap Multi-Factor Index ETF	PSC	NAS CM	C-	C-	C-		27.78	35.73	26.04	Y	US Equity Small Cap (Small Company)
ProShares CDS Short North American HY Credit ETF	WYDE	BATS	D+	D	D+	Up	32.78	33.38	31.52	Y	Fixed Income Misc (Growth & Inc)

★Expanded analysis of this fund is included in Section II: Analysis of All BUY Rated Funds.   ● Expanded analysis of this fund is included in Section III: Analysis of All Rated Funds with Assets over $50 million.

		TOTAL RETURNS & PERFORMANCE							ASSETS		ASSET ALLOCATION & TURNOVER					VALUATION	
3-Month Total Return	6-Month Total Return	1-Year Total Return	3-Year Total Return	5-Year Total Return	Dividend Yield (TTM)	Expense Ratio	3-Yr Std Deviation	Effective Duration	NAV	Total Assets (MIL)	%Cash	%Stocks	%Bonds	%Other	Turnover Ratio	Premium/ Discount 1-Year Avg	Inception Date
-10.88						0.6			23.27	2.6	1	99	0	0		-0.14	Jul-18
-11.25	-10.01	-13.34			2.22	0.65			24.18	26.5	0	100	0	0		1.12	Jun-17
-9.02	-5.19	-7.56			3.59	0.6			27.99	192.2	0	100	0	0	76	0.15	Feb-16
-13.49	-6.54					0.6			23.75	2.6	0	100	0	0		0.57	Apr-18
-9.27	-2.12	8.83	38.15		0.3	0.65	13.05		32.67	331.0	100	0	0	0	3	0.16	Jun-15
-3.65	-7.78	-15.97	2.72		0.73	0.66			25.06	158.0	100	0	0	0	228	0.10	Dec-15
-7.98	-0.97	1.67	28.66		0.96	0.6	9.27		28.76	1,376	100	0	0	0	12	0.11	Jun-15
-5.89	-3.25	0.06	36.01		0.67	0.62	8.59		30.84	647.8	100	0	0	0	66	0.11	Jun-15
-15.91	-12.26	-9.30			1.43	0.49			25.77	184.1	0	100	0	0	101	0.21	Dec-16
-17.71						0.6			20.90	2.3	0	100	0	0		0.03	Jul-18
-17.98	-19.02	-9.72			1.31	0.59			23.17	23.2	0	100	0	0		0.22	Jun-17
-9.71	-7.87	-2.88				0.6			24.14	90.7	100	0	0	0		0.14	Dec-17
7.73						0.18			12.81	71.2	0	0	0	100		-0.44	Jul-18
-5.09						0.53		4.07	37.75	25.3	1	0	99	0		1.28	Sep-18
0.43	1.09					0.15		0.20	49.90	118.9	32	0	67	0	145	0.02	Apr-18
-4.00	-1.61	-0.55	20.55	15.44	4.82	0.56	3.82	2.07	95.44	1,369	-12	0	102	10	42	-0.32	Jun-11
1.25	1.44	1.42	2.40	3.33	1.58	0.16	0.76	1.86	50.15	55.0	1	0	99	0	54	-0.04	Jun-09
-0.26	-0.28	0.18	3.84	2.00	2.4	0.2	1.54	3.04	50.85	822.3	0	0	100	0	32	0.00	Aug-09
-1.80	-6.31	-7.38	10.99	20.87	3.41	0.2	8.4	21.71	62.33	199.5	0	0	100	0	10	-0.05	Sep-09
6.22	-0.19	-4.28	10.73	57.21	2.97	0.15	14.37	27.37	112.45	153.8	0	0	100	0	19	0.03	Oct-09
1.38	1.66	0.16	8.19	16.47	3.43	0.76	2.64	5.65	102.65	1,928	-32	0	131	0	142	-0.12	Feb-12
-0.24	-1.55	-1.72	6.39	8.69	2.43	0.21	3.46	8.02	55.96	54.8	1	0	99	0	8	0.04	Sep-09
0.21	0.96	1.33	6.45		2.77	1.02	0.9	1.48	98.65	222.4	-84	0	182	1	326	0.07	Jan-14
0.21	0.86	1.71	5.71	6.83	2.14	0.42	0.29	0.33	100.96	12,147	14	0	85	0	86	0.00	Nov-09
1.43	1.36	1.11	5.49	13.99	2.55	0.35	2.85	5.14	52.76	278.5	7	0	93	0	27	0.02	Nov-09
-0.21	0.81	-2.70	9.87	17.50	3.43	0.2	3.78	6.75	99.11	774.8	-11	0	111	0	10	-0.08	Sep-10
-7.10	-4.57	-12.73			1.37	0.49			22.07	345.9	2	98	0	0	52	0.29	Aug-17
-12.31	-10.21	-13.56			2.8	0.39			22.38	26.7	1	99	0	0	36	0.12	Aug-17
-14.79	-9.22	-6.58			1.83	0.29			25.21	71.0	1	99	0	0	56	0.18	Aug-17
0.79	0.84	1.37	3.12	4.90	1.64	0.35	1.13	1.90	49.80	80.1	5	0	95	0	87	-0.08	Feb-10
-16.17	-12.50	-14.30			0.43	0.72			23.37	35.3	1	99	0	0		0.26	Sep-17
-16.87	-14.35					0.47			19.85	21.5	14	87	0	-1		0.43	Feb-18
-10.90	-10.18					0.49			18.88	20.3	2	97	0	0		0.36	Feb-18
-17.23	-9.62	-6.86	35.50		1.93	0.37	11.77		32.75	78.2	0	100	0	0	92	-0.24	Jan-15
-20.65	-17.83					0.4			21.31	25.0	9	91	0	0		0.19	Feb-18
-23.45	-21.63	-11.67	31.37		2.15	0.49	18.37		30.76	7.3	10	90	0	0	300	0.51	Jan-15
-5.59	-5.02					0.53			25.88	90.9	0	100	0	0		-0.17	Mar-18
-6.37	-3.10	-3.13			1.39	0.95		1.88	28.69	33.2	7	8	85	0	195	0.06	Oct-16
-13.17	-9.48	-10.35			2.87	0.58			24.30	682.4	0	100	0	0	22	0.39	May-17
-17.01	-13.32	-13.49			1.4	0.29			22.39	3.8	0	100	0	0	62	-0.84	Oct-17
-6.19	-4.48	-4.87	19.75		4.78	0.65	5.41	4.44	37.22	292.6	3	21	69	0	11	0.22	Jul-15
-23.61	-21.07	-11.20			0.13	0.42			27.77	49.3	0	100	0	0	34	0.05	Aug-16
-13.61	-11.70	-14.40			2.56	0.39			84.73	13.4	0	100	0	0	54	4.09	Nov-17
-1.23	-0.77					0.26			24.00	222.6	1	0	99	0	48	0.32	Apr-18
-17.90	-14.22	-7.89			0.55	0.45			31.40	18.6	0	100	0	0	36	0.35	Aug-16
-10.54	-5.61	-1.43			1.15	0.29			31.22	17.1	0	100	0	0	64	0.06	Mar-16
-16.43	-13.05	-12.48			1.84	0.29			27.80	14.2	0	100	0	0	56	0.08	Mar-16
-4.40	-2.99	-6.09			5.35	0.55			89.28	50.4	1	0	80	0	41	0.59	Jul-17
-18.21	-12.66	-5.42			0.79	0.29			24.47	5.3	0	100	0	0	158	-0.79	Oct-17
-10.69	-2.02	-1.76			1.68	0.12			25.11	1,563	0	100	0	0	40	0.37	Oct-17
-19.36	-16.87	-9.22			0.97	0.38			27.78	347.6	0	100	0	0	76	0.63	Sep-16
4.42	1.23	1.39	-14.31		0	0.5	3.38		32.79	6.4	198	0	-98	0		0.80	Aug-14

Fund Name	Ticker Symbol	Traded On	Overall Rating	Reward Rating	Risk Rating	Recent Up/ Downgrade	Price as of 12/31/2018	52-Week High	52-Week Low	Open to New Investors	Category & (Prospectus Objective)
ProShares Decline of the Retail Store ETF	EMTY	NYSE Arca	C-	D+	D+		36.98	39.26	29.66	Y	Trading Tools (Unaligned)
ProShares DJ Brookfield Global Infrastructure ETF	TOLZ	NYSE Arca	C-	C-	C-	Down	38.15	44.06	37.16	Y	Infrastructure Sector Equity (Utility)
ProShares Equities for Rising Rates ETF	EQRR	NAS CM	C-	C	D+	Down	37.22	51.20	35.96	Y	US Equity Large Cap Blend (Growth & Inc)
ProShares Global Listed Private Equity ETF	PEX	BATS	C-	C	D+	Down	29.79	37.80	29.48	Y	Financials Sector Equity (Growth)
ProShares Hedge Replication ETF	HDG	NYSE Arca	D+	D+	D+	Down	43.07	46.26	42.69	Y	Multialternative (Growth)
● ProShares High Yield—Interest Rate Hedged	HYHG	BATS	C-	C-	C-	Down	62.09	68.99	61.54	Y	Fixed Income Misc (Income)
ProShares Inflation Expectations ETF	RINF	NYSE Arca	C-	C-	D+		26.88	30.08	26.82	Y	Fixed Income Misc (Govt Bond - Treasury)
● ProShares Investment Grade—Interest Rate Hedged	IGHG	BATS	C-	C-	C-		71.13	78.65	71.10	Y	Fixed Income Misc (Worldwide Bond)
ProShares K-1 Free Crude Oil Strategy ETF	OILK	BATS	D+	C-	D+	Down	17.13	28.66	16.55	Y	Commodities Specified (Natl Res)
● ProShares Large Cap Core Plus	CSM	BATS	C-	C-	C-	Down	60.62	72.75	57.18	Y	US Equity Large Cap Blend (Growth)
ProShares Long Online/Short Stores ETF	CLIX	NYSE Arca	C	B-	D		41.79	51.59	39.30	Y	Long/Short Equity (Growth & Inc)
ProShares Managed Futures Strategy ETF	FUT	BATS	D+	C-	D	Up	40.15	41.01	39.00	Y	Alternative Misc (Growth & Inc)
ProShares Merger ETF	MRGR	BATS	C-	C	D+	Up	36.98	37.56	34.74	Y	Market Neutral (Growth)
ProShares Morningstar Alternatives Solution ETF	ALTS	BATS	D+	D+	D+	Down	36.24	38.58	36.03	Y	Multialternative (Growth & Inc)
● ProShares MSCI EAFE Dividend Growers ETF	EFAD	BATS	D+	D+	C-	Down	33.39	40.39	32.66	Y	Global Equity Large Cap (Equity-Income)
ProShares MSCI Emerging Markets Dividend Growers ETF	EMDV	BATS	D+	D+	D+	Down	53.54	64.06	49.57	Y	Global Emerg Mkts Equity (Div Emerg Mkts)
ProShares MSCI Europe Dividend Growers ETF	EUDV	BATS	D	D+	D	Down	36.40	43.92	35.69	Y	Europe Equity Large Cap (Growth & Inc)
ProShares Online Retail ETF	ONLN	BATS	U	U	U		30.25	40.52	27.71	Y	Consumer Goods & Svcs (Growth)
ProShares RAFI® Long/Short	RALS	NYSE Arca	D	D	D+		35.85	37.73	35.08	Y	Market Neutral (Growth)
● ProShares Russell 2000 Dividend Growers ETF	SMDV	BATS	C	C	C-		53.83	60.04	51.53	Y	US Equity Small Cap (Growth)
● ProShares S&P 500 Dividend Aristocrats ETF	NOBL	BATS	C	C	C+	Down	60.54	68.36	57.62	Y	US Equity Large Cap Blend (Growth)
ProShares S&P 500® Bond ETF	SPXB	NYSE Arca	U	U	U		79.09	81.35	78.16	Y	US Fixed Income (Corp Bond - Gen)
ProShares S&P 500® ex-Energy ETF	SPXE	NYSE Arca	C-	C	D	Down	52.55	61.51	49.98	Y	US Equity Large Cap Blend (Growth & Inc)
ProShares S&P 500® ex-Financials ETF	SPXN	NYSE Arca	D+	C	E+	Down	51.33	59.89	48.75	Y	US Equity Large Cap Blend (Growth & Inc)
ProShares S&P 500® ex-Health Care ETF	SPXV	NYSE Arca	C-	C	D		51.22	60.55	48.72	Y	US Equity Large Cap Blend (Growth & Inc)
ProShares S&P 500® ex-Technology ETF	SPXT	NYSE Arca	D+	C	D	Down	47.67	56.14	45.42	Y	US Equity Large Cap Blend (Growth & Inc)
● ProShares S&P MidCap 400 Dividend Aristocrats ETF	REGL	BATS	C	C	C-		51.73	58.39	49.63	Y	US Equity Mid Cap (Growth)
● ProShares Short 20+ Year Treasury	TBF	NYSE Arca	C	D+	C		22.39	24.42	21.87	Y	Trading Tools (Govt Bond - Treasury)
ProShares Short 7-10 Year Treasury	TBX	NYSE Arca	C	C-	C-		28.47	29.77	28.31	Y	Trading Tools (Govt Bond - Treasury)
ProShares Short Basic Materials	SBM	NYSE Arca	D+	D	D	Up	20.77	22.08	16.90	Y	Trading Tools (Unaligned)
● ProShares Short Dow30	DOG	NYSE Arca	D	D	D-		61.34	65.91	54.07	Y	Trading Tools (Growth)
ProShares Short Euro	EUFX	NYSE Arca	C-	D+	D+	Up	43.08	43.57	38.37	Y	Trading Tools (Income)
ProShares Short Financials	SEF	NYSE Arca	D	D	D		25.43	26.98	21.74	Y	Trading Tools (Financial)
ProShares Short FTSE China 50	YXI	NYSE Arca	C-	D+	D	Up	21.04	21.84	16.42	Y	Trading Tools (Pacific Stock)
● ProShares Short High Yield	SJB	NYSE Arca	D+	D	D+		23.52	24.12	22.48	Y	Trading Tools (Corp Bond-High Yld)
ProShares Short MidCap400	MYY	NYSE Arca	D+	D	D+	Up	50.34	53.51	41.35	Y	Trading Tools (Growth)
ProShares Short MSCI EAFE	EFZ	NYSE Arca	C-	D	C-	Up	29.52	30.59	23.81	Y	Trading Tools (Foreign Stock)
● ProShares Short MSCI Emerging Markets	EUM	NYSE Arca	C-	D+	D+	Up	20.39	21.51	16.23	Y	Trading Tools (Div Emerg Mkts)
ProShares Short Oil & Gas	DDG	NYSE Arca	D+	D	D+	Up	27.56	29.53	20.67	Y	Trading Tools (Natl Res)
● ProShares Short QQQ	PSQ	NYSE Arca	D	D	D-		34.40	37.20	29.21	Y	Trading Tools (Growth)
ProShares Short Real Estate	REK	NYSE Arca	D+	D	D	Up	16.48	17.81	15.03	Y	Trading Tools (Real Estate)
● ProShares Short Russell2000	RWM	NYSE Arca	D	D	D		46.70	49.87	36.87	Y	Trading Tools (Small Company)
● ProShares Short S&P500	SH	NYSE Arca	D	D	D		31.33	33.59	27.20	Y	Trading Tools (Growth)
ProShares Short SmallCap600	SBB	NYSE Arca	D	D	D		37.12	39.49	29.00	Y	Trading Tools (Small Company)
ProShares Short Term USD Emerging Markets Bond ETF	EMSH	BATS	D+	C-	D		73.65	78.63	73.00	Y	Emerging Mkts Fixed Inc (Div Emerg Mkts)
● ProShares Short VIX Short-Term Futures ETF	SVXY	NYSE Arca	C-	C-	D	Up	42.30	138.21	9.58	Y	Alternative Misc (Growth)
ProShares Ultra 20+ Year Treasury	UBT	NYSE Arca	D	D	D	Down	76.87	83.58	65.19	Y	Trading Tools (Govt Bond - Treasury)
● ProShares Ultra 7-10 Year Treasury	UST	NYSE Arca	D	D	C-		55.79	57.41	51.24	Y	Trading Tools (Govt Bond - Treasury)
ProShares Ultra Basic Materials	UYM	NYSE Arca	C-	C	D+	Down	47.24	82.35	42.31	Y	Trading Tools (Unaligned)
● ProShares Ultra Bloomberg Crude Oil	UCO	NYSE Arca	D+	D+	D	Down	13.30	38.61	12.43	Y	Trading Tools (Natl Res)
ProShares Ultra Bloomberg Natural Gas	BOIL	NYSE Arca	D+	D+	D+	Up	25.82	71.96	25.20	Y	Trading Tools (Natl Res)
ProShares Ultra Consumer Goods	UGE	NYSE Arca	C-	C-	D+		34.00	51.94	31.84	Y	Trading Tools (Unaligned)

★ Expanded analysis of this fund is included in Section II: Analysis of All BUY Rated Funds. ● Expanded analysis of this fund is included in Section III: Analysis of All Rated Funds with Assets over $50 million.

			TOTAL RETURNS & PERFORMANCE						ASSETS		ASSET ALLOCATION & TURNOVER					VALUATION	
3-Month Total Return	6-Month Total Return	1-Year Total Return	3-Year Total Return	5-Year Total Return	Dividend Yield (TTM)	Expense Ratio	3-Yr Std Deviation	Effective Duration	NAV	Total Assets (MIL)	%Cash	%Stocks	%Bonds	%Other	Turnover Ratio	Premium/ Discount 1-Year Avg	Inception Date
21.63	15.12	10.60			0.51	0.65			36.89	5.7	200	-100	0	0		-0.32	Nov-17
-7.83	-6.61	-7.97	16.49		3.45	0.46	9.48		38.12	46.6	0	99	0	1		0.09	Mar-14
-24.34	-20.91	-17.87			1.86	0.35			37.39	7.7	0	100	0	0		0.33	Jul-17
-15.62	-13.16	-13.20	10.84	12.69	20.46	2.78	11.5		29.89	19.8	3	76	0	21		0.31	Feb-13
-4.90	-3.84	-4.20	3.27	3.86	0.32	0.95	3.52		43.18	43.4	60	40	0	0		-0.07	Jul-11
-8.08	-4.25	-2.82	16.29	2.59	6.02	0.5	5.64		62.09	187.2	2	0	98	0		0.01	May-13
-7.69	-6.39	-1.32	1.31	-19.42	2.84	0.3	6.8		26.86	14.3	-148	0	248	0		-0.14	Jan-12
-5.31	-2.09	-4.73	7.94	3.58	3.83	0.3	5.18		71.00	457.0	52	0	48	0		0.01	Nov-13
-39.83	-36.54	-21.39			6.95	0.65			16.96	27.8	0	0	0	100		0.17	Sep-16
-15.73	-9.60	-7.83	28.46	48.49	1.28	0.45	9.5		60.64	806.8	0	100	0	0		0.06	Jul-09
-11.49	-15.30	6.98			0	0.65			41.99	47.6	50	50	0	0		0.03	Nov-17
-1.40	0.63	0.63			0.32	0.75			40.14	3.1	122	0	-12	-10		0.09	Feb-16
2.05	4.63	3.72	4.55	1.57	1.46	0.75	2.62		36.97	3.7	39	83	0	-22		0.13	Dec-12
-4.19	-2.77	-3.68	0.77		3.26	0.95	3.38		36.09	7.5	25	43	37	-5		-0.10	Oct-14
-11.95	-10.03	-11.49	0.04		3.06	0.5	10.51		33.52	109.3	1	97	0	2		-0.03	Aug-14
-0.93	-1.23	-6.71	36.58		2.25	0.6			54.00	20.4	1	99	0	0		0.08	Jan-16
-12.86	-10.96	-11.22	0.06		2.78	0.55	11.52		36.45	10.6	1	96	0	3		-0.02	Sep-15
-20.58						0.58			30.25	28.9	0	100	0	0		0.12	Jul-18
0.23	-0.54	-2.94	-2.94	-9.04	1.62	0.95	3.18		35.80	10.9	100	0	0	0		0.02	Dec-10
-6.96	-5.53	-0.70	40.93		1.75	0.4	10.97		53.80	463.0	0	100	0	0		0.01	Feb-15
-9.11	-1.42	-3.17	30.78	51.59	2.1	0.35	9.31		60.53	3,799	0	100	0	0		0.00	Oct-13
-0.06	1.26					0.15			78.85	27.4	1	0	99	0		0.16	May-18
-13.13	-6.25	-3.75	31.13		1.39	0.27	9.42		52.81	7.3	1	99	0	0		0.25	Sep-15
-14.14	-6.80	-3.03	30.26		1.55	0.27	9.31		51.59	1.4	1	99	0	0		-0.43	Sep-15
-14.62	-9.03	-6.38	29.74		1.64	0.27	9.36		51.46	1.4	0	100	0	0		0.31	Sep-15
-12.78	-6.43	-6.19	22.18		1.69	0.27	9.5		47.90	2.7	1	99	0	0		0.07	Sep-15
-7.92	-4.31	-3.15	38.73		1.91	0.4	10.26		51.74	417.8	0	100	0	0		0.04	Feb-15
-4.01	-0.05	3.81	-8.24	-31.07	0.46	0.91	9.71		22.49	508.1	150	0	3	-53	0	0.09	Aug-09
-3.03	-1.62	1.30	-2.87	-15.07	0.44	0.95	4.68		28.47	41.7	160	0	0	-60	0	-0.01	Apr-11
16.82	15.66	17.64	-25.42	-23.73	0.17	0.95	14.8		20.68	0.97	200	0	0	-100		-0.63	Mar-10
13.06	3.15	3.48	-31.49	-40.70	0.64	0.95	9.67		61.33	224.3	148	-51	3	0	0	-0.02	Jun-06
2.11	3.17	7.69	-1.51	20.91	0	0.97	6.98			8.7	100	0	0	0		-0.17	Jun-12
13.09	9.55	9.64	-24.98	-38.36	0.15	0.95	11.68		25.31	24.6	200	0	0	-100		-0.12	Jun-08
7.44	4.11	9.40	-27.71	-37.07	0.01	0.95	18.02		21.04	6.0	201	-101	0	0		0.03	Mar-10
5.08	2.06	2.47	-17.27	-19.43	0.42	0.95	4.04		23.53	124.8	160	0	0	-60		-0.02	Mar-11
19.44	16.58	12.51	-22.29	-31.62	0.26	0.95	11.78		50.35	17.7	200	-100	0	0	77,384	-0.10	Jun-06
14.62	12.09	16.31	-11.73	-10.88	0.09	0.95	10.52		29.51	44.1	164	-36	0	-28		-0.02	Oct-07
7.22	6.71	14.60	-30.16	-21.89	0.23	0.95	14.73		20.39	237.9	158	-58	0	0	0	-0.02	Oct-07
33.38	28.48	19.74	-11.06	11.88	0	0.95	18.66		27.59	1.8	200	0	0	-100		-0.10	Jun-08
18.29	10.00	-2.20	-33.33	-52.28	0.71	0.95	12.5		34.45	420.9	148	-51	4	0		-0.03	Jun-06
5.27	5.41	4.35	-14.55	-37.70	0.15	0.95	11.31		16.48	9.2	200	0	0	-100		0.03	Mar-10
22.46	21.29	11.50	-23.95	-30.07	0.73	0.95	14.5		46.69	245.4	150	-54	4	0	0	-0.01	Jan-07
15.58	7.98	4.86	-24.04	-37.16	0.84	0.89	9.1		31.36	1,639	147	-51	4	0		-0.01	Jun-06
22.25	19.92	8.10	-28.31	-35.64	0	0.95	14.42		37.03	3.9	200	-100	0	0	0	0.04	Jan-07
0.07	0.97	-0.76	10.62	15.15	3.38	0.5	2.46		73.94	7.4	0	0	100	0		-0.32	Nov-13
-29.90	224.92	-67.37	63.47	23.06	0	1.38	72.09			410.8	150	-50	0	0		-0.12	Oct-11
8.70	0.41	-7.51	6.59	59.09	1.69	0.95	19.1		76.12	29.2	-101	0	86	115	48	-0.20	Jan-10
7.04	4.43	-1.29	2.28	22.41	1.45	0.95	9.24		55.67	58.6	-100	0	67	132	188	-0.03	Jan-10
-29.63	-28.94	-34.96	34.66	0.52	0.65	0.95	29.56		47.65	44.7	-100	104	0	96		0.07	Jan-07
-65.60	-61.26	-45.11	-48.36	-95.95	0	0.95	55.22			347.6	-100	0	0	200	0	-0.17	Nov-08
-2.84	10.78	-4.52	-66.43	-95.98	0	1.31	72.63			37.5	-100	0	0	200		-0.02	Oct-11
-20.19	-18.30	-29.18	0.93	33.89	0.57	0.95	16.79		34.35	7.4	-100	92	0	108		0.09	Jan-07

Fund Name	Ticker Symbol	Traded On	Overall Rating	Reward Rating	Risk Rating	Recent Up/Downgrade	Price as of 12/31/2018	52-Week High	52-Week Low	Open to New Investors	Category & (Prospectus Objective)
ProShares Ultra Consumer Services	UCC	NYSE Arca	C	C	D+	Down	77.29	110.40	68.00	Y	Trading Tools (Unaligned)
● ProShares Ultra Dow30	DDM	NYSE Arca	C+	C	C+	Down	37.82	50.80	33.20	Y	Trading Tools (Growth)
ProShares Ultra Euro	ULE	NYSE Arca	D	D	D+	Down	15.12	18.87	14.69	Y	Trading Tools (Worldwide Bond)
● ProShares Ultra Financials	UYG	NYSE Arca	C	C	C-		32.62	47.70	29.07	Y	Trading Tools (Financial)
ProShares Ultra FTSE China 50	XPP	NYSE Arca	D+	C-	D+	Down	56.73	113.72	54.73	Y	Trading Tools (Pacific Stock)
ProShares Ultra FTSE Europe	UPV	NYSE Arca	D+	D+	D		37.95	66.51	36.85	Y	Trading Tools (Europe Stock)
● ProShares Ultra Gold	UGL	NYSE Arca	D	D	D	Down	37.41	43.96	31.97	Y	Trading Tools (Prec Metals)
ProShares Ultra Gold Miners	GDXX	NYSE Arca	D	D	D-		31.61	47.24	22.59	Y	Trading Tools (Prec Metals)
● ProShares Ultra Health Care	RXL	NYSE Arca	C	C	C-		90.92	117.11	80.30	Y	Trading Tools (Health)
ProShares Ultra High Yield	UJB	NYSE Arca	D	C-	E+	Down	59.69	68.43	58.33	Y	Trading Tools (Corp Bond-High Yld)
ProShares Ultra Industrials	UXI	NYSE Arca	C-	C	D+		52.30	83.08	46.66	Y	Trading Tools (Unaligned)
● ProShares Ultra MidCap400	MVV	NYSE Arca	C	C	C		30.40	46.96	27.06	Y	Trading Tools (Growth)
ProShares Ultra MSCI Brazil Capped	UBR	NYSE Arca	C-	C	D+	Up	63.09	105.40	42.40	Y	Trading Tools (Foreign Stock)
ProShares Ultra MSCI EAFE	EFO	NYSE Arca	D	D+	D	Down	30.51	50.21	28.88	Y	Trading Tools (Foreign Stock)
ProShares Ultra MSCI Emerging Markets	EET	NYSE Arca	D+	C-	D+	Down	62.06	114.44	57.30	Y	Trading Tools (Div Emerg Mkts)
ProShares Ultra MSCI Japan	EZJ	NYSE Arca	D+	D+	D+		28.63	50.10	28.10	Y	Trading Tools (Pacific Stock)
● ProShares Ultra Nasdaq Biotechnology	BIB	NAS CM	D+	D+	D+	Down	42.09	70.14	36.42	Y	Trading Tools (Technology)
● ProShares Ultra Oil & Gas	DIG	NYSE Arca	C-	C-	D	Down	23.33	46.73	20.85	Y	Trading Tools (Natl Res)
● ProShares Ultra QQQ	QLD	NYSE Arca	C	C	C	Down	67.19	101.71	58.52	Y	Trading Tools (Growth)
● ProShares Ultra Real Estate	URE	NYSE Arca	C-	C-	C-	Down	56.01	69.69	51.57	Y	Trading Tools (Real Estate)
● ProShares Ultra Russell2000	UWM	NYSE Arca	C	C	C-	Down	52.13	88.97	46.50	Y	Trading Tools (Small Company)
● ProShares Ultra S&P500	SSO	NYSE Arca	C	C	C+	Down	92.82	129.09	81.81	Y	Trading Tools (Growth)
ProShares Ultra Semiconductors	USD	NYSE Arca	C	C	C-	Down	29.61	53.17	25.73	Y	Trading Tools (Technology)
● ProShares Ultra Silver	AGQ	NYSE Arca	D-	D-	D-	Down	26.37	36.22	21.84	Y	Trading Tools (Prec Metals)
ProShares Ultra SmallCap600	SAA	NYSE Arca	C-	C	D+	Down	77.30	134.04	69.10	Y	Trading Tools (Small Company)
● ProShares Ultra Technology	ROM	NYSE Arca	C+	C+	C	Down	78.85	123.16	68.54	Y	Trading Tools (Technology)
ProShares Ultra Telecommunications	LTL	NYSE Arca	D	D+	D	Down	32.38	45.86	30.18	Y	Trading Tools (Comm)
ProShares Ultra Utilities	UPW	NYSE Arca	C	C+	D+		47.16	54.82	39.28	Y	Trading Tools (Utility)
● ProShares Ultra VIX Short-Term Futures ETF	UVXY	NYSE Arca	C-	C	D	Up	81.73	88.08	8.67	Y	Alternative Misc (Growth)
ProShares Ultra Yen	YCL	NYSE Arca	D	D	D		57.55	65.73	53.53	Y	Trading Tools (Worldwide Bond)
● ProShares UltraPro 3x Crude Oil ETF	OILU	NYSE Arca	D+	D+	D	Down	13.47	73.04	12.37	Y	Trading Tools (Growth & Inc)
ProShares UltraPro 3x Short Crude Oil ETF	OILD	NYSE Arca	D	D	D		48.43	59.09	14.50	Y	Trading Tools (Growth & Inc)
● ProShares UltraPro Dow30	UDOW	NYSE Arca	C	C	C	Down	71.31	116.82	59.11	Y	Trading Tools (Growth)
ProShares UltraPro Financial Select Sector	FINU	NYSE Arca	C-	C	C-	Down	56.48	132.33	47.72	Y	Trading Tools (Financial)
ProShares UltraPro MidCap400	UMDD	NYSE Arca	C-	C	D+	Down	69.51	138.30	59.31	Y	Trading Tools (Growth)
ProShares UltraPro Nasdaq Biotechnology	UBIO	NAS CM	D+	D+	D	Down	20.00	45.49	16.09	Y	Trading Tools (Technology)
● ProShares UltraPro QQQ	TQQQ	NAS CM	C	C	C-	Down	37.04	72.50	30.39	Y	Trading Tools (Growth)
● ProShares UltraPro Russell2000	URTY	NYSE Arca	C-	C	D+	Down	49.58	113.67	41.91	Y	Trading Tools (Small Company)
● ProShares UltraPro S&P500	UPRO	NYSE Arca	C	C	C	Down	34.78	58.37	29.00	Y	Trading Tools (Growth)
● ProShares UltraPro Short 20+ Year Treasury	TTT	NYSE Arca	C-	D+	D+	Up	25.73	32.97	24.30	Y	Trading Tools (Govt Bond - Treasury)
● ProShares UltraPro Short Dow30	SDOW	NYSE Arca	D-	E+	D-		19.20	23.89	13.73	Y	Trading Tools (Growth)
ProShares UltraPro Short Financial Select Sector	FINZ	NYSE Arca	D	D-	D	Up	10.67	12.91	6.46	Y	Trading Tools (Financial)
ProShares UltraPro Short MidCap400	SMDD	NYSE Arca	D	D-	D	Up	13.38	16.18	7.67	Y	Trading Tools (Growth)
ProShares UltraPro Short Nasdaq Biotechnology	ZBIO	NAS CM	D	D-	D		21.98	28.33	12.79	Y	Trading Tools (Technology)
● ProShares UltraPro Short QQQ	SQQQ	NAS CM	D	E+	D-	Up	16.76	21.77	11.08	Y	Trading Tools (Growth)
ProShares UltraPro Short Russell2000	SRTY	NYSE Arca	D	D-	D	Up	39.56	48.34	20.48	Y	Trading Tools (Small Company)
● ProShares UltraPro Short S&P500	SPXU	NYSE Arca	D	D-	D-	Up	46.54	57.55	31.83	Y	Trading Tools (Growth)
● ProShares UltraShort 20+ Year Treasury	TBT	NYSE Arca	C	D+	C	Up	35.13	41.62	33.78	Y	Trading Tools (Govt Bond - Treasury)
● ProShares UltraShort 7-10 Year Treasury	PST	NYSE Arca	C	C-	C-		21.78	23.88	21.55	Y	Trading Tools (Govt Bond - Treasury)
ProShares UltraShort Australian Dollar	CROC	NYSE Arca	C	C-	D+	Up	54.92	55.41	42.26	Y	Trading Tools (Income)
ProShares UltraShort Basic Materials	SMN	NYSE Arca	D+	D	D	Up	35.02	39.32	23.62	Y	Trading Tools (Unaligned)
● ProShares UltraShort Bloomberg Crude Oil	SCO	NYSE Arca	D	D-	D		29.28	33.13	12.52	Y	Trading Tools (Natl Res)

★ Expanded analysis of this fund is included in Section II: Analysis of All BUY Rated Funds.   ● Expanded analysis of this fund is included in Section III: Analysis of All Rated Funds with Assets over $50 million.

3-Month Total Return	6-Month Total Return	1-Year Total Return	3-Year Total Return	5-Year Total Return	Dividend Yield (TTM)	Expense Ratio	3-Yr Std Deviation	Effective Duration	NAV	Total Assets (MIL)	%Cash	%Stocks	%Bonds	%Other	Turnover Ratio	Premium/Discount 1-Year Avg	Inception Date
-28.51	-15.85	-3.21	47.11	103.84	0.12	0.95	23.58		78.02	21.5	-100	96	0	104		0.04	Jan-07
-24.59	-9.24	-13.35	81.33	106.86	0.72	0.95	20.69		37.76	398.1	-100	54	0	146		0.05	Jun-06
-3.57	-5.36	-13.63	-2.89	-42.14	0	1.01	13.86			7.4	100	0	0	0	0	-0.03	Nov-08
-24.15	-19.26	-22.52	41.55	73.00	0.87	0.95	24.62		32.63	810.6	-100	107	0	93		-0.02	Jan-07
-17.85	-15.87	-31.43	18.87	-0.68	0	0.95	37.49		56.73	27.8	-100	200	0	0		-0.01	Jun-09
-26.12	-25.07	-32.28	-0.99	-22.91	0	0.95	24.67		37.98	6.6	-100	200	0	0	0	0.43	Apr-10
13.94	2.23	-6.87	24.91	-9.99	0	0.95	26.02			76.1	-41	0	0	141	0	0.33	Dec-08
26.15	-13.33	-24.91	50.42		0	1.28	78.99		31.56	7.8	-100	72	0	127		0.08	Feb-15
-21.33	1.85	5.39	40.14	130.10	0.24	0.95	25.71		91.97	151.4	-100	103	0	97		0.29	Jan-07
-9.80	-4.52	-5.99	32.14	20.49	2.94	1.31	8.1	3.78	59.66	3.2	-100	0	61	138	12	0.39	Apr-11
-34.30	-22.03	-26.79	50.18	54.52	0.23	0.95	25.09		52.87	18.3	-100	84	0	116		0.36	Jan-07
-32.12	-28.75	-25.65	35.91	45.24	0.42	0.95	23.8		30.30	120.1	-100	200	0	0		0.06	Jun-06
26.26	35.09	-18.70	150.43	-53.12	0	0.95	70.25		63.30	7.9	-100	200	0	0	0	-0.13	Apr-10
-25.42	-22.64	-30.42	2.70	-18.14	0	0.95	21.4		30.66	6.9	-100	200	0	0	145	-0.17	Jun-09
-16.87	-18.14	-33.79	38.48	-18.20	0	0.95	31.18		62.05	23.5	-100	200	0	0	163	0.13	Jun-09
-29.86	-21.71	-30.46	3.46	-0.23	0	0.95	21.05		28.52	6.2	-101	201	0	0		0.20	Jun-09
-38.17	-27.13	-24.36	-40.62	12.62	0	0.95	44.74		42.41	316.2	-100	121	0	78		0.00	Apr-10
-47.41	-44.06	-40.03	-18.12	-64.17	1.73	0.95	37.61		23.35	92.4	-100	100	0	99		0.01	Jan-07
-33.54	-23.50	-8.37	71.88	171.23	0	0.95	26.87		67.10	1,834	-100	200	0	0		0.04	Jun-06
-11.84	-12.68	-13.52	11.26	75.04	1.28	0.95	23.82		56.17	138.2	-100	104	0	96		-0.04	Jan-07
-36.22	-35.11	-25.75	32.73	23.87	0.17	0.95	29.29		52.23	180.9	-100	200	0	0		0.00	Jan-07
-27.57	-16.76	-14.43	49.60	85.89	0.56	0.9	19.09		92.74	2,472	-100	200	0	0		0.02	Jun-06
-33.91	-31.83	-26.27	110.95	244.28	0.63	0.95	37.67		29.77	45.2	-100	74	0	126		0.04	Jan-07
8.55	-11.46	-23.00	-4.54	-59.20	0	0.95	39.17			173.3	-100	0	0	200	0	0.30	Dec-08
-35.98	-33.87	-21.59	47.60	47.43	0.01	0.95	29.78		77.82	28.1	-100	200	0	0		0.36	Jan-07
-34.74	-24.84	-10.04	102.75	189.67	0.17	0.95	30.24		78.86	298.8	-100	102	0	98		0.03	Jan-07
-22.86	-11.47	-21.87	-18.45	-22.69	0.81	0.95	26.41		32.84	1.0	-100	88	0	113		0.41	Mar-08
0.40	1.77	2.67	64.84	127.42	1.78	0.95	23.77		47.44	15.7	-100	98	0	102		-0.13	Jan-07
139.15	608.76	738.37	-96.91	-99.74	0	1.65	83.73			259.3	-50	150	0	0		0.40	Oct-11
5.48	-1.39	-0.68	3.98	-23.60	0	1.01	20.65			2.7	100	0	0	0	0	0.17	Nov-08
-81.61	-78.57	-65.64			0	0.49				62.8	-200	0	0	300		-0.25	Mar-17
233.67	151.14	18.56			0	0.49				28.2	400	0	0	-300		0.27	Mar-17
-35.82	-15.77	-23.51	123.64	157.66	0.44	0.95	31.7		71.37	534.5	-200	300	0	0		0.10	Feb-10
-39.27	-33.51	-45.49	47.13	85.91	0.44	0.95	46.98		57.33	40.2	-200	81	0	219		0.12	Jul-12
-45.29	-41.47	-38.91	42.89	50.60	0.03	0.95	35.89		70.12	31.1	-200	300	0	0		0.50	Feb-10
-53.50	-41.17	-40.36	-65.27		0	0.95	65.15		20.06	34.2	-200	77	0	223		-0.02	Jun-15
-48.16	-36.46	-19.64	95.08	259.19	0	0.95	41.14		37.08	4,353	-200	300	0	0		0.07	Feb-10
-50.51	-49.52	-39.52	34.17	12.51	0	0.95	44.08		49.75	120.2	-200	300	0	0		-0.02	Feb-10
-39.82	-26.18	-24.91	67.31	119.24	0.24	0.92	29.06		34.73	1,516	-200	300	0	0		0.12	Jun-09
-12.91	-2.74	6.46	-31.01	-72.75	0.15	0.95	29.2		25.83	83.0	401	0	-2	-299		0.28	Mar-12
37.74	3.70	-0.69	-72.54	-83.47	0.98	0.95	27.51		19.20	166.1	247	-151	5	0		-0.11	Feb-10
43.63	26.58	27.66	-71.96	-86.00	0.17	0.95	40.29		10.50	1.1	400	0	0	-300		-0.37	Jul-12
62.97	49.95	29.43	-61.17	-75.74	0	0.95	35.04		13.32	2.1	400	-300	0	0	0	-1.17	Feb-10
67.00	24.47	-4.05	-46.46		0	0.95	78.92		21.89	3.3	400	0	0	-300		-0.11	Jun-15
52.20	20.45	-20.93	-77.18	-92.56	1.29	0.95	35.35		16.75	581.8	238	-145	7	0		-0.10	Feb-10
73.27	65.76	23.14	-65.85	-76.74	0.61	0.95	43.15		39.50	49.8	283	-183	0	0		0.06	Feb-10
46.86	18.61	3.75	-62.53	-80.34	1.31	0.91	26.26		46.62	419.3	245	-152	7	0	0	-0.08	Jun-09
-8.32	-1.05	5.85	-18.80	-54.99	0.51	0.89	19.42		35.36	1,554	206	0	3	-110		0.20	Apr-08
-6.28	-3.71	1.85	-5.70	-27.26	0.28	0.95	9.37		21.84	116.3	211	0	0	-111	0	0.07	Apr-08
5.10	7.66	20.88	-5.43	18.81	0	1.03	18.61			7.7	100	0	0	0		0.07	Jul-12
33.73	29.73	30.61	-49.53	-49.32	0	0.95	29.47		34.67	6.7	300	0	0	-200	0	-0.32	Jan-07
133.38	96.03	23.16	-55.04	88.75	0	0.95	60.1			121.5	300	0	0	-200	0	0.17	Nov-08

Fund Name	Ticker Symbol	Traded On	Overall Rating	Reward Rating	Risk Rating	Recent Up/ Downgrade	Price as of 12/31/2018	52-Week High	52-Week Low	Open to New Investors	Category & (Prospectus Objective)
ProShares UltraShort Bloomberg Natural Gas	KOLD	NYSE Arca	D	E+	D-	Down	21.22	47.05	11.00	Y	Trading Tools (Natl Res)
ProShares UltraShort Consumer Goods	SZK	NYSE Arca	C-	D	D+	Up	18.09	19.55	12.92	Y	Trading Tools (Unaligned)
ProShares UltraShort Consumer Services	SCC	NYSE Arca	D	D	D-		21.93	25.29	16.52	Y	Trading Tools (Unaligned)
● ProShares UltraShort Dow30	DXD	NYSE Arca	D	D-	D-		35.40	40.95	27.91	Y	Trading Tools (Growth)
● ProShares UltraShort Euro	EUO	NYSE Arca	C	D+	C	Up	24.25	25.00	19.54	Y	Trading Tools (Worldwide Bond)
ProShares UltraShort Financials	SKF	NYSE Arca	D	D	D		24.32	27.57	18.00	Y	Trading Tools (Financial)
ProShares UltraShort FTSE China 50	FXP	NYSE Arca	D	D	D		76.80	84.08	49.48	Y	Trading Tools (Pacific Stock)
ProShares UltraShort FTSE Europe	EPV	NYSE Arca	C-	D	D+	Up	40.89	43.90	26.89	Y	Trading Tools (Europe Stock)
ProShares UltraShort Gold	GLL	NYSE Arca	C-	D+	D+	Up	72.84	86.19	63.71	Y	Trading Tools (Prec Metals)
ProShares UltraShort Gold Miners	GDXS	NYSE Arca	D+	D	D	Up	14.37	22.48	12.36	Y	Trading Tools (Prec Metals)
ProShares UltraShort Health Care	RXD	NYSE Arca	D	D-	D-		25.72	31.64	21.42	Y	Trading Tools (Health)
ProShares UltraShort Industrials	SIJ	NYSE Arca	D	D-	D		20.21	23.04	13.84	Y	Trading Tools (Unaligned)
ProShares UltraShort MidCap400	MZZ	NYSE Arca	D	D	D		22.89	25.98	15.62	Y	Trading Tools (Growth)
ProShares UltraShort MSCI Brazil Capped	BZQ	NYSE Arca	D	E+	D		35.85	66.75	32.15	Y	Trading Tools (Foreign Stock)
ProShares UltraShort MSCI EAFE	EFU	NYSE Arca	D+	D	D+	Up	30.10	32.08	19.90	Y	Trading Tools (Foreign Stock)
ProShares UltraShort MSCI Emerging Markets	EEV	NYSE Arca	D+	D+	D	Up	51.72	57.72	34.15	Y	Trading Tools (Div Emerg Mkts)
ProShares UltraShort MSCI Japan	EWV	NYSE Arca	D+	D	D	Up	34.36	36.47	22.81	Y	Trading Tools (Pacific Stock)
ProShares UltraShort Nasdaq Biotechnology	BIS	NAS CM	D	D	D		23.10	27.27	15.60	Y	Trading Tools (Technology)
ProShares UltraShort Oil & Gas	DUG	NYSE Arca	D+	D	D+	Up	50.24	57.58	28.25	Y	Trading Tools (Natl Res)
● ProShares UltraShort QQQ	QID	NYSE Arca	D	D-	D-	Up	47.54	55.66	35.18	Y	Trading Tools (Growth)
ProShares UltraShort Real Estate	SRS	NYSE Arca	D	D	D		30.84	36.90	25.85	Y	Trading Tools (Real Estate)
● ProShares UltraShort Russell2000	TWM	NYSE Arca	D	D-	D		20.62	23.50	13.04	Y	Trading Tools (Small Company)
● ProShares UltraShort S&P500	SDS	NYSE Arca	D	D-	D-		42.92	49.43	32.86	Y	Trading Tools (Growth)
ProShares UltraShort Semiconductors	SSG	NYSE Arca	D	D-	D	Up	20.45	23.66	13.82	Y	Trading Tools (Technology)
ProShares UltraShort Silver	ZSL	NYSE Arca	C	C-	D+	Up	37.10	45.45	29.20	Y	Trading Tools (Prec Metals)
ProShares UltraShort SmallCap600	SDD	NYSE Arca	D	D-	D	Up	17.70	20.11	10.94	Y	Trading Tools (Small Company)
ProShares UltraShort Technology	REW	NYSE Arca	D	D-	D-	Up	14.73	17.36	10.58	Y	Trading Tools (Technology)
ProShares UltraShort Utilities	SDP	NYSE Arca	D	D-	D-		22.87	30.89	20.04	Y	Trading Tools (Utility)
● ProShares UltraShort Yen	YCS	NYSE Arca	C	C-	C-	Up	73.86	79.20	65.13	Y	Trading Tools (Worldwide Bond)
ProShares VIX Mid-Term Futures ETF	VIXM	NYSE Arca	D	D-	D	Up	26.74	27.48	19.99	Y	Alternative Misc (Growth)
● ProShares VIX Short-Term Futures ETF	VIXY	NYSE Arca	D-	E+	D	Up	38.61	45.77	21.43	Y	Alternative Misc (Growth)
ProSports Sponsors ETF	FANZ	BATS	D	D+	E+	Down	20.39	23.77	19.45	Y	Consumer Goods & Svcs (Growth & Inc)
QuantX Dynamic Beta US Equity ETF	XUSA	BATS	C	C	C	Up	26.76	31.05	25.74	Y	US Equity Large Cap Blend (Equity-Income)
QUANTX Risk Managed Growth ETF	QXGG	BATS	D+	D+	D+		27.31	29.14	26.87	Y	Global Equity Large Cap (Growth)
QUANTX Risk Managed Multi-Asset Total Return ETF	QXTR	BATS	D+	D+	D+		23.80	26.83	23.37	Y	Moderate Allocation (Multi-Asset Global)
Reality Shares Divcon Dividend Defender ETF	DFND	BATS	C-	C-	D+		26.62	28.63	25.91	Y	Long/Short Equity (Income)
Reality Shares Divcon Dividend Guard ETF	GARD	BATS	C-	C-	C-	Down	24.02	26.84	23.39	Y	Long/Short Equity (Income)
Reality Shares Divcon Leaders Dividend ETF	LEAD	BATS	C	C	C-		29.44	34.84	27.76	Y	US Equity Large Cap Growth (Growth & Inc)
● Reality Shares DIVS ETF	DIVY	NYSE Arca	C-	C-	C-	Down	25.00	27.50	24.84	Y	Multialternative (Growth)
Reality Shares Nasdaq NexGen Economy China ETF	BCNA	NAS CM	U	U	U		18.09	24.20	17.92	Y	Greater China Equity (Growth)
Reality Shares Nasdaq NexGen Economy ETF	BLCN	NAS CM	U	U	U		19.40	25.03	18.83	Y	Technology Sector Equity (Growth)
★ Reaves Utilities ETF	UTES	NYSE Arca	B	B	C+	Up	33.52	36.09	29.65	Y	Utilities Sector Equity (Utility)
Reinhart Intermediate Bond NextShares	RPIBC	NAS CM	U	U	U		20.06	100.03	19.73	Y	US Fixed Income (Corp Bond - Gen)
Renaissance International IPO ETF	IPOS	NYSE Arca	D	D+	D	Down	18.77	26.58	18.10	Y	Global Eq Mid/Small Cap (Foreign Stock)
Renaissance IPO ETF	IPO	NYSE Arca	C-	C-	D+	Down	23.26	31.62	21.70	Y	US Equity Mid Cap (Growth)
Reverse Cap Weighted U.S. Large Cap ETF	RVRS	BATS	D	D	D+		14.11	17.15	13.59	Y	US Equity Large Cap Blend (Growth & Inc)
REX BKCM ETF	BKC	NYSE Arca	U	U	U		18.85	25.81	18.20	Y	Technology Sector Equity (Growth & Inc)
● RiverFront Dynamic Core Income ETF	RFCI	NYSE Arca	D+	D+	C-		23.72	24.70	23.48	Y	US Fixed Income (Income)
RiverFront Dynamic Unconstrained Income ETF	RFUN	NYSE Arca	D+	D+	C-	Down	23.87	26.16	23.55	Y	Fixed Income Misc (Income)
● RiverFront Dynamic US Dividend Advantage ETF	RFDA	NYSE Arca	C-	C-	C-		28.12	33.90	26.47	Y	US Equity Large Cap Blend (Growth & Inc)
● RiverFront Dynamic US Flex-Cap ETF	RFFC	NYSE Arca	C-	C	C-		29.02	36.35	27.40	Y	US Equity Large Cap Blend (Growth)
● RiverFront Strategic Income Fund	RIGS	NYSE Arca	C	C	C-		24.03	25.25	23.90	Y	Global Fixed Income (Income)

★ Expanded analysis of this fund is included in Section II: Analysis of All BUY Rated Funds. ● Expanded analysis of this fund is included in Section III: Analysis of All Rated Funds with Assets over $50 million.

3-Month Total Return	6-Month Total Return	1-Year Total Return	3-Year Total Return	5-Year Total Return	Dividend Yield (TTM)	Expense Ratio	3-Yr Std Deviation	Effective Duration	NAV	Total Assets (MIL)	%Cash	%Stocks	%Bonds	%Other	Turnover Ratio	Premium/Discount 1-Year Avg	Inception Date
-45.84	-54.67	-53.96	-60.93	-22.05	0	1.54	74			23.8	300	0	0	-200		0.00	Oct-11
22.18	18.46	31.06	-17.90	-48.10	0.35	0.95	16.09		17.96	1.7	300	-20	0	-180	73	-0.23	Jan-07
29.18	8.86	-10.33	-48.22	-69.89	0.63	0.95	22.02		21.66	1.1	300	-4	0	-195		0.27	Jan-07
25.66	4.16	2.78	-55.51	-67.27	1.01	0.95	18.84		35.41	136.0	205	-109	4	0	0	-0.03	Jul-06
3.75	5.56	14.60	-4.82	42.49	0	0.95	13.92			163.1	100	0	0	0	0	0.00	Nov-08
26.00	17.63	15.66	-47.25	-65.22	0	0.95	22.92		24.23	26.2	300	0	0	-200		-0.23	Jan-07
13.17	4.94	12.42	-54.23	-68.60	0	0.95	35.44		76.78	34.3	285	-80	0	-105	0	-0.05	Nov-07
30.08	25.80	31.88	-30.06	-32.20	0	0.95	23.33		40.90	20.0	300	-200	0	0		-0.07	Jun-09
-12.94	-3.60	3.94	-36.78	-29.23	0	0.95	25.45			19.9	253	0	0	-153	0	-0.33	Dec-08
-28.25	-2.04	2.93	-86.67		0	0.95	66.03		14.40	3.0	300	0	0	-200		-0.21	Feb-15
20.46	-7.50	-15.81	-46.27	-75.19	0.01	0.95	25.27		25.62	1.3	300	-14	0	-186		-0.61	Jan-07
42.66	19.20	19.37	-50.26	-61.69	0.26	0.95	24.7		20.01	3.1	300	0	0	-200		-0.39	Jan-07
40.41	33.29	22.33	-43.34	-57.00	0.34	0.95	23.46		22.83	3.7	300	-200	0	0		-0.02	Jul-06
-31.26	-43.12	-21.66	-91.17	-82.04	0	0.95	62.09		35.82	32.2	300	-200	0	0		0.01	Jun-09
29.82	23.59	31.70	-26.83	-28.00	0.04	0.95	20.81		30.04	3.7	300	-200	0	0	0	-0.08	Oct-07
12.77	10.54	24.04	-56.52	-48.49	0.15	0.95	28.73		51.71	20.1	300	-200	0	0	25	-0.03	Oct-07
38.21	21.89	29.59	-29.81	-45.81	0	0.95	20.58		34.29	6.6	299	-199	0	0	27	-0.26	Nov-07
45.52	20.73	4.95	-19.57	-77.66	0.1	0.95	50.92		23.03	26.8	286	0	0	-186		-0.06	Apr-10
73.71	60.04	35.64	-30.03	2.09	0.05	0.95	37.29		50.11	20.1	300	-4	0	-196	0	-0.05	Jan-07
35.98	16.82	-9.91	-59.33	-79.83	1.11	0.95	24.3		47.57	250.7	189	-94	5	0	0	-0.03	Jul-06
9.38	9.27	5.87	-30.96	-64.10	0.24	0.95	22.31		30.82	22.6	300	-7	0	-193		-0.01	Jan-07
46.88	43.09	18.95	-47.01	-56.78	0.61	0.95	28.88		20.58	69.6	208	-108	0	0	0	-0.02	Jan-07
31.24	14.08	5.86	-45.26	-63.25	1.13	0.9	17.88		42.97	775.5	197	-103	6	0		-0.03	Jul-06
31.60	23.96	-2.21	-75.46	-89.91	0.38	0.95	34.59		20.25	3.4	300	0	0	-200	0	0.01	Jan-07
-9.84	8.41	19.64	-41.23	-15.46	0	1.62	36.89			20.5	300	0	0	-200	0	-0.36	Dec-08
46.75	40.69	12.75	-52.42	-62.90	0.37	0.95	28.5		17.63	3.1	300	-200	0	0	16	-0.63	Jan-07
36.83	16.85	-11.33	-67.92	-82.89	0.35	0.95	27		14.64	4.8	300	-9	0	-191		-0.12	Jan-07
-2.39	-6.44	-9.36	-51.94	-72.46	0.85	0.95	22.82		22.79	4.0	300	0	0	-200	45	-0.16	Jan-07
-5.13	1.35	-0.35	-15.09	5.37	0	0.95	20.94			66.9	100	0	0	0	0	-0.05	Nov-08
31.30	16.94	26.80	-49.96	-65.02	0	0.87	25.65			46.5	0	100	0	0		0.09	Jan-11
84.74	32.27	72.11	-84.83	-92.96	0	0.87	54.97			111.2	0	100	0	0		0.20	Jan-11
-11.75	-9.40	-6.58				0.69				8.1	0	100	0	0	21	0.20	Jul-17
-11.26	-8.29	-2.69			0.78	0.59			26.82	26.7	0	100	0	0	898	0.29	Jan-17
-5.00	-2.96	-0.77			0.59	1.17		7.41	27.35	48.0	0	86	14	0	225	-0.18	Jan-17
-9.81	-8.00	-7.90			1.57	1.45		7.68	23.86	33.3	12	60	27	0	431	-0.02	Jan-17
-5.97	-1.37	-0.84	16.02		0.26	1.38			26.69	4.9	30	51	19	0	37	0.24	Jan-16
-7.67	-5.05	-2.98	9.02		0.64	1.41			23.97	12.5	55	0	45	0	309	0.40	Jan-16
-13.65	-8.22	-6.01	27.54		0.89	0.43			29.55	45.4	0	100	0	0	0	0.15	Jan-16
-5.86	-4.52	-2.70	9.99		0.83	0.85	4.46		25.23	71.7	54	5	48	-7	0	0.10	Dec-14
-14.64	-19.71					0.78			18.04	1.9	2	98	0	0		-0.08	Jun-18
-17.38	-12.53					0.68			19.56	87.5	1	99	0	0		-0.03	Jan-18
0.51	1.56	5.42	38.46		1.96	0.95	11.6		33.58	14.2	4	96	0	0	29	-0.06	Sep-15
1.64	1.74					0.3			20.06	5.0	4	0	96	0		0.00	Feb-18
-11.46	-12.83	-17.30	4.83		1.06	0.8	14.66		19.08	2.0	1	99	0	0	107	0.34	Oct-14
-22.62	-21.75	-17.12	13.07	10.24	0.43	0.6	15.54		23.26	15.9	0	100	0	0	192	0.01	Oct-13
-14.73	-10.99	-9.41			0.32	0.29			14.20	8.0	0	100	0	0	36	0.17	Oct-17
-22.06	-19.17					0.88				5.5	1	99	0	0		0.10	May-18
0.65	1.17	-0.76			2.79	0.52			23.78	150.5	6	0	93	0	18	0.14	Jun-16
-4.14	-1.27	-3.22			4.78	0.52			23.96	24.5	7	0	93	0	30	0.23	Jun-16
-14.84	-11.87	-8.89			2.14	0.52			28.18	151.3	0	100	0	0	54	0.18	Jun-16
-18.65	-14.10	-9.66			1.15	0.52			29.15	152.5	0	100	0	0	86	0.13	Jun-16
-0.99	0.87	-0.04	13.84	18.03	4.44	0.47	2.03		24.05	152.9	7	0	93	0	32	-0.10	Oct-13

Fund Name	Ticker Symbol	Traded On	Overall Rating	Reward Rating	Risk Rating	Recent Up/Downgrade	Price as of 12/31/2018	52-Week High	52-Week Low	Open to New Investors	Category & (Prospectus Objective)
● Robo Global® Robotics and Automation Index ETF	ROBO	NAS CM	C-	C-	C	Down	32.55	46.16	30.86	Y	Global Eq Mid/Small Cap (Growth)
Rogers AI Global Macro ETF	BIKR	NYSE Arca	U	U	U		23.26	25.39	22.93	Y	Allocation Misc (Technology)
Saba Closed-End Funds ETF	CEFS	BATS	D	D	D+	Down	17.56	21.82	16.83	Y	Long/Short Credit (Growth & Inc)
Sage ESG Intermediate Credit ETF	GUDB	BATS	D	D	E+		48.20	49.69	47.92	Y	US Fixed Income (Growth & Inc)
Salt truBeta™ High Exposure ETF	SLT	BATS	U	U	U		20.58	25.79	18.98	Y	US Equity Large Cap Blend (Growth & Inc)
● Schwab 1000 Index ETF	SCHK	NYSE Arca	C-	D+	C		24.52	28.89	23.02	Y	US Equity Large Cap Blend (Growth & Inc)
● Schwab Emerging Markets Equity ETF™	SCHE	NYSE Arca	C-	C-	C	Down	23.53	31.08	22.96	Y	Global Emerg Mkts Equity (Div Emerg Mkts)
● Schwab Fundamental Emerg Mkts Large Company Ind ETF	FNDE	NYSE Arca	C	C-	C		25.83	33.12	25.30	Y	Global Emerg Mkts Equity (Div Emerg Mkts)
● Schwab Fundamental International Large Company Index ETF	FNDF	NYSE Arca	C-	D+	C-	Down	25.22	32.48	24.38	Y	Global Equity Large Cap (World Stock)
● Schwab Fundamental International Small Company Index ETF	FNDC	NYSE Arca	C-	D+	C-	Down	28.35	38.20	27.19	Y	Global Eq Mid/Small Cap (World Stock)
● Schwab Fundamental U.S. Broad Market Index ETF	FNDB	NYSE Arca	C	C	C-		33.49	40.14	31.73	Y	US Equity Large Cap Value (Growth & Inc)
● Schwab Fundamental U.S. Large Company Index ETF	FNDX	NYSE Arca	C	C	C+	Down	33.98	40.30	32.01	Y	US Equity Large Cap Value (Growth & Inc)
● Schwab Fundamental U.S. Small Company Index ETF	FNDA	NYSE Arca	C	C-	C+	Down	32.84	41.72	31.04	Y	US Equity Small Cap (Small Company)
● Schwab Intermediate-Term U.S. Treasury ETF™	SCHR	NYSE Arca	C-	D	C	Up	52.95	53.32	51.34	Y	US Fixed Income (Govt Bond - Treasury)
● Schwab International Equity ETF™	SCHF	NYSE Arca	C-	D+	C	Down	28.35	36.35	27.44	Y	Global Equity Large Cap (Foreign Stock)
● Schwab International Small-Cap Equity ETF™	SCHC	NYSE Arca	D+	D+	C-	Down	29.10	39.11	27.92	Y	Global Eq Mid/Small Cap (Small Company)
● Schwab Short-Term U.S. Treasury ETF™	SCHO	NYSE Arca	C	C-	C+	Up	49.91	50.04	49.42	Y	US Fixed Income (Govt Bond - Treasury)
● Schwab U.S. Aggregate Bond ETF™	SCHZ	NYSE Arca	C-	D+	C+	Down	50.59	52.04	49.51	Y	US Fixed Income (Multisector Bond)
● Schwab U.S. Broad Market ETF™	SCHB	NYSE Arca	C	C	C+	Down	59.93	71.11	56.21	Y	US Equity Large Cap Blend (Growth)
★ Schwab U.S. Dividend Equity ETF™	SCHD	NYSE Arca	B-	B	C		46.97	54.58	44.23	Y	US Equity Large Cap Value (Equity-Income)
● Schwab U.S. Large-Cap ETF™	SCHX	NYSE Arca	C	C	C+	Down	59.70	70.26	56.03	Y	US Equity Large Cap Blend (Growth)
● Schwab U.S. Large-Cap Growth ETF™	SCHG	NYSE Arca	C	C	C+	Down	68.93	82.25	64.30	Y	US Equity Large Cap Growth (Growth)
● Schwab U.S. Large-Cap Value ETF™	SCHV	NYSE Arca	C	C	C+	Down	49.29	58.00	46.58	Y	US Equity Large Cap Value (Growth)
● Schwab U.S. Mid-Cap ETF™	SCHM	NYSE Arca	C	C-	C+	Down	47.93	58.75	45.02	Y	US Equity Mid Cap (Growth)
● Schwab U.S. REIT ETF™	SCHH	NYSE Arca	C	C	C	Down	38.51	43.28	36.34	Y	Real Estate Sector Equity (Real Estate)
● Schwab U.S. Small-Cap ETF™	SCHA	NYSE Arca	C	C-	C+	Down	60.68	78.22	57.06	Y	US Equity Small Cap (Small Company)
● Schwab U.S. TIPS ETF™	SCHP	NYSE Arca	C-	D+	C	Down	53.25	55.43	52.79	Y	US Fixed Income (Govt Bond - Treasury)
SerenityShares Impact ETF	ICAN	NYSE Arca	D+	C-	D	Down	25.51	29.77	24.13	Y	US Equity Large Cap Growth (Growth & Inc)
● Sit Rising Rate ETF	RISE	NYSE Arca	C-	C-	C-	Down	24.09	25.49	23.70	Y	Fixed Income Misc (Govt Bond - Treasury)
● SPDR S&P® North American Natural Resources ETF	NANR	NYSE Arca	C-	C	D+	Down	28.98	37.64	27.82	Y	Natural Resources (Natl Res)
● SPDR® Blackstone / GSO Senior Loan ETF	SRLN	NYSE Arca	C	C-	C+		44.70	47.65	44.46	Y	US Fixed Income (Income)
● SPDR® Bloomberg Barclays 1-10 Year TIPS ETF	TIPX	NYSE Arca	C-	D+	C-		18.87	19.29	18.75	Y	US Fixed Income (Govt Bond - Treasury)
● SPDR® Bloomberg Barclays 1-3 Month T-Bill ETF	BIL	NYSE Arca	C	C-	C+		91.46	91.61	91.37	Y	US Fixed Income (Govt Bond - Treasury)
● SPDR® Bloomberg Barclays Convertible Securities ETF	CWB	NYSE Arca	C	C-	C+	Down	46.79	54.93	45.13	Y	Convertibles (Convertible Bond)
SPDR® Bloomberg Barclays Corporate Bond ETF	CBND	NYSE Arca	D+	D+	D+	Down	30.57	32.25	30.11	Y	US Fixed Income (Growth)
● SPDR® Bloomberg Barclays Emerging Markets Local Bond ETF	EBND	NYSE Arca	C-	C-	C-		26.52	30.76	25.51	Y	Emerging Mkts Fixed Inc (Worldwide Bond)
● SPDR® Bloomberg Barclays High Yield Bond ETF	JNK	NYSE Arca	C+	C-	B+		33.59	37.03	32.95	Y	US Fixed Income (Corp Bond-High Yld)
● SPDR® Bloomberg Barclays Intermediate Term Treasury ETF	ITE	NYSE Arca	D+	D+	C-	Down	59.55	59.55	57.65	Y	US Fixed Income (Govt Bond - Treasury)
● SPDR® Bloomberg Barclays International Corporate Bond ETF	IBND	NYSE Arca	D+	D+	C-	Down	32.94	36.74	32.28	Y	Global Fixed Income (Worldwide Bond)
● SPDR® Bloomberg Barclays International Treasury Bond ETF	BWX	NYSE Arca	C-	D+	C	Down	27.61	29.61	26.76	Y	Global Fixed Income (Worldwide Bond)
● SPDR® Bloomberg Barclays Investm Grade Floating Rate ETF	FLRN	NYSE Arca	C	C	C+		30.37	30.79	30.32	Y	US Fixed Income (Corp Bond-High Yld)
● SPDR® Bloomberg Barclays Mortgage Backed Bond ETF	MBG	NYSE Arca	D+	D+	C-		25.41	26.02	24.78	Y	US Fixed Income (Govt Bond - Mortgage)
● SPDR® Bloomberg Barclays Short Term High Yield Bond ETF	SJNK	NYSE Arca	C+	C	B		26.03	27.82	25.68	Y	US Fixed Income (Corp Bond-High Yld)
● SPDR® Bloomberg Barclays Short Term Intl Treasury Bond ETF	BWZ	NYSE Arca	C-	D+	C-	Down	30.70	33.46	30.42	Y	Global Fixed Income (Worldwide Bond)
● SPDR® Bloomberg Barclays TIPS ETF	IPE	NYSE Arca	C-	D	C	Down	53.89	56.25	53.29	Y	US Fixed Income (Govt Bond - Treasury)
● SPDR® Dorsey Wright Fixed Income Allocation ETF	DWFI	NAS CM	D+	D+	C-		22.21	25.82	22.07	Y	Cautious Allocation (Growth & Inc)
● SPDR® DoubleLine Short Duration Total Return Tactical ETF	STOT	BATS	C-	C-	D+		48.64	49.40	48.39	Y	US Fixed Income (Income)
● SPDR® DoubleLine Total Return Tactical ETF	TOTL	NYSE Arca	C	C-	C+		47.37	48.64	46.68	Y	US Fixed Income (Growth & Inc)
● SPDR® DoubleLine® Emerging Markets Fixed Income ETF	EMTL	BATS	D+	D+	C-	Down	47.60	50.40	47.34	Y	Emerging Mkts Fixed Inc (Income)
● SPDR® Dow Jones Global Real Estate ETF	RWO	NYSE Arca	C	C-	C+		44.26	49.36	42.86	Y	Real Estate Sector Equity (Real Estate)
★ SPDR® Dow Jones Industrial Average ETF	DIA	NYSE Arca	B-	B	C+	Down	233.20	267.95	218.10	Y	US Equity Large Cap Value (Growth)
● SPDR® Dow Jones International Real Estate ETF	RWX	NYSE Arca	C-	D+	C-	Down	35.34	42.45	34.74	Y	Real Estate Sector Equity (Real Estate)

★ Expanded analysis of this fund is included in Section II: Analysis of All BUY Rated Funds. ● Expanded analysis of this fund is included in Section III: Analysis of All Rated Funds with Assets over $50 million.

			TOTAL RETURNS & PERFORMANCE						ASSETS		ASSET ALLOCATION & TURNOVER					VALUATION	
3-Month Total Return	6-Month Total Return	1-Year Total Return	3-Year Total Return	5-Year Total Return	Dividend Yield (TTM)	Expense Ratio	3-Yr Std Deviation	Effective Duration	NAV	Total Assets (MIL)	%Cash	%Stocks	%Bonds	%Other	Turnover Ratio	Premium/ Discount 1-Year Avg	Inception Date
-21.90	-17.70	-20.43	35.18	22.57	0.03	0.95	16.28		32.72	1,534	0	100	0	0	30	-0.13	Oct-13
-5.97	-4.90					1.18		1.88	23.30	4.8	2	56	42	0	93	-0.13	Jun-18
-10.57	-7.94	-10.40			9.5	2.62		3.81	17.49	26.1	-14	20	89	-5	83	0.30	Mar-17
0.86	1.46	-0.27			2.54	0.35		3.84	48.34	14.4	0	0	99	0	65	-0.12	Oct-17
-18.87	-13.46					0.5			20.69	8.7	0	100	0	0		0.42	May-18
-14.07	-7.77	-4.89			1.5	0.05			24.53	591.1	0	100	0	0		0.06	Oct-17
-6.00	-6.29	-13.31	29.21	9.99	2.61	0.13	14.61		23.54	4,797	0	99	0	0	18	0.15	Jan-10
-7.64	-2.93	-10.01	50.25	8.05	2.22	0.39	17.18		25.87	2,194	0	98	0	0	14	0.00	Aug-13
-12.81	-10.57	-14.18	14.42	3.05	2.56	0.25	11.19		25.24	3,876	0	100	0	0	10	0.09	Aug-13
-15.42	-14.85	-18.76	14.12	15.09	2.23	0.39	11.49		28.46	1,781	0	100	0	0	18	0.08	Aug-13
-14.54	-8.75	-7.64	26.01	36.72	2.1	0.25	9.58		33.64	266.6	0	100	0	0	10	0.09	Aug-13
-14.24	-7.99	-7.31	26.32	37.71	2.08	0.25	9.39		33.95	4,652	0	100	0	0	9	0.00	Aug-13
-18.08	-17.10	-12.09	22.49	25.36	1.35	0.25	13.02		32.84	3,252	0	100	0	0	21	-0.01	Aug-13
2.96	2.62	1.28	4.02	10.22	2.04	0.06	3.06	5.13	52.89	3,152	0	0	100	0	30	0.00	Aug-10
-12.83	-10.45	-14.39	10.82	3.32	2.6	0.06	11.03		28.36	15,779	0	100	0	0	5	0.05	Nov-09
-16.55	-15.91	-18.64	8.55	4.13	3.14	0.12	12.1		29.11	2,070	0	99	0	0	16	0.04	Jan-10
1.29	1.51	1.49	2.64	3.66	1.66	0.06	0.76	1.93	49.88	3,774	0	0	100	0	65	0.02	Aug-10
1.71	1.71	-0.09	5.94	12.89	2.75	0.04	2.74	6.01	50.59	5,361	3	0	97	0	101	-0.04	Jul-11
-14.44	-8.50	-5.24	29.23	46.26	1.77	0.03	9.81		59.90	13,057	0	100	0	0	4	0.00	Nov-09
-10.84	-3.07	-5.46	32.84	48.02	2.67	0.07	9.05		46.98	8,275	0	100	0	0	23	0.01	Oct-11
-13.94	-7.47	-4.52	30.10	48.94	1.79	0.03	9.54		59.63	14,635	0	100	0	0	3	0.01	Nov-09
-15.75	-8.82	-1.34	34.85	61.16	0.87	0.04	11.13		68.89	6,456	1	99	0	0	5	0.01	Dec-09
-11.73	-5.92	-7.23	25.84	38.11	2.67	0.04	8.8		49.27	4,903	0	100	0	0	8	0.02	Dec-09
-16.22	-12.04	-8.68	24.96	37.73	1.37	0.05	11.3		47.94	5,147	0	100	0	0	13	0.02	Jan-11
-5.73	-5.29	-4.20	5.71	45.53	2.89	0.07	12.66		38.49	4,897	0	100	0	0	8	0.01	Jan-11
-18.86	-17.23	-11.75	21.70	24.16	1.34	0.05	13.71		60.69	7,650	0	100	0	0	9	0.02	Nov-09
-0.27	-1.34	-1.31	6.26	8.39	2.79	0.05	3.13	7.47	53.27	5,831	0	0	100	0	19	-0.02	Aug-10
-12.96	-8.34	-3.89			1.18	0.5			25.63	4.3	0	100	0	0	21	0.20	Apr-17
-4.33	-2.61	1.71	-0.63		0	1	5.2		24.06	67.9	390	0	-290	0		0.06	Feb-15
-14.96	-18.42	-16.50	26.57		1.6	0.35			29.06	664.0	0	100	0	0	20	-0.02	Dec-15
-3.50	-1.68	-0.25	10.42	10.46	4.59	0.7	1.92		44.92	3,194	4	0	96	0	68	-0.01	Apr-13
-0.02	-0.59	-0.42	5.22	5.28	2.83	0.15	2.4	5.08	18.85	307.6	0	0	100	0	21	0.00	May-13
0.35	0.80	1.51	2.34	2.13	1.47	0.14	0.2	0.17	91.44	7,043	100	0	0	0	625	0.01	May-07
-9.35	-7.75	-2.31	25.47	34.06	3.7	0.4	8.04		46.68	4,356	0	12	0	2	32	0.00	Apr-09
-0.03	0.61	-2.31	8.93	15.37	3.55	0.06	3.32	7.09	30.49	42.3	0	0	99	0	36	-0.09	Apr-11
2.30	1.20	-6.58	13.65	-3.96	4.91	0.4	9.79	5.40	26.43	587.7	1	0	99	0	42	0.05	Feb-11
-5.12	-2.20	-3.17	18.30	11.02	5.69	0.4	4.82	4.16	33.55	7,235	1	0	99	0	46	0.05	Nov-07
2.97	2.60	1.94	3.99	7.69	1.93	0.1	2.25	5.11	59.38	637.0	0	0	100	0	25	-0.01	May-07
-1.91	-2.37	-6.32	7.48	-7.89	0.75	0.5	7.5	5.56	32.72	184.4	0	0	99	0	14	0.10	May-10
1.32	-0.14	-2.16	8.87	-1.25	1.08	0.35	7.26	8.15	27.53	1,025	0	0	99	1	25	-0.04	Oct-07
-0.23	0.49	1.58	5.24	5.87	2.28	0.15	0.34	0.11	30.41	4,668	6	0	92	0	16	0.09	Nov-11
2.11	2.05	0.87	4.42	11.96	3.36	0.06	2.09	5.49	25.41	218.4	6	0	94	0	323	-0.02	Jan-09
-3.98	-1.60	-0.25	20.03	11.33	5.52	0.4	4.04	2.44	25.98	2,910	3	0	97	0	57	0.10	Mar-12
-0.06	-0.51	-3.16	5.00	-12.37	0.57	0.35	6.45	1.80	30.74	306.4	1	0	98	1	63	0.03	Jan-09
-0.34	-1.57	-1.61	6.22	8.67	3.75	0.15	3.32	7.88	53.89	1,673	0	0	100	0	18	-0.03	May-07
-3.69	-3.47	-8.69			4.64	0.6		5.73	22.24	127.8	1	0	74	0	71	0.06	Jun-16
0.75	1.13	1.16			2.28	0.45		2.06	48.61	82.5	5	0	94	0	123	0.18	Apr-16
1.06	1.28	0.30	6.87		3.28	0.55	2.05	4.56	47.19	2,841	2	0	98	0	72	-0.10	Feb-15
-0.24	0.88	-1.93			2.99	0.65		4.43	47.60	57.1	4	0	95	0	141	0.36	Apr-16
-5.33	-5.48	-6.06	5.24	26.59	3.74	0.5	10.47		44.25	2,225	0	99	0	0	11	-0.10	May-08
-11.93	-2.94	-3.60	43.44	57.76	2.02	0.17	10.11		233.16	22,258	0	100	0	0	2	0.05	Jan-98
-4.85	-5.76	-8.37	5.91	8.42	3.15	0.59	10.45		35.42	2,460	0	99	0	1	15	-0.19	Dec-06

Fund Name	Ticker Symbol	Traded On	Overall Rating	Reward Rating	Risk Rating	Recent Up/ Downgrade	Price as of 12/31/2018	52-Week High	52-Week Low	Open to New Investors	Category & (Prospectus Objective)
● SPDR® Dow Jones REIT ETF	RWR	NYSE Arca	C	C	C	Down	86.00	97.24	81.89	Y	Real Estate Sector Equity (Real Estate)
● SPDR® EURO STOXX 50 ETF	FEZ	NYSE Arca	C-	C-	D+	Down	33.27	44.21	32.08	Y	Europe Equity Large Cap (Europe Stock)
SPDR® EURO STOXX Small Cap ETF	SMEZ	NYSE Arca	D+	D+	D+	Down	51.17	69.29	49.23	Y	Europe Equity Large Cap (Europe Stock)
● SPDR® FactSet Innovative Technology ETF	XITK	NYSE Arca	C-	C	C-	Down	82.71	105.42	76.98	Y	Technology Sector Equity (Technology)
● SPDR® FTSE Intl Govt Inflation-Protected Bond ETF	WIP	NYSE Arca	C-	D+	C-		52.03	60.04	51.61	Y	Global Fixed Income (Worldwide Bond)
● SPDR® Global Dow ETF	DGT	NYSE Arca	C-	C-	D+	Down	75.49	91.75	72.28	Y	Global Equity Large Cap (World Stock)
SPDR® Gold MiniShares	GLDM	NYSE Arca	U	U	U		12.82	12.82	11.74	Y	Commodities Specified (Prec Metals)
● SPDR® Gold Shares	GLD	NYSE Arca	D+	D	C-	Down	121.25	128.83	111.10	Y	Commodities Specified (Prec Metals)
● SPDR® ICE BofAML Crossover Corporate Bond ETF	CJNK	NYSE Arca	D+	C-	D+	Down	24.69	26.58	24.47	Y	US Fixed Income (Corp Bond-High Yld)
SPDR® Kensho Future Security ETF	XKFS	NYSE Arca	D+	D+	D+		29.24	36.39	27.42	Y	Global Equity Large Cap (Technology)
SPDR® Kensho Intelligent Structures ETF	XKII	NYSE Arca	D+	C-	D		24.47	31.54	23.29	Y	Infrastructure Sector Equity (Technology)
SPDR® Kensho Smart Mobility ETF	XKST	NYSE Arca	D+	C-	D		23.34	32.36	22.36	Y	Industrials Sector Equity (Technology)
SPDR® Long Dollar Gold Trust	GLDW	NYSE Arca	D+	D	D+		125.75	126.22	113.95	Y	Commodities Specified (Prec Metals)
SPDR® MFS Systematic Core Equity ETF	SYE	NYSE Arca	C+	B	C	Down	70.55	82.01	66.60	Y	US Equity Large Cap Value (Growth)
SPDR® MFS Systematic Growth Equity ETF	SYG	NYSE Arca	C+	B	C-	Down	70.67	86.96	66.16	Y	US Equity Large Cap Growth (Growth)
SPDR® MFS Systematic Value Equity ETF	SYV	NYSE Arca	C	C	C-		59.35	70.44	56.35	Y	US Equity Large Cap Value (Growth)
● SPDR® MSCI ACWI ex-US ETF	CWI	NYSE Arca	C-	D+	C	Down	32.74	42.01	31.78	Y	Global Equity Large Cap (Foreign Stock)
● SPDR® MSCI ACWI IMI ETF	ACIM	NYSE Arca	C-	C-	C-	Down	69.62	83.96	66.46	Y	Global Equity Large Cap (World Stock)
● SPDR® MSCI ACWI Low Carbon Target ETF	LOWC	NYSE Arca	C-	C-	D+	Down	79.08	96.40	75.73	Y	Global Equity Large Cap (World Stock)
SPDR® MSCI China A Shares IMI ETF	XINA	NYSE Arca	D	D	D	Down	16.55	26.30	16.12	Y	Greater China Equity (Pacific Stock)
● SPDR® MSCI EAFE Fossil Fuel Free ETF	EFAX	NYSE Arca	D	D	D	Down	60.41	77.72	58.71	Y	Global Equity Large Cap (Growth & Inc)
● SPDR® MSCI EAFE StrategicFactors ETF	QEFA	NYSE Arca	D+	D+	C-	Down	56.53	68.89	54.70	Y	Global Equity Large Cap (World Stock)
SPDR® MSCI Emerging Markets Fossil Fuel Free ETF	EEMX	NYSE Arca	D	D	D	Down	56.78	76.80	55.74	Y	Global Emerg Mkts Equity (Growth & Inc)
● SPDR® MSCI Emerging Markets StrategicFactors ETF	QEMM	NYSE Arca	D+	C-	D+	Down	54.37	69.72	52.90	Y	Global Emerg Mkts Equity (World Stock)
● SPDR® MSCI USA StrategicFactors ETF	QUS	NYSE Arca	C	C	C-		72.89	84.64	69.01	Y	US Equity Large Cap Blend (Growth & Inc)
SPDR® MSCI World StrategicFactors ETF	QWLD	NYSE Arca	C-	C-	D+		68.57	79.62	65.50	Y	Global Equity Large Cap (World Stock)
● SPDR® Nuveen Bloomberg Barclays Municipal Bond ETF	TFI	NYSE Arca	C	D+	C		48.12	48.97	46.65	Y	US Muni Fixed Inc (Muni Bond - Natl)
● SPDR® Nuveen Bloomberg Barclays Short Term Muni Bond ETF	SHM	NYSE Arca	C-	D+	C		48.06	48.14	47.43	Y	US Muni Fixed Inc (Muni Bond - Natl)
● SPDR® Nuveen S&P High Yield Municipal Bond ETF	HYMB	NYSE Arca	C	C	C+		56.08	56.84	55.15	Y	US Muni Fixed Inc (Muni Bond - Natl)
● SPDR® NYSE Technology ETF	XNTK	NYSE Arca	C+	B	C	Down	59.53	97.94	54.51	Y	Technology Sector Equity (Technology)
● SPDR® Portfolio Aggregate Bond ETF	SPAB	NYSE Arca	C-	D+	C+	Down	27.85	28.74	27.25	Y	US Fixed Income (Multisector Bond)
● SPDR® Portfolio Developed World ex-US ETF	SPDW	NYSE Arca	C-	D+	C	Down	26.45	33.82	25.64	Y	Global Equity Large Cap (Foreign Stock)
● SPDR® Portfolio Emerging Markets ETF	SPEM	NYSE Arca	C-	C-	C	Down	32.36	42.45	31.29	Y	Global Emerg Mkts Equity (Div Emerg Mkts)
● SPDR® Portfolio Intermediate Term Corporate Bond ETF	SPIB	NYSE Arca	C	C-	C+		33.04	34.22	32.78	Y	US Fixed Income (Corp Bond - Gen)
● SPDR® Portfolio Large Cap ETF	SPLG	NYSE Arca	C	C	C+	Down	29.21	34.45	27.32	Y	US Equity Large Cap Blend (Growth & Inc)
● SPDR® Portfolio Long Term Corporate Bond ETF	SPLB	NYSE Arca	C-	D+	C	Down	25.38	28.61	24.89	Y	US Fixed Income (Corp Bond - Gen)
● SPDR® Portfolio Long Term Treasury ETF	SPTL	NYSE Arca	D+	D	C-	Down	35.04	36.59	32.31	Y	US Fixed Income (Govt Bond - Treasury)
● SPDR® Portfolio Mid Cap ETF	SPMD	NYSE Arca	C	C-	C+	Down	29.42	36.97	27.71	Y	US Equity Mid Cap (Growth)
● SPDR® Portfolio S&P 500 Growth ETF	SPYG	NYSE Arca	C	C	C+	Down	32.50	38.37	30.33	Y	US Equity Large Cap Growth (Growth)
● SPDR® Portfolio S&P 500 High Dividend ETF	SPYD	NYSE Arca	C	C-	C+		34.07	38.74	32.59	Y	US Equity Large Cap Value (Growth & Inc)
● SPDR® Portfolio S&P 500 Value ETF	SPYV	NYSE Arca	C	C	C+	Down	27.16	32.54	25.59	Y	US Equity Large Cap Value (Growth)
● SPDR® Portfolio Short Term Corporate Bond ETF	SPSB	NYSE Arca	C	C	C+		30.14	30.43	29.99	Y	US Fixed Income (Corp Bond - Gen)
● SPDR® Portfolio Short Term Treasury ETF	SPTS	NYSE Arca	C-	D+	C		29.58	29.87	29.34	Y	US Fixed Income (Govt Bond - Treasury)
● SPDR® Portfolio Small Cap ETF	SPSM	NYSE Arca	C	C-	C+	Down	26.36	34.10	24.83	Y	US Equity Small Cap (Growth)
● SPDR® Portfolio Total Stock Market ETF	SPTM	NYSE Arca	C	C	C+	Down	30.91	36.58	28.90	Y	US Equity Large Cap Blend (Growth)
● SPDR® Russell 1000 Low Volatility Focus ETF	ONEV	NYSE Arca	C-	C-	D+	Down	67.37	78.06	64.20	Y	US Equity Mid Cap (Growth & Inc)
● SPDR® Russell 1000 Momentum Focus ETF	ONEO	NYSE Arca	C-	C-	D+	Down	62.73	77.42	59.44	Y	US Equity Mid Cap (Growth & Inc)
● SPDR® Russell 1000® Yield Focus ETF	ONEY	NYSE Arca	C-	C-	D+	Down	61.85	74.19	59.15	Y	US Equity Mid Cap (Growth & Inc)
SPDR® S&P 1500 Momentum Tilt ETF	MMTM	NYSE Arca	C-	C	D+	Down	107.83	128.95	100.85	Y	US Equity Large Cap Blend (Growth)
SPDR® S&P 1500 Value Tilt ETF	VLU	NYSE Arca	D+	C	D	Down	91.78	109.69	86.88	Y	US Equity Large Cap Value (Growth)
● SPDR® S&P 400 Mid Cap Growth ETF	MDYG	NYSE Arca	D-	E+	D		45.85	165.57	43.09	Y	US Equity Mid Cap (Growth)
● SPDR® S&P 400 Mid Cap Value ETF	MDYV	NYSE Arca	D-	D-	D		44.36	106.43	41.80	Y	US Equity Mid Cap (Growth)

★ Expanded analysis of this fund is included in Section II: Analysis of All BUY Rated Funds. ● Expanded analysis of this fund is included in Section III: Analysis of All Rated Funds with Assets over $50 million.

				TOTAL RETURNS & PERFORMANCE					ASSETS		ASSET ALLOCATION & TURNOVER					VALUATION	
3-Month Total Return	6-Month Total Return	1-Year Total Return	3-Year Total Return	5-Year Total Return	Dividend Yield (TTM)	Expense Ratio	3-Yr Std Deviation	Effective Duration	NAV	Total Assets (MIL)	%Cash	%Stocks	%Bonds	%Other	Turnover Ratio	Premium/ Discount 1-Year Avg	Inception Date
-5.68	-5.28	-4.30	5.34	44.49	3.38	0.25	12.64		86.04	2,709	0	100	0	0	9	0.01	Apr-01
-12.99	-11.89	-16.05	5.35	-7.56	3.29	0.29	14.52		33.30	2,743	0	100	0	0	7	-0.15	Oct-02
-13.00	-11.06	-17.37	12.69		2.12	0.45	15.09		51.30	21.7	0	99	0	1	61	-0.10	Jun-14
-17.33	-12.88	8.37	83.91		0.28	0.45			82.95	68.7	0	100	0	0	78	0.30	Jan-16
0.12	-1.63	-5.90	10.46	-1.42	3.86	0.5	7.93		52.12	441.7	1	0	98	1	42	-0.07	Mar-08
-11.98	-6.68	-9.20	25.29	23.15	2.24	0.5	10.4		75.68	89.8	0	100	0	0	10	-0.02	Sep-00
7.71	2.62					0.18			12.80	307.8	0	0	0	100		0.22	Jun-18
7.65	2.50	-1.54	19.22	4.56	0	0.4	12.62		121.16	29,809	0	0	0	100	0	0.12	Nov-04
-1.87	-0.11	-2.80	14.36	18.91	4.25	0.3	3.75	5.41	24.62	69.6	1	0	98	0	24	0.13	Jun-12
-16.97	-10.63	-0.63				0.46				9.7	0	100	0	0		0.25	Dec-17
-20.07	-15.21	-18.04				0.46				5.5	0	100	0	0		0.26	Dec-17
-21.23	-19.67	-19.36				0.46				5.5	0	100	0	0		-0.04	Dec-17
10.09	5.31	4.85			0	0.5			126.14	27.7	0	0	0	100		0.34	Jan-17
-12.65	-5.28	-2.93	29.57	60.27	1.31	0.6	9.23		70.91	27.5	1	99	0	0	67	0.28	Jan-14
-16.68	-10.50	-8.11	23.64	60.01	0.89	0.61	11.35		71.15	35.7	1	99	0	0	55	0.22	Jan-14
-12.92	-7.89	-7.22	25.14	46.14	1.65	0.6	10.34		59.53	36.7	1	99	0	0	64	0.29	Jan-14
-11.34	-9.48	-14.03	14.17	5.23	2.58	0.3	11.09		32.73	1,490	1	99	0	0	3	-0.04	Jan-07
-13.18	-8.25	-9.54	22.05	26.84	2.31	0.25	9.7		69.82	106.5	0	100	0	0	4	0.17	Feb-12
-12.77	-8.56	-9.45	20.57		2.11	0.2	9.67		79.49	147.2	0	99	0	0	17	0.01	Nov-14
-10.80	-14.20	-30.31	-34.53		0	0.65	22.8		16.54	2.6	2	98	0	0	84	0.19	Oct-15
-12.30	-9.98	-14.35			2.5	0.2			60.53	71.0	0	100	0	0	5	0.41	Oct-16
-10.18	-7.42	-10.22	11.59		2.63	0.3	9.84		56.52	233.1	0	100	0	0	6	0.07	Jun-14
-7.35	-8.34	-15.86			1.04	0.3			57.06	32.8	1	98	0	0	8	-0.07	Oct-16
-6.05	-5.46	-12.10	25.20		2.28	0.3	12.85		54.80	256.2	1	99	0	0	30	0.04	Jun-14
-11.76	-5.13	-3.18	31.15		1.26	0.15	8.46		72.93	145.3	0	100	0	0	23	0.23	Apr-15
-11.49	-6.12	-6.39	23.22		1.97	0.3	8.24		68.66	29.9	1	99	0	0	18	0.40	Jun-14
1.92	1.40	0.43	5.86	19.50	2.25	0.23	3.98	7.23	48.14	2,771	0	0	100	0	23	-0.17	Sep-07
1.13	0.88	1.38	2.20	4.29	1.19	0.2	1.76	2.84	48.05	3,681	0	0	100	0	32	-0.04	Oct-07
0.22	1.06	3.80	10.14	33.01	4.01	0.35	3.95	8.15	55.83	634.3	0	0	100	0	11	-0.23	Apr-11
-17.73	-16.92	-6.25	49.00	82.06	0.67	0.35	14.78		59.56	727.1	0	100	0	0	14	0.04	Sep-00
1.68	1.70	-0.13	6.02	12.77	2.95	0.04	2.74	6.00	27.83	3,250	5	0	95	0	46	0.04	May-07
-12.96	-10.66	-14.23	10.79	4.39	2.7	0.04	10.99		26.47	3,132	0	100	0	0	3	0.01	Apr-07
-5.51	-6.64	-13.06	30.00	11.60	1.77	0.11	14.52		32.43	1,761	1	99	0	0	10	0.11	Mar-07
0.53	1.36	-0.35	7.63	13.10	3.05	0.07	2.33	4.33	33.06	3,913	0	0	98	0	33	0.01	Feb-09
-14.04	-7.60	-4.70	29.79	48.08	1.97	0.03	9.52		29.20	1,727	0	100	0	0	4	0.03	Nov-05
-1.63	-0.61	-7.43	15.29	27.24	4.61	0.07	7.13	13.40	25.30	365.0	0	0	100	0	20	-0.09	Mar-09
4.77	1.29	-1.88	7.68	32.68	2.87	0.06	9.18	16.86	34.87	1,209	1	0	99	0	10	-0.06	May-07
-17.30	-15.07	-10.28	22.25	26.81	1.58	0.05	13.13		29.43	1,159	0	100	0	0	37	0.03	Nov-05
-14.96	-7.31	-0.02	35.73	63.95	1.38	0.04	10.52		32.48	3,567	0	100	0	0	13	0.04	Sep-00
-8.09	-5.98	-4.77	33.74		4.14	0.07	8.74		34.05	840.8	0	100	0	0	40	0.03	Oct-15
-12.33	-6.84	-8.92	22.92	33.38	2.56	0.04	9.52		27.15	2,615	0	100	0	0	21	0.04	Sep-00
0.73	1.46	1.46	5.36	7.14	2.32	0.07	0.85	1.85	30.13	4,476	1	0	98	0	67	0.02	Dec-09
1.30	1.50	1.07	2.59	4.56	1.91	0.06	1.31	1.91	29.58	651.2	3	0	97	0	33	0.02	Nov-11
-19.04	-17.83	-11.07	24.65	25.14	1.67	0.05	14.44		26.37	1,413	0	100	0	0	20	0.01	Jul-13
-14.41	-8.51	-5.25	29.46	46.28	1.76	0.03	9.71		30.87	2,597	1	99	0	0	8	0.00	Oct-00
-11.02	-6.36	-4.98	29.89		1.87	0.2			67.54	462.0	0	100	0	0	37	0.04	Dec-15
-16.73	-13.06	-11.97	19.55		1.51	0.2			62.92	460.9	0	100	0	0	101	0.15	Dec-15
-12.99	-9.87	-7.95	30.64		3.19	0.2			62.09	417.2	0	100	0	0	42	0.17	Dec-15
-15.74	-8.81	-3.83	29.09	49.22	1.46	0.12	10.05		108.05	41.8	0	100	0	0	75	0.37	Oct-12
-14.03	-8.50	-7.74	27.94	39.18	2.21	0.13	9.95		91.78	25.7	0	100	0	0	14	0.18	Oct-12
-16.93	-14.63	-70.14	-59.02	-55.13	1.22	0.15	11.58		45.84	1,285	0	100	0	0	54	0.03	Nov-05
-16.31	-13.74	-55.97	-37.61	-34.93	1.94	0.15	12.61		44.34	1,007	0	100	0	0	51	0.03	Nov-05

Fund Name	Ticker Symbol	Traded On	Overall Rating	Reward Rating	Risk Rating	Recent Up/Downgrade	Price as of 12/31/2018	52-Week High	52-Week Low	Open to New Investors	Category & (Prospectus Objective)
SPDR® S&P 500 Buyback ETF	SPYB	NYSE Arca	C-	C	D+	Down	56.79	67.86	53.41	Y	US Equity Large Cap Blend (Growth)
● SPDR® S&P 500 ETF	SPY	NYSE Arca	C+	C	B	Down	249.92	293.58	234.34	Y	US Equity Large Cap Blend (Growth)
● SPDR® S&P 500 Fossil Fuel Reserves Free ETF	SPYX	NYSE Arca	C	C	C-		60.94	71.48	57.18	Y	US Equity Large Cap Blend (Growth & Inc)
● SPDR® S&P 600 Small Cap ETF	SLY	NYSE Arca	D-	D-	D		59.97	139.00	56.32	Y	US Equity Small Cap (Small Company)
● SPDR® S&P 600 Small Cap Growth ETF	SLYG	NYSE Arca	D-	E+	D	Up	53.94	241.89	50.63	Y	US Equity Small Cap (Small Company)
● SPDR® S&P 600 Small Cap Value ETF	SLYV	NYSE Arca	D-	D-	D		53.82	130.78	50.73	Y	US Equity Small Cap (Small Company)
★ SPDR® S&P Aerospace & Defense ETF	XAR	NYSE Arca	B-	B	C	Down	78.92	100.89	74.15	Y	Industrials Sector Equity (Technology)
● SPDR® S&P Bank ETF	KBE	NYSE Arca	C-	C-	C	Down	37.35	51.86	35.17	Y	Financials Sector Equity (Financial)
● SPDR® S&P Biotech ETF	XBI	NYSE Arca	C-	C-	C	Down	71.75	101.15	65.42	Y	Healthcare Sector Equity (Health)
● SPDR® S&P Capital Markets ETF	KCE	NYSE Arca	C	C	C-		47.77	62.39	44.84	Y	Financials Sector Equity (Financial)
● SPDR® S&P China ETF	GXC	NYSE Arca	C-	C-	C-	Down	84.81	123.84	82.62	Y	Greater China Equity (Pacific Stock)
● SPDR® S&P Dividend ETF	SDY	NYSE Arca	C	C	C+	Down	89.52	100.02	84.76	Y	US Equity Large Cap Value (Growth & Inc)
● SPDR® S&P Emerging Asia Pacific ETF	GMF	NYSE Arca	C-	C-	C-		87.76	116.07	84.71	Y	Asia ex-Japan Equity (Pacific Stock)
● SPDR® S&P Emerging Markets Dividend ETF	EDIV	NYSE Arca	C-	C-	C-		29.85	36.54	27.94	Y	Global Emerg Mkts Equity (Div Emerg Mkts)
● SPDR® S&P Emerging Markets Small Cap ETF	EWX	NYSE Arca	D+	C-	D+	Down	40.97	55.78	40.07	Y	Global Emerg Mkts Equity (Div Emerg Mkts)
● SPDR® S&P Global Dividend ETF	WDIV	NYSE Arca	C-	C-	C-	Down	61.99	73.93	60.00	Y	Global Equity Large Cap (Growth & Inc)
● SPDR® S&P Global Infrastructure ETF	GII	NYSE Arca	C-	C-	C-	Down	45.13	53.01	43.84	Y	Infrastructure Sector Equity (Utility)
● SPDR® S&P Global Natural Resources ETF	GNR	NYSE Arca	C	C	C+	Down	41.24	53.06	39.53	Y	Natural Resources (Natl Res)
● SPDR® S&P Health Care Equipment ETF	XHE	NYSE Arca	C	C	C+	Down	70.07	88.81	63.69	Y	Healthcare Sector Equity (Health)
● SPDR® S&P Health Care Services ETF	XHS	NYSE Arca	C	C	C-		62.59	76.74	59.72	Y	Healthcare Sector Equity (Health)
● SPDR® S&P Homebuilders ETF	XHB	NYSE Arca	C	B-	D+	Down	32.52	46.75	30.74	Y	Consumer Goods & Svcs (Real Estate)
● SPDR® S&P Insurance ETF	KIE	NYSE Arca	C	C	C+	Down	28.37	32.75	26.73	Y	Financials Sector Equity (Financial)
● SPDR® S&P International Dividend ETF	DWX	NYSE Arca	C-	C-	C-	Down	34.96	42.91	33.98	Y	Global Equity Large Cap (Foreign Stock)
● SPDR® S&P International Small Cap ETF	GWX	NYSE Arca	D+	D+	C-	Down	27.92	37.98	26.70	Y	Global Eq Mid/Small Cap (Foreign Stock)
● SPDR® S&P Internet ETF	XWEB	NYSE Arca	C	C	C-		76.06	99.61	68.10	Y	Technology Sector Equity (Technology)
● SPDR® S&P Metals and Mining ETF	XME	NYSE Arca	C	C+	D+		26.19	39.17	25.28	Y	Natural Resources (Natl Res)
● SPDR® S&P MidCap 400 ETF	MDY	NYSE Arca	C	C-	C+	Down	302.67	373.52	284.96	Y	US Equity Mid Cap (Growth)
● SPDR® S&P Oil & Gas Equipment & Services ETF	XES	NYSE Arca	D+	C-	D		9.01	19.19	8.33	Y	Energy Sector Equity (Natl Res)
● SPDR® S&P Oil & Gas Exploration & Production ETF	XOP	NYSE Arca	D+	C-	D+	Down	26.53	44.57	24.12	Y	Energy Sector Equity (Natl Res)
● SPDR® S&P Pharmaceuticals ETF	XPH	NYSE Arca	C	C	D+	Up	36.62	49.96	34.77	Y	Healthcare Sector Equity (Health)
● SPDR® S&P Regional Banking ETF	KRE	NYSE Arca	C	C	C	Down	46.79	65.74	44.22	Y	Financials Sector Equity (Financial)
● SPDR® S&P Retail ETF	XRT	NYSE Arca	C-	C-	C-	Down	40.99	52.50	38.45	Y	Consumer Goods & Svcs (Unaligned)
● SPDR® S&P Semiconductor ETF	XSD	NYSE Arca	C	B-	C-	Down	64.70	79.33	60.13	Y	Technology Sector Equity (Technology)
● SPDR® S&P Software & Services ETF	XSW	NYSE Arca	C	C	C-	Down	74.54	92.64	69.45	Y	Technology Sector Equity (Technology)
SPDR® S&P Technology Hardware ETF	XTH	NYSE Arca	C-	C	D+	Up	61.63	82.19	57.48	Y	Technology Sector Equity (Technology)
● SPDR® S&P Telecom ETF	XTL	NYSE Arca	C	C	C-		62.76	77.14	58.72	Y	Communications Sector Equity (Comm)
● SPDR® S&P Transportation ETF	XTN	NYSE Arca	C	C	C-		53.44	69.32	50.73	Y	Industrials Sector Equity (Utility)
SPDR® Solactive Canada ETF	ZCAN	NYSE Arca	C-	C-	D+	Down	49.63	62.73	48.13	Y	Equity Misc (Foreign Stock)
SPDR® Solactive Germany ETF	ZDEU	NYSE Arca	D	D+	D	Down	51.90	70.09	50.04	Y	Equity Misc (Europe Stock)
SPDR® Solactive Hong Kong ETF	ZHOK	NYSE Arca	U	U	U		57.13	61.41	54.02	Y	Greater China Equity (Pacific Stock)
SPDR® Solactive Japan ETF	ZJPN	NYSE Arca	D+	C-	D+		67.07	83.53	64.75	Y	Japan Equity (Pacific Stock)
SPDR® Solactive United Kingdom ETF	ZGBR	NYSE Arca	D+	D+	D+	Down	44.44	56.39	43.78	Y	Equity Misc (Foreign Stock)
● SPDR® SSGA Gender Diversity Index ETF	SHE	NYSE Arca	C	C	C-		63.73	78.05	60.07	Y	US Equity Large Cap Blend (Growth & Inc)
● SPDR® SSgA Global Allocation ETF	GAL	NYSE Arca	C-	C-	C-	Down	34.52	40.37	33.88	Y	Moderate Allocation (Growth)
● SPDR® SSgA Income Allocation ETF	INKM	NYSE Arca	C-	C-	D+	Down	30.61	34.45	30.39	Y	Moderate Allocation (Income)
● SPDR® SSgA Multi-Asset Real Return ETF	RLY	NYSE Arca	C-	C-	C-	Down	22.75	27.48	22.58	Y	Moderate Allocation (Growth & Inc)
● SPDR® SSgA Ultra Short Term Bond ETF	ULST	NYSE Arca	C-	C	C-		40.15	40.34	40.10	Y	US Fixed Income (Growth & Inc)
● SPDR® SSGA US Large Cap Low Volatility Index ETF	LGLV	NYSE Arca	C	C	C-		89.04	98.45	84.44	Y	US Equity Large Cap Blend (Income)
● SPDR® SSGA US Small Cap Low Volatility Index ETF	SMLV	NYSE Arca	C-	C-	D+	Down	82.88	99.77	79.55	Y	US Equity Small Cap (Income)
● SPDR® STOXX Europe 50 ETF	FEU	NYSE Arca	D+	D+	C-	Down	29.89	38.40	28.95	Y	Europe Equity Large Cap (Europe Stock)
● SPDR® Wells Fargo Preferred Stock ETF	PSK	NYSE Arca	D+	D+	C-	Down	39.56	44.04	38.67	Y	US Fixed Income (Growth & Inc)
● Sprott Gold Miners ETF	SGDM	NYSE Arca	C	C	D		17.48	22.42	14.90	Y	Prec Metals (Prec Metals)

★Expanded analysis of this fund is included in Section II: Analysis of All BUY Rated Funds. ● Expanded analysis of this fund is included in Section III: Analysis of All Rated Funds with Assets over $50 million.

		TOTAL RETURNS & PERFORMANCE							ASSETS		ASSET ALLOCATION & TURNOVER					VALUATION	
3-Month Total Return	6-Month Total Return	1-Year Total Return	3-Year Total Return	5-Year Total Return	Dividend Yield (TTM)	Expense Ratio	3-Yr Std Deviation	Effective Duration	NAV	Total Assets (MIL)	%Cash	%Stocks	%Bonds	%Other	Turnover Ratio	Premium/Discount 1-Year Avg	Inception Date
-14.33	-9.09	-7.45	29.50		1.86	0.35	11.7		56.86	22.3	0	100	0	0	97	0.09	Feb-15
-13.79	-7.14	-4.44	29.99	49.57	1.82	0.09	9.38		249.92	269,244	1	99	0	0	3	0.01	Jan-93
-13.75	-6.75	-4.32	30.39		1.72	0.2	9.49		60.74	301.9	0	100	0	0	4	0.17	Nov-15
-18.91	-15.19	-54.24	-34.51	-32.22	1.37	0.15	14.7		59.95	1,110	0	100	0	0	22	0.07	Nov-05
-18.42	-15.00	-76.02	-66.46	-64.24	0.94	0.15	14.85		53.98	1,948	0	100	0	0	59	0.05	Sep-00
-19.39	-19.12	-56.68	-36.65	-36.55	1.76	0.15	14.86		53.81	1,699	0	100	0	0	53	0.06	Sep-00
-20.35	-8.79	-4.45	54.02	70.02	1.02	0.35	14.32		78.94	1,385	3	97	0	0	36	0.04	Sep-11
-18.89	-20.60	-19.58	16.03	22.28	1.73	0.35	20.52		37.34	2,961	0	100	0	0	35	-0.02	Nov-05
-23.73	-25.20	-14.90	3.40	69.95	0.28	0.35	30.87		72.03	4,384	0	100	0	0	59	-0.08	Jan-06
-14.17	-16.89	-15.04	18.53	6.54	2.28	0.35	19.26		47.84	72.1	0	100	0	0	43	0.26	Nov-05
-10.29	-17.34	-18.67	23.18	23.48	2.46	0.59	18.63		85.71	970.9	0	100	0	0	3	-0.12	Mar-07
-7.82	-2.08	-2.71	35.42	53.03	2.4	0.35	9.05		89.47	16,480	0	100	0	0	32	-0.01	Nov-05
-7.92	-10.11	-13.66	26.51	28.96	2.05	0.49	14.52		88.13	417.2	0	100	0	0	5	0.02	Mar-07
-2.65	-0.57	-6.46	39.93	-6.28	3.45	0.49	16.49		29.96	410.3	0	100	0	0	55	-0.11	Feb-11
-6.83	-11.62	-18.48	16.98	1.14	3.44	0.65	13.6		40.96	460.3	1	98	0	0	24	0.03	May-08
-7.27	-5.39	-8.85	22.91	18.43	3.77	0.4	10.18		61.87	201.4	0	100	0	0	39	0.04	May-13
-5.40	-6.56	-10.05	19.86	18.69	3.34	0.4	9.78		45.13	279.9	0	100	0	0	21	0.06	Jan-07
-17.08	-14.72	-13.11	39.42	-5.19	2.8	0.4	15.42		41.25	1,384	0	100	0	0	19	-0.05	Sep-10
-19.26	-10.70	9.28	60.03	102.97	0.04	0.35	16.22		70.12	686.1	0	100	0	0	40	0.15	Jan-11
-17.39	-9.88	2.61	10.34	42.70	0.26	0.35	14.9		62.75	135.3	2	98	0	0	34	0.18	Sep-11
-14.69	-17.10	-25.64	-2.33	1.34	1.05	0.35	16.9		32.52	662.6	0	100	0	0	26	0.04	Jan-06
-10.36	-4.02	-5.86	28.94	47.12	1.78	0.35	11.46		28.40	741.7	0	100	0	0	26	-0.02	Nov-05
-6.44	-6.27	-11.19	19.63	-5.65	4.44	0.45	10.88		34.95	805.4	0	99	0	0	47	-0.24	Feb-08
-16.57	-15.28	-19.11	11.32	10.51	2.85	0.4	12.44		27.92	787.1	1	98	0	1	29	-0.16	Apr-07
-19.43	-12.54	14.68			0.01	0.35			76.35	51.0	0	100	0	0	63	0.16	Jun-16
-23.44	-25.57	-26.16	83.00	-32.32	2.62	0.35	33.17		26.22	523.9	0	100	0	0	51	0.00	Jun-06
-16.65	-14.23	-11.27	23.72	32.12	1.23	0.24	11.82		302.54	19,245	0	100	0	0	23	0.01	May-95
-46.55	-45.07	-47.04	-46.95	-78.00	1.07	0.35	35.45		9.00	275.7	0	100	0	0	34	0.02	Jun-06
-39.11	-36.85	-28.21	-9.98	-59.18	0.8	0.35	32.22		26.54	2,704	0	100	0	0	3	0.02	Jun-06
-21.21	-14.25	-14.70	-26.62	-3.42	0.55	0.35	18.84		36.67	305.5	0	100	0	0	41	0.01	Jun-06
-19.89	-23.11	-18.97	17.46	25.62	1.76	0.35	21.22		46.78	3,971	0	100	0	0	52	0.03	Jun-06
-18.73	-14.81	-8.01	-1.02	-0.78	1.4	0.35	15.81		41.01	634.6	0	100	0	0	33	0.00	Jun-06
-14.05	-10.68	-6.25	51.72	119.17	0.95	0.35	18.3		64.74	244.1	0	100	0	0	37	0.01	Jan-06
-16.02	-8.40	8.89	52.01	70.71	0.17	0.35	14.45		75.13	129.8	0	100	0	0	29	0.15	Sep-11
-19.56	-16.40	-13.30			0.77	0.35			61.79	3.5	0	100	0	0	45	0.54	Jun-16
-15.73	-12.77	-6.03	18.44	21.76	2.2	0.35	12.62		63.08	116.8	0	100	0	0	46	0.08	Jan-11
-19.47	-15.39	-17.00	28.13	36.80	0.79	0.35	17.36		53.63	194.3	0	100	0	0	29	-0.01	Jan-11
-15.22	-13.07	-16.51	20.80		2.18	0.14	12.27		49.84	23.5	0	99	0	1	29	-0.11	Jun-14
-15.19	-12.48	-19.48	6.04		2.89	0.14	14.02		51.43	8.2	0	100	0	0	28	0.23	Jun-14
-5.25						0.14			57.42	5.8	0	100	0	0	0	0.21	Sep-18
-13.91	-9.68	-11.61	9.84		1.8	0.14	9.85		67.68	14.8	0	100	0	0	53	0.02	Jun-14
-11.93	-11.65	-13.37	2.04		3.89	0.14	11.23		44.95	9.6	1	99	0	0	50	0.09	Jun-14
-10.82	-4.71	-1.59			2.21	0.2			63.69	365.6	0	100	0	0	49	0.19	Mar-16
-9.30	-6.50	-7.25	13.34	16.51	2.29	0.35	6.89	7.24	34.64	255.2	10	65	24	0	86	0.11	Apr-12
-3.78	-2.65	-5.24	14.83	18.72	3.33	0.5	5.58	9.53	30.60	92.9	2	37	52	0	47	0.02	Apr-12
-13.18	-11.81	-11.06	9.85	-12.98	2.34	0.5	10.09	7.88	22.87	129.6	16	58	26	0	25	0.09	Apr-12
0.49	1.13	2.10	5.10	5.52	1.9	0.2	0.26	0.24	40.13	108.7	12	0	88	0	83	0.03	Oct-13
-7.49	-0.34	0.54	31.79	57.38	1.92	0.12	8.37		88.93	150.2	0	100	0	0	108	0.33	Feb-13
-12.19	-11.43	-6.01	29.20	42.74	2.68	0.12	13.02		83.16	184.9	0	100	0	0	158	0.14	Feb-13
-10.90	-9.13	-14.34	3.48	-7.66	3.77	0.29	11.96		29.83	175.0	0	100	0	0	5	-0.21	Oct-02
-4.10	-5.68	-4.58	4.91	32.20	6.66	0.45	5.2		39.55	624.6	0	0	0	0	31	0.08	Sep-09
12.86	-8.02	-14.99	39.31		0.78	0.57	38.74		17.53	123.6	0	100	0	0	101	-0.03	Jul-14

Fund Name	Ticker Symbol	Traded On	Overall Rating	Reward Rating	Risk Rating	Recent Up/ Downgrade	Price as of 12/31/2018	52-Week High	52-Week Low	Open to New Investors	Category & (Prospectus Objective)
● Strategy Shares EcoLogical Strategy ETF	HECO	NYSE Arca	C	C	C-		39.24	44.36	39.06	Y	Equity Misc (Growth)
Strategy Shares Nasdaq 7 Handl™ Index ETF	HNDL	NAS CM	U	U	U		22.22	25.16	21.80	Y	Cautious Allocation (Growth & Inc)
● Strategy Shares US Market Rotation Strategy ETF	HUSE	NYSE Arca	C-	C	C-	Down	33.53	41.49	33.49	Y	US Equity Large Cap Blend (Growth)
★ Technology Select Sector SPDR® Fund	XLK	NYSE Arca	B	B	C+		61.98	75.93	57.62	Y	Technology Sector Equity (Technology)
Teucrium Agricultural Fund	TAGS	NYSE Arca	D-	D	E	Down	20.53	25.70	20.04	Y	Commodities Specified (Natl Res)
● Teucrium Corn Fund	CORN	NYSE Arca	D	D	D		16.05	18.48	15.40	Y	Commodities Specified (Unaligned)
Teucrium Soybean	SOYB	NYSE Arca	D	D	D		16.18	19.45	15.30	Y	Commodities Specified (Natl Res)
Teucrium Sugar	CANE	NYSE Arca	D	D	D	Up	7.09	9.94	6.50	Y	Commodities Specified (Unaligned)
● Teucrium Wheat	WEAT	NYSE Arca	D	D	D		5.93	7.18	5.88	Y	Commodities Specified (Unaligned)
The 3D Printing ETF	PRNT	BATS	D+	D+	D+		19.87	27.01	19.04	Y	Technology Sector Equity (Technology)
The Long-Term Care ETF	OLD	NAS CM	C	B-	C-	Up	25.12	27.70	21.66	Y	Real Estate Sector Equity (Health)
The Obesity ETF	SLIM	NAS CM	C-	C	D+	Down	32.14	39.12	29.72	Y	Healthcare Sector Equity (Health)
The Organics ETF	ORG	NAS CM	D+	D+	D+		24.49	35.72	24.10	Y	Consumer Goods & Svcs (Growth & Inc)
★ The Real Estate Select Sector SPDR Fund	XLRE	NYSE Arca	B-	B	C		31.00	34.48	29.40	Y	Real Estate Sector Equity (Real Estate)
Tortoise Global Water ESG Fund	TBLU	BATS	D+	D+	D		25.68	30.56	25.07	Y	Natural Resources (Unaligned)
● Tortoise North American Pipeline Fund	TPYP	NYSE Arca	C	C	C	Down	19.91	24.62	19.22	Y	Energy Sector Equity (Unaligned)
TrimTabs All Cap International Free-Cash-Flow ETF	TTAI	BATS	D	D	D		22.20	28.65	21.86	Y	Global Equity Large Cap (Growth & Inc)
● TrimTabs All Cap U.S. Free-Cash-Flow ETF	TTAC	BATS	C-	C	C-	Down	31.42	38.69	29.75	Y	US Equity Large Cap Blend (Growth & Inc)
U.S. Global GO GOLD and Precious Metal Miners ETF	GOAU	NYSE Arca	D+	D+	D	Down	11.41	13.35	10.05	Y	Commodities Specified (Prec Metals)
● U.S. Global Jets ETF	JETS	NYSE Arca	C+	B-	C-		27.88	34.66	26.85	Y	Industrials Sector Equity (Growth)
● UBS AG FI Enhanced Europe 50 ETN	FIEE	NYSE Arca	D+	D+	D	Down	124.40	201.25	116.52	Y	Europe Equity Large Cap (Europe Stock)
● UBS AG FI Enhanced Global High Yield ETN	FIHD	NYSE Arca	C-	D+	C-		141.51	190.81	129.64	Y	Global Equity Large Cap (Convertible Bond)
● UBS AG FI Enhanced Large Cap Growth ETN	FBGX	NYSE Arca	C-	C	D+	Down	189.53	301.54	167.50	Y	US Equity Large Cap Growth (Growth)
UBS ETRACS - ProShares Daily 3x Inverse Crude ETN	WTID	NYSE Arca	D	D	D		17.32	21.15	5.16	Y	Trading Tools (Natl Res)
UBS ETRACS - ProShares Daily 3x Long Crude ETN	WTIU	NYSE Arca	D	D+	D	Down	8.59	46.94	7.91	Y	Trading Tools (Natl Res)
UBS ETRACS 2×Lev Long ETRACS Wells Fargo® Bus Dev Co Ind E	LBDC	NYSE Arca	D+	D+	D+		11.64	16.52	10.88	Y	Trading Tools (Growth & Inc)
● UBS ETRACS 2xLev Long Wells Fargo Bus Dev Company Ind ETN	BDCL	NYSE Arca	C	C-	C		11.55	16.59	11.01	Y	Trading Tools (Growth)
● UBS ETRACS 2xMonthly Lev Alerian MLP Infrastr Ind ETN SerB	MLPQ	NYSE Arca	D	D	D	Down	23.33	44.09	21.00	Y	Trading Tools (Growth & Inc)
UBS ETRACS 2xMonthly Leveraged S&P MLP Index ETN Series B	MLPZ	NYSE Arca	D	D	D		26.56	49.75	24.14	Y	Trading Tools (Growth & Inc)
● UBS ETRACS Alerian MLP Index ETN	AMU	NYSE Arca	D+	D+	C-		14.00	19.04	13.39	Y	Energy Sector Equity (Income)
UBS ETRACS Alerian MLP Index ETN Series B	AMUB	NYSE Arca	D-	D	E	Down	13.97	18.61	13.34	Y	Energy Sector Equity (Growth & Inc)
● UBS ETRACS Alerian MLP Infrastructure Index ETN	MLPI	NYSE Arca	D+	D+	D+	Up	19.77	26.41	18.86	Y	Energy Sector Equity (Natl Res)
UBS ETRACS Alerian MLP Infrastructure Index ETN Series B	MLPB	NYSE Arca	D	D+	E		19.78	26.40	18.88	Y	Energy Sector Equity (Utility)
UBS ETRACS Alerian Natural Gas MLP Index ETN	MLPG	NYSE Arca	D+	C-	D	Up	19.82	26.14	18.95	Y	Energy Sector Equity (Natl Res)
● UBS ETRACS Bloomberg Commodity Index Total Return ETN	DJCI	NYSE Arca	D+	D+	C-		14.14	16.86	14.14	Y	Commodities Broad Basket (Natl Res)
UBS ETRACS CMCI Agriculture Total Return ETN	UAG	NYSE Arca	D-	D	E		16.17	18.85	15.98	Y	Commodities Specified (Natl Res)
UBS ETRACS CMCI Food Total Return ETN	FUD	NYSE Arca	D	D	D		16.63	18.92	15.90	Y	Commodities Specified (Natl Res)
UBS ETRACS CMCI Gold Total Return ETN	UBG	NYSE Arca	D	D	D		32.25	34.63	29.92	Y	Commodities Specified (Prec Metals)
UBS ETRACS CMCI Silver Total Return ETN	USV	NYSE Arca	D-	D-	E	Down	19.31	22.46	17.25	Y	Commodities Specified (Prec Metals)
● UBS ETRACS CMCI Total Return ETN	UCI	NYSE Arca	C-	C-	C-		13.50	16.32	13.50	Y	Commodities Broad Basket (Natl Res)
● UBS ETRACS - Wells Fargo Business Dev Company Ind ETN	BDCS	NYSE Arca	C-	C-	C-	Down	17.69	21.03	17.15	Y	Financials Sector Equity (Growth)
● UBS ETRACS Monthly Pay 2xLeveraged Closed-End Fund ETN	CEFL	NYSE Arca	C-	D+	C	Down	11.94	18.22	11.05	Y	Trading Tools (Growth & Inc)
UBS ETRACS Monthly Pay 2xLeveraged Div High Income ETN	DVHL	NYSE Arca	C-	C-	D+	Down	15.60	20.97	14.60	Y	Trading Tools (Income)
UBS ETRACS Monthly Pay 2xLev Dow Jones Select Div Ind ETN	DVYL	NYSE Arca	C-	C	D+	Down	56.70	77.77	51.35	Y	Trading Tools (Equity-Income)
● UBS ETRACS Monthly Pay 2xLeveraged Mortgage REIT ETN	MORL	NYSE Arca	C	C	C+	Down	12.71	17.65	11.70	Y	Trading Tools (Real Estate)
● UBS ETRACS Monthly Pay 2xLev Mortg REIT ETN Ser B	MRRL	NYSE Arca	C-	C-	C-	Down	12.57	17.71	11.53	Y	Trading Tools (Real Estate)
UBS ETRACS Monthly Pay 2xLeveraged MSCI US REIT Index ETN	LRET	NYSE Arca	D	D+	D		20.95	26.59	18.85	Y	Trading Tools (Real Estate)
UBS ETRACS Monthly Pay 2xLeveraged S&P Dividend ETN	SDYL	NYSE Arca	C-	C	D	Down	72.64	92.66	64.58	Y	Trading Tools (Equity-Income)
UBS ETRACS Monthly Pay 2xLeveraged US High Div Low Vol ETN	HDLV	NYSE Arca	D+	C-	D+		22.24	32.19	20.61	Y	Trading Tools (Growth & Inc)
● UBS ETRACS Monthly Pay 2xLev US Small Cap High Div ETN	SMHD	NYSE Arca	C-	C-	C-	Down	13.13	20.72	12.00	Y	Trading Tools (Growth)
UBS ETRACS Monthly Pay 2xLev Wells Fargo MLP Ex-Energy ETN	LMLP	NYSE Arca	C-	C	C-	Down	10.45	18.86	9.55	Y	Trading Tools (Income)
UBS ETRACS Month Reset 2xLev ISE Exclusively Homebuilders	HOML	NYSE Arca	D	D+	D	Down	23.91	68.21	21.59	Y	Trading Tools (Real Estate)

★ Expanded analysis of this fund is included in Section II: Analysis of All BUY Rated Funds. ● Expanded analysis of this fund is included in Section III: Analysis of All Rated Funds with Assets over $50 million.

3-Month Total Return	6-Month Total Return	1-Year Total Return	3-Year Total Return	5-Year Total Return	Dividend Yield (TTM)	Expense Ratio	3-Yr Std Deviation	Effective Duration	NAV	Total Assets (MIL)	%Cash	%Stocks	%Bonds	%Other	Turnover Ratio	Premium/ Discount 1-Year Avg	Inception Date
-9.39	-3.08	-3.27	31.80	43.66	1.03	0.98	9.28		39.31	70.0	40	60	0	0	16	0.38	Jun-12
-5.49	-3.26					0.96		6.01	22.31	9.2	12	31	53	0	18	0.14	Jan-18
-15.31	-13.21	-9.56	9.55	25.76	0.02	1.13	9.29		33.56	216.9	33	66	0	1	1,989	0.14	Jul-12
-17.71	-10.86	-1.55	51.75	88.73	1.42	0.13	13.02		61.98	19,121	0	100	0	0	19	0.03	Dec-98
-0.26	-0.74	-10.63	-23.54	-46.39	0	1	11.51		20.33	1.6	0	0	0	100		0.05	Mar-12
-0.67	0.87	-3.83	-24.16	-47.43	0	1	13.3		16.11	62.7	-1	0	0	101		-0.01	Jun-10
0.98	0.83	-9.25	-6.58	-29.43	0	1	16.22		16.20	28.6	0	0	0	100		-0.01	Sep-11
3.12	-3.04	-27.80	-29.46	-49.88	0	1	23.9		7.07	12.2	1	0	0	99		0.08	Sep-11
-5.21	-3.02	-0.73	-35.01	-59.92	0	1	19.95		5.95	56.6	-1	0	0	101		0.07	Sep-11
-22.48	-18.33	-17.19			0.43	0.66			19.96	41.0	0	100	0	0	53	0.78	Jul-16
-4.07	0.20	6.36			2.02	0.35			25.07	8.2	0	100	0	0	19	-0.36	Jun-16
-15.51	-12.51	4.20			0.44	0.35			32.00	10.2	0	100	0	0	44	0.32	Jun-16
-21.75	-22.60	-27.10			1.21	0.35			24.71	10.9	0	100	0	0	86	1.11	Jun-16
-3.02	-2.53	-2.27	11.58		3.44	0.13	12.14		31.00	2,786	0	100	0	0	7	0.00	Oct-15
-8.15	-7.36	-11.86			1.12	0.4			25.84	4.1	0	100	0	0	22	-0.01	Feb-17
-15.07	-11.94	-10.85	25.23		4.21	0.4	13.3		19.92	188.0	1	99	0	0	28	0.14	Jun-15
-16.13	-13.92	-16.76			0.3	0.59			22.23	10.6	1	99	0	0	83	0.95	Jun-17
-16.70	-11.54	-5.99			0.39	0.59			31.48	129.9	0	100	0	0	42	0.16	Sep-16
8.91	-9.44	-10.45			0.17	0.6			11.40	10.3	0	100	0	0		0.31	Jun-17
-12.39	-3.93	-14.22	14.91		0.42	0.6	19.51		27.94	97.2	0	100	0	0	36	-0.03	Apr-15
-22.84	-20.57	-30.43			0	0.95			124.32	471.9						-0.32	Feb-16
-18.27	-9.67	-17.41			0	0.8			141.86	1,542						0.13	Feb-16
-36.38	-25.79	-15.29	54.91		0	0.85	22.04		191.23	1,470						0.23	Jun-14
231.66	149.62	18.53			0	1.85			17.84	6.0						0.34	Jan-17
-81.42	-78.32	-65.00			0	1.45			8.37	7.5						-0.38	Jan-17
-24.70	-19.28	-16.36	19.94		17.18	0.85	24.86		11.59	5.7						1.02	Oct-15
-24.71	-19.28	-16.36	19.94	-11.04	17.18	0.85	24.86		11.59	204.7						0.21	May-11
-34.14	-20.86	-28.16			18.03	0.85			23.33	69.6						0.21	Feb-16
-36.55	-24.62	-30.12			13.32	0.95			26.69	27.9						0.47	Feb-16
-19.25	-11.37	-13.03	-5.22	-34.00	7.65	0.8	17.56		14.02	255.3						-0.15	Jul-12
-20.71	-14.45	-18.98	-11.70		0	0.8	17.75		14.02	6.2						2.10	Oct-15
-18.14	-9.74	-12.40	-6.91	-32.26	7.42	0.85	18.2		19.83	1,387						-0.03	Apr-10
-18.14	-9.74	-12.40	-6.91		7.42	0.85	18.21		19.83	8.6						0.04	Oct-15
-17.92	-8.99	-11.59	6.82	-26.69	6.92	0.85	19.92		20.02	8.8						0.16	Jul-10
-11.44	-10.37	-12.42	-0.78	-39.75	0	0.5	9.52		14.10	51.2					0	-0.01	Oct-09
1.14	-1.43	-9.35	-12.18	-34.17	0	0.65	13.15		16.14	3.0					0	-0.13	Apr-08
1.06	0.08	-8.87	-11.56	-31.23	0	0.65	11.58		16.48	3.6					0	-0.35	Apr-08
7.83	2.87	-3.02	18.54	2.76	0	0.3	13.12		32.26	6.2					0	0.44	Apr-08
7.23	-2.58	-11.19	7.64	-26.58	0	0.4	21.87		19.46	3.5					0	1.79	Apr-08
-12.74	-11.32	-11.59	12.13	-33.60	0	0.55	10.99		13.56	86.8					0	0.01	Apr-08
-12.55	-9.17	-6.95	13.38	-0.93	8.81	0.85	12.49		17.69	82.6						0.18	Apr-11
-20.71	-15.39	-21.53	30.60	11.22	19.96	0.5	18.07		11.97	220.6						0.44	Dec-13
-17.80	-11.47	-10.98	42.26	24.50	15.37	0.85	18.16		15.65	20.0						0.10	Nov-13
-20.11	-15.56	-14.46	61.45	101.31	7.76	0.35	14.95		57.19	41.4						0.46	May-12
-14.25	-13.01	-12.25	77.05	91.11	21.59	0.4	20.92		12.54	443.2						0.43	Oct-12
-14.25	-13.01	-12.25	77.05		21.59	0.4	20.92		12.54	59.6						0.28	Oct-15
-13.12	-12.78	-14.51	2.18		8.17	0.85	25.23		20.54	5.7						-0.06	May-15
-16.71	-6.72	-9.22	70.03	111.63	5.28	0.3	18.11		73.23	16.7						-0.09	May-12
-11.60	-9.95	-21.90	15.96		10.73	0.85	19.17		22.41	17.2						0.33	Sep-14
-28.50	-31.65	-25.15	43.43		21.47	0.85	28.76		12.13	56.2						0.74	Feb-15
-35.61	-30.87	-23.54	22.63		15.64	0.85	33.57		10.49	24.6						0.11	Jun-14
-30.06	-47.27	-60.08	8.37		0	0.85	43.19		24.06	5.9						2.67	Mar-15

Fund Name	Ticker Symbol	Traded On	Overall Rating	Reward Rating	Risk Rating	Recent Up/Downgrade	Price as of 12/31/2018	52-Week High	52-Week Low	Open to New Investors	Category & (Prospectus Objective)
UBS ETRACS NYSE® Pickens Core Midstream™ Index ETN	PYPE	NYSE Arca	U	U	U		19.61	25.02	18.69	Y	Energy Sector Equity (Growth)
UBS ETRACS S&P GSCI Crude Oil Total Return Index ETN	OILX	NYSE Arca	D+	C-	D	Down	27.70	45.07	26.60	Y	Commodities Specified (Growth & Inc)
UBS ETRACS UBS Bloomberg Constant Maturity Commod Ind (CMC	UCIB	NYSE Arca	D	C-	E		13.58	16.21	13.55	Y	Commodities Broad Basket (Growth & Inc)
UBS ETRACS Wells Fargo® Business Dev Company Ind ETN	BDCZ	NYSE Arca	D	C-	E+		17.70	20.90	16.97	Y	Financials Sector Equity (Growth & Inc)
United States 12 Month Natural Gas Fund, LP	UNL	NYSE Arca	D+	D+	C-	Up	10.33	11.67	8.91	Y	Commodities Specified (Natl Res)
● United States 12 Month Oil Fund, LP	USL	NYSE Arca	C-	C-	C-	Down	17.96	28.28	17.20	Y	Commodities Specified (Natl Res)
United States 3x Oil Fund	USOU	NYSE Arca	D+	D+	D		16.30	91.11	15.10	Y	Trading Tools (Growth & Inc)
United States 3x Short Oil Fund	USOD	NYSE Arca	D+	D	D	Up	12.52	15.27	3.68	Y	Trading Tools (Growth & Inc)
● United States Brent Oil Fund, LP	BNO	NYSE Arca	C-	C-	C-	Down	15.33	24.21	14.70	Y	Commodities Specified (Natl Res)
● United States Commodity Index Fund, LP	USCI	NYSE Arca	D+	D	C-	Down	37.53	45.26	37.49	Y	Commodities Broad Basket (Natl Res)
United States Copper Index Fund, LP	CPER	NYSE Arca	C-	C-	D+		16.44	21.06	16.32	Y	Commodities Specified (Prec Metals)
United States Gasoline Fund, LP	UGA	NYSE Arca	D+	D+	D	Down	22.91	36.91	22.18	Y	Commodities Specified (Natl Res)
● United States Natural Gas Fund, LP	UNG	NYSE Arca	D+	D+	D+	Up	24.71	39.32	21.67	Y	Commodities Specified (Natl Res)
● United States Oil Fund, LP	USO	NYSE Arca	D+	D+	D+	Down	9.66	16.08	9.29	Y	Commodities Specified (Natl Res)
● USAA Core Intermediate-Term Bond ETF	UITB	NYSE Arca	D+	D+	C-		48.08	50.19	47.60	Y	US Fixed Income (Income)
● USAA Core Short-Term Bond ETF	USTB	NYSE Arca	D+	D	D+		49.46	50.08	49.24	Y	US Fixed Income (Income)
● USAA MSCI Emerging Markets Value Momentum Blend Index ETF	UEVM	NYSE Arca	D	D	D		41.73	56.13	40.85	Y	Global Emerg Mkts Equity (Div Emerg Mkts)
● USAA MSCI International Value Momentum Blend Index ETF	UIVM	NYSE Arca	D	D	D		41.46	55.50	40.20	Y	Global Equity Large Cap (Growth & Inc)
● USAA MSCI USA Small Cap Value Momentum Blend Index ETF	USVM	NYSE Arca	D	D	D		45.39	57.27	42.68	Y	US Equity Small Cap (Small Company)
● USAA MSCI USA Value Momentum Blend Index ETF	ULVM	NYSE Arca	D	D	D		45.06	55.24	42.49	Y	US Equity Large Cap Blend (Growth & Inc)
USCF SummerHaven Dynamic Commodity Strategy No K-1 Fund	SDCI	NYSE Arca	U	U	U		18.85	22.77	18.85	Y	Commodities Broad Basket (Growth & Inc)
USCF SummerHaven SHPEI Index Fund	BUY	NYSE Arca	D	D	E		18.66	28.68	18.33	Y	US Equity Large Cap Blend (Growth & Inc)
USCF SummerHaven SHPEN Index Fund	BUYN	NYSE Arca	D	D	E+		16.57	28.10	16.39	Y	Natural Resources (Growth & Inc)
★ Utilities Select Sector SPDR® Fund	XLU	NYSE Arca	B	B-	B	Up	52.92	56.93	47.56	Y	Utilities Sector Equity (Utility)
Validea Market Legends ETF	VALX	NAS CM	D+	C-	D	Down	23.91	30.43	23.35	Y	US Equity Mid Cap (Growth & Inc)
● VanEck Merk Gold Trust	OUNZ	NYSE Arca	D+	D	C-		12.59	13.37	11.53	Y	Commodities Specified (Prec Metals)
● VanEck Vectors Africa Index ETF	AFK	NYSE Arca	D+	D+	D	Down	19.66	27.04	19.22	Y	Equity Misc (Growth)
● VanEck Vectors Agribusiness ETF	MOO	NYSE Arca	C	C	C-		56.92	66.33	54.16	Y	Natural Resources (Unaligned)
★ VanEck Vectors AMT-Free Intermediate Municipal Index ETF	ITM	BATS	B	A	C+	Up	47.47	47.53	23.26	Y	US Muni Fixed Inc (Muni Bond - Natl)
● VanEck Vectors AMT-Free Long Municipal Index ETF	MLN	BATS	D+	D+	C-	Down	19.56	20.33	18.91	Y	US Muni Fixed Inc (Muni Bond - Natl)
● VanEck Vectors AMT-Free Short Municipal Index ETF	SMB	BATS	C-	D+	C-		17.30	17.35	17.05	Y	US Muni Fixed Inc (Muni Bond - Natl)
● VanEck Vectors BDC Income ETF	BIZD	NYSE Arca	C+	B	C-	Down	14.04	17.40	14.04	Y	Financials Sector Equity (Income)
● VanEck Vectors Biotech ETF	BBH	NAS CM	C	C	D+		110.72	136.04	103.76	Y	Healthcare Sector Equity (Unaligned)
● VanEck Vectors Brazil Small-Cap ETF	BRF	NYSE Arca	C-	C	D+		20.02	25.87	16.00	Y	Latin America Equity (Growth)
● VanEck Vectors CEF Municipal Income ETF	XMPT	BATS	D+	D	C-		23.88	26.84	23.37	Y	US Muni Fixed Inc (Muni Bond - Natl)
VanEck Vectors ChinaAMC China Bond ETF	CBON	NYSE Arca	D+	C-	D		22.39	24.24	22.06	Y	Emerging Mkts Fixed Inc (Govt Bond - Gen)
● VanEck Vectors ChinaAMC CSI 300 ETF	PEK	NYSE Arca	D	D	D	Down	31.50	54.20	31.39	Y	Greater China Equity (Pacific Stock)
VanEck Vectors ChinaAMC SME-ChiNext ETF	CNXT	NYSE Arca	D-	D-	D	Down	20.94	36.77	20.94	Y	Greater China Equity (Pacific Stock)
● VanEck Vectors Coal ETF	KOL	NYSE Arca	C-	C	C-	Down	12.56	18.39	12.27	Y	Equity Misc (Natl Res)
VanEck Vectors Egypt Index ETF	EGPT	NYSE Arca	D	D	D	Down	27.69	40.42	26.91	Y	Equity Misc (Growth)
VanEck Vectors Emerging Markets Aggregate Bond ETF	EMAG	NYSE Arca	D+	C-	D+	Down	20.06	22.35	19.73	Y	Emerging Mkts Fixed Inc (Income)
● VanEck Vectors Emerging Markets High Yield Bond ETF	HYEM	NYSE Arca	C	C-	C+		22.38	24.64	22.05	Y	Emerging Mkts Fixed Inc (Corp Bond-High Yld)
★ VanEck Vectors Environmental Services ETF	EVX	NYSE Arca	B-	B	C		83.26	99.64	78.68	Y	Industrials Sector Equity (Unaligned)
● VanEck Vectors Fallen Angel High Yield Bond ETF	ANGL	NYSE Arca	C	C-	C+		26.67	30.31	26.29	Y	US Fixed Income (Corp Bond-High Yld)
VanEck Vectors Gaming ETF	BJK	NYSE Arca	D+	C-	D	Down	33.03	50.29	31.53	Y	Consumer Goods & Svcs (Unaligned)
VanEck Vectors Generic Drugs ETF	GNRX	NAS CM	D+	C-	D		20.70	26.55	20.18	Y	Healthcare Sector Equity (Unaligned)
● VanEck Vectors Global Alternative Energy ETF	GEX	NYSE Arca	C-	C-	D+		54.60	64.43	51.82	Y	Equity Misc (Natl Res)
● VanEck Vectors Gold Miners ETF	GDX	NYSE Arca	D+	C-	D	Down	21.09	24.60	17.57	Y	Prec Metals (Prec Metals)
VanEck Vectors Green Bond ETF	GRNB	NYSE Arca	D	D	D+	Down	25.59	27.50	25.14	Y	Global Fixed Income (Growth & Inc)
VanEck Vectors High Income Infrastructure MLP ETF	YMLI	NYSE Arca	C	B-	D		11.05	14.84	10.67	Y	Energy Sector Equity (Utility)
VanEck Vectors High Income MLP ETF	YMLP	NYSE Arca	C	B-	D+		17.15	25.45	16.27	Y	Energy Sector Equity (Natl Res)
★ VanEck Vectors High-Yield Municipal Index ETF	HYD	BATS	B+	A	C+	Up	61.04	63.06	30.64	Y	US Muni Fixed Inc (Muni Bond - Natl)

★ Expanded analysis of this fund is included in Section II: Analysis of All BUY Rated Funds. ● Expanded analysis of this fund is included in Section III: Analysis of All Rated Funds with Assets over $50 million.

3-Month Total Return	6-Month Total Return	1-Year Total Return	3-Year Total Return	5-Year Total Return	Dividend Yield (TTM)	Expense Ratio	3-Yr Std Deviation	Effective Duration	NAV	Total Assets (MIL)	%Cash	%Stocks	%Bonds	%Other	Turnover Ratio	Premium/ Discount 1-Year Avg	Inception Date
-19.34						0.85			19.68	21.7						0.10	Aug-18
-39.71	-36.31	-20.89			0				27.43	12.3						-1.80	Feb-16
-12.74	-11.32	-11.59	12.13		0	0.55	10.99		13.56	5.7						-0.02	Oct-15
-12.55	-9.17	-6.95	13.48		8.81	0.85	12.49		17.69	7.8						0.18	Oct-15
7.05	9.49	10.78	5.52	-44.00	0	0.9	22.22		10.26	6.3	33	0	13	53		-0.22	Nov-09
-36.21	-28.33	-15.31	4.87	-58.38	0	0.86	24.18		17.82	55.6	36	0	18	46	50	-0.17	Dec-07
-81.87	-79.48	-64.68			0	0.95			15.83	9.9	30	0	2	68		-0.08	Jul-17
236.00	159.96	14.91			0	1			12.88	2.7						-0.42	Jul-17
-36.51	-29.95	-16.51	24.21	-65.35	0	0.9	27.98		15.18	80.6	34	0	18	48		-0.12	Jun-10
-12.55	-12.89	-11.73	-7.45	-33.11	0	1.04	8.7		37.49	509.8	41	0	11	49		-0.02	Aug-10
-6.04	-11.52	-21.92	15.44	-28.29	0	0.8	19.1		16.44	11.3	36	0	14	50		0.02	Nov-11
-38.26	-32.86	-29.02	-22.40	-62.03	0	0.75	29.41		22.74	31.8	35	0	18	48	0	-0.12	Feb-08
-4.78	4.92	4.34	-29.93	-70.43	0	1.3	39.66		24.35	368.9	36	0	16	48		0.00	Apr-07
-39.73	-36.01	-20.64	-13.05	-72.79	0	0.77	28.92		9.59	1,570	35	0	19	46	0	-0.10	Apr-06
0.88	1.18	-0.88			2.98	0.4		5.84	48.14	167.0	2	0	96	0	10	0.14	Oct-17
0.89	1.57	1.43			2.24	0.35		1.81	49.47	64.1	7	0	93	0	22	0.15	Oct-17
-7.46	-8.06	-16.62			1	0.45			41.76	166.6	1	98	0	0		0.28	Oct-17
-13.84	-11.90	-17.44			1.54	0.35			41.43	289.6	0	100	0	0		0.30	Oct-17
-16.77	-15.49	-9.26			0.9	0.25			45.40	85.0	0	100	0	0		0.08	Oct-17
-15.51	-11.73	-12.10			1.33	0.2			44.99	392.8	0	100	0	0		0.18	Oct-17
-12.46	-12.81					0.8			18.84	5.8					19	0.06	May-18
-19.22	-20.05	-12.67				0.95			18.70	2.5	1	99	0	0	3	0.48	Dec-17
-39.00	-39.85	-36.43				0.95			16.61	2.4	0	100	0	0	1	-0.21	Dec-17
1.62	2.92	4.01	35.13	65.41	3.26	0.13	12		52.92	8,176	0	100	0	0	5	-0.01	Dec-98
-16.10	-16.16	-15.03	8.38		0.96	0.81	11.84		24.16	24.9	1	99	0	0	133	0.32	Dec-14
7.64	2.49	-1.54	19.21		0	0.4	12.62		12.58	134.0	0	0	0	100		0.11	May-14
-5.31	-11.97	-17.22	18.92	-26.75	2.4	0.84	16.06		20.08	59.6	0	100	0	0	38	-0.14	Jul-08
-11.83	-6.12	-5.87	29.14	17.23	1.41	0.54	9.25		57.11	816.3	0	100	0	0	22	-0.11	Aug-07
1.95	103.37	100.88	112.15	139.61	2.34	0.24	4.34	6.90	47.44	1,649	0	0	100	0	9	-0.21	Dec-07
1.41	0.33	-0.98	7.66	29.74	3.1	0.24	5.13		19.62	140.8	0	0	100	0	33	-0.33	Jan-08
1.07	0.88	1.42	2.67	5.21	1.56	0.2	1.83	3.24	17.34	199.3	0	0	100	0	41	-0.31	Feb-08
-12.38	-8.75	-5.53	18.46	4.92	9.61	9.41	12.55		14.22	198.6	-1	101	0	0	19	0.04	Feb-13
-17.28	-7.11	-10.21	-11.01	27.82	0.55	0.35	21.39		111.33	428.3	0	100	0	0	30	0.02	Dec-11
23.15	15.80	-11.79	115.75	-17.51	5.24	0.6	32.58		20.09	89.2	1	99	0	0	53	-0.08	May-09
-1.93	-3.26	-6.31	3.02	31.57	5.07	1.56	7.76	8.73	23.89	118.0	-9	0	111	-2	9	-0.04	Jul-11
1.65	0.11	0.99	1.05		3.29	0.5	5.11	3.11	22.55	4.5	16	0	84	0	39	-0.58	Nov-14
-18.41	-19.46	-33.78	-26.78	9.29	1.46	0.78	21.56		31.58	61.1	0	99	0	0	37	0.19	Oct-10
-16.68	-26.93	-39.72	-49.66		0.29	0.82	26.08		20.97	16.9	1	99	0	0	37	0.50	Jul-14
-13.21	-13.43	-15.27	127.50	-21.42	4.09	0.6	27.12		12.66	61.3	0	100	0	0	39	-0.32	Jan-08
-5.81	-19.51	-11.88	-25.12	-44.07	0.87	0.94	28.93		28.28	35.7	-1	101	0	0	41	-0.78	Feb-10
0.07	0.88	-3.51	13.96	7.19	4.7	0.35	6.01	4.79	20.24	15.1	1	0	99	0	20	-0.49	May-11
-1.21	0.36	-4.01	19.32	20.13	5.73	0.4	5.29	3.66	22.37	269.9	1	0	98	1	40	-0.24	May-12
-12.67	-7.64	-3.12	45.80	34.12	0.87	0.55	11.09		83.47	23.4	0	100	0	0	24	0.35	Oct-06
-6.41	-4.02	-5.43	29.58	32.07	5.62	0.35	6.89	5.90	26.87	865.6	0	0	97	0	20	-0.32	Apr-12
-12.88	-22.58	-25.67	16.25	-24.39	3.8	0.65	16.83		33.16	27.2	0	100	0	0	31	-0.01	Jan-08
-17.60	-16.21	-14.84	-10.73		0.68	0.57			20.84	3.6	1	99	0	0	15	-0.09	Jan-16
-5.35	-4.03	-8.96	5.14	3.42	1.29	0.63	13.55		55.10	88.1	0	100	0	0	21	0.09	May-07
14.29	-3.98	-8.85	56.12	2.78	0.92	0.53	37.22		21.07	8,936	0	100	0	0	12	0.06	May-06
-0.50	-0.92	-4.15			1.48	0.3		6.41	25.50	25.2	0	0	100	0	26	0.11	Mar-17
-17.33	-8.92	-11.29	10.91	-24.41	8.01	0.83	22.13		11.10	19.8	0	100	0	0	53	-0.18	Feb-13
-21.47	-17.79	-20.27	-2.82	-68.86	9.98	0.82	23.29		17.14	46.1	0	100	0	0	40	-0.18	Mar-12
-0.88	98.78	103.45	125.71	169.30	4.42	0.35	4.61	7.46	61.23	2,339	0	0	100	0	14	-0.15	Feb-09

Fund Name	Ticker Symbol	Traded On	Overall Rating	Reward Rating	Risk Rating	Recent Up/ Downgrade	Price as of 12/31/2018	52-Week High	52-Week Low	Open to New Investors	Category & (Prospectus Objective)
● VanEck Vectors India Small-Cap Index ETF	SCIF	NYSE Arca	D	D	D	Down	42.40	72.50	36.72	Y	India Equity (Small Company)
VanEck Vectors Indonesia Index ETF	IDX	NYSE Arca	D+	D+	D+		21.76	26.88	18.81	Y	Equity Misc (Growth)
● VanEck Vectors International High Yield Bond ETF	IHY	NYSE Arca	C-	C-	C-		23.41	26.11	23.30	Y	Global Fixed Income (Corp Bond-High Yld)
● VanEck Vectors Investment Grade Floating Rate ETF	FLTR	NYSE Arca	C	C-	C+		24.69	25.40	24.69	Y	US Fixed Income (Income)
● VanEck Vectors Israel ETF	ISRA	NYSE Arca	C-	C	D+	Down	28.03	34.34	26.75	Y	Equity Misc (Growth)
★ VanEck Vectors J.P. Morgan EM Local Currency Bond ETF	EMLC	NYSE Arca	B	A	C+	Up	33.00	33.10	16.16	Y	Emerging Mkts Fixed Inc (Div Emerg Mkts)
● VanEck Vectors Junior Gold Miners ETF	GDXJ	NYSE Arca	D	D+	D	Down	30.22	35.74	26.17	Y	Prec Metals (Prec Metals)
● VanEck Vectors Morningstar International Moat ETF	MOTI	NYSE Arca	C-	C-	C-		28.32	36.79	27.71	Y	Global Equity Large Cap (Foreign Stock)
● VanEck Vectors Morningstar Wide Moat ETF	MOAT	NYSE Arca	C	C	C	Down	41.17	47.20	38.89	Y	US Equity Large Cap Blend (Growth)
● VanEck Vectors Mortgage REIT Income ETF	MORT	NYSE Arca	C+	B-	C	Down	21.31	24.70	21.00	Y	Real Estate Sector Equity (Real Estate)
● VanEck Vectors Natural Resources ETF	HAP	NYSE Arca	C-	C	D+	Down	32.23	39.65	30.80	Y	Natural Resources (Natl Res)
● VanEck Vectors Oil Refiners ETF	CRAK	NYSE Arca	C	C	C-		26.84	36.07	25.55	Y	Energy Sector Equity (Unaligned)
● VanEck Vectors Oil Services ETF	OIH	NYSE Arca	C-	C	D		14.03	29.51	13.32	Y	Energy Sector Equity (Natl Res)
● VanEck Vectors Pharmaceutical ETF	PPH	NAS CM	C	C+	C-		54.79	64.61	52.66	Y	Healthcare Sector Equity (Health)
VanEck Vectors Poland ETF	PLND	NYSE Arca	C-	C-	D+	Up	16.26	21.68	15.23	Y	Equity Misc (Growth)
● VanEck Vectors Preferred Securities ex Financials ETF	PFXF	NYSE Arca	C	C-	C+		17.72	19.82	17.35	Y	US Fixed Income (Income)
VanEck Vectors Pre-Refunded Municipal Index ETF	PRB	BATS	D+	D+	D+	Up	24.41	24.52	24.08	Y	US Muni Fixed Inc (Muni Bond - Natl)
● VanEck Vectors Rare Earth/Strategic Metals ETF	REMX	NYSE Arca	D+	C-	D	Down	13.56	32.55	13.21	Y	Prec Metals (Natl Res)
VanEck Vectors Real Asset Allocation ETF	RAAX	NYSE Arca	U	U	U		24.82	26.56	24.58	Y	Moderate Allocation (Growth & Inc)
● VanEck Vectors Retail ETF	RTH	NYSE Arca	C+	B	C-	Down	93.91	111.97	87.33	Y	Consumer Goods & Svcs (Unaligned)
● VanEck Vectors Russia ETF	RSX	NYSE Arca	C	C	C		18.75	24.31	18.44	Y	Equity Misc (Growth)
VanEck Vectors Russia Small-Cap ETF	RSXJ	NYSE Arca	D+	D+	D+	Down	27.33	43.92	26.88	Y	Equity Misc (Growth)
● VanEck Vectors Semiconductor ETF	SMH	NYSE Arca	C+	B	C	Down	87.28	113.07	80.96	Y	Technology Sector Equity (Technology)
● VanEck Vectors Short High-Yield Municipal Index ETF	SHYD	BATS	C-	C	C-	Down	24.20	24.60	23.89	Y	US Muni Fixed Inc (Muni Bond - Natl)
● VanEck Vectors Steel ETF	SLX	NYSE Arca	C+	B	C-	Down	34.84	51.70	33.83	Y	Natural Resources (Unaligned)
● VanEck Vectors Unconventional Oil & Gas ETF	FRAK	NYSE Arca	C	C+	D+		10.92	17.99	10.14	Y	Energy Sector Equity (Natl Res)
VanEck Vectors Uranium+Nuclear Energy ETF	NLR	NYSE Arca	C	C+	C-		49.57	53.81	45.92	Y	Utilities Sector Equity (Natl Res)
● VanEck Vectors Vietnam ETF	VNM	NYSE Arca	C-	C-	C-		14.75	20.39	14.49	Y	Asia ex-Japan Equity (Growth)
● VanEck Vectors® NDR CMG Long/Flat Allocation ETF	LFEQ	NYSE Arca	D+	D+	C-		24.59	28.45	23.52	Y	US Equity Large Cap Blend (Growth & Inc)
● Vanguard Communication Services Index Fund ETF Shares	VOX	NYSE Arca	C+	B	C-	Up	74.07	92.99	69.56	Y	Communications Sector Equity (Comm)
● Vanguard Consumer Discretionary Index Fund ETF Shares	VCR	NYSE Arca	C	C	C-	Down	150.52	181.57	139.59	Y	Consumer Goods & Svcs (Unaligned)
● Vanguard Consumer Staples Index Fund ETF Shares	VDC	NYSE Arca	C+	B	C	Up	131.17	150.85	125.78	Y	Consumer Goods & Svcs (Unaligned)
● Vanguard Dividend Appreciation Index Fund ETF Shares	VIG	NYSE Arca	C+	C	C+		97.95	112.45	92.08	Y	US Equity Large Cap Blend (Equity-Income)
● Vanguard Emerg Mkts Govt Bond Ind Fund ETF Shares	VWOB	NAS CM	C	C-	C+	Up	74.54	80.61	73.40	Y	Emerging Mkts Fixed Inc (Govt Bond - Gen)
● Vanguard Energy Index Fund ETF Shares	VDE	NYSE Arca	C	C	C-	Down	77.11	108.92	72.37	Y	Energy Sector Equity (Natl Res)
Vanguard ESG International Stock ETF	VSGX	BATS	U	U	U		44.50	51.27	43.28	Y	Global Equity Large Cap (Foreign Stock)
Vanguard ESG U.S. Stock ETF	ESGV	BATS	U	U	U		43.00	50.49	40.33	Y	US Equity Large Cap Blend (Growth & Inc)
● Vanguard Extended Duration Treasury Index Fund ETF Shares	EDV	NYSE Arca	D+	D	C-	Down	113.46	120.99	101.75	Y	US Fixed Income (Govt Bond - Treasury)
● Vanguard Extended Market Index Fund ETF Shares	VXF	NYSE Arca	C	C-	C+	Down	99.81	125.16	93.42	Y	US Equity Mid Cap (Growth)
● Vanguard Financials Index Fund ETF Shares	VFH	NYSE Arca	C	C	C+	Down	59.36	75.13	55.73	Y	Financials Sector Equity (Financial)
● Vanguard FTSE All-World ex-US Index Fund ETF Shares	VEU	NYSE Arca	C-	D+	C	Down	45.58	58.89	44.23	Y	Global Equity Large Cap (Foreign Stock)
● Vanguard FTSE All-World ex-US Small-Cap Ind ETF Shares	VSS	NYSE Arca	D+	D+	C-	Down	94.68	127.14	91.12	Y	Global Eq Mid/Small Cap (Foreign Stock)
● Vanguard FTSE Developed Markets Index Fund ETF Shares	VEA	NYSE Arca	C-	D+	C	Down	37.10	47.88	35.84	Y	Global Equity Large Cap (Foreign Stock)
● Vanguard FTSE Emerging Markets Index Fund ETF Shares	VWO	NYSE Arca	C-	C-	C-	Down	38.10	50.98	36.68	Y	Global Emerg Mkts Equity (Div Emerg Mkts)
● Vanguard FTSE Europe Index Fund ETF Shares	VGK	NYSE Arca	C-	D+	C-	Down	48.62	63.49	46.99	Y	Europe Equity Large Cap (Europe Stock)
● Vanguard FTSE Pacific Index Fund ETF Shares	VPL	NYSE Arca	C-	D+	C	Down	60.63	77.85	58.71	Y	Asia Equity (Pacific Stock)
● Vanguard Global ex-U.S. Real Estate Index Fund ETF Shares	VNQI	NAS CM	C-	D+	C	Down	52.41	65.14	51.24	Y	Real Estate Sector Equity (Real Estate)
● Vanguard Growth Index Fund ETF Shares	VUG	NYSE Arca	C	C	C+	Down	134.33	161.48	124.85	Y	US Equity Large Cap Growth (Growth)
● Vanguard Health Care Index Fund ETF Shares	VHT	NYSE Arca	C+	C+	C+		160.60	180.89	149.65	Y	Healthcare Sector Equity (Health)
● Vanguard High Dividend Yield Index Fund ETF Shares	VYM	NYSE Arca	C	C	C+	Down	77.99	90.91	73.71	Y	US Equity Large Cap Value (Equity-Income)
● Vanguard Industrials Index Fund ETF Shares	VIS	NYSE Arca	C	C	C+	Down	120.41	150.77	112.87	Y	Industrials Sector Equity (Unaligned)
● Vanguard Information Technology Index Fund ETF Shares	VGT	NYSE Arca	C+	C+	C+	Down	166.83	203.56	154.81	Y	Technology Sector Equity (Unaligned)

★Expanded analysis of this fund is included in Section II: Analysis of All BUY Rated Funds.   ● Expanded analysis of this fund is included in Section III: Analysis of All Rated Funds with Assets over $50 million.

			TOTAL RETURNS & PERFORMANCE						ASSETS		ASSET ALLOCATION & TURNOVER					VALUATION	
3-Month Total Return	6-Month Total Return	1-Year Total Return	3-Year Total Return	5-Year Total Return	Dividend Yield (TTM)	Expense Ratio	3-Yr Std Deviation	Effective Duration	NAV	Total Assets (MIL)	%Cash	%Stocks	%Bonds	%Other	Turnover Ratio	Premium/ Discount 1-Year Avg	Inception Date
7.39	-11.49	-37.99	-1.42	43.18	0.17	0.72	28.54		42.36	184.7	0	50	0	50	42	0.11	Aug-10
7.49	8.80	-9.44	25.88	15.25	2.08	0.57	16.36		21.85	44.3	0	100	0	0	14	-0.21	Jan-09
-3.15	-1.46	-4.96	17.96	9.99	4.68	0.4	5.85	3.85	23.39	127.1	2	0	97	0	41	-0.19	Apr-12
-1.52	-0.66	0.36	5.40	5.85	2.44	0.14	0.74	0.09	24.75	711.0	0	0	99	0	28	0.07	Apr-11
-14.56	-10.04	-6.96	1.27	0.80	1.48	0.59	11.52		28.05	52.6	0	100	0	0	21	0.31	Jun-13
1.88	100.66	83.81	127.88	83.59	6.45	0.3	11.08	4.99	32.96	4,544	0	0	100	0	28	-0.04	Jul-10
10.64	-6.36	-11.47	66.01	4.84	0.04	0.54	42.02		30.11	3,916	0	100	0	0	67	-0.11	Nov-09
-10.58	-8.53	-13.17	18.40		3.08	0.56	12.23		28.48	81.3	0	100	0	0	112	0.02	Jul-15
-10.48	-4.08	-1.39	47.87	53.71	0.99	0.48	11.43		41.14	1,737	0	100	0	0	56	0.18	Apr-12
-6.95	-5.88	-4.45	38.85	47.27	8.12	0.41	10.56		21.28	147.2	0	100	0	0	21	0.09	Aug-11
-12.51	-9.47	-10.67	30.76	-2.71	2.15	0.5	11.83		32.20	85.7	0	100	0	0	34	0.08	Aug-08
-24.18	-13.13	-10.93	43.97		1.23	0.59	15.85		26.95	55.7	0	100	0	0	24	0.23	Aug-15
-43.38	-43.56	-44.58	-43.16	-67.24	3.75	0.35	29.41		14.03	1,090	0	100	0	0	34	0.01	Dec-11
-13.77	-5.95	-5.52	-10.36	14.08	1.64	0.35	13.52		55.02	278.5	0	100	0	0	18	0.02	Dec-11
-3.50	6.03	-16.07	34.35	-15.04	5.87	0.66	22.22		16.33	13.3	2	94	0	4	28	-0.12	Nov-09
-6.67	-7.02	-4.78	8.72	24.48	6.32	0.41	5.34		17.70	511.5	0	10	0	7	47	0.10	Jul-12
1.00	0.88	1.36	2.42	4.05	1.39	0.24	1.22	2.90	24.37	14.6	3	0	97	0	47	0.01	Feb-09
-24.09	-33.34	-48.31	18.53	-51.90	4.68	0.61	26.81		13.56	128.8	1	99	0	0	57	-0.35	Oct-10
-2.04	-1.65					0.74			24.79	14.8	100	0	0	0		0.15	Apr-18
-14.96	-5.21	3.76	26.04	65.29	1.38	0.35	13.59		93.97	136.8	0	100	0	0	16	0.05	Dec-11
-8.28	-5.98	-6.02	43.39	-20.75	4.44	0.67	18.48		18.79	1,479	0	100	0	0	15	0.07	Apr-07
-10.55	-19.36	-28.80	58.96	-24.42	4.74	0.76	22.34		27.61	36.6	0	98	0	3	39	-0.37	Apr-11
-17.03	-14.10	-9.46	69.56	120.17	1.46	0.35	18.56		87.33	902.5	0	100	0	0	23	0.04	Dec-11
0.14	0.36	2.16	5.80		3.15	0.35	2.93	4.73	24.18	154.5	0	0	100	0	27	-0.12	Jan-14
-20.70	-18.73	-20.08	94.12	-16.96	2.78	0.56	32.89		34.87	76.3	0	100	0	0	31	0.01	Oct-06
-36.73	-35.58	-29.93	-15.84	-59.22	0.83	0.54	28.87		10.93	64.0	0	100	0	0	17	-0.08	Feb-12
-1.77	0.99	5.14	23.73	23.19	4.53	0.61	9.64		49.67	27.2	0	100	0	0	19	-0.16	Aug-07
-10.33	-5.11	-14.13	5.11	-11.08	1.29	0.66	14.88		14.84	333.5	0	100	0	0	50	0.42	Aug-09
-12.05	-6.47	-4.98			0.77	0.59			24.69	52.2	1	99	0	0	28	0.13	Oct-17
-14.55	-12.92	-16.95	-3.87	2.68	3.58	0.1	11.37			1,510	1	99	0	0	84	0.05	Sep-04
-16.93	-11.56	-3.19	26.79	47.51	1.21	0.1	12.16			3,130	1	99	0	0	28	0.03	Jan-04
-5.92	-0.92	-8.12	9.19	34.02	2.51	0.1	9.4			5,194	0	100	0	0	8	0.01	Jan-04
-12.17	-3.74	-3.01	32.56	43.05	1.86	0.08	8.87			39,092	0	100	0	0	14	0.01	Apr-06
-0.19	1.45	-2.89	15.68	23.54	4.6	0.32	4.88	6.24		1,330	0	0	98	2	19	0.22	May-13
-27.40	-24.61	-20.30	0.29	-30.62	2.8	0.1	19.66			4,209	1	99	0	0	5	-0.02	Sep-04
-11.99						0.15				42.4						0.40	Sep-18
-14.88						0.12				68.7						0.08	Sep-18
5.74	0.04	-3.77	10.89	54.32	3.16	0.07	13.5	24.02		1,808	0	0	100	0	18	0.56	Dec-07
-18.23	-15.77	-10.20	23.18	28.15	1.52	0.08	12.82			65,136	3	97	0	0	0	0.01	Dec-01
-14.67	-12.34	-14.24	28.38	45.62	1.95	0.1	14.49			8,084	0	100	0	0	3	0.02	Jan-04
-11.83	-10.98	-14.32	14.23	4.49	3.11	0.11	11			35,373	3	97	0	0	4	0.09	Mar-07
-15.23	-16.27	-19.03	10.07	4.72	3.06	0.13	11.55			6,132	7	91	0	1	14	0.14	Apr-09
-13.55	-11.60	-14.88	10.31	3.79	3.25	0.07	10.78			104,457	4	95	0	1	3	0.05	Jul-07
-6.75	-7.87	-14.90	24.93	6.39	2.65	0.14	14.46			77,643	3	96	0	0	6	0.05	Mar-05
-13.41	-12.86	-15.27	7.01	-1.87	3.74	0.1	12.04			19,810	1	98	0	1	4	0.00	Mar-05
-13.08	-10.29	-14.08	16.36	13.73	2.81	0.1	11.04			6,983	3	97	0	0	3	-0.07	Mar-05
-4.53	-6.87	-9.96	15.91	17.39	5.33	0.14	11.38			6,189	2	96	0	2	6	0.08	Nov-10
-17.24	-10.91	-4.16	29.98	52.58	1.17	0.05	11.12			79,909	1	99	0	0	8	0.00	Jan-04
-12.18	-0.35	4.02	24.04	66.75	1.22	0.1	13.2			10,515	0	100	0	0	6	0.01	Jan-04
-10.67	-5.19	-6.59	27.08	44.68	2.96	0.08	8.26			30,925	0	100	0	0	9	0.02	Nov-06
-19.26	-11.65	-14.80	24.60	30.36	1.66	0.1	13.34			3,832	0	100	0	0	4	-0.02	Sep-04
-18.29	-9.19	1.53	58.28	96.17	1.07	0.1	14.36			21,690	0	100	0	0	7	0.02	Jan-04

I. Index of Exchange-Traded Funds

Fund Name	Ticker Symbol	Traded On	Overall Rating	Reward Rating	Risk Rating	Recent Up/Downgrade	Price as of 12/31/2018	52-Week High	52-Week Low	Open to New Investors	Category & (Prospectus Objective)
● Vanguard Intermediate-Term Bond Index Fund ETF Shares	BIV	NYSE Arca	C-	D	C		81.29	83.83	79.35	Y	US Fixed Income (Income)
● Vanguard Intermediate-Term Corp Bond Ind Fund ETF Shares	VCIT	NAS CM	C	D+	C+		82.86	87.39	82.02	Y	US Fixed Income (Corp Bond - Gen)
● Vanguard Intermediate-Term Treasury Index Fund ETF Shares	VGIT	NAS CM	C-	D	C	Up	63.47	63.94	61.57	Y	US Fixed Income (Govt Bond - Gen)
● Vanguard Intl Dividend Appreciation Ind Fund ETF Shares	VIGI	NAS CM	D+	D+	C-	Down	57.60	70.39	55.63	Y	Global Equity Large Cap (Foreign Stock)
● Vanguard Intl High Dividend Yield Ind Fund ETF Shares	VYMI	NAS CM	C-	D+	C	Down	56.27	72.13	54.56	Y	Global Equity Large Cap (Foreign Stock)
● Vanguard Large-Cap Index Fund ETF Shares	VV	NYSE Arca	C	C	C+	Down	114.86	134.91	107.63	Y	US Equity Large Cap Blend (Growth)
● Vanguard Long-Term Bond Index Fund ETF Shares	BLV	NYSE Arca	D+	D	C	Down	87.51	95.08	83.53	Y	US Fixed Income (Income)
● Vanguard Long-Term Corporate Bond Index Fund ETF Shares	VCLT	NAS CM	C-	D+	C	Down	85.18	95.75	83.50	Y	US Fixed Income (Corp Bond - Gen)
● Vanguard Long-Term Treasury Index Fund ETF Shares	VGLT	NAS CM	D+	D	C-	Down	74.71	78.00	69.06	Y	US Fixed Income (Govt Bond - Gen)
● Vanguard Materials Index Fund ETF Shares	VAW	NYSE Arca	C	C	C		110.83	144.53	104.05	Y	Natural Resources (Unaligned)
● Vanguard Mega Cap Growth Index Fund ETF Shares	MGK	NYSE Arca	C	C	C+	Down	107.01	128.70	99.52	Y	US Equity Large Cap Growth (Growth)
● Vanguard Mega Cap Index Fund ETF Shares	MGC	NYSE Arca	C	C	C-		86.88	101.45	81.34	Y	US Equity Large Cap Blend (Growth)
● Vanguard Mega Cap Value Index Fund ETF Shares	MGV	NYSE Arca	C	C	C+		71.47	81.87	67.32	Y	US Equity Large Cap Value (Growth & Inc)
● Vanguard Mid-Cap Growth Index Fund ETF Shares	VOT	NYSE Arca	C	C	C+	Down	119.69	143.70	111.81	Y	US Equity Mid Cap (Growth)
● Vanguard Mid-Cap Index Fund ETF Shares	VO	NYSE Arca	C	C-	C+	Down	138.18	166.55	129.93	Y	US Equity Mid Cap (Growth)
● Vanguard Mid-Cap Value Index Fund ETF Shares	VOE	NYSE Arca	C	C-	C+	Down	95.26	117.78	90.18	Y	US Equity Mid Cap (Growth)
● Vanguard Mortgage-Backed Securities Index Fund ETF Shares	VMBS	NAS CM	C	D+	C+	Up	51.49	52.44	50.20	Y	US Fixed Income (Govt Bond - Mortgage)
● Vanguard Real Estate Index Fund ETF Shares	VNQ	NYSE Arca	C+	C	B	Up	74.57	84.26	71.74	Y	Real Estate Sector Equity (Real Estate)
● Vanguard Russell 1000 Growth Index Fund ETF Shares	VONG	NAS CM	C	C	C+	Down	134.49	160.23	124.90	Y	US Equity Large Cap Growth (Growth)
● Vanguard Russell 1000 Index Fund ETF Shares	VONE	NAS CM	C	C	C-		114.50	134.87	107.21	Y	US Equity Large Cap Blend (Growth)
● Vanguard Russell 1000 Value Index Fund ETF Shares	VONV	NAS CM	C	C	C-		97.10	114.75	91.61	Y	US Equity Large Cap Value (Growth & Inc)
● Vanguard Russell 2000 Growth Index Fund ETF Shares	VTWG	NAS CM	C-	C-	C-	Down	121.95	160.14	114.04	Y	US Equity Small Cap (Small Company)
● Vanguard Russell 2000 Index Fund ETF Shares	VTWO	NAS CM	C	C-	C+		107.37	139.10	101.52	Y	US Equity Small Cap (Small Company)
● Vanguard Russell 2000 Value Index Fund ETF Shares	VTWV	NAS CM	C-	C-	D+	Down	93.33	119.34	88.80	Y	US Equity Small Cap (Small Company)
● Vanguard Russell 3000 Index Fund ETF Shares	VTHR	NAS CM	C-	C	D+	Down	113.93	135.17	106.85	Y	US Equity Large Cap Blend (Growth)
● Vanguard S&P 500 ETF	VOO	NYSE Arca	C+	C	B	Down	229.81	269.75	215.07	Y	US Equity Large Cap Blend (Growth)
● Vanguard S&P 500 Growth Index Fund ETF Shares	VOOG	NYSE Arca	C	C	C-	Down	135.00	159.32	125.87	Y	US Equity Large Cap Growth (Growth & Inc)
● Vanguard S&P 500 Value Index Fund ETF Shares	VOOV	NYSE Arca	C	C	C-		97.57	116.66	92.00	Y	US Equity Large Cap Value (Growth & Inc)
● Vanguard S&P Mid-Cap 400 Growth Index Fund ETF Shares	IVOG	NYSE Arca	C-	C-	C-	Down	117.88	147.22	111.15	Y	US Equity Mid Cap (Growth & Inc)
● Vanguard S&P Mid-Cap 400 Index Fund ETF Shares	IVOO	NYSE Arca	C-	C-	C-	Down	111.86	138.42	105.39	Y	US Equity Mid Cap (Growth & Inc)
● Vanguard S&P Mid-Cap 400 Value Index Fund ETF Shares	IVOV	NYSE Arca	C-	C-	D+	Down	105.16	130.76	99.28	Y	US Equity Mid Cap (Growth & Inc)
● Vanguard S&P Small-Cap 600 Growth Index Fund ETF Shares	VIOG	NYSE Arca	C-	C	C-	Down	138.33	179.40	129.95	Y	US Equity Small Cap (Growth & Inc)
● Vanguard S&P Small-Cap 600 Index Fund ETF Shares	VIOO	NYSE Arca	C-	C-	C-	Down	125.76	164.63	118.22	Y	US Equity Small Cap (Growth & Inc)
● Vanguard S&P Small-Cap 600 Value Index Fund ETF Shares	VIOV	NYSE Arca	C-	C-	C-	Down	113.62	149.47	107.15	Y	US Equity Small Cap (Growth & Inc)
● Vanguard Short-Term Bond Index Fund ETF Shares	BSV	NYSE Arca	C	D+	C+	Up	78.57	79.10	77.67	Y	US Fixed Income (Income)
● Vanguard Short-Term Corporate Bond Index Fund ETF Shares	VCSH	NAS CM	C	C	C+		77.94	79.30	77.54	Y	US Fixed Income (Corp Bond - Gen)
● Vanguard Sh-Term Inflation-Prot Securities Ind ETF Shares	VTIP	NAS CM	C	C-	C+		47.92	49.05	47.71	Y	US Fixed Income (Govt Bond - Treasury)
● Vanguard Short-Term Treasury Index Fund ETF Shares	VGSH	NAS CM	C	C-	C+	Up	60.12	60.28	59.55	Y	US Fixed Income (Govt Bond - Gen)
● Vanguard Small-Cap Growth Index Fund ETF Shares	VBK	NYSE Arca	C	C-	C+	Down	150.59	190.00	140.03	Y	US Equity Small Cap (Small Company)
● Vanguard Small-Cap Index Fund ETF Shares	VB	NYSE Arca	C	C-	C+	Down	131.99	165.82	123.92	Y	US Equity Small Cap (Small Company)
● Vanguard Small-Cap Value Index Fund ETF Shares	VBR	NYSE Arca	C	C-	C+	Down	114.06	142.94	107.94	Y	US Equity Small Cap (Small Company)
● Vanguard Tax-Exempt Bond Index Fund ETF Shares	VTEB	NYSE Arca	C	C-	C+		51.05	51.68	49.85	Y	US Muni Fixed Inc (Muni Bond - Natl)
● Vanguard Total Bond Market Index Fund ETF Shares	BND	NYSE Arca	C	D+	C+		79.21	81.57	77.49	Y	US Fixed Income (Income)
● Vanguard Total Corporate Bond ETF ETF Shares	VTC	NAS CM	D+	D+	D+		80.00	85.00	79.04	Y	US Fixed Income (Corp Bond - Gen)
● Vanguard Total International Bond Index Fund ETF Shares	BNDX	NAS CM	C	C	C+		54.25	55.31	53.88	Y	Global Fixed Income (Worldwide Bond)
● Vanguard Total International Stock Index Fund ETF Shares	VXUS	NAS CM	C-	D+	C	Down	47.22	61.17	45.72	Y	Global Equity Large Cap (Foreign Stock)
● Vanguard Total Stock Market Index Fund ETF Shares	VTI	NYSE Arca	C+	C	B		127.63	151.31	119.70	Y	US Equity Large Cap Blend (Growth)
Vanguard Total World Bond ETF	BNDW	NAS CM	U	U	U		74.79	75.48	74.05	Y	Global Fixed Income (Worldwide Bond)
● Vanguard Total World Stock Index Fund ETF Shares	VT	NYSE Arca	C	C-	C+	Down	65.46	79.73	62.33	Y	Global Equity Large Cap (World Stock)
Vanguard U.S. Liquidity Factor ETF ETF Shares	VFLQ	BATS	U	U	U		69.48	84.80	65.86	Y	US Equity Mid Cap (Growth)
Vanguard U.S. Minimum Volatility ETF ETF Shares	VFMV	BATS	U	U	U		74.02	85.72	70.84	Y	US Equity Mid Cap (Growth)
Vanguard U.S. Momentum Factor ETF ETF Shares	VFMO	BATS	U	U	U		68.15	87.83	63.67	Y	US Equity Mid Cap (Growth)

★ Expanded analysis of this fund is included in Section II: Analysis of All BUY Rated Funds. ● Expanded analysis of this fund is included in Section III: Analysis of All Rated Funds with Assets over $50 million.

3-Month Total Return	6-Month Total Return	1-Year Total Return	3-Year Total Return	5-Year Total Return	Dividend Yield (TTM)	Expense Ratio	3-Yr Std Deviation	Effective Duration	NAV	Total Assets (MIL)	%Cash	%Stocks	%Bonds	%Other	Turnover Ratio	Premium/Discount 1-Year Avg	Inception Date
1.92	2.01	-0.33	6.40	15.25	2.88	0.07	3.55	6.17		30,879	1	0	98	0	55	0.03	Apr-07
0.22	1.05	-1.96	8.91	18.06	3.6	0.07	3.55	5.96		19,848	0	0	98	0	65	0.12	Nov-09
2.81	2.40	1.08	3.84	10.00	2.01	0.07	3.09	5.13		4,898	0	0	100	0	31	0.03	Nov-09
-10.80	-10.99	-11.80			1.95	0.25				1,078	0	100	0	0	9	0.18	Feb-16
-10.02	-7.61	-12.75			4.02	0.32				1,097	1	99	0	0	8	0.16	Feb-16
-14.54	-8.05	-5.25	29.09	47.94	1.83	0.05	9.5			20,461	1	99	0	0	3	0.01	Jan-04
1.26	0.31	-4.75	12.50	30.23	4.08	0.07	7.28	14.65		10,331	1	0	99	0	41	0.14	Apr-07
-1.40	-0.36	-7.21	15.33	28.41	4.64	0.07	7.17	13.31		3,260	1	0	99	0	48	0.24	Nov-09
4.86	1.16	-1.93	7.97	33.18	2.87	0.07	9.23	16.89		1,897	1	0	99	0	19	0.05	Nov-09
-16.32	-15.30	-18.07	23.01	17.09	1.8	0.1	14.68			2,800	0	100	0	0	5	0.01	Jan-04
-17.49	-10.88	-3.67	32.68	56.41	1.29	0.07	11.17			3,890	2	98	0	0	9	0.02	Dec-07
-14.24	-7.14	-4.24	31.17	50.85	1.85	0.07	9.38			1,628	0	100	0	0	4	0.03	Dec-07
-11.37	-3.81	-4.87	29.56	46.10	2.34	0.07	9.09			2,326	0	100	0	0	8	0.04	Dec-07
-16.39	-11.63	-6.50	21.59	36.62	0.71	0.07	11.65			12,233	0	100	0	0	23	0.01	Aug-06
-16.00	-12.41	-10.02	19.34	33.94	1.61	0.05	10.71			96,609	0	100	0	0	14	0.02	Jan-04
-15.57	-13.18	-13.13	17.19	31.17	2.32	0.07	10.35			17,866	0	100	0	0	17	0.01	Aug-06
1.91	1.72	0.71	4.58	12.24	2.64	0.07	2.03	6.32		8,043	5	0	96	0	279	0.05	Nov-09
-5.77	-5.66	-6.13	6.90	42.58	4.23	0.12	12.58			59,164	1	99	0	0	6	-0.01	Sep-04
-16.91	-9.62	-2.56	35.56	61.54	1.33	0.12	11.02			4,899	1	99	0	0	15	0.04	Sep-10
-14.81	-8.26	-5.70	28.07	46.03	1.75	0.12	9.58			2,905	0	100	0	0	9	0.04	Sep-10
-12.68	-7.46	-9.05	20.85	31.60	2.27	0.12	9.31			3,255	0	100	0	0	16	0.04	Sep-10
-21.27	-18.97	-10.28	22.06	27.21	0.62	0.2	15.34			757.6	2	98	0	0	35	0.03	Sep-10
-19.70	-18.57	-11.68	22.90	23.26	1.28	0.15	14.58			2,366	2	98	0	0	19	0.03	Sep-10
-18.07	-18.20	-13.35	22.84	18.14	1.89	0.2	14.52			341.3	2	98	0	0	30	0.09	Sep-10
-15.18	-9.34	-6.15	27.66	44.01	1.67	0.15	9.79			1,241	0	100	0	0	14	0.09	Sep-10
-14.56	-7.93	-5.23	29.17	48.77	1.82	0.04	9.4			441,304	1	99	0	0	3	0.02	Sep-10
-15.82	-8.27	-1.11	34.27	62.34	1.31	0.15	10.53			2,259	1	99	0	0	19	0.01	Sep-10
-13.08	-7.64	-9.77	21.83	32.25	2.32	0.15	9.54			999.7	0	100	0	0	20	0.04	Sep-10
-17.92	-15.65	-11.53	21.32	32.68	0.92	0.2	11.58			1,016	0	100	0	0	43	0.02	Sep-10
-17.50	-15.08	-12.09	23.04	31.80	1.44	0.15	11.84			2,120	1	99	0	0	12	0.02	Sep-10
-17.05	-14.50	-12.75	23.52	28.82	1.56	0.2	12.63			919.2	0	99	0	0	36	0.06	Sep-10
-18.98	-15.59	-4.81	33.06	41.45	0.73	0.2	14.88			469.4	1	99	0	0	37	0.10	Sep-10
-19.39	-17.63	-9.08	30.25	34.74	1.06	0.15	14.71			1,924	1	99	0	0	13	0.04	Sep-10
-19.81	-19.55	-13.16	26.90	26.87	1.55	0.2	14.93			409.7	1	99	0	0	34	0.12	Sep-10
1.36	1.63	1.22	3.89	6.23	1.93	0.07	1.28	2.66		50,658	1	0	99	0	0	0.02	Apr-07
0.63	1.34	0.77	5.96	9.38	2.59	0.07	1.39	2.65		25,894	0	0	99	0	56	0.04	Nov-09
-0.31	-0.24	0.45	4.02	2.66	3.24	0.06	1.29	2.67		27,052	3	0	97	0	25	0.07	Oct-12
1.24	1.44	1.41	2.58	3.65	1.68	0.07	0.77	1.93		6,541	0	0	100	0	67	0.04	Nov-09
-19.35	-15.39	-6.82	25.77	27.54	0.78	0.07	13.5			22,703	2	98	0	0	19	0.01	Jan-04
-18.27	-15.53	-10.15	23.56	27.99	1.51	0.05	12.83			87,322	2	98	0	0	0	0.00	Jan-04
-17.36	-15.66	-12.82	21.61	28.17	2.1	0.07	12.81			29,528	1	99	0	0	19	0.03	Jan-04
1.55	1.28	0.90	6.24		2.22	0.09	3.24	5.84		3,912	2	0	98	0	18	0.02	Aug-15
1.58	1.49	-0.23	6.03	12.78	2.77	0.05	2.82	6.24		200,719	1	0	99	0	55	0.02	Apr-07
-0.30	0.69	-2.69			3.52	0.07		6.95		75.2	0	0	99	0	4	0.06	Nov-17
1.97	1.58	2.96	10.35	21.39	2.24	0.11	2.41	7.58		112,106	0	0	100	0	19	0.21	May-13
-12.14	-10.78	-14.79	13.77	4.36	3.08	0.11	11			342,022	3	96	0	1	12	0.15	Jan-11
-15.11	-9.25	-5.95	28.38	45.08	1.81	0.04	9.81			726,364	1	99	0	0	3	0.02	May-01
1.69						0.09		6.95		59.7	1	0	99	0		0.06	Sep-18
-13.77	-9.94	-10.27	21.20	23.65	2.34	0.1	9.71			16,947	2	98	0	0	10	0.08	Jun-08
-16.11	-13.74					0.13				15.7	1	99	0	0		0.19	Feb-18
-12.01	-8.41					0.13				22.5	1	99	0	0		0.09	Feb-18
-21.37	-16.65					0.13				32.6	0	100	0	0		0.20	Feb-18

Fund Name	Ticker Symbol	Traded On	Overall Rating	Reward Rating	Risk Rating	Recent Up/ Downgrade	Price as of 12/31/2018	52-Week High	52-Week Low	Open to New Investors	Category & (Prospectus Objective)
Vanguard U.S. Multifactor ETF Shares	VFMF	BATS	U	U	U		67.54	84.05	63.72	Y	US Equity Mid Cap (Growth)
Vanguard U.S. Quality Factor ETF ETF Shares	VFQY	BATS	U	U	U		69.81	87.04	65.83	Y	US Equity Mid Cap (Growth)
Vanguard U.S. Value Factor ETF ETF Shares	VFVA	BATS	U	U	U		63.95	82.20	60.57	Y	US Equity Mid Cap (Growth)
★ Vanguard Utilities Index Fund ETF Shares	VPU	NYSE Arca	B-	B-	C+		117.83	126.42	105.16	Y	Utilities Sector Equity (Utility)
● Vanguard Value Index Fund ETF Shares	VTV	NYSE Arca	C	C	C+	Down	97.95	113.26	92.30	Y	US Equity Large Cap Value (Growth)
VelocityShares 1x Daily Inverse VSTOXX Futures ETN	EXIV	BATS	D	D	D	Down	20.95	58.92	20.26	Y	Alternative Misc (Growth & Inc)
VelocityShares 1x Long VSTOXX Futures ETN	EVIX	BATS	D	D	D-	Up	12.50	17.62	8.23	Y	Alternative Misc (Growth & Inc)
VelocityShares 3x Inverse Crude Oil ETN - S&P GSCI® Crude	DWTIF	OTC BB	D	E+	D	Up	34.20	39.00	10.35	Y	Trading Tools (Natl Res)
● VelocityShares 3x Inverse Crude Oil ETNs - S&P GSCI® Crude	DWT	NYSE Arca	D	D	D		15.94	19.42	4.67	Y	Trading Tools (Growth & Inc)
VelocityShares 3x Inverse Gold ETN - S&P GSCI® Gold Ind ER	DGLD	NAS CM	C-	D+	D+	Up	46.75	60.52	38.67	Y	Trading Tools (Prec Metals)
● VelocityShares 3x Inverse Natural Gas ETN - S&P GSCI® Natu	DGAZ	NYSE Arca	C+	B	D+	Up	118.32	337.40	17.93	Y	Trading Tools (Natl Res)
VelocityShares 3x Inverse Silver ETN - S&P GSCI® Silver In	DSLV	NAS CM	C-	C-	D+	Up	28.00	38.47	21.16	Y	Trading Tools (Prec Metals)
VelocityShares 3x Long Crude Oil ETN - S&P GSCI® Crude Oil			D	D+	D	Down	24.62			Y	Trading Tools (Natl Res)
● VelocityShares 3x Long Crude Oil ETNs - S&P GSCI® Crude Oi	UWT	NYSE Arca	D	D+	D	Down	8.90	49.34	8.22	Y	Trading Tools (Growth & Inc)
★ VelocityShares 3x Long Gold ETN - S&P GSCI® Gold Ind ER	UGLD	NAS CM	B	A-	D+	Up	95.41	95.41	7.59	Y	Trading Tools (Prec Metals)
● VelocityShares 3x Long Natural Gas ETN - S&P GSCI® Natural	UGAZ	NYSE Arca	D	D	D	Up	40.31	253.10	40.31	Y	Trading Tools (Natl Res)
★ VelocityShares 3x Long Silver ETN - S&P GSCI® Silver Ind E	USLV	NAS CM	B-	A-	D+	Up	74.10	74.10	6.39	Y	Trading Tools (Prec Metals)
● VelocityShares Daily 2x VIX Short-Term ETN	TVIX	NAS CM	C-	C	D	Up	70.91	78.72	4.73	Y	Alternative Misc (Growth)
● VelocityShares Daily Inverse VIX Medium-Term ETN	ZIV	NAS CM	C	C-	C-	Down	60.41	93.87	59.11	Y	Alternative Misc (Growth)
VelocityShares Long LIBOR ETN	ULBR	NYSE Arca	D+	C-	D		33.21	40.76	29.54	Y	Trading Tools (Growth & Inc)
VelocityShares Short LIBOR ETN	DLBR	NYSE Arca	D	D	E		19.44	21.20	16.42	Y	Trading Tools (Growth & Inc)
VelocityShares VIX Short-Term ETN	VIIX	NAS CM	D-	E+	D	Up	19.86	23.35	10.92	Y	Alternative Misc (Growth)
Vesper U.S. Large Cap Short-Term Reversal Strategy ETF	UTRN	NYSE Arca	U	U	U		21.28	25.09	20.20	Y	US Equity Large Cap Value (Growth & Inc)
● VictoryShares Developed Enhanced Volatility Wtd ETF	CIZ	NAS CM	D+	D+	C-	Down	30.72	37.46	30.47	Y	Global Equity Large Cap (Income)
VictoryShares Dividend Accelerator ETF	VSDA	NAS CM	C-	C-	C-		27.60	31.45	26.21	Y	US Equity Large Cap Value (Equity-Income)
VictoryShares Emerging Market High Div Volatility Wtd ETF	CEY	NAS CM	D	D	D		21.97	28.35	21.58	Y	Global Emerg Mkts Equity (Div Emerg Mkts)
VictoryShares Emerging Market Volatility Wtd ETF	CEZ	NAS CM	D+	D+	D+	Down	24.15	31.99	23.56	Y	Global Emerg Mkts Equity (Div Emerg Mkts)
VictoryShares International High Div Volatility Wtd ETF	CID	NAS CM	D+	D+	D+	Down	29.89	38.00	29.45	Y	Global Equity Large Cap (Foreign Stock)
VictoryShares International Volatility Wtd ETF	CIL	NAS CM	D+	D+	D+	Down	34.36	43.31	33.54	Y	Global Equity Large Cap (Foreign Stock)
● VictoryShares US 500 Enhanced Volatility Wtd ETF	CFO	NAS CM	C	C-	C+		43.91	52.53	41.40	Y	US Equity Large Cap Blend (Income)
● VictoryShares US 500 Volatility Wtd ETF	CFA	NAS CM	C-	C-	C-	Down	43.98	52.58	41.41	Y	US Equity Large Cap Blend (Income)
● VictoryShares US Discovery Enhanced Volatility Wtd ETF	CSF	NAS CM	C-	C-	C-	Down	39.41	50.28	37.54	Y	US Equity Small Cap (Income)
● VictoryShares US EQ Income Enhanced Volatility Wtd ETF	CDC	NAS CM	C	C	C-		42.32	48.75	40.65	Y	US Equity Large Cap Value (Income)
● VictoryShares US Large Cap High Div Volatility Wtd ETF	CDL	NAS CM	C	C	C-		41.36	47.42	39.56	Y	US Equity Large Cap Value (Growth)
VictoryShares US Multi-Factor Minimum Volatility ETF	VSMV	NAS CM	C	C	C		26.65	30.39	25.31	Y	US Equity Large Cap Blend (Growth & Inc)
● VictoryShares US Small Cap High Div Volatility Wtd ETF	CSB	NAS CM	C-	C	D+	Down	40.15	48.67	38.78	Y	US Equity Small Cap (Small Company)
VictoryShares US Small Cap Volatility Wtd ETF	CSA	NAS CM	C-	C-	D+	Down	40.53	51.56	39.16	Y	US Equity Small Cap (Small Company)
● Vident Core U.S. Bond Strategy ETF™	VBND	NYSE Arca	D+	D	C-		47.39	49.21	46.86	Y	US Fixed Income (Growth & Inc)
● Vident Core U.S. Equity Fund™	VUSE	NYSE Arca	C-	C-	C-	Down	27.92	35.53	26.41	Y	US Equity Mid Cap (Growth & Inc)
● Vident International Equity Fund™	VIDI	NYSE Arca	C-	C-	C-		22.50	30.29	22.04	Y	Global Equity Large Cap (Foreign Stock)
Virtus Cumberland Municipal Bond ETF	CUMB	NYSE Arca	D	D	D+	Down	24.84	25.48	24.18	Y	US Muni Fixed Inc (Muni Bond - Natl)
Virtus Glovista Emerging Markets ETF	EMEM	NYSE Arca	D	D	D		20.86	28.54	20.49	Y	Global Emerg Mkts Equity (Div Emerg Mkts)
Virtus InfraCap U.S. Preferred Stock ETF	PFFA	NYSE Arca	U	U	U		22.13	26.32	21.26	Y	US Fixed Income (Income)
Virtus LifeSci Biotech Clinical Trials ETF	BBC	NYSE Arca	D+	C-	D+	Down	23.23	35.79	20.92	Y	Healthcare Sector Equity (Technology)
Virtus LifeSci Biotech Products ETF	BBP	NYSE Arca	D+	C-	D+	Down	34.90	46.70	31.99	Y	Healthcare Sector Equity (Technology)
● Virtus Newfleet Dynamic Credit ETF	BLHY	NYSE Arca	D+	D+	C-	Down	23.04	25.08	22.92	Y	US Fixed Income (Growth & Inc)
● Virtus Newfleet Multi-Sector Bond ETF	NFLT	NYSE Arca	C-	D+	C-		23.44	25.32	23.27	Y	US Fixed Income (Income)
Virtus WMC Global Factor Opportunities ETF	VGFO	NYSE Arca	D	D+	E+		22.51	27.82	21.46	Y	Global Equity Large Cap (Growth & Inc)
Volshares Large Cap ETF	VSL	NYSE Arca	U	U	U		22.29	25.83	21.31	Y	US Equity Large Cap Blend (Growth)
● WBI BullBear Global High Income ETF	WBIH	NYSE Arca	D+	D+	C-	Down	21.88	25.39	21.71	Y	Cautious Allocation (Income)
● WBI BullBear Global Income ETF	WBII	NYSE Arca	C-	D+	C-	Up	24.04	25.38	23.26	Y	Cautious Allocation (Income)
WBI BullBear Global Rotation ETF	WBIR	NYSE Arca	D+	D+	C-		22.89	26.78	22.87	Y	Moderate Allocation (Growth)

★ Expanded analysis of this fund is included in Section II: Analysis of All BUY Rated Funds. ● Expanded analysis of this fund is included in Section III: Analysis of All Rated Funds with Assets over $50 million.

3-Month Total Return	6-Month Total Return	1-Year Total Return	3-Year Total Return	5-Year Total Return	Dividend Yield (TTM)	Expense Ratio	3-Yr Std Deviation	Effective Duration	NAV	Total Assets (MIL)	%Cash	%Stocks	%Bonds	%Other	Turnover Ratio	Premium/Discount 1-Year Avg	Inception Date
-17.67	-14.55					0.18				76.1	1	99	0	0		0.08	Feb-18
-18.05	-14.22					0.13				17.7	1	99	0	0		0.24	Feb-18
-19.38	-18.05					0.13				37.2	1	99	0	0		0.13	Feb-18
0.82	2.19	4.09	37.65	66.26	3.01	0.1	11.63			4,276	0	100	0	0	4	0.00	Jan-04
-12.01	-5.40	-6.17	28.43	44.08	2.4	0.05	9.17			75,151	0	100	0	0	9	0.03	Jan-04
-44.63	-34.61	-58.68			0	1.35			20.14	11.6							-0.59	May-17
53.29	17.76	6.37			0	1.35			12.86	3.7							1.03	May-17
238.58	166.96	18.43	-83.18	2.93	0	1.35	93.72		33.41	10.8						1.27	Feb-12
238.46	166.76	18.25			0	1.5			16.38	142.5							0.17	Dec-16
-19.68	-7.59	8.93	-50.29	-43.73	0	1.35	37.6		47.07	19.1						-0.08	Oct-11
-63.74	415.33	348.31	99.82	175.31	0	1.65	119.33		123.89	362.4						-0.10	Feb-12
-20.17	1.63	21.43	-61.11	-48.57	0	1.65	59.09		27.96	17.2						0.26	Oct-11
-81.84	-79.74	-65.09	-78.50	-99.72	0	1.35	82.97		8.56	33.1						-14.77	Feb-12
-81.84	-79.76	-65.15			0	1.5			8.67	310.9							-0.24	Dec-16
21.65	942.92	742.64	1,185.54	640.19	0	1.35	38.75		94.74	126.8						0.04	Oct-11
-49.69	-36.27	-47.12	-93.74	-99.85	0	1.65	106.58		38.61	760.2						-0.02	Feb-12
17.30	766.90	521.72	659.22	65.14	0	1.65	65.42		74.10	233.4						-0.23	Oct-11
177.37	35.26	1,151.86	-95.41	-99.61	0	1.65	92.1		70.65	448.4						0.90	Nov-10
-24.81	-16.20	-31.31	45.66	56.82	0	1.35	27.75		60.57	103.7						-0.14	Nov-10
-15.16	-11.77	10.33			0	1.5			33.47	15.3							-0.43	Aug-17
17.44	12.71	-10.22			0	1.5			19.30	2.5							0.90	Aug-17
77.53	27.42	66.72	-85.29	-93.11	0	0.89	55.07		19.82	21.5						0.22	Nov-10
-12.94						0.75			21.36	2.3	0	100	0	0		0.04	Sep-18
-8.95	-6.45	-9.46	4.63		2.79	0.45	9.62		30.87	151.7	75	25	0	0	164	0.33	Sep-14
-10.19	-1.66	-0.69			1.67	0.35			27.68	9.1	0	100	0	0		-0.19	Apr-17
-5.09	-3.65	-10.32			4.84	0.5			22.18	21.7	0	100	0	0		0.16	Oct-17
-4.24	-2.94	-11.70			2.18	0.5			24.36	18.3	1	99	0	0		-0.44	Mar-16
-8.91	-9.01	-13.28	4.48		4.78	0.45	10.56		29.90	43.7	0	99	0	1	69	0.73	Aug-15
-12.68	-10.27	-13.27	9.16		2.87	0.45	10.9		34.22	19.8	0	99	0	1	46	0.87	Aug-15
-14.44	-10.31	-8.61	27.96		1.34	0.35	9.94		43.93	1,104	0	100	0	0	26	0.06	Jul-14
-14.46	-10.32	-8.61	27.95		1.35	0.35	9.95		43.96	668.6	0	100	0	0	26	0.03	Jul-14
-16.96	-17.04	-11.27	18.20		1.15	0.35	13.68		39.45	127.5	75	25	0	0	50	0.14	Jul-14
-9.27	-6.31	-5.52	31.78		3.1	0.35	7.82		42.47	877.6	0	100	0	0	49	0.05	Jul-14
-9.27	-6.31	-5.54	31.85		3.12	0.35	7.8		41.36	157.2	0	100	0	0		0.12	Jul-15
-10.72	-1.88	-0.24			2.05	0.35			26.73	45.2	0	100	0	0		0.27	Jun-17
-12.70	-11.97	-7.05	34.79		3.14	0.35	12.82		40.13	53.8	1	99	0	0	65	0.16	Jul-15
-16.21	-16.29	-10.48	28.33		1.16	0.35	14.28		40.71	39.1	1	99	0	0	47	0.25	Jul-15
1.49	1.36	-0.77	4.47		2.36	0.43	3.16		47.43	488.6	20	0	80	0	324	-0.08	Oct-14
-17.53	-15.89	-14.73	17.82		1.31	0.5	12.19		28.05	537.4	0	100	0	0	63	0.12	Jan-14
-10.37	-9.17	-17.30	19.21	4.08	2.77	0.61	12.09		22.66	578.0	0	100	0	0	66	-0.18	Oct-13
1.05	0.39	-0.43			3.71	0.59			24.85	11.1	1	0	99	0		-0.52	Jan-17
-4.75	-2.28	-15.20			0.39	0.68			20.89	13.4	3	97	0	0		-0.07	Nov-17
-10.79	-10.22					1.36		10.89	22.07	5.8	-31	5	3	2		0.24	May-18
-30.77	-29.78	-17.49	-18.56		1.08	0.79	38.07		23.39	34.3	3	97	0	0	45	0.21	Dec-14
-21.24	-21.36	-13.79	13.63		0.19	0.79	28.31		34.91	28.8	1	99	0	0	34	0.26	Dec-14
-4.42	-2.36	-1.89			5.44	0.68			23.22	64.8	4	0	96	0	96	-0.44	Dec-16
-2.12	-0.70	-2.84	11.05		4.85	0.8	2.6		23.40	76.6	8	0	91	0	113	-0.10	Aug-15
-15.98	-11.80	-12.27			0.38	0.49			22.46	5.1	0	99	0	0		0.21	Oct-17
-11.59	-9.86					0.65			22.34	0.59	0	100	0	0		1.41	Feb-18
-7.36	-6.71	-9.48	1.25		3.48	1.23	4.3	14.99	21.89	208.3	19	32	47	0		-0.03	Aug-14
1.27	3.12	-1.45	5.39		3.62	1.28	2.85	13.02	24.08	77.1	3	0	90	0		-0.08	Aug-14
-8.40	-6.53	-8.83			1.63	1.64		5.02	22.89	45.6	32	36	28	0		0.08	Jul-16

Fund Name	Ticker Symbol	Traded On	Overall Rating	Reward Rating	Risk Rating	Recent Up/ Downgrade	Price as of 12/31/2018	52-Week High	52-Week Low	Open to New Investors	Category & (Prospectus Objective)
WBI BullBear Quality 1000 ETF	WBIL	NYSE Arca	C	C	C-	Down	24.61	29.15	24.60	Y	US Equity Large Cap Blend (Growth & Inc)
WBI BullBear Quality 2000 ETF	WBID	NYSE Arca	D+	C-	D+	Down	20.98	25.58	20.97	Y	US Equity Mid Cap (Growth & Inc)
WBI BullBear Rising Income 1000 ETF	WBIE	NYSE Arca	C	C	C	Down	24.97	28.42	24.97	Y	US Equity Large Cap Growth (Growth & Inc)
WBI BullBear Rising Income 2000 ETF	WBIA	NYSE Arca	D+	D+	D+	Down	21.14	26.44	21.12	Y	US Equity Mid Cap (Growth & Inc)
WBI BullBear Value 1000 ETF	WBIF	NYSE Arca	C	C	C-	Down	27.37	31.00	27.34	Y	US Equity Large Cap Blend (Growth & Inc)
WBI BullBear Value 2000 ETF	WBIB	NYSE Arca	D	D	D+	Down	20.86	27.31	20.84	Y	US Equity Mid Cap (Growth & Inc)
● WBI BullBear Yield 1000 ETF	WBIG	NYSE Arca	C	C	C	Down	23.41	27.95	23.41	Y	US Equity Large Cap Blend (Growth & Inc)
● WBI BullBear Yield 2000 ETF	WBIC	NYSE Arca	C-	C-	C-	Down	19.91	24.13	19.88	Y	US Equity Mid Cap (Growth & Inc)
● WBI Power Factor™ High Dividend ETF	WBIY	NYSE Arca	C	C+	D+		22.15	27.99	21.81	Y	US Equity Large Cap Value (Equity-Income)
Western Asset Total Return ETF	WBND	NAS CM	U	U	U		25.12	25.22	24.68	Y	US Fixed Income (Growth & Inc)
WisdomTree 90/60 U.S. Balanced Fund	NTSX	NYSE Arca	U	U	U		22.78	25.96	21.56	Y	US Equity Large Cap Blend (Balanced)
WisdomTree Asia Local Debt Fund	ALD	NYSE Arca	D	D+	D	Down	43.63	46.88	41.78	Y	Emerging Mkts Fixed Inc (Worldwide Bond)
WisdomTree Asia Pacific ex-Japan Fund	AXJL	NYSE Arca	D+	D+	D+	Down	61.17	75.33	59.95	Y	Asia ex-Japan Equity (Pacific Stock)
WisdomTree Australia Dividend Fund	AUSE	NYSE Arca	D+	D+	C-	Down	47.59	61.99	45.99	Y	Equity Misc (Pacific Stock)
WisdomTree Balanced Income Fund	WBAL	NYSE Arca	D	D	D+		22.49	25.73	22.10	Y	Moderate Allocation (Balanced)
● WisdomTree Bloomberg U.S. Dollar Bullish Fund	USDU	NYSE Arca	C	C	C-	Up	27.05	27.72	24.82	Y	Currency (Money Mkt - Gen)
WisdomTree Brazilian Real Strategy Fund	BZF	NYSE Arca	D+	C-	D+		16.44	19.34	14.95	Y	Currency (Worldwide Bond)
WisdomTree CBOE Russell 2000 PutWrite Strategy Fund	RPUT	BATS	U	U	U		17.99	26.70	17.24	Y	Long/Short Equity (Growth & Inc)
● WisdomTree CBOE S&P 500 PutWrite Strategy Fund	PUTW	NYSE Arca	C-	C-	C-	Down	25.45	30.73	24.52	Y	Long/Short Equity (Growth)
● WisdomTree China ex-State-Owned Enterprises Fund	CXSE	NAS CM	C-	C-	D+	Down	60.89	96.79	60.00	Y	Greater China Equity (Pacific Stock)
WisdomTree Chinese Yuan Strategy Fund	CYB	NYSE Arca	D+	D+	D+	Down	25.11	27.51	24.88	Y	Currency (Worldwide Bond)
● WisdomTree Continuous Commodity Index Fund	GCC	NYSE Arca	D	D	C-	Down	17.55	19.79	17.52	Y	Commodities Broad Basket (Natl Res)
WisdomTree Dynamic Bearish U.S. Equity Fund	DYB	BATS	D+	C-	D+	Down	24.81	26.83	24.56	Y	Alternative Misc (Equity-Income)
WisdomTree Dynamic Currency Hedged Europe Equity Fund	DDEZ	BATS	D	D+	D	Down	25.54	33.87	24.83	Y	Europe Equity Large Cap (Foreign Stock)
● WisdomTree Dynamic Currency Hedged Intl Equity Fund	DDWM	BATS	D+	D+	C-	Down	25.91	31.95	25.36	Y	Global Equity Large Cap (Foreign Stock)
WisdomTree Dynamic Curr Hedg Intl Quality Div Growth Fund	DHDG	BATS	D	D	C-	Down	20.41	26.16	19.80	Y	Global Equity Large Cap (World Stock)
WisdomTree Dynamic Currency Hedg Intl SmallCap Equity Fund	DDLS	BATS	D+	D+	D+	Down	27.43	34.73	26.31	Y	Global Eq Mid/Small Cap (Small Company)
WisdomTree Dynamic Currency Hedged Japan Equity Fund	DDJP	BATS	D	D+	D		24.47	31.29	23.65	Y	Japan Equity (Pacific Stock)
● WisdomTree Dynamic Long/Short U.S. Equity Fund	DYLS	BATS	C-	C	C-	Down	28.97	35.90	27.33	Y	Long/Short Equity (Equity-Income)
WisdomTree Emerging Currency Strategy Fund	CEW	NYSE Arca	D+	D+	D+	Down	18.10	20.04	17.72	Y	Currency (Worldwide Bond)
WisdomTree Emerging Markets Consumer Growth Fund	EMCG	NAS CM	D	D	D	Down	19.89	28.83	19.02	Y	Global Emerg Mkts Equity (Div Emerg Mkts)
WisdomTree Emerging Markets Corporate Bond Fund	EMCB	NAS CM	D+	C-	D+		68.00	73.62	67.08	Y	Emerging Mkts Fixed Inc (Div Emerg Mkts)
WisdomTree Emerging Markets Dividend Fund	DVEM	BATS	D+	D+	D+	Down	28.48	36.70	28.00	Y	Global Emerg Mkts Equity (Div Emerg Mkts)
● WisdomTree Emerg Mkts ex-State-Owned Enterprises Fund	XSOE	NYSE Arca	C-	C-	C-		25.56	35.07	24.50	Y	Global Emerg Mkts Equity (Div Emerg Mkts)
● WisdomTree Emerging Markets High Dividend Fund	DEM	NYSE Arca	C	C-	C+		40.15	50.28	39.27	Y	Global Emerg Mkts Equity (Div Emerg Mkts)
● WisdomTree Emerging Markets Local Debt Fund	ELD	NYSE Arca	D+	D+	C-		33.50	40.02	31.80	Y	Emerging Mkts Fixed Inc (Income)
WisdomTree Emerging Markets Multifactor Fund	EMMF	NYSE Arca	U	U	U		22.76	24.92	22.41	Y	Global Emerg Mkts Equity (Div Emerg Mkts)
● WisdomTree Emerging Markets Quality Dividend Growth Fund	DGRE	NAS CM	C-	C-	C-		22.22	28.90	21.16	Y	Global Emerg Mkts Equity (Div Emerg Mkts)
● WisdomTree Emerging Markets SmallCap Dividend Fund	DGS	NYSE Arca	C-	C-	C-	Down	41.89	56.97	40.12	Y	Global Emerg Mkts Equity (Div Emerg Mkts)
WisdomTree Europe Domestic Economy Fund	EDOM	BATS	D	D+	D	Down	22.01	34.16	21.23	Y	Europe Equity Large Cap (Europe Stock)
● WisdomTree Europe Hedged Equity Fund	HEDJ	NYSE Arca	C-	D+	C	Down	56.44	67.39	54.71	Y	Europe Equity Large Cap (Foreign Stock)
● WisdomTree Europe Hedged SmallCap Equity Fund	EUSC	NYSE Arca	D+	D+	C-	Down	26.42	32.82	25.52	Y	Europe Equity Large Cap (Small Company)
● WisdomTree Europe Quality Dividend Growth Fund	EUDG	NYSE Arca	D+	D+	C-	Down	22.27	28.38	21.53	Y	Europe Equity Large Cap (Growth)
● WisdomTree Europe SmallCap Dividend Fund	DFE	NYSE Arca	D+	D+	D+	Down	53.36	75.54	51.32	Y	Europe Equity Large Cap (Europe Stock)
● WisdomTree Floating Rate Treasury Fund	USFR	NYSE Arca	C	C-	C+		25.08	25.13	25.00	Y	US Fixed Income (Govt Bond - Treasury)
WisdomTree Fundamental U.S. Corporate Bond Fund	WFIG	BATS	D	D+	D		47.40	49.96	47.00	Y	US Fixed Income (Corp Bond - Gen)
WisdomTree Fundamental U.S. High Yield Corporate Bond Fund	WFHY	BATS	C-	C-	D+	Up	47.53	50.82	46.78	Y	US Fixed Income (Corp Bond-High Yld)
WisdomTree Fundamental U.S. Short-Term Corporate Bond Fund	SFIG	BATS	D	C-	E+	Down	49.00	49.41	48.54	Y	US Fixed Income (Corp Bond - Gen)
WisdomTree Fundmnt U.S. Sh-Term High Yld Corp Bond Fund	SFHY	BATS	C-	C-	D+	Up	48.30	50.66	47.78	Y	US Fixed Income (Corp Bond-High Yld)
● WisdomTree Germany Hedged Equity Fund	DXGE	NAS CM	D+	D+	D+	Down	26.48	33.93	25.70	Y	Europe Equity Large Cap (Europe Stock)
WisdomTree Global ex-Mexico Equity Fund	XMX	NYSE Arca	C-	D+	C		26.09	31.68	24.90	Y	Global Equity Large Cap (World Stock)
● WisdomTree Global ex-U.S. Quality Dividend Growth Fund	DNL	NYSE Arca	C-	D+	C-		49.33	62.78	47.65	Y	Global Equity Large Cap (Foreign Stock)

★ Expanded analysis of this fund is included in Section II: Analysis of All BUY Rated Funds. ● Expanded analysis of this fund is included in Section III: Analysis of All Rated Funds with Assets over $50 million.

		TOTAL RETURNS & PERFORMANCE							ASSETS		ASSET ALLOCATION & TURNOVER					VALUATION	
3-Month Total Return	6-Month Total Return	1-Year Total Return	3-Year Total Return	5-Year Total Return	Dividend Yield (TTM)	Expense Ratio	3-Yr Std Deviation	Effective Duration	NAV	Total Assets (MIL)	%Cash	%Stocks	%Bonds	%Other	Turnover Ratio	Premium/ Discount 1-Year Avg	Inception Date
-12.87	-5.31	-9.39	12.45		0.86	1.07	9.9		24.63	38.2	44	56	0	0		0.07	Aug-14
-11.96	-10.69	-13.13	0.96		0.79	1.06	11.54		21.01	35.7	50	50	0	0		0.17	Aug-14
-10.67	-3.44	-2.86	10.79		0.72	1.05	9.77		24.99	47.6	41	59	0	0		0.05	Aug-14
-12.62	-12.89	-14.69	-4.84		0.94	1.08	12.72		21.17	39.8	68	32	0	0		0.13	Aug-14
-10.82	-2.42	-4.14	23.14		0.78	1.05	9.8		27.35	40.6	44	56	0	0		0.04	Aug-14
-10.90	-13.63	-19.60	-6.16		0.81	1.06	11.06		20.90	34.7	57	43	0	0		0.12	Aug-14
-12.37	-8.73	-7.98	12.49		1.26	1.04	9.48		23.46	72.8	37	63	0	0		0.01	Aug-14
-10.65	-12.02	-9.44	-3.81		1.47	1.06	9.08		19.93	61.0	58	42	0	0		0.10	Aug-14
-16.41	-15.60	-12.65			3.95	0.7			22.24	137.2	6	94	0	0		0.08	Dec-16
2.21						0.45			25.40	24.7	36	0	64	0		0.41	Oct-18
-11.05						0.2			22.85	4.9	0	58	42	0		0.10	Aug-18
2.66	1.69	-2.90	7.27	0.98	1.83	0.55	6.26	3.88	43.74	17.5	9	0	90	1	46	-0.24	Mar-11
-8.54	-4.16	-8.44	24.08	10.76	4.1	0.48	12.16		61.66	34.9	0	100	0	0	26	-0.06	Jun-06
-11.89	-10.66	-16.46	19.49	0.27	4.66	0.58	14.21		47.87	21.6	0	100	0	0	28	-0.02	Jun-06
-6.03	-3.33	-6.55				0.35		6.32	22.51	2.4	5	60	34	0		0.25	Dec-17
1.82	2.22	5.53	-0.30	17.76	0	0.5	6.33	0.02	27.07	85.3	96	0	4	0	0	0.03	Dec-13
5.13	3.30	-10.26	28.54	-5.69	0	0.45	16.2	0.02	16.21	12.3	96	0	4	0	0	-0.44	May-08
-15.51	-13.36					0.43			18.04	1.2	102	-2	0	0	0	0.39	Feb-18
-9.87	-6.08	-4.81	16.67		0.19	0.38			25.57	227.6	101	-1	0	0	0	0.05	Feb-16
-13.99	-24.03	-27.92	26.78	27.01	1.25	0.32	20.22		61.37	159.8	0	100	0	0	20	0.07	Sep-12
1.09	-1.67	-1.99	5.26	0.85	0	0.45	4.98	0.02	25.34	30.4	96	0	4	0	0	-0.02	May-08
-4.01	-5.23	-9.09	-5.72	-31.92	0	0.75	7.5		17.50	151.7	50	0	0	51		-0.12	Jan-08
-5.22	-4.24	-4.35	1.47		0	0.48			24.86	15.4	0	101	0	-1		0.08	Dec-15
-11.16	-10.38	-13.29	27.49		3.22	0.43			25.63	15.3	0	100	0	0		-0.21	Jan-16
-11.05	-7.91	-11.05	26.26		3.87	0.35			26.08	206.6	0	100	0	0		0.11	Jan-16
-14.19	-12.92	-13.99			0.66	0.48			20.47	21.8	0	100	0	0		0.29	Nov-16
-13.66	-12.25	-16.60	26.03		1.92	0.43			27.35	19.0	0	99	0	1		0.76	Jan-16
-15.95	-9.77	-15.96	19.00		2.7	0.43			24.66	2.7	0	100	0	0		0.43	Jan-16
-15.60	-10.35	-8.38	22.91		0.97	0.48			29.11	172.4	0	100	0	0		0.00	Dec-15
0.98	-0.33	-5.00	10.11	-7.71	0	0.55	7.44	0.02	18.12	24.0	96	0	4	0	0	-0.15	May-09
-6.26	-9.34	-22.82	11.01	-8.23	3.34	0.32	16.24		19.89	25.9	0	100	0	0	63	0.41	Sep-13
-0.08	0.96	-2.53	17.08	14.39	4.2	0.6	4.5	4.29	68.29	40.7	0	0	100	0	36	-0.22	Mar-12
-8.29	-4.60	-10.69			3.41	0.32			28.62	35.4	0	100	0	0		0.35	Apr-16
-9.03	-11.37	-18.62	28.01		1.61	0.32	14.93		25.55	175.5	0	100	0	0	68	0.25	Dec-14
-7.81	-3.11	-7.30	41.83	-2.12	4.5	0.63	14.6		40.24	1,915	0	100	0	0	41	-0.07	Jul-07
3.19	0.65	-7.71	14.06	-6.85	6.35	0.55	10.53	4.52	33.49	173.2	8	0	92	0	39	-0.13	Aug-10
-7.60						0.48			22.67	14.1	0	100	0	0		0.35	Aug-18
-6.41	-8.03	-15.19	23.12	3.60	2.14	0.32	13.84		22.37	69.5	0	99	0	0	62	0.01	Aug-13
-7.32	-9.24	-15.39	31.73	8.55	3.91	0.63	15.06		42.27	1,293	0	100	0	0	48	-0.19	Oct-07
-18.56	-18.49	-23.86	0.19		7.79	0.48	16.94		22.07	4.7	0	99	0	1		-0.14	Oct-15
-11.04	-9.97	-9.26	12.63	27.05	2.89	0.58	11.83		56.60	4,409	0	100	0	0	20	-0.15	Dec-09
-12.91	-11.56	-13.41	14.21		2.2	0.58	11.93		26.50	141.8	0	100	0	0	37	-0.22	Mar-15
-12.87	-11.01	-15.04	5.77		2.37	0.58	11.89		22.28	50.3	0	100	0	0	18	0.00	May-14
-15.51	-16.71	-21.43	5.68	9.84	4.63	0.58	14.74		53.42	773.9	0	99	0	1	33	-0.25	Jun-06
0.48	0.98	1.81	3.47		1.62	0.15	0.2	0.02	25.07	829.9	0	0	100	0	160	0.03	Feb-14
-0.28	1.00	-2.72			3.3	0.18		6.96	47.44	4.7	1	0	99	0		-0.73	Apr-16
-4.38	-1.35	-1.74			5.68	0.38		4.06	47.53	9.8	0	0	100	0		-1.19	Apr-16
0.72	1.46	1.07			2.23	0.18		2.33	49.11	4.9	0	0	100	0		-0.67	Apr-16
-3.16	-0.54	1.89			4.92	0.38		2.34	48.29	14.8	3	0	97	0		-0.78	Apr-16
-12.56	-11.14	-15.96	6.97	21.03	2.8	0.48	12.35		26.40	61.7	0	100	0	0	20	-0.13	Oct-13
-12.88	-8.28	-8.18			2.23	0.2			26.16	26.0	0	100	0	0		0.23	Feb-17
-13.20	-11.61	-14.25	16.76	8.43	2.15	0.58	11.39		49.47	62.7	0	100	0	0	67	-0.02	Jun-06

Fund Name	Ticker Symbol	Traded On	Overall Rating	Reward Rating	Risk Rating	Recent Up/ Downgrade	Price as of 12/31/2018	52-Week High	52-Week Low	Open to New Investors	Category & (Prospectus Objective)
● WisdomTree Global ex-US Real Estate Fund	DRW	NYSE Arca	C-	D+	C-		27.77	34.83	27.14	Y	Real Estate Sector Equity (Real Estate)
WisdomTree Global Hedged SmallCap Dividend Fund	HGSD	BATS	D	D+	D	Down	22.61	26.78	21.77	Y	Global Eq Mid/Small Cap (Small Company)
● WisdomTree Global High Dividend Fund	DEW	NYSE Arca	C-	C-	C-	Down	41.74	51.07	40.24	Y	Global Equity Large Cap (Equity-Income)
WisdomTree Global SmallCap Dividend Fund	GSD	BATS	D+	D+	D+	Down	27.28	35.24	26.34	Y	Global Eq Mid/Small Cap (Small Company)
WisdomTree ICBCCS S&P China 500 Fund	WCHN	NYSE Arca	D	D	D		23.28	35.30	22.87	Y	Greater China Equity (Pacific Stock)
● WisdomTree India Earnings Fund	EPI	NYSE Arca	C-	C-	C-	Down	24.80	29.40	21.83	Y	India Equity (Foreign Stock)
● WisdomTree Interest Rate Hedged High Yield Bond Fund	HYZD	NAS CM	C	C-	C+	Down	22.42	24.33	22.16	Y	Fixed Income Misc (Corp Bond-High Yld)
● WisdomTree Interest Rate Hedged U.S. Aggregate Bond Fund	AGZD	NAS CM	C-	C	C-		47.26	48.57	47.26	Y	Fixed Income Misc (Growth & Inc)
● WisdomTree International Dividend ex-Financials Fund	DOO	NYSE Arca	D+	D+	D+	Down	37.90	46.31	36.91	Y	Global Equity Large Cap (Foreign Stock)
● WisdomTree International Equity Fund	DWM	NYSE Arca	D+	D+	C-	Down	46.60	59.63	44.98	Y	Global Equity Large Cap (Foreign Stock)
● WisdomTree Intl Hedged Quality Dividend Growth Fund	IHDG	NYSE Arca	D+	D+	C-	Down	27.82	33.03	26.92	Y	Global Equity Large Cap (Growth)
● WisdomTree International High Dividend Fund	DTH	NYSE Arca	D+	D+	C-	Down	37.11	47.36	36.10	Y	Global Equity Large Cap (Foreign Stock)
● WisdomTree International LargeCap Dividend Fund	DOL	NYSE Arca	D+	D+	C-	Down	42.52	54.08	41.44	Y	Global Equity Large Cap (Foreign Stock)
● WisdomTree International MidCap Dividend Fund	DIM	NYSE Arca	D+	D+	C-	Down	56.75	73.67	54.86	Y	Global Eq Mid/Small Cap (Foreign Stock)
WisdomTree International Multifactor Fund	DWMF	NYSE Arca	U	U	U		22.67	25.12	22.06	Y	Global Equity Large Cap (Foreign Stock)
● WisdomTree International Quality Dividend Growth Fund	IQDG	BATS	D+	D+	C-	Down	25.09	32.75	24.23	Y	Global Equity Large Cap (Growth & Inc)
● WisdomTree International SmallCap Dividend Fund	DLS	NYSE Arca	C-	D+	C-		60.32	81.55	58.00	Y	Global Eq Mid/Small Cap (Foreign Stock)
● WisdomTree Japan Hedged Equity Fund	DXJ	NYSE Arca	C-	D+	C	Down	46.39	62.63	44.87	Y	Japan Equity (Pacific Stock)
WisdomTree Japan Hedged Financials Fund	DXJF	NYSE Arca	D+	D+	C-	Down	20.19	27.51	19.58	Y	Japan Equity (Pacific Stock)
WisdomTree Japan Hedged Quality Dividend Growth Fund	JHDG	NYSE Arca	D+	D+	D+	Down	23.70	30.34	22.90	Y	Japan Equity (Pacific Stock)
● WisdomTree Japan Hedged SmallCap Equity Fund	DXJS	NAS CM	C-	D+	C-	Down	36.85	47.76	35.05	Y	Japan Equity (Pacific Stock)
● WisdomTree Japan SmallCap Dividend Fund	DFJ	NYSE Arca	C-	D+	C	Down	64.39	85.46	60.90	Y	Japan Equity (Pacific Stock)
● WisdomTree Managed Futures Strategy Fund	WTMF	NYSE Arca	D+	D+	C-		38.76	41.50	38.76	Y	Alternative Misc (Growth & Inc)
WisdomTree Middle East Dividend Fund	GULF	NAS CM	C	C	C-		18.77	20.03	17.62	Y	Equity Misc (Div Emerg Mkts)
● WisdomTree Negative Duration High Yield Bond Fund	HYND	NAS CM	C	C	C-		19.35	21.79	19.35	Y	Fixed Income Misc (Govt Bond - Treasury)
WisdomTree Negative Duration U.S. Aggregate Bond Fund	AGND	NAS CM	C-	C	C-	Down	42.51	44.54	42.51	Y	Fixed Income Misc (Growth)
● WisdomTree U.S. Dividend ex-Financials Fund	DTN	NYSE Arca	C	C	C-		76.98	92.93	73.26	Y	US Equity Large Cap Value (Growth & Inc)
● WisdomTree U.S. Earnings 500 Fund	EPS	NYSE Arca	C	C	C-		28.20	33.13	26.55	Y	US Equity Large Cap Blend (Growth & Inc)
● WisdomTree U.S. High Dividend Fund	DHS	NYSE Arca	C	C	C-		65.12	75.26	62.15	Y	US Equity Large Cap Value (Growth & Inc)
● WisdomTree U.S. LargeCap Dividend Fund	DLN	NYSE Arca	C	C	C-		84.45	97.25	79.69	Y	US Equity Large Cap Value (Growth & Inc)
● WisdomTree U.S. MidCap Dividend Fund	DON	NYSE Arca	C	C-	C+	Down	31.63	37.50	29.98	Y	US Equity Mid Cap (Growth & Inc)
● WisdomTree U.S. MidCap Earnings Fund	EZM	NYSE Arca	C-	C-	C-	Down	34.29	42.42	32.31	Y	US Equity Mid Cap (Growth & Inc)
● WisdomTree U.S. Multifactor Fund	USMF	BATS	C-	D+	C-	Up	26.12	31.09	24.84	Y	US Equity Large Cap Blend (Growth & Inc)
● WisdomTree U.S. Quality Dividend Growth Fund	DGRW	NAS CM	C	C	C+	Down	38.33	44.81	36.09	Y	US Equity Large Cap Blend (Growth & Inc)
WisdomTree U.S. Quality Shareholder Yield Fund	QSY	NYSE Arca	D+	C-	D	Down	74.27	88.83	69.78	Y	US Equity Large Cap Value (Growth & Inc)
● WisdomTree U.S. SmallCap Dividend Fund	DES	NYSE Arca	C	C-	C+	Down	24.53	30.66	23.32	Y	US Equity Small Cap (Small Company)
● WisdomTree U.S. SmallCap Earnings Fund	EES	NYSE Arca	C-	C-	C-	Down	32.04	40.77	30.28	Y	US Equity Small Cap (Small Company)
● WisdomTree U.S. SmallCap Quality Dividend Growth Fund	DGRS	NAS CM	C-	C	C-	Down	31.15	38.67	29.46	Y	US Equity Small Cap (Small Company)
● WisdomTree U.S. Total Dividend Fund	DTD	NYSE Arca	C	C	C-		84.62	97.65	79.60	Y	US Equity Large Cap Value (Growth & Inc)
● WisdomTree U.S. Total Earnings Fund	EXT	NYSE Arca	C	C	C-		28.44	34.05	26.85	Y	US Equity Large Cap Blend (Growth & Inc)
● WisdomTree Yield Enhanced U.S. Aggregate Bond Fund	AGGY	NYSE Arca	D+	D+	C-	Down	48.22	50.72	47.36	Y	US Fixed Income (Growth & Inc)
WisdomTree Yield Enhanc U.S. Short-Term Aggreg Bond Fund	SHAG	BATS	D	D	D+	Down	48.87	49.74	48.47	Y	US Fixed Income (Growth & Inc)
Workplace Equality Portfolio	EQLT	NYSE Arca	C-	C-	D+		32.37	38.79	30.64	Y	US Equity Large Cap Blend (Growth)
Xtrackers Barclays International Corporate Bond Hedged ETF	IFIX	BATS	D	D+	D		49.46	50.24	49.36	Y	Global Fixed Income (Income)
Xtrackers Barclays International Treasury Bond Hedged ETF	IGVT	BATS	D	D+	D		49.06	49.70	48.34	Y	Global Fixed Income (Income)
Xtrackers Emerging Markets Bond - Interest Rate Hedged ETF	EMIH	BATS	D+	C	D		22.72	25.64	22.72	Y	Fixed Income Misc (Govt Bond - Treasury)
Xtrackers Eurozone Equity ETF	EURZ	BATS	D+	D+	D+	Up	19.53	26.11	18.89	Y	Europe Equity Large Cap (Europe Stock)
● Xtrackers FTSE Developed ex US Comprehensive Factor ETF	DEEF	NYSE Arca	D+	D+	C-	Down	25.04	31.67	24.42	Y	Global Equity Large Cap (Foreign Stock)
Xtrackers FTSE Emerging Comprehensive Factor ETF	DEMG	NYSE Arca	D	D+	D	Down	23.17	30.95	22.84	Y	Global Emerg Mkts Equity (Div Emerg Mkts)
Xtrackers Germany Equity ETF	GRMY	BATS	D	D+	E+		18.56	26.22	17.95	Y	Equity Misc (Europe Stock)
● Xtrackers Harvest CSI 300 China A-Shares ETF	ASHR	NYSE Arca	D	D	D	Down	21.93	34.85	21.68	Y	Greater China Equity (Pacific Stock)
Xtrackers Harvest CSI 500 China-A Shares Small Cap ETF	ASHS	NYSE Arca	D-	D-	D-	Down	22.33	36.99	21.21	Y	Greater China Equity (Pacific Stock)

★ Expanded analysis of this fund is included in Section II: Analysis of All BUY Rated Funds. ● Expanded analysis of this fund is included in Section III: Analysis of All Rated Funds with Assets over $50 million.

				TOTAL RETURNS & PERFORMANCE					ASSETS		ASSET ALLOCATION & TURNOVER					VALUATION	
3-Month Total Return	6-Month Total Return	1-Year Total Return	3-Year Total Return	5-Year Total Return	Dividend Yield (TTM)	Expense Ratio	3-Yr Std Deviation	Effective Duration	NAV	Total Assets (MIL)	%Cash	%Stocks	%Bonds	%Other	Turnover Ratio	Premium/ Discount 1-Year Avg	Inception Date
-5.01	-6.68	-10.97	24.43	31.65	7.42	0.58	13.12		27.83	98.4	0	98	0	1	23	-0.12	Jun-07
-13.83	-12.28	-12.35	22.27		2.1	0.43	10.51		22.59	8.7	0	100	0	0		0.27	Nov-15
-9.53	-6.16	-9.83	18.51	7.68	3.79	0.58	8.66		41.96	95.3	0	99	0	1	21	-0.01	Jun-06
-13.71	-12.67	-13.81	23.36		3.25	0.43	11.22		27.42	15.2	0	100	0	0		0.10	Nov-15
-11.39	-15.70	-23.12				0.55			23.38	13.5	0	100	0	0		0.60	Dec-17
2.73	0.04	-10.44	27.31	50.85	1.15	0.84	19.45		24.76	1,499	0	100	0	0	22	-0.02	Feb-08
-5.09	-2.45	-0.72	20.64	13.67	5.14	0.43	3.97	0.00	22.63	297.7	84	0	16	0	57	0.01	Dec-13
-0.62	0.37	0.58	5.30	4.23	2.6	0.23	1.29	0.35	47.24	71.1	105	0	-5	0	187	0.14	Dec-13
-8.92	-7.03	-9.35	11.01	-2.31	4.19	0.58	10.56		37.97	166.7	0	100	0	0	35	-0.17	Jun-06
-11.72	-9.44	-13.55	9.81	3.19	3.65	0.48	10.85		46.62	828.5	0	100	0	0	19	-0.04	Jun-06
-13.38	-11.64	-11.69	9.03		0.2	0.58	8.46		27.90	471.0	0	100	0	0	42	-0.04	May-14
-10.16	-7.91	-12.56	10.56	-1.75	4.39	0.58	10.9		37.25	269.5	0	100	0	0	26	-0.15	Jun-06
-10.92	-8.62	-12.49	9.33	-0.34	3.85	0.48	10.75		42.74	383.7	0	100	0	0	16	-0.05	Jun-06
-12.48	-10.56	-15.07	11.20	12.37	3.09	0.58	11.75		57.01	252.5	0	100	0	0	23	0.00	Jun-06
-8.86						0.38			22.66	2.4	0	100	0	0		0.21	Aug-18
-14.53	-13.84	-17.05			1.59	0.38			25.10	64.6	0	100	0	0	39	0.24	Apr-16
-14.31	-13.69	-18.69	13.92	13.16	3.56	0.58	12.38		60.53	1,635	0	100	0	0	28	-0.06	Jun-06
-18.68	-11.38	-18.80	-0.65	18.70	3	0.48	16.6		46.95	4,698	0	100	0	0	18	-0.09	Jun-06
-19.22	-11.92	-19.64	-18.00		2.16	0.48	23.59		20.39	24.7	0	100	0	0	30	0.07	Apr-14
-17.06	-11.38	-15.95	2.25		2.08	0.43	13.09		23.97	13.3	0	100	0	0	30	0.08	Apr-15
-17.40	-13.03	-17.82	13.69	47.69	2.18	0.58	14.99		37.29	118.0	0	100	0	0	30	-0.21	Jun-13
-14.72	-13.20	-17.61	20.40	39.51	1.79	0.58	11.59		65.09	900.5	0	100	0	0	18	-0.14	Jun-06
-1.69	0.54	0.32	-3.87	-3.10	0	0.65	4.47		38.79	221.0	128	0	-15	-13	0	0.01	Jan-11
-1.25	1.63	11.76	24.20	16.05	4.03	0.88	11.54		18.89	17.0	0	100	0	0	46	-0.20	Jul-08
-7.48	-3.68	0.26	16.05	-2.01	5.03	0.48	6.38	-7.37	19.66	64.7	115	0	-16	0	71	0.11	Dec-13
-2.20	-0.18	1.27	2.88	-6.08	2.59	0.28	3.59	-5.18	42.62	43.5	108	0	-8	0	209	0.15	Dec-13
-14.19	-8.92	-9.39	21.75	32.77	3.54	0.38	8.46		77.04	798.8	0	100	0	0	34	0.02	Jun-06
-13.31	-7.23	-7.31	29.33	44.36	1.74	0.28	9.47		28.19	222.2	0	100	0	0	17	0.05	Feb-07
-8.97	-4.67	-7.25	22.07	39.68	3.42	0.38	8.08		65.18	950.3	0	100	0	0	17	-0.02	Jun-06
-11.23	-4.58	-5.77	28.51	44.74	2.6	0.28	8.26		84.39	1,996	0	100	0	0	10	0.00	Jun-06
-13.34	-10.18	-8.27	26.73	44.66	2.36	0.38	9.76		31.61	3,301	0	100	0	0	27	0.01	Jun-06
-15.92	-13.98	-12.28	23.07	27.27	1.32	0.38	12.2		34.26	1,105	0	100	0	0	45	0.09	Feb-07
-13.94	-8.82	-4.24			1.17	0.28			26.16	132.6	0	100	0	0	143	0.24	Jun-17
-13.24	-5.44	-5.22	34.70	52.94	2.07	0.28	9.84		38.33	2,458	0	100	0	0	29	0.06	May-13
-14.03	-8.53	-8.03	22.95	38.58	1.63	0.38	9.95		74.32	37.2	0	100	0	0	82	0.06	Feb-07
-15.51	-15.85	-12.75	24.26	26.23	3.32	0.38	13.44		24.53	2,036	0	100	0	0	36	0.04	Jun-06
-18.11	-17.19	-9.96	31.70	25.04	1.41	0.38	15.56		32.02	703.1	0	100	0	0	48	0.12	Feb-07
-15.66	-14.37	-10.29	25.45	21.73	2.37	0.38	13.94		31.15	112.4	0	100	0	0	51	0.10	Jul-13
-11.46	-5.68	-6.35	28.01	44.10	2.66	0.28	8.42		84.56	620.9	0	100	0	0	11	0.03	Jun-06
-13.66	-8.15	-7.79	28.78	41.98	1.79	0.28	9.65		28.54	91.2	0	100	0	0	22	0.28	Feb-07
0.72	1.28	-1.72	7.64		3.31	0.12	3.34	6.79	48.15	384.8	0	0	100	0	134	0.00	Jul-15
1.07	1.62	0.89			2.47	0.12		2.67	48.81	38.8	2	0	98	0	44	0.18	May-17
-13.55	-9.08	-8.67	26.55		1.16	0.75	10.15		32.41	21.9	1	99	0	0	22	0.56	Feb-14
0.31	0.54	0.84			2.15	0.3				5.0	0	0	100	0		0.07	Oct-16
0.99	0.33	1.61			1.39	0.25				4.9	0	0	100	0		0.07	Oct-16
-4.81	-1.13	-4.00	13.03		4.22	0.45	4.93			8.4	101	0	-1	0	48	-0.01	Mar-15
-14.69	-13.67	-17.52	-3.98		2.8	0.09	16.57			4.1	0	100	0	0	93	0.36	Aug-15
-11.98	-10.32	-13.93	11.24		3	0.35	10.4			67.2	1	98	0	0	45	0.11	Nov-15
-7.17	-5.87	-15.51			3.55	0.5				6.1	0	100	0	0	48	0.10	Apr-16
-16.21	-15.21	-22.75	-12.22		2.43	0.09	17.84			2.0	0	100	0	0	113	1.38	Aug-15
-12.22	-13.04	-28.18	-19.60	20.44	1.13	0.66	21.3			1,139	0	100	0	0	65	0.41	Nov-13
-12.51	-20.20	-36.43	-47.22		0	0.65	24.97			21.9	0	100	0	0	29	0.81	May-14

Fund Name	Ticker Symbol	Traded On	Overall Rating	Reward Rating	Risk Rating	Recent Up/ Downgrade	Price as of 12/31/2018	52-Week High	52-Week Low	Open to New Investors	Category & (Prospectus Objective)
Xtrackers High Beta High Yield Bond ETF	HYUP	NYSE Arca	U	U	U		45.05	50.16	44.26	Y	US Fixed Income (Corp Bond-High Yld)
Xtrackers High Yield Corp Bond - Interest Rate Hedged ETF	HYIH	BATS	C-	C-	D+	Down	21.29	23.52	20.96	Y	Fixed Income Misc (Corp Bond-High Yld)
Xtrackers Investment Grade Bond - Interest Rate Hedged ETF	IGIH	BATS	C-	C-	D+		22.47	24.64	22.47	Y	Fixed Income Misc (Corp Bond - Gen)
Xtrackers Japan JPX-Nikkei 400 Equity ETF	JPN	NYSE Arca	C-	D+	C	Down	24.73	31.58	23.94	Y	Japan Equity (Growth & Inc)
Xtrackers Low Beta High Yield Bond ETF	HYDW	NYSE Arca	U	U	U		47.42	50.05	46.81	Y	US Fixed Income (Corp Bond-High Yld)
Xtrackers MSCI All China Equity ETF	CN	NYSE Arca	D+	C-	D	Down	28.38	42.36	27.93	Y	Greater China Equity (Pacific Stock)
● Xtrackers MSCI All World ex U.S. Hedged Equity ETF	DBAW	NYSE Arca	D+	D+	C-	Down	24.23	29.07	23.68	Y	Global Equity Large Cap (World Stock)
Xtrackers MSCI All World ex US High Div Yield Hedg Eq ETF	HDAW	NYSE Arca	C-	C-	C-		22.27	27.42	21.92	Y	Global Equity Large Cap (Growth & Inc)
Xtrackers MSCI Asia Pacific ex Japan Hedged Equity ETF	DBAP	NYSE Arca	D	D+	D	Down	25.35	31.10	24.80	Y	Asia ex-Japan Equity (Pacific Stock)
Xtrackers MSCI China A Inclusion Equity ETF	ASHX	NYSE Arca	D	D	D	Down	15.84	24.14	15.62	Y	Greater China Equity (Pacific Stock)
Xtrackers MSCI EAFE ESG Leaders Equity ETF	EASG	NYSE Arca	U	U	U		22.28	31.77	21.59	Y	Global Equity Large Cap (Foreign Stock)
● Xtrackers MSCI EAFE Hedged Equity ETF	DBEF	NYSE Arca	C	C-	C+	Down	27.90	33.02	27.10	Y	Global Equity Large Cap (World Stock)
● Xtrackers MSCI EAFE High Dividend Yield Equity ETF	HDEF	NYSE Arca	C-	D+	C-	Down	20.64	25.38	20.25	Y	Global Equity Large Cap (Growth & Inc)
● Xtrackers MSCI Europe Hedged Equity ETF	DBEU	NYSE Arca	C	D+	C+	Down	25.17	29.69	24.49	Y	Europe Equity Large Cap (Europe Stock)
Xtrackers MSCI Eurozone Hedged Equity ETF	DBEZ	NYSE Arca	D+	D+	D+	Down	26.46	32.16	25.66	Y	Europe Equity Large Cap (Europe Stock)
Xtrackers MSCI Germany Hedged Equity ETF	DBGR	NYSE Arca	D+	D+	D+	Down	23.30	29.77	22.54	Y	Equity Misc (Foreign Stock)
● Xtrackers MSCI Japan Hedged Equity ETF	DBJP	NYSE Arca	C	C-	C+		36.30	46.50	35.24	Y	Japan Equity (Pacific Stock)
Xtrackers MSCI South Korea Hedged Equity ETF	DBKO	NYSE Arca	D+	C-	D+	Down	25.46	32.94	25.28	Y	Equity Misc (Pacific Stock)
Xtrackers MSCI United Kingdom Hedged Equity ETF	DBUK	NYSE Arca	D	C-	E+	Down	19.31	22.41	18.83	Y	Equity Misc (Europe Stock)
● Xtrackers Municipal Infrastructure Revenue Bond ETF	RVNU	NYSE Arca	D+	C-	D+	Down	26.27	27.16	25.58	Y	US Muni Fixed Inc (Muni Bond - Natl)
● Xtrackers Russell 1000 Comprehensive Factor ETF	DEUS	NYSE Arca	C-	C-	C-	Down	28.67	34.12	27.13	Y	US Equity Mid Cap (Growth & Inc)
Xtrackers Russell 1000 US QARP ETF	QARP	NYSE Arca	U	U	U		23.42	27.66	22.66	Y	US Equity Large Cap Blend (Growth & Inc)
Xtrackers Russell 2000 Comprehensive Factor ETF	DESC	NYSE Arca	D+	C-	D		29.97	38.02	28.41	Y	US Equity Small Cap (Growth & Inc)
Xtrackers Short Duration High Yield Bond ETF	SHYL	NYSE Arca	U	U	U		47.05	50.25	46.49	Y	US Fixed Income (Corp Bond-High Yld)
● Xtrackers USD High Yield Corporate Bond ETF	HYLB	NYSE Arca	C-	D+	C+	Down	46.79	50.89	45.99	Y	US Fixed Income (Corp Bond-High Yld)
● YieldShares High Income ETF	YYY	NYSE Arca	D+	D+	C-	Down	16.04	19.60	15.44	Y	Moderate Allocation (Income)

★ Expanded analysis of this fund is included in Section II: Analysis of All BUY Rated Funds.   ● Expanded analysis of this fund is included in Section III: Analysis of All Rated Funds with Assets over $50 million.

			TOTAL RETURNS & PERFORMANCE							ASSETS		ASSET ALLOCATION & TURNOVER					VALUATION	
3-Month Total Return	6-Month Total Return	1-Year Total Return	3-Year Total Return	5-Year Total Return	Dividend Yield (TTM)	Expense Ratio	3-Yr Std Deviation	Effective Duration	NAV	Total Assets (MIL)	%Cash	%Stocks	%Bonds	%Other	Turnover Ratio	Premium/ Discount 1-Year Avg	Inception Date
-6.86	-3.50					0.35				143.6	1	0	99	0		-0.18	Jan-18
-6.32	-2.61	-1.12	17.73		7.32	0.35	4.86			6.7	102	0	-2	0	50	0.39	Mar-15
-4.37	-1.76	-3.56	6.43		3.42	0.25	4.06			9.3	102	0	-3	0	33	0.06	Mar-15
-15.03	-10.74	-14.74	8.23		1.25	0.09	11.07			30.9	0	100	0	0	78	0.09	Jun-15
-2.28	0.08					0.25				137.8	2	0	98	0		-0.08	Jan-18
-11.24	-16.24	-22.61	4.70		0.98	0.5	19.27			35.3	0	100	0	0	3	0.04	Apr-14
-10.73	-8.32	-9.70	13.88		2.35	0.4	8.71			99.4	5	94	0	0	11	-0.10	Jan-14
-9.74	-6.61	-12.23	9.49		3.32	0.2	8.12			23.7	0	99	0	0	76	0.09	Aug-15
-8.66	-9.08	-11.04	21.26	19.62	2.6	0.6	10.73			3.9	7	93	0	0	24	0.28	Oct-13
-11.59	-12.07	-27.94	-22.98		3.33	0.6	19.75			11.5	0	99	0	1	3	0.21	Oct-15
-12.49						0.14				7.1	0	100	0	0		2.25	Sep-18
-11.88	-8.38	-9.43	11.66	22.83	2.24	0.35	9.32			5,466	2	98	0	0	10	-0.14	Jun-11
-10.38	-8.31	-13.48	6.02		2.46	0.2	8.62			199.0	0	99	0	1	56	0.42	Aug-15
-10.98	-8.55	-8.75	13.10	23.10	2.98	0.45	9.08			940.1	2	97	0	0	11	-0.10	Oct-13
-13.11	-11.40	-11.29	8.76		2.23	0.45	11.78			38.2	3	97	0	0	14	-0.13	Dec-14
-14.01	-12.45	-16.04	2.30	12.59	2.85	0.45	12.88			27.3	2	98	0	0	17	-0.01	Jun-11
-17.00	-9.62	-14.01	1.81	19.71	2.5	0.46	14.58			981.8	2	98	0	0	12	-0.06	Jun-11
-11.63	-9.43	-16.15	17.28		3.07	0.58	12.28			10.5	1	99	0	0	32	-0.66	Jan-14
-8.90	-8.27	-7.90	22.03	18.18	5.62	0.45	9.42			2.1	0	99	0	1	18	-0.34	Oct-13
1.37	0.71	-0.46	8.06	30.44	2.75	0.15	4.72			57.2	0	0	100	0	28	0.06	Jun-13
-14.78	-10.48	-9.59	22.29		1.62	0.17	9.17			165.8	0	100	0	0	67	0.09	Nov-15
-14.52	-7.98					0.19				67.6	0	100	0	0		0.15	Apr-18
-17.35	-17.52	-10.25			1.45	0.3				10.2	1	99	0	0	53	0.33	Jun-16
-3.86	-1.33	-0.72				0.2				46.1	2	0	98	0		0.00	Jan-18
-4.74	-1.79	-2.07			5.6	0.2				1,976	1	0	99	0		-0.26	Dec-16
-10.32	-7.08	-9.96	18.49	9.82	9.14	2.02	9.08	4.00	16.09	191.9	-8	25	86	-6	34	0.15	Jun-12

Section II:
Analysis of All BUY-Rated Funds

Detailed analysis of all BUY-Rated funds. Funds are listed in alphabetical order.

Section II: Contents

This section contains an expanded analysis of all BUY-Rated funds, with current and historical Weiss Investment Ratings, key rating factors, summary financial data and performance charts. Funds are listed in alphabetical order.

TOP ROW

Fund Name
Describes the fund's assets, regions of investments and investment strategies. Many funds have similar names, so you want to make sure the fund you look up is really the one you are interested in evaluating.

Overall Rating
The Weiss rating measured on a scale from A to E based on each fund's risk and performance. See the preceding section, "What Our Ratings Mean," for an explanation of each letter grade rating.

BUY-HOLD-SELL Recommendation
Funds that are rated in the A or B range are, in our opinion, a potential BUY. Funds in the C range will indicate a HOLD status. Funds in the D or E range will indicate a SELL status.

Ticker Symbol
An arrangement of characters (usually letters) representing a particular security listed on an exchange or otherwise traded publicly. When a company issues securities to the public marketplace, it selects an available ticker symbol for its securities which investors use to place trade orders. Every listed security has a unique ticker symbol, facilitating the vast array of trade orders that flow through the financial markets every day.

Traded On (Exchange)
The stock exchange on which the fund is listed. The core function of a stock exchange is to ensure fair and orderly trading, as well as efficient dissemination of price information. Exchanges such as: NYSE (New York Stock Exchange), AMEX (American Stock Exchange), NNM (NASDAQ National Market), and NASQ (NASDAQ Small Cap) give companies, governments and other groups a platform to sell securities to the investing public. NASDAQ is abbreviated as NAS.

NAV (Net Asset Value)

A fund's price per share. The value is calculated by dividing the total value of all the securities in the portfolio, less any liabilities, by the number of fund shares outstanding.

Total Assets ($)

The total of all assets listed on the institution's balance sheet. This figure primarily consists of loans, investments, and fixed assets. Total Assets are displayed in dollars.

Dividend Yield (TTM)

Trailing twelve months dividends paid out relative to the share price. Expressed as a percentage and measures how much cash flow an investor is getting for each invested dollar. **Trailing Twelve Months (TTM)** is a representation of a fund's financial performance over the most recent 12 months. TTM uses the latest available financial data from a company's interim, quarterly or annual reports.

Turnover Ratio

The percentage of an exchange-traded fund or other investment vehicle's holdings that have been replaced with other holdings in a given year. Generally, low turnover ratio is favorable, because high turnover equates to higher brokerage transaction fees, which reduce fund returns.

Expense Ratio

A measure of what it costs an investment company to operate an exchange-traded fund. An expense ratio is determined through an annual calculation, where a fund's operating expenses are divided by the average dollar value of its assets under management. Operating expenses may include money spent on administration and management of the fund, advertising, etc. An expense ratio of 1 percent per annum means that each year 1 percent of the fund's total assets will be used to cover expenses.

LEFT COLUMN

Ratings

Reward Rating

This is based on the total return over a period of up to five years, including net asset value and price growth. The total return figure is stated net of the expenses and fees charged by the fund. Based on proprietary modeling the individual components of the risk and reward ratings are calculated and weighted and the final rating is generated.

Risk Rating

This is includes the risk ratings of component stocks where applicable and also includes the financial stability of the fund, turnover where applicable, together with the level of volatility as measured by the fund's daily returns over a period of up to five years. Funds with greater stability are considered less risky and receive a higher risk rating. Funds with greater volatility are considered riskier, and will receive a lower risk rating. In addition to considering the fund's volatility, the risk rating also considers an assessment of the valuation and quality of a fund's holdings.

Recent Upgrade/Downgrade

An "Up" or "Down" indicates that the Weiss Exchange-Traded Fund rating has changed since the publication of the last print edition. If a fund has had a rating change since September 30, 2018, the change is identified with an "Up" or "Down."

Fund Information

Fund Type

Describes the fund's assets, regions of investments and investment strategies.

Category

Identifies funds according to their actual investment styles as measured by their portfolio holdings. This categorization allows investors to spread their money around in a mix of funds with a variety of risk and return characteristics.

Sub-Category

A subdivision of funds, usually with common characteristics as the category.

Prospectus Objective

Gives a general idea of a fund's overall investment approach and goals.

Inception Date

The date on which the fund began its operations. The commencement date indicates when a fund began investing in the market. Many investors prefer funds with longer operating histories. Funds with longer histories have longer track records and can thereby provide investors with a more long-standing picture of their performance.

Open to New Investments

Indicates whether the fund accepts investments from those who are not existing investors. A "Y" in this column identifies that the fund accepts new investors. No data in this column indicates that the fund is closed to new investors. The fund may be closed to new investors because the fund's asset base is getting too large to effectively execute its investing style. Although, the fund may be closed, in most cases, existing investors are able to add to their holdings.

Prices

Price
The price at which the fund is traded on a regular trading day. Prices in this guide are listed as of December 31, 2018.

52-Week High
The highest price that a fund has achieved during the previous 52 weeks.

52-Week Low
The lowest price that a fund has achieved during the previous 52 weeks.

Total Returns (%)

3-Month Total Return
The rate of return on an investment over three months that includes interest, capital gains, dividends and distributions realized.

6-Month Total Return
The rate of return on an investment over six months that includes interest, capital gains, dividends and distributions realized.

1-Year Total Return
The rate of return on an investment over one year that includes interest, capital gains, dividends and distributions realized.

3-Year Total Return
The rate of return on an investment over three years that includes interest, capital gains, dividends and distributions realized.

5-Year Total Return
The rate of return on an investment over five years that includes interest, capital gains, dividends and distributions realized.

3-Year Standard Deviation
A statistical measurement of dispersion about an average, which depicts how widely the returns varied over the past three years. Investors use the standard deviation of historical performance to try to predict the range of returns that are most likely for a given fund. When a fund has a high standard deviation, the predicted range of performance is wide, implying greater volatility. Standard deviation is most appropriate for measuring risk if it is for a fund that is an investor's only holding. The figure cannot be combined for more than one fund because the standard deviation for a portfolio of multiple funds is a function of not only the individual standard

deviations, but also of the degree of correlation among the funds' returns. If a fund's returns follow a normal distribution, then approximately 68 percent of the time they will fall within one standard deviation of the mean return for the fund, and 95 percent of the time within two standard deviations.

Effective Duration

Effective duration for all long fixed income positions in a portfolio. This value gives a better estimation of how the price of bonds with embedded options, which are common in many exchange-traded funds, will change as a result of changes in interest rates. Effective duration takes into account expected mortgage prepayment or the likelihood that embedded options will be exercised if a fund holds futures, other derivative securities, or other funds as assets, the aggregate effective duration should include the weighted impact of those exposures.

Valuation

Premium/Discount 1-Year Average

The annual average premium or discount of the market price to the NAV (Net Asset Value), expressed as a percentage of the NAV. This value provides a year-by-year picture a fund's trading status. A negative number indicates that, on average, the fund's shares sold at a discount to NAV, and a positive number indicates the shares sold at a premium. If the number shown is –10.00, for example, the shares sold at an average 10% discount to NAV during the listed time-period.

Company Information

Provider

The legal company that issues the fund.

Manager/Tenure (Years)

The name of the manager and the number of years spent managing the fund.

Website

The company's web address.

Address

The company's street address.

Phone Number

The company's phone number.

RIGHT COLUMN

Performance Chart
A graphical representation of the fund's total returns over the past year.

Ratings History

Indicates the fund's Overall, Risk and Reward Ratings for the previous four years. Ratings are listed as of December 31, 2018 (Q4-18), June 30, 2018 (Q2-18), December 31, 2017 (Q4-17), December 31, 2016 (Q4-16), and December 31, 2015 (Q4-15).

Overall Rating
The Weiss rating measured on a scale from A to E based on each fund's risk and performance. See the preceding section, "What Our Ratings Mean," for an explanation of each letter grade rating.

Risk Rating
This is includes the risk ratings of component stocks where applicable and also includes the financial stability of the fund, turnover where applicable, together with the level of volatility as measured by the fund's daily returns over a period of up to five years. Funds with greater stability are considered less risky and receive a higher risk rating. Funds with greater volatility are considered riskier, and will receive a lower risk rating. In addition to considering the fund's volatility, the risk rating also considers an assessment of the valuation and quality of a fund's holdings.

Reward Rating
This is based on the total return over a period of up to five years, including net asset value and price growth. The total return figure is stated net of the expenses and fees charged by the fund.   Based on proprietary modeling the individual components of the risk and reward ratings are calculated and weighted and the final rating is generated.

Asset & Performance History
Indicates the fund's NAV (Net Asset Value) and 1-Year Total Return for the previous 6 years.

NAV (Net Asset Value)
A fund's price per share. The value is calculated by dividing the total value of all the securities in the portfolio, less any liabilities, by the number of fund shares outstanding.

1-Year Total Return

The rate of return on an investment over one year that includes interest, capital gains, dividends and distributions realized.

Total Assets ($)

The total of all assets listed on the institution's balance sheet. This figure primarily consists of loans, investments, and fixed assets. Total Assets are displayed in dollars.

Asset Allocation

Indicates the percentage of assets in each category. Used as an investment strategy that attempts to balance risk versus reward by adjusting the percentage of each asset in an investment portfolio according to the investor's risk tolerance, goals and investment time frame. Allocation percentages may not add up to 100%. Negative values reflect short positions.

%Cash

The percentage of the fund's assets invested in short-term obligations, usually less than 90 days, that provide a return in the form of interest payments. This type of investment generally offers a low return compared to other investments but has a low risk level.

%Stocks

The percentage of the fund's assets invested in stock.

%US Stocks

The percentage of the fund's assets invested in U.S. stock.

%Bonds

The percentage of the fund's assets invested in bonds. A bond is an unsecured debt security issued by companies, municipalities, states and sovereign governments to raise funds. When a company issues a bond it borrows money from the bondholder to boost the business, in exchange the bondholder receives the principal amount back plus the interest on the determined maturity date.

%US Bonds

The percentage of the fund's assets invested in U.S. bonds.

%Other

The percentage of the fund's assets invested in other financial instruments.

Services Offered
Services offered by the fund provider. Such services can include:

Systematic Withdrawal Plan
A plan offered by exchange-traded funds that pays specific amounts to shareholders at predetermined intervals.

Institutional Only
This indicates if the fund is offered to institutional clients only (pension funds, mutual funds, money managers, insurance companies, investment banks, commercial trusts, endowment funds, hedge funds, and some hedge fund investors).

Phone Exchange
This indicates that investors can move money between different funds within the same fund family over the phone.

Wire Redemption
This indicates whether or not investors can redeem electronically.

Qualified Investment
Under a qualified plan, an investor may invest in the variable annuity with pretax dollars through an employee pension plan, such as a 401(k) or 403(b). Money builds up on a tax-deferred basis, and when the qualified investor makes a withdrawal or annuitizes, all contributions received are taxable income.

Investment Strategy
A set of rules, behaviors or procedures, designed to guide an investor's selection of an investment portfolio. Individuals have different profit objectives, and their individual skills make different tactics and strategies appropriate.

Top Holdings
The highest amount of publicly traded assets held by a fund. These publicly traded assets may include company stock, mutual funds or other investment vehicles.

Aberdeen Standard Physical Palladium Shares ETF B- BUY

Ticker	Traded On	NAV	Total Assets ($)	Dividend Yield (TTM)	Turnover Ratio	Expense Ratio
PALL	NYSE Arca	119.66	$159,905,958	0		0.6

Ratings
Reward	B+
Risk	C-
Recent Upgrade/Downgrade	Up

Fund Information
Fund Type	Exchange Traded Funds
Category	Commodities Specified
Sub-Category	Commodities Precious Metals
Prospectus Objective	Prec Metals
Inception Date	Jan-10
Open to New Investments	Y

Prices
Price (as of 12/31/2018)	119.05
52-Week High	123.65
52-Week Low	80.32

Total Returns (%)
3-Month	6-Month	1-Year	3-Year	5-Year
19.76	33.81	18.88	126.76	72.37

3-Year Standard Deviation	30.01
Effective Duration	

Valuation
Premium/Discount (1-Year Average)	-0.40

Company Information
Provider	Aberdeen Standard Investments
Manager/Tenure	Management Team (8)
Website	http://www.aberdeenstandardetfs.us
Address	Aberdeen Standard Investments 405 Lexington Avenue New York NY 10174 United States
Phone Number	212-918-4954

PERFORMANCE

Ratings History

Date	Overall Rating	Risk Rating	Reward Rating
Q4-18	B-	C-	B+
Q2-18	C	C-	C
Q4-17	B	C	A
Q4-16	D+	C-	D+
Q4-15	D	D	D

Asset & Performance History

Date	NAV	1-Year Total Return
2017	100.65	55.27
2016	64.82	22.84
2015	52.77	-31.86
2014	77.44	11.56
2013	69.42	1.1
2012	68.66	9.24

Total Assets: $159,905,958

Asset Allocation

Asset	%
Cash	0%
Stocks	0%
US Stocks	0%
Bonds	0%
US Bonds	0%
Other	100%

Services Offered:

Investment Strategy: The investment seeks to reflect the performance of the price of physical palladium, less the expenses of the Trust's operations. The fund is designed for investors who want a cost-effective and convenient way to invest in palladium with minimal credit risk. **Top Holdings:** Physical Palladium Bullion Physical Gold Bullion

---

AdvisorShares Focused Equity ETF B- BUY

Ticker	Traded On	NAV	Total Assets ($)	Dividend Yield (TTM)	Turnover Ratio	Expense Ratio
CWS	NYSE Arca	28.68	$14,731,636	0.27		0.68

Ratings
Reward	B
Risk	C
Recent Upgrade/Downgrade	

Fund Information
Fund Type	Exchange Traded Funds
Category	US Equity Large Cap Blend
Sub-Category	Mid-Cap Growth
Prospectus Objective	Growth
Inception Date	Sep-16
Open to New Investments	Y

Prices
Price (as of 12/31/2018)	28.70
52-Week High	34.55
52-Week Low	28.19

Total Returns (%)
3-Month	6-Month	1-Year	3-Year	5-Year
-14.63	-9.33	-7.38		

3-Year Standard Deviation	
Effective Duration	

Valuation
Premium/Discount (1-Year Average)	0.37

Company Information
Provider	AdvisorShares
Manager/Tenure	Edward J Elfenbein (2)
Website	http://www.advisorshares.com
Address	AdvisorShares 2 Bethesda Metro Center, Suite 1330 Bethesda MD 20814 United States
Phone Number	877-843-3831

PERFORMANCE

Ratings History

Date	Overall Rating	Risk Rating	Reward Rating
Q4-18	B-	C	B
Q2-18	B-	C	B
Q4-17	D	B	C-
Q4-16	U		
Q4-15			

Asset & Performance History

Date	NAV	1-Year Total Return
2017	31.21	20.66
2016	25.94	
2015		
2014		
2013		
2012		

Total Assets: $14,731,636

Asset Allocation

Asset	%
Cash	0%
Stocks	99%
US Stocks	99%
Bonds	0%
US Bonds	0%
Other	1%

Services Offered:

Investment Strategy: The investment seeks long-term capital appreciation. The fund seeks to achieve its investment objective by investing primarily in a focused group of U.S. exchange listed equity securities, including common and preferred stock and American Depositary Receipts. It will invest at least 80% of its net assets (plus any borrowings for investment purposes) in equity securities. The Advisor may use a variety of methods for security selection and will seek to focus on firms that are fundamentally sound and have shown consistency in their financial results and high earnings quality. **Top Holdings:** Church & Dwight Co Inc Hormel Foods Corp RPM International Inc Fiserv Inc FactSet Research Systems Inc

Amplify YieldShares CWP Dividend & Option Income ETF   B-   BUY

Ticker	Traded On	NAV	Total Assets ($)	Dividend Yield (TTM)	Turnover Ratio	Expense Ratio
DIVO	BATS	26.85	$16,063,377	5.6		0.49

Ratings

Reward	B
Risk	C
Recent Upgrade/Downgrade	Down

Fund Information

Fund Type	Exchange Traded Funds
Category	Long/Short Equity
Sub-Category	Large Blend
Prospectus Objective	Growth & Inc
Inception Date	Dec-16
Open to New Investments	Y

Prices

Price (as of 12/31/2018)	26.72
52-Week High	30.53
52-Week Low	25.34

Total Returns (%)

3-Month	6-Month	1-Year	3-Year	5-Year
-9.46	-2.43	-2.47		

3-Year Standard Deviation	
Effective Duration	

Valuation

Premium/Discount (1-Year Average)	0.20

Company Information

Provider	Amplifyetfs
Manager/Tenure	Anand Desai (1), Dustin Lewellyn (1), Kevin G. Simpson (1), 2 others
Website	http://www.amplifyetfs.com
Address	3250 Lacey Road, Suite 130 Downers Grove Downers Grove IL 60515 United States
Phone Number	630-487-2530

PERFORMANCE

Ratings History

Date	Overall Rating	Risk Rating	Reward Rating
Q4-18	B-	C	B
Q2-18	B	C	B
Q4-17	D	A-	D+
Q4-16			
Q4-15			

Asset & Performance History

Date	NAV	1-Year Total Return
2017	28.93	21.3
2016	24.84	
2015		
2014		
2013		
2012		

Total Assets: $16,063,377

Asset Allocation

Asset	%
Cash	8%
Stocks	92%
US Stocks	92%
Bonds	0%
US Bonds	0%
Other	0%

Services Offered:

Investment Strategy: The investment seeks to provide current income as its primary investment objective and to provide capital appreciation as its secondary investment objective. Under normal circumstances, the fund invests at least 80% of its total assets in dividend-paying U.S. exchange-traded equity securities ("Equity Securities") and will opportunistically utilize an "option strategy" consisting of writing (selling) U.S. exchange-traded covered call options on such Equity Securities. The fund is non-diversified. **Top Holdings:** UnitedHealth Group Inc   Johnson & Johnson   American Express Co   Visa Inc Class A   Walt Disney Co

---

Aptus Behavioral Momentum ETF   B-   BUY

Ticker	Traded On	NAV	Total Assets ($)	Dividend Yield (TTM)	Turnover Ratio	Expense Ratio
BEMO	BATS	28.26	$75,910,288	0.31	124	0.79

Ratings

Reward	B
Risk	C
Recent Upgrade/Downgrade	Down

Fund Information

Fund Type	Exchange Traded Funds
Category	US Equity Large Cap Blend
Sub-Category	Large Growth
Prospectus Objective	Growth & Inc
Inception Date	Jun-16
Open to New Investments	Y

Prices

Price (as of 12/31/2018)	28.25
52-Week High	37.07
52-Week Low	28.17

Total Returns (%)

3-Month	6-Month	1-Year	3-Year	5-Year
-23.09	-16.53	-5.88		

3-Year Standard Deviation	
Effective Duration	

Valuation

Premium/Discount (1-Year Average)	0.08

Company Information

Provider	Aptus Capital Advisors
Manager/Tenure	John D. Gardner (1), Beckham D. Wyrick (1)
Website	
Address	407 Johnson Avenue, Fairhope, Alabama 36532 United States
Phone Number	

PERFORMANCE

Ratings History

Date	Overall Rating	Risk Rating	Reward Rating
Q4-18	B-	C	B
Q2-18	B-	C-	B
Q4-17	D+	B	C
Q4-16	U		
Q4-15			

Asset & Performance History

Date	NAV	1-Year Total Return
2017	30.28	17.28
2016	25.9	
2015		
2014		
2013		
2012		

Total Assets: $75,910,288

Asset Allocation

Asset	%
Cash	0%
Stocks	100%
US Stocks	100%
Bonds	0%
US Bonds	0%
Other	0%

Services Offered:

Investment Strategy: The investment seeks to track the performance, before fees and expenses, of the Aptus Behavioral Momentum Index. The index uses an objective, rules-based methodology to implement a systematic trend-following strategy that directs 100% of its exposure to either equity exposure or treasure exposure. The fund invests at least 80% of its total assets in the component securities of the index. The fund generally may invest up to 20% of its total assets (exclusive of any collateral held from securities lending) in securities or other investments not included in the index, but which the Adviser believes will help the fund track the index. It is non-diversified. **Top Holdings:** HCA Healthcare Inc   Church & Dwight Co Inc   Clorox Co   Merck & Co Inc   McCormick & Co Inc Non-Voting

Consumer Discretionary Select Sector SPDR® Fund   B-   BUY

Ticker	Traded On	NAV	Total Assets ($)	Dividend Yield (TTM)	Turnover Ratio	Expense Ratio
XLY	NYSE Arca	98.99	$13,593,260,414	1.19	23	0.13

Ratings
Reward   B
Risk   C
Recent Upgrade/Downgrade   Down

Fund Information
Fund Type   Exchange Traded Funds
Category   Consumer Goods & Svcs
Sub-Category   Consumer Cyclical
Prospectus Objective   Unaligned
Inception Date   Dec-98
Open to New Investments   Y

Prices
Price (as of 12/31/2018)   99.01
52-Week High   117.79
52-Week Low   91.98

Total Returns (%)

3-Month	6-Month	1-Year	3-Year	5-Year
-14.98	-8.93	1.66	32.14	59.04

3-Year Standard Deviation   12.2
Effective Duration

Valuation
Premium/Discount (1-Year Average)   0.01

Company Information
Provider   SPDR State Street Global Advisors
Manager/Tenure Michael J. Feehily (7), Karl A.
                Schneider (3), Kala O'Donnell (1)
Website   http://www.spdrs.com
Address   SPDR State Street Global Advisors
                State Street Financial Center, 1
                Lincoln Street Boston MA 02111-2900
                United States
Phone Number   617-786-3000

PERFORMANCE

Ratings History

Date	Overall Rating	Risk Rating	Reward Rating
Q4-18	B-	C	B
Q2-18	B	C	B
Q4-17	B	A	B
Q4-16	B	B	B
Q4-15	B	A-	B

Asset & Performance History

Date	NAV	1-Year Total Return
2017	98.6	22.76
2016	81.36	5.79
2015	78.2	9.92
2014	72.18	9.49
2013	66.84	42.74
2012	47.44	23.59

Total Assets: $13,593,260,414

Asset Allocation

Asset	%
Cash	0%
Stocks	100%
US Stocks	100%
Bonds	0%
US Bonds	0%
Other	0%

Services Offered: Dividend Investment Plan, CashInvestment Plan

Investment Strategy: The investment seeks investment results that, before expenses, correspond to the price and yield performance of publicly traded equity securities of companies in the Consumer Discretionary Select Sector Index. The fund employs a replication strategy. It generally invests substantially all, but at least 95%, of its total assets in the securities comprising the index. The index includes securities of companies from the following industries: media; retail; hotels, restaurants and leisure; textiles, apparel and luxury goods; household durables; automobiles; auto components; distributors; leisure products; and diversified consumer services. It is non-diversified. **Top Holdings:** Amazon.com Inc The Home Depot Inc McDonald's Corp Nike Inc B Starbucks Corp

ETFMG Prime Mobile Payments ETF   B-   BUY

Ticker	Traded On	NAV	Total Assets ($)	Dividend Yield (TTM)	Turnover Ratio	Expense Ratio
IPAY	NYSE Arca	35.02	$419,802,911	0.02	16	0.8

Ratings
Reward   B
Risk   C+
Recent Upgrade/Downgrade   Up

Fund Information
Fund Type   Exchange Traded Funds
Category   Equity Misc
Sub-Category   Miscellaneous Sector
Prospectus Objective   Growth & Inc
Inception Date   Jul-15
Open to New Investments   Y

Prices
Price (as of 12/31/2018)   34.95
52-Week High   43.27
52-Week Low   32.45

Total Returns (%)

3-Month	6-Month	1-Year	3-Year	5-Year
-17.99	-9.31	1.33	44.41	

3-Year Standard Deviation   13.84
Effective Duration

Valuation
Premium/Discount (1-Year Average)   0.09

Company Information
Provider   Pure Funds
Manager/Tenure Samuel R. Masucci (0), James B.
                Francis (0), Devin Ryder (0), 1 other
Website   http://www.etfmgfunds.com
Address
Phone Number

PERFORMANCE

Ratings History

Date	Overall Rating	Risk Rating	Reward Rating
Q4-18	B-	C+	B
Q2-18	C+	C	B-
Q4-17	C	B	B-
Q4-16	D	C	B-
Q4-15	U		

Asset & Performance History

Date	NAV	1-Year Total Return
2017	34.8	36.87
2016	25.43	3.42
2015	24.55	
2014		
2013		
2012		

Total Assets: $419,802,911

Asset Allocation

Asset	%
Cash	0%
Stocks	100%
US Stocks	77%
Bonds	0%
US Bonds	0%
Other	0%

Services Offered:

Investment Strategy: The investment seeks to provide investment results that correspond generally to the Prime Mobile Payments Index. The fund invests at least 80% of its total assets in the component securities of the index and in ADRs and GDRs based on the component securities in the index. The index tracks the performance of the exchange-listed equity securities of companies across the globe that (i) engage in providing payment processing services or applications, (ii) provide payment solutions, (iii) build or provide payment industry architecture, infrastructure or software, or (iv) provide services as a credit card network. The fund is non-diversified. **Top Holdings:** American Express Co Visa Inc Class A PayPal Holdings Inc Mastercard Inc A Fidelity National Information Services Inc

Fidelity® MSCI Utilities Index ETF   B-   BUY

Ticker	Traded On	NAV	Total Assets ($)	Dividend Yield (TTM)	Turnover Ratio	Expense Ratio
FUTY	NYSE Arca	34.86	$488,756,480	3.02	6	0.08

Ratings
Reward	B-
Risk	C+
Recent Upgrade/Downgrade	

Fund Information
Fund Type	Exchange Traded Funds
Category	Utilities Sector Equity
Sub-Category	Utilities
Prospectus Objective	Utility
Inception Date	Oct-13
Open to New Investments	Y

Prices
Price (as of 12/31/2018)	34.88
52-Week High	37.49
52-Week Low	31.11

Total Returns (%)
3-Month	6-Month	1-Year	3-Year	5-Year
1.14	2.56	4.40	37.72	66.31

3-Year Standard Deviation	11.59
Effective Duration	

Valuation
Premium/Discount (1-Year Average)	0.02

Company Information
Provider	Fidelity Investments
Manager/Tenure	Jennifer Hsui (5), Greg Savage (5), Alan Mason (2), 2 others
Website	http://www.institutional.fidelity.com
Address	Fidelity Investments 82 Devonshire Street Boston MA 2109 United States
Phone Number	617-563-7000

PERFORMANCE

Ratings History
Date	Overall Rating	Risk Rating	Reward Rating
Q4-18	B-	C+	B-
Q2-18	C+	C	B
Q4-17	B	B	B
Q4-16	B-	C+	B
Q4-15	C-	C	B

Asset & Performance History
Date	NAV	1-Year Total Return
2017	34.47	12.32
2016	31.61	17.44
2015	27.83	-4.79
2014	30.52	26.83
2013	24.87	
2012		

Total Assets: $488,756,480

Asset Allocation
Asset	%
Cash	0%
Stocks	100%
US Stocks	100%
Bonds	0%
US Bonds	0%
Other	0%

Services Offered:

Investment Strategy: The investment seeks to provide investment returns that correspond, before fees and expenses, generally to the performance of the MSCI USA IMI Utilities Index. The fund invests at least 80% of assets in securities included in the fund's underlying index. The fund's underlying index is the MSCI USA IMI Utilities Index, which represents the performance of the utilities sector in the U.S. equity market. It may or may not hold all of the securities in the MSCI USA IMI Utilities Index. The fund is non-diversified. **Top Holdings:** NextEra Energy Inc Duke Energy Corp Dominion Energy Inc Southern Co Exelon Corp

---

First Trust Dow 30 Equal Weight ETF   B-   BUY

Ticker	Traded On	NAV	Total Assets ($)	Dividend Yield (TTM)	Turnover Ratio	Expense Ratio
EDOW	NYSE Arca	21.43	$51,577,674	1.78	20	0.5

Ratings
Reward	B
Risk	C
Recent Upgrade/Downgrade	Up

Fund Information
Fund Type	Exchange Traded Funds
Category	US Equity Large Cap Value
Sub-Category	Large Value
Prospectus Objective	Growth & Inc
Inception Date	Aug-17
Open to New Investments	Y

Prices
Price (as of 12/31/2018)	21.31
52-Week High	23.87
52-Week Low	20.09

Total Returns (%)
3-Month	6-Month	1-Year	3-Year	5-Year
-9.34	-0.24	-0.89		

3-Year Standard Deviation	
Effective Duration	

Valuation
Premium/Discount (1-Year Average)	0.30

Company Information
Provider	First Trust
Manager/Tenure	Jon C. Erickson (1), Daniel J. Lindquist (1), David G. McGarel (1), 3 others
Website	http://www.ftportfolios.com/
Address	First Trust 120 E. Liberty Drive, Suite 400 Wheaton IL 60187 United States
Phone Number	800-621-1675

PERFORMANCE

Ratings History
Date	Overall Rating	Risk Rating	Reward Rating
Q4-18	B-	C	B
Q2-18	U		
Q4-17	U		
Q4-16			
Q4-15			

Asset & Performance History
Date	NAV	1-Year Total Return
2017	22	
2016		
2015		
2014		
2013		
2012		

Total Assets: $51,577,674

Asset Allocation
Asset	%
Cash	0%
Stocks	100%
US Stocks	100%
Bonds	0%
US Bonds	0%
Other	0%

Services Offered:

Investment Strategy: The investment seeks investment results that correspond generally to the price and yield of an equity index called the Dow Jones Industrial Average Equal Weight Index. The fund will normally invest at least 90% of its net assets (including investment borrowings) in common stocks that comprise the index. The index consists of an equally weighted portfolio of the 30 securities that comprise the Dow Jones Industrial Average (TM) (the "DJIA"). The 30 securities comprising the DJIA are domestic, blue-chip companies covering all industries, with the exception of transportation and utilities. The fund is non-diversified. **Top Holdings:** Walgreens Boots Alliance Inc McDonald's Corp Merck & Co Inc Procter & Gamble Co Verizon Communications Inc

First Trust Nasdaq Bank ETF

B-   BUY

Ticker	Traded On	NAV	Total Assets ($)	Dividend Yield (TTM)	Turnover Ratio	Expense Ratio
FTXO	NAS CM	22.28	$222,633,375	1.58	39	0.6

Ratings

Reward	B
Risk	C
Recent Upgrade/Downgrade	Down

Fund Information

Fund Type	Exchange Traded Funds
Category	Financials Sector Equity
Sub-Category	Financial
Prospectus Objective	Financial
Inception Date	Sep-16
Open to New Investments	Y

Prices

Price (as of 12/31/2018)	22.26
52-Week High	32.18
52-Week Low	21.01

Total Returns (%)

3-Month	6-Month	1-Year	3-Year	5-Year
-18.17	-20.50	-21.57		

3-Year Standard Deviation
Effective Duration

Valuation

Premium/Discount (1-Year Average)	0.02

Company Information

Provider	First Trust
Manager/Tenure	Jon C. Erickson (2), Daniel J. Lindquist (2), David G. McGarel (2), 3 others
Website	http://www.ftportfolios.com/
Address	First Trust 120 E. Liberty Drive, Suite 400 Wheaton IL 60187 United States
Phone Number	800-621-1675

PERFORMANCE

Ratings History

Date	Overall Rating	Risk Rating	Reward Rating
Q4-18	B-	C	B
Q2-18	B	C	B+
Q4-17	D	B	C
Q4-16	U		
Q4-15			

Asset & Performance History

Date	NAV	1-Year Total Return
2017	29.32	13.95
2016	26.02	
2015		
2014		
2013		
2012		

Total Assets: $222,633,375

Asset Allocation

Asset	%
Cash	0%
Stocks	100%
US Stocks	100%
Bonds	0%
US Bonds	0%
Other	0%

Services Offered:

Investment Strategy: The investment seeks investment results that correspond generally to the price and yield (before the fund's fees and expenses) of an equity index called the Nasdaq US Smart Banks Index. The fund will normally invest at least 90% of its net assets (including investment borrowings) in common stocks that comprise the underlying index. The underlying index is designed to select bank stocks from the NASDAQ US Benchmark Index based on a ranking methodology of three price factors which aims to select companies. The fund is non-diversified. **Top Holdings:** US Bancorp JPMorgan Chase & Co PNC Financial Services Group Inc Huntington Bancshares Inc SunTrust Banks Inc

---

First Trust Nasdaq Food & Beverage ETF

B-   BUY

Ticker	Traded On	NAV	Total Assets ($)	Dividend Yield (TTM)	Turnover Ratio	Expense Ratio
FTXG	NAS CM	18.05	$998,962	1.35	76	0.6

Ratings

Reward	B
Risk	C
Recent Upgrade/Downgrade	

Fund Information

Fund Type	Exchange Traded Funds
Category	Consumer Goods & Svcs
Sub-Category	Consumer Defensive
Prospectus Objective	Unaligned
Inception Date	Sep-16
Open to New Investments	Y

Prices

Price (as of 12/31/2018)	18.04
52-Week High	21.28
52-Week Low	17.50

Total Returns (%)

3-Month	6-Month	1-Year	3-Year	5-Year
-6.36	-7.60	-12.38		

3-Year Standard Deviation
Effective Duration

Valuation

Premium/Discount (1-Year Average)	-0.03

Company Information

Provider	First Trust
Manager/Tenure	Jon C. Erickson (2), Daniel J. Lindquist (2), David G. McGarel (2), 3 others
Website	http://www.ftportfolios.com/
Address	First Trust 120 E. Liberty Drive, Suite 400 Wheaton IL 60187 United States
Phone Number	800-621-1675

PERFORMANCE

Ratings History

Date	Overall Rating	Risk Rating	Reward Rating
Q4-18	B-	C	B
Q2-18	B-	C	B
Q4-17	D	B	D+
Q4-16	U		
Q4-15			

Asset & Performance History

Date	NAV	1-Year Total Return
2017	20.87	6.09
2016	19.99	
2015		
2014		
2013		
2012		

Total Assets: $998,962

Asset Allocation

Asset	%
Cash	0%
Stocks	100%
US Stocks	96%
Bonds	0%
US Bonds	0%
Other	0%

Services Offered:

Investment Strategy: The investment seeks investment results that correspond generally to the price and yield (before the fund's fees and expenses) of an equity index called the Nasdaq US Smart Food & Beverage Index. The fund will normally invest at least 90% of its net assets (including investment borrowings) in common stocks that comprise the underlying index. The underlying index is designed to select food and beverage stocks from the NASDAQ US Benchmark Index based on a ranking methodology of three price factors which aims to select companies. The fund is non-diversified. **Top Holdings:** Lamb Weston Holdings Inc Coca-Cola Co Post Holdings Inc Archer-Daniels Midland Co McCormick & Co Inc Non-Voting

First Trust Nasdaq Retail ETF   B-   BUY

Ticker	Traded On	NAV	Total Assets ($)	Dividend Yield (TTM)	Turnover Ratio	Expense Ratio
FTXD	NAS CM	20.86	$9,144,260	0.85	126	0.6

Ratings

Reward	B
Risk	C
Recent Upgrade/Downgrade	

Fund Information

Fund Type	Exchange Traded Funds
Category	Consumer Goods & Svcs
Sub-Category	Consumer Cyclical
Prospectus Objective	Unaligned
Inception Date	Sep-16
Open to New Investments	Y

Prices

Price (as of 12/31/2018)	20.84
52-Week High	24.94
52-Week Low	19.60

Total Returns (%)

3-Month	6-Month	1-Year	3-Year	5-Year
-14.32	-7.72	-2.06		

3-Year Standard Deviation

Effective Duration

Valuation

Premium/Discount (1-Year Average)	0.29

Company Information

Provider	First Trust
Manager/Tenure	Jon C. Erickson (2), Daniel J. Lindquist (2), David G. McGarel (2), 3 others
Website	http://www.ftportfolios.com/
Address	First Trust 120 E. Liberty Drive, Suite 400 Wheaton IL 60187 United States
Phone Number	800-621-1675

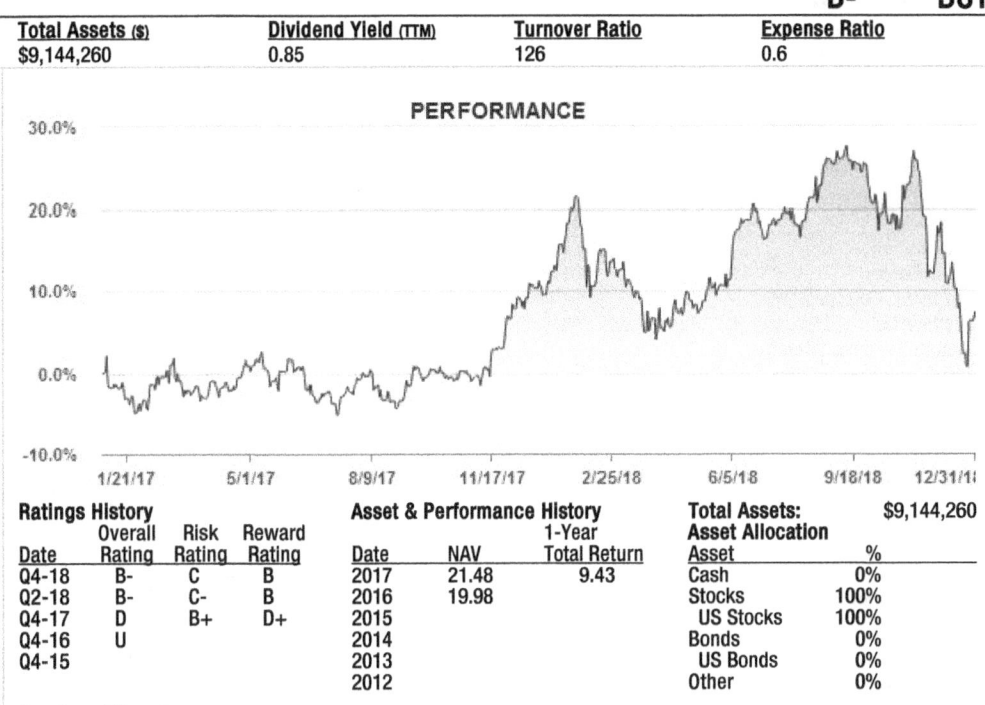

PERFORMANCE

Ratings History

Date	Overall Rating	Risk Rating	Reward Rating
Q4-18	B-	C	B
Q2-18	B-	C-	B
Q4-17	D	B+	D+
Q4-16	U		
Q4-15			

Asset & Performance History

Date	NAV	1-Year Total Return
2017	21.48	9.43
2016	19.98	
2015		
2014		
2013		
2012		

Total Assets: $9,144,260

Asset Allocation

Asset	%
Cash	0%
Stocks	100%
US Stocks	100%
Bonds	0%
US Bonds	0%
Other	0%

Services Offered:

Investment Strategy: The investment seeks investment results that correspond generally to the price and yield (before the fund's fees and expenses) of the Nasdaq US Smart Retail Index. The fund will normally invest at least 90% of its net assets (including investment borrowings) in common stocks that comprise the index. The index is designed to select retail stocks from the NASDAQ US Benchmark Index based on a ranking methodology of three price factors which aims to select companies that exhibit: strong growth through high average 3-, 6-, 9- and 12-month price return; value; and low expected volatility based on historical stock price fluctuation. It is non-diversified. **Top Holdings:** Kohl's Corp   TJX Companies Inc   Costco Wholesale Corp   The Kroger Co   Target Corp

---

First Trust Nasdaq Transportation ETF   B-   BUY

Ticker	Traded On	NAV	Total Assets ($)	Dividend Yield (TTM)	Turnover Ratio	Expense Ratio
FTXR	NAS CM	21.65	$2,521,555	1.32	78	0.6

Ratings

Reward	B
Risk	C
Recent Upgrade/Downgrade	

Fund Information

Fund Type	Exchange Traded Funds
Category	Industrials Sector Equity
Sub-Category	Industrials
Prospectus Objective	Unaligned
Inception Date	Sep-16
Open to New Investments	Y

Prices

Price (as of 12/31/2018)	21.64
52-Week High	27.50
52-Week Low	21.05

Total Returns (%)

3-Month	6-Month	1-Year	3-Year	5-Year
-14.52	-11.05	-15.00		

3-Year Standard Deviation

Effective Duration

Valuation

Premium/Discount (1-Year Average)	0.03

Company Information

Provider	First Trust
Manager/Tenure	Jon C. Erickson (2), Daniel J. Lindquist (2), David G. McGarel (2), 3 others
Website	http://www.ftportfolios.com/
Address	First Trust 120 E. Liberty Drive, Suite 400 Wheaton IL 60187 United States
Phone Number	800-621-1675

PERFORMANCE

Ratings History

Date	Overall Rating	Risk Rating	Reward Rating
Q4-18	B-	C	B
Q2-18	B-	C	B
Q4-17	D	B+	C-
Q4-16	U		
Q4-15			

Asset & Performance History

Date	NAV	1-Year Total Return
2017	25.87	15.63
2016	22.66	
2015		
2014		
2013		
2012		

Total Assets: $2,521,555

Asset Allocation

Asset	%
Cash	0%
Stocks	100%
US Stocks	100%
Bonds	0%
US Bonds	0%
Other	0%

Services Offered:

Investment Strategy: The investment seeks investment results that correspond generally to the price and yield (before the fund's fees and expenses) of the Nasdaq US Smart Transportation Index. The fund invests at least 90% of its net assets (including investment borrowings) in common stocks that comprise the index. The index is designed to select transportation stocks from the NASDAQ US Benchmark Index based on a ranking methodology of three price factors which aims to select companies that exhibit: strong growth through high average 3-, 6-, 9- and 12-month price return; value; and low expected volatility based on historical stock price fluctuation. It is non-diversified. **Top Holdings:** United Continental Holdings Inc   Delta Air Lines Inc   Union Pacific Corp   Norfolk Southern Corp   CSX Corp

First Trust Utilities AlphaDEX® Fund | B | BUY

Ticker	Traded On	NAV		Total Assets ($)	Dividend Yield (TTM)	Turnover Ratio	Expense Ratio
FXU	NYSE Arca	26.80		$390,453,640	3.04		0.63

Ratings
Reward   B+
Risk   C+
Recent Upgrade/Downgrade   Up

Fund Information
Fund Type   Exchange Traded Funds
Category   Utilities Sector Equity
Sub-Category   Utilities
Prospectus Objective   Utility
Inception Date   May-07
Open to New Investments   Y

Prices
Price (as of 12/31/2018)   26.78
52-Week High   28.86
52-Week Low   23.56

Total Returns (%)

3-Month	6-Month	1-Year	3-Year	5-Year
-1.89	3.65	5.59	30.61	53.40

3-Year Standard Deviation   10.38
Effective Duration

Valuation
Premium/Discount (1-Year Average)   0.01

Company Information
Provider   First Trust
Manager/Tenure   Jon C. Erickson (11), Daniel J. Lindquist (11), David G. McGarel (11), 3 others
Website   http://www.ftportfolios.com/
Address   First Trust 120 E. Liberty Drive, Suite 400 Wheaton IL 60187 United States
Phone Number   800-621-1675

PERFORMANCE

Ratings History

Date	Overall Rating	Risk Rating	Reward Rating
Q4-18	B	C+	B+
Q2-18	C+	C	B
Q4-17	C+	B	C
Q4-16	B-	C	B
Q4-15	B-	C	B

Asset & Performance History

Date	NAV	1-Year Total Return
2017	26	0.93
2016	26.73	22.54
2015	22.4	-6.42
2014	24.87	25.5
2013	20.27	17.6
2012	17.99	3.64

Total Assets: $390,453,640

Asset Allocation

Asset	%
Cash	0%
Stocks	100%
US Stocks	100%
Bonds	0%
US Bonds	0%
Other	0%

Services Offered:

Investment Strategy: The investment seeks investment results that correspond generally to the price and yield (before the fund's fees and expenses) of an equity index called the StrataQuant® Utilities Index. The fund will normally invest at least 90% of its net assets (including investment borrowings) in common stocks that comprise the index. The index is a modified equal-dollar weighted index designed by IDI to objectively identify and select stocks from the Russell 1000® Index in the utilities sector that may generate positive alpha relative to traditional passive-style indices through the use of the AlphaDEX® selection methodology. **Top Holdings:** Telephone and Data Systems Inc   Verizon Communications Inc   NextEra Energy Inc   CenturyLink Inc   Sprint Corp

Health Care Select Sector SPDR® Fund | B- | BUY

Ticker	Traded On	NAV		Total Assets ($)	Dividend Yield (TTM)	Turnover Ratio	Expense Ratio
XLV	NYSE Arca	86.43		$19,896,594,302	1.38	5	0.13

Ratings
Reward   B
Risk   C+
Recent Upgrade/Downgrade

Fund Information
Fund Type   Exchange Traded Funds
Category   Healthcare Sector Equity
Sub-Category   Health
Prospectus Objective   Health
Inception Date   Dec-98
Open to New Investments   Y

Prices
Price (as of 12/31/2018)   86.51
52-Week High   95.87
52-Week Low   79.55

Total Returns (%)

3-Month	6-Month	1-Year	3-Year	5-Year
-9.19	4.11	6.29	25.69	68.07

3-Year Standard Deviation   12.5
Effective Duration

Valuation
Premium/Discount (1-Year Average)   0.12

Company Information
Provider   SPDR State Street Global Advisors
Manager/Tenure   Michael J. Feehily (7), Karl A. Schneider (3), Dwayne Hancock (1)
Website   http://www.spdrs.com
Address   SPDR State Street Global Advisors State Street Financial Center, 1 Lincoln Street Boston MA 02111-2900 United States
Phone Number   617-786-3000

PERFORMANCE

Ratings History

Date	Overall Rating	Risk Rating	Reward Rating
Q4-18	B-	C+	B
Q2-18	C+	C	B-
Q4-17	B	B	B-
Q4-16	B-	C+	B
Q4-15	B	B	B

Asset & Performance History

Date	NAV	1-Year Total Return
2017	82.59	21.7
2016	68.91	-3.34
2015	72.05	6.82
2014	68.41	25.17
2013	55.45	41.24
2012	39.93	17.55

Total Assets: $19,896,594,302

Asset Allocation

Asset	%
Cash	1%
Stocks	99%
US Stocks	99%
Bonds	0%
US Bonds	0%
Other	0%

Services Offered: Dividend Investment Plan, CashInvestment Plan

Investment Strategy: The investment seeks investment results that, before expenses, correspond generally to the price and yield performance of publicly traded equity securities of companies in the Health Care Select Sector Index. In seeking to track the performance of the index, the fund employs a replication strategy. It generally invests substantially all, but at least 95%, of its total assets in the securities comprising the index. The index includes companies from the following industries: pharmaceuticals; health care equipment & supplies; health care providers & services; biotechnology; life sciences tools & services; and health care technology. The fund is non-diversified. **Top Holdings:** Johnson & Johnson   Pfizer Inc   UnitedHealth Group Inc   Merck & Co Inc   AbbVie Inc

Invesco Aerospace & Defense ETF   B-   BUY

Ticker	Traded On	NAV		Total Assets ($)	Dividend Yield (TTM)	Turnover Ratio	Expense Ratio
PPA	NYSE Arca	49.50		$906,058,436	0.56	7	0.6

Ratings
Reward	B
Risk	C+
Recent Upgrade/Downgrade	Down

Fund Information
Fund Type	Exchange Traded Funds
Category	Industrials Sector Equity
Sub-Category	Industrials
Prospectus Objective	Unaligned
Inception Date	Oct-05
Open to New Investments	Y

Prices
Price (as of 12/31/2018)	49.45
52-Week High	61.91
52-Week Low	46.46

Total Returns (%)
3-Month	6-Month	1-Year	3-Year	5-Year
-19.45	-9.86	-7.35	43.58	68.74

3-Year Standard Deviation	13.63
Effective Duration	

Valuation
Premium/Discount (1-Year Average)	0.03

Company Information
Provider	Invesco
Manager/Tenure	Peter Hubbard (11), Michael Jeanette (10), Tony Seisser (4), 1 other
Website	http://www.invesco.com/us
Address	Invesco 11 Greenway Plaza, Ste. 2500 Houston TX 77046 United States
Phone Number	800-659-1005

PERFORMANCE

Ratings History
Date	Overall Rating	Risk Rating	Reward Rating
Q4-18	B-	C+	B
Q2-18	B	C+	B
Q4-17	B+	B-	A+
Q4-16	B	C+	B+
Q4-15	B	B	B

Asset & Performance History
Date	NAV	1-Year Total Return
2017	53.87	30.02
2016	41.74	19.2
2015	35.66	4.23
2014	34.7	12.74
2013	30.98	49.81
2012	20.98	17.85

Total Assets: $906,058,436
Asset Allocation
Asset	%
Cash	0%
Stocks	100%
US Stocks	99%
Bonds	0%
US Bonds	0%
Other	0%

Services Offered:

Investment Strategy: The investment seeks to track the investment results (before fees and expenses) of the SPADE® Defense Index. The fund generally will invest at least 90% of its total assets in common stocks of that comprise the underlying index. The underlying index was composed of common stocks of 54 U.S. companies whose shares are listed on the New York Stock Exchange ("NYSE") or the NASDAQ. These companies are engaged principally in the development, manufacture, operation and support of U.S. defense, military, homeland security and space operations. The fund is non-diversified. **Top Holdings:** United Technologies Corp   Boeing Co   Lockheed Martin Corp   Honeywell International Inc   General Dynamics Corp

Invesco DWA Consumer Staples Momentum ETF   B-   BUY

Ticker	Traded On	NAV		Total Assets ($)	Dividend Yield (TTM)	Turnover Ratio	Expense Ratio
PSL	NAS CM	65.44		$184,133,626	0.46	80	0.6

Ratings
Reward	B
Risk	C
Recent Upgrade/Downgrade	Down

Fund Information
Fund Type	Exchange Traded Funds
Category	Consumer Goods & Svcs
Sub-Category	Consumer Defensive
Prospectus Objective	Unaligned
Inception Date	Oct-06
Open to New Investments	Y

Prices
Price (as of 12/31/2018)	65.21
52-Week High	73.71
52-Week Low	62.43

Total Returns (%)
3-Month	6-Month	1-Year	3-Year	5-Year
-8.03	-6.89	1.51	18.93	56.25

3-Year Standard Deviation	6.89
Effective Duration	

Valuation
Premium/Discount (1-Year Average)	0.09

Company Information
Provider	Invesco
Manager/Tenure	Peter Hubbard (11), Michael Jeanette (10), Tony Seisser (4), 1 other
Website	http://www.invesco.com/us
Address	Invesco 11 Greenway Plaza, Ste. 2500 Houston TX 77046 United States
Phone Number	800-659-1005

PERFORMANCE

Ratings History
Date	Overall Rating	Risk Rating	Reward Rating
Q4-18	B-	C	B
Q2-18	B	C	B+
Q4-17	B	B	B
Q4-16	B	C+	B
Q4-15	B+	B	A

Asset & Performance History
Date	NAV	1-Year Total Return
2017	64.93	21.4
2016	53.68	-3.49
2015	56.77	13.48
2014	50.64	15.77
2013	44.19	34.53
2012	33.3	9.5

Total Assets: $184,133,626
Asset Allocation
Asset	%
Cash	0%
Stocks	100%
US Stocks	96%
Bonds	0%
US Bonds	0%
Other	0%

Services Offered:

Investment Strategy: The investment seeks to track the investment results (before fees and expenses) of the Dorsey Wright® Consumer Staples Technical Leaders Index (the "underlying index"). The fund generally will invest at least 90% of its total assets in the securities that comprise the underlying index. The underlying index is composed of at least 30 securities of companies in the consumer staples sector that have powerful relative strength or "momentum" characteristics. **Top Holdings:** Church & Dwight Co Inc   McCormick & Co Inc Non-Voting   Grand Canyon Education Inc   Hormel Foods Corp   Rollins Inc

Invesco DWA Utilities Momentum ETF   B   BUY

Ticker	Traded On	NAV	Total Assets ($)	Dividend Yield (TTM)	Turnover Ratio	Expense Ratio
PUI	NAS CM	28.91	$69,831,641	2.27	41	0.6

Ratings
Reward	B
Risk	C+
Recent Upgrade/Downgrade	Up

Fund Information
Fund Type	Exchange Traded Funds
Category	Utilities Sector Equity
Sub-Category	Utilities
Prospectus Objective	Utility
Inception Date	Oct-05
Open to New Investments	Y

Prices
Price (as of 12/31/2018)	28.96
52-Week High	31.29
52-Week Low	24.57

Total Returns (%)
3-Month	6-Month	1-Year	3-Year	5-Year
1.57	4.92	6.10	41.06	60.02

3-Year Standard Deviation   12.27
Effective Duration

Valuation
Premium/Discount (1-Year Average)   0.04

Company Information
Provider	Invesco
Manager/Tenure	Peter Hubbard (11), Michael Jeanette (10), Tony Seisser (4), 1 other
Website	http://www.invesco.com/us
Address	Invesco 11 Greenway Plaza, Ste. 2500 Houston TX 77046 United States
Phone Number	800-659-1005

PERFORMANCE

Ratings History
Date	Overall Rating	Risk Rating	Reward Rating
Q4-18	B	C+	B
Q2-18	B-	C	B
Q4-17	B-	B	B-
Q4-16	B-	C	B
Q4-15	B	C+	B

Asset & Performance History
Date	NAV	1-Year Total Return
2017	27.79	11.64
2016	25.63	19.07
2015	22.25	-2.98
2014	23.61	16.92
2013	20.64	21.93
2012	17.39	10.04

Total Assets: $69,831,641

Asset Allocation
Asset	%
Cash	0%
Stocks	100%
US Stocks	100%
Bonds	0%
US Bonds	0%
Other	0%

Services Offered:

Investment Strategy: The investment seeks to track the investment results (before fees and expenses) of the Dorsey Wright® Utilities Technical Leaders Index (the "underlying index"). The fund generally will invest at least 90% of its total assets in the securities that comprise the underlying index. The underlying index is composed of at least 30 securities of companies in the utilities sector that have powerful relative strength or "momentum" characteristics. **Top Holdings:** Xcel Energy Inc NRG Energy Inc American Water Works Co Inc DTE Energy Co Pinnacle West Capital Corp

---

Invesco Dynamic Food & Beverage ETF   B-   BUY

Ticker	Traded On	NAV	Total Assets ($)	Dividend Yield (TTM)	Turnover Ratio	Expense Ratio
PBJ	NYSE Arca	29.80	$74,307,640	0.99	147	0.63

Ratings
Reward	B
Risk	C
Recent Upgrade/Downgrade	

Fund Information
Fund Type	Exchange Traded Funds
Category	Consumer Goods & Svcs
Sub-Category	Consumer Defensive
Prospectus Objective	Unaligned
Inception Date	Jun-05
Open to New Investments	Y

Prices
Price (as of 12/31/2018)	29.67
52-Week High	34.92
52-Week Low	28.60

Total Returns (%)
3-Month	6-Month	1-Year	3-Year	5-Year
-7.27	-8.89	-10.77	-4.01	20.34

3-Year Standard Deviation   8.76
Effective Duration

Valuation
Premium/Discount (1-Year Average)   0.03

Company Information
Provider	Invesco
Manager/Tenure	Peter Hubbard (11), Michael Jeanette (10), Tony Seisser (4), 1 other
Website	http://www.invesco.com/us
Address	Invesco 11 Greenway Plaza, Ste. 2500 Houston TX 77046 United States
Phone Number	800-659-1005

PERFORMANCE

Ratings History
Date	Overall Rating	Risk Rating	Reward Rating
Q4-18	B-	C	B
Q2-18	C+	C	B
Q4-17	B-	B	C
Q4-16	B	C+	B
Q4-15	B	B	B+

Asset & Performance History
Date	NAV	1-Year Total Return
2017	33.84	1.57
2016	33.56	5.91
2015	32.19	6.82
2014	30.51	17.37
2013	26.36	33.38
2012	19.94	5.59

Total Assets: $74,307,640

Asset Allocation
Asset	%
Cash	0%
Stocks	100%
US Stocks	94%
Bonds	0%
US Bonds	0%
Other	0%

Services Offered:

Investment Strategy: The investment seeks to track the investment results (before fees and expenses) of the Dynamic Food & Beverage IntellidexSM Index. The fund generally will invest at least 90% of its total assets in common stocks of food and beverage companies that comprise the underlying intellidex. The underlying intellidex was composed of common stocks of 30 U.S. food and beverage companies. These companies are engaged principally in the manufacture, sale or distribution of food and beverage products, agricultural products and products related to the development of new food technologies. The fund is non-diversified. **Top Holdings:** Keurig Dr Pepper Inc Yum Brands Inc PepsiCo Inc Mondelez International Inc Class A Monster Beverage Corp

Invesco KBW Bank ETF   B-   BUY

Ticker	Traded On	NAV	Total Assets ($)	Dividend Yield (TTM)	Turnover Ratio	Expense Ratio
KBWB	NAS CM	44.12	$864,659,499	1.93		0.35

Ratings
Reward	B
Risk	C
Recent Upgrade/Downgrade	Down

Fund Information
Fund Type	Exchange Traded Funds
Category	Financials Sector Equity
Sub-Category	Financial
Prospectus Objective	Financial
Inception Date	Nov-11
Open to New Investments	

Prices
Price (as of 12/31/2018)	43.98
52-Week High	60.11
52-Week Low	41.50

Total Returns (%)
3-Month	6-Month	1-Year	3-Year	5-Year
-17.72	-17.18	-17.95	24.12	35.44

3-Year Standard Deviation	19.88
Effective Duration	

Valuation
Premium/Discount (1-Year Average)	0.03

Company Information
Provider	Invesco
Manager/Tenure	Peter Hubbard (7), Michael Jeanette (7), Tony Seisser (4), 1 other
Website	http://www.invesco.com/us
Address	Invesco 11 Greenway Plaza, Ste. 2500 Houston TX 77046 United States
Phone Number	800-659-1005

PERFORMANCE

Ratings History
Date	Overall Rating	Risk Rating	Reward Rating
Q4-18	B-	C	B
Q2-18	B-	C	B
Q4-17	B+	B-	A
Q4-16	B	C	B+
Q4-15	A-	A-	B+

Asset & Performance History
Date	NAV	1-Year Total Return
2017	54.98	18.15
2016	47.21	28.03
2015	37.57	0.13
2014	38.1	8.97
2013	35.51	37.25
2012	26.28	32.41

Total Assets: $864,659,499

Asset Allocation
Asset	%
Cash	0%
Stocks	100%
US Stocks	100%
Bonds	0%
US Bonds	0%
Other	0%

Services Offered:

Investment Strategy: The investment seeks to track the investment results (before fees and expenses) of the KBW Nasdaq Bank Index (the "underlying index"). The fund generally will invest at least 90% of its total assets in securities of national money centers, regional banks and thrift institutions that are listed on a U.S. national securities exchange and that comprise the underlying index. The underlying index is a modified-market capitalization-weighted index that seeks to reflect the performance of national money centers, regional banks and thrift institutions that are publicly traded in the U.S. The fund is non-diversified. **Top Holdings:** US Bancorp JPMorgan Chase & Co Wells Fargo & Co Citigroup Inc Bank of America Corporation

---

Invesco KBW Property & Casualty Insurance ETF   B-   BUY

Ticker	Traded On	NAV	Total Assets ($)	Dividend Yield (TTM)	Turnover Ratio	Expense Ratio
KBWP	NAS CM	56.92	$64,004,295	2.3		0.35

Ratings
Reward	B
Risk	C
Recent Upgrade/Downgrade	

Fund Information
Fund Type	Exchange Traded Funds
Category	Financials Sector Equity
Sub-Category	Financial
Prospectus Objective	Growth
Inception Date	Dec-10
Open to New Investments	

Prices
Price (as of 12/31/2018)	56.62
52-Week High	64.80
52-Week Low	53.39

Total Returns (%)
3-Month	6-Month	1-Year	3-Year	5-Year
-8.79	-2.99	-2.24	26.85	61.23

3-Year Standard Deviation	10.28
Effective Duration	

Valuation
Premium/Discount (1-Year Average)	0.19

Company Information
Provider	Invesco
Manager/Tenure	Peter Hubbard (8), Michael Jeanette (8), Tony Seisser (4), 1 other
Website	http://www.invesco.com/us
Address	Invesco 11 Greenway Plaza, Ste. 2500 Houston TX 77046 United States
Phone Number	800-659-1005

PERFORMANCE

Ratings History
Date	Overall Rating	Risk Rating	Reward Rating
Q4-18	B-	C	B
Q2-18	B	C+	B
Q4-17	B+	A	B
Q4-16	B	B	A-
Q4-15	B	C	A-

Asset & Performance History
Date	NAV	1-Year Total Return
2017	59.42	8.96
2016	55.59	19.09
2015	47.76	14.24
2014	42.4	11.25
2013	39.22	33.88
2012	29.83	20.16

Total Assets: $64,004,295

Asset Allocation
Asset	%
Cash	0%
Stocks	100%
US Stocks	92%
Bonds	0%
US Bonds	0%
Other	0%

Services Offered:

Investment Strategy: The investment seeks to track the investment results (before fees and expenses) of the KBW Nasdaq Property & Casualty Index (the "underlying index"). The fund generally will invest at least 90% of its total assets in the securities of property and casualty insurance companies that comprise the underlying index. It generally invests in all of the securities comprising the underlying index in proportion to their weightings in the underlying index. The fund is non-diversified. **Top Holdings:** The Travelers Companies Inc Chubb Ltd Progressive Corp Allstate Corp American International Group Inc

Invesco QQQ Trust   B-   BUY

Ticker	Traded On	NAV	Total Assets ($)	Dividend Yield (TTM)	Turnover Ratio	Expense Ratio
QQQ	NAS CM	154.14	$65,965,236,262	0.78		0.2

Ratings
Reward   C+
Risk   B
Recent Upgrade/Downgrade   Down

Fund Information
Fund Type   Exchange Traded Funds
Category   US Equity Large Cap Growth
Sub-Category   Large Growth
Prospectus Objective   Growth
Inception Date   Mar-99
Open to New Investments   Y

Prices
Price (as of 12/31/2018)   154.26
52-Week High   186.74
52-Week Low   143.50

Total Returns (%)

3-Month	6-Month	1-Year	3-Year	5-Year
-16.95	-9.64	-0.14	41.79	85.01

3-Year Standard Deviation   13.13
Effective Duration

Valuation
Premium/Discount (1-Year Average)   0.06

Company Information
Provider   Invesco
Manager/Tenure   Management Team (19)
Website   http://www.invesco.com/us
Address   Invesco 11 Greenway Plaza, Ste. 2500
                  Houston TX 77046 United States
Phone Number   800-659-1005

PERFORMANCE

Ratings History

Date	Overall Rating	Risk Rating	Reward Rating
Q4-18	B-	B	C+
Q2-18	B	B	B
Q4-17	A-	B	A-
Q4-16	B+	B	A-
Q4-15	B	A-	B

Asset & Performance History

Date	NAV	1-Year Total Return
2017	155.68	32.7
2016	118.39	7.01
2015	111.87	9.54
2014	103.17	19.11
2013	87.94	36.6
2012	65.13	18.09

Total Assets: $65,965,236,262

Asset Allocation

Asset	%
Cash	0%
Stocks	100%
US Stocks	97%
Bonds	0%
US Bonds	0%
Other	0%

Services Offered: Dividend Investment Plan, CashInvestment Plan

Investment Strategy: The investment seeks investment results that generally correspond to the price and yield performance of the index. To maintain the correspondence between the composition and weights of the securities in the trust (the "securities") and the stocks in the Nasdaq-100 Index®, the adviser adjusts the securities from time to time to conform to periodic changes in the identity and/or relative weights of index securities. The composition and weighting of the securities portion of a portfolio deposit are also adjusted to conform to changes in the index. **Top Holdings:** Apple Inc Microsoft Corp Amazon.com Inc Alphabet Inc Class C Facebook Inc A

Invesco S&P 500® Equal Weight Utilities ETF   B-   BUY

Ticker	Traded On	NAV	Total Assets ($)	Dividend Yield (TTM)	Turnover Ratio	Expense Ratio
RYU	NYSE Arca	88.83	$268,818,860	3.08		0.4

Ratings
Reward   B
Risk   C
Recent Upgrade/Downgrade   Up

Fund Information
Fund Type   Exchange Traded Funds
Category   Utilities Sector Equity
Sub-Category   Utilities
Prospectus Objective   Utility
Inception Date   Nov-06
Open to New Investments   Y

Prices
Price (as of 12/31/2018)   88.76
52-Week High   95.55
52-Week Low   77.51

Total Returns (%)

3-Month	6-Month	1-Year	3-Year	5-Year
2.16	5.08	6.95	34.57	65.37

3-Year Standard Deviation   10.85
Effective Duration

Valuation
Premium/Discount (1-Year Average)   -0.03

Company Information
Provider   Invesco
Manager/Tenure   Peter Hubbard (0), Michael Jeanette
                  (0), Jonathan Nixon (0), 1 other
Website   http://www.invesco.com/us
Address   Invesco 11 Greenway Plaza, Ste. 2500
                  Houston TX 77046 United States
Phone Number   800-659-1005

PERFORMANCE

Ratings History

Date	Overall Rating	Risk Rating	Reward Rating
Q4-18	B-	C	B
Q2-18	C+	C	B-
Q4-17	B	B	B
Q4-16	C	C	C+
Q4-15	B-	C	B

Asset & Performance History

Date	NAV	1-Year Total Return
2017	85.81	9.01
2016	80.8	14.67
2015	72.37	-4.02
2014	78.58	28.03
2013	63.32	13.33
2012	58.01	8.3

Total Assets: $268,818,860

Asset Allocation

Asset	%
Cash	0%
Stocks	100%
US Stocks	100%
Bonds	0%
US Bonds	0%
Other	0%

Services Offered:

Investment Strategy: The investment seeks to track the investment results (before fees and expenses) of the S&P 500® Equal Weight Telecommunications Services & Utilities Index. The fund generally will invest at least 90% of its total assets in the securities that comprise the underlying index. The underlying index is an equal-weighted version of the S&P 500® Utilities Index. Strictly in accordance with its guidelines and mandated procedures, the index provider compiles, maintains and calculates the underlying index, which is comprised of common stocks of companies in the utilities sector and telecommunication services of the S&P 500® Index. It is non-diversified. **Top Holdings:** SCANA Corp The AES Corp Pinnacle West Capital Corp Duke Energy Corp Xcel Energy Inc

Invesco S&P 500® Low Volatility ETF   B   BUY

Ticker	Traded On	NAV	Total Assets ($)	Dividend Yield (TTM)	Turnover Ratio	Expense Ratio
SPLV	NYSE Arca	46.64	$8,397,903,033	1.99		0.25

Ratings

Reward	C
Risk	A
Recent Upgrade/Downgrade	Up

Fund Information

Fund Type	Exchange Traded Funds
Category	US Equity Large Cap Value
Sub-Category	Large Blend
Prospectus Objective	Growth
Inception Date	May-11
Open to New Investments	

Prices

Price (as of 12/31/2018)	46.65
52-Week High	50.45
52-Week Low	44.55

Total Returns (%)

3-Month	6-Month	1-Year	3-Year	5-Year
-5.11	-0.69	0.03	28.92	57.22

3-Year Standard Deviation	8.02
Effective Duration	

Valuation

Premium/Discount (1-Year Average)	0.02

Company Information

Provider	Invesco
Manager/Tenure	Peter Hubbard (7), Michael Jeanette (7), Tony Seisser (4), 1 other
Website	http://www.invesco.com/us
Address	Invesco 11 Greenway Plaza, Ste. 2500 Houston TX 77046 United States
Phone Number	800-659-1005

PERFORMANCE

Ratings History

Date	Overall Rating	Risk Rating	Reward Rating
Q4-18	B	A	C
Q2-18	C	C+	C
Q4-17	B+	A+	B
Q4-16	C	C+	C
Q4-15	B-	C+	B

Asset & Performance History

Date	NAV	1-Year Total Return
2017	47.63	17.07
2016	41.57	10.09
2015	38.56	4.06
2014	37.93	17.18
2013	33.16	23.24
2012	27.66	10.04

Total Assets: $8,397,903,033

Asset Allocation

Asset	%
Cash	0%
Stocks	100%
US Stocks	99%
Bonds	0%
US Bonds	0%
Other	0%

Services Offered:

Investment Strategy: The investment seeks to track the investment results (before fees and expenses) of the S&P 500® Low Volatility Index (the "underlying index"). The fund generally will invest at least 90% of its total assets in common stocks that comprise the underlying index. Volatility is a statistical measurement of the magnitude of up and down asset price fluctuations (increases or decreases in a stock's price) over time. It generally invests in all of the securities comprising the underlying index in proportion to their weightings in the underlying index. **Top Holdings:** Coca-Cola Co Republic Services Inc Class A Duke Energy Corp Ecolab Inc WEC Energy Group Inc

Invesco Water Resources ETF   B-   BUY

Ticker	Traded On	NAV	Total Assets ($)	Dividend Yield (TTM)	Turnover Ratio	Expense Ratio
PHO	NAS CM	28.24	$813,452,773	0.34	23	0.62

Ratings

Reward	B
Risk	C
Recent Upgrade/Downgrade	

Fund Information

Fund Type	Exchange Traded Funds
Category	Industrials Sector Equity
Sub-Category	Miscellaneous Sector
Prospectus Objective	Utility
Inception Date	Dec-05
Open to New Investments	Y

Prices

Price (as of 12/31/2018)	28.21
52-Week High	32.43
52-Week Low	26.56

Total Returns (%)

3-Month	6-Month	1-Year	3-Year	5-Year
-10.71	-6.49	-6.26	31.87	10.59

3-Year Standard Deviation	11.32
Effective Duration	

Valuation

Premium/Discount (1-Year Average)	0.00

Company Information

Provider	Invesco
Manager/Tenure	Peter Hubbard (11), Michael Jeanette (10), Tony Seisser (4), 1 other
Website	http://www.invesco.com/us
Address	Invesco 11 Greenway Plaza, Ste. 2500 Houston TX 77046 United States
Phone Number	800-659-1005

PERFORMANCE

Ratings History

Date	Overall Rating	Risk Rating	Reward Rating
Q4-18	B-	C	B
Q2-18	B-	C+	B
Q4-17	C+	C	B-
Q4-16	B-	C	B
Q4-15	B-	C+	B

Asset & Performance History

Date	NAV	1-Year Total Return
2017	30.26	23.55
2016	24.58	13.86
2015	21.69	-15.2
2014	25.76	-1.1
2013	26.2	26.97
2012	20.75	24.05

Total Assets: $813,452,773

Asset Allocation

Asset	%
Cash	0%
Stocks	100%
US Stocks	98%
Bonds	0%
US Bonds	0%
Other	0%

Services Offered:

Investment Strategy: The investment seeks to track the investment results (before fees and expenses) of the NASDAQ OMX US Water IndexSM (the "underlying index"). The fund generally will invest at least 90% of its total assets in securities of companies in the water industry that comprise the underlying index. The underlying index seeks to track the performance of U.S. exchange-listed companies that create products designed to conserve and purify water for homes, businesses and industries. The fund is non-diversified. **Top Holdings:** Waters Corp Ecolab Inc Danaher Corp Roper Technologies Inc Xylem Inc

iPath® Global Carbon ETN
B-   **BUY**

Ticker	Traded On	NAV	Total Assets ($)	Dividend Yield (TTM)	Turnover Ratio	Expense Ratio
GRNTF	NYSE Arca		$10,363,630	0	0	0.75

Ratings
Reward	A+
Risk	E
Recent Upgrade/Downgrade	Down

Fund Information
Fund Type	Exchange Traded Funds
Category	Commodities Specified
Sub-Category	Commodities Energy
Prospectus Objective	Natl Res
Inception Date	Jun-08
Open to New Investments	Y

Prices
Price (as of 12/31/2018)	17.90
52-Week High	18.23
52-Week Low	9.49

Total Returns (%)
3-Month	6-Month	1-Year	3-Year	5-Year
15.58	67.22	225.95	221.73	445.54

3-Year Standard Deviation	62.25
Effective Duration	

Valuation
Premium/Discount (1-Year Average)	-12.64

Company Information
Provider	Milleis Investissements Funds
Manager/Tenure	No Manager (10)
Website	
Address	2-4, rue Eugène Ruppert L-2453 Luxembourg Luxembourg L-2453 Luxembourg
Phone Number	

PERFORMANCE

Ratings History
Date	Overall Rating	Risk Rating	Reward Rating
Q4-18	B-	E	A+
Q2-18	C+	E	A-
Q4-17	C	D+	B
Q4-16	D	D	D
Q4-15	D+	D+	D+

Asset & Performance History
Date	NAV	1-Year Total Return
2017	10.18	33.16
2016	7.95	-25.48
2015	10.31	13.13
2014	9.12	49.87
2013	6.08	-28.71
2012	8.53	-27.43

Total Assets: $10,363,630

Asset Allocation
Asset	%
Cash	%
Stocks	%
US Stocks	%
Bonds	%
US Bonds	%
Other	%

Services Offered:

Investment Strategy: The investment seeks to provide investors with exposure to the Barclays Global Carbon Index Total Return™.
The Barclays Global Carbon Index Total Return™ (the "index") is designed to measure the performance of the most liquid carbon-related credit plans. Each carbon-related credit plan included in the index is represented by the most liquid instrument available in the marketplace. The index expects to incorporate new carbon-related credit plans as they develop around the world. **Top Holdings:**

iShares Cohen & Steers REIT ETF
B-   **BUY**

Ticker	Traded On	NAV	Total Assets ($)	Dividend Yield (TTM)	Turnover Ratio	Expense Ratio
ICF	BATS	95.71	$2,021,392,989	3.09	12	0.34

Ratings
Reward	B
Risk	C
Recent Upgrade/Downgrade	

Fund Information
Fund Type	Exchange Traded Funds
Category	Real Estate Sector Equity
Sub-Category	Real Estate
Prospectus Objective	Real Estate
Inception Date	Jan-01
Open to New Investments	Y

Prices
Price (as of 12/31/2018)	95.70
52-Week High	106.05
52-Week Low	88.56

Total Returns (%)
3-Month	6-Month	1-Year	3-Year	5-Year
-2.94	-2.18	-2.45	7.05	52.09

3-Year Standard Deviation	12.62
Effective Duration	

Valuation
Premium/Discount (1-Year Average)	-0.03

Company Information
Provider	iShares
Manager/Tenure	Diane Hsiung (10), Greg Savage (10), Jennifer Hsui (6), 3 others
Website	http://www.ishares.com
Address	iShares 400 Howard Street San Francisco CA 94105 United States
Phone Number	800-474-2737

PERFORMANCE

Ratings History
Date	Overall Rating	Risk Rating	Reward Rating
Q4-18	B-	C	B
Q2-18	C+	C-	B
Q4-17	B-	B	C+
Q4-16	B-	C	B
Q4-15	B	C+	B+

Asset & Performance History
Date	NAV	1-Year Total Return
2017	101.27	4.95
2016	99.55	4.57
2015	99.21	5.96
2014	96.87	34.07
2013	74.66	-1.8
2012	78.53	15.25

Total Assets: $2,021,392,989

Asset Allocation
Asset	%
Cash	0%
Stocks	100%
US Stocks	100%
Bonds	0%
US Bonds	0%
Other	0%

Services Offered: CashInvestment Plan

Investment Strategy: The investment seeks to track the investment results of the Cohen & Steers Realty Majors Index composed of U.S. real estate investment trusts ("REITs"). The fund generally invests at least 90% of its assets in securities of the underlying index and in depositary receipts representing securities of the underlying index. The objective of the underlying index is to represent relatively large and liquid REITs that may benefit from future consolidation and securitization of the U.S. real estate industry. The fund is non-diversified. **Top Holdings:** American Tower Corp   Prologis Inc   Simon Property Group Inc   Public Storage   Equinix Inc

iShares Core High Dividend ETF **B- BUY**

Ticker	Traded On	NAV	Total Assets ($)	Dividend Yield (TTM)	Turnover Ratio	Expense Ratio
HDV	NYSE Arca	84.33	$6,671,828,776	3.42	46	0.08

Ratings
Reward	B
Risk	C
Recent Upgrade/Downgrade	Up

Fund Information
Fund Type	Exchange Traded Funds
Category	US Equity Large Cap Value
Sub-Category	Large Value
Prospectus Objective	Equity-Income
Inception Date	Mar-11
Open to New Investments	Y

Prices
Price (as of 12/31/2018)	84.38
52-Week High	94.20
52-Week Low	80.00

Total Returns (%)
3-Month	6-Month	1-Year	3-Year	5-Year
-6.58	1.27	-2.92	27.41	43.02

3-Year Standard Deviation	8
Effective Duration	

Valuation
Premium/Discount (1-Year Average)	0.00

Company Information
Provider	iShares
Manager/Tenure	Diane Hsiung (7), Greg Savage (7), Jennifer Hsui (6), 3 others
Website	http://www.ishares.com
Address	iShares 400 Howard Street San Francisco CA 94105 United States
Phone Number	800-474-2737

PERFORMANCE

Ratings History
Date	Overall Rating	Risk Rating	Reward Rating
Q4-18	B-	C	B
Q2-18	C+	C-	B-
Q4-17	B	B	B-
Q4-16	B-	C	B
Q4-15	B-	C	B

Asset & Performance History
Date	NAV	1-Year Total Return
2017	90.04	13.35
2016	82.2	15.78
2015	73.41	-0.26
2014	76.54	12.54
2013	70.26	23.6
2012	58.76	9.71

Total Assets: $6,671,828,776

Asset Allocation
Asset	%
Cash	0%
Stocks	100%
US Stocks	100%
Bonds	0%
US Bonds	0%
Other	0%

Services Offered:

Investment Strategy: The investment seeks to track the investment results of the Morningstar® Dividend Yield Focus IndexSM composed of relatively high dividend paying U.S. equities. The fund generally will invest at least 90% of its assets in the component securities of the underlying index and may invest up to 10% of its assets in certain futures, options and swap contracts, cash and cash equivalents. The underlying index is comprised of qualified income paying securities that are screened for superior company quality and financial health as determined by Morningstar, Inc.'s ("Morningstar" or the "index provider") proprietary index methodology. The fund is non-diversified. **Top Holdings:** Exxon Mobil Corp Verizon Communications Inc Johnson & Johnson Chevron Corp Pfizer Inc

iShares Edge MSCI Min Vol USA ETF **B BUY**

Ticker	Traded On	NAV	Total Assets ($)	Dividend Yield (TTM)	Turnover Ratio	Expense Ratio
USMV	BATS	52.39	$19,372,615,794	1.81	22	0.15

Ratings
Reward	C
Risk	A
Recent Upgrade/Downgrade	Up

Fund Information
Fund Type	Exchange Traded Funds
Category	US Equity Large Cap Blend
Sub-Category	Large Blend
Prospectus Objective	Growth
Inception Date	Oct-11
Open to New Investments	Y

Prices
Price (as of 12/31/2018)	52.40
52-Week High	57.58
52-Week Low	49.77

Total Returns (%)
3-Month	6-Month	1-Year	3-Year	5-Year
-7.51	-0.53	1.35	33.24	63.54

3-Year Standard Deviation	7.79
Effective Duration	

Valuation
Premium/Discount (1-Year Average)	-0.02

Company Information
Provider	iShares
Manager/Tenure	Diane Hsiung (7), Greg Savage (7), Jennifer Hsui (6), 3 others
Website	http://www.ishares.com
Address	iShares 400 Howard Street San Francisco CA 94105 United States
Phone Number	800-474-2737

PERFORMANCE

Ratings History
Date	Overall Rating	Risk Rating	Reward Rating
Q4-18	B	A	C
Q2-18	C+	C+	C
Q4-17	B+	A+	B-
Q4-16	C	C+	C
Q4-15	B-	C+	B-

Asset & Performance History
Date	NAV	1-Year Total Return
2017	52.77	18.97
2016	45.19	10.49
2015	41.82	5.5
2014	40.46	16.33
2013	35.48	25.1
2012	29.02	11.04

Total Assets: $19,372,615,794

Asset Allocation
Asset	%
Cash	0%
Stocks	100%
US Stocks	99%
Bonds	0%
US Bonds	0%
Other	0%

Services Offered:

Investment Strategy: The investment seeks the investment results of the MSCI USA Minimum Volatility (USD) Index. The fund will invest at least 90% of its assets in the component securities of the index and may invest up to 10% of its assets in certain futures, options and swap contracts, cash and cash equivalents. The index measures the performance of large and mid-capitalization equity securities listed on stock exchanges in the U.S. that, in the aggregate, have lower volatility relative to the broader U.S. equity market. **Top Holdings:** Visa Inc Class A Pfizer Inc Coca-Cola Co McDonald's Corp Waste Management Inc

iShares Mortgage Real Estate Capped ETF   B-   BUY

Ticker	Traded On	NAV	Total Assets ($)	Dividend Yield (TTM)	Turnover Ratio	Expense Ratio
REM	BATS	39.96	$1,236,463,669	10.11	31	0.48

Ratings
Reward	B
Risk	C
Recent Upgrade/Downgrade	

Fund Information
Fund Type	Exchange Traded Funds
Category	Real Estate Sector Equity
Sub-Category	Real Estate
Prospectus Objective	Real Estate
Inception Date	May-07
Open to New Investments	Y

Prices
Price (as of 12/31/2018)	39.94
52-Week High	45.65
52-Week Low	38.44

Total Returns (%)
3-Month	6-Month	1-Year	3-Year	5-Year
-5.62	-4.16	-2.95	40.34	48.51

3-Year Standard Deviation	10.27
Effective Duration	

Valuation
Premium/Discount (1-Year Average)	-0.02

Company Information
Provider	iShares
Manager/Tenure	Diane Hsiung (10), Greg Savage (10), Jennifer Hsui (6), 3 others
Website	http://www.ishares.com
Address	iShares 400 Howard Street San Francisco CA 94105 United States
Phone Number	800-474-2737

PERFORMANCE

Ratings History
Date	Overall Rating	Risk Rating	Reward Rating
Q4-18	B-	C	B
Q2-18	C+	C-	B
Q4-17	B-	C+	B-
Q4-16	C	C-	B-
Q4-15	C	C	B-

Asset & Performance History
Date	NAV	1-Year Total Return
2017	45.21	18.56
2016	42.06	21.96
2015	38.24	-9.31
2014	46.88	16.69
2013	46.16	-2.46
2012	54.68	21.9

Total Assets: $1,236,463,669

Asset Allocation
Asset	%
Cash	0%
Stocks	100%
US Stocks	100%
Bonds	0%
US Bonds	0%
Other	0%

Services Offered:

Investment Strategy: The investment seeks to track the investment results of the FTSE Nareit All Mortgage Capped Index composed of U.S. real estate investment trusts ("REITs") that hold U.S. residential and commercial mortgages. The fund generally will invest at least 90% of its assets in the component securities of the underlying index and may invest up to 10% of its assets in certain futures, options and swap contracts, cash and cash equivalents. The underlying index measures the performance of the residential and commercial mortgage real estate, mortgage finance and savings associations sectors of the U.S. equity market. The fund is non-diversified. **Top Holdings:** Annaly Capital Management Inc   AGNC Investment Corp   New Residential Investment Corp   Starwood Property Trust Inc   Blackstone Mortgage Trust Inc A

---

iShares PHLX Semiconductor ETF   B-   BUY

Ticker	Traded On	NAV	Total Assets ($)	Dividend Yield (TTM)	Turnover Ratio	Expense Ratio
SOXX	NAS CM	156.88	$1,287,515,970	1.26	20	0.47

Ratings
Reward	B
Risk	C-
Recent Upgrade/Downgrade	Down

Fund Information
Fund Type	Exchange Traded Funds
Category	Technology Sector Equity
Sub-Category	Technology
Prospectus Objective	Technology
Inception Date	Jul-01
Open to New Investments	Y

Prices
Price (as of 12/31/2018)	156.91
52-Week High	196.31
52-Week Low	145.00

Total Returns (%)
3-Month	6-Month	1-Year	3-Year	5-Year
-15.31	-11.93	-6.47	81.00	130.26

3-Year Standard Deviation	19.04
Effective Duration	

Valuation
Premium/Discount (1-Year Average)	-0.01

Company Information
Provider	iShares
Manager/Tenure	Diane Hsiung (10), Greg Savage (10), Jennifer Hsui (6), 3 others
Website	http://www.ishares.com
Address	iShares 400 Howard Street San Francisco CA 94105 United States
Phone Number	800-474-2737

PERFORMANCE

Ratings History
Date	Overall Rating	Risk Rating	Reward Rating
Q4-18	B-	C-	B
Q2-18	B	C	A-
Q4-17	A-	B	A+
Q4-16	C	C	C
Q4-15	B	B-	B

Asset & Performance History
Date	NAV	1-Year Total Return
2017	169.77	39.82
2016	122.66	38.4
2015	89.76	-2.06
2014	92.86	29.89
2013	72.66	41.25
2012	52.12	6.72

Total Assets: $1,287,515,970

Asset Allocation
Asset	%
Cash	0%
Stocks	100%
US Stocks	87%
Bonds	0%
US Bonds	0%
Other	0%

Services Offered: CashInvestment Plan

Investment Strategy: The investment seeks to track the investment results of the PHLX Semiconductor Sector Index composed of U.S. equities in the semiconductor sector. The fund generally invests at least 90% of its assets in securities of the underlying index and in depositary receipts representing securities of the underlying index. The underlying index measures the performance of U.S.-traded securities of companies engaged in the semiconductor business. The fund is non-diversified. **Top Holdings:** Broadcom Inc   Intel Corp   Texas Instruments Inc   Qualcomm Inc   NVIDIA Corp

iShares Transportation Average ETF   B   BUY

Ticker	Traded On	NAV	Total Assets ($)	Dividend Yield (TTM)	Turnover Ratio	Expense Ratio
IYT	BATS	164.99	$732,085,862	1.08	5	0.43

Ratings
Reward   B+
Risk   C
Recent Upgrade/Downgrade

Fund Information
Fund Type	Exchange Traded Funds
Category	Industrials Sector Equity
Sub-Category	Industrials
Prospectus Objective	Unaligned
Inception Date	Oct-03
Open to New Investments	Y

Prices
Price (as of 12/31/2018)	165.01
52-Week High	208.48
52-Week Low	155.39

Total Returns (%)
3-Month	6-Month	1-Year	3-Year	5-Year
-19.31	-11.76	-12.82	26.54	31.81

3-Year Standard Deviation   16.49
Effective Duration

Valuation
Premium/Discount (1-Year Average)   -0.01

Company Information
Provider	iShares
Manager/Tenure	Diane Hsiung (10), Greg Savage (10), Jennifer Hsui (6), 3 others
Website	http://www.ishares.com
Address	iShares 400 Howard Street San Francisco CA 94105 United States
Phone Number	800-474-2737

PERFORMANCE

Ratings History				Asset & Performance History			Total Assets:	$732,085,862
Date	Overall Rating	Risk Rating	Reward Rating	Date	NAV	1-Year Total Return	Asset Allocation	
Q4-18	B	C	B+	2017	191.53	18.93	Asset	%
Q2-18	B	C	B+	2016	162.7	22.05	Cash	0%
Q4-17	C+	C+	B-	2015	134.74	-16.88	Stocks	100%
Q4-16	B-	C	B	2014	164.04	25.32	US Stocks	100%
Q4-15	B	B-	B+	2013	131.91	41.18	Bonds	0%
				2012	94.35	6.61	US Bonds	0%
							Other	0%

Services Offered: CashInvestment Plan

Investment Strategy: The investment seeks to track the investment results of the Dow Jones Transportation Average Index composed of U.S. equities in the transportation sector. The fund generally invests at least 90% of its assets in securities of the underlying index and in depositary receipts representing securities of the underlying index. The underlying index measures the performance of large, well-known companies within the transportation sector of the U.S. equity market. The fund is non-diversified. **Top Holdings:** FedEx Corp   Norfolk Southern Corp   Union Pacific Corp   United Parcel Service Inc Class B   JB Hunt Transport Services Inc

---

iShares U.S. Aerospace & Defense ETF   B-   BUY

Ticker	Traded On	NAV	Total Assets ($)	Dividend Yield (TTM)	Turnover Ratio	Expense Ratio
ITA	BATS	172.98	$5,339,268,639	1.06	14	0.43

Ratings
Reward   B
Risk   C+
Recent Upgrade/Downgrade   Down

Fund Information
Fund Type	Exchange Traded Funds
Category	Industrials Sector Equity
Sub-Category	Industrials
Prospectus Objective	Growth
Inception Date	May-06
Open to New Investments	Y

Prices
Price (as of 12/31/2018)	172.86
52-Week High	217.63
52-Week Low	162.03

Total Returns (%)
3-Month	6-Month	1-Year	3-Year	5-Year
-20.18	-9.87	-7.15	51.10	72.68

3-Year Standard Deviation   14.06
Effective Duration

Valuation
Premium/Discount (1-Year Average)   0.01

Company Information
Provider	iShares
Manager/Tenure	Diane Hsiung (10), Greg Savage (10), Jennifer Hsui (6), 3 others
Website	http://www.ishares.com
Address	iShares 400 Howard Street San Francisco CA 94105 United States
Phone Number	800-474-2737

PERFORMANCE

Ratings History				Asset & Performance History			Total Assets:	$5,339,268,639
Date	Overall Rating	Risk Rating	Reward Rating	Date	NAV	1-Year Total Return	Asset Allocation	
Q4-18	B-	C+	B	2017	188.14	35.17	Asset	%
Q2-18	B	B-	B+	2016	140.62	20.4	Cash	0%
Q4-17	A-	B-	A+	2015	118.16	4.03	Stocks	100%
Q4-16	B	C+	B+	2014	114.76	9.85	US Stocks	100%
Q4-15	B	B	B	2013	105.79	57.07	Bonds	0%
				2012	68.27	14.07	US Bonds	0%
							Other	0%

Services Offered:

Investment Strategy: The investment seeks to track the investment results of the Dow Jones U.S. Select Aerospace & Defense Index composed of U.S. equities in the aerospace and defense sector. The fund generally invests at least 90% of its assets in securities of the underlying index and in depositary receipts representing securities of the underlying index. The underlying index measures the performance of the aerospace and defense sector of the U.S. equity market. Aerospace companies in the index include manufacturers, assemblers and distributors of aircraft and aircraft parts. The fund is non-diversified. **Top Holdings:** Boeing Co   United Technologies Corp   Lockheed Martin Corp   General Dynamics Corp   Raytheon Co

iShares U.S. Broker-Dealers & Securities Exchanges ETF

B- BUY

Ticker	Traded On	NAV	Total Assets ($)	Dividend Yield (TTM)	Turnover Ratio	Expense Ratio
IAI	NYSE Arca	56.08	$251,510,352	1.43	13	0.43

Ratings

Reward	B
Risk	C
Recent Upgrade/Downgrade	

Fund Information

Fund Type	Exchange Traded Funds
Category	Financials Sector Equity
Sub-Category	Financial
Prospectus Objective	Financial
Inception Date	May-06
Open to New Investments	Y

Prices

Price (as of 12/31/2018)	56.03
52-Week High	70.28
52-Week Low	52.67

Total Returns (%)

3-Month	6-Month	1-Year	3-Year	5-Year
-9.67	-12.38	-9.29	42.19	56.17

3-Year Standard Deviation	17.92
Effective Duration	

Valuation

Premium/Discount (1-Year Average)	0.02

Company Information

Provider	iShares
Manager/Tenure	Diane Hsiung (10), Greg Savage (10), Jennifer Hsui (6), 3 others
Website	http://www.ishares.com
Address	iShares 400 Howard Street San Francisco CA 94105 United States
Phone Number	800-474-2737

PERFORMANCE

Ratings History

Date	Overall Rating	Risk Rating	Reward Rating
Q4-18	B-	C	B
Q2-18	B	C+	B
Q4-17	A-	B	A
Q4-16	B-	C	B
Q4-15	B	B+	B

Asset & Performance History

Date	NAV	1-Year Total Return
2017	62.72	28.78
2016	49.47	21.73
2015	41.38	-1.59
2014	42.6	11.6
2013	38.63	65.61
2012	23.63	16.51

Total Assets: $251,510,352

Asset Allocation

Asset	%
Cash	0%
Stocks	100%
US Stocks	100%
Bonds	0%
US Bonds	0%
Other	0%

Services Offered:

Investment Strategy: The investment seeks to track the investment results of the Dow Jones U.S. Select Investment Services Index composed of U.S. equities in the investment services sector. The fund generally invests at least 90% of its assets in securities of the underlying index and in depositary receipts representing securities of the underlying index. The underlying index measures the performance of the investment services sector of the U.S. equity market. The fund may invest the remainder of its assets in certain futures, options and swap contracts, cash and cash equivalents. It is non-diversified. **Top Holdings:** CME Group Inc Class A Morgan Stanley Goldman Sachs Group Inc Intercontinental Exchange Inc Charles Schwab Corp

---

iShares U.S. Financial Services ETF

B- BUY

Ticker	Traded On	NAV	Total Assets ($)	Dividend Yield (TTM)	Turnover Ratio	Expense Ratio
IYG	NYSE Arca	112.32	$1,683,477,109	1.48	4	0.43

Ratings

Reward	B
Risk	C+
Recent Upgrade/Downgrade	Down

Fund Information

Fund Type	Exchange Traded Funds
Category	Financials Sector Equity
Sub-Category	Financial
Prospectus Objective	Financial
Inception Date	Jun-00
Open to New Investments	Y

Prices

Price (as of 12/31/2018)	112.27
52-Week High	141.49
52-Week Low	105.05

Total Returns (%)

3-Month	6-Month	1-Year	3-Year	5-Year
-15.50	-13.08	-12.44	30.59	43.84

3-Year Standard Deviation	16.77
Effective Duration	

Valuation

Premium/Discount (1-Year Average)	0.03

Company Information

Provider	iShares
Manager/Tenure	Diane Hsiung (10), Greg Savage (10), Jennifer Hsui (6), 3 others
Website	http://www.ishares.com
Address	iShares 400 Howard Street San Francisco CA 94105 United States
Phone Number	800-474-2737

PERFORMANCE

Ratings History

Date	Overall Rating	Risk Rating	Reward Rating
Q4-18	B-	C+	B
Q2-18	B	C	B
Q4-17	B+	B	A
Q4-16	B-	C	B
Q4-15	B+	B	B+

Asset & Performance History

Date	NAV	1-Year Total Return
2017	130.36	24.41
2016	106.23	19.88
2015	89.97	-0.71
2014	91.82	10.93
2013	83.76	42.83
2012	59.33	32.95

Total Assets: $1,683,477,109

Asset Allocation

Asset	%
Cash	0%
Stocks	100%
US Stocks	100%
Bonds	0%
US Bonds	0%
Other	0%

Services Offered: CashInvestment Plan

Investment Strategy: The investment seeks to track the investment results of the Dow Jones U.S. Financial Services Index composed of U.S. equities in the financial services sector. The fund generally invests at least 90% of its assets in securities of the underlying index and in depositary receipts representing securities of the underlying index. The underlying index measures the performance of the financial services sector of the U.S. equity market. The fund is non-diversified. **Top Holdings:** JPMorgan Chase & Co Bank of America Corporation Visa Inc Class A Wells Fargo & Co Mastercard Inc A

iShares U.S. Healthcare Providers ETF   B   BUY

Ticker	Traded On	NAV	Total Assets ($)	Dividend Yield (TTM)	Turnover Ratio	Expense Ratio
IHF	NYSE Arca	165.15	$1,209,557,588	0.2	20	0.43

Ratings
Reward   B
Risk   C+
Recent Upgrade/Downgrade

Fund Information
Fund Type   Exchange Traded Funds
Category   Healthcare Sector Equity
Sub-Category   Health
Prospectus Objective   Health
Inception Date   May-06
Open to New Investments   Y

Prices
Price (as of 12/31/2018)   165.19
52-Week High   201.83
52-Week Low   155.72

Total Returns (%)

3-Month	6-Month	1-Year	3-Year	5-Year
-14.25	-2.95	9.60	38.77	85.89

3-Year Standard Deviation   12.95
Effective Duration

Valuation
Premium/Discount (1-Year Average)   0.09

Company Information
Provider   iShares
Manager/Tenure   Diane Hsiung (10), Greg Savage (10),
                  Jennifer Hsui (6), 3 others
Website   http://www.ishares.com
Address   iShares 400 Howard Street San
                  Francisco CA 94105 United States
Phone Number   800-474-2737

PERFORMANCE

Ratings History

Date	Overall Rating	Risk Rating	Reward Rating
Q4-18	B	C+	B
Q2-18	B	C	B
Q4-17	B	B	B-
Q4-16	B-	C+	B
Q4-15	B+	B	B+

Asset & Performance History

Date	NAV	1-Year Total Return
2017	156.76	25.48
2016	125.18	0.9
2015	124.38	5.3
2014	118.35	27.21
2013	93.22	36.71
2012	68.36	17.25

Total Assets: $1,209,557,588

Asset Allocation

Asset	%
Cash	0%
Stocks	100%
US Stocks	99%
Bonds	0%
US Bonds	0%
Other	0%

Services Offered:

Investment Strategy: The investment seeks to track the investment results of the Dow Jones U.S. Select Health Care Providers Index composed of U.S. equities in the healthcare providers sector. The fund generally invests at least 90% of its assets in securities of the underlying index and in depositary receipts representing securities of the underlying index. The underlying index measures the performance of the healthcare providers sector of the U.S. equity market. The fund may invest the remainder of its assets in certain futures, options and swap contracts, cash and cash equivalents. It is non-diversified. **Top Holdings:** UnitedHealth Group Inc CVS Health Corp Anthem Inc Cigna Corp Express Scripts Holding Co

---

iShares U.S. Medical Devices ETF   B-   BUY

Ticker	Traded On	NAV	Total Assets ($)	Dividend Yield (TTM)	Turnover Ratio	Expense Ratio
IHI	NYSE Arca	199.77	$3,073,886,054	0.23	15	0.43

Ratings
Reward   B
Risk   C
Recent Upgrade/Downgrade

Fund Information
Fund Type   Exchange Traded Funds
Category   Healthcare Sector Equity
Sub-Category   Health
Prospectus Objective   Health
Inception Date   May-06
Open to New Investments   Y

Prices
Price (as of 12/31/2018)   199.81
52-Week High   227.72
52-Week Low   172.67

Total Returns (%)

3-Month	6-Month	1-Year	3-Year	5-Year
-12.11	-0.50	15.46	65.06	122.04

3-Year Standard Deviation   13.98
Effective Duration

Valuation
Premium/Discount (1-Year Average)   0.03

Company Information
Provider   iShares
Manager/Tenure   Diane Hsiung (10), Greg Savage (10),
                  Jennifer Hsui (6), 3 others
Website   http://www.ishares.com
Address   iShares 400 Howard Street San
                  Francisco CA 94105 United States
Phone Number   800-474-2737

PERFORMANCE

Ratings History

Date	Overall Rating	Risk Rating	Reward Rating
Q4-18	B-	C	B
Q2-18	B-	C	B
Q4-17	B+	A-	B+
Q4-16	B-	C+	B
Q4-15	C	C	C

Asset & Performance History

Date	NAV	1-Year Total Return
2017	173.46	30.93
2016	132.99	9.18
2015	122.47	9.68
2014	113.11	22.64
2013	92.87	37.75
2012	67.65	15.9

Total Assets: $3,073,886,054

Asset Allocation

Asset	%
Cash	0%
Stocks	100%
US Stocks	100%
Bonds	0%
US Bonds	0%
Other	0%

Services Offered:

Investment Strategy: The investment seeks to track the investment results of the Dow Jones U.S. Select Medical Equipment Index composed of U.S. equities in the medical devices sector. The fund generally invests at least 90% of its assets in securities of the underlying index and in depositary receipts representing securities of the underlying index. The underlying index includes medical equipment companies, including manufacturers and distributors of medical devices such as magnetic resonance imaging (MRI) scanners, prosthetics, pacemakers, X-ray machines, and other non-disposable medical devices. The fund is non-diversified. **Top Holdings:** Abbott Laboratories Medtronic PLC Thermo Fisher Scientific Inc Danaher Corp Becton, Dickinson and Co

iShares U.S. Regional Banks ETF
B- BUY

Ticker	Traded On	NAV
IAT	NYSE Arca	39.86

Total Assets ($)	Dividend Yield (TTM)	Turnover Ratio	Expense Ratio
$691,335,073	1.87	4	0.43

Ratings
Reward	B
Risk	C
Recent Upgrade/Downgrade	Down

Fund Information
Fund Type	Exchange Traded Funds
Category	Financials Sector Equity
Sub-Category	Financial
Prospectus Objective	Financial
Inception Date	May-06
Open to New Investments	Y

Prices
Price (as of 12/31/2018)	39.84
52-Week High	54.54
52-Week Low	37.63

Total Returns (%)

3-Month	6-Month	1-Year	3-Year	5-Year
-17.54	-18.50	-17.38	20.70	32.11

3-Year Standard Deviation	18.71
Effective Duration	

Valuation
Premium/Discount (1-Year Average)	-0.01

Company Information
Provider	iShares
Manager/Tenure	Diane Hsiung (10), Greg Savage (10), Jennifer Hsui (6), 3 others
Website	http://www.ishares.com
Address	iShares 400 Howard Street San Francisco CA 94105 United States
Phone Number	800-474-2737

PERFORMANCE

Ratings History

Date	Overall Rating	Risk Rating	Reward Rating
Q4-18	B-	C	B
Q2-18	B	C+	B+
Q4-17	B+	B-	A
Q4-16	B	C+	B+
Q4-15	B+	B+	B+

Asset & Performance History

Date	NAV	1-Year Total Return
2017	49.29	10.53
2016	45.33	32.18
2015	34.96	1.73
2014	34.97	7.58
2013	33.06	37.59
2012	24.44	17.88

Total Assets: $691,335,073

Asset Allocation

Asset	%
Cash	0%
Stocks	100%
US Stocks	99%
Bonds	0%
US Bonds	0%
Other	0%

Services Offered:

Investment Strategy: The investment seeks to track the investment results of the Dow Jones U.S. Select Regional Banks Index. The fund generally invests at least 90% of its assets in securities of the index and in depositary receipts representing securities of the index. The underlying index measures the performance of the regional bank sector of the U.S. equity market and is a subset of the Dow Jones U.S. Bank Index. The fund is non-diversified. **Top Holdings:** US Bancorp PNC Financial Services Group Inc BB&T Corp SunTrust Banks Inc M&T Bank Corp

---

iShares U.S. Technology ETF
B- BUY

Ticker	Traded On	NAV
IYW	NYSE Arca	159.77

Total Assets ($)	Dividend Yield (TTM)	Turnover Ratio	Expense Ratio
$3,733,774,705	0.82	15	0.43

Ratings
Reward	B
Risk	C
Recent Upgrade/Downgrade	Down

Fund Information
Fund Type	Exchange Traded Funds
Category	Technology Sector Equity
Sub-Category	Technology
Prospectus Objective	Technology
Inception Date	May-00
Open to New Investments	Y

Prices
Price (as of 12/31/2018)	159.93
52-Week High	195.97
52-Week Low	148.42

Total Returns (%)

3-Month	6-Month	1-Year	3-Year	5-Year
-17.60	-11.10	-0.96	53.78	90.48

3-Year Standard Deviation	14.71
Effective Duration	

Valuation
Premium/Discount (1-Year Average)	0.01

Company Information
Provider	iShares
Manager/Tenure	Diane Hsiung (10), Greg Savage (10), Jennifer Hsui (6), 3 others
Website	http://www.ishares.com
Address	iShares 400 Howard Street San Francisco CA 94105 United States
Phone Number	800-474-2737

PERFORMANCE

Ratings History

Date	Overall Rating	Risk Rating	Reward Rating
Q4-18	B-	C	B
Q2-18	B	C+	A-
Q4-17	A-	B	A+
Q4-16	B	C+	A-
Q4-15	B	B	B

Asset & Performance History

Date	NAV	1-Year Total Return
2017	162.67	36.58
2016	120.2	13.68
2015	107.02	3.66
2014	104.42	19.49
2013	88.43	26.47
2012	70.76	11.77

Total Assets: $3,733,774,705

Asset Allocation

Asset	%
Cash	0%
Stocks	100%
US Stocks	99%
Bonds	0%
US Bonds	0%
Other	0%

Services Offered: CashInvestment Plan

Investment Strategy: The investment seeks to track the investment results of the Dow Jones U.S. Technology Index. The fund generally invests at least 90% of its assets in securities of the underlying index and in depositary receipts representing securities of the underlying index. The underlying index measures the performance of the technology sector of the U.S. equity market and may include large-, mid- or small-capitalization companies. The fund is non-diversified. **Top Holdings:** Microsoft Corp Apple Inc Facebook Inc A Alphabet Inc Class C Alphabet Inc A

iShares U.S. Utilities ETF   B-   BUY

Ticker	Traded On	NAV	Total Assets ($)	Dividend Yield (TTM)	Turnover Ratio	Expense Ratio
IDU	NYSE Arca	134.18	$795,681,341	2.53	5	0.43

Ratings
Reward   B-
Risk   C+
Recent Upgrade/Downgrade

Fund Information
Fund Type   Exchange Traded Funds
Category   Utilities Sector Equity
Sub-Category   Utilities
Prospectus Objective   Utility
Inception Date   Jun-00
Open to New Investments   Y

Prices
Price (as of 12/31/2018)   134.22
52-Week High   144.20
52-Week Low   119.94

Total Returns (%)

3-Month	6-Month	1-Year	3-Year	5-Year
1.01	2.27	3.91	35.55	64.15

3-Year Standard Deviation   11.73
Effective Duration

Valuation
Premium/Discount (1-Year Average)   0.00

Company Information
Provider   iShares
Manager/Tenure   Diane Hsiung (10), Greg Savage (10),
                  Jennifer Hsui (6), 3 others
Website   http://www.ishares.com
Address   iShares 400 Howard Street San
                  Francisco CA 94105 United States
Phone Number   800-474-2737

Ratings History

Date	Overall Rating	Risk Rating	Reward Rating
Q4-18	B-	C+	B-
Q2-18	C+	C	B
Q4-17	B	B	B
Q4-16	B-	C+	B
Q4-15	B-	C+	B

Asset & Performance History

Date	NAV	1-Year Total Return
2017	132.88	11.95
2016	121.83	16.51
2015	107.87	-4.97
2014	118.4	27.43
2013	95.84	14.69
2012	86.44	1.3

Total Assets: $795,681,341
Asset Allocation

Asset	%
Cash	0%
Stocks	100%
US Stocks	100%
Bonds	0%
US Bonds	0%
Other	0%

Services Offered: CashInvestment Plan

Investment Strategy: The investment seeks to track the investment results of the Dow Jones U.S. Utilities Index. The fund generally invests at least 90% of its assets in securities of the underlying index and in depositary receipts representing securities of the underlying index. The underlying index measures the performance of the utilities sector of the U.S. equity market and may include large-, mid- or small-capitalization companies. The fund is non-diversified. **Top Holdings:** NextEra Energy Inc   Duke Energy Corp   Dominion Energy Inc   Southern Co   Exelon Corp

---

Ivy Focused Growth NextShares™   B   BUY

Ticker	Traded On	NAV	Total Assets ($)	Dividend Yield (TTM)	Turnover Ratio	Expense Ratio
IVFGC	NAS CM	26.09	$12,753,170	0.23	25	0.78

Ratings
Reward   B+
Risk   C+
Recent Upgrade/Downgrade

Fund Information
Fund Type   Exchange Traded Funds
Category   US Equity Large Cap Growth
Sub-Category   Large Growth
Prospectus Objective   Growth
Inception Date   Oct-16
Open to New Investments   Y

Prices
Price (as of 12/31/2018)   26.09
52-Week High   100.02
52-Week Low   24.17

Total Returns (%)

3-Month	6-Month	1-Year	3-Year	5-Year
-15.03	-7.37	5.18		

3-Year Standard Deviation
Effective Duration

Valuation
Premium/Discount (1-Year Average)   0.00

Company Information
Provider   Ivy Funds
Manager/Tenure   Bradley M. Klapmeyer (2)
Website   http://www.ivyfunds.com
Address   Ivy Funds 6300 Lamar Avenue, P.O.
                  Box 29217 Overland Park KS 66202
                  United States
Phone Number   800-777-6472

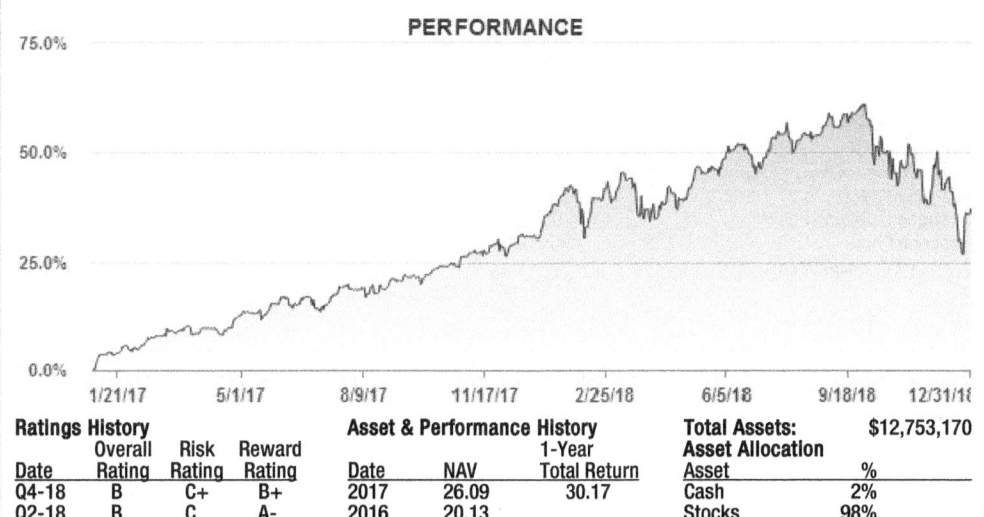

Ratings History

Date	Overall Rating	Risk Rating	Reward Rating
Q4-18	B	C+	B+
Q2-18	B	C	A-
Q4-17	D	A-	D+
Q4-16	U		
Q4-15			

Asset & Performance History

Date	NAV	1-Year Total Return
2017	26.09	30.17
2016	20.13	
2015		
2014		
2013		
2012		

Total Assets: $12,753,170
Asset Allocation

Asset	%
Cash	2%
Stocks	98%
US Stocks	98%
Bonds	0%
US Bonds	0%
Other	0%

Services Offered:

Investment Strategy: The investment seeks to provide growth of capital.
The fund seeks to achieve its objective by investing primarily in a portfolio of common stocks issued by large-capitalization, growth-oriented companies with above-average levels of profitability and that the fund's investment manager, believes have the ability to sustain growth over the long term. Although it primarily invests in securities issued by large capitalization companies, it may invest in securities issued by companies of any size. Growth-oriented companies are those whose earnings IICO believes are likely to grow faster than the economy. The fund is non-diversified. **Top Holdings:** Microsoft Corp   Apple Inc   Mastercard Inc A   Amazon.com Inc   Alphabet Inc Class C

NuShares Short-Term REIT ETF   B-   BUY

Ticker	Traded On	NAV	Total Assets ($)	Dividend Yield (TTM)	Turnover Ratio	Expense Ratio
NURE	BATS	25.05	$32,918,031	3.21	20	0.35

Ratings
Reward   B
Risk   C
Recent Upgrade/Downgrade

Fund Information
Fund Type   Exchange Traded Funds
Category   Real Estate Sector Equity
Sub-Category   Real Estate
Prospectus Objective   Real Estate
Inception Date   Dec-16
Open to New Investments   Y

Prices
Price (as of 12/31/2018)   24.99
52-Week High   28.09
52-Week Low   23.69

Total Returns (%)

3-Month	6-Month	1-Year	3-Year	5-Year
-6.90	-6.76	-2.09		

3-Year Standard Deviation
Effective Duration

Valuation
Premium/Discount (1-Year Average)   -0.40

Company Information
Provider   Nuveen
Manager/Tenure   Philip James(Jim) Campagna (1), Lei Liao (1)
Website   http://www.nuveen.com
Address   Nuveen Investment Trust John Nuveen & Co. Inc. Chicago IL 60606 United States
Phone Number   312-917-8146

PERFORMANCE

Ratings History

Date	Overall Rating	Risk Rating	Reward Rating
Q4-18	B-	C	B
Q2-18	C+	C	B
Q4-17	D-	B+	D+
Q4-16			
Q4-15			

Asset & Performance History

Date	NAV	1-Year Total Return
2017	26.35	7.07
2016	25.49	
2015		
2014		
2013		
2012		

Total Assets: $32,918,031
Asset Allocation

Asset	%
Cash	0%
Stocks	100%
US Stocks	100%
Bonds	0%
US Bonds	0%
Other	0%

Services Offered:

Investment Strategy: The investment seeks to track the investment results of the Dow Jones U.S. Select Short-Term REIT Index. The fund invests at least 80% of the sum of its net assets and the amount of any borrowings for investment purposes in REITs. The index is a subset of the Dow Jones U.S. Select REIT Index, which generally includes equity REITs traded on a national securities exchange in the U.S. that derive at least 75% of their total revenue from the ownership and operation of real estate assets and that have a minimum total market capitalization of $200 million at the time of their inclusion. It is non-diversified. **Top Holdings:** Extra Space Storage Inc Essex Property Trust Inc UDR Inc Equity Residential AvalonBay Communities Inc

Reaves Utilities ETF   B   BUY

Ticker	Traded On	NAV	Total Assets ($)	Dividend Yield (TTM)	Turnover Ratio	Expense Ratio
UTES	NYSE Arca	33.58	$14,248,117	1.96	29	0.95

Ratings
Reward   B
Risk   C+
Recent Upgrade/Downgrade   Up

Fund Information
Fund Type   Exchange Traded Funds
Category   Utilities Sector Equity
Sub-Category   Utilities
Prospectus Objective   Utility
Inception Date   Sep-15
Open to New Investments   Y

Prices
Price (as of 12/31/2018)   33.52
52-Week High   36.09
52-Week Low   29.65

Total Returns (%)

3-Month	6-Month	1-Year	3-Year	5-Year
0.51	1.56	5.42	38.46	

3-Year Standard Deviation   11.6
Effective Duration

Valuation
Premium/Discount (1-Year Average)   -0.06

Company Information
Provider   Virtus
Manager/Tenure   John P. Bartlett (3), Joseph (Jay) Rhame (3)
Website   http://www.virtus.com
Address   Virtus Opportunities Trust 101 Munson Street Greenfield MA 1301 United States
Phone Number   800-243-1574

PERFORMANCE

Ratings History

Date	Overall Rating	Risk Rating	Reward Rating
Q4-18	B	C+	B
Q2-18	B-	C	B
Q4-17	C	B	C
Q4-16	D	C+	B
Q4-15			

Asset & Performance History

Date	NAV	1-Year Total Return
2017	32.53	12.86
2016	29.48	14.83
2015	26.36	
2014		
2013		
2012		

Total Assets: $14,248,117
Asset Allocation

Asset	%
Cash	4%
Stocks	96%
US Stocks	93%
Bonds	0%
US Bonds	0%
Other	0%

Services Offered:

Investment Strategy: The investment seeks to provide total return through a combination of capital appreciation and income. The fund invests not less than 80% of its net assets (plus the amount of any borrowings for investment purposes) in equity securities of companies in the Utility Sector ("Utility Sector Companies"). The manager considers a company to be a "Utility Sector Company" if at least 50% of the company's assets or customers are committed to, or at least 50% of the company's revenues, gross income or profits derive from, the provision of products, services or equipment for the generation or distribution of electricity, gas or water. The fund is non-diversified. **Top Holdings:** NextEra Energy Inc Sempra Energy NextEra Energy Partners LP DTE Energy Co NiSource Inc

Schwab U.S. Dividend Equity ETF™   B-   BUY

Ticker	Traded On	NAV	Total Assets ($)	Dividend Yield (TTM)	Turnover Ratio	Expense Ratio
SCHD	NYSE Arca	46.98	$8,275,438,716	2.67	23	0.07

Ratings
Reward	B
Risk	C
Recent Upgrade/Downgrade	

Fund Information
Fund Type	Exchange Traded Funds
Category	US Equity Large Cap Value
Sub-Category	Large Value
Prospectus Objective	Equity-Income
Inception Date	Oct-11
Open to New Investments	Y

Prices
Price (as of 12/31/2018)	46.97
52-Week High	54.58
52-Week Low	44.23

Total Returns (%)
3-Month	6-Month	1-Year	3-Year	5-Year
-10.84	-3.07	-5.46	32.84	48.02

3-Year Standard Deviation	9.05
Effective Duration	

Valuation
Premium/Discount (1-Year Average)	0.01

Company Information
Provider	Schwab ETFs
Manager/Tenure	Ferian Juwono (7), Christopher Bliss (1), Sabya Sinha (1), 1 other
Website	http://www.schwabetfs.com
Address	Schwab ETFs United States
Phone Number	800-435-4000

PERFORMANCE

Ratings History
Date	Overall Rating	Risk Rating	Reward Rating
Q4-18	B-	C	B
Q2-18	B-	C	B
Q4-17	B	B	B
Q4-16	B-	C	B
Q4-15	C+	C+	C+

Asset & Performance History
Date	NAV	1-Year Total Return
2017	51.13	20.67
2016	43.52	16.23
2015	38.58	-0.21
2014	39.83	11.66
2013	36.65	32.9
2012	28.33	11.39

Total Assets: $8,275,438,716

Asset Allocation
Asset	%
Cash	0%
Stocks	100%
US Stocks	100%
Bonds	0%
US Bonds	0%
Other	0%

Services Offered:

Investment Strategy: The investment seeks to track as closely as possible, before fees and expenses, the total return of the Dow Jones U.S. Dividend 100™ Index. To pursue its goal, the fund generally invests in stocks that are included in the index. The fund invests at least 90% of its net assets in stocks that are included in the index. The index is designed to measure the performance of high dividend yielding stocks issued by U.S. companies that have a record of consistently paying dividends, selected for fundamental strength relative to their peers, based on financial ratios. **Top Holdings:** Procter & Gamble Co Intel Corp Verizon Communications Inc Pfizer Inc PepsiCo Inc

---

SPDR® Dow Jones Industrial Average ETF   B-   BUY

Ticker	Traded On	NAV	Total Assets ($)	Dividend Yield (TTM)	Turnover Ratio	Expense Ratio
DIA	NYSE Arca	233.16	$22,257,558,363	2.02	2	0.17

Ratings
Reward	B
Risk	C+
Recent Upgrade/Downgrade	Down

Fund Information
Fund Type	Exchange Traded Funds
Category	US Equity Large Cap Value
Sub-Category	Large Value
Prospectus Objective	Growth
Inception Date	Jan-98
Open to New Investments	Y

Prices
Price (as of 12/31/2018)	233.20
52-Week High	267.95
52-Week Low	218.10

Total Returns (%)
3-Month	6-Month	1-Year	3-Year	5-Year
-11.93	-2.94	-3.60	43.44	57.76

3-Year Standard Deviation	10.11
Effective Duration	

Valuation
Premium/Discount (1-Year Average)	0.05

Company Information
Provider	SPDR State Street Global Advisors
Manager/Tenure	Management Team (20)
Website	http://www.spdrs.com
Address	SPDR State Street Global Advisors State Street Financial Center, 1 Lincoln Street Boston MA 02111-2900 United States
Phone Number	617-786-3000

PERFORMANCE

Ratings History
Date	Overall Rating	Risk Rating	Reward Rating
Q4-18	B-	C+	B
Q2-18	B	C+	B
Q4-17	B+	B	A-
Q4-16	B-	C	B
Q4-15	B	B	B

Asset & Performance History
Date	NAV	1-Year Total Return
2017	246.98	27.97
2016	197.36	15.42
2015	174	0.09
2014	177.91	9.87
2013	165.4	29.41
2012	130.75	10.03

Total Assets: $22,257,558,363

Asset Allocation
Asset	%
Cash	0%
Stocks	100%
US Stocks	100%
Bonds	0%
US Bonds	0%
Other	0%

Services Offered: Dividend Investment Plan, CashInvestment Plan

Investment Strategy: O investimento destina-se a fornecer os resultados do investimento que, antes das despesas, geralmente corresponde ao preço de desempenho produtivo e do Dow Jones Industrial Average (DJIA). O fundo tem a carteira e dinheiro, e não está activa "administrado" pelos métodos tradicionais. **Top Holdings:** Boeing Co UnitedHealth Group Inc 3M Co Goldman Sachs Group Inc McDonald's Corp

SPDR® S&P Aerospace & Defense ETF   B-   BUY

Ticker	Traded On	NAV	Total Assets ($)	Dividend Yield (TTM)	Turnover Ratio	Expense Ratio
XAR	NYSE Arca	78.94	$1,385,208,986	1.02	36	0.35

Ratings
Reward   B
Risk   C
Recent Upgrade/Downgrade   Down

Fund Information
Fund Type   Exchange Traded Funds
Category   Industrials Sector Equity
Sub-Category   Industrials
Prospectus Objective   Technology
Inception Date   Sep-11
Open to New Investments   Y

Prices
Price (as of 12/31/2018)   78.92
52-Week High   100.89
52-Week Low   74.15

Total Returns (%)

3-Month	6-Month	1-Year	3-Year	5-Year
-20.35	-8.79	-4.45	54.02	70.02

3-Year Standard Deviation   14.32
Effective Duration

Valuation
Premium/Discount (1-Year Average)   0.04

Company Information
Provider   SPDR State Street Global Advisors
Manager/Tenure Michael J. Feehily (7), Karl A.
                Schneider (4), Keith Richardson (1)
Website   http://www.spdrs.com
Address   SPDR State Street Global Advisors
                State Street Financial Center, 1
                Lincoln Street Boston MA 02111-2900
                United States
Phone Number   617-786-3000

PERFORMANCE

Ratings History

Date	Overall Rating	Risk Rating	Reward Rating
Q4-18	B-	C	B
Q2-18	B	C+	B
Q4-17	B+	C+	A+
Q4-16	B	C	B
Q4-15	B	B	B

Asset & Performance History

Date	NAV	1-Year Total Return
2017	83.47	32.82
2016	63.38	21.16
2015	52.84	-0.32
2014	54.24	10.75
2013	49.53	58.65
2012	31.91	17.47

Total Assets: $1,385,208,986
Asset Allocation

Asset	%
Cash	3%
Stocks	97%
US Stocks	97%
Bonds	0%
US Bonds	0%
Other	0%

Services Offered:

Investment Strategy: The investment seeks to provide investment results that, before fees and expenses, correspond generally to the total return performance of the S&P Aerospace & Defense Select Industry Index. In seeking to track the performance of the S&P Aerospace & Defense Select Industry Index (the "index"), the fund employs a sampling strategy. It generally invests substantially all, but at least 80%, of its total assets in the securities comprising the index. The index represents the aerospace and defense segment of the S&P Total Market Index ("S&P TMI"). The fund is non-diversified. **Top Holdings:** United Technologies Corp TransDigm Group Inc Boeing Co Arconic Inc Spirit AeroSystems Holdings Inc

---

Technology Select Sector SPDR® Fund   B   BUY

Ticker	Traded On	NAV	Total Assets ($)	Dividend Yield (TTM)	Turnover Ratio	Expense Ratio
XLK	NYSE Arca	61.98	$19,121,099,208	1.42	19	0.13

Ratings
Reward   B
Risk   C+
Recent Upgrade/Downgrade

Fund Information
Fund Type   Exchange Traded Funds
Category   Technology Sector Equity
Sub-Category   Technology
Prospectus Objective   Technology
Inception Date   Dec-98
Open to New Investments   Y

Prices
Price (as of 12/31/2018)   61.98
52-Week High   75.93
52-Week Low   57.62

Total Returns (%)

3-Month	6-Month	1-Year	3-Year	5-Year
-17.71	-10.86	-1.55	51.75	88.73

3-Year Standard Deviation   13.02
Effective Duration

Valuation
Premium/Discount (1-Year Average)   0.03

Company Information
Provider   SPDR State Street Global Advisors
Manager/Tenure Michael J. Feehily (7), Karl A.
                Schneider (3), David Chin (1)
Website   http://www.spdrs.com
Address   SPDR State Street Global Advisors
                State Street Financial Center, 1
                Lincoln Street Boston MA 02111-2900
                United States
Phone Number   617-786-3000

PERFORMANCE

Ratings History

Date	Overall Rating	Risk Rating	Reward Rating
Q4-18	B	C+	B
Q2-18	B	B-	B+
Q4-17	A-	B	A
Q4-16	B+	B-	A-
Q4-15	B	B	B

Asset & Performance History

Date	NAV	1-Year Total Return
2017	63.89	34.27
2016	48.3	14.28
2015	42.86	5.61
2014	41.33	17.75
2013	35.75	25.98
2012	28.92	15.46

Total Assets: $19,121,099,208
Asset Allocation

Asset	%
Cash	0%
Stocks	100%
US Stocks	100%
Bonds	0%
US Bonds	0%
Other	0%

Services Offered: Dividend Investment Plan, CashInvestment Plan

Investment Strategy: The investment seeks investment results that, before expenses, correspond generally to the price and yield performance of publicly traded equity securities of companies in the Technology Select Sector Index. In seeking to track the performance of the index, the fund employs a replication strategy, which means that the fund typically invests in substantially all of the securities represented in the index in approximately the same proportions as the index. It generally invests substantially all, but at least 95%, of its total assets in the securities comprising the index. The fund is non-diversified. **Top Holdings:** Microsoft Corp Apple Inc Visa Inc Class A Intel Corp Cisco Systems Inc

The Real Estate Select Sector SPDR Fund   B-   BUY

Ticker	Traded On	NAV	Total Assets ($)	Dividend Yield (TTM)	Turnover Ratio	Expense Ratio
XLRE	NYSE Arca	31.00	$2,786,343,478	3.44	7	0.13

Ratings
Reward	B
Risk	C
Recent Upgrade/Downgrade	

Fund Information
Fund Type	Exchange Traded Funds
Category	Real Estate Sector Equity
Sub-Category	Real Estate
Prospectus Objective	Real Estate
Inception Date	Oct-15
Open to New Investments	Y

Prices
Price (as of 12/31/2018)	31.00
52-Week High	34.48
52-Week Low	29.40

Total Returns (%)
3-Month	6-Month	1-Year	3-Year	5-Year
-3.02	-2.53	-2.27	11.58	

3-Year Standard Deviation	12.14
Effective Duration	

Valuation
Premium/Discount (1-Year Average)	0.00

Company Information
Provider	SPDR State Street Global Advisors
Manager/Tenure	Michael J. Feehily (3), Karl A. Schneider (3), Amy Cheng (1)
Website	http://www.spdrs.com
Address	SPDR State Street Global Advisors State Street Financial Center, 1 Lincoln Street Boston MA 02111-2900 United States
Phone Number	617-786-3000

PERFORMANCE

Ratings History
Date	Overall Rating	Risk Rating	Reward Rating
Q4-18	B-	C	B
Q2-18	C+	C-	B
Q4-17	C	B-	C
Q4-16	D	C	B
Q4-15			

Asset & Performance History
Date	NAV	1-Year Total Return
2017	32.92	10.66
2016	30.74	3.17
2015	31.04	
2014		
2013		
2012		

Total Assets: $2,786,343,478

Asset Allocation
Asset	%
Cash	0%
Stocks	100%
US Stocks	100%
Bonds	0%
US Bonds	0%
Other	0%

Services Offered:

Investment Strategy: The investment seeks to provide investment results that, before expenses, correspond generally to the price and yield performance of publicly traded equity securities of companies in the Real Estate Select Sector Index (the "index"). Under normal market conditions, the fund generally invests substantially all, but at least 95%, of its total assets in the securities comprising the index. The index includes securities of companies from the following industries: real estate management and development and REITs, excluding mortgage REITs. The fund is non-diversified. **Top Holdings:** American Tower Corp   Simon Property Group Inc   Crown Castle International Corp   Prologis Inc   Public Storage

---

Utilities Select Sector SPDR® Fund   B   BUY

Ticker	Traded On	NAV	Total Assets ($)	Dividend Yield (TTM)	Turnover Ratio	Expense Ratio
XLU	NYSE Arca	52.92	$8,175,737,375	3.26	5	0.13

Ratings
Reward	B-
Risk	B
Recent Upgrade/Downgrade	Up

Fund Information
Fund Type	Exchange Traded Funds
Category	Utilities Sector Equity
Sub-Category	Utilities
Prospectus Objective	Utility
Inception Date	Dec-98
Open to New Investments	Y

Prices
Price (as of 12/31/2018)	52.92
52-Week High	56.93
52-Week Low	47.56

Total Returns (%)
3-Month	6-Month	1-Year	3-Year	5-Year
1.62	2.92	4.01	35.13	65.41

3-Year Standard Deviation	12
Effective Duration	

Valuation
Premium/Discount (1-Year Average)	-0.01

Company Information
Provider	SPDR State Street Global Advisors
Manager/Tenure	Michael J. Feehily (7), Karl A. Schneider (3), Dwayne Hancock (1)
Website	http://www.spdrs.com
Address	SPDR State Street Global Advisors State Street Financial Center, 1 Lincoln Street Boston MA 02111-2900 United States
Phone Number	617-786-3000

PERFORMANCE

Ratings History
Date	Overall Rating	Risk Rating	Reward Rating
Q4-18	B	B	B-
Q2-18	B-	C	B
Q4-17	B	B	B
Q4-16	B	C+	B
Q4-15	B	C+	B

Asset & Performance History
Date	NAV	1-Year Total Return
2017	52.65	11.94
2016	48.58	15.4
2015	43.29	-4.85
2014	47.2	28.65
2013	37.98	13.01
2012	34.94	1.11

Total Assets: $8,175,737,375

Asset Allocation
Asset	%
Cash	0%
Stocks	100%
US Stocks	100%
Bonds	0%
US Bonds	0%
Other	0%

Services Offered: Dividend Investment Plan, CashInvestment Plan

Investment Strategy: The investment seeks to provide investment results that, before expenses, correspond generally to the price and yield performance of publicly traded equity securities of companies in the Utilities Select Sector Index. In seeking to track the performance of the index, the fund employs a replication strategy. It generally invests substantially all, but at least 95%, of its total assets in the securities comprising the index. The index includes securities of companies from the following industries: electric utilities; water utilities; multi-utilities; independent power and renewable electricity producers; and gas utilities. The fund is non-diversified. **Top Holdings:** NextEra Energy Inc   Duke Energy Corp   Dominion Energy Inc   Southern Co   Exelon Corp

VanEck Vectors AMT-Free Intermediate Municipal Index ETF   B   BUY

Ticker	Traded On	NAV	Total Assets ($)	Dividend Yield (TTM)	Turnover Ratio	Expense Ratio
ITM	BATS	47.44	$1,648,898,391	2.34	9	0.24

Ratings
Reward	A
Risk	C+
Recent Upgrade/Downgrade	Up

Fund Information
Fund Type	Exchange Traded Funds
Category	US Muni Fixed Inc
Sub-Category	Muni National Long
Prospectus Objective	Muni Bond - Natl
Inception Date	Dec-07
Open to New Investments	Y

Prices
Price (as of 12/31/2018)	47.47
52-Week High	47.53
52-Week Low	23.26

Total Returns (%)
3-Month	6-Month	1-Year	3-Year	5-Year
1.95	103.37	100.88	112.15	139.61

3-Year Standard Deviation	4.34
Effective Duration	6.90

Valuation
Premium/Discount (1-Year Average)	-0.21

Company Information
Provider	VanEck
Manager/Tenure	James T. Colby (11)
Website	http://www.vaneck.com
Address	Van Eck Associates Corporation 666 Third Avenue New York NY 10017 United States
Phone Number	800-826-1115

PERFORMANCE

Ratings History
Date	Overall Rating	Risk Rating	Reward Rating
Q4-18	B	C+	A
Q2-18	C	C+	C
Q4-17	B-	B	C
Q4-16	C	C+	C
Q4-15	C	C+	C

Asset & Performance History
Date	NAV	1-Year Total Return
2017	24.13	6.21
2016	23.23	-0.56
2015	23.88	3.64
2014	23.58	8.97
2013	22.18	-3.51
2012	23.58	6.11

Total Assets: $1,648,898,391

Asset Allocation
Asset	%
Cash	0%
Stocks	0%
US Stocks	0%
Bonds	100%
US Bonds	100%
Other	0%

Services Offered:

Investment Strategy: The investment seeks to replicate as closely as possible, before fees and expenses, the price and yield performance of the Bloomberg Barclays AMT-Free Intermediate Continuous Municipal Index. The fund normally invests at least 80% of its total assets in fixed income securities that comprise the index. The index is comprised of publicly traded municipal bonds that cover the U.S. dollar denominated intermediate term tax-exempt bond market. **Top Holdings:** GEORGIA ST 5% HAWAII ST 5% NEW MEXICO FIN AUTH 5% SALES TAX ASSET RECEIVABLE CORP N Y 5% PENNSYLVANIA ST 5%

VanEck Vectors Environmental Services ETF   B-   BUY

Ticker	Traded On	NAV	Total Assets ($)	Dividend Yield (TTM)	Turnover Ratio	Expense Ratio
EVX	NYSE Arca	83.47	$23,370,549	0.87	24	0.55

Ratings
Reward	B
Risk	C
Recent Upgrade/Downgrade	

Fund Information
Fund Type	Exchange Traded Funds
Category	Industrials Sector Equity
Sub-Category	Industrials
Prospectus Objective	Unaligned
Inception Date	Oct-06
Open to New Investments	Y

Prices
Price (as of 12/31/2018)	83.26
52-Week High	99.64
52-Week Low	78.68

Total Returns (%)
3-Month	6-Month	1-Year	3-Year	5-Year
-12.67	-7.64	-3.12	45.80	34.12

3-Year Standard Deviation	11.09
Effective Duration	

Valuation
Premium/Discount (1-Year Average)	0.35

Company Information
Provider	VanEck
Manager/Tenure	Hao-Hung (Peter) Liao (12), Guo Hua (Jason) Jin (0)
Website	http://www.vaneck.com
Address	Van Eck Associates Corporation 666 Third Avenue New York NY 10017 United States
Phone Number	800-826-1115

PERFORMANCE

Ratings History
Date	Overall Rating	Risk Rating	Reward Rating
Q4-18	B-	C	B
Q2-18	B-	C+	B
Q4-17	B	C+	A-
Q4-16	C+	C-	B
Q4-15	B	B-	B

Asset & Performance History
Date	NAV	1-Year Total Return
2017	86.5	15.77
2016	75.42	29.99
2015	58.42	-10.31
2014	65.91	2.56
2013	65.29	28.72
2012	51.31	11.79

Total Assets: $23,370,549

Asset Allocation
Asset	%
Cash	0%
Stocks	100%
US Stocks	90%
Bonds	0%
US Bonds	0%
Other	0%

Services Offered:

Investment Strategy: The investment seeks to replicate as closely as possible, before fees and expenses, the price and yield performance of the NYSE Arca Environmental Services Index. The fund normally invests at least 80% of its total assets in common stocks and ADRs of companies involved in the environmental services industry. The index is comprised of companies that engage in business activities that may benefit from the global increase in demand for consumer waste disposal, removal and storage of industrial by-products, and the management of associated resources and includes securities of companies related environmental services. It is non-diversified. **Top Holdings:** STERIS PLC Republic Services Inc Class A Waste Management Inc Waste Connections Inc Darling Ingredients Inc

VanEck Vectors High-Yield Municipal Index ETF   B+   BUY

Ticker	Traded On	NAV	Total Assets ($)	Dividend Yield (TTM)	Turnover Ratio	Expense Ratio
HYD	BATS	61.23	$2,339,027,872	4.42	14	0.35

Ratings

Reward	A
Risk	C+
Recent Upgrade/Downgrade	Up

Fund Information

Fund Type	Exchange Traded Funds
Category	US Muni Fixed Inc
Sub-Category	High Yield Muni
Prospectus Objective	Muni Bond - Natl
Inception Date	Feb-09
Open to New Investments	Y

Prices

Price (as of 12/31/2018)	61.04
52-Week High	63.06
52-Week Low	30.64

Total Returns (%)

3-Month	6-Month	1-Year	3-Year	5-Year
-0.88	98.78	103.45	125.71	169.30

3-Year Standard Deviation	4.61
Effective Duration	7.46

Valuation

Premium/Discount (1-Year Average)	-0.15

Company Information

Provider	VanEck
Manager/Tenure	James T. Colby (9)
Website	http://www.vaneck.com
Address	Van Eck Associates Corporation 666 Third Avenue New York NY 10017 United States
Phone Number	800-826-1115

PERFORMANCE

Ratings History

Date	Overall Rating	Risk Rating	Reward Rating
Q4-18	B+	C+	A
Q2-18	C+	C+	C
Q4-17	B	A	C+
Q4-16	C	C+	C
Q4-15	C+	C+	C

Asset & Performance History

Date	NAV	1-Year Total Return
2017	31.31	10.49
2016	29.59	0.4
2015	30.78	4.81
2014	30.82	13.82
2013	28.49	-8.13
2012	32.88	16.74

Total Assets: $2,339,027,872

Asset Allocation

Asset	%
Cash	0%
Stocks	0%
US Stocks	0%
Bonds	100%
US Bonds	98%
Other	0%

Services Offered:

Investment Strategy: The investment seeks to replicate as closely as possible, before fees and expenses, the price and yield performance of the Bloomberg Barclays Municipal Custom High Yield Composite Index. The fund normally invests at least 80% of its total assets in securities that comprise the benchmark index. The index is comprised of publicly traded municipal bonds that cover the U.S. dollar denominated high yield long-term tax-exempt bond market. **Top Holdings:** NEW YORK LIBERTY DEV CORP 5% BUCKEYE OHIO TOB SETTLEMENT FING AUTH 5.88% PUBLIC FIN AUTH WIS 7% BUCKEYE OHIO TOB SETTLEMENT FING AUTH 5.12% CHICAGO ILL BRD ED 7%

VanEck Vectors J.P. Morgan EM Local Currency Bond ETF   B   BUY

Ticker	Traded On	NAV	Total Assets ($)	Dividend Yield (TTM)	Turnover Ratio	Expense Ratio
EMLC	NYSE Arca	32.96	$4,543,859,143	6.45	28	0.3

Ratings

Reward	A
Risk	C+
Recent Upgrade/Downgrade	Up

Fund Information

Fund Type	Exchange Traded Funds
Category	Emerging Mkts Fixed Inc
Sub-Category	Emerging-Markets Local-Currency Bond
Prospectus Objective	Div Emerg Mkts
Inception Date	Jul-10
Open to New Investments	Y

Prices

Price (as of 12/31/2018)	33.00
52-Week High	33.10
52-Week Low	16.16

Total Returns (%)

3-Month	6-Month	1-Year	3-Year	5-Year
1.88	100.66	83.81	127.88	83.59

3-Year Standard Deviation	11.08
Effective Duration	4.99

Valuation

Premium/Discount (1-Year Average)	-0.04

Company Information

Provider	VanEck
Manager/Tenure	Francis G. Rodilosso (6)
Website	http://www.vaneck.com
Address	Van Eck Associates Corporation 666 Third Avenue New York NY 10017 United States
Phone Number	800-826-1115

PERFORMANCE

Ratings History

Date	Overall Rating	Risk Rating	Reward Rating
Q4-18	B	C+	A
Q2-18	C	B	C-
Q4-17	C	C	C
Q4-16	D+	D+	D
Q4-15	D	D	D

Asset & Performance History

Date	NAV	1-Year Total Return
2017	18.96	13.98
2016	17.56	8.76
2015	17	-14.63
2014	21.06	-5.62
2013	23.57	-8.76
2012	27.12	16.23

Total Assets: $4,543,859,143

Asset Allocation

Asset	%
Cash	0%
Stocks	0%
US Stocks	0%
Bonds	100%
US Bonds	0%
Other	0%

Services Offered:

Investment Strategy: The investment seeks to replicate as closely as possible, before fees and expenses, the price and yield performance of the J.P. Morgan GBI-EM Global Core Index. The fund normally invests at least 80% of its total assets in securities that comprise the fund's benchmark index. The index is comprised of bonds issued by emerging market governments and denominated in the local currency of the issuer. It may concentrate its investments in a particular industry or group of industries to the extent that the index concentrates in an industry or group of industries. The fund is non-diversified. **Top Holdings:** Dominican Republic 8.9% Secretaria Tesouro Nacional 0% Uruguay (Republic of) 9.88% Brazil (Federative Republic) 9.86% Philippines (Republic Of) 6.25%

Vanguard Utilities Index Fund ETF Shares   B-   BUY

Ticker	Traded On	NAV	Total Assets ($)	Dividend Yield (TTM)	Turnover Ratio	Expense Ratio
VPU	NYSE Arca		$4,275,829,936	3.01	4	0.1

Ratings
Reward   B-
Risk   C+
Recent Upgrade/Downgrade

Fund Information
Fund Type	Exchange Traded Funds
Category	Utilities Sector Equity
Sub-Category	Utilities
Prospectus Objective	Utility
Inception Date	Jan-04
Open to New Investments	Y

Prices
Price (as of 12/31/2018)	117.83
52-Week High	126.42
52-Week Low	105.16

Total Returns (%)

3-Month	6-Month	1-Year	3-Year	5-Year
0.82	2.19	4.09	37.65	66.26

3-Year Standard Deviation   11.63
Effective Duration

Valuation
Premium/Discount (1-Year Average)   0.00

Company Information
Provider	Vanguard
Manager/Tenure	Michael A. Johnson (3), Awais Khan (1)
Website	http://www.vanguard.com
Address	Vanguard 100 Vanguard Boulevard Malvern PA 19355 United States
Phone Number	877-662-7447

PERFORMANCE

Ratings History

Date	Overall Rating	Risk Rating	Reward Rating
Q4-18	B-	C+	B-
Q2-18	B-	C	B
Q4-17	B	B	B
Q4-16	B-	C+	B
Q4-15	B-	C+	B

Asset & Performance History

Date	NAV	1-Year Total Return
2017	116.57	11.94
2016	106.94	16.84
2015	93.93	-4.83
2014	102.36	26.92
2013	83.33	14.93
2012	75.31	1.94

Total Assets: $4,275,829,936
Asset Allocation

Asset	%
Cash	0%
Stocks	100%
US Stocks	100%
Bonds	0%
US Bonds	0%
Other	0%

Services Offered:

Investment Strategy: The investment seeks to track the performance of a benchmark index. The fund employs an indexing investment approach designed to track the performance of the MSCI US Investable Market Index (IMI)/Utilities 25/50, an index made up of stocks of large, mid-size, and small U.S. companies within the utilities sector, as classified under the Global Industry Classification Standard (GICS). The Advisor attempts to replicate the target index by seeking to invest all, or substantially all, of its assets in the stocks that make up the index, in order to hold each stock in approximately the same proportion as its weighting in the index. The fund is non-diversified.
Top Holdings: NextEra Energy Inc Duke Energy Corp Dominion Energy Inc Southern Co Exelon Corp

---

VelocityShares 3x Long Gold ETN Linked to the S&P GSCI® Gold Index ER   B   BUY

Ticker	Traded On	NAV	Total Assets ($)	Dividend Yield (TTM)	Turnover Ratio	Expense Ratio
UGLD	NAS CM	94.74	$126,825,558	0		1.35

Ratings
Reward   A-
Risk   D+
Recent Upgrade/Downgrade   Up

Fund Information
Fund Type	Exchange Traded Funds
Category	Trading Tools
Sub-Category	Trading--Leveraged Commodities
Prospectus Objective	Prec Metals
Inception Date	Oct-11
Open to New Investments	Y

Prices
Price (as of 12/31/2018)	95.41
52-Week High	95.41
52-Week Low	7.59

Total Returns (%)

3-Month	6-Month	1-Year	3-Year	5-Year
21.65	942.92	742.64	1,185.54	640.19

3-Year Standard Deviation   38.75
Effective Duration

Valuation
Premium/Discount (1-Year Average)   0.04

Company Information
Provider	Credit Suisse AG
Manager/Tenure	Management Team (7)
Website	
Address	Kilmore House Park Lane Dublin Ireland
Phone Number	

PERFORMANCE

Ratings History

Date	Overall Rating	Risk Rating	Reward Rating
Q4-18	B	D+	A-
Q2-18	D+	D+	D+
Q4-17	D+	D	C-
Q4-16	D	D	D+
Q4-15	E+	D-	E+

Asset & Performance History

Date	NAV	1-Year Total Return
2017	11.24	28.67
2016	8.36	15.48
2015	7.37	-34.6
2014	11.27	-11.95
2013	12.8	-69.52
2012	42	8.58

Total Assets: $126,825,558
Asset Allocation

Asset	%
Cash	
Stocks	
US Stocks	
Bonds	
US Bonds	
Other	

Services Offered:

Investment Strategy: The investment seeks to replicate, net of expenses, three times the S&P GSCI Gold index ER. The index comprises futures contracts on a single commodity. The fluctuations in the values of it are intended generally to correlate with changes in the price of gold in global markets. **Top Holdings:**

VelocityShares 3x Long Silver ETN Linked to the S&P GSCI® Silver Index ER   B-   BUY

Ticker	Traded On	NAV	Total Assets ($)	Dividend Yield (TTM)	Turnover Ratio	Expense Ratio
USLV	NAS CM	74.10	$233,410,220	0		1.65

Ratings

Reward	A-
Risk	D+
Recent Upgrade/Downgrade	Up

Fund Information

Fund Type	Exchange Traded Funds
Category	Trading Tools
Sub-Category	Trading--Leveraged Commodities
Prospectus Objective	Prec Metals
Inception Date	Oct-11
Open to New Investments	Y

Prices

Price (as of 12/31/2018)	74.10
52-Week High	74.10
52-Week Low	6.39

Total Returns (%)

3-Month	6-Month	1-Year	3-Year	5-Year
17.30	766.90	521.72	659.22	65.14

3-Year Standard Deviation	65.42
Effective Duration	

Valuation

Premium/Discount (1-Year Average)	-0.23

Company Information

Provider	Credit Suisse AG
Manager/Tenure	Management Team (7)
Website	
Address	Kilmore House Park Lane Dublin Ireland
Phone Number	

PERFORMANCE

Ratings History

Date	Overall Rating	Risk Rating	Reward Rating
Q4-18	B-	D+	A-
Q2-18	D-	D-	D-
Q4-17	D-	D-	D-
Q4-16	D	D-	D
Q4-15	E	E+	E

Asset & Performance History

Date	NAV	1-Year Total Return
2017	11.92	-4.04
2016	11.44	21.31
2015	9.76	-47.55
2014	18.61	-58.52
2013	44.87	-82.54
2012	257.1	-8.92

Total Assets: $233,410,220

Asset Allocation

Asset	%
Cash	%
Stocks	%
US Stocks	%
Bonds	%
US Bonds	%
Other	%

Services Offered:

Investment Strategy: The investment seeks to replicate, net of expenses, three times the S&P GSCI Silver index ER.
The index comprises futures contracts on a single commodity. The fluctuations in the values of it are intended generally to correlate with changes in the price of silver in global markets. **Top Holdings:**

Section III:
Analysis of All Rated Funds with Assets over 50 Million

Detailed analysis of all rated funds with assets over 50 million. Funds are listed in order by asset size.

Section III: Contents

This section contains an expanded analysis of all rated funds with assets over 50 million, with current and historical Weiss Investment Ratings, key rating factors, summary financial data and performance charts. Funds are listed in order by asset size.

TOP ROW

Fund Name
Describes the fund's assets, regions of investments and investment strategies. Many funds have similar names, so you want to make sure the fund you look up is really the one you are interested in evaluating.

Overall Rating
The Weiss rating measured on a scale from A to E based on each fund's risk and performance. See the preceding section, "What Our Ratings Mean," for an explanation of each letter grade rating.

BUY-HOLD-SELL Recommendation
Funds that are rated in the A or B range are, in our opinion, a potential BUY. Funds in the C range will indicate a HOLD status. Funds in the D or E range will indicate a SELL status.

Ticker Symbol
An arrangement of characters (usually letters) representing a particular security listed on an exchange or otherwise traded publicly. When a company issues securities to the public marketplace, it selects an available ticker symbol for its securities which investors use to place trade orders. Every listed security has a unique ticker symbol, facilitating the vast array of trade orders that flow through the financial markets every day.

Traded On (Exchange)
The stock exchange on which the fund is listed. The core function of a stock exchange is to ensure fair and orderly trading, as well as efficient dissemination of price information. Exchanges such as: NYSE (New York Stock Exchange), AMEX (American Stock Exchange), NNM (NASDAQ National Market), and NASQ (NASDAQ Small Cap) give companies, governments and other groups a platform to sell securities to the investing public. NASDAQ is abbreviated as NAS.

NAV (Net Asset Value)

A fund's price per share. The value is calculated by dividing the total value of all the securities in the portfolio, less any liabilities, by the number of fund shares outstanding.

Total Assets ($)

The total of all assets listed on the institution's balance sheet. This figure primarily consists of loans, investments, and fixed assets. Total Assets are displayed in dollars.

Dividend Yield (TTM)

Trailing twelve months dividends paid out relative to the share price. Expressed as a percentage and measures how much cash flow an investor is getting for each invested dollar. **Trailing Twelve Months (TTM)** is a representation of a fund's financial performance over the most recent 12 months. TTM uses the latest available financial data from a company's interim, quarterly or annual reports.

Turnover Ratio

The percentage of an exchange-traded fund or other investment vehicle's holdings that have been replaced with other holdings in a given year. Generally, low turnover ratio is favorable, because high turnover equates to higher brokerage transaction fees, which reduce fund returns.

Expense Ratio

A measure of what it costs an investment company to operate an exchange-traded fund. An expense ratio is determined through an annual calculation, where a fund's operating expenses are divided by the average dollar value of its assets under management. Operating expenses may include money spent on administration and management of the fund, advertising, etc. An expense ratio of 1 percent per annum means that each year 1 percent of the fund's total assets will be used to cover expenses.

LEFT COLUMN

Ratings

Reward Rating

This is based on the total return over a period of up to five years, including net asset value and price growth. The total return figure is stated net of the expenses and fees charged by the fund. Based on proprietary modeling the individual components of the risk and reward ratings are calculated and weighted and the final rating is generated.

Risk Rating
This is includes the risk ratings of component stocks where applicable and also includes the financial stability of the fund, turnover where applicable, together with the level of volatility as measured by the fund's daily returns over a period of up to five years. Funds with greater stability are considered less risky and receive a higher risk rating. Funds with greater volatility are considered riskier, and will receive a lower risk rating. In addition to considering the fund's volatility, the risk rating also considers an assessment of the valuation and quality of a fund's holdings.

Recent Upgrade/Downgrade
An "Up" or "Down" indicates that the Weiss Exchange-Traded Fund rating has changed since the publication of the last print edition. If a fund has had a rating change since September 30, 2018, the change is identified with an "Up" or "Down."

Fund Information

Fund Type
Describes the fund's assets, regions of investments and investment strategies.

Category
Identifies funds according to their actual investment styles as measured by their portfolio holdings. This categorization allows investors to spread their money around in a mix of funds with a variety of risk and return characteristics.

Sub-Category
A subdivision of funds, usually with common characteristics as the category.

Prospectus Objective
Gives a general idea of a fund's overall investment approach and goals.

Inception Date
The date on which the fund began its operations. The commencement date indicates when a fund began investing in the market. Many investors prefer funds with longer operating histories. Funds with longer histories have longer track records and can thereby provide investors with a more long-standing picture of their performance.

Open to New Investments
Indicates whether the fund accepts investments from those who are not existing investors. A "Y" in this column identifies that the fund accepts new investors. No data in this column indicates that the fund is closed to new investors. The fund may be closed to new investors because the fund's asset base is getting too large to effectively execute its investing style. Although, the fund may be closed, in most cases, existing investors are able to add to their holdings.

Prices

Price
The price at which the fund is traded on a regular trading day. Prices in this guide are listed as of December 31, 2018.

52-Week High
The highest price that a fund has achieved during the previous 52 weeks.

52-Week Low
The lowest price that a fund has achieved during the previous 52 weeks.

Total Returns (%)

3-Month Total Return
The rate of return on an investment over three months that includes interest, capital gains, dividends and distributions realized.

6-Month Total Return
The rate of return on an investment over six months that includes interest, capital gains, dividends and distributions realized.

1-Year Total Return
The rate of return on an investment over one year that includes interest, capital gains, dividends and distributions realized.

3-Year Total Return
The rate of return on an investment over three years that includes interest, capital gains, dividends and distributions realized.

5-Year Total Return
The rate of return on an investment over five years that includes interest, capital gains, dividends and distributions realized.

3-Year Standard Deviation
A statistical measurement of dispersion about an average, which depicts how widely the returns varied over the past three years. Investors use the standard deviation of historical performance to try to predict the range of returns that are most likely for a given fund. When a fund has a high standard deviation, the predicted range of performance is wide, implying greater volatility. Standard deviation is most appropriate for measuring risk if it is for a fund that is an investor's only holding. The figure cannot be combined for more than one fund because the standard deviation

for a portfolio of multiple funds is a function of not only the individual standard deviations, but also of the degree of correlation among the funds' returns. If a fund's returns follow a normal distribution, then approximately 68 percent of the time they will fall within one standard deviation of the mean return for the fund, and 95 percent of the time within two standard deviations.

Effective Duration
Effective duration for all long fixed income positions in a portfolio. This value gives a better estimation of how the price of bonds with embedded options, which are common in many exchange-traded funds, will change as a result of changes in interest rates. Effective duration takes into account expected mortgage prepayment or the likelihood that embedded options will be exercised if a fund holds futures, other derivative securities, or other funds as assets, the aggregate effective duration should include the weighted impact of those exposures.

Valuation

Premium/Discount 1-Year Average
The annual average premium or discount of the market price to the NAV (Net Asset Value), expressed as a percentage of the NAV. This value provides a year-by-year picture a fund's trading status. A negative number indicates that, on average, the fund's shares sold at a discount to NAV, and a positive number indicates the shares sold at a premium. If the number shown is –10.00, for example, the shares sold at an average 10% discount to NAV during the listed time-period.

Company Information

Provider
The legal company that issues the fund.

Manager/Tenure (Years)
The name of the manager and the number of years spent managing the fund.

Website
The company's web address.

Address
The company's street address.

Phone Number
The company's phone number.

RIGHT COLUMN

Performance Chart
A graphical representation of the fund's total returns over the past year.

Ratings History

Indicates the fund's Overall, Risk and Reward Ratings for the previous four years. Ratings are listed as of December 31, 2018 (Q4-18), June 30, 2018 (Q2-18), December 31, 2017 (Q4-17), December 31, 2016 (Q4-16), and December 31, 2015 (Q4-15).

Overall Rating
The Weiss rating measured on a scale from A to E based on each fund's risk and performance. See the preceding section, "What Our Ratings Mean," for an explanation of each letter grade rating.

Risk Rating
This is includes the risk ratings of component stocks where applicable and also includes the financial stability of the fund, turnover where applicable, together with the level of volatility as measured by the fund's daily returns over a period of up to five years. Funds with greater stability are considered less risky and receive a higher risk rating. Funds with greater volatility are considered riskier, and will receive a lower risk rating. In addition to considering the fund's volatility, the risk rating also considers an assessment of the valuation and quality of a fund's holdings.

Reward Rating
This is based on the total return over a period of up to five years, including net asset value and price growth. The total return figure is stated net of the expenses and fees charged by the fund. Based on proprietary modeling the individual components of the risk and reward ratings are calculated and weighted and the final rating is generated.

Asset & Performance History
Indicates the fund's NAV (Net Asset Value) and 1-Year Total Return for the previous 6 years.

NAV (Net Asset Value)
A fund's price per share. The value is calculated by dividing the total value of all the securities in the portfolio, less any liabilities, by the number of fund shares outstanding.

1-Year Total Return
The rate of return on an investment over one year that includes interest, capital gains, dividends and distributions realized.

Total Assets ($)
The total of all assets listed on the institution's balance sheet. This figure primarily consists of loans, investments, and fixed assets. Total Assets are displayed in dollars.

Asset Allocation
Indicates the percentage of assets in each category. Used as an investment strategy that attempts to balance risk versus reward by adjusting the percentage of each asset in an investment portfolio according to the investor's risk tolerance, goals and investment time frame. Allocation percentages may not add up to 100%. Negative values reflect short positions.

%Cash
The percentage of the fund's assets invested in short-term obligations, usually less than 90 days, that provide a return in the form of interest payments. This type of investment generally offers a low return compared to other investments but has a low risk level.

%Stocks
The percentage of the fund's assets invested in stock.

%US Stocks
The percentage of the fund's assets invested in U.S. stock.

%Bonds
The percentage of the fund's assets invested in bonds. A bond is an unsecured debt security issued by companies, municipalities, states and sovereign governments to raise funds. When a company issues a bond it borrows money from the bondholder to boost the business, in exchange the bondholder receives the principal amount back plus the interest on the determined maturity date.

%US Bonds
The percentage of the fund's assets invested in U.S. bonds.

%Other
The percentage of the fund's assets invested in other financial instruments.

Services Offered
Services offered by the fund provider. Such services can include:

Systematic Withdrawal Plan
A plan offered by exchange-traded funds that pays specific amounts to shareholders at predetermined intervals.

Institutional Only
This indicates if the fund is offered to institutional clients only (pension funds, mutual funds, money managers, insurance companies, investment banks, commercial trusts, endowment funds, hedge funds, and some hedge fund investors).

Phone Exchange
This indicates that investors can move money between different funds within the same fund family over the phone.

Wire Redemption
This indicates whether or not investors can redeem electronically.

Qualified Investment
Under a qualified plan, an investor may invest in the variable annuity with pretax dollars through an employee pension plan, such as a 401(k) or 403(b). Money builds up on a tax-deferred basis, and when the qualified investor makes a withdrawal or annuitizes, all contributions received are taxable income.

Investment Strategy
A set of rules, behaviors or procedures, designed to guide an investor's selection of an investment portfolio. Individuals have different profit objectives, and their individual skills make different tactics and strategies appropriate.

Top Holdings
The highest amount of publicly traded assets held by a fund. These publicly traded assets may include company stock, mutual funds or other investment vehicles.

Vanguard Total Stock Market Index Fund ETF Shares   C+   HOLD

Ticker	Traded On	NAV	Total Assets ($)	Dividend Yield (TTM)	Turnover Ratio	Expense Ratio
VTI	NYSE Arca		$726,364,000,000	1.81	3	0.04

Ratings
Reward	C
Risk	B
Recent Upgrade/Downgrade	

Fund Information
Fund Type	Exchange Traded Funds
Category	US Equity Large Cap Blend
Sub-Category	Large Blend
Prospectus Objective	Growth
Inception Date	May-01
Open to New Investments	Y

Prices
Price (as of 12/31/2018)	127.63
52-Week High	151.31
52-Week Low	119.70

Total Returns (%)
3-Month	6-Month	1-Year	3-Year	5-Year
-15.11	-9.25	-5.95	28.38	45.08

3-Year Standard Deviation	9.81
Effective Duration	

Valuation
Premium/Discount (1-Year Average)	0.02

Company Information
Provider	Vanguard
Manager/Tenure	Gerard C. O'Reilly (23), Walter Nejman (2)
Website	http://www.vanguard.com
Address	Vanguard 100 Vanguard Boulevard Malvern PA 19355 United States
Phone Number	877-662-7447

PERFORMANCE

Ratings History
Date	Overall Rating	Risk Rating	Reward Rating
Q4-18	C+	B	C
Q2-18	C+	C+	C+
Q4-17	B	B	B
Q4-16	B-	C+	B
Q4-15	C+	B-	C

Asset & Performance History
Date	NAV	1-Year Total Return
2017	137.06	21.28
2016	115.21	12.13
2015	104.34	0.39
2014	106	12.55
2013	95.91	33.51
2012	73.24	16.4

Total Assets: $726,364,000,000
Asset Allocation
Asset	%
Cash	1%
Stocks	99%
US Stocks	98%
Bonds	0%
US Bonds	0%
Other	0%

Services Offered:

Investment Strategy: The investment seeks to track the performance of a benchmark index that measures the investment return of the overall stock market. The fund employs an indexing investment approach designed to track the performance of the CRSP US Total Market Index, which represents approximately 100% of the investable U.S. stock market and includes large-, mid-, small-, and micro-cap stocks regularly traded on the New York Stock Exchange and Nasdaq. It invests by sampling the index, meaning that it holds a broadly diversified collection of securities that, in the aggregate, approximates the full index in terms of key characteristics. **Top Holdings:** Apple Inc   Microsoft Corp   Amazon.com Inc   Berkshire Hathaway Inc B   Johnson & Johnson

---

Vanguard S&P 500 ETF   C+   HOLD

Ticker	Traded On	NAV	Total Assets ($)	Dividend Yield (TTM)	Turnover Ratio	Expense Ratio
VOO	NYSE Arca		$441,304,000,000	1.82	3	0.04

Ratings
Reward	C
Risk	B
Recent Upgrade/Downgrade	Down

Fund Information
Fund Type	Exchange Traded Funds
Category	US Equity Large Cap Blend
Sub-Category	Large Blend
Prospectus Objective	Growth
Inception Date	Sep-10
Open to New Investments	Y

Prices
Price (as of 12/31/2018)	229.81
52-Week High	269.75
52-Week Low	215.07

Total Returns (%)
3-Month	6-Month	1-Year	3-Year	5-Year
-14.56	-7.93	-5.23	29.17	48.77

3-Year Standard Deviation	9.4
Effective Duration	

Valuation
Premium/Discount (1-Year Average)	0.02

Company Information
Provider	Vanguard
Manager/Tenure	Donald M. Butler (2), Michelle Louie (1)
Website	http://www.vanguard.com
Address	Vanguard 100 Vanguard Boulevard Malvern PA 19355 United States
Phone Number	877-662-7447

PERFORMANCE

Ratings History
Date	Overall Rating	Risk Rating	Reward Rating
Q4-18	C+	B	C
Q2-18	C+	C+	C
Q4-17	B	B	B
Q4-16	B-	C+	B
Q4-15	C+	C+	C

Asset & Performance History
Date	NAV	1-Year Total Return
2017	244.94	21.84
2016	205	11.39
2015	187.05	1.35
2014	188.45	13.63
2013	169.07	32.33
2012	130.38	15.97

Total Assets: $441,304,000,000
Asset Allocation
Asset	%
Cash	1%
Stocks	99%
US Stocks	99%
Bonds	0%
US Bonds	0%
Other	0%

Services Offered:

Investment Strategy: The investment seeks to track the performance of a benchmark index that measures the investment return of large-capitalization stocks. The fund employs an indexing investment approach designed to track the performance of the Standard & Poor's 500 Index, a widely recognized benchmark of U.S. stock market performance that is dominated by the stocks of large U.S. companies. The advisor attempts to replicate the target index by investing all, or substantially all, of its assets in the stocks that make up the index, holding each stock in approximately the same proportion as its weighting in the index. **Top Holdings:** Apple Inc   Microsoft Corp   Amazon.com Inc   Berkshire Hathaway Inc B   Johnson & Johnson

Vanguard Total International Stock Index Fund ETF Shares   C-   HOLD

Ticker	Traded On	NAV	Total Assets ($)	Dividend Yield (TTM)	Turnover Ratio	Expense Ratio
VXUS	NAS CM		$342,022,000,000	3.08	12	0.11

Ratings
Reward   D+
Risk   C
Recent Upgrade/Downgrade   Down

Fund Information
Fund Type   Exchange Traded Funds
Category   Global Equity Large Cap
Sub-Category   Foreign Large Blend
Prospectus Objective   Foreign Stock
Inception Date   Jan-11
Open to New Investments   Y

Prices
Price (as of 12/31/2018)   47.22
52-Week High   61.17
52-Week Low   45.72

Total Returns (%)

3-Month	6-Month	1-Year	3-Year	5-Year
-12.14	-10.78	-14.79	13.77	4.36

3-Year Standard Deviation   11
Effective Duration

Valuation
Premium/Discount (1-Year Average)   0.15

Company Information
Provider   Vanguard
Manager/Tenure   Michael Perre (10), Christine D. Franquin (1)
Website   http://www.vanguard.com
Address   Vanguard 100 Vanguard Boulevard Malvern PA 19355 United States
Phone Number   877-662-7447

PERFORMANCE

Ratings History

Date	Overall Rating	Risk Rating	Reward Rating
Q4-18	C-	C	D+
Q2-18	C	C+	C
Q4-17	B-	B-	B-
Q4-16	C-	C	D+
Q4-15	C	C+	C-

Asset & Performance History

Date	NAV	1-Year Total Return
2017	56.75	27.67
2016	45.81	3.75
2015	45.08	-4.28
2014	48.36	-4.16
2013	52.09	15.15
2012	46.59	18.21

Total Assets: $342,022,000,000

Asset Allocation

Asset	%
Cash	3%
Stocks	96%
US Stocks	1%
Bonds	0%
US Bonds	0%
Other	1%

Services Offered:

Investment Strategy: The investment seeks to track the performance of a benchmark index that measures the investment return of stocks issued by companies located in developed and emerging markets, excluding the United States. The fund employs an indexing investment approach designed to track the performance of the FTSE Global All Cap ex US Index, a float-adjusted market-capitalization-weighted index designed to measure equity market performance of companies located in developed and emerging markets, excluding the United States. The index includes approximately 5,800 stocks of companies located in over 45 countries. **Top Holdings:** Nestle SA Tencent Holdings Ltd Novartis AG Taiwan Semiconductor Manufacturing Co Ltd Samsung Electronics Co Ltd

---

SPDR® S&P 500 ETF   C+   HOLD

Ticker	Traded On	NAV	Total Assets ($)	Dividend Yield (TTM)	Turnover Ratio	Expense Ratio
SPY	NYSE Arca	249.92	$269,244,000,000	1.82	3	0.09

Ratings
Reward   C
Risk   B
Recent Upgrade/Downgrade   Down

Fund Information
Fund Type   Exchange Traded Funds
Category   US Equity Large Cap Blend
Sub-Category   Large Blend
Prospectus Objective   Growth
Inception Date   Jan-93
Open to New Investments   Y

Prices
Price (as of 12/31/2018)   249.92
52-Week High   293.58
52-Week Low   234.34

Total Returns (%)

3-Month	6-Month	1-Year	3-Year	5-Year
-13.79	-7.14	-4.44	29.99	49.57

3-Year Standard Deviation   9.38
Effective Duration

Valuation
Premium/Discount (1-Year Average)   0.01

Company Information
Provider   SPDR State Street Global Advisors
Manager/Tenure   Management Team (25)
Website   http://www.spdrs.com
Address   SPDR State Street Global Advisors State Street Financial Center, 1 Lincoln Street Boston MA 02111-2900 United States
Phone Number   617-786-3000

PERFORMANCE

Ratings History

Date	Overall Rating	Risk Rating	Reward Rating
Q4-18	C+	B	C
Q2-18	B	A-	C
Q4-17	B	B	B
Q4-16	B	B	B
Q4-15	C+	B-	C

Asset & Performance History

Date	NAV	1-Year Total Return
2017	266.55	21.69
2016	223.28	11.25
2015	204.02	1.34
2014	205.5	13.53
2013	184.54	32.21
2012	142.4	15.83

Total Assets: $269,244,000,000

Asset Allocation

Asset	%
Cash	1%
Stocks	99%
US Stocks	99%
Bonds	0%
US Bonds	0%
Other	0%

Services Offered: Dividend Investment Plan, CashInvestment Plan

Investment Strategy: The investment seeks to provide investment results that, before expenses, generally correspond to the price and yield performance of the S&P 500 Index. The Trust holds the Portfolio and cash and is not actively "managed" by traditional methods. To maintain the correspondence between the composition and weightings of Portfolio Securities and component stocks of the S&P 500 Index ("Index Securities"), the Trustee adjusts the Portfolio from time to time to conform to periodic changes in the identity and/or relative weightings of Index Securities. **Top Holdings:** Microsoft Corp Apple Inc Amazon.com Inc Berkshire Hathaway Inc B Johnson & Johnson

Vanguard Total Bond Market Index Fund ETF Shares

C **HOLD**

Ticker	Traded On	NAV	Total Assets ($)	Dividend Yield (TTM)	Turnover Ratio	Expense Ratio
BND	NYSE Arca		$200,719,000,000	2.77	55	0.05

Ratings

Reward	D+
Risk	C+
Recent Upgrade/Downgrade	

Performance Chart Unavailable

Fund Information

Fund Type	Exchange Traded Funds
Category	US Fixed Income
Sub-Category	Intermediate-Term Bond
Prospectus Objective	Income
Inception Date	Apr-07
Open to New Investments	Y

Prices

Price (as of 12/31/2018)	79.21
52-Week High	81.57
52-Week Low	77.49

Total Returns (%)

3-Month	6-Month	1-Year	3-Year	5-Year
1.58	1.49	-0.23	6.03	12.78

3-Year Standard Deviation	2.82
Effective Duration	6.24

Valuation

Premium/Discount (1-Year Average)	0.02

Company Information

Provider	Vanguard
Manager/Tenure	Joshua C. Barrickman (5)
Website	http://www.vanguard.com
Address	Vanguard 100 Vanguard Boulevard Malvern PA 19355 United States
Phone Number	877-662-7447

Ratings History

Date	Overall Rating	Risk Rating	Reward Rating
Q4-18	C	C+	D+
Q2-18	C-	C	C-
Q4-17	B-	A-	C
Q4-16	C	C+	C
Q4-15	C	C+	C

Asset & Performance History

Date	NAV	1-Year Total Return
2017	81.46	3.62
2016	80.64	2.5
2015	80.58	0.38
2014	82.33	5.95
2013	79.91	-2.14
2012	83.92	4.04

Total Assets: $200,719,000,000

Asset Allocation

Asset	%
Cash	1%
Stocks	0%
US Stocks	0%
Bonds	99%
US Bonds	90%
Other	0%

Services Offered:

Investment Strategy: The investment seeks the performance of Bloomberg Barclays U.S. Aggregate Float Adjusted Index. Bloomberg Barclays U.S. Aggregate Float Adjusted Index represents a wide spectrum of public, investment-grade, taxable, fixed income securities in the United States-including government, corporate, and international dollar-denominated bonds, as well as mortgage-backed and asset-backed securities-all with maturities of more than 1 year. All of its investments will be selected through the sampling process, and at least 80% of its assets will be invested in bonds held in the index. **Top Holdings:** United States Treasury Notes 2.12% United States Treasury Notes 2.88% United States Treasury Notes 2.62% United States Treasury Notes 1.38% United States Treasury Notes 2.12%

---

iShares Core S&P 500 ETF

C+ **HOLD**

Ticker	Traded On	NAV	Total Assets ($)	Dividend Yield (TTM)	Turnover Ratio	Expense Ratio
IVV	NYSE Arca	251.40	$162,725,000,000	1.82	4	0.04

Ratings

Reward	C
Risk	B
Recent Upgrade/Downgrade	Down

Fund Information

Fund Type	Exchange Traded Funds
Category	US Equity Large Cap Blend
Sub-Category	Large Blend
Prospectus Objective	Growth
Inception Date	May-00
Open to New Investments	Y

Prices

Price (as of 12/31/2018)	251.61
52-Week High	295.76
52-Week Low	236.09

PERFORMANCE

Total Returns (%)

3-Month	6-Month	1-Year	3-Year	5-Year
-13.95	-7.27	-4.54	30.09	49.78

3-Year Standard Deviation	9.4
Effective Duration	

Valuation

Premium/Discount (1-Year Average)	0.03

Company Information

Provider	iShares
Manager/Tenure	Diane Hsiung (10), Greg Savage (10), Jennifer Hsui (6), 3 others
Website	http://www.ishares.com
Address	iShares 400 Howard Street San Francisco CA 94105 United States
Phone Number	800-474-2737

Ratings History

Date	Overall Rating	Risk Rating	Reward Rating
Q4-18	C+	B	C
Q2-18	B	A-	C
Q4-17	B	B	B
Q4-16	B	B	B
Q4-15	C+	C+	C

Asset & Performance History

Date	NAV	1-Year Total Return
2017	268.5	21.79
2016	224.64	11.89
2015	205.02	1.33
2014	206.94	13.62
2013	185.62	32.3
2012	143.11	15.91

Total Assets: $162,725,000,000

Asset Allocation

Asset	%
Cash	0%
Stocks	100%
US Stocks	99%
Bonds	0%
US Bonds	0%
Other	0%

Services Offered: CashInvestment Plan

Investment Strategy: The investment seeks to track the investment results of the S&P 500 (the "underlying index"), which measures the performance of the large-capitalization sector of the U.S. equity market. The fund generally invests at least 90% of its assets in securities of the underlying index and in depositary receipts representing securities of the underlying index. It may invest the remainder of its assets in certain futures, options and swap contracts, cash and cash equivalents, as well as in securities not included in the underlying index, but which the advisor believes will help the fund track the underlying index. **Top Holdings:** Microsoft Corp Apple Inc Amazon.com Inc Berkshire Hathaway Inc B Johnson & Johnson

Vanguard Total International Bond Index Fund ETF Shares　　　　　　C　　HOLD

Ticker	Traded On	NAV	Total Assets ($)	Dividend Yield (TTM)	Turnover Ratio	Expense Ratio
BNDX	NAS CM		$112,106,000,000	2.24	19	0.11

Ratings
Reward　　　　　　　　　　　　　　C
Risk　　　　　　　　　　　　　　C+
Recent Upgrade/Downgrade

Fund Information
Fund Type　　　　　　　　Exchange Traded Funds
Category　　　　　　　　Global Fixed Income
Sub-Category　　　　　　　　World Bond
Prospectus Objective　　　　Worldwide Bond
Inception Date　　　　　　　　May-13
Open to New Investments　　　　Y

Prices
Price (as of 12/31/2018)　　　　54.25
52-Week High　　　　　　　　55.31
52-Week Low　　　　　　　　53.88

Total Returns (%)

3-Month	6-Month	1-Year	3-Year	5-Year
1.97	1.58	2.96	10.35	21.39

3-Year Standard Deviation　　　　2.41
Effective Duration　　　　　　7.58

Valuation
Premium/Discount (1-Year Average)　　0.21

Company Information
Provider　　　　Vanguard
Manager/Tenure　Joshua C. Barrickman (5)
Website　　　　http://www.vanguard.com
Address　　　　Vanguard 100 Vanguard Boulevard
　　　　　　　Malvern PA 19355 United States
Phone Number　877-662-7447

PERFORMANCE

Ratings History

Date	Overall Rating	Risk Rating	Reward Rating
Q4-18	C	C+	C
Q2-18	C	C+	C
Q4-17	B	A	C
Q4-16	C	C+	C
Q4-15	C	C+	C-

Asset & Performance History

Date	NAV	1-Year Total Return
2017	54.19	2.28
2016	54.11	4.82
2015	52.68	1.07
2014	52.97	8.83
2013	49.45	
2012		

Total Assets: $112,106,000,000
Asset Allocation

Asset	%
Cash	0%
Stocks	0%
US Stocks	0%
Bonds	100%
US Bonds	3%
Other	0%

Services Offered:

Investment Strategy: The investment seeks to track the performance of a benchmark index that measures the investment return of non-U.S. dollar-denominated investment-grade bonds. The fund employs an indexing investment approach designed to track the performance of the Bloomberg Barclays Global Aggregate ex-USD Float Adjusted RIC Capped Index (USD Hedged). This index provides a broad-based measure of the global, investment-grade, fixed-rate debt markets. It is non-diversified. **Top Holdings:** France(Govt Of) 1% Bundesschatzanw Japan(Govt Of) 0.1% France(Govt Of) 0% Japan(Govt Of) 0.1%

Vanguard FTSE Developed Markets Index Fund ETF Shares　　　　　C-　　HOLD

Ticker	Traded On	NAV	Total Assets ($)	Dividend Yield (TTM)	Turnover Ratio	Expense Ratio
VEA	NYSE Arca		$104,457,000,000	3.25	3	0.07

Ratings
Reward　　　　　　　　　　　　　　D+
Risk　　　　　　　　　　　　　　C
Recent Upgrade/Downgrade　　　　Down

Fund Information
Fund Type　　　　　　　　Exchange Traded Funds
Category　　　　　　　　Global Equity Large Cap
Sub-Category　　　　　　　　Foreign Large Blend
Prospectus Objective　　　　Foreign Stock
Inception Date　　　　　　　　Jul-07
Open to New Investments　　　　Y

Prices
Price (as of 12/31/2018)　　　　37.10
52-Week High　　　　　　　　47.88
52-Week Low　　　　　　　　35.84

Total Returns (%)

3-Month	6-Month	1-Year	3-Year	5-Year
-13.55	-11.60	-14.88	10.31	3.79

3-Year Standard Deviation　　　　10.78
Effective Duration

Valuation
Premium/Discount (1-Year Average)　　0.05

Company Information
Provider　　　　Vanguard
Manager/Tenure　Christine D. Franquin (5), Michael
　　　　　　　Perre (1)
Website　　　　http://www.vanguard.com
Address　　　　Vanguard 100 Vanguard Boulevard
　　　　　　　Malvern PA 19355 United States
Phone Number　877-662-7447

PERFORMANCE

Ratings History

Date	Overall Rating	Risk Rating	Reward Rating
Q4-18	C-	C	D+
Q2-18	C	B-	C
Q4-17	B	B	B-
Q4-16	C-	C	D+
Q4-15	C	C	C-

Asset & Performance History

Date	NAV	1-Year Total Return
2017	44.83	26.77
2016	36.51	1.28
2015	36.75	-0.21
2014	37.85	-5.7
2013	41.53	22.12
2012	35.02	18.59

Total Assets: $104,457,000,000
Asset Allocation

Asset	%
Cash	4%
Stocks	95%
US Stocks	1%
Bonds	0%
US Bonds	0%
Other	1%

Services Offered:

Investment Strategy: The investment seeks to track the performance of the FTSE Developed All Cap ex US Index. The fund employs an indexing investment approach designed to track the performance of the FTSE Developed All Cap ex US Index, a market-capitalization-weighted index that is made up of approximately 3,790 common stocks of large-, mid-, and small-cap companies located in Canada and the major markets of Europe and the Pacific region. The adviser attempts to replicate the target index by investing all, or substantially all, of its assets in the stocks that make up the index, holding each stock in approximately the same proportion as its weighting in the index. **Top Holdings:** Nestle SA Novartis AG Roche Holding AG Dividend Right Cert. HSBC Holdings PLC Samsung Electronics Co Ltd

Vanguard Mid-Cap Index Fund ETF Shares   C   HOLD

Ticker	Traded On	NAV	Total Assets ($)	Dividend Yield (TTM)	Turnover Ratio	Expense Ratio
VO	NYSE Arca		$96,609,369,976	1.61	14	0.05

Ratings
Reward   C-
Risk   C+
Recent Upgrade/Downgrade   Down

Fund Information
Fund Type   Exchange Traded Funds
Category   US Equity Mid Cap
Sub-Category   Mid-Cap Blend
Prospectus Objective   Growth
Inception Date   Jan-04
Open to New Investments   Y

Prices
Price (as of 12/31/2018)   138.18
52-Week High   166.55
52-Week Low   129.93

Total Returns (%)

3-Month	6-Month	1-Year	3-Year	5-Year
-16.00	-12.41	-10.02	19.34	33.94

3-Year Standard Deviation   10.71
Effective Duration

Valuation
Premium/Discount (1-Year Average)   0.02

Company Information
Provider   Vanguard
Manager/Tenure   Donald M. Butler (20), Michael A. Johnson (2)
Website   http://www.vanguard.com
Address   Vanguard 100 Vanguard Boulevard Malvern PA 19355 United States
Phone Number   877-662-7447

PERFORMANCE

Ratings History

Date	Overall Rating	Risk Rating	Reward Rating
Q4-18	C	C+	C-
Q2-18	C+	C+	C+
Q4-17	B-	B-	B-
Q4-16	B-	C+	B
Q4-15	C	C+	C

Asset & Performance History

Date	NAV	1-Year Total Return
2017	154.65	19.57
2016	131.55	10.85
2015	120.07	-1.33
2014	123.5	13.75
2013	109.96	35.14
2012	82.33	15.97

Total Assets: $96,609,369,976

Asset Allocation

Asset	%
Cash	0%
Stocks	100%
US Stocks	99%
Bonds	0%
US Bonds	0%
Other	0%

Services Offered:

Investment Strategy: The investment seeks to track the performance of a benchmark index that measures the investment return of mid-capitalization stocks. The fund employs an indexing investment approach designed to track the performance of the CRSP US Mid Cap Index, a broadly diversified index of stocks of mid-size U.S. companies. The advisor attempts to replicate the target index by investing all, or substantially all, of its assets in the stocks that make up the index, holding each stock in approximately the same proportion as its weighting in the index. **Top Holdings:** Fiserv Inc   Edwards Lifesciences Corp   Red Hat Inc   Roper Technologies Inc   Autodesk Inc

---

Vanguard Small-Cap Index Fund ETF Shares   C   HOLD

Ticker	Traded On	NAV	Total Assets ($)	Dividend Yield (TTM)	Turnover Ratio	Expense Ratio
VB	NYSE Arca		$87,322,089,500	1.51	0	0.05

Ratings
Reward   C-
Risk   C+
Recent Upgrade/Downgrade   Down

Fund Information
Fund Type   Exchange Traded Funds
Category   US Equity Small Cap
Sub-Category   Small Blend
Prospectus Objective   Small Company
Inception Date   Jan-04
Open to New Investments   Y

Prices
Price (as of 12/31/2018)   131.99
52-Week High   165.82
52-Week Low   123.92

Total Returns (%)

3-Month	6-Month	1-Year	3-Year	5-Year
-18.27	-15.53	-10.15	23.56	27.99

3-Year Standard Deviation   12.83
Effective Duration

Valuation
Premium/Discount (1-Year Average)   0.00

Company Information
Provider   Vanguard
Manager/Tenure   William A. Coleman (2), Gerard C. O'Reilly (2)
Website   http://www.vanguard.com
Address   Vanguard 100 Vanguard Boulevard Malvern PA 19355 United States
Phone Number   877-662-7447

PERFORMANCE

Ratings History

Date	Overall Rating	Risk Rating	Reward Rating
Q4-18	C	C+	C-
Q2-18	C+	C+	C+
Q4-17	B	B	B
Q4-16	B-	C+	B
Q4-15	C	C+	C

Asset & Performance History

Date	NAV	1-Year Total Return
2017	147.71	16.5
2016	128.9	17.67
2015	110.71	-3.65
2014	116.61	7.51
2013	110.02	37.8
2012	80.89	18.22

Total Assets: $87,322,089,500

Asset Allocation

Asset	%
Cash	2%
Stocks	98%
US Stocks	97%
Bonds	0%
US Bonds	0%
Other	0%

Services Offered:

Investment Strategy: The investment seeks to track the performance of a benchmark index that measures the investment return of small-capitalization stocks. The fund employs an indexing investment approach designed to track the performance of the CRSP US Small Cap Index, a broadly diversified index of stocks of small U.S. companies. The advisor attempts to replicate the target index by investing all, or substantially all, of its assets in the stocks that make up the index, holding each stock in approximately the same proportion as its weighting in the index. **Top Holdings:** Burlington Stores Inc   NRG Energy Inc   Atmos Energy Corp   Leidos Holdings Inc   IDEX Corp

Vanguard Growth Index Fund ETF Shares   C   HOLD

Ticker	Traded On	NAV	Total Assets ($)	Dividend Yield (TTM)	Turnover Ratio	Expense Ratio
VUG	NYSE Arca		$79,908,714,213	1.17	8	0.05

Ratings

Reward	C
Risk	C+
Recent Upgrade/Downgrade	Down

Fund Information

Fund Type	Exchange Traded Funds
Category	US Equity Large Cap Growth
Sub-Category	Large Growth
Prospectus Objective	Growth
Inception Date	Jan-04
Open to New Investments	Y

Prices

Price (as of 12/31/2018)	134.33
52-Week High	161.48
52-Week Low	124.85

Total Returns (%)

3-Month	6-Month	1-Year	3-Year	5-Year
-17.24	-10.91	-4.16	29.98	52.58

3-Year Standard Deviation	11.12
Effective Duration	

Valuation

Premium/Discount (1-Year Average)	0.00

Company Information

Provider	Vanguard
Manager/Tenure	Gerard C. O'Reilly (23), Walter Nejman (2)
Website	http://www.vanguard.com
Address	Vanguard 100 Vanguard Boulevard Malvern PA 19355 United States
Phone Number	877-662-7447

PERFORMANCE

Ratings History

Date	Overall Rating	Risk Rating	Reward Rating
Q4-18	C	C+	C
Q2-18	B-	C+	B-
Q4-17	B+	A-	B
Q4-16	B-	C+	B-
Q4-15	C+	C+	C+

Asset & Performance History

Date	NAV	1-Year Total Return
2017	140.55	27.7
2016	111.33	5.76
2015	106.4	3.31
2014	104.33	13.61
2013	92.99	32.37
2012	71.19	17.03

Total Assets: $79,908,714,213

Asset Allocation

Asset	%
Cash	1%
Stocks	99%
US Stocks	99%
Bonds	0%
US Bonds	0%
Other	0%

Services Offered:

Investment Strategy: The investment seeks to track the performance of a benchmark index that measures the investment return of large-capitalization growth stocks. The fund employs an indexing investment approach designed to track the performance of the CRSP US Large Cap Growth Index, a broadly diversified index predominantly made up of growth stocks of large U.S. companies. The advisor attempts to replicate the target index by investing all, or substantially all, of its assets in the stocks that make up the index, holding each stock in approximately the same proportion as its weighting in the index. **Top Holdings:** Apple Inc Amazon.com Inc Facebook Inc A Alphabet Inc A Alphabet Inc Class C

Vanguard FTSE Emerging Markets Index Fund ETF Shares   C-   HOLD

Ticker	Traded On	NAV	Total Assets ($)	Dividend Yield (TTM)	Turnover Ratio	Expense Ratio
VWO	NYSE Arca		$77,643,210,441	2.65	6	0.14

Ratings

Reward	C-
Risk	C-
Recent Upgrade/Downgrade	Down

Fund Information

Fund Type	Exchange Traded Funds
Category	Global Emerg Mkts Equity
Sub-Category	Diversified Emerging Mkts
Prospectus Objective	Div Emerg Mkts
Inception Date	Mar-05
Open to New Investments	Y

Prices

Price (as of 12/31/2018)	38.10
52-Week High	50.98
52-Week Low	36.68

Total Returns (%)

3-Month	6-Month	1-Year	3-Year	5-Year
-6.75	-7.87	-14.90	24.93	6.39

3-Year Standard Deviation	14.46
Effective Duration	

Valuation

Premium/Discount (1-Year Average)	0.05

Company Information

Provider	Vanguard
Manager/Tenure	Michael Perre (10), Jeffrey D. Miller (2)
Website	http://www.vanguard.com
Address	Vanguard 100 Vanguard Boulevard Malvern PA 19355 United States
Phone Number	877-662-7447

PERFORMANCE

Ratings History

Date	Overall Rating	Risk Rating	Reward Rating
Q4-18	C-	C-	C-
Q2-18	C	C+	C
Q4-17	C+	C	B-
Q4-16	C-	C	D+
Q4-15	C-	C-	C-

Asset & Performance History

Date	NAV	1-Year Total Return
2017	45.9	30.96
2016	35.8	11.86
2015	32.86	-15.34
2014	39.98	0.59
2013	40.83	-5
2012	44.23	18.83

Total Assets: $77,643,210,441

Asset Allocation

Asset	%
Cash	3%
Stocks	96%
US Stocks	1%
Bonds	0%
US Bonds	0%
Other	0%

Services Offered:

Investment Strategy: The investment seeks to track the performance of a benchmark index that measures the investment return of stocks issued by companies located in emerging market countries. The fund employs an indexing investment approach designed to track the performance of the FTSE Emerging Markets All Cap China A Inclusion Index, a market-capitalization-weighted index that is made up of approximately 4,032 common stocks of large-, mid-, and small-cap companies located in emerging markets around the world. **Top Holdings:** Tencent Holdings Ltd Alibaba Group Holding Ltd ADR Taiwan Semiconductor Manufacturing Co Ltd Naspers Ltd Class N Taiwan Semiconductor Manufacturing Co Ltd ADR

Vanguard Value Index Fund ETF Shares C HOLD

Ticker	Traded On	NAV
VTV	NYSE Arca	

Total Assets ($)	Dividend Yield (TTM)	Turnover Ratio	Expense Ratio
$75,150,880,921	2.4	9	0.05

Ratings
Reward — C
Risk — C+
Recent Upgrade/Downgrade — Down

Fund Information
Fund Type — Exchange Traded Funds
Category — US Equity Large Cap Value
Sub-Category — Large Value
Prospectus Objective — Growth
Inception Date — Jan-04
Open to New Investments — Y

Prices
Price (as of 12/31/2018) — 97.95
52-Week High — 113.26
52-Week Low — 92.30

Total Returns (%)

3-Month	6-Month	1-Year	3-Year	5-Year
-12.01	-5.40	-6.17	28.43	44.08

3-Year Standard Deviation — 9.17
Effective Duration —

Valuation
Premium/Discount (1-Year Average) — 0.03

Company Information
Provider — Vanguard
Manager/Tenure — Gerard C. O'Reilly (23), Walter Nejman (2)
Website — http://www.vanguard.com
Address — Vanguard 100 Vanguard Boulevard Malvern PA 19355 United States
Phone Number — 877-662-7447

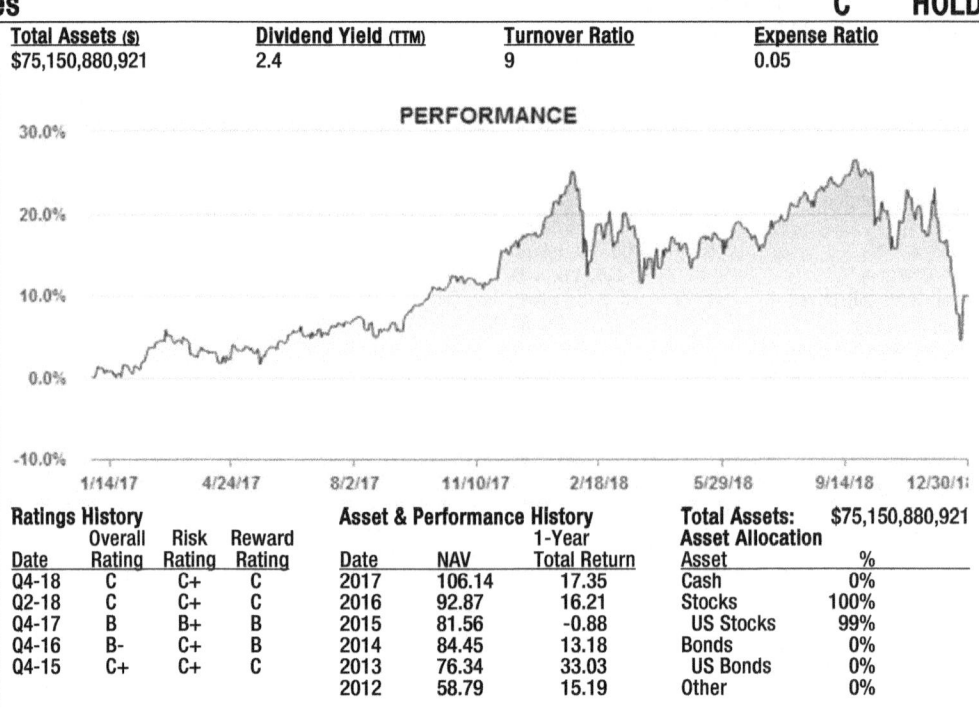

Ratings History

Date	Overall Rating	Risk Rating	Reward Rating
Q4-18	C	C+	C
Q2-18	C	C+	C
Q4-17	B	B+	B
Q4-16	B-	C+	B
Q4-15	C+	C+	C

Asset & Performance History

Date	NAV	1-Year Total Return
2017	106.14	17.35
2016	92.87	16.21
2015	81.56	-0.88
2014	84.45	13.18
2013	76.34	33.03
2012	58.79	15.19

Total Assets: $75,150,880,921
Asset Allocation

Asset	%
Cash	0%
Stocks	100%
US Stocks	99%
Bonds	0%
US Bonds	0%
Other	0%

Services Offered:

Investment Strategy: The investment seeks to track the performance of a benchmark index that measures the investment return of large-capitalization value stocks. The fund employs an indexing investment approach designed to track the performance of the CRSP US Large Cap Value Index, a broadly diversified index predominantly made up of value stocks of large U.S. companies. The advisor attempts to replicate the target index by investing all, or substantially all, of its assets in the stocks that make up the index, holding each stock in approximately the same proportion as its weighting in the index. **Top Holdings:** Microsoft Corp Berkshire Hathaway Inc B Johnson & Johnson JPMorgan Chase & Co Exxon Mobil Corp

---

Invesco QQQ Trust B- BUY

Ticker	Traded On	NAV
QQQ	NAS CM	154.14

Total Assets ($)	Dividend Yield (TTM)	Turnover Ratio	Expense Ratio
$65,965,236,262	0.78		0.2

Ratings
Reward — C+
Risk — B
Recent Upgrade/Downgrade — Down

Fund Information
Fund Type — Exchange Traded Funds
Category — US Equity Large Cap Growth
Sub-Category — Large Growth
Prospectus Objective — Growth
Inception Date — Mar-99
Open to New Investments — Y

Prices
Price (as of 12/31/2018) — 154.26
52-Week High — 186.74
52-Week Low — 143.50

Total Returns (%)

3-Month	6-Month	1-Year	3-Year	5-Year
-16.95	-9.64	-0.14	41.79	85.01

3-Year Standard Deviation — 13.13
Effective Duration —

Valuation
Premium/Discount (1-Year Average) — 0.06

Company Information
Provider — Invesco
Manager/Tenure — Management Team (19)
Website — http://www.invesco.com/us
Address — Invesco 11 Greenway Plaza, Ste. 2500 Houston TX 77046 United States
Phone Number — 800-659-1005

Ratings History

Date	Overall Rating	Risk Rating	Reward Rating
Q4-18	B-	B	C+
Q2-18	B	B	B
Q4-17	A-	B	A-
Q4-16	B+	B	A-
Q4-15	B	A-	B

Asset & Performance History

Date	NAV	1-Year Total Return
2017	155.68	32.7
2016	118.39	7.01
2015	111.87	9.54
2014	103.17	19.11
2013	87.94	36.6
2012	65.13	18.09

Total Assets: $65,965,236,262
Asset Allocation

Asset	%
Cash	0%
Stocks	100%
US Stocks	97%
Bonds	0%
US Bonds	0%
Other	0%

Services Offered: Dividend Investment Plan, CashInvestment Plan

Investment Strategy: The investment seeks investment results that generally correspond to the price and yield performance of the index. To maintain the correspondence between the composition and weights of the securities in the trust (the "securities") and the stocks in the Nasdaq-100 Index®, the adviser adjusts the securities from time to time to conform to periodic changes in the identity and/or relative weights of index securities. The composition and weighting of the securities portion of a portfolio deposit are also adjusted to conform to changes in the index. **Top Holdings:** Apple Inc Microsoft Corp Amazon.com Inc Alphabet Inc Class C Facebook Inc A

Vanguard Extended Market Index Fund ETF Shares   C   HOLD

Ticker	Traded On	NAV	Total Assets ($)	Dividend Yield (TTM)	Turnover Ratio	Expense Ratio
VXF	NYSE Arca		$65,135,785,901	1.52	0	0.08

Ratings
Reward	C-
Risk	C+
Recent Upgrade/Downgrade	Down

Fund Information
Fund Type	Exchange Traded Funds
Category	US Equity Mid Cap
Sub-Category	Mid-Cap Blend
Prospectus Objective	Growth
Inception Date	Dec-01
Open to New Investments	Y

Prices
Price (as of 12/31/2018)	99.81
52-Week High	125.16
52-Week Low	93.42

Total Returns (%)
3-Month	6-Month	1-Year	3-Year	5-Year
-18.23	-15.77	-10.20	23.18	28.15

3-Year Standard Deviation	12.82
Effective Duration	

Valuation
Premium/Discount (1-Year Average)	0.01

Company Information
Provider	Vanguard
Manager/Tenure	Donald M. Butler (20), William A. Coleman (1)
Website	http://www.vanguard.com
Address	Vanguard 100 Vanguard Boulevard Malvern PA 19355 United States
Phone Number	877-662-7447

PERFORMANCE

Ratings History
Date	Overall Rating	Risk Rating	Reward Rating
Q4-18	C	C+	C-
Q2-18	C+	C+	C+
Q4-17	B	B	B
Q4-16	B-	C+	B-
Q4-15	C	C+	C

Asset & Performance History
Date	NAV	1-Year Total Return
2017	111.72	18.44
2016	95.86	15.67
2015	83.8	-3.26
2014	87.79	7.54
2013	82.71	38.37
2012	60.46	18.48

Total Assets: $65,135,785,901

Asset Allocation
Asset	%
Cash	3%
Stocks	97%
US Stocks	95%
Bonds	0%
US Bonds	0%
Other	0%

Services Offered:

Investment Strategy: The investment seeks to track a benchmark index that measures the investment return of small- and mid-capitalization stocks. The fund employs an indexing investment approach designed to track the performance of S&P Completion Index, a broadly diversified index of stocks of small and mid-size U.S. companies. It invests by sampling the index, meaning that it holds a broadly diversified collection of securities that, in the aggregate, approximates the full index in terms of key characteristics. These characteristics include industry weightings and market capitalization, as well as certain financial measures, such as price/earnings ratio and dividend yield. **Top Holdings:** Tesla Inc ServiceNow Inc Worldpay Inc Class A Square Inc A T-Mobile US Inc

---

iShares MSCI EAFE ETF   C-   HOLD

Ticker	Traded On	NAV	Total Assets ($)	Dividend Yield (TTM)	Turnover Ratio	Expense Ratio
EFA	NYSE Arca	58.91	$64,666,263,639	3.35	4	0.31

Ratings
Reward	D+
Risk	C
Recent Upgrade/Downgrade	Down

Fund Information
Fund Type	Exchange Traded Funds
Category	Global Equity Large Cap
Sub-Category	Foreign Large Blend
Prospectus Objective	Foreign Stock
Inception Date	Aug-01
Open to New Investments	Y

Prices
Price (as of 12/31/2018)	58.78
52-Week High	75.25
52-Week Low	56.89

Total Returns (%)
3-Month	6-Month	1-Year	3-Year	5-Year
-12.43	-10.12	-13.82	8.70	2.28

3-Year Standard Deviation	11.06
Effective Duration	

Valuation
Premium/Discount (1-Year Average)	-0.15

Company Information
Provider	iShares
Manager/Tenure	Diane Hsiung (10), Greg Savage (10), Jennifer Hsui (6), 3 others
Website	http://www.ishares.com
Address	iShares 400 Howard Street San Francisco CA 94105 United States
Phone Number	800-474-2737

PERFORMANCE

Ratings History
Date	Overall Rating	Risk Rating	Reward Rating
Q4-18	C-	C	D+
Q2-18	C	C+	C
Q4-17	B	B	B
Q4-16	D+	C-	D
Q4-15	C	C	C-

Asset & Performance History
Date	NAV	1-Year Total Return
2017	70.49	24.94
2016	57.95	0.96
2015	59.18	-0.9
2014	61.26	-5.04
2013	66.75	22.62
2012	56.01	17.22

Total Assets: $64,666,263,639

Asset Allocation
Asset	%
Cash	1%
Stocks	99%
US Stocks	2%
Bonds	0%
US Bonds	0%
Other	0%

Services Offered: CashInvestment Plan

Investment Strategy: The investment seeks to track the investment results of the MSCI EAFE Index composed of large- and mid-capitalization developed market equities, excluding the U.S. and Canada. The fund generally invests at least 90% of its assets in securities of the underlying index and in depositary receipts representing securities of the underlying index. The index measures the equity market performance of developed markets outside of the U.S. and Canada. The underlying index may include large- or mid-capitalization companies. **Top Holdings:** Nestle SA Novartis AG Roche Holding AG Dividend Right Cert. HSBC Holdings PLC Royal Dutch Shell PLC Class A

Vanguard Real Estate Index Fund ETF Shares   C+   HOLD

Ticker	Traded On	NAV	Total Assets ($)	Dividend Yield (TTM)	Turnover Ratio	Expense Ratio
VNQ	NYSE Arca		$59,163,669,767	4.23	6	0.12

Ratings
Reward   C
Risk   B
Recent Upgrade/Downgrade   Up

Fund Information
Fund Type   Exchange Traded Funds
Category   Real Estate Sector Equity
Sub-Category   Real Estate
Prospectus Objective   Real Estate
Inception Date   Sep-04
Open to New Investments   Y

Prices
Price (as of 12/31/2018)   74.57
52-Week High   84.26
52-Week Low   71.74

Total Returns (%)

3-Month	6-Month	1-Year	3-Year	5-Year
-5.77	-5.66	-6.13	6.90	42.58

3-Year Standard Deviation   12.58
Effective Duration

Valuation
Premium/Discount (1-Year Average)   -0.01

Company Information
Provider   Vanguard
Manager/Tenure   Gerard C. O'Reilly (22), Walter Nejman (2)
Website   http://www.vanguard.com
Address   Vanguard 100 Vanguard Boulevard Malvern PA 19355 United States
Phone Number   877-662-7447

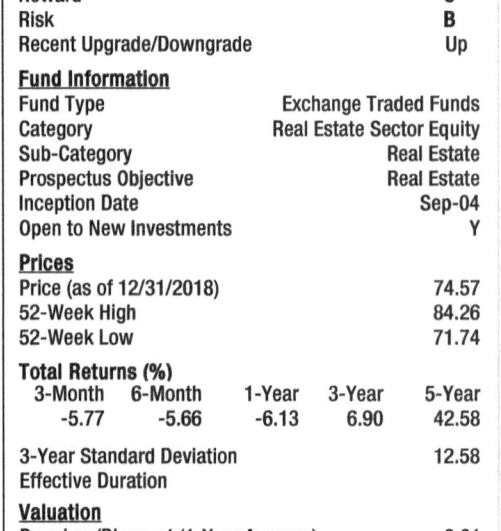

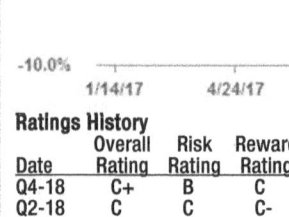

PERFORMANCE

Ratings History

Date	Overall Rating	Risk Rating	Reward Rating
Q4-18	C+	B	C
Q2-18	C	C	C-
Q4-17	B-	B	C+
Q4-16	C+	B-	C+
Q4-15	C+	B-	C+

Asset & Performance History

Date	NAV	1-Year Total Return
2017	82.94	6.31
2016	82.46	6.32
2015	79.72	2.36
2014	81.03	30.29
2013	64.62	2.41
2012	65.79	17.67

Total Assets: $59,163,669,767

Asset Allocation

Asset	%
Cash	1%
Stocks	99%
US Stocks	99%
Bonds	0%
US Bonds	0%
Other	0%

Services Offered:

Investment Strategy: The investment seeks to provide a high level of income and moderate long-term capital appreciation by tracking the performance of the MSCI US Investable Market Real Estate 25/50 Index that measures the performance of publicly traded equity REITs and other real estate-related investments. The advisor attempts to track the index by investing all, or substantially all, of its assets-either directly or indirectly through a wholly owned subsidiary, which is itself a registered investment company-in the stocks that make up the index, holding each stock in approximately the same proportion as its weighting in the index. The fund is non-diversified. **Top Holdings:** Vanguard Real Estate II Index American Tower Corp Simon Property Group Inc Crown Castle International Corp Prologis Inc

---

iShares Core MSCI EAFE ETF   C-   HOLD

Ticker	Traded On	NAV	Total Assets ($)	Dividend Yield (TTM)	Turnover Ratio	Expense Ratio
IEFA	BATS	55.05	$54,938,432,077	3.2	2	0.08

Ratings
Reward   D+
Risk   C
Recent Upgrade/Downgrade   Down

Fund Information
Fund Type   Exchange Traded Funds
Category   Global Equity Large Cap
Sub-Category   Foreign Large Blend
Prospectus Objective   Growth & Inc
Inception Date   Oct-12
Open to New Investments   Y

Prices
Price (as of 12/31/2018)   55.00
52-Week High   70.84
52-Week Low   53.06

Total Returns (%)

3-Month	6-Month	1-Year	3-Year	5-Year
-12.91	-10.78	-14.20	9.94	5.19

3-Year Standard Deviation   11.21
Effective Duration

Valuation
Premium/Discount (1-Year Average)   -0.01

Company Information
Provider   iShares
Manager/Tenure   Diane Hsiung (6), Jennifer Hsui (6), Greg Savage (6), 3 others
Website   http://www.ishares.com
Address   iShares 400 Howard Street San Francisco CA 94105 United States
Phone Number   800-474-2737

PERFORMANCE

Ratings History

Date	Overall Rating	Risk Rating	Reward Rating
Q4-18	C-	C	D+
Q2-18	C	B-	C
Q4-17	B	B	B
Q4-16	C-	C	D+
Q4-15	C	C+	D+

Asset & Performance History

Date	NAV	1-Year Total Return
2017	66.21	26.42
2016	53.8	1.36
2015	54.67	0.52
2014	55.73	-4.82
2013	60.26	23.73
2012	49.9	

Total Assets: $54,938,432,077

Asset Allocation

Asset	%
Cash	1%
Stocks	99%
US Stocks	1%
Bonds	0%
US Bonds	0%
Other	0%

Services Offered:

Investment Strategy: The investment seeks to track the investment results of the MSCI EAFE IMI Index composed of large-, mid- and small-capitalization developed market equities, excluding the U.S. and Canada. The fund generally will invest at least 90% of its assets in the component securities of the underlying index and in investments that have economic characteristics that are substantially identical to the component securities of the underlying index. The index is designed to measure large-, mid- and small-capitalization equity market performance and includes stocks from Europe, Australasia and the Far East. **Top Holdings:** Nestle SA Novartis AG Roche Holding AG Dividend Right Cert. HSBC Holdings PLC Royal Dutch Shell PLC Class A

iShares Core U.S. Aggregate Bond ETF   C   HOLD

Ticker	Traded On	NAV	Total Assets ($)	Dividend Yield (TTM)	Turnover Ratio	Expense Ratio
AGG	NYSE Arca	106.27	$53,587,879,207	2.57	252	0.05

Ratings
Reward	D+
Risk	C+
Recent Upgrade/Downgrade	

Fund Information
Fund Type	Exchange Traded Funds
Category	US Fixed Income
Sub-Category	Intermediate-Term Bond
Prospectus Objective	Corp Bond - Gen
Inception Date	Sep-03
Open to New Investments	Y

Prices
Price (as of 12/31/2018)	106.49
52-Week High	109.33
52-Week Low	104.01

Total Returns (%)

3-Month	6-Month	1-Year	3-Year	5-Year
1.69	1.71	-0.04	6.12	13.07

3-Year Standard Deviation	2.72
Effective Duration	5.91

Valuation
Premium/Discount (1-Year Average)	0.02

Company Information
Provider	iShares
Manager/Tenure	Scott Radell (8), James Mauro (7)
Website	http://www.ishares.com
Address	iShares 400 Howard Street San Francisco CA 94105 United States
Phone Number	800-474-2737

PERFORMANCE

Ratings History				Asset & Performance History			Total Assets:	$53,587,879,207
Date	Overall Rating	Risk Rating	Reward Rating	Date	NAV	1-Year Total Return	Asset Allocation Asset	%
Q4-18	C	C+	D+	2017	109.26	3.58	Cash	3%
Q2-18	C-	C	C-	2016	108.02	2.55	Stocks	0%
Q4-17	B-	A-	C	2015	107.82	0.47	US Stocks	0%
Q4-16	C	B-	C	2014	109.93	6.03	Bonds	96%
Q4-15	C	C+	C	2013	106.21	-2.14	US Bonds	89%
				2012	111.05	4.04	Other	0%

Services Offered: Dividend Investment Plan, CashInvestment Plan

Investment Strategy: The investment seeks to track the investment results of the Bloomberg Barclays U.S. Aggregate Bond Index. The index measures the performance of the total U.S. investment-grade bond market. The fund generally invests at least 90% of its net assets in component securities of its underlying index and in investments that have economic characteristics that are substantially identical to the economic characteristics of the component securities of its underlying index. **Top Holdings:** Fnma 30yr 2016 Production   Gnma2 30yr 2017 Production   Gnma2 30yr 2016 Production   Fgold 30yr 2016 Production   United States Treasury Notes 2.13%

Vanguard Short-Term Bond Index Fund ETF Shares   C   HOLD

Ticker	Traded On	NAV	Total Assets ($)	Dividend Yield (TTM)	Turnover Ratio	Expense Ratio
BSV	NYSE Arca		$50,657,847,119	1.93	0	0.07

Ratings
Reward	D+
Risk	C+
Recent Upgrade/Downgrade	Up

Fund Information
Fund Type	Exchange Traded Funds
Category	US Fixed Income
Sub-Category	Short-Term Bond
Prospectus Objective	Income
Inception Date	Apr-07
Open to New Investments	Y

Prices
Price (as of 12/31/2018)	78.57
52-Week High	79.10
52-Week Low	77.67

Total Returns (%)

3-Month	6-Month	1-Year	3-Year	5-Year
1.36	1.63	1.22	3.89	6.23

3-Year Standard Deviation	1.28
Effective Duration	2.66

Valuation
Premium/Discount (1-Year Average)	0.02

Company Information
Provider	Vanguard
Manager/Tenure	Joshua C. Barrickman (5)
Website	http://www.vanguard.com
Address	Vanguard 100 Vanguard Boulevard Malvern PA 19355 United States
Phone Number	877-662-7447

PERFORMANCE

Ratings History				Asset & Performance History			Total Assets:	$50,657,847,119
Date	Overall Rating	Risk Rating	Reward Rating	Date	NAV	1-Year Total Return	Asset Allocation Asset	%
Q4-18	C	C+	D+	2017	79.09	1.2	Cash	1%
Q2-18	C-	C	D+	2016	79.44	1.41	Stocks	0%
Q4-17	C	B	C	2015	79.49	0.92	US Stocks	0%
Q4-16	C	C+	C	2014	79.87	1.32	Bonds	99%
Q4-15	C	C+	C	2013	79.89	0.17	US Bonds	87%
				2012	80.94	1.98	Other	0%

Services Offered:

Investment Strategy: The investment seeks to track the performance of Bloomberg Barclays U.S. 1-5 Year Government/Credit Float Adjusted Index. Bloomberg Barclays U.S. 1-5 Year Government/Credit Float Adjusted Index includes all medium and larger issues of U.S. government, investment-grade corporate, and investment-grade international dollar-denominated bonds that have maturities between 1 and 5 years and are publicly issued. All of its investments will be selected through the sampling process, and at least 80% of its assets will be invested in bonds held in the index. **Top Holdings:** United States Treasury Notes 1.25%   United States Treasury Notes 1.25%   United States Treasury Notes 1.5%   United States Treasury Notes 1.38%   United States Treasury Notes 1.38%

iShares Core MSCI Emerging Markets ETF

C-   HOLD

Ticker	Traded On	NAV	Total Assets ($)	Dividend Yield (TTM)	Turnover Ratio	Expense Ratio
IEMG	NYSE Arca	47.21	$49,952,654,546	2.87	6	0.14

Ratings
Reward	C-
Risk	C-
Recent Upgrade/Downgrade	Down

Fund Information
Fund Type	Exchange Traded Funds
Category	Global Emerg Mkts Equity
Sub-Category	Diversified Emerging Mkts
Prospectus Objective	Div Emerg Mkts
Inception Date	Oct-12
Open to New Investments	Y

Prices
Price (as of 12/31/2018)	47.15
52-Week High	62.69
52-Week Low	45.85

Total Returns (%)

3-Month	6-Month	1-Year	3-Year	5-Year
-7.19	-7.72	-14.69	28.32	8.29

3-Year Standard Deviation	14.58
Effective Duration	

Valuation
Premium/Discount (1-Year Average)	0.07

Company Information
Provider	iShares
Manager/Tenure	Diane Hsiung (6), Jennifer Hsui (6), Greg Savage (6), 1 other
Website	http://www.ishares.com
Address	iShares 400 Howard Street San Francisco CA 94105 United States
Phone Number	800-474-2737

PERFORMANCE

Ratings History

Date	Overall Rating	Risk Rating	Reward Rating
Q4-18	C-	C-	C-
Q2-18	C	C+	C
Q4-17	B-	C	B
Q4-16	D+	C-	D+
Q4-15	D+	D+	D+

Asset & Performance History

Date	NAV	1-Year Total Return
2017	56.82	36.77
2016	42.58	9.97
2015	39.62	-13.85
2014	47.06	-2.03
2013	49.14	-2.16
2012	51.17	

Total Assets: $49,952,654,546

Asset Allocation

Asset	%
Cash	0%
Stocks	100%
US Stocks	0%
Bonds	0%
US Bonds	0%
Other	0%

Services Offered:

Investment Strategy: The investment seeks to track the investment results of the MSCI Emerging Markets Investable Market Index. The fund generally will invest at least 90% of its assets in the component securities of the underlying index and in investments that have economic characteristics that are substantially identical to the component securities of the underlying index. The index is designed to measure large-, mid- and small-cap equity market performance in the global emerging markets. **Top Holdings:** Tencent Holdings Ltd   Alibaba Group Holding Ltd ADR   Taiwan Semiconductor Manufacturing Co Ltd   Samsung Electronics Co Ltd   Naspers Ltd Class N

---

iShares Core S&P Mid-Cap ETF

C   HOLD

Ticker	Traded On	NAV	Total Assets ($)	Dividend Yield (TTM)	Turnover Ratio	Expense Ratio
IJH	NYSE Arca	166.03	$47,619,802,367	1.54	10	0.07

Ratings
Reward	C-
Risk	C+
Recent Upgrade/Downgrade	Down

Fund Information
Fund Type	Exchange Traded Funds
Category	US Equity Mid Cap
Sub-Category	Mid-Cap Blend
Prospectus Objective	Growth
Inception Date	May-00
Open to New Investments	Y

Prices
Price (as of 12/31/2018)	166.06
52-Week High	204.98
52-Week Low	156.48

Total Returns (%)

3-Month	6-Month	1-Year	3-Year	5-Year
-16.65	-14.22	-11.14	24.54	33.50

3-Year Standard Deviation	11.85
Effective Duration	

Valuation
Premium/Discount (1-Year Average)	0.00

Company Information
Provider	iShares
Manager/Tenure	Diane Hsiung (10), Greg Savage (10), Jennifer Hsui (6), 3 others
Website	http://www.ishares.com
Address	iShares 400 Howard Street San Francisco CA 94105 United States
Phone Number	800-474-2737

PERFORMANCE

Ratings History

Date	Overall Rating	Risk Rating	Reward Rating
Q4-18	C	C+	C-
Q2-18	C+	C+	C+
Q4-17	B	B	B
Q4-16	B	C+	B
Q4-15	C	C+	C

Asset & Performance History

Date	NAV	1-Year Total Return
2017	189.67	16.18
2016	165.35	20.63
2015	139.44	-2.22
2014	144.77	9.63
2013	133.87	33.4
2012	101.79	17.75

Total Assets: $47,619,802,367

Asset Allocation

Asset	%
Cash	0%
Stocks	100%
US Stocks	100%
Bonds	0%
US Bonds	0%
Other	0%

Services Offered: CashInvestment Plan

Investment Strategy: The investment seeks to track the investment results of the S&P MidCap 400® (the "underlying index"), which measures the performance of the mid-capitalization sector of the U.S. equity market. The fund generally invests at least 90% of its assets in securities of the underlying index and in depositary receipts representing securities of the underlying index. It may invest the remainder of its assets in certain futures, options and swap contracts, cash and cash equivalents, as well as in securities not included in the underlying index, but which the advisor believes will help the fund track the underlying index. **Top Holdings:** Teleflex Inc   Domino's Pizza Inc   Atmos Energy Corp   IDEX Corp   STERIS PLC

iShares Russell 2000 ETF   C   HOLD

Ticker	Traded On	NAV	Total Assets ($)	Dividend Yield (TTM)	Turnover Ratio	Expense Ratio
IWM	NYSE Arca	134.01	$45,632,468,069	1.3	16	0.19

Ratings
Reward	C-
Risk	B-
Recent Upgrade/Downgrade	Down

Fund Information
Fund Type	Exchange Traded Funds
Category	US Equity Small Cap
Sub-Category	Small Blend
Prospectus Objective	Small Company
Inception Date	May-00
Open to New Investments	Y

Prices
Price (as of 12/31/2018)	133.90
52-Week High	173.02
52-Week Low	125.88

Total Returns (%)
3-Month	6-Month	1-Year	3-Year	5-Year
-19.08	-17.95	-11.02	23.80	24.30

3-Year Standard Deviation	14.59
Effective Duration	

Valuation
Premium/Discount (1-Year Average)	-0.01

Company Information
Provider	iShares
Manager/Tenure	Diane Hsiung (10), Greg Savage (10), Jennifer Hsui (6), 3 others
Website	http://www.ishares.com
Address	iShares 400 Howard Street San Francisco CA 94105 United States
Phone Number	800-474-2737

PERFORMANCE

Ratings History
Date	Overall Rating	Risk Rating	Reward Rating
Q4-18	C	B-	C-
Q2-18	B-	B	C+
Q4-17	B+	B	A-
Q4-16	B-	C+	B
Q4-15	C	C	C

Asset & Performance History
Date	NAV	1-Year Total Return
2017	152.44	14.65
2016	134.75	21.36
2015	112.76	-4.33
2014	119.6	4.94
2013	115.44	38.85
2012	84.28	16.38

Total Assets: $45,632,468,069
Asset Allocation
Asset	%
Cash	0%
Stocks	100%
US Stocks	99%
Bonds	0%
US Bonds	0%
Other	0%

Services Offered: CashInvestment Plan

Investment Strategy: The investment seeks to track the investment results of the Russell 2000® Index, which measures the performance of the small-capitalization sector of the U.S. equity market. The fund generally invests at least 90% of its assets in securities of the underlying index and in depositary receipts representing securities of the underlying index. It may invest the remainder of its assets in certain futures, options and swap contracts, cash and cash equivalents, as well as in securities not included in the underlying index, but which the advisor believes will help the fund track the underlying index. **Top Holdings:** Etsy Inc Integrated Device Technology Inc Five Below Inc Haemonetics Corp HubSpot Inc

---

iShares Core S&P Small-Cap ETF   C   HOLD

Ticker	Traded On	NAV	Total Assets ($)	Dividend Yield (TTM)	Turnover Ratio	Expense Ratio
IJR	NYSE Arca	69.35	$42,978,854,042	1.31	12	0.07

Ratings
Reward	C-
Risk	B-
Recent Upgrade/Downgrade	Down

Fund Information
Fund Type	Exchange Traded Funds
Category	US Equity Small Cap
Sub-Category	Small Blend
Prospectus Objective	Small Company
Inception Date	May-00
Open to New Investments	Y

Prices
Price (as of 12/31/2018)	69.32
52-Week High	90.31
52-Week Low	65.14

Total Returns (%)
3-Month	6-Month	1-Year	3-Year	5-Year
-18.92	-16.30	-12.23	25.67	30.14

3-Year Standard Deviation	14.71
Effective Duration	

Valuation
Premium/Discount (1-Year Average)	0.01

Company Information
Provider	iShares
Manager/Tenure	Diane Hsiung (10), Greg Savage (10), Jennifer Hsui (6), 3 others
Website	http://www.ishares.com
Address	iShares 400 Howard Street San Francisco CA 94105 United States
Phone Number	800-474-2737

PERFORMANCE

Ratings History
Date	Overall Rating	Risk Rating	Reward Rating
Q4-18	C	B-	C-
Q2-18	B	B+	B
Q4-17	A-	B	A
Q4-16	B	C+	B+
Q4-15	C+	C+	C

Asset & Performance History
Date	NAV	1-Year Total Return
2017	76.79	13.19
2016	68.72	26.49
2015	55.07	-1.99
2014	57	5.66
2013	54.63	41.36
2012	39.09	16.27

Total Assets: $42,978,854,042
Asset Allocation
Asset	%
Cash	0%
Stocks	100%
US Stocks	99%
Bonds	0%
US Bonds	0%
Other	0%

Services Offered: CashInvestment Plan

Investment Strategy: The investment seeks to track the investment results of the S&P SmallCap 600 (the "underlying index"), which measures the performance of the small-capitalization sector of the U.S. equity market. The fund generally invests at least 90% of its assets in securities of the underlying index and in depositary receipts representing securities of the underlying index. It may invest the remainder of its assets in certain futures, options and swap contracts, cash and cash equivalents, as well as in securities not included in the underlying index, but which the advisor believes will help the fund track the underlying index. **Top Holdings:** First Financial Bankshares Inc Ingevity Corp Spire Inc Amedisys Inc FirstCash Inc

iShares Russell 1000 Growth ETF
C   HOLD

Ticker	Traded On	NAV	Total Assets ($)	Dividend Yield (TTM)	Turnover Ratio	Expense Ratio
IWF	NYSE Arca	130.78	$41,687,846,120	1.13	13	0.2

Ratings
Reward   C
Risk   C+
Recent Upgrade/Downgrade   Down

Fund Information
Fund Type	Exchange Traded Funds
Category	US Equity Large Cap Growth
Sub-Category	Large Growth
Prospectus Objective	Growth
Inception Date	May-00
Open to New Investments	Y

Prices
Price (as of 12/31/2018)	130.91
52-Week High	156.36
52-Week Low	121.77

Total Returns (%)
3-Month	6-Month	1-Year	3-Year	5-Year
-16.13	-8.78	-1.69	36.58	62.57

3-Year Standard Deviation   11.01
Effective Duration

Valuation
Premium/Discount (1-Year Average)   -0.01

Company Information
Provider	iShares
Manager/Tenure	Diane Hsiung (10), Greg Savage (10), Jennifer Hsui (6), 3 others
Website	http://www.ishares.com
Address	iShares 400 Howard Street San Francisco CA 94105 United States
Phone Number	800-474-2737

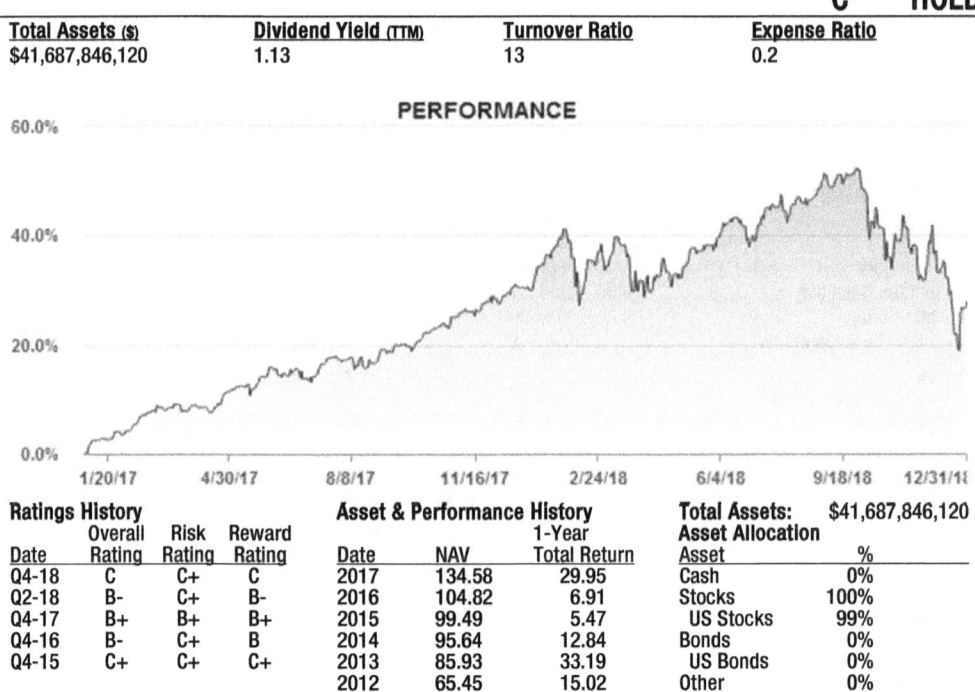

PERFORMANCE

Ratings History

Date	Overall Rating	Risk Rating	Reward Rating
Q4-18	C	C+	C
Q2-18	B-	C+	B-
Q4-17	B+	B+	B+
Q4-16	B-	C+	B
Q4-15	C+	C+	C+

Asset & Performance History

Date	NAV	1-Year Total Return
2017	134.58	29.95
2016	104.82	6.91
2015	99.49	5.47
2014	95.64	12.84
2013	85.93	33.19
2012	65.45	15.02

Total Assets: $41,687,846,120
Asset Allocation

Asset	%
Cash	0%
Stocks	100%
US Stocks	99%
Bonds	0%
US Bonds	0%
Other	0%

Services Offered: CashInvestment Plan

Investment Strategy: The investment seeks to track the investment results of the Russell 1000® Growth Index, which measures the performance of large- and mid-capitalization growth sectors of the U.S. equity market. The fund generally invests at least 90% of its assets in securities of the underlying index and in depositary receipts representing securities of the underlying index. It may invest the remainder of its assets in certain futures, options and swap contracts, cash and cash equivalents, as well as in securities not included in the underlying index, but which the advisor believes will help the fund track the underlying index. **Top Holdings:** Apple Inc   Microsoft Corp   Amazon.com Inc   Facebook Inc A   Alphabet Inc Class C

---

iShares Russell 1000 Value ETF
C+   HOLD

Ticker	Traded On	NAV	Total Assets ($)	Dividend Yield (TTM)	Turnover Ratio	Expense Ratio
IWD	NYSE Arca	110.94	$39,099,203,872	2.28	15	0.2

Ratings
Reward   C
Risk   B
Recent Upgrade/Downgrade

Fund Information
Fund Type	Exchange Traded Funds
Category	US Equity Large Cap Value
Sub-Category	Large Value
Prospectus Objective	Growth
Inception Date	May-00
Open to New Investments	Y

Prices
Price (as of 12/31/2018)	111.05
52-Week High	131.54
52-Week Low	104.79

Total Returns (%)
3-Month	6-Month	1-Year	3-Year	5-Year
-12.01	-6.77	-8.39	21.70	32.34

3-Year Standard Deviation   9.31
Effective Duration

Valuation
Premium/Discount (1-Year Average)   0.01

Company Information
Provider	iShares
Manager/Tenure	Diane Hsiung (10), Greg Savage (10), Jennifer Hsui (6), 3 others
Website	http://www.ishares.com
Address	iShares 400 Howard Street San Francisco CA 94105 United States
Phone Number	800-474-2737

PERFORMANCE

Ratings History

Date	Overall Rating	Risk Rating	Reward Rating
Q4-18	C+	B	C
Q2-18	C	C+	C
Q4-17	B-	B	B-
Q4-16	B	B-	B
Q4-15	C+	C+	C

Asset & Performance History

Date	NAV	1-Year Total Return
2017	124.19	13.46
2016	111.88	17.09
2015	97.87	-3.94
2014	104.39	13.2
2013	94.13	32.17
2012	72.74	17.27

Total Assets: $39,099,203,872
Asset Allocation

Asset	%
Cash	0%
Stocks	100%
US Stocks	98%
Bonds	0%
US Bonds	0%
Other	0%

Services Offered: CashInvestment Plan

Investment Strategy: The investment seeks to track the investment results of the Russell 1000® Value Index (the "underlying index"), which measures the performance of large- and mid- capitalization value sectors of the U.S. equity market. The fund generally invests at least 90% of its assets in securities of the underlying index and in depositary receipts representing securities of the underlying index. It may invest the remainder of its assets in certain futures, options and swap contracts, cash and cash equivalents, as well as in securities not included in the underlying index, but which the advisor believes will help the fund track the underlying index. **Top Holdings:** JPMorgan Chase & Co   Berkshire Hathaway Inc B   Exxon Mobil Corp   Johnson & Johnson   Pfizer Inc

Vanguard Dividend Appreciation Index Fund ETF Shares   C+   HOLD

Ticker	Traded On	NAV	Total Assets ($)	Dividend Yield (TTM)	Turnover Ratio	Expense Ratio
VIG	NYSE Arca		$39,092,161,585	1.86	14	0.08

Ratings
Reward   C
Risk   C+
Recent Upgrade/Downgrade

Fund Information
Fund Type   Exchange Traded Funds
Category   US Equity Large Cap Blend
Sub-Category   Large Blend
Prospectus Objective Equity-Income
Inception Date   Apr-06
Open to New Investments Y

Prices
Price (as of 12/31/2018)   97.95
52-Week High   112.45
52-Week Low   92.08

Total Returns (%)

3-Month	6-Month	1-Year	3-Year	5-Year
-12.17	-3.74	-3.01	32.56	43.05

3-Year Standard Deviation   8.87
Effective Duration

Valuation
Premium/Discount (1-Year Average)   0.01

Company Information
Provider   Vanguard
Manager/Tenure Walter Nejman (2), Gerard C. O'Reilly (2)
Website   http://www.vanguard.com
Address   Vanguard 100 Vanguard Boulevard
                Malvern PA 19355 United States
Phone Number   877-662-7447

PERFORMANCE

Ratings History

Date	Overall Rating	Risk Rating	Reward Rating
Q4-18	C+	C+	C
Q2-18	C+	C+	C
Q4-17	B	B+	B
Q4-16	B-	C+	B-
Q4-15	C+	C+	C+

Asset & Performance History

Date	NAV	1-Year Total Return
2017	101.93	22.06
2016	85.1	11.17
2015	77.78	-1.94
2014	81.18	10.05
2013	75.27	28.98
2012	59.54	11.61

Total Assets: $39,092,161,585
Asset Allocation

Asset	%
Cash	0%
Stocks	100%
US Stocks	99%
Bonds	0%
US Bonds	0%
Other	0%

Services Offered:

Investment Strategy: The investment seeks to track the performance of a benchmark index that measures the investment return of common stocks of companies that have a record of increasing dividends over time. The fund employs an indexing investment approach designed to track the performance of the Nasdaq US Dividend Achievers Select Index, which consists of common stocks of companies that have a record of increasing dividends over time. The adviser attempts to replicate the target index by investing all, or substantially all, of its assets in the stocks that make up the index, holding each stock in approximately the same proportion as its weighting in the index. **Top Holdings:** Microsoft Corp Walmart Inc Johnson & Johnson PepsiCo Inc McDonald's Corp

---

Vanguard FTSE All-World ex-US Index Fund ETF Shares   C-   HOLD

Ticker	Traded On	NAV	Total Assets ($)	Dividend Yield (TTM)	Turnover Ratio	Expense Ratio
VEU	NYSE Arca		$35,373,181,875	3.11	4	0.11

Ratings
Reward   D+
Risk   C
Recent Upgrade/Downgrade   Down

Fund Information
Fund Type   Exchange Traded Funds
Category   Global Equity Large Cap
Sub-Category   Foreign Large Blend
Prospectus Objective Foreign Stock
Inception Date   Mar-07
Open to New Investments Y

Prices
Price (as of 12/31/2018)   45.58
52-Week High   58.89
52-Week Low   44.23

Total Returns (%)

3-Month	6-Month	1-Year	3-Year	5-Year
-11.83	-10.98	-14.32	14.23	4.49

3-Year Standard Deviation   11
Effective Duration

Valuation
Premium/Discount (1-Year Average)   0.09

Company Information
Provider   Vanguard
Manager/Tenure Christine D. Franquin (2), Justin E. Hales (2)
Website   http://www.vanguard.com
Address   Vanguard 100 Vanguard Boulevard
                Malvern PA 19355 United States
Phone Number   877-662-7447

PERFORMANCE

Ratings History

Date	Overall Rating	Risk Rating	Reward Rating
Q4-18	C-	C	D+
Q2-18	C	C+	C
Q4-17	B-	B-	B-
Q4-16	C-	C	D+
Q4-15	C	C+	C-

Asset & Performance History

Date	NAV	1-Year Total Return
2017	54.64	27.44
2016	44.16	3.81
2015	43.45	-4.67
2014	46.85	-4.04
2013	50.46	14.49
2012	45.38	18.54

Total Assets: $35,373,181,875
Asset Allocation

Asset	%
Cash	3%
Stocks	97%
US Stocks	1%
Bonds	0%
US Bonds	0%
Other	0%

Services Offered:

Investment Strategy: The investment seeks to track the performance of a benchmark index that measures the investment return of stocks of companies located in developed and emerging markets outside of the United States. The fund employs an indexing investment approach designed to track the performance of the FTSE All-World ex US Index, a float-adjusted, market-capitalization-weighted index designed to measure equity market performance of international markets, excluding the United States. The index included 2,539 stocks of companies located in 46 countries, including both developed and emerging markets. **Top Holdings:** Nestle SA Tencent Holdings Ltd Novartis AG Roche Holding AG Dividend Right Cert. HSBC Holdings PLC

Vanguard High Dividend Yield Index Fund ETF Shares   C   HOLD

Ticker	Traded On	NAV	Total Assets ($)	Dividend Yield (TTM)	Turnover Ratio	Expense Ratio
VYM	NYSE Arca		$30,925,412,462	2.96	9	0.08

Ratings

Reward	C
Risk	C+
Recent Upgrade/Downgrade	Down

Fund Information

Fund Type	Exchange Traded Funds
Category	US Equity Large Cap Value
Sub-Category	Large Value
Prospectus Objective	Equity-Income
Inception Date	Nov-06
Open to New Investments	Y

Prices

Price (as of 12/31/2018)	77.99
52-Week High	90.91
52-Week Low	73.71

Total Returns (%)

3-Month	6-Month	1-Year	3-Year	5-Year
-10.67	-5.19	-6.59	27.08	44.68

3-Year Standard Deviation	8.26
Effective Duration	

Valuation

Premium/Discount (1-Year Average)	0.02

Company Information

Provider	Vanguard
Manager/Tenure	William A. Coleman (2), Gerard C. O'Reilly (2)
Website	http://www.vanguard.com
Address	Vanguard 100 Vanguard Boulevard Malvern PA 19355 United States
Phone Number	877-662-7447

PERFORMANCE

Ratings History

Date	Overall Rating	Risk Rating	Reward Rating
Q4-18	C	C+	C
Q2-18	C	C+	C
Q4-17	B	B+	B-
Q4-16	B-	C+	B
Q4-15	C+	C+	C+

Asset & Performance History

Date	NAV	1-Year Total Return
2017	85.53	16.47
2016	75.68	16.19
2015	66.77	0.33
2014	68.73	13.47
2013	62.33	30.26
2012	49.32	12.67

Total Assets: $30,925,412,462

Asset Allocation

Asset	%
Cash	0%
Stocks	100%
US Stocks	98%
Bonds	0%
US Bonds	0%
Other	0%

Services Offered:

Investment Strategy: The investment seeks to track the performance of a benchmark index that measures the investment return of common stocks of companies that are characterized by high dividend yield. The fund employs an indexing investment approach designed to track the performance of the FTSE High Dividend Yield Index, which consists of common stocks of companies that pay dividends that generally are higher than average. The adviser attempts to replicate the target index by investing all, or substantially all, of its assets in the stocks that make up the index, holding each stock in approximately the same proportion as its weighting in the index. **Top Holdings:** Johnson & Johnson JPMorgan Chase & Co Exxon Mobil Corp Pfizer Inc Verizon Communications Inc

---

Vanguard Intermediate-Term Bond Index Fund ETF Shares   C-   HOLD

Ticker	Traded On	NAV	Total Assets ($)	Dividend Yield (TTM)	Turnover Ratio	Expense Ratio
BIV	NYSE Arca		$30,879,308,623	2.88	55	0.07

Ratings

Reward	D
Risk	C
Recent Upgrade/Downgrade	

Fund Information

Fund Type	Exchange Traded Funds
Category	US Fixed Income
Sub-Category	Intermediate-Term Bond
Prospectus Objective	Income
Inception Date	Apr-07
Open to New Investments	Y

Prices

Price (as of 12/31/2018)	81.29
52-Week High	83.83
52-Week Low	79.35

Total Returns (%)

3-Month	6-Month	1-Year	3-Year	5-Year
1.92	2.01	-0.33	6.40	15.25

3-Year Standard Deviation	3.55
Effective Duration	6.17

Valuation

Premium/Discount (1-Year Average)	0.03

Company Information

Provider	Vanguard
Manager/Tenure	Joshua C. Barrickman (10)
Website	http://www.vanguard.com
Address	Vanguard 100 Vanguard Boulevard Malvern PA 19355 United States
Phone Number	877-662-7447

PERFORMANCE

Ratings History

Date	Overall Rating	Risk Rating	Reward Rating
Q4-18	C-	C	D
Q2-18	C-	C	D+
Q4-17	B-	B+	C
Q4-16	C	C+	C
Q4-15	C	C+	C

Asset & Performance History

Date	NAV	1-Year Total Return
2017	83.73	3.76
2016	82.86	2.43
2015	82.95	1.22
2014	84.41	6.99
2013	81.65	-3.43
2012	88.07	7.01

Total Assets: $30,879,308,623

Asset Allocation

Asset	%
Cash	1%
Stocks	0%
US Stocks	0%
Bonds	98%
US Bonds	89%
Other	0%

Services Offered:

Investment Strategy: The investment seeks the performance of the Bloomberg Barclays U.S. 5-10 Year Government/Credit Float Adjusted Index. Bloomberg Barclays U.S. 5-10 Year Government/Credit Float Adjusted Index includes all medium and larger issues of U.S. government, investment-grade corporate and investment-grade international dollar-denominated bonds that have maturities between 5 and 10 years and are publicly issued. All of its investments will be selected through the sampling process, and at least 80% of its assets will be invested in bonds held in the index. **Top Holdings:** United States Treasury Notes 2.12% United States Treasury Notes 2.88% United States Treasury Notes 2.5% United States Treasury Notes 2.25% United States Treasury Notes 1.62%

iShares iBoxx $ Investment Grade Corporate Bond ETF   C   HOLD

Ticker	Traded On	NAV	Total Assets ($)	Dividend Yield (TTM)	Turnover Ratio	Expense Ratio
LQD	NYSE Arca	112.69	$29,908,019,302	3.6	10	0.15

Ratings
Reward	D+
Risk	C+
Recent Upgrade/Downgrade	

Fund Information
Fund Type	Exchange Traded Funds
Category	US Fixed Income
Sub-Category	Corporate Bond
Prospectus Objective	Corp Bond - Gen
Inception Date	Jul-02
Open to New Investments	Y

Prices
Price (as of 12/31/2018)	112.82
52-Week High	121.56
52-Week Low	111.35

Total Returns (%)
3-Month	6-Month	1-Year	3-Year	5-Year
-0.51	0.67	-3.75	9.29	17.37

3-Year Standard Deviation	4.51
Effective Duration	8.27

Valuation
Premium/Discount (1-Year Average)	0.04

Company Information
Provider	iShares
Manager/Tenure	Scott Radell (8), James Mauro (7)
Website	http://www.ishares.com
Address	iShares 400 Howard Street San Francisco CA 94105 United States
Phone Number	800-474-2737

PERFORMANCE

Ratings History
Date	Overall Rating	Risk Rating	Reward Rating
Q4-18	C	C+	D+
Q2-18	C	C	C-
Q4-17	B-	B+	C
Q4-16	B-	B+	C
Q4-15	C	C	C

Asset & Performance History
Date	NAV	1-Year Total Return
2017	121.39	7.15
2016	116.91	5.97
2015	114.01	-1.07
2014	119.2	8.56
2013	113.62	-2.49
2012	121	11.68

Total Assets: $29,908,019,302

Asset Allocation
Asset	%
Cash	0%
Stocks	0%
US Stocks	0%
Bonds	99%
US Bonds	85%
Other	0%

Services Offered:

Investment Strategy: The investment seeks to track the investment results of the Markit iBoxx® USD Liquid Investment Grade Index composed of U.S. dollar-denominated, investment-grade corporate bonds. The fund generally invests at least 90% of its assets in securities of the underlying index and at least 95% of its assets in investment-grade corporate bonds. The underlying index is designed to provide a broad representation of the U.S. dollar-denominated liquid investment-grade corporate bond market. **Top Holdings:** Verizon Communications Inc. 4.33% Anheuser-Busch Companies LLC / Anheuser-Busch InBev Worldwide Inc 3.65% Anheuser-Busch Companies LLC / Anheuser-Busch InBev Worldwide Inc 4.9% GE Capital International Funding Company Unlimited Company 4.42% CVS Health Corp 4.3%

---

iShares MSCI Emerging Markets ETF   C-   HOLD

Ticker	Traded On	NAV	Total Assets ($)	Dividend Yield (TTM)	Turnover Ratio	Expense Ratio
EEM	NYSE Arca	39.17	$29,838,462,577	2.41	16	0.67

Ratings
Reward	C-
Risk	C-
Recent Upgrade/Downgrade	Down

Fund Information
Fund Type	Exchange Traded Funds
Category	Global Emerg Mkts Equity
Sub-Category	Diversified Emerging Mkts
Prospectus Objective	Div Emerg Mkts
Inception Date	Apr-03
Open to New Investments	Y

Prices
Price (as of 12/31/2018)	39.06
52-Week High	52.08
52-Week Low	38.00

Total Returns (%)
3-Month	6-Month	1-Year	3-Year	5-Year
-7.43	-7.79	-14.98	28.17	5.35

3-Year Standard Deviation	14.77
Effective Duration	

Valuation
Premium/Discount (1-Year Average)	-0.02

Company Information
Provider	iShares
Manager/Tenure	Diane Hsiung (10), Greg Savage (10), Jennifer Hsui (5), 1 other
Website	http://www.ishares.com
Address	iShares 400 Howard Street San Francisco CA 94105 United States
Phone Number	800-474-2737

PERFORMANCE

Ratings History
Date	Overall Rating	Risk Rating	Reward Rating
Q4-18	C-	C-	C-
Q2-18	C	C+	C
Q4-17	B-	C	B
Q4-16	D+	C-	D+
Q4-15	D+	D+	D+

Asset & Performance History
Date	NAV	1-Year Total Return
2017	47.07	36.42
2016	35.19	10.51
2015	32.46	-15.41
2014	39.26	-2.82
2013	41.3	-3.13
2012	43.58	17.32

Total Assets: $29,838,462,577

Asset Allocation
Asset	%
Cash	0%
Stocks	100%
US Stocks	0%
Bonds	0%
US Bonds	0%
Other	0%

Services Offered: Dividend Investment Plan, CashInvestment Plan

Investment Strategy: The investment seeks to track the investment results of the MSCI Emerging Markets Index. The fund generally invests at least 90% of its assets in the securities of its underlying index and in depositary receipts representing securities in its underlying index. The index is designed to measure equity market performance in the global emerging markets. It may invest the remainder of its assets in other securities, including securities not in the underlying index, but which BFA believes will help the fund track the index, and in other investments, including futures contracts, options on futures contracts, other types of options and swaps related to its index. **Top Holdings:** Tencent Holdings Ltd Alibaba Group Holding Ltd ADR Taiwan Semiconductor Manufacturing Co Ltd Samsung Electronics Co Ltd Naspers Ltd Class N

SPDR® Gold Shares   D+   SELL

Ticker	Traded On	NAV
GLD	NYSE Arca	121.16

Total Assets ($)	Dividend Yield (TTM)	Turnover Ratio	Expense Ratio
$29,808,972,862	0	0	0.4

Ratings
Reward	D
Risk	C-
Recent Upgrade/Downgrade	Down

Fund Information
Fund Type	Exchange Traded Funds
Category	Commodities Specified
Sub-Category	Commodities Precious Metals
Prospectus Objective	Prec Metals
Inception Date	Nov-04
Open to New Investments	Y

Prices
Price (as of 12/31/2018)	121.25
52-Week High	128.83
52-Week Low	111.10

Total Returns (%)
3-Month	6-Month	1-Year	3-Year	5-Year
7.65	2.50	-1.54	19.22	4.56

3-Year Standard Deviation	12.62
Effective Duration	

Valuation
Premium/Discount (1-Year Average)	0.12

Company Information
Provider	SPDR State Street Global Advisors
Manager/Tenure	Management Team (14)
Website	http://www.spdrs.com
Address	SPDR State Street Global Advisors
	State Street Financial Center, 1
	Lincoln Street Boston MA 02111-2900
	United States
Phone Number	617-786-3000

PERFORMANCE

Ratings History
Date	Overall Rating	Risk Rating	Reward Rating
Q4-18	D+	C-	D
Q2-18	C	B-	C-
Q4-17	C-	C-	C-
Q4-16	C-	D+	C-
Q4-15	D	D	D

Asset & Performance History
Date	NAV	1-Year Total Return
2017	123.06	11.41
2016	110.45	8.68
2015	101.62	-11.78
2014	115.2	-0.58
2013	115.87	-28.09
2012	161.14	5.26

Total Assets: $29,808,972,862

Asset Allocation
Asset	%
Cash	0%
Stocks	0%
US Stocks	0%
Bonds	0%
US Bonds	0%
Other	100%

Services Offered:

Investment Strategy: **Top Holdings:** Gold Trust

Vanguard Small-Cap Value Index Fund ETF Shares   C   HOLD

Ticker	Traded On	NAV
VBR	NYSE Arca	

Total Assets ($)	Dividend Yield (TTM)	Turnover Ratio	Expense Ratio
$29,528,383,381	2.1	19	0.07

Ratings
Reward	C-
Risk	C+
Recent Upgrade/Downgrade	Down

Fund Information
Fund Type	Exchange Traded Funds
Category	US Equity Small Cap
Sub-Category	Small Value
Prospectus Objective	Small Company
Inception Date	Jan-04
Open to New Investments	Y

Prices
Price (as of 12/31/2018)	114.06
52-Week High	142.94
52-Week Low	107.94

Total Returns (%)
3-Month	6-Month	1-Year	3-Year	5-Year
-17.36	-15.66	-12.82	21.61	28.17

3-Year Standard Deviation	12.81
Effective Duration	

Valuation
Premium/Discount (1-Year Average)	0.03

Company Information
Provider	Vanguard
Manager/Tenure	William A. Coleman (2), Gerard C. O'Reilly (2)
Website	http://www.vanguard.com
Address	Vanguard 100 Vanguard Boulevard
	Malvern PA 19355 United States
Phone Number	877-662-7447

PERFORMANCE

Ratings History
Date	Overall Rating	Risk Rating	Reward Rating
Q4-18	C	C+	C-
Q2-18	C+	C+	C+
Q4-17	B	B	B
Q4-16	B	C+	B
Q4-15	C	C+	C

Asset & Performance History
Date	NAV	1-Year Total Return
2017	132.71	12.03
2016	120.95	24.08
2015	98.81	-4.66
2014	105.71	10.55
2013	97.32	36.57
2012	72.6	18.77

Total Assets: $29,528,383,381

Asset Allocation
Asset	%
Cash	1%
Stocks	99%
US Stocks	98%
Bonds	0%
US Bonds	0%
Other	0%

Services Offered:

Investment Strategy: The investment seeks to track the performance of a benchmark index that measures the investment return of small-capitalization value stocks. The fund employs an indexing investment approach designed to track the performance of the CRSP US Small Cap Value Index, a broadly diversified index of value stocks of small U.S. companies. The advisor attempts to replicate the target index by investing all, or substantially all, of its assets in the stocks that make up the index, holding each stock in approximately the same proportion as its weighting in the index. **Top Holdings:** NRG Energy Inc Atmos Energy Corp Leidos Holdings Inc IDEX Corp PerkinElmer Inc

Financial Select Sector SPDR® Fund

C+   HOLD

Ticker	Traded On	NAV	Total Assets ($)	Dividend Yield (TTM)	Turnover Ratio	Expense Ratio
XLF	NYSE Arca	23.82	$29,463,234,036	1.77	3	0.13

Ratings
Reward   C
Risk   C+
Recent Upgrade/Downgrade   Down

Fund Information
Fund Type	Exchange Traded Funds
Category	Financials Sector Equity
Sub-Category	Financial
Prospectus Objective	Financial
Inception Date	Dec-98
Open to New Investments	Y

Prices
Price (as of 12/31/2018)	23.82
52-Week High	30.17
52-Week Low	22.31

Total Returns (%)
3-Month	6-Month	1-Year	3-Year	5-Year
-13.38	-9.92	-13.08	29.98	47.11

3-Year Standard Deviation   14.88
Effective Duration

Valuation
Premium/Discount (1-Year Average)   0.00

Company Information
Provider   SPDR State Street Global Advisors
Manager/Tenure Michael J. Feehily (7), Karl A.
Schneider (3), Melissa Kapitulik (1)
Website   http://www.spdrs.com
Address   SPDR State Street Global Advisors
State Street Financial Center, 1
Lincoln Street Boston MA 02111-2900
United States
Phone Number   617-786-3000

PERFORMANCE

Ratings History
Date	Overall Rating	Risk Rating	Reward Rating
Q4-18	C+	C+	C
Q2-18	B-	C+	B
Q4-17	A-	B	A
Q4-16	B	C+	B
Q4-15	B	A	B

Asset & Performance History
Date	NAV	1-Year Total Return
2017	27.92	22.02
2016	23.26	21.15
2015	19.36	-1.6
2014	20.06	15.02
2013	17.74	35.36
2012	13.32	28.53

Total Assets: $29,463,234,036
Asset Allocation
Asset	%
Cash	0%
Stocks	100%
US Stocks	98%
Bonds	0%
US Bonds	0%
Other	0%

Services Offered: Dividend Investment Plan, CashInvestment Plan

Investment Strategy: The investment seeks investment results that, before expenses, correspond generally to the price and yield performance of publicly traded equity securities of companies in the Financial Select Sector Index. The fund generally invests substantially all, but at least 95%, of its total assets in the securities comprising the index. The index includes securities of companies from the following industries: diversified financial services; insurance; banks; capital markets; mortgage real estate investment trusts ("REITs"); consumer finance; and thrifts and mortgage finance. The fund is non-diversified. **Top Holdings:** Berkshire Hathaway Inc B JPMorgan Chase & Co Bank of America Corporation Wells Fargo & Co Citigroup Inc

---

Vanguard Short-Term Inflation-Protected Securities Index Fund ETF Shares

C   HOLD

Ticker	Traded On	NAV	Total Assets ($)	Dividend Yield (TTM)	Turnover Ratio	Expense Ratio
VTIP	NAS CM		$27,051,625,088	3.24	25	0.06

Ratings
Reward   C-
Risk   C+
Recent Upgrade/Downgrade

Fund Information
Fund Type	Exchange Traded Funds
Category	US Fixed Income
Sub-Category	Inflation-Protected Bond
Prospectus Objective	Govt Bond - Treasury
Inception Date	Oct-12
Open to New Investments	Y

Prices
Price (as of 12/31/2018)	47.92
52-Week High	49.05
52-Week Low	47.71

Total Returns (%)
3-Month	6-Month	1-Year	3-Year	5-Year
-0.31	-0.24	0.45	4.02	2.66

3-Year Standard Deviation   1.29
Effective Duration   2.67

Valuation
Premium/Discount (1-Year Average)   0.07

Company Information
Provider   Vanguard
Manager/Tenure Joshua C. Barrickman (6)
Website   http://www.vanguard.com
Address   Vanguard 100 Vanguard Boulevard
Malvern PA 19355 United States
Phone Number   877-662-7447

PERFORMANCE

Ratings History
Date	Overall Rating	Risk Rating	Reward Rating
Q4-18	C	C+	C-
Q2-18	C	C+	C
Q4-17	C	B-	C
Q4-16	C	C+	C
Q4-15	D+	C	D

Asset & Performance History
Date	NAV	1-Year Total Return
2017	48.77	0.77
2016	49.11	2.75
2015	48.18	-0.14
2014	48.25	-1.16
2013	49.22	-1.55
2012	50.02	

Total Assets: $27,051,625,088
Asset Allocation
Asset	%
Cash	3%
Stocks	0%
US Stocks	0%
Bonds	97%
US Bonds	97%
Other	0%

Services Offered:

Investment Strategy: The investment seeks to track the performance of a benchmark index that measures the investment return of inflation-protected public obligations of the U.S. Treasury with remaining maturities of less than 5 years. The fund employs an indexing investment approach designed to track the performance of the Bloomberg Barclays U.S. Treasury Inflation-Protected Securities (TIPS) 0-5 Year Index. The index is a market-capitalization-weighted index that includes all inflation-protected public obligations issued by the U.S. Treasury with remaining maturities of less than 5 years. **Top Holdings:** United States Treasury Notes 0.12% United States Treasury Notes 0.12% United States Treasury Notes 0.12% United States Treasury Notes 0.12% United States Treasury Notes 0.12% United States Treasury Notes 0.12%

Vanguard Short-Term Corporate Bond Index Fund ETF Shares   C   HOLD

Ticker	Traded On	NAV	Total Assets ($)	Dividend Yield (TTM)	Turnover Ratio	Expense Ratio
VCSH	NAS CM		$25,894,200,688	2.59	56	0.07

Ratings
Reward   C
Risk   C+
Recent Upgrade/Downgrade

Fund Information
Fund Type	Exchange Traded Funds
Category	US Fixed Income
Sub-Category	Short-Term Bond
Prospectus Objective	Corp Bond - Gen
Inception Date	Nov-09
Open to New Investments	Y

Prices
Price (as of 12/31/2018)	77.94
52-Week High	79.30
52-Week Low	77.54

Total Returns (%)
3-Month	6-Month	1-Year	3-Year	5-Year
0.63	1.34	0.77	5.96	9.38

3-Year Standard Deviation	1.39
Effective Duration	2.65

Valuation
Premium/Discount (1-Year Average)	0.04

Company Information
Provider	Vanguard
Manager/Tenure	Joshua C. Barrickman (9)
Website	http://www.vanguard.com
Address	Vanguard 100 Vanguard Boulevard
	Malvern PA 19355 United States
Phone Number	877-662-7447

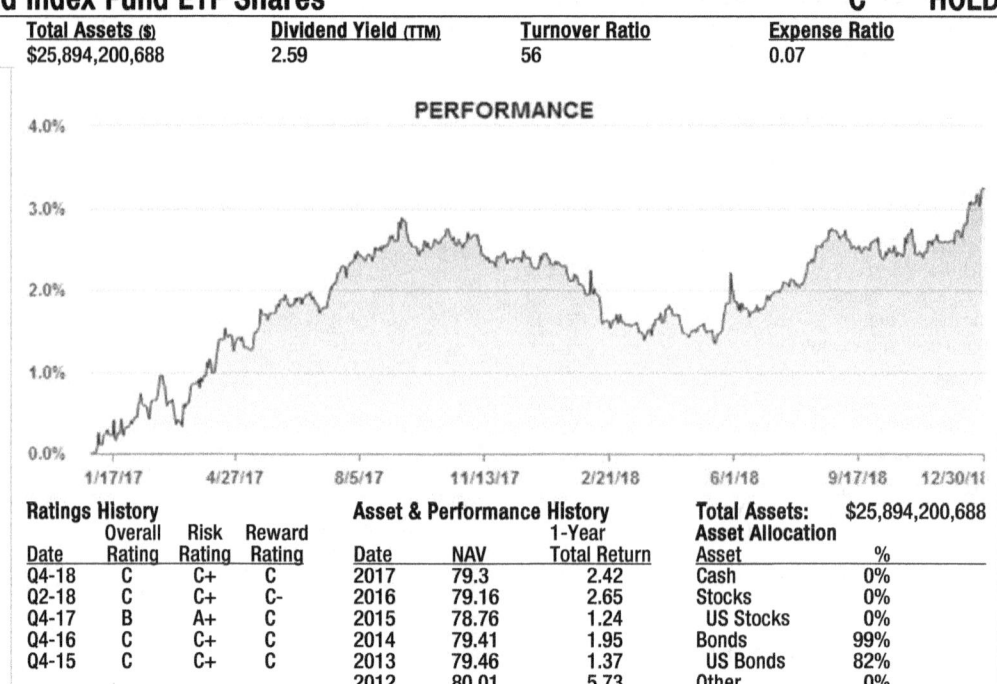

PERFORMANCE

Ratings History
Date	Overall Rating	Risk Rating	Reward Rating
Q4-18	C	C+	C
Q2-18	C	C+	C-
Q4-17	B	A+	C
Q4-16	C	C+	C
Q4-15	C	C+	C

Asset & Performance History
Date	NAV	1-Year Total Return
2017	79.3	2.42
2016	79.16	2.65
2015	78.76	1.24
2014	79.41	1.95
2013	79.46	1.37
2012	80.01	5.73

Total Assets: $25,894,200,688

Asset Allocation
Asset	%
Cash	0%
Stocks	0%
US Stocks	0%
Bonds	99%
US Bonds	82%
Other	0%

Services Offered:

Investment Strategy: The investment seeks to track the performance of a market-weighted corporate bond index with a short-term dollar-weighted average maturity. The fund employs an indexing investment approach designed to track the performance of the Bloomberg Barclays U.S. 1-5 Year Corporate Bond Index. This index includes U.S. dollar-denominated, investment-grade, fixed-rate, taxable securities issued by industrial, utility, and financial companies, with maturities between 1 and 5 years. Under normal circumstances, at least 80% of the fund's assets will be invested in bonds included in the index. **Top Holdings:** Anheuser-Busch InBev Finance Inc. 2.65%   CVS Health Corp 3.7%   Anheuser-Busch InBev Finance Inc. 3.3%   Bank of America Corporation 3%   GE Capital International Funding Company Unlimited Company 2.34%

Vanguard Small-Cap Growth Index Fund ETF Shares   C   HOLD

Ticker	Traded On	NAV	Total Assets ($)	Dividend Yield (TTM)	Turnover Ratio	Expense Ratio
VBK	NYSE Arca		$22,703,440,767	0.78	19	0.07

Ratings
Reward   C-
Risk   C+
Recent Upgrade/Downgrade   Down

Fund Information
Fund Type	Exchange Traded Funds
Category	US Equity Small Cap
Sub-Category	Small Growth
Prospectus Objective	Small Company
Inception Date	Jan-04
Open to New Investments	Y

Prices
Price (as of 12/31/2018)	150.59
52-Week High	190.00
52-Week Low	140.03

Total Returns (%)
3-Month	6-Month	1-Year	3-Year	5-Year
-19.35	-15.39	-6.82	25.77	27.54

3-Year Standard Deviation	13.5
Effective Duration	

Valuation
Premium/Discount (1-Year Average)	0.01

Company Information
Provider	Vanguard
Manager/Tenure	Gerard C. O'Reilly (13), William A. Coleman (2)
Website	http://www.vanguard.com
Address	Vanguard 100 Vanguard Boulevard
	Malvern PA 19355 United States
Phone Number	877-662-7447

PERFORMANCE

Ratings History
Date	Overall Rating	Risk Rating	Reward Rating
Q4-18	C	C+	C-
Q2-18	C+	C+	C+
Q4-17	B	B	B
Q4-16	C+	C+	C+
Q4-15	C+	C+	C

Asset & Performance History
Date	NAV	1-Year Total Return
2017	160.81	22.19
2016	133.07	10.19
2015	121.53	-2.5
2014	125.88	4.02
2013	122.23	38.18
2012	89.03	17.67

Total Assets: $22,703,440,767

Asset Allocation
Asset	%
Cash	2%
Stocks	98%
US Stocks	98%
Bonds	0%
US Bonds	0%
Other	0%

Services Offered:

Investment Strategy: The investment seeks to track the performance of a benchmark index that measures the investment return of small-capitalization growth stocks. The fund employs an indexing investment approach designed to track the performance of the CRSP US Small Cap Growth Index, a broadly diversified index of growth stocks of small U.S. companies. The advisor attempts to replicate the target index by investing all, or substantially all, of its assets in the stocks that make up the index, holding each stock in approximately the same proportion as its weighting in the index. **Top Holdings:** Burlington Stores Inc   Neurocrine Biosciences Inc   Zebra Technologies Corp   PTC Inc   Exact Sciences Corp

SPDR® Dow Jones Industrial Average ETF　　　　　　　　　　　　　　　　　　B-　　BUY

Ticker	Traded On	NAV	Total Assets ($)	Dividend Yield (TTM)	Turnover Ratio	Expense Ratio
DIA	NYSE Arca	233.16	$22,257,558,363	2.02	2	0.17

Ratings
Reward	B
Risk	C+
Recent Upgrade/Downgrade	Down

Fund Information
Fund Type	Exchange Traded Funds
Category	US Equity Large Cap Value
Sub-Category	Large Value
Prospectus Objective	Growth
Inception Date	Jan-98
Open to New Investments	Y

Prices
Price (as of 12/31/2018)	233.20
52-Week High	267.95
52-Week Low	218.10

Total Returns (%)
3-Month	6-Month	1-Year	3-Year	5-Year
-11.93	-2.94	-3.60	43.44	57.76

3-Year Standard Deviation	10.11
Effective Duration	

Valuation
Premium/Discount (1-Year Average)	0.05

Company Information
Provider	SPDR State Street Global Advisors
Manager/Tenure	Management Team (20)
Website	http://www.spdrs.com
Address	SPDR State Street Global Advisors State Street Financial Center, 1 Lincoln Street Boston MA 02111-2900 United States
Phone Number	617-786-3000

PERFORMANCE

Ratings History

Date	Overall Rating	Risk Rating	Reward Rating
Q4-18	B-	C+	B
Q2-18	B	C+	B
Q4-17	B+	B	A-
Q4-16	B-	C	B
Q4-15	B	B	B

Asset & Performance History

Date	NAV	1-Year Total Return
2017	246.98	27.97
2016	197.36	15.42
2015	174	0.09
2014	177.91	9.87
2013	165.4	29.41
2012	130.75	10.03

Total Assets: $22,257,558,363

Asset Allocation

Asset	%
Cash	0%
Stocks	100%
US Stocks	100%
Bonds	0%
US Bonds	0%
Other	0%

Services Offered: Dividend Investment Plan, CashInvestment Plan

Investment Strategy: O investimento destina-se a fornecer os resultados do investimento que, antes das despesas, geralmente corresponde ao preço de desempenho produtivo e do Dow Jones Industrial Average (DJIA). O fundo tem a carteira e dinheiro, e não está activa "administrado" pelos métodos tradicionais. **Top Holdings:** Boeing Co　UnitedHealth Group Inc　3M Co　Goldman Sachs Group Inc　McDonald's Corp

---

iShares TIPS Bond ETF　　　　　　　　　　　　　　　　　　　　　　　　　C-　　HOLD

Ticker	Traded On	NAV	Total Assets ($)	Dividend Yield (TTM)	Turnover Ratio	Expense Ratio
TIP	NYSE Arca	109.46	$21,828,548,539	3	32	0.2

Ratings
Reward	D
Risk	C
Recent Upgrade/Downgrade	Down

Fund Information
Fund Type	Exchange Traded Funds
Category	US Fixed Income
Sub-Category	Inflation-Protected Bond
Prospectus Objective	Govt Bond - Treasury
Inception Date	Dec-03
Open to New Investments	Y

Prices
Price (as of 12/31/2018)	109.51
52-Week High	114.08
52-Week Low	108.28

Total Returns (%)
3-Month	6-Month	1-Year	3-Year	5-Year
-0.34	-1.46	-1.43	6.07	8.03

3-Year Standard Deviation	3.13
Effective Duration	7.29

Valuation
Premium/Discount (1-Year Average)	0.00

Company Information
Provider	iShares
Manager/Tenure	Scott Radell (8), James Mauro (7)
Website	http://www.ishares.com
Address	iShares 400 Howard Street San Francisco CA 94105 United States
Phone Number	800-474-2737

PERFORMANCE

Ratings History

Date	Overall Rating	Risk Rating	Reward Rating
Q4-18	C-	C	D
Q2-18	C	C+	C
Q4-17	C	B-	C
Q4-16	C	C+	C
Q4-15	D+	C	D+

Asset & Performance History

Date	NAV	1-Year Total Return
2017	114.04	2.91
2016	113.13	4.55
2015	109.77	-1.58
2014	111.91	3.49
2013	109.91	-8.65
2012	121.64	6.79

Total Assets: $21,828,548,539

Asset Allocation

Asset	%
Cash	0%
Stocks	0%
US Stocks	0%
Bonds	100%
US Bonds	100%
Other	0%

Services Offered: Dividend Investment Plan

Investment Strategy: The investment seeks to track the investment results of Bloomberg Barclays U.S. Treasury Inflation Protected Securities (TIPS) Index (Series-L) which composed of inflation-protected U.S. Treasury bonds. The fund generally invests at least 90% of its assets in the bonds of the underlying index and at least 95% of its assets in U.S. government bonds. It may invest up to 10% of its assets in U.S. government bonds not included in the underlying index, but which BFA believes will help the fund track the underlying index. It also may invest up to 5% of its assets in repurchase agreements collateralized by U.S. government obligations and in cash and cash equivalents. **Top Holdings:** United States Treasury Notes 0.13%　United States Treasury Notes 0.13%　United States Treasury Notes 0.63%　United States Treasury Notes 0.38%　United States Treasury Notes 0.13%

Vanguard Information Technology Index Fund ETF Shares   C+   HOLD

Ticker	Traded On	NAV	Total Assets ($)	Dividend Yield (TTM)	Turnover Ratio	Expense Ratio
VGT	NYSE Arca		$21,689,512,718	1.07	7	0.1

Ratings
Reward	C+
Risk	C+
Recent Upgrade/Downgrade	Down

Fund Information
Fund Type	Exchange Traded Funds
Category	Technology Sector Equity
Sub-Category	Technology
Prospectus Objective	Unaligned
Inception Date	Jan-04
Open to New Investments	Y

Prices
Price (as of 12/31/2018)	166.83
52-Week High	203.56
52-Week Low	154.81

Total Returns (%)
3-Month	6-Month	1-Year	3-Year	5-Year
-18.29	-9.19	1.53	58.28	96.17

3-Year Standard Deviation	14.36
Effective Duration	

Valuation
Premium/Discount (1-Year Average)	0.02

Company Information
Provider	Vanguard
Manager/Tenure	Walter Nejman (2), Michael A. Johnson (1)
Website	http://www.vanguard.com
Address	Vanguard 100 Vanguard Boulevard Malvern PA 19355 United States
Phone Number	877-662-7447

PERFORMANCE

Ratings History
Date	Overall Rating	Risk Rating	Reward Rating
Q4-18	C+	C+	C+
Q2-18	B	C+	B+
Q4-17	A-	B	A+
Q4-16	C+	C+	C+
Q4-15	B-	B-	B-

Asset & Performance History
Date	NAV	1-Year Total Return
2017	164.64	36.62
2016	121.44	13.22
2015	108.27	5.02
2014	104.48	18.01
2013	89.52	30.91
2012	69.12	14.04

Total Assets: $21,689,512,718
Asset Allocation
Asset	%
Cash	0%
Stocks	100%
US Stocks	99%
Bonds	0%
US Bonds	0%
Other	0%

Services Offered:

Investment Strategy: The investment seeks to track the performance of a benchmark index. The fund employs an indexing investment approach designed to track the performance of the MSCI US Investable Market Index/Information Technology 25/50, an index made up of stocks of large, mid-size, and small U.S. companies within the information technology sector, as classified under the Global Industry Classification Standard. The Advisor attempts to replicate the target index by seeking to invest all, or substantially all, of its assets in the stocks that make up the index, in order to hold each stock in approximately the same proportion as its weighting in the index. It is non-diversified. **Top Holdings:** Apple Inc Microsoft Corp Visa Inc Class A Intel Corp Cisco Systems Inc

---

iShares S&P 500 Growth ETF   C   HOLD

Ticker	Traded On	NAV	Total Assets ($)	Dividend Yield (TTM)	Turnover Ratio	Expense Ratio
IVW	NYSE Arca	150.56	$21,444,344,999	1.18	21	0.18

Ratings
Reward	C
Risk	C+
Recent Upgrade/Downgrade	Down

Fund Information
Fund Type	Exchange Traded Funds
Category	US Equity Large Cap Growth
Sub-Category	Large Growth
Prospectus Objective	Growth
Inception Date	May-00
Open to New Investments	Y

Prices
Price (as of 12/31/2018)	150.67
52-Week High	177.72
52-Week Low	140.58

Total Returns (%)
3-Month	6-Month	1-Year	3-Year	5-Year
-15.00	-7.39	-0.17	35.53	63.70

3-Year Standard Deviation	10.52
Effective Duration	

Valuation
Premium/Discount (1-Year Average)	0.01

Company Information
Provider	iShares
Manager/Tenure	Diane Hsiung (10), Greg Savage (10), Jennifer Hsui (6), 3 others
Website	http://www.ishares.com
Address	iShares 400 Howard Street San Francisco CA 94105 United States
Phone Number	800-474-2737

PERFORMANCE

Ratings History
Date	Overall Rating	Risk Rating	Reward Rating
Q4-18	C	C+	C
Q2-18	B-	C+	B
Q4-17	B	B+	B
Q4-16	B-	C+	B
Q4-15	C+	B-	C+

Asset & Performance History
Date	NAV	1-Year Total Return
2017	152.63	27.19
2016	121.7	6.73
2015	115.8	5.33
2014	111.64	14.66
2013	98.76	32.47
2012	75.76	14.39

Total Assets: $21,444,344,999
Asset Allocation
Asset	%
Cash	0%
Stocks	100%
US Stocks	99%
Bonds	0%
US Bonds	0%
Other	0%

Services Offered: CashInvestment Plan

Investment Strategy: The investment seeks to track the investment results of the S&P 500 Growth IndexTM, which measures the performance of the large-capitalization growth sector of the U.S. equity market. The fund generally invests at least 90% of its assets in securities of the underlying index and in depositary receipts representing securities of the underlying index. It may invest the remainder of its assets in certain futures, options and swap contracts, cash and cash equivalents, as well as in securities not included in the underlying index, but which BFA believes will help the fund track the underlying index. **Top Holdings:** Microsoft Corp Apple Inc Amazon.com Inc Facebook Inc A Alphabet Inc Class C

Vanguard Large-Cap Index Fund ETF Shares   C   HOLD

Ticker	Traded On	NAV	Total Assets ($)	Dividend Yield (TTM)	Turnover Ratio	Expense Ratio
VV	NYSE Arca		$20,461,011,268	1.83	3	0.05

Ratings
Reward   C
Risk   C+
Recent Upgrade/Downgrade   Down

Fund Information
Fund Type   Exchange Traded Funds
Category   US Equity Large Cap Blend
Sub-Category   Large Blend
Prospectus Objective   Growth
Inception Date   Jan-04
Open to New Investments   Y

Prices
Price (as of 12/31/2018)   114.86
52-Week High   134.91
52-Week Low   107.63

Total Returns (%)

3-Month	6-Month	1-Year	3-Year	5-Year
-14.54	-8.05	-5.25	29.09	47.94

3-Year Standard Deviation   9.5
Effective Duration

Valuation
Premium/Discount (1-Year Average)   0.01

Company Information
Provider   Vanguard
Manager/Tenure   Michael A. Johnson (2), Walter Nejman (2)
Website   http://www.vanguard.com
Address   Vanguard 100 Vanguard Boulevard Malvern PA 19355 United States
Phone Number   877-662-7447

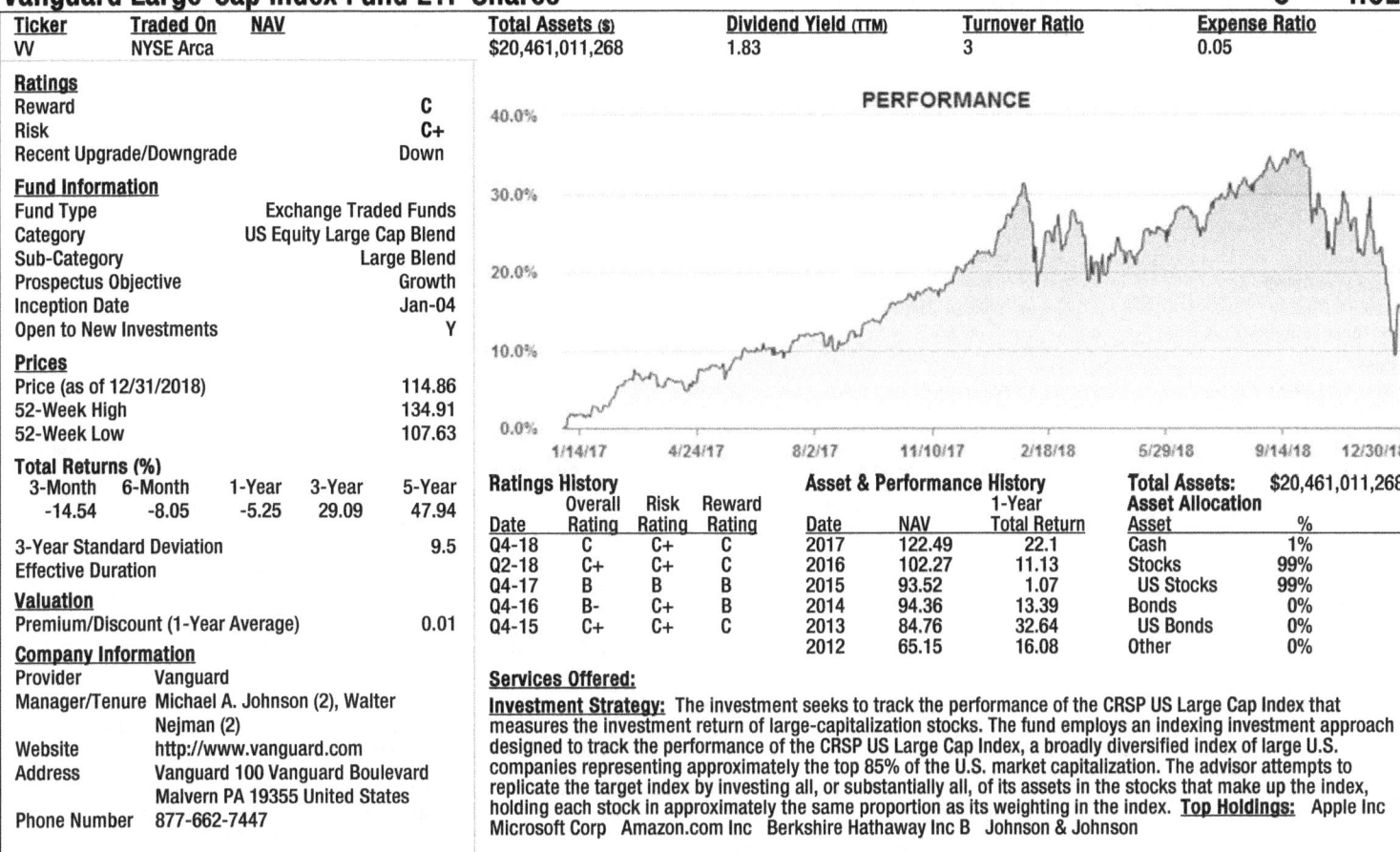

PERFORMANCE

Ratings History

Date	Overall Rating	Risk Rating	Reward Rating
Q4-18	C	C+	C
Q2-18	C+	C+	C
Q4-17	B	B	B
Q4-16	B-	C+	B
Q4-15	C+	C+	C

Asset & Performance History

Date	NAV	1-Year Total Return
2017	122.49	22.1
2016	102.27	11.13
2015	93.52	1.07
2014	94.36	13.39
2013	84.76	32.64
2012	65.15	16.08

Total Assets: $20,461,011,268

Asset Allocation

Asset	%
Cash	1%
Stocks	99%
US Stocks	99%
Bonds	0%
US Bonds	0%
Other	0%

Services Offered:

Investment Strategy: The investment seeks to track the performance of the CRSP US Large Cap Index that measures the investment return of large-capitalization stocks. The fund employs an indexing investment approach designed to track the performance of the CRSP US Large Cap Index, a broadly diversified index of large U.S. companies representing approximately the top 85% of the U.S. market capitalization. The advisor attempts to replicate the target index by investing all, or substantially all, of its assets in the stocks that make up the index, holding each stock in approximately the same proportion as its weighting in the index. **Top Holdings:** Apple Inc Microsoft Corp Amazon.com Inc Berkshire Hathaway Inc B Johnson & Johnson

---

Health Care Select Sector SPDR® Fund   B-   BUY

Ticker	Traded On	NAV	Total Assets ($)	Dividend Yield (TTM)	Turnover Ratio	Expense Ratio
XLV	NYSE Arca	86.43	$19,896,594,302	1.38	5	0.13

Ratings
Reward   B
Risk   C+
Recent Upgrade/Downgrade

Fund Information
Fund Type   Exchange Traded Funds
Category   Healthcare Sector Equity
Sub-Category   Health
Prospectus Objective   Health
Inception Date   Dec-98
Open to New Investments   Y

Prices
Price (as of 12/31/2018)   86.51
52-Week High   95.87
52-Week Low   79.55

Total Returns (%)

3-Month	6-Month	1-Year	3-Year	5-Year
-9.19	4.11	6.29	25.69	68.07

3-Year Standard Deviation   12.5
Effective Duration

Valuation
Premium/Discount (1-Year Average)   0.12

Company Information
Provider   SPDR State Street Global Advisors
Manager/Tenure   Michael J. Feehily (7), Karl A. Schneider (3), Dwayne Hancock (1)
Website   http://www.spdrs.com
Address   SPDR State Street Global Advisors State Street Financial Center, 1 Lincoln Street Boston MA 02111-2900 United States
Phone Number   617-786-3000

PERFORMANCE

Ratings History

Date	Overall Rating	Risk Rating	Reward Rating
Q4-18	B-	C+	B
Q2-18	C+	C	B-
Q4-17	B	B	B-
Q4-16	B-	C+	B
Q4-15	B	B	B

Asset & Performance History

Date	NAV	1-Year Total Return
2017	82.59	21.7
2016	68.91	-3.34
2015	72.05	6.82
2014	68.41	25.17
2013	55.45	41.24
2012	39.93	17.55

Total Assets: $19,896,594,302

Asset Allocation

Asset	%
Cash	1%
Stocks	99%
US Stocks	99%
Bonds	0%
US Bonds	0%
Other	0%

Services Offered: Dividend Investment Plan, CashInvestment Plan

Investment Strategy: The investment seeks investment results that, before expenses, correspond generally to the price and yield performance of publicly traded equity securities of companies in the Health Care Select Sector Index. In seeking to track the performance of the index, the fund employs a replication strategy. It generally invests substantially all, but at least 95%, of its total assets in the securities comprising the index. The index includes companies from the following industries: pharmaceuticals; health care equipment & supplies; health care providers & services; biotechnology; life sciences tools & services; and health care technology. The fund is non-diversified. **Top Holdings:** Johnson & Johnson Pfizer Inc UnitedHealth Group Inc Merck & Co Inc AbbVie Inc

Vanguard Intermediate-Term Corporate Bond Index Fund ETF Shares | C | HOLD

Ticker	Traded On	NAV	Total Assets ($)	Dividend Yield (TTM)	Turnover Ratio	Expense Ratio
VCIT	NAS CM		$19,847,895,059	3.6	65	0.07

Ratings
Reward	D+
Risk	C+
Recent Upgrade/Downgrade	

Fund Information
Fund Type	Exchange Traded Funds
Category	US Fixed Income
Sub-Category	Corporate Bond
Prospectus Objective	Corp Bond - Gen
Inception Date	Nov-09
Open to New Investments	Y

Prices
Price (as of 12/31/2018)	82.86
52-Week High	87.39
52-Week Low	82.02

Total Returns (%)
3-Month	6-Month	1-Year	3-Year	5-Year
0.22	1.05	-1.96	8.91	18.06

3-Year Standard Deviation	3.55
Effective Duration	5.96

Valuation
Premium/Discount (1-Year Average)	0.12

Company Information
Provider	Vanguard
Manager/Tenure	Joshua C. Barrickman (9)
Website	http://www.vanguard.com
Address	Vanguard 100 Vanguard Boulevard Malvern PA 19355 United States
Phone Number	877-662-7447

PERFORMANCE

Ratings History
Date	Overall Rating	Risk Rating	Reward Rating
Q4-18	C	C+	D+
Q2-18	C	C	C-
Q4-17	B	A	C
Q4-16	C	C+	C
Q4-15	C	C+	C

Asset & Performance History
Date	NAV	1-Year Total Return
2017	87.21	5.56
2016	85.37	5.27
2015	83.74	0.87
2014	85.78	7.46
2013	82.55	-1.8
2012	87.38	11.35

Total Assets: $19,847,895,059
Asset Allocation
Asset	%
Cash	0%
Stocks	0%
US Stocks	0%
Bonds	98%
US Bonds	86%
Other	0%

Services Offered:

Investment Strategy: The investment seeks to track the performance of a market-weighted corporate bond index with an intermediate-term dollar-weighted average maturity. The fund employs an indexing investment approach designed to track the performance of the Bloomberg Barclays U.S. 5-10 Year Corporate Bond Index. This index includes U.S. dollar-denominated, investment-grade, fixed-rate, taxable securities issued by industrial, utility, and financial companies, with maturities between 5 and 10 years. Under normal circumstances, at least 80% of the fund's assets will be invested in bonds included in the index. **Top Holdings:** Anheuser-Busch InBev Finance Inc. 3.65% CVS Health Corp 4.3% Bank of America Corporation 3.42% Broadcom Corporation/Broadcom Cayman Finance Ltd 3.88% CVS Health Corp 4.1%

Vanguard FTSE Europe Index Fund ETF Shares | C- | HOLD

Ticker	Traded On	NAV	Total Assets ($)	Dividend Yield (TTM)	Turnover Ratio	Expense Ratio
VGK	NYSE Arca		$19,810,444,623	3.74	4	0.1

Ratings
Reward	D+
Risk	C-
Recent Upgrade/Downgrade	Down

Fund Information
Fund Type	Exchange Traded Funds
Category	Europe Equity Large Cap
Sub-Category	Europe Stock
Prospectus Objective	Europe Stock
Inception Date	Mar-05
Open to New Investments	Y

Prices
Price (as of 12/31/2018)	48.62
52-Week High	63.49
52-Week Low	46.99

Total Returns (%)
3-Month	6-Month	1-Year	3-Year	5-Year
-13.41	-12.86	-15.27	7.01	-1.87

3-Year Standard Deviation	12.04
Effective Duration	

Valuation
Premium/Discount (1-Year Average)	0.00

Company Information
Provider	Vanguard
Manager/Tenure	Christine D. Franquin (2), Justin E. Hales (2)
Website	http://www.vanguard.com
Address	Vanguard 100 Vanguard Boulevard Malvern PA 19355 United States
Phone Number	877-662-7447

PERFORMANCE

Ratings History
Date	Overall Rating	Risk Rating	Reward Rating
Q4-18	C-	C-	D+
Q2-18	C	C+	C
Q4-17	B-	B	B-
Q4-16	D	C-	D
Q4-15	C-	C-	C-

Asset & Performance History
Date	NAV	1-Year Total Return
2017	59.17	27.56
2016	47.93	-2.25
2015	49.98	-1.87
2014	52.48	-6.55
2013	58.54	24.93
2012	48.41	21

Total Assets: $19,810,444,623
Asset Allocation
Asset	%
Cash	1%
Stocks	98%
US Stocks	2%
Bonds	0%
US Bonds	0%
Other	1%

Services Offered:

Investment Strategy: The investment seeks to track the performance of a benchmark index that measures the investment return of stocks issued by companies located in the major markets of Europe. The fund employs an indexing investment approach by investing all, or substantially all, of its assets in the common stocks included in the FTSE Developed Europe All Cap Index. The FTSE Developed Europe All Cap Index is a market-capitalization-weighted index that is made up of approximately 1,258 common stocks of large-, mid-, and small-cap companies located in 16 European countries-mostly companies in the United Kingdom, France, and Germany. **Top Holdings:** Nestle SA Novartis AG Roche Holding AG Dividend Right Cert. HSBC Holdings PLC Total SA

iShares Edge MSCI Min Vol USA ETF　　　　　　　　　　　　　　　　　　B　　BUY

Ticker	Traded On	NAV		Total Assets ($)	Dividend Yield (TTM)	Turnover Ratio	Expense Ratio
USMV	BATS	52.39		$19,372,615,794	1.81	22	0.15

Ratings
Reward　　　　　　　　　　　　C
Risk　　　　　　　　　　　　　A
Recent Upgrade/Downgrade　　Up

Fund Information
Fund Type　　　　　　　Exchange Traded Funds
Category　　　　　　　US Equity Large Cap Blend
Sub-Category　　　　　Large Blend
Prospectus Objective　　Growth
Inception Date　　　　　Oct-11
Open to New Investments　Y

Prices
Price (as of 12/31/2018)　52.40
52-Week High　　　　　57.58
52-Week Low　　　　　49.77

Total Returns (%)

3-Month	6-Month	1-Year	3-Year	5-Year
-7.51	-0.53	1.35	33.24	63.54

3-Year Standard Deviation　　　　　7.79
Effective Duration

Valuation
Premium/Discount (1-Year Average)　　-0.02

Company Information
Provider　　　iShares
Manager/Tenure　Diane Hsiung (7), Greg Savage (7),
　　　　　　　　Jennifer Hsui (6), 3 others
Website　　　http://www.ishares.com
Address　　　iShares 400 Howard Street San
　　　　　　　Francisco CA 94105 United States
Phone Number　800-474-2737

PERFORMANCE

Ratings History

Date	Overall Rating	Risk Rating	Reward Rating
Q4-18	B	A	C
Q2-18	C+	C+	C
Q4-17	B+	A+	B-
Q4-16	C	C+	C
Q4-15	B-	C+	B-

Asset & Performance History

Date	NAV	1-Year Total Return
2017	52.77	18.97
2016	45.19	10.49
2015	41.82	5.5
2014	40.46	16.33
2013	35.48	25.1
2012	29.02	11.04

Total Assets: $19,372,615,794
Asset Allocation

Asset	%
Cash	0%
Stocks	100%
US Stocks	99%
Bonds	0%
US Bonds	0%
Other	0%

Services Offered:

Investment Strategy: The investment seeks the investment results of the MSCI USA Minimum Volatility (USD) Index. The fund will invest at least 90% of its assets in the component securities of the index and may invest up to 10% of its assets in certain futures, options and swap contracts, cash and cash equivalents. The index measures the performance of large and mid-capitalization equity securities listed on stock exchanges in the U.S. that, in the aggregate, have lower volatility relative to the broader U.S. equity market. **Top Holdings:** Visa Inc Class A　Pfizer Inc　Coca-Cola Co　McDonald's Corp　Waste Management Inc

SPDR® S&P MidCap 400 ETF　　　　　　　　　　　　　　　　　　C　　HOLD

Ticker	Traded On	NAV		Total Assets ($)	Dividend Yield (TTM)	Turnover Ratio	Expense Ratio
MDY	NYSE Arca	302.54		$19,244,760,604	1.23	23	0.24

Ratings
Reward　　　　　　　　　　　　C-
Risk　　　　　　　　　　　　　C+
Recent Upgrade/Downgrade　　Down

Fund Information
Fund Type　　　　　　　Exchange Traded Funds
Category　　　　　　　US Equity Mid Cap
Sub-Category　　　　　Mid-Cap Blend
Prospectus Objective　　Growth
Inception Date　　　　　May-95
Open to New Investments　Y

Prices
Price (as of 12/31/2018)　302.67
52-Week High　　　　　373.52
52-Week Low　　　　　284.96

Total Returns (%)

3-Month	6-Month	1-Year	3-Year	5-Year
-16.65	-14.23	-11.27	23.72	32.12

3-Year Standard Deviation　　　　　11.82
Effective Duration

Valuation
Premium/Discount (1-Year Average)　　0.01

Company Information
Provider　　　SPDR State Street Global Advisors
Manager/Tenure　Management Team (23)
Website　　　http://www.spdrs.com
Address　　　SPDR State Street Global Advisors
　　　　　　　State Street Financial Center, 1
　　　　　　　Lincoln Street Boston MA 02111-2900
　　　　　　　United States
Phone Number　617-786-3000

PERFORMANCE

Ratings History

Date	Overall Rating	Risk Rating	Reward Rating
Q4-18	C	C+	C-
Q2-18	C+	C+	C+
Q4-17	B	B	B
Q4-16	B	C+	B
Q4-15	C	C+	C

Asset & Performance History

Date	NAV	1-Year Total Return
2017	345.24	15.88
2016	301.68	20.33
2015	254.27	-2.4
2014	263.93	9.41
2013	244.1	33.08
2012	185.6	17.57

Total Assets: $19,244,760,604
Asset Allocation

Asset	%
Cash	0%
Stocks	100%
US Stocks	100%
Bonds	0%
US Bonds	0%
Other	0%

Services Offered: Dividend Investment Plan, CashInvestment Plan

Investment Strategy: The investment seeks to provide investment results that, before expenses, generally correspond to the price and yield performance of the S&P MidCap 400 Index. The Trust holds the Portfolio and cash and is not actively "managed" by traditional methods. To maintain the correspondence between the composition and weightings of Portfolio Securities and component stocks of the S&P MidCap 400 Index, the Trustee adjusts the Portfolio from time to time to conform to periodic changes in the identity and/or relative weightings of Index Securities. **Top Holdings:** Jack Henry & Associates Inc　Lamb Weston Holdings Inc　Domino's Pizza Inc　Teleflex Inc　Keysight Technologies Inc

Technology Select Sector SPDR® Fund

B   **BUY**

Ticker	Traded On	NAV	Total Assets ($)	Dividend Yield (TTM)	Turnover Ratio	Expense Ratio
XLK	NYSE Arca	61.98	$19,121,099,208	1.42	19	0.13

Ratings
Reward	B
Risk	C+
Recent Upgrade/Downgrade	

Fund Information
Fund Type	Exchange Traded Funds
Category	Technology Sector Equity
Sub-Category	Technology
Prospectus Objective	Technology
Inception Date	Dec-98
Open to New Investments	Y

Prices
Price (as of 12/31/2018)	61.98
52-Week High	75.93
52-Week Low	57.62

Total Returns (%)
3-Month	6-Month	1-Year	3-Year	5-Year
-17.71	-10.86	-1.55	51.75	88.73

3-Year Standard Deviation	13.02
Effective Duration	

Valuation
Premium/Discount (1-Year Average)	0.03

Company Information
Provider	SPDR State Street Global Advisors
Manager/Tenure	Michael J. Feehily (7), Karl A. Schneider (3), David Chin (1)
Website	http://www.spdrs.com
Address	SPDR State Street Global Advisors State Street Financial Center, 1 Lincoln Street Boston MA 02111-2900 United States
Phone Number	617-786-3000

PERFORMANCE

Ratings History
Date	Overall Rating	Risk Rating	Reward Rating
Q4-18	B	C+	B
Q2-18	B	B-	B+
Q4-17	A-	B	A
Q4-16	B+	B-	A-
Q4-15	B	B	B

Asset & Performance History
Date	NAV	1-Year Total Return
2017	63.89	34.27
2016	48.3	14.28
2015	42.86	5.61
2014	41.33	17.75
2013	35.75	25.98
2012	28.92	15.46

Total Assets: $19,121,099,208

Asset Allocation
Asset	%
Cash	0%
Stocks	100%
US Stocks	100%
Bonds	0%
US Bonds	0%
Other	0%

Services Offered: Dividend Investment Plan, CashInvestment Plan

Investment Strategy: The investment seeks investment results that, before expenses, correspond generally to the price and yield performance of publicly traded equity securities of companies in the Technology Select Sector Index. In seeking to track the performance of the index, the fund employs a replication strategy, which means that the fund typically invests in substantially all of the securities represented in the index in approximately the same proportions as the index. It generally invests substantially all, but at least 95%, of its total assets in the securities comprising the index. The fund is non-diversified. **Top Holdings:** Microsoft Corp Apple Inc Visa Inc Class A Intel Corp Cisco Systems Inc

---

Vanguard Mid-Cap Value Index Fund ETF Shares

C   **HOLD**

Ticker	Traded On	NAV	Total Assets ($)	Dividend Yield (TTM)	Turnover Ratio	Expense Ratio
VOE	NYSE Arca		$17,866,104,617	2.32	17	0.07

Ratings
Reward	C-
Risk	C+
Recent Upgrade/Downgrade	Down

Fund Information
Fund Type	Exchange Traded Funds
Category	US Equity Mid Cap
Sub-Category	Mid-Cap Value
Prospectus Objective	Growth
Inception Date	Aug-06
Open to New Investments	Y

Prices
Price (as of 12/31/2018)	95.26
52-Week High	117.78
52-Week Low	90.18

Total Returns (%)
3-Month	6-Month	1-Year	3-Year	5-Year
-15.57	-13.18	-13.13	17.19	31.17

3-Year Standard Deviation	10.35
Effective Duration	

Valuation
Premium/Discount (1-Year Average)	0.01

Company Information
Provider	Vanguard
Manager/Tenure	Donald M. Butler (12), Michael A. Johnson (2)
Website	http://www.vanguard.com
Address	Vanguard 100 Vanguard Boulevard Malvern PA 19355 United States
Phone Number	877-662-7447

PERFORMANCE

Ratings History
Date	Overall Rating	Risk Rating	Reward Rating
Q4-18	C	C+	C-
Q2-18	C	C+	C
Q4-17	B	B+	B
Q4-16	B	C+	B
Q4-15	C	C+	C

Asset & Performance History
Date	NAV	1-Year Total Return
2017	111.47	17.34
2016	97.12	14.81
2015	85.99	-1.8
2014	89.39	13.98
2013	79.73	37.65
2012	58.82	16.03

Total Assets: $17,866,104,617

Asset Allocation
Asset	%
Cash	0%
Stocks	100%
US Stocks	99%
Bonds	0%
US Bonds	0%
Other	0%

Services Offered:

Investment Strategy: The investment seeks to track the performance of the CRSP US Mid Cap Value Index that measures the investment return of mid-capitalization value stocks. The fund employs an indexing investment approach designed to track the performance of the CRSP US Mid Cap Value Index, a broadly diversified index of value stocks of mid-size U.S. companies. The advisor attempts to replicate the target index by investing all, or substantially all, of its assets in the stocks that make up the index, holding each stock in approximately the same proportion as its weighting in the index. **Top Holdings:** WEC Energy Group Inc M&T Bank Corp DTE Energy Co NetApp Inc CenturyLink Inc

iShares Russell Mid-Cap ETF   E+   SELL

Ticker	Traded On	NAV
IWR	NYSE Arca	46.46

Total Assets ($)	Dividend Yield (TTM)	Turnover Ratio	Expense Ratio
$17,591,751,442	1.8	10	0.2

Ratings
Reward	E
Risk	D
Recent Upgrade/Downgrade	Down

Fund Information
Fund Type	Exchange Traded Funds
Category	US Equity Mid Cap
Sub-Category	Mid-Cap Blend
Prospectus Objective	Growth
Inception Date	Jul-01
Open to New Investments	Y

Prices
Price (as of 12/31/2018)	46.48
52-Week High	224.09
52-Week Low	43.70

Total Returns (%)
3-Month	6-Month	1-Year	3-Year	5-Year
-15.04	-77.81	-77.28	-69.46	-66.37

3-Year Standard Deviation	10.62
Effective Duration	

Valuation
Premium/Discount (1-Year Average)	0.01

Company Information
Provider	iShares
Manager/Tenure	Diane Hsiung (10), Greg Savage (10), Jennifer Hsui (6), 3 others
Website	http://www.ishares.com
Address	iShares 400 Howard Street San Francisco CA 94105 United States
Phone Number	800-474-2737

PERFORMANCE

Ratings History
Date	Overall Rating	Risk Rating	Reward Rating
Q4-18	E+	D	E
Q2-18	C+	C+	C
Q4-17	B	B	B
Q4-16	B-	C+	B-
Q4-15	C	C+	C

Asset & Performance History
Date	NAV	1-Year Total Return
2017	208.15	18.32
2016	178.78	13.57
2015	160.27	-2.57
2014	167.06	13.03
2013	150.02	34.49
2012	113.16	17.12

Total Assets: $17,591,751,442
Asset Allocation
Asset	%
Cash	0%
Stocks	100%
US Stocks	99%
Bonds	0%
US Bonds	0%
Other	0%

Services Offered: CashInvestment Plan

Investment Strategy: The investment seeks to track the investment results of the Russell Midcap Index, which measures the performance of the mid-capitalization sector of the U.S. equity market. The fund generally invests at least 90% of its assets in securities of the underlying index and in depositary receipts representing securities of the underlying index. It may invest the remainder of its assets in certain futures, options and swap contracts, cash and cash equivalents, as well as in securities not included in the underlying index, but which the advisor believes will help the fund track the underlying index. **Top Holdings:** Fidelity National Information Services Inc Edwards Lifesciences Corp Analog Devices Inc ServiceNow Inc Ross Stores Inc

---

iShares Russell 1000 ETF   C   HOLD

Ticker	Traded On	NAV
IWB	NYSE Arca	138.54

Total Assets ($)	Dividend Yield (TTM)	Turnover Ratio	Expense Ratio
$17,406,504,765	1.76	4	0.15

Ratings
Reward	C
Risk	C+
Recent Upgrade/Downgrade	Down

Fund Information
Fund Type	Exchange Traded Funds
Category	US Equity Large Cap Blend
Sub-Category	Large Blend
Prospectus Objective	Growth
Inception Date	May-00
Open to New Investments	Y

Prices
Price (as of 12/31/2018)	138.69
52-Week High	163.43
52-Week Low	129.86

Total Returns (%)
3-Month	6-Month	1-Year	3-Year	5-Year
-14.07	-7.75	-4.90	29.33	47.45

3-Year Standard Deviation	9.57
Effective Duration	

Valuation
Premium/Discount (1-Year Average)	0.00

Company Information
Provider	iShares
Manager/Tenure	Diane Hsiung (10), Greg Savage (10), Jennifer Hsui (6), 3 others
Website	http://www.ishares.com
Address	iShares 400 Howard Street San Francisco CA 94105 United States
Phone Number	800-474-2737

PERFORMANCE

Ratings History
Date	Overall Rating	Risk Rating	Reward Rating
Q4-18	C	C+	C
Q2-18	C+	C+	C
Q4-17	B	B	B
Q4-16	B-	C+	B
Q4-15	C+	C+	C

Asset & Performance History
Date	NAV	1-Year Total Return
2017	148.5	21.52
2016	124.37	11.91
2015	113.35	0.82
2014	114.63	13.08
2013	103.17	32.93
2012	79.06	16.27

Total Assets: $17,406,504,765
Asset Allocation
Asset	%
Cash	1%
Stocks	99%
US Stocks	98%
Bonds	0%
US Bonds	0%
Other	0%

Services Offered: CashInvestment Plan

Investment Strategy: The investment seeks to track the investment results of the Russell 1000® Index, which measures the performance of the large- and mid- capitalization sectors of the U.S. equity market. The fund generally invests at least 90% of its assets in securities of the underlying index and in depositary receipts representing securities of the underlying index. It may invest the remainder of its assets in certain futures, options and swap contracts, cash and cash equivalents, as well as in securities not included in the underlying index, but which the advisor believes will help the fund track the underlying index. **Top Holdings:** Apple Inc Microsoft Corp Amazon.com Inc Berkshire Hathaway Inc B Johnson & Johnson

iShares Short Treasury Bond ETF   C   HOLD

Ticker	Traded On	NAV	Total Assets ($)	Dividend Yield (TTM)	Turnover Ratio	Expense Ratio
SHV	NAS CM	110.29	$17,316,991,591	1.47	47	0.15

Ratings
Reward	C-
Risk	C+
Recent Upgrade/Downgrade	

Fund Information
Fund Type	Exchange Traded Funds
Category	US Fixed Income
Sub-Category	Ultrashort Bond
Prospectus Objective	Govt Bond - Treasury
Inception Date	Jan-07
Open to New Investments	Y

Prices
Price (as of 12/31/2018)	110.30
52-Week High	110.47
52-Week Low	110.20

Total Returns (%)
3-Month	6-Month	1-Year	3-Year	5-Year
0.57	1.02	1.74	2.84	2.84

3-Year Standard Deviation	0.19
Effective Duration	0.39

Valuation
Premium/Discount (1-Year Average)	0.02

Company Information
Provider	iShares
Manager/Tenure	Scott Radell (8), James Mauro (7)
Website	http://www.ishares.com
Address	iShares 400 Howard Street San Francisco CA 94105 United States
Phone Number	800-474-2737

PERFORMANCE

Ratings History
Date	Overall Rating	Risk Rating	Reward Rating
Q4-18	C	C+	C-
Q2-18	C	C+	C-
Q4-17	C	C+	C-
Q4-16	C	C+	C-
Q4-15	C	C+	C-

Asset & Performance History
Date	NAV	1-Year Total Return
2017	110.21	0.65
2016	110.29	0.42
2015	110.19	0
2014	110.23	0
2013	110.23	0.01
2012	110.22	0.02

Total Assets: $17,316,991,591

Asset Allocation
Asset	%
Cash	44%
Stocks	0%
US Stocks	0%
Bonds	56%
US Bonds	56%
Other	0%

Services Offered:

Investment Strategy: The investment seeks to track the investment results of the ICE U.S. Treasury Short Bond Index. The fund generally invests at least 90% of its assets in the bonds of the underlying index and at least 95% of its assets in U.S. government bonds. The index measures the performance of public obligations of the U.S. Treasury that have a remaining maturity of equal to or greater than one month and less than one year. It may invest up to 10% of its assets in U.S. government bonds not included in the underlying index, but which BFA believes will help the fund track the underlying index. **Top Holdings:** United States Treasury Notes 1.63% United States Treasury Notes 1.63% United States Treasury Notes 1.63% United States Treasury Notes 3.63% United States Treasury Notes 1.63%

---

iShares 1-3 Year Treasury Bond ETF   C   HOLD

Ticker	Traded On	NAV	Total Assets ($)	Dividend Yield (TTM)	Turnover Ratio	Expense Ratio
SHY	NAS CM	83.60	$17,171,100,037	1.62	85	0.15

Ratings
Reward	C-
Risk	C+
Recent Upgrade/Downgrade	Up

Fund Information
Fund Type	Exchange Traded Funds
Category	US Fixed Income
Sub-Category	Short Government
Prospectus Objective	Govt Bond - Treasury
Inception Date	Jul-02
Open to New Investments	Y

Prices
Price (as of 12/31/2018)	83.62
52-Week High	83.85
52-Week Low	82.85

Total Returns (%)
3-Month	6-Month	1-Year	3-Year	5-Year
1.28	1.48	1.45	2.49	3.42

3-Year Standard Deviation	0.76
Effective Duration	1.88

Valuation
Premium/Discount (1-Year Average)	0.02

Company Information
Provider	iShares
Manager/Tenure	Scott Radell (8), James Mauro (7)
Website	http://www.ishares.com
Address	iShares 400 Howard Street San Francisco CA 94105 United States
Phone Number	800-474-2737

PERFORMANCE

Ratings History
Date	Overall Rating	Risk Rating	Reward Rating
Q4-18	C	C+	C-
Q2-18	C-	C	D+
Q4-17	C	C	C-
Q4-16	C	C+	C
Q4-15	C	C+	C

Asset & Performance History
Date	NAV	1-Year Total Return
2017	83.84	0.27
2016	84.43	0.74
2015	84.4	0.42
2014	84.49	0.48
2013	84.39	0.22
2012	84.42	0.31

Total Assets: $17,171,100,037

Asset Allocation
Asset	%
Cash	0%
Stocks	0%
US Stocks	0%
Bonds	100%
US Bonds	100%
Other	0%

Services Offered:

Investment Strategy: The investment seeks to track the investment results of the ICE U.S. Treasury 1-3 Year Bond Index (the "underlying index"). The fund generally invests at least 90% of its assets in the bonds of the underlying index and at least 95% of its assets in U.S. government bonds. The underlying index measures the performance of public obligations of the U.S. Treasury that have a remaining maturity of greater than one year and less than or equal to three years. **Top Holdings:** United States Treasury Notes 2.25% United States Treasury Notes 2.13% United States Treasury Notes 1.25% United States Treasury Notes 1.63% United States Treasury Notes 1.5%

iShares Select Dividend ETF   C   HOLD

Ticker	Traded On	NAV	Total Assets ($)	Dividend Yield (TTM)	Turnover Ratio	Expense Ratio
DVY	NAS CM	89.29	$17,114,645,467	3.31	28	0.39

Ratings
Reward   C
Risk   C+
Recent Upgrade/Downgrade   Down

Fund Information
Fund Type   Exchange Traded Funds
Category   US Equity Large Cap Value
Sub-Category   Large Value
Prospectus Objective   Equity-Income
Inception Date   Nov-03
Open to New Investments   Y

Prices
Price (as of 12/31/2018)   89.31
52-Week High   102.32
52-Week Low   85.20

Total Returns (%)

3-Month	6-Month	1-Year	3-Year	5-Year
-9.95	-7.04	-6.30	30.82	47.25

3-Year Standard Deviation   7.49
Effective Duration

Valuation
Premium/Discount (1-Year Average)   0.01

Company Information
Provider   iShares
Manager/Tenure   Diane Hsiung (10), Greg Savage (10),
                  Jennifer Hsui (6), 3 others
Website   http://www.ishares.com
Address   iShares 400 Howard Street San
                  Francisco CA 94105 United States
Phone Number   800-474-2737

PERFORMANCE

Ratings History

Date	Overall Rating	Risk Rating	Reward Rating
Q4-18	C	C+	C
Q2-18	C	C+	C
Q4-17	B	B	B
Q4-16	B	C+	B
Q4-15	C+	C+	C

Asset & Performance History

Date	NAV	1-Year Total Return
2017	98.52	14.95
2016	88.44	21.45
2015	75.16	-2.02
2014	79.38	14.89
2013	71.31	28.71
2012	57.27	10.51

Total Assets: $17,114,645,467
Asset Allocation

Asset	%
Cash	0%
Stocks	100%
US Stocks	98%
Bonds	0%
US Bonds	0%
Other	0%

Services Offered: CashInvestment Plan

Investment Strategy: The investment seeks to track the investment results of the Dow Jones U.S. Select Dividend Index composed of relatively high dividend paying U.S. equities. The fund generally invests at least 90% of its assets in securities of the underlying index and in depositary receipts representing securities of the underlying index. The underlying index measures the performance of a selected group of equity securities issued by companies that have provided relatively high dividend yields on a consistent basis over time. **Top Holdings:** CenturyLink Inc   PPL Corp   ONEOK Inc   FirstEnergy Corp   Entergy Corp

Vanguard Total World Stock Index Fund ETF Shares   C   HOLD

Ticker	Traded On	NAV	Total Assets ($)	Dividend Yield (TTM)	Turnover Ratio	Expense Ratio
VT	NYSE Arca		$16,946,990,252	2.34	10	0.1

Ratings
Reward   C-
Risk   C+
Recent Upgrade/Downgrade   Down

Fund Information
Fund Type   Exchange Traded Funds
Category   Global Equity Large Cap
Sub-Category   World Large Stock
Prospectus Objective   World Stock
Inception Date   Jun-08
Open to New Investments   Y

Prices
Price (as of 12/31/2018)   65.46
52-Week High   79.73
52-Week Low   62.33

Total Returns (%)

3-Month	6-Month	1-Year	3-Year	5-Year
-13.77	-9.94	-10.27	21.20	23.65

3-Year Standard Deviation   9.71
Effective Duration

Valuation
Premium/Discount (1-Year Average)   0.08

Company Information
Provider   Vanguard
Manager/Tenure   Christine D. Franquin (5), Scott E.
                  Geiger (1)
Website   http://www.vanguard.com
Address   Vanguard 100 Vanguard Boulevard
                  Malvern PA 19355 United States
Phone Number   877-662-7447

PERFORMANCE

Ratings History

Date	Overall Rating	Risk Rating	Reward Rating
Q4-18	C	C+	C-
Q2-18	C	C+	C
Q4-17	B-	C+	B-
Q4-16	C	C+	C
Q4-15	C	C+	C

Asset & Performance History

Date	NAV	1-Year Total Return
2017	74.15	24.3
2016	61.06	8.05
2015	57.54	-1.88
2014	60.05	3.97
2013	59.16	22.97
2012	49.21	17.33

Total Assets: $16,946,990,252
Asset Allocation

Asset	%
Cash	2%
Stocks	98%
US Stocks	55%
Bonds	0%
US Bonds	0%
Other	0%

Services Offered:

Investment Strategy: The investment seeks to track the performance of a benchmark index that measures the investment return of stocks of companies located in developed and emerging markets around the world. The fund employs an indexing investment approach designed to track the performance of the FTSE Global All Cap Index, a float-adjusted, market-capitalization-weighted index designed to measure the market performance of large-, mid-, and small-capitalization stocks of companies located around the world. The index included 7,781 stocks of companies located in 41 countries, including both developed and emerging markets. **Top Holdings:** Apple Inc   Microsoft Corp   Amazon.com Inc   Johnson & Johnson   JPMorgan Chase & Co

iShares MSCI Japan ETF   C   HOLD

Ticker	Traded On	NAV	Total Assets ($)	Dividend Yield (TTM)	Turnover Ratio	Expense Ratio
EWJ	NYSE Arca	51.20	$16,799,028,720	1.55	4	0.47

Ratings
Reward   D+
Risk   C+
Recent Upgrade/Downgrade

Fund Information
Fund Type   Exchange Traded Funds
Category   Japan Equity
Sub-Category   Japan Stock
Prospectus Objective   Pacific Stock
Inception Date   Mar-96
Open to New Investments   Y

Prices
Price (as of 12/31/2018)   50.69
52-Week High   64.67
52-Week Low   49.12

Total Returns (%)

3-Month	6-Month	1-Year	3-Year	5-Year
-14.13	-9.49	-13.17	9.38	14.29

3-Year Standard Deviation   11.07
Effective Duration

Valuation
Premium/Discount (1-Year Average)   -0.07

Company Information
Provider   iShares
Manager/Tenure Diane Hsiung (10), Greg Savage (10), Jennifer Hsui (5), 1 other
Website   http://www.ishares.com
Address   iShares 400 Howard Street San Francisco CA 94105 United States
Phone Number   800-474-2737

PERFORMANCE

Ratings History

Date	Overall Rating	Risk Rating	Reward Rating
Q4-18	C	C+	D+
Q2-18	C	C+	C
Q4-17	B+	B	A-
Q4-16	B-	C+	B-
Q4-15	B-	B+	C

Asset & Performance History

Date	NAV	1-Year Total Return
2017	59.89	23.55
2016	49.11	1.95
2015	49.12	9.33
2014	45.48	-4.42
2013	48.2	26.47
2012	38.56	7.63

Total Assets: $16,799,028,720

Asset Allocation

Asset	%
Cash	1%
Stocks	99%
US Stocks	0%
Bonds	0%
US Bonds	0%
Other	0%

Services Offered: CashInvestment Plan

Investment Strategy: The investment seeks to track the investment results of the MSCI Japan Index. The fund will at all times invest at least 90% of its assets in the securities of its underlying index and in depositary receipts representing securities in its underlying index. The underlying index consists of stocks traded primarily on the Tokyo Stock Exchange. It may include large- or mid-capitalization companies. **Top Holdings:** Toyota Motor Corp SoftBank Group Corp Sony Corp Mitsubishi UFJ Financial Group Inc Keyence Corp

---

SPDR® S&P Dividend ETF   C   HOLD

Ticker	Traded On	NAV	Total Assets ($)	Dividend Yield (TTM)	Turnover Ratio	Expense Ratio
SDY	NYSE Arca	89.47	$16,480,268,671	2.4	32	0.35

Ratings
Reward   C
Risk   C+
Recent Upgrade/Downgrade   Down

Fund Information
Fund Type   Exchange Traded Funds
Category   US Equity Large Cap Value
Sub-Category   Large Value
Prospectus Objective   Growth & Inc
Inception Date   Nov-05
Open to New Investments   Y

Prices
Price (as of 12/31/2018)   89.52
52-Week High   100.02
52-Week Low   84.76

Total Returns (%)

3-Month	6-Month	1-Year	3-Year	5-Year
-7.82	-2.08	-2.71	35.42	53.03

3-Year Standard Deviation   9.05
Effective Duration

Valuation
Premium/Discount (1-Year Average)   -0.01

Company Information
Provider   SPDR State Street Global Advisors
Manager/Tenure Michael J. Feehily (7), Karl A. Schneider (4), Emiliano Rabinovich (1)
Website   http://www.spdrs.com
Address   SPDR State Street Global Advisors State Street Financial Center, 1 Lincoln Street Boston MA 02111-2900 United States
Phone Number   617-786-3000

PERFORMANCE

Ratings History

Date	Overall Rating	Risk Rating	Reward Rating
Q4-18	C	C+	C
Q2-18	C	C+	C
Q4-17	B	A-	B
Q4-16	B-	C+	B
Q4-15	C+	C+	C

Asset & Performance History

Date	NAV	1-Year Total Return
2017	94.42	14.17
2016	85.46	19.21
2015	73.55	-0.69
2014	78.76	13.79
2013	72.58	30.08
2012	58.12	11.5

Total Assets: $16,480,268,671

Asset Allocation

Asset	%
Cash	0%
Stocks	100%
US Stocks	98%
Bonds	0%
US Bonds	0%
Other	0%

Services Offered: Dividend Investment Plan, CashInvestment Plan

Investment Strategy: The investment seeks to provide investment results that, before fees and expenses, correspond generally to the total return performance of the S&P High Yield Dividend Aristocrats Index. The fund generally invests substantially all, but at least 80%, of its total assets in the securities comprising the index. The index is designed to measure the performance of the highest dividend yielding S&P Composite 1500® Index constituents that have followed a managed-dividends policy of consistently increasing dividends every year for at least 20 consecutive years. The fund is non-diversified. **Top Holdings:** AT&T Inc Realty Income Corp AbbVie Inc National Retail Properties Inc People's United Financial Inc

iShares Core S&P Total U.S. Stock Market ETF   C   HOLD

Ticker	Traded On	NAV	Total Assets ($)	Dividend Yield (TTM)	Turnover Ratio	Expense Ratio
ITOT	NYSE Arca	56.69	$15,844,567,420	1.76	8	0.03

Ratings

Reward	C
Risk	C+
Recent Upgrade/Downgrade	Down

Fund Information

Fund Type	Exchange Traded Funds
Category	US Equity Large Cap Blend
Sub-Category	Large Blend
Prospectus Objective	Growth
Inception Date	Jan-04
Open to New Investments	Y

Prices

Price (as of 12/31/2018)	56.76
52-Week High	67.36
52-Week Low	53.25

Total Returns (%)

3-Month	6-Month	1-Year	3-Year	5-Year
-14.54	-8.64	-5.36	29.16	47.37

3-Year Standard Deviation	9.8
Effective Duration	

Valuation

Premium/Discount (1-Year Average)	0.02

Company Information

Provider	iShares
Manager/Tenure	Diane Hsiung (10), Greg Savage (10), Jennifer Hsui (6), 3 others
Website	http://www.ishares.com
Address	iShares 400 Howard Street San Francisco CA 94105 United States
Phone Number	800-474-2737

PERFORMANCE

Ratings History

Date	Overall Rating	Risk Rating	Reward Rating
Q4-18	C	C+	C
Q2-18	C+	C+	C+
Q4-17	B	B	B
Q4-16	B-	C+	B
Q4-15	C+	C+	C

Asset & Performance History

Date	NAV	1-Year Total Return
2017	61.04	21.22
2016	51.27	12.59
2015	46.42	0.96
2014	46.91	13
2013	42.26	32.66
2012	32.45	15.98

Total Assets: $15,844,567,420

Asset Allocation

Asset	%
Cash	0%
Stocks	100%
US Stocks	99%
Bonds	0%
US Bonds	0%
Other	0%

Services Offered: CashInvestment Plan

Investment Strategy: The investment seeks to track the investment results of the S&P Total Market Index™ (TMI), which is comprised of the common equities included in the S&P 500® and the S&P Completion Index™. The fund generally invests at least 90% of its assets in securities of the underlying index and in depositary receipts representing securities of the underlying index. It may invest the remainder of its assets in certain futures, options and swap contracts, cash and cash equivalents, including shares of money market funds advised by BFA or its affiliates, as well as in securities not included in the underlying index. **Top Holdings:** Microsoft Corp Apple Inc Amazon.com Inc Berkshire Hathaway Inc B   Johnson & Johnson

Schwab International Equity ETF™   C-   HOLD

Ticker	Traded On	NAV	Total Assets ($)	Dividend Yield (TTM)	Turnover Ratio	Expense Ratio
SCHF	NYSE Arca	28.36	$15,779,469,972	2.6	5	0.06

Ratings

Reward	D+
Risk	C
Recent Upgrade/Downgrade	Down

Fund Information

Fund Type	Exchange Traded Funds
Category	Global Equity Large Cap
Sub-Category	Foreign Large Blend
Prospectus Objective	Foreign Stock
Inception Date	Nov-09
Open to New Investments	Y

Prices

Price (as of 12/31/2018)	28.35
52-Week High	36.35
52-Week Low	27.44

Total Returns (%)

3-Month	6-Month	1-Year	3-Year	5-Year
-12.83	-10.45	-14.39	10.82	3.32

3-Year Standard Deviation	11.03
Effective Duration	

Valuation

Premium/Discount (1-Year Average)	0.05

Company Information

Provider	Schwab ETFs
Manager/Tenure	Chuck Craig (5), Christopher Bliss (1), Jane Qin (1), 1 other
Website	http://www.schwabetfs.com
Address	Schwab ETFs United States
Phone Number	800-435-4000

PERFORMANCE

Ratings History

Date	Overall Rating	Risk Rating	Reward Rating
Q4-18	C-	C	D+
Q2-18	C	C+	C
Q4-17	B	B	B
Q4-16	D+	C	D+
Q4-15	C	C+	C-

Asset & Performance History

Date	NAV	1-Year Total Return
2017	34.11	25.88
2016	27.75	2.88
2015	27.67	-2.43
2014	29.01	-4.44
2013	31.23	20.02
2012	26.61	17.11

Total Assets: $15,779,469,972

Asset Allocation

Asset	%
Cash	0%
Stocks	100%
US Stocks	2%
Bonds	0%
US Bonds	0%
Other	0%

Services Offered:

Investment Strategy: The investment seeks to track as closely as possible, before fees and expenses, the total return of the FTSE Developed ex US Index. The fund will invest at least 90% of its net assets in stocks, including depositary receipts representing securities of the index; such depositary receipts may be in the form of American Depositary receipts, Global Depositary receipts and European Depositary receipts. The index is comprised of large and mid capitalization companies in developed countries outside the United States, as defined by the index provider. The index defines the large and mid capitalization universe as approximately the top 90% of the eligible universe. **Top Holdings:** Nestle SA Novartis AG Roche Holding AG Dividend Right Cert. Samsung Electronics Co Ltd GDR HSBC Holdings PLC

iShares S&P 500 Value ETF   C   HOLD

Ticker	Traded On	NAV	Total Assets ($)	Dividend Yield (TTM)	Turnover Ratio	Expense Ratio
IVE	NYSE Arca	101.11	$15,474,902,037	2.37	23	0.18

Ratings

Reward	C
Risk	C+
Recent Upgrade/Downgrade	Down

Fund Information

Fund Type	Exchange Traded Funds
Category	US Equity Large Cap Value
Sub-Category	Large Value
Prospectus Objective	Growth
Inception Date	May-00
Open to New Investments	Y

Prices

Price (as of 12/31/2018)	101.14
52-Week High	121.11
52-Week Low	95.36

Total Returns (%)

3-Month	6-Month	1-Year	3-Year	5-Year
-12.42	-6.95	-9.09	22.69	33.14

3-Year Standard Deviation	9.55
Effective Duration	

Valuation

Premium/Discount (1-Year Average)	0.01

Company Information

Provider	iShares
Manager/Tenure	Diane Hsiung (10), Greg Savage (10), Jennifer Hsui (6), 3 others
Website	http://www.ishares.com
Address	iShares 400 Howard Street San Francisco CA 94105 United States
Phone Number	800-474-2737

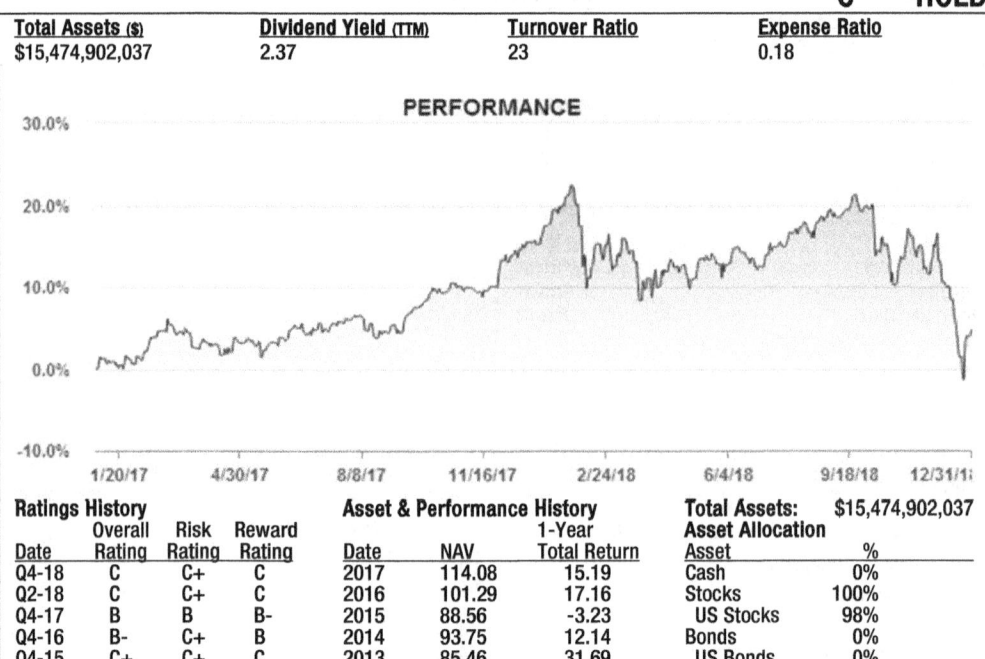

PERFORMANCE

Ratings History

Date	Overall Rating	Risk Rating	Reward Rating
Q4-18	C	C+	C
Q2-18	C	C+	C
Q4-17	B	B	B-
Q4-16	B-	C+	B
Q4-15	C+	C+	C

Asset & Performance History

Date	NAV	1-Year Total Return
2017	114.08	15.19
2016	101.29	17.16
2015	88.56	-3.23
2014	93.75	12.14
2013	85.46	31.69
2012	66.35	17.45

Total Assets: $15,474,902,037

Asset Allocation

Asset	%
Cash	0%
Stocks	100%
US Stocks	98%
Bonds	0%
US Bonds	0%
Other	0%

Services Offered: CashInvestment Plan

Investment Strategy: The investment seeks to track the investment results of the S&P 500 Value IndexTM, which measures the performance of the large-capitalization value sector of the U.S. equity market. The fund generally invests at least 90% of its assets in securities of the underlying index and in depositary receipts representing securities of the underlying index. It may invest the remainder of its assets in certain futures, options and swap contracts, cash and cash equivalents, as well as in securities not included in the underlying index, but which the advisor believes will help the fund track the underlying index. **Top Holdings:** Berkshire Hathaway Inc B JPMorgan Chase & Co Exxon Mobil Corp Verizon Communications Inc Wells Fargo & Co

---

Energy Select Sector SPDR® Fund   C   HOLD

Ticker	Traded On	NAV	Total Assets ($)	Dividend Yield (TTM)	Turnover Ratio	Expense Ratio
XLE	NYSE Arca	57.33	$15,446,648,069	2.96	8	0.13

Ratings

Reward	B-
Risk	C-
Recent Upgrade/Downgrade	Down

Fund Information

Fund Type	Exchange Traded Funds
Category	Energy Sector Equity
Sub-Category	Equity Energy
Prospectus Objective	Natl Res
Inception Date	Dec-98
Open to New Investments	Y

Prices

Price (as of 12/31/2018)	57.35
52-Week High	78.91
52-Week Low	53.84

Total Returns (%)

3-Month	6-Month	1-Year	3-Year	5-Year
-24.68	-22.08	-18.10	3.72	-25.55

3-Year Standard Deviation	18.54
Effective Duration	

Valuation

Premium/Discount (1-Year Average)	0.03

Company Information

Provider	SPDR State Street Global Advisors
Manager/Tenure	Michael J. Feehily (7), Karl A. Schneider (3), David Chin (1)
Website	http://www.spdrs.com
Address	SPDR State Street Global Advisors State Street Financial Center, 1 Lincoln Street Boston MA 02111-2900 United States
Phone Number	617-786-3000

PERFORMANCE

Ratings History

Date	Overall Rating	Risk Rating	Reward Rating
Q4-18	C	C-	B-
Q2-18	C	C-	B-
Q4-17	C-	C	C-
Q4-16	C-	D	C
Q4-15	C+	C	C+

Asset & Performance History

Date	NAV	1-Year Total Return
2017	72.15	-1.01
2016	75.29	28.92
2015	60.32	-21.46
2014	79.16	-8.6
2013	88.42	26.15
2012	71.4	5.17

Total Assets: $15,446,648,069

Asset Allocation

Asset	%
Cash	0%
Stocks	100%
US Stocks	99%
Bonds	0%
US Bonds	0%
Other	0%

Services Offered: Dividend Investment Plan, CashInvestment Plan

Investment Strategy: The investment seeks to provide investment results that, before expenses, correspond generally to the price and yield performance of publicly traded equity securities of companies in the Energy Select Sector Index. In seeking to track the performance of the index, the fund employs a replication strategy. It generally invests substantially all, but at least 95%, of its total assets in the securities comprising the index. The index includes securities of companies from the following industries: oil, gas and consumable fuels; and energy equipment and services. The fund is non-diversified. **Top Holdings:** Exxon Mobil Corp Chevron Corp ConocoPhillips Occidental Petroleum Corp EOG Resources Inc

iShares J.P. Morgan USD Emerging Markets Bond ETF   C-   HOLD

Ticker	Traded On	NAV	Total Assets ($)	Dividend Yield (TTM)	Turnover Ratio	Expense Ratio
EMB	NAS CM	103.17	$14,971,955,332	4.77	26	0.4

Ratings
Reward	D+
Risk	C
Recent Upgrade/Downgrade	Down

Fund Information
Fund Type	Exchange Traded Funds
Category	Emerging Mkts Fixed Inc
Sub-Category	Emerging Markets Bond
Prospectus Objective	Div Emerg Mkts
Inception Date	Dec-07
Open to New Investments	Y

Prices
Price (as of 12/31/2018)	103.91
52-Week High	116.72
52-Week Low	102.36

Total Returns (%)
3-Month	6-Month	1-Year	3-Year	5-Year
-1.56	0.73	-5.67	13.50	21.62

3-Year Standard Deviation	6
Effective Duration	7.04

Valuation
Premium/Discount (1-Year Average)	0.16

Company Information
Provider	iShares
Manager/Tenure	Scott Radell (8), James Mauro (7)
Website	http://www.ishares.com
Address	iShares 400 Howard Street San Francisco CA 94105 United States
Phone Number	800-474-2737

PERFORMANCE

Ratings History
Date	Overall Rating	Risk Rating	Reward Rating
Q4-18	C-	C	D+
Q2-18	C	B-	C-
Q4-17	B	B+	C+
Q4-16	C	C+	C
Q4-15	C	C	C-

Asset & Performance History
Date	NAV	1-Year Total Return
2017	115.53	9.97
2016	110	9.41
2015	105.44	0.43
2014	110.03	6.69
2013	107.84	-7.42
2012	121.96	17.64

Total Assets: $14,971,955,332

Asset Allocation
Asset	%
Cash	0%
Stocks	0%
US Stocks	0%
Bonds	100%
US Bonds	1%
Other	0%

Services Offered:

Investment Strategy: The investment seeks to track the investment results of the J.P. Morgan EMBI® Global Core Index composed of U.S. dollar-denominated, emerging market bonds. The fund generally will invest at least 90% of its assets in the component securities of the underlying index and may invest up to 10% of its assets in certain futures, options and swap contracts, cash and cash equivalents, as well as in securities not included in the underlying index. The index is a broad, diverse U.S. dollar-denominated emerging markets debt benchmark that tracks the total return of actively traded external debt instruments in emerging market countries. The fund is non-diversified. **Top Holdings:** Uruguay (Republic of) 5.1% Poland (Republic of) 5% Russian Federation 5.25% The Republic of Peru 8.75% The Republic of Peru 5.63%

Invesco S&P 500® Equal Weight ETF   C   HOLD

Ticker	Traded On	NAV	Total Assets ($)	Dividend Yield (TTM)	Turnover Ratio	Expense Ratio
RSP	NYSE Arca	91.39	$14,753,649,664	1.74		0.2

Ratings
Reward	C-
Risk	C+
Recent Upgrade/Downgrade	Down

Fund Information
Fund Type	Exchange Traded Funds
Category	US Equity Large Cap Blend
Sub-Category	Large Blend
Prospectus Objective	Growth
Inception Date	Apr-03
Open to New Investments	Y

Prices
Price (as of 12/31/2018)	91.40
52-Week High	108.58
52-Week Low	86.19

Total Returns (%)
3-Month	6-Month	1-Year	3-Year	5-Year
-13.92	-9.31	-7.76	24.98	38.84

3-Year Standard Deviation	9.95
Effective Duration	

Valuation
Premium/Discount (1-Year Average)	-0.01

Company Information
Provider	Invesco
Manager/Tenure	Peter Hubbard (0), Michael Jeanette (0), Jonathan Nixon (0), 1 other
Website	http://www.invesco.com/us
Address	Invesco 11 Greenway Plaza, Ste. 2500 Houston TX 77046 United States
Phone Number	800-659-1005

PERFORMANCE

Ratings History
Date	Overall Rating	Risk Rating	Reward Rating
Q4-18	C	C+	C-
Q2-18	C	C+	C
Q4-17	B-	B-	B-
Q4-16	B-	C+	B
Q4-15	C	C+	C

Asset & Performance History
Date	NAV	1-Year Total Return
2017	100.96	18.68
2016	86.57	13.97
2015	76.69	-2.57
2014	80.03	14.01
2013	71.26	35.59
2012	53.3	17.05

Total Assets: $14,753,649,664

Asset Allocation
Asset	%
Cash	0%
Stocks	100%
US Stocks	99%
Bonds	0%
US Bonds	0%
Other	0%

Services Offered: Dividend Investment Plan

Investment Strategy: The investment seeks to track the investment results (before fees and expenses) of the S&P 500® Equal Weight Index (the "underlying index"). The fund generally invests in all of the securities comprising the underlying index in proportion to their weightings in the underlying index. Strictly in accordance with its guidelines and mandated procedures, the index provider compiles, maintains and calculates the underlying index, which is an equal-weighted version of the S&P 500® Index. The fund is non-diversified. **Top Holdings:** CVS Health Corp SCANA Corp TripAdvisor Inc Starbucks Corp Foot Locker Inc

Schwab U.S. Large-Cap ETF™

C   **HOLD**

Ticker	Traded On	NAV
SCHX	NYSE Arca	59.63

Total Assets ($)	Dividend Yield (TTM)	Turnover Ratio	Expense Ratio
$14,635,170,685	1.79	3	0.03

Ratings
Reward   C
Risk   C+
Recent Upgrade/Downgrade   Down

Fund Information
Fund Type	Exchange Traded Funds
Category	US Equity Large Cap Blend
Sub-Category	Large Blend
Prospectus Objective	Growth
Inception Date	Nov-09
Open to New Investments	Y

Prices
Price (as of 12/31/2018)	59.70
52-Week High	70.26
52-Week Low	56.03

Total Returns (%)
3-Month	6-Month	1-Year	3-Year	5-Year
-13.94	-7.47	-4.52	30.10	48.94

3-Year Standard Deviation	9.54
Effective Duration	

Valuation
Premium/Discount (1-Year Average)	0.01

Company Information
Provider	Schwab ETFs
Manager/Tenure	Ferian Juwono (8), Christopher Bliss (1), Sabya Sinha (1), 1 other
Website	http://www.schwabetfs.com
Address	Schwab ETFs United States
Phone Number	800-435-4000

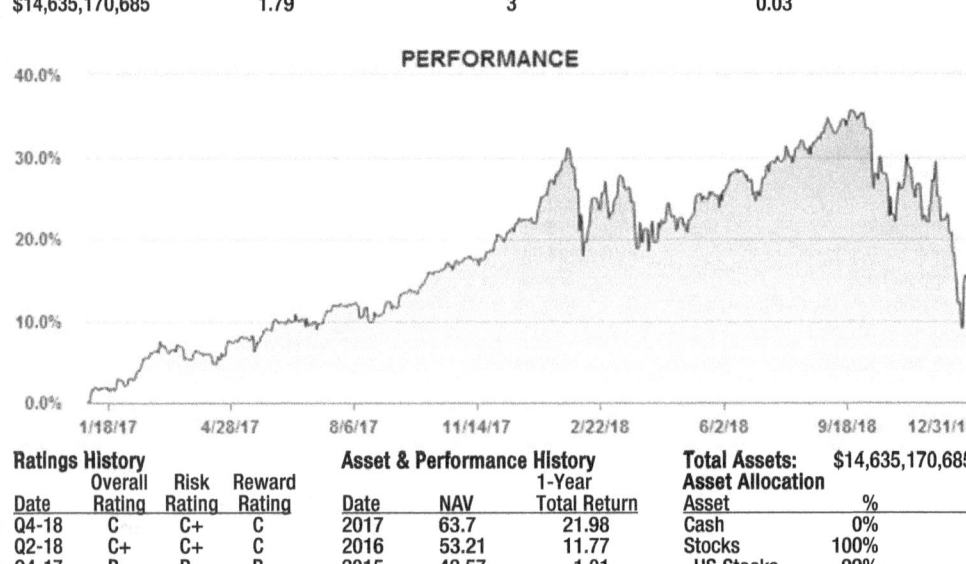

PERFORMANCE

Ratings History
Date	Overall Rating	Risk Rating	Reward Rating
Q4-18	C	C+	C
Q2-18	C+	C+	C
Q4-17	B	B	B
Q4-16	B-	C+	B
Q4-15	C+	C+	C

Asset & Performance History
Date	NAV	1-Year Total Return
2017	63.7	21.98
2016	53.21	11.77
2015	48.57	1.01
2014	49.06	13.33
2013	44.09	32.54
2012	33.88	16.05

Total Assets: $14,635,170,685

Asset Allocation
Asset	%
Cash	0%
Stocks	100%
US Stocks	99%
Bonds	0%
US Bonds	0%
Other	0%

Services Offered:

Investment Strategy: The investment seeks to track as closely as possible, before fees and expenses, the total return of the Dow Jones U.S. Large-Cap Total Stock Market Index. To pursue its goal, the fund generally invests in stocks that are included in the Dow Jones U.S. Large-Cap Total Stock Market Index. The index includes the large-cap portion of the Dow Jones U.S. Total Stock Market Index actually available to investors in the marketplace. The Dow Jones U.S. Large-Cap Total Stock Market Index includes the components ranked 1-750 by full market capitalization. The index is a float-adjusted market capitalization weighted index. **Top Holdings:** Microsoft Corp Apple Inc Amazon.com Inc Berkshire Hathaway Inc B Johnson & Johnson

---

iShares U.S. Preferred Stock ETF

C-   **HOLD**

Ticker	Traded On	NAV
PFF	NAS CM	34.26

Total Assets ($)	Dividend Yield (TTM)	Turnover Ratio	Expense Ratio
$14,577,805,163	5.79	22	0.46

Ratings
Reward   D+
Risk   C
Recent Upgrade/Downgrade   Down

Fund Information
Fund Type	Exchange Traded Funds
Category	US Fixed Income
Sub-Category	Preferred Stock
Prospectus Objective	Growth & Inc
Inception Date	Mar-07
Open to New Investments	Y

Prices
Price (as of 12/31/2018)	34.23
52-Week High	38.19
52-Week Low	33.41

Total Returns (%)
3-Month	6-Month	1-Year	3-Year	5-Year
-5.34	-6.13	-4.77	4.45	23.96

3-Year Standard Deviation	4.45
Effective Duration	4.61

Valuation
Premium/Discount (1-Year Average)	-0.01

Company Information
Provider	iShares
Manager/Tenure	Diane Hsiung (10), Greg Savage (10), Jennifer Hsui (6), 3 others
Website	http://www.ishares.com
Address	iShares 400 Howard Street San Francisco CA 94105 United States
Phone Number	800-474-2737

PERFORMANCE

Ratings History
Date	Overall Rating	Risk Rating	Reward Rating
Q4-18	C-	C	D+
Q2-18	C	C+	C
Q4-17	B	A	C+
Q4-16	C	C	C
Q4-15	C+	C+	C+

Asset & Performance History
Date	NAV	1-Year Total Return
2017	38.16	8.32
2016	37.22	1.25
2015	38.88	4.61
2014	39.34	13.44
2013	36.95	-0.59
2012	39.59	18.24

Total Assets: $14,577,805,163

Asset Allocation
Asset	%
Cash	1%
Stocks	0%
US Stocks	0%
Bonds	0%
US Bonds	0%
Other	0%

Services Offered:

Investment Strategy: The investment seeks to track the investment results of the S&P U.S. Preferred Stock Index, which measures the performance of a select group of preferred stocks listed on the New York Stock Exchange, NYSE Arca, NYSE Amex, NASDAQ Global Select Market, NASDAQ Select Market or NASDAQ Capital Market. The fund generally will invest at least 90% of its assets in the component securities of the index and may invest up to 10% of its assets in certain futures, options and swap contracts, cash and cash equivalents, as well as in securities not included in the index, but which the advisor believes will help the fund track the index. **Top Holdings:** Becton, Dickinson and Co Pfd GMAC Capital Trust I Pfd Secs 2011-15.2.40 Gtd Series 2 Barclays Bank PLC 8 1/8 % Non Cum Callable Dollar Pref Shs Sp Am Dep Receip Citigroup Capital XIII Floating Rate Trust Pfd Secs Registered 2010-30.10.4 Sempra Energy 6% PRF CONVERT 15/01/2021 USD 100

iShares iBoxx $ High Yield Corporate Bond ETF   C+   HOLD

Ticker	Traded On	NAV	Total Assets ($)	Dividend Yield (TTM)	Turnover Ratio	Expense Ratio
HYG	NYSE Arca	80.90	$14,220,040,513	5.34	17	0.49

Ratings
Reward   C-
Risk   A-
Recent Upgrade/Downgrade   Down

Fund Information
Fund Type   Exchange Traded Funds
Category   US Fixed Income
Sub-Category   High Yield Bond
Prospectus Objective   Corp Bond-High Yld
Inception Date   Apr-07
Open to New Investments   Y

Prices
Price (as of 12/31/2018)   81.10
52-Week High   87.97
52-Week Low   79.63

Total Returns (%)

3-Month	6-Month	1-Year	3-Year	5-Year
-4.58	-1.76	-1.93	18.52	14.18

3-Year Standard Deviation   4.16
Effective Duration   3.78

Valuation
Premium/Discount (1-Year Average)   0.15

Company Information
Provider   iShares
Manager/Tenure   Scott Radell (8), James Mauro (7)
Website   http://www.ishares.com
Address   iShares 400 Howard Street San Francisco CA 94105 United States
Phone Number   800-474-2737

PERFORMANCE

Ratings History

Date	Overall Rating	Risk Rating	Reward Rating
Q4-18	C+	A-	C-
Q2-18	B-	B	C
Q4-17	B-	B	C+
Q4-16	C+	B	C
Q4-15	C	C	C-

Asset & Performance History

Date	NAV	1-Year Total Return
2017	86.97	6.08
2016	86.26	13.92
2015	79.97	-5.54
2014	89.43	2
2013	92.62	5.89
2012	92.97	13.82

Total Assets: $14,220,040,513
Asset Allocation

Asset	%
Cash	1%
Stocks	0%
US Stocks	0%
Bonds	99%
US Bonds	86%
Other	0%

Services Offered:

Investment Strategy: The investment seeks to track the investment results of the Markit iBoxx® USD Liquid High Yield Index (the "underlying index"). The underlying index is a rules-based index consisting of liquid, U.S. dollar-denominated, high yield corporate bonds for sale in the United States. The fund generally will invest at least 90% of its assets in the component securities of the underlying index and may invest up to 10% of its assets in certain futures, options and swap contracts, cash and cash equivalents, as well as in securities not included in the underlying index. **Top Holdings:** ALTICE FRANCE S.A 7.38% Sprint Corporation 7.88% First Data Corporation 7% CCO Holdings, LLC/ CCO Holdings Capital Corp. 5.13% Bausch Health Companies Inc 5.88%

Consumer Discretionary Select Sector SPDR® Fund   B-   BUY

Ticker	Traded On	NAV	Total Assets ($)	Dividend Yield (TTM)	Turnover Ratio	Expense Ratio
XLY	NYSE Arca	98.99	$13,593,260,414	1.19	23	0.13

Ratings
Reward   B
Risk   C
Recent Upgrade/Downgrade   Down

Fund Information
Fund Type   Exchange Traded Funds
Category   Consumer Goods & Svcs
Sub-Category   Consumer Cyclical
Prospectus Objective   Unaligned
Inception Date   Dec-98
Open to New Investments   Y

Prices
Price (as of 12/31/2018)   99.01
52-Week High   117.79
52-Week Low   91.98

Total Returns (%)

3-Month	6-Month	1-Year	3-Year	5-Year
-14.98	-8.93	1.66	32.14	59.04

3-Year Standard Deviation   12.2
Effective Duration

Valuation
Premium/Discount (1-Year Average)   0.01

Company Information
Provider   SPDR State Street Global Advisors
Manager/Tenure   Michael J. Feehily (7), Karl A. Schneider (3), Kala O'Donnell (1)
Website   http://www.spdrs.com
Address   SPDR State Street Global Advisors State Street Financial Center, 1 Lincoln Street Boston MA 02111-2900 United States
Phone Number   617-786-3000

PERFORMANCE

Ratings History

Date	Overall Rating	Risk Rating	Reward Rating
Q4-18	B-	C	B
Q2-18	B	C	B
Q4-17	B	A	B
Q4-16	B	B	B
Q4-15	B	A-	B

Asset & Performance History

Date	NAV	1-Year Total Return
2017	98.6	22.76
2016	81.36	5.79
2015	78.2	9.92
2014	72.18	9.49
2013	66.84	42.74
2012	47.44	23.59

Total Assets: $13,593,260,414
Asset Allocation

Asset	%
Cash	0%
Stocks	100%
US Stocks	100%
Bonds	0%
US Bonds	0%
Other	0%

Services Offered: Dividend Investment Plan, CashInvestment Plan

Investment Strategy: The investment seeks investment results that, before expenses, correspond to the price and yield performance of publicly traded equity securities of companies in the Consumer Discretionary Select Sector Index. The fund employs a replication strategy. It generally invests substantially all, but at least 95%, of its total assets in the securities comprising the index. The index includes securities of companies from the following industries: media; retail; hotels, restaurants and leisure; textiles, apparel and luxury goods; household durables; automobiles; auto components; distributors; leisure products; and diversified consumer services. It is non-diversified. **Top Holdings:** Amazon.com Inc The Home Depot Inc McDonald's Corp Nike Inc B Starbucks Corp

Schwab U.S. Broad Market ETF™ | C | HOLD

Ticker	Traded On	NAV	Total Assets ($)	Dividend Yield (TTM)	Turnover Ratio	Expense Ratio
SCHB	NYSE Arca	59.90	$13,057,476,034	1.77	4	0.03

Ratings
Reward	C
Risk	C+
Recent Upgrade/Downgrade	Down

Fund Information
Fund Type	Exchange Traded Funds
Category	US Equity Large Cap Blend
Sub-Category	Large Blend
Prospectus Objective	Growth
Inception Date	Nov-09
Open to New Investments	Y

Prices
Price (as of 12/31/2018)	59.93
52-Week High	71.11
52-Week Low	56.21

Total Returns (%)
3-Month	6-Month	1-Year	3-Year	5-Year
-14.44	-8.50	-5.24	29.23	46.26

3-Year Standard Deviation	9.81
Effective Duration	

Valuation
Premium/Discount (1-Year Average)	0.00

Company Information
Provider	Schwab ETFs
Manager/Tenure	Ferian Juwono (8), Christopher Bliss (1), Sabya Sinha (1), 1 other
Website	http://www.schwabetfs.com
Address	Schwab ETFs United States
Phone Number	800-435-4000

PERFORMANCE

Ratings History
Date	Overall Rating	Risk Rating	Reward Rating
Q4-18	C	C+	C
Q2-18	C+	C+	C+
Q4-17	B	B	B
Q4-16	B-	C+	B
Q4-15	C+	C+	C

Asset & Performance History
Date	NAV	1-Year Total Return
2017	64.45	21.29
2016	54.13	12.54
2015	49.04	0.45
2014	49.79	12.67
2013	44.99	33.37
2012	34.35	16.21

Total Assets: $13,057,476,034

Asset Allocation
Asset	%
Cash	0%
Stocks	100%
US Stocks	99%
Bonds	0%
US Bonds	0%
Other	0%

Services Offered:

Investment Strategy: The investment seeks to track as closely as possible, before fees and expenses, the total return of the Dow Jones U.S. Broad Stock Market Index. To pursue its goal, the fund generally invests in stocks that are included in the index. The fund will invest at least 90% of its net assets in these stocks. The index includes the largest 2,500 publicly traded U.S. companies for which pricing information is readily available. The index is a float-adjusted market capitalization weighted index that reflects the shares of securities actually available to investors in the marketplace. **Top Holdings:** Microsoft Corp Apple Inc Amazon.com Inc Berkshire Hathaway Inc B Johnson & Johnson

---

iShares Core MSCI Total International Stock ETF | C- | HOLD

Ticker	Traded On	NAV	Total Assets ($)	Dividend Yield (TTM)	Turnover Ratio	Expense Ratio
IXUS	NAS CM	52.49	$12,421,488,118	2.99	2	0.1

Ratings
Reward	D+
Risk	C
Recent Upgrade/Downgrade	Down

Fund Information
Fund Type	Exchange Traded Funds
Category	Global Equity Large Cap
Sub-Category	Foreign Large Blend
Prospectus Objective	Foreign Stock
Inception Date	Oct-12
Open to New Investments	Y

Prices
Price (as of 12/31/2018)	52.53
52-Week High	67.91
52-Week Low	50.85

Total Returns (%)
3-Month	6-Month	1-Year	3-Year	5-Year
-11.83	-10.33	-14.55	14.53	4.91

3-Year Standard Deviation	11.34
Effective Duration	

Valuation
Premium/Discount (1-Year Average)	0.08

Company Information
Provider	iShares
Manager/Tenure	Diane Hsiung (6), Jennifer Hsui (6), Greg Savage (6), 3 others
Website	http://www.ishares.com
Address	iShares 400 Howard Street San Francisco CA 94105 United States
Phone Number	800-474-2737

PERFORMANCE

Ratings History
Date	Overall Rating	Risk Rating	Reward Rating
Q4-18	C-	C	D+
Q2-18	C	C+	C
Q4-17	B	B-	B
Q4-16	C-	C	D+
Q4-15	C	C+	D+

Asset & Performance History
Date	NAV	1-Year Total Return
2017	63.15	28.07
2016	50.57	4.65
2015	49.59	-4.61
2014	53.36	-3.96
2013	57.13	15.84
2012	50.48	

Total Assets: $12,421,488,118

Asset Allocation
Asset	%
Cash	1%
Stocks	99%
US Stocks	1%
Bonds	0%
US Bonds	0%
Other	0%

Services Offered:

Investment Strategy: The investment seeks to track the investment results of the MSCI ACWI ex USA IMI composed of large-, mid- and small-capitalization non-U.S. equities. The fund generally will invest at least 90% of its assets in the component securities of the underlying index and in investments that have economic characteristics that are substantially identical to the component securities of the underlying index. The index is a free float-adjusted market capitalization index designed to measure the combined equity market performance of developed and emerging markets countries, excluding the United States. **Top Holdings:** Nestle SA Tencent Holdings Ltd Alibaba Group Holding Ltd ADR Novartis AG Roche Holding AG Dividend Right Cert.

iShares Floating Rate Bond ETF　　　　　　　　　　　　　　　　　C　　HOLD

Ticker	Traded On	NAV	Total Assets ($)	Dividend Yield (TTM)	Turnover Ratio	Expense Ratio
FLOT	BATS	50.42	$12,404,096,632	2.18	21	0.2

Ratings

Reward	C
Risk	C+
Recent Upgrade/Downgrade	

Fund Information

Fund Type	Exchange Traded Funds
Category	US Fixed Income
Sub-Category	Ultrashort Bond
Prospectus Objective	Worldwide Bond
Inception Date	Jun-11
Open to New Investments	Y

Prices

Price (as of 12/31/2018)	50.36
52-Week High	51.06
52-Week Low	50.22

Total Returns (%)

3-Month	6-Month	1-Year	3-Year	5-Year
-0.21	0.51	1.56	5.01	5.45

3-Year Standard Deviation	0.33
Effective Duration	0.15

Valuation

Premium/Discount (1-Year Average)	0.08

Company Information

Provider	iShares
Manager/Tenure	James Mauro (7), Scott Radell (7)
Website	http://www.ishares.com
Address	iShares 400 Howard Street San Francisco CA 94105 United States
Phone Number	800-474-2737

PERFORMANCE

Ratings History

Date	Overall Rating	Risk Rating	Reward Rating
Q4-18	C	C+	C
Q2-18	C	C+	C
Q4-17	B-	A-	C
Q4-16	C	C+	C
Q4-15	C	C+	C

Asset & Performance History

Date	NAV	1-Year Total Return
2017	50.84	1.82
2016	50.66	1.54
2015	50.38	0.11
2014	50.59	0.3
2013	50.66	1.11
2012	50.34	4.08

Total Assets: $12,404,096,632

Asset Allocation

Asset	%
Cash	6%
Stocks	0%
US Stocks	0%
Bonds	92%
US Bonds	53%
Other	0%

Services Offered:

Investment Strategy: The investment seeks to track the investment results of the Bloomberg Barclays US Floating Rate Note < 5 Years Index (the "underlying index"), which measures the performance of U.S. dollar-denominated, investment-grade floating rate notes. The fund generally will invest at least 90% of its assets in the component securities of the underlying index and may invest up to 10% of its assets in certain futures, options and swap contracts, cash and cash equivalents, as well as in securities not included in the underlying index, but which BFA believes will help the fund track the underlying index. **Top Holdings:** Morgan Stanley 3.41% Morgan Stanley 3.65% Asian Development Bank 2.52% Inter-American Development Bank 2.64% International Finance Corporation 2.4%

Vanguard Mid-Cap Growth Index Fund ETF Shares　　　　　　　　　C　　HOLD

Ticker	Traded On	NAV	Total Assets ($)	Dividend Yield (TTM)	Turnover Ratio	Expense Ratio
VOT	NYSE Arca		$12,232,703,847	0.71	23	0.07

Ratings

Reward	C
Risk	C+
Recent Upgrade/Downgrade	Down

Fund Information

Fund Type	Exchange Traded Funds
Category	US Equity Mid Cap
Sub-Category	Mid-Cap Growth
Prospectus Objective	Growth
Inception Date	Aug-06
Open to New Investments	Y

Prices

Price (as of 12/31/2018)	119.69
52-Week High	143.70
52-Week Low	111.81

Total Returns (%)

3-Month	6-Month	1-Year	3-Year	5-Year
-16.39	-11.63	-6.50	21.59	36.62

3-Year Standard Deviation	11.65
Effective Duration	

Valuation

Premium/Discount (1-Year Average)	0.01

Company Information

Provider	Vanguard
Manager/Tenure	Donald M. Butler (5), Michael A. Johnson (2)
Website	http://www.vanguard.com
Address	Vanguard 100 Vanguard Boulevard Malvern PA 19355 United States
Phone Number	877-662-7447

PERFORMANCE

Ratings History

Date	Overall Rating	Risk Rating	Reward Rating
Q4-18	C	C+	C
Q2-18	C+	C+	C+
Q4-17	B-	C+	B
Q4-16	C	C-	B-
Q4-15	C+	C+	C

Asset & Performance History

Date	NAV	1-Year Total Return
2017	127.67	22.18
2016	105.6	6.46
2015	99.75	-0.99
2014	101.57	13.49
2013	90.2	32.22
2012	68.64	15.94

Total Assets: $12,232,703,847

Asset Allocation

Asset	%
Cash	0%
Stocks	100%
US Stocks	99%
Bonds	0%
US Bonds	0%
Other	0%

Services Offered:

Investment Strategy: The investment seeks to track the performance of the CRSP US Mid Cap Growth Index that measures the investment return of mid-capitalization growth stocks. The fund employs an indexing investment approach designed to track the performance of the CRSP US Mid Cap Growth Index, a broadly diversified index of growth stocks of mid-size U.S. companies. The advisor attempts to replicate the target index by investing all, or substantially all, of its assets in the stocks that make up the index, holding each stock in approximately the same proportion as its weighting in the index. **Top Holdings:** Fiserv Inc Edwards Lifesciences Corp Red Hat Inc Roper Technologies Inc Autodesk Inc

PIMCO Enhanced Short Maturity Active Exchange-Traded Fund   C   HOLD

Ticker	Traded On	NAV
MINT	NYSE Arca	100.96

Total Assets ($)	Dividend Yield (TTM)	Turnover Ratio	Expense Ratio
$12,147,252,092	2.14	86	0.42

Ratings
Reward   C
Risk   C+
Recent Upgrade/Downgrade

Fund Information
Fund Type   Exchange Traded Funds
Category   US Fixed Income
Sub-Category   Ultrashort Bond
Prospectus Objective   Income
Inception Date   Nov-09
Open to New Investments   Y

Prices
Price (as of 12/31/2018)   100.95
52-Week High   101.71
52-Week Low   100.95

Total Returns (%)

3-Month	6-Month	1-Year	3-Year	5-Year
0.21	0.86	1.71	5.71	6.83

3-Year Standard Deviation   0.29
Effective Duration   0.33

Valuation
Premium/Discount (1-Year Average)   0.00

Company Information
Provider   PIMCO
Manager/Tenure   Jerome M. Schneider (9)
Website   http://www.pimco.com
Address   PIMCO 840 Newport Center Drive,
                    Suite 100 Newport Beach CA 92660
                    United States
Phone Number   866-746-2602

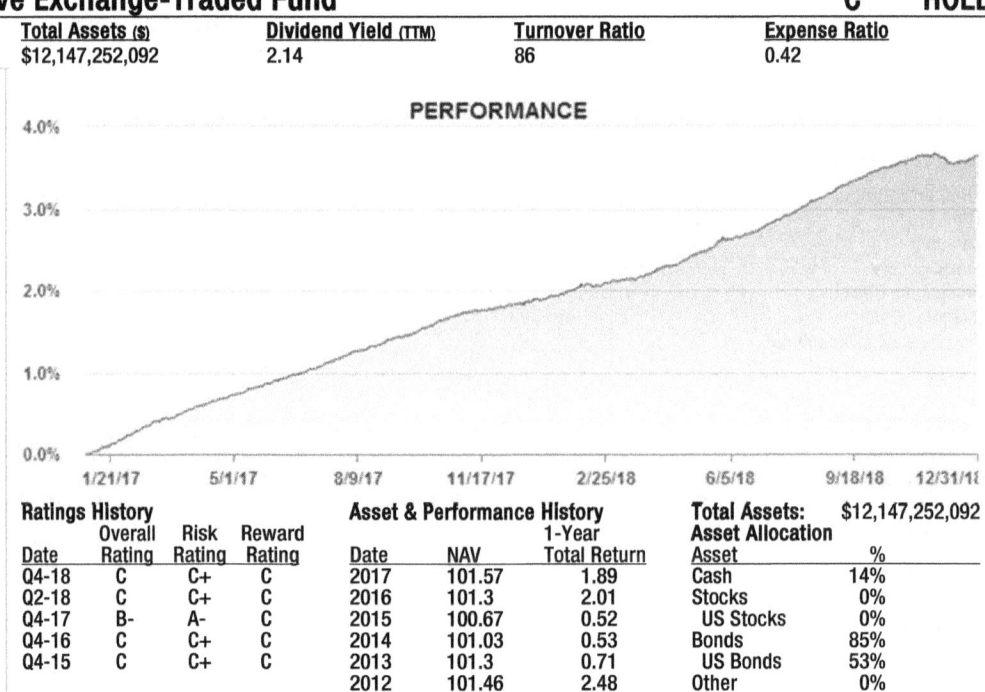

PERFORMANCE

Ratings History

Date	Overall Rating	Risk Rating	Reward Rating
Q4-18	C	C+	C
Q2-18	C	C+	C
Q4-17	B-	A-	C
Q4-16	C	C+	C
Q4-15	C	C+	C

Asset & Performance History

Date	NAV	1-Year Total Return
2017	101.57	1.89
2016	101.3	2.01
2015	100.67	0.52
2014	101.03	0.53
2013	101.3	0.71
2012	101.46	2.48

Total Assets: $12,147,252,092
Asset Allocation

Asset	%
Cash	14%
Stocks	0%
US Stocks	0%
Bonds	85%
US Bonds	53%
Other	0%

Services Offered:

Investment Strategy: The investment seeks maximum current income, consistent with preservation of capital and daily liquidity. The fund invests at least 80% of its net assets in a diversified portfolio of Fixed Income Instruments of varying maturities, which may be represented by forwards. "Fixed Income Instruments" include bonds, debt securities and other similar instruments issued by various U.S. and non-U.S. public- or private-sector entities. The average portfolio duration of this fund will vary based on PIMCO's market forecasts and will normally not exceed one year. **Top Holdings:** Diamond 1 Finance Corporation/Diamond 2 Finance Corporation 3.48% Shire Acquisitions Investments Ireland DAC 1.9% Time Warner Cable Inc. 8.25% Barclays PLC 2.75% NTT Finance Corp 2.92%

Industrial Select Sector SPDR® Fund   C   HOLD

Ticker	Traded On	NAV
XLI	NYSE Arca	64.43

Total Assets ($)	Dividend Yield (TTM)	Turnover Ratio	Expense Ratio
$11,901,074,404	1.92	6	0.13

Ratings
Reward   C
Risk   C+
Recent Upgrade/Downgrade   Down

Fund Information
Fund Type   Exchange Traded Funds
Category   Industrials Sector Equity
Sub-Category   Industrials
Prospectus Objective   Unaligned
Inception Date   Dec-98
Open to New Investments   Y

Prices
Price (as of 12/31/2018)   64.41
52-Week High   80.66
52-Week Low   60.34

Total Returns (%)

3-Month	6-Month	1-Year	3-Year	5-Year
-18.00	-9.21	-13.09	29.07	36.47

3-Year Standard Deviation   13.16
Effective Duration

Valuation
Premium/Discount (1-Year Average)   0.01

Company Information
Provider   SPDR State Street Global Advisors
Manager/Tenure   Michael J. Feehily (7), Karl A.
                    Schneider (3), Emiliano Rabinovich (1)
Website   http://www.spdrs.com
Address   SPDR State Street Global Advisors
                    State Street Financial Center, 1
                    Lincoln Street Boston MA 02111-2900
                    United States
Phone Number   617-786-3000

PERFORMANCE

Ratings History

Date	Overall Rating	Risk Rating	Reward Rating
Q4-18	C	C+	C
Q2-18	B-	B	C+
Q4-17	B-	B-	B+
Q4-16	B	B-	B
Q4-15	B-	B	C+

Asset & Performance History

Date	NAV	1-Year Total Return
2017	75.58	23.84
2016	62.2	19.53
2015	53.03	-4.27
2014	56.58	10.44
2013	52.22	40.44
2012	37.9	14.85

Total Assets: $11,901,074,404
Asset Allocation

Asset	%
Cash	1%
Stocks	99%
US Stocks	99%
Bonds	0%
US Bonds	0%
Other	0%

Services Offered: Dividend Investment Plan, CashInvestment Plan

Investment Strategy: The investment seeks to provide investment results that, before expenses, correspond generally to the price and yield performance of publicly traded equity securities of companies in the Industrial Select Sector Index. Under normal market conditions, the fund generally invests substantially all, but at least 95%, of its total assets in the securities comprising the index. The index includes securities of companies from the following industries: aerospace and defense; industrial conglomerates; marine; transportation infrastructure; machinery; road and rail; air freight and logistics; commercial services and supplies; etc. It is non-diversified. **Top Holdings:** Boeing Co 3M Co Union Pacific Corp Honeywell International Inc United Technologies Corp

iShares MBS ETF   C-   HOLD

Ticker	Traded On	NAV
MBB	NAS CM	104.60

Total Assets ($)	Dividend Yield (TTM)	Turnover Ratio	Expense Ratio
$11,639,111,426	2.56	745	0.09

Ratings
Reward   D+
Risk   C+
Recent Upgrade/Downgrade

Fund Information
Fund Type   Exchange Traded Funds
Category   US Fixed Income
Sub-Category   Intermediate Government
Prospectus Objective   Govt Bond - Mortgage
Inception Date   Mar-07
Open to New Investments   Y

Prices
Price (as of 12/31/2018)   104.65
52-Week High   106.59
52-Week Low   101.79

Total Returns (%)

3-Month	6-Month	1-Year	3-Year	5-Year
2.10	2.04	0.81	4.52	12.38

3-Year Standard Deviation   2.11
Effective Duration   5.43

Valuation
Premium/Discount (1-Year Average)   0.03

Company Information
Provider   iShares
Manager/Tenure   Scott Radell (8), James Mauro (7)
Website   http://www.ishares.com
Address   iShares 400 Howard Street San
                               Francisco CA 94105 United States
Phone Number   800-474-2737

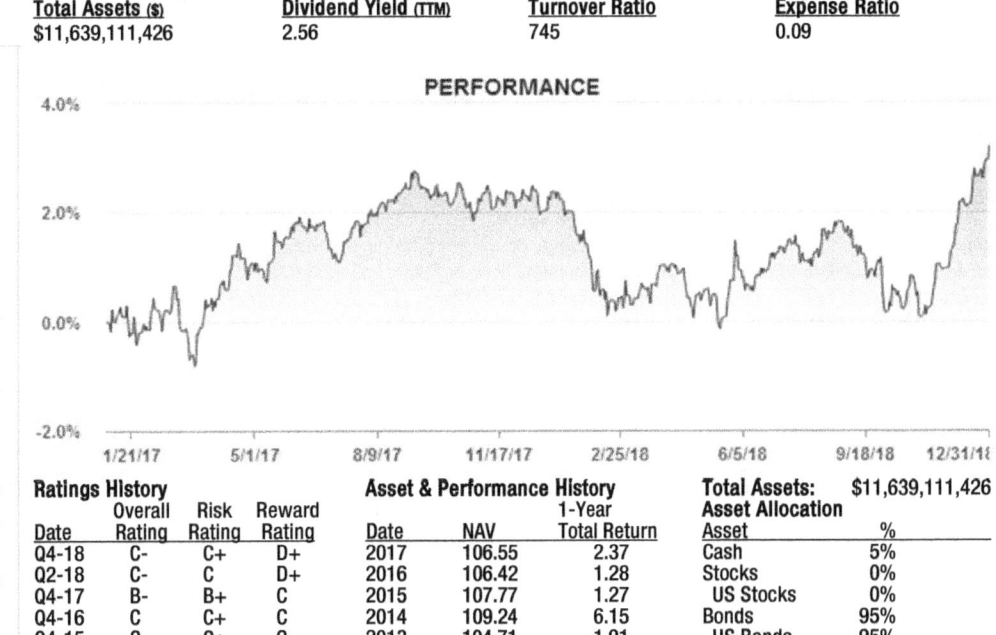

PERFORMANCE

Ratings History

Date	Overall Rating	Risk Rating	Reward Rating
Q4-18	C-	C+	D+
Q2-18	C-	C	D+
Q4-17	B-	B+	C
Q4-16	C	C+	C
Q4-15	C	C+	C

Asset & Performance History

Date	NAV	1-Year Total Return
2017	106.55	2.37
2016	106.42	1.28
2015	107.77	1.27
2014	109.24	6.15
2013	104.71	-1.91
2012	108.1	2.23

Total Assets: $11,639,111,426
Asset Allocation

Asset	%
Cash	5%
Stocks	0%
US Stocks	0%
Bonds	95%
US Bonds	95%
Other	0%

Services Offered:

Investment Strategy: The investment seeks to track the investment results of the Bloomberg Barclays U.S. MBS Index. The fund seeks to track the performance of the underlying index by investing at least 90% of its assets in the securities of the underlying index and in investments that provide substantially similar exposure to securities in the underlying index. The index measures the performance of investment-grade mortgage-backed pass-through securities ("MBS") issued or guaranteed by U.S. government agencies. **Top Holdings:** Fnma 30yr 2016 Production Gnma2 30yr 2017 Production Gnma2 30yr 2016 Production Gnma2 30yr 2016 Production Fgold 30yr 2016 Production

---

iShares Russell Mid-Cap Value ETF   C   HOLD

Ticker	Traded On	NAV
IWS	NYSE Arca	76.34

Total Assets ($)	Dividend Yield (TTM)	Turnover Ratio	Expense Ratio
$11,177,198,855	2.28	20	0.25

Ratings
Reward   C-
Risk   C+
Recent Upgrade/Downgrade   Down

Fund Information
Fund Type   Exchange Traded Funds
Category   US Equity Mid Cap
Sub-Category   Mid-Cap Value
Prospectus Objective   Growth
Inception Date   Jul-01
Open to New Investments   Y

Prices
Price (as of 12/31/2018)   76.35
52-Week High   92.83
52-Week Low   72.26

Total Returns (%)

3-Month	6-Month	1-Year	3-Year	5-Year
-14.70	-12.07	-12.36	18.63	29.12

3-Year Standard Deviation   10.45
Effective Duration

Valuation
Premium/Discount (1-Year Average)   0.00

Company Information
Provider   iShares
Manager/Tenure   Diane Hsiung (10), Greg Savage (10),
                               Jennifer Hsui (6), 3 others
Website   http://www.ishares.com
Address   iShares 400 Howard Street San
                               Francisco CA 94105 United States
Phone Number   800-474-2737

PERFORMANCE

Ratings History

Date	Overall Rating	Risk Rating	Reward Rating
Q4-18	C	C+	C-
Q2-18	C	C+	C
Q4-17	B	B	B-
Q4-16	B-	C+	B
Q4-15	C	C+	C

Asset & Performance History

Date	NAV	1-Year Total Return
2017	89.09	13.09
2016	80.41	19.69
2015	68.7	-4.93
2014	73.77	14.49
2013	65.66	33.1
2012	50.25	18.27

Total Assets: $11,177,198,855
Asset Allocation

Asset	%
Cash	0%
Stocks	100%
US Stocks	99%
Bonds	0%
US Bonds	0%
Other	0%

Services Offered: CashInvestment Plan

Investment Strategy: The investment seeks to track the investment results of the Russell Midcap Value Index, which measures the performance of the mid-capitalization value sector of the U.S. equity market. The fund generally invests at least 90% of its assets in securities of the underlying index and in depositary receipts representing securities of the underlying index. It may invest the remainder of its assets in certain futures, options and swap contracts, cash and cash equivalents, as well as in securities not included in the underlying index, but which the advisor believes will help the fund track the underlying index. **Top Holdings:** Fidelity National Information Services Inc Sempra Energy Williams Companies Inc SunTrust Banks Inc Analog Devices Inc

iShares Gold Trust   D+   SELL

Ticker	Traded On	NAV	Total Assets ($)	Dividend Yield (TTM)	Turnover Ratio	Expense Ratio
IAU	NYSE Arca	12.28	$10,635,318,199	0	0	0.25

Ratings
Reward	D+
Risk	C-
Recent Upgrade/Downgrade	Down

Fund Information
Fund Type	Exchange Traded Funds
Category	Commodities Specified
Sub-Category	Commodities Precious Metals
Prospectus Objective	Prec Metals
Inception Date	Jan-05
Open to New Investments	Y

Prices
Price (as of 12/31/2018)	12.29
52-Week High	13.05
52-Week Low	11.26

Total Returns (%)
3-Month	6-Month	1-Year	3-Year	5-Year
7.69	2.58	-1.37	19.79	5.30

3-Year Standard Deviation	12.62
Effective Duration	

Valuation
Premium/Discount (1-Year Average)	0.13

Company Information
Provider	iShares
Manager/Tenure	Management Team (13)
Website	http://www.ishares.com
Address	iShares 400 Howard Street San Francisco CA 94105 United States
Phone Number	800-474-2737

PERFORMANCE

Ratings History				Asset & Performance History			Total Assets:	$10,635,318,199
Date	Overall Rating	Risk Rating	Reward Rating	Date	NAV	1-Year Total Return	Asset Allocation Asset	%
Q4-18	D+	C-	D+	2017	12.45	11.55	Cash	0%
Q2-18	C	B-	C-	2016	11.16	8.87	Stocks	0%
Q4-17	C-	C-	C-	2015	10.25	-11.71	US Stocks	0%
Q4-16	C-	D+	C-	2014	11.61	-0.42	Bonds	0%
Q4-15	D	D	D	2013	11.66	-27.93	US Bonds	0%
				2012	16.18	8.37	Other	100%

Services Offered:

Investment Strategy: The investment seeks to reflect generally the performance of the price of gold. The Trust seeks to reflect such performance before payment of the Trust's expenses and liabilities. It is not actively managed. The Trust does not engage in any activities designed to obtain a profit from, or to ameliorate losses caused by, changes in the price of gold. The advisor intends to constitute a simple and cost-effective means of making an investment similar to an investment in gold. An investment in physical gold requires expensive and sometimes complicated arrangements in connection with the assay, transportation, warehousing and insurance of the metal. **Top Holdings:** Gold

---

iShares National Muni Bond ETF   C   HOLD

Ticker	Traded On	NAV	Total Assets ($)	Dividend Yield (TTM)	Turnover Ratio	Expense Ratio
MUB	NYSE Arca	108.73	$10,565,480,737	2.45	10	0.07

Ratings
Reward	C-
Risk	C+
Recent Upgrade/Downgrade	

Fund Information
Fund Type	Exchange Traded Funds
Category	US Muni Fixed Inc
Sub-Category	Muni National Interm
Prospectus Objective	Muni Bond - Natl
Inception Date	Sep-07
Open to New Investments	Y

Prices
Price (as of 12/31/2018)	109.04
52-Week High	110.74
52-Week Low	106.42

Total Returns (%)
3-Month	6-Month	1-Year	3-Year	5-Year
1.60	1.27	0.86	5.57	18.10

3-Year Standard Deviation	3.21
Effective Duration	6.16

Valuation
Premium/Discount (1-Year Average)	0.06

Company Information
Provider	iShares
Manager/Tenure	Scott Radell (8), James Mauro (7)
Website	http://www.ishares.com
Address	iShares 400 Howard Street San Francisco CA 94105 United States
Phone Number	800-474-2737

PERFORMANCE

Ratings History				Asset & Performance History			Total Assets:	$10,565,480,737
Date	Overall Rating	Risk Rating	Reward Rating	Date	NAV	1-Year Total Return	Asset Allocation Asset	%
Q4-18	C	C+	C-	2017	110.5	4.42	Cash	1%
Q2-18	C	C+	C	2016	108.06	0.05	Stocks	0%
Q4-17	B-	B+	C	2015	110.34	2.99	US Stocks	0%
Q4-16	C	C+	C	2014	109.88	8.61	Bonds	99%
Q4-15	C+	C+	C	2013	104.01	-3.26	US Bonds	99%
				2012	110.71	6.13	Other	0%

Services Offered:

Investment Strategy: The investment seeks to track the investment results of the S&P National AMT-Free Municipal Bond IndexTM. The fund generally will invest at least 90% of its assets in the component securities of the underlying index and may invest up to 10% of its assets in certain futures, options and swap contracts, cash and cash equivalents. The index measures the performance of the investment-grade segment of the U.S. municipal bond market. **Top Holdings:** UNIVERSITY CALIF 5% SAN FRANCISCO CALIF CITY & CNTY PUB UTILS COMMN 4% CALIFORNIA ST 5% WASHINGTON ST 5% NEW YORK N Y CITY MUN WTR FIN AUTH 4%

Vanguard Health Care Index Fund ETF Shares   C+   HOLD

Ticker	Traded On	NAV	Total Assets ($)	Dividend Yield (TTM)	Turnover Ratio	Expense Ratio
VHT	NYSE Arca		$10,515,260,012	1.22	6	0.1

Ratings
Reward   C+
Risk   C+
Recent Upgrade/Downgrade

Fund Information
Fund Type   Exchange Traded Funds
Category   Healthcare Sector Equity
Sub-Category   Health
Prospectus Objective   Health
Inception Date   Jan-04
Open to New Investments   Y

Prices
Price (as of 12/31/2018)   160.60
52-Week High   180.89
52-Week Low   149.65

Total Returns (%)

3-Month	6-Month	1-Year	3-Year	5-Year
-12.18	-0.35	4.02	24.04	66.75

3-Year Standard Deviation   13.2
Effective Duration

Valuation
Premium/Discount (1-Year Average)   0.01

Company Information
Provider   Vanguard
Manager/Tenure   Walter Nejman (2), Michelle Louie (1)
Website   http://www.vanguard.com
Address   Vanguard 100 Vanguard Boulevard
     Malvern PA 19355 United States
Phone Number   877-662-7447

PERFORMANCE

Ratings History

Date	Overall Rating	Risk Rating	Reward Rating
Q4-18	C+	C+	C+
Q2-18	C	C	C+
Q4-17	B	B	B-
Q4-16	C+	C+	C+
Q4-15	B	B-	B

Asset & Performance History

Date	NAV	1-Year Total Return
2017	154.1	23.84
2016	126.65	-3.82
2015	132.91	7.21
2014	125.5	25.37
2013	101.1	42.66
2012	71.67	19.09

Total Assets: $10,515,260,012
Asset Allocation

Asset	%
Cash	0%
Stocks	100%
US Stocks	100%
Bonds	0%
US Bonds	0%
Other	0%

Services Offered:

Investment Strategy: The investment seeks to track the performance of a benchmark index. The fund employs an indexing investment approach designed to track the performance of the MSCI US Investable Market Index (IMI)/Health Care 25/50, an index made up of stocks of large, mid-size, and small U.S. companies within the health care sector, as classified under the Global Industry Classification Standard (GICS). The Advisor attempts to replicate the target index by seeking to invest all, or substantially all, of its assets in the stocks that make up the index, in order to hold each stock in approximately the same proportion as its weighting in the index. The fund is non-diversified. **Top Holdings:** Johnson & Johnson   Pfizer Inc   UnitedHealth Group Inc   Merck & Co Inc   Amgen Inc

---

Vanguard Long-Term Bond Index Fund ETF Shares   D+   SELL

Ticker	Traded On	NAV	Total Assets ($)	Dividend Yield (TTM)	Turnover Ratio	Expense Ratio
BLV	NYSE Arca		$10,331,224,647	4.08	41	0.07

Ratings
Reward   D
Risk   C
Recent Upgrade/Downgrade   Down

Fund Information
Fund Type   Exchange Traded Funds
Category   US Fixed Income
Sub-Category   Long-Term Bond
Prospectus Objective   Income
Inception Date   Apr-07
Open to New Investments   Y

Prices
Price (as of 12/31/2018)   87.51
52-Week High   95.08
52-Week Low   83.53

Total Returns (%)

3-Month	6-Month	1-Year	3-Year	5-Year
1.26	0.31	-4.75	12.50	30.23

3-Year Standard Deviation   7.28
Effective Duration   14.65

Valuation
Premium/Discount (1-Year Average)   0.14

Company Information
Provider   Vanguard
Manager/Tenure   Joshua C. Barrickman (5)
Website   http://www.vanguard.com
Address   Vanguard 100 Vanguard Boulevard
     Malvern PA 19355 United States
Phone Number   877-662-7447

PERFORMANCE

Ratings History

Date	Overall Rating	Risk Rating	Reward Rating
Q4-18	D+	C	D
Q2-18	C	C	C-
Q4-17	B-	B	C+
Q4-16	C	C+	C
Q4-15	C	C-	C

Asset & Performance History

Date	NAV	1-Year Total Return
2017	94.91	10.99
2016	88.86	6.37
2015	86.8	-3.44
2014	93.73	19.88
2013	81.45	-9.02
2012	93.73	8.49

Total Assets: $10,331,224,647
Asset Allocation

Asset	%
Cash	1%
Stocks	0%
US Stocks	0%
Bonds	99%
US Bonds	90%
Other	0%

Services Offered:

Investment Strategy: The investment seeks to track the performance of the Bloomberg Barclays U.S. Long Government/Credit Float Adjusted Index. Bloomberg Barclays U.S. Long Government/Credit Float Adjusted Index includes all medium and larger issues of U.S. government, investment-grade corporate, and investment-grade international dollar-denominated bonds that have maturities of greater than 10 years and are publicly issued. All of its investments will be selected through the sampling process, and at least 80% of the fund's assets will be invested in bonds held in the index. **Top Holdings:** United States Treasury Bonds 3%   United States Treasury Bonds 3.62%   United States Treasury Bonds 3.75%   United States Treasury Bonds 3.38%   United States Treasury Bonds 3%

Consumer Staples Select Sector SPDR® Fund   C+   HOLD

Ticker	Traded On	NAV	Total Assets ($)	Dividend Yield (TTM)	Turnover Ratio	Expense Ratio
XLP	NYSE Arca	50.78	$10,299,870,118	2.66	12	0.13

Ratings
Reward   B
Risk   C
Recent Upgrade/Downgrade

Fund Information
Fund Type   Exchange Traded Funds
Category   Consumer Goods & Svcs
Sub-Category   Consumer Defensive
Prospectus Objective   Unaligned
Inception Date   Dec-98
Open to New Investments   Y

Prices
Price (as of 12/31/2018)   50.78
52-Week High   58.71
52-Week Low   48.73

Total Returns (%)

3-Month	6-Month	1-Year	3-Year	5-Year
-4.88	0.73	-8.01	9.04	34.98

3-Year Standard Deviation   9.91
Effective Duration

Valuation
Premium/Discount (1-Year Average)   -0.02

Company Information
Provider   SPDR State Street Global Advisors
Manager/Tenure   Michael J. Feehily (7), Karl A.
                  Schneider (3), David Chin (1)
Website   http://www.spdrs.com
Address   SPDR State Street Global Advisors
                  State Street Financial Center, 1
                  Lincoln Street Boston MA 02111-2900
                  United States
Phone Number   617-786-3000

PERFORMANCE

Ratings History

Date	Overall Rating	Risk Rating	Reward Rating
Q4-18	C+	C	B
Q2-18	C+	C-	B-
Q4-17	B	A	C+
Q4-16	B-	C+	B
Q4-15	B	B-	B

Asset & Performance History

Date	NAV	1-Year Total Return
2017	56.86	12.9
2016	51.72	4.34
2015	50.49	6.84
2014	48.51	15.86
2013	42.95	26.27
2012	34.88	10.74

Total Assets: $10,299,870,118
Asset Allocation

Asset	%
Cash	0%
Stocks	100%
US Stocks	100%
Bonds	0%
US Bonds	0%
Other	0%

Services Offered: Dividend Investment Plan, CashInvestment Plan

Investment Strategy: The investment seeks to provide investment results that, before expenses, correspond generally to the price and yield performance of publicly traded equity securities of companies in the Consumer Staples Select Sector Index. In seeking to track the performance of the index, the fund employs a replication strategy. It generally invests substantially all, but at least 95%, of its total assets in the securities comprising the index. The index includes securities of companies from the following industries: food and staples retailing; household products; food products; beverages; tobacco; and personal products. The fund is non-diversified. **Top Holdings:** Procter & Gamble Co Coca-Cola Co PepsiCo Inc Walmart Inc Philip Morris International Inc

---

iShares Short-Term Corporate Bond ETF   E+   SELL

Ticker	Traded On	NAV	Total Assets ($)	Dividend Yield (TTM)	Turnover Ratio	Expense Ratio
IGSB	NAS CM	51.67	$10,219,756,157	2.23	46	0.06

Ratings
Reward   E+
Risk   D-
Recent Upgrade/Downgrade   Down

Fund Information
Fund Type   Exchange Traded Funds
Category   US Fixed Income
Sub-Category   Short-Term Bond
Prospectus Objective   Growth & Inc
Inception Date   Jan-07
Open to New Investments   Y

Prices
Price (as of 12/31/2018)   51.64
52-Week High   104.54
52-Week Low   51.35

Total Returns (%)

3-Month	6-Month	1-Year	3-Year	5-Year
0.73	1.33	-49.33	-47.70	-46.95

3-Year Standard Deviation   0.84
Effective Duration   2.70

Valuation
Premium/Discount (1-Year Average)   0.01

Company Information
Provider   iShares
Manager/Tenure   Scott Radell (8), James Mauro (7)
Website   http://www.ishares.com
Address   iShares 400 Howard Street San
                  Francisco CA 94105 United States
Phone Number   800-474-2737

PERFORMANCE

Ratings History

Date	Overall Rating	Risk Rating	Reward Rating
Q4-18	E+	D-	E+
Q2-18	C	C+	C-
Q4-17	B-	B+	C
Q4-16	C	C+	C
Q4-15	C	C+	C

Asset & Performance History

Date	NAV	1-Year Total Return
2017	104.51	1.26
2016	104.77	1.77
2015	104.45	0.7
2014	104.95	0.73
2013	105.16	1.03
2012	105.31	3.27

Total Assets: $10,219,756,157
Asset Allocation

Asset	%
Cash	1%
Stocks	0%
US Stocks	0%
Bonds	98%
US Bonds	72%
Other	0%

Services Offered:

Investment Strategy: The investment seeks to track the investment results of the ICE BofAML 1-5 Year US Corporate Index. The fund generally invests at least 90% of its assets in securities of the underlying index. The underlying index measures the performance of investment-grade corporate bonds that are U.S. dollar-denominated and have a remaining maturity of greater than or equal to one year and less than five years. **Top Holdings:** Anheuser-Busch InBev Finance Inc. 2.65% GE Capital International Funding Company Unlimited Company 2.34% Shire Acquisitions Investments Ireland DAC 2.4% Bank of America Corporation 2.63% CVS Health Corp 2.8%

iShares Russell 2000 Value ETF   C   HOLD

Ticker	Traded On	NAV	Total Assets ($)	Dividend Yield (TTM)	Turnover Ratio	Expense Ratio
IWN	NYSE Arca	107.57	$9,644,844,362	1.91	23	0.24

Ratings
Reward   C-
Risk   C+
Recent Upgrade/Downgrade   Down

Fund Information
Fund Type   Exchange Traded Funds
Category   US Equity Small Cap
Sub-Category   Small Value
Prospectus Objective   Growth
Inception Date   Jul-00
Open to New Investments   Y

Prices
Price (as of 12/31/2018)   107.54
52-Week High   137.10
52-Week Low   102.04

Total Returns (%)

3-Month	6-Month	1-Year	3-Year	5-Year
-17.67	-17.82	-12.93	23.46	18.88

3-Year Standard Deviation   14.53
Effective Duration

Valuation
Premium/Discount (1-Year Average)   0.00

Company Information
Provider   iShares
Manager/Tenure   Diane Hsiung (10), Greg Savage (10), Jennifer Hsui (6), 3 others
Website   http://www.ishares.com
Address   iShares 400 Howard Street San Francisco CA 94105 United States
Phone Number   800-474-2737

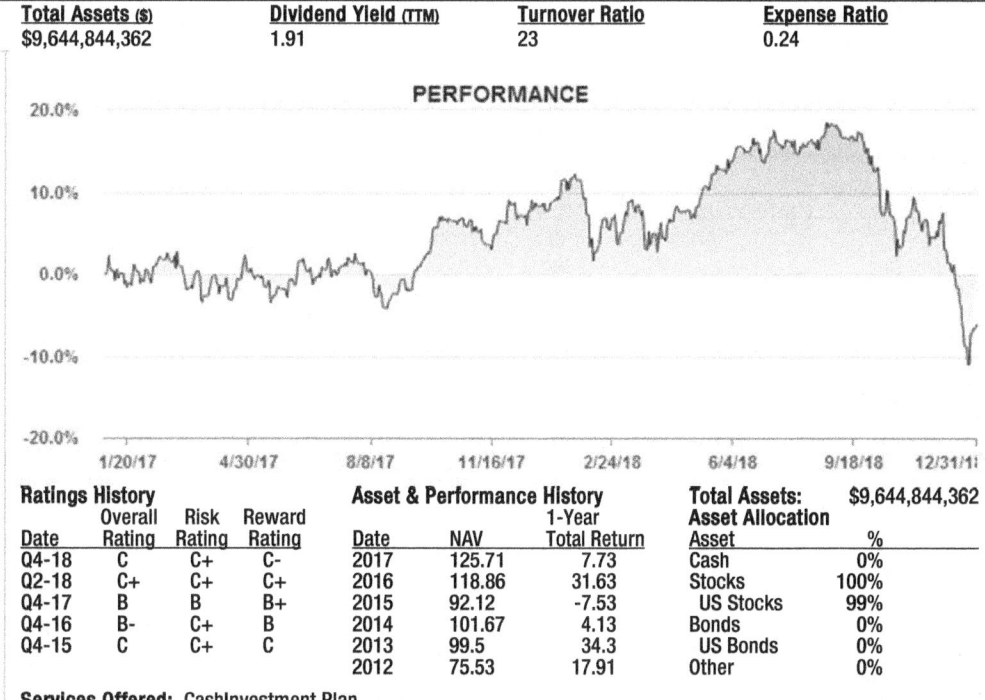

PERFORMANCE

Ratings History

Date	Overall Rating	Risk Rating	Reward Rating
Q4-18	C	C+	C-
Q2-18	C+	C+	C+
Q4-17	B	B	B+
Q4-16	B-	C+	B
Q4-15	C	C+	C

Asset & Performance History

Date	NAV	1-Year Total Return
2017	125.71	7.73
2016	118.86	31.63
2015	92.12	-7.53
2014	101.67	4.13
2013	99.5	34.3
2012	75.53	17.91

Total Assets: $9,644,844,362
Asset Allocation

Asset	%
Cash	0%
Stocks	100%
US Stocks	99%
Bonds	0%
US Bonds	0%
Other	0%

Services Offered: CashInvestment Plan

Investment Strategy: The investment seeks to track the investment results of the Russell 2000 Value Index, which measures the performance of the small-capitalization value sector of the U.S. equity market. The fund generally invests at least 90% of its assets in securities of the underlying index and in depositary receipts representing securities of the underlying index. It may invest the remainder of its assets in certain futures, options and swap contracts, cash and cash equivalents, as well as in securities not included in the underlying index, but which the advisor believes will help the fund track the underlying index. **Top Holdings:** Idacorp Inc   Ciena Corp   Cree Inc   ONE Gas Inc   Spirit Airlines Inc

---

iShares Edge MSCI USA Momentum Factor ETF   C+   HOLD

Ticker	Traded On	NAV	Total Assets ($)	Dividend Yield (TTM)	Turnover Ratio	Expense Ratio
MTUM	BATS	100.06	$9,501,079,984	1.09	104	0.15

Ratings
Reward   C+
Risk   C+
Recent Upgrade/Downgrade   Down

Fund Information
Fund Type   Exchange Traded Funds
Category   US Equity Large Cap Growth
Sub-Category   Large Growth
Prospectus Objective   Growth
Inception Date   Apr-13
Open to New Investments   Y

Prices
Price (as of 12/31/2018)   100.23
52-Week High   119.62
52-Week Low   92.80

Total Returns (%)

3-Month	6-Month	1-Year	3-Year	5-Year
-15.97	-8.60	-1.76	41.78	77.11

3-Year Standard Deviation   11.14
Effective Duration

Valuation
Premium/Discount (1-Year Average)   0.02

Company Information
Provider   iShares
Manager/Tenure   Diane Hsiung (5), Jennifer Hsui (5), Greg Savage (5), 3 others
Website   http://www.ishares.com
Address   iShares 400 Howard Street San Francisco CA 94105 United States
Phone Number   800-474-2737

PERFORMANCE

Ratings History

Date	Overall Rating	Risk Rating	Reward Rating
Q4-18	C+	C+	C+
Q2-18	B	C+	B
Q4-17	A	A	A
Q4-16	B-	B-	B-
Q4-15	C	B-	C+

Asset & Performance History

Date	NAV	1-Year Total Return
2017	103.07	37.6
2016	75.76	4.89
2015	73.27	9.12
2014	67.92	14.47
2013	59.98	
2012		

Total Assets: $9,501,079,984
Asset Allocation

Asset	%
Cash	0%
Stocks	100%
US Stocks	100%
Bonds	0%
US Bonds	0%
Other	0%

Services Offered:

Investment Strategy: The investment seeks to track the investment results of the MSCI USA Momentum Index. The fund generally will invest at least 90% of its assets in the component securities of the underlying index and may invest up to 10% of its assets in certain futures, options and swap contracts, cash and cash equivalents. The index consists of stocks exhibiting relatively higher momentum characteristics than the traditional market capitalization-weighted parent index, the MSCI USA Index, which includes U.S. large- and mid-capitalization stocks. **Top Holdings:** Amazon.com Inc   Microsoft Corp   Apple Inc   Merck & Co Inc   Pfizer Inc

iShares MSCI ACWI ETF   C   HOLD

Ticker	Traded On	NAV	Total Assets ($)	Dividend Yield (TTM)	Turnover Ratio	Expense Ratio
ACWI	NAS CM	64.19	$9,456,232,949	2.11	4	0.32

Ratings
Reward	C-
Risk	C+
Recent Upgrade/Downgrade	Down

Fund Information
Fund Type	Exchange Traded Funds
Category	Global Equity Large Cap
Sub-Category	World Large Stock
Prospectus Objective	World Stock
Inception Date	Mar-08
Open to New Investments	Y

Prices
Price (as of 12/31/2018)	64.16
52-Week High	77.54
52-Week Low	61.18

Total Returns (%)
3-Month	6-Month	1-Year	3-Year	5-Year
-12.92	-8.59	-9.21	22.17	24.79

3-Year Standard Deviation	9.65
Effective Duration	

Valuation
Premium/Discount (1-Year Average)	-0.04

Company Information
Provider	iShares
Manager/Tenure	Diane Hsiung (10), Greg Savage (10), Jennifer Hsui (6), 3 others
Website	http://www.ishares.com
Address	iShares 400 Howard Street San Francisco CA 94105 United States
Phone Number	800-474-2737

PERFORMANCE

Ratings History				Asset & Performance History			Total Assets:	$9,456,232,949
Date	Overall Rating	Risk Rating	Reward Rating	Date	NAV	1-Year Total Return	Asset Allocation	
							Asset	%
Q4-18	C	C+	C-	2017	72.15	24.34	Cash	1%
Q2-18	C	C+	C	2016	59.22	8.21	Stocks	99%
Q4-17	B-	C+	B-	2015	55.96	-2.38	US Stocks	55%
Q4-16	C	C+	C	2014	58.75	4.64	Bonds	0%
Q4-15	C	C+	C	2013	57.41	22.9	US Bonds	0%
				2012	47.69	15.98	Other	0%

Services Offered:

Investment Strategy: The investment seeks to track the investment results of the MSCI ACWI composed of large- and mid-capitalization developed and emerging market equities. The fund generally will invest at least 90% of its assets in the component securities of the underlying index and in investments that have economic characteristics that are substantially identical to the component securities of the underlying index. The index is a free float-adjusted market capitalization index designed to measure the combined equity market performance of developed and emerging markets countries. **Top Holdings:** Apple Inc   Microsoft Corp   Amazon.com Inc   iShares MSCI India ETF   Johnson & Johnson

iShares Russell 2000 Growth ETF   C   HOLD

Ticker	Traded On	NAV	Total Assets ($)	Dividend Yield (TTM)	Turnover Ratio	Expense Ratio
IWO	NYSE Arca	168.12	$9,405,114,927	0.69	26	0.24

Ratings
Reward	C-
Risk	C+
Recent Upgrade/Downgrade	Down

Fund Information
Fund Type	Exchange Traded Funds
Category	US Equity Small Cap
Sub-Category	Small Growth
Prospectus Objective	Growth
Inception Date	Jul-00
Open to New Investments	Y

Prices
Price (as of 12/31/2018)	168.00
52-Week High	220.33
52-Week Low	156.33

Total Returns (%)
3-Month	6-Month	1-Year	3-Year	5-Year
-20.43	-18.11	-9.33	23.55	29.06

3-Year Standard Deviation	15.35
Effective Duration	

Valuation
Premium/Discount (1-Year Average)	0.00

Company Information
Provider	iShares
Manager/Tenure	Diane Hsiung (10), Greg Savage (10), Jennifer Hsui (6), 3 others
Website	http://www.ishares.com
Address	iShares 400 Howard Street San Francisco CA 94105 United States
Phone Number	800-474-2737

PERFORMANCE

Ratings History				Asset & Performance History			Total Assets:	$9,405,114,927
Date	Overall Rating	Risk Rating	Reward Rating	Date	NAV	1-Year Total Return	Asset Allocation	
							Asset	%
Q4-18	C	C+	C-	2017	186.64	22.24	Cash	0%
Q2-18	C+	C+	C+	2016	153.9	11.47	Stocks	100%
Q4-17	B+	B	A-	2015	139.51	-1.18	US Stocks	99%
Q4-16	B-	C+	B-	2014	142.4	5.72	Bonds	0%
Q4-15	C+	C+	C+	2013	135.7	43.43	US Bonds	0%
				2012	95.37	14.74	Other	0%

Services Offered: CashInvestment Plan

Investment Strategy: The investment seeks to track the investment results of the Russell 2000 Growth Index, which measures the performance of the small-capitalization growth sector of the U.S. equity market. The fund generally invests at least 90% of its assets in securities of the underlying index and in depositary receipts representing securities of the underlying index. It may invest the remainder of its assets in certain futures, options and swap contracts, cash and cash equivalents, as well as in securities not included in the underlying index, but which the advisor believes will help the fund track the underlying index. **Top Holdings:** Etsy Inc   Integrated Device Technology Inc   Five Below Inc   Haemonetics Corp   HubSpot Inc

iShares 7-10 Year Treasury Bond ETF   D+   SELL

Ticker	Traded On	NAV		Total Assets ($)	Dividend Yield (TTM)	Turnover Ratio	Expense Ratio
IEF	NAS CM	104.02		$9,264,501,962	2.2	46	0.15

Ratings
Reward	D
Risk	C
Recent Upgrade/Downgrade	

Fund Information
Fund Type	Exchange Traded Funds
Category	US Fixed Income
Sub-Category	Long Government
Prospectus Objective	Govt Bond - Treasury
Inception Date	Jul-02
Open to New Investments	Y

Prices
Price (as of 12/31/2018)	104.20
52-Week High	105.57
52-Week Low	99.72

Total Returns (%)
3-Month	6-Month	1-Year	3-Year	5-Year
3.87	3.01	0.82	4.34	15.40

3-Year Standard Deviation	4.63
Effective Duration	7.41

Valuation
Premium/Discount (1-Year Average)	0.00

Company Information
Provider	iShares
Manager/Tenure	Scott Radell (8), James Mauro (7)
Website	http://www.ishares.com
Address	iShares 400 Howard Street San Francisco CA 94105 United States
Phone Number	800-474-2737

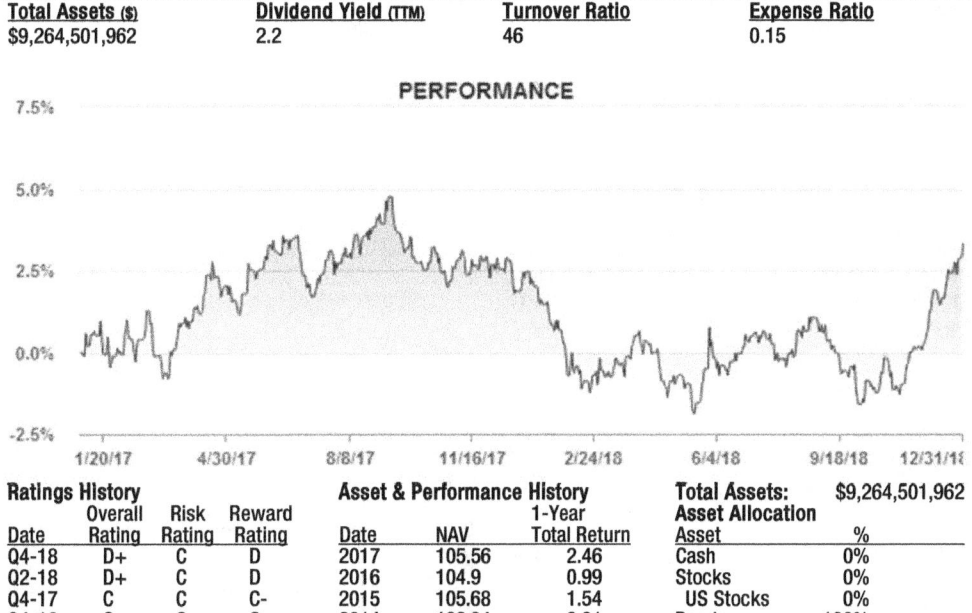
PERFORMANCE

Ratings History
Date	Overall Rating	Risk Rating	Reward Rating
Q4-18	D+	C	D
Q2-18	D+	C	D
Q4-17	C	C	C-
Q4-16	C	C+	C
Q4-15	C	C+	C

Asset & Performance History
Date	NAV	1-Year Total Return
2017	105.56	2.46
2016	104.9	0.99
2015	105.68	1.54
2014	106.04	8.91
2013	99.42	-6.11
2012	107.72	4.06

Total Assets: $9,264,501,962
Asset Allocation
Asset	%
Cash	0%
Stocks	0%
US Stocks	0%
Bonds	100%
US Bonds	100%
Other	0%

Services Offered:

Investment Strategy: The investment seeks to track the investment results of the ICE U.S. Treasury 7-10 Year Bond Index. The fund generally invests at least 90% of its assets in the bonds of the underlying index and at least 95% of its assets in U.S. government bonds. The underlying index measures the performance of public obligations of the U.S. Treasury that have a remaining maturity of greater than seven years and less than or equal to ten years. **Top Holdings:** United States Treasury Notes 2.38% United States Treasury Notes 1.63% United States Treasury Notes 2.25% United States Treasury Notes 2.25% United States Treasury Notes 2.75%

---

iShares MSCI EAFE Small-Cap ETF   C-   HOLD

Ticker	Traded On	NAV		Total Assets ($)	Dividend Yield (TTM)	Turnover Ratio	Expense Ratio
SCZ	NAS CM	51.79		$9,070,964,311	2.71	8	0.39

Ratings
Reward	D+
Risk	C-
Recent Upgrade/Downgrade	Down

Fund Information
Fund Type	Exchange Traded Funds
Category	Global Eq Mid/Small Cap
Sub-Category	Foreign Small/Mid Blend
Prospectus Objective	Small Company
Inception Date	Dec-07
Open to New Investments	Y

Prices
Price (as of 12/31/2018)	51.82
52-Week High	69.19
52-Week Low	49.58

Total Returns (%)
3-Month	6-Month	1-Year	3-Year	5-Year
-15.82	-15.12	-17.64	11.77	15.89

3-Year Standard Deviation	12.37
Effective Duration	

Valuation
Premium/Discount (1-Year Average)	-0.06

Company Information
Provider	iShares
Manager/Tenure	Diane Hsiung (10), Greg Savage (10), Jennifer Hsui (6), 3 others
Website	http://www.ishares.com
Address	iShares 400 Howard Street San Francisco CA 94105 United States
Phone Number	800-474-2737

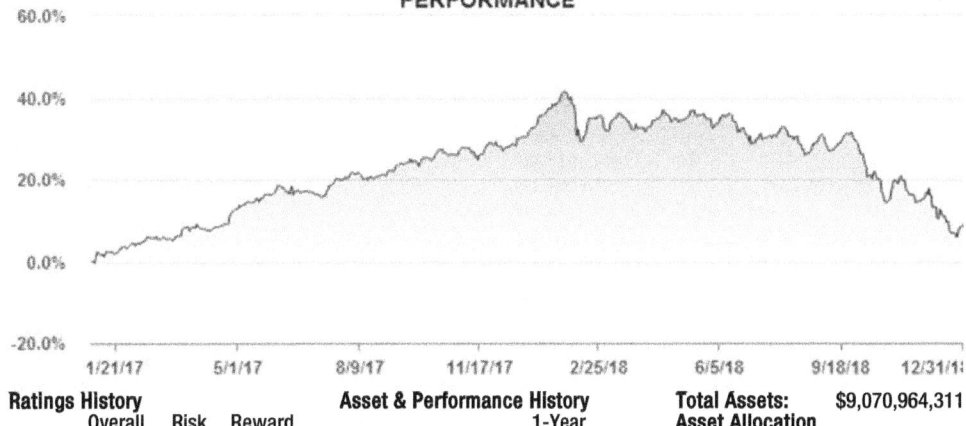
PERFORMANCE

Ratings History
Date	Overall Rating	Risk Rating	Reward Rating
Q4-18	C-	C-	D+
Q2-18	C+	C+	C+
Q4-17	A-	A-	A-
Q4-16	C	C+	C
Q4-15	C	C+	C

Asset & Performance History
Date	NAV	1-Year Total Return
2017	64.6	32.51
2016	50	2.42
2015	50.21	9.16
2014	46.93	-5.01
2013	50.66	29.21
2012	40.27	19.84

Total Assets: $9,070,964,311
Asset Allocation
Asset	%
Cash	1%
Stocks	99%
US Stocks	1%
Bonds	0%
US Bonds	0%
Other	0%

Services Offered:

Investment Strategy: The investment seeks to track the investment results of the MSCI EAFE Small Cap Index composed of small-capitalization developed market equities, excluding the U.S. and Canada. The fund generally will invest at least 90% of its assets in the component securities of the underlying index and in investments that have economic characteristics that are substantially identical to the component securities of the underlying index. The index represents the small-capitalization segment of the MSCI EAFE IMI Index. **Top Holdings:** Rentokil Initial PLC LEG Immobilien AG Halma PLC Hiscox Ltd ASR Nederland NV

iShares Edge MSCI Min Vol EAFE ETF   C   HOLD

Ticker	Traded On	NAV	Total Assets ($)	Dividend Yield (TTM)	Turnover Ratio	Expense Ratio
EFAV	BATS	66.60	$9,032,501,045	2.66	23	0.2

Ratings
Reward	C-
Risk	C
Recent Upgrade/Downgrade	

Fund Information
Fund Type	Exchange Traded Funds
Category	Global Equity Large Cap
Sub-Category	Foreign Large Blend
Prospectus Objective	Foreign Stock
Inception Date	Oct-11
Open to New Investments	Y

Prices
Price (as of 12/31/2018)	66.66
52-Week High	76.47
52-Week Low	65.01

Total Returns (%)
3-Month	6-Month	1-Year	3-Year	5-Year
-7.11	-4.27	-5.80	12.38	26.77

3-Year Standard Deviation	8.68
Effective Duration	

Valuation
Premium/Discount (1-Year Average)	-0.03

Company Information
Provider	iShares
Manager/Tenure	Diane Hsiung (7), Greg Savage (7), Jennifer Hsui (6), 3 others
Website	http://www.ishares.com
Address	iShares 400 Howard Street San Francisco CA 94105 United States
Phone Number	800-474-2737

PERFORMANCE

Ratings History
Date	Overall Rating	Risk Rating	Reward Rating
Q4-18	C	C	C-
Q2-18	C+	C+	C+
Q4-17	B	B	B-
Q4-16	C	C	C
Q4-15	C+	C+	C

Asset & Performance History
Date	NAV	1-Year Total Return
2017	72.98	21.56
2016	61.57	-1.85
2015	65.16	7.83
2014	61.92	4.6
2013	61.27	16.51
2012	54.01	11.51

Total Assets: $9,032,501,045

Asset Allocation
Asset	%
Cash	1%
Stocks	99%
US Stocks	0%
Bonds	0%
US Bonds	0%
Other	0%

Services Offered:

Investment Strategy: The investment seeks the investment results of the MSCI EAFE Minimum Volatility (USD) Index composed of developed market equities that, in the aggregate, have lower volatility characteristics relative to the broader developed equity markets, excluding the U.S. and Canada. The fund generally will invest at least 90% of its assets in the component securities of the index and in investments that have economic characteristics that are substantially identical to the component securities of the index. The index measures the performance of international equity securities that in the aggregate have lower volatility relative to the MSCI EAFE Index. **Top Holdings:** Nestle SA Novartis AG Hong Kong and China Gas Co Ltd CLP Holdings Ltd Roche Holding AG Dividend Right Cert.

VanEck Vectors Gold Miners ETF   D+   SELL

Ticker	Traded On	NAV	Total Assets ($)	Dividend Yield (TTM)	Turnover Ratio	Expense Ratio
GDX	NYSE Arca	21.07	$8,935,893,177	0.92	12	0.53

Ratings
Reward	C-
Risk	D
Recent Upgrade/Downgrade	Down

Fund Information
Fund Type	Exchange Traded Funds
Category	Prec Metals
Sub-Category	Equity Precious Metals
Prospectus Objective	Prec Metals
Inception Date	May-06
Open to New Investments	Y

Prices
Price (as of 12/31/2018)	21.09
52-Week High	24.60
52-Week Low	17.57

Total Returns (%)
3-Month	6-Month	1-Year	3-Year	5-Year
14.29	-3.98	-8.85	56.12	2.78

3-Year Standard Deviation	37.22
Effective Duration	

Valuation
Premium/Discount (1-Year Average)	0.06

Company Information
Provider	VanEck
Manager/Tenure	Hao-Hung (Peter) Liao (12), Guo Hua (Jason) Jin (0)
Website	http://www.vaneck.com
Address	Van Eck Associates Corporation 666 Third Avenue New York NY 10017 United States
Phone Number	800-826-1115

PERFORMANCE

Ratings History
Date	Overall Rating	Risk Rating	Reward Rating
Q4-18	D+	D	C-
Q2-18	C-	C-	C
Q4-17	C-	D	C
Q4-16	C-	D	C
Q4-15	D+	D+	C-

Asset & Performance History
Date	NAV	1-Year Total Return
2017	23.25	12.02
2016	20.92	52.91
2015	13.72	-24.92
2014	18.43	-12.3
2013	21.16	-53.88
2012	46.32	-9.14

Total Assets: $8,935,893,177

Asset Allocation
Asset	%
Cash	0%
Stocks	100%
US Stocks	15%
Bonds	0%
US Bonds	0%
Other	0%

Services Offered:

Investment Strategy: The investment seeks to replicate as closely as possible, before fees and expenses, the price and yield performance of the NYSE Arca Gold Miners Index. The fund normally invests at least 80% of its total assets in common stocks and depositary receipts of companies involved in the gold mining industry. The index is a modified market-capitalization weighted index primarily comprised of publicly traded companies involved in the mining for gold and silver. The fund is non-diversified. **Top Holdings:** Newmont Mining Corp Barrick Gold Corp Franco-Nevada Corp Newcrest Mining Ltd Agnico Eagle Mines Ltd

iShares Russell Mid-Cap Growth ETF   C   HOLD

Ticker	Traded On	NAV	Total Assets ($)	Dividend Yield (TTM)	Turnover Ratio	Expense Ratio
IWP	NYSE Arca	113.63	$8,870,866,673	0.94	24	0.25

Ratings
Reward	C-
Risk	C+
Recent Upgrade/Downgrade	Down

Fund Information
Fund Type	Exchange Traded Funds
Category	US Equity Mid Cap
Sub-Category	Mid-Cap Growth
Prospectus Objective	Growth
Inception Date	Jul-01
Open to New Investments	Y

Prices
Price (as of 12/31/2018)	113.71
52-Week High	137.48
52-Week Low	106.03

Total Returns (%)
3-Month	6-Month	1-Year	3-Year	5-Year
-15.60	-10.10	-4.94	27.28	41.60

3-Year Standard Deviation	11.76
Effective Duration	

Valuation
Premium/Discount (1-Year Average)	0.00

Company Information
Provider	iShares
Manager/Tenure	Diane Hsiung (10), Greg Savage (10), Jennifer Hsui (6), 3 others
Website	http://www.ishares.com
Address	iShares 400 Howard Street San Francisco CA 94105 United States
Phone Number	800-474-2737

PERFORMANCE

Ratings History

Date	Overall Rating	Risk Rating	Reward Rating
Q4-18	C	C+	C-
Q2-18	C+	C+	C+
Q4-17	B	B-	B
Q4-16	C+	C+	B-
Q4-15	C	C+	C

Asset & Performance History

Date	NAV	1-Year Total Return
2017	120.65	24.98
2016	97.36	7.14
2015	91.96	-0.38
2014	93.21	11.68
2013	84.35	35.43
2012	62.83	15.61

Total Assets: $8,870,866,673

Asset Allocation

Asset	%
Cash	0%
Stocks	100%
US Stocks	99%
Bonds	0%
US Bonds	0%
Other	0%

Services Offered: CashInvestment Plan

Investment Strategy: The investment seeks to track the investment results of the Russell Midcap Growth Index, which measures the performance of the mid-capitalization growth sector of the U.S. equity market. The fund generally invests at least 90% of its assets in securities of the underlying index and in depositary receipts representing securities of the underlying index. It may invest the remainder of its assets in certain futures, options and swap contracts, cash and cash equivalents, as well as in securities not included in the underlying index, but which the advisor believes will help the fund track the underlying index. **Top Holdings:** Edwards Lifesciences Corp Ross Stores Inc ServiceNow Inc Fiserv Inc Red Hat Inc

---

Alerian MLP ETF   C   HOLD

Ticker	Traded On	NAV	Total Assets ($)	Dividend Yield (TTM)	Turnover Ratio	Expense Ratio
AMLP	NYSE Arca	8.75	$8,701,659,236	8.49	23	0.85

Ratings
Reward	B-
Risk	D
Recent Upgrade/Downgrade	

Fund Information
Fund Type	Exchange Traded Funds
Category	Energy Sector Equity
Sub-Category	Energy Limited Partnership
Prospectus Objective	Natl Res
Inception Date	Aug-10
Open to New Investments	Y

Prices
Price (as of 12/31/2018)	8.73
52-Week High	11.83
52-Week Low	8.32

Total Returns (%)
3-Month	6-Month	1-Year	3-Year	5-Year
-18.00	-10.04	-12.71	-6.97	-27.75

3-Year Standard Deviation	17.65
Effective Duration	

Valuation
Premium/Discount (1-Year Average)	-0.08

Company Information
Provider	ALPS
Manager/Tenure	Ryan Mischker (3), Andrew Hicks (2)
Website	http://www.alpsfunds.com
Address	ALPS 1290 Broadway, Suite 1100 Denver CO 80203 United States
Phone Number	866-759-5679

PERFORMANCE

Ratings History

Date	Overall Rating	Risk Rating	Reward Rating
Q4-18	C	D	B-
Q2-18	C	D	B-
Q4-17	D	D	D
Q4-16	D	D	D
Q4-15	B-	C	B

Asset & Performance History

Date	NAV	1-Year Total Return
2017	10.82	-7.92
2016	12.64	15.75
2015	11.99	-25.91
2014	17.49	4.82
2013	17.76	18.2
2012	15.97	2.23

Total Assets: $8,701,659,236

Asset Allocation

Asset	%
Cash	0%
Stocks	100%
US Stocks	100%
Bonds	0%
US Bonds	0%
Other	0%

Services Offered:

Investment Strategy: The investment seeks investment results that correspond (before fees and expenses) generally to the price and yield performance of its underlying index, the Alerian MLP Infrastructure Index. The fund will normally invest at least 90% of its total assets in securities that comprise the underlying index. The underlying index is comprised of energy infrastructure MLPs that earn a majority of their cash flow from the transportation, storage and processing of energy commodities. It is non-diversified. **Top Holdings:** Magellan Midstream Partners LP Enterprise Products Partners LP Plains All American Pipeline LP Energy Transfer LP MPLX LP Partnership Units

iShares Russell 3000 ETF

C **HOLD**

Ticker	Traded On	NAV
IWV	NYSE Arca	146.82

Total Assets ($)	Dividend Yield (TTM)	Turnover Ratio	Expense Ratio
$8,603,357,365	1.67	4	0.2

Ratings
Reward	C
Risk	C+
Recent Upgrade/Downgrade	Down

Fund Information
Fund Type	Exchange Traded Funds
Category	US Equity Large Cap Blend
Sub-Category	Large Blend
Prospectus Objective	Growth
Inception Date	May-00
Open to New Investments	Y

Prices
Price (as of 12/31/2018)	146.92
52-Week High	174.15
52-Week Low	137.69

Total Returns (%)
3-Month	6-Month	1-Year	3-Year	5-Year
-14.44	-8.56	-5.39	28.79	45.21

3-Year Standard Deviation	9.79
Effective Duration	

Valuation
Premium/Discount (1-Year Average)	0.00

Company Information
Provider	iShares
Manager/Tenure	Diane Hsiung (10), Greg Savage (10), Jennifer Hsui (6), 3 others
Website	http://www.ishares.com
Address	iShares 400 Howard Street San Francisco CA 94105 United States
Phone Number	800-474-2737

PERFORMANCE

Ratings History
Date	Overall Rating	Risk Rating	Reward Rating
Q4-18	C	C+	C
Q2-18	C+	C+	C+
Q4-17	B	B	B
Q4-16	B-	C+	B
Q4-15	C+	C+	C

Asset & Performance History
Date	NAV	1-Year Total Return
2017	158.03	20.94
2016	132.89	12.55
2015	120.32	0.34
2014	122.29	12.35
2013	110.68	33.25
2012	84.55	16.22

Total Assets: $8,603,357,365

Asset Allocation
Asset	%
Cash	0%
Stocks	100%
US Stocks	99%
Bonds	0%
US Bonds	0%
Other	0%

Services Offered: CashInvestment Plan

Investment Strategy: The investment seeks to track the investment results of the Russell 3000® Index, which measures the performance of the broad U.S. equity market. The fund generally invests at least 90% of its assets in securities of the underlying index and in depositary receipts representing securities of the underlying index. It may invest the remainder of its assets in certain futures, options and swap contracts, cash and cash equivalents, including shares of money market funds advised by the advisor or its affiliates, as well as in securities not included in the underlying index, but which the advisor believes will help the fund track the underlying index. **Top Holdings:** Apple Inc   Microsoft Corp   Amazon.com Inc   Berkshire Hathaway Inc B   Johnson & Johnson

---

Invesco S&P 500® Low Volatility ETF

B **BUY**

Ticker	Traded On	NAV
SPLV	NYSE Arca	46.64

Total Assets ($)	Dividend Yield (TTM)	Turnover Ratio	Expense Ratio
$8,397,903,033	1.99		0.25

Ratings
Reward	C
Risk	A
Recent Upgrade/Downgrade	Up

Fund Information
Fund Type	Exchange Traded Funds
Category	US Equity Large Cap Value
Sub-Category	Large Blend
Prospectus Objective	Growth
Inception Date	May-11
Open to New Investments	

Prices
Price (as of 12/31/2018)	46.65
52-Week High	50.45
52-Week Low	44.55

Total Returns (%)
3-Month	6-Month	1-Year	3-Year	5-Year
-5.11	-0.69	0.03	28.92	57.22

3-Year Standard Deviation	8.02
Effective Duration	

Valuation
Premium/Discount (1-Year Average)	0.02

Company Information
Provider	Invesco
Manager/Tenure	Peter Hubbard (7), Michael Jeanette (7), Tony Seisser (4), 1 other
Website	http://www.invesco.com/us
Address	Invesco 11 Greenway Plaza, Ste. 2500 Houston TX 77046 United States
Phone Number	800-659-1005

PERFORMANCE

Ratings History
Date	Overall Rating	Risk Rating	Reward Rating
Q4-18	B	A	C
Q2-18	C	C+	C
Q4-17	B+	A+	B
Q4-16	C	C+	C
Q4-15	B-	C+	B

Asset & Performance History
Date	NAV	1-Year Total Return
2017	47.63	17.07
2016	41.57	10.09
2015	38.56	4.06
2014	37.93	17.18
2013	33.16	23.24
2012	27.66	10.04

Total Assets: $8,397,903,033

Asset Allocation
Asset	%
Cash	0%
Stocks	100%
US Stocks	99%
Bonds	0%
US Bonds	0%
Other	0%

Services Offered:

Investment Strategy: The investment seeks to track the investment results (before fees and expenses) of the S&P 500® Low Volatility Index (the "underlying index"). The fund generally will invest at least 90% of its total assets in common stocks that comprise the underlying index. Volatility is a statistical measurement of the magnitude of up and down asset price fluctuations (increases or decreases in a stock's price) over time. It generally invests in all of the securities comprising the underlying index in proportion to their weightings in the underlying index. **Top Holdings:** Coca-Cola Co   Republic Services Inc Class A   Duke Energy Corp   Ecolab Inc   WEC Energy Group Inc

iShares Nasdaq Biotechnology ETF   C   HOLD

Ticker	Traded On	NAV	Total Assets ($)	Dividend Yield (TTM)	Turnover Ratio	Expense Ratio
IBB	NAS CM	96.83	$8,352,522,520	0.29	26	0.47

Ratings
Reward	C
Risk	C-
Recent Upgrade/Downgrade	

Fund Information
Fund Type	Exchange Traded Funds
Category	Healthcare Sector Equity
Sub-Category	Health
Prospectus Objective	Technology
Inception Date	Feb-01
Open to New Investments	Y

Prices
Price (as of 12/31/2018)	96.43
52-Week High	122.19
52-Week Low	89.61

Total Returns (%)
3-Month	6-Month	1-Year	3-Year	5-Year
-19.94	-12.54	-9.13	-13.58	29.19

3-Year Standard Deviation	23.08
Effective Duration	

Valuation
Premium/Discount (1-Year Average)	0.01

Company Information
Provider	iShares
Manager/Tenure	Diane Hsiung (10), Greg Savage (10), Jennifer Hsui (6), 3 others
Website	http://www.ishares.com
Address	iShares 400 Howard Street San Francisco CA 94105 United States
Phone Number	800-474-2737

PERFORMANCE

Ratings History
Date	Overall Rating	Risk Rating	Reward Rating
Q4-18	C	C-	C
Q2-18	C-	D+	C
Q4-17	C	C	C-
Q4-16	C	D+	C+
Q4-15	B	C+	B

Asset & Performance History
Date	NAV	1-Year Total Return
2017	106.75	21.2
2016	88.35	-21.53
2015	112.81	11.46
2014	101.23	34.12
2013	75.6	65.47
2012	45.71	31.95

Total Assets: $8,352,522,520

Asset Allocation
Asset	%
Cash	0%
Stocks	100%
US Stocks	98%
Bonds	0%
US Bonds	0%
Other	0%

Services Offered: Dividend Investment Plan

Investment Strategy: The investment seeks to track the investment results of the NASDAQ Biotechnology Index, which contains securities of companies listed on NASDAQ that are classified according to the Industry Classification Benchmark as either biotechnology or pharmaceuticals and that also meet other eligibility criteria determined by Nasdaq, Inc. The fund generally invests at least 90% of its assets in securities of the index and in depositary receipts representing securities of the index. It may invest the remainder of its assets in certain futures, options and swap contracts, cash and cash equivalents. It is non-diversified. **Top Holdings:** Amgen Inc   Gilead Sciences Inc   Biogen Inc   Celgene Corp   Illumina Inc

---

Schwab U.S. Dividend Equity ETF™   B-   BUY

Ticker	Traded On	NAV	Total Assets ($)	Dividend Yield (TTM)	Turnover Ratio	Expense Ratio
SCHD	NYSE Arca	46.98	$8,275,438,716	2.67	23	0.07

Ratings
Reward	B
Risk	C
Recent Upgrade/Downgrade	

Fund Information
Fund Type	Exchange Traded Funds
Category	US Equity Large Cap Value
Sub-Category	Large Value
Prospectus Objective	Equity-Income
Inception Date	Oct-11
Open to New Investments	Y

Prices
Price (as of 12/31/2018)	46.97
52-Week High	54.58
52-Week Low	44.23

Total Returns (%)
3-Month	6-Month	1-Year	3-Year	5-Year
-10.84	-3.07	-5.46	32.84	48.02

3-Year Standard Deviation	9.05
Effective Duration	

Valuation
Premium/Discount (1-Year Average)	0.01

Company Information
Provider	Schwab ETFs
Manager/Tenure	Ferian Juwono (7), Christopher Bliss (1), Sabya Sinha (1), 1 other
Website	http://www.schwabetfs.com
Address	Schwab ETFs United States
Phone Number	800-435-4000

PERFORMANCE

Ratings History
Date	Overall Rating	Risk Rating	Reward Rating
Q4-18	B-	C	B
Q2-18	B-	C	B
Q4-17	B	B	B
Q4-16	B-	C	B
Q4-15	C+	C+	C+

Asset & Performance History
Date	NAV	1-Year Total Return
2017	51.13	20.67
2016	43.52	16.23
2015	38.58	-0.21
2014	39.83	11.66
2013	36.65	32.9
2012	28.33	11.39

Total Assets: $8,275,438,716

Asset Allocation
Asset	%
Cash	0%
Stocks	100%
US Stocks	100%
Bonds	0%
US Bonds	0%
Other	0%

Services Offered:

Investment Strategy: The investment seeks to track as closely as possible, before fees and expenses, the total return of the Dow Jones U.S. Dividend 100™ Index. To pursue its goal, the fund generally invests in stocks that are included in the index. The fund invests at least 90% of its net assets in stocks that are included in the index. The index is designed to measure the performance of high dividend yielding stocks issued by U.S. companies that have a record of consistently paying dividends, selected for fundamental strength relative to their peers, based on financial ratios. **Top Holdings:** Procter & Gamble Co   Intel Corp   Verizon Communications Inc   Pfizer Inc   PepsiCo Inc

Utilities Select Sector SPDR® Fund   B   BUY

Ticker	Traded On	NAV	Total Assets ($)	Dividend Yield (TTM)	Turnover Ratio	Expense Ratio
XLU	NYSE Arca	52.92	$8,175,737,375	3.26	5	0.13

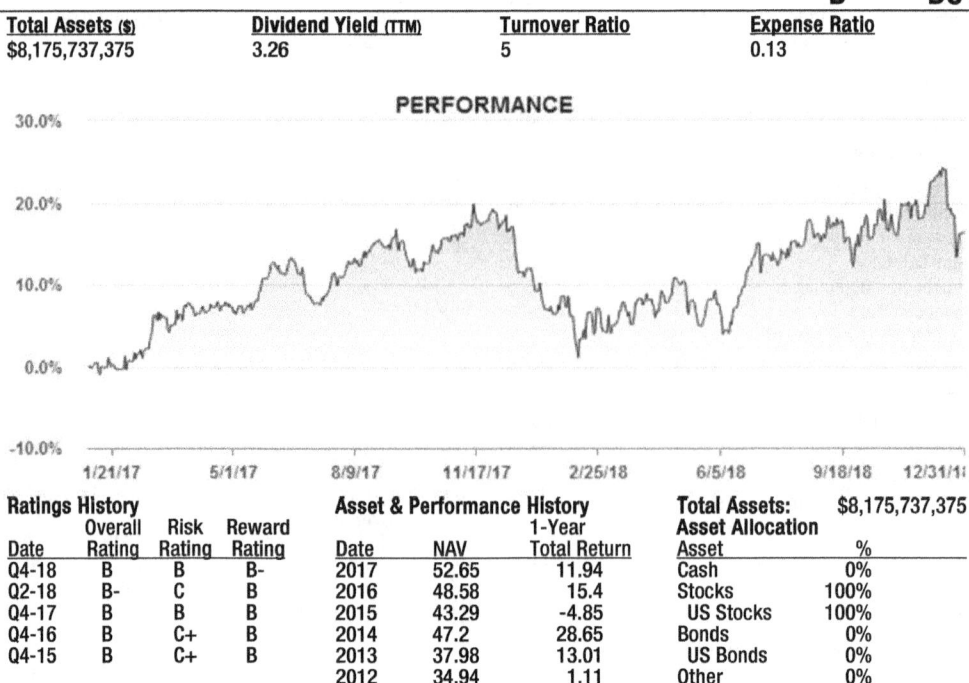

Ratings

Reward	B-
Risk	B
Recent Upgrade/Downgrade	Up

Fund Information

Fund Type	Exchange Traded Funds
Category	Utilities Sector Equity
Sub-Category	Utilities
Prospectus Objective	Utility
Inception Date	Dec-98
Open to New Investments	Y

Prices

Price (as of 12/31/2018)	52.92
52-Week High	56.93
52-Week Low	47.56

Total Returns (%)

3-Month	6-Month	1-Year	3-Year	5-Year
1.62	2.92	4.01	35.13	65.41

3-Year Standard Deviation	12
Effective Duration	

Valuation

Premium/Discount (1-Year Average)	-0.01

Company Information

Provider	SPDR State Street Global Advisors
Manager/Tenure	Michael J. Feehily (7), Karl A. Schneider (3), Dwayne Hancock (1)
Website	http://www.spdrs.com
Address	SPDR State Street Global Advisors State Street Financial Center, 1 Lincoln Street Boston MA 02111-2900 United States
Phone Number	617-786-3000

Ratings History

Date	Overall Rating	Risk Rating	Reward Rating
Q4-18	B-	B	B-
Q2-18	B-	C	B
Q4-17	B	B	B
Q4-16	B	C+	B
Q4-15	B	C+	B

Asset & Performance History

Date	NAV	1-Year Total Return
2017	52.65	11.94
2016	48.58	15.4
2015	43.29	-4.85
2014	47.2	28.65
2013	37.98	13.01
2012	34.94	1.11

Total Assets: $8,175,737,375

Asset Allocation

Asset	%
Cash	0%
Stocks	100%
US Stocks	100%
Bonds	0%
US Bonds	0%
Other	0%

Services Offered: Dividend Investment Plan, CashInvestment Plan

Investment Strategy: The investment seeks to provide investment results that, before expenses, correspond generally to the price and yield performance of publicly traded equity securities of companies in the Utilities Select Sector Index. In seeking to track the performance of the index, the fund employs a replication strategy. It generally invests substantially all, but at least 95%, of its total assets in the securities comprising the index. The index includes securities of companies from the following industries: electric utilities; water utilities; multi-utilities; independent power and renewable electricity producers; and gas utilities. The fund is non-diversified. **Top Holdings:** NextEra Energy Inc Duke Energy Corp Dominion Energy Inc Southern Co Exelon Corp

Vanguard Financials Index Fund ETF Shares   C   HOLD

Ticker	Traded On	NAV	Total Assets ($)	Dividend Yield (TTM)	Turnover Ratio	Expense Ratio
VFH	NYSE Arca		$8,084,060,323	1.95	3	0.1

Ratings

Reward	C
Risk	C+
Recent Upgrade/Downgrade	Down

Fund Information

Fund Type	Exchange Traded Funds
Category	Financials Sector Equity
Sub-Category	Financial
Prospectus Objective	Financial
Inception Date	Jan-04
Open to New Investments	Y

Prices

Price (as of 12/31/2018)	59.36
52-Week High	75.13
52-Week Low	55.73

Total Returns (%)

3-Month	6-Month	1-Year	3-Year	5-Year
-14.67	-12.34	-14.24	28.38	45.62

3-Year Standard Deviation	14.49
Effective Duration	

Valuation

Premium/Discount (1-Year Average)	0.02

Company Information

Provider	Vanguard
Manager/Tenure	William A. Coleman (2), Michelle Louie (1)
Website	http://www.vanguard.com
Address	Vanguard 100 Vanguard Boulevard Malvern PA 19355 United States
Phone Number	877-662-7447

Ratings History

Date	Overall Rating	Risk Rating	Reward Rating
Q4-18	C	C+	C
Q2-18	C+	C+	C+
Q4-17	A-	B	A
Q4-16	B	C+	B+
Q4-15	B-	B-	B-

Asset & Performance History

Date	NAV	1-Year Total Return
2017	70.01	21.13
2016	59.28	23.33
2015	48.46	-0.45
2014	49.66	13.95
2013	44.43	33
2012	34.07	26.25

Total Assets: $8,084,060,323

Asset Allocation

Asset	%
Cash	0%
Stocks	100%
US Stocks	98%
Bonds	0%
US Bonds	0%
Other	0%

Services Offered:

Investment Strategy: The investment seeks to track the performance of a benchmark index. The fund employs an indexing investment approach designed to track the performance of the MSCI US Investable Market Index (IMI)/Financials 25/50, an index made up of stocks of large, mid-size, and small U.S. companies within the financials sector, as classified under the Global Industry Classification Standard (GICS). The Advisor attempts to replicate the target index by seeking to invest all, or substantially all, of its assets in the stocks that make up the index, in order to hold each stock in approximately the same proportion as its weighting in the index. The fund is non-diversified. **Top Holdings:** JPMorgan Chase & Co Bank of America Corporation Berkshire Hathaway Inc B Wells Fargo & Co Citigroup Inc

Vanguard Mortgage-Backed Securities Index Fund ETF Shares   C   HOLD

Ticker	Traded On	NAV	Total Assets ($)	Dividend Yield (TTM)	Turnover Ratio	Expense Ratio
VMBS	NAS CM		$8,042,946,757	2.64	279	0.07

Ratings
Reward	D+
Risk	C+
Recent Upgrade/Downgrade	Up

Fund Information
Fund Type	Exchange Traded Funds
Category	US Fixed Income
Sub-Category	Intermediate Government
Prospectus Objective	Govt Bond - Mortgage
Inception Date	Nov-09
Open to New Investments	Y

Prices
Price (as of 12/31/2018)	51.49
52-Week High	52.44
52-Week Low	50.20

Total Returns (%)
3-Month	6-Month	1-Year	3-Year	5-Year
1.91	1.72	0.71	4.58	12.24

3-Year Standard Deviation	2.03
Effective Duration	6.32

Valuation
Premium/Discount (1-Year Average)	0.05

Company Information
Provider	Vanguard
Manager/Tenure	William D. Baird (9), Joshua C. Barrickman (5)
Website	http://www.vanguard.com
Address	Vanguard 100 Vanguard Boulevard Malvern PA 19355 United States
Phone Number	877-662-7447

PERFORMANCE

Ratings History
Date	Overall Rating	Risk Rating	Reward Rating
Q4-18	C	C+	D+
Q2-18	C-	C	C-
Q4-17	B-	A-	C
Q4-16	C	C+	C
Q4-15	C	C+	C

Asset & Performance History
Date	NAV	1-Year Total Return
2017	52.44	2.45
2016	52.34	1.07
2015	52.68	1.42
2014	52.98	5.81
2013	51.04	-1.27
2012	52.21	2.47

Total Assets: $8,042,946,757
Asset Allocation
Asset	%
Cash	5%
Stocks	0%
US Stocks	0%
Bonds	96%
US Bonds	96%
Other	0%

Services Offered:

Investment Strategy: The investment seeks to track the performance of a market-weighted mortgage-backed securities index. The fund employs an indexing investment approach designed to track the performance of the Bloomberg Barclays U.S. MBS Float Adjusted Index. This index covers U.S. agency mortgage-backed pass-through securities. To be included in the index, pool aggregates must have at least $250 million currently outstanding and a weighted average maturity of at least 1 year. All of the fund's investments will be selected through the sampling process, and under normal circumstances, at least 80% of the fund's assets will be invested in bonds included in the index. **Top Holdings:** Federal Home Loan Mortgage Corporation 3% Government National Mortgage Association 4.5% Federal National Mortgage Association 3% Federal National Mortgage Association 3.5% Government National Mortgage Association 4%

---

iShares 3-7 Year Treasury Bond ETF   C-   HOLD

Ticker	Traded On	NAV	Total Assets ($)	Dividend Yield (TTM)	Turnover Ratio	Expense Ratio
IEI	NAS CM	121.36	$7,798,737,387	1.9	66	0.15

Ratings
Reward	D
Risk	C
Recent Upgrade/Downgrade	Up

Fund Information
Fund Type	Exchange Traded Funds
Category	US Fixed Income
Sub-Category	Intermediate Government
Prospectus Objective	Govt Bond - Treasury
Inception Date	Jan-07
Open to New Investments	Y

Prices
Price (as of 12/31/2018)	121.40
52-Week High	122.16
52-Week Low	118.21

Total Returns (%)
3-Month	6-Month	1-Year	3-Year	5-Year
2.71	2.48	1.35	3.80	8.85

3-Year Standard Deviation	2.64
Effective Duration	4.47

Valuation
Premium/Discount (1-Year Average)	0.02

Company Information
Provider	iShares
Manager/Tenure	Scott Radell (8), James Mauro (7)
Website	http://www.ishares.com
Address	iShares 400 Howard Street San Francisco CA 94105 United States
Phone Number	800-474-2737

PERFORMANCE

Ratings History
Date	Overall Rating	Risk Rating	Reward Rating
Q4-18	C-	C	D
Q2-18	D+	C	D
Q4-17	C	C	C
Q4-16	C	C+	C
Q4-15	C	C+	C

Asset & Performance History
Date	NAV	1-Year Total Return
2017	122.13	1.18
2016	122.52	1.21
2015	122.63	1.67
2014	122.29	3.14
2013	120.04	-1.95
2012	123.37	2.09

Total Assets: $7,798,737,387
Asset Allocation
Asset	%
Cash	0%
Stocks	0%
US Stocks	0%
Bonds	100%
US Bonds	100%
Other	0%

Services Offered:

Investment Strategy: The investment seeks to track the investment results of the ICE U.S. Treasury 3-7 Year Bond Index (the "underlying index"). The fund generally invests at least 90% of its assets in the bonds of the underlying index and at least 95% of its assets in U.S. government bonds. The underlying index measures the performance of public obligations of the U.S. Treasury that have a remaining maturity of greater than three years and less than or equal to seven years. **Top Holdings:** United States Treasury Notes 2.38% United States Treasury Notes 1.88% United States Treasury Notes 2.25% United States Treasury Notes 2% United States Treasury Notes 2.5%

iShares 20+ Year Treasury Bond ETF
D+ **SELL**

Ticker	Traded On	NAV	Total Assets ($)	Dividend Yield (TTM)	Turnover Ratio	Expense Ratio
TLT	NAS CM	121.01	$7,781,932,111	2.75	25	0.15

Ratings
Reward	D
Risk	C-
Recent Upgrade/Downgrade	Down

Fund Information
Fund Type	Exchange Traded Funds
Category	US Fixed Income
Sub-Category	Long Government
Prospectus Objective	Govt Bond - Treasury
Inception Date	Jul-02
Open to New Investments	Y

Prices
Price (as of 12/31/2018)	121.51
52-Week High	126.86
52-Week Low	112.00

Total Returns (%)
3-Month	6-Month	1-Year	3-Year	5-Year
4.74	1.10	-2.07	8.11	35.42

3-Year Standard Deviation	9.58
Effective Duration	17.03

Valuation
Premium/Discount (1-Year Average)	-0.08

Company Information
Provider	iShares
Manager/Tenure	Scott Radell (8), James Mauro (7)
Website	http://www.ishares.com
Address	iShares 400 Howard Street San Francisco CA 94105 United States
Phone Number	800-474-2737

PERFORMANCE

Ratings History
Date	Overall Rating	Risk Rating	Reward Rating
Q4-18	D+	C-	D
Q2-18	C-	C	D+
Q4-17	C	C	C
Q4-16	C+	B	C
Q4-15	C	C-	C

Asset & Performance History
Date	NAV	1-Year Total Return
2017	126.94	8.69
2016	119.49	1.36
2015	120.73	-1.64
2014	125.9	27.35
2013	101.8	-13.91
2012	121.87	3.24

Total Assets: $7,781,932,111
Asset Allocation
Asset	%
Cash	0%
Stocks	0%
US Stocks	0%
Bonds	100%
US Bonds	100%
Other	0%

Services Offered:

Investment Strategy: The investment seeks to track the investment results of the ICE U.S. Treasury 20+ Year Bond Index (the "underlying index"). The fund generally invests at least 90% of its assets in the bonds of the underlying index and at least 95% of its assets in U.S. government bonds. The underlying index measures the performance of public obligations of the U.S. Treasury that have a remaining maturity greater than twenty years.
Top Holdings: United States Treasury Bonds 2.5%   United States Treasury Bonds 2.5%   United States Treasury Bonds 3%   United States Treasury Bonds 3.13%   United States Treasury Bonds 2.88%

First Trust Dow Jones Internet Index Fund
C+ **HOLD**

Ticker	Traded On	NAV	Total Assets ($)	Dividend Yield (TTM)	Turnover Ratio	Expense Ratio
FDN	NYSE Arca	116.65	$7,705,993,163	0	22	0.53

Ratings
Reward	B
Risk	C-
Recent Upgrade/Downgrade	Down

Fund Information
Fund Type	Exchange Traded Funds
Category	Technology Sector Equity
Sub-Category	Technology
Prospectus Objective	Technology
Inception Date	Jun-06
Open to New Investments	Y

Prices
Price (as of 12/31/2018)	116.66
52-Week High	147.65
52-Week Low	107.21

Total Returns (%)
3-Month	6-Month	1-Year	3-Year	5-Year
-17.02	-16.47	6.22	56.30	94.93

3-Year Standard Deviation	15.62
Effective Duration	

Valuation
Premium/Discount (1-Year Average)	0.01

Company Information
Provider	First Trust
Manager/Tenure	Jon C. Erickson (12), Daniel J. Lindquist (12), David G. McGarel (12), 3 others
Website	http://www.ftportfolios.com/
Address	First Trust 120 E. Liberty Drive, Suite 400 Wheaton IL 60187 United States
Phone Number	800-621-1675

PERFORMANCE

Ratings History
Date	Overall Rating	Risk Rating	Reward Rating
Q4-18	C+	C-	B
Q2-18	B-	C	B+
Q4-17	A-	B	A
Q4-16	B-	C	B
Q4-15	B	C	B+

Asset & Performance History
Date	NAV	1-Year Total Return
2017	109.81	37.62
2016	79.79	6.91
2015	74.63	21.76
2014	61.29	2.42
2013	59.84	53.39
2012	39.01	20.84

Total Assets: $7,705,993,163
Asset Allocation
Asset	%
Cash	0%
Stocks	100%
US Stocks	100%
Bonds	0%
US Bonds	0%
Other	0%

Services Offered:

Investment Strategy: The investment seeks investment results that correspond generally to the price and yield (before the fund's fees and expenses) of an equity index called the Dow Jones Internet Composite Index (SM) (the "index"). The fund will normally invest at least 90% of its net assets (including investment borrowings) in common stocks that comprise the index. The index is designed to include only companies whose primary focus is Internet-related. To be eligible for inclusion in the index, a company must generate at least 50% of its revenues from Internet commerce or services. It is non-diversified. **Top Holdings:** Amazon.com Inc   Facebook Inc A   Alphabet Inc Class C   Salesforce.com Inc   Netflix Inc

Schwab U.S. Small-Cap ETF™   C   HOLD

Ticker	Traded On	NAV	Total Assets ($)	Dividend Yield (TTM)	Turnover Ratio	Expense Ratio
SCHA	NYSE Arca	60.69	$7,650,044,979	1.34	9	0.05

Ratings
Reward   C-
Risk   C+
Recent Upgrade/Downgrade   Down

Fund Information
Fund Type   Exchange Traded Funds
Category   US Equity Small Cap
Sub-Category   Small Blend
Prospectus Objective   Small Company
Inception Date   Nov-09
Open to New Investments   Y

Prices
Price (as of 12/31/2018)   60.68
52-Week High   78.22
52-Week Low   57.06

Total Returns (%)

3-Month	6-Month	1-Year	3-Year	5-Year
-18.86	-17.23	-11.75	21.70	24.16

3-Year Standard Deviation   13.71
Effective Duration

Valuation
Premium/Discount (1-Year Average)   0.02

Company Information
Provider   Schwab ETFs
Manager/Tenure   Ferian Juwono (8), Christopher Bliss (1), Sabya Sinha (1), 1 other
Website   http://www.schwabetfs.com
Address   Schwab ETFs United States
Phone Number   800-435-4000

PERFORMANCE

Ratings History

Date	Overall Rating	Risk Rating	Reward Rating
Q4-18	C	C+	C-
Q2-18	C+	C+	C+
Q4-17	B	B	B+
Q4-16	B-	C+	B
Q4-15	C	C+	C

Asset & Performance History

Date	NAV	1-Year Total Return
2017	69.74	15.41
2016	61.42	19.88
2015	52.07	-4.23
2014	55.14	6.53
2013	52.53	39.58
2012	38.12	18.24

Total Assets: $7,650,044,979

Asset Allocation

Asset	%
Cash	0%
Stocks	100%
US Stocks	99%
Bonds	0%
US Bonds	0%
Other	0%

Services Offered:

Investment Strategy: The investment seeks to track as closely as possible, before fees and expenses, the total return of the Dow Jones U.S. Small-Cap Total Stock Market Index. To pursue its goal, the fund generally invests in stocks that are included in the index. The fund will invest at least 90% of its net assets in these stocks. The index includes the small-cap portion of the Dow Jones U.S. Total Stock Market Index actually available to investors in the marketplace. The Dow Jones U.S. Small-Cap Total Stock Market Index includes the components ranked 751-2500 by full market capitalization. The index is a float-adjusted market capitalization weighted index. **Top Holdings:** Exact Sciences Corp   Twilio Inc A   Pool Corp   Etsy Inc   AptarGroup Inc

iShares S&P Mid-Cap 400 Growth ETF   C   HOLD

Ticker	Traded On	NAV	Total Assets ($)	Dividend Yield (TTM)	Turnover Ratio	Expense Ratio
IJK	NYSE Arca	191.20	$7,586,427,222	1.09	40	0.25

Ratings
Reward   C-
Risk   C+
Recent Upgrade/Downgrade   Down

Fund Information
Fund Type   Exchange Traded Funds
Category   US Equity Mid Cap
Sub-Category   Mid-Cap Growth
Prospectus Objective   Growth
Inception Date   Jul-00
Open to New Investments   Y

Prices
Price (as of 12/31/2018)   191.23
52-Week High   237.87
52-Week Low   179.90

Total Returns (%)

3-Month	6-Month	1-Year	3-Year	5-Year
-16.99	-14.69	-10.53	22.59	34.04

3-Year Standard Deviation   11.58
Effective Duration

Valuation
Premium/Discount (1-Year Average)   0.00

Company Information
Provider   iShares
Manager/Tenure   Diane Hsiung (10), Greg Savage (10), Jennifer Hsui (6), 3 others
Website   http://www.ishares.com
Address   iShares 400 Howard Street San Francisco CA 94105 United States
Phone Number   800-474-2737

PERFORMANCE

Ratings History

Date	Overall Rating	Risk Rating	Reward Rating
Q4-18	C	C+	C-
Q2-18	B-	C+	B-
Q4-17	B+	B+	B
Q4-16	B-	C+	B
Q4-15	C+	C+	C+

Asset & Performance History

Date	NAV	1-Year Total Return
2017	215.84	19.65
2016	182.19	14.51
2015	161.03	1.8
2014	159.9	7.39
2013	150.28	32.51
2012	114.52	17.08

Total Assets: $7,586,427,222

Asset Allocation

Asset	%
Cash	0%
Stocks	100%
US Stocks	100%
Bonds	0%
US Bonds	0%
Other	0%

Services Offered: CashInvestment Plan

Investment Strategy: The investment seeks to track the investment results of the S&P MidCap 400 Growth IndexTM, which measures the performance of the mid-capitalization growth sector of the U.S. equity market. The fund generally invests at least 90% of its assets in securities of the underlying index and in depositary receipts representing securities of the underlying index. It may invest the remainder of its assets in certain futures, options and swap contracts, cash and cash equivalents, as well as in securities not included in the underlying index, but which the advisor believes will help the fund track the underlying index. **Top Holdings:** Teleflex Inc   Domino's Pizza Inc   IDEX Corp   Zebra Technologies Corp   Trimble Inc

iShares MSCI Eurozone ETF   D+   SELL

Ticker	Traded On	NAV		Total Assets ($)	Dividend Yield (TTM)	Turnover Ratio	Expense Ratio
EZU	BATS	35.07		$7,570,497,712	3.28	5	0.47

Ratings
Reward	D+
Risk	D+
Recent Upgrade/Downgrade	Down

Fund Information
Fund Type	Exchange Traded Funds
Category	Europe Equity Large Cap
Sub-Category	Europe Stock
Prospectus Objective	Europe Stock
Inception Date	Jul-00
Open to New Investments	Y

Prices
Price (as of 12/31/2018)	35.06
52-Week High	47.11
52-Week Low	33.85

Total Returns (%)
3-Month	6-Month	1-Year	3-Year	5-Year
-14.22	-13.19	-16.97	7.58	-3.15

3-Year Standard Deviation	14.06
Effective Duration	

Valuation
Premium/Discount (1-Year Average)	-0.19

Company Information
Provider	iShares
Manager/Tenure	Diane Hsiung (10), Greg Savage (10), Jennifer Hsui (5), 1 other
Website	http://www.ishares.com
Address	iShares 400 Howard Street San Francisco CA 94105 United States
Phone Number	800-474-2737

PERFORMANCE

Ratings History
Date	Overall Rating	Risk Rating	Reward Rating
Q4-18	D+	D+	D+
Q2-18	C	C+	C
Q4-17	B	B	B
Q4-16	D	C-	D
Q4-15	C	B	C-

Asset & Performance History
Date	NAV	1-Year Total Return
2017	43.52	27.92
2016	34.71	1.29
2015	35.35	-1.62
2014	36.64	-8.5
2013	41.11	28.75
2012	32.81	21.19

Total Assets: $7,570,497,712

Asset Allocation
Asset	%
Cash	0%
Stocks	100%
US Stocks	2%
Bonds	0%
US Bonds	0%
Other	0%

Services Offered: CashInvestment Plan

Investment Strategy: The investment seeks to track the investment results of the MSCI EMU Index composed of large- and mid-capitalization equities from developed market countries that use the euro as their official currency. The fund generally invests at least 95% of its assets in the securities of its underlying index and in depositary receipts representing securities in its underlying index. The index consists of stocks from the following 10 developed market countries: Austria, Belgium, Finland, France, Germany, Ireland, Italy, the Netherlands, Portugal and Spain. **Top Holdings:** Total SA Sanofi SA SAP SE Allianz SE Siemens AG

---

iShares MSCI Brazil Capped ETF   C   HOLD

Ticker	Traded On	NAV		Total Assets ($)	Dividend Yield (TTM)	Turnover Ratio	Expense Ratio
EWZ	NYSE Arca	38.32		$7,354,893,501	2.4	30	0.59

Ratings
Reward	C
Risk	C-
Recent Upgrade/Downgrade	Up

Fund Information
Fund Type	Exchange Traded Funds
Category	Latin America Equity
Sub-Category	Latin America Stock
Prospectus Objective	Foreign Stock
Inception Date	Jul-00
Open to New Investments	Y

Prices
Price (as of 12/31/2018)	38.20
52-Week High	47.33
52-Week Low	30.72

Total Returns (%)
3-Month	6-Month	1-Year	3-Year	5-Year
15.79	22.04	-1.78	96.23	-1.49

3-Year Standard Deviation	34.48
Effective Duration	

Valuation
Premium/Discount (1-Year Average)	-0.03

Company Information
Provider	iShares
Manager/Tenure	Diane Hsiung (10), Greg Savage (10), Jennifer Hsui (5), 1 other
Website	http://www.ishares.com
Address	iShares 400 Howard Street San Francisco CA 94105 United States
Phone Number	800-474-2737

PERFORMANCE

Ratings History
Date	Overall Rating	Risk Rating	Reward Rating
Q4-18	C	C-	C
Q2-18	C-	C-	C
Q4-17	C	C-	C
Q4-16	D+	D+	D+
Q4-15	D-	D-	D-

Asset & Performance History
Date	NAV	1-Year Total Return
2017	40.26	21.9
2016	33.66	63.91
2015	20.95	-41.28
2014	36.76	-14.5
2013	44.38	-17
2012	55.23	-0.6

Total Assets: $7,354,893,501

Asset Allocation
Asset	%
Cash	0%
Stocks	100%
US Stocks	0%
Bonds	0%
US Bonds	0%
Other	0%

Services Offered: CashInvestment Plan

Investment Strategy: The investment seeks to track the investment results of the MSCI Brazil 25/50 Index. The fund invests at least 95% of its assets in the securities of its underlying index and in depositary receipts representing securities in its underlying index. The index, consists of stocks traded primarily on B3 (the largest Brazilian exchange), is a free float-adjusted market capitalization-weighted index with a capping methodology applied to issuer weights so that no single issuer of a component exceeds 25% of the underlying index weight, and all issuers with weight above 5% do not cumulatively exceed 50% of the underlying index weight. The fund is non-diversified. **Top Holdings:** Itau Unibanco Holding SA Participating Preferred Vale SA Bank Bradesco SA Participating Preferred Petroleo Brasileiro SA Petrobras Participating Preferred Petroleo Brasileiro SA Petrobras

SPDR® Bloomberg Barclays High Yield Bond ETF   C+   HOLD

Ticker	Traded On	NAV	Total Assets ($)	Dividend Yield (TTM)	Turnover Ratio	Expense Ratio
JNK	NYSE Arca	33.55	$7,235,078,068	5.69	46	0.4

Ratings
Reward   C-
Risk   B+
Recent Upgrade/Downgrade

Fund Information
Fund Type	Exchange Traded Funds
Category	US Fixed Income
Sub-Category	High Yield Bond
Prospectus Objective	Corp Bond-High Yld
Inception Date	Nov-07
Open to New Investments	Y

Prices
Price (as of 12/31/2018)	33.59
52-Week High	37.03
52-Week Low	32.95

Total Returns (%)
3-Month	6-Month	1-Year	3-Year	5-Year
-5.12	-2.20	-3.17	18.30	11.02

3-Year Standard Deviation   4.82
Effective Duration   4.16

Valuation
Premium/Discount (1-Year Average)   0.05

Company Information
Provider	SPDR State Street Global Advisors
Manager/Tenure	Michael J. Brunell (11), Kyle Kelly (5), Bradley J. Sullivan (2)
Website	http://www.spdrs.com
Address	SPDR State Street Global Advisors State Street Financial Center, 1 Lincoln Street Boston MA 02111-2900 United States
Phone Number	617-786-3000

PERFORMANCE

Ratings History

Date	Overall Rating	Risk Rating	Reward Rating
Q4-18	C+	B+	C-
Q2-18	C+	B	C
Q4-17	C+	B	C+
Q4-16	C+	B-	C
Q4-15	C-	C-	C-

Asset & Performance History

Date	NAV	1-Year Total Return
2017	36.64	6
2016	36.37	14.74
2015	33.75	-7.21
2014	38.62	1.15
2013	40.42	5.89
2012	40.56	14.34

Total Assets: $7,235,078,068
Asset Allocation

Asset	%
Cash	1%
Stocks	0%
US Stocks	0%
Bonds	99%
US Bonds	85%
Other	0%

Services Offered:

Investment Strategy: The investment seeks to provide investment results that correspond generally to the price and yield performance of the Bloomberg Barclays High Yield Very Liquid Index. The fund generally invests substantially all, but at least 80%, of its total assets in the securities comprising the index or in securities that the Adviser determines have economic characteristics that are substantially identical to the economic characteristics of the securities that comprise the index. The index is designed to measure the performance of publicly issued U.S. dollar denominated high yield corporate bonds with above-average liquidity. The fund is non-diversified. **Top Holdings:** ALTICE FRANCE S.A 7.38% Sprint Corporation 7.88% First Data Corporation 7% CCO Holdings, LLC/ CCO Holdings Capital Corp. 5.12% Community Health Systems Incorporated 6.25%

SPDR® Bloomberg Barclays 1-3 Month T-Bill ETF   C   HOLD

Ticker	Traded On	NAV	Total Assets ($)	Dividend Yield (TTM)	Turnover Ratio	Expense Ratio
BIL	NYSE Arca	91.44	$7,043,462,965	1.47	625	0.14

Ratings
Reward   C-
Risk   C+
Recent Upgrade/Downgrade

Fund Information
Fund Type	Exchange Traded Funds
Category	US Fixed Income
Sub-Category	Ultrashort Bond
Prospectus Objective	Govt Bond - Treasury
Inception Date	May-07
Open to New Investments	Y

Prices
Price (as of 12/31/2018)	91.46
52-Week High	91.61
52-Week Low	91.37

Total Returns (%)
3-Month	6-Month	1-Year	3-Year	5-Year
0.35	0.80	1.51	2.34	2.13

3-Year Standard Deviation   0.2
Effective Duration   0.17

Valuation
Premium/Discount (1-Year Average)   0.01

Company Information
Provider	SPDR State Street Global Advisors
Manager/Tenure	Todd Bean (11), Sean Lussier (2)
Website	http://www.spdrs.com
Address	SPDR State Street Global Advisors State Street Financial Center, 1 Lincoln Street Boston MA 02111-2900 United States
Phone Number	617-786-3000

PERFORMANCE

Ratings History

Date	Overall Rating	Risk Rating	Reward Rating
Q4-18	C	C+	C-
Q2-18	C	C+	C-
Q4-17	C	C+	C-
Q4-16	C-	C	D+
Q4-15	D+	C	D

Asset & Performance History

Date	NAV	1-Year Total Return
2017	91.42	0.68
2016	91.42	0.12
2015	91.37	-0.1
2014	91.47	-0.09
2013	91.56	-0.07
2012	91.62	-0.03

Total Assets: $7,043,462,965
Asset Allocation

Asset	%
Cash	100%
Stocks	0%
US Stocks	0%
Bonds	0%
US Bonds	0%
Other	0%

Services Offered:

Investment Strategy: The investment seeks to provide investment results that correspond generally to the price and yield performance of the Bloomberg Barclays 1-3 Month U.S. Treasury Bill Index. The fund invests substantially all, but at least 80%, of its total assets in the securities comprising the index or in securities that the Adviser determines have economic characteristics that are substantially identical to the economic characteristics of the securities that comprise the index. The index measures the performance of public obligations of the U.S. Treasury that have a remaining maturity of greater than or equal to 1 month and less than 3 months. It is non-diversified. **Top Holdings:** Ssi Us Gov Money Market Class State Street Inst Us Gov Ssi Us Gov Money Market Class State Street Inst Us Gov

Vanguard FTSE Pacific Index Fund ETF Shares   C-   HOLD

Ticker	Traded On	NAV	Total Assets ($)	Dividend Yield (TTM)	Turnover Ratio	Expense Ratio
VPL	NYSE Arca		$6,983,038,034	2.81	3	0.1

Ratings
Reward   D+
Risk   C
Recent Upgrade/Downgrade   Down

Fund Information
Fund Type   Exchange Traded Funds
Category   Asia Equity
Sub-Category   Diversified Pacific/Asia
Prospectus Objective   Pacific Stock
Inception Date   Mar-05
Open to New Investments   Y

Prices
Price (as of 12/31/2018)   60.63
52-Week High   77.85
52-Week Low   58.71

Total Returns (%)

3-Month	6-Month	1-Year	3-Year	5-Year
-13.08	-10.29	-14.08	16.36	13.73

3-Year Standard Deviation   11.04
Effective Duration

Valuation
Premium/Discount (1-Year Average)   -0.07

Company Information
Provider   Vanguard
Manager/Tenure Jeffrey D. Miller (2), Michael Perre (2)
Website   http://www.vanguard.com
Address   Vanguard 100 Vanguard Boulevard
                Malvern PA 19355 United States
Phone Number   877-662-7447

PERFORMANCE

Ratings History

Date	Overall Rating	Risk Rating	Reward Rating
Q4-18	C-	C	D+
Q2-18	C	C+	C
Q4-17	B	B	B
Q4-16	C	C+	C
Q4-15	C	C+	C

Asset & Performance History

Date	NAV	1-Year Total Return
2017	72.74	28.82
2016	58.11	4.79
2015	56.68	2.42
2014	56.66	-4.57
2013	60.92	17.55
2012	53.2	15.6

Total Assets: $6,983,038,034
Asset Allocation

Asset	%
Cash	3%
Stocks	97%
US Stocks	0%
Bonds	0%
US Bonds	0%
Other	0%

Services Offered:

Investment Strategy: The investment seeks to track the performance of a benchmark index that measures the investment return of stocks issued by companies located in the major markets of the Pacific region. The fund employs an indexing investment approach by investing all, or substantially all, of its assets in the common stocks included in the FTSE Developed Asia Pacific All Cap Index. The FTSE Developed Asia Pacific All Cap Index is a market-capitalization-weighted index that is made up of approximately 2,256 common stocks of large-, mid-, and small-cap companies located in Japan, Australia, South Korea, Hong Kong, and Singapore. **Top Holdings:** Samsung Electronics Co Ltd Toyota Motor Corp AIA Group Ltd Commonwealth Bank of Australia Mitsubishi UFJ Financial Group Inc

---

iShares Edge MSCI USA Quality Factor ETF   C   HOLD

Ticker	Traded On	NAV	Total Assets ($)	Dividend Yield (TTM)	Turnover Ratio	Expense Ratio
QUAL	BATS	76.65	$6,871,576,058	1.78	41	0.15

Ratings
Reward   C
Risk   C+
Recent Upgrade/Downgrade   Down

Fund Information
Fund Type   Exchange Traded Funds
Category   US Equity Large Cap Blend
Sub-Category   Large Blend
Prospectus Objective   Growth
Inception Date   Jul-13
Open to New Investments   Y

Prices
Price (as of 12/31/2018)   76.76
52-Week High   91.26
52-Week Low   71.91

Total Returns (%)

3-Month	6-Month	1-Year	3-Year	5-Year
-15.02	-7.31	-5.77	25.78	48.20

3-Year Standard Deviation   9.2
Effective Duration

Valuation
Premium/Discount (1-Year Average)   0.00

Company Information
Provider   iShares
Manager/Tenure Diane Hsiung (5), Jennifer Hsui (5),
                Greg Savage (5), 3 others
Website   http://www.ishares.com
Address   iShares 400 Howard Street San
                Francisco CA 94105 United States
Phone Number   800-474-2737

PERFORMANCE

Ratings History

Date	Overall Rating	Risk Rating	Reward Rating
Q4-18	C	C+	C
Q2-18	C+	C+	C+
Q4-17	B	B+	B
Q4-16	B	C+	B
Q4-15	C	C	C

Asset & Performance History

Date	NAV	1-Year Total Return
2017	82.86	22.26
2016	69.07	9.17
2015	64.56	5.56
2014	62.18	11.61
2013	56.5	
2012		

Total Assets: $6,871,576,058
Asset Allocation

Asset	%
Cash	0%
Stocks	100%
US Stocks	100%
Bonds	0%
US Bonds	0%
Other	0%

Services Offered:

Investment Strategy: The investment seeks to track the investment results of the MSCI USA Sector Neutral Quality Index composed of U.S. large- and mid-capitalization stocks with quality characteristics as identified through certain fundamental metrics. The fund generally will invest at least 90% of its assets in the component securities of the underlying index and may invest up to 10% of its assets in certain futures, options and swap contracts, cash and cash equivalents. The index is based on a traditional market capitalization-weighted parent index, the MSCI USA Index. **Top Holdings:** Johnson & Johnson Apple Inc Facebook Inc A Exxon Mobil Corp Mastercard Inc A

iShares U.S. Treasury Bond ETF   C-   HOLD

Ticker	Traded On	NAV		Total Assets ($)	Dividend Yield (TTM)	Turnover Ratio	Expense Ratio
GOVT	BATS	24.78		$6,793,751,566	1.95	47	0.15

Ratings
Reward   D
Risk   C
Recent Upgrade/Downgrade

Fund Information
Fund Type   Exchange Traded Funds
Category   US Fixed Income
Sub-Category   Intermediate Government
Prospectus Objective   Govt Bond - Treasury
Inception Date   Feb-12
Open to New Investments   Y

Prices
Price (as of 12/31/2018)   24.65
52-Week High   25.08
52-Week Low   24.07

Total Returns (%)

3-Month	6-Month	1-Year	3-Year	5-Year
2.68	1.99	0.74	3.90	9.91

3-Year Standard Deviation   3.19
Effective Duration   5.79

Valuation
Premium/Discount (1-Year Average)   0.01

Company Information
Provider   iShares
Manager/Tenure   James Mauro (6), Scott Radell (6)
Website   http://www.ishares.com
Address   iShares 400 Howard Street San
                    Francisco CA 94105 United States
Phone Number   800-474-2737

PERFORMANCE

Ratings History

Date	Overall Rating	Risk Rating	Reward Rating
Q4-18	C-	C	D
Q2-18	C-	C	D+
Q4-17	C	C	C
Q4-16	C	C+	C
Q4-15	C	C+	C

Asset & Performance History

Date	NAV	1-Year Total Return
2017	25.09	2.04
2016	24.94	0.92
2015	25.05	0.76
2014	25.17	4.98
2013	24.26	-2.84
2012	25.2	

Total Assets: $6,793,751,566
Asset Allocation

Asset	%
Cash	0%
Stocks	0%
US Stocks	0%
Bonds	100%
US Bonds	100%
Other	0%

Services Offered:

Investment Strategy: The investment seeks to track the investment results of the ICE U.S. Treasury Core Bond Index (the "underlying index"). The fund generally will invest at least 90% of its assets in the component securities of the underlying index and may invest up to 10% of its assets in certain futures, options and swap contracts, cash and cash equivalents, as well as in securities not included in the underlying index, but which the advisor believes will help the fund track the index. The underlying index measures the performance of public obligations of the U.S. Treasury that have a remaining maturity greater than one year and less than or equal to thirty years. **Top Holdings:** United States Treasury Notes 2.38% United States Treasury Notes 2% United States Treasury Notes 2.25% United States Treasury Notes 1.5% United States Treasury Notes 2.25%

---

iShares Core High Dividend ETF   B-   BUY

Ticker	Traded On	NAV		Total Assets ($)	Dividend Yield (TTM)	Turnover Ratio	Expense Ratio
HDV	NYSE Arca	84.33		$6,671,828,776	3.42	46	0.08

Ratings
Reward   B
Risk   C
Recent Upgrade/Downgrade   Up

Fund Information
Fund Type   Exchange Traded Funds
Category   US Equity Large Cap Value
Sub-Category   Large Value
Prospectus Objective   Equity-Income
Inception Date   Mar-11
Open to New Investments   Y

Prices
Price (as of 12/31/2018)   84.38
52-Week High   94.20
52-Week Low   80.00

Total Returns (%)

3-Month	6-Month	1-Year	3-Year	5-Year
-6.58	1.27	-2.92	27.41	43.02

3-Year Standard Deviation   8
Effective Duration

Valuation
Premium/Discount (1-Year Average)   0.00

Company Information
Provider   iShares
Manager/Tenure   Diane Hsiung (7), Greg Savage (7),
                    Jennifer Hsui (6), 3 others
Website   http://www.ishares.com
Address   iShares 400 Howard Street San
                    Francisco CA 94105 United States
Phone Number   800-474-2737

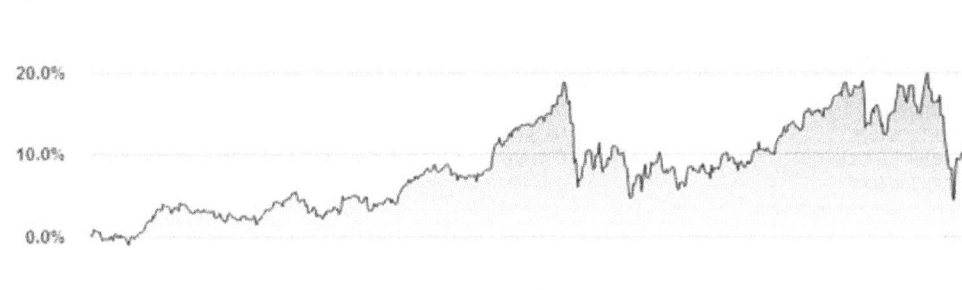
PERFORMANCE

Ratings History

Date	Overall Rating	Risk Rating	Reward Rating
Q4-18	B-	C	B
Q2-18	C+	C-	B-
Q4-17	B	B	B-
Q4-16	B-	C	B
Q4-15	B-	C	B

Asset & Performance History

Date	NAV	1-Year Total Return
2017	90.04	13.35
2016	82.2	15.78
2015	73.41	-0.26
2014	76.54	12.54
2013	70.26	23.6
2012	58.76	9.71

Total Assets: $6,671,828,776
Asset Allocation

Asset	%
Cash	0%
Stocks	100%
US Stocks	100%
Bonds	0%
US Bonds	0%
Other	0%

Services Offered:

Investment Strategy: The investment seeks to track the investment results of the Morningstar® Dividend Yield Focus IndexSM composed of relatively high dividend paying U.S. equities. The fund generally will invest at least 90% of its assets in the component securities of the underlying index and may invest up to 10% of its assets in certain futures, options and swap contracts, cash and cash equivalents. The underlying index is comprised of qualified income paying securities that are screened for superior company quality and financial health as determined by Morningstar, Inc.'s ("Morningstar" or the "index provider") proprietary index methodology. The fund is non-diversified. **Top Holdings:** Exxon Mobil Corp Verizon Communications Inc Johnson & Johnson Chevron Corp Pfizer Inc

Vanguard Short-Term Treasury Index Fund ETF Shares   C   HOLD

Ticker	Traded On	NAV	Total Assets ($)	Dividend Yield (TTM)	Turnover Ratio	Expense Ratio
VGSH	NAS CM		$6,540,986,016	1.68	67	0.07

Ratings
Reward   C-
Risk   C+
Recent Upgrade/Downgrade   Up

Fund Information
Fund Type   Exchange Traded Funds
Category   US Fixed Income
Sub-Category   Short Government
Prospectus Objective   Govt Bond - Gen
Inception Date   Nov-09
Open to New Investments   Y

Prices
Price (as of 12/31/2018)   60.12
52-Week High   60.28
52-Week Low   59.55

Total Returns (%)

3-Month	6-Month	1-Year	3-Year	5-Year
1.24	1.44	1.41	2.58	3.65

3-Year Standard Deviation   0.77
Effective Duration   1.93

Valuation
Premium/Discount (1-Year Average)   0.04

Company Information
Provider   Vanguard
Manager/Tenure   Joshua C. Barrickman (5)
Website   http://www.vanguard.com
Address   Vanguard 100 Vanguard Boulevard
                  Malvern PA 19355 United States
Phone Number   877-662-7447

PERFORMANCE

Ratings History

Date	Overall Rating	Risk Rating	Reward Rating
Q4-18	C	C+	C-
Q2-18	C-	C	D+
Q4-17	C	C+	C
Q4-16	C	C-	C
Q4-15	C	C+	C

Asset & Performance History

Date	NAV	1-Year Total Return
2017	60.27	0.36
2016	60.7	0.78
2015	60.73	0.5
2014	60.85	0.52
2013	60.81	0.25
2012	60.86	0.42

Total Assets: $6,540,986,016
Asset Allocation

Asset	%
Cash	0%
Stocks	0%
US Stocks	0%
Bonds	100%
US Bonds	100%
Other	0%

Services Offered:

Investment Strategy: The investment seeks to track the performance of a market-weighted government bond index with a short-term dollar-weighted average maturity. The fund employs an indexing investment approach designed to track the performance of the Bloomberg Barclays US Treasury 1-3 Year Bond Index. This index includes fixed income securities issued by the U.S. Treasury (not including inflation-protected securities), all with maturities between 1 and 3 years. At least 80% of the fund's assets will be invested in bonds included in the index. **Top Holdings:** United States Treasury Notes 2.25% United States Treasury Notes 1.5% United States Treasury Notes 2.62% United States Treasury Notes 1.38% United States Treasury Notes 1.38%

Schwab U.S. Large-Cap Growth ETF™   C   HOLD

Ticker	Traded On	NAV	Total Assets ($)	Dividend Yield (TTM)	Turnover Ratio	Expense Ratio
SCHG	NYSE Arca	68.89	$6,455,866,891	0.87	5	0.04

Ratings
Reward   C
Risk   C+
Recent Upgrade/Downgrade   Down

Fund Information
Fund Type   Exchange Traded Funds
Category   US Equity Large Cap Growth
Sub-Category   Large Growth
Prospectus Objective   Growth
Inception Date   Dec-09
Open to New Investments   Y

Prices
Price (as of 12/31/2018)   68.93
52-Week High   82.25
52-Week Low   64.30

Total Returns (%)

3-Month	6-Month	1-Year	3-Year	5-Year
-15.75	-8.82	-1.34	34.85	61.16

3-Year Standard Deviation   11.13
Effective Duration

Valuation
Premium/Discount (1-Year Average)   0.01

Company Information
Provider   Schwab ETFs
Manager/Tenure   Ferian Juwono (8), Christopher Bliss
                  (1), Sabya Sinha (1), 1 other
Website   http://www.schwabetfs.com
Address   Schwab ETFs United States
Phone Number   800-435-4000

PERFORMANCE

Ratings History

Date	Overall Rating	Risk Rating	Reward Rating
Q4-18	C	C+	C
Q2-18	B-	C+	B-
Q4-17	B	B	B
Q4-16	B-	C+	B
Q4-15	C+	B-	C+

Asset & Performance History

Date	NAV	1-Year Total Return
2017	70.66	28.05
2016	55.79	6.75
2015	52.82	3.25
2014	51.77	15.73
2013	45.25	33.96
2012	34.19	17.02

Total Assets: $6,455,866,891
Asset Allocation

Asset	%
Cash	1%
Stocks	99%
US Stocks	98%
Bonds	0%
US Bonds	0%
Other	0%

Services Offered:

Investment Strategy: The investment seeks to track as closely as possible, before fees and expenses, the total return of the Dow Jones U.S. Large-Cap Growth Total Stock Market Index. To pursue its goal, the fund generally invests in stocks that are included in the Dow Jones U.S. Large-Cap Growth Total Stock Market Index. The index includes the large-cap growth portion of the Dow Jones U.S. Total Stock Market Index actually available to investors in the marketplace. The Dow Jones U.S. Large-Cap Growth Total Stock Market Index includes the components ranked 1-750 by full market capitalization and that are classified as "growth" based on a number of factors. **Top Holdings:** Microsoft Corp Apple Inc Amazon.com Inc Berkshire Hathaway Inc B Facebook Inc A

Vanguard Global ex-U.S. Real Estate Index Fund ETF Shares   C-   HOLD

Ticker	Traded On	NAV	Total Assets ($)	Dividend Yield (TTM)	Turnover Ratio	Expense Ratio
VNQI	NAS CM		$6,188,940,790	5.33	6	0.14

Ratings

Reward	D+
Risk	C
Recent Upgrade/Downgrade	Down

Fund Information

Fund Type	Exchange Traded Funds
Category	Real Estate Sector Equity
Sub-Category	Global Real Estate
Prospectus Objective	Real Estate
Inception Date	Nov-10
Open to New Investments	Y

Prices

Price (as of 12/31/2018)	52.41
52-Week High	65.14
52-Week Low	51.24

Total Returns (%)

3-Month	6-Month	1-Year	3-Year	5-Year
-4.53	-6.87	-9.96	15.91	17.39

3-Year Standard Deviation	11.38
Effective Duration	

Valuation

Premium/Discount (1-Year Average)	0.08

Company Information

Provider	Vanguard
Manager/Tenure	Justin E. Hales (3), Michael Perre (3)
Website	http://www.vanguard.com
Address	Vanguard 100 Vanguard Boulevard Malvern PA 19355 United States
Phone Number	877-662-7447

PERFORMANCE

Ratings History

Date	Overall Rating	Risk Rating	Reward Rating
Q4-18	C-	C	D+
Q2-18	C+	C+	C
Q4-17	B-	B	B-
Q4-16	C	C	C
Q4-15	C	C+	C

Asset & Performance History

Date	NAV	1-Year Total Return
2017	60.53	27.22
2016	49.75	0.47
2015	51.41	-1.33
2014	53.57	2.64
2013	54.31	3.33
2012	54.32	41.59

Total Assets: $6,188,940,790

Asset Allocation

Asset	%
Cash	2%
Stocks	96%
US Stocks	0%
Bonds	0%
US Bonds	0%
Other	2%

Services Offered:

Investment Strategy: The investment seeks to track the performance of a benchmark index. The fund employs an indexing investment approach designed to track the performance of the S&P Global ex-U.S. Property Index, a float-adjusted, market-capitalization-weighted index that measures the equity market performance of international real estate stocks in both developed and emerging markets. The index is composed of stocks of publicly traded equity real estate investment trusts (known as REITs) and certain real estate management and development companies (REMDs). **Top Holdings:** Unibail-Rodamco-Westfield Vonovia SE Mitsui Fudosan Co Ltd Mitsubishi Estate Co Ltd Daiwa House Industry Co Ltd

---

iShares S&P Small-Cap 600 Growth ETF   C   HOLD

Ticker	Traded On	NAV	Total Assets ($)	Dividend Yield (TTM)	Turnover Ratio	Expense Ratio
IJT	NAS CM	161.56	$6,150,801,841	0.79	47	0.25

Ratings

Reward	C
Risk	C+
Recent Upgrade/Downgrade	Down

Fund Information

Fund Type	Exchange Traded Funds
Category	US Equity Small Cap
Sub-Category	Small Growth
Prospectus Objective	Small Company
Inception Date	Jul-00
Open to New Investments	Y

Prices

Price (as of 12/31/2018)	161.33
52-Week High	209.07
52-Week Low	151.48

Total Returns (%)

3-Month	6-Month	1-Year	3-Year	5-Year
-18.46	-15.05	-4.28	33.79	42.44

3-Year Standard Deviation	14.88
Effective Duration	

Valuation

Premium/Discount (1-Year Average)	0.00

Company Information

Provider	iShares
Manager/Tenure	Diane Hsiung (10), Greg Savage (10), Jennifer Hsui (6), 3 others
Website	http://www.ishares.com
Address	iShares 400 Howard Street San Francisco CA 94105 United States
Phone Number	800-474-2737

PERFORMANCE

Ratings History

Date	Overall Rating	Risk Rating	Reward Rating
Q4-18	C	C+	C
Q2-18	B	C+	B
Q4-17	A-	B+	A
Q4-16	B	C+	B+
Q4-15	C+	C+	C+

Asset & Performance History

Date	NAV	1-Year Total Return
2017	170.2	14.57
2016	149.91	22
2015	124.3	2.64
2014	122.44	3.71
2013	119	42.62
2012	84.1	14.47

Total Assets: $6,150,801,841

Asset Allocation

Asset	%
Cash	0%
Stocks	100%
US Stocks	99%
Bonds	0%
US Bonds	0%
Other	0%

Services Offered: CashInvestment Plan

Investment Strategy: The investment seeks to track the investment results of the S&P SmallCap 600 Growth IndexTM, which measures the performance of the small-capitalization growth sector of the U.S. equity market. The fund generally invests at least 90% of its assets in securities of the underlying index and in depositary receipts representing securities of the underlying index. It may invest the remainder of its assets in certain futures, options and swap contracts, cash and cash equivalents, as well as in securities not included in the underlying index, but which the advisor believes will help the fund track the underlying index. **Top Holdings:** Ingevity Corp Green Dot Corp FirstCash Inc Amedisys Inc Trex Co Inc

Vanguard FTSE All-World ex-US Small-Cap Index Fund ETF Shares

D+   SELL

Ticker	Traded On	NAV		Total Assets ($)	Dividend Yield (TTM)	Turnover Ratio	Expense Ratio
VSS	NYSE Arca			$6,132,310,166	3.06	14	0.13

Ratings
Reward	D+
Risk	C-
Recent Upgrade/Downgrade	Down

Fund Information
Fund Type	Exchange Traded Funds
Category	Global Eq Mid/Small Cap
Sub-Category	Foreign Small/Mid Blend
Prospectus Objective	Foreign Stock
Inception Date	Apr-09
Open to New Investments	Y

Prices
Price (as of 12/31/2018)	94.68
52-Week High	127.14
52-Week Low	91.12

Total Returns (%)
3-Month	6-Month	1-Year	3-Year	5-Year
-15.23	-16.27	-19.03	10.07	4.72

3-Year Standard Deviation	11.55
Effective Duration	

Valuation
Premium/Discount (1-Year Average)	0.14

Company Information
Provider	Vanguard
Manager/Tenure	Jeffrey D. Miller (3), Michael Perre (2)
Website	http://www.vanguard.com
Address	Vanguard 100 Vanguard Boulevard Malvern PA 19355 United States
Phone Number	877-662-7447

PERFORMANCE

Ratings History
Date	Overall Rating	Risk Rating	Reward Rating
Q4-18	D+	C-	D+
Q2-18	C+	C+	C+
Q4-17	B	B	B
Q4-16	C-	C-	C-
Q4-15	C	C+	C-

Asset & Performance History
Date	NAV	1-Year Total Return
2017	118.89	30.34
2016	94.01	3.45
2015	92.75	-0.2
2014	95.38	-4.66
2013	102.61	17.72
2012	89.74	19.12

Total Assets: $6,132,310,166
Asset Allocation
Asset	%
Cash	7%
Stocks	91%
US Stocks	1%
Bonds	0%
US Bonds	0%
Other	1%

Services Offered:

Investment Strategy: The investment seeks to track the performance of a benchmark index that measures the investment return of stocks of international small-cap companies. The fund employs an indexing investment approach designed to track the performance of the FTSE Global Small Cap ex US Index, a float-adjusted, market-capitalization-weighted index designed to measure equity market performance of international small-capitalization stocks. The index included 3,363 stocks of companies located in 46 countries, including both developed and emerging markets. **Top Holdings:** Open Text Corp   First Quantum Minerals Ltd   Canopy Growth Corp   CCL Industries Inc B- Non-Voting   Gildan Activewear Inc

---

Invesco Senior Loan ETF

C   HOLD

Ticker	Traded On	NAV		Total Assets ($)	Dividend Yield (TTM)	Turnover Ratio	Expense Ratio
BKLN	NYSE Arca	21.97		$6,124,334,467	4.04	74	0.65

Ratings
Reward	C-
Risk	B
Recent Upgrade/Downgrade	Down

Fund Information
Fund Type	Exchange Traded Funds
Category	US Fixed Income
Sub-Category	Bank Loan
Prospectus Objective	Income
Inception Date	Mar-11
Open to New Investments	Y

Prices
Price (as of 12/31/2018)	21.78
52-Week High	23.27
52-Week Low	21.59

Total Returns (%)
3-Month	6-Month	1-Year	3-Year	5-Year
-3.92	-1.94	-0.55	10.88	8.46

3-Year Standard Deviation	2.61
Effective Duration	

Valuation
Premium/Discount (1-Year Average)	-0.10

Company Information
Provider	Invesco
Manager/Tenure	Scott Baskind (7), Philip Fang (7), Peter Hubbard (7), 4 others
Website	http://www.invesco.com/us
Address	Invesco 11 Greenway Plaza, Ste. 2500 Houston TX 77046 United States
Phone Number	800-659-1005

PERFORMANCE

Ratings History
Date	Overall Rating	Risk Rating	Reward Rating
Q4-18	C	B	C-
Q2-18	B-	B	C
Q4-17	C+	B	C
Q4-16	B-	B	C
Q4-15	C	C+	C-

Asset & Performance History
Date	NAV	1-Year Total Return
2017	23.06	2.38
2016	23.32	8.89
2015	22.43	-2.85
2014	24.01	0.69
2013	24.82	4.32
2012	24.86	10.21

Total Assets: $6,124,334,467
Asset Allocation
Asset	%
Cash	6%
Stocks	0%
US Stocks	0%
Bonds	92%
US Bonds	61%
Other	0%

Services Offered:

Investment Strategy: The investment seeks to track the investment results (before fees and expenses) of the S&P/LSTA U.S. Leveraged Loan 100 Index (the "underlying index"). The fund generally will invest at least 80% of its net assets (plus any borrowings for investment purposes) in senior loans that comprise the underlying index. Banks and other lending institutions generally issue senior loans to corporations, partnerships or other entities ("borrowers"). These borrowers operate in a variety of industries and geographic regions, including foreign countries. **Top Holdings:** Burger King 2/17 Cov-Lite 02/16/24   Charter Communications Operating 04/13/25   Centurylink, Inc. 01/31/2025   Grifols Worldwide 01/31/25   Caesars Resort Collection 10/02/24

iShares S&P Small-Cap 600 Value ETF   C   HOLD

Ticker	Traded On	NAV	Total Assets ($)	Dividend Yield (TTM)	Turnover Ratio	Expense Ratio
IJS	NYSE Arca	131.84	$6,063,159,716	1.54	39	0.25

Ratings
Reward   C-
Risk   C+
Recent Upgrade/Downgrade   Down

Fund Information
Fund Type   Exchange Traded Funds
Category   US Equity Small Cap
Sub-Category   Small Value
Prospectus Objective   Small Company
Inception Date   Jul-00
Open to New Investments Y

Prices
Price (as of 12/31/2018)   131.85
52-Week High   173.25
52-Week Low   124.11

Total Returns (%)

3-Month	6-Month	1-Year	3-Year	5-Year
-19.52	-19.25	-12.79	27.37	27.29

3-Year Standard Deviation   14.94
Effective Duration

Valuation
Premium/Discount (1-Year Average)   0.00

Company Information
Provider   iShares
Manager/Tenure Diane Hsiung (10), Greg Savage (10),
                Jennifer Hsui (6), 3 others
Website   http://www.ishares.com
Address   iShares 400 Howard Street San
                Francisco CA 94105 United States
Phone Number   800-474-2737

PERFORMANCE

Ratings History

Date	Overall Rating	Risk Rating	Reward Rating
Q4-18	C	C+	C-
Q2-18	C+	C-	B
Q4-17	B+	B	A-
Q4-16	B	C+	B+
Q4-15	C	C+	C

Asset & Performance History

Date	NAV	1-Year Total Return
2017	153.49	11.35
2016	139.93	31.17
2015	108.16	-6.84
2014	117.87	7.27
2013	111.49	39.71
2012	80.86	18.1

Total Assets: $6,063,159,716

Asset Allocation

Asset	%
Cash	0%
Stocks	100%
US Stocks	98%
Bonds	0%
US Bonds	0%
Other	0%

Services Offered: CashInvestment Plan

Investment Strategy: The investment seeks to track the investment results of the S&P SmallCap 600 Value IndexTM, which measures the performance of the small-capitalization value sector of the U.S. equity market. The fund generally invests at least 90% of its assets in securities of the underlying index and in depositary receipts representing securities of the underlying index. It may invest the remainder of its assets in certain futures, options and swap contracts, cash and cash equivalents, as well as in securities not included in the underlying index, but which the advisor believes will help the fund track the underlying index. **Top Holdings:** Spire Inc Community Bank System Inc Wolverine World Wide Inc American Equity Investment Life Holding Co SkyWest Inc

---

iShares S&P Mid-Cap 400 Value ETF   C   HOLD

Ticker	Traded On	NAV	Total Assets ($)	Dividend Yield (TTM)	Turnover Ratio	Expense Ratio
IJJ	NYSE Arca	138.26	$5,872,991,885	1.77	37	0.25

Ratings
Reward   C-
Risk   C+
Recent Upgrade/Downgrade

Fund Information
Fund Type   Exchange Traded Funds
Category   US Equity Mid Cap
Sub-Category   Mid-Cap Value
Prospectus Objective   Growth
Inception Date   Jul-00
Open to New Investments Y

Prices
Price (as of 12/31/2018)   138.34
52-Week High   170.48
52-Week Low   130.36

Total Returns (%)

3-Month	6-Month	1-Year	3-Year	5-Year
-16.38	-13.82	-12.07	24.34	29.65

3-Year Standard Deviation   12.62
Effective Duration

Valuation
Premium/Discount (1-Year Average)   0.00

Company Information
Provider   iShares
Manager/Tenure Diane Hsiung (10), Greg Savage (10),
                Jennifer Hsui (6), 3 others
Website   http://www.ishares.com
Address   iShares 400 Howard Street San
                Francisco CA 94105 United States
Phone Number   800-474-2737

PERFORMANCE

Ratings History

Date	Overall Rating	Risk Rating	Reward Rating
Q4-18	C	C+	C-
Q2-18	C	C-	C
Q4-17	B	B	B
Q4-16	B	C+	B
Q4-15	C	C-	C

Asset & Performance History

Date	NAV	1-Year Total Return
2017	160.08	12.05
2016	145.17	26.2
2015	117.15	-6.8
2014	127.9	11.87
2013	116.27	33.97
2012	88.2	18.29

Total Assets: $5,872,991,885

Asset Allocation

Asset	%
Cash	0%
Stocks	100%
US Stocks	99%
Bonds	0%
US Bonds	0%
Other	0%

Services Offered: CashInvestment Plan

Investment Strategy: The investment seeks to track the investment results of the S&P MidCap 400 Value IndexTM, which measures the performance of the mid-capitalization value sector of the U.S. equity market. The fund generally invests at least 90% of its assets in securities of the underlying index and in depositary receipts representing securities of the underlying index. It may invest the remainder of its assets in certain futures, options and swap contracts, cash and cash equivalents, as well as in securities not included in the underlying index, but which the advisor believes will help the fund track the underlying index. **Top Holdings:** Atmos Energy Corp UGI Corp Leidos Holdings Inc Reinsurance Group of America Inc Alleghany Corp

iShares China Large-Cap ETF

C-   HOLD

Ticker	Traded On	NAV		Total Assets ($)	Dividend Yield (TTM)	Turnover Ratio	Expense Ratio
FXI	NYSE Arca	39.47		$5,836,552,913	3.6	18	0.74

Ratings
Reward	C-
Risk	C
Recent Upgrade/Downgrade	Down

Fund Information
Fund Type	Exchange Traded Funds
Category	Greater China Equity
Sub-Category	China Region
Prospectus Objective	Pacific Stock
Inception Date	Oct-04
Open to New Investments	Y

Prices
Price (as of 12/31/2018)	39.08
52-Week High	54.00
52-Week Low	38.26

Total Returns (%)
3-Month	6-Month	1-Year	3-Year	5-Year
-7.07	-7.67	-12.40	19.84	18.28

3-Year Standard Deviation	18.37
Effective Duration	

Valuation
Premium/Discount (1-Year Average)	0.01

Company Information
Provider	iShares
Manager/Tenure	Diane Hsiung (10), Greg Savage (10), Jennifer Hsui (6), 3 others
Website	http://www.ishares.com
Address	iShares 400 Howard Street San Francisco CA 94105 United States
Phone Number	800-474-2737

PERFORMANCE

Ratings History
Date	Overall Rating	Risk Rating	Reward Rating
Q4-18	C-	C	C-
Q2-18	C	C	C
Q4-17	B	C	A-
Q4-16	C-	C-	C
Q4-15	C	C	C

Asset & Performance History
Date	NAV	1-Year Total Return
2017	46.18	34.47
2016	35.17	1.74
2015	35.52	-11.9
2014	41.41	12.02
2013	37.98	-1.2
2012	39.66	16.95

Total Assets: $5,836,552,913
Asset Allocation
Asset	%
Cash	0%
Stocks	100%
US Stocks	0%
Bonds	0%
US Bonds	0%
Other	0%

Services Offered: Dividend Investment Plan, CashInvestment Plan

Investment Strategy: The investment seeks to track the investment results of the FTSE China 50 Index composed of large-capitalization Chinese equities that trade on the Hong Kong Stock Exchange. The fund generally invests at least 90% of its assets in securities of the underlying index and in depositary receipts representing securities of the underlying index. The index designed to measure the performance of the largest companies in the Chinese equity market that trade on the Stock Exchange of Hong Kong ("SEHK") and are available to international investors, as determined by FTSE International Limited (the "Index Provider" or "FTSE"). The fund is non-diversified. **Top Holdings:** China Construction Bank Corp H Tencent Holdings Ltd Industrial And Commercial Bank Of China Ltd H China Mobile Ltd Ping An Insurance (Group) Co. of China Ltd H

Schwab U.S. TIPS ETF™

C-   HOLD

Ticker	Traded On	NAV		Total Assets ($)	Dividend Yield (TTM)	Turnover Ratio	Expense Ratio
SCHP	NYSE Arca	53.27		$5,830,879,832	2.79	19	0.05

Ratings
Reward	D+
Risk	C
Recent Upgrade/Downgrade	Down

Fund Information
Fund Type	Exchange Traded Funds
Category	US Fixed Income
Sub-Category	Inflation-Protected Bond
Prospectus Objective	Govt Bond - Treasury
Inception Date	Aug-10
Open to New Investments	Y

Prices
Price (as of 12/31/2018)	53.25
52-Week High	55.43
52-Week Low	52.79

Total Returns (%)
3-Month	6-Month	1-Year	3-Year	5-Year
-0.27	-1.34	-1.31	6.26	8.39

3-Year Standard Deviation	3.13
Effective Duration	7.47

Valuation
Premium/Discount (1-Year Average)	-0.02

Company Information
Provider	Schwab ETFs
Manager/Tenure	Matthew Hastings (8), Mark R. McKissick (1)
Website	http://www.schwabetfs.com
Address	Schwab ETFs United States
Phone Number	800-435-4000

PERFORMANCE

Ratings History
Date	Overall Rating	Risk Rating	Reward Rating
Q4-18	C-	C	D+
Q2-18	C	C+	C
Q4-17	C	B-	C
Q4-16	C	C+	C
Q4-15	D+	C-	D+

Asset & Performance History
Date	NAV	1-Year Total Return
2017	55.39	3.06
2016	54.84	4.59
2015	53.15	-1.5
2014	54.11	3.56
2013	52.92	-8.66
2012	58.31	6.82

Total Assets: $5,830,879,832
Asset Allocation
Asset	%
Cash	0%
Stocks	0%
US Stocks	0%
Bonds	100%
US Bonds	100%
Other	0%

Services Offered:

Investment Strategy: The investment seeks to track as closely as possible, before fees and expenses, the total return of the Bloomberg Barclays US Treasury Inflation-Linked Bond Index (Series-L). The fund will invest at least 90% of its net assets in securities included in the index. The index includes all publicly-issued U.S. Treasury Inflation-Protected Securities (TIPS) that have at least one year remaining to maturity, are rated investment grade and have $500 million or more of outstanding face value. The TIPS in the index must be denominated in U.S. dollars and must be fixed-rate and non-convertible. **Top Holdings:** United States Treasury Notes 0.12% United States Treasury Notes 0.12% United States Treasury Notes 0.12% United States Treasury Notes 0.62% United States Treasury Notes 0.38%

iShares MSCI EAFE Value ETF   D+   SELL

Ticker	Traded On	NAV	Total Assets ($)	Dividend Yield (TTM)	Turnover Ratio	Expense Ratio
EFV	BATS	45.23	$5,652,413,106	4.58	22	0.38

Ratings
Reward   D+
Risk   C-
Recent Upgrade/Downgrade   Down

Fund Information
Fund Type   Exchange Traded Funds
Category   Global Equity Large Cap
Sub-Category   Foreign Large Value
Prospectus Objective   Foreign Stock
Inception Date   Aug-05
Open to New Investments   Y

Prices
Price (as of 12/31/2018)   45.22
52-Week High   59.57
52-Week Low   43.66

Total Returns (%)

3-Month	6-Month	1-Year	3-Year	5-Year
-11.46	-9.50	-14.87	8.20	-3.91

3-Year Standard Deviation   11.91
Effective Duration

Valuation
Premium/Discount (1-Year Average)   -0.06

Company Information
Provider   iShares
Manager/Tenure   Diane Hsiung (10), Greg Savage (10),
                      Jennifer Hsui (6), 3 others
Website   http://www.ishares.com
Address   iShares 400 Howard Street San
                      Francisco CA 94105 United States
Phone Number   800-474-2737

PERFORMANCE

Ratings History

Date	Overall Rating	Risk Rating	Reward Rating
Q4-18	D+	C-	D+
Q2-18	C	C	C
Q4-17	C+	C	C+
Q4-16	D+	C-	D
Q4-15	C	C+	C-

Asset & Performance History

Date	NAV	1-Year Total Return
2017	55.37	21.22
2016	47.4	4.86
2015	46.75	-5.88
2014	51.3	-5.65
2013	56.82	22.6
2012	48.03	17.51

Total Assets: $5,652,413,106
Asset Allocation

Asset	%
Cash	1%
Stocks	99%
US Stocks	1%
Bonds	0%
US Bonds	0%
Other	0%

Services Offered:

Investment Strategy: The investment seeks to track the investment results of the MSCI EAFE Value Index composed of developed market equities, excluding the U.S. and Canada, that exhibit value characteristics. The fund generally invests at least 90% of its assets in securities of the underlying index and in depositary receipts representing securities of the underlying index. The underlying index is a subset of the MSCI EAFE Index. Constituents of the underlying index include securities from Europe, Australasia and the Far East. **Top Holdings:** HSBC Holdings PLC   Royal Dutch Shell PLC Class A   Toyota Motor Corp   Total SA   Royal Dutch Shell PLC B

---

iShares Short Maturity Bond ETF   C   HOLD

Ticker	Traded On	NAV	Total Assets ($)	Dividend Yield (TTM)	Turnover Ratio	Expense Ratio
NEAR	BATS	49.87	$5,644,410,037	2.11	56	0.25

Ratings
Reward   C
Risk   C+
Recent Upgrade/Downgrade

Fund Information
Fund Type   Exchange Traded Funds
Category   US Fixed Income
Sub-Category   Ultrashort Bond
Prospectus Objective   Income
Inception Date   Sep-13
Open to New Investments   Y

Prices
Price (as of 12/31/2018)   49.85
52-Week High   50.24
52-Week Low   49.82

Total Returns (%)

3-Month	6-Month	1-Year	3-Year	5-Year
0.20	0.85	1.71	4.75	6.27

3-Year Standard Deviation   0.2
Effective Duration   0.48

Valuation
Premium/Discount (1-Year Average)   0.04

Company Information
Provider   iShares
Manager/Tenure   Thomas F. Musmanno (5), Scott
                      Radell (5)
Website   http://www.ishares.com
Address   iShares 400 Howard Street San
                      Francisco CA 94105 United States
Phone Number   800-474-2737

PERFORMANCE

Ratings History

Date	Overall Rating	Risk Rating	Reward Rating
Q4-18	C	C+	C
Q2-18	C	C+	C
Q4-17	B-	A-	C
Q4-16	C	C+	C
Q4-15	C-	C+	D+

Asset & Performance History

Date	NAV	1-Year Total Return
2017	50.14	1.55
2016	50.13	1.41
2015	49.96	0.69
2014	50.04	0.75
2013	50.09	
2012		

Total Assets: $5,644,410,037
Asset Allocation

Asset	%
Cash	13%
Stocks	0%
US Stocks	0%
Bonds	87%
US Bonds	67%
Other	0%

Services Offered:

Investment Strategy: The investment seeks to maximize current income. The fund seeks to achieve its investment objective by investing, under normal circumstances, at least 80% of its net assets in a portfolio of U.S. dollar-denominated investment-grade fixed-income securities. Under normal circumstances, the effective duration of its portfolio is expected to be one year or less, as calculated by the management team. It is an actively managed exchange-traded fund ("ETF") that does not seek to replicate the performance of a specified index. The fund is non-diversified. **Top Holdings:** Allergan Funding SCS 3%   General Motors Financial Company Inc 3.2%   Shire Acquisitions Investments Ireland DAC 1.9%   Dowdupont Inc 3.42%   AMERICREDIT AUTOMOBILE RECEIVABLES TRUST 3.11%

iShares Intermediate-Term Corporate Bond ETF

D- SELL

Ticker	Traded On	NAV	Total Assets ($)	Dividend Yield (TTM)	Turnover Ratio	Expense Ratio
IGIB	NAS CM	52.49	$5,512,706,404	3.13	21	0.06

Ratings
Reward	E+
Risk	D-
Recent Upgrade/Downgrade	Down

Fund Information
Fund Type	Exchange Traded Funds
Category	US Fixed Income
Sub-Category	Corporate Bond
Prospectus Objective	Growth & Inc
Inception Date	Jan-07
Open to New Investments	Y

Prices
Price (as of 12/31/2018)	52.42
52-Week High	109.21
52-Week Low	52.01

Total Returns (%)
3-Month	6-Month	1-Year	3-Year	5-Year
0.38	1.03	-50.25	-46.78	-44.34

3-Year Standard Deviation	2.28
Effective Duration	6.13

Valuation
Premium/Discount (1-Year Average)	0.01

Company Information
Provider	iShares
Manager/Tenure	Scott Radell (8), James Mauro (7)
Website	http://www.ishares.com
Address	iShares 400 Howard Street San Francisco CA 94105 United States
Phone Number	800-474-2737

PERFORMANCE

Ratings History
Date	Overall Rating	Risk Rating	Reward Rating
Q4-18	D-	D-	E+
Q2-18	C	C	C-
Q4-17	B	A	C
Q4-16	C	C+	C
Q4-15	C	C+	C

Asset & Performance History
Date	NAV	1-Year Total Return
2017	109.15	3.3
2016	108.14	3.37
2015	107.18	0.68
2014	109.12	3.88
2013	107.65	-0.38
2012	111.02	7.81

Total Assets: $5,512,706,404
Asset Allocation
Asset	%
Cash	1%
Stocks	0%
US Stocks	0%
Bonds	98%
US Bonds	74%
Other	0%

Services Offered:

Investment Strategy: The investment seeks to track the investment results of the ICE BofAML 5-10 Year US Corporate Index. The fund generally invests at least 90% of its assets in securities of the underlying index. The index measures the performance of investment-grade corporate bonds that are U.S. dollar-denominated and have a remaining maturity of greater than or equal to five years and less than ten years. The fund may invest the remainder of its assets in certain futures, options and swap contracts, cash and cash equivalents. **Top Holdings:** CVS Health Corp 4.1% BNP Paribas 3.38% Anheuser-Busch Companies LLC / Anheuser-Busch InBev Worldwide Inc 3.65% Vodafone Group plc 3.75% Wells Fargo & Company 3%

Xtrackers MSCI EAFE Hedged Equity ETF

C HOLD

Ticker	Traded On	NAV	Total Assets ($)	Dividend Yield (TTM)	Turnover Ratio	Expense Ratio
DBEF	NYSE Arca		$5,466,167,742	2.24	10	0.35

Ratings
Reward	C-
Risk	C+
Recent Upgrade/Downgrade	Down

Fund Information
Fund Type	Exchange Traded Funds
Category	Global Equity Large Cap
Sub-Category	Foreign Large Blend
Prospectus Objective	World Stock
Inception Date	Jun-11
Open to New Investments	Y

Prices
Price (as of 12/31/2018)	27.90
52-Week High	33.02
52-Week Low	27.10

Total Returns (%)
3-Month	6-Month	1-Year	3-Year	5-Year
-11.88	-8.38	-9.43	11.66	22.83

3-Year Standard Deviation	9.32
Effective Duration	

Valuation
Premium/Discount (1-Year Average)	-0.14

Company Information
Provider	Deutsche Asset Management
Manager/Tenure	Charlotte Cipolletti (1), Patrick Dwyer (1), Bryan Richards (1), 2 others
Website	http://www.deutsche-etfs.com
Address	Deutsche Asset & Wealth Management 345 Park Avenue New York NY 10154 United States
Phone Number	844-851-4255

PERFORMANCE

Ratings History
Date	Overall Rating	Risk Rating	Reward Rating
Q4-18	C	C+	C-
Q2-18	C	C+	C
Q4-17	B	B	B
Q4-16	C+	C+	C
Q4-15	C	C+	C

Asset & Performance History
Date	NAV	1-Year Total Return
2017	31.84	16.59
2016	28.15	5.74
2015	27.38	4.5
2014	27.11	5.26
2013	27.07	25.9
2012	21.87	18.14

Total Assets: $5,466,167,742
Asset Allocation
Asset	%
Cash	2%
Stocks	98%
US Stocks	1%
Bonds	0%
US Bonds	0%
Other	0%

Services Offered:

Investment Strategy: The investment seeks investment results that correspond generally to the performance, before fees and expenses, of the MSCI EAFE US Dollar Hedged Index. The fund, using a "passive" or indexing investment approach, seeks investment results that correspond generally to the performance, before fees and expenses, of the underlying index, which is designed to track developed market performance while mitigating exposure to fluctuations between the value of the U.S. dollar and the currencies of the countries included in the underlying index. It will invest at least 80% of its total assets in component securities of the underlying index. **Top Holdings:** Nestle SA Novartis AG Roche Holding AG Dividend Right Cert. HSBC Holdings PLC Royal Dutch Shell PLC Class A

iShares Core S&P U.S. Growth ETF   C   HOLD

Ticker	Traded On	NAV	Total Assets ($)	Dividend Yield (TTM)	Turnover Ratio	Expense Ratio
IUSG	NAS CM	52.64	$5,462,244,900	1.2	24	0.04

Ratings
Reward   C
Risk   C+
Recent Upgrade/Downgrade   Down

Fund Information
Fund Type   Exchange Traded Funds
Category   US Equity Large Cap Growth
Sub-Category   Large Growth
Prospectus Objective   Growth
Inception Date   Jul-00
Open to New Investments   Y

Prices
Price (as of 12/31/2018)   52.70
52-Week High   62.28
52-Week Low   49.22

Total Returns (%)

3-Month	6-Month	1-Year	3-Year	5-Year
-15.13	-7.85	-0.79	35.23	59.55

3-Year Standard Deviation   10.73
Effective Duration

Valuation
Premium/Discount (1-Year Average)   0.05

Company Information
Provider   iShares
Manager/Tenure   Diane Hsiung (10), Greg Savage (10), Jennifer Hsui (6), 3 others
Website   http://www.ishares.com
Address   iShares 400 Howard Street San Francisco CA 94105 United States
Phone Number   800-474-2737

PERFORMANCE

Ratings History

Date	Overall Rating	Risk Rating	Reward Rating
Q4-18	C	C+	C
Q2-18	B-	C+	B
Q4-17	B	B	B
Q4-16	B-	C+	B
Q4-15	C	C	C+

Asset & Performance History

Date	NAV	1-Year Total Return
2017	53.72	26.93
2016	42.91	7.39
2015	40.57	5.05
2014	39.13	12.3
2013	35.28	33.93
2012	26.71	14.96

Total Assets: $5,462,244,900
Asset Allocation

Asset	%
Cash	0%
Stocks	100%
US Stocks	99%
Bonds	0%
US Bonds	0%
Other	0%

Services Offered: CashInvestment Plan

Investment Strategy: The investment seeks to track the investment results of the S&P 900 Growth Index (the "underlying index"). The fund generally invests at least 90% of its assets in securities of the underlying index and in depositary receipts representing securities of the underlying index. The underlying index measures the performance of the large- and mid- capitalization growth sector of the U.S. equity market. **Top Holdings:** Microsoft Corp   Apple Inc   Amazon.com Inc   Facebook Inc A   Alphabet Inc Class C

Schwab U.S. Aggregate Bond ETF™   C-   HOLD

Ticker	Traded On	NAV	Total Assets ($)	Dividend Yield (TTM)	Turnover Ratio	Expense Ratio
SCHZ	NYSE Arca	50.59	$5,360,959,052	2.75	101	0.04

Ratings
Reward   D+
Risk   C+
Recent Upgrade/Downgrade   Down

Fund Information
Fund Type   Exchange Traded Funds
Category   US Fixed Income
Sub-Category   Intermediate-Term Bond
Prospectus Objective   Multisector Bond
Inception Date   Jul-11
Open to New Investments   Y

Prices
Price (as of 12/31/2018)   50.59
52-Week High   52.04
52-Week Low   49.51

Total Returns (%)

3-Month	6-Month	1-Year	3-Year	5-Year
1.71	1.71	-0.09	5.94	12.89

3-Year Standard Deviation   2.74
Effective Duration   6.01

Valuation
Premium/Discount (1-Year Average)   -0.04

Company Information
Provider   Schwab ETFs
Manager/Tenure   Matthew Hastings (7), Steven Hung (7), Alfonso Portillo (7), 1 other
Website   http://www.schwabetfs.com
Address   Schwab ETFs United States
Phone Number   800-435-4000

PERFORMANCE

Ratings History

Date	Overall Rating	Risk Rating	Reward Rating
Q4-18	C-	C+	D+
Q2-18	C-	C	C-
Q4-17	B-	B+	C
Q4-16	C	C+	C
Q4-15	C	C+	C

Asset & Performance History

Date	NAV	1-Year Total Return
2017	52.07	3.56
2016	51.55	2.49
2015	51.41	0.55
2014	52.2	5.97
2013	50.28	-2.18
2012	52.43	3.9

Total Assets: $5,360,959,052
Asset Allocation

Asset	%
Cash	3%
Stocks	0%
US Stocks	0%
Bonds	97%
US Bonds	89%
Other	0%

Services Offered:

Investment Strategy: The investment seeks to track as closely as possible, before fees and expenses, the total return of the Bloomberg Barclays US Aggregate Bond Index. The fund will invest at least 90% of its net assets in securities included in the index. The index is a broad-based benchmark measuring the performance of the U.S. investment grade, taxable bond market, including U.S. Treasuries, government-related and corporate bonds, mortgage pass-through securities, commercial mortgage-backed securities, and asset-backed securities that are publicly available for sale in the United States. **Top Holdings:** United States Treasury Notes 2.88%   United States Treasury Notes 2.12%   United States Treasury Notes 2.88%   United States Treasury Notes 2.62%   United States Treasury Notes 2%

iShares U.S. Aerospace & Defense ETF   B-   BUY

Ticker	Traded On	NAV
ITA	BATS	172.98

Total Assets ($)	Dividend Yield (TTM)	Turnover Ratio	Expense Ratio
$5,339,268,639	1.06	14	0.43

Ratings
Reward	B
Risk	C+
Recent Upgrade/Downgrade	Down

Fund Information
Fund Type	Exchange Traded Funds
Category	Industrials Sector Equity
Sub-Category	Industrials
Prospectus Objective	Growth
Inception Date	May-06
Open to New Investments	Y

Prices
Price (as of 12/31/2018)	172.86
52-Week High	217.63
52-Week Low	162.03

Total Returns (%)
3-Month	6-Month	1-Year	3-Year	5-Year
-20.18	-9.87	-7.15	51.10	72.68

3-Year Standard Deviation	14.06
Effective Duration	

Valuation
Premium/Discount (1-Year Average)	0.01

Company Information
Provider	iShares
Manager/Tenure	Diane Hsiung (10), Greg Savage (10), Jennifer Hsui (6), 3 others
Website	http://www.ishares.com
Address	iShares 400 Howard Street San Francisco CA 94105 United States
Phone Number	800-474-2737

PERFORMANCE

Ratings History
Date	Overall Rating	Risk Rating	Reward Rating
Q4-18	B-	C+	B
Q2-18	B	B-	B+
Q4-17	A-	B-	A+
Q4-16	B	C+	B+
Q4-15	B	B	B

Asset & Performance History
Date	NAV	1-Year Total Return
2017	188.14	35.17
2016	140.62	20.4
2015	118.16	4.03
2014	114.76	9.85
2013	105.79	57.07
2012	68.27	14.07

Total Assets: $5,339,268,639

Asset Allocation
Asset	%
Cash	0%
Stocks	100%
US Stocks	100%
Bonds	0%
US Bonds	0%
Other	0%

Services Offered:

Investment Strategy: The investment seeks to track the investment results of the Dow Jones U.S. Select Aerospace & Defense Index composed of U.S. equities in the aerospace and defense sector. The fund generally invests at least 90% of its assets in securities of the underlying index and in depositary receipts representing securities of the underlying index. The underlying index measures the performance of the aerospace and defense sector of the U.S. equity market. Aerospace companies in the index include manufacturers, assemblers and distributors of aircraft and aircraft parts. The fund is non-diversified. **Top Holdings:** Boeing Co United Technologies Corp Lockheed Martin Corp General Dynamics Corp Raytheon Co

---

FlexShares Morningstar Global Upstream Natural Resources Index Fund   C   HOLD

Ticker	Traded On	NAV
GUNR	NYSE Arca	29.36

Total Assets ($)	Dividend Yield (TTM)	Turnover Ratio	Expense Ratio
$5,332,588,875	2.78		0.46

Ratings
Reward	C
Risk	C+
Recent Upgrade/Downgrade	

Fund Information
Fund Type	Exchange Traded Funds
Category	Natural Resources
Sub-Category	Natural Resources
Prospectus Objective	Natl Res
Inception Date	Sep-11
Open to New Investments	Y

Prices
Price (as of 12/31/2018)	29.28
52-Week High	35.42
52-Week Low	28.13

Total Returns (%)
3-Month	6-Month	1-Year	3-Year	5-Year
-12.79	-10.70	-9.21	40.77	-1.58

3-Year Standard Deviation	14.39
Effective Duration	

Valuation
Premium/Discount (1-Year Average)	0.06

Company Information
Provider	Flexshares Trust
Manager/Tenure	Robert Anstine (5), Brendan Sullivan (2)
Website	http://www.flexshares.com
Address	50 South LaSalle Street Chicago, Illinois 60603 Chicago Illinois 60603 United States
Phone Number	855-353-9383

PERFORMANCE

Ratings History
Date	Overall Rating	Risk Rating	Reward Rating
Q4-18	C	C+	C
Q2-18	C+	C+	C+
Q4-17	C+	C	C+
Q4-16	C-	D+	C-
Q4-15	D	D	D

Asset & Performance History
Date	NAV	1-Year Total Return
2017	33.31	18.45
2016	28.75	30.91
2015	22.38	-24.47
2014	30.93	-7.43
2013	34.33	-0.45
2012	35.19	8.47

Total Assets: $5,332,588,875

Asset Allocation
Asset	%
Cash	1%
Stocks	99%
US Stocks	34%
Bonds	0%
US Bonds	0%
Other	0%

Services Offered:

Investment Strategy: The investment seeks investment results that correspond generally to the price and yield performance, before fees and expenses, of the Morningstar® Global Upstream Natural Resources IndexSM. The fund will invest at least 80% of its total assets (exclusive of collateral held from securities lending) in the securities of the index and in ADRs and GDRs based on the securities in the index. The index reflects the performance of a selection of equity securities that are traded in or are issued by companies domiciled in global developed or emerging markets, as determined by the index provider pursuant to its index methodology. It is non-diversified. **Top Holdings:** BHP Group Ltd Exxon Mobil Corp Chevron Corp Nutrien Ltd Archer-Daniels Midland Co

Vanguard Consumer Staples Index Fund ETF Shares   C+   HOLD

Ticker	Traded On	NAV
VDC	NYSE Arca	

Total Assets ($)	Dividend Yield (TTM)	Turnover Ratio	Expense Ratio
$5,194,072,044	2.51	8	0.1

Ratings
Reward   B
Risk   C
Recent Upgrade/Downgrade   Up

Fund Information
Fund Type   Exchange Traded Funds
Category   Consumer Goods & Svcs
Sub-Category   Consumer Defensive
Prospectus Objective   Unaligned
Inception Date   Jan-04
Open to New Investments   Y

Prices
Price (as of 12/31/2018)   131.17
52-Week High   150.85
52-Week Low   125.78

Total Returns (%)

3-Month	6-Month	1-Year	3-Year	5-Year
-5.92	-0.92	-8.12	9.19	34.02

3-Year Standard Deviation   9.4
Effective Duration

Valuation
Premium/Discount (1-Year Average)   0.01

Company Information
Provider   Vanguard
Manager/Tenure Michael A. Johnson (7), Awais Khan (1)
Website   http://www.vanguard.com
Address   Vanguard 100 Vanguard Boulevard
                Malvern PA 19355 United States
Phone Number   877-662-7447

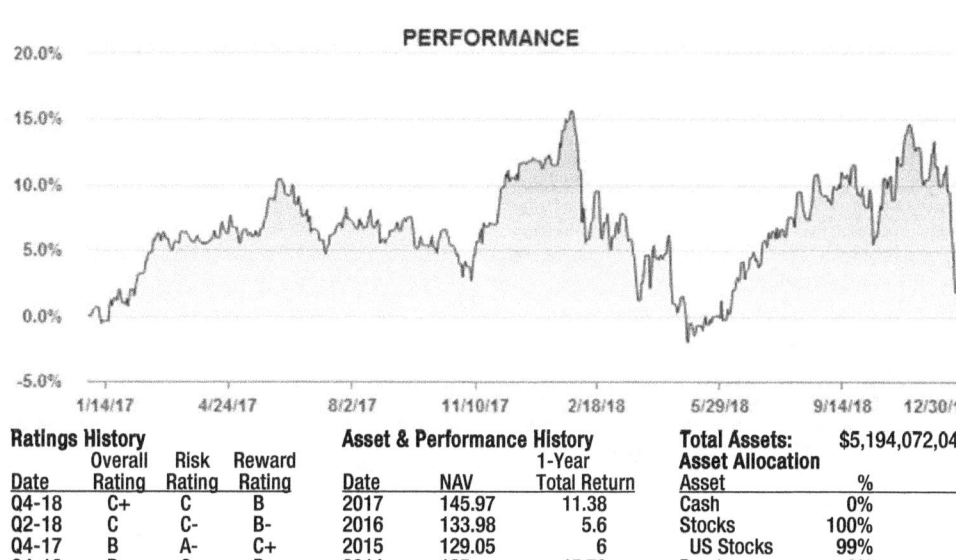

PERFORMANCE

Ratings History

Date	Overall Rating	Risk Rating	Reward Rating
Q4-18	C+	C	B
Q2-18	C	C-	B-
Q4-17	B	A-	C+
Q4-16	B-	C+	B
Q4-15	B	C+	B

Asset & Performance History

Date	NAV	1-Year Total Return
2017	145.97	11.38
2016	133.98	5.6
2015	129.05	6
2014	125	15.78
2013	110.04	27.99
2012	87.89	11.07

Total Assets: $5,194,072,044
Asset Allocation

Asset	%
Cash	0%
Stocks	100%
US Stocks	99%
Bonds	0%
US Bonds	0%
Other	0%

Services Offered:

Investment Strategy: The investment seeks to track the performance of a benchmark index. The fund employs an indexing investment approach designed to track the performance of the MSCI US Investable Market Index/Consumer Staples 25/50, an index made up of stocks of large, mid-size, and small U.S. companies within the consumer staples sector, as classified under the Global Industry Classification Standard. The Advisor attempts to replicate the target index by seeking to invest all, or substantially all, of its assets in the stocks that make up the index, in order to hold each stock in approximately the same proportion as its weighting in the index. The fund is non-diversified. **Top Holdings:** Procter & Gamble Co Coca-Cola Co PepsiCo Inc Walmart Inc Philip Morris International Inc

---

Schwab U.S. Mid-Cap ETF™   C   HOLD

Ticker	Traded On	NAV
SCHM	NYSE Arca	47.94

Total Assets ($)	Dividend Yield (TTM)	Turnover Ratio	Expense Ratio
$5,147,064,974	1.37	13	0.05

Ratings
Reward   C-
Risk   C+
Recent Upgrade/Downgrade   Down

Fund Information
Fund Type   Exchange Traded Funds
Category   US Equity Mid Cap
Sub-Category   Mid-Cap Blend
Prospectus Objective   Growth
Inception Date   Jan-11
Open to New Investments   Y

Prices
Price (as of 12/31/2018)   47.93
52-Week High   58.75
52-Week Low   45.02

Total Returns (%)

3-Month	6-Month	1-Year	3-Year	5-Year
-16.22	-12.04	-8.68	24.96	37.73

3-Year Standard Deviation   11.3
Effective Duration

Valuation
Premium/Discount (1-Year Average)   0.02

Company Information
Provider   Schwab ETFs
Manager/Tenure Ferian Juwono (7), Christopher Bliss (1), Sabya Sinha (1), 1 other
Website   http://www.schwabetfs.com
Address   Schwab ETFs United States
Phone Number   800-435-4000

PERFORMANCE

Ratings History

Date	Overall Rating	Risk Rating	Reward Rating
Q4-18	C	C+	C-
Q2-18	C+	C+	C+
Q4-17	B	B+	B
Q4-16	B-	C+	B
Q4-15	C	C+	C

Asset & Performance History

Date	NAV	1-Year Total Return
2017	53.23	19.89
2016	45.12	14.43
2015	40.06	-0.01
2014	40.66	10.23
2013	37.45	36.36
2012	27.86	17.44

Total Assets: $5,147,064,974
Asset Allocation

Asset	%
Cash	0%
Stocks	100%
US Stocks	98%
Bonds	0%
US Bonds	0%
Other	0%

Services Offered:

Investment Strategy: The investment seeks to track as closely as possible, before fees and expenses, the total return of the Dow Jones U.S. Mid-Cap Total Stock Market Index. The fund will invest at least 90% of its net assets in securities that are included in the index. The index includes the mid-cap portion of the Dow Jones U.S. Total Stock Market Index actually available to investors in the marketplace. The Dow Jones U.S. Mid-Cap Total Stock Market Index includes the components ranked 501-1000 by full market capitalization. The index is a float-adjusted market capitalization weighted index. **Top Holdings:** Diamondback Energy Inc International Flavors & Fragrances Inc Arthur J. Gallagher & Co CDW Corp Gartner Inc A

iShares Core Dividend Growth ETF   C   HOLD

Ticker	Traded On	NAV		Total Assets ($)	Dividend Yield (TTM)	Turnover Ratio	Expense Ratio
DGRO	NYSE Arca	33.16		$5,128,131,269	2.21	24	0.08

Ratings
Reward	C
Risk	C+
Recent Upgrade/Downgrade	Down

Fund Information
Fund Type	Exchange Traded Funds
Category	US Equity Large Cap Value
Sub-Category	Large Value
Prospectus Objective	Equity-Income
Inception Date	Jun-14
Open to New Investments	Y

Prices
Price (as of 12/31/2018)	33.18
52-Week High	37.86
52-Week Low	31.18

Total Returns (%)
3-Month	6-Month	1-Year	3-Year	5-Year
-10.22	-2.31	-2.24	38.42	

3-Year Standard Deviation	8.95
Effective Duration	

Valuation
Premium/Discount (1-Year Average)	0.06

Company Information
Provider	iShares
Manager/Tenure	Diane Hsiung (4), Jennifer Hsui (4), Greg Savage (4), 3 others
Website	http://www.ishares.com
Address	iShares 400 Howard Street San Francisco CA 94105 United States
Phone Number	800-474-2737

PERFORMANCE

Ratings History
Date	Overall Rating	Risk Rating	Reward Rating
Q4-18	C	C+	C
Q2-18	C	C+	C
Q4-17	B	B	B
Q4-16	C	C+	C+
Q4-15	D	C-	D+

Asset & Performance History
Date	NAV	1-Year Total Return
2017	34.72	22.83
2016	28.89	15.27
2015	25.67	-0.62
2014	26.49	
2013		
2012		

Total Assets: $5,128,131,269
Asset Allocation
Asset	%
Cash	0%
Stocks	100%
US Stocks	99%
Bonds	0%
US Bonds	0%
Other	0%

Services Offered:

Investment Strategy: The investment seeks to track the investment results of the Morningstar® US Dividend Growth IndexSM. The fund generally will invest at least 90% of its assets in the component securities of the underlying index. The underlying index is a subset of the Morningstar® US Market IndexSM, which is a diversified broad market index that represents approximately 97% of the market capitalization of publicly-traded U.S. stocks. **Top Holdings:** Pfizer Inc Johnson & Johnson Microsoft Corp Procter & Gamble Co JPMorgan Chase & Co

---

Invesco FTSE RAFI US 1000 ETF   C   HOLD

Ticker	Traded On	NAV		Total Assets ($)	Dividend Yield (TTM)	Turnover Ratio	Expense Ratio
PRF	NYSE Arca	101.56		$5,117,466,708	1.99	9	0.39

Ratings
Reward	C
Risk	C+
Recent Upgrade/Downgrade	Down

Fund Information
Fund Type	Exchange Traded Funds
Category	US Equity Large Cap Value
Sub-Category	Large Value
Prospectus Objective	Growth
Inception Date	Dec-05
Open to New Investments	Y

Prices
Price (as of 12/31/2018)	101.57
52-Week High	120.82
52-Week Low	95.78

Total Returns (%)
3-Month	6-Month	1-Year	3-Year	5-Year
-14.13	-8.76	-8.56	24.22	35.43

3-Year Standard Deviation	9.66
Effective Duration	

Valuation
Premium/Discount (1-Year Average)	0.00

Company Information
Provider	Invesco
Manager/Tenure	Peter Hubbard (11), Michael Jeanette (10), Jonathan Nixon (5), 1 other
Website	http://www.invesco.com/us
Address	Invesco 11 Greenway Plaza, Ste. 2500 Houston TX 77046 United States
Phone Number	800-659-1005

PERFORMANCE

Ratings History
Date	Overall Rating	Risk Rating	Reward Rating
Q4-18	C	C+	C
Q2-18	C	C+	C
Q4-17	B	B	B
Q4-16	B-	C+	B
Q4-15	C+	C+	C

Asset & Performance History
Date	NAV	1-Year Total Return
2017	113.42	15.94
2016	99.46	17.18
2015	86.84	-2.83
2014	91.38	12.2
2013	82.89	35.13
2012	62.4	16.77

Total Assets: $5,117,466,708
Asset Allocation
Asset	%
Cash	0%
Stocks	100%
US Stocks	99%
Bonds	0%
US Bonds	0%
Other	0%

Services Offered:

Investment Strategy: The investment seeks to track the investment results (before fees and expenses) of the FTSE RAFI™ US 1000 Index (the "underlying index"). The fund generally will invest at least 90% of its total assets in common stocks that comprise the underlying index. The underlying index is composed of 1,000 common stocks that FTSE International Limited and Research Affiliates LLC strictly in accordance with their guidelines and mandated procedures, include to track the performance of the largest U.S. companies based on the following four fundamental measures: book value, cash flow, sales and dividends. **Top Holdings:** Exxon Mobil Corp Apple Inc Berkshire Hathaway Inc B Chevron Corp JPMorgan Chase & Co

Schwab U.S. Large-Cap Value ETF™   C   HOLD

Ticker	Traded On	NAV	Total Assets ($)	Dividend Yield (TTM)	Turnover Ratio	Expense Ratio
SCHV	NYSE Arca	49.27	$4,902,673,769	2.67	8	0.04

Ratings
Reward	C
Risk	C+
Recent Upgrade/Downgrade	Down

Fund Information
Fund Type	Exchange Traded Funds
Category	US Equity Large Cap Value
Sub-Category	Large Value
Prospectus Objective	Growth
Inception Date	Dec-09
Open to New Investments	Y

Prices
Price (as of 12/31/2018)	49.29
52-Week High	58.00
52-Week Low	46.58

Total Returns (%)
3-Month	6-Month	1-Year	3-Year	5-Year
-11.73	-5.92	-7.23	25.84	38.11

3-Year Standard Deviation   8.8
Effective Duration

Valuation
Premium/Discount (1-Year Average)   0.02

Company Information
Provider	Schwab ETFs
Manager/Tenure	Ferian Juwono (8), Christopher Bliss (1), Sabya Sinha (1), 1 other
Website	http://www.schwabetfs.com
Address	Schwab ETFs United States
Phone Number	800-435-4000

PERFORMANCE

Ratings History
Date	Overall Rating	Risk Rating	Reward Rating
Q4-18	C	C+	C
Q2-18	C	C+	C
Q4-17	B-	B	B-
Q4-16	B-	C+	B
Q4-15	C+	C+	C

Asset & Performance History
Date	NAV	1-Year Total Return
2017	54.61	16.64
2016	48.05	16.42
2015	42.44	-1.08
2014	44.07	10.96
2013	40.7	30.98
2012	31.82	15.04

Total Assets: $4,902,673,769

Asset Allocation
Asset	%
Cash	0%
Stocks	100%
US Stocks	99%
Bonds	0%
US Bonds	0%
Other	0%

Services Offered:

Investment Strategy: The investment seeks to track as closely as possible, before fees and expenses, the total return of the Dow Jones U.S. Large-Cap Value Total Stock Market Index. To pursue its goal, the fund generally invests in stocks that are included in the Dow Jones U.S. Large-Cap Value Total Stock Market Index. The index includes the large-cap value portion of the Dow Jones U.S. Total Stock Market Index actually available to investors in the marketplace. The Dow Jones U.S. Large-Cap Value Total Stock Market Index includes the components ranked 1-750 by full market capitalization and that are classified as "value" based on a number of factors. **Top Holdings:** Johnson & Johnson   JPMorgan Chase & Co   Exxon Mobil Corp   Pfizer Inc   Bank of America Corporation

---

Vanguard Russell 1000 Growth Index Fund ETF Shares   C   HOLD

Ticker	Traded On	NAV	Total Assets ($)	Dividend Yield (TTM)	Turnover Ratio	Expense Ratio
VONG	NAS CM		$4,898,617,969	1.33	15	0.12

Ratings
Reward	C
Risk	C+
Recent Upgrade/Downgrade	Down

Fund Information
Fund Type	Exchange Traded Funds
Category	US Equity Large Cap Growth
Sub-Category	Large Growth
Prospectus Objective	Growth
Inception Date	Sep-10
Open to New Investments	Y

Prices
Price (as of 12/31/2018)	134.49
52-Week High	160.23
52-Week Low	124.90

Total Returns (%)
3-Month	6-Month	1-Year	3-Year	5-Year
-16.91	-9.62	-2.56	35.56	61.54

3-Year Standard Deviation   11.02
Effective Duration

Valuation
Premium/Discount (1-Year Average)   0.04

Company Information
Provider	Vanguard
Manager/Tenure	Michael A. Johnson (8), Walter Nejman (2)
Website	http://www.vanguard.com
Address	Vanguard 100 Vanguard Boulevard Malvern PA 19355 United States
Phone Number	877-662-7447

PERFORMANCE

Ratings History
Date	Overall Rating	Risk Rating	Reward Rating
Q4-18	C	C+	C
Q2-18	C+	C-	B
Q4-17	B+	B+	B+
Q4-16	C+	C-	B
Q4-15	C	C	C+

Asset & Performance History
Date	NAV	1-Year Total Return
2017	137.93	29.89
2016	107.44	6.58
2015	101.97	5.52
2014	98.07	12.93
2013	88.15	33.28
2012	67.09	15.1

Total Assets: $4,898,617,969

Asset Allocation
Asset	%
Cash	1%
Stocks	99%
US Stocks	98%
Bonds	0%
US Bonds	0%
Other	0%

Services Offered:

Investment Strategy: The investment seeks to track the performance of a benchmark index that measures the investment return of large-capitalization growth stocks in the United States. The fund employs an indexing investment approach designed to track the performance of the Russell 1000® Growth Index. The index is designed to measure the performance of large-capitalization growth stocks in the United States. The Advisor attempts to replicate the target index by investing all, or substantially all, of its assets in the stocks that make up the index, holding each stock in approximately the same proportion as its weighting in the index. **Top Holdings:** Apple Inc Microsoft Corp   Amazon.com Inc   Facebook Inc A   Alphabet Inc Class C

Vanguard Intermediate-Term Treasury Index Fund ETF Shares   C-   HOLD

Ticker	Traded On	NAV	Total Assets ($)	Dividend Yield (TTM)	Turnover Ratio	Expense Ratio
VGIT	NAS CM		$4,898,444,910	2.01	31	0.07

Ratings
Reward   D
Risk   C
Recent Upgrade/Downgrade   Up

Fund Information
Fund Type   Exchange Traded Funds
Category   US Fixed Income
Sub-Category   Intermediate Government
Prospectus Objective   Govt Bond - Gen
Inception Date   Nov-09
Open to New Investments   Y

Prices
Price (as of 12/31/2018)   63.47
52-Week High   63.94
52-Week Low   61.57

Total Returns (%)

3-Month	6-Month	1-Year	3-Year	5-Year
2.81	2.40	1.08	3.84	10.00

3-Year Standard Deviation   3.09
Effective Duration   5.13

Valuation
Premium/Discount (1-Year Average)   0.03

Company Information
Provider   Vanguard
Manager/Tenure   Joshua C. Barrickman (5)
Website   http://www.vanguard.com
Address   Vanguard 100 Vanguard Boulevard
Malvern PA 19355 United States
Phone Number   877-662-7447

Ratings History

Date	Overall Rating	Risk Rating	Reward Rating
Q4-18	C-	C	D
Q2-18	D+	C	D
Q4-17	C	C	C
Q4-16	C	C+	C
Q4-15	C	C-	C

Asset & Performance History

Date	NAV	1-Year Total Return
2017	63.9	1.62
2016	63.95	0.99
2015	64.29	1.63
2014	64.33	4.22
2013	62.69	-2.73
2012	65.49	2.63

Total Assets: $4,898,444,910
Asset Allocation

Asset	%
Cash	0%
Stocks	0%
US Stocks	0%
Bonds	100%
US Bonds	100%
Other	0%

Services Offered:

Investment Strategy: The investment seeks to track the performance of a market-weighted government bond index with an intermediate-term dollar-weighted average maturity. The fund employs an indexing investment approach designed to track the performance of the Bloomberg Barclays US Treasury 3-10 Year Bond Index. This index includes fixed income securities issued by the U.S. Treasury (not including inflation-protected bonds), with maturities between 3 and 10 years. At least 80% of the fund's assets will be invested in bonds included in the index. **Top Holdings:** United States Treasury Notes 2.75% United States Treasury Notes 2% United States Treasury Notes 2.5% United States Treasury Notes 2% United States Treasury Notes 2.38%

Schwab U.S. REIT ETF™   C   HOLD

Ticker	Traded On	NAV	Total Assets ($)	Dividend Yield (TTM)	Turnover Ratio	Expense Ratio
SCHH	NYSE Arca	38.49	$4,896,978,133	2.89	8	0.07

Ratings
Reward   C
Risk   C
Recent Upgrade/Downgrade   Down

Fund Information
Fund Type   Exchange Traded Funds
Category   Real Estate Sector Equity
Sub-Category   Real Estate
Prospectus Objective   Real Estate
Inception Date   Jan-11
Open to New Investments   Y

Prices
Price (as of 12/31/2018)   38.51
52-Week High   43.28
52-Week Low   36.34

Total Returns (%)

3-Month	6-Month	1-Year	3-Year	5-Year
-5.73	-5.29	-4.20	5.71	45.53

3-Year Standard Deviation   12.66
Effective Duration

Valuation
Premium/Discount (1-Year Average)   0.01

Company Information
Provider   Schwab ETFs
Manager/Tenure   Ferian Juwono (7), Christopher Bliss (1), Sabya Sinha (1)
Website   http://www.schwabetfs.com
Address   Schwab ETFs United States
Phone Number   800-435-4000

Ratings History

Date	Overall Rating	Risk Rating	Reward Rating
Q4-18	C	C	C
Q2-18	C	C	C
Q4-17	B-	B+	C+
Q4-16	C+	C	C+
Q4-15	C+	C+	B-

Asset & Performance History

Date	NAV	1-Year Total Return
2017	41.59	5.08
2016	41	6.42
2015	39.62	4.35
2014	38.94	31.92
2013	30.23	1.11
2012	30.66	16.9

Total Assets: $4,896,978,133
Asset Allocation

Asset	%
Cash	0%
Stocks	100%
US Stocks	100%
Bonds	0%
US Bonds	0%
Other	0%

Services Offered:

Investment Strategy: The investment seeks to track as closely as possible, before fees and expenses, the total return of the Dow Jones U.S. Select REIT Index™. The fund invests at least 90% of its net assets (including, for this purpose, any borrowings for investment purposes) in securities included in the index. It will generally give the same weight to a given security as the index does. The index is a float-adjusted market capitalization weighted index comprised of real estate investment trusts ("REITs"). The fund may invest up to 10% of its net assets in securities not included in its index. **Top Holdings:** Simon Property Group Inc Prologis Inc Public Storage Welltower Inc AvalonBay Communities Inc

iShares Core S&P U.S. Value ETF   C   HOLD

Ticker	Traded On	NAV	Total Assets ($)	Dividend Yield (TTM)	Turnover Ratio	Expense Ratio
IUSV	NAS CM	49.09	$4,864,475,415	2.24	27	0.04

Ratings

Reward	C
Risk	C+
Recent Upgrade/Downgrade	Down

Fund Information

Fund Type	Exchange Traded Funds
Category	US Equity Large Cap Value
Sub-Category	Large Value
Prospectus Objective	Growth
Inception Date	Jul-00
Open to New Investments	Y

Prices

Price (as of 12/31/2018)	49.09
52-Week High	58.63
52-Week Low	46.36

Total Returns (%)

3-Month	6-Month	1-Year	3-Year	5-Year
-12.60	-7.30	-9.08	23.79	33.53

3-Year Standard Deviation	9.84
Effective Duration	

Valuation

Premium/Discount (1-Year Average)	0.02

Company Information

Provider	iShares
Manager/Tenure	Diane Hsiung (10), Greg Savage (10), Jennifer Hsui (6), 3 others
Website	http://www.ishares.com
Address	iShares 400 Howard Street San Francisco CA 94105 United States
Phone Number	800-474-2737

PERFORMANCE

Ratings History

Date	Overall Rating	Risk Rating	Reward Rating
Q4-18	C	C+	C
Q2-18	C	C+	C
Q4-17	B	B	B-
Q4-16	B-	C+	B
Q4-15	C	C	C

Asset & Performance History

Date	NAV	1-Year Total Return
2017	55.34	15.07
2016	49.09	18.32
2015	42.48	-4.12
2014	45.42	12.51
2013	41.15	32.33
2012	31.76	17.27

Total Assets: $4,864,475,415

Asset Allocation

Asset	%
Cash	0%
Stocks	100%
US Stocks	99%
Bonds	0%
US Bonds	0%
Other	0%

Services Offered: CashInvestment Plan

Investment Strategy: The investment seeks to track the investment results of the S&P 900 Value Index (the "underlying index"), which measures the performance of the large- and mid-capitalization value sector of the U.S. equity market. The fund generally invests at least 90% of its assets in securities of the underlying index and in depositary receipts representing securities of the underlying index. It may invest the remainder of its assets in certain futures, options and swap contracts, cash and cash equivalents, as well as in securities not included in the underlying index, but which the advisor believes will help the fund track the underlying index. **Top Holdings:** Berkshire Hathaway Inc B   JPMorgan Chase & Co   Exxon Mobil Corp   Verizon Communications Inc   Wells Fargo & Co

---

Schwab Emerging Markets Equity ETF™   C-   HOLD

Ticker	Traded On	NAV	Total Assets ($)	Dividend Yield (TTM)	Turnover Ratio	Expense Ratio
SCHE	NYSE Arca	23.54	$4,796,627,637	2.61	18	0.13

Ratings

Reward	C-
Risk	C
Recent Upgrade/Downgrade	Down

Fund Information

Fund Type	Exchange Traded Funds
Category	Global Emerg Mkts Equity
Sub-Category	Diversified Emerging Mkts
Prospectus Objective	Div Emerg Mkts
Inception Date	Jan-10
Open to New Investments	Y

Prices

Price (as of 12/31/2018)	23.53
52-Week High	31.08
52-Week Low	22.96

Total Returns (%)

3-Month	6-Month	1-Year	3-Year	5-Year
-6.00	-6.29	-13.31	29.21	9.99

3-Year Standard Deviation	14.61
Effective Duration	

Valuation

Premium/Discount (1-Year Average)	0.15

Company Information

Provider	Schwab ETFs
Manager/Tenure	Chuck Craig (5), Christopher Bliss (1), Jane Qin (1), 1 other
Website	http://www.schwabetfs.com
Address	Schwab ETFs United States
Phone Number	800-435-4000

PERFORMANCE

Ratings History

Date	Overall Rating	Risk Rating	Reward Rating
Q4-18	C-	C	C-
Q2-18	C	C+	C
Q4-17	B-	C	B
Q4-16	C-	C	D+
Q4-15	C-	C-	C-

Asset & Performance History

Date	NAV	1-Year Total Return
2017	27.88	32.08
2016	21.62	12.9
2015	19.59	-15.8
2014	23.85	1.1
2013	24.27	-3.83
2012	25.9	16.94

Total Assets: $4,796,627,637

Asset Allocation

Asset	%
Cash	0%
Stocks	99%
US Stocks	0%
Bonds	0%
US Bonds	0%
Other	0%

Services Offered:

Investment Strategy: The investment seeks to track as closely as possible, before fees and expenses, the total return of the FTSE Emerging Index. The fund will invest at least 90% of its net assets (net assets plus borrowings for investment purposes) in these stocks, including depositary receipts representing securities of the index; such depositary receipts may be in the form of ADRs, GDRs and EDRs. It generally invests in stocks that are included in the FTSE Emerging Index. The index is comprised of large and mid capitalization companies in emerging market countries, as defined by the index provider. **Top Holdings:** Tencent Holdings Ltd   Taiwan Semiconductor Manufacturing Co Ltd   Alibaba Group Holding Ltd ADR   Naspers Ltd Class N   China Construction Bank Corp H

iShares S&P 100 ETF   C   HOLD

Ticker	Traded On	NAV	Total Assets ($)	Dividend Yield (TTM)	Turnover Ratio	Expense Ratio
OEF	NYSE Arca	111.47	$4,772,415,411	1.85	4	0.2

Ratings
Reward	C
Risk	C+
Recent Upgrade/Downgrade	Down

Fund Information
Fund Type	Exchange Traded Funds
Category	US Equity Large Cap Blend
Sub-Category	Large Blend
Prospectus Objective	Growth
Inception Date	Oct-00
Open to New Investments	Y

Prices
Price (as of 12/31/2018)	111.53
52-Week High	130.65
52-Week Low	104.34

Total Returns (%)
3-Month	6-Month	1-Year	3-Year	5-Year
-13.94	-6.24	-4.05	29.87	49.74

3-Year Standard Deviation	9.41
Effective Duration	

Valuation
Premium/Discount (1-Year Average)	0.02

Company Information
Provider	iShares
Manager/Tenure	Diane Hsiung (10), Greg Savage (10), Jennifer Hsui (6), 3 others
Website	http://www.ishares.com
Address	iShares 400 Howard Street San Francisco CA 94105 United States
Phone Number	800-474-2737

PERFORMANCE

Ratings History
Date	Overall Rating	Risk Rating	Reward Rating
Q4-18	C	C+	C
Q2-18	C+	C+	C+
Q4-17	B	B+	B
Q4-16	B-	C+	B
Q4-15	C+	B-	C+

Asset & Performance History
Date	NAV	1-Year Total Return
2017	118.47	21.76
2016	99.21	11.16
2015	91.2	2.49
2014	90.9	12.49
2013	82.36	30.05
2012	64.7	15.79

Total Assets: $4,772,415,411

Asset Allocation
Asset	%
Cash	0%
Stocks	100%
US Stocks	100%
Bonds	0%
US Bonds	0%
Other	0%

Services Offered: CashInvestment Plan

Investment Strategy: The investment seeks to track the investment results of the S&P 100®, which measures the performance of the large-capitalization sector of the U.S. equity market. The fund generally invests at least 90% of its assets in securities of the underlying index and in depositary receipts representing securities of the underlying index. It may invest the remainder of its assets in certain futures, options and swap contracts, cash and cash equivalents, including shares of money market funds advised by BFA or its affiliates, as well as in securities not included in the underlying index, but which the advisor believes will help the fund track the underlying index. **Top Holdings:** Microsoft Corp Apple Inc Amazon.com Inc Berkshire Hathaway Inc B Johnson & Johnson

---

iShares Edge MSCI Min Vol Emerging Markets ETF   C   HOLD

Ticker	Traded On	NAV	Total Assets ($)	Dividend Yield (TTM)	Turnover Ratio	Expense Ratio
EEMV	BATS	55.73	$4,733,488,750	2.63	22	0.25

Ratings
Reward	D+
Risk	C+
Recent Upgrade/Downgrade	

Fund Information
Fund Type	Exchange Traded Funds
Category	Global Emerg Mkts Equity
Sub-Category	Diversified Emerging Mkts
Prospectus Objective	Div Emerg Mkts
Inception Date	Oct-11
Open to New Investments	Y

Prices
Price (as of 12/31/2018)	55.87
52-Week High	65.47
52-Week Low	53.54

Total Returns (%)
3-Month	6-Month	1-Year	3-Year	5-Year
-4.44	-2.06	-6.07	23.06	9.08

3-Year Standard Deviation	11
Effective Duration	

Valuation
Premium/Discount (1-Year Average)	-0.09

Company Information
Provider	iShares
Manager/Tenure	Diane Hsiung (7), Greg Savage (7), Jennifer Hsui (5), 1 other
Website	http://www.ishares.com
Address	iShares 400 Howard Street San Francisco CA 94105 United States
Phone Number	800-474-2737

PERFORMANCE

Ratings History
Date	Overall Rating	Risk Rating	Reward Rating
Q4-18	C	C+	D+
Q2-18	C	C+	C
Q4-17	C+	C	C+
Q4-16	D+	C-	D
Q4-15	C-	C-	C-

Asset & Performance History
Date	NAV	1-Year Total Return
2017	60.78	26.32
2016	49.3	3.72
2015	48.85	-12.12
2014	56.91	0.87
2013	57.95	-0.28
2012	59.62	21.98

Total Assets: $4,733,488,750

Asset Allocation
Asset	%
Cash	1%
Stocks	99%
US Stocks	0%
Bonds	0%
US Bonds	0%
Other	0%

Services Offered:

Investment Strategy: The investment seeks to track the investment results of the MSCI Emerging Markets Minimum Volatility (USD) Index. The fund generally will invest at least 90% of its assets in the component securities of the underlying index and in investments that have economic characteristics that are substantially identical to the component securities of the underlying index. The index measures the performance of equity securities in global emerging markets that, in the aggregate, have lower volatility relative to the broader global emerging markets. **Top Holdings:** PT Bank Central Asia Tbk Chunghwa Telecom Co Ltd Taiwan Cooperative Financial Holding Co Ltd Public Bank Bhd China Mobile Ltd

iShares MSCI India ETF   C-   HOLD

Ticker	Traded On	NAV	Total Assets ($)	Dividend Yield (TTM)	Turnover Ratio	Expense Ratio
INDA	BATS	33.16	$4,699,173,610	0.94	10	0.68

Ratings
Reward	D+
Risk	C-
Recent Upgrade/Downgrade	Down

Fund Information
Fund Type	Exchange Traded Funds
Category	India Equity
Sub-Category	India Equity
Prospectus Objective	Pacific Stock
Inception Date	Feb-12
Open to New Investments	Y

Prices
Price (as of 12/31/2018)	33.34
52-Week High	38.06
52-Week Low	29.30

Total Returns (%)
3-Month	6-Month	1-Year	3-Year	5-Year
2.45	1.33	-7.44	23.23	41.90

3-Year Standard Deviation	18.1
Effective Duration	

Valuation
Premium/Discount (1-Year Average)	-0.13

Company Information
Provider	iShares
Manager/Tenure	Diane Hsiung (6), Greg Savage (6), Jennifer Hsui (5), 1 other
Website	http://www.ishares.com
Address	iShares 400 Howard Street San Francisco CA 94105 United States
Phone Number	800-474-2737

Ratings History
Date	Overall Rating	Risk Rating	Reward Rating
Q4-18	C-	C-	D+
Q2-18	C	C	C-
Q4-17	B-	C	B
Q4-16	C	C	C
Q4-15	C	C+	C

Asset & Performance History
Date	NAV	1-Year Total Return
2017	36.17	36.19
2016	26.86	-2.23
2015	27.72	-6.62
2014	30.03	23.31
2013	24.51	-4.23
2012	25.76	

Total Assets: $4,699,173,610
Asset Allocation
Asset	%
Cash	0%
Stocks	100%
US Stocks	0%
Bonds	0%
US Bonds	0%
Other	0%

Services Offered:

Investment Strategy: The investment seeks to track the investment results of the MSCI India Index composed of Indian equities. The fund generally will collectively invest at least 90% of its assets in the component securities of the index and in investments that have economic characteristics that are substantially identical to the component securities of the index. The index measures the performance of equity securities of companies whose market capitalization, as calculated by the index provider, represents the top 85% of companies in the Indian securities market. The fund is non-diversified. **Top Holdings:** Reliance Industries Ltd   Housing Development Finance Corp Ltd   Infosys Ltd   Tata Consultancy Services Ltd   Hindustan Unilever Ltd

---

WisdomTree Japan Hedged Equity Fund   C-   HOLD

Ticker	Traded On	NAV	Total Assets ($)	Dividend Yield (TTM)	Turnover Ratio	Expense Ratio
DXJ	NYSE Arca	46.95	$4,698,419,363	3	18	0.48

Ratings
Reward	D+
Risk	C
Recent Upgrade/Downgrade	Down

Fund Information
Fund Type	Exchange Traded Funds
Category	Japan Equity
Sub-Category	Japan Stock
Prospectus Objective	Pacific Stock
Inception Date	Jun-06
Open to New Investments	Y

Prices
Price (as of 12/31/2018)	46.39
52-Week High	62.63
52-Week Low	44.87

Total Returns (%)
3-Month	6-Month	1-Year	3-Year	5-Year
-18.68	-11.38	-18.80	-0.65	18.70

3-Year Standard Deviation	16.6
Effective Duration	

Valuation
Premium/Discount (1-Year Average)	-0.09

Company Information
Provider	WisdomTree
Manager/Tenure	Richard A. Brown (10), Thomas J. Durante (10), Karen Q. Wong (10)
Website	http://www.wisdomtree.com
Address	WisdomTree 245 Park Avenue, 35th floor New York NY 10167 United States
Phone Number	866-909-9473

Ratings History
Date	Overall Rating	Risk Rating	Reward Rating
Q4-18	C-	C	D+
Q2-18	C	C	C-
Q4-17	B	C+	A-
Q4-16	C	C	C-
Q4-15	B	B+	C+

Asset & Performance History
Date	NAV	1-Year Total Return
2017	59.32	22.25
2016	49.75	0.07
2015	50.8	8.15
2014	49.73	10.47
2013	50.24	41.85
2012	36.34	17.07

Total Assets: $4,698,419,363
Asset Allocation
Asset	%
Cash	0%
Stocks	100%
US Stocks	0%
Bonds	0%
US Bonds	0%
Other	0%

Services Offered:

Investment Strategy: The investment seeks to track the price and yield performance, before fees and expenses, of the WisdomTree Japan Hedged Equity Index. Under normal circumstances, at least 95% of the fund's total assets (exclusive of collateral held from securities lending) will be invested in the component securities of the index and investments that have economic characteristics that are substantially identical to the economic characteristics of such component securities. The index is designed to provide exposure to Japanese equity markets while at the same time neutralizing exposure to fluctuations of the Japanese yen relative to the U.S. dollar. The fund is non-diversified. **Top Holdings:** Toyota Motor Corp   Japan Tobacco Inc   Mitsubishi UFJ Financial Group Inc   Sumitomo Mitsui Financial Group Inc   Nissan Motor Co Ltd

First Trust Value Line® Dividend Index Fund

C   HOLD

Ticker	Traded On	NAV	Total Assets ($)	Dividend Yield (TTM)	Turnover Ratio	Expense Ratio
FVD	NYSE Arca	29.07	$4,677,751,303	2.2	50	0.7

Ratings
Reward	C
Risk	C+
Recent Upgrade/Downgrade	Down

Fund Information
Fund Type	Exchange Traded Funds
Category	US Equity Large Cap Value
Sub-Category	Large Value
Prospectus Objective	Growth & Inc
Inception Date	Aug-03
Open to New Investments	Y

Prices
Price (as of 12/31/2018)	29.08
52-Week High	32.16
52-Week Low	27.80

Total Returns (%)
3-Month	6-Month	1-Year	3-Year	5-Year
-7.21	-2.67	-3.45	30.27	52.93

3-Year Standard Deviation	7.56
Effective Duration	

Valuation
Premium/Discount (1-Year Average)	0.03

Company Information
Provider	First Trust
Manager/Tenure	Jon C. Erickson (15), David G. McGarel (15), Roger F. Testin (15), 3 others
Website	http://www.ftportfolios.com/
Address	First Trust 120 E. Liberty Drive, Suite 400 Wheaton IL 60187 United States
Phone Number	800-621-1675

PERFORMANCE

Ratings History
Date	Overall Rating	Risk Rating	Reward Rating
Q4-18	C	C+	C
Q2-18	C	C+	C
Q4-17	B	A+	B-
Q4-16	B	C+	B
Q4-15	B-	C+	B-

Asset & Performance History
Date	NAV	1-Year Total Return
2017	30.84	12.48
2016	28.02	19.95
2015	23.86	1.24
2014	24.13	15.95
2013	21.36	26.6
2012	17.29	11.18

Total Assets: $4,677,751,303

Asset Allocation
Asset	%
Cash	0%
Stocks	100%
US Stocks	86%
Bonds	0%
US Bonds	0%
Other	0%

Services Offered:

Investment Strategy: The investment seeks investment results that correspond generally to the price and yield (before the fund's fees and expenses) of an equity index called the Value Line® Dividend Index. The fund will normally invest at least 90% of its net assets (including investment borrowings) in common stocks that comprise the index. The index is a modified equal-dollar weighted index comprised of U.S. exchange-listed securities of companies that pay above-average dividends and have potential for capital appreciation. **Top Holdings:** Boeing Co Infosys Ltd ADR Union Pacific Corp Altria Group Inc Pfizer Inc

---

SPDR® Bloomberg Barclays Investment Grade Floating Rate ETF

C   HOLD

Ticker	Traded On	NAV	Total Assets ($)	Dividend Yield (TTM)	Turnover Ratio	Expense Ratio
FLRN	NYSE Arca	30.41	$4,668,341,427	2.28	16	0.15

Ratings
Reward	C
Risk	C+
Recent Upgrade/Downgrade	

Fund Information
Fund Type	Exchange Traded Funds
Category	US Fixed Income
Sub-Category	Ultrashort Bond
Prospectus Objective	Corp Bond-High Yld
Inception Date	Nov-11
Open to New Investments	Y

Prices
Price (as of 12/31/2018)	30.37
52-Week High	30.79
52-Week Low	30.32

Total Returns (%)
3-Month	6-Month	1-Year	3-Year	5-Year
-0.23	0.49	1.58	5.24	5.87

3-Year Standard Deviation	0.34
Effective Duration	0.11

Valuation
Premium/Discount (1-Year Average)	0.09

Company Information
Provider	SPDR State Street Global Advisors
Manager/Tenure	Christopher DiStefano (5), Kyle Kelly (4), Frank Miethe (0)
Website	http://www.spdrs.com
Address	SPDR State Street Global Advisors State Street Financial Center, 1 Lincoln Street Boston MA 02111-2900 United States
Phone Number	617-786-3000

PERFORMANCE

Ratings History
Date	Overall Rating	Risk Rating	Reward Rating
Q4-18	C	C+	C
Q2-18	C	C+	C
Q4-17	B-	A-	C
Q4-16	C	C-	C
Q4-15	C	C-	C

Asset & Performance History
Date	NAV	1-Year Total Return
2017	30.65	1.74
2016	30.55	1.59
2015	30.4	0.2
2014	30.52	0.39
2013	30.57	1.1
2012	30.45	3.46

Total Assets: $4,668,341,427

Asset Allocation
Asset	%
Cash	6%
Stocks	0%
US Stocks	0%
Bonds	92%
US Bonds	52%
Other	0%

Services Offered:

Investment Strategy: The investment seeks to provide investment results that, before fees and expenses, correspond generally to the price and yield performance of the Bloomberg Barclays U.S. Dollar Floating Rate Note < 5 Years Index. The fund generally invests substantially all, but at least 80%, of its total assets in the securities comprising the index or in securities that the Adviser determines have economic characteristics that are substantially identical to the economic characteristics of the securities that comprise the index. The index is designed to measure the performance of U.S. dollar-denominated, investment grade floating rate notes. The fund is non-diversified. **Top Holdings:** Morgan Stanley 3.41% Nederlandse Waterschapsbank N.V. 2.62% Inter-American Development Bank 2.32% Morgan Stanley 3.65% Morgan Stanley 3.17%

Schwab Fundamental U.S. Large Company Index ETF　　　　　　　　C　　HOLD

Ticker	Traded On	NAV	Total Assets ($)	Dividend Yield (TTM)	Turnover Ratio	Expense Ratio
FNDX	NYSE Arca	33.95	$4,651,673,720	2.08	9	0.25

Ratings
Reward　　　　　　　　　　　　　　C
Risk　　　　　　　　　　　　　　　C+
Recent Upgrade/Downgrade　　　　Down

Fund Information
Fund Type　　　　　Exchange Traded Funds
Category　　　　　US Equity Large Cap Value
Sub-Category　　　　　　　　Large Value
Prospectus Objective　　　　Growth & Inc
Inception Date　　　　　　　　Aug-13
Open to New Investments　　　　　　Y

Prices
Price (as of 12/31/2018)　　　　　33.98
52-Week High　　　　　　　　　40.30
52-Week Low　　　　　　　　　32.01

Total Returns (%)

3-Month	6-Month	1-Year	3-Year	5-Year
-14.24	-7.99	-7.31	26.32	37.71

3-Year Standard Deviation　　　　9.39
Effective Duration

Valuation
Premium/Discount (1-Year Average)　　0.00

Company Information
Provider　　　　Schwab ETFs
Manager/Tenure　Christopher Bliss (1), Ferian Juwono (1), Sabya Sinha (1)
Website　　　　http://www.schwabetfs.com
Address　　　　Schwab ETFs United States
Phone Number　800-435-4000

PERFORMANCE

Ratings History

Date	Overall Rating	Risk Rating	Reward Rating
Q4-18	C	C+	C
Q2-18	C	C+	C
Q4-17	B	B	B-
Q4-16	B-	C+	B
Q4-15	C-	C+	C-

Asset & Performance History

Date	NAV	1-Year Total Return
2017	37.43	17.15
2016	32.61	16.41
2015	28.62	-2.92
2014	30.08	12.29
2013	27.24	
2012		

Total Assets: $4,651,673,720
Asset Allocation

Asset	%
Cash	0%
Stocks	100%
US Stocks	99%
Bonds	0%
US Bonds	0%
Other	0%

Services Offered:

Investment Strategy: The investment seeks to track as closely as possible, before fees and expenses, the total return of the Russell RAFI™ US Large Company Index. The fund normally will invest at least 90% of its net assets (including, for this purpose, any borrowings for investment purposes) in stocks included in the index. The index measures the performance of the large company size segment by fundamental overall company scores, which are created using as the universe the companies included in the Russell 3000® Index. It may invest up to 10% of its net assets in securities not included in the index. **Top Holdings:** Exxon Mobil Corp　Apple Inc　Chevron Corp　Microsoft Corp　AT&T Inc

---

Invesco Preferred ETF　　　　　　　　　　　　　　　　　　　C-　　HOLD

Ticker	Traded On	NAV	Total Assets ($)	Dividend Yield (TTM)	Turnover Ratio	Expense Ratio
PGX	NYSE Arca	13.49	$4,604,690,866	5.98		0.51

Ratings
Reward　　　　　　　　　　　　　　D+
Risk　　　　　　　　　　　　　　　C
Recent Upgrade/Downgrade　　　　Down

Fund Information
Fund Type　　　　　Exchange Traded Funds
Category　　　　　　　US Fixed Income
Sub-Category　　　　　　Preferred Stock
Prospectus Objective　　　　Growth & Inc
Inception Date　　　　　　　　Jan-08
Open to New Investments　　　　　　Y

Prices
Price (as of 12/31/2018)　　　　　13.47
52-Week High　　　　　　　　　14.86
52-Week Low　　　　　　　　　13.18

Total Returns (%)

3-Month	6-Month	1-Year	3-Year	5-Year
-3.82	-4.93	-4.24	7.39	33.81

3-Year Standard Deviation　　　　4.81
Effective Duration

Valuation
Premium/Discount (1-Year Average)　　0.01

Company Information
Provider　　　　Invesco
Manager/Tenure　Philip Fang (10), Peter Hubbard (10), Jeffrey W. Kernagis (10), 2 others
Website　　　　http://www.invesco.com/us
Address　　　　Invesco 11 Greenway Plaza, Ste. 2500 Houston TX 77046 United States
Phone Number　800-659-1005

PERFORMANCE

Ratings History

Date	Overall Rating	Risk Rating	Reward Rating
Q4-18	C-	C	D+
Q2-18	C+	C+	C
Q4-17	B	A	C+
Q4-16	C	C+	C
Q4-15	B-	C+	B-

Asset & Performance History

Date	NAV	1-Year Total Return
2017	14.92	10.84
2016	14.24	1.19
2015	14.91	8.07
2014	14.64	15.28
2013	13.5	-1.82
2012	14.66	14.5

Total Assets: $4,604,690,866
Asset Allocation

Asset	%
Cash	0%
Stocks	0%
US Stocks	0%
Bonds	0%
US Bonds	0%
Other	1%

Services Offered:

Investment Strategy: The investment seeks to track the investment results (before fees and expenses) of the ICE BofAML Core Plus Fixed Rate Preferred Securities Index (the "underlying index"). The fund generally will invest at least 80% of its total assets in fixed rate U.S. dollar-denominated preferred securities that comprise the underlying index. The underlying index is a market capitalization-weighted index designed to reflect the total return performance of the fixed rate U.S. dollar-denominated preferred securities market. It is non-diversified. **Top Holdings:** Citigroup Inc Deposit Shs Repr 1/1000th 6 7/8 % Non-Cum Perp Pfd Shs Series　BB&T Corp Deposit Shs Repr 1/1000th Non Cum Perp Pfd Shs Series -E-　Deutsche Bank Conting Cp-8 05 PC Tr Pfd Secs 08-Without Fixed Maturity Pfd　PNC Financial Services Group Inc Perpetual Preferred Share class-P　Bank of America Corporation Deposit Shs Repr 1/1000th 6 1/2 % Non-Cum Pfd S

iShares Silver Trust
D   SELL

Ticker	Traded On	NAV		Total Assets ($)	Dividend Yield (TTM)	Turnover Ratio	Expense Ratio
SLV	NYSE Arca	14.52		$4,577,279,161	0		0.5

Ratings
Reward   D-
Risk   D
Recent Upgrade/Downgrade   Down

Fund Information
Fund Type   Exchange Traded Funds
Category   Commodities Specified
Sub-Category   Commodities Precious Metals
Prospectus Objective   Prec Metals
Inception Date   Apr-06
Open to New Investments   Y

Prices
Price (as of 12/31/2018)   14.52
52-Week High   16.56
52-Week Low   13.15

Total Returns (%)

3-Month	6-Month	1-Year	3-Year	5-Year
6.15	-3.48	-8.76	10.21	-22.66

3-Year Standard Deviation   19.28
Effective Duration

Valuation
Premium/Discount (1-Year Average)   0.15

Company Information
Provider   iShares
Manager/Tenure   Management Team (12)
Website   http://www.ishares.com
Address   iShares 400 Howard Street San Francisco CA 94105 United States
Phone Number   800-474-2737

PERFORMANCE

Ratings History

Date	Overall Rating	Risk Rating	Reward Rating
Q4-18	D	D	D-
Q2-18	D+	C-	D
Q4-17	D+	D+	D+
Q4-16	D+	D	C-
Q4-15	D-	E+	D-

Asset & Performance History

Date	NAV	1-Year Total Return
2017	15.91	3.31
2016	15.4	16.93
2015	13.17	-13.86
2014	15.29	-18.54
2013	18.77	-35.22
2012	28.98	5.74

Total Assets: $4,577,279,161

Asset Allocation

Asset	%
Cash	0%
Stocks	0%
US Stocks	0%
Bonds	0%
US Bonds	0%
Other	100%

Services Offered:

Investment Strategy: The investment seeks to reflect generally the performance of the price of silver. The Trust seeks to reflect such performance before payment of the Trust's expenses and liabilities. It is not actively managed. The Trust does not engage in any activities designed to obtain a profit from, or to ameliorate losses caused by, changes in the price of silver. The Trust seeks to reflect generally the performance of the price of silver. The Trust seeks to reflect such performance before payment of the Trust's expenses and liabilities. **Top Holdings:** Silver

---

VanEck Vectors J.P. Morgan EM Local Currency Bond ETF
B   BUY

Ticker	Traded On	NAV		Total Assets ($)	Dividend Yield (TTM)	Turnover Ratio	Expense Ratio
EMLC	NYSE Arca	32.96		$4,543,859,143	6.45	28	0.3

Ratings
Reward   A
Risk   C+
Recent Upgrade/Downgrade   Up

Fund Information
Fund Type   Exchange Traded Funds
Category   Emerging Mkts Fixed Inc
Sub-Category   Emerging-Markets Local-Currency Bond
Prospectus Objective   Div Emerg Mkts
Inception Date   Jul-10
Open to New Investments   Y

Prices
Price (as of 12/31/2018)   33.00
52-Week High   33.10
52-Week Low   16.16

Total Returns (%)

3-Month	6-Month	1-Year	3-Year	5-Year
1.88	100.66	83.81	127.88	83.59

3-Year Standard Deviation   11.08
Effective Duration   4.99

Valuation
Premium/Discount (1-Year Average)   -0.04

Company Information
Provider   VanEck
Manager/Tenure   Francis G. Rodilosso (6)
Website   http://www.vaneck.com
Address   Van Eck Associates Corporation 666 Third Avenue New York NY 10017 United States
Phone Number   800-826-1115

PERFORMANCE

Ratings History

Date	Overall Rating	Risk Rating	Reward Rating
Q4-18	B	C+	A
Q2-18	C	B	A-
Q4-17	C	C	C
Q4-16	D+	D+	D
Q4-15	D	D	D

Asset & Performance History

Date	NAV	1-Year Total Return
2017	18.96	13.98
2016	17.56	8.76
2015	17	-14.63
2014	21.06	-5.62
2013	23.57	-8.76
2012	27.12	16.23

Total Assets: $4,543,859,143

Asset Allocation

Asset	%
Cash	0%
Stocks	0%
US Stocks	0%
Bonds	100%
US Bonds	0%
Other	0%

Services Offered:

Investment Strategy: The investment seeks to replicate as closely as possible, before fees and expenses, the price and yield performance of the J.P. Morgan GBI-EM Global Core Index. The fund normally invests at least 80% of its total assets in securities that comprise the fund's benchmark index. The index is comprised of bonds issued by emerging market governments and denominated in the local currency of the issuer. It may concentrate its investments in a particular industry or group of industries to the extent that the index concentrates in an industry or group of industries. The fund is non-diversified. **Top Holdings:** Dominican Republic 8.9% Secretaria Tesouro Nacional 0% Uruguay (Republic of) 9.88% Brazil (Federative Republic) 9.86% Philippines (Republic Of) 6.25%

SPDR® Portfolio Short Term Corporate Bond ETF　　　　　　　　　　C　　HOLD

Ticker	Traded On	NAV	Total Assets ($)	Dividend Yield (TTM)	Turnover Ratio	Expense Ratio
SPSB	NYSE Arca	30.13	$4,476,443,422	2.32	67	0.07

Ratings

Reward	C
Risk	C+
Recent Upgrade/Downgrade	

Fund Information

Fund Type	Exchange Traded Funds
Category	US Fixed Income
Sub-Category	Short-Term Bond
Prospectus Objective	Corp Bond - Gen
Inception Date	Dec-09
Open to New Investments	Y

Prices

Price (as of 12/31/2018)	30.14
52-Week High	30.43
52-Week Low	29.99

Total Returns (%)

3-Month	6-Month	1-Year	3-Year	5-Year
0.73	1.46	1.46	5.36	7.14

3-Year Standard Deviation	0.85
Effective Duration	1.85

Valuation

Premium/Discount (1-Year Average)	0.02

Company Information

Provider	SPDR State Street Global Advisors
Manager/Tenure	Kyle Kelly (6), Christopher DiStefano (4), Frank Miethe (2)
Website	http://www.spdrs.com
Address	SPDR State Street Global Advisors State Street Financial Center, 1 Lincoln Street Boston MA 02111-2900 United States
Phone Number	617-786-3000

PERFORMANCE

Ratings History

Date	Overall Rating	Risk Rating	Reward Rating
Q4-18	C	C+	C
Q2-18	C	C+	C-
Q4-17	B	A+	C
Q4-16	C	C+	C
Q4-15	C	C+	C

Asset & Performance History

Date	NAV	1-Year Total Return
2017	30.4	1.43
2016	30.47	2.1
2015	30.34	0.8
2014	30.53	0.87
2013	30.65	1.37
2012	30.66	3.64

Total Assets: $4,476,443,422

Asset Allocation

Asset	%
Cash	1%
Stocks	0%
US Stocks	0%
Bonds	98%
US Bonds	79%
Other	0%

Services Offered:

Investment Strategy: The investment seeks to provide investment results that, before fees and expenses, correspond generally to the price and yield performance of the Bloomberg Barclays U.S. 1-3 Year Corporate Bond Index. The fund generally invests substantially all, but at least 80%, of its total assets in the securities comprising the index or in securities that the Adviser determines have economic characteristics that are substantially identical to the economic characteristics of the securities that comprise the index. The index is designed to measure the performance of the short term U.S. corporate bond market. The fund is non-diversified. **Top Holdings:** GE Capital International Funding Company Unlimited Company 2.34% Anheuser-Busch InBev Finance Inc. 2.65% Oracle Corporation 1.9% Allergan Funding SCS 3% Wells Fargo Bank, National Association 2.6%

WisdomTree Europe Hedged Equity Fund　　　　　　　　　　　　C-　　HOLD

Ticker	Traded On	NAV	Total Assets ($)	Dividend Yield (TTM)	Turnover Ratio	Expense Ratio
HEDJ	NYSE Arca	56.60	$4,408,854,666	2.89	20	0.58

Ratings

Reward	D+
Risk	C
Recent Upgrade/Downgrade	Down

Fund Information

Fund Type	Exchange Traded Funds
Category	Europe Equity Large Cap
Sub-Category	Europe Stock
Prospectus Objective	Foreign Stock
Inception Date	Dec-09
Open to New Investments	Y

Prices

Price (as of 12/31/2018)	56.44
52-Week High	67.39
52-Week Low	54.71

Total Returns (%)

3-Month	6-Month	1-Year	3-Year	5-Year
-11.04	-9.97	-9.26	12.63	27.05

3-Year Standard Deviation	11.83
Effective Duration	

Valuation

Premium/Discount (1-Year Average)	-0.15

Company Information

Provider	WisdomTree
Manager/Tenure	Richard A. Brown (8), Thomas J. Durante (8), Karen Q. Wong (8)
Website	http://www.wisdomtree.com
Address	WisdomTree 245 Park Avenue, 35th floor New York NY 10167 United States
Phone Number	866-909-9473

PERFORMANCE

Ratings History

Date	Overall Rating	Risk Rating	Reward Rating
Q4-18	C-	C	D+
Q2-18	C	C	C
Q4-17	B	B	B
Q4-16	C+	C	C+
Q4-15	B-	B+	C

Asset & Performance History

Date	NAV	1-Year Total Return
2017	63.91	13.89
2016	57.55	9.3
2015	54.25	5.86
2014	56.03	6.54
2013	55.64	21.5
2012	46.78	17.17

Total Assets: $4,408,854,666

Asset Allocation

Asset	%
Cash	0%
Stocks	100%
US Stocks	1%
Bonds	0%
US Bonds	0%
Other	0%

Services Offered:

Investment Strategy: The investment seeks to track the price and yield performance, before fees and expenses, of the WisdomTree Europe Hedged Equity Index. The fund invests at least 95% of its total assets (exclusive of collateral held from securities lending) in component securities of the index and investments that have economic characteristics that are substantially identical to the economic characteristics of such component securities. The index provides exposure to European equity securities, particularly shares of European exporters, while at the same time neutralizing exposure to fluctuations between the value of the U.S. dollar and the euro. The fund is non-diversified. **Top Holdings:** Sanofi SA Anheuser-Busch InBev SA/NV Unilever NV DR Banco Santander SA Telefonica SA

SPDR® S&P Biotech ETF   C-   HOLD

Ticker	Traded On	NAV	Total Assets ($)	Dividend Yield (TTM)	Turnover Ratio	Expense Ratio
XBI	NYSE Arca	72.03	$4,384,283,571	0.28	59	0.35

Ratings
Reward   C-
Risk   C
Recent Upgrade/Downgrade   Down

Fund Information
Fund Type   Exchange Traded Funds
Category   Healthcare Sector Equity
Sub-Category   Health
Prospectus Objective   Health
Inception Date   Jan-06
Open to New Investments   Y

Prices
Price (as of 12/31/2018)   71.75
52-Week High   101.15
52-Week Low   65.42

Total Returns (%)

3-Month	6-Month	1-Year	3-Year	5-Year
-23.73	-25.20	-14.90	3.40	69.95

3-Year Standard Deviation   30.87
Effective Duration

Valuation
Premium/Discount (1-Year Average)   -0.08

Company Information
Provider   SPDR State Street Global Advisors
Manager/Tenure   Michael J. Feehily (7), Karl A. Schneider (4), Raymond V. Donofrio (1)
Website   http://www.spdrs.com
Address   SPDR State Street Global Advisors State Street Financial Center, 1 Lincoln Street Boston MA 02111-2900 United States
Phone Number   617-786-3000

PERFORMANCE

Ratings History

Date	Overall Rating	Risk Rating	Reward Rating
Q4-18	C-	C	C-
Q2-18	C	C	C+
Q4-17	B-	C	B
Q4-16	C-	D+	C
Q4-15	B-	C+	B

Asset & Performance History

Date	NAV	1-Year Total Return
2017	84.83	43.69
2016	59.19	-15.45
2015	70.2	13.6
2014	62.13	44.66
2013	43.48	48.5
2012	29.33	32.85

Total Assets: $4,384,283,571
Asset Allocation

Asset	%
Cash	0%
Stocks	100%
US Stocks	100%
Bonds	0%
US Bonds	0%
Other	0%

Services Offered: Dividend Investment Plan, CashInvestment Plan

Investment Strategy: The investment seeks to provide investment results that, before fees and expenses, correspond generally to the total return performance of the S&P Biotechnology Select Industry Index derived from the biotechnology segment of a U.S. total market composite index. In seeking to track the performance of the S&P Biotechnology Select Industry Index (the "index"), the fund employs a sampling strategy. It generally invests substantially all, but at least 80%, of its total assets in the securities comprising the index. The index represents the biotechnology segment of the S&P Total Market Index ("S&P TMI"). The fund is non-diversified. **Top Holdings:** ACADIA Pharmaceuticals Inc Tesaro Inc Ionis Pharmaceuticals Inc Exelixis Inc Array BioPharma Inc

---

JPMorgan Ultra-Short Income ETF   C   HOLD

Ticker	Traded On	NAV	Total Assets ($)	Dividend Yield (TTM)	Turnover Ratio	Expense Ratio
JPST	BATS	50.09	$4,361,893,788	1.99		0.18

Ratings
Reward   D+
Risk   C+
Recent Upgrade/Downgrade   Up

Fund Information
Fund Type   Exchange Traded Funds
Category   US Fixed Income
Sub-Category   Ultrashort Bond
Prospectus Objective   Growth & Inc
Inception Date   May-17
Open to New Investments   Y

Prices
Price (as of 12/31/2018)   50.13
52-Week High   50.27
52-Week Low   50.02

Total Returns (%)

3-Month	6-Month	1-Year	3-Year	5-Year
0.49	1.20	2.19		

3-Year Standard Deviation
Effective Duration   0.51

Valuation
Premium/Discount (1-Year Average)   0.06

Company Information
Provider   JPMorgan
Manager/Tenure   Cecilia Junker (1), David N. Martucci (1), James McNerny (1), 1 other
Website   http://www.jpmorganfunds.com
Address   JPMorgan 270 Park Avenue New York NY 10017-2070 United States
Phone Number   800-480-4111

PERFORMANCE

Ratings History

Date	Overall Rating	Risk Rating	Reward Rating
Q4-18	C	C+	D+
Q2-18	C-	C+	D
Q4-17	U		
Q4-16			
Q4-15			

Asset & Performance History

Date	NAV	1-Year Total Return
2017	50.04	
2016		
2015		
2014		
2013		
2012		

Total Assets: $4,361,893,788
Asset Allocation

Asset	%
Cash	26%
Stocks	0%
US Stocks	0%
Bonds	73%
US Bonds	40%
Other	0%

Services Offered:

Investment Strategy: The investment seeks to provide current income while seeking to maintain a low volatility of principal. Under normal circumstances, the fund seeks to achieve its investment objective by investing at least 80% of its Assets in investment grade, U.S. dollar denominated short-term fixed, variable and floating rate debt. "Assets" means net assets, plus the amount of borrowings for investment purposes. As part of its principal investment strategy, it may invest in corporate securities, asset-backed securities, mortgage-backed and mortgage-related securities, and high quality money market instruments such as commercial paper and certificates of deposit. **Top Holdings:** United States Treasury Notes 1% Canadian Imperial Bank of Commerce New York Branch 3.08% ABN AMRO Bank N.V. 1.8% Aviation Capital Group LLC 0% Standard Chartered plc 2.1%

SPDR® Bloomberg Barclays Convertible Securities ETF   C   HOLD

Ticker	Traded On	NAV
CWB	NYSE Arca	46.68

Total Assets ($)	Dividend Yield (TTM)	Turnover Ratio	Expense Ratio
$4,356,461,928	3.7	32	0.4

Ratings
Reward	C-
Risk	C+
Recent Upgrade/Downgrade	Down

Fund Information
Fund Type	Exchange Traded Funds
Category	Convertibles
Sub-Category	Convertibles
Prospectus Objective	Convertible Bond
Inception Date	Apr-09
Open to New Investments	Y

Prices
Price (as of 12/31/2018)	46.79
52-Week High	54.93
52-Week Low	45.13

Total Returns (%)
3-Month	6-Month	1-Year	3-Year	5-Year
-9.35	-7.75	-2.31	25.47	34.06

3-Year Standard Deviation	8.04
Effective Duration	

Valuation
Premium/Discount (1-Year Average)	0.00

Company Information
Provider	SPDR State Street Global Advisors
Manager/Tenure	Michael J. Brunell (9), Christopher DiStefano (2)
Website	http://www.spdrs.com
Address	SPDR State Street Global Advisors State Street Financial Center, 1 Lincoln Street Boston MA 02111-2900 United States
Phone Number	617-786-3000

PERFORMANCE

Ratings History
Date	Overall Rating	Risk Rating	Reward Rating
Q4-18	C	C+	C-
Q2-18	B-	C+	B-
Q4-17	B-	B-	B-
Q4-16	C+	C+	C+
Q4-15	C	C+	C

Asset & Performance History
Date	NAV	1-Year Total Return
2017	50.67	14.54
2016	45.5	10.83
2015	43.16	-0.6
2014	46.66	7.5
2013	46.61	20.79
2012	40.1	15.19

Total Assets: $4,356,461,928
Asset Allocation
Asset	%
Cash	0%
Stocks	12%
US Stocks	12%
Bonds	0%
US Bonds	0%
Other	2%

Services Offered:

Investment Strategy: The investment seeks to provide investment results that, before fees and expenses, correspond generally to the price and yield performance of the Bloomberg Barclays U.S. Convertible Liquid Bond Index. The fund generally invests substantially all, but at least 80%, of its total assets in the securities comprising the index or in securities that the Adviser determines have economic characteristics that are substantially identical to the economic characteristics of the securities that comprise the index. The index is designed to represent the market of U.S. convertible securities, such as convertible bonds and convertible preferred stock. It is non-diversified. **Top Holdings:** Mandatory Exchangeable Trust Wells Fargo & Co 7 1/2 % Non Cum Perp Conv Pfd Shs -A- Series -L- Bank of America Corporation 7 1/4 % Non-Cum Perp Conv Pfd Shs Series -L- Becton Dickinson DISH Network Corporation 3.38%

ProShares UltraPro QQQ   C   HOLD

Ticker	Traded On	NAV
TQQQ	NAS CM	37.08

Total Assets ($)	Dividend Yield (TTM)	Turnover Ratio	Expense Ratio
$4,352,909,223	0		0.95

Ratings
Reward	C
Risk	C-
Recent Upgrade/Downgrade	Down

Fund Information
Fund Type	Exchange Traded Funds
Category	Trading Tools
Sub-Category	Trading--Leveraged Equity
Prospectus Objective	Growth
Inception Date	Feb-10
Open to New Investments	Y

Prices
Price (as of 12/31/2018)	37.04
52-Week High	72.50
52-Week Low	30.39

Total Returns (%)
3-Month	6-Month	1-Year	3-Year	5-Year
-48.16	-36.46	-19.64	95.08	259.19

3-Year Standard Deviation	41.14
Effective Duration	

Valuation
Premium/Discount (1-Year Average)	0.07

Company Information
Provider	ProShares
Manager/Tenure	Michael Neches (5), Devin Sullivan (0)
Website	http://www.proshares.com
Address	ProShares 7501 Wisconsin Avenue, Suite 1000 Bethesda MD 20814 United States
Phone Number	866-776-5125

PERFORMANCE

Ratings History
Date	Overall Rating	Risk Rating	Reward Rating
Q4-18	C	C-	C
Q2-18	B	C	B+
Q4-17	B	C	A
Q4-16	C+	C-	B-
Q4-15	B-	C+	B-

Asset & Performance History
Date	NAV	1-Year Total Return
2017	46.2	118.64
2016	21.13	11.04
2015	19.03	17.41
2014	16.21	56.81
2013	10.34	139.98
2012	4.31	51.94

Total Assets: $4,352,909,223
Asset Allocation
Asset	%
Cash	-200%
Stocks	300%
US Stocks	293%
Bonds	0%
US Bonds	0%
Other	0%

Services Offered:

Investment Strategy: The investment seeks daily investment results, before fees and expenses, that correspond to three times (3x) the daily performance of the NASDAQ-100 Index®. The fund invests in financial instruments that ProShare Advisors believes, in combination, should produce daily returns consistent with the fund's investment objective. The index includes 100 of the largest domestic and international non-financial companies listed on The Nasdaq Stock Market based on market capitalization. The fund is non-diversified. **Top Holdings:** Nasdaq 100 Index Swap Societe Generale Nasdaq 100 Index Swap Ubs Ag Nasdaq 100 Index Swap Deutsche Bank Ag Nasdaq 100 Index Swap Citibank, N.A. Nasdaq 100 Index Swap Bnp Paribas

Vanguard Utilities Index Fund ETF Shares
B- BUY

Ticker	Traded On	NAV	Total Assets ($)	Dividend Yield (TTM)	Turnover Ratio	Expense Ratio
VPU	NYSE Arca		$4,275,829,936	3.01	4	0.1

Ratings
Reward	B-
Risk	C+
Recent Upgrade/Downgrade	

Fund Information
Fund Type	Exchange Traded Funds
Category	Utilities Sector Equity
Sub-Category	Utilities
Prospectus Objective	Utility
Inception Date	Jan-04
Open to New Investments	Y

Prices
Price (as of 12/31/2018)	117.83
52-Week High	126.42
52-Week Low	105.16

Total Returns (%)
3-Month	6-Month	1-Year	3-Year	5-Year
0.82	2.19	4.09	37.65	66.26

3-Year Standard Deviation	11.63
Effective Duration	

Valuation
Premium/Discount (1-Year Average)	0.00

Company Information
Provider	Vanguard
Manager/Tenure	Michael A. Johnson (3), Awais Khan (1)
Website	http://www.vanguard.com
Address	Vanguard 100 Vanguard Boulevard Malvern PA 19355 United States
Phone Number	877-662-7447

PERFORMANCE

Ratings History

Date	Overall Rating	Risk Rating	Reward Rating
Q4-18	B-	C+	B-
Q2-18	B-	C	B
Q4-17	B	B	B
Q4-16	B-	C+	B
Q4-15	B-	C+	B

Asset & Performance History

Date	NAV	1-Year Total Return
2017	116.57	11.94
2016	106.94	16.84
2015	93.93	-4.83
2014	102.36	26.92
2013	83.33	14.93
2012	75.31	1.94

Total Assets: $4,275,829,936
Asset Allocation

Asset	%
Cash	0%
Stocks	100%
US Stocks	100%
Bonds	0%
US Bonds	0%
Other	0%

Services Offered:

Investment Strategy: The investment seeks to track the performance of a benchmark index. The fund employs an indexing investment approach designed to track the performance of the MSCI US Investable Market Index (IMI)/Utilities 25/50, an index made up of stocks of large, mid-size, and small U.S. companies within the utilities sector, as classified under the Global Industry Classification Standard (GICS). The Advisor attempts to replicate the target index by seeking to invest all, or substantially all, of its assets in the stocks that make up the index, in order to hold each stock in approximately the same proportion as its weighting in the index. The fund is non-diversified.
Top Holdings: NextEra Energy Inc Duke Energy Corp Dominion Energy Inc Southern Co Exelon Corp

---

Vanguard Energy Index Fund ETF Shares
C HOLD

Ticker	Traded On	NAV	Total Assets ($)	Dividend Yield (TTM)	Turnover Ratio	Expense Ratio
VDE	NYSE Arca		$4,209,131,814	2.8	5	0.1

Ratings
Reward	C
Risk	C-
Recent Upgrade/Downgrade	Down

Fund Information
Fund Type	Exchange Traded Funds
Category	Energy Sector Equity
Sub-Category	Equity Energy
Prospectus Objective	Natl Res
Inception Date	Sep-04
Open to New Investments	Y

Prices
Price (as of 12/31/2018)	77.11
52-Week High	108.92
52-Week Low	72.37

Total Returns (%)
3-Month	6-Month	1-Year	3-Year	5-Year
-27.40	-24.61	-20.30	0.29	-30.62

3-Year Standard Deviation	19.66
Effective Duration	

Valuation
Premium/Discount (1-Year Average)	-0.02

Company Information
Provider	Vanguard
Manager/Tenure	William A. Coleman (2), Awais Khan (1)
Website	http://www.vanguard.com
Address	Vanguard 100 Vanguard Boulevard Malvern PA 19355 United States
Phone Number	877-662-7447

PERFORMANCE

Ratings History

Date	Overall Rating	Risk Rating	Reward Rating
Q4-18	C	C-	C
Q2-18	C	C-	C+
Q4-17	C-	C	D+
Q4-16	C-	D	C
Q4-15	C	C	C

Asset & Performance History

Date	NAV	1-Year Total Return
2017	98.92	-2.3
2016	104.54	29.99
2015	83.16	-23.21
2014	111.66	-9.91
2013	126.44	25.77
2012	102.31	3.45

Total Assets: $4,209,131,814
Asset Allocation

Asset	%
Cash	1%
Stocks	99%
US Stocks	98%
Bonds	0%
US Bonds	0%
Other	0%

Services Offered:

Investment Strategy: The investment seeks to track the performance of a benchmark index. The fund employs an indexing investment approach designed to track the performance of the MSCI US Investable Market Index (IMI)/Energy 25/50, an index made up of stocks of large, mid-size, and small U.S. companies within the energy sector, as classified under the Global Industry Classification Standard (GICS). The Advisor attempts to replicate the target index by seeking to invest all, or substantially all, of its assets in the stocks that make up the index, in order to hold each stock in approximately the same proportion as its weighting in the index. The fund is non-diversified.
Top Holdings: Exxon Mobil Corp Chevron Corp ConocoPhillips Schlumberger Ltd EOG Resources Inc

iShares Edge MSCI USA Value Factor ETF   C   HOLD

Ticker	Traded On	NAV		Total Assets ($)	Dividend Yield (TTM)	Turnover Ratio	Expense Ratio
VLUE	BATS	72.47		$4,165,031,334	2.26	18	0.15

Ratings
Reward	C
Risk	C
Recent Upgrade/Downgrade	Down

Fund Information
Fund Type	Exchange Traded Funds
Category	US Equity Large Cap Value
Sub-Category	Large Value
Prospectus Objective	Growth
Inception Date	Apr-13
Open to New Investments	Y

Prices
Price (as of 12/31/2018)	72.57
52-Week High	89.39
52-Week Low	68.64

Total Returns (%)
3-Month	6-Month	1-Year	3-Year	5-Year
-17.15	-11.33	-11.18	25.31	35.73

3-Year Standard Deviation	10.8
Effective Duration	

Valuation
Premium/Discount (1-Year Average)	0.02

Company Information
Provider	iShares
Manager/Tenure	Diane Hsiung (5), Jennifer Hsui (5), Greg Savage (5), 3 others
Website	http://www.ishares.com
Address	iShares 400 Howard Street San Francisco CA 94105 United States
Phone Number	800-474-2737

PERFORMANCE

Ratings History
Date	Overall Rating	Risk Rating	Reward Rating
Q4-18	C	C	C
Q2-18	C+	C+	C+
Q4-17	B	B	B
Q4-16	B-	C	B
Q4-15	C	C	C

Asset & Performance History
Date	NAV	1-Year Total Return
2017	83.58	21.96
2016	70.15	15.68
2015	62.03	-3.54
2014	65.83	12.29
2013	59.63	
2012		

Total Assets: $4,165,031,334

Asset Allocation
Asset	%
Cash	0%
Stocks	100%
US Stocks	99%
Bonds	0%
US Bonds	0%
Other	0%

Services Offered:

Investment Strategy: The investment seeks to track the investment results of the MSCI USA Enhanced Value Index composed of U.S. large- and mid-capitalization stocks with value characteristics and relatively lower valuations. The fund generally will invest at least 90% of its assets in the component securities of the underlying index and may invest up to 10% of its assets in certain futures, options and swap contracts, cash and cash equivalents. The index is based on a traditional market capitalization-weighted parent index, the MSCI USA Index (the "parent index"). The parent index includes U.S. large- and mid- capitalization stocks. **Top Holdings:** AT&T Inc   Intel Corp   Pfizer Inc   Bank of America Corporation   Chevron Corp

---

iShares International Select Dividend ETF   C   HOLD

Ticker	Traded On	NAV		Total Assets ($)	Dividend Yield (TTM)	Turnover Ratio	Expense Ratio
IDV	BATS	28.76		$4,157,353,602	5.22	24	0.5

Ratings
Reward	D+
Risk	C+
Recent Upgrade/Downgrade	

Fund Information
Fund Type	Exchange Traded Funds
Category	Global Equity Large Cap
Sub-Category	Foreign Large Value
Prospectus Objective	Foreign Stock
Inception Date	Jun-07
Open to New Investments	Y

Prices
Price (as of 12/31/2018)	28.71
52-Week High	35.88
52-Week Low	27.96

Total Returns (%)
3-Month	6-Month	1-Year	3-Year	5-Year
-10.56	-7.04	-10.49	15.28	-2.32

3-Year Standard Deviation	10.93
Effective Duration	

Valuation
Premium/Discount (1-Year Average)	-0.18

Company Information
Provider	iShares
Manager/Tenure	Diane Hsiung (10), Greg Savage (10), Jennifer Hsui (6), 3 others
Website	http://www.ishares.com
Address	iShares 400 Howard Street San Francisco CA 94105 United States
Phone Number	800-474-2737

PERFORMANCE

Ratings History
Date	Overall Rating	Risk Rating	Reward Rating
Q4-18	C	C+	D+
Q2-18	C	C+	C
Q4-17	C+	C+	C+
Q4-16	D+	D+	D+
Q4-15	C-	D+	C

Asset & Performance History
Date	NAV	1-Year Total Return
2017	33.91	19.58
2016	29.71	7.71
2015	28.92	-10.91
2014	34.02	-4.89
2013	37.75	20.01
2012	33.09	17.72

Total Assets: $4,157,353,602

Asset Allocation
Asset	%
Cash	1%
Stocks	99%
US Stocks	0%
Bonds	0%
US Bonds	0%
Other	0%

Services Offered:

Investment Strategy: The investment seeks to track the investment results of the Dow Jones EPAC Select Dividend Index composed of relatively high dividend paying equities in non-U.S. developed markets. The fund generally will invest at least 90% of its assets in the component securities of the underlying index and in investments that have economic characteristics that are substantially identical to the component securities of the underlying index. The underlying index measures the performance of a select group of equity securities issued by companies that have provided relatively high dividend yields on a consistent basis over time. **Top Holdings:** AstraZeneca PLC   Macquarie Group Ltd   Commonwealth Bank of Australia   Royal Dutch Shell PLC Class A   SalMar ASA

Goldman Sachs ActiveBeta® U.S. Large Cap Equity ETF   C   HOLD

Ticker	Traded On	NAV	Total Assets ($)	Dividend Yield (TTM)	Turnover Ratio	Expense Ratio
GSLC	NYSE Arca	50.26	$4,066,844,094	1.67	16	0.09

Ratings
Reward   C
Risk   C+
Recent Upgrade/Downgrade   Down

Fund Information
Fund Type   Exchange Traded Funds
Category   US Equity Large Cap Blend
Sub-Category   Large Blend
Prospectus Objective   Growth
Inception Date   Sep-15
Open to New Investments   Y

Prices
Price (as of 12/31/2018)   50.29
52-Week High   59.25
52-Week Low   47.19

Total Returns (%)

3-Month	6-Month	1-Year	3-Year	5-Year
-14.10	-7.57	-4.01	27.75	

3-Year Standard Deviation   9.35
Effective Duration

Valuation
Premium/Discount (1-Year Average)   0.04

Company Information
Provider   Goldman Sachs
Manager/Tenure Raj Garigipati (3), Jamie McGregor (2)
Website   http://www.gsamfunds.com
Address   Goldman Sachs 200 West Stree New
                York NY 10282 United States
Phone Number   800-526-7384

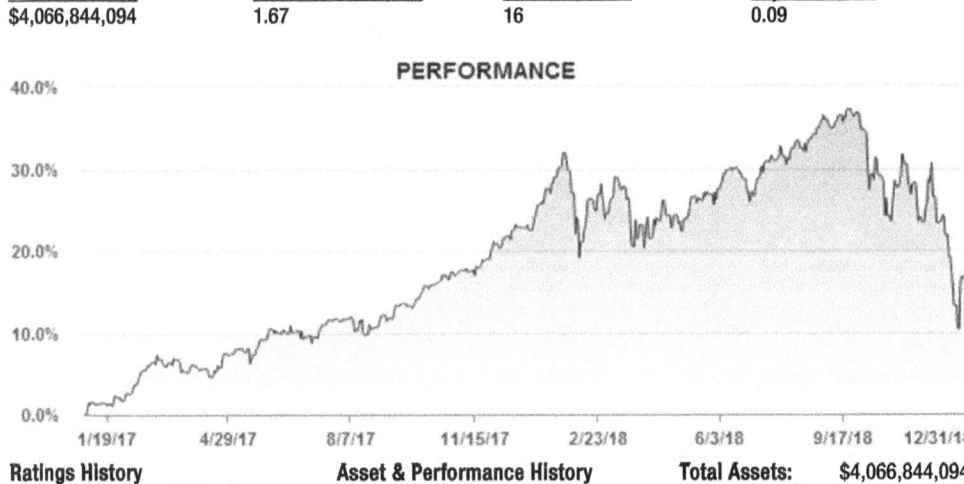

PERFORMANCE

Ratings History

Date	Overall Rating	Risk Rating	Reward Rating
Q4-18	C	C+	C
Q2-18	C+	C+	C
Q4-17	C	B	C+
Q4-16	D	C+	D+
Q4-15			

Asset & Performance History

Date	NAV	1-Year Total Return
2017	53.31	22.52
2016	44.32	8.1
2015	41.5	
2014		
2013		
2012		

Total Assets: $4,066,844,094

Asset Allocation

Asset	%
Cash	0%
Stocks	100%
US Stocks	100%
Bonds	0%
US Bonds	0%
Other	0%

Services Offered:

Investment Strategy: The investment seeks to provide investment results that closely correspond, before fees and expenses, to the performance of the Goldman Sachs ActiveBeta® U.S. Large Cap Equity Index. The fund seeks to achieve its investment objective by investing at least 80% of its assets (exclusive of collateral held from securities lending) in securities included in its underlying index, in depositary receipts representing securities included in its underlying index and in underlying stocks in respect of depositary receipts included in its underlying index. The index is designed to deliver exposure to equity securities of large capitalization U.S. issuers. **Top Holdings:** Microsoft Corp Apple Inc Amazon.com Inc Johnson & Johnson JPMorgan Chase & Co

---

Materials Select Sector SPDR® Fund   C   HOLD

Ticker	Traded On	NAV	Total Assets ($)	Dividend Yield (TTM)	Turnover Ratio	Expense Ratio
XLB	NYSE Arca	50.53	$4,034,542,626	1.98	17	0.13

Ratings
Reward   B-
Risk   C-
Recent Upgrade/Downgrade   Down

Fund Information
Fund Type   Exchange Traded Funds
Category   Natural Resources
Sub-Category   Natural Resources
Prospectus Objective   Natl Res
Inception Date   Dec-98
Open to New Investments   Y

Prices
Price (as of 12/31/2018)   50.52
52-Week High   64.09
52-Week Low   47.34

Total Returns (%)

3-Month	6-Month	1-Year	3-Year	5-Year
-13.07	-11.55	-14.77	23.21	20.84

3-Year Standard Deviation   14.07
Effective Duration

Valuation
Premium/Discount (1-Year Average)   0.00

Company Information
Provider   SPDR State Street Global Advisors
Manager/Tenure Michael J. Feehily (7), Karl A.
                Schneider (3), Ted Janowsky (1)
Website   http://www.spdrs.com
Address   SPDR State Street Global Advisors
                State Street Financial Center, 1
                Lincoln Street Boston MA 02111-2900
                United States
Phone Number   617-786-3000

PERFORMANCE

Ratings History

Date	Overall Rating	Risk Rating	Reward Rating
Q4-18	C	C-	B-
Q2-18	C+	C	B
Q4-17	B	C	B
Q4-16	C+	C	B
Q4-15	B	B-	B

Asset & Performance History

Date	NAV	1-Year Total Return
2017	60.48	23.95
2016	49.68	16.6
2015	43.46	-8.6
2014	48.59	7.31
2013	46.17	25.81
2012	37.55	14.74

Total Assets: $4,034,542,626

Asset Allocation

Asset	%
Cash	0%
Stocks	100%
US Stocks	85%
Bonds	0%
US Bonds	0%
Other	0%

Services Offered: Dividend Investment Plan, CashInvestment Plan

Investment Strategy: The investment seeks to provide investment results that, before expenses, correspond generally to the price and yield performance of publicly traded equity securities of companies in the Materials Select Sector Index. In seeking to track the performance of the index, the fund employs a replication strategy. It generally invests substantially all, but at least 95%, of its total assets in the securities comprising the index. The index includes securities of companies from the following industries: chemicals; metals and mining; paper and forest products; containers and packaging; and construction materials. The fund is non-diversified. **Top Holdings:** DowDuPont Inc Linde PLC Ecolab Inc Sherwin-Williams Co PPG Industries Inc

SPDR® S&P Regional Banking ETF   C   HOLD

Ticker	Traded On	NAV	Total Assets ($)	Dividend Yield (TTM)	Turnover Ratio	Expense Ratio
KRE	NYSE Arca	46.78	$3,971,386,770	1.76	52	0.35

Ratings
Reward   C
Risk   C
Recent Upgrade/Downgrade   Down

Fund Information
Fund Type   Exchange Traded Funds
Category   Financials Sector Equity
Sub-Category   Financial
Prospectus Objective   Financial
Inception Date   Jun-06
Open to New Investments   Y

Prices
Price (as of 12/31/2018)   46.79
52-Week High   65.74
52-Week Low   44.22

Total Returns (%)

3-Month	6-Month	1-Year	3-Year	5-Year
-19.89	-23.11	-18.97	17.46	25.62

3-Year Standard Deviation   21.22
Effective Duration

Valuation
Premium/Discount (1-Year Average)   0.03

Company Information
Provider   SPDR State Street Global Advisors
Manager/Tenure   Michael J. Feehily (7), Karl A.
                 Schneider (4), Payal Kapoor Gupta (1)
Website   http://www.spdrs.com
Address   SPDR State Street Global Advisors
                 State Street Financial Center, 1
                 Lincoln Street Boston MA 02111-2900
                 United States
Phone Number   617-786-3000

PERFORMANCE

Ratings History

Date	Overall Rating	Risk Rating	Reward Rating
Q4-18	C	C	C
Q2-18	B	B-	B
Q4-17	B+	C+	A
Q4-16	C	C	C
Q4-15	B+	A-	B

Asset & Performance History

Date	NAV	1-Year Total Return
2017	58.83	7.52
2016	55.53	33.02
2015	41.94	4.9
2014	40.71	1.95
2013	40.57	47.34
2012	27.97	16.91

Total Assets: $3,971,386,770
Asset Allocation

Asset	%
Cash	0%
Stocks	100%
US Stocks	97%
Bonds	0%
US Bonds	0%
Other	0%

Services Offered:

Investment Strategy: The investment seeks to provide investment results that, before fees and expenses, correspond generally to the total return performance of an index derived from the regional banking segment of the U.S. banking industry. In seeking to track the performance of the S&P Regional Banks Select Industry Index (the "index"), the fund employs a sampling strategy. It generally invests substantially all, but at least 80%, of its total assets in the securities comprising the index. The index represents the regional banks segment of the S&P Total Market Index ("S&P TMI"). The fund is non-diversified. **Top Holdings:** Signature Bank BB&T Corp First Republic Bank M&T Bank Corp PNC Financial Services Group Inc

---

VanEck Vectors Junior Gold Miners ETF   D   SELL

Ticker	Traded On	NAV	Total Assets ($)	Dividend Yield (TTM)	Turnover Ratio	Expense Ratio
GDXJ	NYSE Arca	30.11	$3,916,434,751	0.04	67	0.54

Ratings
Reward   D+
Risk   D
Recent Upgrade/Downgrade   Down

Fund Information
Fund Type   Exchange Traded Funds
Category   Prec Metals
Sub-Category   Equity Precious Metals
Prospectus Objective   Prec Metals
Inception Date   Nov-09
Open to New Investments   Y

Prices
Price (as of 12/31/2018)   30.22
52-Week High   35.74
52-Week Low   26.17

Total Returns (%)

3-Month	6-Month	1-Year	3-Year	5-Year
10.64	-6.36	-11.47	66.01	4.84

3-Year Standard Deviation   42.02
Effective Duration

Valuation
Premium/Discount (1-Year Average)   -0.11

Company Information
Provider   VanEck
Manager/Tenure   Hao-Hung (Peter) Liao (9), Guo Hua
                 (Jason) Jin (0)
Website   http://www.vaneck.com
Address   Van Eck Associates Corporation 666
                 Third Avenue New York NY 10017
                 United States
Phone Number   800-826-1115

PERFORMANCE

Ratings History

Date	Overall Rating	Risk Rating	Reward Rating
Q4-18	D	D	D+
Q2-18	C	C-	C
Q4-17	C-	D	C
Q4-16	C-	D+	C
Q4-15	D-	D-	D-

Asset & Performance History

Date	NAV	1-Year Total Return
2017	34.21	7.88
2016	31.72	73.83
2015	19.22	-19.47
2014	24.04	-21.57
2013	30.9	-60.94
2012	79.12	-15.95

Total Assets: $3,916,434,751
Asset Allocation

Asset	%
Cash	0%
Stocks	100%
US Stocks	3%
Bonds	0%
US Bonds	0%
Other	0%

Services Offered:

Investment Strategy: The investment seeks to replicate as closely as possible, before fees and expenses, the price and yield performance of the MVIS® Global Junior Gold Miners Index. The fund normally invests at least 80% of its total assets in securities that comprise the index. The index includes companies that generate at least 50% of their revenues from gold and/or silver mining/royalties/streaming or have mining projects with the potential to generate at least 50% of their revenues from gold and/or silver when developed. It is non-diversified. **Top Holdings:** Anglogold Ashanti Ltd ADR Evolution Mining Ltd Northern Star Resources Ltd Gold Fields Ltd ADR Pan American Silver Corp

SPDR® Portfolio Intermediate Term Corporate Bond ETF   C   HOLD

Ticker	Traded On	NAV	Total Assets ($)	Dividend Yield (TTM)	Turnover Ratio	Expense Ratio
SPIB	NYSE Arca	33.06	$3,912,886,145	3.05	33	0.07

Ratings
Reward   C-
Risk   C+
Recent Upgrade/Downgrade

Fund Information
Fund Type	Exchange Traded Funds
Category	US Fixed Income
Sub-Category	Corporate Bond
Prospectus Objective	Corp Bond - Gen
Inception Date	Feb-09
Open to New Investments	Y

Prices
Price (as of 12/31/2018)	33.04
52-Week High	34.22
52-Week Low	32.78

Total Returns (%)
3-Month	6-Month	1-Year	3-Year	5-Year
0.53	1.36	-0.35	7.63	13.10

3-Year Standard Deviation   2.33
Effective Duration   4.33

Valuation
Premium/Discount (1-Year Average)   0.01

Company Information
Provider	SPDR State Street Global Advisors
Manager/Tenure	Kyle Kelly (6), Christopher DiStefano (4), Frank Miethe (2)
Website	http://www.spdrs.com
Address	SPDR State Street Global Advisors State Street Financial Center, 1 Lincoln Street Boston MA 02111-2900 United States
Phone Number	617-786-3000

PERFORMANCE

Ratings History
Date	Overall Rating	Risk Rating	Reward Rating
Q4-18	C	C+	C-
Q2-18	C	C+	C-
Q4-17	B	A	C
Q4-16	C	C+	C
Q4-15	C	C+	C

Asset & Performance History
Date	NAV	1-Year Total Return
2017	34.2	3.48
2016	33.87	4.01
2015	33.43	0.91
2014	34.01	4.12
2013	33.54	-0.19
2012	34.63	8.6

Total Assets: $3,912,886,145
Asset Allocation
Asset	%
Cash	0%
Stocks	0%
US Stocks	0%
Bonds	98%
US Bonds	84%
Other	0%

Services Offered:

Investment Strategy: The investment seeks to provide investment results that correspond generally to the price and yield performance of the Bloomberg Barclays U.S. Intermediate Corporate Bond Index. The fund invests substantially all, but at least 80%, of its total assets in the securities comprising the index or in securities that the Adviser determines have economic characteristics that are substantially identical to the economic characteristics of the securities that comprise the index. The index is designed to measure the performance of U.S. corporate bonds that have a maturity of greater than or equal to 1 year and less than 10 years. It is non-diversified. **Top Holdings:** Anheuser-Busch InBev Finance Inc. 3.3% Anheuser-Busch Companies LLC / Anheuser-Busch InBev Worldwide Inc 3.65% CVS Health Corp 4.3% Anheuser-Busch InBev Finance Inc. 2.65% JPMorgan Chase & Co. 4.02%

Vanguard Tax-Exempt Bond Index Fund ETF Shares   C   HOLD

Ticker	Traded On	NAV	Total Assets ($)	Dividend Yield (TTM)	Turnover Ratio	Expense Ratio
VTEB	NYSE Arca		$3,911,728,869	2.22	18	0.09

Ratings
Reward   C-
Risk   C+
Recent Upgrade/Downgrade

Fund Information
Fund Type	Exchange Traded Funds
Category	US Muni Fixed Inc
Sub-Category	Muni National Interm
Prospectus Objective	Muni Bond - Natl
Inception Date	Aug-15
Open to New Investments	Y

Prices
Price (as of 12/31/2018)	51.05
52-Week High	51.68
52-Week Low	49.85

Total Returns (%)
3-Month	6-Month	1-Year	3-Year	5-Year
1.55	1.28	0.90	6.24	

3-Year Standard Deviation   3.24
Effective Duration   5.84

Valuation
Premium/Discount (1-Year Average)   0.02

Company Information
Provider	Vanguard
Manager/Tenure	Adam M. Ferguson (3)
Website	http://www.vanguard.com
Address	Vanguard 100 Vanguard Boulevard Malvern PA 19355 United States
Phone Number	877-662-7447

PERFORMANCE

Ratings History
Date	Overall Rating	Risk Rating	Reward Rating
Q4-18	C	C+	C-
Q2-18	C	C+	C-
Q4-17	C	B	C
Q4-16	D	C	D+
Q4-15	U		

Asset & Performance History
Date	NAV	1-Year Total Return
2017	51.61	4.98
2016	50.15	0.27
2015	50.81	
2014		
2013		
2012		

Total Assets: $3,911,728,869
Asset Allocation
Asset	%
Cash	2%
Stocks	0%
US Stocks	0%
Bonds	98%
US Bonds	98%
Other	0%

Services Offered:

Investment Strategy: The investment seeks to track the Standard & Poor's National AMT-Free Municipal Bond Index, which measures the performance of the investment-grade segment of the U.S. municipal bond market. This index includes municipal bonds from issuers that are primarily state or local governments or agencies whose interest is exempt from U.S. federal income taxes and the federal alternative minimum tax (AMT). All of the fund's investments will be selected through the sampling process, and at least 80% of the fund's assets will be invested in securities held in the index. **Top Holdings:** METROPOLITAN TRANSN AUTH N Y 5% NEW JERSEY ST TRANSN TR FD AUTH 5.88% LOS ANGELES CALIF 5% NEW YORK N Y 5% CALIFORNIA ST 5%

iShares MSCI All Country Asia ex Japan ETF   C-   HOLD

Ticker	Traded On	NAV	Total Assets ($)	Dividend Yield (TTM)	Turnover Ratio	Expense Ratio
AAXJ	NAS CM	63.65	$3,891,710,286	2.47	13	0.69

Ratings
Reward	C-
Risk	C-
Recent Upgrade/Downgrade	Down

Fund Information
Fund Type	Exchange Traded Funds
Category	Asia ex-Japan Equity
Sub-Category	Pacific/Asia ex-Japan Stk
Prospectus Objective	Pacific Stock
Inception Date	Aug-08
Open to New Investments	Y

Prices
Price (as of 12/31/2018)	63.53
52-Week High	83.50
52-Week Low	61.12

Total Returns (%)
3-Month	6-Month	1-Year	3-Year	5-Year
-8.70	-9.69	-14.81	25.48	17.56

3-Year Standard Deviation	14.63
Effective Duration	

Valuation
Premium/Discount (1-Year Average)	-0.15

Company Information
Provider	iShares
Manager/Tenure	Diane Hsiung (10), Greg Savage (10), Jennifer Hsui (6), 3 others
Website	http://www.ishares.com
Address	iShares 400 Howard Street San Francisco CA 94105 United States
Phone Number	800-474-2737

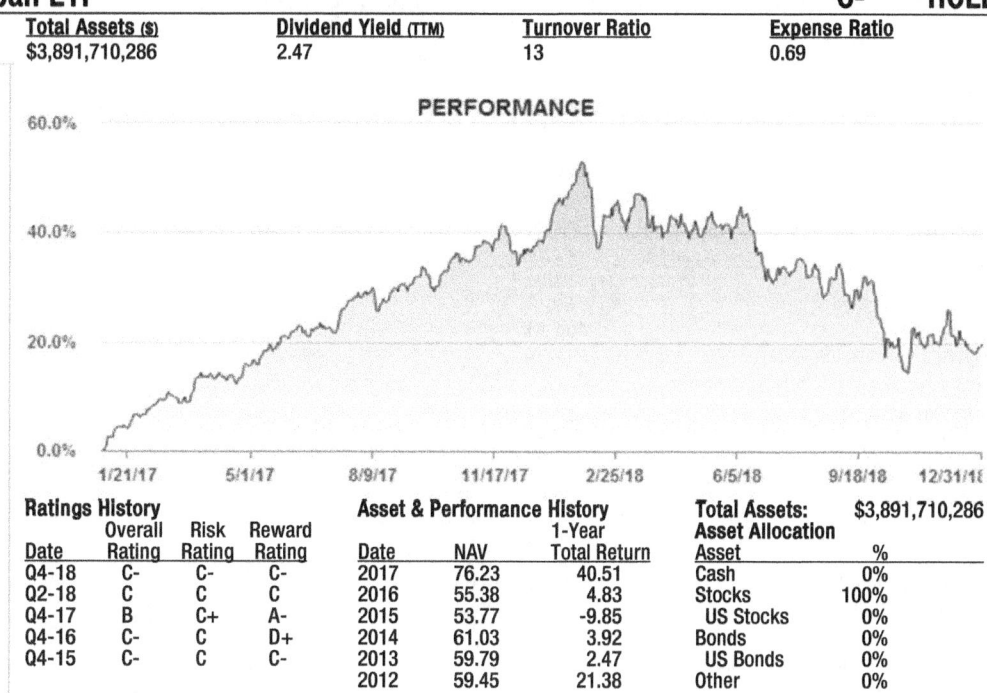

PERFORMANCE

Ratings History
Date	Overall Rating	Risk Rating	Reward Rating
Q4-18	C-	C-	C-
Q2-18	C	C	C
Q4-17	B	C+	A-
Q4-16	C-	C	D+
Q4-15	C-	C	C-

Asset & Performance History
Date	NAV	1-Year Total Return
2017	76.23	40.51
2016	55.38	4.83
2015	53.77	-9.85
2014	61.03	3.92
2013	59.79	2.47
2012	59.45	21.38

Total Assets: $3,891,710,286
Asset Allocation
Asset	%
Cash	0%
Stocks	100%
US Stocks	0%
Bonds	0%
US Bonds	0%
Other	0%

Services Offered:

Investment Strategy: The investment seeks to track the investment results of the MSCI AC Asia ex Japan Index. The fund will invest at least 90% of its assets in the component securities of the index and in investments that have economic characteristics that are substantially identical to the component securities of the index. The index is a free float-adjusted market capitalization index designed to measure equity market performance of securities from the following 11 developed, emerging and frontier market countries or regions: China, Hong Kong, India, Indonesia, Malaysia, Pakistan, the Philippines, Singapore, South Korea, Taiwan and Thailand. **Top Holdings:** Tencent Holdings Ltd Alibaba Group Holding Ltd ADR Taiwan Semiconductor Manufacturing Co Ltd Samsung Electronics Co Ltd AIA Group Ltd

---

Vanguard Mega Cap Growth Index Fund ETF Shares   C   HOLD

Ticker	Traded On	NAV	Total Assets ($)	Dividend Yield (TTM)	Turnover Ratio	Expense Ratio
MGK	NYSE Arca		$3,890,158,110	1.29	9	0.07

Ratings
Reward	C
Risk	C+
Recent Upgrade/Downgrade	Down

Fund Information
Fund Type	Exchange Traded Funds
Category	US Equity Large Cap Growth
Sub-Category	Large Growth
Prospectus Objective	Growth
Inception Date	Dec-07
Open to New Investments	Y

Prices
Price (as of 12/31/2018)	107.01
52-Week High	128.70
52-Week Low	99.52

Total Returns (%)
3-Month	6-Month	1-Year	3-Year	5-Year
-17.49	-10.88	-3.67	32.68	56.41

3-Year Standard Deviation	11.17
Effective Duration	

Valuation
Premium/Discount (1-Year Average)	0.02

Company Information
Provider	Vanguard
Manager/Tenure	Gerard C. O'Reilly (3), Michael A. Johnson (2)
Website	http://www.vanguard.com
Address	Vanguard 100 Vanguard Boulevard Malvern PA 19355 United States
Phone Number	877-662-7447

PERFORMANCE

Ratings History
Date	Overall Rating	Risk Rating	Reward Rating
Q4-18	C	C+	C
Q2-18	B-	C+	B
Q4-17	B	B	B
Q4-16	C+	C-	B-
Q4-15	C+	B-	C+

Asset & Performance History
Date	NAV	1-Year Total Return
2017	111.2	29.26
2016	87.02	6.03
2015	83.07	3.71
2014	81.24	13.65
2013	72.42	32.48
2012	55.46	17.23

Total Assets: $3,890,158,110
Asset Allocation
Asset	%
Cash	2%
Stocks	98%
US Stocks	97%
Bonds	0%
US Bonds	0%
Other	0%

Services Offered:

Investment Strategy: The investment seeks to track the performance of a benchmark index. The fund employs an indexing investment approach designed to track the performance of the CRSP US Mega Cap Growth Index. The index is a float-adjusted, market-capitalization-weighted index designed to measure equity market performance of mega-capitalization growth stocks in the United States. The Advisor attempts to replicate the target index by investing all, or substantially all, of its assets in the stocks that make up the index, holding each stock in approximately the same proportion as its weighting in the index. **Top Holdings:** Apple Inc Amazon.com Inc Facebook Inc A Alphabet Inc A Alphabet Inc Class C

Schwab Fundamental International Large Company Index ETF   C-   HOLD

Ticker	Traded On	NAV	Total Assets ($)	Dividend Yield (TTM)	Turnover Ratio	Expense Ratio
FNDF	NYSE Arca	25.24	$3,876,309,581	2.56	10	0.25

Ratings
Reward	D+
Risk	C-
Recent Upgrade/Downgrade	Down

Fund Information
Fund Type	Exchange Traded Funds
Category	Global Equity Large Cap
Sub-Category	Foreign Large Value
Prospectus Objective	World Stock
Inception Date	Aug-13
Open to New Investments	Y

Prices
Price (as of 12/31/2018)	25.22
52-Week High	32.48
52-Week Low	24.38

Total Returns (%)
3-Month	6-Month	1-Year	3-Year	5-Year
-12.81	-10.57	-14.18	14.42	3.05

3-Year Standard Deviation	11.19
Effective Duration	

Valuation
Premium/Discount (1-Year Average)	0.09

Company Information
Provider	Schwab ETFs
Manager/Tenure	Chuck Craig (5), Jane Qin (5), Christopher Bliss (1), 1 other
Website	http://www.schwabetfs.com
Address	Schwab ETFs United States
Phone Number	800-435-4000

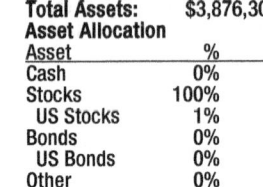

PERFORMANCE

Ratings History
Date	Overall Rating	Risk Rating	Reward Rating
Q4-18	C-	C-	D+
Q2-18	C	C+	C
Q4-17	B-	C	B
Q4-16	C-	C-	D+
Q4-15	C-	C+	D

Asset & Performance History
Date	NAV	1-Year Total Return
2017	30.4	23.85
2016	25.13	7.7
2015	23.9	-5.14
2014	25.73	-5.04
2013	27.59	
2012		

Total Assets: $3,876,309,581
Asset Allocation
Asset	%
Cash	0%
Stocks	100%
US Stocks	1%
Bonds	0%
US Bonds	0%
Other	0%

Services Offered:

Investment Strategy: The investment seeks to track as closely as possible, before fees and expenses, the total return of the Russell RAFI™ Developed ex US Large Company Index. The fund will invest at least 90% of its net assets in stocks included in the index, including depositary receipts representing securities of the index; which may be in the form of American Depositary receipts, Global Depositary receipts and European Depositary receipts. The index measures the performance of the large company size segment by fundamental overall company scores, which are created using as the universe the companies included in the Russell Developed ex US Index. **Top Holdings:** BP PLC Total SA Royal Dutch Shell PLC B Toyota Motor Corp Royal Dutch Shell PLC Class A

---

iShares MSCI South Korea Capped ETF   D+   SELL

Ticker	Traded On	NAV	Total Assets ($)	Dividend Yield (TTM)	Turnover Ratio	Expense Ratio
EWY	NYSE Arca	58.86	$3,838,243,274	3.6	18	0.62

Ratings
Reward	C-
Risk	D+
Recent Upgrade/Downgrade	Down

Fund Information
Fund Type	Exchange Traded Funds
Category	Korea Equity
Sub-Category	Miscellaneous Region
Prospectus Objective	Pacific Stock
Inception Date	May-00
Open to New Investments	Y

Prices
Price (as of 12/31/2018)	58.86
52-Week High	79.04
52-Week Low	56.85

Total Returns (%)
3-Month	6-Month	1-Year	3-Year	5-Year
-12.36	-9.53	-20.30	23.28	1.29

3-Year Standard Deviation	18.12
Effective Duration	

Valuation
Premium/Discount (1-Year Average)	-0.03

Company Information
Provider	iShares
Manager/Tenure	Diane Hsiung (10), Greg Savage (10), Jennifer Hsui (5), 1 other
Website	http://www.ishares.com
Address	iShares 400 Howard Street San Francisco CA 94105 United States
Phone Number	800-474-2737

PERFORMANCE

Ratings History
Date	Overall Rating	Risk Rating	Reward Rating
Q4-18	D+	D+	C-
Q2-18	C+	B	C
Q4-17	B	C	A
Q4-16	D+	C-	D+
Q4-15	D	D	D

Asset & Performance History
Date	NAV	1-Year Total Return
2017	74.86	44.4
2016	53.38	7.12
2015	50.43	-6.72
2014	55.36	-11.9
2013	63.6	3.49
2012	62.34	19.9

Total Assets: $3,838,243,274
Asset Allocation
Asset	%
Cash	0%
Stocks	100%
US Stocks	0%
Bonds	0%
US Bonds	0%
Other	0%

Services Offered: CashInvestment Plan

Investment Strategy: The investment seeks to track the investment results of the MSCI Korea 25/50 Index. The fund will at all times invest at least 80% of its assets in the securities of its underlying index and in depositary receipts representing securities in its underlying index. The underlying index is a free float-adjusted market capitalization-weighted index with a capping methodology applied to issuer weights so that no single issuer of a component exceeds 25% of the underlying index weight, and all issuers with a weight above 5% do not cumulatively exceed 50% of the underlying index weight. The fund is non-diversified. **Top Holdings:** Samsung Electronics Co Ltd SK Hynix Inc Celltrion Inc POSCO KB Financial Group Inc

---

Vanguard Industrials Index Fund ETF Shares C HOLD

Ticker	Traded On	NAV	Total Assets ($)	Dividend Yield (TTM)	Turnover Ratio	Expense Ratio
VIS	NYSE Arca		$3,832,388,967	1.66	4	0.1

Ratings
Reward C
Risk C+
Recent Upgrade/Downgrade Down

Fund Information
Fund Type Exchange Traded Funds
Category Industrials Sector Equity
Sub-Category Industrials
Prospectus Objective Unaligned
Inception Date Sep-04
Open to New Investments Y

Prices
Price (as of 12/31/2018) 120.41
52-Week High 150.77
52-Week Low 112.87

Total Returns (%)

3-Month	6-Month	1-Year	3-Year	5-Year
-19.26	-11.65	-14.80	24.60	30.36

3-Year Standard Deviation 13.34
Effective Duration

Valuation
Premium/Discount (1-Year Average) -0.02

Company Information
Provider Vanguard
Manager/Tenure Walter Nejman (2), Michelle Louie (1)
Website http://www.vanguard.com
Address Vanguard 100 Vanguard Boulevard
Malvern PA 19355 United States
Phone Number 877-662-7447

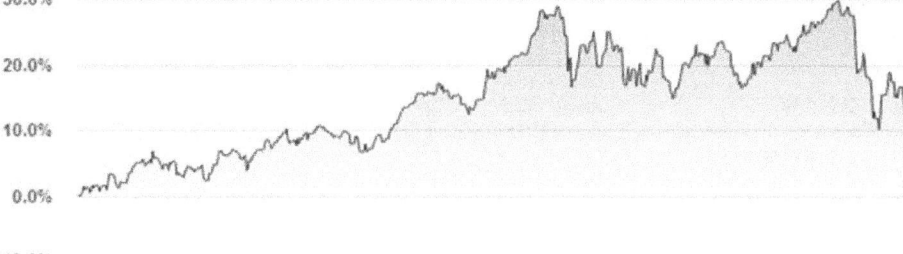

PERFORMANCE

Ratings History

Date	Overall Rating	Risk Rating	Reward Rating
Q4-18	C	C+	C
Q2-18	C	C+	C
Q4-17	B	B-	B+
Q4-16	B-	C	B
Q4-15	C	C	C+

Asset & Performance History

Date	NAV	1-Year Total Return
2017	142.27	21.38
2016	119.15	20.04
2015	100.94	-3.58
2014	106.81	8.5
2013	99.99	41.93
2012	71.21	17.09

Total Assets: $3,832,388,967
Asset Allocation

Asset	%
Cash	0%
Stocks	100%
US Stocks	99%
Bonds	0%
US Bonds	0%
Other	0%

Services Offered:

Investment Strategy: The investment seeks to track the performance of a benchmark index. The fund employs an indexing investment approach designed to track the performance of the MSCI US Investable Market Index (IMI)/Industrials 25/50, an index made up of stocks of large, mid-size, and small U.S. companies within the industrials sector, as classified under the Global Industry Classification Standard (GICS). The Advisor attempts to replicate the target index by seeking to invest all, or substantially all, of its assets in the stocks that make up the index, in order to hold each stock in approximately the same proportion as its weighting in the index. The fund is non-diversified. **Top Holdings:** Boeing Co Union Pacific Corp 3M Co Honeywell International Inc United Technologies Corp

---

ProShares S&P 500 Dividend Aristocrats ETF C HOLD

Ticker	Traded On	NAV	Total Assets ($)	Dividend Yield (TTM)	Turnover Ratio	Expense Ratio
NOBL	BATS	60.53	$3,799,193,573	2.1		0.35

Ratings
Reward C
Risk C+
Recent Upgrade/Downgrade Down

Fund Information
Fund Type Exchange Traded Funds
Category US Equity Large Cap Blend
Sub-Category Large Blend
Prospectus Objective Growth
Inception Date Oct-13
Open to New Investments Y

Prices
Price (as of 12/31/2018) 60.54
52-Week High 68.36
52-Week Low 57.62

Total Returns (%)

3-Month	6-Month	1-Year	3-Year	5-Year
-9.11	-1.42	-3.17	30.78	51.59

3-Year Standard Deviation 9.31
Effective Duration

Valuation
Premium/Discount (1-Year Average) 0.00

Company Information
Provider ProShares
Manager/Tenure Michael Neches (5), Devin Sullivan (0)
Website http://www.proshares.com
Address ProShares 7501 Wisconsin Avenue,
Suite 1000 Bethesda MD 20814
United States
Phone Number 866-776-5125

PERFORMANCE

Ratings History

Date	Overall Rating	Risk Rating	Reward Rating
Q4-18	C	C+	C
Q2-18	C	C+	C
Q4-17	B	B	B
Q4-16	C+	C+	C+
Q4-15	C-	C+	C

Asset & Performance History

Date	NAV	1-Year Total Return
2017	63.96	21.22
2016	53.75	11.42
2015	49.28	0.46
2014	50.06	15.38
2013	44.13	
2012		

Total Assets: $3,799,193,573
Asset Allocation

Asset	%
Cash	0%
Stocks	100%
US Stocks	98%
Bonds	0%
US Bonds	0%
Other	0%

Services Offered:

Investment Strategy: The investment seeks investment results, before fees and expenses, that track the performance of the S&P 500® Dividend Aristocrats® Index (the "index"). The fund will invest at least 80% of its total assets in component securities (i.e., securities of the index and comparable securities that have economic characteristics that are substantially identical to the economic characteristics of the securities of the index). The index contains a minimum of 40 stocks, which are equally weighted, and no single sector is allowed to comprise more than 30% of the index weight. **Top Holdings:** Franklin Resources Inc AbbVie Inc Illinois Tool Works Inc Stanley Black & Decker Inc W.W. Grainger Inc

iShares MSCI China ETF

C-   **HOLD**

Ticker	Traded On	NAV	Total Assets ($)	Dividend Yield (TTM)	Turnover Ratio	Expense Ratio
MCHI	NAS CM	52.96	$3,793,426,706	2.04	14	0.59

Ratings
Reward	C-
Risk	D+
Recent Upgrade/Downgrade	Down

Fund Information
Fund Type	Exchange Traded Funds
Category	Greater China Equity
Sub-Category	China Region
Prospectus Objective	Pacific Stock
Inception Date	Mar-11
Open to New Investments	Y

Prices
Price (as of 12/31/2018)	52.62
52-Week High	76.72
52-Week Low	51.05

Total Returns (%)
3-Month	6-Month	1-Year	3-Year	5-Year
-10.56	-17.58	-19.18	24.16	22.42

3-Year Standard Deviation	18.88
Effective Duration	

Valuation
Premium/Discount (1-Year Average)	0.07

Company Information
Provider	iShares
Manager/Tenure	Diane Hsiung (7), Greg Savage (7), Jennifer Hsui (5), 1 other
Website	http://www.ishares.com
Address	iShares 400 Howard Street San Francisco CA 94105 United States
Phone Number	800-474-2737

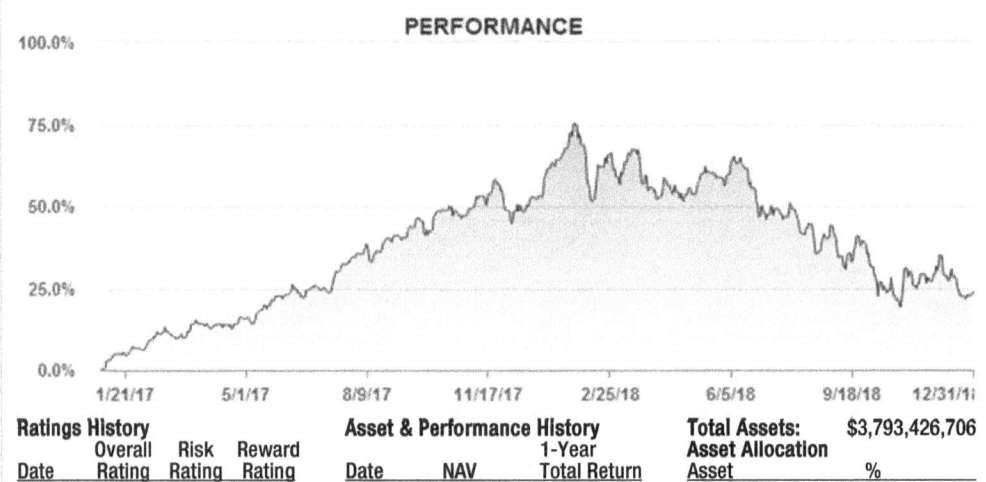

PERFORMANCE

Ratings History
Date	Overall Rating	Risk Rating	Reward Rating
Q4-18	C-	D+	C-
Q2-18	C	C	C
Q4-17	B+	C	A
Q4-16	C	C-	C
Q4-15	C	C	C

Asset & Performance History
Date	NAV	1-Year Total Return
2017	66.48	53.02
2016	44.16	0.4
2015	44.73	-8.25
2014	49.95	7.46
2013	47.67	3.11
2012	47.51	21.93

Total Assets: $3,793,426,706

Asset Allocation
Asset	%
Cash	0%
Stocks	100%
US Stocks	0%
Bonds	0%
US Bonds	0%
Other	0%

Services Offered:

Investment Strategy: The investment seeks to track the investment results of the MSCI China Index. The fund generally will invest at least 90% of its assets in the component securities of the underlying index and in investments that have economic characteristics that are substantially identical to the component securities of the underlying index. The index is a free float-adjusted market capitalization-weighted index designed to measure the performance of equity securities in the top 85% in market capitalization of the Chinese equity securities markets, as represented by the H-Shares and B-Shares markets. The fund is non-diversified. **Top Holdings:** Tencent Holdings Ltd Alibaba Group Holding Ltd ADR China Construction Bank Corp H China Mobile Ltd Baidu Inc ADR

Schwab Short-Term U.S. Treasury ETF™

C   **HOLD**

Ticker	Traded On	NAV	Total Assets ($)	Dividend Yield (TTM)	Turnover Ratio	Expense Ratio
SCHO	NYSE Arca	49.88	$3,773,504,792	1.66	65	0.06

Ratings
Reward	C-
Risk	C+
Recent Upgrade/Downgrade	Up

Fund Information
Fund Type	Exchange Traded Funds
Category	US Fixed Income
Sub-Category	Short Government
Prospectus Objective	Govt Bond - Treasury
Inception Date	Aug-10
Open to New Investments	Y

Prices
Price (as of 12/31/2018)	49.91
52-Week High	50.04
52-Week Low	49.42

Total Returns (%)
3-Month	6-Month	1-Year	3-Year	5-Year
1.29	1.51	1.49	2.64	3.66

3-Year Standard Deviation	0.76
Effective Duration	1.93

Valuation
Premium/Discount (1-Year Average)	0.02

Company Information
Provider	Schwab ETFs
Manager/Tenure	Matthew Hastings (8), Mark R. McKissick (1)
Website	http://www.schwabetfs.com
Address	Schwab ETFs United States
Phone Number	800-435-4000

PERFORMANCE

Ratings History
Date	Overall Rating	Risk Rating	Reward Rating
Q4-18	C	C+	C-
Q2-18	C-	C	D+
Q4-17	C	C	C-
Q4-16	C	C+	C
Q4-15	C	C+	C

Asset & Performance History
Date	NAV	1-Year Total Return
2017	50.03	0.35
2016	50.41	0.78
2015	50.43	0.43
2014	50.55	0.54
2013	50.51	0.25
2012	50.53	0.35

Total Assets: $3,773,504,792

Asset Allocation
Asset	%
Cash	0%
Stocks	0%
US Stocks	0%
Bonds	100%
US Bonds	100%
Other	0%

Services Offered:

Investment Strategy: The investment seeks to track as closely as possible, before fees and expenses, the total return of the Bloomberg Barclays US Treasury 1-3 Year Index. The fund will invest at least 90% of its net assets (including, for this purpose, any borrowings for investment purposes) in securities included in the index. The index includes all publicly-issued U.S. Treasury securities that have a remaining maturity of greater than or equal to one year and less than three years, are rated investment grade, and have $300 million or more of outstanding face value. The securities in the index must be denominated in U.S. dollars and must be fixed-rate and non-convertible. **Top Holdings:** United States Treasury Notes 2.88% United States Treasury Notes 2.75% United States Treasury Notes 2.88% United States Treasury Notes 2% United States Treasury Notes 2.62%

iShares U.S. Technology ETF   B-   BUY

Ticker	Traded On	NAV	Total Assets ($)	Dividend Yield (TTM)	Turnover Ratio	Expense Ratio
IYW	NYSE Arca	159.77	$3,733,774,705	0.82	15	0.43

Ratings

Reward	B
Risk	C
Recent Upgrade/Downgrade	Down

Fund Information

Fund Type	Exchange Traded Funds
Category	Technology Sector Equity
Sub-Category	Technology
Prospectus Objective	Technology
Inception Date	May-00
Open to New Investments	Y

Prices

Price (as of 12/31/2018)	159.93
52-Week High	195.97
52-Week Low	148.42

Total Returns (%)

3-Month	6-Month	1-Year	3-Year	5-Year
-17.60	-11.10	-0.96	53.78	90.48

3-Year Standard Deviation	14.71
Effective Duration	

Valuation

Premium/Discount (1-Year Average)	0.01

Company Information

Provider	iShares
Manager/Tenure	Diane Hsiung (10), Greg Savage (10), Jennifer Hsui (6), 3 others
Website	http://www.ishares.com
Address	iShares 400 Howard Street San Francisco CA 94105 United States
Phone Number	800-474-2737

PERFORMANCE

Ratings History

Date	Overall Rating	Risk Rating	Reward Rating
Q4-18	B-	C	B
Q2-18	B	C+	A-
Q4-17	A-	B	A+
Q4-16	B	C+	A-
Q4-15	B	B	B

Asset & Performance History

Date	NAV	1-Year Total Return
2017	162.67	36.58
2016	120.2	13.68
2015	107.02	3.66
2014	104.42	19.49
2013	88.43	26.47
2012	70.76	11.77

Total Assets: $3,733,774,705

Asset Allocation

Asset	%
Cash	0%
Stocks	100%
US Stocks	99%
Bonds	0%
US Bonds	0%
Other	0%

Services Offered: CashInvestment Plan

Investment Strategy: The investment seeks to track the investment results of the Dow Jones U.S. Technology Index. The fund generally invests at least 90% of its assets in securities of the underlying index and in depositary receipts representing securities of the underlying index. The underlying index measures the performance of the technology sector of the U.S. equity market and may include large-, mid- or small-capitalization companies. The fund is non-diversified. **Top Holdings:** Microsoft Corp Apple Inc Facebook Inc A Alphabet Inc Class C Alphabet Inc A

Invesco Emerging Markets Sovereign Debt ETF   C-   HOLD

Ticker	Traded On	NAV	Total Assets ($)	Dividend Yield (TTM)	Turnover Ratio	Expense Ratio
PCY	NYSE Arca	26.38	$3,686,787,232	4.87	30	0.5

Ratings

Reward	D
Risk	C
Recent Upgrade/Downgrade	

Fund Information

Fund Type	Exchange Traded Funds
Category	Emerging Mkts Fixed Inc
Sub-Category	Emerging Markets Bond
Prospectus Objective	Worldwide Bond
Inception Date	Oct-07
Open to New Investments	Y

Prices

Price (as of 12/31/2018)	26.42
52-Week High	29.71
52-Week Low	25.56

Total Returns (%)

3-Month	6-Month	1-Year	3-Year	5-Year
-1.12	1.92	-6.14	11.94	24.65

3-Year Standard Deviation	6.87
Effective Duration	9.31

Valuation

Premium/Discount (1-Year Average)	-0.20

Company Information

Provider	Invesco
Manager/Tenure	Philip Fang (11), Peter Hubbard (11), Jeffrey W. Kernagis (11), 2 others
Website	http://www.invesco.com/us
Address	Invesco 11 Greenway Plaza, Ste. 2500 Houston TX 77046 United States
Phone Number	800-659-1005

PERFORMANCE

Ratings History

Date	Overall Rating	Risk Rating	Reward Rating
Q4-18	C-	C	D
Q2-18	C-	C	D+
Q4-17	B	A	C+
Q4-16	C+	C+	C
Q4-15	C	C	C

Asset & Performance History

Date	NAV	1-Year Total Return
2017	29.49	9.43
2016	28.28	8.99
2015	27.31	1.98
2014	28.24	9.18
2013	27.07	-9.78
2012	31.36	20.97

Total Assets: $3,686,787,232

Asset Allocation

Asset	%
Cash	0%
Stocks	0%
US Stocks	0%
Bonds	100%
US Bonds	0%
Other	0%

Services Offered:

Investment Strategy: The investment seeks to track the investment results (before fees and expenses) of the DBIQ Emerging Market USD Liquid Balanced Index (the "underlying index"). The fund generally will invest at least 80% of its total assets in U.S. dollar-denominated government bonds from emerging market countries that comprise the underlying index. The underlying index measures potential returns of a theoretical portfolio of liquid emerging market U.S. dollar-denominated government bonds. **Top Holdings:** China (People's Republic Of) 3.5% Trinidad & Tobago 4.5% Republika Slovenija 5.25% Croatia (Republic Of) 6% Croatia (Republic Of) 5.5%

SPDR® Nuveen Bloomberg Barclays Short Term Municipal Bond ETF   C-   HOLD

Ticker	Traded On	NAV	Total Assets ($)	Dividend Yield (TTM)	Turnover Ratio	Expense Ratio
SHM	NYSE Arca	48.05	$3,681,013,644	1.19	32	0.2

Ratings
Reward   D+
Risk   C
Recent Upgrade/Downgrade

Fund Information
Fund Type   Exchange Traded Funds
Category   US Muni Fixed Inc
Sub-Category   Muni National Short
Prospectus Objective   Muni Bond - Natl
Inception Date   Oct-07
Open to New Investments   Y

Prices
Price (as of 12/31/2018)   48.06
52-Week High   48.14
52-Week Low   47.43

Total Returns (%)

3-Month	6-Month	1-Year	3-Year	5-Year
1.13	0.88	1.38	2.20	4.29

3-Year Standard Deviation   1.76
Effective Duration   2.84

Valuation
Premium/Discount (1-Year Average)   -0.04

Company Information
Provider   SPDR State Street Global Advisors
Manager/Tenure Timothy T. Ryan (11), Steven M.
                Hlavin (8)
Website   http://www.spdrs.com
Address   SPDR State Street Global Advisors
                State Street Financial Center, 1
                Lincoln Street Boston MA 02111-2900
                United States
Phone Number   617-786-3000

PERFORMANCE

Ratings History

Date	Overall Rating	Risk Rating	Reward Rating
Q4-18	C-	C	D+
Q2-18	C-	C	D+
Q4-17	C	C	C
Q4-16	C	C	C-
Q4-15	C	C+	C

Asset & Performance History

Date	NAV	1-Year Total Return
2017	47.99	1.17
2016	47.89	-0.46
2015	48.59	1.11
2014	48.49	0.91
2013	48.5	0.89
2012	48.54	1.29

Total Assets: $3,681,013,644
Asset Allocation

Asset	%
Cash	0%
Stocks	0%
US Stocks	0%
Bonds	100%
US Bonds	100%
Other	0%

Services Offered:

Investment Strategy: The investment seeks to provide investment results that, before fees and expenses, correspond generally to the price and yield performance of the Bloomberg Barclays Managed Money Municipal Short Term Index. The fund invests substantially all, but at least 80%, of its total assets in the securities comprising the index or in securities that the Sub-Adviser determines have economic characteristics that are substantially identical to the economic characteristics of the securities that comprise the index. The index tracks the short term tax exempt municipal bond market and provides income that is exempt from federal income taxes. The fund is non-diversified. **Top Holdings:** CONNECTICUT ST HEALTH & EDL FACS AUTH 5%   SAN DIEGO CNTY CALIF WTR AUTH 5%   CALIFORNIA ST 5%   LOS ANGELES CALIF UNI SCH DIST 5%   CALIFORNIA ST 5%

iShares MSCI EAFE Growth ETF   C-   HOLD

Ticker	Traded On	NAV	Total Assets ($)	Dividend Yield (TTM)	Turnover Ratio	Expense Ratio
EFG	BATS	69.02	$3,619,488,909	1.83	22	0.4

Ratings
Reward   D+
Risk   C
Recent Upgrade/Downgrade   Down

Fund Information
Fund Type   Exchange Traded Funds
Category   Global Equity Large Cap
Sub-Category   Foreign Large Growth
Prospectus Objective   Foreign Stock
Inception Date   Aug-05
Open to New Investments   Y

Prices
Price (as of 12/31/2018)   69.07
52-Week High   85.74
52-Week Low   66.77

Total Returns (%)

3-Month	6-Month	1-Year	3-Year	5-Year
-13.41	-10.83	-13.01	8.04	6.87

3-Year Standard Deviation   11.15
Effective Duration

Valuation
Premium/Discount (1-Year Average)   -0.07

Company Information
Provider   iShares
Manager/Tenure Diane Hsiung (10), Greg Savage (10),
                Jennifer Hsui (6), 3 others
Website   http://www.ishares.com
Address   iShares 400 Howard Street San
                Francisco CA 94105 United States
Phone Number   800-474-2737

PERFORMANCE

Ratings History

Date	Overall Rating	Risk Rating	Reward Rating
Q4-18	C-	C	D+
Q2-18	C	C-	C
Q4-17	B	B	B
Q4-16	C-	C	C-
Q4-15	C	C+	C

Asset & Performance History

Date	NAV	1-Year Total Return
2017	80.78	28.49
2016	63.91	-3.33
2015	67.54	3.74
2014	66.19	-4.64
2013	70.96	22.15
2012	59.31	16.54

Total Assets: $3,619,488,909
Asset Allocation

Asset	%
Cash	1%
Stocks	99%
US Stocks	2%
Bonds	0%
US Bonds	0%
Other	0%

Services Offered:

Investment Strategy: The investment seeks to track the investment results of the MSCI EAFE Growth Index composed of developed market equities, excluding the U.S. and Canada, that exhibit growth characteristics. The fund generally invests at least 90% of its assets in securities of the underlying index and in depositary receipts representing securities of the underlying index. The index is a subset of the MSCI EAFE Index. Constituents of the underlying index include securities of companies located in Europe, Australasia and the Far East. **Top Holdings:** Nestle SA   Roche Holding AG Dividend Right Cert.   SAP SE   Novartis AG   AIA Group Ltd

iShares Edge MSCI Min Vol Global ETF   C   HOLD

Ticker	Traded On	NAV		Total Assets ($)	Dividend Yield (TTM)	Turnover Ratio	Expense Ratio
ACWV	BATS	81.21		$3,598,562,726	2.04	23	0.2

Ratings
Reward   C
Risk   C+
Recent Upgrade/Downgrade

Fund Information
Fund Type	Exchange Traded Funds
Category	Global Equity Large Cap
Sub-Category	World Large Stock
Prospectus Objective	World Stock
Inception Date	Oct-11
Open to New Investments	Y

Prices
Price (as of 12/31/2018)	81.26
52-Week High	88.19
52-Week Low	78.32

Total Returns (%)
3-Month	6-Month	1-Year	3-Year	5-Year
-6.46	-0.79	-1.34	25.57	43.80

3-Year Standard Deviation   7.71
Effective Duration

Valuation
Premium/Discount (1-Year Average)   -0.05

Company Information
Provider	iShares
Manager/Tenure	Diane Hsiung (7), Greg Savage (7), Jennifer Hsui (5), 1 other
Website	http://www.ishares.com
Address	iShares 400 Howard Street San Francisco CA 94105 United States
Phone Number	800-474-2737

PERFORMANCE

Ratings History
Date	Overall Rating	Risk Rating	Reward Rating
Q4-18	C	C+	C
Q2-18	C	C-	C
Q4-17	B	B+	B-
Q4-16	C	C+	C
Q4-15	C	C+	C

Asset & Performance History
Date	NAV	1-Year Total Return
2017	84.21	18.17
2016	72.76	7.7
2015	69.28	3.04
2014	68.77	11.12
2013	63.31	17.27
2012	55.38	10.31

Total Assets: $3,598,562,726
Asset Allocation
Asset	%
Cash	1%
Stocks	99%
US Stocks	57%
Bonds	0%
US Bonds	0%
Other	0%

Services Offered:

Investment Strategy: The investment seeks to track the investment results of the MSCI ACWI Minimum Volatility (USD) Index. The fund generally will invest at least 90% of its assets in the component securities of the underlying index and in investments that have economic characteristics that are substantially identical to the component securities of the underlying index. The index measures the combined performance of equity securities in both developed and emerging markets that, in the aggregate, have lower volatility relative to the broader developed and emerging markets. **Top Holdings:** Johnson & Johnson   Waste Management Inc   Consolidated Edison Inc   McDonald's Corp   Verizon Communications Inc

---

iShares U.S. Real Estate ETF   C+   HOLD

Ticker	Traded On	NAV		Total Assets ($)	Dividend Yield (TTM)	Turnover Ratio	Expense Ratio
IYR	NYSE Arca	74.91		$3,568,464,349	3.73	13	0.43

Ratings
Reward   C
Risk   B
Recent Upgrade/Downgrade

Fund Information
Fund Type	Exchange Traded Funds
Category	Real Estate Sector Equity
Sub-Category	Real Estate
Prospectus Objective	Real Estate
Inception Date	Jun-00
Open to New Investments	Y

Prices
Price (as of 12/31/2018)	74.94
52-Week High	83.29
52-Week Low	71.79

Total Returns (%)
3-Month	6-Month	1-Year	3-Year	5-Year
-5.11	-5.03	-4.28	12.00	44.12

3-Year Standard Deviation   11.71
Effective Duration

Valuation
Premium/Discount (1-Year Average)   0.03

Company Information
Provider	iShares
Manager/Tenure	Diane Hsiung (10), Greg Savage (10), Jennifer Hsui (6), 3 others
Website	http://www.ishares.com
Address	iShares 400 Howard Street San Francisco CA 94105 United States
Phone Number	800-474-2737

PERFORMANCE

Ratings History
Date	Overall Rating	Risk Rating	Reward Rating
Q4-18	C+	B	C
Q2-18	C	C	C
Q4-17	B	B	B-
Q4-16	C+	B-	C+
Q4-15	C+	B-	C+

Asset & Performance History
Date	NAV	1-Year Total Return
2017	80.97	9.37
2016	76.88	7
2015	75.04	1.61
2014	76.81	26.61
2013	63.09	1.04
2012	64.75	18.35

Total Assets: $3,568,464,349
Asset Allocation
Asset	%
Cash	0%
Stocks	100%
US Stocks	100%
Bonds	0%
US Bonds	0%
Other	0%

Services Offered: CashInvestment Plan

Investment Strategy: The investment seeks to track the investment results of the Dow Jones U.S. Real Estate Index. The fund generally invests at least 90% of its assets in securities of the underlying index and in depositary receipts representing securities of the underlying index. The underlying fund measures the performance of the real estate sector of the U.S. equity market and may include large-, mid- or small-capitalization companies. **Top Holdings:** American Tower Corp   Simon Property Group Inc   Crown Castle International Corp   Prologis Inc   Public Storage

SPDR® Portfolio S&P 500 Growth ETF   C   HOLD

Ticker	Traded On	NAV	Total Assets ($)	Dividend Yield (TTM)	Turnover Ratio	Expense Ratio
SPYG	NYSE Arca	32.48	$3,567,151,474	1.38	13	0.04

Ratings
Reward	C
Risk	C+
Recent Upgrade/Downgrade	Down

Fund Information
Fund Type	Exchange Traded Funds
Category	US Equity Large Cap Growth
Sub-Category	Large Growth
Prospectus Objective	Growth
Inception Date	Sep-00
Open to New Investments	Y

Prices
Price (as of 12/31/2018)	32.50
52-Week High	38.37
52-Week Low	30.33

Total Returns (%)
3-Month	6-Month	1-Year	3-Year	5-Year
-14.96	-7.31	-0.02	35.73	63.95

3-Year Standard Deviation	10.52
Effective Duration	

Valuation
Premium/Discount (1-Year Average)	0.04

Company Information
Provider	SPDR State Street Global Advisors
Manager/Tenure	Michael J. Feehily (7), Karl A. Schneider (4), Mark Krivitsky (1)
Website	http://www.spdrs.com
Address	SPDR State Street Global Advisors State Street Financial Center, 1 Lincoln Street Boston MA 02111-2900 United States
Phone Number	617-786-3000

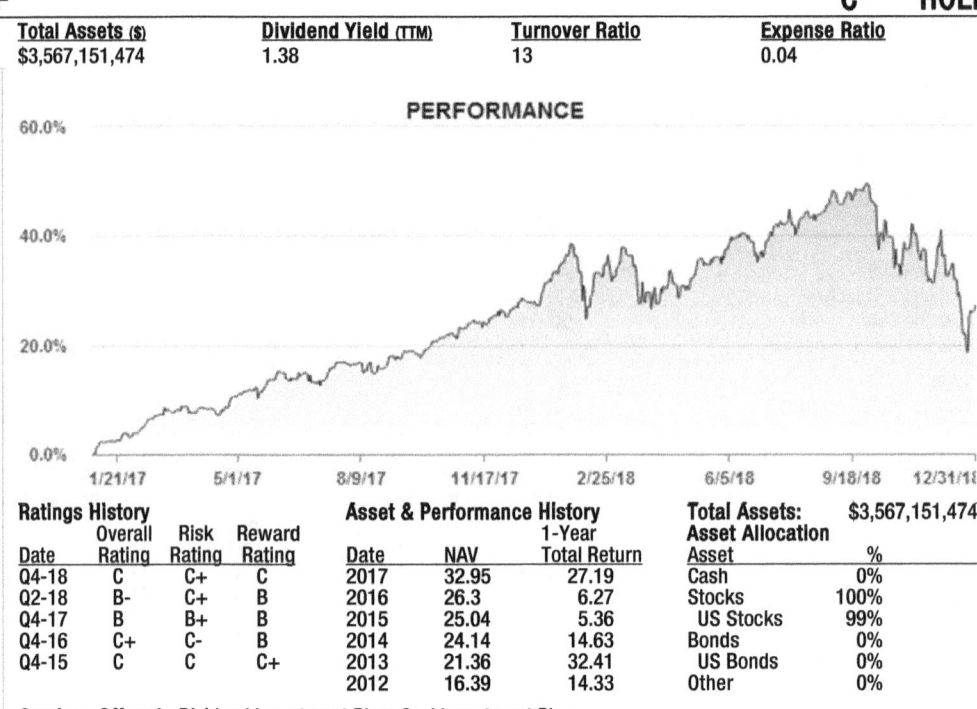

PERFORMANCE

Ratings History
Date	Overall Rating	Risk Rating	Reward Rating
Q4-18	C	C+	C
Q2-18	B-	C+	B
Q4-17	B	B+	B
Q4-16	C+	C-	B
Q4-15	C	C	C+

Asset & Performance History
Date	NAV	1-Year Total Return
2017	32.95	27.19
2016	26.3	6.27
2015	25.04	5.36
2014	24.14	14.63
2013	21.36	32.41
2012	16.39	14.33

Total Assets: $3,567,151,474
Asset Allocation
Asset	%
Cash	0%
Stocks	100%
US Stocks	99%
Bonds	0%
US Bonds	0%
Other	0%

Services Offered: Dividend Investment Plan, CashInvestment Plan

Investment Strategy: The investment seeks to provide investment results that, before fees and expenses, correspond generally to the total return performance of the S&P 500 Growth Index that tracks the performance of large capitalization exchange traded U.S. equity securities exhibiting "growth" characteristics. The fund generally invests substantially all, but at least 80%, of its total assets in the securities comprising the index. The index measures the performance of the large-capitalization growth segment of the U.S. equity market. It is non-diversified. **Top Holdings:** Microsoft Corp   Apple Inc   Amazon.com Inc   Facebook Inc A   Alphabet Inc Class C

---

iShares MSCI ACWI ex U.S. ETF   C-   HOLD

Ticker	Traded On	NAV	Total Assets ($)	Dividend Yield (TTM)	Turnover Ratio	Expense Ratio
ACWX	NAS CM	41.96	$3,538,273,687	2.84	6	0.32

Ratings
Reward	D+
Risk	C
Recent Upgrade/Downgrade	Down

Fund Information
Fund Type	Exchange Traded Funds
Category	Global Equity Large Cap
Sub-Category	Foreign Large Blend
Prospectus Objective	Foreign Stock
Inception Date	Mar-08
Open to New Investments	Y

Prices
Price (as of 12/31/2018)	41.96
52-Week High	53.74
52-Week Low	40.69

Total Returns (%)
3-Month	6-Month	1-Year	3-Year	5-Year
-11.44	-9.60	-14.08	13.85	3.09

3-Year Standard Deviation	11.24
Effective Duration	

Valuation
Premium/Discount (1-Year Average)	-0.14

Company Information
Provider	iShares
Manager/Tenure	Diane Hsiung (10), Greg Savage (10), Jennifer Hsui (6), 3 others
Website	http://www.ishares.com
Address	iShares 400 Howard Street San Francisco CA 94105 United States
Phone Number	800-474-2737

PERFORMANCE

Ratings History
Date	Overall Rating	Risk Rating	Reward Rating
Q4-18	C-	C	D+
Q2-18	C	C+	C
Q4-17	B-	B-	B-
Q4-16	D+	C-	D
Q4-15	C	C+	C-

Asset & Performance History
Date	NAV	1-Year Total Return
2017	50.04	27.04
2016	40.4	4.32
2015	39.82	-5.72
2014	43.21	-3.96
2013	46.35	15.21
2012	41.43	16.29

Total Assets: $3,538,273,687
Asset Allocation
Asset	%
Cash	1%
Stocks	99%
US Stocks	1%
Bonds	0%
US Bonds	0%
Other	0%

Services Offered:

Investment Strategy: The investment seeks to track the investment results of the MSCI ACWI ex USA Index composed of large- and mid-capitalization non-U.S. equities. The fund generally will invest at least 90% of its assets in the component securities of the underlying index and in investments that have economic characteristics that are substantially identical to the component securities of the underlying index. The index is a free float-adjusted market capitalization-weighted index designed to measure the combined equity market performance of developed and emerging markets countries, excluding the United States. **Top Holdings:** iShares MSCI India ETF   Nestle SA   Tencent Holdings Ltd   Alibaba Group Holding Ltd ADR   Novartis AG

First Trust Enhanced Short Maturity ETF   C   HOLD

Ticker	Traded On	NAV	Total Assets ($)	Dividend Yield (TTM)	Turnover Ratio	Expense Ratio
FTSM	NAS CM	59.83	$3,495,632,516	2.06	56	0.35

Ratings
Reward   C
Risk   C+
Recent Upgrade/Downgrade

Fund Information
Fund Type	Exchange Traded Funds
Category	US Fixed Income
Sub-Category	Ultrashort Bond
Prospectus Objective	Income
Inception Date	Aug-14
Open to New Investments	Y

Prices
Price (as of 12/31/2018)	59.85
52-Week High	60.10
52-Week Low	59.79

Total Returns (%)
3-Month	6-Month	1-Year	3-Year	5-Year
0.30	0.92	1.85	4.58	

3-Year Standard Deviation	0.16
Effective Duration	0.28

Valuation
Premium/Discount (1-Year Average)	0.01

Company Information
Provider	First Trust
Manager/Tenure	Jeremiah Charles (4), Todd W. Larson (4), James W. Snyder (4), 1 other
Website	http://www.ftportfolios.com/
Address	First Trust 120 E. Liberty Drive, Suite 400 Wheaton IL 60187 United States
Phone Number	800-621-1675

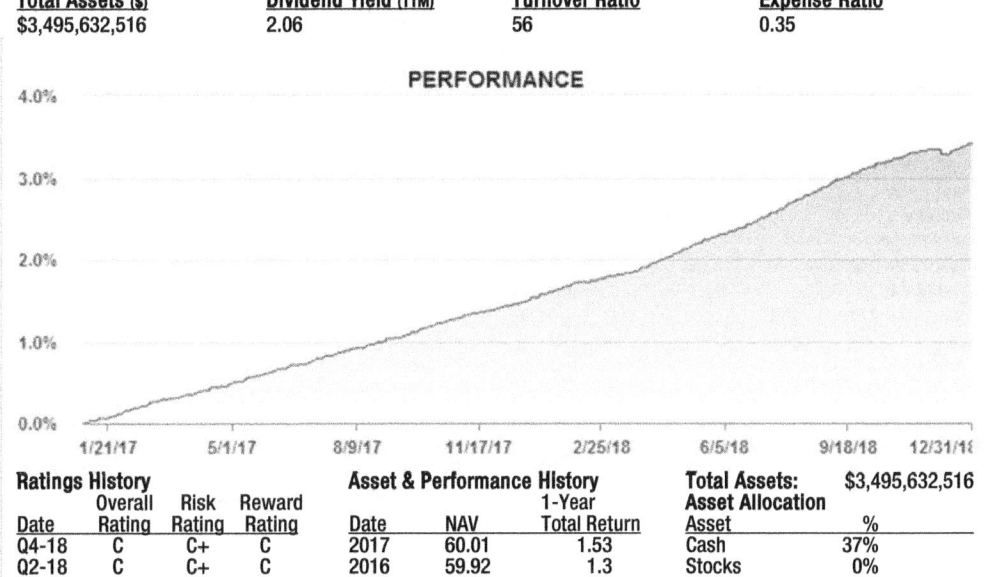

Ratings History
Date	Overall Rating	Risk Rating	Reward Rating
Q4-18	C	C+	C
Q2-18	C	C+	C
Q4-17	C+	B+	C
Q4-16	C	C+	C
Q4-15	D-	C+	D+

Asset & Performance History
Date	NAV	1-Year Total Return
2017	60.01	1.53
2016	59.92	1.3
2015	59.86	0.33
2014	59.95	
2013		
2012		

Total Assets: $3,495,632,516

Asset Allocation
Asset	%
Cash	37%
Stocks	0%
US Stocks	0%
Bonds	62%
US Bonds	50%
Other	0%

Services Offered:

Investment Strategy: The investment seeks current income, consistent with preservation of capital and daily liquidity. Under normal market conditions, the Advisor intends to achieve its investment objective by investing at least 80% of its net assets in a portfolio of U.S. dollar-denominated fixed- and variable-rate instruments (collectively, "Fixed Income Securities") issued by U.S. and non-U.S. public and private sector entities. It is non-diversified. **Top Holdings:** United States Treasury Notes 0.88%   United States Treasury Notes 0.88%   United States Treasury Notes 0.88%   Canadian Pacer Auto Receivables Trust 2017-1 3%   United States Treasury Notes 1%

---

iShares MSCI Taiwan Capped ETF   C-   HOLD

Ticker	Traded On	NAV	Total Assets ($)	Dividend Yield (TTM)	Turnover Ratio	Expense Ratio
EWT	NYSE Arca	31.74	$3,480,151,901	3.06	12	0.62

Ratings
Reward   D+
Risk   C
Recent Upgrade/Downgrade   Down

Fund Information
Fund Type	Exchange Traded Funds
Category	Greater China Equity
Sub-Category	China Region
Prospectus Objective	Pacific Stock
Inception Date	Jun-00
Open to New Investments	Y

Prices
Price (as of 12/31/2018)	31.62
52-Week High	39.32
52-Week Low	30.86

Total Returns (%)
3-Month	6-Month	1-Year	3-Year	5-Year
-13.76	-8.46	-9.59	33.13	26.98

3-Year Standard Deviation	13.76
Effective Duration	

Valuation
Premium/Discount (1-Year Average)	-0.24

Company Information
Provider	iShares
Manager/Tenure	Diane Hsiung (10), Greg Savage (10), Jennifer Hsui (5), 1 other
Website	http://www.ishares.com
Address	iShares 400 Howard Street San Francisco CA 94105 United States
Phone Number	800-474-2737

Ratings History
Date	Overall Rating	Risk Rating	Reward Rating
Q4-18	C-	C	D+
Q2-18	B-	C+	B-
Q4-17	C+	C+	C+
Q4-16	B-	C	B
Q4-15	C	C+	C-

Asset & Performance History
Date	NAV	1-Year Total Return
2017	36.22	25.51
2016	29.69	17.33
2015	25.9	-12.27
2014	30.44	8.72
2013	28.56	8.57
2012	26.8	16.35

Total Assets: $3,480,151,901

Asset Allocation
Asset	%
Cash	0%
Stocks	100%
US Stocks	0%
Bonds	0%
US Bonds	0%
Other	0%

Services Offered: CashInvestment Plan

Investment Strategy: The investment seeks to track the investment results of the MSCI Taiwan 25/50 Index. The fund will at all times invest at least 80% of its assets in the securities of its underlying index and in depositary receipts representing securities in its underlying index. The index is designed to measure the performance of the large- and mid-cap segments of the Taiwanese market. A capping methodology is applied that limits the weight of any single component to a maximum of 25% of the underlying index. The fund is non-diversified. **Top Holdings:** Taiwan Semiconductor Manufacturing Co Ltd   Hon Hai Precision Industry Co Ltd   Formosa Plastics Corp Chunghwa Telecom Co Ltd   Cathay Financial Holding Co Ltd

WisdomTree U.S. MidCap Dividend Fund   C   HOLD

Ticker	Traded On	NAV	Total Assets ($)	Dividend Yield (TTM)	Turnover Ratio	Expense Ratio
DON	NYSE Arca	31.61	$3,301,267,953	2.36	27	0.38

Ratings
Reward	C-
Risk	C+
Recent Upgrade/Downgrade	Down

Fund Information
Fund Type	Exchange Traded Funds
Category	US Equity Mid Cap
Sub-Category	Mid-Cap Value
Prospectus Objective	Growth & Inc
Inception Date	Jun-06
Open to New Investments	Y

Prices
Price (as of 12/31/2018)	31.63
52-Week High	37.50
52-Week Low	29.98

Total Returns (%)
3-Month	6-Month	1-Year	3-Year	5-Year
-13.34	-10.18	-8.27	26.73	44.66

3-Year Standard Deviation	9.76
Effective Duration	

Valuation
Premium/Discount (1-Year Average)	0.01

Company Information
Provider	WisdomTree
Manager/Tenure	Richard A. Brown (10), Thomas J. Durante (10), Karen Q. Wong (10)
Website	http://www.wisdomtree.com
Address	WisdomTree 245 Park Avenue, 35th floor New York NY 10167 United States
Phone Number	866-909-9473

PERFORMANCE

Ratings History
Date	Overall Rating	Risk Rating	Reward Rating
Q4-18	C	C+	C-
Q2-18	C	C+	C
Q4-17	B	B+	B
Q4-16	B	C+	B
Q4-15	C	C-	C

Asset & Performance History
Date	NAV	1-Year Total Return
2017	35.27	14.86
2016	31.45	20.29
2015	26.84	-0.97
2014	27.88	15.27
2013	24.85	32.98
2012	19.16	14.83

Total Assets: $3,301,267,953

Asset Allocation
Asset	%
Cash	0%
Stocks	100%
US Stocks	100%
Bonds	0%
US Bonds	0%
Other	0%

Services Offered:

Investment Strategy: The investment seeks to track the price and yield performance, before fees and expenses, of the WisdomTree U.S. MidCap Dividend Index. Under normal circumstances, at least 95% of the fund's total assets (exclusive of collateral held from securities lending) will be invested in component securities of the index and investments that have economic characteristics that are substantially identical to the economic characteristics of such component securities. The index is a fundamentally weighted index that is comprised of the mid-capitalization segment of the U.S. dividend-paying market. The fund is non-diversified. **Top Holdings:** Targa Resources Corp Macy's Inc Kohl's Corp Evergy Inc The AES Corp

---

First Trust Preferred Securities and Income ETF   C   HOLD

Ticker	Traded On	NAV	Total Assets ($)	Dividend Yield (TTM)	Turnover Ratio	Expense Ratio
FPE	NYSE Arca	17.98	$3,282,045,670	5.94	13	0.85

Ratings
Reward	D+
Risk	C+
Recent Upgrade/Downgrade	

Fund Information
Fund Type	Exchange Traded Funds
Category	US Fixed Income
Sub-Category	Preferred Stock
Prospectus Objective	Income
Inception Date	Feb-13
Open to New Investments	Y

Prices
Price (as of 12/31/2018)	17.95
52-Week High	20.07
52-Week Low	17.82

Total Returns (%)
3-Month	6-Month	1-Year	3-Year	5-Year
-4.22	-2.71	-4.68	13.00	33.12

3-Year Standard Deviation	4.02
Effective Duration	4.06

Valuation
Premium/Discount (1-Year Average)	0.01

Company Information
Provider	First Trust
Manager/Tenure	Scott T. Fleming (5), Robert Wolf (5)
Website	http://www.ftportfolios.com/
Address	First Trust 120 E. Liberty Drive, Suite 400 Wheaton IL 60187 United States
Phone Number	800-621-1675

PERFORMANCE

Ratings History
Date	Overall Rating	Risk Rating	Reward Rating
Q4-18	C	C+	D+
Q2-18	C	C+	C
Q4-17	B	A-	C+
Q4-16	C	C+	C
Q4-15	C	C+	C

Asset & Performance History
Date	NAV	1-Year Total Return
2017	19.99	11.35
2016	18.95	6.46
2015	18.89	6.21
2014	18.79	10.91
2013	17.98	
2012		

Total Assets: $3,282,045,670

Asset Allocation
Asset	%
Cash	0%
Stocks	0%
US Stocks	0%
Bonds	39%
US Bonds	23%
Other	0%

Services Offered:

Investment Strategy: The investment seeks total return and to provide current income. Under normal market conditions, the fund invests at least 80% of its net assets (including investment borrowings) in preferred securities ("Preferred Securities") and income-producing debt securities ("Income Securities"). The fund invests in securities that are traded over-the-counter or listed on an exchange. **Top Holdings:** Enel - Societa per Azioni 8.75% Enbridge Energy Partners L.P. 6.19% GMAC Capital Trust I Pfd Secs 2011-15.2.40 Gtd Series 2 Barclays PLC 7.88% EMERA INCORPORATED 6.75%

Vanguard Long-Term Corporate Bond Index Fund ETF Shares   C-   HOLD

Ticker	Traded On	NAV	Total Assets ($)	Dividend Yield (TTM)	Turnover Ratio	Expense Ratio
VCLT	NAS CM		$3,259,541,706	4.64	48	0.07

Ratings
Reward   D+
Risk   C
Recent Upgrade/Downgrade   Down

Fund Information
Fund Type   Exchange Traded Funds
Category   US Fixed Income
Sub-Category   Corporate Bond
Prospectus Objective   Corp Bond - Gen
Inception Date   Nov-09
Open to New Investments   Y

Prices
Price (as of 12/31/2018)   85.18
52-Week High   95.75
52-Week Low   83.50

Total Returns (%)

3-Month	6-Month	1-Year	3-Year	5-Year
-1.40	-0.36	-7.21	15.33	28.41

3-Year Standard Deviation   7.17
Effective Duration   13.31

Valuation
Premium/Discount (1-Year Average)   0.24

Company Information
Provider   Vanguard
Manager/Tenure   Joshua C. Barrickman (9)
Website   http://www.vanguard.com
Address   Vanguard 100 Vanguard Boulevard
                  Malvern PA 19355 United States
Phone Number   877-662-7447

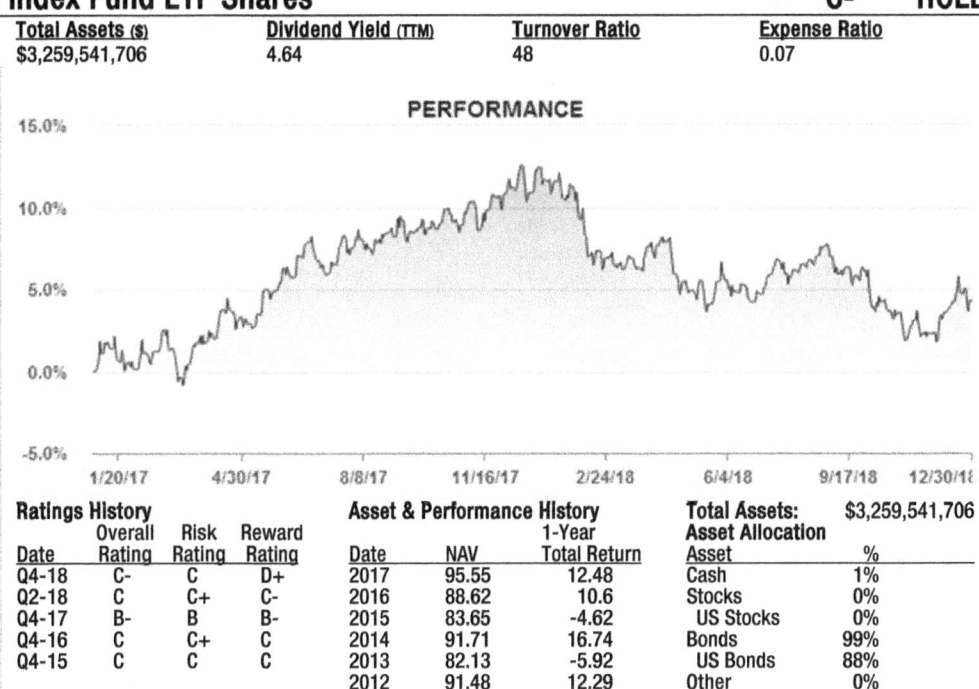

PERFORMANCE

Ratings History

Date	Overall Rating	Risk Rating	Reward Rating
Q4-18	C-	C	D+
Q2-18	C	C+	C-
Q4-17	B-	B	B-
Q4-16	C	C+	C
Q4-15	C	C	C

Asset & Performance History

Date	NAV	1-Year Total Return
2017	95.55	12.48
2016	88.62	10.6
2015	83.65	-4.62
2014	91.71	16.74
2013	82.13	-5.92
2012	91.48	12.29

Total Assets: $3,259,541,706

Asset Allocation

Asset	%
Cash	1%
Stocks	0%
US Stocks	0%
Bonds	99%
US Bonds	88%
Other	0%

Services Offered:

Investment Strategy: The investment seeks to track the performance of a market-weighted corporate bond index with a long-term dollar-weighted average maturity. The fund employs an indexing investment approach designed to track the performance of the Bloomberg Barclays U.S. 10+ Year Corporate Bond Index. This index includes U.S. dollar-denominated, investment-grade, fixed-rate, taxable securities issued by industrial, utility, and financial companies, with maturities greater than 10 years. Under normal circumstances, at least 80% of the fund's assets will be invested in bonds included in the index. **Top Holdings:** Anheuser-Busch InBev Finance Inc. 4.9% GE Capital International Funding Company Unlimited Company 4.42% CVS Health Corp 5.05% Goldman Sachs Group, Inc. 6.75% Anheuser-Busch InBev Finance Inc. 4.7%

Vanguard Russell 1000 Value Index Fund ETF Shares   C   HOLD

Ticker	Traded On	NAV	Total Assets ($)	Dividend Yield (TTM)	Turnover Ratio	Expense Ratio
VONV	NAS CM		$3,255,302,400	2.27	16	0.12

Ratings
Reward   C
Risk   C-
Recent Upgrade/Downgrade

Fund Information
Fund Type   Exchange Traded Funds
Category   US Equity Large Cap Value
Sub-Category   Large Value
Prospectus Objective   Growth & Inc
Inception Date   Sep-10
Open to New Investments   Y

Prices
Price (as of 12/31/2018)   97.10
52-Week High   114.75
52-Week Low   91.61

Total Returns (%)

3-Month	6-Month	1-Year	3-Year	5-Year
-12.68	-7.46	-9.05	20.85	31.60

3-Year Standard Deviation   9.31
Effective Duration

Valuation
Premium/Discount (1-Year Average)   0.04

Company Information
Provider   Vanguard
Manager/Tenure   Michael A. Johnson (8), Walter
                  Nejman (2)
Website   http://www.vanguard.com
Address   Vanguard 100 Vanguard Boulevard
                  Malvern PA 19355 United States
Phone Number   877-662-7447

PERFORMANCE

Ratings History

Date	Overall Rating	Risk Rating	Reward Rating
Q4-18	C	C-	C
Q2-18	C	C-	C
Q4-17	B	B	B-
Q4-16	C+	C-	B
Q4-15	C	C	C

Asset & Performance History

Date	NAV	1-Year Total Return
2017	108.44	13.84
2016	97.71	16.42
2015	85.64	-3.89
2014	91.22	13.3
2013	82.27	32.31
2012	63.5	17.35

Total Assets: $3,255,302,400

Asset Allocation

Asset	%
Cash	0%
Stocks	100%
US Stocks	99%
Bonds	0%
US Bonds	0%
Other	0%

Services Offered:

Investment Strategy: The investment seeks to track the performance of a benchmark index that measures the investment return of large-capitalization value stocks in the United States. The fund employs an indexing investment approach designed to track the performance of the Russell 1000® Value Index. The index is designed to measure the performance of large-capitalization value stocks in the United States. The Advisor attempts to replicate the target index by investing all, or substantially all, of its assets in the stocks that make up the index, holding each stock in approximately the same proportion as its weighting in the index. **Top Holdings:** JPMorgan Chase & Co Berkshire Hathaway Inc B Exxon Mobil Corp Johnson & Johnson Bank of America Corporation

Schwab Fundamental U.S. Small Company Index ETF

C   HOLD

Ticker	Traded On	NAV	Total Assets ($)	Dividend Yield (TTM)	Turnover Ratio	Expense Ratio
FNDA	NYSE Arca	32.84	$3,251,724,480	1.35	21	0.25

Ratings
Reward	C-
Risk	C+
Recent Upgrade/Downgrade	Down

Fund Information
Fund Type	Exchange Traded Funds
Category	US Equity Small Cap
Sub-Category	Small Blend
Prospectus Objective	Small Company
Inception Date	Aug-13
Open to New Investments	Y

Prices
Price (as of 12/31/2018)	32.84
52-Week High	41.72
52-Week Low	31.04

Total Returns (%)
3-Month	6-Month	1-Year	3-Year	5-Year
-18.08	-17.10	-12.09	22.49	25.36

3-Year Standard Deviation	13.02
Effective Duration	

Valuation
Premium/Discount (1-Year Average)	-0.01

Company Information
Provider	Schwab ETFs
Manager/Tenure	Christopher Bliss (1), Ferian Juwono (1), Sabya Sinha (1)
Website	http://www.schwabetfs.com
Address	Schwab ETFs United States
Phone Number	800-435-4000

PERFORMANCE

Ratings History
Date	Overall Rating	Risk Rating	Reward Rating
Q4-18	C	C+	C-
Q2-18	C+	C+	C+
Q4-17	B	B	B+
Q4-16	B-	C+	B
Q4-15	C-	C+	D+

Asset & Performance History
Date	NAV	1-Year Total Return
2017	37.9	13.06
2016	34.05	23.47
2015	27.94	-5.04
2014	29.81	7.78
2013	27.96	
2012		

Total Assets: $3,251,724,480

Asset Allocation
Asset	%
Cash	0%
Stocks	100%
US Stocks	99%
Bonds	0%
US Bonds	0%
Other	0%

Services Offered:

Investment Strategy: The investment seeks to track as closely as possible, before fees and expenses, the total return of the Russell RAFI™ US Small Company Index. The fund normally will invest at least 90% of its net assets (including, for this purpose, any borrowings for investment purposes) in stocks included in the index. The index measures the performance of the small company size segment by fundamental overall company scores, which are created using as the universe the companies included in the Russell 3000® Index. It may invest up to 10% of its net assets in securities not included in the index. **Top Holdings:** Adtalem Global Education Inc Delek US Holdings Inc Deckers Outdoor Corp Cleveland-Cliffs Inc Lamb Weston Holdings Inc

---

SPDR® Portfolio Aggregate Bond ETF

C-   HOLD

Ticker	Traded On	NAV	Total Assets ($)	Dividend Yield (TTM)	Turnover Ratio	Expense Ratio
SPAB	NYSE Arca	27.83	$3,249,963,355	2.95	46	0.04

Ratings
Reward	D+
Risk	C+
Recent Upgrade/Downgrade	Down

Fund Information
Fund Type	Exchange Traded Funds
Category	US Fixed Income
Sub-Category	Intermediate-Term Bond
Prospectus Objective	Multisector Bond
Inception Date	May-07
Open to New Investments	Y

Prices
Price (as of 12/31/2018)	27.85
52-Week High	28.74
52-Week Low	27.25

Total Returns (%)
3-Month	6-Month	1-Year	3-Year	5-Year
1.68	1.70	-0.13	6.02	12.77

3-Year Standard Deviation	2.74
Effective Duration	6.00

Valuation
Premium/Discount (1-Year Average)	0.04

Company Information
Provider	SPDR State Street Global Advisors
Manager/Tenure	Marc DiCosimo (5), Michael Przygoda (4), Nicholas Fischer (0)
Website	http://www.spdrs.com
Address	SPDR State Street Global Advisors State Street Financial Center, 1 Lincoln Street Boston MA 02111-2900 United States
Phone Number	617-786-3000

PERFORMANCE

Ratings History
Date	Overall Rating	Risk Rating	Reward Rating
Q4-18	C-	C+	D+
Q2-18	C-	C-	C-
Q4-17	B-	B+	C
Q4-16	C	C-	C
Q4-15	C	C-	C

Asset & Performance History
Date	NAV	1-Year Total Return
2017	28.7	3.27
2016	28.48	2.5
2015	28.49	0.49
2014	29.08	5.84
2013	28.16	-2.07
2012	29.33	3.94

Total Assets: $3,249,963,355

Asset Allocation
Asset	%
Cash	5%
Stocks	0%
US Stocks	0%
Bonds	95%
US Bonds	88%
Other	0%

Services Offered:

Investment Strategy: The investment seeks to provide investment results that, before fees and expenses, correspond generally to the price and yield performance of the Bloomberg Barclays U.S. Aggregate Bond Index. The fund generally invests substantially all, but at least 80%, of its total assets in the securities comprising the index or in securities that the Adviser determines have economic characteristics that are substantially identical to the economic characteristics of the securities that comprise the index. The index is designed to measure the performance of the U.S. dollar denominated investment grade bond market. The fund is non-diversified. **Top Holdings:** United States Treasury Notes 2% United States Treasury Notes 2.88% United States Treasury Notes 2.75% United States Treasury Notes 2.25% United States Treasury Notes 2.88%

SPDR® Blackstone / GSO Senior Loan ETF   C   HOLD

Ticker	Traded On	NAV	Total Assets ($)	Dividend Yield (TTM)	Turnover Ratio	Expense Ratio
SRLN	NYSE Arca	44.92	$3,194,274,452	4.59	68	0.7

Ratings
Reward	C-
Risk	C+
Recent Upgrade/Downgrade	

Fund Information
Fund Type	Exchange Traded Funds
Category	US Fixed Income
Sub-Category	Bank Loan
Prospectus Objective	Income
Inception Date	Apr-13
Open to New Investments	Y

Prices
Price (as of 12/31/2018)	44.70
52-Week High	47.65
52-Week Low	44.46

Total Returns (%)
3-Month	6-Month	1-Year	3-Year	5-Year
-3.50	-1.68	-0.25	10.42	10.46

3-Year Standard Deviation	1.92
Effective Duration	

Valuation
Premium/Discount (1-Year Average)	-0.01

Company Information
Provider	SPDR State Street Global Advisors
Manager/Tenure	Gordon McKemie (3), Daniel T. McMullen (3)
Website	http://www.spdrs.com
Address	SPDR State Street Global Advisors State Street Financial Center, 1 Lincoln Street Boston MA 02111-2900 United States
Phone Number	617-786-3000

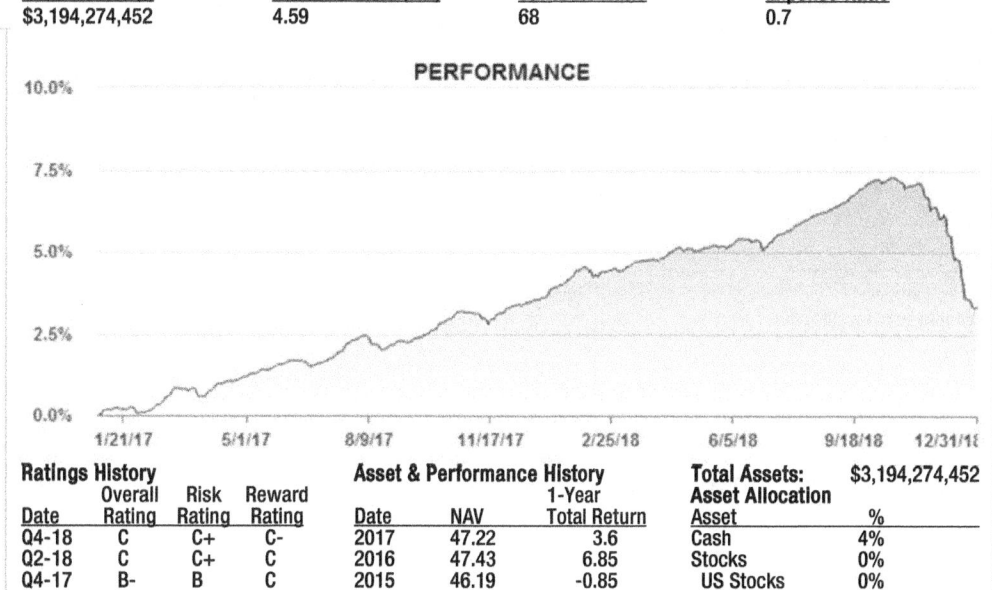

PERFORMANCE

Ratings History
Date	Overall Rating	Risk Rating	Reward Rating
Q4-18	C	C+	C-
Q2-18	C	C+	C
Q4-17	B-	B	C
Q4-16	C	C+	C
Q4-15	C	C+	C

Asset & Performance History
Date	NAV	1-Year Total Return
2017	47.22	3.6
2016	47.43	6.85
2015	46.19	-0.85
2014	48.6	0.89
2013	49.93	
2012		

Total Assets: $3,194,274,452

Asset Allocation
Asset	%
Cash	4%
Stocks	0%
US Stocks	0%
Bonds	96%
US Bonds	94%
Other	0%

Services Offered:

Investment Strategy: The investment seeks to provide current income consistent with the preservation of capital. Under normal circumstances, the fund invests substantially all of its assets in the Blackstone / GSO Senior Loan Portfolio, a separate series of the SSGA Master Trust with an identical investment objective as the fund. As a result, the fund invests indirectly through the Portfolio. In pursuing its investment objective, the Portfolio seeks to outperform the Markit iBoxx USD Liquid Leveraged Loan Index and the S&P/LSTA U.S. Leveraged Loan 100 Index by normally investing at least 80% of its net assets (plus any borrowings for investment purposes) in Senior Loans.
Top Holdings: Centurylink Escrow Llc Term Loan B   Valeant Pharmaceuticals Intl I Initial Term   Asurion Llc Second Lien   Banff Merger Sub Inc Initial Dollar Term Loan   Bass Pro Group Llc Term Loan B

---

iShares Currency Hedged MSCI EAFE ETF   C   HOLD

Ticker	Traded On	NAV	Total Assets ($)	Dividend Yield (TTM)	Turnover Ratio	Expense Ratio
HEFA	BATS	25.82	$3,180,091,754	3.16	12	0.35

Ratings
Reward	C-
Risk	C+
Recent Upgrade/Downgrade	Down

Fund Information
Fund Type	Exchange Traded Funds
Category	Global Equity Large Cap
Sub-Category	Foreign Large Blend
Prospectus Objective	Foreign Stock
Inception Date	Jan-14
Open to New Investments	Y

Prices
Price (as of 12/31/2018)	25.81
52-Week High	30.85
52-Week Low	25.29

Total Returns (%)
3-Month	6-Month	1-Year	3-Year	5-Year
-12.53	-9.01	-9.69	12.30	

3-Year Standard Deviation	8.98
Effective Duration	

Valuation
Premium/Discount (1-Year Average)	0.00

Company Information
Provider	iShares
Manager/Tenure	Diane Hsiung (4), Jennifer Hsui (4), Orlando Montalvo (4), 2 others
Website	http://www.ishares.com
Address	iShares 400 Howard Street San Francisco CA 94105 United States
Phone Number	800-474-2737

PERFORMANCE

Ratings History
Date	Overall Rating	Risk Rating	Reward Rating
Q4-18	C	C+	C-
Q2-18	C	C+	C
Q4-17	B	B	B
Q4-16	C	C+	C
Q4-15	D+	C+	C-

Asset & Performance History
Date	NAV	1-Year Total Return
2017	29.68	16.69
2016	26.11	6.57
2015	25.35	4.44
2014	25.1	
2013		
2012		

Total Assets: $3,180,091,754

Asset Allocation
Asset	%
Cash	1%
Stocks	99%
US Stocks	1%
Bonds	0%
US Bonds	0%
Other	0%

Services Offered:

Investment Strategy: The investment seeks to track the investment results of the MSCI EAFE® 100% Hedged to USD Index. The fund generally will invest at least 90% of its assets in the component securities (including indirect investments through the underlying fund) and other instruments of the underlying index and in investments that have economic characteristics that are substantially identical to the component securities of the underlying index. The index is composed of large- and mid-capitalization equities in Europe, Australasia, and the Far East while mitigating exposure to fluctuations between the value of the component currencies and the U.S. dollar. **Top Holdings:** iShares MSCI EAFE ETF

Schwab Intermediate-Term U.S. Treasury ETF™   C-   HOLD

Ticker	Traded On	NAV	Total Assets ($)	Dividend Yield (TTM)	Turnover Ratio	Expense Ratio
SCHR	NYSE Arca	52.89	$3,151,930,362	2.04	30	0.06

Ratings
Reward	D
Risk	C
Recent Upgrade/Downgrade	Up

Fund Information
Fund Type	Exchange Traded Funds
Category	US Fixed Income
Sub-Category	Intermediate Government
Prospectus Objective	Govt Bond - Treasury
Inception Date	Aug-10
Open to New Investments	Y

Prices
Price (as of 12/31/2018)	52.95
52-Week High	53.32
52-Week Low	51.34

Total Returns (%)
3-Month	6-Month	1-Year	3-Year	5-Year
2.96	2.62	1.28	4.02	10.22

3-Year Standard Deviation	3.06
Effective Duration	5.13

Valuation
Premium/Discount (1-Year Average)	0.00

Company Information
Provider	Schwab ETFs
Manager/Tenure	Matthew Hastings (8), Mark R. McKissick (1)
Website	http://www.schwabetfs.com
Address	Schwab ETFs United States
Phone Number	800-435-4000

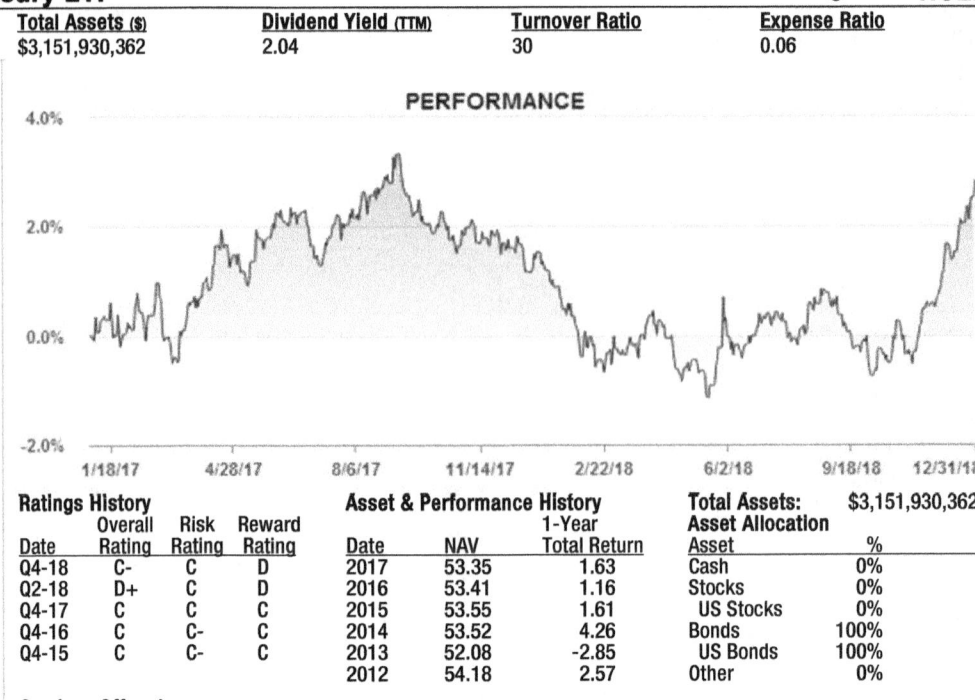

Ratings History
Date	Overall Rating	Risk Rating	Reward Rating
Q4-18	C-	C	D
Q2-18	D+	C	D
Q4-17	C	C	C
Q4-16	C	C-	C
Q4-15	C	C-	C

Asset & Performance History
Date	NAV	1-Year Total Return
2017	53.35	1.63
2016	53.41	1.16
2015	53.55	1.61
2014	53.52	4.26
2013	52.08	-2.85
2012	54.18	2.57

Total Assets: $3,151,930,362
Asset Allocation
Asset	%
Cash	0%
Stocks	0%
US Stocks	0%
Bonds	100%
US Bonds	100%
Other	0%

Services Offered:

Investment Strategy: The investment seeks to track as closely as possible, before fees and expenses, the total return of the Bloomberg Barclays US Treasury 3-10 Year Index. The fund will invest at least 90% of its net assets (including, for this purpose, any borrowings for investment purposes) in securities included in the index. The index includes all publicly-issued U.S. Treasury securities that have a remaining maturity of greater than or equal to three years and less than ten years, are rated investment grade, and have $300 million or more of outstanding face value. The securities in the index must be denominated in U.S. dollars and must be fixed-rate and non-convertible. **Top Holdings:** United States Treasury Notes 2.88% United States Treasury Notes 2.88% United States Treasury Notes 2% United States Treasury Notes 2.75% United States Treasury Notes 2.62%

SPDR® Portfolio Developed World ex-US ETF   C-   HOLD

Ticker	Traded On	NAV	Total Assets ($)	Dividend Yield (TTM)	Turnover Ratio	Expense Ratio
SPDW	NYSE Arca	26.47	$3,132,235,619	2.7	3	0.04

Ratings
Reward	D+
Risk	C
Recent Upgrade/Downgrade	Down

Fund Information
Fund Type	Exchange Traded Funds
Category	Global Equity Large Cap
Sub-Category	Foreign Large Blend
Prospectus Objective	Foreign Stock
Inception Date	Apr-07
Open to New Investments	Y

Prices
Price (as of 12/31/2018)	26.45
52-Week High	33.82
52-Week Low	25.64

Total Returns (%)
3-Month	6-Month	1-Year	3-Year	5-Year
-12.96	-10.66	-14.23	10.79	4.39

3-Year Standard Deviation	10.99
Effective Duration	

Valuation
Premium/Discount (1-Year Average)	0.01

Company Information
Provider	SPDR State Street Global Advisors
Manager/Tenure	Michael J. Feehily (7), Karl A. Schneider (3), Kala O'Donnell (1)
Website	http://www.spdrs.com
Address	SPDR State Street Global Advisors State Street Financial Center, 1 Lincoln Street Boston MA 02111-2900 United States
Phone Number	617-786-3000

Ratings History
Date	Overall Rating	Risk Rating	Reward Rating
Q4-18	C-	C	D+
Q2-18	C	C+	C
Q4-17	B	B	B
Q4-16	C-	C	D+
Q4-15	C	C+	C-

Asset & Performance History
Date	NAV	1-Year Total Return
2017	31.73	25.55
2016	25.78	1.85
2015	25.86	-1.79
2014	27.03	-4.04
2013	29.1	19.52
2012	25	16.91

Total Assets: $3,132,235,619
Asset Allocation
Asset	%
Cash	0%
Stocks	100%
US Stocks	2%
Bonds	0%
US Bonds	0%
Other	0%

Services Offered:

Investment Strategy: The investment seeks investment results that, before fees and expenses, correspond generally to the total return performance of the S&P Developed Ex-U.S.BMI Index. The fund generally invests substantially all, but at least 80%, of its total assets in the securities comprising the index and in depositary receipts based on securities comprising the index. The index is a market capitalization weighted index designed to define and measure the investable universe of publicly traded companies domiciled in developed countries outside the United States. The fund is non-diversified. **Top Holdings:** Nestle SA Novartis AG Samsung Electronics Co Ltd GDR Roche Holding AG Dividend Right Cert. HSBC Holdings PLC

Vanguard Consumer Discretionary Index Fund ETF Shares   C   HOLD

Ticker	Traded On	NAV	Total Assets ($)	Dividend Yield (TTM)	Turnover Ratio	Expense Ratio
VCR	NYSE Arca		$3,129,592,927	1.21	28	0.1

Ratings
Reward   C
Risk   C-
Recent Upgrade/Downgrade   Down

Fund Information
Fund Type   Exchange Traded Funds
Category   Consumer Goods & Svcs
Sub-Category   Consumer Cyclical
Prospectus Objective   Unaligned
Inception Date   Jan-04
Open to New Investments   Y

Prices
Price (as of 12/31/2018)   150.52
52-Week High   181.57
52-Week Low   139.59

Total Returns (%)

3-Month	6-Month	1-Year	3-Year	5-Year
-16.93	-11.56	-3.19	26.79	47.51

3-Year Standard Deviation   12.16
Effective Duration

Valuation
Premium/Discount (1-Year Average)   0.03

Company Information
Provider   Vanguard
Manager/Tenure   Michael A. Johnson (7), Awais Khan (1)
Website   http://www.vanguard.com
Address   Vanguard 100 Vanguard Boulevard Malvern PA 19355 United States
Phone Number   877-662-7447

PERFORMANCE

Ratings History

Date	Overall Rating	Risk Rating	Reward Rating
Q4-18	C	C-	C
Q2-18	C+	C-	B
Q4-17	B	A-	B
Q4-16	C+	C-	B
Q4-15	B-	B-	B-

Asset & Performance History

Date	NAV	1-Year Total Return
2017	155.87	22.67
2016	128.56	6.64
2015	122.54	6.35
2014	116.77	9.39
2013	108.08	43.56
2012	75.93	24.71

Total Assets: $3,129,592,927
Asset Allocation

Asset	%
Cash	1%
Stocks	99%
US Stocks	98%
Bonds	0%
US Bonds	0%
Other	0%

Services Offered:

Investment Strategy: The investment seeks to track the performance of a benchmark index. The fund employs an indexing investment approach designed to track the performance of the MSCI US Investable Market Index/Consumer Discretionary 25/50, an index made up of stocks of large, mid-size, and small U.S. companies within the consumer discretionary sector, as classified under the Global Industry Classification Standard. The Advisor attempts to replicate the target index by seeking to invest all, or substantially all, of its assets in the stocks that make up the index, in order to hold each stock in approximately the same proportion as its weighting in the index. It is non-diversified. **Top Holdings:** Amazon.com Inc The Home Depot Inc McDonald's Corp Nike Inc B Booking Holdings Inc

---

iShares U.S. Medical Devices ETF   B-   BUY

Ticker	Traded On	NAV	Total Assets ($)	Dividend Yield (TTM)	Turnover Ratio	Expense Ratio
IHI	NYSE Arca	199.77	$3,073,886,054	0.23	15	0.43

Ratings
Reward   B
Risk   C
Recent Upgrade/Downgrade

Fund Information
Fund Type   Exchange Traded Funds
Category   Healthcare Sector Equity
Sub-Category   Health
Prospectus Objective   Health
Inception Date   May-06
Open to New Investments   Y

Prices
Price (as of 12/31/2018)   199.81
52-Week High   227.72
52-Week Low   172.67

Total Returns (%)

3-Month	6-Month	1-Year	3-Year	5-Year
-12.11	-0.50	15.46	65.06	122.04

3-Year Standard Deviation   13.98
Effective Duration

Valuation
Premium/Discount (1-Year Average)   0.03

Company Information
Provider   iShares
Manager/Tenure   Diane Hsiung (10), Greg Savage (10), Jennifer Hsui (6), 3 others
Website   http://www.ishares.com
Address   iShares 400 Howard Street San Francisco CA 94105 United States
Phone Number   800-474-2737

PERFORMANCE

Ratings History

Date	Overall Rating	Risk Rating	Reward Rating
Q4-18	B-	C	B
Q2-18	B-	C	B
Q4-17	B+	A-	B+
Q4-16	B-	C+	B
Q4-15	C	C	C

Asset & Performance History

Date	NAV	1-Year Total Return
2017	173.46	30.93
2016	132.99	9.18
2015	122.47	9.68
2014	113.11	22.64
2013	92.87	37.75
2012	67.65	15.9

Total Assets: $3,073,886,054
Asset Allocation

Asset	%
Cash	0%
Stocks	100%
US Stocks	100%
Bonds	0%
US Bonds	0%
Other	0%

Services Offered:

Investment Strategy: The investment seeks to track the investment results of the Dow Jones U.S. Select Medical Equipment Index composed of U.S. equities in the medical devices sector. The fund generally invests at least 90% of its assets in securities of the underlying index and in depositary receipts representing securities of the underlying index. The underlying index includes medical equipment companies, including manufacturers and distributors of medical devices such as magnetic resonance imaging (MRI) scanners, prosthetics, pacemakers, X-ray machines, and other non-disposable medical devices. The fund is non-diversified. **Top Holdings:** Abbott Laboratories Medtronic PLC Thermo Fisher Scientific Inc Danaher Corp Becton, Dickinson and Co

SPDR® S&P Bank ETF
C-   HOLD

Ticker	Traded On	NAV	Total Assets ($)	Dividend Yield (TTM)	Turnover Ratio	Expense Ratio
KBE	NYSE Arca	37.34	$2,961,119,979	1.73	35	0.35

Ratings
Reward	C-
Risk	C
Recent Upgrade/Downgrade	Down

Fund Information
Fund Type	Exchange Traded Funds
Category	Financials Sector Equity
Sub-Category	Financial
Prospectus Objective	Financial
Inception Date	Nov-05
Open to New Investments	Y

Prices
Price (as of 12/31/2018)	37.35
52-Week High	51.86
52-Week Low	35.17

Total Returns (%)
3-Month	6-Month	1-Year	3-Year	5-Year
-18.89	-20.60	-19.58	16.03	22.28

3-Year Standard Deviation	20.52
Effective Duration	

Valuation
Premium/Discount (1-Year Average)	-0.02

Company Information
Provider	SPDR State Street Global Advisors
Manager/Tenure	Michael J. Feehily (7), Karl A. Schneider (4), Melissa Kapitulik (0)
Website	http://www.spdrs.com
Address	SPDR State Street Global Advisors State Street Financial Center, 1 Lincoln Street Boston MA 02111-2900 United States
Phone Number	617-786-3000

PERFORMANCE

Ratings History
Date	Overall Rating	Risk Rating	Reward Rating
Q4-18	C-	C	C-
Q2-18	C+	C+	C+
Q4-17	B+	C+	A
Q4-16	B-	C	B
Q4-15	B	B-	B

Asset & Performance History
Date	NAV	1-Year Total Return
2017	47.31	10.35
2016	43.49	29.17
2015	33.85	2.64
2014	33.54	2.67
2013	33.18	41.53
2012	23.81	22.71

Total Assets: $2,961,119,979

Asset Allocation
Asset	%
Cash	0%
Stocks	100%
US Stocks	98%
Bonds	0%
US Bonds	0%
Other	0%

Services Offered: Dividend Investment Plan, CashInvestment Plan

Investment Strategy: The investment seeks to provide investment results that, before fees and expenses, correspond generally to the total return performance of the S&P Banks Select Industry Index. The fund generally invests substantially all, but at least 80%, of its total assets in the securities comprising the index. The index tracks the performance of publicly traded national money centers and leading regional banks. It may invest in equity securities that are not included in the index, cash and cash equivalents or money market instruments, such as repurchase agreements and money market funds. The fund is non-diversified. **Top Holdings:** LendingTree Inc Signature Bank BB&T Corp US Bancorp Bank of New York Mellon Corp

---

iShares Core MSCI Europe ETF
D+   SELL

Ticker	Traded On	NAV	Total Assets ($)	Dividend Yield (TTM)	Turnover Ratio	Expense Ratio
IEUR	NYSE Arca	41.27	$2,929,254,453	4.03	3	0.1

Ratings
Reward	D+
Risk	C-
Recent Upgrade/Downgrade	Down

Fund Information
Fund Type	Exchange Traded Funds
Category	Europe Equity Large Cap
Sub-Category	Europe Stock
Prospectus Objective	Europe Stock
Inception Date	Jun-14
Open to New Investments	Y

Prices
Price (as of 12/31/2018)	41.33
52-Week High	53.89
52-Week Low	40.03

Total Returns (%)
3-Month	6-Month	1-Year	3-Year	5-Year
-13.33	-11.70	-15.24	7.07	

3-Year Standard Deviation	12.22
Effective Duration	

Valuation
Premium/Discount (1-Year Average)	-0.06

Company Information
Provider	iShares
Manager/Tenure	Diane Hsiung (4), Jennifer Hsui (4), Greg Savage (4), 3 others
Website	http://www.ishares.com
Address	iShares 400 Howard Street San Francisco CA 94105 United States
Phone Number	800-474-2737

PERFORMANCE

Ratings History
Date	Overall Rating	Risk Rating	Reward Rating
Q4-18	D+	C-	D+
Q2-18	C	C+	C
Q4-17	B	B	B
Q4-16	D+	C-	D
Q4-15	D	C+	D

Asset & Performance History
Date	NAV	1-Year Total Return
2017	50.34	26.85
2016	40.79	-0.41
2015	42.27	-1.14
2014	43.87	
2013		
2012		

Total Assets: $2,929,254,453

Asset Allocation
Asset	%
Cash	1%
Stocks	99%
US Stocks	2%
Bonds	0%
US Bonds	0%
Other	0%

Services Offered:

Investment Strategy: The investment seeks to track the investment results of the MSCI Europe IMI. The fund generally will invest at least 90% of its assets in the component securities of the underlying index and in investments that have economic characteristics that are substantially identical to the component securities of the underlying index. The index is a free float-adjusted market capitalization-weighted index which consists of securities from the following 15 developed market countries or regions: Austria, Belgium, Denmark, Finland, France, Germany, Ireland, Italy, the Netherlands, Norway, Portugal, Spain, Sweden, Switzerland and the United Kingdom. **Top Holdings:** Nestle SA Novartis AG Roche Holding AG Dividend Right Cert. HSBC Holdings PLC Royal Dutch Shell PLC Class A

JPMorgan Alerian MLP Index ETN   D+   SELL

Ticker	Traded On	NAV
AMJ	NYSE Arca	

Total Assets ($)	Dividend Yield (TTM)	Turnover Ratio	Expense Ratio
$2,925,020,000	7.61	0	0.85

Ratings

Reward	D+
Risk	C-
Recent Upgrade/Downgrade	

Fund Information

Fund Type	Exchange Traded Funds
Category	Energy Sector Equity
Sub-Category	Energy Limited Partnership
Prospectus Objective	Unaligned
Inception Date	Apr-09
Open to New Investments	Y

Prices

Price (as of 12/31/2018)	22.32
52-Week High	30.57
52-Week Low	21.22

Total Returns (%)

3-Month	6-Month	1-Year	3-Year	5-Year
-17.14	-12.24	-13.19	-5.90	-33.78

3-Year Standard Deviation	18.13
Effective Duration	

Valuation

Premium/Discount (1-Year Average)	-0.31

Company Information

Provider	JPMorgan
Manager/Tenure	No Manager (9)
Website	http://www.jpmorganfunds.com
Address	JPMorgan 270 Park Avenue New York NY 10017-2070 United States
Phone Number	800-480-4111

PERFORMANCE

Ratings History

Date	Overall Rating	Risk Rating	Reward Rating
Q4-18	D+	C-	D+
Q2-18	D	D	D
Q4-17	D	D	D
Q4-16	D	D	D
Q4-15	D+	D	D+

Asset & Performance History

Date	NAV	1-Year Total Return
2017	27.48	-7.07
2016	31.58	17.15
2015	28.96	-32.94
2014	45.92	3.76
2013	46.35	28.5
2012	37.85	2.27

Total Assets: $2,925,020,000

Asset Allocation

Asset	%
Cash	%
Stocks	%
US Stocks	%
Bonds	%
US Bonds	%
Other	%

Services Offered:

Investment Strategy: The investment seeks to replicate, net of expenses, the Alerian MLP Index. The index tracks the performance of midstream energy Master Limited Partnerships. **Top Holdings:**

SPDR® Bloomberg Barclays Short Term High Yield Bond ETF   C+   HOLD

Ticker	Traded On	NAV
SJNK	NYSE Arca	25.98

Total Assets ($)	Dividend Yield (TTM)	Turnover Ratio	Expense Ratio
$2,909,740,772	5.52	57	0.4

Ratings

Reward	C
Risk	B
Recent Upgrade/Downgrade	

Fund Information

Fund Type	Exchange Traded Funds
Category	US Fixed Income
Sub-Category	High Yield Bond
Prospectus Objective	Corp Bond-High Yld
Inception Date	Mar-12
Open to New Investments	Y

Prices

Price (as of 12/31/2018)	26.03
52-Week High	27.82
52-Week Low	25.68

Total Returns (%)

3-Month	6-Month	1-Year	3-Year	5-Year
-3.98	-1.60	-0.25	20.03	11.33

3-Year Standard Deviation	4.04
Effective Duration	2.44

Valuation

Premium/Discount (1-Year Average)	0.10

Company Information

Provider	SPDR State Street Global Advisors
Manager/Tenure	Michael J. Brunell (6), Kyle Kelly (5), Bradley J. Sullivan (2)
Website	http://www.spdrs.com
Address	SPDR State Street Global Advisors State Street Financial Center, 1 Lincoln Street Boston MA 02111-2900 United States
Phone Number	617-786-3000

PERFORMANCE

Ratings History

Date	Overall Rating	Risk Rating	Reward Rating
Q4-18	C+	B	C
Q2-18	C+	C+	C
Q4-17	C+	B-	C+
Q4-16	C	C+	C
Q4-15	C	C+	C-

Asset & Performance History

Date	NAV	1-Year Total Return
2017	27.51	4.85
2016	27.62	14.27
2015	25.62	-6.56
2014	28.93	-0.73
2013	30.7	6.85
2012	30.32	

Total Assets: $2,909,740,772

Asset Allocation

Asset	%
Cash	3%
Stocks	0%
US Stocks	0%
Bonds	97%
US Bonds	85%
Other	0%

Services Offered:

Investment Strategy: The investment seeks to provide investment results that correspond generally to the price and yield performance of the Bloomberg Barclays US High Yield 350mn Cash Pay 0-5 Yr 2% Capped Index. The fund generally invests substantially all, but at least 80%, of its total assets in the securities comprising the index or in securities that the Adviser determines have economic characteristics that are substantially identical to the economic characteristics of the securities that comprise the index. The index is designed to measure the performance of short-term publicly issued U.S. dollar-denominated high yield corporate bonds. It is non-diversified. **Top Holdings:** Reynolds Group Issuer LLC. 5.75% Prime Securities Services Borrower, LLC and Prime Finance, Inc. 9.25% Community Health Systems Incorporated 6.25% Bausch Health Companies Inc 5.88% HCA Inc. 6.5%

Vanguard Russell 1000 Index Fund ETF Shares

C   HOLD

Ticker	Traded On	NAV	Total Assets ($)	Dividend Yield (TTM)	Turnover Ratio	Expense Ratio
VONE	NAS CM		$2,905,250,138	1.75	9	0.12

Ratings
Reward	C
Risk	C-
Recent Upgrade/Downgrade	

Fund Information
Fund Type	Exchange Traded Funds
Category	US Equity Large Cap Blend
Sub-Category	Large Blend
Prospectus Objective	Growth
Inception Date	Sep-10
Open to New Investments	Y

Prices
Price (as of 12/31/2018)	114.50
52-Week High	134.87
52-Week Low	107.21

Total Returns (%)

3-Month	6-Month	1-Year	3-Year	5-Year
-14.81	-8.26	-5.70	28.07	46.03

3-Year Standard Deviation	9.58
Effective Duration	

Valuation
Premium/Discount (1-Year Average)	0.04

Company Information
Provider	Vanguard
Manager/Tenure	Michael A. Johnson (2), Walter Nejman (2)
Website	http://www.vanguard.com
Address	Vanguard 100 Vanguard Boulevard Malvern PA 19355 United States
Phone Number	877-662-7447

PERFORMANCE

Ratings History

Date	Overall Rating	Risk Rating	Reward Rating
Q4-18	C	C-	C
Q2-18	C	C-	C
Q4-17	B	B	B
Q4-16	C+	C-	B
Q4-15	C	C	C

Asset & Performance History

Date	NAV	1-Year Total Return
2017	122.43	21.61
2016	102.57	11.24
2015	93.62	0.81
2014	94.61	13.1
2013	85.12	32.92
2012	65.25	16.3

Total Assets: $2,905,250,138
Asset Allocation

Asset	%
Cash	0%
Stocks	100%
US Stocks	99%
Bonds	0%
US Bonds	0%
Other	0%

Services Offered:

Investment Strategy: The investment seeks to track the performance of a benchmark index that measures the investment return of large-capitalization stocks in the United States. The fund employs an indexing investment approach designed to track the performance of the Russell 1000® Index. The index is designed to measure the performance of large-capitalization stocks in the United States. The Advisor attempts to replicate the target index by investing all, or substantially all, of its assets in the stocks that make up the index, holding each stock in approximately the same proportion as its weighting in the index. **Top Holdings:** Apple Inc Microsoft Corp Amazon.com Inc Berkshire Hathaway Inc B Johnson & Johnson

---

iShares 0-5 Year High Yield Corporate Bond ETF

C   HOLD

Ticker	Traded On	NAV	Total Assets ($)	Dividend Yield (TTM)	Turnover Ratio	Expense Ratio
SHYG	NYSE Arca	44.54	$2,849,064,856	5.53	35	0.3

Ratings
Reward	C
Risk	C+
Recent Upgrade/Downgrade	Down

Fund Information
Fund Type	Exchange Traded Funds
Category	US Fixed Income
Sub-Category	High Yield Bond
Prospectus Objective	Corp Bond-High Yld
Inception Date	Oct-13
Open to New Investments	Y

Prices
Price (as of 12/31/2018)	44.55
52-Week High	47.44
52-Week Low	43.90

Total Returns (%)

3-Month	6-Month	1-Year	3-Year	5-Year
-3.30	-1.07	0.43	18.88	15.02

3-Year Standard Deviation	3.04
Effective Duration	2.43

Valuation
Premium/Discount (1-Year Average)	0.19

Company Information
Provider	iShares
Manager/Tenure	James Mauro (5), Scott Radell (5)
Website	http://www.ishares.com
Address	iShares 400 Howard Street San Francisco CA 94105 United States
Phone Number	800-474-2737

PERFORMANCE

Ratings History

Date	Overall Rating	Risk Rating	Reward Rating
Q4-18	C	C+	C
Q2-18	C+	C+	C
Q4-17	B-	B	C+
Q4-16	C	C+	C
Q4-15	C-	C+	D

Asset & Performance History

Date	NAV	1-Year Total Return
2017	46.93	5.4
2016	47.02	12.3
2015	44.33	-3.73
2014	48.35	0.5
2013	50.18	
2012		

Total Assets: $2,849,064,856
Asset Allocation

Asset	%
Cash	2%
Stocks	0%
US Stocks	0%
Bonds	98%
US Bonds	85%
Other	0%

Services Offered:

Investment Strategy: The investment seeks to track the investment results of the Markit iBoxx® USD Liquid High Yield 0-5 Index composed of U.S. dollar-denominated, high yield corporate bonds with remaining maturities of less than five years. The fund generally invests at least 90% of its assets in the component securities of the index and may invest up to 10% of its assets in certain futures, options and swap contracts, cash and cash equivalents. The index is designed to reflect the performance of U.S. dollar-denominated high yield corporate debt. **Top Holdings:** Sprint Corporation 7.88% Bausch Health Companies Inc 5.88% Reynolds Group Issuer LLC. 5.75% Community Health Systems Incorporated 6.25% Tenet Healthcare Corporation 8.13%

SPDR® DoubleLine Total Return Tactical ETF   C   HOLD

Ticker	Traded On	NAV	Total Assets ($)	Dividend Yield (TTM)	Turnover Ratio	Expense Ratio
TOTL	NYSE Arca	47.19	$2,841,392,426	3.28	72	0.55

Ratings
Reward   C-
Risk   C+
Recent Upgrade/Downgrade

Fund Information
Fund Type   Exchange Traded Funds
Category   US Fixed Income
Sub-Category   Intermediate-Term Bond
Prospectus Objective   Growth & Inc
Inception Date   Feb-15
Open to New Investments   Y

Prices
Price (as of 12/31/2018)   47.37
52-Week High   48.64
52-Week Low   46.68

Total Returns (%)

3-Month	6-Month	1-Year	3-Year	5-Year
1.06	1.28	0.30	6.87	

3-Year Standard Deviation   2.05
Effective Duration   4.56

Valuation
Premium/Discount (1-Year Average)   -0.10

Company Information
Provider   SPDR State Street Global Advisors
Manager/Tenure Philip A. Barach (3), Jeffrey E.
                Gundlach (3), Jeffrey J. Sherman (3)
Website   http://www.spdrs.com
Address   SPDR State Street Global Advisors
                State Street Financial Center, 1
                Lincoln Street Boston MA 02111-2900
                United States
Phone Number   617-786-3000

PERFORMANCE

Ratings History

Date	Overall Rating	Risk Rating	Reward Rating
Q4-18	C	C+	C-
Q2-18	C	C+	C
Q4-17	C+	B+	C
Q4-16	C-	C+	D+
Q4-15	U		

Asset & Performance History

Date	NAV	1-Year Total Return
2017	48.67	3.42
2016	48.48	3.02
2015	48.58	
2014		
2013		
2012		

Total Assets: $2,841,392,426

Asset Allocation

Asset	%
Cash	2%
Stocks	0%
US Stocks	0%
Bonds	98%
US Bonds	89%
Other	0%

Services Offered:

Investment Strategy: The investment seeks to maximize total return. Under normal circumstances, the Sub-Adviser will invest at least 80% of the fund's net assets in a portfolio of fixed income securities of any credit quality. The fund may invest up to 25% of its net assets in corporate high yield securities (commonly known as "junk bonds"). It may invest up to 15% of its net assets in securities denominated in foreign currencies, and may invest beyond this limit in U.S. dollar-denominated securities of foreign issuers. The fund is non-diversified. **Top Holdings:** United States Treasury Notes 2.5% United States Treasury Notes 1.5% United States Treasury Notes 2.12% United States Treasury Bills 0% Federal National Mortgage Association 3%

Vanguard Materials Index Fund ETF Shares   C   HOLD

Ticker	Traded On	NAV	Total Assets ($)	Dividend Yield (TTM)	Turnover Ratio	Expense Ratio
VAW	NYSE Arca		$2,799,580,804	1.8	5	0.1

Ratings
Reward   C
Risk   C
Recent Upgrade/Downgrade

Fund Information
Fund Type   Exchange Traded Funds
Category   Natural Resources
Sub-Category   Natural Resources
Prospectus Objective   Unaligned
Inception Date   Jan-04
Open to New Investments   Y

Prices
Price (as of 12/31/2018)   110.83
52-Week High   144.53
52-Week Low   104.05

Total Returns (%)

3-Month	6-Month	1-Year	3-Year	5-Year
-16.32	-15.30	-18.07	23.01	17.09

3-Year Standard Deviation   14.68
Effective Duration

Valuation
Premium/Discount (1-Year Average)   0.01

Company Information
Provider   Vanguard
Manager/Tenure William A. Coleman (3), Michelle Louie
                (1)
Website   http://www.vanguard.com
Address   Vanguard 100 Vanguard Boulevard
                Malvern PA 19355 United States
Phone Number   877-662-7447

PERFORMANCE

Ratings History

Date	Overall Rating	Risk Rating	Reward Rating
Q4-18	C	C	C
Q2-18	C	C-	C
Q4-17	B	C+	B+
Q4-16	C	C-	B-
Q4-15	C	C	C

Asset & Performance History

Date	NAV	1-Year Total Return
2017	136.55	23.04
2016	112.41	21.47
2015	94.23	-10.11
2014	107.36	5.9
2013	103.18	24.91
2012	84.16	17.25

Total Assets: $2,799,580,804

Asset Allocation

Asset	%
Cash	0%
Stocks	100%
US Stocks	89%
Bonds	0%
US Bonds	0%
Other	0%

Services Offered:

Investment Strategy: The investment seeks to track the performance of a benchmark index. The fund employs an indexing investment approach designed to track the performance of the MSCI US Investable Market Index (IMI)/Materials 25/50, an index made up of stocks of large, mid-size, and small U.S. companies within the materials sector, as classified under the Global Industry Classification Standard (GICS). The Advisor attempts to replicate the target index by seeking to invest all, or substantially all, of its assets in the stocks that make up the index, in order to hold each stock in approximately the same proportion as its weighting in the index. The fund is non-diversified. **Top Holdings:** DowDuPont Inc Praxair Ecolab Inc Air Products & Chemicals Inc Sherwin-Williams Co

The Real Estate Select Sector SPDR Fund   B-   BUY

Ticker	Traded On	NAV	Total Assets ($)	Dividend Yield (TTM)	Turnover Ratio	Expense Ratio
XLRE	NYSE Arca	31.00	$2,786,343,478	3.44	7	0.13

Ratings
Reward   B
Risk   C
Recent Upgrade/Downgrade

Fund Information
Fund Type   Exchange Traded Funds
Category   Real Estate Sector Equity
Sub-Category   Real Estate
Prospectus Objective   Real Estate
Inception Date   Oct-15
Open to New Investments   Y

Prices
Price (as of 12/31/2018)   31.00
52-Week High   34.48
52-Week Low   29.40

Total Returns (%)

3-Month	6-Month	1-Year	3-Year	5-Year
-3.02	-2.53	-2.27	11.58	

3-Year Standard Deviation   12.14
Effective Duration

Valuation
Premium/Discount (1-Year Average)   0.00

Company Information
Provider   SPDR State Street Global Advisors
Manager/Tenure   Michael J. Feehily (3), Karl A. Schneider (3), Amy Cheng (1)
Website   http://www.spdrs.com
Address   SPDR State Street Global Advisors State Street Financial Center, 1 Lincoln Street Boston MA 02111-2900 United States
Phone Number   617-786-3000

PERFORMANCE

Ratings History

Date	Overall Rating	Risk Rating	Reward Rating
Q4-18	B-	C	B
Q2-18	C+	C-	B
Q4-17	C	B-	C
Q4-16	D	C	B
Q4-15			

Asset & Performance History

Date	NAV	1-Year Total Return
2017	32.92	10.66
2016	30.74	3.17
2015	31.04	
2014		
2013		
2012		

Total Assets: $2,786,343,478
Asset Allocation

Asset	%
Cash	0%
Stocks	100%
US Stocks	100%
Bonds	0%
US Bonds	0%
Other	0%

Services Offered:

Investment Strategy: The investment seeks to provide investment results that, before expenses, correspond generally to the price and yield performance of publicly traded equity securities of companies in the Real Estate Select Sector Index (the "index"). Under normal market conditions, the fund generally invests substantially all, but at least 95%, of its total assets in the securities comprising the index. The index includes securities of companies from the following industries: real estate management and development and REITs, excluding mortgage REITs. The fund is non-diversified. **Top Holdings:** American Tower Corp   Simon Property Group Inc   Crown Castle International Corp   Prologis Inc   Public Storage

---

First Trust NYSE Arca Biotechnology Index Fund   C   HOLD

Ticker	Traded On	NAV	Total Assets ($)	Dividend Yield (TTM)	Turnover Ratio	Expense Ratio
FBT	NYSE Arca	124.25	$2,779,420,284	0	36	0.56

Ratings
Reward   C
Risk   D+
Recent Upgrade/Downgrade

Fund Information
Fund Type   Exchange Traded Funds
Category   Healthcare Sector Equity
Sub-Category   Health
Prospectus Objective   Health
Inception Date   Jun-06
Open to New Investments   Y

Prices
Price (as of 12/31/2018)   124.20
52-Week High   159.14
52-Week Low   114.50

Total Returns (%)

3-Month	6-Month	1-Year	3-Year	5-Year
-21.08	-12.15	-0.20	9.90	80.05

3-Year Standard Deviation   25.71
Effective Duration

Valuation
Premium/Discount (1-Year Average)   0.03

Company Information
Provider   First Trust
Manager/Tenure   Jon C. Erickson (12), Daniel J. Lindquist (12), David G. McGarel (12), 3 others
Website   http://www.ftportfolios.com/
Address   First Trust 120 E. Liberty Drive, Suite 400 Wheaton IL 60187 United States
Phone Number   800-621-1675

PERFORMANCE

Ratings History

Date	Overall Rating	Risk Rating	Reward Rating
Q4-18	C	D+	C
Q2-18	C-	D	C
Q4-17	B	C+	B
Q4-16	C	D+	C
Q4-15	C+	C	B-

Asset & Performance History

Date	NAV	1-Year Total Return
2017	124.51	36.98
2016	90.89	-19.6
2015	113.05	10.96
2014	101.99	47.63
2013	69.12	50.09
2012	46.05	40.91

Total Assets: $2,779,420,284
Asset Allocation

Asset	%
Cash	0%
Stocks	100%
US Stocks	96%
Bonds	0%
US Bonds	0%
Other	0%

Services Offered:

Investment Strategy: The investment seeks investment results that correspond generally to the price and yield (before the fund's fees and expenses) of an equity index called the NYSE Arca Biotechnology IndexSM. The fund will normally invest at least 90% of its net assets (including investment borrowings) in common stocks that comprise the index. The index is an equal-dollar weighted index designed to measure the performance of a cross section of companies in the biotechnology industry that are primarily involved in the use of biological processes to develop products or provide services. **Top Holdings:** Ionis Pharmaceuticals Inc   Exelixis Inc   Intercept Pharmaceuticals Inc   Charles River Laboratories International Inc   Illumina Inc

SPDR® Nuveen Bloomberg Barclays Municipal Bond ETF   C   HOLD

Ticker	Traded On	NAV	Total Assets ($)	Dividend Yield (TTM)	Turnover Ratio	Expense Ratio
TFI	NYSE Arca	48.14	$2,771,419,350	2.25	23	0.23

Ratings
Reward   D+
Risk   C
Recent Upgrade/Downgrade

Fund Information
Fund Type   Exchange Traded Funds
Category   US Muni Fixed Inc
Sub-Category   Muni National Long
Prospectus Objective   Muni Bond - Natl
Inception Date   Sep-07
Open to New Investments   Y

Prices
Price (as of 12/31/2018)   48.12
52-Week High   48.97
52-Week Low   46.65

Total Returns (%)

3-Month	6-Month	1-Year	3-Year	5-Year
1.92	1.40	0.43	5.86	19.50

3-Year Standard Deviation   3.98
Effective Duration   7.23

Valuation
Premium/Discount (1-Year Average)   -0.17

Company Information
Provider   SPDR State Street Global Advisors
Manager/Tenure Timothy T. Ryan (11), Steven M.
                Hlavin (8)
Website   http://www.spdrs.com
Address   SPDR State Street Global Advisors
                State Street Financial Center, 1
                Lincoln Street Boston MA 02111-2900
                United States
Phone Number   617-786-3000

PERFORMANCE

Ratings History

Date	Overall Rating	Risk Rating	Reward Rating
Q4-18	C	C	D+
Q2-18	C	C+	C
Q4-17	B-	B	C
Q4-16	C	C+	C
Q4-15	C+	C+	C

Asset & Performance History

Date	NAV	1-Year Total Return
2017	49.03	5.4
2016	47.46	-0.24
2015	48.65	3.33
2014	48.24	9.24
2013	45.24	-3.59
2012	48.47	6.31

Total Assets: $2,771,419,350
Asset Allocation

Asset	%
Cash	0%
Stocks	0%
US Stocks	0%
Bonds	100%
US Bonds	100%
Other	0%

Services Offered:

Investment Strategy: The investment seeks investment results that correspond generally to the price and yield performance of the Bloomberg Barclays Municipal Managed Money 1-25 Years Index. The fund invests substantially all, but at least 80%, of its total assets in the securities comprising the index or in securities that the Sub-Adviser determines have economic characteristics that are substantially identical to the economic characteristics of the securities that comprise the index. The index is designed to track the U.S. fully tax-exempt bond market. It is non-diversified. **Top Holdings:** NEW YORK N Y CITY TRANSITIONAL FIN AUTH 5% NEW YORK N Y CITY TRANSITIONAL FIN AUTH 5% METROPOLITAN TRANSN AUTH N Y 5% PRINCE GEORGES CNTY MD 5% EAST BAY CALIF MUN UTIL DIST 5%

Goldman Sachs Access Treasury 0-1 Year ETF   C   HOLD

Ticker	Traded On	NAV	Total Assets ($)	Dividend Yield (TTM)	Turnover Ratio	Expense Ratio
GBIL	NYSE Arca	100.03	$2,745,066,723	1.51		0.12

Ratings
Reward   C-
Risk   C+
Recent Upgrade/Downgrade   Up

Fund Information
Fund Type   Exchange Traded Funds
Category   US Fixed Income
Sub-Category   Ultrashort Bond
Prospectus Objective   Govt Bond - Treasury
Inception Date   Sep-16
Open to New Investments   Y

Prices
Price (as of 12/31/2018)   100.05
52-Week High   100.23
52-Week Low   99.95

Total Returns (%)

3-Month	6-Month	1-Year	3-Year	5-Year
0.37	0.84	1.58		

3-Year Standard Deviation
Effective Duration

Valuation
Premium/Discount (1-Year Average)   0.02

Company Information
Provider   Goldman Sachs
Manager/Tenure Dave Fishman (2), Jason Singer (1),
                David Westbrook (0)
Website   http://www.gsamfunds.com
Address   Goldman Sachs 200 West Stree New
                York NY 10282 United States
Phone Number   800-526-7384

PERFORMANCE

Ratings History

Date	Overall Rating	Risk Rating	Reward Rating
Q4-18	C	C+	C-
Q2-18	C-	C+	D+
Q4-17	D	C+	D+
Q4-16	U		
Q4-15			

Asset & Performance History

Date	NAV	1-Year Total Return
2017	99.97	0.7
2016	100	
2015		
2014		
2013		
2012		

Total Assets: $2,745,066,723
Asset Allocation

Asset	%
Cash	44%
Stocks	0%
US Stocks	0%
Bonds	56%
US Bonds	56%
Other	0%

Services Offered:

Investment Strategy: The investment seeks to provide investment results that closely correspond, before fees and expenses, to the performance of the FTSE US Treasury 0-1 Year Composite Select Index. The fund seeks to achieve its investment objective by investing at least 80% of its assets (exclusive of collateral held from securities lending) in securities included in its underlying index. The index is designed to measure the performance of U.S. Treasury Securities with a maximum remaining maturity of 12 months. The investment adviser uses a representative sampling strategy to manage the fund. **Top Holdings:** United States Treasury Bills 0% United States Treasury Notes 1.25% United States Treasury Notes 0.88% United States Treasury Notes 1% United States Treasury Notes 1%

SPDR® EURO STOXX 50 ETF   C-   HOLD

Ticker	Traded On	NAV	Total Assets ($)	Dividend Yield (TTM)	Turnover Ratio	Expense Ratio
FEZ	NYSE Arca	33.30	$2,743,209,467	3.29	7	0.29

Ratings

Reward	C-
Risk	D+
Recent Upgrade/Downgrade	Down

Fund Information

Fund Type	Exchange Traded Funds
Category	Europe Equity Large Cap
Sub-Category	Europe Stock
Prospectus Objective	Europe Stock
Inception Date	Oct-02
Open to New Investments	Y

Prices

Price (as of 12/31/2018)	33.27
52-Week High	44.21
52-Week Low	32.08

Total Returns (%)

3-Month	6-Month	1-Year	3-Year	5-Year
-12.99	-11.89	-16.05	5.35	-7.56

3-Year Standard Deviation	14.52
Effective Duration	

Valuation

Premium/Discount (1-Year Average)	-0.15

Company Information

Provider	SPDR State Street Global Advisors
Manager/Tenure	Michael J. Feehily (7), Karl A. Schneider (3), Mark Krivitsky (1)
Website	http://www.spdrs.com
Address	SPDR State Street Global Advisors State Street Financial Center, 1 Lincoln Street Boston MA 02111-2900 United States
Phone Number	617-786-3000

PERFORMANCE

Ratings History

Date	Overall Rating	Risk Rating	Reward Rating
Q4-18	C-	D+	C-
Q2-18	C	C	C
Q4-17	B-	C	B
Q4-16	D+	D+	D
Q4-15	C+	B	C

Asset & Performance History

Date	NAV	1-Year Total Return
2017	40.85	24.39
2016	33.68	-1.31
2015	34.58	-4.25
2014	37.13	-8.36
2013	41.88	27.42
2012	33.97	20.47

Total Assets: $2,743,209,467

Asset Allocation

Asset	%
Cash	0%
Stocks	100%
US Stocks	1%
Bonds	0%
US Bonds	0%
Other	0%

Services Offered: Dividend Investment Plan

Investment Strategy: The investment seeks investment results that, before fees and expenses, correspond generally to the total return performance of the EURO STOXX 50® Index. The fund employs a sampling strategy, which means that the fund is not required to purchase all of the securities represented in the index. It generally invests substantially all, but at least 80%, of its total assets in the securities comprising the index. The index is designed to represent the performance of some of the largest companies across components of the 19 EURO STOXX Supersector Indexes. The EURO STOXX Supersector Indexes are subsets of the EURO STOXX Index. It is non-diversified. **Top Holdings:** Total SA SAP SE Sanofi SA Siemens AG Allianz SE

SPDR® Dow Jones REIT ETF   C   HOLD

Ticker	Traded On	NAV	Total Assets ($)	Dividend Yield (TTM)	Turnover Ratio	Expense Ratio
RWR	NYSE Arca	86.04	$2,708,692,708	3.38	9	0.25

Ratings

Reward	C
Risk	C
Recent Upgrade/Downgrade	Down

Fund Information

Fund Type	Exchange Traded Funds
Category	Real Estate Sector Equity
Sub-Category	Real Estate
Prospectus Objective	Real Estate
Inception Date	Apr-01
Open to New Investments	Y

Prices

Price (as of 12/31/2018)	86.00
52-Week High	97.24
52-Week Low	81.89

Total Returns (%)

3-Month	6-Month	1-Year	3-Year	5-Year
-5.68	-5.28	-4.30	5.34	44.49

3-Year Standard Deviation	12.64
Effective Duration	

Valuation

Premium/Discount (1-Year Average)	0.01

Company Information

Provider	SPDR State Street Global Advisors
Manager/Tenure	Michael J. Feehily (5), Karl A. Schneider (4), Daniel TenPas (1)
Website	http://www.spdrs.com
Address	SPDR State Street Global Advisors State Street Financial Center, 1 Lincoln Street Boston MA 02111-2900 United States
Phone Number	617-786-3000

PERFORMANCE

Ratings History

Date	Overall Rating	Risk Rating	Reward Rating
Q4-18	C	C	C
Q2-18	C	C	C
Q4-17	B-	B+	C+
Q4-16	C+	C	C+
Q4-15	C+	C+	B-

Asset & Performance History

Date	NAV	1-Year Total Return
2017	93.64	3.49
2016	93.27	4.07
2015	91.59	4.17
2014	90.82	31.66
2013	71.29	0.95
2012	72.97	16.81

Total Assets: $2,708,692,708

Asset Allocation

Asset	%
Cash	0%
Stocks	100%
US Stocks	100%
Bonds	0%
US Bonds	0%
Other	0%

Services Offered:

Investment Strategy: The investment seeks to provide investment results that, before fees and expenses, correspond generally to the total return performance of the Dow Jones U.S. Select REIT Index. The fund generally invests substantially all, but at least 80%, of its total assets in the securities comprising the index. The index is designed to provide a measure of real estate securities that serve as proxies for direct real estate investing, in part by excluding securities whose value is not always closely tied to the value of the underlying real estate. The fund is non-diversified. **Top Holdings:** Simon Property Group Inc Prologis Inc Public Storage Welltower Inc AvalonBay Communities Inc

SPDR® S&P Oil & Gas Exploration & Production ETF   D+   SELL

Ticker	Traded On	NAV	Total Assets ($)	Dividend Yield (TTM)	Turnover Ratio	Expense Ratio
XOP	NYSE Arca	26.54	$2,704,346,448	0.8	3	0.35

Ratings
Reward   C-
Risk   D+
Recent Upgrade/Downgrade   Down

Fund Information
Fund Type   Exchange Traded Funds
Category   Energy Sector Equity
Sub-Category   Equity Energy
Prospectus Objective   Natl Res
Inception Date   Jun-06
Open to New Investments   Y

Prices
Price (as of 12/31/2018)   26.53
52-Week High   44.57
52-Week Low   24.12

Total Returns (%)

3-Month	6-Month	1-Year	3-Year	5-Year
-39.11	-36.85	-28.21	-9.98	-59.18

3-Year Standard Deviation   32.22
Effective Duration

Valuation
Premium/Discount (1-Year Average)   0.02

Company Information
Provider   SPDR State Street Global Advisors
Manager/Tenure   Michael J. Feehily (7), Karl A.
                  Schneider (4), Olga Winner (1)
Website   http://www.spdrs.com
Address   SPDR State Street Global Advisors
                  State Street Financial Center, 1
                  Lincoln Street Boston MA 02111-2900
                  United States
Phone Number   617-786-3000

PERFORMANCE

Ratings History

Date	Overall Rating	Risk Rating	Reward Rating
Q4-18	D+	D+	C-
Q2-18	C	D+	C
Q4-17	D	D	D
Q4-16	D+	D	D+
Q4-15	D	D	D

Asset & Performance History

Date	NAV	1-Year Total Return
2017	37.25	-9.31
2016	41.43	42.4
2015	30.23	-35.73
2014	47.85	-29.44
2013	68.53	27.92
2012	54.07	3.93

Total Assets: $2,704,346,448
Asset Allocation

Asset	%
Cash	0%
Stocks	100%
US Stocks	99%
Bonds	0%
US Bonds	0%
Other	0%

Services Offered:

Investment Strategy: The investment seeks to provide investment results that, before fees and expenses, correspond generally to the total return performance of an index derived from the oil and gas exploration and production segment of a U.S. total market composite index. In seeking to track the performance of the S&P Oil & Gas Exploration & Production Select Industry Index, the fund employs a sampling strategy. It generally invests substantially all, but at least 80%, of its total assets in the securities comprising the index. The index represents the oil and gas exploration and production segment of the S&P Total Market Index ("S&P TMI"). The fund is non-diversified. **Top Holdings:** Diamondback Energy Inc Cabot Oil & Gas Corp Class A Murphy Oil Corp Chevron Corp Southwestern Energy Co

---

Invesco S&P 500® High Dividend Low Volatility ETF   C   HOLD

Ticker	Traded On	NAV	Total Assets ($)	Dividend Yield (TTM)	Turnover Ratio	Expense Ratio
SPHD	NYSE Arca	38.18	$2,682,232,307	3.97		0.3

Ratings
Reward   C
Risk   C+
Recent Upgrade/Downgrade   Down

Fund Information
Fund Type   Exchange Traded Funds
Category   US Equity Large Cap Value
Sub-Category   Large Value
Prospectus Objective   Income
Inception Date   Oct-12
Open to New Investments

Prices
Price (as of 12/31/2018)   38.20
52-Week High   43.25
52-Week Low   36.52

Total Returns (%)

3-Month	6-Month	1-Year	3-Year	5-Year
-6.88	-4.53	-6.12	28.51	62.02

3-Year Standard Deviation   8.96
Effective Duration

Valuation
Premium/Discount (1-Year Average)   0.01

Company Information
Provider   Invesco
Manager/Tenure   Peter Hubbard (6), Michael Jeanette
                  (6), Tony Seisser (4), 1 other
Website   http://www.invesco.com/us
Address   Invesco 11 Greenway Plaza, Ste. 2500
                  Houston TX 77046 United States
Phone Number   800-659-1005

PERFORMANCE

Ratings History

Date	Overall Rating	Risk Rating	Reward Rating
Q4-18	C	C+	C
Q2-18	C	C	C
Q4-17	B+	A+	B
Q4-16	B-	C+	B
Q4-15	C+	C+	C+

Asset & Performance History

Date	NAV	1-Year Total Return
2017	42.4	11.93
2016	39.14	22.3
2015	33.32	5.2
2014	32.82	19.83
2013	28.37	20.84
2012	24.39	

Total Assets: $2,682,232,307
Asset Allocation

Asset	%
Cash	0%
Stocks	100%
US Stocks	100%
Bonds	0%
US Bonds	0%
Other	0%

Services Offered:

Investment Strategy: The investment seeks to track the investment results (before fees and expenses) of the S&P 500® Low Volatility High Dividend Index (the "underlying index"). The fund generally will invest at least 90% of its total assets in securities that comprise the underlying index. S&P Dow Jones Indices LLC compiles, maintains and calculates the underlying index, which is composed of 50 securities in the S&P 500® Index that historically have provided high dividend yields with lower volatility. **Top Holdings:** HCP Inc Welltower Inc PPL Corp Iron Mountain Inc Ventas Inc

iShares MSCI Canada ETF

C   HOLD

Ticker	Traded On	NAV	Total Assets ($)	Dividend Yield (TTM)	Turnover Ratio	Expense Ratio
EWC	NYSE Arca	24.00	$2,677,466,636	2.23	3	0.47

Ratings
Reward	C
Risk	C
Recent Upgrade/Downgrade	Down

Fund Information
Fund Type	Exchange Traded Funds
Category	Canadian Equity Large Cap
Sub-Category	Miscellaneous Region
Prospectus Objective	Foreign Stock
Inception Date	Mar-96
Open to New Investments	Y

Prices
Price (as of 12/31/2018)	23.96
52-Week High	30.42
52-Week Low	23.10

Total Returns (%)
3-Month	6-Month	1-Year	3-Year	5-Year
-16.03	-14.29	-17.21	19.36	-8.40

3-Year Standard Deviation	12.32
Effective Duration	

Valuation
Premium/Discount (1-Year Average)	-0.03

Company Information
Provider	iShares
Manager/Tenure	Diane Hsiung (10), Greg Savage (10), Jennifer Hsui (5), 1 other
Website	http://www.ishares.com
Address	iShares 400 Howard Street San Francisco CA 94105 United States
Phone Number	800-474-2737

PERFORMANCE

Ratings History
Date	Overall Rating	Risk Rating	Reward Rating
Q4-18	C	C	C
Q2-18	C+	C+	C
Q4-17	C	C	C+
Q4-16	C	C-	C
Q4-15	C-	D+	C

Asset & Performance History
Date	NAV	1-Year Total Return
2017	29.71	15.97
2016	26.16	24.32
2015	21.42	-24.29
2014	28.9	1.36
2013	29.12	5.4
2012	28.33	8.84

Total Assets: $2,677,466,636

Asset Allocation
Asset	%
Cash	0%
Stocks	100%
US Stocks	0%
Bonds	0%
US Bonds	0%
Other	0%

Services Offered: CashInvestment Plan

Investment Strategy: The investment seeks to track the investment results of the MSCI Canada Custom Capped Index. The fund will at all times invest at least 90% of its assets in the securities of its underlying index and in depositary receipts representing securities in its underlying index. The underlying index is designed to measure broad-based equity performance in Canada. The underlying index uses a capping methodology to limit the weight of any single component to a maximum of 25% of the underlying index. The underlying index may include large- or mid-capitalization companies. **Top Holdings:** Royal Bank of Canada The Toronto-Dominion Bank Bank of Nova Scotia Canadian National Railway Co Enbridge Inc

---

iShares Global Infrastructure ETF

C   HOLD

Ticker	Traded On	NAV	Total Assets ($)	Dividend Yield (TTM)	Turnover Ratio	Expense Ratio
IGF	NAS CM	39.31	$2,635,966,310	3.13	11	0.47

Ratings
Reward	C-
Risk	C
Recent Upgrade/Downgrade	

Fund Information
Fund Type	Exchange Traded Funds
Category	Infrastructure Sector Equity
Sub-Category	Infrastructure
Prospectus Objective	Utility
Inception Date	Dec-07
Open to New Investments	Y

Prices
Price (as of 12/31/2018)	39.38
52-Week High	46.35
52-Week Low	38.21

Total Returns (%)
3-Month	6-Month	1-Year	3-Year	5-Year
-5.45	-6.59	-10.19	19.46	17.93

3-Year Standard Deviation	9.78
Effective Duration	

Valuation
Premium/Discount (1-Year Average)	-0.04

Company Information
Provider	iShares
Manager/Tenure	Diane Hsiung (10), Greg Savage (10), Jennifer Hsui (6), 3 others
Website	http://www.ishares.com
Address	iShares 400 Howard Street San Francisco CA 94105 United States
Phone Number	800-474-2737

PERFORMANCE

Ratings History
Date	Overall Rating	Risk Rating	Reward Rating
Q4-18	C	C	C-
Q2-18	C	C+	C
Q4-17	C+	C+	C+
Q4-16	C	C	C
Q4-15	C	C+	C

Asset & Performance History
Date	NAV	1-Year Total Return
2017	45.27	19.25
2016	39.11	11.54
2015	36.1	-11.97
2014	42.28	12.14
2013	38.82	13.99
2012	35.36	11.08

Total Assets: $2,635,966,310

Asset Allocation
Asset	%
Cash	0%
Stocks	100%
US Stocks	39%
Bonds	0%
US Bonds	0%
Other	0%

Services Offered:

Investment Strategy: The investment seeks to track the S&P Global Infrastructure IndexTM. The fund generally invests at least 90% of its assets in the component securities of the index and in investments that have economic characteristics that are substantially identical to the component securities and may invest up to 10% of its assets in certain futures, options and swap contracts, cash and cash equivalents. The index is designed to track performance of the stocks of large infrastructure companies in developed or emerging markets that must be domiciled in developed markets, or whose stocks are listed on developed market exchanges around the world. **Top Holdings:** Transurban Group Aena SME SA NextEra Energy Inc Enbridge Inc Atlantia SpA

SPDR® Portfolio S&P 500 Value ETF

C   HOLD

Ticker	Traded On	NAV	Total Assets ($)	Dividend Yield (TTM)	Turnover Ratio	Expense Ratio
SPYV	NYSE Arca	27.15	$2,614,792,083	2.56	21	0.04

Ratings
Reward	C
Risk	C+
Recent Upgrade/Downgrade	Down

Fund Information
Fund Type	Exchange Traded Funds
Category	US Equity Large Cap Value
Sub-Category	Large Value
Prospectus Objective	Growth
Inception Date	Sep-00
Open to New Investments	Y

Prices
Price (as of 12/31/2018)	27.16
52-Week High	32.54
52-Week Low	25.59

Total Returns (%)
3-Month	6-Month	1-Year	3-Year	5-Year
-12.33	-6.84	-8.92	22.92	33.38

3-Year Standard Deviation	9.52
Effective Duration	

Valuation
Premium/Discount (1-Year Average)	0.04

Company Information
Provider	SPDR State Street Global Advisors
Manager/Tenure	Michael J. Feehily (7), Karl A. Schneider (4), Mark Krivitsky (1)
Website	http://www.spdrs.com
Address	SPDR State Street Global Advisors State Street Financial Center, 1 Lincoln Street Boston MA 02111-2900 United States
Phone Number	617-786-3000

PERFORMANCE

Ratings History
Date	Overall Rating	Risk Rating	Reward Rating
Q4-18	C	C+	C
Q2-18	C	C+	C
Q4-17	B	B	B-
Q4-16	C+	C-	B
Q4-15	C	C-	C

Asset & Performance History
Date	NAV	1-Year Total Return
2017	30.65	15.18
2016	27.39	16.54
2015	23.97	-3.2
2014	25.4	12.1
2013	23.17	31.63
2012	17.98	17.39

Total Assets: $2,614,792,083
Asset Allocation
Asset	%
Cash	0%
Stocks	100%
US Stocks	98%
Bonds	0%
US Bonds	0%
Other	0%

Services Offered: Dividend Investment Plan, CashInvestment Plan

Investment Strategy: The investment seeks to provide investment results that, before fees and expenses, correspond generally to the total return performance of the S&P 500 Value Index that tracks the performance of large capitalization exchange traded U.S. equity securities exhibiting "value" characteristics. The fund employs a sampling strategy in seeking to track the performance of the S&P 500 Value Index. It generally invests substantially all, but at least 80%, of its total assets in the securities comprising the index. The index measures the performance of the large-capitalization value segment of the U.S. equity market. The fund is non-diversified. **Top Holdings:** Berkshire Hathaway Inc B   JPMorgan Chase & Co   Exxon Mobil Corp   Verizon Communications Inc   Wells Fargo & Co

SPDR® Portfolio Total Stock Market ETF

C   HOLD

Ticker	Traded On	NAV	Total Assets ($)	Dividend Yield (TTM)	Turnover Ratio	Expense Ratio
SPTM	NYSE Arca	30.87	$2,597,157,565	1.76	8	0.03

Ratings
Reward	C
Risk	C+
Recent Upgrade/Downgrade	Down

Fund Information
Fund Type	Exchange Traded Funds
Category	US Equity Large Cap Blend
Sub-Category	Large Blend
Prospectus Objective	Growth
Inception Date	Oct-00
Open to New Investments	Y

Prices
Price (as of 12/31/2018)	30.91
52-Week High	36.58
52-Week Low	28.90

Total Returns (%)
3-Month	6-Month	1-Year	3-Year	5-Year
-14.41	-8.51	-5.25	29.46	46.28

3-Year Standard Deviation	9.71
Effective Duration	

Valuation
Premium/Discount (1-Year Average)	0.00

Company Information
Provider	SPDR State Street Global Advisors
Manager/Tenure	Michael J. Feehily (7), Karl A. Schneider (4), Kathleen Morgan (0)
Website	http://www.spdrs.com
Address	SPDR State Street Global Advisors State Street Financial Center, 1 Lincoln Street Boston MA 02111-2900 United States
Phone Number	617-786-3000

PERFORMANCE

Ratings History
Date	Overall Rating	Risk Rating	Reward Rating
Q4-18	C	C+	C
Q2-18	C+	C+	C+
Q4-17	B	B	B
Q4-16	C+	C-	B
Q4-15	C	C-	C

Asset & Performance History
Date	NAV	1-Year Total Return
2017	33.15	21.14
2016	27.86	12.25
2015	25.2	0.45
2014	25.57	12.48
2013	23.23	33.29
2012	17.74	15.95

Total Assets: $2,597,157,565
Asset Allocation
Asset	%
Cash	1%
Stocks	99%
US Stocks	99%
Bonds	0%
US Bonds	0%
Other	0%

Services Offered: Dividend Investment Plan, CashInvestment Plan

Investment Strategy: The investment seeks to provide investment results that, before fees and expenses, correspond generally to the total return performance of the SSGA Total Stock Market Index that tracks a broad universe of exchange traded U.S. equity securities. The fund generally invests substantially all, but at least 80%, of its total assets in the securities comprising the index. It may invest in equity securities that are not included in the index (including common stock, preferred stock, depositary receipts and shares of other investment companies), cash and cash equivalents or money market instruments. The fund is non-diversified. **Top Holdings:** Microsoft Corp   Apple Inc   Amazon.com Inc   Johnson & Johnson   JPMorgan Chase & Co

iShares U.S. Healthcare ETF   C+   HOLD

Ticker	Traded On	NAV		Total Assets ($)	Dividend Yield (TTM)	Turnover Ratio	Expense Ratio
IYH	NYSE Arca	180.79		$2,539,834,696	1.03	7	0.43

Ratings
Reward   C+
Risk   C
Recent Upgrade/Downgrade   Up

Fund Information
Fund Type   Exchange Traded Funds
Category   Healthcare Sector Equity
Sub-Category   Health
Prospectus Objective   Health
Inception Date   Jun-00
Open to New Investments   Y

Prices
Price (as of 12/31/2018)   180.81
52-Week High   204.02
52-Week Low   168.20

Total Returns (%)

3-Month	6-Month	1-Year	3-Year	5-Year
-10.98	1.72	5.02	24.84	65.86

3-Year Standard Deviation   12.83
Effective Duration

Valuation
Premium/Discount (1-Year Average)   0.02

Company Information
Provider   iShares
Manager/Tenure   Diane Hsiung (10), Greg Savage (10), Jennifer Hsui (6), 3 others
Website   http://www.ishares.com
Address   iShares 400 Howard Street San Francisco CA 94105 United States
Phone Number   800-474-2737

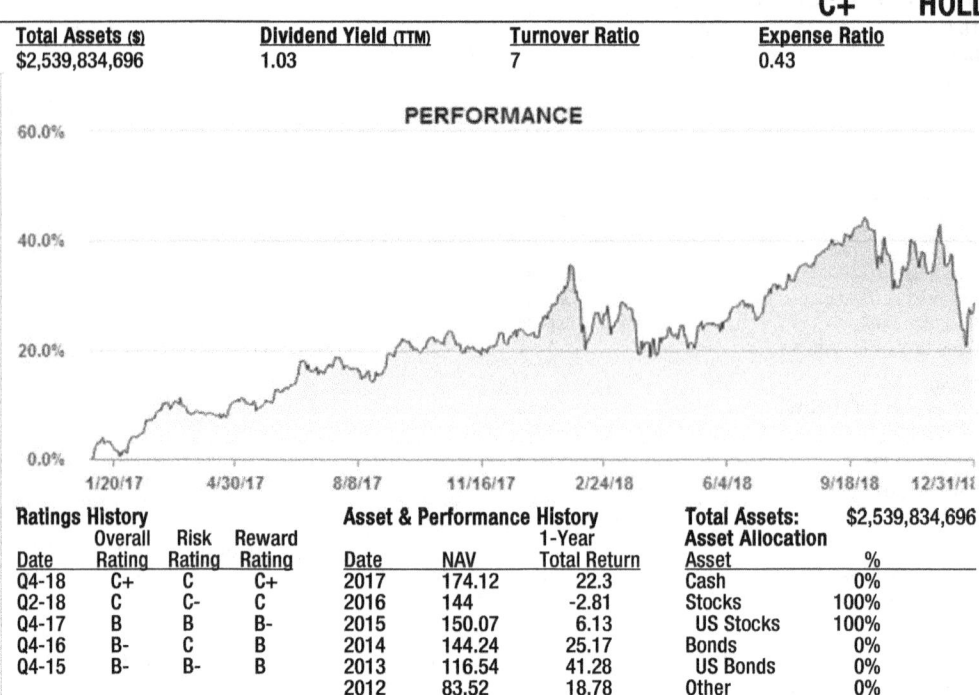

PERFORMANCE

Ratings History

Date	Overall Rating	Risk Rating	Reward Rating
Q4-18	C+	C	C+
Q2-18	C	C-	C
Q4-17	B	B	B-
Q4-16	B-	C	B
Q4-15	B-	B-	B

Asset & Performance History

Date	NAV	1-Year Total Return
2017	174.12	22.3
2016	144	-2.81
2015	150.07	6.13
2014	144.24	25.17
2013	116.54	41.28
2012	83.52	18.78

Total Assets: $2,539,834,696
Asset Allocation

Asset	%
Cash	0%
Stocks	100%
US Stocks	100%
Bonds	0%
US Bonds	0%
Other	0%

Services Offered: CashInvestment Plan

Investment Strategy: The investment seeks to track the investment results of the Dow Jones U.S. Health Care Index composed of U.S. equities in the healthcare sector. The fund generally invests at least 90% of its assets in securities of the underlying index and in depositary receipts representing securities of the underlying index. The underlying index measures the performance of the healthcare sector of the U.S. equity market. The fund is non-diversified. **Top Holdings:** Johnson & Johnson Pfizer Inc UnitedHealth Group Inc Merck & Co Inc AbbVie Inc

---

iShares Global Tech ETF   C+   HOLD

Ticker	Traded On	NAV		Total Assets ($)	Dividend Yield (TTM)	Turnover Ratio	Expense Ratio
IXN	NYSE Arca	144.24		$2,516,413,584	0.87	5	0.47

Ratings
Reward   C+
Risk   C+
Recent Upgrade/Downgrade   Down

Fund Information
Fund Type   Exchange Traded Funds
Category   Technology Sector Equity
Sub-Category   Technology
Prospectus Objective   Technology
Inception Date   Nov-01
Open to New Investments   Y

Prices
Price (as of 12/31/2018)   144.03
52-Week High   177.45
52-Week Low   134.75

Total Returns (%)

3-Month	6-Month	1-Year	3-Year	5-Year
-17.62	-12.15	-5.13	51.83	82.93

3-Year Standard Deviation   13.82
Effective Duration

Valuation
Premium/Discount (1-Year Average)   0.05

Company Information
Provider   iShares
Manager/Tenure   Diane Hsiung (10), Greg Savage (10), Jennifer Hsui (6), 3 others
Website   http://www.ishares.com
Address   iShares 400 Howard Street San Francisco CA 94105 United States
Phone Number   800-474-2737

PERFORMANCE

Ratings History

Date	Overall Rating	Risk Rating	Reward Rating
Q4-18	C+	C+	C+
Q2-18	B-	C	B
Q4-17	A-	B	A+
Q4-16	C	B	C+
Q4-15	C+	C	C+

Asset & Performance History

Date	NAV	1-Year Total Return
2017	153.38	40.77
2016	110.04	13.69
2015	97.85	4.37
2014	94.8	15.43
2013	83.1	25.03
2012	67.22	15.69

Total Assets: $2,516,413,584
Asset Allocation

Asset	%
Cash	0%
Stocks	100%
US Stocks	79%
Bonds	0%
US Bonds	0%
Other	0%

Services Offered: CashInvestment Plan

Investment Strategy: The investment seeks to track the investment results of the S&P Global 1200 Information Technology IndexTM. The fund generally invests at least 90% of its assets in securities of the index and in depositary receipts representing securities of the index. It may invest the remainder of its assets in certain futures, options and swap contracts, cash and cash equivalents, as well as in securities not included in the index. The index measures the performance of companies that the index provider deems to be part of the information technology sector of the economy and that the index provider believes are important to global markets. It is non-diversified. **Top Holdings:** Microsoft Corp Apple Inc Visa Inc Class A Intel Corp Cisco Systems Inc

ProShares Ultra S&P500　　　　　　　　　　　　　　　　C　　HOLD

Ticker	Traded On	NAV	Total Assets ($)	Dividend Yield (TTM)	Turnover Ratio	Expense Ratio
SSO	NYSE Arca	92.74	$2,472,266,421	0.56		0.9

Ratings

Reward	C
Risk	C+
Recent Upgrade/Downgrade	Down

Fund Information

Fund Type	Exchange Traded Funds
Category	Trading Tools
Sub-Category	Trading--Leveraged Equity
Prospectus Objective	Growth
Inception Date	Jun-06
Open to New Investments	Y

Prices

Price (as of 12/31/2018)	92.82
52-Week High	129.09
52-Week Low	81.81

Total Returns (%)

3-Month	6-Month	1-Year	3-Year	5-Year
-27.57	-16.76	-14.43	49.60	85.89

3-Year Standard Deviation	19.09
Effective Duration	

Valuation

Premium/Discount (1-Year Average)	0.02

Company Information

Provider	ProShares
Manager/Tenure	Michael Neches (5), Devin Sullivan (0)
Website	http://www.proshares.com
Address	ProShares 7501 Wisconsin Avenue, Suite 1000 Bethesda MD 20814 United States
Phone Number	866-776-5125

PERFORMANCE

Ratings History

Date	Overall Rating	Risk Rating	Reward Rating
Q4-18	C	C+	C
Q2-18	C	C+	C
Q4-17	B+	C+	A+
Q4-16	B	C+	B+
Q4-15	B-	B+	C

Asset & Performance History

Date	NAV	1-Year Total Return
2017	109.1	44.2
2016	75.99	21.24
2015	63.03	-1.09
2014	64.12	25.63
2013	51.21	70.45
2012	30.14	30.74

Total Assets: $2,472,266,421

Asset Allocation

Asset	%
Cash	-100%
Stocks	200%
US Stocks	198%
Bonds	0%
US Bonds	0%
Other	0%

Services Offered:

Investment Strategy: The investment seeks daily investment results, before fees and expenses, that correspond to two times (2x) the daily performance of the S&P 500® Index. The fund invests in financial instruments that ProShare Advisors believes, in combination, should produce daily returns consistent with the fund's investment objective. The index is a measure of large-cap U.S. stock market performance. It is a float-adjusted, market capitalization-weighted index of 500 U.S. operating companies and real estate investment trusts selected through a process that factors in criteria such as liquidity, price, market capitalization and financial viability. The fund is non-diversified. **Top Holdings:** Spdr S&P 500 (Spy) Swap Goldman Sachs International S&P 500 Index Swap Credit Suisse International S&P 500 Index Swap Societe Generale S&P 500 Index Swap Bank Of America Na S&P500 Emini 12/21/2018 (Esz8)

SPDR® Dow Jones International Real Estate ETF　　　　　C-　　HOLD

Ticker	Traded On	NAV	Total Assets ($)	Dividend Yield (TTM)	Turnover Ratio	Expense Ratio
RWX	NYSE Arca	35.42	$2,459,621,634	3.15	15	0.59

Ratings

Reward	D+
Risk	C-
Recent Upgrade/Downgrade	Down

Fund Information

Fund Type	Exchange Traded Funds
Category	Real Estate Sector Equity
Sub-Category	Global Real Estate
Prospectus Objective	Real Estate
Inception Date	Dec-06
Open to New Investments	Y

Prices

Price (as of 12/31/2018)	35.34
52-Week High	42.45
52-Week Low	34.74

Total Returns (%)

3-Month	6-Month	1-Year	3-Year	5-Year
-4.85	-5.76	-8.37	5.91	8.42

3-Year Standard Deviation	10.45
Effective Duration	

Valuation

Premium/Discount (1-Year Average)	-0.19

Company Information

Provider	SPDR State Street Global Advisors
Manager/Tenure	Michael J. Feehily (5), Karl A. Schneider (3), Keith Richardson (1)
Website	http://www.spdrs.com
Address	SPDR State Street Global Advisors State Street Financial Center, 1 Lincoln Street Boston MA 02111-2900 United States
Phone Number	617-786-3000

PERFORMANCE

Ratings History

Date	Overall Rating	Risk Rating	Reward Rating
Q4-18	C-	C-	D+
Q2-18	C	C+	C
Q4-17	C+	B-	C
Q4-16	C-	C-	D+
Q4-15	C	C+	C

Asset & Performance History

Date	NAV	1-Year Total Return
2017	40.63	15.26
2016	36.28	-1.53
2015	39.34	-3.29
2014	41.83	5.84
2013	40.87	5.07
2012	40.75	36.41

Total Assets: $2,459,621,634

Asset Allocation

Asset	%
Cash	0%
Stocks	99%
US Stocks	0%
Bonds	0%
US Bonds	0%
Other	1%

Services Offered:

Investment Strategy: The investment seeks to provide investment results, before fees and expenses, correspond generally to the total return performance of the Dow Jones Global ex-U.S. Select Real Estate Securities Indexsm. The fund generally invests substantially all, but at least 80%, of its total assets in the securities comprising the index and in depositary receipts based on securities comprising the index. The index is a float-adjusted market capitalization index designed to measure the performance of publicly traded real estate securities in countries excluding the United States. The fund is non-diversified. **Top Holdings:** Mitsui Fudosan Co Ltd Link Real Estate Investment Trust Deutsche Wohnen SE Scentre Group Unibail-Rodamco-Westfield

WisdomTree U.S. Quality Dividend Growth Fund   C   HOLD

Ticker	Traded On	NAV	Total Assets ($)	Dividend Yield (TTM)	Turnover Ratio	Expense Ratio
DGRW	NAS CM	38.33	$2,457,594,793	2.07	29	0.28

Ratings
Reward	C
Risk	C+
Recent Upgrade/Downgrade	Down

Fund Information
Fund Type	Exchange Traded Funds
Category	US Equity Large Cap Blend
Sub-Category	Large Blend
Prospectus Objective	Growth & Inc
Inception Date	May-13
Open to New Investments	Y

Prices
Price (as of 12/31/2018)	38.33
52-Week High	44.81
52-Week Low	36.09

Total Returns (%)
3-Month	6-Month	1-Year	3-Year	5-Year
-13.24	-5.44	-5.22	34.70	52.94

3-Year Standard Deviation	9.84
Effective Duration	

Valuation
Premium/Discount (1-Year Average)	0.06

Company Information
Provider	WisdomTree
Manager/Tenure	Richard A. Brown (5), Thomas J. Durante (5), Karen Q. Wong (5)
Website	http://www.wisdomtree.com
Address	WisdomTree 245 Park Avenue, 35th floor New York NY 10167 United States
Phone Number	866-909-9473

PERFORMANCE

Ratings History
Date	Overall Rating	Risk Rating	Reward Rating
Q4-18	C	C+	C
Q2-18	C	C+	C
Q4-17	B	B	B
Q4-16	B-	C+	B
Q4-15	C	C+	C+

Asset & Performance History
Date	NAV	1-Year Total Return
2017	41.37	26.94
2016	33.22	11.61
2015	30.34	-0.01
2014	31	13.55
2013	27.83	
2012		

Total Assets: $2,457,594,793

Asset Allocation
Asset	%
Cash	0%
Stocks	100%
US Stocks	100%
Bonds	0%
US Bonds	0%
Other	0%

Services Offered:

Investment Strategy: The investment seeks to track the price and yield performance, before fees and expenses, of the WisdomTree U.S. Quality Dividend Growth Index. Under normal circumstances, at least 80% of the fund's total assets (exclusive of collateral held from securities lending) will be invested in component securities of the index and investments that have economic characteristics that are substantially identical to the economic characteristics of such component securities. The index is a fundamentally weighted index that consists of dividend-paying U.S. common stocks with growth characteristics. The fund is non-diversified. **Top Holdings:** Exxon Mobil Corp Johnson & Johnson Microsoft Corp Apple Inc Wells Fargo & Co

---

First Trust Dorsey Wright Focus 5 ETF   C-   HOLD

Ticker	Traded On	NAV	Total Assets ($)	Dividend Yield (TTM)	Turnover Ratio	Expense Ratio
FV	NAS CM	25.31	$2,445,867,364	0.58	44	0.89

Ratings
Reward	C-
Risk	C
Recent Upgrade/Downgrade	Down

Fund Information
Fund Type	Exchange Traded Funds
Category	US Equity Mid Cap
Sub-Category	Mid-Cap Growth
Prospectus Objective	Growth & Inc
Inception Date	Mar-14
Open to New Investments	Y

Prices
Price (as of 12/31/2018)	25.25
52-Week High	31.75
52-Week Low	23.41

Total Returns (%)
3-Month	6-Month	1-Year	3-Year	5-Year
-17.84	-14.90	-8.06	9.78	

3-Year Standard Deviation	13.29
Effective Duration	

Valuation
Premium/Discount (1-Year Average)	-0.03

Company Information
Provider	First Trust
Manager/Tenure	Jon C. Erickson (4), Daniel J. Lindquist (4), David G. McGarel (4), 3 others
Website	http://www.ftportfolios.com/
Address	First Trust 120 E. Liberty Drive, Suite 400 Wheaton IL 60187 United States
Phone Number	800-621-1675

PERFORMANCE

Ratings History
Date	Overall Rating	Risk Rating	Reward Rating
Q4-18	C-	C	C-
Q2-18	C+	C+	C+
Q4-17	B	C+	B
Q4-16	C	C+	C-
Q4-15	D	C+	C

Asset & Performance History
Date	NAV	1-Year Total Return
2017	27.57	19.84
2016	23.16	-0.34
2015	23.47	6.81
2014	22	
2013		
2012		

Total Assets: $2,445,867,364

Asset Allocation
Asset	%
Cash	0%
Stocks	100%
US Stocks	96%
Bonds	0%
US Bonds	0%
Other	0%

Services Offered:

Investment Strategy: The investment seeks investment results that correspond generally to the price and yield (before the fund's fees and expenses) of an index called the Dorsey Wright Focus Five Index (the "index"). The fund will normally invest at least 90% of its net assets (including investment borrowings) in the exchange-traded funds ("ETFs") that comprise the index. The index is designed to provide targeted exposure to the five First Trust sector-based ETFs that the index provider believes offer the greatest potential to outperform the other ETFs in the selection universe and that satisfy certain trading volume and liquidity requirements. The fund is non-diversified. **Top Holdings:** First Trust Technology AlphaDEX® ETF First Trust Health Care AlphaDEX® ETF First Trust NASDAQ-100-Tech Sector ETF First Trust Dow Jones Internet ETF First Trust NYSE Arca Biotech ETF

iShares Core Total USD Bond Market ETF   C   HOLD

Ticker	Traded On	NAV	Total Assets ($)	Dividend Yield (TTM)	Turnover Ratio	Expense Ratio
IUSB	NAS CM	49.14	$2,445,475,742	2.85	264	0.06

Ratings
Reward	D+
Risk	C+
Recent Upgrade/Downgrade	Up

Fund Information
Fund Type	Exchange Traded Funds
Category	US Fixed Income
Sub-Category	Intermediate-Term Bond
Prospectus Objective	Corp Bond - Gen
Inception Date	Jun-14
Open to New Investments	Y

Prices
Price (as of 12/31/2018)	49.25
52-Week High	50.87
52-Week Low	48.37

Total Returns (%)
3-Month	6-Month	1-Year	3-Year	5-Year
1.17	1.49	-0.37	7.57	

3-Year Standard Deviation	2.65
Effective Duration	5.72

Valuation
Premium/Discount (1-Year Average)	0.11

Company Information
Provider	iShares
Manager/Tenure	James Mauro (4), Scott Radell (4)
Website	http://www.ishares.com
Address	iShares 400 Howard Street San Francisco CA 94105 United States
Phone Number	800-474-2737

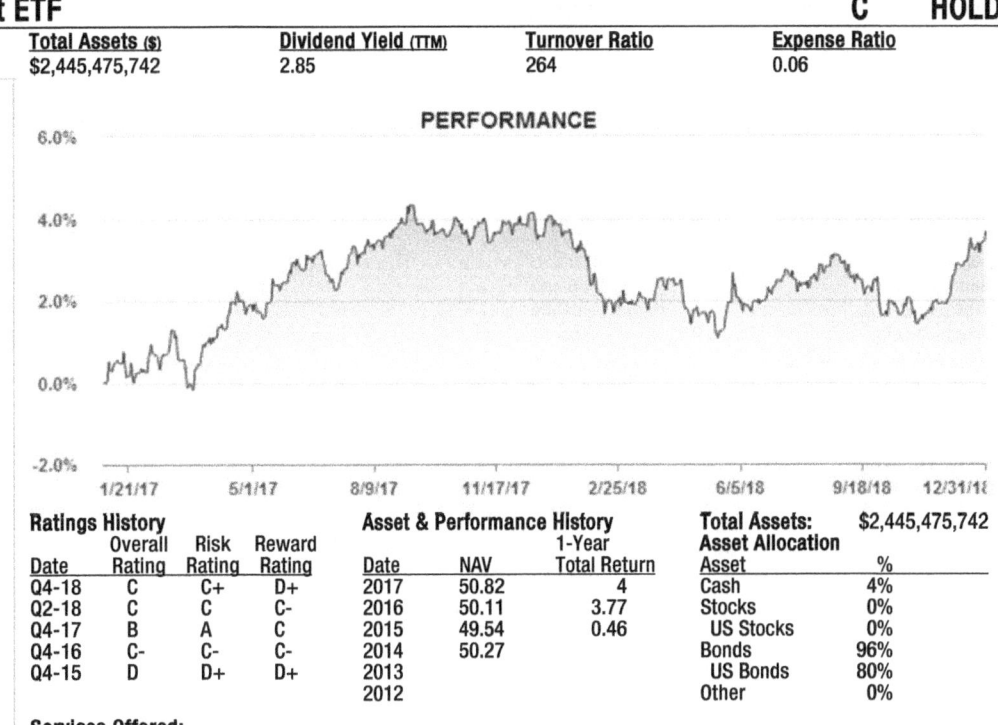

PERFORMANCE

Ratings History
Date	Overall Rating	Risk Rating	Reward Rating
Q4-18	C	C+	D+
Q2-18	C	C	C-
Q4-17	B	A	C
Q4-16	C-	C-	C-
Q4-15	D	D+	D+

Asset & Performance History
Date	NAV	1-Year Total Return
2017	50.82	4
2016	50.11	3.77
2015	49.54	0.46
2014	50.27	
2013		
2012		

Total Assets: $2,445,475,742
Asset Allocation
Asset	%
Cash	4%
Stocks	0%
US Stocks	0%
Bonds	96%
US Bonds	80%
Other	0%

Services Offered:

Investment Strategy: The investment seeks to track the investment results of the Bloomberg Barclays U.S. Universal Index. The fund generally will invest at least 90% of its assets in the component securities of the underlying index and may invest up to 10% of its assets in certain futures, options and swap contracts, cash and cash equivalents, including shares of money market funds advised by BFA or its affiliates, as well as in securities not included in the underlying index, but which BFA believes will help the fund track the underlying index. The index measures the performance of U.S. dollar-denominated taxable bonds that are rated either investment-grade or high yield. Top Holdings: Fnma 30yr 2016 Production Gnma2 30yr 2016 Production United States Treasury Notes 2.63% United States Treasury Notes 1.88% Gnma2 30yr 2016 Production

---

iShares MSCI Germany ETF   D+   SELL

Ticker	Traded On	NAV	Total Assets ($)	Dividend Yield (TTM)	Turnover Ratio	Expense Ratio
EWG	NYSE Arca	25.17	$2,420,951,911	3.1	6	0.47

Ratings
Reward	C-
Risk	D+
Recent Upgrade/Downgrade	Down

Fund Information
Fund Type	Exchange Traded Funds
Category	Europe Equity Large Cap
Sub-Category	Miscellaneous Region
Prospectus Objective	Europe Stock
Inception Date	Mar-96
Open to New Investments	Y

Prices
Price (as of 12/31/2018)	25.35
52-Week High	35.65
52-Week Low	24.44

Total Returns (%)
3-Month	6-Month	1-Year	3-Year	5-Year
-16.04	-15.19	-22.29	1.57	-10.95

3-Year Standard Deviation	15.06
Effective Duration	

Valuation
Premium/Discount (1-Year Average)	-0.14

Company Information
Provider	iShares
Manager/Tenure	Diane Hsiung (10), Greg Savage (10), Jennifer Hsui (5), 1 other
Website	http://www.ishares.com
Address	iShares 400 Howard Street San Francisco CA 94105 United States
Phone Number	800-474-2737

PERFORMANCE

Ratings History
Date	Overall Rating	Risk Rating	Reward Rating
Q4-18	D+	D+	C-
Q2-18	C	C+	C-
Q4-17	B	B-	A-
Q4-16	D+	D+	D+
Q4-15	C	B	C-

Asset & Performance History
Date	NAV	1-Year Total Return
2017	33.18	27.44
2016	26.61	2.58
2015	26.58	-2.06
2014	27.61	-10.49
2013	31.47	31.18
2012	24.41	30.72

Total Assets: $2,420,951,911
Asset Allocation
Asset	%
Cash	1%
Stocks	99%
US Stocks	1%
Bonds	0%
US Bonds	0%
Other	0%

Services Offered: CashInvestment Plan

Investment Strategy: The investment seeks to track the investment results of the MSCI Germany Index. The fund will at all times invest at least 80% of its assets in the securities of its underlying index and in depositary receipts representing securities in its underlying index. The underlying index consists of stocks traded primarily on the Frankfurt Stock Exchange. It may include large- or mid-capitalization companies. The fund is non-diversified. Top Holdings: SAP SE Allianz SE Siemens AG Bayer AG Basf SE

Vanguard Russell 2000 Index Fund ETF Shares

C   HOLD

Ticker	Traded On	NAV
VTWO	NAS CM	

Total Assets ($)	Dividend Yield (TTM)	Turnover Ratio	Expense Ratio
$2,366,144,099	1.28	19	0.15

Ratings
Reward	C-
Risk	C+
Recent Upgrade/Downgrade	

Fund Information
Fund Type	Exchange Traded Funds
Category	US Equity Small Cap
Sub-Category	Small Blend
Prospectus Objective	Small Company
Inception Date	Sep-10
Open to New Investments	Y

Prices
Price (as of 12/31/2018)	107.37
52-Week High	139.10
52-Week Low	101.52

Total Returns (%)
3-Month	6-Month	1-Year	3-Year	5-Year
-19.70	-18.57	-11.68	22.90	23.26

3-Year Standard Deviation	14.58
Effective Duration	

Valuation
Premium/Discount (1-Year Average)	0.03

Company Information
Provider	Vanguard
Manager/Tenure	Walter Nejman (3), Michael A. Johnson (2)
Website	http://www.vanguard.com
Address	Vanguard 100 Vanguard Boulevard Malvern PA 19355 United States
Phone Number	877-662-7447

PERFORMANCE

Ratings History
Date	Overall Rating	Risk Rating	Reward Rating
Q4-18	C	C+	C-
Q2-18	C	C-	C+
Q4-17	B+	B	A-
Q4-16	C+	C-	B
Q4-15	C	C-	C

Asset & Performance History
Date	NAV	1-Year Total Return
2017	122.3	15.17
2016	107.96	20.42
2015	90.23	-4.41
2014	95.55	4.92
2013	92.09	38.81
2012	67.03	16.25

Total Assets: $2,366,144,099

Asset Allocation
Asset	%
Cash	2%
Stocks	98%
US Stocks	97%
Bonds	0%
US Bonds	0%
Other	0%

Services Offered:

Investment Strategy: The investment seeks to track the performance of a benchmark index that measures the investment return of small-capitalization stocks in the United States. The fund employs an indexing investment approach designed to track the performance of the Russell 2000® Index. The index is designed to measure the performance of small-capitalization stocks in the United States. The advisor attempts to replicate the target index by investing all, or substantially all, of its assets in the stocks that make up the index, holding each stock in approximately the same proportion as its weighting in the index. **Top Holdings:** Five Below Inc Integrated Device Technology Inc LivaNova PLC Haemonetics Corp Etsy Inc

---

First Trust Health Care AlphaDEX® Fund

C   HOLD

Ticker	Traded On	NAV
FXH	NYSE Arca	68.89

Total Assets ($)	Dividend Yield (TTM)	Turnover Ratio	Expense Ratio
$2,352,619,657	0	112	0.63

Ratings
Reward	C
Risk	C+
Recent Upgrade/Downgrade	

Fund Information
Fund Type	Exchange Traded Funds
Category	Healthcare Sector Equity
Sub-Category	Health
Prospectus Objective	Health
Inception Date	May-07
Open to New Investments	Y

Prices
Price (as of 12/31/2018)	68.87
52-Week High	84.88
52-Week Low	64.01

Total Returns (%)
3-Month	6-Month	1-Year	3-Year	5-Year
-18.50	-7.69	-1.26	13.99	43.28

3-Year Standard Deviation	14.41
Effective Duration	

Valuation
Premium/Discount (1-Year Average)	0.04

Company Information
Provider	First Trust
Manager/Tenure	Jon C. Erickson (11), Daniel J. Lindquist (11), David G. McGarel (11), 3 others
Website	http://www.ftportfolios.com/
Address	First Trust 120 E. Liberty Drive, Suite 400 Wheaton IL 60187 United States
Phone Number	800-621-1675

PERFORMANCE

Ratings History
Date	Overall Rating	Risk Rating	Reward Rating
Q4-18	C	C+	C
Q2-18	C	C-	C+
Q4-17	C+	B-	C+
Q4-16	C	C	C
Q4-15	B-	C+	B-

Asset & Performance History
Date	NAV	1-Year Total Return
2017	69.77	21.78
2016	57.29	-5.19
2015	60.43	0.23
2014	60.29	25.39
2013	48.08	47.46
2012	32.61	20.8

Total Assets: $2,352,619,657

Asset Allocation
Asset	%
Cash	0%
Stocks	100%
US Stocks	100%
Bonds	0%
US Bonds	0%
Other	0%

Services Offered:

Investment Strategy: The investment seeks investment results that correspond generally to the price and yield (before the fund's fees and expenses) of an equity index called the StrataQuant® Health Care Index. The fund will normally invest at least 90% of its net assets (including investment borrowings) in common stocks that comprise the index. The index is a modified equal-dollar weighted index designed by IDI to objectively identify and select stocks from the Russell 1000® Index in the health care sector that may generate positive alpha relative to traditional passive-style indices through the use of the AlphaDEX® selection methodology. **Top Holdings:** HCA Healthcare Inc PRA Health Sciences Inc Centene Corp Exact Sciences Corp Encompass Health Corp

iShares Exponential Technologies ETF   C   HOLD

Ticker	Traded On	NAV	Total Assets ($)	Dividend Yield (TTM)	Turnover Ratio	Expense Ratio
XT	NAS CM	33.32	$2,344,502,539	1.08	19	0.47

Ratings
Reward	C
Risk	C+
Recent Upgrade/Downgrade	Down

Fund Information
Fund Type	Exchange Traded Funds
Category	Equity Misc
Sub-Category	Miscellaneous Sector
Prospectus Objective	Technology
Inception Date	Mar-15
Open to New Investments	Y

Prices
Price (as of 12/31/2018)	33.26
52-Week High	39.12
52-Week Low	31.56

Total Returns (%)
3-Month	6-Month	1-Year	3-Year	5-Year
-13.78	-7.44	-4.67	38.96	

3-Year Standard Deviation	12.11
Effective Duration	

Valuation
Premium/Discount (1-Year Average)	0.03

Company Information
Provider	iShares
Manager/Tenure	Diane Hsiung (3), Jennifer Hsui (3), Greg Savage (3), 3 others
Website	http://www.ishares.com
Address	iShares 400 Howard Street San Francisco CA 94105 United States
Phone Number	800-474-2737

PERFORMANCE

Ratings History
Date	Overall Rating	Risk Rating	Reward Rating
Q4-18	C	C+	C
Q2-18	C+	C+	C+
Q4-17	B-	B-	B-
Q4-16	D+	C-	C-
Q4-15	U		

Asset & Performance History
Date	NAV	1-Year Total Return
2017	35.41	33.7
2016	26.76	9.03
2015	24.9	
2014		
2013		
2012		

Total Assets: $2,344,502,539

Asset Allocation
Asset	%
Cash	0%
Stocks	100%
US Stocks	65%
Bonds	0%
US Bonds	0%
Other	0%

Services Offered:

Investment Strategy: The investment seeks to track the investment results of the Morningstar® Exponential Technologies IndexSM which composed of stocks of developed and emerging market companies that create or use exponential technologies. The fund generally will invest at least 90% of its assets in the component securities of the underlying index and in investments that have economic characteristics that are substantially identical to the component securities of the underlying index. The underlying index is a subset of the Morningstar US Market Index and the Morningstar Global Markets ex-US Index family. **Top Holdings:** Advanced Micro Devices Inc Intercept Pharmaceuticals Inc Tableau Software Inc A Swedish Orphan Biovitrum AB Illumina Inc

---

VanEck Vectors High-Yield Municipal Index ETF   B+   BUY

Ticker	Traded On	NAV	Total Assets ($)	Dividend Yield (TTM)	Turnover Ratio	Expense Ratio
HYD	BATS	61.23	$2,339,027,872	4.42	14	0.35

Ratings
Reward	A
Risk	C+
Recent Upgrade/Downgrade	Up

Fund Information
Fund Type	Exchange Traded Funds
Category	US Muni Fixed Inc
Sub-Category	High Yield Muni
Prospectus Objective	Muni Bond - Natl
Inception Date	Feb-09
Open to New Investments	Y

Prices
Price (as of 12/31/2018)	61.04
52-Week High	63.06
52-Week Low	30.64

Total Returns (%)
3-Month	6-Month	1-Year	3-Year	5-Year
-0.88	98.78	103.45	125.71	169.30

3-Year Standard Deviation	4.61
Effective Duration	7.46

Valuation
Premium/Discount (1-Year Average)	-0.15

Company Information
Provider	VanEck
Manager/Tenure	James T. Colby (9)
Website	http://www.vaneck.com
Address	Van Eck Associates Corporation 666 Third Avenue New York NY 10017 United States
Phone Number	800-826-1115

PERFORMANCE

Ratings History
Date	Overall Rating	Risk Rating	Reward Rating
Q4-18	B+	C+	A
Q2-18	C+	C+	C
Q4-17	B	A	C+
Q4-16	C	C+	C
Q4-15	C+	C+	C

Asset & Performance History
Date	NAV	1-Year Total Return
2017	31.31	10.49
2016	29.59	0.4
2015	30.78	4.81
2014	30.82	13.82
2013	28.49	-8.13
2012	32.88	16.74

Total Assets: $2,339,027,872

Asset Allocation
Asset	%
Cash	0%
Stocks	0%
US Stocks	0%
Bonds	100%
US Bonds	98%
Other	0%

Services Offered:

Investment Strategy: The investment seeks to replicate as closely as possible, before fees and expenses, the price and yield performance of the Bloomberg Barclays Municipal Custom High Yield Composite Index. The fund normally invests at least 80% of its total assets in securities that comprise the benchmark index. The index is comprised of publicly traded municipal bonds that cover the U.S. dollar denominated high yield long-term tax-exempt bond market. **Top Holdings:** NEW YORK LIBERTY DEV CORP 5% BUCKEYE OHIO TOB SETTLEMENT FING AUTH 5.88% PUBLIC FIN AUTH WIS 7% BUCKEYE OHIO TOB SETTLEMENT FING AUTH 5.12% CHICAGO ILL BRD ED 7%

Vanguard Mega Cap Value Index Fund ETF Shares   C   HOLD

Ticker	Traded On	NAV	Total Assets ($)	Dividend Yield (TTM)	Turnover Ratio	Expense Ratio
MGV	NYSE Arca		$2,325,811,949	2.34	8	0.07

Ratings
Reward   C
Risk   C+
Recent Upgrade/Downgrade

Fund Information
Fund Type   Exchange Traded Funds
Category   US Equity Large Cap Value
Sub-Category   Large Value
Prospectus Objective   Growth & Inc
Inception Date   Dec-07
Open to New Investments   Y

Prices
Price (as of 12/31/2018)   71.47
52-Week High   81.87
52-Week Low   67.32

Total Returns (%)

3-Month	6-Month	1-Year	3-Year	5-Year
-11.37	-3.81	-4.87	29.56	46.10

3-Year Standard Deviation   9.09
Effective Duration

Valuation
Premium/Discount (1-Year Average)   0.04

Company Information
Provider   Vanguard
Manager/Tenure   Gerard C. O'Reilly (3), Michael A. Johnson (2)
Website   http://www.vanguard.com
Address   Vanguard 100 Vanguard Boulevard Malvern PA 19355 United States
Phone Number   877-662-7447

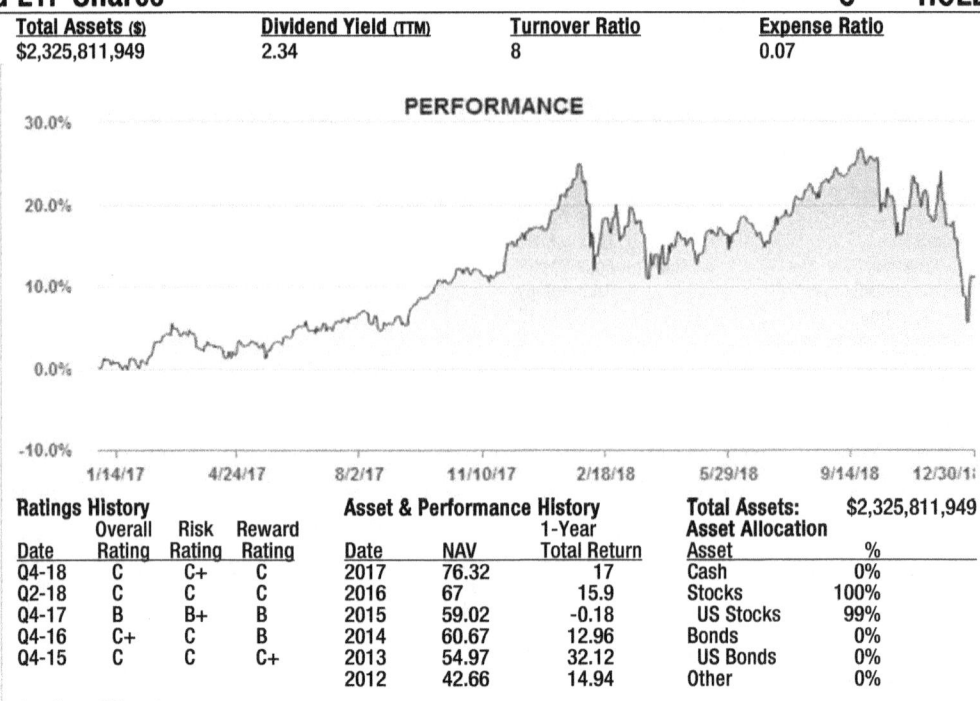

Ratings History

Date	Overall Rating	Risk Rating	Reward Rating
Q4-18	C	C+	C
Q2-18	C	C	C
Q4-17	B	B+	B
Q4-16	C+	C	B
Q4-15	C	C	C+

Asset & Performance History

Date	NAV	1-Year Total Return
2017	76.32	17
2016	67	15.9
2015	59.02	-0.18
2014	60.67	12.96
2013	54.97	32.12
2012	42.66	14.94

Total Assets: $2,325,811,949
Asset Allocation

Asset	%
Cash	0%
Stocks	100%
US Stocks	99%
Bonds	0%
US Bonds	0%
Other	0%

Services Offered:

Investment Strategy: The investment seeks the performance of a benchmark index. The fund employs an indexing investment approach designed to track the performance of the CRSP US Mega Cap Value Index. The index is a float-adjusted, market-capitalization-weighted index designed to measure equity market performance of mega-capitalization value stocks in the United States. The Advisor attempts to replicate the target index by investing all, or substantially all, of its assets in the stocks that make up the index, holding each stock in approximately the same proportion as its weighting in the index. **Top Holdings:** Microsoft Corp Berkshire Hathaway Inc B Johnson & Johnson JPMorgan Chase & Co Exxon Mobil Corp

---

iShares 0-5 Year TIPS Bond ETF   C   HOLD

Ticker	Traded On	NAV	Total Assets ($)	Dividend Yield (TTM)	Turnover Ratio	Expense Ratio
STIP	NYSE Arca	97.99	$2,296,378,505	2.69	27	0.06

Ratings
Reward   C-
Risk   C+
Recent Upgrade/Downgrade

Fund Information
Fund Type   Exchange Traded Funds
Category   US Fixed Income
Sub-Category   Inflation-Protected Bond
Prospectus Objective   Govt Bond - Treasury
Inception Date   Dec-10
Open to New Investments   Y

Prices
Price (as of 12/31/2018)   98.02
52-Week High   100.14
52-Week Low   97.69

Total Returns (%)

3-Month	6-Month	1-Year	3-Year	5-Year
-0.32	-0.17	0.49	4.10	2.67

3-Year Standard Deviation   1.23
Effective Duration   2.57

Valuation
Premium/Discount (1-Year Average)   0.03

Company Information
Provider   iShares
Manager/Tenure   Scott Radell (8), James Mauro (7)
Website   http://www.ishares.com
Address   iShares 400 Howard Street San Francisco CA 94105 United States
Phone Number   800-474-2737

Ratings History

Date	Overall Rating	Risk Rating	Reward Rating
Q4-18	C	C+	C-
Q2-18	C-	C-	C
Q4-17	C	B-	C
Q4-16	C	C-	C
Q4-15	D+	C-	D

Asset & Performance History

Date	NAV	1-Year Total Return
2017	99.88	0.68
2016	100.67	2.77
2015	98.83	-0.1
2014	98.93	-1.28
2013	100.94	-1.73
2012	103.03	2.19

Total Assets: $2,296,378,505
Asset Allocation

Asset	%
Cash	1%
Stocks	0%
US Stocks	0%
Bonds	99%
US Bonds	99%
Other	0%

Services Offered:

Investment Strategy: The investment seeks to track the investment results of the Bloomberg Barclays U.S. Treasury Inflation-Protected Securities (TIPS) 0-5 Years Index (Series-L). The fund generally will invest at least 90% of its assets in the component securities of the underlying index and may invest up to 10% of its assets in certain futures, options and swap contracts, cash and cash equivalents. The index measures the performance of the inflation-protected public obligations of the U.S. Treasury, commonly known as "TIPS," that have a remaining maturity of less than five years. **Top Holdings:** United States Treasury Notes 0.13% United States Treasury Notes 0.63% United States Treasury Notes 0.13% United States Treasury Notes 1.38% United States Treasury Notes 1.25%

Invesco S&P 500® Pure Growth ETF   C   HOLD

Ticker	Traded On	NAV		Total Assets ($)	Dividend Yield (TTM)	Turnover Ratio	Expense Ratio
RPG	NYSE Arca	99.58		$2,292,656,565	0.38		0.35

Ratings
Reward	C
Risk	C+
Recent Upgrade/Downgrade	Down

Fund Information
Fund Type	Exchange Traded Funds
Category	US Equity Large Cap Growth
Sub-Category	Large Growth
Prospectus Objective	Growth
Inception Date	Mar-06
Open to New Investments	Y

Prices
Price (as of 12/31/2018)	99.65
52-Week High	121.33
52-Week Low	93.15

Total Returns (%)
3-Month	6-Month	1-Year	3-Year	5-Year
-17.03	-13.38	-4.58	25.16	45.85

3-Year Standard Deviation	11.93
Effective Duration	

Valuation
Premium/Discount (1-Year Average)	0.01

Company Information
Provider	Invesco
Manager/Tenure	Peter Hubbard (0), Michael Jeanette (0), Jonathan Nixon (0), 1 other
Website	http://www.invesco.com/us
Address	Invesco 11 Greenway Plaza, Ste. 2500 Houston TX 77046 United States
Phone Number	800-659-1005

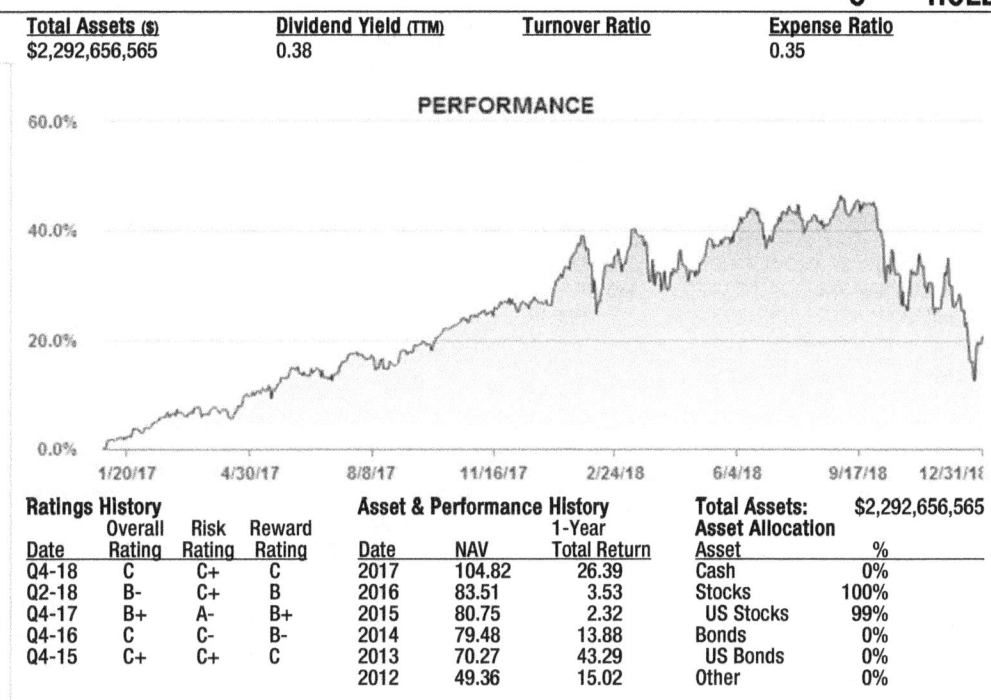

PERFORMANCE

Ratings History
Date	Overall Rating	Risk Rating	Reward Rating
Q4-18	C	C+	C
Q2-18	B-	C+	B
Q4-17	B+	A-	B+
Q4-16	C	C-	B-
Q4-15	C+	C+	C

Asset & Performance History
Date	NAV	1-Year Total Return
2017	104.82	26.39
2016	83.51	3.53
2015	80.75	2.32
2014	79.48	13.88
2013	70.27	43.29
2012	49.36	15.02

Total Assets: $2,292,656,565
Asset Allocation
Asset	%
Cash	0%
Stocks	100%
US Stocks	99%
Bonds	0%
US Bonds	0%
Other	0%

Services Offered:

Investment Strategy: The investment seeks to track the investment results (before fees and expenses) of the S&P 500® Pure Growth Index (the "underlying index"). The fund generally will invest at least 90% of its total assets in the securities that comprise the underlying index. The underlying index includes securities that exhibit the strongest growth characteristics as measured using three factors: three-year sales per share growth, three-year ratio of earnings per share change to price per share, and momentum (12-month percentage price change) as selected by the index provider strictly in accordance with its guidelines and mandated procedures. The fund is non-diversified. **Top Holdings:** Adobe Inc   Netflix Inc   Centene Corp   Red Hat Inc   Amazon.com Inc

---

iShares MSCI Hong Kong ETF   C-   HOLD

Ticker	Traded On	NAV		Total Assets ($)	Dividend Yield (TTM)	Turnover Ratio	Expense Ratio
EWH	NYSE Arca	22.72		$2,270,788,869	4.78	7	0.48

Ratings
Reward	D+
Risk	C
Recent Upgrade/Downgrade	Down

Fund Information
Fund Type	Exchange Traded Funds
Category	Greater China Equity
Sub-Category	China Region
Prospectus Objective	Pacific Stock
Inception Date	Mar-96
Open to New Investments	Y

Prices
Price (as of 12/31/2018)	22.57
52-Week High	26.90
52-Week Low	21.26

Total Returns (%)
3-Month	6-Month	1-Year	3-Year	5-Year
-4.68	-5.54	-8.26	26.56	30.51

3-Year Standard Deviation	15.02
Effective Duration	

Valuation
Premium/Discount (1-Year Average)	-0.21

Company Information
Provider	iShares
Manager/Tenure	Diane Hsiung (10), Greg Savage (10), Jennifer Hsui (5), 1 other
Website	http://www.ishares.com
Address	iShares 400 Howard Street San Francisco CA 94105 United States
Phone Number	800-474-2737

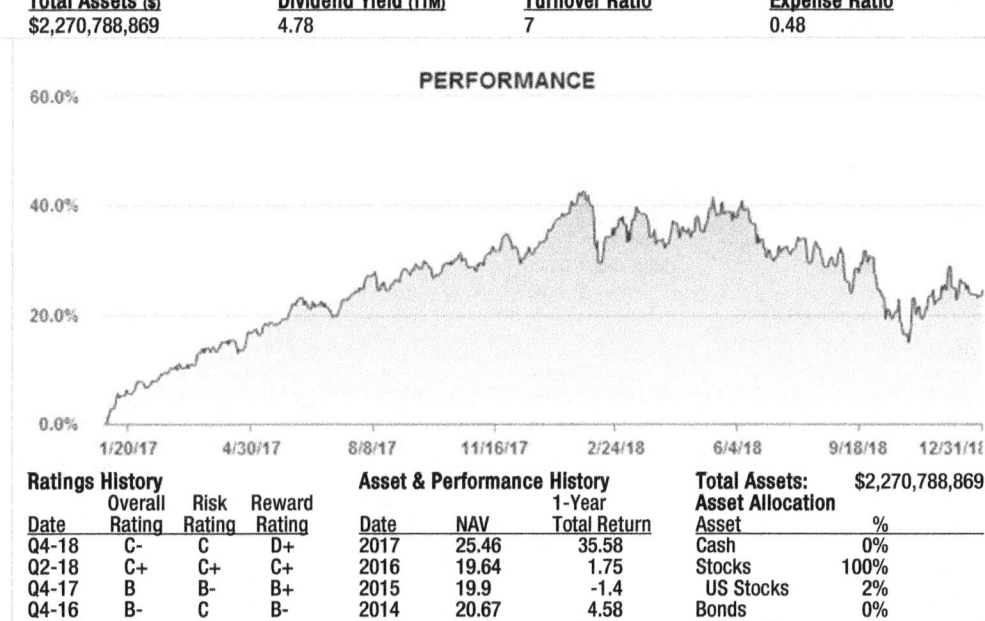

PERFORMANCE

Ratings History
Date	Overall Rating	Risk Rating	Reward Rating
Q4-18	C-	C	D+
Q2-18	C+	C+	C+
Q4-17	B	B-	B+
Q4-16	B-	C	B-
Q4-15	C+	B	C

Asset & Performance History
Date	NAV	1-Year Total Return
2017	25.46	35.58
2016	19.64	1.75
2015	19.9	-1.4
2014	20.67	4.58
2013	20.47	10.44
2012	19.14	27.62

Total Assets: $2,270,788,869
Asset Allocation
Asset	%
Cash	0%
Stocks	100%
US Stocks	2%
Bonds	0%
US Bonds	0%
Other	0%

Services Offered: CashInvestment Plan

Investment Strategy: The investment seeks to track the investment results of the MSCI Hong Kong Index. The fund will at all times invest at least 80% of its assets in the securities of its underlying index and in depositary receipts representing securities in its underlying index. The underlying index consists of stocks traded primarily on the Stock Exchange of Hong Kong Limited (SEHK). It may include large- or mid-capitalization companies. The fund is non-diversified. **Top Holdings:** AIA Group Ltd   Hong Kong Exchanges and Clearing Ltd   CK Hutchison Holdings Ltd   Sun Hung Kai Properties Ltd   Link Real Estate Investment Trust

Vanguard S&P 500 Growth Index Fund ETF Shares   C   HOLD

Ticker	Traded On	NAV	Total Assets ($)	Dividend Yield (TTM)	Turnover Ratio	Expense Ratio
VOOG	NYSE Arca		$2,258,982,500	1.31	19	0.15

Ratings
Reward   C
Risk   C-
Recent Upgrade/Downgrade   Down

Fund Information
Fund Type   Exchange Traded Funds
Category   US Equity Large Cap Growth
Sub-Category   Large Growth
Prospectus Objective   Growth & Inc
Inception Date   Sep-10
Open to New Investments   Y

Prices
Price (as of 12/31/2018)   135.00
52-Week High   159.32
52-Week Low   125.87

Total Returns (%)

3-Month	6-Month	1-Year	3-Year	5-Year
-15.82	-8.27	-1.11	34.27	62.34

3-Year Standard Deviation   10.53
Effective Duration

Valuation
Premium/Discount (1-Year Average)   0.01

Company Information
Provider   Vanguard
Manager/Tenure   Donald M. Butler (2), Michelle Louie (1)
Website   http://www.vanguard.com
Address   Vanguard 100 Vanguard Boulevard
                    Malvern PA 19355 United States
Phone Number   877-662-7447

PERFORMANCE

Ratings History

Date	Overall Rating	Risk Rating	Reward Rating
Q4-18	C	C-	C
Q2-18	C+	C	B
Q4-17	B	B+	B
Q4-16	C+	C-	B
Q4-15	C	C	C+

Asset & Performance History

Date	NAV	1-Year Total Return
2017	136.87	27.08
2016	109.13	6.27
2015	103.78	5.38
2014	100.03	14.72
2013	88.37	32.57
2012	67.76	14.44

Total Assets: $2,258,982,500

Asset Allocation

Asset	%
Cash	1%
Stocks	99%
US Stocks	98%
Bonds	0%
US Bonds	0%
Other	0%

Services Offered:

Investment Strategy: The investment seeks to track the performance of a benchmark index that measures the investment return of large-capitalization growth stocks in the United States. The fund employs an indexing investment approach designed to track the performance of the S&P 500® Growth Index, which represents the growth companies, as determined by the index sponsor, of the S&P 500 Index. The index measures the performance of large-capitalization growth stocks in the United States. **Top Holdings:** Apple Inc Microsoft Corp Amazon.com Inc Facebook Inc A Alphabet Inc A

---

iShares Core 1-5 Year USD Bond ETF   C   HOLD

Ticker	Traded On	NAV	Total Assets ($)	Dividend Yield (TTM)	Turnover Ratio	Expense Ratio
ISTB	NAS CM	49.03	$2,255,494,208	2.43	124	0.06

Ratings
Reward   C-
Risk   C+
Recent Upgrade/Downgrade

Fund Information
Fund Type   Exchange Traded Funds
Category   US Fixed Income
Sub-Category   Short-Term Bond
Prospectus Objective   Multisector Bond
Inception Date   Oct-12
Open to New Investments   Y

Prices
Price (as of 12/31/2018)   49.06
52-Week High   49.83
52-Week Low   48.64

Total Returns (%)

3-Month	6-Month	1-Year	3-Year	5-Year
1.11	1.59	1.18	5.76	7.78

3-Year Standard Deviation   1.26
Effective Duration   2.70

Valuation
Premium/Discount (1-Year Average)   0.09

Company Information
Provider   iShares
Manager/Tenure   James Mauro (6), Scott Radell (6)
Website   http://www.ishares.com
Address   iShares 400 Howard Street San
                    Francisco CA 94105 United States
Phone Number   800-474-2737

PERFORMANCE

Ratings History

Date	Overall Rating	Risk Rating	Reward Rating
Q4-18	C	C+	C-
Q2-18	C	C+	C-
Q4-17	B	A+	C
Q4-16	C	C-	C
Q4-15	C	C-	C

Asset & Performance History

Date	NAV	1-Year Total Return
2017	49.72	1.73
2016	49.84	2.64
2015	49.48	0.83
2014	49.85	1.06
2013	49.85	0.12
2012	50.09	

Total Assets: $2,255,494,208

Asset Allocation

Asset	%
Cash	2%
Stocks	0%
US Stocks	0%
Bonds	97%
US Bonds	77%
Other	0%

Services Offered:

Investment Strategy: The investment seeks to track the investment results of the Bloomberg Barclays U.S. Universal 1-5 Year Index, which measures the performance of U.S. dollar-denominated taxable bonds that are rated either investment-grade or high yield with remaining effective maturities between one and five years. The fund invests at least 90% of its assets in the component securities of the index and in investments that have economic characteristics that are substantially identical to the component securities and may invest up to 10% of its assets in certain futures, options and swap contracts, cash and cash equivalents, as well as in securities not included in the index. **Top Holdings:** United States Treasury Notes 1.38% United States Treasury Notes 1.5% United States Treasury Notes 2.13% United States Treasury Notes 2% United States Treasury Notes 2.13%

First Trust NASDAQ-100-Technology Sector Index Fund   C   HOLD

Ticker	Traded On	NAV	Total Assets ($)	Dividend Yield (TTM)	Turnover Ratio	Expense Ratio
QTEC	NAS CM	67.97	$2,239,929,808	0.83	21	0.58

Ratings
Reward   C+
Risk   C
Recent Upgrade/Downgrade   Down

Fund Information
Fund Type   Exchange Traded Funds
Category   Technology Sector Equity
Sub-Category   Technology
Prospectus Objective   Technology
Inception Date   Apr-06
Open to New Investments   Y

Prices
Price (as of 12/31/2018)   68.06
52-Week High   82.65
52-Week Low   63.38

Total Returns (%)

3-Month	6-Month	1-Year	3-Year	5-Year
-14.08	-11.99	-4.71	64.56	102.57

3-Year Standard Deviation   15.04
Effective Duration

Valuation
Premium/Discount (1-Year Average)   0.03

Company Information
Provider   First Trust
Manager/Tenure   Jon C. Erickson (12), Daniel J.
                  Lindquist (12), David G. McGarel (12),
                  3 others
Website   http://www.ftportfolios.com/
Address   First Trust 120 E. Liberty Drive, Suite
                  400 Wheaton IL 60187 United States
Phone Number   800-621-1675

PERFORMANCE

Ratings History

Date	Overall Rating	Risk Rating	Reward Rating
Q4-18	C	C	C+
Q2-18	B	C+	B+
Q4-17	A-	B	A+
Q4-16	C+	C	C+
Q4-15	C	C	C+

Asset & Performance History

Date	NAV	1-Year Total Return
2017	71.92	37.85
2016	52.62	25.29
2015	42.64	-1.38
2014	43.67	24.81
2013	35.43	38.13
2012	25.86	8

Total Assets: $2,239,929,808
Asset Allocation

Asset	%
Cash	0%
Stocks	100%
US Stocks	86%
Bonds	0%
US Bonds	0%
Other	0%

Services Offered:

Investment Strategy: The investment seeks investment results that correspond generally to the price and yield (before the fund's fees and expenses) of an equity index called the NASDAQ-100 Technology Sector IndexSM. The fund will normally invest at least 90% of its net assets (including investment borrowings) in common stocks that comprise the index. The index is an equal-weighted index based on the securities of the NASDAQ-100 Index® that are classified as "technology" according to the Industry Classification Benchmark classification system. **Top Holdings:** Xilinx Inc Symantec Corp Workday Inc Class A NetEase Inc ADR Intel Corp

---

First Trust North American Energy Infrastructure Fund   C   HOLD

Ticker	Traded On	NAV	Total Assets ($)	Dividend Yield (TTM)	Turnover Ratio	Expense Ratio
EMLP	NYSE Arca	21.44	$2,233,385,393	3.98	24	0.95

Ratings
Reward   C
Risk   C+
Recent Upgrade/Downgrade

Fund Information
Fund Type   Exchange Traded Funds
Category   Energy Sector Equity
Sub-Category   Energy Limited Partnership
Prospectus Objective   Utility
Inception Date   Jun-12
Open to New Investments   Y

Prices
Price (as of 12/31/2018)   21.45
52-Week High   24.98
52-Week Low   20.55

Total Returns (%)

3-Month	6-Month	1-Year	3-Year	5-Year
-8.13	-5.69	-8.52	19.86	10.83

3-Year Standard Deviation   10.41
Effective Duration

Valuation
Premium/Discount (1-Year Average)   0.02

Company Information
Provider   First Trust
Manager/Tenure   James J. Murchie (6), Eva Pao (6),
                  John K. Tysseland (2)
Website   http://www.ftportfolios.com/
Address   First Trust 120 E. Liberty Drive, Suite
                  400 Wheaton IL 60187 United States
Phone Number   800-621-1675

PERFORMANCE

Ratings History

Date	Overall Rating	Risk Rating	Reward Rating
Q4-18	C	C+	C
Q2-18	C-	D+	C
Q4-17	C	C-	C
Q4-16	C	C-	C
Q4-15	C	C	C

Asset & Performance History

Date	NAV	1-Year Total Return
2017	24.51	1.06
2016	25.19	29.66
2015	20.18	-25.2
2014	28.08	23.63
2013	23.47	16.9
2012	20.77	

Total Assets: $2,233,385,393
Asset Allocation

Asset	%
Cash	9%
Stocks	91%
US Stocks	74%
Bonds	0%
US Bonds	0%
Other	0%

Services Offered:

Investment Strategy: The investment seeks total return. The fund invests at least 80% of its net assets in equity securities of companies deemed by the sub-advisor to be engaged in the energy infrastructure sector. These companies principally include publicly-traded MLPs and limited liability companies taxed as partnerships, MLP affiliates, pipeline companies, utilities, and other companies that derive the majority of their revenues from operating or providing services in support of infrastructure assets such as pipelines, power transmission and petroleum and natural gas storage in the petroleum, natural gas and power generation industries. It is non-diversified. **Top Holdings:** TransCanada Corp Enterprise Products Partners LP Kinder Morgan Inc P Exelon Corp NextEra Energy Partners LP

iShares Broad USD Investment Grade Corporate Bond ETF   D-   SELL

Ticker	Traded On	NAV	Total Assets ($)	Dividend Yield (TTM)	Turnover Ratio	Expense Ratio
USIG	NAS CM	52.81	$2,228,734,618	3.37	11	0.06

Ratings
Reward   E+
Risk   D-
Recent Upgrade/Downgrade   Down

Fund Information
Fund Type   Exchange Traded Funds
Category   US Fixed Income
Sub-Category   Corporate Bond
Prospectus Objective   Income
Inception Date   Jan-07
Open to New Investments   Y

Prices
Price (as of 12/31/2018)   52.95
52-Week High   112.03
52-Week Low   52.37

Total Returns (%)

3-Month	6-Month	1-Year	3-Year	5-Year
-0.03	0.69	-51.20	-45.45	-42.00

3-Year Standard Deviation   3.55
Effective Duration   6.77

Valuation
Premium/Discount (1-Year Average)   0.03

Company Information
Provider   iShares
Manager/Tenure   Scott Radell (8), James Mauro (7)
Website   http://www.ishares.com
Address   iShares 400 Howard Street San
                    Francisco CA 94105 United States
Phone Number   800-474-2737

PERFORMANCE

Ratings History

Date	Overall Rating	Risk Rating	Reward Rating
Q4-18	D-	D-	E+
Q2-18	C-	C-	C-
Q4-17	B-	B+	C
Q4-16	C	C-	C
Q4-15	C	C-	C

Asset & Performance History

Date	NAV	1-Year Total Return
2017	111.96	5.74
2016	108.91	5.45
2015	106.52	-0.97
2014	111.02	7.37
2013	106.93	-2.33
2012	113.33	9.12

Total Assets: $2,228,734,618
Asset Allocation

Asset	%
Cash	3%
Stocks	0%
US Stocks	0%
Bonds	97%
US Bonds	76%
Other	0%

Services Offered:

Investment Strategy: The investment seeks to track the investment results of the ICE BofAML US Corporate Index (the "underlying index"). The fund generally invests at least 90% of its assets in securities of the underlying index. It may invest the remainder of its assets in certain futures, options and swap contracts, cash and cash equivalents, as well as in securities not included in the underlying index. The underlying index measures the performance of investment-grade corporate bonds that are U.S. dollar-denominated. **Top Holdings:** Bank of Nova Scotia 2.45% Anheuser-Busch Companies LLC / Anheuser-Busch InBev Worldwide Inc 3.65% GE Capital International Funding Company Unlimited Company 4.42% Bank of America Corporation 3% Westpac Banking Corporation 2.65%

SPDR® Dow Jones Global Real Estate ETF   C   HOLD

Ticker	Traded On	NAV	Total Assets ($)	Dividend Yield (TTM)	Turnover Ratio	Expense Ratio
RWO	NYSE Arca	44.25	$2,225,184,066	3.74	11	0.5

Ratings
Reward   C-
Risk   C+
Recent Upgrade/Downgrade

Fund Information
Fund Type   Exchange Traded Funds
Category   Real Estate Sector Equity
Sub-Category   Global Real Estate
Prospectus Objective   Real Estate
Inception Date   May-08
Open to New Investments   Y

Prices
Price (as of 12/31/2018)   44.26
52-Week High   49.36
52-Week Low   42.86

Total Returns (%)

3-Month	6-Month	1-Year	3-Year	5-Year
-5.33	-5.48	-6.06	5.24	26.59

3-Year Standard Deviation   10.47
Effective Duration

Valuation
Premium/Discount (1-Year Average)   -0.10

Company Information
Provider   SPDR State Street Global Advisors
Manager/Tenure   Michael J. Feehily (5), Karl A.
                    Schneider (3), Keith Richardson (1)
Website   http://www.spdrs.com
Address   SPDR State Street Global Advisors
                    State Street Financial Center, 1
                    Lincoln Street Boston MA 02111-2900
                    United States
Phone Number   617-786-3000

PERFORMANCE

Ratings History

Date	Overall Rating	Risk Rating	Reward Rating
Q4-18	C	C+	C-
Q2-18	C	C+	C
Q4-17	B-	B	C+
Q4-16	C	C+	C
Q4-15	C+	C+	C

Asset & Performance History

Date	NAV	1-Year Total Return
2017	48.89	7.78
2016	46.87	1.85
2015	46.79	0.96
2014	47.74	19.13
2013	41.38	2.85
2012	41.77	25.08

Total Assets: $2,225,184,066
Asset Allocation

Asset	%
Cash	0%
Stocks	99%
US Stocks	59%
Bonds	0%
US Bonds	0%
Other	0%

Services Offered:

Investment Strategy: The investment seeks to provide investment results that, before fees and expenses, correspond generally to the total return performance of the Dow Jones Global Select Real Estate Securities Indexsm based upon the global real estate market. The fund generally invests substantially all, but at least 80%, of its total assets in the securities comprising the index and in depositary receipts based on securities comprising the index. The index is a float-adjusted market capitalization index designed to measure the performance of publicly traded global real estate securities. The fund is non-diversified. **Top Holdings:** Simon Property Group Inc Prologis Inc Public Storage Welltower Inc AvalonBay Communities Inc

Fidelity® MSCI Information Technology Index ETF — C+ HOLD

Ticker	Traded On	NAV	Total Assets ($)	Dividend Yield (TTM)	Turnover Ratio	Expense Ratio
FTEC	NYSE Arca	49.33	$2,224,744,528	0.99	4	0.08

Ratings

Reward	C+
Risk	C+
Recent Upgrade/Downgrade	Down

Fund Information

Fund Type	Exchange Traded Funds
Category	Technology Sector Equity
Sub-Category	Technology
Prospectus Objective	Technology
Inception Date	Oct-13
Open to New Investments	Y

Prices

Price (as of 12/31/2018)	49.24
52-Week High	60.66
52-Week Low	45.74

Total Returns (%)

3-Month	6-Month	1-Year	3-Year	5-Year
-17.85	-11.06	-0.17	55.70	93.22

3-Year Standard Deviation	14.2
Effective Duration	

Valuation

Premium/Discount (1-Year Average)	0.02

Company Information

Provider	Fidelity Investments
Manager/Tenure	Jennifer Hsui (5), Greg Savage (5), Alan Mason (2), 2 others
Website	http://www.institutional.fidelity.com
Address	Fidelity Investments 82 Devonshire Street Boston MA 2109 United States
Phone Number	617-563-7000

PERFORMANCE

Ratings History

Date	Overall Rating	Risk Rating	Reward Rating
Q4-18	C+	C+	C+
Q2-18	B	C+	B+
Q4-17	A-	B	A+
Q4-16	B-	C+	B
Q4-15	C-	B-	C

Asset & Performance History

Date	NAV	1-Year Total Return
2017	49.96	37.07
2016	36.83	13.78
2015	32.81	5.03
2014	31.64	18.15
2013	27.09	
2012		

Total Assets: $2,224,744,528

Asset Allocation

Asset	%
Cash	0%
Stocks	100%
US Stocks	99%
Bonds	0%
US Bonds	0%
Other	0%

Services Offered:

Investment Strategy: The investment seeks to provide investment returns that correspond, before fees and expenses, generally to the performance of the MSCI USA IMI Information Technology Index. The fund invests at least 80% of assets in securities included in the fund's underlying index. The fund's underlying index is the MSCI USA IMI Information Technology Index, which represents the performance of the information technology sector in the U.S. equity market. It may or may not hold all of the securities in the MSCI USA IMI Information Technology Index. The fund is non-diversified. **Top Holdings:** Apple Inc Microsoft Corp Alphabet Inc Class C Facebook Inc A Alphabet Inc A

Schwab Fundamental Emerging Markets Large Company Index ETF — C HOLD

Ticker	Traded On	NAV	Total Assets ($)	Dividend Yield (TTM)	Turnover Ratio	Expense Ratio
FNDE	NYSE Arca	25.87	$2,193,877,298	2.22	14	0.39

Ratings

Reward	C-
Risk	C
Recent Upgrade/Downgrade	

Fund Information

Fund Type	Exchange Traded Funds
Category	Global Emerg Mkts Equity
Sub-Category	Diversified Emerging Mkts
Prospectus Objective	Div Emerg Mkts
Inception Date	Aug-13
Open to New Investments	Y

Prices

Price (as of 12/31/2018)	25.83
52-Week High	33.12
52-Week Low	25.30

Total Returns (%)

3-Month	6-Month	1-Year	3-Year	5-Year
-7.64	-2.93	-10.01	50.25	8.05

3-Year Standard Deviation	17.18
Effective Duration	

Valuation

Premium/Discount (1-Year Average)	0.00

Company Information

Provider	Schwab ETFs
Manager/Tenure	Chuck Craig (5), Jane Qin (5), Christopher Bliss (1), 1 other
Website	http://www.schwabetfs.com
Address	Schwab ETFs United States
Phone Number	800-435-4000

PERFORMANCE

Ratings History

Date	Overall Rating	Risk Rating	Reward Rating
Q4-18	C	C	C-
Q2-18	C	C+	C
Q4-17	B	C	B+
Q4-16	C-	C-	C-
Q4-15	D	D	D

Asset & Performance History

Date	NAV	1-Year Total Return
2017	29.61	26.18
2016	23.96	32.3
2015	18.41	-19.11
2014	23.22	-11.09
2013	26.47	
2012		

Total Assets: $2,193,877,298

Asset Allocation

Asset	%
Cash	0%
Stocks	98%
US Stocks	0%
Bonds	0%
US Bonds	0%
Other	0%

Services Offered:

Investment Strategy: The investment seeks to track as closely as possible, before fees and expenses, the total return of the Russell RAFI™ Emerging Markets Large Company Index. The fund will invest at least 80% of its net assets in stocks included in the index, including depositary receipts representing securities of the index; which may be in the form of American Depositary Receipts, Global Depositary Receipts and European Depositary Receipts. The index measures the performance of the large company size segment by fundamental overall company scores, which are created using as the universe the companies included in the Russell Emerging Markets Index. **Top Holdings:** Samsung Electronics Co Ltd Gazprom PJSC Oil Co Lukoil Pjsc China Construction Bank Corp H China Mobile Ltd

ALPS Sector Dividend Dogs ETF

C   HOLD

Ticker	Traded On	NAV	Total Assets ($)	Dividend Yield (TTM)	Turnover Ratio	Expense Ratio
SDOG	NYSE Arca	39.14	$2,166,708,507	3.58	48	0.4

Ratings
Reward	C
Risk	C
Recent Upgrade/Downgrade	Down

Fund Information
Fund Type	Exchange Traded Funds
Category	US Equity Large Cap Value
Sub-Category	Large Value
Prospectus Objective	Income
Inception Date	Jun-12
Open to New Investments	Y

Prices
Price (as of 12/31/2018)	39.13
52-Week High	49.24
52-Week Low	37.25

Total Returns (%)
3-Month	6-Month	1-Year	3-Year	5-Year
-14.23	-10.04	-11.29	22.32	36.10

3-Year Standard Deviation	10.59
Effective Duration	

Valuation
Premium/Discount (1-Year Average)	0.00

Company Information
Provider	ALPS
Manager/Tenure	Ryan Mischker (3), Andrew Hicks (2)
Website	http://www.alpsfunds.com
Address	ALPS 1290 Broadway, Suite 1100 Denver CO 80203 United States
Phone Number	866-759-5679

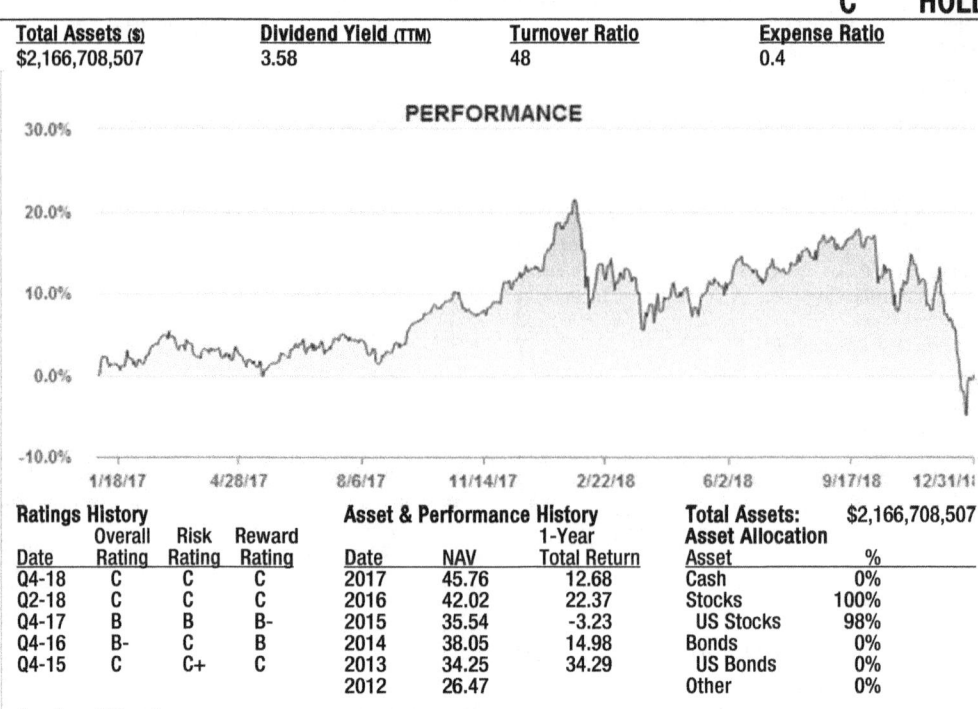

Ratings History
Date	Overall Rating	Risk Rating	Reward Rating
Q4-18	C	C	C
Q2-18	C	C	C
Q4-17	B	B	B-
Q4-16	B-	C	B
Q4-15	C	C+	C

Asset & Performance History
Date	NAV	1-Year Total Return
2017	45.76	12.68
2016	42.02	22.37
2015	35.54	-3.23
2014	38.05	14.98
2013	34.25	34.29
2012	26.47	

Total Assets: $2,166,708,507
Asset Allocation
Asset	%
Cash	0%
Stocks	100%
US Stocks	98%
Bonds	0%
US Bonds	0%
Other	0%

Services Offered:

Investment Strategy: The investment seeks investment results that replicate as closely as possible, before fees and expenses, the performance of the S-Network® Sector Dividend Dogs Index. The underlying index generally consists of 50 stocks on each annual reconstitution date, which is the third Friday of December each year. The underlying index's stocks must be constituents of the S&P 500 Index, the leading benchmark index for U.S. large capitalization stocks. The underlying index methodology selects the five stocks in each of the ten GICS sectors that make up the S&P 500 which offer the highest dividend yields as of the last business day of November. **Top Holdings:** SCANA Corp The AES Corp L Brands Inc Merck & Co Inc Eli Lilly and Co

iShares MSCI Pacific ex Japan ETF

C-   HOLD

Ticker	Traded On	NAV	Total Assets ($)	Dividend Yield (TTM)	Turnover Ratio	Expense Ratio
EPP	NYSE Arca	40.85	$2,161,114,588	4.89	6	0.48

Ratings
Reward	D+
Risk	C
Recent Upgrade/Downgrade	Down

Fund Information
Fund Type	Exchange Traded Funds
Category	Asia ex-Japan Equity
Sub-Category	Pacific/Asia ex-Japan Stk
Prospectus Objective	Pacific Stock
Inception Date	Oct-01
Open to New Investments	Y

Prices
Price (as of 12/31/2018)	40.70
52-Week High	50.31
52-Week Low	39.46

Total Returns (%)
3-Month	6-Month	1-Year	3-Year	5-Year
-7.57	-7.82	-10.68	20.29	8.67

3-Year Standard Deviation	13.25
Effective Duration	

Valuation
Premium/Discount (1-Year Average)	-0.18

Company Information
Provider	iShares
Manager/Tenure	Diane Hsiung (10), Greg Savage (10), Jennifer Hsui (5), 1 other
Website	http://www.ishares.com
Address	iShares 400 Howard Street San Francisco CA 94105 United States
Phone Number	800-474-2737

Ratings History
Date	Overall Rating	Risk Rating	Reward Rating
Q4-18	C-	C	D+
Q2-18	C	C+	C
Q4-17	B-	C	B
Q4-16	D+	C-	D+
Q4-15	C-	D+	C-

Asset & Performance History
Date	NAV	1-Year Total Return
2017	47.94	25.43
2016	39.89	7.38
2015	38.64	-8.88
2014	44.38	-0.85
2013	46.68	5.03
2012	46.38	23.99

Total Assets: $2,161,114,588
Asset Allocation
Asset	%
Cash	1%
Stocks	99%
US Stocks	1%
Bonds	0%
US Bonds	0%
Other	0%

Services Offered: CashInvestment Plan

Investment Strategy: The investment seeks to track the investment results of the MSCI Pacific ex Japan Index. The fund normally invests at least 95% of its total assets in the securities of its underlying index and in depositary receipts representing securities in its underlying index. It will at all times invest at least 90% of its total assets in such securities. The underlying index consists of stocks from the following four countries or regions: Australia, Hong Kong, New Zealand and Singapore. It may include large- or mid-capitalization companies. **Top Holdings:** AIA Group Ltd Commonwealth Bank of Australia BHP Group Ltd Westpac Banking Corp CSL Ltd

Vanguard S&P Mid-Cap 400 Index Fund ETF Shares   C-   HOLD

Ticker	Traded On	NAV	Total Assets ($)	Dividend Yield (TTM)	Turnover Ratio	Expense Ratio
IVOO	NYSE Arca		$2,120,497,689	1.44	12	0.15

Ratings

Reward	C-
Risk	C-
Recent Upgrade/Downgrade	Down

Fund Information

Fund Type	Exchange Traded Funds
Category	US Equity Mid Cap
Sub-Category	Mid-Cap Blend
Prospectus Objective	Growth & Inc
Inception Date	Sep-10
Open to New Investments	Y

Prices

Price (as of 12/31/2018)	111.86
52-Week High	138.42
52-Week Low	105.39

Total Returns (%)

3-Month	6-Month	1-Year	3-Year	5-Year
-17.50	-15.08	-12.09	23.04	31.80

3-Year Standard Deviation	11.84
Effective Duration	

Valuation

Premium/Discount (1-Year Average)	0.02

Company Information

Provider	Vanguard
Manager/Tenure	William A. Coleman (2), Awais Khan (1)
Website	http://www.vanguard.com
Address	Vanguard 100 Vanguard Boulevard Malvern PA 19355 United States
Phone Number	877-662-7447

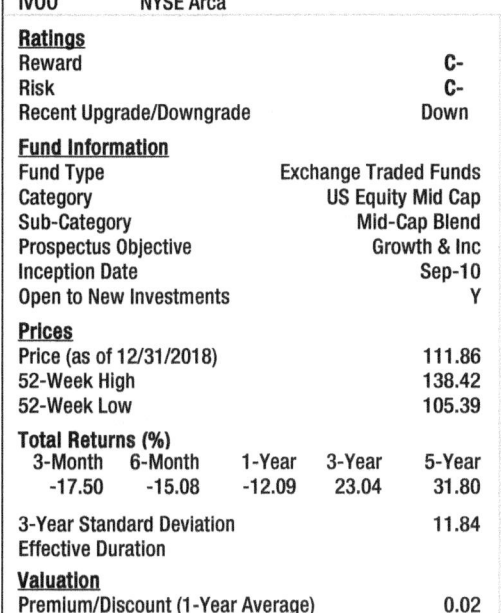

PERFORMANCE

Ratings History

Date	Overall Rating	Risk Rating	Reward Rating
Q4-18	C-	C-	C-
Q2-18	C	C-	C+
Q4-17	B	B	B
Q4-16	C+	C-	B
Q4-15	C	C-	C

Asset & Performance History

Date	NAV	1-Year Total Return
2017	127.79	16.26
2016	111.48	19.8
2015	93.82	-2.29
2014	97.41	9.64
2013	89.96	33.3
2012	68.12	17.74

Total Assets: $2,120,497,689

Asset Allocation

Asset	%
Cash	1%
Stocks	99%
US Stocks	99%
Bonds	0%
US Bonds	0%
Other	0%

Services Offered:

Investment Strategy: The investment seeks to track the performance of a benchmark index that measures the investment return of mid-capitalization stocks in the United States. The fund employs an indexing investment approach designed to track the performance of the S&P MidCap 400® Index. The index measures the performance of mid-capitalization stocks in the United States. The Advisor attempts to replicate the target index by investing all, or substantially all, of its assets in the stocks that make up the index, holding each stock in approximately the same proportion as its weighting in the index. **Top Holdings:** Jack Henry & Associates Inc   Lamb Weston Holdings Inc   Domino's Pizza Inc   Teleflex Inc   Keysight Technologies Inc

---

iShares Europe ETF   D+   SELL

Ticker	Traded On	NAV	Total Assets ($)	Dividend Yield (TTM)	Turnover Ratio	Expense Ratio
IEV	NYSE Arca	39.15	$2,117,858,275	3.3	3	0.6

Ratings

Reward	D+
Risk	C-
Recent Upgrade/Downgrade	Down

Fund Information

Fund Type	Exchange Traded Funds
Category	Europe Equity Large Cap
Sub-Category	Europe Stock
Prospectus Objective	Europe Stock
Inception Date	Jul-00
Open to New Investments	Y

Prices

Price (as of 12/31/2018)	39.12
52-Week High	50.71
52-Week Low	37.89

Total Returns (%)

3-Month	6-Month	1-Year	3-Year	5-Year
-12.71	-10.90	-15.01	5.69	-4.05

3-Year Standard Deviation	12.02
Effective Duration	

Valuation

Premium/Discount (1-Year Average)	-0.20

Company Information

Provider	iShares
Manager/Tenure	Diane Hsiung (10), Greg Savage (10), Jennifer Hsui (6), 3 others
Website	http://www.ishares.com
Address	iShares 400 Howard Street San Francisco CA 94105 United States
Phone Number	800-474-2737

PERFORMANCE

Ratings History

Date	Overall Rating	Risk Rating	Reward Rating
Q4-18	D+	C-	D+
Q2-18	C	C+	C
Q4-17	B-	B-	B-
Q4-16	D	C-	D
Q4-15	C	C+	C-

Asset & Performance History

Date	NAV	1-Year Total Return
2017	47.5	24.94
2016	38.98	-0.45
2015	40.37	-3.36
2014	42.84	-6.07
2013	47.16	25.17
2012	38.74	18.64

Total Assets: $2,117,858,275

Asset Allocation

Asset	%
Cash	1%
Stocks	99%
US Stocks	2%
Bonds	0%
US Bonds	0%
Other	0%

Services Offered: CashInvestment Plan

Investment Strategy: The investment seeks to track the investment results of the S&P Europe 350TM, which measures the performance of the stocks of leading companies in the following countries: Austria, Belgium, Denmark, Finland, France, Germany, Ireland, Italy, Luxembourg, the Netherlands, Norway, Portugal, Spain, Sweden, Switzerland and the United Kingdom. The fund generally invests at least 90% of its assets in securities of the index and in depositary receipts representing securities of the index. It may invest the remainder of its assets in certain futures, options and swap contracts, cash and cash equivalents, as well as in securities not included in the index. **Top Holdings:** Nestle SA   Novartis AG   Roche Holding AG Dividend Right Cert.   HSBC Holdings PLC   Total SA

Invesco Optimum Yield Diversified Commodity Strategy No K-1 ETF   C-   HOLD

Ticker	Traded On	NAV	Total Assets ($)	Dividend Yield (TTM)	Turnover Ratio	Expense Ratio
PDBC	NAS CM	15.02	$2,099,233,293	4.22		0.59

Ratings
Reward	C-
Risk	C
Recent Upgrade/Downgrade	Down

Fund Information
Fund Type	Exchange Traded Funds
Category	Commodities Broad Basket
Sub-Category	Commodities Broad Basket
Prospectus Objective	Growth
Inception Date	Nov-14
Open to New Investments	Y

Prices
Price (as of 12/31/2018)	15.07
52-Week High	19.39
52-Week Low	14.98

Total Returns (%)
3-Month	6-Month	1-Year	3-Year	5-Year
-20.64	-16.07	-13.19	8.53	

3-Year Standard Deviation	13.46
Effective Duration	

Valuation
Premium/Discount (1-Year Average)	-0.06

Company Information
Provider	Invesco
Manager/Tenure	Peter Hubbard (4), Theodore Samulowitz (4), David Hemming (2)
Website	http://www.invesco.com/us
Address	Invesco 11 Greenway Plaza, Ste. 2500 Houston TX 77046 United States
Phone Number	800-659-1005

PERFORMANCE

Ratings History
Date	Overall Rating	Risk Rating	Reward Rating
Q4-18	C-	C	C-
Q2-18	C	C	C
Q4-17	C	C	C
Q4-16	D	D	D+
Q4-15	U		

Asset & Performance History
Date	NAV	1-Year Total Return
2017	17.48	5.27
2016	17.27	18.76
2015	15.5	-27.02
2014	21.24	
2013		
2012		

Total Assets: $2,099,233,293

Asset Allocation
Asset	%
Cash	71%
Stocks	0%
US Stocks	0%
Bonds	29%
US Bonds	29%
Other	0%

Services Offered:

Investment Strategy: The investment seeks long term capital appreciation. The fund is an actively managed exchange-traded fund ("ETF") that seeks to achieve its investment objective by investing in a combination of financial instruments that are economically linked to the world's most heavily traded commodities. Commodities are assets that have tangible properties, such as oil, agricultural produce or raw metals. It is non-diversified. **Top Holdings:** United States Treasury Bills 0% United States Treasury Bills 0% United States Treasury Bills 0% US Treasury Bill Ny Harb Ulsd Fut Jun16

Schwab International Small-Cap Equity ETF™   D+   SELL

Ticker	Traded On	NAV	Total Assets ($)	Dividend Yield (TTM)	Turnover Ratio	Expense Ratio
SCHC	NYSE Arca	29.11	$2,069,523,836	3.14	16	0.12

Ratings
Reward	D+
Risk	C-
Recent Upgrade/Downgrade	Down

Fund Information
Fund Type	Exchange Traded Funds
Category	Global Eq Mid/Small Cap
Sub-Category	Foreign Small/Mid Blend
Prospectus Objective	Small Company
Inception Date	Jan-10
Open to New Investments	Y

Prices
Price (as of 12/31/2018)	29.10
52-Week High	39.11
52-Week Low	27.92

Total Returns (%)
3-Month	6-Month	1-Year	3-Year	5-Year
-16.55	-15.91	-18.64	8.55	4.13

3-Year Standard Deviation	12.1
Effective Duration	

Valuation
Premium/Discount (1-Year Average)	0.04

Company Information
Provider	Schwab ETFs
Manager/Tenure	Chuck Craig (5), Christopher Bliss (1), Jane Qin (1), 1 other
Website	http://www.schwabetfs.com
Address	Schwab ETFs United States
Phone Number	800-435-4000

PERFORMANCE

Ratings History
Date	Overall Rating	Risk Rating	Reward Rating
Q4-18	D+	C-	D+
Q2-18	C+	C+	C+
Q4-17	B	B	B+
Q4-16	C	C	C-
Q4-15	C	C+	C-

Asset & Performance History
Date	NAV	1-Year Total Return
2017	36.65	29.36
2016	29.13	3.16
2015	28.81	1.85
2014	28.96	-5.82
2013	31.55	21.91
2012	26.63	17.49

Total Assets: $2,069,523,836

Asset Allocation
Asset	%
Cash	0%
Stocks	99%
US Stocks	1%
Bonds	0%
US Bonds	0%
Other	0%

Services Offered:

Investment Strategy: The investment seeks to track as closely as possible, before fees and expenses, the total return of the FTSE Developed Small Cap ex US Liquid Index. The fund will invest at least 90% of its net assets in stocks, including depositary receipts representing securities of the index; such depositary receipts may be in the form of American Depositary receipts, Global Depositary receipts and European Depositary receipts. The index is comprised of small capitalization companies in developed countries outside the United States. **Top Holdings:** Open Text Corp Gildan Activewear, Inc. Class A First Quantum Minerals Ltd CCL Industries Inc. Class A Canopy Growth Corp

WisdomTree U.S. SmallCap Dividend Fund   C   HOLD

Ticker	Traded On	NAV	Total Assets ($)	Dividend Yield (TTM)	Turnover Ratio	Expense Ratio
DES	NYSE Arca	24.53	$2,035,983,314	3.32	36	0.38

Ratings

Reward	C-
Risk	C+
Recent Upgrade/Downgrade	Down

Fund Information

Fund Type	Exchange Traded Funds
Category	US Equity Small Cap
Sub-Category	Small Value
Prospectus Objective	Small Company
Inception Date	Jun-06
Open to New Investments	Y

Prices

Price (as of 12/31/2018)	24.53
52-Week High	30.66
52-Week Low	23.32

Total Returns (%)

3-Month	6-Month	1-Year	3-Year	5-Year
-15.51	-15.85	-12.75	24.26	26.23

3-Year Standard Deviation	13.44
Effective Duration	

Valuation

Premium/Discount (1-Year Average)	0.04

Company Information

Provider	WisdomTree
Manager/Tenure	Richard A. Brown (10), Thomas J. Durante (10), Karen Q. Wong (10)
Website	http://www.wisdomtree.com
Address	WisdomTree 245 Park Avenue, 35th floor New York NY 10167 United States
Phone Number	866-909-9473

PERFORMANCE

Ratings History

Date	Overall Rating	Risk Rating	Reward Rating
Q4-18	C	C+	C-
Q2-18	C+	C+	C+
Q4-17	B+	B	A-
Q4-16	C	C-	C
Q4-15	C	C-	C

Asset & Performance History

Date	NAV	1-Year Total Return
2017	29.02	8.68
2016	27.54	31.05
2015	21.67	-5.53
2014	23.63	7.54
2013	22.59	36.85
2012	16.96	18.38

Total Assets: $2,035,983,314

Asset Allocation

Asset	%
Cash	0%
Stocks	100%
US Stocks	100%
Bonds	0%
US Bonds	0%
Other	0%

Services Offered:

Investment Strategy: The investment seeks to track the price and yield performance, before fees and expenses, of the WisdomTree U.S. SmallCap Dividend Index. Under normal circumstances, at least 95% of the fund's total assets (exclusive of collateral held from securities lending) will be invested in component securities of the index and investments that have economic characteristics that are substantially identical to the economic characteristics of such component securities. The index is a fundamentally weighted index measuring the performance of the small-capitalization segment of the U.S. dividend-paying market. The fund is non-diversified. **Top Holdings:** CVR Energy Inc Pattern Energy Group Inc Class A Covanta Holding Corp Vector Group Ltd Uniti Group Inc

---

iShares Cohen & Steers REIT ETF   B-   BUY

Ticker	Traded On	NAV	Total Assets ($)	Dividend Yield (TTM)	Turnover Ratio	Expense Ratio
ICF	BATS	95.71	$2,021,392,989	3.09	12	0.34

Ratings

Reward	B
Risk	C
Recent Upgrade/Downgrade	

Fund Information

Fund Type	Exchange Traded Funds
Category	Real Estate Sector Equity
Sub-Category	Real Estate
Prospectus Objective	Real Estate
Inception Date	Jan-01
Open to New Investments	Y

Prices

Price (as of 12/31/2018)	95.70
52-Week High	106.05
52-Week Low	88.56

Total Returns (%)

3-Month	6-Month	1-Year	3-Year	5-Year
-2.94	-2.18	-2.45	7.05	52.09

3-Year Standard Deviation	12.62
Effective Duration	

Valuation

Premium/Discount (1-Year Average)	-0.03

Company Information

Provider	iShares
Manager/Tenure	Diane Hsiung (10), Greg Savage (10), Jennifer Hsui (6), 3 others
Website	http://www.ishares.com
Address	iShares 400 Howard Street San Francisco CA 94105 United States
Phone Number	800-474-2737

PERFORMANCE

Ratings History

Date	Overall Rating	Risk Rating	Reward Rating
Q4-18	B-	C	B
Q2-18	C+	C-	B
Q4-17	B-	B	C+
Q4-16	B-	C	B
Q4-15	B	C+	B+

Asset & Performance History

Date	NAV	1-Year Total Return
2017	101.27	4.95
2016	99.55	4.57
2015	99.21	5.96
2014	96.87	34.07
2013	74.66	-1.8
2012	78.53	15.25

Total Assets: $2,021,392,989

Asset Allocation

Asset	%
Cash	0%
Stocks	100%
US Stocks	100%
Bonds	0%
US Bonds	0%
Other	0%

Services Offered: CashInvestment Plan

Investment Strategy: The investment seeks to track the investment results of the Cohen & Steers Realty Majors Index composed of U.S. real estate investment trusts ("REITs"). The fund generally invests at least 90% of its assets in securities of the underlying index and in depositary receipts representing securities of the underlying index. The objective of the underlying index is to represent relatively large and liquid REITs that may benefit from future consolidation and securitization of the U.S. real estate industry. The fund is non-diversified. **Top Holdings:** American Tower Corp Prologis Inc Simon Property Group Inc Public Storage Equinix Inc

Invesco DB Commodity Index Tracking Fund

C   HOLD

Ticker	Traded On	NAV	Total Assets ($)	Dividend Yield (TTM)	Turnover Ratio	Expense Ratio
DBC	NYSE Arca	14.44	$2,020,116,547	0	0	0.85

Ratings
Reward	C-
Risk	C
Recent Upgrade/Downgrade	

Fund Information
Fund Type	Exchange Traded Funds
Category	Commodities Broad Basket
Sub-Category	Commodities Broad Basket
Prospectus Objective	Natl Res
Inception Date	Feb-06
Open to New Investments	Y

Prices
Price (as of 12/31/2018)	14.49
52-Week High	18.54
52-Week Low	14.39

Total Returns (%)
3-Month	6-Month	1-Year	3-Year	5-Year
-20.04	-15.44	-12.02	9.59	-42.87

3-Year Standard Deviation	13.2
Effective Duration	

Valuation
Premium/Discount (1-Year Average)	-0.06

Company Information
Provider	Invesco
Manager/Tenure	Management Team (12)
Website	http://www.invesco.com/us
Address	Invesco 11 Greenway Plaza, Ste. 2500 Houston TX 77046 United States
Phone Number	800-659-1005

PERFORMANCE

Ratings History
Date	Overall Rating	Risk Rating	Reward Rating
Q4-18	C	C	C-
Q2-18	C	C	C
Q4-17	C-	D+	C
Q4-16	D	D	D
Q4-15	D-	D-	D-

Asset & Performance History
Date	NAV	1-Year Total Return
2017	16.63	4.82
2016	15.83	19.12
2015	13.35	-27.41
2014	18.4	-28.18
2013	25.62	-7.57
2012	27.72	3.31

Total Assets: $2,020,116,547
Asset Allocation
Asset	%
Cash	35%
Stocks	0%
US Stocks	0%
Bonds	15%
US Bonds	15%
Other	45%

Services Offered:

Investment Strategy: The investment seeks to track changes, whether positive or negative, in the level of the DBIQ Optimum Yield Diversified Commodity Index Excess Return™.
The fund pursues its investment objective by investing in index commodities. The index commodities are Light Sweet Crude Oil (WTI), Heating Oil, RBOB Gasoline, Natural Gas, Brent Crude, Gold, Silver, Aluminum, Zinc, Copper Grade A, Corn, Wheat, Soybeans, and Sugar. The index is composed of notional amounts of each of these commodities. **Top Holdings:** United States Treasury Bills 0% Invesco Treasury Collateral ETF   Gasoline Rbob Fut Jan19 Ny Harb Ulsd Fut Jun19 Brent Crude Futr Jan20

WisdomTree U.S. LargeCap Dividend Fund

C   HOLD

Ticker	Traded On	NAV	Total Assets ($)	Dividend Yield (TTM)	Turnover Ratio	Expense Ratio
DLN	NYSE Arca	84.39	$1,995,967,465	2.6	10	0.28

Ratings
Reward	C
Risk	C-
Recent Upgrade/Downgrade	

Fund Information
Fund Type	Exchange Traded Funds
Category	US Equity Large Cap Value
Sub-Category	Large Value
Prospectus Objective	Growth & Inc
Inception Date	Jun-06
Open to New Investments	Y

Prices
Price (as of 12/31/2018)	84.45
52-Week High	97.25
52-Week Low	79.69

Total Returns (%)
3-Month	6-Month	1-Year	3-Year	5-Year
-11.23	-4.58	-5.77	28.51	44.74

3-Year Standard Deviation	8.26
Effective Duration	

Valuation
Premium/Discount (1-Year Average)	0.00

Company Information
Provider	WisdomTree
Manager/Tenure	Richard A. Brown (10), Thomas J. Durante (10), Karen Q. Wong (10)
Website	http://www.wisdomtree.com
Address	WisdomTree 245 Park Avenue, 35th floor New York NY 10167 United States
Phone Number	866-909-9473

PERFORMANCE

Ratings History
Date	Overall Rating	Risk Rating	Reward Rating
Q4-18	C	C-	C
Q2-18	C	C-	C
Q4-17	B-	B	B-
Q4-16	C+	C-	B
Q4-15	C	C	C

Asset & Performance History
Date	NAV	1-Year Total Return
2017	92.03	18.21
2016	79.83	15.38
2015	71.16	-1.26
2014	74.08	14.07
2013	66.57	27.35
2012	53.66	12.87

Total Assets: $1,995,967,465
Asset Allocation
Asset	%
Cash	0%
Stocks	100%
US Stocks	100%
Bonds	0%
US Bonds	0%
Other	0%

Services Offered:

Investment Strategy: The investment seeks to track the price and yield performance, before fees and expenses, of the WisdomTree U.S. LargeCap Dividend Index. Under normal circumstances, at least 95% of the fund's total assets (exclusive of collateral held from securities lending) will be invested in component securities of the index and investments that have economic characteristics that are substantially identical to the economic characteristics of such component securities. The index is a fundamentally weighted index that is comprised of the large-capitalization segment of the U.S. dividend-paying market. The fund is non-diversified. **Top Holdings:** Microsoft Corp Apple Inc Exxon Mobil Corp Verizon Communications Inc AT&T Inc

Credit Suisse FI Large Cap Growth Enhanced ETN   C-   HOLD

Ticker	Traded On	NAV	Total Assets ($)	Dividend Yield (TTM)	Turnover Ratio	Expense Ratio
FLGE	NYSE Arca		$1,984,774,675	0		0.85

Ratings
Reward   C
Risk   D+
Recent Upgrade/Downgrade   Down

Fund Information
Fund Type   Exchange Traded Funds
Category   US Equity Large Cap Growth
Sub-Category   Large Growth
Prospectus Objective   Growth
Inception Date   Jun-14
Open to New Investments   Y

Prices
Price (as of 12/31/2018)   189.34
52-Week High   300.04
52-Week Low   167.09

Total Returns (%)
3-Month	6-Month	1-Year	3-Year	5-Year
-37.20	-26.78	-16.81	52.43	

3-Year Standard Deviation   21.96
Effective Duration

Valuation
Premium/Discount (1-Year Average)   0.37

Company Information
Provider   Credit Suisse AG
Manager/Tenure   Not Disclosed (4)
Website
Address   Kilmore House Park Lane Dublin
                         Ireland
Phone Number

PERFORMANCE

Ratings History
Date	Overall Rating	Risk Rating	Reward Rating
Q4-18	C-	D+	C
Q2-18	C+	D+	B
Q4-17	A	B	A+
Q4-16	C	C-	C+
Q4-15	D	D+	D

Asset & Performance History
Date	NAV	1-Year Total Return
2017	226.42	62.43
2016	138.96	11.77
2015	123.56	8.95
2014	113.4	
2013		
2012		

Total Assets: $1,984,774,675

Asset Allocation
Asset	%
Cash	%
Stocks	%
US Stocks	%
Bonds	%
US Bonds	%
Other	%

Services Offered:

Investment Strategy: The investment seeks a leveraged return linked to the performance of the Russell 1000® Growth Index Total Return (the "index"), an index that seeks to track the performance of the large-cap growth segment of the U.S. equity market.
The ETNs are subject to a leverage factor of 2.0, but the effective leverage will vary with changes in the Closing Indicative Value of the ETNs since the previous Rebalance Event. **Top Holdings:**

Xtrackers USD High Yield Corporate Bond ETF   C-   HOLD

Ticker	Traded On	NAV	Total Assets ($)	Dividend Yield (TTM)	Turnover Ratio	Expense Ratio
HYLB	NYSE Arca		$1,975,928,660	5.6		0.2

Ratings
Reward   D+
Risk   C+
Recent Upgrade/Downgrade   Down

Fund Information
Fund Type   Exchange Traded Funds
Category   US Fixed Income
Sub-Category   High Yield Bond
Prospectus Objective   Corp Bond-High Yld
Inception Date   Dec-16
Open to New Investments   Y

Prices
Price (as of 12/31/2018)   46.79
52-Week High   50.89
52-Week Low   45.99

Total Returns (%)
3-Month	6-Month	1-Year	3-Year	5-Year
-4.74	-1.79	-2.07		

3-Year Standard Deviation
Effective Duration

Valuation
Premium/Discount (1-Year Average)   -0.26

Company Information
Provider   Deutsche Asset Management
Manager/Tenure   Alexander Bridgeforth (1), Tanuj Dora
                         (1), Brandon Matsui (1), 1 other
Website   http://www.deutsche-etfs.com
Address   Deutsche Asset & Wealth
                         Management 345 Park Avenue New
                         York NY 10154 United States
Phone Number   844-851-4255

PERFORMANCE

Ratings History
Date	Overall Rating	Risk Rating	Reward Rating
Q4-18	C-	C+	D+
Q2-18	C	C+	D+
Q4-17	D	A	D+
Q4-16			
Q4-15			

Asset & Performance History
Date	NAV	1-Year Total Return
2017	50.48	5.96
2016	50.47	
2015		
2014		
2013		
2012		

Total Assets: $1,975,928,660

Asset Allocation
Asset	%
Cash	1%
Stocks	0%
US Stocks	0%
Bonds	99%
US Bonds	86%
Other	0%

Services Offered:

Investment Strategy: The investment seeks investment results that correspond generally to the performance, before fees and expenses, of the Solactive USD High Yield Corporates Total Market Index (the "underlying index"). The fund will normally invest at least 80% of its net assets, plus the amount of any borrowings for investment purposes, in high yield corporate bonds. The index comprised of U.S. dollar-denominated high yield corporate bonds. It will concentrate its investments (i.e., hold 25% or more of its total assets) in a particular industry or group of industries to the extent that its underlying index is concentrated. The fund is non-diversified. **Top Holdings:** ALTICE FRANCE S.A 7.38%   Sprint Corporation 7.88%   First Data Corporation 7%   HCA Inc. 6.5%   Bausch Health Companies Inc 5.88%

Invesco FTSE RAFI US 1500 Small-Mid ETF   C-   HOLD

Ticker	Traded On	NAV	Total Assets ($)	Dividend Yield (TTM)	Turnover Ratio	Expense Ratio
PRFZ	NAS CM	113.68	$1,961,633,247	1.22	26	0.39

Ratings
Reward   C-
Risk   C-
Recent Upgrade/Downgrade   Down

Fund Information
Fund Type   Exchange Traded Funds
Category   US Equity Small Cap
Sub-Category   Small Blend
Prospectus Objective   Growth
Inception Date   Sep-06
Open to New Investments   Y

Prices
Price (as of 12/31/2018)   113.66
52-Week High   146.04
52-Week Low   107.24

Total Returns (%)

3-Month	6-Month	1-Year	3-Year	5-Year
-18.78	-18.10	-11.39	25.62	23.76

3-Year Standard Deviation   13.68
Effective Duration

Valuation
Premium/Discount (1-Year Average)   0.03

Company Information
Provider   Invesco
Manager/Tenure Peter Hubbard (11), Michael Jeanette (10), Jonathan Nixon (5), 1 other
Website   http://www.invesco.com/us
Address   Invesco 11 Greenway Plaza, Ste. 2500 Houston TX 77046 United States
Phone Number   800-659-1005

PERFORMANCE

Ratings History

Date	Overall Rating	Risk Rating	Reward Rating
Q4-18	C-	C-	C-
Q2-18	C	C-	B-
Q4-17	B+	B	A-
Q4-16	C+	C-	B
Q4-15	C	C-	C

Asset & Performance History

Date	NAV	1-Year Total Return
2017	129.88	13.95
2016	115.14	24.42
2015	93.84	-5.7
2014	100.86	4.47
2013	97.66	41.8
2012	69.6	18.28

Total Assets: $1,961,633,247

Asset Allocation

Asset	%
Cash	0%
Stocks	100%
US Stocks	97%
Bonds	0%
US Bonds	0%
Other	0%

Services Offered:

Investment Strategy: The investment seeks to track the investment results (before fees and expenses) of the FTSE RAFI™ US Mid Small 1500 Index. The fund generally will invest at least 90% of its total assets in common stocks that comprise the underlying index. The underlying index is composed of 1,500 common stocks that the index provider strictly in accordance with its guidelines and mandated procedures, include to track the performance of small- and medium-sized U.S. companies based on the following four fundamental measures of firm size: book value, cash flow, sales and dividends. **Top Holdings:** Intelsat SA FTI Consulting Inc Guess? Inc Helen Of Troy Ltd TripAdvisor Inc

iShares Intermediate Government/Credit Bond ETF   C   HOLD

Ticker	Traded On	NAV	Total Assets ($)	Dividend Yield (TTM)	Turnover Ratio	Expense Ratio
GVI	BATS	108.15	$1,961,108,516	2.15	19	0.2

Ratings
Reward   D+
Risk   C+
Recent Upgrade/Downgrade   Up

Fund Information
Fund Type   Exchange Traded Funds
Category   US Fixed Income
Sub-Category   Intermediate-Term Bond
Prospectus Objective   Income
Inception Date   Jan-07
Open to New Investments   Y

Prices
Price (as of 12/31/2018)   108.22
52-Week High   109.76
52-Week Low   106.45

Total Returns (%)

3-Month	6-Month	1-Year	3-Year	5-Year
1.63	1.84	0.70	4.61	8.60

3-Year Standard Deviation   2.01
Effective Duration   3.86

Valuation
Premium/Discount (1-Year Average)   0.02

Company Information
Provider   iShares
Manager/Tenure Scott Radell (8), James Mauro (7)
Website   http://www.ishares.com
Address   iShares 400 Howard Street San Francisco CA 94105 United States
Phone Number   800-474-2737

PERFORMANCE

Ratings History

Date	Overall Rating	Risk Rating	Reward Rating
Q4-18	C	C+	D+
Q2-18	D+	C-	D+
Q4-17	C+	B	C
Q4-16	C	C-	C
Q4-15	C	C-	C

Asset & Performance History

Date	NAV	1-Year Total Return
2017	109.76	1.76
2016	109.72	1.89
2015	109.57	0.85
2014	110.54	2.93
2013	109.25	-1.04
2012	112.36	3.64

Total Assets: $1,961,108,516

Asset Allocation

Asset	%
Cash	1%
Stocks	0%
US Stocks	0%
Bonds	99%
US Bonds	88%
Other	0%

Services Offered:

Investment Strategy: The investment seeks to track the investment results of the Bloomberg Barclays U.S. Intermediate Government/Credit Bond Index. The fund generally invests at least 90% of its assets in securities of the underlying index. The index measures the performance of U.S. dollar-denominated U.S. Treasury bonds, government-related bonds (i.e., U.S. and non-U.S. agencies, sovereign, supranational and local authority debt) and investment-grade U.S. corporate bonds that have a remaining maturity of greater than one year and less than or equal to ten years. **Top Holdings:** United States Treasury Notes 2.25% United States Treasury Notes 2.75% United States Treasury Notes 1.5% United States Treasury Notes 3.5% United States Treasury Notes 2.25%

SPDR® S&P 600 Small Cap Growth ETF   D-   SELL

Ticker	Traded On	NAV	Total Assets ($)	Dividend Yield (TTM)	Turnover Ratio	Expense Ratio
SLYG	NYSE Arca	53.98	$1,948,264,002	0.94	59	0.15

Ratings
Reward	E+
Risk	D
Recent Upgrade/Downgrade	Up

Fund Information
Fund Type	Exchange Traded Funds
Category	US Equity Small Cap
Sub-Category	Small Growth
Prospectus Objective	Small Company
Inception Date	Sep-00
Open to New Investments	Y

Prices
Price (as of 12/31/2018)	53.94
52-Week High	241.89
52-Week Low	50.63

Total Returns (%)
3-Month	6-Month	1-Year	3-Year	5-Year
-18.42	-15.00	-76.02	-66.46	-64.24

3-Year Standard Deviation	14.85
Effective Duration	

Valuation
Premium/Discount (1-Year Average)	0.05

Company Information
Provider	SPDR State Street Global Advisors
Manager/Tenure	Michael J. Feehily (7), Karl A. Schneider (4), David Chin (0)
Website	http://www.spdrs.com
Address	SPDR State Street Global Advisors State Street Financial Center, 1 Lincoln Street Boston MA 02111-2900 United States
Phone Number	617-786-3000

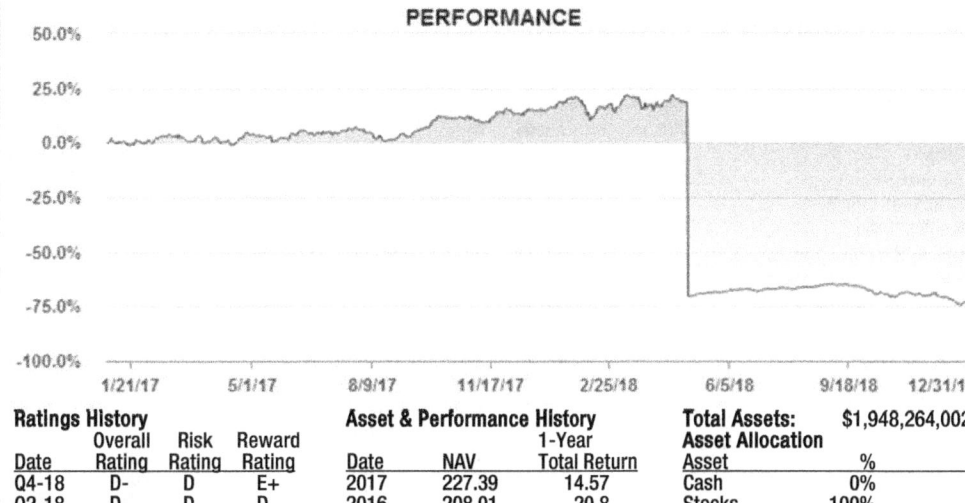

PERFORMANCE

Ratings History
Date	Overall Rating	Risk Rating	Reward Rating
Q4-18	D-	D	E+
Q2-18	D	D	D-
Q4-17	A-	B+	A
Q4-16	C	C-	C
Q4-15	C	C-	C+

Asset & Performance History
Date	NAV	1-Year Total Return
2017	227.39	14.57
2016	208.01	20.8
2015	172.55	2.77
2014	177.57	3.73
2013	178.89	42.45
2012	126.46	14.41

Total Assets: $1,948,264,002

Asset Allocation
Asset	%
Cash	0%
Stocks	100%
US Stocks	99%
Bonds	0%
US Bonds	0%
Other	0%

Services Offered: Dividend Investment Plan, CashInvestment Plan

Investment Strategy: The investment seeks to provide investment results that, before fees and expenses, correspond generally to the total return performance of the S&P SmallCap 600 Growth Index. The fund generally invests substantially all, but at least 80%, of its total assets in the securities comprising the index. The index measures the performance of the small-capitalization growth segment of the U.S. equity market. It may purchase a subset of the securities in the index in an effort to hold a portfolio of securities with generally the same risk and return characteristics of the index. The fund is non-diversified. **Top Holdings:** Ingevity Corp FirstCash Inc Amedisys Inc Green Dot Corp Trex Co Inc

---

First Trust Technology AlphaDEX® Fund   C   HOLD

Ticker	Traded On	NAV	Total Assets ($)	Dividend Yield (TTM)	Turnover Ratio	Expense Ratio
FXL	NYSE Arca	52.52	$1,941,689,574	0.12	115	0.63

Ratings
Reward	C
Risk	C+
Recent Upgrade/Downgrade	Down

Fund Information
Fund Type	Exchange Traded Funds
Category	Technology Sector Equity
Sub-Category	Technology
Prospectus Objective	Technology
Inception Date	May-07
Open to New Investments	Y

Prices
Price (as of 12/31/2018)	52.55
52-Week High	64.60
52-Week Low	48.15

Total Returns (%)
3-Month	6-Month	1-Year	3-Year	5-Year
-16.69	-7.64	2.57	60.77	80.91

3-Year Standard Deviation	16.08
Effective Duration	

Valuation
Premium/Discount (1-Year Average)	0.03

Company Information
Provider	First Trust
Manager/Tenure	Jon C. Erickson (11), Daniel J. Lindquist (11), David G. McGarel (11), 3 others
Website	http://www.ftportfolios.com/
Address	First Trust 120 E. Liberty Drive, Suite 400 Wheaton IL 60187 United States
Phone Number	800-621-1675

PERFORMANCE

Ratings History
Date	Overall Rating	Risk Rating	Reward Rating
Q4-18	C	C+	C
Q2-18	B	C	B+
Q4-17	B+	C+	A+
Q4-16	B	C+	A-
Q4-15	C+	C+	C

Asset & Performance History
Date	NAV	1-Year Total Return
2017	51.31	35.79
2016	37.9	15.42
2015	33.23	-3.3
2014	34.49	16.37
2013	29.83	37.74
2012	21.74	8.97

Total Assets: $1,941,689,574

Asset Allocation
Asset	%
Cash	0%
Stocks	100%
US Stocks	99%
Bonds	0%
US Bonds	0%
Other	0%

Services Offered:

Investment Strategy: The investment seeks investment results that correspond generally to the price and yield (before the fund's fees and expenses) of an equity index called the StrataQuant® Technology Index. The fund will normally invest at least 90% of its net assets (including investment borrowings) in common stocks that comprise the index. The index is a modified equal-dollar weighted index designed by IDI to objectively identify and select stocks from the Russell 1000® Index in the technology sector that may generate positive alpha relative to traditional passive-style indices through the use of the AlphaDEX® selection methodology. **Top Holdings:** Dell-VMWare Tracking Stock V Twilio Inc A Gartner Inc A Broadcom Inc Hewlett Packard Enterprise Co

PIMCO Active Bond Exchange-Traded Fund

C   HOLD

Ticker	Traded On	NAV	Total Assets ($)	Dividend Yield (TTM)	Turnover Ratio	Expense Ratio
BOND	NYSE Arca	102.65	$1,928,426,721	3.43	142	0.76

Ratings

Reward	D+
Risk	C+
Recent Upgrade/Downgrade	Up

Fund Information

Fund Type	Exchange Traded Funds
Category	US Fixed Income
Sub-Category	Intermediate-Term Bond
Prospectus Objective	Income
Inception Date	Feb-12
Open to New Investments	Y

Prices

Price (as of 12/31/2018)	102.77
52-Week High	106.05
52-Week Low	100.83

Total Returns (%)

3-Month	6-Month	1-Year	3-Year	5-Year
1.38	1.66	0.16	8.19	16.47

3-Year Standard Deviation	2.64
Effective Duration	5.65

Valuation

Premium/Discount (1-Year Average)	-0.12

Company Information

Provider	PIMCO
Manager/Tenure	David Braun (1), Daniel Herbert Hyman (1), Jerome M. Schneider (1)
Website	http://www.pimco.com
Address	PIMCO 840 Newport Center Drive, Suite 100 Newport Beach CA 92660 United States
Phone Number	866-746-2602

PERFORMANCE

Ratings History

Date	Overall Rating	Risk Rating	Reward Rating
Q4-18	C	C+	D+
Q2-18	C	C+	C+
Q4-17	B-	A-	C
Q4-16	C	C-	C
Q4-15	C	C+	C

Asset & Performance History

Date	NAV	1-Year Total Return
2017	106.09	4.75
2016	104.22	2.92
2015	103.95	0.73
2014	107.45	6.86
2013	104.72	-1.17
2012	108.94	

Total Assets: $1,928,426,721

Asset Allocation

Asset	%
Cash	-32%
Stocks	0%
US Stocks	0%
Bonds	131%
US Bonds	117%
Other	0%

Services Offered:

Investment Strategy: The investment seeks current income and long-term capital appreciation, consistent with prudent investment management. The fund normally invests at least 80% of its assets in a diversified portfolio of Fixed Income Instruments of varying maturities, which may be represented by forwards or derivatives such as options, futures contracts, or swap agreement. It invests primarily in investment grade debt securities, but may invest up to 30% of its total assets in high yield securities, as rated by Moody's, S&P or Fitch, or, if unrated, as determined by PIMCO. **Top Holdings:** Irs Usd 1.75000 06/20/18-2y Cme Federal Home Loan Mortgage Corporation 4% United States Treasury Notes 3% United States Treasury Notes 3.12% Federal Home Loan Mortgage Corporation 3.5%

Vanguard S&P Small-Cap 600 Index Fund ETF Shares

C-   HOLD

Ticker	Traded On	NAV	Total Assets ($)	Dividend Yield (TTM)	Turnover Ratio	Expense Ratio
VIOO	NYSE Arca		$1,924,353,965	1.06	13	0.15

Ratings

Reward	C-
Risk	C-
Recent Upgrade/Downgrade	Down

Fund Information

Fund Type	Exchange Traded Funds
Category	US Equity Small Cap
Sub-Category	Small Blend
Prospectus Objective	Growth & Inc
Inception Date	Sep-10
Open to New Investments	Y

Prices

Price (as of 12/31/2018)	125.76
52-Week High	164.63
52-Week Low	118.22

Total Returns (%)

3-Month	6-Month	1-Year	3-Year	5-Year
-19.39	-17.63	-9.08	30.25	34.74

3-Year Standard Deviation	14.71
Effective Duration	

Valuation

Premium/Discount (1-Year Average)	0.04

Company Information

Provider	Vanguard
Manager/Tenure	William A. Coleman (5), Donald M. Butler (2)
Website	http://www.vanguard.com
Address	Vanguard 100 Vanguard Boulevard Malvern PA 19355 United States
Phone Number	877-662-7447

PERFORMANCE

Ratings History

Date	Overall Rating	Risk Rating	Reward Rating
Q4-18	C-	C-	C-
Q2-18	C+	C-	B
Q4-17	A-	B	A
Q4-16	C	C-	C
Q4-15	C	D+	C

Asset & Performance History

Date	NAV	1-Year Total Return
2017	139.31	13.69
2016	124.31	25.28
2015	99.25	-2.04
2014	102.6	5.6
2013	98.19	41.04
2012	70.22	16.18

Total Assets: $1,924,353,965

Asset Allocation

Asset	%
Cash	1%
Stocks	99%
US Stocks	98%
Bonds	0%
US Bonds	0%
Other	0%

Services Offered:

Investment Strategy: The investment seeks to track the performance of a benchmark index that measures the investment return of small-capitalization stocks in the United States. The fund employs an indexing investment approach designed to track the performance of the S&P SmallCap 600® Index. The Advisor attempts to replicate the target index by investing all, or substantially all, of its assets in the stocks that make up the index, holding each stock in approximately the same proportion as its weighting in the index. **Top Holdings:** CACI International Inc Class A Insperity Inc First Financial Bankshares Inc Ingevity Corp Selective Insurance Group Inc

iShares Expanded Tech-Software Sector ETF

C+   **HOLD**

Ticker	Traded On	NAV	Total Assets ($)	Dividend Yield (TTM)	Turnover Ratio	Expense Ratio
IGV	BATS	173.45	$1,921,747,514	0.03	12	0.47

Ratings

Reward	B-
Risk	C
Recent Upgrade/Downgrade	Down

Fund Information

Fund Type	Exchange Traded Funds
Category	Technology Sector Equity
Sub-Category	Technology
Prospectus Objective	Technology
Inception Date	Jul-01
Open to New Investments	Y

Prices

Price (as of 12/31/2018)	173.53
52-Week High	205.52
52-Week Low	154.57

Total Returns (%)

3-Month	6-Month	1-Year	3-Year	5-Year
-15.02	-6.52	12.43	69.21	114.83

3-Year Standard Deviation	15.18
Effective Duration	

Valuation

Premium/Discount (1-Year Average)	0.02

Company Information

Provider	iShares
Manager/Tenure	Diane Hsiung (10), Greg Savage (10), Jennifer Hsui (6), 3 others
Website	http://www.ishares.com
Address	iShares 400 Howard Street San Francisco CA 94105 United States
Phone Number	800-474-2737

PERFORMANCE

Ratings History

Date	Overall Rating	Risk Rating	Reward Rating
Q4-18	C+	C	B-
Q2-18	B	C	B+
Q4-17	A-	B+	A+
Q4-16	B-	C	B
Q4-15	B-	C	B

Asset & Performance History

Date	NAV	1-Year Total Return
2017	154.52	42.16
2016	108.81	5.86
2015	103.7	11.96
2014	92.83	13.39
2013	82.12	30.59
2012	63.11	16.94

Total Assets: $1,921,747,514

Asset Allocation

Asset	%
Cash	0%
Stocks	100%
US Stocks	98%
Bonds	0%
US Bonds	0%
Other	0%

Services Offered: CashInvestment Plan

Investment Strategy: The investment seeks to track the investment results of an index composed of North American equities in the software industry and select North American equities from interactive home entertainment and interactive media and services industries. The fund generally invests at least 90% of its assets in securities of the underlying index and in depositary receipts representing securities of the underlying index. The index measures the performance of U.S.-traded stocks from the software industry and select companies from the interactive home entertainment and interactive media and services industries in the U.S. and Canada. The fund is non-diversified.

Top Holdings: Oracle Corp   Microsoft Corp   Adobe Inc   Salesforce.com Inc   Intuit Inc

---

iShares Global 100 ETF

C   **HOLD**

Ticker	Traded On	NAV	Total Assets ($)	Dividend Yield (TTM)	Turnover Ratio	Expense Ratio
100	NYSE Arca	42.49	$1,921,546,847	2.26	8	0.4

Ratings

Reward	C
Risk	C+
Recent Upgrade/Downgrade	Down

Fund Information

Fund Type	Exchange Traded Funds
Category	Global Equity Large Cap
Sub-Category	World Large Stock
Prospectus Objective	World Stock
Inception Date	Dec-00
Open to New Investments	Y

Prices

Price (as of 12/31/2018)	42.40
52-Week High	49.46
52-Week Low	40.41

Total Returns (%)

3-Month	6-Month	1-Year	3-Year	5-Year
-12.64	-6.07	-6.19	25.88	26.47

3-Year Standard Deviation	9.28
Effective Duration	

Valuation

Premium/Discount (1-Year Average)	-0.07

Company Information

Provider	iShares
Manager/Tenure	Diane Hsiung (10), Greg Savage (10), Jennifer Hsui (6), 3 others
Website	http://www.ishares.com
Address	iShares 400 Howard Street San Francisco CA 94105 United States
Phone Number	800-474-2737

PERFORMANCE

Ratings History

Date	Overall Rating	Risk Rating	Reward Rating
Q4-18	C	C+	C
Q2-18	C	C-	C+
Q4-17	B-	B-	B-
Q4-16	C	C-	C+
Q4-15	C	C	C

Asset & Performance History

Date	NAV	1-Year Total Return
2017	46.4	23.39
2016	38.49	8.76
2015	36.41	-1.94
2014	38.17	2.46
2013	38.54	24.62
2012	31.75	12.59

Total Assets: $1,921,546,847

Asset Allocation

Asset	%
Cash	1%
Stocks	99%
US Stocks	65%
Bonds	0%
US Bonds	0%
Other	0%

Services Offered: CashInvestment Plan

Investment Strategy: The investment seeks to track the investment results of the S&P Global 100TM (the "underlying index"), which is designed to measure the performance of the stocks of 100 large-capitalization global companies. The fund generally invests at least 90% of its assets in securities of the underlying index and in depositary receipts representing securities of the underlying index. It may invest the remainder of its assets in certain futures, options and swap contracts, cash and cash equivalents, as well as in securities not included in the underlying index, but which the advisor believes will help the fund track the underlying index. **Top Holdings:** Microsoft Corp   Apple Inc   Amazon.com Inc   Johnson & Johnson   JPMorgan Chase & Co

WisdomTree Emerging Markets High Dividend Fund   C   HOLD

Ticker	Traded On	NAV	Total Assets ($)	Dividend Yield (TTM)	Turnover Ratio	Expense Ratio
DEM	NYSE Arca	40.24	$1,914,862,507	4.5	41	0.63

Ratings

Reward	C-
Risk	C+
Recent Upgrade/Downgrade	

Fund Information

Fund Type	Exchange Traded Funds
Category	Global Emerg Mkts Equity
Sub-Category	Diversified Emerging Mkts
Prospectus Objective	Div Emerg Mkts
Inception Date	Jul-07
Open to New Investments	Y

Prices

Price (as of 12/31/2018)	40.15
52-Week High	50.28
52-Week Low	39.27

Total Returns (%)

3-Month	6-Month	1-Year	3-Year	5-Year
-7.81	-3.11	-7.30	41.83	-2.12

3-Year Standard Deviation	14.6
Effective Duration	

Valuation

Premium/Discount (1-Year Average)	-0.07

Company Information

Provider	WisdomTree
Manager/Tenure	Richard A. Brown (10), Thomas J. Durante (10), Karen Q. Wong (10)
Website	http://www.wisdomtree.com
Address	WisdomTree 245 Park Avenue, 35th floor New York NY 10167 United States
Phone Number	866-909-9473

PERFORMANCE

Ratings History

Date	Overall Rating	Risk Rating	Reward Rating
Q4-18	C	C+	C-
Q2-18	C	C+	C
Q4-17	C+	C	C+
Q4-16	D+	D+	D+
Q4-15	D	D	D

Asset & Performance History

Date	NAV	1-Year Total Return
2017	45.26	24.88
2016	37.68	22.53
2015	31.9	-21.95
2014	42.77	-11.58
2013	50.75	-5.61
2012	56.06	14.02

Total Assets: $1,914,862,507

Asset Allocation

Asset	%
Cash	0%
Stocks	100%
US Stocks	0%
Bonds	0%
US Bonds	0%
Other	0%

Services Offered:

Investment Strategy: The investment seeks to track the price and yield performance, before fees and expenses, of the WisdomTree Emerging Markets High Dividend Index. Under normal circumstances, at least 95% of the fund's total assets (exclusive of collateral held from securities lending) will be invested in component securities of the index and investments that have economic characteristics that are substantially identical to the economic characteristics of such component securities. The index is a fundamentally weighted index that is comprised of the highest dividend-yielding common stocks selected from the WisdomTree Emerging Markets Dividend Index. The fund is non-diversified. **Top Holdings:** China Construction Bank Corp H   China Mobile Ltd   Tatneft PJSC ADR   Gazprom PJSC ADR   MMC Norilsk Nickel JSC ADR

First Trust Low Duration Opportunities ETF   C   HOLD

Ticker	Traded On	NAV	Total Assets ($)	Dividend Yield (TTM)	Turnover Ratio	Expense Ratio
LMBS	NAS CM	50.97	$1,905,479,029	2.69	190	0.68

Ratings

Reward	C
Risk	C+
Recent Upgrade/Downgrade	

Fund Information

Fund Type	Exchange Traded Funds
Category	US Fixed Income
Sub-Category	Short-Term Bond
Prospectus Objective	Govt Bond - Mortgage
Inception Date	Nov-14
Open to New Investments	Y

Prices

Price (as of 12/31/2018)	51.05
52-Week High	51.74
52-Week Low	50.81

Total Returns (%)

3-Month	6-Month	1-Year	3-Year	5-Year
0.59	0.84	1.24	10.08	

3-Year Standard Deviation	1.16
Effective Duration	2.45

Valuation

Premium/Discount (1-Year Average)	0.12

Company Information

Provider	First Trust
Manager/Tenure	Jeremiah Charles (4), James W. Snyder (4)
Website	http://www.ftportfolios.com/
Address	First Trust 120 E. Liberty Drive, Suite 400 Wheaton IL 60187 United States
Phone Number	800-621-1675

PERFORMANCE

Ratings History

Date	Overall Rating	Risk Rating	Reward Rating
Q4-18	C	C+	C
Q2-18	C	C+	C
Q4-17	B-	A	C
Q4-16	C	C+	C-
Q4-15	U		

Asset & Performance History

Date	NAV	1-Year Total Return
2017	51.64	1.76
2016	52.14	6.84
2015	50.22	2.37
2014	50.57	
2013		
2012		

Total Assets: $1,905,479,029

Asset Allocation

Asset	%
Cash	18%
Stocks	0%
US Stocks	0%
Bonds	82%
US Bonds	82%
Other	0%

Services Offered:

Investment Strategy: The investment seeks to generate current income with a secondary objective of capital appreciation. Under normal market conditions, the fund will seek to achieve its investment objectives by investing at least 80% of its net assets (including investment borrowings) in mortgage-related debt securities and other mortgage-related instruments (collectively, "Mortgage-Related Investments"). The advisor normally expects to invest in Mortgage-Related Investments tied to residential and commercial mortgages. It is non-diversified. **Top Holdings:** US 5 Year Note (CBT) Dec18   2 Year US Treasury Note Future Dec18   Us 10yr Ultra Fut Dec18   Federal National Mortgage Association 5%   Federal National Mortgage Association 3%

Vanguard Long-Term Treasury Index Fund ETF Shares   D+   SELL

Ticker	Traded On	NAV	Total Assets ($)	Dividend Yield (TTM)	Turnover Ratio	Expense Ratio
VGLT	NAS CM		$1,896,765,623	2.87	19	0.07

Ratings
Reward	D
Risk	C-
Recent Upgrade/Downgrade	Down

Fund Information
Fund Type	Exchange Traded Funds
Category	US Fixed Income
Sub-Category	Long Government
Prospectus Objective	Govt Bond - Gen
Inception Date	Nov-09
Open to New Investments	Y

Prices
Price (as of 12/31/2018)	74.71
52-Week High	78.00
52-Week Low	69.06

Total Returns (%)
3-Month	6-Month	1-Year	3-Year	5-Year
4.86	1.16	-1.93	7.97	33.18

3-Year Standard Deviation	9.23
Effective Duration	16.89

Valuation
Premium/Discount (1-Year Average)	0.05

Company Information
Provider	Vanguard
Manager/Tenure	Joshua C. Barrickman (5)
Website	http://www.vanguard.com
Address	Vanguard 100 Vanguard Boulevard Malvern PA 19355 United States
Phone Number	877-662-7447

PERFORMANCE

Ratings History
Date	Overall Rating	Risk Rating	Reward Rating
Q4-18	D+	C-	D
Q2-18	C-	C	D+
Q4-17	C	C	C
Q4-16	C	C-	C
Q4-15	C	C-	C

Asset & Performance History
Date	NAV	1-Year Total Return
2017	77.99	8.77
2016	73.67	1.39
2015	74.52	-1.35
2014	77.62	25.04
2013	63.96	-12.73
2012	75.48	3.49

Total Assets: $1,896,765,623

Asset Allocation
Asset	%
Cash	1%
Stocks	0%
US Stocks	0%
Bonds	99%
US Bonds	99%
Other	0%

Services Offered:

Investment Strategy: The investment seeks to track the performance of a market-weighted government bond index with a long-term dollar-weighted average maturity. The fund employs an indexing investment approach designed to track the performance of the Bloomberg Barclays US Long Treasury Bond Index. This index includes fixed income securities issued by the U.S. Treasury (not including inflation-protected bonds), with maturities greater than 10 years. Under normal circumstances, at least 80% of the fund's assets will be invested in bonds included in the index. **Top Holdings:** United States Treasury Bonds 3.75% United States Treasury Bonds 3% United States Treasury Bonds 3.38% United States Treasury Bonds 3.12% United States Treasury Bonds 2.88%

First Trust Senior Loan Fund   C   HOLD

Ticker	Traded On	NAV	Total Assets ($)	Dividend Yield (TTM)	Turnover Ratio	Expense Ratio
FTSL	NAS CM	45.73	$1,895,372,645	4.18	110	0.88

Ratings
Reward	C-
Risk	C+
Recent Upgrade/Downgrade	

Fund Information
Fund Type	Exchange Traded Funds
Category	US Fixed Income
Sub-Category	Bank Loan
Prospectus Objective	Income
Inception Date	May-13
Open to New Investments	Y

Prices
Price (as of 12/31/2018)	45.52
52-Week High	48.38
52-Week Low	45.42

Total Returns (%)
3-Month	6-Month	1-Year	3-Year	5-Year
-3.66	-2.05	-0.83	9.23	11.65

3-Year Standard Deviation	2.04
Effective Duration	0.47

Valuation
Premium/Discount (1-Year Average)	0.12

Company Information
Provider	First Trust
Manager/Tenure	Scott D. Fries (5), William Housey (5)
Website	http://www.ftportfolios.com/
Address	First Trust 120 E. Liberty Drive, Suite 400 Wheaton IL 60187 United States
Phone Number	800-621-1675

PERFORMANCE

Ratings History
Date	Overall Rating	Risk Rating	Reward Rating
Q4-18	C	C+	C-
Q2-18	C	C+	C
Q4-17	B-	B	C
Q4-16	C	C-	C
Q4-15	C	C-	C

Asset & Performance History
Date	NAV	1-Year Total Return
2017	48.04	2.85
2016	48.43	7.09
2015	46.95	0.31
2014	48.62	1.9
2013	49.5	
2012		

Total Assets: $1,895,372,645

Asset Allocation
Asset	%
Cash	7%
Stocks	0%
US Stocks	0%
Bonds	93%
US Bonds	82%
Other	1%

Services Offered:

Investment Strategy: The investment seeks to provide high current income; the fund's secondary investment objective is the preservation of capital. Under normal market conditions, the fund seeks to outperform each of the primary index and secondary index by investing at least 80% of its net assets (including investment borrowings) in first lien senior floating rate bank loans ("Senior Loans"). **Top Holdings:** First Trust Enhanced Short Maturity ETF Valeant Pharma Vrxcn Tl 06/02/25 Caesars Resort Collectio 12/23/24 Stars Group Holdings Bv Tsgicn Tl 07/10/25 Alixpartners Llp Alixpa Tl 04/04/24

ProShares Ultra QQQ
C   HOLD

Ticker	Traded On	NAV	Total Assets ($)	Dividend Yield (TTM)	Turnover Ratio	Expense Ratio
QLD	NYSE Arca	67.10	$1,834,097,633	0		0.95

Ratings
Reward   C
Risk   C
Recent Upgrade/Downgrade   Down

Fund Information
Fund Type   Exchange Traded Funds
Category   Trading Tools
Sub-Category   Trading--Leveraged Equity
Prospectus Objective   Growth
Inception Date   Jun-06
Open to New Investments   Y

Prices
Price (as of 12/31/2018)   67.19
52-Week High   101.71
52-Week Low   58.52

Total Returns (%)

3-Month	6-Month	1-Year	3-Year	5-Year
-33.54	-23.50	-8.37	71.88	171.23

3-Year Standard Deviation   26.87
Effective Duration

Valuation
Premium/Discount (1-Year Average)   0.04

Company Information
Provider   ProShares
Manager/Tenure Michael Neches (5), Devin Sullivan (0)
Website   http://www.proshares.com
Address   ProShares 7501 Wisconsin Avenue,
                     Suite 1000 Bethesda MD 20814
                     United States
Phone Number   866-776-5125

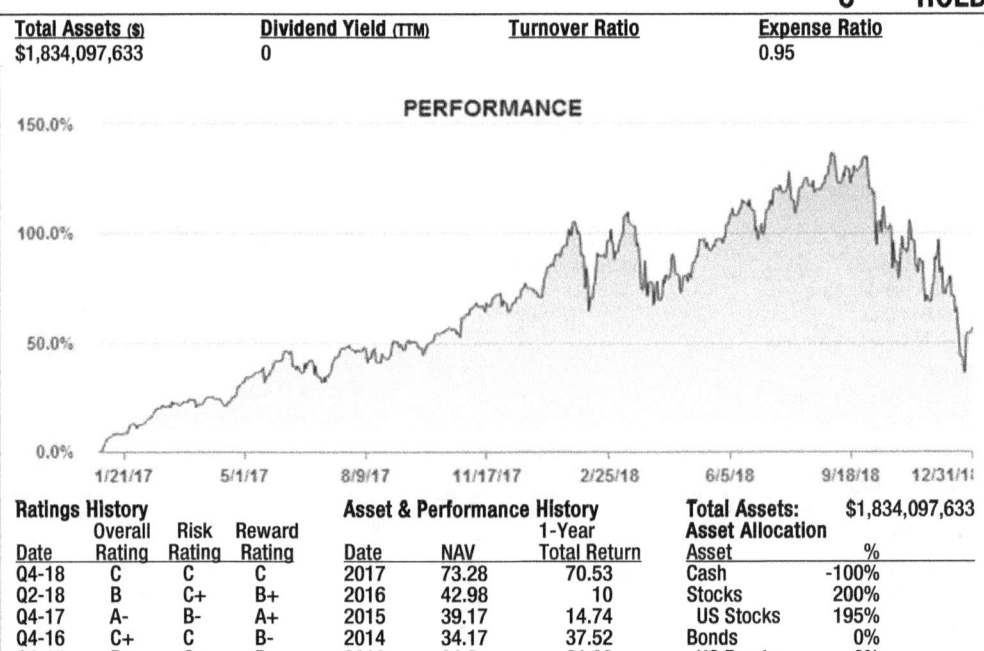

PERFORMANCE

Ratings History

Date	Overall Rating	Risk Rating	Reward Rating
Q4-18	C	C	C
Q2-18	B	C+	B+
Q4-17	A-	B-	A+
Q4-16	C+	C	B-
Q4-15	B-	C+	B-

Asset & Performance History

Date	NAV	1-Year Total Return
2017	73.28	70.53
2016	42.98	10
2015	39.17	14.74
2014	34.17	37.52
2013	24.9	81.83
2012	13.73	34.97

Total Assets: $1,834,097,633
Asset Allocation

Asset	%
Cash	-100%
Stocks	200%
US Stocks	195%
Bonds	0%
US Bonds	0%
Other	0%

Services Offered:

Investment Strategy: The investment seeks daily investment results, before fees and expenses, that correspond to two times (2x) the daily performance of the NASDAQ-100 Index®. The fund invests in financial instruments that ProShare Advisors believes, in combination, should produce daily returns consistent with the fund's investment objective. The index includes 100 of the largest domestic and international non-financial companies listed on The Nasdaq Stock Market based on market capitalization. The fund is non-diversified. **Top Holdings:** Powershares Qqq (Qqq) Swap Morgan Stanley & Co. International Plc   Nasdaq 100 Index Swap Goldman Sachs International   Nasdaq 100 Index Swap Ubs Ag   Nasdaq 100 Index Swap Societe Generale   Nasdaq 100 Index Swap Bnp Paribas

---

iShares U.S. Financials ETF
C   HOLD

Ticker	Traded On	NAV	Total Assets ($)	Dividend Yield (TTM)	Turnover Ratio	Expense Ratio
IYF	NYSE Arca	106.38	$1,814,553,598	1.7	6	0.43

Ratings
Reward   C
Risk   C+
Recent Upgrade/Downgrade   Down

Fund Information
Fund Type   Exchange Traded Funds
Category   Financials Sector Equity
Sub-Category   Financial
Prospectus Objective   Financial
Inception Date   May-00
Open to New Investments   Y

Prices
Price (as of 12/31/2018)   106.37
52-Week High   126.31
52-Week Low   100.04

Total Returns (%)

3-Month	6-Month	1-Year	3-Year	5-Year
-11.93	-8.73	-9.25	26.72	44.16

3-Year Standard Deviation   12.07
Effective Duration

Valuation
Premium/Discount (1-Year Average)   0.01

Company Information
Provider   iShares
Manager/Tenure Diane Hsiung (10), Greg Savage (10),
                     Jennifer Hsui (6), 3 others
Website   http://www.ishares.com
Address   iShares 400 Howard Street San
                     Francisco CA 94105 United States
Phone Number   800-474-2737

PERFORMANCE

Ratings History

Date	Overall Rating	Risk Rating	Reward Rating
Q4-18	C	C+	C
Q2-18	C+	C+	C+
Q4-17	B+	B	A-
Q4-16	B-	C+	B
Q4-15	B-	B-	B-

Asset & Performance History

Date	NAV	1-Year Total Return
2017	119.29	19.54
2016	101.38	16.81
2015	88.41	-0.3
2014	90.16	14.11
2013	80.17	33.59
2012	60.88	26.28

Total Assets: $1,814,553,598
Asset Allocation

Asset	%
Cash	0%
Stocks	100%
US Stocks	99%
Bonds	0%
US Bonds	0%
Other	0%

Services Offered: CashInvestment Plan

Investment Strategy: The investment seeks to track the investment results of the Dow Jones U.S. Financials Index composed of U.S. equities in the financial sector. The fund generally invests at least 90% of its assets in securities of the underlying index and in depositary receipts representing securities of the underlying index. The underlying index measures the performance of the financial sector of the U.S. equity market. **Top Holdings:** Berkshire Hathaway Inc B   JPMorgan Chase & Co   Bank of America Corporation   Visa Inc Class A   Wells Fargo & Co

Vanguard Extended Duration Treasury Index Fund ETF Shares   D+   SELL

Ticker	Traded On	NAV	Total Assets ($)	Dividend Yield (TTM)	Turnover Ratio	Expense Ratio
EDV	NYSE Arca		$1,807,724,114	3.16	18	0.07

Ratings
Reward   D
Risk   C-
Recent Upgrade/Downgrade   Down

Fund Information
Fund Type   Exchange Traded Funds
Category   US Fixed Income
Sub-Category   Long Government
Prospectus Objective   Govt Bond - Treasury
Inception Date   Dec-07
Open to New Investments   Y

Prices
Price (as of 12/31/2018)   113.46
52-Week High   120.99
52-Week Low   101.75

Total Returns (%)

3-Month	6-Month	1-Year	3-Year	5-Year
5.74	0.04	-3.77	10.89	54.32

3-Year Standard Deviation   13.5
Effective Duration   24.02

Valuation
Premium/Discount (1-Year Average)   0.56

Company Information
Provider   Vanguard
Manager/Tenure   William D. Baird (5), Joshua C.
                       Barrickman (5)
Website   http://www.vanguard.com
Address   Vanguard 100 Vanguard Boulevard
                       Malvern PA 19355 United States
Phone Number   877-662-7447

PERFORMANCE

Ratings History

Date	Overall Rating	Risk Rating	Reward Rating
Q4-18	D+	C-	D
Q2-18	D+	C-	D+
Q4-17	C	C	C
Q4-16	C	C-	C
Q4-15	C	D+	C

Asset & Performance History

Date	NAV	1-Year Total Return
2017	120.15	13.72
2016	109.1	1.6
2015	113.04	-4.44
2014	123.28	45.63
2013	87.72	-20.94
2012	116.21	3.18

Total Assets: $1,807,724,114

Asset Allocation

Asset	%
Cash	0%
Stocks	0%
US Stocks	0%
Bonds	100%
US Bonds	100%
Other	0%

Services Offered:

Investment Strategy: The investment seeks to track the performance of an index of extended-duration zero-coupon U.S. Treasury securities. The fund employs an indexing investment approach designed to track the performance of the Bloomberg Barclays U.S. Treasury STRIPS 20-30 Year Equal Par Bond Index. This index includes zero-coupon U.S. Treasury securities (Treasury STRIPS), which are backed by the full faith and credit of the U.S. government, with maturities ranging from 20 to 30 years. The fund invests by sampling the index. At least 80% of the fund's assets will be invested in U.S. Treasury securities held in the index. **Top Holdings:** U.S. Treasury Security Stripped Interest Security 0%   U.S. Treasury Security Stripped Interest Security 0%   U.S. Treasury Security Stripped Interest Security 0%   U.S. Treasury Bond Stripped Principal Payment 0%   U.S. Treasury Security Stripped Interest Security 0%

Invesco Ultra Short Duration ETF   C   HOLD

Ticker	Traded On	NAV	Total Assets ($)	Dividend Yield (TTM)	Turnover Ratio	Expense Ratio
GSY	NYSE Arca	50.07	$1,805,801,478	2.62	56	0.25

Ratings
Reward   C
Risk   C+
Recent Upgrade/Downgrade

Fund Information
Fund Type   Exchange Traded Funds
Category   US Fixed Income
Sub-Category   Ultrashort Bond
Prospectus Objective   Income
Inception Date   Feb-08
Open to New Investments   Y

Prices
Price (as of 12/31/2018)   50.07
52-Week High   50.34
52-Week Low   50.04

Total Returns (%)

3-Month	6-Month	1-Year	3-Year	5-Year
0.39	1.03	2.16	5.99	7.92

3-Year Standard Deviation   0.25
Effective Duration

Valuation
Premium/Discount (1-Year Average)   0.00

Company Information
Provider   Invesco
Manager/Tenure   Laurie F. Brignac (0), Joseph S.
                       Madrid (0), Marques Mercier (0)
Website   http://www.invesco.com/us
Address   Invesco 11 Greenway Plaza, Ste. 2500
                       Houston TX 77046 United States
Phone Number   800-659-1005

PERFORMANCE

Ratings History

Date	Overall Rating	Risk Rating	Reward Rating
Q4-18	C	C+	C
Q2-18	C	C+	C
Q4-17	B-	A	C
Q4-16	C	C+	C
Q4-15	C	C+	C

Asset & Performance History

Date	NAV	1-Year Total Return
2017	50.14	1.91
2016	50.09	1.68
2015	49.85	1.03
2014	49.92	0.78
2013	50.17	1.38
2012	50.06	1.5

Total Assets: $1,805,801,478

Asset Allocation

Asset	%
Cash	37%
Stocks	0%
US Stocks	0%
Bonds	62%
US Bonds	47%
Other	0%

Services Offered:

Investment Strategy: The investment seeks maximum current income, consistent with preservation of capital and daily liquidity. The fund will invest at least 80% of its net assets in fixed income securities and in ETFs and closed-end funds that invest substantially all of their assets in fixed income securities. It uses a low duration strategy to seek to outperform the ICE BofAML US Treasury Bill Index in addition to providing returns in excess of those available in U.S. Treasury bills, government repurchase agreements, and money market funds, while seeking to provide preservation of capital and daily liquidity. The fund is non-diversified. **Top Holdings:** United States Treasury Notes 2.62%   United States Treasury Notes 2.5%   Comcast Corporation 2.85%   United States Treasury Notes 2.62%   The Bank of New York Mellon Corporation 0%

iShares MSCI United Kingdom ETF   C-   HOLD

Ticker	Traded On	NAV	Total Assets ($)	Dividend Yield (TTM)	Turnover Ratio	Expense Ratio
EWU	NYSE Arca	29.48	$1,798,055,247	4.75	5	0.49

Ratings
Reward   D+
Risk   C-
Recent Upgrade/Downgrade   Down

Fund Information
Fund Type   Exchange Traded Funds
Category   UK Equity Large Cap
Sub-Category   Miscellaneous Region
Prospectus Objective   Europe Stock
Inception Date   Mar-96
Open to New Investments   Y

Prices
Price (as of 12/31/2018)   29.35
52-Week High   37.88
52-Week Low   28.56

Total Returns (%)

3-Month	6-Month	1-Year	3-Year	5-Year
-11.73	-11.96	-14.60	3.29	-10.52

3-Year Standard Deviation   11.38
Effective Duration

Valuation
Premium/Discount (1-Year Average)   -0.14

Company Information
Provider   iShares
Manager/Tenure   Diane Hsiung (10), Greg Savage (10),
                  Jennifer Hsui (5), 1 other
Website   http://www.ishares.com
Address   iShares 400 Howard Street San
                  Francisco CA 94105 United States
Phone Number   800-474-2737

PERFORMANCE

Ratings History

Date	Overall Rating	Risk Rating	Reward Rating
Q4-18	C-	C-	D+
Q2-18	C	C	C
Q4-17	C+	B-	C
Q4-16	D+	D+	D+
Q4-15	C	B-	C-

Asset & Performance History

Date	NAV	1-Year Total Return
2017	36.12	21.7
2016	30.92	-0.61
2015	32.32	-7.98
2014	36.48	-5.86
2013	41.48	20
2012	35.5	14.57

Total Assets: $1,798,055,247
Asset Allocation

Asset	%
Cash	1%
Stocks	99%
US Stocks	4%
Bonds	0%
US Bonds	0%
Other	0%

Services Offered: CashInvestment Plan

Investment Strategy: The investment seeks to track the investment results of the MSCI United Kingdom Index. The fund will at all times invest at least 90% of its assets in the securities of its underlying index and in depositary receipts representing securities in its underlying index. The underlying index consists of stocks traded primarily on the London Stock Exchange. The underlying index may include large- or mid-capitalization companies. The fund is non-diversified. **Top Holdings:** HSBC Holdings PLC Royal Dutch Shell PLC Class A BP PLC Royal Dutch Shell PLC B GlaxoSmithKline PLC

iShares Short-Term National Muni Bond ETF   C   HOLD

Ticker	Traded On	NAV	Total Assets ($)	Dividend Yield (TTM)	Turnover Ratio	Expense Ratio
SUB	NYSE Arca	105.05	$1,797,532,954	1.25	21	0.07

Ratings
Reward   C-
Risk   C
Recent Upgrade/Downgrade   Up

Fund Information
Fund Type   Exchange Traded Funds
Category   US Muni Fixed Inc
Sub-Category   Muni National Short
Prospectus Objective   Muni Bond - Natl
Inception Date   Nov-08
Open to New Investments   Y

Prices
Price (as of 12/31/2018)   105.40
52-Week High   105.40
52-Week Low   104.30

Total Returns (%)

3-Month	6-Month	1-Year	3-Year	5-Year
0.94	0.91	1.56	2.44	3.69

3-Year Standard Deviation   1.12
Effective Duration   2.00

Valuation
Premium/Discount (1-Year Average)   0.07

Company Information
Provider   iShares
Manager/Tenure   Scott Radell (8), James Mauro (7)
Website   http://www.ishares.com
Address   iShares 400 Howard Street San
                  Francisco CA 94105 United States
Phone Number   800-474-2737

PERFORMANCE

Ratings History

Date	Overall Rating	Risk Rating	Reward Rating
Q4-18	C	C	C-
Q2-18	C-	C-	D+
Q4-17	C	C	C
Q4-16	C-	C-	C
Q4-15	C	C-	C

Asset & Performance History

Date	NAV	1-Year Total Return
2017	104.81	0.77
2016	104.86	-0.03
2015	105.68	0.64
2014	105.81	0.56
2013	106.01	0.7
2012	106.15	0.94

Total Assets: $1,797,532,954
Asset Allocation

Asset	%
Cash	5%
Stocks	0%
US Stocks	0%
Bonds	95%
US Bonds	95%
Other	0%

Services Offered:

Investment Strategy: The investment seeks to track the investment results of the S&P Short Term National AMT-Free Municipal Bond IndexTM. The fund generally will invest at least 90% of its assets in the component securities of the underlying index and may invest up to 10% of its assets in certain futures, options and swap contracts, cash and cash equivalents. The index measures the performance of the short-term investment-grade segment of the U.S. municipal bond market. **Top Holdings:** NEW YORK ST TWY AUTH 5% MASSACHUSETTS ST 5% NEW JERSEY ST TPK AUTH 5% MICHIGAN FIN AUTH 5% CALIFORNIA ST 5%

iShares Global Healthcare ETF   C   HOLD

Ticker	Traded On	NAV	Total Assets ($)	Dividend Yield (TTM)	Turnover Ratio	Expense Ratio
IXJ	NYSE Arca	56.69	$1,781,712,981	1.36	4	0.47

Ratings
Reward   C
Risk   C
Recent Upgrade/Downgrade

Fund Information
Fund Type   Exchange Traded Funds
Category   Healthcare Sector Equity
Sub-Category   Health
Prospectus Objective   Health
Inception Date   Nov-01
Open to New Investments Y

Prices
Price (as of 12/31/2018)   56.65
52-Week High   63.41
52-Week Low   53.92

Total Returns (%)

3-Month	6-Month	1-Year	3-Year	5-Year
-9.98	1.21	2.24	15.43	43.85

3-Year Standard Deviation   11.61
Effective Duration

Valuation
Premium/Discount (1-Year Average)   -0.03

Company Information
Provider   iShares
Manager/Tenure   Diane Hsiung (10), Greg Savage (10),
                  Jennifer Hsui (6), 3 others
Website   http://www.ishares.com
Address   iShares 400 Howard Street San
                  Francisco CA 94105 United States
Phone Number   800-474-2737

PERFORMANCE

Ratings History

Date	Overall Rating	Risk Rating	Reward Rating
Q4-18	C	C	C
Q2-18	C	C-	C
Q4-17	B-	B	C+
Q4-16	C	C-	C
Q4-15	B-	C+	B-

Asset & Performance History

Date	NAV	1-Year Total Return
2017	56.29	20.34
2016	47.48	-6.18
2015	51.47	5.91
2014	49.96	17.65
2013	43.07	36.15
2012	32.18	17.41

Total Assets: $1,781,712,981

Asset Allocation

Asset	%
Cash	1%
Stocks	99%
US Stocks	71%
Bonds	0%
US Bonds	0%
Other	0%

Services Offered: CashInvestment Plan

Investment Strategy: The investment seeks to track the S&P Global 1200 Health Care IndexTM. The fund generally invests at least 90% of its assets in securities of the underlying index and in depositary receipts representing securities of the underlying index. It may invest the remainder of its assets in certain futures, options and swap contracts, cash and cash equivalents, as well as in securities not included in the underlying index. The index measures the performance of companies that the index provider deems to be a part of the healthcare sector of the economy and that the index provider believes are important to global markets. **Top Holdings:** Johnson & Johnson UnitedHealth Group Inc Pfizer Inc Novartis AG Merck & Co Inc

Schwab Fundamental International Small Company Index ETF   C-   HOLD

Ticker	Traded On	NAV	Total Assets ($)	Dividend Yield (TTM)	Turnover Ratio	Expense Ratio
FNDC	NYSE Arca	28.46	$1,781,318,272	2.23	18	0.39

Ratings
Reward   D+
Risk   C-
Recent Upgrade/Downgrade   Down

Fund Information
Fund Type   Exchange Traded Funds
Category   Global Eq Mid/Small Cap
Sub-Category   Foreign Small/Mid Blend
Prospectus Objective   World Stock
Inception Date   Aug-13
Open to New Investments Y

Prices
Price (as of 12/31/2018)   28.35
52-Week High   38.20
52-Week Low   27.19

Total Returns (%)

3-Month	6-Month	1-Year	3-Year	5-Year
-15.42	-14.85	-18.76	14.12	15.09

3-Year Standard Deviation   11.49
Effective Duration

Valuation
Premium/Discount (1-Year Average)   0.08

Company Information
Provider   Schwab ETFs
Manager/Tenure   Chuck Craig (5), Jane Qin (5),
                  Christopher Bliss (1), 1 other
Website   http://www.schwabetfs.com
Address   Schwab ETFs United States
Phone Number   800-435-4000

PERFORMANCE

Ratings History

Date	Overall Rating	Risk Rating	Reward Rating
Q4-18	C-	C-	D+
Q2-18	C+	C+	C
Q4-17	B+	B+	A-
Q4-16	C	C-	C+
Q4-15	D+	C-	D

Asset & Performance History

Date	NAV	1-Year Total Return
2017	35.94	29
2016	28.4	8.88
2015	26.6	5.12
2014	25.64	-4.06
2013	27.16	
2012		

Total Assets: $1,781,318,272

Asset Allocation

Asset	%
Cash	0%
Stocks	100%
US Stocks	1%
Bonds	0%
US Bonds	0%
Other	0%

Services Offered:

Investment Strategy: The investment seeks to track as closely as possible, before fees and expenses, the total return of the Russell RAFI™ Developed ex US Small Company Index. The fund will invest at least 90% of its net assets in stocks included in the index, including depositary receipts representing securities of the index, which may be in the form of American Depositary receipts, Global Depositary receipts and European Depositary receipts. The index measures the performance of the small company size segment by fundamental overall company scores, which are created using as the universe the companies included in the Russell Developed ex US Index. **Top Holdings:** Msci Eafe Dec18 Ifus 20181221 Melrose Industries PLC Sumitomo Dainippon Pharma Co Ltd FamilyMart UNY Holdings Co Ltd Taisho Pharmaceutical Holding Co Ltd

KraneShares CSI China Internet ETF   C-   HOLD

Ticker	Traded On	NAV		Total Assets ($)	Dividend Yield (TTM)	Turnover Ratio	Expense Ratio
KWEB	NYSE Arca	37.67		$1,772,547,457	0.78	29	0.7

Ratings
Reward	C
Risk	D
Recent Upgrade/Downgrade	Down

Fund Information
Fund Type	Exchange Traded Funds
Category	Greater China Equity
Sub-Category	China Region
Prospectus Objective	Pacific Stock
Inception Date	Jul-13
Open to New Investments	Y

Prices
Price (as of 12/31/2018)	37.50
52-Week High	68.34
52-Week Low	37.50

Total Returns (%)
3-Month	6-Month	1-Year	3-Year	5-Year
-19.93	-34.50	-33.51	3.11	20.69

3-Year Standard Deviation	23.26
Effective Duration	

Valuation
Premium/Discount (1-Year Average)	0.12

Company Information
Provider	KraneShares
Manager/Tenure	Mark Schlarbaum (3), Jonathan Shelon (0)
Website	http://www.kraneshares.com
Address	1350 Avenue of the Americas Second Floor New York NY 10019 United States
Phone Number	855-857-2638

PERFORMANCE

Ratings History
Date	Overall Rating	Risk Rating	Reward Rating
Q4-18	C-	D	C
Q2-18	C+	C	B-
Q4-17	B+	C	A+
Q4-16	D+	D+	D+
Q4-15	C	C	C

Asset & Performance History
Date	NAV	1-Year Total Return
2017	58.56	69.25
2016	34.77	-8.41
2015	38.43	17.82
2014	32.68	-0.61
2013	33.15	
2012		

Total Assets: $1,772,547,457

Asset Allocation
Asset	%
Cash	1%
Stocks	99%
US Stocks	0%
Bonds	0%
US Bonds	0%
Other	0%

Services Offered:

Investment Strategy: The investment seeks to provide investment results that, before fees and expenses, correspond generally to the price and yield performance of the CSI Overseas China Internet Index (the "underlying index"). The fund will normally invest at least 80% of its total assets in equity securities of the underlying index, or in depositary receipts representing securities of the underlying index. The underlying index is designed to measure the performance of the investable universe of publicly traded China-based companies whose primary business or businesses are in the Internet and Internet-related sectors. The fund is non-diversified. **Top Holdings:** Tencent Holdings Ltd   Alibaba Group Holding Ltd ADR   Baidu Inc ADR   NetEase Inc ADR   Meituan Dianping

---

FlexShares Quality Dividend Index Fund   C   HOLD

Ticker	Traded On	NAV		Total Assets ($)	Dividend Yield (TTM)	Turnover Ratio	Expense Ratio
QDF	NYSE Arca	39.78		$1,771,112,760	2.73		0.37

Ratings
Reward	C
Risk	C+
Recent Upgrade/Downgrade	Down

Fund Information
Fund Type	Exchange Traded Funds
Category	US Equity Large Cap Value
Sub-Category	Large Value
Prospectus Objective	Income
Inception Date	Dec-12
Open to New Investments	Y

Prices
Price (as of 12/31/2018)	39.81
52-Week High	48.07
52-Week Low	37.39

Total Returns (%)
3-Month	6-Month	1-Year	3-Year	5-Year
-15.43	-10.56	-9.13	24.72	38.37

3-Year Standard Deviation	9.52
Effective Duration	

Valuation
Premium/Discount (1-Year Average)	0.04

Company Information
Provider	Flexshares Trust
Manager/Tenure	Robert Anstine (5), Brendan Sullivan (2)
Website	http://www.flexshares.com
Address	50 South LaSalle Street Chicago, Illinois 60603 Chicago Illinois 60603 United States
Phone Number	855-353-9383

PERFORMANCE

Ratings History
Date	Overall Rating	Risk Rating	Reward Rating
Q4-18	C	C+	C
Q2-18	C+	C+	C
Q4-17	B	B+	B-
Q4-16	C+	C-	B
Q4-15	C	C	C

Asset & Performance History
Date	NAV	1-Year Total Return
2017	44.97	17.15
2016	39.49	17.16
2015	34.81	-0.94
2014	36.19	12
2013	33.22	35.65
2012	25.04	

Total Assets: $1,771,112,760

Asset Allocation
Asset	%
Cash	1%
Stocks	99%
US Stocks	99%
Bonds	0%
US Bonds	0%
Other	0%

Services Offered:

Investment Strategy: The investment seeks investment results that correspond generally to the price and yield performance, before fees and expenses, of the Northern Trust Quality Dividend IndexSM. Under normal circumstances, the fund will invest at least 80% of its total assets (exclusive of collateral held from securities lending) in the securities of the underlying index. The underlying index is designed to provide exposure to a high-quality, income-oriented portfolio of U.S. equity securities, with an emphasis on long-term capital growth and a targeted overall volatility similar to that of the Northern Trust 1250 IndexSM. **Top Holdings:** Microsoft Corp   Johnson & Johnson   Apple Inc   Exxon Mobil Corp   Walmart Inc

First Trust Cloud Computing ETF   C+   HOLD

Ticker	Traded On	NAV		Total Assets ($)	Dividend Yield (TTM)	Turnover Ratio	Expense Ratio
SKYY	NAS CM	48.25		$1,766,087,978	0.29	7	0.6

Ratings

Reward	B
Risk	C-
Recent Upgrade/Downgrade	Down

Fund Information

Fund Type	Exchange Traded Funds
Category	Technology Sector Equity
Sub-Category	Technology
Prospectus Objective	Technology
Inception Date	Jul-11
Open to New Investments	Y

Prices

Price (as of 12/31/2018)	48.47
52-Week High	56.87
52-Week Low	45.20

Total Returns (%)

3-Month	6-Month	1-Year	3-Year	5-Year
-14.63	-10.41	5.62	62.60	84.94

3-Year Standard Deviation	13.21
Effective Duration	

Valuation

Premium/Discount (1-Year Average)	0.04

Company Information

Provider	First Trust
Manager/Tenure	Jon C. Erickson (7), Daniel J. Lindquist (7), David G. McGarel (7), 3 others
Website	http://www.ftportfolios.com/
Address	First Trust 120 E. Liberty Drive, Suite 400 Wheaton IL 60187 United States
Phone Number	800-621-1675

PERFORMANCE

Ratings History

Date	Overall Rating	Risk Rating	Reward Rating
Q4-18	C+	C-	B
Q2-18	B-	C-	B
Q4-17	A-	B	A
Q4-16	C-	C-	C-
Q4-15	C+	C	B

Asset & Performance History

Date	NAV	1-Year Total Return
2017	45.84	33.38
2016	34.47	15.41
2015	29.98	5.88
2014	28.43	7.42
2013	26.51	33.35
2012	19.88	15.53

Total Assets: $1,766,087,978

Asset Allocation

Asset	%
Cash	0%
Stocks	100%
US Stocks	90%
Bonds	0%
US Bonds	0%
Other	0%

Services Offered:

Investment Strategy: The investment seeks investment results that correspond generally to the price and yield, before the fund's fees and expenses, of an equity index called the ISE Cloud Computing™ Index. The fund will normally invest at least 90% of its net assets (including investment borrowings) in common stocks or in depositary receipts representing securities in the index. The index is designed to provide a benchmark for investors interested in tracking companies actively involved in the cloud computing industry. **Top Holdings:** VMware Inc Cisco Systems Inc Red Hat Inc Salesforce.com Inc Juniper Networks Inc

---

SPDR® Portfolio Emerging Markets ETF   C-   HOLD

Ticker	Traded On	NAV		Total Assets ($)	Dividend Yield (TTM)	Turnover Ratio	Expense Ratio
SPEM	NYSE Arca	32.43		$1,760,937,526	1.77	10	0.11

Ratings

Reward	C-
Risk	C
Recent Upgrade/Downgrade	Down

Fund Information

Fund Type	Exchange Traded Funds
Category	Global Emerg Mkts Equity
Sub-Category	Diversified Emerging Mkts
Prospectus Objective	Div Emerg Mkts
Inception Date	Mar-07
Open to New Investments	Y

Prices

Price (as of 12/31/2018)	32.36
52-Week High	42.45
52-Week Low	31.29

Total Returns (%)

3-Month	6-Month	1-Year	3-Year	5-Year
-5.51	-6.64	-13.06	30.00	11.60

3-Year Standard Deviation	14.52
Effective Duration	

Valuation

Premium/Discount (1-Year Average)	0.11

Company Information

Provider	SPDR State Street Global Advisors
Manager/Tenure	Michael J. Feehily (7), Karl A. Schneider (3), Dwayne Hancock (1)
Website	http://www.spdrs.com
Address	SPDR State Street Global Advisors State Street Financial Center, 1 Lincoln Street Boston MA 02111-2900 United States
Phone Number	617-786-3000

PERFORMANCE

Ratings History

Date	Overall Rating	Risk Rating	Reward Rating
Q4-18	C-	C	C-
Q2-18	C	C+	C
Q4-17	B-	C	B
Q4-16	D+	C-	D+
Q4-15	C-	C-	C-

Asset & Performance History

Date	NAV	1-Year Total Return
2017	38.15	34.48
2016	28.71	11.03
2015	26.23	-15.21
2014	31.62	1.24
2013	31.93	-1.67
2012	33.15	16.83

Total Assets: $1,760,937,526

Asset Allocation

Asset	%
Cash	1%
Stocks	99%
US Stocks	1%
Bonds	0%
US Bonds	0%
Other	0%

Services Offered:

Investment Strategy: The investment seeks investment results that, before fees and expenses, correspond generally to the total return performance of the S&P Emerging BMI Index. The fund generally invests substantially all, but at least 80%, of its total assets in the securities comprising the index and in depositary receipts based on securities comprising the index. The index is a market capitalization weighted index designed to define and measure the investable universe of publicly traded companies domiciled in emerging markets. The fund is non-diversified. **Top Holdings:** Tencent Holdings Ltd Alibaba Group Holding Ltd ADR Taiwan Semiconductor Manufacturing Co Ltd Naspers Ltd Class N China Construction Bank Corp H

Invesco S&P MidCap Low Volatility ETF

C HOLD

Ticker	Traded On	NAV	Total Assets ($)	Dividend Yield (TTM)	Turnover Ratio	Expense Ratio
XMLV	NYSE Arca	44.38	$1,747,424,901	2.3		0.25

Ratings
Reward   C
Risk   C+
Recent Upgrade/Downgrade Down

Fund Information
Fund Type   Exchange Traded Funds
Category   US Equity Mid Cap
Sub-Category   Mid-Cap Value
Prospectus Objective   Income
Inception Date   Feb-13
Open to New Investments

Prices
Price (as of 12/31/2018)   44.39
52-Week High   49.42
52-Week Low   42.36

Total Returns (%)
3-Month	6-Month	1-Year	3-Year	5-Year
-7.10	-4.44	-0.19	38.10	72.01

3-Year Standard Deviation   8.86
Effective Duration

Valuation
Premium/Discount (1-Year Average) 0.01

Company Information
Provider   Invesco
Manager/Tenure Peter Hubbard (5), Michael Jeanette
                (5), Tony Seisser (4), 1 other
Website   http://www.invesco.com/us
Address   Invesco 11 Greenway Plaza, Ste. 2500
                Houston TX 77046 United States
Phone Number   800-659-1005

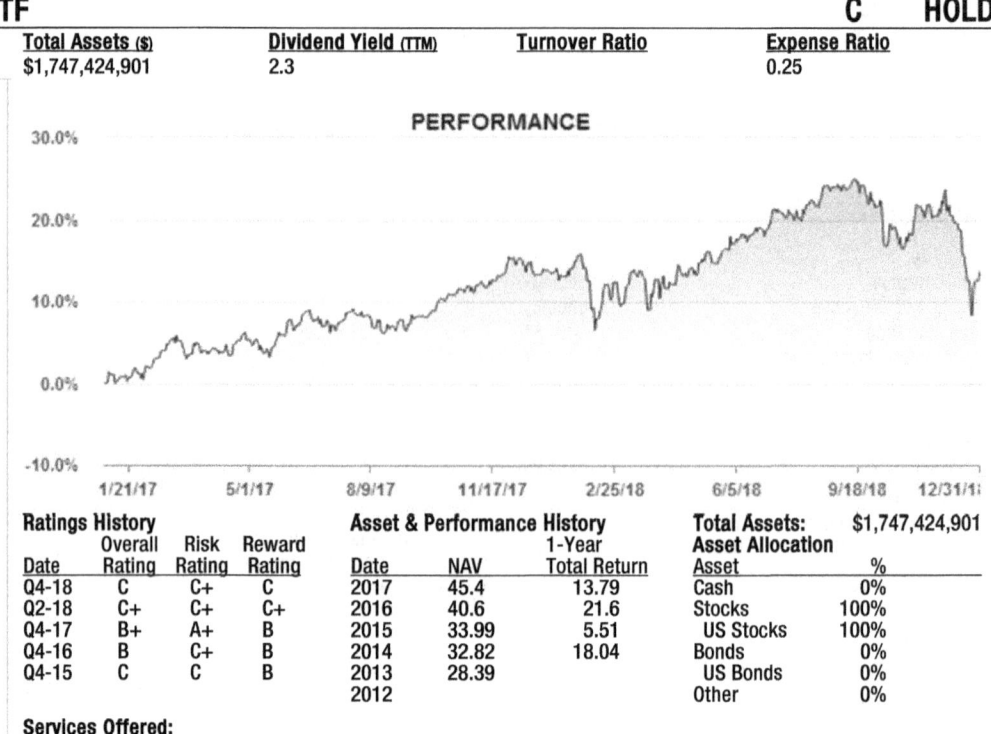

PERFORMANCE

Ratings History
Date	Overall Rating	Risk Rating	Reward Rating
Q4-18	C	C+	C
Q2-18	C+	C+	C+
Q4-17	B+	A+	B
Q4-16	B	C+	B
Q4-15	C	C	B

Asset & Performance History
Date	NAV	1-Year Total Return
2017	45.4	13.79
2016	40.6	21.6
2015	33.99	5.51
2014	32.82	18.04
2013	28.39	
2012		

Total Assets: $1,747,424,901
Asset Allocation
Asset	%
Cash	0%
Stocks	100%
US Stocks	100%
Bonds	0%
US Bonds	0%
Other	0%

Services Offered:

Investment Strategy: The investment seeks to track the investment results (before fees and expenses) of the S&P MidCap 400® Low Volatility Index (the "underlying index"). The fund generally will invest at least 90% of its total assets in common stocks that comprise the underlying index. Strictly in accordance with its procedures and mandated guidelines, the index provider selects for inclusion in the underlying index the 80 securities that it has determined have the lowest volatility over the past 12 months out of the 400 medium capitalization securities that are contained in the S&P MidCap 400® Index. **Top Holdings:** Hawaiian Electric Industries Inc Vectren Corp UGI Corp Brown & Brown Inc WR Berkley Corp

---

VanEck Vectors Morningstar Wide Moat ETF

C HOLD

Ticker	Traded On	NAV	Total Assets ($)	Dividend Yield (TTM)	Turnover Ratio	Expense Ratio
MOAT	NYSE Arca	41.14	$1,736,989,966	0.99	56	0.48

Ratings
Reward   C
Risk   C
Recent Upgrade/Downgrade Down

Fund Information
Fund Type   Exchange Traded Funds
Category   US Equity Large Cap Blend
Sub-Category   Large Blend
Prospectus Objective   Growth
Inception Date   Apr-12
Open to New Investments   Y

Prices
Price (as of 12/31/2018)   41.17
52-Week High   47.20
52-Week Low   38.89

Total Returns (%)
3-Month	6-Month	1-Year	3-Year	5-Year
-10.48	-4.08	-1.39	47.87	53.71

3-Year Standard Deviation   11.43
Effective Duration

Valuation
Premium/Discount (1-Year Average) 0.18

Company Information
Provider   VanEck
Manager/Tenure Hao-Hung (Peter) Liao (6), Guo Hua
                (Jason) Jin (0)
Website   http://www.vaneck.com
Address   Van Eck Associates Corporation 666
                Third Avenue New York NY 10017
                United States
Phone Number   800-826-1115

PERFORMANCE

Ratings History
Date	Overall Rating	Risk Rating	Reward Rating
Q4-18	C	C	C
Q2-18	C	C	C
Q4-17	B	B-	B
Q4-16	C+	C-	B
Q4-15	B-	C	B

Asset & Performance History
Date	NAV	1-Year Total Return
2017	42.42	23.19
2016	34.8	21.73
2015	28.92	-4.85
2014	31.06	9.25
2013	28.81	30.88
2012	22.19	

Total Assets: $1,736,989,966
Asset Allocation
Asset	%
Cash	0%
Stocks	100%
US Stocks	100%
Bonds	0%
US Bonds	0%
Other	0%

Services Offered:

Investment Strategy: The investment seeks to replicate as closely as possible, before fees and expenses, the price and yield performance of the Morningstar® Wide Moat Focus IndexSM. The fund normally invests at least 80% of its total assets in securities that comprise the fund's benchmark index. The index is comprised of securities issued by companies that Morningstar, Inc. ("Morningstar") determines to have sustainable competitive advantages based on a proprietary methodology that considers quantitative and qualitative factors ("wide moat companies"). The fund is non-diversified. **Top Holdings:** Starbucks Corp Pfizer Inc Procter & Gamble Co Comcast Corp Class A PepsiCo Inc

SPDR® Portfolio Large Cap ETF   C   HOLD

Ticker	Traded On	NAV	Total Assets ($)	Dividend Yield (TTM)	Turnover Ratio	Expense Ratio
SPLG	NYSE Arca	29.20	$1,727,043,062	1.97	4	0.03

Ratings
Reward   C
Risk   C+
Recent Upgrade/Downgrade   Down

Fund Information
Fund Type   Exchange Traded Funds
Category   US Equity Large Cap Blend
Sub-Category   Large Blend
Prospectus Objective   Growth & Inc
Inception Date   Nov-05
Open to New Investments   Y

Prices
Price (as of 12/31/2018)   29.21
52-Week High   34.45
52-Week Low   27.32

Total Returns (%)

3-Month	6-Month	1-Year	3-Year	5-Year
-14.04	-7.60	-4.70	29.79	48.08

3-Year Standard Deviation   9.52
Effective Duration

Valuation
Premium/Discount (1-Year Average)   0.03

Company Information
Provider   SPDR State Street Global Advisors
Manager/Tenure   Michael J. Feehily (7), Karl A.
                  Schneider (4), Eric Viliott (1)
Website   http://www.spdrs.com
Address   SPDR State Street Global Advisors
                  State Street Financial Center, 1
                  Lincoln Street Boston MA 02111-2900
                  United States
Phone Number   617-786-3000

PERFORMANCE

Ratings History

Date	Overall Rating	Risk Rating	Reward Rating
Q4-18	C	C+	C
Q2-18	C+	C+	C
Q4-17	B	B	B
Q4-16	C+	D+	B
Q4-15	C	C-	C

Asset & Performance History

Date	NAV	1-Year Total Return
2017	31.27	21.6
2016	26.2	11.49
2015	23.89	0.84
2014	24.16	13.13
2013	21.76	32.78
2012	16.7	15.91

Total Assets: $1,727,043,062
Asset Allocation

Asset	%
Cash	0%
Stocks	100%
US Stocks	99%
Bonds	0%
US Bonds	0%
Other	0%

Services Offered: Dividend Investment Plan, CashInvestment Plan

Investment Strategy: The investment seeks to provide investment results that, before fees and expenses, correspond generally to the total return performance of the SSGA Large Cap Index. The fund generally invests substantially all, but at least 80%, of its total assets in the securities comprising the index. The index is designed to measure the performance of the large-capitalization segment of the U.S. equity market. The fund may purchase a subset of the securities in the index in an effort to hold a portfolio of securities with generally the same risk and return characteristics of the index. It is non-diversified. **Top Holdings:** Microsoft Corp Apple Inc Amazon.com Inc Johnson & Johnson JPMorgan Chase & Co

Global X Robotics & Artificial Intelligence ETF   D+   SELL

Ticker	Traded On	NAV	Total Assets ($)	Dividend Yield (TTM)	Turnover Ratio	Expense Ratio
BOTZ	NAS CM	16.87	$1,726,206,524	0.01	15	0.68

Ratings
Reward   D+
Risk   D+
Recent Upgrade/Downgrade   Down

Fund Information
Fund Type   Exchange Traded Funds
Category   Equity Misc
Sub-Category   Miscellaneous Sector
Prospectus Objective   Technology
Inception Date   Sep-16
Open to New Investments   Y

Prices
Price (as of 12/31/2018)   16.74
52-Week High   27.38
52-Week Low   16.06

Total Returns (%)

3-Month	6-Month	1-Year	3-Year	5-Year
-25.66	-21.89	-27.79		

3-Year Standard Deviation
Effective Duration

Valuation
Premium/Discount (1-Year Average)   -0.09

Company Information
Provider   Global X Funds
Manager/Tenure   Chang Kim (2), James Ong (2), Nam
                  To (0)
Website   http://www.globalxfunds.com
Address   Global X Funds 600 Lexington Avenue,
                  20th Floor New York NY 10022 United
                  States
Phone Number   888-493-8631

PERFORMANCE

Ratings History

Date	Overall Rating	Risk Rating	Reward Rating
Q4-18	D+	D+	D+
Q2-18	C	C+	C-
Q4-17	D	B	C
Q4-16	U		
Q4-15			

Asset & Performance History

Date	NAV	1-Year Total Return
2017	23.7	58.53
2016	14.95	
2015		
2014		
2013		
2012		

Total Assets: $1,726,206,524
Asset Allocation

Asset	%
Cash	0%
Stocks	100%
US Stocks	31%
Bonds	0%
US Bonds	0%
Other	0%

Services Offered:

Investment Strategy: The investment seeks to provide investment results that correspond generally to the price and yield performance, before fees and expenses, of the Indxx Global Robotics & Artificial Intelligence Thematic Index. The fund invests at least 80% of its total assets in the securities of the underlying index. The underlying index is designed to provide exposure to exchange-listed companies in developed markets that are involved in the development of robotics and/or artificial intelligence as defined by Indxx, the provider of the underlying index. The fund is non-diversified. **Top Holdings:** Intuitive Surgical Inc Mitsubishi Electric Corp ABB Ltd Keyence Corp Fanuc Corp

Direxion Daily Financial Bull 3X Shares

C   HOLD

Ticker	Traded On	NAV		Total Assets ($)	Dividend Yield (TTM)	Turnover Ratio	Expense Ratio
FAS	NYSE Arca	44.80		$1,708,053,421	0.89	4	1.02

Ratings
Reward	C
Risk	C-
Recent Upgrade/Downgrade	

Fund Information
Fund Type	Exchange Traded Funds
Category	Trading Tools
Sub-Category	Trading--Leveraged Equity
Prospectus Objective	Financial
Inception Date	Nov-08
Open to New Investments	Y

Prices
Price (as of 12/31/2018)	44.77
52-Week High	81.71
52-Week Low	37.55

Total Returns (%)
3-Month	6-Month	1-Year	3-Year	5-Year
-36.04	-29.22	-33.59	55.90	100.55

3-Year Standard Deviation	36.88
Effective Duration	

Valuation
Premium/Discount (1-Year Average)	0.02

Company Information
Provider	Direxion Funds
Manager/Tenure	Paul Brigandi (10), Tony Ng (3)
Website	http://www.direxionfunds.com
Address	Direxion Funds 1301 Avenue Of The Americas (6th Avenue) New York NY 10019 United States
Phone Number	646-572-3390

PERFORMANCE

Ratings History
Date	Overall Rating	Risk Rating	Reward Rating
Q4-18	C	C-	C
Q2-18	C	C-	C
Q4-17	B	C-	A-
Q4-16	C	D+	B-
Q4-15	A	B+	A+

Asset & Performance History
Date	NAV	1-Year Total Return
2017	68.17	66.94
2016	40.88	40.62
2015	29.07	-8.49
2014	31.77	40.57
2013	22.6	125.93
2012	10	85.15

Total Assets: $1,708,053,421

Asset Allocation
Asset	%
Cash	29%
Stocks	71%
US Stocks	70%
Bonds	0%
US Bonds	0%
Other	0%

Services Offered:

Investment Strategy: The investment seeks daily investment results, before fees and expenses, of 300% of the daily performance of the Russell 1000® Financial Services Index. The fund invests at least 80% of its net assets (plus borrowing for investment purposes) in securities of the index, exchange-traded funds ("ETFs") that track the index and other financial instruments that provide daily leveraged exposure to the index or ETFs that track the index. The index is a subset of the Russell 1000® Index that measures the performance of the securities classified in the financial services sector of the large-capitalization U.S. equity market. It is non-diversified. **Top Holdings:** Russ 1000 Finan Indx Swap Berkshire Hathaway Inc B JPMorgan Chase & Co Bank of America Corporation Visa Inc Class A

SPDR® S&P 600 Small Cap Value ETF

D-   SELL

Ticker	Traded On	NAV		Total Assets ($)	Dividend Yield (TTM)	Turnover Ratio	Expense Ratio
SLYV	NYSE Arca	53.81		$1,699,475,897	1.76	53	0.15

Ratings
Reward	D-
Risk	D
Recent Upgrade/Downgrade	

Fund Information
Fund Type	Exchange Traded Funds
Category	US Equity Small Cap
Sub-Category	Small Value
Prospectus Objective	Small Company
Inception Date	Sep-00
Open to New Investments	Y

Prices
Price (as of 12/31/2018)	53.82
52-Week High	130.78
52-Week Low	50.73

Total Returns (%)
3-Month	6-Month	1-Year	3-Year	5-Year
-19.39	-19.12	-56.68	-36.65	-36.55

3-Year Standard Deviation	14.86
Effective Duration	

Valuation
Premium/Discount (1-Year Average)	0.06

Company Information
Provider	SPDR State Street Global Advisors
Manager/Tenure	Michael J. Feehily (7), Karl A. Schneider (4), David Chin (0)
Website	http://www.spdrs.com
Address	SPDR State Street Global Advisors State Street Financial Center, 1 Lincoln Street Boston MA 02111-2900 United States
Phone Number	617-786-3000

PERFORMANCE

Ratings History
Date	Overall Rating	Risk Rating	Reward Rating
Q4-18	D-	D	D-
Q2-18	D	D	D+
Q4-17	B+	B	A-
Q4-16	C	C-	C
Q4-15	C	C-	C

Asset & Performance History
Date	NAV	1-Year Total Return
2017	125.58	11.5
2016	119.03	30.15
2015	92.91	-6.65
2014	106.08	7.31
2013	106.38	39.65
2012	77.49	18.02

Total Assets: $1,699,475,897

Asset Allocation
Asset	%
Cash	0%
Stocks	100%
US Stocks	98%
Bonds	0%
US Bonds	0%
Other	0%

Services Offered: Dividend Investment Plan, CashInvestment Plan

Investment Strategy: The investment seeks to provide investment results that, before fees and expenses, correspond generally to the total return performance of the S&P SmallCap 600 Value Index. The fund generally invests substantially all, but at least 80%, of its total assets in the securities comprising the index. The index measures the performance of the small-capitalization value segment of the U.S. equity market. It may purchase a subset of the securities in the index in an effort to hold a portfolio of securities with generally the same risk and return characteristics of the index. The fund is non-diversified. **Top Holdings:** CACI International Inc Class A Spire Inc Community Bank System Inc Wolverine World Wide Inc American Equity Investment Life Holding Co

Fidelity® NASDAQ Composite Index® Tracking Stock Fund　　　　　　　　C　　HOLD

Ticker	Traded On	NAV	Total Assets ($)	Dividend Yield (TTM)	Turnover Ratio	Expense Ratio
ONEQ	NAS CM	259.98	$1,698,602,700	0.93	12	0.21

Ratings
Reward　　　　　　　　　　　　　　　C
Risk　　　　　　　　　　　　　　　　C-
Recent Upgrade/Downgrade　　　　Down

Fund Information
Fund Type　　　　　　　　Exchange Traded Funds
Category　　　　　　　　US Equity Large Cap Growth
Sub-Category　　　　　　　　　Large Growth
Prospectus Objective　　　　　　　　Growth
Inception Date　　　　　　　　　　Sep-03
Open to New Investments　　　　　　　　Y

Prices
Price (as of 12/31/2018)　　　　　259.96
52-Week High　　　　　　　　　318.63
52-Week Low　　　　　　　　　243.03

Total Returns (%)

3-Month	6-Month	1-Year	3-Year	5-Year
-17.13	-11.15	-3.06	36.43	67.09

3-Year Standard Deviation　　　　　　12.44
Effective Duration

Valuation
Premium/Discount (1-Year Average)　　0.07

Company Information
Provider　　　　　Fidelity Investments
Manager/Tenure　Patrick Waddell (14), Louis Bottari (9), Peter Matthew (6), 3 others
Website　　　　　http://www.institutional.fidelity.com
Address　　　　　Fidelity Investments 82 Devonshire Street Boston MA 2109 United States
Phone Number　　617-563-7000

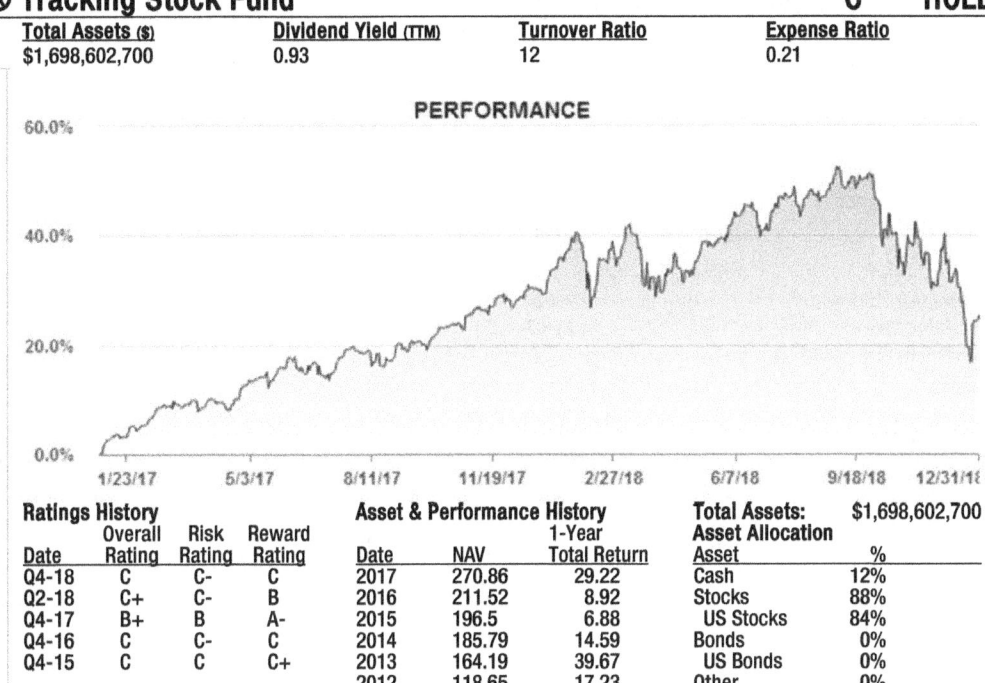

PERFORMANCE

Ratings History

Date	Overall Rating	Risk Rating	Reward Rating
Q4-18	C	C-	C
Q2-18	C+	C-	B
Q4-17	B+	B	A-
Q4-16	C	C-	C
Q4-15	C	C	C+

Asset & Performance History

Date	NAV	1-Year Total Return
2017	270.86	29.22
2016	211.52	8.92
2015	196.5	6.88
2014	185.79	14.59
2013	164.19	39.67
2012	118.65	17.23

Total Assets: $1,698,602,700
Asset Allocation

Asset	%
Cash	12%
Stocks	88%
US Stocks	84%
Bonds	0%
US Bonds	0%
Other	0%

Services Offered:

Investment Strategy: The investment seeks to provide investment returns that closely correspond to the price and yield performance of the Nasdaq Composite Index ®. The fund normally invests at least 80% of assets in common stocks included in the index. It uses statistical sampling techniques that take into account such factors as capitalization, industry exposures, dividend yield, price/earnings (P/E) ratio, price/book (P/B) ratio, and earnings growth to create a portfolio of securities listed in the Nasdaq Composite Index that have a similar investment profile to the entire index. **Top Holdings:** Nasdaq 100 E-Mini Dec18 Nqz8　Apple Inc　Microsoft Corp　Amazon.com Inc　Alphabet Inc Class C

---

iShares U.S. Financial Services ETF　　　　　　　　　　　　　　B-　　BUY

Ticker	Traded On	NAV	Total Assets ($)	Dividend Yield (TTM)	Turnover Ratio	Expense Ratio
IYG	NYSE Arca	112.32	$1,683,477,109	1.48	4	0.43

Ratings
Reward　　　　　　　　　　　　　　　B
Risk　　　　　　　　　　　　　　　　C+
Recent Upgrade/Downgrade　　　　Down

Fund Information
Fund Type　　　　　　　　Exchange Traded Funds
Category　　　　　　　　Financials Sector Equity
Sub-Category　　　　　　　　　Financial
Prospectus Objective　　　　　　　　Financial
Inception Date　　　　　　　　　　Jun-00
Open to New Investments　　　　　　　　Y

Prices
Price (as of 12/31/2018)　　　　　112.27
52-Week High　　　　　　　　　141.49
52-Week Low　　　　　　　　　105.05

Total Returns (%)

3-Month	6-Month	1-Year	3-Year	5-Year
-15.50	-13.08	-12.44	30.59	43.84

3-Year Standard Deviation　　　　　　16.77
Effective Duration

Valuation
Premium/Discount (1-Year Average)　　0.03

Company Information
Provider　　　　　iShares
Manager/Tenure　Diane Hsiung (10), Greg Savage (10), Jennifer Hsui (6), 3 others
Website　　　　　http://www.ishares.com
Address　　　　　iShares 400 Howard Street San Francisco CA 94105 United States
Phone Number　　800-474-2737

PERFORMANCE

Ratings History

Date	Overall Rating	Risk Rating	Reward Rating
Q4-18	B-	C+	B
Q2-18	B	C	B
Q4-17	B+	B	A
Q4-16	B-	C	B
Q4-15	B+	B	B+

Asset & Performance History

Date	NAV	1-Year Total Return
2017	130.36	24.41
2016	106.23	19.88
2015	89.97	-0.71
2014	91.82	10.93
2013	83.76	42.83
2012	59.33	32.95

Total Assets: $1,683,477,109
Asset Allocation

Asset	%
Cash	0%
Stocks	100%
US Stocks	100%
Bonds	0%
US Bonds	0%
Other	0%

Services Offered: CashInvestment Plan

Investment Strategy: The investment seeks to track the investment results of the Dow Jones U.S. Financial Services Index composed of U.S. equities in the financial services sector. The fund generally invests at least 90% of its assets in securities of the underlying index and in depositary receipts representing securities of the underlying index. The underlying index measures the performance of the financial services sector of the U.S. equity market. The fund is non-diversified. **Top Holdings:** JPMorgan Chase & Co　Bank of America Corporation　Visa Inc Class A　Wells Fargo & Co　Mastercard Inc A

SPDR® Bloomberg Barclays TIPS ETF   C-   HOLD

Ticker	Traded On	NAV	Total Assets ($)	Dividend Yield (TTM)	Turnover Ratio	Expense Ratio
IPE	NYSE Arca	53.89	$1,672,615,422	3.75	18	0.15

Ratings
Reward	D
Risk	C
Recent Upgrade/Downgrade	Down

Fund Information
Fund Type	Exchange Traded Funds
Category	US Fixed Income
Sub-Category	Inflation-Protected Bond
Prospectus Objective	Govt Bond - Treasury
Inception Date	May-07
Open to New Investments	Y

Prices
Price (as of 12/31/2018)	53.89
52-Week High	56.25
52-Week Low	53.29

Total Returns (%)
3-Month	6-Month	1-Year	3-Year	5-Year
-0.34	-1.57	-1.61	6.22	8.67

3-Year Standard Deviation	3.32
Effective Duration	7.88

Valuation
Premium/Discount (1-Year Average)	-0.03

Company Information
Provider	SPDR State Street Global Advisors
Manager/Tenure	Cynthia Moy (4), James Kramer (2), Orhan Imer (1)
Website	http://www.spdrs.com
Address	SPDR State Street Global Advisors State Street Financial Center, 1 Lincoln Street Boston MA 02111-2900 United States
Phone Number	617-786-3000

PERFORMANCE

Ratings History
Date	Overall Rating	Risk Rating	Reward Rating
Q4-18	C-	C	D
Q2-18	C	C+	C
Q4-17	C	C+	C
Q4-16	C-	C-	C
Q4-15	D+	C-	D+

Asset & Performance History
Date	NAV	1-Year Total Return
2017	56.3	2.38
2016	56.25	4.6
2015	54.73	-1.86
2014	55.85	4.25
2013	54.45	-9.42
2012	60.76	7.07

Total Assets: $1,672,615,422
Asset Allocation
Asset	%
Cash	0%
Stocks	0%
US Stocks	0%
Bonds	100%
US Bonds	100%
Other	0%

Services Offered:

Investment Strategy: The investment seeks to provide investment results that correspond generally to the price and yield performance of the Bloomberg Barclays U.S. Government Inflation-Linked Bond Index. The fund generally invests substantially all, but at least 80%, of its total assets in the securities comprising the index or in securities that the adviser determines have economic characteristics that are substantially identical to the economic characteristics of the securities that comprise the index. The index is designed to measure the performance of the inflation protected public obligations of the U.S. Treasury, commonly known as "TIPS." It is non-diversified. **Top Holdings:** United States Treasury Notes 0.12% United States Treasury Notes 0.12% United States Treasury Notes 0.12% United States Treasury Notes 0.12% United States Treasury Notes 0.62%

Invesco Variable Rate Preferred ETF   C   HOLD

Ticker	Traded On	NAV	Total Assets ($)	Dividend Yield (TTM)	Turnover Ratio	Expense Ratio
VRP	NYSE Arca	23.05	$1,662,110,567	4.97		0.5

Ratings
Reward	D+
Risk	C+
Recent Upgrade/Downgrade	

Fund Information
Fund Type	Exchange Traded Funds
Category	US Fixed Income
Sub-Category	Preferred Stock
Prospectus Objective	Growth & Inc
Inception Date	May-14
Open to New Investments	Y

Prices
Price (as of 12/31/2018)	22.82
52-Week High	25.70
52-Week Low	22.45

Total Returns (%)
3-Month	6-Month	1-Year	3-Year	5-Year
-6.25	-5.14	-5.69	10.49	

3-Year Standard Deviation	4.82
Effective Duration	

Valuation
Premium/Discount (1-Year Average)	-0.12

Company Information
Provider	Invesco
Manager/Tenure	Philip Fang (4), Peter Hubbard (4), Gary Jones (4), 2 others
Website	http://www.invesco.com/us
Address	Invesco 11 Greenway Plaza, Ste. 2500 Houston TX 77046 United States
Phone Number	800-659-1005

PERFORMANCE

Ratings History
Date	Overall Rating	Risk Rating	Reward Rating
Q4-18	C	C+	D+
Q2-18	C	C+	C
Q4-17	B	A+	C
Q4-16	C	C+	C
Q4-15	D	C+	D+

Asset & Performance History
Date	NAV	1-Year Total Return
2017	25.66	9.7
2016	24.51	6.8
2015	24.16	2.99
2014	24.65	
2013		
2012		

Total Assets: $1,662,110,567
Asset Allocation
Asset	%
Cash	1%
Stocks	0%
US Stocks	0%
Bonds	63%
US Bonds	60%
Other	0%

Services Offered:

Investment Strategy: The investment seeks to track the investment results (before fees and expenses) of the Wells Fargo® Hybrid and Preferred Securities Floating and Variable Rate Index. The fund will invest at least 90% of its total assets in the securities that comprise the underlying index. The underlying index is a market capitalization-weighted index designed to track the performance of preferred stock, as well as certain types of "hybrid securities" that are functionally equivalent to preferred stocks, that are issued by U.S.-based or foreign issuers and that pay a floating or variable rate dividend or coupon. It is non-diversified. **Top Holdings:** General Electric Company 5% JPMorgan Chase & Co. 5.99% Wells Fargo & Company 6.1% GMAC Capital Trust I Pfd Secs 2011-15.2.40 Gtd Series 2 JPMorgan Chase & Co. 5%

Fidelity® MSCI Health Care Index ETF   C+   HOLD

Ticker	Traded On	NAV	Total Assets ($)	Dividend Yield (TTM)	Turnover Ratio	Expense Ratio
FHLC	NYSE Arca	41.31	$1,661,393,450	1.26	8	0.08

Ratings
Reward   C+
Risk   C
Recent Upgrade/Downgrade

Fund Information
Fund Type	Exchange Traded Funds
Category	Healthcare Sector Equity
Sub-Category	Health
Prospectus Objective	Health
Inception Date	Oct-13
Open to New Investments	Y

Prices
Price (as of 12/31/2018)	41.32
52-Week High	46.93
52-Week Low	38.79

Total Returns (%)
3-Month	6-Month	1-Year	3-Year	5-Year
-10.88	1.12	5.52	25.80	68.65

3-Year Standard Deviation	13.18
Effective Duration	

Valuation
Premium/Discount (1-Year Average)	0.05

Company Information
Provider	Fidelity Investments
Manager/Tenure	Jennifer Hsui (5), Greg Savage (5), Alan Mason (2), 2 others
Website	http://www.institutional.fidelity.com
Address	Fidelity Investments 82 Devonshire Street Boston MA 2109 United States
Phone Number	617-563-7000

PERFORMANCE

Ratings History

Date	Overall Rating	Risk Rating	Reward Rating
Q4-18	C+	C	C+
Q2-18	C	C	C+
Q4-17	B	B	B-
Q4-16	C+	C+	C+
Q4-15	C-	B-	C+

Asset & Performance History

Date	NAV	1-Year Total Return
2017	39.98	23.3
2016	32.89	-3.31
2015	34.5	7.05
2014	32.88	25.22
2013	26.55	
2012		

Total Assets: $1,661,393,450
Asset Allocation

Asset	%
Cash	0%
Stocks	100%
US Stocks	100%
Bonds	0%
US Bonds	0%
Other	0%

Services Offered:

Investment Strategy: The investment seeks to provide investment returns that correspond, before fees and expenses, generally to the performance of the MSCI USA IMI Health Care Index. The fund invests at least 80% of assets in securities included in the fund's underlying index. The fund's underlying index is the MSCI USA IMI Health Care Index, which represents the performance of the health care sector in the U.S. equity market. It may or may not hold all of the securities in the MSCI USA IMI Health Care Index. The fund is non-diversified. **Top Holdings:** Johnson & Johnson   Pfizer Inc   UnitedHealth Group Inc   Merck & Co Inc   AbbVie Inc

---

VanEck Vectors AMT-Free Intermediate Municipal Index ETF   B   BUY

Ticker	Traded On	NAV	Total Assets ($)	Dividend Yield (TTM)	Turnover Ratio	Expense Ratio
ITM	BATS	47.44	$1,648,898,391	2.34	9	0.24

Ratings
Reward   A
Risk   C+
Recent Upgrade/Downgrade   Up

Fund Information
Fund Type	Exchange Traded Funds
Category	US Muni Fixed Inc
Sub-Category	Muni National Long
Prospectus Objective	Muni Bond - Natl
Inception Date	Dec-07
Open to New Investments	Y

Prices
Price (as of 12/31/2018)	47.47
52-Week High	47.53
52-Week Low	23.26

Total Returns (%)
3-Month	6-Month	1-Year	3-Year	5-Year
1.95	103.37	100.88	112.15	139.61

3-Year Standard Deviation	4.34
Effective Duration	6.90

Valuation
Premium/Discount (1-Year Average)	-0.21

Company Information
Provider	VanEck
Manager/Tenure	James T. Colby (11)
Website	http://www.vaneck.com
Address	Van Eck Associates Corporation 666 Third Avenue New York NY 10017 United States
Phone Number	800-826-1115

PERFORMANCE

Ratings History

Date	Overall Rating	Risk Rating	Reward Rating
Q4-18	B	C+	A
Q2-18	C	C+	C
Q4-17	B-	B	C
Q4-16	C	C+	C
Q4-15	C	C+	C

Asset & Performance History

Date	NAV	1-Year Total Return
2017	24.13	6.21
2016	23.23	-0.56
2015	23.88	3.64
2014	23.58	8.97
2013	22.18	-3.51
2012	23.58	6.11

Total Assets: $1,648,898,391
Asset Allocation

Asset	%
Cash	0%
Stocks	0%
US Stocks	0%
Bonds	100%
US Bonds	100%
Other	0%

Services Offered:

Investment Strategy: The investment seeks to replicate as closely as possible, before fees and expenses, the price and yield performance of the Bloomberg Barclays AMT-Free Intermediate Continuous Municipal Index. The fund normally invests at least 80% of its total assets in fixed income securities that comprise the index. The index is comprised of publicly traded municipal bonds that cover the U.S. dollar denominated intermediate term tax-exempt bond market. **Top Holdings:** GEORGIA ST 5%   HAWAII ST 5%   NEW MEXICO FIN AUTH 5%   SALES TAX ASSET RECEIVABLE CORP N Y 5%   PENNSYLVANIA ST 5%

ProShares Short S&P500   D   SELL

Ticker	Traded On	NAV	Total Assets ($)	Dividend Yield (TTM)	Turnover Ratio	Expense Ratio
SH	NYSE Arca	31.36	$1,639,081,214	0.84		0.89

Ratings

Reward	D
Risk	D
Recent Upgrade/Downgrade	

Fund Information

Fund Type	Exchange Traded Funds
Category	Trading Tools
Sub-Category	Trading--Inverse Equity
Prospectus Objective	Growth
Inception Date	Jun-06
Open to New Investments	Y

Prices

Price (as of 12/31/2018)	31.33
52-Week High	33.59
52-Week Low	27.20

Total Returns (%)

3-Month	6-Month	1-Year	3-Year	5-Year
15.58	7.98	4.86	-24.04	-37.16

3-Year Standard Deviation	9.1
Effective Duration	

Valuation

Premium/Discount (1-Year Average)	-0.01

Company Information

Provider	ProShares
Manager/Tenure	Michael Neches (5), Devin Sullivan (0)
Website	http://www.proshares.com
Address	ProShares 7501 Wisconsin Avenue, Suite 1000 Bethesda MD 20814 United States
Phone Number	866-776-5125

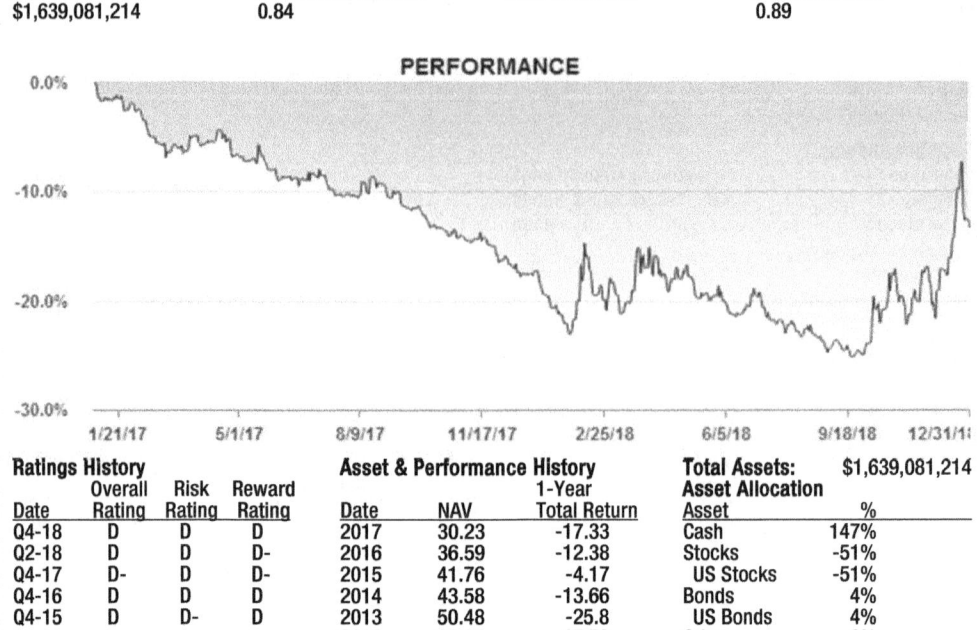

PERFORMANCE

Ratings History

Date	Overall Rating	Risk Rating	Reward Rating
Q4-18	D	D	D
Q2-18	D	D	D-
Q4-17	D-	D	D-
Q4-16	D	D	D
Q4-15	D	D-	D

Asset & Performance History

Date	NAV	1-Year Total Return
2017	30.23	-17.33
2016	36.59	-12.38
2015	41.76	-4.17
2014	43.58	-13.66
2013	50.48	-25.8
2012	68.04	-15.79

Total Assets: $1,639,081,214

Asset Allocation

Asset	%
Cash	147%
Stocks	-51%
US Stocks	-51%
Bonds	4%
US Bonds	4%
Other	0%

Services Offered:

Investment Strategy: The investment seeks daily investment results that correspond to the inverse (-1x) of the daily performance of the S&P 500® Index. The fund invests in financial instruments that ProShare Advisors believes, in combination, should produce daily returns consistent with the fund's investment objective. The index is a measure of large-cap U.S. stock market performance. It is a float-adjusted, market capitalization-weighted index of 500 U.S. operating companies and real estate investment trusts selected through a process that factors in criteria such as liquidity, price, market capitalization and financial viability. The fund is non-diversified. **Top Holdings:** United States Treasury Bills S&P 500 Index Swap Societe Generale United States Treasury Bills S&P500 Emini 12/21/2018 (Esz8) United States Treasury Bills

---

WisdomTree International SmallCap Dividend Fund   C-   HOLD

Ticker	Traded On	NAV	Total Assets ($)	Dividend Yield (TTM)	Turnover Ratio	Expense Ratio
DLS	NYSE Arca	60.53	$1,635,191,337	3.56	28	0.58

Ratings

Reward	D+
Risk	C-
Recent Upgrade/Downgrade	

Fund Information

Fund Type	Exchange Traded Funds
Category	Global Eq Mid/Small Cap
Sub-Category	Foreign Small/Mid Value
Prospectus Objective	Foreign Stock
Inception Date	Jun-06
Open to New Investments	Y

Prices

Price (as of 12/31/2018)	60.32
52-Week High	81.55
52-Week Low	58.00

Total Returns (%)

3-Month	6-Month	1-Year	3-Year	5-Year
-14.31	-13.69	-18.69	13.92	13.16

3-Year Standard Deviation	12.38
Effective Duration	

Valuation

Premium/Discount (1-Year Average)	-0.06

Company Information

Provider	WisdomTree
Manager/Tenure	Richard A. Brown (10), Thomas J. Durante (10), Karen Q. Wong (10)
Website	http://www.wisdomtree.com
Address	WisdomTree 245 Park Avenue, 35th floor New York NY 10167 United States
Phone Number	866-909-9473

PERFORMANCE

Ratings History

Date	Overall Rating	Risk Rating	Reward Rating
Q4-18	C-	C-	D+
Q2-18	C	C-	C
Q4-17	B+	B+	A-
Q4-16	C	C-	C
Q4-15	C-	C-	C-

Asset & Performance History

Date	NAV	1-Year Total Return
2017	76.83	30.95
2016	60.45	7
2015	58.39	6.94
2014	56.06	-7.11
2013	62.35	27.4
2012	51.17	21.49

Total Assets: $1,635,191,337

Asset Allocation

Asset	%
Cash	0%
Stocks	100%
US Stocks	0%
Bonds	0%
US Bonds	0%
Other	0%

Services Offered:

Investment Strategy: The investment seeks to track the price and yield performance, before fees and expenses, of the WisdomTree International SmallCap Dividend Index. Under normal circumstances, at least 95% of the fund's total assets (exclusive of collateral held from securities lending) will be invested in component securities of the index and investments that have economic characteristics that are substantially identical to the economic characteristics of such component securities. The index is comprised of the small-capitalization segment of the dividend-paying market in the industrialized world outside the U.S. and Canada. The fund is non-diversified. **Top Holdings:** Austevoll Seafood ASA StarHub Ltd Delek Group Ltd Nos Sgps SA Hutchison Port Holdings Trust

Vanguard Mega Cap Index Fund ETF Shares   C   HOLD

Ticker	Traded On	NAV	Total Assets ($)	Dividend Yield (TTM)	Turnover Ratio	Expense Ratio
MGC	NYSE Arca		$1,628,201,682	1.85	4	0.07

Ratings
Reward   C
Risk   C-
Recent Upgrade/Downgrade

Fund Information
Fund Type	Exchange Traded Funds
Category	US Equity Large Cap Blend
Sub-Category	Large Blend
Prospectus Objective	Growth
Inception Date	Dec-07
Open to New Investments	Y

Prices
Price (as of 12/31/2018)	86.88
52-Week High	101.45
52-Week Low	81.34

Total Returns (%)
3-Month	6-Month	1-Year	3-Year	5-Year
-14.24	-7.14	-4.24	31.17	50.85

3-Year Standard Deviation   9.38
Effective Duration

Valuation
Premium/Discount (1-Year Average)   0.03

Company Information
Provider	Vanguard
Manager/Tenure	Michael A. Johnson (2), Gerard C. O'Reilly (2)
Website	http://www.vanguard.com
Address	Vanguard 100 Vanguard Boulevard Malvern PA 19355 United States
Phone Number	877-662-7447

PERFORMANCE

Ratings History

Date	Overall Rating	Risk Rating	Reward Rating
Q4-18	C	C-	C
Q2-18	C	C-	C
Q4-17	B	B	B
Q4-16	C+	C-	B
Q4-15	C	C	C

Asset & Performance History

Date	NAV	1-Year Total Return
2017	91.67	22.59
2016	76.27	11.23
2015	69.77	1.53
2014	70.17	13.26
2013	63.13	32.1
2012	48.78	16.1

Total Assets: $1,628,201,682
Asset Allocation

Asset	%
Cash	0%
Stocks	100%
US Stocks	99%
Bonds	0%
US Bonds	0%
Other	0%

Services Offered:

Investment Strategy: The investment seeks to track the performance of a benchmark index that measures the investment return of large-capitalization stocks in the United States. The fund employs an indexing investment approach designed to track the performance of the CRSP US Mega Cap Index. The index is a float-adjusted, market-capitalization-weighted index designed to measure equity market performance of mega-capitalization stocks in the United States. The Advisor attempts to replicate the target index by investing all, or substantially all, of its assets in the stocks that make up the index, holding each stock in approximately the same proportion as its weighting in the index. **Top Holdings:** Apple Inc   Microsoft Corp   Amazon.com Inc   Berkshire Hathaway Inc B   Johnson & Johnson

---

Goldman Sachs ActiveBeta® Emerging Markets Equity ETF   C-   HOLD

Ticker	Traded On	NAV	Total Assets ($)	Dividend Yield (TTM)	Turnover Ratio	Expense Ratio
GEM	NYSE Arca	30.24	$1,609,677,020	2.29	28	0.45

Ratings
Reward   C-
Risk   C
Recent Upgrade/Downgrade   Down

Fund Information
Fund Type	Exchange Traded Funds
Category	Global Emerg Mkts Equity
Sub-Category	Diversified Emerging Mkts
Prospectus Objective	Div Emerg Mkts
Inception Date	Sep-15
Open to New Investments	Y

Prices
Price (as of 12/31/2018)	30.12
52-Week High	39.44
52-Week Low	28.94

Total Returns (%)
3-Month	6-Month	1-Year	3-Year	5-Year
-6.98	-7.33	-13.51	28.38	

3-Year Standard Deviation   14.25
Effective Duration

Valuation
Premium/Discount (1-Year Average)   0.03

Company Information
Provider	Goldman Sachs
Manager/Tenure	Raj Garigipati (3), Jamie McGregor (2)
Website	http://www.gsamfunds.com
Address	Goldman Sachs 200 West Stree New York NY 10282 United States
Phone Number	800-526-7384

PERFORMANCE

Ratings History

Date	Overall Rating	Risk Rating	Reward Rating
Q4-18	C-	C	C-
Q2-18	C	C+	C-
Q4-17	C	B-	C+
Q4-16	D	C-	D+
Q4-15			

Asset & Performance History

Date	NAV	1-Year Total Return
2017	35.65	35.45
2016	26.81	9.43
2015	24.97	
2014		
2013		
2012		

Total Assets: $1,609,677,020
Asset Allocation

Asset	%
Cash	0%
Stocks	100%
US Stocks	0%
Bonds	0%
US Bonds	0%
Other	0%

Services Offered:

Investment Strategy: The investment seeks to provide investment results that closely correspond, before fees and expenses, to the performance of the Goldman Sachs ActiveBeta® Emerging Markets Equity Index. The fund invests at least 80% of its assets (exclusive of collateral held from securities lending) in securities included in its underlying index, in depositary receipts representing securities included in its underlying index and in underlying stocks in respect of depositary receipts included in its underlying index. The index is designed to deliver exposure to equity securities of emerging market issuers. **Top Holdings:** Tencent Holdings Ltd   Samsung Electronics Co Ltd   Taiwan Semiconductor Manufacturing Co Ltd   Alibaba Group Holding Ltd ADR   China Construction Bank Corp H

FlexShares iBoxx 3-Year Target Duration TIPS Index Fund   C-   HOLD

Ticker	Traded On	NAV	Total Assets ($)	Dividend Yield (TTM)	Turnover Ratio	Expense Ratio
TDTT	NYSE Arca	23.82	$1,592,021,004	2.79		0.18

Ratings
Reward   D+
Risk   C
Recent Upgrade/Downgrade   Down

Fund Information
Fund Type   Exchange Traded Funds
Category   US Fixed Income
Sub-Category   Inflation-Protected Bond
Prospectus Objective   Govt Bond - Treasury
Inception Date   Sep-11
Open to New Investments   Y

Prices
Price (as of 12/31/2018)   23.82
52-Week High   24.41
52-Week Low   23.71

Total Returns (%)

3-Month	6-Month	1-Year	3-Year	5-Year
-0.09	-0.39	0.12	3.58	1.74

3-Year Standard Deviation   1.51
Effective Duration

Valuation
Premium/Discount (1-Year Average)   -0.02

Company Information
Provider   Flexshares Trust
Manager/Tenure   Michael R. Chico (7), Brandon P. Ferguson (7), Daniel J. Personette (7)
Website   http://www.flexshares.com
Address   50 South LaSalle Street Chicago, Illinois 60603 Chicago Illinois 60603 United States
Phone Number   855-353-9383

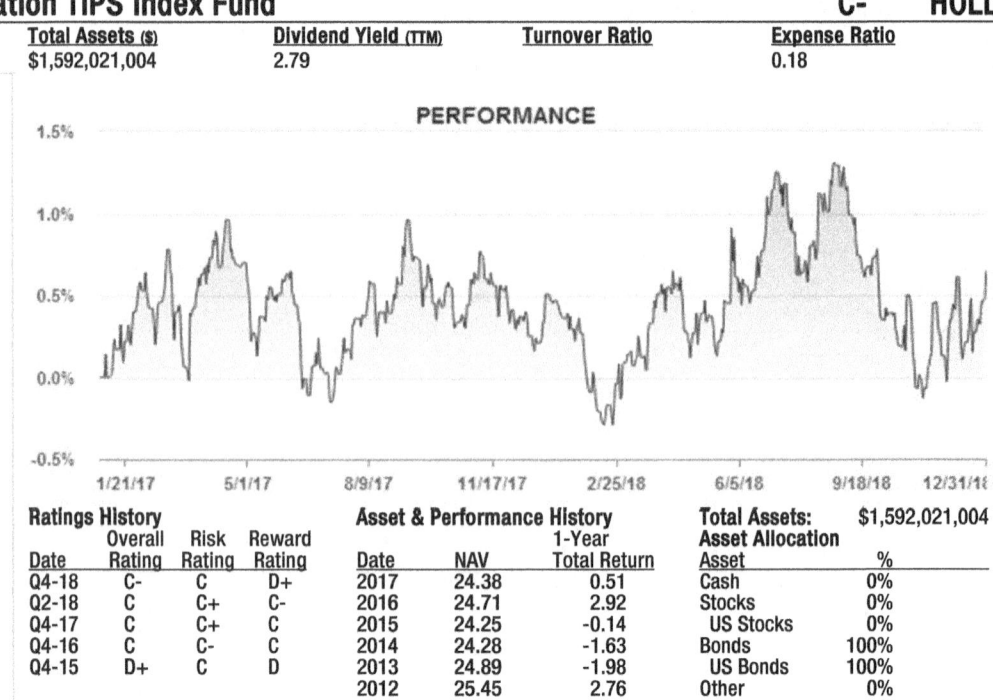

PERFORMANCE

Ratings History

Date	Overall Rating	Risk Rating	Reward Rating
Q4-18	C-	C	D+
Q2-18	C	C+	C-
Q4-17	C	C+	C
Q4-16	C	C-	C
Q4-15	D+	C	D

Asset & Performance History

Date	NAV	1-Year Total Return
2017	24.38	0.51
2016	24.71	2.92
2015	24.25	-0.14
2014	24.28	-1.63
2013	24.89	-1.98
2012	25.45	2.76

Total Assets: $1,592,021,004

Asset Allocation

Asset	%
Cash	0%
Stocks	0%
US Stocks	0%
Bonds	100%
US Bonds	100%
Other	0%

Services Offered:

Investment Strategy: The investment seeks to provide investment results that, before fees and expenses, correspond generally to the price and yield performance of the iBoxx 3-Year Target Duration TIPS Index. Under normal circumstances, the fund will invest at least 80% of its total assets (exclusive of collateral held from securities lending) in the securities of the underlying index. The underlying index reflects the performance of a selection of inflation protected public obligations of the U.S. Treasury, commonly known as "TIPS," with a targeted average modified adjusted duration, as defined by the underlying index, of approximately three years. The fund is non-diversified. **Top Holdings:** United States Treasury Notes 0.12% United States Treasury Notes 0.12% United States Treasury Notes 0.12% United States Treasury Notes 0.12% United States Treasury Notes 0.62%

United States Oil Fund, LP   D+   SELL

Ticker	Traded On	NAV	Total Assets ($)	Dividend Yield (TTM)	Turnover Ratio	Expense Ratio
USO	NYSE Arca	9.59	$1,570,429,872	0	0	0.77

Ratings
Reward   D+
Risk   D+
Recent Upgrade/Downgrade   Down

Fund Information
Fund Type   Exchange Traded Funds
Category   Commodities Specified
Sub-Category   Commodities Energy
Prospectus Objective   Natl Res
Inception Date   Apr-06
Open to New Investments   Y

Prices
Price (as of 12/31/2018)   9.66
52-Week High   16.08
52-Week Low   9.29

Total Returns (%)

3-Month	6-Month	1-Year	3-Year	5-Year
-39.73	-36.01	-20.64	-13.05	-72.79

3-Year Standard Deviation   28.92
Effective Duration

Valuation
Premium/Discount (1-Year Average)   -0.10

Company Information
Provider   USCF Investments
Manager/Tenure   Management Team (12)
Website   http://www.uscfinvestments.com
Address   USCF 1290 Broadway, Suite 1100 Denver CO 80203 United States
Phone Number

PERFORMANCE

Ratings History

Date	Overall Rating	Risk Rating	Reward Rating
Q4-18	D+	D+	D+
Q2-18	C	D+	C
Q4-17	D	D	D+
Q4-16	D-	D-	D-
Q4-15	D-	D-	D-

Asset & Performance History

Date	NAV	1-Year Total Return
2017	12.08	3.18
2016	11.71	6.17
2015	11.02	-45.29
2014	20.15	-42.79
2013	35.23	5.41
2012	33.42	-12.22

Total Assets: $1,570,429,872

Asset Allocation

Asset	%
Cash	35%
Stocks	0%
US Stocks	0%
Bonds	19%
US Bonds	19%
Other	46%

Services Offered:

Investment Strategy: The investment seeks the daily changes in percentage terms of its shares' per share net asset value ("NAV") to reflect the daily changes in percentage terms of the spot price of light, sweet crude oil delivered to Cushing, Oklahoma, as measured by the daily changes in the price of a specified short-term futures contract on light, sweet crude oil called the "Benchmark Oil Futures Contract," less USO's expenses.
USO seeks to achieve its investment objective by investing primarily in futures contracts for light, sweet crude oil, other types of crude oil, diesel-heating oil, gasoline, natural gas, and other petroleum-based fuels. **Top Holdings:** Future Contract On Wti Crude Future Jan19 United States Treasury Bills United States Treasury Bills United States Treasury Bills United States Treasury Bills

Principal U.S. Mega-Cap Multi-Factor Index ETF   C-   HOLD

Ticker	Traded On	NAV	Total Assets ($)	Dividend Yield (TTM)	Turnover Ratio	Expense Ratio
USMC	NAS CM	25.11	$1,563,047,304	1.68	40	0.12

Ratings
Reward   C
Risk   C-
Recent Upgrade/Downgrade

Fund Information
Fund Type   Exchange Traded Funds
Category   US Equity Large Cap Blend
Sub-Category   Large Blend
Prospectus Objective   Growth & Inc
Inception Date   Oct-17
Open to New Investments   Y

Prices
Price (as of 12/31/2018)   25.11
52-Week High   28.47
52-Week Low   23.78

Total Returns (%)

3-Month	6-Month	1-Year	3-Year	5-Year
-10.69	-2.02	-1.76		

3-Year Standard Deviation
Effective Duration

Valuation
Premium/Discount (1-Year Average)   0.37

Company Information
Provider   Principal Funds
Manager/Tenure   Paul S. Kim (1), Mark R. Nebelung (1), Jeffrey A. Schwarte (1)
Website   http://www.principalfunds.com
Address   Principal Funds 30 Dan Road Canton MA 2021 United States
Phone Number   800-787-1621

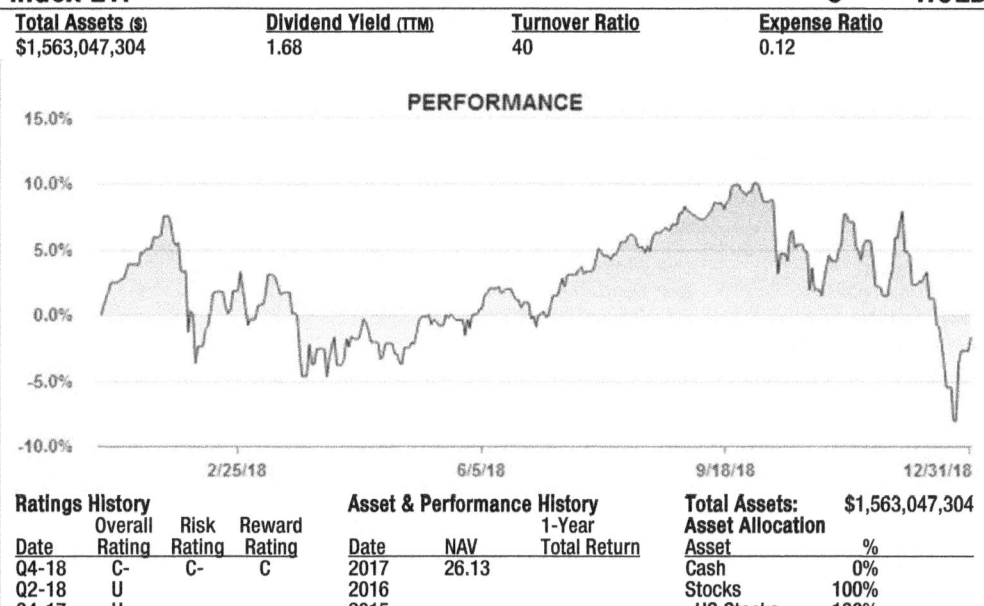

PERFORMANCE

Ratings History

Date	Overall Rating	Risk Rating	Reward Rating
Q4-18	C-	C-	C
Q2-18	U		
Q4-17	U		
Q4-16			
Q4-15			

Asset & Performance History

Date	NAV	1-Year Total Return
2017	26.13	
2016		
2015		
2014		
2013		
2012		

Total Assets: $1,563,047,304

Asset Allocation

Asset	%
Cash	0%
Stocks	100%
US Stocks	100%
Bonds	0%
US Bonds	0%
Other	0%

Services Offered:

Investment Strategy: The investment seeks to provide investment results that closely correspond, before expenses, to the performance of the Nasdaq U.S. Mega Cap Select Leaders Index (the "index"). Under normal circumstances, the fund invests at least 80% of its net assets, plus any borrowings for investment purposes, in equity securities that compose the index at the time of purchase. The index uses a quantitative model designed to identify equity securities of companies in the Nasdaq US 500 Large Cap Index (the "parent index") that have the largest market capitalizations, with higher weights given to less volatile securities. **Top Holdings:** Procter & Gamble Co   Verizon Communications Inc   McDonald's Corp   Merck & Co Inc   Apple Inc

---

ETFMG Prime Cyber Security ETF   C   HOLD

Ticker	Traded On	NAV	Total Assets ($)	Dividend Yield (TTM)	Turnover Ratio	Expense Ratio
HACK	NYSE Arca	33.85	$1,560,598,680	0.01	41	0.64

Ratings
Reward   C
Risk   C
Recent Upgrade/Downgrade

Fund Information
Fund Type   Exchange Traded Funds
Category   Technology Sector Equity
Sub-Category   Technology
Prospectus Objective   Growth
Inception Date   Nov-14
Open to New Investments   Y

Prices
Price (as of 12/31/2018)   33.70
52-Week High   40.58
52-Week Low   30.95

Total Returns (%)

3-Month	6-Month	1-Year	3-Year	5-Year
-14.24	-9.24	7.06	32.19	

3-Year Standard Deviation   16.29
Effective Duration

Valuation
Premium/Discount (1-Year Average)   -0.01

Company Information
Provider   Pure Funds
Manager/Tenure   Samuel R. Masucci (0), James B. Francis (0), Devin Ryder (0), 1 other
Website   http://www.etfmgfunds.com
Address
Phone Number

PERFORMANCE

Ratings History

Date	Overall Rating	Risk Rating	Reward Rating
Q4-18	C	C	C
Q2-18	C	C	B-
Q4-17	C	C	C
Q4-16	C-	C-	C
Q4-15	U		

Asset & Performance History

Date	NAV	1-Year Total Return
2017	31.68	19.6
2016	26.49	2.6
2015	25.98	-1.66
2014	26.42	
2013		
2012		

Total Assets: $1,560,598,680

Asset Allocation

Asset	%
Cash	0%
Stocks	100%
US Stocks	87%
Bonds	0%
US Bonds	0%
Other	0%

Services Offered:

Investment Strategy: The investment seeks investment results that, before fees and expenses, correspond generally to the price and yield performance of the Prime Cyber Defense Index. The fund invests at least 80% of its total assets in the component securities of the index and in ADRs and GDRs based on the component securities in the index. The index tracks the performance of the exchange-listed equity securities of companies across the globe that (i) engage in providing cyber security applications or services as a vital component of its overall business or (ii) provide hardware or software for cyber security activities as a vital component of its overall business. **Top Holdings:** Cisco Systems Inc   FireEye Inc   Imperva Inc   Symantec Corp   Juniper Networks Inc

ProShares UltraShort 20+ Year Treasury   C   HOLD

Ticker	Traded On	NAV	Total Assets ($)	Dividend Yield (TTM)	Turnover Ratio	Expense Ratio
TBT	NYSE Arca	35.36	$1,553,765,402	0.51		0.89

Ratings
Reward	D+
Risk	C
Recent Upgrade/Downgrade	Up

Fund Information
Fund Type	Exchange Traded Funds
Category	Trading Tools
Sub-Category	Trading--Inverse Debt
Prospectus Objective	Govt Bond - Treasury
Inception Date	Apr-08
Open to New Investments	Y

Prices
Price (as of 12/31/2018)	35.13
52-Week High	41.62
52-Week Low	33.78

Total Returns (%)
3-Month	6-Month	1-Year	3-Year	5-Year
-8.32	-1.05	5.85	-18.80	-54.99

3-Year Standard Deviation	19.42
Effective Duration	

Valuation
Premium/Discount (1-Year Average)	0.20

Company Information
Provider	ProShares
Manager/Tenure	Michelle Liu (10), Jeffrey Ploshnick (2)
Website	http://www.proshares.com
Address	ProShares 7501 Wisconsin Avenue, Suite 1000 Bethesda MD 20814 United States
Phone Number	866-776-5125

PERFORMANCE

Ratings History
Date	Overall Rating	Risk Rating	Reward Rating
Q4-18	C	C	D+
Q2-18	C-	D+	D+
Q4-17	D	D	D
Q4-16	D	D-	D
Q4-15	D	D	D

Asset & Performance History
Date	NAV	1-Year Total Return
2017	33.72	-16.82
2016	40.54	-7.77
2015	43.96	-5.42
2014	46.48	-41.39
2013	79.31	26.55
2012	62.67	-13.29

Total Assets: $1,553,765,402
Asset Allocation
Asset	%
Cash	206%
Stocks	0%
US Stocks	0%
Bonds	3%
US Bonds	3%
Other	-110%

Services Offered:

Investment Strategy: The investment seeks daily investment results, before fees and expenses, that correspond to two times the inverse (-2x) of the daily performance of the ICE U.S. Treasury 20+ Year Bond Index. The fund invests in financial instruments that ProShare Advisors believes, in combination, should produce daily returns consistent with the fund's investment objective. The index includes publicly-issued U.S. Treasury securities that have a remaining maturity greater than twenty years and have $300 million or more of outstanding face value, excluding amounts held by the Federal Reserve. The fund is non-diversified. **Top Holdings:** Ice 20+ Year U.S. Treasury Index Swap Bank Of America Na   Ice 20+ Year U.S. Treasury Index Swap Goldman Sachs International   Ice 20+ Year U.S. Treasury Index Swap Societe Generale   Ice 20+ Year U.S. Treasury Index Swap Citibank Na   United States Treasury Bills

---

UBS AG FI Enhanced Global High Yield ETN   C-   HOLD

Ticker	Traded On	NAV	Total Assets ($)	Dividend Yield (TTM)	Turnover Ratio	Expense Ratio
FIHD	NYSE Arca	141.86	$1,542,107,237	0		0.8

Ratings
Reward	D+
Risk	C-
Recent Upgrade/Downgrade	

Fund Information
Fund Type	Exchange Traded Funds
Category	Global Equity Large Cap
Sub-Category	World Large Stock
Prospectus Objective	Convertible Bond
Inception Date	Feb-16
Open to New Investments	Y

Prices
Price (as of 12/31/2018)	141.51
52-Week High	190.81
52-Week Low	129.64

Total Returns (%)
3-Month	6-Month	1-Year	3-Year	5-Year
-18.27	-9.67	-17.41		

3-Year Standard Deviation	
Effective Duration	

Valuation
Premium/Discount (1-Year Average)	0.13

Company Information
Provider	UBS Group AG
Manager/Tenure	No Manager (2)
Website	http://www.ubs.com
Address	Bahnhofstrasse 45 Zurich 8098 Switzerland
Phone Number	412-037-1952

PERFORMANCE

Ratings History
Date	Overall Rating	Risk Rating	Reward Rating
Q4-18	C-	C-	D+
Q2-18	C-	C-	C-
Q4-17	C-	B	C
Q4-16	U		
Q4-15			

Asset & Performance History
Date	NAV	1-Year Total Return
2017	171.78	37.38
2016	125.18	
2015		
2014		
2013		
2012		

Total Assets: $1,542,107,237
Asset Allocation
Asset	%
Cash	%
Stocks	%
US Stocks	%
Bonds	%
US Bonds	%
Other	%

Services Offered:

Investment Strategy: The investment seeks a return linked to the MSCI World High Dividend Yield USD Gross Total Return Index.
The ETN is a series of FI Enhanced ETNs. The Securities are senior unsecured debt securities issued by UBS AG. The Securities are designed to provide a two times leveraged long exposure to the performance of the index compounded on a quarterly basis, reduced by the Accrued Fees. The index is designed to track the performance of large- and mid-cap stocks (excluding REITS) across 23 developed markets countries tracked by the MSCI World Index with higher than average dividend yields that are potentially both sustainable and persistent. **Top Holdings:**

Robo Global® Robotics and Automation Index ETF   C-   HOLD

Ticker	Traded On	NAV	Total Assets ($)	Dividend Yield (TTM)	Turnover Ratio	Expense Ratio
ROBO	NAS CM	32.72	$1,533,735,736	0.03	30	0.95

Ratings
Reward   C-
Risk   C
Recent Upgrade/Downgrade   Down

Fund Information
Fund Type   Exchange Traded Funds
Category   Global Eq Mid/Small Cap
Sub-Category   World Small/Mid Stock
Prospectus Objective Growth
Inception Date   Oct-13
Open to New Investments Y

Prices
Price (as of 12/31/2018)   32.55
52-Week High   46.16
52-Week Low   30.86

Total Returns (%)

3-Month	6-Month	1-Year	3-Year	5-Year
-21.90	-17.70	-20.43	35.18	22.57

3-Year Standard Deviation   16.28
Effective Duration

Valuation
Premium/Discount (1-Year Average)   -0.13

Company Information
Provider   Robo Global
Manager/Tenure   Denise M. Krisko (3), Rafael Zayas (0)
Website   http://www.roboglobaletfs.com
Address   Robo Global United States
Phone Number

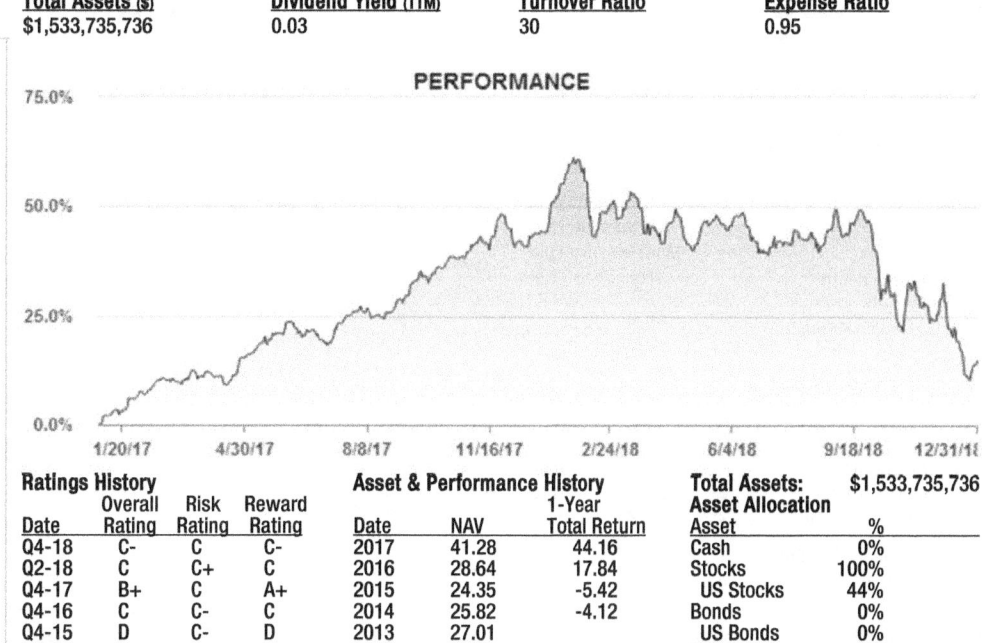

Ratings History

Date	Overall Rating	Risk Rating	Reward Rating
Q4-18	C-	C	C-
Q2-18	C	C+	C
Q4-17	B+	C	A+
Q4-16	C	C-	C
Q4-15	D	C-	D

Asset & Performance History

Date	NAV	1-Year Total Return
2017	41.28	44.16
2016	28.64	17.84
2015	24.35	-5.42
2014	25.82	-4.12
2013	27.01	
2012		

Total Assets: $1,533,735,736
Asset Allocation

Asset	%
Cash	0%
Stocks	100%
US Stocks	44%
Bonds	0%
US Bonds	0%
Other	0%

Services Offered:

Investment Strategy: The investment seeks to provide investment results that, before fees and expenses, correspond generally to the price and yield performance of the ROBO Global® Robotics and Automation Index. The fund will normally invest at least 80% of its total assets in securities of the index or in depositary receipts representing securities of the index. The index is designed to measure the performance of robotics-related and/or automation-related companies. The fund may invest up to 20% of its assets in investments that are not included in the index, but which the Adviser and Sub-Adviser believe will help it track the index. It is non-diversified. **Top Holdings:** Nabtesco Corp Daifuku Co Ltd Zebra Technologies Corp YASKAWA Electric Corp OMRON Corp

---

iShares Global Energy ETF   C   HOLD

Ticker	Traded On	NAV	Total Assets ($)	Dividend Yield (TTM)	Turnover Ratio	Expense Ratio
IXC	NYSE Arca	29.43	$1,531,115,760	3.16	4	0.47

Ratings
Reward   C
Risk   C
Recent Upgrade/Downgrade   Down

Fund Information
Fund Type   Exchange Traded Funds
Category   Energy Sector Equity
Sub-Category   Equity Energy
Prospectus Objective Natl Res
Inception Date   Nov-01
Open to New Investments Y

Prices
Price (as of 12/31/2018)   29.35
52-Week High   39.39
52-Week Low   27.97

Total Returns (%)

3-Month	6-Month	1-Year	3-Year	5-Year
-21.61	-18.69	-14.59	15.31	-20.58

3-Year Standard Deviation   16.32
Effective Duration

Valuation
Premium/Discount (1-Year Average)   -0.06

Company Information
Provider   iShares
Manager/Tenure   Diane Hsiung (10), Greg Savage (10),
                  Jennifer Hsui (6), 3 others
Website   http://www.ishares.com
Address   iShares 400 Howard Street San
                  Francisco CA 94105 United States
Phone Number   800-474-2737

Ratings History

Date	Overall Rating	Risk Rating	Reward Rating
Q4-18	C	C	C
Q2-18	C+	C	C+
Q4-17	C	C	C
Q4-16	C-	D	C
Q4-15	D+	D+	D+

Asset & Performance History

Date	NAV	1-Year Total Return
2017	35.55	5.45
2016	34.83	28.03
2015	28.02	-22.09
2014	37.2	-11.6
2013	43.2	16.23
2012	38.18	2.56

Total Assets: $1,531,115,760
Asset Allocation

Asset	%
Cash	1%
Stocks	99%
US Stocks	53%
Bonds	0%
US Bonds	0%
Other	0%

Services Offered: CashInvestment Plan

Investment Strategy: The investment seeks to track the S&P Global 1200 Energy IndexTM. The fund generally invests at least 90% of its assets in securities of the underlying index and in depositary receipts representing securities of the underlying index. It may invest the remainder of its assets in certain futures, options and swap contracts, cash and cash equivalents, as well as in securities not included in the underlying index. The index measures the performance of companies that the index provider deems to be part of the energy sector of the economy and that the index provider believes are important to global markets. The fund is non-diversified. **Top Holdings:** Exxon Mobil Corp Chevron Corp Total SA Royal Dutch Shell PLC Class A BP PLC

Invesco National AMT-Free Municipal Bond ETF

C   HOLD

Ticker	Traded On	NAV	Total Assets ($)	Dividend Yield (TTM)	Turnover Ratio	Expense Ratio
PZA	NYSE Arca	25.02	$1,519,896,588	3.22		0.28

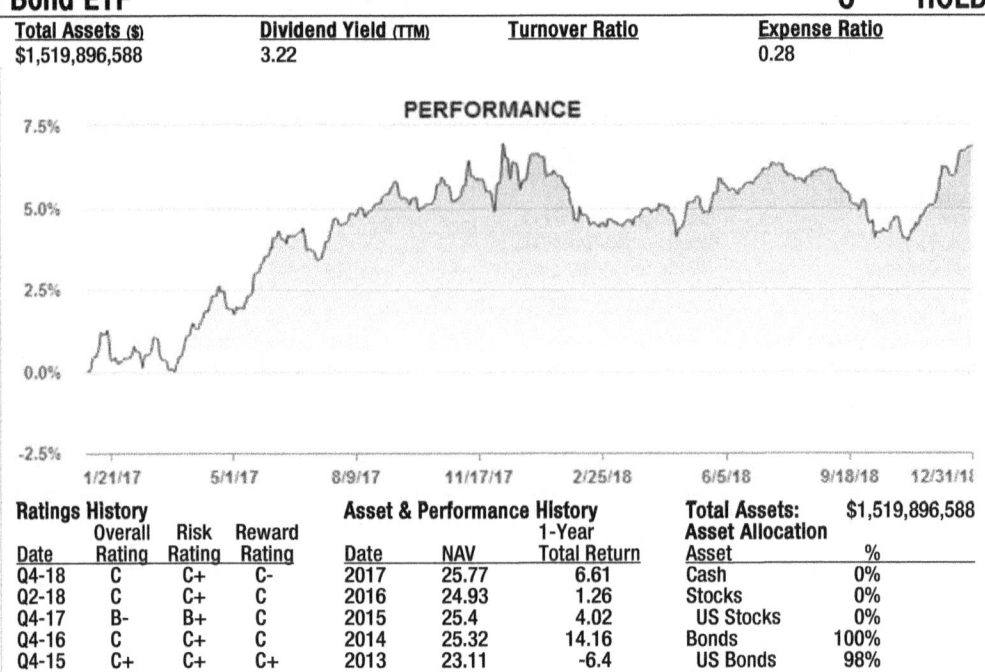

Ratings
Reward	C-
Risk	C+
Recent Upgrade/Downgrade	

Fund Information
Fund Type	Exchange Traded Funds
Category	US Muni Fixed Inc
Sub-Category	Muni National Long
Prospectus Objective	Muni Bond - Natl
Inception Date	Oct-07
Open to New Investments	Y

Prices
Price (as of 12/31/2018)	24.98
52-Week High	25.81
52-Week Low	24.38

Total Returns (%)
3-Month	6-Month	1-Year	3-Year	5-Year
1.57	0.88	0.22	8.20	28.50

3-Year Standard Deviation	3.7
Effective Duration	8.04

Valuation
Premium/Discount (1-Year Average)	-0.11

Company Information
Provider	Invesco
Manager/Tenure	Philip Fang (11), Peter Hubbard (11), Jeffrey W. Kernagis (11), 2 others
Website	http://www.invesco.com/us
Address	Invesco 11 Greenway Plaza, Ste. 2500 Houston TX 77046 United States
Phone Number	800-659-1005

Ratings History

Date	Overall Rating	Risk Rating	Reward Rating
Q4-18	C	C+	C-
Q2-18	C	C+	C
Q4-17	B-	B+	C
Q4-16	C	C+	C
Q4-15	C+	C+	C+

Asset & Performance History

Date	NAV	1-Year Total Return
2017	25.77	6.61
2016	24.93	1.26
2015	25.4	4.02
2014	25.32	14.16
2013	23.11	-6.4
2012	25.71	9.8

Total Assets: $1,519,896,588

Asset Allocation

Asset	%
Cash	0%
Stocks	0%
US Stocks	0%
Bonds	100%
US Bonds	98%
Other	0%

Services Offered:

Investment Strategy: The investment seeks to track the investment results (before fees and expenses) of the ICE BofAML National Long-Term Core Plus Municipal Securities Index (the "underlying index"). The fund generally will invest at least 80% of its total assets in municipal securities that comprise the underlying index and that also are exempt from the federal alternative minimum tax ("AMT"). The underlying index is composed of U.S. dollar-denominated, investment grade, tax-exempt debt publicly issued by U.S. states and territories or their political subdivisions, in the U.S. domestic market with a term of at least 15 years remaining to final maturity. **Top Holdings:** CHICAGO ILL 5% HILLSBOROUGH CNTY FLA AVIATION AUTH 5% GRAND PARKWAY TRANSN CORP TEX SYS 5% JASPER ALA 5% PORT AUTH N Y & N J 5%

Invesco S&P 500® Equal Weight Technology ETF

C   HOLD

Ticker	Traded On	NAV	Total Assets ($)	Dividend Yield (TTM)	Turnover Ratio	Expense Ratio
RYT	NYSE Arca	140.89	$1,517,736,085	0.88		0.4

Ratings
Reward	C
Risk	C+
Recent Upgrade/Downgrade	Down

Fund Information
Fund Type	Exchange Traded Funds
Category	Technology Sector Equity
Sub-Category	Technology
Prospectus Objective	Technology
Inception Date	Nov-06
Open to New Investments	Y

Prices
Price (as of 12/31/2018)	140.83
52-Week High	170.41
52-Week Low	131.48

Total Returns (%)
3-Month	6-Month	1-Year	3-Year	5-Year
-15.91	-11.39	-0.57	57.38	93.16

3-Year Standard Deviation	13.38
Effective Duration	

Valuation
Premium/Discount (1-Year Average)	0.00

Company Information
Provider	Invesco
Manager/Tenure	Peter Hubbard (0), Michael Jeanette (0), Jonathan Nixon (0), 1 other
Website	http://www.invesco.com/us
Address	Invesco 11 Greenway Plaza, Ste. 2500 Houston TX 77046 United States
Phone Number	800-659-1005

Ratings History

Date	Overall Rating	Risk Rating	Reward Rating
Q4-18	C	C+	C
Q2-18	B	C-	B+
Q4-17	A-	B	A+
Q4-16	C+	C+	B-
Q4-15	C+	C+	C

Asset & Performance History

Date	NAV	1-Year Total Return
2017	142.97	32.8
2016	108.47	18.57
2015	92.33	2.95
2014	90.76	19.2
2013	77.06	40.17
2012	55.48	12.24

Total Assets: $1,517,736,085

Asset Allocation

Asset	%
Cash	0%
Stocks	100%
US Stocks	99%
Bonds	0%
US Bonds	0%
Other	0%

Services Offered:

Investment Strategy: The investment seeks to track the investment results (before fees and expenses) of the S&P 500® Equal Weight Information Technology Index (the "underlying index"). The fund generally will invest at least 90% of its total assets in the securities that comprise the underlying index. The underlying index is an equal-weighted version of the S&P 500® Information Technology Index. Strictly in accordance with its guidelines and mandated procedures, the index provider compiles, maintains and calculates the underlying index, which is comprised of common stocks of companies in the information technology sector of the S&P 500® Index. The fund is non-diversified. **Top Holdings:** Red Hat Inc Xilinx Inc Symantec Corp Intel Corp Keysight Technologies Inc

ProShares UltraPro S&P500   C   HOLD

Ticker	Traded On	NAV
UPRO	NYSE Arca	34.73

Total Assets ($)	Dividend Yield (TTM)	Turnover Ratio	Expense Ratio
$1,515,857,719	0.24		0.92

Ratings
Reward	C
Risk	C
Recent Upgrade/Downgrade	Down

Fund Information
Fund Type	Exchange Traded Funds
Category	Trading Tools
Sub-Category	Trading--Leveraged Equity
Prospectus Objective	Growth
Inception Date	Jun-09
Open to New Investments	Y

Prices
Price (as of 12/31/2018)	34.78
52-Week High	58.37
52-Week Low	29.00

Total Returns (%)
3-Month	6-Month	1-Year	3-Year	5-Year
-39.82	-26.18	-24.91	67.31	119.24

3-Year Standard Deviation	29.06
Effective Duration	

Valuation
Premium/Discount (1-Year Average)	0.12

Company Information
Provider	ProShares
Manager/Tenure	Michael Neches (5), Devin Sullivan (0)
Website	http://www.proshares.com
Address	ProShares 7501 Wisconsin Avenue, Suite 1000 Bethesda MD 20814 United States
Phone Number	866-776-5125

PERFORMANCE

Ratings History

Date	Overall Rating	Risk Rating	Reward Rating
Q4-18	C	C	C
Q2-18	C	C	C
Q4-17	B+	C	A+
Q4-16	C	C	C
Q4-15	C+	B	C

Asset & Performance History

Date	NAV	1-Year Total Return
2017	46.5	71.26
2016	27.15	30.1
2015	20.9	-5.04
2014	22.08	38
2013	16.04	118.55
2012	7.35	46.28

Total Assets: $1,515,857,719

Asset Allocation
Asset	%
Cash	-200%
Stocks	300%
US Stocks	298%
Bonds	0%
US Bonds	0%
Other	0%

Services Offered:

Investment Strategy: The investment seeks daily investment results, before fees and expenses, that correspond to three times (3x) the daily performance of the S&P 500® Index. The fund invests in financial instruments that ProShare Advisors believes, in combination, should produce daily returns consistent with the fund's investment objective. The index is a measure of large-cap U.S. stock market performance. The fund is non-diversified. **Top Holdings:** S&P 500 Index Swap Credit Suisse International S&P 500 Index Swap Societe Generale S&P 500 Index Swap Bnp Paribas S&P 500 Index Swap Citibank Na S&P 500 Index Swap Bank Of America Na

---

First Trust Morningstar Dividend Leaders Index Fund   C   HOLD

Ticker	Traded On	NAV
FDL	NYSE Arca	27.24

Total Assets ($)	Dividend Yield (TTM)	Turnover Ratio	Expense Ratio
$1,513,042,374	3.39	43	0.45

Ratings
Reward	C
Risk	C
Recent Upgrade/Downgrade	Down

Fund Information
Fund Type	Exchange Traded Funds
Category	US Equity Large Cap Value
Sub-Category	Large Value
Prospectus Objective	Growth & Inc
Inception Date	Mar-06
Open to New Investments	Y

Prices
Price (as of 12/31/2018)	27.24
52-Week High	31.14
52-Week Low	25.99

Total Returns (%)
3-Month	6-Month	1-Year	3-Year	5-Year
-7.79	-2.45	-5.86	27.20	47.56

3-Year Standard Deviation	8.14
Effective Duration	

Valuation
Premium/Discount (1-Year Average)	0.01

Company Information
Provider	First Trust
Manager/Tenure	Jon C. Erickson (12), Daniel J. Lindquist (12), David G. McGarel (12), 3 others
Website	http://www.ftportfolios.com/
Address	First Trust 120 E. Liberty Drive, Suite 400 Wheaton IL 60187 United States
Phone Number	800-621-1675

PERFORMANCE

Ratings History

Date	Overall Rating	Risk Rating	Reward Rating
Q4-18	C	C	C
Q2-18	C+	C	B
Q4-17	B	A	B-
Q4-16	B	C	B
Q4-15	B-	C	B

Asset & Performance History

Date	NAV	1-Year Total Return
2017	30.06	11.97
2016	27.74	20.68
2015	23.69	2.71
2014	23.94	12.94
2013	21.93	22.76
2012	18.46	9.22

Total Assets: $1,513,042,374

Asset Allocation
Asset	%
Cash	0%
Stocks	100%
US Stocks	100%
Bonds	0%
US Bonds	0%
Other	0%

Services Offered:

Investment Strategy: The investment seeks investment results that correspond generally to the price and yield (before the fund's fees and expenses) of an equity index called the Morningstar® Dividend Leaders IndexSM. The fund will normally invest at least 90% of its net assets (including investment borrowings) in common stocks that comprise the index. The objective of the index is to offer investors a benchmark for dividend portfolios as well as a means to invest in a portfolio of stocks that have a consistent record of growing dividends as well as the ability to sustain them. It is non-diversified. **Top Holdings:** AT&T Inc Exxon Mobil Corp Verizon Communications Inc Chevron Corp Pfizer Inc

Vanguard Communication Services Index Fund ETF Shares   C+   HOLD

Ticker	Traded On	NAV	Total Assets ($)	Dividend Yield (TTM)	Turnover Ratio	Expense Ratio
VOX	NYSE Arca		$1,509,685,264	3.58	84	0.1

Ratings
Reward   B
Risk   C-
Recent Upgrade/Downgrade   Up

Fund Information
Fund Type   Exchange Traded Funds
Category   Communications Sector Equity
Sub-Category   Communications
Prospectus Objective   Comm
Inception Date   Sep-04
Open to New Investments   Y

Prices
Price (as of 12/31/2018)   74.07
52-Week High   92.99
52-Week Low   69.56

Total Returns (%)

3-Month	6-Month	1-Year	3-Year	5-Year
-14.55	-12.92	-16.95	-3.87	2.68

3-Year Standard Deviation   11.37
Effective Duration

Valuation
Premium/Discount (1-Year Average)   0.05

Company Information
Provider   Vanguard
Manager/Tenure   Walter Nejman (2), Awais Khan (1)
Website   http://www.vanguard.com
Address   Vanguard 100 Vanguard Boulevard
                     Malvern PA 19355 United States
Phone Number   877-662-7447

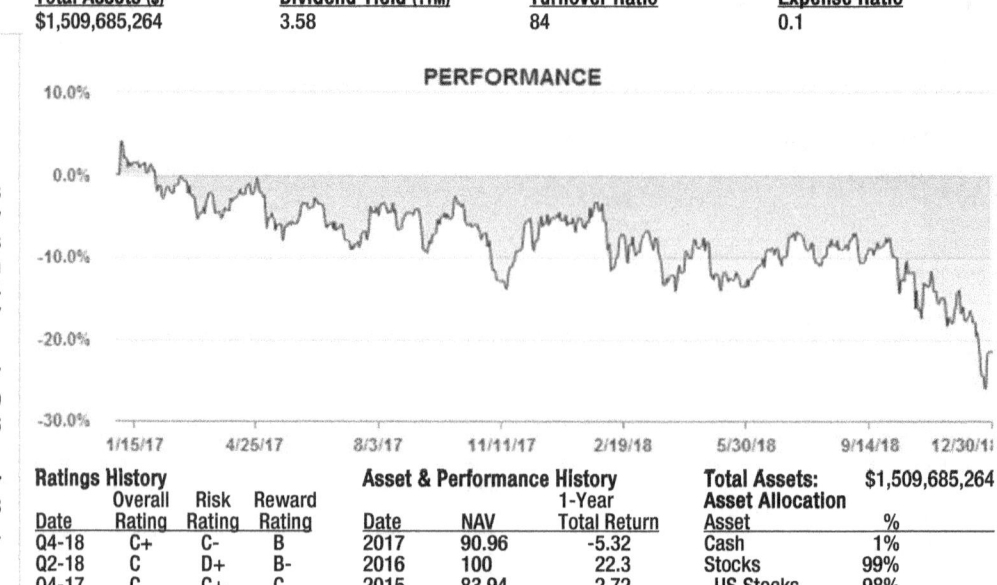

Ratings History

Date	Overall Rating	Risk Rating	Reward Rating
Q4-18	C+	C-	B
Q2-18	C	D+	B-
Q4-17	C	C+	C
Q4-16	B-	C	B
Q4-15	C+	C	B-

Asset & Performance History

Date	NAV	1-Year Total Return
2017	90.96	-5.32
2016	100	22.3
2015	83.94	2.72
2014	84.73	3.98
2013	83.66	24.31
2012	69.97	16.53

Total Assets: $1,509,685,264

Asset Allocation

Asset	%
Cash	1%
Stocks	99%
US Stocks	98%
Bonds	0%
US Bonds	0%
Other	0%

Services Offered:

Investment Strategy: The investment seeks to track the performance of a benchmark index. The fund employs an indexing investment approach designed to track the performance of the MSCI US Investable Market Index (IMI)/Communication Services 25/50, an index made up of stocks of large, mid-size, and small U.S. companies within the communication services sector, as classified under the GICS. The Advisor attempts to replicate the target index by seeking to invest all, or substantially all, of its assets in the stocks that make up the index, in order to hold each stock in approximately the same proportion as its weighting in the index. It is non-diversified. **Top Holdings:** Facebook Inc A   Alphabet Inc Class C   Alphabet Inc A   AT&T Inc   Comcast Corp Class A

Invesco BuyBack Achievers ETF   C   HOLD

Ticker	Traded On	NAV	Total Assets ($)	Dividend Yield (TTM)	Turnover Ratio	Expense Ratio
PKW	NAS CM	52.20	$1,509,527,468	0.99	66	0.63

Ratings
Reward   C
Risk   C
Recent Upgrade/Downgrade

Fund Information
Fund Type   Exchange Traded Funds
Category   US Equity Large Cap Blend
Sub-Category   Large Blend
Prospectus Objective   Unaligned
Inception Date   Dec-06
Open to New Investments   Y

Prices
Price (as of 12/31/2018)   52.17
52-Week High   63.28
52-Week Low   49.25

Total Returns (%)

3-Month	6-Month	1-Year	3-Year	5-Year
-13.80	-7.81	-10.42	19.05	28.46

3-Year Standard Deviation   10.79
Effective Duration

Valuation
Premium/Discount (1-Year Average)   0.03

Company Information
Provider   Invesco
Manager/Tenure   Peter Hubbard (11), Michael Jeanette
                     (10), Tony Seisser (4), 1 other
Website   http://www.invesco.com/us
Address   Invesco 11 Greenway Plaza, Ste. 2500
                     Houston TX 77046 United States
Phone Number   800-659-1005

Ratings History

Date	Overall Rating	Risk Rating	Reward Rating
Q4-18	C	C	C
Q2-18	C	C-	C
Q4-17	B	B	B-
Q4-16	C+	C-	B-
Q4-15	C+	B-	C+

Asset & Performance History

Date	NAV	1-Year Total Return
2017	58.98	17.8
2016	50.41	12.81
2015	45.44	-4.31
2014	48.02	12.77
2013	43.04	45.58
2012	29.77	13.8

Total Assets: $1,509,527,468

Asset Allocation

Asset	%
Cash	0%
Stocks	100%
US Stocks	99%
Bonds	0%
US Bonds	0%
Other	0%

Services Offered:

Investment Strategy: The investment seeks to track the investment results (before fees and expenses) of the NASDAQ US BuyBack AchieversTM Index. The fund generally will invest at least 90% of its total assets in common stocks that comprise the underlying index. The NASDAQ includes common stocks in the underlying index pursuant to a proprietary selection methodology that identifies a universe of "BuyBack Achievers TM". **Top Holdings:** Procter & Gamble Co   American Express Co   Walt Disney Co   CVS Health Corp   Walgreens Boots Alliance Inc

Invesco DWA Momentum ETF   C   HOLD

Ticker	Traded On	NAV	Total Assets ($)	Dividend Yield (TTM)	Turnover Ratio	Expense Ratio
PDP	NAS CM	48.49	$1,499,989,228	0.08	68	0.63

Ratings
Reward   C
Risk   C+
Recent Upgrade/Downgrade   Down

Fund Information
Fund Type   Exchange Traded Funds
Category   US Equity Mid Cap
Sub-Category   Mid-Cap Growth
Prospectus Objective   Growth
Inception Date   Mar-07
Open to New Investments   Y

Prices
Price (as of 12/31/2018)   48.47
52-Week High   60.08
52-Week Low   45.29

Total Returns (%)

3-Month	6-Month	1-Year	3-Year	5-Year
-18.27	-12.64	-5.88	18.62	34.74

3-Year Standard Deviation   11.92
Effective Duration

Valuation
Premium/Discount (1-Year Average)   0.01

Company Information
Provider   Invesco
Manager/Tenure   Peter Hubbard (11), Michael Jeanette (10), Tony Seisser (4), 1 other
Website   http://www.invesco.com/us
Address   Invesco 11 Greenway Plaza, Ste. 2500 Houston TX 77046 United States
Phone Number   800-659-1005

PERFORMANCE

Ratings History

Date	Overall Rating	Risk Rating	Reward Rating
Q4-18	C	C+	C
Q2-18	C+	C+	C+
Q4-17	B	B+	B-
Q4-16	C+	C+	C+
Q4-15	C+	B-	C+

Asset & Performance History

Date	NAV	1-Year Total Return
2017	51.61	23.36
2016	41.96	2.17
2015	41.4	1.3
2014	41.02	12.12
2013	36.64	31.79
2012	27.89	17.89

Total Assets: $1,499,989,228
Asset Allocation

Asset	%
Cash	0%
Stocks	100%
US Stocks	100%
Bonds	0%
US Bonds	0%
Other	0%

Services Offered:

Investment Strategy: The investment seeks to track the investment results (before fees and expenses) of the Dorsey Wright® Technical Leaders Index. The fund generally will invest at least 90% of its total assets in securities that comprise the underlying index. The underlying index is composed of approximately 100 securities from an eligible universe of approximately 1,000 securities of the largest constituents by market capitalization within the NASDAQ US Benchmark Index. **Top Holdings:** O'Reilly Automotive Inc   Domino's Pizza Inc   Rollins Inc   Apple Inc Mastercard Inc A

WisdomTree India Earnings Fund   C-   HOLD

Ticker	Traded On	NAV	Total Assets ($)	Dividend Yield (TTM)	Turnover Ratio	Expense Ratio
EPI	NYSE Arca	24.76	$1,499,351,812	1.15	22	0.84

Ratings
Reward   C-
Risk   C-
Recent Upgrade/Downgrade   Down

Fund Information
Fund Type   Exchange Traded Funds
Category   India Equity
Sub-Category   India Equity
Prospectus Objective   Foreign Stock
Inception Date   Feb-08
Open to New Investments   Y

Prices
Price (as of 12/31/2018)   24.80
52-Week High   29.40
52-Week Low   21.83

Total Returns (%)

3-Month	6-Month	1-Year	3-Year	5-Year
2.73	0.04	-10.44	27.31	50.85

3-Year Standard Deviation   19.45
Effective Duration

Valuation
Premium/Discount (1-Year Average)   -0.02

Company Information
Provider   WisdomTree
Manager/Tenure   Richard A. Brown (10), Thomas J. Durante (10), Karen Q. Wong (10)
Website   http://www.wisdomtree.com
Address   WisdomTree 245 Park Avenue, 35th floor New York NY 10167 United States
Phone Number   866-909-9473

PERFORMANCE

Ratings History

Date	Overall Rating	Risk Rating	Reward Rating
Q4-18	C-	C-	C-
Q2-18	C	C+	C
Q4-17	B-	C	B
Q4-16	C	C	C+
Q4-15	C	C	C-

Asset & Performance History

Date	NAV	1-Year Total Return
2017	27.97	39.01
2016	20.31	2.26
2015	20.07	-8.68
2014	22.23	29.75
2013	17.32	-8.74
2012	19.14	23.81

Total Assets: $1,499,351,812
Asset Allocation

Asset	%
Cash	0%
Stocks	100%
US Stocks	0%
Bonds	0%
US Bonds	0%
Other	0%

Services Offered:

Investment Strategy: The investment seeks to track the price and yield performance, before fees and expenses, of the WisdomTree India Earnings Index. Under normal circumstances, at least 95% of the fund's total assets (exclusive of collateral held from securities lending) will be invested in component securities of the index and investments that have economic characteristics that are substantially identical to the economic characteristics of such component securities. The index is comprised of companies incorporated and traded in India that are profitable and that are eligible to be purchased by foreign investors as of the annual index screening date. It is non-diversified. **Top Holdings:** Housing Development Finance Corp Ltd   Reliance Industries Ltd   Infosys Ltd   Tata Consultancy Services Ltd   ICICI Bank Ltd

SPDR® MSCI ACWI ex-US ETF

C-   HOLD

Ticker	Traded On	NAV
CWI	NYSE Arca	32.73

Total Assets ($)	Dividend Yield (TTM)	Turnover Ratio	Expense Ratio
$1,490,279,313	2.58	3	0.3

Ratings

Reward	D+
Risk	C
Recent Upgrade/Downgrade	Down

Fund Information

Fund Type	Exchange Traded Funds
Category	Global Equity Large Cap
Sub-Category	Foreign Large Blend
Prospectus Objective	Foreign Stock
Inception Date	Jan-07
Open to New Investments	Y

Prices

Price (as of 12/31/2018)	32.74
52-Week High	42.01
52-Week Low	31.78

Total Returns (%)

3-Month	6-Month	1-Year	3-Year	5-Year
-11.34	-9.48	-14.03	14.17	5.23

3-Year Standard Deviation	11.09
Effective Duration	

Valuation

Premium/Discount (1-Year Average)	-0.04

Company Information

Provider	SPDR State Street Global Advisors
Manager/Tenure	Michael J. Feehily (7), Karl A. Schneider (3), Michael Finocchi (1)
Website	http://www.spdrs.com
Address	SPDR State Street Global Advisors State Street Financial Center, 1 Lincoln Street Boston MA 02111-2900 United States
Phone Number	617-786-3000

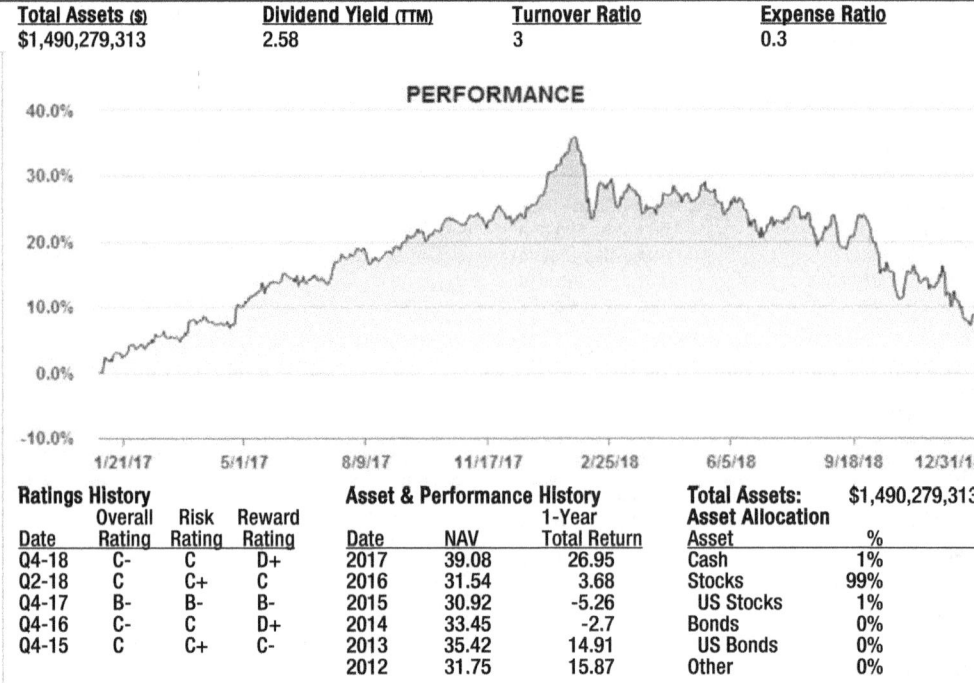

PERFORMANCE

Ratings History

Date	Overall Rating	Risk Rating	Reward Rating
Q4-18	C-	C	D+
Q2-18	C	C+	C
Q4-17	B-	B-	B-
Q4-16	C-	C	D+
Q4-15	C	C+	C-

Asset & Performance History

Date	NAV	1-Year Total Return
2017	39.08	26.95
2016	31.54	3.68
2015	30.92	-5.26
2014	33.45	-2.7
2013	35.42	14.91
2012	31.75	15.87

Total Assets: $1,490,279,313

Asset Allocation

Asset	%
Cash	1%
Stocks	99%
US Stocks	1%
Bonds	0%
US Bonds	0%
Other	0%

Services Offered:

Investment Strategy: The investment seeks investment results that, before fees and expenses, correspond generally to the total return performance of the MSCI All Country World Index ex USA Index. The fund generally invests substantially all, but at least 80%, of its total assets in the securities comprising the index and in depositary receipts based on securities comprising the index. The index is a free float-adjusted market capitalization index that is designed to measure the combined equity market performance of large- and mid-cap securities in developed and emerging market countries excluding the United States. The fund is non-diversified. **Top Holdings:** Nestle SA   Tencent Holdings Ltd   Novartis AG   Samsung Electronics Co Ltd GDR   Taiwan Semiconductor Manufacturing Co Ltd ADR

VanEck Vectors Russia ETF

C   HOLD

Ticker	Traded On	NAV
RSX	NYSE Arca	18.79

Total Assets ($)	Dividend Yield (TTM)	Turnover Ratio	Expense Ratio
$1,479,243,502	4.44	15	0.67

Ratings

Reward	C
Risk	C
Recent Upgrade/Downgrade	

Fund Information

Fund Type	Exchange Traded Funds
Category	Equity Misc
Sub-Category	Miscellaneous Region
Prospectus Objective	Growth
Inception Date	Apr-07
Open to New Investments	Y

Prices

Price (as of 12/31/2018)	18.75
52-Week High	24.31
52-Week Low	18.44

Total Returns (%)

3-Month	6-Month	1-Year	3-Year	5-Year
-8.28	-5.98	-6.02	43.39	-20.75

3-Year Standard Deviation	18.48
Effective Duration	

Valuation

Premium/Discount (1-Year Average)	0.07

Company Information

Provider	VanEck
Manager/Tenure	Hao-Hung (Peter) Liao (11), Guo Hua (Jason) Jin (0)
Website	http://www.vaneck.com
Address	Van Eck Associates Corporation 666 Third Avenue New York NY 10017 United States
Phone Number	800-826-1115

PERFORMANCE

Ratings History

Date	Overall Rating	Risk Rating	Reward Rating
Q4-18	C	C	C
Q2-18	C	C	C
Q4-17	B-	C	B
Q4-16	C-	D+	C-
Q4-15	D	D	D

Asset & Performance History

Date	NAV	1-Year Total Return
2017	21.14	4.57
2016	21.09	45.91
2015	14.69	0.31
2014	15.17	-44.9
2013	28.69	-0.63
2012	29.63	15.42

Total Assets: $1,479,243,502

Asset Allocation

Asset	%
Cash	0%
Stocks	100%
US Stocks	0%
Bonds	0%
US Bonds	0%
Other	0%

Services Offered:

Investment Strategy: The investment seeks to replicate as closely as possible, before fees and expenses, the price and yield performance of the MVIS® Russia Index. The fund normally invests at least 80% of its total assets in securities that comprise the fund's benchmark index. The index includes securities, which may include depositary receipts, of Russian companies. A company is generally considered to be a Russian company if it is incorporated in Russia or is incorporated outside of Russia but has at least 50% of its revenues/related assets in Russia. Such companies may include medium-capitalization companies. It is non-diversified. **Top Holdings:** Gazprom PJSC ADR   Sberbank of Russia PJSC ADR   PJSC Lukoil ADR   Mining and Metallurgical Company NORILSK NICKEL PJSC ADR   NOVATEK PJSC GDR

UBS AG FI Enhanced Large Cap Growth ETN   C-   HOLD

Ticker	Traded On	NAV	Total Assets ($)	Dividend Yield (TTM)	Turnover Ratio	Expense Ratio
FBGX	NYSE Arca	191.23	$1,470,338,813	0		0.85

Ratings
Reward	C
Risk	D+
Recent Upgrade/Downgrade	Down

Fund Information
Fund Type	Exchange Traded Funds
Category	US Equity Large Cap Growth
Sub-Category	Large Growth
Prospectus Objective	Growth
Inception Date	Jun-14
Open to New Investments	Y

Prices
Price (as of 12/31/2018)	189.53
52-Week High	301.54
52-Week Low	167.50

Total Returns (%)
3-Month	6-Month	1-Year	3-Year	5-Year
-36.38	-25.79	-15.29	54.91	

3-Year Standard Deviation	22.04
Effective Duration	

Valuation
Premium/Discount (1-Year Average)	0.23

Company Information
Provider	UBS Group AG
Manager/Tenure	No Manager (4)
Website	http://www.ubs.com
Address	Bahnhofstrasse 45 Zurich 8098 Switzerland
Phone Number	412-037-1952

PERFORMANCE

Ratings History
Date	Overall Rating	Risk Rating	Reward Rating
Q4-18	C-	D+	C
Q2-18	C+	D+	B
Q4-17	A	B	A+
Q4-16	C	D+	C+
Q4-15	D	C-	D

Asset & Performance History
Date	NAV	1-Year Total Return
2017	225.75	62.42
2016	138.55	12.24
2015	123.44	8.88
2014	113.36	
2013		
2012		

Total Assets: $1,470,338,813
Asset Allocation
Asset	%
Cash	%
Stocks	%
US Stocks	%
Bonds	%
US Bonds	%
Other	%

Services Offered:

Investment Strategy: The investment seeks a return linked to the Russell 1000® Growth Total Return Index (the "index").
The UBS AG FI Enhanced Large Cap Growth ETN due June 19, 2024 (the "Securities") are a series of FI Enhanced ETNs. The level of the index reflects both the price performance of the index constituent Securities and the reinvestment of dividends on the index constituent securities. The Securities are two times leveraged with respect to the index and, as a result, may benefit from two times any positive, but will be exposed to two times any negative, quarterly performance of the index. **Top Holdings:**

---

iShares Expanded Tech Sector ETF   C   HOLD

Ticker	Traded On	NAV	Total Assets ($)	Dividend Yield (TTM)	Turnover Ratio	Expense Ratio
IGM	NYSE Arca	172.02	$1,461,171,895	0.51	6	0.47

Ratings
Reward	C+
Risk	C
Recent Upgrade/Downgrade	Down

Fund Information
Fund Type	Exchange Traded Funds
Category	Technology Sector Equity
Sub-Category	Technology
Prospectus Objective	Technology
Inception Date	Mar-01
Open to New Investments	Y

Prices
Price (as of 12/31/2018)	171.71
52-Week High	210.69
52-Week Low	159.35

Total Returns (%)
3-Month	6-Month	1-Year	3-Year	5-Year
-17.85	-11.50	2.53	58.91	99.52

3-Year Standard Deviation	14.47
Effective Duration	

Valuation
Premium/Discount (1-Year Average)	0.03

Company Information
Provider	iShares
Manager/Tenure	Diane Hsiung (10), Greg Savage (10), Jennifer Hsui (6), 3 others
Website	http://www.ishares.com
Address	iShares 400 Howard Street San Francisco CA 94105 United States
Phone Number	800-474-2737

PERFORMANCE

Ratings History
Date	Overall Rating	Risk Rating	Reward Rating
Q4-18	C	C	C+
Q2-18	B	C	A-
Q4-17	A-	B	A+
Q4-16	C	C	C+
Q4-15	C+	C	B-

Asset & Performance History
Date	NAV	1-Year Total Return
2017	168.64	37.11
2016	123.78	13.03
2015	110.57	9.41
2014	101.89	14.74
2013	89.61	33.94
2012	67.49	14.71

Total Assets: $1,461,171,895
Asset Allocation
Asset	%
Cash	0%
Stocks	100%
US Stocks	99%
Bonds	0%
US Bonds	0%
Other	0%

Services Offered: CashInvestment Plan

Investment Strategy: The investment seeks to track the investment results of an index composed of North American equities in the technology sector and select North American equities from communication services and consumer discretionary sectors. The fund invests at least 90% of its assets in securities of the index and in depositary receipts representing securities of the index. The index measures the performance of U.S.-traded stocks from the technology sector and select technology-related companies from the communication services and consumer discretionary sectors in the U.S. and Canada. The fund is non-diversified. **Top Holdings:** Microsoft Corp Amazon.com Inc Apple Inc Facebook Inc A Alphabet Inc Class C

iShares Currency Hedged MSCI Eurozone ETF   C-   HOLD

Ticker	Traded On	NAV	Total Assets ($)	Dividend Yield (TTM)	Turnover Ratio	Expense Ratio
HEZU	NYSE Arca	25.96	$1,442,993,876	3.2	11	0.52

Ratings

Reward	D+
Risk	C
Recent Upgrade/Downgrade	Down

Fund Information

Fund Type	Exchange Traded Funds
Category	Europe Equity Large Cap
Sub-Category	Europe Stock
Prospectus Objective	Europe Stock
Inception Date	Jul-14
Open to New Investments	Y

Prices

Price (as of 12/31/2018)	25.94
52-Week High	31.54
52-Week Low	25.39

Total Returns (%)

3-Month	6-Month	1-Year	3-Year	5-Year
-12.76	-11.39	-10.68	8.90	

3-Year Standard Deviation	11.37
Effective Duration	

Valuation

Premium/Discount (1-Year Average)	0.01

Company Information

Provider	iShares
Manager/Tenure	Diane Hsiung (4), Jennifer Hsui (4), Orlando Montalvo (4), 2 others
Website	http://www.ishares.com
Address	iShares 400 Howard Street San Francisco CA 94105 United States
Phone Number	800-474-2737

PERFORMANCE

Ratings History

Date	Overall Rating	Risk Rating	Reward Rating
Q4-18	C-	C	D+
Q2-18	C	C+	C
Q4-17	B	B	B
Q4-16	C	C+	C-
Q4-15	D	C+	D

Asset & Performance History

Date	NAV	1-Year Total Return
2017	29.82	14.27
2016	26.61	6.7
2015	25.83	8.15
2014	24.49	
2013		
2012		

Total Assets: $1,442,993,876

Asset Allocation

Asset	%
Cash	0%
Stocks	100%
US Stocks	2%
Bonds	0%
US Bonds	0%
Other	0%

Services Offered:

Investment Strategy: The investment seeks to track the investment results of the MSCI EMU 100% Hedged to USD Index. The fund generally will invest at least 90% of its assets in the component securities (including indirect investments through the underlying fund) and other instruments of the underlying index and in investments that have economic characteristics that are substantially identical to the component securities of the underlying index. The index is an equity benchmark for the Economic and Monetary Union countries with the currency risk inherent in the securities included in the underlying index hedged to the U.S. dollar on a monthly basis. **Top Holdings:** iShares MSCI Eurozone ETF

SPDR® Portfolio Small Cap ETF   C   HOLD

Ticker	Traded On	NAV	Total Assets ($)	Dividend Yield (TTM)	Turnover Ratio	Expense Ratio
SPSM	NYSE Arca	26.37	$1,413,420,112	1.67	20	0.05

Ratings

Reward	C-
Risk	C+
Recent Upgrade/Downgrade	Down

Fund Information

Fund Type	Exchange Traded Funds
Category	US Equity Small Cap
Sub-Category	Small Blend
Prospectus Objective	Growth
Inception Date	Jul-13
Open to New Investments	Y

Prices

Price (as of 12/31/2018)	26.36
52-Week High	34.10
52-Week Low	24.83

Total Returns (%)

3-Month	6-Month	1-Year	3-Year	5-Year
-19.04	-17.83	-11.07	24.65	25.14

3-Year Standard Deviation	14.44
Effective Duration	

Valuation

Premium/Discount (1-Year Average)	0.01

Company Information

Provider	SPDR State Street Global Advisors
Manager/Tenure	Michael J. Feehily (5), Karl A. Schneider (4), Teddy Wong (1)
Website	http://www.spdrs.com
Address	SPDR State Street Global Advisors State Street Financial Center, 1 Lincoln Street Boston MA 02111-2900 United States
Phone Number	617-786-3000

PERFORMANCE

Ratings History

Date	Overall Rating	Risk Rating	Reward Rating
Q4-18	C	C+	C-
Q2-18	C+	C+	B-
Q4-17	B+	B	A-
Q4-16	C+	C-	B
Q4-15	C-	D+	C-

Asset & Performance History

Date	NAV	1-Year Total Return
2017	30.14	15.39
2016	26.54	21.47
2015	22.21	-4.34
2014	23.76	4.95
2013	23.03	
2012		

Total Assets: $1,413,420,112

Asset Allocation

Asset	%
Cash	0%
Stocks	100%
US Stocks	99%
Bonds	0%
US Bonds	0%
Other	0%

Services Offered:

Investment Strategy: The investment seeks to provide investment results that, before fees and expenses, correspond generally to the total return performance of the SSGA Small Cap Index that tracks the performance of small capitalization exchange traded U.S. equity securities. The fund generally invests substantially all, but at least 80%, of its total assets in the securities comprising the index. It may purchase a subset of the securities in the index in an effort to hold a portfolio of securities with generally the same risk and return characteristics of the index. The fund is non-diversified. **Top Holdings:** Mr. Cooper Group Inc   Grand Canyon Education Inc   Popular Inc   The Trade Desk Inc A   ITT Inc

JPMorgan Diversified Return International Equity ETF　　　　C-　HOLD

Ticker	Traded On	NAV	Total Assets ($)	Dividend Yield (TTM)	Turnover Ratio	Expense Ratio
JPIN	NYSE Arca	51.07	$1,409,564,542	4.3	29	0.38

Ratings
Reward	D+
Risk	C
Recent Upgrade/Downgrade	Down

Fund Information
Fund Type	Exchange Traded Funds
Category	Global Equity Large Cap
Sub-Category	Foreign Large Blend
Prospectus Objective	Growth & Inc
Inception Date	Nov-14
Open to New Investments	Y

Prices
Price (as of 12/31/2018)	50.89
52-Week High	63.18
52-Week Low	49.33

Total Returns (%)
3-Month	6-Month	1-Year	3-Year	5-Year
-11.52	-8.97	-12.50	10.59	

3-Year Standard Deviation	10.34
Effective Duration	

Valuation
Premium/Discount (1-Year Average)	0.20

Company Information
Provider	JPMorgan
Manager/Tenure	Kartik Aiyar (1), Wei (Victor) Li (1), Yazann Romahi (1), 1 other
Website	http://www.jpmorganfunds.com
Address	JPMorgan 270 Park Avenue New York NY 10017-2070 United States
Phone Number	800-480-4111

PERFORMANCE

Ratings History
Date	Overall Rating	Risk Rating	Reward Rating
Q4-18	C-	C	D+
Q2-18	C	C-	C
Q4-17	C+	B-	C+
Q4-16	D+	C-	D+
Q4-15	U		

Asset & Performance History
Date	NAV	1-Year Total Return
2017	59.84	25.25
2016	48.8	0.91
2015	49.17	2.93
2014	48.81	
2013		
2012		

Total Assets: $1,409,564,542
Asset Allocation
Asset	%
Cash	0%
Stocks	100%
US Stocks	1%
Bonds	0%
US Bonds	0%
Other	0%

Services Offered:

Investment Strategy: The investment seeks investment results that closely correspond, before fees and expenses, to the performance of the JP Morgan Diversified Factor International Equity Index. The fund will invest at least 80% of its net assets in securities included in the underlying index. The underlying index is comprised of equity securities across developed global markets (excluding North America) selected to represent a diversified set of factor characteristics: value, price momentum and quality. **Top Holdings:** SK Telecom Co Ltd Marine Harvest ASA Mochida Pharmaceutical Co Ltd AstraZeneca PLC GlaxoSmithKline PLC

Invesco Financial Preferred ETF　　　　C　HOLD

Ticker	Traded On	NAV	Total Assets ($)	Dividend Yield (TTM)	Turnover Ratio	Expense Ratio
PGF	NYSE Arca	17.38	$1,409,312,904	5.66	5	0.63

Ratings
Reward	C-
Risk	C+
Recent Upgrade/Downgrade	Down

Fund Information
Fund Type	Exchange Traded Funds
Category	US Fixed Income
Sub-Category	Preferred Stock
Prospectus Objective	Financial
Inception Date	Dec-06
Open to New Investments	Y

Prices
Price (as of 12/31/2018)	17.36
52-Week High	18.87
52-Week Low	17.04

Total Returns (%)
3-Month	6-Month	1-Year	3-Year	5-Year
-2.50	-3.50	-2.71	8.92	35.62

3-Year Standard Deviation	4.45
Effective Duration	

Valuation
Premium/Discount (1-Year Average)	-0.02

Company Information
Provider	Invesco
Manager/Tenure	Peter Hubbard (11), Jeffrey W. Kernagis (11), Philip Fang (8), 2 others
Website	http://www.invesco.com/us
Address	Invesco 11 Greenway Plaza, Ste. 2500 Houston TX 77046 United States
Phone Number	800-659-1005

PERFORMANCE

Ratings History
Date	Overall Rating	Risk Rating	Reward Rating
Q4-18	C	C+	C-
Q2-18	C+	C+	C
Q4-17	B	A	C+
Q4-16	C	C+	C
Q4-15	B-	C+	B-

Asset & Performance History
Date	NAV	1-Year Total Return
2017	18.87	10.62
2016	17.99	1.2
2015	18.82	9.2
2014	18.25	14.02
2013	17	-0.88
2012	18.27	20.67

Total Assets: $1,409,312,904
Asset Allocation
Asset	%
Cash	0%
Stocks	0%
US Stocks	0%
Bonds	0%
US Bonds	0%
Other	1%

Services Offered:

Investment Strategy: The investment seeks to track the investment results (before fees and expenses) of the Wells Fargo® Hybrid and Preferred Securities Financial Index. The fund generally will invest at least 90% of its total assets in preferred securities of financial institutions that comprise the underlying index. The underlying index is a market capitalization weighted index designed to track the performance of preferred securities and securities that the index provider believes are functionally equivalent to preferred securities, including, but not limited to, depositary preferred securities, perpetual subordinated debt and certain capital securities. It is non-diversified. **Top Holdings:** PNC Financial Services Group Inc Perpetual Preferred Share class-P Barclays Bank PLC 8 1/8 % Non Cum Callable Dollar Pref Shs Sp Am Dep Receip BB&T Corp Deposit Shs Repr 1/1000th Non Cum Perp Pfd Shs Series -E- Wells Fargo & Co Deposit Shs Repr 1/1000th 5.85 % Non-Cum Perp Pfd Shs -A- JPMorgan Chase & Co Deposit Shs Repr 1/40th 6.15 % Non-Cum Pfd Shs Series -

Invesco BulletShares 2020 Corporate Bond ETF   C   HOLD

Ticker	Traded On	NAV	Total Assets ($)	Dividend Yield (TTM)	Turnover Ratio	Expense Ratio
BSCK	NYSE Arca	21.02	$1,408,149,933	2.28	1	0.1

Ratings

Reward	C
Risk	C+
Recent Upgrade/Downgrade	

Fund Information

Fund Type	Exchange Traded Funds
Category	US Fixed Income
Sub-Category	Short-Term Bond
Prospectus Objective	Corp Bond - Gen
Inception Date	Mar-12
Open to New Investments	Y

Prices

Price (as of 12/31/2018)	21.07
52-Week High	21.29
52-Week Low	20.97

Total Returns (%)

3-Month	6-Month	1-Year	3-Year	5-Year
0.68	1.44	1.14	7.67	15.16

3-Year Standard Deviation	1.91
Effective Duration	1.64

Valuation

Premium/Discount (1-Year Average)	0.25

Company Information

Provider	Invesco
Manager/Tenure	Jeremy Neisewander (2), Peter Hubbard (0), Jeffrey W. Kernagis (0), 1 other
Website	http://www.invesco.com/us
Address	Invesco 11 Greenway Plaza, Ste. 2500 Houston TX 77046 United States
Phone Number	800-659-1005

PERFORMANCE

Ratings History

Date	Overall Rating	Risk Rating	Reward Rating
Q4-18	C	C+	C
Q2-18	C	C+	C
Q4-17	B	A+	C
Q4-16	C	C+	C
Q4-15	C+	C+	C

Asset & Performance History

Date	NAV	1-Year Total Return
2017	21.24	2.21
2016	21.17	3.86
2015	20.84	1.83
2014	20.97	5.02
2013	20.49	-0.72
2012	21.18	

Total Assets: $1,408,149,933

Asset Allocation

Asset	%
Cash	0%
Stocks	0%
US Stocks	0%
Bonds	100%
US Bonds	85%
Other	0%

Services Offered:

Investment Strategy: The investment seeks investment results that correspond generally to the performance, before the fund's fees and expenses, of an investment grade corporate bond index called the Nasdaq BulletShares® USD Corporate Bond 2020 Index. The fund normally invests at least 80% of its total assets in component securities that comprise the index. The index is designed to represent the performance of a held-to-maturity portfolio of U.S. dollar-denominated investment-grade corporate bonds with effective maturities in the year 2020. The fund is non-diversified. **Top Holdings:** GE Capital International Funding Company Unlimited Company 2.34% JPMorgan Chase & Co. 2.25% AbbVie Inc. 2.5% Allergan Funding SCS 3% HCA Inc. 6.5%

FlexShares Morningstar US Market Factors Tilt Index Fund   C-   HOLD

Ticker	Traded On	NAV	Total Assets ($)	Dividend Yield (TTM)	Turnover Ratio	Expense Ratio
TILT	BATS	100.18	$1,406,186,461	1.76		0.25

Ratings

Reward	C-
Risk	C-
Recent Upgrade/Downgrade	Down

Fund Information

Fund Type	Exchange Traded Funds
Category	US Equity Large Cap Blend
Sub-Category	Large Blend
Prospectus Objective	Growth
Inception Date	Sep-11
Open to New Investments	Y

Prices

Price (as of 12/31/2018)	100.12
52-Week High	121.21
52-Week Low	94.13

Total Returns (%)

3-Month	6-Month	1-Year	3-Year	5-Year
-15.55	-11.05	-8.51	26.10	35.71

3-Year Standard Deviation	10.76
Effective Duration	

Valuation

Premium/Discount (1-Year Average)	0.08

Company Information

Provider	Flexshares Trust
Manager/Tenure	Robert Anstine (5), Brendan Sullivan (2)
Website	http://www.flexshares.com
Address	50 South LaSalle Street Chicago, Illinois 60603 Chicago Illinois 60603 United States
Phone Number	855-353-9383

PERFORMANCE

Ratings History

Date	Overall Rating	Risk Rating	Reward Rating
Q4-18	C-	C-	C-
Q2-18	C	C-	C
Q4-17	B	B	B
Q4-16	D+	D+	D+
Q4-15	C	C-	C

Asset & Performance History

Date	NAV	1-Year Total Return
2017	111.48	17.84
2016	96.18	16.97
2015	83.63	-2.1
2014	87.09	9.92
2013	80.27	35.75
2012	59.72	16.41

Total Assets: $1,406,186,461

Asset Allocation

Asset	%
Cash	2%
Stocks	98%
US Stocks	97%
Bonds	0%
US Bonds	0%
Other	0%

Services Offered:

Investment Strategy: The investment seeks investment results that correspond generally to the price and yield performance, before fees and expenses, of the Morningstar® US Market Factor Tilt IndexSM. The fund will invest at least 80% of its total assets (exclusive of collateral held from securities lending) in the securities of the underlying index. The underlying index reflects the performance of a selection of U.S. equity securities that is designed to provide broad exposure to the overall U.S. equities market, with increased exposure (or a "tilt") to small-capitalization stocks and value stocks. It may also invest up to 20% of its assets in cash and cash equivalents. **Top Holdings:** Apple Inc Microsoft Corp Amazon.com Inc Berkshire Hathaway Inc B JPMorgan Chase & Co

Invesco S&P SmallCap Low Volatility ETF   C   HOLD

Ticker	Traded On	NAV	Total Assets ($)	Dividend Yield (TTM)	Turnover Ratio	Expense Ratio
XSLV	NYSE Arca	42.64	$1,399,759,127	2.17		0.25

Ratings

Reward	C-
Risk	C+
Recent Upgrade/Downgrade	Down

Fund Information

Fund Type	Exchange Traded Funds
Category	US Equity Small Cap
Sub-Category	Small Value
Prospectus Objective	Income
Inception Date	Feb-13
Open to New Investments	

Prices

Price (as of 12/31/2018)	42.64
52-Week High	51.11
52-Week Low	40.81

Total Returns (%)

3-Month	6-Month	1-Year	3-Year	5-Year
-11.35	-10.91	-5.33	35.14	53.89

3-Year Standard Deviation	12.05
Effective Duration	

Valuation

Premium/Discount (1-Year Average)	0.03

Company Information

Provider	Invesco
Manager/Tenure	Peter Hubbard (5), Michael Jeanette (5), Tony Seisser (4), 1 other
Website	http://www.invesco.com/us
Address	Invesco 11 Greenway Plaza, Ste. 2500 Houston TX 77046 United States
Phone Number	800-659-1005

PERFORMANCE

Ratings History

Date	Overall Rating	Risk Rating	Reward Rating
Q4-18	C	C+	C-
Q2-18	C+	C+	B-
Q4-17	A	A	A
Q4-16	B	C+	A
Q4-15	C	C-	C+

Asset & Performance History

Date	NAV	1-Year Total Return
2017	46.23	8.68
2016	43.35	31.34
2015	33.72	2.77
2014	33.55	10.8
2013	31.04	
2012		

Total Assets: $1,399,759,127

Asset Allocation

Asset	%
Cash	0%
Stocks	100%
US Stocks	100%
Bonds	0%
US Bonds	0%
Other	0%

Services Offered:

Investment Strategy: The investment seeks to track the investment results (before fees and expenses) of the S&P SmallCap 600® Low Volatility Index (the "underlying index"). The fund generally will invest at least 90% of its total assets in common stocks that comprise the underlying index. Strictly in accordance with its procedures and mandated guidelines, S&P DJI selects for inclusion in the underlying index the 120 securities that it has determined have the lowest volatility over the past 12 months out of the 600 small capitalization securities that are contained in the S&P SmallCap 600® Index. **Top Holdings:** Apollo Commercial Real Estate Finance Inc   ARMOUR Residential REIT Inc   Invesco Mortgage Capital Inc   Redwood Trust Inc   Granite Point Mortgage Trust Inc

---

First Trust Large Cap Core AlphaDEX® Fund   C   HOLD

Ticker	Traded On	NAV	Total Assets ($)	Dividend Yield (TTM)	Turnover Ratio	Expense Ratio
FEX	NAS CM	52.13	$1,394,468,734	1.11	90	0.61

Ratings

Reward	C-
Risk	C+
Recent Upgrade/Downgrade	

Fund Information

Fund Type	Exchange Traded Funds
Category	US Equity Large Cap Blend
Sub-Category	Large Blend
Prospectus Objective	Growth
Inception Date	May-07
Open to New Investments	Y

Prices

Price (as of 12/31/2018)	52.12
52-Week High	63.04
52-Week Low	48.95

Total Returns (%)

3-Month	6-Month	1-Year	3-Year	5-Year
-16.17	-11.63	-9.81	25.05	35.03

3-Year Standard Deviation	10.38
Effective Duration	

Valuation

Premium/Discount (1-Year Average)	0.02

Company Information

Provider	First Trust
Manager/Tenure	Jon C. Erickson (11), Daniel J. Lindquist (11), David G. McGarel (11), 3 others
Website	http://www.ftportfolios.com/
Address	First Trust 120 E. Liberty Drive, Suite 400 Wheaton IL 60187 United States
Phone Number	800-621-1675

PERFORMANCE

Ratings History

Date	Overall Rating	Risk Rating	Reward Rating
Q4-18	C	C+	C-
Q2-18	C	C-	C
Q4-17	B-	B-	B
Q4-16	B-	C+	B-
Q4-15	C	C+	C

Asset & Performance History

Date	NAV	1-Year Total Return
2017	58.51	21.52
2016	48.7	14.11
2015	43.26	-3.88
2014	45.59	12.33
2013	41.13	35.78
2012	30.64	14.4

Total Assets: $1,394,468,734

Asset Allocation

Asset	%
Cash	0%
Stocks	100%
US Stocks	99%
Bonds	0%
US Bonds	0%
Other	0%

Services Offered:

Investment Strategy: The investment seeks investment results that correspond generally to the price and yield (before the fund's fees and expenses) of an equity index called the Nasdaq AlphaDEX® Large Cap Core Index. The fund will normally invest at least 90% of its net assets (including investment borrowings) in common stocks that comprise the index. The index is designed to select stocks from the NASDAQ US 500 Large Cap Index (the "base index") that may generate positive alpha, or risk-adjusted returns, relative to traditional indices through the use of the AlphaDEX® selection methodology. **Top Holdings:** Newell Brands Inc   Verizon Communications Inc   Comcast Corp Class A   Dell-VMWare Tracking Stock V   Dollar Tree Inc

iShares 0-5 Year Investment Grade Corporate Bond ETF   C   HOLD

Ticker	Traded On	NAV	Total Assets ($)	Dividend Yield (TTM)	Turnover Ratio	Expense Ratio
SLQD	NAS CM	49.48	$1,391,516,318	2.38	20	0.06

Ratings
Reward	C
Risk	C+
Recent Upgrade/Downgrade	

Fund Information
Fund Type	Exchange Traded Funds
Category	US Fixed Income
Sub-Category	Short-Term Bond
Prospectus Objective	Corp Bond - Gen
Inception Date	Oct-13
Open to New Investments	Y

Prices
Price (as of 12/31/2018)	49.53
52-Week High	50.26
52-Week Low	49.20

Total Returns (%)
3-Month	6-Month	1-Year	3-Year	5-Year
0.73	1.43	1.15	5.53	8.16

3-Year Standard Deviation	1.16
Effective Duration	2.26

Valuation
Premium/Discount (1-Year Average)	0.12

Company Information
Provider	iShares
Manager/Tenure	James Mauro (5), Scott Radell (5)
Website	http://www.ishares.com
Address	iShares 400 Howard Street San Francisco CA 94105 United States
Phone Number	800-474-2737

PERFORMANCE

Ratings History
Date	Overall Rating	Risk Rating	Reward Rating
Q4-18	C	C+	C
Q2-18	C-	C-	C-
Q4-17	B	A+	C
Q4-16	C-	C-	C-
Q4-15	C-	C-	D+

Asset & Performance History
Date	NAV	1-Year Total Return
2017	50.18	2.13
2016	50.11	2.14
2015	49.95	1.11
2014	50.11	1.36
2013	50.05	
2012		

Total Assets: $1,391,516,318

Asset Allocation
Asset	%
Cash	5%
Stocks	0%
US Stocks	0%
Bonds	95%
US Bonds	77%
Other	0%

Services Offered:

Investment Strategy: The investment seeks to track the investment results of the Markit iBoxx® USD Liquid Investment Grade 0-5 Index composed of U.S. dollar-denominated, investment-grade corporate bonds with remaining maturities of less than five years. The fund generally will invest at least 90% of its assets in the component securities of the underlying index and may invest up to 10% of its assets in certain futures, options and swap contracts, cash and cash equivalents. The index is designed to reflect the performance of U.S. dollar-denominated investment-grade corporate debt. **Top Holdings:** Anheuser-Busch InBev Finance Inc. 2.65% CVS Health Corp 3.7% GE Capital International Funding Company Unlimited Company 2.34% Exxon Mobil Corporation 2.22% Diamond 1 Finance Corporation/Diamond 2 Finance Corporation 4.42%

UBS ETRACS Alerian MLP Infrastructure Index ETN   D+   SELL

Ticker	Traded On	NAV	Total Assets ($)	Dividend Yield (TTM)	Turnover Ratio	Expense Ratio
MLPI	NYSE Arca	19.83	$1,387,328,799	7.42		0.85

Ratings
Reward	D+
Risk	D+
Recent Upgrade/Downgrade	Up

Fund Information
Fund Type	Exchange Traded Funds
Category	Energy Sector Equity
Sub-Category	Energy Limited Partnership
Prospectus Objective	Natl Res
Inception Date	Apr-10
Open to New Investments	Y

Prices
Price (as of 12/31/2018)	19.77
52-Week High	26.41
52-Week Low	18.86

Total Returns (%)
3-Month	6-Month	1-Year	3-Year	5-Year
-18.14	-9.74	-12.40	-6.91	-32.26

3-Year Standard Deviation	18.2
Effective Duration	

Valuation
Premium/Discount (1-Year Average)	-0.03

Company Information
Provider	UBS Group AG
Manager/Tenure	No Manager (8)
Website	http://www.ubs.com
Address	Bahnhofstrasse 45 Zurich 8098 Switzerland
Phone Number	412-037-1952

PERFORMANCE

Ratings History
Date	Overall Rating	Risk Rating	Reward Rating
Q4-18	D+	D+	D+
Q2-18	D	D	D
Q4-17	D	D	D
Q4-16	D	D	D+
Q4-15	D+	D+	C-

Asset & Performance History
Date	NAV	1-Year Total Return
2017	24.23	-9.08
2016	28.47	17.39
2015	26.13	-31.91
2014	40.52	6.86
2013	39.64	27.78
2012	32.52	3.36

Total Assets: $1,387,328,799

Asset Allocation
Asset	%
Cash	%
Stocks	%
US Stocks	%
Bonds	%
US Bonds	%
Other	%

Services Offered:

Investment Strategy: The investment seeks to replicate, net of expenses, the Alerian MLP Infrastructure Index. The index provides exposure to the infrastructure component of the Master Limited Partnership asset class. Its constituents each earn at least 50% of their EBITDA from assets that are not directly exposed to changes in commodity prices. The index is a composite of 25 energy infrastructure MLPs. **Top Holdings:**

SPDR® S&P Aerospace & Defense ETF   B-   BUY

Ticker	Traded On	NAV	Total Assets ($)	Dividend Yield (TTM)	Turnover Ratio	Expense Ratio
XAR	NYSE Arca	78.94	$1,385,208,986	1.02	36	0.35

Ratings

Reward	B
Risk	C
Recent Upgrade/Downgrade	Down

Fund Information

Fund Type	Exchange Traded Funds
Category	Industrials Sector Equity
Sub-Category	Industrials
Prospectus Objective	Technology
Inception Date	Sep-11
Open to New Investments	Y

Prices

Price (as of 12/31/2018)	78.92
52-Week High	100.89
52-Week Low	74.15

Total Returns (%)

3-Month	6-Month	1-Year	3-Year	5-Year
-20.35	-8.79	-4.45	54.02	70.02

3-Year Standard Deviation	14.32
Effective Duration	

Valuation

Premium/Discount (1-Year Average)	0.04

Company Information

Provider	SPDR State Street Global Advisors
Manager/Tenure	Michael J. Feehily (7), Karl A. Schneider (4), Keith Richardson (1)
Website	http://www.spdrs.com
Address	SPDR State Street Global Advisors State Street Financial Center, 1 Lincoln Street Boston MA 02111-2900 United States
Phone Number	617-786-3000

PERFORMANCE

Ratings History

Date	Overall Rating	Risk Rating	Reward Rating
Q4-18	B-	C	B
Q2-18	B	C+	B
Q4-17	B+	C+	A+
Q4-16	B	C	B
Q4-15	B	B	B

Asset & Performance History

Date	NAV	1-Year Total Return
2017	83.47	32.82
2016	63.38	21.16
2015	52.84	-0.32
2014	54.24	10.75
2013	49.53	58.65
2012	31.91	17.47

Total Assets: $1,385,208,986

Asset Allocation

Asset	%
Cash	3%
Stocks	97%
US Stocks	97%
Bonds	0%
US Bonds	0%
Other	0%

Services Offered:

Investment Strategy: The investment seeks to provide investment results that, before fees and expenses, correspond generally to the total return performance of the S&P Aerospace & Defense Select Industry Index. In seeking to track the performance of the S&P Aerospace & Defense Select Industry Index (the "index"), the fund employs a sampling strategy. It generally invests substantially all, but at least 80%, of its total assets in the securities comprising the index. The index represents the aerospace and defense segment of the S&P Total Market Index ("S&P TMI"). The fund is non-diversified. **Top Holdings:** United Technologies Corp TransDigm Group Inc Boeing Co Arconic Inc Spirit AeroSystems Holdings Inc

SPDR® S&P Global Natural Resources ETF   C   HOLD

Ticker	Traded On	NAV	Total Assets ($)	Dividend Yield (TTM)	Turnover Ratio	Expense Ratio
GNR	NYSE Arca	41.25	$1,384,379,534	2.8	19	0.4

Ratings

Reward	C
Risk	C+
Recent Upgrade/Downgrade	Down

Fund Information

Fund Type	Exchange Traded Funds
Category	Natural Resources
Sub-Category	Natural Resources
Prospectus Objective	Natl Res
Inception Date	Sep-10
Open to New Investments	Y

Prices

Price (as of 12/31/2018)	41.24
52-Week High	53.06
52-Week Low	39.53

Total Returns (%)

3-Month	6-Month	1-Year	3-Year	5-Year
-17.08	-14.72	-13.11	39.42	-5.19

3-Year Standard Deviation	15.42
Effective Duration	

Valuation

Premium/Discount (1-Year Average)	-0.05

Company Information

Provider	SPDR State Street Global Advisors
Manager/Tenure	Michael J. Feehily (7), Karl A. Schneider (3), David Chin (1)
Website	http://www.spdrs.com
Address	SPDR State Street Global Advisors State Street Financial Center, 1 Lincoln Street Boston MA 02111-2900 United States
Phone Number	617-786-3000

PERFORMANCE

Ratings History

Date	Overall Rating	Risk Rating	Reward Rating
Q4-18	C	C+	C
Q2-18	C+	C+	C+
Q4-17	C+	C	B-
Q4-16	C-	D+	C-
Q4-15	D	D	D

Asset & Performance History

Date	NAV	1-Year Total Return
2017	49.04	22.16
2016	41.22	31.35
2015	32.08	-24.31
2014	44.09	-10.15
2013	50.22	0.96
2012	51.08	6.4

Total Assets: $1,384,379,534

Asset Allocation

Asset	%
Cash	0%
Stocks	100%
US Stocks	33%
Bonds	0%
US Bonds	0%
Other	0%

Services Offered:

Investment Strategy: The investment seeks investment results that, before fees and expenses, correspond generally to the total return performance of the S&P Global Natural Resources Index. The fund generally invests substantially all, but at least 80%, of its total assets in the securities comprising the index and in depositary receipts based on securities comprising the index. The index is comprised of 90 of the largest U.S. and foreign publicly traded companies, based on market capitalization, in natural resources and commodities businesses that meet certain investability requirements. The fund is non-diversified. **Top Holdings:** Bhp Billiton Limited Common Stock Nutrien Ltd Exxon Mobil Corp Total SA Royal Dutch Shell PLC Class A

Pacer Trendpilot™ US Large Cap ETF   C   HOLD

Ticker	Traded On	NAV	Total Assets ($)	Dividend Yield (TTM)	Turnover Ratio	Expense Ratio
PTLC	BATS	28.76	$1,376,475,868	0.96	12	0.6

Ratings
Reward   C-
Risk   C+
Recent Upgrade/Downgrade   Down

Fund Information
Fund Type   Exchange Traded Funds
Category   US Equity Large Cap Blend
Sub-Category   Large Blend
Prospectus Objective   Growth
Inception Date   Jun-15
Open to New Investments   Y

Prices
Price (as of 12/31/2018)   28.77
52-Week High   31.65
52-Week Low   27.65

Total Returns (%)

3-Month	6-Month	1-Year	3-Year	5-Year
-7.98	-0.97	1.67	28.66	

3-Year Standard Deviation   9.27
Effective Duration

Valuation
Premium/Discount (1-Year Average)   0.11

Company Information
Provider   Pacer
Manager/Tenure   Bruce Kavanaugh (3), Michael Mack (3)
Website   http://www.paceretfs.com
Address   Pacer 16 Industrial Blvd, Suite 201 Paoli PA 19301 United States
Phone Number

PERFORMANCE

Ratings History

Date	Overall Rating	Risk Rating	Reward Rating
Q4-18	C	C+	C-
Q2-18	C	C+	C
Q4-17	C	B-	C+
Q4-16	D	C-	D+
Q4-15	U		

Asset & Performance History

Date	NAV	1-Year Total Return
2017	28.57	21
2016	23.84	4.07
2015	23.04	
2014		
2013		
2012		

Total Assets: $1,376,475,868

Asset Allocation

Asset	%
Cash	100%
Stocks	0%
US Stocks	0%
Bonds	0%
US Bonds	0%
Other	0%

Services Offered:

Investment Strategy: The investment seeks to track the total return performance, before fees and expenses, of the Pacer Trendpilot US Large Cap Index. The fund invests at least 80% of its total assets (exclusive of collateral held from securities lending) in the component securities of the index. The index uses an objective, rules-based methodology to implement a systematic trend-following strategy that directs exposure (i) 100% to the S&P 500, (ii) 50% to the S&P 500 and 50% to 3-Month U.S. Treasury bills, or (iii) 100% to 3-Month U.S. Treasury bills, depending on the relative performance of the S&P 500 TR and its 200-business day historical simple moving average. **Top Holdings:** Resideo Technologies Inc Microsoft Corp Amazon.com Inc Berkshire Hathaway Inc B Facebook Inc A

PIMCO 0-5 Year High Yield Corporate Bond Index Exchange-Traded Fund   C   HOLD

Ticker	Traded On	NAV	Total Assets ($)	Dividend Yield (TTM)	Turnover Ratio	Expense Ratio
HYS	NYSE Arca	95.44	$1,369,079,399	4.82	42	0.56

Ratings
Reward   C-
Risk   C+
Recent Upgrade/Downgrade   Down

Fund Information
Fund Type   Exchange Traded Funds
Category   US Fixed Income
Sub-Category   High Yield Bond
Prospectus Objective   Corp Bond-High Yld
Inception Date   Jun-11
Open to New Investments   Y

Prices
Price (as of 12/31/2018)   95.12
52-Week High   101.41
52-Week Low   94.14

Total Returns (%)

3-Month	6-Month	1-Year	3-Year	5-Year
-4.00	-1.61	-0.55	20.55	15.44

3-Year Standard Deviation   3.82
Effective Duration   2.07

Valuation
Premium/Discount (1-Year Average)   -0.32

Company Information
Provider   PIMCO
Manager/Tenure   Matthew P. Dorsten (2), Mitchell Handa (0), Graham A. Rennison (0)
Website   http://www.pimco.com
Address   PIMCO 840 Newport Center Drive, Suite 100 Newport Beach CA 92660 United States
Phone Number   866-746-2602

PERFORMANCE

Ratings History

Date	Overall Rating	Risk Rating	Reward Rating
Q4-18	C	C+	C-
Q2-18	C+	C+	C
Q4-17	B-	B	C+
Q4-16	C+	C+	C
Q4-15	C	C+	C-

Asset & Performance History

Date	NAV	1-Year Total Return
2017	100.64	5.83
2016	99.93	14.61
2015	92.02	-4.7
2014	101.36	0.49
2013	106.26	8.26
2012	102.82	12.22

Total Assets: $1,369,079,399

Asset Allocation

Asset	%
Cash	-12%
Stocks	0%
US Stocks	0%
Bonds	102%
US Bonds	87%
Other	10%

Services Offered:

Investment Strategy: The investment seeks to provide total return that closely corresponds, before fees and expenses, to the total return of the ICE BofAML 0-5 Year US High Yield Constrained Index. The fund invests under normal circumstances at least 80% of its total assets (exclusive of collateral held from securities lending) in the component securities of the ICE BofAML 0-5 Year US High Yield Constrained Index. The underlying index is an unmanaged index comprised of U.S. dollar denominated below investment grade corporate debt securities publicly issued in the U.S. domestic market with remaining maturities of less than 5 years. **Top Holdings:** Cdx Hy30 5y Ice Fin Fut Us 5yr Cbt 03/29/19 Trs Iboxhy /3ml Indx 03/20/19 Jpm Cdx Hy31 5y Ice Trs Iboxhy /3ml Indx 03/20/19 Bnp

First Trust Capital Strength ETF   C   HOLD

Ticker	Traded On	NAV	Total Assets ($)	Dividend Yield (TTM)	Turnover Ratio	Expense Ratio
FTCS	NAS CM	48.28	$1,363,740,322	1.02	85	0.61

Ratings

Reward	C
Risk	C+
Recent Upgrade/Downgrade	Down

Fund Information

Fund Type	Exchange Traded Funds
Category	US Equity Large Cap Blend
Sub-Category	Large Blend
Prospectus Objective	Growth
Inception Date	Jul-06
Open to New Investments	Y

Prices

Price (as of 12/31/2018)	48.28
52-Week High	55.82
52-Week Low	45.20

Total Returns (%)

3-Month	6-Month	1-Year	3-Year	5-Year
-12.50	-4.98	-4.09	31.70	54.53

3-Year Standard Deviation	8.7
Effective Duration	

Valuation

Premium/Discount (1-Year Average)	0.03

Company Information

Provider	First Trust
Manager/Tenure	Jon C. Erickson (12), Daniel J. Lindquist (12), David G. McGarel (12), 3 others
Website	http://www.ftportfolios.com/
Address	First Trust 120 E. Liberty Drive, Suite 400 Wheaton IL 60187 United States
Phone Number	800-621-1675

PERFORMANCE

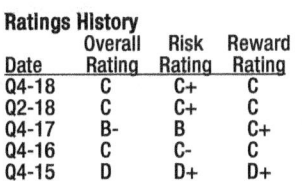

Ratings History

Date	Overall Rating	Risk Rating	Reward Rating
Q4-18	C	C+	C
Q2-18	C+	C+	C+
Q4-17	B	B	B
Q4-16	C+	C	B
Q4-15	C	C	C

Asset & Performance History

Date	NAV	1-Year Total Return
2017	50.95	26.48
2016	40.79	8.57
2015	38.12	1.63
2014	38.08	15.44
2013	33.69	35.9
2012	25.16	17.47

Total Assets: $1,363,740,322

Asset Allocation

Asset	%
Cash	0%
Stocks	100%
US Stocks	100%
Bonds	0%
US Bonds	0%
Other	0%

Services Offered:

Investment Strategy: The investment seeks investment results that correspond generally to the price and yield (before the fund's fees and expenses) of an equity index called the Capital Strength Index(SM). The fund will normally invest at least 90% of its net assets in common stocks that comprise the index. In constructing the index, the index provider begins with the largest 500 U.S. companies included in the NASDAQ US Benchmark Index and excludes the following: companies with less than $1 billion in cash and short term investments; companies with long-term debt divided by market capitalization greater than 30%; and companies with return on equity less than 15%. **Top Holdings:** Expeditors International of Washington Inc Starbucks Corp The Estee Lauder Companies Inc Class A Intercontinental Exchange Inc Marsh & McLennan Companies Inc

---

iShares Global REIT ETF   C   HOLD

Ticker	Traded On	NAV	Total Assets ($)	Dividend Yield (TTM)	Turnover Ratio	Expense Ratio
REET	NYSE Arca	23.50	$1,336,759,350	5.33	7	0.14

Ratings

Reward	C
Risk	C+
Recent Upgrade/Downgrade	

Fund Information

Fund Type	Exchange Traded Funds
Category	Real Estate Sector Equity
Sub-Category	Real Estate
Prospectus Objective	Real Estate
Inception Date	Jul-14
Open to New Investments	Y

Prices

Price (as of 12/31/2018)	23.42
52-Week High	26.45
52-Week Low	22.86

Total Returns (%)

3-Month	6-Month	1-Year	3-Year	5-Year
-5.03	-4.81	-4.89	8.64	

3-Year Standard Deviation	10.77
Effective Duration	

Valuation

Premium/Discount (1-Year Average)	0.03

Company Information

Provider	iShares
Manager/Tenure	Diane Hsiung (4), Jennifer Hsui (4), Greg Savage (4), 3 others
Website	http://www.ishares.com
Address	iShares 400 Howard Street San Francisco CA 94105 United States
Phone Number	800-474-2737

PERFORMANCE

Ratings History

Date	Overall Rating	Risk Rating	Reward Rating
Q4-18	C	C+	C
Q2-18	C	C+	C
Q4-17	B-	B	C+
Q4-16	C	C-	C
Q4-15	D	D+	D+

Asset & Performance History

Date	NAV	1-Year Total Return
2017	26.08	7.57
2016	25.21	6.19
2015	25.01	0.24
2014	25.86	
2013		
2012		

Total Assets: $1,336,759,350

Asset Allocation

Asset	%
Cash	0%
Stocks	99%
US Stocks	66%
Bonds	0%
US Bonds	0%
Other	1%

Services Offered:

Investment Strategy: The investment seeks to track the investment results of the FTSE EPRA Nareit Global REITS Index. The index is designed to track the performance of publicly-listed real estate investment trusts ("REITs") (or their local equivalents) in both developed and emerging markets. The fund generally will invest at least 90% of its assets in the component securities of the underlying index and in investments that have economic characteristics that are substantially identical to the component securities of the underlying index and may invest up to 10% of its assets in certain futures, options and swap contracts, cash and cash equivalents. **Top Holdings:** Simon Property Group Inc Prologis Inc Public Storage Welltower Inc AvalonBay Communities Inc

Vanguard Emerging Markets Government Bond Index Fund ETF Shares

C HOLD

Ticker	Traded On	NAV	Total Assets ($)	Dividend Yield (TTM)	Turnover Ratio	Expense Ratio
VWOB	NAS CM		$1,330,445,879	4.6	19	0.32

Ratings
Reward	C-
Risk	C+
Recent Upgrade/Downgrade	Up

Fund Information
Fund Type	Exchange Traded Funds
Category	Emerging Mkts Fixed Inc
Sub-Category	Emerging Markets Bond
Prospectus Objective	Govt Bond - Gen
Inception Date	May-13
Open to New Investments	Y

Prices
Price (as of 12/31/2018)	74.54
52-Week High	80.61
52-Week Low	73.40

Total Returns (%)
3-Month	6-Month	1-Year	3-Year	5-Year
-0.19	1.45	-2.89	15.68	23.54

3-Year Standard Deviation	4.88
Effective Duration	6.24

Valuation
Premium/Discount (1-Year Average)	0.22

Company Information
Provider	Vanguard
Manager/Tenure	Joshua C. Barrickman (5)
Website	http://www.vanguard.com
Address	Vanguard 100 Vanguard Boulevard Malvern PA 19355 United States
Phone Number	877-662-7447

PERFORMANCE

Ratings History
Date	Overall Rating	Risk Rating	Reward Rating
Q4-18	C	C+	C-
Q2-18	C	C+	C-
Q4-17	B	A	C+
Q4-16	C	C-	C
Q4-15	D+	C-	D+

Asset & Performance History
Date	NAV	1-Year Total Return
2017	79.97	8.48
2016	77.24	9.8
2015	73.69	1.58
2014	76.1	5.12
2013	75.63	
2012		

Total Assets: $1,330,445,879

Asset Allocation
Asset	%
Cash	0%
Stocks	0%
US Stocks	0%
Bonds	98%
US Bonds	2%
Other	2%

Services Offered:

Investment Strategy: The investment seeks to track the performance of a benchmark index that measures the investment return of U.S. dollar-denominated bonds issued by governments and government-related issuers in emerging market countries. The fund employs an indexing investment approach designed to track the performance of the Bloomberg Barclays USD Emerging Markets Government RIC Capped Index. All of the fund's investments will be selected through the sampling process, and under normal circumstances at least 80% of the fund's assets will be invested in bonds included in the index. It is non-diversified. **Top Holdings:** Petroleos Mexicanos 6.75% Petrobras Global Finance B.V. 6% Argentina (Republic of) 7.5% State of Qatar 5.1% Russia Fedn Ministry Fin 4.88% 4.88%

Invesco S&P 500® Quality ETF

C+ HOLD

Ticker	Traded On	NAV	Total Assets ($)	Dividend Yield (TTM)	Turnover Ratio	Expense Ratio
SPHQ	NYSE Arca	27.80	$1,325,554,890	1.75	60	0.15

Ratings
Reward	C
Risk	C+
Recent Upgrade/Downgrade	Down

Fund Information
Fund Type	Exchange Traded Funds
Category	US Equity Large Cap Blend
Sub-Category	Large Blend
Prospectus Objective	Growth
Inception Date	Dec-05
Open to New Investments	Y

Prices
Price (as of 12/31/2018)	27.81
52-Week High	32.91
52-Week Low	25.94

Total Returns (%)
3-Month	6-Month	1-Year	3-Year	5-Year
-15.05	-6.66	-6.98	26.50	49.31

3-Year Standard Deviation	8.86
Effective Duration	

Valuation
Premium/Discount (1-Year Average)	-0.01

Company Information
Provider	Invesco
Manager/Tenure	Peter Hubbard (11), Michael Jeanette (10), Tony Seisser (4), 1 other
Website	http://www.invesco.com/us
Address	Invesco 11 Greenway Plaza, Ste. 2500 Houston TX 77046 United States
Phone Number	800-659-1005

PERFORMANCE

Ratings History
Date	Overall Rating	Risk Rating	Reward Rating
Q4-18	C+	C+	C
Q2-18	C+	C+	C+
Q4-17	B	B+	B
Q4-16	B-	C+	B
Q4-15	C+	C+	B-

Asset & Performance History
Date	NAV	1-Year Total Return
2017	30.41	19.12
2016	25.95	14.17
2015	23.12	1.66
2014	23.27	16.09
2013	20.4	32.04
2012	15.74	14.62

Total Assets: $1,325,554,890

Asset Allocation
Asset	%
Cash	0%
Stocks	100%
US Stocks	100%
Bonds	0%
US Bonds	0%
Other	0%

Services Offered:

Investment Strategy: The investment seeks to track the investment results (before fees and expenses) of the S&P 500® Quality Index. The fund generally will invest at least 90% of its total assets in securities that comprise the underlying index. In selecting constituent securities for the underlying index, the index provider first calculates the quality score of each security in the S&P 500® Index, then selects the 100 stocks with the highest quality score for inclusion in the underlying index. **Top Holdings:** Procter & Gamble Co Visa Inc Class A Mastercard Inc A Apple Inc Walt Disney Co

ARK Innovation ETF   C-   HOLD

Ticker	Traded On	NAV	Total Assets ($)	Dividend Yield (TTM)	Turnover Ratio	Expense Ratio
ARKK	NYSE Arca	37.18	$1,315,395,063	0.11	89	0.75

Ratings
Reward	C
Risk	D+
Recent Upgrade/Downgrade	Down

Fund Information
Fund Type	Exchange Traded Funds
Category	Technology Sector Equity
Sub-Category	Technology
Prospectus Objective	Unaligned
Inception Date	Oct-14
Open to New Investments	Y

Prices
Price (as of 12/31/2018)	37.19
52-Week High	49.70
52-Week Low	35.34

Total Returns (%)
3-Month	6-Month	1-Year	3-Year	5-Year
-21.36	-18.20	0.56	84.74	

3-Year Standard Deviation	23.78
Effective Duration	

Valuation
Premium/Discount (1-Year Average)	0.07

Company Information
Provider	ARK ETF Trust
Manager/Tenure	Catherine D. Wood (4)
Website	http://www.ark-funds.com
Address	ARK ETF Trust 155 West 19th Street, 5th Floor New York New York 10011 United States
Phone Number	212-426-7040

PERFORMANCE

Ratings History
Date	Overall Rating	Risk Rating	Reward Rating
Q4-18	C-	D+	C
Q2-18	C	D+	B-
Q4-17	B-	C+	B
Q4-16	D+	D+	C-
Q4-15	U		

Asset & Performance History
Date	NAV	1-Year Total Return
2017	37.05	87.38
2016	20.03	-1.95
2015	20.43	3.75
2014	20.13	
2013		
2012		

Total Assets: $1,315,395,063

Asset Allocation
Asset	%
Cash	0%
Stocks	100%
US Stocks	80%
Bonds	0%
US Bonds	0%
Other	0%

Services Offered:

Investment Strategy: The investment seeks long-term growth of capital. The fund is an actively-managed exchange-traded fund ("ETF") that will invest under normal circumstances primarily (at least 65% of its assets) in domestic and foreign equity securities of companies that are relevant to the fund's investment theme of disruptive innovation. Its investments in foreign equity securities will be in both developed and emerging markets. It may invest in foreign securities (including investments in American Depositary Receipts ("ADRs") and Global Depositary Receipts ("GDRs")) and securities listed on local foreign exchanges. The fund is non-diversified. **Top Holdings:** Tesla Inc Stratasys Ltd Invitae Corp Twitter Inc Intellia Therapeutics Inc

---

First Trust Tactical High Yield ETF   C   HOLD

Ticker	Traded On	NAV	Total Assets ($)	Dividend Yield (TTM)	Turnover Ratio	Expense Ratio
HYLS	NAS CM	45.07	$1,305,826,568	5.76	75	1.1

Ratings
Reward	C-
Risk	C+
Recent Upgrade/Downgrade	

Fund Information
Fund Type	Exchange Traded Funds
Category	US Fixed Income
Sub-Category	High Yield Bond
Prospectus Objective	Corp Bond-High Yld
Inception Date	Feb-13
Open to New Investments	Y

Prices
Price (as of 12/31/2018)	44.85
52-Week High	48.97
52-Week Low	44.51

Total Returns (%)
3-Month	6-Month	1-Year	3-Year	5-Year
-4.30	-1.69	-1.79	13.11	15.68

3-Year Standard Deviation	2.94
Effective Duration	2.78

Valuation
Premium/Discount (1-Year Average)	-0.07

Company Information
Provider	First Trust
Manager/Tenure	Scott D. Fries (5), William Housey (5), Orlando Purpura (2)
Website	http://www.ftportfolios.com/
Address	First Trust 120 E. Liberty Drive, Suite 400 Wheaton IL 60187 United States
Phone Number	800-621-1675

PERFORMANCE

Ratings History
Date	Overall Rating	Risk Rating	Reward Rating
Q4-18	C	C+	C-
Q2-18	C	C-	C-
Q4-17	B	A-	C+
Q4-16	C	C+	C
Q4-15	C	C-	C

Asset & Performance History
Date	NAV	1-Year Total Return
2017	48.48	6.08
2016	48.28	8.55
2015	46.95	-0.15
2014	49.83	2.42
2013	51.43	
2012		

Total Assets: $1,305,826,568

Asset Allocation
Asset	%
Cash	-5%
Stocks	0%
US Stocks	0%
Bonds	105%
US Bonds	95%
Other	0%

Services Offered:

Investment Strategy: The investment seeks current income; capital appreciation is the secondary objective. Under normal market conditions, the fund invests at least 80% of its net assets (including investment borrowings) in high yield debt securities that are rated below investment grade at the time of purchase or unrated securities deemed by the fund's advisor to be of comparable quality. **Top Holdings:** Tenet Healthcare Corporation 8.12% Stars Group Holdings Bv Tsgicn Tl 07/10/25 MPH Acquisition Holdings LLC 7.12% Valeant Pharma Vrxcn Tl 06/02/25 Gray Television, Inc. 5.88%

Invesco FTSE RAFI Developed Markets ex-U.S. ETF   C-   HOLD

Ticker	Traded On	NAV	Total Assets ($)	Dividend Yield (TTM)	Turnover Ratio	Expense Ratio
PXF	NYSE Arca	37.51	$1,303,239,941	3.51	13	0.45

Ratings

Reward	D+
Risk	C-
Recent Upgrade/Downgrade	Down

Fund Information

Fund Type	Exchange Traded Funds
Category	Global Equity Large Cap
Sub-Category	Foreign Large Value
Prospectus Objective	Foreign Stock
Inception Date	Jun-07
Open to New Investments	

Prices

Price (as of 12/31/2018)	37.52
52-Week High	48.66
52-Week Low	36.29

Total Returns (%)

3-Month	6-Month	1-Year	3-Year	5-Year
-12.72	-10.39	-15.12	12.79	0.69

3-Year Standard Deviation	11.87
Effective Duration	

Valuation

Premium/Discount (1-Year Average)	0.04

Company Information

Provider	Invesco
Manager/Tenure	Peter Hubbard (11), Jonathan Nixon (4), Michael Jeanette (3), 1 other
Website	http://www.invesco.com/us
Address	Invesco 11 Greenway Plaza, Ste. 2500 Houston TX 77046 United States
Phone Number	800-659-1005

PERFORMANCE

Ratings History

Date	Overall Rating	Risk Rating	Reward Rating
Q4-18	C-	C-	D+
Q2-18	C	C-	C
Q4-17	C+	C	B-
Q4-16	D+	C-	D+
Q4-15	C	C+	C-

Asset & Performance History

Date	NAV	1-Year Total Return
2017	45.55	24.77
2016	37.59	6.5
2015	36.5	-4.83
2014	39.46	-6.19
2013	43.63	23.44
2012	36.29	15.58

Total Assets: $1,303,239,941

Asset Allocation

Asset	%
Cash	0%
Stocks	99%
US Stocks	1%
Bonds	0%
US Bonds	0%
Other	0%

Services Offered:

Investment Strategy: The investment seeks to track the investment results (before fees and expenses) of the FTSE RAFI Developed ex U.S. 1000 Index (the "underlying index"). The fund will invest at least 90% of its total assets in the securities of companies originating in countries that are classified as "developed" within the country classification definition of FTSE International Limited, excluding the United States, and that comprise the underlying index, as well as American depositary receipts ("ADRs") and global depositary receipts ("GDRs") that are based on the securities in the underlying index. **Top Holdings:** BP PLC   Royal Dutch Shell PLC Class A   HSBC Holdings PLC Total SA   Royal Dutch Shell PLC B

WisdomTree Emerging Markets SmallCap Dividend Fund   C-   HOLD

Ticker	Traded On	NAV	Total Assets ($)	Dividend Yield (TTM)	Turnover Ratio	Expense Ratio
DGS	NYSE Arca	42.27	$1,293,079,701	3.91	48	0.63

Ratings

Reward	C-
Risk	C-
Recent Upgrade/Downgrade	Down

Fund Information

Fund Type	Exchange Traded Funds
Category	Global Emerg Mkts Equity
Sub-Category	Diversified Emerging Mkts
Prospectus Objective	Div Emerg Mkts
Inception Date	Oct-07
Open to New Investments	Y

Prices

Price (as of 12/31/2018)	41.89
52-Week High	56.97
52-Week Low	40.12

Total Returns (%)

3-Month	6-Month	1-Year	3-Year	5-Year
-7.32	-9.24	-15.39	31.73	8.55

3-Year Standard Deviation	15.06
Effective Duration	

Valuation

Premium/Discount (1-Year Average)	-0.19

Company Information

Provider	WisdomTree
Manager/Tenure	Richard A. Brown (10), Thomas J. Durante (10), Karen Q. Wong (10)
Website	http://www.wisdomtree.com
Address	WisdomTree 245 Park Avenue, 35th floor New York NY 10167 United States
Phone Number	866-909-9473

PERFORMANCE

Ratings History

Date	Overall Rating	Risk Rating	Reward Rating
Q4-18	C-	C-	C-
Q2-18	C	C-	C
Q4-17	B-	C	B
Q4-16	C-	C	D+
Q4-15	D	D+	D

Asset & Performance History

Date	NAV	1-Year Total Return
2017	51.92	35.47
2016	39.51	14.92
2015	35.56	-15.94
2014	43.56	-1.96
2013	45.77	-2.56
2012	48.63	22.26

Total Assets: $1,293,079,701

Asset Allocation

Asset	%
Cash	0%
Stocks	100%
US Stocks	0%
Bonds	0%
US Bonds	0%
Other	0%

Services Offered:

Investment Strategy: The investment seeks to track the price and yield performance, before fees and expenses, of the WisdomTree Emerging Markets SmallCap Dividend Index. Under normal circumstances, at least 95% of the fund's total assets (exclusive of collateral held from securities lending) will be invested in component securities of the index and investments that have economic characteristics that are substantially identical to the economic characteristics of such component securities. The index is a fundamentally weighted index that is comprised of small cap common stocks selected from the WisdomTree Emerging Markets Dividend Index. The fund is non-diversified. **Top Holdings:** Transmissora Alianca de Energia Eletrica SA Unit   Guangzhou R&F Properties Co Ltd H Truworths International Ltd   Hyprop Investments Ltd ADR   Foschini Group Ltd

iShares PHLX Semiconductor ETF   B-   BUY

Ticker	Traded On	NAV	Total Assets ($)	Dividend Yield (TTM)	Turnover Ratio	Expense Ratio
SOXX	NAS CM	156.88	$1,287,515,970	1.26	20	0.47

Ratings

Reward	B
Risk	C-
Recent Upgrade/Downgrade	Down

Fund Information

Fund Type	Exchange Traded Funds
Category	Technology Sector Equity
Sub-Category	Technology
Prospectus Objective	Technology
Inception Date	Jul-01
Open to New Investments	Y

Prices

Price (as of 12/31/2018)	156.91
52-Week High	196.31
52-Week Low	145.00

Total Returns (%)

3-Month	6-Month	1-Year	3-Year	5-Year
-15.31	-11.93	-6.47	81.00	130.26

3-Year Standard Deviation	19.04
Effective Duration	

Valuation

Premium/Discount (1-Year Average)	-0.01

Company Information

Provider	iShares
Manager/Tenure	Diane Hsiung (10), Greg Savage (10), Jennifer Hsui (6), 3 others
Website	http://www.ishares.com
Address	iShares 400 Howard Street San Francisco CA 94105 United States
Phone Number	800-474-2737

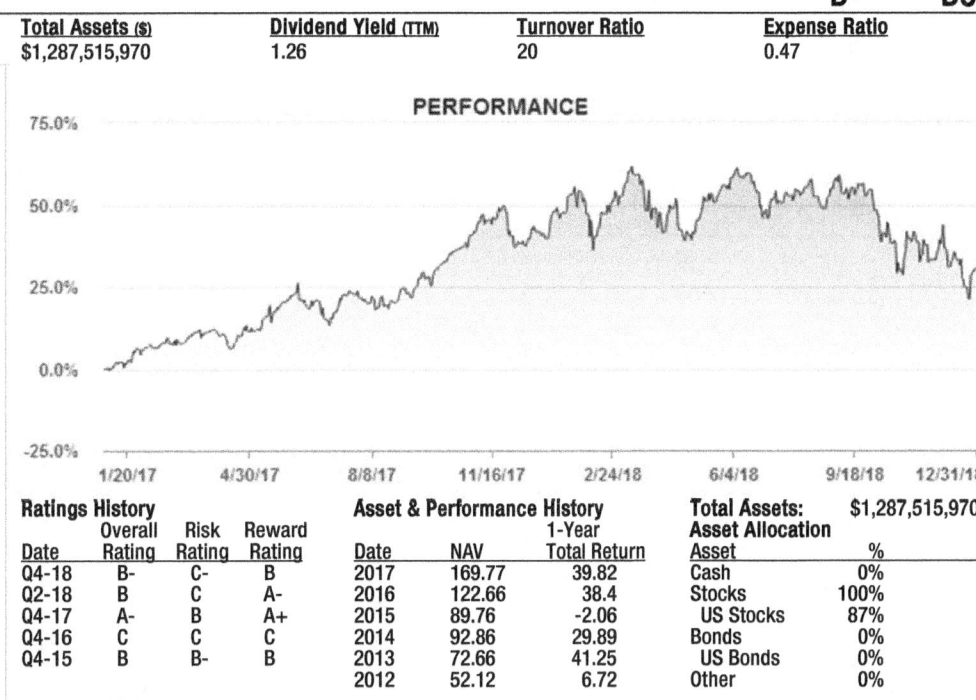

PERFORMANCE

Ratings History

Date	Overall Rating	Risk Rating	Reward Rating
Q4-18	B-	C-	B
Q2-18	B	C	A-
Q4-17	A-	B	A+
Q4-16	C	C	C
Q4-15	B	B-	B

Asset & Performance History

Date	NAV	1-Year Total Return
2017	169.77	39.82
2016	122.66	38.4
2015	89.76	-2.06
2014	92.86	29.89
2013	72.66	41.25
2012	52.12	6.72

Total Assets: $1,287,515,970

Asset Allocation

Asset	%
Cash	0%
Stocks	100%
US Stocks	87%
Bonds	0%
US Bonds	0%
Other	0%

Services Offered: CashInvestment Plan

Investment Strategy: The investment seeks to track the investment results of the PHLX Semiconductor Sector Index composed of U.S. equities in the semiconductor sector. The fund generally invests at least 90% of its assets in securities of the underlying index and in depositary receipts representing securities of the underlying index. The underlying index measures the performance of U.S.-traded securities of companies engaged in the semiconductor business. The fund is non-diversified. **Top Holdings:** Broadcom Inc Intel Corp Texas Instruments Inc Qualcomm Inc NVIDIA Corp

---

SPDR® S&P 400 Mid Cap Growth ETF   D-   SELL

Ticker	Traded On	NAV	Total Assets ($)	Dividend Yield (TTM)	Turnover Ratio	Expense Ratio
MDYG	NYSE Arca	45.84	$1,284,572,233	1.22	54	0.15

Ratings

Reward	E+
Risk	D
Recent Upgrade/Downgrade	

Fund Information

Fund Type	Exchange Traded Funds
Category	US Equity Mid Cap
Sub-Category	Mid-Cap Growth
Prospectus Objective	Growth
Inception Date	Nov-05
Open to New Investments	Y

Prices

Price (as of 12/31/2018)	45.85
52-Week High	165.57
52-Week Low	43.09

Total Returns (%)

3-Month	6-Month	1-Year	3-Year	5-Year
-16.93	-14.63	-70.14	-59.02	-55.13

3-Year Standard Deviation	11.58
Effective Duration	

Valuation

Premium/Discount (1-Year Average)	0.03

Company Information

Provider	SPDR State Street Global Advisors
Manager/Tenure	Michael J. Feehily (7), Karl A. Schneider (4), Dave Swallow (1)
Website	http://www.spdrs.com
Address	SPDR State Street Global Advisors State Street Financial Center, 1 Lincoln Street Boston MA 02111-2900 United States
Phone Number	617-786-3000

PERFORMANCE

Ratings History

Date	Overall Rating	Risk Rating	Reward Rating
Q4-18	D-	D	E+
Q2-18	D	D	D-
Q4-17	B+	B+	B+
Q4-16	C+	C-	B
Q4-15	C	C-	C+

Asset & Performance History

Date	NAV	1-Year Total Return
2017	155.44	19.73
2016	132.81	13.84
2015	117.43	1.96
2014	118.05	7.38
2013	111.71	32.45
2012	85.12	17.05

Total Assets: $1,284,572,233

Asset Allocation

Asset	%
Cash	0%
Stocks	100%
US Stocks	100%
Bonds	0%
US Bonds	0%
Other	0%

Services Offered: Dividend Investment Plan, CashInvestment Plan

Investment Strategy: The investment seeks to provide investment results that, before fees and expenses, correspond generally to the total return performance of the S&P MidCap 400 Growth Index that tracks the performance of medium capitalization exchange traded U.S. equity securities exhibiting "growth" characteristics. The fund generally invests substantially all, but at least 80%, of its total assets in the securities comprising the index. The index measures the performance of the mid-capitalization growth segment of the U.S. equity market. The fund is non-diversified. **Top Holdings:** Teleflex Inc Domino's Pizza Inc Lamb Weston Holdings Inc IDEX Corp Zebra Technologies Corp

Fidelity® MSCI Financials Index ETF

C   HOLD

Ticker	Traded On	NAV	Total Assets ($)	Dividend Yield (TTM)	Turnover Ratio	Expense Ratio
FNCL	NYSE Arca	34.54	$1,278,102,093	1.95	5	0.08

Ratings
Reward	C
Risk	C+
Recent Upgrade/Downgrade	Down

Fund Information
Fund Type	Exchange Traded Funds
Category	Financials Sector Equity
Sub-Category	Financial
Prospectus Objective	Financial
Inception Date	Oct-13
Open to New Investments	Y

Prices
Price (as of 12/31/2018)	34.56
52-Week High	43.73
52-Week Low	32.43

Total Returns (%)
3-Month	6-Month	1-Year	3-Year	5-Year
-13.82	-11.47	-13.36	29.65	46.84

3-Year Standard Deviation	14.46
Effective Duration	

Valuation
Premium/Discount (1-Year Average)	0.03

Company Information
Provider	Fidelity Investments
Manager/Tenure	Jennifer Hsui (5), Greg Savage (5), Alan Mason (2), 2 others
Website	http://www.institutional.fidelity.com
Address	Fidelity Investments 82 Devonshire Street Boston MA 2109 United States
Phone Number	617-563-7000

PERFORMANCE

Ratings History
Date	Overall Rating	Risk Rating	Reward Rating
Q4-18	C	C+	C
Q2-18	C+	C+	C+
Q4-17	A-	B	A
Q4-16	C+	C+	B-
Q4-15	C-	B-	C

Asset & Performance History
Date	NAV	1-Year Total Return
2017	40.72	19.97
2016	34.54	24.72
2015	28.3	-0.62
2014	29.1	13.97
2013	26.01	
2012		

Total Assets: $1,278,102,093

Asset Allocation
Asset	%
Cash	0%
Stocks	100%
US Stocks	98%
Bonds	0%
US Bonds	0%
Other	0%

Services Offered:

Investment Strategy: The investment seeks to provide investment returns that correspond, before fees and expenses, generally to the performance of the MSCI USA IMI Financials Index. The fund invests at least 80% of assets in securities included in the fund's underlying index. The fund's underlying index is the MSCI USA IMI Financials Index, which represents the performance of the financial sector in the U.S. equity market. It may or may not hold all of the securities in the MSCI USA IMI Financials Index. The fund is non-diversified. **Top Holdings:** JPMorgan Chase & Co Berkshire Hathaway Inc B Bank of America Corporation Wells Fargo & Co Citigroup Inc

---

Invesco Dynamic Large Cap Value ETF

C   HOLD

Ticker	Traded On	NAV	Total Assets ($)	Dividend Yield (TTM)	Turnover Ratio	Expense Ratio
PWV	NYSE Arca	32.65	$1,263,392,149	2.14	128	0.56

Ratings
Reward	C
Risk	C
Recent Upgrade/Downgrade	

Fund Information
Fund Type	Exchange Traded Funds
Category	US Equity Large Cap Value
Sub-Category	Large Value
Prospectus Objective	Growth
Inception Date	Mar-05
Open to New Investments	Y

Prices
Price (as of 12/31/2018)	32.63
52-Week High	40.51
52-Week Low	30.83

Total Returns (%)
3-Month	6-Month	1-Year	3-Year	5-Year
-12.25	-7.40	-13.93	19.50	27.87

3-Year Standard Deviation	9.68
Effective Duration	

Valuation
Premium/Discount (1-Year Average)	0.03

Company Information
Provider	Invesco
Manager/Tenure	Peter Hubbard (11), Michael Jeanette (10), Tony Seisser (4), 1 other
Website	http://www.invesco.com/us
Address	Invesco 11 Greenway Plaza, Ste. 2500 Houston TX 77046 United States
Phone Number	800-659-1005

PERFORMANCE

Ratings History
Date	Overall Rating	Risk Rating	Reward Rating
Q4-18	C	C	C
Q2-18	C	C-	C
Q4-17	B	B	B
Q4-16	C+	C-	B
Q4-15	B-	B-	C+

Asset & Performance History
Date	NAV	1-Year Total Return
2017	38.76	16.99
2016	33.67	18.68
2015	29.09	-4.68
2014	31.25	12.26
2013	28.39	32.65
2012	21.83	16.17

Total Assets: $1,263,392,149

Asset Allocation
Asset	%
Cash	0%
Stocks	100%
US Stocks	100%
Bonds	0%
US Bonds	0%
Other	0%

Services Offered:

Investment Strategy: The investment seeks to track the investment results (before fees and expenses) of the Dynamic Large Cap Value IntellidexSM Index. The fund generally will invest at least 90% of its total assets in common stocks of large capitalization companies that comprise the underlying intellidex. The underlying intellidex for the fund is composed of 50 large capitalization U.S. value stocks that, strictly in accordance with its guidelines and mandated procedures, the intellidex provider includes principally on the basis of their capital appreciation potential. **Top Holdings:** United Continental Holdings Inc Coca-Cola Co Mondelez International Inc Class A Walt Disney Co T-Mobile US Inc

iShares S&P GSCI Commodity-Indexed Trust   C-   HOLD

Ticker	Traded On	NAV	Total Assets ($)	Dividend Yield (TTM)	Turnover Ratio	Expense Ratio
GSG	NYSE Arca	13.99	$1,246,236,034	0	0	0.75

Ratings
Reward	C-
Risk	C
Recent Upgrade/Downgrade	Down

Fund Information
Fund Type	Exchange Traded Funds
Category	Commodities Broad Basket
Sub-Category	Commodities Broad Basket
Prospectus Objective	Unaligned
Inception Date	Jul-06
Open to New Investments	Y

Prices
Price (as of 12/31/2018)	14.02
52-Week High	18.72
52-Week Low	13.86

Total Returns (%)
3-Month	6-Month	1-Year	3-Year	5-Year
-24.33	-20.64	-14.27	-1.54	-56.51

3-Year Standard Deviation	15.63
Effective Duration	

Valuation
Premium/Discount (1-Year Average)	-0.09

Company Information
Provider	iShares
Manager/Tenure	Management Team (12)
Website	http://www.ishares.com
Address	iShares 400 Howard Street San Francisco CA 94105 United States
Phone Number	800-474-2737

PERFORMANCE

Ratings History
Date	Overall Rating	Risk Rating	Reward Rating
Q4-18	C-	C	C-
Q2-18	C	C	C
Q4-17	D	D	D+
Q4-16	D-	D	D-
Q4-15	D-	D	D-

Asset & Performance History
Date	NAV	1-Year Total Return
2017	16.32	4.48
2016	15.62	9.92
2015	14.21	-33.47
2014	21.36	-33.6
2013	32.17	-2.04
2012	32.84	-0.6

Total Assets: $1,246,236,034
Asset Allocation
Asset	%
Cash	100%
Stocks	0%
US Stocks	0%
Bonds	0%
US Bonds	0%
Other	0%

Services Offered:

Investment Strategy: The investment seeks investment results, through the Trust's investment in the Investing Pool, that correspond generally, but are not necessarily identical, to the performance of the S&P GSCI™ Total Return Index, before the payment of expenses and liabilities of the Trust and the Investing Pool. The Investing Pool holds long positions in CERFs, which are futures contracts listed on the CME, whose settlement at expiration is based on the value of the S&P GSCI-ER, at that time. The Investing Pool also earns interest on the assets used to collateralize its holdings of CERFs. **Top Holdings:** US Treasury Bill

---

Invesco BulletShares 2019 Corporate Bond ETF   C   HOLD

Ticker	Traded On	NAV	Total Assets ($)	Dividend Yield (TTM)	Turnover Ratio	Expense Ratio
BSCJ	NYSE Arca	21.01	$1,241,980,654	2	3	0.1

Ratings
Reward	C
Risk	C+
Recent Upgrade/Downgrade	

Fund Information
Fund Type	Exchange Traded Funds
Category	US Fixed Income
Sub-Category	Short-Term Bond
Prospectus Objective	Corp Bond - Gen
Inception Date	Mar-12
Open to New Investments	Y

Prices
Price (as of 12/31/2018)	21.06
52-Week High	21.11
52-Week Low	20.94

Total Returns (%)
3-Month	6-Month	1-Year	3-Year	5-Year
0.48	1.26	1.71	6.77	12.73

3-Year Standard Deviation	1.33
Effective Duration	0.73

Valuation
Premium/Discount (1-Year Average)	0.16

Company Information
Provider	Invesco
Manager/Tenure	Jeremy Neisewander (2), Peter Hubbard (0), Jeffrey W. Kernagis (0), 1 other
Website	http://www.invesco.com/us
Address	Invesco 11 Greenway Plaza, Ste. 2500 Houston TX 77046 United States
Phone Number	800-659-1005

PERFORMANCE

Ratings History
Date	Overall Rating	Risk Rating	Reward Rating
Q4-18	C	C+	C
Q2-18	C	C+	C
Q4-17	B	A+	C
Q4-16	C	C+	C
Q4-15	C	C-	C

Asset & Performance History
Date	NAV	1-Year Total Return
2017	21.06	1.53
2016	21.08	3.14
2015	20.82	1.6
2014	20.91	3.91
2013	20.56	-0.1
2012	21.01	

Total Assets: $1,241,980,654
Asset Allocation
Asset	%
Cash	21%
Stocks	0%
US Stocks	0%
Bonds	79%
US Bonds	63%
Other	0%

Services Offered:

Investment Strategy: The investment seeks investment results that correspond generally to the performance, before the fund's fees and expenses, of an investment grade corporate bond index called the Nasdaq BulletShares® USD Corporate Bond 2019 Index. The fund will invest at least 80% of its total assets in component securities that comprise the index. The index is designed to represent the performance of a held-to-maturity portfolio of U.S. dollar-denominated investment-grade corporate bonds with effective maturities in the year 2019. The fund is non-diversified. **Top Holdings:** Shire Acquisitions Investments Ireland DAC 1.9% Morgan Stanley 5.62% JPMorgan Chase & Co. 6.3% Credit Suisse AG New York Branch 2.3% Morgan Stanley 7.3%

Vanguard Russell 3000 Index Fund ETF Shares   C-   HOLD

Ticker	Traded On	NAV	Total Assets ($)	Dividend Yield (TTM)	Turnover Ratio	Expense Ratio
VTHR	NAS CM		$1,241,267,564	1.67	14	0.15

Ratings
Reward	C
Risk	D+
Recent Upgrade/Downgrade	Down

Fund Information
Fund Type	Exchange Traded Funds
Category	US Equity Large Cap Blend
Sub-Category	Large Blend
Prospectus Objective	Growth
Inception Date	Sep-10
Open to New Investments	Y

Prices
Price (as of 12/31/2018)	113.93
52-Week High	135.17
52-Week Low	106.85

Total Returns (%)
3-Month	6-Month	1-Year	3-Year	5-Year
-15.18	-9.34	-6.15	27.66	44.01

3-Year Standard Deviation	9.79
Effective Duration	

Valuation
Premium/Discount (1-Year Average)	0.09

Company Information
Provider	Vanguard
Manager/Tenure	Michael A. Johnson (2), Walter Nejman (2)
Website	http://www.vanguard.com
Address	Vanguard 100 Vanguard Boulevard Malvern PA 19355 United States
Phone Number	877-662-7447

PERFORMANCE

Ratings History
Date	Overall Rating	Risk Rating	Reward Rating
Q4-18	C-	D+	C
Q2-18	C	D+	C+
Q4-17	B	B	B
Q4-16	C+	C-	B
Q4-15	C	C-	C

Asset & Performance History
Date	NAV	1-Year Total Return
2017	122.41	21.06
2016	102.99	11.92
2015	93.33	0.35
2014	94.71	12.41
2013	85.72	33.34
2012	65.41	16.23

Total Assets: $1,241,267,564

Asset Allocation
Asset	%
Cash	0%
Stocks	100%
US Stocks	99%
Bonds	0%
US Bonds	0%
Other	0%

Services Offered:

Investment Strategy: The investment seeks to track the performance of a benchmark index that measures the investment return of the broad U.S. stock market. The fund employs an indexing investment approach designed to track the performance of the Russell 3000® Index, which represents approximately 98% of the U.S. equity market and comprises the 3,000 largest companies in the United States. The Advisor attempts to replicate the target index by investing all, or substantially all, of its assets in the stocks that make up the index, holding each stock in approximately the same proportion as its weighting in the index. **Top Holdings:** Apple Inc Microsoft Corp Amazon.com Inc Berkshire Hathaway Inc B Johnson & Johnson

iShares MSCI KLD 400 Social ETF   C   HOLD

Ticker	Traded On	NAV	Total Assets ($)	Dividend Yield (TTM)	Turnover Ratio	Expense Ratio
DSI	NYSE Arca	92.98	$1,238,023,267	1.42	11	0.25

Ratings
Reward	C
Risk	C-
Recent Upgrade/Downgrade	

Fund Information
Fund Type	Exchange Traded Funds
Category	US Equity Large Cap Blend
Sub-Category	Large Blend
Prospectus Objective	Growth
Inception Date	Nov-06
Open to New Investments	Y

Prices
Price (as of 12/31/2018)	93.00
52-Week High	107.67
52-Week Low	87.24

Total Returns (%)
3-Month	6-Month	1-Year	3-Year	5-Year
-12.81	-7.42	-3.80	28.39	44.66

3-Year Standard Deviation	10.02
Effective Duration	

Valuation
Premium/Discount (1-Year Average)	0.02

Company Information
Provider	iShares
Manager/Tenure	Diane Hsiung (10), Greg Savage (10), Jennifer Hsui (6), 3 others
Website	http://www.ishares.com
Address	iShares 400 Howard Street San Francisco CA 94105 United States
Phone Number	800-474-2737

PERFORMANCE

Ratings History
Date	Overall Rating	Risk Rating	Reward Rating
Q4-18	C	C-	C
Q2-18	C	C-	C+
Q4-17	B	B	B
Q4-16	C+	C-	B
Q4-15	C	C	C

Asset & Performance History
Date	NAV	1-Year Total Return
2017	98.14	20.96
2016	82.25	10.34
2015	75.72	0.46
2014	76.48	12.14
2013	69.09	35.49
2012	51.71	12.65

Total Assets: $1,238,023,267

Asset Allocation
Asset	%
Cash	0%
Stocks	100%
US Stocks	98%
Bonds	0%
US Bonds	0%
Other	0%

Services Offered:

Investment Strategy: The investment seeks to track the investment results of the MSCI KLD 400 Social Index composed of U.S. companies that have positive environmental, social and governance characteristics as identified by the index provider. The fund generally invests at least 90% of its assets in securities of the underlying index and in depositary receipts representing securities of the underlying index. The underlying index is a free float-adjusted market capitalization index designed to target U.S. companies that have positive environmental, social and governance ("ESG") characteristics. **Top Holdings:** Microsoft Corp Alphabet Inc Class C Facebook Inc A Alphabet Inc A Verizon Communications Inc

iShares Russell Top 200 Growth ETF   C   HOLD

Ticker	Traded On	NAV	Total Assets ($)	Dividend Yield (TTM)	Turnover Ratio	Expense Ratio
IWY	NYSE Arca	71.62	$1,237,004,540	1.22	11	0.2

Ratings
Reward   C+
Risk   C
Recent Upgrade/Downgrade   Down

Fund Information
Fund Type   Exchange Traded Funds
Category   US Equity Large Cap Growth
Sub-Category   Large Growth
Prospectus Objective   Growth
Inception Date   Sep-09
Open to New Investments   Y

Prices
Price (as of 12/31/2018)   71.75
52-Week High   85.82
52-Week Low   66.58

Total Returns (%)

3-Month	6-Month	1-Year	3-Year	5-Year
-16.20	-8.26	-0.76	39.45	70.62

3-Year Standard Deviation   10.99
Effective Duration

Valuation
Premium/Discount (1-Year Average)   0.05

Company Information
Provider   iShares
Manager/Tenure   Diane Hsiung (9), Greg Savage (9),
                    Jennifer Hsui (6), 3 others
Website   http://www.ishares.com
Address   iShares 400 Howard Street San
                    Francisco CA 94105 United States
Phone Number   800-474-2737

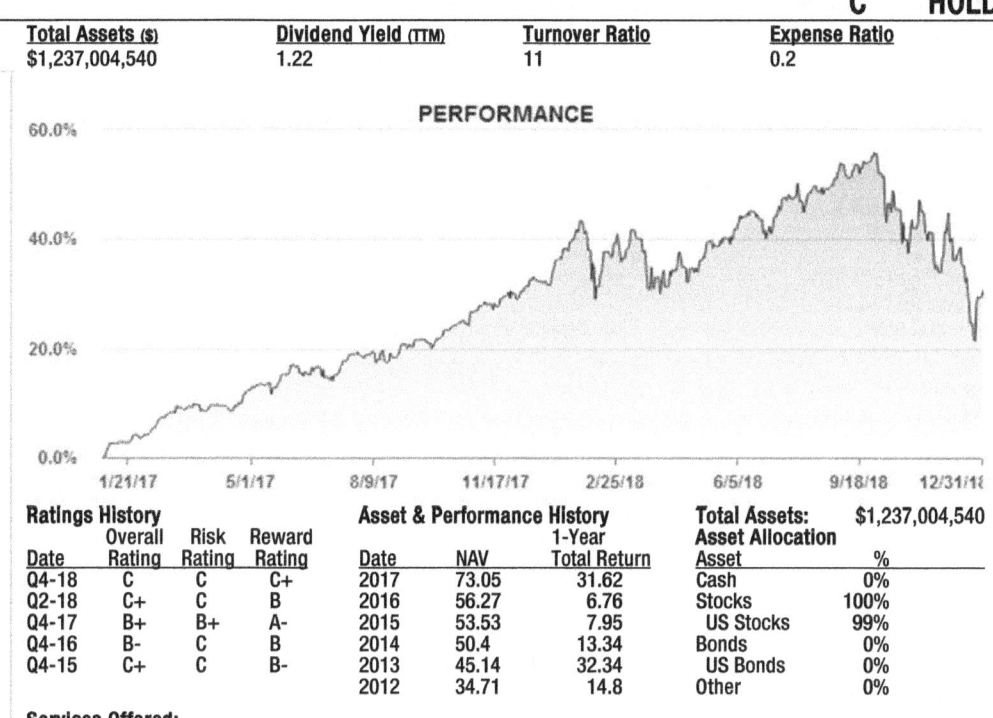

PERFORMANCE

Ratings History

Date	Overall Rating	Risk Rating	Reward Rating
Q4-18	C	C	C+
Q2-18	C+	C	B
Q4-17	B+	B+	A-
Q4-16	B-	C	B
Q4-15	C+	C	B-

Asset & Performance History

Date	NAV	1-Year Total Return
2017	73.05	31.62
2016	56.27	6.76
2015	53.53	7.95
2014	50.4	13.34
2013	45.14	32.34
2012	34.71	14.8

Total Assets: $1,237,004,540
Asset Allocation

Asset	%
Cash	0%
Stocks	100%
US Stocks	99%
Bonds	0%
US Bonds	0%
Other	0%

Services Offered:

Investment Strategy: The investment seeks to track the investment results of the Russell Top 200 Growth Index, which measures the performance of the largest capitalization growth sector of the U.S. equity market. The fund generally will invest at least 90% of its assets in the component securities of the underlying index and may invest up to 10% of its assets in certain futures, options and swap contracts, cash and cash equivalents, as well as in securities not included in the underlying index, but which the advisor believes will help the fund track the underlying index. **Top Holdings:** Apple Inc Microsoft Corp Amazon.com Inc Facebook Inc A Visa Inc Class A

---

iShares Mortgage Real Estate Capped ETF   B-   BUY

Ticker	Traded On	NAV	Total Assets ($)	Dividend Yield (TTM)	Turnover Ratio	Expense Ratio
REM	BATS	39.96	$1,236,463,669	10.11	31	0.48

Ratings
Reward   B
Risk   C
Recent Upgrade/Downgrade

Fund Information
Fund Type   Exchange Traded Funds
Category   Real Estate Sector Equity
Sub-Category   Real Estate
Prospectus Objective   Real Estate
Inception Date   May-07
Open to New Investments   Y

Prices
Price (as of 12/31/2018)   39.94
52-Week High   45.65
52-Week Low   38.44

Total Returns (%)

3-Month	6-Month	1-Year	3-Year	5-Year
-5.62	-4.16	-2.95	40.34	48.51

3-Year Standard Deviation   10.27
Effective Duration

Valuation
Premium/Discount (1-Year Average)   -0.02

Company Information
Provider   iShares
Manager/Tenure   Diane Hsiung (10), Greg Savage (10),
                    Jennifer Hsui (6), 3 others
Website   http://www.ishares.com
Address   iShares 400 Howard Street San
                    Francisco CA 94105 United States
Phone Number   800-474-2737

PERFORMANCE

Ratings History

Date	Overall Rating	Risk Rating	Reward Rating
Q4-18	B-	C	B
Q2-18	C+	C-	B
Q4-17	B-	C+	B-
Q4-16	C	C-	B-
Q4-15	C	C	B-

Asset & Performance History

Date	NAV	1-Year Total Return
2017	45.21	18.56
2016	42.06	21.96
2015	38.24	-9.31
2014	46.88	16.69
2013	46.16	-2.46
2012	54.68	21.9

Total Assets: $1,236,463,669
Asset Allocation

Asset	%
Cash	0%
Stocks	100%
US Stocks	100%
Bonds	0%
US Bonds	0%
Other	0%

Services Offered:

Investment Strategy: The investment seeks to track the investment results of the FTSE Nareit All Mortgage Capped Index composed of U.S. real estate investment trusts ("REITs") that hold U.S. residential and commercial mortgages. The fund generally will invest at least 90% of its assets in the component securities of the underlying index and may invest up to 10% of its assets in certain futures, options and swap contracts, cash and cash equivalents. The underlying index measures the performance of the residential and commercial mortgage real estate, mortgage finance and savings associations sectors of the U.S. equity market. The fund is non-diversified. **Top Holdings:** Annaly Capital Management Inc AGNC Investment Corp New Residential Investment Corp Starwood Property Trust Inc Blackstone Mortgage Trust Inc A

Oppenheimer S&P Ultra Dividend Revenue ETF
C   HOLD

Ticker	Traded On	NAV	Total Assets ($)	Dividend Yield (TTM)	Turnover Ratio	Expense Ratio
RDIV	NYSE Arca	33.53	$1,213,445,157	4.17		0.39

Ratings
Reward   C
Risk   C
Recent Upgrade/Downgrade   Down

Fund Information
Fund Type   Exchange Traded Funds
Category   US Equity Large Cap Value
Sub-Category   Large Value
Prospectus Objective   Growth
Inception Date   Sep-13
Open to New Investments   Y

Prices
Price (as of 12/31/2018)   33.48
52-Week High   39.77
52-Week Low   32.38

Total Returns (%)

3-Month	6-Month	1-Year	3-Year	5-Year
-12.85	-9.91	-4.47	36.82	57.67

3-Year Standard Deviation   10.86
Effective Duration

Valuation
Premium/Discount (1-Year Average)   0.04

Company Information
Provider   OppenheimerFunds
Manager/Tenure   Frank Vallario (1), Donal Bishnoi (0)
Website   http://www.oppenheimerfunds.com
Address   OppenheimerFunds 12100 East Iliff
                  Avenue, Suite 300, Aurora, Colorado
                  Aurora CO 80217-5270 United States
Phone Number   800-225-5677

PERFORMANCE

Ratings History

Date	Overall Rating	Risk Rating	Reward Rating
Q4-18	C	C	C
Q2-18	C	D+	B
Q4-17	B	B	B+
Q4-16	C	D+	B-
Q4-15	C-	C	B

Asset & Performance History

Date	NAV	1-Year Total Return
2017	36.51	11.49
2016	34.24	28.5
2015	27.56	-5.21
2014	30.34	21.4
2013	25.87	
2012		

Total Assets: $1,213,445,157

Asset Allocation

Asset	%
Cash	0%
Stocks	100%
US Stocks	100%
Bonds	0%
US Bonds	0%
Other	0%

Services Offered:

Investment Strategy: The investment seeks to provide investment results that correspond generally, before fees and expenses, to the performance of the S&P 900 Dividend Revenue-Weighted Index (the "underlying index"). The fund will normally invest at least 80% of its net assets, plus any borrowings for investment purposes, in the securities of companies included in the underlying index. The underlying index is constructed using a rules-based methodology that starts with the S&P 900® Index (the "parent index"), subject to a maximum 5% per company weighting. The fund is non-diversified. **Top Holdings:** General Motors Co Chevron Corp Verizon Communications Inc Exxon Mobil Corp International Business Machines Corp

---

iShares Edge MSCI Multifactor USA ETF
C   HOLD

Ticker	Traded On	NAV	Total Assets ($)	Dividend Yield (TTM)	Turnover Ratio	Expense Ratio
LRGF	NYSE Arca	27.83	$1,212,771,462	1.69	46	0.2

Ratings
Reward   C
Risk   C+
Recent Upgrade/Downgrade   Down

Fund Information
Fund Type   Exchange Traded Funds
Category   US Equity Large Cap Value
Sub-Category   Large Value
Prospectus Objective   Growth & Inc
Inception Date   Apr-15
Open to New Investments   Y

Prices
Price (as of 12/31/2018)   27.86
52-Week High   34.13
52-Week Low   26.57

Total Returns (%)

3-Month	6-Month	1-Year	3-Year	5-Year
-16.84	-12.27	-10.96	22.41	

3-Year Standard Deviation   9.98
Effective Duration

Valuation
Premium/Discount (1-Year Average)   -0.07

Company Information
Provider   iShares
Manager/Tenure   Diane Hsiung (3), Jennifer Hsui (3),
                  Greg Savage (3), 3 others
Website   http://www.ishares.com
Address   iShares 400 Howard Street San
                  Francisco CA 94105 United States
Phone Number   800-474-2737

PERFORMANCE

Ratings History

Date	Overall Rating	Risk Rating	Reward Rating
Q4-18	C	C+	C
Q2-18	C+	C+	C+
Q4-17	B-	B	C+
Q4-16	D+	C-	C-
Q4-15	U		

Asset & Performance History

Date	NAV	1-Year Total Return
2017	31.81	21.25
2016	26.71	13.39
2015	23.95	
2014		
2013		
2012		

Total Assets: $1,212,771,462

Asset Allocation

Asset	%
Cash	0%
Stocks	100%
US Stocks	99%
Bonds	0%
US Bonds	0%
Other	0%

Services Offered:

Investment Strategy: The investment seeks to track the investment results of the MSCI USA Diversified Multiple-Factor Index. The fund generally will invest at least 90% of its assets in the component securities of the underlying index and may invest up to 10% of its assets in certain futures, options and swap contracts, cash and cash equivalents. The underlying index is designed to select equity securities from the MSCI USA Index (the "parent index") that have high exposure to four investment style factors: value, quality, momentum and low size, while maintaining a level of risk similar to that of the parent index. **Top Holdings:** AT&T Inc Anthem Inc Express Scripts Holding Co Cigna Corp Intuit Inc

iShares U.S. Healthcare Providers ETF   B   BUY

Ticker	Traded On	NAV	Total Assets ($)	Dividend Yield (TTM)	Turnover Ratio	Expense Ratio
IHF	NYSE Arca	165.15	$1,209,557,588	0.2	20	0.43

Ratings
Reward   B
Risk   C+
Recent Upgrade/Downgrade

Fund Information
Fund Type   Exchange Traded Funds
Category   Healthcare Sector Equity
Sub-Category   Health
Prospectus Objective   Health
Inception Date   May-06
Open to New Investments   Y

Prices
Price (as of 12/31/2018)   165.19
52-Week High   201.83
52-Week Low   155.72

Total Returns (%)

3-Month	6-Month	1-Year	3-Year	5-Year
-14.25	-2.95	9.60	38.77	85.89

3-Year Standard Deviation   12.95
Effective Duration

Valuation
Premium/Discount (1-Year Average)   0.09

Company Information
Provider   iShares
Manager/Tenure   Diane Hsiung (10), Greg Savage (10),
                 Jennifer Hsui (6), 3 others
Website   http://www.ishares.com
Address   iShares 400 Howard Street San
                 Francisco CA 94105 United States
Phone Number   800-474-2737

PERFORMANCE

Ratings History

Date	Overall Rating	Risk Rating	Reward Rating
Q4-18	B	C+	B
Q2-18	B	C	B
Q4-17	B	B	B-
Q4-16	B-	C+	B
Q4-15	B+	B	B+

Asset & Performance History

Date	NAV	1-Year Total Return
2017	156.76	25.48
2016	125.18	0.9
2015	124.38	5.3
2014	118.35	27.21
2013	93.22	36.71
2012	68.36	17.25

Total Assets: $1,209,557,588

Asset Allocation

Asset	%
Cash	0%
Stocks	100%
US Stocks	99%
Bonds	0%
US Bonds	0%
Other	0%

Services Offered:

Investment Strategy: The investment seeks to track the investment results of the Dow Jones U.S. Select Health Care Providers Index composed of U.S. equities in the healthcare providers sector. The fund generally invests at least 90% of its assets in securities of the underlying index and in depositary receipts representing securities of the underlying index. The underlying index measures the performance of the healthcare providers sector of the U.S. equity market. The fund may invest the remainder of its assets in certain futures, options and swap contracts, cash and cash equivalents. It is non-diversified. **Top Holdings:** UnitedHealth Group Inc   CVS Health Corp   Anthem Inc   Cigna Corp   Express Scripts Holding Co

---

SPDR® Portfolio Long Term Treasury ETF   D+   SELL

Ticker	Traded On	NAV	Total Assets ($)	Dividend Yield (TTM)	Turnover Ratio	Expense Ratio
SPTL	NYSE Arca	34.87	$1,209,253,481	2.87	10	0.06

Ratings
Reward   D
Risk   C-
Recent Upgrade/Downgrade   Down

Fund Information
Fund Type   Exchange Traded Funds
Category   US Fixed Income
Sub-Category   Long Government
Prospectus Objective   Govt Bond - Treasury
Inception Date   May-07
Open to New Investments   Y

Prices
Price (as of 12/31/2018)   35.04
52-Week High   36.59
52-Week Low   32.31

Total Returns (%)

3-Month	6-Month	1-Year	3-Year	5-Year
4.77	1.29	-1.88	7.68	32.68

3-Year Standard Deviation   9.18
Effective Duration   16.86

Valuation
Premium/Discount (1-Year Average)   -0.06

Company Information
Provider   SPDR State Street Global Advisors
Manager/Tenure   Joanna Madden (4), Cynthia Moy (2),
                 Orhan Imer (1)
Website   http://www.spdrs.com
Address   SPDR State Street Global Advisors
                 State Street Financial Center, 1
                 Lincoln Street Boston MA 02111-2900
                 United States
Phone Number   617-786-3000

PERFORMANCE

Ratings History

Date	Overall Rating	Risk Rating	Reward Rating
Q4-18	D+	C-	D
Q2-18	C-	C	D+
Q4-17	C	C	C
Q4-16	C	C-	C
Q4-15	C	C-	C

Asset & Performance History

Date	NAV	1-Year Total Return
2017	36.53	8.13
2016	34.58	1.12
2015	34.97	-1.32
2014	36.35	24.87
2013	29.95	-12.75
2012	35.3	3.43

Total Assets: $1,209,253,481

Asset Allocation

Asset	%
Cash	1%
Stocks	0%
US Stocks	0%
Bonds	99%
US Bonds	99%
Other	0%

Services Offered:

Investment Strategy: The investment seeks to provide investment results that correspond generally to the price and yield performance of the Bloomberg Barclays Long U.S. Treasury Index. The fund generally invests substantially all, but at least 80%, of its total assets in the securities comprising the index or in securities that the adviser determines have economic characteristics that are substantially identical to the economic characteristics of the securities that comprise the index. The index is designed to measure the performance of public obligations of the U.S. Treasury that have a remaining maturity of 10 years or more. The fund is non-diversified. **Top Holdings:** United States Treasury Bonds 3%   United States Treasury Bonds 3.62%   United States Treasury Bonds 3.75%   United States Treasury Bonds 3.12%   United States Treasury Bonds 3.38%

Invesco FTSE RAFI Emerging Markets ETF — C — HOLD

Ticker	Traded On	NAV	Total Assets ($)	Dividend Yield (TTM)	Turnover Ratio	Expense Ratio
PXH	NYSE Arca	19.83	$1,197,189,419	3.47	24	0.5

Ratings
Reward — C-
Risk — C
Recent Upgrade/Downgrade

Fund Information
Fund Type	Exchange Traded Funds
Category	Global Emerg Mkts Equity
Sub-Category	Diversified Emerging Mkts
Prospectus Objective	Div Emerg Mkts
Inception Date	Sep-07
Open to New Investments	

Prices
Price (as of 12/31/2018)	19.77
52-Week High	25.30
52-Week Low	19.25

Total Returns (%)
3-Month	6-Month	1-Year	3-Year	5-Year
-5.61	-1.40	-8.12	52.93	12.42

3-Year Standard Deviation — 18.06
Effective Duration

Valuation
Premium/Discount (1-Year Average) — 0.14

Company Information
Provider	Invesco
Manager/Tenure	Peter Hubbard (11), Jonathan Nixon (4), Michael Jeanette (3), 1 other
Website	http://www.invesco.com/us
Address	Invesco 11 Greenway Plaza, Ste. 2500 Houston TX 77046 United States
Phone Number	800-659-1005

PERFORMANCE

Ratings History
Date	Overall Rating	Risk Rating	Reward Rating
Q4-18	C	C	C-
Q2-18	C	C	C
Q4-17	B-	C	B
Q4-16	C-	C-	C-
Q4-15	D	D	D

Asset & Performance History
Date	NAV	1-Year Total Return
2017	22.27	25.69
2016	18.23	32.43
2015	14.06	-22.68
2014	18.75	-4.91
2013	20.29	-7.65
2012	22.6	14.67

Total Assets: $1,197,189,419
Asset Allocation
Asset	%
Cash	0%
Stocks	100%
US Stocks	0%
Bonds	0%
US Bonds	0%
Other	0%

Services Offered:

Investment Strategy: The investment seeks to track the investment results (before fees and expenses) of the FTSE RAFI Emerging Markets Index (the "underlying index"). The fund will invest at least 90% of its total assets in securities of companies domiciled in countries that are classified as emerging markets within the country classification definition of FTSE International Limited that comprise the underlying index, as well as ADRs and GDRs that are based on the securities in the underlying index. The underlying index is designed to track the performance of securities of companies domiciled in emerging market countries with the highest ranking cumulative score. **Top Holdings:** China Construction Bank Corp H Taiwan Semiconductor Manufacturing Co Ltd Gazprom PJSC ADR China Mobile Ltd Industrial And Commercial Bank Of China Ltd H

---

iShares MSCI Australia ETF — C- — HOLD

Ticker	Traded On	NAV	Total Assets ($)	Dividend Yield (TTM)	Turnover Ratio	Expense Ratio
EWA	NYSE Arca	19.25	$1,195,303,823	4.79	3	0.47

Ratings
Reward — C-
Risk — C
Recent Upgrade/Downgrade — Down

Fund Information
Fund Type	Exchange Traded Funds
Category	Australia & New Zealand Equity
Sub-Category	Miscellaneous Region
Prospectus Objective	Pacific Stock
Inception Date	Mar-96
Open to New Investments	Y

Prices
Price (as of 12/31/2018)	19.25
52-Week High	24.11
52-Week Low	18.42

Total Returns (%)
3-Month	6-Month	1-Year	3-Year	5-Year
-9.41	-10.02	-12.31	16.41	0.44

3-Year Standard Deviation — 13.93
Effective Duration

Valuation
Premium/Discount (1-Year Average) — -0.17

Company Information
Provider	iShares
Manager/Tenure	Diane Hsiung (10), Greg Savage (10), Jennifer Hsui (5), 1 other
Website	http://www.ishares.com
Address	iShares 400 Howard Street San Francisco CA 94105 United States
Phone Number	800-474-2737

PERFORMANCE

Ratings History
Date	Overall Rating	Risk Rating	Reward Rating
Q4-18	C-	C	C-
Q2-18	C	C+	C
Q4-17	C+	C	B-
Q4-16	D+	D+	C-
Q4-15	D	D	D+

Asset & Performance History
Date	NAV	1-Year Total Return
2017	23.25	19.55
2016	20.36	11.04
2015	19.09	-10.31
2014	22.41	-3.79
2013	24.42	3.74
2012	24.72	21.55

Total Assets: $1,195,303,823
Asset Allocation
Asset	%
Cash	1%
Stocks	99%
US Stocks	1%
Bonds	0%
US Bonds	0%
Other	0%

Services Offered: CashInvestment Plan

Investment Strategy: The investment seeks to track the investment results of the MSCI Australia Index composed of Australian equities. The fund generally invests at least 90% of its assets in the securities of its underlying index and in depositary receipts representing securities in its underlying index. The underlying index consists of stocks traded primarily on the Australian Stock Exchange. It may include large- or mid-capitalization companies. The fund is non-diversified. **Top Holdings:** Commonwealth Bank of Australia BHP Group Ltd Westpac Banking Corp CSL Ltd Australia and New Zealand Banking Group Ltd

IQ Hedge Multi-Strategy Tracker ETF　　　　　　　　　　　　　　　　C-　　HOLD

Ticker	Traded On	NAV
QAI	NYSE Arca	28.92

Total Assets ($)	Dividend Yield (TTM)	Turnover Ratio	Expense Ratio
$1,193,854,483	0		0.79

Ratings
Reward	D+
Risk	C
Recent Upgrade/Downgrade	Down

Fund Information
Fund Type	Exchange Traded Funds
Category	Multialternative
Sub-Category	Multialternative
Prospectus Objective	Growth
Inception Date	Mar-09
Open to New Investments	Y

Prices
Price (as of 12/31/2018)	28.88
52-Week High	31.25
52-Week Low	28.81

Total Returns (%)
3-Month	6-Month	1-Year	3-Year	5-Year
-4.06	-2.89	-3.21	3.55	3.73

3-Year Standard Deviation	3.38
Effective Duration	2.96

Valuation
Premium/Discount (1-Year Average)	0.03

Company Information
Provider	IndexIQ
Manager/Tenure	Greg Barrato (7), James Harrison (0)
Website	http://www.indexiq.com
Address	IndexIQ 800 Westchester Avenue, Suite N-611 Rye Brook NY 10573 United States
Phone Number	888-934-0777

Ratings History
Date	Overall Rating	Risk Rating	Reward Rating
Q4-18	C-	C	D+
Q2-18	C	C-	C
Q4-17	B-	B+	C
Q4-16	C-	C	D+
Q4-15	C	C+	C

Asset & Performance History
Date	NAV	1-Year Total Return
2017	30.45	6.24
2016	28.66	0.7
2015	28.46	-2.53
2014	29.34	2.77
2013	28.93	5.15
2012	27.86	4.06

Total Assets: $1,193,854,483
Asset Allocation
Asset	%
Cash	27%
Stocks	25%
US Stocks	8%
Bonds	43%
US Bonds	38%
Other	3%

Services Offered:

Investment Strategy: The investment seeks investment results that correspond generally to the price and yield performance of its underlying index, the IQ Hedge Multi-Strategy Index. The fund is a "fund of funds" which means it invests, under normal circumstances, at least 80% of its net assets, plus the amount of any borrowings for investment purposes, in the investments included in its underlying index, which includes underlying funds. The underlying index consists of a number of components ("underlying index Components") selected in accordance with IndexIQ's rules-based methodology of such underlying index. **Top Holdings:** iShares Short Treasury Bond ETF SPDR® Blmbg Barclays 1-3 Mth T-Bill ETF Vanguard Interm-Term Corp Bd ETF Invesco Senior Loan ETF iShares MSCI EAFE Small-Cap ETF

---

iShares Dow Jones U.S. ETF　　　　　　　　　　　　　　　　　　C　　HOLD

Ticker	Traded On	NAV
IYY	NYSE Arca	124.41

Total Assets ($)	Dividend Yield (TTM)	Turnover Ratio	Expense Ratio
$1,192,661,301	1.64	4	0.2

Ratings
Reward	C
Risk	C-
Recent Upgrade/Downgrade	

Fund Information
Fund Type	Exchange Traded Funds
Category	US Equity Large Cap Blend
Sub-Category	Large Blend
Prospectus Objective	Growth
Inception Date	Jun-00
Open to New Investments	Y

Prices
Price (as of 12/31/2018)	124.45
52-Week High	147.06
52-Week Low	116.74

Total Returns (%)
3-Month	6-Month	1-Year	3-Year	5-Year
-14.27	-8.09	-5.22	28.73	45.87

3-Year Standard Deviation	9.64
Effective Duration	

Valuation
Premium/Discount (1-Year Average)	0.00

Company Information
Provider	iShares
Manager/Tenure	Diane Hsiung (10), Greg Savage (10), Jennifer Hsui (6), 3 others
Website	http://www.ishares.com
Address	iShares 400 Howard Street San Francisco CA 94105 United States
Phone Number	800-474-2737

Ratings History
Date	Overall Rating	Risk Rating	Reward Rating
Q4-18	C	C-	C
Q2-18	C	C-	C
Q4-17	B	B	B
Q4-16	C+	C-	B
Q4-15	C	C	C

Asset & Performance History
Date	NAV	1-Year Total Return
2017	133.54	21.23
2016	112.07	12.03
2015	101.95	0.51
2014	103.43	12.74
2013	93.33	32.64
2012	71.63	16.11

Total Assets: $1,192,661,301
Asset Allocation
Asset	%
Cash	0%
Stocks	100%
US Stocks	99%
Bonds	0%
US Bonds	0%
Other	0%

Services Offered: CashInvestment Plan

Investment Strategy: The investment seeks to track the investment results of the Dow Jones U.S. Index composed of U.S. equities. The fund generally invests at least 90% of its assets in securities of the underlying index and in depositary receipts representing securities of the underlying index. The underlying index aims to consistently represent the top 95% of U.S. companies based on a float-adjusted market capitalization, excluding the very smallest and least liquid stocks. **Top Holdings:** Microsoft Corp Apple Inc Amazon.com Inc Berkshire Hathaway Inc B Johnson & Johnson

Invesco S&P SmallCap Health Care ETF   C   HOLD

Ticker	Traded On	NAV	Total Assets ($)	Dividend Yield (TTM)	Turnover Ratio	Expense Ratio
PSCH	NAS CM	107.89	$1,169,996,001	0		0.29

Ratings
Reward   C+
Risk   C-
Recent Upgrade/Downgrade   Down

Fund Information
Fund Type	Exchange Traded Funds
Category	Healthcare Sector Equity
Sub-Category	Health
Prospectus Objective	Health
Inception Date	Apr-10
Open to New Investments	

Prices
Price (as of 12/31/2018)	107.53
52-Week High	144.96
52-Week Low	98.52

Total Returns (%)

3-Month	6-Month	1-Year	3-Year	5-Year
-21.96	-16.83	9.69	50.33	100.77

3-Year Standard Deviation	18.55
Effective Duration	

Valuation
Premium/Discount (1-Year Average)	0.16

Company Information
Provider	Invesco
Manager/Tenure	Peter Hubbard (8), Michael Jeanette (8), Tony Seisser (4), 1 other
Website	http://www.invesco.com/us
Address	Invesco 11 Greenway Plaza, Ste. 2500 Houston TX 77046 United States
Phone Number	800-659-1005

PERFORMANCE

Ratings History

Date	Overall Rating	Risk Rating	Reward Rating
Q4-18	C	C-	C+
Q2-18	B	C-	A-
Q4-17	A-	B+	A
Q4-16	C	C-	B-
Q4-15	C	C	C+

Asset & Performance History

Date	NAV	1-Year Total Return
2017	98.36	34.42
2016	73.17	1.94
2015	71.79	20.29
2014	59.68	11.02
2013	55.1	55.57
2012	35.43	13.11

Total Assets: $1,169,996,001
Asset Allocation

Asset	%
Cash	0%
Stocks	100%
US Stocks	100%
Bonds	0%
US Bonds	0%
Other	0%

Services Offered:

Investment Strategy: The investment seeks to track the investment results (before fees and expenses) of the S&P SmallCap 600® Capped Health Care Index (the "underlying index"). The fund generally will invest at least 90% of its total assets in common stocks of small capitalization U.S. healthcare companies that comprise the underlying index. These companies are principally engaged in the business of providing healthcare-related products, facilities and services, including biotechnology, pharmaceuticals, medical technology and supplies. **Top Holdings:** Amedisys Inc   Merit Medical Systems Inc   Neogen Corp   Emergent BioSolutions Inc   LHC Group Inc

---

Hartford Multifactor Developed Markets (ex-US) ETF   C   HOLD

Ticker	Traded On	NAV	Total Assets ($)	Dividend Yield (TTM)	Turnover Ratio	Expense Ratio
RODM	NYSE Arca	25.77	$1,165,061,523	2.32	47	0.29

Ratings
Reward   D+
Risk   C+
Recent Upgrade/Downgrade

Fund Information
Fund Type	Exchange Traded Funds
Category	Global Equity Large Cap
Sub-Category	Foreign Large Blend
Prospectus Objective	Foreign Stock
Inception Date	Feb-15
Open to New Investments	Y

Prices
Price (as of 12/31/2018)	25.80
52-Week High	30.81
52-Week Low	25.02

Total Returns (%)

3-Month	6-Month	1-Year	3-Year	5-Year
-10.21	-7.10	-9.73	17.18	

3-Year Standard Deviation	9.81
Effective Duration	

Valuation
Premium/Discount (1-Year Average)	0.21

Company Information
Provider	Hartford Funds
Manager/Tenure	Richard A. Brown (3), Thomas J. Durante (3), Karen Q. Wong (3)
Website	http://www.hartfordfunds.com
Address	690 Lee Road Wayne PA 19087 United States
Phone Number	800-456-7526

PERFORMANCE

Ratings History

Date	Overall Rating	Risk Rating	Reward Rating
Q4-18	C	C+	D+
Q2-18	C+	C+	C
Q4-17	C+	B-	C+
Q4-16	D+	D+	D+
Q4-15	U		

Asset & Performance History

Date	NAV	1-Year Total Return
2017	29.1	25.76
2016	23.69	3.22
2015	23.69	
2014		
2013		
2012		

Total Assets: $1,165,061,523
Asset Allocation

Asset	%
Cash	2%
Stocks	98%
US Stocks	3%
Bonds	0%
US Bonds	0%
Other	0%

Services Offered:

Investment Strategy: The investment seeks to provide investment results that, before fees and expenses, correspond to the total return performance of the Hartford Risk-Optimized Multifactor Developed Markets (ex-US) Index. The fund generally invests at least 80% of its assets in securities included in the index and in depositary receipts representing securities included in the index. The index is designed to address risks and opportunities within developed international economies outside the U.S. by selecting equity securities of companies domiciled within developed international equity markets exhibiting a favorable combination of factor characteristics. **Top Holdings:** Swiss Life Holding AG   Kyushu Railway Co   Metro Ag Common Stock   Icon PLC   Essity Aktiebolag B Common Stock Sek3.35

SPDR® Portfolio Mid Cap ETF   C   HOLD

Ticker	Traded On	NAV	Total Assets ($)	Dividend Yield (TTM)	Turnover Ratio	Expense Ratio
SPMD	NYSE Arca	29.43	$1,159,094,003	1.58	37	0.05

Ratings

Reward	C-
Risk	C+
Recent Upgrade/Downgrade	Down

Fund Information

Fund Type	Exchange Traded Funds
Category	US Equity Mid Cap
Sub-Category	Mid-Cap Blend
Prospectus Objective	Growth
Inception Date	Nov-05
Open to New Investments	Y

Prices

Price (as of 12/31/2018)	29.42
52-Week High	36.97
52-Week Low	27.71

Total Returns (%)

3-Month	6-Month	1-Year	3-Year	5-Year
-17.30	-15.07	-10.28	22.25	26.81

3-Year Standard Deviation	13.13
Effective Duration	

Valuation

Premium/Discount (1-Year Average)	0.03

Company Information

Provider	SPDR State Street Global Advisors
Manager/Tenure	Michael J. Feehily (7), Karl A. Schneider (4), Mark Krivitsky (1)
Website	http://www.spdrs.com
Address	SPDR State Street Global Advisors State Street Financial Center, 1 Lincoln Street Boston MA 02111-2900 United States
Phone Number	617-786-3000

PERFORMANCE

Ratings History

Date	Overall Rating	Risk Rating	Reward Rating
Q4-18	C	C+	C-
Q2-18	C+	C+	C+
Q4-17	B	B	B
Q4-16	C	D+	B-
Q4-15	C	D+	C

Asset & Performance History

Date	NAV	1-Year Total Return
2017	33.35	15.27
2016	29.53	17.69
2015	25.56	-3.4
2014	27.87	7.39
2013	27.46	38.13
2012	22.07	17.31

Total Assets: $1,159,094,003

Asset Allocation

Asset	%
Cash	0%
Stocks	100%
US Stocks	99%
Bonds	0%
US Bonds	0%
Other	0%

Services Offered: Dividend Investment Plan, CashInvestment Plan

Investment Strategy: The investment seeks to provide investment results that, before fees and expenses, correspond generally to the total return performance of the S&P 1000 Index. The fund generally invests substantially all, but at least 80%, of its total assets in the securities comprising the index. The index measures the performance of the small- and mid-capitalization segments of the U.S. equity market. The fund is non-diversified.
Top Holdings: Teleflex Inc   Domino's Pizza Inc   Lamb Weston Holdings Inc   Atmos Energy Corp   IDEX Corp

First Trust Large Cap Value AlphaDEX® Fund   C-   HOLD

Ticker	Traded On	NAV	Total Assets ($)	Dividend Yield (TTM)	Turnover Ratio	Expense Ratio
FTA	NAS CM	46.21	$1,157,675,545	1.86	72	0.61

Ratings

Reward	C-
Risk	C-
Recent Upgrade/Downgrade	Down

Fund Information

Fund Type	Exchange Traded Funds
Category	US Equity Large Cap Value
Sub-Category	Large Value
Prospectus Objective	Growth
Inception Date	May-07
Open to New Investments	Y

Prices

Price (as of 12/31/2018)	46.23
52-Week High	57.69
52-Week Low	43.92

Total Returns (%)

3-Month	6-Month	1-Year	3-Year	5-Year
-13.96	-10.61	-13.58	26.84	26.17

3-Year Standard Deviation	11.11
Effective Duration	

Valuation

Premium/Discount (1-Year Average)	0.03

Company Information

Provider	First Trust
Manager/Tenure	Jon C. Erickson (11), Daniel J. Lindquist (11), David G. McGarel (11), 3 others
Website	http://www.ftportfolios.com/
Address	First Trust 120 E. Liberty Drive, Suite 400 Wheaton IL 60187 United States
Phone Number	800-621-1675

PERFORMANCE

Ratings History

Date	Overall Rating	Risk Rating	Reward Rating
Q4-18	C-	C-	C-
Q2-18	C-	C-	C
Q4-17	B	B-	B
Q4-16	C	C-	B-
Q4-15	C	C+	C

Asset & Performance History

Date	NAV	1-Year Total Return
2017	54.59	18.45
2016	46.84	23.92
2015	38.45	-10.28
2014	43.7	10.87
2013	40.14	33.94
2012	30.48	17.27

Total Assets: $1,157,675,545

Asset Allocation

Asset	%
Cash	0%
Stocks	100%
US Stocks	99%
Bonds	0%
US Bonds	0%
Other	0%

Services Offered:

Investment Strategy: The investment seeks investment results that correspond generally to the price and yield (before the fund's fees and expenses) of an equity index called the Nasdaq AlphaDEX® Large Cap Value Index. The fund will normally invest at least 90% of its net assets (including investment borrowings) in common stocks that comprise the index. The index is designed to select value stocks from the NASDAQ US 500 Large Cap Index (the "base index") that may generate positive alpha, or risk-adjusted returns, relative to traditional indices through the use of the AlphaDEX® selection methodology. **Top Holdings:** Newell Brands Inc   Verizon Communications Inc   Comcast Corp Class A   Dollar Tree Inc   Symantec Corp

iShares Latin America 40 ETF
C   HOLD

Ticker	Traded On	NAV
ILF	NYSE Arca	30.86

Total Assets ($)	Dividend Yield (TTM)	Turnover Ratio	Expense Ratio
$1,155,819,044	2.55	16	0.48

Ratings
Reward	C
Risk	C
Recent Upgrade/Downgrade	

Fund Information
Fund Type	Exchange Traded Funds
Category	Latin America Equity
Sub-Category	Latin America Stock
Prospectus Objective	Growth
Inception Date	Oct-01
Open to New Investments	Y

Prices
Price (as of 12/31/2018)	30.82
52-Week High	39.50
52-Week Low	28.72

Total Returns (%)
3-Month	6-Month	1-Year	3-Year	5-Year
-0.63	7.26	-6.71	54.90	-5.95

3-Year Standard Deviation	25.68
Effective Duration	

Valuation
Premium/Discount (1-Year Average)	0.05

Company Information
Provider	iShares
Manager/Tenure	Diane Hsiung (10), Greg Savage (10), Jennifer Hsui (6), 3 others
Website	http://www.ishares.com
Address	iShares 400 Howard Street San Francisco CA 94105 United States
Phone Number	800-474-2737

PERFORMANCE

Ratings History
Date	Overall Rating	Risk Rating	Reward Rating
Q4-18	C	C	C
Q2-18	C	C	C
Q4-17	C	C	C
Q4-16	D+	D+	C-
Q4-15	D	D	D

Asset & Performance History
Date	NAV	1-Year Total Return
2017	34.16	25.84
2016	27.68	31.95
2015	21.33	-31.42
2014	31.97	-11.46
2013	36.88	-12.52
2012	43.63	5.33

Total Assets: $1,155,819,044

Asset Allocation
Asset	%
Cash	0%
Stocks	100%
US Stocks	1%
Bonds	0%
US Bonds	0%
Other	0%

Services Offered: CashInvestment Plan

Investment Strategy: The investment seeks to track the investment results of the S&P Latin America 40TM composed of 40 of the largest Latin American equities. The fund generally invests at least 90% of its assets in securities of the underlying index and in depositary receipts representing securities of the underlying index. It seeks to track the investment results of the S&P Latin America 40TM (the "underlying index"), which is comprised of selected equities trading on the exchanges of five Latin American countries. The fund is non-diversified. **Top Holdings:** Itau Unibanco Holding SA ADR   Vale SA ADR   Bank Bradesco SA ADR   Petroleo Brasileiro SA Petrobras ADR   Petroleo Brasileiro SA Petrobras ADR

---

iShares Core Growth Allocation ETF
C   HOLD

Ticker	Traded On	NAV
AOR	NYSE Arca	41.25

Total Assets ($)	Dividend Yield (TTM)	Turnover Ratio	Expense Ratio
$1,151,207,456	2.08	44	0.25

Ratings
Reward	C-
Risk	C+
Recent Upgrade/Downgrade	

Fund Information
Fund Type	Exchange Traded Funds
Category	Moderate Allocation
Sub-Category	Allocation--50% to 70% Equity
Prospectus Objective	Asset Allocation
Inception Date	Nov-08
Open to New Investments	Y

Prices
Price (as of 12/31/2018)	41.31
52-Week High	46.74
52-Week Low	40.34

Total Returns (%)
3-Month	6-Month	1-Year	3-Year	5-Year
-7.62	-4.86	-5.83	16.38	22.29

3-Year Standard Deviation	6.13
Effective Duration	5.97

Valuation
Premium/Discount (1-Year Average)	0.05

Company Information
Provider	iShares
Manager/Tenure	Diane Hsiung (10), Greg Savage (10), Jennifer Hsui (6), 3 others
Website	http://www.ishares.com
Address	iShares 400 Howard Street San Francisco CA 94105 United States
Phone Number	800-474-2737

PERFORMANCE

Ratings History
Date	Overall Rating	Risk Rating	Reward Rating
Q4-18	C	C+	C-
Q2-18	C	C-	C
Q4-17	B	A-	C+
Q4-16	C	C-	C
Q4-15	C	C-	C

Asset & Performance History
Date	NAV	1-Year Total Return
2017	44.86	15.87
2016	40.5	6.66
2015	38.81	-1.07
2014	40.05	6.21
2013	38.51	15.92
2012	33.9	11.35

Total Assets: $1,151,207,456

Asset Allocation
Asset	%
Cash	2%
Stocks	60%
US Stocks	32%
Bonds	37%
US Bonds	27%
Other	0%

Services Offered:

Investment Strategy: The investment seeks to track the investment results of the S&P Target Risk Growth Index composed of a portfolio of underlying equity and fixed income funds intended to represent a growth allocation target risk strategy. The fund is a fund of funds and seeks its investment objective by investing primarily in other iShares Underlying Funds that themselves seek investment results corresponding to their own respective underlying indexes. It generally will invest at least 90% of its assets in the component securities of the underlying index. The index measures the performance of the S&P Dow Jones Indices LLC proprietary allocation model. **Top Holdings:** iShares Core Total USD Bond Market ETF   iShares Core S&P 500 ETF   iShares Core MSCI Intl Dev Mkts ETF   iShares Core MSCI Emerging Markets ETF   iShares Core International Aggt Bd ETF

Invesco BulletShares 2019 High Yield Corporate Bond ETF   C   HOLD

Ticker	Traded On	NAV	Total Assets ($)	Dividend Yield (TTM)	Turnover Ratio	Expense Ratio
BSJJ	NYSE Arca	23.70	$1,148,511,357	4.41	25	0.42

Ratings
Reward	C
Risk	C+
Recent Upgrade/Downgrade	

Fund Information
Fund Type	Exchange Traded Funds
Category	US Fixed Income
Sub-Category	High Yield Bond
Prospectus Objective	Corp Bond-High Yld
Inception Date	Sep-13
Open to New Investments	Y

Prices
Price (as of 12/31/2018)	23.64
52-Week High	24.51
52-Week Low	23.46

Total Returns (%)
3-Month	6-Month	1-Year	3-Year	5-Year
-1.06	0.50	1.55	19.26	15.74

3-Year Standard Deviation	3.36
Effective Duration	0.73

Valuation
Premium/Discount (1-Year Average)	-0.02

Company Information
Provider	Invesco
Manager/Tenure	Jeremy Neisewander (2), Peter Hubbard (0), Jeffrey W. Kernagis (0), 1 other
Website	http://www.invesco.com/us
Address	Invesco 11 Greenway Plaza, Ste. 2500 Houston TX 77046 United States
Phone Number	800-659-1005

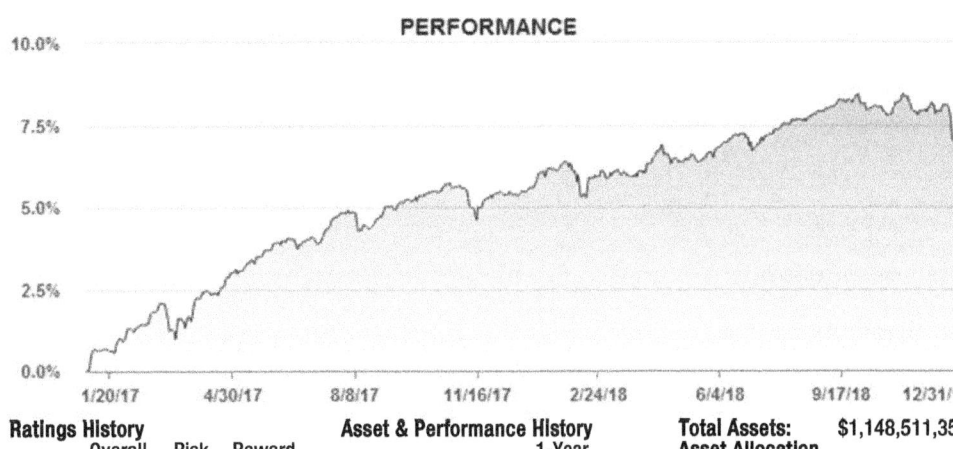

PERFORMANCE

Ratings History
Date	Overall Rating	Risk Rating	Reward Rating
Q4-18	C	C+	C
Q2-18	C+	C+	C
Q4-17	C+	B	C
Q4-16	C	C+	C
Q4-15	D+	C-	D

Asset & Performance History
Date	NAV	1-Year Total Return
2017	24.33	5.64
2016	24.08	11.04
2015	22.79	-3.74
2014	24.86	0.82
2013	25.74	
2012		

Total Assets: $1,148,511,357
Asset Allocation
Asset	%
Cash	8%
Stocks	0%
US Stocks	0%
Bonds	92%
US Bonds	87%
Other	0%

Services Offered:

Investment Strategy: The investment seeks investment results that correspond generally to the performance, before the fund's fees and expenses, of a high yield corporate bond index called the Nasdaq BulletShares® USD High Yield Corporate Bond 2019 Index. The fund will invest at least 80% of its total assets in component securities that comprise the index. The index is designed to represent the performance of a held-to-maturity portfolio of U.S. dollar-denominated high yield corporate bonds with effective maturities in the year 2019. The fund is non-diversified. **Top Holdings:** Prime Securities Services Borrower, LLC and Prime Finance, Inc. 9.25% Neptune Finco Corp 10.12% Solera, LLC / Solera Finance, Inc. 10.5% Scientific Games International, Inc. 10% Dynegy Inc 7.38%

Xtrackers Harvest CSI 300 China A-Shares ETF   D   SELL

Ticker	Traded On	NAV	Total Assets ($)	Dividend Yield (TTM)	Turnover Ratio	Expense Ratio
ASHR	NYSE Arca		$1,139,002,280	1.13	65	0.66

Ratings
Reward	D
Risk	D
Recent Upgrade/Downgrade	Down

Fund Information
Fund Type	Exchange Traded Funds
Category	Greater China Equity
Sub-Category	China Region
Prospectus Objective	Pacific Stock
Inception Date	Nov-13
Open to New Investments	Y

Prices
Price (as of 12/31/2018)	21.93
52-Week High	34.85
52-Week Low	21.68

Total Returns (%)
3-Month	6-Month	1-Year	3-Year	5-Year
-12.22	-13.04	-28.18	-19.60	20.44

3-Year Standard Deviation	21.3
Effective Duration	

Valuation
Premium/Discount (1-Year Average)	0.41

Company Information
Provider	Deutsche Asset Management
Manager/Tenure	Teresa Zheng (2)
Website	http://www.deutsche-etfs.com
Address	Deutsche Asset & Wealth Management 345 Park Avenue New York NY 10154 United States
Phone Number	844-851-4255

PERFORMANCE

Ratings History
Date	Overall Rating	Risk Rating	Reward Rating
Q4-18	D	D	D
Q2-18	D+	D+	C-
Q4-17	B	C	A-
Q4-16	C-	D+	C
Q4-15	D+	C	C

Asset & Performance History
Date	NAV	1-Year Total Return
2017	30.96	31.8
2016	23.69	-15.06
2015	28.09	0.07
2014	36.54	49.69
2013	24.48	
2012		

Total Assets: $1,139,002,280
Asset Allocation
Asset	%
Cash	0%
Stocks	100%
US Stocks	0%
Bonds	0%
US Bonds	0%
Other	0%

Services Offered:

Investment Strategy: The investment seeks investment results that correspond generally to the performance, before fees and expenses, of the CSI 300 Index. The fund will normally invest at least 80% of its total assets in securities of issuers that comprise the underlying index. The underlying index is designed to reflect the price fluctuation and performance of the China A-Share market and is composed of the 300 largest and most liquid stocks in the China A-Share market. The underlying index includes small-cap, mid-cap, and large-cap stocks. **Top Holdings:** Ping An Insurance (Group) Co. of China Ltd China Merchants Bank Co Ltd Kweichow Moutai Co Ltd Industrial Bank Co Ltd Midea Group Co Ltd Class A

Direxion Daily S&P500® Bull 3X Shares

C   **HOLD**

Ticker	Traded On	NAV
SPXL	NYSE Arca	32.86

Total Assets ($)	Dividend Yield (TTM)	Turnover Ratio	Expense Ratio
$1,123,736,445	0.52	99	1.04

Ratings
Reward	C
Risk	C
Recent Upgrade/Downgrade	Down

Fund Information
Fund Type	Exchange Traded Funds
Category	Trading Tools
Sub-Category	Trading--Leveraged Equity
Prospectus Objective	Growth
Inception Date	Nov-08
Open to New Investments	Y

Prices
Price (as of 12/31/2018)	32.90
52-Week High	55.38
52-Week Low	27.54

Total Returns (%)
3-Month	6-Month	1-Year	3-Year	5-Year
-39.74	-25.99	-24.86	66.11	116.39

3-Year Standard Deviation	29.08
Effective Duration	

Valuation
Premium/Discount (1-Year Average)	0.04

Company Information
Provider	Direxion Funds
Manager/Tenure	Paul Brigandi (10), Tony Ng (3)
Website	http://www.direxionfunds.com
Address	Direxion Funds 1301 Avenue Of The Americas (6th Avenue) New York NY 10019 United States
Phone Number	646-572-3390

PERFORMANCE

Ratings History
Date	Overall Rating	Risk Rating	Reward Rating
Q4-18	C	C	C
Q2-18	C	C	C
Q4-17	B+	C	A+
Q4-16	C	C	C
Q4-15	C	C+	C

Asset & Performance History
Date	NAV	1-Year Total Return
2017	44.12	70.88
2016	26.84	29.37
2015	20.74	-5.47
2014	21.95	37.82
2013	15.92	117.94
2012	7.31	44

Total Assets: $1,123,736,445

Asset Allocation
Asset	%
Cash	23%
Stocks	77%
US Stocks	77%
Bonds	0%
US Bonds	0%
Other	0%

Services Offered:

Investment Strategy: The investment seeks daily investment results, before fees and expenses, of 300% of the daily performance of the S&P 500® Index. The fund, under normal circumstances, invests at least 80% of its net assets (plus borrowing for investment purposes) in securities of the index, exchange-traded funds ("ETFs") that track the index and other financial instruments that provide daily leveraged exposure to the index or ETFs that track the index. The index is a float-adjusted, market capitalization-weighted index. The fund is non-diversified. **Top Holdings:** iShares Core S&P 500 ETF S&P 500 Index Swap S&P 500 Index Swap S&P 500 Index Swap S&P 500 Index Swap

---

Invesco BulletShares 2021 Corporate Bond ETF

C   **HOLD**

Ticker	Traded On	NAV
BSCL	NYSE Arca	20.69

Total Assets ($)	Dividend Yield (TTM)	Turnover Ratio	Expense Ratio
$1,118,177,442	2.58	3	0.1

Ratings
Reward	C-
Risk	C+
Recent Upgrade/Downgrade	

Fund Information
Fund Type	Exchange Traded Funds
Category	US Fixed Income
Sub-Category	Corporate Bond
Prospectus Objective	Corp Bond - Gen
Inception Date	Jul-13
Open to New Investments	Y

Prices
Price (as of 12/31/2018)	20.75
52-Week High	21.13
52-Week Low	20.62

Total Returns (%)
3-Month	6-Month	1-Year	3-Year	5-Year
0.74	1.53	0.66	9.02	17.98

3-Year Standard Deviation	2.52
Effective Duration	2.51

Valuation
Premium/Discount (1-Year Average)	0.23

Company Information
Provider	Invesco
Manager/Tenure	Jeremy Neisewander (2), Peter Hubbard (0), Jeffrey W. Kernagis (0), 1 other
Website	http://www.invesco.com/us
Address	Invesco 11 Greenway Plaza, Ste. 2500 Houston TX 77046 United States
Phone Number	800-659-1005

PERFORMANCE

Ratings History
Date	Overall Rating	Risk Rating	Reward Rating
Q4-18	C	C+	C-
Q2-18	C	C+	C
Q4-17	B	A	C
Q4-16	C	C+	C
Q4-15	C-	C-	D+

Asset & Performance History
Date	NAV	1-Year Total Return
2017	21.07	2.81
2016	20.95	5.01
2015	20.44	0.99
2014	20.78	7.15
2013	19.94	
2012		

Total Assets: $1,118,177,442

Asset Allocation
Asset	%
Cash	0%
Stocks	0%
US Stocks	0%
Bonds	100%
US Bonds	79%
Other	0%

Services Offered:

Investment Strategy: The investment seeks investment results that correspond generally to the performance, before the fund's fees and expenses, of an investment grade corporate bond index called the Nasdaq BulletShares® USD Corporate Bond 2021 Index. The fund will invest at least 80% of its total assets in component securities that comprise the index. The index is designed to represent the performance of a held-to-maturity portfolio of U.S. dollar-denominated investment-grade corporate bonds with effective maturities in the year 2021. The fund is non-diversified. **Top Holdings:** Anheuser-Busch InBev Finance Inc. 2.65% Oracle Corporation 1.9% Goldman Sachs Group, Inc. 5.25% Deutsche Bank AG New York Branch 4.25% JPMorgan Chase & Co. 4.35%

SPDR® S&P 600 Small Cap ETF   D-   SELL

Ticker	Traded On	NAV	Total Assets ($)	Dividend Yield (TTM)	Turnover Ratio	Expense Ratio
SLY	NYSE Arca	59.95	$1,109,925,987	1.37	22	0.15

Ratings
Reward	D-
Risk	D
Recent Upgrade/Downgrade	

Fund Information
Fund Type	Exchange Traded Funds
Category	US Equity Small Cap
Sub-Category	Small Blend
Prospectus Objective	Small Company
Inception Date	Nov-05
Open to New Investments	Y

Prices
Price (as of 12/31/2018)	59.97
52-Week High	139.00
52-Week Low	56.32

Total Returns (%)
3-Month	6-Month	1-Year	3-Year	5-Year
-18.91	-15.19	-54.24	-34.51	-32.22

3-Year Standard Deviation	14.7
Effective Duration	

Valuation
Premium/Discount (1-Year Average)	0.07

Company Information
Provider	SPDR State Street Global Advisors
Manager/Tenure	Michael J. Feehily (7), Karl A. Schneider (4), Mark Krivitsky (1)
Website	http://www.spdrs.com
Address	SPDR State Street Global Advisors State Street Financial Center, 1 Lincoln Street Boston MA 02111-2900 United States
Phone Number	617-786-3000

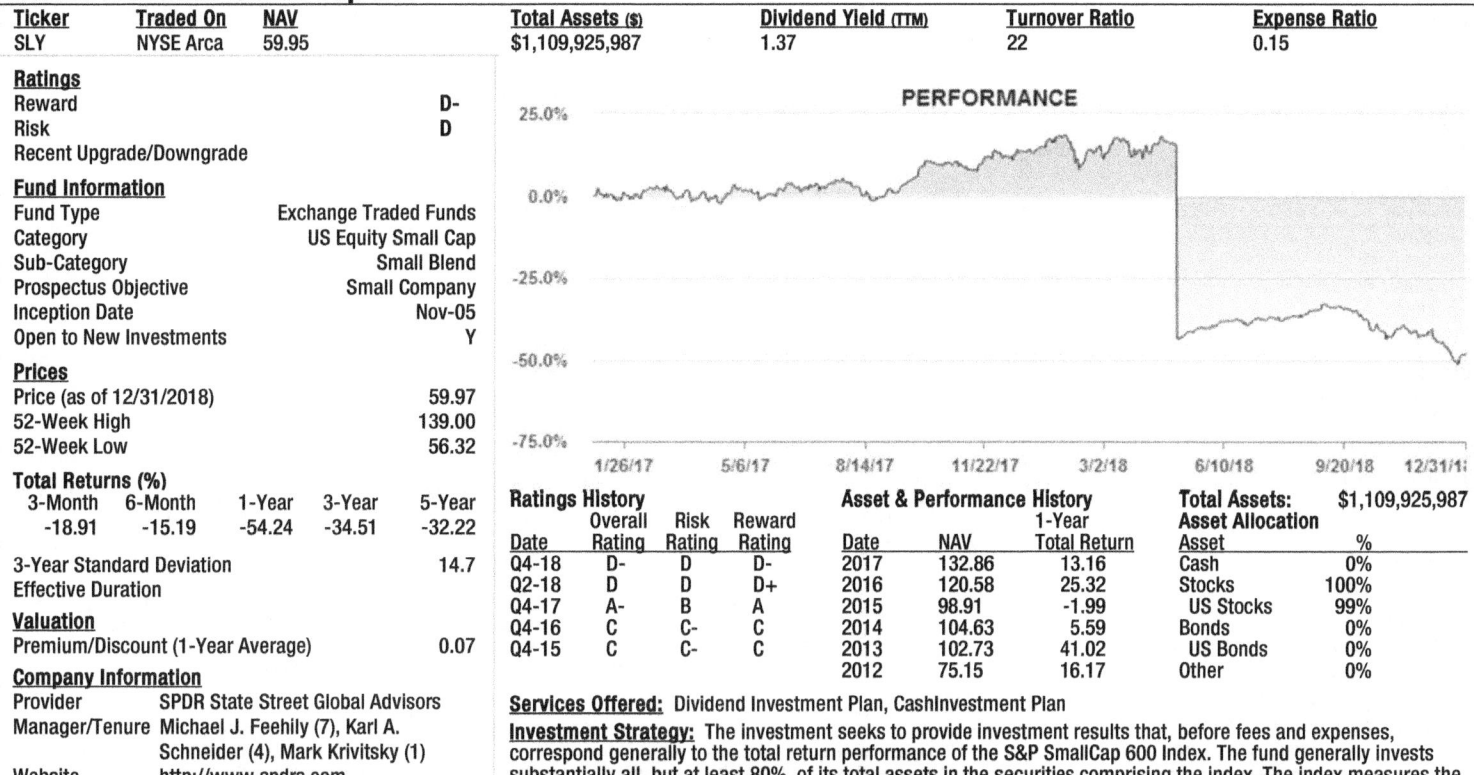

PERFORMANCE

Ratings History
Date	Overall Rating	Risk Rating	Reward Rating
Q4-18	D-	D	D-
Q2-18	D	D	D+
Q4-17	A-	B	A
Q4-16	C	C-	C
Q4-15	C	C-	C

Asset & Performance History
Date	NAV	1-Year Total Return
2017	132.86	13.16
2016	120.58	25.32
2015	98.91	-1.99
2014	104.63	5.59
2013	102.73	41.02
2012	75.15	16.17

Total Assets: $1,109,925,987

Asset Allocation
Asset	%
Cash	0%
Stocks	100%
US Stocks	99%
Bonds	0%
US Bonds	0%
Other	0%

Services Offered: Dividend Investment Plan, CashInvestment Plan

Investment Strategy: The investment seeks to provide investment results that, before fees and expenses, correspond generally to the total return performance of the S&P SmallCap 600 Index. The fund generally invests substantially all, but at least 80%, of its total assets in the securities comprising the index. The index measures the performance of the small-capitalization segment of the U.S. equity market. It may purchase a subset of the securities in the index in an effort to hold a portfolio of securities with generally the same risk and return characteristics of the index. The fund is non-diversified. **Top Holdings:** First Financial Bankshares Inc   Ingevity Corp   CACI International Inc Class A   Spire Inc   Glacier Bancorp Inc

iShares Core MSCI International Developed Markets ETF   D   SELL

Ticker	Traded On	NAV	Total Assets ($)	Dividend Yield (TTM)	Turnover Ratio	Expense Ratio
IDEV	NYSE Arca	48.84	$1,108,263,346	2.45	6	0.05

Ratings
Reward	D
Risk	D+
Recent Upgrade/Downgrade	Down

Fund Information
Fund Type	Exchange Traded Funds
Category	Global Equity Large Cap
Sub-Category	Foreign Large Blend
Prospectus Objective	Foreign Stock
Inception Date	Mar-17
Open to New Investments	Y

Prices
Price (as of 12/31/2018)	48.85
52-Week High	62.47
52-Week Low	47.08

Total Returns (%)
3-Month	6-Month	1-Year	3-Year	5-Year
-13.06	-10.91	-14.31		

3-Year Standard Deviation	
Effective Duration	

Valuation
Premium/Discount (1-Year Average)	-0.04

Company Information
Provider	iShares
Manager/Tenure	Diane Hsiung (1), Jennifer Hsui (1), Alan Mason (1), 3 others
Website	http://www.ishares.com
Address	iShares 400 Howard Street San Francisco CA 94105 United States
Phone Number	800-474-2737

PERFORMANCE

Ratings History
Date	Overall Rating	Risk Rating	Reward Rating
Q4-18	D	D+	D
Q2-18	C-	C-	D+
Q4-17	U		
Q4-16			
Q4-15			

Asset & Performance History
Date	NAV	1-Year Total Return
2017	58.65	
2016		
2015		
2014		
2013		
2012		

Total Assets: $1,108,263,346

Asset Allocation
Asset	%
Cash	1%
Stocks	99%
US Stocks	1%
Bonds	0%
US Bonds	0%
Other	0%

Services Offered:

Investment Strategy: The investment seeks to track the investment results of the MSCI World ex USA Investable Market Index. The fund generally will invest at least 90% of its assets in the component securities of the underlying index and in investments that have economic characteristics that are substantially identical to the component securities of the underlying index. The underlying index is free float adjusted, market cap weighted, and is designed to measure large-, mid- and small-capitalization equity market performance and includes stocks from North America, Europe, Australasia and the Far East. The fund is non-diversified. **Top Holdings:** Nestle SA Novartis AG   Roche Holding AG Dividend Right Cert.   HSBC Holdings PLC   Royal Dutch Shell PLC Class A

WisdomTree U.S. MidCap Earnings Fund

C-   HOLD

Ticker	Traded On	NAV	Total Assets ($)	Dividend Yield (TTM)	Turnover Ratio	Expense Ratio
EZM	NYSE Arca	34.26	$1,104,853,177	1.32	45	0.38

Ratings
Reward	C-
Risk	C-
Recent Upgrade/Downgrade	Down

Fund Information
Fund Type	Exchange Traded Funds
Category	US Equity Mid Cap
Sub-Category	Mid-Cap Blend
Prospectus Objective	Growth & Inc
Inception Date	Feb-07
Open to New Investments	Y

Prices
Price (as of 12/31/2018)	34.29
52-Week High	42.42
52-Week Low	32.31

Total Returns (%)
3-Month	6-Month	1-Year	3-Year	5-Year
-15.92	-13.98	-12.28	23.07	27.27

3-Year Standard Deviation	12.2
Effective Duration	

Valuation
Premium/Discount (1-Year Average)	0.09

Company Information
Provider	WisdomTree
Manager/Tenure	Richard A. Brown (10), Thomas J. Durante (10), Karen Q. Wong (10)
Website	http://www.wisdomtree.com
Address	WisdomTree 245 Park Avenue, 35th floor New York NY 10167 United States
Phone Number	866-909-9473

PERFORMANCE

Ratings History
Date	Overall Rating	Risk Rating	Reward Rating
Q4-18	C-	C-	C-
Q2-18	C	C-	C
Q4-17	B	B	B
Q4-16	C+	C-	B
Q4-15	C	C-	C

Asset & Performance History
Date	NAV	1-Year Total Return
2017	39.63	17.2
2016	34.22	19.71
2015	29.07	-4.63
2014	30.86	8.43
2013	28.8	40.19
2012	20.77	17.83

Total Assets: $1,104,853,177

Asset Allocation
Asset	%
Cash	0%
Stocks	100%
US Stocks	100%
Bonds	0%
US Bonds	0%
Other	0%

Services Offered:

Investment Strategy: The investment seeks to track the price and yield performance, before fees and expenses, of the WisdomTree U.S. MidCap Earnings Index. Under normal circumstances, at least 95% of the fund's total assets (exclusive of collateral held from securities lending) will be invested in component securities of the index and investments that have economic characteristics that are substantially identical to the economic characteristics of such component securities. The index is a fundamentally weighted index that is comprised of earnings-generating companies within the mid-capitalization segment of the U.S. stock market. The fund is non-diversified.
Top Holdings: Park Hotels & Resorts Inc   Discovery Inc Class A   Macy's Inc   First Data Corp Class A   Foot Locker Inc

---

VictoryShares US 500 Enhanced Volatility Wtd ETF

C   HOLD

Ticker	Traded On	NAV	Total Assets ($)	Dividend Yield (TTM)	Turnover Ratio	Expense Ratio
CFO	NAS CM	43.93	$1,103,562,437	1.34	26	0.35

Ratings
Reward	C-
Risk	C+
Recent Upgrade/Downgrade	

Fund Information
Fund Type	Exchange Traded Funds
Category	US Equity Large Cap Blend
Sub-Category	Large Blend
Prospectus Objective	Income
Inception Date	Jul-14
Open to New Investments	Y

Prices
Price (as of 12/31/2018)	43.91
52-Week High	52.53
52-Week Low	41.40

Total Returns (%)
3-Month	6-Month	1-Year	3-Year	5-Year
-14.44	-10.31	-8.61	27.96	

3-Year Standard Deviation	9.94
Effective Duration	

Valuation
Premium/Discount (1-Year Average)	0.06

Company Information
Provider	VictoryShares
Manager/Tenure	Stephen Hammers (4), Mannik Dhillon (0)
Website	http://www.VictorySharesLiterature.com
Address	Victory Shares 4249 Easton Way, Suite 400 Columbus OH 43219 United States
Phone Number	

PERFORMANCE

Ratings History
Date	Overall Rating	Risk Rating	Reward Rating
Q4-18	C	C+	C-
Q2-18	C	C-	C+
Q4-17	B	B	B
Q4-16	C	C-	C
Q4-15	D	C-	D

Asset & Performance History
Date	NAV	1-Year Total Return
2017	48.72	22.39
2016	40.32	13.87
2015	35.75	-0.55
2014	36.42	
2013		
2012		

Total Assets: $1,103,562,437

Asset Allocation
Asset	%
Cash	0%
Stocks	100%
US Stocks	99%
Bonds	0%
US Bonds	0%
Other	0%

Services Offered:

Investment Strategy: The investment seeks to provide investment results that track the performance of the Nasdaq Victory US Large Cap 500 Long/Cash Volatility Weighted Index before fees and expenses. The fund seeks to achieve its investment objective by investing, under normal market conditions, at least 80% of its assets directly or indirectly in the securities included in the Nasdaq Victory US Large Cap 500 Long/Cash Volatility Weighted Index, an unmanaged, volatility weighted index maintained exclusively by the index provider. The index identifies the 500 largest U.S. stocks by market capitalization measured at the time the index's constituent securities are determined.
Top Holdings: UGI Corp   NextEra Energy Inc   Exelon Corp   Procter & Gamble Co   Pfizer Inc

Vanguard International High Dividend Yield Index Fund ETF Shares   C-   HOLD

Ticker	Traded On	NAV	Total Assets ($)	Dividend Yield (TTM)	Turnover Ratio	Expense Ratio
VYMI	NAS CM		$1,097,297,195	4.02	8	0.32

Ratings
Reward	D+
Risk	C
Recent Upgrade/Downgrade	Down

Fund Information
Fund Type	Exchange Traded Funds
Category	Global Equity Large Cap
Sub-Category	Foreign Large Value
Prospectus Objective	Foreign Stock
Inception Date	Feb-16
Open to New Investments	Y

Prices
Price (as of 12/31/2018)	56.27
52-Week High	72.13
52-Week Low	54.56

Total Returns (%)
3-Month	6-Month	1-Year	3-Year	5-Year
-10.02	-7.61	-12.75		

3-Year Standard Deviation	
Effective Duration	

Valuation
Premium/Discount (1-Year Average)	0.16

Company Information
Provider	Vanguard
Manager/Tenure	Justin E. Hales (2), Michael Perre (2)
Website	http://www.vanguard.com
Address	Vanguard 100 Vanguard Boulevard Malvern PA 19355 United States
Phone Number	877-662-7447

PERFORMANCE

Ratings History
Date	Overall Rating	Risk Rating	Reward Rating
Q4-18	C-	C	D+
Q2-18	C-	C-	C-
Q4-17	C-	B+	C
Q4-16	U		
Q4-15			

Asset & Performance History
Date	NAV	1-Year Total Return
2017	66.78	22.55
2016	56.44	
2015		
2014		
2013		
2012		

Total Assets: $1,097,297,195

Asset Allocation
Asset	%
Cash	1%
Stocks	99%
US Stocks	0%
Bonds	0%
US Bonds	0%
Other	0%

Services Offered:

Investment Strategy: The investment seeks to track the performance of FTSE All-World ex US High Dividend Yield Index that measures the investment return of non-U.S. companies that are characterized by high dividend yield. The fund invests by sampling the index, meaning that it holds a broadly diversified collection of securities that, in the aggregate, approximates the full index in terms of key characteristics. The index focuses on companies located in developed and emerging markets, excluding the United States, that are forecasted to have above-average dividend yields. **Top Holdings:** Nestle SA Novartis AG Tsmc Roche Holding AG Dividend Right Cert. HSBC Holdings PLC

Goldman Sachs ActiveBeta® International Equity ETF   C-   HOLD

Ticker	Traded On	NAV	Total Assets ($)	Dividend Yield (TTM)	Turnover Ratio	Expense Ratio
GSIE	NYSE Arca	25.42	$1,091,258,216	2.57	16	0.25

Ratings
Reward	D+
Risk	C
Recent Upgrade/Downgrade	Down

Fund Information
Fund Type	Exchange Traded Funds
Category	Global Equity Large Cap
Sub-Category	Foreign Large Blend
Prospectus Objective	Foreign Stock
Inception Date	Nov-15
Open to New Investments	Y

Prices
Price (as of 12/31/2018)	25.36
52-Week High	31.92
52-Week Low	24.56

Total Returns (%)
3-Month	6-Month	1-Year	3-Year	5-Year
-13.06	-11.16	-12.92	11.32	

3-Year Standard Deviation	10.69
Effective Duration	

Valuation
Premium/Discount (1-Year Average)	0.25

Company Information
Provider	Goldman Sachs
Manager/Tenure	Raj Garigipati (3), Jamie McGregor (2)
Website	http://www.gsamfunds.com
Address	Goldman Sachs 200 West Stree New York NY 10282 United States
Phone Number	800-526-7384

PERFORMANCE

Ratings History
Date	Overall Rating	Risk Rating	Reward Rating
Q4-18	C-	C	D+
Q2-18	C	C+	C
Q4-17	C	B+	C
Q4-16	D	C-	D
Q4-15			

Asset & Performance History
Date	NAV	1-Year Total Return
2017	29.91	26.01
2016	24.38	0.48
2015	24.49	
2014		
2013		
2012		

Total Assets: $1,091,258,216

Asset Allocation
Asset	%
Cash	0%
Stocks	100%
US Stocks	2%
Bonds	0%
US Bonds	0%
Other	0%

Services Offered:

Investment Strategy: The investment seeks to provide investment results that closely correspond, before fees and expenses, to the performance of the Goldman Sachs ActiveBeta® International Equity Index. The fund invests at least 80% of its assets (exclusive of collateral held from securities lending) in securities included in its underlying index, in depositary receipts representing securities included in its underlying index and in underlying stocks in respect of depositary receipts included in its underlying index. The index is designed to deliver exposure to equity securities of developed market issuers outside of the United States. **Top Holdings:** Nestle SA Roche Holding AG Dividend Right Cert. Novartis AG HSBC Holdings PLC Royal Bank of Canada

VanEck Vectors Oil Services ETF   C-   HOLD

Ticker	Traded On	NAV	Total Assets ($)	Dividend Yield (TTM)	Turnover Ratio	Expense Ratio
OIH	NYSE Arca	14.03	$1,090,195,842	3.75	34	0.35

Ratings
Reward   C
Risk   D
Recent Upgrade/Downgrade

Fund Information
Fund Type	Exchange Traded Funds
Category	Energy Sector Equity
Sub-Category	Equity Energy
Prospectus Objective	Natl Res
Inception Date	Dec-11
Open to New Investments	Y

Prices
Price (as of 12/31/2018)	14.03
52-Week High	29.51
52-Week Low	13.32

Total Returns (%)

3-Month	6-Month	1-Year	3-Year	5-Year
-43.38	-43.56	-44.58	-43.16	-67.24

3-Year Standard Deviation   29.41
Effective Duration

Valuation
Premium/Discount (1-Year Average)   0.01

Company Information
Provider	VanEck
Manager/Tenure	Hao-Hung (Peter) Liao (6), Guo Hua (Jason) Jin (0)
Website	http://www.vaneck.com
Address	Van Eck Associates Corporation 666 Third Avenue New York NY 10017 United States
Phone Number	800-826-1115

PERFORMANCE

Ratings History

Date	Overall Rating	Risk Rating	Reward Rating
Q4-18	C-	D	C
Q2-18	C-	D	C
Q4-17	D	D	D
Q4-16	D+	D	C-
Q4-15	C	C	C+

Asset & Performance History

Date	NAV	1-Year Total Return
2017	26.02	-19.82
2016	33.36	27.92
2015	26.44	-24.51
2014	35.89	-23.63
2013	48.1	25.92
2012	38.64	1.99

Total Assets: $1,090,195,842

Asset Allocation

Asset	%
Cash	0%
Stocks	100%
US Stocks	87%
Bonds	0%
US Bonds	0%
Other	0%

Services Offered:

Investment Strategy: The investment seeks to replicate as closely as possible, before fees and expenses, the price and yield performance of the MVIS® US Listed Oil Services 25 Index. The fund normally invests at least 80% of its total assets in securities that comprise the fund's benchmark index. The index includes common stocks and depositary receipts of U.S. exchange-listed companies in the oil services sector. Such companies may include small- and medium-capitalization companies and foreign companies that are listed on a U.S. exchange. The fund is non-diversified. **Top Holdings:** Schlumberger Ltd   Halliburton Co   Helmerich & Payne Inc   Baker Hughes, a GE Co Class A   TechnipFMC PLC

Vanguard International Dividend Appreciation Index Fund ETF Shares   D+   SELL

Ticker	Traded On	NAV	Total Assets ($)	Dividend Yield (TTM)	Turnover Ratio	Expense Ratio
VIGI	NAS CM		$1,078,283,262	1.95	9	0.25

Ratings
Reward   D+
Risk   C-
Recent Upgrade/Downgrade   Down

Fund Information
Fund Type	Exchange Traded Funds
Category	Global Equity Large Cap
Sub-Category	Foreign Large Growth
Prospectus Objective	Foreign Stock
Inception Date	Feb-16
Open to New Investments	Y

Prices
Price (as of 12/31/2018)	57.60
52-Week High	70.39
52-Week Low	55.63

Total Returns (%)

3-Month	6-Month	1-Year	3-Year	5-Year
-10.80	-10.99	-11.80		

3-Year Standard Deviation
Effective Duration

Valuation
Premium/Discount (1-Year Average)   0.18

Company Information
Provider	Vanguard
Manager/Tenure	Justin E. Hales (2), Michael Perre (2)
Website	http://www.vanguard.com
Address	Vanguard 100 Vanguard Boulevard Malvern PA 19355 United States
Phone Number	877-662-7447

PERFORMANCE

Ratings History

Date	Overall Rating	Risk Rating	Reward Rating
Q4-18	D+	C-	D+
Q2-18	C	C-	C
Q4-17	C-	B-	C
Q4-16	U		
Q4-15			

Asset & Performance History

Date	NAV	1-Year Total Return
2017	66.19	27.72
2016	52.77	
2015		
2014		
2013		
2012		

Total Assets: $1,078,283,262

Asset Allocation

Asset	%
Cash	0%
Stocks	100%
US Stocks	2%
Bonds	0%
US Bonds	0%
Other	0%

Services Offered:

Investment Strategy: The investment seeks to track the performance of Nasdaq International Dividend Achievers Select Index that measures the investment return of non-U.S. companies that have a history of increasing dividends. The index focuses on high-quality companies located in developed and emerging markets, excluding the U.S., that have both the ability and the commitment to grow their dividends over time. The manager attempts to replicate the target index by investing all, or substantially all, of its assets in the broadly diversified collection of securities that make up the index, holding each stock in approximately the same proportion as its weighting in the index. **Top Holdings:** Nestle SA   SAP SE   L'Oreal SA   Tencent Holdings Ltd   Tata Consultancy Services Ltd

---

First Trust Developed Markets Ex-US AlphaDEX® Fund   D+   SELL

Ticker	Traded On	NAV	Total Assets ($)	Dividend Yield (TTM)	Turnover Ratio	Expense Ratio
FDT	NAS CM	49.24	$1,072,400,207	2.57	104	0.8

Ratings
Reward	D+
Risk	C-
Recent Upgrade/Downgrade	Down

Fund Information
Fund Type	Exchange Traded Funds
Category	Global Equity Large Cap
Sub-Category	Foreign Large Blend
Prospectus Objective	Foreign Stock
Inception Date	Apr-11
Open to New Investments	Y

Prices
Price (as of 12/31/2018)	49.02
52-Week High	67.08
52-Week Low	47.63

Total Returns (%)
3-Month	6-Month	1-Year	3-Year	5-Year
-16.98	-15.88	-19.52	11.30	5.32

3-Year Standard Deviation	12.59
Effective Duration	

Valuation
Premium/Discount (1-Year Average)	0.05

Company Information
Provider	First Trust
Manager/Tenure	Jon C. Erickson (7), Daniel J. Lindquist (7), David G. McGarel (7), 3 others
Website	http://www.ftportfolios.com/
Address	First Trust 120 E. Liberty Drive, Suite 400 Wheaton IL 60187 United States
Phone Number	800-621-1675

PERFORMANCE

Ratings History
Date	Overall Rating	Risk Rating	Reward Rating
Q4-18	D+	C-	D+
Q2-18	C+	C+	C
Q4-17	B	B	B+
Q4-16	C-	C-	C-
Q4-15	C-	C-	C-

Asset & Performance History
Date	NAV	1-Year Total Return
2017	62.31	33.58
2016	47.43	3.56
2015	46.63	0.63
2014	47.14	-5.97
2013	50.96	18.41
2012	43.93	17.02

Total Assets: $1,072,400,207
Asset Allocation
Asset	%
Cash	0%
Stocks	99%
US Stocks	1%
Bonds	0%
US Bonds	0%
Other	0%

Services Offered:

Investment Strategy: The investment seeks results that correspond generally to the price and yield (before the fund's fees and expenses) of an equity index called the NASDAQ AlphaDEX® Developed Markets Ex-US Index. The fund will normally invest at least 90% of its net assets (including investment borrowings) in common stocks and/or depositary receipts that comprise the index. The index is designed to select stocks from the NASDAQ Developed Markets Ex-US Index that may generate positive alpha, or risk-adjusted returns, relative to traditional indices through the use of the AlphaDEX® selection methodology. **Top Holdings:** Tokyo Electric Power Co Holdings Sumitomo Dainippon Pharma Co Ltd Toshiba Corp Alimentation Couche-Tard Inc B Henderson Land Development Co Ltd

---

Direxion Daily Gold Miners Index Bull 3X Shares   E+   SELL

Ticker	Traded On	NAV	Total Assets ($)	Dividend Yield (TTM)	Turnover Ratio	Expense Ratio
NUGT	NYSE Arca	17.45	$1,066,766,954	0.49	234	1.2

Ratings
Reward	E+
Risk	D-
Recent Upgrade/Downgrade	Down

Fund Information
Fund Type	Exchange Traded Funds
Category	Trading Tools
Sub-Category	Trading--Leveraged Equity
Prospectus Objective	Prec Metals
Inception Date	Dec-10
Open to New Investments	Y

Prices
Price (as of 12/31/2018)	17.50
52-Week High	36.98
52-Week Low	11.14

Total Returns (%)
3-Month	6-Month	1-Year	3-Year	5-Year
34.91	-26.40	-44.78	-10.01	-92.02

3-Year Standard Deviation	123.28
Effective Duration	

Valuation
Premium/Discount (1-Year Average)	0.17

Company Information
Provider	Direxion Funds
Manager/Tenure	Paul Brigandi (7), Tony Ng (3)
Website	http://www.direxionfunds.com
Address	Direxion Funds 1301 Avenue Of The Americas (6th Avenue) New York NY 10019 United States
Phone Number	646-572-3390

PERFORMANCE

Ratings History
Date	Overall Rating	Risk Rating	Reward Rating
Q4-18	E+	D-	E+
Q2-18	D	D	D-
Q4-17	D	D-	D
Q4-16	D	D-	D
Q4-15	E+	E+	E

Asset & Performance History
Date	NAV	1-Year Total Return
2017	31.76	3.25
2016	30.76	57.83
2015	19.49	-78.09
2014	88.96	-59.53
2013	219.84	-95
2012	4,404.00	-43.48

Total Assets: $1,066,766,954
Asset Allocation
Asset	%
Cash	80%
Stocks	28%
US Stocks	4%
Bonds	0%
US Bonds	0%
Other	-8%

Services Offered:

Investment Strategy: The investment seeks daily investment results, before fees and expenses, of 300% of the daily performance of the NYSE Arca Gold Miners Index. The fund invests at least 80% of its net assets (plus borrowing for investment purposes) in securities of the index, ETFs that track the index and other financial instruments that provide daily leveraged exposure to the index or ETFs that track the index. The index is a modified market capitalization weighted index comprised of publicly traded companies that operate globally in both developed and emerging markets, and are involved primarily in mining for gold and, in mining for silver. It is non-diversified. **Top Holdings:** VanEck Vectors Gold Miners ETF Solactive Cust Gld Miners Solactive Cust Gld Miners Ve Vectors Gld Miners Ve Vectors Gld Miners

First Trust US Equity Opportunities ETF

C   HOLD

Ticker	Traded On	NAV	Total Assets ($)	Dividend Yield (TTM)	Turnover Ratio	Expense Ratio
FPX	NYSE Arca	62.07	$1,066,614,485	0.74	31	0.59

Ratings
Reward	C
Risk	C
Recent Upgrade/Downgrade	

Fund Information
Fund Type	Exchange Traded Funds
Category	US Equity Large Cap Growth
Sub-Category	Large Growth
Prospectus Objective	Growth
Inception Date	Apr-06
Open to New Investments	Y

Prices
Price (as of 12/31/2018)	62.06
52-Week High	75.93
52-Week Low	57.83

Total Returns (%)
3-Month	6-Month	1-Year	3-Year	5-Year
-15.90	-13.25	-8.23	24.32	42.16

3-Year Standard Deviation	11.8
Effective Duration	

Valuation
Premium/Discount (1-Year Average)	0.04

Company Information
Provider	First Trust
Manager/Tenure	Jon C. Erickson (12), Daniel J. Lindquist (12), David G. McGarel (12), 3 others
Website	http://www.ftportfolios.com/
Address	First Trust 120 E. Liberty Drive, Suite 400 Wheaton IL 60187 United States
Phone Number	800-621-1675

PERFORMANCE

Ratings History	Overall Rating	Risk Rating	Reward Rating
Date			
Q4-18	C	C	C
Q2-18	C	C-	B-
Q4-17	B	B-	A-
Q4-16	C+	C	B
Q4-15	C+	C+	B-

Asset & Performance History		
Date	NAV	1-Year Total Return
2017	68.17	26.96
2016	54.1	6.7
2015	51.11	2.18
2014	50.32	11.9
2013	45.34	47.98
2012	30.82	30

Total Assets: $1,066,614,485

Asset Allocation	
Asset	%
Cash	0%
Stocks	100%
US Stocks	97%
Bonds	0%
US Bonds	0%
Other	0%

Services Offered:

Investment Strategy: The investment seeks investment results that correspond generally to the price and yield (before the fund's fees and expenses) of an equity index called the IPOX®-100 U.S. Index. The fund will normally invest at least 90% of its net assets (including investment borrowings) in common stocks that comprise the index. The index is an applied, market-cap weighted price index measuring the performance of the top U.S. companies ranked quarterly by market capitalization in the IPOX® U.S. Composite Index, a sub-index of the IPOX® Global Composite Index. It is non-diversified. **Top Holdings:** PayPal Holdings Inc Verizon Communications Inc The Kraft Heinz Co Shire PLC ADR Thermo Fisher Scientific Inc

---

iShares Morningstar Large-Cap Growth ETF

C   HOLD

Ticker	Traded On	NAV	Total Assets ($)	Dividend Yield (TTM)	Turnover Ratio	Expense Ratio
JKE	NYSE Arca	158.44	$1,064,896,545	0.73	48	0.25

Ratings
Reward	C
Risk	C
Recent Upgrade/Downgrade	Down

Fund Information
Fund Type	Exchange Traded Funds
Category	US Equity Large Cap Growth
Sub-Category	Large Growth
Prospectus Objective	Growth
Inception Date	Jun-04
Open to New Investments	Y

Prices
Price (as of 12/31/2018)	158.53
52-Week High	186.55
52-Week Low	147.58

Total Returns (%)
3-Month	6-Month	1-Year	3-Year	5-Year
-14.91	-8.91	2.08	35.43	66.00

3-Year Standard Deviation	11.76
Effective Duration	

Valuation
Premium/Discount (1-Year Average)	0.14

Company Information
Provider	iShares
Manager/Tenure	Diane Hsiung (10), Greg Savage (10), Jennifer Hsui (6), 3 others
Website	http://www.ishares.com
Address	iShares 400 Howard Street San Francisco CA 94105 United States
Phone Number	800-474-2737

PERFORMANCE

Ratings History	Overall Rating	Risk Rating	Reward Rating
Date			
Q4-18	C	C	C
Q2-18	B-	C	B
Q4-17	B+	A-	B+
Q4-16	C+	C	B-
Q4-15	C+	C	B-

Asset & Performance History		
Date	NAV	1-Year Total Return
2017	156.38	30.61
2016	120.9	1.56
2015	120.19	7.44
2014	112.99	14.07
2013	99.96	32.06
2012	76.5	17.73

Total Assets: $1,064,896,545

Asset Allocation	
Asset	%
Cash	0%
Stocks	100%
US Stocks	100%
Bonds	0%
US Bonds	0%
Other	0%

Services Offered:

Investment Strategy: The investment seeks to track the investment results of the Morningstar® Large Growth IndexSM composed of large-capitalization U.S. equities that exhibit growth characteristics. The fund generally invests at least 90% of its assets in securities of the underlying index and in depositary receipts representing securities of the underlying index. The underlying index measures the performance of stocks issued by large-capitalization companies that have exhibited above-average "growth" characteristics as determined by Morningstar, Inc.'s ("Morningstar" or the "index provider") proprietary index methodology. **Top Holdings:** Microsoft Corp Amazon.com Inc Facebook Inc A Alphabet Inc Class C Alphabet Inc A

iShares Currency Hedged MSCI Japan ETF   C   HOLD

Ticker	Traded On	NAV	Total Assets ($)	Dividend Yield (TTM)	Turnover Ratio	Expense Ratio
HEWJ	NYSE Arca	28.02	$1,059,615,791	1.48	9	0.49

Ratings
Reward   C-
Risk   C+
Recent Upgrade/Downgrade

Fund Information
Fund Type   Exchange Traded Funds
Category   Japan Equity
Sub-Category   Japan Stock
Prospectus Objective   Pacific Stock
Inception Date   Jan-14
Open to New Investments   Y

Prices
Price (as of 12/31/2018)   28.09
52-Week High   35.21
52-Week Low   27.38

Total Returns (%)

3-Month	6-Month	1-Year	3-Year	5-Year
-19.01	-11.04	-15.28	1.96	

3-Year Standard Deviation   15.6
Effective Duration

Valuation
Premium/Discount (1-Year Average)   0.03

Company Information
Provider   iShares
Manager/Tenure   Diane Hsiung (4), Jennifer Hsui (4),
                    Orlando Montalvo (4), 2 others
Website   http://www.ishares.com
Address   iShares 400 Howard Street San
                    Francisco CA 94105 United States
Phone Number   800-474-2737

PERFORMANCE

Ratings History

Date	Overall Rating	Risk Rating	Reward Rating
Q4-18	C	C+	C-
Q2-18	C	C	C-
Q4-17	B	B-	A-
Q4-16	C	C	C-
Q4-15	D+	C+	C

Asset & Performance History

Date	NAV	1-Year Total Return
2017	33.36	21.5
2016	27.81	-0.93
2015	28.66	9.04
2014	27.1	
2013		
2012		

Total Assets: $1,059,615,791

Asset Allocation

Asset	%
Cash	1%
Stocks	99%
US Stocks	0%
Bonds	0%
US Bonds	0%
Other	0%

Services Offered:

Investment Strategy: The investment seeks to track the investment results of the MSCI Japan 100% Hedged to USD Index. The fund generally will invest at least 90% of its assets in the component securities (including indirect investments through the underlying fund) and other instruments of the underlying index and in investments that have economic characteristics that are substantially identical to the component securities of the underlying index. The index consists of stocks traded primarily on the Tokyo Stock Exchange with the currency risk inherent in the securities included in the underlying index hedged to the U.S. dollar on a monthly basis. **Top Holdings:** iShares MSCI Japan ETF

First Trust Financials AlphaDEX® Fund   C   HOLD

Ticker	Traded On	NAV	Total Assets ($)	Dividend Yield (TTM)	Turnover Ratio	Expense Ratio
FXO	NYSE Arca	27.01	$1,051,603,130	2.05	80	0.63

Ratings
Reward   C-
Risk   C+
Recent Upgrade/Downgrade   Down

Fund Information
Fund Type   Exchange Traded Funds
Category   Financials Sector Equity
Sub-Category   Financial
Prospectus Objective   Financial
Inception Date   May-07
Open to New Investments   Y

Prices
Price (as of 12/31/2018)   27.01
52-Week High   32.91
52-Week Low   25.49

Total Returns (%)

3-Month	6-Month	1-Year	3-Year	5-Year
-14.34	-12.73	-11.65	23.10	35.42

3-Year Standard Deviation   11.97
Effective Duration

Valuation
Premium/Discount (1-Year Average)   -0.01

Company Information
Provider   First Trust
Manager/Tenure   Jon C. Erickson (11), Daniel J.
                    Lindquist (11), David G. McGarel (11),
                    3 others
Website   http://www.ftportfolios.com/
Address   First Trust 120 E. Liberty Drive, Suite
                    400 Wheaton IL 60187 United States
Phone Number   800-621-1675

PERFORMANCE

Ratings History

Date	Overall Rating	Risk Rating	Reward Rating
Q4-18	C	C+	C-
Q2-18	C+	C	C+
Q4-17	B+	B+	B
Q4-16	B	C+	B
Q4-15	B-	C+	B

Asset & Performance History

Date	NAV	1-Year Total Return
2017	31.3	17.93
2016	27	18.15
2015	23.19	1.19
2014	23.26	8.7
2013	21.74	40.43
2012	15.69	21.25

Total Assets: $1,051,603,130

Asset Allocation

Asset	%
Cash	0%
Stocks	100%
US Stocks	99%
Bonds	0%
US Bonds	0%
Other	0%

Services Offered:

Investment Strategy: The investment seeks investment results that correspond generally to the price and yield (before the fund's fees and expenses) of an equity index called the StrataQuant® Financials Index. The fund will normally invest at least 90% of its net assets (including investment borrowings) in common stocks that comprise the index. The index is a modified equal-dollar weighted index designed by IDI to objectively identify and select stocks from the Russell 1000® Index in the financial services sector that may generate positive alpha relative to traditional passive-style indices through the use of the AlphaDEX® selection methodology. **Top Holdings:** Euronet Worldwide Inc   Chimera Investment Corp   Reinsurance Group of America Inc   Berkshire Hathaway Inc B   Torchmark Corp

iShares MSCI Mexico Capped ETF   D   SELL

Ticker	Traded On	NAV	Total Assets ($)	Dividend Yield (TTM)	Turnover Ratio	Expense Ratio
EWW	NYSE Arca	41.20	$1,048,457,370	2.68	7	0.47

Ratings
Reward   D
Risk   D
Recent Upgrade/Downgrade

Fund Information
Fund Type	Exchange Traded Funds
Category	Mexico Equity
Sub-Category	Miscellaneous Region
Prospectus Objective	Foreign Stock
Inception Date	Mar-96
Open to New Investments	Y

Prices
Price (as of 12/31/2018)	41.18
52-Week High	54.16
52-Week Low	37.76

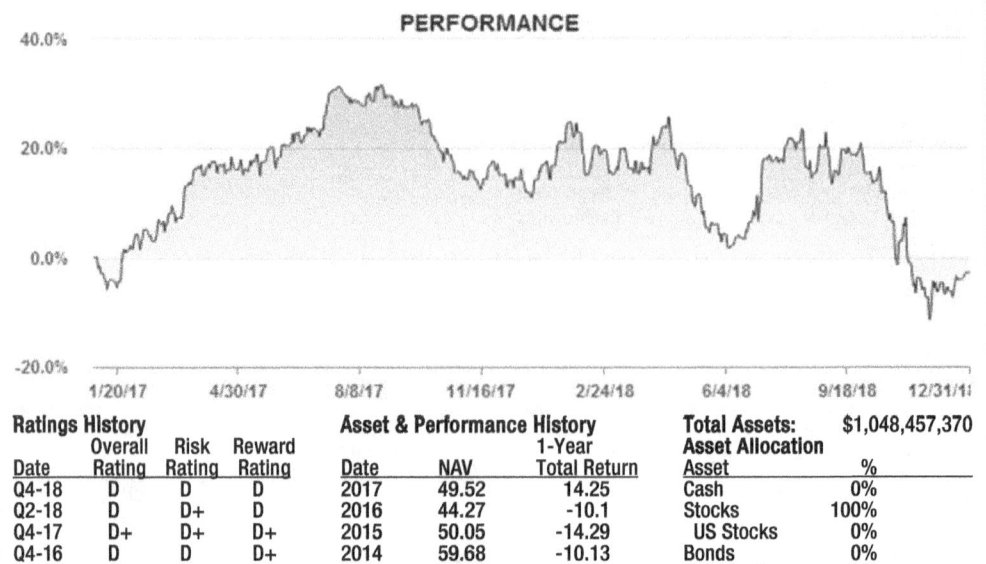

Total Returns (%)
3-Month	6-Month	1-Year	3-Year	5-Year
-19.61	-8.88	-14.93	-12.63	-32.71

3-Year Standard Deviation   22.32
Effective Duration

Valuation
Premium/Discount (1-Year Average)   0.05

Company Information
Provider	iShares
Manager/Tenure	Diane Hsiung (10), Greg Savage (10), Jennifer Hsui (5), 1 other
Website	http://www.ishares.com
Address	iShares 400 Howard Street San Francisco CA 94105 United States
Phone Number	800-474-2737

Ratings History

Date	Overall Rating	Risk Rating	Reward Rating
Q4-18	D	D	D
Q2-18	D	D+	D
Q4-17	D+	D+	D+
Q4-16	D	D	D+
Q4-15	D	D	D

Asset & Performance History

Date	NAV	1-Year Total Return
2017	49.52	14.25
2016	44.27	-10.1
2015	50.05	-14.29
2014	59.68	-10.13
2013	67.23	-1.47
2012	69.63	31.24

Total Assets: $1,048,457,370
Asset Allocation

Asset	%
Cash	0%
Stocks	100%
US Stocks	0%
Bonds	0%
US Bonds	0%
Other	0%

Services Offered: CashInvestment Plan

Investment Strategy: The investment seeks to track the investment results of the MSCI Mexico IMI 25/50 Index. The fund will at all times invest at least 80% of its assets in the securities of its underlying index and in depositary receipts representing securities in its underlying index. The underlying index is a free float-adjusted market capitalization-weighted index with a capping methodology applied to issuer weights so that no single issuer of a component exceeds 25% of the underlying index weight, and all issuers with a weight above 5% do not cumulatively exceed 50% of the underlying index weight. The fund is non-diversified. **Top Holdings:** America Movil SAB de CV Class L   Fomento Economico Mexicano SAB de CV Units (1 Series B, 4 Series D)   Wal - Mart de Mexico SAB de CV Class V   Grupo Financiero Banorte SAB de CV Class O   Cemex SAB de CV CPO Terms:2 Shs-A- & 1 Shs-B-

---

Oppenheimer S&P 500 Revenue ETF   C   HOLD

Ticker	Traded On	NAV	Total Assets ($)	Dividend Yield (TTM)	Turnover Ratio	Expense Ratio
RWL	NYSE Arca	46.51	$1,032,480,155	1.69		0.39

Ratings
Reward   C
Risk   C-
Recent Upgrade/Downgrade

Fund Information
Fund Type	Exchange Traded Funds
Category	US Equity Large Cap Value
Sub-Category	Large Value
Prospectus Objective	Growth
Inception Date	Feb-08
Open to New Investments	Y

Prices
Price (as of 12/31/2018)	46.54
52-Week High	55.26
52-Week Low	44.16

Total Returns (%)
3-Month	6-Month	1-Year	3-Year	5-Year
-13.89	-7.35	-7.57	24.35	39.25

3-Year Standard Deviation   9.89
Effective Duration

Valuation
Premium/Discount (1-Year Average)   0.08

Company Information
Provider	OppenheimerFunds
Manager/Tenure	Frank Vallario (1), Donal Bishnoi (0)
Website	http://www.oppenheimerfunds.com
Address	OppenheimerFunds 12100 East Iliff Avenue, Suite 300, Aurora, Colorado Aurora CO 80217-5270 United States
Phone Number	800-225-5677

Ratings History

Date	Overall Rating	Risk Rating	Reward Rating
Q4-18	C	C-	C
Q2-18	C	C-	C
Q4-17	B-	B-	B
Q4-16	C+	C-	B-
Q4-15	C	C	C

Asset & Performance History

Date	NAV	1-Year Total Return
2017	51.25	19.88
2016	43.49	12.23
2015	39.45	-1.2
2014	40.71	13.38
2013	36.45	37.63
2012	26.95	18.07

Total Assets: $1,032,480,155
Asset Allocation

Asset	%
Cash	1%
Stocks	99%
US Stocks	99%
Bonds	0%
US Bonds	0%
Other	0%

Services Offered:

Investment Strategy: The investment seeks to provide investment results that correspond generally, before fees and expenses, to the performance of the S&P 500 Revenue-Weighted Index (the "underlying index"). The fund normally will invest at least 80% of its net assets, plus any borrowings for investment purposes, in the securities of large capitalization companies included in the underlying index. The underlying index is constructed by using a rules-based methodology that re-weights the constituent securities of the S&P 500® Index (the "parent index") according to the revenue earned by the companies in the parent index, subject to a maximum 5% per company weighting. **Top Holdings:** Walmart Inc   Berkshire Hathaway Inc B   Exxon Mobil Corp   UnitedHealth Group Inc   CVS Health Corp

iShares California Muni Bond ETF   C   HOLD

Ticker	Traded On	NAV	Total Assets ($)	Dividend Yield (TTM)	Turnover Ratio	Expense Ratio
CMF	NYSE Arca	58.22	$1,031,608,088	2.16	32	0.25

Ratings
Reward   C-
Risk   C+
Recent Upgrade/Downgrade

Fund Information
Fund Type   Exchange Traded Funds
Category   US Muni Fixed Inc
Sub-Category   Muni California Long
Prospectus Objective   Muni Bond - Single State
Inception Date   Oct-07
Open to New Investments   Y

Prices
Price (as of 12/31/2018)   58.45
52-Week High   59.30
52-Week Low   56.95

Total Returns (%)

3-Month	6-Month	1-Year	3-Year	5-Year
1.34	0.84	0.68	5.34	19.70

3-Year Standard Deviation   3.42
Effective Duration   6.28

Valuation
Premium/Discount (1-Year Average)   0.14

Company Information
Provider   iShares
Manager/Tenure   Scott Radell (8), James Mauro (7)
Website   http://www.ishares.com
Address   iShares 400 Howard Street San Francisco CA 94105 United States
Phone Number   800-474-2737

PERFORMANCE

Ratings History

Date	Overall Rating	Risk Rating	Reward Rating
Q4-18	C	C+	C-
Q2-18	C	C+	C
Q4-17	B-	B+	C
Q4-16	C	C-	C
Q4-15	C	C-	C+

Asset & Performance History

Date	NAV	1-Year Total Return
2017	59.1	4.67
2016	57.57	-0.2
2015	58.94	3.3
2014	58.55	9.99
2013	54.78	-1.93
2012	57.58	7.73

Total Assets: $1,031,608,088

Asset Allocation

Asset	%
Cash	0%
Stocks	0%
US Stocks	0%
Bonds	100%
US Bonds	100%
Other	0%

Services Offered:

Investment Strategy: The investment seeks to track the investment results of the S&P California AMT-Free Municipal Bond IndexTM. The index measures the performance of the investment-grade segment of the California municipal bond market. The fund generally will invest at least 90% of its assets in the component securities of the index and may invest up to 10% of its assets in certain futures, options and swap contracts, cash and cash equivalents, including shares of money market funds advised by BFA or its affiliates, as well as in securities not included in the index, but which BFA believes will help the fund track the index. It is non-diversified. **Top Holdings:** SAN JOAQUIN HILLS CALIF TRANSN CORRIDOR AGY 5% CALIFORNIA ST 5.5% LOS ANGELES CALIF DEPT WTR & PWR 5% CALIFORNIA ST 5% LOS ANGELES CALIF CMNTY COLLEGE DIST 5%

SPDR® Bloomberg Barclays International Treasury Bond ETF   C-   HOLD

Ticker	Traded On	NAV	Total Assets ($)	Dividend Yield (TTM)	Turnover Ratio	Expense Ratio
BWX	NYSE Arca	27.53	$1,024,602,190	1.08	25	0.35

Ratings
Reward   D+
Risk   C
Recent Upgrade/Downgrade   Down

Fund Information
Fund Type   Exchange Traded Funds
Category   Global Fixed Income
Sub-Category   World Bond
Prospectus Objective   Worldwide Bond
Inception Date   Oct-07
Open to New Investments   Y

Prices
Price (as of 12/31/2018)   27.61
52-Week High   29.61
52-Week Low   26.76

Total Returns (%)

3-Month	6-Month	1-Year	3-Year	5-Year
1.32	-0.14	-2.16	8.87	-1.25

3-Year Standard Deviation   7.26
Effective Duration   8.15

Valuation
Premium/Discount (1-Year Average)   -0.04

Company Information
Provider   SPDR State Street Global Advisors
Manager/Tenure   Joanna Madden (4), James Kramer (2), Orhan Imer (1)
Website   http://www.spdrs.com
Address   SPDR State Street Global Advisors State Street Financial Center, 1 Lincoln Street Boston MA 02111-2900 United States
Phone Number   617-786-3000

PERFORMANCE

Ratings History

Date	Overall Rating	Risk Rating	Reward Rating
Q4-18	C-	C	D+
Q2-18	C	C+	C-
Q4-17	C	C	C
Q4-16	D+	C-	D+
Q4-15	D	D+	D

Asset & Performance History

Date	NAV	1-Year Total Return
2017	28.47	10.14
2016	25.96	0.57
2015	25.7	-6.99
2014	27.63	-2.48
2013	28.82	-3.66
2012	30.48	5.84

Total Assets: $1,024,602,190

Asset Allocation

Asset	%
Cash	0%
Stocks	0%
US Stocks	0%
Bonds	99%
US Bonds	0%
Other	1%

Services Offered:

Investment Strategy: The investment seeks to provide investment results that, before fees and expenses, correspond generally to the price and yield performance of the Bloomberg Barclays Global Treasury ex-US Capped Index. The fund generally invests substantially all, but at least 80%, of its total assets in the securities comprising the index or in securities that the Adviser determines have economic characteristics that are substantially identical to the economic characteristics of the securities that comprise the index. The index is designed to track the fixed-rate local currency sovereign debt of investment grade countries outside the United States. The fund is non-diversified. **Top Holdings:** Denmark(Kingdom) 4.5% Indonesia Government Sr Unsecured 05/28 6.125 Japan(Govt Of) 0.1% Belgium(Kingdom) 5% Netherlands (Kingdom of) 3.75%

iShares Edge MSCI Multifactor Intl ETF   C-   HOLD

Ticker	Traded On	NAV
INTF	NYSE Arca	23.77

Total Assets ($)	Dividend Yield (TTM)	Turnover Ratio	Expense Ratio
$1,016,793,150	3.5	39	0.3

Ratings
Reward	D+
Risk	C
Recent Upgrade/Downgrade	Down

Fund Information
Fund Type	Exchange Traded Funds
Category	Global Equity Large Cap
Sub-Category	Foreign Large Blend
Prospectus Objective	Growth & Inc
Inception Date	Apr-15
Open to New Investments	Y

Prices
Price (as of 12/31/2018)	23.71
52-Week High	31.08
52-Week Low	22.95

Total Returns (%)
3-Month	6-Month	1-Year	3-Year	5-Year
-14.52	-11.89	-15.66	7.85	

3-Year Standard Deviation	11.46
Effective Duration	

Valuation
Premium/Discount (1-Year Average)	0.02

Company Information
Provider	iShares
Manager/Tenure	Diane Hsiung (3), Jennifer Hsui (3), Greg Savage (3), 3 others
Website	http://www.ishares.com
Address	iShares 400 Howard Street San Francisco CA 94105 United States
Phone Number	800-474-2737

PERFORMANCE

Ratings History
Date	Overall Rating	Risk Rating	Reward Rating
Q4-18	C-	C	D+
Q2-18	C	C+	C
Q4-17	B-	B-	C+
Q4-16	D+	D+	D+
Q4-15	U		

Asset & Performance History
Date	NAV	1-Year Total Return
2017	28.86	28.15
2016	23.3	-0.2
2015	23.74	
2014		
2013		
2012		

Total Assets: $1,016,793,150

Asset Allocation
Asset	%
Cash	1%
Stocks	99%
US Stocks	0%
Bonds	0%
US Bonds	0%
Other	1%

Services Offered:

Investment Strategy: The investment seeks to track the investment results of the MSCI World ex USA Diversified Multiple-Factor Index. The fund generally will invest at least 90% of its assets in the component securities of the underlying index and in investments that have economic characteristics that are substantially identical to the component securities of the underlying index. The index is designed to select equity securities from the MSCI World ex USA Index (the "parent index") that have high exposure to four investment style factors: value, quality, momentum and low size, while maintaining a level of risk similar to that of the parent index. **Top Holdings:** Amadeus IT Group SA A   AXA SA   Astellas Pharma Inc   Hitachi Ltd   Woolworths Group Ltd

---

Vanguard S&P Mid-Cap 400 Growth Index Fund ETF Shares   C-   HOLD

Ticker	Traded On	NAV
IVOG	NYSE Arca	

Total Assets ($)	Dividend Yield (TTM)	Turnover Ratio	Expense Ratio
$1,016,272,692	0.92	43	0.2

Ratings
Reward	C-
Risk	C-
Recent Upgrade/Downgrade	Down

Fund Information
Fund Type	Exchange Traded Funds
Category	US Equity Mid Cap
Sub-Category	Mid-Cap Growth
Prospectus Objective	Growth & Inc
Inception Date	Sep-10
Open to New Investments	Y

Prices
Price (as of 12/31/2018)	117.88
52-Week High	147.22
52-Week Low	111.15

Total Returns (%)
3-Month	6-Month	1-Year	3-Year	5-Year
-17.92	-15.65	-11.53	21.32	32.68

3-Year Standard Deviation	11.58
Effective Duration	

Valuation
Premium/Discount (1-Year Average)	0.02

Company Information
Provider	Vanguard
Manager/Tenure	William A. Coleman (2), Awais Khan (1)
Website	http://www.vanguard.com
Address	Vanguard 100 Vanguard Boulevard Malvern PA 19355 United States
Phone Number	877-662-7447

PERFORMANCE

Ratings History
Date	Overall Rating	Risk Rating	Reward Rating
Q4-18	C-	C-	C-
Q2-18	B-	C+	B-
Q4-17	B+	B+	B
Q4-16	C+	C-	B
Q4-15	C	C-	C

Asset & Performance History
Date	NAV	1-Year Total Return
2017	133.06	19.97
2016	112.17	13.77
2015	98.92	1.85
2014	98.14	7.37
2013	92.13	32.49
2012	70	17.1

Total Assets: $1,016,272,692

Asset Allocation
Asset	%
Cash	0%
Stocks	100%
US Stocks	100%
Bonds	0%
US Bonds	0%
Other	0%

Services Offered:

Investment Strategy: The investment seeks to track the performance of a benchmark index that measures the investment return of mid-capitalization growth stocks in the United States. The fund employs an indexing investment approach designed to track the performance of the S&P MidCap 400® Growth Index, which represents the growth companies, as determined by the index sponsor, of the S&P MidCap 400 Index. The Advisor attempts to replicate the target index by investing all, or substantially all, of its assets in the stocks that make up the index, holding each stock in approximately the same proportion as its weighting in the index. **Top Holdings:** Jack Henry & Associates Inc   Lamb Weston Holdings Inc   Domino's Pizza Inc   Teleflex Inc   IDEX Corp

SPDR® S&P 400 Mid Cap Value ETF

D-   **SELL**

Ticker	Traded On	NAV	Total Assets ($)	Dividend Yield (TTM)	Turnover Ratio	Expense Ratio
MDYV	NYSE Arca	44.34	$1,007,059,701	1.94	51	0.15

Ratings
Reward	D-
Risk	D
Recent Upgrade/Downgrade	

Fund Information
Fund Type	Exchange Traded Funds
Category	US Equity Mid Cap
Sub-Category	Mid-Cap Value
Prospectus Objective	Growth
Inception Date	Nov-05
Open to New Investments	Y

Prices
Price (as of 12/31/2018)	44.36
52-Week High	106.43
52-Week Low	41.80

Total Returns (%)
3-Month	6-Month	1-Year	3-Year	5-Year
-16.31	-13.74	-55.97	-37.61	-34.93

3-Year Standard Deviation	12.61
Effective Duration	

Valuation
Premium/Discount (1-Year Average)	0.03

Company Information
Provider	SPDR State Street Global Advisors
Manager/Tenure	Michael J. Feehily (7), Karl A. Schneider (4), Dave Swallow (1)
Website	http://www.spdrs.com
Address	SPDR State Street Global Advisors State Street Financial Center, 1 Lincoln Street Boston MA 02111-2900 United States
Phone Number	617-786-3000

PERFORMANCE

Ratings History
Date	Overall Rating	Risk Rating	Reward Rating
Q4-18	D-	D	D-
Q2-18	D	D	D
Q4-17	B	B	B
Q4-16	C-	C-	C-
Q4-15	C	D+	C

Asset & Performance History
Date	NAV	1-Year Total Return
2017	102.83	12.17
2016	94.05	25.58
2015	75.95	-6.72
2014	84.92	11.82
2013	79.08	33.86
2012	59.99	18.3

Total Assets: $1,007,059,701

Asset Allocation
Asset	%
Cash	0%
Stocks	100%
US Stocks	100%
Bonds	0%
US Bonds	0%
Other	0%

Services Offered: Dividend Investment Plan, CashInvestment Plan

Investment Strategy: The investment seeks to provide investment results that, before fees and expenses, correspond generally to the total return performance of the S&P MidCap 400 Value Index. The fund generally invests substantially all, but at least 80%, of its total assets in the securities comprising the index. The index measures the performance of the mid-capitalization value segment of the U.S. equity market. It may purchase a subset of the securities in the index in an effort to hold a portfolio of securities with generally the same risk and return characteristics of the index. The fund is non-diversified. **Top Holdings:** Atmos Energy Corp   UGI Corp   Reinsurance Group of America Inc   Leidos Holdings Inc   Alleghany Corp

---

iShares Core Moderate Allocation ETF

C   **HOLD**

Ticker	Traded On	NAV	Total Assets ($)	Dividend Yield (TTM)	Turnover Ratio	Expense Ratio
AOM	NYSE Arca	35.69	$999,732,694	2.18	40	0.25

Ratings
Reward	C-
Risk	C+
Recent Upgrade/Downgrade	

Fund Information
Fund Type	Exchange Traded Funds
Category	Cautious Allocation
Sub-Category	Allocation--30% to 50% Equity
Prospectus Objective	Asset Allocation
Inception Date	Nov-08
Open to New Investments	Y

Prices
Price (as of 12/31/2018)	35.68
52-Week High	39.00
52-Week Low	35.24

Total Returns (%)
3-Month	6-Month	1-Year	3-Year	5-Year
-4.69	-2.72	-3.85	13.48	17.13

3-Year Standard Deviation	4.51
Effective Duration	5.97

Valuation
Premium/Discount (1-Year Average)	0.06

Company Information
Provider	iShares
Manager/Tenure	Diane Hsiung (10), Greg Savage (10), Jennifer Hsui (6), 3 others
Website	http://www.ishares.com
Address	iShares 400 Howard Street San Francisco CA 94105 United States
Phone Number	800-474-2737

PERFORMANCE

Ratings History
Date	Overall Rating	Risk Rating	Reward Rating
Q4-18	C	C+	C-
Q2-18	C	C-	C-
Q4-17	B	A-	C+
Q4-16	C	C-	C
Q4-15	C	C-	C

Asset & Performance History
Date	NAV	1-Year Total Return
2017	38.04	11.69
2016	35.21	5.67
2015	34.04	-1.18
2014	35.12	4.44
2013	34.33	10.41
2012	31.7	8.49

Total Assets: $999,732,694

Asset Allocation
Asset	%
Cash	3%
Stocks	40%
US Stocks	22%
Bonds	57%
US Bonds	40%
Other	0%

Services Offered:

Investment Strategy: The investment seeks to track the investment results of the S&P Target Risk Moderate Index composed of a portfolio of underlying equity and fixed income funds intended to represent a moderate target risk allocation strategy. The fund is a fund of funds and seeks its investment objective by investing primarily in other iShares Underlying Funds that themselves seek investment results corresponding to their own respective underlying indexes. It generally will invest at least 90% of its assets in the component securities of the underlying index. The index measures the performance of the S&P Dow Jones Indices LLC proprietary allocation model. **Top Holdings:** iShares Core Total USD Bond Market ETF   iShares Core S&P 500 ETF   iShares Core MSCI Intl Dev Mkts ETF   iShares Core International Aggt Bd ETF   iShares Core MSCI Emerging Markets ETF

Vanguard S&P 500 Value Index Fund ETF Shares   C   HOLD

Ticker	Traded On	NAV	Total Assets ($)	Dividend Yield (TTM)	Turnover Ratio	Expense Ratio
VOOV	NYSE Arca		$999,710,338	2.32	20	0.15

Ratings
Reward   C
Risk   C-
Recent Upgrade/Downgrade

Fund Information
Fund Type   Exchange Traded Funds
Category   US Equity Large Cap Value
Sub-Category   Large Value
Prospectus Objective   Growth & Inc
Inception Date   Sep-10
Open to New Investments   Y

Prices
Price (as of 12/31/2018)   97.57
52-Week High   116.66
52-Week Low   92.00

Total Returns (%)

3-Month	6-Month	1-Year	3-Year	5-Year
-13.08	-7.64	-9.77	21.83	32.25

3-Year Standard Deviation   9.54
Effective Duration

Valuation
Premium/Discount (1-Year Average)   0.04

Company Information
Provider   Vanguard
Manager/Tenure   Donald M. Butler (2), Michelle Louie (1)
Website   http://www.vanguard.com
Address   Vanguard 100 Vanguard Boulevard Malvern PA 19355 United States
Phone Number   877-662-7447

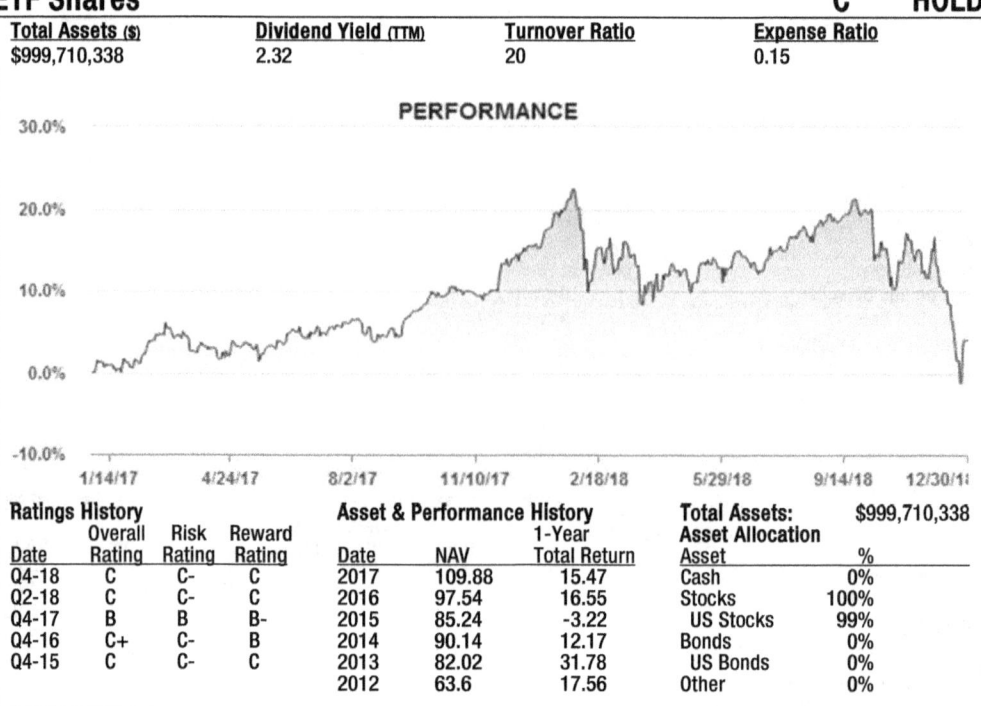

Ratings History

Date	Overall Rating	Risk Rating	Reward Rating
Q4-18	C	C-	C
Q2-18	C	C-	C
Q4-17	B	B	B-
Q4-16	C+	C-	B
Q4-15	C	C-	C

Asset & Performance History

Date	NAV	1-Year Total Return
2017	109.88	15.47
2016	97.54	16.55
2015	85.24	-3.22
2014	90.14	12.17
2013	82.02	31.78
2012	63.6	17.56

Total Assets: $999,710,338
Asset Allocation

Asset	%
Cash	0%
Stocks	100%
US Stocks	99%
Bonds	0%
US Bonds	0%
Other	0%

Services Offered:

Investment Strategy: The investment seeks to track the performance of a benchmark index that measures the investment return of large-capitalization value stocks in the United States. The fund employs an indexing investment approach designed to track the performance of the S&P 500® Value Index, which represents the value companies, as determined by the index sponsor, of the S&P 500 Index. The index measures the performance of large-capitalization value stocks in the United States. **Top Holdings:** Berkshire Hathaway Inc B   JPMorgan Chase & Co   Exxon Mobil Corp   Verizon Communications Inc   Wells Fargo & Co

---

iShares MSCI Spain Capped ETF   D+   SELL

Ticker	Traded On	NAV	Total Assets ($)	Dividend Yield (TTM)	Turnover Ratio	Expense Ratio
EWP	NYSE Arca	26.96	$991,522,381	3.69	21	0.49

Ratings
Reward   C-
Risk   D+
Recent Upgrade/Downgrade   Down

Fund Information
Fund Type   Exchange Traded Funds
Category   Europe Equity Large Cap
Sub-Category   Miscellaneous Region
Prospectus Objective   Europe Stock
Inception Date   Mar-96
Open to New Investments   Y

Prices
Price (as of 12/31/2018)   26.82
52-Week High   36.24
52-Week Low   26.26

Total Returns (%)

3-Month	6-Month	1-Year	3-Year	5-Year
-7.45	-8.71	-15.07	5.48	-15.39

3-Year Standard Deviation   18.69
Effective Duration

Valuation
Premium/Discount (1-Year Average)   -0.22

Company Information
Provider   iShares
Manager/Tenure   Diane Hsiung (10), Greg Savage (10), Jennifer Hsui (5), 1 other
Website   http://www.ishares.com
Address   iShares 400 Howard Street San Francisco CA 94105 United States
Phone Number   800-474-2737

Ratings History

Date	Overall Rating	Risk Rating	Reward Rating
Q4-18	D+	D+	C-
Q2-18	C	C	C
Q4-17	C	C	C
Q4-16	D	D	D
Q4-15	C	C	C

Asset & Performance History

Date	NAV	1-Year Total Return
2017	32.85	26.96
2016	26.58	-2.17
2015	28.45	-15.84
2014	34.99	-4.68
2013	38.33	34.26
2012	29.54	3.08

Total Assets: $991,522,381
Asset Allocation

Asset	%
Cash	0%
Stocks	100%
US Stocks	0%
Bonds	0%
US Bonds	0%
Other	0%

Services Offered: CashInvestment Plan

Investment Strategy: The investment seeks to track the investment results of the MSCI Spain 25/50 Index. The fund will at all times invest at least 80% of its assets in the securities of its underlying index and in depositary receipts representing securities in its underlying index. The underlying index is a free float-adjusted market capitalization-weighted index with a capping methodology applied to issuer weights so that no single issuer of a component exceeds 25% of the underlying index weight, and all issuers with a weight above 5% do not cumulatively exceed 50% of the underlying index weight. The fund is non-diversified. **Top Holdings:** Banco Santander SA   Iberdrola SA   Telefonica SA   Banco Bilbao Vizcaya Argentaria SA   Repsol SA

Xtrackers MSCI Japan Hedged Equity ETF   C   HOLD

Ticker	Traded On	NAV	Total Assets ($)	Dividend Yield (TTM)	Turnover Ratio	Expense Ratio
DBJP	NYSE Arca		$981,823,206	2.5	12	0.46

Ratings
Reward   C-
Risk   C+
Recent Upgrade/Downgrade

Fund Information
Fund Type	Exchange Traded Funds
Category	Japan Equity
Sub-Category	Japan Stock
Prospectus Objective	Pacific Stock
Inception Date	Jun-11
Open to New Investments	Y

Prices
Price (as of 12/31/2018)	36.30
52-Week High	46.50
52-Week Low	35.24

Total Returns (%)
3-Month	6-Month	1-Year	3-Year	5-Year
-17.00	-9.62	-14.01	1.81	19.71

3-Year Standard Deviation   14.58
Effective Duration

Valuation
Premium/Discount (1-Year Average)   -0.06

Company Information
Provider	Deutsche Asset Management
Manager/Tenure	Charlotte Cipolletti (1), Patrick Dwyer (1), Bryan Richards (1), 2 others
Website	http://www.deutsche-etfs.com
Address	Deutsche Asset & Wealth Management 345 Park Avenue New York NY 10154 United States
Phone Number	844-851-4255

PERFORMANCE

Ratings History
Date	Overall Rating	Risk Rating	Reward Rating
Q4-18	C	C+	C-
Q2-18	C	C	C-
Q4-17	B	B-	A-
Q4-16	C	C	C-
Q4-15	B-	C+	B-

Asset & Performance History
Date	NAV	1-Year Total Return
2017	44.08	20.82
2016	37.34	-2
2015	38.6	9.07
2014	37.36	7.79
2013	38.32	51.68
2012	25.81	19.56

Total Assets: $981,823,206
Asset Allocation
Asset	%
Cash	2%
Stocks	98%
US Stocks	0%
Bonds	0%
US Bonds	0%
Other	0%

Services Offered:

Investment Strategy: The investment seeks investment results that correspond generally to the performance, of the MSCI Japan US Dollar Hedged Index. The fund, using a "passive" or indexing investment approach, seeks investment results that correspond generally to the performance, of the underlying index, which is designed to track the performance of the Japanese equity market while mitigating exposure to fluctuations between the value of the U.S. dollar and the Japanese yen. It will invest at least 80% of its total assets in component securities (including depositary receipts in respect of such securities) of the underlying index. **Top Holdings:** Toyota Motor Corp Topix Indx Futr Dec18 SoftBank Group Corp Sony Corp Mitsubishi UFJ Financial Group Inc

---

iShares MSCI Europe Financials ETF   D+   SELL

Ticker	Traded On	NAV	Total Assets ($)	Dividend Yield (TTM)	Turnover Ratio	Expense Ratio
EUFN	NAS CM	16.99	$977,265,373	5.32	3	0.48

Ratings
Reward   D+
Risk   D
Recent Upgrade/Downgrade   Down

Fund Information
Fund Type	Exchange Traded Funds
Category	Financials Sector Equity
Sub-Category	Financial
Prospectus Objective	Financial
Inception Date	Jan-10
Open to New Investments	Y

Prices
Price (as of 12/31/2018)	16.95
52-Week High	25.83
52-Week Low	16.38

Total Returns (%)
3-Month	6-Month	1-Year	3-Year	5-Year
-14.53	-13.76	-23.18	-5.36	-17.17

3-Year Standard Deviation   18.89
Effective Duration

Valuation
Premium/Discount (1-Year Average)   -0.22

Company Information
Provider	iShares
Manager/Tenure	Diane Hsiung (8), Greg Savage (8), Jennifer Hsui (6), 3 others
Website	http://www.ishares.com
Address	iShares 400 Howard Street San Francisco CA 94105 United States
Phone Number	800-474-2737

PERFORMANCE

Ratings History
Date	Overall Rating	Risk Rating	Reward Rating
Q4-18	D+	D	D+
Q2-18	C	C	C-
Q4-17	C+	C	B-
Q4-16	D+	D	D+
Q4-15	C	C+	C-

Asset & Performance History
Date	NAV	1-Year Total Return
2017	23.38	27.16
2016	18.99	-3.11
2015	20.44	-5.01
2014	22.22	-7.86
2013	24.86	30.48
2012	19.42	33.14

Total Assets: $977,265,373
Asset Allocation
Asset	%
Cash	1%
Stocks	99%
US Stocks	0%
Bonds	0%
US Bonds	0%
Other	1%

Services Offered:

Investment Strategy: The investment seeks to track the investment results of the MSCI Europe Financials Index composed of developed market European equities in the financials sector. The fund generally will invest at least 90% of its assets in the component securities of the underlying index and in investments that have economic characteristics that are substantially identical to the component securities of the underlying index. The index is a free float-adjusted market capitalization-weighted index designed to measure the combined equity market performance of the financials sector of developed market countries in Europe. **Top Holdings:** HSBC Holdings PLC Allianz SE Banco Santander SA BNP Paribas UBS Group AG

SPDR® S&P China ETF

C- **HOLD**

Ticker	Traded On	NAV
GXC	NYSE Arca	85.71

Total Assets ($)	Dividend Yield (TTM)	Turnover Ratio	Expense Ratio
$970,949,112	2.46	3	0.59

Ratings
Reward	C-
Risk	C-
Recent Upgrade/Downgrade	Down

Fund Information
Fund Type	Exchange Traded Funds
Category	Greater China Equity
Sub-Category	China Region
Prospectus Objective	Pacific Stock
Inception Date	Mar-07
Open to New Investments	Y

Prices
Price (as of 12/31/2018)	84.81
52-Week High	123.84
52-Week Low	82.62

Total Returns (%)
3-Month	6-Month	1-Year	3-Year	5-Year
-10.29	-17.34	-18.67	23.18	23.48

3-Year Standard Deviation	18.63
Effective Duration	

Valuation
Premium/Discount (1-Year Average)	-0.12

Company Information
Provider	SPDR State Street Global Advisors
Manager/Tenure	Michael J. Feehily (7), Juan Acevedo (1), Thomas Coleman (1)
Website	http://www.spdrs.com
Address	SPDR State Street Global Advisors State Street Financial Center, 1 Lincoln Street Boston MA 02111-2900 United States
Phone Number	617-786-3000

PERFORMANCE

Ratings History
Date	Overall Rating	Risk Rating	Reward Rating
Q4-18	C-	C-	C-
Q2-18	C	C-	C+
Q4-17	B+	C+	A
Q4-16	C	C	C
Q4-15	C	C+	C

Asset & Performance History
Date	NAV	1-Year Total Return
2017	107.37	50.5
2016	72.73	0
2015	73.79	-4.56
2014	79.41	5.03
2013	77.29	9.33
2012	72.6	19.42

Total Assets: $970,949,112

Asset Allocation
Asset	%
Cash	0%
Stocks	100%
US Stocks	1%
Bonds	0%
US Bonds	0%
Other	0%

Services Offered:

Investment Strategy: The investment seeks investment results that, before fees and expenses, correspond generally to the total return performance of the S&P China BMI Index. The fund generally invests substantially all, but at least 80%, of its total assets in the securities comprising the index and in depositary receipts based on securities comprising the index. The index is a market capitalization weighted index designed to define and measure the investable universe of publicly traded companies domiciled in China available to foreign investors. The fund is non-diversified. **Top Holdings:** Tencent Holdings Ltd Alibaba Group Holding Ltd ADR China Construction Bank Corp H Industrial And Commercial Bank Of China Ltd H China Mobile Ltd

---

Invesco BulletShares 2020 High Yield Corporate Bond ETF

C **HOLD**

Ticker	Traded On	NAV
BSJK	NYSE Arca	23.46

Total Assets ($)	Dividend Yield (TTM)	Turnover Ratio	Expense Ratio
$966,148,555	5.05	27	0.42

Ratings
Reward	C
Risk	C+
Recent Upgrade/Downgrade	Down

Fund Information
Fund Type	Exchange Traded Funds
Category	US Fixed Income
Sub-Category	High Yield Bond
Prospectus Objective	Corp Bond-High Yld
Inception Date	Sep-13
Open to New Investments	Y

Prices
Price (as of 12/31/2018)	23.43
52-Week High	24.69
52-Week Low	23.23

Total Returns (%)
3-Month	6-Month	1-Year	3-Year	5-Year
-2.15	-0.27	0.46	20.32	16.63

3-Year Standard Deviation	3.78
Effective Duration	1.48

Valuation
Premium/Discount (1-Year Average)	-0.02

Company Information
Provider	Invesco
Manager/Tenure	Jeremy Neisewander (2), Peter Hubbard (0), Jeffrey W. Kernagis (0), 1 other
Website	http://www.invesco.com/us
Address	Invesco 11 Greenway Plaza, Ste. 2500 Houston TX 77046 United States
Phone Number	800-659-1005

PERFORMANCE

Ratings History
Date	Overall Rating	Risk Rating	Reward Rating
Q4-18	C	C+	C
Q2-18	C+	C+	C
Q4-17	C+	B-	C+
Q4-16	C	C+	C
Q4-15	D+	C-	D

Asset & Performance History
Date	NAV	1-Year Total Return
2017	24.49	5.88
2016	24.24	13.11
2015	22.58	-5.34
2014	25.11	2.41
2013	25.66	
2012		

Total Assets: $966,148,555

Asset Allocation
Asset	%
Cash	2%
Stocks	0%
US Stocks	0%
Bonds	98%
US Bonds	86%
Other	0%

Services Offered:

Investment Strategy: The investment seeks investment results that correspond generally to the performance, before the fund's fees and expenses, of a high yield corporate bond index called the Nasdaq BulletShares® USD High Yield Corporate Bond 2020 Index. The fund will invest at least 80% of its total assets in component securities that comprise the index. The index is designed to represent the performance of a held-to-maturity portfolio of U.S. dollar-denominated high yield corporate bonds with effective maturities in the year 2020. The fund is non-diversified. **Top Holdings:** Reynolds Group Issuer LLC. 5.75% Bausch Health Companies Inc 7% EMC Corporation 2.65% Clear Channel Worldwide Holdings Inc. 7.62% Tenet Healthcare Corporation 6%

FlexShares Morningstar Developed Markets ex-US Factor Tilt Index Fund   D+   SELL

Ticker	Traded On	NAV
TLTD	NYSE Arca	55.62

Total Assets ($)	Dividend Yield (TTM)	Turnover Ratio	Expense Ratio
$962,704,541	3.59		0.39

Ratings
Reward	D+
Risk	C-
Recent Upgrade/Downgrade	Down

Fund Information
Fund Type	Exchange Traded Funds
Category	Global Equity Large Cap
Sub-Category	Foreign Large Blend
Prospectus Objective	Foreign Stock
Inception Date	Sep-12
Open to New Investments	Y

Prices
Price (as of 12/31/2018)	55.51
52-Week High	73.66
52-Week Low	53.42

Total Returns (%)
3-Month	6-Month	1-Year	3-Year	5-Year
-14.04	-12.45	-17.24	9.84	2.63

3-Year Standard Deviation	11.56
Effective Duration	

Valuation
Premium/Discount (1-Year Average)	0.01

Company Information
Provider	Flexshares Trust
Manager/Tenure	Robert Anstine (5), Brendan Sullivan (2)
Website	http://www.flexshares.com
Address	50 South LaSalle Street Chicago, Illinois 60603 Chicago Illinois 60603 United States
Phone Number	855-353-9383

PERFORMANCE

Ratings History
Date	Overall Rating	Risk Rating	Reward Rating
Q4-18	D+	C-	D+
Q2-18	C	C-	C
Q4-17	B-	C+	B
Q4-16	C-	C-	C-
Q4-15	C-	C-	D+

Asset & Performance History
Date	NAV	1-Year Total Return
2017	69.08	25.92
2016	56.46	5.4
2015	55.19	-2.03
2014	57.78	-4.61
2013	62.45	21.96
2012	51.8	

Total Assets: $962,704,541

Asset Allocation
Asset	%
Cash	2%
Stocks	98%
US Stocks	1%
Bonds	0%
US Bonds	0%
Other	0%

Services Offered:

Investment Strategy: The investment seeks investment results that correspond generally to the price and yield performance, before fees and expenses, of the Morningstar® Developed Markets ex-US Factor Tilt IndexSM. The fund will invest at least 80% of its total assets (exclusive of collateral held from securities lending) in the securities of the index and in American ADRs and GDRs based on the securities in the index. The underlying index reflects the performance of a selection of equity securities designed to provide broad exposure to the global developed equities markets, excluding the U.S., with increased exposure (or a "tilt") to small-capitalization stocks and value stocks.
Top Holdings: Toyota Motor Corp   Nestle SA   Total SA   Royal Dutch Shell PLC Class A   Novartis AG

WisdomTree U.S. High Dividend Fund   C   HOLD

Ticker	Traded On	NAV
DHS	NYSE Arca	65.18

Total Assets ($)	Dividend Yield (TTM)	Turnover Ratio	Expense Ratio
$950,329,804	3.42	17	0.38

Ratings
Reward	C
Risk	C-
Recent Upgrade/Downgrade	

Fund Information
Fund Type	Exchange Traded Funds
Category	US Equity Large Cap Value
Sub-Category	Large Value
Prospectus Objective	Growth & Inc
Inception Date	Jun-06
Open to New Investments	Y

Prices
Price (as of 12/31/2018)	65.12
52-Week High	75.26
52-Week Low	62.15

Total Returns (%)
3-Month	6-Month	1-Year	3-Year	5-Year
-8.97	-4.67	-7.25	22.07	39.68

3-Year Standard Deviation	8.08
Effective Duration	

Valuation
Premium/Discount (1-Year Average)	-0.02

Company Information
Provider	WisdomTree
Manager/Tenure	Richard A. Brown (10), Thomas J. Durante (10), Karen Q. Wong (10)
Website	http://www.wisdomtree.com
Address	WisdomTree 245 Park Avenue, 35th floor New York NY 10167 United States
Phone Number	866-909-9473

PERFORMANCE

Ratings History
Date	Overall Rating	Risk Rating	Reward Rating
Q4-18	C	C-	C
Q2-18	C	C-	C
Q4-17	B	B+	B-
Q4-16	C+	C-	B-
Q4-15	C	C	C+

Asset & Performance History
Date	NAV	1-Year Total Return
2017	72.8	11.68
2016	67.27	17.85
2015	59.05	-0.6
2014	61.52	15.12
2013	55.1	24.44
2012	45.8	11.31

Total Assets: $950,329,804

Asset Allocation
Asset	%
Cash	0%
Stocks	100%
US Stocks	100%
Bonds	0%
US Bonds	0%
Other	0%

Services Offered:

Investment Strategy: The investment seeks to track the price and yield performance, before fees and expenses, of the WisdomTree U.S. High Dividend Index. Under normal circumstances, at least 95% of the fund's total assets (exclusive of collateral held from securities lending) will be invested in component securities of the index and investments that have economic characteristics that are substantially identical to the economic characteristics of such component securities. The index is a fundamentally weighted index that is comprised of companies with high dividend yields selected from the WisdomTree U.S. Dividend Index. The fund is non-diversified. **Top Holdings:** Exxon Mobil Corp   Verizon Communications Inc   AT&T Inc   Pfizer Inc   Johnson & Johnson

Direxion Daily Small Cap Bull 3X Shares   C-   HOLD

Ticker	Traded On	NAV	Total Assets ($)	Dividend Yield (TTM)	Turnover Ratio	Expense Ratio
TNA	NYSE Arca	42.19	$949,863,345	0.19	185	1.1

Ratings
Reward   C
Risk   D+
Recent Upgrade/Downgrade   Down

Fund Information
Fund Type   Exchange Traded Funds
Category   Trading Tools
Sub-Category   Trading--Leveraged Equity
Prospectus Objective   Small Company
Inception Date   Nov-08
Open to New Investments   Y

Prices
Price (as of 12/31/2018)   42.09
52-Week High   96.51
52-Week Low   35.43

Total Returns (%)

3-Month	6-Month	1-Year	3-Year	5-Year
-50.77	-49.78	-39.94	32.41	9.74

3-Year Standard Deviation   44.13
Effective Duration

Valuation
Premium/Discount (1-Year Average)   -0.02

Company Information
Provider   Direxion Funds
Manager/Tenure   Paul Brigandi (10), Tony Ng (3)
Website   http://www.direxionfunds.com
Address   Direxion Funds 1301 Avenue Of The
                   Americas (6th Avenue) New York NY
                   10019 United States
Phone Number   646-572-3390

PERFORMANCE

Ratings History

Date	Overall Rating	Risk Rating	Reward Rating
Q4-18	C-	D+	C
Q2-18	C+	C-	B
Q4-17	B	C-	A+
Q4-16	C	D+	C+
Q4-15	C	C+	C

Asset & Performance History

Date	NAV	1-Year Total Return
2017	70.26	39.58
2016	50.41	57.95
2015	31.92	-21.09
2014	40.45	5.02
2013	38.76	151.22
2012	15.98	42.19

Total Assets: $949,863,345
Asset Allocation

Asset	%
Cash	40%
Stocks	60%
US Stocks	59%
Bonds	0%
US Bonds	0%
Other	0%

Services Offered:

Investment Strategy: The investment seeks daily investment results, before fees and expenses, of 300% of the daily performance of the Russell 2000® Index. The fund invests at least 80% of its net assets (plus borrowing for investment purposes) in securities of the index, exchange-traded funds ("ETFs") that track the index and other financial instruments that provide daily leveraged exposure to the index or ETFs that track the index. The index measures the performance of approximately 2,000 small-capitalization companies in the Russell 3000® Index, based on a combination of their market capitalization and current index membership. The fund is non-diversified. **Top Holdings:** iShares Russell 2000 ETF Russ 2000 Indx Small Swap Russ 2000 Indx Small Swap Russ 2000 Indx Small Swap Russ 2000 Indx Small Swap

iShares U.S. Industrials ETF   C   HOLD

Ticker	Traded On	NAV	Total Assets ($)	Dividend Yield (TTM)	Turnover Ratio	Expense Ratio
IYJ	BATS	128.56	$941,576,890	1.24	7	0.43

Ratings
Reward   C
Risk   C+
Recent Upgrade/Downgrade

Fund Information
Fund Type   Exchange Traded Funds
Category   Industrials Sector Equity
Sub-Category   Industrials
Prospectus Objective   Unaligned
Inception Date   Jun-00
Open to New Investments   Y

Prices
Price (as of 12/31/2018)   128.53
52-Week High   159.01
52-Week Low   120.07

Total Returns (%)

3-Month	6-Month	1-Year	3-Year	5-Year
-17.85	-10.09	-11.59	30.36	36.38

3-Year Standard Deviation   12.46
Effective Duration

Valuation
Premium/Discount (1-Year Average)   0.01

Company Information
Provider   iShares
Manager/Tenure   Diane Hsiung (10), Greg Savage (10),
                   Jennifer Hsui (6), 3 others
Website   http://www.ishares.com
Address   iShares 400 Howard Street San
                   Francisco CA 94105 United States
Phone Number   800-474-2737

PERFORMANCE

Ratings History

Date	Overall Rating	Risk Rating	Reward Rating
Q4-18	C	C+	C
Q2-18	C	C	C
Q4-17	B	B-	A-
Q4-16	B-	C	B
Q4-15	C	C	C

Asset & Performance History

Date	NAV	1-Year Total Return
2017	147.29	23.96
2016	120.51	18.94
2015	102.82	-2.09
2014	106.62	6.85
2013	101.28	39.92
2012	73.33	17.35

Total Assets: $941,576,890
Asset Allocation

Asset	%
Cash	0%
Stocks	100%
US Stocks	99%
Bonds	0%
US Bonds	0%
Other	0%

Services Offered: CashInvestment Plan

Investment Strategy: The investment seeks to track the investment results of the Dow Jones U.S. Industrials Index composed of U.S. equities in the industrials sector. The fund generally invests at least 90% of its assets in securities of the underlying index and in depositary receipts representing securities of the underlying index. The underlying index measures the performance of the industrials sector of the U.S. equity market. **Top Holdings:** Boeing Co 3M Co Union Pacific Corp Honeywell International Inc Accenture PLC A

Xtrackers MSCI Europe Hedged Equity ETF   C   HOLD

Ticker	Traded On	NAV		Total Assets ($)	Dividend Yield (TTM)	Turnover Ratio	Expense Ratio
DBEU	NYSE Arca			$940,100,447	2.98	11	0.45

Ratings
Reward   D+
Risk   C+
Recent Upgrade/Downgrade   Down

Fund Information
Fund Type   Exchange Traded Funds
Category   Europe Equity Large Cap
Sub-Category   Europe Stock
Prospectus Objective   Europe Stock
Inception Date   Oct-13
Open to New Investments   Y

Prices
Price (as of 12/31/2018)   25.17
52-Week High   29.69
52-Week Low   24.49

Total Returns (%)

3-Month	6-Month	1-Year	3-Year	5-Year
-10.98	-8.55	-8.75	13.10	23.10

3-Year Standard Deviation   9.08
Effective Duration

Valuation
Premium/Discount (1-Year Average)   -0.10

Company Information
Provider   Deutsche Asset Management
Manager/Tenure   Charlotte Cipolletti (1), Patrick Dwyer
                  (1), Bryan Richards (1), 2 others
Website   http://www.deutsche-etfs.com
Address   Deutsche Asset & Wealth
                  Management 345 Park Avenue New
                  York NY 10154 United States
Phone Number   844-851-4255

PERFORMANCE

Ratings History

Date	Overall Rating	Risk Rating	Reward Rating
Q4-18	C	C+	D+
Q2-18	C+	C+	C
Q4-17	B	B	B-
Q4-16	C	C	C
Q4-15	C-	C+	C-

Asset & Performance History

Date	NAV	1-Year Total Return
2017	28.5	14.61
2016	25.44	8.14
2015	25.97	4.2
2014	26.21	4.45
2013	26.2	
2012		

Total Assets: $940,100,447
Asset Allocation

Asset	%
Cash	2%
Stocks	97%
US Stocks	2%
Bonds	0%
US Bonds	0%
Other	0%

Services Offered:

Investment Strategy: The investment seeks investment results that correspond generally to the performance, before fees and expenses, of the MSCI Europe US Dollar Hedged Index. The fund, using a "passive" or indexing investment approach, seeks investment results that correspond generally to the performance, of the underlying index, which is designed to track the performance of the developed markets in Europe, while mitigating exposure to fluctuations between the value of the U.S. dollar and the currencies of the countries included in the underlying index. It will invest at least 80% of its total assets in component securities of the underlying index. **Top Holdings:** Nestle SA Novartis AG Roche Holding AG Dividend Right Cert. HSBC Holdings PLC Royal Dutch Shell PLC Class A

---

iShares Asia 50 ETF   C-   HOLD

Ticker	Traded On	NAV		Total Assets ($)	Dividend Yield (TTM)	Turnover Ratio	Expense Ratio
AIA	NAS CM	55.43		$936,841,354	1.9	16	0.5

Ratings
Reward   C-
Risk   C-
Recent Upgrade/Downgrade   Down

Fund Information
Fund Type   Exchange Traded Funds
Category   Asia ex-Japan Equity
Sub-Category   Pacific/Asia ex-Japan Stk
Prospectus Objective   Pacific Stock
Inception Date   Nov-07
Open to New Investments   Y

Prices
Price (as of 12/31/2018)   55.30
52-Week High   72.96
52-Week Low   53.63

Total Returns (%)

3-Month	6-Month	1-Year	3-Year	5-Year
-9.96	-9.68	-13.94	38.10	30.58

3-Year Standard Deviation   15.5
Effective Duration

Valuation
Premium/Discount (1-Year Average)   -0.06

Company Information
Provider   iShares
Manager/Tenure   Diane Hsiung (10), Greg Savage (10),
                  Jennifer Hsui (6), 3 others
Website   http://www.ishares.com
Address   iShares 400 Howard Street San
                  Francisco CA 94105 United States
Phone Number   800-474-2737

PERFORMANCE

Ratings History

Date	Overall Rating	Risk Rating	Reward Rating
Q4-18	C-	C-	C-
Q2-18	C+	C+	C+
Q4-17	B+	C+	A
Q4-16	C	C-	C
Q4-15	C	C-	C

Asset & Performance History

Date	NAV	1-Year Total Return
2017	65.98	43.51
2016	46.68	11.82
2015	42.72	-6.45
2014	46.93	1.07
2013	47.48	2.64
2012	47.32	22.71

Total Assets: $936,841,354
Asset Allocation

Asset	%
Cash	0%
Stocks	100%
US Stocks	0%
Bonds	0%
US Bonds	0%
Other	0%

Services Offered:

Investment Strategy: The investment seeks to track the S&P Asia 50TM, which is a total float-adjusted, market capitalization-weighted index that is designed to measure the performance of the 50 leading companies listed in four Asian countries or regions: Hong Kong, Singapore, South Korea and Taiwan. The fund generally will invest at least 90% of its assets in the component securities of the index and in investments that have economic characteristics that are substantially identical to the component securities and may invest up to 10% of its assets in certain futures, options and swap contracts, cash and cash equivalents. It is non-diversified. **Top Holdings:** Tencent Holdings Ltd Samsung Electronics Co Ltd Taiwan Semiconductor Manufacturing Co Ltd AIA Group Ltd China Construction Bank Corp H

Invesco S&P 500® Pure Value ETF   C   HOLD

Ticker	Traded On	NAV		Total Assets ($)	Dividend Yield (TTM)	Turnover Ratio	Expense Ratio
RPV	NYSE Arca	56.82		$932,578,334	1.94		0.35

Ratings
Reward   C
Risk   C+
Recent Upgrade/Downgrade

Fund Information
Fund Type	Exchange Traded Funds
Category	US Equity Large Cap Value
Sub-Category	Large Value
Prospectus Objective	Growth
Inception Date	Mar-06
Open to New Investments	Y

Prices
Price (as of 12/31/2018)	56.86
52-Week High	71.10
52-Week Low	53.85

Total Returns (%)
3-Month	6-Month	1-Year	3-Year	5-Year
-16.74	-12.30	-12.26	22.54	26.16

3-Year Standard Deviation   12.14
Effective Duration

Valuation
Premium/Discount (1-Year Average)   0.02

Company Information
Provider	Invesco
Manager/Tenure	Peter Hubbard (0), Michael Jeanette (0), Jonathan Nixon (0), 1 other
Website	http://www.invesco.com/us
Address	Invesco 11 Greenway Plaza, Ste. 2500 Houston TX 77046 United States
Phone Number	800-659-1005

PERFORMANCE

Ratings History

Date	Overall Rating	Risk Rating	Reward Rating
Q4-18	C	C+	C
Q2-18	C	C-	C
Q4-17	B-	B-	B
Q4-16	C	C-	B-
Q4-15	C+	B-	C

Asset & Performance History

Date	NAV	1-Year Total Return
2017	66.22	17.65
2016	57.55	18.79
2015	49.24	-8.29
2014	54.93	12.26
2013	49.72	47.46
2012	34.17	25

Total Assets: $932,578,334
Asset Allocation

Asset	%
Cash	0%
Stocks	100%
US Stocks	98%
Bonds	0%
US Bonds	0%
Other	0%

Services Offered:

Investment Strategy: The investment seeks to track the investment results (before fees and expenses) of the S&P 500® Pure Value Index (the "underlying index"). The fund generally will invest at least 90% of its total assets in the securities that comprise the underlying index. The underlying index includes securities that exhibit the strongest value characteristics as measured using three factors: book to value price ratio, earnings to price ratio, and sales to price ratio, as selected by the index provider strictly in accordance with its guidelines and mandated procedures. The fund is non-diversified. **Top Holdings:** CenturyLink Inc   Berkshire Hathaway Inc B   Kohl's Corp   Macy's Inc   Archer-Daniels Midland Co

---

iShares Morningstar Large-Cap ETF   C   HOLD

Ticker	Traded On	NAV		Total Assets ($)	Dividend Yield (TTM)	Turnover Ratio	Expense Ratio
JKD	NYSE Arca	142.58		$926,549,889	1.9	46	0.2

Ratings
Reward   C
Risk   C-
Recent Upgrade/Downgrade

Fund Information
Fund Type	Exchange Traded Funds
Category	US Equity Large Cap Blend
Sub-Category	Large Blend
Prospectus Objective	Growth
Inception Date	Jun-04
Open to New Investments	Y

Prices
Price (as of 12/31/2018)	142.53
52-Week High	169.91
52-Week Low	133.93

Total Returns (%)
3-Month	6-Month	1-Year	3-Year	5-Year
-15.30	-6.66	-8.39	27.05	46.79

3-Year Standard Deviation   8.97
Effective Duration

Valuation
Premium/Discount (1-Year Average)   0.02

Company Information
Provider	iShares
Manager/Tenure	Diane Hsiung (10), Greg Savage (10), Jennifer Hsui (6), 3 others
Website	http://www.ishares.com
Address	iShares 400 Howard Street San Francisco CA 94105 United States
Phone Number	800-474-2737

PERFORMANCE

Ratings History

Date	Overall Rating	Risk Rating	Reward Rating
Q4-18	C	C-	C
Q2-18	C	C-	C
Q4-17	B	B	B
Q4-16	B-	C	B
Q4-15	C+	C	C+

Asset & Performance History

Date	NAV	1-Year Total Return
2017	158.79	22.11
2016	132.56	13.58
2015	119.15	-1.12
2014	123.46	16.84
2013	107.75	34.13
2012	82	17.3

Total Assets: $926,549,889
Asset Allocation

Asset	%
Cash	0%
Stocks	100%
US Stocks	98%
Bonds	0%
US Bonds	0%
Other	0%

Services Offered:

Investment Strategy: The investment seeks to track the investment results of the Morningstar® Large Core IndexSM composed of large-capitalization U.S. equities. The fund generally invests at least 90% of its assets in securities of the underlying index and in depositary receipts representing securities of the underlying index. The underlying index measures the performance of stocks issued by large-capitalization companies that have exhibited average "growth" and "value" characteristics as determined by Morningstar, Inc.'s ("Morningstar" or the "index provider") proprietary index methodology. **Top Holdings:** Apple Inc   Johnson & Johnson   Bank of America Corporation   Chevron Corp   Comcast Corp Class A

---

iShares Micro-Cap ETF   C-   HOLD

Ticker	Traded On	NAV		Total Assets ($)	Dividend Yield (TTM)	Turnover Ratio	Expense Ratio
IWC	NYSE Arca	82.37		$920,686,791	1.11	22	0.6

Ratings
Reward	C-
Risk	C-
Recent Upgrade/Downgrade	Down

Fund Information
Fund Type	Exchange Traded Funds
Category	US Equity Small Cap
Sub-Category	Small Blend
Prospectus Objective	Growth
Inception Date	Aug-05
Open to New Investments	Y

Prices
Price (as of 12/31/2018)	82.45
52-Week High	109.91
52-Week Low	77.77

Total Returns (%)
3-Month	6-Month	1-Year	3-Year	5-Year
-21.01	-22.34	-13.07	18.10	16.10

3-Year Standard Deviation	16.01
Effective Duration	

Valuation
Premium/Discount (1-Year Average)	0.03

Company Information
Provider	iShares
Manager/Tenure	Diane Hsiung (10), Greg Savage (10), Jennifer Hsui (6), 3 others
Website	http://www.ishares.com
Address	iShares 400 Howard Street San Francisco CA 94105 United States
Phone Number	800-474-2737

PERFORMANCE

Ratings History
Date	Overall Rating	Risk Rating	Reward Rating
Q4-18	C-	C-	C-
Q2-18	C	C-	B-
Q4-17	B+	B	A-
Q4-16	C	C-	B-
Q4-15	C	C-	C

Asset & Performance History
Date	NAV	1-Year Total Return
2017	95.57	12.72
2016	85.76	20.53
2015	72.1	-5.04
2014	77.02	3.53
2013	75.24	45.38
2012	52.34	19.42

Total Assets: $920,686,791
Asset Allocation
Asset	%
Cash	0%
Stocks	100%
US Stocks	99%
Bonds	0%
US Bonds	0%
Other	0%

Services Offered:

Investment Strategy: The investment seeks to track the investment results of the Russell Microcap Index, which measures the performance of the microcap sector of the U.S. equity market. The fund generally invests at least 90% of its assets in securities of the underlying index and in depositary receipts representing securities of the underlying index. It may invest the remainder of its assets in certain futures, options and swap contracts, cash and cash equivalents, as well as in securities not included in the underlying index, but which the advisor believes will help the fund track the underlying index. **Top Holdings:** Tandem Diabetes Care Inc Crocs Inc Staar Surgical Co Endocyte Inc Heritage Financial Corp

---

Vanguard S&P Mid-Cap 400 Value Index Fund ETF Shares   C-   HOLD

Ticker	Traded On	NAV		Total Assets ($)	Dividend Yield (TTM)	Turnover Ratio	Expense Ratio
IVOV	NYSE Arca			$919,188,341	1.56	36	0.2

Ratings
Reward	C-
Risk	D+
Recent Upgrade/Downgrade	Down

Fund Information
Fund Type	Exchange Traded Funds
Category	US Equity Mid Cap
Sub-Category	Mid-Cap Value
Prospectus Objective	Growth & Inc
Inception Date	Sep-10
Open to New Investments	Y

Prices
Price (as of 12/31/2018)	105.16
52-Week High	130.76
52-Week Low	99.28

Total Returns (%)
3-Month	6-Month	1-Year	3-Year	5-Year
-17.05	-14.50	-12.75	23.52	28.82

3-Year Standard Deviation	12.63
Effective Duration	

Valuation
Premium/Discount (1-Year Average)	0.06

Company Information
Provider	Vanguard
Manager/Tenure	William A. Coleman (2), Awais Khan (1)
Website	http://www.vanguard.com
Address	Vanguard 100 Vanguard Boulevard Malvern PA 19355 United States
Phone Number	877-662-7447

PERFORMANCE

Ratings History
Date	Overall Rating	Risk Rating	Reward Rating
Q4-18	C-	D+	C-
Q2-18	C	D+	C
Q4-17	B	B	B
Q4-16	C-	C-	C-
Q4-15	C	D+	C

Asset & Performance History
Date	NAV	1-Year Total Return
2017	121.62	12.23
2016	110.15	25.52
2015	88.4	-6.77
2014	96.41	11.86
2013	87.45	33.93
2012	65.86	18.35

Total Assets: $919,188,341
Asset Allocation
Asset	%
Cash	0%
Stocks	99%
US Stocks	99%
Bonds	0%
US Bonds	0%
Other	0%

Services Offered:

Investment Strategy: The investment seeks to track the performance of a benchmark index that measures the investment return of mid-capitalization value stocks in the United States. The fund employs an indexing investment approach designed to track the performance of the S&P MidCap 400® Value Index, which represents the value companies, as determined by the index sponsor, of the S&P MidCap 400 Index. The Advisor attempts to replicate the target index by investing all, or substantially all, of its assets in the stocks that make up the index, holding each stock in approximately the same proportion as its weighting in the index. **Top Holdings:** Atmos Energy Corp Leidos Holdings Inc Steel Dynamics Inc UGI Corp Reinsurance Group of America Inc

iShares Core International Aggregate Bond ETF   C-   HOLD

Ticker	Traded On	NAV		Total Assets ($)	Dividend Yield (TTM)	Turnover Ratio	Expense Ratio
IAGG	BATS	52.03		$919,015,092	1.6	20	0.09

Ratings
Reward   C
Risk   C-
Recent Upgrade/Downgrade

Fund Information
Fund Type   Exchange Traded Funds
Category   Global Fixed Income
Sub-Category   World Bond
Prospectus Objective   Worldwide Bond
Inception Date   Nov-15
Open to New Investments   Y

Prices
Price (as of 12/31/2018) 52.21
52-Week High   52.91
52-Week Low   51.58

Total Returns (%)

3-Month	6-Month	1-Year	3-Year	5-Year
1.92	1.54	2.92	10.76	

3-Year Standard Deviation   2.62
Effective Duration   7.29

Valuation
Premium/Discount (1-Year Average)   0.13

Company Information
Provider   iShares
Manager/Tenure   Scott Radell (3), Sid Swaminathan (0)
Website   http://www.ishares.com
Address   iShares 400 Howard Street San
                  Francisco CA 94105 United States
Phone Number   800-474-2737

PERFORMANCE

Ratings History

Date	Overall Rating	Risk Rating	Reward Rating
Q4-18	C-	C-	C
Q2-18	C-	C-	C
Q4-17	C	B+	D+
Q4-16	D	C+	D
Q4-15			

Asset & Performance History

Date	NAV	1-Year Total Return
2017	52.1	2.51
2016	51.72	4.98
2015	50.04	
2014		
2013		
2012		

Total Assets: $919,015,092

Asset Allocation

Asset	%
Cash	0%
Stocks	0%
US Stocks	0%
Bonds	100%
US Bonds	3%
Other	0%

Services Offered:

Investment Strategy: The investment seeks to track the investment results of the Bloomberg Barclays Global Aggregate ex USD 10% Issuer Capped (Hedged) Index composed of global non-U.S. dollar-denominated investment-grade bonds that mitigates exposure to fluctuations between the value of the component currencies and the U.S. dollar. The fund generally will invest at least 90% of its assets in the component securities and other instruments of the underlying index. The index measures the performance of the global investment-grade bond market. The fund is non-diversified. **Top Holdings:** Germany (Federal Republic Of) 2.25% Germany (Federal Republic Of) 0% France (Republic Of) 0.5% Canada (Government of) 0.75% Japan (Government Of) 0.1%

Global X SuperDividend™ ETF   C-   HOLD

Ticker	Traded On	NAV		Total Assets ($)	Dividend Yield (TTM)	Turnover Ratio	Expense Ratio
SDIV	NYSE Arca	17.20		$914,121,343	8.1	67	0.58

Ratings
Reward   C-
Risk   C
Recent Upgrade/Downgrade Down

Fund Information
Fund Type   Exchange Traded Funds
Category   Global Eq Mid/Small Cap
Sub-Category   World Small/Mid Stock
Prospectus Objective   Equity-Income
Inception Date   Jun-11
Open to New Investments   Y

Prices
Price (as of 12/31/2018) 17.10
52-Week High   22.55
52-Week Low   16.68

Total Returns (%)

3-Month	6-Month	1-Year	3-Year	5-Year
-13.26	-13.69	-15.36	6.82	3.35

3-Year Standard Deviation   10.53
Effective Duration

Valuation
Premium/Discount (1-Year Average)   0.00

Company Information
Provider   Global X Funds
Manager/Tenure   Chang Kim (4), James Ong (2), Nam
                  To (0)
Website   http://www.globalxfunds.com
Address   Global X Funds 600 Lexington Avenue,
                  20th Floor New York NY 10022 United
                  States
Phone Number   888-493-8631

PERFORMANCE

Ratings History

Date	Overall Rating	Risk Rating	Reward Rating
Q4-18	C-	C	C-
Q2-18	C	C+	C
Q4-17	C+	C+	C+
Q4-16	C	C	C-
Q4-15	C	C	C-

Asset & Performance History

Date	NAV	1-Year Total Return
2017	21.81	11.54
2016	20.91	13.16
2015	19.84	-8.54
2014	23.19	5.78
2013	23.3	14.73
2012	21.8	15.29

Total Assets: $914,121,343

Asset Allocation

Asset	%
Cash	0%
Stocks	100%
US Stocks	59%
Bonds	0%
US Bonds	0%
Other	0%

Services Offered: Retirement Investment

Investment Strategy: The investment seeks investment results that correspond generally to the price and yield performance, before fees and expenses, of the Solactive Global SuperDividend® Index. The fund invests at least 80% of its total assets in the securities of the underlying index and in American Depositary Receipts ("ADRs") and Global Depositary Receipts ("GDRs") based on the securities in the underlying index. The underlying index tracks the performance of 100 equally-weighted companies that rank among the highest dividend yielding equity securities in the world, including emerging market countries. **Top Holdings:** Two Harbors Investment Corp Omega Healthcare Investors Inc Arbor Realty Trust Inc Medical Properties Trust Inc Uniti Group Inc

First Trust Large Cap Growth AlphaDEX® Fund   C   HOLD

Ticker	Traded On	NAV	Total Assets ($)	Dividend Yield (TTM)	Turnover Ratio	Expense Ratio
FTC	NAS CM	57.26	$910,557,933	0.32	148	0.61

Ratings

Reward	C-
Risk	C+
Recent Upgrade/Downgrade	Down

Fund Information

Fund Type	Exchange Traded Funds
Category	US Equity Large Cap Growth
Sub-Category	Large Growth
Prospectus Objective	Growth
Inception Date	May-07
Open to New Investments	Y

Prices

Price (as of 12/31/2018)	57.32
52-Week High	70.61
52-Week Low	53.12

Total Returns (%)

3-Month	6-Month	1-Year	3-Year	5-Year
-18.68	-13.33	-5.98	20.69	44.07

3-Year Standard Deviation	11.54
Effective Duration	

Valuation

Premium/Discount (1-Year Average)	0.09

Company Information

Provider	First Trust
Manager/Tenure	Jon C. Erickson (11), Daniel J. Lindquist (11), David G. McGarel (11), 3 others
Website	http://www.ftportfolios.com/
Address	First Trust 120 E. Liberty Drive, Suite 400 Wheaton IL 60187 United States
Phone Number	800-621-1675

PERFORMANCE

Ratings History

Date	Overall Rating	Risk Rating	Reward Rating
Q4-18	C	C+	C-
Q2-18	C+	C-	B
Q4-17	B+	A	B
Q4-16	C	C-	C+
Q4-15	B	C+	B

Asset & Performance History

Date	NAV	1-Year Total Return
2017	61.1	25.18
2016	49.02	2.55
2015	48.21	4.28
2014	46.47	14.46
2013	40.92	37.71
2012	29.87	9.97

Total Assets: $910,557,933

Asset Allocation

Asset	%
Cash	0%
Stocks	100%
US Stocks	100%
Bonds	0%
US Bonds	0%
Other	0%

Services Offered:

Investment Strategy: The investment seeks investment results that correspond generally to the price and yield (before the fund's fees and expenses) of an equity index called the Nasdaq AlphaDEX® Large Cap Growth Index. The fund will normally invest at least 90% of its net assets (including investment borrowings) in common stocks that comprise the index. The index is designed to select growth stocks from the NASDAQ US 500 Large Cap Index (the "base index") that may generate positive alpha, or risk-adjusted returns, relative to traditional indices through the use of the AlphaDEX® selection methodology. **Top Holdings:** Dell-VMWare Tracking Stock V   Ulta Beauty Inc   HCA Healthcare Inc   Burlington Stores Inc   O'Reilly Automotive Inc

Invesco Aerospace & Defense ETF   B-   BUY

Ticker	Traded On	NAV	Total Assets ($)	Dividend Yield (TTM)	Turnover Ratio	Expense Ratio
PPA	NYSE Arca	49.50	$906,058,436	0.56	7	0.6

Ratings

Reward	B
Risk	C+
Recent Upgrade/Downgrade	Down

Fund Information

Fund Type	Exchange Traded Funds
Category	Industrials Sector Equity
Sub-Category	Industrials
Prospectus Objective	Unaligned
Inception Date	Oct-05
Open to New Investments	Y

Prices

Price (as of 12/31/2018)	49.45
52-Week High	61.91
52-Week Low	46.46

Total Returns (%)

3-Month	6-Month	1-Year	3-Year	5-Year
-19.45	-9.86	-7.35	43.58	68.74

3-Year Standard Deviation	13.63
Effective Duration	

Valuation

Premium/Discount (1-Year Average)	0.03

Company Information

Provider	Invesco
Manager/Tenure	Peter Hubbard (11), Michael Jeanette (10), Tony Seisser (4), 1 other
Website	http://www.invesco.com/us
Address	Invesco 11 Greenway Plaza, Ste. 2500 Houston TX 77046 United States
Phone Number	800-659-1005

PERFORMANCE

Ratings History

Date	Overall Rating	Risk Rating	Reward Rating
Q4-18	B-	C+	B
Q2-18	B	C+	B
Q4-17	B+	B-	A+
Q4-16	B	C+	B+
Q4-15	B	B	B

Asset & Performance History

Date	NAV	1-Year Total Return
2017	53.87	30.02
2016	41.74	19.2
2015	35.66	4.23
2014	34.7	12.74
2013	30.98	49.81
2012	20.98	17.85

Total Assets: $906,058,436

Asset Allocation

Asset	%
Cash	0%
Stocks	100%
US Stocks	99%
Bonds	0%
US Bonds	0%
Other	0%

Services Offered:

Investment Strategy: The investment seeks to track the investment results (before fees and expenses) of the SPADE® Defense Index. The fund generally will invest at least 90% of its total assets in common stocks of that comprise the underlying index. The underlying index was composed of common stocks of 54 U.S. companies whose shares are listed on the New York Stock Exchange ("NYSE") or the NASDAQ. These companies are engaged principally in the development, manufacture, operation and support of U.S. defense, military, homeland security and space operations. The fund is non-diversified. **Top Holdings:** United Technologies Corp   Boeing Co   Lockheed Martin Corp   Honeywell International Inc   General Dynamics Corp

iShares MSCI Switzerland Capped ETF

C   HOLD

Ticker	Traded On	NAV
EWL	NYSE Arca	31.35

Total Assets ($)	Dividend Yield (TTM)	Turnover Ratio	Expense Ratio
$903,238,097	2.44	9	0.49

Ratings
Reward	D+
Risk	C+
Recent Upgrade/Downgrade	

Fund Information
Fund Type	Exchange Traded Funds
Category	Europe Equity Large Cap
Sub-Category	Miscellaneous Region
Prospectus Objective	Europe Stock
Inception Date	Mar-96
Open to New Investments	Y

Prices
Price (as of 12/31/2018)	31.52
52-Week High	37.74
52-Week Low	30.43

Total Returns (%)
3-Month	6-Month	1-Year	3-Year	5-Year
-9.86	-3.09	-9.77	7.91	7.58

3-Year Standard Deviation	10.96
Effective Duration	

Valuation
Premium/Discount (1-Year Average)	-0.22

Company Information
Provider	iShares
Manager/Tenure	Diane Hsiung (10), Greg Savage (10), Jennifer Hsui (5), 1 other
Website	http://www.ishares.com
Address	iShares 400 Howard Street San Francisco CA 94105 United States
Phone Number	800-474-2737

PERFORMANCE

Ratings History
Date	Overall Rating	Risk Rating	Reward Rating
Q4-18	C	C+	D+
Q2-18	C	C	C-
Q4-17	B-	B	C+
Q4-16	C-	C-	C-
Q4-15	C	C+	C

Asset & Performance History
Date	NAV	1-Year Total Return
2017	35.62	23.36
2016	29.49	-3.04
2015	31.24	0.51
2014	31.82	-0.81
2013	32.82	26.47
2012	26.5	20.23

Total Assets: $903,238,097
Asset Allocation
Asset	%
Cash	1%
Stocks	99%
US Stocks	0%
Bonds	0%
US Bonds	0%
Other	0%

Services Offered: CashInvestment Plan

Investment Strategy: The investment seeks to track the investment results of the MSCI Switzerland 25/50 Index. The fund will at all times invest at least 80% of its assets in the securities of its underlying index and in depositary receipts representing securities in its underlying index. The underlying index is a free float-adjusted market capitalization-weighted index with a capping methodology applied to issuer weights so that no single issuer of a component exceeds 25% of the underlying index weight, and all issuers with a weight above 5% do not cumulatively exceed 50% of the underlying index weight. The fund is non-diversified. **Top Holdings:** Nestle SA Novartis AG Roche Holding AG Dividend Right Cert. Zurich Insurance Group AG UBS Group AG

VanEck Vectors Semiconductor ETF

C+   HOLD

Ticker	Traded On	NAV
SMH	NYSE Arca	87.33

Total Assets ($)	Dividend Yield (TTM)	Turnover Ratio	Expense Ratio
$902,469,961	1.46	23	0.35

Ratings
Reward	B
Risk	C
Recent Upgrade/Downgrade	Down

Fund Information
Fund Type	Exchange Traded Funds
Category	Technology Sector Equity
Sub-Category	Technology
Prospectus Objective	Technology
Inception Date	Dec-11
Open to New Investments	Y

Prices
Price (as of 12/31/2018)	87.28
52-Week High	113.07
52-Week Low	80.96

Total Returns (%)
3-Month	6-Month	1-Year	3-Year	5-Year
-17.03	-14.10	-9.46	69.56	120.17

3-Year Standard Deviation	18.56
Effective Duration	

Valuation
Premium/Discount (1-Year Average)	0.04

Company Information
Provider	VanEck
Manager/Tenure	Hao-Hung (Peter) Liao (6), Guo Hua (Jason) Jin (0)
Website	http://www.vaneck.com
Address	Van Eck Associates Corporation 666 Third Avenue New York NY 10017 United States
Phone Number	800-826-1115

PERFORMANCE

Ratings History
Date	Overall Rating	Risk Rating	Reward Rating
Q4-18	C+	C	B
Q2-18	B	C	B+
Q4-17	B+	C+	A+
Q4-16	C+	C	C+
Q4-15	B	B	B

Asset & Performance History
Date	NAV	1-Year Total Return
2017	97.77	38.31
2016	71.68	35.4
2015	53.36	-0.11
2014	54.56	29.99
2013	42.45	33.7
2012	32.25	8.28

Total Assets: $902,469,961
Asset Allocation
Asset	%
Cash	0%
Stocks	100%
US Stocks	75%
Bonds	0%
US Bonds	0%
Other	0%

Services Offered:

Investment Strategy: The investment seeks to replicate as closely as possible, before fees and expenses, the price and yield performance of the MVIS® US Listed Semiconductor 25 Index. The fund normally invests at least 80% of its total assets in securities that comprise the fund's benchmark index. The index includes common stocks and depositary receipts of U.S. exchange-listed companies in the semiconductor sector. Such companies may include medium-capitalization companies and foreign companies that are listed on a U.S. exchange. The fund is non-diversified. **Top Holdings:** Intel Corp Taiwan Semiconductor Manufacturing Co Ltd ADR Broadcom Inc ASML Holding NV ADR NVIDIA Corp

WisdomTree Japan SmallCap Dividend Fund   C-   HOLD

Ticker	Traded On	NAV	Total Assets ($)	Dividend Yield (TTM)	Turnover Ratio	Expense Ratio
DFJ	NYSE Arca	65.09	$900,523,027	1.79	18	0.58

Ratings
Reward	D+
Risk	C
Recent Upgrade/Downgrade	Down

Fund Information
Fund Type	Exchange Traded Funds
Category	Japan Equity
Sub-Category	Japan Stock
Prospectus Objective	Pacific Stock
Inception Date	Jun-06
Open to New Investments	Y

Prices
Price (as of 12/31/2018)	64.39
52-Week High	85.46
52-Week Low	60.90

Total Returns (%)
3-Month	6-Month	1-Year	3-Year	5-Year
-14.72	-13.20	-17.61	20.40	39.51

3-Year Standard Deviation	11.59
Effective Duration	

Valuation
Premium/Discount (1-Year Average)	-0.14

Company Information
Provider	WisdomTree
Manager/Tenure	Richard A. Brown (10), Thomas J. Durante (10), Karen Q. Wong (10)
Website	http://www.wisdomtree.com
Address	WisdomTree 245 Park Avenue, 35th floor New York NY 10167 United States
Phone Number	866-909-9473

PERFORMANCE

Ratings History
Date	Overall Rating	Risk Rating	Reward Rating
Q4-18	C-	C	D+
Q2-18	C	C-	C+
Q4-17	A-	B	A
Q4-16	C	C-	C+
Q4-15	C+	C-	B

Asset & Performance History
Date	NAV	1-Year Total Return
2017	80.4	31.6
2016	62.14	11.04
2015	56.99	17.68
2014	49.03	-1.53
2013	50.57	20.08
2012	43.12	5.48

Total Assets: $900,523,027
Asset Allocation
Asset	%
Cash	0%
Stocks	100%
US Stocks	0%
Bonds	0%
US Bonds	0%
Other	0%

Services Offered:

Investment Strategy: The investment seeks to track the price and yield performance, before fees and expenses, of the WisdomTree Japan SmallCap Dividend Index. Under normal circumstances, at least 95% of the fund's total assets (exclusive of collateral held from securities lending) will be invested in the component securities of the index and investments that have economic characteristics that are substantially identical to the economic characteristics of such component securities. The index is comprised of dividend-paying small capitalization companies in Japan. The fund is non-diversified. **Top Holdings:** Sankyo Co Ltd   Matsui Securities Co Ltd WisdomTree Japan Hedged Equity ETF   DIC Corp   Mitsubishi Materials Corp

---

Invesco BulletShares 2022 Corporate Bond ETF   C   HOLD

Ticker	Traded On	NAV	Total Assets ($)	Dividend Yield (TTM)	Turnover Ratio	Expense Ratio
BSCM	NYSE Arca	20.56	$895,307,224	2.81	0	0.1

Ratings
Reward	C-
Risk	C+
Recent Upgrade/Downgrade	

Fund Information
Fund Type	Exchange Traded Funds
Category	US Fixed Income
Sub-Category	Corporate Bond
Prospectus Objective	Corp Bond - Gen
Inception Date	Jul-13
Open to New Investments	Y

Prices
Price (as of 12/31/2018)	20.61
52-Week High	21.17
52-Week Low	20.47

Total Returns (%)
3-Month	6-Month	1-Year	3-Year	5-Year
0.73	1.54	0.03	9.97	19.17

3-Year Standard Deviation	3.09
Effective Duration	3.37

Valuation
Premium/Discount (1-Year Average)	0.24

Company Information
Provider	Invesco
Manager/Tenure	Jeremy Neisewander (2), Peter Hubbard (0), Jeffrey W. Kernagis (0), 1 other
Website	http://www.invesco.com/us
Address	Invesco 11 Greenway Plaza, Ste. 2500 Houston TX 77046 United States
Phone Number	800-659-1005

PERFORMANCE

Ratings History
Date	Overall Rating	Risk Rating	Reward Rating
Q4-18	C	C+	C-
Q2-18	C	C+	C-
Q4-17	B	A	C
Q4-16	C	C-	C
Q4-15	C-	C-	D+

Asset & Performance History
Date	NAV	1-Year Total Return
2017	21.12	3.63
2016	20.86	5.8
2015	20.23	0.57
2014	20.67	7.74
2013	19.79	
2012		

Total Assets: $895,307,224
Asset Allocation
Asset	%
Cash	0%
Stocks	0%
US Stocks	0%
Bonds	100%
US Bonds	84%
Other	0%

Services Offered:

Investment Strategy: The investment seeks investment results that correspond generally to the performance, before the fund's fees and expenses, of an investment grade corporate bond index called the Nasdaq BulletShares® USD Corporate Bond 2022 Index. The fund will invest at least 80% of its total assets in component securities that comprise the index. The index is designed to represent the performance of a held-to-maturity portfolio of U.S. dollar-denominated investment-grade corporate bonds with effective maturities in the year 2022. The fund is non-diversified. **Top Holdings:** Goldman Sachs Group, Inc. 5.75%   JPMorgan Chase & Co. 4.5% Barclays Bank plc 7.62%   Goldman Sachs Group, Inc. 3%   Morgan Stanley 2.75%

First Trust NASDAQ Technology Dividend Index Fund

C+   **HOLD**

Ticker	Traded On	NAV	Total Assets ($)	Dividend Yield (TTM)	Turnover Ratio	Expense Ratio
TDIV	NAS CM	33.16	$888,182,080	2.41	27	0.5

Ratings
Reward	B
Risk	C
Recent Upgrade/Downgrade	Down

Fund Information
Fund Type	Exchange Traded Funds
Category	Technology Sector Equity
Sub-Category	Technology
Prospectus Objective	Technology
Inception Date	Aug-12
Open to New Investments	Y

Prices
Price (as of 12/31/2018)	33.16
52-Week High	38.63
52-Week Low	31.20

Total Returns (%)
3-Month	6-Month	1-Year	3-Year	5-Year
-12.97	-5.36	-3.04	41.44	53.64

3-Year Standard Deviation	12.25
Effective Duration	

Valuation
Premium/Discount (1-Year Average)	0.07

Company Information
Provider	First Trust
Manager/Tenure	Jon C. Erickson (6), Daniel J. Lindquist (6), David G. McGarel (6), 3 others
Website	http://www.ftportfolios.com/
Address	First Trust 120 E. Liberty Drive, Suite 400 Wheaton IL 60187 United States
Phone Number	800-621-1675

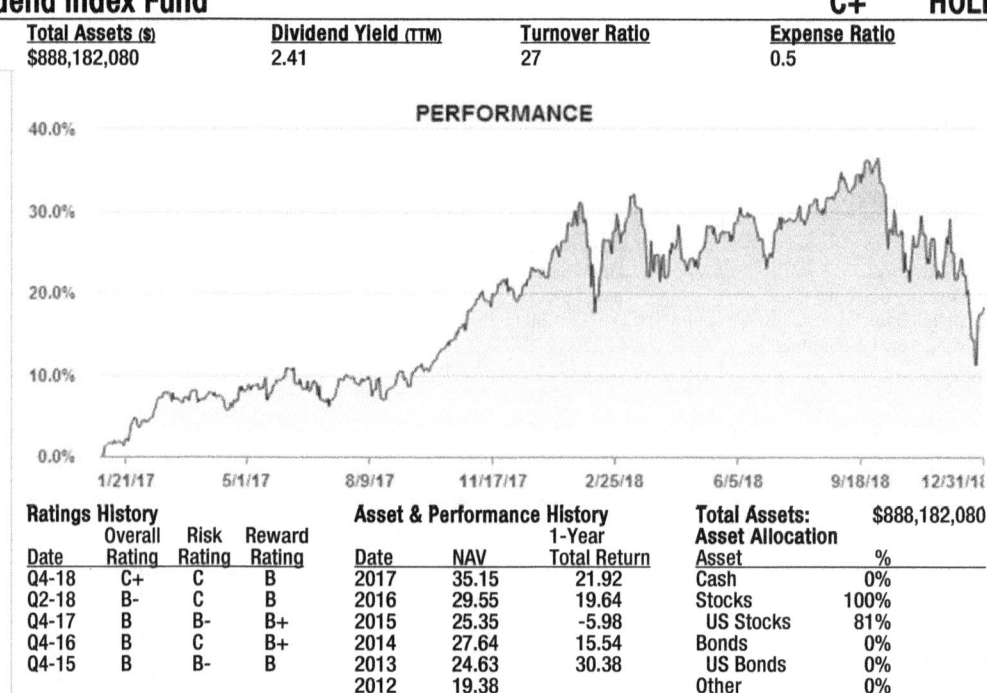

PERFORMANCE

Ratings History
Date	Overall Rating	Risk Rating	Reward Rating
Q4-18	C+	C	B
Q2-18	B-	C	B
Q4-17	B	B-	B+
Q4-16	B	C	B+
Q4-15	B	B-	B

Asset & Performance History
Date	NAV	1-Year Total Return
2017	35.15	21.92
2016	29.55	19.64
2015	25.35	-5.98
2014	27.64	15.54
2013	24.63	30.38
2012	19.38	

Total Assets: $888,182,080

Asset Allocation
Asset	%
Cash	0%
Stocks	100%
US Stocks	81%
Bonds	0%
US Bonds	0%
Other	0%

Services Offered:

Investment Strategy: The investment seeks investment results that correspond generally to the price and yield (before the fund's fees and expenses) of an equity index called the NASDAQ Technology Dividend IndexSM. The fund will normally invest at least 90% of its net assets (including investment borrowings) in the common stocks and/or depositary receipts included in the index. The index is owned and was developed by Nasdaq, Inc. (the "index provider"). The index is calculated and maintained by the index Provider. The index includes up to 100 technology and telecommunications companies that pay a regular or common dividend. The fund is non-diversified.
Top Holdings: Intel Corp Cisco Systems Inc Microsoft Corp International Business Machines Corp Apple Inc

---

iShares U.S. Consumer Services ETF

C   **HOLD**

Ticker	Traded On	NAV	Total Assets ($)	Dividend Yield (TTM)	Turnover Ratio	Expense Ratio
IYC	NYSE Arca	180.89	$887,998,741	0.81	10	0.43

Ratings
Reward	C+
Risk	C
Recent Upgrade/Downgrade	Down

Fund Information
Fund Type	Exchange Traded Funds
Category	Consumer Goods & Svcs
Sub-Category	Consumer Cyclical
Prospectus Objective	Unaligned
Inception Date	Jun-00
Open to New Investments	Y

Prices
Price (as of 12/31/2018)	180.90
52-Week High	211.88
52-Week Low	168.12

Total Returns (%)
3-Month	6-Month	1-Year	3-Year	5-Year
-14.09	-6.36	1.79	28.78	55.95

3-Year Standard Deviation	11.55
Effective Duration	

Valuation
Premium/Discount (1-Year Average)	0.03

Company Information
Provider	iShares
Manager/Tenure	Diane Hsiung (10), Greg Savage (10), Jennifer Hsui (6), 3 others
Website	http://www.ishares.com
Address	iShares 400 Howard Street San Francisco CA 94105 United States
Phone Number	800-474-2737

PERFORMANCE

Ratings History
Date	Overall Rating	Risk Rating	Reward Rating
Q4-18	C	C	C+
Q2-18	C+	C-	B
Q4-17	B	A-	B-
Q4-16	C+	C	B
Q4-15	C+	C	B-

Asset & Performance History
Date	NAV	1-Year Total Return
2017	179.19	19.88
2016	150.97	5.52
2015	144.68	6.18
2014	137.68	14.04
2013	121.76	41.48
2012	86.82	23.6

Total Assets: $887,998,741

Asset Allocation
Asset	%
Cash	0%
Stocks	100%
US Stocks	99%
Bonds	0%
US Bonds	0%
Other	0%

Services Offered: CashInvestment Plan

Investment Strategy: The investment seeks to track the investment results of the Dow Jones U.S. Consumer Services Index composed of U.S. equities in the consumer services sector. The fund generally invests at least 90% of its assets in securities of the underlying index and in depositary receipts representing securities of the underlying index. The underlying index measures the performance of the consumer services sector of the U.S. equity market. **Top Holdings:** Amazon.com Inc Comcast Corp Class A The Home Depot Inc Walt Disney Co McDonald's Corp

iShares Core Aggressive Allocation ETF   C   HOLD

Ticker	Traded On	NAV	Total Assets ($)	Dividend Yield (TTM)	Turnover Ratio	Expense Ratio
AOA	NYSE Arca	48.56	$882,420,253	1.98	40	0.25

Ratings
Reward   C-
Risk   C+
Recent Upgrade/Downgrade

Fund Information
Fund Type   Exchange Traded Funds
Category   Aggressive Allocation
Sub-Category   Allocation--70% to 85% Equity
Prospectus Objective Asset Allocation
Inception Date   Nov-08
Open to New Investments   Y

Prices
Price (as of 12/31/2018)   48.55
52-Week High   56.92
52-Week Low   47.04

Total Returns (%)

3-Month	6-Month	1-Year	3-Year	5-Year
-10.45	-6.93	-7.76	19.16	25.08

3-Year Standard Deviation   7.82
Effective Duration   5.97

Valuation
Premium/Discount (1-Year Average)   0.04

Company Information
Provider   iShares
Manager/Tenure   Diane Hsiung (10), Greg Savage (10),
                 Jennifer Hsui (6), 3 others
Website   http://www.ishares.com
Address   iShares 400 Howard Street San
                 Francisco CA 94105 United States
Phone Number   800-474-2737

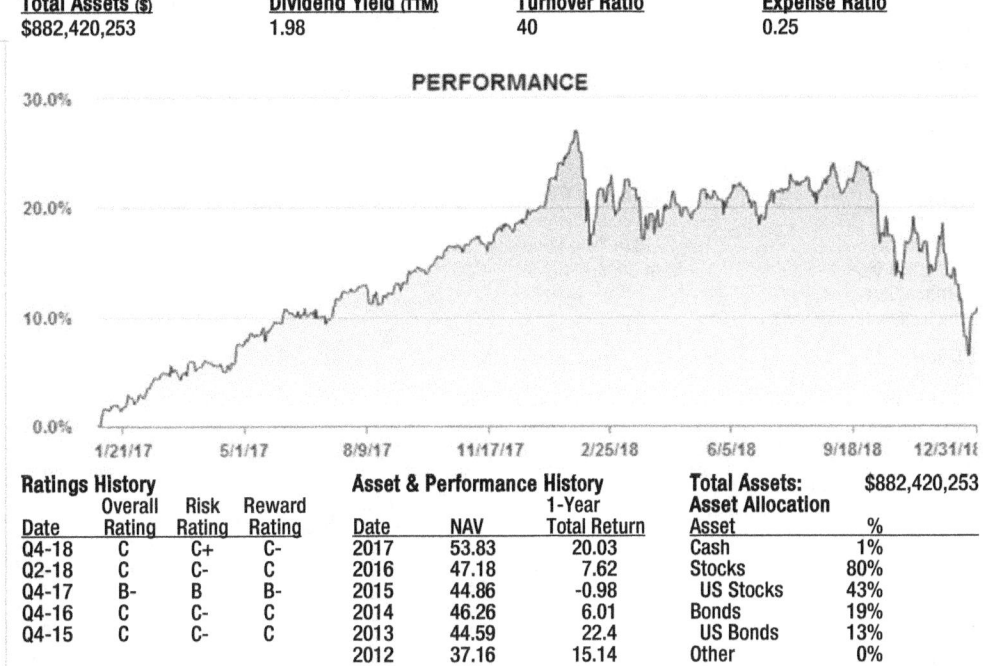

PERFORMANCE

Ratings History

Date	Overall Rating	Risk Rating	Reward Rating
Q4-18	C	C+	C-
Q2-18	C	C-	C
Q4-17	B-	B	B-
Q4-16	C	C-	C
Q4-15	C	C-	C

Asset & Performance History

Date	NAV	1-Year Total Return
2017	53.83	20.03
2016	47.18	7.62
2015	44.86	-0.98
2014	46.26	6.01
2013	44.59	22.4
2012	37.16	15.14

Total Assets: $882,420,253

Asset Allocation

Asset	%
Cash	1%
Stocks	80%
US Stocks	43%
Bonds	19%
US Bonds	13%
Other	0%

Services Offered:

Investment Strategy: The investment seeks to track the investment results of the S&P Target Risk Aggressive Index composed of a portfolio of underlying equity and fixed income funds intended to represent an aggressive target risk allocation strategy. The fund is a fund of funds and seeks its investment objective by investing primarily in other iShares Underlying Funds that themselves seek investment results corresponding to their own respective underlying indexes. It generally will invest at least 90% of its assets in the component securities of the underlying index. The index measures the performance of the S&P Dow Jones Indices LLC proprietary allocation model. **Top Holdings:** iShares Core S&P 500 ETF iShares Core MSCI Intl Dev Mkts ETF iShares Core Total USD Bond Market ETF iShares Core MSCI Emerging Markets ETF iShares Core International Aggt Bd ETF

VictoryShares US EQ Income Enhanced Volatility Wtd ETF   C   HOLD

Ticker	Traded On	NAV	Total Assets ($)	Dividend Yield (TTM)	Turnover Ratio	Expense Ratio
CDC	NAS CM	42.47	$877,566,951	3.1	49	0.35

Ratings
Reward   C
Risk   C-
Recent Upgrade/Downgrade

Fund Information
Fund Type   Exchange Traded Funds
Category   US Equity Large Cap Value
Sub-Category   Large Value
Prospectus Objective Income
Inception Date   Jul-14
Open to New Investments   Y

Prices
Price (as of 12/31/2018)   42.32
52-Week High   48.75
52-Week Low   40.65

Total Returns (%)

3-Month	6-Month	1-Year	3-Year	5-Year
-9.27	-6.31	-5.52	31.78	

3-Year Standard Deviation   7.82
Effective Duration

Valuation
Premium/Discount (1-Year Average)   0.05

Company Information
Provider   VictoryShares
Manager/Tenure   Stephen Hammers (4), Mannik Dhillon
                 (0)
Website   http://www.VictorySharesLiterature.com
Address   Victory Shares 4249 Easton Way,
                 Suite 400 Columbus OH 43219 United
                 States
Phone Number

PERFORMANCE

Ratings History

Date	Overall Rating	Risk Rating	Reward Rating
Q4-18	C	C-	C
Q2-18	C	C-	C
Q4-17	B	B+	B
Q4-16	C	C-	B-
Q4-15	D	C	D+

Asset & Performance History

Date	NAV	1-Year Total Return
2017	46.38	15.73
2016	41.28	19.77
2015	35.37	-0.52
2014	36.69	
2013		
2012		

Total Assets: $877,566,951

Asset Allocation

Asset	%
Cash	0%
Stocks	100%
US Stocks	99%
Bonds	0%
US Bonds	0%
Other	0%

Services Offered:

Investment Strategy: The investment seeks to provide investment results that track the performance of the Nasdaq Victory US Large Cap High Dividend 100 Long/Cash Volatility Weighted Index before fees and expenses. The fund seeks to achieve its investment objective by investing, under normal market conditions, at least 80% of its assets directly or indirectly in the securities included in the Nasdaq Victory US Large Cap 100 High Dividend Long/Cash Volatility Weighted Index. The index identifies the 100 highest dividend yielding stocks in the Nasdaq Victory US Large Cap 500 Volatility Weighted Index. **Top Holdings:** NextEra Energy Inc Exelon Corp Procter & Gamble Co Pfizer Inc DTE Energy Co

Invesco Fundamental High Yield® Corporate Bond ETF   C   HOLD

Ticker	Traded On	NAV	Total Assets ($)	Dividend Yield (TTM)	Turnover Ratio	Expense Ratio
PHB	NYSE Arca	17.72	$875,368,862	4.26		0.5

Ratings
Reward   C
Risk   C+
Recent Upgrade/Downgrade

Fund Information
Fund Type   Exchange Traded Funds
Category   US Fixed Income
Sub-Category   High Yield Bond
Prospectus Objective   Corp Bond-High Yld
Inception Date   Nov-07
Open to New Investments   Y

Prices
Price (as of 12/31/2018) 17.67
52-Week High   19.03
52-Week Low   17.49

Total Returns (%)

3-Month	6-Month	1-Year	3-Year	5-Year
-3.50	-1.36	-2.37	15.73	14.77

3-Year Standard Deviation   3.86
Effective Duration   3.55

Valuation
Premium/Discount (1-Year Average)   -0.23

Company Information
Provider   Invesco
Manager/Tenure Philip Fang (11), Peter Hubbard (11),
                Jeffrey W. Kernagis (11), 2 others
Website   http://www.invesco.com/us
Address   Invesco 11 Greenway Plaza, Ste. 2500
                Houston TX 77046 United States
Phone Number   800-659-1005

PERFORMANCE

Ratings History

Date	Overall Rating	Risk Rating	Reward Rating
Q4-18	C	C+	C
Q2-18	C	C+	C
Q4-17	B-	B	C+
Q4-16	C+	C+	C
Q4-15	C	C+	C-

Asset & Performance History

Date	NAV	1-Year Total Return
2017	18.94	5.11
2016	18.78	12.78
2015	17.46	-2.62
2014	18.74	1.83
2013	19.22	4.3
2012	19.3	11.98

Total Assets: $875,368,862
Asset Allocation

Asset	%
Cash	0%
Stocks	0%
US Stocks	0%
Bonds	100%
US Bonds	100%
Other	0%

Services Offered:

Investment Strategy: The investment seeks to track the investment results (before fees and expenses) of the RAFI® Bonds U.S. High Yield 1-10 Index (the "underlying index"). The fund generally will invest at least 80% of its total assets in high-yield corporate bonds that comprise the underlying index. The underlying index is comprised of U.S. dollar-denominated bonds that are SEC-registered securities or Rule 144A securities with registration rights (issued after July 31, 2013) and whose issuers are public companies listed on a major U.S. stock exchange. **Top Holdings:** United Continental Holdings, Inc. 4.25% Ally Financial Inc. 8% Micron Technology Inc. 5.5% Hess Corporation 4.3% YUM Brands Inc 3.75%

---

iShares U.S. Energy ETF   C   HOLD

Ticker	Traded On	NAV	Total Assets ($)	Dividend Yield (TTM)	Turnover Ratio	Expense Ratio
IYE	NYSE Arca	31.17	$874,704,454	2.63	6	0.43

Ratings
Reward   C
Risk   C-
Recent Upgrade/Downgrade Down

Fund Information
Fund Type   Exchange Traded Funds
Category   Energy Sector Equity
Sub-Category   Equity Energy
Prospectus Objective   Natl Res
Inception Date   Jun-00
Open to New Investments   Y

Prices
Price (as of 12/31/2018) 31.16
52-Week High   43.43
52-Week Low   29.27

Total Returns (%)

3-Month	6-Month	1-Year	3-Year	5-Year
-26.21	-23.43	-19.20	-0.49	-30.06

3-Year Standard Deviation   18.72
Effective Duration

Valuation
Premium/Discount (1-Year Average)   0.02

Company Information
Provider   iShares
Manager/Tenure Diane Hsiung (10), Greg Savage (10),
                Jennifer Hsui (6), 3 others
Website   http://www.ishares.com
Address   iShares 400 Howard Street San
                Francisco CA 94105 United States
Phone Number   800-474-2737

PERFORMANCE

Ratings History

Date	Overall Rating	Risk Rating	Reward Rating
Q4-18	C	C-	C
Q2-18	C	C-	B-
Q4-17	C-	C	D+
Q4-16	C-	D	C
Q4-15	C	C	C+

Asset & Performance History

Date	NAV	1-Year Total Return
2017	39.59	-1.94
2016	41.54	25.6
2015	33.85	-22.21
2014	44.82	-9.64
2013	50.5	25.7
2012	40.85	4.28

Total Assets: $874,704,454
Asset Allocation

Asset	%
Cash	1%
Stocks	99%
US Stocks	99%
Bonds	0%
US Bonds	0%
Other	0%

Services Offered: CashInvestment Plan

Investment Strategy: The investment seeks to track the investment results of the Dow Jones U.S. Oil & Gas Index composed of U.S. equities in the energy sector. The fund generally invests at least 90% of its assets in securities of the underlying index and in depositary receipts representing securities of the underlying index. The underlying index measures the performance of the oil and gas sector of the U.S. equity market. The fund is non-diversified.
Top Holdings: Exxon Mobil Corp Chevron Corp ConocoPhillips Schlumberger Ltd EOG Resources Inc

VanEck Vectors Fallen Angel High Yield Bond ETF   C   HOLD

Ticker	Traded On	NAV	Total Assets ($)	Dividend Yield (TTM)	Turnover Ratio	Expense Ratio
ANGL	NYSE Arca	26.87	$865,649,228	5.62	20	0.35

Ratings
Reward   C-
Risk   C+
Recent Upgrade/Downgrade

Fund Information
Fund Type	Exchange Traded Funds
Category	US Fixed Income
Sub-Category	High Yield Bond
Prospectus Objective	Corp Bond-High Yld
Inception Date	Apr-12
Open to New Investments	Y

Prices
Price (as of 12/31/2018)	26.67
52-Week High	30.31
52-Week Low	26.29

Total Returns (%)
3-Month	6-Month	1-Year	3-Year	5-Year
-6.41	-4.02	-5.43	29.58	32.07

3-Year Standard Deviation	6.89
Effective Duration	5.90

Valuation
Premium/Discount (1-Year Average)   -0.32

Company Information
Provider	VanEck
Manager/Tenure	Francis G. Rodilosso (6)
Website	http://www.vaneck.com
Address	Van Eck Associates Corporation 666 Third Avenue New York NY 10017 United States
Phone Number	800-826-1115

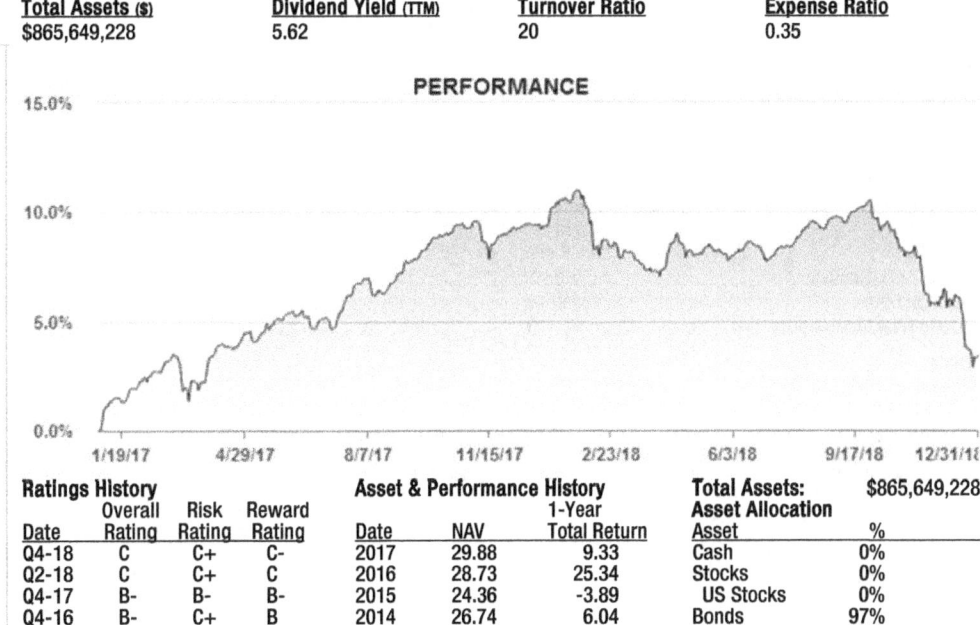

PERFORMANCE

Ratings History
Date	Overall Rating	Risk Rating	Reward Rating
Q4-18	C	C+	C-
Q2-18	C	C+	C
Q4-17	B-	B-	B-
Q4-16	B-	C+	B
Q4-15	C	C-	C

Asset & Performance History
Date	NAV	1-Year Total Return
2017	29.88	9.33
2016	28.73	25.34
2015	24.36	-3.89
2014	26.74	6.04
2013	26.89	6.88
2012	26.75	

Total Assets: $865,649,228
Asset Allocation
Asset	%
Cash	0%
Stocks	0%
US Stocks	0%
Bonds	97%
US Bonds	83%
Other	0%

Services Offered:

Investment Strategy: The investment seeks to replicate as closely as possible, before fees and expenses, the price and yield performance of the ICE BofAML US Fallen Angel High Yield Index (the "Fallen Angel Index"). The fund normally invests at least 80% of its total assets in securities that comprise the fund's benchmark index. The index is comprised of below investment grade corporate bonds denominated in U.S. dollars that were rated investment grade at the time of issuance. **Top Holdings:** Sprint Capital Corporation 6.88% Sprint Capital Corporation 8.75% EMC Corporation 2.65% FREEPORT-MCMORAN INC 3.55% FREEPORT-MCMORAN INC 3.88%

Invesco KBW Bank ETF   B-   BUY

Ticker	Traded On	NAV	Total Assets ($)	Dividend Yield (TTM)	Turnover Ratio	Expense Ratio
KBWB	NAS CM	44.12	$864,659,499	1.93		0.35

Ratings
Reward   B
Risk   C
Recent Upgrade/Downgrade   Down

Fund Information
Fund Type	Exchange Traded Funds
Category	Financials Sector Equity
Sub-Category	Financial
Prospectus Objective	Financial
Inception Date	Nov-11
Open to New Investments	

Prices
Price (as of 12/31/2018)	43.98
52-Week High	60.11
52-Week Low	41.50

Total Returns (%)
3-Month	6-Month	1-Year	3-Year	5-Year
-17.72	-17.18	-17.95	24.12	35.44

3-Year Standard Deviation	19.88
Effective Duration	

Valuation
Premium/Discount (1-Year Average)   0.03

Company Information
Provider	Invesco
Manager/Tenure	Peter Hubbard (7), Michael Jeanette (7), Tony Seisser (4), 1 other
Website	http://www.invesco.com/us
Address	Invesco 11 Greenway Plaza, Ste. 2500 Houston TX 77046 United States
Phone Number	800-659-1005

PERFORMANCE

Ratings History
Date	Overall Rating	Risk Rating	Reward Rating
Q4-18	B-	C	B
Q2-18	B-	C	B
Q4-17	B+	B-	A
Q4-16	B	C	B+
Q4-15	A-	A-	B+

Asset & Performance History
Date	NAV	1-Year Total Return
2017	54.98	18.15
2016	47.21	28.03
2015	37.57	0.13
2014	38.1	8.97
2013	35.51	37.25
2012	26.28	32.41

Total Assets: $864,659,499
Asset Allocation
Asset	%
Cash	0%
Stocks	100%
US Stocks	100%
Bonds	0%
US Bonds	0%
Other	0%

Services Offered:

Investment Strategy: The investment seeks to track the investment results (before fees and expenses) of the KBW Nasdaq Bank Index (the "underlying index"). The fund generally will invest at least 90% of its total assets in securities of national money centers, regional banks and thrift institutions that are listed on a U.S. national securities exchange and that comprise the underlying index. The underlying index is a modified-market capitalization-weighted index that seeks to reflect the performance of national money centers, regional banks and thrift institutions that are publicly traded in the U.S. The fund is non-diversified. **Top Holdings:** US Bancorp JPMorgan Chase & Co Wells Fargo & Co Citigroup Inc Bank of America Corporation

iShares MSCI USA ESG Select ETF
C   HOLD

Ticker	Traded On	NAV		Total Assets ($)	Dividend Yield (TTM)	Turnover Ratio	Expense Ratio
SUSA	NYSE Arca	103.16		$862,156,871	1.51	13	0.25

Ratings

Reward	C
Risk	C
Recent Upgrade/Downgrade	

Fund Information

Fund Type	Exchange Traded Funds
Category	US Equity Large Cap Blend
Sub-Category	Large Blend
Prospectus Objective	Growth
Inception Date	Jan-05
Open to New Investments	Y

Prices

Price (as of 12/31/2018)	103.14
52-Week High	120.97
52-Week Low	96.94

Total Returns (%)

3-Month	6-Month	1-Year	3-Year	5-Year
-13.68	-7.75	-5.56	29.87	44.62

3-Year Standard Deviation	9.94
Effective Duration	

Valuation

Premium/Discount (1-Year Average)	0.09

Company Information

Provider	iShares
Manager/Tenure	Diane Hsiung (10), Greg Savage (10), Jennifer Hsui (6), 3 others
Website	http://www.ishares.com
Address	iShares 400 Howard Street San Francisco CA 94105 United States
Phone Number	800-474-2737

PERFORMANCE

Ratings History

Date	Overall Rating	Risk Rating	Reward Rating
Q4-18	C	C	C
Q2-18	C	C	C+
Q4-17	B-	B-	B
Q4-16	C+	C	B
Q4-15	C	C	C+

Asset & Performance History

Date	NAV	1-Year Total Return
2017	110.99	22.52
2016	91.95	12.24
2015	83.25	-1.88
2014	86.06	13.49
2013	76.79	30.86
2012	59.51	10.23

Total Assets: $862,156,871

Asset Allocation

Asset	%
Cash	0%
Stocks	100%
US Stocks	99%
Bonds	0%
US Bonds	0%
Other	0%

Services Offered:

Investment Strategy: The investment seeks to track the investment results of the MSCI USA Extended ESG Select Index composed of U.S. companies that have positive environmental, social and governance characteristics as identified by the index provider. The fund generally invests at least 90% of its assets in securities of the underlying index and in depositary receipts representing securities of the underlying index. The underlying index is an optimized index designed to maximize exposure to favorable environmental, social and governance ("ESG") characteristics, while exhibiting risk and return characteristics similar to the MSCI USA Index. **Top Holdings:** Microsoft Corp   Ecolab Inc   Apple Inc   3M Co   Accenture PLC A

---

iShares U.S. Home Construction ETF
C   HOLD

Ticker	Traded On	NAV		Total Assets ($)	Dividend Yield (TTM)	Turnover Ratio	Expense Ratio
ITB	BATS	29.99		$859,630,679	0.49	18	0.43

Ratings

Reward	B-
Risk	D+
Recent Upgrade/Downgrade	Down

Fund Information

Fund Type	Exchange Traded Funds
Category	Consumer Goods & Svcs
Sub-Category	Consumer Cyclical
Prospectus Objective	Real Estate
Inception Date	May-06
Open to New Investments	Y

Prices

Price (as of 12/31/2018)	30.04
52-Week High	46.25
52-Week Low	28.55

Total Returns (%)

3-Month	6-Month	1-Year	3-Year	5-Year
-14.64	-21.07	-30.96	12.05	23.15

3-Year Standard Deviation	18.63
Effective Duration	

Valuation

Premium/Discount (1-Year Average)	0.04

Company Information

Provider	iShares
Manager/Tenure	Diane Hsiung (10), Greg Savage (10), Jennifer Hsui (6), 3 others
Website	http://www.ishares.com
Address	iShares 400 Howard Street San Francisco CA 94105 United States
Phone Number	800-474-2737

PERFORMANCE

Ratings History

Date	Overall Rating	Risk Rating	Reward Rating
Q4-18	C	D+	B-
Q2-18	B-	C	B
Q4-17	A-	B	A+
Q4-16	B-	C	B
Q4-15	B	B	B+

Asset & Performance History

Date	NAV	1-Year Total Return
2017	43.68	59.44
2016	27.49	1.8
2015	27.12	4.98
2014	25.92	4.68
2013	24.85	17.81
2012	21.12	78.87

Total Assets: $859,630,679

Asset Allocation

Asset	%
Cash	0%
Stocks	100%
US Stocks	100%
Bonds	0%
US Bonds	0%
Other	0%

Services Offered:

Investment Strategy: The investment seeks to track the investment results of the Dow Jones U.S. Select Home Construction Index composed of U.S. equities in the home construction sector. The fund generally invests at least 90% of its assets in securities of the underlying index and in depositary receipts representing securities of the underlying index. The underlying index measures the performance of the home construction sector of the U.S. equity market. The fund may invest the remainder of its assets in certain futures, options and swap contracts, cash and cash equivalents. It is non-diversified. **Top Holdings:** D.R. Horton Inc   Lennar Corp   NVR Inc   PulteGroup Inc   Toll Brothers Inc

iShares iBonds Dec 2021 Term Corporate ETF   C   HOLD

Ticker	Traded On	NAV	Total Assets ($)	Dividend Yield (TTM)	Turnover Ratio	Expense Ratio
IBDM	NYSE Arca	24.30	$857,762,953	2.54	3	0.1

Ratings
Reward   C-
Risk   C+
Recent Upgrade/Downgrade

Fund Information
Fund Type   Exchange Traded Funds
Category   US Fixed Income
Sub-Category   Corporate Bond
Prospectus Objective   Corp Bond - Gen
Inception Date   Mar-15
Open to New Investments   Y

Prices
Price (as of 12/31/2018)   24.36
52-Week High   24.80
52-Week Low   24.16

Total Returns (%)

3-Month	6-Month	1-Year	3-Year	5-Year
0.82	1.57	0.81	8.55	

3-Year Standard Deviation   2.32
Effective Duration   2.42

Valuation
Premium/Discount (1-Year Average)   0.22

Company Information
Provider   iShares
Manager/Tenure   James Mauro (3), Scott Radell (3)
Website   http://www.ishares.com
Address   iShares 400 Howard Street San
                        Francisco CA 94105 United States
Phone Number   800-474-2737

PERFORMANCE

Ratings History

Date	Overall Rating	Risk Rating	Reward Rating
Q4-18	C	C+	C-
Q2-18	C	C+	C
Q4-17	C+	B+	C
Q4-16	D+	C-	D+
Q4-15	U		

Asset & Performance History

Date	NAV	1-Year Total Return
2017	24.74	2.97
2016	24.58	4.41
2015	24.13	
2014		
2013		
2012		

Total Assets: $857,762,953

Asset Allocation

Asset	%
Cash	0%
Stocks	0%
US Stocks	0%
Bonds	99%
US Bonds	77%
Other	0%

Services Offered:

Investment Strategy: The investment seeks to track the investment results of the Bloomberg Barclays December 2021 Maturity Corporate Index which composed of U.S. dollar-denominated, investment-grade corporate bonds maturing in 2021. The fund generally will invest at least 90% of its assets in the component securities of the underlying index. The underlying index is composed of U.S. dollar-denominated, taxable, investment-grade corporate bonds scheduled to mature after December 31, 2020 and before December 16, 2021. The fund is non-diversified. **Top Holdings:** Anheuser-Busch InBev Finance Inc. 2.65% Diamond 1 Finance Corporation/Diamond 2 Finance Corporation 4.42% Deutsche Bank AG New York Branch 3.15% Oracle Corporation 1.9% Morgan Stanley 5.5%

---

iShares iBonds Dec 2020 Term Corporate ETF   C   HOLD

Ticker	Traded On	NAV	Total Assets ($)	Dividend Yield (TTM)	Turnover Ratio	Expense Ratio
IBDL	NYSE Arca	24.97	$856,290,816	2.28	4	0.1

Ratings
Reward   C
Risk   C+
Recent Upgrade/Downgrade

Fund Information
Fund Type   Exchange Traded Funds
Category   US Fixed Income
Sub-Category   Short-Term Bond
Prospectus Objective   Corp Bond - Gen
Inception Date   Dec-14
Open to New Investments   Y

Prices
Price (as of 12/31/2018)   24.98
52-Week High   25.33
52-Week Low   24.92

Total Returns (%)

3-Month	6-Month	1-Year	3-Year	5-Year
0.68	1.42	1.17	7.70	

3-Year Standard Deviation   1.79
Effective Duration   1.54

Valuation
Premium/Discount (1-Year Average)   0.18

Company Information
Provider   iShares
Manager/Tenure   James Mauro (4), Scott Radell (4)
Website   http://www.ishares.com
Address   iShares 400 Howard Street San
                        Francisco CA 94105 United States
Phone Number   800-474-2737

PERFORMANCE

Ratings History

Date	Overall Rating	Risk Rating	Reward Rating
Q4-18	C	C+	C
Q2-18	C	C+	C
Q4-17	B-	A-	C
Q4-16	C-	C-	D+
Q4-15	U		

Asset & Performance History

Date	NAV	1-Year Total Return
2017	25.27	2.53
2016	25.15	3.69
2015	24.81	1.76
2014	24.98	
2013		
2012		

Total Assets: $856,290,816

Asset Allocation

Asset	%
Cash	2%
Stocks	0%
US Stocks	0%
Bonds	98%
US Bonds	82%
Other	0%

Services Offered:

Investment Strategy: The investment seeks to track the investment results of the Bloomberg Barclays December 2020 Maturity Corporate Index (the "underlying index"). The fund generally will invest at least 90% of its assets in the component securities of the underlying index. The underlying index is composed of U.S. dollar-denominated, taxable, investment-grade corporate bonds scheduled to mature after December 31, 2019 and before December 16, 2020. **Top Holdings:** GE Capital International Funding Company Unlimited Company 2.34% Allergan Funding SCS 3% CVS Health Corp 2.8% JPMorgan Chase & Co. 2.25% AbbVie Inc. 2.5%

iShares Core MSCI Pacific ETF

D+ **SELL**

Ticker	Traded On	NAV	Total Assets ($)	Dividend Yield (TTM)	Turnover Ratio	Expense Ratio
IPAC	NYSE Arca	50.95	$852,858,650	3.4	5	0.1

Ratings
Reward	D+
Risk	C-
Recent Upgrade/Downgrade	Down

Fund Information
Fund Type	Exchange Traded Funds
Category	Asia Equity
Sub-Category	Diversified Pacific/Asia
Prospectus Objective	Pacific Stock
Inception Date	Jun-14
Open to New Investments	Y

Prices
Price (as of 12/31/2018)	50.62
52-Week High	63.85
52-Week Low	49.08

Total Returns (%)
3-Month	6-Month	1-Year	3-Year	5-Year
-11.95	-9.14	-12.37	15.26	

3-Year Standard Deviation	11.12
Effective Duration	

Valuation
Premium/Discount (1-Year Average)	-0.01

Company Information
Provider	iShares
Manager/Tenure	Diane Hsiung (4), Jennifer Hsui (4), Greg Savage (4), 3 others
Website	http://www.ishares.com
Address	iShares 400 Howard Street San Francisco CA 94105 United States
Phone Number	800-474-2737

PERFORMANCE

Ratings History
Date	Overall Rating	Risk Rating	Reward Rating
Q4-18	D+	C-	D+
Q2-18	C	C-	C
Q4-17	B+	B	A-
Q4-16	C	C-	C
Q4-15	D	C+	D

Asset & Performance History
Date	NAV	1-Year Total Return
2017	59.75	25.83
2016	48.97	4.54
2015	48.11	3.35
2014	47.72	
2013		
2012		

Total Assets: $852,858,650

Asset Allocation
Asset	%
Cash	1%
Stocks	99%
US Stocks	0%
Bonds	0%
US Bonds	0%
Other	0%

Services Offered:

Investment Strategy: The investment seeks to track the investment results of the MSCI Pacific IMI (the "underlying index"). The fund generally will invest at least 90% of its assets in the component securities of the underlying index and in investments that have economic characteristics that are substantially identical to the component securities of the underlying index. The index is a free float-adjusted market capitalization-weighted index which consists of securities from the following five countries or regions: Australia, Hong Kong, Japan, New Zealand and Singapore. **Top Holdings:** Toyota Motor Corp AIA Group Ltd Commonwealth Bank of Australia SoftBank Group Corp BHP Group Ltd

---

First Trust Mid Cap Core AlphaDEX® Fund

C- **HOLD**

Ticker	Traded On	NAV	Total Assets ($)	Dividend Yield (TTM)	Turnover Ratio	Expense Ratio
FNX	NAS CM	57.83	$847,130,443	0.88		0.62

Ratings
Reward	C-
Risk	C-
Recent Upgrade/Downgrade	Down

Fund Information
Fund Type	Exchange Traded Funds
Category	US Equity Mid Cap
Sub-Category	Mid-Cap Blend
Prospectus Objective	Growth
Inception Date	May-07
Open to New Investments	Y

Prices
Price (as of 12/31/2018)	57.82
52-Week High	73.03
52-Week Low	54.08

Total Returns (%)
3-Month	6-Month	1-Year	3-Year	5-Year
-18.16	-14.88	-11.11	24.07	20.36

3-Year Standard Deviation	12.78
Effective Duration	

Valuation
Premium/Discount (1-Year Average)	0.04

Company Information
Provider	First Trust
Manager/Tenure	Jon C. Erickson (11), Daniel J. Lindquist (11), David G. McGarel (11), 3 others
Website	http://www.ftportfolios.com/
Address	First Trust 120 E. Liberty Drive, Suite 400 Wheaton IL 60187 United States
Phone Number	800-621-1675

PERFORMANCE

Ratings History
Date	Overall Rating	Risk Rating	Reward Rating
Q4-18	C-	C-	C-
Q2-18	C	C-	C+
Q4-17	B	B	B
Q4-16	C	C-	C+
Q4-15	C	C+	C

Asset & Performance History
Date	NAV	1-Year Total Return
2017	65.65	17.62
2016	56.35	18.67
2015	48.03	-8.1
2014	52.79	5.55
2013	50.4	37.46
2012	36.95	14.23

Total Assets: $847,130,443

Asset Allocation
Asset	%
Cash	0%
Stocks	100%
US Stocks	99%
Bonds	0%
US Bonds	0%
Other	0%

Services Offered:

Investment Strategy: The investment seeks investment results that correspond generally to the price and yield (before the fund's fees and expenses) of an equity index called the Nasdaq AlphaDEX® Mid Cap Core Index. The fund will normally invest at least 90% of its net assets (including investment borrowings) in common stocks that comprise the index. The index is designed to select stocks from the NASDAQ US 600 Mid Cap Index (the "base index") that may generate positive alpha, or risk-adjusted returns, relative to traditional indices through the use of the AlphaDEX® selection methodology. **Top Holdings:** Spirit Airlines Inc Pilgrims Pride Corp Amedisys Inc PulteGroup Inc Twilio Inc A

SPDR® Portfolio S&P 500 High Dividend ETF   C   HOLD

Ticker	Traded On	NAV	Total Assets ($)	Dividend Yield (TTM)	Turnover Ratio	Expense Ratio
SPYD	NYSE Arca	34.05	$840,780,737	4.14	40	0.07

Ratings
Reward   C-
Risk   C+
Recent Upgrade/Downgrade

Fund Information
Fund Type	Exchange Traded Funds
Category	US Equity Large Cap Value
Sub-Category	Large Value
Prospectus Objective	Growth & Inc
Inception Date	Oct-15
Open to New Investments	Y

Prices
Price (as of 12/31/2018)	34.07
52-Week High	38.74
52-Week Low	32.59

Total Returns (%)
3-Month	6-Month	1-Year	3-Year	5-Year
-8.09	-5.98	-4.77	33.74	

3-Year Standard Deviation	8.74
Effective Duration	

Valuation
Premium/Discount (1-Year Average)	0.03

Company Information
Provider	SPDR State Street Global Advisors
Manager/Tenure	Michael J. Feehily (3), Karl A. Schneider (3), John Law (0)
Website	http://www.spdrs.com
Address	SPDR State Street Global Advisors State Street Financial Center, 1 Lincoln Street Boston MA 02111-2900 United States
Phone Number	617-786-3000

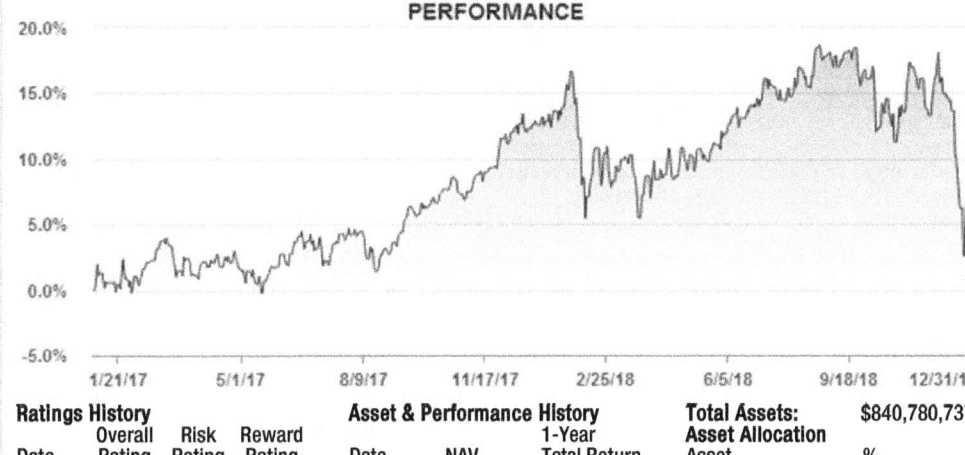

PERFORMANCE

Ratings History
Date	Overall Rating	Risk Rating	Reward Rating
Q4-18	C	C+	C-
Q2-18	C	C+	C
Q4-17	C	B+	C-
Q4-16	D	C-	D+
Q4-15			

Asset & Performance History
Date	NAV	1-Year Total Return
2017	37.39	12.58
2016	34.83	24.74
2015	29.19	
2014		
2013		
2012		

Total Assets: $840,780,737
Asset Allocation
Asset	%
Cash	0%
Stocks	100%
US Stocks	99%
Bonds	0%
US Bonds	0%
Other	0%

Services Offered:

Investment Strategy: The investment seeks to track the performance of the S&P 500 High Dividend Index. Under normal market conditions, the fund generally invests substantially all, but at least 80%, of its total assets in the securities comprising the index. The index is designed to measure the performance of 80 high dividend-yielding companies within the S&P 500® Index. The S&P 500 Index focuses on the large capitalization U.S. equity market, including common stock and real estate investment trusts ("REITs"). The fund is non-diversified. **Top Holdings:** Pfizer Inc   Procter & Gamble Co   The AES Corp   Verizon Communications Inc   UDR Inc

---

FlexShares iBoxx 5-Year Target Duration TIPS Index Fund   C-   HOLD

Ticker	Traded On	NAV	Total Assets ($)	Dividend Yield (TTM)	Turnover Ratio	Expense Ratio
TDTF	NYSE Arca	24.09	$833,455,723	2.93		0.18

Ratings
Reward   D
Risk   C
Recent Upgrade/Downgrade   Down

Fund Information
Fund Type	Exchange Traded Funds
Category	US Fixed Income
Sub-Category	Inflation-Protected Bond
Prospectus Objective	Govt Bond - Treasury
Inception Date	Sep-11
Open to New Investments	Y

Prices
Price (as of 12/31/2018)	24.12
52-Week High	24.95
52-Week Low	23.80

Total Returns (%)
3-Month	6-Month	1-Year	3-Year	5-Year
0.13	-0.92	-0.87	5.33	4.64

3-Year Standard Deviation	2.77
Effective Duration	

Valuation
Premium/Discount (1-Year Average)	0.00

Company Information
Provider	Flexshares Trust
Manager/Tenure	Michael R. Chico (7), Brandon P. Ferguson (7), Daniel J. Personette (7)
Website	http://www.flexshares.com
Address	50 South LaSalle Street Chicago, Illinois 60603 Chicago Illinois 60603 United States
Phone Number	855-353-9383

PERFORMANCE

Ratings History
Date	Overall Rating	Risk Rating	Reward Rating
Q4-18	C-	C	D
Q2-18	C-	C-	C-
Q4-17	C	B-	C
Q4-16	C	C-	C
Q4-15	D+	C-	D

Asset & Performance History
Date	NAV	1-Year Total Return
2017	24.93	1.78
2016	24.99	4.22
2015	24.34	-0.17
2014	24.43	-0.48
2013	24.85	-5.02
2012	26.2	5.28

Total Assets: $833,455,723
Asset Allocation
Asset	%
Cash	0%
Stocks	0%
US Stocks	0%
Bonds	100%
US Bonds	100%
Other	0%

Services Offered:

Investment Strategy: The investment seeks to provide investment results that, before fees and expenses, correspond generally to the price and yield performance of the iBoxx 5-Year Target Duration TIPS Index. Under normal circumstances, the fund will invest at least 80% of its total assets (exclusive of collateral held from securities lending) in the securities of the underlying index. The underlying index reflects the performance of a selection of inflation protected public obligations of the U.S. Treasury, commonly known as "TIPS," with a targeted average modified adjusted duration, as defined by the underlying index, of approximately five years. The fund is non-diversified. **Top Holdings:** United States Treasury Notes 0.62%   United States Treasury Notes 0.38%   United States Treasury Notes 0.12%   United States Treasury Bonds 2%   United States Treasury Notes 0.62%

Invesco Taxable Municipal Bond ETF   C   HOLD

Ticker	Traded On	NAV	Total Assets ($)	Dividend Yield (TTM)	Turnover Ratio	Expense Ratio
BAB	NYSE Arca	29.51	$833,229,638	4.26		0.28

Ratings
Reward	C-
Risk	C+
Recent Upgrade/Downgrade	

Fund Information
Fund Type	Exchange Traded Funds
Category	US Fixed Income
Sub-Category	Long-Term Bond
Prospectus Objective	Muni Bond - Natl
Inception Date	Nov-09
Open to New Investments	Y

Prices
Price (as of 12/31/2018)	29.69
52-Week High	30.69
52-Week Low	28.54

Total Returns (%)
3-Month	6-Month	1-Year	3-Year	5-Year
2.30	1.48	0.63	14.62	33.83

3-Year Standard Deviation	4.26
Effective Duration	8.09

Valuation
Premium/Discount (1-Year Average)	-0.32

Company Information
Provider	Invesco
Manager/Tenure	Philip Fang (9), Peter Hubbard (9), Jeffrey W. Kernagis (9), 2 others
Website	http://www.invesco.com/us
Address	Invesco 11 Greenway Plaza, Ste. 2500 Houston TX 77046 United States
Phone Number	800-659-1005

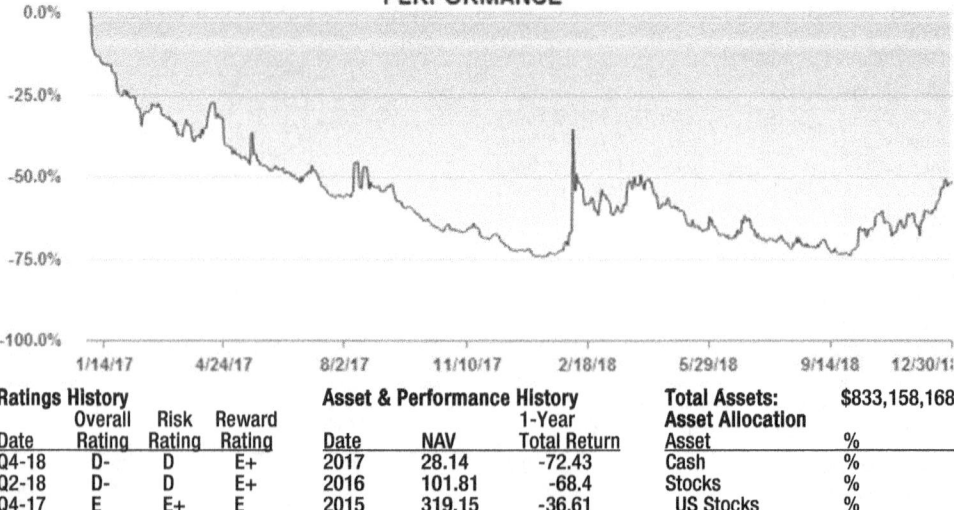

PERFORMANCE

Ratings History
Date	Overall Rating	Risk Rating	Reward Rating
Q4-18	C	C+	C-
Q2-18	C	C-	C
Q4-17	B	A-	C+
Q4-16	C	C+	C
Q4-15	C	C-	C

Asset & Performance History
Date	NAV	1-Year Total Return
2017	30.59	8.2
2016	29.44	5.27
2015	29.13	0.91
2014	30.23	15.69
2013	27.41	-5.09
2012	30.33	11.35

Total Assets: $833,229,638
Asset Allocation
Asset	%
Cash	0%
Stocks	0%
US Stocks	0%
Bonds	100%
US Bonds	100%
Other	0%

Services Offered:

Investment Strategy: The investment seeks to track the investment results (before fees and expenses) of the ICE BofAML US Taxable Municipal Securities Plus Index (the "underlying index"). The fund generally will invest at least 80% of its total assets in taxable municipal securities that comprise the underlying index. The underlying index is designed to track the performance of U.S. dollar-denominated taxable municipal debt publicly issued by U.S. states and territories, and their political subdivisions, in the U.S. market. **Top Holdings:** CALIFORNIA ST 6.51% ILLINOIS ST 5.56% CALIFORNIA ST 7.95% TEXAS TRANSN COMMN ST HWY FD 5.18% MISSOURI JT MUN ELEC UTIL COMMN PWR 6.89%

---

iPath® S&P 500 VIX Short-Term Futures™ ETN   D-   SELL

Ticker	Traded On	NAV	Total Assets ($)	Dividend Yield (TTM)	Turnover Ratio	Expense Ratio
VXX	NYSE Arca		$833,158,168	0	0	0.89

Ratings
Reward	E+
Risk	D
Recent Upgrade/Downgrade	Up

Fund Information
Fund Type	Exchange Traded Funds
Category	Alternative Misc
Sub-Category	Volatility
Prospectus Objective	Growth
Inception Date	Jan-09
Open to New Investments	Y

Prices
Price (as of 12/31/2018)	46.88
52-Week High	55.24
52-Week Low	25.84

Total Returns (%)
3-Month	6-Month	1-Year	3-Year	5-Year
84.82	32.62	73.51	-84.69	-92.83

3-Year Standard Deviation	55.06
Effective Duration	

Valuation
Premium/Discount (1-Year Average)	0.15

Company Information
Provider	Milleis Investissements Funds
Manager/Tenure	No Manager (9)
Website	
Address	2-4, rue Eugène Ruppert L-2453 Luxembourg Luxembourg L-2453 Luxembourg
Phone Number	

PERFORMANCE

Ratings History
Date	Overall Rating	Risk Rating	Reward Rating
Q4-18	D-	D	E+
Q2-18	D-	D	E+
Q4-17	E	E+	E
Q4-16	E+	D-	E
Q4-15	E+	E+	E+

Asset & Performance History
Date	NAV	1-Year Total Return
2017	28.14	-72.43
2016	101.81	-68.4
2015	319.15	-36.61
2014	503.5	-26.16
2013	681.92	-66.02
2012	2,007.30	-78.11

Total Assets: $833,158,168
Asset Allocation
Asset	%
Cash	%
Stocks	%
US Stocks	%
Bonds	%
US Bonds	%
Other	%

Services Offered:

Investment Strategy: Der S&P 500 VIX Short -Term Futures™ Index Total Return macht die Aktienmarktvolatilität mit Hilfe von Terminkontrakten auf den CBOE Volatility Index® handelbar. Er ermöglicht Anlegern ein Engagement in eine rollierende Long-Position in VIX-Terminkontrakte mit ein- und zweimonatiger Laufzeit, und spiegelt die implizite Volatilität des S&P 500® Index an verschiedenen Punkten der Volatilitäts-Forwardkurve wider. Die Index-Futures werden kontinuierlich im Monatsrhythmus vom VIX-Terminkontrakt mit einmonatiger Laufzeit in den Zwei-Monats-Kontrakt gerollt. Eine Direktanlage in den VIX ist nicht möglich. **Top Holdings:**

Global X MLP ETF　　　　　　　　　　　　　　　　　　　　　　　　C　　HOLD

Ticker	Traded On	NAV	Total Assets ($)	Dividend Yield (TTM)	Turnover Ratio	Expense Ratio
MLPA	NYSE Arca	7.68	$830,328,506	8.98	35	0.46

Ratings
Reward　　　　　　　　　　　　　　B-
Risk　　　　　　　　　　　　　　　D
Recent Upgrade/Downgrade

Fund Information
Fund Type	Exchange Traded Funds
Category	Energy Sector Equity
Sub-Category	Energy Limited Partnership
Prospectus Objective	Utility
Inception Date	Apr-12
Open to New Investments	Y

Prices
Price (as of 12/31/2018)	7.67
52-Week High	10.80
52-Week Low	7.33

Total Returns (%)
3-Month	6-Month	1-Year	3-Year	5-Year
-19.83	-11.93	-15.47	-6.32	-31.83

3-Year Standard Deviation　　　18.17
Effective Duration

Valuation
Premium/Discount (1-Year Average)　　0.08

Company Information
Provider	Global X Funds
Manager/Tenure	Chang Kim (4), James Ong (2), Nam To (0)
Website	http://www.globalxfunds.com
Address	Global X Funds 600 Lexington Avenue, 20th Floor New York NY 10022 United States
Phone Number	888-493-8631

PERFORMANCE

Ratings History
Date	Overall Rating	Risk Rating	Reward Rating
Q4-18	C	D	B-
Q2-18	C	D	B-
Q4-17	D	D	D
Q4-16	D	D	D
Q4-15	B-	C	B

Asset & Performance History
Date	NAV	1-Year Total Return
2017	9.85	-8.5
2016	11.58	21.12
2015	10.36	-30.13
2014	15.92	4.15
2013	16.16	17.82
2012	14.52	

Total Assets: $830,328,506
Asset Allocation
Asset	%
Cash	0%
Stocks	100%
US Stocks	100%
Bonds	0%
US Bonds	0%
Other	0%

Services Offered:

Investment Strategy: The investment seeks to provide investment results that correspond generally to the price and yield performance, before fees and expenses, of the Solactive MLP Infrastructure Index ("underlying index"). The fund invests at least 80% of its net assets in the securities of the underlying index. Moreover, at least 80% of the fund's net assets will be invested in securities that have economic characteristics of the Master Limited Partnership ("MLP") asset class. The underlying index is intended to give investors a means of tracking the performance of the energy infrastructure MLP asset class in the United States. The fund is non-diversified. **Top Holdings:** Enterprise Products Partners LP　Energy Transfer LP　Magellan Midstream Partners LP　Plains All American Pipeline LP　MPLX LP Partnership Units

---

WisdomTree Floating Rate Treasury Fund　　　　　　　　　　　　　C　　HOLD

Ticker	Traded On	NAV	Total Assets ($)	Dividend Yield (TTM)	Turnover Ratio	Expense Ratio
USFR	NYSE Arca	25.07	$829,889,206	1.62	160	0.15

Ratings
Reward　　　　　　　　　　　　　　C-
Risk　　　　　　　　　　　　　　　C+
Recent Upgrade/Downgrade

Fund Information
Fund Type	Exchange Traded Funds
Category	US Fixed Income
Sub-Category	Short Government
Prospectus Objective	Govt Bond - Treasury
Inception Date	Feb-14
Open to New Investments	Y

Prices
Price (as of 12/31/2018)	25.08
52-Week High	25.13
52-Week Low	25.00

Total Returns (%)
3-Month	6-Month	1-Year	3-Year	5-Year
0.48	0.98	1.81	3.47	

3-Year Standard Deviation　　　0.2
Effective Duration　　　　　　　0.02

Valuation
Premium/Discount (1-Year Average)　　0.03

Company Information
Provider	WisdomTree
Manager/Tenure	Paul L. Benson (3), Stephanie Shu (3)
Website	http://www.wisdomtree.com
Address	WisdomTree 245 Park Avenue, 35th floor New York NY 10167 United States
Phone Number	866-909-9473

PERFORMANCE

Ratings History
Date	Overall Rating	Risk Rating	Reward Rating
Q4-18	C	C+	C-
Q2-18	C	C+	C-
Q4-17	C	B-	C-
Q4-16	C-	D+	C-
Q4-15	D	D+	D

Asset & Performance History
Date	NAV	1-Year Total Return
2017	25.04	1.03
2016	25.04	0.58
2015	24.96	-0.07
2014	24.98	
2013		
2012		

Total Assets: $829,889,206
Asset Allocation
Asset	%
Cash	0%
Stocks	0%
US Stocks	0%
Bonds	100%
US Bonds	100%
Other	0%

Services Offered:

Investment Strategy: The investment seeks to track the price and yield performance, before fees and expenses, of the Bloomberg U.S. Treasury Floating Rate Bond Index (the "index"). The fund invests at least 80% of its total assets (exclusive of collateral held from securities lending) in the component securities of the index and investments that have economic characteristics that are substantially identical to the economic characteristics of such component securities. The index is designed to measure the performance of floating rate public obligations of the U.S. Treasury. The fund is non-diversified. **Top Holdings:** United States Treasury Notes 2.43%　United States Treasury Notes 2.42%　United States Treasury Notes 2.38%　United States Treasury Notes 2.43%

WisdomTree International Equity Fund   D+   SELL

Ticker	Traded On	NAV	Total Assets ($)	Dividend Yield (TTM)	Turnover Ratio	Expense Ratio
DWM	NYSE Arca	46.62	$828,504,186	3.65	19	0.48

Ratings
Reward	D+
Risk	C-
Recent Upgrade/Downgrade	Down

Fund Information
Fund Type	Exchange Traded Funds
Category	Global Equity Large Cap
Sub-Category	Foreign Large Value
Prospectus Objective	Foreign Stock
Inception Date	Jun-06
Open to New Investments	Y

Prices
Price (as of 12/31/2018)	46.60
52-Week High	59.63
52-Week Low	44.98

Total Returns (%)
3-Month	6-Month	1-Year	3-Year	5-Year
-11.72	-9.44	-13.55	9.81	3.19

3-Year Standard Deviation	10.85
Effective Duration	

Valuation
Premium/Discount (1-Year Average)	-0.04

Company Information
Provider	WisdomTree
Manager/Tenure	Richard A. Brown (10), Thomas J. Durante (10), Karen Q. Wong (10)
Website	http://www.wisdomtree.com
Address	WisdomTree 245 Park Avenue, 35th floor New York NY 10167 United States
Phone Number	866-909-9473

PERFORMANCE

Ratings History
Date	Overall Rating	Risk Rating	Reward Rating
Q4-18	D+	C-	D+
Q2-18	C	C-	C
Q4-17	B-	B-	B-
Q4-16	D+	C-	D+
Q4-15	C-	C-	C-

Asset & Performance History
Date	NAV	1-Year Total Return
2017	55.82	23.45
2016	46.67	2.89
2015	46.95	-2.6
2014	49.8	-3.52
2013	53.9	21.74
2012	45.96	16.37

Total Assets: $828,504,186
Asset Allocation
Asset	%
Cash	0%
Stocks	100%
US Stocks	0%
Bonds	0%
US Bonds	0%
Other	0%

Services Offered:

Investment Strategy: The investment seeks to track the price and yield performance, before fees and expenses, of the WisdomTree International Equity Index. At least 95% of the fund's total assets (exclusive of collateral held from securities lending) will be invested in component securities of the index and investments that have economic characteristics that are substantially identical to the economic characteristics of such component securities. The index is a fundamentally weighted index that is comprised of dividend-paying companies in the industrialized world, excluding Canada and the United States, that pay regular cash dividends. It is non-diversified. **Top Holdings:** China Mobile Ltd Novartis AG Nestle SA HSBC Holdings PLC Roche Holding AG Dividend Right Cert.

Bitcoin Investment Trust   D+   SELL

Ticker	Traded On	NAV	Total Assets ($)	Dividend Yield (TTM)	Turnover Ratio	Expense Ratio
GBTC	OTC BB	3.72	$826,269,056	0		2

Ratings
Reward	C-
Risk	D+
Recent Upgrade/Downgrade	Down

Fund Information
Fund Type	Exchange Traded Funds
Category	Trading Tools
Sub-Category	Trading--Miscellaneous
Prospectus Objective	Growth & Inc
Inception Date	Sep-13
Open to New Investments	Y

Prices
Price (as of 12/31/2018)	3.97
52-Week High	25.69
52-Week Low	3.84

Total Returns (%)
3-Month	6-Month	1-Year	3-Year	5-Year
-43.01	-42.55	-74.61	732.52	344.57

3-Year Standard Deviation	91.94
Effective Duration	

Valuation
Premium/Discount (1-Year Average)	42.55

Company Information
Provider	Grayscale
Manager/Tenure	Management Team (5)
Website	http://grayscale.co/bitcoin-investment-trust/#overview
Address	Grayscale 636 Avenue of the Americas New York New York 10011 United States
Phone Number	212-668-5920

PERFORMANCE

Ratings History
Date	Overall Rating	Risk Rating	Reward Rating
Q4-18	D+	D+	C-
Q2-18	C-	D+	C
Q4-17	B+	C	A+
Q4-16	D+	D+	D+
Q4-15			

Asset & Performance History
Date	NAV	1-Year Total Return
2017	14.65	1,391.43
2016	0.98	119.87
2015	0.45	33.36
2014	0.33	-59.95
2013	0.84	
2012		

Total Assets: $826,269,056
Asset Allocation
Asset	%
Cash	-55%
Stocks	0%
US Stocks	0%
Bonds	0%
US Bonds	0%
Other	155%

Services Offered:

Investment Strategy: The investment objective of the Trust is for the NAV per Share to track the Bitcoin Market Price per Share, less the Trust's liabilities (including estimated accrued expenses). **Top Holdings:** Bitcoin

iShares International Treasury Bond ETF   D+   SELL

Ticker	Traded On	NAV	Total Assets ($)	Dividend Yield (TTM)	Turnover Ratio	Expense Ratio
IGOV	NAS CM	48.35	$822,792,861	0.04	9	0.35

Ratings
Reward	D+
Risk	C-
Recent Upgrade/Downgrade	Down

Fund Information
Fund Type	Exchange Traded Funds
Category	Global Fixed Income
Sub-Category	World Bond
Prospectus Objective	Worldwide Bond
Inception Date	Jan-09
Open to New Investments	Y

Prices
Price (as of 12/31/2018)	48.47
52-Week High	52.07
52-Week Low	47.13

Total Returns (%)
3-Month	6-Month	1-Year	3-Year	5-Year
1.00	-1.03	-2.68	9.29	-0.71

3-Year Standard Deviation	7.26
Effective Duration	8.31

Valuation
Premium/Discount (1-Year Average)	0.01

Company Information
Provider	iShares
Manager/Tenure	Scott Radell (8), James Mauro (7)
Website	http://www.ishares.com
Address	iShares 400 Howard Street San Francisco CA 94105 United States
Phone Number	800-474-2737

PERFORMANCE

Ratings History
Date	Overall Rating	Risk Rating	Reward Rating
Q4-18	D+	C-	D+
Q2-18	C	C+	C-
Q4-17	C	C+	C
Q4-16	D+	C-	D+
Q4-15	D	D+	D

Asset & Performance History
Date	NAV	1-Year Total Return
2017	49.84	10.9
2016	45.01	1.22
2015	44.77	-6.89
2014	48.14	-2.43
2013	49.95	-1.55
2012	51.41	7.39

Total Assets: $822,792,861

Asset Allocation
Asset	%
Cash	2%
Stocks	0%
US Stocks	0%
Bonds	98%
US Bonds	0%
Other	0%

Services Offered:

Investment Strategy: The investment seeks to track the investment results of the S&P International Sovereign Ex-U.S. Bond Index. The fund generally will invest at least 90% of its assets in the component securities of the underlying index and may invest up to 10% of its assets in certain futures, options and swap contracts, cash and cash equivalents. The underlying index is a broad, diverse, market value-weighted index designed to measure the performance of sovereign bonds issued in local currencies by developed market countries, as classified by SPDJI, outside the U.S. The fund is non-diversified. **Top Holdings:** Denmark (Kingdom Of) 4.5% Sweden (Kingdom Of) 3.5% Ireland (Republic Of) 5.4% Denmark (Kingdom Of) 1.75% Portugal (Republic Of) 5.65%

PIMCO 1-5 Year U.S. TIPS Index Exchange-Traded Fund   C-   HOLD

Ticker	Traded On	NAV	Total Assets ($)	Dividend Yield (TTM)	Turnover Ratio	Expense Ratio
STPZ	NYSE Arca	50.85	$822,278,575	2.4	32	0.2

Ratings
Reward	C-
Risk	C-
Recent Upgrade/Downgrade	

Fund Information
Fund Type	Exchange Traded Funds
Category	US Fixed Income
Sub-Category	Inflation-Protected Bond
Prospectus Objective	Govt Bond - Treasury
Inception Date	Aug-09
Open to New Investments	Y

Prices
Price (as of 12/31/2018)	50.84
52-Week High	51.99
52-Week Low	50.72

Total Returns (%)
3-Month	6-Month	1-Year	3-Year	5-Year
-0.26	-0.28	0.18	3.84	2.00

3-Year Standard Deviation	1.54
Effective Duration	3.04

Valuation
Premium/Discount (1-Year Average)	0.00

Company Information
Provider	PIMCO
Manager/Tenure	Matthew P. Dorsten (2), Mitchell Handa (0), Graham A. Rennison (0)
Website	http://www.pimco.com
Address	PIMCO 840 Newport Center Drive, Suite 100 Newport Beach CA 92660 United States
Phone Number	866-746-2602

PERFORMANCE

Ratings History
Date	Overall Rating	Risk Rating	Reward Rating
Q4-18	C-	C-	C-
Q2-18	C-	C-	C-
Q4-17	C	C+	C
Q4-16	C	C-	C
Q4-15	D+	C-	D

Asset & Performance History
Date	NAV	1-Year Total Return
2017	51.97	0.64
2016	52.42	2.95
2015	51.23	-0.44
2014	51.71	-1.32
2013	52.84	-2.12
2012	54.04	2.39

Total Assets: $822,278,575

Asset Allocation
Asset	%
Cash	0%
Stocks	0%
US Stocks	0%
Bonds	100%
US Bonds	100%
Other	0%

Services Offered:

Investment Strategy: The investment seeks to provide total return that closely corresponds, before fees and expenses, to the total return of the ICE BofAML 1-5 Year US Inflation-Linked Treasury Index. The fund invests at least 80% of its total assets (exclusive of collateral held from securities lending) in the component securities of the ICE BofAML 1-5 Year US Inflation-Linked Treasury Index (the "underlying index"). The underlying index is an unmanaged index comprised of Treasury Inflation-Protected Securities ("TIPS") with a maturity of at least 1 year and less than 5 years. **Top Holdings:** United States Treasury Notes 0.12% United States Treasury Notes 0.12% United States Treasury Notes 0.12% United States Treasury Notes 0.38% United States Treasury Notes 1.12%

iPath® Bloomberg Commodity Index Total Return(SM) ETN   D+   SELL

Ticker	Traded On	NAV	Total Assets ($)	Dividend Yield (TTM)	Turnover Ratio	Expense Ratio
DJP	NYSE Arca		$820,124,982	0	0	0.75

Ratings
Reward	D
Risk	C-
Recent Upgrade/Downgrade	Down

Fund Information
Fund Type	Exchange Traded Funds
Category	Commodities Broad Basket
Sub-Category	Commodities Broad Basket
Prospectus Objective	Natl Res
Inception Date	Jun-06
Open to New Investments	Y

Prices
Price (as of 12/31/2018)	21.22
52-Week High	25.68
52-Week Low	21.22

Total Returns (%)
3-Month	6-Month	1-Year	3-Year	5-Year
-11.29	-10.18	-12.51	-0.30	-41.73

3-Year Standard Deviation	10.32
Effective Duration	

Valuation
Premium/Discount (1-Year Average)	-0.04

Company Information
Provider	Milleis Investissements Funds
Manager/Tenure	No Manager (12)
Website	
Address	2-4, rue Eugène Ruppert L-2453 Luxembourg Luxembourg L-2453 Luxembourg
Phone Number	

PERFORMANCE

Ratings History
Date	Overall Rating	Risk Rating	Reward Rating
Q4-18	D+	C-	D
Q2-18	C	C	C-
Q4-17	D+	D	D+
Q4-16	D	D	D
Q4-15	D-	D	D-

Asset & Performance History
Date	NAV	1-Year Total Return
2017	24.48	0.34
2016	24.19	13.64
2015	21.48	-27.81
2014	29.75	-19.04
2013	36.75	-10.81
2012	41.2	-1.9

Total Assets: $820,124,982

Asset Allocation
Asset	%
Cash	%
Stocks	%
US Stocks	%
Bonds	%
US Bonds	%
Other	%

Services Offered:

Investment Strategy: The investment seeks to provide investors with exposure to the Dow Jones-UBS Commodity Index Total ReturnService Mark.
The Dow Jones-UBS Commodity Index Total ReturnService Mark (the "index") reflects the returns that are potentially available through an unleveraged investment in the futures contracts on physical commodities comprising the index plus the rate of interest that could be earned on cash collateral invested in specified Treasury Bills. The index is a rolling index rebalancing annually. **Top Holdings:**

VanEck Vectors Agribusiness ETF   C   HOLD

Ticker	Traded On	NAV	Total Assets ($)	Dividend Yield (TTM)	Turnover Ratio	Expense Ratio
MOO	NYSE Arca	57.11	$816,311,775	1.41	22	0.54

Ratings
Reward	C
Risk	C-
Recent Upgrade/Downgrade	

Fund Information
Fund Type	Exchange Traded Funds
Category	Natural Resources
Sub-Category	Natural Resources
Prospectus Objective	Unaligned
Inception Date	Aug-07
Open to New Investments	Y

Prices
Price (as of 12/31/2018)	56.92
52-Week High	66.33
52-Week Low	54.16

Total Returns (%)
3-Month	6-Month	1-Year	3-Year	5-Year
-11.83	-6.12	-5.87	29.14	17.23

3-Year Standard Deviation	9.25
Effective Duration	

Valuation
Premium/Discount (1-Year Average)	-0.11

Company Information
Provider	VanEck
Manager/Tenure	Hao-Hung (Peter) Liao (11), Guo Hua (Jason) Jin (0)
Website	http://www.vaneck.com
Address	Van Eck Associates Corporation 666 Third Avenue New York NY 10017 United States
Phone Number	800-826-1115

PERFORMANCE

Ratings History
Date	Overall Rating	Risk Rating	Reward Rating
Q4-18	C	C-	C
Q2-18	C	C-	C+
Q4-17	B-	B-	B-
Q4-16	C	C	C
Q4-15	C+	C+	C+

Asset & Performance History
Date	NAV	1-Year Total Return
2017	61.63	21.68
2016	51.38	12.75
2015	46.55	-8.9
2014	52.59	-0.34
2013	54.44	4.82
2012	52.94	14.22

Total Assets: $816,311,775

Asset Allocation
Asset	%
Cash	0%
Stocks	100%
US Stocks	54%
Bonds	0%
US Bonds	0%
Other	0%

Services Offered:

Investment Strategy: The investment seeks to replicate as closely as possible, before fees and expenses, the price and yield performance of the MVIS® Global Agribusiness Index. The fund normally invests at least 80% of its total assets in securities that comprise the fund's benchmark index. The index includes equity securities of companies that generate at least 50% of their revenues from agri-chemicals, animal health and fertilizers, seeds and traits, from farm/irrigation equipment and farm machinery, aquaculture and fishing, livestock, cultivation and plantations and trading of agricultural products. It is non-diversified. **Top Holdings:** Zoetis Inc Class A Deere & Co Nutrien Ltd Archer-Daniels Midland Co Kubota Corp

Invesco Water Resources ETF   B-   BUY

Ticker	Traded On	NAV	Total Assets ($)	Dividend Yield (TTM)	Turnover Ratio	Expense Ratio
PHO	NAS CM	28.24	$813,452,773	0.34	23	0.62

Ratings
Reward	B
Risk	C
Recent Upgrade/Downgrade	

Fund Information
Fund Type	Exchange Traded Funds
Category	Industrials Sector Equity
Sub-Category	Miscellaneous Sector
Prospectus Objective	Utility
Inception Date	Dec-05
Open to New Investments	Y

Prices
Price (as of 12/31/2018)	28.21
52-Week High	32.43
52-Week Low	26.56

Total Returns (%)
3-Month	6-Month	1-Year	3-Year	5-Year
-10.71	-6.49	-6.26	31.87	10.59

3-Year Standard Deviation	11.32
Effective Duration	

Valuation
Premium/Discount (1-Year Average)	0.00

Company Information
Provider	Invesco
Manager/Tenure	Peter Hubbard (11), Michael Jeanette (10), Tony Seisser (4), 1 other
Website	http://www.invesco.com/us
Address	Invesco 11 Greenway Plaza, Ste. 2500 Houston TX 77046 United States
Phone Number	800-659-1005

PERFORMANCE

Ratings History
Date	Overall Rating	Risk Rating	Reward Rating
Q4-18	B-	C	B
Q2-18	B-	C+	B
Q4-17	C+	C	B-
Q4-16	B-	C	B
Q4-15	B-	C+	B

Asset & Performance History
Date	NAV	1-Year Total Return
2017	30.26	23.55
2016	24.58	13.86
2015	21.69	-15.2
2014	25.76	-1.1
2013	26.2	26.97
2012	20.75	24.05

Total Assets: $813,452,773
Asset Allocation
Asset	%
Cash	0%
Stocks	100%
US Stocks	98%
Bonds	0%
US Bonds	0%
Other	0%

Services Offered:

Investment Strategy: The investment seeks to track the investment results (before fees and expenses) of the NASDAQ OMX US Water IndexSM (the "underlying index"). The fund generally will invest at least 90% of its total assets in securities of companies in the water industry that comprise the underlying index. The underlying index seeks to track the performance of U.S. exchange-listed companies that create products designed to conserve and purify water for homes, businesses and industries. The fund is non-diversified. **Top Holdings:** Waters Corp Ecolab Inc Danaher Corp Roper Technologies Inc Xylem Inc

---

iShares North American Natural Resources ETF   C-   HOLD

Ticker	Traded On	NAV	Total Assets ($)	Dividend Yield (TTM)	Turnover Ratio	Expense Ratio
IGE	BATS	27.20	$812,404,642	2.15	7	0.47

Ratings
Reward	C-
Risk	C-
Recent Upgrade/Downgrade	Down

Fund Information
Fund Type	Exchange Traded Funds
Category	Natural Resources
Sub-Category	Natural Resources
Prospectus Objective	Natl Res
Inception Date	Oct-01
Open to New Investments	Y

Prices
Price (as of 12/31/2018)	27.18
52-Week High	38.04
52-Week Low	25.63

Total Returns (%)
3-Month	6-Month	1-Year	3-Year	5-Year
-24.60	-24.06	-21.44	2.94	-30.22

3-Year Standard Deviation	18.51
Effective Duration	

Valuation
Premium/Discount (1-Year Average)	0.02

Company Information
Provider	iShares
Manager/Tenure	Diane Hsiung (10), Greg Savage (10), Jennifer Hsui (6), 3 others
Website	http://www.ishares.com
Address	iShares 400 Howard Street San Francisco CA 94105 United States
Phone Number	800-474-2737

PERFORMANCE

Ratings History
Date	Overall Rating	Risk Rating	Reward Rating
Q4-18	C-	C-	C-
Q2-18	C	C	C
Q4-17	C-	C	C-
Q4-16	C-	D+	C-
Q4-15	C-	D+	C-

Asset & Performance History
Date	NAV	1-Year Total Return
2017	35.41	0.71
2016	35.96	30.12
2015	28.14	-24.51
2014	38.3	-10.21
2013	43.35	15.89
2012	38.01	1.7

Total Assets: $812,404,642
Asset Allocation
Asset	%
Cash	0%
Stocks	100%
US Stocks	80%
Bonds	0%
US Bonds	0%
Other	0%

Services Offered: CashInvestment Plan

Investment Strategy: The investment seeks to track the investment results of the S&P North American Natural Resources Sector Index composed of North American equities in the natural resources sector. The fund generally invests at least 90% of its assets in securities of the underlying index and in depositary receipts representing securities of the underlying index. The underlying index measures the performance of U.S.-traded stocks of natural resource-related companies in the U.S. and Canada. The fund is non-diversified. **Top Holdings:** Chevron Corp Exxon Mobil Corp ConocoPhillips Schlumberger Ltd EOG Resources Inc

ProShares Ultra Financials

C HOLD

Ticker	Traded On	NAV	Total Assets ($)	Dividend Yield (TTM)	Turnover Ratio	Expense Ratio
UYG	NYSE Arca	32.63	$810,619,570	0.87		0.95

Ratings
Reward	C
Risk	C-
Recent Upgrade/Downgrade	

Fund Information
Fund Type	Exchange Traded Funds
Category	Trading Tools
Sub-Category	Trading--Leveraged Equity
Prospectus Objective	Financial
Inception Date	Jan-07
Open to New Investments	Y

Prices
Price (as of 12/31/2018)	32.62
52-Week High	47.70
52-Week Low	29.07

Total Returns (%)
3-Month	6-Month	1-Year	3-Year	5-Year
-24.15	-19.26	-22.52	41.55	73.00

3-Year Standard Deviation	24.62
Effective Duration	

Valuation
Premium/Discount (1-Year Average)	-0.02

Company Information
Provider	ProShares
Manager/Tenure	Michael Neches (5), Tarak Davé (0)
Website	http://www.proshares.com
Address	ProShares 7501 Wisconsin Avenue, Suite 1000 Bethesda MD 20814 United States
Phone Number	866-776-5125

PERFORMANCE

Ratings History
Date	Overall Rating	Risk Rating	Reward Rating
Q4-18	C	C-	C
Q2-18	C	C+	C
Q4-17	B+	C+	A+
Q4-16	C	C-	C+
Q4-15	C+	C	B-

Asset & Performance History
Date	NAV	1-Year Total Return
2017	42.59	39.28
2016	30.77	31.18
2015	23.67	-4.06
2014	24.85	27.39
2013	19.63	74.3
2012	11.3	54.16

Total Assets: $810,619,570

Asset Allocation
Asset	%
Cash	-100%
Stocks	107%
US Stocks	106%
Bonds	0%
US Bonds	0%
Other	93%

Services Offered:

Investment Strategy: The investment seeks daily investment results, before fees and expenses, that correspond to two times (2x) the daily performance of the Dow Jones U.S. FinancialsSM Index. The fund invests in financial instruments that ProShare Advisors believes, in combination, should produce daily returns consistent with the fund's investment objective. The index seeks to measure the performance of certain companies in the financial services sector of the U.S. equity market. The fund is non-diversified. **Top Holdings:** Dj U.S. Financials Index Swap Credit Suisse International   Dj U.S. Financials Index Swap Deutsche Bank Ag   Ishares U.S. Financials (lyf)   Swap Morgan Stanley & Co. International Plc   Dj U.S. Financials Index Swap Ubs Ag   Dj U.S. Financials Index Swap Goldman Sachs International

ProShares Large Cap Core Plus

C- HOLD

Ticker	Traded On	NAV	Total Assets ($)	Dividend Yield (TTM)	Turnover Ratio	Expense Ratio
CSM	BATS	60.64	$806,750,587	1.28		0.45

Ratings
Reward	C-
Risk	C-
Recent Upgrade/Downgrade	Down

Fund Information
Fund Type	Exchange Traded Funds
Category	US Equity Large Cap Blend
Sub-Category	Large Blend
Prospectus Objective	Growth
Inception Date	Jul-09
Open to New Investments	Y

Prices
Price (as of 12/31/2018)	60.62
52-Week High	72.75
52-Week Low	57.18

Total Returns (%)
3-Month	6-Month	1-Year	3-Year	5-Year
-15.73	-9.60	-7.83	28.46	48.49

3-Year Standard Deviation	9.5
Effective Duration	

Valuation
Premium/Discount (1-Year Average)	0.06

Company Information
Provider	ProShares
Manager/Tenure	Michael Neches (5), Tarak Davé (0)
Website	http://www.proshares.com
Address	ProShares 7501 Wisconsin Avenue, Suite 1000 Bethesda MD 20814 United States
Phone Number	866-776-5125

PERFORMANCE

Ratings History
Date	Overall Rating	Risk Rating	Reward Rating
Q4-18	C-	C-	C-
Q2-18	C	C-	C
Q4-17	B	B	B
Q4-16	B-	C+	B
Q4-15	C	C-	C

Asset & Performance History
Date	NAV	1-Year Total Return
2017	66.73	22.5
2016	55.23	13.78
2015	49.31	-0.45
2014	50.38	16.12
2013	44.02	35.78
2012	32.86	16.27

Total Assets: $806,750,587

Asset Allocation
Asset	%
Cash	0%
Stocks	100%
US Stocks	100%
Bonds	0%
US Bonds	0%
Other	0%

Services Offered:

Investment Strategy: The investment seeks investment results, before fees and expenses, that track the performance of the Credit Suisse 130/30 Large Cap Index (the "index"). The fund invests in financial instruments that ProShare Advisors believes, in combination, should track the performance of the index. The index is designed to replicate an investment strategy that establishes either long or short positions in the stocks of 500 leading large-cap U.S. companies (the "Universe") by applying a rules-based ranking and weighting methodology. The fund is non-diversified. **Top Holdings:** Credit Suisse 130/30 Large Cap Short Sub-Index Swap Deutsche Bank Ag   Credit Suisse 130/30 Large Cap Long Sub-Index Swap Societe Generale   Credit Suisse 130/30 Large Cap Long Sub-Index Swap Ubs Ag   Microsoft Corp   Apple Inc

Janus Henderson Short Duration Income ETF   C   HOLD

Ticker	Traded On	NAV	Total Assets ($)	Dividend Yield (TTM)	Turnover Ratio	Expense Ratio
VNLA	NYSE Arca	49.05	$805,872,859	2.43	44	0.35

Ratings

Reward	D+
Risk	C+
Recent Upgrade/Downgrade	

Fund Information

Fund Type	Exchange Traded Funds
Category	US Fixed Income
Sub-Category	Ultrashort Bond
Prospectus Objective	Multisector Bond
Inception Date	Nov-16
Open to New Investments	Y

Prices

Price (as of 12/31/2018)	49.00
52-Week High	50.23
52-Week Low	49.00

Total Returns (%)

3-Month	6-Month	1-Year	3-Year	5-Year
0.08	0.85	1.57		

3-Year Standard Deviation	
Effective Duration	

Valuation

Premium/Discount (1-Year Average)	0.10

Company Information

Provider	Janus Henderson
Manager/Tenure	Nick Maroutsos (2), Daniel Siluk (2), Jason England (0)
Website	http://www.janus.com
Address	Janus 151 Detroit Street Denver CO 80206 United States
Phone Number	877-335-2687

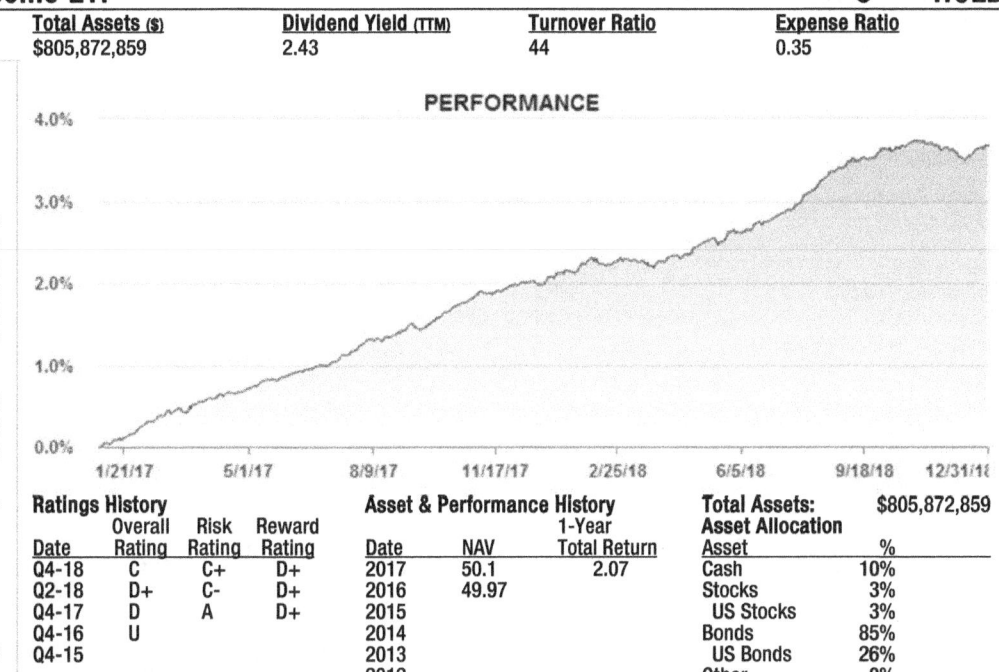

Ratings History

Date	Overall Rating	Risk Rating	Reward Rating
Q4-18	C	C+	D+
Q2-18	D+	C-	D+
Q4-17	D	A	D+
Q4-16	U		
Q4-15			

Asset & Performance History

Date	NAV	1-Year Total Return
2017	50.1	2.07
2016	49.97	
2015		
2014		
2013		
2012		

Total Assets: $805,872,859

Asset Allocation

Asset	%
Cash	10%
Stocks	3%
US Stocks	3%
Bonds	85%
US Bonds	26%
Other	0%

Services Offered:

Investment Strategy: The investment seeks to provide a steady income stream with capital preservation across various market cycles and consistently outperform the FTSE 3-Month US Treasury Bill Index by a moderate amount through various market cycles while at the same time providing low volatility. The fund normally invests its net assets in a portfolio of fixed income instruments of varying maturities. It may invest up to 25% in asset-backed securities that are rated investment grade or of similar quality as determined by Janus Capital. The average portfolio duration of the fund generally will be within 0-2 years of the index. **Top Holdings:** Us 5yr Note (Cbt) Mar19 Xcbt 20190329   S20224830 Irs Nzd P V 03mnzdbb 1620224830_flo Ccpvanilla   S20224830 Irs Nzd R F 2.58000 1620224830_fix Ccpvanilla   S10497552 Irs Usd P V 03mlibor 1610497552_flo Ccpvanilla   S10497552 Irs Usd R F 2.82950 1610497552_fix Ccpvanilla

---

SPDR® S&P International Dividend ETF   C-   HOLD

Ticker	Traded On	NAV	Total Assets ($)	Dividend Yield (TTM)	Turnover Ratio	Expense Ratio
DWX	NYSE Arca	34.95	$805,446,673	4.44	47	0.45

Ratings

Reward	C-
Risk	C-
Recent Upgrade/Downgrade	Down

Fund Information

Fund Type	Exchange Traded Funds
Category	Global Equity Large Cap
Sub-Category	Foreign Large Value
Prospectus Objective	Foreign Stock
Inception Date	Feb-08
Open to New Investments	Y

Prices

Price (as of 12/31/2018)	34.96
52-Week High	42.91
52-Week Low	33.98

Total Returns (%)

3-Month	6-Month	1-Year	3-Year	5-Year
-6.44	-6.27	-11.19	19.63	-5.65

3-Year Standard Deviation	10.88
Effective Duration	

Valuation

Premium/Discount (1-Year Average)	-0.24

Company Information

Provider	SPDR State Street Global Advisors
Manager/Tenure	Michael J. Feehily (7), Karl A. Schneider (3), Ted Janowsky (1)
Website	http://www.spdrs.com
Address	SPDR State Street Global Advisors State Street Financial Center, 1 Lincoln Street Boston MA 02111-2900 United States
Phone Number	617-786-3000

Ratings History

Date	Overall Rating	Risk Rating	Reward Rating
Q4-18	C-	C-	C-
Q2-18	C	C+	C-
Q4-17	C	C	C+
Q4-16	D+	D+	D+
Q4-15	D+	D+	D+

Asset & Performance History

Date	NAV	1-Year Total Return
2017	41.25	18.43
2016	36.24	12.84
2015	33.62	-16.59
2014	42.42	-5.44
2013	47.3	7.65
2012	47.19	8.56

Total Assets: $805,446,673

Asset Allocation

Asset	%
Cash	0%
Stocks	99%
US Stocks	1%
Bonds	0%
US Bonds	0%
Other	0%

Services Offered:

Investment Strategy: The investment seeks to provide investment results that, before fees and expenses, correspond generally to the total return performance of the S&P International Dividend Opportunities® Index. The fund generally invests substantially all, but at least 80%, of its total assets in the securities comprising the index and in depositary receipts based on securities comprising the index. The index is designed to measure the performance of 100 high-yielding international common stocks. The fund is non-diversified. **Top Holdings:** National Australia Bank Ltd   Vodacom Group Ltd   Bce Inc Common Stock   Westpac Banking Corp   Commonwealth Bank of Australia

FlexShares STOXX Global Broad Infrastructure Index Fund   C-   HOLD

Ticker	Traded On	NAV		Total Assets ($)	Dividend Yield (TTM)	Turnover Ratio	Expense Ratio
NFRA	NYSE Arca	43.67		$802,071,004	3.02		0.47

Ratings
Reward	C-
Risk	C-
Recent Upgrade/Downgrade	Down

Fund Information
Fund Type	Exchange Traded Funds
Category	Infrastructure Sector Equity
Sub-Category	Infrastructure
Prospectus Objective	Utility
Inception Date	Oct-13
Open to New Investments	Y

Prices
Price (as of 12/31/2018)	43.69
52-Week High	49.97
52-Week Low	42.10

Total Returns (%)
3-Month	6-Month	1-Year	3-Year	5-Year
-5.90	-2.90	-7.92	15.93	19.08

3-Year Standard Deviation	8.65
Effective Duration	

Valuation
Premium/Discount (1-Year Average)	-0.07

Company Information
Provider	Flexshares Trust
Manager/Tenure	Robert Anstine (5), Brendan Sullivan (2)
Website	http://www.flexshares.com
Address	50 South LaSalle Street Chicago, Illinois 60603 Chicago Illinois 60603 United States
Phone Number	855-353-9383

PERFORMANCE

Ratings History
Date	Overall Rating	Risk Rating	Reward Rating
Q4-18	C-	C-	C-
Q2-18	C-	C-	C
Q4-17	C+	B-	C+
Q4-16	C-	C-	C-
Q4-15	C-	C-	D+

Asset & Performance History
Date	NAV	1-Year Total Return
2017	48.83	16.05
2016	43.3	8.49
2015	41.1	-6.86
2014	45.17	10.28
2013	42.21	
2012		

Total Assets: $802,071,004

Asset Allocation
Asset	%
Cash	1%
Stocks	99%
US Stocks	40%
Bonds	0%
US Bonds	0%
Other	0%

Services Offered:

Investment Strategy: The investment seeks investment results that correspond generally to the price and yield performance, before fees and expenses, of the STOXX® Global Broad Infrastructure Index. The fund will invest at least 80% of its total assets (exclusive of collateral held from securities lending) in the securities of the underlying index and in ADRs and GDRs based on the securities in the underlying index. The underlying index reflects the performance of a selection of equity securities of infrastructure-related companies that are domiciled or traded in developed and emerging markets around the world (including the U.S.). The fund is non-diversified. **Top Holdings:** Verizon Communications Inc   AT&T Inc   Comcast Corp Class A   Canadian National Railway Co   Enbridge Inc

---

WisdomTree U.S. Dividend ex-Financials Fund   C   HOLD

Ticker	Traded On	NAV		Total Assets ($)	Dividend Yield (TTM)	Turnover Ratio	Expense Ratio
DTN	NYSE Arca	77.04		$798,822,987	3.54	34	0.38

Ratings
Reward	C
Risk	C-
Recent Upgrade/Downgrade	

Fund Information
Fund Type	Exchange Traded Funds
Category	US Equity Large Cap Value
Sub-Category	Large Value
Prospectus Objective	Growth & Inc
Inception Date	Jun-06
Open to New Investments	Y

Prices
Price (as of 12/31/2018)	76.98
52-Week High	92.93
52-Week Low	73.26

Total Returns (%)
3-Month	6-Month	1-Year	3-Year	5-Year
-14.19	-8.92	-9.39	21.75	32.77

3-Year Standard Deviation	8.46
Effective Duration	

Valuation
Premium/Discount (1-Year Average)	0.02

Company Information
Provider	WisdomTree
Manager/Tenure	Richard A. Brown (10), Thomas J. Durante (10), Karen Q. Wong (10)
Website	http://www.wisdomtree.com
Address	WisdomTree 245 Park Avenue, 35th floor New York NY 10167 United States
Phone Number	866-909-9473

PERFORMANCE

Ratings History
Date	Overall Rating	Risk Rating	Reward Rating
Q4-18	C	C-	C
Q2-18	C	C-	C
Q4-17	B-	B	B-
Q4-16	C+	C-	B
Q4-15	C	C-	C

Asset & Performance History
Date	NAV	1-Year Total Return
2017	88.33	13.78
2016	80.25	18.1
2015	70.26	-5.23
2014	76.63	15.06
2013	68.77	27.64
2012	55.57	11.79

Total Assets: $798,822,987

Asset Allocation
Asset	%
Cash	0%
Stocks	100%
US Stocks	100%
Bonds	0%
US Bonds	0%
Other	0%

Services Offered:

Investment Strategy: The investment seeks to track the price and yield performance, before fees and expenses, of the WisdomTree U.S. Dividend ex-Financials Index. The fund normally invests at least 95% of its total assets (exclusive of collateral held from securities lending) in component securities of the index and investments that have economic characteristics that are substantially identical to the economic characteristics of such component securities. The index is comprised of the 10 highest dividend-yielding companies in each sector, selected from the three hundred largest companies by market value in the WisdomTree U.S. Dividend Index. The fund is non-diversified. **Top Holdings:** CenturyLink Inc   Targa Resources Corp   ONEOK Inc   Verizon Communications Inc   Merck & Co Inc

Aberdeen Standard Physical Swiss Gold Shares ETF   D+   SELL

Ticker	Traded On	NAV	Total Assets ($)	Dividend Yield (TTM)	Turnover Ratio	Expense Ratio
SGOL	NYSE Arca	123.61	$798,612,798	0	11	0.39

Ratings
Reward   D
Risk   C-
Recent Upgrade/Downgrade   Down

Fund Information
Fund Type   Exchange Traded Funds
Category   Commodities Specified
Sub-Category   Commodities Precious Metals
Prospectus Objective   Prec Metals
Inception Date   Sep-09
Open to New Investments   Y

Prices
Price (as of 12/31/2018)   123.68
52-Week High   131.40
52-Week Low   113.37

Total Returns (%)

3-Month	6-Month	1-Year	3-Year	5-Year
7.67	2.53	-1.51	19.27	4.62

3-Year Standard Deviation   12.62
Effective Duration

Valuation
Premium/Discount (1-Year Average)   0.17

Company Information
Provider   Aberdeen Standard Investments
Manager/Tenure   Management Team (9)
Website   http://www.aberdeenstandardetfs.us
Address   Aberdeen Standard Investments 405 Lexington Avenue New York NY 10174 United States
Phone Number   212-918-4954

PERFORMANCE

Ratings History

Date	Overall Rating	Risk Rating	Reward Rating
Q4-18	D+	C-	D
Q2-18	C-	C-	C-
Q4-17	C-	C-	C-
Q4-16	C-	D+	C-
Q4-15	D	D	D

Asset & Performance History

Date	NAV	1-Year Total Return
2017	125.51	11.41
2016	112.65	8.69
2015	103.64	-11.76
2014	117.46	-0.57
2013	118.14	-28.07
2012	164.26	5.27

Total Assets: $798,612,798
Asset Allocation

Asset	%
Cash	0%
Stocks	0%
US Stocks	0%
Bonds	0%
US Bonds	0%
Other	100%

Services Offered:

Investment Strategy: The investment seeks to reflect the performance of the price of gold bullion, less the Trust's expenses.
The Shares are intended to constitute a simple and cost-effective means of making an investment similar to an investment in physical gold. An investment in physical gold requires expensive and sometimes complicated arrangements in connection with the assay, transportation, warehousing and insurance of the metal. Although the Shares are not the exact equivalent of an investment in gold, they provide investors with an alternative that allows a level of participation in the gold market through the securities market. **Top Holdings:** Physical Gold Bullion

---

iShares U.S. Utilities ETF   B-   BUY

Ticker	Traded On	NAV	Total Assets ($)	Dividend Yield (TTM)	Turnover Ratio	Expense Ratio
IDU	NYSE Arca	134.18	$795,681,341	2.53	5	0.43

Ratings
Reward   B-
Risk   C+
Recent Upgrade/Downgrade

Fund Information
Fund Type   Exchange Traded Funds
Category   Utilities Sector Equity
Sub-Category   Utilities
Prospectus Objective   Utility
Inception Date   Jun-00
Open to New Investments   Y

Prices
Price (as of 12/31/2018)   134.22
52-Week High   144.20
52-Week Low   119.94

Total Returns (%)

3-Month	6-Month	1-Year	3-Year	5-Year
1.01	2.27	3.91	35.55	64.15

3-Year Standard Deviation   11.73
Effective Duration

Valuation
Premium/Discount (1-Year Average)   0.00

Company Information
Provider   iShares
Manager/Tenure   Diane Hsiung (10), Greg Savage (10), Jennifer Hsui (6), 3 others
Website   http://www.ishares.com
Address   iShares 400 Howard Street San Francisco CA 94105 United States
Phone Number   800-474-2737

PERFORMANCE

Ratings History

Date	Overall Rating	Risk Rating	Reward Rating
Q4-18	B-	C+	B-
Q2-18	C+	C	B
Q4-17	B	B	B
Q4-16	B-	C+	B
Q4-15	B-	C+	B

Asset & Performance History

Date	NAV	1-Year Total Return
2017	132.88	11.95
2016	121.83	16.51
2015	107.87	-4.97
2014	118.4	27.43
2013	95.84	14.69
2012	86.44	1.3

Total Assets: $795,681,341
Asset Allocation

Asset	%
Cash	0%
Stocks	100%
US Stocks	100%
Bonds	0%
US Bonds	0%
Other	0%

Services Offered: CashInvestment Plan

Investment Strategy: The investment seeks to track the investment results of the Dow Jones U.S. Utilities Index. The fund generally invests at least 90% of its assets in securities of the underlying index and in depositary receipts representing securities of the underlying index. The underlying index measures the performance of the utilities sector of the U.S. equity market and may include large-, mid- or small-capitalization companies. The fund is non-diversified. **Top Holdings:** NextEra Energy Inc   Duke Energy Corp   Dominion Energy Inc   Southern Co   Exelon Corp

Invesco S&P 500® Top 50 ETF

C   HOLD

Ticker	Traded On	NAV		Total Assets ($)	Dividend Yield (TTM)	Turnover Ratio	Expense Ratio
XLG	NYSE Arca	179.73		$792,852,424	1.79		0.2

Ratings
Reward	C+
Risk	C
Recent Upgrade/Downgrade	Down

Fund Information
Fund Type	Exchange Traded Funds
Category	US Equity Large Cap Blend
Sub-Category	Large Blend
Prospectus Objective	Growth
Inception Date	May-05
Open to New Investments	Y

Prices
Price (as of 12/31/2018)	179.82
52-Week High	210.70
52-Week Low	167.99

Total Returns (%)
3-Month	6-Month	1-Year	3-Year	5-Year
-14.03	-6.17	-3.48	31.90	53.18

3-Year Standard Deviation	9.29
Effective Duration	

Valuation
Premium/Discount (1-Year Average)	0.09

Company Information
Provider	Invesco
Manager/Tenure	Peter Hubbard (0), Michael Jeanette (0), Jonathan Nixon (0), 1 other
Website	http://www.invesco.com/us
Address	Invesco 11 Greenway Plaza, Ste. 2500 Houston TX 77046 United States
Phone Number	800-659-1005

PERFORMANCE

Ratings History
Date	Overall Rating	Risk Rating	Reward Rating
Q4-18	C	C	C+
Q2-18	C+	C	B-
Q4-17	B	B+	B
Q4-16	B-	C	B
Q4-15	C+	C	C+

Asset & Performance History
Date	NAV	1-Year Total Return
2017	189.75	23.05
2016	157.39	10.49
2015	144.63	4.23
2014	141.75	11.41
2013	129.85	28.78
2012	103.04	15.35

Total Assets: $792,852,424

Asset Allocation
Asset	%
Cash	0%
Stocks	100%
US Stocks	100%
Bonds	0%
US Bonds	0%
Other	0%

Services Offered:

Investment Strategy: The investment seeks to track the investment results (before fees and expenses) of the S&P 500® Top 50 Index (the "underlying index"). The fund generally will invest at least 90% of its total assets in the securities that comprise the underlying index. The index provider compiles, maintains and calculates the underlying index, which includes 50 of the largest capitalization members of the S&P 500® Index. The underlying index's components are weighted by float-adjusted market capitalization. The fund is non-diversified. **Top Holdings:** Microsoft Corp Apple Inc Amazon.com Inc Berkshire Hathaway Inc B Johnson & Johnson

---

SPDR® S&P International Small Cap ETF

D+   SELL

Ticker	Traded On	NAV		Total Assets ($)	Dividend Yield (TTM)	Turnover Ratio	Expense Ratio
GWX	NYSE Arca	27.92		$787,140,105	2.85	29	0.4

Ratings
Reward	D+
Risk	C-
Recent Upgrade/Downgrade	Down

Fund Information
Fund Type	Exchange Traded Funds
Category	Global Eq Mid/Small Cap
Sub-Category	Foreign Small/Mid Blend
Prospectus Objective	Foreign Stock
Inception Date	Apr-07
Open to New Investments	Y

Prices
Price (as of 12/31/2018)	27.92
52-Week High	37.98
52-Week Low	26.70

Total Returns (%)
3-Month	6-Month	1-Year	3-Year	5-Year
-16.57	-15.28	-19.11	11.32	10.51

3-Year Standard Deviation	12.44
Effective Duration	

Valuation
Premium/Discount (1-Year Average)	-0.16

Company Information
Provider	SPDR State Street Global Advisors
Manager/Tenure	Michael J. Feehily (7), Karl A. Schneider (3), Teddy Wong (1)
Website	http://www.spdrs.com
Address	SPDR State Street Global Advisors State Street Financial Center, 1 Lincoln Street Boston MA 02111-2900 United States
Phone Number	617-786-3000

PERFORMANCE

Ratings History
Date	Overall Rating	Risk Rating	Reward Rating
Q4-18	D+	C-	D+
Q2-18	C	C-	C+
Q4-17	B+	B	B+
Q4-16	C	C-	C
Q4-15	C	C+	C

Asset & Performance History
Date	NAV	1-Year Total Return
2017	35.53	28.33
2016	29.17	6.57
2015	28.36	5.67
2014	27.56	-6.05
2013	33.29	21.82
2012	28.22	15.76

Total Assets: $787,140,105

Asset Allocation
Asset	%
Cash	1%
Stocks	98%
US Stocks	1%
Bonds	0%
US Bonds	0%
Other	1%

Services Offered:

Investment Strategy: The investment seeks investment results that, before fees and expenses, correspond generally to the total return performance of the S&P Developed Ex-U.S. under USD2 Billion Index. The fund generally invests substantially all, but at least 80%, of its total assets in the securities comprising the index and in depositary receipts based on securities comprising the index. The index is a market capitalization weighted index designed to define and measure the investable universe of publicly traded small-cap companies, as defined by the index, domiciled in developed countries outside the United States. It is non-diversified. **Top Holdings:** NIKKON Holdings Co Ltd Wihlborgs Fastigheter AB NIPPON REIT Investment Corp Iwatani Corp Toagosei Co Ltd

iShares Core U.S. REIT ETF   C   HOLD

Ticker	Traded On	NAV	Total Assets ($)	Dividend Yield (TTM)	Turnover Ratio	Expense Ratio
USRT	NYSE Arca	44.86	$784,540,201	5.2	8	0.08

Ratings

Reward	C
Risk	C+
Recent Upgrade/Downgrade	

Fund Information

Fund Type	Exchange Traded Funds
Category	Real Estate Sector Equity
Sub-Category	Real Estate
Prospectus Objective	Real Estate
Inception Date	May-07
Open to New Investments	Y

Prices

Price (as of 12/31/2018)	44.85
52-Week High	51.10
52-Week Low	43.17

Total Returns (%)

3-Month	6-Month	1-Year	3-Year	5-Year
-5.83	-4.95	-4.55	8.49	44.41

3-Year Standard Deviation	12.39
Effective Duration	

Valuation

Premium/Discount (1-Year Average)	0.02

Company Information

Provider	iShares
Manager/Tenure	Diane Hsiung (10), Greg Savage (10), Jennifer Hsui (6), 3 others
Website	http://www.ishares.com
Address	iShares 400 Howard Street San Francisco CA 94105 United States
Phone Number	800-474-2737

PERFORMANCE

Ratings History

Date	Overall Rating	Risk Rating	Reward Rating
Q4-18	C	C+	C
Q2-18	C	C	C
Q4-17	B	B+	C+
Q4-16	C+	C-	B
Q4-15	B-	C	B

Asset & Performance History

Date	NAV	1-Year Total Return
2017	49.59	5.16
2016	48.81	8.08
2015	46.98	3.86
2014	46.93	28.15
2013	38.02	-1.06
2012	39.86	17.45

Total Assets: $784,540,201

Asset Allocation

Asset	%
Cash	0%
Stocks	100%
US Stocks	100%
Bonds	0%
US Bonds	0%
Other	0%

Services Offered:

Investment Strategy: The investment seeks to track the investment results of the FTSE Nareit Equity REITS Index composed of U.S. real estate equities. The fund generally will invest at least 90% of its assets in the component securities of the underlying index and may invest up to 10% of its assets in certain futures, options and swap contracts, cash and cash equivalents. The index measures the performance of U.S. listed equity real estate investment trusts ("REITs"), excluding infrastructure REITs, mortgage REITs, and timber REITs. **Top Holdings:** Simon Property Group Inc   Prologis Inc   Public Storage   Equinix Inc   Welltower Inc

---

iShares India 50 ETF   C-   HOLD

Ticker	Traded On	NAV	Total Assets ($)	Dividend Yield (TTM)	Turnover Ratio	Expense Ratio
INDY	NAS CM	35.29	$783,332,651	0.37	14	0.92

Ratings

Reward	D+
Risk	C
Recent Upgrade/Downgrade	Down

Fund Information

Fund Type	Exchange Traded Funds
Category	India Equity
Sub-Category	India Equity
Prospectus Objective	Foreign Stock
Inception Date	Nov-09
Open to New Investments	Y

Prices

Price (as of 12/31/2018)	35.32
52-Week High	39.29
52-Week Low	31.33

Total Returns (%)

3-Month	6-Month	1-Year	3-Year	5-Year
3.30	1.43	-4.48	30.19	54.62

3-Year Standard Deviation	18.08
Effective Duration	

Valuation

Premium/Discount (1-Year Average)	-0.15

Company Information

Provider	iShares
Manager/Tenure	Diane Hsiung (9), Greg Savage (9), Jennifer Hsui (6), 3 others
Website	http://www.ishares.com
Address	iShares 400 Howard Street San Francisco CA 94105 United States
Phone Number	800-474-2737

PERFORMANCE

Ratings History

Date	Overall Rating	Risk Rating	Reward Rating
Q4-18	C-	C	D+
Q2-18	C	C+	C-
Q4-17	B-	C	B
Q4-16	C	C	C
Q4-15	C	C+	C

Asset & Performance History

Date	NAV	1-Year Total Return
2017	37.15	35.31
2016	27.53	0.73
2015	27.46	-7.82
2014	29.95	28.84
2013	23.37	-4.69
2012	24.72	25.67

Total Assets: $783,332,651

Asset Allocation

Asset	%
Cash	0%
Stocks	100%
US Stocks	0%
Bonds	0%
US Bonds	0%
Other	0%

Services Offered:

Investment Strategy: The investment seeks to track the investment results of the Nifty 50 IndexTM composed of 50 of the largest Indian equities. The Subsidiary and the fund will collectively invest at least 90% of the fund's assets in the component securities of the underlying index and in investments that have economic characteristics that are substantially identical to the component securities of the underlying index. The underlying index measures the equity performance of the top 50 companies by free float market capitalization whose equity securities trade in the Indian securities markets. The fund is non-diversified. **Top Holdings:** Reliance Industries Ltd   HDFC Bank Ltd   Housing Development Finance Corp Ltd   Infosys Ltd   ITC Ltd

ProShares UltraShort S&P500   D   SELL

Ticker	Traded On	NAV	Total Assets ($)	Dividend Yield (TTM)	Turnover Ratio	Expense Ratio
SDS	NYSE Arca	42.97	$775,521,303	1.13		0.9

Ratings

Reward	D-
Risk	D-
Recent Upgrade/Downgrade	

Fund Information

Fund Type	Exchange Traded Funds
Category	Trading Tools
Sub-Category	Trading--Inverse Equity
Prospectus Objective	Growth
Inception Date	Jul-06
Open to New Investments	Y

Prices

Price (as of 12/31/2018)	42.92
52-Week High	49.43
52-Week Low	32.86

Total Returns (%)

3-Month	6-Month	1-Year	3-Year	5-Year
31.24	14.08	5.86	-45.26	-63.25

3-Year Standard Deviation	17.88
Effective Duration	

Valuation

Premium/Discount (1-Year Average)	-0.03

Company Information

Provider	ProShares
Manager/Tenure	Michael Neches (5), Devin Sullivan (0)
Website	http://www.proshares.com
Address	ProShares 7501 Wisconsin Avenue, Suite 1000 Bethesda MD 20814 United States
Phone Number	866-776-5125

PERFORMANCE

Ratings History

Date	Overall Rating	Risk Rating	Reward Rating
Q4-18	D	D-	D-
Q2-18	D	D-	D-
Q4-17	D-	D-	E+
Q4-16	D	D-	D-
Q4-15	D	E+	D-

Asset & Performance History

Date	NAV	1-Year Total Return
2017	41.18	-31.94
2016	60.56	-24.03
2015	79.72	-9.61
2014	88.2	-25.73
2013	118.76	-45.16
2012	216.56	-29.79

Total Assets: $775,521,303

Asset Allocation

Asset	%
Cash	197%
Stocks	-103%
US Stocks	-103%
Bonds	6%
US Bonds	6%
Other	0%

Services Offered:

Investment Strategy: The investment seeks daily investment results, before fees and expenses, that correspond to two times the inverse (-2x) of the daily performance of the S&P 500® Index. The fund invests in financial instruments that ProShare Advisors believes, in combination, should produce daily returns consistent with the fund's investment objective. The index is a measure of large-cap U.S. stock market performance. The fund is non-diversified. **Top Holdings:** S&P 500 Index Swap Deutsche Bank Ag S&P 500 Index Swap Citibank Na S&P 500 Index Swap Goldman Sachs International S&P 500 Index Swap Credit Suisse International S&P 500 Index Swap Bnp Paribas

---

PIMCO Investment Grade Corporate Bond Index Exchange-Traded Fund   C-   HOLD

Ticker	Traded On	NAV	Total Assets ($)	Dividend Yield (TTM)	Turnover Ratio	Expense Ratio
CORP	NYSE Arca	99.11	$774,771,583	3.43	10	0.2

Ratings

Reward	D+
Risk	C-
Recent Upgrade/Downgrade	

Fund Information

Fund Type	Exchange Traded Funds
Category	US Fixed Income
Sub-Category	Corporate Bond
Prospectus Objective	Corp Bond - High Quality
Inception Date	Sep-10
Open to New Investments	Y

Prices

Price (as of 12/31/2018)	99.05
52-Week High	105.67
52-Week Low	97.96

Total Returns (%)

3-Month	6-Month	1-Year	3-Year	5-Year
-0.21	0.81	-2.70	9.87	17.50

3-Year Standard Deviation	3.78
Effective Duration	6.75

Valuation

Premium/Discount (1-Year Average)	-0.08

Company Information

Provider	PIMCO
Manager/Tenure	Matthew P. Dorsten (2), Mitchell Handa (0), Graham A. Rennison (0)
Website	http://www.pimco.com
Address	PIMCO 840 Newport Center Drive, Suite 100 Newport Beach CA 92660 United States
Phone Number	866-746-2602

PERFORMANCE

Ratings History

Date	Overall Rating	Risk Rating	Reward Rating
Q4-18	C-	C-	D+
Q2-18	C-	C-	C-
Q4-17	B-	B+	C
Q4-16	C	C-	C
Q4-15	C	C-	C

Asset & Performance History

Date	NAV	1-Year Total Return
2017	105.43	6.38
2016	102.24	6.17
2015	99.11	-0.46
2014	102.66	7.43
2013	99.02	-1.62
2012	108.03	10.15

Total Assets: $774,771,583

Asset Allocation

Asset	%
Cash	-11%
Stocks	0%
US Stocks	0%
Bonds	111%
US Bonds	85%
Other	0%

Services Offered:

Investment Strategy: The investment seeks to provide total return that closely corresponds, before fees and expenses, to the total return of the ICE BofAML US Corporate Index. The fund invests at least 80% of its total assets (exclusive of collateral held from securities lending) in the component securities of the ICE BofAML US Corporate Index (the "underlying index"). The underlying index is an unmanaged index comprised of U.S. dollar denominated investment grade corporate debt securities publicly issued in the U.S. domestic market with at least one year remaining term to final maturity. **Top Holdings:** Cdx Ig31 5y Ice Fin Fut Us 10yr Cbt 03/20/19 Fin Fut Us 30yr Cbt 03/20/19 Fin Fut Us 2yr Cbt 03/29/19 Fin Fut Us 5yr Cbt 03/29/19

WisdomTree Europe SmallCap Dividend Fund   D+   SELL

Ticker	Traded On	NAV	Total Assets ($)	Dividend Yield (TTM)	Turnover Ratio	Expense Ratio
DFE	NYSE Arca	53.42	$773,914,224	4.63	33	0.58

Ratings
Reward	D+
Risk	D+
Recent Upgrade/Downgrade	Down

Fund Information
Fund Type	Exchange Traded Funds
Category	Europe Equity Large Cap
Sub-Category	Europe Stock
Prospectus Objective	Europe Stock
Inception Date	Jun-06
Open to New Investments	Y

Prices
Price (as of 12/31/2018)	53.36
52-Week High	75.54
52-Week Low	51.32

Total Returns (%)
3-Month	6-Month	1-Year	3-Year	5-Year
-15.51	-16.71	-21.43	5.68	9.84

3-Year Standard Deviation	14.74
Effective Duration	

Valuation
Premium/Discount (1-Year Average)	-0.25

Company Information
Provider	WisdomTree
Manager/Tenure	Richard A. Brown (10), Thomas J. Durante (10), Karen Q. Wong (10)
Website	http://www.wisdomtree.com
Address	WisdomTree 245 Park Avenue, 35th floor New York NY 10167 United States
Phone Number	866-909-9473

PERFORMANCE

Ratings History
Date	Overall Rating	Risk Rating	Reward Rating
Q4-18	D+	D+	D+
Q2-18	C	C-	C
Q4-17	B+	A-	B+
Q4-16	C	C-	C
Q4-15	C	C+	C

Asset & Performance History
Date	NAV	1-Year Total Return
2017	70.84	32.46
2016	54.95	1.56
2015	56.29	10.96
2014	52.1	-6.33
2013	57.1	47.17
2012	40.06	27.96

Total Assets: $773,914,224
Asset Allocation
Asset	%
Cash	0%
Stocks	99%
US Stocks	0%
Bonds	0%
US Bonds	0%
Other	1%

Services Offered:

Investment Strategy: The investment seeks to track the price and yield performance, before fees and expenses, of the WisdomTree Europe SmallCap Dividend Index. Under normal circumstances, at least 95% of the fund's total assets (exclusive of collateral held from securities lending) will be invested in the component securities of the index and investments that have economic characteristics that are substantially identical to the economic characteristics of such component securities. The index is a fundamentally weighted index that is comprised of the small-capitalization segment of the European dividend-paying market. The fund is non-diversified. **Top Holdings:** BE Semiconductor Industries NV ADR Gaztransport et technigaz SA REN-Redes Energeticas Nacionais Sgps SA Aurelius Equity Opportunities Se & Co KGaA Peab AB B

John Hancock Multifactor Large Cap ETF   C-   HOLD

Ticker	Traded On	NAV	Total Assets ($)	Dividend Yield (TTM)	Turnover Ratio	Expense Ratio
JHML	NYSE Arca	32.02	$769,851,151	1.44	5	0.35

Ratings
Reward	C-
Risk	C-
Recent Upgrade/Downgrade	Down

Fund Information
Fund Type	Exchange Traded Funds
Category	US Equity Large Cap Blend
Sub-Category	Large Blend
Prospectus Objective	Growth
Inception Date	Sep-15
Open to New Investments	Y

Prices
Price (as of 12/31/2018)	32.05
52-Week High	37.87
52-Week Low	30.10

Total Returns (%)
3-Month	6-Month	1-Year	3-Year	5-Year
-14.05	-8.32	-6.33	27.94	

3-Year Standard Deviation	9.59
Effective Duration	

Valuation
Premium/Discount (1-Year Average)	0.05

Company Information
Provider	John Hancock
Manager/Tenure	Joel P. Schneider (3), Lukas J. Smart (3), Joseph F. Hohn (0)
Website	http://jhinvestments.com
Address	601 Congress Street, Boston MA 02210 United States
Phone Number	800-225-5913

PERFORMANCE

Ratings History
Date	Overall Rating	Risk Rating	Reward Rating
Q4-18	C-	C-	C-
Q2-18	C	C-	C
Q4-17	C	B	C+
Q4-16	D	C-	D+
Q4-15			

Asset & Performance History
Date	NAV	1-Year Total Return
2017	34.72	21.24
2016	29.07	12.67
2015	26.17	
2014		
2013		
2012		

Total Assets: $769,851,151
Asset Allocation
Asset	%
Cash	2%
Stocks	98%
US Stocks	98%
Bonds	0%
US Bonds	0%
Other	0%

Services Offered:

Investment Strategy: The investment seeks to provide investment results that closely correspond, before fees and expenses, to the performance of the John Hancock Dimensional Large Cap Index. The fund normally invests at least 80% of its net assets (plus any borrowings for investment purposes) in securities that compose the fund's benchmark index. The index is designed to comprise a subset of securities in the U.S. Universe issued by companies whose market capitalizations are larger than that of the 801st largest U.S. company at the time of reconstitution. **Top Holdings:** Apple Inc Microsoft Corp Amazon.com Inc Alphabet Inc A Berkshire Hathaway Inc B

VelocityShares 3x Long Natural Gas ETN Linked to the S&P GSCI® Natural Gas Index ER   D   SELL

Ticker	Traded On	NAV
UGAZ	NYSE Arca	38.61

Total Assets ($)	Dividend Yield (TTM)	Turnover Ratio	Expense Ratio
$760,159,266	0		1.65

Ratings
Reward	D
Risk	D
Recent Upgrade/Downgrade	Up

Fund Information
Fund Type	Exchange Traded Funds
Category	Trading Tools
Sub-Category	Trading--Leveraged Commodities
Prospectus Objective	Natl Res
Inception Date	Feb-12
Open to New Investments	Y

Prices
Price (as of 12/31/2018)	40.31
52-Week High	253.10
52-Week Low	40.31

Total Returns (%)
3-Month	6-Month	1-Year	3-Year	5-Year
-49.69	-36.27	-47.12	-93.74	-99.85

3-Year Standard Deviation	106.58
Effective Duration	

Valuation
Premium/Discount (1-Year Average)	-0.02

Company Information
Provider	Credit Suisse AG
Manager/Tenure	Management Team (6)
Website	
Address	Kilmore House Park Lane Dublin Ireland
Phone Number	

PERFORMANCE

Ratings History
Date	Overall Rating	Risk Rating	Reward Rating
Q4-18	D	D	D
Q2-18	E+	D-	E
Q4-17	C-	D	C
Q4-16	E+	D-	E
Q4-15	E+	E+	E

Asset & Performance History
Date	NAV	1-Year Total Return
2017	73.04	44.62
2016	455.6	-7.96
2015	617.5	-87.06
2014	4,775.00	-81.82
2013	26,275.00	-3.31
2012	27,175.00	

Total Assets: $760,159,266
Asset Allocation
Asset	%
Cash	%
Stocks	%
US Stocks	%
Bonds	%
US Bonds	%
Other	%

Services Offered:

Investment Strategy: The investment seeks to replicate, net of expenses, three times the performance of the S&P GSCI Natural Gas Index ER.
The index comprises futures contracts on a single commodity and is calculated according to the methodology of the S&P GSCI Index. **Top Holdings:**

IQ Merger Arbitrage ETF   C+   HOLD

Ticker	Traded On	NAV
MNA	NYSE Arca	31.68

Total Assets ($)	Dividend Yield (TTM)	Turnover Ratio	Expense Ratio
$757,681,640	0		0.78

Ratings
Reward	C+
Risk	C
Recent Upgrade/Downgrade	Up

Fund Information
Fund Type	Exchange Traded Funds
Category	Market Neutral
Sub-Category	Market Neutral
Prospectus Objective	Growth
Inception Date	Nov-09
Open to New Investments	Y

Prices
Price (as of 12/31/2018)	31.71
52-Week High	32.06
52-Week Low	30.32

Total Returns (%)
3-Month	6-Month	1-Year	3-Year	5-Year
-0.01	3.08	2.08	13.33	20.83

3-Year Standard Deviation	3.34
Effective Duration	

Valuation
Premium/Discount (1-Year Average)	0.22

Company Information
Provider	IndexIQ
Manager/Tenure	Greg Barrato (7), James Harrison (0)
Website	http://www.indexiq.com
Address	IndexIQ 800 Westchester Avenue, Suite N-611 Rye Brook NY 10573 United States
Phone Number	888-934-0777

PERFORMANCE

Ratings History
Date	Overall Rating	Risk Rating	Reward Rating
Q4-18	C+	C	C+
Q2-18	C	C+	C
Q4-17	C+	B	C
Q4-16	C	C-	C+
Q4-15	C	C	C

Asset & Performance History
Date	NAV	1-Year Total Return
2017	31.03	5.86
2016	29.31	4.86
2015	28.01	1.27
2014	27.9	5.28
2013	26.5	7.65
2012	24.86	0.6

Total Assets: $757,681,640
Asset Allocation
Asset	%
Cash	7%
Stocks	80%
US Stocks	68%
Bonds	11%
US Bonds	11%
Other	3%

Services Offered:

Investment Strategy: The investment seeks investment results that correspond generally to the price and yield performance of its underlying index, the IQ Merger Arbitrage Index. The fund invests at least 80% of its net assets, plus the amount of any borrowings for investment purposes, in the investments included in its underlying index. The underlying index seeks to employ a systematic investment process designed to identify opportunities in companies whose equity securities trade in developed markets, including the U.S., and which are involved in announced mergers, acquisitions and other buyout-related transactions. The fund is non-diversified. **Top Holdings:** Morgan Stanley Ilf/Treas/Inst Red Hat Inc Express Scripts Holding Co Payb Xli Short Ms Recv Xli Short Ms

Vanguard Russell 2000 Growth Index Fund ETF Shares   C-   HOLD

Ticker	Traded On	NAV	Total Assets ($)	Dividend Yield (TTM)	Turnover Ratio	Expense Ratio
VTWG	NAS CM		$757,558,802	0.62	35	0.2

Ratings

Reward	C-
Risk	C-
Recent Upgrade/Downgrade	Down

Fund Information

Fund Type	Exchange Traded Funds
Category	US Equity Small Cap
Sub-Category	Small Growth
Prospectus Objective	Small Company
Inception Date	Sep-10
Open to New Investments	Y

Prices

Price (as of 12/31/2018)	121.95
52-Week High	160.14
52-Week Low	114.04

Total Returns (%)

3-Month	6-Month	1-Year	3-Year	5-Year
-21.27	-18.97	-10.28	22.06	27.21

3-Year Standard Deviation	15.34
Effective Duration	

Valuation

Premium/Discount (1-Year Average)	0.03

Company Information

Provider	Vanguard
Manager/Tenure	Walter Nejman (3), Michael A. Johnson (2)
Website	http://www.vanguard.com
Address	Vanguard 100 Vanguard Boulevard Malvern PA 19355 United States
Phone Number	877-662-7447

PERFORMANCE

Ratings History

Date	Overall Rating	Risk Rating	Reward Rating
Q4-18	C-	C-	C-
Q2-18	C	C-	C+
Q4-17	B+	B	A-
Q4-16	C	D+	B-
Q4-15	C	C-	C+

Asset & Performance History

Date	NAV	1-Year Total Return
2017	135.43	22.62
2016	111.66	10.56
2015	101.26	-1.35
2014	103.38	5.64
2013	98.46	43.3
2012	69.09	14.45

Total Assets: $757,558,802

Asset Allocation

Asset	%
Cash	2%
Stocks	98%
US Stocks	97%
Bonds	0%
US Bonds	0%
Other	0%

Services Offered:

Investment Strategy: The investment seeks to track the performance of a benchmark index that measures the investment return of small-capitalization growth stocks in the United States. The fund employs an indexing investment approach designed to track the performance of the Russell 2000® Growth Index. The index is designed to measure the performance of small-capitalization growth stocks in the United States. The advisor attempts to replicate the target index by investing all, or substantially all, of its assets in the stocks that make up the index, holding each stock in approximately the same proportion as its weighting in the index. **Top Holdings:** Five Below Inc   Integrated Device Technology Inc   Haemonetics Corp   Etsy Inc   HealthEquity Inc

---

FlexShares International Quality Dividend Index Fund   D+   SELL

Ticker	Traded On	NAV	Total Assets ($)	Dividend Yield (TTM)	Turnover Ratio	Expense Ratio
IQDF	NYSE Arca	21.10	$755,990,138	5.71		0.47

Ratings

Reward	C-
Risk	D+
Recent Upgrade/Downgrade	Down

Fund Information

Fund Type	Exchange Traded Funds
Category	Global Equity Large Cap
Sub-Category	Foreign Large Value
Prospectus Objective	World Stock
Inception Date	Apr-13
Open to New Investments	Y

Prices

Price (as of 12/31/2018)	21.04
52-Week High	28.63
52-Week Low	20.28

Total Returns (%)

3-Month	6-Month	1-Year	3-Year	5-Year
-11.43	-10.19	-16.94	10.61	-3.59

3-Year Standard Deviation	11.11
Effective Duration	

Valuation

Premium/Discount (1-Year Average)	-0.08

Company Information

Provider	Flexshares Trust
Manager/Tenure	Robert Anstine (5), Brendan Sullivan (2)
Website	http://www.flexshares.com
Address	50 South LaSalle Street Chicago, Illinois 60603 Chicago Illinois 60603 United States
Phone Number	855-353-9383

PERFORMANCE

Ratings History

Date	Overall Rating	Risk Rating	Reward Rating
Q4-18	D+	D+	C-
Q2-18	C-	C-	C-
Q4-17	C+	C	C+
Q4-16	D+	C-	D
Q4-15	C-	C-	D+

Asset & Performance History

Date	NAV	1-Year Total Return
2017	26.75	23.59
2016	22.53	7.75
2015	21.72	-9.53
2014	24.95	-3.66
2013	26.93	
2012		

Total Assets: $755,990,138

Asset Allocation

Asset	%
Cash	0%
Stocks	99%
US Stocks	0%
Bonds	0%
US Bonds	0%
Other	0%

Services Offered:

Investment Strategy: The investment seeks investment results that correspond generally to the price and yield performance, before fees and expenses, of the Northern Trust International Quality Dividend IndexSM. The fund will invest at least 80% of its total assets in the securities of the index and in ADRs and GDRs based on the securities in the index. The index is designed to provide exposure to a high-quality, income-oriented portfolio of international equity securities issued by non-U.S.-based companies, with an emphasis on long-term capital growth and a targeted overall volatility similar to that of the Northern Trust International Large Cap IndexSM. **Top Holdings:** GlaxoSmithKline PLC   Unilever NV DR   BP PLC   Total SA   HSBC Holdings PLC

Invesco High Yield Equity Dividend Achievers™ ETF   C   HOLD

Ticker	Traded On	NAV	Total Assets ($)	Dividend Yield (TTM)	Turnover Ratio	Expense Ratio
PEY	NAS CM	15.85	$745,043,461	3.95	38	0.54

Ratings

Reward	C
Risk	C+
Recent Upgrade/Downgrade	

Fund Information

Fund Type	Exchange Traded Funds
Category	US Equity Mid Cap
Sub-Category	Mid-Cap Value
Prospectus Objective	Growth & Inc
Inception Date	Dec-04
Open to New Investments	Y

Prices

Price (as of 12/31/2018)	15.84
52-Week High	18.61
52-Week Low	15.14

Total Returns (%)

3-Month	6-Month	1-Year	3-Year	5-Year
-10.49	-7.96	-7.35	32.42	59.88

3-Year Standard Deviation	9.72
Effective Duration	

Valuation

Premium/Discount (1-Year Average)	-0.01

Company Information

Provider	Invesco
Manager/Tenure	Peter Hubbard (11), Michael Jeanette (10), Tony Seisser (4), 1 other
Website	http://www.invesco.com/us
Address	Invesco 11 Greenway Plaza, Ste. 2500 Houston TX 77046 United States
Phone Number	800-659-1005

PERFORMANCE

Ratings History

Date	Overall Rating	Risk Rating	Reward Rating
Q4-18	C	C+	C
Q2-18	C	C	C
Q4-17	B+	A	B
Q4-16	B	C+	B+
Q4-15	B-	C+	B-

Asset & Performance History

Date	NAV	1-Year Total Return
2017	17.8	8.64
2016	16.94	31.56
2015	13.34	2.44
2014	13.48	17.84
2013	11.85	30.4
2012	9.42	6.47

Total Assets: $745,043,461

Asset Allocation

Asset	%
Cash	0%
Stocks	100%
US Stocks	100%
Bonds	0%
US Bonds	0%
Other	0%

Services Offered:

Investment Strategy: The investment seeks to track the investment results (before fees and expenses) of the NASDAQ US Dividend AchieversTM 50 Index (the "underlying index"). The fund generally will invest at least 90% of its total assets in common stocks of companies that comprise the underlying index. Strictly in accordance with its guidelines and mandated procedures, Nasdaq, Inc. includes common stocks in the underlying index that have a consistent record of dividend increases, principally on the basis of dividend yield and consistent growth in dividends. **Top Holdings:** Vector Group Ltd AT&T Inc Southern Co PPL Corp Mercury General Corp

---

SPDR® S&P Insurance ETF   C   HOLD

Ticker	Traded On	NAV	Total Assets ($)	Dividend Yield (TTM)	Turnover Ratio	Expense Ratio
KIE	NYSE Arca	28.40	$741,705,686	1.78	26	0.35

Ratings

Reward	C
Risk	C+
Recent Upgrade/Downgrade	Down

Fund Information

Fund Type	Exchange Traded Funds
Category	Financials Sector Equity
Sub-Category	Financial
Prospectus Objective	Financial
Inception Date	Nov-05
Open to New Investments	Y

Prices

Price (as of 12/31/2018)	28.37
52-Week High	32.75
52-Week Low	26.73

Total Returns (%)

3-Month	6-Month	1-Year	3-Year	5-Year
-10.36	-4.02	-5.86	28.94	47.12

3-Year Standard Deviation	11.46
Effective Duration	

Valuation

Premium/Discount (1-Year Average)	-0.02

Company Information

Provider	SPDR State Street Global Advisors
Manager/Tenure	Michael J. Feehily (7), Karl A. Schneider (4), Raymond V. Donofrio (1)
Website	http://www.spdrs.com
Address	SPDR State Street Global Advisors State Street Financial Center, 1 Lincoln Street Boston MA 02111-2900 United States
Phone Number	617-786-3000

PERFORMANCE

Ratings History

Date	Overall Rating	Risk Rating	Reward Rating
Q4-18	C	C+	C
Q2-18	C+	C+	C+
Q4-17	B+	A-	B
Q4-16	C	C	C
Q4-15	B+	B-	A

Asset & Performance History

Date	NAV	1-Year Total Return
2017	30.7	12.89
2016	27.63	19.97
2015	23.17	6.01
2014	22.22	7.61
2013	21.04	45.57
2012	14.68	20.85

Total Assets: $741,705,686

Asset Allocation

Asset	%
Cash	0%
Stocks	100%
US Stocks	98%
Bonds	0%
US Bonds	0%
Other	0%

Services Offered: Dividend Investment Plan, CashInvestment Plan

Investment Strategy: The investment seeks to provide investment results that, before fees and expenses, correspond generally to the total return performance of an index that tracks the performance of publicly traded companies in the insurance industry. In seeking to track the performance of the S&P Insurance Select Industry Index (the "index"), the fund employs a sampling strategy. It generally invests substantially all, but at least 80%, of its total assets in the securities comprising the index. The index represents the insurance segment of the S&P Total Market Index ("S&P TMI"). The fund is non-diversified. **Top Holdings:** Aon PLC Willis Towers Watson PLC Cincinnati Financial Corp Arthur J. Gallagher & Co Reinsurance Group of America Inc

Invesco S&P 500® Equal Weight Health Care ETF   C   HOLD

Ticker	Traded On	NAV		Total Assets ($)	Dividend Yield (TTM)	Turnover Ratio	Expense Ratio
RYH	NYSE Arca	177.68		$739,541,288	0.45		0.4

Ratings

Reward	C
Risk	C-
Recent Upgrade/Downgrade	

Fund Information

Fund Type	Exchange Traded Funds
Category	Healthcare Sector Equity
Sub-Category	Health
Prospectus Objective	Health
Inception Date	Nov-06
Open to New Investments	Y

Prices

Price (as of 12/31/2018)	177.53
52-Week High	206.09
52-Week Low	165.92

Total Returns (%)

3-Month	6-Month	1-Year	3-Year	5-Year
-13.71	-2.87	-0.33	17.46	64.98

3-Year Standard Deviation	13.21
Effective Duration	

Valuation

Premium/Discount (1-Year Average)	0.13

Company Information

Provider	Invesco
Manager/Tenure	Peter Hubbard (0), Michael Jeanette (0), Jonathan Nixon (0), 1 other
Website	http://www.invesco.com/us
Address	Invesco 11 Greenway Plaza, Ste. 2500 Houston TX 77046 United States
Phone Number	800-659-1005

PERFORMANCE

Ratings History

Date	Overall Rating	Risk Rating	Reward Rating
Q4-18	C	C-	C
Q2-18	C	C-	C
Q4-17	B	B	B-
Q4-16	C	C-	C
Q4-15	C+	C	B-

Asset & Performance History

Date	NAV	1-Year Total Return
2017	179.18	24.01
2016	145.92	-4.98
2015	153.51	8.2
2014	142.55	29.79
2013	110.35	40.75
2012	78.77	20.44

Total Assets: $739,541,288

Asset Allocation

Asset	%
Cash	1%
Stocks	99%
US Stocks	99%
Bonds	0%
US Bonds	0%
Other	0%

Services Offered:

Investment Strategy: The investment seeks to track the investment results (before fees and expenses) of the S&P 500® Equal Weight Health Care Index (the "underlying index"). The fund generally will invest at least 90% of its total assets in the securities that comprise the underlying index. The underlying index is an equal-weighted version of the S&P 500® Health Care Index. Strictly in accordance with its guidelines and mandated procedures, the index provider compiles, maintains and calculates the underlying index, which is comprised of common stocks of companies in the health care sector of the S&P 500® Index. The fund is non-diversified. **Top Holdings:** CVS Health Corp   Cigna Corp   Merck & Co Inc   Eli Lilly and Co   Hologic Inc

---

Global X Lithium & Battery Tech ETF   C   HOLD

Ticker	Traded On	NAV		Total Assets ($)	Dividend Yield (TTM)	Turnover Ratio	Expense Ratio
LIT	NYSE Arca	27.17		$738,477,860	4.01	68	0.75

Ratings

Reward	C
Risk	C-
Recent Upgrade/Downgrade	

Fund Information

Fund Type	Exchange Traded Funds
Category	Natural Resources
Sub-Category	Natural Resources
Prospectus Objective	Unaligned
Inception Date	Jul-10
Open to New Investments	Y

Prices

Price (as of 12/31/2018)	26.98
52-Week High	41.08
52-Week Low	26.49

Total Returns (%)

3-Month	6-Month	1-Year	3-Year	5-Year
-17.96	-16.01	-29.84	41.59	10.96

3-Year Standard Deviation	17.76
Effective Duration	

Valuation

Premium/Discount (1-Year Average)	-0.29

Company Information

Provider	Global X Funds
Manager/Tenure	Chang Kim (4), James Ong (2), Nam To (0)
Website	http://www.globalxfunds.com
Address	Global X Funds 600 Lexington Avenue, 20th Floor New York NY 10022 United States
Phone Number	888-493-8631

PERFORMANCE

Ratings History

Date	Overall Rating	Risk Rating	Reward Rating
Q4-18	C	C-	C
Q2-18	C	C	C
Q4-17	B+	C	A+
Q4-16	C-	D+	C-
Q4-15	D	D	D

Asset & Performance History

Date	NAV	1-Year Total Return
2017	38.73	63.36
2016	24.48	23.55
2015	20.24	-10.07
2014	22.56	-12.85
2013	26.16	-9.06
2012	28.86	2.3

Total Assets: $738,477,860

Asset Allocation

Asset	%
Cash	0%
Stocks	100%
US Stocks	45%
Bonds	0%
US Bonds	0%
Other	0%

Services Offered:

Investment Strategy: The investment seeks to provide investment results that correspond generally to the price and yield performance, before fees and expenses, of the Solactive Global Lithium Index. The fund invests at least 80% of its total assets in the securities of the underlying index and in American Depositary Receipts ("ADRs") and Global Depositary Receipts ("GDRs") based on the securities in the underlying index. The underlying index is designed to measure broad-based equity market performance of global companies involved in the lithium industry. The fund is non-diversified. **Top Holdings:** Albemarle Corp   FMC Corp   Sociedad Quimica Y Minera De Chile SA ADR   Tesla Inc   BYD Co Ltd H

Invesco International Dividend Achievers ETF   C   HOLD

Ticker	Traded On	NAV	Total Assets ($)	Dividend Yield (TTM)	Turnover Ratio	Expense Ratio
PID	NAS CM	14.17	$737,721,777	3.78	55	0.55

Ratings
Reward   C-
Risk   C
Recent Upgrade/Downgrade

Fund Information
Fund Type   Exchange Traded Funds
Category   Global Equity Large Cap
Sub-Category   Foreign Large Value
Prospectus Objective   Foreign Stock
Inception Date   Sep-05
Open to New Investments   Y

Prices
Price (as of 12/31/2018)   14.13
52-Week High   17.36
52-Week Low   13.74

Total Returns (%)

3-Month	6-Month	1-Year	3-Year	5-Year
-9.81	-6.35	-11.08	16.34	-6.95

3-Year Standard Deviation   12.21
Effective Duration

Valuation
Premium/Discount (1-Year Average)   -0.04

Company Information
Provider   Invesco
Manager/Tenure   Peter Hubbard (11), Michael Jeanette (10), Tony Seisser (4), 1 other
Website   http://www.invesco.com/us
Address   Invesco 11 Greenway Plaza, Ste. 2500 Houston TX 77046 United States
Phone Number   800-659-1005

PERFORMANCE

Ratings History

Date	Overall Rating	Risk Rating	Reward Rating
Q4-18	C	C	C-
Q2-18	C	C	C
Q4-17	C	C	C
Q4-16	D+	D+	D+
Q4-15	C-	C-	C-

Asset & Performance History

Date	NAV	1-Year Total Return
2017	16.52	19.03
2016	14.39	9.92
2015	13.62	-19.09
2014	17.51	-1.14
2013	18.39	18.71
2012	15.86	12.25

Total Assets: $737,721,777

Asset Allocation

Asset	%
Cash	0%
Stocks	100%
US Stocks	4%
Bonds	0%
US Bonds	0%
Other	0%

Services Offered:

Investment Strategy: The investment seeks to track the investment results (before fees and expenses) of the NASDAQ International Dividend AchieversTM Index. The fund generally will invest at least 90% of its total assets in dividend-paying common stocks and other securities that comprise the underlying index. The underlying index is composed of Global Depositary Receipts ("GDRs") and American Depositary Receipts ("ADRs") that are listed on the London Stock Exchange ("LSE") or the London International Exchange, in addition to ADRs and non-U.S. common or ordinary stocks traded on NYSE, NASDAQ or NYSE American. **Top Holdings:** BT Group PLC ADR Novolipetsk Steel PJSC GDR Vodafone Group PLC ADR Micro Focus International PLC ADR BCE Inc

---

First Trust NASDAQ Cybersecurity ETF   C   HOLD

Ticker	Traded On	NAV	Total Assets ($)	Dividend Yield (TTM)	Turnover Ratio	Expense Ratio
CIBR	NAS CM	23.44	$736,998,963	0.07	56	0.6

Ratings
Reward   C+
Risk   C-
Recent Upgrade/Downgrade   Down

Fund Information
Fund Type   Exchange Traded Funds
Category   Technology Sector Equity
Sub-Category   Technology
Prospectus Objective   Technology
Inception Date   Jul-15
Open to New Investments   Y

Prices
Price (as of 12/31/2018)   23.42
52-Week High   28.89
52-Week Low   21.94

Total Returns (%)

3-Month	6-Month	1-Year	3-Year	5-Year
-16.47	-11.96	1.91	33.71	

3-Year Standard Deviation   14.93
Effective Duration

Valuation
Premium/Discount (1-Year Average)   0.15

Company Information
Provider   First Trust
Manager/Tenure   Jon C. Erickson (3), Daniel J. Lindquist (3), David G. McGarel (3), 3 others
Website   http://www.ftportfolios.com/
Address   First Trust 120 E. Liberty Drive, Suite 400 Wheaton IL 60187 United States
Phone Number   800-621-1675

PERFORMANCE

Ratings History

Date	Overall Rating	Risk Rating	Reward Rating
Q4-18	C	C-	C+
Q2-18	C+	C	C+
Q4-17	C	B-	C+
Q4-16	D	D+	C+
Q4-15	U		

Asset & Performance History

Date	NAV	1-Year Total Return
2017	23.05	18.32
2016	19.5	10.88
2015	17.74	
2014		
2013		
2012		

Total Assets: $736,998,963

Asset Allocation

Asset	%
Cash	0%
Stocks	100%
US Stocks	89%
Bonds	0%
US Bonds	0%
Other	0%

Services Offered:

Investment Strategy: The investment seeks investment results that correspond generally to the price and yield (before the fund's fees and expenses) of an equity index called the Nasdaq CTA Cybersecurity IndexSM (the "index"). The fund will normally invest at least 90% of its net assets (including investment borrowings) in common stocks or in depositary receipts that comprise the index. The index will include securities of companies classified as "cyber security" companies by the CTA. The fund is non-diversified. **Top Holdings:** Symantec Corp Cisco Systems Inc Raytheon Co Splunk Inc Palo Alto Networks Inc

iShares Transportation Average ETF   B   BUY

Ticker	Traded On	NAV	Total Assets ($)	Dividend Yield (TTM)	Turnover Ratio	Expense Ratio
IYT	BATS	164.99	$732,085,862	1.08	5	0.43

Ratings
Reward   B+
Risk   C
Recent Upgrade/Downgrade

Fund Information
Fund Type	Exchange Traded Funds
Category	Industrials Sector Equity
Sub-Category	Industrials
Prospectus Objective	Unaligned
Inception Date	Oct-03
Open to New Investments	Y

Prices
Price (as of 12/31/2018)	165.01
52-Week High	208.48
52-Week Low	155.39

Total Returns (%)
3-Month	6-Month	1-Year	3-Year	5-Year
-19.31	-11.76	-12.82	26.54	31.81

3-Year Standard Deviation	16.49
Effective Duration	

Valuation
Premium/Discount (1-Year Average)	-0.01

Company Information
Provider	iShares
Manager/Tenure	Diane Hsiung (10), Greg Savage (10), Jennifer Hsui (6), 3 others
Website	http://www.ishares.com
Address	iShares 400 Howard Street San Francisco CA 94105 United States
Phone Number	800-474-2737

Ratings History

Date	Overall Rating	Risk Rating	Reward Rating
Q4-18	B	C	B+
Q2-18	B	C	B+
Q4-17	C+	C+	B-
Q4-16	B-	C	B
Q4-15	B	B-	B+

Asset & Performance History

Date	NAV	1-Year Total Return
2017	191.53	18.93
2016	162.7	22.05
2015	134.74	-16.88
2014	164.04	25.32
2013	131.91	41.18
2012	94.35	6.61

Total Assets: $732,085,862

Asset Allocation

Asset	%
Cash	0%
Stocks	100%
US Stocks	100%
Bonds	0%
US Bonds	0%
Other	0%

Services Offered: CashInvestment Plan

Investment Strategy: The investment seeks to track the investment results of the Dow Jones Transportation Average Index composed of U.S. equities in the transportation sector. The fund generally invests at least 90% of its assets in securities of the underlying index and in depositary receipts representing securities of the underlying index. The underlying index measures the performance of large, well-known companies within the transportation sector of the U.S. equity market. The fund is non-diversified. **Top Holdings:** FedEx Corp Norfolk Southern Corp Union Pacific Corp United Parcel Service Inc Class B JB Hunt Transport Services Inc

---

SPDR® NYSE Technology ETF   C+   HOLD

Ticker	Traded On	NAV	Total Assets ($)	Dividend Yield (TTM)	Turnover Ratio	Expense Ratio
XNTK	NYSE Arca	59.56	$727,083,925	0.67	14	0.35

Ratings
Reward   B
Risk   C
Recent Upgrade/Downgrade   Down

Fund Information
Fund Type	Exchange Traded Funds
Category	Technology Sector Equity
Sub-Category	Technology
Prospectus Objective	Technology
Inception Date	Sep-00
Open to New Investments	Y

Prices
Price (as of 12/31/2018)	59.53
52-Week High	97.94
52-Week Low	54.51

Total Returns (%)
3-Month	6-Month	1-Year	3-Year	5-Year
-17.73	-16.92	-6.25	49.00	82.06

3-Year Standard Deviation	14.78
Effective Duration	

Valuation
Premium/Discount (1-Year Average)	0.04

Company Information
Provider	SPDR State Street Global Advisors
Manager/Tenure	Michael J. Feehily (7), Karl A. Schneider (4), Kathleen Morgan (0)
Website	http://www.spdrs.com
Address	SPDR State Street Global Advisors State Street Financial Center, 1 Lincoln Street Boston MA 02111-2900 United States
Phone Number	617-786-3000

Ratings History

Date	Overall Rating	Risk Rating	Reward Rating
Q4-18	C+	C	B
Q2-18	B	C	A-
Q4-17	A-	B	A+
Q4-16	C	C	C+
Q4-15	C+	C	B-

Asset & Performance History

Date	NAV	1-Year Total Return
2017	83.77	40.25
2016	60.53	12.91
2015	53.88	7.76
2014	50.48	13.38
2013	44.93	33.21
2012	34.13	17.61

Total Assets: $727,083,925

Asset Allocation

Asset	%
Cash	0%
Stocks	100%
US Stocks	87%
Bonds	0%
US Bonds	0%
Other	0%

Services Offered: Dividend Investment Plan, CashInvestment Plan

Investment Strategy: The investment seeks to provide investment results that, before fees and expenses, correspond generally to the total return performance of the NYSE Technology Index that tracks the performance of publicly traded technology companies. The fund generally invests substantially all, but at least 80%, of its total assets in the securities comprising the index. It may invest in equity securities that are not included in the index, cash and cash equivalents or money market instruments, such as repurchase agreements and money market funds. The index is composed of 35 leading U.S.-listed technology-related companies. The fund is non-diversified. **Top Holdings:** Netflix Inc Amazon.com Inc Adobe Inc Salesforce.com Inc VMware Inc

Fidelity® MSCI Consumer Discretionary Index ETF

C   **HOLD**

Ticker	Traded On	NAV	Total Assets ($)	Dividend Yield (TTM)	Turnover Ratio	Expense Ratio
FDIS	NYSE Arca	38.32	$724,206,329	0.99	5	0.08

Ratings
Reward	C+
Risk	C
Recent Upgrade/Downgrade	Down

Fund Information
Fund Type	Exchange Traded Funds
Category	Consumer Goods & Svcs
Sub-Category	Consumer Cyclical
Prospectus Objective	Unaligned
Inception Date	Oct-13
Open to New Investments	Y

Prices
Price (as of 12/31/2018)	38.32
52-Week High	45.63
52-Week Low	35.51

Total Returns (%)
3-Month	6-Month	1-Year	3-Year	5-Year
-15.27	-9.91	-0.73	29.94	51.11

3-Year Standard Deviation	11.77
Effective Duration	

Valuation
Premium/Discount (1-Year Average)	0.07

Company Information
Provider	Fidelity Investments
Manager/Tenure	Jennifer Hsui (5), Greg Savage (5), Alan Mason (2), 2 others
Website	http://www.institutional.fidelity.com
Address	Fidelity Investments 82 Devonshire Street Boston MA 2109 United States
Phone Number	617-563-7000

PERFORMANCE

Ratings History
Date	Overall Rating	Risk Rating	Reward Rating
Q4-18	C	C	C+
Q2-18	B-	C	B
Q4-17	B	A-	B
Q4-16	C+	C+	C+
Q4-15	C-	C+	C

Asset & Performance History
Date	NAV	1-Year Total Return
2017	39.07	22.78
2016	32.17	6.62
2015	30.67	6.4
2014	29.19	9.29
2013	26.99	
2012		

Total Assets: $724,206,329
Asset Allocation
Asset	%
Cash	0%
Stocks	100%
US Stocks	99%
Bonds	0%
US Bonds	0%
Other	0%

Services Offered:

Investment Strategy: The investment seeks to provide investment returns that correspond, before fees and expenses, generally to the performance of the MSCI USA IMI Consumer Discretionary Index. The fund invests at least 80% of assets in securities included in the fund's underlying index. The fund's underlying index is the MSCI USA IMI Consumer Discretionary Index, which represents the performance of the consumer discretionary sector in the U.S. equity market. It may or may not hold all of the securities in the MSCI USA IMI Consumer Discretionary Index. The fund is non-diversified. **Top Holdings:** Amazon.com Inc The Home Depot Inc Comcast Corp Class A Walt Disney Co McDonald's Corp

---

John Hancock Multifactor Mid Cap ETF

C   **HOLD**

Ticker	Traded On	NAV	Total Assets ($)	Dividend Yield (TTM)	Turnover Ratio	Expense Ratio
JHMM	NYSE Arca	30.44	$720,525,623	0.93	11	0.45

Ratings
Reward	C-
Risk	C+
Recent Upgrade/Downgrade	

Fund Information
Fund Type	Exchange Traded Funds
Category	US Equity Mid Cap
Sub-Category	Mid-Cap Blend
Prospectus Objective	Growth
Inception Date	Sep-15
Open to New Investments	Y

Prices
Price (as of 12/31/2018)	30.44
52-Week High	36.91
52-Week Low	28.59

Total Returns (%)
3-Month	6-Month	1-Year	3-Year	5-Year
-15.43	-11.80	-9.62	23.73	

3-Year Standard Deviation	10.86
Effective Duration	

Valuation
Premium/Discount (1-Year Average)	0.10

Company Information
Provider	John Hancock
Manager/Tenure	Joel P. Schneider (3), Lukas J. Smart (3), Joseph F. Hohn (0)
Website	http://jhinvestments.com
Address	601 Congress Street, Boston MA 02210 United States
Phone Number	800-225-5913

PERFORMANCE

Ratings History
Date	Overall Rating	Risk Rating	Reward Rating
Q4-18	C	C+	C-
Q2-18	C	C-	C
Q4-17	C	B	C+
Q4-16	D	D+	D+
Q4-15			

Asset & Performance History
Date	NAV	1-Year Total Return
2017	34.14	20.06
2016	28.7	14.02
2015	25.47	
2014		
2013		
2012		

Total Assets: $720,525,623
Asset Allocation
Asset	%
Cash	3%
Stocks	97%
US Stocks	96%
Bonds	0%
US Bonds	0%
Other	0%

Services Offered:

Investment Strategy: The investment seeks to provide investment results that closely correspond, before fees and expenses, to the performance of the John Hancock Dimensional Mid Cap Index. The fund normally invests at least 80% of its net assets (plus any borrowings for investment purposes) in securities that compose the fund's benchmark index. The index is designed to comprise a subset of securities in the U.S. Universe issued by companies whose market capitalizations are between the 200th and 951st largest U.S. company at the time of reconstitution. **Top Holdings:** United Continental Holdings Inc Centene Corp Edwards Lifesciences Corp Xcel Energy Inc Parker Hannifin Corp

iShares iBonds Dec 2019 Term Corporate ETF   C   HOLD

Ticker	Traded On	NAV	Total Assets ($)	Dividend Yield (TTM)	Turnover Ratio	Expense Ratio
IBDK	NYSE Arca	24.74	$719,412,921	2	7	0.1

Ratings
Reward   C
Risk   C+
Recent Upgrade/Downgrade

Fund Information
Fund Type   Exchange Traded Funds
Category   US Fixed Income
Sub-Category   Short-Term Bond
Prospectus Objective   Corp Bond - Gen
Inception Date   Mar-15
Open to New Investments   Y

Prices
Price (as of 12/31/2018)   24.80
52-Week High   24.87
52-Week Low   24.71

Total Returns (%)

3-Month	6-Month	1-Year	3-Year	5-Year
0.54	1.28	1.82	7.07	

3-Year Standard Deviation   1.22
Effective Duration   0.60

Valuation
Premium/Discount (1-Year Average)   0.16

Company Information
Provider   iShares
Manager/Tenure   James Mauro (3), Scott Radell (3)
Website   http://www.ishares.com
Address   iShares 400 Howard Street San
                      Francisco CA 94105 United States
Phone Number   800-474-2737

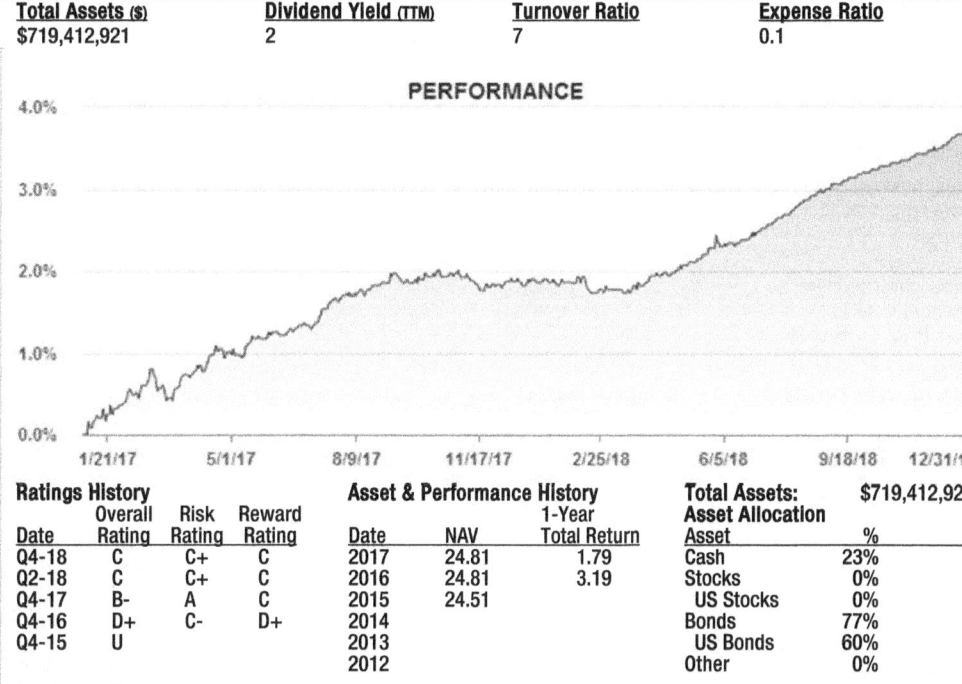

PERFORMANCE

Ratings History

Date	Overall Rating	Risk Rating	Reward Rating
Q4-18	C	C+	C
Q2-18	C	C+	C
Q4-17	B-	A	C
Q4-16	D+	C-	D+
Q4-15	U		

Asset & Performance History

Date	NAV	1-Year Total Return
2017	24.81	1.79
2016	24.81	3.19
2015	24.51	
2014		
2013		
2012		

Total Assets: $719,412,921
Asset Allocation

Asset	%
Cash	23%
Stocks	0%
US Stocks	0%
Bonds	77%
US Bonds	60%
Other	0%

Services Offered:

Investment Strategy: The investment seeks to track the investment results of the Bloomberg Barclays December 2019 Maturity Corporate Index which composed of U.S. dollar-denominated, investment-grade corporate bonds maturing in 2019. The fund generally will invest at least 90% of its assets in the component securities of the underlying index. The underlying index includes U.S. dollar-denominated, investment-grade securities publicly issued by U.S. and non-U.S. corporate issuers that have $300 million or more of outstanding face value at the time of inclusion. **Top Holdings:** Diamond 1 Finance Corporation/Diamond 2 Finance Corporation 3.48% Shire Acquisitions Investments Ireland DAC 1.9% Morgan Stanley 5.63% Morgan Stanley 2.38% JPMorgan Chase & Co. 6.3%

VanEck Vectors Investment Grade Floating Rate ETF   C   HOLD

Ticker	Traded On	NAV	Total Assets ($)	Dividend Yield (TTM)	Turnover Ratio	Expense Ratio
FLTR	NYSE Arca	24.75	$710,993,987	2.44	28	0.14

Ratings
Reward   C-
Risk   C+
Recent Upgrade/Downgrade

Fund Information
Fund Type   Exchange Traded Funds
Category   US Fixed Income
Sub-Category   Ultrashort Bond
Prospectus Objective   Income
Inception Date   Apr-11
Open to New Investments   Y

Prices
Price (as of 12/31/2018)   24.69
52-Week High   25.40
52-Week Low   24.69

Total Returns (%)

3-Month	6-Month	1-Year	3-Year	5-Year
-1.52	-0.66	0.36	5.40	5.85

3-Year Standard Deviation   0.74
Effective Duration   0.09

Valuation
Premium/Discount (1-Year Average)   0.07

Company Information
Provider   VanEck
Manager/Tenure   Francis G. Rodilosso (6)
Website   http://www.vaneck.com
Address   Van Eck Associates Corporation 666
                      Third Avenue New York NY 10017
                      United States
Phone Number   800-826-1115

PERFORMANCE

Ratings History

Date	Overall Rating	Risk Rating	Reward Rating
Q4-18	C	C+	C-
Q2-18	C	C+	C
Q4-17	B-	A-	C
Q4-16	C-	D+	C
Q4-15	C	C-	C

Asset & Performance History

Date	NAV	1-Year Total Return
2017	25.24	2.84
2016	24.96	2.11
2015	24.73	0.01
2014	24.9	0.41
2013	24.96	1.62
2012	24.72	6.48

Total Assets: $710,993,987
Asset Allocation

Asset	%
Cash	0%
Stocks	0%
US Stocks	0%
Bonds	99%
US Bonds	65%
Other	0%

Services Offered:

Investment Strategy: The investment seeks to replicate as closely as possible, before fees and expenses, the price and yield performance of the MVIS® US Investment Grade Floating Rate Index (the "Floating Rate Index"). The fund normally invests at least 80% of its total assets in securities that comprise the fund's benchmark index. The index is comprised of U.S. dollar-denominated floating rate notes issued by corporate entities or similar commercial entities that are public reporting companies in the United States and rated investment grade. The fund is non-diversified. **Top Holdings:** AT&T Inc 3.51% Morgan Stanley 3.65% Goldman Sachs Group, Inc. 3.43% Morgan Stanley 3.89% Citigroup Inc. 4.17%

iShares Morningstar Mid-Cap ETF   C-   HOLD

Ticker	Traded On	NAV		Total Assets ($)	Dividend Yield (TTM)	Turnover Ratio	Expense Ratio
JKG	NYSE Arca	161.81		$706,688,215	1.62	50	0.25

Ratings
Reward   C
Risk   D+
Recent Upgrade/Downgrade   Down

Fund Information
Fund Type   Exchange Traded Funds
Category   US Equity Mid Cap
Sub-Category   Mid-Cap Blend
Prospectus Objective   Growth
Inception Date   Jun-04
Open to New Investments   Y

Prices
Price (as of 12/31/2018)   161.64
52-Week High   194.75
52-Week Low   152.72

Total Returns (%)

3-Month	6-Month	1-Year	3-Year	5-Year
-14.02	-10.99	-11.41	18.78	35.15

3-Year Standard Deviation   10.73
Effective Duration

Valuation
Premium/Discount (1-Year Average)   0.06

Company Information
Provider   iShares
Manager/Tenure   Diane Hsiung (10), Greg Savage (10), Jennifer Hsui (6), 3 others
Website   http://www.ishares.com
Address   iShares 400 Howard Street San Francisco CA 94105 United States
Phone Number   800-474-2737

PERFORMANCE

Ratings History

Date	Overall Rating	Risk Rating	Reward Rating
Q4-18	C-	D+	C
Q2-18	C	D+	C
Q4-17	B	B+	B
Q4-16	C+	C-	B-
Q4-15	C	C-	C

Asset & Performance History

Date	NAV	1-Year Total Return
2017	185.63	19.57
2016	157.42	12.13
2015	143.01	-1.6
2014	147.45	15.63
2013	129.37	32.47
2012	98.95	17.73

Total Assets: $706,688,215
Asset Allocation

Asset	%
Cash	0%
Stocks	100%
US Stocks	99%
Bonds	0%
US Bonds	0%
Other	0%

Services Offered:

Investment Strategy: The investment seeks to track the investment results of the Morningstar® Mid Core IndexSM composed of mid-capitalization U.S. equities. The fund generally invests at least 90% of its assets in securities of the underlying index and in depositary receipts representing securities of the underlying index. The underlying index measures the performance of stocks issued by mid-capitalization companies that have exhibited average "growth" and "value" characteristics as determined by Morningstar, Inc.'s ("Morningstar" or the "index provider") proprietary index methodology. **Top Holdings:** Centene Corp Ingersoll-Rand PLC Xilinx Inc Agilent Technologies Inc Ventas Inc

---

WisdomTree U.S. SmallCap Earnings Fund   C-   HOLD

Ticker	Traded On	NAV		Total Assets ($)	Dividend Yield (TTM)	Turnover Ratio	Expense Ratio
EES	NYSE Arca	32.02		$703,134,873	1.41	48	0.38

Ratings
Reward   C-
Risk   C-
Recent Upgrade/Downgrade   Down

Fund Information
Fund Type   Exchange Traded Funds
Category   US Equity Small Cap
Sub-Category   Small Blend
Prospectus Objective   Small Company
Inception Date   Feb-07
Open to New Investments   Y

Prices
Price (as of 12/31/2018)   32.04
52-Week High   40.77
52-Week Low   30.28

Total Returns (%)

3-Month	6-Month	1-Year	3-Year	5-Year
-18.11	-17.19	-9.96	31.70	25.04

3-Year Standard Deviation   15.56
Effective Duration

Valuation
Premium/Discount (1-Year Average)   0.12

Company Information
Provider   WisdomTree
Manager/Tenure   Richard A. Brown (10), Thomas J. Durante (10), Karen Q. Wong (10)
Website   http://www.wisdomtree.com
Address   WisdomTree 245 Park Avenue, 35th floor New York NY 10167 United States
Phone Number   866-909-9473

PERFORMANCE

Ratings History

Date	Overall Rating	Risk Rating	Reward Rating
Q4-18	C-	C-	C-
Q2-18	C+	C-	B-
Q4-17	B+	B	A-
Q4-16	C	D+	B-
Q4-15	C	C-	C

Asset & Performance History

Date	NAV	1-Year Total Return
2017	36.14	12.56
2016	32.43	29.95
2015	25.25	-7.08
2014	27.53	2.19
2013	27.22	45.41
2012	18.88	15.41

Total Assets: $703,134,873
Asset Allocation

Asset	%
Cash	0%
Stocks	100%
US Stocks	99%
Bonds	0%
US Bonds	0%
Other	0%

Services Offered:

Investment Strategy: The investment seeks to track the price and yield performance, before fees and expenses, of the WisdomTree U.S. SmallCap Earnings Index. Under normal circumstances, at least 95% of the fund's total assets (exclusive of collateral held from securities lending) will be invested in component securities of the index and investments that have economic characteristics that are substantially identical to the economic characteristics of such component securities. The index is a fundamentally weighted index that is comprised of earnings-generating companies within the small-capitalization segment of the U.S. stock market. The fund is non-diversified. **Top Holdings:** Match Group Inc Premier Inc Class A Kemet Corp EnPro Industries Inc Warrior Met Coal Inc

First Trust Rising Dividend Achievers ETF   C   HOLD

Ticker	Traded On	NAV	Total Assets ($)	Dividend Yield (TTM)	Turnover Ratio	Expense Ratio
RDVY	NAS CM	26.53	$697,688,721	1.32	40	0.5

Ratings

Reward	C
Risk	C+
Recent Upgrade/Downgrade	Down

Fund Information

Fund Type	Exchange Traded Funds
Category	US Equity Large Cap Value
Sub-Category	Large Value
Prospectus Objective	Income
Inception Date	Jan-14
Open to New Investments	Y

Prices

Price (as of 12/31/2018)	26.51
52-Week High	31.91
52-Week Low	24.76

Total Returns (%)

3-Month	6-Month	1-Year	3-Year	5-Year
-15.51	-10.55	-9.72	34.84	46.00

3-Year Standard Deviation	11.51
Effective Duration	

Valuation

Premium/Discount (1-Year Average)	0.09

Company Information

Provider	First Trust
Manager/Tenure	Jon C. Erickson (4), Daniel J. Lindquist (4), David G. McGarel (4), 3 others
Website	http://www.ftportfolios.com/
Address	First Trust 120 E. Liberty Drive, Suite 400 Wheaton IL 60187 United States
Phone Number	800-621-1675

PERFORMANCE

Ratings History

Date	Overall Rating	Risk Rating	Reward Rating
Q4-18	C	C+	C
Q2-18	C+	C+	C+
Q4-17	B	B	B+
Q4-16	C	C-	C+
Q4-15	D+	C-	C

Asset & Performance History

Date	NAV	1-Year Total Return
2017	29.84	22.56
2016	24.67	21.88
2015	20.73	-2.88
2014	21.79	11.5
2013		
2012		

Total Assets: $697,688,721

Asset Allocation

Asset	%
Cash	0%
Stocks	100%
US Stocks	100%
Bonds	0%
US Bonds	0%
Other	0%

Services Offered:

Investment Strategy: The investment seeks investment results that correspond generally to the price and yield (before the fees and expenses) of the NASDAQ US Rising Dividend Achievers Index. The fund will normally invest at least 90% of its net assets (including investment borrowings) in securities that comprise the index. The index is composed of the securities of 50 companies with a history of raising their dividends and exhibit the characteristics to continue to do so in the future ("index securities"). The index is designed to provide access to a diversified portfolio of small, mid and large capitalization income producing securities. **Top Holdings:** Foot Locker Inc Starbucks Corp Sanderson Farms Inc Hormel Foods Corp Omnicom Group Inc

---

First Trust Europe AlphaDEX® Fund   D+   SELL

Ticker	Traded On	NAV	Total Assets ($)	Dividend Yield (TTM)	Turnover Ratio	Expense Ratio
FEP	NAS CM	31.11	$694,352,049	2.84	100	0.8

Ratings

Reward	D+
Risk	C-
Recent Upgrade/Downgrade	Down

Fund Information

Fund Type	Exchange Traded Funds
Category	Europe Equity Large Cap
Sub-Category	Europe Stock
Prospectus Objective	Foreign Stock
Inception Date	Apr-11
Open to New Investments	Y

Prices

Price (as of 12/31/2018)	30.98
52-Week High	42.36
52-Week Low	30.01

Total Returns (%)

3-Month	6-Month	1-Year	3-Year	5-Year
-18.59	-17.31	-18.66	11.60	4.15

3-Year Standard Deviation	14.07
Effective Duration	

Valuation

Premium/Discount (1-Year Average)	0.02

Company Information

Provider	First Trust
Manager/Tenure	Jon C. Erickson (7), Daniel J. Lindquist (7), David G. McGarel (7), 3 others
Website	http://www.ftportfolios.com/
Address	First Trust 120 E. Liberty Drive, Suite 400 Wheaton IL 60187 United States
Phone Number	800-621-1675

PERFORMANCE

Ratings History

Date	Overall Rating	Risk Rating	Reward Rating
Q4-18	D+	C-	D+
Q2-18	C+	C+	B-
Q4-17	B+	B	A-
Q4-16	D+	C-	D
Q4-15	C	C+	C-

Asset & Performance History

Date	NAV	1-Year Total Return
2017	39.07	35.68
2016	29.32	1.23
2015	29.61	2.46
2014	29.5	-8.91
2013	33.1	31.33
2012	25.68	22.08

Total Assets: $694,352,049

Asset Allocation

Asset	%
Cash	0%
Stocks	99%
US Stocks	1%
Bonds	0%
US Bonds	0%
Other	1%

Services Offered:

Investment Strategy: The investment seeks investment results that correspond generally to the price and yield (before the fund's fees and expenses) of an equity index called the NASDAQ AlphaDEX® Europe Index (the "index"). The fund will normally invest at least 90% of its net assets (including investment borrowings) in common stocks and/or depositary receipts that comprise the index. The index is designed to select stocks from the NASDAQ Europe Index (the "base index") that may generate positive alpha, or risk-adjusted returns, relative to traditional indices through the use of the AlphaDEX® selection methodology. **Top Holdings:** Acciona SA Polymetal International PLC Hufvudstaden AB A Deutsche Lufthansa AG Porsche Automobil Holding SE Participating Preferred

iShares U.S. Regional Banks ETF

B- **BUY**

Ticker	Traded On	NAV
IAT	NYSE Arca	39.86

Total Assets ($)	Dividend Yield (TTM)	Turnover Ratio	Expense Ratio
$691,335,073	1.87	4	0.43

Ratings
Reward	B
Risk	C
Recent Upgrade/Downgrade	Down

Fund Information
Fund Type	Exchange Traded Funds
Category	Financials Sector Equity
Sub-Category	Financial
Prospectus Objective	Financial
Inception Date	May-06
Open to New Investments	Y

Prices
Price (as of 12/31/2018)	39.84
52-Week High	54.54
52-Week Low	37.63

Total Returns (%)
3-Month	6-Month	1-Year	3-Year	5-Year
-17.54	-18.50	-17.38	20.70	32.11

3-Year Standard Deviation	18.71
Effective Duration	

Valuation
Premium/Discount (1-Year Average)	-0.01

Company Information
Provider	iShares
Manager/Tenure	Diane Hsiung (10), Greg Savage (10), Jennifer Hsui (6), 3 others
Website	http://www.ishares.com
Address	iShares 400 Howard Street San Francisco CA 94105 United States
Phone Number	800-474-2737

PERFORMANCE

Ratings History
Date	Overall Rating	Risk Rating	Reward Rating
Q4-18	B-	C	B
Q2-18	B	C+	B+
Q4-17	B+	B-	A
Q4-16	B	C+	B+
Q4-15	B+	B+	B+

Asset & Performance History
Date	NAV	1-Year Total Return
2017	49.29	10.53
2016	45.33	32.18
2015	34.96	1.73
2014	34.97	7.58
2013	33.06	37.59
2012	24.44	17.88

Total Assets: $691,335,073
Asset Allocation
Asset	%
Cash	0%
Stocks	100%
US Stocks	99%
Bonds	0%
US Bonds	0%
Other	0%

Services Offered:

Investment Strategy: The investment seeks to track the investment results of the Dow Jones U.S. Select Regional Banks Index. The fund generally invests at least 90% of its assets in securities of the index and in depositary receipts representing securities of the index. The underlying index measures the performance of the regional bank sector of the U.S. equity market and is a subset of the Dow Jones U.S. Bank Index. The fund is non-diversified. **Top Holdings:** US Bancorp PNC Financial Services Group Inc BB&T Corp SunTrust Banks Inc M&T Bank Corp

---

Fidelity® MSCI Real Estate Index ETF

C **HOLD**

Ticker	Traded On	NAV
FREL	NYSE Arca	22.37

Total Assets ($)	Dividend Yield (TTM)	Turnover Ratio	Expense Ratio
$690,700,119	5.19	8	0.08

Ratings
Reward	C
Risk	C+
Recent Upgrade/Downgrade	Down

Fund Information
Fund Type	Exchange Traded Funds
Category	Real Estate Sector Equity
Sub-Category	Real Estate
Prospectus Objective	Real Estate
Inception Date	Feb-15
Open to New Investments	Y

Prices
Price (as of 12/31/2018)	22.39
52-Week High	25.35
52-Week Low	21.52

Total Returns (%)
3-Month	6-Month	1-Year	3-Year	5-Year
-5.52	-5.45	-4.49	12.40	

3-Year Standard Deviation	11.81
Effective Duration	

Valuation
Premium/Discount (1-Year Average)	0.02

Company Information
Provider	Fidelity Investments
Manager/Tenure	Jennifer Hsui (3), Greg Savage (3), Alan Mason (2), 2 others
Website	http://www.institutional.fidelity.com
Address	Fidelity Investments 82 Devonshire Street Boston MA 2109 United States
Phone Number	617-563-7000

PERFORMANCE

Ratings History
Date	Overall Rating	Risk Rating	Reward Rating
Q4-18	C	C+	C
Q2-18	C	C-	C
Q4-17	B-	B	C
Q4-16	C-	C	C
Q4-15	U		

Asset & Performance History
Date	NAV	1-Year Total Return
2017	24.68	8.91
2016	23.42	8.06
2015	22.55	
2014		
2013		
2012		

Total Assets: $690,700,119
Asset Allocation
Asset	%
Cash	0%
Stocks	100%
US Stocks	100%
Bonds	0%
US Bonds	0%
Other	0%

Services Offered:

Investment Strategy: The investment seeks to provide investment returns that correspond, before fees and expenses, generally to the performance of the MSCI USA IMI Real Estate Index. The fund invests at least 80% of assets in securities included in the fund's underlying index. The fund's underlying index is the MSCI USA IMI Real Estate Index, which represents the performance of the real estate sector in the U.S. equity market. It may or may not hold all of the securities in the MSCI USA IMI Real Estate Index. **Top Holdings:** American Tower Corp Simon Property Group Inc Crown Castle International Corp Prologis Inc Public Storage

---

iShares Ultra Short-Term Bond ETF   C   HOLD

Ticker	Traded On	NAV	Total Assets ($)	Dividend Yield (TTM)	Turnover Ratio	Expense Ratio
ICSH	BATS	50.05	$689,379,769	2.01	11	0.08

Ratings
Reward C
Risk C+
Recent Upgrade/Downgrade

Fund Information
Fund Type	Exchange Traded Funds
Category	US Fixed Income
Sub-Category	Ultrashort Bond
Prospectus Objective	Income
Inception Date	Dec-13
Open to New Investments	Y

Prices
Price (as of 12/31/2018)	50.08
52-Week High	50.21
52-Week Low	50.00

Total Returns (%)
3-Month	6-Month	1-Year	3-Year	5-Year
0.57	1.26	2.26	5.06	5.70

3-Year Standard Deviation 0.27
Effective Duration 0.39

Valuation
Premium/Discount (1-Year Average) 0.05

Company Information
Provider	iShares
Manager/Tenure	Richard Mejzak (4), Scott Radell (4)
Website	http://www.ishares.com
Address	iShares 400 Howard Street San Francisco CA 94105 United States
Phone Number	800-474-2737

PERFORMANCE

Ratings History				Asset & Performance History			Total Assets:	$689,379,769
Date	Overall Rating	Risk Rating	Reward Rating	Date	NAV	1-Year Total Return	Asset Allocation Asset	%
Q4-18	C	C+	C	2017	50.03	1.53	Cash	63%
Q2-18	C-	C-	C	2016	49.95	1.18	Stocks	0%
Q4-17	B-	A-	C	2015	49.8	0.17	US Stocks	0%
Q4-16	C-	D+	C	2014	49.98	0.43	Bonds	36%
Q4-15	D+	D+	D+	2013	49.99		US Bonds	18%
				2012			Other	0%

Services Offered:

Investment Strategy: The investment seeks to provide current income consistent with preservation of capital. The fund seeks to achieve its investment objective by investing, under normal circumstances, at least 80% of its net assets in a portfolio of U.S. dollar-denominated investment-grade fixed- and floating-rate debt securities that are rated BBB- or higher by S&P Global Ratings and/or Fitch Ratings, Inc. ("Fitch"), or Baa3 or higher by Moody's Investors Service, Inc. ("Moody's"), or, if unrated, determined by BFA to be of equivalent quality. **Top Holdings:** Suncorp-Metway Limited 2.98%   Jackson National Life Global Funding 2.74%   American Honda Finance Corporation 2.59%   Volkswagen Group of America Finance LLC 3.88%   Morgan Stanley 2.38%

SPDR® S&P Health Care Equipment ETF   C   HOLD

Ticker	Traded On	NAV	Total Assets ($)	Dividend Yield (TTM)	Turnover Ratio	Expense Ratio
XHE	NYSE Arca	70.12	$686,130,387	0.04	40	0.35

Ratings
Reward C
Risk C+
Recent Upgrade/Downgrade Down

Fund Information
Fund Type	Exchange Traded Funds
Category	Healthcare Sector Equity
Sub-Category	Health
Prospectus Objective	Health
Inception Date	Jan-11
Open to New Investments	Y

Prices
Price (as of 12/31/2018)	70.07
52-Week High	88.81
52-Week Low	63.69

Total Returns (%)
3-Month	6-Month	1-Year	3-Year	5-Year
-19.26	-10.70	9.28	60.03	102.97

3-Year Standard Deviation 16.22
Effective Duration

Valuation
Premium/Discount (1-Year Average) 0.15

Company Information
Provider	SPDR State Street Global Advisors
Manager/Tenure	Michael J. Feehily (7), Karl A. Schneider (4), Kala O'Donnell (1)
Website	http://www.spdrs.com
Address	SPDR State Street Global Advisors State Street Financial Center, 1 Lincoln Street Boston MA 02111-2900 United States
Phone Number	617-786-3000

PERFORMANCE

Ratings History				Asset & Performance History			Total Assets:	$686,130,387
Date	Overall Rating	Risk Rating	Reward Rating	Date	NAV	1-Year Total Return	Asset Allocation Asset	%
Q4-18	C	C+	C	2017	64.22	29.99	Cash	0%
Q2-18	B	C-	A-	2016	49.79	11.71	Stocks	100%
Q4-17	A-	B+	A-	2015	44.28	9.09	US Stocks	100%
Q4-16	C	C-	B-	2014	43.59	16.25	Bonds	0%
Q4-15	C	C-	C+	2013	38.19	36.31	US Bonds	0%
				2012	28.08	16.53	Other	0%

Services Offered:

Investment Strategy: The investment seeks to provide investment results that, before fees and expenses, correspond generally to the total return performance of an index derived from the health care equipment and supplies segment of a U.S. total market composite index. In seeking to track the performance of the S&P Health Care Equipment Select Industry Index (the "index"), the fund employs a sampling strategy. It generally invests substantially all, but at least 80%, of its total assets in the securities comprising the index. The index represents the health care equipment segment of the S&P Total Market Index ("S&P TMI"). The fund is non-diversified. **Top Holdings:** Hologic Inc   Varian Medical Systems Inc   Edwards Lifesciences Corp   Orthofix Medical Inc   Abbott Laboratories

Principal Active Global Dividend Income ETF

D+ SELL

Ticker	Traded On	NAV	Total Assets ($)	Dividend Yield (TTM)	Turnover Ratio	Expense Ratio
GDVD	BATS	24.30	$682,374,107	2.87	22	0.58

Ratings
Reward	D+
Risk	D+
Recent Upgrade/Downgrade	

Fund Information
Fund Type	Exchange Traded Funds
Category	Global Equity Large Cap
Sub-Category	World Large Stock
Prospectus Objective	Growth & Inc
Inception Date	May-17
Open to New Investments	Y

Prices
Price (as of 12/31/2018)	24.25
52-Week High	29.52
52-Week Low	23.59

Total Returns (%)
3-Month	6-Month	1-Year	3-Year	5-Year
-13.17	-9.48	-10.35		

3-Year Standard Deviation	
Effective Duration	

Valuation
Premium/Discount (1-Year Average)	0.39

Company Information
Provider	Principal Funds
Manager/Tenure	Daniel R. Coleman (1), Paul S. Kim (1), Cliff Remily (1), 1 other
Website	http://www.principalfunds.com
Address	Principal Funds 30 Dan Road Canton MA 2021 United States
Phone Number	800-787-1621

PERFORMANCE

Ratings History
Date	Overall Rating	Risk Rating	Reward Rating
Q4-18	D+	D+	D+
Q2-18	D+	D	C-
Q4-17	U		
Q4-16			
Q4-15			

Asset & Performance History
Date	NAV	1-Year Total Return
2017	27.84	
2016		
2015		
2014		
2013		
2012		

Total Assets: $682,374,107

Asset Allocation
Asset	%
Cash	0%
Stocks	100%
US Stocks	43%
Bonds	0%
US Bonds	0%
Other	0%

Services Offered:

Investment Strategy: The investment seeks current income and long-term growth of income and capital. The fund is an actively managed ETF that seeks to achieve its investment objective by investing, under normal circumstances, at least 80% of its net assets, plus any borrowings for investment purposes, in dividend-paying equity securities at the time of purchase. It invests in equity securities of small, medium and large market capitalization companies and in growth and value stocks. **Top Holdings:** Microsoft Corp Taiwan Semiconductor Manufacturing Co Ltd ADR Pfizer Inc Roche Holding AG Dividend Right Cert. JPMorgan Chase & Co

---

Invesco CEF Income Composite ETF

C HOLD

Ticker	Traded On	NAV	Total Assets ($)	Dividend Yield (TTM)	Turnover Ratio	Expense Ratio
PCEF	NYSE Arca	20.20	$680,971,954	7.81		2.07

Ratings
Reward	D+
Risk	C+
Recent Upgrade/Downgrade	

Fund Information
Fund Type	Exchange Traded Funds
Category	Cautious Allocation
Sub-Category	Allocation--30% to 50% Equity
Prospectus Objective	Income
Inception Date	Feb-10
Open to New Investments	Y

Prices
Price (as of 12/31/2018)	20.23
52-Week High	24.17
52-Week Low	19.45

Total Returns (%)
3-Month	6-Month	1-Year	3-Year	5-Year
-9.73	-7.84	-8.89	18.68	22.81

3-Year Standard Deviation	6.91
Effective Duration	

Valuation
Premium/Discount (1-Year Average)	0.11

Company Information
Provider	Invesco
Manager/Tenure	Peter Hubbard (8), Michael Jeanette (8), Tony Seisser (4), 1 other
Website	http://www.invesco.com/us
Address	Invesco 11 Greenway Plaza, Ste. 2500 Houston TX 77046 United States
Phone Number	800-659-1005

PERFORMANCE

Ratings History
Date	Overall Rating	Risk Rating	Reward Rating
Q4-18	C	C+	D+
Q2-18	C	C-	C
Q4-17	B-	B	B-
Q4-16	C	C-	C
Q4-15	C	C+	C-

Asset & Performance History
Date	NAV	1-Year Total Return
2017	23.87	14.18
2016	22.44	14.08
2015	21.31	-1.56
2014	23.6	5.12
2013	24.25	4.22
2012	25.2	15.76

Total Assets: $680,971,954

Asset Allocation
Asset	%
Cash	-1%
Stocks	27%
US Stocks	20%
Bonds	67%
US Bonds	47%
Other	-2%

Services Offered:

Investment Strategy: The investment seeks to track the investment results (before fees and expenses) of the S-Network Composite Closed-End Fund IndexSM. The fund generally invests at least 90% of its total assets in securities of U.S.-listed closed-end funds that comprise the underlying index. It is a "fund of funds," as it invests its assets in the common shares of funds included in the underlying index rather than in individual securities (the "underlying funds"). **Top Holdings:** Nuveen Pref & Income Securities Fund EV Limited Duration Income BlackRock Enhanced Equity Div BlackRock Credit Allocation Inc EV Tax-Mgd Gbl Div Equity Income

Direxion Daily S&P Biotech Bull 3X Shares   D   SELL

Ticker	Traded On	NAV	Total Assets ($)	Dividend Yield (TTM)	Turnover Ratio	Expense Ratio
LABU	NYSE Arca	33.03	$677,547,521	0.22	642	1.08

Ratings

Reward	D
Risk	D
Recent Upgrade/Downgrade	Down

Fund Information

Fund Type	Exchange Traded Funds
Category	Trading Tools
Sub-Category	Trading--Leveraged Equity
Prospectus Objective	Technology
Inception Date	May-15
Open to New Investments	Y

Prices

Price (as of 12/31/2018)	32.86
52-Week High	114.79
52-Week Low	25.21

Total Returns (%)

3-Month	6-Month	1-Year	3-Year	5-Year
-62.76	-66.28	-57.27	-60.71	

3-Year Standard Deviation	86.13
Effective Duration	

Valuation

Premium/Discount (1-Year Average)	0.02

Company Information

Provider	Direxion Funds
Manager/Tenure	Paul Brigandi (3), Tony Ng (3)
Website	http://www.direxionfunds.com
Address	Direxion Funds 1301 Avenue Of The Americas (6th Avenue) New York NY 10019 United States
Phone Number	646-572-3390

PERFORMANCE

Ratings History

Date	Overall Rating	Risk Rating	Reward Rating
Q4-18	D	D	D
Q2-18	C	D+	C
Q4-17	C-	D+	C
Q4-16	D	D-	D
Q4-15	U		

Asset & Performance History

Date	NAV	1-Year Total Return
2017	77.65	148.69
2016	31.28	-63.02
2015	84.6	
2014		
2013		
2012		

Total Assets: $677,547,521

Asset Allocation

Asset	%
Cash	96%
Stocks	4%
US Stocks	4%
Bonds	0%
US Bonds	0%
Other	0%

Services Offered:

Investment Strategy: The investment seeks daily investment results, before fees and expenses, of 300% of the daily performance of the S&P Biotechnology Select Industry Index ("index"). The fund invests at least 80% of its net assets (plus borrowing for investment purposes) in securities of the index, exchange-traded funds ("ETFs") that track the index and other financial instruments that provide daily leveraged exposure to the index or ETFs that track the index. The index is designed to measure the performance of the biotechnology sub-industry based on the Global Industry Classification Standards ("GICS"). The fund is non-diversified. **Top Holdings:** SPDR® S&P Biotech ETF   S&P Biotechnology Select   S&P Biotechnology Select   S&P Biotechnology Select   Morgan Stanley Ilf/Treas/

Invesco Dynamic Large Cap Growth ETF   C   HOLD

Ticker	Traded On	NAV	Total Assets ($)	Dividend Yield (TTM)	Turnover Ratio	Expense Ratio
PWB	NYSE Arca	41.49	$672,400,334	0.67	119	0.57

Ratings

Reward	C+
Risk	C
Recent Upgrade/Downgrade	Down

Fund Information

Fund Type	Exchange Traded Funds
Category	US Equity Large Cap Growth
Sub-Category	Large Growth
Prospectus Objective	Growth
Inception Date	Mar-05
Open to New Investments	Y

Prices

Price (as of 12/31/2018)	41.47
52-Week High	48.53
52-Week Low	38.42

Total Returns (%)

3-Month	6-Month	1-Year	3-Year	5-Year
-14.19	-7.46	1.06	35.80	66.13

3-Year Standard Deviation	9.93
Effective Duration	

Valuation

Premium/Discount (1-Year Average)	0.07

Company Information

Provider	Invesco
Manager/Tenure	Peter Hubbard (11), Michael Jeanette (10), Tony Seisser (4), 1 other
Website	http://www.invesco.com/us
Address	Invesco 11 Greenway Plaza, Ste. 2500 Houston TX 77046 United States
Phone Number	800-659-1005

PERFORMANCE

Ratings History

Date	Overall Rating	Risk Rating	Reward Rating
Q4-18	C	C	C+
Q2-18	B-	C	B+
Q4-17	A-	B	A
Q4-16	C+	C	B
Q4-15	B-	C	B

Asset & Performance History

Date	NAV	1-Year Total Return
2017	41.44	30.54
2016	31.93	2.93
2015	31.28	7.78
2014	29.22	13.5
2013	25.86	37.32
2012	18.92	18.63

Total Assets: $672,400,334

Asset Allocation

Asset	%
Cash	0%
Stocks	100%
US Stocks	100%
Bonds	0%
US Bonds	0%
Other	0%

Services Offered:

Investment Strategy: The investment seeks to track the investment results (before fees and expenses) of the Dynamic Large Cap Growth IntellidexSM Index. The fund generally will invest at least 90% of its total assets in common stocks of large capitalization companies that comprise the underlying intellidex. The intellidex provider. considers a company to be a large capitalization company if it falls within the underlying intellidex model. The underlying intellidex for the fund is composed of 50 large capitalization U.S. growth stocks that the intellidex provider includes principally on the basis of their capital appreciation potential. **Top Holdings:** Abbott Laboratories   UnitedHealth Group Inc   Dollar General Corp   American Express Co   Automatic Data Processing Inc

VictoryShares US 500 Volatility Wtd ETF   C-   HOLD

Ticker	Traded On	NAV	Total Assets ($)	Dividend Yield (TTM)	Turnover Ratio	Expense Ratio
CFA	NAS CM	43.96	$668,594,992	1.35	26	0.35

Ratings
Reward	C-
Risk	C-
Recent Upgrade/Downgrade	Down

Fund Information
Fund Type	Exchange Traded Funds
Category	US Equity Large Cap Blend
Sub-Category	Large Blend
Prospectus Objective	Income
Inception Date	Jul-14
Open to New Investments	Y

Prices
Price (as of 12/31/2018)	43.98
52-Week High	52.58
52-Week Low	41.41

Total Returns (%)
3-Month	6-Month	1-Year	3-Year	5-Year
-14.46	-10.32	-8.61	27.95	

3-Year Standard Deviation	9.95
Effective Duration	

Valuation
Premium/Discount (1-Year Average)	0.03

Company Information
Provider	VictoryShares
Manager/Tenure	Stephen Hammers (4), Mannik Dhillon (0)
Website	http://www.VictorySharesLiterature.com
Address	Victory Shares 4249 Easton Way, Suite 400 Columbus OH 43219 United States
Phone Number	

PERFORMANCE

Ratings History
Date	Overall Rating	Risk Rating	Reward Rating
Q4-18	C-	C-	C-
Q2-18	C	C-	C
Q4-17	B	B	B
Q4-16	C	C-	C
Q4-15	D	D+	D

Asset & Performance History
Date	NAV	1-Year Total Return
2017	48.76	22.38
2016	40.34	13.84
2015	35.78	-0.51
2014	36.43	
2013		
2012		

Total Assets: $668,594,992
Asset Allocation
Asset	%
Cash	0%
Stocks	100%
US Stocks	99%
Bonds	0%
US Bonds	0%
Other	0%

Services Offered:

Investment Strategy: The investment seeks to provide investment results that track the performance of the Nasdaq Victory US Large Cap 500 Volatility Weighted Index before fees and expenses. The fund seeks to achieve its investment objective by investing, under normal market conditions, at least 80% of its net assets directly or indirectly in the securities included in the Nasdaq Victory US Large Cap 500 Volatility Weighted Index, an unmanaged, volatility weighted index maintained exclusively by the index provider. The index identifies the 500 largest U.S. stocks by market capitalization measured at the time the index's constituent securities are determined.
Top Holdings: UGI Corp NextEra Energy Inc Exelon Corp Procter & Gamble Co Pfizer Inc

---

iShares 10-20 Year Treasury Bond ETF   D   SELL

Ticker	Traded On	NAV	Total Assets ($)	Dividend Yield (TTM)	Turnover Ratio	Expense Ratio
TLH	NYSE Arca	132.92	$668,403,104	2.21	27	0.15

Ratings
Reward	D
Risk	C-
Recent Upgrade/Downgrade	Down

Fund Information
Fund Type	Exchange Traded Funds
Category	US Fixed Income
Sub-Category	Long Government
Prospectus Objective	Govt Bond - Treasury
Inception Date	Jan-07
Open to New Investments	Y

Prices
Price (as of 12/31/2018)	133.51
52-Week High	136.01
52-Week Low	125.72

Total Returns (%)
3-Month	6-Month	1-Year	3-Year	5-Year
4.52	2.58	-0.10	4.89	21.56

3-Year Standard Deviation	5.9
Effective Duration	10.54

Valuation
Premium/Discount (1-Year Average)	0.01

Company Information
Provider	iShares
Manager/Tenure	Scott Radell (8), James Mauro (7)
Website	http://www.ishares.com
Address	iShares 400 Howard Street San Francisco CA 94105 United States
Phone Number	800-474-2737

PERFORMANCE

Ratings History
Date	Overall Rating	Risk Rating	Reward Rating
Q4-18	D	C-	D
Q2-18	D+	C-	D
Q4-17	C	C	C
Q4-16	C	C-	C
Q4-15	C	C-	C

Asset & Performance History
Date	NAV	1-Year Total Return
2017	136.05	4.05
2016	133.17	0.9
2015	134.37	1.27
2014	135.49	14.42
2013	121.06	-8.48
2012	135.34	4.08

Total Assets: $668,403,104
Asset Allocation
Asset	%
Cash	0%
Stocks	0%
US Stocks	0%
Bonds	100%
US Bonds	100%
Other	0%

Services Offered:

Investment Strategy: The investment seeks to track the investment results of the ICE U.S. Treasury 10-20 Year Bond Index. The fund generally invests at least 90% of its assets in the bonds of its underlying index and at least 95% of its assets in U.S. government bonds. It seeks to track the investment results of the underlying index which measures the performance of public obligations of the U.S. Treasury that have a remaining maturity of greater than ten years and less than or equal to twenty years. **Top Holdings:** United States Treasury Bonds 4.5% United States Treasury Bonds 4.38% United States Treasury Bonds 5% United States Treasury Bonds 6.25% United States Treasury Bonds 6.13%

SPDR S&P® North American Natural Resources ETF   C-   HOLD

Ticker	Traded On	NAV	Total Assets ($)	Dividend Yield (TTM)	Turnover Ratio	Expense Ratio
NANR	NYSE Arca	29.06	$664,029,188	1.6	20	0.35

Ratings
Reward   C
Risk   D+
Recent Upgrade/Downgrade   Down

Fund Information
Fund Type   Exchange Traded Funds
Category   Natural Resources
Sub-Category   Natural Resources
Prospectus Objective   Natl Res
Inception Date   Dec-15
Open to New Investments Y

Prices
Price (as of 12/31/2018)   28.98
52-Week High   37.64
52-Week Low   27.82

Total Returns (%)

3-Month	6-Month	1-Year	3-Year	5-Year
-14.96	-18.42	-16.50	26.57	

3-Year Standard Deviation
Effective Duration

Valuation
Premium/Discount (1-Year Average)   -0.02

Company Information
Provider   SPDR State Street Global Advisors
Manager/Tenure Michael J. Feehily (2), Karl A.
                Schneider (2), Emiliano Rabinovich (1)
Website   http://www.spdrs.com
Address   SPDR State Street Global Advisors
                State Street Financial Center, 1
                Lincoln Street Boston MA 02111-2900
                United States
Phone Number   617-786-3000

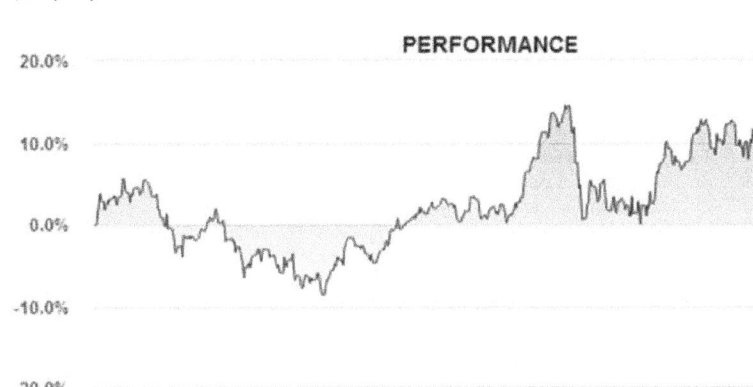

PERFORMANCE

Ratings History

Date	Overall Rating	Risk Rating	Reward Rating
Q4-18	C-	D+	C
Q2-18	C	C-	C+
Q4-17	C	B	D+
Q4-16	D	D+	D+
Q4-15			

Asset & Performance History

Date	NAV	1-Year Total Return
2017	35.44	7.98
2016	33.48	34.59
2015	25.06	
2014		
2013		
2012		

Total Assets: $664,029,188

Asset Allocation

Asset	%
Cash	0%
Stocks	100%
US Stocks	63%
Bonds	0%
US Bonds	0%
Other	0%

Services Offered:

Investment Strategy: The investment seeks to track the performance of the S&P BMI North American Natural Resources Index. The fund generally invests substantially all, but at least 80%, of its total assets in the securities comprising the index. The index comprises publicly traded large- and mid-capitalization U.S. and Canadian companies in the natural resources and commodities businesses that meet certain investability requirements and are classified within the sub-industries of one of three natural resources categories: energy, metals & mining or agriculture. The fund is non-diversified. **Top Holdings:** Exxon Mobil Corp   Chevron Corp   Nutrien Ltd   Newmont Mining Corp   Freeport-McMoRan Inc

---

SPDR® S&P Homebuilders ETF   C   HOLD

Ticker	Traded On	NAV	Total Assets ($)	Dividend Yield (TTM)	Turnover Ratio	Expense Ratio
XHB	NYSE Arca	32.52	$662,554,082	1.05	26	0.35

Ratings
Reward   B-
Risk   D+
Recent Upgrade/Downgrade   Down

Fund Information
Fund Type   Exchange Traded Funds
Category   Consumer Goods & Svcs
Sub-Category   Consumer Cyclical
Prospectus Objective   Real Estate
Inception Date   Jan-06
Open to New Investments Y

Prices
Price (as of 12/31/2018)   32.52
52-Week High   46.75
52-Week Low   30.74

Total Returns (%)

3-Month	6-Month	1-Year	3-Year	5-Year
-14.69	-17.10	-25.64	-2.33	1.34

3-Year Standard Deviation   16.9
Effective Duration

Valuation
Premium/Discount (1-Year Average)   0.04

Company Information
Provider   SPDR State Street Global Advisors
Manager/Tenure Michael J. Feehily (7), Karl A.
                Schneider (4), Raymond V. Donofrio (1)
Website   http://www.spdrs.com
Address   SPDR State Street Global Advisors
                State Street Financial Center, 1
                Lincoln Street Boston MA 02111-2900
                United States
Phone Number   617-786-3000

PERFORMANCE

Ratings History

Date	Overall Rating	Risk Rating	Reward Rating
Q4-18	C	D+	B-
Q2-18	B-	C	B
Q4-17	B+	B	A-
Q4-16	B-	C	B
Q4-15	B+	B	A-

Asset & Performance History

Date	NAV	1-Year Total Return
2017	44.22	31.65
2016	33.86	-0.28
2015	34.17	0.59
2014	34.13	3.15
2013	33.27	25.5
2012	26.6	57.53

Total Assets: $662,554,082

Asset Allocation

Asset	%
Cash	0%
Stocks	100%
US Stocks	96%
Bonds	0%
US Bonds	0%
Other	0%

Services Offered: Dividend Investment Plan, CashInvestment Plan

Investment Strategy: The investment seeks to provide investment results that, before fees and expenses, correspond generally to the total return performance of an index derived from the homebuilding segment of a U.S. total market composite index. In seeking to track the performance of the S&P Homebuilders Select Industry Index (the "index"), the fund employs a sampling strategy. It generally invests substantially all, but at least 80%, of its total assets in the securities comprising the index. The index represents the homebuilders segment of the S&P Total Market Index ("S&P TMI"). The fund is non-diversified. **Top Holdings:** Whirlpool Corp   PulteGroup Inc   NVR Inc   Johnson Controls International PLC   Toll Brothers Inc

SPDR® Portfolio Short Term Treasury ETF   C-   HOLD

Ticker	Traded On	NAV	Total Assets ($)	Dividend Yield (TTM)	Turnover Ratio	Expense Ratio
SPTS	NYSE Arca	29.58	$651,224,479	1.91	33	0.06

Ratings
Reward   D+
Risk   C
Recent Upgrade/Downgrade

Fund Information
Fund Type   Exchange Traded Funds
Category   US Fixed Income
Sub-Category   Short Government
Prospectus Objective   Govt Bond - Treasury
Inception Date   Nov-11
Open to New Investments   Y

Prices
Price (as of 12/31/2018)   29.58
52-Week High   29.87
52-Week Low   29.34

Total Returns (%)

3-Month	6-Month	1-Year	3-Year	5-Year
1.30	1.50	1.07	2.59	4.56

3-Year Standard Deviation   1.31
Effective Duration   1.91

Valuation
Premium/Discount (1-Year Average)   0.02

Company Information
Provider   SPDR State Street Global Advisors
Manager/Tenure Joanna Madden (4), Cynthia Moy (2),
                Orhan Imer (1)
Website   http://www.spdrs.com
Address   SPDR State Street Global Advisors
                State Street Financial Center, 1
                Lincoln Street Boston MA 02111-2900
                United States
Phone Number   617-786-3000

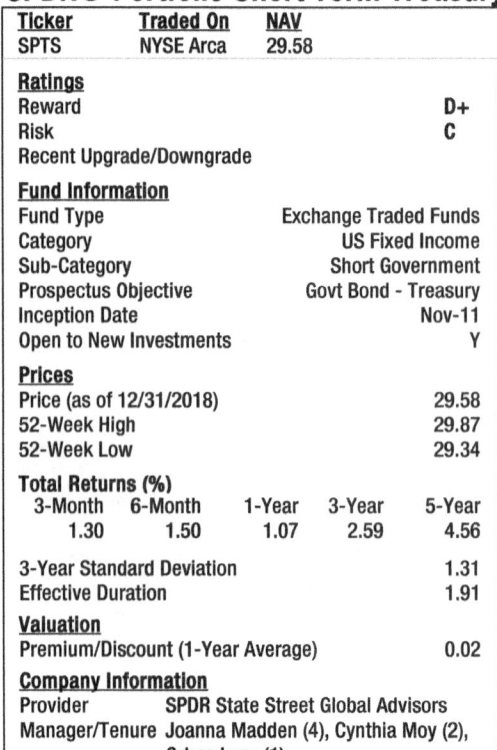

PERFORMANCE

Ratings History

Date	Overall Rating	Risk Rating	Reward Rating
Q4-18	C-	C	D+
Q2-18	C-	C	D
Q4-17	C	C	C
Q4-16	C	C-	C
Q4-15	C	C-	C

Asset & Performance History

Date	NAV	1-Year Total Return
2017	29.87	0.42
2016	30.06	0.89
2015	30.07	0.81
2014	30.07	1.09
2013	29.95	-0.26
2012	30.15	0.78

Total Assets: $651,224,479

Asset Allocation

Asset	%
Cash	3%
Stocks	0%
US Stocks	0%
Bonds	97%
US Bonds	97%
Other	0%

Services Offered:

Investment Strategy: The investment seeks to provide investment results that correspond generally to the price and yield performance of the Bloomberg Barclays 1-3 Year U.S. Treasury Index. The fund invests at least 80%, of its total assets in the securities comprising the index or in securities that the Adviser determines have economic characteristics that are substantially identical to the economic characteristics of the securities that comprise the index. The index is designed to measure the performance of short term (1-3 years) public obligations of the U.S. Treasury. The fund is non-diversified. **Top Holdings:** United States Treasury Notes 2.62% United States Treasury Notes 3.62% United States Treasury Notes 3.62% United States Treasury Notes 2.88% United States Treasury Notes 2.25%

ETFMG Alternative Harvest ETF   C   HOLD

Ticker	Traded On	NAV	Total Assets ($)	Dividend Yield (TTM)	Turnover Ratio	Expense Ratio
MJ	NYSE Arca	24.87	$650,695,358	0.69	97	0.75

Ratings
Reward   C-
Risk   C
Recent Upgrade/Downgrade   Up

Fund Information
Fund Type   Exchange Traded Funds
Category   Misc
Sub-Category   Miscellaneous Sector
Prospectus Objective   Unaligned
Inception Date   Dec-15
Open to New Investments   Y

Prices
Price (as of 12/31/2018)   24.94
52-Week High   43.01
52-Week Low   23.66

Total Returns (%)

3-Month	6-Month	1-Year	3-Year	5-Year
-38.51	-15.66	-23.00	27.67	

3-Year Standard Deviation
Effective Duration

Valuation
Premium/Discount (1-Year Average)   0.02

Company Information
Provider   ETF Managers Trust
Manager/Tenure Timothy J Collins (1), James B.
                Francis (0), Devin Ryder (0), 1 other
Website   http://www.ise.com/
Address   FACTORSHARES TRUST 35
                Beechwood Road, Suite. 2B Summit
                NJ 07901 United States
Phone Number   877-756-

PERFORMANCE

Ratings History

Date	Overall Rating	Risk Rating	Reward Rating
Q4-18	C	C	C-
Q2-18	C	C	C-
Q4-17	C	B	C-
Q4-16	D	D	D
Q4-15			

Asset & Performance History

Date	NAV	1-Year Total Return
2017	32.46	29.91
2016	24.18	9.65
2015	23.57	
2014		
2013		
2012		

Total Assets: $650,695,358

Asset Allocation

Asset	%
Cash	0%
Stocks	100%
US Stocks	17%
Bonds	0%
US Bonds	0%
Other	0%

Services Offered:

Investment Strategy: The investment seeks to provide investment results that, before fees and expenses, correspond generally to the total return performance of the Prime Alternative Harvest Index. The fund will invest at least 80% of its total assets, exclusive of collateral held from securities lending, in the component securities of the index and in ADRs and GDRs based on the component securities in the index. The index is concentrated in the Pharmaceuticals and Tobacco industries and tracks the performance of the exchange-listed common stock (or corresponding ADRs or GDRs) of companies across the globe. The fund is non-diversified. **Top Holdings:** Canopy Growth Corp Cronos Group Inc Tilray Inc Aurora Cannabis Inc GW Pharmaceuticals PLC ADR

Pacer Trendpilot™ US Mid Cap ETF   C-   HOLD

Ticker	Traded On	NAV	Total Assets ($)	Dividend Yield (TTM)	Turnover Ratio	Expense Ratio
PTMC	BATS	30.84	$647,765,164	0.67	66	0.62

Ratings
Reward	C-
Risk	C-
Recent Upgrade/Downgrade	Down

Fund Information
Fund Type	Exchange Traded Funds
Category	US Equity Mid Cap
Sub-Category	Mid-Cap Blend
Prospectus Objective	Growth
Inception Date	Jun-15
Open to New Investments	Y

Prices
Price (as of 12/31/2018)	30.84
52-Week High	33.83
52-Week Low	29.35

Total Returns (%)
3-Month	6-Month	1-Year	3-Year	5-Year
-5.89	-3.25	0.06	36.01	

3-Year Standard Deviation	8.59
Effective Duration	

Valuation
Premium/Discount (1-Year Average)	0.11

Company Information
Provider	Pacer
Manager/Tenure	Bruce Kavanaugh (3), Michael Mack (3)
Website	http://www.paceretfs.com
Address	Pacer 16 Industrial Blvd, Suite 201 Paoli PA 19301 United States
Phone Number	

PERFORMANCE

Ratings History
Date	Overall Rating	Risk Rating	Reward Rating
Q4-18	C-	C-	C-
Q2-18	C	C-	C
Q4-17	C	B	C+
Q4-16	D	C-	C-
Q4-15	U		

Asset & Performance History
Date	NAV	1-Year Total Return
2017	31.09	17.57
2016	26.62	15.99
2015	23.18	
2014		
2013		
2012		

Total Assets: $647,765,164
Asset Allocation
Asset	%
Cash	100%
Stocks	0%
US Stocks	0%
Bonds	0%
US Bonds	0%
Other	0%

Services Offered:

Investment Strategy: The investment seeks to track the total return performance, before fees and expenses, of the Pacer Trendpilot US Mid Cap Index. The fund invests at least 80% of its total assets (exclusive of collateral held from securities lending) in the component securities of the index. The index implements a systematic trend-following strategy that directs exposure (i) 100% to the &P MidCap 400, (ii) 50% to the S&P MidCap 400 and 50% to 3-Month U.S. Treasury bills, or (iii) 100% to 3-Month U.S. Treasury bills, depending on the relative performance of the S&P MidCap 400 TR and its 200-business day historical simple moving average. **Top Holdings:** PotlatchDeltic Corp   Domino's Pizza Inc   Keysight Technologies Inc   Jack Henry & Associates Inc   Teleflex Inc

---

SPDR® Bloomberg Barclays Intermediate Term Treasury ETF   D+   SELL

Ticker	Traded On	NAV	Total Assets ($)	Dividend Yield (TTM)	Turnover Ratio	Expense Ratio
ITE	NYSE Arca	59.38	$636,986,455	1.93	25	0.1

Ratings
Reward	D+
Risk	C-
Recent Upgrade/Downgrade	Down

Fund Information
Fund Type	Exchange Traded Funds
Category	US Fixed Income
Sub-Category	Intermediate Government
Prospectus Objective	Govt Bond - Treasury
Inception Date	May-07
Open to New Investments	Y

Prices
Price (as of 12/31/2018)	59.55
52-Week High	59.55
52-Week Low	57.65

Total Returns (%)
3-Month	6-Month	1-Year	3-Year	5-Year
2.97	2.60	1.94	3.99	7.69

3-Year Standard Deviation	2.25
Effective Duration	5.11

Valuation
Premium/Discount (1-Year Average)	-0.01

Company Information
Provider	SPDR State Street Global Advisors
Manager/Tenure	Joanna Madden (4), Cynthia Moy (2), Orhan Imer (1)
Website	http://www.spdrs.com
Address	SPDR State Street Global Advisors State Street Financial Center, 1 Lincoln Street Boston MA 02111-2900 United States
Phone Number	617-786-3000

PERFORMANCE

Ratings History
Date	Overall Rating	Risk Rating	Reward Rating
Q4-18	D+	C-	D+
Q2-18	D+	C-	D
Q4-17	C	C	C
Q4-16	C-	C-	C
Q4-15	C	C-	C

Asset & Performance History
Date	NAV	1-Year Total Return
2017	59.43	0.85
2016	59.67	0.91
2015	59.83	1.07
2014	59.89	2.45
2013	59.08	-1.45
2012	60.83	1.61

Total Assets: $636,986,455
Asset Allocation
Asset	%
Cash	0%
Stocks	0%
US Stocks	0%
Bonds	100%
US Bonds	100%
Other	0%

Services Offered:

Investment Strategy: The investment seeks to provide investment results that correspond generally to the price and yield performance of the Bloomberg Barclays 3-10 Year U.S. Treasury Index. The fund generally invests substantially all, but at least 80%, of its total assets in the securities comprising the index or in securities that the Adviser determines have economic characteristics that are substantially identical to the economic characteristics of the securities that comprise the index. The index is designed to measure the performance of intermediate term (3-10 years) public obligations of the U.S. Treasury. It is non-diversified. **Top Holdings:** United States Treasury Notes 2.88%   United States Treasury Notes 2.5%   United States Treasury Notes 2.88%   United States Treasury Notes 2.25%   United States Treasury Notes 2%

SPDR® S&P Retail ETF

C- HOLD

Ticker	Traded On	NAV		Total Assets ($)	Dividend Yield (TTM)	Turnover Ratio	Expense Ratio
XRT	NYSE Arca	41.01		$634,606,794	1.4	33	0.35

Ratings
Reward	C-
Risk	C-
Recent Upgrade/Downgrade	Down

Fund Information
Fund Type	Exchange Traded Funds
Category	Consumer Goods & Svcs
Sub-Category	Consumer Cyclical
Prospectus Objective	Unaligned
Inception Date	Jun-06
Open to New Investments	Y

Prices
Price (as of 12/31/2018)	40.99
52-Week High	52.50
52-Week Low	38.45

Total Returns (%)
3-Month	6-Month	1-Year	3-Year	5-Year
-18.73	-14.81	-8.01	-1.02	-0.78

3-Year Standard Deviation	15.81
Effective Duration	

Valuation
Premium/Discount (1-Year Average)	0.00

Company Information
Provider	SPDR State Street Global Advisors
Manager/Tenure	Michael J. Feehily (7), Karl A. Schneider (4), Ted Janowsky (1)
Website	http://www.spdrs.com
Address	SPDR State Street Global Advisors State Street Financial Center, 1 Lincoln Street Boston MA 02111-2900 United States
Phone Number	617-786-3000

PERFORMANCE

Ratings History
Date	Overall Rating	Risk Rating	Reward Rating
Q4-18	C-	C-	C-
Q2-18	C	C	C
Q4-17	D+	C	D
Q4-16	C	C	C
Q4-15	C+	C+	C

Asset & Performance History
Date	NAV	1-Year Total Return
2017	45.19	4.16
2016	44.1	2.97
2015	43.28	-8.8
2014	48.02	9.92
2013	44.04	42.16
2012	31.18	20.73

Total Assets: $634,606,794

Asset Allocation
Asset	%
Cash	0%
Stocks	100%
US Stocks	100%
Bonds	0%
US Bonds	0%
Other	0%

Services Offered:

Investment Strategy: The investment seeks to provide investment results that, before fees and expenses, correspond generally to the total return performance of an index derived from the retail segment of a U.S. total market composite index. In seeking to track the performance of the S&P Retail Select Industry Index (the "index"), the fund employs a sampling strategy. It generally invests substantially all, but at least 80%, of its total assets in the securities comprising the index. The index represents the retail segment of the S&P Total Market Index ("S&P TMI"). The fund is non-diversified. **Top Holdings:** Foot Locker Inc Walgreens Boots Alliance Inc Sally Beauty Holdings Inc Monro Inc L Brands Inc

---

SPDR® Nuveen S&P High Yield Municipal Bond ETF

C HOLD

Ticker	Traded On	NAV		Total Assets ($)	Dividend Yield (TTM)	Turnover Ratio	Expense Ratio
HYMB	NYSE Arca	55.83		$634,310,884	4.01	11	0.35

Ratings
Reward	C
Risk	C+
Recent Upgrade/Downgrade	

Fund Information
Fund Type	Exchange Traded Funds
Category	US Muni Fixed Inc
Sub-Category	High Yield Muni
Prospectus Objective	Muni Bond - Natl
Inception Date	Apr-11
Open to New Investments	Y

Prices
Price (as of 12/31/2018)	56.08
52-Week High	56.84
52-Week Low	55.15

Total Returns (%)
3-Month	6-Month	1-Year	3-Year	5-Year
0.22	1.06	3.80	10.14	33.01

3-Year Standard Deviation	3.95
Effective Duration	8.15

Valuation
Premium/Discount (1-Year Average)	-0.23

Company Information
Provider	SPDR State Street Global Advisors
Manager/Tenure	Steven M. Hlavin (7), Timothy T. Ryan (7)
Website	http://www.spdrs.com
Address	SPDR State Street Global Advisors State Street Financial Center, 1 Lincoln Street Boston MA 02111-2900 United States
Phone Number	617-786-3000

PERFORMANCE

Ratings History
Date	Overall Rating	Risk Rating	Reward Rating
Q4-18	C	C+	C
Q2-18	C	C-	C
Q4-17	C+	B+	C
Q4-16	C	C-	C
Q4-15	C	C-	C

Asset & Performance History
Date	NAV	1-Year Total Return
2017	56	3.51
2016	55.96	2.17
2015	56.96	3.7
2014	57.48	16.44
2013	51.71	-7
2012	58.34	16.79

Total Assets: $634,310,884

Asset Allocation
Asset	%
Cash	0%
Stocks	0%
US Stocks	0%
Bonds	100%
US Bonds	94%
Other	0%

Services Offered:

Investment Strategy: The investment seeks to provide investment results that correspond generally to the price and yield performance of the S&P Municipal Yield Index. The fund generally invests substantially all, but at least 80%, of its total assets in the securities comprising the index or in securities that the Sub-Adviser determines have economic characteristics that are substantially identical to the economic characteristics of the securities that comprise the index. The index tracks the U.S. high yield municipal bond market and to provide income that is exempt from federal income taxes. The fund is non-diversified. **Top Holdings:** GOLDEN ST TOB SECURITIZATION CORP CALIF 5.25% TOBACCO SETTLEMENT FING CORP VA 5% BUCKEYE OHIO TOB SETTLEMENT FING AUTH 5.88% NEW YORK LIBERTY DEV CORP 5% BUCKEYE OHIO TOB SETTLEMENT FING AUTH 5.75%

iShares Global Consumer Staples ETF   C-   HOLD

Ticker	Traded On	NAV
KXI	NYSE Arca	46.08

Total Assets ($)	Dividend Yield (TTM)	Turnover Ratio	Expense Ratio
$630,690,204	2.45	5	0.47

Ratings
Reward   C-
Risk   C-
Recent Upgrade/Downgrade

Fund Information
Fund Type   Exchange Traded Funds
Category   Consumer Goods & Svcs
Sub-Category   Consumer Defensive
Prospectus Objective   Unaligned
Inception Date   Sep-06
Open to New Investments   Y

Prices
Price (as of 12/31/2018)   45.97
52-Week High   54.53
52-Week Low   44.53

Total Returns (%)

3-Month	6-Month	1-Year	3-Year	5-Year
-6.99	-3.79	-10.59	6.35	20.46

3-Year Standard Deviation   9.11
Effective Duration

Valuation
Premium/Discount (1-Year Average)   -0.05

Company Information
Provider   iShares
Manager/Tenure   Diane Hsiung (10), Greg Savage (10),
                 Jennifer Hsui (6), 3 others
Website   http://www.ishares.com
Address   iShares 400 Howard Street San
                 Francisco CA 94105 United States
Phone Number   800-474-2737

PERFORMANCE

Ratings History

Date	Overall Rating	Risk Rating	Reward Rating
Q4-18	C-	C-	C-
Q2-18	C-	C-	C-
Q4-17	B-	B	C+
Q4-16	C	C	C+
Q4-15	C	C	C

Asset & Performance History

Date	NAV	1-Year Total Return
2017	53.04	17.37
2016	46.19	1.34
2015	46.61	6.11
2014	44.91	6.73
2013	43.06	19.93
2012	36.69	13.39

Total Assets: $630,690,204
Asset Allocation

Asset	%
Cash	0%
Stocks	100%
US Stocks	53%
Bonds	0%
US Bonds	0%
Other	0%

Services Offered:

Investment Strategy: The investment seeks to track the S&P Global 1200 Consumer Staples IndexTM. The fund generally invests at least 90% of its assets in securities of the underlying index and in depositary receipts representing securities of the underlying index. It may invest the remainder of its assets in certain futures, options and swap contracts, cash and cash equivalents, as well as in securities not included in the underlying index. The index measures the performance of companies that the index provider deems to be part of the consumer staples sector of the economy and that the index provider believes are important to global markets. **Top Holdings:** Nestle SA   Procter & Gamble Co   Coca-Cola Co   PepsiCo Inc   Walmart Inc

---

Direxion Daily Technology Bull 3X Shares   C   HOLD

Ticker	Traded On	NAV
TECL	NYSE Arca	84.92

Total Assets ($)	Dividend Yield (TTM)	Turnover Ratio	Expense Ratio
$626,679,072	0.44	0	1.09

Ratings
Reward   C
Risk   C-
Recent Upgrade/Downgrade   Down

Fund Information
Fund Type   Exchange Traded Funds
Category   Trading Tools
Sub-Category   Trading--Leveraged Equity
Prospectus Objective   Technology
Inception Date   Dec-08
Open to New Investments   Y

Prices
Price (as of 12/31/2018)   85.00
52-Week High   171.14
52-Week Low   68.96

Total Returns (%)

3-Month	6-Month	1-Year	3-Year	5-Year
-49.94	-38.03	-24.04	133.94	272.89

3-Year Standard Deviation   41.3
Effective Duration

Valuation
Premium/Discount (1-Year Average)   0.01

Company Information
Provider   Direxion Funds
Manager/Tenure   Paul Brigandi (9), Tony Ng (3)
Website   http://www.direxionfunds.com
Address   Direxion Funds 1301 Avenue Of The
                 Americas (6th Avenue) New York NY
                 10019 United States
Phone Number   646-572-3390

PERFORMANCE

Ratings History

Date	Overall Rating	Risk Rating	Reward Rating
Q4-18	C	C-	C
Q2-18	B	C+	A
Q4-17	B+	C+	A
Q4-16	C+	C-	B
Q4-15	C	C+	C

Asset & Performance History

Date	NAV	1-Year Total Return
2017	112.09	124.97
2016	49.87	36.89
2015	36.43	4.77
2014	34.77	52.13
2013	22.86	88.02
2012	12.16	33.2

Total Assets: $626,679,072
Asset Allocation

Asset	%
Cash	28%
Stocks	74%
US Stocks	74%
Bonds	-2%
US Bonds	-2%
Other	0%

Services Offered:

Investment Strategy: The investment seeks daily investment results, before fees and expenses, of 300% of the daily performance of the Technology Select Sector Index. The fund invests at least 80% of its net assets (plus borrowing for investment purposes) in securities of the index, ETFs that track the index and other financial instruments that provide daily leveraged exposure to the index or ETFs that track the index. The index includes domestic companies from the technology sector. It is non-diversified. **Top Holdings:** Technology Select Sector SPDR® ETF   Technology Select Sector   Technology Select Sector   Technology Select Sector   Technology Select Sector

First Trust Multi-Asset Diversified Income Index Fund

C   **HOLD**

Ticker	Traded On	NAV	Total Assets ($)	Dividend Yield (TTM)	Turnover Ratio	Expense Ratio
MDIV	NAS CM	16.84	$626,595,563	6.44	84	0.79

Ratings
Reward   C-
Risk   C+
Recent Upgrade/Downgrade

Fund Information
Fund Type   Exchange Traded Funds
Category   Moderate Allocation
Sub-Category   Allocation--50% to 70% Equity
Prospectus Objective   Income
Inception Date   Aug-12
Open to New Investments   Y

Prices
Price (as of 12/31/2018)   16.83
52-Week High   19.42
52-Week Low   16.21

Total Returns (%)
3-Month	6-Month	1-Year	3-Year	5-Year
-7.74	-5.20	-5.75	10.62	10.45

3-Year Standard Deviation   7.24
Effective Duration   2.68

Valuation
Premium/Discount (1-Year Average)   -0.03

Company Information
Provider   First Trust
Manager/Tenure   Jon C. Erickson (6), Daniel J. Lindquist (6), David G. McGarel (6), 3 others
Website   http://www.ftportfolios.com/
Address   First Trust 120 E. Liberty Drive, Suite 400 Wheaton IL 60187 United States
Phone Number   800-621-1675

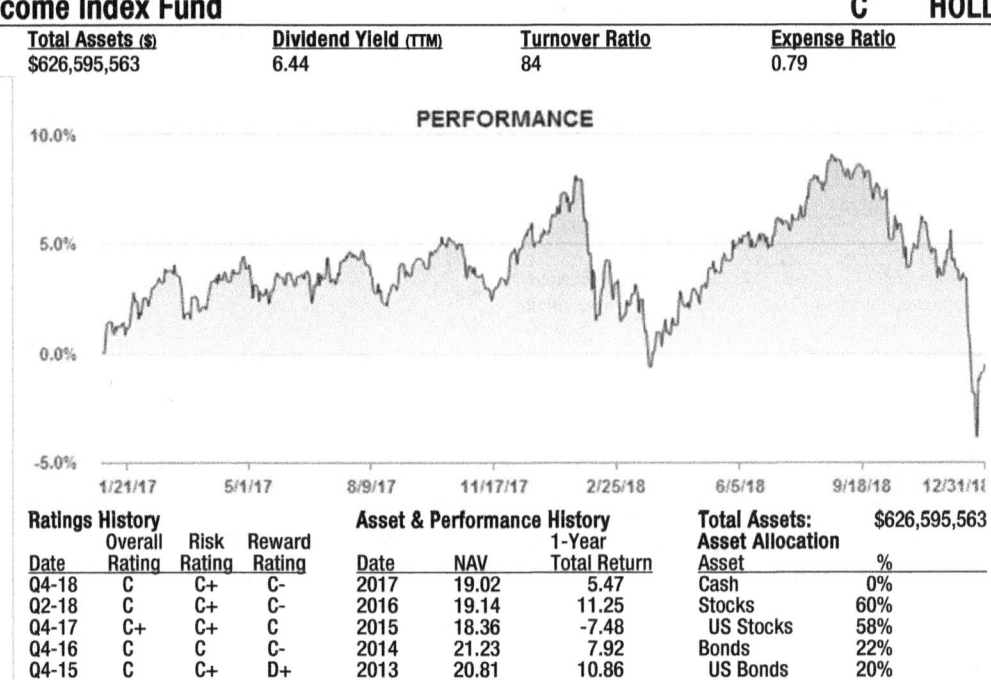

PERFORMANCE

Ratings History
Date	Overall Rating	Risk Rating	Reward Rating
Q4-18	C	C+	C-
Q2-18	C	C+	C-
Q4-17	C+	C+	C
Q4-16	C	C	C-
Q4-15	C	C+	D+

Asset & Performance History
Date	NAV	1-Year Total Return
2017	19.02	5.47
2016	19.14	11.25
2015	18.36	-7.48
2014	21.23	7.92
2013	20.81	10.86
2012	19.85	

Total Assets: $626,595,563
Asset Allocation
Asset	%
Cash	0%
Stocks	60%
US Stocks	58%
Bonds	22%
US Bonds	20%
Other	0%

Services Offered:

Investment Strategy: The investment seeks investment results that correspond generally to the price and yield (before the fund's fees and expenses) of an index called the NASDAQ US Multi-Asset Diversified Income IndexSM. The fund will normally invest at least 90% of its net assets (including investment borrowings) in the common stocks and/or depositary receipts (20%), real estate investment trusts ("REITs") (20%), preferred securities (20%), master limited partnerships ("MLPs") (20%) and an exchange-traded fund ("ETF")(20%) that comprise the index (each, an "index segment"). **Top Holdings:** First Trust Tactical High Yield ETF   Buckeye Partners LP   Chimera Investment Corp   Annaly Capital Management Inc   New Residential Investment Corp

---

First Trust Small Cap Core AlphaDEX® Fund

C-   **HOLD**

Ticker	Traded On	NAV	Total Assets ($)	Dividend Yield (TTM)	Turnover Ratio	Expense Ratio
FYX	NAS CM	54.33	$626,308,818	0.85	111	0.66

Ratings
Reward   C-
Risk   C-
Recent Upgrade/Downgrade   Down

Fund Information
Fund Type   Exchange Traded Funds
Category   US Equity Small Cap
Sub-Category   Small Blend
Prospectus Objective   Small Company
Inception Date   May-07
Open to New Investments   Y

Prices
Price (as of 12/31/2018)   54.15
52-Week High   70.34
52-Week Low   50.98

Total Returns (%)
3-Month	6-Month	1-Year	3-Year	5-Year
-19.73	-17.13	-10.27	26.01	16.28

3-Year Standard Deviation   15.42
Effective Duration

Valuation
Premium/Discount (1-Year Average)   0.05

Company Information
Provider   First Trust
Manager/Tenure   Jon C. Erickson (11), Daniel J. Lindquist (11), David G. McGarel (11), 3 others
Website   http://www.ftportfolios.com/
Address   First Trust 120 E. Liberty Drive, Suite 400 Wheaton IL 60187 United States
Phone Number   800-621-1675

PERFORMANCE

Ratings History
Date	Overall Rating	Risk Rating	Reward Rating
Q4-18	C-	C-	C-
Q2-18	C	C-	C+
Q4-17	B	B-	B+
Q4-16	C	C-	C+
Q4-15	C	C+	C

Asset & Performance History
Date	NAV	1-Year Total Return
2017	61.13	14.45
2016	53.75	22.71
2015	44.24	-8.91
2014	48.97	1.31
2013	48.62	43.15
2012	34.1	15.41

Total Assets: $626,308,818
Asset Allocation
Asset	%
Cash	0%
Stocks	100%
US Stocks	100%
Bonds	0%
US Bonds	0%
Other	0%

Services Offered:

Investment Strategy: The investment seeks investment results that correspond generally to the price and yield (before the fund's fees and expenses) of an equity index called the Nasdaq AlphaDEX® Small Cap Core Index. The fund will normally invest at least 90% of its net assets (including investment borrowings) in common stocks that comprise the index. The index is designed to select stocks from the NASDAQ US 700 Small Cap Index (the "base index") that may generate positive alpha, or risk-adjusted returns, relative to traditional indices through the use of the AlphaDEX® selection methodology. **Top Holdings:** Crocs Inc   Ensign Group Inc   Telephone and Data Systems Inc   Brinker International Inc   Graham Holdings Co

Invesco BulletShares 2018 Corporate Bond ETF   C   HOLD

Ticker	Traded On	NAV	Total Assets ($)	Dividend Yield (TTM)	Turnover Ratio	Expense Ratio
BSCI	NYSE Arca		$625,697,054	1.85	0	0.1

Ratings
Reward	C
Risk	C+
Recent Upgrade/Downgrade	

Fund Information
Fund Type	Exchange Traded Funds
Category	US Fixed Income
Sub-Category	Corporate Bond
Prospectus Objective	Corp Bond - Gen
Inception Date	Mar-12
Open to New Investments	Y

Prices
Price (as of 12/31/2018)	21.14
52-Week High	21.19
52-Week Low	21.09

Total Returns (%)
3-Month	6-Month	1-Year	3-Year	5-Year
0.49	1.07	1.89	6.02	10.48

3-Year Standard Deviation	0.76
Effective Duration	0.17

Valuation
Premium/Discount (1-Year Average)	-0.08

Company Information
Provider	Invesco
Manager/Tenure	Jeremy Neisewander (2), Peter Hubbard (0), Jeffrey W. Kernagis (0), 1 other
Website	http://www.invesco.com/us
Address	Invesco 11 Greenway Plaza, Ste. 2500 Houston TX 77046 United States
Phone Number	800-659-1005

PERFORMANCE

Ratings History

Date	Overall Rating	Risk Rating	Reward Rating
Q4-18	C	C+	C
Q2-18	C	C+	C
Q4-17	B-	A-	C
Q4-16	C	C+	C
Q4-15	C+	C+	C

Asset & Performance History

Date	NAV	1-Year Total Return
2017	21.14	1.52
2016	21.14	2.46
2015	20.96	1.34
2014	21.03	2.81
2013	20.82	0.64
2012	21.04	

Total Assets: $625,697,054

Asset Allocation

Asset	%
Cash	100%
Stocks	0%
US Stocks	0%
Bonds	0%
US Bonds	0%
Other	0%

Services Offered:

Investment Strategy: The investment seeks investment results that correspond generally to the performance, before the fund's fees and expenses, of an investment grade corporate bond index called the Nasdaq BulletShares® USD Corporate Bond 2018 Index. The fund will invest at least 80% of its total assets in component securities that comprise the index. The index is designed to represent the performance of a held-to-maturity portfolio of U.S. dollar-denominated investment-grade corporate bonds with effective maturities in the year 2018. The fund is non-diversified. **Top Holdings:** MPLX LP 5.5% Citigroup Inc. 2.05% BNP Paribas 2.4% Royal Bank of Canada 2% CVS Health Corp 2.25%

SPDR® Wells Fargo Preferred Stock ETF   D+   SELL

Ticker	Traded On	NAV	Total Assets ($)	Dividend Yield (TTM)	Turnover Ratio	Expense Ratio
PSK	NYSE Arca	39.55	$624,639,994	6.66	31	0.45

Ratings
Reward	D+
Risk	C-
Recent Upgrade/Downgrade	Down

Fund Information
Fund Type	Exchange Traded Funds
Category	US Fixed Income
Sub-Category	Preferred Stock
Prospectus Objective	Growth & Inc
Inception Date	Sep-09
Open to New Investments	Y

Prices
Price (as of 12/31/2018)	39.56
52-Week High	44.04
52-Week Low	38.67

Total Returns (%)
3-Month	6-Month	1-Year	3-Year	5-Year
-4.10	-5.68	-4.58	4.91	32.20

3-Year Standard Deviation	5.2
Effective Duration	

Valuation
Premium/Discount (1-Year Average)	0.08

Company Information
Provider	SPDR State Street Global Advisors
Manager/Tenure	Michael J. Feehily (7), Karl A. Schneider (4), Amy Scofield (1)
Website	http://www.spdrs.com
Address	SPDR State Street Global Advisors State Street Financial Center, 1 Lincoln Street Boston MA 02111-2900 United States
Phone Number	617-786-3000

PERFORMANCE

Ratings History

Date	Overall Rating	Risk Rating	Reward Rating
Q4-18	D+	C-	D+
Q2-18	C	C-	C
Q4-17	B	A	C+
Q4-16	C	C-	C
Q4-15	C+	C+	C+

Asset & Performance History

Date	NAV	1-Year Total Return
2017	44.05	10.5
2016	41.97	-0.48
2015	44.61	8.17
2014	43.54	16.49
2013	39.56	-5.35
2012	44.96	13.56

Total Assets: $624,639,994

Asset Allocation

Asset	%
Cash	0%
Stocks	0%
US Stocks	0%
Bonds	0%
US Bonds	0%
Other	0%

Services Offered:

Investment Strategy: The investment seeks to provide investment results that, before fees and expenses, correspond generally to the total return performance of an index. In seeking to track the performance of Wells Fargo Hybrid and Preferred Securities Aggregate Index (the "index"), the fund employs a sampling strategy. It generally invests substantially all, but at least 80%, of its total assets in the securities comprising the index. The index is a modified market capitalization weighted index designed to measure the performance of non-convertible preferred stock and securities that are functionally equivalent to preferred stock. The fund is non-diversified. **Top Holdings:** PNC Financial Services Group Inc Perpetual Preferred Share class-P HSBC Holdings PLC ADR AT&T Inc 0% US Bancorp Shs Repr 1/1000th Non Cum Perp Pfd Shs Series-F BB&T Corp Deposit Shs Repr 1/1000th Non Cum Perp Pfd Shs Series -E-

WisdomTree U.S. Total Dividend Fund   C   HOLD

Ticker	Traded On	NAV
DTD	NYSE Arca	84.56

Total Assets ($)	Dividend Yield (TTM)	Turnover Ratio	Expense Ratio
$620,873,386	2.66	11	0.28

Ratings

Reward	C
Risk	C-
Recent Upgrade/Downgrade	

Fund Information

Fund Type	Exchange Traded Funds
Category	US Equity Large Cap Value
Sub-Category	Large Value
Prospectus Objective	Growth & Inc
Inception Date	Jun-06
Open to New Investments	Y

Prices

Price (as of 12/31/2018)	84.62
52-Week High	97.65
52-Week Low	79.60

Total Returns (%)

3-Month	6-Month	1-Year	3-Year	5-Year
-11.46	-5.68	-6.35	28.01	44.10

3-Year Standard Deviation	8.42
Effective Duration	

Valuation

Premium/Discount (1-Year Average)	0.03

Company Information

Provider	WisdomTree
Manager/Tenure	Richard A. Brown (10), Thomas J. Durante (10), Karen Q. Wong (10)
Website	http://www.wisdomtree.com
Address	WisdomTree 245 Park Avenue, 35th floor New York NY 10167 United States
Phone Number	866-909-9473

PERFORMANCE

Ratings History

Date	Overall Rating	Risk Rating	Reward Rating
Q4-18	C	C-	C
Q2-18	C	C-	C
Q4-17	B-	B	B-
Q4-16	C+	C-	B
Q4-15	C	C	C

Asset & Performance History

Date	NAV	1-Year Total Return
2017	92.8	17.26
2016	81.18	16.58
2015	71.63	-1.31
2014	74.62	14.06
2013	67.11	28.02
2012	53.8	13.13

Total Assets: $620,873,386

Asset Allocation

Asset	%
Cash	0%
Stocks	100%
US Stocks	100%
Bonds	0%
US Bonds	0%
Other	0%

Services Offered:

Investment Strategy: The investment seeks to track the price and yield performance, before fees and expenses, of the WisdomTree U.S. Dividend Index. The fund invests at least 95% of its total assets (exclusive of collateral held from securities lending) in the component securities of the index and investments that have economic characteristics that are substantially identical to the economic characteristics of such component securities. The index is a fundamentally-weighted index that is comprised of U.S. companies listed on a U.S. stock market that pay regular cash dividends. The fund is non-diversified. **Top Holdings:** Microsoft Corp Apple Inc Exxon Mobil Corp Verizon Communications Inc AT&T Inc

---

Direxion Daily Semiconductor Bull 3X Shares   C   HOLD

Ticker	Traded On	NAV
SOXL	NYSE Arca	83.40

Total Assets ($)	Dividend Yield (TTM)	Turnover Ratio	Expense Ratio
$616,135,772	0.86	17	1.02

Ratings

Reward	C
Risk	D+
Recent Upgrade/Downgrade	Down

Fund Information

Fund Type	Exchange Traded Funds
Category	Trading Tools
Sub-Category	Trading--Leveraged Equity
Prospectus Objective	Technology
Inception Date	Mar-10
Open to New Investments	Y

Prices

Price (as of 12/31/2018)	83.32
52-Week High	201.28
52-Week Low	67.08

Total Returns (%)

3-Month	6-Month	1-Year	3-Year	5-Year
-46.29	-41.69	-38.94	229.33	412.13

3-Year Standard Deviation	59.26
Effective Duration	

Valuation

Premium/Discount (1-Year Average)	0.00

Company Information

Provider	Direxion Funds
Manager/Tenure	Paul Brigandi (8), Tony Ng (3)
Website	http://www.direxionfunds.com
Address	Direxion Funds 1301 Avenue Of The Americas (6th Avenue) New York NY 10019 United States
Phone Number	646-572-3390

PERFORMANCE

Ratings History

Date	Overall Rating	Risk Rating	Reward Rating
Q4-18	C	D+	C
Q2-18	C+	C-	B
Q4-17	B	D+	A-
Q4-16	C	D+	C+
Q4-15	C	C	C

Asset & Performance History

Date	NAV	1-Year Total Return
2017	137.76	141.54
2016	57.08	123.29
2015	26.75	-20.72
2014	33.74	96.15
2013	17.2	155.13
2012	6.74	3.69

Total Assets: $616,135,772

Asset Allocation

Asset	%
Cash	36%
Stocks	64%
US Stocks	55%
Bonds	0%
US Bonds	0%
Other	0%

Services Offered:

Investment Strategy: The investment seeks daily investment results, before fees and expenses, of 300% of the daily performance of the PHLX Semiconductor Sector Index. The fund, under normal circumstances, invests at least 80% of its net assets (plus borrowing for investment purposes) in securities of the index, exchange-traded funds ("ETFs") that track the index and other financial instruments that provide daily leveraged exposure to the index or ETFs that track the index. The index measures the performance of domestic companies engaged in the design, distribution, manufacture and sale of semiconductors. The fund is non-diversified. **Top Holdings:** Phila Semiconductor Index Broadcom Inc Intel Corp Qualcomm Inc Texas Instruments Inc

Legg Mason Low Volatility High Dividend ETF   C   HOLD

Ticker	Traded On	NAV	Total Assets ($)	Dividend Yield (TTM)	Turnover Ratio	Expense Ratio
LVHD	NAS CM	28.76	$605,763,604	3.47	44	0.27

Ratings
Reward   C
Risk   C
Recent Upgrade/Downgrade

Fund Information
Fund Type	Exchange Traded Funds
Category	US Equity Large Cap Value
Sub-Category	Large Value
Prospectus Objective	Income
Inception Date	Dec-15
Open to New Investments	Y

Prices
Price (as of 12/31/2018)	28.68
52-Week High	31.98
52-Week Low	27.85

Total Returns (%)
3-Month	6-Month	1-Year	3-Year	5-Year
-5.14	-1.55	-5.17	28.03	

3-Year Standard Deviation
Effective Duration

Valuation
Premium/Discount (1-Year Average)   0.01

Company Information
Provider	Legg Mason
Manager/Tenure	Michael J. LaBella (2), Russell Shtern (2), Robert Y. Wang (2)
Website	http://www.leggmason.com
Address	Legg Mason/Western 100 International Drive Baltimore MD 21202 United States
Phone Number	877-721-1926

PERFORMANCE

Ratings History

Date	Overall Rating	Risk Rating	Reward Rating
Q4-18	C	C	C
Q2-18	C	C-	C
Q4-17	C-	B+	C-
Q4-16	D-	C	C
Q4-15			

Asset & Performance History

Date	NAV	1-Year Total Return
2017	31.47	13.96
2016	28.54	17.49
2015	24.74	
2014		
2013		
2012		

Total Assets: $605,763,604
Asset Allocation

Asset	%
Cash	0%
Stocks	100%
US Stocks	100%
Bonds	0%
US Bonds	0%
Other	0%

Services Offered:

Investment Strategy: The investment seeks to track the investment results of the QS Low Volatility High Dividend Index (the "underlying index"). The fund will invest at least 80% of its net assets, plus borrowings for investment purposes, if any, in securities that compose the underlying index. The underlying index is composed of equity securities of U.S. companies with relatively high yield and low price and earnings volatility. **Top Holdings:** McDonald's Corp   Duke Energy Corp   Dominion Energy Inc   American Electric Power Co Inc   Ventas Inc

---

iShares Commodities Select Strategy ETF   C   HOLD

Ticker	Traded On	NAV	Total Assets ($)	Dividend Yield (TTM)	Turnover Ratio	Expense Ratio
COMT	NAS CM	30.48	$601,595,430	5.81	44	0.48

Ratings
Reward   C-
Risk   C+
Recent Upgrade/Downgrade

Fund Information
Fund Type	Exchange Traded Funds
Category	Commodities Broad Basket
Sub-Category	Commodities Broad Basket
Prospectus Objective	Growth & Inc
Inception Date	Oct-14
Open to New Investments	Y

Prices
Price (as of 12/31/2018)	30.49
52-Week High	40.38
52-Week Low	29.85

Total Returns (%)
3-Month	6-Month	1-Year	3-Year	5-Year
-15.01	-11.84	-6.59	26.48	

3-Year Standard Deviation   12.72
Effective Duration

Valuation
Premium/Discount (1-Year Average)   0.02

Company Information
Provider	iShares
Manager/Tenure	Greg Savage (4), Robert Shimell (4), Alan Mason (2), 1 other
Website	http://www.ishares.com
Address	iShares 400 Howard Street San Francisco CA 94105 United States
Phone Number	800-474-2737

PERFORMANCE

Ratings History

Date	Overall Rating	Risk Rating	Reward Rating
Q4-18	C	C+	C-
Q2-18	C	C-	C
Q4-17	C	C	C
Q4-16	D+	D	D+
Q4-15	U		

Asset & Performance History

Date	NAV	1-Year Total Return
2017	36.34	6.9
2016	34.28	21.22
2015	28.44	-30.37
2014	41.31	
2013		
2012		

Total Assets: $601,595,430
Asset Allocation

Asset	%
Cash	67%
Stocks	32%
US Stocks	20%
Bonds	1%
US Bonds	0%
Other	0%

Services Offered:

Investment Strategy: The investment seeks total return by providing investors with broad commodity exposure. The fund seeks to achieve its investment objective by investing in a combination of exchange-traded commodity futures contracts, exchange-traded options on commodity-related futures contracts and exchange-cleared commodity-related swaps (together, "Commodity-Linked Investments") and commodity-related equity securities ("Commodity-Related Equities"), thereby obtaining exposure to the commodities markets. It is an actively managed exchange-traded fund ("ETF") that does not seek to replicate the performance of a specified index. **Top Holdings:** Exxon Mobil Corp   Chevron Corp   Deere & Co   Ecolab Inc   Societe Generale S.A. 0%

O'Shares FTSE U.S. Quality Dividend ETF

C   HOLD

Ticker	Traded On	NAV	Total Assets ($)	Dividend Yield (TTM)	Turnover Ratio	Expense Ratio
OUSA	NYSE Arca	30.00	$600,826,021	2.9		0.48

Ratings

Reward	C
Risk	C+
Recent Upgrade/Downgrade	

Fund Information

Fund Type	Exchange Traded Funds
Category	US Equity Large Cap Value
Sub-Category	Large Value
Prospectus Objective	Growth
Inception Date	Jul-15
Open to New Investments	Y

Prices

Price (as of 12/31/2018)	30.02
52-Week High	33.39
52-Week Low	28.55

Total Returns (%)

3-Month	6-Month	1-Year	3-Year	5-Year
-8.36	-0.92	-3.43	28.81	

3-Year Standard Deviation	8.1
Effective Duration	

Valuation

Premium/Discount (1-Year Average)	0.00

Company Information

Provider	O'Shares Investments
Manager/Tenure	William H. DeRoche (3), Philip Lee (3), Josh Belko (0)
Website	http://www.oshares.com
Address	O'Shares Investments 60 State Street, Suite 700 Boston MA 02109 United States
Phone Number	617-855-7670

PERFORMANCE

Ratings History

Date	Overall Rating	Risk Rating	Reward Rating
Q4-18	C	C+	C
Q2-18	C	C-	C
Q4-17	C	B+	C+
Q4-16	D	C	C
Q4-15	U		

Asset & Performance History

Date	NAV	1-Year Total Return
2017	31.87	18.78
2016	27.45	12.3
2015	25.03	
2014		
2013		
2012		

Total Assets: $600,826,021

Asset Allocation

Asset	%
Cash	0%
Stocks	100%
US Stocks	99%
Bonds	0%
US Bonds	0%
Other	0%

Services Offered:

Investment Strategy: The investment seeks to track the performance (before fees and expenses) of the FTSE USA Qual/Vol/Yield Factor 5% Capped Index (the "target index"). The target index is designed to reflect the performance of publicly-listed large capitalization and mid-capitalization dividend-paying issuers in the United States exhibiting high quality, low volatility and high dividend yields, as determined by FTSE-Russell (the "index provider"). Under normal market conditions, the fund will invest at least 80% of its total assets in the components of the target index. **Top Holdings:** Johnson & Johnson Exxon Mobil Corp Cisco Systems Inc Procter & Gamble Co Intel Corp

---

First Trust Dorsey Wright International Focus 5 ETF

D+   SELL

Ticker	Traded On	NAV	Total Assets ($)	Dividend Yield (TTM)	Turnover Ratio	Expense Ratio
IFV	NAS CM	17.46	$598,007,443	2.27	0	1.06

Ratings

Reward	D+
Risk	D+
Recent Upgrade/Downgrade	Down

Fund Information

Fund Type	Exchange Traded Funds
Category	Global Equity Large Cap
Sub-Category	Foreign Large Blend
Prospectus Objective	Growth & Inc
Inception Date	Jul-14
Open to New Investments	Y

Prices

Price (as of 12/31/2018)	17.42
52-Week High	24.22
52-Week Low	16.87

Total Returns (%)

3-Month	6-Month	1-Year	3-Year	5-Year
-13.68	-14.80	-20.25	1.50	

3-Year Standard Deviation	14.21
Effective Duration	

Valuation

Premium/Discount (1-Year Average)	-0.12

Company Information

Provider	First Trust
Manager/Tenure	Jon C. Erickson (4), Daniel J. Lindquist (4), David G. McGarel (4), 3 others
Website	http://www.ftportfolios.com/
Address	First Trust 120 E. Liberty Drive, Suite 400 Wheaton IL 60187 United States
Phone Number	800-621-1675

PERFORMANCE

Ratings History

Date	Overall Rating	Risk Rating	Reward Rating
Q4-18	D+	D+	D+
Q2-18	C	C+	C
Q4-17	B	B-	B
Q4-16	D+	C-	D
Q4-15	D	C-	D

Asset & Performance History

Date	NAV	1-Year Total Return
2017	22.25	32.26
2016	17.07	-3.76
2015	17.93	0.27
2014	18.16	
2013		
2012		

Total Assets: $598,007,443

Asset Allocation

Asset	%
Cash	0%
Stocks	100%
US Stocks	2%
Bonds	0%
US Bonds	0%
Other	0%

Services Offered:

Investment Strategy: The investment seeks investment results that correspond generally to the price and yield (before fees and expenses) of an index called the Dorsey Wright International Focus Five Index. The fund will normally invest at least 90% of its net assets (including investment borrowings) in the ETFs that comprise the index. The ETFs in which the fund invests are advised by First Trust Advisors L.P., the fund's investment advisor. The index is designed to provide targeted exposure to the five First Trust country/region-based ETFs that the index provider believes offer the greatest potential to outperform the other ETFs in the selection universe. It is non-diversified. **Top Holdings:** First Trust BICK ETF First Trust Dev Mkts Ex-US AlphaDEX® ETF First Trust Brazil AlphaDEX® ETF First Trust Germany AlphaDEX® ETF First Trust Switzerland AlphaDEX® ETF

Schwab 1000 Index ETF   C-   HOLD

Ticker	Traded On	NAV		Total Assets ($)	Dividend Yield (TTM)	Turnover Ratio	Expense Ratio
SCHK	NYSE Arca	24.53		$591,082,646	1.5		0.05

Ratings
Reward   D+
Risk   C
Recent Upgrade/Downgrade

Fund Information
Fund Type   Exchange Traded Funds
Category   US Equity Large Cap Blend
Sub-Category   Large Blend
Prospectus Objective   Growth & Inc
Inception Date   Oct-17
Open to New Investments   Y

Prices
Price (as of 12/31/2018)   24.52
52-Week High   28.89
52-Week Low   23.02

Total Returns (%)

3-Month	6-Month	1-Year	3-Year	5-Year
-14.07	-7.77	-4.89		

3-Year Standard Deviation
Effective Duration

Valuation
Premium/Discount (1-Year Average)   0.06

Company Information
Provider   Schwab ETFs
Manager/Tenure   Christopher Bliss (1), Ferian Juwono
                      (1), Sabya Sinha (1), 1 other
Website   http://www.schwabetfs.com
Address   Schwab ETFs United States
Phone Number   800-435-4000

PERFORMANCE

Ratings History

Date	Overall Rating	Risk Rating	Reward Rating
Q4-18	C-	C	D+
Q2-18	U		
Q4-17	U		
Q4-16			
Q4-15			

Asset & Performance History

Date	NAV	1-Year Total Return
2017	26.22	
2016		
2015		
2014		
2013		
2012		

Total Assets: $591,082,646

Asset Allocation

Asset	%
Cash	0%
Stocks	100%
US Stocks	99%
Bonds	0%
US Bonds	0%
Other	0%

Services Offered:

Investment Strategy: The investment seeks to track as closely as possible, before fees and expenses, the total return of the Schwab 1000 Index®. It is the fund's policy that under normal circumstances it will invest at least 90% of its net assets (net assets plus borrowings for investment purposes) in stocks included in the index. The Schwab 1000 Index is a float-adjusted market capitalization weighted index that includes the 1,000 largest stocks of publicly traded companies in the United States, with size being determined by market capitalization (total market value of all shares outstanding). **Top Holdings:** Microsoft Corp Apple Inc Amazon.com Inc Berkshire Hathaway Inc B Johnson & Johnson

---

iShares MSCI France ETF   C-   HOLD

Ticker	Traded On	NAV		Total Assets ($)	Dividend Yield (TTM)	Turnover Ratio	Expense Ratio
EWQ	NYSE Arca	26.60		$588,115,484	2.65	4	0.47

Ratings
Reward   C-
Risk   C-
Recent Upgrade/Downgrade   Down

Fund Information
Fund Type   Exchange Traded Funds
Category   Europe Equity Large Cap
Sub-Category   Miscellaneous Region
Prospectus Objective   Europe Stock
Inception Date   Mar-96
Open to New Investments   Y

Prices
Price (as of 12/31/2018)   26.52
52-Week High   33.73
52-Week Low   25.56

Total Returns (%)

3-Month	6-Month	1-Year	3-Year	5-Year
-15.08	-11.51	-12.68	18.09	6.20

3-Year Standard Deviation   13.21
Effective Duration

Valuation
Premium/Discount (1-Year Average)   -0.13

Company Information
Provider   iShares
Manager/Tenure   Diane Hsiung (10), Greg Savage (10),
                      Jennifer Hsui (5), 1 other
Website   http://www.ishares.com
Address   iShares 400 Howard Street San
                      Francisco CA 94105 United States
Phone Number   800-474-2737

PERFORMANCE

Ratings History

Date	Overall Rating	Risk Rating	Reward Rating
Q4-18	C-	C-	C-
Q2-18	C+	C+	C+
Q4-17	B	C+	A-
Q4-16	D+	C-	D
Q4-15	C	C+	C

Asset & Performance History

Date	NAV	1-Year Total Return
2017	31.25	28.83
2016	24.75	4.97
2015	24.27	-0.16
2014	24.81	-9.91
2013	28.37	26.35
2012	23.1	21.4

Total Assets: $588,115,484

Asset Allocation

Asset	%
Cash	0%
Stocks	100%
US Stocks	1%
Bonds	0%
US Bonds	0%
Other	0%

Services Offered: CashInvestment Plan

Investment Strategy: The investment seeks to track the investment results of the MSCI France Index. The fund will at all times invest at least 80% of its assets in the securities of its underlying index and in depositary receipts representing securities in its underlying index. The underlying index consists of stocks traded primarily on the Paris Stock Exchange. It may include large- or mid-capitalization companies. The fund is non-diversified. **Top Holdings:** Total SA Sanofi SA LVMH Moet Hennessy Louis Vuitton SE Airbus SE L'Oreal SA

SPDR® Bloomberg Barclays Emerging Markets Local Bond ETF

C- **HOLD**

Ticker	Traded On	NAV		Total Assets ($)	Dividend Yield (TTM)	Turnover Ratio	Expense Ratio
EBND	NYSE Arca	26.43		$587,742,911	4.91	42	0.4

Ratings
Reward	C-
Risk	C-
Recent Upgrade/Downgrade	

Fund Information
Fund Type	Exchange Traded Funds
Category	Emerging Mkts Fixed Inc
Sub-Category	Emerging-Markets Local-Currency Bond
Prospectus Objective	Worldwide Bond
Inception Date	Feb-11
Open to New Investments	Y

Prices
Price (as of 12/31/2018)	26.52
52-Week High	30.76
52-Week Low	25.51

Total Returns (%)
3-Month	6-Month	1-Year	3-Year	5-Year
2.30	1.20	-6.58	13.65	-3.96

3-Year Standard Deviation	9.79
Effective Duration	5.40

Valuation
Premium/Discount (1-Year Average)	0.05

Company Information
Provider	SPDR State Street Global Advisors
Manager/Tenure	Abhishek Kumar (7), Peter Spano (3), Richard Jenkins (1)
Website	http://www.spdrs.com
Address	SPDR State Street Global Advisors State Street Financial Center, 1 Lincoln Street Boston MA 02111-2900 United States
Phone Number	617-786-3000

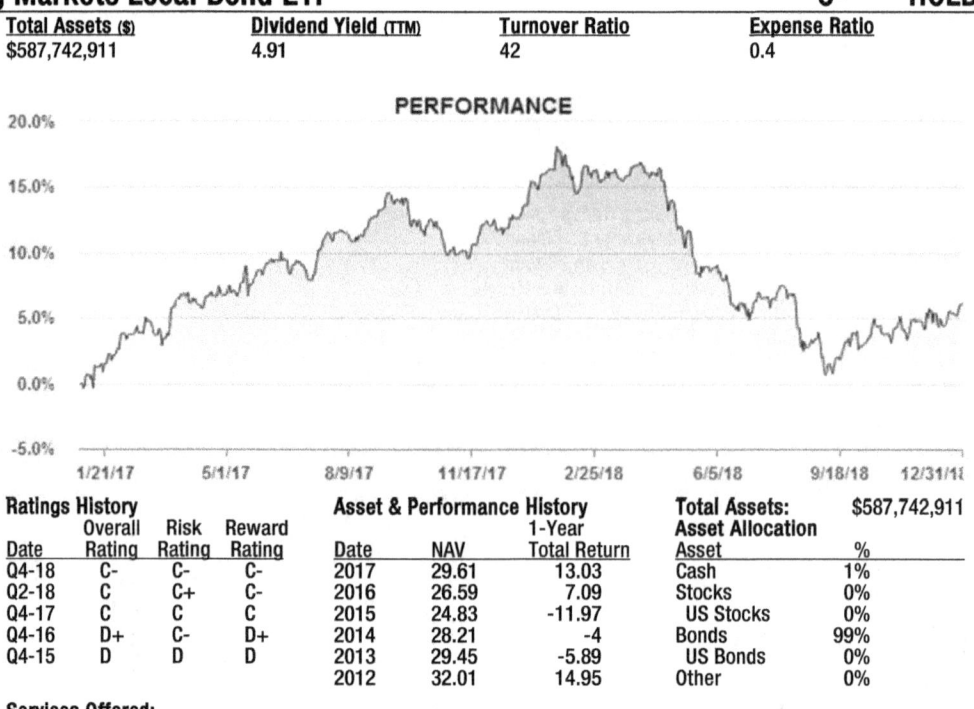

PERFORMANCE

Ratings History
Date	Overall Rating	Risk Rating	Reward Rating
Q4-18	C-	C-	C-
Q2-18	C	C+	C-
Q4-17	C	C	C
Q4-16	D+	C-	D+
Q4-15	D	D	D

Asset & Performance History
Date	NAV	1-Year Total Return
2017	29.61	13.03
2016	26.59	7.09
2015	24.83	-11.97
2014	28.21	-4
2013	29.45	-5.89
2012	32.01	14.95

Total Assets: $587,742,911

Asset Allocation
Asset	%
Cash	1%
Stocks	0%
US Stocks	0%
Bonds	99%
US Bonds	0%
Other	0%

Services Offered:

Investment Strategy: The investment seeks to provide investment results that correspond generally to the price and yield performance of the Bloomberg Barclays EM Local Currency Government Diversified Index. The fund generally invests substantially all, but at least 80%, of its total assets in the securities comprising the index or in securities that the Sub-Adviser determines have economic characteristics that are substantially identical to the economic characteristics of the securities that comprise the index. The index is designed to measure the performance of the fixed-rate local currency sovereign debt of emerging market countries. The fund is non-diversified. **Top Holdings:** Letra Tesouro Nacional Bills 07/20 0.00000 Nota Do Tesouro Nacional Notes 01/23 10 Letra Tesouro Nacional Bills 01/20 0.00000 Colombia Rep 7.5% Letra Tesouro Nacional Bills 07/21 0.00000

Direxion Daily Junior Gold Miners Index Bull 3X Shares

E+ **SELL**

Ticker	Traded On	NAV		Total Assets ($)	Dividend Yield (TTM)	Turnover Ratio	Expense Ratio
JNUG	NYSE Arca	9.20		$583,113,620	0	245	1.18

Ratings
Reward	E+
Risk	D-
Recent Upgrade/Downgrade	Down

Fund Information
Fund Type	Exchange Traded Funds
Category	Trading Tools
Sub-Category	Trading--Leveraged Equity
Prospectus Objective	Prec Metals
Inception Date	Oct-13
Open to New Investments	Y

Prices
Price (as of 12/31/2018)	9.21
52-Week High	19.96
52-Week Low	6.23

Total Returns (%)
3-Month	6-Month	1-Year	3-Year	5-Year
23.89	-30.47	-48.22	-25.84	-96.95

3-Year Standard Deviation	144.57
Effective Duration	

Valuation
Premium/Discount (1-Year Average)	0.13

Company Information
Provider	Direxion Funds
Manager/Tenure	Paul Brigandi (5), Tony Ng (3)
Website	http://www.direxionfunds.com
Address	Direxion Funds 1301 Avenue Of The Americas (6th Avenue) New York NY 10019 United States
Phone Number	646-572-3390

PERFORMANCE

Ratings History
Date	Overall Rating	Risk Rating	Reward Rating
Q4-18	E+	D-	E+
Q2-18	D	D	D-
Q4-17	D-	D-	D
Q4-16	D	D	D+
Q4-15	D-	E+	D-

Asset & Performance History
Date	NAV	1-Year Total Return
2017	17.78	-19.66
2016	22.2	117.82
2015	12.45	-74.34
2014	48.54	-83.96
2013	314.8	
2012		

Total Assets: $583,113,620

Asset Allocation
Asset	%
Cash	107%
Stocks	24%
US Stocks	1%
Bonds	0%
US Bonds	0%
Other	-31%

Services Offered:

Investment Strategy: The investment seeks daily investment results, before fees and expenses, of 300% of the daily performance of the MVIS Global Junior Gold Miners Index. The fund invests at least 80% of its net assets (plus borrowing for investment purposes) in securities of the index, ETFs that track the index and other financial instruments that provide daily leveraged exposure to the index or ETFs that track the index. The index includes companies from markets that are freely investable to foreign investors, including "emerging markets," as that term is defined by the index provider. It is non-diversified. **Top Holdings:** VanEck Vectors Junior Gold Miners ETF Ve Vectors Jr Gld Miners Ve Vectors Jr Gld Miners Ve Vectors Jr Gld Miners Ve Vectors Jr Gld Miners Ve Vectors Jr Gld Miners

ProShares UltraPro Short QQQ   D   SELL

Ticker	Traded On	NAV		Total Assets ($)	Dividend Yield (TTM)	Turnover Ratio	Expense Ratio
SQQQ	NAS CM	16.75		$581,842,646	1.29		0.95

Ratings
Reward   E+
Risk   D-
Recent Upgrade/Downgrade   Up

Fund Information
Fund Type   Exchange Traded Funds
Category   Trading Tools
Sub-Category   Trading--Inverse Equity
Prospectus Objective   Growth
Inception Date   Feb-10
Open to New Investments   Y

Prices
Price (as of 12/31/2018)   16.76
52-Week High   21.77
52-Week Low   11.08

Total Returns (%)

3-Month	6-Month	1-Year	3-Year	5-Year
52.20	20.45	-20.93	-77.18	-92.56

3-Year Standard Deviation   35.35
Effective Duration

Valuation
Premium/Discount (1-Year Average)   -0.10

Company Information
Provider   ProShares
Manager/Tenure   Michael Neches (5), Devin Sullivan (0)
Website   http://www.proshares.com
Address   ProShares 7501 Wisconsin Avenue, Suite 1000 Bethesda MD 20814 United States
Phone Number   866-776-5125

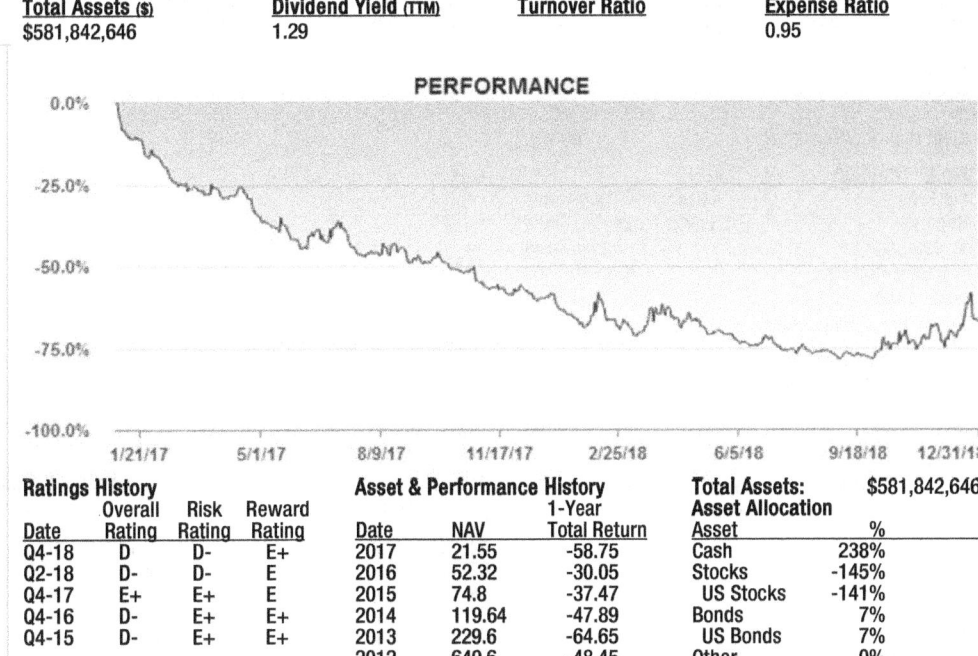

PERFORMANCE

Ratings History

Date	Overall Rating	Risk Rating	Reward Rating
Q4-18	D	D-	E+
Q2-18	D-	D-	E
Q4-17	E+	E+	E
Q4-16	D-	E+	E+
Q4-15	D-	E+	E+

Asset & Performance History

Date	NAV	1-Year Total Return
2017	21.55	-58.75
2016	52.32	-30.05
2015	74.8	-37.47
2014	119.64	-47.89
2013	229.6	-64.65
2012	649.6	-48.45

Total Assets: $581,842,646
Asset Allocation

Asset	%
Cash	238%
Stocks	-145%
US Stocks	-141%
Bonds	7%
US Bonds	7%
Other	0%

Services Offered:

Investment Strategy: The investment seeks daily investment results, before fees and expenses, that correspond to three times the inverse (-3x) of the daily performance of the NASDAQ-100 Index®. The fund invests in financial instruments that ProShare Advisors believes, in combination, should produce daily returns consistent with the fund's investment objective. The index includes 100 of the largest domestic and international non-financial companies listed on The Nasdaq Stock Market based on market capitalization. The fund is non-diversified. **Top Holdings:** Nasdaq 100 Index Swap Societe Generale   Nasdaq 100 Index Swap Bank Of America, Na   Nasdaq 100 Index Swap Credit Suisse International   Nasdaq 100 Index Swap Deutsche Bank Ag   Nasdaq 100 Index Swap Goldman Sachs International

---

Invesco DB Agriculture Fund   D   SELL

Ticker	Traded On	NAV		Total Assets ($)	Dividend Yield (TTM)	Turnover Ratio	Expense Ratio
DBA	NYSE Arca	16.94		$581,554,552	0		0.85

Ratings
Reward   D
Risk   D
Recent Upgrade/Downgrade

Fund Information
Fund Type   Exchange Traded Funds
Category   Commodities Specified
Sub-Category   Commodities Agriculture
Prospectus Objective   Natl Res
Inception Date   Jan-07
Open to New Investments   Y

Prices
Price (as of 12/31/2018)   16.94
52-Week High   19.63
52-Week Low   16.85

Total Returns (%)

3-Month	6-Month	1-Year	3-Year	5-Year
0.61	-2.88	-8.74	-17.15	-29.47

3-Year Standard Deviation   8.98
Effective Duration

Valuation
Premium/Discount (1-Year Average)   -0.04

Company Information
Provider   Invesco
Manager/Tenure   Management Team (11)
Website   http://www.invesco.com/us
Address   Invesco 11 Greenway Plaza, Ste. 2500 Houston TX 77046 United States
Phone Number   800-659-1005

PERFORMANCE

Ratings History

Date	Overall Rating	Risk Rating	Reward Rating
Q4-18	D	D	D
Q2-18	D	D+	D
Q4-17	D	D	D
Q4-16	D	D	D
Q4-15	D	D	D

Asset & Performance History

Date	NAV	1-Year Total Return
2017	18.76	-6.16
2016	19.98	-3.02
2015	20.67	-16.75
2014	24.83	2.26
2013	24.28	-13.17
2012	27.97	-2.93

Total Assets: $581,554,552
Asset Allocation

Asset	%
Cash	33%
Stocks	0%
US Stocks	0%
Bonds	17%
US Bonds	17%
Other	50%

Services Offered:

Investment Strategy: The investment seeks to track changes, whether positive or negative, in the level of the DBIQ Diversified Agriculture Index Excess Return™ (the "index") over time, plus the excess, if any, of the sum of the fund's Treasury Income, Money Market Income and T-Bill ETF Income, over the expenses of the fund. The index, which is comprised of one or more underlying commodities ("index commodities"), is intended to reflect the agricultural sector. **Top Holdings:** United States Treasury Bills 0%   Invesco Treasury Collateral ETF   Live Cattle Futr Feb19   Soybean Future Nov19   Sugar #11 (World) Oct19

JPMorgan Diversified Return U.S. Equity ETF   C-   HOLD

Ticker	Traded On	NAV	Total Assets ($)	Dividend Yield (TTM)	Turnover Ratio	Expense Ratio
JPUS	NYSE Arca	64.88	$578,383,687	2.61	27	0.19

Ratings

Reward   C-
Risk   C-
Recent Upgrade/Downgrade   Down

Fund Information

Fund Type	Exchange Traded Funds
Category	US Equity Large Cap Blend
Sub-Category	Large Blend
Prospectus Objective	Growth & Inc
Inception Date	Sep-15
Open to New Investments	Y

Prices

Price (as of 12/31/2018)	64.87
52-Week High	75.64
52-Week Low	61.37

Total Returns (%)

3-Month	6-Month	1-Year	3-Year	5-Year
-12.37	-7.55	-6.02	27.03	

3-Year Standard Deviation   8.5
Effective Duration

Valuation

Premium/Discount (1-Year Average)   0.09

Company Information

Provider	JPMorgan
Manager/Tenure	Jonathan Msika (2), Yazann Romahi (2), Joe Staines (2), 1 other
Website	http://www.jpmorganfunds.com
Address	JPMorgan 270 Park Avenue New York NY 10017-2070 United States
Phone Number	800-480-4111

PERFORMANCE

Ratings History

Date	Overall Rating	Risk Rating	Reward Rating
Q4-18	C-	C-	C-
Q2-18	C	C-	C
Q4-17	C	B	C+
Q4-16	D	C-	D+
Q4-15			

Asset & Performance History

Date	NAV	1-Year Total Return
2017	70.46	20.6
2016	59.15	12.08
2015	53.18	
2014		
2013		
2012		

Total Assets: $578,383,687

Asset Allocation

Asset	%
Cash	1%
Stocks	99%
US Stocks	98%
Bonds	0%
US Bonds	0%
Other	0%

Services Offered:

Investment Strategy: The investment seeks investment results that closely correspond, before fees and expenses, to the performance of the JP Morgan Diversified Factor US Equity Index. The fund will invest at least 80% of its net assets in securities included in the underlying index. The underlying index is comprised of U.S. equity securities selected to represent a diversified set of factor characteristics: value, momentum, and quality. The fund's securities are large- and mid-cap equity securities of U.S. companies, including common stock, preferred stock and real estate investment trusts (REITs). **Top Holdings:** McCormick & Co Inc Non-Voting Church & Dwight Co Inc The AES Corp Hormel Foods Corp Marathon Petroleum Corp

---

Vident International Equity Fund™   C-   HOLD

Ticker	Traded On	NAV	Total Assets ($)	Dividend Yield (TTM)	Turnover Ratio	Expense Ratio
VIDI	NYSE Arca	22.66	$578,046,349	2.77	66	0.61

Ratings

Reward   C-
Risk   C-
Recent Upgrade/Downgrade

Fund Information

Fund Type	Exchange Traded Funds
Category	Global Equity Large Cap
Sub-Category	Foreign Large Value
Prospectus Objective	Foreign Stock
Inception Date	Oct-13
Open to New Investments	Y

Prices

Price (as of 12/31/2018)	22.50
52-Week High	30.29
52-Week Low	22.04

Total Returns (%)

3-Month	6-Month	1-Year	3-Year	5-Year
-10.37	-9.17	-17.30	19.21	4.08

3-Year Standard Deviation   12.09
Effective Duration

Valuation

Premium/Discount (1-Year Average)   -0.18

Company Information

Provider	Vident Financial
Manager/Tenure	Denise M. Krisko (3), Rafael Zayas (1)
Website	http://www.videntfinancial.com
Address	Vident Financial 201 17th Street, Suite 300 Atlanta GA 30363 United States
Phone Number	800-617-0004

PERFORMANCE

Ratings History

Date	Overall Rating	Risk Rating	Reward Rating
Q4-18	C-	C-	C-
Q2-18	C-	C-	C
Q4-17	B-	C+	B
Q4-16	D+	C-	D+
Q4-15	D	D+	D

Asset & Performance History

Date	NAV	1-Year Total Return
2017	28.11	32.86
2016	21.66	7.88
2015	20.36	-10.76
2014	23.29	-2.15
2013	24.34	
2012		

Total Assets: $578,046,349

Asset Allocation

Asset	%
Cash	0%
Stocks	100%
US Stocks	4%
Bonds	0%
US Bonds	0%
Other	0%

Services Offered:

Investment Strategy: The investment seeks to track the performance, before fees and expenses, of the Vident Core International Equity Index™. The advisor attempts to invest all, or substantially all, of its assets in the common stocks that make up the underlying index. The underlying index is a rules-based, systematic strategy index comprised of equity securities of issuers in developed and emerging markets outside of the United States. **Top Holdings:** Sumitomo Dainippon Pharma Co Ltd Air Canada Class B Petroleo Brasileiro SA Petrobras Participating Preferred China Telecom Corp Ltd H Shares JBS SA

Invesco S&P MidCap 400® Pure Growth ETF   C-   HOLD

Ticker	Traded On	NAV		Total Assets ($)	Dividend Yield (TTM)	Turnover Ratio	Expense Ratio
RFG	NYSE Arca	131.89		$573,363,879	0.7		0.35

Ratings

Reward — C
Risk — D+
Recent Upgrade/Downgrade — Down

Fund Information

Fund Type	Exchange Traded Funds
Category	US Equity Mid Cap
Sub-Category	Mid-Cap Growth
Prospectus Objective	Growth
Inception Date	Mar-06
Open to New Investments	Y

Prices

Price (as of 12/31/2018)	131.71
52-Week High	169.49
52-Week Low	124.17

Total Returns (%)

3-Month	6-Month	1-Year	3-Year	5-Year
-19.12	-18.09	-13.76	8.11	10.40

3-Year Standard Deviation — 12.56
Effective Duration —

Valuation

Premium/Discount (1-Year Average) — 0.20

Company Information

Provider	Invesco
Manager/Tenure	Peter Hubbard (0), Michael Jeanette (0), Jonathan Nixon (0), 1 other
Website	http://www.invesco.com/us
Address	Invesco 11 Greenway Plaza, Ste. 2500 Houston TX 77046 United States
Phone Number	800-659-1005

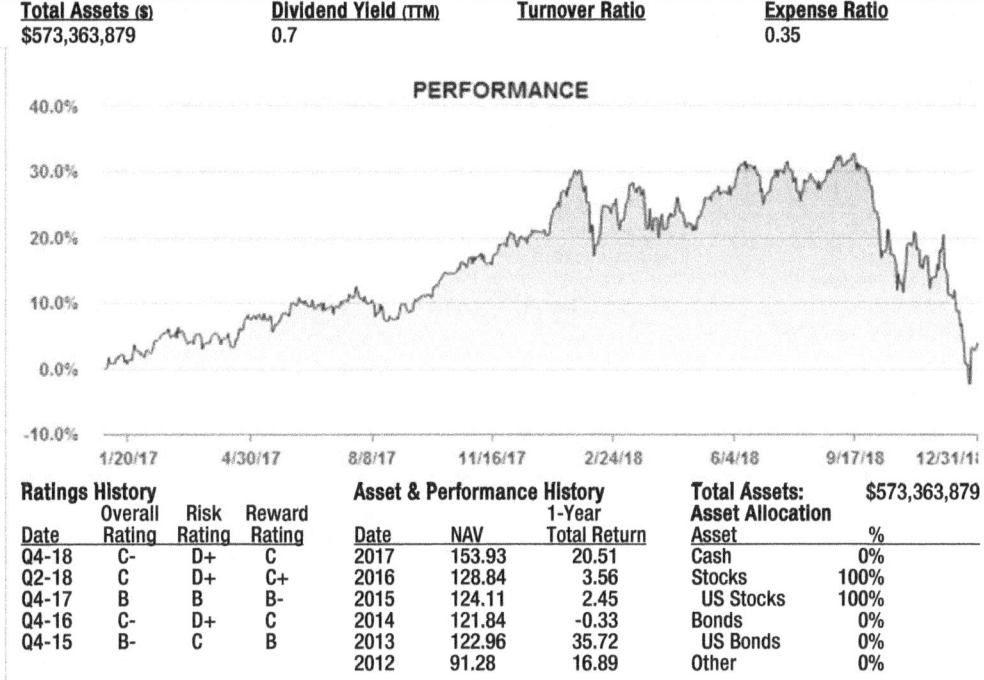

PERFORMANCE

Ratings History

Date	Overall Rating	Risk Rating	Reward Rating
Q4-18	C-	D+	C
Q2-18	C	D+	C+
Q4-17	B	B	B-
Q4-16	C-	D+	C
Q4-15	B-	C	B

Asset & Performance History

Date	NAV	1-Year Total Return
2017	153.93	20.51
2016	128.84	3.56
2015	124.11	2.45
2014	121.84	-0.33
2013	122.96	35.72
2012	91.28	16.89

Total Assets: $573,363,879

Asset Allocation

Asset	%
Cash	0%
Stocks	100%
US Stocks	100%
Bonds	0%
US Bonds	0%
Other	0%

Services Offered:

Investment Strategy: The investment seeks to track the investment results (before fees and expenses) of the S&P MidCap 400® Pure Growth Index (the "underlying index"). The fund generally will invest at least 90% of its total assets in the securities that comprise the underlying index. The underlying index is comprised only those S&P MidCap 400® companies with strong growth characteristics as measured using three factors: three-year sales per share growth, three-year ratio of earnings per share change to price per share, and momentum (12-month percentage price change). The fund is non-diversified. **Top Holdings:** Five Below Inc Medidata Solutions Inc Zebra Technologies Corp LivaNova PLC Integrated Device Technology Inc

---

iShares iBonds Dec 2022 Term Corporate ETF   C   HOLD

Ticker	Traded On	NAV		Total Assets ($)	Dividend Yield (TTM)	Turnover Ratio	Expense Ratio
IBDN	NYSE Arca	24.22		$570,062,540	2.79	7	0.1

Ratings

Reward — C-
Risk — C+
Recent Upgrade/Downgrade — Up

Fund Information

Fund Type	Exchange Traded Funds
Category	US Fixed Income
Sub-Category	Corporate Bond
Prospectus Objective	Corp Bond - Gen
Inception Date	Mar-15
Open to New Investments	Y

Prices

Price (as of 12/31/2018)	24.17
52-Week High	24.98
52-Week Low	24.10

Total Returns (%)

3-Month	6-Month	1-Year	3-Year	5-Year
0.73	1.49	0.08	9.68	

3-Year Standard Deviation — 2.82
Effective Duration — 3.31

Valuation

Premium/Discount (1-Year Average) — 0.22

Company Information

Provider	iShares
Manager/Tenure	James Mauro (3), Scott Radell (3)
Website	http://www.ishares.com
Address	iShares 400 Howard Street San Francisco CA 94105 United States
Phone Number	800-474-2737

PERFORMANCE

Ratings History

Date	Overall Rating	Risk Rating	Reward Rating
Q4-18	C	C+	C-
Q2-18	C-	C-	C
Q4-17	B-	A-	C
Q4-16	D+	C-	D+
Q4-15	U		

Asset & Performance History

Date	NAV	1-Year Total Return
2017	24.9	3.76
2016	24.62	5.45
2015	24.02	
2014		
2013		
2012		

Total Assets: $570,062,540

Asset Allocation

Asset	%
Cash	1%
Stocks	0%
US Stocks	0%
Bonds	99%
US Bonds	85%
Other	0%

Services Offered:

Investment Strategy: The investment seeks to track the investment results of the Bloomberg Barclays December 2022 Maturity Corporate Index which composed of U.S. dollar-denominated, investment-grade corporate bonds maturing in 2022. The fund generally will invest at least 90% of its assets in the component securities of the underlying index. The underlying index is composed of U.S. dollar-denominated, taxable, investment-grade corporate bonds scheduled to mature after December 31, 2021 and before December 16, 2022. **Top Holdings:** Goldman Sachs Group, Inc. 5.75% Goldman Sachs Group, Inc. 3% Cooperatieve Rabobank U.A. 3.88% Broadcom Corporation/Broadcom Cayman Finance Ltd 3% Citigroup Inc. 4.5%

Invesco S&P International Developed Low Volatility ETF   C   HOLD

Ticker	Traded On	NAV	Total Assets ($)	Dividend Yield (TTM)	Turnover Ratio	Expense Ratio
IDLV	NYSE Arca	29.89	$567,248,726	4.17	69	0.25

Ratings
Reward   D+
Risk   C+
Recent Upgrade/Downgrade

Fund Information
Fund Type   Exchange Traded Funds
Category   Global Equity Large Cap
Sub-Category   Foreign Large Blend
Prospectus Objective   Foreign Stock
Inception Date   Jan-12
Open to New Investments

Prices
Price (as of 12/31/2018)   29.84
52-Week High   35.29
52-Week Low   29.12

Total Returns (%)

3-Month	6-Month	1-Year	3-Year	5-Year
-6.83	-4.86	-7.91	15.95	13.19

3-Year Standard Deviation   9.05
Effective Duration

Valuation
Premium/Discount (1-Year Average)   -0.09

Company Information
Provider   Invesco
Manager/Tenure   Peter Hubbard (6), Jonathan Nixon (5),
                    Michael Jeanette (3), 1 other
Website   http://www.invesco.com/us
Address   Invesco 11 Greenway Plaza, Ste. 2500
                    Houston TX 77046 United States
Phone Number   800-659-1005

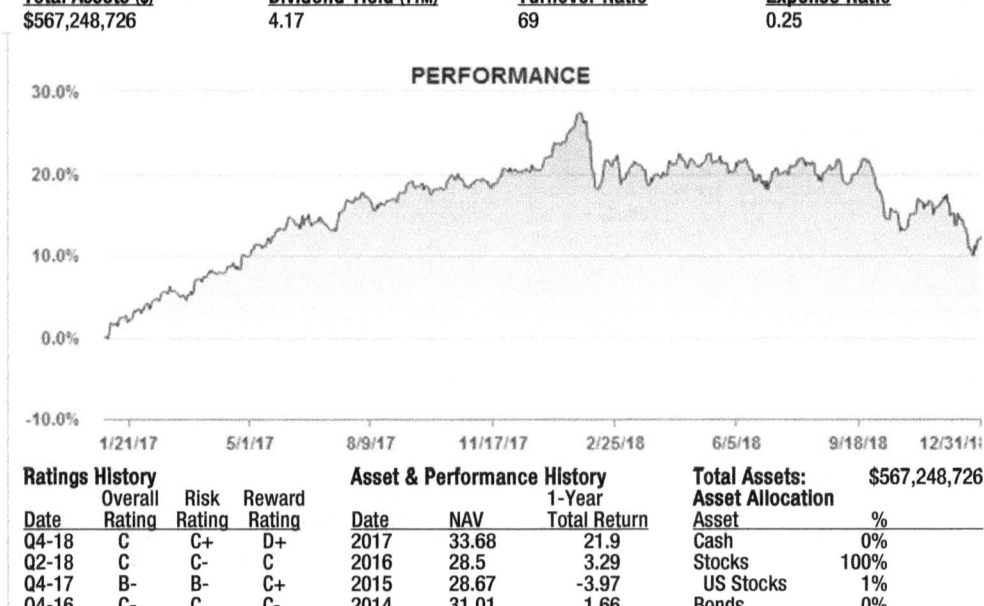

PERFORMANCE

Ratings History

Date	Overall Rating	Risk Rating	Reward Rating
Q4-18	C	C+	D+
Q2-18	C	C-	C
Q4-17	B-	B-	C+
Q4-16	C-	C	C-
Q4-15	C-	C-	C-

Asset & Performance History

Date	NAV	1-Year Total Return
2017	33.68	21.9
2016	28.5	3.29
2015	28.67	-3.97
2014	31.01	1.66
2013	31.47	15.92
2012	27.86	

Total Assets: $567,248,726

Asset Allocation

Asset	%
Cash	0%
Stocks	100%
US Stocks	1%
Bonds	0%
US Bonds	0%
Other	0%

Services Offered:

Investment Strategy: The investment seeks to track the investment results (before fees and expenses) of the S&P BMI International Developed Low VolatilityTM Index (the "underlying index"). The fund will invest at least 90% of its total assets in the securities of companies that comprise the underlying index. S&P Dow Jones Indices ("S&P DJI" or the "index provider") compiles, maintains and calculates the underlying index, which is designed to measure the performance of 200 of the least volatile stocks of the S&P Developed ex-U.S. & South Korea LargeMidCap Index. **Top Holdings:** MAN SE   BCE Inc   H&R Real Estate Investment Trust   Great-West Lifeco Inc   Bank of Montreal

---

iShares Long-Term Corporate Bond ETF   D+   SELL

Ticker	Traded On	NAV	Total Assets ($)	Dividend Yield (TTM)	Turnover Ratio	Expense Ratio
IGLB	NYSE Arca	56.08	$562,799,499	4.62	12	0.06

Ratings
Reward   D+
Risk   C-
Recent Upgrade/Downgrade   Down

Fund Information
Fund Type   Exchange Traded Funds
Category   US Fixed Income
Sub-Category   Corporate Bond
Prospectus Objective   Growth & Inc
Inception Date   Dec-09
Open to New Investments   Y

Prices
Price (as of 12/31/2018)   56.30
52-Week High   63.20
52-Week Low   55.17

Total Returns (%)

3-Month	6-Month	1-Year	3-Year	5-Year
-1.44	-0.66	-7.17	14.34	25.82

3-Year Standard Deviation   6.93
Effective Duration   12.90

Valuation
Premium/Discount (1-Year Average)   -0.02

Company Information
Provider   iShares
Manager/Tenure   Scott Radell (8), James Mauro (7)
Website   http://www.ishares.com
Address   iShares 400 Howard Street San
                    Francisco CA 94105 United States
Phone Number   800-474-2737

PERFORMANCE

Ratings History

Date	Overall Rating	Risk Rating	Reward Rating
Q4-18	D+	C-	D+
Q2-18	C-	C-	C-
Q4-17	B-	B	B-
Q4-16	C	C+	C
Q4-15	C	C	C-

Asset & Performance History

Date	NAV	1-Year Total Return
2017	63.15	11.67
2016	58.7	9.91
2015	55.66	-4.75
2014	61.03	15.54
2013	55.12	-7.05
2012	62.26	12.9

Total Assets: $562,799,499

Asset Allocation

Asset	%
Cash	1%
Stocks	0%
US Stocks	0%
Bonds	99%
US Bonds	83%
Other	0%

Services Offered:

Investment Strategy: The investment seeks to track the investment results of the ICE BofAML 10+ Year US Corporate Index. The fund generally will invest at least 90% of its assets in the component securities of the underlying index and may invest up to 10% of its assets in certain futures, options and swap contracts, cash and cash equivalents. The underlying index measures the performance of U.S. dollar-denominated investment-grade corporate bonds that have a remaining maturity of greater than or equal to ten years. **Top Holdings:** Anheuser-Busch Companies LLC / Anheuser-Busch InBev Worldwide Inc 4.9%   GE Capital International Funding Company Unlimited Company 4.42% CVS Health Corp 5.05%   Goldman Sachs Group, Inc. 6.75%   Anheuser-Busch Companies LLC / Anheuser-Busch InBev Worldwide Inc 4.7%

iShares MSCI Malaysia ETF   C-   HOLD

Ticker	Traded On	NAV		Total Assets ($)	Dividend Yield (TTM)	Turnover Ratio	Expense Ratio
EWM	NYSE Arca	29.92		$559,921,524	7.09	63	0.47

Ratings
Reward	C-
Risk	D+
Recent Upgrade/Downgrade	Down

Fund Information
Fund Type	Exchange Traded Funds
Category	Asia ex-Japan Equity
Sub-Category	Miscellaneous Region
Prospectus Objective	Pacific Stock
Inception Date	Mar-96
Open to New Investments	Y

Prices
Price (as of 12/31/2018)	29.77
52-Week High	36.47
52-Week Low	28.48

Total Returns (%)
3-Month	6-Month	1-Year	3-Year	5-Year
-5.72	-1.96	-6.27	12.08	-20.23

3-Year Standard Deviation	14.65
Effective Duration	

Valuation
Premium/Discount (1-Year Average)	-0.16

Company Information
Provider	iShares
Manager/Tenure	Diane Hsiung (10), Greg Savage (10), Jennifer Hsui (5), 1 other
Website	http://www.ishares.com
Address	iShares 400 Howard Street San Francisco CA 94105 United States
Phone Number	800-474-2737

PERFORMANCE

Ratings History
Date	Overall Rating	Risk Rating	Reward Rating
Q4-18	C-	D+	C-
Q2-18	C	C+	C-
Q4-17	C-	D+	C
Q4-16	D	D	D
Q4-15	D	D	D

Asset & Performance History
Date	NAV	1-Year Total Return
2017	33.14	24.51
2016	28.17	-3.95
2015	31.04	-20.35
2014	54	-10.64
2013	62.76	7.08
2012	60.44	13.61

Total Assets: $559,921,524
Asset Allocation
Asset	%
Cash	0%
Stocks	100%
US Stocks	0%
Bonds	0%
US Bonds	0%
Other	0%

Services Offered: CashInvestment Plan

Investment Strategy: The investment seeks to track the investment results of the MSCI Malaysia Index. The fund will at all times invest at least 90% of its assets in the securities of its underlying index and in depositary receipts representing securities in its underlying index. The underlying index consists of stocks traded primarily on the Kuala Lumpur Stock Exchange. It may include large- or mid-capitalization companies. The fund is non-diversified.
Top Holdings: Public Bank Bhd Tenaga Nasional Bhd Malayan Banking Bhd CIMB Group Holdings Bhd Petronas Chemicals Group Bhd

---

Invesco S&P Global Water Index ETF   C-   HOLD

Ticker	Traded On	NAV		Total Assets ($)	Dividend Yield (TTM)	Turnover Ratio	Expense Ratio
CGW	NYSE Arca	31.23		$552,072,363	1.81	13	0.61

Ratings
Reward	C-
Risk	C-
Recent Upgrade/Downgrade	Down

Fund Information
Fund Type	Exchange Traded Funds
Category	Equity Misc
Sub-Category	Miscellaneous Sector
Prospectus Objective	Natl Res
Inception Date	May-07
Open to New Investments	Y

Prices
Price (as of 12/31/2018)	31.14
52-Week High	36.40
52-Week Low	29.76

Total Returns (%)
3-Month	6-Month	1-Year	3-Year	5-Year
-8.57	-4.52	-10.01	21.64	24.05

3-Year Standard Deviation	10.41
Effective Duration	

Valuation
Premium/Discount (1-Year Average)	-0.04

Company Information
Provider	Invesco
Manager/Tenure	Peter Hubbard (0), Michael Jeanette (0), Jonathan Nixon (0), 1 other
Website	http://www.invesco.com/us
Address	Invesco 11 Greenway Plaza, Ste. 2500 Houston TX 77046 United States
Phone Number	800-659-1005

PERFORMANCE

Ratings History
Date	Overall Rating	Risk Rating	Reward Rating
Q4-18	C-	C-	C-
Q2-18	C	C	C
Q4-17	B	B+	B
Q4-16	C	C-	C
Q4-15	C	C-	C

Asset & Performance History
Date	NAV	1-Year Total Return
2017	35.48	26.76
2016	28.48	5.55
2015	27.14	-1.81
2014	28.1	3.86
2013	27.53	26.21
2012	22.15	20.21

Total Assets: $552,072,363
Asset Allocation
Asset	%
Cash	0%
Stocks	100%
US Stocks	49%
Bonds	0%
US Bonds	0%
Other	0%

Services Offered:

Investment Strategy: The investment seeks investment results that correspond generally to the performance, before the fund's fees and expenses, of an equity index called the S&P Global Water Index. The fund will invest at least 90% of its total assets in common stock and American depositary receipts ("ADRs") that comprise the index and depositary receipts representing common stocks included in the index. At each rebalancing the index is comprised of 50 equity securities selected, based on investment and other criteria, from a universe of companies listed on global developed market exchanges. It is non-diversified. **Top Holdings:** American Water Works Co Inc Xylem Inc Veolia Environnement SA Danaher Corp IDEX Corp

First Trust Dorsey Wright Dynamic Focus 5 ETF   C-   HOLD

Ticker	Traded On	NAV	Total Assets ($)	Dividend Yield (TTM)	Turnover Ratio	Expense Ratio
FVC	NAS CM	23.55	$551,431,244	0.59	42	0.89

Ratings

Reward	C-
Risk	C
Recent Upgrade/Downgrade	Down

Fund Information

Fund Type	Exchange Traded Funds
Category	US Equity Mid Cap
Sub-Category	Large Blend
Prospectus Objective	Growth & Inc
Inception Date	Mar-16
Open to New Investments	Y

Prices

Price (as of 12/31/2018)	23.42
52-Week High	29.60
52-Week Low	21.74

Total Returns (%)

3-Month	6-Month	1-Year	3-Year	5-Year
-17.84	-14.89	-8.05		

3-Year Standard Deviation	
Effective Duration	

Valuation

Premium/Discount (1-Year Average)	0.02

Company Information

Provider	First Trust
Manager/Tenure	Jon C. Erickson (2), Daniel J. Lindquist (2), David G. McGarel (2), 3 others
Website	http://www.ftportfolios.com/
Address	First Trust 120 E. Liberty Drive, Suite 400 Wheaton IL 60187 United States
Phone Number	800-621-1675

PERFORMANCE

Ratings History

Date	Overall Rating	Risk Rating	Reward Rating
Q4-18	C-	C	C-
Q2-18	C	C-	C
Q4-17	D+	B+	C
Q4-16	U		
Q4-15			

Asset & Performance History

Date	NAV	1-Year Total Return
2017	25.67	19.83
2016	21.56	
2015		
2014		
2013		
2012		

Total Assets: $551,431,244

Asset Allocation

Asset	%
Cash	0%
Stocks	100%
US Stocks	96%
Bonds	0%
US Bonds	0%
Other	0%

Services Offered:

Investment Strategy: The investment seeks investment results that correspond to the price and yield of an index called the Dorsey Wright Dynamic Focus Five Index. The fund will normally invest at least 80% of its total assets in the ETFs and cash equivalents that comprise the index. The ETFs in which the fund invests are advised by the fund's investment advisor. The index is designed to provide targeted exposure to the five First Trust sector and industry-based ETFs that the index determines offer the greatest potential to outperform the other First Trust sector and industry-based ETFs and that satisfy certain trading volume and liquidity requirements. It is non-diversified.
Top Holdings: First Trust Technology AlphaDEX® ETF   First Trust Health Care AlphaDEX® ETF   First Trust NASDAQ-100-Tech Sector ETF   First Trust Dow Jones Internet ETF   First Trust NYSE Arca Biotech ETF

---

iShares MSCI World ETF   C   HOLD

Ticker	Traded On	NAV	Total Assets ($)	Dividend Yield (TTM)	Turnover Ratio	Expense Ratio
URTH	NYSE Arca	78.82	$550,985,938	2.18	3	0.24

Ratings

Reward	C-
Risk	C+
Recent Upgrade/Downgrade	

Fund Information

Fund Type	Exchange Traded Funds
Category	Global Equity Large Cap
Sub-Category	World Large Stock
Prospectus Objective	World Stock
Inception Date	Jan-12
Open to New Investments	Y

Prices

Price (as of 12/31/2018)	78.87
52-Week High	94.07
52-Week Low	75.04

Total Returns (%)

3-Month	6-Month	1-Year	3-Year	5-Year
-13.58	-8.72	-8.44	20.95	26.09

3-Year Standard Deviation	9.41
Effective Duration	

Valuation

Premium/Discount (1-Year Average)	0.03

Company Information

Provider	iShares
Manager/Tenure	Diane Hsiung (6), Greg Savage (6), Jennifer Hsui (5), 1 other
Website	http://www.ishares.com
Address	iShares 400 Howard Street San Francisco CA 94105 United States
Phone Number	800-474-2737

PERFORMANCE

Ratings History

Date	Overall Rating	Risk Rating	Reward Rating
Q4-18	C	C+	C-
Q2-18	C	C-	C
Q4-17	B-	B-	B-
Q4-16	C	C-	C+
Q4-15	C	C+	C

Asset & Performance History

Date	NAV	1-Year Total Return
2017	87.88	22.5
2016	73.16	7.83
2015	69.34	-0.62
2014	71.38	4.9
2013	69.63	26.74
2012	55.57	13.59

Total Assets: $550,985,938

Asset Allocation

Asset	%
Cash	1%
Stocks	99%
US Stocks	62%
Bonds	0%
US Bonds	0%
Other	0%

Services Offered:

Investment Strategy: The investment seeks to track the investment results of the MSCI World Index. The fund generally will invest at least 90% of its assets in the component securities of the underlying index and in investments that have economic characteristics that are substantially identical to the component securities of the underlying index. The index is designed to measure the performance of equity securities in the top 85% of equity market capitalization, as calculated by the index provider, in certain developed market countries. **Top Holdings:** Apple Inc   Microsoft Corp   Amazon.com Inc   Johnson & Johnson   JPMorgan Chase & Co

iShares MSCI Turkey ETF   D-   SELL

Ticker	Traded On	NAV	Total Assets ($)	Dividend Yield (TTM)	Turnover Ratio	Expense Ratio
TUR	NAS CM	24.68	$549,902,897	3.96	7	0.62

Ratings
Reward	D-
Risk	D
Recent Upgrade/Downgrade	Down

Fund Information
Fund Type	Exchange Traded Funds
Category	Equity Misc
Sub-Category	Miscellaneous Region
Prospectus Objective	Foreign Stock
Inception Date	Mar-08
Open to New Investments	Y

Prices
Price (as of 12/31/2018)	24.57
52-Week High	46.66
52-Week Low	19.07

Total Returns (%)
3-Month	6-Month	1-Year	3-Year	5-Year
3.80	-17.64	-41.41	-26.14	-40.92

3-Year Standard Deviation	32.69
Effective Duration	

Valuation
Premium/Discount (1-Year Average)	0.15

Company Information
Provider	iShares
Manager/Tenure	Diane Hsiung (10), Greg Savage (10), Jennifer Hsui (5), 1 other
Website	http://www.ishares.com
Address	iShares 400 Howard Street San Francisco CA 94105 United States
Phone Number	800-474-2737

PERFORMANCE

Ratings History
Date	Overall Rating	Risk Rating	Reward Rating
Q4-18	D-	D	D-
Q2-18	D	D	D
Q4-17	D+	D	C-
Q4-16	D	D	D
Q4-15	D	D	D

Asset & Performance History
Date	NAV	1-Year Total Return
2017	43.61	37.44
2016	32.62	-8.28
2015	36.42	-31.46
2014	54.41	16.71
2013	47.36	-26.76
2012	65.89	63.21

Total Assets: $549,902,897
Asset Allocation
Asset	%
Cash	0%
Stocks	100%
US Stocks	0%
Bonds	0%
US Bonds	0%
Other	0%

Services Offered:

Investment Strategy: The investment seeks to track the investment results of the MSCI Turkey Investable Market Index (IMI). The fund generally will invest at least 90% of its assets in the component securities of the underlying index and in investments that have economic characteristics that are substantially identical to the component securities of the underlying index. The underlying index consists of stocks traded primarily on the Istanbul Stock Exchange (ISE). The underlying index may include large-, mid- or small- capitalization companies. The fund is non-diversified. **Top Holdings:** Turkiye Garanti Bankasi AS   Bim Birlesik Magazalar AS   Akbank TAS   Tupras-Turkiye Petrol Rafineleri AS   Turkcell Iletisim Hizmetleri AS

Invesco Dynamic Pharmaceuticals ETF   C   HOLD

Ticker	Traded On	NAV	Total Assets ($)	Dividend Yield (TTM)	Turnover Ratio	Expense Ratio
PJP	NYSE Arca	62.40	$542,125,627	0.61	98	0.57

Ratings
Reward	B-
Risk	D+
Recent Upgrade/Downgrade	

Fund Information
Fund Type	Exchange Traded Funds
Category	Healthcare Sector Equity
Sub-Category	Health
Prospectus Objective	Health
Inception Date	Jun-05
Open to New Investments	Y

Prices
Price (as of 12/31/2018)	62.35
52-Week High	74.14
52-Week Low	58.29

Total Returns (%)
3-Month	6-Month	1-Year	3-Year	5-Year
-13.32	-7.05	-1.69	-8.46	30.21

3-Year Standard Deviation	17.1
Effective Duration	

Valuation
Premium/Discount (1-Year Average)	-0.04

Company Information
Provider	Invesco
Manager/Tenure	Peter Hubbard (11), Michael Jeanette (10), Tony Seisser (4), 1 other
Website	http://www.invesco.com/us
Address	Invesco 11 Greenway Plaza, Ste. 2500 Houston TX 77046 United States
Phone Number	800-659-1005

PERFORMANCE

Ratings History
Date	Overall Rating	Risk Rating	Reward Rating
Q4-18	C	D+	B-
Q2-18	C	D+	B-
Q4-17	C	C	C
Q4-16	C	D+	B-
Q4-15	B	B-	B

Asset & Performance History
Date	NAV	1-Year Total Return
2017	64.18	15.31
2016	56.03	-19.24
2015	69.98	11.05
2014	66.48	28.1
2013	53.45	55.6
2012	34.53	24.72

Total Assets: $542,125,627
Asset Allocation
Asset	%
Cash	0%
Stocks	100%
US Stocks	97%
Bonds	0%
US Bonds	0%
Other	0%

Services Offered:

Investment Strategy: The investment seeks to track the investment results (before fees and expenses) of the Dynamic Pharmaceutical IntellidexSM Index. The fund generally will invest at least 90% of its total assets in common stocks of pharmaceutical companies that comprise the underlying intellidex. The underlying intellidex was composed of common stocks of 23 U.S. pharmaceuticals companies. These companies are engaged principally in the research, development, manufacture, sale or distribution of pharmaceuticals and drugs of all types. The fund is non-diversified. **Top Holdings:** Merck & Co Inc   Eli Lilly and Co   Pfizer Inc   Abbott Laboratories   Johnson & Johnson

Global X MLP & Energy Infrastructure ETF

C   HOLD

Ticker	Traded On	NAV	Total Assets ($)	Dividend Yield (TTM)	Turnover Ratio	Expense Ratio
MLPX	NYSE Arca	10.93	$540,370,789	5.36	40	0.45

Ratings
Reward   B-
Risk   D+
Recent Upgrade/Downgrade

Fund Information
Fund Type   Exchange Traded Funds
Category   Energy Sector Equity
Sub-Category   Energy Limited Partnership
Prospectus Objective   Growth & Inc
Inception Date   Aug-13
Open to New Investments   Y

Prices
Price (as of 12/31/2018)   10.93
52-Week High   14.60
52-Week Low   10.40

Total Returns (%)

3-Month	6-Month	1-Year	3-Year	5-Year
-18.83	-14.70	-15.31	9.83	-17.09

3-Year Standard Deviation   18.96
Effective Duration

Valuation
Premium/Discount (1-Year Average)   -0.34

Company Information
Provider   Global X Funds
Manager/Tenure   Chang Kim (4), James Ong (2), Nam To (0)
Website   http://www.globalxfunds.com
Address   Global X Funds 600 Lexington Avenue, 20th Floor New York NY 10022 United States
Phone Number   888-493-8631

PERFORMANCE

Ratings History

Date	Overall Rating	Risk Rating	Reward Rating
Q4-18	C	D+	B-
Q2-18	C	D	B-
Q4-17	D	D	D+
Q4-16	C	D	C+
Q4-15	C-	C	B

Asset & Performance History

Date	NAV	1-Year Total Return
2017	13.57	-4.75
2016	14.86	36.17
2015	11.62	-35.23
2014	18.56	16.53
2013	16.28	
2012		

Total Assets: $540,370,789
Asset Allocation

Asset	%
Cash	0%
Stocks	100%
US Stocks	81%
Bonds	0%
US Bonds	0%
Other	0%

Services Offered:

Investment Strategy: The investment seeks to provide investment results that correspond generally to the price and yield performance, before fees and expenses, of the Solactive MLP & Energy Infrastructure Index. The fund invests at least 80% of its total assets in the securities of the index. It also invests at least 80% of its total assets in securities of master limited partnerships and energy infrastructure corporations. The fund's 80% investment policies are non-fundamental and require 60 days' prior written notice to shareholders before they can be changed. The index tracks the performance of midstream energy infrastructure MLPs and corporations. It is non-diversified.
Top Holdings: TransCanada Corp   Enbridge Inc   Kinder Morgan Inc P   Williams Companies Inc   Cheniere Energy Inc

iShares Global Financials ETF

C   HOLD

Ticker	Traded On	NAV	Total Assets ($)	Dividend Yield (TTM)	Turnover Ratio	Expense Ratio
IXG	NYSE Arca	57.02	$539,101,191	2.85	4	0.47

Ratings
Reward   C-
Risk   C
Recent Upgrade/Downgrade

Fund Information
Fund Type   Exchange Traded Funds
Category   Financials Sector Equity
Sub-Category   Financial
Prospectus Objective   Financial
Inception Date   Nov-01
Open to New Investments   Y

Prices
Price (as of 12/31/2018)   56.87
52-Week High   75.99
52-Week Low   54.20

Total Returns (%)

3-Month	6-Month	1-Year	3-Year	5-Year
-12.69	-10.03	-15.97	16.43	15.13

3-Year Standard Deviation   13.86
Effective Duration

Valuation
Premium/Discount (1-Year Average)   -0.01

Company Information
Provider   iShares
Manager/Tenure   Diane Hsiung (10), Greg Savage (10), Jennifer Hsui (6), 3 others
Website   http://www.ishares.com
Address   iShares 400 Howard Street San Francisco CA 94105 United States
Phone Number   800-474-2737

PERFORMANCE

Ratings History

Date	Overall Rating	Risk Rating	Reward Rating
Q4-18	C	C	C-
Q2-18	C	C-	C
Q4-17	B	B-	B
Q4-16	C-	C-	C
Q4-15	C	C+	C

Asset & Performance History

Date	NAV	1-Year Total Return
2017	69.82	23.42
2016	57.86	12.26
2015	52.81	-4.39
2014	56.71	3.42
2013	56.13	27.03
2012	45.26	29.42

Total Assets: $539,101,191
Asset Allocation

Asset	%
Cash	0%
Stocks	99%
US Stocks	47%
Bonds	0%
US Bonds	0%
Other	0%

Services Offered: CashInvestment Plan

Investment Strategy: The investment seeks to track the investment results of the S&P Global 1200 Financials IndexTM. The fund generally invests at least 90% of its assets in securities of the underlying index and in depositary receipts representing securities of the underlying index. It may invest the remainder of its assets in certain futures, options and swap contracts, cash and cash equivalents, as well as in securities not included in the underlying index. The index measures the performance of companies that the index provider deems to be part of the financial sector of the economy and that the index provider believes are important to global markets. **Top Holdings:** Berkshire Hathaway Inc B   JPMorgan Chase & Co   Bank of America Corporation   Wells Fargo & Co   HSBC Holdings PLC

Vident Core U.S. Equity Fund™   C-   HOLD

Ticker	Traded On	NAV	Total Assets ($)	Dividend Yield (TTM)	Turnover Ratio	Expense Ratio
VUSE	NYSE Arca	28.05	$537,408,059	1.31	63	0.5

Ratings
Reward   C-
Risk   C-
Recent Upgrade/Downgrade   Down

Fund Information
Fund Type   Exchange Traded Funds
Category   US Equity Mid Cap
Sub-Category   Mid-Cap Value
Prospectus Objective   Growth & Inc
Inception Date   Jan-14
Open to New Investments   Y

Prices
Price (as of 12/31/2018)   27.92
52-Week High   35.53
52-Week Low   26.41

Total Returns (%)

3-Month	6-Month	1-Year	3-Year	5-Year
-17.53	-15.89	-14.73	17.82	

3-Year Standard Deviation   12.19
Effective Duration

Valuation
Premium/Discount (1-Year Average)   0.12

Company Information
Provider   Vident Financial
Manager/Tenure   Denise M. Krisko (3)
Website   http://www.videntfinancial.com
Address   Vident Financial 201 17th Street, Suite
                  300 Atlanta GA 30363 United States
Phone Number   800-617-0004

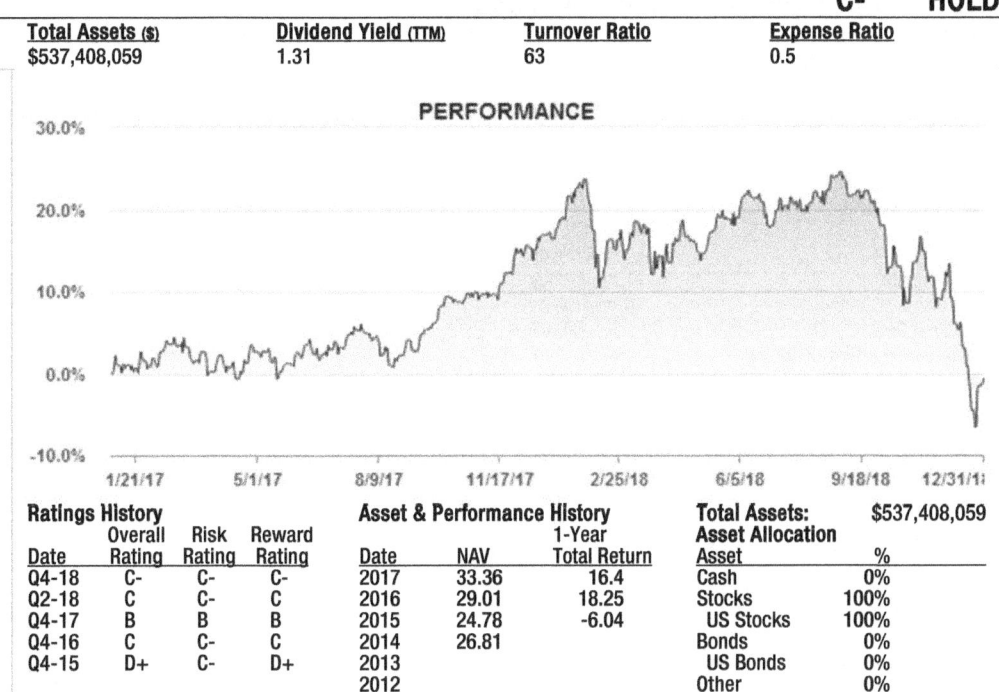

Ratings History

Date	Overall Rating	Risk Rating	Reward Rating
Q4-18	C-	C-	C-
Q2-18	C	C-	C
Q4-17	B	B	B
Q4-16	C	C-	C
Q4-15	D+	C-	D+

Asset & Performance History

Date	NAV	1-Year Total Return
2017	33.36	16.4
2016	29.01	18.25
2015	24.78	-6.04
2014	26.81	
2013		
2012		

Total Assets: $537,408,059
Asset Allocation

Asset	%
Cash	0%
Stocks	100%
US Stocks	100%
Bonds	0%
US Bonds	0%
Other	0%

Services Offered:

Investment Strategy: The investment seeks to track the performance, before fees and expenses, of the Vident Core U.S. Stock IndexTM (the "index"). Under normal circumstances, at least 80% of the fund's total assets (exclusive of collateral held from securities lending) will be invested in the component securities of the index and investments that have economic characteristics that are substantially identical to the economic characteristics of such component securities. The underlying index is a rules-based, systematic strategy index comprised of equity securities of issuers domiciled and traded in the United States. **Top Holdings:** Spirit Airlines Inc Telephone and Data Systems Inc Amedisys Inc Molina Healthcare Inc Walgreens Boots Alliance Inc

---

Fidelity® MSCI Consumer Staples Index ETF   C+   HOLD

Ticker	Traded On	NAV	Total Assets ($)	Dividend Yield (TTM)	Turnover Ratio	Expense Ratio
FSTA	NYSE Arca	30.52	$535,711,254	2.63	24	0.08

Ratings
Reward   B
Risk   C
Recent Upgrade/Downgrade   Up

Fund Information
Fund Type   Exchange Traded Funds
Category   Consumer Goods & Svcs
Sub-Category   Consumer Defensive
Prospectus Objective   Unaligned
Inception Date   Oct-13
Open to New Investments   Y

Prices
Price (as of 12/31/2018)   30.50
52-Week High   35.42
52-Week Low   29.30

Total Returns (%)

3-Month	6-Month	1-Year	3-Year	5-Year
-5.41	-0.27	-8.29	9.26	33.63

3-Year Standard Deviation   9.6
Effective Duration

Valuation
Premium/Discount (1-Year Average)   0.05

Company Information
Provider   Fidelity Investments
Manager/Tenure   Jennifer Hsui (5), Greg Savage (5),
                  Alan Mason (2), 2 others
Website   http://www.institutional.fidelity.com
Address   Fidelity Investments 82 Devonshire
                  Street Boston MA 2109 United States
Phone Number   617-563-7000

Ratings History

Date	Overall Rating	Risk Rating	Reward Rating
Q4-18	C+	C	B
Q2-18	C	C-	B-
Q4-17	B	A-	C+
Q4-16	B-	C	B
Q4-15	C-	B-	B

Asset & Performance History

Date	NAV	1-Year Total Return
2017	34.26	12.5
2016	31.21	5.9
2015	30.21	5.65
2014	29.45	15.75
2013	26.06	
2012		

Total Assets: $535,711,254
Asset Allocation

Asset	%
Cash	0%
Stocks	100%
US Stocks	100%
Bonds	0%
US Bonds	0%
Other	0%

Services Offered:

Investment Strategy: The investment seeks to provide investment returns that correspond, before fees and expenses, generally to the performance of the MSCI USA IMI Consumer Staples Index. The fund invests at least 80% of assets in securities included in the fund's underlying index. The fund's underlying index is the MSCI USA IMI Consumer Staples Index, which represents the performance of the consumer staples sector in the U.S. equity market. It may or may not hold all of the securities in the MSCI USA IMI Consumer Staples Index. The fund is non-diversified. **Top Holdings:** Procter & Gamble Co Coca-Cola Co PepsiCo Inc Walmart Inc Philip Morris International Inc

Invesco DB US Dollar Index Bullish Fund   C   HOLD

Ticker	Traded On	NAV	Total Assets ($)	Dividend Yield (TTM)	Turnover Ratio	Expense Ratio
UUP	NYSE Arca	25.48	$535,132,772	0.09		0.75

Ratings
Reward	C
Risk	C+
Recent Upgrade/Downgrade	Up

Fund Information
Fund Type	Exchange Traded Funds
Category	Currency
Sub-Category	Multicurrency
Prospectus Objective	Growth & Inc
Inception Date	Feb-07
Open to New Investments	Y

Prices
Price (as of 12/31/2018)	25.45
52-Week High	26.04
52-Week Low	23.13

Total Returns (%)
3-Month	6-Month	1-Year	3-Year	5-Year
0.69	2.05	6.29	-0.54	18.54

3-Year Standard Deviation	6.34
Effective Duration	

Valuation
Premium/Discount (1-Year Average)	-0.03

Company Information
Provider	Invesco
Manager/Tenure	Management Team (11)
Website	http://www.invesco.com/us
Address	Invesco 11 Greenway Plaza, Ste. 2500 Houston TX 77046 United States
Phone Number	800-659-1005

PERFORMANCE

Ratings History
Date	Overall Rating	Risk Rating	Reward Rating
Q4-18	C	C+	C
Q2-18	D+	C	D
Q4-17	D+	C	D+
Q4-16	C+	C+	C+
Q4-15	C+	C+	C

Asset & Performance History
Date	NAV	1-Year Total Return
2017	24	-9.05
2016	26.43	3.91
2015	25.65	6.96
2014	23.98	11.43
2013	21.52	-1.33
2012	21.81	-2.81

Total Assets: $535,132,772
Asset Allocation
Asset	%
Cash	38%
Stocks	50%
US Stocks	50%
Bonds	12%
US Bonds	12%
Other	0%

Services Offered:

Investment Strategy: The investment seeks to establish long positions in ICE U.S. Dollar Index futures contracts with a view to tracking the changes, whether positive or negative, in the level of the Deutsche Bank Long USD Currency Portfolio Index — Excess ReturnTM over time, plus the excess, if any, of the sum of the fund's Treasury Income, Money Market Income and T-Bill ETF Income over the expenses of the fund.
The fund invests in futures contracts in an attempt to track its index. The index is calculated to reflect the changes in market value over time, whether positive or negative, of long positions in DX Contracts. **Top Holdings:** Dollar Index Dec18   United States Treasury Bills 0%   Invesco Treasury Collateral ETF   Invesco Treasury Collateral ETF United States Treasury Bills 0%

ProShares UltraPro Dow30   C   HOLD

Ticker	Traded On	NAV	Total Assets ($)	Dividend Yield (TTM)	Turnover Ratio	Expense Ratio
UDOW	NYSE Arca	71.37	$534,516,796	0.44		0.95

Ratings
Reward	C
Risk	C
Recent Upgrade/Downgrade	Down

Fund Information
Fund Type	Exchange Traded Funds
Category	Trading Tools
Sub-Category	Trading--Leveraged Equity
Prospectus Objective	Growth
Inception Date	Feb-10
Open to New Investments	Y

Prices
Price (as of 12/31/2018)	71.31
52-Week High	116.82
52-Week Low	59.11

Total Returns (%)
3-Month	6-Month	1-Year	3-Year	5-Year
-35.82	-15.77	-23.51	123.64	157.66

3-Year Standard Deviation	31.7
Effective Duration	

Valuation
Premium/Discount (1-Year Average)	0.10

Company Information
Provider	ProShares
Manager/Tenure	Michael Neches (5), Devin Sullivan (0)
Website	http://www.proshares.com
Address	ProShares 7501 Wisconsin Avenue, Suite 1000 Bethesda MD 20814 United States
Phone Number	866-776-5125

PERFORMANCE

Ratings History
Date	Overall Rating	Risk Rating	Reward Rating
Q4-18	C	C	C
Q2-18	C	C	C+
Q4-17	B	C	A
Q4-16	C	C	C+
Q4-15	C+	C+	C

Asset & Performance History
Date	NAV	1-Year Total Return
2017	93.9	98.87
2016	47.29	47.02
2015	32.28	-8.35
2014	35.3	25.7
2013	28.22	106.69
2012	13.71	26.4

Total Assets: $534,516,796
Asset Allocation
Asset	%
Cash	-200%
Stocks	300%
US Stocks	300%
Bonds	0%
US Bonds	0%
Other	0%

Services Offered:

Investment Strategy: The investment seeks daily investment results, before fees and expenses, that correspond to three times (3x) the daily performance of the Dow Jones Industrial AverageSM. The fund invests in financial instruments that ProShare Advisors believes, in combination, should produce daily returns consistent with the fund's investment objective. The index is a price-weighted index and includes 30 large-cap, "blue-chip" U.S. stocks, excluding utility and transportation companies. The fund is non-diversified. **Top Holdings:** Dj Industrial Average Swap Societe Generale   Dj Industrial Average Index Swap Bnp Paribas   Dj Industrial Average Swap Bank Of America, Na   Dj Industrial Average Swap Citibank, N.A.   Dj Industrial Average Swap Goldman Sachs International

Invesco S&P 500® Equal Weight Consumer Staples ETF　　　　　　　C+　　HOLD

Ticker	Traded On	NAV		Total Assets ($)	Dividend Yield (TTM)	Turnover Ratio	Expense Ratio
RHS	NYSE Arca	116.47		$533,950,976	2.05		0.4

Ratings
Reward　　　　　　　　　　　　　　B
Risk　　　　　　　　　　　　　　　C
Recent Upgrade/Downgrade　　　　　Up

Fund Information
Fund Type　　　　　　Exchange Traded Funds
Category　　　　　　Consumer Goods & Svcs
Sub-Category　　　　　Consumer Defensive
Prospectus Objective　　　　　Unaligned
Inception Date　　　　　　　　　Nov-06
Open to New Investments　　　　　　Y

Prices
Price (as of 12/31/2018)　　　　　116.48
52-Week High　　　　　　　　　137.38
52-Week Low　　　　　　　　　112.22

Total Returns (%)

3-Month	6-Month	1-Year	3-Year	5-Year
-8.32	-4.74	-10.72	6.69	42.31

3-Year Standard Deviation　　　　　9.86
Effective Duration

Valuation
Premium/Discount (1-Year Average)　　0.02

Company Information
Provider　　　　Invesco
Manager/Tenure　Peter Hubbard (0), Michael Jeanette (0), Jonathan Nixon (0), 1 other
Website　　　　http://www.invesco.com/us
Address　　　　Invesco 11 Greenway Plaza, Ste. 2500 Houston TX 77046 United States
Phone Number　800-659-1005

PERFORMANCE

Ratings History	Overall Rating	Risk Rating	Reward Rating
Date			
Q4-18	C+	C	B
Q2-18	C+	C	B-
Q4-17	B	A-	C+
Q4-16	C	C	C+
Q4-15	B	C	B+

Asset & Performance History		1-Year
Date	NAV	Total Return
2017	133.52	13.6
2016	119.44	4.3
2015	115.93	13.1
2014	104.45	17.92
2013	90.22	32.55
2012	69.2	12.18

Total Assets: $533,950,976
Asset Allocation

Asset	%
Cash	0%
Stocks	100%
US Stocks	100%
Bonds	0%
US Bonds	0%
Other	0%

Services Offered:

Investment Strategy: The investment seeks to track the investment results (before fees and expenses) of the S&P 500® Equal Weight Consumer Staples Index (the "underlying index"). The fund generally will invest at least 90% of its total assets in the securities that comprise the underlying index. The underlying index is an equal-weighted version of the S&P 500® Consumer Staples Index. Strictly in accordance with its guidelines and mandated procedures, the index provider compiles, maintains and calculates the underlying index, which is comprised of common stocks of companies in the consumer staples sector of the S&P 500® Index. The fund is non-diversified. **Top Holdings:** Walgreens Boots Alliance Inc　McCormick & Co Inc Non-Voting　Procter & Gamble Co　Church & Dwight Co Inc　Coca-Cola Co

iShares MSCI Singapore Capped ETF　　　　　　　　　　　　C-　　HOLD

Ticker	Traded On	NAV		Total Assets ($)	Dividend Yield (TTM)	Turnover Ratio	Expense Ratio
EWS	NYSE Arca	22.21		$526,886,552	4.93	26	0.49

Ratings
Reward　　　　　　　　　　　　　C-
Risk　　　　　　　　　　　　　　　C
Recent Upgrade/Downgrade　　　　　Down

Fund Information
Fund Type　　　　　　Exchange Traded Funds
Category　　　　　　Asia ex-Japan Equity
Sub-Category　　　　　Miscellaneous Region
Prospectus Objective　　　　　Pacific Stock
Inception Date　　　　　　　　　Mar-96
Open to New Investments　　　　　　Y

Prices
Price (as of 12/31/2018)　　　　　22.10
52-Week High　　　　　　　　　28.19
52-Week Low　　　　　　　　　21.71

Total Returns (%)

3-Month	6-Month	1-Year	3-Year	5-Year
-6.68	-3.83	-11.00	20.40	1.67

3-Year Standard Deviation　　　　　15.61
Effective Duration

Valuation
Premium/Discount (1-Year Average)　　0.01

Company Information
Provider　　　　iShares
Manager/Tenure　Diane Hsiung (10), Greg Savage (10), Jennifer Hsui (5), 1 other
Website　　　　http://www.ishares.com
Address　　　　iShares 400 Howard Street San Francisco CA 94105 United States
Phone Number　800-474-2737

PERFORMANCE

Ratings History	Overall Rating	Risk Rating	Reward Rating
Date			
Q4-18	C-	C	C-
Q2-18	C	C+	C
Q4-17	C+	C	C+
Q4-16	D	D+	D
Q4-15	D+	D+	D+

Asset & Performance History		1-Year
Date	NAV	Total Return
2017	25.97	33.81
2016	20.11	1.11
2015	20.66	-17.94
2014	26.16	2.91
2013	26.28	0.95
2012	27.06	29.99

Total Assets: $526,886,552
Asset Allocation

Asset	%
Cash	0%
Stocks	100%
US Stocks	0%
Bonds	0%
US Bonds	0%
Other	0%

Services Offered: CashInvestment Plan

Investment Strategy: The investment seeks to track the investment results of the MSCI Singapore 25/50 Index. The fund will at all times invest at least 80% of its assets in the securities of its underlying index and in depositary receipts representing securities in its underlying index. The index is designed to measure the performance of the large- and mid-cap segments of the Singapore market. A capping methodology is applied that limits the weight of any single component to a maximum of 25% of the underlying index. The fund is non-diversified. **Top Holdings:** DBS Group Holdings Ltd　Oversea-Chinese Banking Corp Ltd　United Overseas Bank Ltd　Singapore Telecommunications Ltd　Keppel Corp Ltd

iShares MSCI ACWI Low Carbon Target ETF   C-   HOLD

Ticker	Traded On	NAV	Total Assets ($)	Dividend Yield (TTM)	Turnover Ratio	Expense Ratio
CRBN	NYSE Arca	103.66	$524,047,546	2.26	18	0.2

Ratings
Reward   C-
Risk   C-
Recent Upgrade/Downgrade   Down

Fund Information
Fund Type   Exchange Traded Funds
Category   Global Equity Large Cap
Sub-Category   World Large Stock
Prospectus Objective   World Stock
Inception Date   Dec-14
Open to New Investments   Y

Prices
Price (as of 12/31/2018)   103.02
52-Week High   125.90
52-Week Low   99.00

Total Returns (%)

3-Month	6-Month	1-Year	3-Year	5-Year
-12.76	-8.46	-9.38	20.66	

3-Year Standard Deviation   9.68
Effective Duration

Valuation
Premium/Discount (1-Year Average)   0.01

Company Information
Provider   iShares
Manager/Tenure   Diane Hsiung (3), Jennifer Hsui (3),
                  Greg Savage (3), 3 others
Website   http://www.ishares.com
Address   iShares 400 Howard Street San
                  Francisco CA 94105 United States
Phone Number   800-474-2737

PERFORMANCE

Ratings History

Date	Overall Rating	Risk Rating	Reward Rating
Q4-18	C-	C-	C-
Q2-18	C	D+	C
Q4-17	C+	B-	C+
Q4-16	C-	C-	D+
Q4-15	U		

Asset & Performance History

Date	NAV	1-Year Total Return
2017	117.1	23.71
2016	96.7	7.63
2015	91.94	-1.34
2014	95.04	
2013		
2012		

Total Assets: $524,047,546
Asset Allocation

Asset	%
Cash	1%
Stocks	99%
US Stocks	55%
Bonds	0%
US Bonds	0%
Other	0%

Services Offered:

Investment Strategy: The investment seeks to track the investment results of the MSCI ACWI Low Carbon Target Index. The fund generally will invest at least 90% of its assets in the component securities of the underlying index and in investments that have economic characteristics that are substantially identical to the component securities of the underlying index. The underlying index is designed to address two dimensions of carbon exposure - carbon emissions and potential carbon emissions from fossil fuel reserves. **Top Holdings:** Apple Inc   Microsoft Corp   Amazon.com Inc   Johnson & Johnson   JPMorgan Chase & Co

---

iShares MSCI Russia Capped ETF   C+   HOLD

Ticker	Traded On	NAV	Total Assets ($)	Dividend Yield (TTM)	Turnover Ratio	Expense Ratio
ERUS	NYSE Arca	30.96	$524,009,652	3.25	32	0.59

Ratings
Reward   C+
Risk   C+
Recent Upgrade/Downgrade   Up

Fund Information
Fund Type   Exchange Traded Funds
Category   Equity Misc
Sub-Category   Miscellaneous Region
Prospectus Objective   Foreign Stock
Inception Date   Nov-10
Open to New Investments   Y

Prices
Price (as of 12/31/2018)   30.80
52-Week High   39.23
52-Week Low   30.59

Total Returns (%)

3-Month	6-Month	1-Year	3-Year	5-Year
-8.45	-4.31	-3.66	54.98	-11.81

3-Year Standard Deviation   19.96
Effective Duration

Valuation
Premium/Discount (1-Year Average)   -0.29

Company Information
Provider   iShares
Manager/Tenure   Diane Hsiung (8), Greg Savage (8),
                  Jennifer Hsui (5), 1 other
Website   http://www.ishares.com
Address   iShares 400 Howard Street San
                  Francisco CA 94105 United States
Phone Number   800-474-2737

PERFORMANCE

Ratings History

Date	Overall Rating	Risk Rating	Reward Rating
Q4-18	C+	C+	C+
Q2-18	C	C	C
Q4-17	B	C	A-
Q4-16	C-	D+	C-
Q4-15	D	D	D

Asset & Performance History

Date	NAV	1-Year Total Return
2017	33.61	4.5
2016	33.42	53.94
2015	22.28	3.36
2014	22.38	-44.95
2013	43.12	-3.21
2012	45.92	13.67

Total Assets: $524,009,652
Asset Allocation

Asset	%
Cash	0%
Stocks	100%
US Stocks	0%
Bonds	0%
US Bonds	0%
Other	0%

Services Offered:

Investment Strategy: The investment seeks to track the investment results of the MSCI Russia 25/50 Index. The fund generally will invest at least 90% of its assets in the component securities of the underlying index and in investments that have economic characteristics that are substantially identical to the component securities of the underlying index. The index is designed to measure the performance of equity securities listed on stock exchanges in Russia. The fund is non-diversified. **Top Holdings:** PJSC Lukoil   Gazprom PJSC   Sberbank of Russia PJSC   Mining and Metallurgical Company NORILSK NICKEL PJSC   Sberbank of Russia PJSC ADR

SPDR® S&P Metals and Mining ETF   C   HOLD

Ticker	Traded On	NAV	Total Assets ($)	Dividend Yield (TTM)	Turnover Ratio	Expense Ratio
XME	NYSE Arca	26.22	$523,922,229	2.62	51	0.35

Ratings
Reward	C+
Risk	D+
Recent Upgrade/Downgrade	

Fund Information
Fund Type	Exchange Traded Funds
Category	Natural Resources
Sub-Category	Natural Resources
Prospectus Objective	Natl Res
Inception Date	Jun-06
Open to New Investments	Y

Prices
Price (as of 12/31/2018)	26.19
52-Week High	39.17
52-Week Low	25.28

Total Returns (%)
3-Month	6-Month	1-Year	3-Year	5-Year
-23.44	-25.57	-26.16	83.00	-32.32

3-Year Standard Deviation	33.17
Effective Duration	

Valuation
Premium/Discount (1-Year Average)	0.00

Company Information
Provider	SPDR State Street Global Advisors
Manager/Tenure	Michael J. Feehily (7), Karl A. Schneider (4), Raymond V. Donofrio (1)
Website	http://www.spdrs.com
Address	SPDR State Street Global Advisors State Street Financial Center, 1 Lincoln Street Boston MA 02111-2900 United States
Phone Number	617-786-3000

PERFORMANCE

Ratings History
Date	Overall Rating	Risk Rating	Reward Rating
Q4-18	C	D+	C+
Q2-18	C	C-	C+
Q4-17	C	D+	C+
Q4-16	C	D+	C
Q4-15	C	C-	C

Asset & Performance History
Date	NAV	1-Year Total Return
2017	36.12	20.22
2016	30.44	110.82
2015	14.95	-50.51
2014	30.86	-25.26
2013	42.07	-5.4
2012	45.14	-6.52

Total Assets: $523,922,229
Asset Allocation
Asset	%
Cash	0%
Stocks	100%
US Stocks	99%
Bonds	0%
US Bonds	0%
Other	0%

Services Offered:

Investment Strategy: The investment seeks to provide investment results that, before fees and expenses, correspond generally to the total return performance of an index derived from the metals and mining segment of a U.S. total market composite index. In seeking to track the performance of the S&P Metals & Mining Select Industry Index (the "index"), the fund employs a sampling strategy. It generally invests substantially all, but at least 80%, of its total assets in the securities comprising the index. The index represents the metals and mining segment of the S&P Total Market Index ("S&P TMI"). The fund is non-diversified. **Top Holdings:** Newmont Mining Corp Royal Gold Inc Allegheny Technologies Inc Nucor Corp Reliance Steel & Aluminum Co

---

iShares Emerging Markets Dividend ETF   C   HOLD

Ticker	Traded On	NAV	Total Assets ($)	Dividend Yield (TTM)	Turnover Ratio	Expense Ratio
DVYE	NYSE Arca	37.48	$521,240,094	5.62	55	0.49

Ratings
Reward	C-
Risk	C+
Recent Upgrade/Downgrade	Up

Fund Information
Fund Type	Exchange Traded Funds
Category	Global Emerg Mkts Equity
Sub-Category	Diversified Emerging Mkts
Prospectus Objective	Div Emerg Mkts
Inception Date	Feb-12
Open to New Investments	Y

Prices
Price (as of 12/31/2018)	37.43
52-Week High	46.10
52-Week Low	36.59

Total Returns (%)
3-Month	6-Month	1-Year	3-Year	5-Year
-3.18	-0.91	-5.41	43.01	-1.01

3-Year Standard Deviation	14.05
Effective Duration	

Valuation
Premium/Discount (1-Year Average)	-0.16

Company Information
Provider	iShares
Manager/Tenure	Diane Hsiung (6), Greg Savage (6), Jennifer Hsui (6), 3 others
Website	http://www.ishares.com
Address	iShares 400 Howard Street San Francisco CA 94105 United States
Phone Number	800-474-2737

PERFORMANCE

Ratings History
Date	Overall Rating	Risk Rating	Reward Rating
Q4-18	C	C+	C-
Q2-18	C-	C-	C
Q4-17	C	C	C
Q4-16	D+	D+	D+
Q4-15	D	D	D

Asset & Performance History
Date	NAV	1-Year Total Return
2017	41.83	25.7
2016	34.95	20.28
2015	30.43	-23.77
2014	42.15	-9.2
2013	48.31	-9.51
2012	55.91	

Total Assets: $521,240,094
Asset Allocation
Asset	%
Cash	1%
Stocks	99%
US Stocks	0%
Bonds	0%
US Bonds	0%
Other	0%

Services Offered:

Investment Strategy: The investment seeks to track the investment results of the Dow Jones Emerging Markets Select Dividend Index, which measures the performance of a group of equity securities issued by companies in emerging market countries that have provided relatively high dividend yields on a consistent basis over time. The fund generally will invest at least 90% of its assets in the component securities of the index and in investments that have economic characteristics that are substantially identical to the component securities of the index. **Top Holdings:** Seaspan Corp Farglory Land Development Co Ltd Severstal PAO Highwealth Construction Corp ALROSA PJSC

Invesco NASDAQ Internet ETF   C+   HOLD

Ticker	Traded On	NAV	Total Assets ($)	Dividend Yield (TTM)	Turnover Ratio	Expense Ratio
PNQI	NAS CM	109.84	$519,533,990	0.02	20	0.6

Ratings
Reward	B
Risk	C-
Recent Upgrade/Downgrade	Down

Fund Information
Fund Type	Exchange Traded Funds
Category	Technology Sector Equity
Sub-Category	Technology
Prospectus Objective	Technology
Inception Date	Jun-08
Open to New Investments	Y

Prices
Price (as of 12/31/2018)	109.83
52-Week High	146.88
52-Week Low	102.97

Total Returns (%)
3-Month	6-Month	1-Year	3-Year	5-Year
-17.98	-21.79	-5.02	37.12	61.04

3-Year Standard Deviation	16.2
Effective Duration	

Valuation
Premium/Discount (1-Year Average)	0.04

Company Information
Provider	Invesco
Manager/Tenure	Peter Hubbard (10), Michael Jeanette (10), Tony Seisser (4), 1 other
Website	http://www.invesco.com/us
Address	Invesco 11 Greenway Plaza, Ste. 2500 Houston TX 77046 United States
Phone Number	800-659-1005

PERFORMANCE

Ratings History
Date	Overall Rating	Risk Rating	Reward Rating
Q4-18	C+	C-	B
Q2-18	B-	C-	B+
Q4-17	B+	B	A-
Q4-16	C+	C-	B
Q4-15	B-	C	B

Asset & Performance History
Date	NAV	1-Year Total Return
2017	115.65	39.94
2016	82.66	3.17
2015	80.12	19.36
2014	67.12	-1.61
2013	68.22	64.78
2012	41.4	20.06

Total Assets: $519,533,990

Asset Allocation
Asset	%
Cash	0%
Stocks	100%
US Stocks	82%
Bonds	0%
US Bonds	0%
Other	0%

Services Offered:

Investment Strategy: The investment seeks to track the investment results (before fees and expenses) of the NASDAQ Internet IndexSM. The fund generally will invest at least 90% of its total assets in securities that comprise the underlying index. The underlying index is designed to track the performance of the largest and most liquid U.S.-listed companies engaged in Internet-related businesses that are listed on one of the three major U.S. stock exchanges. The fund is non-diversified. **Top Holdings:** Booking Holdings Inc Alphabet Inc Class C Amazon.com Inc Facebook Inc A Netflix Inc

---

First Trust NASDAQ-100 Equal Weighted Index Fund   C-   HOLD

Ticker	Traded On	NAV	Total Assets ($)	Dividend Yield (TTM)	Turnover Ratio	Expense Ratio
QQEW	NAS CM	54.61	$518,806,728	0.48	26	0.6

Ratings
Reward	C
Risk	C-
Recent Upgrade/Downgrade	Down

Fund Information
Fund Type	Exchange Traded Funds
Category	US Equity Large Cap Growth
Sub-Category	Large Growth
Prospectus Objective	Growth
Inception Date	Apr-06
Open to New Investments	Y

Prices
Price (as of 12/31/2018)	54.60
52-Week High	64.28
52-Week Low	51.19

Total Returns (%)
3-Month	6-Month	1-Year	3-Year	5-Year
-13.80	-9.85	-5.16	27.88	55.71

3-Year Standard Deviation	11.96
Effective Duration	

Valuation
Premium/Discount (1-Year Average)	0.06

Company Information
Provider	First Trust
Manager/Tenure	Jon C. Erickson (12), Daniel J. Lindquist (12), David G. McGarel (12), 3 others
Website	http://www.ftportfolios.com/
Address	First Trust 120 E. Liberty Drive, Suite 400 Wheaton IL 60187 United States
Phone Number	800-621-1675

PERFORMANCE

Ratings History
Date	Overall Rating	Risk Rating	Reward Rating
Q4-18	C-	C-	C
Q2-18	C	C-	C+
Q4-17	B	B+	B
Q4-16	C-	C-	C-
Q4-15	C+	C+	C

Asset & Performance History
Date	NAV	1-Year Total Return
2017	57.88	25.99
2016	46.17	7.02
2015	43.48	2.21
2014	42.8	19.12
2013	36.34	39.95
2012	26.1	14.85

Total Assets: $518,806,728

Asset Allocation
Asset	%
Cash	0%
Stocks	100%
US Stocks	90%
Bonds	0%
US Bonds	0%
Other	0%

Services Offered:

Investment Strategy: The investment seeks investment results that correspond generally to the price and yield (before the fund's fees and expenses) of an equity index called the NASDAQ-100 Equal Weighted IndexSM. The fund will normally invest at least 90% of its net assets (including investment borrowings) in common stocks that comprise the index. The NASDAQ-100 Equal Weighted Index is the equal-weighted version of the NASDAQ-100 Index® which includes 100 of the largest non-financial companies listed on Nasdaq based on market capitalization. **Top Holdings:** Walgreens Boots Alliance Inc Starbucks Corp Xilinx Inc Tesla Inc MercadoLibre Inc

Invesco Treasury Collateral ETF   D+   SELL

Ticker	Traded On	NAV	Total Assets ($)	Dividend Yield (TTM)	Turnover Ratio	Expense Ratio
CLTL	NYSE Arca	105.44	$517,987,317	2.13		0.08

Ratings
Reward	D+
Risk	C-
Recent Upgrade/Downgrade	Up

Fund Information
Fund Type	Exchange Traded Funds
Category	US Fixed Income
Sub-Category	Ultrashort Bond
Prospectus Objective	Govt Bond - Treasury
Inception Date	Jan-17
Open to New Investments	Y

Prices
Price (as of 12/31/2018)	105.44
52-Week High	106.48
52-Week Low	105.29

Total Returns (%)
3-Month	6-Month	1-Year	3-Year	5-Year
0.58	1.05	1.80		

3-Year Standard Deviation	
Effective Duration	

Valuation
Premium/Discount (1-Year Average)	0.02

Company Information
Provider	Invesco
Manager/Tenure	Laurie F. Brignac (1), Peter Hubbard (1), Jeffrey W. Kernagis (1), 3 others
Website	http://www.invesco.com/us
Address	Invesco 11 Greenway Plaza, Ste. 2500 Houston TX 77046 United States
Phone Number	800-659-1005

PERFORMANCE

Ratings History
Date	Overall Rating	Risk Rating	Reward Rating
Q4-18	D+	C-	D+
Q2-18	D+	D+	D+
Q4-17	D-	B-	D
Q4-16			
Q4-15			

Asset & Performance History
Date	NAV	1-Year Total Return
2017	105.33	0.67
2016		
2015		
2014		
2013		
2012		

Total Assets: $517,987,317
Asset Allocation
Asset	%
Cash	51%
Stocks	0%
US Stocks	0%
Bonds	49%
US Bonds	49%
Other	0%

Services Offered:

Investment Strategy: The investment seeks to track the investment results (before fees and expenses) of the ICE U.S. Treasury Short Bond Index. The fund generally will invest at least 80% of its total assets in the components of the index. The index is designed to measure the performance of U.S. Treasury Obligations with a maximum remaining maturity of 12 months. "U.S. Treasury Obligations" refer to securities issued or guaranteed by the U.S. Treasury where the payment of principal and interest is backed by the full faith and credit of the U.S. government. They include U.S. Treasury notes, bills and bonds. It is non-diversified. **Top Holdings:** United States Treasury Bills 0%   United States Treasury Bills 0%   United States Treasury Notes 1.5%   United States Treasury Bills 0%   United States Treasury Bills 0%

Invesco BulletShares 2021 High Yield Corporate Bond ETF   C   HOLD

Ticker	Traded On	NAV	Total Assets ($)	Dividend Yield (TTM)	Turnover Ratio	Expense Ratio
BSJL	NYSE Arca	23.71	$513,459,773	5.07	14	0.42

Ratings
Reward	C
Risk	C+
Recent Upgrade/Downgrade	

Fund Information
Fund Type	Exchange Traded Funds
Category	US Fixed Income
Sub-Category	High Yield Bond
Prospectus Objective	Corp Bond-High Yld
Inception Date	Sep-14
Open to New Investments	Y

Prices
Price (as of 12/31/2018)	23.66
52-Week High	25.08
52-Week Low	23.39

Total Returns (%)
3-Month	6-Month	1-Year	3-Year	5-Year
-2.92	-0.70	0.01	20.74	

3-Year Standard Deviation	3.51
Effective Duration	2.07

Valuation
Premium/Discount (1-Year Average)	-0.07

Company Information
Provider	Invesco
Manager/Tenure	Jeremy Neisewander (2), Peter Hubbard (0), Jeffrey W. Kernagis (0), 1 other
Website	http://www.invesco.com/us
Address	Invesco 11 Greenway Plaza, Ste. 2500 Houston TX 77046 United States
Phone Number	800-659-1005

PERFORMANCE

Ratings History
Date	Overall Rating	Risk Rating	Reward Rating
Q4-18	C	C+	C
Q2-18	C+	C+	C
Q4-17	B-	B	C+
Q4-16	C-	C-	C-
Q4-15	U		

Asset & Performance History
Date	NAV	1-Year Total Return
2017	24.88	5.54
2016	24.67	13.81
2015	22.84	-1.48
2014	24.35	
2013		
2012		

Total Assets: $513,459,773
Asset Allocation
Asset	%
Cash	3%
Stocks	0%
US Stocks	0%
Bonds	97%
US Bonds	88%
Other	0%

Services Offered:

Investment Strategy: The investment seeks investment results that correspond generally to the performance, before the fund's fees and expenses, of a high yield corporate bond index called the Nasdaq BulletShares® USD High Yield Corporate Bond 2021 Index. The fund will invest at least 80% of its total assets in component securities that comprise the index. The index is designed to represent the performance of a held-to-maturity portfolio of U.S. dollar-denominated high yield corporate bonds with effective maturities in the year 2021. The fund is non-diversified. **Top Holdings:** Sprint Corporation 7.25%   T-Mobile USA, Inc. 6.5%   DISH DBS Corporation 6.75%   Blackstone CQP Holdco 6.5%   Bombardier Inc. 8.75%

VanEck Vectors Preferred Securities ex Financials ETF

C   HOLD

Ticker	Traded On	NAV	Total Assets ($)	Dividend Yield (TTM)	Turnover Ratio	Expense Ratio
PFXF	NYSE Arca	17.70	$511,491,198	6.32	47	0.41

Ratings

Reward	C-
Risk	C+
Recent Upgrade/Downgrade	

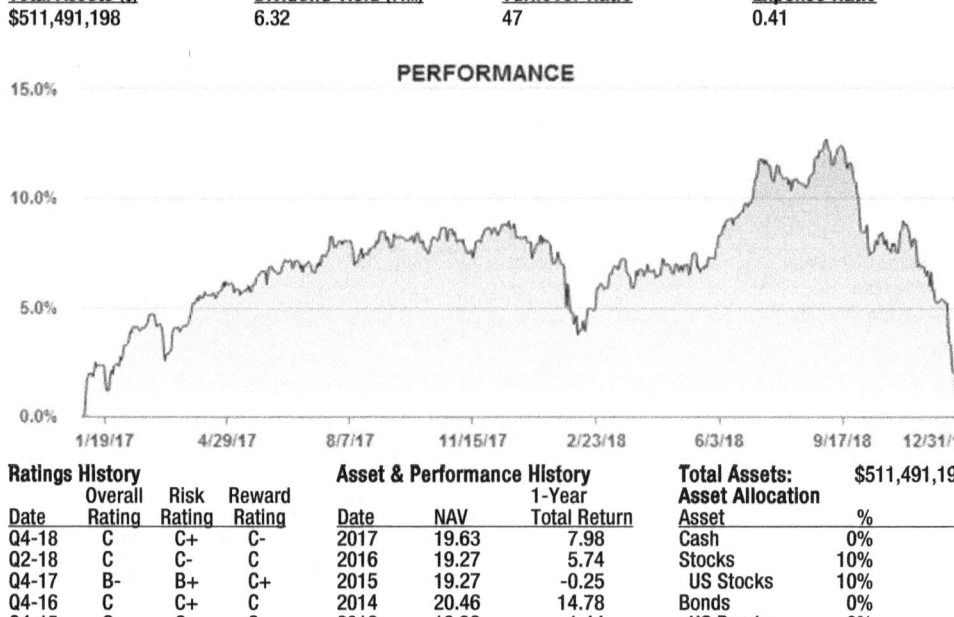

PERFORMANCE

Fund Information

Fund Type	Exchange Traded Funds
Category	US Fixed Income
Sub-Category	Preferred Stock
Prospectus Objective	Income
Inception Date	Jul-12
Open to New Investments	Y

Prices

Price (as of 12/31/2018)	17.72
52-Week High	19.82
52-Week Low	17.35

Total Returns (%)

3-Month	6-Month	1-Year	3-Year	5-Year
-6.67	-7.02	-4.78	8.72	24.48

3-Year Standard Deviation	5.34
Effective Duration	

Valuation

Premium/Discount (1-Year Average)	0.10

Company Information

Provider	VanEck
Manager/Tenure	Hao-Hung (Peter) Liao (6), Guo Hua (Jason) Jin (0)
Website	http://www.vaneck.com
Address	Van Eck Associates Corporation 666 Third Avenue New York NY 10017 United States
Phone Number	800-826-1115

Ratings History

Date	Overall Rating	Risk Rating	Reward Rating
Q4-18	C	C+	C-
Q2-18	C	C-	C
Q4-17	B-	B+	C+
Q4-16	C	C+	C
Q4-15	C	C-	C

Asset & Performance History

Date	NAV	1-Year Total Return
2017	19.63	7.98
2016	19.27	5.74
2015	19.27	-0.25
2014	20.46	14.78
2013	18.92	-1.44
2012	20.43	

Total Assets: $511,491,198

Asset Allocation

Asset	%
Cash	0%
Stocks	10%
US Stocks	10%
Bonds	0%
US Bonds	0%
Other	7%

Services Offered:

Investment Strategy: The investment seeks to replicate as closely as possible, before fees and expenses, the price and yield performance of the Wells Fargo® Hybrid and Preferred Securities ex Financials Index (the "Preferred Securities Index"). The fund normally invests at least 80% of its total assets in securities that comprise the fund's benchmark index. The index is comprised of convertible or exchangeable and non-convertible preferred securities listed on U.S. exchanges. The fund is non-diversified. **Top Holdings:** Becton Dickinson NextEra Energy Inc Unit Sempra Energy 6% PRF CONVERT 15/01/2021 USD 100 Dominion Energy Inc Unit AT&T Inc 0%

United States Commodity Index Fund, LP

D+   SELL

Ticker	Traded On	NAV	Total Assets ($)	Dividend Yield (TTM)	Turnover Ratio	Expense Ratio
USCI	NYSE Arca	37.49	$509,812,503	0		1.04

Ratings

Reward	D
Risk	C-
Recent Upgrade/Downgrade	Down

PERFORMANCE

Fund Information

Fund Type	Exchange Traded Funds
Category	Commodities Broad Basket
Sub-Category	Commodities Broad Basket
Prospectus Objective	Natl Res
Inception Date	Aug-10
Open to New Investments	Y

Prices

Price (as of 12/31/2018)	37.53
52-Week High	45.26
52-Week Low	37.49

Total Returns (%)

3-Month	6-Month	1-Year	3-Year	5-Year
-12.55	-12.89	-11.73	-7.45	-33.11

3-Year Standard Deviation	8.7
Effective Duration	

Valuation

Premium/Discount (1-Year Average)	-0.02

Company Information

Provider	USCF Investments
Manager/Tenure	Management Team (8)
Website	http://www.uscfinvestments.com
Address	USCF 1290 Broadway, Suite 1100 Denver CO 80203 United States
Phone Number	

Ratings History

Date	Overall Rating	Risk Rating	Reward Rating
Q4-18	D+	C-	D
Q2-18	C-	C-	C-
Q4-17	D	D+	D
Q4-16	D	D	D
Q4-15	D	D	D

Asset & Performance History

Date	NAV	1-Year Total Return
2017	42.48	6.14
2016	40.02	-1.22
2015	40.52	-16.01
2014	48.24	-13.95
2013	56.06	-4.1
2012	58.46	-0.02

Total Assets: $509,812,503

Asset Allocation

Asset	%
Cash	41%
Stocks	0%
US Stocks	0%
Bonds	11%
US Bonds	11%
Other	49%

Services Offered:

Investment Strategy: The investment seeks the daily changes in percentage terms of its shares' per share net asset value ("NAV") to reflect the daily changes in percentage terms of the SummerHaven Dynamic Commodity Index Total ReturnSM (the "SDCI"), less USCI's expenses.
The fund seeks to achieve its investment objective by investing to the fullest extent possible in the Benchmark Component Futures Contracts. The index is designed to reflect the performance of a diversified group of commodities. **Top Holdings:** United States Treasury Bills Future Contract On Natural Gas Futr May19 Future Contract On Copper Future Mar19 Future Contract On Gold 100 Oz Futr Feb19 Future Contract On Cotton No.2 Futr Mar19

Invesco BulletShares 2018 High Yield Corporate Bond ETF   C   HOLD

Ticker	Traded On	NAV
BSJI	NYSE Arca	

Total Assets ($)	Dividend Yield (TTM)	Turnover Ratio	Expense Ratio
$509,798,645	2.97	0	0.42

Ratings
Reward	C
Risk	C+
Recent Upgrade/Downgrade	

Fund Information
Fund Type	Exchange Traded Funds
Category	US Fixed Income
Sub-Category	High Yield Bond
Prospectus Objective	Corp Bond-High Yld
Inception Date	Apr-12
Open to New Investments	Y

Prices
Price (as of 12/31/2018)	25.09
52-Week High	25.18
52-Week Low	24.86

Total Returns (%)
3-Month	6-Month	1-Year	3-Year	5-Year
0.28	1.08	2.43	17.85	14.38

3-Year Standard Deviation	2.54
Effective Duration	0.32

Valuation
Premium/Discount (1-Year Average)	-0.15

Company Information
Provider	Invesco
Manager/Tenure	Jeremy Neisewander (2), Peter Hubbard (0), Jeffrey W. Kernagis (0), 1 other
Website	http://www.invesco.com/us
Address	Invesco 11 Greenway Plaza, Ste. 2500 Houston TX 77046 United States
Phone Number	800-659-1005

PERFORMANCE

Ratings History
Date	Overall Rating	Risk Rating	Reward Rating
Q4-18	C	C+	C
Q2-18	C+	C+	C
Q4-17	C+	B	C
Q4-16	C	C+	C
Q4-15	C	C-	C

Asset & Performance History
Date	NAV	1-Year Total Return
2017	25.13	3.68
2016	25.13	10.51
2015	23.75	-3.4
2014	25.73	0.63
2013	26.85	8.28
2012	26.02	

Total Assets: $509,798,645

Asset Allocation
Asset	%
Cash	96%
Stocks	0%
US Stocks	0%
Bonds	4%
US Bonds	4%
Other	0%

Services Offered:

Investment Strategy: The investment seeks investment results that correspond generally to the performance, before the fund's fees and expenses, of a high yield corporate bond index called the Nasdaq BulletShares® USD High Yield Corporate Bond 2018 Index. The fund invests at least 80% of its total assets in component securities that comprise the index. The index is designed to represent the performance of a held-to-maturity portfolio of U.S. dollar-denominated high yield corporate bonds with effective maturities in the year 2018. The fund is non-diversified. **Top Holdings:** Apx Group, Inc. 7.88% Tegna Inc 6.38% Tervita Corp Univision Commmunications Inc. 6.75% Tervita Corp

---

FlexShares Morningstar Emerging Markets Factor Tilt Index Fund   C-   HOLD

Ticker	Traded On	NAV
TLTE	NYSE Arca	48.38

Total Assets ($)	Dividend Yield (TTM)	Turnover Ratio	Expense Ratio
$508,193,923	3.18		0.59

Ratings
Reward	C-
Risk	C-
Recent Upgrade/Downgrade	

Fund Information
Fund Type	Exchange Traded Funds
Category	Global Emerg Mkts Equity
Sub-Category	Diversified Emerging Mkts
Prospectus Objective	Div Emerg Mkts
Inception Date	Sep-12
Open to New Investments	Y

Prices
Price (as of 12/31/2018)	47.98
52-Week High	65.31
52-Week Low	46.27

Total Returns (%)
3-Month	6-Month	1-Year	3-Year	5-Year
-7.25	-8.21	-16.12	24.37	5.94

3-Year Standard Deviation	14.86
Effective Duration	

Valuation
Premium/Discount (1-Year Average)	-0.18

Company Information
Provider	Flexshares Trust
Manager/Tenure	Robert Anstine (5), Brendan Sullivan (2)
Website	http://www.flexshares.com
Address	50 South LaSalle Street Chicago, Illinois 60603 Chicago Illinois 60603 United States
Phone Number	855-353-9383

PERFORMANCE

Ratings History
Date	Overall Rating	Risk Rating	Reward Rating
Q4-18	C-	C-	C-
Q2-18	C-	C-	C
Q4-17	B-	C	B
Q4-16	D+	D+	D+
Q4-15	D+	D+	D+

Asset & Performance History
Date	NAV	1-Year Total Return
2017	59.28	32.36
2016	45.79	12.03
2015	41.83	-12.96
2014	49.02	-2.12
2013	51.11	-2.54
2012	52.89	

Total Assets: $508,193,923

Asset Allocation
Asset	%
Cash	1%
Stocks	99%
US Stocks	0%
Bonds	0%
US Bonds	0%
Other	0%

Services Offered:

Investment Strategy: The investment seeks investment results that correspond generally to the price and yield performance, before fees and expenses, of the Morningstar® Emerging Markets Factor Tilt IndexSM. The fund will invest at least 80% of its total assets (exclusive of collateral held from securities lending) in the securities of the underlying index and in ADRs and GDRs based on the securities in the underlying index. The underlying index reflects the performance of a selection of equity securities designed to provide broad exposure to the global emerging equities markets, with increased exposure (or a "tilt") to small-capitalization stocks and value stocks. **Top Holdings:** Tencent Holdings Ltd Samsung Electronics Co Ltd China Construction Bank Corp H Taiwan Semiconductor Manufacturing Co Ltd Industrial And Commercial Bank Of China Ltd H

ProShares Short 20+ Year Treasury   C   HOLD

Ticker	Traded On	NAV	Total Assets ($)	Dividend Yield (TTM)	Turnover Ratio	Expense Ratio
TBF	NYSE Arca	22.49	$508,106,552	0.46	0	0.91

Ratings
Reward   D+
Risk   C
Recent Upgrade/Downgrade

Fund Information
Fund Type   Exchange Traded Funds
Category   Trading Tools
Sub-Category   Trading--Inverse Debt
Prospectus Objective   Govt Bond - Treasury
Inception Date   Aug-09
Open to New Investments   Y

Prices
Price (as of 12/31/2018)   22.39
52-Week High   24.42
52-Week Low   21.87

Total Returns (%)

3-Month	6-Month	1-Year	3-Year	5-Year
-4.01	-0.05	3.81	-8.24	-31.07

3-Year Standard Deviation   9.71
Effective Duration

Valuation
Premium/Discount (1-Year Average)   0.09

Company Information
Provider   ProShares
Manager/Tenure   Michelle Liu (9), Jeffrey Ploshnick (2)
Website   http://www.proshares.com
Address   ProShares 7501 Wisconsin Avenue,
                    Suite 1000 Bethesda MD 20814
                    United States
Phone Number   866-776-5125

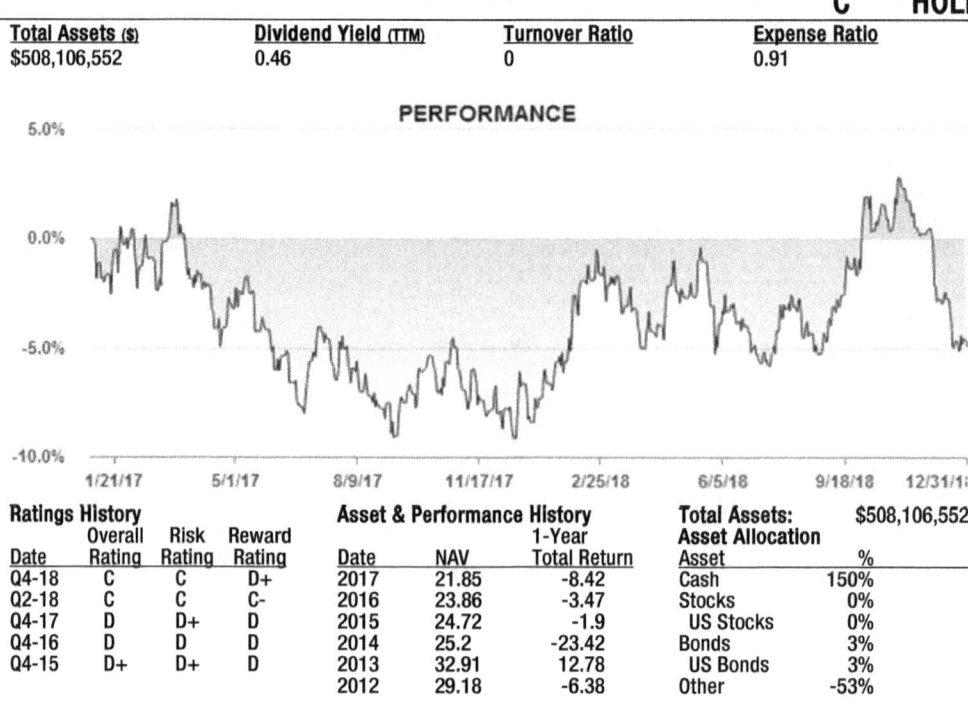

PERFORMANCE

Ratings History

Date	Overall Rating	Risk Rating	Reward Rating
Q4-18	C	C	D+
Q2-18	C	C	C-
Q4-17	D	D+	D
Q4-16	D	D	D
Q4-15	D+	D+	D

Asset & Performance History

Date	NAV	1-Year Total Return
2017	21.85	-8.42
2016	23.86	-3.47
2015	24.72	-1.9
2014	25.2	-23.42
2013	32.91	12.78
2012	29.18	-6.38

Total Assets: $508,106,552
Asset Allocation

Asset	%
Cash	150%
Stocks	0%
US Stocks	0%
Bonds	3%
US Bonds	3%
Other	-53%

Services Offered:

Investment Strategy: The investment seeks daily investment results, before fees and expenses, that correspond to the inverse (-1x) of the daily performance of the ICE U.S. Treasury 20+ Year Bond Index. The fund invests in financial instruments that ProShare Advisors believes, in combination, should produce daily returns consistent with the fund's investment objective. The index includes publicly- issued U.S. Treasury securities that have a remaining maturity greater than twenty years and have $300 million or more of outstanding face value, excluding amounts held by the Federal Reserve. The fund is non-diversified. **Top Holdings:** Ice 20+ Year U.S. Treasury Index Swap Societe Generale Ice 20+ Year U.S. Treasury Index Swap Citibank Na United States Treasury Bills United States Treasury Bills Ice 20+ Year U.S. Treasury Index Swap Goldman Sachs International

---

iShares U.S. Consumer Goods ETF   C   HOLD

Ticker	Traded On	NAV	Total Assets ($)	Dividend Yield (TTM)	Turnover Ratio	Expense Ratio
IYK	NYSE Arca	106.51	$507,078,500	2.46	7	0.43

Ratings
Reward   C
Risk   C-
Recent Upgrade/Downgrade

Fund Information
Fund Type   Exchange Traded Funds
Category   Consumer Goods & Svcs
Sub-Category   Consumer Defensive
Prospectus Objective   Unaligned
Inception Date   Jun-00
Open to New Investments   Y

Prices
Price (as of 12/31/2018)   106.44
52-Week High   130.64
52-Week Low   102.26

Total Returns (%)

3-Month	6-Month	1-Year	3-Year	5-Year
-9.94	-8.45	-13.72	5.42	24.28

3-Year Standard Deviation   8.28
Effective Duration

Valuation
Premium/Discount (1-Year Average)   0.03

Company Information
Provider   iShares
Manager/Tenure   Diane Hsiung (10), Greg Savage (10),
                    Jennifer Hsui (6), 3 others
Website   http://www.ishares.com
Address   iShares 400 Howard Street San
                    Francisco CA 94105 United States
Phone Number   800-474-2737

PERFORMANCE

Ratings History

Date	Overall Rating	Risk Rating	Reward Rating
Q4-18	C	C-	C
Q2-18	C	C-	C
Q4-17	B	A	C+
Q4-16	C	C	C+
Q4-15	C+	C	B-

Asset & Performance History

Date	NAV	1-Year Total Return
2017	126.67	16.52
2016	110.68	4.87
2015	108.3	5.61
2014	104.77	11.61
2013	95.67	29.92
2012	75.1	12.26

Total Assets: $507,078,500
Asset Allocation

Asset	%
Cash	0%
Stocks	100%
US Stocks	99%
Bonds	0%
US Bonds	0%
Other	0%

Services Offered: CashInvestment Plan

Investment Strategy: The investment seeks to track the investment results of the Dow Jones U.S. Consumer Goods Index composed of U.S. equities in the consumer goods sector. The fund generally invests at least 90% of its assets in securities of the underlying index and in depositary receipts representing securities of the underlying index. The underlying index measures the performance of the consumer goods sector of the U.S. equity market. The fund may invest the remainder of its assets in certain futures, options and swap contracts, cash and cash equivalents. It is non-diversified. **Top Holdings:** Procter & Gamble Co Coca-Cola Co PepsiCo Inc Philip Morris International Inc Altria Group Inc

InfraCap MLP ETF   C   HOLD

Ticker	Traded On	NAV	Total Assets ($)	Dividend Yield (TTM)	Turnover Ratio	Expense Ratio
AMZA	NYSE Arca	5.10	$506,603,201	8.98	104	1.93

Ratings
Reward   C+
Risk   D+
Recent Upgrade/Downgrade

Fund Information
Fund Type   Exchange Traded Funds
Category   Energy Sector Equity
Sub-Category   Energy Limited Partnership
Prospectus Objective   Growth & Inc
Inception Date   Oct-14
Open to New Investments   Y

Prices
Price (as of 12/31/2018)   5.02
52-Week High   9.04
52-Week Low   4.76

Total Returns (%)

3-Month	6-Month	1-Year	3-Year	5-Year
-29.20	-22.83	-25.19	-12.92	

3-Year Standard Deviation   25.11
Effective Duration

Valuation
Premium/Discount (1-Year Average)   0.19

Company Information
Provider   Virtus
Manager/Tenure   Jay D. Hatfield (4), Edward F. Ryan (4)
Website   http://www.virtus.com
Address   Virtus Opportunities Trust 101
                    Munson Street Greenfield MA 1301
                    United States
Phone Number   800-243-1574

PERFORMANCE

Ratings History

Date	Overall Rating	Risk Rating	Reward Rating
Q4-18	C	D+	C+
Q2-18	C	D	C+
Q4-17	D	D	D
Q4-16	D	D	D
Q4-15	U		

Asset & Performance History

Date	NAV	1-Year Total Return
2017	8.58	-6.59
2016	11.26	24.62
2015	11.09	-45.85
2014	22.81	
2013		
2012		

Total Assets: $506,603,201
Asset Allocation

Asset	%
Cash	-45%
Stocks	144%
US Stocks	142%
Bonds	0%
US Bonds	0%
Other	1%

Services Offered:

Investment Strategy: The investment seeks total return primarily through investments in equity securities of publicly traded master limited partnerships and limited liability companies taxed as partnerships ("MLPs"). Under normal market conditions, the fund will invest not less than 80% of its net assets (plus the amount of any borrowings for investment purposes) in equity securities of MLPs in the energy infrastructure sector. It is non-diversified. **Top Holdings:** EQM Midstream Partners LP MPLX LP Partnership Units Energy Transfer LP Enterprise Products Partners LP Marathon Petroleum Corp

---

ARK Web x.0 ETF   C   HOLD

Ticker	Traded On	NAV	Total Assets ($)	Dividend Yield (TTM)	Turnover Ratio	Expense Ratio
ARKW	NYSE Arca	42.45	$504,322,523	0.7	68	0.75

Ratings
Reward   C+
Risk   C-
Recent Upgrade/Downgrade   Down

Fund Information
Fund Type   Exchange Traded Funds
Category   Technology Sector Equity
Sub-Category   Technology
Prospectus Objective   Technology
Inception Date   Sep-14
Open to New Investments   Y

Prices
Price (as of 12/31/2018)   42.42
52-Week High   59.90
52-Week Low   42.01

Total Returns (%)

3-Month	6-Month	1-Year	3-Year	5-Year
-25.91	-23.14	-6.34	90.59	

3-Year Standard Deviation   20.21
Effective Duration

Valuation
Premium/Discount (1-Year Average)   0.06

Company Information
Provider   ARK ETF Trust
Manager/Tenure   Catherine D. Wood (4)
Website   http://www.ark-funds.com
Address   ARK ETF Trust 155 West 19th Street,
                    5th Floor New York New York 10011
                    United States
Phone Number   212-426-7040

PERFORMANCE

Ratings History

Date	Overall Rating	Risk Rating	Reward Rating
Q4-18	C	C-	C+
Q2-18	B-	C-	B
Q4-17	B	B	B
Q4-16	C	D+	C
Q4-15	U		

Asset & Performance History

Date	NAV	1-Year Total Return
2017	45.97	87.17
2016	25.06	8.72
2015	23.05	15.28
2014	20.45	
2013		
2012		

Total Assets: $504,322,523
Asset Allocation

Asset	%
Cash	0%
Stocks	99%
US Stocks	79%
Bonds	0%
US Bonds	0%
Other	1%

Services Offered:

Investment Strategy: The investment seeks long-term growth of capital. The fund is an actively-managed exchange-traded fund ("ETF") that will invest under normal circumstances primarily (at least 80% of its assets) in domestic and foreign equity securities of companies that are relevant to the fund's investment theme of Web x.0. Under normal circumstances, substantially all of the fund's assets will be invested in equity securities, including common stocks, partnership interests, business trust shares and other equity investments or ownership interests in business enterprises. The fund is non-diversified. **Top Holdings:** Tesla Inc Twitter Inc Tencent Holdings Ltd ADR Baidu Inc ADR Square Inc A

iShares MSCI Thailand Capped ETF

C   **HOLD**

Ticker	Traded On	NAV	Total Assets ($)	Dividend Yield (TTM)	Turnover Ratio	Expense Ratio
THD	NYSE Arca	82.24	$499,592,209	2.5	10	0.62

Ratings

Reward	C
Risk	C+
Recent Upgrade/Downgrade	

Fund Information

Fund Type	Exchange Traded Funds
Category	Thailand Equity
Sub-Category	Miscellaneous Region
Prospectus Objective	Pacific Stock
Inception Date	Mar-08
Open to New Investments	Y

Prices

Price (as of 12/31/2018)	82.81
52-Week High	101.73
52-Week Low	81.53

Total Returns (%)

3-Month	6-Month	1-Year	3-Year	5-Year
-12.46	0.26	-8.76	50.13	39.72

3-Year Standard Deviation	14.41
Effective Duration	

Valuation

Premium/Discount (1-Year Average)	0.09

Company Information

Provider	iShares
Manager/Tenure	Diane Hsiung (10), Greg Savage (10), Jennifer Hsui (5), 1 other
Website	http://www.ishares.com
Address	iShares 400 Howard Street San Francisco CA 94105 United States
Phone Number	800-474-2737

PERFORMANCE

Ratings History

Date	Overall Rating	Risk Rating	Reward Rating
Q4-18	C	C+	C
Q2-18	C	C+	C
Q4-17	B	C	B
Q4-16	C-	C-	C-
Q4-15	D	D	D

Asset & Performance History

Date	NAV	1-Year Total Return
2017	92.43	30.96
2016	72.31	25.65
2015	59.14	-21.13
2014	77.24	18
2013	67.01	-14.98
2012	80.92	37.65

Total Assets: $499,592,209
Asset Allocation

Asset	%
Cash	0%
Stocks	100%
US Stocks	0%
Bonds	0%
US Bonds	0%
Other	0%

Services Offered:

Investment Strategy: The investment seeks to track the investment results of the MSCI Thailand IMI 25/50 Index. The fund generally will invest at least 90% of its assets in the component securities of the index and in investments that have economic characteristics that are substantially identical to the component securities of the underlying index. The index consists of stocks traded primarily on the Stock Exchange of Thailand. A capping methodology is applied to issuer weights so that no single issuer of a component exceeds 25% of the index weight, and all issuers with weight above 5% do not cumulatively exceed 50% of the index weight. It is non-diversified. **Top Holdings:** Ptt PCL DR CP All PCL DR Airports Of Thailand PLC DR Kasikornbank Public Co Ltd The Siam Commercial Bank PCL DR

---

iShares MSCI Frontier 100 ETF

D+   **SELL**

Ticker	Traded On	NAV	Total Assets ($)	Dividend Yield (TTM)	Turnover Ratio	Expense Ratio
FM	NYSE Arca	26.49	$492,791,374	4.34	35	0.81

Ratings

Reward	C-
Risk	D+
Recent Upgrade/Downgrade	Down

Fund Information

Fund Type	Exchange Traded Funds
Category	Global Emerg Mkts Equity
Sub-Category	Diversified Emerging Mkts
Prospectus Objective	Div Emerg Mkts
Inception Date	Sep-12
Open to New Investments	Y

Prices

Price (as of 12/31/2018)	26.15
52-Week High	36.15
52-Week Low	26.01

Total Returns (%)

3-Month	6-Month	1-Year	3-Year	5-Year
-5.12	-6.12	-17.45	14.15	0.56

3-Year Standard Deviation	12.31
Effective Duration	

Valuation

Premium/Discount (1-Year Average)	-0.40

Company Information

Provider	iShares
Manager/Tenure	Diane Hsiung (6), Jennifer Hsui (6), Greg Savage (6), 1 other
Website	http://www.ishares.com
Address	iShares 400 Howard Street San Francisco CA 94105 United States
Phone Number	800-474-2737

PERFORMANCE

Ratings History

Date	Overall Rating	Risk Rating	Reward Rating
Q4-18	D+	D+	C-
Q2-18	C	C+	C
Q4-17	C+	C	C+
Q4-16	D	D+	D
Q4-15	D+	C-	D+

Asset & Performance History

Date	NAV	1-Year Total Return
2017	33.36	33.66
2016	25.5	3.46
2015	25.18	-15.31
2014	30.46	4.04
2013	33.12	25.6
2012	26.7	

Total Assets: $492,791,374
Asset Allocation

Asset	%
Cash	0%
Stocks	100%
US Stocks	2%
Bonds	0%
US Bonds	0%
Other	0%

Services Offered:

Investment Strategy: The investment seeks to track the investment results of the MSCI Frontier Markets 100 Index. The fund generally will invest at least 90% of its assets in the component securities of the underlying index and in investments that have economic characteristics that are substantially identical to the component securities of the underlying index. The index is designed to measure equity market performance of frontier markets while putting stronger emphasis on tradability compared to the MSCI Frontier Markets IMI (the parent index). **Top Holdings:** National Bank of Kuwait SAK Kuwait Finance House KSC Vietnam Dairy Products JSC Ahli United Bank BSC Vingroup JSC

Aberdeen Standard Physical Platinum Shares ETF   D   SELL

Ticker	Traded On	NAV	Total Assets ($)	Dividend Yield (TTM)	Turnover Ratio	Expense Ratio
PPLT	NYSE Arca	75.22	$492,158,689	0		0.6

Ratings
Reward   D
Risk   D
Recent Upgrade/Downgrade

Fund Information
Fund Type	Exchange Traded Funds
Category	Commodities Specified
Sub-Category	Commodities Precious Metals
Prospectus Objective	Prec Metals
Inception Date	Jan-10
Open to New Investments	Y

Prices
Price (as of 12/31/2018)	75.24
52-Week High	96.81
52-Week Low	72.98

Total Returns (%)
3-Month	6-Month	1-Year	3-Year	5-Year
-2.96	-5.64	-14.86	-10.57	-43.26

3-Year Standard Deviation   19.18
Effective Duration

Valuation
Premium/Discount (1-Year Average)   0.02

Company Information
Provider	Aberdeen Standard Investments
Manager/Tenure	Management Team (8)
Website	http://www.aberdeenstandardetfs.us
Address	Aberdeen Standard Investments 405 Lexington Avenue New York NY 10174 United States
Phone Number	212-918-4954

PERFORMANCE

Ratings History
Date	Overall Rating	Risk Rating	Reward Rating
Q4-18	D	D	D
Q2-18	D	D	D
Q4-17	D	D	D
Q4-16	D	D	D
Q4-15	D-	D-	D-

Asset & Performance History
Date	NAV	1-Year Total Return
2017	88.36	1.59
2016	86.97	3.39
2015	84.12	-28.36
2014	117.43	-11.43
2013	132.59	-11.36
2012	149.59	9.61

Total Assets: $492,158,689

Asset Allocation
Asset	%
Cash	0%
Stocks	0%
US Stocks	0%
Bonds	0%
US Bonds	0%
Other	100%

Services Offered:

Investment Strategy: The investment seeks to reflect the performance of the price of physical platinum, less the expenses of the Trust's operations.
The fund designed for investors who want a cost-effective and convenient way to invest in platinum with minimal credit risk. Advantages of investing in the Shares include Ease and Flexibility of Investment, Expenses, Minimal Credit Risk. **Top Holdings:** Physical Platinum Bullion

---

iShares iBonds Dec 2023 Term Corporate ETF   C-   HOLD

Ticker	Traded On	NAV	Total Assets ($)	Dividend Yield (TTM)	Turnover Ratio	Expense Ratio
IBDO	NYSE Arca	24.17	$489,965,770	3.04	8	0.1

Ratings
Reward   C-
Risk   C-
Recent Upgrade/Downgrade

Fund Information
Fund Type	Exchange Traded Funds
Category	US Fixed Income
Sub-Category	Corporate Bond
Prospectus Objective	Corp Bond - Gen
Inception Date	Mar-15
Open to New Investments	Y

Prices
Price (as of 12/31/2018)	24.19
52-Week High	25.07
52-Week Low	23.99

Total Returns (%)
3-Month	6-Month	1-Year	3-Year	5-Year
0.79	1.69	-0.20	10.55	

3-Year Standard Deviation   3.1
Effective Duration   4.09

Valuation
Premium/Discount (1-Year Average)   0.20

Company Information
Provider	iShares
Manager/Tenure	James Mauro (3), Scott Radell (3)
Website	http://www.ishares.com
Address	iShares 400 Howard Street San Francisco CA 94105 United States
Phone Number	800-474-2737

PERFORMANCE

Ratings History
Date	Overall Rating	Risk Rating	Reward Rating
Q4-18	C-	C-	C-
Q2-18	C-	C-	C
Q4-17	B-	A-	C
Q4-16	D+	C-	D+
Q4-15	U		

Asset & Performance History
Date	NAV	1-Year Total Return
2017	24.98	4.5
2016	24.58	5.82
2015	23.93	
2014		
2013		
2012		

Total Assets: $489,965,770

Asset Allocation
Asset	%
Cash	1%
Stocks	0%
US Stocks	0%
Bonds	99%
US Bonds	84%
Other	0%

Services Offered:

Investment Strategy: The investment seeks to track the investment results of the Bloomberg Barclays December 2023 Maturity Corporate Index which composed of U.S. dollar-denominated, investment-grade corporate bonds maturing in 2023. The fund generally will invest at least 90% of its assets in the component securities of the underlying index. The underlying index is composed of U.S. dollar-denominated, taxable, investment-grade corporate bonds scheduled to mature after December 31, 2022 and before December 16, 2023. **Top Holdings:** Apple Inc. 2.4%   Anheuser-Busch InBev Finance Inc. 3.3%   CVS Health Corp 3.7%   Verizon Communications Inc. 5.15%   Bank of America Corporation 3.3%

Fidelity® MSCI Utilities Index ETF   B-   BUY

Ticker	Traded On	NAV	Total Assets ($)	Dividend Yield (TTM)	Turnover Ratio	Expense Ratio
FUTY	NYSE Arca	34.86	$488,756,480	3.02	6	0.08

Ratings
Reward	B-
Risk	C+
Recent Upgrade/Downgrade	

Fund Information
Fund Type	Exchange Traded Funds
Category	Utilities Sector Equity
Sub-Category	Utilities
Prospectus Objective	Utility
Inception Date	Oct-13
Open to New Investments	Y

Prices
Price (as of 12/31/2018)	34.88
52-Week High	37.49
52-Week Low	31.11

Total Returns (%)
3-Month	6-Month	1-Year	3-Year	5-Year
1.14	2.56	4.40	37.72	66.31

3-Year Standard Deviation	11.59
Effective Duration	

Valuation
Premium/Discount (1-Year Average)	0.02

Company Information
Provider	Fidelity Investments
Manager/Tenure	Jennifer Hsui (5), Greg Savage (5), Alan Mason (2), 2 others
Website	http://www.institutional.fidelity.com
Address	Fidelity Investments 82 Devonshire Street Boston MA 2109 United States
Phone Number	617-563-7000

PERFORMANCE

Ratings History
Date	Overall Rating	Risk Rating	Reward Rating
Q4-18	B-	C+	B-
Q2-18	C+	C	B
Q4-17	B	B	B
Q4-16	B-	C+	B
Q4-15	C-	C	B

Asset & Performance History
Date	NAV	1-Year Total Return
2017	34.47	12.32
2016	31.61	17.44
2015	27.83	-4.79
2014	30.52	26.83
2013	24.87	
2012		

Total Assets: $488,756,480
Asset Allocation
Asset	%
Cash	0%
Stocks	100%
US Stocks	100%
Bonds	0%
US Bonds	0%
Other	0%

Services Offered:

Investment Strategy: The investment seeks to provide investment returns that correspond, before fees and expenses, generally to the performance of the MSCI USA IMI Utilities Index. The fund invests at least 80% of assets in securities included in the fund's underlying index. The fund's underlying index is the MSCI USA IMI Utilities Index, which represents the performance of the utilities sector in the U.S. equity market. It may or may not hold all of the securities in the MSCI USA IMI Utilities Index. The fund is non-diversified. **Top Holdings:** NextEra Energy Inc Duke Energy Corp Dominion Energy Inc Southern Co Exelon Corp

---

Vident Core U.S. Bond Strategy ETF™   D+   SELL

Ticker	Traded On	NAV	Total Assets ($)	Dividend Yield (TTM)	Turnover Ratio	Expense Ratio
VBND	NYSE Arca	47.43	$488,628,753	2.36	324	0.43

Ratings
Reward	D
Risk	C-
Recent Upgrade/Downgrade	

Fund Information
Fund Type	Exchange Traded Funds
Category	US Fixed Income
Sub-Category	Intermediate-Term Bond
Prospectus Objective	Growth & Inc
Inception Date	Oct-14
Open to New Investments	Y

Prices
Price (as of 12/31/2018)	47.39
52-Week High	49.21
52-Week Low	46.86

Total Returns (%)
3-Month	6-Month	1-Year	3-Year	5-Year
1.49	1.36	-0.77	4.47	

3-Year Standard Deviation	3.16
Effective Duration	

Valuation
Premium/Discount (1-Year Average)	-0.08

Company Information
Provider	Vident Financial
Manager/Tenure	Jim Iredale (3), Denise M. Krisko (3)
Website	http://www.videntfinancial.com
Address	Vident Financial 201 17th Street, Suite 300 Atlanta GA 30363 United States
Phone Number	800-617-0004

PERFORMANCE

Ratings History
Date	Overall Rating	Risk Rating	Reward Rating
Q4-18	D+	C-	D
Q2-18	D+	C-	D+
Q4-17	C	B-	C-
Q4-16	D+	C-	D+
Q4-15	U		

Asset & Performance History
Date	NAV	1-Year Total Return
2017	49.16	2.82
2016	48.77	2.25
2015	49.12	0.38
2014	49.66	
2013		
2012		

Total Assets: $488,628,753
Asset Allocation
Asset	%
Cash	20%
Stocks	0%
US Stocks	0%
Bonds	80%
US Bonds	80%
Other	0%

Services Offered:

Investment Strategy: The investment seeks to track the performance, before fees and expenses, of the Vident Core U.S. Bond IndexTM. Under normal circumstances, at least 80% of the fund's total assets (exclusive of collateral held from securities lending) will be invested in the component securities of the index and investments that have economic characteristics that are substantially identical to the economic characteristics of such component securities (such as TBA securities). The index seeks to improve the overall mix of credit quality, interest rate and yield as compared to traditional U.S. core bond indices. **Top Holdings:** Federal Home Loan Mortgage Corporation 5% Federal National Mortgage Association 3% Federal Home Loan Mortgage Corporation 3% United States Treasury Notes 2% United States Treasury Notes 2.12%

Fidelity® MSCI Energy Index ETF   C   HOLD

Ticker	Traded On	NAV	Total Assets ($)	Dividend Yield (TTM)	Turnover Ratio	Expense Ratio
FENY	NYSE Arca	15.61	$487,818,715	2.78	5	0.08

Ratings
Reward	C
Risk	C-
Recent Upgrade/Downgrade	Down

Fund Information
Fund Type	Exchange Traded Funds
Category	Energy Sector Equity
Sub-Category	Equity Energy
Prospectus Objective	Natl Res
Inception Date	Oct-13
Open to New Investments	Y

Prices
Price (as of 12/31/2018)	15.62
52-Week High	22.04
52-Week Low	14.63

Total Returns (%)
3-Month	6-Month	1-Year	3-Year	5-Year
-27.00	-24.19	-19.95	-0.78	-31.09

3-Year Standard Deviation	19.24
Effective Duration	

Valuation
Premium/Discount (1-Year Average)	0.03

Company Information
Provider	Fidelity Investments
Manager/Tenure	Jennifer Hsui (5), Greg Savage (5), Alan Mason (2), 2 others
Website	http://www.institutional.fidelity.com
Address	Fidelity Investments 82 Devonshire Street Boston MA 2109 United States
Phone Number	617-563-7000

PERFORMANCE

Ratings History
Date	Overall Rating	Risk Rating	Reward Rating
Q4-18	C	C-	C
Q2-18	C	C-	C+
Q4-17	C-	C	D+
Q4-16	C-	D	C
Q4-15	C-	C	C

Asset & Performance History
Date	NAV	1-Year Total Return
2017	20.03	-2.43
2016	21.18	27.02
2015	17.1	-23
2014	22.81	-9.79
2013	25.71	
2012		

Total Assets: $487,818,715

Asset Allocation
Asset	%
Cash	0%
Stocks	100%
US Stocks	99%
Bonds	0%
US Bonds	0%
Other	0%

Services Offered:

Investment Strategy: The investment seeks to provide investment returns that correspond, before fees and expenses, generally to the performance of the MSCI USA IMI Energy Index. The fund invests at least 80% of assets in securities included in the fund's underlying index. The fund's underlying index is the MSCI USA IMI Energy Index, which represents the performance of the energy sector in the U.S. equity market. It may or may not hold all of the securities in the MSCI USA IMI Energy Index. The fund is non-diversified. **Top Holdings:** Exxon Mobil Corp Chevron Corp ConocoPhillips Schlumberger Ltd EOG Resources Inc

---

Highland/iBoxx Senior Loan ETF   C   HOLD

Ticker	Traded On	NAV	Total Assets ($)	Dividend Yield (TTM)	Turnover Ratio	Expense Ratio
SNLN	NAS CM	17.16	$487,017,057	4.72	126	0.55

Ratings
Reward	C-
Risk	C+
Recent Upgrade/Downgrade	

Fund Information
Fund Type	Exchange Traded Funds
Category	US Fixed Income
Sub-Category	Bank Loan
Prospectus Objective	Income
Inception Date	Nov-12
Open to New Investments	Y

Prices
Price (as of 12/31/2018)	17.18
52-Week High	18.40
52-Week Low	17.10

Total Returns (%)
3-Month	6-Month	1-Year	3-Year	5-Year
-4.77	-2.85	-1.11	9.16	7.47

3-Year Standard Deviation	2.62
Effective Duration	

Valuation
Premium/Discount (1-Year Average)	0.01

Company Information
Provider	Highland Funds
Manager/Tenure	Mark Okada (1), Allan Smallwood (1), Jon Poglitsch (0), 1 other
Website	http://www.highlandfunds.com
Address	Highland Funds 200 Crescent Court, Suite 700 Dallas TX 75201 United States
Phone Number	877-665-1287

PERFORMANCE

Ratings History
Date	Overall Rating	Risk Rating	Reward Rating
Q4-18	C	C+	C-
Q2-18	C	C+	C
Q4-17	B-	B+	C
Q4-16	C	C+	C
Q4-15	C	C+	C-

Asset & Performance History
Date	NAV	1-Year Total Return
2017	18.2	1.82
2016	18.73	8.41
2015	18.06	-2.25
2014	19.26	0.71
2013	19.96	5.34
2012	19.97	

Total Assets: $487,017,057

Asset Allocation
Asset	%
Cash	8%
Stocks	1%
US Stocks	1%
Bonds	91%
US Bonds	86%
Other	0%

Services Offered:

Investment Strategy: The investment seeks to provide investment results that, before fees and expenses, correspond generally to the price and yield performance of the Markit iBoxx USD Liquid Leveraged Loan Index. The fund will, under normal circumstances, invest at least 80% of its assets (the "80% basket") in component securities of the underlying index. The underlying index is a subset of the Markit iBoxx USD Leveraged Loan Index. "Leveraged Loans" are loans to companies that typically already have a high amount of debt and are often characterized by lower credit ratings or higher interest rates. It is non-diversified. **Top Holdings:** Univision Communications Valeant Pharmaceuticals? Ss&C Technologies First Data Corporation Crown Finance TI

iShares MSCI Indonesia ETF

D+   **SELL**

Ticker	Traded On	NAV
EIDO	NYSE Arca	24.89

Total Assets ($)	Dividend Yield (TTM)	Turnover Ratio	Expense Ratio
$483,814,818	1.92	7	0.62

Ratings
Reward	D+
Risk	D+
Recent Upgrade/Downgrade	

Fund Information
Fund Type	Exchange Traded Funds
Category	Asia ex-Japan Equity
Sub-Category	Miscellaneous Region
Prospectus Objective	Pacific Stock
Inception Date	May-10
Open to New Investments	Y

Prices
Price (as of 12/31/2018)	24.82
52-Week High	30.56
52-Week Low	20.88

Total Returns (%)
3-Month	6-Month	1-Year	3-Year	5-Year
8.47	9.90	-10.57	23.72	19.67

3-Year Standard Deviation	16.42
Effective Duration	

Valuation
Premium/Discount (1-Year Average)	-0.15

Company Information
Provider	iShares
Manager/Tenure	Diane Hsiung (8), Greg Savage (8), Jennifer Hsui (5), 1 other
Website	http://www.ishares.com
Address	iShares 400 Howard Street San Francisco CA 94105 United States
Phone Number	800-474-2737

PERFORMANCE

Ratings History
Date	Overall Rating	Risk Rating	Reward Rating
Q4-18	D+	D+	D+
Q2-18	C-	C-	C-
Q4-17	C	C-	C
Q4-16	C-	D+	C
Q4-15	D	D	D

Asset & Performance History
Date	NAV	1-Year Total Return
2017	28.39	18.43
2016	24.29	16.82
2015	21.04	-22.02
2014	27.39	24.05
2013	22.39	-24.77
2012	30.24	4.09

Total Assets: $483,814,818

Asset Allocation
Asset	%
Cash	0%
Stocks	100%
US Stocks	0%
Bonds	0%
US Bonds	0%
Other	0%

Services Offered:

Investment Strategy: The investment seeks to track the investment results of the MSCI Indonesia Investable Market Index (IMI). The fund generally will invest at least 90% of its assets in the component securities of the underlying index and in investments that have economic characteristics that are substantially identical to the component securities of the underlying index. The index is a free float-adjusted market capitalization-weighted index designed to measure the performance of equity securities listed on stock exchanges in Indonesia. The fund is non-diversified. **Top Holdings:** PT Bank Central Asia Tbk Bank Rakyat Indonesia (Persero) Tbk Class B PT Telekomunikasi Indonesia (Persero) Tbk Class B PT Astra International Tbk PT Bank Mandiri (Persero) Tbk

---

Invesco China Technology ETF

D+   **SELL**

Ticker	Traded On	NAV
CQQQ	NYSE Arca	

Total Assets ($)	Dividend Yield (TTM)	Turnover Ratio	Expense Ratio
$482,990,673	1.96	21	0.7

Ratings
Reward	C-
Risk	D
Recent Upgrade/Downgrade	Down

Fund Information
Fund Type	Exchange Traded Funds
Category	Greater China Equity
Sub-Category	China Region
Prospectus Objective	Technology
Inception Date	Dec-09
Open to New Investments	Y

Prices
Price (as of 12/31/2018)	39.37
52-Week High	66.86
52-Week Low	38.20

Total Returns (%)
3-Month	6-Month	1-Year	3-Year	5-Year
-17.19	-29.13	-34.40	13.14	21.01

3-Year Standard Deviation	21.4
Effective Duration	

Valuation
Premium/Discount (1-Year Average)	0.03

Company Information
Provider	Invesco
Manager/Tenure	Peter Hubbard (0), Michael Jeanette (0), Jonathan Nixon (0), 1 other
Website	http://www.invesco.com/us
Address	Invesco 11 Greenway Plaza, Ste. 2500 Houston TX 77046 United States
Phone Number	800-659-1005

PERFORMANCE

Ratings History
Date	Overall Rating	Risk Rating	Reward Rating
Q4-18	D+	D	C-
Q2-18	C	C-	C
Q4-17	B+	C	A+
Q4-16	C-	C-	C-
Q4-15	C	C-	C

Asset & Performance History
Date	NAV	1-Year Total Return
2017	60.55	72.8
2016	35.59	0.01
2015	36.21	6.74
2014	34.51	0.18
2013	34.79	59.71
2012	21.96	8.81

Total Assets: $482,990,673

Asset Allocation
Asset	%
Cash	0%
Stocks	100%
US Stocks	0%
Bonds	0%
US Bonds	0%
Other	0%

Services Offered:

Investment Strategy: The investment seeks investment results that correspond generally to the performance, before the fund's fees and expenses, of an equity index called the AlphaShares China Technology Index. The fund will invest at least 90% of its total assets in common stocks, ADRs, ADSs, GDRs and IDRs that comprise the index and depositary receipts or shares representing common stocks included in the index. The index is designed to measure and monitor the performance of the universe of publicly-traded companies which are based in mainland China, Hong Kong or Macau, are in the Information Technology Sector. It is non-diversified. **Top Holdings:** Alibaba Group Holding Ltd ADR Tencent Holdings Ltd NetEase Inc ADR Baidu Inc ADR 58.com Inc ADR repr Class A

Oppenheimer S&P SmallCap 600 Revenue ETF   C-   HOLD

Ticker	Traded On	NAV	Total Assets ($)	Dividend Yield (TTM)	Turnover Ratio	Expense Ratio
RWJ	NYSE Arca	57.44	$474,870,515	1.07		0.39

Ratings
Reward   C-
Risk   C-
Recent Upgrade/Downgrade   Down

Fund Information
Fund Type   Exchange Traded Funds
Category   US Equity Small Cap
Sub-Category   Small Value
Prospectus Objective   Small Company
Inception Date   Feb-08
Open to New Investments   Y

Prices
Price (as of 12/31/2018)   57.31
52-Week High   78.89
52-Week Low   54.53

Total Returns (%)

3-Month	6-Month	1-Year	3-Year	5-Year
-22.10	-21.37	-16.87	14.10	11.16

3-Year Standard Deviation   16.93
Effective Duration

Valuation
Premium/Discount (1-Year Average)   -0.01

Company Information
Provider   OppenheimerFunds
Manager/Tenure Frank Vallario (1), Donal Bishnoi (0)
Website   http://www.oppenheimerfunds.com
Address   OppenheimerFunds 12100 East Iliff
                Avenue, Suite 300, Aurora, Colorado
                Aurora CO 80217-5270 United States
Phone Number   800-225-5677

PERFORMANCE

Ratings History

Date	Overall Rating	Risk Rating	Reward Rating
Q4-18	C-	C-	C-
Q2-18	C	C-	C
Q4-17	B	C+	B
Q4-16	C-	C-	C-
Q4-15	C	C-	C

Asset & Performance History

Date	NAV	1-Year Total Return
2017	69.95	5.16
2016	67.14	30.52
2015	51.8	-8.5
2014	57.01	6.3
2013	53.85	45.52
2012	37.52	18.61

Total Assets: $474,870,515
Asset Allocation

Asset	%
Cash	0%
Stocks	100%
US Stocks	98%
Bonds	0%
US Bonds	0%
Other	0%

Services Offered:

Investment Strategy: The investment seeks to provide investment results that correspond generally, before fees and expenses, to the performance of the S&P SmallCap 600 Revenue-Weighted Index (the "underlying index"). The fund will normally invest at least 80% of its net assets, plus any borrowings for investment purposes, in the securities of small capitalization companies included in the underlying index. The underlying index is constructed using a rules-based methodology that re-weights the constituent securities of the S&P SmallCap 600® Index (the "parent index") according to the revenue earned by the companies in the parent index, subject to a maximum 5% per company weighting. **Top Holdings:** Community Health Systems Inc   Core-Mark Holding Co Inc   Lithia Motors Inc Class A   Office Depot Inc   JC Penney Co Inc

---

UBS AG FI Enhanced Europe 50 ETN   D+   SELL

Ticker	Traded On	NAV	Total Assets ($)	Dividend Yield (TTM)	Turnover Ratio	Expense Ratio
FIEE	NYSE Arca	124.32	$471,887,458	0		0.95

Ratings
Reward   D+
Risk   D
Recent Upgrade/Downgrade   Down

Fund Information
Fund Type   Exchange Traded Funds
Category   Europe Equity Large Cap
Sub-Category   Europe Stock
Prospectus Objective   Europe Stock
Inception Date   Feb-16
Open to New Investments   Y

Prices
Price (as of 12/31/2018)   124.40
52-Week High   201.25
52-Week Low   116.52

Total Returns (%)

3-Month	6-Month	1-Year	3-Year	5-Year
-22.84	-20.57	-30.43		

3-Year Standard Deviation
Effective Duration

Valuation
Premium/Discount (1-Year Average)   -0.32

Company Information
Provider   UBS Group AG
Manager/Tenure No Manager (2)
Website   http://www.ubs.com
Address   Bahnhofstrasse 45 Zurich 8098
                Switzerland
Phone Number   412-037-1952

PERFORMANCE

Ratings History

Date	Overall Rating	Risk Rating	Reward Rating
Q4-18	D+	D	D+
Q2-18	C-	D+	C-
Q4-17	C-	C+	C
Q4-16	U		
Q4-15			

Asset & Performance History

Date	NAV	1-Year Total Return
2017	178.7	50.68
2016	119.49	
2015		
2014		
2013		
2012		

Total Assets: $471,887,458
Asset Allocation

Asset	%
Cash	%
Stocks	%
US Stocks	%
Bonds	%
US Bonds	%
Other	%

Services Offered:

Investment Strategy: The investment seeks to provide a two times leveraged long exposure to the performance of the index compounded on a quarterly basis, reduced by the Accrued Fees.
 The UBS AG FI Enhanced Europe 50 ETN are a series of FI Enhanced ETNs linked to the STOXX Europe 50® USD (Gross Return) Index. The Securities are senior unsecured debt securities issued by UBS AG (UBS). The index is derived from the STOXX Europe 600 Index (the "parent index"), which is further subdivided into 19 STOXX Regional Total Market Index (TMI) Supersector Indices (the "Supersector Indices"). The index is composed of 50 European blue-chip companies from within the parent index. **Top Holdings:**

WisdomTree International Hedged Quality Dividend Growth Fund   D+   SELL

Ticker	Traded On	NAV	Total Assets ($)	Dividend Yield (TTM)	Turnover Ratio	Expense Ratio
IHDG	NYSE Arca	27.90	$470,976,067	0.2	42	0.58

Ratings
Reward	D+
Risk	C-
Recent Upgrade/Downgrade	Down

Fund Information
Fund Type	Exchange Traded Funds
Category	Global Equity Large Cap
Sub-Category	Foreign Large Growth
Prospectus Objective	Growth
Inception Date	May-14
Open to New Investments	Y

Prices
Price (as of 12/31/2018)	27.82
52-Week High	33.03
52-Week Low	26.92

Total Returns (%)
3-Month	6-Month	1-Year	3-Year	5-Year
-13.38	-11.64	-11.69	9.03	

3-Year Standard Deviation	8.46
Effective Duration	

Valuation
Premium/Discount (1-Year Average)	-0.04

Company Information
Provider	WisdomTree
Manager/Tenure	Richard A. Brown (4), Thomas J. Durante (4), Karen Q. Wong (4)
Website	http://www.wisdomtree.com
Address	WisdomTree 245 Park Avenue, 35th floor New York NY 10167 United States
Phone Number	866-909-9473

PERFORMANCE

Ratings History

Date	Overall Rating	Risk Rating	Reward Rating
Q4-18	D+	C-	D+
Q2-18	C	C-	C+
Q4-17	B+	A-	B
Q4-16	C	C-	C
Q4-15	D	C+	C-

Asset & Performance History

Date	NAV	1-Year Total Return
2017	31.66	21.43
2016	26.43	1.67
2015	26.51	12.53
2014	24.28	
2013		
2012		

Total Assets: $470,976,067

Asset Allocation

Asset	%
Cash	0%
Stocks	100%
US Stocks	1%
Bonds	0%
US Bonds	0%
Other	0%

Services Offered:

Investment Strategy: The investment seeks to track the price and yield performance of the WisdomTree International Hedged Quality Dividend Growth Index. The fund will invest at least 80% of its total assets in the component securities of the index and investments that have economic characteristics that are substantially identical to the economic characteristics of such component securities. The index consists of dividend-paying common stocks with growth characteristics of companies in the industrialized world, excluding Canada and the U.S., while at the same time neutralizing exposure to fluctuations of the value of foreign currencies relative to the USD. It is non-diversified. **Top Holdings:** Novo Nordisk A/S B Diageo PLC British American Tobacco PLC Industria De Diseno Textil SA China Overseas Land & Investment Ltd

---

Vanguard S&P Small-Cap 600 Growth Index Fund ETF Shares   C-   HOLD

Ticker	Traded On	NAV	Total Assets ($)	Dividend Yield (TTM)	Turnover Ratio	Expense Ratio
VIOG	NYSE Arca		$469,425,250	0.73	37	0.2

Ratings
Reward	C
Risk	C-
Recent Upgrade/Downgrade	Down

Fund Information
Fund Type	Exchange Traded Funds
Category	US Equity Small Cap
Sub-Category	Small Growth
Prospectus Objective	Growth & Inc
Inception Date	Sep-10
Open to New Investments	Y

Prices
Price (as of 12/31/2018)	138.33
52-Week High	179.40
52-Week Low	129.95

Total Returns (%)
3-Month	6-Month	1-Year	3-Year	5-Year
-18.98	-15.59	-4.81	33.06	41.45

3-Year Standard Deviation	14.88
Effective Duration	

Valuation
Premium/Discount (1-Year Average)	0.10

Company Information
Provider	Vanguard
Manager/Tenure	William A. Coleman (5), Donald M. Butler (2)
Website	http://www.vanguard.com
Address	Vanguard 100 Vanguard Boulevard Malvern PA 19355 United States
Phone Number	877-662-7447

PERFORMANCE

Ratings History

Date	Overall Rating	Risk Rating	Reward Rating
Q4-18	C-	C-	C
Q2-18	B-	C-	B
Q4-17	A-	B+	A
Q4-16	C-	D+	C
Q4-15	C	D+	C+

Asset & Performance History

Date	NAV	1-Year Total Return
2017	145.79	15.07
2016	128.4	20.72
2015	106.31	2.57
2014	104.72	3.63
2013	101.78	42.42
2012	71.84	14.37

Total Assets: $469,425,250

Asset Allocation

Asset	%
Cash	1%
Stocks	99%
US Stocks	98%
Bonds	0%
US Bonds	0%
Other	0%

Services Offered:

Investment Strategy: The investment seeks to track the performance of a benchmark index that measures the investment return of small-capitalization growth stocks in the United States. The fund employs an indexing investment approach designed to track the performance of the S&P SmallCap 600® Growth Index, which represents the growth companies, as determined by the index sponsor, of the S&P SmallCap 600 Index. The Advisor attempts to replicate the target index by investing all, or substantially all, of its assets in the stocks that make up the index, holding each stock in approximately the same proportion as its weighting in the index. **Top Holdings:** Insperity Inc Ingevity Corp Trex Co Inc Axon Enterprise Inc Green Dot Corp

iShares MSCI South Africa ETF   D   SELL

Ticker	Traded On	NAV	Total Assets ($)	Dividend Yield (TTM)	Turnover Ratio	Expense Ratio
EZA	NYSE Arca	50.97	$467,144,218	2.81	15	0.62

Ratings
Reward   D+
Risk   D
Recent Upgrade/Downgrade   Down

Fund Information
Fund Type   Exchange Traded Funds
Category   Equity Misc
Sub-Category   Miscellaneous Region
Prospectus Objective   Foreign Stock
Inception Date   Feb-03
Open to New Investments   Y

Prices
Price (as of 12/31/2018)   50.45
52-Week High   75.98
52-Week Low   47.13

Total Returns (%)

3-Month	6-Month	1-Year	3-Year	5-Year
-3.14	-8.00	-24.58	19.16	-7.69

3-Year Standard Deviation   23.64
Effective Duration

Valuation
Premium/Discount (1-Year Average)   -0.03

Company Information
Provider   iShares
Manager/Tenure   Diane Hsiung (10), Greg Savage (10), Jennifer Hsui (5), 1 other
Website   http://www.ishares.com
Address   iShares 400 Howard Street San Francisco CA 94105 United States
Phone Number   800-474-2737

PERFORMANCE

Ratings History

Date	Overall Rating	Risk Rating	Reward Rating
Q4-18	D	D	D+
Q2-18	C	C	C-
Q4-17	C	C	C+
Q4-16	D+	D	D+
Q4-15	D+	D+	C-

Asset & Performance History

Date	NAV	1-Year Total Return
2017	70.11	34.77
2016	52.94	17.24
2015	47.02	-25.92
2014	65.15	4.55
2013	63.71	-6.81
2012	70.2	17.91

Total Assets: $467,144,218
Asset Allocation

Asset	%
Cash	0%
Stocks	99%
US Stocks	0%
Bonds	0%
US Bonds	0%
Other	1%

Services Offered:

Investment Strategy: The investment seeks to track the investment results of the MSCI South Africa 25/50 Index. The fund normally invests at least 95% of its total assets in the securities of its underlying index and in depositary receipts representing securities in its underlying index. The underlying index uses a capping methodology to limit the weight of any single component to a maximum of 25% of the underlying index. The underlying index may include large- or mid-capitalization companies. The fund is non-diversified. **Top Holdings:** Naspers Ltd Class N Standard Bank Group Ltd Firstrand Ltd Sasol Ltd MTN Group Ltd

---

iShares Core Conservative Allocation ETF   C   HOLD

Ticker	Traded On	NAV	Total Assets ($)	Dividend Yield (TTM)	Turnover Ratio	Expense Ratio
AOK	NYSE Arca	32.74	$466,617,477	2.3	41	0.25

Ratings
Reward   C-
Risk   C+
Recent Upgrade/Downgrade

Fund Information
Fund Type   Exchange Traded Funds
Category   Cautious Allocation
Sub-Category   Allocation--30% to 50% Equity
Prospectus Objective   Asset Allocation
Inception Date   Nov-08
Open to New Investments   Y

Prices
Price (as of 12/31/2018)   32.72
52-Week High   35.24
52-Week Low   32.37

Total Returns (%)

3-Month	6-Month	1-Year	3-Year	5-Year
-3.65	-2.10	-3.31	11.42	14.50

3-Year Standard Deviation   3.8
Effective Duration   5.97

Valuation
Premium/Discount (1-Year Average)   0.07

Company Information
Provider   iShares
Manager/Tenure   Diane Hsiung (10), Greg Savage (10), Jennifer Hsui (6), 3 others
Website   http://www.ishares.com
Address   iShares 400 Howard Street San Francisco CA 94105 United States
Phone Number   800-474-2737

PERFORMANCE

Ratings History

Date	Overall Rating	Risk Rating	Reward Rating
Q4-18	C	C+	C-
Q2-18	C	C-	C
Q4-17	B	A-	C+
Q4-16	C	C-	C
Q4-15	C	C-	C

Asset & Performance History

Date	NAV	1-Year Total Return
2017	34.6	9.61
2016	32.51	5.13
2015	31.59	-1.13
2014	32.59	3.94
2013	32.01	6.64
2012	30.58	6.52

Total Assets: $466,617,477
Asset Allocation

Asset	%
Cash	3%
Stocks	31%
US Stocks	16%
Bonds	66%
US Bonds	47%
Other	0%

Services Offered:

Investment Strategy: The investment seeks to track the investment results of the S&P Target Risk Conservative Index composed of a portfolio of underlying equity and fixed income funds intended to represent a conservative target risk allocation strategy. The fund is a fund of funds and seeks its investment objective by investing primarily in other iShares Underlying Funds that themselves seek investment results corresponding to their own respective underlying indexes. It generally will invest at least 90% of its assets in the component securities of the underlying index. The index measures the performance of the S&P Dow Jones Indices LLC proprietary allocation model. **Top Holdings:** iShares Core Total USD Bond Market ETF iShares Core S&P 500 ETF iShares Core MSCI Intl Dev Mkts ETF iShares Core International Aggt Bd ETF iShares Core MSCI Emerging Markets ETF

First Trust Industrials/Producer Durables AlphaDEX® Fund   C   HOLD

Ticker	Traded On	NAV	Total Assets ($)	Dividend Yield (TTM)	Turnover Ratio	Expense Ratio
FXR	NYSE Arca	34.11	$465,115,271	0.71	101	0.62

Ratings
Reward	C
Risk	C+
Recent Upgrade/Downgrade	Down

Fund Information
Fund Type	Exchange Traded Funds
Category	Industrials Sector Equity
Sub-Category	Industrials
Prospectus Objective	Unaligned
Inception Date	May-07
Open to New Investments	Y

Prices
Price (as of 12/31/2018)	34.09
52-Week High	43.14
52-Week Low	32.01

Total Returns (%)
3-Month	6-Month	1-Year	3-Year	5-Year
-18.85	-12.54	-15.02	33.71	25.14

3-Year Standard Deviation	15.79
Effective Duration	

Valuation
Premium/Discount (1-Year Average)	0.01

Company Information
Provider	First Trust
Manager/Tenure	Jon C. Erickson (11), Daniel J. Lindquist (11), David G. McGarel (11), 3 others
Website	http://www.ftportfolios.com/
Address	First Trust 120 E. Liberty Drive, Suite 400 Wheaton IL 60187 United States
Phone Number	800-621-1675

PERFORMANCE

Ratings History
Date	Overall Rating	Risk Rating	Reward Rating
Q4-18	C	C+	C
Q2-18	C	C+	C
Q4-17	B	C+	A-
Q4-16	C+	C	B-
Q4-15	C+	C+	C

Asset & Performance History
Date	NAV	1-Year Total Return
2017	40.57	24.14
2016	32.88	26.75
2015	26.09	-13.44
2014	30.33	8.13
2013	28.36	46.46
2012	19.45	15.45

Total Assets: $465,115,271
Asset Allocation
Asset	%
Cash	0%
Stocks	100%
US Stocks	99%
Bonds	0%
US Bonds	0%
Other	0%

Services Offered:

Investment Strategy: The investment seeks investment results that correspond generally to the price and yield (before the fund's fees and expenses) of an equity index called the StrataQuant® Industrials Index. The fund will normally invest at least 90% of its net assets (including investment borrowings) in common stocks that comprise the index. The index is a modified equal-dollar weighted index designed by IDI to objectively identify and select stocks from the Russell 1000® Index in the industrials and producer durables sectors that may generate positive alpha relative to traditional passive-style indices through the use of the AlphaDEX® selection methodology. **Top Holdings:** Copa Holdings SA Class A Zebra Technologies Corp Knight-Swift Transportation Holdings Inc A JetBlue Airways Corp Donaldson Co Inc

---

iShares International Developed Real Estate ETF   C   HOLD

Ticker	Traded On	NAV	Total Assets ($)	Dividend Yield (TTM)	Turnover Ratio	Expense Ratio
IFGL	NAS CM	26.96	$463,134,422	5.69	8	0.48

Ratings
Reward	C-
Risk	C
Recent Upgrade/Downgrade	

Fund Information
Fund Type	Exchange Traded Funds
Category	Real Estate Sector Equity
Sub-Category	Global Real Estate
Prospectus Objective	Real Estate
Inception Date	Nov-07
Open to New Investments	Y

Prices
Price (as of 12/31/2018)	27.03
52-Week High	31.71
52-Week Low	26.69

Total Returns (%)
3-Month	6-Month	1-Year	3-Year	5-Year
-4.85	-5.54	-6.68	13.07	11.11

3-Year Standard Deviation	10.97
Effective Duration	

Valuation
Premium/Discount (1-Year Average)	-0.20

Company Information
Provider	iShares
Manager/Tenure	Diane Hsiung (10), Greg Savage (10), Jennifer Hsui (6), 3 others
Website	http://www.ishares.com
Address	iShares 400 Howard Street San Francisco CA 94105 United States
Phone Number	800-474-2737

PERFORMANCE

Ratings History
Date	Overall Rating	Risk Rating	Reward Rating
Q4-18	C	C	C-
Q2-18	C	C-	C
Q4-17	B-	B-	C+
Q4-16	C-	C	C-
Q4-15	C	C+	C-

Asset & Performance History
Date	NAV	1-Year Total Return
2017	30.02	19.88
2016	26.33	1.07
2015	28.03	-4.02
2014	30.23	2.38
2013	30.57	5.29
2012	32.62	37.32

Total Assets: $463,134,422
Asset Allocation
Asset	%
Cash	1%
Stocks	97%
US Stocks	0%
Bonds	0%
US Bonds	0%
Other	2%

Services Offered:

Investment Strategy: The investment seeks to track the investment results of the FTSE EPRA Nareit Developed ex-U.S. Index composed of real estate equities in developed non-U.S. markets. The fund generally will invest at least 90% of its assets in the component securities of the underlying index and in investments that have economic characteristics that are substantially identical to the component securities of the underlying index. The underlying index measures the stock performance of companies engaged in the ownership and development of real estate markets in developed countries (except for the United States) as defined by FTSE EPRA/NAREIT. **Top Holdings:** Vonovia SE Unibail-Rodamco-Westfield Mitsui Fudosan Co Ltd Link Real Estate Investment Trust Sun Hung Kai Properties Ltd

ProShares Russell 2000 Dividend Growers ETF   C   HOLD

Ticker	Traded On	NAV	Total Assets ($)	Dividend Yield (TTM)	Turnover Ratio	Expense Ratio
SMDV	BATS	53.80	$463,042,975	1.75		0.4

Ratings
Reward   C
Risk   C-
Recent Upgrade/Downgrade

Fund Information
Fund Type	Exchange Traded Funds
Category	US Equity Small Cap
Sub-Category	Small Value
Prospectus Objective	Growth
Inception Date	Feb-15
Open to New Investments	Y

Prices
Price (as of 12/31/2018)	53.83
52-Week High	60.04
52-Week Low	51.53

Total Returns (%)
3-Month	6-Month	1-Year	3-Year	5-Year
-6.96	-5.53	-0.70	40.93	

3-Year Standard Deviation	10.97
Effective Duration	

Valuation
Premium/Discount (1-Year Average)	0.01

Company Information
Provider	ProShares
Manager/Tenure	Michael Neches (3), Devin Sullivan (0)
Website	http://www.proshares.com
Address	ProShares 7501 Wisconsin Avenue, Suite 1000 Bethesda MD 20814 United States
Phone Number	866-776-5125

PERFORMANCE

Ratings History
Date	Overall Rating	Risk Rating	Reward Rating
Q4-18	C	C-	C
Q2-18	C	C-	C+
Q4-17	B	B+	C+
Q4-16	C-	C-	C
Q4-15	U		

Asset & Performance History
Date	NAV	1-Year Total Return
2017	55.22	4.7
2016	53.73	35.55
2015	40.24	
2014		
2013		
2012		

Total Assets: $463,042,975
Asset Allocation
Asset	%
Cash	0%
Stocks	100%
US Stocks	100%
Bonds	0%
US Bonds	0%
Other	0%

Services Offered:

Investment Strategy: The investment seeks investment results, before fees and expenses, that track the performance of the Russell 2000 Dividend Growth Index (the "index"). Under normal circumstances, the fund will invest at least 80% of its total assets in component securities (i.e., securities of the index and comparable securities that have economic characteristics that are substantially identical to the economic characteristics of the securities of the index). The index contains a minimum of 40 stocks, which are equally weighted, and no single sector is allowed to comprise more than 30% of the index weight. **Top Holdings:** Tootsie Roll Industries Inc Ensign Group Inc   Atrion Corp   Lancaster Colony Corp   Healthcare Services Group Inc

---

SPDR® Russell 1000 Low Volatility Focus ETF   C-   HOLD

Ticker	Traded On	NAV	Total Assets ($)	Dividend Yield (TTM)	Turnover Ratio	Expense Ratio
ONEV	NYSE Arca	67.54	$462,025,330	1.87	37	0.2

Ratings
Reward   C-
Risk   D+
Recent Upgrade/Downgrade   Down

Fund Information
Fund Type	Exchange Traded Funds
Category	US Equity Mid Cap
Sub-Category	Mid-Cap Blend
Prospectus Objective	Growth & Inc
Inception Date	Dec-15
Open to New Investments	Y

Prices
Price (as of 12/31/2018)	67.37
52-Week High	78.06
52-Week Low	64.20

Total Returns (%)
3-Month	6-Month	1-Year	3-Year	5-Year
-11.02	-6.36	-4.98	29.89	

3-Year Standard Deviation	
Effective Duration	

Valuation
Premium/Discount (1-Year Average)	0.04

Company Information
Provider	SPDR State Street Global Advisors
Manager/Tenure	Michael J. Feehily (3), Karl A. Schneider (3), Emiliano Rabinovich (1)
Website	http://www.spdrs.com
Address	SPDR State Street Global Advisors State Street Financial Center, 1 Lincoln Street Boston MA 02111-2900 United States
Phone Number	617-786-3000

PERFORMANCE

Ratings History
Date	Overall Rating	Risk Rating	Reward Rating
Q4-18	C-	D+	C-
Q2-18	C-	D	C
Q4-17	C	B+	C-
Q4-16	D	D+	D+
Q4-15			

Asset & Performance History
Date	NAV	1-Year Total Return
2017	72.53	17.9
2016	65.85	15.94
2015	58.97	
2014		
2013		
2012		

Total Assets: $462,025,330
Asset Allocation
Asset	%
Cash	0%
Stocks	100%
US Stocks	100%
Bonds	0%
US Bonds	0%
Other	0%

Services Offered:

Investment Strategy: The investment seeks to provide investment results that, before fees and expenses, correspond generally to the total return performance of the Russell 1000 Low Volatility Focused Factor Index. Under normal market conditions, the fund generally invests substantially all, but at least 80%, of its total assets in the securities comprising the index. The index is designed to reflect the performance of a segment of large-capitalization U.S. equity securities demonstrating a combination of core factors (high value, high quality, and low size characteristics), with a focus factor comprising low volatility characteristics. The fund is non-diversified. **Top Holdings:** Omnicom Group Inc   Motorola Solutions Inc   Clorox Co   AutoZone Inc   Kimberly-Clark Corp

SPDR® Russell 1000 Momentum Focus ETF

C-   HOLD

Ticker	Traded On	NAV
ONEO	NYSE Arca	62.92

Total Assets ($)	Dividend Yield (TTM)	Turnover Ratio	Expense Ratio
$460,896,556	1.51	101	0.2

Ratings
Reward	C-
Risk	D+
Recent Upgrade/Downgrade	Down

Fund Information
Fund Type	Exchange Traded Funds
Category	US Equity Mid Cap
Sub-Category	Mid-Cap Blend
Prospectus Objective	Growth & Inc
Inception Date	Dec-15
Open to New Investments	Y

Prices
Price (as of 12/31/2018)	62.73
52-Week High	77.42
52-Week Low	59.44

Total Returns (%)
3-Month	6-Month	1-Year	3-Year	5-Year
-16.73	-13.06	-11.97	19.55	

3-Year Standard Deviation	
Effective Duration	

Valuation
Premium/Discount (1-Year Average)	0.15

Company Information
Provider	SPDR State Street Global Advisors
Manager/Tenure	Michael J. Feehily (3), Karl A. Schneider (3), Emiliano Rabinovich (1)
Website	http://www.spdrs.com
Address	SPDR State Street Global Advisors State Street Financial Center, 1 Lincoln Street Boston MA 02111-2900 United States
Phone Number	617-786-3000

PERFORMANCE

Ratings History
Date	Overall Rating	Risk Rating	Reward Rating
Q4-18	C-	D+	C-
Q2-18	C	C-	C
Q4-17	C	B+	C
Q4-16	D	D+	D+
Q4-15			

Asset & Performance History
Date	NAV	1-Year Total Return
2017	72.58	20.75
2016	64.84	12.47
2015	58.75	
2014		
2013		
2012		

Total Assets: $460,896,556

Asset Allocation
Asset	%
Cash	0%
Stocks	100%
US Stocks	98%
Bonds	0%
US Bonds	0%
Other	0%

Services Offered:

Investment Strategy: The investment seeks to provide investment results that, before fees and expenses, correspond generally to the total return performance of the Russell 1000 Momentum Focused Factor Index. Under normal market conditions, the fund generally invests substantially all, but at least 80%, of its total assets in the securities comprising the index. The index is designed to reflect the performance of a segment of large-capitalization U.S. equity securities demonstrating a combination of core factors (high value, high quality, and low size characteristics), with a focus factor comprising high momentum characteristics. The fund is non-diversified. **Top Holdings:** Centene Corp Best Buy Co Inc Marathon Petroleum Corp Kohl's Corp Dollar General Corp

---

First Trust Managed Municipal ETF

C-   HOLD

Ticker	Traded On	NAV
FMB	NAS CM	52.54

Total Assets ($)	Dividend Yield (TTM)	Turnover Ratio	Expense Ratio
$460,867,017	2.59	85	0.5

Ratings
Reward	C
Risk	C-
Recent Upgrade/Downgrade	Down

Fund Information
Fund Type	Exchange Traded Funds
Category	US Muni Fixed Inc
Sub-Category	Muni National Interm
Prospectus Objective	Growth & Inc
Inception Date	May-14
Open to New Investments	Y

Prices
Price (as of 12/31/2018)	52.62
52-Week High	53.59
52-Week Low	51.54

Total Returns (%)
3-Month	6-Month	1-Year	3-Year	5-Year
1.27	1.06	0.88	9.92	

3-Year Standard Deviation	3.57
Effective Duration	6.23

Valuation
Premium/Discount (1-Year Average)	0.11

Company Information
Provider	First Trust
Manager/Tenure	J. Thomas Futrell (4), Johnathan N. Wilhelm (4)
Website	http://www.ftportfolios.com/
Address	First Trust 120 E. Liberty Drive, Suite 400 Wheaton IL 60187 United States
Phone Number	800-621-1675

PERFORMANCE

Ratings History
Date	Overall Rating	Risk Rating	Reward Rating
Q4-18	C-	C-	C
Q2-18	C	C-	C
Q4-17	B	A	C
Q4-16	C	C-	C
Q4-15	D	D+	C-

Asset & Performance History
Date	NAV	1-Year Total Return
2017	53.44	7.4
2016	51.03	1.44
2015	51.75	3.84
2014	51.4	
2013		
2012		

Total Assets: $460,867,017

Asset Allocation
Asset	%
Cash	2%
Stocks	0%
US Stocks	0%
Bonds	98%
US Bonds	98%
Other	0%

Services Offered:

Investment Strategy: The investment seeks to generate current income that is exempt from regular federal income taxes and its secondary objective is long term capital appreciation. Under normal market conditions, the fund seeks to achieve its investment objectives by investing at least 80% of its net assets (including investment borrowings) in municipal debt securities that pay interest that is exempt from regular federal income taxes (collectively, "Municipal Securities"). It is non-diversified. **Top Holdings:** Future Contract On Us 10yr Note (Cbt)dec18 Future Contract On Us 10yr Ultra Fut Dec18 NEW YORK N Y CITY MUN WTR FIN AUTH 1.76% GREAT LAKES WTR AUTH MICH 5% ORANGE CNTY FLA HEALTH FACS AUTH 5%

SPDR® S&P Emerging Markets Small Cap ETF

D+   SELL

Ticker	Traded On	NAV	Total Assets ($)	Dividend Yield (TTM)	Turnover Ratio	Expense Ratio
EWX	NYSE Arca	40.96	$460,254,143	3.44	24	0.65

Ratings
Reward	C-
Risk	D+
Recent Upgrade/Downgrade	Down

Fund Information
Fund Type	Exchange Traded Funds
Category	Global Emerg Mkts Equity
Sub-Category	Diversified Emerging Mkts
Prospectus Objective	Div Emerg Mkts
Inception Date	May-08
Open to New Investments	Y

Prices
Price (as of 12/31/2018)	40.97
52-Week High	55.78
52-Week Low	40.07

Total Returns (%)
3-Month	6-Month	1-Year	3-Year	5-Year
-6.83	-11.62	-18.48	16.98	1.14

3-Year Standard Deviation	13.6
Effective Duration	

Valuation
Premium/Discount (1-Year Average)	0.03

Company Information
Provider	SPDR State Street Global Advisors
Manager/Tenure	Michael J. Feehily (7), Karl A. Schneider (3), Amy Cheng (1)
Website	http://www.spdrs.com
Address	SPDR State Street Global Advisors State Street Financial Center, 1 Lincoln Street Boston MA 02111-2900 United States
Phone Number	617-786-3000

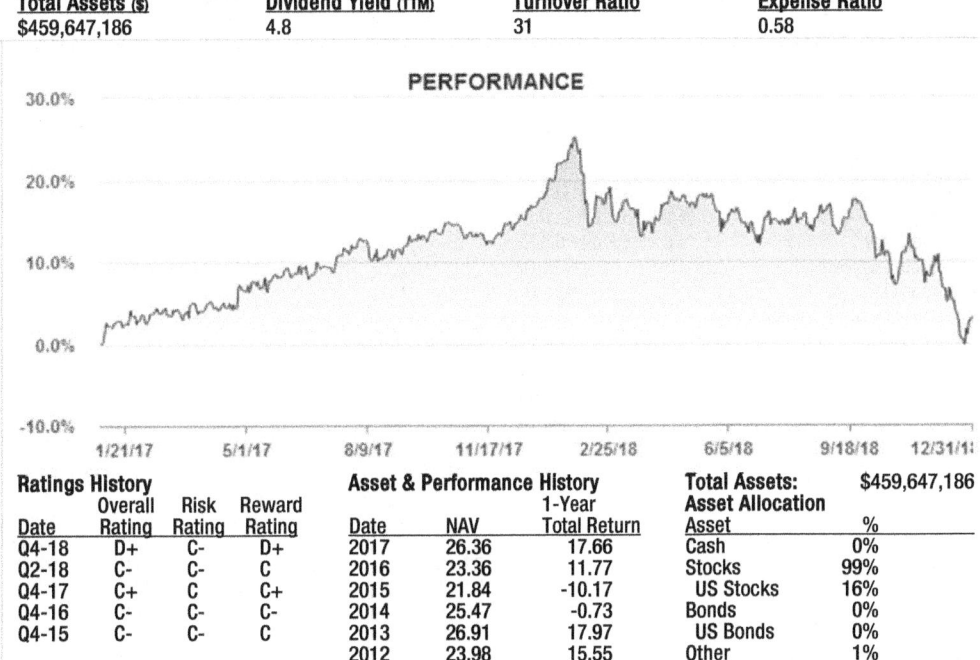

PERFORMANCE

Ratings History
Date	Overall Rating	Risk Rating	Reward Rating
Q4-18	D+	D+	C-
Q2-18	C-	C-	C
Q4-17	C+	C	B-
Q4-16	D+	C-	D+
Q4-15	D+	D+	D+

Asset & Performance History
Date	NAV	1-Year Total Return
2017	51.81	32.07
2016	40.19	8.1
2015	37.9	-12.21
2014	44.45	-1.5
2013	46.35	2.51
2012	46.31	24.3

Total Assets: $460,254,143
Asset Allocation
Asset	%
Cash	1%
Stocks	98%
US Stocks	0%
Bonds	0%
US Bonds	0%
Other	0%

Services Offered:

Investment Strategy: The investment seeks investment results that, before fees and expenses, correspond generally to the total return performance of the S&P Emerging Markets Under USD2 Billion Index. The fund generally invests substantially all, but at least 80%, of its total assets in the securities comprising the index and in depositary receipts based on securities comprising the index. The index is a float-adjusted market capitalization weighted index designed to represent the small capitalization segment of emerging countries included in the S&P Global BMI. The fund is non-diversified. **Top Holdings:** BR Malls Participacoes SA CVC Brasil Operadora e Agencia de Viagens SA Accton Technology Corp Moneta Money Bank AS Estacio Participacoes SA

First Trust Dow Jones Global Select Dividend Index Fund

D+   SELL

Ticker	Traded On	NAV	Total Assets ($)	Dividend Yield (TTM)	Turnover Ratio	Expense Ratio
FGD	NYSE Arca	21.89	$459,647,186	4.8	31	0.58

Ratings
Reward	D+
Risk	C-
Recent Upgrade/Downgrade	Down

Fund Information
Fund Type	Exchange Traded Funds
Category	Global Equity Large Cap
Sub-Category	Foreign Large Value
Prospectus Objective	World Stock
Inception Date	Nov-07
Open to New Investments	Y

Prices
Price (as of 12/31/2018)	21.86
52-Week High	28.07
52-Week Low	21.06

Total Returns (%)
3-Month	6-Month	1-Year	3-Year	5-Year
-11.21	-8.04	-12.40	15.20	2.71

3-Year Standard Deviation	9.34
Effective Duration	

Valuation
Premium/Discount (1-Year Average)	0.07

Company Information
Provider	First Trust
Manager/Tenure	Jon C. Erickson (11), Daniel J. Lindquist (11), David G. McGarel (11), 3 others
Website	http://www.ftportfolios.com/
Address	First Trust 120 E. Liberty Drive, Suite 400 Wheaton IL 60187 United States
Phone Number	800-621-1675

PERFORMANCE

Ratings History
Date	Overall Rating	Risk Rating	Reward Rating
Q4-18	D+	C-	D+
Q2-18	C-	C-	C
Q4-17	C+	C	C+
Q4-16	C-	C-	C-
Q4-15	C-	C-	C

Asset & Performance History
Date	NAV	1-Year Total Return
2017	26.36	17.66
2016	23.36	11.77
2015	21.84	-10.17
2014	25.47	-0.73
2013	26.91	17.97
2012	23.98	15.55

Total Assets: $459,647,186
Asset Allocation
Asset	%
Cash	0%
Stocks	99%
US Stocks	16%
Bonds	0%
US Bonds	0%
Other	1%

Services Offered:

Investment Strategy: The investment seeks investment results that correspond generally to the price and yield (before the fund's fees and expenses) of an equity index called the Dow Jones Global Select Dividend IndexSM. The fund will normally invest at least 90% of its net assets (including investment borrowings) in common stocks or in depositary receipts representing securities in the index. The index is an indicated annual dividend yield weighted index of 100 stocks selected from the developed-market portion of the Dow Jones World IndexSM. **Top Holdings:** CenturyLink Inc Galliford Try PLC Element Fleet Management Corp GameStop Corp Class A Spark New Zealand Ltd

ProShares Investment Grade—Interest Rate Hedged | C- | HOLD

Ticker	Traded On	NAV	Total Assets ($)	Dividend Yield (TTM)	Turnover Ratio	Expense Ratio
IGHG	BATS	71.00	$456,980,172	3.83		0.3

Ratings
Reward   C-
Risk   C-
Recent Upgrade/Downgrade

Fund Information
Fund Type	Exchange Traded Funds
Category	Fixed Income Misc
Sub-Category	Nontraditional Bond
Prospectus Objective	Worldwide Bond
Inception Date	Nov-13
Open to New Investments	Y

Prices
Price (as of 12/31/2018)	71.13
52-Week High	78.65
52-Week Low	71.10

Total Returns (%)
3-Month	6-Month	1-Year	3-Year	5-Year
-5.31	-2.09	-4.73	7.94	3.58

3-Year Standard Deviation   5.18
Effective Duration

Valuation
Premium/Discount (1-Year Average)   0.01

Company Information
Provider	ProShares
Manager/Tenure	Jeffrey Ploshnick (5), Benjamin McAbee (2)
Website	http://www.proshares.com
Address	ProShares 7501 Wisconsin Avenue, Suite 1000 Bethesda MD 20814 United States
Phone Number	866-776-5125

PERFORMANCE

Ratings History
Date	Overall Rating	Risk Rating	Reward Rating
Q4-18	C-	C-	C-
Q2-18	C-	C-	C
Q4-17	B-	B	C
Q4-16	C-	C-	C
Q4-15	D	C-	D

Asset & Performance History
Date	NAV	1-Year Total Return
2017	77.18	5.63
2016	75.59	7.26
2015	72.99	-2.16
2014	77.3	-1.92
2013	81.59	
2012		

Total Assets: $456,980,172
Asset Allocation
Asset	%
Cash	52%
Stocks	0%
US Stocks	0%
Bonds	48%
US Bonds	-1%
Other	0%

Services Offered:

Investment Strategy: The investment seeks investment results, before fees and expenses, that track the performance of the FTSE Corporate Investment Grade (Treasury Rate-Hedged) Index (the "index"). The index is comprised of (a) long positions in USD-denominated investment grade corporate bonds issued by both U.S. and foreign domiciled companies; and (b) short positions in U.S. Treasury notes or bonds ("Treasury Securities") of, in aggregate, approximate equivalent duration to the investment grade bonds. The fund will invest at least 80% of its total assets in component securities (i.e., securities of the index) and invest at least 80% of its total assets in investment grade bonds. **Top Holdings:** U.S. Treasury Bond Mar19   US 10 Year Note (CBT) Mar19   Us 10yr Note Future 03/20/2019 (Tyh9) - Cash Offset   Us Ultra Bond Future 03/20/2019 (Wnh9)   Us Ultra Bond Future 03/20/2019 (Wnh9) - Cash Offset

First Trust RiverFront Dynamic Developed International ETF | D+ | SELL

Ticker	Traded On	NAV	Total Assets ($)	Dividend Yield (TTM)	Turnover Ratio	Expense Ratio
RFDI	NAS CM	51.60	$456,724,052	2.64	106	0.83

Ratings
Reward   D+
Risk   C-
Recent Upgrade/Downgrade   Down

Fund Information
Fund Type	Exchange Traded Funds
Category	Global Equity Large Cap
Sub-Category	Foreign Large Blend
Prospectus Objective	Growth
Inception Date	Apr-16
Open to New Investments	Y

Prices
Price (as of 12/31/2018)	51.24
52-Week High	68.93
52-Week Low	49.45

Total Returns (%)
3-Month	6-Month	1-Year	3-Year	5-Year
-16.13	-12.66	-17.60		

3-Year Standard Deviation
Effective Duration

Valuation
Premium/Discount (1-Year Average)   0.08

Company Information
Provider	First Trust
Manager/Tenure	Adam Grossman (2), Scott Hays (2), Chris Konstantinos (2), 1 other
Website	http://www.ftportfolios.com/
Address	First Trust 120 E. Liberty Drive, Suite 400 Wheaton IL 60187 United States
Phone Number	800-621-1675

PERFORMANCE

Ratings History
Date	Overall Rating	Risk Rating	Reward Rating
Q4-18	D+	C-	D+
Q2-18	C-	C-	D+
Q4-17	D+	B+	C
Q4-16	U		
Q4-15			

Asset & Performance History
Date	NAV	1-Year Total Return
2017	64.03	24.93
2016	52.13	
2015		
2014		
2013		
2012		

Total Assets: $456,724,052
Asset Allocation
Asset	%
Cash	0%
Stocks	99%
US Stocks	1%
Bonds	0%
US Bonds	0%
Other	0%

Services Offered:

Investment Strategy: The investment seeks capital appreciation. The fund will seek to achieve its investment objective by investing at least 80% of its net assets in a portfolio of equity securities of developed market companies, including through investments in common stock, depositary receipts, and common and preferred shares of real estate investment trusts ("REITs"), and forward foreign currency exchange contracts and currency spot transactions used to hedge the fund's exposure to the currencies in which the equity securities of such developed market companies are denominated. It is non-diversified. **Top Holdings:** Nestle SA   Roche Holding AG Dividend Right Cert.   Royal Dutch Shell PLC Class A   LVMH Moet Hennessy Louis Vuitton SE   Royal Dutch Shell PLC B

iShares Agency Bond ETF   C-   HOLD

Ticker	Traded On	NAV
AGZ	NYSE Arca	111.88

Total Assets ($)	Dividend Yield (TTM)	Turnover Ratio	Expense Ratio
$454,085,426	2.05	78	0.2

Ratings

Reward	C-
Risk	C-
Recent Upgrade/Downgrade	Up

Fund Information

Fund Type	Exchange Traded Funds
Category	US Fixed Income
Sub-Category	Short Government
Prospectus Objective	Govt Bond - Gen
Inception Date	Nov-08
Open to New Investments	Y

Prices

Price (as of 12/31/2018)	112.13
52-Week High	113.09
52-Week Low	109.93

Total Returns (%)

3-Month	6-Month	1-Year	3-Year	5-Year
1.96	1.87	1.33	4.54	9.34

3-Year Standard Deviation	1.82
Effective Duration	3.94

Valuation

Premium/Discount (1-Year Average)	0.03

Company Information

Provider	iShares
Manager/Tenure	Scott Radell (8), James Mauro (7)
Website	http://www.ishares.com
Address	iShares 400 Howard Street San Francisco CA 94105 United States
Phone Number	800-474-2737

PERFORMANCE

Ratings History

Date	Overall Rating	Risk Rating	Reward Rating
Q4-18	C-	C-	C-
Q2-18	C-	C-	C-
Q4-17	C+	B	C
Q4-16	C	C-	C
Q4-15	C	C-	C

Asset & Performance History

Date	NAV	1-Year Total Return
2017	112.83	1.68
2016	112.55	1.3
2015	112.78	1
2014	113.11	3.55
2013	110.7	-1.31
2012	113.5	1.98

Total Assets: $454,085,426

Asset Allocation

Asset	%
Cash	0%
Stocks	0%
US Stocks	0%
Bonds	100%
US Bonds	81%
Other	0%

Services Offered:

Investment Strategy: The investment seeks to track the investment results of the Bloomberg Barclays U.S. Agency Bond Index. The underlying index measures the performance of the agency sector of the U.S. government bond market and is comprised of investment-grade U.S. dollar-denominated publicly-issued government agency bonds or debentures. The fund generally will invest at least 90% of its assets in the component securities of the underlying index. **Top Holdings:** Federal Home Loan Mortgage Corporation 1.85% Federal National Mortgage Association 2.88% Israel (State Of) 5.5% Iraq (Republic Of) 2.15% Federal Farm Credit Banks 2.54%

First Trust Emerging Markets AlphaDEX® Fund   C-   HOLD

Ticker	Traded On	NAV
FEM	NAS CM	22.80

Total Assets ($)	Dividend Yield (TTM)	Turnover Ratio	Expense Ratio
$453,439,835	3.99	101	0.8

Ratings

Reward	C-
Risk	C
Recent Upgrade/Downgrade	Down

Fund Information

Fund Type	Exchange Traded Funds
Category	Global Emerg Mkts Equity
Sub-Category	Diversified Emerging Mkts
Prospectus Objective	Div Emerg Mkts
Inception Date	Apr-11
Open to New Investments	Y

Prices

Price (as of 12/31/2018)	22.83
52-Week High	31.30
52-Week Low	22.37

Total Returns (%)

3-Month	6-Month	1-Year	3-Year	5-Year
-9.28	-10.20	-15.44	36.63	6.77

3-Year Standard Deviation	16.28
Effective Duration	

Valuation

Premium/Discount (1-Year Average)	-0.03

Company Information

Provider	First Trust
Manager/Tenure	Jon C. Erickson (7), Daniel J. Lindquist (7), David G. McGarel (7), 3 others
Website	http://www.ftportfolios.com/
Address	First Trust 120 E. Liberty Drive, Suite 400 Wheaton IL 60187 United States
Phone Number	800-621-1675

PERFORMANCE

Ratings History

Date	Overall Rating	Risk Rating	Reward Rating
Q4-18	C-	C	C-
Q2-18	C	C	C
Q4-17	B	C+	B+
Q4-16	D+	C-	D+
Q4-15	D	D+	D

Asset & Performance History

Date	NAV	1-Year Total Return
2017	27.84	39.47
2016	20.5	15.84
2015	18.1	-13.13
2014	21.53	-10.03
2013	24.55	-3.34
2012	26.1	21.1

Total Assets: $453,439,835

Asset Allocation

Asset	%
Cash	0%
Stocks	100%
US Stocks	0%
Bonds	0%
US Bonds	0%
Other	0%

Services Offered:

Investment Strategy: The investment seeks investment results that correspond generally to the price and yield (before the fund's fees and expenses) of an equity index called the NASDAQ AlphaDEX® Emerging Markets Index. The fund will normally invest at least 90% of its net assets (including investment borrowings) in common stocks and/or depositary receipts that comprise the index. The index is designed to select stocks from the NASDAQ Emerging Markets Index (the "base index") that may generate positive alpha, or risk-adjusted returns, relative to traditional indices through the use of the AlphaDEX® selection methodology. **Top Holdings:** Telefonica Brasil SA Participating Preferred IRB Brasil Resseguros SA Tupras-Turkiye Petrol Rafineleri AS Grupa LOTOS SA Nanya Technology Corp

Fidelity® Total Bond ETF

C- **HOLD**

Ticker	Traded On	NAV		Total Assets ($)	Dividend Yield (TTM)	Turnover Ratio	Expense Ratio
FBND	NYSE Arca	48.35		$453,380,601	2.89	91	0.36

Ratings
Reward	D+
Risk	C-
Recent Upgrade/Downgrade	

Fund Information
Fund Type	Exchange Traded Funds
Category	US Fixed Income
Sub-Category	Intermediate-Term Bond
Prospectus Objective	Income
Inception Date	Oct-14
Open to New Investments	Y

Prices
Price (as of 12/31/2018)	48.53
52-Week High	50.25
52-Week Low	47.95

Total Returns (%)
3-Month	6-Month	1-Year	3-Year	5-Year
0.56	0.86	-0.66	10.24	

3-Year Standard Deviation	3
Effective Duration	5.75

Valuation
Premium/Discount (1-Year Average)	0.22

Company Information
Provider	Fidelity Investments
Manager/Tenure	Michael Foggin (4), Ford E. O'Neil (4), Michael Plage (3), 2 others
Website	http://www.institutional.fidelity.com
Address	Fidelity Investments 82 Devonshire Street Boston MA 2109 United States
Phone Number	617-563-7000

PERFORMANCE

Ratings History
Date	Overall Rating	Risk Rating	Reward Rating
Q4-18	C-	C-	D+
Q2-18	C-	C-	C
Q4-17	C+	B	C
Q4-16	D+	C-	D+
Q4-15	U		

Asset & Performance History
Date	NAV	1-Year Total Return
2017	50.12	4.07
2016	49.41	6.64
2015	47.67	-1.43
2014	49.92	
2013		
2012		

Total Assets: $453,380,601

Asset Allocation
Asset	%
Cash	7%
Stocks	0%
US Stocks	0%
Bonds	93%
US Bonds	86%
Other	0%

Services Offered:

Investment Strategy: The investment seeks a high level of current income. Normally, the fund invests at least 80% of assets in debt securities of all types and repurchase agreements for those securities. It uses the Bloomberg Barclays U.S. Universal Bond Index as a guide in allocating assets across the investment-grade, high yield, and emerging market asset classes. The fund invests up to 20% of assets in lower-quality debt securities. It is managed to have similar overall interest rate risk to the index. **Top Holdings:** United States Treasury Notes 2% United States Treasury Notes 1.88% United States Treasury Bonds 3% United States Treasury Notes 2.12% United States Treasury Notes 1.62%

---

iShares U.S. Basic Materials ETF

C **HOLD**

Ticker	Traded On	NAV		Total Assets ($)	Dividend Yield (TTM)	Turnover Ratio	Expense Ratio
IYM	NYSE Arca	84.01		$453,330,367	1.61	6	0.43

Ratings
Reward	C
Risk	C-
Recent Upgrade/Downgrade	Down

Fund Information
Fund Type	Exchange Traded Funds
Category	Natural Resources
Sub-Category	Natural Resources
Prospectus Objective	Natl Res
Inception Date	Jun-00
Open to New Investments	Y

Prices
Price (as of 12/31/2018)	83.96
52-Week High	108.05
52-Week Low	78.95

Total Returns (%)
3-Month	6-Month	1-Year	3-Year	5-Year
-15.09	-14.15	-16.49	24.73	12.01

3-Year Standard Deviation	14.71
Effective Duration	

Valuation
Premium/Discount (1-Year Average)	0.01

Company Information
Provider	iShares
Manager/Tenure	Diane Hsiung (10), Greg Savage (10), Jennifer Hsui (6), 3 others
Website	http://www.ishares.com
Address	iShares 400 Howard Street San Francisco CA 94105 United States
Phone Number	800-474-2737

PERFORMANCE

Ratings History
Date	Overall Rating	Risk Rating	Reward Rating
Q4-18	C	C-	C
Q2-18	C+	C	B-
Q4-17	B-	C	B
Q4-16	C	C-	B-
Q4-15	B-	C+	B

Asset & Performance History
Date	NAV	1-Year Total Return
2017	102.11	24.74
2016	83.15	19.74
2015	70.53	-12.77
2014	82.45	2.95
2013	81.46	19.88
2012	69.33	9.97

Total Assets: $453,330,367

Asset Allocation
Asset	%
Cash	0%
Stocks	100%
US Stocks	85%
Bonds	0%
US Bonds	0%
Other	0%

Services Offered: CashInvestment Plan

Investment Strategy: The investment seeks to track the investment results of the Dow Jones U.S. Basic Materials Index composed of U.S. equities in the basic materials sector. The fund generally invests at least 90% of its assets in securities of the underlying index and in depositary receipts representing securities of the underlying index. The underlying index measures the performance of the basic materials sector of the U.S. equity market. The fund is non-diversified. **Top Holdings:** DowDuPont Inc Linde PLC Ecolab Inc Air Products & Chemicals Inc LyondellBasell Industries NV

Invesco BulletShares 2023 Corporate Bond ETF   C   HOLD

Ticker	Traded On	NAV	Total Assets ($)	Dividend Yield (TTM)	Turnover Ratio	Expense Ratio
BSCN	NYSE Arca	20.13	$452,543,550	3	0	0.1

Ratings
Reward	C-
Risk	C+
Recent Upgrade/Downgrade	Up

Fund Information
Fund Type	Exchange Traded Funds
Category	US Fixed Income
Sub-Category	Corporate Bond
Prospectus Objective	Corp Bond - Gen
Inception Date	Sep-14
Open to New Investments	Y

Prices
Price (as of 12/31/2018)	20.17
52-Week High	20.83
52-Week Low	20.00

Total Returns (%)
3-Month	6-Month	1-Year	3-Year	5-Year
0.75	1.71	-0.35	10.80	

3-Year Standard Deviation	3.22
Effective Duration	4.15

Valuation
Premium/Discount (1-Year Average)	0.22

Company Information
Provider	Invesco
Manager/Tenure	Jeremy Neisewander (2), Peter Hubbard (0), Jeffrey W. Kernagis (0), 1 other
Website	http://www.invesco.com/us
Address	Invesco 11 Greenway Plaza, Ste. 2500 Houston TX 77046 United States
Phone Number	800-659-1005

PERFORMANCE

Ratings History
Date	Overall Rating	Risk Rating	Reward Rating
Q4-18	C	C+	C-
Q2-18	C	C+	C
Q4-17	B	A	C
Q4-16	D+	C-	D+
Q4-15	U		

Asset & Performance History
Date	NAV	1-Year Total Return
2017	20.79	4.41
2016	20.43	6.01
2015	19.86	0.67
2014	20.32	
2013		
2012		

Total Assets: $452,543,550
Asset Allocation
Asset	%
Cash	0%
Stocks	0%
US Stocks	0%
Bonds	100%
US Bonds	85%
Other	0%

Services Offered:

Investment Strategy: The investment seeks investment results that correspond generally to the performance, before the fund's fees and expenses, of an investment grade corporate bond index called the Nasdaq BulletShares® USD Corporate Bond 2023 Index. The fund will invest at least 80% of its total assets in component securities that comprise the index. The index is designed to represent the performance of a held-to-maturity portfolio of U.S. dollar-denominated investment-grade corporate bonds with effective maturities in the year 2023. The fund is non-diversified. **Top Holdings:** Anheuser-Busch InBev Finance Inc. 3.3% Verizon Communications Inc. 5.15% Apple Inc. 2.4% CVS Health Corp 3.7% Bank of America Corporation 3.3%

Invesco Russell 1000 Equal Weight ETF   C-   HOLD

Ticker	Traded On	NAV	Total Assets ($)	Dividend Yield (TTM)	Turnover Ratio	Expense Ratio
EQAL	NYSE Arca	27.92	$451,663,022	1.49		0.2

Ratings
Reward	C-
Risk	C-
Recent Upgrade/Downgrade	Down

Fund Information
Fund Type	Exchange Traded Funds
Category	US Equity Mid Cap
Sub-Category	Mid-Cap Blend
Prospectus Objective	Growth
Inception Date	Dec-14
Open to New Investments	

Prices
Price (as of 12/31/2018)	27.90
52-Week High	33.62
52-Week Low	26.31

Total Returns (%)
3-Month	6-Month	1-Year	3-Year	5-Year
-15.25	-11.24	-8.90	23.89	

3-Year Standard Deviation	10.67
Effective Duration	

Valuation
Premium/Discount (1-Year Average)	0.08

Company Information
Provider	Invesco
Manager/Tenure	Peter Hubbard (3), Michael Jeanette (3), Tony Seisser (3), 1 other
Website	http://www.invesco.com/us
Address	Invesco 11 Greenway Plaza, Ste. 2500 Houston TX 77046 United States
Phone Number	800-659-1005

PERFORMANCE

Ratings History
Date	Overall Rating	Risk Rating	Reward Rating
Q4-18	C-	C-	C-
Q2-18	C+	C+	C
Q4-17	C+	B-	C+
Q4-16	C-	C-	C-
Q4-15	U		

Asset & Performance History
Date	NAV	1-Year Total Return
2017	31.11	17.18
2016	26.88	16.06
2015	23.54	-4.2
2014	24.97	
2013		
2012		

Total Assets: $451,663,022
Asset Allocation
Asset	%
Cash	0%
Stocks	100%
US Stocks	99%
Bonds	0%
US Bonds	0%
Other	0%

Services Offered:

Investment Strategy: The investment seeks to track the investment results (before fees and expenses) of the Russell 1000® Equal Weight Index (the "underlying index"). The fund generally will invest at least 90% of its total assets in common stocks that comprise the underlying index. Strictly in accordance with its guidelines and mandated procedures, Frank Russell Company compiles and maintains the underlying index, which is composed of all of the securities in the Russell 1000® Index (the "Russell 1000") "equally weighted." **Top Holdings:** SCANA Corp United States Cellular Corp Walgreens Boots Alliance Inc CVS Health Corp Marathon Petroleum Corp

iShares MSCI EAFE ESG Optimized ETF   D+   SELL

Ticker	Traded On	NAV	Total Assets ($)	Dividend Yield (TTM)	Turnover Ratio	Expense Ratio
ESGD	NAS CM	57.19	$450,372,191	2.88	24	0.2

Ratings
Reward   D+
Risk   C-
Recent Upgrade/Downgrade   Down

Fund Information
Fund Type   Exchange Traded Funds
Category   Global Equity Large Cap
Sub-Category   Foreign Large Blend
Prospectus Objective   Growth & Inc
Inception Date   Jun-16
Open to New Investments   Y

Prices
Price (as of 12/31/2018)   57.38
52-Week High   72.49
52-Week Low   55.20

Total Returns (%)

3-Month	6-Month	1-Year	3-Year	5-Year
-12.61	-10.03	-13.62		

3-Year Standard Deviation
Effective Duration

Valuation
Premium/Discount (1-Year Average)   0.17

Company Information
Provider   iShares
Manager/Tenure   Diane Hsiung (2), Jennifer Hsui (2),
                  Alan Mason (2), 1 other
Website   http://www.ishares.com
Address   iShares 400 Howard Street San
                  Francisco CA 94105 United States
Phone Number   800-474-2737

PERFORMANCE

Ratings History

Date	Overall Rating	Risk Rating	Reward Rating
Q4-18	D+	C-	D+
Q2-18	C-	C-	D+
Q4-17	D	B	C
Q4-16	U		
Q4-15			

Asset & Performance History

Date	NAV	1-Year Total Return
2017	67.86	25.21
2016	55.72	
2015		
2014		
2013		
2012		

Total Assets: $450,372,191

Asset Allocation

Asset	%
Cash	1%
Stocks	99%
US Stocks	1%
Bonds	0%
US Bonds	0%
Other	0%

Services Offered:

Investment Strategy: The investment seeks to track the investment results of the MSCI EAFE Extended ESG Focus Index. The fund generally will invest at least 90% of its assets in the component securities of the underlying index and in investments that have economic characteristics that are substantially identical to the component securities of the underlying index. The underlying index is composed of large- and mid-capitalization developed market equities, excluding the U.S. and Canada that have positive environmental, social and governance characteristics as identified by the index provider. The fund is non-diversified. **Top Holdings:** Nestle SA Roche Holding AG Dividend Right Cert. BP PLC Total SA Toyota Motor Corp

---

VelocityShares Daily 2x VIX Short-Term ETN   C-   HOLD

Ticker	Traded On	NAV	Total Assets ($)	Dividend Yield (TTM)	Turnover Ratio	Expense Ratio
TVIX	NAS CM	70.65	$448,413,599	0		1.65

Ratings
Reward   C
Risk   D
Recent Upgrade/Downgrade   Up

Fund Information
Fund Type   Exchange Traded Funds
Category   Alternative Misc
Sub-Category   Volatility
Prospectus Objective   Growth
Inception Date   Nov-10
Open to New Investments   Y

Prices
Price (as of 12/31/2018)   70.91
52-Week High   78.72
52-Week Low   4.73

Total Returns (%)

3-Month	6-Month	1-Year	3-Year	5-Year
177.37	35.26	1,151.86	-95.41	-99.61

3-Year Standard Deviation   92.1
Effective Duration

Valuation
Premium/Discount (1-Year Average)   0.90

Company Information
Provider   Credit Suisse AG
Manager/Tenure   Management Team (8)
Website
Address   Kilmore House Park Lane Dublin
                  Ireland
Phone Number

PERFORMANCE

Ratings History

Date	Overall Rating	Risk Rating	Reward Rating
Q4-18	C-	D	C
Q2-18	D	D	D
Q4-17	E	E	E-
Q4-16	E+	D-	E-
Q4-15	E	E+	E

Asset & Performance History

Date	NAV	1-Year Total Return
2017	5.64	-94.05
2016	94.4	-93.98
2015	1,540.00	-77.68
2014	6,900.00	-62.13
2013	18,225.00	-91.68
2012	219,250.00	-97.29

Total Assets: $448,413,599

Asset Allocation

Asset	%
Cash	%
Stocks	%
US Stocks	%
Bonds	%
US Bonds	%
Other	%

Services Offered:

Investment Strategy: The investment seeks to replicate, net of expenses, the returns of twice (2x) the daily performance of the S&P 500 VIX Short-Term Futures index.
The index was designed to provide investors with exposure to one or more maturities of futures contracts on the VIX, which reflects implied volatility of the S&P 500 Index at various points along the volatility forward curve. The ETNs are linked to a multiple (2x) of the daily return of the index and do not represent an investment in the VIX.
Top Holdings:

Invesco Variable Rate Investment Grade ETF   C   HOLD

Ticker	Traded On	NAV	Total Assets ($)	Dividend Yield (TTM)	Turnover Ratio	Expense Ratio
VRIG	NAS CM	24.71	$448,075,421	2.79	23	0.3

Ratings

Reward	C-
Risk	C+
Recent Upgrade/Downgrade	Up

Fund Information

Fund Type	Exchange Traded Funds
Category	US Fixed Income
Sub-Category	Ultrashort Bond
Prospectus Objective	Income
Inception Date	Sep-16
Open to New Investments	Y

Prices

Price (as of 12/31/2018)	24.63
52-Week High	25.26
52-Week Low	24.60

Total Returns (%)

3-Month	6-Month	1-Year	3-Year	5-Year
-0.68	0.13	1.03		

3-Year Standard Deviation	
Effective Duration	

Valuation

Premium/Discount (1-Year Average)	0.07

Company Information

Provider	Invesco
Manager/Tenure	Philip Armstrong (2), Peter Hubbard (2), Jeffrey W. Kernagis (2), 3 others
Website	http://www.invesco.com/us
Address	Invesco 11 Greenway Plaza, Ste. 2500 Houston TX 77046 United States
Phone Number	800-659-1005

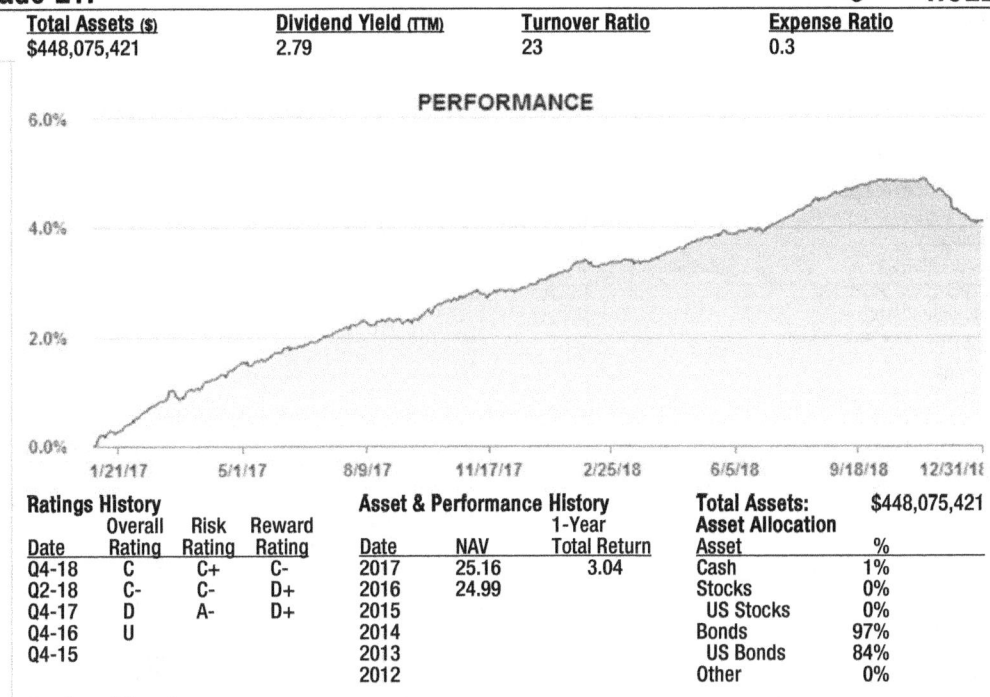

PERFORMANCE

Ratings History

Date	Overall Rating	Risk Rating	Reward Rating
Q4-18	C	C+	C-
Q2-18	C-	C-	D+
Q4-17	D	A-	D+
Q4-16	U		
Q4-15			

Asset & Performance History

Date	NAV	1-Year Total Return
2017	25.16	3.04
2016	24.99	
2015		
2014		
2013		
2012		

Total Assets: $448,075,421
Asset Allocation

Asset	%
Cash	1%
Stocks	0%
US Stocks	0%
Bonds	97%
US Bonds	84%
Other	0%

Services Offered:

Investment Strategy: The investment seeks to generate current income while maintaining low portfolio duration as a primary objective and capital appreciation as a secondary objective. The fund invests at least 80% of its net assets (plus any borrowings for investment purposes) in a portfolio of investment-grade, variable rate or floating rate debt securities. At least 80% of its net assets (plus any borrowings for investment purposes) will be invested in Variable Rate Instruments that are, at the time of purchase, investment grade (or in affiliated ETFs that invest primarily in any or all of the foregoing securities). It is non-diversified. **Top Holdings:** United States Treasury Notes 2.38% United States Treasury Notes 2.43% Federal Home Loan Mortgage Corporation 3.67% Federal Home Loan Mortgage Corporation 5.17% Federal Home Loan Mortgage Corporation 4.27%

---

iShares Morningstar Mid-Cap Value ETF   C-   HOLD

Ticker	Traded On	NAV	Total Assets ($)	Dividend Yield (TTM)	Turnover Ratio	Expense Ratio
JKI	NAS CM	139.05	$445,549,040	2.16	45	0.3

Ratings

Reward	C
Risk	D+
Recent Upgrade/Downgrade	Down

Fund Information

Fund Type	Exchange Traded Funds
Category	US Equity Mid Cap
Sub-Category	Mid-Cap Value
Prospectus Objective	Growth
Inception Date	Jun-04
Open to New Investments	Y

Prices

Price (as of 12/31/2018)	138.81
52-Week High	168.36
52-Week Low	132.21

Total Returns (%)

3-Month	6-Month	1-Year	3-Year	5-Year
-13.20	-11.47	-10.76	25.46	35.52

3-Year Standard Deviation	10.38
Effective Duration	

Valuation

Premium/Discount (1-Year Average)	0.07

Company Information

Provider	iShares
Manager/Tenure	Diane Hsiung (10), Greg Savage (10), Jennifer Hsui (6), 3 others
Website	http://www.ishares.com
Address	iShares 400 Howard Street San Francisco CA 94105 United States
Phone Number	800-474-2737

PERFORMANCE

Ratings History

Date	Overall Rating	Risk Rating	Reward Rating
Q4-18	C-	D+	C
Q2-18	C	D+	C
Q4-17	B	B	B
Q4-16	C	C-	C
Q4-15	C	D+	C

Asset & Performance History

Date	NAV	1-Year Total Return
2017	159.53	12.69
2016	144.39	24.76
2015	118.41	-2.8
2014	124.58	11.13
2013	114.35	41.72
2012	82.38	17.27

Total Assets: $445,549,040
Asset Allocation

Asset	%
Cash	0%
Stocks	100%
US Stocks	98%
Bonds	0%
US Bonds	0%
Other	0%

Services Offered:

Investment Strategy: The investment seeks to track the investment results of the Morningstar® Mid Value IndexSM composed of mid-capitalization U.S. equities that exhibit value characteristics. The fund generally invests at least 90% of its assets in securities of the underlying index and in depositary receipts representing securities of the underlying index. The underlying index measures the performance of stocks issued by mid-capitalization companies that have exhibited "value" characteristics as determined by Morningstar, Inc.'s ("Morningstar" or the "index provider") proprietary index methodology. **Top Holdings:** Welltower Inc The Kroger Co WEC Energy Group Inc United Continental Holdings Inc DTE Energy Co

Hartford Total Return Bond ETF   D+   SELL

Ticker	Traded On	NAV	Total Assets ($)	Dividend Yield (TTM)	Turnover Ratio	Expense Ratio
HTRB	NYSE Arca	38.72	$445,032,295	2.47	46	0.29

Ratings
Reward   D
Risk   C
Recent Upgrade/Downgrade

Fund Information
Fund Type	Exchange Traded Funds
Category	US Fixed Income
Sub-Category	Intermediate-Term Bond
Prospectus Objective	Income
Inception Date	Sep-17
Open to New Investments	Y

Prices
Price (as of 12/31/2018)	38.78
52-Week High	40.06
52-Week Low	38.34

Total Returns (%)
3-Month	6-Month	1-Year	3-Year	5-Year
0.45	0.98	-0.79		

3-Year Standard Deviation
Effective Duration

Valuation
Premium/Discount (1-Year Average)   0.23

Company Information
Provider	Hartford Funds
Manager/Tenure	Robert D. Burn (1), Campe Goodman (1), Joseph F. Marvan (1)
Website	http://www.hartfordfunds.com
Address	690 Lee Road Wayne PA 19087 United States
Phone Number	800-456-7526

PERFORMANCE

Ratings History
Date	Overall Rating	Risk Rating	Reward Rating
Q4-18	D+	C	D
Q2-18	U		
Q4-17	U		
Q4-16			
Q4-15			

Asset & Performance History
Date	NAV	1-Year Total Return
2017	39.96	
2016		
2015		
2014		
2013		
2012		

Total Assets: $445,032,295
Asset Allocation
Asset	%
Cash	16%
Stocks	0%
US Stocks	0%
Bonds	82%
US Bonds	73%
Other	0%

Services Offered:

Investment Strategy: The investment seeks a competitive total return, with income as a secondary objective. The fund invests at least 80% of its net assets in bonds that the sub-adviser considers to be attractive from a total return perspective along with current income. It may invest up to 20% of its net assets in securities rated below investment grade (also known as "junk bonds"). The fund may invest up to 40% of its net assets in debt securities of foreign issuers, including from emerging markets, and up to 20% of its net assets in non-dollar securities. **Top Holdings:** Us 2yr Note (Cbt) Mar19 Xcbt 20190329   Federal National Mortgage Association 4%   Us 10yr Ultra Fut Mar19 Xcbt 20190320   B9d09bc10 Irs Usd R V 03mlibor 99d09bc69 Ccpvanilla   B9d09bc10 Irs Usd P F 2.25000 99d09bc10 Ccpvanilla

---

UBS ETRACS Monthly Pay 2xLeveraged Mortgage REIT ETN   C   HOLD

Ticker	Traded On	NAV	Total Assets ($)	Dividend Yield (TTM)	Turnover Ratio	Expense Ratio
MORL	NYSE Arca	12.54	$443,174,684	21.59		0.4

Ratings
Reward   C
Risk   C+
Recent Upgrade/Downgrade   Down

Fund Information
Fund Type	Exchange Traded Funds
Category	Trading Tools
Sub-Category	Trading--Leveraged Equity
Prospectus Objective	Real Estate
Inception Date	Oct-12
Open to New Investments	Y

Prices
Price (as of 12/31/2018)	12.71
52-Week High	17.65
52-Week Low	11.70

Total Returns (%)
3-Month	6-Month	1-Year	3-Year	5-Year
-14.25	-13.01	-12.25	77.05	91.11

3-Year Standard Deviation   20.92
Effective Duration

Valuation
Premium/Discount (1-Year Average)   0.43

Company Information
Provider	UBS Group AG
Manager/Tenure	No Manager (6)
Website	http://www.ubs.com
Address	Bahnhofstrasse 45 Zurich 8098 Switzerland
Phone Number	412-037-1952

PERFORMANCE

Ratings History
Date	Overall Rating	Risk Rating	Reward Rating
Q4-18	C	C+	C
Q2-18	C	C	C+
Q4-17	B	C	B+
Q4-16	C	C-	B-
Q4-15	C-	D+	C-

Asset & Performance History
Date	NAV	1-Year Total Return
2017	17.61	38.04
2016	15.55	47.29
2015	13.25	-20.5
2014	20.86	35.77
2013	18.93	-3.21
2012	24.48	

Total Assets: $443,174,684
Asset Allocation
Asset	%
Cash	%
Stocks	%
US Stocks	%
Bonds	%
US Bonds	%
Other	%

Services Offered:

Investment Strategy: The investment seeks to link to the Market Vectors® Global Mortgage REITs Index. The index tracks the overall performance of publicly-traded mortgage REITs that derive at least 50% of their revenues from mortgage-related activities. The Securities are senior unsecured debt securities issued by UBS AG (UBS). The Securities provide a monthly compounded two times leveraged long exposure to the performance of the Index, reduced by the Accrued Fees. **Top Holdings:**

IQ Chaikin U.S. Small Cap ETF   D   SELL

Ticker	Traded On	NAV	Total Assets ($)	Dividend Yield (TTM)	Turnover Ratio	Expense Ratio
CSML	NAS CM	22.36	$443,029,128	0.76		0.35

Ratings
Reward	D
Risk	D
Recent Upgrade/Downgrade	Down

Fund Information
Fund Type	Exchange Traded Funds
Category	US Equity Small Cap
Sub-Category	Small Blend
Prospectus Objective	Small Company
Inception Date	May-17
Open to New Investments	Y

Prices
Price (as of 12/31/2018)	22.32
52-Week High	29.80
52-Week Low	21.19

Total Returns (%)
3-Month	6-Month	1-Year	3-Year	5-Year
-19.45	-22.15	-19.51		

3-Year Standard Deviation	
Effective Duration	

Valuation
Premium/Discount (1-Year Average)	0.05

Company Information
Provider	IndexIQ
Manager/Tenure	Greg Barrato (1), James Harrison (0)
Website	http://www.indexiq.com
Address	IndexIQ 800 Westchester Avenue, Suite N-611 Rye Brook NY 10573 United States
Phone Number	888-934-0777

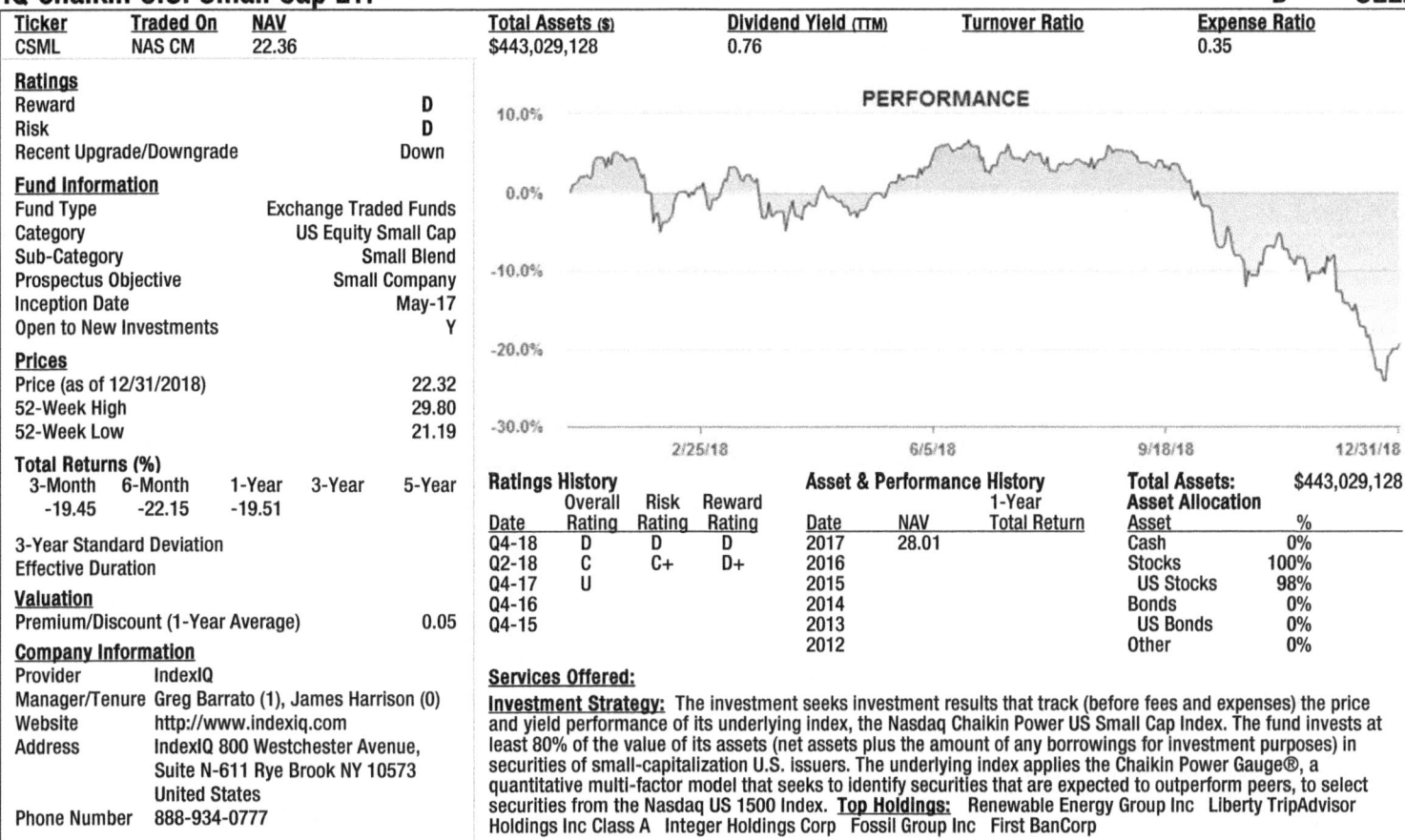

PERFORMANCE

Ratings History
Date	Overall Rating	Risk Rating	Reward Rating
Q4-18	D	D	D
Q2-18	C	C+	D+
Q4-17	U		
Q4-16			
Q4-15			

Asset & Performance History
Date	NAV	1-Year Total Return
2017	28.01	
2016		
2015		
2014		
2013		
2012		

Total Assets: $443,029,128

Asset Allocation
Asset	%
Cash	0%
Stocks	100%
US Stocks	98%
Bonds	0%
US Bonds	0%
Other	0%

Services Offered:

Investment Strategy: The investment seeks investment results that track (before fees and expenses) the price and yield performance of its underlying index, the Nasdaq Chaikin Power US Small Cap Index. The fund invests at least 80% of the value of its assets (net assets plus the amount of any borrowings for investment purposes) in securities of small-capitalization U.S. issuers. The underlying index applies the Chaikin Power Gauge®, a quantitative multi-factor model that seeks to identify securities that are expected to outperform peers, to select securities from the Nasdaq US 1500 Index. **Top Holdings:** Renewable Energy Group Inc Liberty TripAdvisor Holdings Inc Class A Integer Holdings Corp Fossil Group Inc First BanCorp

---

SPDR® FTSE International Government Inflation-Protected Bond ETF   C-   HOLD

Ticker	Traded On	NAV	Total Assets ($)	Dividend Yield (TTM)	Turnover Ratio	Expense Ratio
WIP	NYSE Arca	52.12	$441,714,363	3.86	42	0.5

Ratings
Reward	D+
Risk	C-
Recent Upgrade/Downgrade	

Fund Information
Fund Type	Exchange Traded Funds
Category	Global Fixed Income
Sub-Category	World Bond
Prospectus Objective	Worldwide Bond
Inception Date	Mar-08
Open to New Investments	Y

Prices
Price (as of 12/31/2018)	52.03
52-Week High	60.04
52-Week Low	51.61

Total Returns (%)
3-Month	6-Month	1-Year	3-Year	5-Year
0.12	-1.63	-5.90	10.46	-1.42

3-Year Standard Deviation	7.93
Effective Duration	

Valuation
Premium/Discount (1-Year Average)	-0.07

Company Information
Provider	SPDR State Street Global Advisors
Manager/Tenure	Cynthia Moy (4), James Kramer (2), Orhan Imer (1)
Website	http://www.spdrs.com
Address	SPDR State Street Global Advisors State Street Financial Center, 1 Lincoln Street Boston MA 02111-2900 United States
Phone Number	617-786-3000

PERFORMANCE

Ratings History
Date	Overall Rating	Risk Rating	Reward Rating
Q4-18	C-	C-	D+
Q2-18	C	C+	C-
Q4-17	C	C+	C
Q4-16	D+	C-	D
Q4-15	D	D+	D

Asset & Performance History
Date	NAV	1-Year Total Return
2017	57.58	10.4
2016	52.58	4.76
2015	50.64	-10.43
2014	57.18	-0.36
2013	58.79	-4.82
2012	63.22	14.01

Total Assets: $441,714,363

Asset Allocation
Asset	%
Cash	1%
Stocks	0%
US Stocks	0%
Bonds	98%
US Bonds	0%
Other	1%

Services Offered:

Investment Strategy: The investment seeks to provide investment results that, before fees and expenses, correspond generally to the price and yield performance of the FTSE International Inflation-Linked Securities Select Index. The fund generally invests substantially all, but at least 80%, of its total assets in the securities comprising the index or in securities that the Adviser determines have economic characteristics. The index is designed to measure the total return performance of inflation-linked bonds outside the United States with fixed-rate coupon payments that are linked to an inflation index. It is non-diversified. **Top Holdings:** Brazil Federative Rep 6% Nota Do Tesouro Nacional Notes 08/22 6 France (Govt Of) Bonds Regs 07/27 1.85 Japan(Govt Of) 0.1% Spain I/L Bond Sr Unsecured 144a Regs 11/24 1

iShares ESG MSCI EM ETF

D+   **SELL**

Ticker	Traded On	NAV	Total Assets ($)	Dividend Yield (TTM)	Turnover Ratio	Expense Ratio
ESGE	NAS CM	30.88	$436,590,811	2.17	45	0.25

Ratings
Reward   D+
Risk   D
Recent Upgrade/Downgrade

Fund Information
Fund Type   Exchange Traded Funds
Category   Global Emerg Mkts Equity
Sub-Category   Diversified Emerging Mkts
Prospectus Objective   Div Emerg Mkts
Inception Date   Jun-16
Open to New Investments   Y

Prices
Price (as of 12/31/2018)   30.67
52-Week High   40.80
52-Week Low   29.80

Total Returns (%)

3-Month	6-Month	1-Year	3-Year	5-Year
-6.27	-5.96	-14.31		

3-Year Standard Deviation
Effective Duration

Valuation
Premium/Discount (1-Year Average)   0.33

Company Information
Provider   iShares
Manager/Tenure   Diane Hsiung (2), Jennifer Hsui (2),
                  Alan Mason (2), 1 other
Website   http://www.ishares.com
Address   iShares 400 Howard Street San
                  Francisco CA 94105 United States
Phone Number   800-474-2737

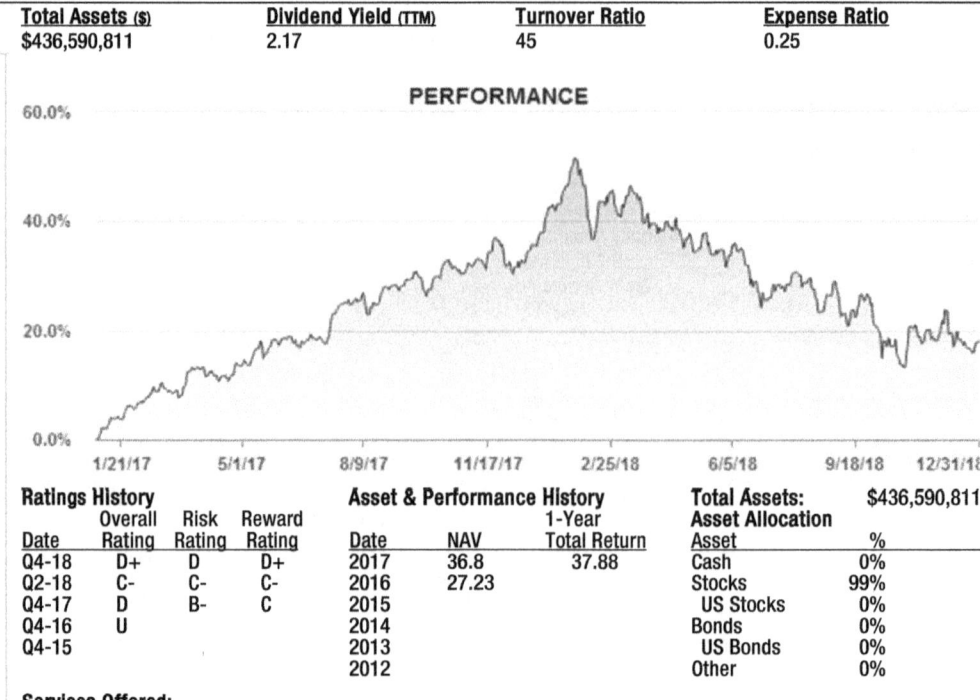

PERFORMANCE

Ratings History

Date	Overall Rating	Risk Rating	Reward Rating
Q4-18	D+	D	D+
Q2-18	C-	C-	C-
Q4-17	D	B-	C
Q4-16	U		
Q4-15			

Asset & Performance History

Date	NAV	1-Year Total Return
2017	36.8	37.88
2016	27.23	
2015		
2014		
2013		
2012		

Total Assets: $436,590,811

Asset Allocation

Asset	%
Cash	0%
Stocks	99%
US Stocks	0%
Bonds	0%
US Bonds	0%
Other	0%

Services Offered:

Investment Strategy: The investment seeks to track the investment results of the MSCI Emerging Markets Extended ESG Focus Index. The fund generally will invest at least 90% of its assets in the component securities of the underlying index and in investments that have economic characteristics that are substantially identical to the component securities of the underlying index. The index is an optimized equity index designed to reflect the equity performance of companies that have favorable ESG characteristics, while exhibiting risk and return characteristics similar to those of the MSCI Market Cap Weighted Index (the "parent index"). The fund is non-diversified. **Top Holdings:** Tencent Holdings Ltd Taiwan Semiconductor Manufacturing Co Ltd Alibaba Group Holding Ltd ADR Samsung Electronics Co Ltd Naspers Ltd Class N

---

iShares MSCI Emerging Markets Asia ETF

C-   **HOLD**

Ticker	Traded On	NAV	Total Assets ($)	Dividend Yield (TTM)	Turnover Ratio	Expense Ratio
EEMA	NAS CM	60.97	$434,766,412	2.11	33	0.5

Ratings
Reward   C-
Risk   C-
Recent Upgrade/Downgrade

Fund Information
Fund Type   Exchange Traded Funds
Category   Asia ex-Japan Equity
Sub-Category   Pacific/Asia ex-Japan Stk
Prospectus Objective   Pacific Stock
Inception Date   Feb-12
Open to New Investments   Y

Prices
Price (as of 12/31/2018)   60.85
52-Week High   81.27
52-Week Low   58.61

Total Returns (%)

3-Month	6-Month	1-Year	3-Year	5-Year
-9.13	-10.27	-15.53	26.58	18.93

3-Year Standard Deviation   14.85
Effective Duration

Valuation
Premium/Discount (1-Year Average)   -0.14

Company Information
Provider   iShares
Manager/Tenure   Diane Hsiung (6), Greg Savage (6),
                  Jennifer Hsui (5), 1 other
Website   http://www.ishares.com
Address   iShares 400 Howard Street San
                  Francisco CA 94105 United States
Phone Number   800-474-2737

PERFORMANCE

Ratings History

Date	Overall Rating	Risk Rating	Reward Rating
Q4-18	C-	C-	C-
Q2-18	C	C	C
Q4-17	B	C+	A
Q4-16	C-	C-	C-
Q4-15	C-	C-	C-

Asset & Performance History

Date	NAV	1-Year Total Return
2017	73.7	41.93
2016	52.87	5.59
2015	50.95	-9.82
2014	57.81	4.2
2013	56.24	1.97
2012	56.57	

Total Assets: $434,766,412

Asset Allocation

Asset	%
Cash	0%
Stocks	100%
US Stocks	0%
Bonds	0%
US Bonds	0%
Other	0%

Services Offered:

Investment Strategy: The investment seeks to track the investment results of the MSCI EM Asia Custom Capped Index. The fund generally will invest at least 90% of its assets in the component securities of the underlying index and in investments that have economic characteristics that are substantially identical to the component securities of the underlying index. The underlying index is designed to measure equity market performance in the emerging market countries of Asia. It may include large- or mid-capitalization companies. **Top Holdings:** Tencent Holdings Ltd Alibaba Group Holding Ltd ADR Taiwan Semiconductor Manufacturing Co Ltd Samsung Electronics Co Ltd China Construction Bank Corp H

iShares MSCI Chile Capped ETF   C-   HOLD

Ticker	Traded On	NAV	Total Assets ($)	Dividend Yield (TTM)	Turnover Ratio	Expense Ratio
ECH	BATS	41.58	$432,774,832	2.25	54	0.59

Ratings
Reward	C-
Risk	C-
Recent Upgrade/Downgrade	Down

Fund Information
Fund Type	Exchange Traded Funds
Category	Equity Misc
Sub-Category	Miscellaneous Region
Prospectus Objective	Foreign Stock
Inception Date	Nov-07
Open to New Investments	Y

Prices
Price (as of 12/31/2018)	41.41
52-Week High	56.17
52-Week Low	40.69

Total Returns (%)
3-Month	6-Month	1-Year	3-Year	5-Year
-8.80	-8.80	-19.13	35.81	-2.86

3-Year Standard Deviation	20.82
Effective Duration	

Valuation
Premium/Discount (1-Year Average)	-0.13

Company Information
Provider	iShares
Manager/Tenure	Diane Hsiung (10), Greg Savage (10), Jennifer Hsui (5), 1 other
Website	http://www.ishares.com
Address	iShares 400 Howard Street San Francisco CA 94105 United States
Phone Number	800-474-2737

PERFORMANCE

Ratings History
Date	Overall Rating	Risk Rating	Reward Rating
Q4-18	C-	C-	C-
Q2-18	C	C+	C
Q4-17	B	C	B+
Q4-16	D+	D+	D+
Q4-15	D-	D-	D-

Asset & Performance History
Date	NAV	1-Year Total Return
2017	52.49	42.59
2016	37.45	17.78
2015	32.4	-18.04
2014	40.26	-12.72
2013	46.84	-23.86
2012	62.31	8.89

Total Assets: $432,774,832

Asset Allocation
Asset	%
Cash	0%
Stocks	100%
US Stocks	0%
Bonds	0%
US Bonds	0%
Other	0%

Services Offered:

Investment Strategy: The investment seeks to track the investment results of the MSCI Chile IMI 25/50 Index. The fund generally will invest at least 90% of its assets in the component securities of the underlying index and in investments that have economic characteristics that are substantially identical to the component securities of the underlying index. The underlying index is a free float-adjusted market capitalization index that is designed to measure broad-based equity market performance in Chile. The fund is non-diversified. **Top Holdings:** Empresas COPEC SA SACI Falabella Sociedad Quimica Y Minera De Chile SA Class B Banco Santander Chile Enel Americas SA

IQ Chaikin U.S. Large Cap ETF   D+   SELL

Ticker	Traded On	NAV	Total Assets ($)	Dividend Yield (TTM)	Turnover Ratio	Expense Ratio
CLRG	NAS CM	21.48	$432,185,693			0.25

Ratings
Reward	D+
Risk	D
Recent Upgrade/Downgrade	

Fund Information
Fund Type	Exchange Traded Funds
Category	US Equity Large Cap Blend
Sub-Category	Large Value
Prospectus Objective	Growth & Inc
Inception Date	Dec-17
Open to New Investments	Y

Prices
Price (as of 12/31/2018)	21.33
52-Week High	27.28
52-Week Low	20.41

Total Returns (%)
3-Month	6-Month	1-Year	3-Year	5-Year
-17.39	-12.45	-13.10		

3-Year Standard Deviation	
Effective Duration	

Valuation
Premium/Discount (1-Year Average)	0.14

Company Information
Provider	IndexIQ
Manager/Tenure	Greg Barrato (0), James Harrison (0)
Website	http://www.indexiq.com
Address	IndexIQ 800 Westchester Avenue, Suite N-611 Rye Brook NY 10573 United States
Phone Number	888-934-0777

PERFORMANCE

Ratings History
Date	Overall Rating	Risk Rating	Reward Rating
Q4-18	D+	D	D+
Q2-18	U		
Q4-17	U		
Q4-16			
Q4-15			

Asset & Performance History
Date	NAV	1-Year Total Return
2017	25.17	
2016		
2015		
2014		
2013		
2012		

Total Assets: $432,185,693

Asset Allocation
Asset	%
Cash	0%
Stocks	100%
US Stocks	98%
Bonds	0%
US Bonds	0%
Other	0%

Services Offered:

Investment Strategy: The investment seeks investment results that track (before fees and expenses) the price and yield performance of the Nasdaq Chaikin Power US Large Cap Index (the "underlying index"). The underlying index is an equally weighted index of large-capitalization securities. The fund generally will invest in all of the securities that comprise its underlying index in proportion to their weightings in the underlying index. It invests, under normal circumstances, at least 80% of the value of its assets (net assets plus the amount of any borrowings for investment purposes) in securities of large-capitalization U.S. issuers. **Top Holdings:** HCA Healthcare Inc Cigna Corp Anthem Inc Pfizer Inc Norfolk Southern Corp

Innovator IBD® 50 ETF
C HOLD

Ticker	Traded On	NAV	Total Assets ($)	Dividend Yield (TTM)	Turnover Ratio	Expense Ratio
FFTY	NYSE	27.65	$432,089,494	0.18		0.8

Ratings
Reward	C+
Risk	C
Recent Upgrade/Downgrade	Down

Fund Information
Fund Type	Exchange Traded Funds
Category	US Equity Mid Cap
Sub-Category	Mid-Cap Growth
Prospectus Objective	Growth
Inception Date	Apr-15
Open to New Investments	Y

Prices
Price (as of 12/31/2018)	27.62
52-Week High	38.44
52-Week Low	25.43

Total Returns (%)
3-Month	6-Month	1-Year	3-Year	5-Year
-27.31	-22.28	-16.62	24.91	

3-Year Standard Deviation	18.13
Effective Duration	

Valuation
Premium/Discount (1-Year Average)	0.02

Company Information
Provider	Innovator ETFs
Manager/Tenure	Anand Desai (1), Dustin Lewellyn (1), Ernesto Tong (1)
Website	http://innovatoretfs.com/
Address	Innovator ETFs 120 N Hale Street, Suite 200 Wheaton IL 60187 United States
Phone Number	800-208-5212

PERFORMANCE

Ratings History
Date	Overall Rating	Risk Rating	Reward Rating
Q4-18	C	C	C+
Q2-18	B	C-	B+
Q4-17	C+	C	B-
Q4-16	D+	C-	C
Q4-15	U		

Asset & Performance History
Date	NAV	1-Year Total Return
2017	33.16	37.31
2016	24.19	8.6
2015	22.17	
2014		
2013		
2012		

Total Assets: $432,089,494
Asset Allocation
Asset	%
Cash	0%
Stocks	100%
US Stocks	94%
Bonds	0%
US Bonds	0%
Other	0%

Services Offered:

Investment Strategy: The investment seeks to track, before fees and expenses, the performance of the IBD® 50 Index (the "index"). The fund will normally invest at least 80% of its net assets (including investment borrowings) in securities that comprise the index. The IBD® 50 Index is a weekly, rules-based, computer-generated stock index compiled and published by Investor's Business Daily® ("IBD" or the "index provider") that seeks to identify the current top 50 growth stocks. **Top Holdings:** The Trade Desk Inc A Atlassian Corporation PLC A BioTelemetry Inc CyberArk Software Ltd Veeva Systems Inc Class A

VanEck Vectors Biotech ETF
C HOLD

Ticker	Traded On	NAV	Total Assets ($)	Dividend Yield (TTM)	Turnover Ratio	Expense Ratio
BBH	NAS CM	111.33	$428,322,493	0.55	30	0.35

Ratings
Reward	C
Risk	D+
Recent Upgrade/Downgrade	

Fund Information
Fund Type	Exchange Traded Funds
Category	Healthcare Sector Equity
Sub-Category	Health
Prospectus Objective	Unaligned
Inception Date	Dec-11
Open to New Investments	Y

Prices
Price (as of 12/31/2018)	110.72
52-Week High	136.04
52-Week Low	103.76

Total Returns (%)
3-Month	6-Month	1-Year	3-Year	5-Year
-17.28	-7.11	-10.21	-11.01	27.82

3-Year Standard Deviation	21.39
Effective Duration	

Valuation
Premium/Discount (1-Year Average)	0.02

Company Information
Provider	VanEck
Manager/Tenure	Hao-Hung (Peter) Liao (6), Guo Hua (Jason) Jin (0)
Website	http://www.vaneck.com
Address	Van Eck Associates Corporation 666 Third Avenue New York NY 10017 United States
Phone Number	800-826-1115

PERFORMANCE

Ratings History
Date	Overall Rating	Risk Rating	Reward Rating
Q4-18	C	D+	C
Q2-18	C-	D	C
Q4-17	C	C+	C
Q4-16	C	D+	B-
Q4-15	B	B-	B

Asset & Performance History
Date	NAV	1-Year Total Return
2017	124.62	16.63
2016	107.43	-15.03
2015	126.82	10.2
2014	115.39	30.35
2013	88.52	65.49
2012	53.49	47.22

Total Assets: $428,322,493
Asset Allocation
Asset	%
Cash	0%
Stocks	100%
US Stocks	97%
Bonds	0%
US Bonds	0%
Other	0%

Services Offered:

Investment Strategy: The investment seeks to replicate as closely as possible, before fees and expenses, the price and yield performance of the MVIS® US Listed Biotech 25 Index. The fund normally invests at least 80% of its total assets in securities that comprise the fund's benchmark index. The Biotech Index includes common stocks and depositary receipts of U.S. exchange-listed companies in the biotechnology sector. Such companies may include medium-capitalization companies and foreign companies that are listed on a U.S. exchange. It is non-diversified. **Top Holdings:** Amgen Inc Gilead Sciences Inc Shire PLC ADR Vertex Pharmaceuticals Inc Biogen Inc

IQ 50 Percent Hedged FTSE International ETF   C-   HOLD

Ticker	Traded On	NAV	Total Assets ($)	Dividend Yield (TTM)	Turnover Ratio	Expense Ratio
HFXI	NYSE Arca	18.25	$422,487,583	3.14		0.2

Ratings
Reward   D+
Risk   C
Recent Upgrade/Downgrade   Down

Fund Information
Fund Type	Exchange Traded Funds
Category	Global Equity Large Cap
Sub-Category	Foreign Large Blend
Prospectus Objective	World Stock
Inception Date	Jul-15
Open to New Investments	Y

Prices
Price (as of 12/31/2018)	18.17
52-Week High	22.78
52-Week Low	17.88

Total Returns (%)
3-Month	6-Month	1-Year	3-Year	5-Year
-13.57	-10.52	-13.26	9.24	

3-Year Standard Deviation   9.91
Effective Duration

Valuation
Premium/Discount (1-Year Average)   0.22

Company Information
Provider	IndexIQ
Manager/Tenure	Greg Barrato (3), James Harrison (0)
Website	http://www.indexiq.com
Address	IndexIQ 800 Westchester Avenue, Suite N-611 Rye Brook NY 10573 United States
Phone Number	888-934-0777

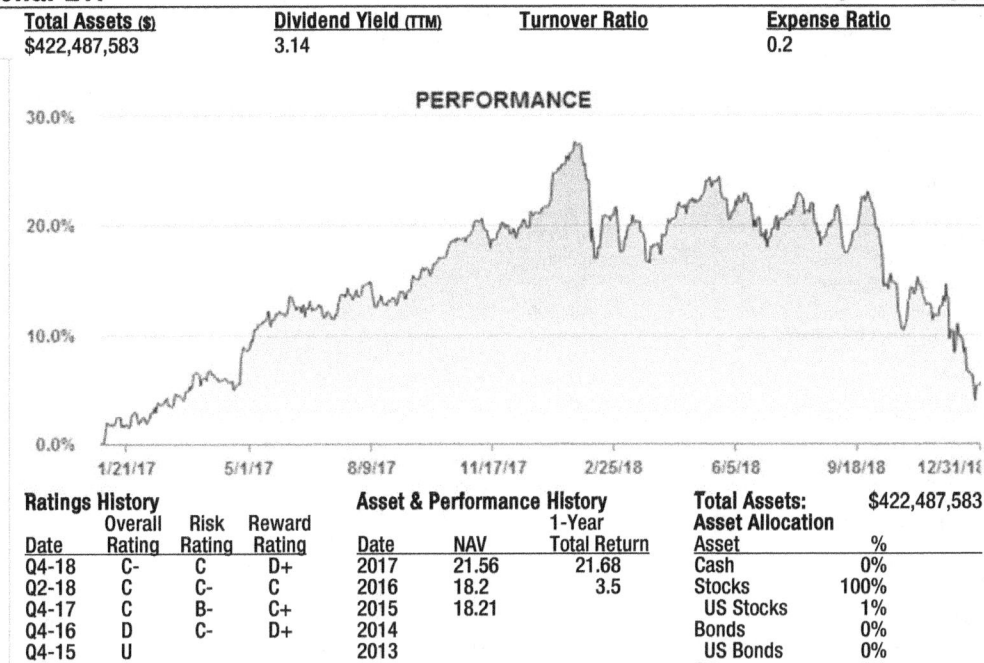

PERFORMANCE

Ratings History
Date	Overall Rating	Risk Rating	Reward Rating
Q4-18	C-	C	D+
Q2-18	C	C-	C
Q4-17	C	B-	C+
Q4-16	D	C-	D+
Q4-15	U		

Asset & Performance History
Date	NAV	1-Year Total Return
2017	21.56	21.68
2016	18.2	3.5
2015	18.21	
2014		
2013		
2012		

Total Assets: $422,487,583
Asset Allocation
Asset	%
Cash	0%
Stocks	100%
US Stocks	1%
Bonds	0%
US Bonds	0%
Other	0%

Services Offered:

Investment Strategy: The investment seeks investment results that correspond generally to the price and yield performance of its underlying index, the FTSE Developed ex North America 50% Hedged to USD Index (the "underlying index"). The underlying index is an equity benchmark of international stocks from developed markets, with approximately half of the currency exposure of the securities included in the underlying index "hedged" against the U.S. dollar on a monthly basis. The fund invests, under normal circumstances, at least 80% of its net assets, plus the amount of any borrowings for investment purposes, in the securities and other instruments included in its underlying index. **Top Holdings:** Nestle SA   Novartis AG   Samsung Electronics Co Ltd   Roche Holding AG Dividend Right Cert.   HSBC Holdings PLC

---

iShares U.S. Telecommunications ETF   C+   HOLD

Ticker	Traded On	NAV	Total Assets ($)	Dividend Yield (TTM)	Turnover Ratio	Expense Ratio
IYZ	BATS	26.34	$421,216,204	2.89	86	0.43

Ratings
Reward   B
Risk   C-
Recent Upgrade/Downgrade   Up

Fund Information
Fund Type	Exchange Traded Funds
Category	Communications Sector Equity
Sub-Category	Communications
Prospectus Objective	Comm
Inception Date	May-00
Open to New Investments	Y

Prices
Price (as of 12/31/2018)	26.35
52-Week High	30.08
52-Week Low	24.71

Total Returns (%)
3-Month	6-Month	1-Year	3-Year	5-Year
-11.07	-4.19	-8.54	-1.24	-0.25

3-Year Standard Deviation   13.1
Effective Duration

Valuation
Premium/Discount (1-Year Average)   -0.02

Company Information
Provider	iShares
Manager/Tenure	Diane Hsiung (10), Greg Savage (10), Jennifer Hsui (6), 3 others
Website	http://www.ishares.com
Address	iShares 400 Howard Street San Francisco CA 94105 United States
Phone Number	800-474-2737

PERFORMANCE

Ratings History
Date	Overall Rating	Risk Rating	Reward Rating
Q4-18	C+	C-	B
Q2-18	C	D+	B-
Q4-17	C-	C-	D+
Q4-16	C	D+	B-
Q4-15	C+	C	B-

Asset & Performance History
Date	NAV	1-Year Total Return
2017	29.39	-11.58
2016	34.38	22.14
2015	28.84	0.47
2014	29.26	0.51
2013	29.76	26.24
2012	24.27	18.48

Total Assets: $421,216,204
Asset Allocation
Asset	%
Cash	0%
Stocks	100%
US Stocks	100%
Bonds	0%
US Bonds	0%
Other	0%

Services Offered: CashInvestment Plan

Investment Strategy: The investment seeks to track the investment results of the Dow Jones U.S. Select Telecommunications Index. The fund generally invests at least 90% of its assets in securities of the underlying index and in depositary receipts representing securities of the underlying index. The underlying index measures the performance of the telecommunications sector of the U.S. equity market and may include large-, mid- or small-capitalization companies. The fund is non-diversified. **Top Holdings:** Verizon Communications Inc   Cisco Systems Inc   AT&T Inc   Motorola Solutions Inc   T-Mobile US Inc

ProShares Short QQQ   D   SELL

Ticker	Traded On	NAV	Total Assets ($)	Dividend Yield (TTM)	Turnover Ratio	Expense Ratio
PSQ	NYSE Arca	34.45	$420,932,315	0.71		0.95

Ratings
Reward   D
Risk   D-
Recent Upgrade/Downgrade

Fund Information
Fund Type   Exchange Traded Funds
Category   Trading Tools
Sub-Category   Trading--Inverse Equity
Prospectus Objective   Growth
Inception Date   Jun-06
Open to New Investments   Y

Prices
Price (as of 12/31/2018)   34.40
52-Week High   37.20
52-Week Low   29.21

Total Returns (%)

3-Month	6-Month	1-Year	3-Year	5-Year
18.29	10.00	-2.20	-33.33	-52.28

3-Year Standard Deviation   12.5
Effective Duration

Valuation
Premium/Discount (1-Year Average)   -0.03

Company Information
Provider   ProShares
Manager/Tenure   Michael Neches (5), Devin Sullivan (0)
Website   http://www.proshares.com
Address   ProShares 7501 Wisconsin Avenue, Suite 1000 Bethesda MD 20814 United States
Phone Number   866-776-5125

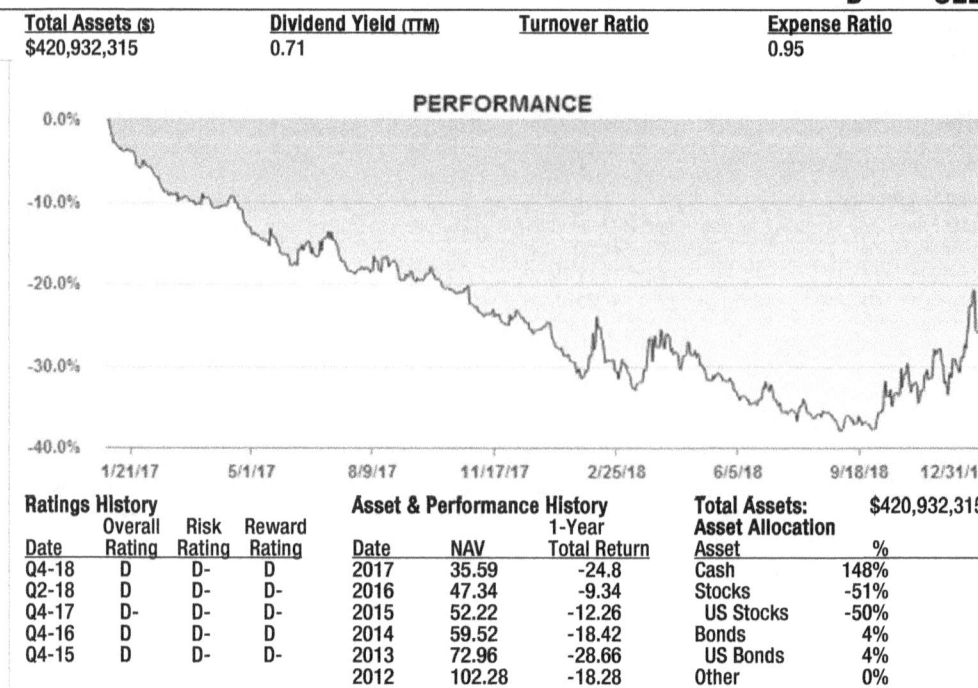

PERFORMANCE

Ratings History

Date	Overall Rating	Risk Rating	Reward Rating
Q4-18	D	D-	D
Q2-18	D	D-	D-
Q4-17	D-	D-	D-
Q4-16	D	D-	D
Q4-15	D	D-	D-

Asset & Performance History

Date	NAV	1-Year Total Return
2017	35.59	-24.8
2016	47.34	-9.34
2015	52.22	-12.26
2014	59.52	-18.42
2013	72.96	-28.66
2012	102.28	-18.28

Total Assets: $420,932,315

Asset Allocation

Asset	%
Cash	148%
Stocks	-51%
US Stocks	-50%
Bonds	4%
US Bonds	4%
Other	0%

Services Offered:

Investment Strategy: The investment seeks daily investment results before fees and expenses that correspond to the inverse (-1x) of the daily performance of the NASDAQ-100 Index®. The fund invests in financial instruments that ProShare Advisors believes, in combination, should produce daily returns consistent with the fund's investment objective. The index includes 100 of the largest domestic and international non-financial companies listed on The Nasdaq Stock Market based on market capitalization. The fund is non-diversified. **Top Holdings:** Nasdaq 100 Index Swap Credit Suisse International   Nasdaq 100 Index Swap Citibank Na   Nasdaq 100 Index Swap Bank Of America Na   United States Treasury Bills   United States Treasury Bills

---

ETFMG Prime Mobile Payments ETF   B-   BUY

Ticker	Traded On	NAV	Total Assets ($)	Dividend Yield (TTM)	Turnover Ratio	Expense Ratio
IPAY	NYSE Arca	35.02	$419,802,911	0.02	16	0.8

Ratings
Reward   B
Risk   C+
Recent Upgrade/Downgrade   Up

Fund Information
Fund Type   Exchange Traded Funds
Category   Equity Misc
Sub-Category   Miscellaneous Sector
Prospectus Objective   Growth & Inc
Inception Date   Jul-15
Open to New Investments   Y

Prices
Price (as of 12/31/2018)   34.95
52-Week High   43.27
52-Week Low   32.45

Total Returns (%)

3-Month	6-Month	1-Year	3-Year	5-Year
-17.99	-9.31	1.33	44.41	

3-Year Standard Deviation   13.84
Effective Duration

Valuation
Premium/Discount (1-Year Average)   0.09

Company Information
Provider   Pure Funds
Manager/Tenure   Samuel R. Masucci (0), James B. Francis (0), Devin Ryder (0), 1 other
Website   http://www.etfmgfunds.com
Address
Phone Number

PERFORMANCE

Ratings History

Date	Overall Rating	Risk Rating	Reward Rating
Q4-18	B-	C+	B
Q2-18	C+	C	B-
Q4-17	C	B	B-
Q4-16	D	C	B-
Q4-15	U		

Asset & Performance History

Date	NAV	1-Year Total Return
2017	34.8	36.87
2016	25.43	3.42
2015	24.55	
2014		
2013		
2012		

Total Assets: $419,802,911

Asset Allocation

Asset	%
Cash	0%
Stocks	100%
US Stocks	77%
Bonds	0%
US Bonds	0%
Other	0%

Services Offered:

Investment Strategy: The investment seeks to provide investment results that correspond generally to the Prime Mobile Payments Index. The fund invests at least 80% of its total assets in the component securities of the index and in ADRs and GDRs based on the component securities in the index. The index tracks the performance of the exchange-listed equity securities of companies across the globe that (i) engage in providing payment processing services or applications, (ii) provide payment solutions, (iii) build or provide payment industry architecture, infrastructure or software, or (iv) provide services as a credit card network. The fund is non-diversified. **Top Holdings:** American Express Co   Visa Inc Class A   PayPal Holdings Inc   Mastercard Inc A   Fidelity National Information Services Inc

ProShares UltraPro Short S&P500

D   SELL

Ticker	Traded On	NAV
SPXU	NYSE Arca	46.62

Total Assets ($)	Dividend Yield (TTM)	Turnover Ratio	Expense Ratio
$419,282,222	1.31	0	0.91

Ratings
Reward	D-
Risk	D-
Recent Upgrade/Downgrade	Up

Fund Information
Fund Type	Exchange Traded Funds
Category	Trading Tools
Sub-Category	Trading--Inverse Equity
Prospectus Objective	Growth
Inception Date	Jun-09
Open to New Investments	Y

Prices
Price (as of 12/31/2018)	46.54
52-Week High	57.55
52-Week Low	31.83

Total Returns (%)
3-Month	6-Month	1-Year	3-Year	5-Year
46.86	18.61	3.75	-62.53	-80.34

3-Year Standard Deviation 26.26
Effective Duration

Valuation
Premium/Discount (1-Year Average) -0.08

Company Information
Provider	ProShares
Manager/Tenure	Michael Neches (5), Devin Sullivan (0)
Website	http://www.proshares.com
Address	ProShares 7501 Wisconsin Avenue, Suite 1000 Bethesda MD 20814 United States
Phone Number	866-776-5125

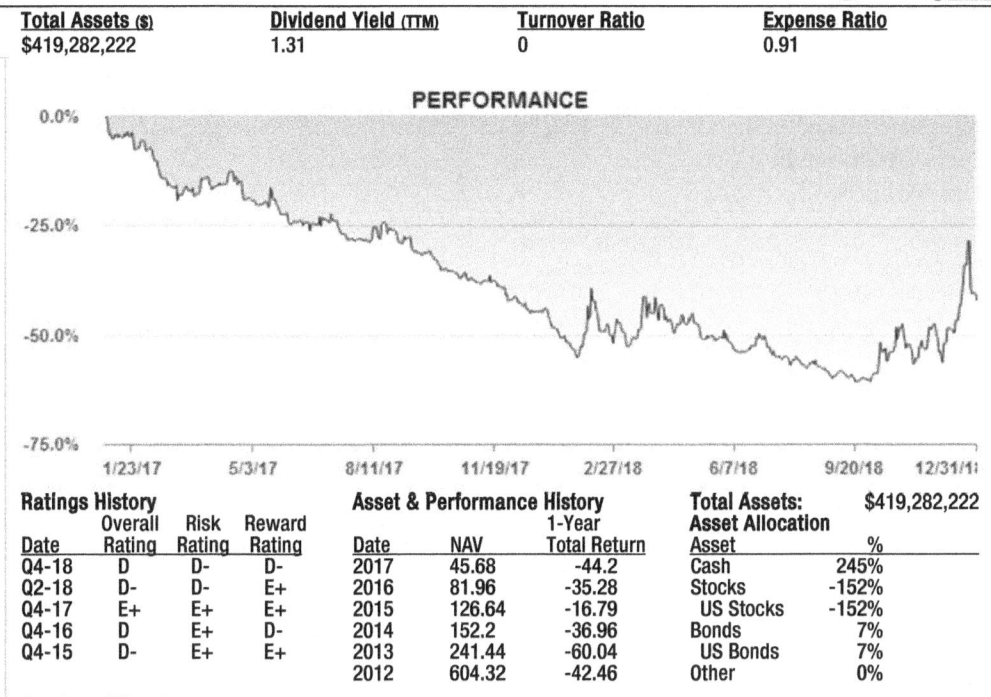

PERFORMANCE

Ratings History
Date	Overall Rating	Risk Rating	Reward Rating
Q4-18	D	D-	D-
Q2-18	D-	D-	E+
Q4-17	E+	E+	E+
Q4-16	D	E+	D-
Q4-15	D-	E+	E+

Asset & Performance History
Date	NAV	1-Year Total Return
2017	45.68	-44.2
2016	81.96	-35.28
2015	126.64	-16.79
2014	152.2	-36.96
2013	241.44	-60.04
2012	604.32	-42.46

Total Assets: $419,282,222
Asset Allocation
Asset	%
Cash	245%
Stocks	-152%
US Stocks	-152%
Bonds	7%
US Bonds	7%
Other	0%

Services Offered:

Investment Strategy: The investment seeks daily investment results before fees and expenses that correspond to three times the inverse (-3x) of the daily performance of the S&P 500® Index. The fund invests in financial instruments that ProShare Advisors believes, in combination, should produce daily returns consistent with the fund's investment objective. The index is a measure of large-cap U.S. stock market performance. The fund is non-diversified. **Top Holdings:** S&P 500 Index Swap Credit Suisse International   S&P 500 Index Swap Bnp Paribas   S&P 500 Index Swap Deutsche Bank Ag   S&P 500 Index Swap Ubs Ag   S&P 500 Index Swap Societe Generale

---

Global X SuperDividend™ U.S. ETF

C   HOLD

Ticker	Traded On	NAV
DIV	NYSE Arca	22.37

Total Assets ($)	Dividend Yield (TTM)	Turnover Ratio	Expense Ratio
$418,293,442	6.38	53	0.45

Ratings
Reward	C
Risk	C-
Recent Upgrade/Downgrade	

Fund Information
Fund Type	Exchange Traded Funds
Category	US Equity Mid Cap
Sub-Category	Mid-Cap Value
Prospectus Objective	Income
Inception Date	Mar-13
Open to New Investments	Y

Prices
Price (as of 12/31/2018)	22.41
52-Week High	25.60
52-Week Low	21.69

Total Returns (%)
3-Month	6-Month	1-Year	3-Year	5-Year
-9.38	-7.29	-6.66	13.41	19.19

3-Year Standard Deviation 6.66
Effective Duration

Valuation
Premium/Discount (1-Year Average) 0.04

Company Information
Provider	Global X Funds
Manager/Tenure	Chang Kim (4), James Ong (2), Nam To (0)
Website	http://www.globalxfunds.com
Address	Global X Funds 600 Lexington Avenue, 20th Floor New York NY 10022 United States
Phone Number	888-493-8631

PERFORMANCE

Ratings History
Date	Overall Rating	Risk Rating	Reward Rating
Q4-18	C	C-	C
Q2-18	C	C-	C
Q4-17	C+	C+	C+
Q4-16	C	C-	C
Q4-15	C	C-	C

Asset & Performance History
Date	NAV	1-Year Total Return
2017	25.57	9.71
2016	24.74	10.75
2015	23.92	-10.52
2014	28.85	17.45
2013	25.93	
2012		

Total Assets: $418,293,442
Asset Allocation
Asset	%
Cash	0%
Stocks	100%
US Stocks	99%
Bonds	0%
US Bonds	0%
Other	0%

Services Offered:

Investment Strategy: The investment seeks to provide investment results that correspond generally to the price and yield performance, before fees and expenses, of the Indxx SuperDividend® U.S. Low Volatility Index ("underlying index"). The fund invests at least 80% of its total assets in the securities of the underlying index. The underlying index tracks the performance of 50 equally-weighted common stocks, including Master Limited Partnerships ("MLPs") and Real Estate Investment Trusts ("REITs") that rank among the highest dividend yielding equity securities in the United States. **Top Holdings:** Annaly Capital Management Inc   Brinker International Inc   Universal Corp   Pfizer Inc   PennyMac Mortgage Investment Trust

ProShares S&P MidCap 400 Dividend Aristocrats ETF

C   **HOLD**

Ticker	Traded On	NAV	Total Assets ($)	Dividend Yield (TTM)	Turnover Ratio	Expense Ratio
REGL	BATS	51.74	$417,789,251	1.91		0.4

Ratings

Reward	C
Risk	C-
Recent Upgrade/Downgrade	

Fund Information

Fund Type	Exchange Traded Funds
Category	US Equity Mid Cap
Sub-Category	Mid-Cap Value
Prospectus Objective	Growth
Inception Date	Feb-15
Open to New Investments	Y

Prices

Price (as of 12/31/2018)	51.73
52-Week High	58.39
52-Week Low	49.63

Total Returns (%)

3-Month	6-Month	1-Year	3-Year	5-Year
-7.92	-4.31	-3.15	38.73	

3-Year Standard Deviation	10.26
Effective Duration	

Valuation

Premium/Discount (1-Year Average)	0.04

Company Information

Provider	ProShares
Manager/Tenure	Michael Neches (3), Devin Sullivan (0)
Website	http://www.proshares.com
Address	ProShares 7501 Wisconsin Avenue, Suite 1000 Bethesda MD 20814 United States
Phone Number	866-776-5125

PERFORMANCE

Ratings History

Date	Overall Rating	Risk Rating	Reward Rating
Q4-18	C	C-	C
Q2-18	C	C	C+
Q4-17	B-	B	C+
Q4-16	C-	C	C
Q4-15	U		

Asset & Performance History

Date	NAV	1-Year Total Return
2017	54.5	10.22
2016	50.29	29.96
2015	39.2	
2014		
2013		
2012		

Total Assets: $417,789,251

Asset Allocation

Asset	%
Cash	0%
Stocks	100%
US Stocks	100%
Bonds	0%
US Bonds	0%
Other	0%

Services Offered:

Investment Strategy: The investment seeks investment results, before fees and expenses, that track the performance of the S&P MidCap 400® Dividend Aristocrats Index (the "index"). Under normal circumstances, the fund will invest at least 80% of its total assets in component securities (i.e., securities of the index and comparable securities that have economic characteristics that are substantially identical to the economic characteristics of the securities of the index). The index contains a minimum of 40 stocks which are equally weighted. No single sector is allowed to comprise more than 30% of the index weight. **Top Holdings:** Graco Inc Telephone and Data Systems Inc Mercury General Corp Prosperity Bancshares Inc Cracker Barrel Old Country Store Inc

---

iShares U.S. Pharmaceuticals ETF

C   **HOLD**

Ticker	Traded On	NAV	Total Assets ($)	Dividend Yield (TTM)	Turnover Ratio	Expense Ratio
IHE	NYSE Arca	140.74	$417,632,712	1.13	23	0.43

Ratings

Reward	C+
Risk	C-
Recent Upgrade/Downgrade	

Fund Information

Fund Type	Exchange Traded Funds
Category	Healthcare Sector Equity
Sub-Category	Health
Prospectus Objective	Health
Inception Date	May-06
Open to New Investments	Y

Prices

Price (as of 12/31/2018)	140.77
52-Week High	169.55
52-Week Low	132.01

Total Returns (%)

3-Month	6-Month	1-Year	3-Year	5-Year
-14.88	-6.68	-7.67	-9.80	27.34

3-Year Standard Deviation	15.16
Effective Duration	

Valuation

Premium/Discount (1-Year Average)	0.06

Company Information

Provider	iShares
Manager/Tenure	Diane Hsiung (10), Greg Savage (10), Jennifer Hsui (6), 3 others
Website	http://www.ishares.com
Address	iShares 400 Howard Street San Francisco CA 94105 United States
Phone Number	800-474-2737

PERFORMANCE

Ratings History

Date	Overall Rating	Risk Rating	Reward Rating
Q4-18	C	C-	C+
Q2-18	C	D+	C
Q4-17	C	C	C
Q4-16	C	D+	C+
Q4-15	C+	C	B-

Asset & Performance History

Date	NAV	1-Year Total Return
2017	154.21	10.65
2016	141.26	-11.72
2015	161.48	8.81
2014	151.23	29.74
2013	118.1	40.52
2012	85.06	13.4

Total Assets: $417,632,712

Asset Allocation

Asset	%
Cash	0%
Stocks	100%
US Stocks	99%
Bonds	0%
US Bonds	0%
Other	0%

Services Offered:

Investment Strategy: The investment seeks to track the investment results of the Dow Jones U.S. Select Pharmaceuticals Index. The fund generally invests at least 90% of its assets in securities of the underlying index and in depositary receipts representing securities of the underlying index. The underlying index measures the performance of the pharmaceuticals sector of the U.S. equity market. The underlying index includes pharmaceutical companies such as manufacturers of prescription or over-the-counter drugs or vaccines, but excludes producers of vitamins. The fund is non-diversified. **Top Holdings:** Johnson & Johnson Pfizer Inc Merck & Co Inc Eli Lilly and Co Bristol-Myers Squibb Company

SPDR® Russell 1000® Yield Focus ETF   C-   HOLD

Ticker	Traded On	NAV	Total Assets ($)	Dividend Yield (TTM)	Turnover Ratio	Expense Ratio
ONEY	NYSE Arca	62.09	$417,220,622	3.19	42	0.2

Ratings

Reward	C-
Risk	D+
Recent Upgrade/Downgrade	Down

Fund Information

Fund Type	Exchange Traded Funds
Category	US Equity Mid Cap
Sub-Category	Mid-Cap Value
Prospectus Objective	Growth & Inc
Inception Date	Dec-15
Open to New Investments	Y

Prices

Price (as of 12/31/2018)	61.85
52-Week High	74.19
52-Week Low	59.15

Total Returns (%)

3-Month	6-Month	1-Year	3-Year	5-Year
-12.99	-9.87	-7.95	30.64	

3-Year Standard Deviation	
Effective Duration	

Valuation

Premium/Discount (1-Year Average)	0.17

Company Information

Provider	SPDR State Street Global Advisors
Manager/Tenure	Michael J. Feehily (3), Karl A. Schneider (3), John Law (1)
Website	http://www.spdrs.com
Address	SPDR State Street Global Advisors State Street Financial Center, 1 Lincoln Street Boston MA 02111-2900 United States
Phone Number	617-786-3000

PERFORMANCE

Ratings History

Date	Overall Rating	Risk Rating	Reward Rating
Q4-18	C-	D+	C-
Q2-18	C-	D	C
Q4-17	C	B+	C-
Q4-16	D	D	D+
Q4-15			

Asset & Performance History

Date	NAV	1-Year Total Return
2017	69.79	15.28
2016	67.23	23.1
2015	58.18	
2014		
2013		
2012		

Total Assets: $417,220,622

Asset Allocation

Asset	%
Cash	0%
Stocks	100%
US Stocks	100%
Bonds	0%
US Bonds	0%
Other	0%

Services Offered:

Investment Strategy: The investment seeks to provide investment results that, before fees and expenses, correspond generally to the total return performance of the Russell 1000 Yield Focused Factor Index. Under normal market conditions, the fund generally invests substantially all, but at least 80%, of its total assets in the securities comprising the index. The index is designed to reflect the performance of a segment of large-capitalization U.S. equity securities demonstrating a combination of core factors (high value, high quality, and low size characteristics), with a focus factor comprising high yield characteristics (the "Factor Characteristics"). It is non-diversified. **Top Holdings:** Cummins Inc Target Corp Omnicom Group Inc PACCAR Inc LyondellBasell Industries NV

SPDR® S&P Emerging Asia Pacific ETF   C-   HOLD

Ticker	Traded On	NAV	Total Assets ($)	Dividend Yield (TTM)	Turnover Ratio	Expense Ratio
GMF	NYSE Arca	88.13	$417,160,948	2.05	5	0.49

Ratings

Reward	C-
Risk	C-
Recent Upgrade/Downgrade	

Fund Information

Fund Type	Exchange Traded Funds
Category	Asia ex-Japan Equity
Sub-Category	Pacific/Asia ex-Japan Stk
Prospectus Objective	Pacific Stock
Inception Date	Mar-07
Open to New Investments	Y

Prices

Price (as of 12/31/2018)	87.76
52-Week High	116.07
52-Week Low	84.71

Total Returns (%)

3-Month	6-Month	1-Year	3-Year	5-Year
-7.92	-10.11	-13.66	26.51	28.96

3-Year Standard Deviation	14.52
Effective Duration	

Valuation

Premium/Discount (1-Year Average)	0.02

Company Information

Provider	SPDR State Street Global Advisors
Manager/Tenure	Michael J. Feehily (7), Karl A. Schneider (3), Teddy Wong (1)
Website	http://www.spdrs.com
Address	SPDR State Street Global Advisors State Street Financial Center, 1 Lincoln Street Boston MA 02111-2900 United States
Phone Number	617-786-3000

PERFORMANCE

Ratings History

Date	Overall Rating	Risk Rating	Reward Rating
Q4-18	C-	C-	C-
Q2-18	C	C-	C-
Q4-17	B	C+	A-
Q4-16	C	C-	C
Q4-15	C	C+	C

Asset & Performance History

Date	NAV	1-Year Total Return
2017	104.32	40.14
2016	75.79	4.1
2015	74.29	-7.85
2014	83.61	10.62
2013	76.78	2.79
2012	76.44	17.63

Total Assets: $417,160,948

Asset Allocation

Asset	%
Cash	0%
Stocks	100%
US Stocks	1%
Bonds	0%
US Bonds	0%
Other	0%

Services Offered:

Investment Strategy: The investment seeks to provide investment results that, before fees and expenses, correspond generally to the total return performance of the S&P Asia Pacific Emerging BMI Index based upon the emerging markets of the Asia Pacific region. The fund generally invests substantially all, but at least 80%, of its total assets in the securities comprising the index and in depositary receipts (including ADRs or GDRs) based on securities comprising the index. The index is a market capitalization weighted index designed to define and measure the investable universe of publicly traded companies domiciled in emerging Asian Pacific markets. The fund is non-diversified. **Top Holdings:** Tencent Holdings Ltd Alibaba Group Holding Ltd ADR Taiwan Semiconductor Manufacturing Co Ltd ADR China Construction Bank Corp H Reliance Industries Ltd ADR

Fidelity® Dividend ETF for Rising Rates

C   HOLD

Ticker	Traded On	NAV	Total Assets ($)	Dividend Yield (TTM)	Turnover Ratio	Expense Ratio
FDRR	NYSE Arca	28.75	$416,758,393	3.03		0.29

Ratings

Reward	C
Risk	C+
Recent Upgrade/Downgrade	Up

Fund Information

Fund Type	Exchange Traded Funds
Category	US Equity Large Cap Value
Sub-Category	Large Value
Prospectus Objective	Growth & Inc
Inception Date	Sep-16
Open to New Investments	Y

Prices

Price (as of 12/31/2018)	28.68
52-Week High	32.73
52-Week Low	27.18

Total Returns (%)

3-Month	6-Month	1-Year	3-Year	5-Year
-10.71	-3.77	-3.23		

3-Year Standard Deviation
Effective Duration

Valuation

Premium/Discount (1-Year Average)	0.13

Company Information

Provider	Fidelity Investments
Manager/Tenure	Louis Bottari (2), Deane Gyllenhaal (2), Peter Matthew (2), 2 others
Website	http://www.institutional.fidelity.com
Address	Fidelity Investments 82 Devonshire Street Boston MA 2109 United States
Phone Number	617-563-7000

PERFORMANCE

Ratings History

Date	Overall Rating	Risk Rating	Reward Rating
Q4-18	C	C+	C
Q2-18	C-	C-	C-
Q4-17	D	B+	C
Q4-16	U		
Q4-15			

Asset & Performance History

Date	NAV	1-Year Total Return
2017	30.61	19.51
2016	26.41	
2015		
2014		
2013		
2012		

Total Assets: $416,758,393

Asset Allocation

Asset	%
Cash	0%
Stocks	100%
US Stocks	92%
Bonds	0%
US Bonds	0%
Other	0%

Services Offered:

Investment Strategy: The investment seeks to provide investment returns that correspond, before fees and expenses, generally to the performance of the Fidelity Dividend Index for Rising Rates?. The fund normally invests at least 80% of assets in securities included in the underlying index and in depository receipts representing securities included in the underlying index. The underlying index is designed to reflect the performance of stocks of large and mid-capitalization dividend-paying companies that are expected to continue to pay and grow their dividends and have a positive correlation of returns to increasing 10-year U.S. Treasury yields. **Top Holdings:** Apple Inc   Microsoft Corp   Johnson & Johnson   Pfizer Inc   Merck & Co Inc

Franklin LibertyQ U.S. Equity ETF

C-   HOLD

Ticker	Traded On	NAV	Total Assets ($)	Dividend Yield (TTM)	Turnover Ratio	Expense Ratio
FLQL	BATS	27.69	$413,499,963	1.58	21	0.25

Ratings

Reward	D+
Risk	C-
Recent Upgrade/Downgrade	

Fund Information

Fund Type	Exchange Traded Funds
Category	US Equity Large Cap Blend
Sub-Category	Large Blend
Prospectus Objective	Growth & Inc
Inception Date	Apr-17
Open to New Investments	Y

Prices

Price (as of 12/31/2018)	27.62
52-Week High	31.54
52-Week Low	26.18

Total Returns (%)

3-Month	6-Month	1-Year	3-Year	5-Year
-11.03	-4.25	-1.97		

3-Year Standard Deviation
Effective Duration

Valuation

Premium/Discount (1-Year Average)	0.24

Company Information

Provider	Franklin Templeton Investments
Manager/Tenure	Dina Ting (1), Louis Hsu (1)
Website	http://www.franklintempleton.com
Address	Franklin Templeton Investments One Franklin Parkway, Building 970, 1st Floor San Mateo CA 94403 United States
Phone Number	650-312-2000

PERFORMANCE

Ratings History

Date	Overall Rating	Risk Rating	Reward Rating
Q4-18	C-	C-	D+
Q2-18	D+	D+	C-
Q4-17	U		
Q4-16			
Q4-15			

Asset & Performance History

Date	NAV	1-Year Total Return
2017	28.74	
2016		
2015		
2014		
2013		
2012		

Total Assets: $413,499,963

Asset Allocation

Asset	%
Cash	0%
Stocks	100%
US Stocks	99%
Bonds	0%
US Bonds	0%
Other	0%

Services Offered:

Investment Strategy: The investment seeks to provide investment results that closely correspond, before fees and expenses, to the performance of the LibertyQ U.S. Large Cap Equity Index (the U.S. Large Cap underlying index). Under normal market conditions, the fund invests at least 80% of its assets in the component securities of the U.S. Large Cap underlying index. The U.S. Large Cap underlying index is based on the Russell 1000® Index using a methodology developed with Franklin Templeton to reflect Franklin Templeton's desired investment strategy. **Top Holdings:** Eli Lilly and Co   Procter & Gamble Co   Pfizer Inc   Verizon Communications Inc   CVS Health Corp

ProShares Short VIX Short-Term Futures ETF　　　　　　　　C-　　HOLD

Ticker	Traded On	NAV	Total Assets ($)	Dividend Yield (TTM)	Turnover Ratio	Expense Ratio
SVXY	NYSE Arca		$410,775,697	0		1.38

Ratings
Reward	C-
Risk	D
Recent Upgrade/Downgrade	Up

Fund Information
Fund Type	Exchange Traded Funds
Category	Alternative Misc
Sub-Category	Volatility
Prospectus Objective	Growth
Inception Date	Oct-11
Open to New Investments	Y

Prices
Price (as of 12/31/2018)	42.30
52-Week High	138.21
52-Week Low	9.58

Total Returns (%)
3-Month	6-Month	1-Year	3-Year	5-Year
-29.90	224.92	-67.37	63.47	23.06

3-Year Standard Deviation	72.09
Effective Duration	

Valuation
Premium/Discount (1-Year Average)	-0.12

Company Information
Provider	ProShares
Manager/Tenure	Management Team (7)
Website	http://www.proshares.com
Address	ProShares 7501 Wisconsin Avenue, Suite 1000 Bethesda MD 20814 United States
Phone Number	866-776-5125

PERFORMANCE

Ratings History
Date	Overall Rating	Risk Rating	Reward Rating
Q4-18	C-	D	C-
Q2-18	D	D	E+
Q4-17	B	D+	A+
Q4-16	C	D+	C
Q4-15	C+	D+	C+

Asset & Performance History
Date	NAV	1-Year Total Return
2017	127.32	179.11
2016	45.62	79.53
2015	25.41	-17.24
2014	30.7	-9.02
2013	33.75	104.05
2012	16.54	155.84

Total Assets: $410,775,697
Asset Allocation
Asset	%
Cash	150%
Stocks	-50%
US Stocks	-50%
Bonds	0%
US Bonds	0%
Other	0%

Services Offered:

Investment Strategy: The investment seeks results (before fees and expenses) that correspond to one-half the inverse (-0.5x) of the performance of the S&P 500 VIX Short-Term Futures Index for a single day. The index seeks to offer exposure to market volatility through publicly traded futures markets and is designed to measure the return from a rolling long position in the first and second month VIX futures contracts. **Top Holdings:** Cboe Vix Future 12/19/2018 (Uxz8)　Cboe Vix Future 01/16/2019 (Uxf9)

---

iShares Morningstar Large-Cap Value ETF　　　　　　　　C　　HOLD

Ticker	Traded On	NAV	Total Assets ($)	Dividend Yield (TTM)	Turnover Ratio	Expense Ratio
JKF	NYSE Arca	96.31	$410,548,521	2.54	24	0.25

Ratings
Reward	C
Risk	C-
Recent Upgrade/Downgrade	

Fund Information
Fund Type	Exchange Traded Funds
Category	US Equity Large Cap Value
Sub-Category	Large Value
Prospectus Objective	Growth
Inception Date	Jun-04
Open to New Investments	Y

Prices
Price (as of 12/31/2018)	96.33
52-Week High	112.57
52-Week Low	91.27

Total Returns (%)
3-Month	6-Month	1-Year	3-Year	5-Year
-9.93	-3.56	-6.10	27.80	37.05

3-Year Standard Deviation	9.06
Effective Duration	

Valuation
Premium/Discount (1-Year Average)	0.10

Company Information
Provider	iShares
Manager/Tenure	Diane Hsiung (10), Greg Savage (10), Jennifer Hsui (6), 3 others
Website	http://www.ishares.com
Address	iShares 400 Howard Street San Francisco CA 94105 United States
Phone Number	800-474-2737

PERFORMANCE

Ratings History
Date	Overall Rating	Risk Rating	Reward Rating
Q4-18	C	C-	C
Q2-18	C	C-	C
Q4-17	B	B	B
Q4-16	C+	C-	B
Q4-15	C	C	C+

Asset & Performance History
Date	NAV	1-Year Total Return
2017	105.45	14.81
2016	94.14	18.54
2015	81.79	-1.55
2014	85.61	8.93
2013	80.56	28.53
2012	64.39	12.55

Total Assets: $410,548,521
Asset Allocation
Asset	%
Cash	0%
Stocks	100%
US Stocks	99%
Bonds	0%
US Bonds	0%
Other	0%

Services Offered:

Investment Strategy: The investment seeks to track the investment results of the Morningstar® Large Value IndexSM composed of large-capitalization U.S. equities that exhibit value characteristics. The fund generally invests at least 90% of its assets in securities of the underlying index and in depositary receipts representing securities of the underlying index. The underlying index measures the performance of stocks issued by large-capitalization companies that have exhibited above-average "value" characteristics as determined by Morningstar, Inc.'s ("Morningstar" or the "index provider") proprietary index methodology. **Top Holdings:** Berkshire Hathaway Inc B　JPMorgan Chase & Co　Exxon Mobil Corp　Pfizer Inc　Verizon Communications Inc

SPDR® S&P Emerging Markets Dividend ETF   C-   HOLD

Ticker	Traded On	NAV	Total Assets ($)	Dividend Yield (TTM)	Turnover Ratio	Expense Ratio
EDIV	NYSE Arca	29.96	$410,341,170	3.45	55	0.49

Ratings
Reward   C-
Risk   C-
Recent Upgrade/Downgrade

Fund Information
Fund Type   Exchange Traded Funds
Category   Global Emerg Mkts Equity
Sub-Category   Diversified Emerging Mkts
Prospectus Objective   Div Emerg Mkts
Inception Date   Feb-11
Open to New Investments   Y

Prices
Price (as of 12/31/2018)   29.85
52-Week High   36.54
52-Week Low   27.94

Total Returns (%)

3-Month	6-Month	1-Year	3-Year	5-Year
-2.65	-0.57	-6.46	39.93	-6.28

3-Year Standard Deviation   16.49
Effective Duration

Valuation
Premium/Discount (1-Year Average)   -0.11

Company Information
Provider   SPDR State Street Global Advisors
Manager/Tenure   Michael J. Feehily (7), Karl A. Schneider (3), Payal Kapoor Gupta (1)
Website   http://www.spdrs.com
Address   SPDR State Street Global Advisors State Street Financial Center, 1 Lincoln Street Boston MA 02111-2900 United States
Phone Number   617-786-3000

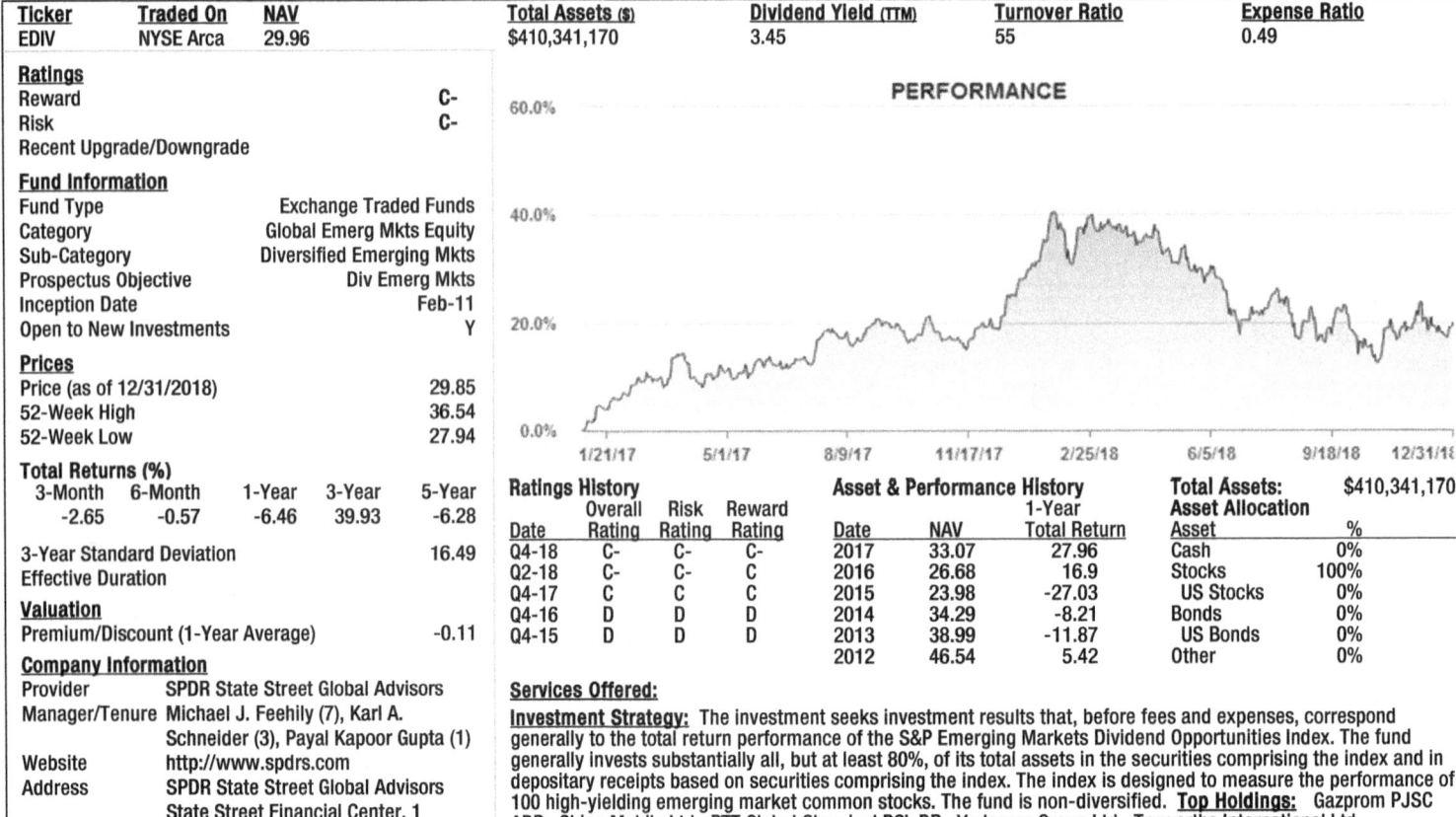

PERFORMANCE

Ratings History

Date	Overall Rating	Risk Rating	Reward Rating
Q4-18	C-	C-	C-
Q2-18	C-	C-	C
Q4-17	C	C	C
Q4-16	D	D	D
Q4-15	D	D	D

Asset & Performance History

Date	NAV	1-Year Total Return
2017	33.07	27.96
2016	26.68	16.9
2015	23.98	-27.03
2014	34.29	-8.21
2013	38.99	-11.87
2012	46.54	5.42

Total Assets: $410,341,170
Asset Allocation

Asset	%
Cash	0%
Stocks	100%
US Stocks	0%
Bonds	0%
US Bonds	0%
Other	0%

Services Offered:

Investment Strategy: The investment seeks investment results that, before fees and expenses, correspond generally to the total return performance of the S&P Emerging Markets Dividend Opportunities Index. The fund generally invests substantially all, but at least 80%, of its total assets in the securities comprising the index and in depositary receipts based on securities comprising the index. The index is designed to measure the performance of 100 high-yielding emerging market common stocks. The fund is non-diversified. **Top Holdings:** Gazprom PJSC ADR   China Mobile Ltd   PTT Global Chemical PCL DR   Vodacom Group Ltd   Truworths International Ltd

Vanguard S&P Small-Cap 600 Value Index Fund ETF Shares   C-   HOLD

Ticker	Traded On	NAV	Total Assets ($)	Dividend Yield (TTM)	Turnover Ratio	Expense Ratio
VIOV	NYSE Arca		$409,732,094	1.55	34	0.2

Ratings
Reward   C-
Risk   C-
Recent Upgrade/Downgrade   Down

Fund Information
Fund Type   Exchange Traded Funds
Category   US Equity Small Cap
Sub-Category   Small Value
Prospectus Objective   Growth & Inc
Inception Date   Sep-10
Open to New Investments   Y

Prices
Price (as of 12/31/2018)   113.62
52-Week High   149.47
52-Week Low   107.15

Total Returns (%)

3-Month	6-Month	1-Year	3-Year	5-Year
-19.81	-19.55	-13.16	26.90	26.87

3-Year Standard Deviation   14.93
Effective Duration

Valuation
Premium/Discount (1-Year Average)   0.12

Company Information
Provider   Vanguard
Manager/Tenure   William A. Coleman (5), Donald M. Butler (2)
Website   http://www.vanguard.com
Address   Vanguard 100 Vanguard Boulevard Malvern PA 19355 United States
Phone Number   877-662-7447

PERFORMANCE

Ratings History

Date	Overall Rating	Risk Rating	Reward Rating
Q4-18	C-	C-	C-
Q2-18	C+	C-	B
Q4-17	B+	B	A-
Q4-16	C	C-	C
Q4-15	C	D+	C

Asset & Performance History

Date	NAV	1-Year Total Return
2017	132.29	11.76
2016	120.45	30.07
2015	93.11	-6.83
2014	101.28	7.3
2013	95.59	39.67
2012	69.07	17.97

Total Assets: $409,732,094
Asset Allocation

Asset	%
Cash	1%
Stocks	99%
US Stocks	98%
Bonds	0%
US Bonds	0%
Other	0%

Services Offered:

Investment Strategy: The investment seeks to track the performance of a benchmark index that measures the investment return of small-capitalization value stocks in the United States. The fund employs an indexing investment approach designed to track the performance of the S&P SmallCap 600® Value Index, which represents the value companies, as determined by the index sponsor, of the S&P SmallCap 600 Index. The Advisor attempts to replicate the target index by investing all, or substantially all, of its assets in the stocks that make up the index, holding each stock in approximately the same proportion as its weighting in the index. **Top Holdings:** CACI International Inc Class A   Spire Inc   Endo International PLC   Wolverine World Wide Inc   KapStone Paper And Packaging Corp

Fidelity® MSCI Industrials Index ETF   C   HOLD

Ticker	Traded On	NAV
FIDU	NYSE Arca	32.74

Total Assets ($)	Dividend Yield (TTM)	Turnover Ratio	Expense Ratio
$409,589,096	1.65	5	0.08

Ratings
Reward	C
Risk	C
Recent Upgrade/Downgrade	Down

Fund Information
Fund Type	Exchange Traded Funds
Category	Industrials Sector Equity
Sub-Category	Industrials
Prospectus Objective	Unaligned
Inception Date	Oct-13
Open to New Investments	Y

Prices
Price (as of 12/31/2018)	32.76
52-Week High	41.16
52-Week Low	30.66

Total Returns (%)
3-Month	6-Month	1-Year	3-Year	5-Year
-18.54	-10.95	-13.81	26.98	30.33

3-Year Standard Deviation	13.24
Effective Duration	

Valuation
Premium/Discount (1-Year Average)	0.02

Company Information
Provider	Fidelity Investments
Manager/Tenure	Jennifer Hsui (5), Greg Savage (5), Alan Mason (2), 2 others
Website	http://www.institutional.fidelity.com
Address	Fidelity Investments 82 Devonshire Street Boston MA 2109 United States
Phone Number	617-563-7000

PERFORMANCE

Ratings History
Date	Overall Rating	Risk Rating	Reward Rating
Q4-18	C	C	C
Q2-18	C	C+	C
Q4-17	B	B-	A-
Q4-16	C	C	C+
Q4-15	C-	C+	C

Asset & Performance History
Date	NAV	1-Year Total Return
2017	38.67	22.1
2016	32.23	20.66
2015	27.18	-3.63
2014	28.76	6.51
2013	27.43	
2012		

Total Assets: $409,589,096
Asset Allocation
Asset	%
Cash	0%
Stocks	100%
US Stocks	99%
Bonds	0%
US Bonds	0%
Other	0%

Services Offered:

Investment Strategy: The investment seeks to provide investment returns that correspond, before fees and expenses, generally to the performance of the MSCI USA IMI Industrials Index. The fund invests at least 80% of assets in securities included in the fund's underlying index. The fund's underlying index is the MSCI USA IMI Industrials Index, which represents the performance of the industrial sector in the U.S. equity market. It may or may not hold all of the securities in the MSCI USA IMI Industrials Index. **Top Holdings:** Boeing Co 3M Co Union Pacific Corp Honeywell International Inc United Technologies Corp

---

Barclays ETN+ Select MLP ETN   C-   HOLD

Ticker	Traded On	NAV
ATMP	NYSE Arca	

Total Assets ($)	Dividend Yield (TTM)	Turnover Ratio	Expense Ratio
$407,834,756	6.04		0.95

Ratings
Reward	D+
Risk	C-
Recent Upgrade/Downgrade	Up

Fund Information
Fund Type	Exchange Traded Funds
Category	Energy Sector Equity
Sub-Category	Energy Limited Partnership
Prospectus Objective	Growth
Inception Date	Mar-13
Open to New Investments	Y

Prices
Price (as of 12/31/2018)	17.73
52-Week High	22.74
52-Week Low	16.98

Total Returns (%)
3-Month	6-Month	1-Year	3-Year	5-Year
-16.22	-10.20	-10.85	12.06	-17.40

3-Year Standard Deviation	17.47
Effective Duration	

Valuation
Premium/Discount (1-Year Average)	0.08

Company Information
Provider	Milleis Investissements Funds
Manager/Tenure	No Manager (5)
Website	
Address	2-4, rue Eugène Ruppert L-2453 Luxembourg Luxembourg L-2453 Luxembourg
Phone Number	

PERFORMANCE

Ratings History
Date	Overall Rating	Risk Rating	Reward Rating
Q4-18	C-	C-	D+
Q2-18	D	D	D+
Q4-17	D	D	D+
Q4-16	C-	D+	C-
Q4-15	D+	D+	D+

Asset & Performance History
Date	NAV	1-Year Total Return
2017	20.77	-6.66
2016	23.44	38.12
2015	18.56	-36.79
2014	30.79	16.59
2013	27.37	
2012		

Total Assets: $407,834,756
Asset Allocation
Asset	%
Cash	%
Stocks	%
US Stocks	%
Bonds	%
US Bonds	%
Other	%

Services Offered:

Investment Strategy: The investment seeks to replicate, net of expenses, the Atlantic Trust Select MLP Index. The index seeks to capture returns that may be available from investing in a basket of direct or indirect interests in master limited partnerships ("MLPs"), limited liability companies ("LLCs") and corporations (collectively, "MLP Interests") that are selected pursuant to the Atlantic Trust Select MLP Strategy. **Top Holdings:**

DeltaShares S&P 500 Managed Risk ETF   D+   SELL

Ticker	Traded On	NAV
DMRL	NYSE Arca	51.23

Total Assets ($)	Dividend Yield (TTM)	Turnover Ratio	Expense Ratio
$405,763,838	1.19	2	0.35

Ratings
Reward D+
Risk D+
Recent Upgrade/Downgrade

Fund Information
Fund Type Exchange Traded Funds
Category US Equity Large Cap Blend
Sub-Category Large Blend
Prospectus Objective Growth
Inception Date Jul-17
Open to New Investments Y

Prices
Price (as of 12/31/2018) 51.10
52-Week High 58.34
52-Week Low 49.51

Total Returns (%)

3-Month	6-Month	1-Year	3-Year	5-Year
-11.51	-4.72	-4.16		

3-Year Standard Deviation
Effective Duration

Valuation
Premium/Discount (1-Year Average) 0.34

Company Information
Provider DeltaShares
Manager/Tenure Blake Graves (1), Charles Lowery (1), Louis Ng (1)
Website http://www.deltashares.com
Address DeltaShares United States
Phone Number

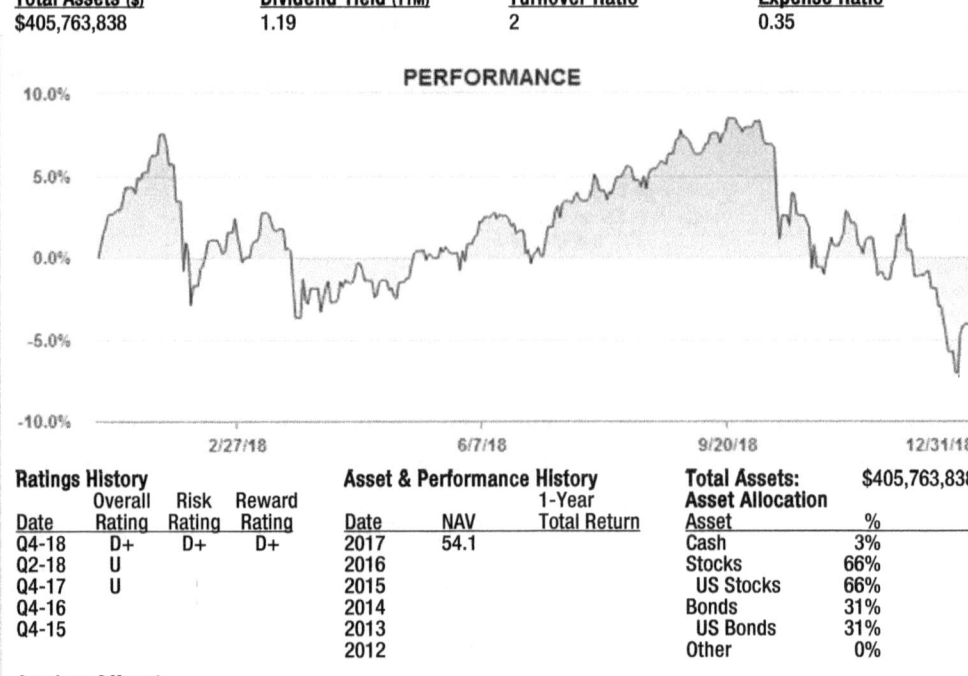

Ratings History

Date	Overall Rating	Risk Rating	Reward Rating
Q4-18	D+	D+	D+
Q2-18	U		
Q4-17	U		
Q4-16			
Q4-15			

Asset & Performance History

Date	NAV	1-Year Total Return
2017	54.1	
2016		
2015		
2014		
2013		
2012		

Total Assets: $405,763,838

Asset Allocation

Asset	%
Cash	3%
Stocks	66%
US Stocks	66%
Bonds	31%
US Bonds	31%
Other	0%

Services Offered:

Investment Strategy: The investment seeks to track the investment results, before fees and expenses, of the S&P 500 Managed Risk 2.0 Index. Under normal market conditions, the fund invests a substantial portion, but at least 80%, of its assets, exclusive of collateral held from securities lending, in securities comprising the S&P 500 Managed Risk 2.0 Index. The underlying index seeks to achieve these objectives by allocating weightings among the S&P 500 Index, the S&P U.S. Treasury Bond Current 5-Year Index and the S&P U.S. Treasury Bill 0-3 Month Index. The fund is non-diversified. **Top Holdings:** United States Treasury Notes 2.88% Apple Inc Microsoft Corp Amazon.com Inc S+p500 Emini Fut Dec18 Xcme 20181221

Main Sector Rotation ETF   D+   SELL

Ticker	Traded On	NAV
SECT	BATS	24.40

Total Assets ($)	Dividend Yield (TTM)	Turnover Ratio	Expense Ratio
$405,731,572	0.94	12	0.78

Ratings
Reward D+
Risk D+
Recent Upgrade/Downgrade

Fund Information
Fund Type Exchange Traded Funds
Category US Equity Large Cap Blend
Sub-Category Large Blend
Prospectus Objective Growth & Inc
Inception Date Sep-17
Open to New Investments Y

Prices
Price (as of 12/31/2018) 24.31
52-Week High 29.53
52-Week Low 23.31

Total Returns (%)

3-Month	6-Month	1-Year	3-Year	5-Year
-15.25	-11.59	-9.30		

3-Year Standard Deviation
Effective Duration

Valuation
Premium/Discount (1-Year Average) 0.25

Company Information
Provider Main Management ETFs
Manager/Tenure Kim D. Arthur (1), James W. Concidine (1), J. Richard Fredericks (1)
Website http://www.mainmgtetfs.com
Address Main Management ETFs 601 California Street, Suite 620 San Francisco CA 94108 United States
Phone Number

Ratings History

Date	Overall Rating	Risk Rating	Reward Rating
Q4-18	D+	D+	D+
Q2-18	U		
Q4-17	U		
Q4-16			
Q4-15			

Asset & Performance History

Date	NAV	1-Year Total Return
2017	27.33	
2016		
2015		
2014		
2013		
2012		

Total Assets: $405,731,572

Asset Allocation

Asset	%
Cash	0%
Stocks	100%
US Stocks	88%
Bonds	0%
US Bonds	0%
Other	0%

Services Offered:

Investment Strategy: The investment seeks to outperform the S&P 500 in rising markets while limiting losses during periods of decline. The fund utilizes a "fund of funds" structure to invest in sector based equity ETFs. It seeks to achieve its objective through dynamic sector rotation. The Adviser focuses its research primarily on sector selection by carefully reviewing the sector, industry, and sub-industries in the fund's portfolio. The Adviser chooses sectors it believes are undervalued and poised to respond favorably to financial market catalysts. The fund will sell a security when it achieves its target price and is, in the opinion of the Adviser, no longer undervalued. **Top Holdings:** Technology Select Sector SPDR® ETF Health Care Select Sector SPDR® ETF Financial Select Sector SPDR® ETF SPDR® S&P Bank ETF Consumer Staples Select Sector SPDR® ETF

First Trust Small Cap Growth AlphaDEX® Fund   C-   HOLD

Ticker	Traded On	NAV	Total Assets ($)	Dividend Yield (TTM)	Turnover Ratio	Expense Ratio
FYC	NAS CM	40.16	$404,391,853	0.15	162	0.7

Ratings
Reward   C
Risk   C-
Recent Upgrade/Downgrade   Down

Fund Information
Fund Type   Exchange Traded Funds
Category   US Equity Small Cap
Sub-Category   Small Growth
Prospectus Objective   Small Company
Inception Date   Apr-11
Open to New Investments   Y

Prices
Price (as of 12/31/2018)   40.12
52-Week High   53.13
52-Week Low   37.33

Total Returns (%)

3-Month	6-Month	1-Year	3-Year	5-Year
-21.85	-17.81	-5.60	32.47	32.61

3-Year Standard Deviation   15.84
Effective Duration

Valuation
Premium/Discount (1-Year Average)   0.13

Company Information
Provider   First Trust
Manager/Tenure   Jon C. Erickson (7), Daniel J. Lindquist
                  (7), David G. McGarel (7), 3 others
Website   http://www.ftportfolios.com/
Address   First Trust 120 E. Liberty Drive, Suite
                  400 Wheaton IL 60187 United States
Phone Number   800-621-1675

PERFORMANCE

Ratings History

Date	Overall Rating	Risk Rating	Reward Rating
Q4-18	C-	C-	C
Q2-18	B-	C-	B+
Q4-17	B+	B	A
Q4-16	C+	C-	B
Q4-15	C+	C-	B-

Asset & Performance History

Date	NAV	1-Year Total Return
2017	42.58	23.19
2016	34.6	13.91
2015	30.47	1.78
2014	30	-1.64
2013	30.51	42.93
2012	21.35	13.08

Total Assets: $404,391,853
Asset Allocation

Asset	%
Cash	0%
Stocks	100%
US Stocks	99%
Bonds	0%
US Bonds	0%
Other	0%

Services Offered:

Investment Strategy: The investment seeks investment results that correspond generally to the price and yield (before the fund's fees and expenses) of an equity index called the Nasdaq AlphaDEX® Small Cap Growth Index. The fund will normally invest at least 90% of its net assets (including investment borrowings) in common stocks that comprise the index. The index is designed to select growth stocks from the NASDAQ US 700 Small Cap Index (the "base index") that may generate positive alpha, or risk-adjusted returns, relative to traditional indices through the use of the AlphaDEX® selection methodology. **Top Holdings:** Crocs Inc Ensign Group Inc BioTelemetry Inc HMS Holdings Corp Iridium Communications Inc

---

iShares J.P. Morgan EM Local Currency Bond ETF   D+   SELL

Ticker	Traded On	NAV	Total Assets ($)	Dividend Yield (TTM)	Turnover Ratio	Expense Ratio
LEMB	NYSE Arca	42.96	$404,330,253	0	97	0.3

Ratings
Reward   D
Risk   D+
Recent Upgrade/Downgrade   Down

Fund Information
Fund Type   Exchange Traded Funds
Category   Emerging Mkts Fixed Inc
Sub-Category   Emerging-Markets Local-Currency Bond
Prospectus Objective   Worldwide Bond
Inception Date   Oct-11
Open to New Investments   Y

Prices
Price (as of 12/31/2018)   43.08
52-Week High   50.76
52-Week Low   41.58

Total Returns (%)

3-Month	6-Month	1-Year	3-Year	5-Year
3.26	1.08	-7.64	11.00	-6.00

3-Year Standard Deviation   10.72
Effective Duration   4.73

Valuation
Premium/Discount (1-Year Average)   0.19

Company Information
Provider   iShares
Manager/Tenure   James Mauro (7), Scott Radell (7)
Website   http://www.ishares.com/
Address   iShares 400 Howard Street San
                  Francisco CA 94105 United States
Phone Number   800-474-2737

PERFORMANCE

Ratings History

Date	Overall Rating	Risk Rating	Reward Rating
Q4-18	D+	D+	D
Q2-18	C	C+	C-
Q4-17	C	C	C
Q4-16	D+	C-	D+
Q4-15	D	D	D

Asset & Performance History

Date	NAV	1-Year Total Return
2017	48.15	12.31
2016	42.87	7.01
2015	40.06	-11.76
2014	45.66	-4.04
2013	48.88	-4.91
2012	52.91	13.76

Total Assets: $404,330,253
Asset Allocation

Asset	%
Cash	1%
Stocks	0%
US Stocks	0%
Bonds	99%
US Bonds	0%
Other	0%

Services Offered:

Investment Strategy: The investment seeks to track the investment results of the J.P. Morgan GBI-EM Global Diversified 15% Cap 4.5% Floor Index composed of local currency denominated, emerging market sovereign bonds. The fund generally will invest at least 90% of its assets in the component securities of the underlying index and may invest up to 10% of its assets in certain futures, options and swap contracts, cash and cash equivalents, including shares of money market funds advised by BFA or its affiliates. The index tracks the performance of local currency-denominated sovereign bond markets of emerging market countries. The fund is non-diversified. **Top Holdings:** Dominican Republic 8.9% Brazil (Federative Republic) 10% Uruguay (Republic of) 9.88% Russian Federation 7% Uruguay (Republic of) 8.5%

ProShares Ultra Dow30   C+   HOLD

Ticker	Traded On	NAV	Total Assets ($)	Dividend Yield (TTM)	Turnover Ratio	Expense Ratio
DDM	NYSE Arca	37.76	$398,057,345	0.72		0.95

Ratings
Reward   C
Risk   C+
Recent Upgrade/Downgrade   Down

Fund Information
Fund Type   Exchange Traded Funds
Category   Trading Tools
Sub-Category   Trading--Leveraged Equity
Prospectus Objective   Growth
Inception Date   Jun-06
Open to New Investments   Y

Prices
Price (as of 12/31/2018)   37.82
52-Week High   50.80
52-Week Low   33.20

Total Returns (%)

3-Month	6-Month	1-Year	3-Year	5-Year
-24.59	-9.24	-13.35	81.33	106.86

3-Year Standard Deviation   20.69
Effective Duration

Valuation
Premium/Discount (1-Year Average)   0.05

Company Information
Provider   ProShares
Manager/Tenure   Michael Neches (5), Devin Sullivan (0)
Website   http://www.proshares.com
Address   ProShares 7501 Wisconsin Avenue, Suite 1000 Bethesda MD 20814 United States
Phone Number   866-776-5125

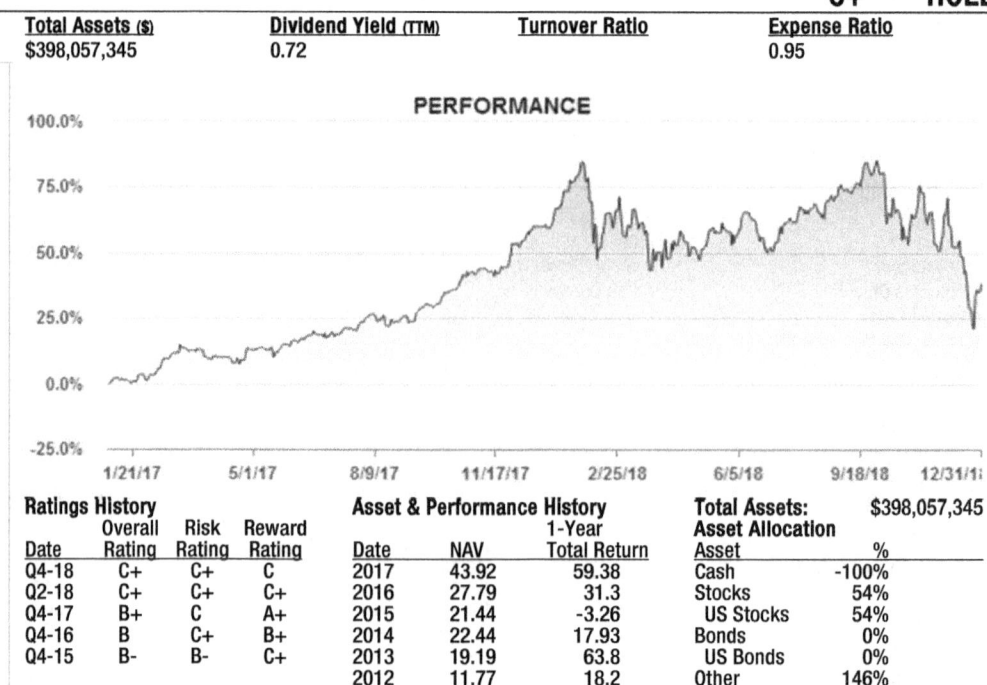

PERFORMANCE

Ratings History

Date	Overall Rating	Risk Rating	Reward Rating
Q4-18	C+	C+	C
Q2-18	C+	C+	C+
Q4-17	B+	C	A+
Q4-16	B	C+	B+
Q4-15	B-	B-	C+

Asset & Performance History

Date	NAV	1-Year Total Return
2017	43.92	59.38
2016	27.79	31.3
2015	21.44	-3.26
2014	22.44	17.93
2013	19.19	63.8
2012	11.77	18.2

Total Assets: $398,057,345
Asset Allocation

Asset	%
Cash	-100%
Stocks	54%
US Stocks	54%
Bonds	0%
US Bonds	0%
Other	146%

Services Offered:

Investment Strategy: The investment seeks daily investment results, before fees and expenses, that correspond to two times (2x) the daily performance of the Dow Jones Industrial AverageSM Index. The fund invests in financial instruments that ProShare Advisors believes, in combination, should produce daily returns consistent with the fund's investment objective. The index is a price-weighted index and includes 30 large-cap, "blue-chip" U.S. stocks, excluding utility and transportation companies. The fund is non-diversified. **Top Holdings:** Spdr Dow Jones Industrial Average (Dia) Swap Morgan Stanley & Co. Internati Dj Industrial Average Swap Citibank Na Dj Industrial Average Swap Bnp Paribas Dj Industrial Average Swap Bank Of America Na Mini DJ Industrial Avg ($5) Future Dec18

---

iShares Treasury Floating Rate Bond ETF   C   HOLD

Ticker	Traded On	NAV	Total Assets ($)	Dividend Yield (TTM)	Turnover Ratio	Expense Ratio
TFLO	NYSE Arca	50.24	$397,560,581	1.63	68	0.15

Ratings
Reward   C-
Risk   C+
Recent Upgrade/Downgrade   Up

Fund Information
Fund Type   Exchange Traded Funds
Category   US Fixed Income
Sub-Category   Short Government
Prospectus Objective   Govt Bond - Treasury
Inception Date   Feb-14
Open to New Investments   Y

Prices
Price (as of 12/31/2018)   50.27
52-Week High   50.35
52-Week Low   50.15

Total Returns (%)

3-Month	6-Month	1-Year	3-Year	5-Year
0.50	0.97	1.82	3.22	

3-Year Standard Deviation   0.19
Effective Duration   0.01

Valuation
Premium/Discount (1-Year Average)   0.06

Company Information
Provider   iShares
Manager/Tenure   James Mauro (4), Scott Radell (4)
Website   http://www.ishares.com
Address   iShares 400 Howard Street San Francisco CA 94105 United States
Phone Number   800-474-2737

PERFORMANCE

Ratings History

Date	Overall Rating	Risk Rating	Reward Rating
Q4-18	C	C+	C-
Q2-18	C-	C-	C-
Q4-17	C	B-	C-
Q4-16	C-	D+	C-
Q4-15	D	D+	D+

Asset & Performance History

Date	NAV	1-Year Total Return
2017	50.16	0.71
2016	50.14	0.46
2015	50.06	0.1
2014	50.08	
2013		
2012		

Total Assets: $397,560,581
Asset Allocation

Asset	%
Cash	19%
Stocks	0%
US Stocks	0%
Bonds	81%
US Bonds	81%
Other	0%

Services Offered:

Investment Strategy: The investment seeks to track the investment results of the Bloomberg Barclays U.S. Treasury Floating Rate Index, which is composed of U.S. Treasury floating rate bonds. The fund generally will invest at least 90% of its assets in the component securities of the underlying index and may invest up to 10% of its assets in certain futures, options and swap contracts, cash and cash equivalents. The underlying index is a market capitalization-weighted index that measures the performance of floating rate public obligations of the U.S. Treasury. **Top Holdings:** United States Treasury Notes 2.44% United States Treasury Notes 2.43% United States Treasury Notes 2.45% United States Treasury Notes 2.42% United States Treasury Notes 2.38%

iShares Morningstar Small-Cap Value ETF   C-   HOLD

Ticker	Traded On	NAV	Total Assets ($)	Dividend Yield (TTM)	Turnover Ratio	Expense Ratio
JKL	NYSE Arca	123.36	$397,527,319	2.11	54	0.3

Ratings
Reward   C-
Risk   D+
Recent Upgrade/Downgrade   Down

Fund Information
Fund Type   Exchange Traded Funds
Category   US Equity Small Cap
Sub-Category   Small Value
Prospectus Objective   Small Company
Inception Date   Jun-04
Open to New Investments   Y

Prices
Price (as of 12/31/2018)   123.17
52-Week High   158.92
52-Week Low   117.04

Total Returns (%)

3-Month	6-Month	1-Year	3-Year	5-Year
-18.55	-17.81	-16.79	14.95	15.15

3-Year Standard Deviation   14.54
Effective Duration

Valuation
Premium/Discount (1-Year Average)   0.11

Company Information
Provider   iShares
Manager/Tenure   Diane Hsiung (10), Greg Savage (10),
                  Jennifer Hsui (6), 3 others
Website   http://www.ishares.com
Address   iShares 400 Howard Street San
                  Francisco CA 94105 United States
Phone Number   800-474-2737

PERFORMANCE

Ratings History

Date	Overall Rating	Risk Rating	Reward Rating
Q4-18	C-	D+	C-
Q2-18	C	C-	C
Q4-17	B	B-	B
Q4-16	D+	D+	C-
Q4-15	C	C-	C

Asset & Performance History

Date	NAV	1-Year Total Return
2017	151.46	8.08
2016	142.73	27.82
2015	114.73	-8.77
2014	128.89	9.8
2013	120.28	35.35
2012	90.65	18.06

Total Assets: $397,527,319

Asset Allocation

Asset	%
Cash	0%
Stocks	100%
US Stocks	98%
Bonds	0%
US Bonds	0%
Other	0%

Services Offered:

Investment Strategy: The investment seeks to track the investment results of the Morningstar® Small Value IndexSM composed of small-capitalization U.S. equities that exhibit value characteristics. The fund generally invests at least 90% of its assets in securities of the underlying index and in depositary receipts representing securities of the underlying index. The underlying index measures the performance of stocks issued by small-capitalization companies that have exhibited "value" characteristics as determined by Morningstar, Inc.'s ("Morningstar" or the "index provider") proprietary index methodology. **Top Holdings:** Popular Inc Dun & Bradstreet Corp EPR Properties Ashland Global Holdings Inc The Hanover Insurance Group Inc

---

iShares Interest Rate Hedged High Yield Bond ETF   C-   HOLD

Ticker	Traded On	NAV	Total Assets ($)	Dividend Yield (TTM)	Turnover Ratio	Expense Ratio
HYGH	NYSE Arca	84.83	$396,605,572	5.57	0	0.54

Ratings
Reward   C-
Risk   C-
Recent Upgrade/Downgrade   Down

Fund Information
Fund Type   Exchange Traded Funds
Category   US Fixed Income
Sub-Category   High Yield Bond
Prospectus Objective   Corp Bond-High Yld
Inception Date   May-14
Open to New Investments   Y

Prices
Price (as of 12/31/2018)   84.77
52-Week High   92.71
52-Week Low   84.42

Total Returns (%)

3-Month	6-Month	1-Year	3-Year	5-Year
-7.12	-3.70	-1.83	18.10	

3-Year Standard Deviation   4.38
Effective Duration   0.23

Valuation
Premium/Discount (1-Year Average)   0.01

Company Information
Provider   iShares
Manager/Tenure   James Mauro (4), Scott Radell (4)
Website   http://www.ishares.com
Address   iShares 400 Howard Street San
                  Francisco CA 94105 United States
Phone Number   800-474-2737

PERFORMANCE

Ratings History

Date	Overall Rating	Risk Rating	Reward Rating
Q4-18	C-	C-	C-
Q2-18	C	C-	C
Q4-17	C+	B-	C+
Q4-16	C-	D+	C
Q4-15	D	D+	D+

Asset & Performance History

Date	NAV	1-Year Total Return
2017	90.93	6.53
2016	89.53	12.93
2015	83.19	-6.32
2014	93.65	
2013		
2012		

Total Assets: $396,605,572

Asset Allocation

Asset	%
Cash	-2%
Stocks	0%
US Stocks	0%
Bonds	102%
US Bonds	88%
Other	0%

Services Offered:

Investment Strategy: The investment seeks to mitigate the interest rate risk of a portfolio composed of U.S. dollar-denominated, high yield corporate bonds. The fund seeks to achieve its investment objective by investing, under normal circumstances, at least 80% of its net assets in U.S. dollar-denominated high yield bonds, in one or more underlying funds that principally invest in high yield bonds, and in U.S. Treasury securities (or cash equivalents). It may also invest in other interest rate futures contracts, including but not limited to, Eurodollar and Federal Funds futures. **Top Holdings:** iShares iBoxx $ High Yield Corp Bd ETF Swp: Usd 2.337500 08-Dec-2036 Swp: Usd 2.300500 18-Sep-2025 Swp: Usd 0.897500 18-Sep-2017 Swp: Usd 2.806500 18-Sep-2045

iShares Russell Top 200 Value ETF   C   HOLD

Ticker	Traded On	NAV	Total Assets ($)	Dividend Yield (TTM)	Turnover Ratio	Expense Ratio
IWX	NYSE Arca	47.71	$394,481,203	2.22	13	0.2

Ratings
Reward   C
Risk   C-
Recent Upgrade/Downgrade

Fund Information
Fund Type   Exchange Traded Funds
Category   US Equity Large Cap Value
Sub-Category   Large Value
Prospectus Objective   Growth
Inception Date   Sep-09
Open to New Investments   Y

Prices
Price (as of 12/31/2018)   47.80
52-Week High   55.81
52-Week Low   44.99

PERFORMANCE

Total Returns (%)

3-Month	6-Month	1-Year	3-Year	5-Year
-10.70	-4.07	-6.40	23.21	33.85

3-Year Standard Deviation   9.09
Effective Duration

Valuation
Premium/Discount (1-Year Average)   0.21

Company Information
Provider	iShares
Manager/Tenure	Diane Hsiung (9), Greg Savage (9), Jennifer Hsui (6), 3 others
Website	http://www.ishares.com
Address	iShares 400 Howard Street San Francisco CA 94105 United States
Phone Number	800-474-2737

Ratings History

Date	Overall Rating	Risk Rating	Reward Rating
Q4-18	C	C-	C
Q2-18	C	C-	C
Q4-17	B-	B	B-
Q4-16	C+	C-	B
Q4-15	C	C	C+

Asset & Performance History

Date	NAV	1-Year Total Return
2017	52.27	13.58
2016	47.06	15.9
2015	41.58	-3.57
2014	44.32	12.65
2013	40.24	31.78
2012	31.17	16.74

Total Assets: $394,481,203
Asset Allocation

Asset	%
Cash	0%
Stocks	100%
US Stocks	98%
Bonds	0%
US Bonds	0%
Other	0%

Services Offered:

Investment Strategy: The investment seeks to track the investment results of the Russell Top 200 Value Index, which measures the performance of the largest capitalization value sector of the U.S. equity market. The fund generally will invest at least 90% of its assets in the component securities of the underlying index and may invest up to 10% of its assets in certain futures, options and swap contracts, cash and cash equivalents, including shares of money market funds advised by BFA or its affiliates, as well as in securities not included in the underlying index, but which BFA believes will help the fund track the underlying index. **Top Holdings:** JPMorgan Chase & Co Berkshire Hathaway Inc B Exxon Mobil Corp Johnson & Johnson Pfizer Inc

---

USAA MSCI USA Value Momentum Blend Index ETF   D   SELL

Ticker	Traded On	NAV	Total Assets ($)	Dividend Yield (TTM)	Turnover Ratio	Expense Ratio
ULVM	NYSE Arca	44.99	$392,835,928	1.33		0.2

Ratings
Reward   D
Risk   D
Recent Upgrade/Downgrade

Fund Information
Fund Type   Exchange Traded Funds
Category   US Equity Large Cap Blend
Sub-Category   Large Blend
Prospectus Objective   Growth & Inc
Inception Date   Oct-17
Open to New Investments   Y

Prices
Price (as of 12/31/2018)   45.06
52-Week High   55.24
52-Week Low   42.49

PERFORMANCE

Total Returns (%)

3-Month	6-Month	1-Year	3-Year	5-Year
-15.51	-11.73	-12.10		

3-Year Standard Deviation
Effective Duration

Valuation
Premium/Discount (1-Year Average)   0.18

Company Information
Provider	USAA
Manager/Tenure	Lance Humphrey (1), Wasif A. Latif (1), John Law (1), 2 others
Website	http://www.usaa.com
Address	USAA P.O. Box 659453 San Antonio TX 78265-9825 United States
Phone Number	800-531-8722

Ratings History

Date	Overall Rating	Risk Rating	Reward Rating
Q4-18	D	D	D
Q2-18	U		
Q4-17	U		
Q4-16			
Q4-15			

Asset & Performance History

Date	NAV	1-Year Total Return
2017	51.94	
2016		
2015		
2014		
2013		
2012		

Total Assets: $392,835,928
Asset Allocation

Asset	%
Cash	0%
Stocks	100%
US Stocks	99%
Bonds	0%
US Bonds	0%
Other	0%

Services Offered:

Investment Strategy: The investment seeks to provide investment results that closely correspond, before fees and expenses, to the performance of the MSCI USA Select Value Momentum Blend Index. Under normal circumstances, the fund seeks to achieve its investment objective by investing at least 80% of its net assets in securities in the index. The index is designed to deliver exposure to equity securities of large- and mid-capitalization U.S. issuers that have higher exposure to value and momentum factors within the MSCI USA Index (the "parent index") while also maintaining moderate index turnover and lower realized volatility than traditional capitalization weighted indexes. **Top Holdings:** Entergy Corp Aflac Inc Public Service Enterprise Group Inc Progressive Corp Mastercard Inc A

First Trust Utilities AlphaDEX® Fund   B   BUY

Ticker	Traded On	NAV	Total Assets ($)	Dividend Yield (TTM)	Turnover Ratio	Expense Ratio
FXU	NYSE Arca	26.80	$390,453,640	3.04		0.63

Ratings

Reward	B+
Risk	C+
Recent Upgrade/Downgrade	Up

Fund Information

Fund Type	Exchange Traded Funds
Category	Utilities Sector Equity
Sub-Category	Utilities
Prospectus Objective	Utility
Inception Date	May-07
Open to New Investments	Y

Prices

Price (as of 12/31/2018)	26.78
52-Week High	28.86
52-Week Low	23.56

Total Returns (%)

3-Month	6-Month	1-Year	3-Year	5-Year
-1.89	3.65	5.59	30.61	53.40

3-Year Standard Deviation	10.38
Effective Duration	

Valuation

Premium/Discount (1-Year Average)	0.01

Company Information

Provider	First Trust
Manager/Tenure	Jon C. Erickson (11), Daniel J. Lindquist (11), David G. McGarel (11), 3 others
Website	http://www.ftportfolios.com/
Address	First Trust 120 E. Liberty Drive, Suite 400 Wheaton IL 60187 United States
Phone Number	800-621-1675

PERFORMANCE

Ratings History

Date	Overall Rating	Risk Rating	Reward Rating
Q4-18	B	C+	B+
Q2-18	C+	C	B
Q4-17	C+	B	C
Q4-16	B-	C	B
Q4-15	B-	C	B

Asset & Performance History

Date	NAV	1-Year Total Return
2017	26	0.93
2016	26.73	22.54
2015	22.4	-6.42
2014	24.87	25.5
2013	20.27	17.6
2012	17.99	3.64

Total Assets: $390,453,640

Asset Allocation

Asset	%
Cash	0%
Stocks	100%
US Stocks	100%
Bonds	0%
US Bonds	0%
Other	0%

Services Offered:

Investment Strategy: The investment seeks investment results that correspond generally to the price and yield (before the fund's fees and expenses) of an equity index called the StrataQuant® Utilities Index. The fund will normally invest at least 90% of its net assets (including investment borrowings) in common stocks that comprise the index. The index is a modified equal-dollar weighted index designed by IDI to objectively identify and select stocks from the Russell 1000® Index in the utilities sector that may generate positive alpha relative to traditional passive-style indices through the use of the AlphaDEX® selection methodology. **Top Holdings:** Telephone and Data Systems Inc   Verizon Communications Inc   NextEra Energy Inc   CenturyLink Inc   Sprint Corp

---

iShares Emerging Markets High Yield Bond ETF   C-   HOLD

Ticker	Traded On	NAV	Total Assets ($)	Dividend Yield (TTM)	Turnover Ratio	Expense Ratio
EMHY	BATS	44.30	$390,074,037	5.27	25	0.5

Ratings

Reward	C-
Risk	C-
Recent Upgrade/Downgrade	Up

Fund Information

Fund Type	Exchange Traded Funds
Category	Emerging Mkts Fixed Inc
Sub-Category	Emerging Markets Bond
Prospectus Objective	Corp Bond-High Yld
Inception Date	Apr-12
Open to New Investments	Y

Prices

Price (as of 12/31/2018)	44.37
52-Week High	50.46
52-Week Low	44.09

Total Returns (%)

3-Month	6-Month	1-Year	3-Year	5-Year
-0.36	1.52	-5.10	18.67	23.27

3-Year Standard Deviation	6.63
Effective Duration	5.29

Valuation

Premium/Discount (1-Year Average)	0.15

Company Information

Provider	iShares
Manager/Tenure	James Mauro (6), Scott Radell (6)
Website	http://www.ishares.com
Address	iShares 400 Howard Street San Francisco CA 94105 United States
Phone Number	800-474-2737

PERFORMANCE

Ratings History

Date	Overall Rating	Risk Rating	Reward Rating
Q4-18	C-	C-	C-
Q2-18	C-	C-	C-
Q4-17	B	A	C+
Q4-16	C	C-	C
Q4-15	C-	C-	C-

Asset & Performance History

Date	NAV	1-Year Total Return
2017	49.85	8.65
2016	48.35	14.71
2015	44.98	1.77
2014	47.26	2.06
2013	49.15	-5.47
2012	55.09	

Total Assets: $390,074,037

Asset Allocation

Asset	%
Cash	1%
Stocks	0%
US Stocks	0%
Bonds	99%
US Bonds	3%
Other	0%

Services Offered:

Investment Strategy: The investment seeks to track the investment results of the Morningstar® Emerging Markets High Yield Bond IndexSM. The fund generally will invest at least 90% of its assets in the component securities of the underlying index and may invest up to 10% of its assets in certain futures, options and swap contracts, cash and cash equivalents, including shares of money market funds advised by BFA or its affiliates. The index tracks the performance of the below-investment-grade U.S. dollar-denominated emerging market sovereign and corporate high yield bond market. The fund is non-diversified. **Top Holdings:** Argentina (Republic of) 7.5% Petrobras Global Finance B.V. 6%   Russian Federation 7.5%   Argentina (Republic of) 6.88%   Russian Federation 12.75%

iShares U.S. Oil & Gas Exploration & Production ETF

C+   HOLD

Ticker	Traded On	NAV	Total Assets ($)	Dividend Yield (TTM)	Turnover Ratio	Expense Ratio
IEO	BATS	51.66	$389,405,325	1.12	17	0.43

Ratings
Reward	B
Risk	C-
Recent Upgrade/Downgrade	Up

Fund Information
Fund Type	Exchange Traded Funds
Category	Energy Sector Equity
Sub-Category	Equity Energy
Prospectus Objective	Natl Res
Inception Date	May-06
Open to New Investments	Y

Prices
Price (as of 12/31/2018)	51.63
52-Week High	78.42
52-Week Low	47.66

Total Returns (%)
3-Month	6-Month	1-Year	3-Year	5-Year
-32.60	-28.70	-19.36	1.16	-33.07

3-Year Standard Deviation	25.96
Effective Duration	

Valuation
Premium/Discount (1-Year Average)	0.00

Company Information
Provider	iShares
Manager/Tenure	Diane Hsiung (10), Greg Savage (10), Jennifer Hsui (6), 3 others
Website	http://www.ishares.com
Address	iShares 400 Howard Street San Francisco CA 94105 United States
Phone Number	800-474-2737

PERFORMANCE

Ratings History
Date	Overall Rating	Risk Rating	Reward Rating
Q4-18	C+	C-	B
Q2-18	C	C-	C+
Q4-17	D+	D+	D+
Q4-16	D+	D	C-
Q4-15	C+	C+	C+

Asset & Performance History
Date	NAV	1-Year Total Return
2017	64.95	0.29
2016	65.45	25.09
2015	52.91	-24.59
2014	71.38	-12.27
2013	82.27	30.63
2012	63.58	4.36

Total Assets: $389,405,325
Asset Allocation
Asset	%
Cash	0%
Stocks	100%
US Stocks	100%
Bonds	0%
US Bonds	0%
Other	0%

Services Offered:

Investment Strategy: The investment seeks to track the investment results of the Dow Jones U.S. Select Oil Exploration & Production Index composed of U.S. equities in the oil and gas exploration and production sector. The fund generally invests at least 90% of its assets in securities of the underlying index and in depositary receipts representing securities of the underlying index. The underlying index measures the performance of the oil exploration and production sector of the U.S. equity market. The fund is non-diversified. **Top Holdings:** ConocoPhillips EOG Resources Inc Marathon Petroleum Corp Phillips 66 Valero Energy Corp

---

Invesco S&P SmallCap Information Technology ETF

C-   HOLD

Ticker	Traded On	NAV	Total Assets ($)	Dividend Yield (TTM)	Turnover Ratio	Expense Ratio
PSCT	NAS CM	69.20	$386,139,045	0.51		0.29

Ratings
Reward	C-
Risk	C-
Recent Upgrade/Downgrade	Down

Fund Information
Fund Type	Exchange Traded Funds
Category	Technology Sector Equity
Sub-Category	Technology
Prospectus Objective	Technology
Inception Date	Apr-10
Open to New Investments	

Prices
Price (as of 12/31/2018)	69.02
52-Week High	89.71
52-Week Low	64.05

Total Returns (%)
3-Month	6-Month	1-Year	3-Year	5-Year
-16.59	-17.05	-9.13	33.53	57.41

3-Year Standard Deviation	15.05
Effective Duration	

Valuation
Premium/Discount (1-Year Average)	0.06

Company Information
Provider	Invesco
Manager/Tenure	Peter Hubbard (8), Michael Jeanette (8), Tony Seisser (4), 1 other
Website	http://www.invesco.com/us
Address	Invesco 11 Greenway Plaza, Ste. 2500 Houston TX 77046 United States
Phone Number	800-659-1005

PERFORMANCE

Ratings History
Date	Overall Rating	Risk Rating	Reward Rating
Q4-18	C-	C-	C-
Q2-18	C	C-	B-
Q4-17	B+	A-	B
Q4-16	C+	C-	B-
Q4-15	C	C	C

Asset & Performance History
Date	NAV	1-Year Total Return
2017	76.47	10.11
2016	69.58	33.46
2015	52.27	4.33
2014	50.17	12.97
2013	44.47	44.44
2012	30.86	11.73

Total Assets: $386,139,045
Asset Allocation
Asset	%
Cash	0%
Stocks	100%
US Stocks	95%
Bonds	0%
US Bonds	0%
Other	0%

Services Offered:

Investment Strategy: The investment seeks to track the investment results (before fees and expenses) of the S&P SmallCap 600® Capped Information Technology Index (the "underlying index"). The fund generally will invest at least 90% of its total assets in common stocks of small capitalization U.S. information technology companies that comprise the underlying index. These companies are principally engaged in the business of providing information technology-related products and services, including computer hardware and software, Internet, electronics and semiconductors, and communication technologies. **Top Holdings:** CACI International Inc Class A Semtech Corp Cabot Microelectronics Corp Finisar Corp Qualys Inc

WisdomTree Yield Enhanced U.S. Aggregate Bond Fund   D+   SELL

Ticker	Traded On	NAV	Total Assets ($)	Dividend Yield (TTM)	Turnover Ratio	Expense Ratio
AGGY	NYSE Arca	48.15	$384,845,990	3.31	134	0.12

Ratings
Reward   D+
Risk   C-
Recent Upgrade/Downgrade   Down

Fund Information
Fund Type   Exchange Traded Funds
Category   US Fixed Income
Sub-Category   Intermediate-Term Bond
Prospectus Objective   Growth & Inc
Inception Date   Jul-15
Open to New Investments   Y

Prices
Price (as of 12/31/2018)   48.22
52-Week High   50.72
52-Week Low   47.36

Total Returns (%)

3-Month	6-Month	1-Year	3-Year	5-Year
0.72	1.28	-1.72	7.64	

3-Year Standard Deviation   3.34
Effective Duration   6.79

Valuation
Premium/Discount (1-Year Average)   0.00

Company Information
Provider   WisdomTree
Manager/Tenure   Paul L. Benson (3), Stephanie Shu (3)
Website   http://www.wisdomtree.com
Address   WisdomTree 245 Park Avenue, 35th floor New York NY 10167 United States
Phone Number   866-909-9473

PERFORMANCE

Ratings History

Date	Overall Rating	Risk Rating	Reward Rating
Q4-18	D+	C-	D+
Q2-18	C-	C-	C-
Q4-17	C	B	C
Q4-16	D	C-	D+
Q4-15	U		

Asset & Performance History

Date	NAV	1-Year Total Return
2017	50.66	5.21
2016	49.52	4.1
2015	49.08	
2014		
2013		
2012		

Total Assets: $384,845,990
Asset Allocation

Asset	%
Cash	0%
Stocks	0%
US Stocks	0%
Bonds	100%
US Bonds	91%
Other	0%

Services Offered:

Investment Strategy: The investment seeks to track the price and yield performance, before fees and expenses, of the Bloomberg Barclays U.S. Aggregate Enhanced Yield Index (the "index"). Under normal circumstances, the fund will invest at least 80% of its total asset in component securities of the index and investments that have economic characteristics that are substantially identical to the economic characteristics of such component securities. The index is designed to broadly capture the U.S. investment grade, fixed income securities market while seeking to enhance yield within desired risk parameters and constraints. The fund is non-diversified. **Top Holdings:** United States Treasury Notes 1.63% United States Treasury Notes 1.13% United States Treasury Notes 1.38% United States Treasury Notes 2.75% United States Treasury Notes 2.88%

First Trust STOXX® European Select Dividend Index Fund   C-   HOLD

Ticker	Traded On	NAV	Total Assets ($)	Dividend Yield (TTM)	Turnover Ratio	Expense Ratio
FDD	NYSE Arca	11.98	$383,983,396	4.69	35	0.6

Ratings
Reward   D+
Risk   C
Recent Upgrade/Downgrade   Down

Fund Information
Fund Type   Exchange Traded Funds
Category   Europe Equity Large Cap
Sub-Category   Europe Stock
Prospectus Objective   Europe Stock
Inception Date   Aug-07
Open to New Investments   Y

Prices
Price (as of 12/31/2018)   11.94
52-Week High   14.77
52-Week Low   11.69

Total Returns (%)

3-Month	6-Month	1-Year	3-Year	5-Year
-7.84	-7.35	-8.80	11.24	7.41

3-Year Standard Deviation   10.55
Effective Duration

Valuation
Premium/Discount (1-Year Average)   -0.04

Company Information
Provider   First Trust
Manager/Tenure   Jon C. Erickson (11), Daniel J. Lindquist (11), David G. McGarel (11), 3 others
Website   http://www.ftportfolios.com/
Address   First Trust 120 E. Liberty Drive, Suite 400 Wheaton IL 60187 United States
Phone Number   800-621-1675

PERFORMANCE

Ratings History

Date	Overall Rating	Risk Rating	Reward Rating
Q4-18	C-	C	D+
Q2-18	C	C+	C
Q4-17	B-	B	C+
Q4-16	D+	C-	D+
Q4-15	C	C+	C

Asset & Performance History

Date	NAV	1-Year Total Return
2017	13.75	19.05
2016	11.89	2.45
2015	12.17	-3.33
2014	13.11	-0.1
2013	13.64	17.19
2012	12.14	10.18

Total Assets: $383,983,396
Asset Allocation

Asset	%
Cash	0%
Stocks	100%
US Stocks	0%
Bonds	0%
US Bonds	0%
Other	0%

Services Offered:

Investment Strategy: The investment seeks investment results that correspond generally to the price and yield (before the fund's fees and expenses) of an equity index called the STOXX® Europe Select Dividend 30 Index. The fund will normally invest at least 90% of its net assets (including investment borrowings) in common stocks or in depositary receipts representing securities in the index. The index consists of 30 high dividend-yielding securities selected from the STOXX® Europe 600 Index, including secondary lines of those companies (where there are multiple lines of equity capital in a company). **Top Holdings:** GlaxoSmithKline PLC SSE PLC National Grid PLC Royal Dutch Shell PLC B United Utilities Group PLC

WisdomTree International LargeCap Dividend Fund   D+   SELL

Ticker	Traded On	NAV	Total Assets ($)	Dividend Yield (TTM)	Turnover Ratio	Expense Ratio
DOL	NYSE Arca	42.74	$383,734,634	3.85	16	0.48

Ratings
Reward   D+
Risk   C-
Recent Upgrade/Downgrade   Down

Fund Information
Fund Type   Exchange Traded Funds
Category   Global Equity Large Cap
Sub-Category   Foreign Large Value
Prospectus Objective   Foreign Stock
Inception Date   Jun-06
Open to New Investments   Y

Prices
Price (as of 12/31/2018)   42.52
52-Week High   54.08
52-Week Low   41.44

Total Returns (%)

3-Month	6-Month	1-Year	3-Year	5-Year
-10.92	-8.62	-12.49	9.33	-0.34

3-Year Standard Deviation   10.75
Effective Duration

Valuation
Premium/Discount (1-Year Average)   -0.05

Company Information
Provider   WisdomTree
Manager/Tenure   Richard A. Brown (10), Thomas J. Durante (10), Karen Q. Wong (10)
Website   http://www.wisdomtree.com
Address   WisdomTree 245 Park Avenue, 35th floor New York NY 10167 United States
Phone Number   866-909-9473

PERFORMANCE

Ratings History

Date	Overall Rating	Risk Rating	Reward Rating
Q4-18	D+	C-	D+
Q2-18	C	C-	C
Q4-17	C+	B-	C+
Q4-16	D+	C-	D
Q4-15	C-	C-	C-

Asset & Performance History

Date	NAV	1-Year Total Return
2017	50.64	21.54
2016	43.08	2.8
2015	43.44	-4.82
2014	47.18	-4.23
2013	51.57	20.74
2012	44.28	15.24

Total Assets: $383,734,634
Asset Allocation

Asset	%
Cash	0%
Stocks	100%
US Stocks	0%
Bonds	0%
US Bonds	0%
Other	0%

Services Offered:

Investment Strategy: The investment seeks to track the price and yield performance, before fees and expenses, of the WisdomTree International LargeCap Dividend Index. The fund normally invests at least 95% of its total assets (exclusive of collateral held from securities lending) in component securities of the index and investments that have economic characteristics that are substantially identical to the economic characteristics of such component securities. The index is a fundamentally weighted index that is comprised of the large-capitalization segment of the dividend-paying market in the industrialized world outside the U.S. and Canada. The fund is non-diversified. **Top Holdings:** China Mobile Ltd Novartis AG Nestle SA Royal Dutch Shell PLC Class A HSBC Holdings PLC

ELEMENTS Linked to the Rogers International Commodity Index - Total Return   C-   HOLD

Ticker	Traded On	NAV	Total Assets ($)	Dividend Yield (TTM)	Turnover Ratio	Expense Ratio
RJI	NYSE Arca		$375,498,200	0	0	0.75

Ratings
Reward   C-
Risk   C
Recent Upgrade/Downgrade   Down

Fund Information
Fund Type   Exchange Traded Funds
Category   Commodities Broad Basket
Sub-Category   Commodities Broad Basket
Prospectus Objective   Natl Res
Inception Date   Oct-07
Open to New Investments   Y

Prices
Price (as of 12/31/2018)   4.89
52-Week High   5.88
52-Week Low   4.87

Total Returns (%)

3-Month	6-Month	1-Year	3-Year	5-Year
-14.38	-12.85	-9.62	6.31	-40.19

3-Year Standard Deviation   11.23
Effective Duration

Valuation
Premium/Discount (1-Year Average)   0.00

Company Information
Provider   ELEMENTS
Manager/Tenure   No Manager (11)
Website   http://www.elementsetn.com
Address   ELEMENTS United States
Phone Number   212-449-2957

PERFORMANCE

Ratings History

Date	Overall Rating	Risk Rating	Reward Rating
Q4-18	C-	C	C-
Q2-18	C	C	C
Q4-17	C-	D+	C
Q4-16	D	D	D
Q4-15	D-	D	D-

Asset & Performance History

Date	NAV	1-Year Total Return
2017	5.4	3.46
2016	5.19	11.37
2015	4.59	-27.14
2014	6.3	-22.79
2013	8.16	-5.33
2012	8.62	1.17

Total Assets: $375,498,200
Asset Allocation

Asset	%
Cash	
Stocks	
US Stocks	
Bonds	
US Bonds	
Other	

Services Offered:

Investment Strategy: The investment seeks to replicate, net of expenses, the Rogers International Commodity Index – Total Return index.
The index represents the value of a basket of 35 commodity futures contracts. **Top Holdings:**

Invesco KBW Premium Yield Equity REIT ETF   C   HOLD

Ticker	Traded On	NAV	Total Assets ($)	Dividend Yield (TTM)	Turnover Ratio	Expense Ratio
KBWY	NAS CM	26.97	$371,808,712	7.58		0.35

Ratings
Reward   B-
Risk   D+
Recent Upgrade/Downgrade

Fund Information
Fund Type   Exchange Traded Funds
Category   Real Estate Sector Equity
Sub-Category   Real Estate
Prospectus Objective   Real Estate
Inception Date   Dec-10
Open to New Investments

Prices
Price (as of 12/31/2018)   26.95
52-Week High   36.70
52-Week Low   26.11

Total Returns (%)

3-Month	6-Month	1-Year	3-Year	5-Year
-17.47	-21.33	-18.04	9.98	25.08

3-Year Standard Deviation   16.03
Effective Duration

Valuation
Premium/Discount (1-Year Average)   0.03

Company Information
Provider   Invesco
Manager/Tenure   Peter Hubbard (8), Michael Jeanette
                  (8), Tony Seisser (4), 1 other
Website   http://www.invesco.com/us
Address   Invesco 11 Greenway Plaza, Ste. 2500
                   Houston TX 77046 United States
Phone Number   800-659-1005

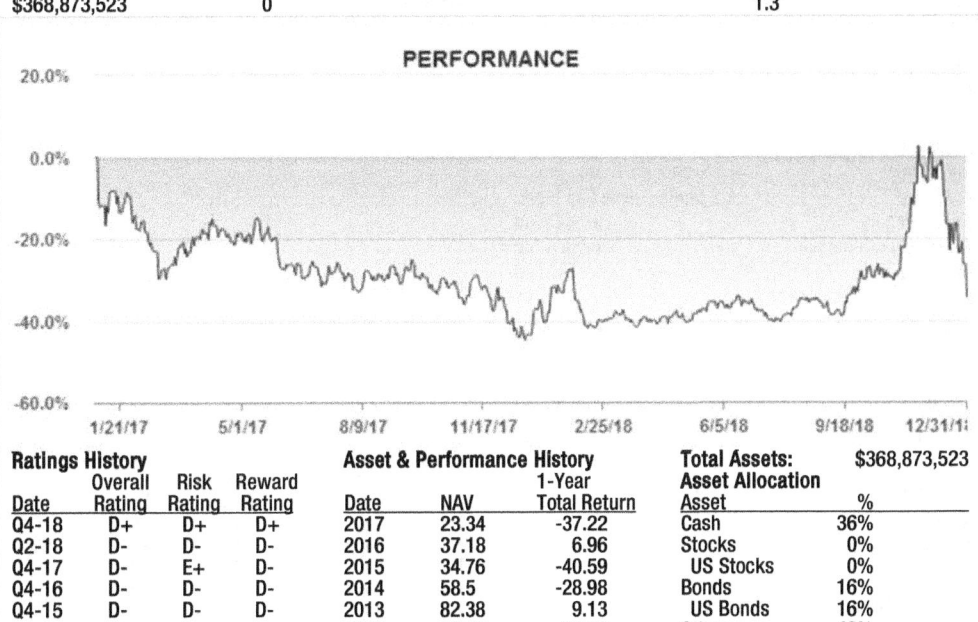

PERFORMANCE

Ratings History

Date	Overall Rating	Risk Rating	Reward Rating
Q4-18	C	D+	B-
Q2-18	C	D	C+
Q4-17	C+	B-	C
Q4-16	C	D+	B-
Q4-15	B-	C	B

Asset & Performance History

Date	NAV	1-Year Total Return
2017	35.38	0.85
2016	37.59	33.04
2015	30.41	-8.17
2014	34.94	23.85
2013	29.66	10.28
2012	28.17	29.17

Total Assets: $371,808,712

Asset Allocation

Asset	%
Cash	0%
Stocks	100%
US Stocks	100%
Bonds	0%
US Bonds	0%
Other	0%

Services Offered:

Investment Strategy: The investment seeks to track the investment results (before fees and expenses) of the KBW Nasdaq Premium Yield Equity REIT Index (the "underlying index"). The fund generally will invest at least 90% of its total assets in the securities of small- and mid-cap equity REITs in the United States that comprise the underlying index. It generally invests in all of the securities comprising the underlying index in proportion to their weightings in the underlying index. **Top Holdings:** Washington Prime Group Inc Global Net Lease Inc SITE Centers Corp Whitestone REIT Class B Medical Properties Trust Inc

---

United States Natural Gas Fund, LP   D+   SELL

Ticker	Traded On	NAV	Total Assets ($)	Dividend Yield (TTM)	Turnover Ratio	Expense Ratio
UNG	NYSE Arca	24.35	$368,873,523	0		1.3

Ratings
Reward   D+
Risk   D+
Recent Upgrade/Downgrade   Up

Fund Information
Fund Type   Exchange Traded Funds
Category   Commodities Specified
Sub-Category   Commodities Energy
Prospectus Objective   Natl Res
Inception Date   Apr-07
Open to New Investments   Y

Prices
Price (as of 12/31/2018)   24.71
52-Week High   39.32
52-Week Low   21.67

Total Returns (%)

3-Month	6-Month	1-Year	3-Year	5-Year
-4.78	4.92	4.34	-29.93	-70.43

3-Year Standard Deviation   39.66
Effective Duration

Valuation
Premium/Discount (1-Year Average)   0.00

Company Information
Provider   USCF Investments
Manager/Tenure   Management Team (11)
Website   http://www.uscfinvestments.com
Address   USCF 1290 Broadway, Suite 1100
                   Denver CO 80203 United States
Phone Number

PERFORMANCE

Ratings History

Date	Overall Rating	Risk Rating	Reward Rating
Q4-18	D+	D+	D+
Q2-18	D-	D-	D-
Q4-17	D-	E+	D-
Q4-16	D-	D-	D-
Q4-15	D-	D-	D-

Asset & Performance History

Date	NAV	1-Year Total Return
2017	23.34	-37.22
2016	37.18	6.96
2015	34.76	-40.59
2014	58.5	-28.98
2013	82.38	9.13
2012	75.48	-27.13

Total Assets: $368,873,523

Asset Allocation

Asset	%
Cash	36%
Stocks	0%
US Stocks	0%
Bonds	16%
US Bonds	16%
Other	48%

Services Offered:

Investment Strategy: The investment seeks to reflect the daily changes in percentage terms of the price of natural gas delivered at the Henry Hub, Louisiana, as measured by the daily changes in the price of a specified short-term futures contract.
The fund invests primarily in futures contracts for natural gas that are traded on the NYMEX, ICE Futures Europe and ICE Futures U.S. (together, "ICE Futures") or other U.S. and foreign exchanges. The Benchmark Futures Contract is the futures contract on natural gas as traded on the New York Mercantile Exchange that is the near month contract to expire, except when the near month contract is within two weeks of expiration. **Top Holdings:** Future Contract On Natural Gas Futr Jan19 Future Contract On Ice Nf Ld1 Jan19 United States Treasury Bills United States Treasury Bills United States Treasury Bills

First Trust Consumer Discretionary AlphaDEX® Fund   C   HOLD

Ticker	Traded On	NAV	Total Assets ($)	Dividend Yield (TTM)	Turnover Ratio	Expense Ratio
FXD	NYSE Arca	36.89	$365,582,719	0.96	93	0.64

Ratings
Reward	C
Risk	C+
Recent Upgrade/Downgrade	

Fund Information
Fund Type	Exchange Traded Funds
Category	Consumer Goods & Svcs
Sub-Category	Consumer Cyclical
Prospectus Objective	Unaligned
Inception Date	May-07
Open to New Investments	Y

Prices
Price (as of 12/31/2018)	36.85
52-Week High	45.22
52-Week Low	34.86

Total Returns (%)
3-Month	6-Month	1-Year	3-Year	5-Year
-14.26	-12.28	-11.43	11.49	19.71

3-Year Standard Deviation	11.49
Effective Duration	

Valuation
Premium/Discount (1-Year Average)	0.01

Company Information
Provider	First Trust
Manager/Tenure	Jon C. Erickson (11), Daniel J. Lindquist (11), David G. McGarel (11), 3 others
Website	http://www.ftportfolios.com/
Address	First Trust 120 E. Liberty Drive, Suite 400 Wheaton IL 60187 United States
Phone Number	800-621-1675

PERFORMANCE

Ratings History
Date	Overall Rating	Risk Rating	Reward Rating
Q4-18	C	C+	C
Q2-18	C	C-	C
Q4-17	B-	B	C+
Q4-16	C+	C+	C+
Q4-15	C+	C+	C

Asset & Performance History
Date	NAV	1-Year Total Return
2017	42.06	19.75
2016	35.48	5.12
2015	34.11	-3.81
2014	35.77	11.63
2013	32.22	42.99
2012	22.62	15.82

Total Assets: $365,582,719
Asset Allocation
Asset	%
Cash	0%
Stocks	100%
US Stocks	99%
Bonds	0%
US Bonds	0%
Other	0%

Services Offered:

Investment Strategy: The investment seeks investment results that correspond generally to the price and yield (before the fund's fees and expenses) of an equity index called the StrataQuant® Consumer Discretionary Index. The fund will normally invest at least 90% of its net assets (including investment borrowings) in common stocks that comprise the index. The index is a modified equal-dollar weighted index designed by IDI to objectively identify and select stocks from the Russell 1000® Index in the consumer discretionary sector that may generate positive alpha relative to traditional passive-style indices through the use of the AlphaDEX® selection methodology. **Top Holdings:** Newell Brands Inc Graham Holdings Co Comcast Corp Class A Tribune Media Co A Live Nation Entertainment Inc

---

SPDR® SSGA Gender Diversity Index ETF   C   HOLD

Ticker	Traded On	NAV	Total Assets ($)	Dividend Yield (TTM)	Turnover Ratio	Expense Ratio
SHE	NYSE Arca	63.69	$365,566,354	2.21	49	0.2

Ratings
Reward	C
Risk	C-
Recent Upgrade/Downgrade	

Fund Information
Fund Type	Exchange Traded Funds
Category	US Equity Large Cap Blend
Sub-Category	Large Blend
Prospectus Objective	Growth & Inc
Inception Date	Mar-16
Open to New Investments	Y

Prices
Price (as of 12/31/2018)	63.73
52-Week High	78.05
52-Week Low	60.07

Total Returns (%)
3-Month	6-Month	1-Year	3-Year	5-Year
-10.82	-4.71	-1.59		

3-Year Standard Deviation	
Effective Duration	

Valuation
Premium/Discount (1-Year Average)	0.19

Company Information
Provider	SPDR State Street Global Advisors
Manager/Tenure	Lynn Blake (2), Melissa Kapitulik (2), Amy Cheng (2)
Website	http://www.spdrs.com
Address	SPDR State Street Global Advisors State Street Financial Center, 1 Lincoln Street Boston MA 02111-2900 United States
Phone Number	617-786-3000

PERFORMANCE

Ratings History
Date	Overall Rating	Risk Rating	Reward Rating
Q4-18	C	C-	C
Q2-18	C	C-	C+
Q4-17	C-	B+	C
Q4-16	U		
Q4-15			

Asset & Performance History
Date	NAV	1-Year Total Return
2017	70.72	19.67
2016	62.35	
2015		
2014		
2013		
2012		

Total Assets: $365,566,354
Asset Allocation
Asset	%
Cash	0%
Stocks	100%
US Stocks	100%
Bonds	0%
US Bonds	0%
Other	0%

Services Offered:

Investment Strategy: The investment seeks to provide investment results that, before fees and expenses, correspond generally to the total return performance of the SSGA Gender Diversity Index, which tracks U.S. companies that are leaders in advancing women through gender diversity on their boards of directors and in management. Under normal market conditions, the fund generally invests substantially all, but at least 80%, of its total assets in the securities comprising the index. In addition, it may invest in equity securities that are not included in the index, cash and cash equivalents or money market instruments. The fund is non-diversified. **Top Holdings:** Johnson & Johnson Coca-Cola Co The Home Depot Inc Wells Fargo & Co Mastercard Inc A

Direxion Daily Energy Bull 3X Shares   D   SELL

Ticker	Traded On	NAV	Total Assets ($)	Dividend Yield (TTM)	Turnover Ratio	Expense Ratio
ERX	NYSE Arca	15.15	$365,372,267	2.55	59	1.1

Ratings
Reward	D
Risk	D
Recent Upgrade/Downgrade	Down

Fund Information
Fund Type	Exchange Traded Funds
Category	Trading Tools
Sub-Category	Trading--Leveraged Equity
Prospectus Objective	Natl Res
Inception Date	Nov-08
Open to New Investments	Y

Prices
Price (as of 12/31/2018)	15.15
52-Week High	43.69
52-Week Low	12.78

Total Returns (%)
3-Month	6-Month	1-Year	3-Year	5-Year
-60.89	-57.97	-55.83	-33.79	-82.69

3-Year Standard Deviation	55.91
Effective Duration	

Valuation
Premium/Discount (1-Year Average)	0.02

Company Information
Provider	Direxion Funds
Manager/Tenure	Paul Brigandi (10), Tony Ng (3)
Website	http://www.direxionfunds.com
Address	Direxion Funds 1301 Avenue Of The Americas (6th Avenue) New York NY 10019 United States
Phone Number	646-572-3390

PERFORMANCE

Ratings History
Date	Overall Rating	Risk Rating	Reward Rating
Q4-18	D	D	D
Q2-18	C-	D+	C
Q4-17	D	D+	D
Q4-16	D	D	D+
Q4-15	D	D	D

Asset & Performance History
Date	NAV	1-Year Total Return
2017	34.85	-11.7
2016	39.87	69.8
2015	23.48	-61.16
2014	60.46	-32.7
2013	89.84	84.89
2012	48.59	3.71

Total Assets: $365,372,267
Asset Allocation
Asset	%
Cash	37%
Stocks	63%
US Stocks	63%
Bonds	0%
US Bonds	0%
Other	0%

Services Offered:

Investment Strategy: The investment seeks daily investment results, before fees and expenses, of 300% of the daily performance of the Energy Select Sector Index. The fund invests at least 80% of its net assets (plus borrowing for investment purposes) in securities of the index, ETFs that track the index and other financial instruments that provide daily leveraged exposure to the index or ETFs that track the index. The index is provided by S&P Dow Jones indices (the "index provider") and includes domestic companies from the energy sector which includes the following industries: oil, gas and consumable fuels; and energy equipment and services. The fund is non-diversified. **Top Holdings:** Energy Select Sector SPDR® ETF   Energy Select Sector   Energy Select Sector Energy Select Sector   Energy Select Sector

---

SPDR® Portfolio Long Term Corporate Bond ETF   C-   HOLD

Ticker	Traded On	NAV	Total Assets ($)	Dividend Yield (TTM)	Turnover Ratio	Expense Ratio
SPLB	NYSE Arca	25.30	$364,980,133	4.61	20	0.07

Ratings
Reward	D+
Risk	C
Recent Upgrade/Downgrade	Down

Fund Information
Fund Type	Exchange Traded Funds
Category	US Fixed Income
Sub-Category	Corporate Bond
Prospectus Objective	Corp Bond - Gen
Inception Date	Mar-09
Open to New Investments	Y

Prices
Price (as of 12/31/2018)	25.38
52-Week High	28.61
52-Week Low	24.89

Total Returns (%)
3-Month	6-Month	1-Year	3-Year	5-Year
-1.63	-0.61	-7.43	15.29	27.24

3-Year Standard Deviation	7.13
Effective Duration	13.40

Valuation
Premium/Discount (1-Year Average)	-0.09

Company Information
Provider	SPDR State Street Global Advisors
Manager/Tenure	Kyle Kelly (6), Christopher DiStefano (4), Frank Miethe (2)
Website	http://www.spdrs.com
Address	SPDR State Street Global Advisors State Street Financial Center, 1 Lincoln Street Boston MA 02111-2900 United States
Phone Number	617-786-3000

PERFORMANCE

Ratings History
Date	Overall Rating	Risk Rating	Reward Rating
Q4-18	C-	C	D+
Q2-18	C	C+	C-
Q4-17	B	B	B-
Q4-16	C	C-	C
Q4-15	C	C	C-

Asset & Performance History
Date	NAV	1-Year Total Return
2017	28.55	11.79
2016	26.54	10.87
2015	24.96	-4.53
2014	27.34	15.61
2013	24.71	-5.9
2012	27.53	11.96

Total Assets: $364,980,133
Asset Allocation
Asset	%
Cash	0%
Stocks	0%
US Stocks	0%
Bonds	100%
US Bonds	89%
Other	0%

Services Offered:

Investment Strategy: The investment seeks to provide investment results that, before fees and expenses, correspond generally to the price and yield performance of the Bloomberg Barclays U.S. Long Term Corporate Bond Index. The fund generally invests substantially all, but at least 80%, of its total assets in the securities comprising the index or in securities that the Adviser determines have economic characteristics that are substantially identical to the economic characteristics of the securities that comprise the index. The index is designed to measure the performance of U.S. corporate bonds that have a maturity of greater than or equal to 10 years. The fund is non-diversified. **Top Holdings:** Anheuser-Busch Companies LLC / Anheuser-Busch InBev Worldwide Inc 4.9% Verizon Communications Inc. 5.01%   CVS Health Corp 5.05%   Verizon Communications Inc. 4.33%   AstraZeneca Plc 6.45%

VelocityShares 3x Inverse Natural Gas ETN Linked to the S&P GSCI® Natural Gas Index ER
C+   HOLD

Ticker	Traded On	NAV	Total Assets ($)	Dividend Yield (TTM)	Turnover Ratio	Expense Ratio
DGAZ	NYSE Arca	123.89	$362,435,397	0		1.65

Ratings
Reward	B
Risk	D+
Recent Upgrade/Downgrade	Up

Fund Information
Fund Type	Exchange Traded Funds
Category	Trading Tools
Sub-Category	Trading--Inverse Commodities
Prospectus Objective	Natl Res
Inception Date	Feb-12
Open to New Investments	Y

Prices
Price (as of 12/31/2018)	118.32
52-Week High	337.40
52-Week Low	17.93

Total Returns (%)
3-Month	6-Month	1-Year	3-Year	5-Year
-63.74	415.33	348.31	99.82	175.31

3-Year Standard Deviation	119.33
Effective Duration	

Valuation
Premium/Discount (1-Year Average)	-0.10

Company Information
Provider	Credit Suisse AG
Manager/Tenure	Management Team (6)
Website	
Address	Kilmore House Park Lane Dublin Ireland
Phone Number	

PERFORMANCE

Ratings History
Date	Overall Rating	Risk Rating	Reward Rating
Q4-18	C+	D+	B
Q2-18	D+	D+	D
Q4-17	C	D+	C+
Q4-16	C-	D	C-
Q4-15	C-	D-	C-

Asset & Performance History
Date	NAV	1-Year Total Return
2017	27.64	98.56
2016	15.4	-80.51
2015	62	48.68
2014	41.7	-7.33
2013	45	-56.6
2012	103.7	

Total Assets: $362,435,397

Asset Allocation
Asset	%
Cash	
Stocks	
US Stocks	
Bonds	
US Bonds	
Other	

Services Offered:

Investment Strategy: The investment seeks to replicate, net of expenses, three times the opposite (inverse) of this GSCI Natural Gas Index ER.
The index comprises futures contracts on a single commodity and is calculated according to the methodology of the S&P GSCI Index. **Top Holdings:**

Oppenheimer S&P MidCap 400 Revenue ETF
C-   HOLD

Ticker	Traded On	NAV	Total Assets ($)	Dividend Yield (TTM)	Turnover Ratio	Expense Ratio
RWK	NYSE Arca	51.27	$362,111,919	1.01		0.39

Ratings
Reward	C-
Risk	C-
Recent Upgrade/Downgrade	Down

Fund Information
Fund Type	Exchange Traded Funds
Category	US Equity Mid Cap
Sub-Category	Mid-Cap Value
Prospectus Objective	Growth
Inception Date	Feb-08
Open to New Investments	Y

Prices
Price (as of 12/31/2018)	51.25
52-Week High	65.07
52-Week Low	48.52

Total Returns (%)
3-Month	6-Month	1-Year	3-Year	5-Year
-17.47	-15.48	-14.49	17.33	21.01

3-Year Standard Deviation	13.21
Effective Duration	

Valuation
Premium/Discount (1-Year Average)	0.04

Company Information
Provider	OppenheimerFunds
Manager/Tenure	Frank Vallario (1), Donal Bishnoi (0)
Website	http://www.oppenheimerfunds.com
Address	OppenheimerFunds 12100 East Iliff Avenue, Suite 300, Aurora, Colorado Aurora CO 80217-5270 United States
Phone Number	800-225-5677

PERFORMANCE

Ratings History
Date	Overall Rating	Risk Rating	Reward Rating
Q4-18	C-	C-	C-
Q2-18	C	C-	C
Q4-17	B	B	B
Q4-16	C+	C-	B
Q4-15	C	C	C

Asset & Performance History
Date	NAV	1-Year Total Return
2017	60.61	12.87
2016	54.11	21.56
2015	45.13	-5.78
2014	48.32	9.47
2013	44.6	40.6
2012	32.16	15.83

Total Assets: $362,111,919

Asset Allocation
Asset	%
Cash	0%
Stocks	100%
US Stocks	100%
Bonds	0%
US Bonds	0%
Other	0%

Services Offered:

Investment Strategy: The investment seeks to provide investment results that correspond generally, before fees and expenses, to the performance of the S&P MidCap 400 Revenue-Weighted Index (the "underlying index"). The fund will normally invest at least 80% of its net assets, plus any borrowings for investment purposes, in the securities of mid capitalization companies included in the underlying index. The underlying index is constructed using a rules-based methodology that re-weights the constituent securities of the S&P MidCap 400® Index (the "parent index") according to the revenue earned by the companies in the parent index, subject to a maximum 5% per company weighting. **Top Holdings:** Tech Data Corp World Fuel Services Corp Arrow Electronics Inc ManpowerGroup Inc AECOM

Amplify Online Retail ETF   C   HOLD

Ticker	Traded On	NAV	Total Assets ($)	Dividend Yield (TTM)	Turnover Ratio	Expense Ratio
IBUY	NAS CM	40.19	$361,231,944	0	11	0.65

Ratings
Reward	C+
Risk	C-
Recent Upgrade/Downgrade	Down

Fund Information
Fund Type	Exchange Traded Funds
Category	Consumer Goods & Svcs
Sub-Category	Consumer Cyclical
Prospectus Objective	Growth & Inc
Inception Date	Apr-16
Open to New Investments	Y

Prices
Price (as of 12/31/2018)	40.09
52-Week High	54.51
52-Week Low	37.41

Total Returns (%)
3-Month	6-Month	1-Year	3-Year	5-Year
-22.09	-21.87	-1.56		

3-Year Standard Deviation

Effective Duration

Valuation
Premium/Discount (1-Year Average)	0.09

Company Information
Provider	Amplifyetfs
Manager/Tenure	Anand Desai (2), Dustin Lewellyn (2), Ernesto Tong (2)
Website	http://www.amplifyetfs.com
Address	3250 Lacey Road, Suite 130 Downers Grove Downers Grove IL 60515 United States
Phone Number	630-487-2530

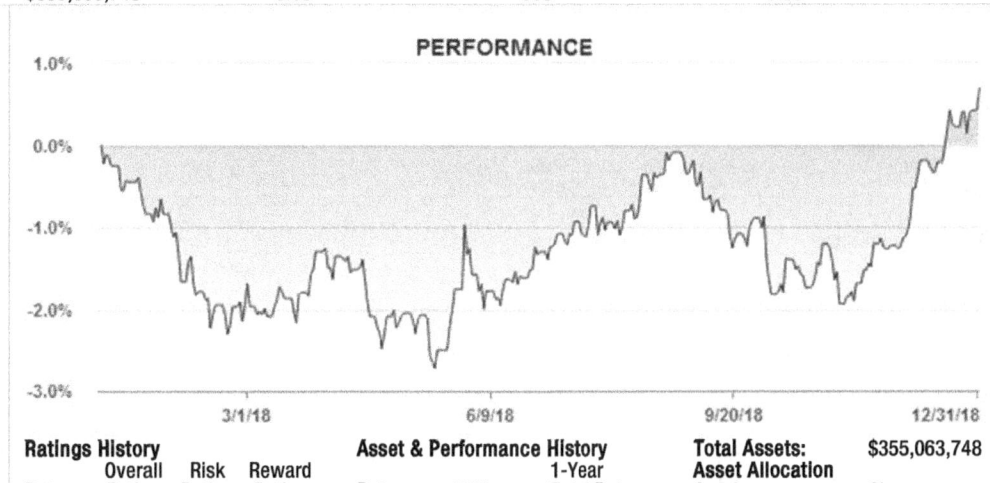

PERFORMANCE

Ratings History
Date	Overall Rating	Risk Rating	Reward Rating
Q4-18	C	C-	C+
Q2-18	C	C-	B-
Q4-17	D+	B+	C
Q4-16	U		
Q4-15			

Asset & Performance History
Date	NAV	1-Year Total Return
2017	40.83	50.16
2016	27.19	
2015		
2014		
2013		
2012		

Total Assets: $361,231,944
Asset Allocation
Asset	%
Cash	0%
Stocks	100%
US Stocks	78%
Bonds	0%
US Bonds	0%
Other	0%

Services Offered:

Investment Strategy: The investment seeks investment results that generally correspond (before fees and expenses) to the price and yield of the EQM Online Retail Index. The fund will invest at least 80% of its total assets in global equity securities that comprise the index, which will primarily include common stocks and/or depositary receipts, such as ADRs and GDRs. The index seeks to measure the performance of global equity securities of publicly traded companies with significant revenue from the online retail business. The index methodology is designed to result in a portfolio that has the potential for capital appreciation. The fund is non-diversified. **Top Holdings:** Lands' End Inc TripAdvisor Inc Wayfair Inc Class A Etsy Inc Nutrisystem Inc

---

First Trust TCW Opportunistic Fixed Income ETF   D+   SELL

Ticker	Traded On	NAV	Total Assets ($)	Dividend Yield (TTM)	Turnover Ratio	Expense Ratio
FIXD	NAS CM	49.37	$355,063,748	3.08	358	0.55

Ratings
Reward	D
Risk	C-
Recent Upgrade/Downgrade	

Fund Information
Fund Type	Exchange Traded Funds
Category	US Fixed Income
Sub-Category	Intermediate-Term Bond
Prospectus Objective	Growth & Inc
Inception Date	Feb-17
Open to New Investments	Y

Prices
Price (as of 12/31/2018)	49.34
52-Week High	50.75
52-Week Low	48.40

Total Returns (%)
3-Month	6-Month	1-Year	3-Year	5-Year
1.72	2.01	0.69		

3-Year Standard Deviation

Effective Duration   6.19

Valuation
Premium/Discount (1-Year Average)	0.03

Company Information
Provider	First Trust
Manager/Tenure	Stephen M. Kane (1), Laird R. Landmann (1), Tad Rivelle (1), 1 other
Website	http://www.ftportfolios.com/
Address	First Trust 120 E. Liberty Drive, Suite 400 Wheaton IL 60187 United States
Phone Number	800-621-1675

PERFORMANCE

Ratings History
Date	Overall Rating	Risk Rating	Reward Rating
Q4-18	D+	C-	D
Q2-18	D+	C-	D+
Q4-17	U		
Q4-16			
Q4-15			

Asset & Performance History
Date	NAV	1-Year Total Return
2017	50.66	
2016		
2015		
2014		
2013		
2012		

Total Assets: $355,063,748
Asset Allocation
Asset	%
Cash	4%
Stocks	0%
US Stocks	0%
Bonds	96%
US Bonds	92%
Other	0%

Services Offered:

Investment Strategy: The investment seeks to maximize long-term total return. The fund pursues its objective by investing at least 80% of its net assets (including investment borrowings) in fixed income securities. It may invest up to 35% of its net assets in corporate, non-U.S. and non-agency debt and other securities rated below investment grade by one or more nationally recognized statistical rating organization ("NRSRO"), or, if unrated, judged to be of comparable quality by the Sub-Advisor. The fund is non-diversified. **Top Holdings:** US 5 Year Note (CBT) Mar19 United States Treasury Notes 2.88% 2 Year US Treasury Note Future Mar19 United States Treasury Bonds 3% United States Treasury Notes 3.12%

Goldman Sachs Access Investment Grade Corporate Bond ETF D SELL

Ticker	Traded On	NAV		Total Assets ($)	Dividend Yield (TTM)	Turnover Ratio	Expense Ratio
GIGB	NYSE Arca	47.26		$353,867,371	3.26	22	0.14

Ratings

Reward	D
Risk	C-
Recent Upgrade/Downgrade	Down

Fund Information

Fund Type	Exchange Traded Funds
Category	Canada Fixed Income
Sub-Category	Corporate Bond
Prospectus Objective	Corp Bond - Gen
Inception Date	Jun-17
Open to New Investments	Y

Prices

Price (as of 12/31/2018)	47.27
52-Week High	50.22
52-Week Low	46.80

Total Returns (%)

3-Month	6-Month	1-Year	3-Year	5-Year
-0.65	0.35	-3.12		

3-Year Standard Deviation	
Effective Duration	

Valuation

Premium/Discount (1-Year Average)	-0.05

Company Information

Provider	Goldman Sachs
Manager/Tenure	Jason Singer (1), David Westbrook (0)
Website	http://www.gsamfunds.com
Address	Goldman Sachs 200 West Stree New York NY 10282 United States
Phone Number	800-526-7384

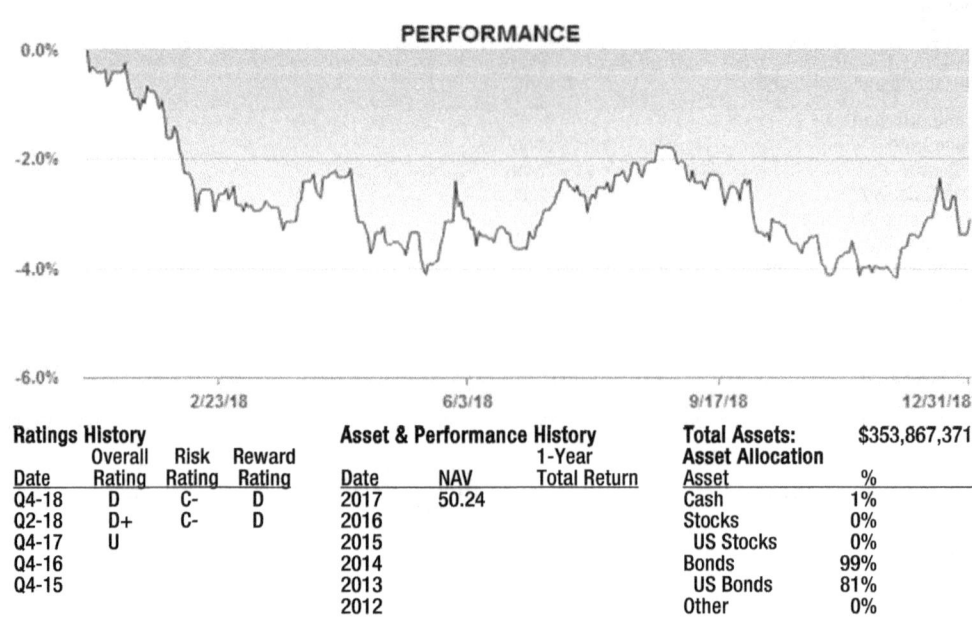

Ratings History

Date	Overall Rating	Risk Rating	Reward Rating
Q4-18	D	C-	D
Q2-18	D+	C-	D
Q4-17	U		
Q4-16			
Q4-15			

Asset & Performance History

Date	NAV	1-Year Total Return
2017	50.24	
2016		
2015		
2014		
2013		
2012		

Total Assets: $353,867,371

Asset Allocation

Asset	%
Cash	1%
Stocks	0%
US Stocks	0%
Bonds	99%
US Bonds	81%
Other	0%

Services Offered:

Investment Strategy: The investment seeks to provide investment results that closely correspond, before fees and expenses, to the performance of the FTSE Goldman Sachs Investment Grade Corporate Bond Index (the "index"). The fund seeks to achieve its investment objective by investing at least 80% of its assets (exclusive of collateral held from securities lending) in securities included in its underlying index. The index is a rules-based index that is designed to measure the performance of investment grade, corporate bonds denominated in U.S. dollars ("USD") that meet certain liquidity and fundamental screening criteria. **Top Holdings:** BP Capital Markets plc 3.56% Credit Suisse AG New York Branch 3.62% Anheuser-Busch InBev Finance Inc. 2.62% Unilever Capital Corporation 4.25% State Street Corporation 3.7%

First Trust Consumer Staples AlphaDEX® Fund C+ HOLD

Ticker	Traded On	NAV		Total Assets ($)	Dividend Yield (TTM)	Turnover Ratio	Expense Ratio
FXG	NYSE Arca	42.20		$352,783,801	2.2	100	0.64

Ratings

Reward	B
Risk	C-
Recent Upgrade/Downgrade	Up

Fund Information

Fund Type	Exchange Traded Funds
Category	Consumer Goods & Svcs
Sub-Category	Consumer Defensive
Prospectus Objective	Unaligned
Inception Date	May-07
Open to New Investments	Y

Prices

Price (as of 12/31/2018)	42.20
52-Week High	51.44
52-Week Low	40.68

Total Returns (%)

3-Month	6-Month	1-Year	3-Year	5-Year
-9.22	-8.10	-11.43	-0.01	28.45

3-Year Standard Deviation	9.26
Effective Duration	

Valuation

Premium/Discount (1-Year Average)	-0.02

Company Information

Provider	First Trust
Manager/Tenure	Jon C. Erickson (11), Daniel J. Lindquist (11), David G. McGarel (11), 3 others
Website	http://www.ftportfolios.com/
Address	First Trust 120 E. Liberty Drive, Suite 400 Wheaton IL 60187 United States
Phone Number	800-621-1675

Ratings History

Date	Overall Rating	Risk Rating	Reward Rating
Q4-18	C+	C-	B
Q2-18	C+	C-	B-
Q4-17	B-	B+	C+
Q4-16	B-	C	B
Q4-15	B+	B	A-

Asset & Performance History

Date	NAV	1-Year Total Return
2017	48.64	7.8
2016	45.75	4.72
2015	44.43	6.13
2014	42.57	21.04
2013	35.64	41.94
2012	25.37	9.39

Total Assets: $352,783,801

Asset Allocation

Asset	%
Cash	0%
Stocks	100%
US Stocks	98%
Bonds	0%
US Bonds	0%
Other	0%

Services Offered:

Investment Strategy: The investment seeks investment results that correspond generally to the price and yield (before the fund's fees and expenses) of an equity index called the StrataQuant® Consumer Staples Index. The fund will normally invest at least 90% of its net assets (including investment borrowings) in common stocks that comprise the index. The index is a modified equal-dollar weighted index designed by IDI to objectively identify and select stocks from the Russell 1000® Index in the consumer staples sector that may generate positive alpha relative to traditional passive-style indices through the use of the AlphaDEX® selection methodology. **Top Holdings:** Pilgrims Pride Corp Molson Coors Brewing Co B JM Smucker Co Sprouts Farmers Market Inc Tyson Foods Inc Class A

Direxion Daily MSCI Brazil Bull 3X Shares   D+   SELL

Ticker	Traded On	NAV	Total Assets ($)	Dividend Yield (TTM)	Turnover Ratio	Expense Ratio
BRZU	NYSE Arca	25.03	$352,111,744	1.46	42	1.29

Ratings
Reward	C-
Risk	D
Recent Upgrade/Downgrade	Up

Fund Information
Fund Type	Exchange Traded Funds
Category	Trading Tools
Sub-Category	Trading--Leveraged Equity
Prospectus Objective	Foreign Stock
Inception Date	Apr-13
Open to New Investments	Y

Prices
Price (as of 12/31/2018)	24.97
52-Week High	63.39
52-Week Low	14.42

Total Returns (%)
3-Month	6-Month	1-Year	3-Year	5-Year
35.55	44.63	-37.21	121.03	-87.40

3-Year Standard Deviation	108.08
Effective Duration	

Valuation
Premium/Discount (1-Year Average)	-0.03

Company Information
Provider	Direxion Funds
Manager/Tenure	Paul Brigandi (5), Tony Ng (3)
Website	http://www.direxionfunds.com
Address	Direxion Funds 1301 Avenue Of The Americas (6th Avenue) New York NY 10019 United States
Phone Number	646-572-3390

PERFORMANCE

Ratings History
Date	Overall Rating	Risk Rating	Reward Rating
Q4-18	D+	D	C-
Q2-18	D+	D	C-
Q4-17	C-	D	C
Q4-16	D	D	D+
Q4-15	D-	D-	D-

Asset & Performance History
Date	NAV	1-Year Total Return
2017	40.36	31.19
2016	31.02	168.34
2015	11.56	-86.92
2014	88.4	-56.43
2013	202.9	
2012		

Total Assets: $352,111,744
Asset Allocation
Asset	%
Cash	21%
Stocks	79%
US Stocks	0%
Bonds	0%
US Bonds	0%
Other	0%

Services Offered:

Investment Strategy: The investment seeks daily investment results, before fees and expenses, of 300% of the daily performance of the MSCI Brazil 25/50 Index. The fund invests at least 80% of its net assets (plus borrowing for investment purposes) in securities of the index, exchange-traded funds ("ETFs") that track the index and other financial instruments that provide daily leveraged exposure to the index or ETFs that track the index. The index is designed to measure the performance of the large- and mid-capitalization segments of the Brazilian equity market, covering approximately 85% of the free float-adjusted market capitalization of Brazilian issuers. It is non-diversified. **Top Holdings:** iShares MSCI Brazil Capped ETF Msci Brazil Index Swap Msci Brazil Index Swap Msci Brazil Index Swap Msci Brazil Index Swap

---

Invesco S&P 500® Equal Weight Financials ETF   C-   HOLD

Ticker	Traded On	NAV	Total Assets ($)	Dividend Yield (TTM)	Turnover Ratio	Expense Ratio
RYF	NYSE Arca	36.36	$348,290,191	1.74		0.4

Ratings
Reward	C
Risk	C-
Recent Upgrade/Downgrade	Down

Fund Information
Fund Type	Exchange Traded Funds
Category	Financials Sector Equity
Sub-Category	Financial
Prospectus Objective	Financial
Inception Date	Nov-06
Open to New Investments	Y

Prices
Price (as of 12/31/2018)	36.35
52-Week High	47.31
52-Week Low	34.13

Total Returns (%)
3-Month	6-Month	1-Year	3-Year	5-Year
-15.00	-13.55	-15.62	26.53	43.31

3-Year Standard Deviation	14.38
Effective Duration	

Valuation
Premium/Discount (1-Year Average)	0.04

Company Information
Provider	Invesco
Manager/Tenure	Peter Hubbard (0), Michael Jeanette (0), Jonathan Nixon (0), 1 other
Website	http://www.invesco.com/us
Address	Invesco 11 Greenway Plaza, Ste. 2500 Houston TX 77046 United States
Phone Number	800-659-1005

PERFORMANCE

Ratings History
Date	Overall Rating	Risk Rating	Reward Rating
Q4-18	C-	C-	C
Q2-18	C	C-	C
Q4-17	A-	B	A
Q4-16	C	C-	C
Q4-15	C	C	C+

Asset & Performance History
Date	NAV	1-Year Total Return
2017	44.06	22.32
2016	36.83	-14.75
2015	30.13	-1.19
2014	31.16	14.63
2013	27.65	37.73
2012	20.43	25.27

Total Assets: $348,290,191
Asset Allocation
Asset	%
Cash	0%
Stocks	100%
US Stocks	99%
Bonds	0%
US Bonds	0%
Other	0%

Services Offered:

Investment Strategy: The investment seeks to track the investment results (before fees and expenses) of the S&P 500® Equal Weight Financials Index (the "underlying index"). The fund generally will invest at least 90% of its total assets in the securities that comprise the underlying index. The underlying index is an equal-weighted version of the S&P 500® Financials Index. Strictly in accordance with its guidelines and mandated procedures, the index provider compiles, maintains and calculates the underlying index, which is comprised of common stocks of companies in the financials sector of the S&P 500® Index. The fund is non-diversified. **Top Holdings:** CME Group Inc Class A Aon PLC Willis Towers Watson PLC Franklin Resources Inc Cincinnati Financial Corp

Principal U.S. Small-Cap Multi-Factor Index ETF   C-   HOLD

Ticker	Traded On	NAV	Total Assets ($)	Dividend Yield (TTM)	Turnover Ratio	Expense Ratio
PSC	NAS CM	27.78	$347,637,574	0.97	76	0.38

Ratings
Reward   C-
Risk   C-
Recent Upgrade/Downgrade

Fund Information
Fund Type   Exchange Traded Funds
Category   US Equity Small Cap
Sub-Category   Small Blend
Prospectus Objective   Small Company
Inception Date   Sep-16
Open to New Investments   Y

Prices
Price (as of 12/31/2018)   27.78
52-Week High   35.73
52-Week Low   26.04

Total Returns (%)
3-Month	6-Month	1-Year	3-Year	5-Year
-19.36	-16.87	-9.22		

3-Year Standard Deviation
Effective Duration

Valuation
Premium/Discount (1-Year Average)   0.63

Company Information
Provider   Principal Funds
Manager/Tenure   Paul S. Kim (2), Mark R. Nebelung (2),
                  Jeffrey A. Schwarte (2)
Website   http://www.principalfunds.com
Address   Principal Funds 30 Dan Road Canton
                  MA 2021 United States
Phone Number   800-787-1621

PERFORMANCE

Ratings History
Date	Overall Rating	Risk Rating	Reward Rating
Q4-18	C-	C-	C-
Q2-18	D+	D	C-
Q4-17	D	B	C
Q4-16	U		
Q4-15			

Asset & Performance History
Date	NAV	1-Year Total Return
2017	30.97	13.4
2016	27.59	
2015		
2014		
2013		
2012		

Total Assets: $347,637,574
Asset Allocation
Asset	%
Cash	0%
Stocks	100%
US Stocks	99%
Bonds	0%
US Bonds	0%
Other	0%

Services Offered:

Investment Strategy: The investment seeks investment results that closely correspond, before expenses, to the performance of the Nasdaq U.S. Small Cap Select Leaders Index. The fund invests at least 80% of its net assets, plus any borrowings for investment purposes, in equity securities of companies that compose the index. The index uses a quantitative model designed to identify equity securities (including growth and value stock) of small-capitalization companies in the Nasdaq US Small Cap Index (the "parent index") that exhibit potential for high degrees of sustainable shareholder yield, pricing power and strong momentum, while adjusting for liquidity and quality. **Top Holdings:** Black Hills Corp Deckers Outdoor Corp Patterson Companies Inc Tanger Factory Outlet Centers Inc Redwood Trust Inc

---

ProShares Ultra Bloomberg Crude Oil   D+   SELL

Ticker	Traded On	NAV	Total Assets ($)	Dividend Yield (TTM)	Turnover Ratio	Expense Ratio
UCO	NYSE Arca		$347,604,375	0	0	0.95

Ratings
Reward   D+
Risk   D
Recent Upgrade/Downgrade   Down

Fund Information
Fund Type   Exchange Traded Funds
Category   Trading Tools
Sub-Category   Trading--Leveraged Commodities
Prospectus Objective   Natl Res
Inception Date   Nov-08
Open to New Investments   Y

Prices
Price (as of 12/31/2018)   13.30
52-Week High   38.61
52-Week Low   12.43

Total Returns (%)
3-Month	6-Month	1-Year	3-Year	5-Year
-65.60	-61.26	-45.11	-48.36	-95.95

3-Year Standard Deviation   55.22
Effective Duration

Valuation
Premium/Discount (1-Year Average)   -0.17

Company Information
Provider   ProShares
Manager/Tenure   Management Team (10)
Website   http://www.proshares.com
Address   ProShares 7501 Wisconsin Avenue,
                  Suite 1000 Bethesda MD 20814
                  United States
Phone Number   866-776-5125

PERFORMANCE

Ratings History
Date	Overall Rating	Risk Rating	Reward Rating
Q4-18	D+	D	D+
Q2-18	C	D+	C
Q4-17	D	D	D
Q4-16	E+	D-	E
Q4-15	E+	D-	E+

Asset & Performance History
Date	NAV	1-Year Total Return
2017	23.67	1.41
2016	23.34	-7.23
2015	25.15	-75.21
2014	101.49	-68.37
2013	320.87	9.16
2012	293.93	-28.1

Total Assets: $347,604,375
Asset Allocation
Asset	%
Cash	-100%
Stocks	0%
US Stocks	0%
Bonds	0%
US Bonds	0%
Other	200%

Services Offered:

Investment Strategy: The investment seeks to provide daily investment results (before fees and expenses) that correspond to twice the daily performance of the Bloomberg WTI Crude Oil SubindexSM.
The "Ultra" funds seek results for a single day that match (before fees and expenses) two times (2x) the daily performance of a benchmark. It does not seek to achieve their stated objective over a period greater than a single day. The Bloomberg WTI Crude Oil SubindexSM is designed to track crude oil futures prices. **Top Holdings:** Bloomberg Wti Crude Oil Subindex Swap - Citibank N Wti Crude Oil Future 12/19/2018 (Clf9) Bloomberg Wti Crude Oil Subindex Swap - Gs Bloomberg Wti Crude Oil Subindex Swap - Ubs Ag Bloomberg Wti Crude Oil Subindex Swap - Rbc

Direxion Daily 20+ Year Treasury Bear 3X Shares   C-   HOLD

Ticker	Traded On	NAV	Total Assets ($)	Dividend Yield (TTM)	Turnover Ratio	Expense Ratio
TMV	NYSE Arca	18.43	$346,006,452	0.25	0	1.02

Ratings
Reward	D+
Risk	D+
Recent Upgrade/Downgrade	Up

Fund Information
Fund Type	Exchange Traded Funds
Category	Trading Tools
Sub-Category	Trading--Inverse Debt
Prospectus Objective	Govt Bond - Treasury
Inception Date	Apr-09
Open to New Investments	Y

Prices
Price (as of 12/31/2018)	18.23
52-Week High	23.66
52-Week Low	17.63

Total Returns (%)
3-Month	6-Month	1-Year	3-Year	5-Year
-13.58	-3.08	5.67	-33.51	-75.01

3-Year Standard Deviation	29.71
Effective Duration	

Valuation
Premium/Discount (1-Year Average)	0.08

Company Information
Provider	Direxion Funds
Manager/Tenure	Paul Brigandi (9), Tony Ng (3)
Website	http://www.direxionfunds.com
Address	Direxion Funds 1301 Avenue Of The Americas (6th Avenue) New York NY 10019 United States
Phone Number	646-572-3390

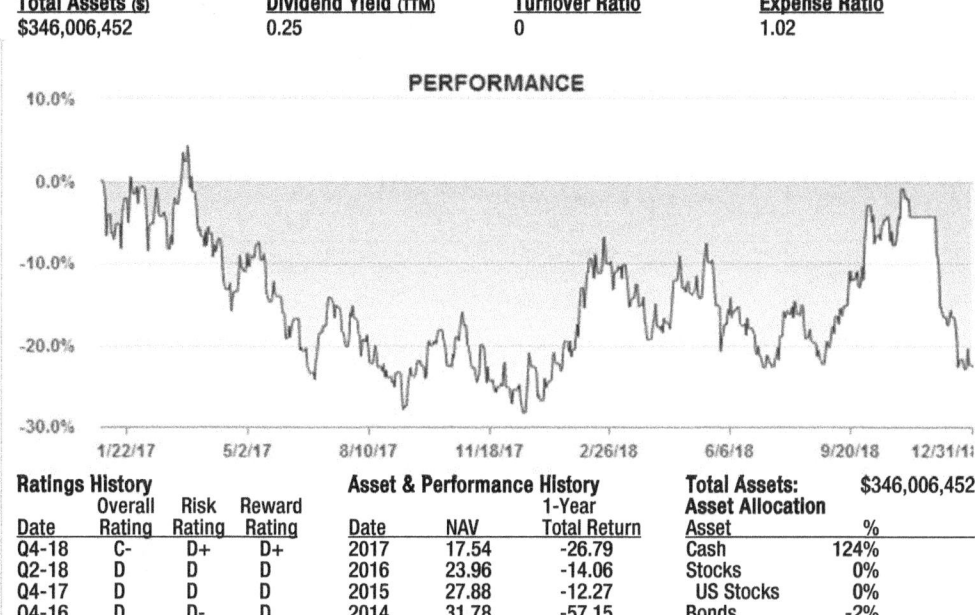

PERFORMANCE

Ratings History
Date	Overall Rating	Risk Rating	Reward Rating
Q4-18	C-	D+	D+
Q2-18	D	D	D
Q4-17	D	D	D
Q4-16	D	D-	D
Q4-15	D	D	D-

Asset & Performance History
Date	NAV	1-Year Total Return
2017	17.54	-26.79
2016	23.96	-14.06
2015	27.88	-12.27
2014	31.78	-57.15
2013	74.17	37.45
2012	53.96	-20.71

Total Assets: $346,006,452
Asset Allocation
Asset	%
Cash	124%
Stocks	0%
US Stocks	0%
Bonds	-2%
US Bonds	-2%
Other	-22%

Services Offered:

Investment Strategy: The investment seeks daily investment results before fees and expenses of 300% of the inverse (or opposite) of the daily performance of the ICE U.S. Treasury 20+ Year Bond Index. The fund, under normal circumstances, invests in swap agreements, futures contracts, short positions or other financial instruments that, in combination, provide inverse (opposite) or short leveraged exposure to the index equal to at least 80% of the fund's net assets (plus borrowing for investment purposes). The index is a market value weighted index that includes publicly issued U.S. Treasury securities that have a remaining maturity of greater than 20 years. It is non-diversified. **Top Holdings:** 20+ Yr Treas Bd Idx Swap   20+ Yr Treas Bd Idx Swap   20+ Yr Treas Bd Idx Swap   20+ Yr Treas Bd Idx Swap   20+ Yr Treas Bd Idx Swap

---

PIMCO RAFI Dynamic Multi-Factor Emerging Markets Equity ETF   D   SELL

Ticker	Traded On	NAV	Total Assets ($)	Dividend Yield (TTM)	Turnover Ratio	Expense Ratio
MFEM	NYSE Arca	22.07	$345,920,055	1.37	52	0.49

Ratings
Reward	D
Risk	D
Recent Upgrade/Downgrade	

Fund Information
Fund Type	Exchange Traded Funds
Category	Global Emerg Mkts Equity
Sub-Category	Diversified Emerging Mkts
Prospectus Objective	Div Emerg Mkts
Inception Date	Aug-17
Open to New Investments	Y

Prices
Price (as of 12/31/2018)	22.10
52-Week High	28.32
52-Week Low	21.67

Total Returns (%)
3-Month	6-Month	1-Year	3-Year	5-Year
-7.10	-4.57	-12.73		

3-Year Standard Deviation	
Effective Duration	

Valuation
Premium/Discount (1-Year Average)	0.29

Company Information
Provider	PIMCO
Manager/Tenure	Thomas C. Seto (1)
Website	http://www.pimco.com
Address	PIMCO 840 Newport Center Drive, Suite 100 Newport Beach CA 92660 United States
Phone Number	866-746-2602

PERFORMANCE

Ratings History
Date	Overall Rating	Risk Rating	Reward Rating
Q4-18	D	D	D
Q2-18	U		
Q4-17	U		
Q4-16			
Q4-15			

Asset & Performance History
Date	NAV	1-Year Total Return
2017	26.03	
2016		
2015		
2014		
2013		
2012		

Total Assets: $345,920,055
Asset Allocation
Asset	%
Cash	2%
Stocks	98%
US Stocks	0%
Bonds	0%
US Bonds	0%
Other	0%

Services Offered:

Investment Strategy: The investment seeks to track the investment results of the RAFI Dynamic Multi-Factor Emerging Markets Index. The fund seeks to achieve its investment objective by investing at least 80% of its total assets (exclusive of collateral held from securities lending) in the component securities of the RAFI Dynamic Multi-Factor Emerging Markets Index. The underlying index is constructed by RAFI Indices, LLC using a rules-based approach to construct factor portfolios within the underlying index. The underlying index consists of "factor portfolios," each of which emphasizes one of the following factors: value, low volatility, quality and momentum. **Top Holdings:** Vale SA ADR   Taiwan Semiconductor Manufacturing Co Ltd ADR   PJSC Lukoil ADR   Infosys Ltd ADR   Gazprom PJSC

Vanguard Russell 2000 Value Index Fund ETF Shares   C-   HOLD

Ticker	Traded On	NAV	Total Assets ($)	Dividend Yield (TTM)	Turnover Ratio	Expense Ratio
VTWV	NAS CM		$341,275,105	1.89	30	0.2

Ratings
Reward	C-
Risk	D+
Recent Upgrade/Downgrade	Down

Fund Information
Fund Type	Exchange Traded Funds
Category	US Equity Small Cap
Sub-Category	Small Value
Prospectus Objective	Small Company
Inception Date	Sep-10
Open to New Investments	Y

Prices
Price (as of 12/31/2018)	93.33
52-Week High	119.34
52-Week Low	88.80

Total Returns (%)
3-Month	6-Month	1-Year	3-Year	5-Year
-18.07	-18.20	-13.35	22.84	18.14

3-Year Standard Deviation	14.52
Effective Duration	

Valuation
Premium/Discount (1-Year Average)	0.09

Company Information
Provider	Vanguard
Manager/Tenure	Walter Nejman (3), Michael A. Johnson (2)
Website	http://www.vanguard.com
Address	Vanguard 100 Vanguard Boulevard Malvern PA 19355 United States
Phone Number	877-662-7447

PERFORMANCE

Ratings History
Date	Overall Rating	Risk Rating	Reward Rating
Q4-18	C-	D+	C-
Q2-18	C	D+	C+
Q4-17	B	B	B+
Q4-16	D+	D+	D+
Q4-15	C	D+	C

Asset & Performance History
Date	NAV	1-Year Total Return
2017	109.12	8.25
2016	102.97	30.55
2015	79.67	-7.58
2014	87.97	4.07
2013	85.98	34.26
2012	64.95	17.8

Total Assets: $341,275,105
Asset Allocation
Asset	%
Cash	2%
Stocks	98%
US Stocks	97%
Bonds	0%
US Bonds	0%
Other	0%

Services Offered:

Investment Strategy: The investment seeks to track the performance of a benchmark index that measures the investment return of small-capitalization value stocks in the United States. The fund employs an indexing investment approach designed to track the performance of the Russell 2000® Value Index. The index is designed to measure the performance of small-capitalization value stocks in the United States. The advisor attempts to replicate the target index by investing all, or substantially all, of its assets in the stocks that make up the index, holding each stock in approximately the same proportion as its weighting in the index. **Top Holdings:** Idacorp Inc Ciena Corp MGIC Investment Corp CACI International Inc Class A Radian Group Inc

---

Invesco DWA SmallCap Momentum ETF   C-   HOLD

Ticker	Traded On	NAV	Total Assets ($)	Dividend Yield (TTM)	Turnover Ratio	Expense Ratio
DWAS	NAS CM	43.66	$338,898,215	0.2		0.6

Ratings
Reward	C-
Risk	C-
Recent Upgrade/Downgrade	Down

Fund Information
Fund Type	Exchange Traded Funds
Category	US Equity Small Cap
Sub-Category	Small Growth
Prospectus Objective	Small Company
Inception Date	Jul-12
Open to New Investments	

Prices
Price (as of 12/31/2018)	43.50
52-Week High	59.39
52-Week Low	40.08

Total Returns (%)
3-Month	6-Month	1-Year	3-Year	5-Year
-22.47	-20.06	-10.18	16.84	11.09

3-Year Standard Deviation	17.6
Effective Duration	

Valuation
Premium/Discount (1-Year Average)	0.08

Company Information
Provider	Invesco
Manager/Tenure	Peter Hubbard (6), Michael Jeanette (6), Tony Seisser (4), 1 other
Website	http://www.invesco.com/us
Address	Invesco 11 Greenway Plaza, Ste. 2500 Houston TX 77046 United States
Phone Number	800-659-1005

PERFORMANCE

Ratings History
Date	Overall Rating	Risk Rating	Reward Rating
Q4-18	C-	C-	C-
Q2-18	C	C-	C+
Q4-17	B	B-	B+
Q4-16	C-	C-	C
Q4-15	C	C-	C

Asset & Performance History
Date	NAV	1-Year Total Return
2017	48.63	20.58
2016	40.41	7.88
2015	37.66	-3.33
2014	39.03	-1.64
2013	39.7	49.19
2012	26.66	

Total Assets: $338,898,215
Asset Allocation
Asset	%
Cash	0%
Stocks	100%
US Stocks	99%
Bonds	0%
US Bonds	0%
Other	0%

Services Offered:

Investment Strategy: The investment seeks to track the investment results (before fees and expenses) of the Dorsey Wright® SmallCap Technical Leaders Index (the "underlying index"). The fund generally will invest at least 90% of its total assets in equity securities of small capitalization companies that comprise the underlying index. The index provider selects such securities pursuant to its proprietary selection methodology, which is designed to identify securities that demonstrate powerful relative strength characteristics. **Top Holdings:** CareDx Inc Endocyte Inc Codexis Inc Heska Corp ePlus Inc

Aberdeen Standard Physical Precious Metals Basket Shares ETF   D+   SELL

Ticker	Traded On	NAV	Total Assets ($)	Dividend Yield (TTM)	Turnover Ratio	Expense Ratio
GLTR	NYSE Arca	63.03	$337,031,257	0		0.6

Ratings
Reward	D
Risk	D+

Recent Upgrade/Downgrade

Fund Information
Fund Type	Exchange Traded Funds
Category	Commodities Specified
Sub-Category	Commodities Precious Metals
Prospectus Objective	Prec Metals
Inception Date	Oct-10
Open to New Investments	Y

Prices
Price (as of 12/31/2018)	63.16
52-Week High	67.81
52-Week Low	56.51

Total Returns (%)
3-Month	6-Month	1-Year	3-Year	5-Year
7.90	3.12	-2.48	20.78	-4.37

3-Year Standard Deviation	13.79
Effective Duration	

Valuation
Premium/Discount (1-Year Average)	0.09

Company Information
Provider	Aberdeen Standard Investments
Manager/Tenure	Management Team (8)
Website	http://www.aberdeenstandardetfs.us
Address	Aberdeen Standard Investments 405 Lexington Avenue New York NY 10174 United States
Phone Number	212-918-4954

PERFORMANCE

Ratings History
Date	Overall Rating	Risk Rating	Reward Rating
Q4-18	D+	D+	D
Q2-18	C-	C-	C
Q4-17	C-	C-	C-
Q4-16	D+	D+	C-
Q4-15	D-	D-	D-

Asset & Performance History
Date	NAV	1-Year Total Return
2017	64.63	11.21
2016	58.11	11.36
2015	52.18	-15.28
2014	61.6	-6.54
2013	65.91	-28.29
2012	91.93	5.72

Total Assets: $337,031,257
Asset Allocation
Asset	%
Cash	0%
Stocks	0%
US Stocks	0%
Bonds	0%
US Bonds	0%
Other	100%

Services Offered:

Investment Strategy: The investment objective of the Trust is for the Shares to reflect the performance of the price of physical gold, silver, platinum and palladium in the proportions held by the Trust, less the expenses of the Trust's operations.
The Shares are designed for investors who want a cost-effective and convenient way to invest in a basket of Bullion with minimal credit risk. **Top Holdings:** Physical Gold Bullion Physical Silver Bullion Physical Palladium Bullion Physical Platinum Bullion

---

John Hancock Multifactor Small Cap ETF   D   SELL

Ticker	Traded On	NAV	Total Assets ($)	Dividend Yield (TTM)	Turnover Ratio	Expense Ratio
JHSC	NYSE Arca	22.63	$336,070,936	0.55	17	0.5

Ratings
Reward	D
Risk	D

Recent Upgrade/Downgrade

Fund Information
Fund Type	Exchange Traded Funds
Category	US Equity Small Cap
Sub-Category	Small Blend
Prospectus Objective	Small Company
Inception Date	Nov-17
Open to New Investments	Y

Prices
Price (as of 12/31/2018)	22.62
52-Week High	28.48
52-Week Low	21.34

Total Returns (%)
3-Month	6-Month	1-Year	3-Year	5-Year
-17.83	-15.64	-12.12		

3-Year Standard Deviation	
Effective Duration	

Valuation
Premium/Discount (1-Year Average)	0.20

Company Information
Provider	John Hancock
Manager/Tenure	Joel P. Schneider (1), Lukas J. Smart (1), Joseph F. Hohn (0)
Website	http://jhinvestments.com
Address	601 Congress Street, Boston MA 02210 United States
Phone Number	800-225-5913

PERFORMANCE

Ratings History
Date	Overall Rating	Risk Rating	Reward Rating
Q4-18	D	D	D
Q2-18	U		
Q4-17	U		
Q4-16			
Q4-15			

Asset & Performance History
Date	NAV	1-Year Total Return
2017	26.01	
2016		
2015		
2014		
2013		
2012		

Total Assets: $336,070,936
Asset Allocation
Asset	%
Cash	7%
Stocks	93%
US Stocks	92%
Bonds	0%
US Bonds	0%
Other	0%

Services Offered:

Investment Strategy: The investment seeks to provide investment results that closely correspond, before fees and expenses, to the performance of the John Hancock Dimensional Small Cap Index (the index). The fund normally invests at least 80% of its net assets (plus any borrowings for investment purposes) in securities that compose the fund's index. The index is designed to comprise a subset of securities in the U.S. Universe issued by companies whose market capitalizations are smaller than the 750th largest U.S. company but excluding the smallest 4% of U.S. companies at the time of reconstitution. **Top Holdings:** Integrated Device Technology Inc Primerica Inc Popular Inc Medical Properties Trust Inc Idacorp Inc

iShares Residential Real Estate Capped ETF

C+ HOLD

Ticker	Traded On	NAV		Total Assets ($)	Dividend Yield (TTM)	Turnover Ratio	Expense Ratio
REZ	NYSE Arca	62.39		$334,624,128	3.35	19	0.48

Ratings

Reward	B
Risk	C
Recent Upgrade/Downgrade	

Fund Information

Fund Type	Exchange Traded Funds
Category	Real Estate Sector Equity
Sub-Category	Real Estate
Prospectus Objective	Real Estate
Inception Date	May-07
Open to New Investments	Y

Prices

Price (as of 12/31/2018)	62.34
52-Week High	68.12
52-Week Low	53.95

Total Returns (%)

3-Month	6-Month	1-Year	3-Year	5-Year
1.18	1.38	4.09	11.63	67.81

3-Year Standard Deviation	13.98
Effective Duration	

Valuation

Premium/Discount (1-Year Average)	0.01

Company Information

Provider	iShares
Manager/Tenure	Diane Hsiung (10), Greg Savage (10), Jennifer Hsui (6), 3 others
Website	http://www.ishares.com
Address	iShares 400 Howard Street San Francisco CA 94105 United States
Phone Number	800-474-2737

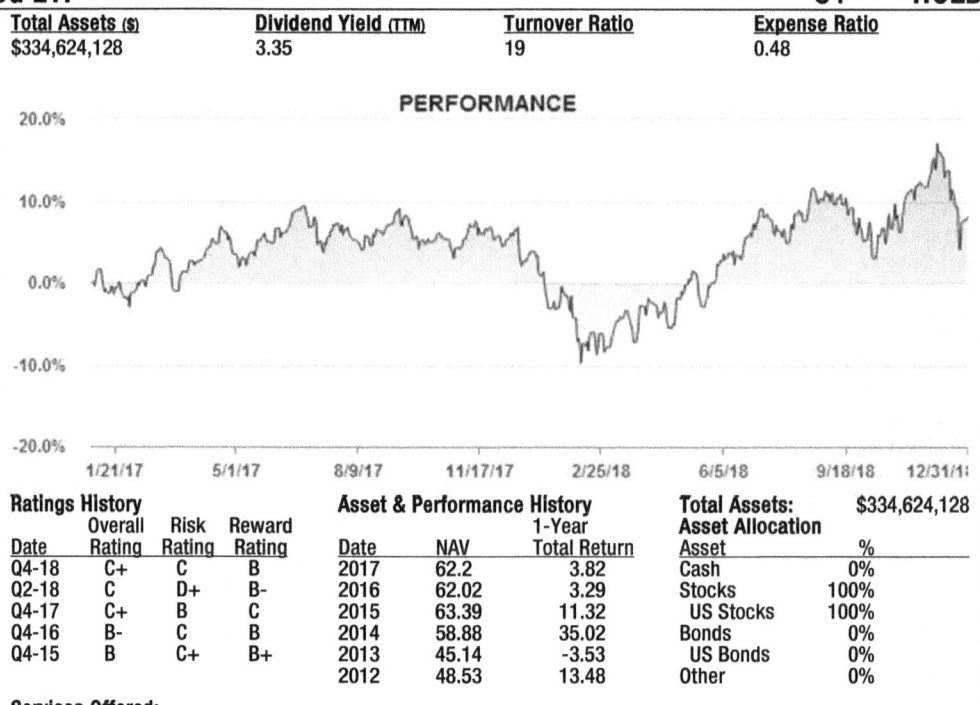

Ratings History

Date	Overall Rating	Risk Rating	Reward Rating
Q4-18	C+	C	B
Q2-18	C	D+	B-
Q4-17	C+	B	C
Q4-16	B-	C	B
Q4-15	B	C+	B+

Asset & Performance History

Date	NAV	1-Year Total Return
2017	62.2	3.82
2016	62.02	3.29
2015	63.39	11.32
2014	58.88	35.02
2013	45.14	-3.53
2012	48.53	13.48

Total Assets: $334,624,128
Asset Allocation

Asset	%
Cash	0%
Stocks	100%
US Stocks	100%
Bonds	0%
US Bonds	0%
Other	0%

Services Offered:

Investment Strategy: The investment seeks to track the investment results of the FTSE Nareit All Residential Capped Index composed of U.S. residential, healthcare and self-storage real estate equities. The fund generally will invest at least 90% of its assets in the component securities of the underlying index and may invest up to 10% of its assets in certain futures, options and swap contracts, cash and cash equivalents. The underlying index measures the performance of the residential apartments, manufactured homes, healthcare and self-storage real estate sectors of the U.S. equity market. The fund is non-diversified. **Top Holdings:** Public Storage Welltower Inc AvalonBay Communities Inc Equity Residential Ventas Inc

---

FlexShares Quality Dividend Defensive Index Fund

C HOLD

Ticker	Traded On	NAV		Total Assets ($)	Dividend Yield (TTM)	Turnover Ratio	Expense Ratio
QDEF	NYSE Arca	39.47		$334,124,760	2.72		0.37

Ratings

Reward	C
Risk	C-
Recent Upgrade/Downgrade	

Fund Information

Fund Type	Exchange Traded Funds
Category	US Equity Large Cap Value
Sub-Category	Large Value
Prospectus Objective	Income
Inception Date	Dec-12
Open to New Investments	Y

Prices

Price (as of 12/31/2018)	39.54
52-Week High	47.54
52-Week Low	37.31

Total Returns (%)

3-Month	6-Month	1-Year	3-Year	5-Year
-15.05	-9.95	-7.96	24.19	40.58

3-Year Standard Deviation	8.56
Effective Duration	

Valuation

Premium/Discount (1-Year Average)	0.13

Company Information

Provider	Flexshares Trust
Manager/Tenure	Robert Anstine (5), Brendan Sullivan (2)
Website	http://www.flexshares.com
Address	50 South LaSalle Street Chicago, Illinois 60603 Chicago Illinois 60603 United States
Phone Number	855-353-9383

Ratings History

Date	Overall Rating	Risk Rating	Reward Rating
Q4-18	C	C-	C
Q2-18	C	C-	C
Q4-17	B-	B	B-
Q4-16	C+	C-	B
Q4-15	C	C	C

Asset & Performance History

Date	NAV	1-Year Total Return
2017	44.05	16.94
2016	38.75	15.39
2015	34.61	-0.19
2014	35.71	13.41
2013	32.32	32.29
2012	24.98	

Total Assets: $334,124,760
Asset Allocation

Asset	%
Cash	2%
Stocks	98%
US Stocks	97%
Bonds	0%
US Bonds	0%
Other	0%

Services Offered:

Investment Strategy: The investment seeks investment results that correspond generally to the price and yield performance, before fees and expenses, of the Northern Trust Quality Dividend Defensive IndexSM. The fund will invest at least 80% of its total assets (exclusive of collateral held from securities lending) in the securities of the underlying index. The underlying index is designed to provide exposure to a high-quality, income-oriented portfolio of U.S. equity securities, with an emphasis on long-term capital growth and a targeted overall volatility that is lower than that of the Northern Trust 1250 IndexSM. **Top Holdings:** Johnson & Johnson Exxon Mobil Corp Cisco Systems Inc Microsoft Corp Walmart Inc

VanEck Vectors Vietnam ETF   C-   HOLD

Ticker	Traded On	NAV	Total Assets ($)	Dividend Yield (TTM)	Turnover Ratio	Expense Ratio
VNM	NYSE Arca	14.84	$333,543,779	1.29	50	0.66

Ratings
Reward   C-
Risk   C-
Recent Upgrade/Downgrade

Fund Information
Fund Type   Exchange Traded Funds
Category   Asia ex-Japan Equity
Sub-Category   Miscellaneous Region
Prospectus Objective   Growth
Inception Date   Aug-09
Open to New Investments   Y

Prices
Price (as of 12/31/2018)   14.75
52-Week High   20.39
52-Week Low   14.49

Total Returns (%)

3-Month	6-Month	1-Year	3-Year	5-Year
-10.33	-5.11	-14.13	5.11	-11.08

3-Year Standard Deviation   14.88
Effective Duration

Valuation
Premium/Discount (1-Year Average)   0.42

Company Information
Provider   VanEck
Manager/Tenure Hao-Hung (Peter) Liao (9), Guo Hua
                (Jason) Jin (0)
Website   http://www.vaneck.com
Address   Van Eck Associates Corporation 666
                Third Avenue New York NY 10017
                United States
Phone Number   800-826-1115

PERFORMANCE

Ratings History

Date	Overall Rating	Risk Rating	Reward Rating
Q4-18	C-	C-	C-
Q2-18	C	C	C
Q4-17	C	C	C
Q4-16	D	D	D
Q4-15	D+	D	D+

Asset & Performance History

Date	NAV	1-Year Total Return
2017	17.45	36.15
2016	12.97	-10.09
2015	14.78	-18.57
2014	18.84	3.89
2013	18.63	12.69
2012	17.06	18.16

Total Assets: $333,543,779
Asset Allocation

Asset	%
Cash	0%
Stocks	100%
US Stocks	3%
Bonds	0%
US Bonds	0%
Other	0%

Services Offered:

Investment Strategy: The investment seeks to replicate as closely as possible, before fees and expenses, the price and yield performance of the MVIS® Vietnam Index. The fund normally invests at least 80% of its total assets in securities that comprise the fund's benchmark index. The index includes securities of Vietnamese companies. A company is generally considered to be a Vietnamese company if it is incorporated in Vietnam or is incorporated outside of Vietnam but has at least 50% of its revenues/related assets in Vietnam. It is non-diversified. **Top Holdings:** Vietnam Dairy Products JSC Vinhomes JSC Vingroup JSC No Va Land Investment Group Corp Ma San Group Corp

---

Columbia Emerging Markets Consumer ETF   D   SELL

Ticker	Traded On	NAV	Total Assets ($)	Dividend Yield (TTM)	Turnover Ratio	Expense Ratio
ECON	NYSE Arca	20.46	$332,155,860	0.46	27	0.59

Ratings
Reward   D
Risk   D
Recent Upgrade/Downgrade   Down

Fund Information
Fund Type   Exchange Traded Funds
Category   Global Emerg Mkts Equity
Sub-Category   Diversified Emerging Mkts
Prospectus Objective   Unaligned
Inception Date   Sep-10
Open to New Investments   Y

Prices
Price (as of 12/31/2018)   20.37
52-Week High   29.85
52-Week Low   19.79

Total Returns (%)

3-Month	6-Month	1-Year	3-Year	5-Year
-7.46	-14.93	-26.72	-2.44	-19.55

3-Year Standard Deviation   15.5
Effective Duration

Valuation
Premium/Discount (1-Year Average)   -0.28

Company Information
Provider   Columbia
Manager/Tenure Christopher Lo (2)
Website   http://www.columbiathreadneedleus.com
Address   Liberty Financial Funds P.O. Box 8081
                Boston MA 02266-8081 United States
Phone Number   800-345-6611

PERFORMANCE

Ratings History

Date	Overall Rating	Risk Rating	Reward Rating
Q4-18	D	D	D
Q2-18	C-	C-	C-
Q4-17	C	C	C
Q4-16	D+	D+	D+
Q4-15	C-	C-	C-

Asset & Performance History

Date	NAV	1-Year Total Return
2017	28.2	26.86
2016	22.31	4.95
2015	21.42	-15.12
2014	25.51	-2.84
2013	26.57	1.66
2012	26.33	20.55

Total Assets: $332,155,860
Asset Allocation

Asset	%
Cash	0%
Stocks	100%
US Stocks	0%
Bonds	0%
US Bonds	0%
Other	0%

Services Offered:

Investment Strategy: The investment seeks investment results that correspond (before fees and expenses) to the price and yield performance of the Dow Jones Emerging Markets Consumer Titans 30TM Index. The fund will invest at least 80% of its net assets in securities of Emerging Markets Consumer companies included in the index and the advisor generally expects to be substantially invested at such times, with at least 95% of its net assets invested in these securities. It is non-diversified. **Top Holdings:** Naspers Ltd Class N Hindustan Unilever Ltd Ambev SA ADR Yum China Holdings Inc PT Astra International Tbk

iShares iBonds Dec 2025 Term Corporate ETF

C-   **HOLD**

Ticker	Traded On	NAV	Total Assets ($)	Dividend Yield (TTM)	Turnover Ratio	Expense Ratio
IBDQ	NYSE Arca	23.68	$331,906,821	3.44	5	0.1

Ratings
Reward	D+
Risk	C-
Recent Upgrade/Downgrade	

Fund Information
Fund Type	Exchange Traded Funds
Category	US Fixed Income
Sub-Category	Corporate Bond
Prospectus Objective	Corp Bond - Gen
Inception Date	Mar-15
Open to New Investments	Y

Prices
Price (as of 12/31/2018)	23.60
52-Week High	25.03
52-Week Low	23.51

Total Returns (%)
3-Month	6-Month	1-Year	3-Year	5-Year
0.34	1.38	-1.69		10.27

3-Year Standard Deviation	3.71
Effective Duration	5.67

Valuation
Premium/Discount (1-Year Average)	0.20

Company Information
Provider	iShares
Manager/Tenure	James Mauro (3), Scott Radell (3)
Website	http://www.ishares.com
Address	iShares 400 Howard Street San Francisco CA 94105 United States
Phone Number	800-474-2737

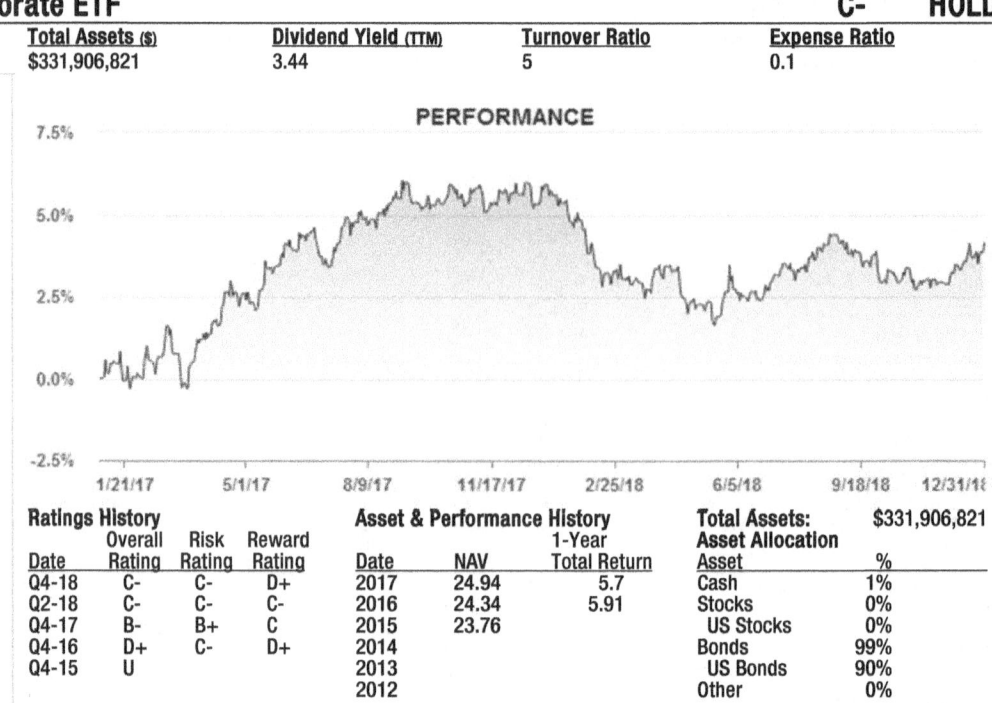

Ratings History

Date	Overall Rating	Risk Rating	Reward Rating
Q4-18	C-	C-	D+
Q2-18	C-	C-	C-
Q4-17	B-	B+	C
Q4-16	D+	C-	D+
Q4-15	U		

Asset & Performance History

Date	NAV	1-Year Total Return
2017	24.94	5.7
2016	24.34	5.91
2015	23.76	
2014		
2013		
2012		

Total Assets: $331,906,821

Asset Allocation

Asset	%
Cash	1%
Stocks	0%
US Stocks	0%
Bonds	99%
US Bonds	90%
Other	0%

Services Offered:

Investment Strategy: The investment seeks to track the investment results of the Bloomberg Barclays December 2025 Maturity Corporate Index which composed of U.S. dollar-denominated, investment-grade corporate bonds maturing in 2025. The fund generally will invest at least 90% of its assets in the component securities of the underlying index. The underlying index is composed of U.S. dollar-denominated, taxable, investment-grade corporate bonds scheduled to mature after December 31, 2024, and before December 16, 2025. **Top Holdings:** AT&T Inc 3.4% CVS Health Corp 4.1% Charter Communications Operating, LLC/Charter Communications Operating Capi Visa Inc 3.15% Medtronic, Inc. 3.5%

Invesco S&P 500 BuyWrite ETF

C   **HOLD**

Ticker	Traded On	NAV	Total Assets ($)	Dividend Yield (TTM)	Turnover Ratio	Expense Ratio
PBP	NYSE Arca	19.80	$331,344,880	1.2	16	0.49

Ratings
Reward	C
Risk	C+
Recent Upgrade/Downgrade	Down

Fund Information
Fund Type	Exchange Traded Funds
Category	Long/Short Equity
Sub-Category	Options-based
Prospectus Objective	Growth
Inception Date	Dec-07
Open to New Investments	Y

Prices
Price (as of 12/31/2018)	19.75
52-Week High	22.88
52-Week Low	19.12

Total Returns (%)
3-Month	6-Month	1-Year	3-Year	5-Year
-11.05	-6.78	-5.26	12.84	23.56

3-Year Standard Deviation	5.78
Effective Duration	

Valuation
Premium/Discount (1-Year Average)	0.08

Company Information
Provider	Invesco
Manager/Tenure	Peter Hubbard (10), Theodore Samulowitz (5), Michael Jeanette (5), 3 others
Website	http://www.invesco.com/us
Address	Invesco 11 Greenway Plaza, Ste. 2500 Houston TX 77046 United States
Phone Number	800-659-1005

Ratings History

Date	Overall Rating	Risk Rating	Reward Rating
Q4-18	C	C+	C
Q2-18	C+	C+	C+
Q4-17	B	B+	C+
Q4-16	C	C-	B-
Q4-15	C+	C+	C+

Asset & Performance History

Date	NAV	1-Year Total Return
2017	21.43	11.5
2016	21.22	6.21
2015	20.5	4.44
2014	20.66	4.83
2013	20.68	12.39
2012	19.67	4.36

Total Assets: $331,344,880

Asset Allocation

Asset	%
Cash	0%
Stocks	100%
US Stocks	99%
Bonds	0%
US Bonds	0%
Other	0%

Services Offered:

Investment Strategy: The investment seeks to track the investment results (before fees and expenses) of the CBOE S&P 500 BuyWrite IndexSM. The fund generally will invest at least 90% of its total assets in securities that comprise the underlying index and will write (sell) call options thereon. The underlying index is a total return benchmark index that is designed to track the performance of a hypothetical "buy-write" strategy on the S&P 500® Index. **Top Holdings:** Microsoft Corp Apple Inc Amazon.com Inc Berkshire Hathaway Inc B Spx 12/21/18 2735 Call

Pacer Trendpilot™ 100 ETF   C   HOLD

Ticker	Traded On	NAV	Total Assets ($)	Dividend Yield (TTM)	Turnover Ratio	Expense Ratio
PTNQ	BATS	32.67	$330,997,576	0.3	3	0.65

Ratings
Reward   C+
Risk   C
Recent Upgrade/Downgrade   Down

Fund Information
Fund Type   Exchange Traded Funds
Category   US Equity Large Cap Growth
Sub-Category   Large Growth
Prospectus Objective   Growth
Inception Date   Jun-15
Open to New Investments   Y

Prices
Price (as of 12/31/2018)   32.68
52-Week High   36.30
52-Week Low   29.80

Total Returns (%)

3-Month	6-Month	1-Year	3-Year	5-Year
-9.27	-2.12	8.83	38.15	

3-Year Standard Deviation   13.05
Effective Duration

Valuation
Premium/Discount (1-Year Average)   0.16

Company Information
Provider   Pacer
Manager/Tenure   Bruce Kavanaugh (3), Michael Mack (3)
Website   http://www.paceretfs.com
Address   Pacer 16 Industrial Blvd, Suite 201 Paoli PA 19301 United States
Phone Number

PERFORMANCE

Ratings History

Date	Overall Rating	Risk Rating	Reward Rating
Q4-18	C	C	C+
Q2-18	C+	C	B-
Q4-17	C	B-	C+
Q4-16	D	C-	C
Q4-15	U		

Asset & Performance History

Date	NAV	1-Year Total Return
2017	30.15	32.08
2016	22.9	-4.01
2015	23.9	
2014		
2013		
2012		

Total Assets: $330,997,576

Asset Allocation

Asset	%
Cash	100%
Stocks	0%
US Stocks	0%
Bonds	0%
US Bonds	0%
Other	0%

Services Offered:

Investment Strategy: The investment seeks to track the total return performance, before fees and expenses, of the Pacer NASDAQ-100 Trendpilot Index. The fund invests at least 80% of its total assets (exclusive of collateral held from securities lending) in the component securities of the index. The index implements a systematic trend-following strategy that directs exposure (i) 100% to the NASDAQ-100, (ii) 50% to the NASDAQ-100 and 50% to 3-Month U.S. Treasury bills, or (iii) 100% to 3-Month U.S. Treasury bills, depending on the relative performance of the NASDAQ-100 TR and its 200-business day historical simple moving average. It is non-diversified. **Top Holdings:** Apple Inc Microsoft Corp Amazon.com Inc Invesco QQQ Trust Alphabet Inc Class C

Global X FinTech ETF   C+   HOLD

Ticker	Traded On	NAV	Total Assets ($)	Dividend Yield (TTM)	Turnover Ratio	Expense Ratio
FINX	NAS CM	22.16	$327,733,185	0.01	12	0.68

Ratings
Reward   B-
Risk   C
Recent Upgrade/Downgrade

Fund Information
Fund Type   Exchange Traded Funds
Category   Technology Sector Equity
Sub-Category   Technology
Prospectus Objective   Technology
Inception Date   Sep-16
Open to New Investments   Y

Prices
Price (as of 12/31/2018)   22.09
52-Week High   29.31
52-Week Low   20.71

Total Returns (%)

3-Month	6-Month	1-Year	3-Year	5-Year
-22.53	-14.92	1.38		

3-Year Standard Deviation
Effective Duration

Valuation
Premium/Discount (1-Year Average)   0.08

Company Information
Provider   Global X Funds
Manager/Tenure   Chang Kim (2), James Ong (2), Nam To (0)
Website   http://www.globalxfunds.com
Address   Global X Funds 600 Lexington Avenue, 20th Floor New York NY 10022 United States
Phone Number   888-493-8631

PERFORMANCE

Ratings History

Date	Overall Rating	Risk Rating	Reward Rating
Q4-18	C+	C	B-
Q2-18	C+	C	B
Q4-17	D	B	C
Q4-16	U		
Q4-15			

Asset & Performance History

Date	NAV	1-Year Total Return
2017	21.86	50.56
2016	14.52	
2015		
2014		
2013		
2012		

Total Assets: $327,733,185

Asset Allocation

Asset	%
Cash	0%
Stocks	100%
US Stocks	71%
Bonds	0%
US Bonds	0%
Other	0%

Services Offered:

Investment Strategy: The investment seeks to provide investment results that correspond generally to the price and yield performance, before fees and expenses, of the Indxx Global Fintech Thematic Index. The fund invests at least 80% of its total assets in the securities of the underlying index. The underlying index is designed to provide exposure to exchange-listed companies in developed markets that provide financial technology products and services, including companies involved in mobile payments, peer-to-peer (P2P) and marketplace lending, financial analytics software and alternative currencies, as defined by the index provider. The fund is non-diversified. **Top Holdings:** Fiserv Inc Square Inc A Intuit Inc Fidelity National Information Services Inc PayPal Holdings Inc

iShares MSCI Japan Small-Cap ETF
C-   HOLD

Ticker	Traded On	NAV		Total Assets ($)	Dividend Yield (TTM)	Turnover Ratio	Expense Ratio
SCJ	NYSE Arca	65.82		$326,365,279	1.32	9	0.47

Ratings
Reward	D+
Risk	C-
Recent Upgrade/Downgrade	Down

Fund Information
Fund Type	Exchange Traded Funds
Category	Japan Equity
Sub-Category	Japan Stock
Prospectus Objective	Pacific Stock
Inception Date	Dec-07
Open to New Investments	Y

Prices
Price (as of 12/31/2018)	65.23
52-Week High	85.22
52-Week Low	61.80

Total Returns (%)
3-Month	6-Month	1-Year	3-Year	5-Year
-14.72	-13.26	-16.35	17.83	33.95

3-Year Standard Deviation	11.57
Effective Duration	

Valuation
Premium/Discount (1-Year Average)	-0.15

Company Information
Provider	iShares
Manager/Tenure	Diane Hsiung (10), Greg Savage (10), Jennifer Hsui (5), 1 other
Website	http://www.ishares.com
Address	iShares 400 Howard Street San Francisco CA 94105 United States
Phone Number	800-474-2737

PERFORMANCE

Ratings History
Date	Overall Rating	Risk Rating	Reward Rating
Q4-18	C-	C-	D+
Q2-18	B-	C+	B-
Q4-17	A	A	A
Q4-16	B	C+	B
Q4-15	C+	C+	C+

Asset & Performance History
Date	NAV	1-Year Total Return
2017	79.73	30.92
2016	61.85	7.6
2015	59.08	14.85
2014	52.23	-1.01
2013	53.97	25.52
2012	43.84	3.85

Total Assets: $326,365,279

Asset Allocation
Asset	%
Cash	1%
Stocks	99%
US Stocks	0%
Bonds	0%
US Bonds	0%
Other	0%

Services Offered:

Investment Strategy: The investment seeks to track the investment results of the MSCI Japan Small Cap Index. The fund generally will invest at least 90% of its assets in the component securities of the underlying index and in investments that have economic characteristics that are substantially identical to the component securities of the underlying index. The index is designed to measure the performance of equity securities of small-capitalization companies in Japan. **Top Holdings:** Sojitz Corp Orix Jreit Inc Advantest Corp PeptiDream Inc GLP J-REIT

Direxion Daily FTSE China Bull 3X Shares
D+   SELL

Ticker	Traded On	NAV		Total Assets ($)	Dividend Yield (TTM)	Turnover Ratio	Expense Ratio
YINN	NYSE Arca	17.42		$325,647,461	2.4	112	1.34

Ratings
Reward	D+
Risk	D+
Recent Upgrade/Downgrade	Down

Fund Information
Fund Type	Exchange Traded Funds
Category	Trading Tools
Sub-Category	Trading--Leveraged Equity
Prospectus Objective	Pacific Stock
Inception Date	Dec-09
Open to New Investments	Y

Prices
Price (as of 12/31/2018)	17.39
52-Week High	53.80
52-Week Low	16.54

Total Returns (%)
3-Month	6-Month	1-Year	3-Year	5-Year
-27.69	-26.61	-48.50	0.22	-40.79

3-Year Standard Deviation	56.74
Effective Duration	

Valuation
Premium/Discount (1-Year Average)	-0.05

Company Information
Provider	Direxion Funds
Manager/Tenure	Paul Brigandi (9), Tony Ng (3)
Website	http://www.direxionfunds.com
Address	Direxion Funds 1301 Avenue Of The Americas (6th Avenue) New York NY 10019 United States
Phone Number	646-572-3390

PERFORMANCE

Ratings History
Date	Overall Rating	Risk Rating	Reward Rating
Q4-18	D+	D+	D+
Q2-18	C-	D+	C
Q4-17	B-	D+	B+
Q4-16	D	D	D
Q4-15	C-	D+	C

Asset & Performance History
Date	NAV	1-Year Total Return
2017	34.1	130.19
2016	14.99	-15.45
2015	17.73	-50.44
2014	35.78	19.21
2013	30.08	60.42
2012	18.75	14.74

Total Assets: $325,647,461

Asset Allocation
Asset	%
Cash	46%
Stocks	54%
US Stocks	0%
Bonds	0%
US Bonds	0%
Other	0%

Services Offered:

Investment Strategy: The investment seeks daily investment results, before fees and expenses, of 300% of the daily performance of the FTSE China 50 Index. The fund, under normal circumstances, invests at least 80% of its net assets (plus borrowing for investment purposes) in securities of the index, exchange-traded funds ("ETFs") that track the index and other financial instruments that provide daily leveraged exposure to the index or ETFs that track the index. The index consists of the 50 largest and most liquid public Chinese companies currently trading on the Hong Kong Stock Exchange ("SEHK"). The fund is non-diversified. **Top Holdings:** iShares China Large-Cap ETF Ishares China Largecap Ishares China Largecap Ishares China Largecap Ishares China Largecap

ARK Genomic Revolution Multi-Sector ETF　　　　　　　　　D+　　SELL

Ticker	Traded On	NAV
ARKG	NYSE Arca	24.04

Total Assets ($)	Dividend Yield (TTM)	Turnover Ratio	Expense Ratio
$324,896,633	0.65	80	0.75

Ratings
Reward	D+
Risk	D
Recent Upgrade/Downgrade	

Fund Information
Fund Type	Exchange Traded Funds
Category	Healthcare Sector Equity
Sub-Category	Health
Prospectus Objective	Unaligned
Inception Date	Oct-14
Open to New Investments	Y

Prices
Price (as of 12/31/2018)	23.98
52-Week High	34.45
52-Week Low	22.36

Total Returns (%)
3-Month	6-Month	1-Year	3-Year	5-Year
-25.58	-18.20	-0.55	17.41	

3-Year Standard Deviation	29.31
Effective Duration	

Valuation
Premium/Discount (1-Year Average)	0.15

Company Information
Provider	ARK ETF Trust
Manager/Tenure	Catherine D. Wood (4)
Website	http://www.ark-funds.com
Address	ARK ETF Trust 155 West 19th Street, 5th Floor New York New York 10011 United States
Phone Number	212-426-7040

PERFORMANCE

Ratings History
Date	Overall Rating	Risk Rating	Reward Rating
Q4-18	D+	D	D+
Q2-18	D+	D	C-
Q4-17	C	C	C
Q4-16	D+	D	C-
Q4-15	U		

Asset & Performance History
Date	NAV	1-Year Total Return
2017	24.38	44.61
2016	16.99	-18.35
2015	20.81	-1.51
2014	21.13	
2013		
2012		

Total Assets: $324,896,633
Asset Allocation
Asset	%
Cash	0%
Stocks	100%
US Stocks	88%
Bonds	0%
US Bonds	0%
Other	0%

Services Offered:

Investment Strategy: The investment seeks long-term growth of capital. The fund is an actively-managed exchange-traded fund ("ETF") that will invest under normal circumstances primarily (at least 80% of its assets) in domestic and foreign equity securities of companies across multiple sectors, including healthcare, information technology, materials, energy and consumer discretionary, that are relevant to the fund's investment theme of the genomics revolution ("Genomics Revolution Companies"). It is non-diversified. **Top Holdings:** Illumina Inc Invitae Corp Intellia Therapeutics Inc Editas Medicine Inc Pacific Biosciences of California Inc

---

Invesco Dividend Achievers™ ETF　　　　　　　　　　　　　C　　HOLD

Ticker	Traded On	NAV
PFM	NAS CM	24.71

Total Assets ($)	Dividend Yield (TTM)	Turnover Ratio	Expense Ratio
$324,132,898	2.08	5	0.55

Ratings
Reward	C
Risk	C-
Recent Upgrade/Downgrade	

Fund Information
Fund Type	Exchange Traded Funds
Category	US Equity Large Cap Value
Sub-Category	Large Value
Prospectus Objective	Equity-Income
Inception Date	Sep-05
Open to New Investments	Y

Prices
Price (as of 12/31/2018)	24.70
52-Week High	28.02
52-Week Low	23.52

Total Returns (%)
3-Month	6-Month	1-Year	3-Year	5-Year
-10.12	-2.42	-4.40	28.61	38.44

3-Year Standard Deviation	8.32
Effective Duration	

Valuation
Premium/Discount (1-Year Average)	0.11

Company Information
Provider	Invesco
Manager/Tenure	Peter Hubbard (11), Michael Jeanette (10), Tony Seisser (4), 1 other
Website	http://www.invesco.com/us
Address	Invesco 11 Greenway Plaza, Ste. 2500 Houston TX 77046 United States
Phone Number	800-659-1005

PERFORMANCE

Ratings History
Date	Overall Rating	Risk Rating	Reward Rating
Q4-18	C	C-	C
Q2-18	C	C-	C
Q4-17	B	B	B-
Q4-16	C+	C-	B-
Q4-15	C	C	C+

Asset & Performance History
Date	NAV	1-Year Total Return
2017	26.42	17.35
2016	22.92	14.64
2015	20.52	-3.13
2014	21.69	11.12
2013	19.91	25.63
2012	16.17	10.82

Total Assets: $324,132,898
Asset Allocation
Asset	%
Cash	0%
Stocks	100%
US Stocks	99%
Bonds	0%
US Bonds	0%
Other	0%

Services Offered:

Investment Strategy: The investment seeks to track the investment results (before fees and expenses) of the NASDAQ US Broad Dividend Achievers™ Index. The fund generally will invest at least 90% of its total assets in common stocks of companies that comprise the underlying index. Strictly in accordance with its guidelines and mandated procedures, Nasdaq, Inc. ("Nasdaq" or the "index provider") includes common stock in the underlying index pursuant to a proprietary selection methodology that identifies a universe of "Dividend Achievers™." **Top Holdings:** Johnson & Johnson Exxon Mobil Corp Microsoft Corp Walmart Inc Verizon Communications Inc

Invesco BulletShares 2024 Corporate Bond ETF
C- HOLD

Ticker	Traded On	NAV	Total Assets ($)	Dividend Yield (TTM)	Turnover Ratio	Expense Ratio
BSCO	NYSE Arca	19.93	$323,477,666	3.36	2	0.1

Ratings
Reward   C-
Risk   C-
Recent Upgrade/Downgrade

Fund Information
Fund Type	Exchange Traded Funds
Category	US Fixed Income
Sub-Category	Corporate Bond
Prospectus Objective	Corp Bond - Gen
Inception Date	Sep-14
Open to New Investments	Y

Prices
Price (as of 12/31/2018)	19.97
52-Week High	20.89
52-Week Low	19.77

Total Returns (%)
3-Month	6-Month	1-Year	3-Year	5-Year
0.52	1.63	-1.06	10.69	

3-Year Standard Deviation	3.62
Effective Duration	4.98

Valuation
Premium/Discount (1-Year Average)	0.29

Company Information
Provider	Invesco
Manager/Tenure	Jeremy Neisewander (2), Peter Hubbard (0), Jeffrey W. Kernagis (0), 1 other
Website	http://www.invesco.com/us
Address	Invesco 11 Greenway Plaza, Ste. 2500 Houston TX 77046 United States
Phone Number	800-659-1005

PERFORMANCE

Ratings History
Date	Overall Rating	Risk Rating	Reward Rating
Q4-18	C-	C-	C-
Q2-18	C-	C-	C-
Q4-17	B	A	C
Q4-16	D+	C-	D+
Q4-15	U		

Asset & Performance History
Date	NAV	1-Year Total Return
2017	20.8	5.56
2016	20.34	6.02
2015	19.77	0.62
2014	20.3	
2013		
2012		

Total Assets: $323,477,666
Asset Allocation
Asset	%
Cash	0%
Stocks	0%
US Stocks	0%
Bonds	100%
US Bonds	87%
Other	0%

Services Offered:

Investment Strategy: The investment seeks investment results that correspond generally to the performance, before the fund's fees and expenses, of an investment grade corporate bond index called the Nasdaq BulletShares® USD Corporate Bond 2024 Index. The fund will invest at least 80% of its total assets in component securities that comprise the index. The index is designed to represent the performance of a held-to-maturity portfolio of U.S. dollar-denominated investment grade corporate bonds with effective maturities in the year 2024. The fund is non-diversified. **Top Holdings:** JPMorgan Chase & Co. 3.88% Morgan Stanley 3.88% Goldman Sachs Group, Inc. 4% Bank of America Corporation 4.2% Morgan Stanley 3.7%

Aberdeen Standard Physical Silver Shares ETF
D SELL

Ticker	Traded On	NAV	Total Assets ($)	Dividend Yield (TTM)	Turnover Ratio	Expense Ratio
SIVR	NYSE Arca	15.03	$322,481,703	0	4	0.3

Ratings
Reward   D-
Risk   D
Recent Upgrade/Downgrade   Down

Fund Information
Fund Type	Exchange Traded Funds
Category	Commodities Specified
Sub-Category	Commodities Precious Metals
Prospectus Objective	Prec Metals
Inception Date	Jul-09
Open to New Investments	Y

Prices
Price (as of 12/31/2018)	15.04
52-Week High	17.12
52-Week Low	13.61

Total Returns (%)
3-Month	6-Month	1-Year	3-Year	5-Year
6.20	-3.36	-8.57	10.89	-21.87

3-Year Standard Deviation	19.28
Effective Duration	

Valuation
Premium/Discount (1-Year Average)	0.16

Company Information
Provider	Aberdeen Standard Investments
Manager/Tenure	Management Team (9)
Website	http://www.aberdeenstandardetfs.us
Address	Aberdeen Standard Investments 405 Lexington Avenue New York NY 10174 United States
Phone Number	212-918-4954

PERFORMANCE

Ratings History
Date	Overall Rating	Risk Rating	Reward Rating
Q4-18	D	D	D-
Q2-18	C-	C	D+
Q4-17	D+	D+	D+
Q4-16	D+	D	C-
Q4-15	D-	E+	D-

Asset & Performance History
Date	NAV	1-Year Total Return
2017	16.44	3.53
2016	15.88	17.15
2015	13.56	-13.72
2014	15.71	-18.34
2013	19.24	-35.08
2012	29.64	5.96

Total Assets: $322,481,703
Asset Allocation
Asset	%
Cash	0%
Stocks	0%
US Stocks	0%
Bonds	0%
US Bonds	0%
Other	100%

Services Offered:

Investment Strategy: The investment seeks to replicate, net of expenses, the price of silver bullion. The shares are backed by physical allocated silver bullion held by the custodian. All physical silver held conforms to the London Bullion Market Association's rules for good delivery. **Top Holdings:** Physical Silver Bullion

iShares Morningstar Mid-Cap Growth ETF   C-   HOLD

Ticker	Traded On	NAV	Total Assets ($)	Dividend Yield (TTM)	Turnover Ratio	Expense Ratio
JKH	NYSE Arca	194.56	$320,773,090	0.34	43	0.3

Ratings

Reward	C
Risk	D+
Recent Upgrade/Downgrade	Down

Fund Information

Fund Type	Exchange Traded Funds
Category	US Equity Mid Cap
Sub-Category	Mid-Cap Growth
Prospectus Objective	Growth
Inception Date	Jun-04
Open to New Investments	Y

Prices

Price (as of 12/31/2018)	194.39
52-Week High	237.43
52-Week Low	180.97

Total Returns (%)

3-Month	6-Month	1-Year	3-Year	5-Year
-16.84	-11.16	-3.38	28.71	39.65

3-Year Standard Deviation	12.66
Effective Duration	

Valuation

Premium/Discount (1-Year Average)	0.12

Company Information

Provider	iShares
Manager/Tenure	Diane Hsiung (10), Greg Savage (10), Jennifer Hsui (6), 3 others
Website	http://www.ishares.com
Address	iShares 400 Howard Street San Francisco CA 94105 United States
Phone Number	800-474-2737

PERFORMANCE

Ratings History

Date	Overall Rating	Risk Rating	Reward Rating
Q4-18	C-	D+	C
Q2-18	C	D+	C+
Q4-17	B	C+	B
Q4-16	C	D+	C+
Q4-15	C	D+	C

Asset & Performance History

Date	NAV	1-Year Total Return
2017	202.03	25.37
2016	161.93	6.25
2015	153.2	-0.93
2014	155.23	9.53
2013	142.6	33.83
2012	106.97	15.51

Total Assets: $320,773,090

Asset Allocation

Asset	%
Cash	0%
Stocks	100%
US Stocks	99%
Bonds	0%
US Bonds	0%
Other	0%

Services Offered:

Investment Strategy: The investment seeks to track the investment results of the Morningstar® Mid Growth IndexSM composed of mid-capitalization U.S. equities that exhibit growth characteristics. The fund generally invests at least 90% of its assets in securities of the underlying index and in depositary receipts representing securities of the underlying index. The underlying index measures the performance of stocks issued by mid-capitalization companies that have exhibited above-average "growth" characteristics as determined by Morningstar, Inc.'s ("Morningstar" or the "index provider") proprietary index methodology. **Top Holdings:** O'Reilly Automotive Inc   Workday Inc Class A   Twitter Inc   Rockwell Automation Inc   Square Inc A

First Trust Water ETF   C+   HOLD

Ticker	Traded On	NAV	Total Assets ($)	Dividend Yield (TTM)	Turnover Ratio	Expense Ratio
FIW	NYSE Arca	43.96	$319,752,925	0.62	24	0.56

Ratings

Reward	B
Risk	C
Recent Upgrade/Downgrade	Down

Fund Information

Fund Type	Exchange Traded Funds
Category	Industrials Sector Equity
Sub-Category	Miscellaneous Sector
Prospectus Objective	Natl Res
Inception Date	May-07
Open to New Investments	Y

Prices

Price (as of 12/31/2018)	43.91
52-Week High	51.62
52-Week Low	41.46

Total Returns (%)

3-Month	6-Month	1-Year	3-Year	5-Year
-12.86	-8.42	-8.88	49.68	35.48

3-Year Standard Deviation	13.03
Effective Duration	

Valuation

Premium/Discount (1-Year Average)	0.08

Company Information

Provider	First Trust
Manager/Tenure	Jon C. Erickson (11), Daniel J. Lindquist (11), David G. McGarel (11), 3 others
Website	http://www.ftportfolios.com/
Address	First Trust 120 E. Liberty Drive, Suite 400 Wheaton IL 60187 United States
Phone Number	800-621-1675

PERFORMANCE

Ratings History

Date	Overall Rating	Risk Rating	Reward Rating
Q4-18	C+	C	B
Q2-18	B-	C	B
Q4-17	B+	C+	A
Q4-16	C+	C-	B
Q4-15	B-	C+	B-

Asset & Performance History

Date	NAV	1-Year Total Return
2017	48.58	24.25
2016	39.6	32.21
2015	30.12	-9.81
2014	33.65	0.35
2013	33.78	30.91
2012	25.99	26.86

Total Assets: $319,752,925

Asset Allocation

Asset	%
Cash	0%
Stocks	100%
US Stocks	98%
Bonds	0%
US Bonds	0%
Other	0%

Services Offered:

Investment Strategy: The investment seeks investment results that correspond generally to the price and yield (before the fund's fees and expenses) of an equity index called the ISE Clean Edge Water Index. The fund will normally invest at least 90% of its net assets (including investment borrowings) in common stocks that comprise the index. The index is a modified market-capitalization weighted portfolio of 36 stocks of companies as of March 29, 2018 that derive a substantial portion of their revenues from the potable and wastewater industries which are generally industrial and utilities companies. **Top Holdings:** Agilent Technologies Inc   American Water Works Co Inc   Ecolab Inc   Danaher Corp   Roper Technologies Inc

EMQQ The Emerging Markets Internet & Ecommerce ETF   C-   HOLD

Ticker	Traded On	NAV	Total Assets ($)	Dividend Yield (TTM)	Turnover Ratio	Expense Ratio
EMQQ	NYSE Arca	26.89	$317,848,491	0.47	33	0.86

Ratings
Reward   C
Risk   D
Recent Upgrade/Downgrade   Down

Fund Information
Fund Type   Exchange Traded Funds
Category   Global Emerg Mkts Equity
Sub-Category   Diversified Emerging Mkts
Prospectus Objective   Div Emerg Mkts
Inception Date   Nov-14
Open to New Investments   Y

Prices
Price (as of 12/31/2018)   26.71
52-Week High   43.50
52-Week Low   26.22

Total Returns (%)

3-Month	6-Month	1-Year	3-Year	5-Year
-15.54	-26.50	-29.21	14.80	

3-Year Standard Deviation   21.14
Effective Duration

Valuation
Premium/Discount (1-Year Average)   -0.04

Company Information
Provider   EMQQ
Manager/Tenure   Dustin Lewellyn (4), Anand Desai (2), Ernesto Tong (2)
Website   http://www.emqqetf.com
Address   EMQQ 1 Freedom Valley Drive Oaks PA 19456 United States
Phone Number   855-888-9892

PERFORMANCE

Ratings History

Date	Overall Rating	Risk Rating	Reward Rating
Q4-18	C-	D	C
Q2-18	C	C	C
Q4-17	B-	C	B
Q4-16	C	D+	C
Q4-15	U		

Asset & Performance History

Date	NAV	1-Year Total Return
2017	37.99	67.16
2016	22.94	-2.97
2015	23.82	5.2
2014	22.66	
2013		
2012		

Total Assets: $317,848,491
Asset Allocation

Asset	%
Cash	0%
Stocks	100%
US Stocks	0%
Bonds	0%
US Bonds	0%
Other	0%

Services Offered:

Investment Strategy: The investment seeks to provide investment results that, before fees and expenses, correspond generally to the price and yield performance of EMQQ The Emerging Markets Internet & Ecommerce IndexTM (the "index"). The fund will normally invest at least 80% of its total assets in securities of the index or in depositary receipts representing securities of the index. The index is designed to measure the performance of an investable universe of publicly-traded, emerging market internet and ecommerce companies. The fund is non-diversified. **Top Holdings:** Tencent Holdings Ltd Alibaba Group Holding Ltd ADR Naspers Ltd Class N MercadoLibre Inc Baidu Inc ADR

---

iShares CMBS ETF   C-   HOLD

Ticker	Traded On	NAV	Total Assets ($)	Dividend Yield (TTM)	Turnover Ratio	Expense Ratio
CMBS	NYSE Arca	50.14	$317,177,547	2.74	19	0.25

Ratings
Reward   D+
Risk   C-
Recent Upgrade/Downgrade   Up

Fund Information
Fund Type   Exchange Traded Funds
Category   US Fixed Income
Sub-Category   Intermediate-Term Bond
Prospectus Objective   Growth
Inception Date   Feb-12
Open to New Investments   Y

Prices
Price (as of 12/31/2018)   50.28
52-Week High   51.27
52-Week Low   49.03

Total Returns (%)

3-Month	6-Month	1-Year	3-Year	5-Year
1.74	2.17	0.59	6.83	11.21

3-Year Standard Deviation   2.77
Effective Duration   5.04

Valuation
Premium/Discount (1-Year Average)   0.17

Company Information
Provider   iShares
Manager/Tenure   James Mauro (6), Scott Radell (6)
Website   http://www.ishares.com
Address   iShares 400 Howard Street San Francisco CA 94105 United States
Phone Number   800-474-2737

PERFORMANCE

Ratings History

Date	Overall Rating	Risk Rating	Reward Rating
Q4-18	C-	C-	D+
Q2-18	C-	C-	C-
Q4-17	B-	A-	C
Q4-16	C	C+	C
Q4-15	C	C-	C

Asset & Performance History

Date	NAV	1-Year Total Return
2017	51.22	2.85
2016	50.95	3.04
2015	50.57	0.6
2014	51.42	3.47
2013	50.77	0.02
2012	51.78	

Total Assets: $317,177,547
Asset Allocation

Asset	%
Cash	0%
Stocks	1%
US Stocks	1%
Bonds	99%
US Bonds	99%
Other	0%

Services Offered:

Investment Strategy: The investment seeks to track the investment results of the Bloomberg Barclays U.S. CMBS (ERISA Only) Index. The index measures the performance of investment-grade commercial mortgage-backed securities ("CMBS"), which are classes of securities (known as "certificates") that represent interests in "pools" of commercial mortgages. The fund generally will invest at least 90% of its assets in the component securities of the underlying index and may invest up to 10% of its assets in certain futures, options and swap contracts, cash and cash equivalents. **Top Holdings:** Federal Home Loan Mortgage Corporation 3.43% Federal Home Loan Mortgage Corporation 4.33% Federal Home Loan Mortgage Corporation 2.75% Morgan Stanley BAML Trust 3.53% Federal Home Loan Mortgage Corporation 3.11%

iShares New York Muni Bond ETF   C-   HOLD

Ticker	Traded On	NAV	Total Assets ($)	Dividend Yield (TTM)	Turnover Ratio	Expense Ratio
NYF	NYSE Arca	54.55	$316,663,401	2.48	31	0.25

Ratings
Reward   C-
Risk   C-
Recent Upgrade/Downgrade   Down

Fund Information
Fund Type   Exchange Traded Funds
Category   US Muni Fixed Inc
Sub-Category   Muni New York Intermediate
Prospectus Objective   Muni Bond - Single State
Inception Date   Oct-07
Open to New Investments   Y

Prices
Price (as of 12/31/2018)   54.77
52-Week High   55.78
52-Week Low   53.49

Total Returns (%)

3-Month	6-Month	1-Year	3-Year	5-Year
1.58	1.12	0.56	5.09	17.85

3-Year Standard Deviation   3.11
Effective Duration   6.16

Valuation
Premium/Discount (1-Year Average)   0.21

Company Information
Provider   iShares
Manager/Tenure   Scott Radell (8), James Mauro (7)
Website   http://www.ishares.com
Address   iShares 400 Howard Street San Francisco CA 94105 United States
Phone Number   800-474-2737

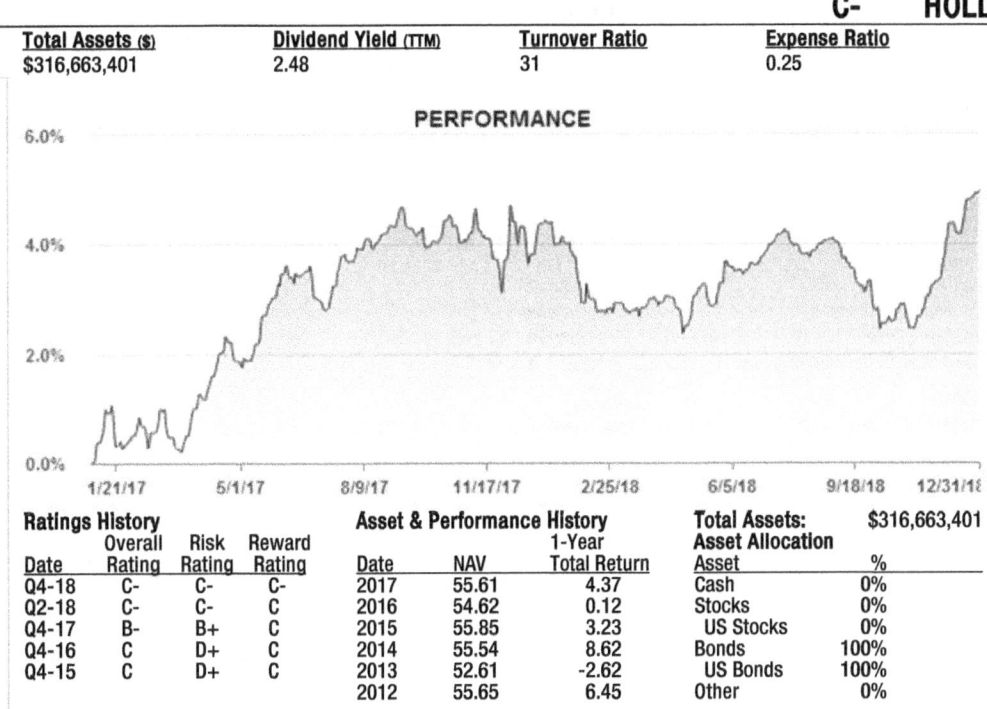

Ratings History

Date	Overall Rating	Risk Rating	Reward Rating
Q4-18	C-	C-	C-
Q2-18	C-	C-	C
Q4-17	B-	B+	C
Q4-16	C	D+	C
Q4-15	C	D+	C

Asset & Performance History

Date	NAV	1-Year Total Return
2017	55.61	4.37
2016	54.62	0.12
2015	55.85	3.23
2014	55.54	8.62
2013	52.61	-2.62
2012	55.65	6.45

Total Assets: $316,663,401
Asset Allocation

Asset	%
Cash	0%
Stocks	0%
US Stocks	0%
Bonds	100%
US Bonds	100%
Other	0%

Services Offered:

Investment Strategy: The investment seeks to track the investment results of the S&P New York AMT-Free Municipal Bond IndexTM. The fund generally will invest at least 90% of its assets in the component securities of the underlying index and may invest up to 10% of its assets in certain futures, options and swap contracts, cash and cash equivalents. The index measures the performance of the investment-grade segment of the New York municipal bond market. The fund is non-diversified. **Top Holdings:** SUFFOLK CNTY N Y WTR AUTH 4% NEW YORK ST TWY AUTH 5.25% NEW YORK ST TWY AUTH 5% LONG IS PWR AUTH N Y 5% UTILITY DEBT SECURITIZATION AUTH N Y 5%

ProShares Ultra Nasdaq Biotechnology   D+   SELL

Ticker	Traded On	NAV	Total Assets ($)	Dividend Yield (TTM)	Turnover Ratio	Expense Ratio
BIB	NAS CM	42.41	$316,225,519	0		0.95

Ratings
Reward   D+
Risk   D+
Recent Upgrade/Downgrade   Down

Fund Information
Fund Type   Exchange Traded Funds
Category   Trading Tools
Sub-Category   Trading--Leveraged Equity
Prospectus Objective   Technology
Inception Date   Apr-10
Open to New Investments   Y

Prices
Price (as of 12/31/2018)   42.09
52-Week High   70.14
52-Week Low   36.42

Total Returns (%)

3-Month	6-Month	1-Year	3-Year	5-Year
-38.17	-27.13	-24.36	-40.62	12.62

3-Year Standard Deviation   44.74
Effective Duration

Valuation
Premium/Discount (1-Year Average)   0.00

Company Information
Provider   ProShares
Manager/Tenure   Michael Neches (5), Tarak Davé (0)
Website   http://www.proshares.com
Address   ProShares 7501 Wisconsin Avenue, Suite 1000 Bethesda MD 20814 United States
Phone Number   866-776-5125

Ratings History

Date	Overall Rating	Risk Rating	Reward Rating
Q4-18	D+	D+	D+
Q2-18	D+	D	C-
Q4-17	D+	D+	D+
Q4-16	C-	D+	C-
Q4-15	B-	C+	B

Asset & Performance History

Date	NAV	1-Year Total Return
2017	56.07	40.73
2016	39.84	-44.22
2015	71.43	13.79
2014	62.77	66.69
2013	37.66	160.13
2012	14.48	67.12

Total Assets: $316,225,519
Asset Allocation

Asset	%
Cash	-100%
Stocks	121%
US Stocks	118%
Bonds	0%
US Bonds	0%
Other	78%

Services Offered:

Investment Strategy: The investment seeks daily investment results that correspond to two times (2x) the daily performance of the Nasdaq Biotechnology Index®. The fund invests in financial instruments that ProShare Advisors believes, in combination, should produce daily returns consistent with the fund's investment objective. The index is a modified capitalization weighted index that includes securities of Nasdaq listed companies that are classified as either biotechnology or pharmaceutical. The fund is non-diversified. **Top Holdings:** Nasdaq Biotechnology Index Swap Deutsche Bank Ag Nasdaq Biotechnology Index Swap Ubs Ag Ishares Biotech (Ibb) Swap Bank Of America Na Nasdaq Biotechnology Index Swap Societe Generale Nasdaq Biotechnology Index Swap Bank Of America Na

iShares iBonds Sep 2020 Term Muni Bond ETF
C-   HOLD

Ticker	Traded On	NAV	Total Assets ($)	Dividend Yield (TTM)	Turnover Ratio	Expense Ratio
IBMI	NYSE Arca	25.35	$314,993,192	1.19	0	0.18

Ratings
Reward	C-
Risk	C-
Recent Upgrade/Downgrade	

Fund Information
Fund Type	Exchange Traded Funds
Category	US Muni Fixed Inc
Sub-Category	Muni National Short
Prospectus Objective	Muni Bond - Natl
Inception Date	Aug-14
Open to New Investments	Y

Prices
Price (as of 12/31/2018)	25.37
52-Week High	25.42
52-Week Low	25.17

Total Returns (%)
3-Month	6-Month	1-Year	3-Year	5-Year
0.75	0.61	1.35	2.95	

3-Year Standard Deviation	2.03
Effective Duration	1.62

Valuation
Premium/Discount (1-Year Average)	0.08

Company Information
Provider	iShares
Manager/Tenure	James Mauro (4), Scott Radell (4)
Website	http://www.ishares.com
Address	iShares 400 Howard Street San Francisco CA 94105 United States
Phone Number	800-474-2737

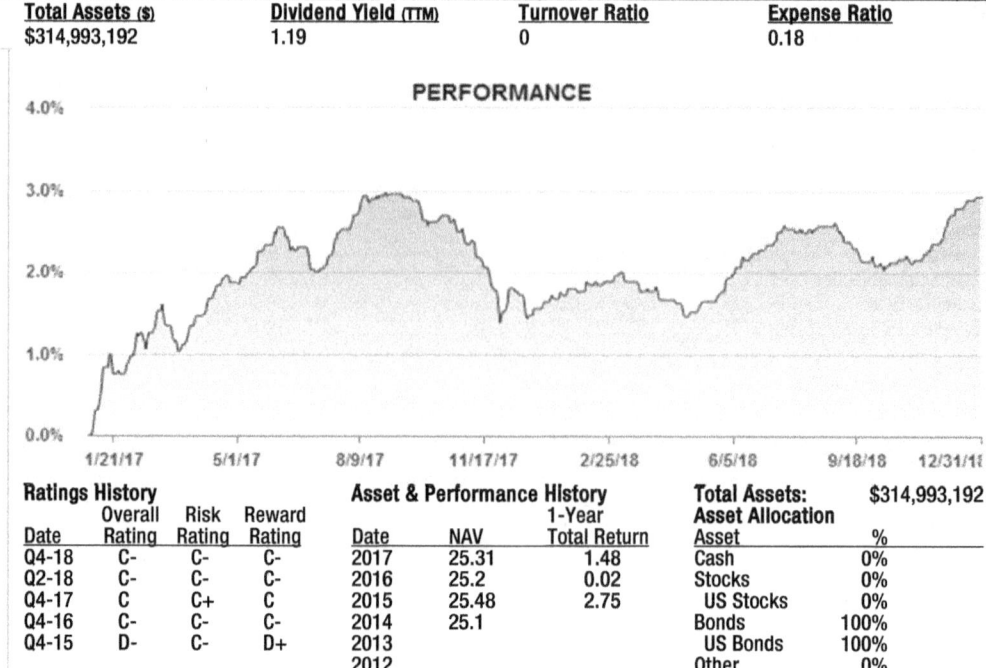
PERFORMANCE

Ratings History
Date	Overall Rating	Risk Rating	Reward Rating
Q4-18	C-	C-	C-
Q2-18	C-	C-	C-
Q4-17	C	C+	C
Q4-16	C-	C-	C-
Q4-15	D-	C-	D+

Asset & Performance History
Date	NAV	1-Year Total Return
2017	25.31	1.48
2016	25.2	0.02
2015	25.48	2.75
2014	25.1	
2013		
2012		

Total Assets: $314,993,192
Asset Allocation
Asset	%
Cash	0%
Stocks	0%
US Stocks	0%
Bonds	100%
US Bonds	100%
Other	0%

Services Offered:

Investment Strategy: The investment seeks to track the investment results of the S&P AMT-Free Municipal Series 2020 IndexTM. The fund generally will invest at least 90% of its assets in the component securities of the underlying index, and may invest up to 10% of its assets in certain futures, options and swap contracts, cash and cash equivalents, as well as in securities not included in the underlying index, but which the advisor believes will help the fund track the underlying index. The underlying index measures the performance of investment-grade, non-callable U.S. municipal bonds maturing in 2020. **Top Holdings:** CALIFORNIA ST 5% MASSACHUSETTS ST 5% WISCONSIN ST 5% DELAWARE ST 5% MARYLAND ST 5%

First Trust NASDAQ® ABA Community Bank Index Fund
C-   HOLD

Ticker	Traded On	NAV	Total Assets ($)	Dividend Yield (TTM)	Turnover Ratio	Expense Ratio
QABA	NAS CM	43.16	$314,942,109	1.42	14	0.6

Ratings
Reward	C-
Risk	C-
Recent Upgrade/Downgrade	Down

Fund Information
Fund Type	Exchange Traded Funds
Category	Financials Sector Equity
Sub-Category	Financial
Prospectus Objective	Financial
Inception Date	Jun-09
Open to New Investments	Y

Prices
Price (as of 12/31/2018)	43.08
52-Week High	58.34
52-Week Low	41.05

Total Returns (%)
3-Month	6-Month	1-Year	3-Year	5-Year
-17.44	-21.10	-16.17	15.98	28.53

3-Year Standard Deviation	19.15
Effective Duration	

Valuation
Premium/Discount (1-Year Average)	0.04

Company Information
Provider	First Trust
Manager/Tenure	Jon C. Erickson (9), Daniel J. Lindquist (9), David G. McGarel (9), 3 others
Website	http://www.ftportfolios.com/
Address	First Trust 120 E. Liberty Drive, Suite 400 Wheaton IL 60187 United States
Phone Number	800-621-1675

PERFORMANCE

Ratings History
Date	Overall Rating	Risk Rating	Reward Rating
Q4-18	C-	C-	C-
Q2-18	C+	C-	B-
Q4-17	B+	B	A
Q4-16	C	C-	C+
Q4-15	C	C	C+

Asset & Performance History
Date	NAV	1-Year Total Return
2017	52.34	0.57
2016	52.81	37.57
2015	38.94	7.88
2014	36.61	2.72
2013	36.11	42.91
2012	25.56	13.54

Total Assets: $314,942,109
Asset Allocation
Asset	%
Cash	0%
Stocks	100%
US Stocks	98%
Bonds	0%
US Bonds	0%
Other	0%

Services Offered:

Investment Strategy: The investment seeks investment results that correspond generally to the price and yield (before the fund's fees and expenses) of an equity index called the NASDAQ OMX® ABA Community Bank IndexSM. The fund will normally invest at least 90% of its net assets (including investment borrowings) in common stocks that comprise the index. The index is a market-capitalization-weighted index. **Top Holdings:** East West Bancorp Inc Commerce Bancshares Inc Popular Inc BOK Financial Corp PacWest Bancorp

Global X Uranium ETF   D   SELL

Ticker	Traded On	NAV	Total Assets ($)	Dividend Yield (TTM)	Turnover Ratio	Expense Ratio
URA	NYSE Arca	11.82	$314,362,165	2.43	12	0.69

Ratings
Reward   D
Risk   D
Recent Upgrade/Downgrade   Down

Fund Information
Fund Type   Exchange Traded Funds
Category   Natural Resources
Sub-Category   Natural Resources
Prospectus Objective   Unaligned
Inception Date   Nov-10
Open to New Investments   Y

Prices
Price (as of 12/31/2018)   11.67
52-Week High   15.83
52-Week Low   11.30

Total Returns (%)

3-Month	6-Month	1-Year	3-Year	5-Year
-12.31	-7.72	-20.51	-7.92	-54.69

3-Year Standard Deviation   33.15
Effective Duration

Valuation
Premium/Discount (1-Year Average)   -0.12

Company Information
Provider   Global X Funds
Manager/Tenure   Chang Kim (4), James Ong (2), Nam
                    To (0)
Website   http://www.globalxfunds.com
Address   Global X Funds 600 Lexington Avenue,
                    20th Floor New York NY 10022 United
                    States
Phone Number   888-493-8631

Ratings History

Date	Overall Rating	Risk Rating	Reward Rating
Q4-18	D	D	D
Q2-18	D+	D	D+
Q4-17	D+	D	C
Q4-16	D	D	D
Q4-15	D+	D+	D+

Asset & Performance History

Date	NAV	1-Year Total Return
2017	14.87	19.04
2016	12.75	-2.69
2015	14.09	-36.63
2014	22.68	-22.33
2013	30.46	-21.58
2012	39.06	-19.47

Total Assets: $314,362,165
Asset Allocation

Asset	%
Cash	-1%
Stocks	101%
US Stocks	6%
Bonds	0%
US Bonds	0%
Other	0%

Services Offered:

Investment Strategy: The investment seeks to provide investment results that correspond generally to the price and yield performance, before fees and expenses, of the Solactive Global Uranium Total Return Index. The fund invests at least 80% of its total assets in the securities of the underlying index and in American Depositary Receipts ("ADRs") and Global Depositary Receipts ("GDRs") based on the securities in the underlying index. The underlying index is designed to measure broad-based equity market performance of global companies involved in the uranium industry. The fund is non-diversified. **Top Holdings:** Cameco Corp NexGen Energy Ltd Uranium Participation Corp Hyundai Engineering & Construction Co Ltd Mitsubishi Heavy Industries Ltd

---

iShares Global Timber & Forestry ETF   C-   HOLD

Ticker	Traded On	NAV	Total Assets ($)	Dividend Yield (TTM)	Turnover Ratio	Expense Ratio
WOOD	NAS CM	57.23	$312,703,831	1.51	31	0.47

Ratings
Reward   C
Risk   D+
Recent Upgrade/Downgrade   Down

Fund Information
Fund Type   Exchange Traded Funds
Category   Natural Resources
Sub-Category   Natural Resources
Prospectus Objective   Natl Res
Inception Date   Jun-08
Open to New Investments   Y

Prices
Price (as of 12/31/2018)   57.13
52-Week High   83.76
52-Week Low   55.24

Total Returns (%)

3-Month	6-Month	1-Year	3-Year	5-Year
-22.95	-25.04	-17.56	25.45	18.92

3-Year Standard Deviation   16.43
Effective Duration

Valuation
Premium/Discount (1-Year Average)   -0.06

Company Information
Provider   iShares
Manager/Tenure   Diane Hsiung (10), Greg Savage (10),
                    Jennifer Hsui (6), 3 others
Website   http://www.ishares.com
Address   iShares 400 Howard Street San
                    Francisco CA 94105 United States
Phone Number   800-474-2737

Ratings History

Date	Overall Rating	Risk Rating	Reward Rating
Q4-18	C-	D+	C
Q2-18	B	C-	A-
Q4-17	B	C	A
Q4-16	C	C-	C+
Q4-15	C	C	C

Asset & Performance History

Date	NAV	1-Year Total Return
2017	71.12	34.28
2016	53.68	13.34
2015	48.23	-7.25
2014	53.01	2.21
2013	52.76	19.95
2012	44.76	22.02

Total Assets: $312,703,831
Asset Allocation

Asset	%
Cash	1%
Stocks	99%
US Stocks	36%
Bonds	0%
US Bonds	0%
Other	0%

Services Offered:

Investment Strategy: The investment seeks to track the investment results of the S&P Global Timber & Forestry IndexTM. The fund generally will invest at least 90% of its assets in the component securities of the underlying index and in investments that have economic characteristics that are substantially identical to the component securities and may invest up to 10% of its assets in certain futures, options and swap contracts, cash and cash equivalents. The index is comprised of approximately 25 of the largest publicly-traded companies engaged in the ownership, management or upstream supply chain of forests and timberlands. The fund is non-diversified. **Top Holdings:** Rayonier Inc Weyerhaeuser Co West Fraser Timber Co.Ltd Svenska Cellulosa AB B PotlatchDeltic Corp

Global X Silver Miners ETF   D   SELL

Ticker	Traded On	NAV	Total Assets ($)	Dividend Yield (TTM)	Turnover Ratio	Expense Ratio
SIL	NYSE Arca	24.98	$311,298,095	0.03	24	0.65

Ratings

Reward	D+
Risk	D
Recent Upgrade/Downgrade	Down

Fund Information

Fund Type	Exchange Traded Funds
Category	Prec Metals
Sub-Category	Equity Precious Metals
Prospectus Objective	Prec Metals
Inception Date	Apr-10
Open to New Investments	Y

Prices

Price (as of 12/31/2018)	25.02
52-Week High	33.93
52-Week Low	22.47

Total Returns (%)

3-Month	6-Month	1-Year	3-Year	5-Year
3.73	-12.01	-23.60	39.19	-22.62

3-Year Standard Deviation	41.54
Effective Duration	

Valuation

Premium/Discount (1-Year Average)	-0.03

Company Information

Provider	Global X Funds
Manager/Tenure	Chang Kim (4), James Ong (2), Nam To (0)
Website	http://www.globalxfunds.com
Address	Global X Funds 600 Lexington Avenue, 20th Floor New York NY 10022 United States
Phone Number	888-493-8631

PERFORMANCE

Ratings History

Date	Overall Rating	Risk Rating	Reward Rating
Q4-18	D	D	D+
Q2-18	D+	D+	D+
Q4-17	C-	D	C
Q4-16	C-	D	C
Q4-15	D	D	D

Asset & Performance History

Date	NAV	1-Year Total Return
2017	32.7	1.03
2016	32.37	80.33
2015	18.56	-33.08
2014	27.84	-16.93
2013	33.54	-50.31
2012	67.95	8.42

Total Assets: $311,298,095

Asset Allocation

Asset	%
Cash	0%
Stocks	100%
US Stocks	8%
Bonds	0%
US Bonds	0%
Other	0%

Services Offered:

Investment Strategy: The investment seeks to provide investment results that correspond generally to the price and yield performance, before fees and expenses, of the Solactive Global Silver Miners Total Return Index. The fund invests at least 80% of its total assets in the securities of the underlying index and in American Depositary Receipts ("ADRs") and Global Depositary Receipts ("GDRs") based on the securities in the underlying index. The underlying index is designed to measure broad-based equity market performance of global companies involved in the silver mining industry. The fund is non-diversified. **Top Holdings:** Korea Zinc Co Ltd Polymetal International PLC Wheaton Precious Metals Corp Pan American Silver Corp Tahoe Resources Inc

VelocityShares 3x Long Crude Oil ETNs linked to the S&P GSCI® Crude Oil Index ER New   D   SELL

Ticker	Traded On	NAV	Total Assets ($)	Dividend Yield (TTM)	Turnover Ratio	Expense Ratio
UWT	NYSE Arca	8.67	$310,865,136	0		1.5

Ratings

Reward	D+
Risk	D
Recent Upgrade/Downgrade	Down

Fund Information

Fund Type	Exchange Traded Funds
Category	Trading Tools
Sub-Category	Trading--Leveraged Commodities
Prospectus Objective	Growth & Inc
Inception Date	Dec-16
Open to New Investments	Y

Prices

Price (as of 12/31/2018)	8.90
52-Week High	49.34
52-Week Low	8.22

Total Returns (%)

3-Month	6-Month	1-Year	3-Year	5-Year
-81.84	-79.76	-65.15		

3-Year Standard Deviation	
Effective Duration	

Valuation

Premium/Discount (1-Year Average)	-0.24

Company Information

Provider	Credit Suisse AG
Manager/Tenure	No Manager (1)
Website	
Address	Kilmore House Park Lane Dublin Ireland
Phone Number	

PERFORMANCE

Ratings History

Date	Overall Rating	Risk Rating	Reward Rating
Q4-18	D	D	D+
Q2-18	C	D+	C
Q4-17	D	D	D+
Q4-16			
Q4-15			

Asset & Performance History

Date	NAV	1-Year Total Return
2017	24.87	-12.7
2016	27.61	
2015		
2014		
2013		
2012		

Total Assets: $310,865,136

Asset Allocation

Asset	%
Cash	%
Stocks	%
US Stocks	%
Bonds	%
US Bonds	%
Other	%

Services Offered:

Investment Strategy: The investment seeks to replicate, net of expenses, three times of the S&P GSCI® Crude Oil Index ER.
The index tracks a hypothetical position in the nearest-to-expiration NYMEX light sweet crude oil futures contract, which is rolled each month into the futures contract expiring in the next month. The value of the index fluctuates with changes in the price of the relevant NYMEX light sweet crude oil futures contracts. **Top Holdings:**

KraneShares Bosera MSCI China A ETF   D   SELL

Ticker	Traded On	NAV		Total Assets ($)	Dividend Yield (TTM)	Turnover Ratio	Expense Ratio
KBA	NYSE Arca	24.58		$309,803,496	0.69	52	0.6

Ratings
Reward   D
Risk   D
Recent Upgrade/Downgrade

Fund Information
Fund Type   Exchange Traded Funds
Category   Greater China Equity
Sub-Category   China Region
Prospectus Objective   Pacific Stock
Inception Date   Mar-14
Open to New Investments   Y

Prices
Price (as of 12/31/2018)   24.46
52-Week High   39.22
52-Week Low   24.29

Total Returns (%)

3-Month	6-Month	1-Year	3-Year	5-Year
-12.01	-12.74	-26.76	-24.04	

3-Year Standard Deviation   21
Effective Duration

Valuation
Premium/Discount (1-Year Average)   0.21

Company Information
Provider   KraneShares
Manager/Tenure   Qiong Wan (2)
Website   http://www.kraneshares.com
Address   1350 Avenue of the Americas Second Floor New York NY 10019 United States
Phone Number   855-857-2638

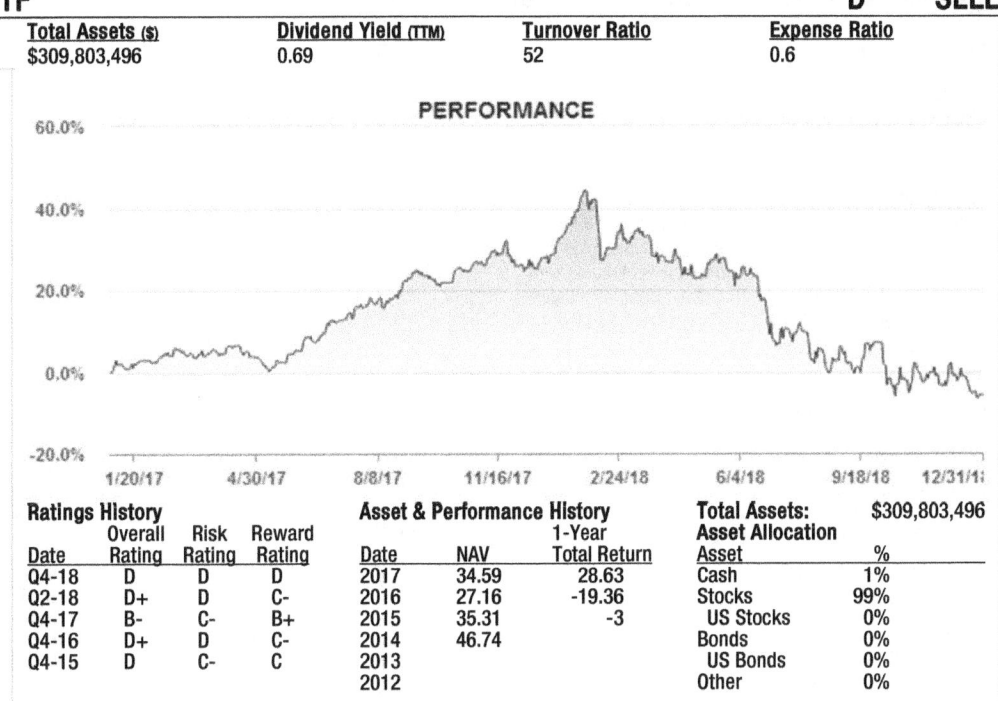

PERFORMANCE

Ratings History

Date	Overall Rating	Risk Rating	Reward Rating
Q4-18	D	D	D
Q2-18	D+	D	C-
Q4-17	B-	C-	B+
Q4-16	D+	D	C-
Q4-15	D	C-	C

Asset & Performance History

Date	NAV	1-Year Total Return
2017	34.59	28.63
2016	27.16	-19.36
2015	35.31	-3
2014	46.74	
2013		
2012		

Total Assets: $309,803,496
Asset Allocation

Asset	%
Cash	1%
Stocks	99%
US Stocks	0%
Bonds	0%
US Bonds	0%
Other	0%

Services Offered:

Investment Strategy: The investment seeks to provide investment results that, before fees and expenses, correspond to the price and yield performance of the MSCI China A Inclusion Index (the "underlying index"). The fund will invest at least 80% of its total assets in securities of the underlying index, depositary receipts representing such securities and securities underlying depositary receipts in the underlying index. The index reflects the Chinese renminbi -denominated equity securities listed on the Shenzhen or Shanghai Stock Exchanges ("A Shares") included in the MSCI Emerging Markets Index assuming that index's methodology permitted the full inclusion of A Shares. **Top Holdings:** Kweichow Moutai Co Ltd   Ping An Insurance (Group) Co. of China Ltd China Merchants Bank Co Ltd   Industrial Bank Co Ltd   Shanghai Pudong Development Bank Co Ltd

---

iShares iBonds Dec 2024 Term Corporate ETF   C-   HOLD

Ticker	Traded On	NAV		Total Assets ($)	Dividend Yield (TTM)	Turnover Ratio	Expense Ratio
IBDP	NYSE Arca	23.88		$308,463,583	3.29	8	0.1

Ratings
Reward   C-
Risk   C-
Recent Upgrade/Downgrade

Fund Information
Fund Type   Exchange Traded Funds
Category   US Fixed Income
Sub-Category   Corporate Bond
Prospectus Objective   Corp Bond - Gen
Inception Date   Mar-15
Open to New Investments   Y

Prices
Price (as of 12/31/2018)   23.90
52-Week High   25.05
52-Week Low   23.69

Total Returns (%)

3-Month	6-Month	1-Year	3-Year	5-Year
0.51	1.59	-1.08	10.69	

3-Year Standard Deviation   3.44
Effective Duration   4.90

Valuation
Premium/Discount (1-Year Average)   0.30

Company Information
Provider   iShares
Manager/Tenure   James Mauro (3), Scott Radell (3)
Website   http://www.ishares.com
Address   iShares 400 Howard Street San Francisco CA 94105 United States
Phone Number   800-474-2737

PERFORMANCE

Ratings History

Date	Overall Rating	Risk Rating	Reward Rating
Q4-18	C-	C-	C-
Q2-18	C-	C-	C-
Q4-17	B-	B+	C
Q4-16	D+	C-	D+
Q4-15	U		

Asset & Performance History

Date	NAV	1-Year Total Return
2017	24.96	5.35
2016	24.41	6.02
2015	23.77	
2014		
2013		
2012		

Total Assets: $308,463,583
Asset Allocation

Asset	%
Cash	1%
Stocks	0%
US Stocks	0%
Bonds	99%
US Bonds	89%
Other	0%

Services Offered:

Investment Strategy: The investment seeks to track the investment results of the Bloomberg Barclays December 2024 Maturity Corporate Index which composed of U.S. dollar-denominated, investment-grade corporate bonds maturing in 2024. The fund generally will invest at least 90% of its assets in the component securities of the underlying index. The underlying index is composed of U.S. dollar-denominated, taxable, investment-grade corporate bonds scheduled to mature after December 31, 2023 and before December 16, 2024. **Top Holdings:** Goldman Sachs Group, Inc. 4%   Morgan Stanley 3.88%   Morgan Stanley 3.7%   Bank of America Corporation 4.2% Credit Suisse AG New York Branch 3.63%

SPDR® Bloomberg Barclays 1-10 Year TIPS ETF   C-   HOLD

Ticker	Traded On	NAV	Total Assets ($)	Dividend Yield (TTM)	Turnover Ratio	Expense Ratio
TIPX	NYSE Arca	18.85	$307,612,028	2.83	21	0.15

Ratings
Reward	D+
Risk	C-
Recent Upgrade/Downgrade	

Fund Information
Fund Type	Exchange Traded Funds
Category	US Fixed Income
Sub-Category	Inflation-Protected Bond
Prospectus Objective	Govt Bond - Treasury
Inception Date	May-13
Open to New Investments	Y

Prices
Price (as of 12/31/2018)	18.87
52-Week High	19.29
52-Week Low	18.75

Total Returns (%)
3-Month	6-Month	1-Year	3-Year	5-Year
-0.02	-0.59	-0.42	5.22	5.28

3-Year Standard Deviation	2.4
Effective Duration	5.08

Valuation
Premium/Discount (1-Year Average)	0.00

Company Information
Provider	SPDR State Street Global Advisors
Manager/Tenure	Cynthia Moy (4), James Kramer (2), Orhan Imer (1)
Website	http://www.spdrs.com
Address	SPDR State Street Global Advisors State Street Financial Center, 1 Lincoln Street Boston MA 02111-2900 United States
Phone Number	617-786-3000

PERFORMANCE

Ratings History
Date	Overall Rating	Risk Rating	Reward Rating
Q4-18	C-	C-	D+
Q2-18	C-	C-	C
Q4-17	C	C	C
Q4-16	C-	D+	C
Q4-15	D+	D+	D+

Asset & Performance History
Date	NAV	1-Year Total Return
2017	19.29	0.85
2016	19.49	3.82
2015	18.97	-0.66
2014	19.11	0.73
2013	19.25	
2012		

Total Assets: $307,612,028
Asset Allocation
Asset	%
Cash	0%
Stocks	0%
US Stocks	0%
Bonds	100%
US Bonds	100%
Other	0%

Services Offered:

Investment Strategy: The investment seeks to provide investment results that correspond generally to the price and yield performance of the Bloomberg Barclays 1-10 Year U.S. Government Inflation-Linked Bond Index that tracks the 1-10 year inflation protected sector of the United States Treasury market. Under normal market conditions, the fund generally invests substantially all, but at least 80%, of its total assets in the securities comprising the index or in securities that the Adviser determines have economic characteristics that are substantially identical to the economic characteristics of the securities that comprise the index. The fund is non-diversified. **Top Holdings:** United States Treasury Notes 0.12% United States Treasury Notes 0.12% United States Treasury Notes 0.12% United States Treasury Notes 0.62% United States Treasury Notes 0.38%

SPDR® Bloomberg Barclays Short Term International Treasury Bond ETF   C-   HOLD

Ticker	Traded On	NAV	Total Assets ($)	Dividend Yield (TTM)	Turnover Ratio	Expense Ratio
BWZ	NYSE Arca	30.74	$306,440,442	0.57	63	0.35

Ratings
Reward	D+
Risk	C-
Recent Upgrade/Downgrade	Down

Fund Information
Fund Type	Exchange Traded Funds
Category	Global Fixed Income
Sub-Category	World Bond
Prospectus Objective	Worldwide Bond
Inception Date	Jan-09
Open to New Investments	Y

Prices
Price (as of 12/31/2018)	30.70
52-Week High	33.46
52-Week Low	30.42

Total Returns (%)
3-Month	6-Month	1-Year	3-Year	5-Year
-0.06	-0.51	-3.16	5.00	-12.37

3-Year Standard Deviation	6.45
Effective Duration	1.80

Valuation
Premium/Discount (1-Year Average)	0.03

Company Information
Provider	SPDR State Street Global Advisors
Manager/Tenure	Joanna Madden (4), James Kramer (2), Orhan Imer (1)
Website	http://www.spdrs.com
Address	SPDR State Street Global Advisors State Street Financial Center, 1 Lincoln Street Boston MA 02111-2900 United States
Phone Number	617-786-3000

PERFORMANCE

Ratings History
Date	Overall Rating	Risk Rating	Reward Rating
Q4-18	C-	C-	D+
Q2-18	C-	C-	C-
Q4-17	C	C	C-
Q4-16	D+	D+	D
Q4-15	D	D+	D

Asset & Performance History
Date	NAV	1-Year Total Return
2017	32.09	9.55
2016	29.31	-1.9
2015	29.76	-7.44
2014	32.17	-9.83
2013	35.75	-2.34
2012	36.64	2.1

Total Assets: $306,440,442
Asset Allocation
Asset	%
Cash	1%
Stocks	0%
US Stocks	0%
Bonds	98%
US Bonds	0%
Other	1%

Services Offered:

Investment Strategy: The investment seeks to provide investment results that correspond generally to the Bloomberg Barclays 1-3 Year Global Treasury ex-US Capped Index. The fund invests substantially all, but at least 80%, of its total assets in the securities comprising the index or in securities that the Adviser determines have economic characteristics that are substantially identical to the economic characteristics of the securities that comprise the index. The index is designed to measure the performance of fixed-rate local currency sovereign debt of investment grade countries outside the United States that have remaining maturities of 1-3 years. The fund is non-diversified. **Top Holdings:** Japan(Govt Of) 0.1% Japan (10 Year Issue) Sr Unsecured 09/21 1.1 Japan (5 Year Issue) Sr Unsecured 09/21 0.1 Australia(Cmnwlth) 5.75% Japan(Govt Of) 0.1%

SPDR® S&P Pharmaceuticals ETF   C   HOLD

Ticker	Traded On	NAV	Total Assets ($)	Dividend Yield (TTM)	Turnover Ratio	Expense Ratio
XPH	NYSE Arca	36.67	$305,489,366	0.55	41	0.35

Ratings
Reward	C
Risk	D+
Recent Upgrade/Downgrade	Up

Fund Information
Fund Type	Exchange Traded Funds
Category	Healthcare Sector Equity
Sub-Category	Health
Prospectus Objective	Health
Inception Date	Jun-06
Open to New Investments	Y

Prices
Price (as of 12/31/2018)	36.62
52-Week High	49.96
52-Week Low	34.77

Total Returns (%)
3-Month	6-Month	1-Year	3-Year	5-Year
-21.21	-14.25	-14.70	-26.62	-3.42

3-Year Standard Deviation	18.84
Effective Duration	

Valuation
Premium/Discount (1-Year Average)	0.01

Company Information
Provider	SPDR State Street Global Advisors
Manager/Tenure	Michael J. Feehily (7), Karl A. Schneider (4), Keith Richardson (1)
Website	http://www.spdrs.com
Address	SPDR State Street Global Advisors State Street Financial Center, 1 Lincoln Street Boston MA 02111-2900 United States
Phone Number	617-786-3000

PERFORMANCE

Ratings History
Date	Overall Rating	Risk Rating	Reward Rating
Q4-18	C	D+	C
Q2-18	C-	D	C
Q4-17	D+	D+	D+
Q4-16	C	D+	C
Q4-15	C	C	C+

Asset & Performance History
Date	NAV	1-Year Total Return
2017	43.49	12.05
2016	39.08	-24.97
2015	51.21	1.61
2014	54	29.52
2013	43.98	60.69
2012	27.97	11.02

Total Assets: $305,489,366

Asset Allocation
Asset	%
Cash	0%
Stocks	100%
US Stocks	99%
Bonds	0%
US Bonds	0%
Other	0%

Services Offered:

Investment Strategy: The investment seeks to provide investment results that, before fees and expenses, correspond generally to the total return performance of an index derived from the pharmaceuticals segment of a U.S. total market composite index. In seeking to track the performance of the S&P Pharmaceuticals Select Industry Index (the "index"), the fund employs a sampling strategy. It generally invests substantially all, but at least 80%, of its total assets in the securities comprising the index. The index represents the pharmaceuticals segment of the S&P Total Market Index ("S&P TMI"). The fund is non-diversified. **Top Holdings:** Merck & Co Inc   Eli Lilly and Co   Pfizer Inc   Zoetis Inc Class A   Johnson & Johnson

---

iShares MSCI Global Metals & Mining Producers ETF   C   HOLD

Ticker	Traded On	NAV	Total Assets ($)	Dividend Yield (TTM)	Turnover Ratio	Expense Ratio
PICK	BATS	27.05	$304,289,542	3.34	14	0.39

Ratings
Reward	C-
Risk	C
Recent Upgrade/Downgrade	

Fund Information
Fund Type	Exchange Traded Funds
Category	Prec Metals
Sub-Category	Equity Precious Metals
Prospectus Objective	Prec Metals
Inception Date	Jan-12
Open to New Investments	Y

Prices
Price (as of 12/31/2018)	26.98
52-Week High	37.82
52-Week Low	26.26

Total Returns (%)
3-Month	6-Month	1-Year	3-Year	5-Year
-14.26	-13.46	-18.50	75.63	-15.48

3-Year Standard Deviation	26.59
Effective Duration	

Valuation
Premium/Discount (1-Year Average)	-0.04

Company Information
Provider	iShares
Manager/Tenure	Diane Hsiung (6), Greg Savage (6), Jennifer Hsui (5), 1 other
Website	http://www.ishares.com
Address	iShares 400 Howard Street San Francisco CA 94105 United States
Phone Number	800-474-2737

PERFORMANCE

Ratings History
Date	Overall Rating	Risk Rating	Reward Rating
Q4-18	C	C	C-
Q2-18	C	C	C+
Q4-17	C+	C-	B
Q4-16	C-	D+	C-
Q4-15	D-	D	D-

Asset & Performance History
Date	NAV	1-Year Total Return
2017	34.67	37.14
2016	26.02	57.16
2015	16.76	-40.25
2014	31.08	-19.45
2013	39.64	-7.53
2012	44.5	

Total Assets: $304,289,542

Asset Allocation
Asset	%
Cash	0%
Stocks	100%
US Stocks	15%
Bonds	0%
US Bonds	0%
Other	0%

Services Offered:

Investment Strategy: The investment seeks to track the investment results of the MSCI ACWI Select Metals & Mining Producers ex Gold and Silver Investable Market Index. The fund generally will invest at least 90% of its assets in the component securities of the index and in investments that have economic characteristics that are substantially identical to the component securities of the index. The index composed of global equities of companies primarily engaged in mining, extraction or production of diversified metals, excluding gold and silver. The fund is non-diversified. **Top Holdings:** BHP Group Ltd   Rio Tinto PLC   Vale SA   Glencore PLC   BHP Group PLC

Invesco KBW High Dividend Yield Financial ETF

C   HOLD

Ticker	Traded On	NAV	Total Assets ($)	Dividend Yield (TTM)	Turnover Ratio	Expense Ratio
KBWD	NAS CM	19.81	$303,547,502	8.57		2.4

Ratings
Reward   B-
Risk   C-
Recent Upgrade/Downgrade

Fund Information
Fund Type   Exchange Traded Funds
Category   Financials Sector Equity
Sub-Category   Financial
Prospectus Objective   Financial
Inception Date   Dec-10
Open to New Investments

Prices
Price (as of 12/31/2018)   19.84
52-Week High   23.79
52-Week Low   18.90

Total Returns (%)

3-Month	6-Month	1-Year	3-Year	5-Year
-10.84	-11.34	-8.77	23.15	19.70

3-Year Standard Deviation   13.48
Effective Duration

Valuation
Premium/Discount (1-Year Average)   0.06

Company Information
Provider   Invesco
Manager/Tenure   Peter Hubbard (8), Michael Jeanette
                  (8), Tony Seisser (4), 1 other
Website   http://www.invesco.com/us
Address   Invesco 11 Greenway Plaza, Ste. 2500
                  Houston TX 77046 United States
Phone Number   800-659-1005

PERFORMANCE

Ratings History				Asset & Performance History			Total Assets:	$303,547,502
Date	Overall Rating	Risk Rating	Reward Rating	Date	NAV	1-Year Total Return	Asset Allocation	%
Q4-18	C	C-	B-	2017	23.6	11.92	Cash	0%
Q2-18	C	D+	B-	2016	23	20.61	Stocks	100%
Q4-17	B-	C+	B-	2015	20.99	-10.19	US Stocks	100%
Q4-16	C	C-	C+	2014	25.26	8.23	Bonds	0%
Q4-15	C	C-	C	2013	25.35	18.2	US Bonds	0%
				2012	23.17	16.76	Other	0%

Services Offered:

Investment Strategy: The investment seeks to track the investment results (before fees and expenses) of the KBW Nasdaq Financial Sector Dividend Yield Index (the "underlying index"). The fund generally will invest at least 90% of its total assets in the securities of financial companies that are listed on a U.S. national securities exchange and are principally engaged in the business of providing financial services and products, including banking, insurance and diversified financial services, in the United States and that comprise the underlying index. **Top Holdings:** Chimera Investment Corp AGNC Investment Corp Dynex Capital Inc Orchid Island Capital Inc AG Mortgage Investment Trust Inc

---

SPDR® S&P 500 Fossil Fuel Reserves Free ETF

C   HOLD

Ticker	Traded On	NAV	Total Assets ($)	Dividend Yield (TTM)	Turnover Ratio	Expense Ratio
SPYX	NYSE Arca	60.74	$301,908,569	1.72	4	0.2

Ratings
Reward   C
Risk   C-
Recent Upgrade/Downgrade

Fund Information
Fund Type   Exchange Traded Funds
Category   US Equity Large Cap Blend
Sub-Category   Large Blend
Prospectus Objective   Growth & Inc
Inception Date   Nov-15
Open to New Investments   Y

Prices
Price (as of 12/31/2018)   60.94
52-Week High   71.48
52-Week Low   57.18

Total Returns (%)

3-Month	6-Month	1-Year	3-Year	5-Year
-13.75	-6.75	-4.32	30.39	

3-Year Standard Deviation   9.49
Effective Duration

Valuation
Premium/Discount (1-Year Average)   0.17

Company Information
Provider   SPDR State Street Global Advisors
Manager/Tenure   Michael J. Feehily (3), Karl A.
                  Schneider (3), Eric Viliott (1)
Website   http://www.spdrs.com
Address   SPDR State Street Global Advisors
                  State Street Financial Center, 1
                  Lincoln Street Boston MA 02111-2900
                  United States
Phone Number   617-786-3000

PERFORMANCE

Ratings History				Asset & Performance History			Total Assets:	$301,908,569
Date	Overall Rating	Risk Rating	Reward Rating	Date	NAV	1-Year Total Return	Asset Allocation	%
Q4-18	C	C-	C	2017	64.65	22.87	Cash	0%
Q2-18	C	D+	C	2016	53.56	10.91	Stocks	100%
Q4-17	C	B+	C	2015	49.27		US Stocks	99%
Q4-16	D	D+	D+	2014			Bonds	0%
Q4-15				2013			US Bonds	0%
				2012			Other	0%

Services Offered:

Investment Strategy: The investment seeks to provide investment results that, before fees and expenses, correspond generally to the total return performance of the S&P 500 Fossil Fuel Free Index. Normally, the fund generally invests substantially all, but at least 80%, of its total assets in the securities comprising the index. In addition, it may invest in equity securities that are not included in the index, cash and cash equivalents or money market instruments. The index is designed to measure the performance of companies in the S&P 500 Index that do not own fossil fuel reserves. The fund is non-diversified. **Top Holdings:** Microsoft Corp Apple Inc Amazon.com Inc Berkshire Hathaway Inc B Johnson & Johnson

iShares Convertible Bond ETF   C-   HOLD

Ticker	Traded On	NAV
ICVT	BATS	52.05

Total Assets ($)	Dividend Yield (TTM)	Turnover Ratio	Expense Ratio
$301,879,417	1.97	14	0.2

Ratings
Reward   C-
Risk   C-
Recent Upgrade/Downgrade   Down

Fund Information
Fund Type   Exchange Traded Funds
Category   Convertibles
Sub-Category   Convertibles
Prospectus Objective   Convertible Bond
Inception Date   Jun-15
Open to New Investments   Y

Prices
Price (as of 12/31/2018)   52.52
52-Week High   60.12
52-Week Low   50.03

Total Returns (%)
3-Month	6-Month	1-Year	3-Year	5-Year
-10.48	-7.55	-1.85	26.13	

3-Year Standard Deviation   8.6
Effective Duration   1.63

Valuation
Premium/Discount (1-Year Average)   0.10

Company Information
Provider   iShares
Manager/Tenure   James Mauro (3), Scott Radell (3)
Website   http://www.ishares.com
Address   iShares 400 Howard Street San Francisco CA 94105 United States
Phone Number   800-474-2737

PERFORMANCE

Ratings History
Date	Overall Rating	Risk Rating	Reward Rating
Q4-18	C-	C-	C-
Q2-18	C	C-	C
Q4-17	C	B	C+
Q4-16	D	D+	C-
Q4-15	U		

Asset & Performance History
Date	NAV	1-Year Total Return
2017	54.91	15.19
2016	48.75	11.13
2015	45.29	
2014		
2013		
2012		

Total Assets: $301,879,417
Asset Allocation
Asset	%
Cash	1%
Stocks	1%
US Stocks	1%
Bonds	0%
US Bonds	0%
Other	0%

Services Offered:

Investment Strategy: The investment seeks to track the investment results of the Bloomberg Barclays U.S. Convertible Cash Pay Bond > $250MM Index (the "underlying index"). The fund generally will invest at least 90% of its assets in the component securities of the underlying index and may invest up to 10% of its assets in certain futures, options and swap contracts, cash and cash equivalents, as well as in securities not included in the underlying index. The underlying index is a subset of the Bloomberg Barclays U.S. Convertibles: Cash Pay Bonds Index, which measures the performance of the U.S. dollar-denominated convertibles market. **Top Holdings:** DISH Network Corporation 3.38% Intel Corporation 3.25% Advanced Micro Devices, Inc. 2.13% Microchip Technology Incorporated 1.63% Microchip Technology Incorporated 1.63%

Invesco California AMT-Free Municipal Bond ETF   C   HOLD

Ticker	Traded On	NAV
PWZ	NYSE Arca	25.76

Total Assets ($)	Dividend Yield (TTM)	Turnover Ratio	Expense Ratio
$300,580,256	2.58		0.28

Ratings
Reward   C-
Risk   C+
Recent Upgrade/Downgrade

Fund Information
Fund Type   Exchange Traded Funds
Category   US Muni Fixed Inc
Sub-Category   Muni California Long
Prospectus Objective   Muni Bond - Single State
Inception Date   Oct-07
Open to New Investments   Y

Prices
Price (as of 12/31/2018)   25.80
52-Week High   26.38
52-Week Low   25.05

Total Returns (%)
3-Month	6-Month	1-Year	3-Year	5-Year
1.49	0.78	0.39	7.99	28.25

3-Year Standard Deviation   4.09
Effective Duration   8.14

Valuation
Premium/Discount (1-Year Average)   -0.05

Company Information
Provider   Invesco
Manager/Tenure   Philip Fang (11), Peter Hubbard (11), Jeffrey W. Kernagis (11), 2 others
Website   http://www.invesco.com/us
Address   Invesco 11 Greenway Plaza, Ste. 2500 Houston TX 77046 United States
Phone Number   800-659-1005

PERFORMANCE

Ratings History
Date	Overall Rating	Risk Rating	Reward Rating
Q4-18	C	C+	C-
Q2-18	C	C-	C
Q4-17	B-	B+	C
Q4-16	C	C-	C
Q4-15	C	C-	C+

Asset & Performance History
Date	NAV	1-Year Total Return
2017	26.32	6.65
2016	25.31	0.86
2015	25.8	4.15
2014	25.58	14.01
2013	23.34	-4.1
2012	25.28	8.78

Total Assets: $300,580,256
Asset Allocation
Asset	%
Cash	0%
Stocks	0%
US Stocks	0%
Bonds	100%
US Bonds	99%
Other	0%

Services Offered:

Investment Strategy: The investment seeks to track the investment results (before fees and expenses) of the ICE BofAML California Long-Term Core Plus Municipal Securities Index. The fund generally will invest at least 80% of its total assets in municipal securities that comprise the underlying index and that also are exempt from the federal AMT. The underlying index is composed of U.S. dollar-denominated, investment grade, tax-exempt debt publicly issued by California or any U.S. territory or their political subdivisions, in the U.S. domestic market with a term of at least 15 years remaining to final maturity. It is non-diversified. **Top Holdings:** SAN DIEGO CALIF UNI SCH DIST 5% CALIFORNIA HEALTH FACS FING AUTH 5% LOS ANGELES CALIF 1.4% SAN FRANCISCO CALIF CITY & CNTY ARPTS COMMN 5% SACRAMENTO CALIF 5%

ProShares Ultra Technology

C+   HOLD

Ticker	Traded On	NAV	Total Assets ($)	Dividend Yield (TTM)	Turnover Ratio	Expense Ratio
ROM	NYSE Arca	78.86	$298,833,409	0.17		0.95

Ratings
Reward   C+
Risk   C
Recent Upgrade/Downgrade   Down

Fund Information
Fund Type   Exchange Traded Funds
Category   Trading Tools
Sub-Category   Trading--Leveraged Equity
Prospectus Objective   Technology
Inception Date   Jan-07
Open to New Investments   Y

Prices
Price (as of 12/31/2018)   78.85
52-Week High   123.16
52-Week Low   68.54

Total Returns (%)

3-Month	6-Month	1-Year	3-Year	5-Year
-34.74	-24.84	-10.04	102.75	189.67

3-Year Standard Deviation   30.24
Effective Duration

Valuation
Premium/Discount (1-Year Average)   0.03

Company Information
Provider   ProShares
Manager/Tenure   Michael Neches (5), Tarak Davé (0)
Website   http://www.proshares.com
Address   ProShares 7501 Wisconsin Avenue,
                  Suite 1000 Bethesda MD 20814
                  United States
Phone Number   866-776-5125

PERFORMANCE

Ratings History

Date	Overall Rating	Risk Rating	Reward Rating
Q4-18	C+	C	C+
Q2-18	B	C	A
Q4-17	A-	B-	A+
Q4-16	C	D+	B-
Q4-15	C	C	C

Asset & Performance History

Date	NAV	1-Year Total Return
2017	87.9	81.2
2016	48.55	24.37
2015	39.13	2.88
2014	38.08	38.86
2013	27.49	55.88
2012	17.64	20.13

Total Assets: $298,833,409
Asset Allocation

Asset	%
Cash	-100%
Stocks	102%
US Stocks	102%
Bonds	0%
US Bonds	0%
Other	98%

Services Offered:

Investment Strategy: The investment seeks daily investment results that correspond to two times (2x) the daily performance of the Dow Jones U.S. TechnologySM Index. The fund invests in financial instruments that ProShare Advisors believes, in combination, should produce daily returns consistent with the fund's investment objective. The index measures the performance of certain companies in the technology sector of the U.S. equity market. Component companies include, among others, those involved in computers and office equipment, software, communications technology, semiconductors, diversified technology services and Internet services. The fund is non-diversified. **Top Holdings:** Dj U.S. Technology Index Swap Goldman Sachs International   Dj U.S. Technology Index Swap Deutsche Bank Ag   Dj U.S. Technology Index Swap Ubs Ag   Microsoft Corp   Apple Inc

---

GraniteShares Gold Trust

D   SELL

Ticker	Traded On	NAV	Total Assets ($)	Dividend Yield (TTM)	Turnover Ratio	Expense Ratio
BAR	NYSE Arca	127.83	$298,783,968	0		0.17

Ratings
Reward   D
Risk   D+
Recent Upgrade/Downgrade

Fund Information
Fund Type   Exchange Traded Funds
Category   Commodities Specified
Sub-Category   Commodities Precious Metals
Prospectus Objective   Prec Metals
Inception Date   Aug-17
Open to New Investments   Y

Prices
Price (as of 12/31/2018)   127.88
52-Week High   135.42
52-Week Low   117.19

Total Returns (%)

3-Month	6-Month	1-Year	3-Year	5-Year
7.71	2.61	-1.33		

3-Year Standard Deviation
Effective Duration

Valuation
Premium/Discount (1-Year Average)   0.18

Company Information
Provider   Graniteshares
Manager/Tenure   Management Team (1)
Website   http://www.graniteshares.com
Address   Graniteshares 30 Vesey Street, 9th
                  Floor New York New York 10007
                  United States
Phone Number

PERFORMANCE

Ratings History

Date	Overall Rating	Risk Rating	Reward Rating
Q4-18	D	D+	D
Q2-18	U		
Q4-17	U		
Q4-16			
Q4-15			

Asset & Performance History

Date	NAV	1-Year Total Return
2017	129.56	
2016		
2015		
2014		
2013		
2012		

Total Assets: $298,783,968
Asset Allocation

Asset	%
Cash	0%
Stocks	0%
US Stocks	0%
Bonds	0%
US Bonds	0%
Other	100%

Services Offered:

Investment Strategy: The investment seeks to reflect generally the performance of the price of gold. The Shares are intended to constitute a simple and cost-effective means of making an investment similar to an investment in gold. **Top Holdings:** Physical Gold Bullion

WisdomTree Interest Rate Hedged High Yield Bond Fund   C   HOLD

Ticker	Traded On	NAV	Total Assets ($)	Dividend Yield (TTM)	Turnover Ratio	Expense Ratio
HYZD	NAS CM	22.63	$297,731,086	5.14	57	0.43

Ratings

Reward	C-
Risk	C+
Recent Upgrade/Downgrade	Down

Fund Information

Fund Type	Exchange Traded Funds
Category	Fixed Income Misc
Sub-Category	Nontraditional Bond
Prospectus Objective	Corp Bond-High Yld
Inception Date	Dec-13
Open to New Investments	Y

Prices

Price (as of 12/31/2018)	22.42
52-Week High	24.33
52-Week Low	22.16

Total Returns (%)

3-Month	6-Month	1-Year	3-Year	5-Year
-5.09	-2.45	-0.72	20.64	13.67

3-Year Standard Deviation	3.97
Effective Duration	0.00

Valuation

Premium/Discount (1-Year Average)	0.01

Company Information

Provider	WisdomTree
Manager/Tenure	Paul L. Benson (3), Stephanie Shu (3)
Website	http://www.wisdomtree.com
Address	WisdomTree 245 Park Avenue, 35th floor New York NY 10167 United States
Phone Number	866-909-9473

PERFORMANCE

Ratings History

Date	Overall Rating	Risk Rating	Reward Rating
Q4-18	C	C+	C-
Q2-18	C	C-	C+
Q4-17	C+	B	C+
Q4-16	C-	D+	C
Q4-15	D	C-	D

Asset & Performance History

Date	NAV	1-Year Total Return
2017	24.02	6.44
2016	23.72	13.58
2015	21.91	-5.32
2014	24.11	-0.47
2013	25.1	
2012		

Total Assets: $297,731,086

Asset Allocation

Asset	%
Cash	84%
Stocks	0%
US Stocks	0%
Bonds	16%
US Bonds	4%
Other	0%

Services Offered:

Investment Strategy: The investment seeks to track the price and yield performance of the BofA Merrill Lynch 0-5 Year U.S. High Yield Constrained, Zero Duration Index. The index is designed to provide long exposure to the BofA Merrill Lynch 0-5 Year U.S. High Yield Constrained Index while seeking to manage interest rate risk through the use of short positions in U.S. Treasury securities. Under normal circumstances, at least 80% of the fund's total assets will be invested in the component securities of the index and investments that have economic characteristics that are substantially identical to the economic characteristics of such component securities. It is non-diversified. **Top Holdings:** Us 2yr Note (Cbt) Mar19 Xcbt 20190329   Us 5yr Note (Cbt) Mar19 Xcbt 20190329   Sprint Corporation 7.88%   Reynolds Group Issuer LLC. 5.75%   Bausch Health Companies Inc 5.88%

Invesco S&P SmallCap 600® Pure Growth ETF   C-   HOLD

Ticker	Traded On	NAV	Total Assets ($)	Dividend Yield (TTM)	Turnover Ratio	Expense Ratio
RZG	NYSE Arca	104.25	$295,711,776	0.42		0.35

Ratings

Reward	C
Risk	D+
Recent Upgrade/Downgrade	Down

Fund Information

Fund Type	Exchange Traded Funds
Category	US Equity Small Cap
Sub-Category	Small Growth
Prospectus Objective	Small Company
Inception Date	Mar-06
Open to New Investments	Y

Prices

Price (as of 12/31/2018)	104.15
52-Week High	139.81
52-Week Low	98.06

Total Returns (%)

3-Month	6-Month	1-Year	3-Year	5-Year
-20.74	-18.42	-7.74	31.15	34.22

3-Year Standard Deviation	16.69
Effective Duration	

Valuation

Premium/Discount (1-Year Average)	0.10

Company Information

Provider	Invesco
Manager/Tenure	Peter Hubbard (0), Michael Jeanette (0), Jonathan Nixon (0), 1 other
Website	http://www.invesco.com/us
Address	Invesco 11 Greenway Plaza, Ste. 2500 Houston TX 77046 United States
Phone Number	800-659-1005

PERFORMANCE

Ratings History

Date	Overall Rating	Risk Rating	Reward Rating
Q4-18	C-	D+	C
Q2-18	C+	C-	B
Q4-17	A-	B	A
Q4-16	D+	D+	D+
Q4-15	C	C	B-

Asset & Performance History

Date	NAV	1-Year Total Return
2017	113.47	18.4
2016	96.73	19.33
2015	80.82	0.88
2014	80.64	1.44
2013	79.78	43.44
2012	55.83	12.64

Total Assets: $295,711,776

Asset Allocation

Asset	%
Cash	0%
Stocks	100%
US Stocks	99%
Bonds	0%
US Bonds	0%
Other	0%

Services Offered:

Investment Strategy: The investment seeks to track the investment results (before fees and expenses) of the S&P SmallCap 600 Pure Growth Index (the "underlying index"). The fund generally will invest at least 90% of its total assets in the securities that comprise the underlying index. Strictly in accordance with its guidelines and mandated procedures, the index provider, compiles, maintains and calculates the underlying index, which is comprised of those S&P SmallCap 600® companies with strong growth characteristics selected by the index provider. The fund is non-diversified. **Top Holdings:** BioTelemetry Inc   Amedisys Inc   Integer Holdings Corp   Qualys Inc   Innoviva Inc

iShares Morningstar Multi-Asset Income ETF

C-   **HOLD**

Ticker	Traded On	NAV	Total Assets ($)	Dividend Yield (TTM)	Turnover Ratio	Expense Ratio
IYLD	BATS	23.25	$294,500,738	5.12	64	0.59

Ratings
Reward	D+
Risk	C-
Recent Upgrade/Downgrade	Down

Fund Information
Fund Type	Exchange Traded Funds
Category	Cautious Allocation
Sub-Category	Allocation--30% to 50% Equity
Prospectus Objective	Multi-Asset Global
Inception Date	Apr-12
Open to New Investments	Y

Prices
Price (as of 12/31/2018)	23.28
52-Week High	25.94
52-Week Low	23.02

Total Returns (%)
3-Month	6-Month	1-Year	3-Year	5-Year
-3.92	-1.95	-4.75	15.94	21.63

3-Year Standard Deviation	5.02
Effective Duration	5.40

Valuation
Premium/Discount (1-Year Average)	0.01

Company Information
Provider	iShares
Manager/Tenure	James Mauro (6), Scott Radell (6)
Website	http://www.ishares.com
Address	iShares 400 Howard Street San Francisco CA 94105 United States
Phone Number	800-474-2737

PERFORMANCE

Ratings History
Date	Overall Rating	Risk Rating	Reward Rating
Q4-18	C-	C-	D+
Q2-18	C-	C-	C
Q4-17	B-	B	C+
Q4-16	C	C-	C
Q4-15	C-	C-	C-

Asset & Performance History
Date	NAV	1-Year Total Return
2017	25.79	10.86
2016	24.28	9.79
2015	23.21	-4.76
2014	25.62	10.16
2013	24.75	0.56
2012	26.16	

Total Assets: $294,500,738
Asset Allocation
Asset	%
Cash	1%
Stocks	35%
US Stocks	15%
Bonds	59%
US Bonds	33%
Other	0%

Services Offered:

Investment Strategy: The investment seeks to track the investment results of the Morningstar® Multi-Asset High Income IndexSM. The fund generally will invest at least 90% of its assets in the component securities of the underlying index and may invest up to 10% of its assets in certain futures, options and swap contracts, cash and cash equivalents. The index is broadly diversified and seeks to deliver high current income while maintaining long-term capital appreciation. The fund is a fund-of-funds and invests primarily in the securities of the underlying funds that themselves seek investment results corresponding to their own underlying indexes. **Top Holdings:** iShares iBoxx $ High Yield Corp Bd ETF   iShares Mortgage Real Estate Capped ETF   iShares International Select Div ETF iShares JP Morgan USD Em Mkts Bd ETF   iShares Intermediate-Term Corp Bd ETF

Invesco Dynamic Biotechnology & Genome ETF

C   **HOLD**

Ticker	Traded On	NAV	Total Assets ($)	Dividend Yield (TTM)	Turnover Ratio	Expense Ratio
PBE	NYSE Arca	47.29	$294,066,877	0	141	0.59

Ratings
Reward	C+
Risk	D+
Recent Upgrade/Downgrade	

Fund Information
Fund Type	Exchange Traded Funds
Category	Healthcare Sector Equity
Sub-Category	Health
Prospectus Objective	Health
Inception Date	Jun-05
Open to New Investments	Y

Prices
Price (as of 12/31/2018)	47.07
52-Week High	60.27
52-Week Low	43.44

Total Returns (%)
3-Month	6-Month	1-Year	3-Year	5-Year
-19.58	-14.69	0.23	-5.53	31.43

3-Year Standard Deviation	24.96
Effective Duration	

Valuation
Premium/Discount (1-Year Average)	0.05

Company Information
Provider	Invesco
Manager/Tenure	Peter Hubbard (11), Michael Jeanette (10), Tony Seisser (4), 1 other
Website	http://www.invesco.com/us
Address	Invesco 11 Greenway Plaza, Ste. 2500 Houston TX 77046 United States
Phone Number	800-659-1005

PERFORMANCE

Ratings History
Date	Overall Rating	Risk Rating	Reward Rating
Q4-18	C	D+	C+
Q2-18	C	D	C
Q4-17	C-	C	D+
Q4-16	C-	D	C
Q4-15	C+	C	B-

Asset & Performance History
Date	NAV	1-Year Total Return
2017	47.18	22.42
2016	38.78	-23.02
2015	50.56	2
2014	50.1	36.39
2013	36.96	61.67
2012	22.86	14.01

Total Assets: $294,066,877
Asset Allocation
Asset	%
Cash	0%
Stocks	100%
US Stocks	97%
Bonds	0%
US Bonds	0%
Other	0%

Services Offered:

Investment Strategy: The investment seeks to track the investment results (before fees and expenses) of the Dynamic Biotech & Genome IntellidexSM Index. The fund generally will invest at least 90% of its total assets in common stocks of biotechnology companies and genome companies that comprise the underlying intellidex. The underlying intellidex was composed of common stocks of 30 U.S. biotechnology and genome companies. These companies are engaged principally in the research, development, manufacture and marketing and distribution of various biotechnological products, services and processes, etc. It is non-diversified. **Top Holdings:** Amgen Inc Vertex Pharmaceuticals Inc   Illumina Inc   Biogen Inc   Qiagen NV

Principal EDGE Active Income ETF   C-   HOLD

Ticker	Traded On	NAV
YLD	NYSE Arca	37.22

Total Assets ($)	Dividend Yield (TTM)	Turnover Ratio	Expense Ratio
$292,637,010	4.78	11	0.65

Ratings

Reward	C-
Risk	D+
Recent Upgrade/Downgrade	

Fund Information

Fund Type	Exchange Traded Funds
Category	Cautious Allocation
Sub-Category	Allocation--30% to 50% Equity
Prospectus Objective	Income
Inception Date	Jul-15
Open to New Investments	Y

Prices

Price (as of 12/31/2018)	37.93
52-Week High	41.70
52-Week Low	37.44

Total Returns (%)

3-Month	6-Month	1-Year	3-Year	5-Year
-6.19	-4.48	-4.87	19.75	

3-Year Standard Deviation	5.41
Effective Duration	4.44

Valuation

Premium/Discount (1-Year Average)	0.22

Company Information

Provider	Principal Funds
Manager/Tenure	Charles D. Averill (3), Todd A. Jablonski (3), Paul S. Kim (3), 2 others
Website	http://www.principalfunds.com
Address	Principal Funds 30 Dan Road Canton MA 2021 United States
Phone Number	800-787-1621

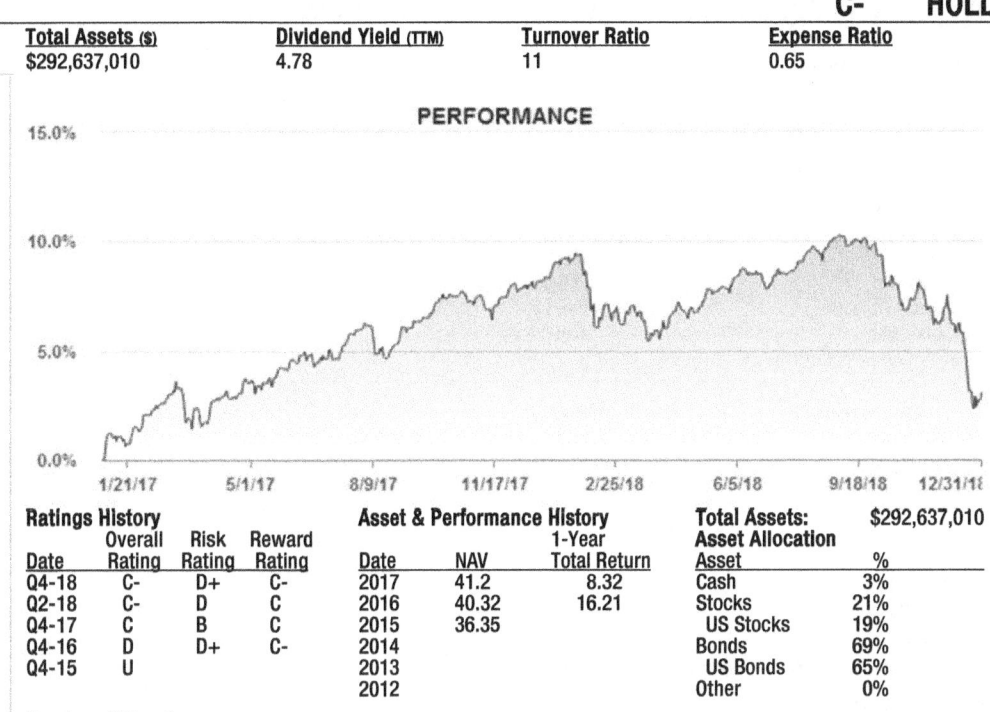

PERFORMANCE

Ratings History

Date	Overall Rating	Risk Rating	Reward Rating
Q4-18	C-	D+	C-
Q2-18	C-	D	C
Q4-17	C	B	C
Q4-16	D	D+	C-
Q4-15	U		

Asset & Performance History

Date	NAV	1-Year Total Return
2017	41.2	8.32
2016	40.32	16.21
2015	36.35	
2014		
2013		
2012		

Total Assets: $292,637,010

Asset Allocation

Asset	%
Cash	3%
Stocks	21%
US Stocks	19%
Bonds	69%
US Bonds	65%
Other	0%

Services Offered:

Investment Strategy: The investment seeks to provide current income. The fund is an actively managed exchange-traded fund ("ETF") that seeks to achieve its investment objective by investing, under normal circumstances, its assets in investment grade and non-investment grade fixed income securities (commonly known as "junk bonds") and in equity securities. The fund's Sub-Advisors, actively and tactically allocates the fund's assets among fixed income securities and equity securities in an effort to take advantage of changing economic conditions that the Advisor believes favors one asset class over another. **Top Holdings:** Hologic Inc 4.62% Gulfport Energy Corporation 6.38% OCI Nv 6.62% Titan International, Inc. 6.5% CBL & Associates Limited Partnership 5.95%

Invesco FTSE RAFI Developed Markets ex-U.S. Small-Mid ETF   C-   HOLD

Ticker	Traded On	NAV
PDN	NYSE Arca	27.66

Total Assets ($)	Dividend Yield (TTM)	Turnover Ratio	Expense Ratio
$292,626,833	3.19	19	0.49

Ratings

Reward	D+
Risk	C-
Recent Upgrade/Downgrade	

Fund Information

Fund Type	Exchange Traded Funds
Category	Global Eq Mid/Small Cap
Sub-Category	Foreign Small/Mid Value
Prospectus Objective	Foreign Stock
Inception Date	Sep-07
Open to New Investments	

Prices

Price (as of 12/31/2018)	27.56
52-Week High	36.59
52-Week Low	26.23

Total Returns (%)

3-Month	6-Month	1-Year	3-Year	5-Year
-14.89	-14.26	-17.71	13.22	11.96

3-Year Standard Deviation	11.49
Effective Duration	

Valuation

Premium/Discount (1-Year Average)	0.25

Company Information

Provider	Invesco
Manager/Tenure	Peter Hubbard (11), Jonathan Nixon (4), Michael Jeanette (3), 1 other
Website	http://www.invesco.com/us
Address	Invesco 11 Greenway Plaza, Ste. 2500 Houston TX 77046 United States
Phone Number	800-659-1005

PERFORMANCE

Ratings History

Date	Overall Rating	Risk Rating	Reward Rating
Q4-18	C-	C-	D+
Q2-18	C	C-	C+
Q4-17	B+	B	B+
Q4-16	C	C-	C
Q4-15	C-	C-	C-

Asset & Performance History

Date	NAV	1-Year Total Return
2017	34.26	29.35
2016	27.17	6.37
2015	26.11	3.6
2014	25.71	-4.55
2013	27.44	20.83
2012	23.24	14.47

Total Assets: $292,626,833

Asset Allocation

Asset	%
Cash	0%
Stocks	100%
US Stocks	1%
Bonds	0%
US Bonds	0%
Other	0%

Services Offered:

Investment Strategy: The investment seeks to track the investment results (before fees and expenses) of the FTSE RAFI Developed ex U.S. Mid-Small 1500 Index (the "underlying index"). The fund will invest at least 90% of its total assets in securities of small-and mid-capitalization companies that are classified as "developed" within the country classification definition of FTSE International Limited ("FTSE"), excluding the United States, and that comprise the underlying index, as well as American depositary receipts ("ADRs") and global depositary receipts ("GDRs") that are based on the securities in the underlying index. **Top Holdings:** MEG Energy Corp Sumitomo Dainippon Pharma Co Ltd TFI International Inc GS Engineering & Construction Corp Taisho Pharmaceutical Holding Co Ltd

Invesco BulletShares 2022 High Yield Corporate Bond ETF   C   HOLD

Ticker	Traded On	NAV	Total Assets ($)	Dividend Yield (TTM)	Turnover Ratio	Expense Ratio
BSJM	NYSE Arca	23.29	$290,336,276	5.66	17	0.42

Ratings
Reward   C
Risk   C+
Recent Upgrade/Downgrade

Fund Information
Fund Type	Exchange Traded Funds
Category	US Fixed Income
Sub-Category	High Yield Bond
Prospectus Objective	Corp Bond-High Yld
Inception Date	Sep-14
Open to New Investments	Y

Prices
Price (as of 12/31/2018)	23.21
52-Week High	25.14
52-Week Low	22.88

Total Returns (%)
3-Month	6-Month	1-Year	3-Year	5-Year
-4.03	-1.69	-1.38	20.31	

3-Year Standard Deviation	3.7
Effective Duration	2.52

Valuation
Premium/Discount (1-Year Average)	-0.06

Company Information
Provider	Invesco
Manager/Tenure	Jeremy Neisewander (2), Peter Hubbard (0), Jeffrey W. Kernagis (0), 1 other
Website	http://www.invesco.com/us
Address	Invesco 11 Greenway Plaza, Ste. 2500 Houston TX 77046 United States
Phone Number	800-659-1005

PERFORMANCE

Ratings History
Date	Overall Rating	Risk Rating	Reward Rating
Q4-18	C	C+	C
Q2-18	C	C-	C
Q4-17	B	B+	C+
Q4-16	C-	C-	C-
Q4-15	U		

Asset & Performance History
Date	NAV	1-Year Total Return
2017	24.9	5.33
2016	24.95	15.87
2015	22.67	-2.32
2014	24.39	
2013		
2012		

Total Assets: $290,336,276

Asset Allocation
Asset	%
Cash	2%
Stocks	0%
US Stocks	0%
Bonds	98%
US Bonds	85%
Other	0%

Services Offered:

Investment Strategy: The investment seeks investment results that correspond generally to the performance, before the fund's fees and expenses, of a high yield corporate bond index called the Nasdaq BulletShares® USD High Yield Corporate Bond 2022 Index. The fund will invest at least 80% of its total assets in component securities that comprise the index. The index is designed to represent the performance of a held-to-maturity portfolio of U.S. dollar-denominated high yield corporate bonds with effective maturities in the year 2022. The fund is non-diversified. **Top Holdings:** Tenet Healthcare Corporation 8.12% Altice Luxembourg S.A. 7.75% Sprint Communications, Inc. 6% HCA Inc. 7.5% Nielsen Finance LLC/Nielsen Finance Co 5%

FlexShares Ready Access Variable Income Fund   C-   HOLD

Ticker	Traded On	NAV	Total Assets ($)	Dividend Yield (TTM)	Turnover Ratio	Expense Ratio
RAVI	NYSE Arca	75.09	$290,126,906	2.04		0.25

Ratings
Reward   C
Risk   C-
Recent Upgrade/Downgrade

Fund Information
Fund Type	Exchange Traded Funds
Category	US Fixed Income
Sub-Category	Ultrashort Bond
Prospectus Objective	Income
Inception Date	Oct-12
Open to New Investments	Y

Prices
Price (as of 12/31/2018)	75.03
52-Week High	75.62
52-Week Low	74.89

Total Returns (%)
3-Month	6-Month	1-Year	3-Year	5-Year
0.23	0.95	1.82	4.38	5.55

3-Year Standard Deviation	0.31
Effective Duration	0.48

Valuation
Premium/Discount (1-Year Average)	0.01

Company Information
Provider	Flexshares Trust
Manager/Tenure	Bilal Memon (6), Peter Yi (6)
Website	http://www.flexshares.com
Address	50 South LaSalle Street Chicago, Illinois 60603 Chicago Illinois 60603 United States
Phone Number	855-353-9383

PERFORMANCE

Ratings History
Date	Overall Rating	Risk Rating	Reward Rating
Q4-18	C-	C-	C
Q2-18	C-	C-	C
Q4-17	C+	B+	C
Q4-16	C	C-	C
Q4-15	C	C-	C

Asset & Performance History
Date	NAV	1-Year Total Return
2017	75.39	1.29
2016	75.38	1.21
2015	75.16	0.38
2014	75.36	0.72
2013	75.32	0.9
2012	74.96	

Total Assets: $290,126,906

Asset Allocation
Asset	%
Cash	19%
Stocks	0%
US Stocks	0%
Bonds	78%
US Bonds	59%
Other	0%

Services Offered:

Investment Strategy: The investment seeks maximum current income consistent with the preservation of capital and liquidity. The fund seeks to achieve its investment objective by investing at least 80% of its total assets in a non-diversified portfolio of fixed-income instruments, including bonds, debt securities and other similar instruments issued by U.S. and non-U.S. public and private sector entities. The dollar-weighted average portfolio maturity of the fund is normally not expected to exceed two years. It may invest up to 20% of its total assets in fixed-income securities and instruments of issuers in emerging markets. The fund is non-diversified. **Top Holdings:** Canadian Pacific Railway Company 7.25% Republic Services, Inc. 5.5% Volkswagen Group of America Finance LLC 3.39% Pfizer Inc. 2.65% United States Treasury Notes 1.5%

USAA MSCI International Value Momentum Blend Index ETF　　　　　　　D　　SELL

Ticker	Traded On	NAV	Total Assets ($)	Dividend Yield (TTM)	Turnover Ratio	Expense Ratio
UIVM	NYSE Arca	41.43	$289,649,180	1.54		0.35

Ratings
Reward　　　　　　　　　　　　　　　D
Risk　　　　　　　　　　　　　　　　D
Recent Upgrade/Downgrade

Fund Information
Fund Type	Exchange Traded Funds
Category	Global Equity Large Cap
Sub-Category	Foreign Large Value
Prospectus Objective	Growth & Inc
Inception Date	Oct-17
Open to New Investments	Y

Prices
Price (as of 12/31/2018)	41.46
52-Week High	55.50
52-Week Low	40.20

Total Returns (%)
3-Month	6-Month	1-Year	3-Year	5-Year
-13.84	-11.90	-17.44		

3-Year Standard Deviation
Effective Duration

Valuation
Premium/Discount (1-Year Average)　　　0.30

Company Information
Provider	USAA
Manager/Tenure	Lance Humphrey (1), Wasif A. Latif (1), Emiliano Rabinovich (1), 2 others
Website	http://www.usaa.com
Address	USAA P.O. Box 659453 San Antonio TX 78265-9825 United States
Phone Number	800-531-8722

PERFORMANCE

Ratings History

Date	Overall Rating	Risk Rating	Reward Rating
Q4-18	D	D	D
Q2-18	U		
Q4-17	U		
Q4-16			
Q4-15			

Asset & Performance History

Date	NAV	1-Year Total Return
2017	51.42	
2016		
2015		
2014		
2013		
2012		

Total Assets: $289,649,180

Asset Allocation

Asset	%
Cash	0%
Stocks	100%
US Stocks	2%
Bonds	0%
US Bonds	0%
Other	0%

Services Offered:

Investment Strategy: The investment seeks to provide investment results that correspond to the MSCI World ex USA Select Value Momentum Blend Index. The fund seeks to achieve its investment objective by investing at least 80% of its net assets in securities in the index, depositary receipts on securities in the index, and securities underlying depositary receipts in the index. The index is designed to deliver exposure to equity market performance in non-U.S. markets and provide higher exposure to value and momentum factors within the MSCI World ex USA Index while also maintaining moderate index turnover and lower realized volatility than traditional capitalization weighted indexes. **Top Holdings:** Swiss Life Holding AG　Bank Hapoalim BM　Mizrahi Tefahot Bank Ltd　Link Real Estate Investment Trust　Koninklijke Ahold Delhaize NV

---

iShares iBonds Sep 2019 Term Muni Bond ETF　　　　　　　　　　　C-　　HOLD

Ticker	Traded On	NAV	Total Assets ($)	Dividend Yield (TTM)	Turnover Ratio	Expense Ratio
IBMH	NYSE Arca	25.37	$289,157,510	1.03	0	0.18

Ratings
Reward　　　　　　　　　　　　　　　C-
Risk　　　　　　　　　　　　　　　　C-
Recent Upgrade/Downgrade

Fund Information
Fund Type	Exchange Traded Funds
Category	US Muni Fixed Inc
Sub-Category	Muni National Short
Prospectus Objective	Muni Bond - Natl
Inception Date	Feb-14
Open to New Investments	Y

Prices
Price (as of 12/31/2018)	25.39
52-Week High	25.43
52-Week Low	25.27

Total Returns (%)
3-Month	6-Month	1-Year	3-Year	5-Year
0.48	0.55	1.33	2.78	

3-Year Standard Deviation　　　1.32
Effective Duration　　　　　　　0.68

Valuation
Premium/Discount (1-Year Average)　　　0.04

Company Information
Provider	iShares
Manager/Tenure	James Mauro (4), Scott Radell (4)
Website	http://www.ishares.com
Address	iShares 400 Howard Street San Francisco CA 94105 United States
Phone Number	800-474-2737

PERFORMANCE

Ratings History

Date	Overall Rating	Risk Rating	Reward Rating
Q4-18	C-	C-	C-
Q2-18	C-	C-	C
Q4-17	C	C	C
Q4-16	C-	C-	C-
Q4-15	D	C-	D+

Asset & Performance History

Date	NAV	1-Year Total Return
2017	25.3	1.08
2016	25.26	0.28
2015	25.44	1.81
2014	25.26	
2013		
2012		

Total Assets: $289,157,510

Asset Allocation

Asset	%
Cash	0%
Stocks	0%
US Stocks	0%
Bonds	100%
US Bonds	100%
Other	0%

Services Offered:

Investment Strategy: The investment seeks to track the investment results of the S&P AMT-Free Municipal Series 2019 IndexTM. The fund generally invests at least 90% of its assets in the component securities of the underlying index, and may invest up to 10% of its assets in certain futures, options and swap contracts, cash and cash equivalents, as well as in securities not included in the underlying index. The underlying index measures the performance of investment-grade, non-callable U.S. municipal bonds maturing in 2019. **Top Holdings:** CALIFORNIA ST 5%　WASHINGTON ST 5%　WASHINGTON ST 5%　ENERGY NORTHWEST WASH 5%　PENNSYLVANIA ECONOMIC DEV FING AUTH 5%

Invesco DB Oil Fund

C-   **HOLD**

Ticker	Traded On	NAV	Total Assets ($)	Dividend Yield (TTM)	Turnover Ratio	Expense Ratio
DBO	NYSE Arca	8.38	$287,854,273	0		0.75

Ratings
Reward	C-
Risk	C-
Recent Upgrade/Downgrade	Down

Fund Information
Fund Type	Exchange Traded Funds
Category	Commodities Specified
Sub-Category	Commodities Energy
Prospectus Objective	Natl Res
Inception Date	Jan-07
Open to New Investments	Y

Prices
Price (as of 12/31/2018)	8.47
52-Week High	14.02
52-Week Low	8.12

Total Returns (%)
3-Month	6-Month	1-Year	3-Year	5-Year
-39.50	-31.42	-17.88	-7.58	-69.72

3-Year Standard Deviation	25.1
Effective Duration	

Valuation
Premium/Discount (1-Year Average)	-0.17

Company Information
Provider	Invesco
Manager/Tenure	Management Team (11)
Website	http://www.invesco.com/us
Address	Invesco 11 Greenway Plaza, Ste. 2500 Houston TX 77046 United States
Phone Number	800-659-1005

PERFORMANCE

Ratings History

Date	Overall Rating	Risk Rating	Reward Rating
Q4-18	C-	C-	C-
Q2-18	C	C-	C
Q4-17	D	D	D+
Q4-16	D-	D-	D-
Q4-15	D-	D-	D-

Asset & Performance History

Date	NAV	1-Year Total Return
2017	10.21	4.41
2016	9.67	8.25
2015	9.07	-41.52
2014	15.51	-43.97
2013	27.69	6.55
2012	25.99	-9

Total Assets: $287,854,273

Asset Allocation

Asset	%
Cash	37%
Stocks	0%
US Stocks	0%
Bonds	12%
US Bonds	12%
Other	51%

Services Offered:

Investment Strategy: The investment seeks to track the DBIQ Optimum Yield Crude Oil Index Excess Return™ (DBIQ-OY CL ER™), which is intended to reflect the changes in market value of crude oil. The single index Commodity consists of Light, Sweet Crude Oil (WTI). **Top Holdings:** Wti Crude Future Mar19 United States Treasury Bills 0% United States Treasury Bills 0% Invesco Treasury Collateral ETF Invesco Treasury Collateral ETF

---

iShares Currency Hedged MSCI Emerging Markets ETF

C-   **HOLD**

Ticker	Traded On	NAV	Total Assets ($)	Dividend Yield (TTM)	Turnover Ratio	Expense Ratio
HEEM	BATS	23.08	$287,824,544	2.45	7	0.69

Ratings
Reward	C-
Risk	C
Recent Upgrade/Downgrade	Down

Fund Information
Fund Type	Exchange Traded Funds
Category	Global Emerg Mkts Equity
Sub-Category	Diversified Emerging Mkts
Prospectus Objective	Div Emerg Mkts
Inception Date	Sep-14
Open to New Investments	Y

Prices
Price (as of 12/31/2018)	23.03
52-Week High	28.95
52-Week Low	22.75

Total Returns (%)
3-Month	6-Month	1-Year	3-Year	5-Year
-9.24	-8.54	-12.30	21.24	

3-Year Standard Deviation	11.1
Effective Duration	

Valuation
Premium/Discount (1-Year Average)	0.02

Company Information
Provider	iShares
Manager/Tenure	Diane Hsiung (4), Jennifer Hsui (4), Orlando Montalvo (4), 2 others
Website	http://www.ishares.com
Address	iShares 400 Howard Street San Francisco CA 94105 United States
Phone Number	800-474-2737

PERFORMANCE

Ratings History

Date	Overall Rating	Risk Rating	Reward Rating
Q4-18	C-	C	C-
Q2-18	C	C-	C
Q4-17	C+	C	C+
Q4-16	D+	C-	D+
Q4-15	U		

Asset & Performance History

Date	NAV	1-Year Total Return
2017	26.51	27.99
2016	21.15	8.02
2015	19.95	-10.02
2014	23.52	
2013		
2012		

Total Assets: $287,824,544

Asset Allocation

Asset	%
Cash	0%
Stocks	100%
US Stocks	0%
Bonds	0%
US Bonds	0%
Other	0%

Services Offered:

Investment Strategy: The investment seeks to track the investment results of the MSCI Emerging Markets 100% Hedged to USD Index. The fund generally will invest at least 90% of its assets in the component securities (including indirect investments through the underlying fund) and other instruments of the underlying index and in investments that have economic characteristics that are substantially identical to the component securities of the underlying index. The index is an equity benchmark for global emerging markets stock performance with the currency risk inherent in the securities included in the index hedged to the U.S. dollar on a monthly basis. **Top Holdings:** iShares MSCI Emerging Markets ETF

ALPS International Sector Dividend Dogs ETF   D+   SELL

Ticker	Traded On	NAV	Total Assets ($)	Dividend Yield (TTM)	Turnover Ratio	Expense Ratio
IDOG	NYSE Arca	23.96	$285,327,147	4.33	37	0.5

Ratings
Reward	D+
Risk	C-
Recent Upgrade/Downgrade	Down

Fund Information
Fund Type	Exchange Traded Funds
Category	Global Equity Large Cap
Sub-Category	Foreign Large Value
Prospectus Objective	Growth
Inception Date	Jun-13
Open to New Investments	Y

Prices
Price (as of 12/31/2018)	23.82
52-Week High	30.21
52-Week Low	23.10

Total Returns (%)
3-Month	6-Month	1-Year	3-Year	5-Year
-9.92	-9.18	-13.08	13.65	0.18

3-Year Standard Deviation	10.96
Effective Duration	

Valuation
Premium/Discount (1-Year Average)	0.03

Company Information
Provider	ALPS
Manager/Tenure	Ryan Mischker (3), Andrew Hicks (2)
Website	http://www.alpsfunds.com
Address	ALPS 1290 Broadway, Suite 1100 Denver CO 80203 United States
Phone Number	866-759-5679

PERFORMANCE

Ratings History
Date	Overall Rating	Risk Rating	Reward Rating
Q4-18	D+	C-	D+
Q2-18	C	C-	C
Q4-17	B-	B-	B-
Q4-16	D+	C-	D+
Q4-15	D	C-	D

Asset & Performance History
Date	NAV	1-Year Total Return
2017	28.7	25.82
2016	23.63	3.93
2015	23.67	-6.23
2014	26.22	-5.99
2013	29.03	
2012		

Total Assets: $285,327,147
Asset Allocation
Asset	%
Cash	1%
Stocks	99%
US Stocks	0%
Bonds	0%
US Bonds	0%
Other	0%

Services Offered:

Investment Strategy: The investment seeks investment results that replicate as closely as possible, before fees and expenses, the performance of the S-Network® International Sector Dividend Dogs Index. The fund seeks investment results that replicate as closely as possible, before fees and expenses, the performance of the underlying index. The underlying index is a rules-based index intended to give investors a means of tracking the overall performance of the highest dividend paying stocks (i.e. "Dividend Dogs") in the S-Network Developed International 1000 Index. **Top Holdings:** Hennes & Mauritz AB B Proximus SA Micro Focus International PLC Fortescue Metals Group Ltd Woolworths Group Ltd

---

FlexShares Global Quality Real Estate Index Fund   D+   SELL

Ticker	Traded On	NAV	Total Assets ($)	Dividend Yield (TTM)	Turnover Ratio	Expense Ratio
GQRE	NYSE Arca	55.36	$282,154,431	3.14		0.45

Ratings
Reward	C-
Risk	D+
Recent Upgrade/Downgrade	Down

Fund Information
Fund Type	Exchange Traded Funds
Category	Real Estate Sector Equity
Sub-Category	Global Real Estate
Prospectus Objective	Real Estate
Inception Date	Nov-13
Open to New Investments	Y

Prices
Price (as of 12/31/2018)	55.51
52-Week High	63.88
52-Week Low	53.78

Total Returns (%)
3-Month	6-Month	1-Year	3-Year	5-Year
-8.21	-8.75	-9.06	7.23	29.86

3-Year Standard Deviation	10.47
Effective Duration	

Valuation
Premium/Discount (1-Year Average)	0.02

Company Information
Provider	Flexshares Trust
Manager/Tenure	Robert Anstine (5), Brendan Sullivan (2)
Website	http://www.flexshares.com
Address	50 South LaSalle Street Chicago, Illinois 60603 Chicago Illinois 60603 United States
Phone Number	855-353-9383

PERFORMANCE

Ratings History
Date	Overall Rating	Risk Rating	Reward Rating
Q4-18	D+	D+	C-
Q2-18	C	D+	C+
Q4-17	B	B	B-
Q4-16	C	C-	C
Q4-15	D+	C-	C-

Asset & Performance History
Date	NAV	1-Year Total Return
2017	62.74	13.42
2016	56.44	3.96
2015	56.55	3.49
2014	55.92	17
2013	49.08	
2012		

Total Assets: $282,154,431
Asset Allocation
Asset	%
Cash	3%
Stocks	96%
US Stocks	51%
Bonds	0%
US Bonds	0%
Other	1%

Services Offered:

Investment Strategy: The investment seeks investment results that correspond generally to the price and yield performance, before fees and expenses, of the Northern Trust Global Quality Real Estate IndexSM. The fund normally will invest at least 80% of its total assets (exclusive of collateral held from securities lending) in the securities of the index and in ADRs and GDRs based on the securities in the index. The index is designed to measure the performance of companies that exhibit certain quality, valuation and momentum characteristics within a universe of publicly-traded equity securities of U.S. and non-U.S. REITs and real estate companies. The fund is non-diversified. **Top Holdings:** Prologis Inc Equity Residential Link Real Estate Investment Trust Weyerhaeuser Co Scentre Group

Franklin LibertyQ Emerging Markets ETF   D+   SELL

Ticker	Traded On	NAV	Total Assets ($)	Dividend Yield (TTM)	Turnover Ratio	Expense Ratio
FLQE	NYSE Arca	28.16	$281,735,344	2.98	33	0.55

Ratings
Reward   D+
Risk   C-
Recent Upgrade/Downgrade   Down

Fund Information
Fund Type   Exchange Traded Funds
Category   Global Emerg Mkts Equity
Sub-Category   Diversified Emerging Mkts
Prospectus Objective   Growth & Inc
Inception Date   Jun-16
Open to New Investments Y

Prices
Price (as of 12/31/2018)   28.22
52-Week High   35.46
52-Week Low   27.64

Total Returns (%)

3-Month	6-Month	1-Year	3-Year	5-Year
-5.73	-3.75	-11.72		

3-Year Standard Deviation
Effective Duration

Valuation
Premium/Discount (1-Year Average)   -0.18

Company Information
Provider   Franklin Templeton Investments
Manager/Tenure Dina Ting (2), Louis Hsu (1)
Website   http://www.franklintempleton.com
Address   Franklin Templeton Investments One
                Franklin Parkway, Building 970, 1st
                Floor San Mateo CA 94403 United
                States
Phone Number   650-312-2000

PERFORMANCE

Ratings History

Date	Overall Rating	Risk Rating	Reward Rating
Q4-18	D+	C-	D+
Q2-18	D+	C-	D+
Q4-17	D+	B-	C
Q4-16	U		
Q4-15			

Asset & Performance History

Date	NAV	1-Year Total Return
2017	33.12	28.36
2016	26.51	
2015		
2014		
2013		
2012		

Total Assets: $281,735,344

Asset Allocation

Asset	%
Cash	1%
Stocks	99%
US Stocks	0%
Bonds	0%
US Bonds	0%
Other	0%

Services Offered:

Investment Strategy: The investment seeks to provide investment results that closely correspond, before fees and expenses, to the performance of the LibertyQ Emerging Markets Index. The fund invests at least 80% of its assets in the component securities of the index and in depositary receipts representing such securities. The index seeks to achieve a lower level of risk and higher risk-adjusted performance than the MSCI Emerging Markets Index over the long term by applying a multi-factor selection process. **Top Holdings:** NOVATEK PJSC GDR Rosneft Oil Co Itausa Investimentos ITAU SA Participating Preferred HCL Technologies Ltd Infosys Ltd

First Trust Energy AlphaDEX® Fund   C   HOLD

Ticker	Traded On	NAV	Total Assets ($)	Dividend Yield (TTM)	Turnover Ratio	Expense Ratio
FXN	NYSE Arca	11.53	$280,160,702	1.07	55	0.63

Ratings
Reward   C
Risk   D+
Recent Upgrade/Downgrade

Fund Information
Fund Type   Exchange Traded Funds
Category   Energy Sector Equity
Sub-Category   Equity Energy
Prospectus Objective   Natl Res
Inception Date   May-07
Open to New Investments Y

Prices
Price (as of 12/31/2018)   11.51
52-Week High   18.18
52-Week Low   10.71

Total Returns (%)

3-Month	6-Month	1-Year	3-Year	5-Year
-34.83	-30.14	-24.64	-13.84	-51.09

3-Year Standard Deviation   26.2
Effective Duration

Valuation
Premium/Discount (1-Year Average)   0.03

Company Information
Provider   First Trust
Manager/Tenure Jon C. Erickson (11), Daniel J.
                Lindquist (11), David G. McGarel (11),
                3 others
Website   http://www.ftportfolios.com/
Address   First Trust 120 E. Liberty Drive, Suite
                400 Wheaton IL 60187 United States
Phone Number   800-621-1675

PERFORMANCE

Ratings History

Date	Overall Rating	Risk Rating	Reward Rating
Q4-18	C	D+	C
Q2-18	C	D+	C
Q4-17	D	D	D
Q4-16	D	D	D+
Q4-15	D+	D	C-

Asset & Performance History

Date	NAV	1-Year Total Return
2017	15.48	-5.08
2016	16.52	20.46
2015	13.87	-32.41
2014	20.91	-16.01
2013	25.26	28.66
2012	19.81	3.7

Total Assets: $280,160,702

Asset Allocation

Asset	%
Cash	0%
Stocks	100%
US Stocks	98%
Bonds	0%
US Bonds	0%
Other	0%

Services Offered:

Investment Strategy: The investment seeks results that correspond generally to the price and yield (before the fund's fees and expenses) of an equity index called the StrataQuant® Energy Index. The fund will normally invest at least 90% of its net assets (including investment borrowings) in common stocks that comprise the index. The index is a modified equal-dollar weighted index designed by IDI to objectively identify and select stocks from the Russell 1000® Index in the energy sector that may generate positive alpha relative to traditional passive-style indices through the use of the AlphaDEX® selection methodology. **Top Holdings:** RPC Inc Helmerich & Payne Inc Cheniere Energy Inc HollyFrontier Corp Phillips 66

SPDR® S&P Global Infrastructure ETF   C-   HOLD

Ticker	Traded On	NAV	Total Assets ($)	Dividend Yield (TTM)	Turnover Ratio	Expense Ratio
GII	NYSE Arca	45.13	$279,907,065	3.34	21	0.4

Ratings

Reward	C-
Risk	C-
Recent Upgrade/Downgrade	Down

Fund Information

Fund Type	Exchange Traded Funds
Category	Infrastructure Sector Equity
Sub-Category	Infrastructure
Prospectus Objective	Utility
Inception Date	Jan-07
Open to New Investments	Y

Prices

Price (as of 12/31/2018)	45.13
52-Week High	53.01
52-Week Low	43.84

Total Returns (%)

3-Month	6-Month	1-Year	3-Year	5-Year
-5.40	-6.56	-10.05	19.86	18.69

3-Year Standard Deviation	9.78
Effective Duration	

Valuation

Premium/Discount (1-Year Average)	0.06

Company Information

Provider	SPDR State Street Global Advisors
Manager/Tenure	Michael J. Feehily (7), Karl A. Schneider (3), Michael Finocchi (1)
Website	http://www.spdrs.com
Address	SPDR State Street Global Advisors State Street Financial Center, 1 Lincoln Street Boston MA 02111-2900 United States
Phone Number	617-786-3000

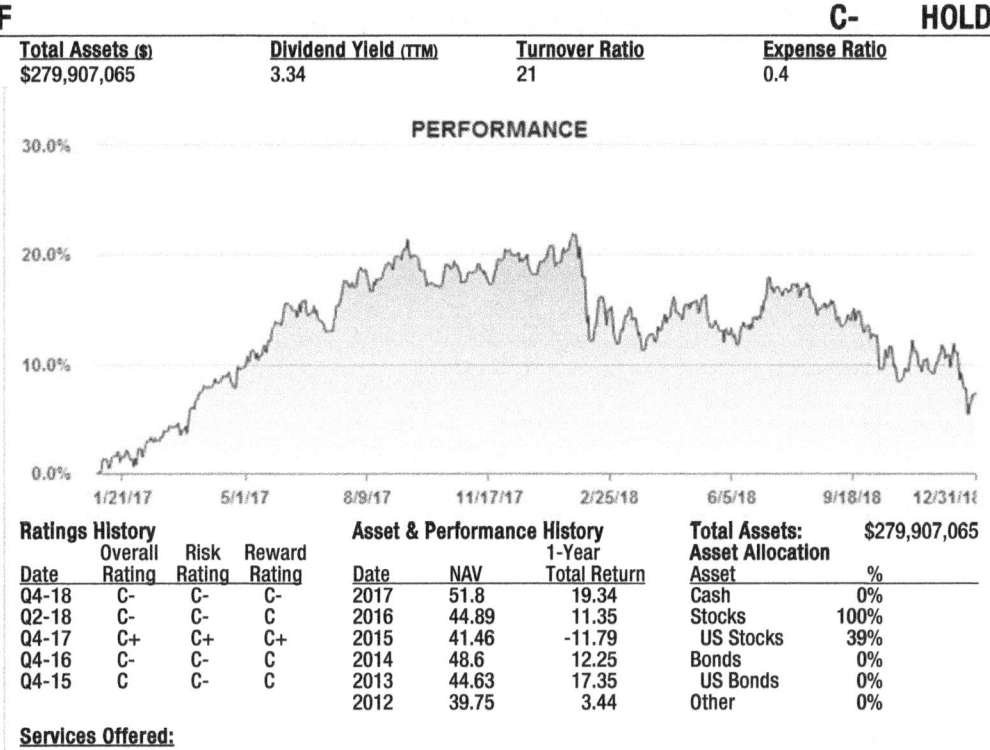

PERFORMANCE

Ratings History

Date	Overall Rating	Risk Rating	Reward Rating
Q4-18	C-	C-	C-
Q2-18	C-	C-	C
Q4-17	C+	C+	C+
Q4-16	C-	C-	C
Q4-15	C	C-	C

Asset & Performance History

Date	NAV	1-Year Total Return
2017	51.8	19.34
2016	44.89	11.35
2015	41.46	-11.79
2014	48.6	12.25
2013	44.63	17.35
2012	39.75	3.44

Total Assets: $279,907,065

Asset Allocation

Asset	%
Cash	0%
Stocks	100%
US Stocks	39%
Bonds	0%
US Bonds	0%
Other	0%

Services Offered:

Investment Strategy: The investment seeks investment results that, before fees and expenses, correspond generally to the total return performance of the S&P Global Infrastructure Index. The fund generally invests substantially all, but at least 80%, of its total assets in the securities comprising the index and in depositary receipts based on securities comprising the index. The index is comprised of 75 of the largest publicly listed infrastructure companies that meet specific investability requirements. The fund is non-diversified. **Top Holdings:** Transurban Group   Aena SME SA   NextEra Energy Inc   Enbridge Inc   Atlantia SpA

Invesco Solar ETF   D+   SELL

Ticker	Traded On	NAV	Total Assets ($)	Dividend Yield (TTM)	Turnover Ratio	Expense Ratio
TAN	NYSE Arca		$278,893,810	2.12	54	0.7

Ratings

Reward	D+
Risk	D
Recent Upgrade/Downgrade	

Fund Information

Fund Type	Exchange Traded Funds
Category	Technology Sector Equity
Sub-Category	Miscellaneous Sector
Prospectus Objective	Natl Res
Inception Date	Apr-08
Open to New Investments	Y

Prices

Price (as of 12/31/2018)	18.55
52-Week High	26.93
52-Week Low	17.70

Total Returns (%)

3-Month	6-Month	1-Year	3-Year	5-Year
-10.48	-20.50	-25.76	-35.01	-41.53

3-Year Standard Deviation	24.64
Effective Duration	

Valuation

Premium/Discount (1-Year Average)	-0.21

Company Information

Provider	Invesco
Manager/Tenure	Peter Hubbard (0), Michael Jeanette (0), Jonathan Nixon (0), 1 other
Website	http://www.invesco.com/us
Address	Invesco 11 Greenway Plaza, Ste. 2500 Houston TX 77046 United States
Phone Number	800-659-1005

PERFORMANCE

Ratings History

Date	Overall Rating	Risk Rating	Reward Rating
Q4-18	D+	D	D+
Q2-18	D+	D	C
Q4-17	C-	D+	C-
Q4-16	D	D-	D
Q4-15	C	C-	C

Asset & Performance History

Date	NAV	1-Year Total Return
2017	25.07	53.1
2016	16.55	-42.7
2015	30.61	-9.37
2014	34.3	-0.71
2013	35.2	129.94
2012	15.51	-31.86

Total Assets: $278,893,810

Asset Allocation

Asset	%
Cash	0%
Stocks	100%
US Stocks	41%
Bonds	0%
US Bonds	0%
Other	0%

Services Offered:

Investment Strategy: The investment seeks investment results that correspond generally to the performance, before the fund's fees and expenses, of an equity index called the MAC Global Solar Energy Index. The fund will invest at least 90% of its total assets in common stock, ADRs and GDRs that comprise the index and depositary receipts representing common stocks included in the index. The index is comprised of equity securities, including ADRs and GDRs, traded in developed markets. The fund is non-diversified. **Top Holdings:** Xinyi Solar Holdings Ltd First Solar Inc   Sunrun Inc   Scatec Solar ASA   SolarEdge Technologies Inc

PIMCO Intermediate Municipal Bond Active Exchange-Traded Fund

C-   HOLD

Ticker	Traded On	NAV	Total Assets ($)	Dividend Yield (TTM)	Turnover Ratio	Expense Ratio
MUNI	NYSE Arca	52.76	$278,510,255	2.55	27	0.35

Ratings

Reward	C-
Risk	C-
Recent Upgrade/Downgrade	Down

Fund Information

Fund Type	Exchange Traded Funds
Category	US Muni Fixed Inc
Sub-Category	Muni National Interm
Prospectus Objective	Muni Bond - Natl
Inception Date	Nov-09
Open to New Investments	Y

Prices

Price (as of 12/31/2018)	52.82
52-Week High	53.65
52-Week Low	51.81

Total Returns (%)

3-Month	6-Month	1-Year	3-Year	5-Year
1.43	1.36	1.11	5.49	13.99

3-Year Standard Deviation	2.85
Effective Duration	5.14

Valuation

Premium/Discount (1-Year Average)	0.02

Company Information

Provider	PIMCO
Manager/Tenure	Julie P. Callahan (3), David Hammer (2)
Website	http://www.pimco.com
Address	PIMCO 840 Newport Center Drive, Suite 100 Newport Beach CA 92660 United States
Phone Number	866-746-2602

PERFORMANCE

Ratings History

Date	Overall Rating	Risk Rating	Reward Rating
Q4-18	C-	C-	C-
Q2-18	C	C-	C
Q4-17	B-	B+	C
Q4-16	C	C-	C
Q4-15	C	C-	C

Asset & Performance History

Date	NAV	1-Year Total Return
2017	53.54	4.54
2016	52.45	-0.19
2015	53.77	2.58
2014	53.59	5.32
2013	51.87	-2.32
2012	54.31	4.77

Total Assets: $278,510,255

Asset Allocation

Asset	%
Cash	7%
Stocks	0%
US Stocks	0%
Bonds	93%
US Bonds	93%
Other	0%

Services Offered:

Investment Strategy: The investment seeks attractive tax-exempt income, consistent with preservation of capital. The fund invests at least 80% of its assets in a diversified portfolio of debt securities whose interest is, in the opinion of bond counsel for the issuer at the time of issuance, exempt from federal income tax ("Municipal Bonds"). It may invest 25% or more of its total assets in Municipal Bonds that finance similar projects, such as those relating to education, health care, housing, transportation, and utilities, and 25% or more of its total assets in industrial development bonds. **Top Holdings:** TOBACCO SETTLEMENT FING CORP RHODE IS 5%   CHICAGO ILL MIDWAY ARPT 5%   NEW YORK N Y CITY TRANSITIONAL FIN AUTH 5%   PENNSYLVANIA ST TPK COMMN 2.57% HARRIS CNTY TEX CULTURAL ED FACS FIN CORP 2.27%

VanEck Vectors Pharmaceutical ETF

C   HOLD

Ticker	Traded On	NAV	Total Assets ($)	Dividend Yield (TTM)	Turnover Ratio	Expense Ratio
PPH	NAS CM	55.02	$278,450,878	1.64	18	0.35

Ratings

Reward	C+
Risk	C-
Recent Upgrade/Downgrade	

Fund Information

Fund Type	Exchange Traded Funds
Category	Healthcare Sector Equity
Sub-Category	Health
Prospectus Objective	Health
Inception Date	Dec-11
Open to New Investments	Y

Prices

Price (as of 12/31/2018)	54.79
52-Week High	64.61
52-Week Low	52.66

Total Returns (%)

3-Month	6-Month	1-Year	3-Year	5-Year
-13.77	-5.95	-5.52	-10.36	14.08

3-Year Standard Deviation	13.52
Effective Duration	

Valuation

Premium/Discount (1-Year Average)	0.02

Company Information

Provider	VanEck
Manager/Tenure	Hao-Hung (Peter) Liao (6), Guo Hua (Jason) Jin (0)
Website	http://www.vaneck.com
Address	Van Eck Associates Corporation 666 Third Avenue New York NY 10017 United States
Phone Number	800-826-1115

PERFORMANCE

Ratings History

Date	Overall Rating	Risk Rating	Reward Rating
Q4-18	C	C-	C+
Q2-18	C	D+	C
Q4-17	D+	C-	D+
Q4-16	C	D+	C+
Q4-15	B	C+	B

Asset & Performance History

Date	NAV	1-Year Total Return
2017	59.34	15.37
2016	52.47	-17.76
2015	65.24	3.41
2014	64.27	23.07
2013	53.16	36.82
2012	39.72	12.94

Total Assets: $278,450,878

Asset Allocation

Asset	%
Cash	0%
Stocks	100%
US Stocks	63%
Bonds	0%
US Bonds	0%
Other	0%

Services Offered:

Investment Strategy: The investment seeks to replicate as closely as possible, before fees and expenses, the price and yield performance of the MVIS® US Listed Pharmaceutical 25 Index. The fund normally invests at least 80% of its total assets in securities that comprise the fund's benchmark index. The index includes common stocks and depositary receipts of U.S. exchange-listed companies in the pharmaceutical sector. Such companies may include medium-capitalization companies and foreign companies that are listed on a U.S. exchange. It is non-diversified. **Top Holdings:** Merck & Co Inc   Pfizer Inc   Novartis AG ADR   GlaxoSmithKline PLC ADR   Johnson & Johnson

iShares Edge MSCI Intl Value Factor ETF   D+   SELL

Ticker	Traded On	NAV	Total Assets ($)	Dividend Yield (TTM)	Turnover Ratio	Expense Ratio
IVLU	NYSE Arca	21.94	$277,429,379	3.32	16	0.3

Ratings
Reward	D+
Risk	C-
Recent Upgrade/Downgrade	Down

Fund Information
Fund Type	Exchange Traded Funds
Category	Global Equity Large Cap
Sub-Category	Foreign Large Value
Prospectus Objective	Foreign Stock
Inception Date	Jun-15
Open to New Investments	Y

Prices
Price (as of 12/31/2018)	21.87
52-Week High	28.41
52-Week Low	21.28

Total Returns (%)
3-Month	6-Month	1-Year	3-Year	5-Year
-12.42	-9.87	-14.71	8.26	

3-Year Standard Deviation	11.88
Effective Duration	

Valuation
Premium/Discount (1-Year Average)	0.15

Company Information
Provider	iShares
Manager/Tenure	Diane Hsiung (3), Jennifer Hsui (3), Greg Savage (3), 3 others
Website	http://www.ishares.com
Address	iShares 400 Howard Street San Francisco CA 94105 United States
Phone Number	800-474-2737

PERFORMANCE

Ratings History
Date	Overall Rating	Risk Rating	Reward Rating
Q4-18	D+	C-	D+
Q2-18	C	C-	C
Q4-17	C	C+	C+
Q4-16	D	D+	D
Q4-15	U		

Asset & Performance History
Date	NAV	1-Year Total Return
2017	26.4	23.1
2016	22.1	3.12
2015	22	
2014		
2013		
2012		

Total Assets: $277,429,379
Asset Allocation
Asset	%
Cash	1%
Stocks	99%
US Stocks	3%
Bonds	0%
US Bonds	0%
Other	0%

Services Offered:

Investment Strategy: The investment seeks to track the investment results of the MSCI World ex USA Enhanced Value Index. The fund generally will invest at least 90% of its assets in the component securities of the underlying index and in investments that have economic characteristics that are substantially identical to the component securities of the underlying index and may invest up to 10% of its assets in certain futures, options and swap contracts, cash and cash equivalents as well as in securities not included in the underlying index. The index is based on a traditional market capitalization-weighted parent index, the MSCI World ex USA Index. **Top Holdings:** Sanofi SA Toyota Motor Corp Novartis AG British American Tobacco PLC HSBC Holdings PLC

SPDR® S&P Oil & Gas Equipment & Services ETF   D+   SELL

Ticker	Traded On	NAV	Total Assets ($)	Dividend Yield (TTM)	Turnover Ratio	Expense Ratio
XES	NYSE Arca	9.00	$275,676,576	1.07	34	0.35

Ratings
Reward	C-
Risk	D
Recent Upgrade/Downgrade	

Fund Information
Fund Type	Exchange Traded Funds
Category	Energy Sector Equity
Sub-Category	Equity Energy
Prospectus Objective	Natl Res
Inception Date	Jun-06
Open to New Investments	Y

Prices
Price (as of 12/31/2018)	9.01
52-Week High	19.19
52-Week Low	8.33

Total Returns (%)
3-Month	6-Month	1-Year	3-Year	5-Year
-46.55	-45.07	-47.04	-46.95	-78.00

3-Year Standard Deviation	35.45
Effective Duration	

Valuation
Premium/Discount (1-Year Average)	0.02

Company Information
Provider	SPDR State Street Global Advisors
Manager/Tenure	Michael J. Feehily (7), Karl A. Schneider (4), Melissa Kapitulik (0)
Website	http://www.spdrs.com
Address	SPDR State Street Global Advisors State Street Financial Center, 1 Lincoln Street Boston MA 02111-2900 United States
Phone Number	617-786-3000

PERFORMANCE

Ratings History
Date	Overall Rating	Risk Rating	Reward Rating
Q4-18	D+	D	C-
Q2-18	D+	D	D+
Q4-17	D	D	D
Q4-16	D	D	D+
Q4-15	D	D	D

Asset & Performance History
Date	NAV	1-Year Total Return
2017	17.13	-21.87
2016	22.33	29.35
2015	17.55	-36.53
2014	28.22	-34.65
2013	43.69	26.99
2012	34.63	0.61

Total Assets: $275,676,576
Asset Allocation
Asset	%
Cash	0%
Stocks	100%
US Stocks	94%
Bonds	0%
US Bonds	0%
Other	0%

Services Offered:

Investment Strategy: The investment seeks to provide investment results that, before fees and expenses, correspond generally to the total return performance of an index derived from the oil and gas equipment and services segment of a U.S. total market composite index. In seeking to track the performance of the S&P Oil & Gas Equipment & Services Select Industry Index, the fund employs a sampling strategy. It generally invests substantially all, but at least 80%, of its total assets in the securities comprising the index. The index represents the oil and gas equipment and services segment of the S&P Total Market Index ("S&P TMI"). The fund is non-diversified. **Top Holdings:** ProPetro Holding Corp Helmerich & Payne Inc RPC Inc Rowan Companies PLC Keane Group Inc

Invesco DWA Healthcare Momentum ETF

C   HOLD

Ticker	Traded On	NAV	Total Assets ($)	Dividend Yield (TTM)	Turnover Ratio	Expense Ratio
PTH	NAS CM	71.48	$274,974,094	0	130	0.6

Ratings
Reward	C
Risk	C-
Recent Upgrade/Downgrade	

Fund Information
Fund Type	Exchange Traded Funds
Category	Healthcare Sector Equity
Sub-Category	Health
Prospectus Objective	Health
Inception Date	Oct-06
Open to New Investments	Y

Prices
Price (as of 12/31/2018)	71.18
52-Week High	98.76
52-Week Low	64.96

Total Returns (%)
3-Month	6-Month	1-Year	3-Year	5-Year
-26.44	-19.29	-0.86	29.61	50.80

3-Year Standard Deviation	25.82
Effective Duration	

Valuation
Premium/Discount (1-Year Average)	0.11

Company Information
Provider	Invesco
Manager/Tenure	Peter Hubbard (11), Michael Jeanette (10), Tony Seisser (4), 1 other
Website	http://www.invesco.com/us
Address	Invesco 11 Greenway Plaza, Ste. 2500 Houston TX 77046 United States
Phone Number	800-659-1005

PERFORMANCE

Ratings History
Date	Overall Rating	Risk Rating	Reward Rating
Q4-18	C	C-	C
Q2-18	C	D+	B-
Q4-17	B	C	A-
Q4-16	C-	D+	C-
Q4-15	C+	C	B

Asset & Performance History
Date	NAV	1-Year Total Return
2017	72.1	50.11
2016	48.03	-12.91
2015	55.15	2.28
2014	53.92	13.75
2013	47.4	44.08
2012	33.02	16.43

Total Assets: $274,974,094

Asset Allocation
Asset	%
Cash	0%
Stocks	100%
US Stocks	99%
Bonds	0%
US Bonds	0%
Other	0%

Services Offered:

Investment Strategy: The investment seeks to track the investment results (before fees and expenses) of the Dorsey Wright® Healthcare Technical Leaders Index (the "underlying index"). The fund generally will invest at least 90% of its total assets in the securities that comprise the underlying index. The underlying index is composed of at least 30 securities of companies in the healthcare sector that have powerful relative strength or "momentum" characteristics. **Top Holdings:** Exact Sciences Corp   PTC Therapeutics Inc   Teladoc Health Inc   CareDx Inc   UnitedHealth Group Inc

---

Invesco CurrencyShares® Euro Currency Trust

C-   HOLD

Ticker	Traded On	NAV	Total Assets ($)	Dividend Yield (TTM)	Turnover Ratio	Expense Ratio
FXE	NYSE Arca	109.25	$272,244,958	0	0	0.4

Ratings
Reward	D+
Risk	C
Recent Upgrade/Downgrade	Down

Fund Information
Fund Type	Exchange Traded Funds
Category	Currency
Sub-Category	Single Currency
Prospectus Objective	Worldwide Bond
Inception Date	Dec-05
Open to New Investments	Y

Prices
Price (as of 12/31/2018)	109.48
52-Week High	120.47
52-Week Low	107.47

Total Returns (%)
3-Month	6-Month	1-Year	3-Year	5-Year
-1.78	-1.90	-5.56	2.73	-19.79

3-Year Standard Deviation	7
Effective Duration	

Valuation
Premium/Discount (1-Year Average)	-0.05

Company Information
Provider	Invesco
Manager/Tenure	Management Team (12)
Website	http://www.invesco.com/us
Address	Invesco 11 Greenway Plaza, Ste. 2500 Houston TX 77046 United States
Phone Number	800-659-1005

PERFORMANCE

Ratings History
Date	Overall Rating	Risk Rating	Reward Rating
Q4-18	C-	C	D+
Q2-18	C	C	C-
Q4-17	C	C+	C
Q4-16	D	D	D
Q4-15	D	D	D

Asset & Performance History
Date	NAV	1-Year Total Return
2017	115.69	12.93
2016	102.45	-3.66
2015	106.34	-10.74
2014	119.14	-12.53
2013	136.22	4.1
2012	130.85	1.19

Total Assets: $272,244,958

Asset Allocation
Asset	%
Cash	100%
Stocks	0%
US Stocks	0%
Bonds	0%
US Bonds	0%
Other	0%

Services Offered:

Investment Strategy: The investment objective of the Trust is for the Shares to reflect the price in USD of the Euro. The Shares are intended to provide institutional and retail investors with a simple, cost-effective means of gaining investment benefits similar to those of holding euro. **Top Holdings:**

iShares Currency Hedged MSCI Germany ETF   D+   SELL

Ticker	Traded On	NAV	Total Assets ($)	Dividend Yield (TTM)	Turnover Ratio	Expense Ratio
HEWG	NAS CM	23.77	$271,801,230	2.88	11	0.53

Ratings
Reward   D+
Risk   C-
Recent Upgrade/Downgrade   Down

Fund Information
Fund Type   Exchange Traded Funds
Category   Equity Misc
Sub-Category   Miscellaneous Region
Prospectus Objective   Foreign Stock
Inception Date   Jan-14
Open to New Investments   Y

Prices
Price (as of 12/31/2018)   23.75
52-Week High   30.33
52-Week Low   22.95

Total Returns (%)

3-Month	6-Month	1-Year	3-Year	5-Year
-13.46	-12.33	-15.17	4.80	

3-Year Standard Deviation   12.72
Effective Duration

Valuation
Premium/Discount (1-Year Average)   -0.01

Company Information
Provider   iShares
Manager/Tenure   Diane Hsiung (4), Jennifer Hsui (4),
                      Orlando Montalvo (4), 2 others
Website   http://www.ishares.com
Address   iShares 400 Howard Street San
                      Francisco CA 94105 United States
Phone Number   800-474-2737

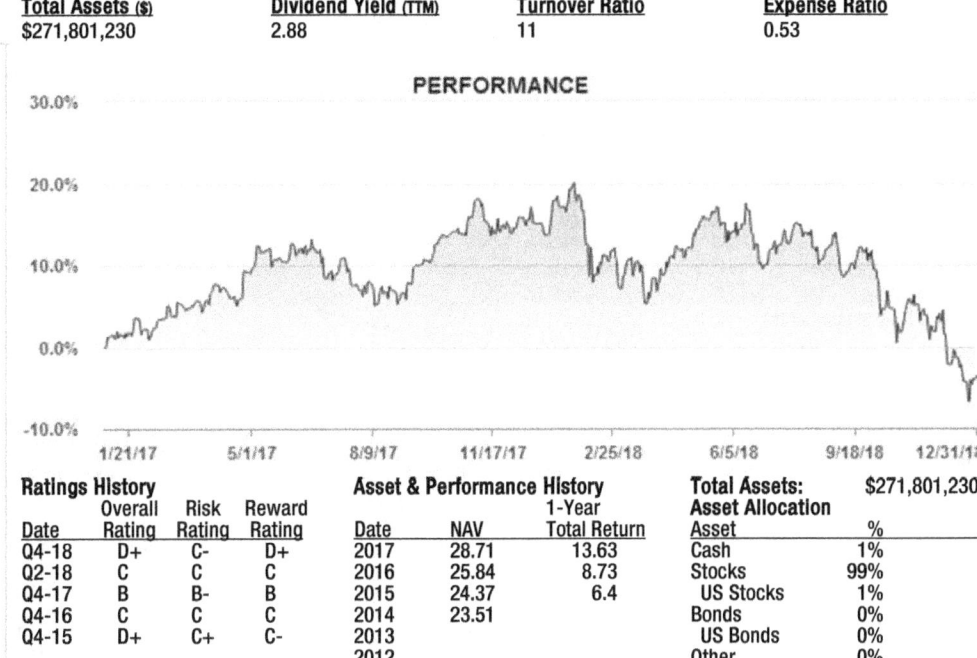

PERFORMANCE

Ratings History

Date	Overall Rating	Risk Rating	Reward Rating
Q4-18	D+	C-	D+
Q2-18	C	C	C
Q4-17	B	B-	B
Q4-16	C	C	C
Q4-15	D+	C+	C-

Asset & Performance History

Date	NAV	1-Year Total Return
2017	28.71	13.63
2016	25.84	8.73
2015	24.37	6.4
2014	23.51	
2013		
2012		

Total Assets: $271,801,230
Asset Allocation

Asset	%
Cash	1%
Stocks	99%
US Stocks	1%
Bonds	0%
US Bonds	0%
Other	0%

Services Offered:

Investment Strategy: The investment seeks to track the investment results of the MSCI Germany 100% Hedged to USD Index. The fund generally will invest at least 90% of its assets in the component securities (including indirect investments through the underlying fund) and other instruments of the underlying index and in investments that have economic characteristics that are substantially identical to the component securities of the underlying index. The index consists of stocks traded primarily on the Frankfurt Stock Exchange with the currency risk inherent in the securities included in the underlying index hedged to the U.S. dollar on a monthly basis. **Top Holdings:** iShares MSCI Germany ETF

VanEck Vectors Emerging Markets High Yield Bond ETF   C   HOLD

Ticker	Traded On	NAV	Total Assets ($)	Dividend Yield (TTM)	Turnover Ratio	Expense Ratio
HYEM	NYSE Arca	22.37	$269,907,914	5.73	40	0.4

Ratings
Reward   C-
Risk   C+
Recent Upgrade/Downgrade

Fund Information
Fund Type   Exchange Traded Funds
Category   Emerging Mkts Fixed Inc
Sub-Category   Emerging Markets Bond
Prospectus Objective   Corp Bond-High Yld
Inception Date   May-12
Open to New Investments   Y

Prices
Price (as of 12/31/2018)   22.38
52-Week High   24.64
52-Week Low   22.05

Total Returns (%)

3-Month	6-Month	1-Year	3-Year	5-Year
-1.21	0.36	-4.01	19.32	20.13

3-Year Standard Deviation   5.29
Effective Duration   3.66

Valuation
Premium/Discount (1-Year Average)   -0.24

Company Information
Provider   VanEck
Manager/Tenure   Francis G. Rodilosso (6)
Website   http://www.vaneck.com
Address   Van Eck Associates Corporation 666
                      Third Avenue New York NY 10017
                      United States
Phone Number   800-826-1115

PERFORMANCE

Ratings History

Date	Overall Rating	Risk Rating	Reward Rating
Q4-18	C	C+	C-
Q2-18	C	C+	C-
Q4-17	B	B+	C+
Q4-16	C	C-	C+
Q4-15	C	C+	C-

Asset & Performance History

Date	NAV	1-Year Total Return
2017	24.5	7.98
2016	24.05	15.12
2015	22.27	2.95
2014	23.25	-2.21
2013	25.28	0.37
2012	26.73	

Total Assets: $269,907,914
Asset Allocation

Asset	%
Cash	1%
Stocks	0%
US Stocks	0%
Bonds	98%
US Bonds	13%
Other	1%

Services Offered:

Investment Strategy: The investment seeks to replicate as closely as possible, before fees and expenses, the price and yield performance of the ICE BofAML Diversified High Yield US Emerging Markets Corporate Plus Index. The fund normally invests at least 80% of its total assets in securities that comprise the fund's benchmark index. The index is comprised of U.S. dollar denominated bonds issued by non-sovereign emerging market issuers that have a below investment grade rating and that are issued in the major domestic and Eurobond markets. **Top Holdings:** Turkiye Is Bankasi A.S. 6% SUB PIDI NTS 24/10/2022 USD (144A) Yapi Ve Kredi Bankasi A.S. 5.5% SUB PIDI BDS 06/12/2022 USD (144A) Provincia De Buenos Aires 9.125% China Evergrande Group 8.75% SNR PIDI NTS 28/06/2025 USD (REGS) YPF Sociedad Anonima 8.5% SNR GMTN 28/07/2025 USD (144A)

WisdomTree International High Dividend Fund   D+   SELL

Ticker	Traded On	NAV	Total Assets ($)	Dividend Yield (TTM)	Turnover Ratio	Expense Ratio
DTH	NYSE Arca	37.25	$269,454,283	4.39	26	0.58

Ratings
Reward   D+
Risk   C-
Recent Upgrade/Downgrade   Down

Fund Information
Fund Type   Exchange Traded Funds
Category   Global Equity Large Cap
Sub-Category   Foreign Large Value
Prospectus Objective   Foreign Stock
Inception Date   Jun-06
Open to New Investments   Y

Prices
Price (as of 12/31/2018)   37.11
52-Week High   47.36
52-Week Low   36.10

Total Returns (%)

3-Month	6-Month	1-Year	3-Year	5-Year
-10.16	-7.91	-12.56	10.56	-1.75

3-Year Standard Deviation   10.9
Effective Duration

Valuation
Premium/Discount (1-Year Average)   -0.15

Company Information
Provider   WisdomTree
Manager/Tenure   Richard A. Brown (10), Thomas J. Durante (10), Karen Q. Wong (10)
Website   http://www.wisdomtree.com
Address   WisdomTree 245 Park Avenue, 35th floor New York NY 10167 United States
Phone Number   866-909-9473

PERFORMANCE

Ratings History

Date	Overall Rating	Risk Rating	Reward Rating
Q4-18	D+	C-	D+
Q2-18	C	C-	C
Q4-17	C+	C	C+
Q4-16	D+	C-	D+
Q4-15	C	C-	C

Asset & Performance History

Date	NAV	1-Year Total Return
2017	44.42	20.31
2016	38.38	5.11
2015	38.07	-6.99
2014	42.57	-4.46
2013	47.01	23.15
2012	39.88	14.71

Total Assets: $269,454,283
Asset Allocation

Asset	%
Cash	0%
Stocks	100%
US Stocks	0%
Bonds	0%
US Bonds	0%
Other	0%

Services Offered:

Investment Strategy: The investment seeks to track the price and yield performance, before fees and expenses, of the WisdomTree International High Dividend Index. Under normal circumstances, at least 95% of the fund's total assets (exclusive of collateral held from securities lending) will be invested in component securities of the index and investments that have economic characteristics that are substantially identical to the economic characteristics of such component securities. The index is a fundamentally weighted index that is comprised of companies with high dividend yields selected from the WisdomTree International Equity Index. The fund is non-diversified. **Top Holdings:** China Mobile Ltd Novartis AG Nestle SA Royal Dutch Shell PLC Class A BP PLC

Invesco S&P 500® Equal Weight Utilities ETF   B-   BUY

Ticker	Traded On	NAV	Total Assets ($)	Dividend Yield (TTM)	Turnover Ratio	Expense Ratio
RYU	NYSE Arca	88.83	$268,818,860	3.08		0.4

Ratings
Reward   B
Risk   C
Recent Upgrade/Downgrade   Up

Fund Information
Fund Type   Exchange Traded Funds
Category   Utilities Sector Equity
Sub-Category   Utilities
Prospectus Objective   Utility
Inception Date   Nov-06
Open to New Investments   Y

Prices
Price (as of 12/31/2018)   88.76
52-Week High   95.55
52-Week Low   77.51

Total Returns (%)

3-Month	6-Month	1-Year	3-Year	5-Year
2.16	5.08	6.95	34.57	65.37

3-Year Standard Deviation   10.85
Effective Duration

Valuation
Premium/Discount (1-Year Average)   -0.03

Company Information
Provider   Invesco
Manager/Tenure   Peter Hubbard (0), Michael Jeanette (0), Jonathan Nixon (0), 1 other
Website   http://www.invesco.com/us
Address   Invesco 11 Greenway Plaza, Ste. 2500 Houston TX 77046 United States
Phone Number   800-659-1005

PERFORMANCE

Ratings History

Date	Overall Rating	Risk Rating	Reward Rating
Q4-18	B-	C	B
Q2-18	C+	C	B-
Q4-17	B	B	B
Q4-16	C	C	C+
Q4-15	B-	C	B

Asset & Performance History

Date	NAV	1-Year Total Return
2017	85.81	9.01
2016	80.8	14.67
2015	72.37	-4.02
2014	78.58	28.03
2013	63.32	13.33
2012	58.01	8.3

Total Assets: $268,818,860
Asset Allocation

Asset	%
Cash	0%
Stocks	100%
US Stocks	100%
Bonds	0%
US Bonds	0%
Other	0%

Services Offered:

Investment Strategy: The investment seeks to track the investment results (before fees and expenses) of the S&P 500® Equal Weight Telecommunications Services & Utilities Index. The fund generally will invest at least 90% of its total assets in the securities that comprise the underlying index. The underlying index is an equal-weighted version of the S&P 500® Utilities Index. Strictly in accordance with its guidelines and mandated procedures, the index provider compiles, maintains and calculates the underlying index, which is comprised of common stocks of companies in the utilities sector and telecommunication services of the S&P 500® Index. It is non-diversified. **Top Holdings:** SCANA Corp The AES Corp Pinnacle West Capital Corp Duke Energy Corp Xcel Energy Inc

iShares Edge MSCI Multifactor Emerging Markets ETF   D+   SELL

Ticker	Traded On	NAV	Total Assets ($)	Dividend Yield (TTM)	Turnover Ratio	Expense Ratio
EMGF	BATS	39.03	$268,622,259	2.47	39	0.45

Ratings

Reward	D+
Risk	D+
Recent Upgrade/Downgrade	Down

Fund Information

Fund Type	Exchange Traded Funds
Category	Global Emerg Mkts Equity
Sub-Category	Diversified Emerging Mkts
Prospectus Objective	Div Emerg Mkts
Inception Date	Dec-15
Open to New Investments	Y

Prices

Price (as of 12/31/2018)	38.73
52-Week High	53.84
52-Week Low	38.00

Total Returns (%)

3-Month	6-Month	1-Year	3-Year	5-Year
-8.39	-13.38	-18.64	24.77	

3-Year Standard Deviation	
Effective Duration	

Valuation

Premium/Discount (1-Year Average)	0.14

Company Information

Provider	iShares
Manager/Tenure	Diane Hsiung (2), Jennifer Hsui (2), Greg Savage (2), 1 other
Website	http://www.ishares.com
Address	iShares 400 Howard Street San Francisco CA 94105 United States
Phone Number	800-474-2737

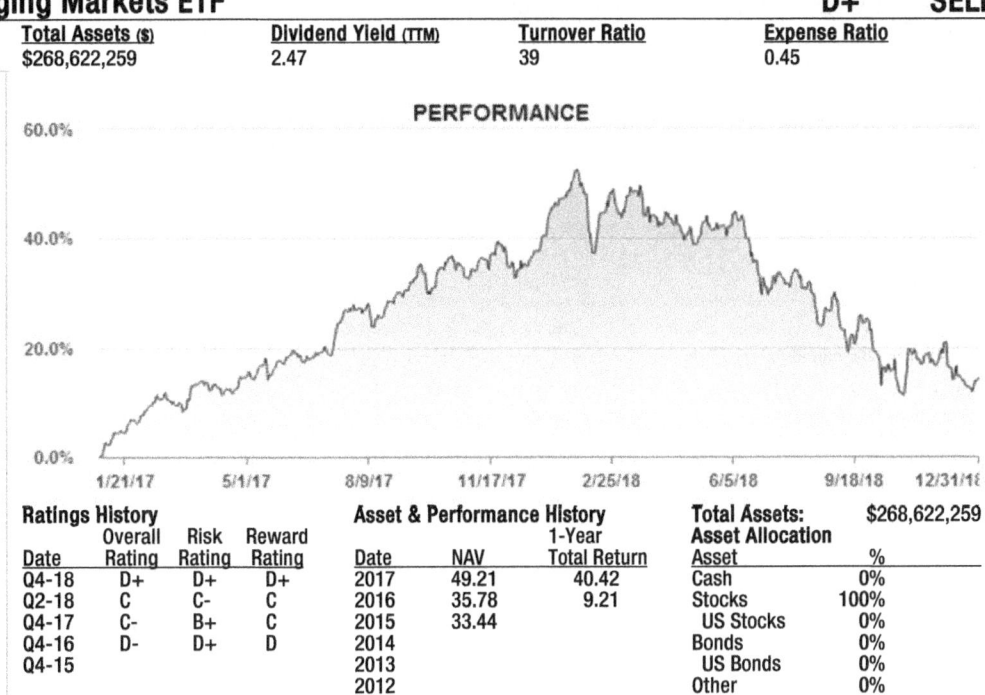

PERFORMANCE

Ratings History

Date	Overall Rating	Risk Rating	Reward Rating
Q4-18	D+	D+	D+
Q2-18	C	C-	C
Q4-17	C-	B+	C
Q4-16	D-	D+	D
Q4-15			

Asset & Performance History

Date	NAV	1-Year Total Return
2017	49.21	40.42
2016	35.78	9.21
2015	33.44	
2014		
2013		
2012		

Total Assets: $268,622,259

Asset Allocation

Asset	%
Cash	0%
Stocks	100%
US Stocks	0%
Bonds	0%
US Bonds	0%
Other	0%

Services Offered:

Investment Strategy: The investment seeks to track the investment results of the MSCI Emerging Markets Diversified Multiple-Factor Index. The underlying index is designed to select equity securities from the MSCI Emerging Markets Index that have high exposure to four investment style factors: value, quality, momentum and low size, while maintaining a level of risk similar to that of the parent index. The fund generally will invest at least 90% of its assets in the component securities of the underlying index and in investments that have economic characteristics that are substantially identical to the component securities of the underlying index. **Top Holdings:** China Mobile Ltd   SK Hynix Inc   Tencent Holdings Ltd   Samsung Electronics Co Ltd   Yum China Holdings Inc

---

Invesco S&P Emerging Markets Low Volatility ETF   C-   HOLD

Ticker	Traded On	NAV	Total Assets ($)	Dividend Yield (TTM)	Turnover Ratio	Expense Ratio
EELV	NYSE Arca	22.77	$267,613,318	4.3	81	0.29

Ratings

Reward	C-
Risk	C-
Recent Upgrade/Downgrade	

Fund Information

Fund Type	Exchange Traded Funds
Category	Global Emerg Mkts Equity
Sub-Category	Diversified Emerging Mkts
Prospectus Objective	Div Emerg Mkts
Inception Date	Jan-12
Open to New Investments	

Prices

Price (as of 12/31/2018)	22.75
52-Week High	27.55
52-Week Low	22.50

Total Returns (%)

3-Month	6-Month	1-Year	3-Year	5-Year
-6.79	-1.35	-5.70	22.97	-3.20

3-Year Standard Deviation	12.11
Effective Duration	

Valuation

Premium/Discount (1-Year Average)	-0.08

Company Information

Provider	Invesco
Manager/Tenure	Peter Hubbard (6), Jonathan Nixon (5), Michael Jeanette (3), 1 other
Website	http://www.invesco.com/us
Address	Invesco 11 Greenway Plaza, Ste. 2500 Houston TX 77046 United States
Phone Number	800-659-1005

PERFORMANCE

Ratings History

Date	Overall Rating	Risk Rating	Reward Rating
Q4-18	C-	C-	C-
Q2-18	C-	C-	C-
Q4-17	C	C	C
Q4-16	D	D+	D
Q4-15	D	D	D

Asset & Performance History

Date	NAV	1-Year Total Return
2017	25.44	24.53
2016	21.05	4.72
2015	20.55	-17.54
2014	25.51	-4.53
2013	27.56	-1.15
2012	28.49	

Total Assets: $267,613,318

Asset Allocation

Asset	%
Cash	0%
Stocks	100%
US Stocks	0%
Bonds	0%
US Bonds	0%
Other	0%

Services Offered:

Investment Strategy: The investment seeks to track the investment results (before fees and expenses) of the S&P BMI Emerging Markets Low Volatility IndexTM (the "underlying index"). The fund will invest at least 90% of its total assets in the securities of companies that comprise the underlying index. S&P Dow Jones Indices LLC ("S&P DJI" or the "index provider") compiles, maintains and calculates the underlying index, which is designed to measure the performance of 200 of the least volatile stocks of the S&P Emerging Plus LargeMidCap Index. **Top Holdings:** Kuala Lumpur Kepong Bhd   Taiwan Cooperative Financial Holding Co Ltd   Hua Nan Financial Holdings Co Ltd Chang Hwa Commercial Bank Ltd   First Financial Holding Co Ltd

Schwab Fundamental U.S. Broad Market Index ETF   C   HOLD

Ticker	Traded On	NAV		Total Assets ($)	Dividend Yield (TTM)	Turnover Ratio	Expense Ratio
FNDB	NYSE Arca	33.64		$266,617,719	2.1	10	0.25

Ratings
Reward   C
Risk   C-
Recent Upgrade/Downgrade

Fund Information
Fund Type	Exchange Traded Funds
Category	US Equity Large Cap Value
Sub-Category	Large Value
Prospectus Objective	Growth & Inc
Inception Date	Aug-13
Open to New Investments	Y

Prices
Price (as of 12/31/2018)	33.49
52-Week High	40.14
52-Week Low	31.73

Total Returns (%)
3-Month	6-Month	1-Year	3-Year	5-Year
-14.54	-8.75	-7.64	26.01	36.72

3-Year Standard Deviation   9.58
Effective Duration

Valuation
Premium/Discount (1-Year Average)   0.09

Company Information
Provider	Schwab ETFs
Manager/Tenure	Christopher Bliss (1), Ferian Juwono (1), Sabya Sinha (1)
Website	http://www.schwabetfs.com
Address	Schwab ETFs United States
Phone Number	800-435-4000

PERFORMANCE

Ratings History
Date	Overall Rating	Risk Rating	Reward Rating
Q4-18	C	C-	C
Q2-18	C	C-	C
Q4-17	B	B	B-
Q4-16	C+	C-	B
Q4-15	C-	C-	C-

Asset & Performance History
Date	NAV	1-Year Total Return
2017	37.22	16.76
2016	32.56	16.96
2015	28.46	-3.07
2014	30.03	11.93
2013	27.29	
2012		

Total Assets: $266,617,719

Asset Allocation
Asset	%
Cash	0%
Stocks	100%
US Stocks	99%
Bonds	0%
US Bonds	0%
Other	0%

Services Offered:

Investment Strategy: The investment seeks to track as closely as possible, before fees and expenses, the total return of the Russell RAFI™ US Index. The fund will invest at least 90% of its net assets (including, for this purpose, any borrowings for investment purposes) in stocks included in the index. The index measures the performance of the constituent companies by fundamental overall company scores, which are created using as the universe the companies included in the Russell 3000® Index. It may invest up to 10% of its net assets in securities not included in the index. **Top Holdings:** Exxon Mobil Corp   Apple Inc   Chevron Corp   Microsoft Corp   AT&T Inc

---

Invesco Dynamic Software ETF   C   HOLD

Ticker	Traded On	NAV		Total Assets ($)	Dividend Yield (TTM)	Turnover Ratio	Expense Ratio
PSJ	NYSE Arca	73.98		$266,359,150	0	145	0.63

Ratings
Reward   C+
Risk   C-
Recent Upgrade/Downgrade   Down

Fund Information
Fund Type	Exchange Traded Funds
Category	Technology Sector Equity
Sub-Category	Technology
Prospectus Objective	Technology
Inception Date	Jun-05
Open to New Investments	Y

Prices
Price (as of 12/31/2018)	73.90
52-Week High	88.71
52-Week Low	63.50

Total Returns (%)
3-Month	6-Month	1-Year	3-Year	5-Year
-13.99	-4.18	16.63	75.07	105.31

3-Year Standard Deviation   15.78
Effective Duration

Valuation
Premium/Discount (1-Year Average)   0.11

Company Information
Provider	Invesco
Manager/Tenure	Peter Hubbard (11), Michael Jeanette (10), Tony Seisser (4), 1 other
Website	http://www.invesco.com/us
Address	Invesco 11 Greenway Plaza, Ste. 2500 Houston TX 77046 United States
Phone Number	800-659-1005

PERFORMANCE

Ratings History
Date	Overall Rating	Risk Rating	Reward Rating
Q4-18	C	C-	C+
Q2-18	B-	C-	B+
Q4-17	A-	B+	A
Q4-16	C-	C-	C-
Q4-15	B-	C	B

Asset & Performance History
Date	NAV	1-Year Total Return
2017	63.43	34.47
2016	47.17	11.62
2015	42.27	7.08
2014	39.53	9.51
2013	36.13	33.12
2012	27.14	16.33

Total Assets: $266,359,150

Asset Allocation
Asset	%
Cash	0%
Stocks	100%
US Stocks	97%
Bonds	0%
US Bonds	0%
Other	0%

Services Offered:

Investment Strategy: The investment seeks to track the investment results (before fees and expenses) of the Dynamic Software IntellidexSM Index. The fund generally will invest at least 90% of its total assets in common stocks of software companies that comprise the underlying intellidex. The underlying intellidex was composed of common stocks of 30 U.S. software companies. These are companies that are principally engaged in the research, design, production or distribution of products or processes that relate to software applications and systems and information-based services. The fund is non-diversified. **Top Holdings:** Liberty Broadband Corp A   Microsoft Corp   Citrix Systems Inc   Intuit Inc   Atlassian Corporation PLC A

Direxion Daily Small Cap Bear 3X Shares   D   SELL

Ticker	Traded On	NAV	Total Assets ($)	Dividend Yield (TTM)	Turnover Ratio	Expense Ratio
TZA	NYSE Arca	15.20	$264,145,852	0.42	0	1.1

Ratings
Reward   D-
Risk   D
Recent Upgrade/Downgrade   Up

Fund Information
Fund Type	Exchange Traded Funds
Category	Trading Tools
Sub-Category	Trading--Inverse Equity
Prospectus Objective	Small Company
Inception Date	Nov-08
Open to New Investments	Y

Prices
Price (as of 12/31/2018)	15.22
52-Week High	18.62
52-Week Low	7.85

Total Returns (%)

3-Month	6-Month	1-Year	3-Year	5-Year
73.87	66.89	24.79	-65.79	-77.40

3-Year Standard Deviation   43.15
Effective Duration

Valuation
Premium/Discount (1-Year Average)   -0.06

Company Information
Provider	Direxion Funds
Manager/Tenure	Paul Brigandi (10), Tony Ng (3)
Website	http://www.direxionfunds.com
Address	Direxion Funds 1301 Avenue Of The Americas (6th Avenue) New York NY 10019 United States
Phone Number	646-572-3390

PERFORMANCE

Ratings History

Date	Overall Rating	Risk Rating	Reward Rating
Q4-18	D	D	D-
Q2-18	D-	D-	E+
Q4-17	E+	E+	E+
Q4-16	D	D-	E+
Q4-15	D-	E+	E+

Asset & Performance History

Date	NAV	1-Year Total Return
2017	12.28	-38.35
2016	19.92	-55.53
2015	44.8	-6.82
2014	48.08	-29.12
2013	67.84	-68.61
2012	216.16	-48.9

Total Assets: $264,145,852
Asset Allocation

Asset	%
Cash	105%
Stocks	-5%
US Stocks	-5%
Bonds	0%
US Bonds	0%
Other	0%

Services Offered:

Investment Strategy: The investment seeks daily investment results, before fees and expenses, of 300% of the inverse (or opposite) of the daily performance of the Russell 2000® Index. The fund invests in swap agreements, futures contracts, short positions or other financial instruments that, in combination, provide inverse (opposite) or short leveraged exposure to the index equal to at least 80% of the fund's net assets (plus borrowing for investment purposes). The index measures the performance of approximately 2,000 small-capitalization companies in the Russell 3000® Index, based on a combination of their market capitalization and current index membership. It is non-diversified. **Top Holdings:** Russ 2000 Indx Small Swap   Russ 2000 Indx Small Swap   Russ 2000 Indx Small Swap   Russ 2000 Indx Small Swap   Russ 2000 Indx Small Swap

---

Invesco Zacks Multi-Asset Income ETF   C-   HOLD

Ticker	Traded On	NAV	Total Assets ($)	Dividend Yield (TTM)	Turnover Ratio	Expense Ratio
CVY	NYSE Arca	19.25	$263,080,908	4.24		0.88

Ratings
Reward   C-
Risk   C-
Recent Upgrade/Downgrade   Down

Fund Information
Fund Type	Exchange Traded Funds
Category	Aggressive Allocation
Sub-Category	Allocation--85%+ Equity
Prospectus Objective	Multi-Asset Global
Inception Date	Sep-06
Open to New Investments	Y

Prices
Price (as of 12/31/2018)	19.22
52-Week High	23.39
52-Week Low	18.31

Total Returns (%)

3-Month	6-Month	1-Year	3-Year	5-Year
-12.31	-10.48	-10.42	20.24	-1.13

3-Year Standard Deviation   9.17
Effective Duration   3.86

Valuation
Premium/Discount (1-Year Average)   -0.09

Company Information
Provider	Invesco
Manager/Tenure	Peter Hubbard (0), Michael Jeanette (0), Jonathan Nixon (0), 1 other
Website	http://www.invesco.com/us
Address	Invesco 11 Greenway Plaza, Ste. 2500 Houston TX 77046 United States
Phone Number	800-659-1005

PERFORMANCE

Ratings History

Date	Overall Rating	Risk Rating	Reward Rating
Q4-18	C-	C-	C-
Q2-18	C	C	C
Q4-17	C+	C	C+
Q4-16	C-	C-	D+
Q4-15	C-	C-	C-

Asset & Performance History

Date	NAV	1-Year Total Return
2017	22.37	15.55
2016	20.19	16.31
2015	18.21	-14.16
2014	22.37	-4.2
2013	24.74	19.62
2012	21.87	13.07

Total Assets: $263,080,908
Asset Allocation

Asset	%
Cash	0%
Stocks	81%
US Stocks	68%
Bonds	9%
US Bonds	5%
Other	-1%

Services Offered:

Investment Strategy: The investment seeks to track the investment results (before fees and expenses) of the Zacks Multi-Asset Income Index (the "underlying index"). The fund generally will invest at least 90% of its total assets in securities that comprise the underlying index and depositary receipts representing securities that comprise the underlying index. The underlying index was comprised of approximately 149 securities selected, based on investment and other criteria, from a universe of domestic and international companies listed on major U.S. exchanges. The fund is non-diversified. **Top Holdings:** Energy Company of Minas Gerais ADR   Starbucks Corp   Omega Healthcare Investors Inc   Broadcom Inc   National Retail Properties Inc

iShares MSCI Poland ETF   C-   HOLD

Ticker	Traded On	NAV	Total Assets ($)	Dividend Yield (TTM)	Turnover Ratio	Expense Ratio
EPOL	NYSE Arca	22.99	$260,716,199	1.92	7	0.63

Ratings
Reward   C-
Risk   C-
Recent Upgrade/Downgrade   Up

Fund Information
Fund Type   Exchange Traded Funds
Category   Europe Equity Mid/Small Cap
Sub-Category   Miscellaneous Region
Prospectus Objective   Europe Stock
Inception Date   May-10
Open to New Investments   Y

Prices
Price (as of 12/31/2018)   23.03
52-Week High   30.00
52-Week Low   21.09

Total Returns (%)

3-Month	6-Month	1-Year	3-Year	5-Year
-2.27	8.51	-14.30	34.44	-12.65

3-Year Standard Deviation   22.84
Effective Duration

Valuation
Premium/Discount (1-Year Average)   -0.23

Company Information
Provider   iShares
Manager/Tenure   Diane Hsiung (8), Greg Savage (8),
                      Jennifer Hsui (5), 1 other
Website   http://www.ishares.com
Address   iShares 400 Howard Street San
                      Francisco CA 94105 United States
Phone Number   800-474-2737

PERFORMANCE

Ratings History

Date	Overall Rating	Risk Rating	Reward Rating
Q4-18	C-	C-	C-
Q2-18	C-	C-	C-
Q4-17	C	C	C+
Q4-16	D	D	D
Q4-15	D	D	D

Asset & Performance History

Date	NAV	1-Year Total Return
2017	27.21	52.69
2016	18.17	2.75
2015	18.07	-23.26
2014	24.08	-15.33
2013	29.35	4.62
2012	29.05	38.25

Total Assets: $260,716,199
Asset Allocation

Asset	%
Cash	0%
Stocks	100%
US Stocks	0%
Bonds	0%
US Bonds	0%
Other	0%

Services Offered:

Investment Strategy: The investment seeks to track the investment results of the MSCI Poland IMI 25/50 Index. The fund generally will invest at least 90% of its assets in the component securities of the index and in investments that have economic characteristics that are substantially identical to the component securities of the index and may invest up to 10% of its assets in certain futures, options and swap contracts, cash and cash equivalents. The index is a free float-adjusted market capitalization-weighted index designed to measure the performance of equity securities listed on stock exchanges in Poland. The fund is non-diversified. **Top Holdings:** PKO Bank Polski SA Polski Koncern Naftowy ORLEN SA Powszechny Zaklad Ubezpieczen SA Bank Polska Kasa Opieki SA Polish Oil and Gas Company (PGNiG) SA

ProShares Ultra VIX Short-Term Futures ETF   C-   HOLD

Ticker	Traded On	NAV	Total Assets ($)	Dividend Yield (TTM)	Turnover Ratio	Expense Ratio
UVXY	NYSE Arca		$259,340,948	0		1.65

Ratings
Reward   C
Risk   D
Recent Upgrade/Downgrade   Up

Fund Information
Fund Type   Exchange Traded Funds
Category   Alternative Misc
Sub-Category   Volatility
Prospectus Objective   Growth
Inception Date   Oct-11
Open to New Investments   Y

Prices
Price (as of 12/31/2018)   81.73
52-Week High   88.08
52-Week Low   8.67

Total Returns (%)

3-Month	6-Month	1-Year	3-Year	5-Year
139.15	608.76	738.37	-96.91	-99.74

3-Year Standard Deviation   83.73
Effective Duration

Valuation
Premium/Discount (1-Year Average)   0.40

Company Information
Provider   ProShares
Manager/Tenure   Management Team (7)
Website   http://www.proshares.com
Address   ProShares 7501 Wisconsin Avenue,
                      Suite 1000 Bethesda MD 20814
                      United States
Phone Number   866-776-5125

PERFORMANCE

Ratings History

Date	Overall Rating	Risk Rating	Reward Rating
Q4-18	C-	D	C
Q2-18	E+	D-	E
Q4-17	E	E	E-
Q4-16	E+	D-	E-
Q4-15	E	E+	E

Asset & Performance History

Date	NAV	1-Year Total Return
2017	10.34	-94.05
2016	173.92	-93.8
2015	2,808.49	-77.61
2014	12,546.68	-62.59
2013	33,541.68	-91.67
2012	402,673.80	-97.28

Total Assets: $259,340,948
Asset Allocation

Asset	%
Cash	-50%
Stocks	150%
US Stocks	150%
Bonds	0%
US Bonds	0%
Other	0%

Services Offered:

Investment Strategy: The investment seeks results (before fees and expenses) that correspond to one and one-half times (1.5x) of the performance of the S&P 500 VIX Short-Term Futures Index for a single day. The index seeks to offer exposure to market volatility through publicly traded futures markets and is designed to measure the return from a rolling long position in the first and second month VIX futures contracts. **Top Holdings:** Cboe Vix Future 12/19/2018 (Uxz8) Cboe Vix Future 01/16/2019 (Uxf9) Ipath S&P 500 Vix Short-Term Fut Swap - Gs S&P 500 Vix Short-Term Futures Index Swap ¿ Deutsche Bank Ag S&P 500 Vix Short-Term Futures Index Swap - Deutsche Bank

Direxion Daily S&P 500® Bear 3X Shares   D   SELL

Ticker	Traded On	NAV	Total Assets ($)	Dividend Yield (TTM)	Turnover Ratio	Expense Ratio
SPXS	NYSE Arca	30.92	$257,341,661	0.32	7	1.1

Ratings

Reward	D-
Risk	D-
Recent Upgrade/Downgrade	Up

Fund Information

Fund Type	Exchange Traded Funds
Category	Trading Tools
Sub-Category	Trading--Inverse Equity
Prospectus Objective	Growth
Inception Date	Nov-08
Open to New Investments	Y

Prices

Price (as of 12/31/2018)	30.79
52-Week High	38.16
52-Week Low	21.06

Total Returns (%)

3-Month	6-Month	1-Year	3-Year	5-Year
46.52	18.34	3.39	-63.19	-81.30

3-Year Standard Deviation	26.22
Effective Duration	

Valuation

Premium/Discount (1-Year Average)	-0.03

Company Information

Provider	Direxion Funds
Manager/Tenure	Paul Brigandi (10), Tony Ng (3)
Website	http://www.direxionfunds.com
Address	Direxion Funds 1301 Avenue Of The Americas (6th Avenue) New York NY 10019 United States
Phone Number	646-572-3390

PERFORMANCE

Ratings History

Date	Overall Rating	Risk Rating	Reward Rating
Q4-18	D	D-	D-
Q2-18	D-	D-	E+
Q4-17	E+	E+	E+
Q4-16	D	E+	D-
Q4-15	D-	E+	E+

Asset & Performance History

Date	NAV	1-Year Total Return
2017	30.1	-44.46
2016	54.2	-35.89
2015	84.55	-18.07
2014	103.2	-37.99
2013	166.45	-60.62
2012	422.75	-42.73

Total Assets: $257,341,661

Asset Allocation

Asset	%
Cash	104%
Stocks	-4%
US Stocks	-4%
Bonds	0%
US Bonds	0%
Other	0%

Services Offered:

Investment Strategy: The investment seeks daily investment results, before fees and expenses, of 300% of the inverse (or opposite) of the daily performance of the S&P 500® Index. The fund, under normal circumstances, invests in swap agreements, futures contracts, short positions or other financial instruments that, in combination, provide inverse (opposite) or short leveraged exposure to the index equal to at least 80% of the fund's net assets (plus borrowing for investment purposes). The index is a float-adjusted, market capitalization-weighted index. The fund is non-diversified. **Top Holdings:** S&P 500 Index Swap   S&P 500 Index Swap   Goldman Finl Sq Trsry Ins S&P 500 Index Swap   S&P 500 Index Swap

---

SPDR® MSCI Emerging Markets StrategicFactors ETF   D+   SELL

Ticker	Traded On	NAV	Total Assets ($)	Dividend Yield (TTM)	Turnover Ratio	Expense Ratio
QEMM	NYSE Arca	54.80	$256,189,777	2.28	30	0.3

Ratings

Reward	C-
Risk	D+
Recent Upgrade/Downgrade	Down

Fund Information

Fund Type	Exchange Traded Funds
Category	Global Emerg Mkts Equity
Sub-Category	Diversified Emerging Mkts
Prospectus Objective	World Stock
Inception Date	Jun-14
Open to New Investments	Y

Prices

Price (as of 12/31/2018)	54.37
52-Week High	69.72
52-Week Low	52.90

Total Returns (%)

3-Month	6-Month	1-Year	3-Year	5-Year
-6.05	-5.46	-12.10	25.20	

3-Year Standard Deviation	12.85
Effective Duration	

Valuation

Premium/Discount (1-Year Average)	0.04

Company Information

Provider	SPDR State Street Global Advisors
Manager/Tenure	Michael J. Feehily (4), Karl A. Schneider (3), Payal Kapoor Gupta (1)
Website	http://www.spdrs.com
Address	SPDR State Street Global Advisors State Street Financial Center, 1 Lincoln Street Boston MA 02111-2900 United States
Phone Number	617-786-3000

PERFORMANCE

Ratings History

Date	Overall Rating	Risk Rating	Reward Rating
Q4-18	D+	D+	C-
Q2-18	C-	D+	C
Q4-17	C+	C	C+
Q4-16	D+	D+	D+
Q4-15	D	D	D

Asset & Performance History

Date	NAV	1-Year Total Return
2017	64.08	30.21
2016	50.33	9.39
2015	46.96	-14.53
2014	56.05	
2013		
2012		

Total Assets: $256,189,777

Asset Allocation

Asset	%
Cash	1%
Stocks	99%
US Stocks	0%
Bonds	0%
US Bonds	0%
Other	0%

Services Offered:

Investment Strategy: The investment seeks to track the performance of the MSCI Emerging Markets (EM) Factor Mix A-Series Index. The fund generally invests substantially all, but at least 80%, of its total assets in the securities comprising the index and in depositary receipts based on securities comprising the index. The index captures large- and mid-cap representation across 23 emerging markets countries and aims to represent the performance of value, low volatility, and quality factor strategies. The fund is non-diversified. **Top Holdings:** Taiwan Semiconductor Manufacturing Co Ltd   Tencent Holdings Ltd   Samsung Electronics Co Ltd   SK Hynix Inc   Tata Consultancy Services Ltd

UBS ETRACS Alerian MLP Index ETN   D+   SELL

Ticker	Traded On	NAV	Total Assets ($)	Dividend Yield (TTM)	Turnover Ratio	Expense Ratio
AMU	NYSE Arca	14.02	$255,321,156	7.65		0.8

Ratings
Reward	D+
Risk	C-
Recent Upgrade/Downgrade	

Fund Information
Fund Type	Exchange Traded Funds
Category	Energy Sector Equity
Sub-Category	Energy Limited Partnership
Prospectus Objective	Income
Inception Date	Jul-12
Open to New Investments	Y

Prices
Price (as of 12/31/2018)	14.00
52-Week High	19.04
52-Week Low	13.39

Total Returns (%)
3-Month	6-Month	1-Year	3-Year	5-Year
-19.25	-11.37	-13.03	-5.22	-34.00

3-Year Standard Deviation	17.56
Effective Duration	

Valuation
Premium/Discount (1-Year Average)	-0.15

Company Information
Provider	UBS Group AG
Manager/Tenure	No Manager (6)
Website	http://www.ubs.com
Address	Bahnhofstrasse 45 Zurich 8098 Switzerland
Phone Number	412-037-1952

PERFORMANCE

Ratings History
Date	Overall Rating	Risk Rating	Reward Rating
Q4-18	D+	C-	D+
Q2-18	D	D	D
Q4-17	D	D	D
Q4-16	D	D	D
Q4-15	D	D	D

Asset & Performance History
Date	NAV	1-Year Total Return
2017	17.31	-6.57
2016	19.89	17.2
2015	18.24	-32.92
2014	28.92	3.82
2013	29.19	26.51
2012	24.23	

Total Assets: $255,321,156
Asset Allocation
Asset	%
Cash	%
Stocks	%
US Stocks	%
Bonds	%
US Bonds	%
Other	%

Services Offered:

Investment Strategy: The investment seeks to replicate, net of expenses, the Alerian MLP Index. The index measures the performance of 50 prominent energy master limited partnerships. It constituents earn the majority of their cash flow from the transportation, storage, processing or production of energy commodities. The Alerian MLP Index is calculated, maintained and published by S&P in consultation with the index sponsor. **Top Holdings:**

SPDR® SSgA Global Allocation ETF   C-   HOLD

Ticker	Traded On	NAV	Total Assets ($)	Dividend Yield (TTM)	Turnover Ratio	Expense Ratio
GAL	NYSE Arca	34.64	$255,228,255	2.29	86	0.35

Ratings
Reward	C-
Risk	C-
Recent Upgrade/Downgrade	Down

Fund Information
Fund Type	Exchange Traded Funds
Category	Moderate Allocation
Sub-Category	Allocation--50% to 70% Equity
Prospectus Objective	Growth
Inception Date	Apr-12
Open to New Investments	Y

Prices
Price (as of 12/31/2018)	34.52
52-Week High	40.37
52-Week Low	33.88

Total Returns (%)
3-Month	6-Month	1-Year	3-Year	5-Year
-9.30	-6.50	-7.25	13.34	16.51

3-Year Standard Deviation	6.89
Effective Duration	7.24

Valuation
Premium/Discount (1-Year Average)	0.11

Company Information
Provider	SPDR State Street Global Advisors
Manager/Tenure	Timothy J. Furbush (5), Michael O. Martel (4), Jeremiah K. Holly (0)
Website	http://www.spdrs.com
Address	SPDR State Street Global Advisors State Street Financial Center, 1 Lincoln Street Boston MA 02111-2900 United States
Phone Number	617-786-3000

PERFORMANCE

Ratings History
Date	Overall Rating	Risk Rating	Reward Rating
Q4-18	C-	C-	C-
Q2-18	C	C-	C
Q4-17	B	B+	C+
Q4-16	C-	C-	C
Q4-15	C	C-	C

Asset & Performance History
Date	NAV	1-Year Total Return
2017	38.22	18.42
2016	33.05	3.2
2015	32.8	-2.28
2014	34.61	5.19
2013	34.01	12.7
2012	30.97	

Total Assets: $255,228,255
Asset Allocation
Asset	%
Cash	10%
Stocks	65%
US Stocks	41%
Bonds	24%
US Bonds	21%
Other	0%

Services Offered:

Investment Strategy: The investment seeks to provide capital appreciation. The Adviser primarily invests the assets of the fund among exchange traded products ("ETPs") that provide balanced exposure to domestic and international debt and equity securities. The fund typically allocates approximately 60% of its assets to equity securities, though this percentage can vary based on the Adviser's tactical decisions. **Top Holdings:** SPDR® S&P 500 ETF SPDR® Portfolio Developed Wld ex-US ETF SPDR® Blmbg Barclays High Yield Bd ETF SPDR® Blmbg Barclays TIPS ETF SPDR® Portfolio Small Cap ETF

iShares MSCI India Small-Cap ETF　　　　　　　　　　D+　SELL

Ticker	Traded On	NAV	Total Assets ($)	Dividend Yield (TTM)	Turnover Ratio	Expense Ratio
SMIN	BATS	38.73	$255,063,199	2.92	49	0.75

Ratings
Reward	D+
Risk	D
Recent Upgrade/Downgrade	Down

Fund Information
Fund Type	Exchange Traded Funds
Category	India Equity
Sub-Category	India Equity
Prospectus Objective	Small Company
Inception Date	Feb-12
Open to New Investments	Y

Prices
Price (as of 12/31/2018)	38.57
52-Week High	55.07
52-Week Low	33.38

Total Returns (%)
3-Month	6-Month	1-Year	3-Year	5-Year
6.34	-7.38	-25.43	20.13	91.53

3-Year Standard Deviation	23.77
Effective Duration	

Valuation
Premium/Discount (1-Year Average)	-0.05

Company Information
Provider	iShares
Manager/Tenure	Diane Hsiung (6), Greg Savage (6), Jennifer Hsui (5), 1 other
Website	http://www.ishares.com
Address	iShares 400 Howard Street San Francisco CA 94105 United States
Phone Number	800-474-2737

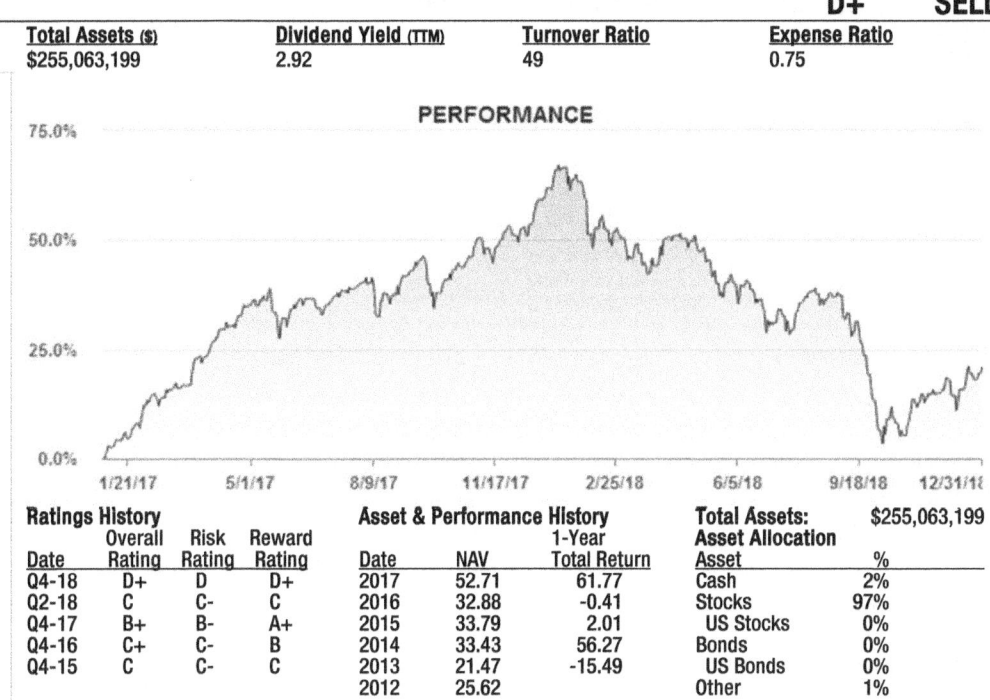

PERFORMANCE

Ratings History
Date	Overall Rating	Risk Rating	Reward Rating
Q4-18	D+	D	D+
Q2-18	C	C-	C
Q4-17	B+	B-	A+
Q4-16	C+	C-	B
Q4-15	C	C-	C

Asset & Performance History
Date	NAV	1-Year Total Return
2017	52.71	61.77
2016	32.88	-0.41
2015	33.79	2.01
2014	33.43	56.27
2013	21.47	-15.49
2012	25.62	

Total Assets: $255,063,199
Asset Allocation
Asset	%
Cash	2%
Stocks	97%
US Stocks	0%
Bonds	0%
US Bonds	0%
Other	1%

Services Offered:

Investment Strategy: The investment seeks to track the investment results of the MSCI India Small Cap Index. The fund generally will collectively invest at least 90% of its assets in the component securities of the underlying index and in investments that have economic characteristics that are substantially identical to the component securities of the underlying index. The index is designed to measure the performance of equity securities of small-capitalization companies whose market capitalization, as calculated by the index provider, represents the bottom 14% of companies in the Indian securities market. **Top Holdings:** The Federal Bank Ltd RBL Bank Ltd Apollo Hospitals Enterprise Ltd Info Edge (India) Ltd MindTree Ltd

---

Global X MSCI Greece ETF　　　　　　　　　　　　　D　SELL

Ticker	Traded On	NAV	Total Assets ($)	Dividend Yield (TTM)	Turnover Ratio	Expense Ratio
GREK	NYSE Arca	6.96	$255,001,446	2.92	22	0.59

Ratings
Reward	D
Risk	D
Recent Upgrade/Downgrade	Down

Fund Information
Fund Type	Exchange Traded Funds
Category	Europe Equity Mid/Small Cap
Sub-Category	Miscellaneous Region
Prospectus Objective	Foreign Stock
Inception Date	Dec-11
Open to New Investments	Y

Prices
Price (as of 12/31/2018)	6.90
52-Week High	11.49
52-Week Low	6.79

Total Returns (%)
3-Month	6-Month	1-Year	3-Year	5-Year
-16.24	-23.34	-31.56	-10.58	-66.46

3-Year Standard Deviation	28.56
Effective Duration	

Valuation
Premium/Discount (1-Year Average)	-0.15

Company Information
Provider	Global X Funds
Manager/Tenure	Chang Kim (4), James Ong (2), Nam To (0)
Website	http://www.globalxfunds.com
Address	Global X Funds 600 Lexington Avenue, 20th Floor New York NY 10022 United States
Phone Number	888-493-8631

PERFORMANCE

Ratings History
Date	Overall Rating	Risk Rating	Reward Rating
Q4-18	D	D	D
Q2-18	C-	D+	C-
Q4-17	D+	D	D+
Q4-16	D	D-	D
Q4-15	D-	D-	D-

Asset & Performance History
Date	NAV	1-Year Total Return
2017	10.17	32.18
2016	7.86	-1.16
2015	8.11	-39.33
2014	13.57	-38.18
2013	22.16	26.92
2012	17.48	23.26

Total Assets: $255,001,446
Asset Allocation
Asset	%
Cash	0%
Stocks	100%
US Stocks	1%
Bonds	0%
US Bonds	0%
Other	0%

Services Offered:

Investment Strategy: The investment seeks to provide investment results that correspond generally to the price and yield performance, before fees and expenses, of the MSCI All Greece Select 25/50 Index. The fund invests at least 80% of its total assets in the securities of the underlying index and in American Depositary Receipts ("ADRs") and Global Depositary Receipts ("GDRs") based on the securities in the underlying index. The underlying index is designed to represent the performance of the broad Greece equity universe. The fund is non-diversified. **Top Holdings:** Hellenic Telecommunication Organization SA Alpha Bank AE Greek Organisation of Football Prognostics SA GasLog Ltd Jumbo SA

iShares Broad USD High Yield Corporate Bond ETF
D+ **SELL**

Ticker	Traded On	NAV	Total Assets ($)	Dividend Yield (TTM)	Turnover Ratio	Expense Ratio
USHY	BATS	45.56	$254,131,392	5.86	0	0.22

Ratings
Reward	D
Risk	C-
Recent Upgrade/Downgrade	

Fund Information
Fund Type	Exchange Traded Funds
Category	US Fixed Income
Sub-Category	High Yield Bond
Prospectus Objective	Corp Bond-High Yld
Inception Date	Oct-17
Open to New Investments	Y

Prices
Price (as of 12/31/2018)	45.84
52-Week High	50.30
52-Week Low	45.07

Total Returns (%)
3-Month	6-Month	1-Year	3-Year	5-Year
-4.90	-2.08	-2.54		

3-Year Standard Deviation	
Effective Duration	4.06

Valuation
Premium/Discount (1-Year Average)	0.39

Company Information
Provider	iShares
Manager/Tenure	James Mauro (1), Scott Radell (1)
Website	http://www.ishares.com
Address	iShares 400 Howard Street San Francisco CA 94105 United States
Phone Number	800-474-2737

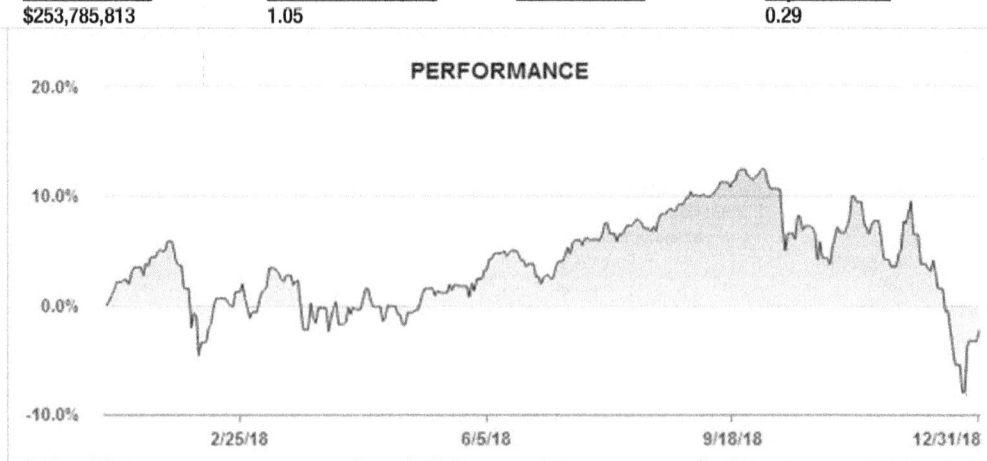

PERFORMANCE

Ratings History
Date	Overall Rating	Risk Rating	Reward Rating
Q4-18	D+	C-	D
Q2-18	U		
Q4-17	U		
Q4-16			
Q4-15			

Asset & Performance History
Date	NAV	1-Year Total Return
2017	49.63	
2016		
2015		
2014		
2013		
2012		

Total Assets: $254,131,392
Asset Allocation
Asset	%
Cash	2%
Stocks	0%
US Stocks	0%
Bonds	98%
US Bonds	84%
Other	0%

Services Offered:

Investment Strategy: The investment seeks to track the investment results of the ICE BofAML US High Yield Constrained Index. The fund generally will invest at least 90% of its assets in the component securities of the underlying index and may invest up to 10% of its assets in certain futures, options and swap contracts, cash and cash equivalents, including shares of money market funds advised by BFA or its affiliates, as well as in securities not included in the underlying index. The underlying index is designed to provide a broad representation of the U.S. dollar-denominated high yield corporate bond market. The fund is non-diversified. **Top Holdings:** ALTICE FRANCE S.A 7.38% Sprint Corporation 7.88% Reynolds Group Issuer LLC. 5.75% First Data Corporation 7% Tenet Healthcare Corporation 8.13%

Oppenheimer Russell 1000 Dynamic Multifactor ETF
C- **HOLD**

Ticker	Traded On	NAV	Total Assets ($)	Dividend Yield (TTM)	Turnover Ratio	Expense Ratio
OMFL	BATS	25.09	$253,785,813	1.05		0.29

Ratings
Reward	C-
Risk	C-
Recent Upgrade/Downgrade	

Fund Information
Fund Type	Exchange Traded Funds
Category	US Equity Large Cap Blend
Sub-Category	Large Blend
Prospectus Objective	Growth
Inception Date	Nov-17
Open to New Investments	Y

Prices
Price (as of 12/31/2018)	25.10
52-Week High	29.21
52-Week Low	23.84

Total Returns (%)
3-Month	6-Month	1-Year	3-Year	5-Year
-13.02	-4.95	-2.30		

3-Year Standard Deviation	
Effective Duration	

Valuation
Premium/Discount (1-Year Average)	0.14

Company Information
Provider	OppenheimerFunds
Manager/Tenure	Frank Vallario (1), Donal Bishnoi (0)
Website	http://www.oppenheimerfunds.com
Address	OppenheimerFunds 12100 East Iliff Avenue, Suite 300, Aurora, Colorado Aurora CO 80217-5270 United States
Phone Number	800-225-5677

PERFORMANCE

Ratings History
Date	Overall Rating	Risk Rating	Reward Rating
Q4-18	C-	C-	C-
Q2-18	U		
Q4-17	U		
Q4-16			
Q4-15			

Asset & Performance History
Date	NAV	1-Year Total Return
2017	26.02	
2016		
2015		
2014		
2013		
2012		

Total Assets: $253,785,813
Asset Allocation
Asset	%
Cash	0%
Stocks	100%
US Stocks	99%
Bonds	0%
US Bonds	0%
Other	0%

Services Offered:

Investment Strategy: The investment seeks to provide investment results that correspond generally, before fees and expenses, to the performance of the Russell 1000 OFI Dynamic Multifactor Index. Under normal circumstances, the fund will invest at least 80% of its net assets, plus any borrowings for investment purposes, in securities of companies included in the underlying index. The underlying index is constructed using a rules-based methodology by selecting equity securities from the Russell 1000 Index (the "parent index"), which measures the performance of the 1,000 largest-capitalization companies in the United States. **Top Holdings:** Johnson & Johnson Apple Inc Exxon Mobil Corp Visa Inc Class A The Home Depot Inc

Invesco Russell MidCap Pure Growth ETF   C   HOLD

Ticker	Traded On	NAV	Total Assets ($)	Dividend Yield (TTM)	Turnover Ratio	Expense Ratio
PXMG	NYSE Arca	45.15	$253,349,241	0.06	29	0.39

Ratings
Reward	C
Risk	C-
Recent Upgrade/Downgrade	Down

Fund Information
Fund Type	Exchange Traded Funds
Category	US Equity Mid Cap
Sub-Category	Mid-Cap Growth
Prospectus Objective	Growth
Inception Date	Mar-05
Open to New Investments	Y

Prices
Price (as of 12/31/2018)	44.97
52-Week High	55.63
52-Week Low	41.61

Total Returns (%)
3-Month	6-Month	1-Year	3-Year	5-Year
-16.46	-8.13	6.81	52.28	59.39

3-Year Standard Deviation	15.67
Effective Duration	

Valuation
Premium/Discount (1-Year Average)	0.16

Company Information
Provider	Invesco
Manager/Tenure	Peter Hubbard (11), Michael Jeanette (10), Jonathan Nixon (5), 2 others
Website	http://www.invesco.com/us
Address	Invesco 11 Greenway Plaza, Ste. 2500 Houston TX 77046 United States
Phone Number	800-659-1005

PERFORMANCE

Ratings History
Date	Overall Rating	Risk Rating	Reward Rating
Q4-18	C	C-	C
Q2-18	B	C-	A-
Q4-17	B	B	A-
Q4-16	C	D+	C
Q4-15	C	C-	C

Asset & Performance History
Date	NAV	1-Year Total Return
2017	42.35	36.52
2016	31.1	4.42
2015	29.85	-4.27
2014	31.37	9.35
2013	29.05	27.34
2012	23.13	15.09

Total Assets: $253,349,241
Asset Allocation
Asset	%
Cash	0%
Stocks	100%
US Stocks	100%
Bonds	0%
US Bonds	0%
Other	0%

Services Offered:

Investment Strategy: The investment seeks to track the investment results (before fees and expenses) of the Russell Midcap® Pure Growth Index (the "underlying index"). The fund generally will invest at least 90% of its total assets in the component securities that comprise the underlying index. The underlying index is composed of a subset of securities from the Russell Midcap® Index, which is composed of the smallest 800 securities of the Russell 1000® Index, an index designed to measure the performance of the largest 1,000 companies in the U.S. equity market. **Top Holdings:** Square Inc A   Ulta Beauty Inc   Chipotle Mexican Grill Inc Class A   O'Reilly Automotive Inc   Paycom Software Inc

---

WisdomTree International MidCap Dividend Fund   D+   SELL

Ticker	Traded On	NAV	Total Assets ($)	Dividend Yield (TTM)	Turnover Ratio	Expense Ratio
DIM	NYSE Arca	57.01	$252,495,189	3.09	23	0.58

Ratings
Reward	D+
Risk	C-
Recent Upgrade/Downgrade	Down

Fund Information
Fund Type	Exchange Traded Funds
Category	Global Eq Mid/Small Cap
Sub-Category	Foreign Small/Mid Value
Prospectus Objective	Foreign Stock
Inception Date	Jun-06
Open to New Investments	Y

Prices
Price (as of 12/31/2018)	56.75
52-Week High	73.67
52-Week Low	54.86

Total Returns (%)
3-Month	6-Month	1-Year	3-Year	5-Year
-12.48	-10.56	-15.07	11.20	12.37

3-Year Standard Deviation	11.75
Effective Duration	

Valuation
Premium/Discount (1-Year Average)	0.00

Company Information
Provider	WisdomTree
Manager/Tenure	Richard A. Brown (10), Thomas J. Durante (10), Karen Q. Wong (10)
Website	http://www.wisdomtree.com
Address	WisdomTree 245 Park Avenue, 35th floor New York NY 10167 United States
Phone Number	866-909-9473

PERFORMANCE

Ratings History
Date	Overall Rating	Risk Rating	Reward Rating
Q4-18	D+	C-	D+
Q2-18	C	C-	C
Q4-17	B	B	B
Q4-16	C-	D+	C-
Q4-15	C	C-	C

Asset & Performance History
Date	NAV	1-Year Total Return
2017	69.1	28.07
2016	55.44	2.23
2015	55.85	2.37
2014	56.02	-1.29
2013	58.61	21.97
2012	49.8	18.89

Total Assets: $252,495,189
Asset Allocation
Asset	%
Cash	0%
Stocks	100%
US Stocks	0%
Bonds	0%
US Bonds	0%
Other	0%

Services Offered:

Investment Strategy: The investment seeks to track the price and yield performance, before fees and expenses, of the WisdomTree International MidCap Dividend Index. The fund normally invests at least 95% of its total assets (exclusive of collateral held from securities lending) in component securities of the index and investments that have economic characteristics that are substantially identical to the economic characteristics of such component securities. The index is a fundamentally weighted index that is comprised of the mid-capitalization segment of the dividend-paying market in the industrialized world outside the U.S. and Canada. The fund is non-diversified. **Top Holdings:** Snam SpA   Telefonica Deutschland Holding AG   Marine Harvest ASA   Centrica PLC   Hannover Rueck SE

iShares U.S. Broker-Dealers & Securities Exchanges ETF

B-   **BUY**

Ticker	Traded On	NAV	Total Assets ($)	Dividend Yield (TTM)	Turnover Ratio	Expense Ratio
IAI	NYSE Arca	56.08	$251,510,352	1.43	13	0.43

Ratings
Reward	B
Risk	C
Recent Upgrade/Downgrade	

Fund Information
Fund Type	Exchange Traded Funds
Category	Financials Sector Equity
Sub-Category	Financial
Prospectus Objective	Financial
Inception Date	May-06
Open to New Investments	Y

Prices
Price (as of 12/31/2018)	56.03
52-Week High	70.28
52-Week Low	52.67

Total Returns (%)
3-Month	6-Month	1-Year	3-Year	5-Year
-9.67	-12.38	-9.29	42.19	56.17

3-Year Standard Deviation	17.92
Effective Duration	

Valuation
Premium/Discount (1-Year Average)	0.02

Company Information
Provider	iShares
Manager/Tenure	Diane Hsiung (10), Greg Savage (10), Jennifer Hsui (6), 3 others
Website	http://www.ishares.com
Address	iShares 400 Howard Street San Francisco CA 94105 United States
Phone Number	800-474-2737

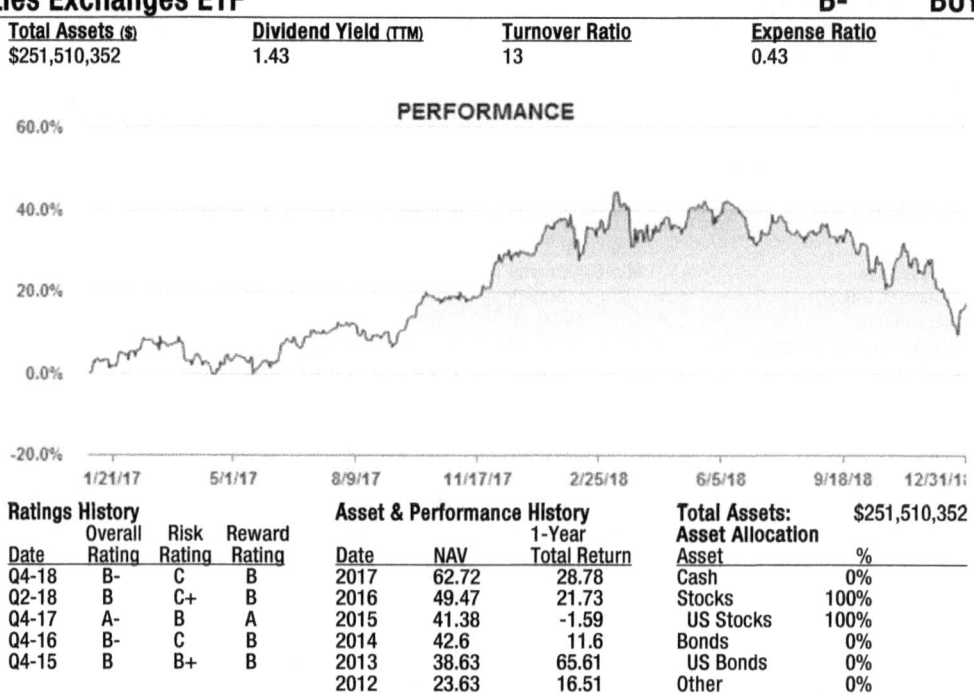

PERFORMANCE

Ratings History
Date	Overall Rating	Risk Rating	Reward Rating
Q4-18	B-	C	B
Q2-18	B	C+	B
Q4-17	A-	B	A
Q4-16	B-	C	B
Q4-15	B	B+	B

Asset & Performance History
Date	NAV	1-Year Total Return
2017	62.72	28.78
2016	49.47	21.73
2015	41.38	-1.59
2014	42.6	11.6
2013	38.63	65.61
2012	23.63	16.51

Total Assets: $251,510,352

Asset Allocation
Asset	%
Cash	0%
Stocks	100%
US Stocks	100%
Bonds	0%
US Bonds	0%
Other	0%

Services Offered:

Investment Strategy: The investment seeks to track the investment results of the Dow Jones U.S. Select Investment Services Index composed of U.S. equities in the investment services sector. The fund generally invests at least 90% of its assets in securities of the underlying index and in depositary receipts representing securities of the underlying index. The underlying index measures the performance of the investment services sector of the U.S. equity market. The fund may invest the remainder of its assets in certain futures, options and swap contracts, cash and cash equivalents. It is non-diversified. **Top Holdings:** CME Group Inc Class A   Morgan Stanley   Goldman Sachs Group Inc   Intercontinental Exchange Inc   Charles Schwab Corp

---

Franklin FTSE Japan ETF

D   **SELL**

Ticker	Traded On	NAV	Total Assets ($)	Dividend Yield (TTM)	Turnover Ratio	Expense Ratio
FLJP	NYSE Arca	22.66	$250,764,597	0.51	1	0.09

Ratings
Reward	D
Risk	D
Recent Upgrade/Downgrade	

Fund Information
Fund Type	Exchange Traded Funds
Category	Japan Equity
Sub-Category	Japan Stock
Prospectus Objective	Foreign Stock
Inception Date	Nov-17
Open to New Investments	Y

Prices
Price (as of 12/31/2018)	22.50
52-Week High	28.53
52-Week Low	21.71

Total Returns (%)
3-Month	6-Month	1-Year	3-Year	5-Year
-14.27	-11.38	-13.10		

3-Year Standard Deviation	
Effective Duration	

Valuation
Premium/Discount (1-Year Average)	0.17

Company Information
Provider	Franklin Templeton Investments
Manager/Tenure	Louis Hsu (1), Dina Ting (1)
Website	http://www.franklintempleton.com
Address	Franklin Templeton Investments One Franklin Parkway, Building 970, 1st Floor San Mateo CA 94403 United States
Phone Number	650-312-2000

PERFORMANCE

Ratings History
Date	Overall Rating	Risk Rating	Reward Rating
Q4-18	D	D	D
Q2-18	U		
Q4-17	U		
Q4-16			
Q4-15			

Asset & Performance History
Date	NAV	1-Year Total Return
2017	26.45	
2016		
2015		
2014		
2013		
2012		

Total Assets: $250,764,597

Asset Allocation
Asset	%
Cash	0%
Stocks	100%
US Stocks	0%
Bonds	0%
US Bonds	0%
Other	0%

Services Offered:

Investment Strategy: The investment seeks to provide investment results that closely correspond, before fees and expenses, to the performance of the FTSE Japan RIC Capped Index (the FTSE Japan Capped Index). Under normal market conditions, the fund invests at least 80% of its assets in the component securities of the FTSE Japan Capped Index and in depositary receipts representing such securities. The FTSE Japan Capped Index is based on the FTSE Japan Index and is designed to measure the performance of Japanese large- and mid-capitalization stocks. **Top Holdings:** Toyota Motor Corp   SoftBank Group Corp   Mitsubishi UFJ Financial Group Inc   Sony Corp   Honda Motor Co Ltd

ProShares UltraShort QQQ　　　　　　　　　　　　　　D　　SELL

Ticker	Traded On	NAV	Total Assets ($)	Dividend Yield (TTM)	Turnover Ratio	Expense Ratio
QID	NYSE Arca	47.57	$250,699,579	1.11	0	0.95

Ratings
Reward	D-
Risk	D-
Recent Upgrade/Downgrade	Up

Fund Information
Fund Type	Exchange Traded Funds
Category	Trading Tools
Sub-Category	Trading--Inverse Equity
Prospectus Objective	Growth
Inception Date	Jul-06
Open to New Investments	Y

Prices
Price (as of 12/31/2018)	47.54
52-Week High	55.66
52-Week Low	35.18

Total Returns (%)

3-Month	6-Month	1-Year	3-Year	5-Year
35.98	16.82	-9.91	-59.33	-79.83

3-Year Standard Deviation	24.3
Effective Duration	

Valuation
Premium/Discount (1-Year Average)	-0.03

Company Information
Provider	ProShares
Manager/Tenure	Michael Neches (5), Devin Sullivan (0)
Website	http://www.proshares.com
Address	ProShares 7501 Wisconsin Avenue, Suite 1000 Bethesda MD 20814 United States
Phone Number	866-776-5125

PERFORMANCE

Ratings History

Date	Overall Rating	Risk Rating	Reward Rating
Q4-18	D	D-	D-
Q2-18	D-	D-	E+
Q4-17	E+	E+	E+
Q4-16	D	D-	D-
Q4-15	D-	E+	E+

Asset & Performance History

Date	NAV	1-Year Total Return
2017	53.64	-44.03
2016	95.92	-19.34
2015	118.92	-24.73
2014	158	-34.12
2013	239.84	-49.4
2012	474.08	-34.34

Total Assets: $250,699,579

Asset Allocation

Asset	%
Cash	189%
Stocks	-94%
US Stocks	-92%
Bonds	5%
US Bonds	5%
Other	0%

Services Offered:

Investment Strategy: The investment seeks daily investment results, before fees and expenses, that correspond to two times the inverse (-2x) of the daily performance of the NASDAQ-100 Index®. The fund invests in financial instruments that ProShare Advisors believes, in combination, should produce daily returns consistent with the fund's investment objective. The index includes 100 of the largest domestic and international non-financial companies listed on The Nasdaq Stock Market based on market capitalization. The fund is non-diversified. **Top Holdings:** Nasdaq 100 Index Swap Deutsche Bank Ag　Nasdaq 100 Index Swap Credit Suisse International　Nasdaq 100 Index Swap Bnp Paribas　United States Treasury Bills　United States Treasury Bills

Invesco Zacks Mid-Cap ETF　　　　　　　　　　　　　　C　　HOLD

Ticker	Traded On	NAV	Total Assets ($)	Dividend Yield (TTM)	Turnover Ratio	Expense Ratio
CZA	NYSE Arca	58.98	$249,909,415	1.1		0.68

Ratings
Reward	C
Risk	C-
Recent Upgrade/Downgrade	

Fund Information
Fund Type	Exchange Traded Funds
Category	US Equity Mid Cap
Sub-Category	Mid-Cap Blend
Prospectus Objective	Growth
Inception Date	Apr-07
Open to New Investments	Y

Prices
Price (as of 12/31/2018)	58.98
52-Week High	69.62
52-Week Low	56.31

Total Returns (%)

3-Month	6-Month	1-Year	3-Year	5-Year
-12.51	-7.80	-8.75	28.56	38.25

3-Year Standard Deviation	10.29
Effective Duration	

Valuation
Premium/Discount (1-Year Average)	0.06

Company Information
Provider	Invesco
Manager/Tenure	Peter Hubbard (0), Michael Jeanette (0), Jonathan Nixon (0), 1 other
Website	http://www.invesco.com/us
Address	Invesco 11 Greenway Plaza, Ste. 2500 Houston TX 77046 United States
Phone Number	800-659-1005

PERFORMANCE

Ratings History

Date	Overall Rating	Risk Rating	Reward Rating
Q4-18	C	C-	C
Q2-18	C	C-	C
Q4-17	B	B-	B
Q4-16	C+	D+	B
Q4-15	C	C	C

Asset & Performance History

Date	NAV	1-Year Total Return
2017	65.5	22.03
2016	54.42	15.17
2015	47.87	-1.78
2014	49.4	9.49
2013	45.45	35.99
2012	33.76	15.25

Total Assets: $249,909,415

Asset Allocation

Asset	%
Cash	0%
Stocks	100%
US Stocks	88%
Bonds	0%
US Bonds	0%
Other	0%

Services Offered:

Investment Strategy: The investment seeks to track the investment results (before fees and expenses) of the Zacks Mid-Cap Core Index (the "underlying index"). The fund generally will invest at least 90% of its total assets in securities that comprise the underlying index and depositary receipts representing securities that comprise the underlying index. The underlying index was comprised of 100 securities selected, according to the investment and other criteria in the underlying index methodology, from a universe of mid-capitalization securities including common stocks, MLPs, ADRs, REITs and BDCs. The fund is non-diversified. **Top Holdings:** Coca-Cola European Partners PLC　Ventas Inc　Agilent Technologies Inc　Eversource Energy　Tyson Foods Inc Class A

Invesco Russell Top 200 Pure Growth ETF   C   HOLD

Ticker	Traded On	NAV
PXLG	NYSE Arca	45.76

Total Assets ($)	Dividend Yield (TTM)	Turnover Ratio	Expense Ratio
$248,883,227	0.73	19	0.39

Ratings
Reward	C+
Risk	C
Recent Upgrade/Downgrade	Down

Fund Information
Fund Type	Exchange Traded Funds
Category	US Equity Large Cap Growth
Sub-Category	Large Growth
Prospectus Objective	Growth
Inception Date	Jun-11
Open to New Investments	Y

Prices
Price (as of 12/31/2018)	45.78
52-Week High	54.72
52-Week Low	42.07

Total Returns (%)
3-Month	6-Month	1-Year	3-Year	5-Year
-16.00	-9.72	1.80	37.60	69.42

3-Year Standard Deviation	12.27
Effective Duration	

Valuation
Premium/Discount (1-Year Average)	0.10

Company Information
Provider	Invesco
Manager/Tenure	Peter Hubbard (7), Michael Jeanette (7), Jonathan Nixon (5), 1 other
Website	http://www.invesco.com/us
Address	Invesco 11 Greenway Plaza, Ste. 2500 Houston TX 77046 United States
Phone Number	800-659-1005

PERFORMANCE

Ratings History
Date	Overall Rating	Risk Rating	Reward Rating
Q4-18	C	C	C+
Q2-18	B-	C	B+
Q4-17	A-	A-	A
Q4-16	C	C-	B-
Q4-15	B-	C	B

Asset & Performance History
Date	NAV	1-Year Total Return
2017	45.36	35.82
2016	33.64	-0.49
2015	34.11	6.18
2014	32.49	15.95
2013	28.46	29.42
2012	22.5	16.59

Total Assets: $248,883,227

Asset Allocation
Asset	%
Cash	0%
Stocks	100%
US Stocks	100%
Bonds	0%
US Bonds	0%
Other	0%

Services Offered:

Investment Strategy: The investment seeks to track the investment results (before fees and expenses) of the Russell Top 200® Pure Growth Index (the "underlying index"). The fund generally will invest at least 90% of its total assets in the component securities that comprise the underlying index. The underlying index is composed of a subset of securities from the Russell Top 200® Index, which is composed of the largest 200 securities of the Russell 3000® Index, an index designed to measure the performance of the largest 3,000 companies in the U.S. equity market. **Top Holdings:** Vertex Pharmaceuticals Inc   Salesforce.com Inc   Amazon.com Inc   Mastercard Inc A   Visa Inc Class A

Fidelity® MSCI Communication Services Index ETF   C+   HOLD

Ticker	Traded On	NAV
FCOM	NYSE Arca	28.43

Total Assets ($)	Dividend Yield (TTM)	Turnover Ratio	Expense Ratio
$248,581,640	2.71	38	0.08

Ratings
Reward	B
Risk	C-
Recent Upgrade/Downgrade	Up

Fund Information
Fund Type	Exchange Traded Funds
Category	Communications Sector Equity
Sub-Category	Communications
Prospectus Objective	Comm
Inception Date	Oct-13
Open to New Investments	Y

Prices
Price (as of 12/31/2018)	28.49
52-Week High	31.90
52-Week Low	26.75

Total Returns (%)
3-Month	6-Month	1-Year	3-Year	5-Year
-9.21	1.12	-5.44	20.64	32.54

3-Year Standard Deviation	12.05
Effective Duration	

Valuation
Premium/Discount (1-Year Average)	0.14

Company Information
Provider	Fidelity Investments
Manager/Tenure	Jennifer Hsui (5), Greg Savage (5), Alan Mason (2), 2 others
Website	http://www.institutional.fidelity.com
Address	Fidelity Investments 82 Devonshire Street Boston MA 2109 United States
Phone Number	617-563-7000

PERFORMANCE

Ratings History
Date	Overall Rating	Risk Rating	Reward Rating
Q4-18	C+	C-	B
Q2-18	C	D+	B-
Q4-17	B-	B	C
Q4-16	B-	C-	B
Q4-15	C-	C	B-

Asset & Performance History
Date	NAV	1-Year Total Return
2017	30.88	-0.53
2016	32.08	23.17
2015	26.68	3.26
2014	26.6	6.39
2013	25.69	
2012		

Total Assets: $248,581,640

Asset Allocation
Asset	%
Cash	1%
Stocks	99%
US Stocks	99%
Bonds	0%
US Bonds	0%
Other	0%

Services Offered:

Investment Strategy: The investment seeks to provide investment returns that correspond, before fees and expenses, generally to the performance of the MSCI USA IMI Communication Services 25/50 Index. The fund invests at least 80% of assets in securities included in the fund's underlying index. The fund's underlying index is the MSCI USA IMI Communication Services 25/50 Index, which represents the performance of the communication services sector in the U.S. equity market. It may or may not hold all of the securities in the MSCI USA IMI Communication Services 25/50 Index. The fund is non-diversified. **Top Holdings:** Verizon Communications Inc   AT&T Inc   T-Mobile US Inc   CenturyLink Inc   pdvWireless Inc

---

ProShares Short Russell2000   D   SELL

Ticker	Traded On	NAV	Total Assets ($)	Dividend Yield (TTM)	Turnover Ratio	Expense Ratio
RWM	NYSE Arca	46.69	$245,375,020	0.73	0	0.95

Ratings

Reward	D
Risk	D
Recent Upgrade/Downgrade	

Fund Information

Fund Type	Exchange Traded Funds
Category	Trading Tools
Sub-Category	Trading--Inverse Equity
Prospectus Objective	Small Company
Inception Date	Jan-07
Open to New Investments	Y

Prices

Price (as of 12/31/2018)	46.70
52-Week High	49.87
52-Week Low	36.87

Total Returns (%)

3-Month	6-Month	1-Year	3-Year	5-Year
22.46	21.29	11.50	-23.95	-30.07

3-Year Standard Deviation	14.5
Effective Duration	

Valuation

Premium/Discount (1-Year Average)	-0.01

Company Information

Provider	ProShares
Manager/Tenure	Michael Neches (5), Devin Sullivan (0)
Website	http://www.proshares.com
Address	ProShares 7501 Wisconsin Avenue, Suite 1000 Bethesda MD 20814 United States
Phone Number	866-776-5125

PERFORMANCE

Ratings History

Date	Overall Rating	Risk Rating	Reward Rating
Q4-18	D	D	D
Q2-18	D	D-	D-
Q4-17	D-	D-	D-
Q4-16	D	D	D
Q4-15	D	D-	D

Asset & Performance History

Date	NAV	1-Year Total Return
2017	42.29	-13.61
2016	48.99	-21.04
2015	62.05	0.4
2014	61.8	-8.41
2013	67.48	-30.57
2012	97.2	-17.93

Total Assets: $245,375,020

Asset Allocation

Asset	%
Cash	150%
Stocks	-54%
US Stocks	-54%
Bonds	4%
US Bonds	4%
Other	0%

Services Offered:

Investment Strategy: The investment seeks daily investment results that correspond to the inverse (-1x) of the daily performance of the Russell 2000® Index. The fund invests in financial instruments that ProShare Advisors believes, in combination, should produce daily returns consistent with the fund's investment objective. It is a float-adjusted, market capitalization-weighted index containing approximately 2000 of the smallest companies in the Russell 3000® Index or approximately 8% of the total market capitalization of the Russell 3000® Index, which in turn represents approximately 98% of the investable U.S. equity market. The fund is non-diversified. **Top Holdings:** Russell 2000 Index Swap Goldman Sachs International United States Treasury Bills United States Treasury Bills Russell 2000 Index Swap Ubs Ag United States Treasury Bills

SPDR® S&P Semiconductor ETF   C   HOLD

Ticker	Traded On	NAV	Total Assets ($)	Dividend Yield (TTM)	Turnover Ratio	Expense Ratio
XSD	NYSE Arca	64.74	$244,102,561	0.95	37	0.35

Ratings

Reward	B-
Risk	C-
Recent Upgrade/Downgrade	Down

Fund Information

Fund Type	Exchange Traded Funds
Category	Technology Sector Equity
Sub-Category	Technology
Prospectus Objective	Technology
Inception Date	Jan-06
Open to New Investments	Y

Prices

Price (as of 12/31/2018)	64.70
52-Week High	79.33
52-Week Low	60.13

Total Returns (%)

3-Month	6-Month	1-Year	3-Year	5-Year
-14.05	-10.68	-6.25	51.72	119.17

3-Year Standard Deviation	18.3
Effective Duration	

Valuation

Premium/Discount (1-Year Average)	0.01

Company Information

Provider	SPDR State Street Global Advisors
Manager/Tenure	Michael J. Feehily (7), Karl A. Schneider (4), Kala O'Donnell (1)
Website	http://www.spdrs.com
Address	SPDR State Street Global Advisors State Street Financial Center, 1 Lincoln Street Boston MA 02111-2900 United States
Phone Number	617-786-3000

PERFORMANCE

Ratings History

Date	Overall Rating	Risk Rating	Reward Rating
Q4-18	C	C-	B-
Q2-18	C+	C-	B
Q4-17	A-	B	A+
Q4-16	C	C-	C
Q4-15	C	C	C+

Asset & Performance History

Date	NAV	1-Year Total Return
2017	69.79	25.23
2016	56.08	29.08
2015	43.71	10.29
2014	39.86	30.97
2013	30.59	36.31
2012	22.57	2.62

Total Assets: $244,102,561

Asset Allocation

Asset	%
Cash	0%
Stocks	100%
US Stocks	97%
Bonds	0%
US Bonds	0%
Other	0%

Services Offered: Dividend Investment Plan, CashInvestment Plan

Investment Strategy: The investment seeks to provide investment results that, before fees and expenses, correspond generally to the total return performance of an index derived from the semiconductor segment of a U.S. total market composite index. In seeking to track the performance of the S&P Semiconductor Select Industry Index (the "Index"), the fund employs a sampling strategy. It generally invests substantially all, but at least 80%, of its total assets in the securities comprising the index. The index represents the semiconductors segment of the S&P Total Market Index ("S&P TMI"). The fund is non-diversified. **Top Holdings:** Xilinx Inc Inphi Corp Intel Corp Cree Inc Integrated Device Technology Inc

iShares MSCI Sweden Capped ETF   C-   HOLD

Ticker	Traded On	NAV	Total Assets ($)	Dividend Yield (TTM)	Turnover Ratio	Expense Ratio
EWD	NYSE Arca	28.17	$240,217,445	6.12	5	0.49

Ratings
Reward	C-
Risk	C-
Recent Upgrade/Downgrade	Down

Fund Information
Fund Type	Exchange Traded Funds
Category	Europe Equity Large Cap
Sub-Category	Miscellaneous Region
Prospectus Objective	Europe Stock
Inception Date	Mar-96
Open to New Investments	Y

Prices
Price (as of 12/31/2018)	28.24
52-Week High	36.58
52-Week Low	26.79

Total Returns (%)
3-Month	6-Month	1-Year	3-Year	5-Year
-13.90	-6.72	-13.22	7.14	-4.50

3-Year Standard Deviation	13.78
Effective Duration	

Valuation
Premium/Discount (1-Year Average)	-0.19

Company Information
Provider	iShares
Manager/Tenure	Diane Hsiung (10), Greg Savage (10), Jennifer Hsui (5), 1 other
Website	http://www.ishares.com
Address	iShares 400 Howard Street San Francisco CA 94105 United States
Phone Number	800-474-2737

Ratings History
Date	Overall Rating	Risk Rating	Reward Rating
Q4-18	C-	C-	C-
Q2-18	C	C+	C-
Q4-17	C+	B-	C
Q4-16	D	D+	D
Q4-15	C	C+	C-

Asset & Performance History
Date	NAV	1-Year Total Return
2017	34.01	21.94
2016	28.81	1.25
2015	29.58	-3.71
2014	31.83	-7.43
2013	35.64	24.66
2012	29.76	22.09

Total Assets: $240,217,445
Asset Allocation
Asset	%
Cash	2%
Stocks	98%
US Stocks	1%
Bonds	0%
US Bonds	0%
Other	0%

Services Offered: CashInvestment Plan

Investment Strategy: The investment seeks to track the investment results of the MSCI Sweden 25/50 Index. The fund will at all times invest at least 80% of its assets in the securities of its underlying index and in depositary receipts representing securities in its underlying index. The underlying index is designed to measure the performance of the large- and mid-cap segments of the Swedish market. A capping methodology is applied that limits the weight of any single component to a maximum of 25% of the underlying index. The fund is non-diversified. **Top Holdings:** Nordea Bank Abp   Telefonaktiebolaget L M Ericsson B   Volvo AB B   Swedbank AB A   Investor AB B

---

iShares iBonds Dec 2021 Term Muni Bond ETF   C-   HOLD

Ticker	Traded On	NAV	Total Assets ($)	Dividend Yield (TTM)	Turnover Ratio	Expense Ratio
IBMJ	NYSE Arca	25.42	$239,281,148	1.31	0	0.18

Ratings
Reward	C-
Risk	C-
Recent Upgrade/Downgrade	Up

Fund Information
Fund Type	Exchange Traded Funds
Category	US Muni Fixed Inc
Sub-Category	Muni National Interm
Prospectus Objective	Muni Bond - Natl
Inception Date	Sep-15
Open to New Investments	Y

Prices
Price (as of 12/31/2018)	25.45
52-Week High	25.54
52-Week Low	25.19

Total Returns (%)
3-Month	6-Month	1-Year	3-Year	5-Year
1.02	0.86	1.35	3.46	

3-Year Standard Deviation	2.72
Effective Duration	2.51

Valuation
Premium/Discount (1-Year Average)	0.08

Company Information
Provider	iShares
Manager/Tenure	James Mauro (3), Scott Radell (3)
Website	http://www.ishares.com
Address	iShares 400 Howard Street San Francisco CA 94105 United States
Phone Number	800-474-2737

Ratings History
Date	Overall Rating	Risk Rating	Reward Rating
Q4-18	C-	C-	C-
Q2-18	C-	C-	C-
Q4-17	C	C	C-
Q4-16	D	C-	D+
Q4-15			

Asset & Performance History
Date	NAV	1-Year Total Return
2017	25.42	2.07
2016	25.19	-0.07
2015	25.51	
2014		
2013		
2012		

Total Assets: $239,281,148
Asset Allocation
Asset	%
Cash	0%
Stocks	0%
US Stocks	0%
Bonds	100%
US Bonds	100%
Other	0%

Services Offered:

Investment Strategy: The investment seeks to track the investment results of the S&P AMT-Free Municipal Series Dec 2021 IndexTM, which measures the performance of investment-grade, non-callable U.S. municipal bonds maturing in 2021. The fund generally will invest at least 90% of its assets in the component securities of the underlying index, and may invest up to 10% of its assets in certain futures, options and swap contracts, cash and cash equivalents, including shares of money market funds advised by BFA or its affiliates, as well as in securities not included in the underlying index, but which BFA believes will help the fund track the underlying index. **Top Holdings:** OHIO ST 5%   MARYLAND ST DEPT TRANSN 5%   ARLINGTON CNTY VA 4%   VIRGINIA COMWLTH TRANSN BRD 5%   KING CNTY WASH 5%

iShares iBonds Dec 2022 Term Muni Bond ETF   C-   HOLD

Ticker	Traded On	NAV	Total Assets ($)	Dividend Yield (TTM)	Turnover Ratio	Expense Ratio
IBMK	NYSE Arca	25.58	$239,100,603	1.5	1	0.18

Ratings
Reward	C-
Risk	C-
Recent Upgrade/Downgrade	Up

Fund Information
Fund Type	Exchange Traded Funds
Category	US Muni Fixed Inc
Sub-Category	Muni National Interm
Prospectus Objective	Muni Bond - Natl
Inception Date	Sep-15
Open to New Investments	Y

Prices
Price (as of 12/31/2018)	25.62
52-Week High	25.76
52-Week Low	25.21

Total Returns (%)
3-Month	6-Month	1-Year	3-Year	5-Year
1.29	1.07	1.25	4.16	

3-Year Standard Deviation	3.28
Effective Duration	3.38

Valuation
Premium/Discount (1-Year Average)	0.10

Company Information
Provider	iShares
Manager/Tenure	James Mauro (3), Scott Radell (3)
Website	http://www.ishares.com
Address	iShares 400 Howard Street San Francisco CA 94105 United States
Phone Number	800-474-2737

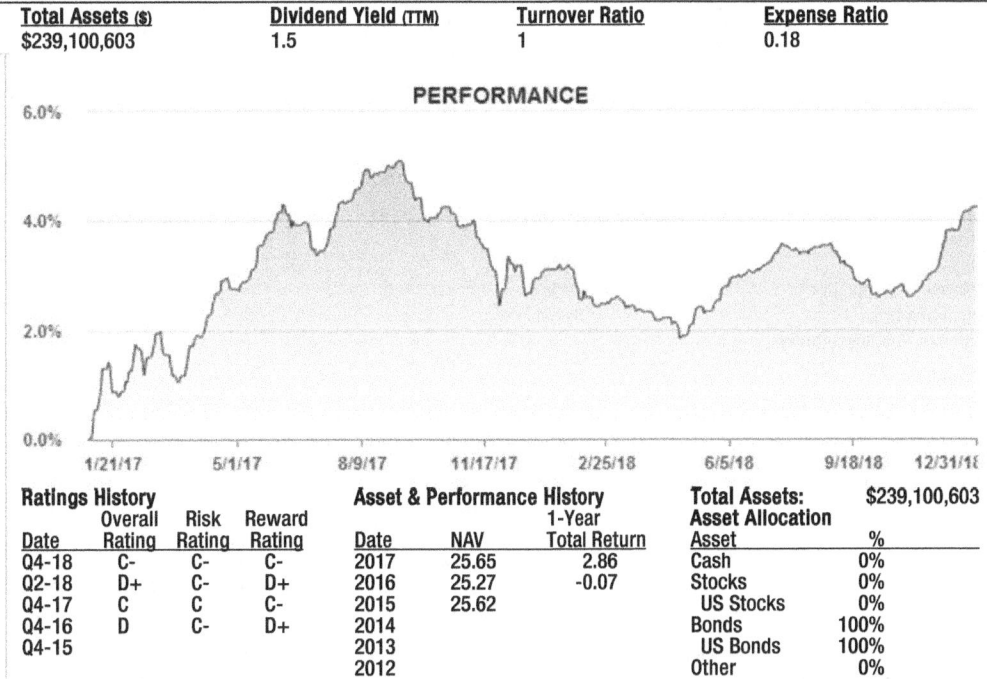

PERFORMANCE

Ratings History
Date	Overall Rating	Risk Rating	Reward Rating
Q4-18	C-	C-	C-
Q2-18	D+	C-	D+
Q4-17	C	C	C-
Q4-16	D	C-	D+
Q4-15			

Asset & Performance History
Date	NAV	1-Year Total Return
2017	25.65	2.86
2016	25.27	-0.07
2015	25.62	
2014		
2013		
2012		

Total Assets: $239,100,603
Asset Allocation
Asset	%
Cash	0%
Stocks	0%
US Stocks	0%
Bonds	100%
US Bonds	100%
Other	0%

Services Offered:

Investment Strategy: The investment seeks to track the investment results of the S&P AMT-Free Municipal Series Dec 2022 IndexTM, which measures the performance of investment-grade, non-callable U.S. municipal bonds maturing in 2022. The fund generally will invest at least 90% of its assets in the component securities of the underlying index, and may invest up to 10% of its assets in certain futures, options and swap contracts, cash and cash equivalents, including shares of money market funds advised by BFA or its affiliates, as well as in securities not included in the underlying index, but which BFA believes will help the fund track the underlying index. **Top Holdings:** GUILFORD CNTY N C 5% NEW JERSEY ST TPK AUTH 5% HONOLULU HAWAII 5% WISCONSIN ST 5% NEW YORK ST DORM AUTH 5%

Fidelity® High Dividend ETF   C   HOLD

Ticker	Traded On	NAV	Total Assets ($)	Dividend Yield (TTM)	Turnover Ratio	Expense Ratio
FDVV	NYSE Arca	27.33	$239,026,048	3.82		0.29

Ratings
Reward	C
Risk	C-
Recent Upgrade/Downgrade	

Fund Information
Fund Type	Exchange Traded Funds
Category	US Equity Large Cap Value
Sub-Category	Large Value
Prospectus Objective	Growth & Inc
Inception Date	Sep-16
Open to New Investments	Y

Prices
Price (as of 12/31/2018)	27.28
52-Week High	31.10
52-Week Low	26.00

Total Returns (%)
3-Month	6-Month	1-Year	3-Year	5-Year
-10.06	-4.60	-0.93		

3-Year Standard Deviation	
Effective Duration	

Valuation
Premium/Discount (1-Year Average)	0.17

Company Information
Provider	Fidelity Investments
Manager/Tenure	Louis Bottari (2), Deane Gyllenhaal (2), Peter Matthew (2), 2 others
Website	http://www.institutional.fidelity.com
Address	Fidelity Investments 82 Devonshire Street Boston MA 2109 United States
Phone Number	617-563-7000

PERFORMANCE

Ratings History
Date	Overall Rating	Risk Rating	Reward Rating
Q4-18	C	C-	C
Q2-18	C	C-	C
Q4-17	D	B	C-
Q4-16	U		
Q4-15			

Asset & Performance History
Date	NAV	1-Year Total Return
2017	28.66	13.76
2016	26.15	
2015		
2014		
2013		
2012		

Total Assets: $239,026,048
Asset Allocation
Asset	%
Cash	0%
Stocks	100%
US Stocks	96%
Bonds	0%
US Bonds	0%
Other	0%

Services Offered:

Investment Strategy: The investment seeks to provide investment returns that correspond, before fees and expenses, generally to the performance of the Fidelity High Dividend Index?. The fund normally invests at least 80% of assets in securities included in the underlying index and in depository receipts representing securities included in the underlying index. The underlying index is designed to reflect the performance of stocks of large and mid-capitalization high-dividend-paying companies that are expected to continue to pay and grow their dividends. **Top Holdings:** Verizon Communications Inc Apple Inc Microsoft Corp Exxon Mobil Corp JPMorgan Chase & Co

Invesco International BuyBack Achievers™ ETF   D+   SELL

Ticker	Traded On	NAV	Total Assets ($)	Dividend Yield (TTM)	Turnover Ratio	Expense Ratio
IPKW	NAS CM	28.98	$238,609,153	2.33	118	0.55

Ratings
Reward	D+
Risk	D+
Recent Upgrade/Downgrade	Down

Fund Information
Fund Type	Exchange Traded Funds
Category	Global Equity Large Cap
Sub-Category	Foreign Large Blend
Prospectus Objective	Growth
Inception Date	Feb-14
Open to New Investments	

Prices
Price (as of 12/31/2018)	28.81
52-Week High	40.11
52-Week Low	28.19

Total Returns (%)
3-Month	6-Month	1-Year	3-Year	5-Year
-14.93	-17.43	-20.97	18.00	

3-Year Standard Deviation	13.2
Effective Duration	

Valuation
Premium/Discount (1-Year Average)	0.04

Company Information
Provider	Invesco
Manager/Tenure	Peter Hubbard (4), Jonathan Nixon (4), Michael Jeanette (3), 1 other
Website	http://www.invesco.com/us
Address	Invesco 11 Greenway Plaza, Ste. 2500 Houston TX 77046 United States
Phone Number	800-659-1005

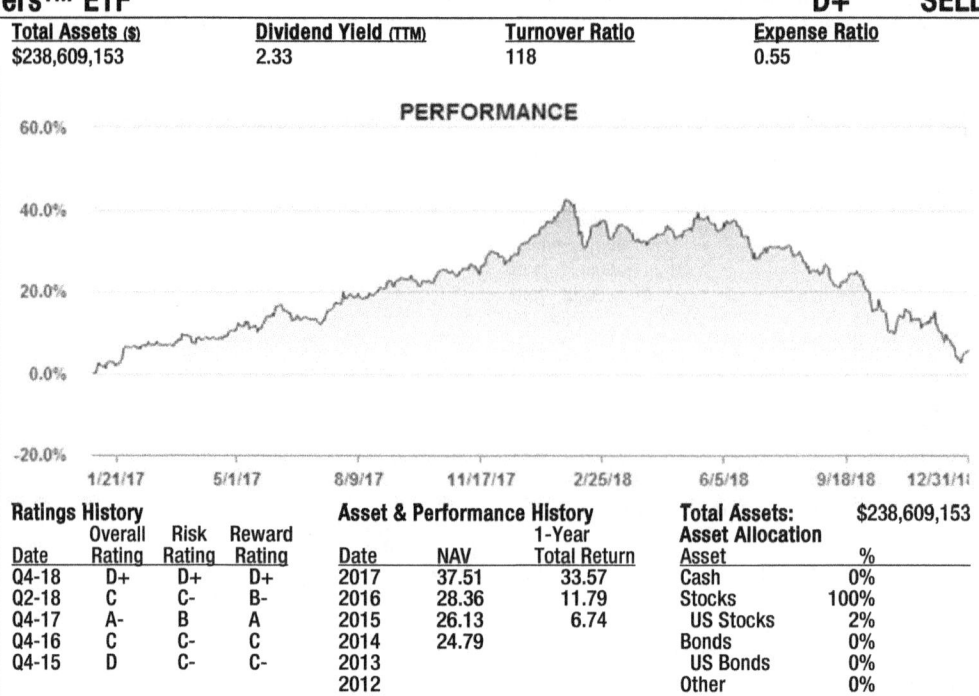

PERFORMANCE

Ratings History
Date	Overall Rating	Risk Rating	Reward Rating
Q4-18	D+	D+	D+
Q2-18	C	C-	B-
Q4-17	A-	B	A
Q4-16	C	C-	C
Q4-15	D	C-	C-

Asset & Performance History
Date	NAV	1-Year Total Return
2017	37.51	33.57
2016	28.36	11.79
2015	26.13	6.74
2014	24.79	
2013		
2012		

Total Assets: $238,609,153
Asset Allocation
Asset	%
Cash	0%
Stocks	100%
US Stocks	2%
Bonds	0%
US Bonds	0%
Other	0%

Services Offered:

Investment Strategy: The investment seeks to track the investment results (before fees and expenses) of the NASDAQ International BuyBack AchieversTM Index (the "underlying index"). The fund generally will invest at least 90% of its total assets in common stocks that comprise the underlying index. Strictly in accordance with its guidelines and mandated procedures, the Nasdaq, Inc. includes in the underlying index common stocks of foreign companies that are classified as "International BuyBack AchieversTM" pursuant to a proprietary selection methodology. It is non-diversified. **Top Holdings:** Bridgestone Corp Rakuten Inc CGI Group Inc A Canadian Tire Corp Ltd Class A Infosys Ltd ADR

ProShares Short MSCI Emerging Markets   C-   HOLD

Ticker	Traded On	NAV	Total Assets ($)	Dividend Yield (TTM)	Turnover Ratio	Expense Ratio
EUM	NYSE Arca	20.39	$237,926,834	0.23	0	0.95

Ratings
Reward	D+
Risk	D+
Recent Upgrade/Downgrade	Up

Fund Information
Fund Type	Exchange Traded Funds
Category	Trading Tools
Sub-Category	Trading--Inverse Equity
Prospectus Objective	Div Emerg Mkts
Inception Date	Oct-07
Open to New Investments	Y

Prices
Price (as of 12/31/2018)	20.39
52-Week High	21.51
52-Week Low	16.23

Total Returns (%)
3-Month	6-Month	1-Year	3-Year	5-Year
7.22	6.71	14.60	-30.16	-21.89

3-Year Standard Deviation	14.73
Effective Duration	

Valuation
Premium/Discount (1-Year Average)	-0.02

Company Information
Provider	ProShares
Manager/Tenure	Alexander V. Ilyasov (9), Scott Hanson (2)
Website	http://www.proshares.com
Address	ProShares 7501 Wisconsin Avenue, Suite 1000 Bethesda MD 20814 United States
Phone Number	866-776-5125

PERFORMANCE

Ratings History
Date	Overall Rating	Risk Rating	Reward Rating
Q4-18	C-	D+	D+
Q2-18	D	D	D
Q4-17	D-	D	D-
Q4-16	D	D	D
Q4-15	C	C	C

Asset & Performance History
Date	NAV	1-Year Total Return
2017	17.95	-28.08
2016	24.96	-15.27
2015	29.46	11.97
2014	26.31	-0.11
2013	26.34	-1.23
2012	26.67	-20.22

Total Assets: $237,926,834
Asset Allocation
Asset	%
Cash	158%
Stocks	-58%
US Stocks	-58%
Bonds	0%
US Bonds	0%
Other	0%

Services Offered:

Investment Strategy: The investment seeks daily investment results, before fees and expenses, that correspond to the inverse (-1x) of the daily performance of the MSCI Emerging Markets Index®. The fund invests in financial instruments that ProShare Advisors believes, in combination, should produce daily returns consistent with the fund's investment objective. The index includes 85% of the free float-adjusted market capitalization in each industry group in emerging market countries. The fund is non-diversified. **Top Holdings:** Ishares Msci Emerging Markets (Eem) Swap Citibank Na Ishares Msci Emerging Markets (Eem) Swap Societe Generale United States Treasury Bills United States Treasury Bills United States Treasury Bills

iShares Morningstar Small-Cap ETF   C-   HOLD

Ticker	Traded On	NAV	Total Assets ($)	Dividend Yield (TTM)	Turnover Ratio	Expense Ratio
JKJ	NYSE Arca	148.04	$235,606,608	1.4	56	0.25

Ratings

Reward	C-
Risk	D+
Recent Upgrade/Downgrade	Down

Fund Information

Fund Type	Exchange Traded Funds
Category	US Equity Small Cap
Sub-Category	Small Blend
Prospectus Objective	Small Company
Inception Date	Jun-04
Open to New Investments	Y

Prices

Price (as of 12/31/2018)	147.86
52-Week High	186.23
52-Week Low	139.81

Total Returns (%)

3-Month	6-Month	1-Year	3-Year	5-Year
-16.48	-16.73	-13.80	20.22	22.95

3-Year Standard Deviation	12.93
Effective Duration	

Valuation

Premium/Discount (1-Year Average)	0.05

Company Information

Provider	iShares
Manager/Tenure	Diane Hsiung (10), Greg Savage (10), Jennifer Hsui (6), 3 others
Website	http://www.ishares.com
Address	iShares 400 Howard Street San Francisco CA 94105 United States
Phone Number	800-474-2737

PERFORMANCE

Ratings History

Date	Overall Rating	Risk Rating	Reward Rating
Q4-18	C-	D+	C-
Q2-18	C	D+	C+
Q4-17	B	B	B
Q4-16	C-	D+	C-
Q4-15	C	D+	C

Asset & Performance History

Date	NAV	1-Year Total Return
2017	174.16	13.01
2016	156.15	23.42
2015	128.72	-5.58
2014	138.15	8.31
2013	129.09	36.06
2012	95.79	16.44

Total Assets: $235,606,608

Asset Allocation

Asset	%
Cash	0%
Stocks	100%
US Stocks	99%
Bonds	0%
US Bonds	0%
Other	0%

Services Offered:

Investment Strategy: The investment seeks to track the investment results of the Morningstar® Small Core IndexSM composed of small-capitalization U.S. equities. The fund generally invests at least 90% of its assets in securities of the underlying index and in depositary receipts representing securities of the underlying index. The underlying index measures the performance of stocks issued by small-capitalization companies that have exhibited average "growth" and "value" characteristics as determined by Morningstar, Inc.'s ("Morningstar" or the "index provider") proprietary index methodology. **Top Holdings:** Molina Healthcare Inc   Haemonetics Corp   Primerica Inc   Genesee & Wyoming Inc Class A   ITT Inc

---

JPMorgan Diversified Return Emerging Markets Equity ETF   C-   HOLD

Ticker	Traded On	NAV	Total Assets ($)	Dividend Yield (TTM)	Turnover Ratio	Expense Ratio
JPEM	NYSE Arca	50.58	$235,468,814	4.7	60	0.47

Ratings

Reward	C-
Risk	C-
Recent Upgrade/Downgrade	

Fund Information

Fund Type	Exchange Traded Funds
Category	Global Emerg Mkts Equity
Sub-Category	Diversified Emerging Mkts
Prospectus Objective	Div Emerg Mkts
Inception Date	Jan-15
Open to New Investments	Y

Prices

Price (as of 12/31/2018)	50.84
52-Week High	64.42
52-Week Low	49.44

Total Returns (%)

3-Month	6-Month	1-Year	3-Year	5-Year
-6.24	-3.95	-10.55	30.58	

3-Year Standard Deviation	13.27
Effective Duration	

Valuation

Premium/Discount (1-Year Average)	0.40

Company Information

Provider	JPMorgan
Manager/Tenure	Kartik Aiyar (1), Yazann Romahi (1), Joe Staines (1)
Website	http://www.jpmorganfunds.com
Address	JPMorgan 270 Park Avenue New York NY 10017-2070 United States
Phone Number	800-480-4111

PERFORMANCE

Ratings History

Date	Overall Rating	Risk Rating	Reward Rating
Q4-18	C-	C-	C-
Q2-18	C-	C-	C
Q4-17	C+	C	C+
Q4-16	D+	C-	D+
Q4-15	U		

Asset & Performance History

Date	NAV	1-Year Total Return
2017	58.06	28.83
2016	46.05	13.3
2015	41.18	-15.04
2014		
2013		
2012		

Total Assets: $235,468,814

Asset Allocation

Asset	%
Cash	1%
Stocks	99%
US Stocks	0%
Bonds	0%
US Bonds	0%
Other	0%

Services Offered:

Investment Strategy: The investment seeks investment results that closely correspond, before fees and expenses, to the performance of the JP Morgan Diversified Factor Emerging Markets Equity Index. The fund will invest at least 80% of its assets in securities included in the underlying index. "Assets" means net assets, plus the amount of borrowing for investment purposes. The underlying index is comprised of equity securities from emerging markets selected to represent a diversified set of factor characteristics. **Top Holdings:** China Mobile Ltd   Taiwan Semiconductor Manufacturing Co Ltd   Vale SA   Baidu Inc ADR   China Construction Bank Corp H

iShares Edge MSCI USA Size Factor ETF   C-   HOLD

Ticker	Traded On	NAV	Total Assets ($)	Dividend Yield (TTM)	Turnover Ratio	Expense Ratio
SIZE	NYSE Arca	76.57	$235,306,584	1.97	17	0.15

Ratings
Reward   C-
Risk   C-
Recent Upgrade/Downgrade   Down

Fund Information
Fund Type   Exchange Traded Funds
Category   US Equity Large Cap Blend
Sub-Category   Large Blend
Prospectus Objective   Growth
Inception Date   Apr-13
Open to New Investments   Y

Prices
Price (as of 12/31/2018)   76.63
52-Week High   89.69
52-Week Low   72.15

Total Returns (%)

3-Month	6-Month	1-Year	3-Year	5-Year
-12.47	-7.79	-6.58	25.84	46.23

3-Year Standard Deviation   8.91
Effective Duration

Valuation
Premium/Discount (1-Year Average)   0.09

Company Information
Provider   iShares
Manager/Tenure   Diane Hsiung (5), Jennifer Hsui (5),
                  Greg Savage (5), 3 others
Website   http://www.ishares.com
Address   iShares 400 Howard Street San
                  Francisco CA 94105 United States
Phone Number   800-474-2737

PERFORMANCE

Ratings History

Date	Overall Rating	Risk Rating	Reward Rating
Q4-18	C-	C-	C-
Q2-18	C	C-	C
Q4-17	B-	B	B-
Q4-16	D+	D+	D+
Q4-15	C	D+	C

Asset & Performance History

Date	NAV	1-Year Total Return
2017	83.75	18.87
2016	71.65	13.32
2015	64.48	0.36
2014	65.51	15.77
2013	57.65	
2012		

Total Assets: $235,306,584
Asset Allocation

Asset	%
Cash	0%
Stocks	100%
US Stocks	98%
Bonds	0%
US Bonds	0%
Other	0%

Services Offered:

Investment Strategy: The investment seeks to track the investment results of the MSCI USA Low Size Index. The fund generally will invest at least 90% of its assets in the component securities of the underlying index and may invest up to 10% of its assets in certain futures, options and swap contracts, cash and cash equivalents. The index is based on a traditional market capitalization-weighted parent index, the MSCI USA Index (the "parent index"). The parent index includes U.S. large- and mid- capitalization stocks. **Top Holdings:** Zillow Group Inc C CVS Health Corp Wayfair Inc Class A Splunk Inc Workday Inc Class A

iShares Global Comm Services ETF   C   HOLD

Ticker	Traded On	NAV	Total Assets ($)	Dividend Yield (TTM)	Turnover Ratio	Expense Ratio
IXP	NYSE Arca	50.33	$235,092,463	4.26	3	0.47

Ratings
Reward   C
Risk   C-
Recent Upgrade/Downgrade   Up

Fund Information
Fund Type   Exchange Traded Funds
Category   Communications Sector Equity
Sub-Category   Communications
Prospectus Objective   Comm
Inception Date   Nov-01
Open to New Investments   Y

Prices
Price (as of 12/31/2018)   50.18
52-Week High   62.51
52-Week Low   48.09

Total Returns (%)

3-Month	6-Month	1-Year	3-Year	5-Year
-11.66	-4.77	-13.54	-2.88	-3.86

3-Year Standard Deviation   10.57
Effective Duration

Valuation
Premium/Discount (1-Year Average)   -0.06

Company Information
Provider   iShares
Manager/Tenure   Diane Hsiung (10), Greg Savage (10),
                  Jennifer Hsui (6), 3 others
Website   http://www.ishares.com
Address   iShares 400 Howard Street San
                  Francisco CA 94105 United States
Phone Number   800-474-2737

PERFORMANCE

Ratings History

Date	Overall Rating	Risk Rating	Reward Rating
Q4-18	C	C-	C
Q2-18	C-	C-	C-
Q4-17	C	C	C
Q4-16	C	C-	B-
Q4-15	C	C-	C

Asset & Performance History

Date	NAV	1-Year Total Return
2017	60.62	6.38
2016	58.96	5.59
2015	58.05	-0.3
2014	60.43	-0.7
2013	68.22	24.43
2012	56.93	7.04

Total Assets: $235,092,463
Asset Allocation

Asset	%
Cash	0%
Stocks	100%
US Stocks	68%
Bonds	0%
US Bonds	0%
Other	0%

Services Offered: CashInvestment Plan

Investment Strategy: The investment seeks to track the investment results of the S&P Global 1200 Communication Services Sector IndexTM. The fund invests at least 90% of its assets in securities of the index and in depositary receipts representing securities of the index. It may invest the remainder of its assets in certain futures, options and swap contracts, cash and cash equivalents, as well as in securities not included in the index. The index measures the performance of companies that the index provider deems to be a part of the communication services sector of the economy and that the index provider believes are important to global markets. The fund is non-diversified. **Top Holdings:** Alphabet Inc Class C Facebook Inc A Alphabet Inc A AT&T Inc Verizon Communications Inc

First Trust Mid Cap Growth AlphaDEX® Fund

C-   **HOLD**

Ticker	Traded On	NAV	Total Assets ($)	Dividend Yield (TTM)	Turnover Ratio	Expense Ratio
FNY	NAS CM	36.24	$233,586,242	0.11	153	0.7

Ratings

Reward	C
Risk	C-
Recent Upgrade/Downgrade	Down

Fund Information

Fund Type	Exchange Traded Funds
Category	US Equity Mid Cap
Sub-Category	Mid-Cap Growth
Prospectus Objective	Growth
Inception Date	Apr-11
Open to New Investments	Y

Prices

Price (as of 12/31/2018)	36.22
52-Week High	47.12
52-Week Low	33.42

Total Returns (%)

3-Month	6-Month	1-Year	3-Year	5-Year
-20.79	-16.52	-7.35	26.63	31.35

3-Year Standard Deviation	13.13
Effective Duration	

Valuation

Premium/Discount (1-Year Average)	0.10

Company Information

Provider	First Trust
Manager/Tenure	Jon C. Erickson (7), Daniel J. Lindquist (7), David G. McGarel (7), 3 others
Website	http://www.ftportfolios.com/
Address	First Trust 120 E. Liberty Drive, Suite 400 Wheaton IL 60187 United States
Phone Number	800-621-1675

PERFORMANCE

Ratings History

Date	Overall Rating	Risk Rating	Reward Rating
Q4-18	C-	C-	C
Q2-18	C+	C-	B
Q4-17	B	B-	A-
Q4-16	C	C-	C+
Q4-15	C	C	C+

Asset & Performance History

Date	NAV	1-Year Total Return
2017	39.14	24.92
2016	31.4	9.42
2015	28.87	-1.19
2014	29.35	4.98
2013	28.02	36.64
2012	20.59	9.9

Total Assets: $233,586,242

Asset Allocation

Asset	%
Cash	0%
Stocks	100%
US Stocks	98%
Bonds	0%
US Bonds	0%
Other	0%

Services Offered:

Investment Strategy: The investment seeks investment results that correspond generally to the price and yield (before the fund's fees and expenses) of an equity index called the Nasdaq AlphaDEX® Mid Cap Growth Index. The fund will normally invest at least 90% of its net assets (including investment borrowings) in common stocks that comprise the index. The index is designed to select growth stocks from the NASDAQ US 600 Mid Cap Index (the "base index") that may generate positive alpha, or risk-adjusted returns, relative to traditional indices through the use of the AlphaDEX® selection methodology. **Top Holdings:** Amedisys Inc   Twilio Inc A   Tractor Supply Co   PRA Health Sciences Inc   Etsy Inc

---

VelocityShares 3x Long Silver ETN Linked to the S&P GSCI® Silver Index ER

B-   **BUY**

Ticker	Traded On	NAV	Total Assets ($)	Dividend Yield (TTM)	Turnover Ratio	Expense Ratio
USLV	NAS CM	74.10	$233,410,220	0		1.65

Ratings

Reward	A-
Risk	D+
Recent Upgrade/Downgrade	Up

Fund Information

Fund Type	Exchange Traded Funds
Category	Trading Tools
Sub-Category	Trading--Leveraged Commodities
Prospectus Objective	Prec Metals
Inception Date	Oct-11
Open to New Investments	Y

Prices

Price (as of 12/31/2018)	74.10
52-Week High	74.10
52-Week Low	6.39

Total Returns (%)

3-Month	6-Month	1-Year	3-Year	5-Year
17.30	766.90	521.72	659.22	65.14

3-Year Standard Deviation	65.42
Effective Duration	

Valuation

Premium/Discount (1-Year Average)	-0.23

Company Information

Provider	Credit Suisse AG
Manager/Tenure	Management Team (7)
Website	
Address	Kilmore House Park Lane Dublin Ireland
Phone Number	

PERFORMANCE

Ratings History

Date	Overall Rating	Risk Rating	Reward Rating
Q4-18	B-	D+	A-
Q2-18	D-	D-	D-
Q4-17	D-	D-	D-
Q4-16	D	D-	D
Q4-15	E	E+	E

Asset & Performance History

Date	NAV	1-Year Total Return
2017	11.92	-4.04
2016	11.44	21.31
2015	9.76	-47.55
2014	18.61	-58.52
2013	44.87	-82.54
2012	257.1	-8.92

Total Assets: $233,410,220

Asset Allocation

Asset	%
Cash	%
Stocks	%
US Stocks	%
Bonds	%
US Bonds	%
Other	%

Services Offered:

Investment Strategy: The investment seeks to replicate, net of expenses, three times the S&P GSCI Silver index ER.

The index comprises futures contracts on a single commodity. The fluctuations in the values of it are intended generally to correlate with changes in the price of silver in global markets. **Top Holdings:**

SPDR® MSCI EAFE StrategicFactors ETF   D+   SELL

Ticker	Traded On	NAV	Total Assets ($)	Dividend Yield (TTM)	Turnover Ratio	Expense Ratio
QEFA	NYSE Arca	56.52	$233,122,225	2.63	6	0.3

Ratings
Reward	D+
Risk	C-
Recent Upgrade/Downgrade	Down

Fund Information
Fund Type	Exchange Traded Funds
Category	Global Equity Large Cap
Sub-Category	Foreign Large Blend
Prospectus Objective	World Stock
Inception Date	Jun-14
Open to New Investments	Y

Prices
Price (as of 12/31/2018)	56.53
52-Week High	68.89
52-Week Low	54.70

Total Returns (%)
3-Month	6-Month	1-Year	3-Year	5-Year
-10.18	-7.42	-10.22	11.59	

3-Year Standard Deviation	9.84
Effective Duration	

Valuation
Premium/Discount (1-Year Average)	0.07

Company Information
Provider	SPDR State Street Global Advisors
Manager/Tenure	Michael J. Feehily (4), Karl A. Schneider (3), David Chin (1)
Website	http://www.spdrs.com
Address	SPDR State Street Global Advisors State Street Financial Center, 1 Lincoln Street Boston MA 02111-2900 United States
Phone Number	617-786-3000

PERFORMANCE

Ratings History
Date	Overall Rating	Risk Rating	Reward Rating
Q4-18	D+	C-	D+
Q2-18	C	C-	C
Q4-17	B	B	B
Q4-16	D+	D+	C-
Q4-15	D	D+	D+

Asset & Performance History
Date	NAV	1-Year Total Return
2017	64.89	23.89
2016	53.66	0.32
2015	54.59	1.76
2014	55.19	
2013		
2012		

Total Assets: $233,122,225

Asset Allocation
Asset	%
Cash	0%
Stocks	100%
US Stocks	1%
Bonds	0%
US Bonds	0%
Other	0%

Services Offered:

Investment Strategy: The investment seeks to track the performance of the MSCI EAFE Factor Mix A-Series Index. The fund generally invests substantially all, but at least 80%, of its total assets in the securities comprising the index and in depositary receipts based on securities comprising the index. The index captures large- and mid-cap representation across 21 developed market Europe, Australasia, and Far East countries and aims to represent the performance of value, low volatility, and quality factor strategies. The fund is non-diversified. **Top Holdings:** Nestle SA   Roche Holding AG Dividend Right Cert.   AstraZeneca PLC   Diageo PLC   Novo Nordisk A/S B

---

iShares MSCI Emerging Markets Small-Cap ETF   D+   SELL

Ticker	Traded On	NAV	Total Assets ($)	Dividend Yield (TTM)	Turnover Ratio	Expense Ratio
EEMS	NYSE Arca	42.04	$230,677,075	3.38	39	0.67

Ratings
Reward	D+
Risk	D+
Recent Upgrade/Downgrade	Down

Fund Information
Fund Type	Exchange Traded Funds
Category	Global Emerg Mkts Equity
Sub-Category	Diversified Emerging Mkts
Prospectus Objective	Div Emerg Mkts
Inception Date	Aug-11
Open to New Investments	Y

Prices
Price (as of 12/31/2018)	41.81
52-Week High	57.26
52-Week Low	39.95

Total Returns (%)
3-Month	6-Month	1-Year	3-Year	5-Year
-6.76	-9.94	-18.19	11.54	2.73

3-Year Standard Deviation	14.12
Effective Duration	

Valuation
Premium/Discount (1-Year Average)	-0.19

Company Information
Provider	iShares
Manager/Tenure	Diane Hsiung (7), Greg Savage (7), Jennifer Hsui (5), 1 other
Website	http://www.ishares.com
Address	iShares 400 Howard Street San Francisco CA 94105 United States
Phone Number	800-474-2737

PERFORMANCE

Ratings History
Date	Overall Rating	Risk Rating	Reward Rating
Q4-18	D+	D+	D+
Q2-18	C-	C-	C
Q4-17	B-	C+	B-
Q4-16	D+	C-	D+
Q4-15	C-	C-	C-

Asset & Performance History
Date	NAV	1-Year Total Return
2017	52.89	33.96
2016	40.53	1.78
2015	40.83	-7.58
2014	45.16	-0.33
2013	46.53	0.96
2012	47.13	21.23

Total Assets: $230,677,075

Asset Allocation
Asset	%
Cash	0%
Stocks	100%
US Stocks	0%
Bonds	0%
US Bonds	0%
Other	0%

Services Offered:

Investment Strategy: The investment seeks to track the investment results of the MSCI Emerging Markets Small Cap Index. The fund generally will invest at least 90% of its assets in the component securities of the underlying index and in investments that have economic characteristics that are substantially identical to the component securities of the underlying index. The index is designed to measure the performance of equity securities of small-capitalization companies whose market capitalization represents the bottom 14% of companies in emerging market countries, as measured by market capitalization. **Top Holdings:** AVI Ltd   CVC Brasil Operadora e Agencia de Viagens SA   Bradespar SA Participating Preferred   Li Ning Co Ltd   The Federal Bank Ltd

Direxion Daily MSCI Emerging Markets Bull 3X Shares   D+   SELL

Ticker	Traded On	NAV	Total Assets ($)	Dividend Yield (TTM)	Turnover Ratio	Expense Ratio
EDC	NYSE Arca	62.73	$228,949,043	1.12	38	1.26

Ratings

Reward	C-
Risk	D
Recent Upgrade/Downgrade	Down

Fund Information

Fund Type	Exchange Traded Funds
Category	Trading Tools
Sub-Category	Trading--Leveraged Equity
Prospectus Objective	Div Emerg Mkts
Inception Date	Dec-08
Open to New Investments	Y

Prices

Price (as of 12/31/2018)	62.79
52-Week High	168.60
52-Week Low	57.53

Total Returns (%)

3-Month	6-Month	1-Year	3-Year	5-Year
-26.10	-28.78	-49.96	37.09	-44.90

3-Year Standard Deviation	47.58
Effective Duration	

Valuation

Premium/Discount (1-Year Average)	0.04

Company Information

Provider	Direxion Funds
Manager/Tenure	Paul Brigandi (9), Tony Ng (3)
Website	http://www.direxionfunds.com
Address	Direxion Funds 1301 Avenue Of The Americas (6th Avenue) New York NY 10019 United States
Phone Number	646-572-3390

PERFORMANCE

Ratings History

Date	Overall Rating	Risk Rating	Reward Rating
Q4-18	D+	D	C-
Q2-18	C	D+	C
Q4-17	B-	D+	A-
Q4-16	D	D	D
Q4-15	D	D	D-

Asset & Performance History

Date	NAV	1-Year Total Return
2017	125.81	138.8
2016	52.83	14.74
2015	46.04	-49.91
2014	91.92	-19.76
2013	114.56	-21.53
2012	146	46.94

Total Assets: $228,949,043

Asset Allocation

Asset	%
Cash	48%
Stocks	52%
US Stocks	-2%
Bonds	0%
US Bonds	0%
Other	0%

Services Offered:

Investment Strategy: The investment seeks daily investment results, before fees and expenses, of 300% of the daily performance of the MSCI Emerging Markets IndexSM. The fund invests at least 80% of its net assets (plus borrowing for investment purposes) in securities of the index, exchange-traded funds ("ETFs") that track the index and other financial instruments that provide daily leveraged exposure to the index or ETFs that track the index. The index is a free float-adjusted market capitalization weighted index that is designed to represent the performance of large- and mid-capitalizations securities across the 24 emerging market countries. The fund is non-diversified.
Top Holdings: iShares MSCI Emerging Markets ETF   Msci Emerg Mkts Idx Swap   Msci Emerg Mkts Idx Swap   Msci Emerg Mkts Idx Swap   Msci Emerg Mkts Idx Swap

---

iPath® S&P GSCI® Crude Oil Total Return Index ETN   D   SELL

Ticker	Traded On	NAV	Total Assets ($)	Dividend Yield (TTM)	Turnover Ratio	Expense Ratio
OILNF	NYSE Arca		$228,853,382	0	0	0.75

Ratings

Reward	D+
Risk	E
Recent Upgrade/Downgrade	Down

Fund Information

Fund Type	Exchange Traded Funds
Category	Commodities Specified
Sub-Category	Commodities Energy
Prospectus Objective	Natl Res
Inception Date	Aug-06
Open to New Investments	Y

Prices

Price (as of 12/31/2018)	9.26
52-Week High	9.49
52-Week Low	6.43

Total Returns (%)

3-Month	6-Month	1-Year	3-Year	5-Year
-49.54	-46.00	-28.64	-17.93	-79.61

3-Year Standard Deviation	39.05
Effective Duration	

Valuation

Premium/Discount (1-Year Average)	6.95

Company Information

Provider	Milleis Investissements Funds
Manager/Tenure	No Manager (12)
Website	
Address	2-4, rue Eugène Ruppert L-2453 Luxembourg Luxembourg L-2453 Luxembourg
Phone Number	

PERFORMANCE

Ratings History

Date	Overall Rating	Risk Rating	Reward Rating
Q4-18	D	E	D+
Q2-18	D+	E	C
Q4-17	D	D	D+
Q4-16	D-	D-	D-
Q4-15	D-	D-	D-

Asset & Performance History

Date	NAV	1-Year Total Return
2017	6.59	3.1
2016	6.3	11.92
2015	5.73	-53.41
2014	12.29	-46.68
2013	23.06	5.61
2012	21.84	-12.93

Total Assets: $228,853,382

Asset Allocation

Asset	%
Cash	%
Stocks	%
US Stocks	%
Bonds	%
US Bonds	%
Other	%

Services Offered:

Investment Strategy: The investment seeks to provide with exposure to the S&P GSCI® Crude Oil Total Return Index.
The S&P GSCI® Crude Oil Total Return Index (the "index") is a sub-index of the S&P GSCI® Commodity Index. The index reflects the returns that are potentially available through an unleveraged investment in the West Texas Intermediate (WTI) crude oil futures contract. **Top Holdings:**

WisdomTree CBOE S&P 500 PutWrite Strategy Fund   C-   HOLD

Ticker	Traded On	NAV	Total Assets ($)	Dividend Yield (TTM)	Turnover Ratio	Expense Ratio
PUTW	NYSE Arca	25.57	$227,591,408	0.19	0	0.38

Ratings
Reward	C-
Risk	C-
Recent Upgrade/Downgrade	Down

Fund Information
Fund Type	Exchange Traded Funds
Category	Long/Short Equity
Sub-Category	Options-based
Prospectus Objective	Growth
Inception Date	Feb-16
Open to New Investments	Y

Prices
Price (as of 12/31/2018)	25.45
52-Week High	30.73
52-Week Low	24.52

Total Returns (%)
3-Month	6-Month	1-Year	3-Year	5-Year
-9.87	-6.08	-4.81	16.67	

3-Year Standard Deviation	
Effective Duration	

Valuation
Premium/Discount (1-Year Average)	0.05

Company Information
Provider	WisdomTree
Manager/Tenure	Vassilis Dagioglu (2), James H. Stavena (2)
Website	http://www.wisdomtree.com
Address	WisdomTree 245 Park Avenue, 35th floor New York NY 10167 United States
Phone Number	866-909-9473

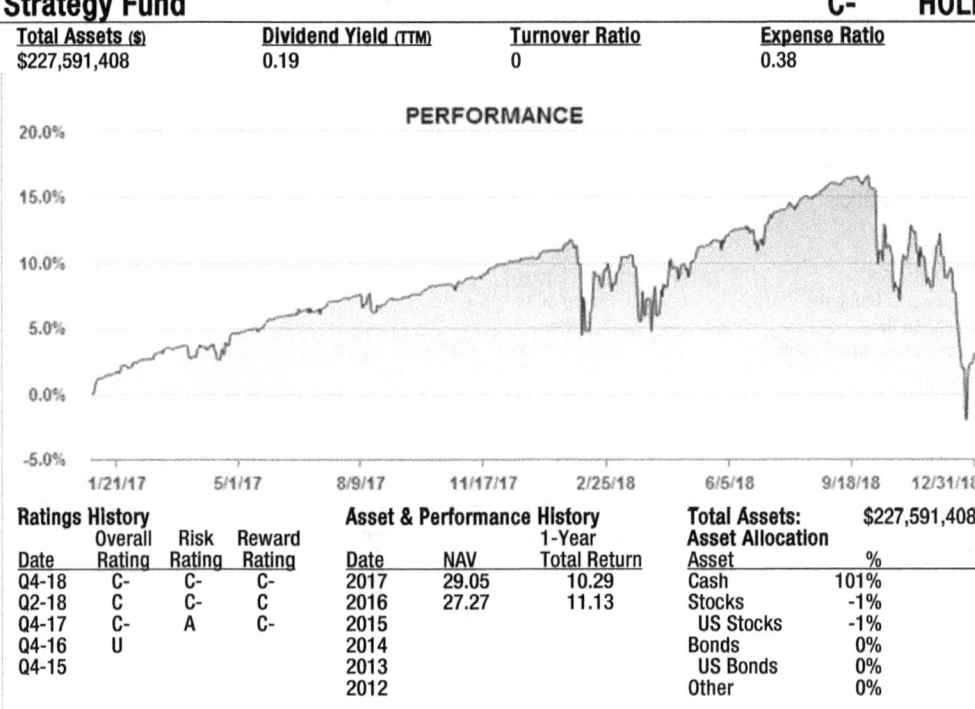

Ratings History
Date	Overall Rating	Risk Rating	Reward Rating
Q4-18	C-	C-	C-
Q2-18	C	C-	C
Q4-17	C-	A	C-
Q4-16	U		
Q4-15			

Asset & Performance History
Date	NAV	1-Year Total Return
2017	29.05	10.29
2016	27.27	11.13
2015		
2014		
2013		
2012		

Total Assets: $227,591,408
Asset Allocation
Asset	%
Cash	101%
Stocks	-1%
US Stocks	-1%
Bonds	0%
US Bonds	0%
Other	0%

Services Offered:

Investment Strategy: The investment seeks to track the price and yield performance, before fees and expenses, of the CBOE S&P 500 PutWrite Index (the "index"). Under normal circumstances, at least 80% of the fund's total assets will be invested in component securities of the index and investments that have economic characteristics that are substantially identical to the economic characteristics of such component securities. The index tracks the value of a cash-secured put option sales strategy, which consists of selling (or "writing") S&P 500 Index put options ("SPX Puts") and investing the sale proceeds in one- and three-month Treasury bills. The fund is non-diversified. **Top Holdings:** S+p 500 Index Dec18 2730 Put

Davis Select Worldwide ETF   D+   SELL

Ticker	Traded On	NAV	Total Assets ($)	Dividend Yield (TTM)	Turnover Ratio	Expense Ratio
DWLD	NAS CM	19.60	$226,011,337	0.08	14	0.65

Ratings
Reward	C-
Risk	D
Recent Upgrade/Downgrade	Down

Fund Information
Fund Type	Exchange Traded Funds
Category	Global Equity Large Cap
Sub-Category	World Large Stock
Prospectus Objective	World Stock
Inception Date	Jan-17
Open to New Investments	Y

Prices
Price (as of 12/31/2018)	19.55
52-Week High	28.88
52-Week Low	19.39

Total Returns (%)
3-Month	6-Month	1-Year	3-Year	5-Year
-20.08	-21.85	-22.09		

3-Year Standard Deviation	
Effective Duration	

Valuation
Premium/Discount (1-Year Average)	0.20

Company Information
Provider	Davis ETFs
Manager/Tenure	Danton Goei (1)
Website	
Address	c/o Davis Selected Advisers, L.P. 2949 E. Elvira Rd., Ste. 101 Tucson Arizona 85756 United States
Phone Number	800-279-0279

Ratings History
Date	Overall Rating	Risk Rating	Reward Rating
Q4-18	D+	D	C-
Q2-18	C	C-	C
Q4-17	D-	B+	D+
Q4-16			
Q4-15			

Asset & Performance History
Date	NAV	1-Year Total Return
2017	26.2	31.16
2016		
2015		
2014		
2013		
2012		

Total Assets: $226,011,337
Asset Allocation
Asset	%
Cash	0%
Stocks	100%
US Stocks	52%
Bonds	0%
US Bonds	0%
Other	0%

Services Offered:

Investment Strategy: The investment seeks long-term growth of capital. The fund's investment adviser, uses the Davis Investment Discipline to invest the fund's portfolio principally in common stocks issued by both United States and foreign companies, including countries with developed or emerging markets. It will invest significantly in issuers (i) organized or located outside of the U.S.; (ii) whose primary trading market is located outside the U.S.; or (iii) doing a substantial amount of business outside the U.S., which the adviser considers to be a company that derives at least 50% of its revenue from business outside the U.S. or has at least 50% of its assets outside the U.S. **Top Holdings:** Alphabet Inc Class C Amazon.com Inc Alibaba Group Holding Ltd ADR   Naspers Ltd N Shs Berkshire Hathaway Inc B

ProShares Short Dow30   D   SELL

Ticker	Traded On	NAV		Total Assets ($)	Dividend Yield (TTM)	Turnover Ratio	Expense Ratio
DOG	NYSE Arca	61.33		$224,339,199	0.64	0	0.95

Ratings
Reward   D
Risk   D-
Recent Upgrade/Downgrade

Fund Information
Fund Type   Exchange Traded Funds
Category   Trading Tools
Sub-Category   Trading--Inverse Equity
Prospectus Objective   Growth
Inception Date   Jun-06
Open to New Investments   Y

Prices
Price (as of 12/31/2018)   61.34
52-Week High   65.91
52-Week Low   54.07

Total Returns (%)

3-Month	6-Month	1-Year	3-Year	5-Year
13.06	3.15	3.48	-31.49	-40.70

3-Year Standard Deviation   9.67
Effective Duration

Valuation
Premium/Discount (1-Year Average)   -0.02

Company Information
Provider   ProShares
Manager/Tenure   Michael Neches (5), Devin Sullivan (0)
Website   http://www.proshares.com
Address   ProShares 7501 Wisconsin Avenue,
                    Suite 1000 Bethesda MD 20814
                    United States
Phone Number   866-776-5125

Ratings History

Date	Overall Rating	Risk Rating	Reward Rating
Q4-18	D	D-	D
Q2-18	D	D-	D-
Q4-17	D-	D-	D-
Q4-16	D	D	D
Q4-15	D	D	D

Asset & Performance History

Date	NAV	1-Year Total Return
2017	59.8	-21.49
2016	76.2	-15.67
2015	90.36	-3.04
2014	93.2	-10.72
2013	104.4	-24.19
2012	137.72	-11.26

Total Assets: $224,339,199

Asset Allocation

Asset	%
Cash	148%
Stocks	-51%
US Stocks	-51%
Bonds	3%
US Bonds	3%
Other	0%

Services Offered:

Investment Strategy: The investment seeks daily investment results, before fees and expenses, that correspond to the inverse (-1x) of the daily performance of the Dow Jones Industrial AverageSM. The fund invests in financial instruments that ProShare Advisors believes, in combination, should produce daily returns consistent with the fund's investment objective. The index is a price-weighted index and includes 30 large-cap, "blue-chip" U.S. stocks, excluding utility and transportation companies. The fund is non-diversified. **Top Holdings:** Dj Industrial Average Swap Goldman Sachs International   United States Treasury Bills   Dj Industrial Average Swap Citibank Na   United States Treasury Bills   Dj Industrial Average Swap Credit Suisse International

---

iShares Global Materials ETF   D+   SELL

Ticker	Traded On	NAV		Total Assets ($)	Dividend Yield (TTM)	Turnover Ratio	Expense Ratio
MXI	NYSE Arca	57.52		$223,512,709	2.2	8	0.47

Ratings
Reward   C-
Risk   D+
Recent Upgrade/Downgrade   Down

Fund Information
Fund Type   Exchange Traded Funds
Category   Natural Resources
Sub-Category   Natural Resources
Prospectus Objective   Natl Res
Inception Date   Sep-06
Open to New Investments   Y

Prices
Price (as of 12/31/2018)   57.37
52-Week High   75.12
52-Week Low   54.93

Total Returns (%)

3-Month	6-Month	1-Year	3-Year	5-Year
-14.08	-12.37	-15.79	34.73	3.39

3-Year Standard Deviation   15.25
Effective Duration

Valuation
Premium/Discount (1-Year Average)   -0.03

Company Information
Provider   iShares
Manager/Tenure   Diane Hsiung (10), Greg Savage (10),
                    Jennifer Hsui (6), 3 others
Website   http://www.ishares.com
Address   iShares 400 Howard Street San
                    Francisco CA 94105 United States
Phone Number   800-474-2737

PERFORMANCE

Ratings History

Date	Overall Rating	Risk Rating	Reward Rating
Q4-18	D+	D+	C-
Q2-18	C	C-	C
Q4-17	B-	C-	B
Q4-16	C-	C-	C-
Q4-15	D+	D+	D+

Asset & Performance History

Date	NAV	1-Year Total Return
2017	70.06	29.55
2016	55.15	23.51
2015	45.28	-16.83
2014	56.19	-7.73
2013	62.21	2.92
2012	61.91	10.99

Total Assets: $223,512,709

Asset Allocation

Asset	%
Cash	0%
Stocks	100%
US Stocks	32%
Bonds	0%
US Bonds	0%
Other	0%

Services Offered:

Investment Strategy: The investment seeks to track the investment results of the S&P Global 1200 Materials IndexTM. The fund generally invests at least 90% of its assets in securities of the underlying index and in depositary receipts representing securities of the underlying index. It may invest the remainder of its assets in certain futures, options and swap contracts, cash and cash equivalents, as well as in securities not included in the underlying index. The index measures the performance of companies that the index provider deems to be part of the materials sector of the economy and that the index provider believes are important to global markets. **Top Holdings:** DowDuPont Inc   Linde PLC   BHP Group Ltd   Basf SE   Rio Tinto PLC

ALPS Medical Breakthroughs ETF

C-   HOLD

Ticker	Traded On	NAV
SBIO	NYSE Arca	28.23

Total Assets ($)	Dividend Yield (TTM)	Turnover Ratio	Expense Ratio
$223,373,506	1.73	43	0.5

Ratings
Reward	C-
Risk	D+
Recent Upgrade/Downgrade	Down

Fund Information
Fund Type	Exchange Traded Funds
Category	Healthcare Sector Equity
Sub-Category	Health
Prospectus Objective	Health
Inception Date	Dec-14
Open to New Investments	Y

Prices
Price (as of 12/31/2018)	28.14
52-Week High	39.37
52-Week Low	25.86

Total Returns (%)
3-Month	6-Month	1-Year	3-Year	5-Year
-24.23	-22.59	-11.19	-6.84	

3-Year Standard Deviation	30.4
Effective Duration	

Valuation
Premium/Discount (1-Year Average)	0.11

Company Information
Provider	ALPS
Manager/Tenure	Ryan Mischker (3), Andrew Hicks (2)
Website	http://www.alpsfunds.com
Address	ALPS 1290 Broadway, Suite 1100 Denver CO 80203 United States
Phone Number	866-759-5679

PERFORMANCE

Ratings History
Date	Overall Rating	Risk Rating	Reward Rating
Q4-18	C-	D+	C-
Q2-18	C	D+	C
Q4-17	C	C	C
Q4-16	D	D	D
Q4-15	U		

Asset & Performance History
Date	NAV	1-Year Total Return
2017	32.7	44.98
2016	22.96	-27.65
2015	31.74	28.07
2014	24.78	
2013		
2012		

Total Assets: $223,373,506

Asset Allocation
Asset	%
Cash	0%
Stocks	100%
US Stocks	89%
Bonds	0%
US Bonds	0%
Other	0%

Services Offered:

Investment Strategy: The investment seeks investment results that correspond (before fees and expenses) generally to the performance of its underlying index, the Poliwogg Medical Breakthroughs IndexSM. The fund employs a "passive management" - or indexing - investment approach designed to track the performance of the underlying index. It will normally invest at least 80% of its net assets in securities that comprise the underlying index. The underlying index is comprised of small- and mid-cap stocks of biotechnology and pharmaceutical companies that have one or more drugs in either Phase II or Phase III U.S. Food and Drug Administration clinical trials. It is non-diversified. **Top Holdings:** Amarin Corp PLC ADR Galapagos NV ADR United Therapeutics Corp Hutchison China Meditech Ltd ADR Loxo Oncology Inc

---

First Trust Nasdaq Bank ETF

B-   BUY

Ticker	Traded On	NAV
FTXO	NAS CM	22.28

Total Assets ($)	Dividend Yield (TTM)	Turnover Ratio	Expense Ratio
$222,633,375	1.58	39	0.6

Ratings
Reward	B
Risk	C
Recent Upgrade/Downgrade	Down

Fund Information
Fund Type	Exchange Traded Funds
Category	Financials Sector Equity
Sub-Category	Financial
Prospectus Objective	Financial
Inception Date	Sep-16
Open to New Investments	Y

Prices
Price (as of 12/31/2018)	22.26
52-Week High	32.18
52-Week Low	21.01

Total Returns (%)
3-Month	6-Month	1-Year	3-Year	5-Year
-18.17	-20.50	-21.57		

3-Year Standard Deviation	
Effective Duration	

Valuation
Premium/Discount (1-Year Average)	0.02

Company Information
Provider	First Trust
Manager/Tenure	Jon C. Erickson (2), Daniel J. Lindquist (2), David G. McGarel (2), 3 others
Website	http://www.ftportfolios.com/
Address	First Trust 120 E. Liberty Drive, Suite 400 Wheaton IL 60187 United States
Phone Number	800-621-1675

PERFORMANCE

Ratings History
Date	Overall Rating	Risk Rating	Reward Rating
Q4-18	B-	C	B
Q2-18	B	C	B+
Q4-17	D	B	C
Q4-16	U		
Q4-15			

Asset & Performance History
Date	NAV	1-Year Total Return
2017	29.32	13.95
2016	26.02	
2015		
2014		
2013		
2012		

Total Assets: $222,633,375

Asset Allocation
Asset	%
Cash	0%
Stocks	100%
US Stocks	100%
Bonds	0%
US Bonds	0%
Other	0%

Services Offered:

Investment Strategy: The investment seeks investment results that correspond generally to the price and yield (before the fund's fees and expenses) of an equity index called the Nasdaq US Smart Banks Index. The fund will normally invest at least 90% of its net assets (including investment borrowings) in common stocks that comprise the underlying index. The underlying index is designed to select bank stocks from the NASDAQ US Benchmark Index based on a ranking methodology of three price factors which aims to select companies. The fund is non-diversified. **Top Holdings:** US Bancorp JPMorgan Chase & Co PNC Financial Services Group Inc Huntington Bancshares Inc SunTrust Banks Inc

PIMCO Enhanced Low Duration Active Exchange-Traded Fund   C   HOLD

Ticker	Traded On	NAV	Total Assets ($)	Dividend Yield (TTM)	Turnover Ratio	Expense Ratio
LDUR	NYSE Arca	98.65	$222,421,881	2.77	326	1.02

Ratings
Reward   C
Risk   C-
Recent Upgrade/Downgrade

Fund Information
Fund Type	Exchange Traded Funds
Category	US Fixed Income
Sub-Category	Short-Term Bond
Prospectus Objective	Income
Inception Date	Jan-14
Open to New Investments	Y

Prices
Price (as of 12/31/2018)	98.76
52-Week High	100.40
52-Week Low	98.71

Total Returns (%)
3-Month	6-Month	1-Year	3-Year	5-Year
0.21	0.96	1.33	6.45	

3-Year Standard Deviation	0.9
Effective Duration	1.48

Valuation
Premium/Discount (1-Year Average)	0.07

Company Information
Provider	PIMCO
Manager/Tenure	Jerome M. Schneider (4), Hozef Arif (1), David Braun (1)
Website	http://www.pimco.com
Address	PIMCO 840 Newport Center Drive, Suite 100 Newport Beach CA 92660 United States
Phone Number	866-746-2602

PERFORMANCE

Ratings History
Date	Overall Rating	Risk Rating	Reward Rating
Q4-18	C	C-	C
Q2-18	C	C-	C
Q4-17	B	A+	C
Q4-16	C-	D+	C
Q4-15	D+	D+	C-

Asset & Performance History
Date	NAV	1-Year Total Return
2017	100.32	2.14
2016	100.27	2.83
2015	99.33	2.04
2014	100.2	
2013		
2012		

Total Assets: $222,421,881

Asset Allocation
Asset	%
Cash	-84%
Stocks	0%
US Stocks	0%
Bonds	182%
US Bonds	152%
Other	1%

Services Offered:

Investment Strategy: The investment seeks maximum total return, consistent with preservation of capital and prudent investment management. The fund seeks to achieve its investment objective by investing at least 80% of its net assets in a diversified portfolio of Fixed Income Instruments of varying maturities, which may be represented by forwards or derivatives such as options, futures contracts, or swap agreements. It invests primarily in investment grade debt securities, but may invest up to 15% of its total assets in high yield securities, as rated by Moody's, S&P or Fitch, or, if unrated, as determined by PIMCO. **Top Holdings:** Fin Fut Us 2yr Cbt 03/29/19 United States Treasury Notes 2.88% Fin Fut Us 5yr Cbt 03/29/19 United States Treasury Notes 2.62% Fin Fut Us 10yr Cbt 03/20/19

WisdomTree U.S. Earnings 500 Fund   C   HOLD

Ticker	Traded On	NAV	Total Assets ($)	Dividend Yield (TTM)	Turnover Ratio	Expense Ratio
EPS	NYSE Arca	28.19	$222,189,812	1.74	17	0.28

Ratings
Reward   C
Risk   C-
Recent Upgrade/Downgrade

Fund Information
Fund Type	Exchange Traded Funds
Category	US Equity Large Cap Blend
Sub-Category	Large Blend
Prospectus Objective	Growth & Inc
Inception Date	Feb-07
Open to New Investments	Y

Prices
Price (as of 12/31/2018)	28.20
52-Week High	33.13
52-Week Low	26.55

Total Returns (%)
3-Month	6-Month	1-Year	3-Year	5-Year
-13.31	-7.23	-7.31	29.33	44.36

3-Year Standard Deviation	9.47
Effective Duration	

Valuation
Premium/Discount (1-Year Average)	0.05

Company Information
Provider	WisdomTree
Manager/Tenure	Richard A. Brown (10), Thomas J. Durante (10), Karen Q. Wong (10)
Website	http://www.wisdomtree.com
Address	WisdomTree 245 Park Avenue, 35th floor New York NY 10167 United States
Phone Number	866-909-9473

PERFORMANCE

Ratings History
Date	Overall Rating	Risk Rating	Reward Rating
Q4-18	C	C-	C
Q2-18	C	C-	C
Q4-17	B	B-	B
Q4-16	C+	D+	B
Q4-15	C	C-	C

Asset & Performance History
Date	NAV	1-Year Total Return
2017	30.99	22.54
2016	25.73	13.87
2015	23.08	-1.65
2014	23.97	13.48
2013	21.49	32.56
2012	16.5	15.27

Total Assets: $222,189,812

Asset Allocation
Asset	%
Cash	0%
Stocks	100%
US Stocks	100%
Bonds	0%
US Bonds	0%
Other	0%

Services Offered:

Investment Strategy: The investment seeks to track the price and yield performance, before fees and expenses, of the WisdomTree U.S. Earnings 500 Index. Under normal circumstances, at least 95% of the fund's total assets (exclusive of collateral held from securities lending) will be invested in component securities of the index and investments that have economic characteristics that are substantially identical to the economic characteristics of such component securities. The index is a fundamentally weighted index that is comprised of earnings-generating companies within the large-capitalization segment of the U.S. Stock Market. The fund is non-diversified. **Top Holdings:** Apple Inc Microsoft Corp JPMorgan Chase & Co Alphabet Inc A Berkshire Hathaway Inc B

WisdomTree Managed Futures Strategy Fund   D+   SELL

Ticker	Traded On	NAV	Total Assets ($)	Dividend Yield (TTM)	Turnover Ratio	Expense Ratio
WTMF	NYSE Arca	38.79	$220,967,699	0	0	0.65

Ratings

Reward	D+
Risk	C-
Recent Upgrade/Downgrade	

Fund Information

Fund Type	Exchange Traded Funds
Category	Alternative Misc
Sub-Category	Managed Futures
Prospectus Objective	Growth & Inc
Inception Date	Jan-11
Open to New Investments	Y

Prices

Price (as of 12/31/2018)	38.76
52-Week High	41.50
52-Week Low	38.76

Total Returns (%)

3-Month	6-Month	1-Year	3-Year	5-Year
-1.69	0.54	0.32	-3.87	-3.10

3-Year Standard Deviation	4.47
Effective Duration	

Valuation

Premium/Discount (1-Year Average)	0.01

Company Information

Provider	WisdomTree
Manager/Tenure	Vassilis Dagioglu (7), James H. Stavena (7)
Website	http://www.wisdomtree.com
Address	WisdomTree 245 Park Avenue, 35th floor New York NY 10167 United States
Phone Number	866-909-9473

PERFORMANCE

Ratings History

Date	Overall Rating	Risk Rating	Reward Rating
Q4-18	D+	C-	D+
Q2-18	D+	C-	D+
Q4-17	D	C-	D
Q4-16	D+	C-	D+
Q4-15	C-	C-	C-

Asset & Performance History

Date	NAV	1-Year Total Return
2017	40.05	-3.21
2016	41.38	-1
2015	41.8	-4.06
2014	43.58	5.07
2013	41.47	2.75
2012	40.36	-11

Total Assets: $220,967,699

Asset Allocation

Asset	%
Cash	128%
Stocks	0%
US Stocks	0%
Bonds	-15%
US Bonds	-15%
Other	-13%

Services Offered:

Investment Strategy: The investment seeks to provide investors with positive total returns in rising or falling markets. The fund normally invests at least 80% of its net assets, plus the amount of any borrowings for investment purposes, in "managed futures". It is an actively managed exchange traded fund ("ETF") that seeks to achieve positive total returns in rising or falling markets that are not directly correlated to broad market equity or fixed income returns. The fund is managed using a quantitative, rules-based strategy designed to provide returns that correspond to the performance of the WisdomTree Managed Futures Index. It is non-diversified. **Top Holdings:** Wt Cayman Managed Futures Mutual Funds   Us Long Bond(Cbt) Mar19 Xcbt 20190320   Us 10yr Note (Cbt)mar19 Xcbt 20190320   Silver Future Mar19 Xcec 20190327   Wheat Future(Cbt) Mar19 Xcbt 20190314

UBS ETRACS Monthly Pay 2xLeveraged Closed-End Fund ETN   C-   HOLD

Ticker	Traded On	NAV	Total Assets ($)	Dividend Yield (TTM)	Turnover Ratio	Expense Ratio
CEFL	NYSE Arca	11.97	$220,555,300	19.96		0.5

Ratings

Reward	D+
Risk	C
Recent Upgrade/Downgrade	Down

Fund Information

Fund Type	Exchange Traded Funds
Category	Trading Tools
Sub-Category	Trading--Miscellaneous
Prospectus Objective	Growth & Inc
Inception Date	Dec-13
Open to New Investments	Y

Prices

Price (as of 12/31/2018)	11.94
52-Week High	18.22
52-Week Low	11.05

Total Returns (%)

3-Month	6-Month	1-Year	3-Year	5-Year
-20.71	-15.39	-21.53	30.60	11.22

3-Year Standard Deviation	18.07
Effective Duration	

Valuation

Premium/Discount (1-Year Average)	0.44

Company Information

Provider	UBS Group AG
Manager/Tenure	No Manager (4)
Website	http://www.ubs.com
Address	Bahnhofstrasse 45 Zurich 8098 Switzerland
Phone Number	412-037-1952

PERFORMANCE

Ratings History

Date	Overall Rating	Risk Rating	Reward Rating
Q4-18	C-	C	D+
Q2-18	C-	C-	C
Q4-17	B-	C	B
Q4-16	C-	C-	D+
Q4-15	D	D	D

Asset & Performance History

Date	NAV	1-Year Total Return
2017	18.08	27.5
2016	16.61	30.37
2015	15.56	-17.03
2014	22.78	2.64
2013	26.42	
2012		

Total Assets: $220,555,300

Asset Allocation

Asset	%
Cash	%
Stocks	%
US Stocks	%
Bonds	%
US Bonds	%
Other	%

Services Offered:

Investment Strategy: The investment seeks a return linked to the performance of the price return version of the ISE High Income™ Index.
The ETRACS Monthly Pay 2xLeveraged Closed-End Fund ETN due December 10, 2043 (the "Securities") are a series of Monthly Pay 2xLeveraged Exchange Traded Access Securities (ETRACS) linked to the price return. The index measures the performance of 30 U.S. closed-end funds, as selected and ranked by the index sponsor in accordance with the index methodology. **Top Holdings:**

SPDR® Bloomberg Barclays Mortgage Backed Bond ETF　　　　　　　D+　　SELL

Ticker	Traded On	NAV	Total Assets ($)	Dividend Yield (TTM)	Turnover Ratio	Expense Ratio
MBG	NYSE Arca	25.41	$218,374,028	3.36	323	0.06

Ratings
Reward　　　　　　　　　　　D+
Risk　　　　　　　　　　　　C-
Recent Upgrade/Downgrade

Fund Information
Fund Type　　　　　　　　Exchange Traded Funds
Category　　　　　　　　　US Fixed Income
Sub-Category　　　　Intermediate Government
Prospectus Objective　　Govt Bond - Mortgage
Inception Date　　　　　　　Jan-09
Open to New Investments　　　　Y

Prices
Price (as of 12/31/2018)　　　25.41
52-Week High　　　　　　　　26.02
52-Week Low　　　　　　　　24.78

Total Returns (%)

3-Month	6-Month	1-Year	3-Year	5-Year
2.11	2.05	0.87	4.42	11.96

3-Year Standard Deviation　　　　2.09
Effective Duration　　　　　　　5.49

Valuation
Premium/Discount (1-Year Average)　　-0.02

Company Information
Provider　　　SPDR State Street Global Advisors
Manager/Tenure　Marc DiCosimo (5), Michael Przygoda
　　　　　　(4), Nicholas Fischer (0)
Website　　　http://www.spdrs.com
Address　　　SPDR State Street Global Advisors
　　　　　　State Street Financial Center, 1
　　　　　　Lincoln Street Boston MA 02111-2900
　　　　　　United States
Phone Number　617-786-3000

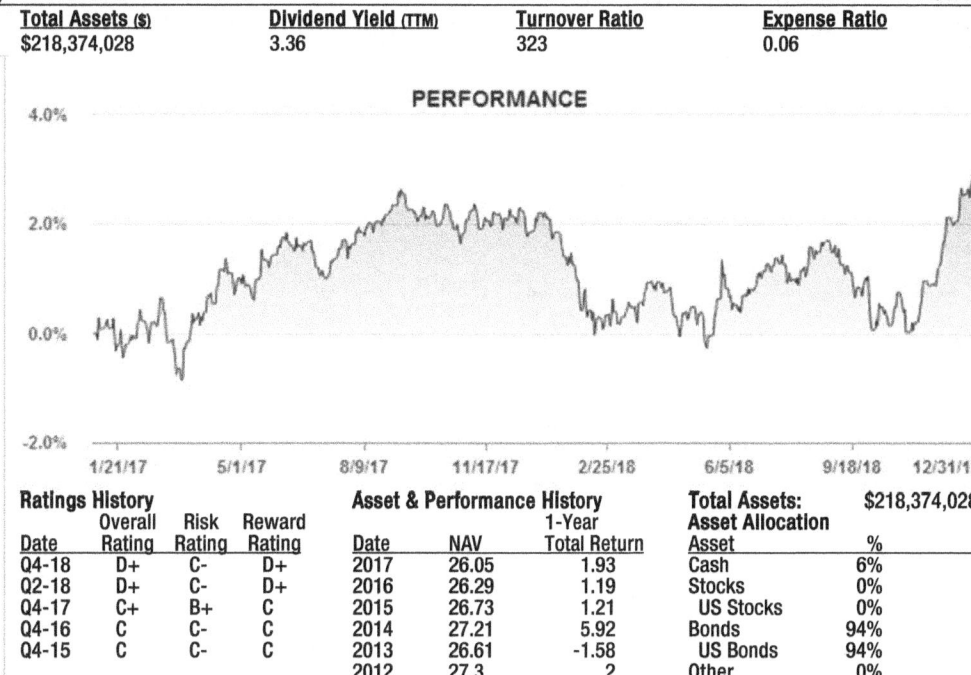
PERFORMANCE

Ratings History

Date	Overall Rating	Risk Rating	Reward Rating
Q4-18	D+	C-	D+
Q2-18	D+	C-	D+
Q4-17	C+	B+	C
Q4-16	C	C-	C
Q4-15	C	C-	C

Asset & Performance History

Date	NAV	1-Year Total Return
2017	26.05	1.93
2016	26.29	1.19
2015	26.73	1.21
2014	27.21	5.92
2013	26.61	-1.58
2012	27.3	2

Total Assets: $218,374,028
Asset Allocation

Asset	%
Cash	6%
Stocks	0%
US Stocks	0%
Bonds	94%
US Bonds	94%
Other	0%

Services Offered:

Investment Strategy: The investment seeks to provide investment results that, before fees and expenses, correspond generally to the price and yield performance of the Bloomberg Barclays U.S. MBS Index. The fund generally invests substantially all, but at least 80%, of its total assets in the securities comprising the index or in securities that the Adviser determines have economic characteristics that are substantially identical to the economic characteristics of the securities that comprise the index. The index is designed to measure the performance of the U.S. agency mortgage pass-through segment of the U.S. investment grade bond market. The fund is non-diversified. **Top Holdings:** Government National Mortgage Association 3.5% Government National Mortgage Association 3% Government National Mortgage Association 4% Federal National Mortgage Association 3% Government National Mortgage Association 3.5%

iShares Global Consumer Discretionary ETF　　　　　　　　　　　　C　　HOLD

Ticker	Traded On	NAV	Total Assets ($)	Dividend Yield (TTM)	Turnover Ratio	Expense Ratio
RXI	NYSE Arca	100.91	$218,027,554	1.52	6	0.47

Ratings
Reward　　　　　　　　　　　C
Risk　　　　　　　　　　　　C-
Recent Upgrade/Downgrade　　Down

Fund Information
Fund Type　　　　　　　　Exchange Traded Funds
Category　　　　　　　Consumer Goods & Svcs
Sub-Category　　　　　Consumer Cyclical
Prospectus Objective　　　　Unaligned
Inception Date　　　　　　　Sep-06
Open to New Investments　　　　Y

Prices
Price (as of 12/31/2018)　　　100.89
52-Week High　　　　　　　　120.77
52-Week Low　　　　　　　　94.89

Total Returns (%)

3-Month	6-Month	1-Year	3-Year	5-Year
-15.35	-10.98	-6.19	18.39	29.77

3-Year Standard Deviation　　　　11.79
Effective Duration

Valuation
Premium/Discount (1-Year Average)　　-0.04

Company Information
Provider　　　iShares
Manager/Tenure　Diane Hsiung (10), Greg Savage (10),
　　　　　　Jennifer Hsui (6), 3 others
Website　　　http://www.ishares.com
Address　　　iShares 400 Howard Street San
　　　　　　Francisco CA 94105 United States
Phone Number　800-474-2737

PERFORMANCE

Ratings History

Date	Overall Rating	Risk Rating	Reward Rating
Q4-18	C	C-	C
Q2-18	C	C-	B-
Q4-17	B	A-	B
Q4-16	C	C-	B-
Q4-15	C	C	C+

Asset & Performance History

Date	NAV	1-Year Total Return
2017	109.29	22.61
2016	90.32	2.94
2015	89.32	5.62
2014	85.53	3.77
2013	83.86	38.44
2012	61.42	24.58

Total Assets: $218,027,554
Asset Allocation

Asset	%
Cash	0%
Stocks	100%
US Stocks	61%
Bonds	0%
US Bonds	0%
Other	0%

Services Offered:

Investment Strategy: The investment seeks to track the S&P Global 1200 Consumer Discretionary IndexTM. The fund generally invests at least 90% of its assets in securities of the underlying index and in depositary receipts representing securities of the underlying index. It may invest the remainder of its assets in certain futures, options and swap contracts, cash and cash equivalents, as well as in securities not included in the underlying index. The index measures the performance of companies that the index provider deems to be part of the consumer discretionary sector of the economy and that the index provider believes are important to global markets. **Top Holdings:** Amazon.com Inc The Home Depot Inc Toyota Motor Corp McDonald's Corp Nike Inc B

iShares MSCI USA Equal Weighted ETF   C-   HOLD

Ticker	Traded On	NAV	Total Assets ($)	Dividend Yield (TTM)	Turnover Ratio	Expense Ratio
EUSA	NYSE Arca	50.00	$217,675,023	1.72	23	0.15

Ratings
Reward   C-
Risk   C-
Recent Upgrade/Downgrade   Down

Fund Information
Fund Type   Exchange Traded Funds
Category   US Equity Large Cap Blend
Sub-Category   Large Blend
Prospectus Objective   Growth
Inception Date   May-10
Open to New Investments   Y

Prices
Price (as of 12/31/2018)   49.79
52-Week High   59.92
52-Week Low   47.02

Total Returns (%)

3-Month	6-Month	1-Year	3-Year	5-Year
-14.74	-10.43	-8.23	24.67	38.04

3-Year Standard Deviation   10.37
Effective Duration

Valuation
Premium/Discount (1-Year Average)   0.05

Company Information
Provider   iShares
Manager/Tenure   Diane Hsiung (8), Greg Savage (8),
                     Jennifer Hsui (5), 1 other
Website   http://www.ishares.com
Address   iShares 400 Howard Street San
                     Francisco CA 94105 United States
Phone Number   800-474-2737

PERFORMANCE

Ratings History

Date	Overall Rating	Risk Rating	Reward Rating
Q4-18	C-	C-	C-
Q2-18	C	C-	C
Q4-17	B-	B-	B-
Q4-16	C+	D+	B
Q4-15	C	C-	C

Asset & Performance History

Date	NAV	1-Year Total Return
2017	55.44	19.09
2016	47.3	14.07
2015	42.16	-2.17
2014	44.04	13.19
2013	39.69	32.38
2012	30.63	15.93

Total Assets: $217,675,023
Asset Allocation

Asset	%
Cash	0%
Stocks	100%
US Stocks	98%
Bonds	0%
US Bonds	0%
Other	0%

Services Offered:

Investment Strategy: The investment seeks to track the investment results of the MSCI USA Equal Weighted Index. The fund generally will invest at least 90% of its assets in the component securities of the underlying index and may invest up to 10% of its assets in certain futures, options and swap contracts, cash and cash equivalents. The index is an equally-weighted securities index that measures the performance of equity securities in the top 85% by market capitalization of equity securities listed on stock exchanges in the United States and which represents an alternative weighting scheme to its market capitalization-weighted parent index, the MSCI USA Index. **Top Holdings:** Workday Inc Class A Splunk Inc Wayfair Inc Class A Salesforce.com Inc Zillow Group Inc C

Invesco S&P 500® Equal Weight Industrials ETF   C   HOLD

Ticker	Traded On	NAV	Total Assets ($)	Dividend Yield (TTM)	Turnover Ratio	Expense Ratio
RGI	NYSE Arca	103.40	$217,436,862	1.08		0.4

Ratings
Reward   C
Risk   C-
Recent Upgrade/Downgrade

Fund Information
Fund Type   Exchange Traded Funds
Category   Industrials Sector Equity
Sub-Category   Industrials
Prospectus Objective   Unaligned
Inception Date   Nov-06
Open to New Investments   Y

Prices
Price (as of 12/31/2018)   103.29
52-Week High   129.25
52-Week Low   96.98

Total Returns (%)

3-Month	6-Month	1-Year	3-Year	5-Year
-17.75	-9.22	-12.98	30.07	35.19

3-Year Standard Deviation   13.79
Effective Duration

Valuation
Premium/Discount (1-Year Average)   0.04

Company Information
Provider   Invesco
Manager/Tenure   Peter Hubbard (0), Michael Jeanette
                     (0), Jonathan Nixon (0), 1 other
Website   http://www.invesco.com/us
Address   Invesco 11 Greenway Plaza, Ste. 2500
                     Houston TX 77046 United States
Phone Number   800-659-1005

PERFORMANCE

Ratings History

Date	Overall Rating	Risk Rating	Reward Rating
Q4-18	C	C-	C
Q2-18	C	C-	C
Q4-17	B+	B	A-
Q4-16	B-	C-	B
Q4-15	C	C-	C

Asset & Performance History

Date	NAV	1-Year Total Return
2017	120.47	22.99
2016	99.08	20.94
2015	82.75	-6.85
2014	90.15	11.58
2013	81.87	39.47
2012	59.3	16.49

Total Assets: $217,436,862
Asset Allocation

Asset	%
Cash	1%
Stocks	99%
US Stocks	97%
Bonds	0%
US Bonds	0%
Other	0%

Services Offered:

Investment Strategy: The investment seeks to track the investment results (before fees and expenses) of the S&P 500® Equal Weight Industrials Index (the "underlying index"). The fund generally will invest at least 90% of its total assets in the securities that comprise the underlying index. The underlying index is an equal-weighted version of the S&P 500® Industrials Index. Strictly in accordance with its guidelines and mandated procedures, the index provider compiles, maintains and calculates the underlying index, which is comprised of common stocks of companies in the industrials sector of the S&P 500® Index. The fund is non-diversified. **Top Holdings:** United Technologies Corp United Continental Holdings Inc Alaska Air Group Inc Cummins Inc Deere & Co

Strategy Shares US Market Rotation Strategy ETF   C-   HOLD

Ticker	Traded On	NAV	Total Assets ($)	Dividend Yield (TTM)	Turnover Ratio	Expense Ratio
HUSE	NYSE Arca	33.56	$216,942,259	0.02	1,989	1.13

Ratings
Reward   C
Risk   C-
Recent Upgrade/Downgrade   Down

Fund Information
Fund Type   Exchange Traded Funds
Category   US Equity Large Cap Blend
Sub-Category   Large Blend
Prospectus Objective Growth
Inception Date   Jul-12
Open to New Investments Y

Prices
Price (as of 12/31/2018)   33.53
52-Week High   41.49
52-Week Low   33.49

Total Returns (%)

3-Month	6-Month	1-Year	3-Year	5-Year
-15.31	-13.21	-9.56	9.55	25.76

3-Year Standard Deviation   9.29
Effective Duration

Valuation
Premium/Discount (1-Year Average)   0.14

Company Information
Provider   Strategy shares
Manager/Tenure   Matthew B. Tuttle (2)
Website
Address   Strategy shares United States
Phone Number

PERFORMANCE

Ratings History

Date	Overall Rating	Risk Rating	Reward Rating
Q4-18	C-	C-	C
Q2-18	C	D+	C+
Q4-17	B	A	C+
Q4-16	C	D+	B-
Q4-15	C-	D	C

Asset & Performance History

Date	NAV	1-Year Total Return
2017	38.25	13.27
2016	36.1	6.62
2015	37.35	2.49
2014	37.39	12
2013	35.02	33.64
2012	26.54	

Total Assets: $216,942,259
Asset Allocation

Asset	%
Cash	33%
Stocks	66%
US Stocks	65%
Bonds	0%
US Bonds	0%
Other	1%

Services Offered:

Investment Strategy: The investment seeks capital appreciation. Under normal circumstances, at least 80% of the fund's net assets, plus any borrowings for investment purposes, will be invested in securities of U.S. companies and/or the U.S. government, or in other investment companies that principally invest in such securities. It will invest in companies within each of the large-cap, mid-cap and small-cap U.S. equity segments (each a "Market Segment"). **Top Holdings:** ServiceNow Inc Booking Holdings Inc Berkshire Hathaway Inc B Comcast Corp Class A JPMorgan Chase & Co

---

Invesco India ETF   D+   SELL

Ticker	Traded On	NAV	Total Assets ($)	Dividend Yield (TTM)	Turnover Ratio	Expense Ratio
PIN	NYSE Arca	24.08	$216,246,449	0	27	0.79

Ratings
Reward   D+
Risk   C-
Recent Upgrade/Downgrade   Down

Fund Information
Fund Type   Exchange Traded Funds
Category   India Equity
Sub-Category   India Equity
Prospectus Objective Foreign Stock
Inception Date   Mar-08
Open to New Investments Y

Prices
Price (as of 12/31/2018)   24.17
52-Week High   27.85
52-Week Low   21.45

Total Returns (%)

3-Month	6-Month	1-Year	3-Year	5-Year
1.07	-0.66	-8.09	26.16	44.69

3-Year Standard Deviation   17.72
Effective Duration

Valuation
Premium/Discount (1-Year Average)   -0.07

Company Information
Provider   Invesco
Manager/Tenure   Peter Hubbard (10), Jonathan Nixon
                    (5), Michael Jeanette (3), 1 other
Website   http://www.invesco.com/us
Address   Invesco 11 Greenway Plaza, Ste. 2500
                    Houston TX 77046 United States
Phone Number   800-659-1005

PERFORMANCE

Ratings History

Date	Overall Rating	Risk Rating	Reward Rating
Q4-18	D+	C-	D+
Q2-18	C-	C-	C
Q4-17	B-	C	B
Q4-16	C	C	C
Q4-15	C	C+	C

Asset & Performance History

Date	NAV	1-Year Total Return
2017	26.46	37.11
2016	19.52	0.11
2015	19.73	-5.91
2014	21.09	21.89
2013	17.48	-4.14
2012	18.33	13.52

Total Assets: $216,246,449
Asset Allocation

Asset	%
Cash	1%
Stocks	99%
US Stocks	0%
Bonds	0%
US Bonds	0%
Other	0%

Services Offered:

Investment Strategy: The investment seeks to track the investment results (before fees and expenses) of the Indus India Index (the "underlying index"). The fund seeks to achieve its investment objective by investing at least 90% of its total assets in securities of Indian companies that comprise the underlying index, as well as American depositary receipts ("ADRs") and global depositary receipts ("GDRs") based on the securities in the underlying index. The underlying index is designed to represent the large-cap segment of the Indian equity markets. The fund is non-diversified. **Top Holdings:** Reliance Industries Ltd Infosys Ltd Housing Development Finance Corp Ltd Hindustan Unilever Ltd Tata Consultancy Services Ltd

Invesco Global Listed Private Equity ETF   C-   HOLD

Ticker	Traded On	NAV	Total Assets ($)	Dividend Yield (TTM)	Turnover Ratio	Expense Ratio
PSP	NYSE Arca	10.04	$213,175,549	9.54	44	2.03

Ratings
Reward   D+
Risk   C-
Recent Upgrade/Downgrade   Down

Fund Information
Fund Type   Exchange Traded Funds
Category   Financials Sector Equity
Sub-Category   World Small/Mid Stock
Prospectus Objective   Growth
Inception Date   Oct-06
Open to New Investments   Y

Prices
Price (as of 12/31/2018)   10.01
52-Week High   13.52
52-Week Low   9.72

Total Returns (%)

3-Month	6-Month	1-Year	3-Year	5-Year
-18.70	-14.22	-14.91	16.29	13.41

3-Year Standard Deviation   13.91
Effective Duration

Valuation
Premium/Discount (1-Year Average)   -0.02

Company Information
Provider   Invesco
Manager/Tenure Peter Hubbard (11), Jonathan Nixon
                (5), Michael Jeanette (3), 1 other
Website   http://www.invesco.com/us
Address   Invesco 11 Greenway Plaza, Ste. 2500
                Houston TX 77046 United States
Phone Number   800-659-1005

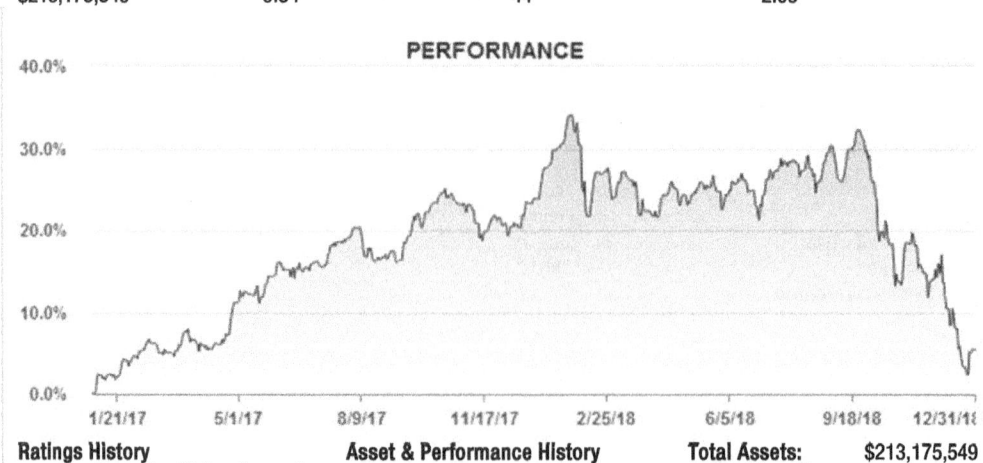

PERFORMANCE

Ratings History

Date	Overall Rating	Risk Rating	Reward Rating
Q4-18	C-	C-	D+
Q2-18	C	C+	C
Q4-17	B	C+	B
Q4-16	C	C-	C
Q4-15	C+	C+	C

Asset & Performance History

Date	NAV	1-Year Total Return
2017	12.46	23.9
2016	11.13	10.31
2015	10.53	1.14
2014	11.01	-3.58
2013	11.97	37.1
2012	10.04	28.41

Total Assets: $213,175,549

Asset Allocation

Asset	%
Cash	12%
Stocks	76%
US Stocks	32%
Bonds	0%
US Bonds	0%
Other	12%

Services Offered:

Investment Strategy: The investment seeks to track the investment results (before fees and expenses) of the Red Rocks Global Listed Private Equity Index. The fund generally will invest at least 90% of its total assets in securities (including American depositary receipts ("ADRs") and global depositary receipts ("GDRs")) that comprise the underlying index. The underlying index is composed of securities, ADRs and GDRs of 40 to 75 private equity companies, including business development companies ("BDCs"), master limited partnerships ("MLPs") and other vehicles. **Top Holdings:** Naspers Ltd Class N Ps Citi Blackstone Trs 10/23/15 Financing Leg Ps Citi Blackstone Trs 10/23/15 Asset Leg Partners Group Holding AG IAC/InterActiveCorp

---

Invesco Global Short Term High Yield Bond ETF   C   HOLD

Ticker	Traded On	NAV	Total Assets ($)	Dividend Yield (TTM)	Turnover Ratio	Expense Ratio
PGHY	NYSE Arca	22.82	$211,618,209	5.4	38	0.35

Ratings
Reward   C
Risk   C-
Recent Upgrade/Downgrade

Fund Information
Fund Type   Exchange Traded Funds
Category   Global Fixed Income
Sub-Category   High Yield Bond
Prospectus Objective   Worldwide Bond
Inception Date   Jun-13
Open to New Investments   Y

Prices
Price (as of 12/31/2018)   22.70
52-Week High   24.03
52-Week Low   22.65

Total Returns (%)

3-Month	6-Month	1-Year	3-Year	5-Year
-1.00	0.09	0.61	17.55	18.65

3-Year Standard Deviation   2.44
Effective Duration   1.25

Valuation
Premium/Discount (1-Year Average)   -0.14

Company Information
Provider   Invesco
Manager/Tenure Philip Fang (5), Peter Hubbard (5),
                Gary Jones (5), 2 others
Website   http://www.invesco.com/us
Address   Invesco 11 Greenway Plaza, Ste. 2500
                Houston TX 77046 United States
Phone Number   800-659-1005

PERFORMANCE

Ratings History

Date	Overall Rating	Risk Rating	Reward Rating
Q4-18	C	C-	C
Q2-18	C	C-	C
Q4-17	B	A-	C+
Q4-16	C	C-	C+
Q4-15	D+	C-	D

Asset & Performance History

Date	NAV	1-Year Total Return
2017	23.91	3.87
2016	24.3	12.48
2015	23.04	3.03
2014	23.39	-2.03
2013	24.9	
2012		

Total Assets: $211,618,209

Asset Allocation

Asset	%
Cash	7%
Stocks	0%
US Stocks	0%
Bonds	92%
US Bonds	43%
Other	1%

Services Offered:

Investment Strategy: The investment seeks investment results that correspond to the DB Global Short Maturity High Yield Bond Index. The fund will invest at least 80% of its total assets in U.S. and foreign short-term, non-investment grade bonds that comprise the index. The index provider selects such bonds issued by corporations, as well as sovereign, sub-sovereign or quasi-government entities, from a universe of eligible securities that: are denominated in USD; are rated below investment grade; have not been marked as defaulted by any rating agency; have three years or less to maturity; have a minimum amount outstanding of $250 million; and have a fixed coupon. **Top Holdings:** China SCE Group Holdings Limited 7.45% Banco Votorantim S.A. 7.38% CSN Islands XI Corp. 6.88% Nine West Holdings Inc 8.25% Controladora Mabe S.A.de CV 7.88%

iShares Interest Rate Hedged Corporate Bond ETF   C-   HOLD

Ticker	Traded On	NAV	Total Assets ($)	Dividend Yield (TTM)	Turnover Ratio	Expense Ratio
LQDH	NYSE Arca	90.86	$211,330,650	3.07	0	0.24

Ratings
Reward   C-
Risk   C-
Recent Upgrade/Downgrade   Down

Fund Information
Fund Type   Exchange Traded Funds
Category   US Fixed Income
Sub-Category   Corporate Bond
Prospectus Objective Growth & Inc
Inception Date   May-14
Open to New Investments   Y

Prices
Price (as of 12/31/2018)   90.67
52-Week High   98.72
52-Week Low   90.67

Total Returns (%)

3-Month	6-Month	1-Year	3-Year	5-Year
-3.96	-1.71	-2.07	9.37	

3-Year Standard Deviation   4.12
Effective Duration   0.12

Valuation
Premium/Discount (1-Year Average)   0.05

Company Information
Provider   iShares
Manager/Tenure James Mauro (4), Scott Radell (4)
Website   http://www.ishares.com
Address   iShares 400 Howard Street San
                Francisco CA 94105 United States
Phone Number   800-474-2737

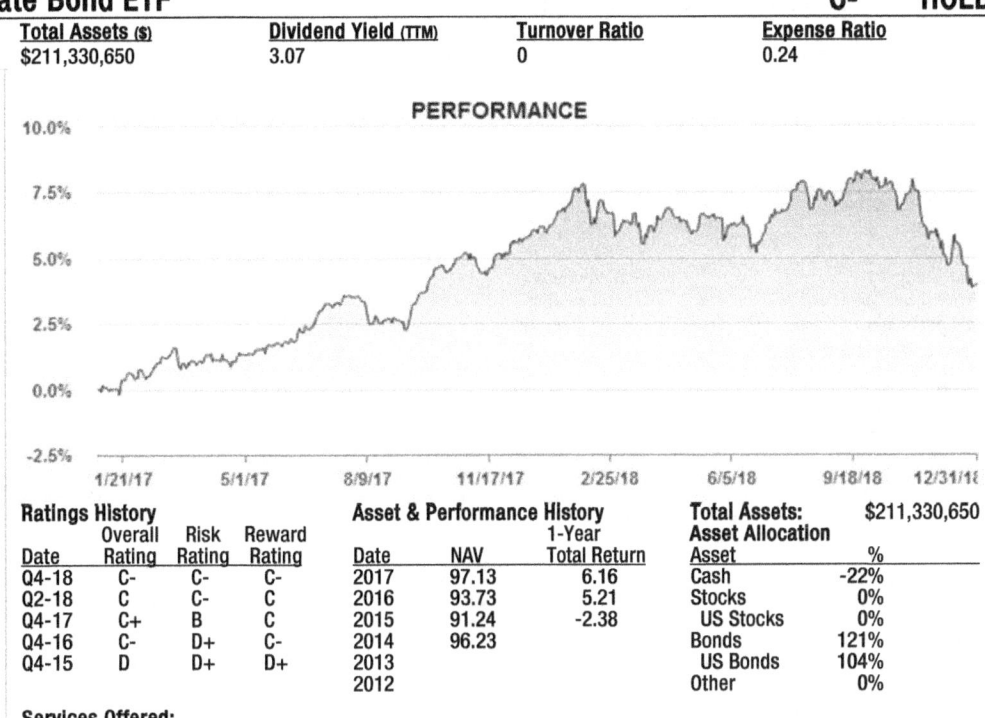

PERFORMANCE

Ratings History

Date	Overall Rating	Risk Rating	Reward Rating
Q4-18	C-	C-	C-
Q2-18	C	C-	C
Q4-17	C+	B	C
Q4-16	C-	D+	C-
Q4-15	D	D+	D+

Asset & Performance History

Date	NAV	1-Year Total Return
2017	97.13	6.16
2016	93.73	5.21
2015	91.24	-2.38
2014	96.23	
2013		
2012		

Total Assets: $211,330,650

Asset Allocation

Asset	%
Cash	-22%
Stocks	0%
US Stocks	0%
Bonds	121%
US Bonds	104%
Other	0%

Services Offered:

Investment Strategy: The investment seeks to mitigate the interest rate risk of a portfolio composed of U.S. dollar-denominated, investment-grade corporate bonds. The fund seeks to invest, at least 80% of its net assets in U.S. dollar-denominated investment-grade bonds, in one or more underlying funds that principally invest in investment-grade bonds, and in U.S. Treasury securities (or cash equivalents). It is an actively managed exchange-traded fund that does not seek to replicate the performance of a specified index. **Top Holdings:** iShares iBoxx $ Invmt Grade Corp Bd ETF Swp: Usd 2.705500 18-Sep-2035 Swp: Usd 2.300500 18-Sep-2025 Swp: Usd 1.638500 18-Sep-2020 Swp: Usd 2.806500 18-Sep-2045

Invesco S&P 500® Equal Weight Energy ETF   C   HOLD

Ticker	Traded On	NAV	Total Assets ($)	Dividend Yield (TTM)	Turnover Ratio	Expense Ratio
RYE	NYSE Arca	43.18	$210,808,144	1.8		0.4

Ratings
Reward   C+
Risk   D+
Recent Upgrade/Downgrade

Fund Information
Fund Type   Exchange Traded Funds
Category   Energy Sector Equity
Sub-Category   Equity Energy
Prospectus Objective Natl Res
Inception Date   Nov-06
Open to New Investments   Y

Prices
Price (as of 12/31/2018)   43.14
52-Week High   64.61
52-Week Low   40.29

Total Returns (%)

3-Month	6-Month	1-Year	3-Year	5-Year
-30.93	-28.85	-24.45	-2.78	-41.00

3-Year Standard Deviation   24.37
Effective Duration

Valuation
Premium/Discount (1-Year Average)   0.03

Company Information
Provider   Invesco
Manager/Tenure Peter Hubbard (0), Michael Jeanette
                (0), Jonathan Nixon (0), 1 other
Website   http://www.invesco.com/us
Address   Invesco 11 Greenway Plaza, Ste. 2500
                Houston TX 77046 United States
Phone Number   800-659-1005

PERFORMANCE

Ratings History

Date	Overall Rating	Risk Rating	Reward Rating
Q4-18	C	D+	C+
Q2-18	C	D+	C
Q4-17	D+	D+	D+
Q4-16	C-	D+	C-
Q4-15	C-	D+	C-

Asset & Performance History

Date	NAV	1-Year Total Return
2017	58.18	-6.49
2016	64.05	40.65
2015	47.09	-28.69
2014	67.58	-14.89
2013	80.71	26.62
2012	64.41	5.92

Total Assets: $210,808,144

Asset Allocation

Asset	%
Cash	0%
Stocks	100%
US Stocks	97%
Bonds	0%
US Bonds	0%
Other	0%

Services Offered:

Investment Strategy: The investment seeks to track the investment results (before fees and expenses) of the S&P 500® Equal Weight Energy Index (the "underlying index"). The fund generally will invest at least 90% of its total assets in the securities that comprise the underlying index. The underlying index is an equal-weighted version of the S&P 500® Energy Index. Strictly in accordance with its guidelines and mandated procedures, the index provider compiles, maintains and calculates the underlying index, which is comprised of common stocks of companies in the energy sector of the S&P 500® Index. The fund is non-diversified. **Top Holdings:** Cabot Oil & Gas Corp Class A Chevron Corp Exxon Mobil Corp Kinder Morgan Inc P Helmerich & Payne Inc

JPMorgan Diversified Alternative ETF
D   SELL

Ticker	Traded On	NAV	Total Assets ($)	Dividend Yield (TTM)	Turnover Ratio	Expense Ratio
JPHF	NYSE Arca	24.04	$209,172,828	0	107	0.85

Ratings
Reward	D
Risk	C-
Recent Upgrade/Downgrade	

Fund Information
Fund Type	Exchange Traded Funds
Category	Multialternative
Sub-Category	Multialternative
Prospectus Objective	Asset Allocation
Inception Date	Sep-16
Open to New Investments	Y

Prices
Price (as of 12/31/2018)	24.00
52-Week High	26.55
52-Week Low	23.72

Total Returns (%)
3-Month	6-Month	1-Year	3-Year	5-Year
-3.60	-3.76	-7.82		

3-Year Standard Deviation	
Effective Duration	

Valuation
Premium/Discount (1-Year Average)	0.15

Company Information
Provider	JPMorgan
Manager/Tenure	Wei (Victor) Li (2), Yazann Romahi (2)
Website	http://www.jpmorganfunds.com
Address	JPMorgan 270 Park Avenue New York NY 10017-2070 United States
Phone Number	800-480-4111

PERFORMANCE

Ratings History

Date	Overall Rating	Risk Rating	Reward Rating
Q4-18	D	C-	D
Q2-18	D	C-	D
Q4-17	D	B+	D+
Q4-16	U		
Q4-15			

Asset & Performance History

Date	NAV	1-Year Total Return
2017	26.08	2.11
2016	25.54	
2015		
2014		
2013		
2012		

Total Assets: $209,172,828

Asset Allocation

Asset	%
Cash	35%
Stocks	66%
US Stocks	61%
Bonds	0%
US Bonds	0%
Other	0%

Services Offered:

Investment Strategy: The investment seeks to provide long-term total return. The fund will seek to achieve its investment objective by allocating assets across several different investment strategies, including traditional and alternative investment strategies, such as those utilized by certain hedge funds. The strategies identified by the adviser for the fund fall into the following broad categories: Equity Long/Short, Event Driven and Macro/Managed Futures strategies. The fund will invest its assets based on a systematic investment process for securities selection and asset allocation. **Top Holdings:** Jpm Div Alts Cs Ltd Twenty-First Century Fox Inc Class A USG Corp Dun & Bradstreet Corp Vectren Corp

---

iShares US & Intl High Yield Corp Bond ETF
C-   HOLD

Ticker	Traded On	NAV	Total Assets ($)	Dividend Yield (TTM)	Turnover Ratio	Expense Ratio
GHYG	BATS	46.00	$208,417,488	5.59	22	0.4

Ratings
Reward	C-
Risk	C-
Recent Upgrade/Downgrade	Down

Fund Information
Fund Type	Exchange Traded Funds
Category	Global Fixed Income
Sub-Category	High Yield Bond
Prospectus Objective	Corp Bond-High Yld
Inception Date	Apr-12
Open to New Investments	Y

Prices
Price (as of 12/31/2018)	46.03
52-Week High	51.59
52-Week Low	45.07

Total Returns (%)
3-Month	6-Month	1-Year	3-Year	5-Year
-4.77	-2.21	-3.67	18.44	10.12

3-Year Standard Deviation	4.88
Effective Duration	3.84

Valuation
Premium/Discount (1-Year Average)	0.26

Company Information
Provider	iShares
Manager/Tenure	James Mauro (6), Scott Radell (6)
Website	http://www.ishares.com
Address	iShares 400 Howard Street San Francisco CA 94105 United States
Phone Number	800-474-2737

PERFORMANCE

Ratings History

Date	Overall Rating	Risk Rating	Reward Rating
Q4-18	C-	C-	C-
Q2-18	C	C-	C
Q4-17	C+	B-	C+
Q4-16	C-	D+	C
Q4-15	C-	D+	C-

Asset & Performance History

Date	NAV	1-Year Total Return
2017	50.36	8.37
2016	48.17	12.29
2015	44.96	-6.4
2014	50.21	-0.66
2013	53.34	7.78
2012	52.36	

Total Assets: $208,417,488

Asset Allocation

Asset	%
Cash	1%
Stocks	0%
US Stocks	0%
Bonds	99%
US Bonds	66%
Other	0%

Services Offered:

Investment Strategy: The investment seeks to track the investment results of the Markit iBoxx Global Developed Markets High Yield Index. The fund generally will invest at least 90% of its assets in the component securities of the underlying index and may invest up to 10% of its assets in certain futures, options and swap contracts, cash and cash equivalents, including shares of money market funds advised by BFA or its affiliates. The index is a rules-based index consisting of high yield corporate bonds denominated in U.S. dollars, euros, British pounds sterling and Canadian dollars. **Top Holdings:** ALTICE FRANCE S.A 7.38% Sprint Corporation 7.88% First Data Corporation 7% Altice Luxembourg S.A. 7.75% Reynolds Group Issuer LLC. 5.75%

WBI BullBear Global High Income ETF   D+   SELL

Ticker	Traded On	NAV	Total Assets ($)	Dividend Yield (TTM)	Turnover Ratio	Expense Ratio
WBIH	NYSE Arca	21.89	$208,349,889	3.48		1.23

Ratings

Reward	D+
Risk	C-
Recent Upgrade/Downgrade	Down

Fund Information

Fund Type	Exchange Traded Funds
Category	Cautious Allocation
Sub-Category	Allocation--15% to 30% Equity
Prospectus Objective	Income
Inception Date	Aug-14
Open to New Investments	Y

Prices

Price (as of 12/31/2018)	21.88
52-Week High	25.39
52-Week Low	21.71

Total Returns (%)

3-Month	6-Month	1-Year	3-Year	5-Year
-7.36	-6.71	-9.48	1.25	

3-Year Standard Deviation	4.3
Effective Duration	14.99

Valuation

Premium/Discount (1-Year Average)	-0.03

Company Information

Provider	WBI Investments
Manager/Tenure	Donald R. Schreiber (4), Gary E. Stroik (4)
Website	http://www.wbishares.com
Address	34 Sycamore Ave Suite 1-E Little Silver NJ 07739 United States
Phone Number	732-842-4920

PERFORMANCE

Ratings History

Date	Overall Rating	Risk Rating	Reward Rating
Q4-18	D+	C-	D+
Q2-18	C-	C-	C-
Q4-17	C+	B	C
Q4-16	C-	C-	C-
Q4-15	D-	C-	D+

Asset & Performance History

Date	NAV	1-Year Total Return
2017	24.94	7.99
2016	23.76	3.48
2015	23.29	-4.17
2014	24.8	
2013		
2012		

Total Assets: $208,349,889

Asset Allocation

Asset	%
Cash	19%
Stocks	32%
US Stocks	32%
Bonds	47%
US Bonds	45%
Other	0%

Services Offered:

Investment Strategy: The investment seeks high current income with the potential for long-term capital appreciation, while also seeking to protect principal during unfavorable market conditions. Under normal market conditions, the fund will invest at least 80% of its net assets, plus the amount of any borrowings for investment purposes, in income-producing debt and equity securities of foreign and domestic issuers, including the securities of foreign and domestic corporate and government entities. **Top Holdings:** Vanguard Long-Term Treasury ETF iShares 20+ Year Treasury Bond ETF Comcast Corp Class A Chevron Corp Verizon Communications Inc

---

DeltaShares S&P International Managed Risk ETF   D   SELL

Ticker	Traded On	NAV	Total Assets ($)	Dividend Yield (TTM)	Turnover Ratio	Expense Ratio
DMRI	NYSE Arca	44.94	$207,892,658	2.68	3	0.5

Ratings

Reward	D
Risk	D
Recent Upgrade/Downgrade	Down

Fund Information

Fund Type	Exchange Traded Funds
Category	Global Equity Large Cap
Sub-Category	Foreign Large Blend
Prospectus Objective	Foreign Stock
Inception Date	Jul-17
Open to New Investments	Y

Prices

Price (as of 12/31/2018)	45.41
52-Week High	56.64
52-Week Low	44.43

Total Returns (%)

3-Month	6-Month	1-Year	3-Year	5-Year
-11.56	-9.22	-13.30		

3-Year Standard Deviation	
Effective Duration	

Valuation

Premium/Discount (1-Year Average)	1.00

Company Information

Provider	DeltaShares
Manager/Tenure	Blake Graves (1), Charles Lowery (1), Louis Ng (1)
Website	http://www.deltashares.com
Address	DeltaShares United States
Phone Number	

PERFORMANCE

Ratings History

Date	Overall Rating	Risk Rating	Reward Rating
Q4-18	D	D	D
Q2-18	U		
Q4-17	U		
Q4-16			
Q4-15			

Asset & Performance History

Date	NAV	1-Year Total Return
2017	53.13	
2016		
2015		
2014		
2013		
2012		

Total Assets: $207,892,658

Asset Allocation

Asset	%
Cash	2%
Stocks	92%
US Stocks	1%
Bonds	7%
US Bonds	7%
Other	0%

Services Offered:

Investment Strategy: The investment seeks to track the investment results, before fees and expenses, of the S&P EPAC Ex. Korea LargeMidCap Managed Risk 2.0 Index. Under normal market conditions, the fund invests a substantial portion, but at least 80%, of its assets, exclusive of collateral held from securities lending, in securities comprising the underlying index. The underlying index seeks to achieve these objectives by allocating weightings among the S&P EPAC Ex. Korea LargeMidCap Index, the S&P U.S. Treasury Bond Current 5-Year Index and the S&P U.S. Treasury Bill 0-3 Month Index. The fund is non-diversified. **Top Holdings:** United States Treasury Notes 2.88% Nestle SA Novartis AG Msci Eafe Dec18 Ifus 20181221 Roche Holding AG Dividend Right Cert.

JPMorgan Diversified Return Global Equity ETF   C-   HOLD

Ticker	Traded On	NAV	Total Assets ($)	Dividend Yield (TTM)	Turnover Ratio	Expense Ratio
JPGE	NYSE Arca	54.49	$207,580,350	3.42	26	0.38

Ratings
Reward   D+
Risk   C-
Recent Upgrade/Downgrade   Down

Fund Information
Fund Type	Exchange Traded Funds
Category	Global Equity Large Cap
Sub-Category	World Large Stock
Prospectus Objective	Growth & Inc
Inception Date	Jun-14
Open to New Investments	Y

Prices
Price (as of 12/31/2018)	54.39
52-Week High	65.59
52-Week Low	52.65

Total Returns (%)
3-Month	6-Month	1-Year	3-Year	5-Year
-10.76	-7.72	-10.33	18.01	

3-Year Standard Deviation	9.16
Effective Duration	

Valuation
Premium/Discount (1-Year Average)	0.11

Company Information
Provider	JPMorgan
Manager/Tenure	Kartik Aiyar (1), Wei (Victor) Li (1), Yazann Romahi (1), 1 other
Website	http://www.jpmorganfunds.com
Address	JPMorgan 270 Park Avenue New York NY 10017-2070 United States
Phone Number	800-480-4111

PERFORMANCE

Ratings History
Date	Overall Rating	Risk Rating	Reward Rating
Q4-18	C-	C-	D+
Q2-18	C	C-	C
Q4-17	B	B+	B-
Q4-16	C-	D+	C
Q4-15	D	D+	D

Asset & Performance History
Date	NAV	1-Year Total Return
2017	62.18	24.41
2016	50.74	5.79
2015	49.03	3.51
2014	48.29	
2013		
2012		

Total Assets: $207,580,350
Asset Allocation
Asset	%
Cash	1%
Stocks	99%
US Stocks	26%
Bonds	0%
US Bonds	0%
Other	0%

Services Offered:

Investment Strategy: The investment seeks investment results that closely correspond, before fees and expenses, to the performance of the JP Morgan Diversified Factor Global Developed Equity Index. The index is comprised of equity securities across developed global markets selected to represent a diversified set of factor characteristics: value, price momentum and quality. The fund will invest at least 80% of its net assets in securities included in the index. **Top Holdings:** Sumitomo Dainippon Pharma Co Ltd Church & Dwight Co Inc Samsung Electronics Co Ltd Pfizer Inc Verizon Communications Inc

---

WisdomTree Dynamic Currency Hedged International Equity Fund   D+   SELL

Ticker	Traded On	NAV	Total Assets ($)	Dividend Yield (TTM)	Turnover Ratio	Expense Ratio
DDWM	BATS	26.08	$206,642,234	3.87		0.35

Ratings
Reward   D+
Risk   C-
Recent Upgrade/Downgrade   Down

Fund Information
Fund Type	Exchange Traded Funds
Category	Global Equity Large Cap
Sub-Category	Foreign Large Value
Prospectus Objective	Foreign Stock
Inception Date	Jan-16
Open to New Investments	Y

Prices
Price (as of 12/31/2018)	25.91
52-Week High	31.95
52-Week Low	25.36

Total Returns (%)
3-Month	6-Month	1-Year	3-Year	5-Year
-11.05	-7.91	-11.05	26.26	

3-Year Standard Deviation	
Effective Duration	

Valuation
Premium/Discount (1-Year Average)	0.11

Company Information
Provider	WisdomTree
Manager/Tenure	Richard A. Brown (2), Thomas J. Durante (2), Karen Q. Wong (2)
Website	http://www.wisdomtree.com
Address	WisdomTree 245 Park Avenue, 35th floor New York NY 10167 United States
Phone Number	866-909-9473

PERFORMANCE

Ratings History
Date	Overall Rating	Risk Rating	Reward Rating
Q4-18	D+	C-	D+
Q2-18	C	C+	C
Q4-17	C-	B+	C
Q4-16	D-	C-	D+
Q4-15			

Asset & Performance History
Date	NAV	1-Year Total Return
2017	30.51	18.53
2016	26.48	14.5
2015		
2014		
2013		
2012		

Total Assets: $206,642,234
Asset Allocation
Asset	%
Cash	0%
Stocks	100%
US Stocks	0%
Bonds	0%
US Bonds	0%
Other	0%

Services Offered:

Investment Strategy: The investment seeks to track the WisdomTree Dynamic Currency Hedged International Equity Index. The fund will invest at least 80% of its total assets in component securities of the index and investments that have economic characteristics that are substantially identical to the economic characteristics of such component securities. The index is a dividend weighted index designed to provide exposure to equity securities in the industrialized world, excluding Canada and the United States, while at the same time dynamically hedging currency exposure to fluctuations between the value of the applicable foreign currencies and the USD. The fund is non-diversified. **Top Holdings:** China Mobile Ltd Novartis AG Nestle SA HSBC Holdings PLC BP PLC

iShares MSCI Saudi Arabia ETF　　　　　　　　　　　　　　C-　　HOLD

Ticker	Traded On	NAV	Total Assets ($)	Dividend Yield (TTM)	Turnover Ratio	Expense Ratio
KSA	NYSE Arca	28.87	$205,666,884	2.17	20	0.74

Ratings
Reward　　　　　　　　　　　　　　　C-
Risk　　　　　　　　　　　　　　　　C-
Recent Upgrade/Downgrade　　　　Down

Fund Information
Fund Type　　　　　　　　Exchange Traded Funds
Category　　　　　　　　　　　　　Equity Misc
Sub-Category　　　　　　Miscellaneous Region
Prospectus Objective　　　　　　　　Growth
Inception Date　　　　　　　　　　　Sep-15
Open to New Investments　　　　　　　　Y

Prices
Price (as of 12/31/2018)　　　　　28.89
52-Week High　　　　　　　　　　31.96
52-Week Low　　　　　　　　　　26.00

Total Returns (%)

3-Month	6-Month	1-Year	3-Year	5-Year
-2.57	-4.60	15.29	32.43	

3-Year Standard Deviation　　　　18.37
Effective Duration

Valuation
Premium/Discount (1-Year Average)　　0.79

Company Information
Provider　　　　iShares
Manager/Tenure　Diane Hsiung (3), Jennifer Hsui (3), Greg Savage (3), 1 other
Website　　　　http://www.ishares.com
Address　　　　iShares 400 Howard Street San Francisco CA 94105 United States
Phone Number　800-474-2737

PERFORMANCE

Ratings History

Date	Overall Rating	Risk Rating	Reward Rating
Q4-18	C-	C-	C-
Q2-18	C+	C+	C+
Q4-17	C	C+	C-
Q4-16	D	D+	D+
Q4-15			

Asset & Performance History

Date	NAV	1-Year Total Return
2017	25.65	5.14
2016	24.98	9.23
2015	23.63	
2014		
2013		
2012		

Total Assets: $205,666,884

Asset Allocation

Asset	%
Cash	0%
Stocks	100%
US Stocks	0%
Bonds	0%
US Bonds	0%
Other	0%

Services Offered:

Investment Strategy: The investment seeks to track the investment results of the MSCI Saudi Arabia IMI 25/50 Index. The fund generally will invest at least 90% of its assets in the component securities of the index and in investments that have economic characteristics that are substantially identical to the component securities of the index. The index is a free float-adjusted market capitalization-weighted index with a capping methodology applied to issuer weights so that no single issuer of a component exceeds 25% of the index weight, and all issuers with a weight above 5% do not cumulatively exceed 50% of the index weight. The fund is non-diversified. **Top Holdings:** Saudi Basic Industries Corp　Al Rajhi Bank　The National Commercial Bank　Samba Financial Group　Saudi Telecom Co

---

iShares Global Industrials ETF　　　　　　　　　　　　　　C-　　HOLD

Ticker	Traded On	NAV	Total Assets ($)	Dividend Yield (TTM)	Turnover Ratio	Expense Ratio
EXI	NYSE Arca	77.91	$205,659,355	1.94	6	0.47

Ratings
Reward　　　　　　　　　　　　　　　C-
Risk　　　　　　　　　　　　　　　　C-
Recent Upgrade/Downgrade　　　　Down

Fund Information
Fund Type　　　　　　　　Exchange Traded Funds
Category　　　　　　　Industrials Sector Equity
Sub-Category　　　　　　　　　　Industrials
Prospectus Objective　　　　　　World Stock
Inception Date　　　　　　　　　　　Sep-06
Open to New Investments　　　　　　　　Y

Prices
Price (as of 12/31/2018)　　　　　77.92
52-Week High　　　　　　　　　　99.02
52-Week Low　　　　　　　　　　73.93

Total Returns (%)

3-Month	6-Month	1-Year	3-Year	5-Year
-16.45	-10.12	-14.31	20.91	20.25

3-Year Standard Deviation　　　　11.41
Effective Duration

Valuation
Premium/Discount (1-Year Average)　　-0.03

Company Information
Provider　　　　iShares
Manager/Tenure　Diane Hsiung (10), Greg Savage (10), Jennifer Hsui (6), 3 others
Website　　　　http://www.ishares.com
Address　　　　iShares 400 Howard Street San Francisco CA 94105 United States
Phone Number　800-474-2737

PERFORMANCE

Ratings History

Date	Overall Rating	Risk Rating	Reward Rating
Q4-18	C-	C-	C-
Q2-18	C	C-	C
Q4-17	B	B-	B
Q4-16	C	C-	C+
Q4-15	C	C	C

Asset & Performance History

Date	NAV	1-Year Total Return
2017	92.77	24.88
2016	75.45	13
2015	67.98	-2.17
2014	70.81	1.66
2013	70.97	31.97
2012	54.72	15.74

Total Assets: $205,659,355

Asset Allocation

Asset	%
Cash	1%
Stocks	99%
US Stocks	54%
Bonds	0%
US Bonds	0%
Other	0%

Services Offered:

Investment Strategy: The investment seeks to track the investment results of the S&P Global 1200 Industrials IndexTM. The fund generally invests at least 90% of its assets in securities of the underlying index and in depositary receipts representing securities of the underlying index. It may invest the remainder of its assets in certain futures, options and swap contracts, cash and cash equivalents, as well as in securities not included in the underlying index. The index measures the performance of companies that the index provider deems to be part of the industrials sector of the economy and that the index provider believes are important to global markets. **Top Holdings:** Boeing Co　3M Co　Union Pacific Corp　Honeywell International Inc　Siemens AG

UBS ETRACS 2xLeveraged Long Wells Fargo Business Development Company Index ETN   C   HOLD

Ticker	Traded On	NAV	Total Assets ($)	Dividend Yield (TTM)	Turnover Ratio	Expense Ratio
BDCL	NYSE Arca	11.59	$204,720,516	17.18		0.85

Ratings
Reward   C-
Risk   C
Recent Upgrade/Downgrade

Fund Information
Fund Type   Exchange Traded Funds
Category   Trading Tools
Sub-Category   Trading--Leveraged Equity
Prospectus Objective   Growth
Inception Date   May-11
Open to New Investments   Y

Prices
Price (as of 12/31/2018)   11.55
52-Week High   16.59
52-Week Low   11.01

Total Returns (%)

3-Month	6-Month	1-Year	3-Year	5-Year
-24.71	-19.28	-16.36	19.94	-11.04

3-Year Standard Deviation   24.86
Effective Duration

Valuation
Premium/Discount (1-Year Average)   0.21

Company Information
Provider   UBS Group AG
Manager/Tenure   No Manager (7)
Website   http://www.ubs.com
Address   Bahnhofstrasse 45 Zurich 8098 Switzerland
Phone Number   412-037-1952

Ratings History

Date	Overall Rating	Risk Rating	Reward Rating
Q4-18	C	C	C-
Q2-18	C	C-	C
Q4-17	C	C	C
Q4-16	C	C-	C+
Q4-15	C-	C-	C-

Asset & Performance History

Date	NAV	1-Year Total Return
2017	16.25	-1.88
2016	19.7	48.65
2015	15.84	-10.88
2014	21.15	-16.77
2013	29.64	31.57
2012	26.11	75.28

Total Assets: $204,720,516
Asset Allocation

Asset	%
Cash	
Stocks	
US Stocks	
Bonds	
US Bonds	
Other	

Services Offered:

Investment Strategy: The investment seeks to replicate, net of expenses, twice the performance of the Wells Fargo Business Development Company Index.
The index is a float adjusted, capitalization-weighted index that is intended to measure the performance of all Business Development Companies ("BDC") that are listed on the New York Stock Exchange or NASDAQ and satisfy specified market capitalization and other eligibility requirements. The BDC business model is to lend to small and midsized companies at high yield equivalent rates while also at times taking equity stakes in such companies. **Top Holdings:**

Invesco DWA Developed Markets Momentum ETF   D+   SELL

Ticker	Traded On	NAV	Total Assets ($)	Dividend Yield (TTM)	Turnover Ratio	Expense Ratio
PIZ	NAS CM	23.03	$204,557,400	1.36	98	0.81

Ratings
Reward   D+
Risk   D+
Recent Upgrade/Downgrade   Down

Fund Information
Fund Type   Exchange Traded Funds
Category   Global Equity Large Cap
Sub-Category   Foreign Large Growth
Prospectus Objective   Foreign Stock
Inception Date   Dec-07
Open to New Investments

Prices
Price (as of 12/31/2018)   22.97
52-Week High   29.67
52-Week Low   22.12

Total Returns (%)

3-Month	6-Month	1-Year	3-Year	5-Year
-16.17	-14.71	-16.17	0.80	-6.03

3-Year Standard Deviation   12.64
Effective Duration

Valuation
Premium/Discount (1-Year Average)   0.05

Company Information
Provider   Invesco
Manager/Tenure   Peter Hubbard (10), Jonathan Nixon (5), Michael Jeanette (3), 1 other
Website   http://www.invesco.com/us
Address   Invesco 11 Greenway Plaza, Ste. 2500 Houston TX 77046 United States
Phone Number   800-659-1005

Ratings History

Date	Overall Rating	Risk Rating	Reward Rating
Q4-18	D+	D+	D+
Q2-18	C	C-	C
Q4-17	B-	B	B-
Q4-16	D	D+	D
Q4-15	C	C+	C-

Asset & Performance History

Date	NAV	1-Year Total Return
2017	27.72	30.7
2016	21.5	-7.99
2015	23.87	-0.15
2014	24.16	-6.64
2013	26.27	36.13
2012	19.88	16.11

Total Assets: $204,557,400
Asset Allocation

Asset	%
Cash	0%
Stocks	100%
US Stocks	1%
Bonds	0%
US Bonds	0%
Other	0%

Services Offered:

Investment Strategy: The investment seeks to track the investment results (before fees and expenses) of the Dorsey Wright® Developed Markets Technical Leaders Index (the "underlying index"). The fund will invest at least 90% of its total assets in the equity securities that comprise the underlying index. The underlying index is comprised of equity securities of large capitalization companies based in countries with developed economies, excluding the United States. **Top Holdings:** Ryman Healthcare Ltd   InterContinental Hotels Group PLC   Constellation Software Inc   Royal UNIBREW A/S   CSL Ltd

First Trust SSI Strategic Convertible Securities ETF   C-   HOLD

Ticker	Traded On	NAV	Total Assets ($)	Dividend Yield (TTM)	Turnover Ratio	Expense Ratio
FCVT	NAS CM	27.65	$204,410,037	2.29	56	0.95

Ratings
Reward	C-
Risk	C-
Recent Upgrade/Downgrade	Down

Fund Information
Fund Type	Exchange Traded Funds
Category	Convertibles
Sub-Category	Convertibles
Prospectus Objective	Convertible Bond
Inception Date	Nov-15
Open to New Investments	Y

Prices
Price (as of 12/31/2018)	27.52
52-Week High	31.05
52-Week Low	26.47

Total Returns (%)
3-Month	6-Month	1-Year	3-Year	5-Year
-9.27	-6.10	-1.54	19.44	

3-Year Standard Deviation	7.55
Effective Duration	1.97

Valuation
Premium/Discount (1-Year Average)	0.24

Company Information
Provider	First Trust
Manager/Tenure	George M. Douglas (3), Florian Eitner (3), Ethan Ganz (3), 2 others
Website	http://www.ftportfolios.com/
Address	First Trust 120 E. Liberty Drive, Suite 400 Wheaton IL 60187 United States
Phone Number	800-621-1675

PERFORMANCE

Ratings History

Date	Overall Rating	Risk Rating	Reward Rating
Q4-18	C-	C-	C-
Q2-18	C	C-	C
Q4-17	C	B+	C-
Q4-16	D	C-	D+
Q4-15			

Asset & Performance History

Date	NAV	1-Year Total Return
2017	28.58	12.78
2016	25.72	6.78
2015	24.56	
2014		
2013		
2012		

Total Assets: $204,410,037

Asset Allocation
Asset	%
Cash	2%
Stocks	4%
US Stocks	4%
Bonds	0%
US Bonds	0%
Other	2%

Services Offered:

Investment Strategy: The investment seeks total return. Under normal market conditions, the fund seeks to achieve its investment objective by investing at least 80% of its net assets (including investment borrowings) in a portfolio of U.S. and non-U.S. convertible securities. In general, convertible securities combine the investment characteristics of bonds and common stocks and typically consist of debt securities or preferred securities that may be converted or exchanged within a specified period of time into a certain amount of common stock or other equity security of the same or a different issuer. The fund is non-diversified. **Top Holdings:** Wells Fargo & Co 7 1/2 % Non Cum Perp Conv Pfd Shs -A- Series -L- Bank of America Corporation 7 1/4 % Non-Cum Perp Conv Pfd Shs Series -L- Becton Dickinson Palo Alto Networks Inc 0.75% Square Inc 0.5%

Hartford Multifactor US Equity ETF   C-   HOLD

Ticker	Traded On	NAV	Total Assets ($)	Dividend Yield (TTM)	Turnover Ratio	Expense Ratio
ROUS	NYSE Arca	27.84	$204,102,008	1.54	36	0.19

Ratings
Reward	C-
Risk	C-
Recent Upgrade/Downgrade	Down

Fund Information
Fund Type	Exchange Traded Funds
Category	US Equity Large Cap Blend
Sub-Category	Large Value
Prospectus Objective	Growth
Inception Date	Feb-15
Open to New Investments	Y

Prices
Price (as of 12/31/2018)	27.80
52-Week High	33.64
52-Week Low	26.23

Total Returns (%)
3-Month	6-Month	1-Year	3-Year	5-Year
-15.00	-10.44	-8.97	24.27	

3-Year Standard Deviation	10.25
Effective Duration	

Valuation
Premium/Discount (1-Year Average)	0.31

Company Information
Provider	Hartford Funds
Manager/Tenure	Richard A. Brown (3), Thomas J. Durante (3), Karen Q. Wong (3)
Website	http://www.hartfordfunds.com
Address	690 Lee Road Wayne PA 19087 United States
Phone Number	800-456-7526

PERFORMANCE

Ratings History

Date	Overall Rating	Risk Rating	Reward Rating
Q4-18	C-	C-	C-
Q2-18	C	C-	C
Q4-17	B-	B-	C+
Q4-16	D+	D+	C-
Q4-15	U		

Asset & Performance History

Date	NAV	1-Year Total Return
2017	31.12	22.58
2016	25.82	11.36
2015	23.68	
2014		
2013		
2012		

Total Assets: $204,102,008

Asset Allocation
Asset	%
Cash	0%
Stocks	100%
US Stocks	98%
Bonds	0%
US Bonds	0%
Other	0%

Services Offered:

Investment Strategy: The investment seeks to provide investment results that, before fees and expenses, correspond to the total return performance of the Hartford Risk-Optimized Multifactor US Equity Index. The fund generally invests at least 80 percent of its assets in securities of the index and in depositary receipts representing securities of the index. The index seeks to improve returns through a market cycle relative to traditional cap-weighted U.S. equity market indices and active U.S. equity market strategies. **Top Holdings:** VMware Inc Express Scripts Holding Co Marathon Petroleum Corp Centene Corp HP Inc

iShares Russell Top 200 ETF
C   HOLD

Ticker	Traded On	NAV	Total Assets ($)	Dividend Yield (TTM)	Turnover Ratio	Expense Ratio
IWL	NYSE Arca	58.34	$202,566,489	1.68	5	0.15

Ratings
Reward   C
Risk   C-
Recent Upgrade/Downgrade

Fund Information
Fund Type   Exchange Traded Funds
Category   US Equity Large Cap Blend
Sub-Category   Large Blend
Prospectus Objective   Growth
Inception Date   Sep-09
Open to New Investments   Y

Prices
Price (as of 12/31/2018)   58.39
52-Week High   68.21
52-Week Low   54.65

Total Returns (%)

3-Month	6-Month	1-Year	3-Year	5-Year
-13.69	-6.35	-3.20	32.09	52.60

3-Year Standard Deviation   9.36
Effective Duration

Valuation
Premium/Discount (1-Year Average)   0.10

Company Information
Provider   iShares
Manager/Tenure   Diane Hsiung (9), Greg Savage (9), Jennifer Hsui (6), 3 others
Website   http://www.ishares.com
Address   iShares 400 Howard Street San Francisco CA 94105 United States
Phone Number   800-474-2737

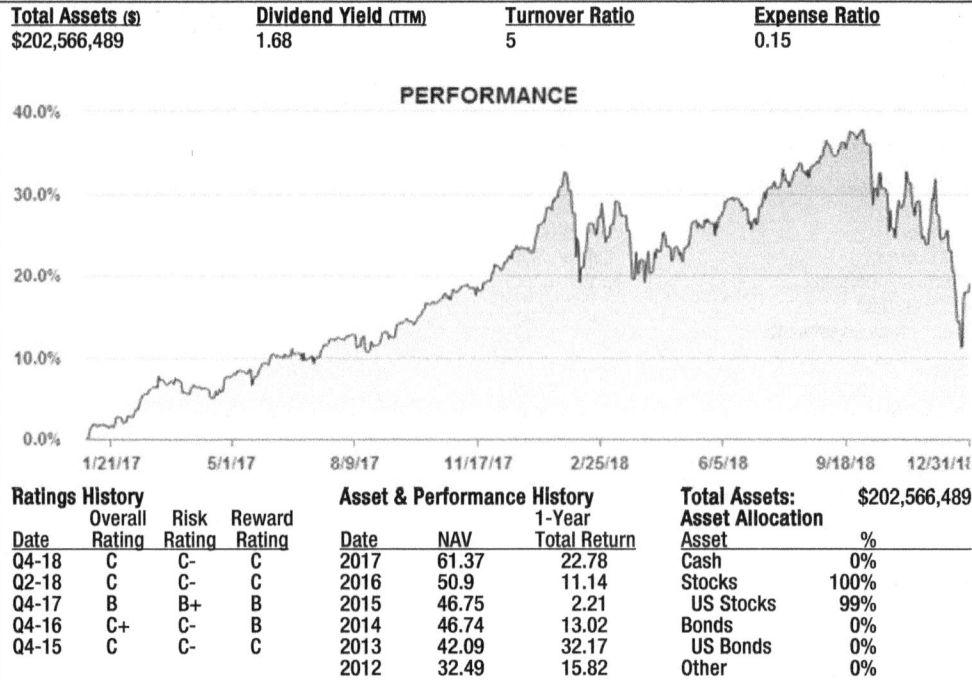
PERFORMANCE

Ratings History

Date	Overall Rating	Risk Rating	Reward Rating
Q4-18	C	C-	C
Q2-18	C	C-	C
Q4-17	B	B+	B
Q4-16	C+	C-	B
Q4-15	C	C-	C

Asset & Performance History

Date	NAV	1-Year Total Return
2017	61.37	22.78
2016	50.9	11.14
2015	46.75	2.21
2014	46.74	13.02
2013	42.09	32.17
2012	32.49	15.82

Total Assets: $202,566,489

Asset Allocation

Asset	%
Cash	0%
Stocks	100%
US Stocks	99%
Bonds	0%
US Bonds	0%
Other	0%

Services Offered:

Investment Strategy: The investment seeks to track the investment results of the Russell Top 200® Index, which measures the performance of the largest capitalization sector of the U.S. equity market. The fund generally will invest at least 90% of its assets in the component securities of the underlying index and may invest up to 10% of its assets in certain futures, options and swap contracts, cash and cash equivalents, including shares of money market funds advised by the advisor or its affiliates, as well as in securities not included in the underlying index, but which the advisor believes will help the fund track the underlying index. **Top Holdings:** Apple Inc Microsoft Corp Amazon.com Inc Berkshire Hathaway Inc B Johnson & Johnson

---

FormulaFolios Tactical Income ETF
D   SELL

Ticker	Traded On	NAV	Total Assets ($)	Dividend Yield (TTM)	Turnover Ratio	Expense Ratio
FFTI	BATS	23.15	$201,460,990	3.6	48	1.05

Ratings
Reward   D
Risk   C-
Recent Upgrade/Downgrade   Down

Fund Information
Fund Type   Exchange Traded Funds
Category   US Fixed Income
Sub-Category   Multisector Bond
Prospectus Objective   Multisector Bond
Inception Date   Jun-17
Open to New Investments   Y

Prices
Price (as of 12/31/2018)   23.12
52-Week High   25.02
52-Week Low   22.89

Total Returns (%)

3-Month	6-Month	1-Year	3-Year	5-Year
-2.82	-1.36	-3.76		

3-Year Standard Deviation
Effective Duration   2.45

Valuation
Premium/Discount (1-Year Average)   0.11

Company Information
Provider   FormulaFolioFunds
Manager/Tenure   Derek Prusa (1), Jason Wenk (1)
Website
Address   89 Ionia NW, Suite 600 Grand Rapids, MI 49503 United States
Phone Number

PERFORMANCE

Ratings History

Date	Overall Rating	Risk Rating	Reward Rating
Q4-18	D	C-	D
Q2-18	D+	C-	D
Q4-17	U		
Q4-16			
Q4-15			

Asset & Performance History

Date	NAV	1-Year Total Return
2017	24.93	
2016		
2015		
2014		
2013		
2012		

Total Assets: $201,460,990

Asset Allocation

Asset	%
Cash	3%
Stocks	0%
US Stocks	0%
Bonds	91%
US Bonds	68%
Other	0%

Services Offered:

Investment Strategy: The investment seeks to provide income. The fund seeks to achieve its investment objective by investing primarily in foreign and domestic fixed income securities through other exchange traded funds ("ETFs"). The fixed income securities in which the fund will invest are U.S. Treasuries, investment grade U.S. bonds, high-yield U.S. bonds, U.S. aggregate bond, and international government bonds of any maturity and duration. The adviser uses its proprietary investment model to rank 5 major fixed income asset classes based on the strongest combination of yield spread and price momentum. **Top Holdings:** SPDR® Blmbg Barclays Inv Grd Flt Rt ETF iShares Floating Rate Bond ETF iShares iBoxx $ High Yield Corp Bd ETF SPDR® Blmbg Barclays High Yield Bd ETF VanEck Vectors High-Yield Municipal ETF

SPDR® S&P Global Dividend ETF   C-   HOLD

Ticker	Traded On	NAV	Total Assets ($)	Dividend Yield (TTM)	Turnover Ratio	Expense Ratio
WDIV	NYSE Arca	61.87	$201,406,071	3.77	39	0.4

Ratings
Reward	C-
Risk	C-
Recent Upgrade/Downgrade	Down

Fund Information
Fund Type	Exchange Traded Funds
Category	Global Equity Large Cap
Sub-Category	World Large Stock
Prospectus Objective	Growth & Inc
Inception Date	May-13
Open to New Investments	Y

Prices
Price (as of 12/31/2018)	61.99
52-Week High	73.93
52-Week Low	60.00

Total Returns (%)
3-Month	6-Month	1-Year	3-Year	5-Year
-7.27	-5.39	-8.85	22.91	18.43

3-Year Standard Deviation	10.18
Effective Duration	

Valuation
Premium/Discount (1-Year Average)	0.04

Company Information
Provider	SPDR State Street Global Advisors
Manager/Tenure	Michael J. Feehily (5), Karl A. Schneider (3), Amy Scofield (1)
Website	http://www.spdrs.com
Address	SPDR State Street Global Advisors State Street Financial Center, 1 Lincoln Street Boston MA 02111-2900 United States
Phone Number	617-786-3000

PERFORMANCE

Ratings History
Date	Overall Rating	Risk Rating	Reward Rating
Q4-18	C-	C-	C-
Q2-18	C	C-	C
Q4-17	B-	B-	B-
Q4-16	C	C-	C
Q4-15	D+	D+	D

Asset & Performance History
Date	NAV	1-Year Total Return
2017	70.76	18.83
2016	61.85	12.38
2015	56.94	-7.94
2014	64.78	4.67
2013	64.77	
2012		

Total Assets: $201,406,071

Asset Allocation
Asset	%
Cash	0%
Stocks	100%
US Stocks	22%
Bonds	0%
US Bonds	0%
Other	0%

Services Offered:

Investment Strategy: The investment seeks to provide investment results that, before fees and expenses, correspond generally to the total return of the S&P Global Dividend Aristocrats Index. The fund generally invests substantially all, but at least 80%, of its total assets in the securities comprising the index and in depositary receipts based on securities comprising the index. The index is designed to measure the performance of high dividend-yield companies included in the S&P Global BMI that have followed a managed-dividends policy of increasing or stable dividends for at least ten consecutive years. The fund is non-diversified. **Top Holdings:** SCANA Corp   GlaxoSmithKline PLC   EDP - Energias de Portugal SA   Fortum Oyj   Greene King PLC

PIMCO 15+ Year U.S. TIPS Index Exchange-Traded Fund   D+   SELL

Ticker	Traded On	NAV	Total Assets ($)	Dividend Yield (TTM)	Turnover Ratio	Expense Ratio
LTPZ	NYSE Arca	62.33	$199,485,936	3.41	10	0.2

Ratings
Reward	D
Risk	C-
Recent Upgrade/Downgrade	Down

Fund Information
Fund Type	Exchange Traded Funds
Category	US Fixed Income
Sub-Category	Inflation-Protected Bond
Prospectus Objective	Govt Bond - Treasury
Inception Date	Sep-09
Open to New Investments	Y

Prices
Price (as of 12/31/2018)	62.39
52-Week High	69.23
52-Week Low	60.38

Total Returns (%)
3-Month	6-Month	1-Year	3-Year	5-Year
-1.80	-6.31	-7.38	10.99	20.87

3-Year Standard Deviation	8.4
Effective Duration	21.71

Valuation
Premium/Discount (1-Year Average)	-0.05

Company Information
Provider	PIMCO
Manager/Tenure	Matthew P. Dorsten (2), Mitchell Handa (0), Graham A. Rennison (0)
Website	http://www.pimco.com
Address	PIMCO 840 Newport Center Drive, Suite 100 Newport Beach CA 92660 United States
Phone Number	866-746-2602

PERFORMANCE

Ratings History
Date	Overall Rating	Risk Rating	Reward Rating
Q4-18	D+	C-	D
Q2-18	C-	C-	C
Q4-17	C+	B-	C
Q4-16	C	C-	C
Q4-15	D+	D+	D+

Asset & Performance History
Date	NAV	1-Year Total Return
2017	69.45	9.44
2016	64.95	8.84
2015	60.65	-8.73
2014	66.91	19.31
2013	57.11	-19.54
2012	71.85	11.81

Total Assets: $199,485,936

Asset Allocation
Asset	%
Cash	0%
Stocks	0%
US Stocks	0%
Bonds	100%
US Bonds	100%
Other	0%

Services Offered:

Investment Strategy: The investment seeks to provide total return that closely corresponds, before fees and expenses, to the total return of the ICE BofAML 15+ Year US Inflation-Linked Treasury Index. The fund invests at least 80% of its total assets (exclusive of collateral held from securities lending) in the component securities of the ICE BofAML 15+ Year US Inflation-Linked Treasury Index (the "underlying index"). The underlying index is an unmanaged index comprised of Treasury Inflation-Protected Securities ("TIPS") with a maturity of at least 15 years. **Top Holdings:** United States Treasury Bonds 2.12%   United States Treasury Bonds 1.38%   United States Treasury Bonds 0.62%   United States Treasury Bonds 0.75%   United States Treasury Bonds 0.75%

VanEck Vectors AMT-Free Short Municipal Index ETF   C-   HOLD

Ticker	Traded On	NAV	Total Assets ($)	Dividend Yield (TTM)	Turnover Ratio	Expense Ratio
SMB	BATS	17.34	$199,286,357	1.56	41	0.2

Ratings
Reward   D+
Risk   C-
Recent Upgrade/Downgrade

Fund Information
Fund Type   Exchange Traded Funds
Category   US Muni Fixed Inc
Sub-Category   Muni National Short
Prospectus Objective   Muni Bond - Natl
Inception Date   Feb-08
Open to New Investments   Y

Prices
Price (as of 12/31/2018)   17.30
52-Week High   17.35
52-Week Low   17.05

Total Returns (%)

3-Month	6-Month	1-Year	3-Year	5-Year
1.07	0.88	1.42	2.67	5.21

3-Year Standard Deviation   1.83
Effective Duration   3.24

Valuation
Premium/Discount (1-Year Average)   -0.31

Company Information
Provider   VanEck
Manager/Tenure   James T. Colby (10)
Website   http://www.vaneck.com
Address   Van Eck Associates Corporation 666
                         Third Avenue New York NY 10017
                         United States
Phone Number   800-826-1115

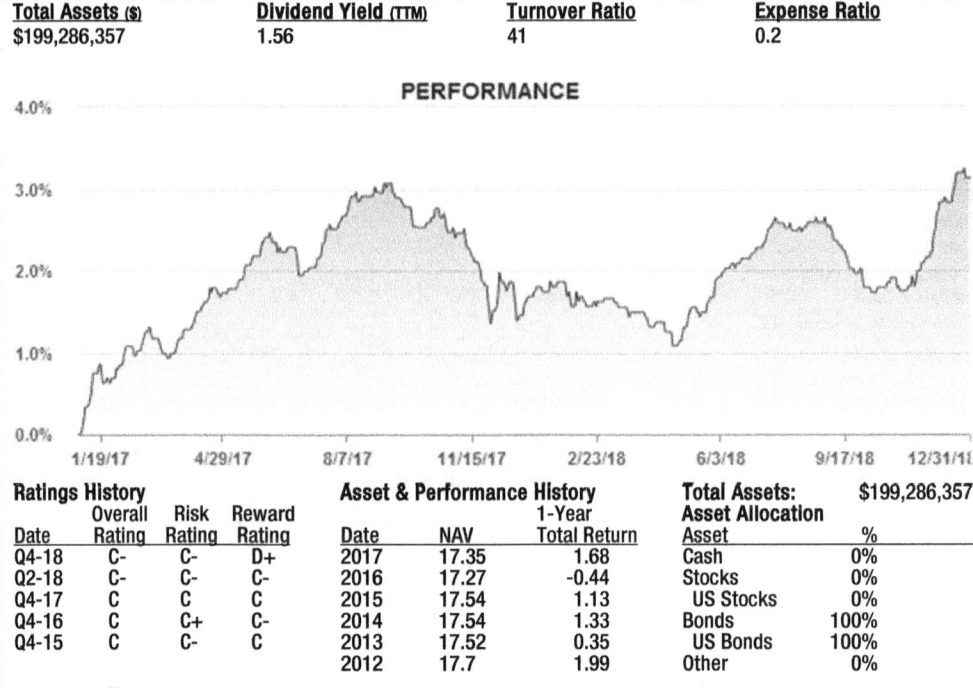

Ratings History

Date	Overall Rating	Risk Rating	Reward Rating
Q4-18	C-	C-	D+
Q2-18	C-	C-	C-
Q4-17	C	C	C
Q4-16	C	C+	C-
Q4-15	C	C-	C

Asset & Performance History

Date	NAV	1-Year Total Return
2017	17.35	1.68
2016	17.27	-0.44
2015	17.54	1.13
2014	17.54	1.33
2013	17.52	0.35
2012	17.7	1.99

Total Assets: $199,286,357
Asset Allocation

Asset	%
Cash	0%
Stocks	0%
US Stocks	0%
Bonds	100%
US Bonds	100%
Other	0%

Services Offered:

Investment Strategy: The investment seeks to replicate as closely as possible, before fees and expenses, the price and yield performance of the Bloomberg Barclays AMT-Free Short Continuous Municipal Index. The fund normally invests at least 80% of its total assets in fixed income securities that comprise the index. The index is comprised of publicly traded municipal bonds that cover the U.S. dollar denominated short-term tax-exempt bond market. **Top Holdings:** MARYLAND ST 5% MASSACHUSETTS ST 5% WASHINGTON ST 5% METROPOLITAN UTILS DIST OMAHA NEB WTR 5% MARYLAND ST 5%

Xtrackers MSCI EAFE High Dividend Yield Equity ETF   C-   HOLD

Ticker	Traded On	NAV	Total Assets ($)	Dividend Yield (TTM)	Turnover Ratio	Expense Ratio
HDEF	NYSE Arca		$198,952,561	2.46	56	0.2

Ratings
Reward   D+
Risk   C-
Recent Upgrade/Downgrade   Down

Fund Information
Fund Type   Exchange Traded Funds
Category   Global Equity Large Cap
Sub-Category   Foreign Large Value
Prospectus Objective   Growth & Inc
Inception Date   Aug-15
Open to New Investments   Y

Prices
Price (as of 12/31/2018)   20.64
52-Week High   25.38
52-Week Low   20.25

Total Returns (%)

3-Month	6-Month	1-Year	3-Year	5-Year
-10.38	-8.31	-13.48	6.02	

3-Year Standard Deviation   8.62
Effective Duration

Valuation
Premium/Discount (1-Year Average)   0.42

Company Information
Provider   Deutsche Asset Management
Manager/Tenure   Charlotte Cipolletti (2), Patrick Dwyer
                         (2), Bryan Richards (2), 2 others
Website   http://www.deutsche-etfs.com
Address   Deutsche Asset & Wealth
                         Management 345 Park Avenue New
                         York NY 10154 United States
Phone Number   844-851-4255

PERFORMANCE

Ratings History

Date	Overall Rating	Risk Rating	Reward Rating
Q4-18	C-	C-	D+
Q2-18	C-	D+	C
Q4-17	C	B	C+
Q4-16	D	D+	C-
Q4-15	U		

Asset & Performance History

Date	NAV	1-Year Total Return
2017	24.67	9.83
2016	23.24	11.58
2015	22.92	
2014		
2013		
2012		

Total Assets: $198,952,561
Asset Allocation

Asset	%
Cash	0%
Stocks	99%
US Stocks	0%
Bonds	0%
US Bonds	0%
Other	1%

Services Offered:

Investment Strategy: The investment seeks investment results that correspond generally to the performance, before fees and expenses, of the MSCI EAFE High Dividend Yield Index. The fund will invest at least 80% of its total assets (but typically far more) in component securities of the underlying index. The underlying index is designed to reflect the performance of equities in its parent index, the MSCI EAFE Index, with higher dividend income and quality characteristics than average dividend yields of equities in the parent index, where such higher dividend income and quality characteristics are both sustainable and persistent. **Top Holdings:** Sanofi SA AstraZeneca PLC GlaxoSmithKline PLC Allianz SE Total SA

VanEck Vectors BDC Income ETF   C+   HOLD

Ticker	Traded On	NAV	Total Assets ($)	Dividend Yield (TTM)	Turnover Ratio	Expense Ratio
BIZD	NYSE Arca	14.22	$198,556,494	9.61	19	9.41

Ratings
Reward   B
Risk   C-
Recent Upgrade/Downgrade   Down

Fund Information
Fund Type   Exchange Traded Funds
Category   Financials Sector Equity
Sub-Category   Financial
Prospectus Objective   Income
Inception Date   Feb-13
Open to New Investments   Y

Prices
Price (as of 12/31/2018)   14.04
52-Week High   17.40
52-Week Low   14.04

Total Returns (%)

3-Month	6-Month	1-Year	3-Year	5-Year
-12.38	-8.75	-5.53	18.46	4.92

3-Year Standard Deviation   12.55
Effective Duration

Valuation
Premium/Discount (1-Year Average)   0.04

Company Information
Provider   VanEck
Manager/Tenure   Hao-Hung (Peter) Liao (5), Guo Hua (Jason) Jin (0)
Website   http://www.vaneck.com
Address   Van Eck Associates Corporation 666 Third Avenue New York NY 10017 United States
Phone Number   800-826-1115

PERFORMANCE

Ratings History

Date	Overall Rating	Risk Rating	Reward Rating
Q4-18	C+	C-	B
Q2-18	C+	C-	B
Q4-17	C	C+	C
Q4-16	C	C-	C+
Q4-15	D+	C-	D+

Asset & Performance History

Date	NAV	1-Year Total Return
2017	16.57	0.04
2016	18.03	25.35
2015	15.73	-4.45
2014	17.92	-7.29
2013	20.9	
2012		

Total Assets: $198,556,494

Asset Allocation

Asset	%
Cash	-1%
Stocks	101%
US Stocks	101%
Bonds	0%
US Bonds	0%
Other	0%

Services Offered:

Investment Strategy: The investment seeks to replicate as closely as possible, before fees and expenses, the price and yield performance of the MVIS® US Business Development Companies Index. The fund normally invests at least 80% of its total assets in securities that comprise the fund's benchmark index. The index is comprised of BDCs. BDCs are vehicles whose principal business is to invest in, lend capital to or provide services to privately-held companies or thinly traded U.S. public companies. **Top Holdings:** Ares Capital Corp   Main Street Capital Corp   Prospect Capital Corp   Corporate Capital Trust Inc Registered form   FS Investment Corp

---

iShares Core 10+ Year USD Bond ETF   D+   SELL

Ticker	Traded On	NAV	Total Assets ($)	Dividend Yield (TTM)	Turnover Ratio	Expense Ratio
ILTB	NYSE Arca	58.86	$194,950,023	4.19	11	0.06

Ratings
Reward   D
Risk   C-
Recent Upgrade/Downgrade   Down

Fund Information
Fund Type   Exchange Traded Funds
Category   US Fixed Income
Sub-Category   Long-Term Bond
Prospectus Objective   Growth
Inception Date   Dec-09
Open to New Investments   Y

Prices
Price (as of 12/31/2018)   59.02
52-Week High   64.77
52-Week Low   57.00

Total Returns (%)

3-Month	6-Month	1-Year	3-Year	5-Year
0.71	0.40	-4.99	13.47	29.74

3-Year Standard Deviation   6.95
Effective Duration   13.94

Valuation
Premium/Discount (1-Year Average)   0.05

Company Information
Provider   iShares
Manager/Tenure   Scott Radell (8), James Mauro (7)
Website   http://www.ishares.com
Address   iShares 400 Howard Street San Francisco CA 94105 United States
Phone Number   800-474-2737

PERFORMANCE

Ratings History

Date	Overall Rating	Risk Rating	Reward Rating
Q4-18	D+	C-	D
Q2-18	C-	C-	C-
Q4-17	B-	B	C+
Q4-16	C	C-	C
Q4-15	C	C-	C

Asset & Performance History

Date	NAV	1-Year Total Return
2017	64.53	10.61
2016	60.58	7.63
2015	58.49	-2.96
2014	62.75	17.83
2013	55.32	-8.72
2012	63.49	8.32

Total Assets: $194,950,023

Asset Allocation

Asset	%
Cash	0%
Stocks	0%
US Stocks	0%
Bonds	99%
US Bonds	82%
Other	0%

Services Offered:

Investment Strategy: The investment seeks to track the investment results of the Bloomberg Barclays U.S. Universal 10+ Year Index (the "underlying index"). The underlying index measures the performance of U.S. dollar-denominated taxable bonds that are rated either investment-grade or high yield with remaining maturities greater than ten years. The fund generally will invest at least 90% of its assets in the component securities of the underlying index and may invest up to 10% of its assets in certain futures, options and swap contracts, cash and cash equivalents, as well as in securities not included in the underlying index. **Top Holdings:** United States Treasury Bonds 3%   United States Treasury Bonds 2.75%   United States Treasury Bonds 2.88%   United States Treasury Bonds 3.63%   United States Treasury Bonds 4.38%

SPDR® S&P Transportation ETF   C   HOLD

Ticker	Traded On	NAV	Total Assets ($)	Dividend Yield (TTM)	Turnover Ratio	Expense Ratio
XTN	NYSE Arca	53.63	$194,317,250	0.79	29	0.35

Ratings

Reward   C
Risk   C-
Recent Upgrade/Downgrade

Fund Information

Fund Type	Exchange Traded Funds
Category	Industrials Sector Equity
Sub-Category	Industrials
Prospectus Objective	Utility
Inception Date	Jan-11
Open to New Investments	Y

Prices

Price (as of 12/31/2018)	53.44
52-Week High	69.32
52-Week Low	50.73

Total Returns (%)

3-Month	6-Month	1-Year	3-Year	5-Year
-19.47	-15.39	-17.00	28.13	36.80

3-Year Standard Deviation	17.36
Effective Duration	

Valuation

Premium/Discount (1-Year Average)	-0.01

Company Information

Provider	SPDR State Street Global Advisors
Manager/Tenure	Michael J. Feehily (7), Karl A. Schneider (4), Michael Finocchi (1)
Website	http://www.spdrs.com
Address	SPDR State Street Global Advisors State Street Financial Center, 1 Lincoln Street Boston MA 02111-2900 United States
Phone Number	617-786-3000

PERFORMANCE

Ratings History

Date	Overall Rating	Risk Rating	Reward Rating
Q4-18	C	C-	C
Q2-18	C	C	C+
Q4-17	B	C+	B+
Q4-16	C+	C-	B
Q4-15	C	C	C+

Asset & Performance History

Date	NAV	1-Year Total Return
2017	65.18	21.63
2016	53.97	27.29
2015	42.84	-20.19
2014	54.21	33.78
2013	40.7	52.01
2012	26.9	20.4

Total Assets: $194,317,250

Asset Allocation

Asset	%
Cash	0%
Stocks	100%
US Stocks	100%
Bonds	0%
US Bonds	0%
Other	0%

Services Offered:

Investment Strategy: The investment seeks to provide investment results that, before fees and expenses, correspond generally to the total return performance of an index derived from the transportation segment of a U.S. total market composite index. In seeking to track the performance of the S&P Transportation Select Industry Index (the "index"), the fund employs a sampling strategy. It generally invests substantially all, but at least 80%, of its total assets in the securities comprising the index. The index represents the transportation segment of the S&P Total Market Index ("S&P TMI"). The fund is non-diversified. **Top Holdings:** Spirit Airlines Inc   Allegiant Travel Co United Continental Holdings Inc   Alaska Air Group Inc   Delta Air Lines Inc

---

First Trust Global Tactical Commodity Strategy Fund   D   SELL

Ticker	Traded On	NAV	Total Assets ($)	Dividend Yield (TTM)	Turnover Ratio	Expense Ratio
FTGC	NAS CM	17.92	$193,915,095	1.39	0	0.95

Ratings

Reward   D
Risk   D+
Recent Upgrade/Downgrade   Down

Fund Information

Fund Type	Exchange Traded Funds
Category	Commodities Broad Basket
Sub-Category	Commodities Broad Basket
Prospectus Objective	Growth & Inc
Inception Date	Oct-13
Open to New Investments	Y

Prices

Price (as of 12/31/2018)	17.93
52-Week High	21.79
52-Week Low	17.93

Total Returns (%)

3-Month	6-Month	1-Year	3-Year	5-Year
-9.96	-11.39	-12.98	-10.04	-38.60

3-Year Standard Deviation	7.54
Effective Duration	

Valuation

Premium/Discount (1-Year Average)	-0.02

Company Information

Provider	First Trust
Manager/Tenure	John W. Gambla (5), Rob A. Guttschow (5)
Website	http://www.ftportfolios.com/
Address	First Trust 120 E. Liberty Drive, Suite 400 Wheaton IL 60187 United States
Phone Number	800-621-1675

PERFORMANCE

Ratings History

Date	Overall Rating	Risk Rating	Reward Rating
Q4-18	D	D+	D
Q2-18	C-	C-	C-
Q4-17	D	D+	D
Q4-16	D	D	D
Q4-15	D	D	D

Asset & Performance History

Date	NAV	1-Year Total Return
2017	20.75	2.84
2016	20.43	0.52
2015	20.32	-22.55
2014	26.24	-11.88
2013	29.78	
2012		

Total Assets: $193,915,095

Asset Allocation

Asset	%
Cash	78%
Stocks	0%
US Stocks	0%
Bonds	10%
US Bonds	10%
Other	13%

Services Offered:

Investment Strategy: The investment seeks to provide total return by providing investors with commodity exposure while seeking a relatively stable risk profile. The fund is an actively managed exchange-traded fund ("ETF") that seeks to achieve attractive risk adjusted return by investing in commodity futures contracts and exchange-traded commodity linked instruments (collectively, "Commodities Instruments") through a wholly-owned subsidiary of the fund organized under the laws of the Cayman Islands (the "Subsidiary"). The advisor expects to gain exposure to these investments exclusively by investing in the Subsidiary. **Top Holdings:** Ft Cayman Subsidiary Ii   United States Treasury Bills   United States Treasury Bills   United States Treasury Bills

---

iShares MSCI Europe Small-Cap ETF   D+   SELL

Ticker	Traded On	NAV
IEUS	NAS CM	45.12

Total Assets ($)	Dividend Yield (TTM)	Turnover Ratio	Expense Ratio
$193,174,591	3.11	15	0.4

Ratings
Reward	D+
Risk	C-
Recent Upgrade/Downgrade	Down

Fund Information
Fund Type	Exchange Traded Funds
Category	Europe Equity Large Cap
Sub-Category	Europe Stock
Prospectus Objective	Small Company
Inception Date	Nov-07
Open to New Investments	Y

Prices
Price (as of 12/31/2018)	44.93
52-Week High	62.07
52-Week Low	43.21

Total Returns (%)
3-Month	6-Month	1-Year	3-Year	5-Year
-17.99	-17.84	-19.82	6.52	14.48

3-Year Standard Deviation	14.72
Effective Duration	

Valuation
Premium/Discount (1-Year Average)	-0.04

Company Information
Provider	iShares
Manager/Tenure	Diane Hsiung (10), Greg Savage (10), Jennifer Hsui (6), 3 others
Website	http://www.ishares.com
Address	iShares 400 Howard Street San Francisco CA 94105 United States
Phone Number	800-474-2737

PERFORMANCE

Ratings History
Date	Overall Rating	Risk Rating	Reward Rating
Q4-18	D+	C-	D+
Q2-18	C	C-	C+
Q4-17	B+	B	A-
Q4-16	C-	C-	C
Q4-15	C	D+	C

Asset & Performance History
Date	NAV	1-Year Total Return
2017	57.85	35.27
2016	43.75	-1.78
2015	45.64	10.85
2014	42.01	-3.04
2013	44.32	27.34
2012	35.81	21.17

Total Assets: $193,174,591

Asset Allocation
Asset	%
Cash	0%
Stocks	99%
US Stocks	1%
Bonds	0%
US Bonds	0%
Other	1%

Services Offered:

Investment Strategy: The investment seeks to track the investment results of the MSCI Europe Small Cap Index composed of small-capitalization developed market equities in Europe. The fund generally will invest at least 90% of its assets in the component securities of the underlying index and in investments that have economic characteristics that are substantially identical to the component securities of the underlying index. The index is a free float-adjusted, market capitalization-weighted index that captures small-capitalization representation across the 15 developed market countries in Europe. **Top Holdings:** Rentokil Initial PLC LEG Immobilien AG Halma PLC Hiscox Ltd ASR Nederland NV

Invesco Defensive Equity ETF   C   HOLD

Ticker	Traded On	NAV
DEF	NYSE Arca	44.00

Total Assets ($)	Dividend Yield (TTM)	Turnover Ratio	Expense Ratio
$192,794,135	1.55	136	0.6

Ratings
Reward	C
Risk	C-
Recent Upgrade/Downgrade	

Fund Information
Fund Type	Exchange Traded Funds
Category	US Equity Large Cap Blend
Sub-Category	Large Blend
Prospectus Objective	Growth
Inception Date	Dec-06
Open to New Investments	Y

Prices
Price (as of 12/31/2018)	44.04
52-Week High	50.42
52-Week Low	41.71

Total Returns (%)
3-Month	6-Month	1-Year	3-Year	5-Year
-10.84	-3.85	-3.73	33.14	43.45

3-Year Standard Deviation	8.62
Effective Duration	

Valuation
Premium/Discount (1-Year Average)	0.10

Company Information
Provider	Invesco
Manager/Tenure	Peter Hubbard (0), Michael Jeanette (0), Jonathan Nixon (0), 1 other
Website	http://www.invesco.com/us
Address	Invesco 11 Greenway Plaza, Ste. 2500 Houston TX 77046 United States
Phone Number	800-659-1005

PERFORMANCE

Ratings History
Date	Overall Rating	Risk Rating	Reward Rating
Q4-18	C	C-	C
Q2-18	C	C-	C
Q4-17	B-	C+	B-
Q4-16	C	D+	C+
Q4-15	C	C-	C

Asset & Performance History
Date	NAV	1-Year Total Return
2017	46.38	20.91
2016	38.91	14.08
2015	34.82	-4.5
2014	37.66	12.82
2013	34.22	22.64
2012	28.55	7.58

Total Assets: $192,794,135

Asset Allocation
Asset	%
Cash	0%
Stocks	100%
US Stocks	99%
Bonds	0%
US Bonds	0%
Other	0%

Services Offered:

Investment Strategy: The investment seeks to track the investment results (before fees and expenses) of the Invesco Defensive Equity Index (the "underlying index"). The fund generally will invest at least 80% of its total assets in the securities that comprise the underlying index. The underlying index is comprised of a subset of securities from the S&P 500® Index (the "S&P 500"). The fund will concentrate its investments in securities of issuers in any one industry or group of industries only to the extent that the underlying index reflects a concentration in that industry or group of industries. The fund is non-diversified. **Top Holdings:** Starbucks Corp Cigna Corp McCormick & Co Inc Non-Voting Ball Corp Merck & Co Inc

Pacer Global Cash Cows Dividend ETF

C- HOLD

Ticker	Traded On	NAV		Total Assets ($)	Dividend Yield (TTM)	Turnover Ratio	Expense Ratio
GCOW	BATS	27.99		$192,198,823	3.59	76	0.6

Ratings

Reward	C-
Risk	C-
Recent Upgrade/Downgrade	Down

Fund Information

Fund Type	Exchange Traded Funds
Category	Global Equity Large Cap
Sub-Category	World Large Stock
Prospectus Objective	Growth & Inc
Inception Date	Feb-16
Open to New Investments	Y

Prices

Price (as of 12/31/2018)	27.92
52-Week High	33.33
52-Week Low	26.95

Total Returns (%)

3-Month	6-Month	1-Year	3-Year	5-Year
-9.02	-5.19	-7.56		

3-Year Standard Deviation	
Effective Duration	

Valuation

Premium/Discount (1-Year Average)	0.15

Company Information

Provider	Pacer
Manager/Tenure	Bruce Kavanaugh (2), Michael Mack (2)
Website	http://www.paceretfs.com
Address	Pacer 16 Industrial Blvd, Suite 201 Paoli PA 19301 United States
Phone Number	

PERFORMANCE

Ratings History

Date	Overall Rating	Risk Rating	Reward Rating
Q4-18	C-	C-	C-
Q2-18	C	C-	C
Q4-17	C-	B	C-
Q4-16	U		
Q4-15			

Asset & Performance History

Date	NAV	1-Year Total Return
2017	31.42	20.62
2016	26.82	
2015		
2014		
2013		
2012		

Total Assets: $192,198,823

Asset Allocation

Asset	%
Cash	0%
Stocks	100%
US Stocks	38%
Bonds	0%
US Bonds	0%
Other	0%

Services Offered:

Investment Strategy: The investment seeks to track the total return performance, before fees and expenses, of the Pacer Global Cash Cows Dividend Index. Under normal circumstances, the fund will invest at least 80% of its total assets (exclusive of collateral held from securities lending) in the components of the index and investments that have economic characteristics that are substantially identical to the economic characteristics of such component securities (e.g., depositary receipts). The index uses an objective, rules-based methodology to provide exposure to global companies with high dividend yields backed by a high free cash flow yield. The fund is non-diversified. **Top Holdings:** Procter & Gamble Co Pfizer Inc Novartis AG ADR Roche Holding AG ADR Sanofi SA ADR

YieldShares High Income ETF

D+ SELL

Ticker	Traded On	NAV		Total Assets ($)	Dividend Yield (TTM)	Turnover Ratio	Expense Ratio
YYY	NYSE Arca	16.09		$191,882,334	9.14	34	2.02

Ratings

Reward	D+
Risk	C-
Recent Upgrade/Downgrade	Down

Fund Information

Fund Type	Exchange Traded Funds
Category	Moderate Allocation
Sub-Category	Tactical Allocation
Prospectus Objective	Income
Inception Date	Jun-12
Open to New Investments	Y

Prices

Price (as of 12/31/2018)	16.04
52-Week High	19.60
52-Week Low	15.44

Total Returns (%)

3-Month	6-Month	1-Year	3-Year	5-Year
-10.32	-7.08	-9.96	18.49	9.82

3-Year Standard Deviation	9.08
Effective Duration	4.00

Valuation

Premium/Discount (1-Year Average)	0.15

Company Information

Provider	YieldShares
Manager/Tenure	Denise M. Krisko (3)
Website	http://www.yieldshares.com
Address	YieldShares 10900 Hefner Pointe Drive, Suite 207 Oklahoma OK 73120 United States
Phone Number	

PERFORMANCE

Ratings History

Date	Overall Rating	Risk Rating	Reward Rating
Q4-18	D+	C-	D+
Q2-18	C-	C-	C
Q4-17	C+	C+	C+
Q4-16	C-	C-	C-
Q4-15	D+	C-	D+

Asset & Performance History

Date	NAV	1-Year Total Return
2017	19.49	14.02
2016	18.55	15.42
2015	17.84	-8.3
2014	21.44	1.07
2013	23.16	8.42
2012	22.5	

Total Assets: $191,882,334

Asset Allocation

Asset	%
Cash	-8%
Stocks	25%
US Stocks	22%
Bonds	86%
US Bonds	58%
Other	-6%

Services Offered:

Investment Strategy: The investment seeks to provide investment results that, before fees and expenses, correspond generally to the price and yield performance of the ISE High Income™ Index (the "index"). The fund will normally invest at least 80% of its total assets in securities of the index. Because the index is comprised of securities issued by other investment companies, the fund operates in a manner that is commonly referred to as a "fund of funds," meaning that it invests its assets in shares of funds included in the index. The index seeks to measure the performance of the top 30 U.S. exchange-listed closed-end funds. **Top Holdings:** EV Risk-Mgd Divers Equity Inc Liberty All-Star Equity Cohen & Steers Qty Inc Realty PGIM Global Short Duration High DoubleLine Income Solutions

iShares U.S. Oil Equipment & Services ETF   D+   SELL

Ticker	Traded On	NAV	Total Assets ($)	Dividend Yield (TTM)	Turnover Ratio	Expense Ratio
IEZ	NYSE Arca	20.40	$190,916,578	1.42	25	0.43

Ratings
Reward   C
Risk   D
Recent Upgrade/Downgrade   Down

Fund Information
Fund Type   Exchange Traded Funds
Category   Energy Sector Equity
Sub-Category   Equity Energy
Prospectus Objective   Natl Res
Inception Date   May-06
Open to New Investments   Y

Prices
Price (as of 12/31/2018)   20.42
52-Week High   40.37
52-Week Low   19.30

Total Returns (%)

3-Month	6-Month	1-Year	3-Year	5-Year
-43.23	-42.21	-42.48	-39.61	-65.57

3-Year Standard Deviation   29.75
Effective Duration

Valuation
Premium/Discount (1-Year Average)   0.02

Company Information
Provider   iShares
Manager/Tenure   Diane Hsiung (10), Greg Savage (10),
                                Jennifer Hsui (6), 3 others
Website   http://www.ishares.com
Address   iShares 400 Howard Street San
                                Francisco CA 94105 United States
Phone Number   800-474-2737

PERFORMANCE

Ratings History

Date	Overall Rating	Risk Rating	Reward Rating
Q4-18	D+	D	C
Q2-18	D+	D	C
Q4-17	D	D	D
Q4-16	D+	D	C-
Q4-15	D+	D+	C-

Asset & Performance History

Date	NAV	1-Year Total Return
2017	35.9	-18.19
2016	45.43	28.35
2015	35.78	-26.97
2014	49.99	-21.93
2013	64.89	28.16
2012	51.04	-1.04

Total Assets: $190,916,578
Asset Allocation

Asset	%
Cash	0%
Stocks	100%
US Stocks	92%
Bonds	0%
US Bonds	0%
Other	0%

Services Offered:

Investment Strategy: The investment seeks to track the investment results of the Dow Jones U.S. Select Oil Equipment & Services Index. The fund generally invests at least 90% of its assets in securities of the underlying index and in depositary receipts representing securities of the underlying index. The underlying fund measures the performance of the oil equipment and services sector of the U.S. equity market and includes companies that are suppliers of equipment or services to oil fields and offshore platforms, such as drilling, exploration, seismic information services and platform construction. The fund is non-diversified. **Top Holdings:** Schlumberger Ltd Halliburton Co Baker Hughes, a GE Co Class A National Oilwell Varco Inc TechnipFMC PLC

Deep Value ETF   C   HOLD

Ticker	Traded On	NAV	Total Assets ($)	Dividend Yield (TTM)	Turnover Ratio	Expense Ratio
DVP	NYSE Arca	30.20	$190,390,884	2.47	126	0.59

Ratings
Reward   B
Risk   D
Recent Upgrade/Downgrade

Fund Information
Fund Type   Exchange Traded Funds
Category   US Equity Mid Cap
Sub-Category   Mid-Cap Value
Prospectus Objective   Growth & Inc
Inception Date   Sep-14
Open to New Investments   Y

Prices
Price (as of 12/31/2018)   30.07
52-Week High   37.21
52-Week Low   28.82

Total Returns (%)

3-Month	6-Month	1-Year	3-Year	5-Year
-12.88	-11.76	-5.48	50.09	

3-Year Standard Deviation   15.26
Effective Duration

Valuation
Premium/Discount (1-Year Average)   0.12

Company Information
Provider   TWM FUNDS
Manager/Tenure   Richard A. Brown (4), Thomas J.
                                Durante (4), Karen Q. Wong (4)
Website   http://www.twmfunds.com/
Address   Tiedemann New York City United
                                States
Phone Number

PERFORMANCE

Ratings History

Date	Overall Rating	Risk Rating	Reward Rating
Q4-18	C	D	B
Q2-18	C+	D+	B
Q4-17	C+	C	C+
Q4-16	C	D	C+
Q4-15	U		

Asset & Performance History

Date	NAV	1-Year Total Return
2017	32.77	27.29
2016	26.3	24.86
2015	21.83	-10.22
2014	25.24	
2013		
2012		

Total Assets: $190,390,884
Asset Allocation

Asset	%
Cash	0%
Stocks	100%
US Stocks	100%
Bonds	0%
US Bonds	0%
Other	0%

Services Offered:

Investment Strategy: The investment seeks to track the price and total return performance, before fees and expenses, of the Deep Value Index. The index is composed of the common stock of typically 20 companies included in the S&P 500® Index that have been selected through a proprietary ranking system developed by Tiedemann Wealth Management, LLC, that evaluates the earnings and cash flows of each company to create a final universe of companies that are deeply undervalued as compared to the S&P 500® Index overall. Under normal circumstances, at least 80% of the fund's total assets will be invested in the component securities of the index. It is non-diversified. **Top Holdings:** Viacom Inc B CVS Health Corp Gap Inc Macy's Inc Western Digital Corp

IQ Global Resources ETF   C-   HOLD

Ticker	Traded On	NAV	Total Assets ($)	Dividend Yield (TTM)	Turnover Ratio	Expense Ratio
GRES	NYSE Arca	25.39	$188,722,964	0		0.78

Ratings
Reward   D+
Risk   C-
Recent Upgrade/Downgrade

Fund Information
Fund Type	Exchange Traded Funds
Category	Natural Resources
Sub-Category	Natural Resources
Prospectus Objective	World Stock
Inception Date	Oct-09
Open to New Investments	Y

Prices
Price (as of 12/31/2018)	25.23
52-Week High	29.23
52-Week Low	25.05

Total Returns (%)
3-Month	6-Month	1-Year	3-Year	5-Year
-6.51	-6.63	-10.23	22.29	-6.45

3-Year Standard Deviation   9.82
Effective Duration

Valuation
Premium/Discount (1-Year Average)   -0.02

Company Information
Provider	IndexIQ
Manager/Tenure	Greg Barrato (7), James Harrison (0)
Website	http://www.indexiq.com
Address	IndexIQ 800 Westchester Avenue, Suite N-611 Rye Brook NY 10573 United States
Phone Number	888-934-0777

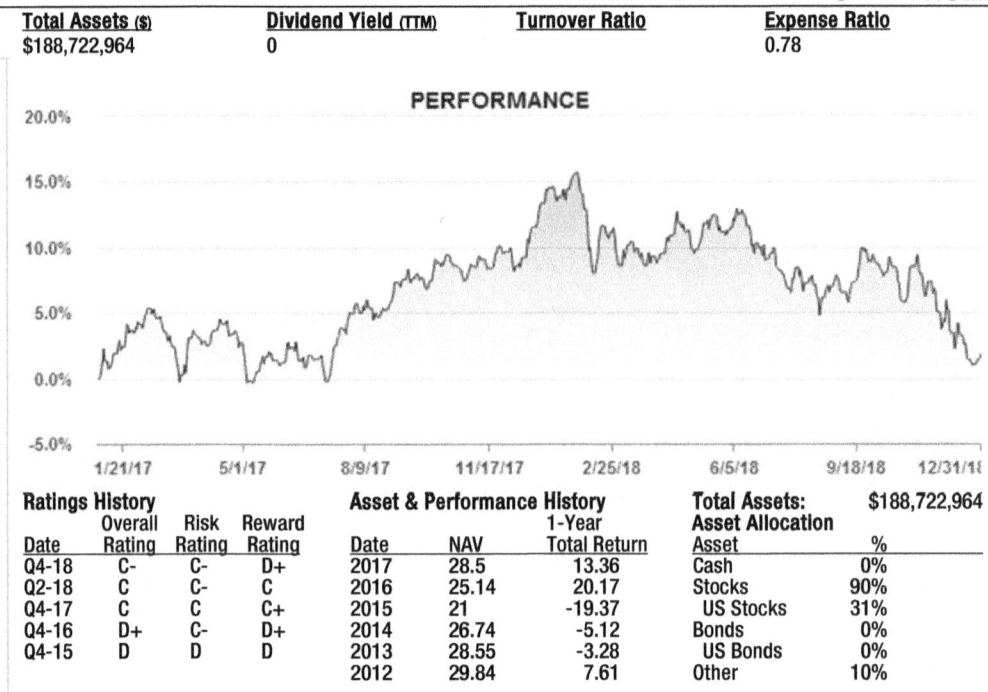

PERFORMANCE

Ratings History
Date	Overall Rating	Risk Rating	Reward Rating
Q4-18	C-	C-	D+
Q2-18	C	C-	C
Q4-17	C	C	C+
Q4-16	D+	C-	D+
Q4-15	D	D	D

Asset & Performance History
Date	NAV	1-Year Total Return
2017	28.5	13.36
2016	25.14	20.17
2015	21	-19.37
2014	26.74	-5.12
2013	28.55	-3.28
2012	29.84	7.61

Total Assets: $188,722,964
Asset Allocation
Asset	%
Cash	0%
Stocks	90%
US Stocks	31%
Bonds	0%
US Bonds	0%
Other	10%

Services Offered:

Investment Strategy: The investment seeks investment results that correspond generally to the price and yield performance of its underlying index, the IQ Global Resources Index. The fund invests at least 80% of its net assets, in the investments included in its underlying index. The underlying index seeks to employ a systematic investment process designed to identify opportunities in markets exhibiting trending or momentum characteristics across commodity asset classes, represented by companies that operate in commodity-specific market segments and whose equity securities trade in developed markets, including the U.S. The fund is non-diversified. **Top Holdings:** Recv Spdr S&P 500 Etf Trus Recv Ishares Msci Eafe Index Fund Swap Payb Ishares Msci Eafe Index Fund Swap Payb Spdr S&P500 Etf Trus Morgan Stanley Ilf/Treas/Inst

---

iShares Morningstar Small-Cap Growth ETF   C-   HOLD

Ticker	Traded On	NAV	Total Assets ($)	Dividend Yield (TTM)	Turnover Ratio	Expense Ratio
JKK	NYSE Arca	166.99	$188,320,126	0.42	51	0.3

Ratings
Reward   C-
Risk   D+
Recent Upgrade/Downgrade   Down

Fund Information
Fund Type	Exchange Traded Funds
Category	US Equity Small Cap
Sub-Category	Small Growth
Prospectus Objective	Small Company
Inception Date	Jun-04
Open to New Investments	Y

Prices
Price (as of 12/31/2018)	166.47
52-Week High	215.87
52-Week Low	154.61

Total Returns (%)
3-Month	6-Month	1-Year	3-Year	5-Year
-20.36	-16.23	-5.79	27.35	30.31

3-Year Standard Deviation   15.12
Effective Duration

Valuation
Premium/Discount (1-Year Average)   0.27

Company Information
Provider	iShares
Manager/Tenure	Diane Hsiung (10), Greg Savage (10), Jennifer Hsui (6), 3 others
Website	http://www.ishares.com
Address	iShares 400 Howard Street San Francisco CA 94105 United States
Phone Number	800-474-2737

PERFORMANCE

Ratings History
Date	Overall Rating	Risk Rating	Reward Rating
Q4-18	C-	D+	C-
Q2-18	C	D+	B-
Q4-17	B+	B	A-
Q4-16	C	D+	C+
Q4-15	C	D+	C

Asset & Performance History
Date	NAV	1-Year Total Return
2017	177.88	23.48
2016	144.88	9.47
2015	133.95	-0.03
2014	134.83	2.36
2013	132.47	41.9
2012	93.91	14.47

Total Assets: $188,320,126
Asset Allocation
Asset	%
Cash	0%
Stocks	100%
US Stocks	99%
Bonds	0%
US Bonds	0%
Other	0%

Services Offered:

Investment Strategy: The investment seeks to track the investment results of the Morningstar® Small Growth IndexSM composed of small-capitalization U.S. equities that exhibit growth characteristics. The fund generally invests at least 90% of its assets in securities of the underlying index and in depositary receipts representing securities of the underlying index. The underlying index measures the performance of stocks issued by small-capitalization companies that have exhibited above-average "growth" characteristics as determined by Morningstar, Inc.'s ("Morningstar" or the "index provider") proprietary index methodology. **Top Holdings:** Sarepta Therapeutics Inc Twilio Inc A Etsy Inc Wayfair Inc Class A Zendesk Inc

Global X U.S. Preferred ETF   D+   SELL

Ticker	Traded On	NAV	Total Assets ($)	Dividend Yield (TTM)	Turnover Ratio	Expense Ratio
PFFD	BATS	22.46	$188,314,439	6.16	4	0.23

Ratings
Reward   D
Risk   C
Recent Upgrade/Downgrade

Fund Information
Fund Type   Exchange Traded Funds
Category   US Fixed Income
Sub-Category   Preferred Stock
Prospectus Objective   Growth & Inc
Inception Date   Sep-17
Open to New Investments   Y

Prices
Price (as of 12/31/2018)   22.54
52-Week High   24.88
52-Week Low   22.14

Total Returns (%)

3-Month	6-Month	1-Year	3-Year	5-Year
-4.97	-5.49	-4.41		

3-Year Standard Deviation
Effective Duration

Valuation
Premium/Discount (1-Year Average)   0.24

Company Information
Provider   Global X Funds
Manager/Tenure   Chang Kim (1), James Ong (1), Nam
                  To (0)
Website   http://www.globalxfunds.com
Address   Global X Funds 600 Lexington Avenue,
                  20th Floor New York NY 10022 United
                  States
Phone Number   888-493-8631

PERFORMANCE

Ratings History

Date	Overall Rating	Risk Rating	Reward Rating
Q4-18	D+	C	D
Q2-18	U		
Q4-17	U		
Q4-16			
Q4-15			

Asset & Performance History

Date	NAV	1-Year Total Return
2017	24.79	
2016		
2015		
2014		
2013		
2012		

Total Assets: $188,314,439
Asset Allocation

Asset	%
Cash	0%
Stocks	1%
US Stocks	1%
Bonds	0%
US Bonds	0%
Other	3%

Services Offered:

Investment Strategy: The investment seeks to provide investment results that correspond generally to the price and yield performance, before fees and expenses, of BofA Merrill Lynch Diversified Core U.S. Preferred Securities Index. The fund invests at least 80% of its total assets in the securities of its underlying index. It also invests at least 80% of its total assets in preferred securities that are domiciled in, principally traded in or whose revenues are primarily from the U.S. The underlying index is designed to track the broad-based performance of the U.S. preferred securities market. It is non-diversified. **Top Holdings:** Wells Fargo & Co 7 1/2 % Non Cum Perp Conv Pfd Shs -A- Series -L- Bank of America Corporation 7 1/4 % Non-Cum Perp Conv Pfd Shs Series -L- Becton Dickinson GMAC Capital Trust I Pfd Secs 2011-15.2.40 Gtd Series 2 Citigroup Capital XIII Floating Rate Trust Pfd Secs Registered 2010-30.10.4

Direxion All Cap Insider Sentiment Shares   C-   HOLD

Ticker	Traded On	NAV	Total Assets ($)	Dividend Yield (TTM)	Turnover Ratio	Expense Ratio
KNOW	NYSE Arca	33.77	$188,276,675	4.25	932	0.59

Ratings
Reward   C
Risk   C-
Recent Upgrade/Downgrade   Down

Fund Information
Fund Type   Exchange Traded Funds
Category   US Equity Mid Cap
Sub-Category   Mid-Cap Blend
Prospectus Objective   Balanced
Inception Date   Dec-11
Open to New Investments   Y

Prices
Price (as of 12/31/2018)   33.66
52-Week High   43.61
52-Week Low   32.19

Total Returns (%)

3-Month	6-Month	1-Year	3-Year	5-Year
-17.22	-15.53	-14.78	13.41	38.40

3-Year Standard Deviation   10.36
Effective Duration

Valuation
Premium/Discount (1-Year Average)   0.03

Company Information
Provider   Direxion Funds
Manager/Tenure   Paul Brigandi (6), Tony Ng (3)
Website   http://www.direxionfunds.com
Address   Direxion Funds 1301 Avenue Of The
                  Americas (6th Avenue) New York NY
                  10019 United States
Phone Number   646-572-3390

PERFORMANCE

Ratings History

Date	Overall Rating	Risk Rating	Reward Rating
Q4-18	C-	C-	C
Q2-18	C	C-	C
Q4-17	B+	A-	B
Q4-16	C-	D+	C-
Q4-15	C	C	C

Asset & Performance History

Date	NAV	1-Year Total Return
2017	41.4	16.43
2016	38.31	14.3
2015	35.46	3.44
2014	34.52	17.96
2013	29.62	36.24
2012	22	16.45

Total Assets: $188,276,675
Asset Allocation

Asset	%
Cash	0%
Stocks	100%
US Stocks	100%
Bonds	0%
US Bonds	0%
Other	0%

Services Offered:

Investment Strategy: The investment seeks investment results before fees and expenses that track the Sabrient Multi-Cap Insider/Analyst Quant-Weighted Index. The fund, under normal circumstances, invests at least 80% of its assets in the securities that comprise the index. The index is composed of 100 stocks selected from the S&P 1500® by the index provider using a quantitative methodology. The fund is non-diversified. **Top Holdings:** General Mills Inc Nordstrom Inc Signet Jewelers Ltd AT&T Inc First Horizon National Corp

Tortoise North American Pipeline Fund   C   HOLD

Ticker	Traded On	NAV	Total Assets ($)	Dividend Yield (TTM)	Turnover Ratio	Expense Ratio
TPYP	NYSE Arca	19.92	$187,992,909	4.21	28	0.4

Ratings
Reward   C
Risk   C
Recent Upgrade/Downgrade   Down

Fund Information
Fund Type   Exchange Traded Funds
Category   Energy Sector Equity
Sub-Category   Energy Limited Partnership
Prospectus Objective   Unaligned
Inception Date   Jun-15
Open to New Investments   Y

Prices
Price (as of 12/31/2018)   19.91
52-Week High   24.62
52-Week Low   19.22

Total Returns (%)

3-Month	6-Month	1-Year	3-Year	5-Year
-15.07	-11.94	-10.85	25.23	

3-Year Standard Deviation   13.3
Effective Duration

Valuation
Premium/Discount (1-Year Average)   0.14

Company Information
Provider   Tortoise Capital Advisors
Manager/Tenure   Matthew Weglarz (3)
Website   http://www.tortoiseadvisors.com/
Address   Tortoise Capital Advisors 11550 Ash Street, Suite 300 Leawood KS 66211 United States
Phone Number   866-362-9331

PERFORMANCE

Ratings History

Date	Overall Rating	Risk Rating	Reward Rating
Q4-18	C	C	C
Q2-18	C	D+	B-
Q4-17	C	C	C
Q4-16	D	D+	C+
Q4-15	U		

Asset & Performance History

Date	NAV	1-Year Total Return
2017	23.29	2.15
2016	23.66	40.05
2015	17.87	
2014		
2013		
2012		

Total Assets: $187,992,909

Asset Allocation

Asset	%
Cash	1%
Stocks	99%
US Stocks	70%
Bonds	0%
US Bonds	0%
Other	0%

Services Offered:

Investment Strategy: The investment seeks investment results that correspond (before fees and expenses) generally to the price and distribution rate (total return) performance of the Tortoise North American Pipeline Index (the "underlying index"). The fund will normally invest at least 80% of its total assets in securities that comprise the underlying index (or depository receipts based on such securities). The underlying index is a proprietary rules-based, capitalization weighted, float adjusted index designed to track the overall performance of equity securities of North American Pipeline Companies. The fund is non-diversified. **Top Holdings:** Enbridge Inc TransCanada Corp ONEOK Inc Kinder Morgan Inc P Williams Companies Inc

---

First Trust Multi Cap Growth AlphaDEX® Fund   C-   HOLD

Ticker	Traded On	NAV	Total Assets ($)	Dividend Yield (TTM)	Turnover Ratio	Expense Ratio
FAD	NAS CM	61.15	$187,797,224	0.18	142	0.69

Ratings
Reward   C-
Risk   C-
Recent Upgrade/Downgrade   Down

Fund Information
Fund Type   Exchange Traded Funds
Category   US Equity Mid Cap
Sub-Category   Mid-Cap Growth
Prospectus Objective   Growth
Inception Date   May-07
Open to New Investments   Y

Prices
Price (as of 12/31/2018)   61.30
52-Week High   77.58
52-Week Low   56.57

Total Returns (%)

3-Month	6-Month	1-Year	3-Year	5-Year
-19.90	-15.16	-6.22	24.91	38.09

3-Year Standard Deviation   12.4
Effective Duration

Valuation
Premium/Discount (1-Year Average)   0.22

Company Information
Provider   First Trust
Manager/Tenure   Jon C. Erickson (11), Daniel J. Lindquist (11), David G. McGarel (11), 3 others
Website   http://www.ftportfolios.com/
Address   First Trust 120 E. Liberty Drive, Suite 400 Wheaton IL 60187 United States
Phone Number   800-621-1675

PERFORMANCE

Ratings History

Date	Overall Rating	Risk Rating	Reward Rating
Q4-18	C-	C-	C-
Q2-18	C+	C-	B
Q4-17	A-	B+	A-
Q4-16	C	C-	B-
Q4-15	C	C-	B-

Asset & Performance History

Date	NAV	1-Year Total Return
2017	65.33	24.68
2016	52.52	6.82
2015	49.48	2.09
2014	48.66	8.28
2013	45.14	38.4
2012	32.73	10.56

Total Assets: $187,797,224

Asset Allocation

Asset	%
Cash	0%
Stocks	100%
US Stocks	99%
Bonds	0%
US Bonds	0%
Other	0%

Services Offered:

Investment Strategy: The investment seeks investment results that correspond generally to the price and yield (before the fund's fees and expenses) of the Nasdaq AlphaDEX® Multi Cap Growth Index. The fund will normally invest at least 90% of its net assets (including investment borrowings) in common stocks that comprise the index. The index is designed to select growth stocks from the NASDAQ US 500 Large Cap Index, NASDAQ US 600 Mid Cap Index and NASDAQ US 700 Small Cap Index that may generate positive alpha, or risk-adjusted returns, relative to traditional indices through the use of the AlphaDEX® selection methodology. **Top Holdings:** Dell-VMWare Tracking Stock V Ulta Beauty Inc HCA Healthcare Inc Burlington Stores Inc O'Reilly Automotive Inc

Direxion NASDAQ-100® Equal Weighted Index Shares   C   HOLD

Ticker	Traded On	NAV	Total Assets ($)	Dividend Yield (TTM)	Turnover Ratio	Expense Ratio
QQQE	NYSE Arca	40.69	$187,686,649	0.7	31	0.35

Ratings
Reward   C
Risk   C-
Recent Upgrade/Downgrade

Fund Information
Fund Type	Exchange Traded Funds
Category	US Equity Large Cap Growth
Sub-Category	Large Growth
Prospectus Objective	Growth
Inception Date	Mar-12
Open to New Investments	Y

Prices
Price (as of 12/31/2018)	40.56
52-Week High	47.92
52-Week Low	38.25

Total Returns (%)
3-Month	6-Month	1-Year	3-Year	5-Year
-13.73	-9.71	-4.92	28.76	57.59

3-Year Standard Deviation   11.94
Effective Duration

Valuation
Premium/Discount (1-Year Average)   0.07

Company Information
Provider	Direxion Funds
Manager/Tenure	Paul Brigandi (6), Tony Ng (3)
Website	http://www.direxionfunds.com
Address	Direxion Funds 1301 Avenue Of The Americas (6th Avenue) New York NY 10019 United States
Phone Number	646-572-3390

PERFORMANCE

Ratings History
Date	Overall Rating	Risk Rating	Reward Rating
Q4-18	C	C-	C
Q2-18	C	C-	C+
Q4-17	B	B+	B
Q4-16	C-	C-	C-
Q4-15	C	C-	C+

Asset & Performance History
Date	NAV	1-Year Total Return
2017	43.11	26.28
2016	34.37	7.24
2015	32.45	2.52
2014	31.83	19.36
2013	27.07	40.23
2012	19.39	

Total Assets: $187,686,649

Asset Allocation
Asset	%
Cash	0%
Stocks	100%
US Stocks	90%
Bonds	0%
US Bonds	0%
Other	0%

Services Offered:

Investment Strategy: The investment seeks investment results before fees and expenses that track the NASDAQ-100® Equal Weighted Index. The fund, under normal circumstances, invests at least 80% of its assets in the securities that comprise the index. The index is the equal weighted version of the NASDAQ-100 Index® which includes 100 of the largest domestic and international non-financial companies listed on the NASDAQ® Stock Market based on market capitalization. The fund is non-diversified. **Top Holdings:** Tesla Inc   Walgreens Boots Alliance Inc   Xilinx Inc   Express Scripts Holding Co   Shire PLC ADR

ProShares High Yield—Interest Rate Hedged   C-   HOLD

Ticker	Traded On	NAV	Total Assets ($)	Dividend Yield (TTM)	Turnover Ratio	Expense Ratio
HYHG	BATS	62.09	$187,169,690	6.02		0.5

Ratings
Reward   C-
Risk   C-
Recent Upgrade/Downgrade   Down

Fund Information
Fund Type	Exchange Traded Funds
Category	Fixed Income Misc
Sub-Category	Nontraditional Bond
Prospectus Objective	Income
Inception Date	May-13
Open to New Investments	Y

Prices
Price (as of 12/31/2018)	62.09
52-Week High	68.99
52-Week Low	61.54

Total Returns (%)
3-Month	6-Month	1-Year	3-Year	5-Year
-8.08	-4.25	-2.82	16.29	2.59

3-Year Standard Deviation   5.64
Effective Duration

Valuation
Premium/Discount (1-Year Average)   0.01

Company Information
Provider	ProShares
Manager/Tenure	Jeffrey Ploshnick (5), Benjamin McAbee (2)
Website	http://www.proshares.com
Address	ProShares 7501 Wisconsin Avenue, Suite 1000 Bethesda MD 20814 United States
Phone Number	866-776-5125

PERFORMANCE

Ratings History
Date	Overall Rating	Risk Rating	Reward Rating
Q4-18	C-	C-	C-
Q2-18	C	C-	C
Q4-17	C+	C+	C
Q4-16	D+	D+	C-
Q4-15	D+	C-	D+

Asset & Performance History
Date	NAV	1-Year Total Return
2017	67.41	4.42
2016	68.19	14.6
2015	63	-9.51
2014	73.73	-2.5
2013	79.65	
2012		

Total Assets: $187,169,690

Asset Allocation
Asset	%
Cash	2%
Stocks	0%
US Stocks	0%
Bonds	98%
US Bonds	81%
Other	0%

Services Offered:

Investment Strategy: The investment seeks investment results, before fees and expenses, that track the performance of the FTSE High Yield (Treasury Rate-Hedged) Index (the "index"). Under normal circumstances, the fund will invest at least 80% of its total assets in high-yield bonds included in the index. The index is comprised of (a) long positions in U.S. dollar-denominated high yield corporate bonds ("high yield bonds") and (b) short positions in U.S. Treasury notes or bonds ("Treasury Securities") of, in aggregate, approximate equivalent duration to the high yield bonds. **Top Holdings:** US 5 Year Note (CBT) Mar19   Us 5 Yr Note Future 03/29/2019 (Fvh9) - Cash Offset   US 10 Year Note (CBT) Mar19   Us 10yr Note Future 03/20/2019 (Tyh9) - Cash Offset   2 Year US Treasury Note Future Mar19

Direxion Daily Healthcare Bull 3X Shares   C   HOLD

Ticker	Traded On	NAV	Total Assets ($)	Dividend Yield (TTM)	Turnover Ratio	Expense Ratio
CURE	NYSE Arca	47.62	$187,100,842	0.42	23	1.09

Ratings
Reward   C
Risk   C
Recent Upgrade/Downgrade

Fund Information
Fund Type   Exchange Traded Funds
Category   Trading Tools
Sub-Category   Trading--Leveraged Equity
Prospectus Objective   Health
Inception Date   Jun-11
Open to New Investments   Y

Prices
Price (as of 12/31/2018)   47.59
52-Week High   67.75
52-Week Low   39.11

Total Returns (%)
3-Month	6-Month	1-Year	3-Year	5-Year
-29.36	4.31	2.91	43.82	178.47

3-Year Standard Deviation   38.02
Effective Duration

Valuation
Premium/Discount (1-Year Average)   -0.03

Company Information
Provider   Direxion Funds
Manager/Tenure   Paul Brigandi (7), Tony Ng (3)
Website   http://www.direxionfunds.com
Address   Direxion Funds 1301 Avenue Of The
                    Americas (6th Avenue) New York NY
                    10019 United States
Phone Number   646-572-3390

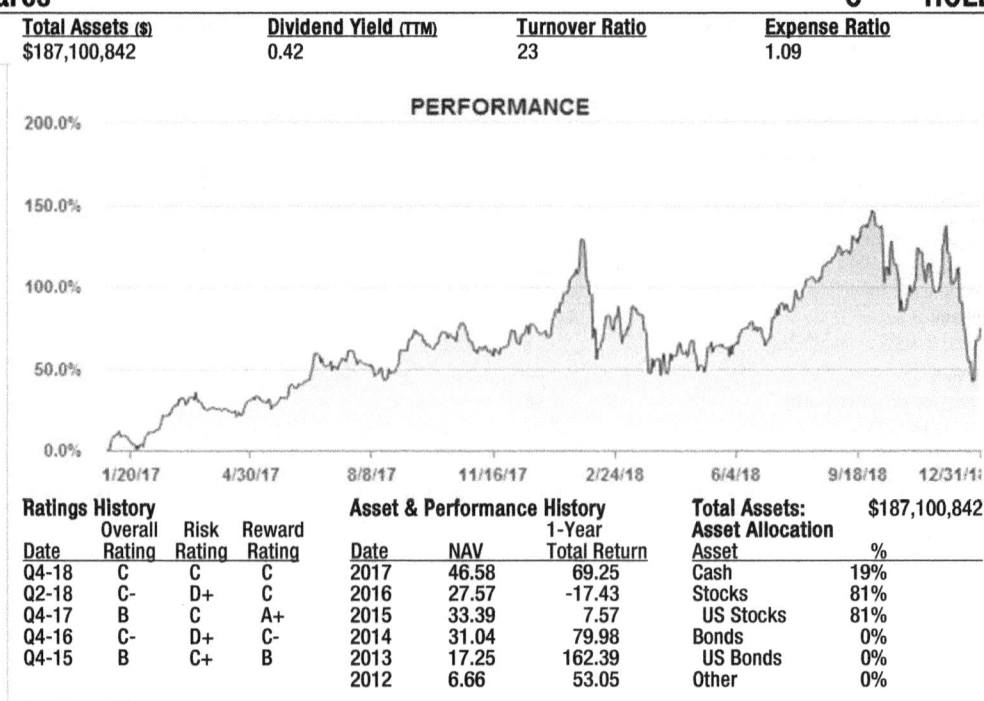

PERFORMANCE

Ratings History

Date	Overall Rating	Risk Rating	Reward Rating
Q4-18	C	C	C
Q2-18	C-	D+	C
Q4-17	B	C	A+
Q4-16	C-	D+	C-
Q4-15	B	C+	B

Asset & Performance History

Date	NAV	1-Year Total Return
2017	46.58	69.25
2016	27.57	-17.43
2015	33.39	7.57
2014	31.04	79.98
2013	17.25	162.39
2012	6.66	53.05

Total Assets: $187,100,842

Asset Allocation

Asset	%
Cash	19%
Stocks	81%
US Stocks	81%
Bonds	0%
US Bonds	0%
Other	0%

Services Offered:

Investment Strategy: The investment seeks daily investment results, before fees and expenses, of 300% of the daily performance of the Health Care Select Sector Index. The fund invests at least 80% of its net assets in securities of the index, ETFs that track the index and other financial instruments that provide daily leveraged exposure to the index or ETFs that track the index. The index includes domestic companies from the healthcare sector, which includes the following industries: pharmaceuticals; health care equipment and supplies; health care providers and services; biotechnology; life sciences tools and services; and health care technology. It is non-diversified. **Top Holdings:** Health Care Select Sector SPDR® ETF   Health Care Sel Sec Index   Health Care Sel Sec Index   Health Care Sel Sec Index   Health Care Sel Sec Index

---

iShares MSCI BRIC ETF   C-   HOLD

Ticker	Traded On	NAV	Total Assets ($)	Dividend Yield (TTM)	Turnover Ratio	Expense Ratio
BKF	NYSE Arca	37.81	$186,600,211	1.87	22	0.67

Ratings
Reward   C-
Risk   C-
Recent Upgrade/Downgrade

Fund Information
Fund Type   Exchange Traded Funds
Category   Global Emerg Mkts Equity
Sub-Category   Diversified Emerging Mkts
Prospectus Objective   Foreign Stock
Inception Date   Nov-07
Open to New Investments   Y

Prices
Price (as of 12/31/2018)   37.51
52-Week High   50.87
52-Week Low   36.50

Total Returns (%)
3-Month	6-Month	1-Year	3-Year	5-Year
-4.96	-9.01	-13.57	35.45	12.91

3-Year Standard Deviation   16.89
Effective Duration

Valuation
Premium/Discount (1-Year Average)   -0.29

Company Information
Provider   iShares
Manager/Tenure   Diane Hsiung (10), Greg Savage (10),
                    Jennifer Hsui (5), 1 other
Website   http://www.ishares.com
Address   iShares 400 Howard Street San
                    Francisco CA 94105 United States
Phone Number   800-474-2737

PERFORMANCE

Ratings History

Date	Overall Rating	Risk Rating	Reward Rating
Q4-18	C-	C-	C-
Q2-18	C	C-	C
Q4-17	B	C+	A
Q4-16	D+	C-	D+
Q4-15	D+	D+	C-

Asset & Performance History

Date	NAV	1-Year Total Return
2017	44.73	40.83
2016	32.27	11.28
2015	29.54	-13.62
2014	35.18	-3.49
2013	37.54	-4.25
2012	40.24	13.51

Total Assets: $186,600,211

Asset Allocation

Asset	%
Cash	0%
Stocks	100%
US Stocks	0%
Bonds	0%
US Bonds	0%
Other	0%

Services Offered:

Investment Strategy: The investment seeks to track the investment results of the MSCI BRIC Index. The fund generally will invest at least 90% of its assets in the component securities of the underlying index and in investments that have economic characteristics that are substantially identical to the component securities of the underlying index. The index is a free float-adjusted market capitalization index that is designed to measure the combined equity market performance in Brazil, Russia, India and China ("BRIC"). **Top Holdings:** Tencent Holdings Ltd   Alibaba Group Holding Ltd ADR   China Construction Bank Corp H   China Mobile Ltd   Baidu Inc ADR

Invesco Dynamic Semiconductors ETF   C+   HOLD

Ticker	Traded On	NAV		Total Assets ($)	Dividend Yield (TTM)	Turnover Ratio	Expense Ratio
PSI	NYSE Arca	44.46		$185,206,674	0.55	65	0.61

Ratings
Reward	B
Risk	C-
Recent Upgrade/Downgrade	Down

Fund Information
Fund Type	Exchange Traded Funds
Category	Technology Sector Equity
Sub-Category	Technology
Prospectus Objective	Technology
Inception Date	Jun-05
Open to New Investments	Y

Prices
Price (as of 12/31/2018)	44.31
52-Week High	57.52
52-Week Low	41.12

Total Returns (%)
3-Month	6-Month	1-Year	3-Year	5-Year
-15.94	-15.39	-11.19	79.64	144.15

3-Year Standard Deviation	21.86
Effective Duration	

Valuation
Premium/Discount (1-Year Average)	0.04

Company Information
Provider	Invesco
Manager/Tenure	Peter Hubbard (11), Michael Jeanette (10), Tony Seisser (4), 1 other
Website	http://www.invesco.com/us
Address	Invesco 11 Greenway Plaza, Ste. 2500 Houston TX 77046 United States
Phone Number	800-659-1005

PERFORMANCE

Ratings History

Date	Overall Rating	Risk Rating	Reward Rating
Q4-18	C+	C-	B
Q2-18	B	C	B+
Q4-17	A-	B	A+
Q4-16	C	C	C+
Q4-15	B	B-	B

Asset & Performance History

Date	NAV	1-Year Total Return
2017	50.44	40.03
2016	36.1	44.44
2015	25.18	-0.78
2014	25.42	36.98
2013	18.9	31.57
2012	14.46	4.67

Total Assets: $185,206,674

Asset Allocation
Asset	%
Cash	0%
Stocks	100%
US Stocks	95%
Bonds	0%
US Bonds	0%
Other	0%

Services Offered:

Investment Strategy: The investment seeks to track the investment results (before fees and expenses) of the Dynamic Semiconductor IntellidexSM Index. The fund generally will invest at least 90% of its total assets in common stocks of semiconductor companies that comprise the underlying intellidex. The underlying intellidex was composed of common stocks of 30 U.S. semiconductor companies. These are companies that are principally engaged in the manufacture of semiconductors. The fund is non-diversified. **Top Holdings:** Xilinx Inc   Intel Corp   Analog Devices Inc   Texas Instruments Inc   Advanced Micro Devices Inc

---

SPDR® SSGA US Small Cap Low Volatility Index ETF   C-   HOLD

Ticker	Traded On	NAV		Total Assets ($)	Dividend Yield (TTM)	Turnover Ratio	Expense Ratio
SMLV	NYSE Arca	83.16		$184,929,785	2.68	158	0.12

Ratings
Reward	C-
Risk	D+
Recent Upgrade/Downgrade	Down

Fund Information
Fund Type	Exchange Traded Funds
Category	US Equity Small Cap
Sub-Category	Small Blend
Prospectus Objective	Income
Inception Date	Feb-13
Open to New Investments	Y

Prices
Price (as of 12/31/2018)	82.88
52-Week High	99.77
52-Week Low	79.55

Total Returns (%)
3-Month	6-Month	1-Year	3-Year	5-Year
-12.19	-11.43	-6.01	29.20	42.74

3-Year Standard Deviation	13.02
Effective Duration	

Valuation
Premium/Discount (1-Year Average)	0.14

Company Information
Provider	SPDR State Street Global Advisors
Manager/Tenure	Michael J. Feehily (5), Karl A. Schneider (4), John Law (0)
Website	http://www.spdrs.com
Address	SPDR State Street Global Advisors State Street Financial Center, 1 Lincoln Street Boston MA 02111-2900 United States
Phone Number	617-786-3000

PERFORMANCE

Ratings History

Date	Overall Rating	Risk Rating	Reward Rating
Q4-18	C-	D+	C-
Q2-18	C	D+	C+
Q4-17	B+	B+	B+
Q4-16	C	C-	C+
Q4-15	C	C-	C

Asset & Performance History

Date	NAV	1-Year Total Return
2017	91.09	5.21
2016	93.49	30.65
2015	73.99	-1.86
2014	77.4	12.58
2013	70.76	
2012		

Total Assets: $184,929,785

Asset Allocation
Asset	%
Cash	0%
Stocks	100%
US Stocks	97%
Bonds	0%
US Bonds	0%
Other	0%

Services Offered:

Investment Strategy: The investment seeks to provide investment results that, before fees and expenses, correspond generally to the total return performance of the SSGA US Small Cap Low Volatility Index. The fund generally invests substantially all, but at least 80%, of its total assets in the securities comprising the index. The index is designed to measure the performance of the stocks of U.S. small capitalization companies that exhibit low volatility. Volatility is a statistical measurement of the magnitude of movements in a stock's price over time. The fund is non-diversified. **Top Holdings:** Apollo Commercial Real Estate Finance Inc   White Mountains Insurance Group Ltd   Capitol Federal Financial Inc   Kearny Financial Corp   Capstead Mortgage Corp

VanEck Vectors India Small-Cap Index ETF   D   SELL

Ticker	Traded On	NAV	Total Assets ($)	Dividend Yield (TTM)	Turnover Ratio	Expense Ratio
SCIF	NYSE Arca	42.36	$184,733,647	0.17	42	0.72

Ratings
Reward	D
Risk	D
Recent Upgrade/Downgrade	Down

Fund Information
Fund Type	Exchange Traded Funds
Category	India Equity
Sub-Category	India Equity
Prospectus Objective	Small Company
Inception Date	Aug-10
Open to New Investments	Y

Prices
Price (as of 12/31/2018)	42.40
52-Week High	72.50
52-Week Low	36.72

Total Returns (%)
3-Month	6-Month	1-Year	3-Year	5-Year
7.39	-11.49	-37.99	-1.42	43.18

3-Year Standard Deviation	28.54
Effective Duration	

Valuation
Premium/Discount (1-Year Average)	0.11

Company Information
Provider	VanEck
Manager/Tenure	Hao-Hung (Peter) Liao (8), Guo Hua (Jason) Jin (0)
Website	http://www.vaneck.com
Address	Van Eck Associates Corporation 666 Third Avenue New York NY 10017 United States
Phone Number	800-826-1115

PERFORMANCE

Ratings History
Date	Overall Rating	Risk Rating	Reward Rating
Q4-18	D	D	D
Q2-18	C-	C-	C
Q4-17	B+	C+	A
Q4-16	C+	C-	B
Q4-15	C	C-	C

Asset & Performance History
Date	NAV	1-Year Total Return
2017	68.4	66.89
2016	41.03	-4.73
2015	43.66	1.12
2014	44.53	43.64
2013	31.31	-28.77
2012	44.16	25.31

Total Assets: $184,733,647
Asset Allocation
Asset	%
Cash	0%
Stocks	50%
US Stocks	1%
Bonds	0%
US Bonds	0%
Other	50%

Services Offered:

Investment Strategy: The investment seeks to replicate as closely as possible, before fees and expenses, the price and yield performance of the MVIS® India Small-Cap Index. The fund invests substantially all of its assets in the Subsidiary, a wholly-owned subsidiary located in the Republic of Mauritius. The Subsidiary in turn will normally invest at least 80% of its total assets in securities that comprise the fund's benchmark index, and depositary receipts based on the securities in the fund's benchmark index. The index includes Indian small-capitalization companies selected on the basis of their relative market capitalizations. **Top Holdings:** India Small Cap Mauritius NCC Ltd Ipca Laboratories Ltd PVR Ltd KPIT Technologies Ltd

---

SPDR® Bloomberg Barclays International Corporate Bond ETF   D+   SELL

Ticker	Traded On	NAV	Total Assets ($)	Dividend Yield (TTM)	Turnover Ratio	Expense Ratio
IBND	NYSE Arca	32.72	$184,363,953	0.75	14	0.5

Ratings
Reward	D+
Risk	C-
Recent Upgrade/Downgrade	Down

Fund Information
Fund Type	Exchange Traded Funds
Category	Global Fixed Income
Sub-Category	World Bond
Prospectus Objective	Worldwide Bond
Inception Date	May-10
Open to New Investments	Y

Prices
Price (as of 12/31/2018)	32.94
52-Week High	36.74
52-Week Low	32.28

Total Returns (%)
3-Month	6-Month	1-Year	3-Year	5-Year
-1.91	-2.37	-6.32	7.48	-7.89

3-Year Standard Deviation	7.5
Effective Duration	5.56

Valuation
Premium/Discount (1-Year Average)	0.10

Company Information
Provider	SPDR State Street Global Advisors
Manager/Tenure	Peter Spano (3), Richard Darby-Dowman (3), Paul Brown (2)
Website	http://www.spdrs.com
Address	SPDR State Street Global Advisors State Street Financial Center, 1 Lincoln Street Boston MA 02111-2900 United States
Phone Number	617-786-3000

PERFORMANCE

Ratings History
Date	Overall Rating	Risk Rating	Reward Rating
Q4-18	D+	C-	D+
Q2-18	C-	C-	C-
Q4-17	C	C+	C
Q4-16	D+	C-	D
Q4-15	D+	D+	D

Asset & Performance History
Date	NAV	1-Year Total Return
2017	35.19	14.76
2016	30.77	-0.01
2015	30.78	-10.28
2014	34.31	-4.48
2013	36.49	5.08
2012	35.17	12.97

Total Assets: $184,363,953
Asset Allocation
Asset	%
Cash	0%
Stocks	0%
US Stocks	0%
Bonds	99%
US Bonds	29%
Other	0%

Services Offered:

Investment Strategy: The investment seeks to provide investment results that correspond generally to the price and yield performance of the Bloomberg Barclays Global Aggregate ex-USD >$1B: Corporate Bond Index. The fund invests substantially all, but at least 80%, of its total assets in the securities comprising the index or in securities that the Adviser determines have economic characteristics that are substantially identical to the economic characteristics of the securities that comprise the index. The index is designed to be a broad based measure of the global investment grade, fixed rate, fixed income corporate markets outside the United States. It is non-diversified. **Top Holdings:** Sanofi Sr Unsecured Regs 09/26 1.75 Deutsche Bank Ag Sr Unsecured Regs 03/25 1.125 Sanofi 0.5% Anheuser-Busch InBev N.V./S.A. 2.75% Panasonic Corp 0.47%

Invesco DWA Consumer Staples Momentum ETF   B-   BUY

Ticker	Traded On	NAV	Total Assets ($)	Dividend Yield (TTM)	Turnover Ratio	Expense Ratio
PSL	NAS CM	65.44	$184,133,626	0.46	80	0.6

Ratings

Reward	B
Risk	C
Recent Upgrade/Downgrade	Down

Fund Information

Fund Type	Exchange Traded Funds
Category	Consumer Goods & Svcs
Sub-Category	Consumer Defensive
Prospectus Objective	Unaligned
Inception Date	Oct-06
Open to New Investments	Y

Prices

Price (as of 12/31/2018)	65.21
52-Week High	73.71
52-Week Low	62.43

Total Returns (%)

3-Month	6-Month	1-Year	3-Year	5-Year
-8.03	-6.89	1.51	18.93	56.25

3-Year Standard Deviation 6.89
Effective Duration

Valuation

Premium/Discount (1-Year Average) 0.09

Company Information

Provider	Invesco
Manager/Tenure	Peter Hubbard (11), Michael Jeanette (10), Tony Seisser (4), 1 other
Website	http://www.invesco.com/us
Address	Invesco 11 Greenway Plaza, Ste. 2500 Houston TX 77046 United States
Phone Number	800-659-1005

PERFORMANCE

Ratings History

Date	Overall Rating	Risk Rating	Reward Rating
Q4-18	B-	C	B
Q2-18	B	C	B+
Q4-17	B	B	B
Q4-16	B	C+	B
Q4-15	B+	B	A

Asset & Performance History

Date	NAV	1-Year Total Return
2017	64.93	21.4
2016	53.68	-3.49
2015	56.77	13.48
2014	50.64	15.77
2013	44.19	34.53
2012	33.3	9.5

Total Assets: $184,133,626

Asset Allocation

Asset	%
Cash	0%
Stocks	100%
US Stocks	96%
Bonds	0%
US Bonds	0%
Other	0%

Services Offered:

Investment Strategy: The investment seeks to track the investment results (before fees and expenses) of the Dorsey Wright® Consumer Staples Technical Leaders Index (the "underlying index"). The fund generally will invest at least 90% of its total assets in the securities that comprise the underlying index. The underlying index is composed of at least 30 securities of companies in the consumer staples sector that have powerful relative strength or "momentum" characteristics. **Top Holdings:** Church & Dwight Co Inc McCormick & Co Inc Non-Voting Grand Canyon Education Inc Hormel Foods Corp Rollins Inc

Pacer US Cash Cows 100 ETF   C-   HOLD

Ticker	Traded On	NAV	Total Assets ($)	Dividend Yield (TTM)	Turnover Ratio	Expense Ratio
COWZ	BATS	25.77	$184,078,814	1.43	101	0.49

Ratings

Reward	C-
Risk	C-
Recent Upgrade/Downgrade	

Fund Information

Fund Type	Exchange Traded Funds
Category	US Equity Large Cap Blend
Sub-Category	Large Value
Prospectus Objective	Growth & Inc
Inception Date	Dec-16
Open to New Investments	Y

Prices

Price (as of 12/31/2018)	25.70
52-Week High	31.30
52-Week Low	24.24

Total Returns (%)

3-Month	6-Month	1-Year	3-Year	5-Year
-15.91	-12.26	-9.30		

3-Year Standard Deviation
Effective Duration

Valuation

Premium/Discount (1-Year Average) 0.21

Company Information

Provider	Pacer
Manager/Tenure	Bruce Kavanaugh (1), Michael Mack (1)
Website	http://www.paceretfs.com
Address	Pacer 16 Industrial Blvd, Suite 201 Paoli PA 19301 United States
Phone Number	

PERFORMANCE

Ratings History

Date	Overall Rating	Risk Rating	Reward Rating
Q4-18	C-	C-	C-
Q2-18	C-	C-	C
Q4-17	D-	B+	D+
Q4-16			
Q4-15			

Asset & Performance History

Date	NAV	1-Year Total Return
2017	28.85	19.54
2016	24.64	
2015		
2014		
2013		
2012		

Total Assets: $184,078,814

Asset Allocation

Asset	%
Cash	0%
Stocks	100%
US Stocks	98%
Bonds	0%
US Bonds	0%
Other	0%

Services Offered:

Investment Strategy: The investment seeks to track the total return performance, before fees and expenses, of the Pacer US Cash Cows 100 Index (the "index"). Under normal circumstances, at least 80% of the fund's total assets (exclusive of collateral held from securities lending) will be invested in the component securities of the index. The index uses an objective, rules-based methodology to provide exposure to large and mid-capitalization U.S. companies with high free cash flow yields. Companies with high free cash flow yields are commonly referred to as "cash cows". The fund is non-diversified. **Top Holdings:** Walgreens Boots Alliance Inc Express Scripts Holding Co VMware Inc Oracle Corp Amgen Inc

Franklin Liberty Short Duration U.S. Government ETF

C-   HOLD

Ticker	Traded On	NAV	Total Assets ($)	Dividend Yield (TTM)	Turnover Ratio	Expense Ratio
FTSD	NYSE Arca	94.37	$183,974,887	2.62	103	0.25

Ratings

Reward   C-
Risk   C-
Recent Upgrade/Downgrade

Fund Information

Fund Type	Exchange Traded Funds
Category	US Fixed Income
Sub-Category	Short Government
Prospectus Objective	Growth
Inception Date	Nov-13
Open to New Investments	Y

Prices

Price (as of 12/31/2018)	94.78
52-Week High	95.86
52-Week Low	94.18

Total Returns (%)

3-Month	6-Month	1-Year	3-Year	5-Year
0.66	0.93	1.19	3.02	3.99

3-Year Standard Deviation	0.43
Effective Duration	

Valuation

Premium/Discount (1-Year Average)   0.05

Company Information

Provider	Franklin Templeton Investments
Manager/Tenure	Roger Bayston (5), Patrick Klein (5)
Website	http://www.franklintempleton.com
Address	Franklin Templeton Investments One Franklin Parkway, Building 970, 1st Floor San Mateo CA 94403 United States
Phone Number	650-312-2000

PERFORMANCE

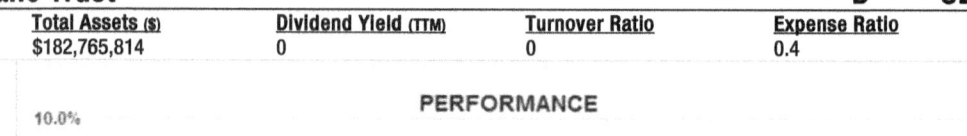

Ratings History

Date	Overall Rating	Risk Rating	Reward Rating
Q4-18	C-	C-	C-
Q2-18	C-	D+	C-
Q4-17	C	B	C
Q4-16	C-	D+	C
Q4-15	D+	C-	D+

Asset & Performance History

Date	NAV	1-Year Total Return
2017	95.74	0.79
2016	97.12	1
2015	98.01	0.34
2014	99.16	0.58
2013	100.47	
2012		

Total Assets: $183,974,887

Asset Allocation

Asset	%
Cash	2%
Stocks	0%
US Stocks	0%
Bonds	98%
US Bonds	94%
Other	0%

Services Offered:

Investment Strategy: The investment seeks a high level of current income as is consistent with prudent investing, while seeking preservation of capital. Under normal market conditions, the fund invests at least 80% of its net assets in securities issued or guaranteed by the U.S. government, its agencies, or instrumentalities. It is an actively managed exchange-traded fund ("ETF") that does not seek to replicate the performance of a specified index. To pursue its investment goal, it may invest in certain interest rate-related derivative transactions, principally U.S. Treasury and fixed income index futures contracts. **Top Holdings:** Federal National Mortgage Association 3% Federal Home Loan Mortgage Corporation 4.18% Government National Mortgage Association 3.5% Federal Home Loan Mortgage Corporation 4% United States Treasury Notes 2.75%

Invesco CurrencyShares® Swiss Franc Trust

D   SELL

Ticker	Traded On	NAV	Total Assets ($)	Dividend Yield (TTM)	Turnover Ratio	Expense Ratio
FXF	NYSE Arca	94.60	$182,765,814	0	0	0.4

Ratings

Reward   D
Risk   C-
Recent Upgrade/Downgrade

Fund Information

Fund Type	Exchange Traded Funds
Category	Currency
Sub-Category	Single Currency
Prospectus Objective	Worldwide Bond
Inception Date	Jun-06
Open to New Investments	Y

Prices

Price (as of 12/31/2018)	94.88
52-Week High	102.20
52-Week Low	92.44

Total Returns (%)

3-Month	6-Month	1-Year	3-Year	5-Year
-1.20	0.19	-2.28	-1.93	-14.12

3-Year Standard Deviation	7.4
Effective Duration	

Valuation

Premium/Discount (1-Year Average)   -0.07

Company Information

Provider	Invesco
Manager/Tenure	Management Team (12)
Website	http://www.invesco.com/us
Address	Invesco 11 Greenway Plaza, Ste. 2500 Houston TX 77046 United States
Phone Number	800-659-1005

PERFORMANCE

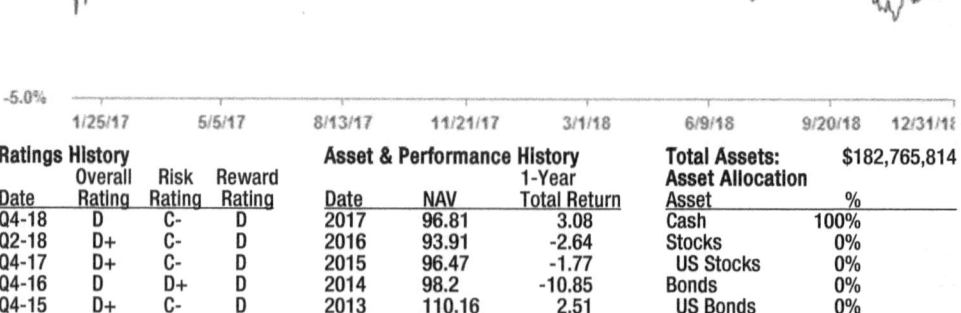

Ratings History

Date	Overall Rating	Risk Rating	Reward Rating
Q4-18	D	C-	D
Q2-18	D+	C-	D
Q4-17	D+	C-	D
Q4-16	D	D+	D
Q4-15	D+	C-	D

Asset & Performance History

Date	NAV	1-Year Total Return
2017	96.81	3.08
2016	93.91	-2.64
2015	96.47	-1.77
2014	98.2	-10.85
2013	110.16	2.51
2012	107.46	1.75

Total Assets: $182,765,814

Asset Allocation

Asset	%
Cash	100%
Stocks	0%
US Stocks	0%
Bonds	0%
US Bonds	0%
Other	0%

Services Offered:

Investment Strategy: The investment seeks to track the price of the Swiss Franc, net of trust expenses. The fund seeks to reflect the price of the Swiss Franc. The sponsor believes that, for many investors, the shares represent a cost-effective investment relative to traditional means of investing in the foreign exchange market. **Top Holdings:**

Invesco Golden Dragon China ETF · C · HOLD

Ticker	Traded On	NAV
PGJ	NAS CM	31.62

Total Assets ($)	Dividend Yield (TTM)	Turnover Ratio	Expense Ratio
$182,398,191	2.05	25	0.7

Ratings
Reward	B-
Risk	D
Recent Upgrade/Downgrade	Down

Fund Information
Fund Type	Exchange Traded Funds
Category	Greater China Equity
Sub-Category	China Region
Prospectus Objective	Pacific Stock
Inception Date	Dec-04
Open to New Investments	Y

Prices
Price (as of 12/31/2018)	31.53
52-Week High	50.87
52-Week Low	30.95

Total Returns (%)
3-Month	6-Month	1-Year	3-Year	5-Year
-17.61	-31.02	-29.15	0.45	10.13

3-Year Standard Deviation	20.24
Effective Duration	

Valuation
Premium/Discount (1-Year Average)	-0.12

Company Information
Provider	Invesco
Manager/Tenure	Peter Hubbard (11), Michael Jeanette (10), Jonathan Nixon (3), 1 other
Website	http://www.invesco.com/us
Address	Invesco 11 Greenway Plaza, Ste. 2500 Houston TX 77046 United States
Phone Number	800-659-1005

PERFORMANCE

Ratings History
Date	Overall Rating	Risk Rating	Reward Rating
Q4-18	C	D	B-
Q2-18	C+	D+	B
Q4-17	B+	C+	A+
Q4-16	C	D+	B
Q4-15	B-	C	B

Asset & Performance History
Date	NAV	1-Year Total Return
2017	44.74	59.96
2016	28.57	-11.35
2015	32.85	18.23
2014	27.89	-7.27
2013	30.33	59.64
2012	19.21	0.12

Total Assets: $182,398,191

Asset Allocation
Asset	%
Cash	0%
Stocks	100%
US Stocks	0%
Bonds	0%
US Bonds	0%
Other	0%

Services Offered:

Investment Strategy: The investment seeks to track the investment results (before fees and expenses) of the NASDAQ Golden Dragon China Index. The fund generally will invest at least 90% of its total assets in equity securities that comprise the underlying index. The underlying index is composed of securities of U.S. exchange-listed companies that are headquartered or incorporated in the People's Republic of China. The fund is non-diversified. **Top Holdings:** NetEase Inc ADR Alibaba Group Holding Ltd ADR Baidu Inc ADR Ctrip.com International Ltd ADR JD.com Inc ADR

---

iShares Edge MSCI Multifactor USA Small-Cap ETF · C- · HOLD

Ticker	Traded On	NAV
SMLF	NYSE Arca	35.75

Total Assets ($)	Dividend Yield (TTM)	Turnover Ratio	Expense Ratio
$181,536,352	1.05	46	0.3

Ratings
Reward	C-
Risk	C-
Recent Upgrade/Downgrade	Down

Fund Information
Fund Type	Exchange Traded Funds
Category	US Equity Small Cap
Sub-Category	Small Blend
Prospectus Objective	Small Company
Inception Date	Apr-15
Open to New Investments	Y

Prices
Price (as of 12/31/2018)	35.82
52-Week High	44.87
52-Week Low	33.54

Total Returns (%)
3-Month	6-Month	1-Year	3-Year	5-Year
-16.65	-14.71	-8.16	26.05	

3-Year Standard Deviation	13.09
Effective Duration	

Valuation
Premium/Discount (1-Year Average)	0.06

Company Information
Provider	iShares
Manager/Tenure	Diane Hsiung (3), Jennifer Hsui (3), Greg Savage (3), 3 others
Website	http://www.ishares.com
Address	iShares 400 Howard Street San Francisco CA 94105 United States
Phone Number	800-474-2737

PERFORMANCE

Ratings History
Date	Overall Rating	Risk Rating	Reward Rating
Q4-18	C-	C-	C-
Q2-18	C	C-	C
Q4-17	B-	B	C+
Q4-16	D+	D+	C-
Q4-15	U		

Asset & Performance History
Date	NAV	1-Year Total Return
2017	39.34	12.06
2016	35.45	22.49
2015	29.19	
2014		
2013		
2012		

Total Assets: $181,536,352

Asset Allocation
Asset	%
Cash	0%
Stocks	100%
US Stocks	98%
Bonds	0%
US Bonds	0%
Other	0%

Services Offered:

Investment Strategy: The investment seeks to track the investment results of the MSCI USA Small Cap Diversified Multiple-Factor Index. The fund generally will invest at least 90% of its assets in the component securities of the underlying index and may invest up to 10% of its assets in certain futures, options and swap contracts, cash and cash equivalents. The underlying index is designed to select equity securities from the MSCI USA Small Cap Index (the "parent index") that have high exposure to four investment style factors: value, quality, momentum and low size, while maintaining a level of risk similar to that of the parent index. **Top Holdings:** Encompass Health Corp Teradyne Inc Integrated Device Technology Inc Aspen Technology Inc National Instruments Corp

JPMorgan Global Bond Opportunities ETF | D+ | SELL

Ticker	Traded On	NAV		Total Assets ($)	Dividend Yield (TTM)	Turnover Ratio	Expense Ratio
JPGB	BATS	47.34		$181,488,015	3.37		0.55

Ratings
Reward   D
Risk   C-
Recent Upgrade/Downgrade

Fund Information
Fund Type	Exchange Traded Funds
Category	US Fixed Income
Sub-Category	Multisector Bond
Prospectus Objective	Multi-Asset Global
Inception Date	Apr-17
Open to New Investments	Y

Prices
Price (as of 12/31/2018)	47.31
52-Week High	51.54
52-Week Low	47.26

Total Returns (%)
3-Month	6-Month	1-Year	3-Year	5-Year
-4.52	-2.79	-4.41		

3-Year Standard Deviation
Effective Duration   3.06

Valuation
Premium/Discount (1-Year Average)   0.16

Company Information
Provider	JPMorgan
Manager/Tenure	Nicholas J. Gartside (1), Robert Michele (1), Iain T. Stealey (1)
Website	http://www.jpmorganfunds.com
Address	JPMorgan 270 Park Avenue New York NY 10017-2070 United States
Phone Number	800-480-4111

PERFORMANCE

Ratings History
Date	Overall Rating	Risk Rating	Reward Rating
Q4-18	D+	C-	D
Q2-18	D+	D+	D+
Q4-17	U		
Q4-16			
Q4-15			

Asset & Performance History
Date	NAV	1-Year Total Return
2017	50.93	
2016		
2015		
2014		
2013		
2012		

Total Assets: $181,488,015
Asset Allocation
Asset	%
Cash	7%
Stocks	0%
US Stocks	0%
Bonds	90%
US Bonds	52%
Other	0%

Services Offered:

Investment Strategy: The investment seeks to provide total return. Under normal circumstances, the fund will invest at least 80% of its assets in bonds. It will invest at least 40% of its assets in countries other than the United States. The fund may invest in developed or emerging markets. It generally invests at least 25% of its assets in securities that, at the time of purchase are rated investment grade or the unrated equivalent. "Assets" means net assets plus the amount of borrowings for investment purposes. The fund may also use currency related transactions involving currency derivatives as part of its primary investment strategy. **Top Holdings:** Republic of South Africa 6.5% Federal Home Loan Mortgage Corporation 3.5% Federal National Mortgage Association 3% Federal Home Loan Mortgage Corporation 4% United States Treasury Notes 2.88%

Fidelity® MSCI Materials Index ETF | C | HOLD

Ticker	Traded On	NAV		Total Assets ($)	Dividend Yield (TTM)	Turnover Ratio	Expense Ratio
FMAT	NYSE Arca	28.37		$181,310,836	1.92	10	0.08

Ratings
Reward   C
Risk   C-
Recent Upgrade/Downgrade   Down

Fund Information
Fund Type	Exchange Traded Funds
Category	Natural Resources
Sub-Category	Natural Resources
Prospectus Objective	Natl Res
Inception Date	Oct-13
Open to New Investments	Y

Prices
Price (as of 12/31/2018)	28.39
52-Week High	37.07
52-Week Low	26.67

Total Returns (%)
3-Month	6-Month	1-Year	3-Year	5-Year
-15.58	-14.57	-17.40	23.82	17.56

3-Year Standard Deviation   14.67
Effective Duration

Valuation
Premium/Discount (1-Year Average)   0.00

Company Information
Provider	Fidelity Investments
Manager/Tenure	Jennifer Hsui (5), Greg Savage (5), Alan Mason (2), 2 others
Website	http://www.institutional.fidelity.com
Address	Fidelity Investments 82 Devonshire Street Boston MA 2109 United States
Phone Number	617-563-7000

PERFORMANCE

Ratings History
Date	Overall Rating	Risk Rating	Reward Rating
Q4-18	C	C-	C
Q2-18	C	C-	C
Q4-17	B	C+	B+
Q4-16	C	C-	C+
Q4-15	C-	C	C-

Asset & Performance History
Date	NAV	1-Year Total Return
2017	35.02	23.41
2016	28.85	21.46
2015	24.21	-10.21
2014	27.52	5.75
2013	26.45	
2012		

Total Assets: $181,310,836
Asset Allocation
Asset	%
Cash	0%
Stocks	100%
US Stocks	89%
Bonds	0%
US Bonds	0%
Other	0%

Services Offered:

Investment Strategy: The investment seeks to provide investment returns that correspond, before fees and expenses, generally to the performance of the MSCI USA IMI Materials Index. The fund invests at least 80% of assets in securities included in the fund's underlying index. The fund's underlying index is the MSCI USA IMI Materials Index, which represents the performance of the materials sector in the U.S. equity market. It may or may not hold all of the securities in the MSCI USA IMI Materials Index. The fund is non-diversified. **Top Holdings:** DowDuPont Inc Linde PLC Ecolab Inc Sherwin-Williams Co Air Products & Chemicals Inc

ProShares Ultra Russell2000   C   HOLD

Ticker	Traded On	NAV	Total Assets ($)	Dividend Yield (TTM)	Turnover Ratio	Expense Ratio
UWM	NYSE Arca	52.23	$180,883,836	0.17		0.95

Ratings
Reward   C
Risk   C-
Recent Upgrade/Downgrade   Down

Fund Information
Fund Type   Exchange Traded Funds
Category   Trading Tools
Sub-Category   Trading--Leveraged Equity
Prospectus Objective   Small Company
Inception Date   Jan-07
Open to New Investments   Y

Prices
Price (as of 12/31/2018)   52.13
52-Week High   88.97
52-Week Low   46.50

Total Returns (%)

3-Month	6-Month	1-Year	3-Year	5-Year
-36.22	-35.11	-25.75	32.73	23.87

3-Year Standard Deviation   29.29
Effective Duration

Valuation
Premium/Discount (1-Year Average)   0.00

Company Information
Provider   ProShares
Manager/Tenure   Michael Neches (5), Devin Sullivan (0)
Website   http://www.proshares.com
Address   ProShares 7501 Wisconsin Avenue,
               Suite 1000 Bethesda MD 20814
               United States
Phone Number   866-776-5125

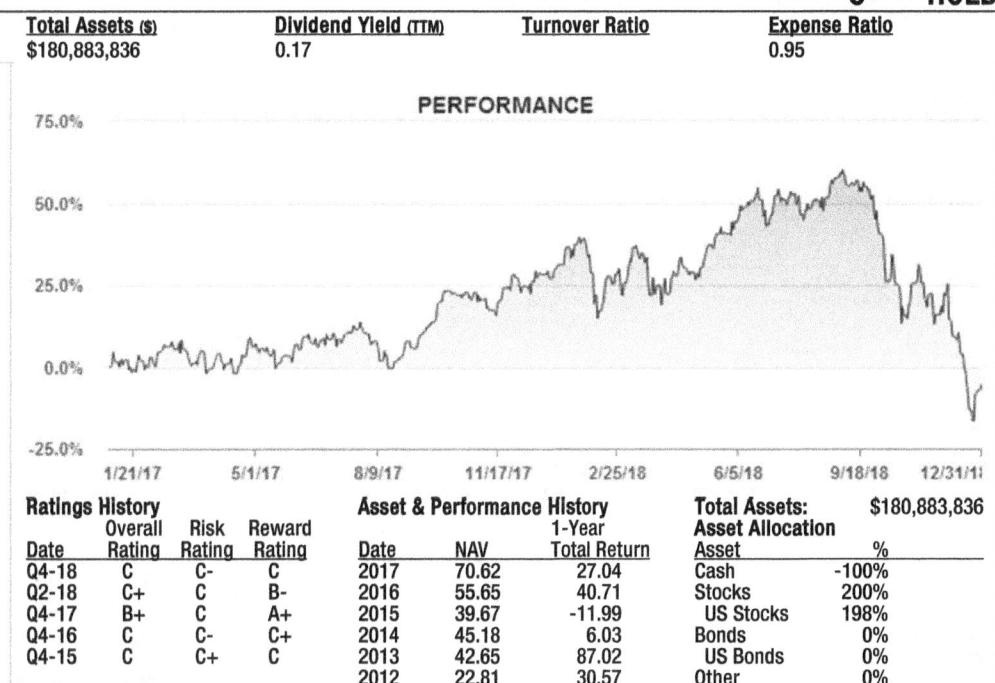

PERFORMANCE

Ratings History

Date	Overall Rating	Risk Rating	Reward Rating
Q4-18	C	C-	C
Q2-18	C+	C	B-
Q4-17	B+	C	A+
Q4-16	C	C-	C+
Q4-15	C	C+	C

Asset & Performance History

Date	NAV	1-Year Total Return
2017	70.62	27.04
2016	55.65	40.71
2015	39.67	-11.99
2014	45.18	6.03
2013	42.65	87.02
2012	22.81	30.57

Total Assets: $180,883,836
Asset Allocation

Asset	%
Cash	-100%
Stocks	200%
US Stocks	198%
Bonds	0%
US Bonds	0%
Other	0%

Services Offered:

Investment Strategy: The investment seeks daily investment results that correspond to two times (2x) the daily performance of the Russell 2000® Index. The fund invests in financial instruments that ProShare Advisors believes, in combination, should produce daily returns consistent with the fund's investment objective. The index is a float-adjusted, market capitalization-weighted index containing approximately 2000 of the smallest companies in the Russell 3000® Index or approximately 8% of the total market capitalization of the Russell 3000® Index, which in turn represents approximately 98% of the investable U.S. equity market. It is non-diversified. **Top Holdings:** Russell 2000 Index Swap Societe Generale   Russell 2000 Index Swap Citibank, N.A.   Russell 2000 Index Swap Deutsche Bank Ag   Russell 2000 Index Swap Bank Of America, Na   Russell 2000 Index Swap Ubs Ag

---

Invesco DWA Emerging Markets Momentum ETF   D+   SELL

Ticker	Traded On	NAV	Total Assets ($)	Dividend Yield (TTM)	Turnover Ratio	Expense Ratio
PIE	NAS CM	15.67	$179,965,414	3.02	174	0.9

Ratings
Reward   D+
Risk   D+
Recent Upgrade/Downgrade   Down

Fund Information
Fund Type   Exchange Traded Funds
Category   Global Emerg Mkts Equity
Sub-Category   Diversified Emerging Mkts
Prospectus Objective   Div Emerg Mkts
Inception Date   Dec-07
Open to New Investments

Prices
Price (as of 12/31/2018)   15.56
52-Week High   22.21
52-Week Low   15.34

Total Returns (%)

3-Month	6-Month	1-Year	3-Year	5-Year
-11.36	-20.34	-21.24	10.02	-7.24

3-Year Standard Deviation   13.4
Effective Duration

Valuation
Premium/Discount (1-Year Average)   -0.17

Company Information
Provider   Invesco
Manager/Tenure   Peter Hubbard (10), Jonathan Nixon
               (5), Michael Jeanette (3), 1 other
Website   http://www.invesco.com/us
Address   Invesco 11 Greenway Plaza, Ste. 2500
               Houston TX 77046 United States
Phone Number   800-659-1005

PERFORMANCE

Ratings History

Date	Overall Rating	Risk Rating	Reward Rating
Q4-18	D+	D+	D+
Q2-18	C+	C	C+
Q4-17	C+	C	B-
Q4-16	D+	D+	D
Q4-15	D+	C-	D

Asset & Performance History

Date	NAV	1-Year Total Return
2017	20.49	39.48
2016	14.94	0.15
2015	15.13	-13.99
2014	17.73	-1.97
2013	18.18	-0.08
2012	18.42	15.99

Total Assets: $179,965,414
Asset Allocation

Asset	%
Cash	-1%
Stocks	101%
US Stocks	0%
Bonds	0%
US Bonds	0%
Other	0%

Services Offered:

Investment Strategy: The investment seeks to track the investment results (before fees and expenses) of the Dorsey Wright® Emerging Markets Technical Leaders Index (the "underlying index"). The fund will invest at least 90% of its total assets in the equity securities that comprise the underlying index. The underlying index is comprised of equity securities of large capitalization companies based in emerging market countries. **Top Holdings:** Hartalega Holdings Bhd   Shenzhou International Group Holdings Ltd   Clicks Group Ltd   Bangkok Dusit Medical Services PCL DR   TISCO Financial Group PCL DR

Global X SuperIncome™ Preferred ETF   D+   SELL

Ticker	Traded On	NAV	Total Assets ($)	Dividend Yield (TTM)	Turnover Ratio	Expense Ratio
SPFF	NYSE Arca	11.06	$179,793,943	7.47	45	0.58

Ratings
Reward	D+
Risk	C-
Recent Upgrade/Downgrade	Down

Fund Information
Fund Type	Exchange Traded Funds
Category	US Fixed Income
Sub-Category	Preferred Stock
Prospectus Objective	Equity-Income
Inception Date	Jul-12
Open to New Investments	Y

Prices
Price (as of 12/31/2018)	11.03
52-Week High	12.33
52-Week Low	10.92

Total Returns (%)
3-Month	6-Month	1-Year	3-Year	5-Year
-4.52	-3.86	-2.62	3.31	7.47

3-Year Standard Deviation	4.59
Effective Duration	

Valuation
Premium/Discount (1-Year Average)	-0.02

Company Information
Provider	Global X Funds
Manager/Tenure	Chang Kim (4), James Ong (2), Nam To (0)
Website	http://www.globalxfunds.com
Address	Global X Funds 600 Lexington Avenue, 20th Floor New York NY 10022 United States
Phone Number	888-493-8631

PERFORMANCE

Ratings History
Date	Overall Rating	Risk Rating	Reward Rating
Q4-18	D+	C-	D+
Q2-18	C-	C-	C-
Q4-17	C	C	C
Q4-16	C-	C-	C
Q4-15	C	C+	C-

Asset & Performance History
Date	NAV	1-Year Total Return
2017	12.2	2.29
2016	12.78	3.72
2015	13.19	-2.66
2014	14.54	6.87
2013	14.54	5
2012	14.89	

Total Assets: $179,793,943
Asset Allocation
Asset	%
Cash	0%
Stocks	0%
US Stocks	0%
Bonds	0%
US Bonds	0%
Other	0%

Services Offered:

Investment Strategy: The investment seeks investment results that correspond generally to the price and yield performance, before fees and expenses, of the S&P Enhanced Yield North American Preferred Stock Index ("underlying index"). The fund will invest at least 80% of its total assets in the securities of the underlying index and in American Depositary Receipts ("ADRs") and Global Depositary Receipts ("GDRs") based on the securities in the underlying index. The underlying index tracks the performance of the highest-yielding preferred securities in the United States and Canada. The fund is non-diversified. **Top Holdings:** Barclays Bank PLC 8 1/8 % Non Cum Callable Dollar Pref Shs Sp Am Dep Receip GMAC Capital Trust I Pfd Secs 2011-15.2.40 Gtd Series 2 HSBC Holdings PLC ADR Sempra Energy 6% PRF CONVERT 15/01/2021 USD 100 US Bancorp Shs Repr 1/1000th Non Cum Perp Pfd Shs Series-F

IQ Enhanced Core Plus Bond U.S. ETF   D+   SELL

Ticker	Traded On	NAV	Total Assets ($)	Dividend Yield (TTM)	Turnover Ratio	Expense Ratio
AGGP	NYSE Arca	18.93	$178,093,210	3.3		0.38

Ratings
Reward	D+
Risk	C-
Recent Upgrade/Downgrade	

Fund Information
Fund Type	Exchange Traded Funds
Category	US Fixed Income
Sub-Category	Intermediate-Term Bond
Prospectus Objective	Income
Inception Date	May-16
Open to New Investments	Y

Prices
Price (as of 12/31/2018)	18.91
52-Week High	19.99
52-Week Low	18.74

Total Returns (%)
3-Month	6-Month	1-Year	3-Year	5-Year
-0.21	0.53	-2.31		

3-Year Standard Deviation	
Effective Duration	3.77

Valuation
Premium/Discount (1-Year Average)	-0.03

Company Information
Provider	IndexIQ
Manager/Tenure	Greg Barrato (2), James Harrison (0)
Website	http://www.indexiq.com
Address	IndexIQ 800 Westchester Avenue, Suite N-611 Rye Brook NY 10573 United States
Phone Number	888-934-0777

PERFORMANCE

Ratings History
Date	Overall Rating	Risk Rating	Reward Rating
Q4-18	D+	C-	D+
Q2-18	D+	C	D
Q4-17	D+	B	D+
Q4-16	U		
Q4-15			

Asset & Performance History
Date	NAV	1-Year Total Return
2017	19.96	4.27
2016	19.73	
2015		
2014		
2013		
2012		

Total Assets: $178,093,210
Asset Allocation
Asset	%
Cash	1%
Stocks	0%
US Stocks	0%
Bonds	99%
US Bonds	92%
Other	0%

Services Offered:

Investment Strategy: The investment seeks to track the price and yield performance of its underlying index, the IQ Enhanced Core Plus Bond U.S. Index. The fund is a "fund of funds" which means it invests, under normal circumstances, at least 80% of its net assets, plus the amount of any borrowings for investment purposes, in the investments included in its underlying index, which includes underlying funds. The underlying index seeks to outperform the U.S. dollar-denominated taxable fixed income universe by using a combination of short- and long-term momentum to overweight and underweight various sectors of the investment grade and high yield fixed income securities market. **Top Holdings:** Vanguard Short-Term Treasury ETF Schwab Short-Term US Treasury ETF™ iShares iBoxx $ High Yield Corp Bd ETF SPDR® Blmbg Barclays High Yield Bd ETF Vanguard Short-Term Corporate Bond ETF

AI Powered Equity ETF   D+   SELL

Ticker	Traded On	NAV
AIEQ	NYSE Arca	21.87

Total Assets ($)	Dividend Yield (TTM)	Turnover Ratio	Expense Ratio
$176,721,281	0.45		0.75

Ratings
Reward   D+
Risk   D+
Recent Upgrade/Downgrade

Fund Information
Fund Type	Exchange Traded Funds
Category	US Equity Large Cap Blend
Sub-Category	Large Blend
Prospectus Objective	Growth & Inc
Inception Date	Oct-17
Open to New Investments	Y

Prices
Price (as of 12/31/2018)	21.82
52-Week High	29.89
52-Week Low	20.35

Total Returns (%)
3-Month	6-Month	1-Year	3-Year	5-Year
-18.74	-14.72	-7.28		

3-Year Standard Deviation
Effective Duration

Valuation
Premium/Discount (1-Year Average)   0.03

Company Information
Provider	Equbot
Manager/Tenure	Timothy J Collins (1), James B. Francis (0), Devin Ryder (0), 1 other
Website	http://www.equbotetf.com
Address	Equbot 450 Townsend St San Francisco United States
Phone Number	650-451-5497

PERFORMANCE

Ratings History

Date	Overall Rating	Risk Rating	Reward Rating
Q4-18	D+	D+	D+
Q2-18	U		
Q4-17	U		
Q4-16			
Q4-15			

Asset & Performance History

Date	NAV	1-Year Total Return
2017	25.87	
2016		
2015		
2014		
2013		
2012		

Total Assets: $176,721,281

Asset Allocation
Asset	%
Cash	4%
Stocks	96%
US Stocks	96%
Bonds	0%
US Bonds	0%
Other	0%

Services Offered:

Investment Strategy: The investment seeks capital appreciation. The fund is actively managed and invests primarily in equity securities listed on a U.S. exchange based on the results of a proprietary, quantitative model (the "EquBot Model") developed by EquBot LLC ("EquBot") that runs on the Watson™ platform. EquBot, the fund's sub-adviser, is a technology based company focused on applying artificial intelligence ("AI") based solutions to investment analyses. The fund is non-diversified. **Top Holdings:** Alphabet Inc A   Forest City Realty Trust Inc Class A   NetApp Inc   Texas Instruments Inc   Amazon.com Inc

---

ARK Industrial Innovation ETF   C   HOLD

Ticker	Traded On	NAV
ARKQ	NYSE Arca	29.52

Total Assets ($)	Dividend Yield (TTM)	Turnover Ratio	Expense Ratio
$176,594,347	0.07	57	0.75

Ratings
Reward   C+
Risk   D+
Recent Upgrade/Downgrade

Fund Information
Fund Type	Exchange Traded Funds
Category	Technology Sector Equity
Sub-Category	Technology
Prospectus Objective	Unaligned
Inception Date	Sep-14
Open to New Investments	Y

Prices
Price (as of 12/31/2018)	29.49
52-Week High	37.37
52-Week Low	28.79

Total Returns (%)
3-Month	6-Month	1-Year	3-Year	5-Year
-19.10	-14.92	-10.16	54.82	

3-Year Standard Deviation   19.43
Effective Duration

Valuation
Premium/Discount (1-Year Average)   0.11

Company Information
Provider	ARK ETF Trust
Manager/Tenure	Catherine D. Wood (4)
Website	http://www.ark-funds.com
Address	ARK ETF Trust 155 West 19th Street, 5th Floor New York New York 10011 United States
Phone Number	212-426-7040

PERFORMANCE

Ratings History

Date	Overall Rating	Risk Rating	Reward Rating
Q4-18	C	D+	C+
Q2-18	C	D+	B-
Q4-17	B-	C	B
Q4-16	C	D+	C+
Q4-15	U		

Asset & Performance History

Date	NAV	1-Year Total Return
2017	32.86	50.22
2016	21.89	14.72
2015	19.08	-2.26
2014	19.71	
2013		
2012		

Total Assets: $176,594,347

Asset Allocation
Asset	%
Cash	0%
Stocks	100%
US Stocks	65%
Bonds	0%
US Bonds	0%
Other	0%

Services Offered:

Investment Strategy: The investment seeks long-term growth of capital. The fund is an actively-managed exchange-traded fund that will invest under normal circumstances primarily (at least 80% of its assets) in domestic and foreign equity securities of companies that are relevant to the fund's investment theme of industrial innovation. Substantially all of the fund's assets will be invested in equity securities, including common stocks, partnership interests, business trust shares and other equity investments or ownership interests in business enterprises. The advisor currently intends to use only ADRs when purchasing foreign securities. The fund is non-diversified. **Top Holdings:** Tesla Inc   Stratasys Ltd   Baidu Inc ADR   Teradyne Inc   Materialise NV ADR

Invesco S&P Spin-Off ETF
C   HOLD

Ticker	Traded On	NAV	Total Assets ($)	Dividend Yield (TTM)	Turnover Ratio	Expense Ratio
CSD	NYSE Arca	42.37	$176,233,514	0.65		0.64

Ratings
Reward	B-
Risk	C-
Recent Upgrade/Downgrade	

Fund Information
Fund Type	Exchange Traded Funds
Category	US Equity Mid Cap
Sub-Category	Mid-Cap Blend
Prospectus Objective	Growth
Inception Date	Dec-06
Open to New Investments	Y

Prices
Price (as of 12/31/2018)	42.36
52-Week High	56.49
52-Week Low	39.90

Total Returns (%)
3-Month	6-Month	1-Year	3-Year	5-Year
-21.70	-21.10	-17.83	13.79	1.40

3-Year Standard Deviation	12.64
Effective Duration	

Valuation
Premium/Discount (1-Year Average)	0.06

Company Information
Provider	Invesco
Manager/Tenure	Peter Hubbard (0), Michael Jeanette (0), Jonathan Nixon (0), 1 other
Website	http://www.invesco.com/us
Address	Invesco 11 Greenway Plaza, Ste. 2500 Houston TX 77046 United States
Phone Number	800-659-1005

PERFORMANCE

Ratings History
Date	Overall Rating	Risk Rating	Reward Rating
Q4-18	C	C-	B-
Q2-18	C	C-	B-
Q4-17	C+	C	B-
Q4-16	B-	C	B
Q4-15	C	C-	C+

Asset & Performance History
Date	NAV	1-Year Total Return
2017	52.11	21.15
2016	43.4	14.18
2015	38.46	-12.09
2014	44.87	1.37
2013	44.98	51.83
2012	29.68	26.95

Total Assets: $176,233,514

Asset Allocation
Asset	%
Cash	0%
Stocks	100%
US Stocks	98%
Bonds	0%
US Bonds	0%
Other	0%

Services Offered:

Investment Strategy: The investment seeks to track the investment results (before the fund's fees and expenses) of the S&P U.S. Spin-Off Index (the "underlying index"). The fund generally will invest at least 90% of its total assets in the securities that comprise the underlying index. The index is designed to measure the performance of U.S. companies that have been spun off from larger corporations within the past four years. The fund is non-diversified. **Top Holdings:** Fortive Corp PayPal Holdings Inc Synchrony Financial Hewlett Packard Enterprise Co Lamb Weston Holdings Inc

---

WisdomTree Emerging Markets ex-State-Owned Enterprises Fund
C-   HOLD

Ticker	Traded On	NAV	Total Assets ($)	Dividend Yield (TTM)	Turnover Ratio	Expense Ratio
XSOE	NYSE Arca	25.55	$175,516,761	1.61	68	0.32

Ratings
Reward	C-
Risk	C-
Recent Upgrade/Downgrade	

Fund Information
Fund Type	Exchange Traded Funds
Category	Global Emerg Mkts Equity
Sub-Category	Diversified Emerging Mkts
Prospectus Objective	Div Emerg Mkts
Inception Date	Dec-14
Open to New Investments	Y

Prices
Price (as of 12/31/2018)	25.56
52-Week High	35.07
52-Week Low	24.50

Total Returns (%)
3-Month	6-Month	1-Year	3-Year	5-Year
-9.03	-11.37	-18.62	28.01	

3-Year Standard Deviation	14.93
Effective Duration	

Valuation
Premium/Discount (1-Year Average)	0.25

Company Information
Provider	WisdomTree
Manager/Tenure	Richard A. Brown (3), Thomas J. Durante (3), Karen Q. Wong (3)
Website	http://www.wisdomtree.com
Address	WisdomTree 245 Park Avenue, 35th floor New York NY 10167 United States
Phone Number	866-909-9473

PERFORMANCE

Ratings History
Date	Overall Rating	Risk Rating	Reward Rating
Q4-18	C-	C-	C-
Q2-18	C	C-	C
Q4-17	C+	C	B-
Q4-16	D+	D+	D+
Q4-15	U		

Asset & Performance History
Date	NAV	1-Year Total Return
2017	31.85	46.5
2016	21.89	7.38
2015	20.67	-12.28
2014	24.38	
2013		
2012		

Total Assets: $175,516,761

Asset Allocation
Asset	%
Cash	0%
Stocks	100%
US Stocks	0%
Bonds	0%
US Bonds	0%
Other	0%

Services Offered:

Investment Strategy: The investment seeks to track the price and yield performance, before fees and expenses, of the WisdomTree Emerging Markets ex-State-Owned Enterprises Index (the "index"). Under normal circumstances, at least 80% of the fund's total assets will be invested in component securities of the index and investments that have economic characteristics that are substantially identical to the economic characteristics of such component securities. The index is a modified float-adjusted market cap weighted index that consists of common stocks in emerging markets, excluding common stocks of "state-owned enterprises." The fund is non-diversified. **Top Holdings:** Tencent Holdings Ltd Alibaba Group Holding Ltd ADR Samsung Electronics Co Ltd Taiwan Semiconductor Manufacturing Co Ltd Naspers Ltd Class N

iShares MSCI Global Gold Miners ETF   D   SELL

Ticker	Traded On	NAV	Total Assets ($)	Dividend Yield (TTM)	Turnover Ratio	Expense Ratio
RING	NAS CM	16.19	$175,191,471	0.8	4	0.39

Ratings
Reward	D+
Risk	D
Recent Upgrade/Downgrade	Down

Fund Information
Fund Type	Exchange Traded Funds
Category	Prec Metals
Sub-Category	Equity Precious Metals
Prospectus Objective	Prec Metals
Inception Date	Jan-12
Open to New Investments	Y

Prices
Price (as of 12/31/2018)	16.22
52-Week High	20.18
52-Week Low	13.59

Total Returns (%)
3-Month	6-Month	1-Year	3-Year	5-Year
13.12	-6.75	-13.57	53.05	-6.63

3-Year Standard Deviation	38.81
Effective Duration	

Valuation
Premium/Discount (1-Year Average)	-0.10

Company Information
Provider	iShares
Manager/Tenure	Diane Hsiung (6), Greg Savage (6), Jennifer Hsui (5), 1 other
Website	http://www.ishares.com
Address	iShares 400 Howard Street San Francisco CA 94105 United States
Phone Number	800-474-2737

PERFORMANCE

Ratings History
Date	Overall Rating	Risk Rating	Reward Rating
Q4-18	D	D	D+
Q2-18	C-	D+	C-
Q4-17	D+	D	C-
Q4-16	C-	D	C
Q4-15	D-	D-	D-

Asset & Performance History
Date	NAV	1-Year Total Return
2017	18.86	9
2016	17.38	62.47
2015	10.86	-26.61
2014	14.92	-16.87
2013	18.08	-52.16
2012	38.36	

Total Assets: $175,191,471

Asset Allocation
Asset	%
Cash	0%
Stocks	100%
US Stocks	15%
Bonds	0%
US Bonds	0%
Other	0%

Services Offered:

Investment Strategy: The investment seeks to track the investment results of the MSCI ACWI Select Gold Miners Investable Market Index. The fund generally will invest at least 90% of its assets in the component securities of the underlying index and in investments that have economic characteristics that are substantially identical to the component securities of the underlying index. The index measures the combined performance of equity securities of companies primarily engaged in the business of gold mining in both developed and emerging markets. The fund is non-diversified. **Top Holdings:** Newmont Mining Corp   Barrick Gold Corp   Newcrest Mining Ltd   Goldcorp Inc   Randgold Resources Ltd

---

SPDR® STOXX Europe 50 ETF   D+   SELL

Ticker	Traded On	NAV	Total Assets ($)	Dividend Yield (TTM)	Turnover Ratio	Expense Ratio
FEU	NYSE Arca	29.83	$174,981,207	3.77	5	0.29

Ratings
Reward	D+
Risk	C-
Recent Upgrade/Downgrade	Down

Fund Information
Fund Type	Exchange Traded Funds
Category	Europe Equity Large Cap
Sub-Category	Europe Stock
Prospectus Objective	Europe Stock
Inception Date	Oct-02
Open to New Investments	Y

Prices
Price (as of 12/31/2018)	29.89
52-Week High	38.40
52-Week Low	28.95

Total Returns (%)
3-Month	6-Month	1-Year	3-Year	5-Year
-10.90	-9.13	-14.34	3.48	-7.66

3-Year Standard Deviation	11.96
Effective Duration	

Valuation
Premium/Discount (1-Year Average)	-0.21

Company Information
Provider	SPDR State Street Global Advisors
Manager/Tenure	Michael J. Feehily (7), Karl A. Schneider (3), Mark Krivitsky (1)
Website	http://www.spdrs.com
Address	SPDR State Street Global Advisors State Street Financial Center, 1 Lincoln Street Boston MA 02111-2900 United States
Phone Number	617-786-3000

PERFORMANCE

Ratings History
Date	Overall Rating	Risk Rating	Reward Rating
Q4-18	D+	C-	D+
Q2-18	C-	C-	C
Q4-17	C+	B-	C+
Q4-16	D+	D+	D+
Q4-15	C-	C-	C-

Asset & Performance History
Date	NAV	1-Year Total Return
2017	36.09	23.66
2016	30.07	-4.21
2015	31.93	-4.37
2014	34.51	-6.68
2013	39	22.36
2012	33.01	14.78

Total Assets: $174,981,207

Asset Allocation
Asset	%
Cash	0%
Stocks	100%
US Stocks	0%
Bonds	0%
US Bonds	0%
Other	0%

Services Offered: Dividend Investment Plan

Investment Strategy: The investment seeks to provide investment results that, before fees and expenses, correspond generally to the total return performance of the STOXX® Europe 50 Index. The fund generally invests substantially all, but at least 80%, of its total assets in the securities comprising the index. It employs a sampling strategy, which means that the fund is not required to purchase all of the securities represented in the index. The index is a market capitalization weighted index designed to represent the performance of some of the largest companies across all components of the 19 STOXX Europe 600 Supersector Indexes. The fund is non-diversified. **Top Holdings:** Nestle SA   Novartis AG   Roche Holding AG Dividend Right Cert.   HSBC Holdings PLC   Total SA

First Trust Switzerland AlphaDEX® Fund
D+ SELL

Ticker	Traded On	NAV	Total Assets ($)	Dividend Yield (TTM)	Turnover Ratio	Expense Ratio
FSZ	NAS CM	43.89	$174,842,907	2.21	50	0.8

Ratings
Reward — D+
Risk — C-
Recent Upgrade/Downgrade — Down

Fund Information
Fund Type — Exchange Traded Funds
Category — Europe Equity Large Cap
Sub-Category — Miscellaneous Region
Prospectus Objective — Europe Stock
Inception Date — Feb-12
Open to New Investments — Y

Prices
Price (as of 12/31/2018) — 43.84
52-Week High — 56.69
52-Week Low — 42.24

Total Returns (%)

3-Month	6-Month	1-Year	3-Year	5-Year
-13.78	-11.76	-15.12	16.03	16.81

3-Year Standard Deviation — 11.59
Effective Duration —

Valuation
Premium/Discount (1-Year Average) — -0.09

Company Information
Provider — First Trust
Manager/Tenure — Jon C. Erickson (6), Daniel J. Lindquist (6), David G. McGarel (6), 3 others
Website — http://www.ftportfolios.com/
Address — First Trust 120 E. Liberty Drive, Suite 400 Wheaton IL 60187 United States
Phone Number — 800-621-1675

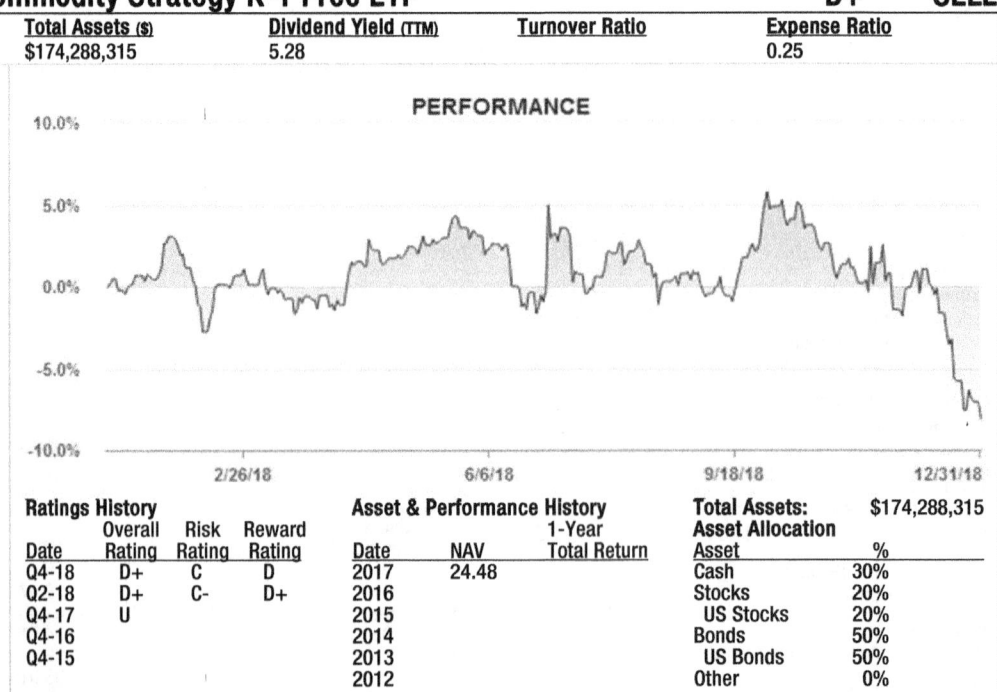

PERFORMANCE

Ratings History

Date	Overall Rating	Risk Rating	Reward Rating
Q4-18	D+	C-	D+
Q2-18	C-	D+	C
Q4-17	B	B+	B
Q4-16	C-	D+	C
Q4-15	C-	C-	C-

Asset & Performance History

Date	NAV	1-Year Total Return
2017	52.73	31.27
2016	40.82	4.2
2015	39.97	6.01
2014	38.09	-5.04
2013	40.79	28.9
2012	32.38	

Total Assets: $174,842,907
Asset Allocation

Asset	%
Cash	0%
Stocks	100%
US Stocks	4%
Bonds	0%
US Bonds	0%
Other	0%

Services Offered:

Investment Strategy: The investment seeks investment results that correspond generally to the price and yield (before the fund's fees and expenses) of an equity index called the NASDAQ AlphaDEX® Switzerland Index. The fund will normally invest at least 90% of its net assets (including investment borrowings) in common stocks and/or depositary receipts that comprise the index. The index is designed to select stocks from the NASDAQ Switzerland Index (the "base index") that may generate positive alpha, or risk-adjusted returns, relative to traditional indices through the use of the AlphaDEX® selection methodology. **Top Holdings:** Sunrise Communications Group AG Swisscom AG Swiss Life Holding AG BKW AG Adecco Group AG

Aberdeen Standard Bloomberg All Commodity Strategy K-1 Free ETF
D+ SELL

Ticker	Traded On	NAV	Total Assets ($)	Dividend Yield (TTM)	Turnover Ratio	Expense Ratio
BCI	NYSE Arca	21.38	$174,288,315	5.28		0.25

Ratings
Reward — D
Risk — C
Recent Upgrade/Downgrade —

Fund Information
Fund Type — Exchange Traded Funds
Category — Commodities Broad Basket
Sub-Category — Commodities Broad Basket
Prospectus Objective — Growth & Inc
Inception Date — Mar-17
Open to New Investments — Y

Prices
Price (as of 12/31/2018) — 21.50
52-Week High — 25.57
52-Week Low — 21.50

Total Returns (%)

3-Month	6-Month	1-Year	3-Year	5-Year
-11.80	-12.47	-8.12		

3-Year Standard Deviation —
Effective Duration —

Valuation
Premium/Discount (1-Year Average) — 0.01

Company Information
Provider — Aberdeen Standard Investments
Manager/Tenure — Denise M. Krisko (1)
Website — http://www.aberdeenstandardetfs.us
Address — Aberdeen Standard Investments 405 Lexington Avenue New York NY 10174 United States
Phone Number — 212-918-4954

PERFORMANCE

Ratings History

Date	Overall Rating	Risk Rating	Reward Rating
Q4-18	D+	C	D
Q2-18	D+	C-	D+
Q4-17	U		
Q4-16			
Q4-15			

Asset & Performance History

Date	NAV	1-Year Total Return
2017	24.48	
2016		
2015		
2014		
2013		
2012		

Total Assets: $174,288,315
Asset Allocation

Asset	%
Cash	30%
Stocks	20%
US Stocks	20%
Bonds	50%
US Bonds	50%
Other	0%

Services Offered:

Investment Strategy: The investment seeks to provide a total return designed to exceed the performance of the Bloomberg Commodity IndexSM which is calculated on an excess return basis. The fund is an actively managed exchange traded fund that seeks to provide a total return designed to exceed the performance of the index. It will generally seek to hold similar interests to those included in the index and will seek exposure to many of the commodities included in the index under the same futures rolling schedule as the index. The fund will also hold short-term fixed-income securities. It is non-diversified. **Top Holdings:** United States Treasury Bills Etfs All Commodities Fund Limited Common Stock Usd United States Treasury Bills United States Treasury Bills United States Treasury Bills

Invesco Raymond James SB-1 Equity ETF   C-   HOLD

Ticker	Traded On	NAV	Total Assets ($)	Dividend Yield (TTM)	Turnover Ratio	Expense Ratio
RYJ	NYSE Arca		$173,755,367	0	82	0.75

Ratings
Reward   C-
Risk   D+
Recent Upgrade/Downgrade   Down

Fund Information
Fund Type   Exchange Traded Funds
Category   US Equity Mid Cap
Sub-Category   Mid-Cap Growth
Prospectus Objective   Growth
Inception Date   May-06
Open to New Investments   Y

Prices
Price (as of 12/31/2018)   36.50
52-Week High   49.48
52-Week Low   34.27

Total Returns (%)

3-Month	6-Month	1-Year	3-Year	5-Year
-24.93	-22.70	-16.59	12.85	10.81

3-Year Standard Deviation   14.13
Effective Duration

Valuation
Premium/Discount (1-Year Average)   0.13

Company Information
Provider   Invesco
Manager/Tenure   Peter Hubbard (0), Michael Jeanette (0), Jonathan Nixon (0), 1 other
Website   http://www.invesco.com/us
Address   Invesco 11 Greenway Plaza, Ste. 2500 Houston TX 77046 United States
Phone Number   800-659-1005

PERFORMANCE

Ratings History

Date	Overall Rating	Risk Rating	Reward Rating
Q4-18	C-	D+	C-
Q2-18	C	D+	C+
Q4-17	B	B	B
Q4-16	C	D+	B-
Q4-15	C	C-	C

Asset & Performance History

Date	NAV	1-Year Total Return
2017	43.39	13.29
2016	38.39	19.5
2015	32.56	-6.17
2014	35.02	4.65
2013	33.55	43.37
2012	23.48	14.93

Total Assets: $173,755,367
Asset Allocation

Asset	%
Cash	0%
Stocks	100%
US Stocks	96%
Bonds	0%
US Bonds	0%
Other	0%

Services Offered:

Investment Strategy: The investment seeks investment results that correspond generally to the performance, before the fund's fees and expenses, of an equity index called the Raymond James SB-1 Equity Index. The fund will invest at least 90% of its total assets in securities that comprise the index and depositary receipts representing securities that comprise the index. Index constituents include equity securities of all market capitalizations, as defined by the index provider, that trade on a U.S. securities exchange, including common stocks, ADRs, REITs, master limited partnerships and business development companies. The fund is non-diversified. **Top Holdings:** Ocular Therapeutix Inc   Spirit Airlines Inc   ServiceNow Inc   RingCentral Inc Class A   Salesforce.com Inc

---

ProShares Ultra Silver   D-   SELL

Ticker	Traded On	NAV	Total Assets ($)	Dividend Yield (TTM)	Turnover Ratio	Expense Ratio
AGQ	NYSE Arca		$173,293,710	0	0	0.95

Ratings
Reward   D-
Risk   D-
Recent Upgrade/Downgrade   Down

Fund Information
Fund Type   Exchange Traded Funds
Category   Trading Tools
Sub-Category   Trading--Leveraged Commodities
Prospectus Objective   Prec Metals
Inception Date   Dec-08
Open to New Investments   Y

Prices
Price (as of 12/31/2018)   26.37
52-Week High   36.22
52-Week Low   21.84

Total Returns (%)

3-Month	6-Month	1-Year	3-Year	5-Year
8.55	-11.46	-23.00	-4.54	-59.20

3-Year Standard Deviation   39.17
Effective Duration

Valuation
Premium/Discount (1-Year Average)   0.30

Company Information
Provider   ProShares
Manager/Tenure   Management Team (10)
Website   http://www.proshares.com
Address   ProShares 7501 Wisconsin Avenue, Suite 1000 Bethesda MD 20814 United States
Phone Number   866-776-5125

PERFORMANCE

Ratings History

Date	Overall Rating	Risk Rating	Reward Rating
Q4-18	D-	D-	D-
Q2-18	D	D	D
Q4-17	D	D	D
Q4-16	D	D-	D+
Q4-15	E+	E+	E+

Asset & Performance History

Date	NAV	1-Year Total Return
2017	33.56	0.33
2016	33.44	23.56
2015	27.06	-31.24
2014	39.37	-37.83
2013	63.33	-63.15
2012	171.88	-0.51

Total Assets: $173,293,710
Asset Allocation

Asset	%
Cash	-100%
Stocks	0%
US Stocks	0%
Bonds	0%
US Bonds	0%
Other	200%

Services Offered:

Investment Strategy: The investment seeks to provide daily investment results (before fees and expenses) that correspond to twice (200%) the daily performance of silver bullion as measured by the U.S. Dollar fixing price for delivery in London.
The "Ultra" funds seek results for a single day that match (before fees and expenses) two times (2x) the daily performance of a benchmark. It does not seek to achieve their stated objective over a period greater than a single day. **Top Holdings:** London Silver Price Forward - Citibank Na   London Silver Price Forward - Goldman Sachs London Silver Price Forward - Ubs Ag   London Silver Price Forward - Societe Generale   Silver Future 03/27/2019 (Slh9)

WisdomTree Emerging Markets Local Debt Fund

D+   **SELL**

Ticker	Traded On	NAV	Total Assets ($)	Dividend Yield (TTM)	Turnover Ratio	Expense Ratio
ELD	NYSE Arca	33.49	$173,152,066	6.35	39	0.55

Ratings
Reward	D+
Risk	C-
Recent Upgrade/Downgrade	

Fund Information
Fund Type	Exchange Traded Funds
Category	Emerging Mkts Fixed Inc
Sub-Category	Emerging-Markets Local-Currency Bond
Prospectus Objective	Income
Inception Date	Aug-10
Open to New Investments	Y

Prices
Price (as of 12/31/2018)	33.50
52-Week High	40.02
52-Week Low	31.80

Total Returns (%)
3-Month	6-Month	1-Year	3-Year	5-Year
3.19	0.65	-7.71	14.06	-6.85

3-Year Standard Deviation	10.53
Effective Duration	4.52

Valuation
Premium/Discount (1-Year Average)	-0.13

Company Information
Provider	WisdomTree
Manager/Tenure	Stephanie Shu (8), Paul L. Benson (3)
Website	http://www.wisdomtree.com
Address	WisdomTree 245 Park Avenue, 35th floor New York NY 10167 United States
Phone Number	866-909-9473

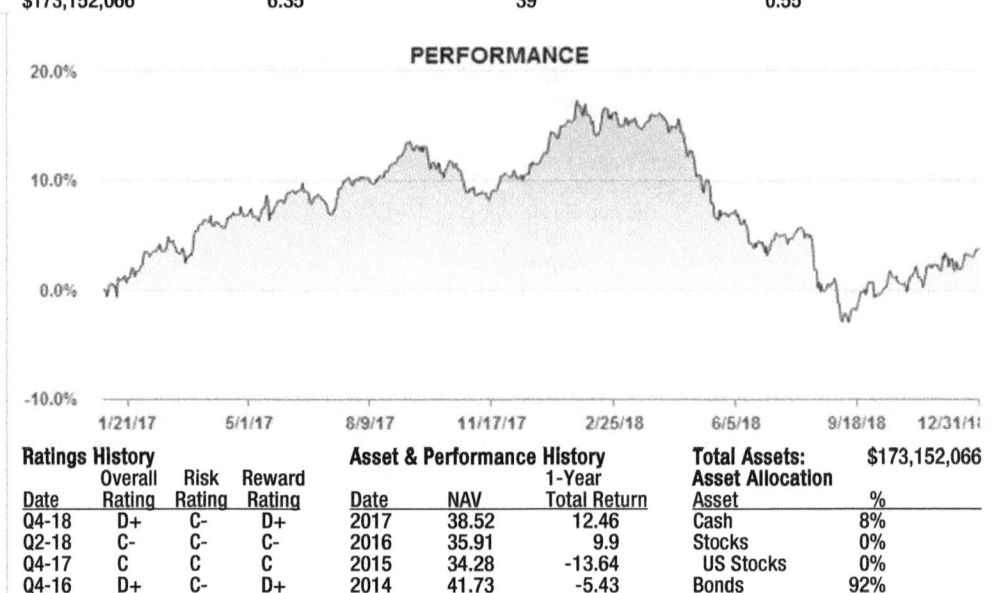

PERFORMANCE

Ratings History
Date	Overall Rating	Risk Rating	Reward Rating
Q4-18	D+	C-	D+
Q2-18	C-	C-	C-
Q4-17	C	C	C
Q4-16	D+	C-	D+
Q4-15	D	D	D

Asset & Performance History
Date	NAV	1-Year Total Return
2017	38.52	12.46
2016	35.91	9.9
2015	34.28	-13.64
2014	41.73	-5.43
2013	45.91	-10.38
2012	53.11	13.27

Total Assets: $173,152,066

Asset Allocation
Asset	%
Cash	8%
Stocks	0%
US Stocks	0%
Bonds	92%
US Bonds	12%
Other	0%

Services Offered:

Investment Strategy: The investment seeks a high level of total return consisting of both income and capital appreciation. The fund seeks to achieve its investment objective through investment in bonds and other debt instruments denominated in the local currencies of emerging market countries. Under normal circumstances, it will invest at least 80% of its net assets, plus the amount of any borrowings for investment purposes, in Local Debt. The Advisor attempts to maintain an aggregate portfolio duration of between two and ten years under normal market conditions. The fund is non-diversified. **Top Holdings:** Massachusetts St Indl Fin Agy Health 10% Indonesia(Rep Of) 8.75% Letra Tesouro Nacional Bills 01/22 0.00000 Indonesia(Rep Of) 8.25% Letra Tesouro Nacional Bills 07/20 0.00000

WisdomTree Dynamic Long/Short U.S. Equity Fund

C-   **HOLD**

Ticker	Traded On	NAV	Total Assets ($)	Dividend Yield (TTM)	Turnover Ratio	Expense Ratio
DYLS	BATS	29.11	$172,382,273	0.97		0.48

Ratings
Reward	C
Risk	C-
Recent Upgrade/Downgrade	Down

Fund Information
Fund Type	Exchange Traded Funds
Category	Long/Short Equity
Sub-Category	Long-Short Equity
Prospectus Objective	Equity-Income
Inception Date	Dec-15
Open to New Investments	Y

Prices
Price (as of 12/31/2018)	28.97
52-Week High	35.90
52-Week Low	27.33

Total Returns (%)
3-Month	6-Month	1-Year	3-Year	5-Year
-15.60	-10.35	-8.38	22.91	

3-Year Standard Deviation	
Effective Duration	

Valuation
Premium/Discount (1-Year Average)	0.00

Company Information
Provider	WisdomTree
Manager/Tenure	Richard A. Brown (2), Thomas J. Durante (2), Karen Q. Wong (2)
Website	http://www.wisdomtree.com
Address	WisdomTree 245 Park Avenue, 35th floor New York NY 10167 United States
Phone Number	866-909-9473

PERFORMANCE

Ratings History
Date	Overall Rating	Risk Rating	Reward Rating
Q4-18	C-	C-	C
Q2-18	C	C-	C+
Q4-17	C-	B+	C-
Q4-16	D-	C-	D+
Q4-15			

Asset & Performance History
Date	NAV	1-Year Total Return
2017	32.5	20.1
2016	27.33	9.51
2015	25.1	
2014		
2013		
2012		

Total Assets: $172,382,273

Asset Allocation
Asset	%
Cash	0%
Stocks	100%
US Stocks	100%
Bonds	0%
US Bonds	0%
Other	0%

Services Offered:

Investment Strategy: The investment seeks to track the price and yield performance, before fees and expenses, of the WisdomTree Dynamic Long/Short U.S. Equity Index (the "index"). Under normal circumstances, at least 80% of the fund's total assets will be invested in component securities of the index and investments that have economic characteristics that are substantially identical to the economic characteristics of such component securities. The index includes long U.S. equity positions (the "Long Equity Basket") and, at times, short U.S. equity positions (the "Short Equity Basket"). The fund is non-diversified. **Top Holdings:** Cracker Barrel Old Country Store Inc VMware Inc Mednax Inc Macy's Inc Encompass Health Corp

High Yield ETF   C-   HOLD

Ticker	Traded On	NAV	Total Assets ($)	Dividend Yield (TTM)	Turnover Ratio	Expense Ratio
HYLD	NYSE Arca	33.93	$172,323,454	7.83		1.25

Ratings
Reward	C-
Risk	C-
Recent Upgrade/Downgrade	Down

Fund Information
Fund Type	Exchange Traded Funds
Category	US Fixed Income
Sub-Category	High Yield Bond
Prospectus Objective	Income
Inception Date	Nov-10
Open to New Investments	Y

Prices
Price (as of 12/31/2018)	33.66
52-Week High	37.18
52-Week Low	33.66

Total Returns (%)
3-Month	6-Month	1-Year	3-Year	5-Year
-5.68	-3.90	-0.29	26.95	-3.36

3-Year Standard Deviation	5.69
Effective Duration	

Valuation
Premium/Discount (1-Year Average)	-0.21

Company Information
Provider	Peritus
Manager/Tenure	Tim Gramatovich (8), Michael DePalma (0), Michael Ning (0)
Website	http://www.hyldetf.com
Address	Peritus 10900 Hefner Pointe Drive, Suite 207 Oklahoma City OK 73120 United States
Phone Number	

PERFORMANCE

Ratings History

Date	Overall Rating	Risk Rating	Reward Rating
Q4-18	C-	C-	C-
Q2-18	C	C-	C+
Q4-17	C	C+	C
Q4-16	D+	C-	D+
Q4-15	D+	C-	D

Asset & Performance History

Date	NAV	1-Year Total Return
2017	36.63	8.63
2016	36.19	17.21
2015	33.08	-13.87
2014	42.09	-11.61
2013	51.67	12.12
2012	49.92	15.1

Total Assets: $172,323,454

Asset Allocation

Asset	%
Cash	6%
Stocks	0%
US Stocks	0%
Bonds	94%
US Bonds	75%
Other	0%

Services Offered:

Investment Strategy: The investment seeks high current income with a secondary goal of capital appreciation. The Sub-Advisor seeks to achieve the fund's investment objective by selecting a focused portfolio of high-yield debt securities, which include senior and subordinated corporate debt obligations (such as loans, bonds, debentures, notes and commercial paper). The fund does not have any portfolio maturity limitation and may invest its assets in instruments with short-term, medium-term or long-term maturities. It invests at least 80% of its net assets (plus any borrowings for investment purposes) in high-yield debt securities. **Top Holdings:** Osum Production 07/31/20 Term Loan Techniplas, LLC. 10% LEE Enterprises Inc 9.5% Compass Group Diversified Holdings LLC 8% Global Ship Lease Inc 9.88%

Invesco Global Water ETF   C-   HOLD

Ticker	Traded On	NAV	Total Assets ($)	Dividend Yield (TTM)	Turnover Ratio	Expense Ratio
PIO	NAS CM	23.19	$171,899,159	1.81	34	0.75

Ratings
Reward	C
Risk	C-
Recent Upgrade/Downgrade	Down

Fund Information
Fund Type	Exchange Traded Funds
Category	Equity Misc
Sub-Category	Miscellaneous Sector
Prospectus Objective	Natl Res
Inception Date	Jun-07
Open to New Investments	

Prices
Price (as of 12/31/2018)	23.08
52-Week High	27.15
52-Week Low	22.13

Total Returns (%)
3-Month	6-Month	1-Year	3-Year	5-Year
-9.75	-5.94	-9.37	15.38	8.58

3-Year Standard Deviation	11.48
Effective Duration	

Valuation
Premium/Discount (1-Year Average)	-0.12

Company Information
Provider	Invesco
Manager/Tenure	Peter Hubbard (11), Jonathan Nixon (5), Michael Jeanette (3), 1 other
Website	http://www.invesco.com/us
Address	Invesco 11 Greenway Plaza, Ste. 2500 Houston TX 77046 United States
Phone Number	800-659-1005

PERFORMANCE

Ratings History

Date	Overall Rating	Risk Rating	Reward Rating
Q4-18	C-	C-	C
Q2-18	C	C-	C
Q4-17	C+	B-	C+
Q4-16	C-	C-	C-
Q4-15	C	C	C

Asset & Performance History

Date	NAV	1-Year Total Return
2017	26.07	26.17
2016	20.88	0.91
2015	20.99	-7.62
2014	23.07	1.87
2013	22.95	29.15
2012	18.07	17.25

Total Assets: $171,899,159

Asset Allocation

Asset	%
Cash	0%
Stocks	100%
US Stocks	50%
Bonds	0%
US Bonds	0%
Other	0%

Services Offered: Wire Redemption

Investment Strategy: The investment seeks to track the investment results (before fees and expenses) of the NASDAQ OMX Global Water IndexSM (the "underlying index"). The fund will invest at least 90% of its total assets in the securities of companies listed on a global exchange that create products designed to conserve and purify water for homes, businesses and industries that comprise the underlying index, as well as American depositary receipts ("ADRs") and global depositary receipts ("GDRs") that are based on the securities in the underlying index. It is non-diversified. **Top Holdings:** Ecolab Inc Danaher Corp Pentair PLC Ferguson Geberit AG

First Trust Emerging Markets Small Cap AlphaDEX® Fund   C-   HOLD

Ticker	Traded On	NAV		Total Assets ($)	Dividend Yield (TTM)	Turnover Ratio	Expense Ratio
FEMS	NAS CM	32.45		$171,326,902	3.6	113	0.8

Ratings
Reward	C-
Risk	D+
Recent Upgrade/Downgrade	Down

Fund Information
Fund Type	Exchange Traded Funds
Category	Global Emerg Mkts Equity
Sub-Category	Diversified Emerging Mkts
Prospectus Objective	Div Emerg Mkts
Inception Date	Feb-12
Open to New Investments	Y

Prices
Price (as of 12/31/2018)	32.19
52-Week High	47.41
52-Week Low	31.64

Total Returns (%)
3-Month	6-Month	1-Year	3-Year	5-Year
-9.94	-13.84	-21.47	30.71	7.61

3-Year Standard Deviation	17.37
Effective Duration	

Valuation
Premium/Discount (1-Year Average)	-0.27

Company Information
Provider	First Trust
Manager/Tenure	Jon C. Erickson (6), Daniel J. Lindquist (6), David G. McGarel (6), 3 others
Website	http://www.ftportfolios.com/
Address	First Trust 120 E. Liberty Drive, Suite 400 Wheaton IL 60187 United States
Phone Number	800-621-1675

PERFORMANCE

Ratings History
Date	Overall Rating	Risk Rating	Reward Rating
Q4-18	C-	D+	C-
Q2-18	C	C-	C
Q4-17	B	C+	B+
Q4-16	C-	C-	C-
Q4-15	C-	C-	C-

Asset & Performance History
Date	NAV	1-Year Total Return
2017	43.02	46.6
2016	30.42	13.53
2015	27.43	-13.41
2014	32.64	-4.91
2013	35.44	5.65
2012	34.17	

Total Assets: $171,326,902

Asset Allocation
Asset	%
Cash	0%
Stocks	100%
US Stocks	0%
Bonds	0%
US Bonds	0%
Other	0%

Services Offered:

Investment Strategy: The investment seeks investment results that correspond generally to the price and yield (before the fund's fees and expenses) of an equity index called the NASDAQ AlphaDEX® Emerging Markets Small Cap Index. The fund will normally invest at least 90% of its net assets in common stocks and/or depositary receipts that comprise the index. The index is designed to select small cap stocks from the NASDAQ Emerging Markets Index (the "base index") that may generate positive alpha, or risk-adjusted returns, relative to traditional indices through the use of the AlphaDEX® selection methodology. **Top Holdings:** Adani Enterprises Ltd ICBC Turkey Bank AS Energy Company of Parana Participating Preferred Dogan Sirketler Grubu Holdings AS Soda Sanayii AS

---

iShares Global Utilities ETF   C   HOLD

Ticker	Traded On	NAV		Total Assets ($)	Dividend Yield (TTM)	Turnover Ratio	Expense Ratio
JXI	NYSE Arca	49.07		$170,694,680	3.3	4	0.47

Ratings
Reward	C
Risk	C
Recent Upgrade/Downgrade	

Fund Information
Fund Type	Exchange Traded Funds
Category	Utilities Sector Equity
Sub-Category	Utilities
Prospectus Objective	Utility
Inception Date	Sep-06
Open to New Investments	Y

Prices
Price (as of 12/31/2018)	49.10
52-Week High	52.26
52-Week Low	45.53

Total Returns (%)
3-Month	6-Month	1-Year	3-Year	5-Year
1.21	1.36	2.02	24.16	33.90

3-Year Standard Deviation	10.97
Effective Duration	

Valuation
Premium/Discount (1-Year Average)	0.00

Company Information
Provider	iShares
Manager/Tenure	Diane Hsiung (10), Greg Savage (10), Jennifer Hsui (6), 3 others
Website	http://www.ishares.com
Address	iShares 400 Howard Street San Francisco CA 94105 United States
Phone Number	800-474-2737

PERFORMANCE

Ratings History
Date	Overall Rating	Risk Rating	Reward Rating
Q4-18	C	C	C
Q2-18	C	C-	C
Q4-17	C+	B-	C+
Q4-16	C	C-	C
Q4-15	C	C-	C

Asset & Performance History
Date	NAV	1-Year Total Return
2017	49.64	14.73
2016	44.83	6.07
2015	44.23	-6.72
2014	49.2	15.61
2013	44.07	12.77
2012	40.87	1.85

Total Assets: $170,694,680

Asset Allocation
Asset	%
Cash	1%
Stocks	99%
US Stocks	62%
Bonds	0%
US Bonds	0%
Other	0%

Services Offered:

Investment Strategy: The investment seeks to track the investment results of the S&P Global 1200 Utilities IndexTM. The fund generally invests at least 90% of its assets in securities of the underlying index and in depositary receipts representing securities of the underlying index. It may invest the remainder of its assets in certain futures, options and swap contracts, cash and cash equivalents, as well as in securities not included in the underlying index. A significant portion of the underlying index is represented by securities of companies in the electric utilities and utilities industries or sectors. **Top Holdings:** NextEra Energy Inc Duke Energy Corp Dominion Energy Inc Southern Co Iberdrola SA

Invesco DB Base Metals Fund   C-   HOLD

Ticker	Traded On	NAV	Total Assets ($)	Dividend Yield (TTM)	Turnover Ratio	Expense Ratio
DBB	NYSE Arca	15.44	$169,669,378	0	0	0.75

Ratings
Reward	C-
Risk	C-
Recent Upgrade/Downgrade	Down

Fund Information
Fund Type	Exchange Traded Funds
Category	Commodities Specified
Sub-Category	Commodities Industrial Metals
Prospectus Objective	Prec Metals
Inception Date	Jan-07
Open to New Investments	Y

Prices
Price (as of 12/31/2018)	15.39
52-Week High	19.89
52-Week Low	15.39

Total Returns (%)
3-Month	6-Month	1-Year	3-Year	5-Year
-8.18	-11.19	-20.37	30.03	-7.98

3-Year Standard Deviation	14.8
Effective Duration	

Valuation
Premium/Discount (1-Year Average)	-0.06

Company Information
Provider	Invesco
Manager/Tenure	Management Team (11)
Website	http://www.invesco.com/us
Address	Invesco 11 Greenway Plaza, Ste. 2500 Houston TX 77046 United States
Phone Number	800-659-1005

PERFORMANCE

Ratings History
Date	Overall Rating	Risk Rating	Reward Rating
Q4-18	C-	C-	C-
Q2-18	C	C+	C
Q4-17	C+	C	B
Q4-16	C-	C-	C-
Q4-15	D	D	D

Asset & Performance History
Date	NAV	1-Year Total Return
2017	19.39	31.91
2016	14.95	22.98
2015	11.87	-25.74
2014	15.99	-4.7
2013	16.78	-12.31
2012	19.13	2.2

Total Assets: $169,669,378

Asset Allocation
Asset	%
Cash	38%
Stocks	0%
US Stocks	0%
Bonds	18%
US Bonds	18%
Other	44%

Services Offered:

Investment Strategy: The investment seeks to track the DBIQ Optimum Yield Industrial Metals Index Excess Return™ (DBIQ-OY Industrial Metals ER™), which is intended to reflect the base metals sector. The index Commodities consist of Aluminum, Zinc and Copper – Grade A. **Top Holdings:** Lme Copper Future Feb19　Lme Zinc Future Jan19　Lme Pri Alum Futr Oct19　Lme Copper Future Feb19　Lme Zinc Future Jan19

Invesco S&P SmallCap Financials ETF   C-   HOLD

Ticker	Traded On	NAV	Total Assets ($)	Dividend Yield (TTM)	Turnover Ratio	Expense Ratio
PSCF	NAS CM	48.11	$167,592,251	2.58		0.29

Ratings
Reward	C
Risk	D+
Recent Upgrade/Downgrade	Down

Fund Information
Fund Type	Exchange Traded Funds
Category	Financials Sector Equity
Sub-Category	Financial
Prospectus Objective	Financial
Inception Date	Apr-10
Open to New Investments	

Prices
Price (as of 12/31/2018)	47.94
52-Week High	60.46
52-Week Low	46.25

Total Returns (%)
3-Month	6-Month	1-Year	3-Year	5-Year
-13.08	-14.18	-8.81	28.51	38.85

3-Year Standard Deviation	15.45
Effective Duration	

Valuation
Premium/Discount (1-Year Average)	0.10

Company Information
Provider	Invesco
Manager/Tenure	Peter Hubbard (8), Michael Jeanette (8), Tony Seisser (4), 1 other
Website	http://www.invesco.com/us
Address	Invesco 11 Greenway Plaza, Ste. 2500 Houston TX 77046 United States
Phone Number	800-659-1005

PERFORMANCE

Ratings History
Date	Overall Rating	Risk Rating	Reward Rating
Q4-18	C-	D+	C
Q2-18	C+	C-	B-
Q4-17	A-	B	A
Q4-16	C	C-	C+
Q4-15	C+	C-	B

Asset & Performance History
Date	NAV	1-Year Total Return
2017	54.28	6.28
2016	52.25	32.06
2015	40.74	0.07
2014	41.68	7.96
2013	39.59	31.45
2012	30.87	17.17

Total Assets: $167,592,251

Asset Allocation
Asset	%
Cash	0%
Stocks	100%
US Stocks	99%
Bonds	0%
US Bonds	0%
Other	0%

Services Offered:

Investment Strategy: The investment seeks to track the investment results (before fees and expenses) of the S&P SmallCap 600® Capped Financials & Real Estate Index (the "underlying index"). The fund generally will invest at least 90% of its total assets in common stocks of small capitalization U.S. financial service companies that comprise the underlying index. These companies are principally engaged in the business of providing financial services and products, including banking, investment services, insurance and real estate finance services. **Top Holdings:** First Financial Bankshares Inc　Glacier Bancorp Inc　FirstCash Inc　Selective Insurance Group Inc　Green Dot Corp

First Trust Materials AlphaDEX® Fund

C   HOLD

Ticker	Traded On	NAV	Total Assets ($)	Dividend Yield (TTM)	Turnover Ratio	Expense Ratio
FXZ	NYSE Arca	33.54	$167,552,870	1.15	84	0.64

Ratings
Reward   C
Risk   C-
Recent Upgrade/Downgrade

Fund Information
Fund Type   Exchange Traded Funds
Category   Natural Resources
Sub-Category   Natural Resources
Prospectus Objective   Unaligned
Inception Date   May-07
Open to New Investments   Y

Prices
Price (as of 12/31/2018) 33.52
52-Week High   46.42
52-Week Low   31.50

Total Returns (%)

3-Month	6-Month	1-Year	3-Year	5-Year
-18.82	-18.99	-22.55	23.73	10.44

3-Year Standard Deviation   15.81
Effective Duration

Valuation
Premium/Discount (1-Year Average)   0.01

Company Information
Provider   First Trust
Manager/Tenure   Jon C. Erickson (11), Daniel J.
                  Lindquist (11), David G. McGarel (11),
                  3 others
Website   http://www.ftportfolios.com/
Address   First Trust 120 E. Liberty Drive, Suite
                  400 Wheaton IL 60187 United States
Phone Number   800-621-1675

PERFORMANCE

Ratings History

Date	Overall Rating	Risk Rating	Reward Rating
Q4-18	C	C-	C
Q2-18	C	C	C+
Q4-17	B	C+	A
Q4-16	B-	C	B
Q4-15	C	C	C

Asset & Performance History

Date	NAV	1-Year Total Return
2017	43.83	23.68
2016	35.83	29.17
2015	28.09	-9.85
2014	31.54	-0.98
2013	32.39	26.73
2012	25.82	25.2

Total Assets: $167,552,870
Asset Allocation

Asset	%
Cash	0%
Stocks	100%
US Stocks	100%
Bonds	0%
US Bonds	0%
Other	0%

Services Offered:

Investment Strategy: The investment seeks investment results that correspond generally to the price and yield (before the fund's fees and expenses) of an equity index called the StrataQuant® Materials Index. The fund will normally invest at least 90% of its net assets (including investment borrowings) in common stocks that comprise the index. The index is a modified equal-dollar weighted index designed by IDI to objectively identify and select stocks from the Russell 1000® Index in the materials and processing sector that may generate positive alpha relative to traditional passive-style indices through the use of the AlphaDEX® selection methodology. **Top Holdings:** Nucor Corp Reliance Steel & Aluminum Co LyondellBasell Industries NV WRKCo Inc A Martin Marietta Materials Inc

---

iShares MSCI Italy Capped ETF

D+   SELL

Ticker	Traded On	NAV	Total Assets ($)	Dividend Yield (TTM)	Turnover Ratio	Expense Ratio
EWI	NYSE Arca	24.15	$167,066,886	3.93	10	0.47

Ratings
Reward   D+
Risk   D
Recent Upgrade/Downgrade Down

Fund Information
Fund Type   Exchange Traded Funds
Category   Europe Equity Large Cap
Sub-Category   Miscellaneous Region
Prospectus Objective   Europe Stock
Inception Date   Mar-96
Open to New Investments   Y

Prices
Price (as of 12/31/2018) 24.21
52-Week High   34.44
52-Week Low   23.28

Total Returns (%)

3-Month	6-Month	1-Year	3-Year	5-Year
-11.14	-14.29	-17.51	-3.99	-9.96

3-Year Standard Deviation   21.01
Effective Duration

Valuation
Premium/Discount (1-Year Average)   -0.12

Company Information
Provider   iShares
Manager/Tenure   Diane Hsiung (10), Greg Savage (10),
                  Jennifer Hsui (5), 1 other
Website   http://www.ishares.com
Address   iShares 400 Howard Street San
                  Francisco CA 94105 United States
Phone Number   800-474-2737

PERFORMANCE

Ratings History

Date	Overall Rating	Risk Rating	Reward Rating
Q4-18	D+	D	D+
Q2-18	C	C	C
Q4-17	C+	C	B
Q4-16	D	D	D
Q4-15	C	C	C

Asset & Performance History

Date	NAV	1-Year Total Return
2017	30.49	28.46
2016	24.3	-9.4
2015	27.84	4
2014	27.32	-9.83
2013	30.94	20.93
2012	26.28	12.62

Total Assets: $167,066,886
Asset Allocation

Asset	%
Cash	0%
Stocks	100%
US Stocks	9%
Bonds	0%
US Bonds	0%
Other	0%

Services Offered: CashInvestment Plan

Investment Strategy: The investment seeks to track the investment results of the MSCI Italy 25/50 Index. The fund will at all times invest at least 80% of its assets in the securities of its underlying index and in depositary receipts representing securities in its underlying index. The underlying index is a free float-adjusted market capitalization-weighted index with a capping methodology applied to issuer weights so that no single issuer of a component exceeds 25% of the underlying index weight, and all issuers with a weight above 5% do not cumulatively exceed 50% of the underlying index weight. The fund is non-diversified. **Top Holdings:** Enel SpA Eni SpA Intesa Sanpaolo UniCredit SpA Assicurazioni Generali

USAA Core Intermediate-Term Bond ETF   D+   SELL

Ticker	Traded On	NAV	Total Assets ($)	Dividend Yield (TTM)	Turnover Ratio	Expense Ratio
UITB	NYSE Arca	48.14	$167,013,658	2.98	10	0.4

Ratings
Reward   D+
Risk   C-
Recent Upgrade/Downgrade

Fund Information
Fund Type   Exchange Traded Funds
Category   US Fixed Income
Sub-Category   Intermediate-Term Bond
Prospectus Objective   Income
Inception Date   Oct-17
Open to New Investments   Y

Prices
Price (as of 12/31/2018)   48.08
52-Week High   50.19
52-Week Low   47.60

Total Returns (%)

3-Month	6-Month	1-Year	3-Year	5-Year
0.88	1.18	-0.88		

3-Year Standard Deviation
Effective Duration   5.84

Valuation
Premium/Discount (1-Year Average)   0.14

Company Information
Provider   USAA
Manager/Tenure   Julianne Bass (1), Kurt Daum (1), Brian W. Smith (1), 1 other
Website   http://www.usaa.com
Address   USAA P.O. Box 659453 San Antonio TX 78265-9825 United States
Phone Number   800-531-8722

PERFORMANCE

Ratings History

Date	Overall Rating	Risk Rating	Reward Rating
Q4-18	D+	C-	D+
Q2-18	U		
Q4-17	U		
Q4-16			
Q4-15			

Asset & Performance History

Date	NAV	1-Year Total Return
2017	50.03	
2016		
2015		
2014		
2013		
2012		

Total Assets: $167,013,658
Asset Allocation

Asset	%
Cash	2%
Stocks	0%
US Stocks	0%
Bonds	96%
US Bonds	86%
Other	0%

Services Offered:

Investment Strategy: The investment seeks high current income without undue risk to principal. Under normal circumstances, the fund invests at least 80% of its net assets (plus any borrowings for investment purposes, exclusive of collateral held from securities lending) in debt securities and in derivatives and other instruments that have economic characteristics similar to such securities. The fund may not invest more than 20% of fixed-income securities (by weight of all fixed-income securities in the portfolio) in non-agency, non-government sponsored entities (GSEs), or privately issued mortgage- or asset-backed securities. **Top Holdings:** United States Treasury Notes 2%   United States Treasury Notes 2.38%   United States Treasury Notes 2.88%   Federal Home Loan Mortgage Corporation 3.5%   United States Treasury Bonds 3%

WisdomTree International Dividend ex-Financials Fund   D+   SELL

Ticker	Traded On	NAV	Total Assets ($)	Dividend Yield (TTM)	Turnover Ratio	Expense Ratio
DOO	NYSE Arca	37.97	$166,663,104	4.19	35	0.58

Ratings
Reward   D+
Risk   D+
Recent Upgrade/Downgrade   Down

Fund Information
Fund Type   Exchange Traded Funds
Category   Global Equity Large Cap
Sub-Category   Foreign Large Value
Prospectus Objective   Foreign Stock
Inception Date   Jun-06
Open to New Investments   Y

Prices
Price (as of 12/31/2018)   37.90
52-Week High   46.31
52-Week Low   36.91

Total Returns (%)

3-Month	6-Month	1-Year	3-Year	5-Year
-8.92	-7.03	-9.35	11.01	-2.31

3-Year Standard Deviation   10.56
Effective Duration

Valuation
Premium/Discount (1-Year Average)   -0.17

Company Information
Provider   WisdomTree
Manager/Tenure   Richard A. Brown (10), Thomas J. Durante (10), Karen Q. Wong (10)
Website   http://www.wisdomtree.com
Address   WisdomTree 245 Park Avenue, 35th floor New York NY 10167 United States
Phone Number   866-909-9473

PERFORMANCE

Ratings History

Date	Overall Rating	Risk Rating	Reward Rating
Q4-18	D+	D+	D+
Q2-18	C	C-	C
Q4-17	C+	C+	C+
Q4-16	D	D+	D
Q4-15	C-	C-	C

Asset & Performance History

Date	NAV	1-Year Total Return
2017	43.53	20.01
2016	37.67	2.04
2015	38.38	-8.26
2014	43.46	-4.08
2013	47.43	19.67
2012	41.31	9.93

Total Assets: $166,663,104
Asset Allocation

Asset	%
Cash	0%
Stocks	100%
US Stocks	0%
Bonds	0%
US Bonds	0%
Other	0%

Services Offered:

Investment Strategy: The investment seeks to track the price and yield performance, before fees and expenses, of the WisdomTree International Dividend ex-Financials Index. Under normal circumstances, at least 95% of the fund's total assets (exclusive of collateral held from securities lending) will be invested in the component securities of the index and investments that have economic characteristics that are substantially identical to the economic characteristics of such component securities. The index is a fundamentally weighted index that is comprised of high dividend-yielding international common stocks outside the financial sector. The fund is non-diversified. **Top Holdings:** BT Group PLC   Hennes & Mauritz AB B   Telstra Corp Ltd   Telefonica Deutschland Holding AG   Endesa SA

USAA MSCI Emerging Markets Value Momentum Blend Index ETF   D   SELL

Ticker	Traded On	NAV	Total Assets ($)	Dividend Yield (TTM)	Turnover Ratio	Expense Ratio
UEVM	NYSE Arca	41.76	$166,645,355	1		0.45

Ratings
Reward   D
Risk   D
Recent Upgrade/Downgrade

Fund Information
Fund Type	Exchange Traded Funds
Category	Global Emerg Mkts Equity
Sub-Category	Diversified Emerging Mkts
Prospectus Objective	Div Emerg Mkts
Inception Date	Oct-17
Open to New Investments	Y

Prices
Price (as of 12/31/2018)	41.73
52-Week High	56.13
52-Week Low	40.85

Total Returns (%)

3-Month	6-Month	1-Year	3-Year	5-Year
-7.46	-8.06	-16.62		

3-Year Standard Deviation
Effective Duration

Valuation
Premium/Discount (1-Year Average)   0.28

Company Information
Provider	USAA
Manager/Tenure	Lance Humphrey (1), Wasif A. Latif (1), Emiliano Rabinovich (1), 2 others
Website	http://www.usaa.com
Address	USAA P.O. Box 659453 San Antonio TX 78265-9825 United States
Phone Number	800-531-8722

PERFORMANCE

Ratings History

Date	Overall Rating	Risk Rating	Reward Rating
Q4-18	D	D	D
Q2-18	U		
Q4-17	U		
Q4-16			
Q4-15			

Asset & Performance History

Date	NAV	1-Year Total Return
2017	51.19	
2016		
2015		
2014		
2013		
2012		

Total Assets: $166,645,355

Asset Allocation

Asset	%
Cash	1%
Stocks	98%
US Stocks	0%
Bonds	0%
US Bonds	0%
Other	0%

Services Offered:

Investment Strategy: The investment seeks to provide investment results that correspond to the MSCI Emerging Markets Select Value Momentum Blend Index. The fund seeks to achieve by investing at least 80% of its net assets in securities in the index, depositary receipts on securities in the index, and securities underlying depositary receipts in the index. The index is designed to deliver exposure to equity market performance in the global emerging markets and provide higher exposure to value and momentum factors within the MSCI Emerging Markets Index while also maintaining moderate index turnover and lower realized volatility than traditional capitalization weighted indexes. **Top Holdings:** Hong Leong Bank Bhd Taiwan Business Bank PPB Group Bhd KT Corp First Financial Holding Co Ltd

Invesco DB Energy Fund   C   HOLD

Ticker	Traded On	NAV	Total Assets ($)	Dividend Yield (TTM)	Turnover Ratio	Expense Ratio
DBE	NYSE Arca	12.33	$166,324,664	0		0.75

Ratings
Reward   C-
Risk   C
Recent Upgrade/Downgrade

Fund Information
Fund Type	Exchange Traded Funds
Category	Commodities Specified
Sub-Category	Commodities Energy
Prospectus Objective	Natl Res
Inception Date	Jan-07
Open to New Investments	Y

Prices
Price (as of 12/31/2018)	12.44
52-Week High	18.74
52-Week Low	12.16

Total Returns (%)

3-Month	6-Month	1-Year	3-Year	5-Year
-32.42	-25.10	-14.06	12.44	-56.99

3-Year Standard Deviation   21.96
Effective Duration

Valuation
Premium/Discount (1-Year Average)   -0.10

Company Information
Provider	Invesco
Manager/Tenure	Management Team (11)
Website	http://www.invesco.com/us
Address	Invesco 11 Greenway Plaza, Ste. 2500 Houston TX 77046 United States
Phone Number	800-659-1005

PERFORMANCE

Ratings History

Date	Overall Rating	Risk Rating	Reward Rating
Q4-18	C	C	C-
Q2-18	C	C-	C
Q4-17	C-	D+	C
Q4-16	D	D	D
Q4-15	D-	D-	D-

Asset & Performance History

Date	NAV	1-Year Total Return
2017	14.59	5.08
2016	13.8	25.69
2015	11.15	-34.87
2014	17.13	-41.27
2013	29.16	4.21
2012	27.99	1.33

Total Assets: $166,324,664

Asset Allocation

Asset	%
Cash	37%
Stocks	0%
US Stocks	0%
Bonds	13%
US Bonds	13%
Other	50%

Services Offered:

Investment Strategy: The investment seeks to track the DBIQ Optimum Yield Energy Index Excess Return™ (DBIQ-OY Energy ER™), which is intended to reflect the energy sector.
The index Commodities consist of Light, Sweet Crude Oil (WTI), Heating Oil, Brent Crude Oil, RBOB Gasoline and Natural Gas. **Top Holdings:** Gasoline Rbob Fut Jan19 Ny Harb Ulsd Fut Jun19 Brent Crude Futr Jan20 Wti Crude Future Mar19 United States Treasury Bills 0%

ProShares UltraPro Short Dow30   D-   SELL

Ticker	Traded On	NAV	Total Assets ($)	Dividend Yield (TTM)	Turnover Ratio	Expense Ratio
SDOW	NYSE Arca	19.20	$166,119,162	0.98		0.95

Ratings
Reward	E+
Risk	D-
Recent Upgrade/Downgrade	

Fund Information
Fund Type	Exchange Traded Funds
Category	Trading Tools
Sub-Category	Trading--Inverse Equity
Prospectus Objective	Growth
Inception Date	Feb-10
Open to New Investments	Y

Prices
Price (as of 12/31/2018)	19.20
52-Week High	23.89
52-Week Low	13.73

Total Returns (%)
3-Month	6-Month	1-Year	3-Year	5-Year
37.74	3.70	-0.69	-72.54	-83.47

3-Year Standard Deviation	27.51
Effective Duration	

Valuation
Premium/Discount (1-Year Average)	-0.11

Company Information
Provider	ProShares
Manager/Tenure	Michael Neches (5), Devin Sullivan (0)
Website	http://www.proshares.com
Address	ProShares 7501 Wisconsin Avenue, Suite 1000 Bethesda MD 20814 United States
Phone Number	866-776-5125

PERFORMANCE

Ratings History
Date	Overall Rating	Risk Rating	Reward Rating
Q4-18	D-	D-	E+
Q2-18	D-	D-	E+
Q4-17	E+	E+	E+
Q4-16	D	D-	D-
Q4-15	D	E+	D-

Asset & Performance History
Date	NAV	1-Year Total Return
2017	19.59	-52.17
2016	41	-42.18
2015	70.92	-13.84
2014	82.32	-30.14
2013	117.84	-56.94
2012	273.72	-32.08

Total Assets: $166,119,162
Asset Allocation
Asset	%
Cash	247%
Stocks	-151%
US Stocks	-151%
Bonds	5%
US Bonds	5%
Other	0%

Services Offered:

Investment Strategy: The investment seeks daily investment results, before fees and expenses, that correspond to three times the inverse (-3x) of the daily performance of the Dow Jones Industrial Average® Index. The fund invests in financial instruments that ProShare Advisors believes, in combination, should produce daily returns consistent with the fund's investment objective. The index is a price-weighted index and includes 30 large-cap, "blue-chip" U.S. stocks, excluding utility and transportation companies. The fund is non-diversified. **Top Holdings:** Dj Industrial Average Swap Societe Generale   Dj Industrial Average Swap Morgan Stanley & Co. International Plc   Dj Industrial Average Swap Citibank, N.A.   United States Treasury Bills   United States Treasury Bills

---

Xtrackers Russell 1000 Comprehensive Factor ETF   C-   HOLD

Ticker	Traded On	NAV	Total Assets ($)	Dividend Yield (TTM)	Turnover Ratio	Expense Ratio
DEUS	NYSE Arca		$165,825,705	1.62	67	0.17

Ratings
Reward	C-
Risk	C-
Recent Upgrade/Downgrade	Down

Fund Information
Fund Type	Exchange Traded Funds
Category	US Equity Mid Cap
Sub-Category	Mid-Cap Blend
Prospectus Objective	Growth & Inc
Inception Date	Nov-15
Open to New Investments	Y

Prices
Price (as of 12/31/2018)	28.67
52-Week High	34.12
52-Week Low	27.13

Total Returns (%)
3-Month	6-Month	1-Year	3-Year	5-Year
-14.78	-10.48	-9.59	22.29	

3-Year Standard Deviation	9.17
Effective Duration	

Valuation
Premium/Discount (1-Year Average)	0.09

Company Information
Provider	Deutsche Asset Management
Manager/Tenure	Bryan Richards (3), Patrick Dwyer (2), Shlomo Bassous (0), 2 others
Website	http://www.deutsche-etfs.com
Address	Deutsche Asset & Wealth Management 345 Park Avenue New York NY 10154 United States
Phone Number	844-851-4255

PERFORMANCE

Ratings History
Date	Overall Rating	Risk Rating	Reward Rating
Q4-18	C-	C-	C-
Q2-18	C	C-	C
Q4-17	C	B+	C
Q4-16	D	C-	D+
Q4-15			

Asset & Performance History
Date	NAV	1-Year Total Return
2017	31.97	19.92
2016	27.03	12.79
2015	24.64	
2014		
2013		
2012		

Total Assets: $165,825,705
Asset Allocation
Asset	%
Cash	0%
Stocks	100%
US Stocks	99%
Bonds	0%
US Bonds	0%
Other	0%

Services Offered:

Investment Strategy: The investment seeks investment results that correspond generally to the performance, before fees and expenses, of the Russell 1000 Comprehensive Factor Index. The fund, using a "passive" or indexing investment approach, seeks investment results that correspond generally to the performance of the underlying index, which is designed to track the equity market performance of companies in the United States selected on the investment style criteria ("factors") of value, momentum, quality, low volatility and size. It will invest at least 80% of its total assets (but typically far more) in component securities of the underlying index. **Top Holdings:** Dollar General Corp   Target Corp   Ross Stores Inc   Torchmark Corp   Centene Corp

Barron's 400 ETF   C-   HOLD

Ticker	Traded On	NAV	Total Assets ($)	Dividend Yield (TTM)	Turnover Ratio	Expense Ratio
BFOR	NYSE Arca	35.52	$165,729,455	0.61	84	0.66

Ratings
Reward   C-
Risk   D+
Recent Upgrade/Downgrade   Down

Fund Information
Fund Type   Exchange Traded Funds
Category   US Equity Mid Cap
Sub-Category   Mid-Cap Growth
Prospectus Objective   Equity-Income
Inception Date   Jun-13
Open to New Investments   Y

Prices
Price (as of 12/31/2018)   35.48
52-Week High   46.14
52-Week Low   33.40

Total Returns (%)

3-Month	6-Month	1-Year	3-Year	5-Year
-19.91	-17.25	-13.43	20.88	23.65

3-Year Standard Deviation   13.01
Effective Duration

Valuation
Premium/Discount (1-Year Average)   0.17

Company Information
Provider   ALPS ETF
Manager/Tenure Ryan Mischker (3), Andrew Hicks (2)
Website   http://www.alpsfunds.com
Address   ALPS ETF PO Box 328 Denver CO
                80201-0328 United States
Phone Number   855-724-0450

PERFORMANCE

Ratings History

Date	Overall Rating	Risk Rating	Reward Rating
Q4-18	C-	D+	C-
Q2-18	C	D+	C+
Q4-17	B	B	B+
Q4-16	C	D+	C+
Q4-15	C-	C-	C-

Asset & Performance History

Date	NAV	1-Year Total Return
2017	41.43	18.93
2016	35.04	17.41
2015	30.07	-3.74
2014	31.51	6.27
2013	29.86	
2012		

Total Assets: $165,729,455

Asset Allocation

Asset	%
Cash	1%
Stocks	99%
US Stocks	99%
Bonds	0%
US Bonds	0%
Other	0%

Services Offered:

Investment Strategy: The investment seeks investment results that correspond generally, before fees and expenses, to the performance of the Barron's 400SM Index (the "underlying index"). The underlying index is a rules-based index intended to give investors a means of tracking the overall performance of high performing equity securities of U.S. companies. The fund will invest at least 80% of its total assets in the equity securities which comprise the underlying index. **Top Holdings:** Electro Scientific Industries Inc   Marathon Petroleum Corp   Cabot Microelectronics Corp   Cracker Barrel Old Country Store Inc   AMN Healthcare Services Inc

---

First Trust Germany AlphaDEX® Fund   D+   SELL

Ticker	Traded On	NAV	Total Assets ($)	Dividend Yield (TTM)	Turnover Ratio	Expense Ratio
FGM	NAS CM	37.57	$165,565,662	2.03	82	0.8

Ratings
Reward   D+
Risk   D+
Recent Upgrade/Downgrade   Down

Fund Information
Fund Type   Exchange Traded Funds
Category   Europe Equity Large Cap
Sub-Category   Miscellaneous Region
Prospectus Objective   Europe Stock
Inception Date   Feb-12
Open to New Investments   Y

Prices
Price (as of 12/31/2018)   37.68
52-Week High   55.25
52-Week Low   36.33

Total Returns (%)

3-Month	6-Month	1-Year	3-Year	5-Year
-19.45	-17.87	-25.41	9.09	-1.72

3-Year Standard Deviation   15.65
Effective Duration

Valuation
Premium/Discount (1-Year Average)   -0.07

Company Information
Provider   First Trust
Manager/Tenure Jon C. Erickson (6), Daniel J. Lindquist
                (6), David G. McGarel (6), 3 others
Website   http://www.ftportfolios.com/
Address   First Trust 120 E. Liberty Drive, Suite
                400 Wheaton IL 60187 United States
Phone Number   800-621-1675

PERFORMANCE

Ratings History

Date	Overall Rating	Risk Rating	Reward Rating
Q4-18	D+	D+	D+
Q2-18	C-	D+	C
Q4-17	A-	B	A
Q4-16	C-	D+	C-
Q4-15	C-	C-	C-

Asset & Performance History

Date	NAV	1-Year Total Return
2017	51.26	43.94
2016	36.47	1.68
2015	36.37	1.9
2014	36.07	-11.59
2013	41.48	26.63
2012	33.42	

Total Assets: $165,565,662

Asset Allocation

Asset	%
Cash	0%
Stocks	100%
US Stocks	2%
Bonds	0%
US Bonds	0%
Other	0%

Services Offered:

Investment Strategy: The investment seeks investment results that correspond generally to the price and yield (before the fund's fees and expenses) of an equity index called the NASDAQ AlphaDEX® Germany Index. The fund will normally invest at least 90% of its net assets (including investment borrowings) in common stocks and/or depositary receipts that comprise the index. The index is designed to select stocks from the NASDAQ Germany Index (the "base index") that may generate positive alpha, or risk-adjusted returns, relative to traditional indices through the use of the AlphaDEX® selection methodology. **Top Holdings:** LEG Immobilien AG   Deutsche Lufthansa AG   Porsche Automobil Holding SE Participating Preferred   Wirecard AG   MorphoSys AG

iShares Global Clean Energy ETF   C-   HOLD

Ticker	Traded On	NAV	Total Assets ($)	Dividend Yield (TTM)	Turnover Ratio	Expense Ratio
ICLN	NAS CM	8.27	$165,474,683	2.38	29	0.47

Ratings
Reward	C-
Risk	C-
Recent Upgrade/Downgrade	

Fund Information
Fund Type	Exchange Traded Funds
Category	Utilities Sector Equity
Sub-Category	Miscellaneous Sector
Prospectus Objective	Natl Res
Inception Date	Jun-08
Open to New Investments	Y

Prices
Price (as of 12/31/2018)	8.26
52-Week High	10.02
52-Week Low	7.91

Total Returns (%)
3-Month	6-Month	1-Year	3-Year	5-Year
-2.06	-4.19	-8.61	-7.46	-8.64

3-Year Standard Deviation	16.98
Effective Duration	

Valuation
Premium/Discount (1-Year Average)	0.13

Company Information
Provider	iShares
Manager/Tenure	Diane Hsiung (10), Greg Savage (10), Jennifer Hsui (6), 3 others
Website	http://www.ishares.com
Address	iShares 400 Howard Street San Francisco CA 94105 United States
Phone Number	800-474-2737

PERFORMANCE

Ratings History
Date	Overall Rating	Risk Rating	Reward Rating
Q4-18	C-	C-	C-
Q2-18	C-	C-	C-
Q4-17	C	C	C-
Q4-16	D	D	D
Q4-15	C-	C-	C-

Asset & Performance History
Date	NAV	1-Year Total Return
2017	9.29	20.47
2016	7.92	-15.95
2015	9.78	2.76
2014	9.72	-3.92
2013	10.39	49.01
2012	7.14	-14.29

Total Assets: $165,474,683
Asset Allocation
Asset	%
Cash	1%
Stocks	99%
US Stocks	35%
Bonds	0%
US Bonds	0%
Other	0%

Services Offered:

Investment Strategy: The investment seeks to track the S&P Global Clean Energy IndexTM. The fund generally invests at least 90% of its assets in the component securities of the index and in investments that have economic characteristics that are substantially identical to the component securities and may invest up to 10% of its assets in certain futures, options and swap contracts, cash and cash equivalents, as well as in securities not included in the index. The index is designed to track the performance of approximately 30 of what are will be the most liquid and tradable securities of global companies involved in clean energy related businesses. The fund is non-diversified. **Top Holdings:** Siemens Gamesa Renewable Energy SA Energy Company of Minas Gerais ADR Vestas Wind Systems A/S Pattern Energy Group Inc Class A Ormat Technologies Inc

---

Invesco MSCI Global Timber ETF   D+   SELL

Ticker	Traded On	NAV	Total Assets ($)	Dividend Yield (TTM)	Turnover Ratio	Expense Ratio
CUT	NYSE Arca	24.20	$164,964,364	1.83	10	0.55

Ratings
Reward	C-
Risk	D+
Recent Upgrade/Downgrade	Down

Fund Information
Fund Type	Exchange Traded Funds
Category	Natural Resources
Sub-Category	Natural Resources
Prospectus Objective	Natl Res
Inception Date	Nov-07
Open to New Investments	Y

Prices
Price (as of 12/31/2018)	24.06
52-Week High	34.52
52-Week Low	23.21

Total Returns (%)
3-Month	6-Month	1-Year	3-Year	5-Year
-21.91	-22.40	-21.10	9.67	5.36

3-Year Standard Deviation	14.99
Effective Duration	

Valuation
Premium/Discount (1-Year Average)	-0.07

Company Information
Provider	Invesco
Manager/Tenure	Peter Hubbard (0), Michael Jeanette (0), Jonathan Nixon (0), 1 other
Website	http://www.invesco.com/us
Address	Invesco 11 Greenway Plaza, Ste. 2500 Houston TX 77046 United States
Phone Number	800-659-1005

PERFORMANCE

Ratings History
Date	Overall Rating	Risk Rating	Reward Rating
Q4-18	D+	D+	C-
Q2-18	C+	C-	B
Q4-17	B	C+	A-
Q4-16	C	C-	C+
Q4-15	C	C-	C

Asset & Performance History
Date	NAV	1-Year Total Return
2017	31.76	29.18
2016	24.86	6.92
2015	23.69	-1.17
2014	24.33	-2.79
2013	25.73	28.73
2012	20.27	23.85

Total Assets: $164,964,364
Asset Allocation
Asset	%
Cash	0%
Stocks	100%
US Stocks	42%
Bonds	0%
US Bonds	0%
Other	0%

Services Offered:

Investment Strategy: The investment seeks to track the investment results (before fees and expenses) of the MSCI ACWI IMI Timber Select Capped Index (the underlying index). The fund generally will invest at least 90% of its total assets in the securities that comprise the underlying index, as well as American depositary receipts ("ADRs") and global depositary receipts ("GDRs") that represent securities in the underlying index. The underlying index is comprised of equity securities of companies that are primarily engaged in the ownership and management of forests and timberlands and the production of finished products that use timber as a raw material. The fund is non-diversified. **Top Holdings:** Amcor Ltd International Paper Co WRKCo Inc A Weyerhaeuser Co UPM-Kymmene Oyj

First Trust BICK Index Fund
C- HOLD

Ticker	Traded On	NAV	Total Assets ($)	Dividend Yield (TTM)	Turnover Ratio	Expense Ratio
BICK	NAS CM	24.78	$163,230,619	1.34	65	0.64

Ratings
Reward   C-
Risk   C-
Recent Upgrade/Downgrade

Fund Information
Fund Type   Exchange Traded Funds
Category   Global Emerg Mkts Equity
Sub-Category   Diversified Emerging Mkts
Prospectus Objective   Foreign Stock
Inception Date   Apr-10
Open to New Investments   Y

Prices
Price (as of 12/31/2018)   24.75
52-Week High   33.60
52-Week Low   23.64

Total Returns (%)

3-Month	6-Month	1-Year	3-Year	5-Year
-5.46	-7.66	-15.89	35.36	7.54

3-Year Standard Deviation   16.14
Effective Duration

Valuation
Premium/Discount (1-Year Average)   0.19

Company Information
Provider   First Trust
Manager/Tenure Jon C. Erickson (8), Daniel J. Lindquist (8), David G. McGarel (8), 3 others
Website   http://www.ftportfolios.com/
Address   First Trust 120 E. Liberty Drive, Suite 400 Wheaton IL 60187 United States
Phone Number   800-621-1675

PERFORMANCE

Chart axis: 60.0%, 40.0%, 20.0%, 0.0% — dates 1/21/17, 5/1/17, 8/9/17, 11/17/17, 2/25/18, 6/5/18, 9/18/18, 12/31/18

Ratings History

Date	Overall Rating	Risk Rating	Reward Rating
Q4-18	C-	C-	C-
Q2-18	C	D+	C
Q4-17	B	C	B
Q4-16	D	D	D+
Q4-15	D+	D	C-

Asset & Performance History

Date	NAV	1-Year Total Return
2017	30.01	37.97
2016	21.98	16.65
2015	19.09	-18.47
2014	23.79	-2.54
2013	24.85	-0.16
2012	25.39	13.03

Total Assets: $163,230,619
Asset Allocation

Asset	%
Cash	0%
Stocks	100%
US Stocks	3%
Bonds	0%
US Bonds	0%
Other	0%

Services Offered:

Investment Strategy: The investment seeks investment results that correspond generally to the price and yield (before the fund's fees and expenses) of an equity index called the ISE BICKTM. The fund will normally invest at least 90% of its net assets (including investment borrowings) in common stocks or in depositary receipts representing securities in the index. The index is designed to provide a benchmark for investors interested in tracking some of the largest and most liquid public companies that are domiciled in Brazil, India, China (including Hong Kong) and South Korea that are accessible for investment by U.S. investors. **Top Holdings:** Dr Reddy's Laboratories Ltd ADR   ICICI Bank Ltd ADR   Larsen & Toubro Ltd ADR   HDFC Bank Ltd ADR   Wipro Ltd ADR

ProShares UltraShort Euro
C HOLD

Ticker	Traded On	NAV	Total Assets ($)	Dividend Yield (TTM)	Turnover Ratio	Expense Ratio
EUO	NYSE Arca		$163,146,797	0	0	0.95

Ratings
Reward   D+
Risk   C
Recent Upgrade/Downgrade   Up

Fund Information
Fund Type   Exchange Traded Funds
Category   Trading Tools
Sub-Category   Trading--Miscellaneous
Prospectus Objective   Worldwide Bond
Inception Date   Nov-08
Open to New Investments   Y

Prices
Price (as of 12/31/2018)   24.25
52-Week High   25.00
52-Week Low   19.54

Total Returns (%)

3-Month	6-Month	1-Year	3-Year	5-Year
3.75	5.56	14.60	-4.82	42.49

3-Year Standard Deviation   13.92
Effective Duration

Valuation
Premium/Discount (1-Year Average)   0.00

Company Information
Provider   ProShares
Manager/Tenure Management Team (10)
Website   http://www.proshares.com
Address   ProShares 7501 Wisconsin Avenue, Suite 1000 Bethesda MD 20814 United States
Phone Number   866-776-5125

PERFORMANCE

Chart axis: 10.0%, 0.0%, -10.0%, -20.0%, -30.0% — dates 1/22/17, 5/2/17, 8/10/17, 11/18/17, 2/26/18, 6/6/18, 9/19/18, 12/31/18

Ratings History

Date	Overall Rating	Risk Rating	Reward Rating
Q4-18	C	C	D+
Q2-18	D+	D+	D
Q4-17	D	D	D
Q4-16	B	C+	B-
Q4-15	C+	C	C

Asset & Performance History

Date	NAV	1-Year Total Return
2017	21.21	-21.68
2016	27.09	6.04
2015	25.54	18.27
2014	21.59	26.57
2013	17.06	-10.28
2012	19.02	-6.49

Total Assets: $163,146,797
Asset Allocation

Asset	%
Cash	100%
Stocks	0%
US Stocks	0%
Bonds	0%
US Bonds	0%
Other	0%

Services Offered:

Investment Strategy: The investment seeks daily results that match (before fees and expenses) twice the inverse (-2x) of the daily performance of the U.S. Dollar price of the Euro.
The "UltraShort" funds seek results for a single day that match (before fees and expenses) two times the inverse (-2x) of the daily performance of a benchmark. It does not seek to achieve their stated objectives over a period greater than a single day. **Top Holdings:**

Global X S&P 500® Catholic Values ETF   C-   HOLD

Ticker	Traded On	NAV	Total Assets ($)	Dividend Yield (TTM)	Turnover Ratio	Expense Ratio
CATH	NAS CM	30.57	$163,076,967	1.19	6	0.29

Ratings
Reward	C
Risk	C-
Recent Upgrade/Downgrade	Down

Fund Information
Fund Type	Exchange Traded Funds
Category	US Equity Large Cap Blend
Sub-Category	Large Blend
Prospectus Objective	Growth & Inc
Inception Date	Apr-16
Open to New Investments	Y

Prices
Price (as of 12/31/2018)	30.40
52-Week High	36.43
52-Week Low	29.28

Total Returns (%)
3-Month	6-Month	1-Year	3-Year	5-Year
-14.26	-7.65	-5.09		

3-Year Standard Deviation	
Effective Duration	

Valuation
Premium/Discount (1-Year Average)	0.18

Company Information
Provider	Global X Funds
Manager/Tenure	Chang Kim (2), James Ong (2), Nam To (0)
Website	http://www.globalxfunds.com
Address	Global X Funds 600 Lexington Avenue, 20th Floor New York NY 10022 United States
Phone Number	888-493-8631

PERFORMANCE

Ratings History
Date	Overall Rating	Risk Rating	Reward Rating
Q4-18	C-	C-	C
Q2-18	C-	D+	C-
Q4-17	D+	B+	C
Q4-16	U		
Q4-15			

Asset & Performance History
Date	NAV	1-Year Total Return
2017	32.81	22.47
2016	27.12	
2015		
2014		
2013		
2012		

Total Assets: $163,076,967
Asset Allocation
Asset	%
Cash	0%
Stocks	100%
US Stocks	99%
Bonds	0%
US Bonds	0%
Other	0%

Services Offered:

Investment Strategy: The investment seeks investment results that correspond generally to the price and yield performance, of the S&P 500® Catholic Values Index. The fund invests at least 80% of its total assets in the securities of the underlying index. The underlying index is based on the S&P 500® Index, and generally comprises approximately 500 or less U.S. listed common stocks. From this starting universe, constituents are screened to exclude companies involved in activities which are perceived to be inconsistent with Catholic values as outlined in the Socially Responsible Investment Guidelines of the United States Conference of Catholic Bishops. **Top Holdings:** Microsoft Corp Apple Inc Amazon.com Inc Berkshire Hathaway Inc B JPMorgan Chase & Co

First Trust Japan AlphaDEX® Fund   D+   SELL

Ticker	Traded On	NAV	Total Assets ($)	Dividend Yield (TTM)	Turnover Ratio	Expense Ratio
FJP	NAS CM	48.55	$163,059,302	1.61	101	0.8

Ratings
Reward	D+
Risk	C-
Recent Upgrade/Downgrade	Down

Fund Information
Fund Type	Exchange Traded Funds
Category	Japan Equity
Sub-Category	Japan Stock
Prospectus Objective	Pacific Stock
Inception Date	Apr-11
Open to New Investments	Y

Prices
Price (as of 12/31/2018)	48.09
52-Week High	63.21
52-Week Low	46.52

Total Returns (%)
3-Month	6-Month	1-Year	3-Year	5-Year
-15.04	-10.24	-17.67	7.35	12.09

3-Year Standard Deviation	12.35
Effective Duration	

Valuation
Premium/Discount (1-Year Average)	0.00

Company Information
Provider	First Trust
Manager/Tenure	Jon C. Erickson (7), Daniel J. Lindquist (7), David G. McGarel (7), 3 others
Website	http://www.ftportfolios.com/
Address	First Trust 120 E. Liberty Drive, Suite 400 Wheaton IL 60187 United States
Phone Number	800-621-1675

PERFORMANCE

Ratings History
Date	Overall Rating	Risk Rating	Reward Rating
Q4-18	D+	C-	D+
Q2-18	C-	C-	C
Q4-17	B+	B	A-
Q4-16	C	C-	C
Q4-15	C	C+	C

Asset & Performance History
Date	NAV	1-Year Total Return
2017	59.8	26.69
2016	47.85	2.92
2015	47.18	5.71
2014	44.99	-1.23
2013	46.02	30.68
2012	35.49	-4.58

Total Assets: $163,059,302
Asset Allocation
Asset	%
Cash	0%
Stocks	100%
US Stocks	0%
Bonds	0%
US Bonds	0%
Other	0%

Services Offered:

Investment Strategy: The investment seeks investment results that correspond generally to the price and yield (before the fund's fees and expenses) of an equity index called the NASDAQ AlphaDEX® Japan Index. The fund will normally invest at least 90% of its net assets (including investment borrowings) in common stocks and/or depositary receipts that comprise the index. The index is designed to select stocks from the NASDAQ Japan Index (the "base index") that may generate positive alpha, or risk-adjusted returns, relative to traditional indices through the use of the AlphaDEX® selection methodology. **Top Holdings:** Sumitomo Dainippon Pharma Co Ltd FamilyMart UNY Holdings Co Ltd Tokyo Electric Power Co Holdings Kuraray Co Ltd Idemitsu Kosan Co Ltd

Invesco Dynamic Market ETF   C   HOLD

Ticker	Traded On	NAV	Total Assets ($)	Dividend Yield (TTM)	Turnover Ratio	Expense Ratio
PWC	NYSE Arca	88.15	$160,342,323	1.94	215	0.6

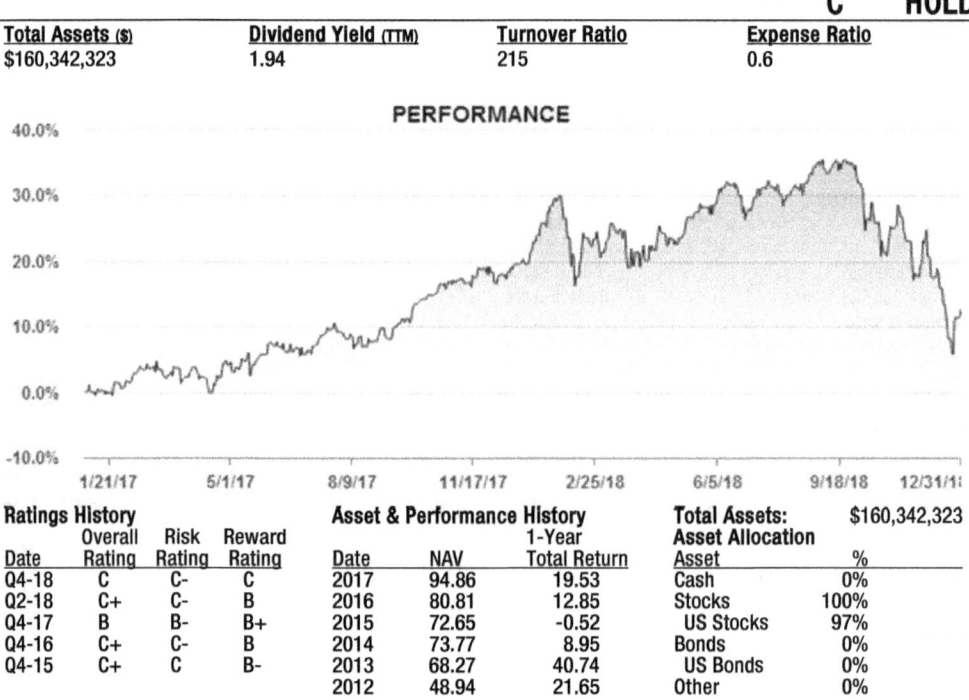

Ratings

Reward	C
Risk	C-
Recent Upgrade/Downgrade	Down

Fund Information

Fund Type	Exchange Traded Funds
Category	US Equity Mid Cap
Sub-Category	Mid-Cap Blend
Prospectus Objective	Growth
Inception Date	May-03
Open to New Investments	Y

Prices

Price (as of 12/31/2018)	88.02
52-Week High	106.71
52-Week Low	83.08

Total Returns (%)

3-Month	6-Month	1-Year	3-Year	5-Year
-16.49	-12.10	-5.84	27.01	37.65

3-Year Standard Deviation	11.15
Effective Duration	

Valuation

Premium/Discount (1-Year Average)	0.07

Company Information

Provider	Invesco
Manager/Tenure	Peter Hubbard (11), Michael Jeanette (10), Tony Seisser (4), 1 other
Website	http://www.invesco.com/us
Address	Invesco 11 Greenway Plaza, Ste. 2500 Houston TX 77046 United States
Phone Number	800-659-1005

Ratings History

Date	Overall Rating	Risk Rating	Reward Rating
Q4-18	C	C-	C
Q2-18	C+	C-	B
Q4-17	B	B-	B+
Q4-16	C+	C-	B
Q4-15	C+	C	B-

Asset & Performance History

Date	NAV	1-Year Total Return
2017	94.86	19.53
2016	80.81	12.85
2015	72.65	-0.52
2014	73.77	8.95
2013	68.27	40.74
2012	48.94	21.65

Total Assets: $160,342,323

Asset Allocation

Asset	%
Cash	0%
Stocks	100%
US Stocks	97%
Bonds	0%
US Bonds	0%
Other	0%

Services Offered:

Investment Strategy: The investment seeks to track the investment results (before fees and expenses) of the Dynamic Market IntellidexSM Index. The fund generally will invest at least 90% of its total assets in common stocks that comprise the underlying intellidex. The underlying intellidex was composed of 100 U.S. stocks that the intellidex provider, strictly in accordance with its guidelines and mandated procedures, included pursuant to a proprietary selection methodology. Stocks are selected from the top of each sector and size category in a manner designed to produce an index with sector and size dispersion similar to the overall broad market. **Top Holdings:** Motorola Solutions Inc Intuit Inc Adobe Inc Mastercard Inc A NetApp Inc

---

Aberdeen Standard Physical Palladium Shares ETF   B-   BUY

Ticker	Traded On	NAV	Total Assets ($)	Dividend Yield (TTM)	Turnover Ratio	Expense Ratio
PALL	NYSE Arca	119.66	$159,905,958	0		0.6

Ratings

Reward	B+
Risk	C-
Recent Upgrade/Downgrade	Up

Fund Information

Fund Type	Exchange Traded Funds
Category	Commodities Specified
Sub-Category	Commodities Precious Metals
Prospectus Objective	Prec Metals
Inception Date	Jan-10
Open to New Investments	Y

Prices

Price (as of 12/31/2018)	119.05
52-Week High	123.65
52-Week Low	80.32

Total Returns (%)

3-Month	6-Month	1-Year	3-Year	5-Year
19.76	33.81	18.88	126.76	72.37

3-Year Standard Deviation	30.01
Effective Duration	

Valuation

Premium/Discount (1-Year Average)	-0.40

Company Information

Provider	Aberdeen Standard Investments
Manager/Tenure	Management Team (8)
Website	http://www.aberdeenstandardetfs.us
Address	Aberdeen Standard Investments 405 Lexington Avenue New York NY 10174 United States
Phone Number	212-918-4954

Ratings History

Date	Overall Rating	Risk Rating	Reward Rating
Q4-18	B-	C-	B+
Q2-18	C	C-	C
Q4-17	B	C	A
Q4-16	D+	C-	D+
Q4-15	D	D	D

Asset & Performance History

Date	NAV	1-Year Total Return
2017	100.65	55.27
2016	64.82	22.84
2015	52.77	-31.86
2014	77.44	11.56
2013	69.42	1.1
2012	68.66	9.24

Total Assets: $159,905,958

Asset Allocation

Asset	%
Cash	0%
Stocks	0%
US Stocks	0%
Bonds	0%
US Bonds	0%
Other	100%

Services Offered:

Investment Strategy: The investment seeks to reflect the performance of the price of physical palladium, less the expenses of the Trust's operations.
The fund is designed for investors who want a cost-effective and convenient way to invest in palladium with minimal credit risk. **Top Holdings:** Physical Palladium Bullion Physical Gold Bullion

WisdomTree China ex-State-Owned Enterprises Fund   C-   HOLD

Ticker	Traded On	NAV	Total Assets ($)	Dividend Yield (TTM)	Turnover Ratio	Expense Ratio
CXSE	NAS CM	61.37	$159,824,556	1.25	20	0.32

Ratings

Reward	C-
Risk	D+
Recent Upgrade/Downgrade	Down

Fund Information

Fund Type	Exchange Traded Funds
Category	Greater China Equity
Sub-Category	China Region
Prospectus Objective	Pacific Stock
Inception Date	Sep-12
Open to New Investments	Y

Prices

Price (as of 12/31/2018)	60.89
52-Week High	96.79
52-Week Low	60.00

Total Returns (%)

3-Month	6-Month	1-Year	3-Year	5-Year
-13.99	-24.03	-27.92	26.78	27.01

3-Year Standard Deviation	20.22
Effective Duration	

Valuation

Premium/Discount (1-Year Average)	0.07

Company Information

Provider	WisdomTree
Manager/Tenure	Richard A. Brown (4), Thomas J. Durante (4), Karen Q. Wong (4)
Website	http://www.wisdomtree.com
Address	WisdomTree 245 Park Avenue, 35th floor New York NY 10167 United States
Phone Number	866-909-9473

PERFORMANCE

Ratings History

Date	Overall Rating	Risk Rating	Reward Rating
Q4-18	C-	D+	C-
Q2-18	C	C-	C+
Q4-17	B+	C+	A+
Q4-16	C-	D	C
Q4-15	C-	D+	C

Asset & Performance History

Date	NAV	1-Year Total Return
2017	86.16	78.03
2016	48.82	-1.19
2015	50.08	-1.43
2014	52.07	1.64
2013	52.41	-1.1
2012	54.61	

Total Assets: $159,824,556

Asset Allocation

Asset	%
Cash	0%
Stocks	100%
US Stocks	1%
Bonds	0%
US Bonds	0%
Other	0%

Services Offered:

Investment Strategy: The investment seeks to track the price and yield performance, before fees and expenses, of the WisdomTree China ex-State-Owned Enterprises Index. Under normal circumstances, at least 80% of the fund's total assets (exclusive of collateral held from securities lending) will be invested in component securities of the index and investments that have economic characteristics that are substantially identical to the economic characteristics of such component securities. The index is a float-adjusted market cap weighted index that consists of common stocks in China, excluding common stocks of "state-owned enterprises." The fund is non-diversified. **Top Holdings:** Alibaba Group Holding Ltd ADR Tencent Holdings Ltd Baidu Inc ADR Ping An Insurance (Group) Co. of China Ltd Ping An Insurance (Group) Co. of China Ltd H

First Trust Horizon Managed Volatility Domestic ETF   C   HOLD

Ticker	Traded On	NAV	Total Assets ($)	Dividend Yield (TTM)	Turnover Ratio	Expense Ratio
HUSV	NYSE Arca	22.21	$159,518,161	1.17	157	0.7

Ratings

Reward	C
Risk	C-
Recent Upgrade/Downgrade	Up

Fund Information

Fund Type	Exchange Traded Funds
Category	US Equity Large Cap Blend
Sub-Category	Large Blend
Prospectus Objective	Growth
Inception Date	Aug-16
Open to New Investments	Y

Prices

Price (as of 12/31/2018)	22.22
52-Week High	24.28
52-Week Low	21.11

Total Returns (%)

3-Month	6-Month	1-Year	3-Year	5-Year
-7.12	-1.54	-2.10		

3-Year Standard Deviation	
Effective Duration	

Valuation

Premium/Discount (1-Year Average)	0.09

Company Information

Provider	First Trust
Manager/Tenure	Steven Clark (2), Michael Dickson (2), Scott E. Ladner (2)
Website	http://www.ftportfolios.com/
Address	First Trust 120 E. Liberty Drive, Suite 400 Wheaton IL 60187 United States
Phone Number	800-621-1675

PERFORMANCE

Ratings History

Date	Overall Rating	Risk Rating	Reward Rating
Q4-18	C	C-	C
Q2-18	C-	C	C-
Q4-17	D	B	C-
Q4-16	U		
Q4-15			

Asset & Performance History

Date	NAV	1-Year Total Return
2017	23.01	16.16
2016	20.08	
2015		
2014		
2013		
2012		

Total Assets: $159,518,161

Asset Allocation

Asset	%
Cash	0%
Stocks	100%
US Stocks	97%
Bonds	0%
US Bonds	0%
Other	0%

Services Offered:

Investment Strategy: The investment seeks to provide capital appreciation. The fund seeks to achieve its investment objective by investing at least 80% of its net assets in common stocks of domestic companies listed and traded on U.S. national securities exchanges that the sub-advisor believes exhibit low future expected volatility. To implement this strategy, the sub-advisor employs volatility forecasting models to forecast future expected volatility. The strategy is largely quantitative and rules-based, but also includes multiple parameters over which the sub-advisor may exercise discretion in connection with its active management of the fund. The fund is non-diversified. **Top Holdings:** Coca-Cola Co Aon PLC AvalonBay Communities Inc Republic Services Inc Class A Arthur J. Gallagher & Co

Invesco Cleantech™ ETF   C-   HOLD

Ticker	Traded On	NAV	Total Assets ($)	Dividend Yield (TTM)	Turnover Ratio	Expense Ratio
PZD	NYSE Arca	36.89	$158,601,372	0.55	17	0.67

Ratings
Reward   C-
Risk   D+
Recent Upgrade/Downgrade   Down

Fund Information
Fund Type   Exchange Traded Funds
Category   Industrials Sector Equity
Sub-Category   Miscellaneous Sector
Prospectus Objective   Technology
Inception Date   Oct-06
Open to New Investments   Y

Prices
Price (as of 12/31/2018)   36.80
52-Week High   45.28
52-Week Low   35.15

Total Returns (%)

3-Month	6-Month	1-Year	3-Year	5-Year
-14.32	-11.55	-12.34	28.87	21.49

3-Year Standard Deviation   13.17
Effective Duration

Valuation
Premium/Discount (1-Year Average)   0.34

Company Information
Provider   Invesco
Manager/Tenure   Peter Hubbard (11), Michael Jeanette (5), Jonathan Nixon (5), 1 other
Website   http://www.invesco.com/us
Address   Invesco 11 Greenway Plaza, Ste. 2500 Houston TX 77046 United States
Phone Number   800-659-1005

PERFORMANCE

Ratings History

Date	Overall Rating	Risk Rating	Reward Rating
Q4-18	C-	D+	C-
Q2-18	C	D+	B-
Q4-17	A-	B	A
Q4-16	C	D+	B-
Q4-15	C-	D+	C

Asset & Performance History

Date	NAV	1-Year Total Return
2017	42.31	30.26
2016	32.79	12.86
2015	29.37	2.59
2014	28.85	-8.1
2013	31.63	37.72
2012	23.2	8.54

Total Assets: $158,601,372

Asset Allocation

Asset	%
Cash	0%
Stocks	100%
US Stocks	57%
Bonds	0%
US Bonds	0%
Other	0%

Services Offered:

Investment Strategy: The investment seeks to track the investment results (before fees and expenses) of The Cleantech IndexTM. The fund generally will invest at least 90% of its total assets in securities that comprise the underlying index, which is designed to track the performance of publicly traded clean technology (or "cleantech") companies. Cleantech considers a company to be a cleantech company when it derives at least 50% of its revenues or operating profits from cleantech businesses. **Top Holdings:** Vestas Wind Systems A/S Siemens Gamesa Renewable Energy SA Intertek Group PLC Autodesk Inc Roper Technologies Inc

Pacer Trendpilot™ European Index ETF   D+   SELL

Ticker	Traded On	NAV	Total Assets ($)	Dividend Yield (TTM)	Turnover Ratio	Expense Ratio
PTEU	BATS	25.06	$158,040,347	0.73	228	0.66

Ratings
Reward   D+
Risk   D+
Recent Upgrade/Downgrade   Down

Fund Information
Fund Type   Exchange Traded Funds
Category   Europe Equity Large Cap
Sub-Category   Europe Stock
Prospectus Objective   Growth & Inc
Inception Date   Dec-15
Open to New Investments   Y

Prices
Price (as of 12/31/2018)   25.05
52-Week High   33.20
52-Week Low   25.05

Total Returns (%)

3-Month	6-Month	1-Year	3-Year	5-Year
-3.65	-7.78	-15.97	2.72	

3-Year Standard Deviation
Effective Duration

Valuation
Premium/Discount (1-Year Average)   0.10

Company Information
Provider   Pacer
Manager/Tenure   Bruce Kavanaugh (2), Michael Mack (2)
Website   http://www.paceretfs.com
Address   Pacer 16 Industrial Blvd, Suite 201 Paoli PA 19301 United States
Phone Number

PERFORMANCE

Ratings History

Date	Overall Rating	Risk Rating	Reward Rating
Q4-18	D+	D+	D+
Q2-18	C-	C-	C
Q4-17	C-	C+	C
Q4-16	D-	D	D
Q4-15			

Asset & Performance History

Date	NAV	1-Year Total Return
2017	30.38	28.04
2016	23.87	-5.2
2015	25	
2014		
2013		
2012		

Total Assets: $158,040,347

Asset Allocation

Asset	%
Cash	100%
Stocks	0%
US Stocks	0%
Bonds	0%
US Bonds	0%
Other	0%

Services Offered:

Investment Strategy: The investment seeks to track the total return performance of the Pacer Trendpilot European Index. Normally the fund will invest at least 80% of its total assets in the component securities of the index and investments that have economic characteristics that are substantially identical to the economic characteristics of such component securities. The index uses an objective, rules-based methodology to implement a systematic trend-following strategy that directs exposure (i) 100% to the FTSE Eurozone Index, (ii) 50% to the FTSE Eurozone Index and 50% to 3-Month U.S. Treasury bills, or (iii) 100% to 3-Month U.S. Treasury bills. It is non-diversified. **Top Holdings:** Folli Follie Commercial Manufacturing And Technical SA SAP SE ADR Siemens AG Sanofi SA ADR Allianz SE

VictoryShares US Large Cap High Div Volatility Wtd ETF   C   HOLD

Ticker	Traded On	NAV	Total Assets ($)	Dividend Yield (TTM)	Turnover Ratio	Expense Ratio
CDL	NAS CM	41.36	$157,217,532	3.12		0.35

Ratings
Reward   C
Risk   C-
Recent Upgrade/Downgrade

Fund Information
Fund Type   Exchange Traded Funds
Category   US Equity Large Cap Value
Sub-Category   Large Value
Prospectus Objective   Growth
Inception Date   Jul-15
Open to New Investments   Y

Prices
Price (as of 12/31/2018)   41.36
52-Week High   47.42
52-Week Low   39.56

Total Returns (%)

3-Month	6-Month	1-Year	3-Year	5-Year
-9.27	-6.31	-5.54	31.85	

3-Year Standard Deviation   7.8
Effective Duration

Valuation
Premium/Discount (1-Year Average)   0.12

Company Information
Provider   VictoryShares
Manager/Tenure   Stephen Hammers (3), Mannik Dhillon (0)
Website   http://www.VictorySharesLiterature.com
Address   Victory Shares 4249 Easton Way, Suite 400 Columbus OH 43219 United States
Phone Number

PERFORMANCE

Ratings History

Date	Overall Rating	Risk Rating	Reward Rating
Q4-18	C	C-	C
Q2-18	C	C-	C
Q4-17	C	B+	C+
Q4-16	D	C-	C
Q4-15	U		

Asset & Performance History

Date	NAV	1-Year Total Return
2017	45.16	15.74
2016	40.22	19.84
2015	34.43	
2014		
2013		
2012		

Total Assets: $157,217,532
Asset Allocation

Asset	%
Cash	0%
Stocks	100%
US Stocks	99%
Bonds	0%
US Bonds	0%
Other	0%

Services Offered:

Investment Strategy: The investment seeks to provide investment results that track the performance of the Nasdaq Victory US Large Cap High Dividend 100 Volatility Weighted Index. The fund seeks to achieve its investment objective by investing at least 80% of its assets directly or indirectly in the securities included in the Nasdaq Victory US Large Cap High Dividend 100 Volatility Weighted Index. The index universe begins with the stocks included in the Nasdaq Victory US Large Cap 500 Volatility Weighted Index, a volatility weighted index comprised of the 500 largest U.S. companies by market capitalization with positive earnings in each of the four most recent quarters.
Top Holdings: NextEra Energy Inc   Exelon Corp   Procter & Gamble Co   Pfizer Inc   DTE Energy Co

First Trust Long/Short Equity ETF   C   HOLD

Ticker	Traded On	NAV	Total Assets ($)	Dividend Yield (TTM)	Turnover Ratio	Expense Ratio
FTLS	NYSE Arca	37.04	$156,911,768	0.62	176	1.48

Ratings
Reward   C
Risk   C-
Recent Upgrade/Downgrade

Fund Information
Fund Type   Exchange Traded Funds
Category   Long/Short Equity
Sub-Category   Long-Short Equity
Prospectus Objective   Growth
Inception Date   Sep-14
Open to New Investments   Y

Prices
Price (as of 12/31/2018)   37.09
52-Week High   41.72
52-Week Low   35.84

Total Returns (%)

3-Month	6-Month	1-Year	3-Year	5-Year
-8.18	-4.60	-4.79	16.03	

3-Year Standard Deviation   7.41
Effective Duration

Valuation
Premium/Discount (1-Year Average)   0.11

Company Information
Provider   First Trust
Manager/Tenure   John W. Gambla (4), Rob A. Guttschow (4)
Website   http://www.ftportfolios.com/
Address   First Trust 120 E. Liberty Drive, Suite 400 Wheaton IL 60187 United States
Phone Number   800-621-1675

PERFORMANCE

Ratings History

Date	Overall Rating	Risk Rating	Reward Rating
Q4-18	C	C-	C
Q2-18	C	C-	C
Q4-17	B	A+	C+
Q4-16	C	C-	C
Q4-15	U		

Asset & Performance History

Date	NAV	1-Year Total Return
2017	39.23	14.09
2016	34.54	6.82
2015	32.68	5.17
2014	31.22	
2013		
2012		

Total Assets: $156,911,768
Asset Allocation

Asset	%
Cash	42%
Stocks	58%
US Stocks	52%
Bonds	0%
US Bonds	0%
Other	0%

Services Offered:

Investment Strategy: The investment seeks to provide investors with long-term total return. The fund pursues its investment objective by establishing long and short positions in a portfolio of U.S. exchange-listed equity securities and/or U.S. exchange-traded funds ("ETFs") that provide exposure to such securities (collectively, "Equity Securities"). Under normal circumstances, at least 80% of the fund's net assets (including investment borrowings) will be exposed to Equity Securities. The fund may invest up to 20% of its net assets (including investment borrowings) in U.S. exchange-listed equity index futures contracts. **Top Holdings:** Berkshire Hathaway Inc B   Apple Inc   Alphabet Inc A   Amgen Inc   Microsoft Corp

Davis Select Financial ETF

C+   HOLD

Ticker	Traded On	NAV	Total Assets ($)	Dividend Yield (TTM)	Turnover Ratio	Expense Ratio
DFNL	NAS CM	20.64	$156,701,865	0.41	13	0.65

Ratings
Reward   B-
Risk   C
Recent Upgrade/Downgrade   Down

Fund Information
Fund Type   Exchange Traded Funds
Category   Financials Sector Equity
Sub-Category   Financial
Prospectus Objective   Financial
Inception Date   Jan-17
Open to New Investments   Y

Prices
Price (as of 12/31/2018)   20.50
52-Week High   25.51
52-Week Low   20.12

Total Returns (%)

3-Month	6-Month	1-Year	3-Year	5-Year
-13.73	-10.34	-10.79		

3-Year Standard Deviation
Effective Duration

Valuation
Premium/Discount (1-Year Average)   0.25

Company Information
Provider   Davis ETFs
Manager/Tenure   Christopher Cullom Davis (1), Pierce Crosbie (0)
Website
Address   c/o Davis Selected Advisers, L.P. 2949 E. Elvira Rd., Ste. 101 Tucson Arizona 85756 United States
Phone Number   800-279-0279

PERFORMANCE

Ratings History

Date	Overall Rating	Risk Rating	Reward Rating
Q4-18	C+	C	B-
Q2-18	B-	C	B
Q4-17	D-	B+	D+
Q4-16			
Q4-15			

Asset & Performance History

Date	NAV	1-Year Total Return
2017	23.87	21.81
2016		
2015		
2014		
2013		
2012		

Total Assets: $156,701,865
Asset Allocation

Asset	%
Cash	0%
Stocks	100%
US Stocks	83%
Bonds	0%
US Bonds	0%
Other	0%

Services Offered:

Investment Strategy: The investment seeks long-term growth of capital. The fund's investment adviser, uses the Davis Investment Discipline to invest, under normal market conditions, at least 80% of its net assets plus any borrowings for investment purposes in securities issued by companies principally engaged in the financial services sector. The fund's portfolio generally contains between 15 and 35 companies. It invests, principally, in common stocks. The fund may invest in large, medium or small companies without regard to market capitalization and may invest in issuers in foreign countries, including countries with developed or emerging markets. It is non-diversified.
Top Holdings: US Bancorp Berkshire Hathaway Inc B American Express Co Capital One Financial Corp Markel Corp

---

Direxion Daily S&P Oil & Gas Exp. & Prod. Bull 3X Shares

D   SELL

Ticker	Traded On	NAV	Total Assets ($)	Dividend Yield (TTM)	Turnover Ratio	Expense Ratio
GUSH	NYSE Arca	7.79	$156,413,744	0.06	350	1.15

Ratings
Reward   D
Risk   D
Recent Upgrade/Downgrade   Down

Fund Information
Fund Type   Exchange Traded Funds
Category   Trading Tools
Sub-Category   Trading--Leveraged Equity
Prospectus Objective   Natl Res
Inception Date   May-15
Open to New Investments   Y

Prices
Price (as of 12/31/2018)   7.80
52-Week High   45.19
52-Week Low   6.21

Total Returns (%)

3-Month	6-Month	1-Year	3-Year	5-Year
-80.87	-78.99	-73.46	-75.74	

3-Year Standard Deviation   97.89
Effective Duration

Valuation
Premium/Discount (1-Year Average)   0.11

Company Information
Provider   Direxion Funds
Manager/Tenure   Paul Brigandi (3), Tony Ng (3)
Website   http://www.direxionfunds.com
Address   Direxion Funds 1301 Avenue Of The Americas (6th Avenue) New York NY 10019 United States
Phone Number   646-572-3390

PERFORMANCE

Ratings History

Date	Overall Rating	Risk Rating	Reward Rating
Q4-18	D	D	D
Q2-18	D+	D	C-
Q4-17	D	D	D
Q4-16	D	D	D
Q4-15	U		

Asset & Performance History

Date	NAV	1-Year Total Return
2017	30.3	-40.18
2016	50.66	57.58
2015	33.15	
2014		
2013		
2012		

Total Assets: $156,413,744
Asset Allocation

Asset	%
Cash	67%
Stocks	33%
US Stocks	32%
Bonds	0%
US Bonds	0%
Other	0%

Services Offered:

Investment Strategy: The investment seeks daily investment results, of 300% of the daily performance of the S&P Oil & Gas Exploration & Production Select Industry Index. The fund, under normal circumstances, invests at least 80% of its net assets (plus borrowing for investment purposes) in securities of the index, exchange-traded funds ("ETFs") that track the index and other financial instruments that provide daily leveraged exposure to the index or ETFs that track the index. The index is designed to measure the performance of a sub-industry or group of sub-industries determined based on the Global Industry Classification Standards ("GICS"). The fund is non-diversified.
Top Holdings: SPDR® S&P Oil & Gas Explor & Prodtn ETF S&P Oil & Gas Exploration S&P Oil & Gas Exploration S&P Oil & Gas Exploration S&P Oil & Gas Exploration

Invesco Russell 1000 Low Beta Equal Weight ETF　　　　　　　　　C-　　HOLD

Ticker	Traded On	NAV	Total Assets ($)	Dividend Yield (TTM)	Turnover Ratio	Expense Ratio
USLB	NAS CM	28.32	$156,258,345	1.7		0.35

Ratings
Reward　　　　　　　　　　　　　　　C-
Risk　　　　　　　　　　　　　　　　D+
Recent Upgrade/Downgrade　　　　　Down

Fund Information
Fund Type　　　　　　　Exchange Traded Funds
Category　　　　　　　　US Equity Mid Cap
Sub-Category　　　　　　Mid-Cap Blend
Prospectus Objective　　　Growth & Inc
Inception Date　　　　　　Nov-15
Open to New Investments

Prices
Price (as of 12/31/2018)　　　　　　28.02
52-Week High　　　　　　　　　　33.45
52-Week Low　　　　　　　　　　27.11

Total Returns (%)

3-Month	6-Month	1-Year	3-Year	5-Year
-13.18	-9.81	-7.37	20.54	

3-Year Standard Deviation　　　　　8.61
Effective Duration

Valuation
Premium/Discount (1-Year Average)　0.20

Company Information
Provider　　　　Invesco
Manager/Tenure　Peter Hubbard (3), Michael Jeanette (3), Jonathan Nixon (3), 1 other
Website　　　　http://www.invesco.com/us
Address　　　　Invesco 11 Greenway Plaza, Ste. 2500 Houston TX 77046 United States
Phone Number　800-659-1005

PERFORMANCE

Ratings History

Date	Overall Rating	Risk Rating	Reward Rating
Q4-18	C-	D+	C-
Q2-18	C	D+	C
Q4-17	C	B+	C-
Q4-16	D	C-	D+
Q4-15			

Asset & Performance History

Date	NAV	1-Year Total Return
2017	31.06	16.29
2016	27.11	11.2
2015	24.63	
2014		
2013		
2012		

Total Assets: $156,258,345

Asset Allocation

Asset	%
Cash	0%
Stocks	100%
US Stocks	99%
Bonds	0%
US Bonds	0%
Other	0%

Services Offered:

Investment Strategy: The investment seeks to track the investment results (before fees and expenses) of the Russell 1000® Low Beta Equal Weight Index (the "underlying index"). The fund generally will invest at least 90% of its total assets in common stocks that comprise the underlying index. Strictly in accordance with its guidelines and mandated procedures, the index provider compiles, maintains and calculates the underlying index, which is designed to provide exposure to constituents of the Russell 1000® Index (the "Russell 1000") that exhibit low beta characteristics. **Top Holdings:** Prologis Inc　Concho Resources Inc　United States Cellular Corp　McCormick & Co Inc Non-Voting　Eli Lilly and Co

---

Invesco S&P SmallCap 600® Pure Value ETF　　　　　　　　　　C-　　HOLD

Ticker	Traded On	NAV	Total Assets ($)	Dividend Yield (TTM)	Turnover Ratio	Expense Ratio
RZV	NYSE Arca	57.81	$155,586,378	1.59		0.35

Ratings
Reward　　　　　　　　　　　　　　　C-
Risk　　　　　　　　　　　　　　　　C-
Recent Upgrade/Downgrade　　　　　Down

Fund Information
Fund Type　　　　　　　Exchange Traded Funds
Category　　　　　　　　US Equity Small Cap
Sub-Category　　　　　　Small Value
Prospectus Objective　　　Small Company
Inception Date　　　　　　Mar-06
Open to New Investments　　　　　　Y

Prices
Price (as of 12/31/2018)　　　　　　57.79
52-Week High　　　　　　　　　　81.41
52-Week Low　　　　　　　　　　55.11

Total Returns (%)

3-Month	6-Month	1-Year	3-Year	5-Year
-23.26	-25.03	-19.52	8.75	-2.25

3-Year Standard Deviation　　　　　19.59
Effective Duration

Valuation
Premium/Discount (1-Year Average)　0.05

Company Information
Provider　　　　Invesco
Manager/Tenure　Peter Hubbard (0), Michael Jeanette (0), Jonathan Nixon (0), 1 other
Website　　　　http://www.invesco.com/us
Address　　　　Invesco 11 Greenway Plaza, Ste. 2500 Houston TX 77046 United States
Phone Number　800-659-1005

PERFORMANCE

Ratings History

Date	Overall Rating	Risk Rating	Reward Rating
Q4-18	C-	C-	C-
Q2-18	C	D+	C
Q4-17	B-	C	B
Q4-16	C	C-	B-
Q4-15	C	C-	C

Asset & Performance History

Date	NAV	1-Year Total Return
2017	73.03	0.87
2016	73.02	34.26
2015	54.95	-12.45
2014	63.47	2.66
2013	62.25	45.1
2012	43.22	21.31

Total Assets: $155,586,378

Asset Allocation

Asset	%
Cash	0%
Stocks	100%
US Stocks	98%
Bonds	0%
US Bonds	0%
Other	0%

Services Offered:

Investment Strategy: The investment seeks to track the investment results (before fees and expenses) of the S&P SmallCap 600® Pure Value Index (the "underlying index"). The fund generally will invest at least 90% of its total assets in the securities that comprise the underlying index. Strictly in accordance with its guidelines and mandated procedures, the index provider, compiles, maintains and calculates the underlying index, which is comprised of those S&P SmallCap 600® companies with strong value characteristics selected by the index provider. The fund is non-diversified. **Top Holdings:** Office Depot Inc　Renewable Energy Group Inc　GameStop Corp Class A　Shoe Carnival Inc　Barnes & Noble Inc

ALPS Equal Sector Weight ETF

C-   HOLD

Ticker	Traded On	NAV	Total Assets ($)	Dividend Yield (TTM)	Turnover Ratio	Expense Ratio
EQL	NYSE Arca	63.90	$154,742,029	2.07	5	0.48

Ratings
Reward   C-
Risk   D+
Recent Upgrade/Downgrade   Down

Fund Information
Fund Type   Exchange Traded Funds
Category   US Equity Large Cap Blend
Sub-Category   Large Blend
Prospectus Objective Growth
Inception Date   Jul-09
Open to New Investments Y

Prices
Price (as of 12/31/2018)   63.85
52-Week High   73.70
52-Week Low   60.34

Total Returns (%)

3-Month	6-Month	1-Year	3-Year	5-Year
-12.00	-6.91	-6.00	25.72	39.74

3-Year Standard Deviation   8.64
Effective Duration

Valuation
Premium/Discount (1-Year Average)   0.06

Company Information
Provider   ALPS
Manager/Tenure   Ryan Mischker (3), Andrew Hicks (2)
Website   http://www.alpsfunds.com
Address   ALPS 1290 Broadway, Suite 1100
                 Denver CO 80203 United States
Phone Number   866-759-5679

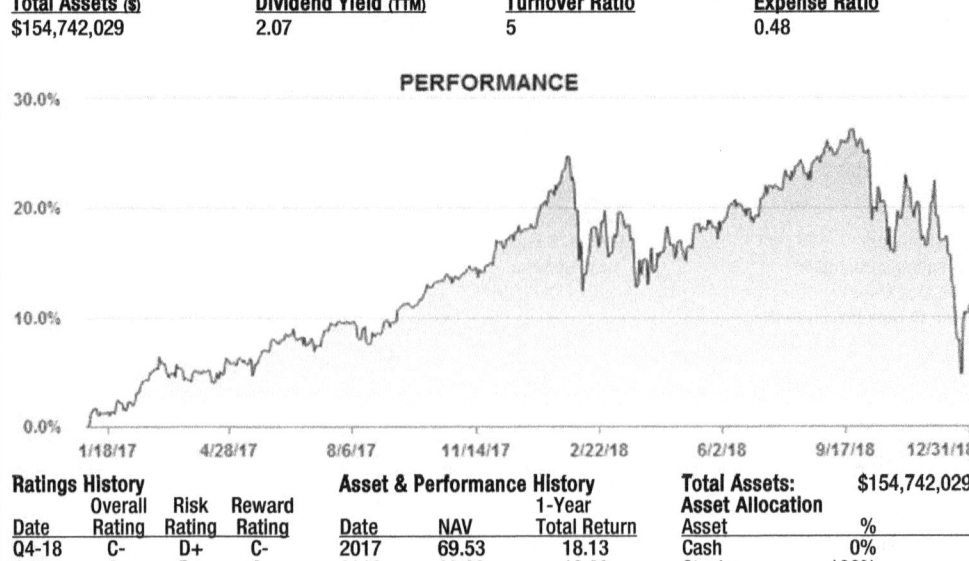

PERFORMANCE

Ratings History

Date	Overall Rating	Risk Rating	Reward Rating
Q4-18	C-	D+	C-
Q2-18	C-	D+	C
Q4-17	B-	B	B-
Q4-16	C	D+	B-
Q4-15	C	D+	C

Asset & Performance History

Date	NAV	1-Year Total Return
2017	69.53	18.13
2016	60.09	12.63
2015	54.65	-1.67
2014	56.73	13.04
2013	51.06	30.17
2012	39.89	14.5

Total Assets: $154,742,029
Asset Allocation

Asset	%
Cash	0%
Stocks	100%
US Stocks	98%
Bonds	0%
US Bonds	0%
Other	0%

Services Offered:

Investment Strategy: The investment seeks investment results that replicate as closely as possible, before fees and expenses, the performance of the NYSE Select Sector Equal Weight Index (the "underlying index"). In order to track the underlying index, the fund will use a "fund of funds" approach, and seek to achieve its investment objective by investing at least 90% of its total assets in the shares of the Underlying Sector ETFs. The underlying index is an index of ETFs comprised of all active Select Sector SPDR® ETFs in an equal weighted portfolio. It is non-diversified. **Top Holdings:** Utilities Select Sector SPDR® ETF Consumer Staples Select Sector SPDR® ETF Real Estate Select Sector SPDR® Health Care Select Sector SPDR® ETF Financial Select Sector SPDR® ETF

VanEck Vectors Short High-Yield Municipal Index ETF

C-   HOLD

Ticker	Traded On	NAV	Total Assets ($)	Dividend Yield (TTM)	Turnover Ratio	Expense Ratio
SHYD	BATS	24.18	$154,490,294	3.15	27	0.35

Ratings
Reward   C
Risk   C-
Recent Upgrade/Downgrade   Down

Fund Information
Fund Type   Exchange Traded Funds
Category   US Muni Fixed Inc
Sub-Category   High Yield Muni
Prospectus Objective Muni Bond - Natl
Inception Date   Jan-14
Open to New Investments Y

Prices
Price (as of 12/31/2018)   24.20
52-Week High   24.60
52-Week Low   23.89

Total Returns (%)

3-Month	6-Month	1-Year	3-Year	5-Year
0.14	0.36	2.16	5.80	

3-Year Standard Deviation   2.93
Effective Duration   4.73

Valuation
Premium/Discount (1-Year Average)   -0.12

Company Information
Provider   VanEck
Manager/Tenure   James T. Colby (4)
Website   http://www.vaneck.com
Address   Van Eck Associates Corporation 666
                 Third Avenue New York NY 10017
                 United States
Phone Number   800-826-1115

PERFORMANCE

Ratings History

Date	Overall Rating	Risk Rating	Reward Rating
Q4-18	C-	C-	C
Q2-18	C-	C-	C
Q4-17	C+	B	C
Q4-16	C-	C-	C-
Q4-15	D+	C-	D+

Asset & Performance History

Date	NAV	1-Year Total Return
2017	24.36	5.52
2016	23.81	-1.86
2015	24.96	1.47
2014	25.39	
2013		
2012		

Total Assets: $154,490,294
Asset Allocation

Asset	%
Cash	0%
Stocks	0%
US Stocks	0%
Bonds	100%
US Bonds	98%
Other	0%

Services Offered:

Investment Strategy: The investment seeks to replicate as closely as possible, before fees and expenses, the price and yield performance of the Bloomberg Barclays Municipal High Yield Short Duration Index. The fund normally invests at least 80% of its total assets in securities that comprise the benchmark index. The index is composed of publicly traded municipal bonds that cover the U.S. dollar denominated high yield short-term tax-exempt bond market. **Top Holdings:** BUCKEYE OHIO TOB SETTLEMENT FING AUTH 5.12% CLEVELAND-CUYAHOGA CNTY OHIO PORT AUTH 5% FOUNTAIN COLO URBAN RENEWAL AUTH 4.5% HOUSTON TEX 5% ILLINOIS ST 5%

PIMCO 25+ Year Zero Coupon U.S. Treasury Index Exchange-Traded Fund   D+   SELL

Ticker	Traded On	NAV	Total Assets ($)	Dividend Yield (TTM)	Turnover Ratio	Expense Ratio
ZROZ	NYSE Arca	112.45	$153,843,612	2.97	19	0.15

Ratings

Reward	D
Risk	D+
Recent Upgrade/Downgrade	Down

Fund Information

Fund Type	Exchange Traded Funds
Category	US Fixed Income
Sub-Category	Long Government
Prospectus Objective	Govt Bond - Treasury
Inception Date	Oct-09
Open to New Investments	Y

Prices

Price (as of 12/31/2018)	112.49
52-Week High	121.42
52-Week Low	100.48

Total Returns (%)

3-Month	6-Month	1-Year	3-Year	5-Year
6.22	-0.19	-4.28	10.73	57.21

3-Year Standard Deviation	14.37
Effective Duration	27.37

Valuation

Premium/Discount (1-Year Average)	0.03

Company Information

Provider	PIMCO
Manager/Tenure	Matthew P. Dorsten (2), Mitchell Handa (0), Graham A. Rennison (0)
Website	http://www.pimco.com
Address	PIMCO 840 Newport Center Drive, Suite 100 Newport Beach CA 92660 United States
Phone Number	866-746-2602

PERFORMANCE

Ratings History

Date	Overall Rating	Risk Rating	Reward Rating
Q4-18	D+	D+	D
Q2-18	D+	C-	D+
Q4-17	C	C	C
Q4-16	C	C-	C
Q4-15	C	D+	C

Asset & Performance History

Date	NAV	1-Year Total Return
2017	120.96	14.06
2016	108.88	1.61
2015	110.24	-4.94
2014	119.36	49.35
2013	82.35	-21.94
2012	109.7	1.81

Total Assets: $153,843,612

Asset Allocation

Asset	%
Cash	0%
Stocks	0%
US Stocks	0%
Bonds	100%
US Bonds	100%
Other	0%

Services Offered:

Investment Strategy: The investment seeks to provide total return that closely corresponds, before fees and expenses, to the total return of the ICE BofAML Long US Treasury Principal STRIPS Index. The fund invests at least 80% of its total assets (exclusive of collateral held from securities lending) in the component securities of the ICE BofAML Long US Treasury Principal STRIPS Index (the "underlying index"). The underlying index is an unmanaged index comprised of long maturity Separate Trading of Registered Interest and Principal of Securities ("STRIPS") representing the final principal payment of U.S. Treasury bonds. **Top Holdings:** U.S. Treasury Bond Stripped Principal Payment 0% U.S. Treasury Bond Stripped Principal Payment 0% U.S. Treasury Bond Stripped Principal Payment 0% U.S. Treasury Bond Stripped Principal Payment 0% U.S. Treasury Bond Stripped Principal Payment 0%

First Trust Brazil AlphaDEX® Fund   C   HOLD

Ticker	Traded On	NAV	Total Assets ($)	Dividend Yield (TTM)	Turnover Ratio	Expense Ratio
FBZ	NAS CM	13.37	$153,725,412	6.67	159	0.8

Ratings

Reward	C
Risk	C-
Recent Upgrade/Downgrade	Up

Fund Information

Fund Type	Exchange Traded Funds
Category	Latin America Equity
Sub-Category	Latin America Stock
Prospectus Objective	Foreign Stock
Inception Date	Apr-11
Open to New Investments	Y

Prices

Price (as of 12/31/2018)	13.24
52-Week High	17.59
52-Week Low	10.52

Total Returns (%)

3-Month	6-Month	1-Year	3-Year	5-Year
20.50	21.70	-1.12	99.55	-2.87

3-Year Standard Deviation	32.34
Effective Duration	

Valuation

Premium/Discount (1-Year Average)	-0.09

Company Information

Provider	First Trust
Manager/Tenure	Jon C. Erickson (7), Daniel J. Lindquist (7), David G. McGarel (7), 3 others
Website	http://www.ftportfolios.com/
Address	First Trust 120 E. Liberty Drive, Suite 400 Wheaton IL 60187 United States
Phone Number	800-621-1675

PERFORMANCE

Ratings History

Date	Overall Rating	Risk Rating	Reward Rating
Q4-18	C	C-	C
Q2-18	C-	D+	C
Q4-17	C	C-	C
Q4-16	D+	D+	D+
Q4-15	D-	D-	D-

Asset & Performance History

Date	NAV	1-Year Total Return
2017	15.51	21.01
2016	13.93	59.84
2015	8.87	-41.76
2014	15.65	-16.42
2013	19.45	-14.69
2012	23.42	5.94

Total Assets: $153,725,412

Asset Allocation

Asset	%
Cash	2%
Stocks	98%
US Stocks	0%
Bonds	0%
US Bonds	0%
Other	0%

Services Offered:

Investment Strategy: The investment seeks investment results that correspond generally to the price and yield (before the fund's fees and expenses) of an equity index called the NASDAQ AlphaDEX® Brazil Index. The fund will normally invest at least 90% of its net assets (including investment borrowings) in common stocks and/or depositary receipts that comprise the index. The index is designed to select stocks from the NASDAQ Brazil Index (the "base index") that may generate positive alpha, or risk-adjusted returns, relative to traditional indices through the use of the AlphaDEX® selection methodology. **Top Holdings:** Energy Company of Parana Participating Preferred Guararapes Confeccoes SA Energy Company of Minas Gerais Participating Preferred Magazine Luiza SA Cia de Transmissao de Energia Eletrica Paulista Participating Preferred

RiverFront Strategic Income Fund

C   **HOLD**

Ticker	Traded On	NAV	Total Assets ($)	Dividend Yield (TTM)	Turnover Ratio	Expense Ratio
RIGS	NYSE Arca	24.05	$152,879,989	4.44	32	0.47

Ratings
Reward	C
Risk	C-
Recent Upgrade/Downgrade	

Fund Information
Fund Type	Exchange Traded Funds
Category	Global Fixed Income
Sub-Category	World Bond
Prospectus Objective	Income
Inception Date	Oct-13
Open to New Investments	Y

Prices
Price (as of 12/31/2018)	24.03
52-Week High	25.25
52-Week Low	23.90

Total Returns (%)
3-Month	6-Month	1-Year	3-Year	5-Year
-0.99	0.87	-0.04	13.84	18.03

3-Year Standard Deviation	2.03
Effective Duration	

Valuation
Premium/Discount (1-Year Average)	-0.10

Company Information
Provider	ALPS
Manager/Tenure	Tim Anderson (5), Rob Glownia (2), Rebecca Felton (0)
Website	http://www.alpsfunds.com
Address	ALPS 1290 Broadway, Suite 1100 Denver CO 80203 United States
Phone Number	866-759-5679

PERFORMANCE

Ratings History
Date	Overall Rating	Risk Rating	Reward Rating
Q4-18	C	C-	C
Q2-18	C	C-	C
Q4-17	B-	B	C+
Q4-16	C	C-	C
Q4-15	C-	C-	D+

Asset & Performance History
Date	NAV	1-Year Total Return
2017	25.16	4.68
2016	25.12	8.79
2015	24.16	0.6
2014	24.87	3.06
2013	24.93	
2012		

Total Assets: $152,879,989

Asset Allocation
Asset	%
Cash	7%
Stocks	0%
US Stocks	0%
Bonds	93%
US Bonds	83%
Other	0%

Services Offered:

Investment Strategy: The investment seeks total return, with an emphasis on income as the source of that total return. The fund seeks to achieve its investment objective by investing in a global portfolio of fixed income securities of various maturities, ratings and currency denominations. The adviser intends to utilize various investment strategies in a broad array of fixed income sectors. The fund may purchase fixed income securities issued by U.S. or foreign corporations or financial institutions, including debt securities of all types and maturities, convertible securities and preferred stocks. It is non-diversified. **Top Holdings:** Sprint Communications, Inc. 7% DISH DBS Corporation 7.88% Cablevision Systems Corporation 8% HCA Inc. 5.88% Dolphin Subsidiary II, Inc. 7.25%

First Trust Chindia ETF

C   **HOLD**

Ticker	Traded On	NAV	Total Assets ($)	Dividend Yield (TTM)	Turnover Ratio	Expense Ratio
FNI	NYSE Arca	30.93	$152,526,963	2.72	35	0.6

Ratings
Reward	C+
Risk	D+
Recent Upgrade/Downgrade	

Fund Information
Fund Type	Exchange Traded Funds
Category	Equity Misc
Sub-Category	Miscellaneous Region
Prospectus Objective	Pacific Stock
Inception Date	May-07
Open to New Investments	Y

Prices
Price (as of 12/31/2018)	30.86
52-Week High	43.90
52-Week Low	29.74

Total Returns (%)
3-Month	6-Month	1-Year	3-Year	5-Year
-9.63	-19.02	-20.71	14.31	16.64

3-Year Standard Deviation	16.67
Effective Duration	

Valuation
Premium/Discount (1-Year Average)	0.03

Company Information
Provider	First Trust
Manager/Tenure	Jon C. Erickson (11), Daniel J. Lindquist (11), David G. McGarel (11), 3 others
Website	http://www.ftportfolios.com/
Address	First Trust 120 E. Liberty Drive, Suite 400 Wheaton IL 60187 United States
Phone Number	800-621-1675

PERFORMANCE

Ratings History
Date	Overall Rating	Risk Rating	Reward Rating
Q4-18	C	D+	C+
Q2-18	C	D+	B-
Q4-17	B	C	A-
Q4-16	C	D+	B-
Q4-15	C+	C	B-

Asset & Performance History
Date	NAV	1-Year Total Return
2017	39.57	47.34
2016	27.39	-2.15
2015	28.36	-0.32
2014	28.63	2.37
2013	28.22	35.83
2012	20.97	17.15

Total Assets: $152,526,963

Asset Allocation
Asset	%
Cash	0%
Stocks	100%
US Stocks	3%
Bonds	0%
US Bonds	0%
Other	0%

Services Offered:

Investment Strategy: The investment seeks investment results that correspond generally to the price and yield (before the fund's fees and expenses) of an equity index called the ISE ChIndiaTM Index. The fund will normally invest at least 90% of its net assets (including investment borrowings) in securities that comprise the index. The index is a modified market capitalization weighted of 50 American Depositary Receipts ("ADRs"), American Depositary Shares ("ADSs") and/or stocks selected from a universe of all listed ADRs, ADSs and/or stocks of companies from China and India currently trading on U.S. exchanges. It is non-diversified. **Top Holdings:** ICICI Bank Ltd ADR Infosys Ltd ADR HDFC Bank Ltd ADR Alibaba Group Holding Ltd ADR Baidu Inc ADR

RiverFront Dynamic US Flex-Cap ETF   C-   HOLD

Ticker	Traded On	NAV	Total Assets ($)	Dividend Yield (TTM)	Turnover Ratio	Expense Ratio
RFFC	NYSE Arca	29.15	$152,464,497	1.15	86	0.52

Ratings
Reward	C
Risk	C-
Recent Upgrade/Downgrade	

Fund Information
Fund Type	Exchange Traded Funds
Category	US Equity Large Cap Blend
Sub-Category	Large Blend
Prospectus Objective	Growth
Inception Date	Jun-16
Open to New Investments	Y

Prices
Price (as of 12/31/2018)	29.02
52-Week High	36.35
52-Week Low	27.40

Total Returns (%)
3-Month	6-Month	1-Year	3-Year	5-Year
-18.65	-14.10	-9.66		

3-Year Standard Deviation	
Effective Duration	

Valuation
Premium/Discount (1-Year Average)	0.13

Company Information
Provider	ALPS
Manager/Tenure	Adam Grossman (2), Scott Hays (2), Chris Konstantinos (2), 1 other
Website	http://www.alpsfunds.com
Address	ALPS 1290 Broadway, Suite 1100 Denver CO 80203 United States
Phone Number	866-759-5679

PERFORMANCE

Ratings History
Date	Overall Rating	Risk Rating	Reward Rating
Q4-18	C-	C-	C
Q2-18	C-	D+	C-
Q4-17	D+	B+	C
Q4-16	U		
Q4-15			

Asset & Performance History
Date	NAV	1-Year Total Return
2017	32.66	20.81
2016	27.31	
2015		
2014		
2013		
2012		

Total Assets: $152,464,497

Asset Allocation
Asset	%
Cash	0%
Stocks	100%
US Stocks	97%
Bonds	0%
US Bonds	0%
Other	0%

Services Offered:

Investment Strategy: The investment seeks to provide capital appreciation. The fund invests at least 65% of its net assets in a portfolio of equity securities of publicly traded U.S. companies. Equity securities include common stocks and common or preferred shares of real estate investment trusts. The fund may invest in small-, mid- and large-capitalization companies. It is non-diversified. **Top Holdings:** Amazon.com Inc Apple Inc Microsoft Corp Johnson & Johnson JPMorgan Chase & Co

---

First Trust RBA American Industrial Renaissance™ ETF   C+   HOLD

Ticker	Traded On	NAV	Total Assets ($)	Dividend Yield (TTM)	Turnover Ratio	Expense Ratio
AIRR	NAS CM	21.73	$152,366,113	0.3	35	0.7

Ratings
Reward	B-
Risk	C-
Recent Upgrade/Downgrade	Down

Fund Information
Fund Type	Exchange Traded Funds
Category	Industrials Sector Equity
Sub-Category	Industrials
Prospectus Objective	Growth & Inc
Inception Date	Mar-14
Open to New Investments	Y

Prices
Price (as of 12/31/2018)	21.69
52-Week High	28.50
52-Week Low	20.46

Total Returns (%)
3-Month	6-Month	1-Year	3-Year	5-Year
-20.98	-18.59	-20.45	32.63	

3-Year Standard Deviation	18.98
Effective Duration	

Valuation
Premium/Discount (1-Year Average)	0.05

Company Information
Provider	First Trust
Manager/Tenure	Jon C. Erickson (4), Daniel J. Lindquist (4), David G. McGarel (4), 3 others
Website	http://www.ftportfolios.com/
Address	First Trust 120 E. Liberty Drive, Suite 400 Wheaton IL 60187 United States
Phone Number	800-621-1675

PERFORMANCE

Ratings History
Date	Overall Rating	Risk Rating	Reward Rating
Q4-18	C+	C-	B-
Q2-18	C	C-	C+
Q4-17	B+	C+	A
Q4-16	C+	C-	B
Q4-15	D	C	C

Asset & Performance History
Date	NAV	1-Year Total Return
2017	27.42	16.33
2016	23.64	43.33
2015	16.51	-9.47
2014	18.32	
2013		
2012		

Total Assets: $152,366,113

Asset Allocation
Asset	%
Cash	0%
Stocks	100%
US Stocks	100%
Bonds	0%
US Bonds	0%
Other	0%

Services Offered:

Investment Strategy: The investment seeks investment results that correspond generally to the price and yield (before the fund's fees and expenses) of an index called the Richard Bernstein Advisors American Industrial Renaissance® Index (the "index"). The fund will normally invest at least 90% of its net assets (including investment borrowings) in U.S. equity securities that comprise the index. The index is designed to measure the performance of small and mid cap U.S. companies in the industrial and community banking sectors. **Top Holdings:** Granite Construction Inc RBC Bearings Inc MasTec Inc EMCOR Group Inc Generac Holdings Inc

Invesco CurrencyShares® Canadian Dollar Trust

D+   SELL

Ticker	Traded On	NAV	Total Assets ($)	Dividend Yield (TTM)	Turnover Ratio	Expense Ratio
FXC	NYSE Arca	72.26	$152,357,014	0.31	0	0.4

Ratings
Reward D+
Risk C-
Recent Upgrade/Downgrade

Fund Information
Fund Type — Exchange Traded Funds
Category — Currency
Sub-Category — Single Currency
Prospectus Objective — Worldwide Bond
Inception Date — Jun-06
Open to New Investments — Y

Prices
Price (as of 12/31/2018) — 72.29
52-Week High — 80.39
52-Week Low — 72.20

Total Returns (%)

3-Month	6-Month	1-Year	3-Year	5-Year
-5.23	-3.16	-7.88	1.55	-22.31

3-Year Standard Deviation — 8.03
Effective Duration —

Valuation
Premium/Discount (1-Year Average) — -0.10

Company Information
Provider — Invesco
Manager/Tenure — Management Team (12)
Website — http://www.invesco.com/us
Address — Invesco 11 Greenway Plaza, Ste. 2500 Houston TX 77046 United States
Phone Number — 800-659-1005

PERFORMANCE

Ratings History

Date	Overall Rating	Risk Rating	Reward Rating
Q4-18	D+	C-	D+
Q2-18	C-	C-	D+
Q4-17	C-	C	D+
Q4-16	D	D+	D
Q4-15	D	D	D

Asset & Performance History

Date	NAV	1-Year Total Return
2017	78.73	6.85
2016	73.7	3.18
2015	71.42	-16.79
2014	85.86	-8.06
2013	93.61	-6.09
2012	99.88	2.38

Total Assets: $152,357,014

Asset Allocation

Asset	%
Cash	100%
Stocks	0%
US Stocks	0%
Bonds	0%
US Bonds	0%
Other	0%

Services Offered:

Investment Strategy: The investment seeks to track the price of the Canadian Dollar, net of trust expenses. The fund seeks to reflect the price of the Canadian Dollar. The sponsor believes that, for many investors, the shares represent a cost-effective investment relative to traditional means of investing in the foreign exchange market. **Top Holdings:**

---

iShares iBonds Dec 2026 Term Corporate ETF

D+   SELL

Ticker	Traded On	NAV	Total Assets ($)	Dividend Yield (TTM)	Turnover Ratio	Expense Ratio
IBDR	NYSE Arca	23.04	$152,181,247	3.46	6	0.1

Ratings
Reward D+
Risk C-
Recent Upgrade/Downgrade

Fund Information
Fund Type — Exchange Traded Funds
Category — US Fixed Income
Sub-Category — Corporate Bond
Prospectus Objective — Corp Bond - Gen
Inception Date — Sep-16
Open to New Investments — Y

Prices
Price (as of 12/31/2018) — 23.03
52-Week High — 24.54
52-Week Low — 22.85

Total Returns (%)

3-Month	6-Month	1-Year	3-Year	5-Year
0.38	1.29	-2.30		

3-Year Standard Deviation —
Effective Duration — 6.44

Valuation
Premium/Discount (1-Year Average) — 0.21

Company Information
Provider — iShares
Manager/Tenure — James Mauro (2), Scott Radell (2)
Website — http://www.ishares.com
Address — iShares 400 Howard Street San Francisco CA 94105 United States
Phone Number — 800-474-2737

PERFORMANCE

Ratings History

Date	Overall Rating	Risk Rating	Reward Rating
Q4-18	D+	C-	D+
Q2-18	D+	C-	D
Q4-17	D	B	D+
Q4-16	U		
Q4-15			

Asset & Performance History

Date	NAV	1-Year Total Return
2017	24.43	5.68
2016	23.84	
2015		
2014		
2013		
2012		

Total Assets: $152,181,247

Asset Allocation

Asset	%
Cash	1%
Stocks	0%
US Stocks	0%
Bonds	99%
US Bonds	85%
Other	0%

Services Offered:

Investment Strategy: The investment seeks to track the investment results of the Bloomberg Barclays December 2026 Maturity Corporate Index composed of U.S. dollar-denominated, investment-grade corporate bonds maturing in 2026. The fund generally will invest at least 90% of its assets in the component securities of the underlying index, and may invest up to 10% of its assets in certain futures, options and swap contracts, cash and cash equivalents. The index includes U.S. dollar-denominated, investment-grade securities publicly issued by U.S. and non-U.S. corporate issuers that have $300 million or more of outstanding face value at the time of inclusion. It is non-diversified. **Top Holdings:** Anheuser-Busch Companies LLC / Anheuser-Busch InBev Worldwide Inc 3.65% Diamond 1 Finance Corporation/Diamond 2 Finance Corporation 6.02% Microsoft Corporation 2.4% JPMorgan Chase & Co. 3.3% Wells Fargo & Company 3%

WisdomTree Continuous Commodity Index Fund   D   SELL

Ticker	Traded On	NAV	Total Assets ($)	Dividend Yield (TTM)	Turnover Ratio	Expense Ratio
GCC	NYSE Arca	17.50	$151,734,692	0		0.75

Ratings
Reward	D
Risk	C-
Recent Upgrade/Downgrade	Down

Fund Information
Fund Type	Exchange Traded Funds
Category	Commodities Broad Basket
Sub-Category	Commodities Broad Basket
Prospectus Objective	Natl Res
Inception Date	Jan-08
Open to New Investments	Y

Prices
Price (as of 12/31/2018)	17.55
52-Week High	19.79
52-Week Low	17.52

Total Returns (%)
3-Month	6-Month	1-Year	3-Year	5-Year
-4.01	-5.23	-9.09	-5.72	-31.92

3-Year Standard Deviation	7.5
Effective Duration	

Valuation
Premium/Discount (1-Year Average)	-0.12

Company Information
Provider	WisdomTree
Manager/Tenure	Management Team (10)
Website	http://www.wisdomtree.com
Address	WisdomTree 245 Park Avenue, 35th floor New York NY 10167 United States
Phone Number	866-909-9473

PERFORMANCE

Ratings History
Date	Overall Rating	Risk Rating	Reward Rating
Q4-18	D	C-	D
Q2-18	C-	C-	C-
Q4-17	D	D+	D
Q4-16	D	D	D
Q4-15	D	D	D

Asset & Performance History
Date	NAV	1-Year Total Return
2017	19.25	-0.53
2016	19.35	4.27
2015	18.56	-18.63
2014	22.81	-11.24
2013	25.7	-10.91
2012	28.85	-3.68

Total Assets: $151,734,692
Asset Allocation
Asset	%
Cash	50%
Stocks	0%
US Stocks	0%
Bonds	0%
US Bonds	0%
Other	51%

Services Offered:

Investment Strategy: The investment seeks, through its investment in the master fund, to reflect the performance of the index, over time, less the expenses of the fund and the master fund's overall operations.
 The master fund invests in a portfolio of index commodities, as well as holding cash and United States Treasury securities and other high credit quality short-term fixed income securities for deposit with the master fund's Commodity Broker as margin. The Continuous Commodity Total Return Index is a broad based commodity index that reflects the price movement of 17 exchange-traded futures contracts. **Top Holdings:** Platinum Future Jul19 Xnym 20190729   Platinum Future Apr19 Xnym 20190426   Coffee \'c\' Future Jul19 Ifus 20190719   Cotton No.2 Futr Jul19 Ifus 20190709   Live Cattle Futr Feb19 Xcme 20190228

VictoryShares Developed Enhanced Volatility Wtd ETF   D+   SELL

Ticker	Traded On	NAV	Total Assets ($)	Dividend Yield (TTM)	Turnover Ratio	Expense Ratio
CIZ	NAS CM	30.87	$151,704,600	2.79	164	0.45

Ratings
Reward	D+
Risk	C-
Recent Upgrade/Downgrade	Down

Fund Information
Fund Type	Exchange Traded Funds
Category	Global Equity Large Cap
Sub-Category	Foreign Large Blend
Prospectus Objective	Income
Inception Date	Sep-14
Open to New Investments	Y

Prices
Price (as of 12/31/2018)	30.72
52-Week High	37.46
52-Week Low	30.47

Total Returns (%)
3-Month	6-Month	1-Year	3-Year	5-Year
-8.95	-6.45	-9.46	4.63	

3-Year Standard Deviation	9.62
Effective Duration	

Valuation
Premium/Discount (1-Year Average)	0.33

Company Information
Provider	VictoryShares
Manager/Tenure	Stephen Hammers (4), Mannik Dhillon (0)
Website	http://www.VictorySharesLiterature.com
Address	Victory Shares 4249 Easton Way, Suite 400 Columbus OH 43219 United States
Phone Number	

PERFORMANCE

Ratings History
Date	Overall Rating	Risk Rating	Reward Rating
Q4-18	D+	C-	D+
Q2-18	C	C-	C
Q4-17	C	C+	C
Q4-16	D	D	D
Q4-15	U		

Asset & Performance History
Date	NAV	1-Year Total Return
2017	34.96	25.66
2016	28.34	-8.73
2015	31.42	-6.64
2014	34.23	
2013		
2012		

Total Assets: $151,704,600
Asset Allocation
Asset	%
Cash	75%
Stocks	25%
US Stocks	0%
Bonds	0%
US Bonds	0%
Other	0%

Services Offered:

Investment Strategy: The investment seeks to track the performance of the Nasdaq Victory International 500 Long/Cash Volatility Weighted Index before fees and expenses. The fund seeks to achieve its investment objective by investing, under normal market conditions, at least 80% of its assets directly or indirectly in the securities included in the Nasdaq Victory International 500 Long/Cash Volatility Weighted Index, an unmanaged, volatility weighted index maintained exclusively by the index provider. The index identifies the 500 largest foreign companies by market capitalization measured at the time the index's constituent securities are determined. **Top Holdings:** Mini Msci Eafe Fut Dec18   Bank of Montreal   TELUS Corp   BCE Inc   Canadian Imperial Bank of Commerce

ProShares Ultra Health Care
C   HOLD

Ticker	Traded On	NAV	Total Assets ($)	Dividend Yield (TTM)	Turnover Ratio	Expense Ratio
RXL	NYSE Arca	91.97	$151,447,055	0.24		0.95

Ratings
Reward   C
Risk   C-
Recent Upgrade/Downgrade

Fund Information
Fund Type	Exchange Traded Funds
Category	Trading Tools
Sub-Category	Trading--Leveraged Equity
Prospectus Objective	Health
Inception Date	Jan-07
Open to New Investments	Y

Prices
Price (as of 12/31/2018)	90.92
52-Week High	117.11
52-Week Low	80.30

Total Returns (%)
3-Month	6-Month	1-Year	3-Year	5-Year
-21.33	1.85	5.39	40.14	130.10

3-Year Standard Deviation   25.71
Effective Duration

Valuation
Premium/Discount (1-Year Average)   0.29

Company Information
Provider	ProShares
Manager/Tenure	Michael Neches (5), Tarak Davé (0)
Website	http://www.proshares.com
Address	ProShares 7501 Wisconsin Avenue, Suite 1000 Bethesda MD 20814 United States
Phone Number	866-776-5125

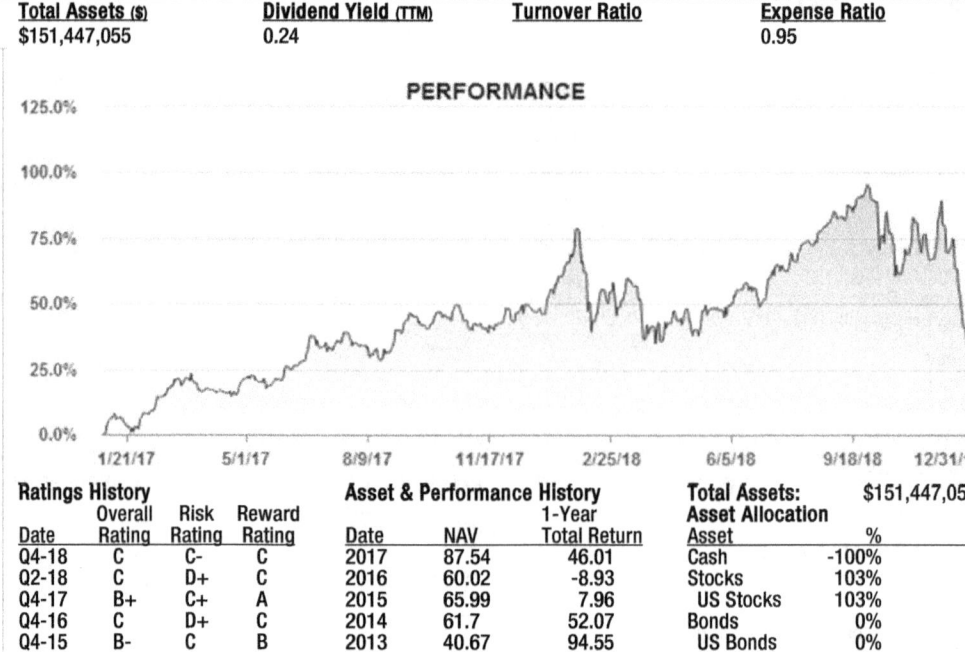

PERFORMANCE

Ratings History
Date	Overall Rating	Risk Rating	Reward Rating
Q4-18	C	C-	C
Q2-18	C	D+	C
Q4-17	B+	C+	A
Q4-16	C	D+	C
Q4-15	B-	C	B

Asset & Performance History
Date	NAV	1-Year Total Return
2017	87.54	46.01
2016	60.02	-8.93
2015	65.99	7.96
2014	61.7	52.07
2013	40.67	94.55
2012	20.96	38.34

Total Assets: $151,447,055
Asset Allocation
Asset	%
Cash	-100%
Stocks	103%
US Stocks	103%
Bonds	0%
US Bonds	0%
Other	97%

Services Offered:

Investment Strategy: The investment seeks daily investment results, before fees and expenses, that correspond to two times (2x) the daily performance of the Dow Jones U.S. Health CareSM Index. The fund invests in financial instruments that ProShare Advisors believes, in combination, should produce daily returns consistent with the fund's investment objective. The index measures the performance of certain companies in the healthcare sector of the U.S. equity market. Component companies include, among others, health care providers, biotechnology companies, medical supplies, advanced medical devices and pharmaceuticals. The fund is non-diversified. **Top Holdings:** Dj U.S. Health Care Index Swap Goldman Sachs International   Dj U.S. Health Care Index Swap Citibank Na   Ishares U.S. Healthcare (Iyh) Swap Bank Of America Na   Dj U.S. Health Care Index Swap Societe Generale   Johnson & Johnson

RiverFront Dynamic US Dividend Advantage ETF
C-   HOLD

Ticker	Traded On	NAV	Total Assets ($)	Dividend Yield (TTM)	Turnover Ratio	Expense Ratio
RFDA	NYSE Arca	28.18	$151,292,628	2.14	54	0.52

Ratings
Reward   C-
Risk   C-
Recent Upgrade/Downgrade

Fund Information
Fund Type	Exchange Traded Funds
Category	US Equity Large Cap Blend
Sub-Category	Large Value
Prospectus Objective	Growth & Inc
Inception Date	Jun-16
Open to New Investments	Y

Prices
Price (as of 12/31/2018)	28.12
52-Week High	33.90
52-Week Low	26.47

Total Returns (%)
3-Month	6-Month	1-Year	3-Year	5-Year
-14.84	-11.87	-8.89		

3-Year Standard Deviation
Effective Duration

Valuation
Premium/Discount (1-Year Average)   0.18

Company Information
Provider	ALPS
Manager/Tenure	Adam Grossman (2), Scott Hays (2), Chris Konstantinos (2), 1 other
Website	http://www.alpsfunds.com
Address	ALPS 1290 Broadway, Suite 1100 Denver CO 80203 United States
Phone Number	866-759-5679

PERFORMANCE

Ratings History
Date	Overall Rating	Risk Rating	Reward Rating
Q4-18	C-	C-	C-
Q2-18	C-	C-	C-
Q4-17	D+	B+	C
Q4-16	U		
Q4-15			

Asset & Performance History
Date	NAV	1-Year Total Return
2017	31.61	19.76
2016	26.95	
2015		
2014		
2013		
2012		

Total Assets: $151,292,628
Asset Allocation
Asset	%
Cash	0%
Stocks	100%
US Stocks	99%
Bonds	0%
US Bonds	0%
Other	0%

Services Offered:

Investment Strategy: The investment seeks to provide capital appreciation and dividend income. The fund invests at least 65% of its net assets in a portfolio of equity securities of publicly traded U.S. companies with the potential for dividend income. Equity securities include common stocks and common or preferred shares of real estate investment trusts. The fund may invest in small-, mid- and large-capitalization companies. It is non-diversified. **Top Holdings:** Amazon.com Inc   Apple Inc   Eli Lilly and Co   JPMorgan Chase & Co   Amgen Inc

RiverFront Dynamic Core Income ETF   D+   SELL

Ticker	Traded On	NAV		Total Assets ($)	Dividend Yield (TTM)	Turnover Ratio	Expense Ratio
RFCI	NYSE Arca	23.78		$150,526,917	2.79	18	0.52

Ratings
Reward	D+
Risk	C-
Recent Upgrade/Downgrade	

Fund Information
Fund Type	Exchange Traded Funds
Category	US Fixed Income
Sub-Category	Intermediate-Term Bond
Prospectus Objective	Income
Inception Date	Jun-16
Open to New Investments	Y

Prices
Price (as of 12/31/2018)	23.72
52-Week High	24.70
52-Week Low	23.48

Total Returns (%)
3-Month	6-Month	1-Year	3-Year	5-Year
0.65	1.17	-0.76		

3-Year Standard Deviation	
Effective Duration	

Valuation
Premium/Discount (1-Year Average)	0.14

Company Information
Provider	ALPS
Manager/Tenure	Tim Anderson (2), Rob Glownia (2), Rebecca Felton (0)
Website	http://www.alpsfunds.com
Address	ALPS 1290 Broadway, Suite 1100 Denver CO 80203 United States
Phone Number	866-759-5679

PERFORMANCE

Ratings History
Date	Overall Rating	Risk Rating	Reward Rating
Q4-18	D+	C-	D+
Q2-18	D+	C-	D
Q4-17	D+	B-	D+
Q4-16	U		
Q4-15			

Asset & Performance History
Date	NAV	1-Year Total Return
2017	24.63	3.27
2016	24.34	
2015		
2014		
2013		
2012		

Total Assets: $150,526,917

Asset Allocation
Asset	%
Cash	6%
Stocks	0%
US Stocks	0%
Bonds	93%
US Bonds	82%
Other	0%

Services Offered:

Investment Strategy: The investment seeks total return, with an emphasis on income as the source of that total return. The fund invests in a global portfolio of fixed income securities of various maturities, ratings and currency denominations. It may purchase fixed income securities issued by U.S. or foreign corporations or financial institutions, including debt securities of all types and maturities, convertible securities and preferred stocks. The fund is non-diversified. **Top Holdings:** United States Treasury Notes 3% United States Treasury Notes 2.88% U.S. Treasury Bond Stripped Principal Payment 0% United States Treasury Notes 2.88% U.S. Treasury Bond Stripped Principal Payment 0%

SPDR® SSGA US Large Cap Low Volatility Index ETF   C   HOLD

Ticker	Traded On	NAV		Total Assets ($)	Dividend Yield (TTM)	Turnover Ratio	Expense Ratio
LGLV	NYSE Arca	88.93		$150,235,447	1.92	108	0.12

Ratings
Reward	C
Risk	C-
Recent Upgrade/Downgrade	

Fund Information
Fund Type	Exchange Traded Funds
Category	US Equity Large Cap Blend
Sub-Category	Large Blend
Prospectus Objective	Income
Inception Date	Feb-13
Open to New Investments	Y

Prices
Price (as of 12/31/2018)	89.04
52-Week High	98.45
52-Week Low	84.44

Total Returns (%)
3-Month	6-Month	1-Year	3-Year	5-Year
-7.49	-0.34	0.54	31.79	57.38

3-Year Standard Deviation	8.37
Effective Duration	

Valuation
Premium/Discount (1-Year Average)	0.33

Company Information
Provider	SPDR State Street Global Advisors
Manager/Tenure	Michael J. Feehily (5), Karl A. Schneider (4), Juan Acevedo (0)
Website	http://www.spdrs.com
Address	SPDR State Street Global Advisors State Street Financial Center, 1 Lincoln Street Boston MA 02111-2900 United States
Phone Number	617-786-3000

PERFORMANCE

Ratings History
Date	Overall Rating	Risk Rating	Reward Rating
Q4-18	C	C-	C
Q2-18	C	C-	C
Q4-17	B+	A+	B-
Q4-16	C	C-	B-
Q4-15	C	C-	C

Asset & Performance History
Date	NAV	1-Year Total Return
2017	90.27	17.82
2016	80.05	11.25
2015	73.84	2.36
2014	74.34	16.65
2013	68.38	
2012		

Total Assets: $150,235,447

Asset Allocation
Asset	%
Cash	0%
Stocks	100%
US Stocks	98%
Bonds	0%
US Bonds	0%
Other	0%

Services Offered:

Investment Strategy: The investment seeks to provide investment results that, before fees and expenses, correspond generally to the total return performance of the SSGA US Large Cap Low Volatility Index. The fund generally invests substantially all, but at least 80%, of its total assets in the securities comprising the index. The index is designed to measure the performance of the stocks of U.S. large capitalization companies that exhibit low volatility. Volatility is a statistical measurement of the magnitude of movements in a stock's price over time. The fund is non-diversified. **Top Holdings:** Republic Services Inc Class A Berkshire Hathaway Inc B Marsh & McLennan Companies Inc PepsiCo Inc US Bancorp

Invesco Dynamic Building & Construction ETF

C+   **HOLD**

Ticker	Traded On	NAV	Total Assets ($)	Dividend Yield (TTM)	Turnover Ratio	Expense Ratio
PKB	NYSE Arca	23.83	$148,627,362	0.4	143	0.58

Ratings

Reward	B
Risk	C-
Recent Upgrade/Downgrade	Down

Fund Information

Fund Type	Exchange Traded Funds
Category	Industrials Sector Equity
Sub-Category	Industrials
Prospectus Objective	Unaligned
Inception Date	Oct-05
Open to New Investments	Y

Prices

Price (as of 12/31/2018)	23.78
52-Week High	36.11
52-Week Low	22.38

Total Returns (%)

3-Month	6-Month	1-Year	3-Year	5-Year
-19.37	-21.73	-30.87	1.25	7.81

3-Year Standard Deviation	17.8
Effective Duration	

Valuation

Premium/Discount (1-Year Average)	-0.05

Company Information

Provider	Invesco
Manager/Tenure	Peter Hubbard (11), Michael Jeanette (10), Tony Seisser (4), 1 other
Website	http://www.invesco.com/us
Address	Invesco 11 Greenway Plaza, Ste. 2500 Houston TX 77046 United States
Phone Number	800-659-1005

PERFORMANCE

Ratings History

Date	Overall Rating	Risk Rating	Reward Rating
Q4-18	C+	C-	B
Q2-18	B-	C	B
Q4-17	A-	B+	A
Q4-16	B-	C	B
Q4-15	B+	B-	A-

Asset & Performance History

Date	NAV	1-Year Total Return
2017	34.64	24.43
2016	27.89	17.71
2015	23.77	10.42
2014	21.55	-3.57
2013	22.37	28.93
2012	17.35	45.62

Total Assets: $148,627,362

Asset Allocation

Asset	%
Cash	0%
Stocks	100%
US Stocks	100%
Bonds	0%
US Bonds	0%
Other	0%

Services Offered:

Investment Strategy: The investment seeks to track the investment results (before fees and expenses) of the Dynamic Building & Construction IntellidexSM Index. The fund generally will invest at least 90% of its total assets in common stocks of building and construction companies that comprise the underlying intellidex. The underlying intellidex was composed of common stocks of 30 U.S. building and construction companies. These companies are engaged primarily in providing construction and related engineering services for building and remodeling residential properties, commercial or industrial buildings, etc. It is non-diversified. **Top Holdings:** Tractor Supply Co   Ingersoll-Rand PLC   Martin Marietta Materials Inc   Vulcan Materials Co   Johnson Controls International PLC

Knowledge Leaders Developed World ETF

C-   **HOLD**

Ticker	Traded On	NAV	Total Assets ($)	Dividend Yield (TTM)	Turnover Ratio	Expense Ratio
KLDW	NYSE Arca	29.26	$147,974,253	0.72	10	0.75

Ratings

Reward	C-
Risk	C-
Recent Upgrade/Downgrade	Down

Fund Information

Fund Type	Exchange Traded Funds
Category	Global Equity Large Cap
Sub-Category	World Large Stock
Prospectus Objective	Growth & Inc
Inception Date	Jul-15
Open to New Investments	Y

Prices

Price (as of 12/31/2018)	29.05
52-Week High	35.72
52-Week Low	27.85

Total Returns (%)

3-Month	6-Month	1-Year	3-Year	5-Year
-15.19	-11.64	-11.43	20.98	

3-Year Standard Deviation	10.3
Effective Duration	

Valuation

Premium/Discount (1-Year Average)	0.31

Company Information

Provider	GaveKal
Manager/Tenure	Andrew Serowik (0), Travis E. Trampe (0)
Website	http://www.gavekalfunds.com
Address	GaveKal United States
Phone Number	

PERFORMANCE

Ratings History

Date	Overall Rating	Risk Rating	Reward Rating
Q4-18	C-	C-	C-
Q2-18	C	D+	C
Q4-17	C	B+	C+
Q4-16	D	D+	D+
Q4-15	U		

Asset & Performance History

Date	NAV	1-Year Total Return
2017	33.37	27.61
2016	26.33	7.04
2015	24.76	
2014		
2013		
2012		

Total Assets: $147,974,253

Asset Allocation

Asset	%
Cash	1%
Stocks	99%
US Stocks	33%
Bonds	0%
US Bonds	0%
Other	0%

Services Offered:

Investment Strategy: The investment seeks to provide investment results that, before fees and expenses, correspond generally to the total return performance of the Knowledge Leaders Developed World Index. The fund will normally invest at least 80% of its total assets in securities of the index. The index is designed to measure the performance of issuers in developed markets countries that are considered to be "Knowledge Leaders," as defined and determined by the index provider, based on a proprietary selection model developed by the index provider and incorporated into the index methodology. The fund is non-diversified. **Top Holdings:** Hoya Corp   Adobe Inc   Nissan Chemical Corp   Kyocera Corp   Modern Times Group MTG AB B

Invesco CurrencyShares® Japanese Yen Trust   D+   SELL

Ticker	Traded On	NAV	Total Assets ($)	Dividend Yield (TTM)	Turnover Ratio	Expense Ratio
FXY	NYSE Arca	87.03	$147,549,952	0	0	0.4

Ratings
Reward	D
Risk	C-
Recent Upgrade/Downgrade	

Fund Information
Fund Type	Exchange Traded Funds
Category	Currency
Sub-Category	Single Currency
Prospectus Objective	Worldwide Bond
Inception Date	Feb-07
Open to New Investments	Y

Prices
Price (as of 12/31/2018)	87.11
52-Week High	91.52
52-Week Low	83.60

Total Returns (%)
3-Month	6-Month	1-Year	3-Year	5-Year
3.39	0.69	2.16	8.04	-6.35

3-Year Standard Deviation	10.3
Effective Duration	

Valuation
Premium/Discount (1-Year Average)	0.01

Company Information
Provider	Invesco
Manager/Tenure	Management Team (11)
Website	http://www.invesco.com/us
Address	Invesco 11 Greenway Plaza, Ste. 2500 Houston TX 77046 United States
Phone Number	800-659-1005

PERFORMANCE

Ratings History
Date	Overall Rating	Risk Rating	Reward Rating
Q4-18	D+	C-	D
Q2-18	C	C+	C
Q4-17	C-	C	D+
Q4-16	C-	C-	C-
Q4-15	D-	D-	D

Asset & Performance History
Date	NAV	1-Year Total Return
2017	85.19	3.02
2016	82.69	2.65
2015	80.55	-0.73
2014	81.15	-12.68
2013	92.94	-18.06
2012	113.42	-11.37

Total Assets: $147,549,952
Asset Allocation
Asset	%
Cash	100%
Stocks	0%
US Stocks	0%
Bonds	0%
US Bonds	0%
Other	0%

Services Offered:

Investment Strategy: The investment seeks to track the price of the Japanese Yen, net of trust expenses. The fund seeks to reflect the price of the Japanese Yen. The sponsor believes that, for many investors, the shares represent a cost-effective investment relative to traditional means of investing in the foreign exchange market.
Top Holdings:

SPDR® MSCI ACWI Low Carbon Target ETF   C-   HOLD

Ticker	Traded On	NAV	Total Assets ($)	Dividend Yield (TTM)	Turnover Ratio	Expense Ratio
LOWC	NYSE Arca	79.49	$147,170,342	2.11	17	0.2

Ratings
Reward	C-
Risk	D+
Recent Upgrade/Downgrade	Down

Fund Information
Fund Type	Exchange Traded Funds
Category	Global Equity Large Cap
Sub-Category	World Large Stock
Prospectus Objective	World Stock
Inception Date	Nov-14
Open to New Investments	Y

Prices
Price (as of 12/31/2018)	79.08
52-Week High	96.40
52-Week Low	75.73

Total Returns (%)
3-Month	6-Month	1-Year	3-Year	5-Year
-12.77	-8.56	-9.45	20.57	

3-Year Standard Deviation	9.67
Effective Duration	

Valuation
Premium/Discount (1-Year Average)	0.01

Company Information
Provider	SPDR State Street Global Advisors
Manager/Tenure	Michael J. Feehily (4), Karl A. Schneider (4), Payal Kapoor Gupta (1)
Website	http://www.spdrs.com
Address	SPDR State Street Global Advisors State Street Financial Center, 1 Lincoln Street Boston MA 02111-2900 United States
Phone Number	617-786-3000

PERFORMANCE

Ratings History
Date	Overall Rating	Risk Rating	Reward Rating
Q4-18	C-	D+	C-
Q2-18	C	D+	C
Q4-17	C+	B-	C+
Q4-16	D+	D	C-
Q4-15	U		

Asset & Performance History
Date	NAV	1-Year Total Return
2017	89.92	23.62
2016	74.43	7.71
2015	70.56	-1.52
2014	73.32	
2013		
2012		

Total Assets: $147,170,342
Asset Allocation
Asset	%
Cash	0%
Stocks	99%
US Stocks	56%
Bonds	0%
US Bonds	0%
Other	0%

Services Offered:

Investment Strategy: The investment seeks to provide investment results that, before fees and expenses, correspond generally to the total return performance of the MSCI ACWI Low Carbon Target Index. The fund generally invests substantially all, but at least 80%, of its total assets in the securities comprising the index and in depositary receipts based on securities comprising the index. The index is designed to address two dimensions of carbon exposure - carbon emissions and fossil fuel reserves, expressed as potential emissions. The fund is non-diversified. **Top Holdings:** Apple Inc   Microsoft Corp   Amazon.com Inc   Johnson & Johnson   Alphabet Inc A

VanEck Vectors Mortgage REIT Income ETF   C+   HOLD

Ticker	Traded On	NAV	Total Assets ($)	Dividend Yield (TTM)	Turnover Ratio	Expense Ratio
MORT	NYSE Arca	21.28	$147,151,703	8.12	21	0.41

Ratings
Reward   B-
Risk   C
Recent Upgrade/Downgrade   Down

Fund Information
Fund Type   Exchange Traded Funds
Category   Real Estate Sector Equity
Sub-Category   Real Estate
Prospectus Objective   Real Estate
Inception Date   Aug-11
Open to New Investments   Y

Prices
Price (as of 12/31/2018)   21.31
52-Week High   24.70
52-Week Low   21.00

Total Returns (%)

3-Month	6-Month	1-Year	3-Year	5-Year
-6.95	-5.88	-4.45	38.85	47.27

3-Year Standard Deviation   10.56
Effective Duration

Valuation
Premium/Discount (1-Year Average)   0.09

Company Information
Provider   VanEck
Manager/Tenure Hao-Hung (Peter) Liao (7), Guo Hua
                (Jason) Jin (0)
Website   http://www.vaneck.com
Address   Van Eck Associates Corporation 666
                Third Avenue New York NY 10017
                United States
Phone Number   800-826-1115

PERFORMANCE

Ratings History

Date	Overall Rating	Risk Rating	Reward Rating
Q4-18	C+	C	B-
Q2-18	C+	C-	B-
Q4-17	B-	C+	B-
Q4-16	C	C-	B-
Q4-15	C	C	B-

Asset & Performance History

Date	NAV	1-Year Total Return
2017	24.04	18.53
2016	21.9	22.61
2015	19.44	-10.06
2014	23.66	17.93
2013	22.13	0.99
2012	25.17	22.34

Total Assets: $147,151,703

Asset Allocation

Asset	%
Cash	0%
Stocks	100%
US Stocks	100%
Bonds	0%
US Bonds	0%
Other	0%

Services Offered:

Investment Strategy: The investment seeks to replicate as closely as possible, before fees and expenses, the price and yield performance of the MVIS® US Mortgage REITs Index (the "Mortgage REITs Index"). The fund normally invests at least 80% of its total assets in securities that comprise the fund's benchmark index. The Mortgage REITs Index may include small-, medium- and large-capitalization companies. The fund is non-diversified. **Top Holdings:** Annaly Capital Management Inc AGNC Investment Corp Starwood Property Trust Inc New Residential Investment Corp Blackstone Mortgage Trust Inc A

---

iShares Edge MSCI Intl Momentum Factor ETF   C-   HOLD

Ticker	Traded On	NAV	Total Assets ($)	Dividend Yield (TTM)	Turnover Ratio	Expense Ratio
IMTM	NYSE Arca	25.68	$147,089,620	2.18	131	0.3

Ratings
Reward   D+
Risk   C-
Recent Upgrade/Downgrade   Down

Fund Information
Fund Type   Exchange Traded Funds
Category   Global Equity Large Cap
Sub-Category   Foreign Large Growth
Prospectus Objective   World Stock
Inception Date   Jan-15
Open to New Investments   Y

Prices
Price (as of 12/31/2018)   25.60
52-Week High   32.95
52-Week Low   24.83

Total Returns (%)

3-Month	6-Month	1-Year	3-Year	5-Year
-15.24	-11.41	-13.96	8.61	

3-Year Standard Deviation   11.04
Effective Duration

Valuation
Premium/Discount (1-Year Average)   0.10

Company Information
Provider   iShares
Manager/Tenure Diane Hsiung (3), Jennifer Hsui (3),
                Greg Savage (3), 3 others
Website   http://www.ishares.com
Address   iShares 400 Howard Street San
                Francisco CA 94105 United States
Phone Number   800-474-2737

PERFORMANCE

Ratings History

Date	Overall Rating	Risk Rating	Reward Rating
Q4-18	C-	C-	D+
Q2-18	C	C-	C
Q4-17	C+	C+	C+
Q4-16	D+	D+	D+
Q4-15	U		

Asset & Performance History

Date	NAV	1-Year Total Return
2017	30.49	25.5
2016	24.79	0.59
2015	25.32	
2014		
2013		
2012		

Total Assets: $147,089,620

Asset Allocation

Asset	%
Cash	1%
Stocks	99%
US Stocks	2%
Bonds	0%
US Bonds	0%
Other	0%

Services Offered:

Investment Strategy: The investment seeks to track the investment results of the MSCI World ex USA Momentum Index that measures the performance of international developed large- and mid-capitalization stocks exhibiting relatively higher momentum characteristics. The fund will invest at least 90% of its assets in the component securities of the index and in investments that have economic characteristics that are substantially identical to the component securities of the index. The index consists of stocks exhibiting relatively higher momentum characteristics than the traditional market capitalization-weighted parent index, the MSCI World ex USA Index. **Top Holdings:** Nestle SA Novartis AG Roche Holding AG Dividend Right Cert. BP PLC AstraZeneca PLC

iShares MSCI Kokusai ETF   C-   HOLD

Ticker	Traded On	NAV		Total Assets ($)	Dividend Yield (TTM)	Turnover Ratio	Expense Ratio
TOK	NYSE Arca	58.37		$146,961,225	2.67	6	0.25

Ratings
Reward   C-
Risk   D+
Recent Upgrade/Downgrade   Down

Fund Information
Fund Type   Exchange Traded Funds
Category   Global Equity Large Cap
Sub-Category   World Large Stock
Prospectus Objective   World Stock
Inception Date   Dec-07
Open to New Investments   Y

Prices
Price (as of 12/31/2018)   58.10
52-Week High   69.65
52-Week Low   55.44

Total Returns (%)

3-Month	6-Month	1-Year	3-Year	5-Year
-13.48	-8.64	-8.11	21.92	27.22

3-Year Standard Deviation   9.52
Effective Duration

Valuation
Premium/Discount (1-Year Average)   -0.27

Company Information
Provider   iShares
Manager/Tenure   Diane Hsiung (10), Greg Savage (10), Jennifer Hsui (6), 3 others
Website   http://www.ishares.com
Address   iShares 400 Howard Street San Francisco CA 94105 United States
Phone Number   800-474-2737

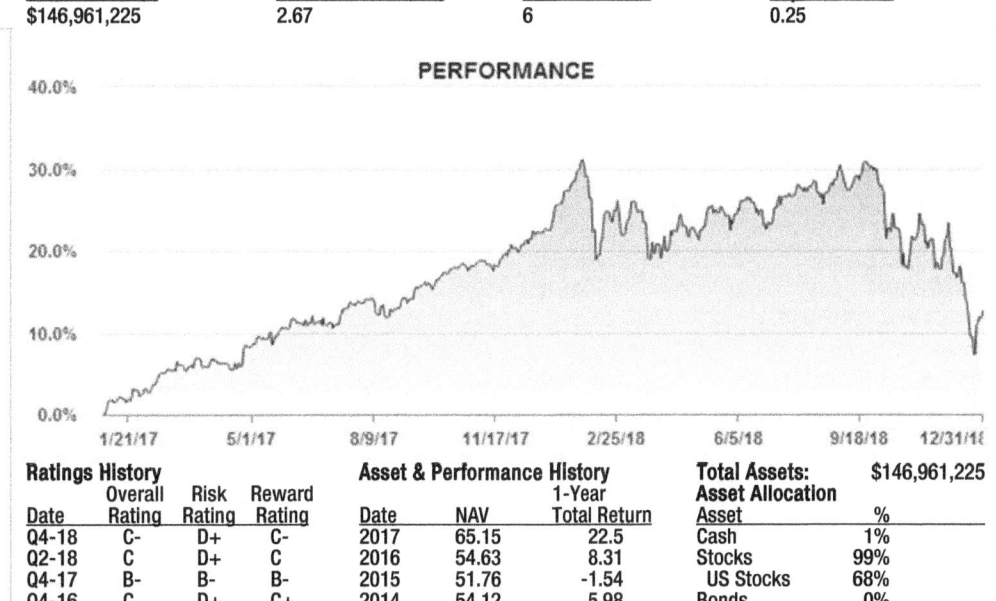

Ratings History

Date	Overall Rating	Risk Rating	Reward Rating
Q4-18	C-	D+	C-
Q2-18	C	D+	C
Q4-17	B-	B-	B-
Q4-16	C	D+	C+
Q4-15	C	D+	C

Asset & Performance History

Date	NAV	1-Year Total Return
2017	65.15	22.5
2016	54.63	8.31
2015	51.76	-1.54
2014	54.12	5.98
2013	52.42	26.87
2012	42.41	16.87

Total Assets: $146,961,225
Asset Allocation

Asset	%
Cash	1%
Stocks	99%
US Stocks	68%
Bonds	0%
US Bonds	0%
Other	0%

Services Offered:

Investment Strategy: The investment seeks to track the investment results of the MSCI Kokusai Index composed of developed market equities, excluding Japan. The fund generally will invest at least 90% of its assets in the component securities of the underlying index and in investments that have economic characteristics that are substantially identical to the component securities of the underlying index. The index is designed to measure equity market performance in those countries that MSCI Inc. (the "index provider" or "MSCI") has classified as having developed economies, excluding Japan ("DEEJ"). **Top Holdings:** Apple Inc   Microsoft Corp   Amazon.com Inc   Johnson & Johnson   JPMorgan Chase & Co

---

iShares MSCI New Zealand ETF   C-   HOLD

Ticker	Traded On	NAV		Total Assets ($)	Dividend Yield (TTM)	Turnover Ratio	Expense Ratio
ENZL	NAS CM	46.15		$146,687,227	3.59	14	0.49

Ratings
Reward   C-
Risk   C-
Recent Upgrade/Downgrade   Down

Fund Information
Fund Type   Exchange Traded Funds
Category   Australia & New Zealand Equity
Sub-Category   Miscellaneous Region
Prospectus Objective   Pacific Stock
Inception Date   Sep-10
Open to New Investments   Y

Prices
Price (as of 12/31/2018)   46.02
52-Week High   50.80
52-Week Low   43.93

Total Returns (%)

3-Month	6-Month	1-Year	3-Year	5-Year
-3.69	-1.42	-0.22	37.23	53.12

3-Year Standard Deviation   16.16
Effective Duration

Valuation
Premium/Discount (1-Year Average)   -0.26

Company Information
Provider   iShares
Manager/Tenure   Diane Hsiung (8), Greg Savage (8), Jennifer Hsui (5), 1 other
Website   http://www.ishares.com
Address   iShares 400 Howard Street San Francisco CA 94105 United States
Phone Number   800-474-2737

Ratings History

Date	Overall Rating	Risk Rating	Reward Rating
Q4-18	C-	C-	C-
Q2-18	C	C	B-
Q4-17	C+	C	C+
Q4-16	C	C-	C
Q4-15	C-	D+	C

Asset & Performance History

Date	NAV	1-Year Total Return
2017	47.88	23.9
2016	40.12	11
2015	37.87	-1.28
2014	40.11	13.03
2013	37.32	13.8
2012	34.18	29.23

Total Assets: $146,687,227
Asset Allocation

Asset	%
Cash	0%
Stocks	100%
US Stocks	0%
Bonds	0%
US Bonds	0%
Other	0%

Services Offered:

Investment Strategy: The investment seeks to track the investment results of the MSCI New Zealand IMI 25/50 Index. The fund generally will invest at least 90% of its assets in the component securities of the underlying index and in investments that have economic characteristics that are substantially identical to the component securities of the underlying index. The index is a free float-adjusted market capitalization-weighted index designed to measure the performance of equity securities in the top 99% by market capitalization of equity securities listed on stock exchanges in New Zealand. The fund is non-diversified. **Top Holdings:** Spark New Zealand Ltd   Fisher & Paykel Healthcare Corp Ltd   The a2 Milk Co Ltd   Auckland International Airport Ltd   Ryman Healthcare Ltd

SPDR® MSCI USA StrategicFactors ETF　　　　　　　　　　C　　HOLD

Ticker	Traded On	NAV	Total Assets ($)	Dividend Yield (TTM)	Turnover Ratio	Expense Ratio
QUS	NYSE Arca	72.93	$145,279,695	1.26	23	0.15

Ratings
Reward　　　　　　　　　　　　C
Risk　　　　　　　　　　　　　C-
Recent Upgrade/Downgrade

Fund Information
Fund Type　　　　　　　Exchange Traded Funds
Category　　　　　　　US Equity Large Cap Blend
Sub-Category　　　　　　　Large Blend
Prospectus Objective　　　　　Growth & Inc
Inception Date　　　　　　　Apr-15
Open to New Investments　　　　Y

Prices
Price (as of 12/31/2018)　　　　72.89
52-Week High　　　　　　　84.64
52-Week Low　　　　　　　69.01

Total Returns (%)

3-Month	6-Month	1-Year	3-Year	5-Year
-11.76	-5.13	-3.18	31.15	

3-Year Standard Deviation　　　　8.46
Effective Duration

Valuation
Premium/Discount (1-Year Average)　　0.23

Company Information
Provider　　　SPDR State Street Global Advisors
Manager/Tenure　Michael J. Feehily (3), Karl A.
　　　　　　　Schneider (3), John Law (0)
Website　　　http://www.spdrs.com
Address　　　SPDR State Street Global Advisors
　　　　　　　State Street Financial Center, 1
　　　　　　　Lincoln Street Boston MA 02111-2900
　　　　　　　United States
Phone Number　617-786-3000

PERFORMANCE

Ratings History

Date	Overall Rating	Risk Rating	Reward Rating
Q4-18	C	C-	C
Q2-18	C	D+	C
Q4-17	B-	B+	C+
Q4-16	D+	D+	C-
Q4-15	U		

Asset & Performance History

Date	NAV	1-Year Total Return
2017	76.92	21.17
2016	64.75	11.79
2015	59.18	
2014		
2013		
2012		

Total Assets: $145,279,695
Asset Allocation

Asset	%
Cash	0%
Stocks	100%
US Stocks	99%
Bonds	0%
US Bonds	0%
Other	0%

Services Offered:

Investment Strategy: The investment seeks to track the performance of the MSCI USA Factor Mix A-Series Capped Index. The fund invests at least 80%, of its total assets in the securities comprising the index. The index is designed to measure the equity market performance of large-and mid-cap companies across the U.S. equity market. It aims to represent the performance of a combination of three factors: value, quality, and low volatility. It is an equal weighted combination of the following three MSCI Factor Indices in a single composite index: the MSCI USA Value Weighted Index, the MSCI USA Quality Index, and the MSCI USA Minimum Volatility Index. The fund is non-diversified. **Top Holdings:** Johnson & Johnson Apple Inc Microsoft Corp Visa Inc Class A Procter & Gamble Co

iShares MSCI All Peru ETF　　　　　　　　　　　　C-　　HOLD

Ticker	Traded On	NAV	Total Assets ($)	Dividend Yield (TTM)	Turnover Ratio	Expense Ratio
EPU	NYSE Arca	35.49	$144,737,010	3.2	11	0.62

Ratings
Reward　　　　　　　　　　　　C
Risk　　　　　　　　　　　　　C-
Recent Upgrade/Downgrade　　　Down

Fund Information
Fund Type　　　　　　　Exchange Traded Funds
Category　　　　　　　　　Equity Misc
Sub-Category　　　　　　Miscellaneous Region
Prospectus Objective　　　　　Foreign Stock
Inception Date　　　　　　　Jun-09
Open to New Investments　　　　Y

Prices
Price (as of 12/31/2018)　　　　35.50
52-Week High　　　　　　　44.95
52-Week Low　　　　　　　34.49

Total Returns (%)

3-Month	6-Month	1-Year	3-Year	5-Year
-3.86	-8.87	-12.18	84.91	16.53

3-Year Standard Deviation　　　　21.89
Effective Duration

Valuation
Premium/Discount (1-Year Average)　　-0.17

Company Information
Provider　　　iShares
Manager/Tenure　Diane Hsiung (9), Greg Savage (9),
　　　　　　　Jennifer Hsui (5), 1 other
Website　　　http://www.ishares.com
Address　　　iShares 400 Howard Street San
　　　　　　　Francisco CA 94105 United States
Phone Number　800-474-2737

PERFORMANCE

Ratings History

Date	Overall Rating	Risk Rating	Reward Rating
Q4-18	C-	C-	C
Q2-18	C+	C-	B
Q4-17	B	C	A
Q4-16	C-	D+	C
Q4-15	D	D	D

Asset & Performance History

Date	NAV	1-Year Total Return
2017	40.98	30.34
2016	32.63	61.55
2015	20.38	-36.12
2014	32.4	-1.33
2013	33.35	-25.83
2012	45.7	21.51

Total Assets: $144,737,010
Asset Allocation

Asset	%
Cash	0%
Stocks	100%
US Stocks	10%
Bonds	0%
US Bonds	0%
Other	0%

Services Offered:

Investment Strategy: The investment seeks to track the investment results of the MSCI All Peru Capped Index. The fund generally will invest at least 90% of its assets in the component securities of the underlying index and in investments that have economic characteristics that are substantially identical to the component securities of the underlying index. The index is an index composed of Peruvian equities. The fund is non-diversified. **Top Holdings:** Credicorp Ltd Southern Copper Corp Buenaventura Mining Co Inc ADR InRetail Peru Corp Intercorp Financial Services Inc

AdvisorShares Dorsey Wright ADR ETF   C   HOLD

Ticker	Traded On	NAV	Total Assets ($)	Dividend Yield (TTM)	Turnover Ratio	Expense Ratio
AADR	NYSE Arca	40.18	$142,949,667	0.97		0.88

Ratings
Reward	C
Risk	D+
Recent Upgrade/Downgrade	

Fund Information
Fund Type	Exchange Traded Funds
Category	Global Equity Large Cap
Sub-Category	Foreign Large Growth
Prospectus Objective	Growth
Inception Date	Jul-10
Open to New Investments	Y

Prices
Price (as of 12/31/2018)	40.07
52-Week High	63.31
52-Week Low	38.43

Total Returns (%)
3-Month	6-Month	1-Year	3-Year	5-Year
-25.37	-24.00	-31.18	6.74	10.49

3-Year Standard Deviation	15.44
Effective Duration	

Valuation
Premium/Discount (1-Year Average)	0.00

Company Information
Provider	AdvisorShares
Manager/Tenure	John G. Lewis (2)
Website	http://www.advisorshares.com
Address	AdvisorShares 2 Bethesda Metro Center, Suite 1330 Bethesda MD 20814 United States
Phone Number	877-843-3831

PERFORMANCE

Ratings History
Date	Overall Rating	Risk Rating	Reward Rating
Q4-18	C	D+	C
Q2-18	C	C-	C+
Q4-17	A-	B+	A+
Q4-16	C	D+	C+
Q4-15	C	D+	C

Asset & Performance History
Date	NAV	1-Year Total Return
2017	58.71	46.92
2016	40.31	5.57
2015	38.41	4.38
2014	37.1	-0.83
2013	37.59	20.87
2012	31.22	12.65

Total Assets: $142,949,667
Asset Allocation
Asset	%
Cash	0%
Stocks	100%
US Stocks	24%
Bonds	0%
US Bonds	0%
Other	0%

Services Offered:

Investment Strategy: The investment seeks long-term capital appreciation above international benchmarks such as the BNY Mellon Classic ADR Index, the fund's primary benchmark, and the MSCI EAFE Index, the fund's secondary benchmark. The fund seeks to achieve the fund's investment objective by selecting primarily a portfolio of U.S.-traded securities of non-U.S. organizations, most often American Depositary Receipts ("ADRs"). It will invest at least 80% of its total assets in ADRs and in securities that have economic characteristics similar to ADRs. **Top Holdings:** Intelsat SA   NICE Ltd ADR   Ecopetrol SA ADR   CNOOC Ltd ADR   Galapagos NV ADR

VelocityShares 3x Inverse Crude Oil ETNs linked to the S&P GSCI® Crude Oil Index ER New   D   SELL

Ticker	Traded On	NAV	Total Assets ($)	Dividend Yield (TTM)	Turnover Ratio	Expense Ratio
DWT	NYSE Arca	16.38	$142,544,817	0		1.5

Ratings
Reward	D
Risk	D
Recent Upgrade/Downgrade	

Fund Information
Fund Type	Exchange Traded Funds
Category	Trading Tools
Sub-Category	Trading--Inverse Commodities
Prospectus Objective	Growth & Inc
Inception Date	Dec-16
Open to New Investments	Y

Prices
Price (as of 12/31/2018)	15.94
52-Week High	19.42
52-Week Low	4.67

Total Returns (%)
3-Month	6-Month	1-Year	3-Year	5-Year
238.46	166.76	18.25		

3-Year Standard Deviation	
Effective Duration	

Valuation
Premium/Discount (1-Year Average)	0.17

Company Information
Provider	Credit Suisse AG
Manager/Tenure	No Manager (1)
Website	
Address	Kilmore House Park Lane Dublin Ireland
Phone Number	

PERFORMANCE

Ratings History
Date	Overall Rating	Risk Rating	Reward Rating
Q4-18	D	D	D
Q2-18	D	D	D-
Q4-17	D	D-	D
Q4-16			
Q4-15			

Asset & Performance History
Date	NAV	1-Year Total Return
2017	13.85	-35.01
2016	22.01	
2015		
2014		
2013		
2012		

Total Assets: $142,544,817
Asset Allocation
Asset	%
Cash	%
Stocks	%
US Stocks	%
Bonds	%
US Bonds	%
Other	%

Services Offered:

Investment Strategy: The investment seeks to replicate, net of expenses, three times the opposite (inverse) of the S&P GSCI® Crude Oil Index ER.
 The index tracks a hypothetical position in the nearest-to-expiration NYMEX light sweet crude oil futures contract, which is rolled each month into the futures contract expiring in the next month. The value of the Index fluctuates with changes in the price of the relevant NYMEX light sweet crude oil futures contracts. **Top Holdings:**

Invesco CurrencyShares® British Pound Sterling Trust   D   SELL

Ticker	Traded On	NAV	Total Assets ($)	Dividend Yield (TTM)	Turnover Ratio	Expense Ratio
FXB	NYSE Arca	123.54	$142,541,228	0	0	0.4

Ratings
Reward	D
Risk	D+
Recent Upgrade/Downgrade	Down

Fund Information
Fund Type	Exchange Traded Funds
Category	Currency
Sub-Category	Single Currency
Prospectus Objective	Worldwide Bond
Inception Date	Jun-06
Open to New Investments	Y

Prices
Price (as of 12/31/2018)	123.65
52-Week High	139.18
52-Week Low	121.25

Total Returns (%)
3-Month	6-Month	1-Year	3-Year	5-Year
-2.34	-3.01	-6.04	-14.39	-24.31

3-Year Standard Deviation	9.21
Effective Duration	

Valuation
Premium/Discount (1-Year Average)	-0.09

Company Information
Provider	Invesco
Manager/Tenure	Management Team (12)
Website	http://www.invesco.com/us
Address	Invesco 11 Greenway Plaza, Ste. 2500 Houston TX 77046 United States
Phone Number	800-659-1005

PERFORMANCE

Ratings History

Date	Overall Rating	Risk Rating	Reward Rating
Q4-18	D	D+	D
Q2-18	D+	C-	D
Q4-17	D+	D+	D+
Q4-16	D	D	D
Q4-15	D+	C-	D+

Asset & Performance History

Date	NAV	1-Year Total Return
2017	131.49	9.05
2016	120.57	-16.45
2015	144.31	-5.77
2014	153.15	-6.17
2013	163.24	1.54
2012	160.76	4.27

Total Assets: $142,541,228
Asset Allocation

Asset	%
Cash	100%
Stocks	0%
US Stocks	0%
Bonds	0%
US Bonds	0%
Other	0%

Services Offered:

Investment Strategy: The investment seeks to reflect the price in USD of the British Pound Sterling. The shares are intended to provide institutional and retail investors with a simple, cost-effective means of gaining investment benefits similar to those of holding British Pounds Sterling. **Top Holdings:**

Cambria Global Value ETF   C-   HOLD

Ticker	Traded On	NAV	Total Assets ($)	Dividend Yield (TTM)	Turnover Ratio	Expense Ratio
GVAL	BATS	21.12	$142,468,454	2.42	14	0.68

Ratings
Reward	C-
Risk	C-
Recent Upgrade/Downgrade	

Fund Information
Fund Type	Exchange Traded Funds
Category	Global Eq Mid/Small Cap
Sub-Category	Foreign Small/Mid Value
Prospectus Objective	Div Emerg Mkts
Inception Date	Mar-14
Open to New Investments	Y

Prices
Price (as of 12/31/2018)	21.00
52-Week High	28.37
52-Week Low	20.97

Total Returns (%)
3-Month	6-Month	1-Year	3-Year	5-Year
-8.70	-7.60	-13.46	29.40	

3-Year Standard Deviation	14.46
Effective Duration	

Valuation
Premium/Discount (1-Year Average)	-0.06

Company Information
Provider	CAMBRIA ETF TRUST
Manager/Tenure	Mebane T. Faber (4)
Website	http://www.cambriafunds.com
Address	CAMBRIA ETF TRUST 2711 Centreville Road Suite 400 Wilmington, DE 19808 Wilmington DE 19808 United States
Phone Number	310-683-5500

PERFORMANCE

Ratings History

Date	Overall Rating	Risk Rating	Reward Rating
Q4-18	C-	C-	C-
Q2-18	C	C-	C
Q4-17	B-	B-	B-
Q4-16	D+	C-	D+
Q4-15	D	D	D

Asset & Performance History

Date	NAV	1-Year Total Return
2017	25.5	28.75
2016	20.23	16.14
2015	17.92	-7.43
2014	19.73	
2013		
2012		

Total Assets: $142,468,454
Asset Allocation

Asset	%
Cash	3%
Stocks	97%
US Stocks	0%
Bonds	0%
US Bonds	0%
Other	0%

Services Offered:

Investment Strategy: The investment seeks investment results that correspond (before fees and expenses) generally to the price and yield performance of its underlying index, the Cambria Global Value Index (the "underlying index"). Under normal market conditions, the fund will invest at least 80% of its total assets in the components of the underlying index and in depositary receipts representing components of the underlying index. The underlying index is comprised of equity securities of issuers located in developed and emerging countries, as well as exchange-traded funds composed of issuers located in such countries. **Top Holdings:** Corticeira Amorim SGPS SA   Banco Santander (Brasil) SA Unit   Motor Oil (Hellas) Corinth Refineries SA   Israel Chemicals Ltd   Teva Pharmaceutical Industries Ltd

First Trust Dow Jones Select MicroCap Index Fund   C-   HOLD

Ticker	Traded On	NAV	Total Assets ($)	Dividend Yield (TTM)	Turnover Ratio	Expense Ratio
FDM	NYSE Arca	40.76	$142,115,580	1	55	0.6

Ratings
Reward   C-
Risk   C-
Recent Upgrade/Downgrade   Down

Fund Information
Fund Type   Exchange Traded Funds
Category   US Equity Small Cap
Sub-Category   Small Value
Prospectus Objective   Growth
Inception Date   Sep-05
Open to New Investments   Y

Prices
Price (as of 12/31/2018)   40.58
52-Week High   53.18
52-Week Low   38.71

Total Returns (%)

3-Month	6-Month	1-Year	3-Year	5-Year
-18.90	-20.13	-12.69	28.26	32.93

3-Year Standard Deviation   15.66
Effective Duration

Valuation
Premium/Discount (1-Year Average)   0.20

Company Information
Provider   First Trust
Manager/Tenure   Jon C. Erickson (13), Daniel J. Lindquist (13), David G. McGarel (13), 3 others
Website   http://www.ftportfolios.com/
Address   First Trust 120 E. Liberty Drive, Suite 400 Wheaton IL 60187 United States
Phone Number   800-621-1675

PERFORMANCE

Ratings History

Date	Overall Rating	Risk Rating	Reward Rating
Q4-18	C-	C-	C-
Q2-18	C+	D+	B
Q4-17	A-	B+	A
Q4-16	C	D+	C+
Q4-15	C	D+	C+

Asset & Performance History

Date	NAV	1-Year Total Return
2017	47.21	8.46
2016	43.98	35.45
2015	32.92	0.54
2014	33.21	3.08
2013	32.47	43.33
2012	22.87	15.88

Total Assets: $142,115,580

Asset Allocation

Asset	%
Cash	0%
Stocks	100%
US Stocks	99%
Bonds	0%
US Bonds	0%
Other	0%

Services Offered:

Investment Strategy: The investment seeks investment results that correspond generally to the price and yield (before the fund's fees and expenses) of an equity index called the Dow Jones Select MicroCap Index(SM). The fund will normally invest at least 90% of its net assets in common stocks that comprise the index. The index is comprised of selected U.S. micro-capitalization companies chosen from all common stocks traded on the New York Stock Exchange, the NYSE MKT and NASDAQ® with limited partnerships excluded. It will normally invest at least 80% of its net assets in common stocks of U.S. micro-capitalization companies which are publicly traded in the United States. **Top Holdings:** CVR Energy Inc   Renewable Energy Group Inc   K12 Inc   TPG RE Finance Trust Inc Marcus & Millichap Inc

---

WisdomTree Europe Hedged SmallCap Equity Fund   D+   SELL

Ticker	Traded On	NAV	Total Assets ($)	Dividend Yield (TTM)	Turnover Ratio	Expense Ratio
EUSC	NYSE Arca	26.50	$141,806,833	2.2	37	0.58

Ratings
Reward   D+
Risk   C-
Recent Upgrade/Downgrade   Down

Fund Information
Fund Type   Exchange Traded Funds
Category   Europe Equity Large Cap
Sub-Category   Europe Stock
Prospectus Objective   Small Company
Inception Date   Mar-15
Open to New Investments   Y

Prices
Price (as of 12/31/2018)   26.42
52-Week High   32.82
52-Week Low   25.52

Total Returns (%)

3-Month	6-Month	1-Year	3-Year	5-Year
-12.91	-11.56	-13.41	14.21	

3-Year Standard Deviation   11.93
Effective Duration

Valuation
Premium/Discount (1-Year Average)   -0.22

Company Information
Provider   WisdomTree
Manager/Tenure   Richard A. Brown (3), Thomas J. Durante (3), Karen Q. Wong (3)
Website   http://www.wisdomtree.com
Address   WisdomTree 245 Park Avenue, 35th floor New York NY 10167 United States
Phone Number   866-909-9473

PERFORMANCE

Ratings History

Date	Overall Rating	Risk Rating	Reward Rating
Q4-18	D+	C-	D+
Q2-18	C+	C+	C
Q4-17	B-	B-	C+
Q4-16	D+	C-	D+
Q4-15	U		

Asset & Performance History

Date	NAV	1-Year Total Return
2017	31.23	22.3
2016	25.92	7.85
2015	24.69	
2014		
2013		
2012		

Total Assets: $141,806,833

Asset Allocation

Asset	%
Cash	0%
Stocks	100%
US Stocks	0%
Bonds	0%
US Bonds	0%
Other	0%

Services Offered:

Investment Strategy: The investment seeks to track the price and yield performance, before fees and expenses, of the WisdomTree Europe Hedged SmallCap Equity Index. Under normal circumstances, at least 80% of the fund's total assets will be invested in component securities of the index and investments that have economic characteristics that are substantially identical to the economic characteristics of such component securities. The index is a dividend weighted index designed to provide exposure to small cap equity securities within Europe, while at the same time neutralizing exposure to fluctuations between the value of the euro and the U.S. dollar. The fund is non-diversified. **Top Holdings:** UnipolSai SPA   Casino Guichard-Perrachon SA   Eutelsat Communications Metro Ag (New)   Banca Mediolanum

Invesco S&P 500® ex-Rate Sensitive Low Volatility ETF   C   HOLD

Ticker	Traded On	NAV	Total Assets ($)	Dividend Yield (TTM)	Turnover Ratio	Expense Ratio
XRLV	NYSE Arca	32.33	$141,487,456	1.52		0.25

Ratings
Reward   C
Risk   C-
Recent Upgrade/Downgrade

Fund Information
Fund Type   Exchange Traded Funds
Category   US Equity Large Cap Blend
Sub-Category   Large Blend
Prospectus Objective   Growth
Inception Date   Apr-15
Open to New Investments

Prices
Price (as of 12/31/2018)   32.31
52-Week High   36.81
52-Week Low   30.55

Total Returns (%)

3-Month	6-Month	1-Year	3-Year	5-Year
-10.44	-3.69	-2.83	33.30	

3-Year Standard Deviation   9.02
Effective Duration

Valuation
Premium/Discount (1-Year Average)   0.09

Company Information
Provider   Invesco
Manager/Tenure   Peter Hubbard (3), Michael Jeanette
                 (3), Jonathan Nixon (3), 1 other
Website   http://www.invesco.com/us
Address   Invesco 11 Greenway Plaza, Ste. 2500
                 Houston TX 77046 United States
Phone Number   800-659-1005

PERFORMANCE

Ratings History

Date	Overall Rating	Risk Rating	Reward Rating
Q4-18	C	C-	C
Q2-18	C	C-	C
Q4-17	B-	B+	C+
Q4-16	D+	C-	C-
Q4-15	U		

Asset & Performance History

Date	NAV	1-Year Total Return
2017	33.83	22.99
2016	27.93	11.54
2015	25.49	
2014		
2013		
2012		

Total Assets: $141,487,456

Asset Allocation

Asset	%
Cash	0%
Stocks	100%
US Stocks	99%
Bonds	0%
US Bonds	0%
Other	0%

Services Offered:

Investment Strategy: The investment seeks to track the investment results (before fees and expenses) of the S&P 500 Low Volatility Rate Response Index (the "underlying index"). The fund generally will invest at least 90% of its total assets in common stocks that comprise the underlying index. The underlying index is designed to include stocks exhibiting low volatility characteristics, after removing stocks that historically have performed poorly in rising interest rate environments. The fund is non-diversified. **Top Holdings:** Coca-Cola Co Republic Services Inc Class A Ecolab Inc Citrix Systems Inc Waste Management Inc

---

Invesco Russell 1000 Enhanced Equal Weight ETF   D+   SELL

Ticker	Traded On	NAV	Total Assets ($)	Dividend Yield (TTM)	Turnover Ratio	Expense Ratio
USEQ	BATS	24.07	$141,236,780	1.55		0.29

Ratings
Reward   D+
Risk   D+
Recent Upgrade/Downgrade

Fund Information
Fund Type   Exchange Traded Funds
Category   US Equity Large Cap Value
Sub-Category   Mid-Cap Blend
Prospectus Objective   Growth & Inc
Inception Date   Jul-17
Open to New Investments   Y

Prices
Price (as of 12/31/2018)   23.97
52-Week High   29.05
52-Week Low   22.78

Total Returns (%)

3-Month	6-Month	1-Year	3-Year	5-Year
-14.20	-10.63	-10.19		

3-Year Standard Deviation
Effective Duration

Valuation
Premium/Discount (1-Year Average)   0.23

Company Information
Provider   Invesco
Manager/Tenure   Peter Hubbard (1), Michael Jeanette
                 (1), Jonathan Nixon (1), 1 other
Website   http://www.invesco.com/us
Address   Invesco 11 Greenway Plaza, Ste. 2500
                 Houston TX 77046 United States
Phone Number   800-659-1005

PERFORMANCE

Ratings History

Date	Overall Rating	Risk Rating	Reward Rating
Q4-18	D+	D+	D+
Q2-18	D+	C-	D+
Q4-17	U		
Q4-16			
Q4-15			

Asset & Performance History

Date	NAV	1-Year Total Return
2017	27.5	
2016		
2015		
2014		
2013		
2012		

Total Assets: $141,236,780

Asset Allocation

Asset	%
Cash	0%
Stocks	100%
US Stocks	98%
Bonds	0%
US Bonds	0%
Other	0%

Services Offered:

Investment Strategy: The investment seeks to track the investment results (before fees and expenses) of the Russell 1000® Enhanced Value Equal Weight Index (the "underlying index"). The fund generally will invest at least 90% of its total assets in securities that comprise the underlying index. The underlying index is a subset of the Russell 1000, which measures the performance of the large-cap segment of the U.S. equity universe. The fund is non-diversified. **Top Holdings:** Concho Resources Inc CVS Health Corp United States Cellular Corp Marathon Petroleum Corp Euronet Worldwide Inc

Innovator Lunt Low Vol/High Beta Tactical ETF   C-   HOLD

Ticker	Traded On	NAV	Total Assets ($)	Dividend Yield (TTM)	Turnover Ratio	Expense Ratio
LVHB	BATS	29.69	$141,229,084	1.07	667	0.49

Ratings
Reward	C-
Risk	D+
Recent Upgrade/Downgrade	

Fund Information
Fund Type	Exchange Traded Funds
Category	US Equity Large Cap Blend
Sub-Category	Large Value
Prospectus Objective	Growth & Inc
Inception Date	Oct-16
Open to New Investments	Y

Prices
Price (as of 12/31/2018)	29.60
52-Week High	34.33
52-Week Low	28.29

Total Returns (%)
3-Month	6-Month	1-Year	3-Year	5-Year
-5.74	-1.88	-7.58		

3-Year Standard Deviation
Effective Duration

Valuation
Premium/Discount (1-Year Average)	0.04

Company Information
Provider	Innovator ETFs
Manager/Tenure	Anand Desai (0), Dustin Lewellyn (0), Ernesto Tong (0)
Website	http://innovatoretfs.com/
Address	Innovator ETFs 120 N Hale Street, Suite 200 Wheaton IL 60187 United States
Phone Number	800-208-5212

PERFORMANCE

Ratings History
Date	Overall Rating	Risk Rating	Reward Rating
Q4-18	C-	D+	C-
Q2-18	C-	C-	D+
Q4-17	D	B	C
Q4-16	U		
Q4-15			

Asset & Performance History
Date	NAV	1-Year Total Return
2017	32.35	15.84
2016	28.38	
2015		
2014		
2013		
2012		

Total Assets: $141,229,084
Asset Allocation
Asset	%
Cash	0%
Stocks	100%
US Stocks	99%
Bonds	0%
US Bonds	0%
Other	0%

Services Offered:

Investment Strategy: The investment seeks investment results that generally correspond (before fees and expenses) to the price and yield of the Lunt Capital U.S. Large Cap Equity Rotation Index. The fund generally will invest at least 80% of its total assets in the U.S.-listed large capitalization common stocks that comprise the index. The index utilizes Lunt Capital's proprietary relative strength methodology to rotate between one of two sub-indices that identify certain components of the S&P 500. The first sub-index is the S&P 500 Low Volatility Index; the second sub-index is the S&P 500 High Beta Index. The fund is non-diversified. **Top Holdings:** Coca-Cola Co Republic Services Inc Class A WEC Energy Group Inc Duke Energy Corp CMS Energy Corp

---

Global X U.S. Infrastructure Development ETF   C   HOLD

Ticker	Traded On	NAV	Total Assets ($)	Dividend Yield (TTM)	Turnover Ratio	Expense Ratio
PAVE	BATS	13.50	$140,914,038	0.32		0.47

Ratings
Reward	C
Risk	C-
Recent Upgrade/Downgrade	

Fund Information
Fund Type	Exchange Traded Funds
Category	Infrastructure Sector Equity
Sub-Category	Infrastructure
Prospectus Objective	Utility
Inception Date	Mar-17
Open to New Investments	Y

Prices
Price (as of 12/31/2018)	13.46
52-Week High	17.72
52-Week Low	12.79

Total Returns (%)
3-Month	6-Month	1-Year	3-Year	5-Year
-20.98	-16.42	-18.62		

3-Year Standard Deviation
Effective Duration

Valuation
Premium/Discount (1-Year Average)	0.15

Company Information
Provider	Global X Funds
Manager/Tenure	Chang Kim (1), James Ong (1), Nam To (0)
Website	http://www.globalxfunds.com
Address	Global X Funds 600 Lexington Avenue, 20th Floor New York NY 10022 United States
Phone Number	888-493-8631

PERFORMANCE

Ratings History
Date	Overall Rating	Risk Rating	Reward Rating
Q4-18	C	C-	C
Q2-18	C	C	C
Q4-17	U		
Q4-16			
Q4-15			

Asset & Performance History
Date	NAV	1-Year Total Return
2017	16.72	
2016		
2015		
2014		
2013		
2012		

Total Assets: $140,914,038
Asset Allocation
Asset	%
Cash	0%
Stocks	100%
US Stocks	99%
Bonds	0%
US Bonds	0%
Other	0%

Services Offered:

Investment Strategy: The investment seeks to provide investment results that correspond generally to the price and yield performance, of the Indxx U.S. Infrastructure Development Index. The fund invests at least 80% of its total assets in the securities of the underlying index. The underlying index is designed to measure the performance of U.S. listed companies that provide exposure to domestic infrastructure development, including companies involved in construction and engineering; production of infrastructure raw materials, composites and products; industrial transportation; and producers/distributors of heavy construction equipment. It is non-diversified. **Top Holdings:** CSX Corp Norfolk Southern Corp Fastenal Co Union Pacific Corp Fortive Corp

VanEck Vectors AMT-Free Long Municipal Index ETF

D+   SELL

Ticker	Traded On	NAV	Total Assets ($)	Dividend Yield (TTM)	Turnover Ratio	Expense Ratio
MLN	BATS	19.62	$140,762,636	3.1	33	0.24

Ratings

Reward	D+
Risk	C-
Recent Upgrade/Downgrade	Down

Fund Information

Fund Type	Exchange Traded Funds
Category	US Muni Fixed Inc
Sub-Category	Muni National Long
Prospectus Objective	Muni Bond - Natl
Inception Date	Jan-08
Open to New Investments	Y

Prices

Price (as of 12/31/2018)	19.56
52-Week High	20.33
52-Week Low	18.91

Total Returns (%)

3-Month	6-Month	1-Year	3-Year	5-Year
1.41	0.33	-0.98	7.66	29.74

3-Year Standard Deviation	5.13
Effective Duration	

Valuation

Premium/Discount (1-Year Average)	-0.33

Company Information

Provider	VanEck
Manager/Tenure	James T. Colby (10)
Website	http://www.vaneck.com
Address	Van Eck Associates Corporation 666 Third Avenue New York NY 10017 United States
Phone Number	800-826-1115

PERFORMANCE

Ratings History

Date	Overall Rating	Risk Rating	Reward Rating
Q4-18	D+	C-	D+
Q2-18	C	C-	C
Q4-17	B-	B	C
Q4-16	C	C-	C
Q4-15	C	C-	C

Asset & Performance History

Date	NAV	1-Year Total Return
2017	20.38	8.55
2016	19.34	0.16
2015	19.9	4.16
2014	19.77	15.69
2013	17.77	-8.18
2012	20.17	10.74

Total Assets: $140,762,636

Asset Allocation

Asset	%
Cash	0%
Stocks	0%
US Stocks	0%
Bonds	100%
US Bonds	100%
Other	0%

Services Offered:

Investment Strategy: The investment seeks to replicate as closely as possible, before fees and expenses, the price and yield performance of the Bloomberg Barclays AMT-Free Long Continuous Municipal Index. The fund normally invests at least 80% of its total assets in fixed income securities that comprise the index. The index is comprised of publicly traded municipal bonds that cover the U.S. dollar denominated long-term tax-exempt bond market. **Top Holdings:** HUDSON YDS INFRASTRUCTURE CORP N Y 5% FRISCO TEX INDPT SCH DIST 4% MIRACOSTA CALIF CMNTY COLLEGE DIST 4% SAN DIEGO CALIF UNI SCH DIST 4% LOS ANGELES CALIF DEPT WTR & PWR 5%

JPMorgan Disciplined High Yield ETF

C-   HOLD

Ticker	Traded On	NAV	Total Assets ($)	Dividend Yield (TTM)	Turnover Ratio	Expense Ratio
JPHY	BATS	47.30	$140,288,034	4.91	23	0.4

Ratings

Reward	C-
Risk	C-
Recent Upgrade/Downgrade	

Fund Information

Fund Type	Exchange Traded Funds
Category	US Fixed Income
Sub-Category	High Yield Bond
Prospectus Objective	Corp Bond-High Yld
Inception Date	Sep-16
Open to New Investments	Y

Prices

Price (as of 12/31/2018)	47.64
52-Week High	51.62
52-Week Low	47.14

Total Returns (%)

3-Month	6-Month	1-Year	3-Year	5-Year
-3.98	-1.01	-2.53		

3-Year Standard Deviation	
Effective Duration	4.20

Valuation

Premium/Discount (1-Year Average)	0.42

Company Information

Provider	JPMorgan
Manager/Tenure	Bhupinder Bahra (2), Frederick Bourgoin (2), William J. Morgan (2), 2 others
Website	http://www.jpmorganfunds.com
Address	JPMorgan 270 Park Avenue New York NY 10017-2070 United States
Phone Number	800-480-4111

PERFORMANCE

Ratings History

Date	Overall Rating	Risk Rating	Reward Rating
Q4-18	C-	C-	C-
Q2-18	D+	D+	D+
Q4-17	D	B	D+
Q4-16	U		
Q4-15			

Asset & Performance History

Date	NAV	1-Year Total Return
2017	50.94	6.11
2016	50.38	
2015		
2014		
2013		
2012		

Total Assets: $140,288,034

Asset Allocation

Asset	%
Cash	2%
Stocks	0%
US Stocks	0%
Bonds	97%
US Bonds	79%
Other	0%

Services Offered:

Investment Strategy: The investment seeks a high level of income; capital appreciation is a secondary objective. The fund invests primarily in high yield, high risk debt securities. Under normal circumstances, it invests at least 80% of its assets in high yield securities. For purposes of this policy, "assets" means net assets plus the amount of borrowings for investment purposes. The fund may invest up to 100% of its total assets in below investment grade or unrated securities. The adviser uses a multi-factor security selection process that uses factors that the adviser believes reflect liquidity and issuer quality. **Top Holdings:** ALTICE FRANCE S.A 7.38% Sprint Corporation 7.88% First Data Corporation 7% CCO Holdings, LLC/ CCO Holdings Capital Corp. 5.12% Bausch Health Companies Inc 5.88%

iShares MSCI Netherlands ETF   C-   HOLD

Ticker	Traded On	NAV		Total Assets ($)	Dividend Yield (TTM)	Turnover Ratio	Expense Ratio
EWN	NYSE Arca	26.42		$140,078,885	2.41	14	0.47

Ratings
Reward	C-
Risk	C-
Recent Upgrade/Downgrade	Down

Fund Information
Fund Type	Exchange Traded Funds
Category	Europe Equity Large Cap
Sub-Category	Miscellaneous Region
Prospectus Objective	Europe Stock
Inception Date	Mar-96
Open to New Investments	Y

Prices
Price (as of 12/31/2018)	26.30
52-Week High	34.04
52-Week Low	25.35

Total Returns (%)
3-Month	6-Month	1-Year	3-Year	5-Year
-12.35	-12.21	-14.99	17.83	13.75

3-Year Standard Deviation	12.88
Effective Duration	

Valuation
Premium/Discount (1-Year Average)	-0.13

Company Information
Provider	iShares
Manager/Tenure	Diane Hsiung (10), Greg Savage (10), Jennifer Hsui (5), 1 other
Website	http://www.ishares.com
Address	iShares 400 Howard Street San Francisco CA 94105 United States
Phone Number	800-474-2737

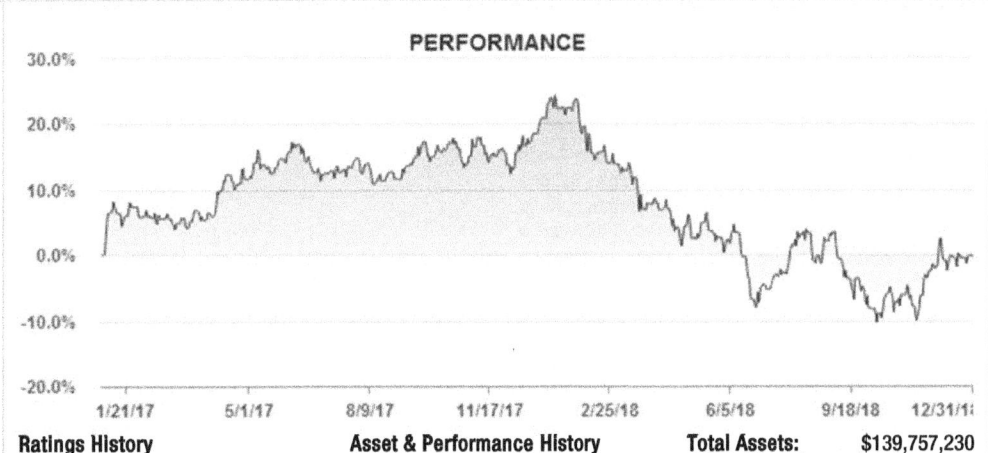

PERFORMANCE

Ratings History
Date	Overall Rating	Risk Rating	Reward Rating
Q4-18	C-	C-	C-
Q2-18	C+	C+	C
Q4-17	B	B	B+
Q4-16	C	C	C
Q4-15	C+	C+	C

Asset & Performance History
Date	NAV	1-Year Total Return
2017	31.74	33.4
2016	24.22	3.91
2015	23.95	1.33
2014	24.06	-4.73
2013	25.81	30.14
2012	20.19	19.75

Total Assets: $140,078,885
Asset Allocation
Asset	%
Cash	0%
Stocks	100%
US Stocks	3%
Bonds	0%
US Bonds	0%
Other	0%

Services Offered: CashInvestment Plan

Investment Strategy: The investment seeks to track the investment results of the MSCI Netherlands IMI 25/50 Index. The fund will at all times invest at least 80% of its assets in the securities of its underlying index and in depositary receipts representing securities in its underlying index. The underlying index uses a capping methodology to limit the weight of any single component to a maximum of 25% of the underlying index. The underlying index may include large-, mid- or small- capitalization companies. The fund is non-diversified. **Top Holdings:** Unilever NV DR ASML Holding NV ING Groep NV Royal Philips NV NXP Semiconductors NV

---

iShares MSCI Philippines ETF   D   SELL

Ticker	Traded On	NAV		Total Assets ($)	Dividend Yield (TTM)	Turnover Ratio	Expense Ratio
EPHE	NYSE Arca	31.90		$139,757,230	0.47	8	0.62

Ratings
Reward	D
Risk	D
Recent Upgrade/Downgrade	

Fund Information
Fund Type	Exchange Traded Funds
Category	Asia ex-Japan Equity
Sub-Category	Miscellaneous Region
Prospectus Objective	Pacific Stock
Inception Date	Sep-10
Open to New Investments	Y

Prices
Price (as of 12/31/2018)	31.88
52-Week High	40.18
52-Week Low	28.20

Total Returns (%)
3-Month	6-Month	1-Year	3-Year	5-Year
6.26	5.07	-17.44	-5.38	6.06

3-Year Standard Deviation	16.53
Effective Duration	

Valuation
Premium/Discount (1-Year Average)	-0.07

Company Information
Provider	iShares
Manager/Tenure	Diane Hsiung (8), Greg Savage (8), Jennifer Hsui (5), 1 other
Website	http://www.ishares.com
Address	iShares 400 Howard Street San Francisco CA 94105 United States
Phone Number	800-474-2737

PERFORMANCE

Ratings History
Date	Overall Rating	Risk Rating	Reward Rating
Q4-18	D	D	D
Q2-18	D	D	D
Q4-17	C	C-	C
Q4-16	C-	C-	D+
Q4-15	C	C	C

Asset & Performance History
Date	NAV	1-Year Total Return
2017	38.82	20.87
2016	32.24	-5.17
2015	34.22	-10.44
2014	38.57	25.18
2013	31.12	-7.92
2012	34.13	45.49

Total Assets: $139,757,230
Asset Allocation
Asset	%
Cash	0%
Stocks	100%
US Stocks	0%
Bonds	0%
US Bonds	0%
Other	0%

Services Offered:

Investment Strategy: The investment seeks to track the investment results of the MSCI Philippines Investable Market Index (IMI). The fund generally will invest at least 90% of its assets in the component securities of the underlying index and in investments that have economic characteristics that are substantially identical to the component securities of the underlying index. The index is a free float-adjusted market capitalization-weighted index designed to measure the performance of the Philippine equity markets. The fund is non-diversified. **Top Holdings:** SM Prime Holdings Inc Ayala Land Inc BDO Unibank Inc Ayala Corporation SM Investments Corp

Davis Select U.S. Equity ETF   C+   HOLD

Ticker	Traded On	NAV		Total Assets ($)	Dividend Yield (TTM)	Turnover Ratio	Expense Ratio
DUSA	NAS CM	20.03		$139,283,215	0.33	6	0.65

Ratings
Reward	B-
Risk	C
Recent Upgrade/Downgrade	Down

Fund Information
Fund Type	Exchange Traded Funds
Category	US Equity Large Cap Blend
Sub-Category	Large Blend
Prospectus Objective	Growth
Inception Date	Jan-17
Open to New Investments	Y

Prices
Price (as of 12/31/2018)	20.02
52-Week High	25.81
52-Week Low	19.43

Total Returns (%)
3-Month	6-Month	1-Year	3-Year	5-Year
-18.78	-14.57	-11.57		

3-Year Standard Deviation	
Effective Duration	

Valuation
Premium/Discount (1-Year Average)	0.33

Company Information
Provider	Davis ETFs
Manager/Tenure	Christopher Cullom Davis (1), Danton Goei (1)
Website	
Address	c/o Davis Selected Advisers, L.P. 2949 E. Elvira Rd., Ste. 101 Tucson Arizona 85756 United States
Phone Number	800-279-0279

PERFORMANCE

Ratings History
Date	Overall Rating	Risk Rating	Reward Rating
Q4-18	C+	C	B-
Q2-18	B-	C	B
Q4-17	D-	B+	D+
Q4-16			
Q4-15			

Asset & Performance History
Date	NAV	1-Year Total Return
2017	23.28	18.19
2016		
2015		
2014		
2013		
2012		

Total Assets: $139,283,215

Asset Allocation
Asset	%
Cash	0%
Stocks	100%
US Stocks	86%
Bonds	0%
US Bonds	0%
Other	0%

Services Offered:

Investment Strategy: The investment seeks long-term capital growth and capital preservation. Under normal market conditions, the fund will invest at least 80% of its net assets plus any borrowings for investment purposes in equity securities issued by U.S. companies. The fund's portfolio generally contains between 15 and 35 companies. It may invest a portion of its assets in financial services companies. The fund may also invest in mid- and small-capitalization companies, which the manager considers to be those companies with less than $10 billion in market capitalization. It may invest up to 20% of net assets in non-U.S. companies. The fund is non-diversified. **Top Holdings:** Berkshire Hathaway Inc B Alphabet Inc Class C Amazon.com Inc Capital One Financial Corp United Technologies Corp

iShares Aaa - A Rated Corporate Bond ETF   D+   SELL

Ticker	Traded On	NAV		Total Assets ($)	Dividend Yield (TTM)	Turnover Ratio	Expense Ratio
QLTA	NYSE Arca	50.00		$138,486,054	3.05	16	0.15

Ratings
Reward	D+
Risk	C-
Recent Upgrade/Downgrade	Down

Fund Information
Fund Type	Exchange Traded Funds
Category	US Fixed Income
Sub-Category	Corporate Bond
Prospectus Objective	Corp Bond - High Quality
Inception Date	Feb-12
Open to New Investments	Y

Prices
Price (as of 12/31/2018)	50.08
52-Week High	52.84
52-Week Low	49.32

Total Returns (%)
3-Month	6-Month	1-Year	3-Year	5-Year
0.45	1.15	-2.29	7.41	15.26

3-Year Standard Deviation	3.38
Effective Duration	6.83

Valuation
Premium/Discount (1-Year Average)	0.05

Company Information
Provider	iShares
Manager/Tenure	James Mauro (6), Scott Radell (6)
Website	http://www.ishares.com
Address	iShares 400 Howard Street San Francisco CA 94105 United States
Phone Number	800-474-2737

PERFORMANCE

Ratings History
Date	Overall Rating	Risk Rating	Reward Rating
Q4-18	D+	C-	D+
Q2-18	C-	C-	C-
Q4-17	B	A	C
Q4-16	C	D+	C
Q4-15	C	C-	C

Asset & Performance History
Date	NAV	1-Year Total Return
2017	52.77	5.23
2016	51.4	4.24
2015	50.58	0.74
2014	51.7	6.5
2013	49.69	-2.19
2012	51.89	

Total Assets: $138,486,054

Asset Allocation
Asset	%
Cash	1%
Stocks	0%
US Stocks	0%
Bonds	98%
US Bonds	80%
Other	0%

Services Offered:

Investment Strategy: The investment seeks to track the investment results of the Bloomberg Barclays U.S. Corporate Aaa - A Capped Index. The fund generally will invest at least 90% of its assets in the component securities of the underlying index and may invest up to 10% of its assets in certain futures, options and swap contracts, cash and cash equivalents. The underlying index is a subset of the Bloomberg Barclays U.S. Corporate Index, which measures the performance of the Aaa - A rated range of the fixed-rate, U.S. dollar-denominated taxable, corporate bond market. **Top Holdings:** Anheuser-Busch Companies LLC / Anheuser-Busch InBev Worldwide Inc 3.65% Anheuser-Busch Companies LLC / Anheuser-Busch InBev Worldwide Inc 4.9% National Australia Bank Limited New York Branch 2.63% Morgan Stanley 2.75% Intel Corporation 3.3%

ProShares Ultra Real Estate   C-   HOLD

Ticker	Traded On	NAV	Total Assets ($)	Dividend Yield (TTM)	Turnover Ratio	Expense Ratio
URE	NYSE Arca	56.17	$138,185,435	1.28		0.95

Ratings
Reward   C-
Risk   C-
Recent Upgrade/Downgrade   Down

Fund Information
Fund Type   Exchange Traded Funds
Category   Trading Tools
Sub-Category   Trading--Leveraged Equity
Prospectus Objective   Real Estate
Inception Date   Jan-07
Open to New Investments   Y

Prices
Price (as of 12/31/2018)   56.01
52-Week High   69.69
52-Week Low   51.57

Total Returns (%)

3-Month	6-Month	1-Year	3-Year	5-Year
-11.84	-12.68	-13.52	11.26	75.04

3-Year Standard Deviation   23.82
Effective Duration

Valuation
Premium/Discount (1-Year Average)   -0.04

Company Information
Provider   ProShares
Manager/Tenure   Michael Neches (5), Tarak Davé (0)
Website   http://www.proshares.com
Address   ProShares 7501 Wisconsin Avenue,
                      Suite 1000 Bethesda MD 20814
                      United States
Phone Number   866-776-5125

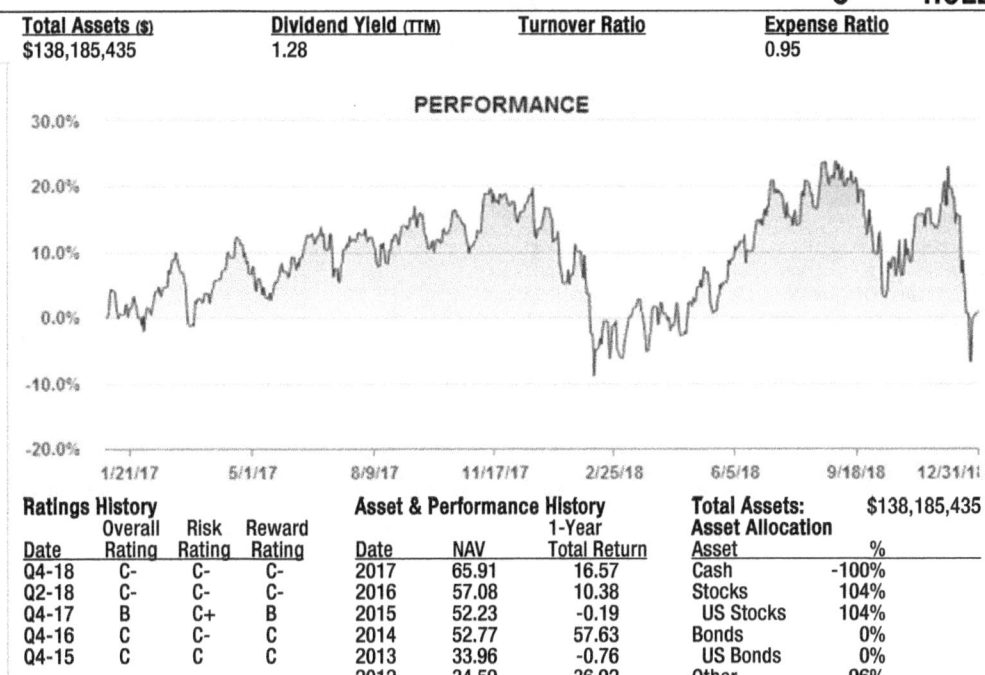

PERFORMANCE

Ratings History

Date	Overall Rating	Risk Rating	Reward Rating
Q4-18	C-	C-	C-
Q2-18	C-	C-	C-
Q4-17	B	C+	B
Q4-16	C	C-	C
Q4-15	C	C	C

Asset & Performance History

Date	NAV	1-Year Total Return
2017	65.91	16.57
2016	57.08	10.38
2015	52.23	-0.19
2014	52.77	57.63
2013	33.96	-0.76
2012	34.59	36.92

Total Assets: $138,185,435

Asset Allocation

Asset	%
Cash	-100%
Stocks	104%
US Stocks	104%
Bonds	0%
US Bonds	0%
Other	96%

Services Offered:

Investment Strategy: The investment seeks daily investment results, before fees and expenses, that correspond to two times (2x) the daily performance of the Dow Jones U.S. Real EstateSM Index. The fund invests in financial instruments that ProShare Advisors believes, in combination, should produce daily returns consistent with the fund's investment objective. The index seeks to measure the performance of certain companies in the real estate sector of the U.S. equity market. Component companies include, among others, real estate holding and development and real estate services companies and real estate investment trusts ("REITs"). The fund is non-diversified. **Top Holdings:** Dj U.S. Real Estate Index Swap Credit Suisse International Ishares U.S. Real Estate (1yr) Swap Bank Of America Na Dj U.S. Real Estate Index Swap Deutsche Bank Ag Dj U.S. Real Estate Index Swap Ubs Ag American Tower Corp

---

Columbia India Consumer ETF   D+   SELL

Ticker	Traded On	NAV	Total Assets ($)	Dividend Yield (TTM)	Turnover Ratio	Expense Ratio
INCO	NYSE Arca	44.12	$137,544,817	0.06	28	0.76

Ratings
Reward   D+
Risk   D+
Recent Upgrade/Downgrade   Down

Fund Information
Fund Type   Exchange Traded Funds
Category   India Equity
Sub-Category   India Equity
Prospectus Objective   Unaligned
Inception Date   Aug-11
Open to New Investments   Y

Prices
Price (as of 12/31/2018)   44.20
52-Week High   51.04
52-Week Low   37.36

Total Returns (%)

3-Month	6-Month	1-Year	3-Year	5-Year
7.24	-3.06	-11.56	36.28	98.18

3-Year Standard Deviation   19.79
Effective Duration

Valuation
Premium/Discount (1-Year Average)   -0.11

Company Information
Provider   Columbia
Manager/Tenure   Christopher Lo (2)
Website   http://www.columbiathreadneedleus.com
Address   Liberty Financial Funds P.O. Box 8081
                      Boston MA 02266-8081 United States
Phone Number   800-345-6611

PERFORMANCE

Ratings History

Date	Overall Rating	Risk Rating	Reward Rating
Q4-18	D+	D+	D+
Q2-18	C	C-	C
Q4-17	B+	B-	A
Q4-16	C	D+	B-
Q4-15	C	C-	C

Asset & Performance History

Date	NAV	1-Year Total Return
2017	49.95	52.88
2016	32.69	0.8
2015	32.46	-0.06
2014	32.48	45.5
2013	22.34	-6.83
2012	23.98	51.77

Total Assets: $137,544,817

Asset Allocation

Asset	%
Cash	0%
Stocks	100%
US Stocks	0%
Bonds	0%
US Bonds	0%
Other	0%

Services Offered:

Investment Strategy: The investment seeks investment results that correspond to the price and yield performance of the Indxx India Consumer Index. The fund will invest at least 80% of its net assets in Indian consumer companies included in the index and the advisor generally expects to be substantially invested at such times, with at least 95% of its net assets invested in these securities. The index is a maximum 30-stock free-float adjusted market capitalization-weighted index designed to measure the market performance of companies in the consumer industry in India, as defined by Indxx's proprietary methodology. It is non-diversified. **Top Holdings:** Nestle India Ltd Hindustan Unilever Ltd Britannia Industries Ltd Titan Co Ltd Godrej Consumer Products Ltd

iShares iBonds Dec 2027 Term Corporate ETF　　　　　　D　SELL

Ticker	Traded On	NAV	Total Assets ($)	Dividend Yield (TTM)	Turnover Ratio	Expense Ratio
IBDS	NYSE Arca	23.26	$137,357,627	3.67	2	0.1

Ratings
Reward	D
Risk	C-
Recent Upgrade/Downgrade	Down

Fund Information
Fund Type	Exchange Traded Funds
Category	US Fixed Income
Sub-Category	Corporate Bond
Prospectus Objective	Corp Bond - Gen
Inception Date	Sep-17
Open to New Investments	Y

Prices
Price (as of 12/31/2018)	23.39
52-Week High	24.94
52-Week Low	23.05

Total Returns (%)
3-Month	6-Month	1-Year	3-Year	5-Year
0.17	1.13	-2.74		

3-Year Standard Deviation	
Effective Duration	7.14

Valuation
Premium/Discount (1-Year Average)	0.28

Company Information
Provider	iShares
Manager/Tenure	James Mauro (1), Scott Radell (1)
Website	http://www.ishares.com
Address	iShares 400 Howard Street San Francisco CA 94105 United States
Phone Number	800-474-2737

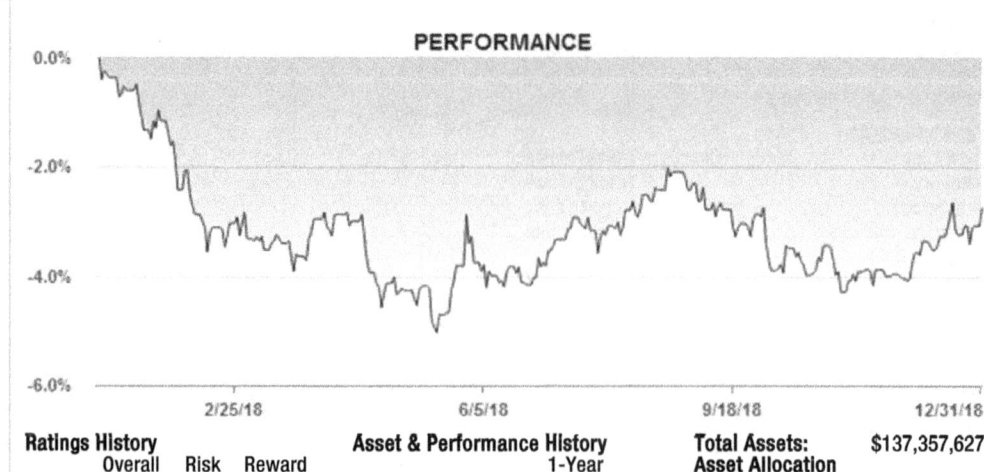

PERFORMANCE

Ratings History
Date	Overall Rating	Risk Rating	Reward Rating
Q4-18	D	C-	D
Q2-18	U		
Q4-17	U		
Q4-16			
Q4-15			

Asset & Performance History
Date	NAV	1-Year Total Return
2017	24.8	
2016		
2015		
2014		
2013		
2012		

Total Assets: $137,357,627
Asset Allocation
Asset	%
Cash	1%
Stocks	0%
US Stocks	0%
Bonds	99%
US Bonds	88%
Other	0%

Services Offered:

Investment Strategy: The investment seeks to meet its investment objective generally by investing in individual securities which satisfy the criteria of the Bloomberg Barclays December 2027 Maturity Corporate Index. The fund generally will invest at least 90% of its assets in the component securities of the underlying index, except during the last months of the fund's operations, and may invest up to 10% of its assets in certain futures, options and swap contracts, cash and cash equivalents, including shares of money market funds. The index is composed of U.S. dollar-denominated, investment-grade corporate bonds maturing in 2027. The fund is non-diversified. **Top Holdings:** Broadcom Corporation/Broadcom Cayman Finance Ltd 3.88% Microsoft Corporation 3.3% Citigroup Inc. 4.45% B.A.T. Capital Corporation 3.56% Verizon Communications Inc. 4.12%

WBI Power Factor™ High Dividend ETF　　　　　　C　HOLD

Ticker	Traded On	NAV	Total Assets ($)	Dividend Yield (TTM)	Turnover Ratio	Expense Ratio
WBIY	NYSE Arca	22.24	$137,247,981	3.95		0.7

Ratings
Reward	C+
Risk	D+
Recent Upgrade/Downgrade	

Fund Information
Fund Type	Exchange Traded Funds
Category	US Equity Large Cap Value
Sub-Category	Large Value
Prospectus Objective	Equity-Income
Inception Date	Dec-16
Open to New Investments	Y

Prices
Price (as of 12/31/2018)	22.15
52-Week High	27.99
52-Week Low	21.81

Total Returns (%)
3-Month	6-Month	1-Year	3-Year	5-Year
-16.41	-15.60	-12.65		

3-Year Standard Deviation	
Effective Duration	

Valuation
Premium/Discount (1-Year Average)	0.08

Company Information
Provider	WBI Investments
Manager/Tenure	Donald R. Schreiber (1), Gary E. Stroik (1)
Website	http://www.wbishares.com
Address	34 Sycamore Ave Suite 1-E Little Silver NJ 07739 United States
Phone Number	732-842-4920

PERFORMANCE

Ratings History
Date	Overall Rating	Risk Rating	Reward Rating
Q4-18	C	D+	C+
Q2-18	C	D+	C+
Q4-17	D-	B	D+
Q4-16			
Q4-15			

Asset & Performance History
Date	NAV	1-Year Total Return
2017	26.49	14.1
2016	24.65	
2015		
2014		
2013		
2012		

Total Assets: $137,247,981
Asset Allocation
Asset	%
Cash	6%
Stocks	94%
US Stocks	91%
Bonds	0%
US Bonds	0%
Other	0%

Services Offered:

Investment Strategy: The investment seeks to provide investment results that correspond to the price and yield of its underlying index, the Solactive Power Factor High Dividend Index. Under normal circumstances the fund will invest at least 80% of its total assets in the securities of the underlying index. The underlying index is designed to select securities from the Solactive US Broad Market Index that exhibit certain yield and fundamental value characteristics. The parent index includes large, mid- and small-cap securities listed in the U.S., including approximately the 3,000 largest U.S. companies that are selected and weighted according to free float market capitalization. **Top Holdings:** International Paper Co Nielsen Holdings PLC LyondellBasell Industries NV General Mills Inc CenterPoint Energy Inc

iShares Short Maturity Municipal Bond ETF   C-   HOLD

Ticker	Traded On	NAV	Total Assets ($)	Dividend Yield (TTM)	Turnover Ratio	Expense Ratio
MEAR	BATS	49.88	$137,184,501	1.31	163	0.25

Ratings
Reward	C-
Risk	C-
Recent Upgrade/Downgrade	

Fund Information
Fund Type	Exchange Traded Funds
Category	US Muni Fixed Inc
Sub-Category	Muni National Short
Prospectus Objective	Muni Bond - Natl
Inception Date	Mar-15
Open to New Investments	Y

Prices
Price (as of 12/31/2018)	49.94
52-Week High	50.03
52-Week Low	49.66

Total Returns (%)
3-Month	6-Month	1-Year	3-Year	5-Year
0.39	0.66	1.44	3.03	

3-Year Standard Deviation	0.49
Effective Duration	0.57

Valuation
Premium/Discount (1-Year Average)	0.00

Company Information
Provider	iShares
Manager/Tenure	William A. Henderson (3), Scott Radell (3)
Website	http://www.ishares.com
Address	iShares 400 Howard Street San Francisco CA 94105 United States
Phone Number	800-474-2737

PERFORMANCE

Ratings History
Date	Overall Rating	Risk Rating	Reward Rating
Q4-18	C-	C-	C-
Q2-18	C-	C-	C-
Q4-17	C	B-	C-
Q4-16	D+	D+	D+
Q4-15	U		

Asset & Performance History
Date	NAV	1-Year Total Return
2017	49.78	0.97
2016	49.8	0.59
2015	49.91	
2014		
2013		
2012		

Total Assets: $137,184,501

Asset Allocation
Asset	%
Cash	7%
Stocks	0%
US Stocks	0%
Bonds	93%
US Bonds	93%
Other	0%

Services Offered:

Investment Strategy: The investment seeks to maximize tax-free current income. The fund normally invests at least 80% of its net assets in municipal securities such that the interest on each bond is exempt from U.S. federal income taxes and the federal alternative minimum tax ("AMT"). It primarily invests in U.S. dollar-denominated investment-grade short-term fixed- and floating-rate municipal securities with remaining maturities of five years or less, such as municipal bonds, municipal notes and variable rate demand obligations, as well as money market instruments and registered investment companies. The fund is an actively managed exchange-traded fund ("ETF"). **Top Holdings:** ILLINOIS FIN AUTH 1.76% LOUDOUN CNTY VA INDL DEV AUTH 1.75% NEW JERSEY ECONOMIC DEV AUTH 5% ALLEN CNTY OHIO 1.71% TEXAS ST 1.75%

Invesco BulletShares 2025 Corporate Bond ETF   C-   HOLD

Ticker	Traded On	NAV	Total Assets ($)	Dividend Yield (TTM)	Turnover Ratio	Expense Ratio
BSCP	NYSE Arca	19.59	$137,069,376	3.43	1	0.1

Ratings
Reward	D+
Risk	C-
Recent Upgrade/Downgrade	

Fund Information
Fund Type	Exchange Traded Funds
Category	US Fixed Income
Sub-Category	Corporate Bond
Prospectus Objective	Corp Bond - Gen
Inception Date	Oct-15
Open to New Investments	Y

Prices
Price (as of 12/31/2018)	19.66
52-Week High	20.70
52-Week Low	19.40

Total Returns (%)
3-Month	6-Month	1-Year	3-Year	5-Year
0.23	1.30	-1.90	9.20	

3-Year Standard Deviation	3.94
Effective Duration	5.72

Valuation
Premium/Discount (1-Year Average)	0.19

Company Information
Provider	Invesco
Manager/Tenure	Jeremy Neisewander (2), Peter Hubbard (0), Jeffrey W. Kernagis (0), 1 other
Website	http://www.invesco.com/us
Address	Invesco 11 Greenway Plaza, Ste. 2500 Houston TX 77046 United States
Phone Number	800-659-1005

PERFORMANCE

Ratings History
Date	Overall Rating	Risk Rating	Reward Rating
Q4-18	C-	C-	D+
Q2-18	D+	C-	D+
Q4-17	C	B	C
Q4-16	D	C-	D
Q4-15			

Asset & Performance History
Date	NAV	1-Year Total Return
2017	20.63	5.82
2016	20.11	5.13
2015	19.68	
2014		
2013		
2012		

Total Assets: $137,069,376

Asset Allocation
Asset	%
Cash	1%
Stocks	0%
US Stocks	0%
Bonds	99%
US Bonds	90%
Other	0%

Services Offered:

Investment Strategy: The investment seeks investment results that correspond generally to the performance of the Nasdaq BulletShares® USD Corporate Bond 2025 Index. The fund will invest at least 80% of its total assets in component securities that comprise the index. The index is designed to represent the performance of a held-to-maturity portfolio of U.S. dollar-denominated investment-grade corporate bonds with effective maturities in the year 2025. The fund is non-diversified. **Top Holdings:** AT&T Inc 3.4% CVS Health Corp 4.1% Charter Communications Operating, LLC/Charter Communications Operating Capi Allergan Funding SCS 3.8% Verizon Communications Inc. 3.38%

VanEck Vectors Retail ETF

C+ **HOLD**

Ticker	Traded On	NAV	Total Assets ($)	Dividend Yield (TTM)	Turnover Ratio	Expense Ratio
RTH	NYSE Arca	93.97	$136,828,908	1.38	16	0.35

Ratings
Reward	B
Risk	C-
Recent Upgrade/Downgrade	Down

Fund Information
Fund Type	Exchange Traded Funds
Category	Consumer Goods & Svcs
Sub-Category	Consumer Cyclical
Prospectus Objective	Unaligned
Inception Date	Dec-11
Open to New Investments	Y

Prices
Price (as of 12/31/2018)	93.91
52-Week High	111.97
52-Week Low	87.33

Total Returns (%)
3-Month	6-Month	1-Year	3-Year	5-Year
-14.96	-5.21	3.76	26.04	65.29

3-Year Standard Deviation	13.59
Effective Duration	

Valuation
Premium/Discount (1-Year Average)	0.05

Company Information
Provider	VanEck
Manager/Tenure	Hao-Hung (Peter) Liao (6), Guo Hua (Jason) Jin (0)
Website	http://www.vaneck.com
Address	Van Eck Associates Corporation 666 Third Avenue New York NY 10017 United States
Phone Number	800-826-1115

PERFORMANCE

Ratings History
Date	Overall Rating	Risk Rating	Reward Rating
Q4-18	C+	C-	B
Q2-18	C+	C-	B
Q4-17	B+	A	B
Q4-16	C+	C-	B
Q4-15	B	C+	B+

Asset & Performance History
Date	NAV	1-Year Total Return
2017	91.31	22.22
2016	75.88	-0.6
2015	77.71	10.84
2014	71.7	18.31
2013	60.85	40.48
2012	43.75	19.7

Total Assets: $136,828,908
Asset Allocation
Asset	%
Cash	0%
Stocks	100%
US Stocks	98%
Bonds	0%
US Bonds	0%
Other	0%

Services Offered:

Investment Strategy: The investment seeks to replicate as closely as possible, before fees and expenses, the price and yield performance of the MVIS® US Listed Retail 25 Index. The fund normally invests at least 80% of its total assets in securities that comprise the fund's benchmark index. The index includes common stocks and depositary receipts of U.S. exchange-listed companies that derive at least 50% of their revenues from (or, in certain circumstances, have at least 50% of their assets related to) retail. The fund is non-diversified. **Top Holdings:** Amazon.com Inc The Home Depot Inc Walmart Inc Walgreens Boots Alliance Inc Costco Wholesale Corp

---

C-Tracks Exchange-Traded Notes Miller/Howard Strategic Dividend Reinvestor

D **SELL**

Ticker	Traded On	NAV	Total Assets ($)	Dividend Yield (TTM)	Turnover Ratio	Expense Ratio
DIVC	NYSE Arca	30.76	$136,712,000	0		0.7

Ratings
Reward	C-
Risk	E+
Recent Upgrade/Downgrade	Down

Fund Information
Fund Type	Exchange Traded Funds
Category	US Equity Large Cap Value
Sub-Category	Large Value
Prospectus Objective	Income
Inception Date	Sep-14
Open to New Investments	Y

Prices
Price (as of 12/31/2018)	30.76
52-Week High	37.34
52-Week Low	29.19

Total Returns (%)
3-Month	6-Month	1-Year	3-Year	5-Year
-15.48	-15.48	-12.12	23.16	

3-Year Standard Deviation	13.85
Effective Duration	

Valuation
Premium/Discount (1-Year Average)	0.00

Company Information
Provider	Citigroup
Manager/Tenure	No Manager (4)
Website	
Address	Citigroup United States
Phone Number	

PERFORMANCE

Ratings History
Date	Overall Rating	Risk Rating	Reward Rating
Q4-18	D	E+	C-
Q2-18	C-	E+	C+
Q4-17	B	B-	B
Q4-16	D+	D	C-
Q4-15	U		

Asset & Performance History
Date	NAV	1-Year Total Return
2017	35	16.39
2016	30.07	20.42
2015	24.97	-2.38
2014	25.58	
2013		
2012		

Total Assets: $136,712,000
Asset Allocation
Asset	%
Cash	
Stocks	
US Stocks	
Bonds	
US Bonds	
Other	

Services Offered:

Investment Strategy: The investment seeks to provide exposure to the performance of the Miller/Howard Strategic Dividend Index Total Return.
 The C-Tracks Exchange-Traded Notes Miller/Howard Strategic Dividend Reinvestor, are unsecured senior debt securities. The index is designed to track the performance of 30 equally weighted stocks traded on U.S. exchanges selected quarterly pursuant to rules based upon certain quantitative fundamental factors, including dividend yield, expected growth of dividend yield, market valuation relative to book value, return on invested capital relative to price-to-earnings ratio and trailing 26-week stock price momentum. **Top Holdings:**

Direxion Daily Russia Bull 3X Shares   D+   SELL

Ticker	Traded On	NAV	Total Assets ($)	Dividend Yield (TTM)	Turnover Ratio	Expense Ratio
RUSL	NYSE Arca	29.82	$136,301,474	3.56	65	1.28

Ratings
Reward	D+
Risk	D+
Recent Upgrade/Downgrade	

Fund Information
Fund Type	Exchange Traded Funds
Category	Trading Tools
Sub-Category	Trading--Leveraged Equity
Prospectus Objective	Foreign Stock
Inception Date	May-11
Open to New Investments	Y

Prices
Price (as of 12/31/2018)	29.81
52-Week High	73.38
52-Week Low	28.52

Total Returns (%)
3-Month	6-Month	1-Year	3-Year	5-Year
-31.73	-28.31	-40.05	36.15	-91.80

3-Year Standard Deviation	56.94
Effective Duration	

Valuation
Premium/Discount (1-Year Average)	0.04

Company Information
Provider	Direxion Funds
Manager/Tenure	Paul Brigandi (7), Tony Ng (3)
Website	http://www.direxionfunds.com
Address	Direxion Funds 1301 Avenue Of The Americas (6th Avenue) New York NY 10019 United States
Phone Number	646-572-3390

PERFORMANCE

Ratings History
Date	Overall Rating	Risk Rating	Reward Rating
Q4-18	D+	D+	D+
Q2-18	D+	D+	C-
Q4-17	C	D+	C+
Q4-16	D	D	D+
Q4-15	E+	D-	E

Asset & Performance History
Date	NAV	1-Year Total Return
2017	50.35	0.4
2016	50.68	126.22
2015	22.4	-31.99
2014	32.94	-91.15
2013	372.6	-15.96
2012	443.4	19.27

Total Assets: $136,301,474
Asset Allocation
Asset	%
Cash	56%
Stocks	44%
US Stocks	-3%
Bonds	0%
US Bonds	0%
Other	0%

Services Offered:

Investment Strategy: The investment seeks daily investment results, before fees and expenses, of 300% of the daily performance of the MVIS Russia Index. The fund invests at least 80% of its net assets in securities of the index, ETFs that track the index and other financial instruments that provide daily leveraged exposure to the index or ETFs that track the index. The index is a rules-based index, intended to represent the overall performance of publically traded companies that are domiciled and primarily listed on an exchange in Russia or that are not Russian companies, but nonetheless generate at least 50% of their revenues in Russia. It is non-diversified. **Top Holdings:** VanEck Vectors Russia ETF   Mrkt Vectors Russia Swap   Mrkt Vectors Russia Swap   Mrkt Vectors Russia Swap   Mrkt Vectors Russia Swap

---

ProShares UltraShort Dow30   D   SELL

Ticker	Traded On	NAV	Total Assets ($)	Dividend Yield (TTM)	Turnover Ratio	Expense Ratio
DXD	NYSE Arca	35.41	$135,952,346	1.01	0	0.95

Ratings
Reward	D-
Risk	D-
Recent Upgrade/Downgrade	

Fund Information
Fund Type	Exchange Traded Funds
Category	Trading Tools
Sub-Category	Trading--Inverse Equity
Prospectus Objective	Growth
Inception Date	Jul-06
Open to New Investments	Y

Prices
Price (as of 12/31/2018)	35.40
52-Week High	40.95
52-Week Low	27.91

Total Returns (%)
3-Month	6-Month	1-Year	3-Year	5-Year
25.66	4.16	2.78	-55.51	-67.27

3-Year Standard Deviation	18.84
Effective Duration	

Valuation
Premium/Discount (1-Year Average)	-0.03

Company Information
Provider	ProShares
Manager/Tenure	Michael Neches (5), Devin Sullivan (0)
Website	http://www.proshares.com
Address	ProShares 7501 Wisconsin Avenue, Suite 1000 Bethesda MD 20814 United States
Phone Number	866-776-5125

PERFORMANCE

Ratings History
Date	Overall Rating	Risk Rating	Reward Rating
Q4-18	D	D-	D-
Q2-18	D	D-	D-
Q4-17	E+	E+	E+
Q4-16	D	D-	D-
Q4-15	D	D-	D

Asset & Performance History
Date	NAV	1-Year Total Return
2017	34.88	-38.55
2016	56.84	-29.54
2015	80.68	-7.39
2014	87.12	-20.56
2013	109.68	-42.64
2012	191.24	-21.93

Total Assets: $135,952,346
Asset Allocation
Asset	%
Cash	205%
Stocks	-109%
US Stocks	-109%
Bonds	4%
US Bonds	4%
Other	0%

Services Offered:

Investment Strategy: The investment seeks daily investment results, before fees and expenses, that correspond to two times the inverse (-2x) of the daily performance of the Dow Jones Industrial Average® Index. The fund invests in financial instruments that ProShare Advisors believes, in combination, should produce daily returns consistent with the fund's investment objective. The index is a price-weighted index and includes 30 large-cap, "blue-chip" U.S. stocks, excluding utility and transportation companies. The fund is non-diversified. **Top Holdings:** Dj Industrial Average Swap Societe Generale   Dj Industrial Average Swap Goldman Sachs International   United States Treasury Bills   Dj Industrial Average Swap Citibank, N.A.   Dj Industrial Average Swap Ubs Ag

SPDR® S&P Health Care Services ETF   C   HOLD

Ticker	Traded On	NAV	Total Assets ($)	Dividend Yield (TTM)	Turnover Ratio	Expense Ratio
XHS	NYSE Arca	62.75	$135,304,425	0.26	34	0.35

Ratings
Reward   C
Risk   C-
Recent Upgrade/Downgrade

Fund Information
Fund Type   Exchange Traded Funds
Category   Healthcare Sector Equity
Sub-Category   Health
Prospectus Objective   Health
Inception Date   Sep-11
Open to New Investments   Y

Prices
Price (as of 12/31/2018)   62.59
52-Week High   76.74
52-Week Low   59.72

Total Returns (%)

3-Month	6-Month	1-Year	3-Year	5-Year
-17.39	-9.88	2.61	10.34	42.70

3-Year Standard Deviation   14.9
Effective Duration

Valuation
Premium/Discount (1-Year Average)   0.18

Company Information
Provider   SPDR State Street Global Advisors
Manager/Tenure   Michael J. Feehily (7), Karl A. Schneider (4), Raymond V. Donofrio (0)
Website   http://www.spdrs.com
Address   SPDR State Street Global Advisors State Street Financial Center, 1 Lincoln Street Boston MA 02111-2900 United States
Phone Number   617-786-3000

PERFORMANCE

Ratings History

Date	Overall Rating	Risk Rating	Reward Rating
Q4-18	C	C-	C
Q2-18	C	D+	C+
Q4-17	C	C	C-
Q4-16	C	C-	C
Q4-15	C	C	C+

Asset & Performance History

Date	NAV	1-Year Total Return
2017	61.34	17.12
2016	52.49	-8.37
2015	57.34	3.22
2014	56.07	25.28
2013	45.29	37.16
2012	33.18	22.65

Total Assets: $135,304,425
Asset Allocation

Asset	%
Cash	2%
Stocks	98%
US Stocks	97%
Bonds	0%
US Bonds	0%
Other	0%

Services Offered:

Investment Strategy: The investment seeks to provide investment results that, before fees and expenses, correspond generally to the total return performance of an index derived from the health care providers and services segment of a U.S. total market composite index. In seeking to track the performance of the S&P Health Care Services Select Industry Index (the "index"), the fund employs a sampling strategy. It generally invests substantially all, but at least 80%, of its total assets in the securities comprising the index. The index represents the health care services segment of the S&P Total Market Index ("S&P TMI"). The fund is non-diversified. **Top Holdings:** CVS Health Corp   AMN Healthcare Services Inc   Tivity Health Inc   Cigna Corp   BioTelemetry Inc

Global X Social Media ETF   C-   HOLD

Ticker	Traded On	NAV	Total Assets ($)	Dividend Yield (TTM)	Turnover Ratio	Expense Ratio
SOCL	NAS CM	27.74	$134,992,907	1.67	41	0.65

Ratings
Reward   C
Risk   C-
Recent Upgrade/Downgrade   Down

Fund Information
Fund Type   Exchange Traded Funds
Category   Technology Sector Equity
Sub-Category   Technology
Prospectus Objective   Technology
Inception Date   Nov-11
Open to New Investments   Y

Prices
Price (as of 12/31/2018)   27.55
52-Week High   38.73
52-Week Low   26.60

Total Returns (%)

3-Month	6-Month	1-Year	3-Year	5-Year
-12.82	-22.66	-16.04	41.20	33.15

3-Year Standard Deviation   17.59
Effective Duration

Valuation
Premium/Discount (1-Year Average)   -0.14

Company Information
Provider   Global X Funds
Manager/Tenure   Chang Kim (4), James Ong (2), Nam To (0)
Website   http://www.globalxfunds.com
Address   Global X Funds 600 Lexington Avenue, 20th Floor New York NY 10022 United States
Phone Number   888-493-8631

PERFORMANCE

Ratings History

Date	Overall Rating	Risk Rating	Reward Rating
Q4-18	C-	C-	C
Q2-18	C	C-	B-
Q4-17	A-	B-	A+
Q4-16	C+	C-	B
Q4-15	C	C-	C+

Asset & Performance History

Date	NAV	1-Year Total Return
2017	33.04	54.71
2016	21.67	8.7
2015	19.97	10.21
2014	18.12	-14.44
2013	21.19	64.39
2012	12.89	-0.53

Total Assets: $134,992,907
Asset Allocation

Asset	%
Cash	0%
Stocks	100%
US Stocks	43%
Bonds	0%
US Bonds	0%
Other	0%

Services Offered:

Investment Strategy: The investment seeks to provide investment results that correspond generally to the price and yield performance, before fees and expenses, of the Solactive Social Media Total Return Index. The fund will invest at least 80% of its total assets in the securities of the underlying index and in American Depositary Receipts and Global Depositary Receipts based on the securities in the underlying index. The underlying index tracks the equity performance of the largest and most liquid companies involved in the social media industry, including companies that provide social networking, file sharing, and other web-based media applications. The fund is non-diversified. **Top Holdings:** Tencent Holdings Ltd   Twitter Inc   Facebook Inc A   NAVER Corp   NetEase Inc ADR

Direxion Daily Financial Bear 3X Shares   D   SELL

Ticker	Traded On	NAV	Total Assets ($)	Dividend Yield (TTM)	Turnover Ratio	Expense Ratio
FAZ	NYSE Arca	13.56	$134,974,083	0.35	0	1.1

Ratings
Reward   D-
Risk   D
Recent Upgrade/Downgrade   Up

Fund Information
Fund Type   Exchange Traded Funds
Category   Trading Tools
Sub-Category   Trading--Inverse Equity
Prospectus Objective   Financial
Inception Date   Nov-08
Open to New Investments   Y

Prices
Price (as of 12/31/2018)   13.57
52-Week High   16.62
52-Week Low   8.88

Total Returns (%)

3-Month	6-Month	1-Year	3-Year	5-Year
39.91	24.25	16.26	-66.83	-84.13

3-Year Standard Deviation   33.08
Effective Duration

Valuation
Premium/Discount (1-Year Average)   -0.05

Company Information
Provider   Direxion Funds
Manager/Tenure   Paul Brigandi (10), Tony Ng (3)
Website   http://www.direxionfunds.com
Address   Direxion Funds 1301 Avenue Of The
                  Americas (6th Avenue) New York NY
                  10019 United States
Phone Number   646-572-3390

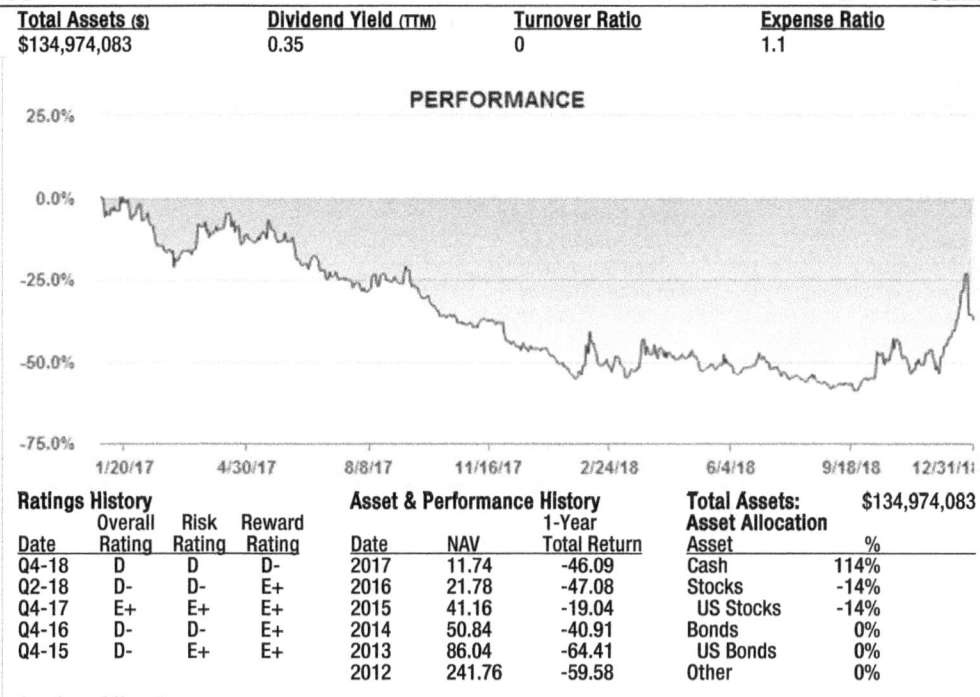

Ratings History

Date	Overall Rating	Risk Rating	Reward Rating
Q4-18	D	D	D-
Q2-18	D-	D-	E+
Q4-17	E+	E+	E+
Q4-16	D-	D-	E+
Q4-15	D-	E+	E+

Asset & Performance History

Date	NAV	1-Year Total Return
2017	11.74	-46.09
2016	21.78	-47.08
2015	41.16	-19.04
2014	50.84	-40.91
2013	86.04	-64.41
2012	241.76	-59.58

Total Assets: $134,974,083
Asset Allocation

Asset	%
Cash	114%
Stocks	-14%
US Stocks	-14%
Bonds	0%
US Bonds	0%
Other	0%

Services Offered:

Investment Strategy: The investment seeks daily investment results, before fees and expenses, of 300% of the inverse (or opposite) of the daily performance of the Russell 1000® Financial Services Index. The fund invests in swap agreements, futures contracts, short positions or other financial instruments that, in combination, provide inverse or short leveraged exposure to the index equal to at least 80% of the fund's net assets (plus borrowing for investment purposes). The index is a subset of the Russell 1000® Index that measures the performance of the securities classified in the financial services sector of the large-capitalization U.S. equity market. It is non-diversified. **Top Holdings:** Russ 1000 Finan Indx Swap   Russ 1000 Finan Indx Swap   Russ 1000 Finan Indx Swap Russ 1000 Finan Indx Swap   Russ 1000 Finan Indx Swap

Invesco S&P 500® Equal Weight Materials ETF   C+   HOLD

Ticker	Traded On	NAV	Total Assets ($)	Dividend Yield (TTM)	Turnover Ratio	Expense Ratio
RTM	NYSE Arca	94.60	$134,838,155	1.48		0.4

Ratings
Reward   B
Risk   C-
Recent Upgrade/Downgrade

Fund Information
Fund Type   Exchange Traded Funds
Category   Natural Resources
Sub-Category   Natural Resources
Prospectus Objective   Unaligned
Inception Date   Nov-06
Open to New Investments   Y

Prices
Price (as of 12/31/2018)   94.52
52-Week High   118.23
52-Week Low   88.78

Total Returns (%)

3-Month	6-Month	1-Year	3-Year	5-Year
-13.02	-10.85	-14.52	30.33	28.02

3-Year Standard Deviation   14.6
Effective Duration

Valuation
Premium/Discount (1-Year Average)   0.02

Company Information
Provider   Invesco
Manager/Tenure   Peter Hubbard (0), Michael Jeanette
                  (0), Jonathan Nixon (0), 1 other
Website   http://www.invesco.com/us
Address   Invesco 11 Greenway Plaza, Ste. 2500
                  Houston TX 77046 United States
Phone Number   800-659-1005

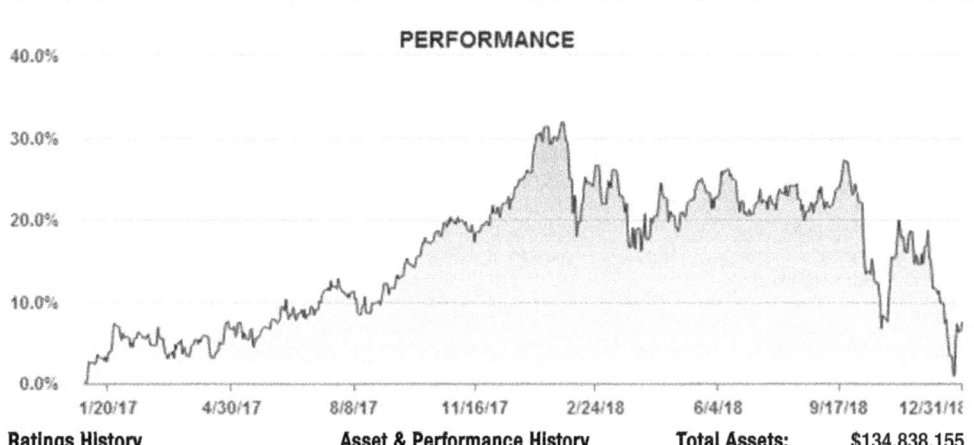

Ratings History

Date	Overall Rating	Risk Rating	Reward Rating
Q4-18	C+	C-	B
Q2-18	B-	C	B
Q4-17	B+	B-	A
Q4-16	C+	C-	B-
Q4-15	B	C+	B

Asset & Performance History

Date	NAV	1-Year Total Return
2017	112.57	24.89
2016	91.05	21.48
2015	76.11	-7.9
2014	83.88	6.65
2013	79.8	24.66
2012	65	17.64

Total Assets: $134,838,155
Asset Allocation

Asset	%
Cash	0%
Stocks	100%
US Stocks	96%
Bonds	0%
US Bonds	0%
Other	0%

Services Offered:

Investment Strategy: The investment seeks to track the investment results (before fees and expenses) of the S&P 500® Equal Weight Materials Index (the "underlying index"). The fund generally will invest at least 90% of its total assets in the securities that comprise the underlying index. The underlying index is an equal-weighted version of the S&P 500® Materials Index. Strictly in accordance with its guidelines and mandated procedures, the index provider compiles, maintains and calculates the underlying index, which is comprised of common stocks of companies in the materials sector of the S&P 500® Index. The fund is non-diversified. **Top Holdings:** The Mosaic Co   Ball Corp   Newmont Mining Corp   International Flavors & Fragrances Inc   Ecolab Inc

Invesco 1-30 Laddered Treasury ETF   D+   SELL

Ticker	Traded On	NAV	Total Assets ($)	Dividend Yield (TTM)	Turnover Ratio	Expense Ratio
PLW	NAS CM	31.94	$134,401,912	2.22		0.25

Ratings
Reward	D
Risk	C-
Recent Upgrade/Downgrade	

Fund Information
Fund Type	Exchange Traded Funds
Category	US Fixed Income
Sub-Category	Long Government
Prospectus Objective	Govt Bond - Treasury
Inception Date	Oct-07
Open to New Investments	Y

Prices
Price (as of 12/31/2018)	31.99
52-Week High	32.79
52-Week Low	30.35

Total Returns (%)
3-Month	6-Month	1-Year	3-Year	5-Year
3.83	1.93	-0.37	5.28	20.93

3-Year Standard Deviation	5.93
Effective Duration	10.64

Valuation
Premium/Discount (1-Year Average)	-0.04

Company Information
Provider	Invesco
Manager/Tenure	Philip Fang (11), Peter Hubbard (11), Jeffrey W. Kernagis (11), 2 others
Website	http://www.invesco.com/us
Address	Invesco 11 Greenway Plaza, Ste. 2500 Houston TX 77046 United States
Phone Number	800-659-1005

PERFORMANCE

Ratings History
Date	Overall Rating	Risk Rating	Reward Rating
Q4-18	D+	C-	D
Q2-18	D+	C-	D+
Q4-17	C	C	C
Q4-16	C	C-	C
Q4-15	C	C+	C

Asset & Performance History
Date	NAV	1-Year Total Return
2017	32.77	4.64
2016	31.96	0.99
2015	32.25	0.11
2014	32.9	14.73
2013	29.38	-8.16
2012	32.74	3.24

Total Assets: $134,401,912
Asset Allocation
Asset	%
Cash	3%
Stocks	0%
US Stocks	0%
Bonds	97%
US Bonds	97%
Other	0%

Services Offered:

Investment Strategy: The investment seeks to track the investment results (before fees and expenses) of the Ryan/NASDAQ U.S. 1-30 Year Treasury Laddered Index (the "underlying index"). The fund generally invests at least 80% of its total assets in U.S. Treasury securities that comprise the underlying index. The index seeks to maintain a continuous maturity laddered portfolio of securities, meaning that securities holdings are scheduled to mature in a proportional, annual sequential pattern. Nasdaq, Inc. (the "index provider") allows a six-month maturity deviation if securities with a desired maturity date are not available. **Top Holdings:** United States Treasury Bonds 5.38% United States Treasury Bonds 4.5% United States Treasury Notes 2% United States Treasury Bonds 5.25% United States Treasury Bonds 4.38%

VanEck Merk Gold Trust   D+   SELL

Ticker	Traded On	NAV	Total Assets ($)	Dividend Yield (TTM)	Turnover Ratio	Expense Ratio
OUNZ	NYSE Arca	12.58	$134,046,425	0		0.4

Ratings
Reward	D
Risk	C-
Recent Upgrade/Downgrade	

Fund Information
Fund Type	Exchange Traded Funds
Category	Commodities Specified
Sub-Category	Commodities Precious Metals
Prospectus Objective	Prec Metals
Inception Date	May-14
Open to New Investments	Y

Prices
Price (as of 12/31/2018)	12.59
52-Week High	13.37
52-Week Low	11.53

Total Returns (%)
3-Month	6-Month	1-Year	3-Year	5-Year
7.64	2.49	-1.54	19.21	

3-Year Standard Deviation	12.62
Effective Duration	

Valuation
Premium/Discount (1-Year Average)	0.11

Company Information
Provider	Merk Funds
Manager/Tenure	Management Team (4)
Website	http://www.merkfund.com
Address	Merk Funds P.O. Box 588 Portland ME 4112 United States
Phone Number	866-637-5386

PERFORMANCE

Ratings History
Date	Overall Rating	Risk Rating	Reward Rating
Q4-18	D+	C-	D
Q2-18	C-	C-	C-
Q4-17	C-	C-	C-
Q4-16	C-	C-	C-
Q4-15	D	D	D

Asset & Performance History
Date	NAV	1-Year Total Return
2017	12.78	12.21
2016	11.47	7.67
2015	10.55	-11.78
2014	11.96	
2013		
2012		

Total Assets: $134,046,425
Asset Allocation
Asset	%
Cash	0%
Stocks	0%
US Stocks	0%
Bonds	0%
US Bonds	0%
Other	100%

Services Offered:

Investment Strategy: The Trust's primary objective is to provide investors with an opportunity to invest in gold through the shares and be able to take delivery of physical gold in exchange for those shares. The Trust's secondary objective is for the shares to reflect the performance of the price of gold less the expenses of the Trust's operations. Each share represents a fractional undivided beneficial interest in the Trust's net assets. The Trust's assets consist principally of gold held on the Trust's behalf in financial institutions for safekeeping. **Top Holdings:** Gold Oz.

JPMorgan Diversified Return U.S. Mid Cap Equity ETF   C-   HOLD

Ticker	Traded On	NAV	Total Assets ($)	Dividend Yield (TTM)	Turnover Ratio	Expense Ratio
JPME	NYSE Arca	57.35	$133,477,579	2.31	31	0.24

Ratings
Reward	C-
Risk	C-
Recent Upgrade/Downgrade	Down

Fund Information
Fund Type	Exchange Traded Funds
Category	US Equity Mid Cap
Sub-Category	Mid-Cap Blend
Prospectus Objective	Growth
Inception Date	May-16
Open to New Investments	Y

Prices
Price (as of 12/31/2018)	57.11
52-Week High	68.32
52-Week Low	54.16

Total Returns (%)
3-Month	6-Month	1-Year	3-Year	5-Year
-13.90	-10.51	-8.42		

3-Year Standard Deviation
Effective Duration

Valuation
Premium/Discount (1-Year Average)	0.14

Company Information
Provider	JPMorgan
Manager/Tenure	Jonathan Msika (2), Yazann Romahi (2), Joe Staines (2), 1 other
Website	http://www.jpmorganfunds.com
Address	JPMorgan 270 Park Avenue New York NY 10017-2070 United States
Phone Number	800-480-4111

PERFORMANCE

Ratings History
Date	Overall Rating	Risk Rating	Reward Rating
Q4-18	C-	C-	C-
Q2-18	D+	D+	C-
Q4-17	D+	B+	C
Q4-16	U		
Q4-15			

Asset & Performance History
Date	NAV	1-Year Total Return
2017	63.67	19.06
2016	54.1	
2015		
2014		
2013		
2012		

Total Assets: $133,477,579
Asset Allocation
Asset	%
Cash	1%
Stocks	99%
US Stocks	99%
Bonds	0%
US Bonds	0%
Other	0%

Services Offered:

Investment Strategy: The investment seeks investment results that closely correspond, before fees and expenses, to the performance of the JP Morgan Diversified Factor US Mid Cap Equity Index. The fund will invest at least 80% of its net assets in securities included in the underlying index. The underlying index is comprised of U.S. equity securities selected to represent a diversified set of factor characteristics: value, momentum, and quality.
Top Holdings: McCormick & Co Inc Non-Voting Church & Dwight Co Inc Clorox Co Eversource Energy Xcel Energy Inc

---

WisdomTree U.S. Multifactor Fund   C-   HOLD

Ticker	Traded On	NAV	Total Assets ($)	Dividend Yield (TTM)	Turnover Ratio	Expense Ratio
USMF	BATS	26.16	$132,622,555	1.17	143	0.28

Ratings
Reward	D+
Risk	C-
Recent Upgrade/Downgrade	Up

Fund Information
Fund Type	Exchange Traded Funds
Category	US Equity Large Cap Blend
Sub-Category	Large Blend
Prospectus Objective	Growth & Inc
Inception Date	Jun-17
Open to New Investments	Y

Prices
Price (as of 12/31/2018)	26.12
52-Week High	31.09
52-Week Low	24.84

Total Returns (%)
3-Month	6-Month	1-Year	3-Year	5-Year
-13.94	-8.82	-4.24		

3-Year Standard Deviation
Effective Duration

Valuation
Premium/Discount (1-Year Average)	0.24

Company Information
Provider	WisdomTree
Manager/Tenure	Richard A. Brown (1), Thomas J. Durante (1), Karen Q. Wong (1)
Website	http://www.wisdomtree.com
Address	WisdomTree 245 Park Avenue, 35th floor New York NY 10167 United States
Phone Number	866-909-9473

PERFORMANCE

Ratings History
Date	Overall Rating	Risk Rating	Reward Rating
Q4-18	C-	C-	D+
Q2-18	D+	C-	D+
Q4-17	U		
Q4-16			
Q4-15			

Asset & Performance History
Date	NAV	1-Year Total Return
2017	27.7	
2016		
2015		
2014		
2013		
2012		

Total Assets: $132,622,555
Asset Allocation
Asset	%
Cash	0%
Stocks	100%
US Stocks	100%
Bonds	0%
US Bonds	0%
Other	0%

Services Offered:

Investment Strategy: The investment seeks to track the price and yield performance, before fees and expenses, of the WisdomTree U.S. Multifactor Index. Under normal circumstances, at least 80% of the fund's total assets will be invested in component securities of the index and investments that have economic characteristics that are substantially identical to the economic characteristics of such component securities. The index is generally comprised of 200 U.S. companies with the highest composite scores based on two fundamental factors (value and quality measures) and two technical factors (momentum and correlation). The fund is non-diversified. **Top Holdings:** Verizon Communications Inc Fiserv Inc Fidelity National Information Services Inc WR Berkley Corp Booz Allen Hamilton Holding Corp

Global X SuperDividend® REIT ETF   C+   HOLD

Ticker	Traded On	NAV	Total Assets ($)	Dividend Yield (TTM)	Turnover Ratio	Expense Ratio
SRET	NAS CM	13.59	$130,131,556	8.86	55	0.55

Ratings
Reward   B
Risk   C
Recent Upgrade/Downgrade   Down

Fund Information
Fund Type   Exchange Traded Funds
Category   Real Estate Sector Equity
Sub-Category   Real Estate
Prospectus Objective   Real Estate
Inception Date   Mar-15
Open to New Investments   Y

Prices
Price (as of 12/31/2018)   13.57
52-Week High   15.83
52-Week Low   13.25

Total Returns (%)

3-Month	6-Month	1-Year	3-Year	5-Year
-7.28	-6.62	-5.14	38.25	

3-Year Standard Deviation   10.96
Effective Duration

Valuation
Premium/Discount (1-Year Average)   0.20

Company Information
Provider   Global X Funds
Manager/Tenure   Chang Kim (3), James Ong (2), Nam To (0)
Website   http://www.globalxfunds.com
Address   Global X Funds 600 Lexington Avenue, 20th Floor New York NY 10022 United States
Phone Number   888-493-8631

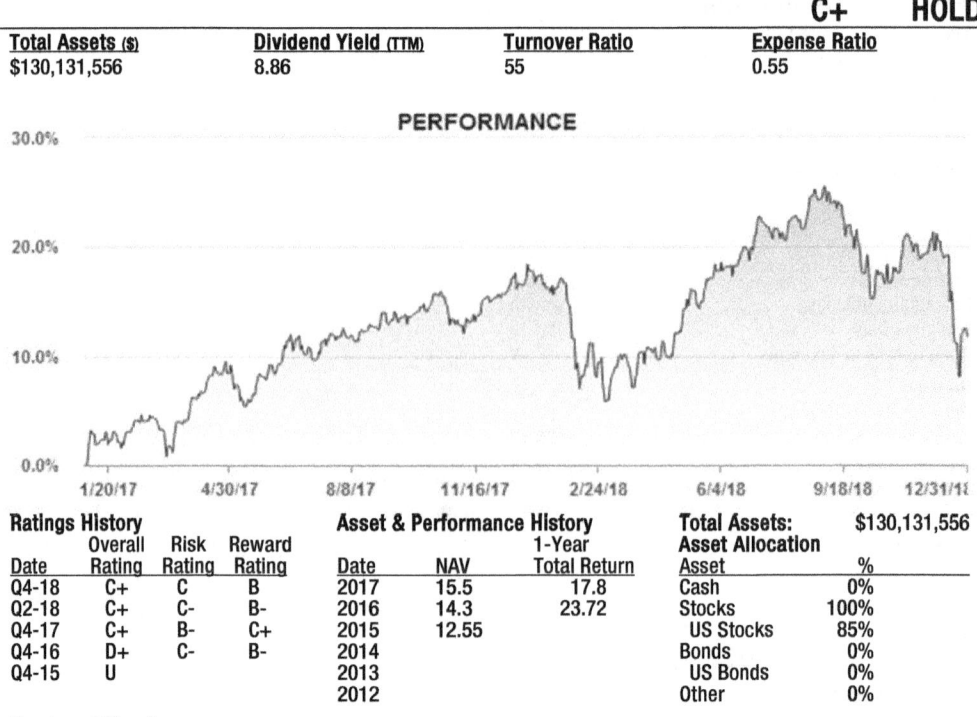

PERFORMANCE

Ratings History

Date	Overall Rating	Risk Rating	Reward Rating
Q4-18	C+	C	B
Q2-18	C+	C-	B-
Q4-17	C+	B-	C+
Q4-16	D+	C-	B-
Q4-15	U		

Asset & Performance History

Date	NAV	1-Year Total Return
2017	15.5	17.8
2016	14.3	23.72
2015	12.55	
2014		
2013		
2012		

Total Assets: $130,131,556
Asset Allocation

Asset	%
Cash	0%
Stocks	100%
US Stocks	85%
Bonds	0%
US Bonds	0%
Other	0%

Services Offered:

Investment Strategy: The investment seeks investment results that correspond generally to the price and yield performance, before fees and expenses, of the Solactive Global SuperDividend® REIT Index. The fund invests at least 80% of its total assets in the securities of the underlying index and in American Depositary Receipts ("ADRs") and Global Depositary Receipts ("GDRs") based on the securities in the underlying index. The underlying index tracks the performance of REITs that rank among the highest yielding REITs globally, as determined by Solactive AG, the provider of the underlying index. The fund is non-diversified. **Top Holdings:** Annaly Capital Management Inc   Medical Properties Trust Inc   EPR Properties   Ladder Capital Corp Class A   Blackstone Mortgage Trust Inc A

AdvisorShares Ranger Equity Bear ETF   D+   SELL

Ticker	Traded On	NAV	Total Assets ($)	Dividend Yield (TTM)	Turnover Ratio	Expense Ratio
HDGE	NYSE Arca	8.43	$130,015,733	0	245	2.72

Ratings
Reward   D
Risk   D+
Recent Upgrade/Downgrade

Fund Information
Fund Type   Exchange Traded Funds
Category   Alternative Misc
Sub-Category   Bear Market
Prospectus Objective   Growth
Inception Date   Jan-11
Open to New Investments   Y

Prices
Price (as of 12/31/2018)   8.43
52-Week High   8.97
52-Week Low   7.24

Total Returns (%)

3-Month	6-Month	1-Year	3-Year	5-Year
13.30	8.21	7.11	-21.58	-33.98

3-Year Standard Deviation   13.96
Effective Duration

Valuation
Premium/Discount (1-Year Average)   -0.01

Company Information
Provider   AdvisorShares
Manager/Tenure   John Del Vecchio (7), Brad H. Lamensdorf (7)
Website   http://www.advisorshares.com
Address   AdvisorShares 2 Bethesda Metro Center, Suite 1330 Bethesda MD 20814 United States
Phone Number   877-843-3831

PERFORMANCE

Ratings History

Date	Overall Rating	Risk Rating	Reward Rating
Q4-18	D+	D+	D
Q2-18	D+	D+	D
Q4-17	D-	D-	D-
Q4-16	D+	D+	D
Q4-15	D	D	D

Asset & Performance History

Date	NAV	1-Year Total Return
2017	7.87	-15.01
2016	9.26	-13.86
2015	10.75	-6.27
2014	11.47	-10.18
2013	12.77	-30.29
2012	18.32	-26.72

Total Assets: $130,015,733
Asset Allocation

Asset	%
Cash	144%
Stocks	-89%
US Stocks	-87%
Bonds	45%
US Bonds	42%
Other	0%

Services Offered:

Investment Strategy: The investment seeks capital appreciation through short sales of domestically traded equity securities. The Sub-Advisor seeks to achieve the fund's investment objective by short selling a portfolio of liquid mid- and large-cap U.S. exchange-traded equity securities, ETFs, ETNs and other exchange-traded products. The fund invests at least 80% of its net assets, plus any borrowings for investment purposes, in short positions in equity securities. The Sub-Advisor implements a bottom-up, fundamental, research driven security selection process. **Top Holdings:** AdvisorShares Sage Core Reserves ETF   Fidelity Instl Govt 657 C   Snap-on Inc   NetScout Systems Inc   Allegiant Travel Co

TrimTabs All Cap U.S. Free-Cash-Flow ETF   C-   HOLD

Ticker	Traded On	NAV	Total Assets ($)	Dividend Yield (TTM)	Turnover Ratio	Expense Ratio
TTAC	BATS	31.48	$129,938,935	0.39	42	0.59

Ratings
Reward	C
Risk	C-
Recent Upgrade/Downgrade	Down

Fund Information
Fund Type	Exchange Traded Funds
Category	US Equity Large Cap Blend
Sub-Category	Mid-Cap Growth
Prospectus Objective	Growth & Inc
Inception Date	Sep-16
Open to New Investments	Y

Prices
Price (as of 12/31/2018)	31.42
52-Week High	38.69
52-Week Low	29.75

Total Returns (%)
3-Month	6-Month	1-Year	3-Year	5-Year
-16.70	-11.54	-5.99		

3-Year Standard Deviation	
Effective Duration	

Valuation
Premium/Discount (1-Year Average)	0.16

Company Information
Provider	TrimTabs
Manager/Tenure	Theodore M. Theodore (2), Janet F. Johnston (1)
Website	http://www.trimtabsfunds.com
Address	TrimTabs 1350 Avenue of the Americas, Suite 248 New York NY 10019 United States
Phone Number	

PERFORMANCE

Ratings History
Date	Overall Rating	Risk Rating	Reward Rating
Q4-18	C-	C-	C
Q2-18	C	C-	C
Q4-17	D	B	C
Q4-16	U		
Q4-15			

Asset & Performance History
Date	NAV	1-Year Total Return
2017	33.7	25.59
2016	26.94	
2015		
2014		
2013		
2012		

Total Assets: $129,938,935

Asset Allocation
Asset	%
Cash	0%
Stocks	100%
US Stocks	100%
Bonds	0%
US Bonds	0%
Other	0%

Services Offered:

Investment Strategy: The investment seeks to generate long-term returns in excess of the total return of the Russell 3000® Index (the "index"), with less volatility than the index. The fund is an actively managed ETF. It seeks to achieve its investment objective by investing in stocks with liquidity and fundamental characteristics that the adviser believes are historically associated with superior long-term performance. Based on extensive historical research, the adviser designed the following quantitative stock selection rules to make allocation decisions and seek to protect against dramatic over- or under-weighting of individual securities in the fund's portfolio. **Top Holdings:** Illumina Inc VeriSign Inc Burlington Stores Inc Rollins Inc Zoetis Inc Class A

SPDR® S&P Software & Services ETF   C   HOLD

Ticker	Traded On	NAV	Total Assets ($)	Dividend Yield (TTM)	Turnover Ratio	Expense Ratio
XSW	NYSE Arca	75.13	$129,847,379	0.17	29	0.35

Ratings
Reward	C
Risk	C-
Recent Upgrade/Downgrade	Down

Fund Information
Fund Type	Exchange Traded Funds
Category	Technology Sector Equity
Sub-Category	Technology
Prospectus Objective	Technology
Inception Date	Sep-11
Open to New Investments	Y

Prices
Price (as of 12/31/2018)	74.54
52-Week High	92.64
52-Week Low	69.45

Total Returns (%)
3-Month	6-Month	1-Year	3-Year	5-Year
-16.02	-8.40	8.89	52.01	70.71

3-Year Standard Deviation	14.45
Effective Duration	

Valuation
Premium/Discount (1-Year Average)	0.15

Company Information
Provider	SPDR State Street Global Advisors
Manager/Tenure	Michael J. Feehily (7), Karl A. Schneider (4), Melissa Kapitulik (0)
Website	http://www.spdrs.com
Address	SPDR State Street Global Advisors State Street Financial Center, 1 Lincoln Street Boston MA 02111-2900 United States
Phone Number	617-786-3000

PERFORMANCE

Ratings History
Date	Overall Rating	Risk Rating	Reward Rating
Q4-18	C	C-	C
Q2-18	B	C-	A-
Q4-17	A-	B	A
Q4-16	C	D+	C
Q4-15	C	D+	C+

Asset & Performance History
Date	NAV	1-Year Total Return
2017	69.2	27.58
2016	54.5	9.41
2015	50.26	7.39
2014	47.05	4.56
2013	45.25	47.84
2012	31.25	15.5

Total Assets: $129,847,379

Asset Allocation
Asset	%
Cash	0%
Stocks	100%
US Stocks	98%
Bonds	0%
US Bonds	0%
Other	0%

Services Offered:

Investment Strategy: The investment seeks to provide investment results that, before fees and expenses, correspond generally to the total return performance of an index derived from the computer software segment of a U.S. total market composite index. In seeking to track the performance of the S&P Software & Services Select Industry Index (the "index"), the fund employs a sampling strategy. It generally invests substantially all, but at least 80%, of its total assets in the securities comprising the index. The index represents the software and services segment of the S&P Total Market Index ("S&P TMI"). The fund is non-diversified. **Top Holdings:** SendGrid Inc FireEye Inc Red Hat Inc Benefitfocus Inc Imperva Inc

Invesco BulletShares 2023 High Yield Corporate Bond ETF

C- **HOLD**

Ticker	Traded On	NAV	Total Assets ($)	Dividend Yield (TTM)	Turnover Ratio	Expense Ratio
BSJN	NYSE Arca	24.63	$129,737,765	5.18	6	0.42

Ratings

Reward	C-
Risk	C-
Recent Upgrade/Downgrade	Down

Fund Information

Fund Type	Exchange Traded Funds
Category	US Fixed Income
Sub-Category	High Yield Bond
Prospectus Objective	Corp Bond-High Yld
Inception Date	Oct-15
Open to New Investments	Y

Prices

Price (as of 12/31/2018)	24.63
52-Week High	26.67
52-Week Low	24.23

Total Returns (%)

3-Month	6-Month	1-Year	3-Year	5-Year
-4.64	-1.97	-1.35	17.39	

3-Year Standard Deviation	3.5
Effective Duration	3.13

Valuation

Premium/Discount (1-Year Average)	-0.07

Company Information

Provider	Invesco
Manager/Tenure	Jeremy Neisewander (2), Peter Hubbard (0), Jeffrey W. Kernagis (0), 1 other
Website	http://www.invesco.com/us
Address	Invesco 11 Greenway Plaza, Ste. 2500 Houston TX 77046 United States
Phone Number	800-659-1005

PERFORMANCE

Ratings History

Date	Overall Rating	Risk Rating	Reward Rating
Q4-18	C-	C-	C-
Q2-18	C	C-	C
Q4-17	C	B	C
Q4-16	D	D+	D+
Q4-15			

Asset & Performance History

Date	NAV	1-Year Total Return
2017	26.33	5.55
2016	26.35	12.6
2015	24.56	
2014		
2013		
2012		

Total Assets: $129,737,765

Asset Allocation

Asset	%
Cash	1%
Stocks	0%
US Stocks	0%
Bonds	98%
US Bonds	85%
Other	0%

Services Offered:

Investment Strategy: The investment seeks investment results that correspond generally to the performance, of a high yield corporate bond index called the Nasdaq BulletShares® USD High Yield Corporate Bond 2023 Index. The fund will invest at least 80% of its total assets in component securities that comprise the index. The index is designed to represent the performance of a held-to-maturity portfolio of U.S. dollar-denominated high yield corporate bonds with effective maturities in 2023. The fund is non-diversified. **Top Holdings:** Sprint Corporation 7.88% Altice Financing S.A. 6.62% First Data Corporation 7% Bausch Health Companies Inc 5.88% Reynolds Group Issuer LLC. 5.12%

SPDR® SSgA Multi-Asset Real Return ETF

C- **HOLD**

Ticker	Traded On	NAV	Total Assets ($)	Dividend Yield (TTM)	Turnover Ratio	Expense Ratio
RLY	NYSE Arca	22.87	$129,605,539	2.34	25	0.5

Ratings

Reward	C-
Risk	C-
Recent Upgrade/Downgrade	Down

Fund Information

Fund Type	Exchange Traded Funds
Category	Moderate Allocation
Sub-Category	Allocation--50% to 70% Equity
Prospectus Objective	Growth & Inc
Inception Date	Apr-12
Open to New Investments	Y

Prices

Price (as of 12/31/2018)	22.75
52-Week High	27.48
52-Week Low	22.58

Total Returns (%)

3-Month	6-Month	1-Year	3-Year	5-Year
-13.18	-11.81	-11.06	9.85	-12.98

3-Year Standard Deviation	10.09
Effective Duration	7.88

Valuation

Premium/Discount (1-Year Average)	0.09

Company Information

Provider	SPDR State Street Global Advisors
Manager/Tenure	Robert Guiliano (6), John A. Gulino (6), Michael O. Martel (4)
Website	http://www.spdrs.com
Address	SPDR State Street Global Advisors State Street Financial Center, 1 Lincoln Street Boston MA 02111-2900 United States
Phone Number	617-786-3000

PERFORMANCE

Ratings History

Date	Overall Rating	Risk Rating	Reward Rating
Q4-18	C-	C-	C-
Q2-18	C	C-	C
Q4-17	C	C	C
Q4-16	D+	D+	D
Q4-15	D	D	D

Asset & Performance History

Date	NAV	1-Year Total Return
2017	26.37	10.24
2016	24.39	12.04
2015	22.23	-15.24
2014	26.66	-6.54
2013	29.02	-3.06
2012	30.6	

Total Assets: $129,605,539

Asset Allocation

Asset	%
Cash	16%
Stocks	58%
US Stocks	29%
Bonds	26%
US Bonds	23%
Other	0%

Services Offered:

Investment Strategy: The investment seeks to achieve real return consisting of capital appreciation and current income. Under normal circumstances, the Adviser invests at least 80% of the net assets of the fund among ETPs that provide exposure to the following primary asset classes: (i) inflation protected securities issued by the United States government, its agencies and/or instrumentalities, as well as inflation protected securities issued by foreign governments, agencies, and/or instrumentalities; (ii) domestic and international real estate securities; (iii) commodities; and (iv) publicly-traded companies in natural resources and/or commodities businesses. **Top Holdings:** SPDR® S&P Global Natural Resources ETF Invesco Optm Yd Dvrs Cdty Stra No K1 ETF SPDR® Blmbg Barclays TIPS ETF SPDR® S&P Global Infrastructure ETF SPDR® Dow Jones International RelEst ETF

Invesco BLDRS Emerging Markets 50 ADR Index Fund   C   HOLD

Ticker	Traded On	NAV	Total Assets ($)	Dividend Yield (TTM)	Turnover Ratio	Expense Ratio
ADRE	NAS CM	36.20	$129,323,221	1.97	10	0.18

Ratings
Reward   B-
Risk   D+
Recent Upgrade/Downgrade   Down

Fund Information
Fund Type   Exchange Traded Funds
Category   Global Emerg Mkts Equity
Sub-Category   Diversified Emerging Mkts
Prospectus Objective   Div Emerg Mkts
Inception Date   Nov-02
Open to New Investments   Y

Prices
Price (as of 12/31/2018)   36.07
52-Week High   48.87
52-Week Low   34.99

Total Returns (%)

3-Month	6-Month	1-Year	3-Year	5-Year
-10.72	-10.14	-14.00	31.06	7.64

3-Year Standard Deviation   16.57
Effective Duration

Valuation
Premium/Discount (1-Year Average)   0.02

Company Information
Provider   Invesco
Manager/Tenure   Management Team (16)
Website   http://www.invesco.com/us
Address   Invesco 11 Greenway Plaza, Ste. 2500
                      Houston TX 77046 United States
Phone Number   800-659-1005

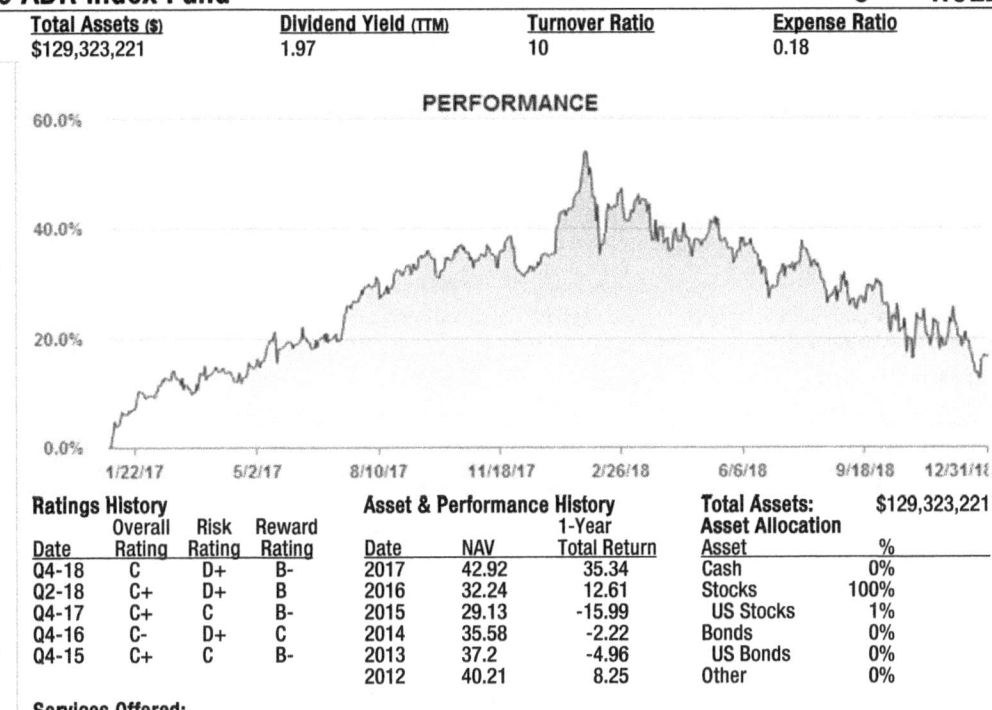

Ratings History

Date	Overall Rating	Risk Rating	Reward Rating
Q4-18	C	D+	B-
Q2-18	C+	D+	B
Q4-17	C+	C	B-
Q4-16	C-	D+	C
Q4-15	C+	C	B-

Asset & Performance History

Date	NAV	1-Year Total Return
2017	42.92	35.34
2016	32.24	12.61
2015	29.13	-15.99
2014	35.58	-2.22
2013	37.2	-4.96
2012	40.21	8.25

Total Assets: $129,323,221
Asset Allocation

Asset	%
Cash	0%
Stocks	100%
US Stocks	1%
Bonds	0%
US Bonds	0%
Other	0%

Services Offered:

Investment Strategy: The investment seeks to provide investment results that correspond generally, before fees and expenses, to the price and yield performance of the Bank of New York Mellon Emerging Markets 50 ADR Index. The fund typically invests substantially all of its assets in the securities that make up the index. The index is intended to give investors a benchmark for tracking the price and yield performance of Emerging Markets Depositary Receipts. the fund is non-diversified. **Top Holdings:** Alibaba Group Holding Ltd ADR   Taiwan Semiconductor Manufacturing Co Ltd ADR   HDFC Bank Ltd ADR   Baidu Inc ADR   China Mobile Ltd ADR

---

iShares International Developed Property ETF   D+   SELL

Ticker	Traded On	NAV	Total Assets ($)	Dividend Yield (TTM)	Turnover Ratio	Expense Ratio
WPS	NYSE Arca	34.61	$129,233,589	4.96	11	0.48

Ratings
Reward   D+
Risk   C-
Recent Upgrade/Downgrade   Down

Fund Information
Fund Type   Exchange Traded Funds
Category   Real Estate Sector Equity
Sub-Category   Global Real Estate
Prospectus Objective   Real Estate
Inception Date   Jul-07
Open to New Investments   Y

Prices
Price (as of 12/31/2018)   34.48
52-Week High   41.74
52-Week Low   34.00

Total Returns (%)

3-Month	6-Month	1-Year	3-Year	5-Year
-4.68	-6.44	-8.89	12.74	15.36

3-Year Standard Deviation   10.66
Effective Duration

Valuation
Premium/Discount (1-Year Average)   -0.22

Company Information
Provider   iShares
Manager/Tenure   Diane Hsiung (10), Greg Savage (10),
                      Jennifer Hsui (6), 3 others
Website   http://www.ishares.com
Address   iShares 400 Howard Street San
                      Francisco CA 94105 United States
Phone Number   800-474-2737

Ratings History

Date	Overall Rating	Risk Rating	Reward Rating
Q4-18	D+	C-	D+
Q2-18	C	C-	C
Q4-17	B	B	B-
Q4-16	C-	C-	C
Q4-15	C-	D+	C

Asset & Performance History

Date	NAV	1-Year Total Return
2017	39.59	22.07
2016	33.91	1.37
2015	35.32	-0.81
2014	36.72	3.17
2013	37	7.59
2012	35.88	37.25

Total Assets: $129,233,589
Asset Allocation

Asset	%
Cash	1%
Stocks	97%
US Stocks	0%
Bonds	0%
US Bonds	0%
Other	2%

Services Offered:

Investment Strategy: The investment seeks to track the investment results of the S&P Developed ex-U.S. Property IndexTM. The fund generally invests at least 90% of its assets in the component securities of the index and in investments that have economic characteristics that are substantially identical to the component securities and may invest up to 10% of its assets in certain futures, options and swap contracts, cash and cash equivalents. The index is a free float-adjusted, market capitalization-weighted index that defines and measures the investable universe of publicly-traded real estate companies domiciled in developed countries outside of the U.S. **Top Holdings:** Vonovia SE   Mitsui Fudosan Co Ltd   Unibail-Rodamco-Westfield   Mitsubishi Estate Co Ltd   Sun Hung Kai Properties Ltd

O'Shares FTSE Russell Small Cap Quality Dividend ETF

C- HOLD

Ticker	Traded On	NAV	Total Assets ($)	Dividend Yield (TTM)	Turnover Ratio	Expense Ratio
OUSM	NYSE Arca	23.67	$128,862,424	2.08		0.48

Ratings

Reward	D+
Risk	C-
Recent Upgrade/Downgrade	

Fund Information

Fund Type	Exchange Traded Funds
Category	US Equity Small Cap
Sub-Category	Small Blend
Prospectus Objective	Small Company
Inception Date	Dec-16
Open to New Investments	Y

Prices

Price (as of 12/31/2018)	23.61
52-Week High	29.15
52-Week Low	22.48

Total Returns (%)

3-Month	6-Month	1-Year	3-Year	5-Year
-15.31	-12.06	-10.29		

3-Year Standard Deviation	
Effective Duration	

Valuation

Premium/Discount (1-Year Average)	0.05

Company Information

Provider	O'Shares Investments
Manager/Tenure	Denise M. Krisko (1), Austin Wen (0)
Website	http://www.oshares.com
Address	O'Shares Investments 60 State Street, Suite 700 Boston MA 02109 United States
Phone Number	617-855-7670

PERFORMANCE

Ratings History

Date	Overall Rating	Risk Rating	Reward Rating
Q4-18	C-	C-	D+
Q2-18	C-	C-	C-
Q4-17	D-	B+	D+
Q4-16			
Q4-15			

Asset & Performance History

Date	NAV	1-Year Total Return
2017	27.01	10.08
2016	24.95	
2015		
2014		
2013		
2012		

Total Assets: $128,862,424

Asset Allocation

Asset	%
Cash	0%
Stocks	100%
US Stocks	99%
Bonds	0%
US Bonds	0%
Other	0%

Services Offered:

Investment Strategy: The investment seeks to track the performance (before fees and expenses) of the FTSE USA Small Cap ex Real Estate 2Qual/Vol/Yield 3% Capped Factor Index. Under normal market conditions, the fund will invest at least 80% of its total assets in the components of the index. The index is constructed using a proprietary, rules-based methodology designed to select equity securities from the FTSE USA Small Cap Index that have exposure to the following three factors: 1) quality, 2) low volatility and 3) yield. **Top Holdings:** Leidos Holdings Inc Lazard Ltd Shs A Eaton Vance Corp OGE Energy Corp Teradyne Inc

---

VanEck Vectors Rare Earth/Strategic Metals ETF

D+ SELL

Ticker	Traded On	NAV	Total Assets ($)	Dividend Yield (TTM)	Turnover Ratio	Expense Ratio
REMX	NYSE Arca	13.56	$128,788,368	4.68	57	0.61

Ratings

Reward	C-
Risk	D
Recent Upgrade/Downgrade	Down

Fund Information

Fund Type	Exchange Traded Funds
Category	Prec Metals
Sub-Category	Equity Precious Metals
Prospectus Objective	Natl Res
Inception Date	Oct-10
Open to New Investments	Y

Prices

Price (as of 12/31/2018)	13.56
52-Week High	32.55
52-Week Low	13.21

Total Returns (%)

3-Month	6-Month	1-Year	3-Year	5-Year
-24.09	-33.34	-48.31	18.53	-51.90

3-Year Standard Deviation	26.81
Effective Duration	

Valuation

Premium/Discount (1-Year Average)	-0.35

Company Information

Provider	VanEck
Manager/Tenure	Hao-Hung (Peter) Liao (8), Guo Hua (Jason) Jin (0)
Website	http://www.vaneck.com
Address	Van Eck Associates Corporation 666 Third Avenue New York NY 10017 United States
Phone Number	800-826-1115

PERFORMANCE

Ratings History

Date	Overall Rating	Risk Rating	Reward Rating
Q4-18	D+	D	C-
Q2-18	C	D+	C
Q4-17	C+	D+	B
Q4-16	D	D	D
Q4-15	D-	E+	D-

Asset & Performance History

Date	NAV	1-Year Total Return
2017	29.75	81.55
2016	16.9	26.3
2015	13.68	-43.59
2014	25.49	-28.06
2013	35.98	-31.84
2012	52.92	-10.82

Total Assets: $128,788,368

Asset Allocation

Asset	%
Cash	1%
Stocks	99%
US Stocks	12%
Bonds	0%
US Bonds	0%
Other	0%

Services Offered:

Investment Strategy: The investment seeks to replicate as closely as possible, before fees and expenses, the price and yield performance of the MVIS® Global Rare Earth/Strategic Metals Index. The fund normally invests at least 80% of its total assets in securities that comprise the fund's benchmark index. The index includes companies primarily engaged in a variety of activities that are related to the producing, refining and recycling of rare earth and strategic metals and minerals. It is non-diversified. **Top Holdings:** Iluka Resources Ltd Pilbara Minerals Ltd Toho Titanium Co Ltd Orocobre Ltd Lynas Corp Ltd

AdvisorShares Newfleet Multi-Sector Income ETF   C-   HOLD

Ticker	Traded On	NAV	Total Assets ($)	Dividend Yield (TTM)	Turnover Ratio	Expense Ratio
MINC	NYSE Arca	47.37	$128,389,797	2.79		0.75

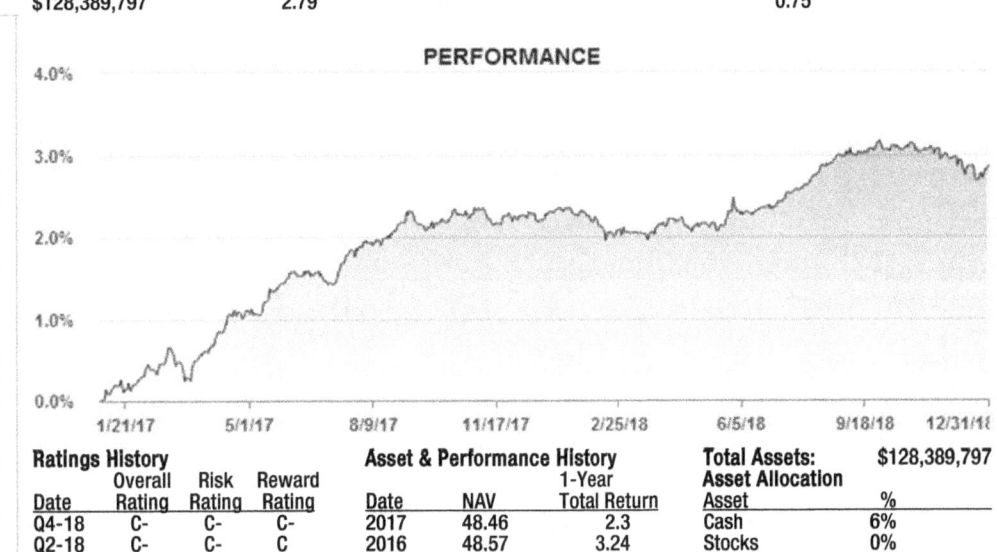

Ratings
Reward	C-
Risk	C-
Recent Upgrade/Downgrade	

Fund Information
Fund Type	Exchange Traded Funds
Category	US Fixed Income
Sub-Category	Short-Term Bond
Prospectus Objective	Income
Inception Date	Mar-13
Open to New Investments	Y

Prices
Price (as of 12/31/2018)	47.33
52-Week High	48.44
52-Week Low	47.16

Total Returns (%)
3-Month	6-Month	1-Year	3-Year	5-Year
-0.27	0.50	0.53	6.19	9.81

3-Year Standard Deviation	0.88
Effective Duration	1.59

Valuation
Premium/Discount (1-Year Average)	-0.13

Company Information
Provider	AdvisorShares
Manager/Tenure	David L. Albrycht (5), Jonathan R. Stanley (5)
Website	http://www.advisorshares.com
Address	AdvisorShares 2 Bethesda Metro Center, Suite 1330 Bethesda MD 20814 United States
Phone Number	877-843-3831

Ratings History
Date	Overall Rating	Risk Rating	Reward Rating
Q4-18	C-	C-	C-
Q2-18	C-	C-	C
Q4-17	B	A+	C
Q4-16	C	C-	C
Q4-15	C	C-	C

Asset & Performance History
Date	NAV	1-Year Total Return
2017	48.46	2.3
2016	48.57	3.24
2015	48.35	1.27
2014	49.07	2.11
2013	49.42	
2012		

Total Assets: $128,389,797
Asset Allocation
Asset	%
Cash	6%
Stocks	0%
US Stocks	0%
Bonds	94%
US Bonds	91%
Other	0%

Services Offered:

Investment Strategy: The investment seeks to provide current income consistent with preservation of capital, while limiting fluctuations in net asset value ("NAV") due to changes in interest rates. The Sub-Advisor applies a time-tested approach and extensive credit research to capitalize on opportunities across undervalued areas of the bond markets. The fund principally invests in investment-grade securities, which are securities with credit ratings within the four highest rating categories of a nationally recognized statistical rating organization or, if unrated, those securities that the Sub-Advisor determines to be of comparable quality. **Top Holdings:** Morgan Stanley 3.89% Exeter Automobile Receivables Trust 2015-2 3.9% CARFINANCE CAPITAL AUTO TRUST 2.91% Hertz Vehicle Financing Llc 2.73% Citigroup Inc. 3.65%

SPDR® Dorsey Wright Fixed Income Allocation ETF   D+   SELL

Ticker	Traded On	NAV	Total Assets ($)	Dividend Yield (TTM)	Turnover Ratio	Expense Ratio
DWFI	NAS CM	22.24	$127,835,160	4.64	71	0.6

Ratings
Reward	D+
Risk	C-
Recent Upgrade/Downgrade	

Fund Information
Fund Type	Exchange Traded Funds
Category	Cautious Allocation
Sub-Category	Allocation--15% to 30% Equity
Prospectus Objective	Growth & Inc
Inception Date	Jun-16
Open to New Investments	Y

Prices
Price (as of 12/31/2018)	22.21
52-Week High	25.82
52-Week Low	22.07

Total Returns (%)
3-Month	6-Month	1-Year	3-Year	5-Year
-3.69	-3.47	-8.69		

3-Year Standard Deviation	
Effective Duration	5.73

Valuation
Premium/Discount (1-Year Average)	0.06

Company Information
Provider	SPDR State Street Global Advisors
Manager/Tenure	Michael J. Feehily (2), Karl A. Schneider (2), Raymond V. Donofrio (1)
Website	http://www.spdrs.com
Address	SPDR State Street Global Advisors State Street Financial Center, 1 Lincoln Street Boston MA 02111-2900 United States
Phone Number	617-786-3000

Ratings History
Date	Overall Rating	Risk Rating	Reward Rating
Q4-18	D+	C-	D+
Q2-18	D+	C-	D+
Q4-17	D+	B	D+
Q4-16	U		
Q4-15			

Asset & Performance History
Date	NAV	1-Year Total Return
2017	25.24	8.92
2016	24.3	
2015		
2014		
2013		
2012		

Total Assets: $127,835,160
Asset Allocation
Asset	%
Cash	1%
Stocks	0%
US Stocks	0%
Bonds	74%
US Bonds	69%
Other	0%

Services Offered:

Investment Strategy: The investment seeks to provide investment results that, before fees and expenses, correspond generally to the price and yield performance of the Dorsey Wright Fixed Income Allocation Index. The index is comprised of exchange-traded funds advised by SSGA Funds Management, Inc. The selection universe for the index includes U.S.-listed fixed income ETFs advised by SSGA FM or its affiliates that are designed to target exposure to fixed income securities. The fund invests at least 80%, of its total assets in securities comprising the index. It is non-diversified. **Top Holdings:** SPDR® Nuveen Blmbg Barclays Muni Bd ETF SPDR® Blackstone / GSO Senior Loan ETF SPDR® Wells Fargo Preferred Stock ETF SPDR® Blmbg Barclays High Yield Bd ETF Ssi Us Gov Money Market Class State Street Inst Us Gov

VictoryShares US Discovery Enhanced Volatility Wtd ETF   C-   HOLD

Ticker	Traded On	NAV	Total Assets ($)	Dividend Yield (TTM)	Turnover Ratio	Expense Ratio
CSF	NAS CM	39.45	$127,457,828	1.15	50	0.35

Ratings
Reward	C-
Risk	C-
Recent Upgrade/Downgrade	Down

Fund Information
Fund Type	Exchange Traded Funds
Category	US Equity Small Cap
Sub-Category	Small Blend
Prospectus Objective	Income
Inception Date	Jul-14
Open to New Investments	Y

Prices
Price (as of 12/31/2018)	39.41
52-Week High	50.28
52-Week Low	37.54

Total Returns (%)
3-Month	6-Month	1-Year	3-Year	5-Year
-16.96	-17.04	-11.27	18.20	

3-Year Standard Deviation	13.68
Effective Duration	

Valuation
Premium/Discount (1-Year Average)	0.14

Company Information
Provider	VictoryShares
Manager/Tenure	Stephen Hammers (4), Mannik Dhillon (0)
Website	http://www.VictorySharesLiterature.com
Address	Victory Shares 4249 Easton Way, Suite 400 Columbus OH 43219 United States
Phone Number	

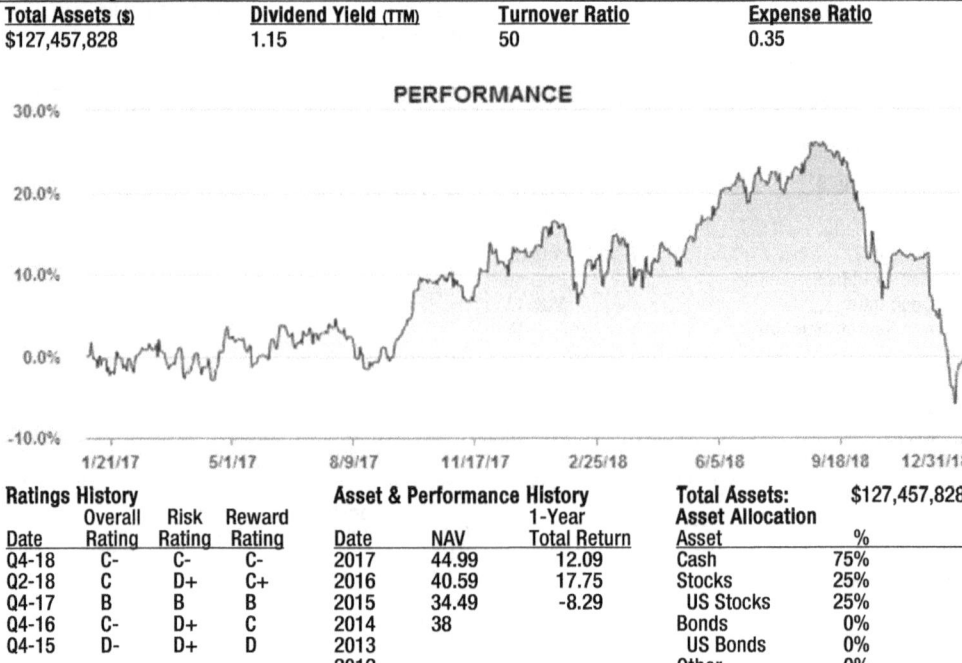

Ratings History
Date	Overall Rating	Risk Rating	Reward Rating
Q4-18	C-	C-	C-
Q2-18	C	D+	C+
Q4-17	B	B	B
Q4-16	C-	D+	C
Q4-15	D-	D+	D

Asset & Performance History
Date	NAV	1-Year Total Return
2017	44.99	12.09
2016	40.59	17.75
2015	34.49	-8.29
2014	38	
2013		
2012		

Total Assets: $127,457,828

Asset Allocation
Asset	%
Cash	75%
Stocks	25%
US Stocks	25%
Bonds	0%
US Bonds	0%
Other	0%

Services Offered:

Investment Strategy: The investment seeks investment results that match the performance of the Nasdaq Victory US Small Cap 500 Long/Cash Volatility Weighted Index before fees and expenses. The fund seeks to achieve its investment objective by investing, under normal market conditions, at least 80% of its assets directly or indirectly in the securities included in the Nasdaq Victory US Small Cap 500 Long/Cash Volatility Weighted Index. The index identifies the 500 largest U.S. companies with market capitalizations of less than $3 billion measured at the time the index's constituent securities are determined. **Top Holdings:** Russ 2000 Idx Fut Dec18 Capitol Federal Financial Inc Northwest Bancshares Inc Four Corners Property Trust Inc Advanced Disposal Services Inc

iShares MSCI Israel Capped ETF   C-   HOLD

Ticker	Traded On	NAV	Total Assets ($)	Dividend Yield (TTM)	Turnover Ratio	Expense Ratio
EIS	NYSE Arca	48.54	$127,456,030	1.92	6	0.59

Ratings
Reward	C
Risk	C-
Recent Upgrade/Downgrade	

Fund Information
Fund Type	Exchange Traded Funds
Category	Equity Misc
Sub-Category	Miscellaneous Region
Prospectus Objective	Foreign Stock
Inception Date	Mar-08
Open to New Investments	Y

Prices
Price (as of 12/31/2018)	48.42
52-Week High	58.28
52-Week Low	46.52

Total Returns (%)
3-Month	6-Month	1-Year	3-Year	5-Year
-13.01	-6.29	-4.98	3.05	9.66

3-Year Standard Deviation	13.24
Effective Duration	

Valuation
Premium/Discount (1-Year Average)	-0.05

Company Information
Provider	iShares
Manager/Tenure	Diane Hsiung (10), Greg Savage (10), Jennifer Hsui (5), 1 other
Website	http://www.ishares.com
Address	iShares 400 Howard Street San Francisco CA 94105 United States
Phone Number	800-474-2737

Ratings History
Date	Overall Rating	Risk Rating	Reward Rating
Q4-18	C-	C-	C
Q2-18	C-	C-	C-
Q4-17	C-	C	C-
Q4-16	C-	C-	C-
Q4-15	B	C+	B+

Asset & Performance History
Date	NAV	1-Year Total Return
2017	51.5	13.08
2016	46.47	-4.08
2015	49.31	7.13
2014	47.18	-0.66
2013	48.34	18.27
2012	41.84	8.49

Total Assets: $127,456,030

Asset Allocation
Asset	%
Cash	0%
Stocks	100%
US Stocks	16%
Bonds	0%
US Bonds	0%
Other	0%

Services Offered:

Investment Strategy: The investment seeks to track the investment results of the MSCI Israel Capped Investable Market Index (IMI). The fund generally will invest at least 90% of its assets in the component securities of the underlying index and in investments that have economic characteristics that are substantially identical to the component securities of the underlying index. The index is a free float-adjusted market capitalization index designed to measure broad-based equity market performance in Israel. The fund is non-diversified. **Top Holdings:** Teva Pharmaceutical Industries Ltd ADR Check Point Software Technologies Ltd Bank Leumi Le-Israel BM Bank Hapoalim BM NICE Ltd

VanEck Vectors International High Yield Bond ETF   C-   HOLD

Ticker	Traded On	NAV	Total Assets ($)	Dividend Yield (TTM)	Turnover Ratio	Expense Ratio
IHY	NYSE Arca	23.39	$127,060,465	4.68	41	0.4

Ratings
Reward   C-
Risk   C-
Recent Upgrade/Downgrade

Fund Information
Fund Type	Exchange Traded Funds
Category	Global Fixed Income
Sub-Category	High Yield Bond
Prospectus Objective	Corp Bond-High Yld
Inception Date	Apr-12
Open to New Investments	Y

Prices
Price (as of 12/31/2018)	23.41
52-Week High	26.11
52-Week Low	23.30

Total Returns (%)
3-Month	6-Month	1-Year	3-Year	5-Year
-3.15	-1.46	-4.96	17.96	9.99

3-Year Standard Deviation	5.85
Effective Duration	3.85

Valuation
Premium/Discount (1-Year Average)	-0.19

Company Information
Provider	VanEck
Manager/Tenure	Francis G. Rodilosso (6)
Website	http://www.vaneck.com
Address	Van Eck Associates Corporation 666 Third Avenue New York NY 10017 United States
Phone Number	800-826-1115

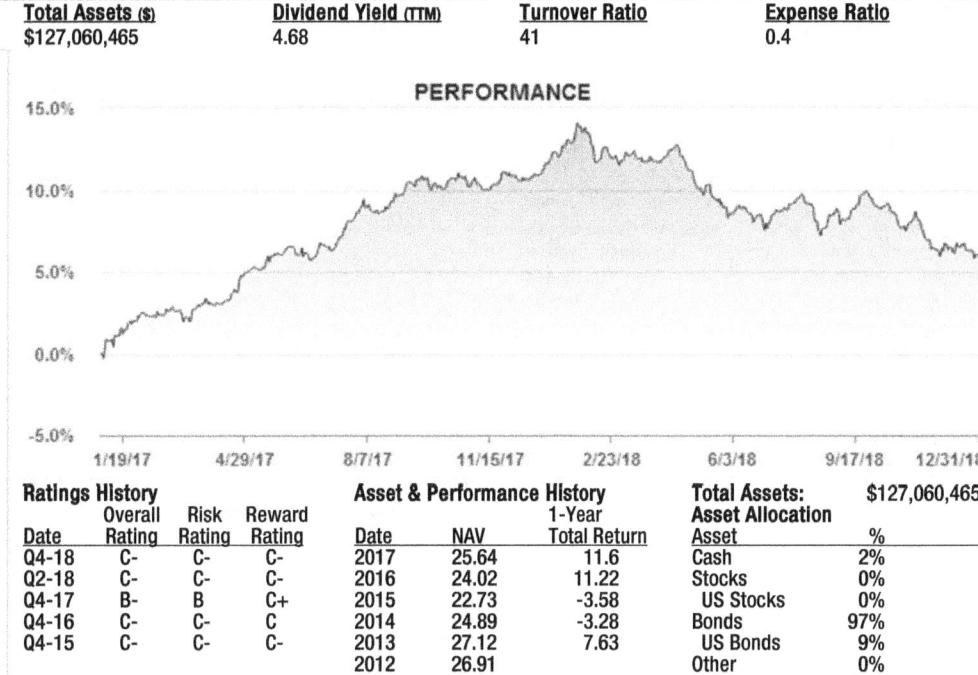

PERFORMANCE

Ratings History
Date	Overall Rating	Risk Rating	Reward Rating
Q4-18	C-	C-	C-
Q2-18	C-	C-	C-
Q4-17	B-	B	C+
Q4-16	C-	C-	C
Q4-15	C-	C-	C-

Asset & Performance History
Date	NAV	1-Year Total Return
2017	25.64	11.6
2016	24.02	11.22
2015	22.73	-3.58
2014	24.89	-3.28
2013	27.12	7.63
2012	26.91	

Total Assets: $127,060,465
Asset Allocation
Asset	%
Cash	2%
Stocks	0%
US Stocks	0%
Bonds	97%
US Bonds	9%
Other	0%

Services Offered:

Investment Strategy: The investment seeks to replicate as closely as possible, before fees and expenses, the price and yield performance of the ICE BofAML Global ex-US Issuers High Yield Constrained Index. The fund normally invests at least 80% of its total assets in securities that comprise the fund's benchmark index. The index is comprised of below investment grade bonds issued by corporations located throughout the world (which may include emerging market countries) excluding the United States denominated in Euros, U.S. dollars, Canadian dollars or pound sterling and issued in the major domestic or Eurobond markets. **Top Holdings:** Softbank Group Corp 6.25% Reynolds Group Issuer LLC. 5.75% ALTICE FRANCE S.A 7.38% Banco do Brasil S.A. (Grand Cayman Branch) 3.88% Altice Luxembourg S.A. 7.75%

---

iShares iBonds Mar 2020 Term Corporate ETF   C   HOLD

Ticker	Traded On	NAV	Total Assets ($)	Dividend Yield (TTM)	Turnover Ratio	Expense Ratio
IBDC	NYSE Arca	25.89	$126,891,643	2.14	7	0.1

Ratings
Reward   C
Risk   C-
Recent Upgrade/Downgrade

Fund Information
Fund Type	Exchange Traded Funds
Category	US Fixed Income
Sub-Category	Short-Term Bond
Prospectus Objective	Corp Bond - Gen
Inception Date	Jul-13
Open to New Investments	Y

Prices
Price (as of 12/31/2018)	25.94
52-Week High	26.08
52-Week Low	25.83

Total Returns (%)
3-Month	6-Month	1-Year	3-Year	5-Year
0.57	1.31	1.60	7.38	14.20

3-Year Standard Deviation	1.4
Effective Duration	0.90

Valuation
Premium/Discount (1-Year Average)	0.11

Company Information
Provider	iShares
Manager/Tenure	James Mauro (5), Scott Radell (5)
Website	http://www.ishares.com
Address	iShares 400 Howard Street San Francisco CA 94105 United States
Phone Number	800-474-2737

PERFORMANCE

Ratings History
Date	Overall Rating	Risk Rating	Reward Rating
Q4-18	C	C-	C
Q2-18	C	C-	C
Q4-17	B	A+	C
Q4-16	C	D+	C
Q4-15	D+	D+	C-

Asset & Performance History
Date	NAV	1-Year Total Return
2017	26.04	1.95
2016	26.04	3.48
2015	25.72	1.49
2014	25.92	4.78
2013	25.39	
2012		

Total Assets: $126,891,643
Asset Allocation
Asset	%
Cash	3%
Stocks	0%
US Stocks	0%
Bonds	97%
US Bonds	77%
Other	0%

Services Offered:

Investment Strategy: The investment seeks to track the investment results of the Bloomberg Barclays 2020 Maturity Corporate Index composed of U.S. dollar-denominated, investment-grade corporate bonds maturing after March 31, 2019 and before April 1, 2020. The fund generally will invest at least 90% of its assets in the component securities (including indirect investments through an underlying fund) of the index, except during the last months of the fund's operations. The index includes U.S. dollar-denominated, investment-grade securities publicly issued by U.S. and non-U.S. corporate issuers that have $300 million or more of outstanding face value at the time of inclusion. **Top Holdings:** iShares iBonds Mar 2020Tm CorpexFncl ETF JPMorgan Chase & Co. 2.25% Apple Inc. 2.1% Wells Fargo & Company 2.15% Goldman Sachs Group, Inc. 5.38%

Invesco Dynamic Leisure and Entertainment ETF | C+ HOLD

Ticker	Traded On	NAV	Total Assets ($)	Dividend Yield (TTM)	Turnover Ratio	Expense Ratio
PEJ	NYSE Arca	39.86	$126,881,588	0.54	177	0.63

Ratings
Reward — B
Risk — C-
Recent Upgrade/Downgrade — Down

Fund Information
Fund Type — Exchange Traded Funds
Category — Consumer Goods & Svcs
Sub-Category — Consumer Cyclical
Prospectus Objective — Unaligned
Inception Date — Jun-05
Open to New Investments — Y

Prices
Price (as of 12/31/2018) — 39.80
52-Week High — 48.32
52-Week Low — 38.07

Total Returns (%)

3-Month	6-Month	1-Year	3-Year	5-Year
-14.04	-13.82	-8.93	10.77	20.78

3-Year Standard Deviation — 13
Effective Duration —

Valuation
Premium/Discount (1-Year Average) — 0.15

Company Information
Provider — Invesco
Manager/Tenure — Peter Hubbard (11), Michael Jeanette (10), Tony Seisser (4), 1 other
Website — http://www.invesco.com/us
Address — Invesco 11 Greenway Plaza, Ste. 2500 Houston TX 77046 United States
Phone Number — 800-659-1005

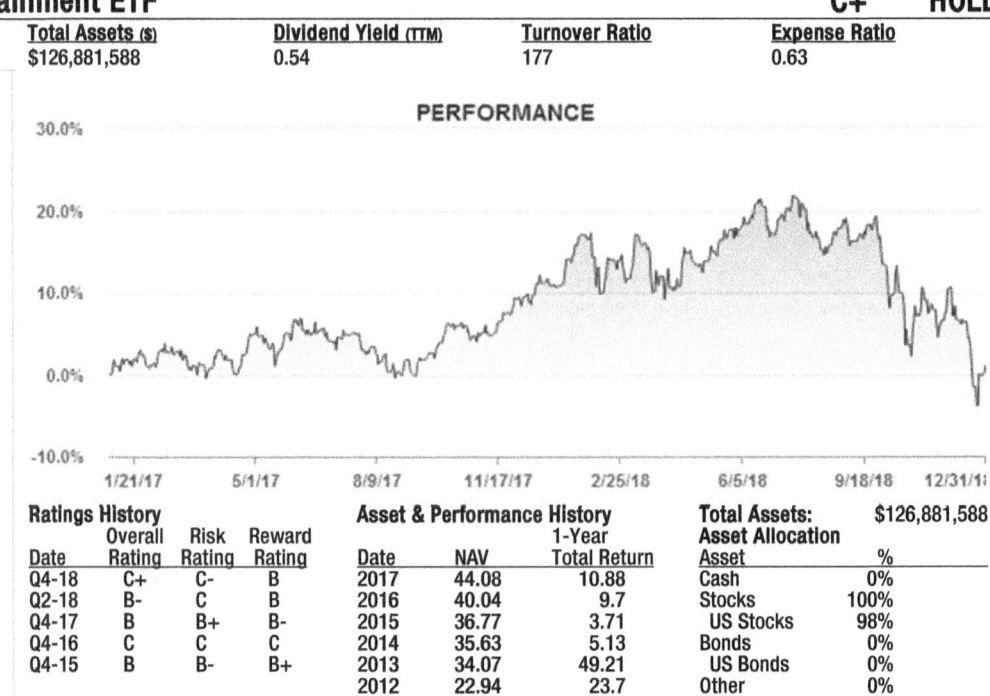

Ratings History

Date	Overall Rating	Risk Rating	Reward Rating
Q4-18	C+	C-	B
Q2-18	B-	C	B
Q4-17	B	B+	B-
Q4-16	C	C	C
Q4-15	B	B-	B+

Asset & Performance History

Date	NAV	1-Year Total Return
2017	44.08	10.88
2016	40.04	9.7
2015	36.77	3.71
2014	35.63	5.13
2013	34.07	49.21
2012	22.94	23.7

Total Assets: $126,881,588

Asset Allocation

Asset	%
Cash	0%
Stocks	100%
US Stocks	98%
Bonds	0%
US Bonds	0%
Other	0%

Services Offered:

Investment Strategy: The investment seeks to track the investment results (before fees and expenses) of the Dynamic Leisure & Entertainment IntellidexSM Index. The fund generally will invest at least 90% of its total assets in common stocks of leisure companies and entertainment companies that comprise the underlying intellidex. The underlying intellidex was composed of common stocks of 30 U.S. leisure and entertainment companies. These companies are engaged principally in the design, production or distribution of goods or services in the leisure and entertainment industries. The fund is non-diversified. **Top Holdings:** United Continental Holdings Inc Yum Brands Inc Walt Disney Co Delta Air Lines Inc Hilton Worldwide Holdings Inc

---

VelocityShares 3x Long Gold ETN Linked to the S&P GSCI® Gold Index ER | B BUY

Ticker	Traded On	NAV	Total Assets ($)	Dividend Yield (TTM)	Turnover Ratio	Expense Ratio
UGLD	NAS CM	94.74	$126,825,558	0		1.35

Ratings
Reward — A-
Risk — D+
Recent Upgrade/Downgrade — Up

Fund Information
Fund Type — Exchange Traded Funds
Category — Trading Tools
Sub-Category — Trading--Leveraged Commodities
Prospectus Objective — Prec Metals
Inception Date — Oct-11
Open to New Investments — Y

Prices
Price (as of 12/31/2018) — 95.41
52-Week High — 95.41
52-Week Low — 7.59

Total Returns (%)

3-Month	6-Month	1-Year	3-Year	5-Year
21.65	942.92	742.64	1,185.54	640.19

3-Year Standard Deviation — 38.75
Effective Duration —

Valuation
Premium/Discount (1-Year Average) — 0.04

Company Information
Provider — Credit Suisse AG
Manager/Tenure — Management Team (7)
Website —
Address — Kilmore House Park Lane Dublin Ireland
Phone Number —

Ratings History

Date	Overall Rating	Risk Rating	Reward Rating
Q4-18	B	D+	A-
Q2-18	D+	D+	D+
Q4-17	D+	D	C-
Q4-16	D	D	D+
Q4-15	E+	D-	E+

Asset & Performance History

Date	NAV	1-Year Total Return
2017	11.24	28.67
2016	8.36	15.48
2015	7.37	-34.6
2014	11.27	-11.95
2013	12.8	-69.52
2012	42	8.58

Total Assets: $126,825,558

Asset Allocation

Asset	%
Cash	%
Stocks	%
US Stocks	%
Bonds	%
US Bonds	%
Other	%

Services Offered:

Investment Strategy: The investment seeks to replicate, net of expenses, three times the S&P GSCI Gold index ER. The index comprises futures contracts on a single commodity. The fluctuations in the values of it are intended generally to correlate with changes in the price of gold in global markets. **Top Holdings:**

Invesco DWA Technology Momentum ETF   C   HOLD

Ticker	Traded On	NAV		Total Assets ($)	Dividend Yield (TTM)	Turnover Ratio	Expense Ratio
PTF	NAS CM	52.94		$124,959,358	0.07	107	0.6

Ratings
Reward	C
Risk	C-
Recent Upgrade/Downgrade	Down

Fund Information
Fund Type	Exchange Traded Funds
Category	Technology Sector Equity
Sub-Category	Technology
Prospectus Objective	Technology
Inception Date	Oct-06
Open to New Investments	Y

Prices
Price (as of 12/31/2018)	52.67
52-Week High	68.61
52-Week Low	48.33

Total Returns (%)
3-Month	6-Month	1-Year	3-Year	5-Year
-18.56	-12.96	0.98	33.87	50.94

3-Year Standard Deviation	18.1
Effective Duration	

Valuation
Premium/Discount (1-Year Average)	0.09

Company Information
Provider	Invesco
Manager/Tenure	Peter Hubbard (11), Michael Jeanette (10), Tony Seisser (4), 1 other
Website	http://www.invesco.com/us
Address	Invesco 11 Greenway Plaza, Ste. 2500 Houston TX 77046 United States
Phone Number	800-659-1005

PERFORMANCE

Ratings History
Date	Overall Rating	Risk Rating	Reward Rating
Q4-18	C	C-	C
Q2-18	C+	C-	B
Q4-17	B+	B	A
Q4-16	C-	C-	C-
Q4-15	B-	C+	B-

Asset & Performance History
Date	NAV	1-Year Total Return
2017	52.46	31.14
2016	40.02	1.09
2015	39.69	3.38
2014	38.39	9.06
2013	35.44	34.62
2012	26.37	15.02

Total Assets: $124,959,358

Asset Allocation
Asset	%
Cash	0%
Stocks	100%
US Stocks	100%
Bonds	0%
US Bonds	0%
Other	0%

Services Offered:

Investment Strategy: The investment seeks to track the investment results (before fees and expenses) of the Dorsey Wright® Technology Technical Leaders Index (the "underlying index"). The fund generally will invest at least 90% of its total assets in the securities that comprise the underlying index. The underlying index is composed of at least 30 securities of companies in the technology sector that have powerful relative strength or "momentum" characteristics. **Top Holdings:** Amphenol Corp Class A Apple Inc Paycom Software Inc Monolithic Power Systems Inc Twilio Inc A

ProShares Short High Yield   D+   SELL

Ticker	Traded On	NAV		Total Assets ($)	Dividend Yield (TTM)	Turnover Ratio	Expense Ratio
SJB	NYSE Arca	23.53		$124,767,984	0.42		0.95

Ratings
Reward	D
Risk	D+
Recent Upgrade/Downgrade	

Fund Information
Fund Type	Exchange Traded Funds
Category	Trading Tools
Sub-Category	Trading--Inverse Debt
Prospectus Objective	Corp Bond-High Yld
Inception Date	Mar-11
Open to New Investments	Y

Prices
Price (as of 12/31/2018)	23.52
52-Week High	24.12
52-Week Low	22.48

Total Returns (%)
3-Month	6-Month	1-Year	3-Year	5-Year
5.08	2.06	2.47	-17.27	-19.43

3-Year Standard Deviation	4.04
Effective Duration	

Valuation
Premium/Discount (1-Year Average)	-0.02

Company Information
Provider	ProShares
Manager/Tenure	Jeffrey Ploshnick (7), Benjamin McAbee (2)
Website	http://www.proshares.com
Address	ProShares 7501 Wisconsin Avenue, Suite 1000 Bethesda MD 20814 United States
Phone Number	866-776-5125

PERFORMANCE

Ratings History
Date	Overall Rating	Risk Rating	Reward Rating
Q4-18	D+	D+	D
Q2-18	D+	D+	D
Q4-17	D	D+	D
Q4-16	D+	D	D
Q4-15	D+	D+	D

Asset & Performance History
Date	NAV	1-Year Total Return
2017	23.13	-6.28
2016	24.68	-13.85
2015	28.65	2.24
2014	28.02	-4.75
2013	29.42	-8.57
2012	32.18	-13.26

Total Assets: $124,767,984

Asset Allocation
Asset	%
Cash	160%
Stocks	0%
US Stocks	0%
Bonds	0%
US Bonds	0%
Other	-60%

Services Offered:

Investment Strategy: The investment seeks daily investment results that correspond to the inverse (-1x) of the daily performance of the Markit iBoxx $ Liquid High Yield Index. The fund invests in financial instruments that ProShare Advisors believes, in combination, should produce daily returns consistent with the fund's investment objective. The index is a market-value weighted index designed to provide a balanced representation of U.S. dollar denominated high yield corporate bonds for sale within the US by means of including the most liquid high yield corporate bonds available as determined by a set of transparent and objective index rules. The fund is non-diversified. **Top Holdings:** Markit Iboxx $ Liquid High Yield Index (Hyg) Swap Goldman Sachs Internation Markit Iboxx $ Liquid High Yield Index (Hyg) Swap Citibank Na United States Treasury Bills United States Treasury Bills United States Treasury Bills

Invesco KBW Regional Banking ETF   C-   HOLD

Ticker	Traded On	NAV	Total Assets ($)	Dividend Yield (TTM)	Turnover Ratio	Expense Ratio
KBWR	NAS CM	44.89	$124,715,418	2.06		0.35

Ratings
Reward	C
Risk	C-
Recent Upgrade/Downgrade	Down

Fund Information
Fund Type	Exchange Traded Funds
Category	Financials Sector Equity
Sub-Category	Financial
Prospectus Objective	Financial
Inception Date	Nov-11
Open to New Investments	

Prices
Price (as of 12/31/2018)	44.80
52-Week High	61.82
52-Week Low	42.37

Total Returns (%)
3-Month	6-Month	1-Year	3-Year	5-Year
-17.84	-21.37	-17.77	15.44	24.31

3-Year Standard Deviation	20.21
Effective Duration	

Valuation
Premium/Discount (1-Year Average)	0.27

Company Information
Provider	Invesco
Manager/Tenure	Peter Hubbard (7), Michael Jeanette (7), Tony Seisser (4), 1 other
Website	http://www.invesco.com/us
Address	Invesco 11 Greenway Plaza, Ste. 2500 Houston TX 77046 United States
Phone Number	800-659-1005

PERFORMANCE

Ratings History
Date	Overall Rating	Risk Rating	Reward Rating
Q4-18	C-	C-	C
Q2-18	C+	C	B-
Q4-17	B	C+	A-
Q4-16	C	C-	C+
Q4-15	B-	C	B

Asset & Performance History
Date	NAV	1-Year Total Return
2017	55.76	1.36
2016	55.91	38.5
2015	41.11	5.52
2014	39.71	2.04
2013	39.63	46.31
2012	27.55	12.91

Total Assets: $124,715,418

Asset Allocation
Asset	%
Cash	0%
Stocks	100%
US Stocks	97%
Bonds	0%
US Bonds	0%
Other	0%

Services Offered:

Investment Strategy: The investment seeks to track the investment results (before fees and expenses) of the KBW Nasdaq Regional Banking Index (the "underlying index"). The fund generally will invest at least 90% of its total assets in securities of publicly traded mid-capitalization companies that do business as regional banks and thrifts listed on U.S. stock markets and that comprise the underlying index. The index provider compile, maintain and calculate the underlying index, which is a modified-market capitalization-weighted index comprised of securities of 50 mid-cap banking companies that are publicly listed in the United States. **Top Holdings:** East West Bancorp Inc   Commerce Bancshares Inc   Signature Bank   Cullen/Frost Bankers Inc   PacWest Bancorp

---

Sprott Gold Miners ETF   C   HOLD

Ticker	Traded On	NAV	Total Assets ($)	Dividend Yield (TTM)	Turnover Ratio	Expense Ratio
SGDM	NYSE Arca	17.53	$123,575,575	0.78	101	0.57

Ratings
Reward	C
Risk	D
Recent Upgrade/Downgrade	

Fund Information
Fund Type	Exchange Traded Funds
Category	Prec Metals
Sub-Category	Equity Precious Metals
Prospectus Objective	Prec Metals
Inception Date	Jul-14
Open to New Investments	Y

Prices
Price (as of 12/31/2018)	17.48
52-Week High	22.42
52-Week Low	14.90

Total Returns (%)
3-Month	6-Month	1-Year	3-Year	5-Year
12.86	-8.02	-14.99	39.31	

3-Year Standard Deviation	38.74
Effective Duration	

Valuation
Premium/Discount (1-Year Average)	-0.03

Company Information
Provider	ALPS
Manager/Tenure	Ryan Mischker (3), Andrew Hicks (2)
Website	http://www.alpsfunds.com
Address	ALPS 1290 Broadway, Suite 1100 Denver CO 80203 United States
Phone Number	866-759-5679

PERFORMANCE

Ratings History
Date	Overall Rating	Risk Rating	Reward Rating
Q4-18	C	D	C
Q2-18	C	D+	C+
Q4-17	D+	D	C-
Q4-16	C-	D	C
Q4-15	D	C-	C

Asset & Performance History
Date	NAV	1-Year Total Return
2017	20.73	10.98
2016	18.78	47.65
2015	12.72	-26.41
2014	17.54	
2013		
2012		

Total Assets: $123,575,575

Asset Allocation
Asset	%
Cash	0%
Stocks	100%
US Stocks	13%
Bonds	0%
US Bonds	0%
Other	0%

Services Offered:

Investment Strategy: The investment seeks results that correspond (before fees and expenses) generally to the performance of the Sprott Zacks Gold Miners Index. The index aims to track the performance of gold and silver mining companies whose stocks are traded on major U.S. exchanges. In addition to common stock or American Depository Receipts of gold mining companies, the index may include common stock or ADRs of silver mining companies. The fund will normally invest at least 90% of its net assets in securities that comprise the index. The fund is non-diversified. **Top Holdings:** Royal Gold Inc   Agnico Eagle Mines Ltd   Goldcorp Inc   Wheaton Precious Metals Corp   Kirkland Lake Gold Ltd

iPath® MSCI India Index(SM) ETN   D+   SELL

Ticker	Traded On	NAV	Total Assets ($)	Dividend Yield (TTM)	Turnover Ratio	Expense Ratio
INPTF	OTC BB		$122,190,159	0	0	0.89

Ratings
Reward	D+
Risk	D+
Recent Upgrade/Downgrade	Down

Fund Information
Fund Type	Exchange Traded Funds
Category	India Equity
Sub-Category	India Equity
Prospectus Objective	Foreign Stock
Inception Date	Dec-06
Open to New Investments	Y

Prices
Price (as of 12/31/2018)	80.92
52-Week High	93.40
52-Week Low	69.81

Total Returns (%)
3-Month	6-Month	1-Year	3-Year	5-Year
1.86	0.30	-9.04	25.09	43.97

3-Year Standard Deviation	19.86
Effective Duration	

Valuation
Premium/Discount (1-Year Average)	-1.32

Company Information
Provider	Milleis Investissements Funds
Manager/Tenure	No Manager (11)
Website	
Address	2-4, rue Eugène Ruppert L-2453 Luxembourg Luxembourg L-2453 Luxembourg
Phone Number	

PERFORMANCE

Ratings History
Date	Overall Rating	Risk Rating	Reward Rating
Q4-18	D+	D+	D+
Q2-18	C-	D+	C-
Q4-17	B-	C	B
Q4-16	C-	D+	C
Q4-15	C	C-	C

Asset & Performance History
Date	NAV	1-Year Total Return
2017	88.82	41.43
2016	62.96	-2.78
2015	64.58	-7.45
2014	69.78	24.36
2013	56.11	-4.93
2012	59.02	26.38

Total Assets: $122,190,159
Asset Allocation
Asset	%
Cash	%
Stocks	%
US Stocks	%
Bonds	%
US Bonds	%
Other	%

Services Offered:

Investment Strategy: The investment seeks to track the performance, before fees and expenses, of the MSCI India Total Return Index.
The index is a free float-adjusted market capitalization index that is designed to measure the market performance of Indian securities. It is currently comprised of the top 68 companies by market capitalization listed on the Nation Stock Exchange of India. **Top Holdings:**

---

iShares iBonds Dec 2023 Term Muni Bond ETF   D+   SELL

Ticker	Traded On	NAV	Total Assets ($)	Dividend Yield (TTM)	Turnover Ratio	Expense Ratio
IBML	BATS	25.05	$121,838,450	1.58	0	0.18

Ratings
Reward	D
Risk	C-
Recent Upgrade/Downgrade	

Fund Information
Fund Type	Exchange Traded Funds
Category	US Muni Fixed Inc
Sub-Category	Muni National Interm
Prospectus Objective	Muni Bond - Natl
Inception Date	Apr-17
Open to New Investments	Y

Prices
Price (as of 12/31/2018)	25.11
52-Week High	25.27
52-Week Low	24.60

Total Returns (%)
3-Month	6-Month	1-Year	3-Year	5-Year
1.64	1.34	1.20		

3-Year Standard Deviation	
Effective Duration	4.15

Valuation
Premium/Discount (1-Year Average)	0.16

Company Information
Provider	iShares
Manager/Tenure	James Mauro (1), Scott Radell (1)
Website	http://www.ishares.com
Address	iShares 400 Howard Street San Francisco CA 94105 United States
Phone Number	800-474-2737

PERFORMANCE

Ratings History
Date	Overall Rating	Risk Rating	Reward Rating
Q4-18	D+	C-	D
Q2-18	D+	C-	D+
Q4-17	U		
Q4-16			
Q4-15			

Asset & Performance History
Date	NAV	1-Year Total Return
2017	25.17	
2016		
2015		
2014		
2013		
2012		

Total Assets: $121,838,450
Asset Allocation
Asset	%
Cash	0%
Stocks	0%
US Stocks	0%
Bonds	100%
US Bonds	100%
Other	0%

Services Offered:

Investment Strategy: The investment seeks to track the investment results of the S&P AMT-Free Municipal Series Dec 2023 IndexTM composed of investment-grade U.S. municipal bonds maturing after December 31, 2022 and before December 2, 2023. The fund generally will invest at least 90% of its assets in the component securities of the index, and may invest up to 10% of its assets in certain futures, options and swap contracts, cash and cash equivalents. The index includes municipal bonds primarily from issuers that are state or local governments or agencies such that the interest on the bonds is exempt from U.S. federal income taxes. The fund is non-diversified. **Top Holdings:** WISCONSIN ST 5% CALIFORNIA ST 5% METROPOLITAN GOVT NASHVILLE & DAVIDSON CNTY TENN 5% VIRGINIA COMWLTH TRANSN BRD 5% VIRGINIA COLLEGE BLDG AUTH VA 5%

ProShares UltraShort Bloomberg Crude Oil   D   SELL

Ticker	Traded On	NAV	Total Assets ($)	Dividend Yield (TTM)	Turnover Ratio	Expense Ratio
SCO	NYSE Arca		$121,483,335	0	0	0.95

Ratings
Reward   D-
Risk   D
Recent Upgrade/Downgrade

Fund Information
Fund Type   Exchange Traded Funds
Category   Trading Tools
Sub-Category   Trading--Inverse Commodities
Prospectus Objective   Natl Res
Inception Date   Nov-08
Open to New Investments   Y

Prices
Price (as of 12/31/2018)   29.28
52-Week High   33.13
52-Week Low   12.52

Total Returns (%)

3-Month	6-Month	1-Year	3-Year	5-Year
133.38	96.03	23.16	-55.04	88.75

3-Year Standard Deviation   60.1
Effective Duration

Valuation
Premium/Discount (1-Year Average)   0.17

Company Information
Provider   ProShares
Manager/Tenure   Management Team (10)
Website   http://www.proshares.com
Address   ProShares 7501 Wisconsin Avenue,
                      Suite 1000 Bethesda MD 20814
                      United States
Phone Number   866-776-5125

PERFORMANCE

Ratings History

Date	Overall Rating	Risk Rating	Reward Rating
Q4-18	D	D	D-
Q2-18	D	D	E+
Q4-17	D	D	D+
Q4-16	C	D+	C-
Q4-15	B-	D+	B

Asset & Performance History

Date	NAV	1-Year Total Return
2017	24.31	-23.29
2016	31.7	-52.4
2015	66.6	70.82
2014	38.99	145.77
2013	15.86	-21.27
2012	20.15	3.83

Total Assets: $121,483,335
Asset Allocation

Asset	%
Cash	300%
Stocks	0%
US Stocks	0%
Bonds	0%
US Bonds	0%
Other	-200%

Services Offered:

Investment Strategy: The investment seeks to provide daily investment results (before fees and expenses) that correspond to twice (200%) the inverse of the daily performance of the Bloomberg WTI Crude Oil SubindexSM. The "UltraShort" funds seek results for a single day that match (before fees and expenses) two times the inverse (-2x) of the daily performance of a benchmark. It does not seek to achieve their stated objectives over a period greater than a single day. The Bloomberg WTI Crude Oil SubindexSM is designed to track crude oil futures prices.
Top Holdings: Bloomberg Wti Crude Oil Subindex Swap - Citibank   Wti Crude Oil Future 12/19/2018 (Clf9) Bloomberg Wti Crude Oil Subindex Swap - Ubs Ag   Bloomberg Wti Crude Oil Subindex Swap - Rbc Bloomberg Wti Crude Oil Subindex Swap - Gs

Cambria Shareholder Yield ETF   C-   HOLD

Ticker	Traded On	NAV	Total Assets ($)	Dividend Yield (TTM)	Turnover Ratio	Expense Ratio
SYLD	BATS	32.48	$120,325,271	2.12	16	0.59

Ratings
Reward   C
Risk   C-
Recent Upgrade/Downgrade   Down

Fund Information
Fund Type   Exchange Traded Funds
Category   US Equity Mid Cap
Sub-Category   Mid-Cap Value
Prospectus Objective   Growth & Inc
Inception Date   May-13
Open to New Investments   Y

Prices
Price (as of 12/31/2018)   32.47
52-Week High   40.83
52-Week Low   30.75

Total Returns (%)

3-Month	6-Month	1-Year	3-Year	5-Year
-17.12	-13.11	-13.36	19.56	31.15

3-Year Standard Deviation   11.68
Effective Duration

Valuation
Premium/Discount (1-Year Average)   0.12

Company Information
Provider   CAMBRIA ETF TRUST
Manager/Tenure   Mebane T. Faber (5)
Website   http://www.cambriafunds.com
Address   CAMBRIA ETF TRUST 2711 Centreville
                      Road Suite 400 Wilmington, DE 19808
                      Wilmington DE 19808 United States
Phone Number   310-683-5500

PERFORMANCE

Ratings History

Date	Overall Rating	Risk Rating	Reward Rating
Q4-18	C-	C-	C
Q2-18	C	C-	C
Q4-17	B	B+	B
Q4-16	C	D+	B-
Q4-15	C	C	C

Asset & Performance History

Date	NAV	1-Year Total Return
2017	38.33	19.73
2016	32.53	15.25
2015	28.82	-1.25
2014	31.2	11.08
2013	29.32	
2012		

Total Assets: $120,325,271
Asset Allocation

Asset	%
Cash	1%
Stocks	99%
US Stocks	98%
Bonds	0%
US Bonds	0%
Other	0%

Services Offered:

Investment Strategy: The investment seeks investment results that correspond (before fees and expenses) generally to the price and yield performance of the Cambria Shareholder Yield Index (the "underlying index"). Under normal market conditions, the fund will invest at least 80% of its total assets in the components of the underlying index. The underlying index is comprised of equity securities issued by U.S.-based issuers. The adviser considers an issuer to be U.S.-based if it is domiciled or incorporated or has substantial business activity in the United States.
Top Holdings: United Continental Holdings Inc   O'Reilly Automotive Inc   Texas Instruments Inc   FTI Consulting Inc   The Home Depot Inc

Fidelity® Quality Factor ETF   C   HOLD

Ticker	Traded On	NAV		Total Assets ($)	Dividend Yield (TTM)	Turnover Ratio	Expense Ratio
FQAL	NYSE Arca	30.05		$120,253,927	1.55		0.29

Ratings
Reward	C
Risk	C-
Recent Upgrade/Downgrade	Up

Fund Information
Fund Type	Exchange Traded Funds
Category	US Equity Large Cap Blend
Sub-Category	Large Growth
Prospectus Objective	Growth & Inc
Inception Date	Sep-16
Open to New Investments	Y

Prices
Price (as of 12/31/2018)	29.92
52-Week High	34.96
52-Week Low	28.26

Total Returns (%)
3-Month	6-Month	1-Year	3-Year	5-Year
-13.10	-6.53	-3.72		

3-Year Standard Deviation	
Effective Duration	

Valuation
Premium/Discount (1-Year Average)	0.08

Company Information
Provider	Fidelity Investments
Manager/Tenure	Louis Bottari (2), Deane Gyllenhaal (2), Peter Matthew (2), 2 others
Website	http://www.institutional.fidelity.com
Address	Fidelity Investments 82 Devonshire Street Boston MA 2109 United States
Phone Number	617-563-7000

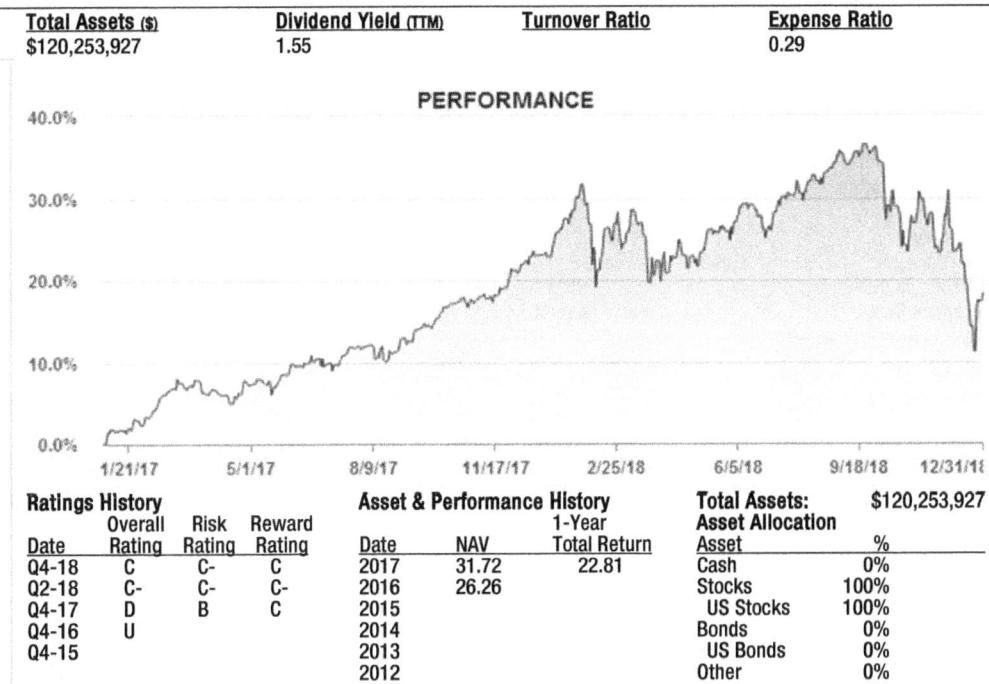

PERFORMANCE

Ratings History
Date	Overall Rating	Risk Rating	Reward Rating
Q4-18	C	C-	C
Q2-18	C-	C-	C-
Q4-17	D	B	C
Q4-16	U		
Q4-15			

Asset & Performance History
Date	NAV	1-Year Total Return
2017	31.72	22.81
2016	26.26	
2015		
2014		
2013		
2012		

Total Assets: $120,253,927
Asset Allocation
Asset	%
Cash	0%
Stocks	100%
US Stocks	100%
Bonds	0%
US Bonds	0%
Other	0%

Services Offered:

Investment Strategy: The investment seeks to provide investment returns that correspond, before fees and expenses, generally to the performance of the Fidelity U.S. Quality Factor Index?. The fund normally invests at least 80% of assets in securities included in the Fidelity U.S. Quality Factor Index?, which is designed to reflect the performance of stocks of large and mid-capitalization U.S. companies with a higher quality profile than the broader market. It may lend securities to earn income for the fund. **Top Holdings:** Microsoft Corp Apple Inc Alphabet Inc A Johnson & Johnson Pfizer Inc

---

ProShares UltraPro Russell2000   C-   HOLD

Ticker	Traded On	NAV		Total Assets ($)	Dividend Yield (TTM)	Turnover Ratio	Expense Ratio
URTY	NYSE Arca	49.75		$120,215,956	0		0.95

Ratings
Reward	C
Risk	D+
Recent Upgrade/Downgrade	Down

Fund Information
Fund Type	Exchange Traded Funds
Category	Trading Tools
Sub-Category	Trading--Leveraged Equity
Prospectus Objective	Small Company
Inception Date	Feb-10
Open to New Investments	Y

Prices
Price (as of 12/31/2018)	49.58
52-Week High	113.67
52-Week Low	41.91

Total Returns (%)
3-Month	6-Month	1-Year	3-Year	5-Year
-50.51	-49.52	-39.52	34.17	12.51

3-Year Standard Deviation	44.08
Effective Duration	

Valuation
Premium/Discount (1-Year Average)	-0.02

Company Information
Provider	ProShares
Manager/Tenure	Michael Neches (5), Devin Sullivan (0)
Website	http://www.proshares.com
Address	ProShares 7501 Wisconsin Avenue, Suite 1000 Bethesda MD 20814 United States
Phone Number	866-776-5125

PERFORMANCE

Ratings History
Date	Overall Rating	Risk Rating	Reward Rating
Q4-18	C-	D+	C
Q2-18	C+	C-	B
Q4-17	B	C-	A+
Q4-16	C	D+	C+
Q4-15	C	C	C

Asset & Performance History
Date	NAV	1-Year Total Return
2017	82.5	39.75
2016	59.03	58.74
2015	37.2	-20.59
2014	46.84	5.6
2013	44.36	148.2
2012	17.87	43.91

Total Assets: $120,215,956
Asset Allocation
Asset	%
Cash	-200%
Stocks	300%
US Stocks	297%
Bonds	0%
US Bonds	0%
Other	0%

Services Offered:

Investment Strategy: The investment seeks daily investment results that correspond to three times (3x) the daily performance of the Russell 2000® Index. The fund invests in financial instruments that ProShare Advisors believes, in combination, should produce daily returns consistent with the fund's investment objective. The index is a measure of small-cap U.S. stock market performance. The fund is non-diversified. **Top Holdings:** Russell 2000 Index Swap Deutsche Bank Ag Russell 2000 Index Swap Goldman Sachs International Russell 2000 Index Swap Citibank, N.A. Russell 2000 Index Swap Bank Of America, Na Russell 2000 Index Swap Credit Suisse International

ProShares Ultra MidCap400   C   HOLD

Ticker	Traded On	NAV	Total Assets ($)	Dividend Yield (TTM)	Turnover Ratio	Expense Ratio
MVV	NYSE Arca	30.30	$120,107,102	0.42		0.95

Ratings
Reward	C
Risk	C
Recent Upgrade/Downgrade	

Fund Information
Fund Type	Exchange Traded Funds
Category	Trading Tools
Sub-Category	Trading--Leveraged Equity
Prospectus Objective	Growth
Inception Date	Jun-06
Open to New Investments	Y

Prices
Price (as of 12/31/2018)	30.40
52-Week High	46.96
52-Week Low	27.06

Total Returns (%)
3-Month	6-Month	1-Year	3-Year	5-Year
-32.12	-28.75	-25.65	35.91	45.24

3-Year Standard Deviation	23.8
Effective Duration	

Valuation
Premium/Discount (1-Year Average)	0.06

Company Information
Provider	ProShares
Manager/Tenure	Michael Neches (5), Devin Sullivan (0)
Website	http://www.proshares.com
Address	ProShares 7501 Wisconsin Avenue, Suite 1000 Bethesda MD 20814 United States
Phone Number	866-776-5125

PERFORMANCE

Ratings History

Date	Overall Rating	Risk Rating	Reward Rating
Q4-18	C	C	C
Q2-18	C	C-	C+
Q4-17	B+	C+	A+
Q4-16	C	C-	C
Q4-15	C	C+	C

Asset & Performance History

Date	NAV	1-Year Total Return
2017	40.97	30.7
2016	31.42	39.86
2015	22.57	-7.81
2014	24.53	15.91
2013	21.16	71.39
2012	12.35	33.58

Total Assets: $120,107,102

Asset Allocation

Asset	%
Cash	-100%
Stocks	200%
US Stocks	200%
Bonds	0%
US Bonds	0%
Other	0%

Services Offered:

Investment Strategy: The investment seeks daily investment results, before fees and expenses, that correspond to two times (2x) the daily performance of the S&P MidCap 400®. The fund invests in financial instruments that ProShare Advisors believes, in combination, should produce daily returns consistent with the fund's investment objective. The index is a float-adjusted, market capitalization-weighted index of 400 U.S. operating companies and real estate investment trusts selected through a process that assesses criteria such as liquidity, price, market capitalization and financial viability. The fund is non-diversified. **Top Holdings:** Spdr S&P Midcap 400 (Mdy) Swap Goldman Sachs International   S&P Midcap 400 Index Swap Societe Generale   S&P Midcap 400 Index Swap Bnp Paribas   S&P Midcap 400 Index Swap Citibank Na   S&P Midcap 400 Index Swap Goldman Sachs International

---

Fidelity® Limited Term Bond ETF   C-   HOLD

Ticker	Traded On	NAV	Total Assets ($)	Dividend Yield (TTM)	Turnover Ratio	Expense Ratio
FLTB	NYSE Arca	49.29	$119,983,879	2.49	113	0.36

Ratings
Reward	C-
Risk	C-
Recent Upgrade/Downgrade	

Fund Information
Fund Type	Exchange Traded Funds
Category	US Fixed Income
Sub-Category	Short-Term Bond
Prospectus Objective	Income
Inception Date	Oct-14
Open to New Investments	Y

Prices
Price (as of 12/31/2018)	49.39
52-Week High	50.11
52-Week Low	49.01

Total Returns (%)
3-Month	6-Month	1-Year	3-Year	5-Year
0.80	1.38	0.87	5.09	

3-Year Standard Deviation	1.35
Effective Duration	2.57

Valuation
Premium/Discount (1-Year Average)	0.04

Company Information
Provider	Fidelity Investments
Manager/Tenure	Robert Galusza (4), David Prothro (4)
Website	http://www.institutional.fidelity.com
Address	Fidelity Investments 82 Devonshire Street Boston MA 2109 United States
Phone Number	617-563-7000

PERFORMANCE

Ratings History

Date	Overall Rating	Risk Rating	Reward Rating
Q4-18	C-	C-	C-
Q2-18	C-	C-	C-
Q4-17	C+	A-	C
Q4-16	C-	C-	D+
Q4-15	U		

Asset & Performance History

Date	NAV	1-Year Total Return
2017	50.1	1.84
2016	50.07	2.28
2015	49.72	1.26
2014	49.9	
2013		
2012		

Total Assets: $119,983,879

Asset Allocation

Asset	%
Cash	1%
Stocks	0%
US Stocks	0%
Bonds	98%
US Bonds	88%
Other	0%

Services Offered:

Investment Strategy: The investment seeks to provide a high rate of income. The fund normally invests at least 80% of assets in investment-grade debt securities (those of medium and high quality) of all types and repurchase agreements for those securities. It is managed to have similar overall interest rate risk to the Fidelity Limited Term Composite Index. Normally, the fund maintains a dollar-weighted average maturity between two and five years. **Top Holdings:** United States Treasury Notes 1.12%   United States Treasury Notes 2.38%   United States Treasury Notes 1.62%   United States Treasury Notes 1.88%   JPMorgan Chase & Co. 2.55%

Barclays ETN+ Shiller Capet ETN   C-   HOLD

Ticker	Traded On	NAV
CAPE	NYSE Arca	

Total Assets ($)	Dividend Yield (TTM)	Turnover Ratio	Expense Ratio
$119,652,312	0		0.45

Ratings
Reward	C
Risk	D+
Recent Upgrade/Downgrade	Down

Fund Information
Fund Type	Exchange Traded Funds
Category	US Equity Large Cap Value
Sub-Category	Large Value
Prospectus Objective	Growth
Inception Date	Oct-12
Open to New Investments	Y

Prices
Price (as of 12/31/2018)	112.41
52-Week High	133.10
52-Week Low	106.83

Total Returns (%)
3-Month	6-Month	1-Year	3-Year	5-Year
-15.75	-6.93	-3.40	38.61	66.95

3-Year Standard Deviation	10.32
Effective Duration	

Valuation
Premium/Discount (1-Year Average)	0.23

Company Information
Provider	Milleis Investissements Funds
Manager/Tenure	No Manager (6)
Website	
Address	2-4, rue Eugène Ruppert L-2453 Luxembourg Luxembourg L-2453 Luxembourg
Phone Number	

PERFORMANCE

x-axis: 1/14/17, 4/24/17, 8/2/17, 11/10/17, 2/18/18, 5/29/18, 9/14/18, 12/30/18
y-axis: 0.0%, 10.0%, 20.0%, 30.0%, 40.0%, 50.0%

Ratings History
Date	Overall Rating	Risk Rating	Reward Rating
Q4-18	C-	D+	C
Q2-18	C	D+	C
Q4-17	B	B+	B
Q4-16	C	D+	C
Q4-15	C	D+	C

Asset & Performance History
Date	NAV	1-Year Total Return
2017	116.2	20.7
2016	96.12	18.29
2015	80.97	4.7
2014	77.33	15.02
2013	67.23	32.88
2012	50.59	

Total Assets: $119,652,312
Asset Allocation
Asset	%
Cash	%
Stocks	%
US Stocks	%
Bonds	%
US Bonds	%
Other	%

Services Offered:

Investment Strategy: The investment seeks to replicate, net of expenses, the Shiller Barclays CAPETM US Core Sector Index.
The index seeks to provide a notional long exposure to the top four relatively undervalued U.S. equity sectors that also exhibit relatively strong price momentum. It incorporates the CAPE (Cyclically Adjusted Price Earnings) ratio to assess equity market valuations of nine sectors on a monthly basis and to identify the relatively undervalued sectors represented in the S&P 500®. **Top Holdings:**

---

iShares Edge U.S. Fixed Income Balanced Risk ETF   D+   SELL

Ticker	Traded On	NAV
FIBR	BATS	95.45

Total Assets ($)	Dividend Yield (TTM)	Turnover Ratio	Expense Ratio
$119,448,600	3.25	683	0.25

Ratings
Reward	C-
Risk	D+
Recent Upgrade/Downgrade	Down

Fund Information
Fund Type	Exchange Traded Funds
Category	Fixed Income Misc
Sub-Category	Intermediate-Term Bond
Prospectus Objective	Income
Inception Date	Feb-15
Open to New Investments	Y

Prices
Price (as of 12/31/2018)	95.77
52-Week High	100.17
52-Week Low	94.77

Total Returns (%)
3-Month	6-Month	1-Year	3-Year	5-Year
-0.48	0.70	-1.01	8.25	

3-Year Standard Deviation	2.33
Effective Duration	5.30

Valuation
Premium/Discount (1-Year Average)	0.10

Company Information
Provider	iShares
Manager/Tenure	James Mauro (3), Scott Radell (3)
Website	http://www.ishares.com
Address	iShares 400 Howard Street San Francisco CA 94105 United States
Phone Number	800-474-2737

PERFORMANCE

x-axis: 1/21/17, 5/1/17, 8/9/17, 11/17/17, 2/25/18, 6/5/18, 9/18/18, 12/31/18
y-axis: -2.0%, 0.0%, 2.0%, 4.0%, 6.0%

Ratings History
Date	Overall Rating	Risk Rating	Reward Rating
Q4-18	D+	D+	C-
Q2-18	C-	D+	C
Q4-17	C+	B	C
Q4-16	D+	D+	D+
Q4-15	U		

Asset & Performance History
Date	NAV	1-Year Total Return
2017	99.93	3.84
2016	98.91	5.31
2015	96.69	
2014		
2013		
2012		

Total Assets: $119,448,600
Asset Allocation
Asset	%
Cash	-11%
Stocks	0%
US Stocks	0%
Bonds	110%
US Bonds	99%
Other	0%

Services Offered:

Investment Strategy: The investment seeks to track the investment results of the Bloomberg Barclays U.S. Fixed Income Balanced Risk Index. The underlying index measures the performance of the corporate and mortgage portion of the Bloomberg Barclays U.S. Universal Index while targeting an equal allocation between interest rate and credit spread risk. The fund generally will invest at least 90% of its assets in the component securities of the underlying index and in investments that have economic characteristics that are substantially identical to the component securities of the underlying index. It is non-diversified. **Top Holdings:** Federal National Mortgage Association 3.5% Government National Mortgage Association 3.5% Fgold 30yr 2016 Production Gnma2 30yr 2017 Production Hewlett Packard Enterprise Company 3.6%

Invesco Fundamental Investment Grade Corporate Bond ETF   C-   HOLD

Ticker	Traded On	NAV	Total Assets ($)	Dividend Yield (TTM)	Turnover Ratio	Expense Ratio
PFIG	NYSE Arca	24.64	$118,377,633	2.86		0.22

Ratings
Reward   D+
Risk   C-
Recent Upgrade/Downgrade

Fund Information
Fund Type   Exchange Traded Funds
Category   US Fixed Income
Sub-Category   Corporate Bond
Prospectus Objective   Corp Bond - High Quality
Inception Date   Sep-11
Open to New Investments   Y

Prices
Price (as of 12/31/2018)   24.65
52-Week High   25.58
52-Week Low   24.40

Total Returns (%)

3-Month	6-Month	1-Year	3-Year	5-Year
0.75	1.54	-0.59	6.98	12.74

3-Year Standard Deviation   2.54
Effective Duration   4.56

Valuation
Premium/Discount (1-Year Average)   0.15

Company Information
Provider   Invesco
Manager/Tenure   Philip Fang (7), Peter Hubbard (7),
                     Jeffrey W. Kernagis (7), 2 others
Website   http://www.invesco.com/us
Address   Invesco 11 Greenway Plaza, Ste. 2500
                     Houston TX 77046 United States
Phone Number   800-659-1005

PERFORMANCE

Ratings History

Date	Overall Rating	Risk Rating	Reward Rating
Q4-18	C-	C-	D+
Q2-18	C-	C-	C-
Q4-17	B	A	C
Q4-16	C	C-	C
Q4-15	C	D+	C

Asset & Performance History

Date	NAV	1-Year Total Return
2017	25.51	3.46
2016	25.29	4.02
2015	24.94	0.75
2014	25.39	4.6
2013	24.86	-1.06
2012	25.67	6.27

Total Assets: $118,377,633

Asset Allocation

Asset	%
Cash	1%
Stocks	0%
US Stocks	0%
Bonds	99%
US Bonds	97%
Other	0%

Services Offered:

Investment Strategy: The investment seeks to track the investment results (before fees and expenses) of the RAFI® Bonds U.S. Investment Grade 1-10 Index (the "underlying index"). The fund generally will invest at least 80% of its total assets in the component securities that comprise the underlying index. The underlying index is comprised of U.S. dollar-denominated bonds which are SEC-registered securities or Rule 144A securities with registration rights (issued after July 31, 2013) and whose issuers are public companies listed on a major U.S. stock exchange. **Top Holdings:** JPMorgan Chase & Co. 2.95% Wells Fargo & Company 2.62% Exxon Mobil Corporation 2.22% The Boeing Company 4.88% Exxon Mobil Corporation 3.04%

Global X Scientific Beta US ETF   C-   HOLD

Ticker	Traded On	NAV	Total Assets ($)	Dividend Yield (TTM)	Turnover Ratio	Expense Ratio
SCIU	NYSE Arca	27.91	$118,291,301	1.44	28	0.19

Ratings
Reward   C-
Risk   C-
Recent Upgrade/Downgrade   Down

Fund Information
Fund Type   Exchange Traded Funds
Category   US Equity Large Cap Blend
Sub-Category   Large Blend
Prospectus Objective   Growth
Inception Date   May-15
Open to New Investments   Y

Prices
Price (as of 12/31/2018)   27.92
52-Week High   33.43
52-Week Low   27.01

Total Returns (%)

3-Month	6-Month	1-Year	3-Year	5-Year
-13.83	-9.26	-7.35	21.92	

3-Year Standard Deviation   8.71
Effective Duration

Valuation
Premium/Discount (1-Year Average)   0.21

Company Information
Provider   Global X Funds
Manager/Tenure   Chang Kim (3), James Ong (2), Nam
                     To (0)
Website   http://www.globalxfunds.com
Address   Global X Funds 600 Lexington Avenue,
                     20th Floor New York NY 10022 United
                     States
Phone Number   888-493-8631

PERFORMANCE

Ratings History

Date	Overall Rating	Risk Rating	Reward Rating
Q4-18	C-	C-	C-
Q2-18	C	C-	C
Q4-17	B-	B	C+
Q4-16	D+	D+	C-
Q4-15	U		

Asset & Performance History

Date	NAV	1-Year Total Return
2017	30.83	18.81
2016	26.33	10.76
2015	24.08	
2014		
2013		
2012		

Total Assets: $118,291,301

Asset Allocation

Asset	%
Cash	0%
Stocks	100%
US Stocks	99%
Bonds	0%
US Bonds	0%
Other	0%

Services Offered:

Investment Strategy: The investment seeks investment results that correspond generally to the price and yield performance, before fees and expenses, of the Scientific Beta United States Multi-Beta Multi-Strategy Four-Factor Equal Risk Contribution (ERC) Index. The fund invests at least 80% of its total assets in the securities of the underlying index. The underlying index generally comprises approximately 500 or less U.S. listed common stocks selected based on a proprietary methodology developed by EDHEC Risk Institute Asia Ltd. **Top Holdings:** NextEra Energy Inc CME Group Inc Class A Centene Corp Occidental Petroleum Corp Walmart Inc

---

VanEck Vectors CEF Municipal Income ETF   D+   SELL

Ticker	Traded On	NAV	Total Assets ($)	Dividend Yield (TTM)	Turnover Ratio	Expense Ratio
XMPT	BATS	23.89	$118,045,423	5.07	9	1.56

Ratings
Reward   D
Risk   C-
Recent Upgrade/Downgrade

Fund Information
Fund Type	Exchange Traded Funds
Category	US Muni Fixed Inc
Sub-Category	Muni National Long
Prospectus Objective	Muni Bond - Natl
Inception Date	Jul-11
Open to New Investments	Y

Prices
Price (as of 12/31/2018)	23.88
52-Week High	26.84
52-Week Low	23.37

Total Returns (%)
3-Month	6-Month	1-Year	3-Year	5-Year
-1.93	-3.26	-6.31	3.02	31.57

3-Year Standard Deviation   7.76
Effective Duration   8.73

Valuation
Premium/Discount (1-Year Average)   -0.04

Company Information
Provider	VanEck
Manager/Tenure	Hao-Hung (Peter) Liao (7), Guo Hua (Jason) Jin (0)
Website	http://www.vaneck.com
Address	Van Eck Associates Corporation 666 Third Avenue New York NY 10017 United States
Phone Number	800-826-1115

PERFORMANCE

Ratings History
Date	Overall Rating	Risk Rating	Reward Rating
Q4-18	D+	C-	D
Q2-18	D+	C-	D+
Q4-17	C+	B	C
Q4-16	C	C-	C
Q4-15	C-	D+	C

Asset & Performance History
Date	NAV	1-Year Total Return
2017	26.65	8.26
2016	25.83	1.56
2015	26.73	7.7
2014	26.19	18.57
2013	23.37	-12.93
2012	28.42	11.67

Total Assets: $118,045,423
Asset Allocation
Asset	%
Cash	-9%
Stocks	0%
US Stocks	0%
Bonds	111%
US Bonds	110%
Other	-2%

Services Offered:

Investment Strategy: The investment seeks to replicate as closely as possible, before fees and expenses, the price and yield performance of the S-Network Municipal Bond Closed-End Fund IndexSM (the "CEFMX Index"). The fund normally invests at least 80% of its total assets in investments the income from which is exempt from U.S. federal income tax (other than federal alternative minimum tax). It normally invests at least 80% of its total assets in securities of issuers that comprise the fund's benchmark index. The CEFMX Index is comprised of shares of U.S.-listed closed-end funds. **Top Holdings:** Nuveen Quality Muni Income Fund   Nuveen AMT-Free Quality Muni Inc   Nuveen AMT-Free Muni Credit Inc   Nuveen Municipal Credit Income   Nuveen Municipal Value

WisdomTree Japan Hedged SmallCap Equity Fund   C-   HOLD

Ticker	Traded On	NAV	Total Assets ($)	Dividend Yield (TTM)	Turnover Ratio	Expense Ratio
DXJS	NAS CM	37.29	$117,962,374	2.18	30	0.58

Ratings
Reward   D+
Risk   C-
Recent Upgrade/Downgrade   Down

Fund Information
Fund Type	Exchange Traded Funds
Category	Japan Equity
Sub-Category	Japan Stock
Prospectus Objective	Pacific Stock
Inception Date	Jun-13
Open to New Investments	Y

Prices
Price (as of 12/31/2018)	36.85
52-Week High	47.76
52-Week Low	35.05

Total Returns (%)
3-Month	6-Month	1-Year	3-Year	5-Year
-17.40	-13.03	-17.82	13.69	47.69

3-Year Standard Deviation   14.99
Effective Duration

Valuation
Premium/Discount (1-Year Average)   -0.21

Company Information
Provider	WisdomTree
Manager/Tenure	Richard A. Brown (5), Thomas J. Durante (5), Karen Q. Wong (5)
Website	http://www.wisdomtree.com
Address	WisdomTree 245 Park Avenue, 35th floor New York NY 10167 United States
Phone Number	866-909-9473

PERFORMANCE

Ratings History
Date	Overall Rating	Risk Rating	Reward Rating
Q4-18	C-	C-	D+
Q2-18	C	C-	C
Q4-17	A-	B	A
Q4-16	C	C-	C
Q4-15	C	C-	C

Asset & Performance History
Date	NAV	1-Year Total Return
2017	46.17	29.46
2016	36.28	6.26
2015	34.6	17.34
2014	30.55	10.71
2013	30.01	
2012		

Total Assets: $117,962,374
Asset Allocation
Asset	%
Cash	0%
Stocks	100%
US Stocks	0%
Bonds	0%
US Bonds	0%
Other	0%

Services Offered:

Investment Strategy: The investment seeks to track the price and yield performance, before fees and expenses, of the WisdomTree Japan Hedged SmallCap Equity Index. The fund normally invests at least 80% of its total assets in component securities of the index and investments that have economic characteristics that are substantially identical to the economic characteristics of such component securities. The index is a dividend weighted index designed to provide exposure to Japanese equity markets while at the same time neutralizing exposure to fluctuations of the value of the Japanese yen relative to the U.S. dollar. The fund is non-diversified. **Top Holdings:** Matsui Securities Co Ltd   Sankyo Co Ltd   DIC Corp   Mitsubishi Materials Corp   Yokohama Rubber Co Ltd

Invesco International Corporate Bond ETF

D+   **SELL**

Ticker	Traded On	NAV	Total Assets ($)	Dividend Yield (TTM)	Turnover Ratio	Expense Ratio
PICB	NYSE Arca	25.14	$117,188,020	1.72	14	0.5

Ratings
Reward   D+
Risk   C-
Recent Upgrade/Downgrade   Down

Fund Information
Fund Type   Exchange Traded Funds
Category   Global Fixed Income
Sub-Category   World Bond
Prospectus Objective   Worldwide Bond
Inception Date   Jun-10
Open to New Investments   Y

Prices
Price (as of 12/31/2018)   25.18
52-Week High   28.56
52-Week Low   24.84

Total Returns (%)

3-Month	6-Month	1-Year	3-Year	5-Year
-2.57	-2.72	-7.39	5.28	-5.49

3-Year Standard Deviation   7.87
Effective Duration   7.23

Valuation
Premium/Discount (1-Year Average)   -0.14

Company Information
Provider   Invesco
Manager/Tenure   Philip Fang (8), Peter Hubbard (8),
                  Jeffrey W. Kernagis (8), 2 others
Website   http://www.invesco.com/us
Address   Invesco 11 Greenway Plaza, Ste. 2500
                  Houston TX 77046 United States
Phone Number   800-659-1005

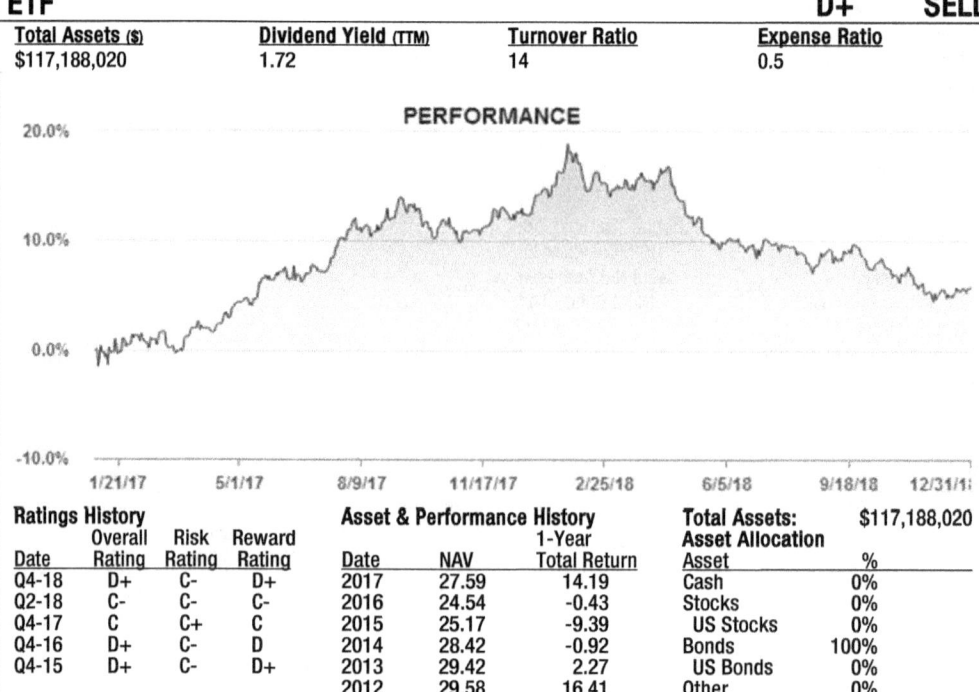

PERFORMANCE

Ratings History

Date	Overall Rating	Risk Rating	Reward Rating
Q4-18	D+	C-	D+
Q2-18	C-	C-	C-
Q4-17	C	C+	C
Q4-16	D+	C-	D
Q4-15	D+	C-	D+

Asset & Performance History

Date	NAV	1-Year Total Return
2017	27.59	14.19
2016	24.54	-0.43
2015	25.17	-9.39
2014	28.42	-0.92
2013	29.42	2.27
2012	29.58	16.41

Total Assets: $117,188,020

Asset Allocation

Asset	%
Cash	0%
Stocks	0%
US Stocks	0%
Bonds	100%
US Bonds	0%
Other	0%

Services Offered:

Investment Strategy: The investment seeks to track the investment results (before fees and expenses) of the S&P International Corporate Bond Index® (the "underlying index"). The fund generally will invest at least 80% of its total assets in investment grade corporate bonds that comprise the underlying index. The underlying index measures the performance of investment grade corporate bonds issued in the following currencies of Group of Ten countries, excluding the U.S. Dollar (USD): Australian Dollar (AUD), British Pound (GBP), Canadian Dollar (CAD), Euro (EUR), Japanese Yen (JPY), New Zealand Dollar (NZD), Norwegian Krone (NOK), Swedish Krona (SEK) and Swiss Franc (SFR). **Top Holdings:** Electricite de France SA 6.12% Panasonic Corp 0.39% The Toronto-Dominion Bank 1.99% Engie 5% Electricite de France SA 6%

SPDR® S&P Telecom ETF

C   **HOLD**

Ticker	Traded On	NAV	Total Assets ($)	Dividend Yield (TTM)	Turnover Ratio	Expense Ratio
XTL	NYSE Arca	63.08	$116,839,620	2.2	46	0.35

Ratings
Reward   C
Risk   C-
Recent Upgrade/Downgrade

Fund Information
Fund Type   Exchange Traded Funds
Category   Communications Sector Equity
Sub-Category   Communications
Prospectus Objective   Comm
Inception Date   Jan-11
Open to New Investments   Y

Prices
Price (as of 12/31/2018)   62.76
52-Week High   77.14
52-Week Low   58.72

Total Returns (%)

3-Month	6-Month	1-Year	3-Year	5-Year
-15.73	-12.77	-6.03	18.44	21.76

3-Year Standard Deviation   12.62
Effective Duration

Valuation
Premium/Discount (1-Year Average)   0.08

Company Information
Provider   SPDR State Street Global Advisors
Manager/Tenure   Michael J. Feehily (7), Karl A.
                  Schneider (4), Michael Finocchi (1)
Website   http://www.spdrs.com
Address   SPDR State Street Global Advisors
                  State Street Financial Center, 1
                  Lincoln Street Boston MA 02111-2900
                  United States
Phone Number   617-786-3000

PERFORMANCE

Ratings History

Date	Overall Rating	Risk Rating	Reward Rating
Q4-18	C	C-	C
Q2-18	C	C-	C+
Q4-17	C+	B-	C
Q4-16	C	D+	C
Q4-15	C	C	C

Asset & Performance History

Date	NAV	1-Year Total Return
2017	68.26	0.44
2016	69.35	25.49
2015	55.95	-1.68
2014	57.69	4.57
2013	55.74	23.21
2012	45.45	12.03

Total Assets: $116,839,620

Asset Allocation

Asset	%
Cash	0%
Stocks	100%
US Stocks	100%
Bonds	0%
US Bonds	0%
Other	0%

Services Offered:

Investment Strategy: The investment seeks to provide investment results that, before fees and expenses, correspond generally to the total return performance of an index derived from the telecommunications segment of a U.S. total market composite index. In seeking to track the performance of the S&P Telecom Select Industry Index (the "index"), the fund employs a sampling strategy. It generally invests substantially all, but at least 80%, of its total assets in the securities comprising the index. The index represents the telecommunications segment of the S&P Total Market Index ("S&P TMI"). The fund is non-diversified. **Top Holdings:** Finisar Corp Iridium Communications Inc ARRIS International PLC Telephone and Data Systems Inc Extreme Networks Inc

ProShares UltraShort 7-10 Year Treasury   C   HOLD

Ticker	Traded On	NAV		Total Assets ($)	Dividend Yield (TTM)	Turnover Ratio	Expense Ratio
PST	NYSE Arca	21.84		$116,331,669	0.28	0	0.95

Ratings

Reward   C-
Risk   C-
Recent Upgrade/Downgrade

Fund Information

Fund Type	Exchange Traded Funds
Category	Trading Tools
Sub-Category	Trading--Inverse Debt
Prospectus Objective	Govt Bond - Treasury
Inception Date	Apr-08
Open to New Investments	Y

Prices

Price (as of 12/31/2018)	21.78
52-Week High	23.88
52-Week Low	21.55

Total Returns (%)

3-Month	6-Month	1-Year	3-Year	5-Year
-6.28	-3.71	1.85	-5.70	-27.26

3-Year Standard Deviation   9.37
Effective Duration

Valuation

Premium/Discount (1-Year Average)   0.07

Company Information

Provider	ProShares
Manager/Tenure	Michelle Liu (10), Jeffrey Ploshnick (2)
Website	http://www.proshares.com
Address	ProShares 7501 Wisconsin Avenue, Suite 1000 Bethesda MD 20814 United States
Phone Number	866-776-5125

PERFORMANCE

Ratings History

Date	Overall Rating	Risk Rating	Reward Rating
Q4-18	C	C-	C-
Q2-18	C	C-	C-
Q4-17	D+	C-	D+
Q4-16	D	D	D
Q4-15	D+	D+	D

Asset & Performance History

Date	NAV	1-Year Total Return
2017	21.58	-4.13
2016	22.51	-3.43
2015	23.31	-6
2014	24.8	-17.93
2013	30.22	10.05
2012	27.46	-10.2

Total Assets: $116,331,669

Asset Allocation

Asset	%
Cash	211%
Stocks	0%
US Stocks	0%
Bonds	0%
US Bonds	0%
Other	-111%

Services Offered:

Investment Strategy: The investment seeks daily investment results that correspond to two times the inverse (-2x) of the daily performance of the ICE U.S. Treasury 7-10 Year Bond Index. The fund invests in financial instruments that ProShare Advisors believes, in combination, should produce daily returns consistent with the fund's investment objective. The index includes publicly-issued U.S. Treasury securities that have a remaining maturity of greater than seven years and less than or equal to ten years and have $300 million or more of outstanding face value, excluding amounts held by the Federal Reserve. The fund is non-diversified. **Top Holdings:** Ice 7-10 Year U.S. Treasury Index Swap Societe Generale   Ice 7-10 Year U.S. Treasury Index Swap Citibank Na   United States Treasury Bills   United States Treasury Bills   United States Treasury Bills

---

iShares JPX-Nikkei 400 ETF   D+   SELL

Ticker	Traded On	NAV		Total Assets ($)	Dividend Yield (TTM)	Turnover Ratio	Expense Ratio
JPXN	NYSE Arca	55.03		$116,246,245	1.66	8	0.48

Ratings

Reward   D+
Risk   D+
Recent Upgrade/Downgrade   Down

Fund Information

Fund Type	Exchange Traded Funds
Category	Japan Equity
Sub-Category	Japan Stock
Prospectus Objective	Pacific Stock
Inception Date	Oct-01
Open to New Investments	Y

Prices

Price (as of 12/31/2018)	54.48
52-Week High	70.06
52-Week Low	52.64

Total Returns (%)

3-Month	6-Month	1-Year	3-Year	5-Year
-14.37	-10.08	-13.94	8.93	14.15

3-Year Standard Deviation   10.9
Effective Duration

Valuation

Premium/Discount (1-Year Average)   0.00

Company Information

Provider	iShares
Manager/Tenure	Diane Hsiung (10), Greg Savage (10), Jennifer Hsui (6), 3 others
Website	http://www.ishares.com
Address	iShares 400 Howard Street San Francisco CA 94105 United States
Phone Number	800-474-2737

PERFORMANCE

Ratings History

Date	Overall Rating	Risk Rating	Reward Rating
Q4-18	D+	D+	D+
Q2-18	C	D+	C
Q4-17	B+	B	A-
Q4-16	C	D+	B-
Q4-15	C	D+	C

Asset & Performance History

Date	NAV	1-Year Total Return
2017	64.89	24
2016	53.15	2.07
2015	53.16	10.63
2014	48.67	-5.28
2013	52.09	26.03
2012	41.86	9.16

Total Assets: $116,246,245

Asset Allocation

Asset	%
Cash	1%
Stocks	99%
US Stocks	0%
Bonds	0%
US Bonds	0%
Other	0%

Services Offered: CashInvestment Plan

Investment Strategy: The investment seeks to track the investment results of the JPX-Nikkei Index 400 composed of Japanese equities. The fund generally invests at least 90% of its assets in securities of the underlying index and in depositary receipts representing securities of the underlying index. The underlying index may include large-, mid- or small-capitalization companies. The currency of the component securities of the underlying index is the Japanese yen ("JPY"). **Top Holdings:** SoftBank Group Corp   Sony Corp   Mitsubishi UFJ Financial Group Inc   Keyence Corp   Honda Motor Co Ltd

Direxion Daily Gold Miners Index Bear 3X Shares   D+   SELL

Ticker	Traded On	NAV	Total Assets ($)	Dividend Yield (TTM)	Turnover Ratio	Expense Ratio
DUST	NYSE Arca	22.95	$115,331,582	0.18	0	1.08

Ratings

Reward	D
Risk	D
Recent Upgrade/Downgrade	Up

Fund Information

Fund Type	Exchange Traded Funds
Category	Trading Tools
Sub-Category	Trading--Inverse Equity
Prospectus Objective	Prec Metals
Inception Date	Dec-10
Open to New Investments	Y

Prices

Price (as of 12/31/2018)	22.86
52-Week High	46.37
52-Week Low	19.61

Total Returns (%)

3-Month	6-Month	1-Year	3-Year	5-Year
-41.18	-7.77	-2.92	-97.20	-98.95

3-Year Standard Deviation	95.37
Effective Duration	

Valuation

Premium/Discount (1-Year Average)	-0.01

Company Information

Provider	Direxion Funds
Manager/Tenure	Paul Brigandi (7), Tony Ng (3)
Website	http://www.direxionfunds.com
Address	Direxion Funds 1301 Avenue Of The Americas (6th Avenue) New York NY 10019 United States
Phone Number	646-572-3390

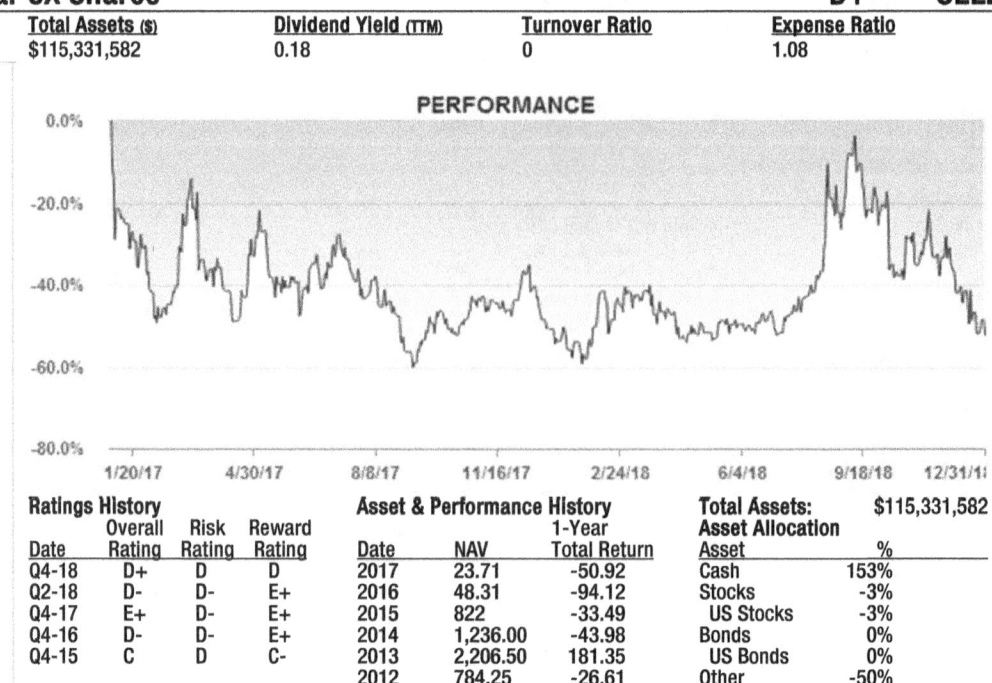

PERFORMANCE

Ratings History

Date	Overall Rating	Risk Rating	Reward Rating
Q4-18	D+	D	D
Q2-18	D-	D-	E+
Q4-17	E+	D-	E+
Q4-16	D-	D-	E+
Q4-15	C	D	C-

Asset & Performance History

Date	NAV	1-Year Total Return
2017	23.71	-50.92
2016	48.31	-94.12
2015	822	-33.49
2014	1,236.00	-43.98
2013	2,206.50	181.35
2012	784.25	-26.61

Total Assets: $115,331,582

Asset Allocation

Asset	%
Cash	153%
Stocks	-3%
US Stocks	-3%
Bonds	0%
US Bonds	0%
Other	-50%

Services Offered:

Investment Strategy: The investment seeks daily investment results before fees and expenses of 300% of the inverse of the daily performance of the NYSE Arca Gold Miners Index. The fund invests in swap agreements, futures contracts, short positions or other financial instruments that, in combination, provide inverse or short leveraged exposure to the index equal to at least 80% of the fund's net assets. The index is a modified market capitalization weighted index comprised of publicly traded companies that operate globally in both developed and emerging markets, and are involved primarily in mining for gold and, to a lesser extent, in mining for silver. It is non-diversified. **Top Holdings:** Ve Vectors Gld Miners Ve Vectors Gld Miners Ve Vectors Gld Miners Ve Vectors Gld Miners Ve Vectors Gld Miners

---

Invesco S&P SmallCap Industrials ETF   C-   HOLD

Ticker	Traded On	NAV	Total Assets ($)	Dividend Yield (TTM)	Turnover Ratio	Expense Ratio
PSCI	NAS CM	56.02	$114,662,170	0.66		0.29

Ratings

Reward	C
Risk	D+
Recent Upgrade/Downgrade	Down

Fund Information

Fund Type	Exchange Traded Funds
Category	Industrials Sector Equity
Sub-Category	Industrials
Prospectus Objective	Unaligned
Inception Date	Apr-10
Open to New Investments	

Prices

Price (as of 12/31/2018)	55.67
52-Week High	75.51
52-Week Low	52.49

Total Returns (%)

3-Month	6-Month	1-Year	3-Year	5-Year
-22.02	-17.82	-12.39	32.50	28.08

3-Year Standard Deviation	17.88
Effective Duration	

Valuation

Premium/Discount (1-Year Average)	0.05

Company Information

Provider	Invesco
Manager/Tenure	Peter Hubbard (8), Michael Jeanette (8), Tony Seisser (4), 1 other
Website	http://www.invesco.com/us
Address	Invesco 11 Greenway Plaza, Ste. 2500 Houston TX 77046 United States
Phone Number	800-659-1005

PERFORMANCE

Ratings History

Date	Overall Rating	Risk Rating	Reward Rating
Q4-18	C-	D+	C
Q2-18	C+	D+	B
Q4-17	A-	B	A
Q4-16	C	C-	C
Q4-15	C	C-	C

Asset & Performance History

Date	NAV	1-Year Total Return
2017	64.32	17.08
2016	55.36	29.18
2015	43.2	-5.55
2014	46.19	2.35
2013	45.51	41.41
2012	32.35	20.99

Total Assets: $114,662,170

Asset Allocation

Asset	%
Cash	0%
Stocks	100%
US Stocks	100%
Bonds	0%
US Bonds	0%
Other	0%

Services Offered:

Investment Strategy: The investment seeks to track the investment results (before fees and expenses) of the S&P SmallCap 600® Capped Industrials Index (the "underlying index"). The fund generally will invest at least 90% of its total assets in common stocks of small capitalization U.S. industrial companies that comprise the underlying index. These companies are principally engaged in the business of providing industrial products and services, including engineering, heavy machinery, construction, electrical equipment, aerospace and defense and general manufacturing. **Top Holdings:** Trex Co Inc Proto Labs Inc Tetra Tech Inc SkyWest Inc Moog Inc A

ELEMENTS Linked to the Rogers International Commodity Index - Agriculture Total Return   D   SELL

Ticker	Traded On	NAV	Total Assets ($)	Dividend Yield (TTM)	Turnover Ratio	Expense Ratio
RJA	NYSE Arca		$114,207,336	0	0	0.75

Ratings
Reward   D
Risk   D
Recent Upgrade/Downgrade

Fund Information
Fund Type   Exchange Traded Funds
Category   Commodities Specified
Sub-Category   Commodities Agriculture
Prospectus Objective   Natl Res
Inception Date   Oct-07
Open to New Investments Y

Prices
Price (as of 12/31/2018)   5.60
52-Week High   6.44
52-Week Low   5.59

Total Returns (%)

3-Month	6-Month	1-Year	3-Year	5-Year
-2.09	-4.41	-6.50	-10.52	-29.78

3-Year Standard Deviation   9.62
Effective Duration

Valuation
Premium/Discount (1-Year Average)   0.00

Company Information
Provider   ELEMENTS
Manager/Tenure   No Manager (11)
Website   http://www.elementsetn.com
Address   ELEMENTS United States
Phone Number   212-449-2957

PERFORMANCE

Ratings History

Date	Overall Rating	Risk Rating	Reward Rating
Q4-18	D	D	D
Q2-18	D+	C-	D
Q4-17	D	D	D
Q4-16	D	D	D
Q4-15	D	D	D

Asset & Performance History

Date	NAV	1-Year Total Return
2017	6	-4.59
2016	6.31	0.63
2015	6.27	-15.04
2014	7.38	-7.63
2013	7.99	-11.9
2012	9.07	1

Total Assets: $114,207,336
Asset Allocation

Asset	%
Cash	%
Stocks	%
US Stocks	%
Bonds	%
US Bonds	%
Other	%

Services Offered:

Investment Strategy: The investment seeks to replicate, net of expenses, the Rogers International Commodity Index – Agriculture Total Return index.
The index represents the value of a basket of 20 agricultural commodity futures contracts. **Top Holdings:**

---

iShares Edge MSCI Intl Quality Factor ETF   D+   SELL

Ticker	Traded On	NAV	Total Assets ($)	Dividend Yield (TTM)	Turnover Ratio	Expense Ratio
IQLT	NYSE Arca	25.80	$114,035,048	2.45	21	0.3

Ratings
Reward   D+
Risk   C-
Recent Upgrade/Downgrade   Down

Fund Information
Fund Type   Exchange Traded Funds
Category   Global Equity Large Cap
Sub-Category   Foreign Large Blend
Prospectus Objective   World Stock
Inception Date   Jan-15
Open to New Investments Y

Prices
Price (as of 12/31/2018)   25.81
52-Week High   31.34
52-Week Low   24.90

Total Returns (%)

3-Month	6-Month	1-Year	3-Year	5-Year
-11.94	-8.37	-10.86	11.27	

3-Year Standard Deviation   10.5
Effective Duration

Valuation
Premium/Discount (1-Year Average)   0.15

Company Information
Provider   iShares
Manager/Tenure   Diane Hsiung (3), Jennifer Hsui (3),
                  Greg Savage (3), 3 others
Website   http://www.ishares.com
Address   iShares 400 Howard Street San
                  Francisco CA 94105 United States
Phone Number   800-474-2737

PERFORMANCE

Ratings History

Date	Overall Rating	Risk Rating	Reward Rating
Q4-18	D+	C-	D+
Q2-18	C	C-	C
Q4-17	C+	B-	C+
Q4-16	D	D	D+
Q4-15	U		

Asset & Performance History

Date	NAV	1-Year Total Return
2017	29.68	24.08
2016	24.52	0.6
2015	25.08	
2014		
2013		
2012		

Total Assets: $114,035,048
Asset Allocation

Asset	%
Cash	0%
Stocks	99%
US Stocks	1%
Bonds	0%
US Bonds	0%
Other	0%

Services Offered:

Investment Strategy: The investment seeks to track the investment results of the MSCI World ex USA Sector Neutral Quality Index. The fund generally will invest at least 90% of its assets in the component securities of the underlying index and in investments that have economic characteristics that are substantially identical to the component securities of the underlying index. The index measures the performance of international developed large- and mid-capitalization stocks exhibiting relatively higher quality characteristics as identified through three fundamental variables: return on equity, earnings variability and debt-to-equity. **Top Holdings:** Total SA   Nestle SA   Roche Holding AG Dividend Right Cert.   AIA Group Ltd   GlaxoSmithKline PLC

First Trust Natural Gas ETF   C-   HOLD

Ticker	Traded On	NAV	Total Assets ($)	Dividend Yield (TTM)	Turnover Ratio	Expense Ratio
FCG	NYSE Arca	14.69	$114,019,468	1.08	53	0.6

Ratings
Reward   C
Risk   D
Recent Upgrade/Downgrade

Fund Information
Fund Type   Exchange Traded Funds
Category   Energy Sector Equity
Sub-Category   Equity Energy
Prospectus Objective   Natl Res
Inception Date   May-07
Open to New Investments   Y

Prices
Price (as of 12/31/2018)   14.70
52-Week High   24.49
52-Week Low   13.59

Total Returns (%)

3-Month	6-Month	1-Year	3-Year	5-Year
-35.10	-35.65	-34.76	-30.96	-83.64

3-Year Standard Deviation   31.79
Effective Duration

Valuation
Premium/Discount (1-Year Average)   0.00

Company Information
Provider   First Trust
Manager/Tenure   Jon C. Erickson (11), Daniel J. Lindquist (11), David G. McGarel (11), 3 others
Website   http://www.ftportfolios.com/
Address   First Trust 120 E. Liberty Drive, Suite 400 Wheaton IL 60187 United States
Phone Number   800-621-1675

PERFORMANCE

Ratings History

Date	Overall Rating	Risk Rating	Reward Rating
Q4-18	C-	D	C
Q2-18	D+	D	C
Q4-17	D	D-	D
Q4-16	D	D	D+
Q4-15	C-	C-	C

Asset & Performance History

Date	NAV	1-Year Total Return
2017	22.75	-11.43
2016	26.15	19.47
2015	22.3	-59.13
2014	56.1	-42.02
2013	97.65	25.12
2012	78.35	-13.47

Total Assets: $114,019,468

Asset Allocation

Asset	%
Cash	0%
Stocks	100%
US Stocks	92%
Bonds	0%
US Bonds	0%
Other	0%

Services Offered:

Investment Strategy: The investment seeks investment results that correspond generally to the price and yield (before the fund's fees and expenses) of an equity index called the ISE-Revere Natural GasTM Index. The fund will normally invest at least 90% of its net assets in equity securities that comprise the index. The index uses a linear-based capitalization-weighted methodology for each of the MLP and non-MLP group of constituents that initially ranks the equity securities based on market capitalization and average daily trading volume, and then adjusts the combined rankings of each equity security by a factor relating to its market capitalization. **Top Holdings:** Cabot Oil & Gas Corp Class A   Cimarex Energy Co   Concho Resources Inc   Murphy Oil Corp   Range Resources Corp

---

Invesco S&P 500® High Beta ETF   C-   HOLD

Ticker	Traded On	NAV	Total Assets ($)	Dividend Yield (TTM)	Turnover Ratio	Expense Ratio
SPHB	NYSE Arca	35.29	$113,890,103	1.67		0.25

Ratings
Reward   C
Risk   C-
Recent Upgrade/Downgrade   Down

Fund Information
Fund Type   Exchange Traded Funds
Category   US Equity Large Cap Blend
Sub-Category   Large Blend
Prospectus Objective   Growth
Inception Date   May-11
Open to New Investments

Prices
Price (as of 12/31/2018)   35.29
52-Week High   45.93
52-Week Low   32.76

Total Returns (%)

3-Month	6-Month	1-Year	3-Year	5-Year
-21.29	-17.52	-15.43	25.60	23.49

3-Year Standard Deviation   18.05
Effective Duration

Valuation
Premium/Discount (1-Year Average)   0.01

Company Information
Provider   Invesco
Manager/Tenure   Peter Hubbard (7), Michael Jeanette (7), Tony Seisser (4), 1 other
Website   http://www.invesco.com/us
Address   Invesco 11 Greenway Plaza, Ste. 2500 Houston TX 77046 United States
Phone Number   800-659-1005

PERFORMANCE

Ratings History

Date	Overall Rating	Risk Rating	Reward Rating
Q4-18	C-	C-	C
Q2-18	C+	C+	C+
Q4-17	B	C	B+
Q4-16	C+	C	B
Q4-15	C+	C+	C

Asset & Performance History

Date	NAV	1-Year Total Return
2017	42.44	17.77
2016	36.57	26.11
2015	29.29	-12.77
2014	34.12	12.72
2013	30.58	40.81
2012	21.88	17.87

Total Assets: $113,890,103

Asset Allocation

Asset	%
Cash	0%
Stocks	100%
US Stocks	99%
Bonds	0%
US Bonds	0%
Other	0%

Services Offered:

Investment Strategy: The investment seeks to track the investment results (before fees and expenses) of the S&P 500® High Beta Index (the "underlying index"). The fund generally will invest at least 90% of its total assets in common stocks that comprise the underlying index. S&P Dow Jones Indices LLC compiles, maintains and calculates the underlying index. **Top Holdings:** Applied Materials Inc   Lam Research Corp   Netflix Inc   Autodesk Inc   Micron Technology Inc

Invesco CurrencyShares® Australian Dollar Trust   D+   SELL

Ticker	Traded On	NAV	Total Assets ($)	Dividend Yield (TTM)	Turnover Ratio	Expense Ratio
FXA	NYSE Arca	70.45	$113,422,246	0.99	0	0.4

Ratings
Reward   D
Risk   C-
Recent Upgrade/Downgrade

Fund Information
Fund Type   Exchange Traded Funds
Category   Currency
Sub-Category   Single Currency
Prospectus Objective   Worldwide Bond
Inception Date   Jun-06
Open to New Investments   Y

Prices
Price (as of 12/31/2018)   70.45
52-Week High   81.14
52-Week Low   70.31

Total Returns (%)

3-Month	6-Month	1-Year	3-Year	5-Year
-2.63	-3.56	-9.13	-0.58	-16.48

3-Year Standard Deviation   9.35
Effective Duration

Valuation
Premium/Discount (1-Year Average)   -0.19

Company Information
Provider   Invesco
Manager/Tenure   Management Team (12)
Website   http://www.invesco.com/us
Address   Invesco 11 Greenway Plaza, Ste. 2500
     Houston TX 77046 United States
Phone Number   800-659-1005

PERFORMANCE

Ratings History

Date	Overall Rating	Risk Rating	Reward Rating
Q4-18	D+	C-	D
Q2-18	C-	C-	C-
Q4-17	C-	C	D+
Q4-16	D+	C-	D
Q4-15	D	D	D

Asset & Performance History

Date	NAV	1-Year Total Return
2017	78.25	8.89
2016	72.47	0.47
2015	72.84	-9.83
2014	81.98	-6.83
2013	89.6	-12.16
2012	104.02	4.32

Total Assets: $113,422,246
Asset Allocation

Asset	%
Cash	100%
Stocks	0%
US Stocks	0%
Bonds	0%
US Bonds	0%
Other	0%

Services Offered:

Investment Strategy: The investment objective of the fund is for the Shares to reflect the price in USD of the Australian Dollar.
The Shares are intended to provide institutional and retail investors with a simple, cost-effective means of gaining investment benefits similar to those of holding Australian Dollars. The costs of purchasing Shares should not exceed the costs associated with purchasing any other publicly-traded equity securities. **Top Holdings:**

Nationwide Risk-Based International Equity ETF   D   SELL

Ticker	Traded On	NAV	Total Assets ($)	Dividend Yield (TTM)	Turnover Ratio	Expense Ratio
RBIN	NYSE Arca	22.80	$112,781,585	0.43		0.42

Ratings
Reward   D
Risk   D
Recent Upgrade/Downgrade

Fund Information
Fund Type   Exchange Traded Funds
Category   Global Equity Large Cap
Sub-Category   Foreign Large Blend
Prospectus Objective   Foreign Stock
Inception Date   Sep-17
Open to New Investments   Y

Prices
Price (as of 12/31/2018)   22.76
52-Week High   27.45
52-Week Low   22.56

Total Returns (%)

3-Month	6-Month	1-Year	3-Year	5-Year
-12.33	-10.04	-11.91		

3-Year Standard Deviation
Effective Duration

Valuation
Premium/Discount (1-Year Average)   0.27

Company Information
Provider   Nationwide
Manager/Tenure   Denise M. Krisko (1), Rafael Zayas (1)
Website
     http://www.nationwide.com/mutualfunds
Address   Nationwide One Nationwide Plaza
     Columbus OH 43215 United States
Phone Number   800-848-0920

PERFORMANCE

Ratings History

Date	Overall Rating	Risk Rating	Reward Rating
Q4-18	D	D	D
Q2-18	U		
Q4-17	U		
Q4-16			
Q4-15			

Asset & Performance History

Date	NAV	1-Year Total Return
2017	25.88	
2016		
2015		
2014		
2013		
2012		

Total Assets: $112,781,585
Asset Allocation

Asset	%
Cash	0%
Stocks	100%
US Stocks	1%
Bonds	0%
US Bonds	0%
Other	0%

Services Offered:

Investment Strategy: The investment seeks to track the total return performance, before fees and expenses, of the Rothschild & Co Risk-Based International Index. At least 80% of its total assets will be invested in the component securities of the index. The index is a rules-based, equal risk-weighted index that is designed to provide exposure to large capitalization companies in developed markets outside the U.S. and Canada with lower volatility, reduced maximum drawdown, and an improved Sharpe ratio as compared to traditional, market capitalization weighted approaches. **Top Holdings:** Jardine Matheson Holdings Ltd   Hongkong Land Holdings Ltd Japan Post Holdings Co Ltd   NTT DOCOMO Inc   Amcor Ltd

Nationwide Risk-Based U.S. Equity ETF   D   SELL

Ticker	Traded On	NAV	Total Assets ($)	Dividend Yield (TTM)	Turnover Ratio	Expense Ratio
RBUS	NYSE Arca	24.44	$112,733,413	0.4		0.3

Ratings
Reward	D+
Risk	D
Recent Upgrade/Downgrade	

Fund Information
Fund Type	Exchange Traded Funds
Category	US Equity Large Cap Blend
Sub-Category	Large Blend
Prospectus Objective	Growth
Inception Date	Sep-17
Open to New Investments	Y

Prices
Price (as of 12/31/2018)	24.41
52-Week High	28.05
52-Week Low	23.93

Total Returns (%)
3-Month	6-Month	1-Year	3-Year	5-Year
-10.13	-5.45	-3.94		

3-Year Standard Deviation
Effective Duration

Valuation
Premium/Discount (1-Year Average)	0.21

Company Information
Provider	Nationwide
Manager/Tenure	Denise M. Krisko (1), Austin Wen (1)
Website	http://www.nationwide.com/mutualfunds
Address	Nationwide One Nationwide Plaza Columbus OH 43215 United States
Phone Number	800-848-0920

PERFORMANCE

Ratings History
Date	Overall Rating	Risk Rating	Reward Rating
Q4-18	D	D	D+
Q2-18	U		
Q4-17	U		
Q4-16			
Q4-15			

Asset & Performance History
Date	NAV	1-Year Total Return
2017	26.07	
2016		
2015		
2014		
2013		
2012		

Total Assets: $112,733,413
Asset Allocation
Asset	%
Cash	1%
Stocks	99%
US Stocks	97%
Bonds	0%
US Bonds	0%
Other	0%

Services Offered:

Investment Strategy: The investment seeks to track the total return performance, before fees and expenses, of the Rothschild & Co Risk-Based US Index (the "index"). The advisor attempts to invest all, or substantially all, of its assets in the component securities that make up the index. Normally, at least 80% of the fund's total assets will be invested in the component securities of the index. The index is a rules-based, equal risk-weighted index that is designed to provide exposure to U.S.-listed large capitalization companies with lower volatility, reduced maximum drawdown, and an improved Sharpe ratio as compared to traditional, market capitalization weighted approaches.
Top Holdings: Southern Co   Newmont Mining Corp   Duke Energy Corp   American Electric Power Co Inc   DTE Energy Co

---

WisdomTree U.S. SmallCap Quality Dividend Growth Fund   C-   HOLD

Ticker	Traded On	NAV	Total Assets ($)	Dividend Yield (TTM)	Turnover Ratio	Expense Ratio
DGRS	NAS CM	31.15	$112,377,640	2.37	51	0.38

Ratings
Reward	C
Risk	C-
Recent Upgrade/Downgrade	Down

Fund Information
Fund Type	Exchange Traded Funds
Category	US Equity Small Cap
Sub-Category	Small Blend
Prospectus Objective	Small Company
Inception Date	Jul-13
Open to New Investments	Y

Prices
Price (as of 12/31/2018)	31.15
52-Week High	38.67
52-Week Low	29.46

Total Returns (%)
3-Month	6-Month	1-Year	3-Year	5-Year
-15.66	-14.37	-10.29	25.45	21.73

3-Year Standard Deviation   13.94
Effective Duration

Valuation
Premium/Discount (1-Year Average)	0.10

Company Information
Provider	WisdomTree
Manager/Tenure	Richard A. Brown (5), Thomas J. Durante (5), Karen Q. Wong (5)
Website	http://www.wisdomtree.com
Address	WisdomTree 245 Park Avenue, 35th floor New York NY 10167 United States
Phone Number	866-909-9473

PERFORMANCE

Ratings History
Date	Overall Rating	Risk Rating	Reward Rating
Q4-18	C-	C-	C
Q2-18	C	C-	C+
Q4-17	B	B	B+
Q4-16	C-	C-	C
Q4-15	C-	D+	C-

Asset & Performance History
Date	NAV	1-Year Total Return
2017	35.55	7.09
2016	33.94	30.08
2015	26.53	-7.02
2014	29.23	4.36
2013	28.61	
2012		

Total Assets: $112,377,640
Asset Allocation
Asset	%
Cash	0%
Stocks	100%
US Stocks	100%
Bonds	0%
US Bonds	0%
Other	0%

Services Offered:

Investment Strategy: The investment seeks to track the price and yield performance, before fees and expenses, of the WisdomTree U.S. SmallCap Quality Dividend Growth Index. The index is a fundamentally weighted index that consists of the small-capitalization segment of dividend-paying U.S. common stocks with growth characteristics. Under normal circumstances, at least 80% of the fund's total assets (exclusive of collateral held from securities lending) will be invested in component securities of the index and investments that have economic characteristics that are substantially identical to the economic characteristics of such component securities. It is non-diversified.
Top Holdings: CoreCivic Inc   Dine Brands Global Inc   GATX Corp   American Eagle Outfitters Inc   South Jersey Industries Inc

---

First Trust S&P REIT Index Fund   C   HOLD

Ticker	Traded On	NAV	Total Assets ($)	Dividend Yield (TTM)	Turnover Ratio	Expense Ratio
FRI	NYSE Arca	21.63	$112,170,193	2.88	7	0.48

Ratings
Reward   C
Risk   C-
Recent Upgrade/Downgrade

Fund Information
Fund Type   Exchange Traded Funds
Category   Real Estate Sector Equity
Sub-Category   Real Estate
Prospectus Objective   Real Estate
Inception Date   May-07
Open to New Investments   Y

Prices
Price (as of 12/31/2018)   21.62
52-Week High   24.29
52-Week Low   20.31

Total Returns (%)

3-Month	6-Month	1-Year	3-Year	5-Year
-5.31	-4.68	-4.23	7.36	41.85

3-Year Standard Deviation   12.82
Effective Duration

Valuation
Premium/Discount (1-Year Average)   -0.06

Company Information
Provider   First Trust
Manager/Tenure   Jon C. Erickson (11), Daniel J.
                    Lindquist (11), David G. McGarel (11),
                    3 others
Website   http://www.ftportfolios.com/
Address   First Trust 120 E. Liberty Drive, Suite
                    400 Wheaton IL 60187 United States
Phone Number   800-621-1675

PERFORMANCE

Ratings History

Date	Overall Rating	Risk Rating	Reward Rating
Q4-18	C	C-	C
Q2-18	C-	C-	C-
Q4-17	B-	B	C+
Q4-16	C+	C	C+
Q4-15	C	C	C+

Asset & Performance History

Date	NAV	1-Year Total Return
2017	23.28	3.81
2016	23.07	8
2015	22.07	1.96
2014	22.24	29.57
2013	17.54	1.83
2012	17.75	17.43

Total Assets: $112,170,193

Asset Allocation

Asset	%
Cash	0%
Stocks	100%
US Stocks	100%
Bonds	0%
US Bonds	0%
Other	0%

Services Offered:

Investment Strategy: The investment seeks investment results that correspond generally to the price and yield (before the fund's fees and expenses) of an equity index called the S&P United States REIT Index. The fund will normally invest at least 90% of its net assets (including investment borrowings) in common stocks that comprise the index. The index is a subset of the S&P Developed REIT Index, which measures the performance of more than 200 REITs or REIT-like structures in 15 developed markets. **Top Holdings:** Simon Property Group Inc   Prologis Inc   Public Storage   Welltower Inc   AvalonBay Communities Inc

---

iShares MSCI USA ESG Optimized ETF   C-   HOLD

Ticker	Traded On	NAV	Total Assets ($)	Dividend Yield (TTM)	Turnover Ratio	Expense Ratio
ESGU	NAS CM	54.78	$112,146,151	1.42	28	0.15

Ratings
Reward   D+
Risk   C-
Recent Upgrade/Downgrade

Fund Information
Fund Type   Exchange Traded Funds
Category   US Equity Large Cap Blend
Sub-Category   Large Blend
Prospectus Objective   Growth & Inc
Inception Date   Dec-16
Open to New Investments   Y

Prices
Price (as of 12/31/2018)   54.93
52-Week High   64.63
52-Week Low   51.48

Total Returns (%)

3-Month	6-Month	1-Year	3-Year	5-Year
-14.06	-7.31	-4.13		

3-Year Standard Deviation
Effective Duration

Valuation
Premium/Discount (1-Year Average)   0.29

Company Information
Provider   iShares
Manager/Tenure   Diane Hsiung (2), Jennifer Hsui (2),
                    Alan Mason (2), 1 other
Website   http://www.ishares.com
Address   iShares 400 Howard Street San
                    Francisco CA 94105 United States
Phone Number   800-474-2737

PERFORMANCE

Ratings History

Date	Overall Rating	Risk Rating	Reward Rating
Q4-18	C-	C-	D+
Q2-18	C-	C-	C-
Q4-17	D	A	D+
Q4-16			
Q4-15			

Asset & Performance History

Date	NAV	1-Year Total Return
2017	58.12	21.25
2016	48.88	
2015		
2014		
2013		
2012		

Total Assets: $112,146,151

Asset Allocation

Asset	%
Cash	0%
Stocks	100%
US Stocks	98%
Bonds	0%
US Bonds	0%
Other	0%

Services Offered:

Investment Strategy: The investment seeks to track the investment results of the MSCI USA Extended ESG Focus Index. The fund generally will invest at least 90% of its assets in the component securities of the underlying index and may invest up to 10% of its assets in certain futures, options and swap contracts, cash and cash equivalents. The underlying index is an optimized equity index designed to reflect the equity performance of U.S. companies that have favorable environmental, social and governance ("ESG") characteristics, while exhibiting risk and return characteristics similar to those of the MSCI USA Index. The fund is non-diversified. **Top Holdings:** Microsoft Corp   Apple Inc   Amazon.com Inc   Johnson & Johnson   JPMorgan Chase & Co

Invesco FTSE International Low Beta Equal Weight ETF   D+   SELL

Ticker	Traded On	NAV	Total Assets ($)	Dividend Yield (TTM)	Turnover Ratio	Expense Ratio
IDLB	NAS CM	25.90	$111,823,261	3.14	39	0.45

Ratings

Reward	D+
Risk	D+
Recent Upgrade/Downgrade	Down

Fund Information

Fund Type	Exchange Traded Funds
Category	Global Equity Large Cap
Sub-Category	Foreign Large Blend
Prospectus Objective	Growth & Inc
Inception Date	Nov-15
Open to New Investments	

Prices

Price (as of 12/31/2018)	25.83
52-Week High	31.82
52-Week Low	25.28

Total Returns (%)

3-Month	6-Month	1-Year	3-Year	5-Year
-11.52	-9.76	-12.55	13.39	

3-Year Standard Deviation	10.55
Effective Duration	

Valuation

Premium/Discount (1-Year Average)	0.06

Company Information

Provider	Invesco
Manager/Tenure	Peter Hubbard (3), Michael Jeanette (3), Jonathan Nixon (3), 1 other
Website	http://www.invesco.com/us
Address	Invesco 11 Greenway Plaza, Ste. 2500 Houston TX 77046 United States
Phone Number	800-659-1005

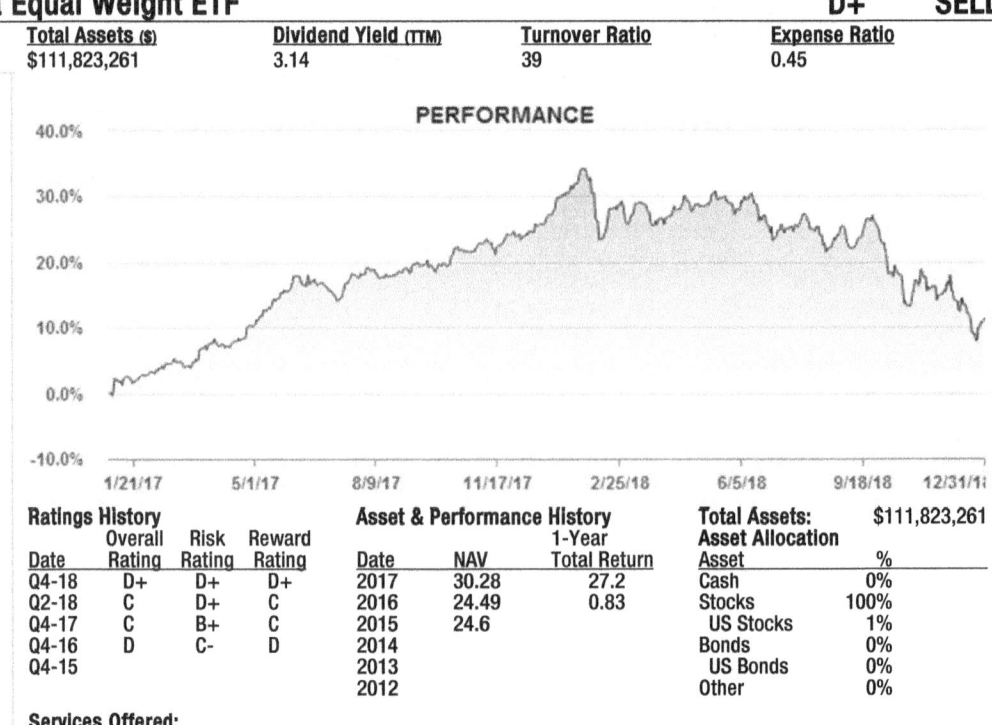

PERFORMANCE

Ratings History

Date	Overall Rating	Risk Rating	Reward Rating
Q4-18	D+	D+	D+
Q2-18	C	D+	C
Q4-17	C	B+	C
Q4-16	D	C-	D
Q4-15			

Asset & Performance History

Date	NAV	1-Year Total Return
2017	30.28	27.2
2016	24.49	0.83
2015	24.6	
2014		
2013		
2012		

Total Assets: $111,823,261

Asset Allocation

Asset	%
Cash	0%
Stocks	100%
US Stocks	1%
Bonds	0%
US Bonds	0%
Other	0%

Services Offered:

Investment Strategy: The investment seeks to track the investment results (before fees and expenses) of the FTSE Developed ex-U.S. Low Beta Equal Weight Index (the "underlying index"). The fund generally will invest at least 90% of its total assets in common stocks that comprise the underlying index. Strictly in accordance with its guidelines and mandated procedures, the index provider compiles, maintains and calculates the underlying index, which is designed to provide exposure to constituents of the FTSE Developed ex US Index that exhibit low beta characteristics. **Top Holdings:** FamilyMart UNY Holdings Co Ltd   Sumitomo Dainippon Pharma Co Ltd   M1 Ltd   Daikyo Inc   NCsoft Corp

---

Invesco DB Precious Metals Fund   D   SELL

Ticker	Traded On	NAV	Total Assets ($)	Dividend Yield (TTM)	Turnover Ratio	Expense Ratio
DBP	NYSE Arca	36.29	$111,500,608	0.13		0.75

Ratings

Reward	D
Risk	D+
Recent Upgrade/Downgrade	Down

Fund Information

Fund Type	Exchange Traded Funds
Category	Commodities Specified
Sub-Category	Commodities Precious Metals
Prospectus Objective	Prec Metals
Inception Date	Jan-07
Open to New Investments	Y

Prices

Price (as of 12/31/2018)	36.37
52-Week High	40.07
52-Week Low	34.00

Total Returns (%)

3-Month	6-Month	1-Year	3-Year	5-Year
5.82	0.11	-6.17	12.57	-7.24

3-Year Standard Deviation	13.79
Effective Duration	

Valuation

Premium/Discount (1-Year Average)	-0.03

Company Information

Provider	Invesco
Manager/Tenure	Management Team (11)
Website	http://www.invesco.com/us
Address	Invesco 11 Greenway Plaza, Ste. 2500 Houston TX 77046 United States
Phone Number	800-659-1005

PERFORMANCE

Ratings History

Date	Overall Rating	Risk Rating	Reward Rating
Q4-18	D	D+	D
Q2-18	C-	C-	C-
Q4-17	C-	C-	C-
Q4-16	D+	D+	C-
Q4-15	D-	D-	D-

Asset & Performance History

Date	NAV	1-Year Total Return
2017	38.68	8.96
2016	34.93	8.95
2015	32.28	-11.78
2014	36.59	-6.58
2013	39.17	-31.39
2012	57.1	5.61

Total Assets: $111,500,608

Asset Allocation

Asset	%
Cash	59%
Stocks	0%
US Stocks	0%
Bonds	31%
US Bonds	31%
Other	10%

Services Offered:

Investment Strategy: The investment seeks to track the DBIQ Optimum Yield Precious Metals Index Excess Return™ (DBIQ-OY Precious Metals ER™), which is intended to reflect the precious metals sector. The index Commodities consist of Gold and Silver. **Top Holdings:** United States Treasury Bills 0%   Silver Future May19   United States Treasury Bills 0%   United States Treasury Bills 0%

ProShares VIX Short-Term Futures ETF D- SELL

Ticker	Traded On	NAV	Total Assets ($)	Dividend Yield (TTM)	Turnover Ratio	Expense Ratio
VIXY	NYSE Arca		$111,194,305	0		0.87

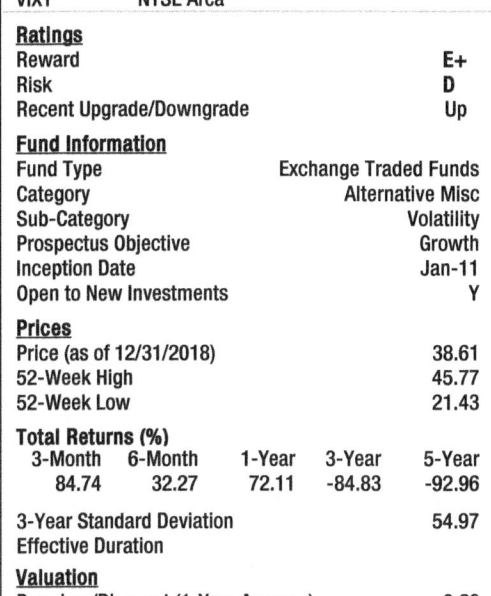

Ratings
Reward	E+
Risk	D
Recent Upgrade/Downgrade	Up

Fund Information
Fund Type	Exchange Traded Funds
Category	Alternative Misc
Sub-Category	Volatility
Prospectus Objective	Growth
Inception Date	Jan-11
Open to New Investments	Y

Prices
Price (as of 12/31/2018)	38.61
52-Week High	45.77
52-Week Low	21.43

Total Returns (%)
3-Month	6-Month	1-Year	3-Year	5-Year
84.74	32.27	72.11	-84.83	-92.96

3-Year Standard Deviation	54.97
Effective Duration	

Valuation
Premium/Discount (1-Year Average)	0.20

Company Information
Provider	ProShares
Manager/Tenure	Management Team (7)
Website	http://www.proshares.com
Address	ProShares 7501 Wisconsin Avenue, Suite 1000 Bethesda MD 20814 United States
Phone Number	866-776-5125

Ratings History
Date	Overall Rating	Risk Rating	Reward Rating
Q4-18	D-	D	E+
Q2-18	D-	D	E+
Q4-17	E	E+	E
Q4-16	E+	D-	E
Q4-15	E+	E+	E+

Asset & Performance History
Date	NAV	1-Year Total Return
2017	23.34	-72.48
2016	84.86	-67.96
2015	264.87	-36.73
2014	418.65	-26.65
2013	570.81	-65.99
2012	1,678.71	-78.02

Total Assets: $111,194,305
Asset Allocation
Asset	%
Cash	0%
Stocks	100%
US Stocks	100%
Bonds	0%
US Bonds	0%
Other	0%

Services Offered:

Investment Strategy: The investment seeks results (before fees and expenses) that, both for a single day and over time, match the performance of the S&P 500 VIX Short-Term Futures Index for a single day. The index seeks to offer exposure to market volatility through publicly traded futures markets and is designed to measure the return from a rolling long position in the first and second month VIX futures contracts. **Top Holdings:** Cboe Vix Future 12/19/2018 (Uxz8) Cboe Vix Future 01/16/2019 (Uxf9)

Global X MSCI Norway ETF C HOLD

Ticker	Traded On	NAV	Total Assets ($)	Dividend Yield (TTM)	Turnover Ratio	Expense Ratio
NORW	NYSE Arca	11.54	$109,458,614	2.89	10	0.5

Ratings
Reward	C
Risk	C+
Recent Upgrade/Downgrade	Down

Fund Information
Fund Type	Exchange Traded Funds
Category	Equity Misc
Sub-Category	Miscellaneous Region
Prospectus Objective	Europe Stock
Inception Date	Nov-10
Open to New Investments	Y

Prices
Price (as of 12/31/2018)	11.54
52-Week High	15.42
52-Week Low	11.43

Total Returns (%)
3-Month	6-Month	1-Year	3-Year	5-Year
-20.86	-14.95	-8.38	31.53	-14.46

3-Year Standard Deviation	15.23
Effective Duration	

Valuation
Premium/Discount (1-Year Average)	-0.27

Company Information
Provider	Global X Funds
Manager/Tenure	Chang Kim (4), James Ong (2), Nam To (0)
Website	http://www.globalxfunds.com
Address	Global X Funds 600 Lexington Avenue, 20th Floor New York NY 10022 United States
Phone Number	888-493-8631

Ratings History
Date	Overall Rating	Risk Rating	Reward Rating
Q4-18	C	C+	C
Q2-18	C+	C-	B-
Q4-17	C	C	C
Q4-16	D+	D	D+
Q4-15	D	D	D

Asset & Performance History
Date	NAV	1-Year Total Return
2017	13.19	22.03
2016	11.12	17.63
2015	9.73	-15.72
2014	11.98	-22.84
2013	16.59	12.79
2012	15.06	23.29

Total Assets: $109,458,614
Asset Allocation
Asset	%
Cash	0%
Stocks	100%
US Stocks	1%
Bonds	0%
US Bonds	0%
Other	0%

Services Offered:

Investment Strategy: The investment seeks investment results that correspond generally to the price and yield performance, before fees and expenses, of the MSCI Norway IMI 25/50 Index. The fund invests at least 80% of its total assets in the securities of the underlying index and in American Depositary Receipts ("ADRs") and Global Depositary Receipts ("GDRs") based on the securities in the underlying index. The underlying index is designed to represent the performance of the broad Norway equity universe. The fund is non-diversified. **Top Holdings:** Equinor ASA DNB ASA Telenor ASA Marine Harvest ASA Yara International ASA

ProShares MSCI EAFE Dividend Growers ETF   D+   SELL

Ticker	Traded On	NAV	Total Assets ($)	Dividend Yield (TTM)	Turnover Ratio	Expense Ratio
EFAD	BATS	33.52	$109,331,332	3.06		0.5

Ratings
Reward	D+
Risk	C-
Recent Upgrade/Downgrade	Down

Fund Information
Fund Type	Exchange Traded Funds
Category	Global Equity Large Cap
Sub-Category	Foreign Large Growth
Prospectus Objective	Equity-Income
Inception Date	Aug-14
Open to New Investments	Y

Prices
Price (as of 12/31/2018)	33.39
52-Week High	40.39
52-Week Low	32.66

Total Returns (%)
3-Month	6-Month	1-Year	3-Year	5-Year
-11.95	-10.03	-11.49	0.04	

3-Year Standard Deviation	10.51
Effective Duration	

Valuation
Premium/Discount (1-Year Average)	-0.03

Company Information
Provider	ProShares
Manager/Tenure	Alexander V. Ilyasov (4), Scott Hanson (2)
Website	http://www.proshares.com
Address	ProShares 7501 Wisconsin Avenue, Suite 1000 Bethesda MD 20814 United States
Phone Number	866-776-5125

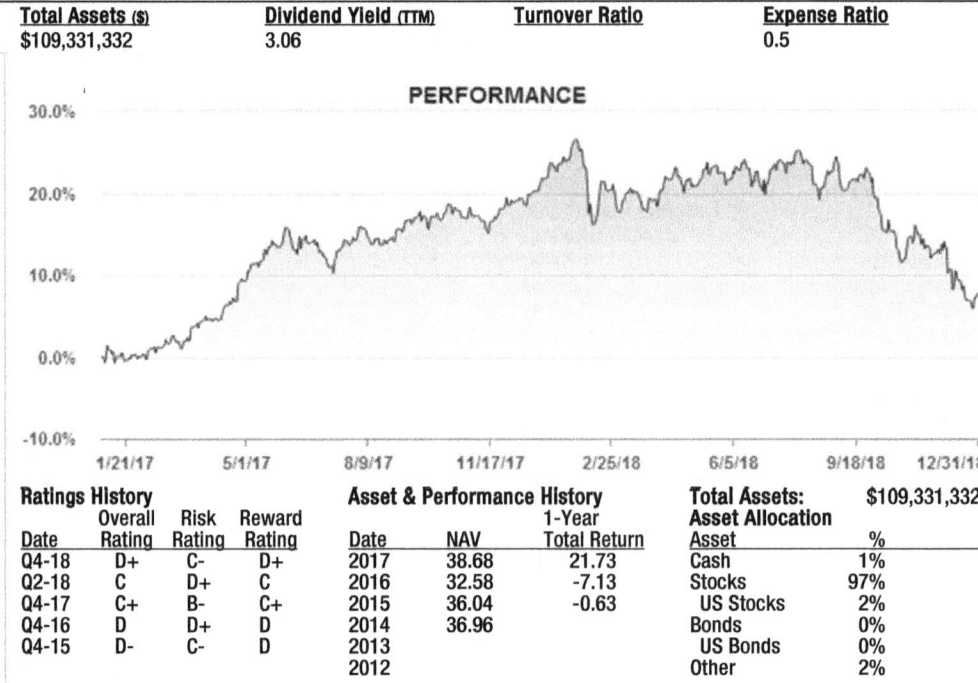

PERFORMANCE

Ratings History
Date	Overall Rating	Risk Rating	Reward Rating
Q4-18	D+	C-	D+
Q2-18	C	D+	C
Q4-17	C+	B-	C+
Q4-16	D	D+	D
Q4-15	D-	C-	D

Asset & Performance History
Date	NAV	1-Year Total Return
2017	38.68	21.73
2016	32.58	-7.13
2015	36.04	-0.63
2014	36.96	
2013		
2012		

Total Assets: $109,331,332

Asset Allocation
Asset	%
Cash	1%
Stocks	97%
US Stocks	2%
Bonds	0%
US Bonds	0%
Other	2%

Services Offered:

Investment Strategy: The investment seeks investment results, before fees and expenses, that track the performance of the MSCI EAFE Dividend Masters Index (the "index"). The index, constructed and maintained by MSCI, targets companies that are currently members of the MSCI EAFE Index ("MSCI EAFE") and have increased dividend payments each year for at least 10 years. The index contains a minimum of 40 stocks, which are equally weighted. Under normal circumstances, the fund will invest at least 80% of its total assets in component securities. **Top Holdings:** SEB SA   Vodafone Group PLC   Fresenius Medical Care AG & Co. KGaA   REA Group Ltd   Novo Nordisk A/S B

Goldman Sachs Hedge Industry VIP ETF   C-   HOLD

Ticker	Traded On	NAV	Total Assets ($)	Dividend Yield (TTM)	Turnover Ratio	Expense Ratio
GVIP	NYSE Arca	49.17	$109,127,604	0.26	1	0.45

Ratings
Reward	C-
Risk	C-
Recent Upgrade/Downgrade	Down

Fund Information
Fund Type	Exchange Traded Funds
Category	US Equity Large Cap Blend
Sub-Category	Large Growth
Prospectus Objective	Growth & Inc
Inception Date	Nov-16
Open to New Investments	Y

Prices
Price (as of 12/31/2018)	49.13
52-Week High	58.76
52-Week Low	46.00

Total Returns (%)
3-Month	6-Month	1-Year	3-Year	5-Year
-15.36	-10.68	-6.66		

3-Year Standard Deviation	
Effective Duration	

Valuation
Premium/Discount (1-Year Average)	0.06

Company Information
Provider	Goldman Sachs
Manager/Tenure	Raj Garigipati (2), Jamie McGregor (2)
Website	http://www.gsamfunds.com
Address	Goldman Sachs 200 West Stree New York NY 10282 United States
Phone Number	800-526-7384

PERFORMANCE

Ratings History
Date	Overall Rating	Risk Rating	Reward Rating
Q4-18	C-	C-	C-
Q2-18	C	C-	C
Q4-17	D	A-	D+
Q4-16	U		
Q4-15			

Asset & Performance History
Date	NAV	1-Year Total Return
2017	52.9	25.72
2016	42.34	
2015		
2014		
2013		
2012		

Total Assets: $109,127,604

Asset Allocation
Asset	%
Cash	0%
Stocks	100%
US Stocks	96%
Bonds	0%
US Bonds	0%
Other	0%

Services Offered:

Investment Strategy: The investment seeks to provide investment results that closely correspond, before fees and expenses, to the performance of the Goldman Sachs Hedge Fund VIP Index™. The fund seeks to achieve its investment objective by investing at least 80% of its assets in securities included in its underlying index, in depositary receipts representing securities included in its underlying index and in underlying stocks in respect of depositary receipts included in its underlying index. The index is designed to deliver exposure to equity securities whose performance is expected to influence the long portfolios of hedge funds. **Top Holdings:** Autodesk Inc   ServiceNow Inc   Salesforce.com Inc   General Motors Co   Delta Air Lines Inc

---

Invesco WilderHill Clean Energy ETF   C   HOLD

Ticker	Traded On	NAV	Total Assets ($)	Dividend Yield (TTM)	Turnover Ratio	Expense Ratio
PBW	NYSE Arca	21.41	$108,813,230	1.47	43	0.7

Ratings

Reward	C+
Risk	D+
Recent Upgrade/Downgrade	

Fund Information

Fund Type	Exchange Traded Funds
Category	Technology Sector Equity
Sub-Category	Miscellaneous Sector
Prospectus Objective	Natl Res
Inception Date	Mar-05
Open to New Investments	Y

Prices

Price (as of 12/31/2018)	21.39
52-Week High	26.92
52-Week Low	20.12

Total Returns (%)

3-Month	6-Month	1-Year	3-Year	5-Year
-13.38	-13.84	-13.71	-4.39	-25.97

3-Year Standard Deviation	16.12
Effective Duration	

Valuation

Premium/Discount (1-Year Average)	0.05

Company Information

Provider	Invesco
Manager/Tenure	Peter Hubbard (11), Michael Jeanette (10), Tony Seisser (4), 1 other
Website	http://www.invesco.com/us
Address	Invesco 11 Greenway Plaza, Ste. 2500 Houston TX 77046 United States
Phone Number	800-659-1005

PERFORMANCE

Ratings History

Date	Overall Rating	Risk Rating	Reward Rating
Q4-18	C	D+	C+
Q2-18	C	C-	C
Q4-17	C	C	C
Q4-16	C-	D	C
Q4-15	C-	C-	C

Asset & Performance History

Date	NAV	1-Year Total Return
2017	25.27	39.78
2016	18.35	-20.74
2015	23.75	-8.58
2014	26.35	-15.29
2013	31.9	59.83
2012	20.45	-16.86

Total Assets: $108,813,230

Asset Allocation

Asset	%
Cash	0%
Stocks	100%
US Stocks	81%
Bonds	0%
US Bonds	0%
Other	0%

Services Offered:

Investment Strategy: The investment seeks to track the investment results (before fees and expenses) of the WilderHill Clean Energy Index (the "underlying index"). The fund generally will invest at least 90% of its total assets in common stocks of companies that comprise the underlying index. The underlying index was composed of the stocks of about 39 companies that are publicly traded companies in the United States that are engaged in the business of the advancement of cleaner energy and conservation. **Top Holdings:** Enphase Energy Inc Canadian Solar Inc Tesla Inc Sunrun Inc Ormat Technologies Inc

---

JPMorgan Diversified Return U.S. Small Cap Equity ETF   D+   SELL

Ticker	Traded On	NAV	Total Assets ($)	Dividend Yield (TTM)	Turnover Ratio	Expense Ratio
JPSE	NYSE Arca	26.89	$108,770,183	1.42		0.29

Ratings

Reward	D+
Risk	C-
Recent Upgrade/Downgrade	Down

Fund Information

Fund Type	Exchange Traded Funds
Category	US Equity Small Cap
Sub-Category	Small Blend
Prospectus Objective	Small Company
Inception Date	Nov-16
Open to New Investments	Y

Prices

Price (as of 12/31/2018)	26.84
52-Week High	33.30
52-Week Low	25.38

Total Returns (%)

3-Month	6-Month	1-Year	3-Year	5-Year
-16.09	-14.45	-8.13		

3-Year Standard Deviation	
Effective Duration	

Valuation

Premium/Discount (1-Year Average)	0.14

Company Information

Provider	JPMorgan
Manager/Tenure	Jonathan Msika (2), Yazann Romahi (2), Joe Staines (2), 1 other
Website	http://www.jpmorganfunds.com
Address	JPMorgan 270 Park Avenue New York NY 10017-2070 United States
Phone Number	800-480-4111

PERFORMANCE

Ratings History

Date	Overall Rating	Risk Rating	Reward Rating
Q4-18	D+	C-	D+
Q2-18	C-	C-	C-
Q4-17	D	B+	D+
Q4-16	U		
Q4-15			

Asset & Performance History

Date	NAV	1-Year Total Return
2017	29.59	14.38
2016	26.06	
2015		
2014		
2013		
2012		

Total Assets: $108,770,183

Asset Allocation

Asset	%
Cash	0%
Stocks	100%
US Stocks	99%
Bonds	0%
US Bonds	0%
Other	0%

Services Offered:

Investment Strategy: The investment seeks investment results that closely correspond, before fees and expenses, to the performance of the JP Morgan Diversified Factor US Small Cap Equity Index. The fund will invest at least 80% of its assets in securities included in the underlying index. "Assets" means net assets, plus the amount of borrowing for investment purposes. The underlying index is comprised of U.S. equity securities selected to represent a diversified set of factor characteristics. The rules based proprietary multi-factor selection process utilizes the following characteristics: relative valuation, momentum and quality. **Top Holdings:** Helen Of Troy Ltd Iridium Communications Inc New Jersey Resources Corp Black Hills Corp Lancaster Colony Corp

SPDR® SSgA Ultra Short Term Bond ETF   C-   HOLD

Ticker	Traded On	NAV	Total Assets ($)	Dividend Yield (TTM)	Turnover Ratio	Expense Ratio
ULST	NYSE Arca	40.13	$108,677,746	1.9	83	0.2

Ratings
Reward   C
Risk   C-
Recent Upgrade/Downgrade

Fund Information
Fund Type   Exchange Traded Funds
Category   US Fixed Income
Sub-Category   Ultrashort Bond
Prospectus Objective   Growth & Inc
Inception Date   Oct-13
Open to New Investments   Y

Prices
Price (as of 12/31/2018)   40.15
52-Week High   40.34
52-Week Low   40.10

Total Returns (%)

3-Month	6-Month	1-Year	3-Year	5-Year
0.49	1.13	2.10	5.10	5.52

3-Year Standard Deviation   0.26
Effective Duration   0.24

Valuation
Premium/Discount (1-Year Average)   0.03

Company Information
Provider   SPDR State Street Global Advisors
Manager/Tenure   Thomas Connelley (5), Karyn Corridan (0)
Website   http://www.spdrs.com
Address   SPDR State Street Global Advisors
State Street Financial Center, 1
Lincoln Street Boston MA 02111-2900
United States
Phone Number   617-786-3000

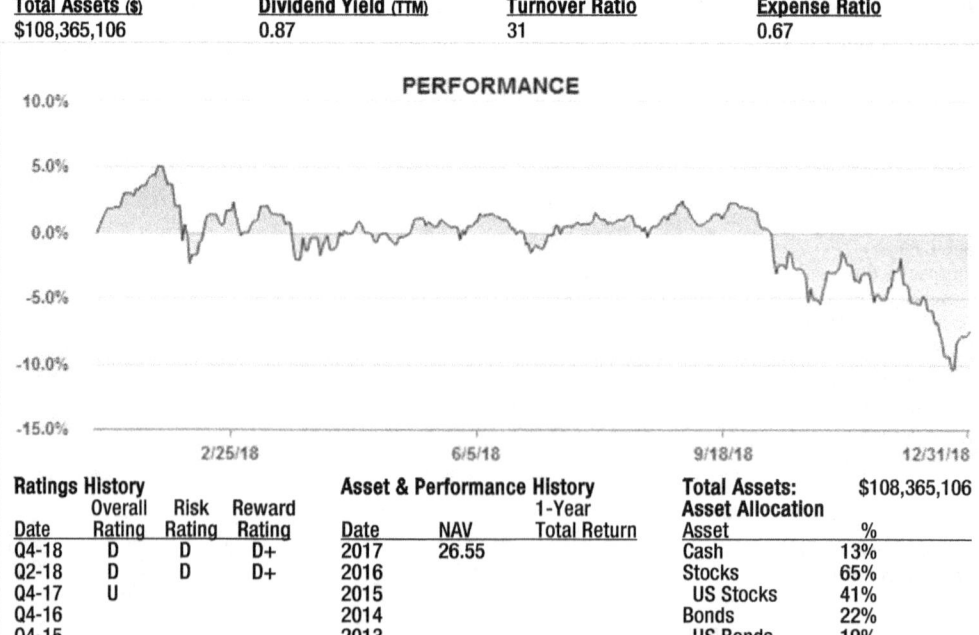

PERFORMANCE

Ratings History

Date	Overall Rating	Risk Rating	Reward Rating
Q4-18	C-	C-	C
Q2-18	C-	D+	C
Q4-17	C+	B+	C
Q4-16	C-	D+	C
Q4-15	D+	D+	D+

Asset & Performance History

Date	NAV	1-Year Total Return
2017	40.22	1.39
2016	40.15	1.52
2015	39.92	0.11
2014	40.02	0.28
2013	40.04	
2012		

Total Assets: $108,677,746

Asset Allocation

Asset	%
Cash	12%
Stocks	0%
US Stocks	0%
Bonds	88%
US Bonds	68%
Other	0%

Services Offered:

Investment Strategy: The investment seeks to provide current income consistent with preservation of capital and daily liquidity through short duration high quality investments. The Adviser invests, under normal circumstances, at least 80% of the fund's net assets (plus the amount of borrowings for investment purposes) in a diversified portfolio of U.S. dollar-denominated investment-grade fixed income securities. The fund may also invest in exchange traded products ("ETPs"). It is non-diversified. **Top Holdings:** United States Treasury Notes 0.88% United States Treasury Notes 2% Citibank Credit Card Issuance Trust 1.74% AmeriCredit Automobile Receivables Trust 2014-2 2.57% American Express Credit Account Master Trust 1.64%

ClearShares OCIO ETF   D   SELL

Ticker	Traded On	NAV	Total Assets ($)	Dividend Yield (TTM)	Turnover Ratio	Expense Ratio
OCIO	NYSE Arca	24.03	$108,365,106	0.87	31	0.67

Ratings
Reward   D+
Risk   D
Recent Upgrade/Downgrade

Fund Information
Fund Type   Exchange Traded Funds
Category   Moderate Allocation
Sub-Category   Allocation--50% to 70% Equity
Prospectus Objective   Growth & Inc
Inception Date   Jun-17
Open to New Investments   Y

Prices
Price (as of 12/31/2018)   23.99
52-Week High   27.77
52-Week Low   23.78

Total Returns (%)

3-Month	6-Month	1-Year	3-Year	5-Year
-9.21	-6.48	-7.52		

3-Year Standard Deviation
Effective Duration   4.24

Valuation
Premium/Discount (1-Year Average)   0.34

Company Information
Provider   ClearShares
Manager/Tenure   Eric J Blasberg (1), Jonathan M Chesshire (1), Mark N Hong (1)
Website   http://www.clear-shares.com
Address   ClearShares United States
Phone Number

PERFORMANCE

Ratings History

Date	Overall Rating	Risk Rating	Reward Rating
Q4-18	D	D	D+
Q2-18	D	D	D+
Q4-17	U		
Q4-16			
Q4-15			

Asset & Performance History

Date	NAV	1-Year Total Return
2017	26.55	
2016		
2015		
2014		
2013		
2012		

Total Assets: $108,365,106

Asset Allocation

Asset	%
Cash	13%
Stocks	65%
US Stocks	41%
Bonds	22%
US Bonds	19%
Other	0%

Services Offered:

Investment Strategy: The investment seeks to outperform a traditional 60/40 mix of global equity and fixed-income investments. The fund is expected to typically invest approximately 40% to 70% of its total assets in underlying funds that principally invest in equity securities of any market capitalization. It is expected to typically invest approximately 20% to 50% of its total assets in underlying funds that principally invest in debt obligations. In addition to the underlying funds, the fund may invest in non-investment company exchange-traded products. **Top Holdings:** Vanguard Total Stock Market ETF ClearShares Ultra-Short Maturity ETF iShares Core S&P 500 ETF Vanguard S&P 500 ETF iShares Edge MSCI USA Value Factor ETF

Cambria Global Momentum ETF   D+   SELL

Ticker	Traded On	NAV
GMOM	BATS	24.45

Total Assets ($)	Dividend Yield (TTM)	Turnover Ratio	Expense Ratio
$108,320,706	1.4	50	1.07

Ratings
Reward	D+
Risk	C-
Recent Upgrade/Downgrade	Down

Fund Information
Fund Type	Exchange Traded Funds
Category	Moderate Allocation
Sub-Category	World Allocation
Prospectus Objective	Growth & Inc
Inception Date	Nov-14
Open to New Investments	Y

Prices
Price (as of 12/31/2018)	24.31
52-Week High	29.35
52-Week Low	24.26

Total Returns (%)
3-Month	6-Month	1-Year	3-Year	5-Year
-7.84	-6.31	-8.72	14.81	

3-Year Standard Deviation	7.6
Effective Duration	4.54

Valuation
Premium/Discount (1-Year Average)	0.18

Company Information
Provider	CAMBRIA ETF TRUST
Manager/Tenure	Mebane T. Faber (4)
Website	http://www.cambriafunds.com
Address	CAMBRIA ETF TRUST 2711 Centreville Road Suite 400 Wilmington, DE 19808 Wilmington DE 19808 United States
Phone Number	310-683-5500

PERFORMANCE (chart from 1/20/17 to 12/31/18)

Ratings History
Date	Overall Rating	Risk Rating	Reward Rating
Q4-18	D+	C-	D+
Q2-18	C	C-	C
Q4-17	C+	C+	C+
Q4-16	D+	C-	D+
Q4-15	U		

Asset & Performance History
Date	NAV	1-Year Total Return
2017	27.28	20.59
2016	23.12	4.3
2015	22.56	-8.51
2014	25.1	
2013		
2012		

Total Assets: $108,320,706
Asset Allocation
Asset	%
Cash	15%
Stocks	37%
US Stocks	32%
Bonds	44%
US Bonds	37%
Other	3%

Services Offered:

Investment Strategy: The investment seeks to preserve and grow capital from investments in the U.S. and foreign equity, fixed income, commodity and currency markets, independent of market direction. The fund is considered a "fund of funds" that seeks to achieve its investment objective by primarily investing in other exchange-traded funds and other exchange traded products including, but not limited to, exchange-traded notes, exchange traded currency trusts, closed-end funds, and real estate investment trusts that offer diversified exposure, including inverse exposure, to global regions, countries, styles and sectors. **Top Holdings:** iShares Residential Real Estate Capd ETF   Vanguard Total Stock Market ETF   Vanguard Real Estate ETF   iShares Mortgage Real Estate Capped ETF   iShares Global Healthcare ETF

Invesco S&P SmallCap Consumer Staples ETF   C+   HOLD

Ticker	Traded On	NAV
PSCC	NAS CM	69.39

Total Assets ($)	Dividend Yield (TTM)	Turnover Ratio	Expense Ratio
$108,217,171	0.98		0.29

Ratings
Reward	B-
Risk	C
Recent Upgrade/Downgrade	Down

Fund Information
Fund Type	Exchange Traded Funds
Category	Consumer Goods & Svcs
Sub-Category	Consumer Defensive
Prospectus Objective	Unaligned
Inception Date	Apr-10
Open to New Investments	

Prices
Price (as of 12/31/2018)	69.15
52-Week High	85.94
52-Week Low	66.72

Total Returns (%)
3-Month	6-Month	1-Year	3-Year	5-Year
-15.05	-13.02	-6.20	31.97	49.44

3-Year Standard Deviation	13.3
Effective Duration	

Valuation
Premium/Discount (1-Year Average)	0.21

Company Information
Provider	Invesco
Manager/Tenure	Peter Hubbard (8), Michael Jeanette (8), Tony Seisser (4), 1 other
Website	http://www.invesco.com/us
Address	Invesco 11 Greenway Plaza, Ste. 2500 Houston TX 77046 United States
Phone Number	800-659-1005

PERFORMANCE (chart from 1/21/17 to 12/31/18)

Ratings History
Date	Overall Rating	Risk Rating	Reward Rating
Q4-18	C+	C	B-
Q2-18	B-	C-	B
Q4-17	A-	A-	A-
Q4-16	B-	C-	B
Q4-15	B	B-	B

Asset & Performance History
Date	NAV	1-Year Total Return
2017	74.65	9.44
2016	69.09	28.56
2015	54.56	1.6
2014	54.42	11.44
2013	49.75	44.11
2012	34.68	11.88

Total Assets: $108,217,171
Asset Allocation
Asset	%
Cash	0%
Stocks	100%
US Stocks	95%
Bonds	0%
US Bonds	0%
Other	0%

Services Offered:

Investment Strategy: The investment seeks to track the investment results (before fees and expenses) of the S&P SmallCap 600® Capped Consumer Staples Index (the "underlying index"). The fund generally will invest at least 90% of its total assets in common stocks of small capitalization U.S. consumer staples companies that comprise the underlying index. These companies are principally engaged in the business of providing consumer goods and services that have non-cyclical characteristics, including tobacco, food and beverage, and non-discretionary retail. The fund is non-diversified. **Top Holdings:** Darling Ingredients Inc   WD-40 Co   J&J Snack Foods Corp   Medifast Inc   United Natural Foods Inc

ETFMG Video Game Tech ETF   D+   SELL

Ticker	Traded On	NAV	Total Assets ($)	Dividend Yield (TTM)	Turnover Ratio	Expense Ratio
GAMR	NYSE Arca	39.19	$107,791,875	1.43	42	0.82

Ratings

Reward	D+
Risk	C-
Recent Upgrade/Downgrade	Down

Fund Information

Fund Type	Exchange Traded Funds
Category	Technology Sector Equity
Sub-Category	Technology
Prospectus Objective	Technology
Inception Date	Mar-16
Open to New Investments	Y

Prices

Price (as of 12/31/2018)	38.90
52-Week High	54.26
52-Week Low	37.44

Total Returns (%)

3-Month	6-Month	1-Year	3-Year	5-Year
-17.36	-19.15	-16.89		

3-Year Standard Deviation	
Effective Duration	

Valuation

Premium/Discount (1-Year Average)	0.04

Company Information

Provider	Pure Funds
Manager/Tenure	Samuel R. Masucci (0), James B. Francis (0), Devin Ryder (0), 1 other
Website	http://www.etfmgfunds.com
Address	
Phone Number	

PERFORMANCE

Ratings History

Date	Overall Rating	Risk Rating	Reward Rating
Q4-18	D+	C-	D+
Q2-18	C	C-	C+
Q4-17	C-	B+	C
Q4-16	U		
Q4-15			

Asset & Performance History

Date	NAV	1-Year Total Return
2017	47.77	59.89
2016	30.02	
2015		
2014		
2013		
2012		

Total Assets: $107,791,875

Asset Allocation

Asset	%
Cash	1%
Stocks	99%
US Stocks	31%
Bonds	0%
US Bonds	0%
Other	0%

Services Offered:

Investment Strategy: The investment seeks to provide investment results that, before fees and expenses, correspond generally to the price and yield performance of the EEFund Video Game Tech Index. The index tracks the performance of the common stock of exchange-listed companies across the globe that are actively engaged in a business activity supporting or utilizing the video gaming industry. The fund normally invests at least 80% of its total assets, exclusive of collateral held from securities lending, in securities, ADRs, or GDRs of Video Gaming Companies. It is non-diversified. **Top Holdings:** NCsoft Corp Glu Mobile Inc Changyou.com Ltd ADR Take-Two Interactive Software Inc GameStop Corp Class A

SPDR® MSCI ACWI IMI ETF   C-   HOLD

Ticker	Traded On	NAV	Total Assets ($)	Dividend Yield (TTM)	Turnover Ratio	Expense Ratio
ACIM	NYSE Arca	69.82	$106,452,237	2.31	4	0.25

Ratings

Reward	C-
Risk	C-
Recent Upgrade/Downgrade	Down

Fund Information

Fund Type	Exchange Traded Funds
Category	Global Equity Large Cap
Sub-Category	World Large Stock
Prospectus Objective	World Stock
Inception Date	Feb-12
Open to New Investments	Y

Prices

Price (as of 12/31/2018)	69.62
52-Week High	83.96
52-Week Low	66.46

Total Returns (%)

3-Month	6-Month	1-Year	3-Year	5-Year
-13.18	-8.25	-9.54	22.05	26.84

3-Year Standard Deviation	9.7
Effective Duration	

Valuation

Premium/Discount (1-Year Average)	0.17

Company Information

Provider	SPDR State Street Global Advisors
Manager/Tenure	Michael J. Feehily (6), Karl A. Schneider (3), Olga Winner (1)
Website	http://www.spdrs.com
Address	SPDR State Street Global Advisors State Street Financial Center, 1 Lincoln Street Boston MA 02111-2900 United States
Phone Number	617-786-3000

PERFORMANCE

Ratings History

Date	Overall Rating	Risk Rating	Reward Rating
Q4-18	C-	C-	C-
Q2-18	C	D+	C
Q4-17	B-	B-	B-
Q4-16	C	D+	C+
Q4-15	C	D+	C

Asset & Performance History

Date	NAV	1-Year Total Return
2017	78.6	23.98
2016	64.92	8.83
2015	60.8	-1.68
2014	64.1	5.7
2013	61.97	23.45
2012	51.17	

Total Assets: $106,452,237

Asset Allocation

Asset	%
Cash	0%
Stocks	100%
US Stocks	56%
Bonds	0%
US Bonds	0%
Other	0%

Services Offered:

Investment Strategy: The investment seeks to provide investment results that, before fees and expenses, correspond generally to the total return performance of the MSCI ACWI IMI Index. The fund generally invests substantially all, but at least 80%, of its total assets in the securities comprising the index and in depositary receipts based on securities comprising the index. The index is a free float-adjusted market capitalization-weighted index that is designed to measure the combined equity market performance of developed and emerging markets. It is non-diversified. **Top Holdings:** Apple Inc Microsoft Corp Amazon.com Inc JPMorgan Chase & Co Visa Inc Class A

DeltaShares S&P 400 Managed Risk ETF   D   SELL

Ticker	Traded On	NAV	Total Assets ($)	Dividend Yield (TTM)	Turnover Ratio	Expense Ratio
DMRM	NYSE Arca	48.30	$106,200,067	1.22	6	0.45

Ratings
Reward   D+
Risk   D
Recent Upgrade/Downgrade   Down

Fund Information
Fund Type   Exchange Traded Funds
Category   US Equity Mid Cap
Sub-Category   Mid-Cap Blend
Prospectus Objective   Growth
Inception Date   Jul-17
Open to New Investments   Y

Prices
Price (as of 12/31/2018)   48.28
52-Week High   56.91
52-Week Low   47.01

Total Returns (%)

3-Month	6-Month	1-Year	3-Year	5-Year
-12.65	-10.16	-9.18		

3-Year Standard Deviation
Effective Duration

Valuation
Premium/Discount (1-Year Average)   0.35

Company Information
Provider   DeltaShares
Manager/Tenure   Blake Graves (1), Charles Lowery (1),
                  Louis Ng (1)
Website   http://www.deltashares.com
Address   DeltaShares United States
Phone Number

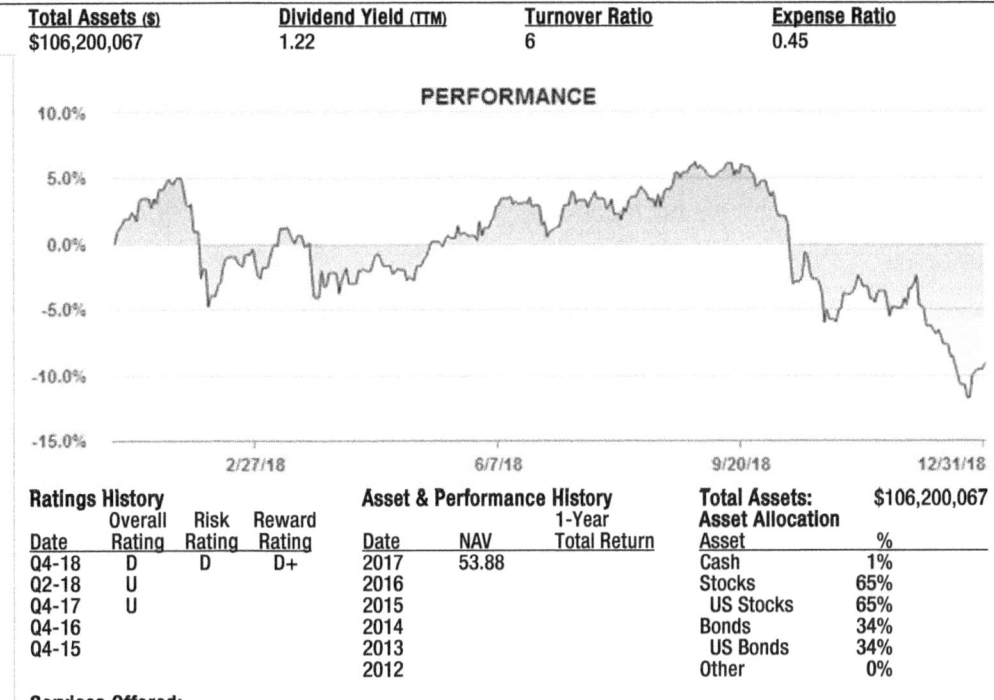

Ratings History

Date	Overall Rating	Risk Rating	Reward Rating
Q4-18	D	D	D+
Q2-18	U		
Q4-17	U		
Q4-16			
Q4-15			

Asset & Performance History

Date	NAV	1-Year Total Return
2017	53.88	
2016		
2015		
2014		
2013		
2012		

Total Assets: $106,200,067
Asset Allocation

Asset	%
Cash	1%
Stocks	65%
US Stocks	65%
Bonds	34%
US Bonds	34%
Other	0%

Services Offered:

Investment Strategy: The investment seeks to track the investment results, before fees and expenses, of the S&P 400 Managed Risk 2.0 Index. Under normal market conditions, the fund invests a substantial portion, but at least 80%, of its assets, exclusive of collateral held from securities lending, in securities comprising the S&P 400 Managed Risk 2.0 Index. The underlying index seeks to achieve these objectives by allocating weightings among the S&P MidCap 400 Index, the S&P U.S. Treasury Bond Current 5-Year Index and the S&P U.S. Treasury Bill 0-3 Month Index. The fund is non-diversified. **Top Holdings:** United States Treasury Notes 2.88% S+p Mid 400 Emini Dec18 Xcme 20181221   Jack Henry & Associates Inc   Lamb Weston Holdings Inc   Domino's Pizza Inc

First Trust RiverFront Dynamic Emerging Markets ETF   D+   SELL

Ticker	Traded On	NAV	Total Assets ($)	Dividend Yield (TTM)	Turnover Ratio	Expense Ratio
RFEM	NAS CM	56.34	$105,776,392	2.14	87	0.95

Ratings
Reward   D+
Risk   D
Recent Upgrade/Downgrade

Fund Information
Fund Type   Exchange Traded Funds
Category   Global Emerg Mkts Equity
Sub-Category   Diversified Emerging Mkts
Prospectus Objective   Div Emerg Mkts
Inception Date   Jun-16
Open to New Investments   Y

Prices
Price (as of 12/31/2018)   55.99
52-Week High   79.03
52-Week Low   54.25

Total Returns (%)

3-Month	6-Month	1-Year	3-Year	5-Year
-9.37	-13.41	-18.07		

3-Year Standard Deviation
Effective Duration

Valuation
Premium/Discount (1-Year Average)   0.07

Company Information
Provider   First Trust
Manager/Tenure   Adam Grossman (2), Scott Hays (2),
                  Chris Konstantinos (2), 1 other
Website   http://www.ftportfolios.com/
Address   First Trust 120 E. Liberty Drive, Suite
                  400 Wheaton IL 60187 United States
Phone Number   800-621-1675

Ratings History

Date	Overall Rating	Risk Rating	Reward Rating
Q4-18	D+	D	D+
Q2-18	D+	D+	C-
Q4-17	D+	B	C
Q4-16	U		
Q4-15			

Asset & Performance History

Date	NAV	1-Year Total Return
2017	70.25	35.57
2016	52.71	
2015		
2014		
2013		
2012		

Total Assets: $105,776,392
Asset Allocation

Asset	%
Cash	0%
Stocks	100%
US Stocks	1%
Bonds	0%
US Bonds	0%
Other	0%

Services Offered:

Investment Strategy: The investment seeks to provide capital appreciation. The fund invests at least 80% of its net assets (including investment borrowings) in a portfolio of equity securities of emerging market companies, including through investments in common stock, depositary receipts, and common and preferred shares of real estate investment trusts, and forward foreign currency exchange contracts and currency spot transactions used to hedge the fund's exposure to the currencies in which the equity securities of such emerging market companies are denominated. The fund may invest in small, mid and large capitalization companies. It is non-diversified. **Top Holdings:** Samsung Electronics Co Ltd   Tencent Holdings Ltd   Taiwan Semiconductor Manufacturing Co Ltd   Alibaba Group Holding Ltd ADR   China Construction Bank Corp H

iShares GNMA Bond ETF   D+   SELL

Ticker	Traded On	NAV	Total Assets ($)	Dividend Yield (TTM)	Turnover Ratio	Expense Ratio
GNMA	NAS CM	48.68	$105,475,009	2.41	917	0.15

Ratings
Reward   D
Risk   C-
Recent Upgrade/Downgrade

Fund Information
Fund Type   Exchange Traded Funds
Category   US Fixed Income
Sub-Category   Intermediate Government
Prospectus Objective   Govt Bond - Mortgage
Inception Date   Feb-12
Open to New Investments   Y

Prices
Price (as of 12/31/2018)   48.70
52-Week High   49.52
52-Week Low   47.32

Total Returns (%)

3-Month	6-Month	1-Year	3-Year	5-Year
1.93	1.89	0.68	3.75	11.05

3-Year Standard Deviation   1.94
Effective Duration   5.26

Valuation
Premium/Discount (1-Year Average)   -0.07

Company Information
Provider   iShares
Manager/Tenure James Mauro (6), Scott Radell (6)
Website   http://www.ishares.com
Address   iShares 400 Howard Street San
                       Francisco CA 94105 United States
Phone Number   800-474-2737

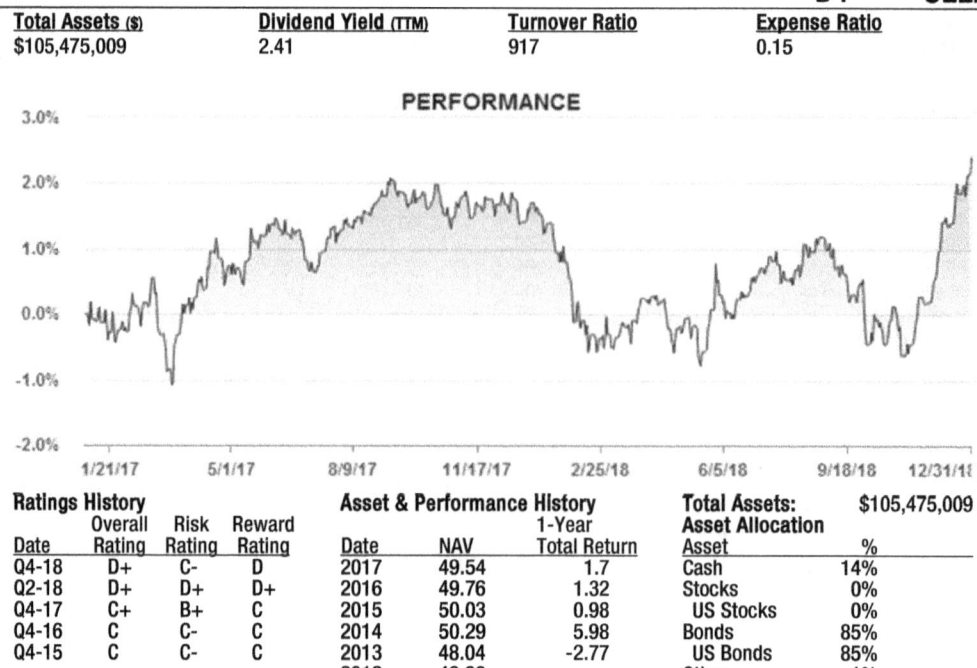

PERFORMANCE

Ratings History

Date	Overall Rating	Risk Rating	Reward Rating
Q4-18	D+	C-	D
Q2-18	D+	D+	D+
Q4-17	C+	B+	C
Q4-16	C	C-	C
Q4-15	C	C-	C

Asset & Performance History

Date	NAV	1-Year Total Return
2017	49.54	1.7
2016	49.76	1.32
2015	50.03	0.98
2014	50.29	5.98
2013	48.04	-2.77
2012	49.93	

Total Assets: $105,475,009
Asset Allocation

Asset	%
Cash	14%
Stocks	0%
US Stocks	0%
Bonds	85%
US Bonds	85%
Other	1%

Services Offered:

Investment Strategy: The investment seeks to track the investment results of the Bloomberg Barclays U.S. GNMA Bond Index. The fund generally will invest at least 90% of its assets in the component securities of the underlying index and in investments that have economic characteristics that are substantially identical to the component securities of the underlying index. The underlying index includes fixed-rate mortgage pass-through securities issued by GNMA that have 30- or 15-year maturities. The index measures the performance of mortgage-backed pass-through securities issued by GNMA. **Top Holdings:** Gnma2 30yr 2016 Production Gnma2 30yr 2016 Production Gnma2 30yr 2017 Production Gnma 30yr 4% Fico <660 2015 Gnma2 30yr 2017 Production

---

iShares MSCI Austria Capped ETF   C-   HOLD

Ticker	Traded On	NAV	Total Assets ($)	Dividend Yield (TTM)	Turnover Ratio	Expense Ratio
EWO	NYSE Arca	18.32	$105,156,797	3.31	19	0.47

Ratings
Reward   C-
Risk   C-
Recent Upgrade/Downgrade   Down

Fund Information
Fund Type   Exchange Traded Funds
Category   Europe Equity Mid/Small Cap
Sub-Category   Miscellaneous Region
Prospectus Objective   Europe Stock
Inception Date   Mar-96
Open to New Investments   Y

Prices
Price (as of 12/31/2018)   18.36
52-Week High   27.26
52-Week Low   17.50

Total Returns (%)

3-Month	6-Month	1-Year	3-Year	5-Year
-19.20	-17.07	-23.19	25.44	5.17

3-Year Standard Deviation   17.05
Effective Duration

Valuation
Premium/Discount (1-Year Average)   -0.25

Company Information
Provider   iShares
Manager/Tenure Diane Hsiung (10), Greg Savage (10),
                       Jennifer Hsui (5), 1 other
Website   http://www.ishares.com
Address   iShares 400 Howard Street San
                       Francisco CA 94105 United States
Phone Number   800-474-2737

PERFORMANCE

Ratings History

Date	Overall Rating	Risk Rating	Reward Rating
Q4-18	C-	C-	C-
Q2-18	C	C+	C
Q4-17	B+	B-	A+
Q4-16	C-	C-	C-
Q4-15	C-	C-	C-

Asset & Performance History

Date	NAV	1-Year Total Return
2017	24.69	52.53
2016	16.56	7.07
2015	15.8	4.9
2014	15.28	-20.07
2013	19.73	13.24
2012	17.83	28.66

Total Assets: $105,156,797
Asset Allocation

Asset	%
Cash	1%
Stocks	99%
US Stocks	0%
Bonds	0%
US Bonds	0%
Other	0%

Services Offered: CashInvestment Plan

Investment Strategy: The investment seeks to track the investment results of the MSCI Austria IMI 25/50 Index. The fund generally invests at least 90% of its assets in the securities of its underlying index and in depositary receipts representing securities in the index. The index is a free float-adjusted market capitalization-weighted index with a capping methodology applied to issuer weights so that no single issuer of a component exceeds 25% of the index weight, and all issuers with a weight above 5% do not cumulatively exceed 50% of the index weight. The fund is non-diversified. **Top Holdings:** Erste Group Bank AG. Omv Ag Raiffeisen Bank International AG Wienerberger AG Immofinanz AG

iShares U.S. Insurance ETF   C   HOLD

Ticker	Traded On	NAV	Total Assets ($)	Dividend Yield (TTM)	Turnover Ratio	Expense Ratio
IAK	NYSE Arca	57.97	$103,979,019	2.13	12	0.43

Ratings
Reward   C
Risk   C-
Recent Upgrade/Downgrade   Down

Fund Information
Fund Type   Exchange Traded Funds
Category   Financials Sector Equity
Sub-Category   Financial
Prospectus Objective   Financial
Inception Date   May-06
Open to New Investments   Y

Prices
Price (as of 12/31/2018)   57.72
52-Week High   69.88
52-Week Low   54.51

Total Returns (%)

3-Month	6-Month	1-Year	3-Year	5-Year
-11.59	-5.09	-11.05	20.12	34.02

3-Year Standard Deviation   12.32
Effective Duration

Valuation
Premium/Discount (1-Year Average)   0.06

Company Information
Provider   iShares
Manager/Tenure   Diane Hsiung (10), Greg Savage (10), Jennifer Hsui (6), 3 others
Website   http://www.ishares.com
Address   iShares 400 Howard Street San Francisco CA 94105 United States
Phone Number   800-474-2737

PERFORMANCE

Ratings History

Date	Overall Rating	Risk Rating	Reward Rating
Q4-18	C	C-	C
Q2-18	C+	C	B-
Q4-17	B+	A-	B+
Q4-16	C	C-	C
Q4-15	B+	B+	B+

Asset & Performance History

Date	NAV	1-Year Total Return
2017	66.59	14.1
2016	59.36	18.36
2015	51.1	3.94
2014	49.98	7.33
2013	47.33	45.17
2012	33.02	18.09

Total Assets: $103,979,019
Asset Allocation

Asset	%
Cash	0%
Stocks	100%
US Stocks	91%
Bonds	0%
US Bonds	0%
Other	0%

Services Offered:

Investment Strategy: The investment seeks to track the investment results of the Dow Jones U.S. Select Insurance Index composed of U.S. equities in the insurance sector. The fund generally invests at least 90% of its assets in securities of the underlying index and in depositary receipts representing securities of the underlying index. The underlying index measures the performance of the insurance sector of the U.S. equity market. The fund is non-diversified. **Top Holdings:** Chubb Ltd MetLife Inc Prudential Financial Inc Progressive Corp American International Group Inc

---

VelocityShares Daily Inverse VIX Medium-Term ETN   C   HOLD

Ticker	Traded On	NAV	Total Assets ($)	Dividend Yield (TTM)	Turnover Ratio	Expense Ratio
ZIV	NAS CM	60.57	$103,725,061	0		1.35

Ratings
Reward   C-
Risk   C-
Recent Upgrade/Downgrade   Down

Fund Information
Fund Type   Exchange Traded Funds
Category   Alternative Misc
Sub-Category   Volatility
Prospectus Objective   Growth
Inception Date   Nov-10
Open to New Investments   Y

Prices
Price (as of 12/31/2018)   60.41
52-Week High   93.87
52-Week Low   59.11

Total Returns (%)

3-Month	6-Month	1-Year	3-Year	5-Year
-24.81	-16.20	-31.31	45.66	56.82

3-Year Standard Deviation   27.75
Effective Duration

Valuation
Premium/Discount (1-Year Average)   -0.14

Company Information
Provider   Credit Suisse AG
Manager/Tenure   Management Team (8)
Website
Address   Kilmore House Park Lane Dublin Ireland
Phone Number

PERFORMANCE

Ratings History

Date	Overall Rating	Risk Rating	Reward Rating
Q4-18	C	C-	C-
Q2-18	C	C-	C
Q4-17	B+	C	A+
Q4-16	C	C-	C-
Q4-15	C+	C-	C+

Asset & Performance History

Date	NAV	1-Year Total Return
2017	88.17	88.67
2016	46.77	12.89
2015	41.58	-0.85
2014	41.94	8.59
2013	38.62	64.83
2012	23.43	88.95

Total Assets: $103,725,061
Asset Allocation

Asset	%
Cash	%
Stocks	%
US Stocks	%
Bonds	%
US Bonds	%
Other	%

Services Offered:

Investment Strategy: The investment seeks to replicate, net of expenses, the inverse of the daily performance of the S&P 500 VIX Mid-Term Futures index.
 The index was designed to provide investors with exposure to one or more maturities of futures contracts on the VIX, which reflects implied volatility of the S&P 500 Index at various points along the volatility forward curve. The calculation of the VIX is based on prices of put and call options on the S&P 500 Index. The ETNs are linked to the daily inverse return of the index and do not represent an investment in the inverse of the VIX. **Top Holdings:**

iShares Government/Credit Bond ETF

D+   **SELL**

Ticker	Traded On	NAV	Total Assets ($)	Dividend Yield (TTM)	Turnover Ratio	Expense Ratio
GBF	NYSE Arca	110.29	$103,379,977	2.67	17	0.2

Ratings
Reward   D
Risk   D+
Recent Upgrade/Downgrade

Fund Information
Fund Type   Exchange Traded Funds
Category   US Fixed Income
Sub-Category   Intermediate-Term Bond
Prospectus Objective   Income
Inception Date   Jan-07
Open to New Investments   Y

Prices
Price (as of 12/31/2018)   110.44
52-Week High   113.94
52-Week Low   108.16

Total Returns (%)

3-Month	6-Month	1-Year	3-Year	5-Year
1.49	1.48	-0.60	6.07	12.29

3-Year Standard Deviation   3.05
Effective Duration   6.20

Valuation
Premium/Discount (1-Year Average)   -0.01

Company Information
Provider   iShares
Manager/Tenure   Scott Radell (8), James Mauro (7)
Website   http://www.ishares.com
Address   iShares 400 Howard Street San Francisco CA 94105 United States
Phone Number   800-474-2737

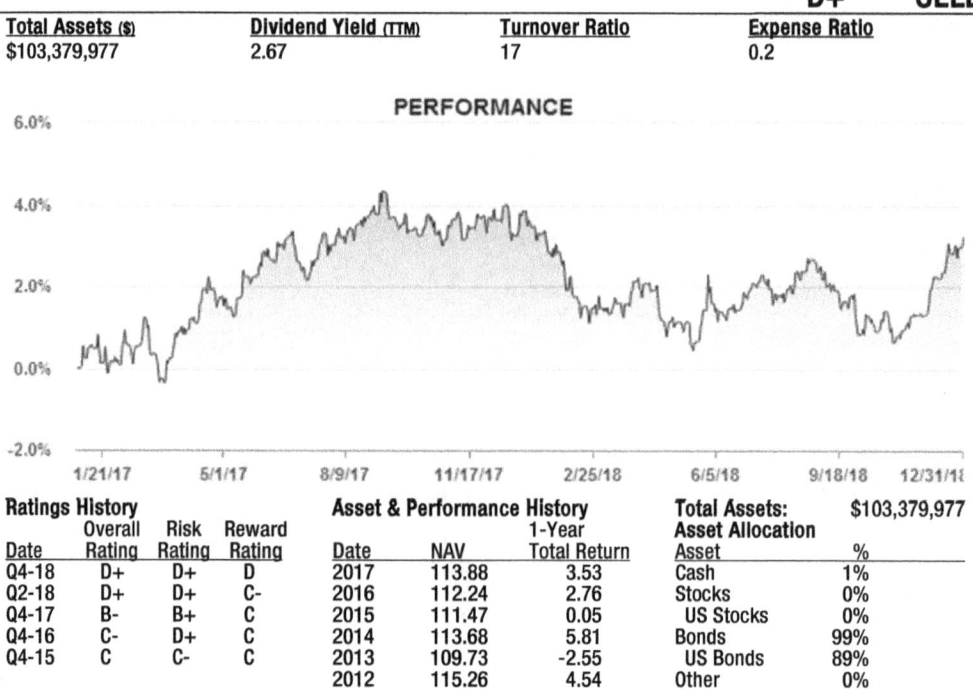

PERFORMANCE

Ratings History

Date	Overall Rating	Risk Rating	Reward Rating
Q4-18	D+	D+	D
Q2-18	D+	D+	C-
Q4-17	B-	B+	C
Q4-16	C-	D+	C
Q4-15	C	C-	C

Asset & Performance History

Date	NAV	1-Year Total Return
2017	113.88	3.53
2016	112.24	2.76
2015	111.47	0.05
2014	113.68	5.81
2013	109.73	-2.55
2012	115.26	4.54

Total Assets: $103,379,977
Asset Allocation

Asset	%
Cash	1%
Stocks	0%
US Stocks	0%
Bonds	99%
US Bonds	89%
Other	0%

Services Offered:

Investment Strategy: The investment seeks to track the investment results of the Bloomberg Barclays U.S. government/Credit Bond Index (the "underlying index"). The underlying index measures the performance of U.S. dollar-denominated U.S. Treasury bonds, government-related bonds and investment-grade U.S. corporate bonds that have a remaining maturity of greater than or equal to one year. The fund generally invests at least 90% of its assets in securities of the underlying index. It may invest the remainder of its assets in certain futures, options and swap contracts, cash and cash equivalents, as well as in securities not included in the underlying index. **Top Holdings:** United States Treasury Notes 1.88% United States Treasury Notes 3.63% United States Treasury Notes 1.5% United States Treasury Notes 1.88% United States Treasury Notes 2.25%

Nationwide Maximum Diversification U.S. Core Equity ETF

D+   **SELL**

Ticker	Traded On	NAV	Total Assets ($)	Dividend Yield (TTM)	Turnover Ratio	Expense Ratio
MXDU	NYSE Arca	24.86	$102,926,142	0.41		0.34

Ratings
Reward   D+
Risk   D+
Recent Upgrade/Downgrade

Fund Information
Fund Type   Exchange Traded Funds
Category   US Equity Large Cap Blend
Sub-Category   Large Blend
Prospectus Objective   Growth
Inception Date   Sep-17
Open to New Investments   Y

Prices
Price (as of 12/31/2018)   24.80
52-Week High   29.79
52-Week Low   23.92

Total Returns (%)

3-Month	6-Month	1-Year	3-Year	5-Year
-14.19	-10.09	-4.37		

3-Year Standard Deviation
Effective Duration

Valuation
Premium/Discount (1-Year Average)   0.09

Company Information
Provider   Nationwide
Manager/Tenure   Denise M. Krisko (1), Austin Wen (1)
Website   http://www.nationwide.com/mutualfunds
Address   Nationwide One Nationwide Plaza Columbus OH 43215 United States
Phone Number   800-848-0920

PERFORMANCE

Ratings History

Date	Overall Rating	Risk Rating	Reward Rating
Q4-18	D+	D+	D+
Q2-18	U		
Q4-17	U		
Q4-16			
Q4-15			

Asset & Performance History

Date	NAV	1-Year Total Return
2017	26.44	
2016		
2015		
2014		
2013		
2012		

Total Assets: $102,926,142
Asset Allocation

Asset	%
Cash	0%
Stocks	100%
US Stocks	99%
Bonds	0%
US Bonds	0%
Other	0%

Services Offered:

Investment Strategy: The investment seeks to track the total return performance, before fees and expenses, of the TOBAM Maximum Diversification USA Index (the "index"). The advisor attempts to invest all, or substantially all, of its assets in the component securities that make up the index. Normally, at least 80% of the fund's total assets will be invested in the component securities of the index. The index is a rules-based index that is designed to create a more diversified equity portfolio of the common and preferred stock of large and mid-capitalization U.S. companies relative to traditional market capitalization weighted benchmarks. **Top Holdings:** Humana Inc The Kroger Co Twitter Inc Amazon.com Inc Newmont Mining Corp

Alpha Architect U.S. Quantitative Value ETF

C HOLD

Ticker	Traded On	NAV
QVAL	BATS	25.18

Total Assets ($)	Dividend Yield (TTM)	Turnover Ratio	Expense Ratio
$102,768,295	1.18	46	0.79

Ratings
Reward	C
Risk	C-
Recent Upgrade/Downgrade	

Fund Information
Fund Type	Exchange Traded Funds
Category	US Equity Mid Cap
Sub-Category	Mid-Cap Value
Prospectus Objective	Growth
Inception Date	Oct-14
Open to New Investments	Y

Prices
Price (as of 12/31/2018)	25.04
52-Week High	33.41
52-Week Low	23.89

Total Returns (%)
3-Month	6-Month	1-Year	3-Year	5-Year
-18.06	-18.13	-16.55	18.28	

3-Year Standard Deviation	14.84
Effective Duration	

Valuation
Premium/Discount (1-Year Average)	0.14

Company Information
Provider	Alpha Architect
Manager/Tenure	Tao Wang (4)
Website	http://www.alphaarchitect.com/funds
Address	Alpha Architect 213 Foxcroft Road Broomall PA 19008 United States
Phone Number	

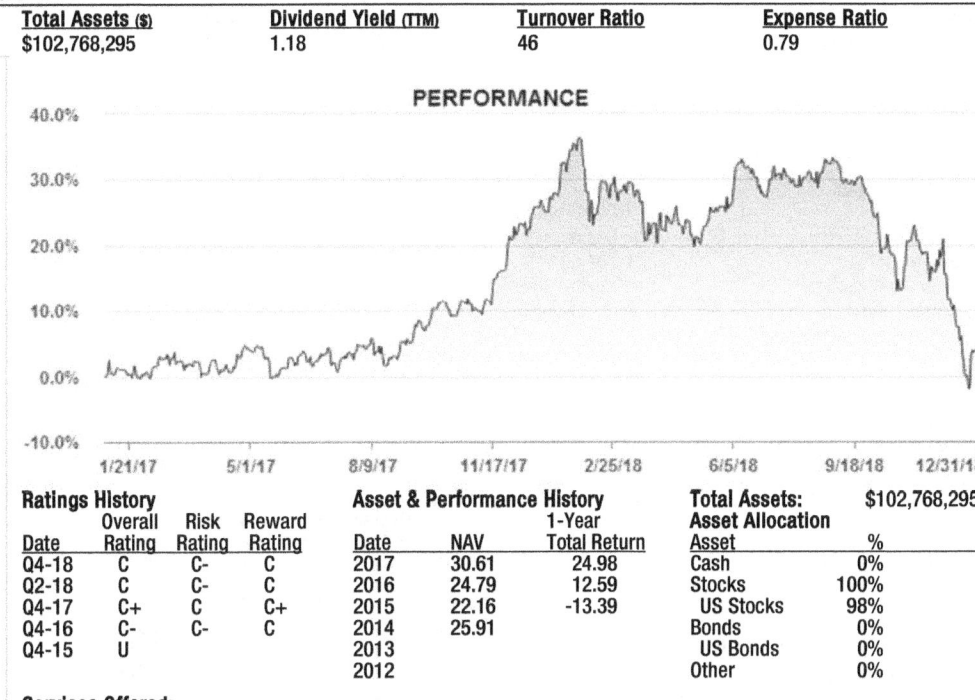

PERFORMANCE

Ratings History
Date	Overall Rating	Risk Rating	Reward Rating
Q4-18	C	C-	C
Q2-18	C	C-	C
Q4-17	C+	C	C+
Q4-16	C-	C-	C
Q4-15	U		

Asset & Performance History
Date	NAV	1-Year Total Return
2017	30.61	24.98
2016	24.79	12.59
2015	22.16	-13.39
2014	25.91	
2013		
2012		

Total Assets: $102,768,295

Asset Allocation
Asset	%
Cash	0%
Stocks	100%
US Stocks	98%
Bonds	0%
US Bonds	0%
Other	0%

Services Offered:

Investment Strategy: The investment seeks to track the total return performance, before fees and expenses, of the Alpha Architect Quantitative Value Index. The fund will normally invest at least 80% of its total assets in the component securities of the index. It may also invest up to 20% of its assets in cash and cash equivalents, other investment companies, as well as securities and other instruments not included in the index but which the Adviser believes will help the fund track the index. The index uses a 5-step, quantitative, rules-based methodology to identify a portfolio of approximately 40-50 undervalued U.S. equity securities with the potential for capital appreciation. **Top Holdings:** Cigna Corp Foot Locker Inc Cummins Inc Viacom Inc B Ingredion Inc

---

Hartford Municipal Opportunities ETF

D SELL

Ticker	Traded On	NAV
HMOP	NYSE Arca	39.84

Total Assets ($)	Dividend Yield (TTM)	Turnover Ratio	Expense Ratio
$102,691,126		37	0.29

Ratings
Reward	D+
Risk	D
Recent Upgrade/Downgrade	

Fund Information
Fund Type	Exchange Traded Funds
Category	US Muni Fixed Inc
Sub-Category	Muni National Interm
Prospectus Objective	Growth & Inc
Inception Date	Dec-17
Open to New Investments	Y

Prices
Price (as of 12/31/2018)	39.89
52-Week High	40.34
52-Week Low	39.08

Total Returns (%)
3-Month	6-Month	1-Year	3-Year	5-Year
1.71	1.61	1.44		

3-Year Standard Deviation	
Effective Duration	

Valuation
Premium/Discount (1-Year Average)	0.14

Company Information
Provider	Hartford Funds
Manager/Tenure	Timothy D. Haney (0), Brad W. Libby (0)
Website	http://www.hartfordfunds.com
Address	690 Lee Road Wayne PA 19087 United States
Phone Number	800-456-7526

PERFORMANCE

Ratings History
Date	Overall Rating	Risk Rating	Reward Rating
Q4-18	D	D	D+
Q2-18	U		
Q4-17	U		
Q4-16			
Q4-15			

Asset & Performance History
Date	NAV	1-Year Total Return
2017	40.18	
2016		
2015		
2014		
2013		
2012		

Total Assets: $102,691,126

Asset Allocation
Asset	%
Cash	7%
Stocks	0%
US Stocks	0%
Bonds	93%
US Bonds	93%
Other	0%

Services Offered:

Investment Strategy: The investment seeks to provide current income that is generally exempt from federal income taxes and long-term total return. The fund invests in investment grade and non-investment grade municipal securities (known as "junk bonds") that the sub-adviser considers to be attractive from a yield perspective while considering total return. At least 80% of the fund's net assets must be invested in municipal securities, and up to 35% of its net assets may be invested in non-investment grade municipal securities. The fund may invest in securities of any maturity or duration. **Top Holdings:** DISTRICT COLUMBIA 5% NEW YORK ST DORM AUTH 5% NEW YORK N Y CITY TRANSITIONAL FIN AUTH 5% NEW YORK N Y CITY TRANSITIONAL FIN AUTH 5% NORTH EAST INDPT SCH DIST TEX 5%

Fidelity® Momentum Factor ETF

C   HOLD

Ticker	Traded On	NAV	Total Assets ($)	Dividend Yield (TTM)	Turnover Ratio	Expense Ratio
FDMO	NYSE Arca	29.71	$102,677,392	1.03		0.29

Ratings
Reward	C
Risk	C-
Recent Upgrade/Downgrade	

Fund Information
Fund Type	Exchange Traded Funds
Category	US Equity Large Cap Growth
Sub-Category	Large Growth
Prospectus Objective	Growth & Inc
Inception Date	Sep-16
Open to New Investments	Y

Prices
Price (as of 12/31/2018)	29.65
52-Week High	35.53
52-Week Low	27.72

Total Returns (%)
3-Month	6-Month	1-Year	3-Year	5-Year
-16.01	-9.04	-3.71		

3-Year Standard Deviation	
Effective Duration	

Valuation
Premium/Discount (1-Year Average)	0.15

Company Information
Provider	Fidelity Investments
Manager/Tenure	Louis Bottari (2), Deane Gyllenhaal (2), Peter Matthew (2), 2 others
Website	http://www.institutional.fidelity.com
Address	Fidelity Investments 82 Devonshire Street Boston MA 2109 United States
Phone Number	617-563-7000

PERFORMANCE

Ratings History
Date	Overall Rating	Risk Rating	Reward Rating
Q4-18	C	C-	C
Q2-18	C	C-	C
Q4-17	D	B	C
Q4-16	U		
Q4-15			

Asset & Performance History
Date	NAV	1-Year Total Return
2017	31.21	23.71
2016	25.53	
2015		
2014		
2013		
2012		

Total Assets: $102,677,392

Asset Allocation
Asset	%
Cash	0%
Stocks	100%
US Stocks	99%
Bonds	0%
US Bonds	0%
Other	0%

Services Offered:

Investment Strategy: The investment seeks to provide investment returns that correspond, before fees and expenses, generally to the performance of the Fidelity U.S. Momentum Factor Index?. The fund normally invests at least 80% of assets in securities included in the Fidelity U.S. Momentum Factor Index?, which is designed to reflect the performance of stocks of large and mid-capitalization U.S. companies that exhibit positive momentum signals. It may lend securities to earn income for the fund. **Top Holdings:** Microsoft Corp Apple Inc Amazon.com Inc Alphabet Inc A Berkshire Hathaway Inc B

Invesco S&P MidCap 400® Pure Value ETF

C-   HOLD

Ticker	Traded On	NAV	Total Assets ($)	Dividend Yield (TTM)	Turnover Ratio	Expense Ratio
RFV	NYSE Arca	56.59	$102,390,740	1.26		0.35

Ratings
Reward	C
Risk	D+
Recent Upgrade/Downgrade	Down

Fund Information
Fund Type	Exchange Traded Funds
Category	US Equity Small Cap
Sub-Category	Small Value
Prospectus Objective	Growth
Inception Date	Mar-06
Open to New Investments	Y

Prices
Price (as of 12/31/2018)	56.16
52-Week High	73.79
52-Week Low	53.74

Total Returns (%)
3-Month	6-Month	1-Year	3-Year	5-Year
-20.32	-18.81	-17.95	23.24	19.11

3-Year Standard Deviation	16.67
Effective Duration	

Valuation
Premium/Discount (1-Year Average)	0.06

Company Information
Provider	Invesco
Manager/Tenure	Peter Hubbard (0), Michael Jeanette (0), Jonathan Nixon (0), 1 other
Website	http://www.invesco.com/us
Address	Invesco 11 Greenway Plaza, Ste. 2500 Houston TX 77046 United States
Phone Number	800-659-1005

PERFORMANCE

Ratings History
Date	Overall Rating	Risk Rating	Reward Rating
Q4-18	C-	D+	C
Q2-18	C-	D+	C
Q4-17	B	B-	B+
Q4-16	C+	C-	B
Q4-15	C	C-	C

Asset & Performance History
Date	NAV	1-Year Total Return
2017	69.79	14.63
2016	61.71	30.54
2015	47.64	-10.79
2014	54.3	8.35
2013	50.73	38.28
2012	37.02	19.04

Total Assets: $102,390,740

Asset Allocation
Asset	%
Cash	0%
Stocks	100%
US Stocks	99%
Bonds	0%
US Bonds	0%
Other	0%

Services Offered:

Investment Strategy: The investment seeks to track the investment results (before fees and expenses) of the S&P MidCap 400® Pure Value Index (the "underlying index"). The fund generally will invest at least 90% of its total assets in the securities that comprise the underlying index. The underlying index is comprised only of those S&P MidCap 400® companies with strong value characteristics as measured using three factors: book to value price ratio, earnings to price ratio, and sales to price ratio. The fund is non-diversified. **Top Holdings:** Genworth Financial Inc Dillard's Inc Avnet Inc Signet Jewelers Ltd NOW Inc

Invesco DWA Industrials Momentum ETF   C   HOLD

Ticker	Traded On	NAV	Total Assets ($)	Dividend Yield (TTM)	Turnover Ratio	Expense Ratio
PRN	NAS CM	51.22	$102,246,079	0.17	106	0.6

Ratings
Reward   C
Risk   C-
Recent Upgrade/Downgrade   Down

Fund Information
Fund Type   Exchange Traded Funds
Category   Industrials Sector Equity
Sub-Category   Industrials
Prospectus Objective   Unaligned
Inception Date   Oct-06
Open to New Investments   Y

Prices
Price (as of 12/31/2018)   50.95
52-Week High   66.35
52-Week Low   47.61

Total Returns (%)

3-Month	6-Month	1-Year	3-Year	5-Year
-19.80	-14.19	-15.54	16.94	9.80

3-Year Standard Deviation   13.77
Effective Duration

Valuation
Premium/Discount (1-Year Average)   0.18

Company Information
Provider   Invesco
Manager/Tenure   Peter Hubbard (11), Michael Jeanette (10), Tony Seisser (4), 1 other
Website   http://www.invesco.com/us
Address   Invesco 11 Greenway Plaza, Ste. 2500 Houston TX 77046 United States
Phone Number   800-659-1005

PERFORMANCE

Ratings History

Date	Overall Rating	Risk Rating	Reward Rating
Q4-18	C	C-	C
Q2-18	C	C	C+
Q4-17	B	B	B+
Q4-16	C	C-	B-
Q4-15	C+	C	B-

Asset & Performance History

Date	NAV	1-Year Total Return
2017	60.81	22.48
2016	49.97	13.05
2015	44.46	-5.7
2014	47.35	-0.42
2013	47.72	48.82
2012	32.19	20.95

Total Assets: $102,246,079
Asset Allocation

Asset	%
Cash	0%
Stocks	100%
US Stocks	100%
Bonds	0%
US Bonds	0%
Other	0%

Services Offered:

Investment Strategy: The investment seeks to track the investment results (before fees and expenses) of the Dorsey Wright® Industrials Technical Leaders Index (the "underlying index"). The fund generally will invest at least 90% of its total assets in the securities that comprise the underlying index. The underlying index is composed of at least 30 securities of companies in the industrials sector that have powerful relative strength or "momentum" characteristics. **Top Holdings:** TransDigm Group Inc   JB Hunt Transport Services Inc   Gartner Inc A   Roper Technologies Inc   Sherwin-Williams Co

Direxion Daily MSCI India Bull 3x Shares   D+   SELL

Ticker	Traded On	NAV	Total Assets ($)	Dividend Yield (TTM)	Turnover Ratio	Expense Ratio
INDL	NYSE Arca	67.54	$102,093,583	0.46	15	1.36

Ratings
Reward   D+
Risk   D
Recent Upgrade/Downgrade

Fund Information
Fund Type   Exchange Traded Funds
Category   Trading Tools
Sub-Category   Trading--Leveraged Equity
Prospectus Objective   Foreign Stock
Inception Date   Mar-10
Open to New Investments   Y

Prices
Price (as of 12/31/2018)   66.96
52-Week High   119.33
52-Week Low   46.97

Total Returns (%)

3-Month	6-Month	1-Year	3-Year	5-Year
3.30	-6.37	-33.91	26.83	23.51

3-Year Standard Deviation   55.16
Effective Duration

Valuation
Premium/Discount (1-Year Average)   -0.10

Company Information
Provider   Direxion Funds
Manager/Tenure   Paul Brigandi (8), Tony Ng (3)
Website   http://www.direxionfunds.com
Address   Direxion Funds 1301 Avenue Of The Americas (6th Avenue) New York NY 10019 United States
Phone Number   646-572-3390

PERFORMANCE

Ratings History

Date	Overall Rating	Risk Rating	Reward Rating
Q4-18	D+	D	D+
Q2-18	C-	D+	C-
Q4-17	C	D+	B-
Q4-16	D	D	D+
Q4-15	C-	D+	C

Asset & Performance History

Date	NAV	1-Year Total Return
2017	102.39	128.21
2016	45.01	-15.9
2015	53.52	-33.33
2014	80.28	46.07
2013	54.96	-31.74
2012	80.52	22.52

Total Assets: $102,093,583
Asset Allocation

Asset	%
Cash	39%
Stocks	61%
US Stocks	0%
Bonds	0%
US Bonds	0%
Other	0%

Services Offered:

Investment Strategy: The investment seeks daily investment results, before fees and expenses, of 300% of the daily performance of the MSCI India Index. The fund, under normal circumstances, invests at least 80% of its net assets (plus borrowing for investment purposes) in securities of the index, exchange-traded funds ("ETFs") that track the index and other financial instruments that provide daily leveraged exposure to the index or ETFs that track the index. The index is designed to measure the performance of the large- and mid-capitalization segments of the Indian equity market, covering approximately 85% of the Indian equity universe. The fund is non-diversified. **Top Holdings:** iShares MSCI India ETF   Ishares Msci India Etf   Ishares Msci India Etf   Ishares Msci India Etf   Dreyfus Govt Cm Inst 289

Fidelity® Value Factor ETF

C   HOLD

Ticker	Traded On	NAV	Total Assets ($)	Dividend Yield (TTM)	Turnover Ratio	Expense Ratio
FVAL	NYSE Arca	29.88	$102,067,369	1.72		0.29

Ratings
Reward	C
Risk	C-
Recent Upgrade/Downgrade	Up

Fund Information
Fund Type	Exchange Traded Funds
Category	US Equity Large Cap Value
Sub-Category	Large Value
Prospectus Objective	Growth & Inc
Inception Date	Sep-16
Open to New Investments	Y

Prices
Price (as of 12/31/2018)	29.71
52-Week High	35.44
52-Week Low	28.19

Total Returns (%)
3-Month	6-Month	1-Year	3-Year	5-Year
-14.06	-7.83	-7.07		

3-Year Standard Deviation	
Effective Duration	

Valuation
Premium/Discount (1-Year Average)	0.14

Company Information
Provider	Fidelity Investments
Manager/Tenure	Louis Bottari (2), Deane Gyllenhaal (2), Peter Matthew (2), 2 others
Website	http://www.institutional.fidelity.com
Address	Fidelity Investments 82 Devonshire Street Boston MA 2109 United States
Phone Number	617-563-7000

PERFORMANCE

Ratings History
Date	Overall Rating	Risk Rating	Reward Rating
Q4-18	C	C-	C
Q2-18	C-	C-	C-
Q4-17	D	B+	C
Q4-16	U		
Q4-15			

Asset & Performance History
Date	NAV	1-Year Total Return
2017	32.77	21.89
2016	27.36	
2015		
2014		
2013		
2012		

Total Assets: $102,067,369

Asset Allocation
Asset	%
Cash	0%
Stocks	100%
US Stocks	99%
Bonds	0%
US Bonds	0%
Other	0%

Services Offered:

Investment Strategy: The investment seeks to provide investment returns that correspond, before fees and expenses, generally to the performance of the Fidelity U.S. Value Factor Index?. The fund normally invests at least 80% of assets in securities included in the Fidelity U.S. Value Factor Index?, which is designed to reflect the performance of stocks of large and mid-capitalization U.S. companies that have attractive valuations. It may lend securities to earn income for the fund. **Top Holdings:** Microsoft Corp Apple Inc Alphabet Inc A Johnson & Johnson Berkshire Hathaway Inc B

Alpha Architect Value Momentum Trend ETF

D   SELL

Ticker	Traded On	NAV	Total Assets ($)	Dividend Yield (TTM)	Turnover Ratio	Expense Ratio
VMOT	BATS	24.23	$101,809,288	1.27	44	0.79

Ratings
Reward	D
Risk	D
Recent Upgrade/Downgrade	Down

Fund Information
Fund Type	Exchange Traded Funds
Category	Long/Short Equity
Sub-Category	Long-Short Equity
Prospectus Objective	Growth & Inc
Inception Date	May-17
Open to New Investments	Y

Prices
Price (as of 12/31/2018)	24.26
52-Week High	31.26
52-Week Low	23.44

Total Returns (%)
3-Month	6-Month	1-Year	3-Year	5-Year
-16.25	-14.97	-15.69		

3-Year Standard Deviation	
Effective Duration	

Valuation
Premium/Discount (1-Year Average)	0.00

Company Information
Provider	Alpha Architect
Manager/Tenure	Tao Wang (1)
Website	http://www.alphaarchitect.com/funds
Address	Alpha Architect 213 Foxcroft Road Broomall PA 19008 United States
Phone Number	

PERFORMANCE

Ratings History
Date	Overall Rating	Risk Rating	Reward Rating
Q4-18	D	D	D
Q2-18	D+	C-	D+
Q4-17	U		
Q4-16			
Q4-15			

Asset & Performance History
Date	NAV	1-Year Total Return
2017	28.97	
2016		
2015		
2014		
2013		
2012		

Total Assets: $101,809,288

Asset Allocation
Asset	%
Cash	77%
Stocks	23%
US Stocks	22%
Bonds	0%
US Bonds	0%
Other	0%

Services Offered:

Investment Strategy: The investment seeks to track the total return performance, before fees and expenses, of the Alpha Architect Value Momentum Trend Index. Under normal circumstances, at least 80% of the fund's total assets (exclusive of collateral held from securities lending) will be invested in the component securities of the index and other instruments of the index. The index will be composed primarily of the other ETFs advised by the Adviser. Currently, there are four Alpha Architect ETFs, which invest in either domestic or international equity securities, and employ either a "momentum" or a "value" investment strategy. The fund is non-diversified. **Top Holdings:** iShares MSCI EAFE ETF Alpha Architect Intl Quant Val ETF SPDR® S&P 500 ETF Alpha Architect US Quantitative Momt ETF Alpha Architect Intl Quant Momt ETF

Invesco S&P MidCap 400® Equal Weight ETF   C-   HOLD

Ticker	Traded On	NAV	Total Assets ($)	Dividend Yield (TTM)	Turnover Ratio	Expense Ratio
EWMC	NYSE Arca	55.72	$101,581,931	1.37		0.4

Ratings
Reward	C-
Risk	D+
Recent Upgrade/Downgrade	Down

Fund Information
Fund Type	Exchange Traded Funds
Category	US Equity Mid Cap
Sub-Category	Mid-Cap Blend
Prospectus Objective	Growth
Inception Date	Dec-10
Open to New Investments	Y

Prices
Price (as of 12/31/2018)	55.57
52-Week High	69.54
52-Week Low	52.58

Total Returns (%)
3-Month	6-Month	1-Year	3-Year	5-Year
-17.32	-15.53	-12.26	21.92	27.16

3-Year Standard Deviation	12.57
Effective Duration	

Valuation
Premium/Discount (1-Year Average)	-0.08

Company Information
Provider	Invesco
Manager/Tenure	Peter Hubbard (0), Michael Jeanette (0), Jonathan Nixon (0), 1 other
Website	http://www.invesco.com/us
Address	Invesco 11 Greenway Plaza, Ste. 2500 Houston TX 77046 United States
Phone Number	800-659-1005

PERFORMANCE

Ratings History
Date	Overall Rating	Risk Rating	Reward Rating
Q4-18	C-	D+	C-
Q2-18	C	D+	C+
Q4-17	B	B	B
Q4-16	D+	D+	D+
Q4-15	C	C-	C

Asset & Performance History
Date	NAV	1-Year Total Return
2017	64.35	13.56
2016	57.4	22.53
2015	47.4	-5.13
2014	50.65	9.93
2013	46.67	35.06
2012	35.22	16.31

Total Assets: $101,581,931

Asset Allocation
Asset	%
Cash	0%
Stocks	100%
US Stocks	100%
Bonds	0%
US Bonds	0%
Other	0%

Services Offered:

Investment Strategy: The investment seeks to track the investment results (before fees and expenses) of the S&P MidCap 400® Equal Weight Index (the "underlying index"). The fund generally will invest at least 90% of its total assets in the securities that comprise the underlying index. The underlying index is an equal-weighted version of the S&P MidCap 400® Index. The index provider compiles, maintains and calculates the underlying index, which consists of U.S. common equities listed on the NYSE and NASDAQ, and also may include equity interests in real estate investment trusts ("REITs") and business development companies ("BDCs"). The fund is non-diversified.
Top Holdings: Esterline Technologies Corp   Adtalem Global Education Inc   Exelixis Inc   Cracker Barrel Old Country Store Inc   Tech Data Corp

---

Invesco Russell Top 200 Pure Value ETF   C   HOLD

Ticker	Traded On	NAV	Total Assets ($)	Dividend Yield (TTM)	Turnover Ratio	Expense Ratio
PXLV	NYSE Arca	34.19	$100,694,395	2.68	25	0.39

Ratings
Reward	C
Risk	C-
Recent Upgrade/Downgrade	

Fund Information
Fund Type	Exchange Traded Funds
Category	US Equity Large Cap Value
Sub-Category	Large Value
Prospectus Objective	Growth
Inception Date	Jun-11
Open to New Investments	Y

Prices
Price (as of 12/31/2018)	34.20
52-Week High	40.69
52-Week Low	32.62

Total Returns (%)
3-Month	6-Month	1-Year	3-Year	5-Year
-11.90	-7.81	-8.59	29.07	35.16

3-Year Standard Deviation	9.58
Effective Duration	

Valuation
Premium/Discount (1-Year Average)	0.22

Company Information
Provider	Invesco
Manager/Tenure	Peter Hubbard (7), Michael Jeanette (7), Jonathan Nixon (5), 1 other
Website	http://www.invesco.com/us
Address	Invesco 11 Greenway Plaza, Ste. 2500 Houston TX 77046 United States
Phone Number	800-659-1005

PERFORMANCE

Ratings History
Date	Overall Rating	Risk Rating	Reward Rating
Q4-18	C	C-	C
Q2-18	C	C-	C
Q4-17	B	B	B
Q4-16	C+	D+	B
Q4-15	C	C	C+

Asset & Performance History
Date	NAV	1-Year Total Return
2017	38.49	13.98
2016	34.36	23.88
2015	28.58	-5.19
2014	30.95	10.46
2013	28.58	33
2012	21.94	18.93

Total Assets: $100,694,395

Asset Allocation
Asset	%
Cash	0%
Stocks	100%
US Stocks	100%
Bonds	0%
US Bonds	0%
Other	0%

Services Offered:

Investment Strategy: The investment seeks to track the investment results (before fees and expenses) of the Russell Top 200® Pure Value Index (the "underlying index"). The fund generally will invest at least 90% of its total assets in the component securities that comprise the underlying index. The underlying index is composed of a subset of securities from the Russell Top 200® Index, which is composed of the largest 200 securities of the Russell 3000® Index, an index designed to measure the performance of the largest 3,000 companies in the U.S. equity market. **Top Holdings:** AT&T Inc   Allergan PLC   Duke Energy Corp   Mondelez International Inc Class A   American Electric Power Co Inc

Invesco DB Gold Fund   D+   SELL

Ticker	Traded On	NAV	Total Assets ($)	Dividend Yield (TTM)	Turnover Ratio	Expense Ratio
DGL	NYSE Arca	39.42	$99,536,605	0.11	0	0.75

Ratings
Reward   D
Risk   D+
Recent Upgrade/Downgrade

Fund Information
Fund Type   Exchange Traded Funds
Category   Commodities Specified
Sub-Category   Commodities Precious Metals
Prospectus Objective   Prec Metals
Inception Date   Jan-07
Open to New Investments   Y

Prices
Price (as of 12/31/2018)   39.54
52-Week High   43.10
52-Week Low   36.93

Total Returns (%)

3-Month	6-Month	1-Year	3-Year	5-Year
5.64	0.78	-5.04	13.76	-2.16

3-Year Standard Deviation   12.78
Effective Duration

Valuation
Premium/Discount (1-Year Average)   0.01

Company Information
Provider   Invesco
Manager/Tenure   Management Team (11)
Website   http://www.invesco.com/us
Address   Invesco 11 Greenway Plaza, Ste. 2500 Houston TX 77046 United States
Phone Number   800-659-1005

PERFORMANCE

Ratings History

Date	Overall Rating	Risk Rating	Reward Rating
Q4-18	D+	D+	D
Q2-18	C-	C-	C-
Q4-17	C-	C-	C-
Q4-16	D+	D+	C-
Q4-15	D	D	D

Asset & Performance History

Date	NAV	1-Year Total Return
2017	41.51	10.53
2016	37.04	7.37
2015	34.69	-11.45
2014	39.17	-2.87
2013	40.33	-29.77
2012	57.44	5.33

Total Assets: $99,536,605
Asset Allocation

Asset	%
Cash	47%
Stocks	0%
US Stocks	0%
Bonds	3%
US Bonds	3%
Other	0%

Services Offered:

Investment Strategy: The investment seeks to track the DBIQ Optimum Yield Gold Index Excess Return™ (DBIQ-OY GC ER™), which is intended to reflect the changes in market value of gold.
The single index Commodity consists of Gold. **Top Holdings:** Goldman Sachs International 0% United States Treasury Bills 0% United States Treasury Bills 0% United States Treasury Bills 0%

Xtrackers MSCI All World ex U.S. Hedged Equity ETF   D+   SELL

Ticker	Traded On	NAV	Total Assets ($)	Dividend Yield (TTM)	Turnover Ratio	Expense Ratio
DBAW	NYSE Arca		$99,369,639	2.35	11	0.4

Ratings
Reward   D+
Risk   C-
Recent Upgrade/Downgrade   Down

Fund Information
Fund Type   Exchange Traded Funds
Category   Global Equity Large Cap
Sub-Category   Foreign Large Blend
Prospectus Objective   World Stock
Inception Date   Jan-14
Open to New Investments   Y

Prices
Price (as of 12/31/2018)   24.23
52-Week High   29.07
52-Week Low   23.68

Total Returns (%)

3-Month	6-Month	1-Year	3-Year	5-Year
-10.73	-8.32	-9.70	13.88	

3-Year Standard Deviation   8.71
Effective Duration

Valuation
Premium/Discount (1-Year Average)   -0.10

Company Information
Provider   Deutsche Asset Management
Manager/Tenure   Charlotte Cipolletti (2), Patrick Dwyer (2), Bryan Richards (2), 2 others
Website   http://www.deutsche-etfs.com
Address   Deutsche Asset & Wealth Management 345 Park Avenue New York NY 10154 United States
Phone Number   844-851-4255

PERFORMANCE

Ratings History

Date	Overall Rating	Risk Rating	Reward Rating
Q4-18	D+	C-	D+
Q2-18	C	C-	C
Q4-17	B-	C+	B
Q4-16	C-	C-	C
Q4-15	D+	C-	C-

Asset & Performance History

Date	NAV	1-Year Total Return
2017	27.74	18.49
2016	24	6.43
2015	23.03	0.33
2014	24.22	
2013		
2012		

Total Assets: $99,369,639
Asset Allocation

Asset	%
Cash	5%
Stocks	94%
US Stocks	2%
Bonds	0%
US Bonds	0%
Other	0%

Services Offered:

Investment Strategy: The investment seeks investment results that correspond generally to the performance, of the MSCI ACWI ex USA US Dollar Hedged Index. The fund, using a "passive" or indexing investment approach, seeks investment results that correspond generally to the performance, of the underlying index, which is designed to track the performance of equity securities in developed and emerging stock markets while mitigating exposure to fluctuations between the value of the USD and the currencies of the countries included in the underlying index. It will invest at least 80% of its total assets in component securities of the underlying index. **Top Holdings:** Msci Eafe Dec18 Sgx Nifty 50 Dec18 Nestle SA Tencent Holdings Ltd Novartis AG

WisdomTree Global ex-US Real Estate Fund   C-   HOLD

Ticker	Traded On	NAV	Total Assets ($)	Dividend Yield (TTM)	Turnover Ratio	Expense Ratio
DRW	NYSE Arca	27.83	$98,399,751	7.42	23	0.58

Ratings
Reward   D+
Risk   C-
Recent Upgrade/Downgrade

Fund Information
Fund Type   Exchange Traded Funds
Category   Real Estate Sector Equity
Sub-Category   Global Real Estate
Prospectus Objective   Real Estate
Inception Date   Jun-07
Open to New Investments   Y

Prices
Price (as of 12/31/2018)   27.77
52-Week High   34.83
52-Week Low   27.14

Total Returns (%)

3-Month	6-Month	1-Year	3-Year	5-Year
-5.01	-6.68	-10.97	24.43	31.65

3-Year Standard Deviation   13.12
Effective Duration

Valuation
Premium/Discount (1-Year Average)   -0.12

Company Information
Provider   WisdomTree
Manager/Tenure   Richard A. Brown (10), Thomas J.
                  Durante (10), Karen Q. Wong (10)
Website   http://www.wisdomtree.com
Address   WisdomTree 245 Park Avenue, 35th
                  floor New York NY 10167 United
                  States
Phone Number   866-909-9473

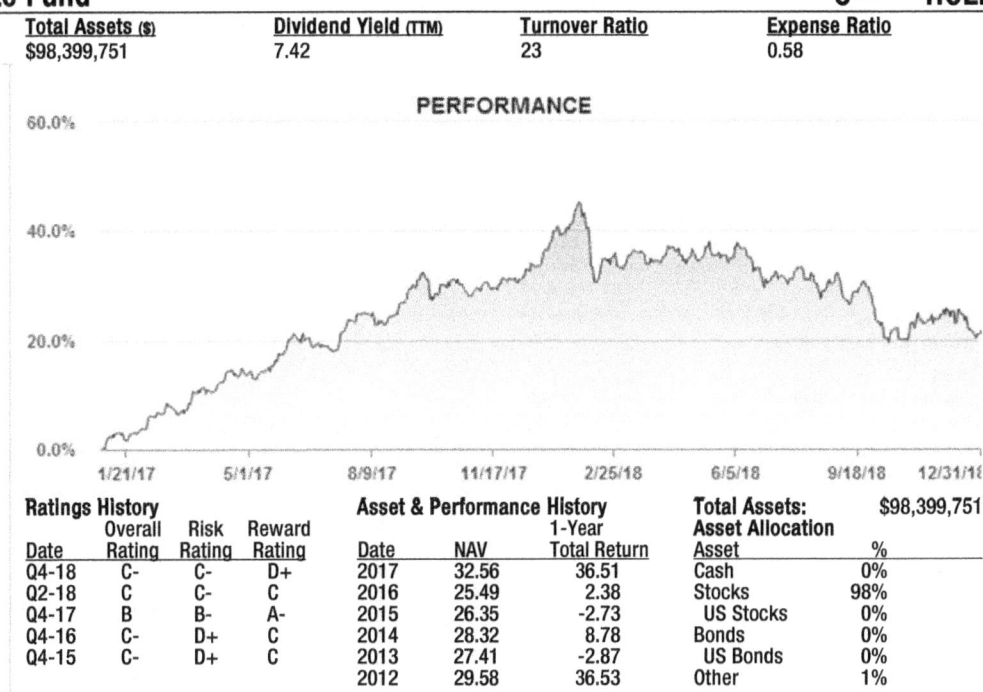

PERFORMANCE

Ratings History

Date	Overall Rating	Risk Rating	Reward Rating
Q4-18	C-	C-	D+
Q2-18	C	C-	C
Q4-17	B	B-	A-
Q4-16	C-	D+	C
Q4-15	C-	D+	C

Asset & Performance History

Date	NAV	1-Year Total Return
2017	32.56	36.51
2016	25.49	2.38
2015	26.35	-2.73
2014	28.32	8.78
2013	27.41	-2.87
2012	29.58	36.53

Total Assets: $98,399,751
Asset Allocation

Asset	%
Cash	0%
Stocks	98%
US Stocks	0%
Bonds	0%
US Bonds	0%
Other	1%

Services Offered:

Investment Strategy: The investment seeks to track the price and yield performance, before fees and expenses, of the WisdomTree Global ex-U.S. Real Estate Index. Under normal circumstances, at least 95% of the fund's total assets will be invested in component securities of the index and investments that have economic characteristics that are substantially identical to the economic characteristics of such component securities. The index is a fundamentally weighted index that is comprised of companies from developed and emerging markets outside of the United States that are classified as being part of the "Global Real Estate" sector. The fund is non-diversified.
Top Holdings: Sun Hung Kai Properties Ltd   Unibail-Rodamco-We 0%   Henderson Land Development Co Ltd   Scentre Group   Vonovia SE

GS Connect S&P GSCI Enhanced Commodity Total Return ETN   D+   SELL

Ticker	Traded On	NAV	Total Assets ($)	Dividend Yield (TTM)	Turnover Ratio	Expense Ratio
GSC	NYSE Arca		$98,256,000	0	0	1.25

Ratings
Reward   C-
Risk   D
Recent Upgrade/Downgrade

Fund Information
Fund Type   Exchange Traded Funds
Category   Commodities Broad Basket
Sub-Category   Commodities Broad Basket
Prospectus Objective   Natl Res
Inception Date   Jul-07
Open to New Investments   Y

Prices
Price (as of 12/31/2018)   19.30
52-Week High   30.97
52-Week Low   17.93

Total Returns (%)

3-Month	6-Month	1-Year	3-Year	5-Year
-35.10	-32.89	-25.35	-10.75	-62.06

3-Year Standard Deviation   18.09
Effective Duration

Valuation
Premium/Discount (1-Year Average)   0.00

Company Information
Provider   Goldman Sachs
Manager/Tenure   No Manager (11)
Website   http://www.gsamfunds.com
Address   Goldman Sachs 200 West Stree New
                  York NY 10282 United States
Phone Number   800-526-7384

PERFORMANCE

Ratings History

Date	Overall Rating	Risk Rating	Reward Rating
Q4-18	D+	D	C-
Q2-18	C-	D+	C
Q4-17	D	D	D+
Q4-16	D	D	D-
Q4-15	D-	D-	D-

Asset & Performance History

Date	NAV	1-Year Total Return
2017	23.98	2.33
2016	23.31	16.69
2015	20.08	-34.05
2014	30.45	-35.01
2013	46.86	-1.92
2012	47.78	-1.72

Total Assets: $98,256,000
Asset Allocation

Asset	%
Cash	%
Stocks	%
US Stocks	%
Bonds	%
US Bonds	%
Other	%

Services Offered:

Investment Strategy: The investment seeks to replicates, net of expenses, the S&P GSCI Enhanced Commodity Total Return Strategy Index.
The index reflects the total returns that are potentially available through an unleveraged investment in the same futures contracts as are included in the S&P GSCI. **Top Holdings:**

U.S. Global Jets ETF   C+   HOLD

Ticker	Traded On	NAV	Total Assets ($)	Dividend Yield (TTM)	Turnover Ratio	Expense Ratio
JETS	NYSE Arca	27.94	$97,211,864	0.42	36	0.6

Ratings
Reward   B-
Risk   C-
Recent Upgrade/Downgrade

Fund Information
Fund Type   Exchange Traded Funds
Category   Industrials Sector Equity
Sub-Category   Miscellaneous Sector
Prospectus Objective   Growth
Inception Date   Apr-15
Open to New Investments   Y

Prices
Price (as of 12/31/2018)   27.88
52-Week High   34.66
52-Week Low   26.85

Total Returns (%)

3-Month	6-Month	1-Year	3-Year	5-Year
-12.39	-3.93	-14.22	14.91	

3-Year Standard Deviation   19.51
Effective Duration

Valuation
Premium/Discount (1-Year Average)   -0.03

Company Information
Provider   U.S. Global Investors
Manager/Tenure   Ralph P. Aldis (3), Frank E. Holmes (3)
Website   http://www.usfunds.com
Address   U.S. Global Investors P.O. Box 781234
                 San Antonio TX 78278-1234 United
                 States
Phone Number   800-873-8637

PERFORMANCE

Ratings History

Date	Overall Rating	Risk Rating	Reward Rating
Q4-18	C+	C-	B-
Q2-18	C+	C-	B
Q4-17	C+	B-	C+
Q4-16	D+	C-	B
Q4-15	U		

Asset & Performance History

Date	NAV	1-Year Total Return
2017	32.61	18.01
2016	27.97	12.37
2015	24.86	
2014		
2013		
2012		

Total Assets: $97,211,864
Asset Allocation

Asset	%
Cash	0%
Stocks	100%
US Stocks	81%
Bonds	0%
US Bonds	0%
Other	0%

Services Offered:

Investment Strategy: The investment seeks to track the performance, before fees and expenses, of the U.S. Global Jets Index. The fund uses a "passive management" (or indexing) approach to track the performance, before fees and expenses, of the index. The index is composed of the exchange-listed common stock (or depository receipts) of U.S. and international passenger airlines, aircraft manufacturers, airports, and terminal services companies (as determined by independent industry listings) across the globe (collectively, "Airline Companies"). The index may include small-, mid-, and large-capitalization companies. The fund is non-diversified. **Top Holdings:** United Continental Holdings Inc   Delta Air Lines Inc   American Airlines Group Inc   Southwest Airlines Co   Spirit Airlines Inc

---

First Trust Institutional Preferred Securities and Income ETF   D   SELL

Ticker	Traded On	NAV	Total Assets ($)	Dividend Yield (TTM)	Turnover Ratio	Expense Ratio
FPEI	NYSE Arca	18.00	$95,343,962	5.55	13	0.85

Ratings
Reward   D
Risk   C-
Recent Upgrade/Downgrade   Down

Fund Information
Fund Type   Exchange Traded Funds
Category   US Fixed Income
Sub-Category   Preferred Stock
Prospectus Objective   Growth & Inc
Inception Date   Aug-17
Open to New Investments   Y

Prices
Price (as of 12/31/2018)   18.24
52-Week High   20.23
52-Week Low   18.05

Total Returns (%)

3-Month	6-Month	1-Year	3-Year	5-Year
-4.26	-2.09	-5.37		

3-Year Standard Deviation
Effective Duration   3.49

Valuation
Premium/Discount (1-Year Average)   0.16

Company Information
Provider   First Trust
Manager/Tenure   Scott T. Fleming (1), Robert Wolf (1)
Website   http://www.ftportfolios.com/
Address   First Trust 120 E. Liberty Drive, Suite
                 400 Wheaton IL 60187 United States
Phone Number   800-621-1675

PERFORMANCE

Ratings History

Date	Overall Rating	Risk Rating	Reward Rating
Q4-18	D	C-	D
Q2-18	U		
Q4-17	U		
Q4-16			
Q4-15			

Asset & Performance History

Date	NAV	1-Year Total Return
2017	20.11	
2016		
2015		
2014		
2013		
2012		

Total Assets: $95,343,962
Asset Allocation

Asset	%
Cash	3%
Stocks	0%
US Stocks	0%
Bonds	57%
US Bonds	37%
Other	0%

Services Offered:

Investment Strategy: The investment seeks total return and to provide current income. The fund invests at least 80% of its net assets (including investment borrowings) in institutional preferred securities and income-producing debt securities ("Income Securities"). Preferred securities are a type of equity security that have preference over common stock in the payment of distributions and the liquidation of a company's assets, but are generally junior to all forms of the company's debt, including both senior and subordinated debt. The fund's investments in preferred securities will primarily be in institutional preferred securities. It is non-diversified. **Top Holdings:** The Hartford Financial Services Group, Inc. 4.74%   Catlin Insurance Company Ltd. 5.42%   EMERA INCORPORATED 6.75%   Credit Agricole S.A. 7.88%   Aercap Global Aviation Trust 6.5%

WisdomTree Global High Dividend Fund   C-   HOLD

Ticker	Traded On	NAV	Total Assets ($)	Dividend Yield (TTM)	Turnover Ratio	Expense Ratio
DEW	NYSE Arca	41.96	$95,277,950	3.79	21	0.58

Ratings

Reward	C-
Risk	C-
Recent Upgrade/Downgrade	Down

Fund Information

Fund Type	Exchange Traded Funds
Category	Global Equity Large Cap
Sub-Category	World Large Stock
Prospectus Objective	Equity-Income
Inception Date	Jun-06
Open to New Investments	Y

Prices

Price (as of 12/31/2018)	41.74
52-Week High	51.07
52-Week Low	40.24

Total Returns (%)

3-Month	6-Month	1-Year	3-Year	5-Year
-9.53	-6.16	-9.83	18.51	7.68

3-Year Standard Deviation	8.66
Effective Duration	

Valuation

Premium/Discount (1-Year Average)	-0.01

Company Information

Provider	WisdomTree
Manager/Tenure	Richard A. Brown (10), Thomas J. Durante (10), Karen Q. Wong (10)
Website	http://www.wisdomtree.com
Address	WisdomTree 245 Park Avenue, 35th floor New York NY 10167 United States
Phone Number	866-909-9473

PERFORMANCE

Ratings History

Date	Overall Rating	Risk Rating	Reward Rating
Q4-18	C-	C-	C-
Q2-18	C-	D+	C
Q4-17	C+	C+	C+
Q4-16	C-	D+	C
Q4-15	C-	C-	C-

Asset & Performance History

Date	NAV	1-Year Total Return
2017	48.37	15.24
2016	43.39	14.05
2015	39.41	-7.1
2014	44.16	-2.19
2013	47.3	14.87
2012	42.86	14.45

Total Assets: $95,277,950

Asset Allocation

Asset	%
Cash	0%
Stocks	99%
US Stocks	57%
Bonds	0%
US Bonds	0%
Other	1%

Services Offered:

Investment Strategy: The investment seeks to track the price and yield performance of the WisdomTree Global High Dividend Index. The fund will invest at least 95% of its total assets in component securities of the index and investments that have economic characteristics that are substantially identical to the economic characteristics of such component securities. The index is a fundamentally weighted index that is comprised of high dividend-yielding companies selected from the WisdomTree Global Dividend Index, which defines the dividend-paying universe of companies in the U.S., developed countries and emerging markets throughout the world. The fund is non-diversified. **Top Holdings:** Exxon Mobil Corp   AT&T Inc   Verizon Communications Inc   Chevron Corp   Pfizer Inc

---

C-Tracks Exchange-Traded Notes Based on the Performance of the Miller/Howard MLP Fundamental Index   D

Ticker	Traded On	NAV	Total Assets ($)	Dividend Yield (TTM)	Turnover Ratio	Expense Ratio
MLPC	NYSE Arca	12.05	$94,360,000	5.09		0.95

Ratings

Reward	D
Risk	D+
Recent Upgrade/Downgrade	

Fund Information

Fund Type	Exchange Traded Funds
Category	Energy Sector Equity
Sub-Category	Energy Limited Partnership
Prospectus Objective	Growth
Inception Date	Sep-13
Open to New Investments	Y

Prices

Price (as of 12/31/2018)	12.05
52-Week High	16.87
52-Week Low	11.82

Total Returns (%)

3-Month	6-Month	1-Year	3-Year	5-Year
-19.32	-15.47	-18.00	-9.38	-40.41

3-Year Standard Deviation	18.01
Effective Duration	

Valuation

Premium/Discount (1-Year Average)	0.00

Company Information

Provider	Citigroup
Manager/Tenure	No Manager (5)
Website	
Address	Citigroup United States
Phone Number	

PERFORMANCE

Ratings History

Date	Overall Rating	Risk Rating	Reward Rating
Q4-18	D	D+	D
Q2-18	D	D	D
Q4-17	D	D	D+
Q4-16	D	D	D
Q4-15	D	D	D

Asset & Performance History

Date	NAV	1-Year Total Return
2017	15.22	-5.08
2016	16.7	14.78
2015	15.46	-35.53
2014	25.5	1.99
2013	26.2	
2012		

Total Assets: $94,360,000

Asset Allocation

Asset	%
Cash	%
Stocks	%
US Stocks	%
Bonds	%
US Bonds	%
Other	%

Services Offered:

Investment Strategy: The investment seeks a return that based on the Performance of the Miller/Howard MLP Fundamental Index (the "index"), which the adviser refer to as the C-Tracks, are unsecured senior debt securities issued by Citigroup Inc.

The index is designed to measure the performance of 25 energy master limited partnerships ("MLPs") selected quarterly by a methodology that is based upon certain quantitative fundamental factors of publicly traded MLPs, including distribution growth, estimated capital expenditures and distribution coverage. **Top Holdings:**

John Hancock Multifactor Developed International ETF
D   SELL

Ticker	Traded On	NAV		Total Assets ($)	Dividend Yield (TTM)	Turnover Ratio	Expense Ratio
JHMD	NYSE Arca	25.61		$94,059,962	2.66	15	0.45

Ratings

Reward	D
Risk	D+
Recent Upgrade/Downgrade	Down

Fund Information

Fund Type	Exchange Traded Funds
Category	Global Equity Large Cap
Sub-Category	Foreign Large Blend
Prospectus Objective	Foreign Stock
Inception Date	Dec-16
Open to New Investments	Y

Prices

Price (as of 12/31/2018)	25.52
52-Week High	32.49
52-Week Low	24.81

Total Returns (%)

3-Month	6-Month	1-Year	3-Year	5-Year
-12.62	-10.22	-13.92		

3-Year Standard Deviation	
Effective Duration	

Valuation

Premium/Discount (1-Year Average)	0.23

Company Information

Provider	John Hancock
Manager/Tenure	Joel P. Schneider (1), Lukas J. Smart (1), Joseph F. Hohn (0)
Website	http://jhinvestments.com
Address	601 Congress Street, Boston MA 02210 United States
Phone Number	800-225-5913

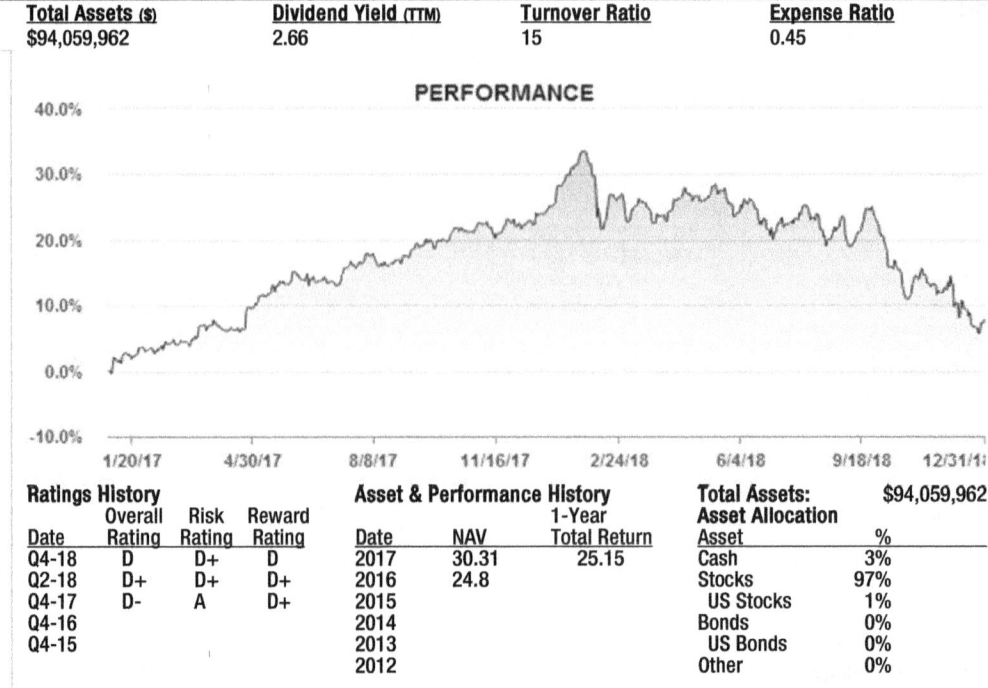

PERFORMANCE

Ratings History

Date	Overall Rating	Risk Rating	Reward Rating
Q4-18	D	D+	D
Q2-18	D+	D+	D+
Q4-17	D-	A	D+
Q4-16			
Q4-15			

Asset & Performance History

Date	NAV	1-Year Total Return
2017	30.31	25.15
2016	24.8	
2015		
2014		
2013		
2012		

Total Assets: $94,059,962

Asset Allocation

Asset	%
Cash	3%
Stocks	97%
US Stocks	1%
Bonds	0%
US Bonds	0%
Other	0%

Services Offered:

Investment Strategy: The investment seeks to provide investment results that closely correspond, before fees and expenses, to the performance of the John Hancock Dimensional Developed International Index. The fund normally invests at least 80% of its net assets (plus any borrowings for investment purposes) in securities included in the fund's benchmark index, in depositary receipts representing securities included in the fund's benchmark index and in underlying stocks in respect of depositary receipts included in the fund's benchmark index. The index is designed to comprise a subset of securities of companies associated with developed markets outside the U.S. and Canada. **Top Holdings:** BP PLC Nestle SA Novartis AG Toyota Motor Corp Roche Holding AG Dividend Right Cert.

Direxion Daily CSI 300 China A Share Bear 1X Shares
C-   HOLD

Ticker	Traded On	NAV		Total Assets ($)	Dividend Yield (TTM)	Turnover Ratio	Expense Ratio
CHAD	NYSE Arca	39.81		$92,981,167	0.52	0	0.85

Ratings

Reward	D+
Risk	C-
Recent Upgrade/Downgrade	Up

Fund Information

Fund Type	Exchange Traded Funds
Category	Trading Tools
Sub-Category	Trading--Inverse Equity
Prospectus Objective	Foreign Stock
Inception Date	Jun-15
Open to New Investments	Y

Prices

Price (as of 12/31/2018)	39.78
52-Week High	41.12
52-Week Low	27.72

Total Returns (%)

3-Month	6-Month	1-Year	3-Year	5-Year
11.58	9.01	28.76	-4.94	

3-Year Standard Deviation	20.29
Effective Duration	

Valuation

Premium/Discount (1-Year Average)	-0.03

Company Information

Provider	Direxion Funds
Manager/Tenure	Paul Brigandi (3), Tony Ng (3)
Website	http://www.direxionfunds.com
Address	Direxion Funds 1301 Avenue Of The Americas (6th Avenue) New York NY 10019 United States
Phone Number	646-572-3390

PERFORMANCE

Ratings History

Date	Overall Rating	Risk Rating	Reward Rating
Q4-18	C-	C-	D+
Q2-18	D	D-	D
Q4-17	D-	D-	D
Q4-16	D	D	D
Q4-15	U		

Asset & Performance History

Date	NAV	1-Year Total Return
2017	31.16	-27.11
2016	42.75	1.27
2015	42.21	
2014		
2013		
2012		

Total Assets: $92,981,167

Asset Allocation

Asset	%
Cash	109%
Stocks	-9%
US Stocks	-9%
Bonds	0%
US Bonds	0%
Other	0%

Services Offered:

Investment Strategy: The investment seeks daily investment results, before fees and expenses, of 100% of the inverse of the daily performance of the CSI 300 Index. The fund, under normal circumstances, invests in swap agreements, futures contracts, short positions or other financial instruments that, in combination, provide inverse (opposite) or short exposure to the index equal to at least 80% of the fund's net assets (plus borrowing for investment purposes). The index is a modified free-float market capitalization weighted index comprised of the largest and most liquid stocks in the Chinese A-share market. The fund is non-diversified. **Top Holdings:** Deutsche X-Trck Harv Swp Deutsche X-Trck Harv Swp Deutsche X-Trck Harv Swp Deutsche X-Trck Harv Swp Deutsche X-Trck Harv Swp

SPDR® SSgA Income Allocation ETF   C-   HOLD

Ticker	Traded On	NAV	Total Assets ($)	Dividend Yield (TTM)	Turnover Ratio	Expense Ratio
INKM	NYSE Arca	30.60	$92,899,492	3.33	47	0.5

Ratings
Reward   C-
Risk   D+
Recent Upgrade/Downgrade   Down

Fund Information
Fund Type	Exchange Traded Funds
Category	Moderate Allocation
Sub-Category	Allocation--30% to 50% Equity
Prospectus Objective	Income
Inception Date	Apr-12
Open to New Investments	Y

Prices
Price (as of 12/31/2018)	30.61
52-Week High	34.45
52-Week Low	30.39

Total Returns (%)
3-Month	6-Month	1-Year	3-Year	5-Year
-3.78	-2.65	-5.24	14.83	18.72

3-Year Standard Deviation   5.58
Effective Duration   9.53

Valuation
Premium/Discount (1-Year Average)   0.02

Company Information
Provider	SPDR State Street Global Advisors
Manager/Tenure	Jeremiah K. Holly (6), Timothy J. Furbush (4), Michael O. Martel (4)
Website	http://www.spdrs.com
Address	SPDR State Street Global Advisors State Street Financial Center, 1 Lincoln Street Boston MA 02111-2900 United States
Phone Number	617-786-3000

PERFORMANCE

Ratings History
Date	Overall Rating	Risk Rating	Reward Rating
Q4-18	C-	D+	C-
Q2-18	C-	D+	C
Q4-17	B-	B	C+
Q4-16	C-	D+	C
Q4-15	C-	C-	C

Asset & Performance History
Date	NAV	1-Year Total Return
2017	33.6	13.65
2016	30.51	6.63
2015	29.58	-4.65
2014	32.08	8.43
2013	30.62	3.04
2012	30.96	

Total Assets: $92,899,492
Asset Allocation
Asset	%
Cash	2%
Stocks	37%
US Stocks	29%
Bonds	52%
US Bonds	44%
Other	0%

Services Offered:

Investment Strategy: The investment seeks to provide total return by focusing on investments in income and yield-generating assets. The Adviser primarily invests the assets of the fund among ETPs that provide exposure to five primary asset classes: (i) domestic and international equity securities; (ii) domestic and international investment-grade and high yield debt securities; (iii) hybrid equity/debt securities; (iv) first lien senior secured floating rate bank loans, commonly referred to as "Senior Loans"; and (v) REITs, including equity REITs and mortgage REITs. **Top Holdings:** SPDR® Portfolio S&P 500 High Div ETF   SPDR® Portfolio Long Term Treasury ETF   SPDR® Blmbg Barclays High Yield Bd ETF   SPDR® Blmbg Barclays Em Mkts Lcl Bd ETF   SPDR® Blackstone / GSO Senior Loan ETF

ProShares Ultra Oil & Gas   C-   HOLD

Ticker	Traded On	NAV	Total Assets ($)	Dividend Yield (TTM)	Turnover Ratio	Expense Ratio
DIG	NYSE Arca	23.35	$92,424,382	1.73		0.95

Ratings
Reward   C-
Risk   D
Recent Upgrade/Downgrade   Down

Fund Information
Fund Type	Exchange Traded Funds
Category	Trading Tools
Sub-Category	Trading--Leveraged Equity
Prospectus Objective	Natl Res
Inception Date	Jan-07
Open to New Investments	Y

Prices
Price (as of 12/31/2018)	23.33
52-Week High	46.73
52-Week Low	20.85

Total Returns (%)
3-Month	6-Month	1-Year	3-Year	5-Year
-47.41	-44.06	-40.03	-18.12	-64.17

3-Year Standard Deviation   37.61
Effective Duration

Valuation
Premium/Discount (1-Year Average)   0.01

Company Information
Provider	ProShares
Manager/Tenure	Michael Neches (5), Tarak Davé (0)
Website	http://www.proshares.com
Address	ProShares 7501 Wisconsin Avenue, Suite 1000 Bethesda MD 20814 United States
Phone Number	866-776-5125

PERFORMANCE

Ratings History
Date	Overall Rating	Risk Rating	Reward Rating
Q4-18	C-	D	C-
Q2-18	C	D+	C
Q4-17	D+	D+	D+
Q4-16	D+	D	D+
Q4-15	D+	D+	C-

Asset & Performance History
Date	NAV	1-Year Total Return
2017	39.55	-7.25
2016	43.49	47.2
2015	29.94	-43.93
2014	53.98	-21.95
2013	69.64	53.13
2012	45.72	4.18

Total Assets: $92,424,382
Asset Allocation
Asset	%
Cash	-100%
Stocks	100%
US Stocks	100%
Bonds	0%
US Bonds	0%
Other	99%

Services Offered:

Investment Strategy: The investment seeks daily investment results that correspond to two times (2x) the daily performance of the Dow Jones U.S. Oil & GasSM Index. The fund invests in financial instruments that ProShare Advisors believes, in combination, should produce daily returns consistent with the fund's investment objective. The index measures the performance of certain companies in the oil and gas sector of the U.S. equity market. Component companies include, among others, exploration and production, integrated oil and gas, oil equipment and services, pipelines, renewable energy equipment companies and alternative fuel producers. The fund is non-diversified. **Top Holdings:** Dj U.S. Oil & Gas Index Swap Ubs Ag   Dj U.S. Oil & Gas Index Swap Bank Of America Na   Exxon Mobil Corp   Dj U.S. Oil & Gas Index Swap Morgan Stanley & Co. International Plc   Chevron Corp

Fidelity® Low Volatility Factor ETF

C   HOLD

Ticker	Traded On	NAV	Total Assets ($)	Dividend Yield (TTM)	Turnover Ratio	Expense Ratio
FDLO	NYSE Arca	30.15	$92,261,245	1.57		0.29

Ratings
Reward	C
Risk	C-
Recent Upgrade/Downgrade	Up

Fund Information
Fund Type	Exchange Traded Funds
Category	US Equity Large Cap Blend
Sub-Category	Large Blend
Prospectus Objective	Growth & Inc
Inception Date	Sep-16
Open to New Investments	Y

Prices
Price (as of 12/31/2018)	30.01
52-Week High	33.98
52-Week Low	28.31

Total Returns (%)
3-Month	6-Month	1-Year	3-Year	5-Year
-10.16	-2.27	0.53		

3-Year Standard Deviation
Effective Duration

Valuation
Premium/Discount (1-Year Average)	0.12

Company Information
Provider	Fidelity Investments
Manager/Tenure	Louis Bottari (2), Deane Gyllenhaal (2), Peter Matthew (2), 2 others
Website	http://www.institutional.fidelity.com
Address	Fidelity Investments 82 Devonshire Street Boston MA 2109 United States
Phone Number	617-563-7000

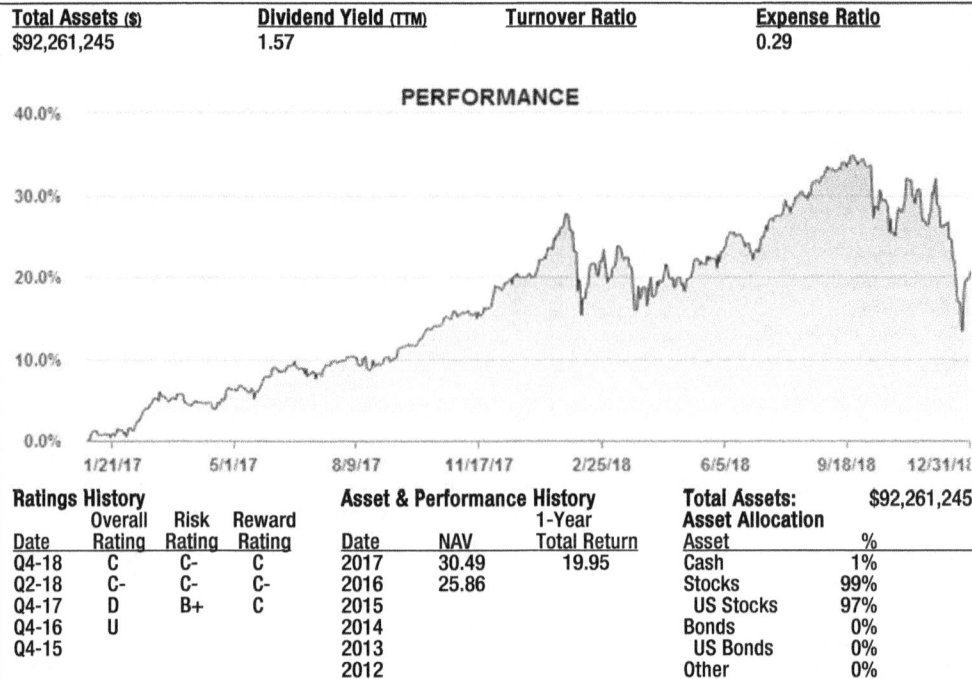

Ratings History

Date	Overall Rating	Risk Rating	Reward Rating
Q4-18	C	C-	C
Q2-18	C-	C-	C-
Q4-17	D	B+	C
Q4-16	U		
Q4-15			

Asset & Performance History

Date	NAV	1-Year Total Return
2017	30.49	19.95
2016	25.86	
2015		
2014		
2013		
2012		

Total Assets: $92,261,245

Asset Allocation
Asset	%
Cash	1%
Stocks	99%
US Stocks	97%
Bonds	0%
US Bonds	0%
Other	0%

Services Offered:

Investment Strategy: The investment seeks to provide investment returns that correspond, before fees and expenses, generally to the performance of the Fidelity U.S. Low Volatility Factor Index?. The fund normally invests at least 80% of assets in securities included in the Fidelity U.S. Low Volatility Factor Index?, which is designed to reflect the performance of stocks of large and mid-capitalization U.S. companies with lower volatility than the broader market. It may lend securities to earn income for the fund. **Top Holdings:** Apple Inc   Alphabet Inc A   Johnson & Johnson   Berkshire Hathaway Inc B   Pfizer Inc

---

Global X MSCI Argentina ETF

C-   HOLD

Ticker	Traded On	NAV	Total Assets ($)	Dividend Yield (TTM)	Turnover Ratio	Expense Ratio
ARGT	NYSE Arca	23.58	$91,792,220	0.68	24	0.59

Ratings
Reward	C
Risk	D
Recent Upgrade/Downgrade	Down

Fund Information
Fund Type	Exchange Traded Funds
Category	Equity Misc
Sub-Category	Miscellaneous Region
Prospectus Objective	Foreign Stock
Inception Date	Mar-11
Open to New Investments	Y

Prices
Price (as of 12/31/2018)	23.47
52-Week High	38.39
52-Week Low	21.88

Total Returns (%)
3-Month	6-Month	1-Year	3-Year	5-Year
-11.58	-11.48	-33.38	32.13	23.61

3-Year Standard Deviation	20.51
Effective Duration	

Valuation
Premium/Discount (1-Year Average)	-0.08

Company Information
Provider	Global X Funds
Manager/Tenure	Chang Kim (4), James Ong (2), Nam To (0)
Website	http://www.globalxfunds.com
Address	Global X Funds 600 Lexington Avenue, 20th Floor New York NY 10022 United States
Phone Number	888-493-8631

Ratings History

Date	Overall Rating	Risk Rating	Reward Rating
Q4-18	C-	D	C
Q2-18	C	D+	C+
Q4-17	B+	C+	A+
Q4-16	C	D+	B-
Q4-15	B-	C+	B-

Asset & Performance History

Date	NAV	1-Year Total Return
2017	35.4	53.86
2016	23.12	28.91
2015	18	-3.66
2014	18.85	-2.88
2013	19.5	13.67
2012	17.26	-17.74

Total Assets: $91,792,220

Asset Allocation
Asset	%
Cash	0%
Stocks	100%
US Stocks	5%
Bonds	0%
US Bonds	0%
Other	0%

Services Offered:

Investment Strategy: The investment seeks to provide investment results that correspond generally to the price and yield performance, before fees and expenses, of the MSCI All Argentina 25/50 Index. The fund invests at least 80% of its total assets in the securities of the underlying index and in American Depositary Receipts ("ADRs") and Global Depositary Receipts ("GDRs") based on the securities in the underlying index. The underlying index is designed to represent the performance of the broad Argentina equity universe, while including a minimum number of constituents. The fund is non-diversified. **Top Holdings:** MercadoLibre Inc   Tenaris SA   Grupo Financiero Galicia SA ADR   Globant SA   Banco Macro SA ADR

First Trust NASDAQ® Clean Edge® Green Energy Index Fund   C   HOLD

Ticker	Traded On	NAV	Total Assets ($)	Dividend Yield (TTM)	Turnover Ratio	Expense Ratio
QCLN	NAS CM	17.63	$91,591,839	0.66	32	0.6

Ratings

Reward	C+
Risk	D+
Recent Upgrade/Downgrade	

Fund Information

Fund Type	Exchange Traded Funds
Category	Technology Sector Equity
Sub-Category	Miscellaneous Sector
Prospectus Objective	Technology
Inception Date	Feb-07
Open to New Investments	Y

Prices

Price (as of 12/31/2018)	17.62
52-Week High	21.55
52-Week Low	16.31

Total Returns (%)

3-Month	6-Month	1-Year	3-Year	5-Year
-10.86	-9.12	-12.23	13.18	2.66

3-Year Standard Deviation	13.54
Effective Duration	

Valuation

Premium/Discount (1-Year Average)	0.07

Company Information

Provider	First Trust
Manager/Tenure	Daniel J. Lindquist (11), David G. McGarel (11), Roger F. Testin (11), 3 others
Website	http://www.ftportfolios.com/
Address	First Trust 120 E. Liberty Drive, Suite 400 Wheaton IL 60187 United States
Phone Number	800-621-1675

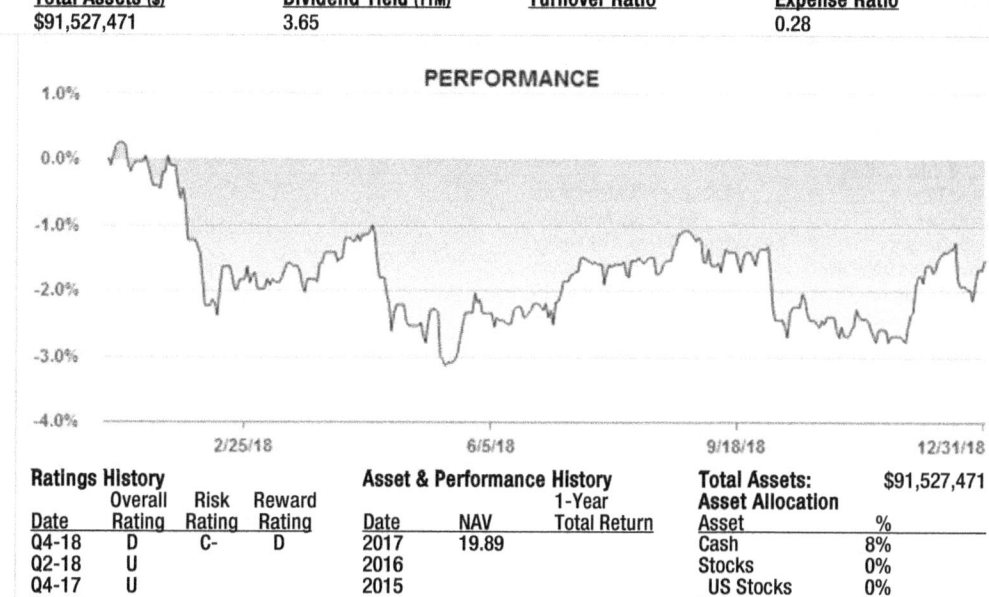

PERFORMANCE

Ratings History

Date	Overall Rating	Risk Rating	Reward Rating
Q4-18	C	D+	C+
Q2-18	C	D+	B-
Q4-17	C+	C	B-
Q4-16	C	D+	C+
Q4-15	C	C	C+

Asset & Performance History

Date	NAV	1-Year Total Return
2017	20.28	31.73
2016	15.47	-2.1
2015	16.01	-6.44
2014	17.23	-3.04
2013	17.9	89.81
2012	9.48	-0.53

Total Assets: $91,591,839

Asset Allocation

Asset	%
Cash	0%
Stocks	100%
US Stocks	94%
Bonds	0%
US Bonds	0%
Other	0%

Services Offered:

Investment Strategy: The investment seeks investment results that correspond generally to the price and yield (before the fund's fees and expenses) of an equity index called the NASDAQ® Clean Edge® Green Energy IndexSM. The fund will normally invest at least 90% of its net assets (including investment borrowings) in common stocks that comprise the index. The index is a modified market capitalization-weighted index designed to track the performance of companies whose securities are listed on NASDAQ, NYSE MKT or NYSE that are primarily manufacturers, developers, distributors or installers of clean-energy technologies. It is non-diversified. **Top Holdings:** Tesla Inc Albemarle Corp ON Semiconductor Corp Hexcel Corp Integrated Device Technology Inc

---

Columbia Diversified Fixed Income Allocation ETF   D   SELL

Ticker	Traded On	NAV	Total Assets ($)	Dividend Yield (TTM)	Turnover Ratio	Expense Ratio
DIAL	NYSE Arca	18.91	$91,527,471	3.65		0.28

Ratings

Reward	D
Risk	C-
Recent Upgrade/Downgrade	

Fund Information

Fund Type	Exchange Traded Funds
Category	US Fixed Income
Sub-Category	Multisector Bond
Prospectus Objective	Growth & Inc
Inception Date	Oct-17
Open to New Investments	Y

Prices

Price (as of 12/31/2018)	18.87
52-Week High	20.01
52-Week Low	18.78

Total Returns (%)

3-Month	6-Month	1-Year	3-Year	5-Year
-0.16	1.02	-1.53		

3-Year Standard Deviation	
Effective Duration	

Valuation

Premium/Discount (1-Year Average)	-0.11

Company Information

Provider	Columbia
Manager/Tenure	David Janssen (1), Gene R. Tannuzzo (1)
Website	http://www.columbiathreadneedleus.com
Address	Liberty Financial Funds P.O. Box 8081 Boston MA 02266-8081 United States
Phone Number	800-345-6611

PERFORMANCE

Ratings History

Date	Overall Rating	Risk Rating	Reward Rating
Q4-18	D	C-	D
Q2-18	U		
Q4-17	U		
Q4-16			
Q4-15			

Asset & Performance History

Date	NAV	1-Year Total Return
2017	19.89	
2016		
2015		
2014		
2013		
2012		

Total Assets: $91,527,471

Asset Allocation

Asset	%
Cash	8%
Stocks	0%
US Stocks	0%
Bonds	92%
US Bonds	60%
Other	0%

Services Offered:

Investment Strategy: The investment seeks investment results that closely correspond to the performance of the Beta Advantage® Multi-Sector Bond Index. The fund invests at least 80% of its assets in securities within the index or in securities, that have economic characteristics that are substantially the same as the economic characteristics of the securities within the index. The index reflects a rules-based multi-sector strategic beta approach to measuring the performance of the debt market through representation of six sectors of the debt market in the index, each focused on yield, quality, and liquidity of the particular eligible universe. **Top Holdings:** Federal National Mortgage Association 3% United States Treasury Bonds 3.75% Federal National Mortgage Association 4% United States Treasury Bonds 3.38% Federal Home Loan Mortgage Corporation 3.5%

WisdomTree U.S. Total Earnings Fund

C   HOLD

Ticker	Traded On	NAV	Total Assets ($)	Dividend Yield (TTM)	Turnover Ratio	Expense Ratio
EXT	NYSE Arca	28.54	$91,184,050	1.79	22	0.28

Ratings
Reward	C
Risk	C-
Recent Upgrade/Downgrade	

Fund Information
Fund Type	Exchange Traded Funds
Category	US Equity Large Cap Blend
Sub-Category	Large Blend
Prospectus Objective	Growth & Inc
Inception Date	Feb-07
Open to New Investments	Y

Prices
Price (as of 12/31/2018)	28.44
52-Week High	34.05
52-Week Low	26.85

Total Returns (%)
3-Month	6-Month	1-Year	3-Year	5-Year
-13.66	-8.15	-7.79	28.78	41.98

3-Year Standard Deviation	9.65
Effective Duration	

Valuation
Premium/Discount (1-Year Average)	0.28

Company Information
Provider	WisdomTree
Manager/Tenure	Richard A. Brown (10), Thomas J. Durante (10), Karen Q. Wong (10)
Website	http://www.wisdomtree.com
Address	WisdomTree 245 Park Avenue, 35th floor New York NY 10167 United States
Phone Number	866-909-9473

PERFORMANCE

Ratings History
Date	Overall Rating	Risk Rating	Reward Rating
Q4-18	C	C-	C
Q2-18	C	D+	C
Q4-17	B	B-	B
Q4-16	C+	D+	B
Q4-15	C	C-	C

Asset & Performance History
Date	NAV	1-Year Total Return
2017	31.8	21.71
2016	26.58	14.75
2015	23.64	-2.07
2014	24.67	12.58
2013	22.27	33.66
2012	16.96	15.4

Total Assets: $91,184,050
Asset Allocation
Asset	%
Cash	0%
Stocks	100%
US Stocks	100%
Bonds	0%
US Bonds	0%
Other	0%

Services Offered:

Investment Strategy: The investment seeks to track the price and yield performance, before fees and expenses, of the WisdomTree U.S. Earnings Index. Under normal circumstances, at least 95% of the fund's total assets (exclusive of collateral held from securities lending) will be invested in component securities of the index and investments that have economic characteristics that are substantially identical to the economic characteristics of such component securities. The index is a fundamentally weighted index that is comprised of earnings-generating companies within the broad U.S. stock market. The fund is non-diversified. **Top Holdings:** Apple Inc Microsoft Corp JPMorgan Chase & Co Alphabet Inc A Berkshire Hathaway Inc B

Pacer WealthShield ETF

D+   SELL

Ticker	Traded On	NAV	Total Assets ($)	Dividend Yield (TTM)	Turnover Ratio	Expense Ratio
PWS	BATS	24.14	$90,662,688			0.6

Ratings
Reward	D+
Risk	D+
Recent Upgrade/Downgrade	

Fund Information
Fund Type	Exchange Traded Funds
Category	Moderate Allocation
Sub-Category	Allocation--50% to 70% Equity
Prospectus Objective	Growth & Inc
Inception Date	Dec-17
Open to New Investments	Y

Prices
Price (as of 12/31/2018)	24.14
52-Week High	27.20
52-Week Low	23.18

Total Returns (%)
3-Month	6-Month	1-Year	3-Year	5-Year
-9.71	-7.87	-2.88		

3-Year Standard Deviation	
Effective Duration	

Valuation
Premium/Discount (1-Year Average)	0.14

Company Information
Provider	Pacer
Manager/Tenure	Bruce Kavanaugh (0), Michael Mack (0)
Website	http://www.paceretfs.com
Address	Pacer 16 Industrial Blvd, Suite 201 Paoli PA 19301 United States
Phone Number	

PERFORMANCE

Ratings History
Date	Overall Rating	Risk Rating	Reward Rating
Q4-18	D+	D+	D+
Q2-18	U		
Q4-17	U		
Q4-16			
Q4-15			

Asset & Performance History
Date	NAV	1-Year Total Return
2017	25.13	
2016		
2015		
2014		
2013		
2012		

Total Assets: $90,662,688
Asset Allocation
Asset	%
Cash	100%
Stocks	0%
US Stocks	0%
Bonds	0%
US Bonds	0%
Other	0%

Services Offered:

Investment Strategy: The investment seeks to track the total return performance, before fees and expenses, of the Pacer WealthShield Index. Under normal circumstances, at least 80% of the fund's total assets (exclusive of collateral held from securities lending) will be invested in (i) the component securities of the index or (ii) ETFs that seek to track the performance of some or all of the component securities of the index in the same approximate weight as such component securities. The index utilizes a systematic risk management strategy that directs the index's exposure to U.S. equity securities, U.S. Treasury securities, or a mix of each. The fund is non-diversified. **Top Holdings:** Amazon.com Inc Exxon Mobil Corp Apple Inc Microsoft Corp Chevron Corp

Direxion Daily 20+ Year Treasury Bull 3X Shares   D   SELL

Ticker	Traded On	NAV	Total Assets ($)	Dividend Yield (TTM)	Turnover Ratio	Expense Ratio
TMF	NYSE Arca	19.22	$90,520,426	1.67	66	1.11

Ratings
Reward   D
Risk   D
Recent Upgrade/Downgrade

Fund Information
Fund Type   Exchange Traded Funds
Category   Trading Tools
Sub-Category   Trading--Leveraged Debt
Prospectus Objective   Govt Bond - Treasury
Inception Date   Apr-09
Open to New Investments   Y

Prices
Price (as of 12/31/2018)   19.37
52-Week High   22.11
52-Week Low   15.21

Total Returns (%)

3-Month	6-Month	1-Year	3-Year	5-Year
13.84	0.33	-12.06	4.40	83.30

3-Year Standard Deviation   28.99
Effective Duration   17.03

Valuation
Premium/Discount (1-Year Average)   -0.10

Company Information
Provider   Direxion Funds
Manager/Tenure   Paul Brigandi (9), Tony Ng (3)
Website   http://www.direxionfunds.com
Address   Direxion Funds 1301 Avenue Of The
                   Americas (6th Avenue) New York NY
                   10019 United States
Phone Number   646-572-3390

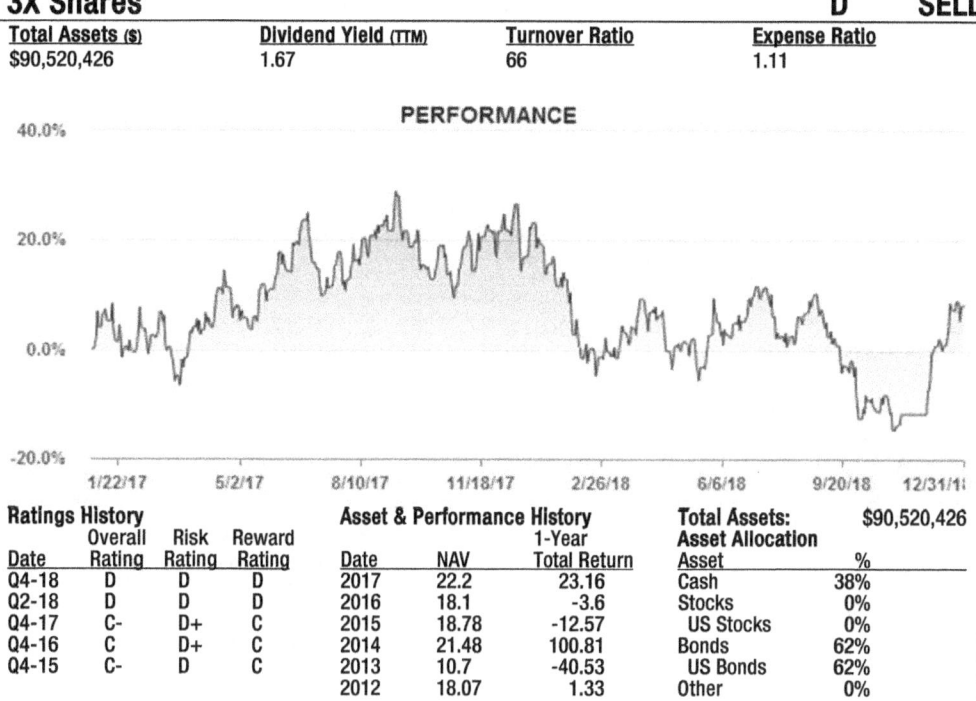

PERFORMANCE

Ratings History

Date	Overall Rating	Risk Rating	Reward Rating
Q4-18	D	D	D
Q2-18	D	D	D
Q4-17	C-	D+	C
Q4-16	C	D+	C
Q4-15	C-	D	C

Asset & Performance History

Date	NAV	1-Year Total Return
2017	22.2	23.16
2016	18.1	-3.6
2015	18.78	-12.57
2014	21.48	100.81
2013	10.7	-40.53
2012	18.07	1.33

Total Assets: $90,520,426
Asset Allocation

Asset	%
Cash	38%
Stocks	0%
US Stocks	0%
Bonds	62%
US Bonds	62%
Other	0%

Services Offered:

Investment Strategy: The investment seeks daily investment results, before fees and expenses, of 300% of the daily performance of the ICE U.S. Treasury 20+ Year Bond Index. The fund, under normal circumstances, invests at least 80% of its net assets (plus borrowing for investment purposes) in securities of the index, exchange-traded funds ("ETFs") that track the index and other financial instruments that provide daily leveraged exposure to the index or ETFs that track the index. The index is a market value weighted index that includes publicly issued U.S. Treasury securities that have a remaining maturity of greater than 20 years. The fund is non-diversified. **Top Holdings:** iShares 20+ Year Treasury Bond ETF 20+ Yr Treas Bd Idx Swap 20+ Yr Treas Bd Idx Swap 20+ Yr Treas Bd Idx Swap 20+ Yr Treas Bd Idx Swap

---

Invesco S&P 500® Equal Weight Consumer Discretionary ETF   C-   HOLD

Ticker	Traded On	NAV	Total Assets ($)	Dividend Yield (TTM)	Turnover Ratio	Expense Ratio
RCD	NYSE Arca	89.92	$90,274,330	1.37		0.4

Ratings
Reward   C
Risk   D+
Recent Upgrade/Downgrade   Down

Fund Information
Fund Type   Exchange Traded Funds
Category   Consumer Goods & Svcs
Sub-Category   Consumer Cyclical
Prospectus Objective   Unaligned
Inception Date   Nov-06
Open to New Investments   Y

Prices
Price (as of 12/31/2018)   89.86
52-Week High   108.34
52-Week Low   84.82

Total Returns (%)

3-Month	6-Month	1-Year	3-Year	5-Year
-14.59	-11.96	-8.48	10.87	19.90

3-Year Standard Deviation   11.7
Effective Duration

Valuation
Premium/Discount (1-Year Average)   0.13

Company Information
Provider   Invesco
Manager/Tenure   Peter Hubbard (0), Michael Jeanette
                   (0), Jonathan Nixon (0), 1 other
Website   http://www.invesco.com/us
Address   Invesco 11 Greenway Plaza, Ste. 2500
                   Houston TX 77046 United States
Phone Number   800-659-1005

PERFORMANCE

Ratings History

Date	Overall Rating	Risk Rating	Reward Rating
Q4-18	C-	D+	C
Q2-18	C-	D+	C
Q4-17	B-	B	C+
Q4-16	C	D+	B-
Q4-15	C	C	C

Asset & Performance History

Date	NAV	1-Year Total Return
2017	99.8	14.67
2016	88.37	5.54
2015	84.73	-2.86
2014	88.38	11.33
2013	80.28	43.18
2012	56.62	21.89

Total Assets: $90,274,330
Asset Allocation

Asset	%
Cash	0%
Stocks	100%
US Stocks	99%
Bonds	0%
US Bonds	0%
Other	0%

Services Offered:

Investment Strategy: The investment seeks to track the investment results (before fees and expenses) of the S&P 500® Equal Weight Consumer Discretionary Index (the "underlying index"). The fund generally will invest at least 90% of its total assets in the securities that comprise the underlying index. The underlying index is an equal-weighted version of the S&P 500® Consumer Discretionary Index. Strictly in accordance with its guidelines and mandated procedures, the index provider compiles, maintains and calculates the underlying index, which is comprised of common stocks of companies in the consumer discretionary sector of the S&P 500® Index. The fund is non-diversified. **Top Holdings:** Starbucks Corp Foot Locker Inc McDonald's Corp L Brands Inc General Motors Co

Alpha Architect International Quantitative Value ETF

D+   **SELL**

Ticker	Traded On	NAV	Total Assets ($)	Dividend Yield (TTM)	Turnover Ratio	Expense Ratio
IVAL	BATS	25.18	$89,847,398	3.14	30	0.79

Ratings
Reward	D+
Risk	D+
Recent Upgrade/Downgrade	Down

Fund Information
Fund Type	Exchange Traded Funds
Category	Global Equity Large Cap
Sub-Category	Foreign Large Value
Prospectus Objective	Growth
Inception Date	Dec-14
Open to New Investments	Y

Prices
Price (as of 12/31/2018)	24.98
52-Week High	34.94
52-Week Low	24.27

Total Returns (%)
3-Month	6-Month	1-Year	3-Year	5-Year
-17.11	-15.87	-21.62	11.38	

3-Year Standard Deviation	13.92
Effective Duration	

Valuation
Premium/Discount (1-Year Average)	0.16

Company Information
Provider	Alpha Architect
Manager/Tenure	Tao Wang (3)
Website	http://www.alphaarchitect.com/funds
Address	Alpha Architect 213 Foxcroft Road Broomall PA 19008 United States
Phone Number	

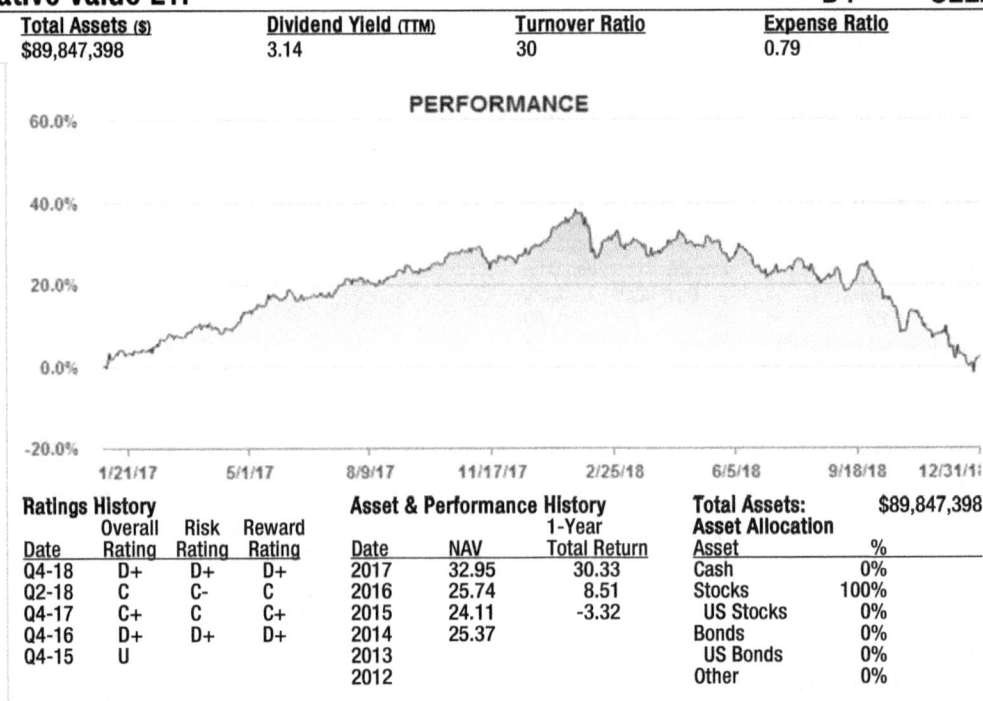

PERFORMANCE

Ratings History
Date	Overall Rating	Risk Rating	Reward Rating
Q4-18	D+	D+	D+
Q2-18	C	C-	C
Q4-17	C+	C	C+
Q4-16	D+	D+	D+
Q4-15	U		

Asset & Performance History
Date	NAV	1-Year Total Return
2017	32.95	30.33
2016	25.74	8.51
2015	24.11	-3.32
2014	25.37	
2013		
2012		

Total Assets: $89,847,398

Asset Allocation
Asset	%
Cash	0%
Stocks	100%
US Stocks	0%
Bonds	0%
US Bonds	0%
Other	0%

Services Offered:

Investment Strategy: The investment seeks to track the total return performance, before fees and expenses, of the Alpha Architect International Quantitative Value Index. The fund normally will invest at least 80% of its total assets in the component securities of the index and investments that have economic characteristics that are substantially identical to the economic characteristics of such component securities. The index uses a 5-step, quantitative, rules-based methodology to identify a portfolio of approximately 40-50 undervalued non-U.S. equity securities or their depositary receipts with the potential for capital appreciation. **Top Holdings:** Nippon Telegraph & Telephone Corp Deutsche Lufthansa AG Qantas Airways Ltd Sumitomo Heavy Industries Ltd Suzuki Motor Corp

---

SPDR® Global Dow ETF

C-   **HOLD**

Ticker	Traded On	NAV	Total Assets ($)	Dividend Yield (TTM)	Turnover Ratio	Expense Ratio
DGT	NYSE Arca	75.68	$89,823,146	2.24	10	0.5

Ratings
Reward	C-
Risk	D+
Recent Upgrade/Downgrade	Down

Fund Information
Fund Type	Exchange Traded Funds
Category	Global Equity Large Cap
Sub-Category	World Large Stock
Prospectus Objective	World Stock
Inception Date	Sep-00
Open to New Investments	Y

Prices
Price (as of 12/31/2018)	75.49
52-Week High	91.75
52-Week Low	72.28

Total Returns (%)
3-Month	6-Month	1-Year	3-Year	5-Year
-11.98	-6.68	-9.20	25.29	23.15

3-Year Standard Deviation	10.4
Effective Duration	

Valuation
Premium/Discount (1-Year Average)	-0.02

Company Information
Provider	SPDR State Street Global Advisors
Manager/Tenure	Michael J. Feehily (7), Karl A. Schneider (4), Kathleen Morgan (0)
Website	http://www.spdrs.com
Address	SPDR State Street Global Advisors State Street Financial Center, 1 Lincoln Street Boston MA 02111-2900 United States
Phone Number	617-786-3000

PERFORMANCE

Ratings History
Date	Overall Rating	Risk Rating	Reward Rating
Q4-18	C-	D+	C-
Q2-18	C-	D+	C
Q4-17	B-	C+	B-
Q4-16	C	D+	C
Q4-15	C	D+	C

Asset & Performance History
Date	NAV	1-Year Total Return
2017	85.29	24.47
2016	69.98	10.04
2015	64.69	-4.41
2014	69.22	2.82
2013	69.09	26.95
2012	55.76	13.54

Total Assets: $89,823,146

Asset Allocation
Asset	%
Cash	0%
Stocks	100%
US Stocks	48%
Bonds	0%
US Bonds	0%
Other	0%

Services Offered: Dividend Investment Plan, CashInvestment Plan

Investment Strategy: The investment seeks to provide investment results that, before fees and expenses, correspond generally to the total return performance of the Global Dow that tracks the performance of multinational blue-chip issuers. The fund generally invests substantially all, but at least 80%, of its total assets in the securities comprising the index. The index is made up of 150 companies from around the world. It may purchase a subset of the securities in the index in an effort to hold a portfolio of securities with generally the same risk and return characteristics of the index. The fund is non-diversified. **Top Holdings:** Petroleo Brasileiro SA Petrobras ADR MTN Group Ltd Starbucks Corp McDonald's Corp Telefonica SA

VanEck Vectors Brazil Small-Cap ETF   C-   HOLD

Ticker	Traded On	NAV	Total Assets ($)	Dividend Yield (TTM)	Turnover Ratio	Expense Ratio
BRF	NYSE Arca	20.09	$89,248,131	5.24	53	0.6

Ratings
Reward   C
Risk   D+
Recent Upgrade/Downgrade

Fund Information
Fund Type   Exchange Traded Funds
Category   Latin America Equity
Sub-Category   Latin America Stock
Prospectus Objective   Growth
Inception Date   May-09
Open to New Investments   Y

Prices
Price (as of 12/31/2018)   20.02
52-Week High   25.87
52-Week Low   16.00

Total Returns (%)

3-Month	6-Month	1-Year	3-Year	5-Year
23.15	15.80	-11.79	115.75	-17.51

3-Year Standard Deviation   32.58
Effective Duration

Valuation
Premium/Discount (1-Year Average)   -0.08

Company Information
Provider   VanEck
Manager/Tenure Hao-Hung (Peter) Liao (9), Guo Hua (Jason) Jin (0)
Website   http://www.vaneck.com
Address   Van Eck Associates Corporation 666 Third Avenue New York NY 10017 United States
Phone Number   800-826-1115

PERFORMANCE

Ratings History

Date	Overall Rating	Risk Rating	Reward Rating
Q4-18	C-	D+	C
Q2-18	C	D+	C
Q4-17	C	D+	C+
Q4-16	D+	D+	D+
Q4-15	E+	E+	E+

Asset & Performance History

Date	NAV	1-Year Total Return
2017	23.33	51.75
2016	16.1	61.17
2015	10.44	-48.87
2014	21.23	-25.21
2013	29.61	-28.52
2012	42.2	17.9

Total Assets: $89,248,131

Asset Allocation

Asset	%
Cash	1%
Stocks	99%
US Stocks	1%
Bonds	0%
US Bonds	0%
Other	0%

Services Offered:

Investment Strategy: The investment seeks to replicate as closely as possible, before fees and expenses, the price and yield performance of the MVIS® Brazil Small-Cap Index. The fund normally invests at least 80% of its total assets in securities that comprise the fund's benchmark index. The index includes securities of Brazilian small-capitalization companies. A company is generally considered to be a Brazilian company if it is incorporated in Brazil or is incorporated outside of Brazil but has at least 50% of its revenues/related assets in Brazil. **Top Holdings:** CVC Brasil Operadora e Agencia de Viagens SA Transmissora Alianca de Energia Eletrica SA Unit CIA Saneamento Do Parana-SANEPAR Units (1 Ord Share & 4 Pref Shares) Metalurgica Gerdau SA Participating Preferred Cosan Ltd

---

VanEck Vectors Global Alternative Energy ETF   C-   HOLD

Ticker	Traded On	NAV	Total Assets ($)	Dividend Yield (TTM)	Turnover Ratio	Expense Ratio
GEX	NYSE Arca	55.10	$88,091,971	1.29	21	0.63

Ratings
Reward   C-
Risk   D+
Recent Upgrade/Downgrade

Fund Information
Fund Type   Exchange Traded Funds
Category   Equity Misc
Sub-Category   Miscellaneous Sector
Prospectus Objective   Natl Res
Inception Date   May-07
Open to New Investments   Y

Prices
Price (as of 12/31/2018)   54.60
52-Week High   64.43
52-Week Low   51.82

Total Returns (%)

3-Month	6-Month	1-Year	3-Year	5-Year
-5.35	-4.03	-8.96	5.14	3.42

3-Year Standard Deviation   13.55
Effective Duration

Valuation
Premium/Discount (1-Year Average)   0.09

Company Information
Provider   VanEck
Manager/Tenure Hao-Hung (Peter) Liao (11), Guo Hua (Jason) Jin (0)
Website   http://www.vaneck.com
Address   Van Eck Associates Corporation 666 Third Avenue New York NY 10017 United States
Phone Number   800-826-1115

PERFORMANCE

Ratings History

Date	Overall Rating	Risk Rating	Reward Rating
Q4-18	C-	D+	C-
Q2-18	C	D+	C
Q4-17	C+	B-	C+
Q4-16	D+	D+	D+
Q4-15	C-	D+	C-

Asset & Performance History

Date	NAV	1-Year Total Return
2017	60.94	21.89
2016	50.62	-5.24
2015	54.57	1.45
2014	54.09	-3.04
2013	55.9	69.71
2012	33.27	3.08

Total Assets: $88,091,971

Asset Allocation

Asset	%
Cash	0%
Stocks	100%
US Stocks	62%
Bonds	0%
US Bonds	0%
Other	0%

Services Offered:

Investment Strategy: The investment seeks to replicate as closely as possible, before fees and expenses, the price and yield performance of the Ardour Global IndexSM (Extra Liquid). The fund normally invests at least 80% of its total assets in stocks of companies primarily engaged in the business of alternative energy. Such companies may include small- and medium-capitalization companies and foreign issuers. Alternative energy refers to the generation of power through environmentally friendly, non traditional sources. It is non-diversified. **Top Holdings:** Tesla Inc Vestas Wind Systems A/S Eaton Corp PLC Cree Inc NIBE Industrier AB B

Inspire Global Hope ETF

D SELL

Ticker	Traded On	NAV		Total Assets ($)	Dividend Yield (TTM)	Turnover Ratio	Expense Ratio
BLES	NYSE Arca	24.31		$87,777,870	1.85		0.61

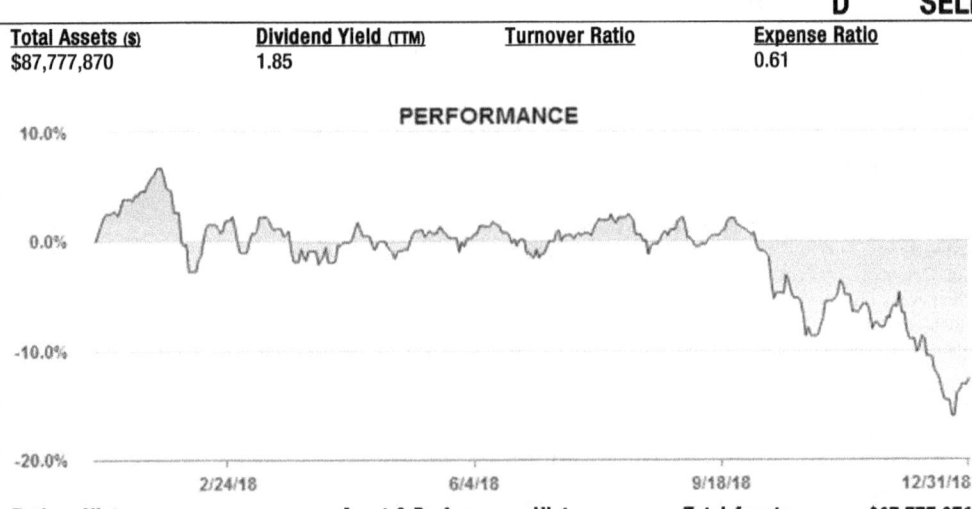

Ratings

Reward	D
Risk	D+
Recent Upgrade/Downgrade	Down

Fund Information

Fund Type	Exchange Traded Funds
Category	Global Equity Large Cap
Sub-Category	World Large Stock
Prospectus Objective	Growth
Inception Date	Feb-17
Open to New Investments	Y

Prices

Price (as of 12/31/2018)	24.24
52-Week High	30.44
52-Week Low	23.44

Total Returns (%)

3-Month	6-Month	1-Year	3-Year	5-Year
-13.35	-11.31	-12.74		

3-Year Standard Deviation	
Effective Duration	

Valuation

Premium/Discount (1-Year Average)	0.66

Company Information

Provider	Inspire
Manager/Tenure	Darrell Jayroe (1), Robert Netzly (1)
Website	
Address	Inspire 650 San Benito Street, Suite 130 Hollister CA 95023 United States
Phone Number	

Ratings History

Date	Overall Rating	Risk Rating	Reward Rating
Q4-18	D	D+	D
Q2-18	C-	C-	D+
Q4-17	U		
Q4-16			
Q4-15			

Asset & Performance History

Date	NAV	1-Year Total Return
2017	28.29	
2016		
2015		
2014		
2013		
2012		

Total Assets: $87,777,870

Asset Allocation

Asset	%
Cash	0%
Stocks	100%
US Stocks	54%
Bonds	0%
US Bonds	0%
Other	0%

Services Offered:

Investment Strategy: The investment seeks to replicate investment results that generally correspond to the Inspire Global Hope Large Cap Index. The fund will invest at least 80% of its total assets in the component securities of the index. The index provider selects foreign and domestic equity securities included in the Russell 1,000 Index, MSCI EAFE Index, and MSCI EM Large Cap Index using the index provider's Inspire Impact Score®, a proprietary selection methodology that is designed to assign a score to a particular security based on the security's alignment with biblical values and the positive impact that company has on the world through various ESG criterion. **Top Holdings:** Energy Company of Minas Gerais Participating Preferred Natura Cosmeticos SA SCANA Corp Petroleo Brasileiro SA Petrobras Participating Preferred Xilinx Inc

First Trust Multi Cap Value AlphaDEX® Fund

C- HOLD

Ticker	Traded On	NAV		Total Assets ($)	Dividend Yield (TTM)	Turnover Ratio	Expense Ratio
FAB	NAS CM	47.94		$87,119,664	1.66	81	0.71

Ratings

Reward	C-
Risk	D+
Recent Upgrade/Downgrade	Down

Fund Information

Fund Type	Exchange Traded Funds
Category	US Equity Mid Cap
Sub-Category	Mid-Cap Value
Prospectus Objective	Growth
Inception Date	May-07
Open to New Investments	Y

Prices

Price (as of 12/31/2018)	47.81
52-Week High	59.21
52-Week Low	45.89

Total Returns (%)

3-Month	6-Month	1-Year	3-Year	5-Year
-15.48	-13.35	-13.97	23.54	16.63

3-Year Standard Deviation	12.41
Effective Duration	

Valuation

Premium/Discount (1-Year Average)	0.19

Company Information

Provider	First Trust
Manager/Tenure	Jon C. Erickson (11), Daniel J. Lindquist (11), David G. McGarel (11), 3 others
Website	http://www.ftportfolios.com/
Address	First Trust 120 E. Liberty Drive, Suite 400 Wheaton IL 60187 United States
Phone Number	800-621-1675

Ratings History

Date	Overall Rating	Risk Rating	Reward Rating
Q4-18	C-	D+	C-
Q2-18	C-	D+	C
Q4-17	B-	B-	B
Q4-16	C	D+	C+
Q4-15	C	C-	C

Asset & Performance History

Date	NAV	1-Year Total Return
2017	56.71	14.11
2016	50.45	25.84
2015	40.71	-12.46
2014	47.22	7.86
2013	44.4	37.02
2012	32.79	17.19

Total Assets: $87,119,664

Asset Allocation

Asset	%
Cash	0%
Stocks	100%
US Stocks	99%
Bonds	0%
US Bonds	0%
Other	0%

Services Offered:

Investment Strategy: The investment seeks investment results that correspond generally to the price and yield (before the fund's fees and expenses) of the Nasdaq AlphaDEX® Multi Cap Value Index. The fund will normally invest at least 90% of its net assets (including investment borrowings) in common stocks that comprise the index. The index is designed to select value stocks from the NASDAQ US 500 Large Cap Index, NASDAQ US 600 Mid Cap Index and NASDAQ US 700 Small Cap Index that may generate positive alpha, or risk-adjusted returns, relative to traditional indices through the use of the AlphaDEX® selection methodology. **Top Holdings:** Newell Brands Inc Verizon Communications Inc Comcast Corp Class A Dollar Tree Inc Symantec Corp

Direxion Daily MSCI Emerging Markets Bear 3X Shares   D+   SELL

Ticker	Traded On	NAV	Total Assets ($)	Dividend Yield (TTM)	Turnover Ratio	Expense Ratio
EDZ	NYSE Arca	59.80	$87,056,920	0.29	0	1.12

Ratings
Reward   D
Risk   D
Recent Upgrade/Downgrade   Up

Fund Information
Fund Type   Exchange Traded Funds
Category   Trading Tools
Sub-Category   Trading--Inverse Equity
Prospectus Objective   Div Emerg Mkts
Inception Date   Dec-08
Open to New Investments   Y

Prices
Price (as of 12/31/2018)   59.74
52-Week High   70.95
52-Week Low   33.35

Total Returns (%)

3-Month	6-Month	1-Year	3-Year	5-Year
17.32	13.43	32.61	-74.43	-69.97

3-Year Standard Deviation   42.16
Effective Duration

Valuation
Premium/Discount (1-Year Average)   0.00

Company Information
Provider   Direxion Funds
Manager/Tenure   Paul Brigandi (9), Tony Ng (3)
Website   http://www.direxionfunds.com
Address   Direxion Funds 1301 Avenue Of The
                  Americas (6th Avenue) New York NY
                  10019 United States
Phone Number   646-572-3390

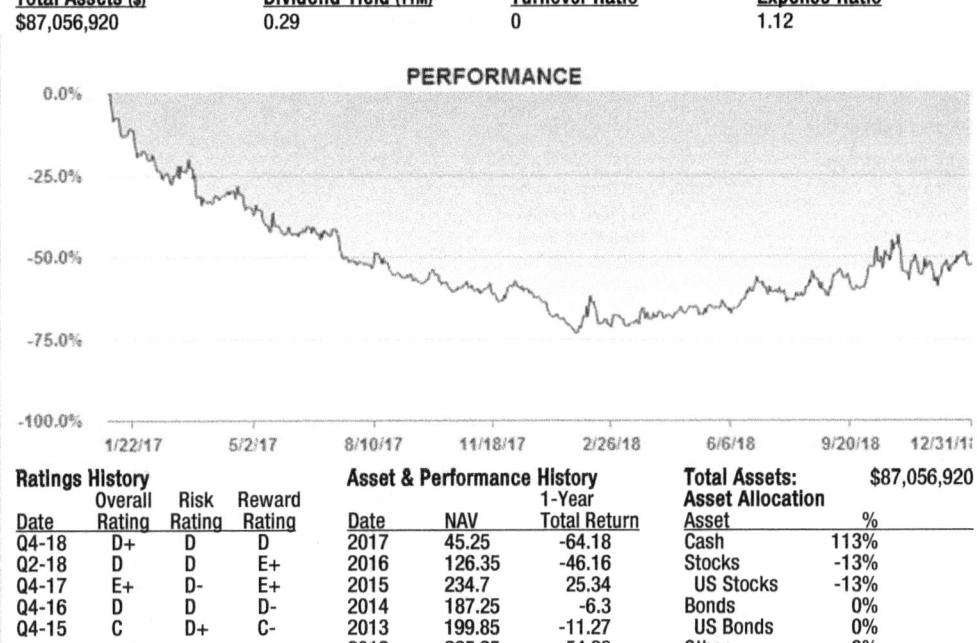

PERFORMANCE

Ratings History

Date	Overall Rating	Risk Rating	Reward Rating
Q4-18	D+	D	D
Q2-18	D	D	E+
Q4-17	E+	D-	E+
Q4-16	D	D	D-
Q4-15	C	D+	C-

Asset & Performance History

Date	NAV	1-Year Total Return
2017	45.25	-64.18
2016	126.35	-46.16
2015	234.7	25.34
2014	187.25	-6.3
2013	199.85	-11.27
2012	225.25	-54.28

Total Assets: $87,056,920
Asset Allocation

Asset	%
Cash	113%
Stocks	-13%
US Stocks	-13%
Bonds	0%
US Bonds	0%
Other	0%

Services Offered:

Investment Strategy: The investment seeks daily investment results, before fees and expenses, of 300% of the inverse of the daily performance of the MSCI Emerging Markets IndexSM. The fund invests in swap agreements, futures contracts, short positions or other financial instruments that, in combination, provide inverse or short leveraged exposure to the index equal to at least 80% of the fund's net assets (plus borrowing for investment purposes). The index is a free float-adjusted market capitalization weighted index that is designed to represent the performance of large- and mid-capitalizations securities across the 24 emerging market countries. The fund is non-diversified. **Top Holdings:** Msci Emerg Mkts Idx Swap   Msci Emerg Mkts Idx Swap   Msci Emerg Mkts Idx Swap   Msci Emerg Mkts Idx Swap   Msci Emerg Mkts Idx Swap

---

UBS ETRACS CMCI Total Return ETN   C-   HOLD

Ticker	Traded On	NAV	Total Assets ($)	Dividend Yield (TTM)	Turnover Ratio	Expense Ratio
UCI	NYSE Arca	13.56	$86,767,950	0	0	0.55

Ratings
Reward   C-
Risk   C-
Recent Upgrade/Downgrade

Fund Information
Fund Type   Exchange Traded Funds
Category   Commodities Broad Basket
Sub-Category   Commodities Broad Basket
Prospectus Objective   Natl Res
Inception Date   Apr-08
Open to New Investments   Y

Prices
Price (as of 12/31/2018)   13.50
52-Week High   16.32
52-Week Low   13.50

Total Returns (%)

3-Month	6-Month	1-Year	3-Year	5-Year
-12.74	-11.32	-11.59	12.13	-33.60

3-Year Standard Deviation   10.99
Effective Duration

Valuation
Premium/Discount (1-Year Average)   0.01

Company Information
Provider   UBS Group AG
Manager/Tenure   No Manager (10)
Website   http://www.ubs.com
Address   Bahnhofstrasse 45 Zurich 8098
                  Switzerland
Phone Number   412-037-1952

PERFORMANCE

Ratings History

Date	Overall Rating	Risk Rating	Reward Rating
Q4-18	C-	C-	C-
Q2-18	C	C-	C
Q4-17	C-	D+	C
Q4-16	D	D	D+
Q4-15	D-	D	D-

Asset & Performance History

Date	NAV	1-Year Total Return
2017	15.34	7.96
2016	14.19	17.28
2015	12.1	-26.01
2014	16.35	-19.97
2013	20.43	-7.26
2012	22.03	2.22

Total Assets: $86,767,950
Asset Allocation

Asset	%
Cash	%
Stocks	%
US Stocks	%
Bonds	%
US Bonds	%
Other	%

Services Offered:

Investment Strategy: The investment seeks to track the price and performance yield, before fees and expenses, of the UBS Bloomberg Constant Maturity Commodity index.
The fund is designed to be a diversified benchmark for commodities as an asset class. The index is comprised of 28 futures contracts with up to five different maturities for each individual commodity. **Top Holdings:**

IQ S&P High Yield Low Volatility Bond ETF

D SELL

Ticker	Traded On	NAV	Total Assets ($)	Dividend Yield (TTM)	Turnover Ratio	Expense Ratio
HYLV	NYSE Arca	23.29	$85,692,651	4.31		0.4

Ratings

Reward	D
Risk	D+
Recent Upgrade/Downgrade	Down

Fund Information

Fund Type	Exchange Traded Funds
Category	US Fixed Income
Sub-Category	High Yield Bond
Prospectus Objective	Corp Bond-High Yld
Inception Date	Feb-17
Open to New Investments	Y

Prices

Price (as of 12/31/2018)	23.28
52-Week High	25.37
52-Week Low	23.07

Total Returns (%)

3-Month	6-Month	1-Year	3-Year	5-Year
-3.39	-0.96	-3.38		

3-Year Standard Deviation	
Effective Duration	

Valuation

Premium/Discount (1-Year Average)	0.11

Company Information

Provider	IndexIQ
Manager/Tenure	Scott Dolph (1), Dan C. Roberts (1), Alexandra Wilson-Elizondo (1)
Website	http://www.indexiq.com
Address	IndexIQ 800 Westchester Avenue, Suite N-611 Rye Brook NY 10573 United States
Phone Number	888-934-0777

PERFORMANCE

Ratings History

Date	Overall Rating	Risk Rating	Reward Rating
Q4-18	D	D+	D
Q2-18	D+	C-	D+
Q4-17	U		
Q4-16			
Q4-15			

Asset & Performance History

Date	NAV	1-Year Total Return
2017	25.07	
2016		
2015		
2014		
2013		
2012		

Total Assets: $85,692,651

Asset Allocation

Asset	%
Cash	0%
Stocks	0%
US Stocks	0%
Bonds	99%
US Bonds	90%
Other	1%

Services Offered:

Investment Strategy: The investment seeks investment results that track (before fees and expenses) the price and yield performance of its underlying index, the S&P U.S. High Yield Low Volatility Corporate Bond Index. The fund uses a "Representative Sampling" strategy in seeking to track the performance of the underlying index. The underlying index is comprised of U.S. dollar denominated high yield corporate bonds that have been selected in accordance with a rules-based methodology that seeks to identify securities that, in the aggregate, are expected to have lower volatility relative to the broad U.S. dollar denominated high yield corporate bond market. **Top Holdings:** Blackrock Treasury Trust Instl 62   1011778 B.C. Unlimited Liability Company / New Red Finance, Inc. 5%   CCO Holdings, LLC/ CCO Holdings Capital Corp. 5.75%   Ally Financial Inc. 8%   Bausch Health Companies Inc 7%

Direxion Daily FTSE China Bear 3X Shares

D SELL

Ticker	Traded On	NAV	Total Assets ($)	Dividend Yield (TTM)	Turnover Ratio	Expense Ratio
YANG	NYSE Arca	66.66	$85,669,786	0.3	0	1.09

Ratings

Reward	D-
Risk	D
Recent Upgrade/Downgrade	

Fund Information

Fund Type	Exchange Traded Funds
Category	Trading Tools
Sub-Category	Trading--Inverse Equity
Prospectus Objective	Pacific Stock
Inception Date	Dec-09
Open to New Investments	Y

Prices

Price (as of 12/31/2018)	66.67
52-Week High	77.18
52-Week Low	36.30

Total Returns (%)

3-Month	6-Month	1-Year	3-Year	5-Year
18.14	4.82	12.95	-73.01	-87.24

3-Year Standard Deviation	52.32
Effective Duration	

Valuation

Premium/Discount (1-Year Average)	0.09

Company Information

Provider	Direxion Funds
Manager/Tenure	Paul Brigandi (9), Tony Ng (3)
Website	http://www.direxionfunds.com
Address	Direxion Funds 1301 Avenue Of The Americas (6th Avenue) New York NY 10019 United States
Phone Number	646-572-3390

PERFORMANCE

Ratings History

Date	Overall Rating	Risk Rating	Reward Rating
Q4-18	D	D	D-
Q2-18	D	D	E+
Q4-17	E+	D-	E+
Q4-16	D	D	E+
Q4-15	D-	D-	E+

Asset & Performance History

Date	NAV	1-Year Total Return
2017	59.2	-64.94
2016	168.9	-31.84
2015	247.83	-13.04
2014	285	-45.63
2013	524.25	-59.55
2012	1,296.25	-45.67

Total Assets: $85,669,786

Asset Allocation

Asset	%
Cash	108%
Stocks	-8%
US Stocks	-8%
Bonds	0%
US Bonds	0%
Other	0%

Services Offered:

Investment Strategy: The investment seeks daily investment results, before fees and expenses, of 300% of the inverse (or opposite) of the daily performance of the FTSE China 50 Index. The fund, under normal circumstances, invests in swap agreements, futures contracts, short positions or other financial instruments that, in combination, provide inverse (opposite) or short leveraged exposure to the index equal to at least 80% of the fund's net assets (plus borrowing for investment purposes). The index consists of the 50 largest and most liquid public Chinese companies currently trading on the Hong Kong Stock Exchange ("SEHK"). The fund is non-diversified. **Top Holdings:** Ishares China Largecap   Ishares China Largecap   Ishares China Largecap   Ishares China Largecap Goldman Finl Sq Trsry Ins

VanEck Vectors Natural Resources ETF   C-   HOLD

Ticker	Traded On	NAV	Total Assets ($)	Dividend Yield (TTM)	Turnover Ratio	Expense Ratio
HAP	NYSE Arca	32.20	$85,654,282	2.15	34	0.5

Ratings
Reward   C
Risk   D+
Recent Upgrade/Downgrade   Down

Fund Information
Fund Type   Exchange Traded Funds
Category   Natural Resources
Sub-Category   Natural Resources
Prospectus Objective   Natl Res
Inception Date   Aug-08
Open to New Investments Y

Prices
Price (as of 12/31/2018)   32.23
52-Week High   39.65
52-Week Low   30.80

Total Returns (%)

3-Month	6-Month	1-Year	3-Year	5-Year
-12.51	-9.47	-10.67	30.76	-2.71

3-Year Standard Deviation   11.83
Effective Duration

Valuation
Premium/Discount (1-Year Average)   0.08

Company Information
Provider   VanEck
Manager/Tenure Hao-Hung (Peter) Liao (10), Guo Hua
                (Jason) Jin (0)
Website   http://www.vaneck.com
Address   Van Eck Associates Corporation 666
                Third Avenue New York NY 10017
                United States
Phone Number   800-826-1115

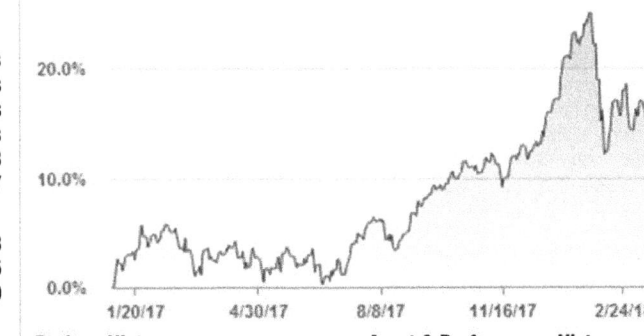

PERFORMANCE

Ratings History

Date	Overall Rating	Risk Rating	Reward Rating
Q4-18	C-	D+	C
Q2-18	C	D+	C
Q4-17	C+	C	C+
Q4-16	C-	D+	C-
Q4-15	D+	D+	D+

Asset & Performance History

Date	NAV	1-Year Total Return
2017	37.09	17.17
2016	32.31	24.93
2015	26.38	-19.39
2014	33.73	-7.7
2013	37.46	6.58
2012	35.94	9.01

Total Assets: $85,654,282
Asset Allocation

Asset	%
Cash	0%
Stocks	100%
US Stocks	49%
Bonds	0%
US Bonds	0%
Other	0%

Services Offered:

Investment Strategy: The investment seeks to replicate as closely as possible, before fees and expenses, the price and yield performance of the VanEck® Natural Resources Index. The fund normally invests at least 80% of its total assets in securities that comprise the fund's benchmark index. The index is comprised of publicly traded companies engaged (derive greater than 50% of revenues from applicable sources) in the production and distribution of commodities and commodity-related products and services in the following sectors: 1) Agriculture; 2) Alternatives (Water & Alternative Energy); 3) Base and Industrial Metals; 4) Energy; 5) Forest Products; and 6) Precious Metals. **Top Holdings:** Deere & Co Nutrien Ltd Archer-Daniels Midland Co Tyson Foods Inc Class A Exxon Mobil Corp

First Trust NASDAQ-100 Ex-Technology Sector Index Fund   C-   HOLD

Ticker	Traded On	NAV	Total Assets ($)	Dividend Yield (TTM)	Turnover Ratio	Expense Ratio
QQXT	NAS CM	45.66	$85,569,820	0.26	25	0.6

Ratings
Reward   C
Risk   D+
Recent Upgrade/Downgrade   Down

Fund Information
Fund Type   Exchange Traded Funds
Category   US Equity Large Cap Growth
Sub-Category   Large Growth
Prospectus Objective   Growth
Inception Date   Feb-07
Open to New Investments Y

Prices
Price (as of 12/31/2018)   45.66
52-Week High   53.38
52-Week Low   43.14

Total Returns (%)

3-Month	6-Month	1-Year	3-Year	5-Year
-13.66	-8.67	-5.58	11.26	34.42

3-Year Standard Deviation   11.74
Effective Duration

Valuation
Premium/Discount (1-Year Average)   0.15

Company Information
Provider   First Trust
Manager/Tenure Jon C. Erickson (11), Daniel J.
                Lindquist (11), David G. McGarel (11),
                3 others
Website   http://www.ftportfolios.com/
Address   First Trust 120 E. Liberty Drive, Suite
                400 Wheaton IL 60187 United States
Phone Number   800-621-1675

PERFORMANCE

Ratings History

Date	Overall Rating	Risk Rating	Reward Rating
Q4-18	C-	D+	C
Q2-18	C-	D+	C
Q4-17	B-	B	C+
Q4-16	C	D+	C+
Q4-15	C	C	C+

Asset & Performance History

Date	NAV	1-Year Total Return
2017	48.53	20.4
2016	40.44	-2.13
2015	41.45	4.74
2014	39.73	15.35
2013	34.77	41.24
2012	24.69	20.3

Total Assets: $85,569,820
Asset Allocation

Asset	%
Cash	0%
Stocks	100%
US Stocks	93%
Bonds	0%
US Bonds	0%
Other	0%

Services Offered:

Investment Strategy: The investment seeks investment results that correspond generally to the price and yield (before the fund's fees and expenses) of an equity index called the NASDAQ-100 Ex-Tech Sector IndexSM. The fund will normally invest at least 90% of its net assets (including investment borrowings) in common stocks that comprise the index. The index is an equal-weighted index based on the securities of the NASDAQ-100 Index® that are not classified as "technology" according to the Industry Classification Benchmark ("ICB") classification system and, as a result, is a subset of the NASDAQ-100 Index®. **Top Holdings:** Walgreens Boots Alliance Inc Starbucks Corp Tesla Inc MercadoLibre Inc Hologic Inc

iShares iBonds Mar 2020 Term Corporate ex-Financials ETF

C-   HOLD

Ticker	Traded On	NAV	Total Assets ($)	Dividend Yield (TTM)	Turnover Ratio	Expense Ratio
IBCD	NYSE Arca	24.37	$85,257,638	1.88	11	0.1

Ratings

Reward	C
Risk	D+
Recent Upgrade/Downgrade	

Fund Information

Fund Type	Exchange Traded Funds
Category	US Fixed Income
Sub-Category	Short-Term Bond
Prospectus Objective	Corp Bond - High Quality
Inception Date	Apr-13
Open to New Investments	Y

Prices

Price (as of 12/31/2018)	24.39
52-Week High	24.52
52-Week Low	24.26

Total Returns (%)

3-Month	6-Month	1-Year	3-Year	5-Year
0.56	1.26	1.50	6.42	12.86

3-Year Standard Deviation	1.42
Effective Duration	0.92

Valuation

Premium/Discount (1-Year Average)	0.11

Company Information

Provider	iShares
Manager/Tenure	James Mauro (5), Scott Radell (5)
Website	http://www.ishares.com
Address	iShares 400 Howard Street San Francisco CA 94105 United States
Phone Number	800-474-2737

PERFORMANCE

Ratings History

Date	Overall Rating	Risk Rating	Reward Rating
Q4-18	C-	D+	C
Q2-18	C-	D+	C
Q4-17	B	A+	C
Q4-16	C	D+	C
Q4-15	D+	D	C

Asset & Performance History

Date	NAV	1-Year Total Return
2017	24.47	1.63
2016	24.49	3.01
2015	24.25	1.54
2014	24.4	4.43
2013	23.87	
2012		

Total Assets: $85,257,638

Asset Allocation

Asset	%
Cash	4%
Stocks	0%
US Stocks	0%
Bonds	96%
US Bonds	84%
Other	0%

Services Offered:

Investment Strategy: The investment seeks to track the investment results of the Bloomberg Barclays 2020 Maturity High Quality Corporate Index which is composed of U.S. dollar-denominated, investment-grade corporate bonds, excluding financials, maturing after March 31, 2019 and before April 1, 2020. The fund generally will invest at least 90% of its assets in the component securities of the underlying index, and may invest up to 10% of its assets in certain futures, options and swap contracts, cash and cash equivalents, as well as in securities not included in the underlying index. **Top Holdings:** America Movil S.A.B. de C.V. 5% Medtronic, Inc. 2.5% Cisco Systems, Inc. 4.45% Alibaba Group Holding Ltd 2.5% Oracle Corporation 2.25%

WisdomTree Bloomberg U.S. Dollar Bullish Fund

C   HOLD

Ticker	Traded On	NAV	Total Assets ($)	Dividend Yield (TTM)	Turnover Ratio	Expense Ratio
USDU	NYSE Arca	27.07	$85,255,036	0	0	0.5

Ratings

Reward	C
Risk	C-
Recent Upgrade/Downgrade	Up

Fund Information

Fund Type	Exchange Traded Funds
Category	Currency
Sub-Category	Multicurrency
Prospectus Objective	Money Mkt - Gen
Inception Date	Dec-13
Open to New Investments	Y

Prices

Price (as of 12/31/2018)	27.05
52-Week High	27.72
52-Week Low	24.82

Total Returns (%)

3-Month	6-Month	1-Year	3-Year	5-Year
1.82	2.22	5.53	-0.30	17.76

3-Year Standard Deviation	6.33
Effective Duration	0.02

Valuation

Premium/Discount (1-Year Average)	0.03

Company Information

Provider	WisdomTree
Manager/Tenure	Paul L. Benson (3), Stephanie Shu (3)
Website	http://www.wisdomtree.com
Address	WisdomTree 245 Park Avenue, 35th floor New York NY 10167 United States
Phone Number	866-909-9473

PERFORMANCE

Ratings History

Date	Overall Rating	Risk Rating	Reward Rating
Q4-18	C	C-	C
Q2-18	D+	C-	D
Q4-17	C-	C	D+
Q4-16	C	C-	C
Q4-15	D+	C+	C

Asset & Performance History

Date	NAV	1-Year Total Return
2017	25.88	-7.9
2016	28.1	2.57
2015	27.39	7.97
2014	27.01	9.39
2013	25.08	
2012		

Total Assets: $85,255,036

Asset Allocation

Asset	%
Cash	96%
Stocks	0%
US Stocks	0%
Bonds	4%
US Bonds	4%
Other	0%

Services Offered:

Investment Strategy: The investment seeks to provide total returns, before fees and expenses, that exceed the performance of the Bloomberg Dollar Total Return Index (the "index"). The fund is an actively managed ETF that seeks to provide total returns, before fees and expenses, that exceed the performance of the index. The index is structured to potentially benefit as the U.S. dollar appreciates relative to a basket of global currencies. The fund will seek exposure to both the U.S. dollar and global currencies held by the index through investing, under normal circumstances, at least 80% of its assets in money market securities and other liquid securities. It is non-diversified. **Top Holdings:** WisdomTree Floating Rate Treasury ETF

First Trust RiverFront Dynamic Europe ETF   D+   SELL

Ticker	Traded On	NAV	Total Assets ($)	Dividend Yield (TTM)	Turnover Ratio	Expense Ratio
RFEU	NAS CM	52.68	$85,245,125	2.78	110	0.83

Ratings
Reward	D+
Risk	C-
Recent Upgrade/Downgrade	Down

Fund Information
Fund Type	Exchange Traded Funds
Category	Europe Equity Large Cap
Sub-Category	Europe Stock
Prospectus Objective	Growth
Inception Date	Apr-16
Open to New Investments	Y

Prices
Price (as of 12/31/2018)	52.61
52-Week High	70.57
52-Week Low	50.49

Total Returns (%)
3-Month	6-Month	1-Year	3-Year	5-Year
-16.93	-12.87	-17.27		

3-Year Standard Deviation

Effective Duration

Valuation
Premium/Discount (1-Year Average)	0.08

Company Information
Provider	First Trust
Manager/Tenure	Adam Grossman (2), Scott Hays (2), Chris Konstantinos (2), 1 other
Website	http://www.ftportfolios.com/
Address	First Trust 120 E. Liberty Drive, Suite 400 Wheaton IL 60187 United States
Phone Number	800-621-1675

PERFORMANCE

Ratings History
Date	Overall Rating	Risk Rating	Reward Rating
Q4-18	D+	C-	D+
Q2-18	D+	D+	C-
Q4-17	D+	B+	C
Q4-16	U		
Q4-15			

Asset & Performance History
Date	NAV	1-Year Total Return
2017	65.22	27.27
2016	51.99	
2015		
2014		
2013		
2012		

Total Assets: $85,245,125

Asset Allocation
Asset	%
Cash	0%
Stocks	99%
US Stocks	2%
Bonds	0%
US Bonds	0%
Other	1%

Services Offered:

Investment Strategy: The investment seeks capital appreciation. The fund seeks to achieve its investment objective by investing at least 80% of its net assets (including investment borrowings) in a portfolio of equity securities of European companies, including through investments in common stock, depositary receipts, and common and preferred shares of real estate investment trusts ("REITs"), and forward foreign currency exchange contracts and currency spot transactions used to hedge the fund's exposure to the currencies in which the equity securities of such European companies are denominated. It is non-diversified. **Top Holdings:** Nestle SA   Roche Holding AG Dividend Right Cert.   Royal Dutch Shell PLC Class A   LVMH Moet Hennessy Louis Vuitton SE   Royal Dutch Shell PLC B

USAA MSCI USA Small Cap Value Momentum Blend Index ETF   D   SELL

Ticker	Traded On	NAV	Total Assets ($)	Dividend Yield (TTM)	Turnover Ratio	Expense Ratio
USVM	NYSE Arca	45.40	$84,990,245	0.9		0.25

Ratings
Reward	D
Risk	D
Recent Upgrade/Downgrade	

Fund Information
Fund Type	Exchange Traded Funds
Category	US Equity Small Cap
Sub-Category	Small Blend
Prospectus Objective	Small Company
Inception Date	Oct-17
Open to New Investments	Y

Prices
Price (as of 12/31/2018)	45.39
52-Week High	57.27
52-Week Low	42.68

Total Returns (%)
3-Month	6-Month	1-Year	3-Year	5-Year
-16.77	-15.49	-9.26		

3-Year Standard Deviation

Effective Duration

Valuation
Premium/Discount (1-Year Average)	0.08

Company Information
Provider	USAA
Manager/Tenure	Lance Humphrey (1), Wasif A. Latif (1), Emiliano Rabinovich (1), 2 others
Website	http://www.usaa.com
Address	USAA P.O. Box 659453 San Antonio TX 78265-9825 United States
Phone Number	800-531-8722

PERFORMANCE

Ratings History
Date	Overall Rating	Risk Rating	Reward Rating
Q4-18	D	D	D
Q2-18	U		
Q4-17	U		
Q4-16			
Q4-15			

Asset & Performance History
Date	NAV	1-Year Total Return
2017	50.67	
2016		
2015		
2014		
2013		
2012		

Total Assets: $84,990,245

Asset Allocation
Asset	%
Cash	0%
Stocks	100%
US Stocks	97%
Bonds	0%
US Bonds	0%
Other	0%

Services Offered:

Investment Strategy: The investment seeks to provide investment results that closely correspond, before fees and expenses, to the performance of the MSCI USA Small Cap Select Value Momentum Blend Index. Under normal circumstances, the fund seeks to achieve its investment objective by investing at least 80% of its net assets in securities in the index. The index is designed to deliver exposure to equity securities of small-capitalization U.S. issuers that have higher exposure to value and momentum factors within the MSCI USA Small Cap Index while also maintaining moderate Index turnover and lower realized volatility than traditional capitalization weighted indexes. **Top Holdings:** Hawaiian Electric Industries Inc   Portland General Electric Co   Apollo Commercial Real Estate Finance Inc   Arbor Realty Trust Inc   ALLETE Inc

NuShares ESG Small-Cap ETF

D+   SELL

Ticker	Traded On	NAV	Total Assets ($)	Dividend Yield (TTM)	Turnover Ratio	Expense Ratio
NUSC	BATS	24.80	$84,029,852	0.64	36	0.4

Ratings
Reward	D+
Risk	C-
Recent Upgrade/Downgrade	Down

Fund Information
Fund Type	Exchange Traded Funds
Category	US Equity Small Cap
Sub-Category	Small Blend
Prospectus Objective	Small Company
Inception Date	Dec-16
Open to New Investments	Y

Prices
Price (as of 12/31/2018)	24.74
52-Week High	32.42
52-Week Low	24.25

Total Returns (%)
3-Month	6-Month	1-Year	3-Year	5-Year
-18.34	-16.66	-10.23		

3-Year Standard Deviation
Effective Duration

Valuation
Premium/Discount (1-Year Average)	0.10

Company Information
Provider	Nuveen
Manager/Tenure	Philip James(Jim) Campagna (1), Lei Liao (1)
Website	http://www.nuveen.com
Address	Nuveen Investment Trust John Nuveen & Co. Inc. Chicago IL 60606 United States
Phone Number	312-917-8146

PERFORMANCE

Ratings History
Date	Overall Rating	Risk Rating	Reward Rating
Q4-18	D+	C-	D+
Q2-18	C-	C-	C-
Q4-17	D	B+	D+
Q4-16			
Q4-15			

Asset & Performance History
Date	NAV	1-Year Total Return
2017	28.43	15.87
2016	24.61	
2015		
2014		
2013		
2012		

Total Assets: $84,029,852

Asset Allocation
Asset	%
Cash	0%
Stocks	100%
US Stocks	99%
Bonds	0%
US Bonds	0%
Other	0%

Services Offered:

Investment Strategy: The investment seeks to track the investment results, before fees and expenses, of the TIAA ESG USA Small-Cap Index (the "index"). Under normal market conditions, the fund invests at least 80% of the sum of its net assets and the amount of any borrowings for investment purposes in component securities of the index. The index is comprised of equity securities issued by small-capitalization companies listed on U.S. exchanges that meet certain environmental, social, and governance ("ESG") criteria. **Top Holdings:** Booz Allen Hamilton Holding Corp Pool Corp First American Financial Corp WEX Inc Starwood Property Trust Inc

Direxion Daily CSI 300 China A Share Bull 2X Shares

D   SELL

Ticker	Traded On	NAV	Total Assets ($)	Dividend Yield (TTM)	Turnover Ratio	Expense Ratio
CHAU	NYSE Arca	14.41	$83,838,096	0.38	1,747	1.04

Ratings
Reward	D-
Risk	D
Recent Upgrade/Downgrade	Down

Fund Information
Fund Type	Exchange Traded Funds
Category	Trading Tools
Sub-Category	Trading--Leveraged Equity
Prospectus Objective	Growth
Inception Date	Apr-15
Open to New Investments	Y

Prices
Price (as of 12/31/2018)	14.44
52-Week High	37.42
52-Week Low	14.17

Total Returns (%)
3-Month	6-Month	1-Year	3-Year	5-Year
-24.83	-25.98	-51.17	-37.29	

3-Year Standard Deviation   41.16
Effective Duration

Valuation
Premium/Discount (1-Year Average)	0.04

Company Information
Provider	Direxion Funds
Manager/Tenure	Paul Brigandi (3), Tony Ng (3)
Website	http://www.direxionfunds.com
Address	Direxion Funds 1301 Avenue Of The Americas (6th Avenue) New York NY 10019 United States
Phone Number	646-572-3390

PERFORMANCE

Ratings History
Date	Overall Rating	Risk Rating	Reward Rating
Q4-18	D	D	D-
Q2-18	C-	D+	C
Q4-17	C	D+	B-
Q4-16	D	D	D
Q4-15	U		

Asset & Performance History
Date	NAV	1-Year Total Return
2017	29.73	75.29
2016	16.96	-26.73
2015	23.15	
2014		
2013		
2012		

Total Assets: $83,838,096

Asset Allocation
Asset	%
Cash	93%
Stocks	7%
US Stocks	-15%
Bonds	0%
US Bonds	0%
Other	0%

Services Offered:

Investment Strategy: The investment seeks daily investment results, before fees and expenses, of 200% of the daily performance of the CSI 300 Index. The fund invests at least 80% of its net assets (plus borrowing for investment purposes) in securities of the index, ETFs that track the index and other financial instruments that provide daily leveraged exposure to the index or ETFs that track the index. The index is a modified free-float market capitalization weighted index comprised of the largest and most liquid stocks in the Chinese A-share market. The fund is non-diversified. **Top Holdings:** Xtrackers Harvest CSI 300 China A ETF Deutsche X-Trck Harv Swp Deutsche X-Trck Harv Swp Deutsche X-Trck Harv Swp Deutsche X-Trck Harv Swp

Aptus Fortified Value ETF   D+   SELL

Ticker	Traded On	NAV	Total Assets ($)	Dividend Yield (TTM)	Turnover Ratio	Expense Ratio
FTVA	BATS	23.73	$83,557,397	0.12		0.79

Ratings
Reward   C-
Risk   D
Recent Upgrade/Downgrade

Fund Information
Fund Type   Exchange Traded Funds
Category   Long/Short Equity
Sub-Category   Options-based
Prospectus Objective   Growth & Inc
Inception Date   Oct-17
Open to New Investments   Y

Prices
Price (as of 12/31/2018)   23.66
52-Week High   29.57
52-Week Low   23.23

Total Returns (%)

3-Month	6-Month	1-Year	3-Year	5-Year
-17.53	-14.33	-12.13		

3-Year Standard Deviation
Effective Duration

Valuation
Premium/Discount (1-Year Average)   0.14

Company Information
Provider   Aptus Capital Advisors
Manager/Tenure   John D. Gardner (1), Beckham D. Wyrick (1)
Website
Address   407 Johnson Avenue, Fairhope, Alabama 36532 United States
Phone Number

PERFORMANCE

Ratings History

Date	Overall Rating	Risk Rating	Reward Rating
Q4-18	D+	D	C-
Q2-18	U		
Q4-17	U		
Q4-16			
Q4-15			

Asset & Performance History

Date	NAV	1-Year Total Return
2017	27.1	
2016		
2015		
2014		
2013		
2012		

Total Assets: $83,557,397

Asset Allocation

Asset	%
Cash	0%
Stocks	100%
US Stocks	99%
Bonds	0%
US Bonds	0%
Other	0%

Services Offered:

Investment Strategy: The investment seeks to track the performance, before fees and expenses, of the Aptus Fortified Value Index (the "index"). Under normal circumstances, at least 80% of the fund's total assets (exclusive of any collateral held from securities lending) will be invested in the component securities of the index. The index is a rules-based, equal-weighted index that is designed to gain exposure to 50 of the most undervalued U.S.-listed common stocks and real estate investment trusts ("REITs"), while hedging against significant U.S. equity market declines when the market is overvalued. The fund is non-diversified. **Top Holdings:** Gentex Corp   CVS Health Corp   NVR Inc   Lam Research Corp   Applied Materials Inc

---

ProShares UltraPro Short 20+ Year Treasury   C-   HOLD

Ticker	Traded On	NAV	Total Assets ($)	Dividend Yield (TTM)	Turnover Ratio	Expense Ratio
TTT	NYSE Arca	25.83	$83,040,566	0.15		0.95

Ratings
Reward   D+
Risk   D+
Recent Upgrade/Downgrade   Up

Fund Information
Fund Type   Exchange Traded Funds
Category   Trading Tools
Sub-Category   Trading--Inverse Debt
Prospectus Objective   Govt Bond - Treasury
Inception Date   Mar-12
Open to New Investments   Y

Prices
Price (as of 12/31/2018)   25.73
52-Week High   32.97
52-Week Low   24.30

Total Returns (%)

3-Month	6-Month	1-Year	3-Year	5-Year
-12.91	-2.74	6.46	-31.01	-72.75

3-Year Standard Deviation   29.2
Effective Duration

Valuation
Premium/Discount (1-Year Average)   0.28

Company Information
Provider   ProShares
Manager/Tenure   Michelle Liu (6), Jeffrey Ploshnick (2)
Website   http://www.proshares.com
Address   ProShares 7501 Wisconsin Avenue, Suite 1000 Bethesda MD 20814 United States
Phone Number   866-776-5125

PERFORMANCE

Ratings History

Date	Overall Rating	Risk Rating	Reward Rating
Q4-18	C-	D+	D+
Q2-18	D+	D	D
Q4-17	D	D	D
Q4-16	D	D-	D
Q4-15	D	D	D-

Asset & Performance History

Date	NAV	1-Year Total Return
2017	24.3	-25.23
2016	32.5	-13.33
2015	37.5	-11.01
2014	42.14	-55.61
2013	94.94	39.45
2012	68.08	

Total Assets: $83,040,566

Asset Allocation

Asset	%
Cash	401%
Stocks	0%
US Stocks	0%
Bonds	-2%
US Bonds	-2%
Other	-299%

Services Offered:

Investment Strategy: The investment seeks daily investment results, before fees and expenses, that correspond to three times the inverse (-3x) of the daily performance of the ICE U.S. Treasury 20+ Year Bond Index. The fund invests in financial instruments that ProShare Advisors believes, in combination, should produce daily returns consistent with the fund's investment objective. The index includes publicly- issued U.S. Treasury securities that have a remaining maturity greater than twenty years and have $300 million or more of outstanding face value, excluding amounts held by the Federal Reserve. The fund is non-diversified. **Top Holdings:** Ice 20+ Year U.S. Treasury Index Swap Societe Generale   Ice 20+ Year U.S. Treasury Index Swap Citibank Na   Ice 20+ Year U.S. Treasury Index Swap Goldman Sachs International   Ice 20+ Year U.S. Treasury Index Swap Bank Of America Na   Ice 20+ Year U.S. Treasury Index Swap Morgan Stanley & Co. International Pl

Global X Internet of Things ETF   C   HOLD

Ticker	Traded On	NAV	Total Assets ($)	Dividend Yield (TTM)	Turnover Ratio	Expense Ratio
SNSR	NAS CM	16.19	$82,983,333	0.6	25	0.68

Ratings
Reward   C
Risk   C-
Recent Upgrade/Downgrade

Fund Information
Fund Type   Exchange Traded Funds
Category   Technology Sector Equity
Sub-Category   Technology
Prospectus Objective   Technology
Inception Date   Sep-16
Open to New Investments   Y

Prices
Price (as of 12/31/2018)   16.14
52-Week High   21.29
52-Week Low   15.40

Total Returns (%)

3-Month	6-Month	1-Year	3-Year	5-Year
-18.80	-15.49	-16.44		

3-Year Standard Deviation
Effective Duration

Valuation
Premium/Discount (1-Year Average)   0.09

Company Information
Provider   Global X Funds
Manager/Tenure   Chang Kim (2), James Ong (2), Nam To (0)
Website   http://www.globalxfunds.com
Address   Global X Funds 600 Lexington Avenue, 20th Floor New York NY 10022 United States
Phone Number   888-493-8631

PERFORMANCE

Ratings History

Date	Overall Rating	Risk Rating	Reward Rating
Q4-18	C	C-	C
Q2-18	C	C-	C
Q4-17	D	B	C
Q4-16	U		
Q4-15			

Asset & Performance History

Date	NAV	1-Year Total Return
2017	19.62	26.7
2016	15.57	
2015		
2014		
2013		
2012		

Total Assets: $82,983,333
Asset Allocation

Asset	%
Cash	0%
Stocks	100%
US Stocks	74%
Bonds	0%
US Bonds	0%
Other	0%

Services Offered:

Investment Strategy: The investment seeks to provide investment results that correspond generally to the price and yield performance, before fees and expenses, of the Indxx Global Internet of Things Thematic Index. The fund invests at least 80% of its total assets in the securities of the underlying index. The underlying index is designed to provide exposure to exchange-listed companies in developed markets that facilitate the Internet of Things industry, including companies involved in wearable technology, home automation, connected automotive technology, sensors, networking infrastructure/software, smart metering and energy control devices. The fund is non-diversified. **Top Holdings:** DexCom Inc Garmin Ltd Sensata Technologies Holding PLC Skyworks Solutions Inc ADT Inc

Invesco S&P SmallCap Consumer Discretionary ETF   C-   HOLD

Ticker	Traded On	NAV	Total Assets ($)	Dividend Yield (TTM)	Turnover Ratio	Expense Ratio
PSCD	NAS CM	55.02	$82,781,875	1.11		0.29

Ratings
Reward   C
Risk   D+
Recent Upgrade/Downgrade   Down

Fund Information
Fund Type   Exchange Traded Funds
Category   Consumer Goods & Svcs
Sub-Category   Consumer Cyclical
Prospectus Objective   Unaligned
Inception Date   Apr-10
Open to New Investments

Prices
Price (as of 12/31/2018)   54.78
52-Week High   71.63
52-Week Low   51.80

Total Returns (%)

3-Month	6-Month	1-Year	3-Year	5-Year
-18.27	-15.96	-8.21	24.29	18.42

3-Year Standard Deviation   15.64
Effective Duration

Valuation
Premium/Discount (1-Year Average)   0.28

Company Information
Provider   Invesco
Manager/Tenure   Peter Hubbard (8), Michael Jeanette (8), Tony Seisser (4), 1 other
Website   http://www.invesco.com/us
Address   Invesco 11 Greenway Plaza, Ste. 2500 Houston TX 77046 United States
Phone Number   800-659-1005

PERFORMANCE

Ratings History

Date	Overall Rating	Risk Rating	Reward Rating
Q4-18	C-	D+	C
Q2-18	C	D+	C+
Q4-17	B	B-	B
Q4-16	C	D+	C
Q4-15	C	C-	C+

Asset & Performance History

Date	NAV	1-Year Total Return
2017	60.71	17.06
2016	52.41	15.68
2015	45.8	-8.96
2014	50.81	4.65
2013	48.9	48.2
2012	33.16	23.88

Total Assets: $82,781,875
Asset Allocation

Asset	%
Cash	0%
Stocks	100%
US Stocks	99%
Bonds	0%
US Bonds	0%
Other	0%

Services Offered:

Investment Strategy: The investment seeks to track the investment results (before fees and expenses) of the S&P SmallCap 600® Capped Consumer Discretionary Index (the "underlying index"). The fund generally will invest at least 90% of its total assets in common stocks of small capitalization U.S. consumer discretionary companies that comprise the underlying index. These companies are principally engaged in the businesses of providing consumer goods and services that are cyclical in nature, including, but not limited to, household durables, leisure products and services, apparel and luxury goods, computers and electronics, automobiles, etc. **Top Holdings:** Wolverine World Wide Inc Strategic Education Inc Stamps.com Inc Monro Inc iRobot Corp

UBS ETRACS Linked to the Wells Fargo Business Development Company Index ETN   C-   HOLD

Ticker	Traded On	NAV	Total Assets ($)	Dividend Yield (TTM)	Turnover Ratio	Expense Ratio
BDCS	NYSE Arca	17.69	$82,631,674	8.81		0.85

Ratings

Reward	C-
Risk	C-
Recent Upgrade/Downgrade	Down

Fund Information

Fund Type	Exchange Traded Funds
Category	Financials Sector Equity
Sub-Category	Financial
Prospectus Objective	Growth
Inception Date	Apr-11
Open to New Investments	Y

Prices

Price (as of 12/31/2018)	17.69
52-Week High	21.03
52-Week Low	17.15

Total Returns (%)

3-Month	6-Month	1-Year	3-Year	5-Year
-12.55	-9.17	-6.95	13.38	-0.93

3-Year Standard Deviation	12.49
Effective Duration	

Valuation

Premium/Discount (1-Year Average)	0.18

Company Information

Provider	UBS Group AG
Manager/Tenure	No Manager (7)
Website	http://www.ubs.com
Address	Bahnhofstrasse 45 Zurich 8098 Switzerland
Phone Number	412-037-1952

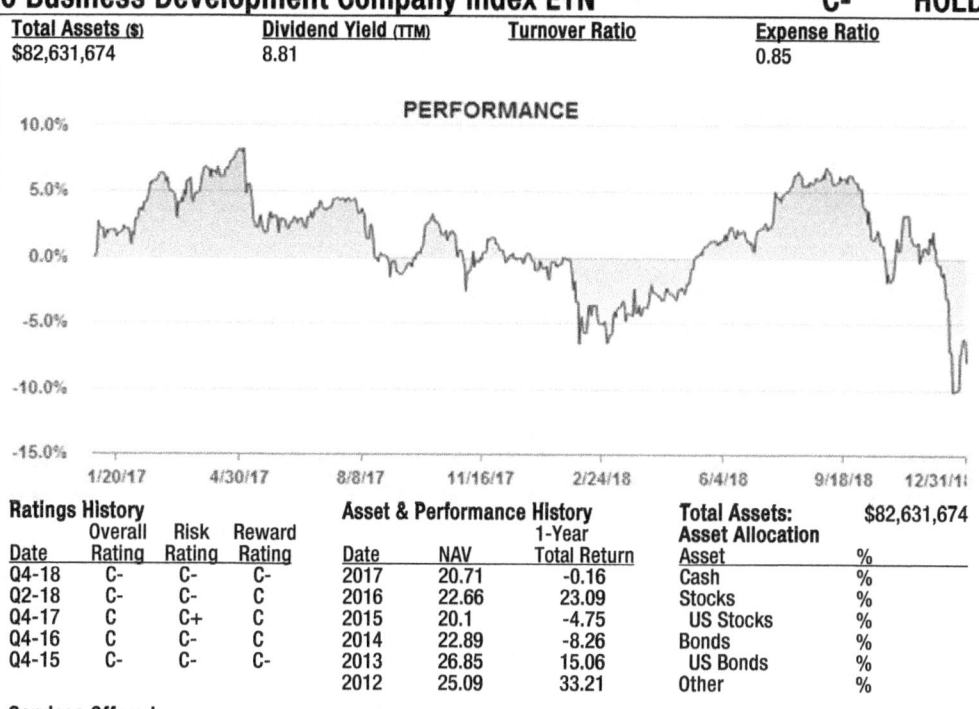

PERFORMANCE

Ratings History

Date	Overall Rating	Risk Rating	Reward Rating
Q4-18	C-	C-	C-
Q2-18	C-	C-	C
Q4-17	C	C+	C
Q4-16	C	C-	C
Q4-15	C-	C-	C-

Asset & Performance History

Date	NAV	1-Year Total Return
2017	20.71	-0.16
2016	22.66	23.09
2015	20.1	-4.75
2014	22.89	-8.26
2013	26.85	15.06
2012	25.09	33.21

Total Assets: $82,631,674
Asset Allocation

Asset	%
Cash	%
Stocks	%
US Stocks	%
Bonds	%
US Bonds	%
Other	%

Services Offered:

Investment Strategy: The investment seeks to replicate, net of expenses, the performance of the Wells Fargo Business Development Company Index.
The index is a float adjusted, capitalization-weighted index that is intended to measure the performance of all Business Development Companies ("BDC") that are listed on the New York Stock Exchange or NASDAQ and satisfy specified market capitalization and other eligibility requirements. The BDC business model is to lend to small and midsized companies at high yield equivalent rates while also at times taking equity stakes in such companies. **Top Holdings:**

SPDR® DoubleLine Short Duration Total Return Tactical ETF   C-   HOLD

Ticker	Traded On	NAV	Total Assets ($)	Dividend Yield (TTM)	Turnover Ratio	Expense Ratio
STOT	BATS	48.61	$82,536,700	2.28	123	0.45

Ratings

Reward	C-
Risk	D+
Recent Upgrade/Downgrade	

Fund Information

Fund Type	Exchange Traded Funds
Category	US Fixed Income
Sub-Category	Short-Term Bond
Prospectus Objective	Income
Inception Date	Apr-16
Open to New Investments	Y

Prices

Price (as of 12/31/2018)	48.64
52-Week High	49.40
52-Week Low	48.39

Total Returns (%)

3-Month	6-Month	1-Year	3-Year	5-Year
0.75	1.13	1.16		

3-Year Standard Deviation	
Effective Duration	2.06

Valuation

Premium/Discount (1-Year Average)	0.18

Company Information

Provider	SPDR State Street Global Advisors
Manager/Tenure	Philip A. Barach (2), Jeffrey E. Gundlach (2), Jeffrey J. Sherman (2)
Website	http://www.spdrs.com
Address	SPDR State Street Global Advisors State Street Financial Center, 1 Lincoln Street Boston MA 02111-2900 United States
Phone Number	617-786-3000

PERFORMANCE

Ratings History

Date	Overall Rating	Risk Rating	Reward Rating
Q4-18	C-	D+	C-
Q2-18	D+	C-	D+
Q4-17	D+	B-	D+
Q4-16	U		
Q4-15			

Asset & Performance History

Date	NAV	1-Year Total Return
2017	49.27	1.62
2016	49.43	
2015		
2014		
2013		
2012		

Total Assets: $82,536,700
Asset Allocation

Asset	%
Cash	5%
Stocks	0%
US Stocks	0%
Bonds	94%
US Bonds	83%
Other	0%

Services Offered:

Investment Strategy: The investment seeks to maximize current income with a dollar-weighted average effective duration between one and three years. Under normal circumstances, the fund will invest at least 80% of its net assets in a diversified portfolio of fixed income securities of any credit quality. Fixed income securities in which the fund principally invests are defined as securities issued or guaranteed by the U.S. government or its agencies, instrumentalities or sponsored corporations; TIPS; municipal bonds (the fund may invest up to 20% of its portfolio in municipal bonds); asset-backed securities; etc. **Top Holdings:** United States Treasury Notes 2.75% United States Treasury Notes 2.12% United States Treasury Notes 2% United States Treasury Notes 1.5% Federal National Mortgage Association 2%

First Trust Strategic Income ETF

C-   HOLD

Ticker	Traded On	NAV	Total Assets ($)	Dividend Yield (TTM)	Turnover Ratio	Expense Ratio
FDIV	NAS CM	46.35	$82,295,126	5.35	119	0.88

Ratings
Reward	C-
Risk	C-
Recent Upgrade/Downgrade	Down

Fund Information
Fund Type	Exchange Traded Funds
Category	Cautious Allocation
Sub-Category	Allocation--30% to 50% Equity
Prospectus Objective	Income
Inception Date	Aug-14
Open to New Investments	Y

Prices
Price (as of 12/31/2018)	46.26
52-Week High	52.01
52-Week Low	45.32

Total Returns (%)
3-Month	6-Month	1-Year	3-Year	5-Year
-4.50	-2.10	-4.05	14.12	

3-Year Standard Deviation	4.66
Effective Duration	3.10

Valuation
Premium/Discount (1-Year Average)	0.03

Company Information
Provider	First Trust
Manager/Tenure	Richard Bernstein (4), Jeremiah Charles (4), Jon C. Erickson (4), 19 others
Website	http://www.ftportfolios.com/
Address	First Trust 120 E. Liberty Drive, Suite 400 Wheaton IL 60187 United States
Phone Number	800-621-1675

PERFORMANCE

Ratings History
Date	Overall Rating	Risk Rating	Reward Rating
Q4-18	C-	C-	C-
Q2-18	C-	C-	C-
Q4-17	B-	B	C+
Q4-16	C-	D+	C
Q4-15	D-	D+	D

Asset & Performance History
Date	NAV	1-Year Total Return
2017	51.13	6.47
2016	49.9	11.71
2015	46.46	-4.38
2014	50.54	
2013		
2012		

Total Assets: $82,295,126

Asset Allocation
Asset	%
Cash	3%
Stocks	46%
US Stocks	40%
Bonds	44%
US Bonds	29%
Other	0%

Services Offered:

Investment Strategy: The investment seeks risk-adjusted income; capital appreciation is the secondary objective. The fund is a multi-manager, multi-strategy actively managed ETF. Its investment categories will be: (i) high yield corporate bonds, and first lien senior secured floating rate bank loans; (ii) mortgage-related investments; (iii) preferred securities; (iv) international sovereign bonds, including emerging markets debt; (v) equity securities of Energy Infrastructure Companies, certain of which are referred to as master limited partnerships; and (vi) dividend paying U.S. exchange-traded equity securities of companies and depositary receipts. It is non-diversified. **Top Holdings:** First Trust Senior Loan ETF   First Trust Preferred Sec & Inc ETF   iShares MBS ETF   First Trust Emerging Mkts Lcl Ccy Bd ETF   First Trust Instl Pref Secs and Inc ETF

Global X MSCI Colombia ETF

D+   SELL

Ticker	Traded On	NAV	Total Assets ($)	Dividend Yield (TTM)	Turnover Ratio	Expense Ratio
GXG	NYSE Arca	7.87	$82,182,183	2.14	41	0.61

Ratings
Reward	D+
Risk	D
Recent Upgrade/Downgrade	Down

Fund Information
Fund Type	Exchange Traded Funds
Category	Equity Misc
Sub-Category	Miscellaneous Region
Prospectus Objective	Foreign Stock
Inception Date	Feb-09
Open to New Investments	Y

Prices
Price (as of 12/31/2018)	7.79
52-Week High	11.47
52-Week Low	7.75

Total Returns (%)
3-Month	6-Month	1-Year	3-Year	5-Year
-19.10	-22.87	-19.26	12.15	-51.55

3-Year Standard Deviation	20.64
Effective Duration	

Valuation
Premium/Discount (1-Year Average)	0.06

Company Information
Provider	Global X Funds
Manager/Tenure	Chang Kim (4), James Ong (2), Nam To (0)
Website	http://www.globalxfunds.com
Address	Global X Funds 600 Lexington Avenue, 20th Floor New York NY 10022 United States
Phone Number	888-493-8631

PERFORMANCE

Ratings History
Date	Overall Rating	Risk Rating	Reward Rating
Q4-18	D+	D	D+
Q2-18	C	C	C
Q4-17	D+	D	C-
Q4-16	D	D	D
Q4-15	D-	D	D-

Asset & Performance History
Date	NAV	1-Year Total Return
2017	10.04	12.34
2016	9.1	23.64
2015	7.47	-41.26
2014	12.92	-26.45
2013	18.13	-14.41
2012	22.06	25.46

Total Assets: $82,182,183

Asset Allocation
Asset	%
Cash	0%
Stocks	99%
US Stocks	0%
Bonds	0%
US Bonds	0%
Other	0%

Services Offered:

Investment Strategy: The investment seeks to provide investment results that correspond generally to the price and yield performance, before fees and expenses, of the MSCI All Colombia Select 25/50 Index. The fund invests at least 80% of its total assets in the securities of the underlying index and in American Depositary Receipts ("ADRs") and Global Depositary Receipts ("GDRs") based on the securities in the underlying index. It also invests at least 80% of its total assets in securities of companies that are economically tied to Colombia. The underlying index is designed to represent the performance of the broad Colombia equity universe. The fund is non-diversified. **Top Holdings:** Ecopetrol SA ADR   BanColombia SA ADR   Grupo de Inversiones Suramericana SA   BanColombia SA   Grupo Nutresa SA

ClearBridge All Cap Growth ETF

C-   HOLD

Ticker	Traded On	NAV	Total Assets ($)	Dividend Yield (TTM)	Turnover Ratio	Expense Ratio
CACG	NAS CM	26.82	$81,392,360	0.23	15	0.53

Ratings
Reward   C-
Risk   C-
Recent Upgrade/Downgrade   Down

Fund Information
Fund Type   Exchange Traded Funds
Category   US Equity Large Cap Growth
Sub-Category   Large Growth
Prospectus Objective   Growth
Inception Date   May-17
Open to New Investments   Y

Prices
Price (as of 12/31/2018)   26.73
52-Week High   31.81
52-Week Low   25.40

Total Returns (%)

3-Month	6-Month	1-Year	3-Year	5-Year
-14.17	-9.71	-2.92		

3-Year Standard Deviation
Effective Duration

Valuation
Premium/Discount (1-Year Average)   0.17

Company Information
Provider   Legg Mason
Manager/Tenure   Evan Bauman (1), Peter Bourbeau (1),
                          Richard A. Freeman (1), 1 other
Website   http://www.leggmason.com
Address   Legg Mason/Western 100
                          International Drive Baltimore MD
                          21202 United States
Phone Number   877-721-1926

PERFORMANCE

Ratings History

Date	Overall Rating	Risk Rating	Reward Rating
Q4-18	C-	C-	C-
Q2-18	C-	C-	C-
Q4-17	U		
Q4-16			
Q4-15			

Asset & Performance History

Date	NAV	1-Year Total Return
2017	27.79	
2016		
2015		
2014		
2013		
2012		

Total Assets: $81,392,360

Asset Allocation

Asset	%
Cash	2%
Stocks	98%
US Stocks	93%
Bonds	0%
US Bonds	0%
Other	0%

Services Offered:

Investment Strategy: The investment seeks to achieve long-term capital appreciation. The fund seeks to invest in a diversified portfolio of large, medium and small capitalization stocks that have the potential for above-average long-term earnings and/or cash flow growth. The fund's subadviser uses a bottom-up investment process that seeks to find inefficiently priced companies with strong fundamentals, incentive-driven management teams, dominant positions in niche markets and/or goods and services that are in high customer demand. **Top Holdings:** UnitedHealth Group Inc Amazon.com Inc Comcast Corp Class A Biogen Inc Microsoft Corp

---

Invesco DWA Basic Materials Momentum ETF

C   HOLD

Ticker	Traded On	NAV	Total Assets ($)	Dividend Yield (TTM)	Turnover Ratio	Expense Ratio
PYZ	NAS CM	53.48	$81,365,167	0.99	75	0.6

Ratings
Reward   C
Risk   D+
Recent Upgrade/Downgrade   Down

Fund Information
Fund Type   Exchange Traded Funds
Category   Natural Resources
Sub-Category   Natural Resources
Prospectus Objective   Unaligned
Inception Date   Oct-06
Open to New Investments   Y

Prices
Price (as of 12/31/2018)   52.93
52-Week High   75.00
52-Week Low   50.28

Total Returns (%)

3-Month	6-Month	1-Year	3-Year	5-Year
-22.04	-20.50	-23.31	12.96	10.18

3-Year Standard Deviation   18.18
Effective Duration

Valuation
Premium/Discount (1-Year Average)   0.16

Company Information
Provider   Invesco
Manager/Tenure   Peter Hubbard (11), Michael Jeanette
                          (10), Tony Seisser (4), 1 other
Website   http://www.invesco.com/us
Address   Invesco 11 Greenway Plaza, Ste. 2500
                          Houston TX 77046 United States
Phone Number   800-659-1005

PERFORMANCE

Ratings History

Date	Overall Rating	Risk Rating	Reward Rating
Q4-18	C	D+	C
Q2-18	B-	C	B
Q4-17	B	C	A-
Q4-16	C+	C	B
Q4-15	B	B-	B

Asset & Performance History

Date	NAV	1-Year Total Return
2017	70.46	19.43
2016	59.33	23.33
2015	48.64	-6.1
2014	52.45	3.88
2013	50.99	27.71
2012	40.35	28.54

Total Assets: $81,365,167

Asset Allocation

Asset	%
Cash	0%
Stocks	100%
US Stocks	100%
Bonds	0%
US Bonds	0%
Other	0%

Services Offered:

Investment Strategy: The investment seeks to track the investment results (before fees and expenses) of the Dorsey Wright® Basic Materials Technical Leaders Index (the "underlying index"). The fund generally will invest at least 90% of its total assets in the securities that comprise the underlying index. The underlying index is composed of at least 30 securities of companies in the basic materials sector that have powerful relative strength or "momentum" characteristics. **Top Holdings:** FMC Corp LyondellBasell Industries NV Avery Dennison Corp RPM International Inc Air Products & Chemicals Inc

VanEck Vectors Morningstar International Moat ETF   C-   HOLD

Ticker	Traded On	NAV	Total Assets ($)	Dividend Yield (TTM)	Turnover Ratio	Expense Ratio
MOTI	NYSE Arca	28.48	$81,265,005	3.08	112	0.56

Ratings

Reward	C-
Risk	C-
Recent Upgrade/Downgrade	

Fund Information

Fund Type	Exchange Traded Funds
Category	Global Equity Large Cap
Sub-Category	Foreign Large Blend
Prospectus Objective	Foreign Stock
Inception Date	Jul-15
Open to New Investments	Y

Prices

Price (as of 12/31/2018)	28.32
52-Week High	36.79
52-Week Low	27.71

Total Returns (%)

3-Month	6-Month	1-Year	3-Year	5-Year
-10.58	-8.53	-13.17	18.40	

3-Year Standard Deviation	12.23
Effective Duration	

Valuation

Premium/Discount (1-Year Average)	0.02

Company Information

Provider	VanEck
Manager/Tenure	Hao-Hung (Peter) Liao (3), Guo Hua (Jason) Jin (0)
Website	http://www.vaneck.com
Address	Van Eck Associates Corporation 666 Third Avenue New York NY 10017 United States
Phone Number	800-826-1115

PERFORMANCE

Ratings History

Date	Overall Rating	Risk Rating	Reward Rating
Q4-18	C-	C-	C-
Q2-18	C-	C-	C
Q4-17	C	B	C
Q4-16	D	C-	D+
Q4-15	U		

Asset & Performance History

Date	NAV	1-Year Total Return
2017	34.1	26.03
2016	27.85	5.11
2015	26.85	
2014		
2013		
2012		

Total Assets: $81,265,005

Asset Allocation

Asset	%
Cash	0%
Stocks	100%
US Stocks	4%
Bonds	0%
US Bonds	0%
Other	0%

Services Offered:

Investment Strategy: The investment seeks to replicate as closely as possible, before fees and expenses, the price and yield performance of the Morningstar® Global ex-US Moat Focus IndexSM. The fund normally invests at least 80% of its total assets in securities that comprise the fund's benchmark index. The index is comprised of securities issued by companies that Morningstar, Inc. ("Morningstar") determines have sustainable competitive advantages based on a proprietary methodology that considers quantitative and qualitative factors ("wide and narrow moat companies"). It is non-diversified. **Top Holdings:** Cameco Corp CapitaLand Mall Trust Orange SA Millicom International Cellular SA DR ANTA Sports Products Ltd

Cambria Core Equity ETF   C-   HOLD

Ticker	Traded On	NAV	Total Assets ($)	Dividend Yield (TTM)	Turnover Ratio	Expense Ratio
CCOR	NYSE Arca	26.63	$80,693,193	1.98	8	1.21

Ratings

Reward	C-
Risk	C-
Recent Upgrade/Downgrade	

Fund Information

Fund Type	Exchange Traded Funds
Category	Long/Short Equity
Sub-Category	Options-based
Prospectus Objective	Growth & Inc
Inception Date	May-17
Open to New Investments	Y

Prices

Price (as of 12/31/2018)	26.58
52-Week High	26.61
52-Week Low	24.37

Total Returns (%)

3-Month	6-Month	1-Year	3-Year	5-Year
5.34	10.20	4.86		

3-Year Standard Deviation	
Effective Duration	

Valuation

Premium/Discount (1-Year Average)	-0.08

Company Information

Provider	CAMBRIA ETF TRUST
Manager/Tenure	Mebane T. Faber (1), David C. Pursell (1)
Website	http://www.cambriafunds.com
Address	CAMBRIA ETF TRUST 2711 Centreville Road Suite 400 Wilmington, DE 19808 Wilmington DE 19808 United States
Phone Number	310-683-5500

PERFORMANCE

Ratings History

Date	Overall Rating	Risk Rating	Reward Rating
Q4-18	C-	C-	C-
Q2-18	C-	C	C-
Q4-17	U		
Q4-16			
Q4-15			

Asset & Performance History

Date	NAV	1-Year Total Return
2017	25.81	
2016		
2015		
2014		
2013		
2012		

Total Assets: $80,693,193

Asset Allocation

Asset	%
Cash	3%
Stocks	97%
US Stocks	95%
Bonds	0%
US Bonds	0%
Other	0%

Services Offered:

Investment Strategy: The investment seeks capital appreciation and capital preservation with a low correlation to the broader U.S. equity market. Under normal market conditions, at least 80% of the value of the fund's net assets (plus borrowings for investment purposes) will be invested in equity securities. It invests primarily in U.S. equity securities that tend to offer current dividends. The fund focuses on high-quality companies that have prospects for long-term total returns as a result of their ability to grow earnings and their willingness to increase dividends over time. **Top Holdings:** Spx Us 03/15/19 P2700 Starbucks Corp McDonald's Corp Merck & Co Inc Procter & Gamble Co

United States Brent Oil Fund, LP   C-   HOLD

Ticker	Traded On	NAV	Total Assets ($)	Dividend Yield (TTM)	Turnover Ratio	Expense Ratio
BNO	NYSE Arca	15.18	$80,566,509	0		0.9

Ratings

Reward	C-
Risk	C-
Recent Upgrade/Downgrade	Down

Fund Information

Fund Type	Exchange Traded Funds
Category	Commodities Specified
Sub-Category	Commodities Energy
Prospectus Objective	Natl Res
Inception Date	Jun-10
Open to New Investments	Y

Prices

Price (as of 12/31/2018)	15.33
52-Week High	24.21
52-Week Low	14.70

Total Returns (%)

3-Month	6-Month	1-Year	3-Year	5-Year
-36.51	-29.95	-16.51	24.21	-65.35

3-Year Standard Deviation	27.98
Effective Duration	

Valuation

Premium/Discount (1-Year Average)	-0.12

Company Information

Provider	USCF Investments
Manager/Tenure	Management Team (8)
Website	http://www.uscfinvestments.com
Address	USCF 1290 Broadway, Suite 1100 Denver CO 80203 United States
Phone Number	

PERFORMANCE

Ratings History

Date	Overall Rating	Risk Rating	Reward Rating
Q4-18	C-	C-	C-
Q2-18	C	D+	C
Q4-17	C-	D+	C
Q4-16	D-	D	D-
Q4-15	D-	D-	D-

Asset & Performance History

Date	NAV	1-Year Total Return
2017	18.18	15.82
2016	15.7	28.45
2015	12.22	-45.42
2014	22.39	-48.89
2013	43.81	6.92
2012	40.98	9.94

Total Assets: $80,566,509

Asset Allocation

Asset	%
Cash	34%
Stocks	0%
US Stocks	0%
Bonds	18%
US Bonds	18%
Other	48%

Services Offered:

Investment Strategy: The investment seeks the daily changes in percentage terms of its shares' per share net asset value ("NAV") to reflect the daily changes in percentage terms of the spot price of Brent crude oil. The Benchmark Futures Contract is the futures contract on Brent crude oil as traded on the Ice Futures Europe Exchange that is the near month contract to expire, except when the near month contract is within two weeks of expiration, in which case it will be measured by the futures contract that is the next month contract to expire. **Top Holdings:** Future Contract On Brent Crude Futr Feb19 United States Treasury Bills United States Treasury Bills United States Treasury Bills United States Treasury Bills

---

PIMCO Short Term Municipal Bond Active Exchange-Traded Fund   C-   HOLD

Ticker	Traded On	NAV	Total Assets ($)	Dividend Yield (TTM)	Turnover Ratio	Expense Ratio
SMMU	NYSE Arca	49.80	$80,089,954	1.64	87	0.35

Ratings

Reward	C-
Risk	D+
Recent Upgrade/Downgrade	

Fund Information

Fund Type	Exchange Traded Funds
Category	US Muni Fixed Inc
Sub-Category	Muni National Short
Prospectus Objective	Muni Bond - Natl
Inception Date	Feb-10
Open to New Investments	Y

Prices

Price (as of 12/31/2018)	49.83
52-Week High	50.19
52-Week Low	49.50

Total Returns (%)

3-Month	6-Month	1-Year	3-Year	5-Year
0.79	0.84	1.37	3.12	4.90

3-Year Standard Deviation	1.13
Effective Duration	1.90

Valuation

Premium/Discount (1-Year Average)	-0.08

Company Information

Provider	PIMCO
Manager/Tenure	Julie P. Callahan (4), David Hammer (3)
Website	http://www.pimco.com
Address	PIMCO 840 Newport Center Drive, Suite 100 Newport Beach CA 92660 United States
Phone Number	866-746-2602

PERFORMANCE

Ratings History

Date	Overall Rating	Risk Rating	Reward Rating
Q4-18	C-	D+	C-
Q2-18	C-	D+	C
Q4-17	C	B-	C
Q4-16	C-	C-	C
Q4-15	C-	D+	C

Asset & Performance History

Date	NAV	1-Year Total Return
2017	49.98	1.98
2016	49.7	-0.23
2015	50.33	0.88
2014	50.33	0.82
2013	50.25	0.31
2012	50.38	0.93

Total Assets: $80,089,954

Asset Allocation

Asset	%
Cash	5%
Stocks	0%
US Stocks	0%
Bonds	95%
US Bonds	95%
Other	0%

Services Offered:

Investment Strategy: The investment seeks attractive tax-exempt income, consistent with preservation of capital. The fund invests at least 80% of its assets in a diversified portfolio of debt securities whose interest is, in the opinion of bond counsel for the issuer at the time of issuance, exempt from federal income tax ("Municipal Bonds"). Municipal Bonds generally are issued by or on behalf of states and local governments and their agencies, authorities and other instrumentalities. It may only invest in U.S. dollar-denominated investment grade debt securities, rated Baa or higher. **Top Holdings:** NEW YORK ST TWY AUTH 5% SOUTHEASTERN PA TRANSN AUTH PA 5% RAILSPLITTER TOB SETTLEMENT AUTH 5.25% CONNECTICUT ST 5% PORT SEATTLE WASH 5%

Invesco Russell 2000 Pure Growth ETF   C-   HOLD

Ticker	Traded On	NAV	Total Assets ($)	Dividend Yield (TTM)	Turnover Ratio	Expense Ratio
PXSG	NYSE Arca	30.93	$78,580,511	0.5	43	0.39

Ratings
Reward	C
Risk	C-
Recent Upgrade/Downgrade	Down

Fund Information
Fund Type	Exchange Traded Funds
Category	US Equity Small Cap
Sub-Category	Small Growth
Prospectus Objective	Growth
Inception Date	Mar-05
Open to New Investments	Y

Prices
Price (as of 12/31/2018)	30.85
52-Week High	40.72
52-Week Low	28.65

Total Returns (%)
3-Month	6-Month	1-Year	3-Year	5-Year
-20.84	-15.92	-2.88	28.45	34.72

3-Year Standard Deviation 16.22
Effective Duration

Valuation
Premium/Discount (1-Year Average) 0.16

Company Information
Provider	Invesco
Manager/Tenure	Peter Hubbard (11), Michael Jeanette (10), Jonathan Nixon (5), 2 others
Website	http://www.invesco.com/us
Address	Invesco 11 Greenway Plaza, Ste. 2500 Houston TX 77046 United States
Phone Number	800-659-1005

PERFORMANCE

Ratings History
Date	Overall Rating	Risk Rating	Reward Rating
Q4-18	C-	C-	C
Q2-18	C+	C-	B-
Q4-17	B	B	B+
Q4-16	C	D+	C+
Q4-15	C	D+	C+

Asset & Performance History
Date	NAV	1-Year Total Return
2017	32.03	23.42
2016	26.03	7.16
2015	24.37	0.32
2014	24.37	4.53
2013	23.62	32.33
2012	18.03	14.55

Total Assets: $78,580,511
Asset Allocation
Asset	%
Cash	0%
Stocks	100%
US Stocks	99%
Bonds	0%
US Bonds	0%
Other	0%

Services Offered:

Investment Strategy: The investment seeks to track the investment results (before fees and expenses) of the Russell 2000® Pure Growth Index (the "underlying index"). The fund generally will invest at least 90% of its total assets in the component securities that comprise the underlying index. The underlying index is composed of a subset of securities from the Russell 2000® Index, which is composed of the smallest 2,000 securities of the Russell 3000® Index, an index designed to measure the performance of the largest 3,000 companies in the U.S. equity market. **Top Holdings:** Pacira Pharmaceuticals Inc Tandem Diabetes Care Inc Shenandoah Telecommunications Co NeoGenomics Inc HealthEquity Inc

---

FlexShares STOXX Global ESG Impact Index Fund   C-   HOLD

Ticker	Traded On	NAV	Total Assets ($)	Dividend Yield (TTM)	Turnover Ratio	Expense Ratio
ESGG	NAS CM	85.05	$78,313,091	1.84		0.42

Ratings
Reward	C
Risk	D+
Recent Upgrade/Downgrade	

Fund Information
Fund Type	Exchange Traded Funds
Category	Global Equity Large Cap
Sub-Category	World Large Stock
Prospectus Objective	Growth & Inc
Inception Date	Jul-16
Open to New Investments	Y

Prices
Price (as of 12/31/2018)	85.32
52-Week High	101.95
52-Week Low	80.43

Total Returns (%)
3-Month	6-Month	1-Year	3-Year	5-Year
-13.93	-8.20	-8.49		

3-Year Standard Deviation
Effective Duration

Valuation
Premium/Discount (1-Year Average) 0.55

Company Information
Provider	Flexshares Trust
Manager/Tenure	Robert Anstine (2), Brendan Sullivan (2)
Website	http://www.flexshares.com
Address	50 South LaSalle Street Chicago, Illinois 60603 Chicago Illinois 60603 United States
Phone Number	855-353-9383

PERFORMANCE

Ratings History
Date	Overall Rating	Risk Rating	Reward Rating
Q4-18	C-	D+	C
Q2-18	C-	D+	C-
Q4-17	D	B	C
Q4-16	U		
Q4-15			

Asset & Performance History
Date	NAV	1-Year Total Return
2017	94.75	23.86
2016	77.92	
2015		
2014		
2013		
2012		

Total Assets: $78,313,091
Asset Allocation
Asset	%
Cash	2%
Stocks	98%
US Stocks	58%
Bonds	0%
US Bonds	0%
Other	0%

Services Offered:

Investment Strategy: The investment seeks investment results that correspond generally to the price and yield performance, before fees and expenses, of the STOXX® Global ESG Impact Index. The fund will invest at least 80% of its total assets (exclusive of collateral held from securities lending) in the securities of the index and in ADRs and GDRs based on the securities in the index. The index is an optimized index designed to provide broad market exposure that is tilted toward global companies that score better with respect to a small set of ESG characteristics and to provide the potential for attractive risk-adjusted performance relative to the STOXX® Global 1800 Index. **Top Holdings:** Microsoft Corp Amazon.com Inc Apple Inc Alphabet Inc Class C Bank of America Corporation

PortfolioPlus S&P 500® ETF   C-   HOLD

Ticker	Traded On	NAV
PPLC	NYSE Arca	32.75

Total Assets ($)	Dividend Yield (TTM)	Turnover Ratio	Expense Ratio
$78,246,876	1.93	92	0.37

Ratings
Reward	C
Risk	D+
Recent Upgrade/Downgrade	Down

Fund Information
Fund Type	Exchange Traded Funds
Category	Trading Tools
Sub-Category	Trading--Leveraged Equity
Prospectus Objective	Growth
Inception Date	Jan-15
Open to New Investments	Y

Prices
Price (as of 12/31/2018)	32.66
52-Week High	40.60
52-Week Low	30.45

Total Returns (%)
3-Month	6-Month	1-Year	3-Year	5-Year
-17.23	-9.62	-6.86	35.50	

3-Year Standard Deviation	11.77
Effective Duration	

Valuation
Premium/Discount (1-Year Average)	-0.24

Company Information
Provider	Direxion Funds
Manager/Tenure	Paul Brigandi (3), Tony Ng (3)
Website	http://www.direxionfunds.com
Address	Direxion Funds 1301 Avenue Of The Americas (6th Avenue) New York NY 10019 United States
Phone Number	646-572-3390

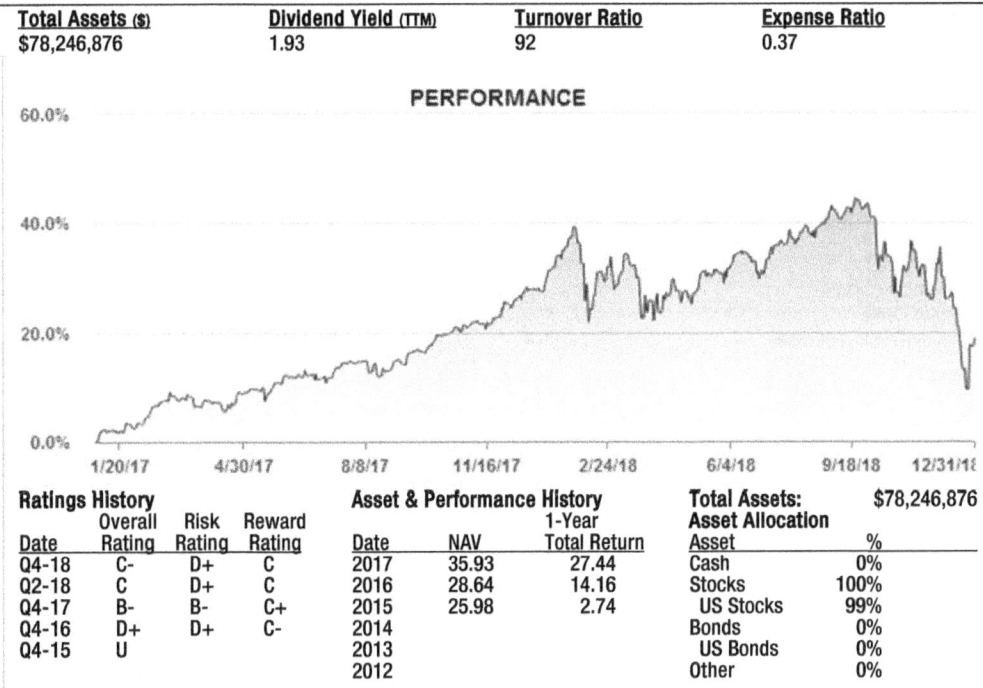

PERFORMANCE

Ratings History
Date	Overall Rating	Risk Rating	Reward Rating
Q4-18	C-	D+	C
Q2-18	C	D+	C
Q4-17	B-	B-	C+
Q4-16	D+	D+	C-
Q4-15	U		

Asset & Performance History
Date	NAV	1-Year Total Return
2017	35.93	27.44
2016	28.64	14.16
2015	25.98	2.74
2014		
2013		
2012		

Total Assets: $78,246,876
Asset Allocation
Asset	%
Cash	0%
Stocks	100%
US Stocks	99%
Bonds	0%
US Bonds	0%
Other	0%

Services Offered:

Investment Strategy: The investment seeks daily investment results, before fees and expenses, of 125% of the daily performance of the S&P 500® Index. The fund, under normal circumstances, invests at least 80% of its net assets (plus borrowing for investment purposes) in securities of the index, exchange-traded funds ("ETFs") that track the index and other financial instruments that provide daily leveraged exposure to the index or ETFs that track the index The index is a float-adjusted, market capitalization-weighted index. The fund is non-diversified. The fund is non-diversified. **Top Holdings:** iShares Core S&P 500 ETF   S&P 500 Index Swap   S&P 500 Index Swap   S&P 500 Index Swap

---

DB Gold Double Long ETN   D   SELL

Ticker	Traded On	NAV
DGP	NYSE Arca	

Total Assets ($)	Dividend Yield (TTM)	Turnover Ratio	Expense Ratio
$77,453,016	0	0	0.75

Ratings
Reward	D
Risk	D
Recent Upgrade/Downgrade	Down

Fund Information
Fund Type	Exchange Traded Funds
Category	Trading Tools
Sub-Category	Trading--Leveraged Commodities
Prospectus Objective	Prec Metals
Inception Date	Feb-08
Open to New Investments	Y

Prices
Price (as of 12/31/2018)	23.12
52-Week High	27.04
52-Week Low	19.73

Total Returns (%)
3-Month	6-Month	1-Year	3-Year	5-Year
14.59	3.93	-8.29	26.87	-7.93

3-Year Standard Deviation	25.54
Effective Duration	

Valuation
Premium/Discount (1-Year Average)	0.02

Company Information
Provider	Deutsche Bank AG
Manager/Tenure	No Manager (10)
Website	
Address	Theodor-Heuss-Allee 72 Frankfurt am Main 60486 Germany
Phone Number	

PERFORMANCE

Ratings History
Date	Overall Rating	Risk Rating	Reward Rating
Q4-18	D	D	D
Q2-18	C-	C-	C-
Q4-17	D+	D	C-
Q4-16	D+	D	C-
Q4-15	D-	D-	D-

Asset & Performance History
Date	NAV	1-Year Total Return
2017	25.16	21.35
2016	20.13	11.97
2015	18.18	-22.79
2014	23.55	-6.01
2013	25.06	-51.96
2012	52.17	9.29

Total Assets: $77,453,016
Asset Allocation
Asset	%
Cash	%
Stocks	%
US Stocks	%
Bonds	%
US Bonds	%
Other	%

Services Offered:

Investment Strategy: The investment seeks to replicate, net of expenses, twice the daily performance of the Deutsche Bank Liquid Commodity index - Optimum Yield Gold Excess Return.
The index is intended to reflect changes in the market value of certain gold futures contracts and is comprised of a single unfunded gold futures contract. **Top Holdings:**

WBI BullBear Global Income ETF   C-   HOLD

Ticker	Traded On	NAV	Total Assets ($)	Dividend Yield (TTM)	Turnover Ratio	Expense Ratio
WBII	NYSE Arca	24.08	$77,074,673	3.62		1.28

Ratings
Reward   D+
Risk   C-
Recent Upgrade/Downgrade   Up

Fund Information
Fund Type   Exchange Traded Funds
Category   Cautious Allocation
Sub-Category   Allocation--15% to 30% Equity
Prospectus Objective   Income
Inception Date   Aug-14
Open to New Investments   Y

Prices
Price (as of 12/31/2018)   24.04
52-Week High   25.38
52-Week Low   23.26

Total Returns (%)

3-Month	6-Month	1-Year	3-Year	5-Year
1.27	3.12	-1.45		5.39

3-Year Standard Deviation   2.85
Effective Duration   13.02

Valuation
Premium/Discount (1-Year Average)   -0.08

Company Information
Provider   WBI Investments
Manager/Tenure   Donald R. Schreiber (4), Gary E. Stroik (4)
Website   http://www.wbishares.com
Address   34 Sycamore Ave Suite 1-E Little Silver NJ 07739 United States
Phone Number   732-842-4920

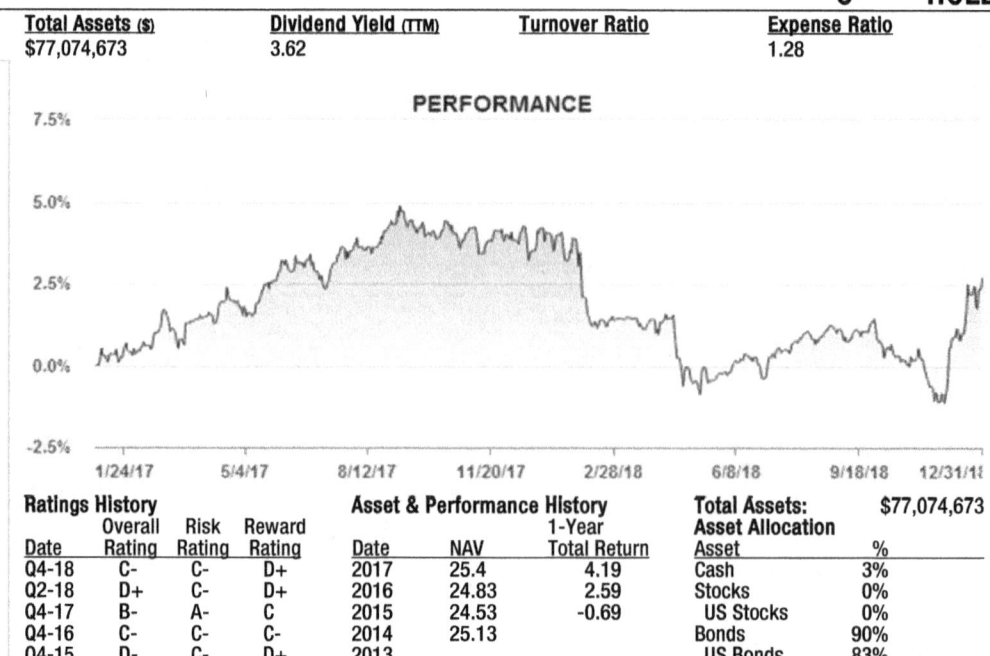

PERFORMANCE

Ratings History

Date	Overall Rating	Risk Rating	Reward Rating
Q4-18	C-	C-	D+
Q2-18	D+	C-	D+
Q4-17	B-	A-	C
Q4-16	C-	C-	C-
Q4-15	D-	C-	D+

Asset & Performance History

Date	NAV	1-Year Total Return
2017	25.4	4.19
2016	24.83	2.59
2015	24.53	-0.69
2014	25.13	
2013		
2012		

Total Assets: $77,074,673

Asset Allocation

Asset	%
Cash	3%
Stocks	0%
US Stocks	0%
Bonds	90%
US Bonds	83%
Other	0%

Services Offered:

Investment Strategy: The investment seeks current income with the potential for long-term capital appreciation, while also seeking to protect principal during unfavorable market conditions. Under normal market conditions, the fund will invest at least 80% of its net assets, plus the amount of any borrowings for investment purposes, in income-producing debt and equity securities of foreign and domestic issuers, including the securities of foreign and domestic corporate and government entities. **Top Holdings:** iShares 20+ Year Treasury Bond ETF Vanguard Long-Term Treasury ETF iShares Intermediate-Term Corp Bd ETF First Trust Preferred Sec & Inc ETF iShares iBoxx $ Invmt Grade Corp Bd ETF

IQ U.S. Real Estate Small Cap ETF   C-   HOLD

Ticker	Traded On	NAV	Total Assets ($)	Dividend Yield (TTM)	Turnover Ratio	Expense Ratio
ROOF	NYSE Arca	21.94	$76,793,134	5.81		0.7

Ratings
Reward   C
Risk   D+
Recent Upgrade/Downgrade   Down

Fund Information
Fund Type   Exchange Traded Funds
Category   Real Estate Sector Equity
Sub-Category   Real Estate
Prospectus Objective   Real Estate
Inception Date   Jun-11
Open to New Investments   Y

Prices
Price (as of 12/31/2018)   21.93
52-Week High   27.39
52-Week Low   21.70

Total Returns (%)

3-Month	6-Month	1-Year	3-Year	5-Year
-12.50	-13.59	-11.19	8.04	21.35

3-Year Standard Deviation   13.99
Effective Duration

Valuation
Premium/Discount (1-Year Average)   0.02

Company Information
Provider   IndexIQ
Manager/Tenure   Greg Barrato (7), James Harrison (0)
Website   http://www.indexiq.com
Address   IndexIQ 800 Westchester Avenue, Suite N-611 Rye Brook NY 10573 United States
Phone Number   888-934-0777

PERFORMANCE

Ratings History

Date	Overall Rating	Risk Rating	Reward Rating
Q4-18	C-	D+	C
Q2-18	C-	D+	C
Q4-17	C+	B-	C
Q4-16	C	C-	C+
Q4-15	C	C-	C

Asset & Performance History

Date	NAV	1-Year Total Return
2017	26.28	2.07
2016	27.19	19.19
2015	24.23	-6.92
2014	27.49	20.67
2013	24.07	15.14
2012	22.51	34.08

Total Assets: $76,793,134

Asset Allocation

Asset	%
Cash	0%
Stocks	99%
US Stocks	99%
Bonds	0%
US Bonds	0%
Other	0%

Services Offered:

Investment Strategy: The investment seeks investment results that correspond generally to the price and yield performance of its underlying index, the IQ U.S. Real Estate Small Cap Index. The fund invests at least 80% of its net assets, plus the amount of any borrowings for investment purposes, in the investments included in its index. The index is a rules based, modified capitalization weighted, float adjusted index intended to give investors a means of tracking the overall performance of the small capitalization sector of publicly traded companies domiciled and primarily listed on an exchange in the U.S. and that invest in real estate. The fund is non-diversified. **Top Holdings:** Physicians Realty Trust Rexford Industrial Realty Inc Stag Industrial Inc Empire State Realty Trust Inc Class A Brandywine Realty Trust

Goldman Sachs Equal Weight U.S. Large Cap Equity ETF   D+   SELL

Ticker	Traded On	NAV	Total Assets ($)	Dividend Yield (TTM)	Turnover Ratio	Expense Ratio
GSEW	BATS	39.58	$76,658,326	1.64	34	0.09

Ratings

Reward   D+
Risk   C-
Recent Upgrade/Downgrade

Fund Information

Fund Type	Exchange Traded Funds
Category	US Equity Large Cap Blend
Sub-Category	Large Blend
Prospectus Objective	Growth & Inc
Inception Date	Sep-17
Open to New Investments	Y

Prices

Price (as of 12/31/2018)	39.39
52-Week High	46.90
52-Week Low	37.41

Total Returns (%)

3-Month	6-Month	1-Year	3-Year	5-Year
-13.97	-9.08	-7.28		

3-Year Standard Deviation
Effective Duration

Valuation

Premium/Discount (1-Year Average)   0.16

Company Information

Provider	Goldman Sachs
Manager/Tenure	Raj Garigipati (1), Jamie McGregor (1)
Website	http://www.gsamfunds.com
Address	Goldman Sachs 200 West Stree New York NY 10282 United States
Phone Number	800-526-7384

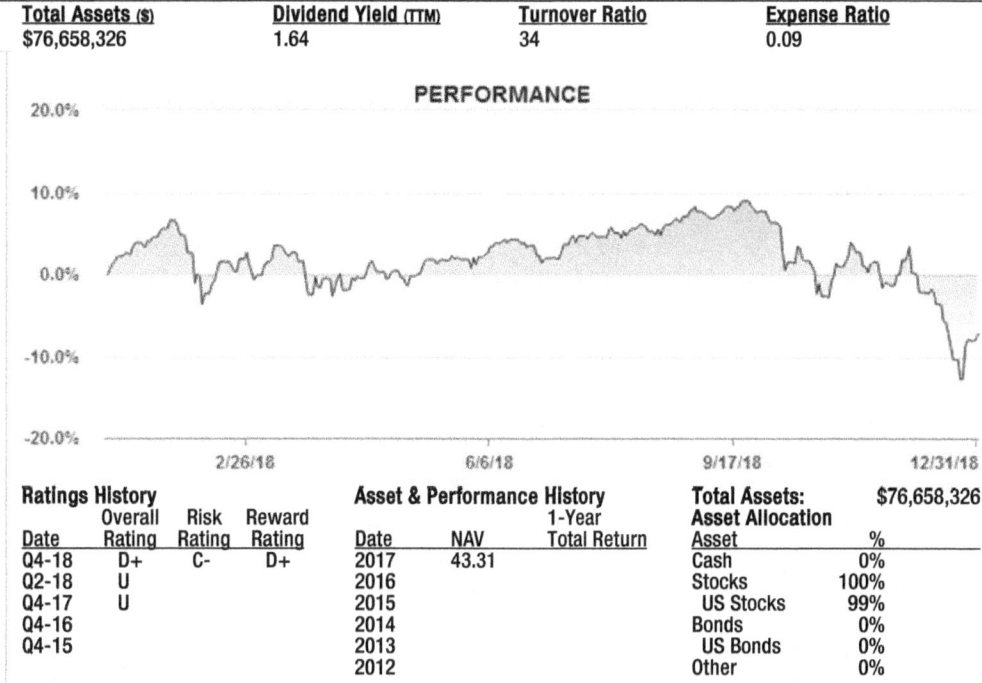

PERFORMANCE

Ratings History

Date	Overall Rating	Risk Rating	Reward Rating
Q4-18	D+	C-	D+
Q2-18	U		
Q4-17	U		
Q4-16			
Q4-15			

Asset & Performance History

Date	NAV	1-Year Total Return
2017	43.31	
2016		
2015		
2014		
2013		
2012		

Total Assets: $76,658,326
Asset Allocation

Asset	%
Cash	0%
Stocks	100%
US Stocks	99%
Bonds	0%
US Bonds	0%
Other	0%

Services Offered:

Investment Strategy: The investment seeks to provide investment results that closely correspond, before fees and expenses, to the performance of the Solactive US Large Cap Equal Weight Index (GTR). The fund seeks to achieve its investment objective by investing at least 80% of its assets (exclusive of collateral held from securities lending) in securities included in its underlying index. The index consists of equity securities of large capitalization U.S. issuers. The index is an equal-weight version of the Solactive US Large Cap Index, a market capitalization-weighted index that includes equity securities of approximately 500 of the largest U.S. companies. **Top Holdings:** CVS Health Corp United Technologies Corp Workday Inc Class A Splunk Inc VMware Inc

---

Virtus Newfleet Multi-Sector Bond ETF   C-   HOLD

Ticker	Traded On	NAV	Total Assets ($)	Dividend Yield (TTM)	Turnover Ratio	Expense Ratio
NFLT	NYSE Arca	23.40	$76,575,019	4.85	113	0.8

Ratings

Reward   D+
Risk   C-
Recent Upgrade/Downgrade

Fund Information

Fund Type	Exchange Traded Funds
Category	US Fixed Income
Sub-Category	Multisector Bond
Prospectus Objective	Income
Inception Date	Aug-15
Open to New Investments	Y

Prices

Price (as of 12/31/2018)	23.44
52-Week High	25.32
52-Week Low	23.27

Total Returns (%)

3-Month	6-Month	1-Year	3-Year	5-Year
-2.12	-0.70	-2.84	11.05	

3-Year Standard Deviation   2.6
Effective Duration

Valuation

Premium/Discount (1-Year Average)   -0.10

Company Information

Provider	Virtus
Manager/Tenure	David L. Albrycht (3), Jonathan R. Stanley (3)
Website	http://www.virtus.com
Address	Virtus Opportunities Trust 101 Munson Street Greenfield MA 1301 United States
Phone Number	800-243-1574

PERFORMANCE

Ratings History

Date	Overall Rating	Risk Rating	Reward Rating
Q4-18	C-	C-	D+
Q2-18	C-	C-	C-
Q4-17	C	B	C
Q4-16	D	C-	D+
Q4-15	U		

Asset & Performance History

Date	NAV	1-Year Total Return
2017	25.23	4.13
2016	25.31	7.85
2015	24.73	
2014		
2013		
2012		

Total Assets: $76,575,019
Asset Allocation

Asset	%
Cash	8%
Stocks	0%
US Stocks	0%
Bonds	91%
US Bonds	69%
Other	0%

Services Offered:

Investment Strategy: The investment seeks to provide a high level of current income and, secondarily, capital appreciation. Under normal market conditions, the fund will invest not less than 80% of its net assets (plus the amount of any borrowings for investment purposes) in bonds. The Sub-Adviser seeks to select securities using a sector rotation approach and seeks to adjust the proportion of fund investments in various sectors and sub-sectors in an effort to obtain higher relative returns. **Top Holdings:** United States Treasury Notes 2.38% United States Treasury Notes 2% Federal National Mortgage Association 4% Indonesia (Republic of) 8.5% United States Treasury Bonds 2.5%

AdvisorShares DoubleLine Value Equity ETF

C- HOLD

Ticker	Traded On	NAV	Total Assets ($)	Dividend Yield (TTM)	Turnover Ratio	Expense Ratio
DBLV	NYSE Arca	59.26	$76,470,559	0.7		0.9

Ratings

Reward	C
Risk	D+
Recent Upgrade/Downgrade	

Fund Information

Fund Type	Exchange Traded Funds
Category	US Equity Mid Cap
Sub-Category	Mid-Cap Value
Prospectus Objective	Growth
Inception Date	Oct-11
Open to New Investments	Y

Prices

Price (as of 12/31/2018)	58.54
52-Week High	75.63
52-Week Low	56.67

Total Returns (%)

3-Month	6-Month	1-Year	3-Year	5-Year
-14.41	-11.73	-15.78	12.91	27.79

3-Year Standard Deviation	11.14
Effective Duration	

Valuation

Premium/Discount (1-Year Average)	0.01

Company Information

Provider	AdvisorShares
Manager/Tenure	Emidio Checcone (0), Brian C. Ear (0)
Website	http://www.advisorshares.com
Address	AdvisorShares 2 Bethesda Metro Center, Suite 1330 Bethesda MD 20814 United States
Phone Number	877-843-3831

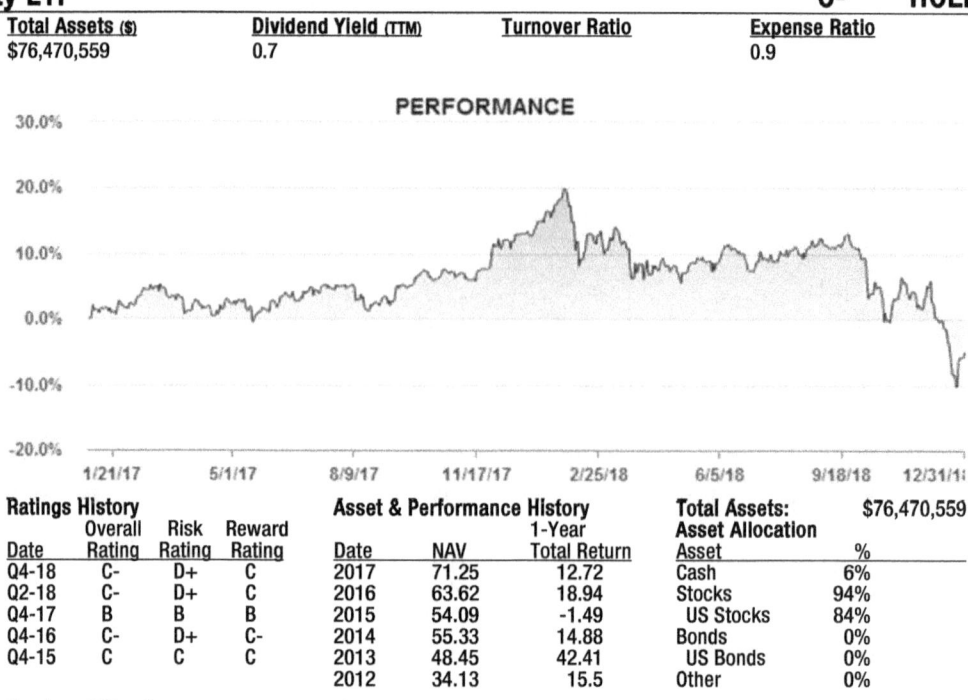

PERFORMANCE

Ratings History

Date	Overall Rating	Risk Rating	Reward Rating
Q4-18	C-	D+	C
Q2-18	C-	D+	C
Q4-17	B	B	B
Q4-16	C-	D+	C-
Q4-15	C	C	C

Asset & Performance History

Date	NAV	1-Year Total Return
2017	71.25	12.72
2016	63.62	18.94
2015	54.09	-1.49
2014	55.33	14.88
2013	48.45	42.41
2012	34.13	15.5

Total Assets: $76,470,559

Asset Allocation

Asset	%
Cash	6%
Stocks	94%
US Stocks	84%
Bonds	0%
US Bonds	0%
Other	0%

Services Offered:

Investment Strategy: The investment seeks to generate long-term capital appreciation. The fund is an actively managed exchange-traded fund that seeks to achieve its investment objective by primarily investing in the broad U.S. equity market. It invests in stocks with liquidity and fundamental characteristics that are historically associated with superior long-term performance. The fund invests at least 80% of its net assets (plus any borrowings for investment purposes) in equity securities. **Top Holdings:** Verizon Communications Inc JPMorgan Chase & Co Bank of America Corporation Comcast Corp Class A Citigroup Inc

---

VanEck Vectors Steel ETF

C+ HOLD

Ticker	Traded On	NAV	Total Assets ($)	Dividend Yield (TTM)	Turnover Ratio	Expense Ratio
SLX	NYSE Arca	34.87	$76,279,081	2.78	31	0.56

Ratings

Reward	B
Risk	C-
Recent Upgrade/Downgrade	Down

Fund Information

Fund Type	Exchange Traded Funds
Category	Natural Resources
Sub-Category	Natural Resources
Prospectus Objective	Unaligned
Inception Date	Oct-06
Open to New Investments	Y

Prices

Price (as of 12/31/2018)	34.84
52-Week High	51.70
52-Week Low	33.83

Total Returns (%)

3-Month	6-Month	1-Year	3-Year	5-Year
-20.70	-18.73	-20.08	94.12	-16.96

3-Year Standard Deviation	32.89
Effective Duration	

Valuation

Premium/Discount (1-Year Average)	0.01

Company Information

Provider	VanEck
Manager/Tenure	Hao-Hung (Peter) Liao (12), Guo Hua (Jason) Jin (0)
Website	http://www.vaneck.com
Address	Van Eck Associates Corporation 666 Third Avenue New York NY 10017 United States
Phone Number	800-826-1115

PERFORMANCE

Ratings History

Date	Overall Rating	Risk Rating	Reward Rating
Q4-18	C+	C-	B
Q2-18	B-	C-	B
Q4-17	B-	D+	B
Q4-16	C	D	C
Q4-15	C	C-	C

Asset & Performance History

Date	NAV	1-Year Total Return
2017	45.74	24.07
2016	37.82	95.78
2015	19.52	-41.89
2014	35.45	-26.38
2013	49.76	3.93
2012	48.85	4.86

Total Assets: $76,279,081

Asset Allocation

Asset	%
Cash	0%
Stocks	100%
US Stocks	40%
Bonds	0%
US Bonds	0%
Other	0%

Services Offered:

Investment Strategy: The investment seeks to replicate as closely as possible, before fees and expenses, the price and yield performance of the NYSE Arca Steel Index. The fund normally invests at least 80% of its total assets in common stocks and depositary receipts of companies involved in the steel sector. Such companies may include small- and medium-capitalization companies and foreign and emerging market issuers. It may concentrate its investments in a particular industry or group of industries to the extent that the Steel Index concentrates in an industry or group of industries. The fund is non-diversified. **Top Holdings:** Rio Tinto PLC ADR Vale SA ADR Ternium SA ADR Vedanta Ltd ADR Gerdau SA ADR

iPath® Series B S&P GSCI® Crude Oil Total Return Index ETN   D+   SELL

Ticker	Traded On	NAV	Total Assets ($)	Dividend Yield (TTM)	Turnover Ratio	Expense Ratio
OIL	NYSE Arca		$76,227,984	0		0.75

Ratings
Reward   D+
Risk   D
Recent Upgrade/Downgrade   Down

Fund Information
Fund Type	Exchange Traded Funds
Category	Commodities Specified
Sub-Category	Commodities Energy
Prospectus Objective	Natl Res
Inception Date	Nov-16
Open to New Investments	Y

Prices
Price (as of 12/31/2018)	47.46
52-Week High	79.07
52-Week Low	45.57

Total Returns (%)
3-Month	6-Month	1-Year	3-Year	5-Year
-39.82	-36.42	-21.00		

3-Year Standard Deviation
Effective Duration

Valuation
Premium/Discount (1-Year Average)   0.15

Company Information
Provider	Milleis Investissements Funds
Manager/Tenure	No Manager (2)
Website	
Address	2-4, rue Eugène Ruppert L-2453
	Luxembourg Luxembourg L-2453
	Luxembourg
Phone Number	

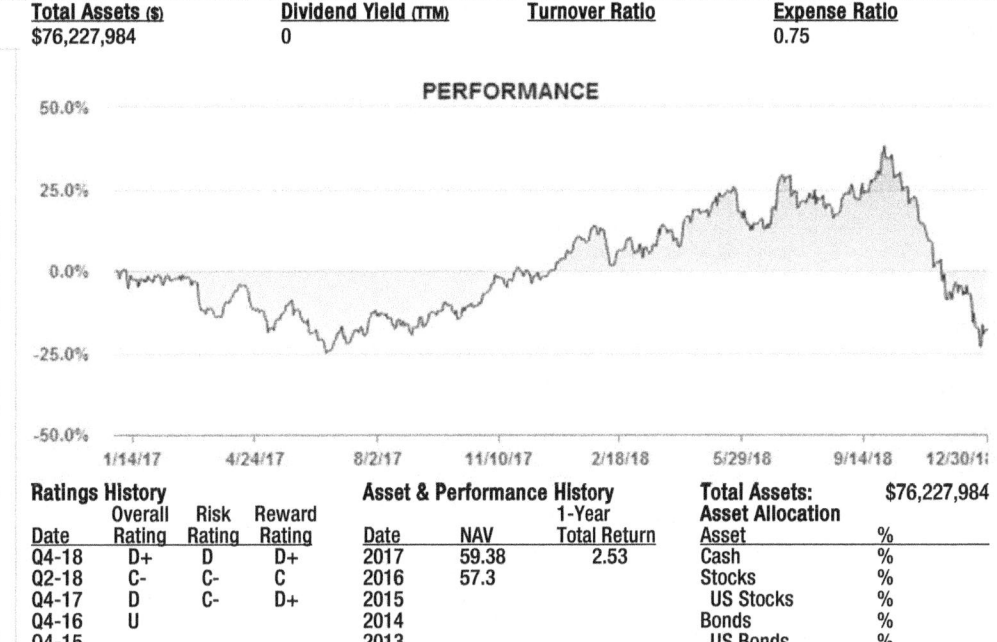

PERFORMANCE

Ratings History
Date	Overall Rating	Risk Rating	Reward Rating
Q4-18	D+	D	D+
Q2-18	C-	C-	C
Q4-17	D	C-	D+
Q4-16	U		
Q4-15			

Asset & Performance History
Date	NAV	1-Year Total Return
2017	59.38	2.53
2016	57.3	
2015		
2014		
2013		
2012		

Total Assets: $76,227,984

Asset Allocation
Asset	%
Cash	%
Stocks	%
US Stocks	%
Bonds	%
US Bonds	%
Other	%

Services Offered:

Investment Strategy: The investment seeks to provide investors with exposure to the performance of the S&P GSCI® Crude Oil Total Return Index.
The underlying index is a sub-index of the S&P GSCI® Commodity Index and reflects the excess returns that are potentially available through an unleveraged investment in the commodities futures contracts comprising the Index, plus the Treasury Bill rate of interest that could be earned on funds committed to the trading of the underlying futures contracts. **Top Holdings:**

---

iShares 1-3 Year International Treasury Bond ETF   D+   SELL

Ticker	Traded On	NAV	Total Assets ($)	Dividend Yield (TTM)	Turnover Ratio	Expense Ratio
ISHG	NAS CM	79.69	$76,134,951	0.49	48	0.35

Ratings
Reward   D+
Risk   D+
Recent Upgrade/Downgrade

Fund Information
Fund Type	Exchange Traded Funds
Category	Global Fixed Income
Sub-Category	World Bond
Prospectus Objective	Worldwide Bond
Inception Date	Jan-09
Open to New Investments	Y

Prices
Price (as of 12/31/2018)	79.76
52-Week High	87.66
52-Week Low	78.94

Total Returns (%)
3-Month	6-Month	1-Year	3-Year	5-Year
-0.18	-1.10	-3.67	4.69	-13.69

3-Year Standard Deviation   6.48
Effective Duration   1.84

Valuation
Premium/Discount (1-Year Average)   -0.02

Company Information
Provider	iShares
Manager/Tenure	Scott Radell (8), James Mauro (7)
Website	http://www.ishares.com
Address	iShares 400 Howard Street San
	Francisco CA 94105 United States
Phone Number	800-474-2737

PERFORMANCE

Ratings History
Date	Overall Rating	Risk Rating	Reward Rating
Q4-18	D+	D+	D+
Q2-18	C-	D+	C-
Q4-17	C	C	C-
Q4-16	D	D+	D
Q4-15	D	D	D

Asset & Performance History
Date	NAV	1-Year Total Return
2017	84.23	9.51
2016	76.91	-1.22
2015	77.86	-7.49
2014	84.24	-10.88
2013	94.9	-1.92
2012	96.96	1.74

Total Assets: $76,134,951

Asset Allocation
Asset	%
Cash	1%
Stocks	0%
US Stocks	0%
Bonds	99%
US Bonds	0%
Other	0%

Services Offered:

Investment Strategy: The investment seeks to track the investment results of the S&P International Sovereign Ex-U.S. 1-3 Year Bond Index. The fund will invest at least 90% of its assets in the component securities of the index and may invest up to 10% of its assets in certain futures, options and swap contracts, cash and cash equivalents. The index is a broad, market value weighted index designed to measure the performance of sovereign bonds issued in local currencies by developed market countries, as classified by SPDJI, outside the U.S. The fund is non-diversified. **Top Holdings:** Japan (Government Of) 0.1% Japan (Government Of) 0.1% Belgium (Kingdom Of) 3.75% Japan (Government Of) 0.1% Netherlands (Kingdom Of) 3.5%

ProShares Ultra Gold   D   SELL

Ticker	Traded On	NAV	Total Assets ($)	Dividend Yield (TTM)	Turnover Ratio	Expense Ratio
UGL	NYSE Arca		$76,121,139	0	0	0.95

Ratings
Reward	D
Risk	D
Recent Upgrade/Downgrade	Down

Fund Information
Fund Type	Exchange Traded Funds
Category	Trading Tools
Sub-Category	Trading--Leveraged Commodities
Prospectus Objective	Prec Metals
Inception Date	Dec-08
Open to New Investments	Y

Prices
Price (as of 12/31/2018)	37.41
52-Week High	43.96
52-Week Low	31.97

Total Returns (%)
3-Month	6-Month	1-Year	3-Year	5-Year
13.94	2.23	-6.87	24.91	-9.99

3-Year Standard Deviation	26.02
Effective Duration	

Valuation
Premium/Discount (1-Year Average)	0.33

Company Information
Provider	ProShares
Manager/Tenure	Management Team (10)
Website	http://www.proshares.com
Address	ProShares 7501 Wisconsin Avenue, Suite 1000 Bethesda MD 20814 United States
Phone Number	866-776-5125

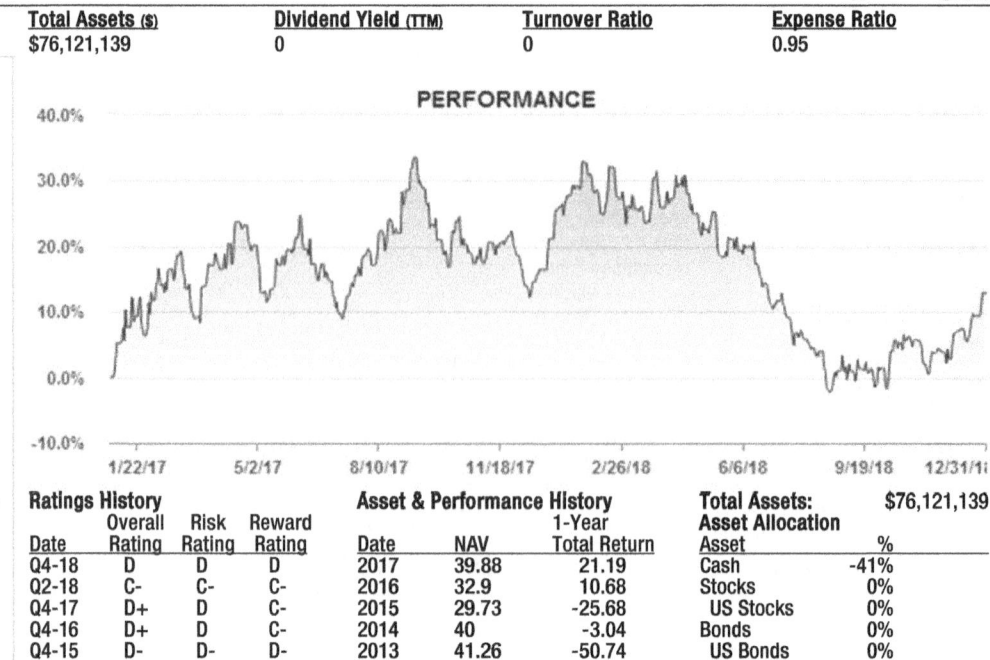

PERFORMANCE

Ratings History
Date	Overall Rating	Risk Rating	Reward Rating
Q4-18	D	D	D
Q2-18	C-	C-	C-
Q4-17	D+	D	C-
Q4-16	D+	D	C-
Q4-15	D-	D-	D-

Asset & Performance History
Date	NAV	1-Year Total Return
2017	39.88	21.19
2016	32.9	10.68
2015	29.73	-25.68
2014	40	-3.04
2013	41.26	-50.74
2012	83.76	10.34

Total Assets: $76,121,139

Asset Allocation
Asset	%
Cash	-41%
Stocks	0%
US Stocks	0%
Bonds	0%
US Bonds	0%
Other	141%

Services Offered:

Investment Strategy: The investment seeks to provide daily investment results (before fees and expenses) that correspond to twice (200%) the daily performance of gold bullion as measured by the U.S. Dollar p.m. fixing price for delivery in London.
The "Ultra" funds seek results for a single day that match (before fees and expenses) two times (2x) the daily performance of a benchmark. It does not seek to achieve their stated objective over a period greater than a single day. **Top Holdings:** London Gold Price Forward - Citibank Na   London Gold Price Forward - Ubs Ag   London Gold Price Forward - Societe Generale   Gold 100 Oz Future 02/26/2019 (Gcg9)   Gold 100 Oz Future 12/27/2018 (Gcz8)

Aptus Behavioral Momentum ETF   B-   BUY

Ticker	Traded On	NAV	Total Assets ($)	Dividend Yield (TTM)	Turnover Ratio	Expense Ratio
BEMO	BATS	28.26	$75,910,288	0.31	124	0.79

Ratings
Reward	B
Risk	C
Recent Upgrade/Downgrade	Down

Fund Information
Fund Type	Exchange Traded Funds
Category	US Equity Large Cap Blend
Sub-Category	Large Growth
Prospectus Objective	Growth & Inc
Inception Date	Jun-16
Open to New Investments	Y

Prices
Price (as of 12/31/2018)	28.25
52-Week High	37.07
52-Week Low	28.17

Total Returns (%)
3-Month	6-Month	1-Year	3-Year	5-Year
-23.09	-16.53	-5.88		

3-Year Standard Deviation	
Effective Duration	

Valuation
Premium/Discount (1-Year Average)	0.08

Company Information
Provider	Aptus Capital Advisors
Manager/Tenure	John D. Gardner (1), Beckham D. Wyrick (1)
Website	
Address	407 Johnson Avenue, Fairhope, Alabama 36532 United States
Phone Number	

PERFORMANCE

Ratings History
Date	Overall Rating	Risk Rating	Reward Rating
Q4-18	B-	C	B
Q2-18	B-	C-	B
Q4-17	D+	B	C
Q4-16	U		
Q4-15			

Asset & Performance History
Date	NAV	1-Year Total Return
2017	30.28	17.28
2016	25.9	
2015		
2014		
2013		
2012		

Total Assets: $75,910,288

Asset Allocation
Asset	%
Cash	0%
Stocks	100%
US Stocks	100%
Bonds	0%
US Bonds	0%
Other	0%

Services Offered:

Investment Strategy: The investment seeks to track the performance, before fees and expenses, of the Aptus Behavioral Momentum Index. The index uses an objective, rules-based methodology to implement a systematic trend-following strategy that directs 100% of its exposure to either equity exposure or treasure exposure. The fund invests at least 80% of its total assets in the component securities of the index. The fund generally may invest up to 20% of its total assets (exclusive of any collateral held from securities lending) in securities or other investments not included in the index, but which the Adviser believes will help the fund track the index. It is non-diversified.
Top Holdings: HCA Healthcare Inc   Church & Dwight Co Inc   Clorox Co   Merck & Co Inc   McCormick & Co Inc Non-Voting

Invesco S&P SmallCap Utilities & Communication Services ETF   C+   HOLD

Ticker	Traded On	NAV	Total Assets ($)	Dividend Yield (TTM)	Turnover Ratio	Expense Ratio
PSCU	NAS CM	49.27	$75,731,998	2.96		0.29

Ratings
Reward   B-
Risk   C-
Recent Upgrade/Downgrade

Fund Information
Fund Type	Exchange Traded Funds
Category	Utilities Sector Equity
Sub-Category	Utilities
Prospectus Objective	Utility
Inception Date	Apr-10
Open to New Investments	

Prices
Price (as of 12/31/2018)	49.20
52-Week High	58.10
52-Week Low	46.95

Total Returns (%)
3-Month	6-Month	1-Year	3-Year	5-Year
-13.03	-7.88	-4.46	33.42	66.46

3-Year Standard Deviation   12.21
Effective Duration

Valuation
Premium/Discount (1-Year Average)   0.15

Company Information
Provider	Invesco
Manager/Tenure	Peter Hubbard (8), Michael Jeanette (8), Tony Seisser (4), 1 other
Website	http://www.invesco.com/us
Address	Invesco 11 Greenway Plaza, Ste. 2500 Houston TX 77046 United States
Phone Number	800-659-1005

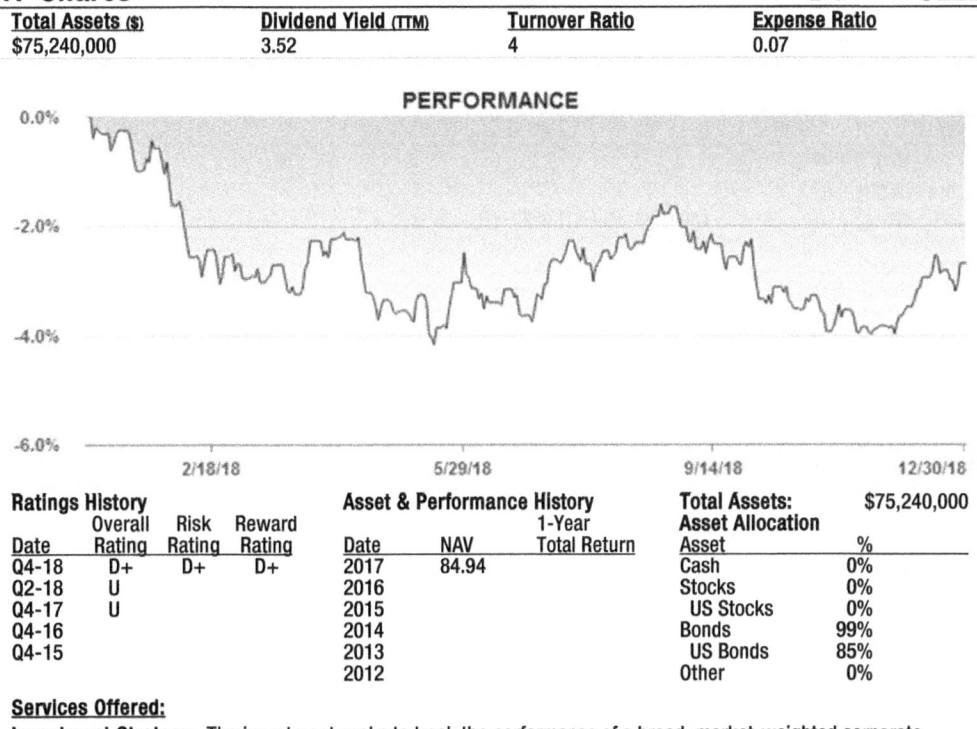

PERFORMANCE

Ratings History
Date	Overall Rating	Risk Rating	Reward Rating
Q4-18	C+	C-	B-
Q2-18	C+	C-	B-
Q4-17	A-	A-	B+
Q4-16	B-	C	B
Q4-15	B-	C	B-

Asset & Performance History
Date	NAV	1-Year Total Return
2017	52.72	11.91
2016	47.96	20.43
2015	41.14	7.04
2014	39.67	16.55
2013	34.94	20.35
2012	29.93	1.58

Total Assets: $75,731,998
Asset Allocation
Asset	%
Cash	0%
Stocks	100%
US Stocks	100%
Bonds	0%
US Bonds	0%
Other	0%

Services Offered:

Investment Strategy: The investment seeks to track the investment results (before fees and expenses) of the S&P SmallCap 600® Capped Utilities & Communication Services Index (the "underlying index"). The fund generally will invest at least 90% of its total assets in common stocks of small capitalization U.S. utility companies that comprise the underlying index. These companies are principally engaged in providing either energy, water, electric or natural gas utilities. The fund is non-diversified. **Top Holdings:** Spire Inc Avista Corp South Jersey Industries Inc Vonage Holdings Corp El Paso Electric Co

---

Vanguard Total Corporate Bond ETF ETF Shares   D+   SELL

Ticker	Traded On	NAV	Total Assets ($)	Dividend Yield (TTM)	Turnover Ratio	Expense Ratio
VTC	NAS CM		$75,240,000	3.52	4	0.07

Ratings
Reward   D+
Risk   D+
Recent Upgrade/Downgrade

Fund Information
Fund Type	Exchange Traded Funds
Category	US Fixed Income
Sub-Category	Corporate Bond
Prospectus Objective	Corp Bond - Gen
Inception Date	Nov-17
Open to New Investments	Y

Prices
Price (as of 12/31/2018)	80.00
52-Week High	85.00
52-Week Low	79.04

Total Returns (%)
3-Month	6-Month	1-Year	3-Year	5-Year
-0.30	0.69	-2.69		

3-Year Standard Deviation
Effective Duration   6.95

Valuation
Premium/Discount (1-Year Average)   0.06

Company Information
Provider	Vanguard
Manager/Tenure	Joshua C. Barrickman (1)
Website	http://www.vanguard.com
Address	Vanguard 100 Vanguard Boulevard Malvern PA 19355 United States
Phone Number	877-662-7447

PERFORMANCE

Ratings History
Date	Overall Rating	Risk Rating	Reward Rating
Q4-18	D+	D+	D+
Q2-18	U		
Q4-17	U		
Q4-16			
Q4-15			

Asset & Performance History
Date	NAV	1-Year Total Return
2017	84.94	
2016		
2015		
2014		
2013		
2012		

Total Assets: $75,240,000
Asset Allocation
Asset	%
Cash	0%
Stocks	0%
US Stocks	0%
Bonds	99%
US Bonds	85%
Other	0%

Services Offered:

Investment Strategy: The investment seeks to track the performance of a broad, market-weighted corporate bond index. The fund is a fund of funds and employs an indexing investment approach designed to track the performance of the Bloomberg Barclays U.S. Corporate Bond Index, which measures the investment-grade, fixed-rate, taxable corporate bond market. The index includes U.S. dollar-denominated securities that are publicly issued by industrial, utility, and financial issuers. **Top Holdings:** Vanguard Short-Term Corporate Bond ETF Vanguard Long-Term Corporate Bd ETF Vanguard Interm-Term Corp Bd ETF

FlexShares Credit-Scored US Corporate Bond Index Fund   C-   HOLD

Ticker	Traded On	NAV	Total Assets ($)	Dividend Yield (TTM)	Turnover Ratio	Expense Ratio
SKOR	NAS CM	48.81	$75,096,971	2.86		0.22

Ratings
Reward   D+
Risk   C-
Recent Upgrade/Downgrade   Up

Fund Information
Fund Type   Exchange Traded Funds
Category   US Fixed Income
Sub-Category   Corporate Bond
Prospectus Objective   Convertible Bond
Inception Date   Nov-14
Open to New Investments   Y

Prices
Price (as of 12/31/2018)   48.85
52-Week High   50.89
52-Week Low   48.38

Total Returns (%)

3-Month	6-Month	1-Year	3-Year	5-Year
0.68	1.46	-0.82	5.98	

3-Year Standard Deviation   2.53
Effective Duration   4.65

Valuation
Premium/Discount (1-Year Average)   0.05

Company Information
Provider   Flexshares Trust
Manager/Tenure   Bradley Camden (4), Michael T. Doyle (4), Brandon P. Ferguson (4)
Website   http://www.flexshares.com
Address   50 South LaSalle Street Chicago, Illinois 60603 Chicago Illinois 60603 United States
Phone Number   855-353-9383

PERFORMANCE

Ratings History

Date	Overall Rating	Risk Rating	Reward Rating
Q4-18	C-	C-	D+
Q2-18	D+	D+	D+
Q4-17	C+	B+	C
Q4-16	D+	D+	D+
Q4-15	U		

Asset & Performance History

Date	NAV	1-Year Total Return
2017	50.63	3.3
2016	50.03	2.6
2015	49.79	1.64
2014	50.09	
2013		
2012		

Total Assets: $75,096,971

Asset Allocation

Asset	%
Cash	0%
Stocks	0%
US Stocks	0%
Bonds	99%
US Bonds	83%
Other	0%

Services Offered:

Investment Strategy: The investment seeks the price and yield performance, before fees and expenses, of the Northern Trust Credit-Scored US Corporate Bond IndexSM. The fund generally will invest under normal circumstances at least 80% of its total assets (exclusive of collateral held from securities lending) in the securities of its underlying index. The underlying index is designed to outperform the parent index on a risk-adjusted basis, as measured by a combination of yield return and price appreciation. Securities included in the underlying index are component securities of the Parent Index. The fund is non-diversified. **Top Holdings:** Goldman Sachs Group, Inc. 5.75% JPMorgan Chase & Co. 3.78% Morgan Stanley 5% Bank of America Corporation 2.5% Comcast Corporation 3.95%

Invesco Dynamic Food & Beverage ETF   B-   BUY

Ticker	Traded On	NAV	Total Assets ($)	Dividend Yield (TTM)	Turnover Ratio	Expense Ratio
PBJ	NYSE Arca	29.80	$74,307,640	0.99	147	0.63

Ratings
Reward   B
Risk   C
Recent Upgrade/Downgrade

Fund Information
Fund Type   Exchange Traded Funds
Category   Consumer Goods & Svcs
Sub-Category   Consumer Defensive
Prospectus Objective   Unaligned
Inception Date   Jun-05
Open to New Investments   Y

Prices
Price (as of 12/31/2018)   29.67
52-Week High   34.92
52-Week Low   28.60

Total Returns (%)

3-Month	6-Month	1-Year	3-Year	5-Year
-7.27	-8.89	-10.77	-4.01	20.34

3-Year Standard Deviation   8.76
Effective Duration

Valuation
Premium/Discount (1-Year Average)   0.03

Company Information
Provider   Invesco
Manager/Tenure   Peter Hubbard (11), Michael Jeanette (10), Tony Seisser (4), 1 other
Website   http://www.invesco.com/us
Address   Invesco 11 Greenway Plaza, Ste. 2500 Houston TX 77046 United States
Phone Number   800-659-1005

PERFORMANCE

Ratings History

Date	Overall Rating	Risk Rating	Reward Rating
Q4-18	B-	C	B
Q2-18	C+	C	B
Q4-17	B-	B	C
Q4-16	B	C+	B
Q4-15	B	B	B+

Asset & Performance History

Date	NAV	1-Year Total Return
2017	33.84	1.57
2016	33.56	5.91
2015	32.19	6.82
2014	30.51	17.37
2013	26.36	33.38
2012	19.94	5.59

Total Assets: $74,307,640

Asset Allocation

Asset	%
Cash	0%
Stocks	100%
US Stocks	94%
Bonds	0%
US Bonds	0%
Other	0%

Services Offered:

Investment Strategy: The investment seeks to track the investment results (before fees and expenses) of the Dynamic Food & Beverage IntellidexSM Index. The fund generally will invest at least 90% of its total assets in common stocks of food and beverage companies that comprise the underlying intellidex. The underlying intellidex was composed of common stocks of 30 U.S. food and beverage companies. These companies are engaged principally in the manufacture, sale or distribution of food and beverage products, agricultural products and products related to the development of new food technologies. The fund is non-diversified. **Top Holdings:** Keurig Dr Pepper Inc Yum Brands Inc PepsiCo Inc Mondelez International Inc Class A Monster Beverage Corp

FlexShares International Quality Dividend Defensive Index Fund   C-   HOLD

Ticker	Traded On	NAV	Total Assets ($)	Dividend Yield (TTM)	Turnover Ratio	Expense Ratio
IQDE	NYSE Arca	20.38	$73,264,370	5.91		0.47

Ratings
Reward   C-
Risk   C-
Recent Upgrade/Downgrade

Fund Information
Fund Type   Exchange Traded Funds
Category   Global Equity Large Cap
Sub-Category   Foreign Large Value
Prospectus Objective   World Stock
Inception Date   Apr-13
Open to New Investments   Y

Prices
Price (as of 12/31/2018)   20.47
52-Week High   26.98
52-Week Low   19.98

Total Returns (%)

3-Month	6-Month	1-Year	3-Year	5-Year
-10.31	-8.91	-16.12	8.69	-4.55

3-Year Standard Deviation   10.7
Effective Duration

Valuation
Premium/Discount (1-Year Average)   0.02

Company Information
Provider   Flexshares Trust
Manager/Tenure   Robert Anstine (5), Brendan Sullivan (2)
Website   http://www.flexshares.com
Address   50 South LaSalle Street Chicago, Illinois 60603 Chicago Illinois 60603 United States
Phone Number   855-353-9383

PERFORMANCE

Ratings History

Date	Overall Rating	Risk Rating	Reward Rating
Q4-18	C-	C-	C-
Q2-18	C-	D+	C-
Q4-17	C+	C+	C+
Q4-16	D+	D+	D+
Q4-15	D+	D+	D+

Asset & Performance History

Date	NAV	1-Year Total Return
2017	25.44	21.68
2016	21.9	6.5
2015	21.33	-8.61
2014	24.41	-3.91
2013	26.34	
2012		

Total Assets: $73,264,370

Asset Allocation

Asset	%
Cash	1%
Stocks	99%
US Stocks	0%
Bonds	0%
US Bonds	0%
Other	0%

Services Offered:

Investment Strategy: The investment seeks investment results that correspond generally to the price and yield performance, before fees and expenses, of the Northern Trust International Quality Dividend Defensive IndexSM. The fund will invest at least 80% of its total assets in the securities of the index and in ADRs and GDRs based on the securities in the index. The index is designed to provide exposure to a high-quality, income-oriented portfolio of international equity securities issued by non-U.S.-based companies, with an emphasis on long-term capital growth and a targeted overall volatility that is lower than that of the Northern Trust International Large Cap IndexSM. **Top Holdings:** GlaxoSmithKline PLC   Nestle SA   BP PLC   Toyota Motor Corp   Total SA

Invesco Dynamic Energy Exploration & Production ETF   C+   HOLD

Ticker	Traded On	NAV	Total Assets ($)	Dividend Yield (TTM)	Turnover Ratio	Expense Ratio
PXE	NYSE Arca	17.40	$72,792,307	1.07	87	0.65

Ratings
Reward   B
Risk   C-
Recent Upgrade/Downgrade   Up

Fund Information
Fund Type   Exchange Traded Funds
Category   Energy Sector Equity
Sub-Category   Equity Energy
Prospectus Objective   Natl Res
Inception Date   Oct-05
Open to New Investments   Y

Prices
Price (as of 12/31/2018)   17.37
52-Week High   28.22
52-Week Low   15.89

Total Returns (%)

3-Month	6-Month	1-Year	3-Year	5-Year
-36.87	-34.34	-23.16	-12.02	-42.03

3-Year Standard Deviation   30.39
Effective Duration

Valuation
Premium/Discount (1-Year Average)   0.06

Company Information
Provider   Invesco
Manager/Tenure   Peter Hubbard (11), Michael Jeanette (10), Tony Seisser (4), 1 other
Website   http://www.invesco.com/us
Address   Invesco 11 Greenway Plaza, Ste. 2500 Houston TX 77046 United States
Phone Number   800-659-1005

PERFORMANCE

Ratings History

Date	Overall Rating	Risk Rating	Reward Rating
Q4-18	C+	C-	B
Q2-18	C	D+	C+
Q4-17	D+	D+	D
Q4-16	D+	D	C-
Q4-15	B	B-	B

Asset & Performance History

Date	NAV	1-Year Total Return
2017	22.89	0.78
2016	23.12	13.61
2015	21.9	-19.19
2014	27.72	-18.47
2013	34.57	29.99
2012	27.11	23.59

Total Assets: $72,792,307

Asset Allocation

Asset	%
Cash	0%
Stocks	100%
US Stocks	94%
Bonds	0%
US Bonds	0%
Other	0%

Services Offered:

Investment Strategy: The investment seeks to track the investment results (before fees and expenses) of the Dynamic Energy Exploration & Production IntellidexSM Index. The fund invests at least 90% of its total assets in common stocks of companies engaged in energy exploration and production that comprise the underlying intellidex. The intellidex was composed of common stocks of 30 U.S. companies involved in the exploration and production of natural resources used to produce energy. These companies are engaged principally in exploration, extraction and production of crude oil and natural gas from land-based or offshore wells. The fund is non-diversified. **Top Holdings:** Marathon Petroleum Corp   ConocoPhillips   EOG Resources Inc   Occidental Petroleum Corp   Phillips 66

WBI BullBear Yield 1000 ETF

C **HOLD**

Ticker	Traded On	NAV		Total Assets ($)	Dividend Yield (TTM)	Turnover Ratio	Expense Ratio
WBIG	NYSE Arca	23.46		$72,750,602	1.26		1.04

Ratings

Reward	C
Risk	C
Recent Upgrade/Downgrade	Down

Fund Information

Fund Type	Exchange Traded Funds
Category	US Equity Large Cap Blend
Sub-Category	Large Blend
Prospectus Objective	Growth & Inc
Inception Date	Aug-14
Open to New Investments	Y

Prices

Price (as of 12/31/2018)	23.41
52-Week High	27.95
52-Week Low	23.41

Total Returns (%)

3-Month	6-Month	1-Year	3-Year	5-Year
-12.37	-8.73	-7.98	12.49	

3-Year Standard Deviation	9.48
Effective Duration	

Valuation

Premium/Discount (1-Year Average)	0.01

Company Information

Provider	WBI Investments
Manager/Tenure	Donald R. Schreiber (4), Gary E. Stroik (4)
Website	http://www.wbishares.com
Address	34 Sycamore Ave Suite 1-E Little Silver NJ 07739 United States
Phone Number	732-842-4920

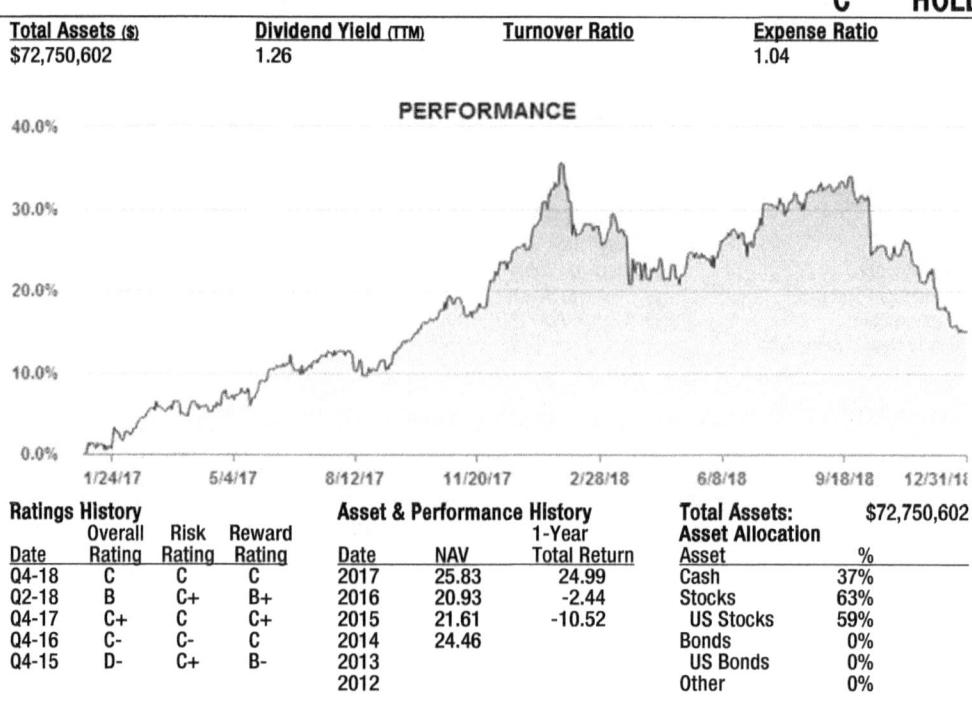

PERFORMANCE

Ratings History

Date	Overall Rating	Risk Rating	Reward Rating
Q4-18	C	C	C
Q2-18	B	C+	B+
Q4-17	C+	C	C+
Q4-16	C-	C-	C
Q4-15	D-	C+	B-

Asset & Performance History

Date	NAV	1-Year Total Return
2017	25.83	24.99
2016	20.93	-2.44
2015	21.61	-10.52
2014	24.46	
2013		
2012		

Total Assets: $72,750,602

Asset Allocation

Asset	%
Cash	37%
Stocks	63%
US Stocks	59%
Bonds	0%
US Bonds	0%
Other	0%

Services Offered:

Investment Strategy: The investment seeks long-term capital appreciation and the potential for current income, while also seeking to protect principal during unfavorable market conditions. The fund will seek to invest in the dividend-paying equity securities of large capitalization domestic and foreign companies that WBI Investments, Inc., the sub-advisor ("Sub-Advisor") to the fund and an affiliate of Millington Securities Inc., the advisor ("Advisor"), believes display attractive dividend payment prospects, and in other tactical investment opportunities. It may invest up to 50% of its net assets in the securities of issuers in emerging markets. **Top Holdings:** Verizon Communications Inc Exelon Corp Delta Air Lines Inc Coca-Cola European Partners PLC Mondelez International Inc Class A

FormulaFolios Hedged Growth ETF

D+ **SELL**

Ticker	Traded On	NAV		Total Assets ($)	Dividend Yield (TTM)	Turnover Ratio	Expense Ratio
FFHG	BATS	26.01		$72,679,398	0.58	138	1.16

Ratings

Reward	D+
Risk	D+
Recent Upgrade/Downgrade	

Fund Information

Fund Type	Exchange Traded Funds
Category	Long/Short Equity
Sub-Category	Long-Short Equity
Prospectus Objective	Growth
Inception Date	Jun-17
Open to New Investments	Y

Prices

Price (as of 12/31/2018)	26.00
52-Week High	30.27
52-Week Low	24.91

Total Returns (%)

3-Month	6-Month	1-Year	3-Year	5-Year
-11.74	-7.56	-5.41		

3-Year Standard Deviation	
Effective Duration	

Valuation

Premium/Discount (1-Year Average)	0.15

Company Information

Provider	FormulaFolioFunds
Manager/Tenure	Derek Prusa (1), Jason Wenk (1)
Website	
Address	89 Ionia NW, Suite 600 Grand Rapids, MI 49503 United States
Phone Number	

PERFORMANCE

Ratings History

Date	Overall Rating	Risk Rating	Reward Rating
Q4-18	D+	D+	D+
Q2-18	D+	C-	D+
Q4-17	U		
Q4-16			
Q4-15			

Asset & Performance History

Date	NAV	1-Year Total Return
2017	27.58	
2016		
2015		
2014		
2013		
2012		

Total Assets: $72,679,398

Asset Allocation

Asset	%
Cash	-10%
Stocks	110%
US Stocks	109%
Bonds	0%
US Bonds	0%
Other	0%

Services Offered:

Investment Strategy: The investment seeks to provide capital growth. The fund seeks to achieve its investment objective by investing primarily in domestic equity securities of any market capitalization and U.S. Treasuries through other unaffiliated exchange traded funds ("ETFs") (including leveraged ETFs and inverse ETFs). The adviser allocates the fund's assets equally between two proprietary investment models. The adviser's first investment model identifies trends in the equity markets. The adviser's second investment model uses two sub-strategies. **Top Holdings:** iShares Core S&P Small-Cap ETF Financial Select Sector SPDR® ETF iShares S&P 100 ETF iShares Core S&P 500 ETF iShares Core S&P Mid-Cap ETF

SPDR® S&P Capital Markets ETF   C   HOLD

Ticker	Traded On	NAV	Total Assets ($)	Dividend Yield (TTM)	Turnover Ratio	Expense Ratio
KCE	NYSE Arca	47.84	$72,050,266	2.28	43	0.35

Ratings
Reward   C
Risk   C-
Recent Upgrade/Downgrade

Fund Information
Fund Type   Exchange Traded Funds
Category   Financials Sector Equity
Sub-Category   Financial
Prospectus Objective   Financial
Inception Date   Nov-05
Open to New Investments   Y

Prices
Price (as of 12/31/2018)   47.77
52-Week High   62.39
52-Week Low   44.84

Total Returns (%)

3-Month	6-Month	1-Year	3-Year	5-Year
-14.17	-16.89	-15.04	18.53	6.54

3-Year Standard Deviation   19.26
Effective Duration

Valuation
Premium/Discount (1-Year Average)   0.26

Company Information
Provider   SPDR State Street Global Advisors
Manager/Tenure   Michael J. Feehily (7), Karl A. Schneider (4), Kala O'Donnell (1)
Website   http://www.spdrs.com
Address   SPDR State Street Global Advisors State Street Financial Center, 1 Lincoln Street Boston MA 02111-2900 United States
Phone Number   617-786-3000

PERFORMANCE

Ratings History

Date	Overall Rating	Risk Rating	Reward Rating
Q4-18	C	C-	C
Q2-18	C+	C-	B-
Q4-17	B-	C+	B
Q4-16	C-	D+	C-
Q4-15	C+	C	C+

Asset & Performance History

Date	NAV	1-Year Total Return
2017	57.64	31.43
2016	44.84	5.28
2015	43.32	-12.38
2014	50.58	2.59
2013	50.11	50.04
2012	34.08	26.82

Total Assets: $72,050,266

Asset Allocation

Asset	%
Cash	0%
Stocks	100%
US Stocks	100%
Bonds	0%
US Bonds	0%
Other	0%

Services Offered: Dividend Investment Plan, CashInvestment Plan

Investment Strategy: The investment seeks to provide investment results that, before fees and expenses, correspond generally to the total return performance of the S&P Capital Markets Select Industry Index. The fund generally invests substantially all, but at least 80%, of its total assets in the securities comprising the index. The index represents the capital markets segment of the S&P Total Market Index ("S&P TMI") and tracks the performance of publicly traded companies that do business as broker-dealers, asset managers, trust and custody banks or exchanges. The fund is non-diversified. **Top Holdings:** MarketAxess Holdings Inc   Virtu Financial Inc A   Federated Investors Inc Class B   CME Group Inc Class A   Franklin Resources Inc

FlexShares Disciplined Duration MBS Index Fund   D+   SELL

Ticker	Traded On	NAV	Total Assets ($)	Dividend Yield (TTM)	Turnover Ratio	Expense Ratio
MBSD	NAS CM	22.92	$71,933,914	3.2		0.2

Ratings
Reward   D
Risk   C-
Recent Upgrade/Downgrade   Up

Fund Information
Fund Type   Exchange Traded Funds
Category   US Fixed Income
Sub-Category   Intermediate Government
Prospectus Objective   Income
Inception Date   Sep-14
Open to New Investments   Y

Prices
Price (as of 12/31/2018)   22.90
52-Week High   23.69
52-Week Low   22.69

Total Returns (%)

3-Month	6-Month	1-Year	3-Year	5-Year
1.17	1.08	0.07	2.09	

3-Year Standard Deviation   1.67
Effective Duration   4.38

Valuation
Premium/Discount (1-Year Average)   0.07

Company Information
Provider   Flexshares Trust
Manager/Tenure   Bradley Camden (4), James O'Shaughnessy (2)
Website   http://www.flexshares.com
Address   50 South LaSalle Street Chicago, Illinois 60603 Chicago Illinois 60603 United States
Phone Number   855-353-9383

PERFORMANCE

Ratings History

Date	Overall Rating	Risk Rating	Reward Rating
Q4-18	D+	C-	D
Q2-18	D+	D+	D
Q4-17	C	B-	C-
Q4-16	C-	D+	C-
Q4-15	U		

Asset & Performance History

Date	NAV	1-Year Total Return
2017	23.65	0.93
2016	24.14	1.06
2015	24.53	1.2
2014	25.08	
2013		
2012		

Total Assets: $71,933,914

Asset Allocation

Asset	%
Cash	3%
Stocks	0%
US Stocks	0%
Bonds	97%
US Bonds	97%
Other	0%

Services Offered:

Investment Strategy: The investment seeks investment results that correspond generally to the price and yield performance, before fees and expenses, of the BofA Merrill Lynch Constrained Duration US Mortgage Backed Securities IndexSM. The fund generally will invest under normal circumstances at least 80% of its total assets (exclusive of collateral held from securities lending) in the securities of the underlying index and in "TBA Transactions" that represent securities in the underlying index. The underlying index reflects the performance of a selection of investment-grade U.S. agency residential mortgage-backed pass-through securities. **Top Holdings:** Federal Home Loan Mortgage Corporation 6%   Government National Mortgage Association 4%   Federal National Mortgage Association 3%   Government National Mortgage Association 3%   Federal National Mortgage Association 3.5%

Reality Shares DIVS ETF

C- HOLD

Ticker	Traded On	NAV	Total Assets ($)	Dividend Yield (TTM)	Turnover Ratio	Expense Ratio
DIVY	NYSE Arca	25.23	$71,724,642	0.83	0	0.85

Ratings
Reward	C-
Risk	C-
Recent Upgrade/Downgrade	Down

Fund Information
Fund Type	Exchange Traded Funds
Category	Multialternative
Sub-Category	Multialternative
Prospectus Objective	Growth
Inception Date	Dec-14
Open to New Investments	Y

Prices
Price (as of 12/31/2018)	25.00
52-Week High	27.50
52-Week Low	24.84

Total Returns (%)
3-Month	6-Month	1-Year	3-Year	5-Year
-5.86	-4.52	-2.70	9.99	

3-Year Standard Deviation	4.46
Effective Duration	

Valuation
Premium/Discount (1-Year Average)	0.10

Company Information
Provider	Reality Shares ETF Trust
Manager/Tenure	Eric Ervin (3)
Website	http://www.realityshares.com
Address	Reality Shares ETF Trust 402 West Broadway, Suite 2800 San Diego CA 92101 United States
Phone Number	619-487-1445

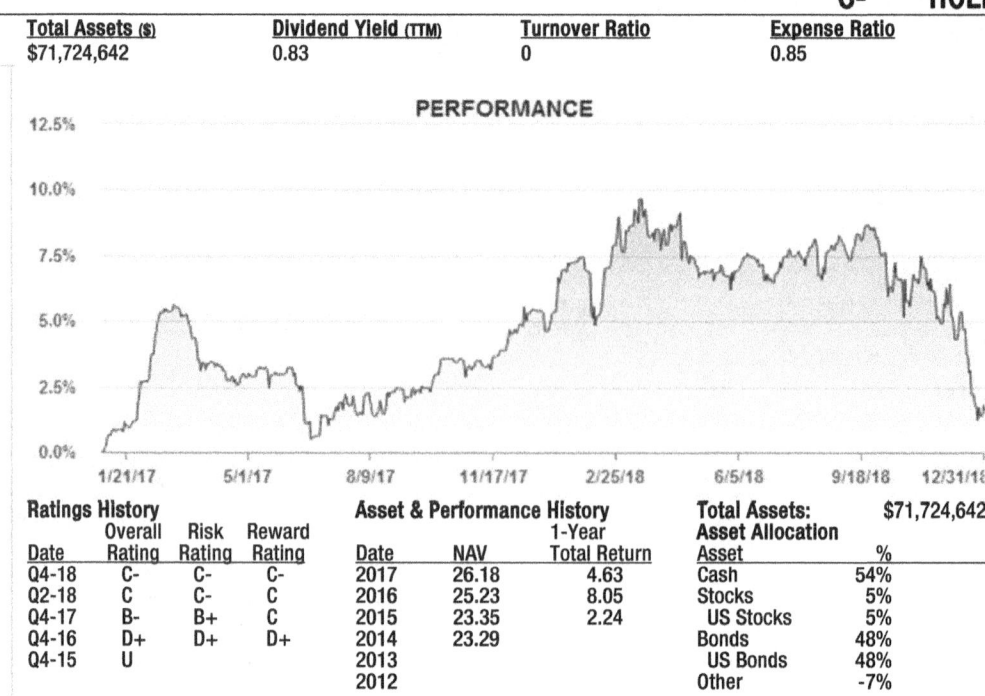

PERFORMANCE

Ratings History
Date	Overall Rating	Risk Rating	Reward Rating
Q4-18	C-	C-	C-
Q2-18	C	C-	C
Q4-17	B-	B+	C
Q4-16	D+	D+	D+
Q4-15	U		

Asset & Performance History
Date	NAV	1-Year Total Return
2017	26.18	4.63
2016	25.23	8.05
2015	23.35	2.24
2014	23.29	
2013		
2012		

Total Assets: $71,724,642
Asset Allocation
Asset	%
Cash	54%
Stocks	5%
US Stocks	5%
Bonds	48%
US Bonds	48%
Other	-7%

Services Offered:

Investment Strategy: The investment seeks to produce long-term capital appreciation. The fund's principal investment strategy is designed to provide exposure to the aggregate value of ordinary dividends expected to be paid on a portfolio of large capitalization equity securities listed for trading in the U.S. ("Large Cap Securities"). The fund may use a variety of investment strategies to achieve this objective. Under normal circumstances, it generally invests in a combination of dividend swaps, dividend futures and forwards on indexes of Large Cap Securities ("Large Cap Securities Indexes"). The fund is non-diversified. **Top Holdings:** Recv Bnppsp500 D18dvdswap Payb Bnppsp500 D18dvdswap Payb Bnppspx D21dvdswap Payb Bnppspx D22dvdswap Recv Bnppspx D21dvdswap

---

First Trust Global Wind Energy ETF

C- HOLD

Ticker	Traded On	NAV	Total Assets ($)	Dividend Yield (TTM)	Turnover Ratio	Expense Ratio
FAN	NYSE Arca	11.51	$71,594,777	2.06	22	0.6

Ratings
Reward	C-
Risk	C-
Recent Upgrade/Downgrade	

Fund Information
Fund Type	Exchange Traded Funds
Category	Utilities Sector Equity
Sub-Category	Miscellaneous Sector
Prospectus Objective	Natl Res
Inception Date	Jun-08
Open to New Investments	Y

Prices
Price (as of 12/31/2018)	11.46
52-Week High	14.07
52-Week Low	11.09

Total Returns (%)
3-Month	6-Month	1-Year	3-Year	5-Year
-6.65	-7.44	-11.12	13.06	19.51

3-Year Standard Deviation	14.84
Effective Duration	

Valuation
Premium/Discount (1-Year Average)	-0.11

Company Information
Provider	First Trust
Manager/Tenure	Jon C. Erickson (10), Daniel J. Lindquist (10), David G. McGarel (10), 3 others
Website	http://www.ftportfolios.com/
Address	First Trust 120 E. Liberty Drive, Suite 400 Wheaton IL 60187 United States
Phone Number	800-621-1675

PERFORMANCE

Ratings History
Date	Overall Rating	Risk Rating	Reward Rating
Q4-18	C-	C-	C-
Q2-18	C	C-	C
Q4-17	B-	B+	C
Q4-16	C	C-	C
Q4-15	C	C-	C

Asset & Performance History
Date	NAV	1-Year Total Return
2017	13.27	16.28
2016	11.72	4.31
2015	11.37	13.21
2014	10.28	-6.62
2013	11.27	64.53
2012	6.91	-12.22

Total Assets: $71,594,777
Asset Allocation
Asset	%
Cash	0%
Stocks	100%
US Stocks	14%
Bonds	0%
US Bonds	0%
Other	0%

Services Offered:

Investment Strategy: The investment seeks investment results that correspond generally to the price and yield (before the fund's fees and expenses) of an equity index called the ISE Clean Edge Global Wind Energy Index. The fund will normally invest at least 90% of its net assets (including investment borrowings) in common stocks or in depositary receipts representing securities in the index. The index provides a benchmark for investors interested in tracking public companies throughout the world that are active in the wind energy industry based on analysis of the products and services offered by those companies. The fund is non-diversified. **Top Holdings:** Vestas Wind Systems A/S Orsted A/S Siemens Gamesa Renewable Energy SA China Longyuan Power Group Corp Ltd H Boralex Inc Class A

NuShares Enhanced Yield U.S. Aggregate Bond ETF   D+   SELL

Ticker	Traded On	NAV	Total Assets ($)	Dividend Yield (TTM)	Turnover Ratio	Expense Ratio
NUAG	NYSE Arca	23.19	$71,200,369	3.93	123	0.2

Ratings
Reward   D+
Risk   D+
Recent Upgrade/Downgrade

Fund Information
Fund Type   Exchange Traded Funds
Category   US Fixed Income
Sub-Category   Intermediate-Term Bond
Prospectus Objective   Corp Bond - Gen
Inception Date   Sep-16
Open to New Investments   Y

Prices
Price (as of 12/31/2018)   23.18
52-Week High   24.46
52-Week Low   22.81

Total Returns (%)

3-Month	6-Month	1-Year	3-Year	5-Year
0.25	0.61	-1.86		

3-Year Standard Deviation
Effective Duration   6.29

Valuation
Premium/Discount (1-Year Average)   0.03

Company Information
Provider   Nuveen
Manager/Tenure   Lijun (Kevin) Chen (2), Yong (Mark) Zheng (0)
Website   http://www.nuveen.com
Address   Nuveen Investment Trust John Nuveen & Co. Inc. Chicago IL 60606 United States
Phone Number   312-917-8146

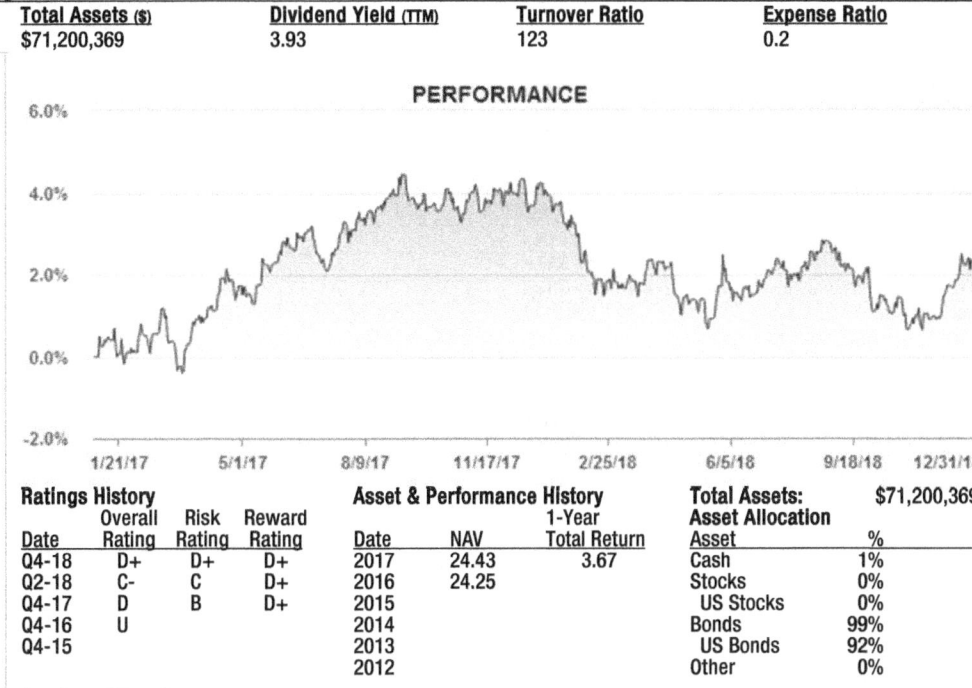

Ratings History

Date	Overall Rating	Risk Rating	Reward Rating
Q4-18	D+	D+	D+
Q2-18	C-	C	D+
Q4-17	D	B	D+
Q4-16	U		
Q4-15			

Asset & Performance History

Date	NAV	1-Year Total Return
2017	24.43	3.67
2016	24.25	
2015		
2014		
2013		
2012		

Total Assets: $71,200,369
Asset Allocation

Asset	%
Cash	1%
Stocks	0%
US Stocks	0%
Bonds	99%
US Bonds	92%
Other	0%

Services Offered:

Investment Strategy: The investment seeks to track the investment results, before fees and expenses, of the ICE BofAML Enhanced Yield US Broad Bond Index (the "index"). Under normal market conditions, the fund invests at least 80% of its assets, exclusive of collateral held from securities lending, in component securities of the index. The index consists of U.S. dollar-denominated, investment grade taxable debt securities with fixed rate coupons that have at least one year to final maturity. **Top Holdings:** United States Treasury Notes 2% United States Treasury Notes 1.75% Federal National Mortgage Association 4% Federal National Mortgage Association 3.5% Government National Mortgage Association 3.5%

WisdomTree Interest Rate Hedged U.S. Aggregate Bond Fund   C-   HOLD

Ticker	Traded On	NAV	Total Assets ($)	Dividend Yield (TTM)	Turnover Ratio	Expense Ratio
AGZD	NAS CM	47.24	$71,145,333	2.6	187	0.23

Ratings
Reward   C
Risk   C-
Recent Upgrade/Downgrade

Fund Information
Fund Type   Exchange Traded Funds
Category   Fixed Income Misc
Sub-Category   Nontraditional Bond
Prospectus Objective   Growth & Inc
Inception Date   Dec-13
Open to New Investments   Y

Prices
Price (as of 12/31/2018)   47.26
52-Week High   48.57
52-Week Low   47.26

Total Returns (%)

3-Month	6-Month	1-Year	3-Year	5-Year
-0.62	0.37	0.58	5.30	4.23

3-Year Standard Deviation   1.29
Effective Duration   0.35

Valuation
Premium/Discount (1-Year Average)   0.14

Company Information
Provider   WisdomTree
Manager/Tenure   Paul L. Benson (3), Stephanie Shu (3)
Website   http://www.wisdomtree.com
Address   WisdomTree 245 Park Avenue, 35th floor New York NY 10167 United States
Phone Number   866-909-9473

Ratings History

Date	Overall Rating	Risk Rating	Reward Rating
Q4-18	C-	C-	C
Q2-18	C-	D+	C
Q4-17	C+	B+	C
Q4-16	C-	D+	C-
Q4-15	D+	C-	D

Asset & Performance History

Date	NAV	1-Year Total Return
2017	48.2	2.55
2016	48.12	1.87
2015	48	-1.13
2014	49.36	0.12
2013	50.13	
2012		

Total Assets: $71,145,333
Asset Allocation

Asset	%
Cash	105%
Stocks	0%
US Stocks	0%
Bonds	-5%
US Bonds	-12%
Other	0%

Services Offered:

Investment Strategy: The investment seeks to track the price and yield performance, before fees and expenses, of the Bloomberg Barclays Rate Hedged U.S. Aggregate Bond Index, Zero Duration (the "index"). The index is designed to provide long exposure to the Bloomberg Barclays U.S. Aggregate Bond Index while seeking to manage interest rate risk through the use of short positions in U.S. Treasury securities. The fund normally invests at least 80% of its total assets in the component securities of the index and investments that have economic characteristics that are substantially identical to the economic characteristics of such component securities. It is non-diversified. **Top Holdings:** Us 5yr Note (Cbt) Mar19 Xcbt 20190329 Us 2yr Note (Cbt) Mar19 Xcbt 20190329 Us 10yr Ultra Fut Mar19 Xcbt 20190320 Us Ultra Bond Cbt Mar19 Xcbt 20190320 United States Treasury Notes 1.75%

Franklin FTSE Europe ETF

D **SELL**

Ticker	Traded On	NAV
FLEE	NYSE Arca	20.96

Total Assets ($)	Dividend Yield (TTM)	Turnover Ratio	Expense Ratio
$71,080,419	2.54	1	0.09

Ratings
Reward	D
Risk	D
Recent Upgrade/Downgrade	

Fund Information
Fund Type	Exchange Traded Funds
Category	Europe Equity Large Cap
Sub-Category	Europe Stock
Prospectus Objective	Foreign Stock
Inception Date	Nov-17
Open to New Investments	Y

Prices
Price (as of 12/31/2018)	20.95
52-Week High	27.21
52-Week Low	20.33

Total Returns (%)
3-Month	6-Month	1-Year	3-Year	5-Year
-12.75	-12.14	-14.80		

3-Year Standard Deviation
Effective Duration

Valuation
Premium/Discount (1-Year Average)	0.14

Company Information
Provider	Franklin Templeton Investments
Manager/Tenure	Louis Hsu (1), Dina Ting (1)
Website	http://www.franklintempleton.com
Address	Franklin Templeton Investments One Franklin Parkway, Building 970, 1st Floor San Mateo CA 94403 United States
Phone Number	650-312-2000

PERFORMANCE

Ratings History
Date	Overall Rating	Risk Rating	Reward Rating
Q4-18	D	D	D
Q2-18	U		
Q4-17	U		
Q4-16			
Q4-15			

Asset & Performance History
Date	NAV	1-Year Total Return
2017	25.47	
2016		
2015		
2014		
2013		
2012		

Total Assets: $71,080,419
Asset Allocation
Asset	%
Cash	1%
Stocks	98%
US Stocks	1%
Bonds	0%
US Bonds	0%
Other	0%

Services Offered:

Investment Strategy: The investment seeks to provide investment results that closely correspond, before fees and expenses, to the performance of the FTSE Developed Europe RIC Capped Index (the FTSE Developed Europe Capped Index). Under normal market conditions, the fund invests at least 80% of its assets in the component securities of the FTSE Developed Europe Capped Index and in depositary receipts representing such securities. The FTSE Developed Europe Capped Index is based on the FTSE Developed Europe Index and is designed to measure the performance of large- and mid-capitalization stocks from developed European countries. **Top Holdings:** Nestle SA Novartis AG Roche Holding AG Dividend Right Cert. HSBC Holdings PLC Total SA

Arrow Reserve Capital Management ETF

D **SELL**

Ticker	Traded On	NAV
ARCM	BATS	99.72

Total Assets ($)	Dividend Yield (TTM)	Turnover Ratio	Expense Ratio
$71,078,517	1.63	66	0.42

Ratings
Reward	D+
Risk	D
Recent Upgrade/Downgrade	

Fund Information
Fund Type	Exchange Traded Funds
Category	US Fixed Income
Sub-Category	Ultrashort Bond
Prospectus Objective	Growth & Inc
Inception Date	Mar-17
Open to New Investments	Y

Prices
Price (as of 12/31/2018)	99.65
52-Week High	100.76
52-Week Low	99.63

Total Returns (%)
3-Month	6-Month	1-Year	3-Year	5-Year
0.19	0.72	1.57		

3-Year Standard Deviation
Effective Duration

Valuation
Premium/Discount (1-Year Average)	-0.05

Company Information
Provider	ArrowShares
Manager/Tenure	Joseph Barrato (1), Steven Boyd (1), Adam Cohn (1), 3 others
Website	http://www.ArrowShares.com
Address	c/o Gemini Fund Services, LLC 17605 Wright Street, Suite 2 Omaha NE 68130 United States
Phone Number	877-277-6933

PERFORMANCE

Ratings History
Date	Overall Rating	Risk Rating	Reward Rating
Q4-18	D	D	D+
Q2-18	D	D	D+
Q4-17	U		
Q4-16			
Q4-15			

Asset & Performance History
Date	NAV	1-Year Total Return
2017	100.05	
2016		
2015		
2014		
2013		
2012		

Total Assets: $71,078,517
Asset Allocation
Asset	%
Cash	23%
Stocks	0%
US Stocks	0%
Bonds	77%
US Bonds	73%
Other	0%

Services Offered:

Investment Strategy: The investment seeks to preserve capital while maximizing current income. The fund invests in a variety of domestic fixed income securities. It will invest in fixed income instruments with a dollar-weighted average effective maturity of 0 to 2 years issued by U.S. Dollar-denominated issuers, including mortgage- or asset-backed securities, rated Baa- or higher by Moody's, or equivalently rated by S&P or Fitch, or, if unrated, determined by the Sub-Advisor. It may also invest in interest rate futures and forwards. The Sub-Advisor attempts to maximize income by identifying securities that offer an acceptable yield for a given level of credit risk and maturity. **Top Holdings:** Honeywell International Inc. 2.56% The Walt Disney Company 2.45% Bank of Montreal 3.09% Medtronic, Inc. 3.13% MARTIN MARIETTA MATERIALS INC 2.84%

iShares J.P. Morgan EM Corporate Bond ETF   D+   SELL

Ticker	Traded On	NAV	Total Assets ($)	Dividend Yield (TTM)	Turnover Ratio	Expense Ratio
CEMB	BATS	47.34	$71,072,646	4.49	62	0.5

Ratings
Reward   C-
Risk   D+
Recent Upgrade/Downgrade   Down

Fund Information
Fund Type   Exchange Traded Funds
Category   Emerging Mkts Fixed Inc
Sub-Category   Emerging Markets Bond
Prospectus Objective   Income
Inception Date   Apr-12
Open to New Investments   Y

Prices
Price (as of 12/31/2018)   47.47
52-Week High   51.40
52-Week Low   47.04

Total Returns (%)

3-Month	6-Month	1-Year	3-Year	5-Year
-0.25	0.85	-2.82	16.30	18.63

3-Year Standard Deviation   4.28
Effective Duration   4.93

Valuation
Premium/Discount (1-Year Average)   0.17

Company Information
Provider   iShares
Manager/Tenure James Mauro (6), Scott Radell (6)
Website   http://www.ishares.com
Address   iShares 400 Howard Street San
                Francisco CA 94105 United States
Phone Number   800-474-2737

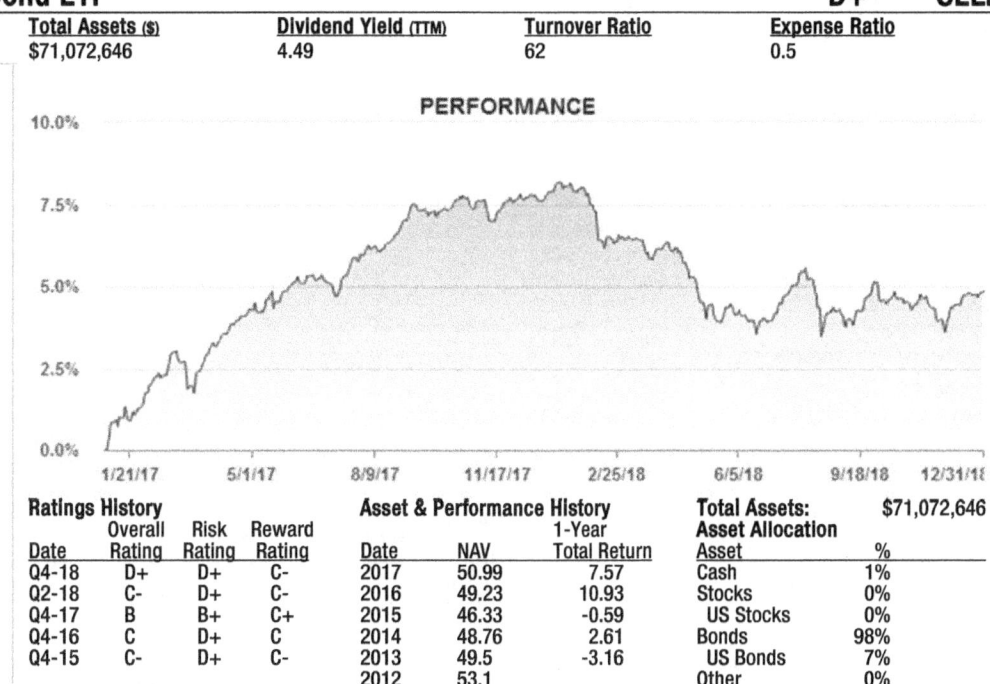

PERFORMANCE

Ratings History

Date	Overall Rating	Risk Rating	Reward Rating
Q4-18	D+	D+	C-
Q2-18	C-	D+	C-
Q4-17	B	B+	C+
Q4-16	C	D+	C
Q4-15	C-	D+	C-

Asset & Performance History

Date	NAV	1-Year Total Return
2017	50.99	7.57
2016	49.23	10.93
2015	46.33	-0.59
2014	48.76	2.61
2013	49.5	-3.16
2012	53.1	

Total Assets: $71,072,646
Asset Allocation

Asset	%
Cash	1%
Stocks	0%
US Stocks	0%
Bonds	98%
US Bonds	7%
Other	0%

Services Offered:

Investment Strategy: The investment seeks to track the investment results of the J.P. Morgan CEMBI Broad Diversified Core Index composed of U.S. dollar-denominated, emerging market corporate bonds. The fund generally will invest at least 90% of its assets in the component securities of the underlying index and may invest up to 10% of its assets in certain futures, options and swap contracts, cash and cash equivalents. The index tracks the performance of the U.S. dollar-denominated emerging market corporate bond market. **Top Holdings:** Saudi Electricity Global Sukuk Company 3 4%   First Quantum Minerals Ltd. 7.25%   CK Hutchison International (16) Limited 2.75%   Reliance Industries Limited 4.13%   Singtel Group Treasury Pte Ltd 3.25%

ERShares Entrepreneur 30 ETF   C+   HOLD

Ticker	Traded On	NAV	Total Assets ($)	Dividend Yield (TTM)	Turnover Ratio	Expense Ratio
ENTR	NYSE Arca	14.04	$71,040,552	0.08	32	0.49

Ratings
Reward   B
Risk   C-
Recent Upgrade/Downgrade

Fund Information
Fund Type   Exchange Traded Funds
Category   US Equity Large Cap Growth
Sub-Category   Large Growth
Prospectus Objective   Growth & Inc
Inception Date   Nov-17
Open to New Investments   Y

Prices
Price (as of 12/31/2018)   14.01
52-Week High   18.84
52-Week Low   13.02

Total Returns (%)

3-Month	6-Month	1-Year	3-Year	5-Year
-19.57	-14.63	-1.66		

3-Year Standard Deviation
Effective Duration

Valuation
Premium/Discount (1-Year Average)   0.23

Company Information
Provider   EntrepreneurShares
Manager/Tenure Joel M. Shulman (1)
Website   http://www.ershares.com
Address   EntrepreneurShares 175 Federal
                Street, Suite #875 Boston MA 02110
                United States
Phone Number

PERFORMANCE

Ratings History

Date	Overall Rating	Risk Rating	Reward Rating
Q4-18	C+	C-	B
Q2-18	U		
Q4-17	U		
Q4-16			
Q4-15			

Asset & Performance History

Date	NAV	1-Year Total Return
2017	15.26	
2016		
2015		
2014		
2013		
2012		

Total Assets: $71,040,552
Asset Allocation

Asset	%
Cash	1%
Stocks	99%
US Stocks	99%
Bonds	0%
US Bonds	0%
Other	0%

Services Offered:

Investment Strategy: The investment seeks investment results that correspond (before fees and expenses) generally to the performance of its underlying index, the Entrepreneur 30 Index. Under normal circumstances, the fund will invest at least 80% of its net assets, plus any borrowings for investment purposes, in securities of companies included in the Entrepreneur 30 Index. The index comprises 30 U.S. Companies with the highest market capitalizations and composite scores based on six criteria. The fund is non-diversified. **Top Holdings:** Amazon.com Inc   Facebook Inc A   Alphabet Inc A   FedEx Corp   Microchip Technology Inc

SPDR® MSCI EAFE Fossil Fuel Free ETF   D   SELL

Ticker	Traded On	NAV	Total Assets ($)	Dividend Yield (TTM)	Turnover Ratio	Expense Ratio
EFAX	NYSE Arca	60.53	$71,008,490	2.5	5	0.2

Ratings

Reward	D
Risk	D
Recent Upgrade/Downgrade	Down

Fund Information

Fund Type	Exchange Traded Funds
Category	Global Equity Large Cap
Sub-Category	Foreign Large Blend
Prospectus Objective	Growth & Inc
Inception Date	Oct-16
Open to New Investments	Y

Prices

Price (as of 12/31/2018)	60.41
52-Week High	77.72
52-Week Low	58.71

Total Returns (%)

3-Month	6-Month	1-Year	3-Year	5-Year
-12.30	-9.98	-14.35		

3-Year Standard Deviation	
Effective Duration	

Valuation

Premium/Discount (1-Year Average)	0.41

Company Information

Provider	SPDR State Street Global Advisors
Manager/Tenure	Michael J. Feehily (2), Karl A. Schneider (2), John Law (0)
Website	http://www.spdrs.com
Address	SPDR State Street Global Advisors State Street Financial Center, 1 Lincoln Street Boston MA 02111-2900 United States
Phone Number	617-786-3000

PERFORMANCE

Ratings History

Date	Overall Rating	Risk Rating	Reward Rating
Q4-18	D	D	D
Q2-18	D+	D+	D+
Q4-17	D	A	D+
Q4-16	U		
Q4-15			

Asset & Performance History

Date	NAV	1-Year Total Return
2017	72.65	24.69
2016	60.06	
2015		
2014		
2013		
2012		

Total Assets: $71,008,490

Asset Allocation

Asset	%
Cash	0%
Stocks	100%
US Stocks	1%
Bonds	0%
US Bonds	0%
Other	0%

Services Offered:

Investment Strategy: The investment seeks to provide investment results that, before fees and expenses, correspond generally to the total return performance of the MSCI EAFE ex Fossil Fuels Index. Under normal market conditions, the fund generally invests substantially all, but at least 80%, of its total assets in the securities comprising the index and in depositary receipts based on securities comprising the index. The index is designed to measure the performance of companies in the MSCI EAFE Index that are "fossil fuel reserves free," which are defined as companies that do not own fossil fuel reserves. The fund is non-diversified. **Top Holdings:** Nestle SA Novartis AG Roche Holding AG Dividend Right Cert. HSBC Holdings PLC Toyota Motor Corp

PIMCO RAFI Dynamic Multi-Factor U.S. Equity ETF   D+   SELL

Ticker	Traded On	NAV	Total Assets ($)	Dividend Yield (TTM)	Turnover Ratio	Expense Ratio
MFUS	NYSE Arca	25.21	$70,951,032	1.83	56	0.29

Ratings

Reward	D+
Risk	D+
Recent Upgrade/Downgrade	

Fund Information

Fund Type	Exchange Traded Funds
Category	US Equity Large Cap Blend
Sub-Category	Large Blend
Prospectus Objective	Growth & Inc
Inception Date	Aug-17
Open to New Investments	Y

Prices

Price (as of 12/31/2018)	25.21
52-Week High	30.12
52-Week Low	24.14

Total Returns (%)

3-Month	6-Month	1-Year	3-Year	5-Year
-14.79	-9.22	-6.58		

3-Year Standard Deviation	
Effective Duration	

Valuation

Premium/Discount (1-Year Average)	0.18

Company Information

Provider	PIMCO
Manager/Tenure	Thomas C. Seto (1)
Website	http://www.pimco.com
Address	PIMCO 840 Newport Center Drive, Suite 100 Newport Beach CA 92660 United States
Phone Number	866-746-2602

PERFORMANCE

Ratings History

Date	Overall Rating	Risk Rating	Reward Rating
Q4-18	D+	D+	D+
Q2-18	U		
Q4-17	U		
Q4-16			
Q4-15			

Asset & Performance History

Date	NAV	1-Year Total Return
2017	27.5	
2016		
2015		
2014		
2013		
2012		

Total Assets: $70,951,032

Asset Allocation

Asset	%
Cash	1%
Stocks	99%
US Stocks	98%
Bonds	0%
US Bonds	0%
Other	0%

Services Offered:

Investment Strategy: The investment seeks to track the investment results of the RAFI Dynamic Multi-Factor U.S. Index. The fund seeks to achieve its investment objective by investing at least 80% of its total assets (exclusive of collateral held from securities lending) in the component securities of the RAFI Dynamic Multi-Factor U.S. Index. The underlying index is constructed by RAFI Indices, LLC (the "index provider") using a rules-based approach to construct factor portfolios within the underlying index. The underlying index consists of "factor portfolios," each of which emphasizes one of the following factors: value, low volatility, quality, momentum and size. **Top Holdings:** Apple Inc Walmart Inc Verizon Communications Inc CVS Health Corp International Business Machines Corp

iPath® Bloomberg Coffee Subindex Total Return(SM) ETN   D-   SELL

Ticker	Traded On	NAV	Total Assets ($)	Dividend Yield (TTM)	Turnover Ratio	Expense Ratio
JJOFF	OTC BB		$70,881,811	0	0	0.75

Ratings
Reward	D-
Risk	D
Recent Upgrade/Downgrade	

Fund Information
Fund Type	Exchange Traded Funds
Category	Commodities Specified
Sub-Category	Commodities Agriculture
Prospectus Objective	Natl Res
Inception Date	Jun-08
Open to New Investments	Y

Prices
Price (as of 12/31/2018)	10.71
52-Week High	16.31
52-Week Low	10.35

Total Returns (%)
3-Month	6-Month	1-Year	3-Year	5-Year
-4.96	-17.29	-32.41	-46.44	-50.86

3-Year Standard Deviation	26.95
Effective Duration	

Valuation
Premium/Discount (1-Year Average)	-0.40

Company Information
Provider	Milleis Investissements Funds
Manager/Tenure	No Manager (10)
Website	
Address	2-4, rue Eugène Ruppert L-2453
	Luxembourg Luxembourg L-2453
	Luxembourg
Phone Number	

PERFORMANCE

Ratings History
Date	Overall Rating	Risk Rating	Reward Rating
Q4-18	D-	D	D-
Q2-18	D-	D-	D-
Q4-17	D-	D-	D-
Q4-16	C-	D+	C
Q4-15	D-	D-	D-

Asset & Performance History
Date	NAV	1-Year Total Return
2017	15.77	-18.82
2016	19.44	-0.98
2015	19.91	-34.34
2014	30.32	39.72
2013	21.7	-32.71
2012	32.25	-43.11

Total Assets: $70,881,811
Asset Allocation
Asset	%
Cash	%
Stocks	%
US Stocks	%
Bonds	%
US Bonds	%
Other	%

Services Offered:

Investment Strategy: The investment seeks to provide investors with exposure to the Dow Jones-UBS Coffee Subindex Total ReturnService Mark.
The Dow Jones-UBS Coffee Subindex Total ReturnService Mark (the "index") reflects the returns that are potentially available through an unleveraged investment in the futures contracts on coffee. The index currently consists of one futures contract on the commodity of coffee which is included in the Dow Jones-UBS Commodity Index Total ReturnService. **Top Holdings:**

Invesco Dynamic Networking ETF   C   HOLD

Ticker	Traded On	NAV	Total Assets ($)	Dividend Yield (TTM)	Turnover Ratio	Expense Ratio
PXQ	NYSE Arca	48.44	$70,627,002	0.46	79	0.63

Ratings
Reward	B-
Risk	D+
Recent Upgrade/Downgrade	Down

Fund Information
Fund Type	Exchange Traded Funds
Category	Technology Sector Equity
Sub-Category	Technology
Prospectus Objective	Technology
Inception Date	Jun-05
Open to New Investments	Y

Prices
Price (as of 12/31/2018)	48.37
52-Week High	58.89
52-Week Low	45.28

Total Returns (%)
3-Month	6-Month	1-Year	3-Year	5-Year
-14.82	-8.37	6.36	43.98	57.16

3-Year Standard Deviation	15.48
Effective Duration	

Valuation
Premium/Discount (1-Year Average)	0.16

Company Information
Provider	Invesco
Manager/Tenure	Peter Hubbard (11), Michael Jeanette (10), Tony Seisser (4), 1 other
Website	http://www.invesco.com/us
Address	Invesco 11 Greenway Plaza, Ste. 2500
	Houston TX 77046 United States
Phone Number	800-659-1005

PERFORMANCE

Ratings History
Date	Overall Rating	Risk Rating	Reward Rating
Q4-18	C	D+	B-
Q2-18	C+	D+	B
Q4-17	B	B	B
Q4-16	C	C-	C
Q4-15	C+	C	B

Asset & Performance History
Date	NAV	1-Year Total Return
2017	46.09	14.89
2016	40.39	17.82
2015	34.46	-0.94
2014	34.79	10.19
2013	31.57	25.05
2012	25.42	4.85

Total Assets: $70,627,002
Asset Allocation
Asset	%
Cash	0%
Stocks	100%
US Stocks	100%
Bonds	0%
US Bonds	0%
Other	0%

Services Offered:

Investment Strategy: The investment seeks to track the investment results (before fees and expenses) of the Dynamic Networking IntellidexSM Index. The fund generally will invest at least 90% of its total assets in common stocks of networking companies that comprise the underlying intellidex. The underlying intellidex was composed of common stocks of 30 U.S. networking companies. These are companies that are principally engaged in the development, manufacture, sale or distribution of products, services or technologies that support the flow of electronic information, including voice, data, images and commercial transactions. It is non-diversified. **Top Holdings:** VMware Inc Motorola Solutions Inc Cisco Systems Inc Amphenol Corp Class A Qualcomm Inc

Invesco Chinese Yuan Dim Sum Bond ETF
D+ **SELL**

Ticker	Traded On	NAV	Total Assets ($)	Dividend Yield (TTM)	Turnover Ratio	Expense Ratio
DSUM	NYSE Arca	21.86	$70,444,051	4.17	60	0.45

Ratings
Reward	D+
Risk	C-
Recent Upgrade/Downgrade	Down

Fund Information
Fund Type	Exchange Traded Funds
Category	Emerging Mkts Fixed Inc
Sub-Category	Emerging-Markets Local-Currency Bond
Prospectus Objective	Worldwide Bond
Inception Date	Sep-11
Open to New Investments	Y

Prices
Price (as of 12/31/2018)	21.62
52-Week High	24.65
52-Week Low	21.23

Total Returns (%)
3-Month	6-Month	1-Year	3-Year	5-Year
0.86	-2.34	-3.12	6.30	2.63

3-Year Standard Deviation	5.42
Effective Duration	1.80

Valuation
Premium/Discount (1-Year Average)	-0.49

Company Information
Provider	Invesco
Manager/Tenure	Philip Fang (7), Peter Hubbard (7), Jeffrey W. Kernagis (7), 2 others
Website	http://www.invesco.com/us
Address	Invesco 11 Greenway Plaza, Ste. 2500 Houston TX 77046 United States
Phone Number	800-659-1005

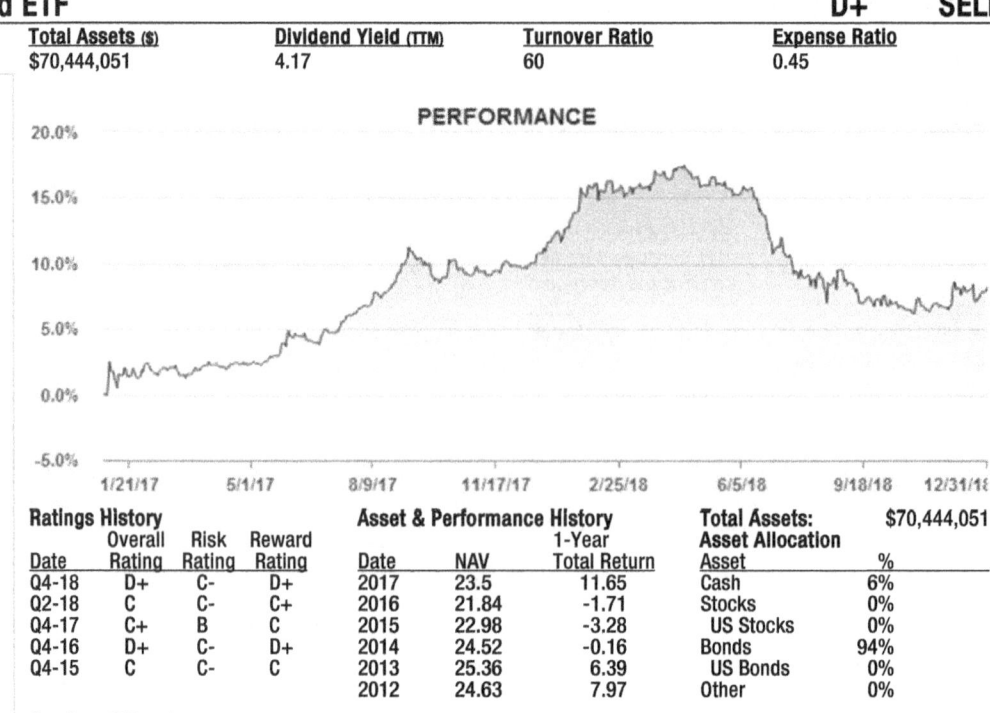

Ratings History

Date	Overall Rating	Risk Rating	Reward Rating
Q4-18	D+	C-	D+
Q2-18	C	C-	C+
Q4-17	C+	B	C
Q4-16	D+	C-	D+
Q4-15	C	C-	C

Asset & Performance History

Date	NAV	1-Year Total Return
2017	23.5	11.65
2016	21.84	-1.71
2015	22.98	-3.28
2014	24.52	-0.16
2013	25.36	6.39
2012	24.63	7.97

Total Assets: $70,444,051
Asset Allocation

Asset	%
Cash	6%
Stocks	0%
US Stocks	0%
Bonds	94%
US Bonds	0%
Other	0%

Services Offered:

Investment Strategy: The investment seeks to track the investment results (before fees and expenses) of the FTSE Custom Dim Sum (Offshore CNY) Bond Index (the "underlying index"). The fund generally invests at least 80% of its total assets in Chinese Renminbi ("RMB")-denominated bonds that comprise the underlying index. The underlying index measures the performance of RMB-denominated "Dim Sum" bonds that are issued and settled outside of mainland China. Dim Sum bonds are RMB-denominated and generally are issued in Hong Kong by a variety of entities ranging from governments to corporations. **Top Holdings:** Lenovo Group Ltd 4.95% Commonwealth Bank of Australia 4.2% Sinochem Offshore Capital Company Ltd. 4.4% Chongqing Grain Group Co., Ltd 4.02% CNI CAPITAL LIMITED 4.3%

Invesco Russell 2000 Pure Value ETF
C- **HOLD**

Ticker	Traded On	NAV	Total Assets ($)	Dividend Yield (TTM)	Turnover Ratio	Expense Ratio
PXSV	NYSE Arca	26.42	$70,015,766	2.29	56	0.39

Ratings
Reward	C-
Risk	D+
Recent Upgrade/Downgrade	Down

Fund Information
Fund Type	Exchange Traded Funds
Category	US Equity Small Cap
Sub-Category	Small Value
Prospectus Objective	Growth
Inception Date	Mar-05
Open to New Investments	Y

Prices
Price (as of 12/31/2018)	26.39
52-Week High	33.59
52-Week Low	25.28

Total Returns (%)
3-Month	6-Month	1-Year	3-Year	5-Year
-16.89	-16.92	-11.81	23.29	18.25

3-Year Standard Deviation	16.06
Effective Duration	

Valuation
Premium/Discount (1-Year Average)	0.11

Company Information
Provider	Invesco
Manager/Tenure	Peter Hubbard (11), Michael Jeanette (10), Jonathan Nixon (5), 2 others
Website	http://www.invesco.com/us
Address	Invesco 11 Greenway Plaza, Ste. 2500 Houston TX 77046 United States
Phone Number	800-659-1005

Ratings History

Date	Overall Rating	Risk Rating	Reward Rating
Q4-18	C-	D+	C-
Q2-18	C	D+	C+
Q4-17	B	B-	B
Q4-16	C-	D+	C-
Q4-15	C	D+	C

Asset & Performance History

Date	NAV	1-Year Total Return
2017	30.66	3.16
2016	30.3	35.52
2015	22.93	-8.84
2014	25.81	5.22
2013	24.86	44.14
2012	17.47	21.28

Total Assets: $70,015,766
Asset Allocation

Asset	%
Cash	0%
Stocks	100%
US Stocks	98%
Bonds	0%
US Bonds	0%
Other	0%

Services Offered:

Investment Strategy: The investment seeks to track the investment results (before fees and expenses) of the Russell 2000® Pure Value Index (the "underlying index"). The fund generally will invest at least 90% of its total assets in the component securities that comprise the underlying index. The underlying index is composed of a subset of securities from the Russell 2000® Index, which is composed of the smallest 2,000 securities of the Russell 3000® Index, an index designed to measure the performance of the largest 3,000 companies in the U.S. equity market. **Top Holdings:** Iridium Communications Inc Natural Grocers by Vitamin Cottage Inc Mallinckrodt PLC Genworth Financial Inc Esterline Technologies Corp

---

Strategy Shares EcoLogical Strategy ETF   C   HOLD

Ticker	Traded On	NAV	Total Assets ($)	Dividend Yield (TTM)	Turnover Ratio	Expense Ratio
HECO	NYSE Arca	39.31	$70,010,964	1.03	16	0.98

Ratings
Reward	C
Risk	C-
Recent Upgrade/Downgrade	

Fund Information
Fund Type	Exchange Traded Funds
Category	Equity Misc
Sub-Category	Miscellaneous Sector
Prospectus Objective	Growth
Inception Date	Jun-12
Open to New Investments	Y

Prices
Price (as of 12/31/2018)	39.24
52-Week High	44.36
52-Week Low	39.06

Total Returns (%)
3-Month	6-Month	1-Year	3-Year	5-Year
-9.39	-3.08	-3.27	31.80	43.66

3-Year Standard Deviation	9.28
Effective Duration	

Valuation
Premium/Discount (1-Year Average)	0.38

Company Information
Provider	Strategy shares
Manager/Tenure	Matthew B. Tuttle (0)
Website	
Address	Strategy shares United States
Phone Number	

PERFORMANCE

Ratings History

Date	Overall Rating	Risk Rating	Reward Rating
Q4-18	C	C-	C
Q2-18	C	D+	C+
Q4-17	B-	B	B-
Q4-16	D+	D+	D+
Q4-15	C	D	C

Asset & Performance History

Date	NAV	1-Year Total Return
2017	41.47	20.85
2016	36.34	12.05
2015	35.48	0.95
2014	36.61	7.95
2013	34.34	29.57
2012	26.77	

Total Assets: $70,010,964

Asset Allocation

Asset	%
Cash	40%
Stocks	60%
US Stocks	52%
Bonds	0%
US Bonds	0%
Other	0%

Services Offered:

Investment Strategy: The investment seeks capital appreciation. The fund is an actively managed exchange-traded fund ("ETF") and, under normal conditions, will invest at least 80% of its net assets (plus borrowings for investment purposes), directly or indirectly through mutual funds and ETFs, in the equity and fixed income securities of ecologically-focused companies and/or green bonds. It may also invest up to 20% of its net assets in cash and cash equivalents including U.S. government securities. The fund may invest in domestic and foreign securities of companies of any market capitalization. **Top Holdings:** Humana Inc   W.W. Grainger Inc   Nike Inc B   Anthem Inc   Union Pacific Corp

---

Invesco DWA Utilities Momentum ETF   B   BUY

Ticker	Traded On	NAV	Total Assets ($)	Dividend Yield (TTM)	Turnover Ratio	Expense Ratio
PUI	NAS CM	28.91	$69,831,641	2.27	41	0.6

Ratings
Reward	B
Risk	C+
Recent Upgrade/Downgrade	Up

Fund Information
Fund Type	Exchange Traded Funds
Category	Utilities Sector Equity
Sub-Category	Utilities
Prospectus Objective	Utility
Inception Date	Oct-05
Open to New Investments	Y

Prices
Price (as of 12/31/2018)	28.96
52-Week High	31.29
52-Week Low	24.57

Total Returns (%)
3-Month	6-Month	1-Year	3-Year	5-Year
1.57	4.92	6.10	41.06	60.02

3-Year Standard Deviation	12.27
Effective Duration	

Valuation
Premium/Discount (1-Year Average)	0.04

Company Information
Provider	Invesco
Manager/Tenure	Peter Hubbard (11), Michael Jeanette (10), Tony Seisser (4), 1 other
Website	http://www.invesco.com/us
Address	Invesco 11 Greenway Plaza, Ste. 2500 Houston TX 77046 United States
Phone Number	800-659-1005

PERFORMANCE

Ratings History

Date	Overall Rating	Risk Rating	Reward Rating
Q4-18	B	C+	B
Q2-18	B-	C	B
Q4-17	B-	B	B-
Q4-16	B-	C	B
Q4-15	B	C+	B

Asset & Performance History

Date	NAV	1-Year Total Return
2017	27.79	11.64
2016	25.63	19.07
2015	22.25	-2.98
2014	23.61	16.92
2013	20.64	21.93
2012	17.39	10.04

Total Assets: $69,831,641

Asset Allocation

Asset	%
Cash	0%
Stocks	100%
US Stocks	100%
Bonds	0%
US Bonds	0%
Other	0%

Services Offered:

Investment Strategy: The investment seeks to track the investment results (before fees and expenses) of the Dorsey Wright® Utilities Technical Leaders Index (the "underlying index"). The fund generally will invest at least 90% of its total assets in the securities that comprise the underlying index. The underlying index is composed of at least 30 securities of companies in the utilities sector that have powerful relative strength or "momentum" characteristics. **Top Holdings:** Xcel Energy Inc   NRG Energy Inc   American Water Works Co Inc   DTE Energy Co   Pinnacle West Capital Corp

SPDR® ICE BofAML Crossover Corporate Bond ETF — D+ SELL

Ticker	Traded On	NAV		Total Assets ($)	Dividend Yield (TTM)	Turnover Ratio	Expense Ratio
CJNK	NYSE Arca	24.62		$69,632,420	4.25	24	0.3

Ratings
Reward — C-
Risk — D+
Recent Upgrade/Downgrade — Down

Fund Information
Fund Type — Exchange Traded Funds
Category — US Fixed Income
Sub-Category — Corporate Bond
Prospectus Objective — Corp Bond-High Yld
Inception Date — Jun-12
Open to New Investments — Y

Prices
Price (as of 12/31/2018) — 24.69
52-Week High — 26.58
52-Week Low — 24.47

Total Returns (%)

3-Month	6-Month	1-Year	3-Year	5-Year
-1.87	-0.11	-2.80	14.36	18.91

3-Year Standard Deviation — 3.75
Effective Duration — 5.41

Valuation
Premium/Discount (1-Year Average) — 0.13

Company Information
Provider — SPDR State Street Global Advisors
Manager/Tenure — Michael J. Brunell (6), Kyle Kelly (5), Bradley J. Sullivan (3)
Website — http://www.spdrs.com
Address — SPDR State Street Global Advisors State Street Financial Center, 1 Lincoln Street Boston MA 02111-2900 United States
Phone Number — 617-786-3000

PERFORMANCE

Ratings History

Date	Overall Rating	Risk Rating	Reward Rating
Q4-18	D+	D+	C-
Q2-18	C-	C-	C
Q4-17	B-	B+	C+
Q4-16	C	D+	C
Q4-15	C-	D+	C-

Asset & Performance History

Date	NAV	1-Year Total Return
2017	26.36	5.83
2016	25.86	10.42
2015	24.45	-1.94
2014	25.97	6.04
2013	25.47	1.06
2012	26.31	

Total Assets: $69,632,420

Asset Allocation

Asset	%
Cash	1%
Stocks	0%
US Stocks	0%
Bonds	98%
US Bonds	85%
Other	0%

Services Offered:

Investment Strategy: The investment seeks investment results that, before fees and expenses, correspond generally to the price and yield performance of the ICE BofAML US Diversified Crossover Corporate Index. The fund invests substantially all, but at least 80%, of its total assets in the securities comprising the index or in securities that the Adviser determines have economic characteristics that are substantially identical to the economic characteristics of the securities that comprise the index. The index is designed to measure the performance of U.S. dollar denominated BBB and BB corporate debt publicly issued in the U.S. domestic market. The fund is non-diversified. **Top Holdings:** Verizon Communications Inc. 4.33% Ally Financial Inc. 5.75% HCA Inc. 5.88% The AES Corporation 6% Bausch Health Companies Inc 6.5%

ProShares UltraShort Russell2000 — D SELL

Ticker	Traded On	NAV		Total Assets ($)	Dividend Yield (TTM)	Turnover Ratio	Expense Ratio
TWM	NYSE Arca	20.58		$69,583,175	0.61	0	0.95

Ratings
Reward — D-
Risk — D
Recent Upgrade/Downgrade

Fund Information
Fund Type — Exchange Traded Funds
Category — Trading Tools
Sub-Category — Trading--Inverse Equity
Prospectus Objective — Small Company
Inception Date — Jan-07
Open to New Investments — Y

Prices
Price (as of 12/31/2018) — 20.62
52-Week High — 23.50
52-Week Low — 13.04

Total Returns (%)

3-Month	6-Month	1-Year	3-Year	5-Year
46.88	43.09	18.95	-47.01	-56.78

3-Year Standard Deviation — 28.88
Effective Duration —

Valuation
Premium/Discount (1-Year Average) — -0.02

Company Information
Provider — ProShares
Manager/Tenure — Michael Neches (5), Devin Sullivan (0)
Website — http://www.proshares.com
Address — ProShares 7501 Wisconsin Avenue, Suite 1000 Bethesda MD 20814 United States
Phone Number — 866-776-5125

PERFORMANCE

Ratings History

Date	Overall Rating	Risk Rating	Reward Rating
Q4-18	D	D	D-
Q2-18	D	D-	E+
Q4-17	E+	E+	E+
Q4-16	D	D	D-
Q4-15	D	E+	D-

Asset & Performance History

Date	NAV	1-Year Total Return
2017	17.46	-26.51
2016	23.77	-39.39
2015	39.22	-1.03
2014	39.63	-17.57
2013	48.08	-52.5
2012	101.24	-34.15

Total Assets: $69,583,175

Asset Allocation

Asset	%
Cash	208%
Stocks	-108%
US Stocks	-108%
Bonds	0%
US Bonds	0%
Other	0%

Services Offered:

Investment Strategy: The investment seeks daily investment results that correspond to two times the inverse (-2x) of the daily performance of the Russell 2000® Index. The fund invests in financial instruments that ProShare Advisors believes, in combination, should produce daily returns consistent with the fund's investment objective. The index is a measure of small-cap U.S. stock market performance. The fund is non-diversified. **Top Holdings:** Russell 2000 Index Swap Morgan Stanley & Co. International Plc Russell 2000 Index Swap Citibank, N.A. United States Treasury Bills United States Treasury Bills Russell 2000 Index Swap Deutsche Bank Ag

UBS ETRACS 2xMonthly Leveraged Alerian MLP Infrastructure Index ETN SeriesB   D   SELL

Ticker	Traded On	NAV	Total Assets ($)	Dividend Yield (TTM)	Turnover Ratio	Expense Ratio
MLPQ	NYSE Arca	23.33	$69,574,073	18.03		0.85

Ratings
Reward	D
Risk	D
Recent Upgrade/Downgrade	Down

Fund Information
Fund Type	Exchange Traded Funds
Category	Trading Tools
Sub-Category	Trading--Leveraged Equity
Prospectus Objective	Growth & Inc
Inception Date	Feb-16
Open to New Investments	Y

Prices
Price (as of 12/31/2018)	23.33
52-Week High	44.09
52-Week Low	21.00

Total Returns (%)
3-Month	6-Month	1-Year	3-Year	5-Year
-34.14	-20.86	-28.16		

3-Year Standard Deviation	
Effective Duration	

Valuation
Premium/Discount (1-Year Average)	0.21

Company Information
Provider	UBS Group AG
Manager/Tenure	No Manager (2)
Website	http://www.ubs.com
Address	Bahnhofstrasse 45 Zurich 8098 Switzerland
Phone Number	412-037-1952

PERFORMANCE

Ratings History
Date	Overall Rating	Risk Rating	Reward Rating
Q4-18	D	D	D
Q2-18	D	D	D
Q4-17	D	D	D
Q4-16	U		
Q4-15			

Asset & Performance History
Date	NAV	1-Year Total Return
2017	37.66	-19.42
2016	53.92	
2015		
2014		
2013		
2012		

Total Assets: $69,574,073

Asset Allocation
Asset	%
Cash	%
Stocks	%
US Stocks	%
Bonds	%
US Bonds	%
Other	%

Services Offered:

Investment Strategy: The investment seeks to provide two times leveraged long exposure to the compounded monthly performance of the Alerian MLP Infrastructure Index (the "index").
The index, comprising 22 energy infrastructure master limited partnerships, is a subset of the Alerian MLP Infrastructure Index. The index constituent securities earn the majority of their cash flow from the transportation, storage, and processing of energy commodities. **Top Holdings:**

WisdomTree Emerging Markets Quality Dividend Growth Fund   C-   HOLD

Ticker	Traded On	NAV	Total Assets ($)	Dividend Yield (TTM)	Turnover Ratio	Expense Ratio
DGRE	NAS CM	22.37	$69,473,191	2.14	62	0.32

Ratings
Reward	C-
Risk	C-
Recent Upgrade/Downgrade	

Fund Information
Fund Type	Exchange Traded Funds
Category	Global Emerg Mkts Equity
Sub-Category	Diversified Emerging Mkts
Prospectus Objective	Div Emerg Mkts
Inception Date	Aug-13
Open to New Investments	Y

Prices
Price (as of 12/31/2018)	22.22
52-Week High	28.90
52-Week Low	21.16

Total Returns (%)
3-Month	6-Month	1-Year	3-Year	5-Year
-6.41	-8.03	-15.19	23.12	3.60

3-Year Standard Deviation	13.84
Effective Duration	

Valuation
Premium/Discount (1-Year Average)	0.01

Company Information
Provider	WisdomTree
Manager/Tenure	Richard A. Brown (5), Thomas J. Durante (5), Karen Q. Wong (5)
Website	http://www.wisdomtree.com
Address	WisdomTree 245 Park Avenue, 35th floor New York NY 10167 United States
Phone Number	866-909-9473

PERFORMANCE

Ratings History
Date	Overall Rating	Risk Rating	Reward Rating
Q4-18	C-	C-	C-
Q2-18	C-	C-	C
Q4-17	C+	C	B-
Q4-16	D+	D+	D+
Q4-15	D	D	D

Asset & Performance History
Date	NAV	1-Year Total Return
2017	27.05	29.9
2016	21.3	11.12
2015	19.66	-16.86
2014	24.3	1.21
2013	24.57	
2012		

Total Assets: $69,473,191

Asset Allocation
Asset	%
Cash	0%
Stocks	99%
US Stocks	0%
Bonds	0%
US Bonds	0%
Other	0%

Services Offered:

Investment Strategy: The investment seeks income and capital appreciation. The fund seeks to achieve its investment objective by investing primarily in emerging market dividend-paying common stocks with growth characteristics. The adviser, using a disciplined model-based process focused on a long-term approach to investing, seeks to identify dividend-paying companies with strong corporate profitability and sustainable growth characteristics. The fund is non-diversified. **Top Holdings:** Tencent Holdings Ltd Taiwan Semiconductor Manufacturing Co Ltd Samsung Electronics Co Ltd China Mobile Ltd Ping An Insurance (Group) Co. of China Ltd H

Invesco Insider Sentiment ETF   C-   HOLD

Ticker	Traded On	NAV	Total Assets ($)	Dividend Yield (TTM)	Turnover Ratio	Expense Ratio
NFO	NYSE Arca	56.63	$69,072,117	1.46		0.6

Ratings
Reward   C
Risk   D+
Recent Upgrade/Downgrade   Down

Fund Information
Fund Type   Exchange Traded Funds
Category   US Equity Mid Cap
Sub-Category   Mid-Cap Blend
Prospectus Objective   Growth
Inception Date   Sep-06
Open to New Investments   Y

Prices
Price (as of 12/31/2018)   56.52
52-Week High   67.06
52-Week Low   53.28

Total Returns (%)

3-Month	6-Month	1-Year	3-Year	5-Year
-13.95	-11.07	-7.35	27.38	29.86

3-Year Standard Deviation   10.49
Effective Duration

Valuation
Premium/Discount (1-Year Average)   0.18

Company Information
Provider   Invesco
Manager/Tenure Peter Hubbard (0), Michael Jeanette
                (0), Jonathan Nixon (0), 1 other
Website   http://www.invesco.com/us
Address   Invesco 11 Greenway Plaza, Ste. 2500
                Houston TX 77046 United States
Phone Number   800-659-1005

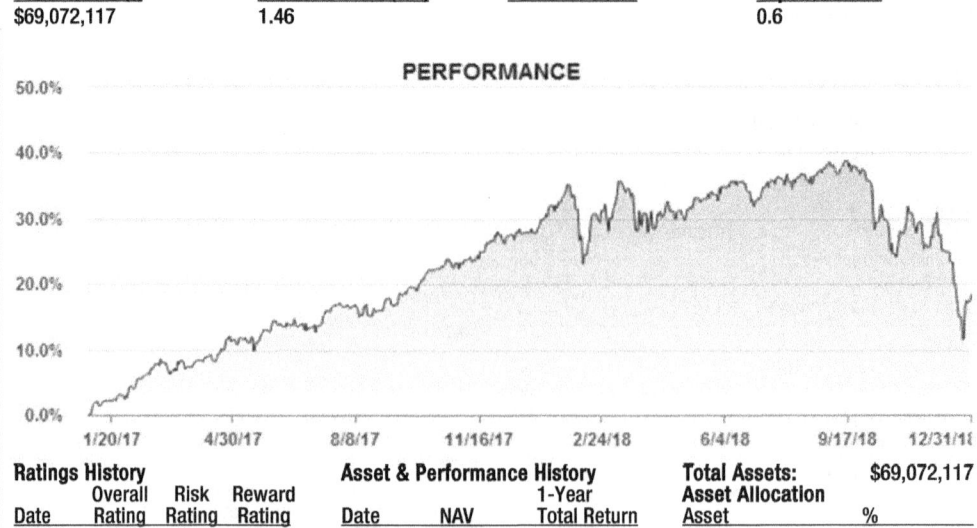

PERFORMANCE

Ratings History

Date	Overall Rating	Risk Rating	Reward Rating
Q4-18	C-	D+	C
Q2-18	C	D+	B-
Q4-17	B	B	B
Q4-16	C	D+	C+
Q4-15	C	C	C

Asset & Performance History

Date	NAV	1-Year Total Return
2017	61.8	27.96
2016	49.08	7.36
2015	46.45	-3.73
2014	48.99	5.89
2013	46.81	35.38
2012	34.9	15.31

Total Assets: $69,072,117

Asset Allocation

Asset	%
Cash	0%
Stocks	100%
US Stocks	98%
Bonds	0%
US Bonds	0%
Other	0%

Services Offered:

Investment Strategy: The investment seeks to track the investment results (before fees and expenses) of the Nasdaq US Insider Sentiment Index. The fund will invest at least 90% of its total assets in securities that comprise the underlying index and depositary receipts representing common stocks included in the underlying index (or underlying securities representing depositary receipts included in the underlying index). The companies eligible for the underlying index are derived from its starting universe, the Nasdaq US Large Mid Cap Index, which is designed to track the performance of mid- to large-capitalization U.S. companies. The fund is non-diversified. **Top Holdings:** Medical Properties Trust Inc Verizon Communications Inc Xcel Energy Inc The Mosaic Co The AES Corp

---

JPMorgan Diversified Return Europe Equity ETF   D+   SELL

Ticker	Traded On	NAV	Total Assets ($)	Dividend Yield (TTM)	Turnover Ratio	Expense Ratio
JPEU	NYSE Arca	50.67	$68,701,898	5.67	18	0.38

Ratings
Reward   D+
Risk   D+
Recent Upgrade/Downgrade   Down

Fund Information
Fund Type   Exchange Traded Funds
Category   Europe Equity Large Cap
Sub-Category   Europe Stock
Prospectus Objective   Europe Stock
Inception Date   Dec-15
Open to New Investments   Y

Prices
Price (as of 12/31/2018)   50.70
52-Week High   64.29
52-Week Low   49.14

Total Returns (%)

3-Month	6-Month	1-Year	3-Year	5-Year
-12.80	-11.55	-13.55	7.74	

3-Year Standard Deviation
Effective Duration

Valuation
Premium/Discount (1-Year Average)   0.27

Company Information
Provider   JPMorgan
Manager/Tenure Kartik Aiyar (1), Wei (Victor) Li (1),
                Jonathan Msika (1), 2 others
Website   http://www.jpmorganfunds.com
Address   JPMorgan 270 Park Avenue New York
                NY 10017-2070 United States
Phone Number   800-480-4111

PERFORMANCE

Ratings History

Date	Overall Rating	Risk Rating	Reward Rating
Q4-18	D+	D+	D+
Q2-18	C	D+	C
Q4-17	C-	B-	C
Q4-16	D-	D+	D
Q4-15			

Asset & Performance History

Date	NAV	1-Year Total Return
2017	60.14	26.74
2016	48.75	-1.66
2015	50.72	
2014		
2013		
2012		

Total Assets: $68,701,898

Asset Allocation

Asset	%
Cash	0%
Stocks	100%
US Stocks	1%
Bonds	0%
US Bonds	0%
Other	0%

Services Offered:

Investment Strategy: The investment seeks investment results that closely correspond, before fees and expenses, to the performance of the JP Morgan Diversified Factor Europe Equity Index. The fund will invest at least 80% of its net assets in securities included in the underlying index. The underlying index is comprised of equity securities across developed Europe selected to represent a diversified set of factor characteristics: value, momentum, and quality. The fund may invest in depositary receipts representing securities included in the underlying index. **Top Holdings:** Neste Corp Capgemini SE Novartis AG BT Group PLC Nestle SA

SPDR® FactSet Innovative Technology ETF   C-   HOLD

Ticker	Traded On	NAV	Total Assets ($)	Dividend Yield (TTM)	Turnover Ratio	Expense Ratio
XITK	NYSE Arca	82.95	$68,687,598	0.28	78	0.45

Ratings
Reward	C
Risk	C-
Recent Upgrade/Downgrade	Down

Fund Information
Fund Type	Exchange Traded Funds
Category	Technology Sector Equity
Sub-Category	Technology
Prospectus Objective	Technology
Inception Date	Jan-16
Open to New Investments	Y

Prices
Price (as of 12/31/2018)	82.71
52-Week High	105.42
52-Week Low	76.98

Total Returns (%)
3-Month	6-Month	1-Year	3-Year	5-Year
-17.33	-12.88	8.37	83.91	

3-Year Standard Deviation	
Effective Duration	

Valuation
Premium/Discount (1-Year Average)	0.30

Company Information
Provider	SPDR State Street Global Advisors
Manager/Tenure	Michael J. Feehily (2), Karl A. Schneider (2), Michael Finocchi (1)
Website	http://www.spdrs.com
Address	SPDR State Street Global Advisors State Street Financial Center, 1 Lincoln Street Boston MA 02111-2900 United States
Phone Number	617-786-3000

PERFORMANCE

Ratings History
Date	Overall Rating	Risk Rating	Reward Rating
Q4-18	C-	C-	C
Q2-18	C	D+	C+
Q4-17	C-	B+	C
Q4-16	D-	D+	D+
Q4-15			

Asset & Performance History
Date	NAV	1-Year Total Return
2017	77.78	35.55
2016	58.37	19.97
2015		
2014		
2013		
2012		

Total Assets: $68,687,598
Asset Allocation
Asset	%
Cash	0%
Stocks	100%
US Stocks	89%
Bonds	0%
US Bonds	0%
Other	0%

Services Offered:

Investment Strategy: The investment seeks to provide investment results that, before fees and expenses, correspond generally to the total return performance of the FactSet Innovative Technology Index. The index is designed to represent the performance of U.S.-listed stock and American Depository Receipts of Technology companies and Technology-related companies within the most innovative segments of the Technology sector and Electronic Media sub-sector of the Media sector, as defined by FactSet Research Systems, Inc. The fund generally invests substantially all, but at least 80%, of its total assets in the securities comprising the index. It is non-diversified. **Top Holdings:** Twilio Inc A The Trade Desk Inc A Okta Inc A Alteryx Inc A Everbridge Inc

Global X Copper Miners ETF   D+   SELL

Ticker	Traded On	NAV	Total Assets ($)	Dividend Yield (TTM)	Turnover Ratio	Expense Ratio
COPX	NYSE Arca	18.45	$68,091,394	2.17	44	0.65

Ratings
Reward	C-
Risk	D
Recent Upgrade/Downgrade	Down

Fund Information
Fund Type	Exchange Traded Funds
Category	Natural Resources
Sub-Category	Natural Resources
Prospectus Objective	Natl Res
Inception Date	Apr-10
Open to New Investments	Y

Prices
Price (as of 12/31/2018)	18.31
52-Week High	29.10
52-Week Low	18.14

Total Returns (%)
3-Month	6-Month	1-Year	3-Year	5-Year
-17.07	-23.12	-32.41	59.61	-30.12

3-Year Standard Deviation	36.41
Effective Duration	

Valuation
Premium/Discount (1-Year Average)	-0.10

Company Information
Provider	Global X Funds
Manager/Tenure	Chang Kim (4), James Ong (2), Nam To (0)
Website	http://www.globalxfunds.com
Address	Global X Funds 600 Lexington Avenue, 20th Floor New York NY 10022 United States
Phone Number	888-493-8631

PERFORMANCE

Ratings History
Date	Overall Rating	Risk Rating	Reward Rating
Q4-18	D+	D	C-
Q2-18	C	D+	C
Q4-17	C	D+	C+
Q4-16	D+	D	C-
Q4-15	D	D	D

Asset & Performance History
Date	NAV	1-Year Total Return
2017	27.3	36.79
2016	20.27	72.64
2015	11.81	-46.67
2014	22.41	-17.9
2013	27.93	-27.86
2012	39	4.37

Total Assets: $68,091,394
Asset Allocation
Asset	%
Cash	0%
Stocks	100%
US Stocks	9%
Bonds	0%
US Bonds	0%
Other	0%

Services Offered:

Investment Strategy: The investment seeks to provide investment results that correspond generally to the price and yield performance, before fees and expenses, of the Solactive Global Copper Miners Total Return Index. The fund invests at least 80% of its total assets in the securities of the underlying index and in American Depositary Receipts ("ADRs") and Global Depositary Receipts ("GDRs") based on the securities in the underlying index. The underlying index is designed to measure broad-based equity market performance of global companies involved in the copper mining industry. The fund is non-diversified. **Top Holdings:** KAZ Minerals PLC Vedanta Ltd ADR KGHM Polska Miedz SA Zijin Mining Group Co Ltd H Oz Minerals Ltd

iShares Edge Investment Grade Enhanced Bond ETF   D   SELL

Ticker	Traded On	NAV		Total Assets ($)	Dividend Yield (TTM)	Turnover Ratio	Expense Ratio
IGEB	BATS	47.14		$67,897,017	3.69	36	0.18

Ratings
Reward	D
Risk	C-
Recent Upgrade/Downgrade	

Fund Information
Fund Type	Exchange Traded Funds
Category	US Fixed Income
Sub-Category	Corporate Bond
Prospectus Objective	Corp Bond - Gen
Inception Date	Jul-17
Open to New Investments	Y

Prices
Price (as of 12/31/2018)	47.39
52-Week High	50.40
52-Week Low	46.87

Total Returns (%)
3-Month	6-Month	1-Year	3-Year	5-Year
-0.14	1.03	-3.06		

3-Year Standard Deviation	
Effective Duration	6.86

Valuation
Premium/Discount (1-Year Average)	0.30

Company Information
Provider	iShares
Manager/Tenure	James Mauro (1), Scott Radell (1)
Website	http://www.ishares.com
Address	iShares 400 Howard Street San Francisco CA 94105 United States
Phone Number	800-474-2737

PERFORMANCE

Ratings History
Date	Overall Rating	Risk Rating	Reward Rating
Q4-18	D	C-	D
Q2-18	D	D	D
Q4-17	U		
Q4-16			
Q4-15			

Asset & Performance History
Date	NAV	1-Year Total Return
2017	50.39	
2016		
2015		
2014		
2013		
2012		

Total Assets: $67,897,017

Asset Allocation
Asset	%
Cash	1%
Stocks	0%
US Stocks	0%
Bonds	98%
US Bonds	90%
Other	0%

Services Offered:

Investment Strategy: The investment seeks to track the investment results of the BlackRock Investment Grade Enhanced Bond Index. The fund will invest at least 80% of its assets in the component securities of the underlying index and may invest up to 20% of its assets in certain index futures, options, options on index futures, swap contracts or other derivatives, cash and cash equivalents, other investment companies, as well as in securities and other instruments not included in the underlying index, but which BFA believes will help the fund track the underlying index. The index consists of U.S. dollar-denominated, investment-grade corporate bonds. **Top Holdings:** Discover Bank 3.1% Conagra Brands Inc 3.2% Verizon Communications Inc. 4.13% HSBC Holdings plc 3.6% Charter Communications Operating, LLC/Charter Communications Operating Capi

---

Sit Rising Rate ETF   C-   HOLD

Ticker	Traded On	NAV		Total Assets ($)	Dividend Yield (TTM)	Turnover Ratio	Expense Ratio
RISE	NYSE Arca	24.06		$67,852,100	0		1

Ratings
Reward	C-
Risk	C-
Recent Upgrade/Downgrade	Down

Fund Information
Fund Type	Exchange Traded Funds
Category	Fixed Income Misc
Sub-Category	Nontraditional Bond
Prospectus Objective	Govt Bond - Treasury
Inception Date	Feb-15
Open to New Investments	Y

Prices
Price (as of 12/31/2018)	24.09
52-Week High	25.49
52-Week Low	23.70

Total Returns (%)
3-Month	6-Month	1-Year	3-Year	5-Year
-4.33	-2.61	1.71	-0.63	

3-Year Standard Deviation	5.2
Effective Duration	

Valuation
Premium/Discount (1-Year Average)	0.06

Company Information
Provider	RISE
Manager/Tenure	Management Team (3)
Website	http://www.risingrateetf.com/
Address	RISE 35 Beechwood Road NJ 07901 United States
Phone Number	

PERFORMANCE

Ratings History
Date	Overall Rating	Risk Rating	Reward Rating
Q4-18	C-	C-	C-
Q2-18	C	C-	C
Q4-17	C	B-	D+
Q4-16	D	D+	D
Q4-15	U		

Asset & Performance History
Date	NAV	1-Year Total Return
2017	23.65	-0.12
2016	23.68	-2.14
2015	24.21	
2014		
2013		
2012		

Total Assets: $67,852,100

Asset Allocation
Asset	%
Cash	390%
Stocks	0%
US Stocks	0%
Bonds	-290%
US Bonds	-290%
Other	0%

Services Offered:

Investment Strategy: The investment seeks to profit from rising interest rates by tracking the performance of a portfolio consisting of exchange traded futures contracts and options on futures on 2, 5 and 10-year U.S. Treasury securities weighted to achieve a targeted negative 10 year average effective portfolio duration. The weighting of the Treasury Instruments constituting the Benchmark Component Instruments will be based on each maturity's duration contribution. The expected range for the duration weighted percentage of the 2 year and 5 year maturity Treasury Instruments will be from 30% to 70%. **Top Holdings:** 2 Year US Treasury Note Future Mar19 US 5 Year Note (CBT) Mar19 Us 10yr Fut Optn Mar19p 118.5 Us 5yr Futr Optn Jan19c 112.5 Us 10yr Fut Optn Aug18p 120

Xtrackers FTSE Developed ex US Comprehensive Factor ETF

D+   **SELL**

Ticker	Traded On	NAV	Total Assets ($)	Dividend Yield (TTM)	Turnover Ratio	Expense Ratio
DEEF	NYSE Arca		$67,171,584	3	45	0.35

Ratings
Reward	D+
Risk	C-
Recent Upgrade/Downgrade	Down

Fund Information
Fund Type	Exchange Traded Funds
Category	Global Equity Large Cap
Sub-Category	Foreign Large Blend
Prospectus Objective	Foreign Stock
Inception Date	Nov-15
Open to New Investments	Y

Prices
Price (as of 12/31/2018)	25.04
52-Week High	31.67
52-Week Low	24.42

Total Returns (%)
3-Month	6-Month	1-Year	3-Year	5-Year
-11.98	-10.32	-13.93	11.24	

3-Year Standard Deviation	10.4
Effective Duration	

Valuation
Premium/Discount (1-Year Average)	0.11

Company Information
Provider	Deutsche Asset Management
Manager/Tenure	Bryan Richards (3), Patrick Dwyer (2), Shlomo Bassous (0), 2 others
Website	http://www.deutsche-etfs.com
Address	Deutsche Asset & Wealth Management 345 Park Avenue New York NY 10154 United States
Phone Number	844-851-4255

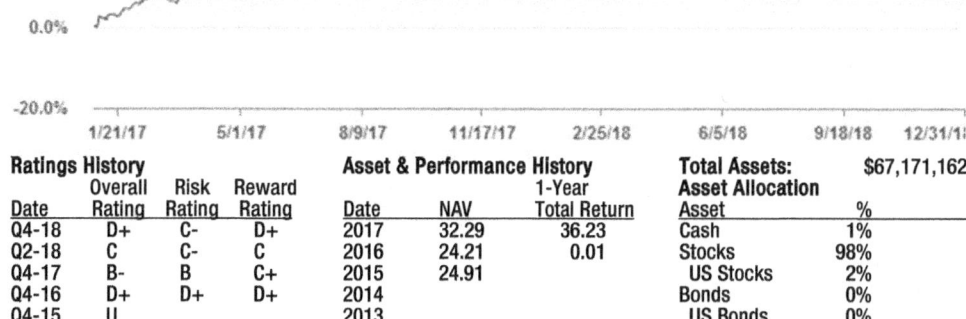

PERFORMANCE

Ratings History
Date	Overall Rating	Risk Rating	Reward Rating
Q4-18	D+	C-	D+
Q2-18	C	D+	C
Q4-17	C	B+	C
Q4-16	D	C-	D
Q4-15			

Asset & Performance History
Date	NAV	1-Year Total Return
2017	29.88	27.58
2016	24.08	1.3
2015	24.78	
2014		
2013		
2012		

Total Assets: $67,171,584

Asset Allocation
Asset	%
Cash	1%
Stocks	98%
US Stocks	1%
Bonds	0%
US Bonds	0%
Other	0%

Services Offered:

Investment Strategy: The investment seeks investment results that correspond generally to the performance, before fees and expenses, of the FTSE Developed ex US Comprehensive Factor Index. The fund will normally invest at least 80% of its net assets, plus the amount of any borrowings for investment purposes, in equity securities of issuers from developed markets countries other than the United States. The index is designed to track the equity market performance of companies in developed countries selected on the investment style criteria of value, momentum, quality, low volatility and size. **Top Holdings:** Link Real Estate Investment Trust   Koninklijke Ahold Delhaize NV   Dexus   Scentre Group   Segro PLC

---

iShares Edge MSCI Multifactor Intl Small-Cap ETF

D+   **SELL**

Ticker	Traded On	NAV	Total Assets ($)	Dividend Yield (TTM)	Turnover Ratio	Expense Ratio
ISCF	NYSE Arca	25.92	$67,171,162	2.43	44	0.4

Ratings
Reward	D+
Risk	C-
Recent Upgrade/Downgrade	Down

Fund Information
Fund Type	Exchange Traded Funds
Category	Global Eq Mid/Small Cap
Sub-Category	Foreign Small/Mid Blend
Prospectus Objective	Small Company
Inception Date	Apr-15
Open to New Investments	Y

Prices
Price (as of 12/31/2018)	25.87
52-Week High	34.65
52-Week Low	24.74

Total Returns (%)
3-Month	6-Month	1-Year	3-Year	5-Year
-16.50	-15.77	-18.18	11.47	

3-Year Standard Deviation	12.55
Effective Duration	

Valuation
Premium/Discount (1-Year Average)	0.53

Company Information
Provider	iShares
Manager/Tenure	Diane Hsiung (3), Jennifer Hsui (3), Greg Savage (3), 3 others
Website	http://www.ishares.com
Address	iShares 400 Howard Street San Francisco CA 94105 United States
Phone Number	800-474-2737

PERFORMANCE

Ratings History
Date	Overall Rating	Risk Rating	Reward Rating
Q4-18	D+	C-	D+
Q2-18	C	C-	C
Q4-17	B-	B	C+
Q4-16	D+	D+	D+
Q4-15	U		

Asset & Performance History
Date	NAV	1-Year Total Return
2017	32.29	36.23
2016	24.21	0.01
2015	24.91	
2014		
2013		
2012		

Total Assets: $67,171,162

Asset Allocation
Asset	%
Cash	1%
Stocks	98%
US Stocks	2%
Bonds	0%
US Bonds	0%
Other	1%

Services Offered:

Investment Strategy: The investment seeks to track the investment results of the MSCI World ex USA Small Cap Diversified Multiple-Factor Index. The fund generally will invest at least 90% of its assets in the component securities of the underlying index and in investments that have economic characteristics that are substantially identical to the component securities of the underlying index. The underlying index is designed to select equity securities from the MSCI World ex USA Small Cap Index that have high exposure to four investment style factors: value, quality, momentum and low size, while maintaining a level of risk similar to that of the parent index. **Top Holdings:** ASR Nederland NV   Logitech International SA   GN Store Nord A/S   Northern Star Resources Ltd   Euronext NV

AdvisorShares Sage Core Reserves ETF — C- HOLD

Ticker	Traded On	NAV	Total Assets ($)	Dividend Yield (TTM)	Turnover Ratio	Expense Ratio
HOLD	NYSE Arca	99.09	$66,952,006	1.87		0.35

Ratings

Reward	C
Risk	D+
Recent Upgrade/Downgrade	

Fund Information

Fund Type	Exchange Traded Funds
Category	US Fixed Income
Sub-Category	Ultrashort Bond
Prospectus Objective	Income
Inception Date	Jan-14
Open to New Investments	Y

Prices

Price (as of 12/31/2018)	99.11
52-Week High	99.59
52-Week Low	99.04

Total Returns (%)

3-Month	6-Month	1-Year	3-Year	5-Year
0.32	0.96	1.75	4.38	

3-Year Standard Deviation	0.34
Effective Duration	0.41

Valuation

Premium/Discount (1-Year Average)	0.00

Company Information

Provider	AdvisorShares
Manager/Tenure	Mark Cordes MacQueen (4), Thomas Hideo Urano (4)
Website	http://www.advisorshares.com
Address	AdvisorShares 2 Bethesda Metro Center, Suite 1330 Bethesda MD 20814 United States
Phone Number	877-843-3831

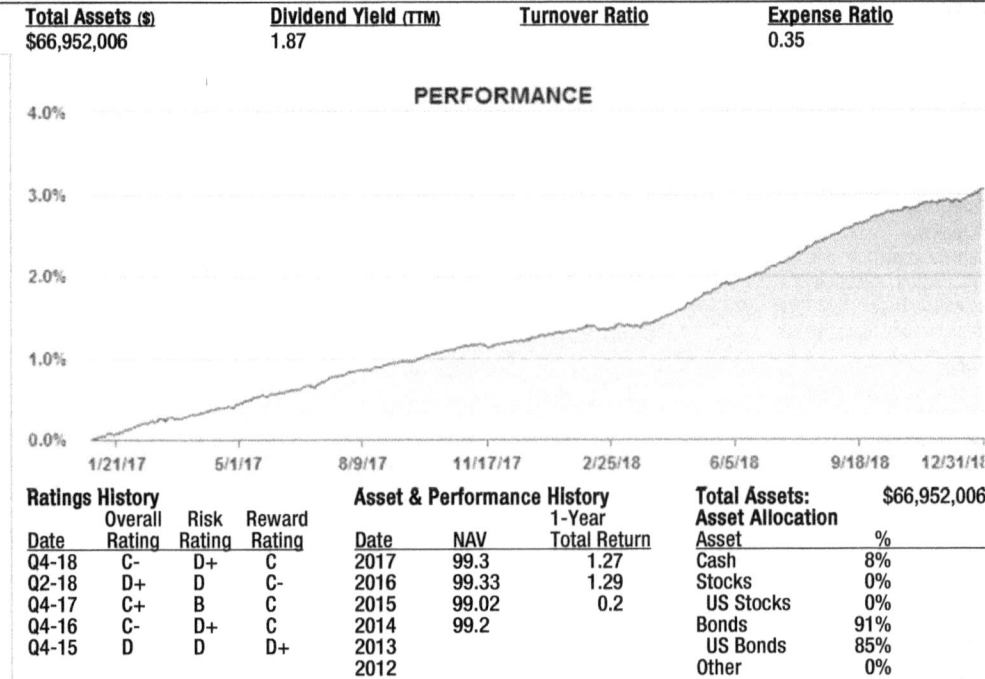

PERFORMANCE

Ratings History

Date	Overall Rating	Risk Rating	Reward Rating
Q4-18	C-	D+	C
Q2-18	D+	D	C-
Q4-17	C+	B	C
Q4-16	C-	D+	C
Q4-15	D	D	D+

Asset & Performance History

Date	NAV	1-Year Total Return
2017	99.3	1.27
2016	99.33	1.29
2015	99.02	0.2
2014	99.2	
2013		
2012		

Total Assets: $66,952,006

Asset Allocation

Asset	%
Cash	8%
Stocks	0%
US Stocks	0%
Bonds	91%
US Bonds	85%
Other	0%

Services Offered:

Investment Strategy: The investment seeks to preserve capital while maximizing income. Sage Advisory Services, Ltd. Co. (the "Sub-Advisor") seeks to achieve the fund's investment objective by investing in a variety of fixed income securities, including bonds, forwards and instruments issued by U.S. and foreign issuers. It will invest in U.S. dollar-denominated investment grade debt securities, including mortgage- or asset-backed securities, rated Baa- or higher by Moody's Investors Service, Inc. ("Moody's"), or equivalently rated by Standard & Poor's Ratings Services ("S&P") or Fitch, Inc. ("Fitch"), or, if unrated, determined by the Sub-Advisor to be of comparable quality. **Top Holdings:** United States Treasury Notes 0.88% United States Treasury Notes 1.62% Chase Issuance Trust 1.37% Ally Master Owner Trust 1.83% Capital One Multi Asset Execution Trust 1.34%

First Trust Eurozone AlphaDEX® ETF — D+ SELL

Ticker	Traded On	NAV	Total Assets ($)	Dividend Yield (TTM)	Turnover Ratio	Expense Ratio
FEUZ	NAS CM	34.43	$66,949,895	2.25	77	0.8

Ratings

Reward	D+
Risk	D+
Recent Upgrade/Downgrade	Down

Fund Information

Fund Type	Exchange Traded Funds
Category	Europe Equity Large Cap
Sub-Category	Europe Stock
Prospectus Objective	Income
Inception Date	Oct-14
Open to New Investments	Y

Prices

Price (as of 12/31/2018)	34.17
52-Week High	48.11
52-Week Low	33.28

Total Returns (%)

3-Month	6-Month	1-Year	3-Year	5-Year
-17.88	-17.56	-19.82	15.07	

3-Year Standard Deviation	14.82
Effective Duration	

Valuation

Premium/Discount (1-Year Average)	0.10

Company Information

Provider	First Trust
Manager/Tenure	Jon C. Erickson (4), Daniel J. Lindquist (4), David G. McGarel (4), 3 others
Website	http://www.ftportfolios.com/
Address	First Trust 120 E. Liberty Drive, Suite 400 Wheaton IL 60187 United States
Phone Number	800-621-1675

PERFORMANCE

Ratings History

Date	Overall Rating	Risk Rating	Reward Rating
Q4-18	D+	D+	D+
Q2-18	C	C-	C
Q4-17	B-	C+	B-
Q4-16	D+	D+	D+
Q4-15	U		

Asset & Performance History

Date	NAV	1-Year Total Return
2017	43.81	36.16
2016	32.64	5.48
2015	31.65	3.51
2014	30.89	
2013		
2012		

Total Assets: $66,949,895

Asset Allocation

Asset	%
Cash	0%
Stocks	100%
US Stocks	2%
Bonds	0%
US Bonds	0%
Other	0%

Services Offered:

Investment Strategy: The investment seeks investment results that correspond generally to the price and yield of an index called the NASDAQ® AlphaDEX® Eurozone Index. The fund will normally invest at least 90% of its net assets (including investment borrowings) in common stocks and/or depositary receipts that comprise the index. The index is designed to select stocks from the NASDAQ Eurozone Index that may generate positive alpha, or risk-adjusted returns, relative to traditional passive-style indices through the use of the AlphaDEX® selection methodology. **Top Holdings:** Telecom Italia SpA SCOR SE Acciona SA TAG Immobilien AG Deutsche Lufthansa AG

ProShares UltraShort Yen   C   HOLD

Ticker	Traded On	NAV
YCS	NYSE Arca	

Total Assets ($)	Dividend Yield (TTM)	Turnover Ratio	Expense Ratio
$66,873,364	0	0	0.95

Ratings
Reward   C-
Risk   C-
Recent Upgrade/Downgrade   Up

Fund Information
Fund Type	Exchange Traded Funds
Category	Trading Tools
Sub-Category	Trading--Miscellaneous
Prospectus Objective	Worldwide Bond
Inception Date	Nov-08
Open to New Investments	Y

Prices
Price (as of 12/31/2018)	73.86
52-Week High	79.20
52-Week Low	65.13

Total Returns (%)
3-Month	6-Month	1-Year	3-Year	5-Year
-5.13	1.35	-0.35	-15.09	5.37

3-Year Standard Deviation   20.94
Effective Duration

Valuation
Premium/Discount (1-Year Average)   -0.05

Company Information
Provider	ProShares
Manager/Tenure	Management Team (10)
Website	http://www.proshares.com
Address	ProShares 7501 Wisconsin Avenue, Suite 1000 Bethesda MD 20814 United States
Phone Number	866-776-5125

PERFORMANCE

Ratings History
Date	Overall Rating	Risk Rating	Reward Rating
Q4-18	C	C-	C-
Q2-18	D	D	D
Q4-17	C-	C-	D+
Q4-16	D+	D	D
Q4-15	C	C-	C

Asset & Performance History
Date	NAV	1-Year Total Return
2017	74.94	-6.61
2016	80.24	-8.75
2015	87.95	-1.54
2014	89.33	26.06
2013	70.86	39.6
2012	50.76	23.92

Total Assets: $66,873,364
Asset Allocation
Asset	%
Cash	100%
Stocks	0%
US Stocks	0%
Bonds	0%
US Bonds	0%
Other	0%

Services Offered:

Investment Strategy: The investment seeks to provide daily investment results (before fees and expenses) that correspond to twice (200%) the inverse of the daily performance of the U.S. Dollar price of the Japanese Yen. The "UltraShort" funds seek results for a single day that match (before fees and expenses) two times the inverse (-2x) of the daily performance of a benchmark. It does not seek to achieve their stated objectives over a period greater than a single day. **Top Holdings:**

Invesco DWA Consumer Cyclicals Momentum ETF   C+   HOLD

Ticker	Traded On	NAV
PEZ	NAS CM	46.82

Total Assets ($)	Dividend Yield (TTM)	Turnover Ratio	Expense Ratio
$66,432,819	0.34	185	0.6

Ratings
Reward   B
Risk   C-
Recent Upgrade/Downgrade   Down

Fund Information
Fund Type	Exchange Traded Funds
Category	Consumer Goods & Svcs
Sub-Category	Consumer Cyclical
Prospectus Objective	Unaligned
Inception Date	Oct-06
Open to New Investments	Y

Prices
Price (as of 12/31/2018)	46.67
52-Week High	60.10
52-Week Low	43.46

Total Returns (%)
3-Month	6-Month	1-Year	3-Year	5-Year
-20.83	-14.26	-6.30	8.10	16.02

3-Year Standard Deviation   14.35
Effective Duration

Valuation
Premium/Discount (1-Year Average)   0.20

Company Information
Provider	Invesco
Manager/Tenure	Peter Hubbard (11), Michael Jeanette (10), Tony Seisser (4), 1 other
Website	http://www.invesco.com/us
Address	Invesco 11 Greenway Plaza, Ste. 2500 Houston TX 77046 United States
Phone Number	800-659-1005

PERFORMANCE

Ratings History
Date	Overall Rating	Risk Rating	Reward Rating
Q4-18	C+	C-	B
Q2-18	C	C-	B-
Q4-17	C+	B-	C+
Q4-16	B-	C	B
Q4-15	B	B-	B+

Asset & Performance History
Date	NAV	1-Year Total Return
2017	50.15	19.33
2016	42.21	-3.31
2015	44.02	-0.7
2014	44.6	8.07
2013	41.33	39.87
2012	29.7	18.62

Total Assets: $66,432,819
Asset Allocation
Asset	%
Cash	0%
Stocks	100%
US Stocks	100%
Bonds	0%
US Bonds	0%
Other	0%

Services Offered:

Investment Strategy: The investment seeks to track the investment results (before fees and expenses) of the Dorsey Wright® Consumer Cyclicals Technical Leaders Index (the "underlying index"). The fund generally will invest at least 90% of its total assets in the securities that comprise the underlying index. The underlying index is composed of at least 30 securities of companies in the consumer discretionary (or cyclicals) sector that have powerful relative strength or "momentum" characteristics. **Top Holdings:** O'Reilly Automotive Inc   Etsy Inc   Domino's Pizza Inc   Ross Stores Inc   The Trade Desk Inc A

iShares MSCI Brazil Small-Cap ETF   C-   HOLD

Ticker	Traded On	NAV	Total Assets ($)	Dividend Yield (TTM)	Turnover Ratio	Expense Ratio
EWZS	NAS CM	14.36	$66,377,117	4.91	67	0.59

Ratings
Reward   C
Risk   D+
Recent Upgrade/Downgrade

Fund Information
Fund Type   Exchange Traded Funds
Category   Latin America Equity
Sub-Category   Latin America Stock
Prospectus Objective   Foreign Stock
Inception Date   Sep-10
Open to New Investments   Y

Prices
Price (as of 12/31/2018)   14.43
52-Week High   18.06
52-Week Low   11.01

Total Returns (%)

3-Month	6-Month	1-Year	3-Year	5-Year
26.52	20.12	-7.17	131.21	-13.08

3-Year Standard Deviation   35.47
Effective Duration

Valuation
Premium/Discount (1-Year Average)   -0.08

Company Information
Provider   iShares
Manager/Tenure   Diane Hsiung (8), Greg Savage (8),
                         Jennifer Hsui (5), 1 other
Website   http://www.ishares.com
Address   iShares 400 Howard Street San
                         Francisco CA 94105 United States
Phone Number   800-474-2737

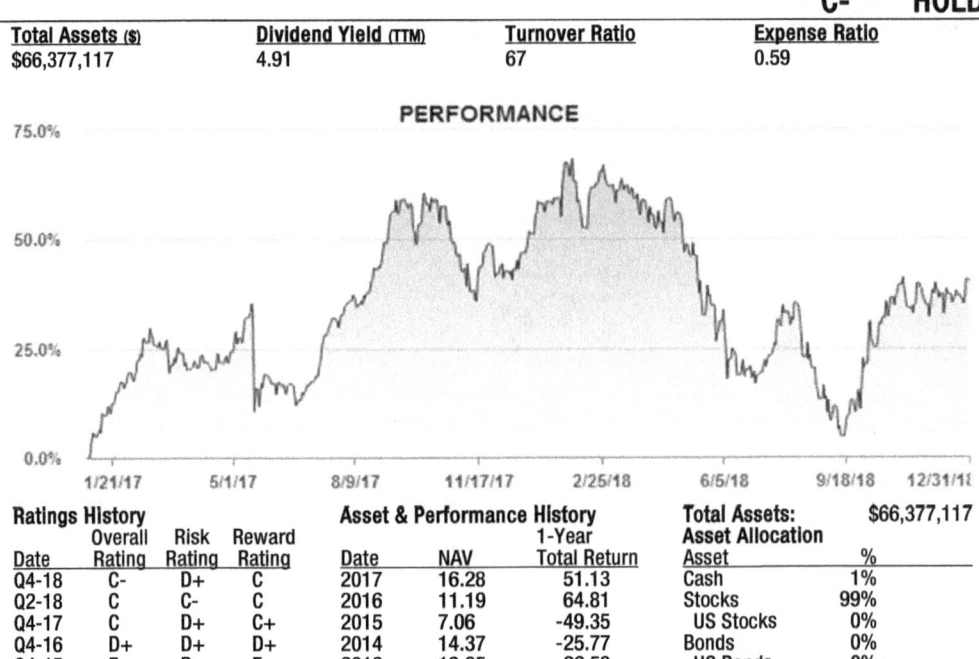

Ratings History

Date	Overall Rating	Risk Rating	Reward Rating
Q4-18	C-	D+	C
Q2-18	C	C-	C
Q4-17	C	D+	C+
Q4-16	D+	D+	D+
Q4-15	E+	D-	E+

Asset & Performance History

Date	NAV	1-Year Total Return
2017	16.28	51.13
2016	11.19	64.81
2015	7.06	-49.35
2014	14.37	-25.77
2013	19.85	-26.52
2012	27.49	28.07

Total Assets: $66,377,117
Asset Allocation

Asset	%
Cash	1%
Stocks	99%
US Stocks	0%
Bonds	0%
US Bonds	0%
Other	0%

Services Offered:

Investment Strategy: The investment seeks to track the investment results of the MSCI Brazil Small Cap Index. The fund generally will invest at least 90% of its assets in the component securities of the underlying index and in investments that have economic characteristics that are substantially identical to the component securities of the underlying index. The index is a free float-adjusted market capitalization-weighted index designed to measure the performance of equity securities in the bottom 14% by market capitalization of equity securities listed on stock exchanges in Brazil. **Top Holdings:** CVC Brasil Operadora e Agencia de Viagens SA Bradespar SA Participating Preferred Estacio Participacoes SA Transmissora Alianca de Energia Eletrica SA Unit Metalurgica Gerdau SA Participating Preferred

---

Invesco China Small Cap ETF   D+   SELL

Ticker	Traded On	NAV	Total Assets ($)	Dividend Yield (TTM)	Turnover Ratio	Expense Ratio
HAO	NYSE Arca		$66,211,584	4.12	34	0.75

Ratings
Reward   D+
Risk   D+
Recent Upgrade/Downgrade   Down

Fund Information
Fund Type   Exchange Traded Funds
Category   Greater China Equity
Sub-Category   China Region
Prospectus Objective   Pacific Stock
Inception Date   Jan-08
Open to New Investments   Y

Prices
Price (as of 12/31/2018)   22.73
52-Week High   33.19
52-Week Low   22.03

Total Returns (%)

3-Month	6-Month	1-Year	3-Year	5-Year
-16.74	-25.37	-25.07	-2.05	-3.64

3-Year Standard Deviation   18.14
Effective Duration

Valuation
Premium/Discount (1-Year Average)   -0.54

Company Information
Provider   Invesco
Manager/Tenure   Peter Hubbard (0), Michael Jeanette
                         (0), Jonathan Nixon (0), 1 other
Website   http://www.invesco.com/us
Address   Invesco 11 Greenway Plaza, Ste. 2500
                         Houston TX 77046 United States
Phone Number   800-659-1005

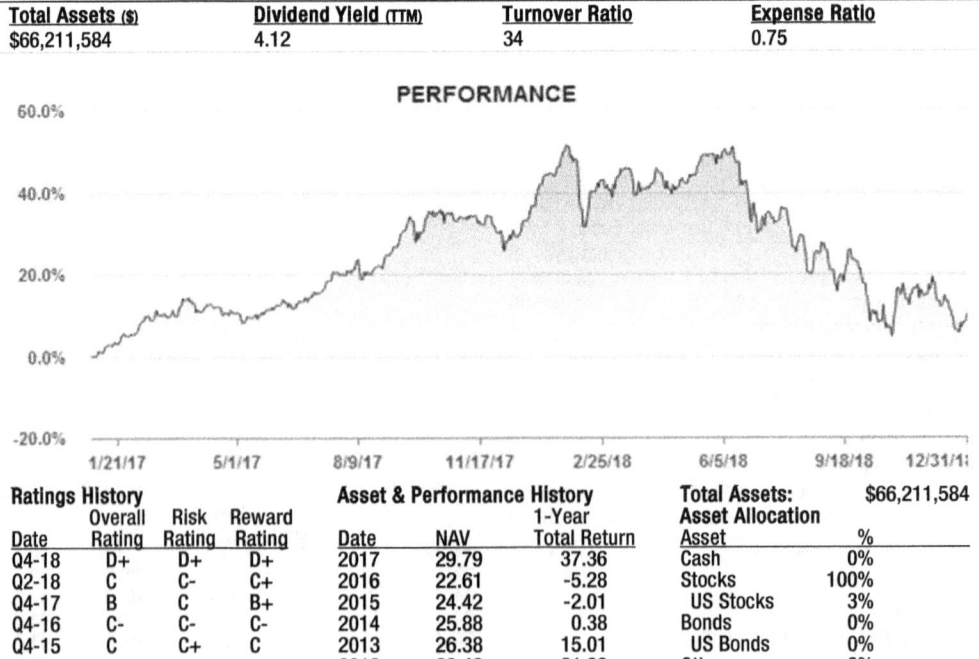

Ratings History

Date	Overall Rating	Risk Rating	Reward Rating
Q4-18	D+	D+	D+
Q2-18	C	C-	C+
Q4-17	B	C	B+
Q4-16	C-	C-	C-
Q4-15	C	C+	C

Asset & Performance History

Date	NAV	1-Year Total Return
2017	29.79	37.36
2016	22.61	-5.28
2015	24.42	-2.01
2014	25.88	0.38
2013	26.38	15.01
2012	23.42	21.99

Total Assets: $66,211,584
Asset Allocation

Asset	%
Cash	0%
Stocks	100%
US Stocks	3%
Bonds	0%
US Bonds	0%
Other	0%

Services Offered:

Investment Strategy: The investment seeks to track investment results (before fees and expenses) of the AlphaShares China Small Cap Index (the "underlying index"). The fund generally will invest at least 90% of its total assets in the securities (including American depositary receipts ("ADRs") and global depositary receipts ("GDRs")) that comprise the underlying index. The underlying index is comprised of equity securities of publicly-traded mainland China companies of small capitalization. The fund is non-diversified. **Top Holdings:** Momo Inc ADR WuXi Biologics (Cayman) Inc Registered Shs Unitary 144A/Reg S Zall Smart Commerce Group Ltd Shandong Weigao Group Medical Polymer Co Ltd H Zijin Mining Group Co Ltd H

Alpha Architect U.S. Quantitative Momentum ETF　　　　　　　C-　　HOLD

Ticker	Traded On	NAV	Total Assets ($)	Dividend Yield (TTM)	Turnover Ratio	Expense Ratio
QMOM	BATS	25.30	$66,050,232	0	91	0.79

Ratings
Reward　　　　　　　　　　　　　　C
Risk　　　　　　　　　　　　　　　D+
Recent Upgrade/Downgrade　　　Down

Fund Information
Fund Type　　　　　　　　Exchange Traded Funds
Category　　　　　　　　　US Equity Mid Cap
Sub-Category　　　　　　　Mid-Cap Growth
Prospectus Objective　　　Growth
Inception Date　　　　　　Dec-15
Open to New Investments　Y

Prices
Price (as of 12/31/2018)　25.23
52-Week High　　　　　　34.22
52-Week Low　　　　　　23.31

Total Returns (%)

3-Month	6-Month	1-Year	3-Year	5-Year
-25.02	-18.36	-11.03	8.12	

3-Year Standard Deviation
Effective Duration

Valuation
Premium/Discount (1-Year Average)　0.31

Company Information
Provider　　　　　Alpha Architect
Manager/Tenure　Tao Wang (3)
Website　　　　　http://www.alphaarchitect.com/funds
Address　　　　　Alpha Architect 213 Foxcroft Road
　　　　　　　　　Broomall PA 19008 United States
Phone Number

PERFORMANCE

Ratings History

Date	Overall Rating	Risk Rating	Reward Rating
Q4-18	C-	D+	C
Q2-18	C	D+	C+
Q4-17	C	B	C-
Q4-16	D	C-	C-
Q4-15			

Asset & Performance History

Date	NAV	1-Year Total Return
2017	28.45	15.62
2016	24.64	5.19
2015	23.52	
2014		
2013		
2012		

Total Assets:　$66,050,232

Asset Allocation

Asset	%
Cash	0%
Stocks	100%
US Stocks	98%
Bonds	0%
US Bonds	0%
Other	0%

Services Offered:

Investment Strategy: The investment seeks to track the total return performance, before fees and expenses, of the Alpha Architect Quantitative Momentum Index. The fund will normally invest at least 80% of its total assets in the component securities of the index. The fund may also invest up to 20% of its assets in cash and cash equivalents, other investment companies, as well as securities and other instruments not included in the index but which the Adviser believes will help the fund track the index. The index uses a 5-step, quantitative, rules-based methodology to identify a portfolio of approximately 40-50 U.S. equity securities with positive momentum. It is non-diversified. **Top Holdings:** Okta Inc A　Wayfair Inc Class A　HubSpot Inc　World Wrestling Entertainment Inc Class A　Coupa Software Inc

---

iShares Fallen Angels USD Bond ETF　　　　　　　　　　　C-　　HOLD

Ticker	Traded On	NAV	Total Assets ($)	Dividend Yield (TTM)	Turnover Ratio	Expense Ratio
FALN	NAS CM	24.47	$65,662,099	5.55	31	0.25

Ratings
Reward　　　　　　　　　　　　　　C-
Risk　　　　　　　　　　　　　　　C-
Recent Upgrade/Downgrade

Fund Information
Fund Type　　　　　　　　Exchange Traded Funds
Category　　　　　　　　　US Fixed Income
Sub-Category　　　　　　　High Yield Bond
Prospectus Objective　　　Corp Bond-High Yld
Inception Date　　　　　　Jun-16
Open to New Investments　Y

Prices
Price (as of 12/31/2018)　24.40
52-Week High　　　　　　27.77
52-Week Low　　　　　　24.12

Total Returns (%)

3-Month	6-Month	1-Year	3-Year	5-Year
-5.96	-3.58	-4.36		

3-Year Standard Deviation
Effective Duration　　　5.92

Valuation
Premium/Discount (1-Year Average)　0.13

Company Information
Provider　　　　　iShares
Manager/Tenure　James Mauro (2), Scott Radell (2)
Website　　　　　http://www.ishares.com
Address　　　　　iShares 400 Howard Street San
　　　　　　　　　Francisco CA 94105 United States
Phone Number　　800-474-2737

PERFORMANCE

Ratings History

Date	Overall Rating	Risk Rating	Reward Rating
Q4-18	C-	C-	C-
Q2-18	C-	C-	D+
Q4-17	D+	A-	C-
Q4-16	U		
Q4-15			

Asset & Performance History

Date	NAV	1-Year Total Return
2017	27.05	8.88
2016	26.54	
2015		
2014		
2013		
2012		

Total Assets:　$65,662,099

Asset Allocation

Asset	%
Cash	0%
Stocks	0%
US Stocks	0%
Bonds	98%
US Bonds	81%
Other	0%

Services Offered:

Investment Strategy: The investment seeks to track the investment results of the Bloomberg Barclays US High Yield Fallen Angel 3% Capped Index composed of U.S. dollar-denominated, high yield corporate bonds that were previously rated investment grade. The fund generally will invest at least 90% of its assets in the component securities of the index and may invest up to 10% of its assets in certain futures, options and swap contracts, cash and cash equivalents. The index is designed to reflect the performance of U.S. dollar denominated, high yield corporate bonds that were previously rated investment grade. The fund is non-diversified. **Top Holdings:** Sprint Capital Corporation 6.88%　Intesa Sanpaolo S.p.A. 5.02%　Sprint Capital Corporation 8.75%　EMC Corporation 2.65%　Deutsche Bank AG New York Branch 4.3%

iShares Edge MSCI Multifactor Global ETF   C-   HOLD

Ticker	Traded On	NAV	Total Assets ($)	Dividend Yield (TTM)	Turnover Ratio	Expense Ratio
ACWF	NYSE Arca	25.97	$65,440,922	1.98	46	0.35

Ratings
Reward   C-
Risk   C-
Recent Upgrade/Downgrade   Down

Fund Information
Fund Type   Exchange Traded Funds
Category   Global Equity Large Cap
Sub-Category   World Large Stock
Prospectus Objective   Growth & Inc
Inception Date   Apr-15
Open to New Investments   Y

Prices
Price (as of 12/31/2018)   25.97
52-Week High   33.19
52-Week Low   24.98

Total Returns (%)

3-Month	6-Month	1-Year	3-Year	5-Year
-14.87	-12.32	-13.38	18.03	

3-Year Standard Deviation   10.44
Effective Duration

Valuation
Premium/Discount (1-Year Average)   0.64

Company Information
Provider   iShares
Manager/Tenure   Diane Hsiung (3), Jennifer Hsui (3), Greg Savage (3), 3 others
Website   http://www.ishares.com
Address   iShares 400 Howard Street San Francisco CA 94105 United States
Phone Number   800-474-2737

PERFORMANCE

Ratings History

Date	Overall Rating	Risk Rating	Reward Rating
Q4-18	C-	C-	C-
Q2-18	C	C-	C
Q4-17	B-	B-	C+
Q4-16	D+	D	C-
Q4-15	U		

Asset & Performance History

Date	NAV	1-Year Total Return
2017	30.35	29.62
2016	23.9	5.12
2015	23.19	
2014		
2013		
2012		

Total Assets: $65,440,922

Asset Allocation

Asset	%
Cash	0%
Stocks	99%
US Stocks	59%
Bonds	0%
US Bonds	0%
Other	0%

Services Offered:

Investment Strategy: The investment seeks to track the investment results of the MSCI ACWI Diversified Multiple-Factor Index. The fund generally will invest at least 90% of its assets in the component securities of the underlying index and in investments that have economic characteristics that are substantially identical to the component securities of the underlying index. The underlying index is designed to contain equity securities from the MSCI ACWI Index (the "parent index") that have high exposure to four investment style factors: value, quality, momentum and low size, while maintaining a level of risk similar to that of the parent index. **Top Holdings:** Accenture PLC A China Construction Bank Corp H Anthem Inc Intuitive Surgical Inc Biogen Inc

---

Virtus Newfleet Dynamic Credit ETF   D+   SELL

Ticker	Traded On	NAV	Total Assets ($)	Dividend Yield (TTM)	Turnover Ratio	Expense Ratio
BLHY	NYSE Arca	23.22	$64,802,152	5.44	96	0.68

Ratings
Reward   D+
Risk   C-
Recent Upgrade/Downgrade   Down

Fund Information
Fund Type   Exchange Traded Funds
Category   US Fixed Income
Sub-Category   High Yield Bond
Prospectus Objective   Growth & Inc
Inception Date   Dec-16
Open to New Investments   Y

Prices
Price (as of 12/31/2018)   23.04
52-Week High   25.08
52-Week Low   22.92

Total Returns (%)

3-Month	6-Month	1-Year	3-Year	5-Year
-4.42	-2.36	-1.89		

3-Year Standard Deviation
Effective Duration

Valuation
Premium/Discount (1-Year Average)   -0.44

Company Information
Provider   Virtus
Manager/Tenure   David L. Albrycht (1), Francesco Ossino (1), Jonathan R. Stanley (1)
Website   http://www.virtus.com
Address   Virtus Opportunities Trust 101 Munson Street Greenfield MA 1301 United States
Phone Number   800-243-1574

PERFORMANCE

Ratings History

Date	Overall Rating	Risk Rating	Reward Rating
Q4-18	D+	C-	D+
Q2-18	D+	D+	D+
Q4-17	D+	A+	D+
Q4-16			
Q4-15			

Asset & Performance History

Date	NAV	1-Year Total Return
2017	24.99	3.47
2016	25.02	
2015		
2014		
2013		
2012		

Total Assets: $64,802,152

Asset Allocation

Asset	%
Cash	4%
Stocks	0%
US Stocks	0%
Bonds	96%
US Bonds	87%
Other	0%

Services Offered:

Investment Strategy: The investment seeks to provide a high level of current income and, secondarily, capital appreciation. Under normal market conditions, the fund will invest not less than 80% of its net assets (plus the amount of any borrowings for investment purposes) in credit investments, and in derivatives and other instruments that have economic characteristics similar to such investments. Credit investments include corporate and sovereign bonds, including U.S. Treasury securities; loans (including, without limitation, through loan participations and assignments); and securitized instruments. **Top Holdings:** Level 3 Financin 02/22/24 Term Loan Vf Holding Corp 7/02/25 Term Loan Caesars Resort Collectio 12/23/2024 Term Loan Enterprise Merger Sub In 10/10/25 Term Loan Wex Inc 06/30/23 Term Loan

WisdomTree Negative Duration High Yield Bond Fund   C   HOLD

Ticker	Traded On	NAV	Total Assets ($)	Dividend Yield (TTM)	Turnover Ratio	Expense Ratio
HYND	NAS CM	19.66	$64,661,173	5.03	71	0.48

Ratings
Reward   C
Risk   C-
Recent Upgrade/Downgrade

Fund Information
Fund Type   Exchange Traded Funds
Category   Fixed Income Misc
Sub-Category   Nontraditional Bond
Prospectus Objective   Govt Bond - Treasury
Inception Date   Dec-13
Open to New Investments   Y

Prices
Price (as of 12/31/2018)   19.35
52-Week High   21.79
52-Week Low   19.35

Total Returns (%)

3-Month	6-Month	1-Year	3-Year	5-Year
-7.48	-3.68	0.26	16.05	-2.01

3-Year Standard Deviation   6.38
Effective Duration   -7.37

Valuation
Premium/Discount (1-Year Average)   0.11

Company Information
Provider   WisdomTree
Manager/Tenure   Paul L. Benson (3), Stephanie Shu (3)
Website   http://www.wisdomtree.com
Address   WisdomTree 245 Park Avenue, 35th
                  floor New York NY 10167 United
                  States
Phone Number   866-909-9473

PERFORMANCE

Ratings History

Date	Overall Rating	Risk Rating	Reward Rating
Q4-18	C	C-	C
Q2-18	C	C-	C+
Q4-17	B-	B	C
Q4-16	D+	D+	C-
Q4-15	D	D+	D

Asset & Performance History

Date	NAV	1-Year Total Return
2017	20.65	3.32
2016	20.99	11.43
2015	19.72	-5.01
2014	21.59	-11.11
2013	25.24	
2012		

Total Assets: $64,661,173
Asset Allocation

Asset	%
Cash	115%
Stocks	0%
US Stocks	0%
Bonds	-16%
US Bonds	-26%
Other	0%

Services Offered:

Investment Strategy: The investment seeks to track the price and yield performance, before fees and expenses, of the BofA Merrill Lynch 0-5 Year U.S. High Yield Constrained, Negative Seven Duration Index. The index is designed to provide long exposure to the BofA Merrill Lynch 0-5 Year US High Yield Constrained Index while seeking to manage interest rate risk through the use of short positions in U.S. Treasury securities. The fund normally invests at least 80% of its total assets in the component securities of the index and investments that have economic characteristics that are substantially identical to such component securities. It is non-diversified. **Top Holdings:** Us 10yr Ultra Fut Mar19 Xcbt 20190320 Us 5yr Note (Cbt) Mar19 Xcbt 20190329 Us Ultra Bond Cbt Mar19 Xcbt 20190320 Sprint Corporation 7.88% Bausch Health Companies Inc 5.88%

iShares International High Yield Bond ETF   D+   SELL

Ticker	Traded On	NAV	Total Assets ($)	Dividend Yield (TTM)	Turnover Ratio	Expense Ratio
HYXU	BATS	48.01	$64,639,978	0	49	0.4

Ratings
Reward   D+
Risk   C-
Recent Upgrade/Downgrade   Down

Fund Information
Fund Type   Exchange Traded Funds
Category   Global Fixed Income
Sub-Category   High Yield Bond
Prospectus Objective   Corp Bond-High Yld
Inception Date   Apr-12
Open to New Investments   Y

Prices
Price (as of 12/31/2018)   48.30
52-Week High   56.93
52-Week Low   47.72

Total Returns (%)

3-Month	6-Month	1-Year	3-Year	5-Year
-4.84	-3.05	-8.03	14.82	-4.19

3-Year Standard Deviation   8.98
Effective Duration   3.96

Valuation
Premium/Discount (1-Year Average)   0.14

Company Information
Provider   iShares
Manager/Tenure   James Mauro (6), Scott Radell (6)
Website   http://www.ishares.com
Address   iShares 400 Howard Street San
                  Francisco CA 94105 United States
Phone Number   800-474-2737

PERFORMANCE

Ratings History

Date	Overall Rating	Risk Rating	Reward Rating
Q4-18	D+	C-	D+
Q2-18	C-	C-	C-
Q4-17	B-	B-	B-
Q4-16	D+	C-	D
Q4-15	D+	D+	D+

Asset & Performance History

Date	NAV	1-Year Total Return
2017	54.32	19.65
2016	45.75	4.35
2015	44.59	-9.47
2014	50.79	-7.84
2013	57.43	12.84
2012	53.67	

Total Assets: $64,639,978
Asset Allocation

Asset	%
Cash	0%
Stocks	0%
US Stocks	0%
Bonds	100%
US Bonds	11%
Other	0%

Services Offered:

Investment Strategy: The investment seeks to track the investment results of the Markit iBoxx Global Developed Markets ex-US High Yield Index. The fund generally will invest at least 90% of its assets in the component securities of the underlying index and may invest up to 10% of its assets in certain futures, options and swap contracts, cash and cash equivalents, including shares of money market funds advised by BFA or its affiliates. The index is a rules-based index consisting of high yield corporate bonds denominated in euros, British pounds sterling and Canadian dollars. **Top Holdings:** Altice Luxembourg S.A. 7.25% Wind Tre S.p.A. 3.13% UniCredit S.p.A. 6.95% Intrum Ab 2.75% Softbank Group Corp 3.13%

Invesco DWA Tactical Sector Rotation ETF

C- **HOLD**

Ticker	Traded On	NAV
DWTR	NAS CM	24.70

Total Assets ($)	Dividend Yield (TTM)	Turnover Ratio	Expense Ratio
$64,583,619	0.28		0.75

Ratings
Reward	C-
Risk	C-
Recent Upgrade/Downgrade	Down

Fund Information
Fund Type	Exchange Traded Funds
Category	US Equity Mid Cap
Sub-Category	Mid-Cap Growth
Prospectus Objective	Growth & Inc
Inception Date	Oct-15
Open to New Investments	Y

Prices
Price (as of 12/31/2018)	24.59
52-Week High	32.22
52-Week Low	22.70

Total Returns (%)
3-Month	6-Month	1-Year	3-Year	5-Year
-21.07	-16.28	-12.61	-0.50	

3-Year Standard Deviation	13.62
Effective Duration	

Valuation
Premium/Discount (1-Year Average)	-0.22

Company Information
Provider	Invesco
Manager/Tenure	Peter Hubbard (3), Michael Jeanette (3), Jonathan Nixon (3), 1 other
Website	http://www.invesco.com/us
Address	Invesco 11 Greenway Plaza, Ste. 2500 Houston TX 77046 United States
Phone Number	800-659-1005

PERFORMANCE

Ratings History
Date	Overall Rating	Risk Rating	Reward Rating
Q4-18	C-	C-	C-
Q2-18	C	D+	C
Q4-17	C	B-	C
Q4-16	D	C-	D
Q4-15			

Asset & Performance History
Date	NAV	1-Year Total Return
2017	28.28	16.68
2016	24.36	-2.84
2015	25.18	
2014		
2013		
2012		

Total Assets: $64,583,619
Asset Allocation
Asset	%
Cash	0%
Stocks	100%
US Stocks	100%
Bonds	0%
US Bonds	0%
Other	0%

Services Offered:

Investment Strategy: The investment seeks investment results that generally correspond (before fees and expenses) of the Dorsey Wright® Sector 4 Index (the "underlying index"). The fund generally will invest at least 90% of its total assets in securities that comprise the underlying index. It is a "fund of funds," meaning that it invests its assets in the shares of other exchange-traded funds ("ETFs") eligible for inclusion in the underlying index. The underlying index seeks to gain exposure to the sectors of the U.S. equity markets that display the strongest relative strength, as evaluated on a monthly basis. The fund is non-diversified. **Top Holdings:** Invesco DWA Industrials Momentum ETF Invesco DWA Technology Momentum ETF Invesco DWA Consumer Cyclicals Mom ETF Invesco DWA Healthcare Momentum ETF

WisdomTree International Quality Dividend Growth Fund

D+ **SELL**

Ticker	Traded On	NAV
IQDG	BATS	25.10

Total Assets ($)	Dividend Yield (TTM)	Turnover Ratio	Expense Ratio
$64,556,326	1.59	39	0.38

Ratings
Reward	D+
Risk	C-
Recent Upgrade/Downgrade	Down

Fund Information
Fund Type	Exchange Traded Funds
Category	Global Equity Large Cap
Sub-Category	Foreign Large Growth
Prospectus Objective	Growth & Inc
Inception Date	Apr-16
Open to New Investments	Y

Prices
Price (as of 12/31/2018)	25.09
52-Week High	32.75
52-Week Low	24.23

Total Returns (%)
3-Month	6-Month	1-Year	3-Year	5-Year
-14.53	-13.84	-17.05		

3-Year Standard Deviation	
Effective Duration	

Valuation
Premium/Discount (1-Year Average)	0.24

Company Information
Provider	WisdomTree
Manager/Tenure	Richard A. Brown (2), Thomas J. Durante (2), Karen Q. Wong (2)
Website	http://www.wisdomtree.com
Address	WisdomTree 245 Park Avenue, 35th floor New York NY 10167 United States
Phone Number	866-909-9473

PERFORMANCE

Ratings History
Date	Overall Rating	Risk Rating	Reward Rating
Q4-18	D+	C-	D+
Q2-18	C	C-	C
Q4-17	D+	B-	C
Q4-16	U		
Q4-15			

Asset & Performance History
Date	NAV	1-Year Total Return
2017	30.79	31.39
2016	23.87	
2015		
2014		
2013		
2012		

Total Assets: $64,556,326
Asset Allocation
Asset	%
Cash	0%
Stocks	100%
US Stocks	1%
Bonds	0%
US Bonds	0%
Other	0%

Services Offered:

Investment Strategy: The investment seeks to track the price and yield performance, before fees and expenses, of the WisdomTree International Quality Dividend Growth Index. Under normal circumstances, at least 80% of the fund's total assets (exclusive of collateral held from securities lending) will be invested in component securities of the index and investments that have economic characteristics that are substantially identical to the economic characteristics of such component securities. The index consists of dividend-paying common stocks with growth characteristics of companies in the industrialized world, excluding Canada and the United States. The fund is non-diversified. **Top Holdings:** Novo Nordisk A/S B Diageo PLC British American Tobacco PLC Industria De Diseno Textil SA China Overseas Land & Investment Ltd

Direxion Daily Mid Cap Bull 3X Shares   C-   HOLD

Ticker	Traded On	NAV
MIDU	NYSE Arca	28.12

Total Assets ($)	Dividend Yield (TTM)	Turnover Ratio	Expense Ratio
$64,504,406	0.24	130	1.08

Ratings
Reward	C
Risk	C-
Recent Upgrade/Downgrade	Down

Fund Information
Fund Type	Exchange Traded Funds
Category	Trading Tools
Sub-Category	Trading--Leveraged Equity
Prospectus Objective	Growth
Inception Date	Jan-09
Open to New Investments	Y

Prices
Price (as of 12/31/2018)	28.04
52-Week High	55.59
52-Week Low	23.80

Total Returns (%)
3-Month	6-Month	1-Year	3-Year	5-Year
-45.26	-41.54	-38.94	41.71	48.29

3-Year Standard Deviation	35.88
Effective Duration	

Valuation
Premium/Discount (1-Year Average)	0.02

Company Information
Provider	Direxion Funds
Manager/Tenure	Paul Brigandi (9), Tony Ng (3)
Website	http://www.direxionfunds.com
Address	Direxion Funds 1301 Avenue Of The Americas (6th Avenue) New York NY 10019 United States
Phone Number	646-572-3390

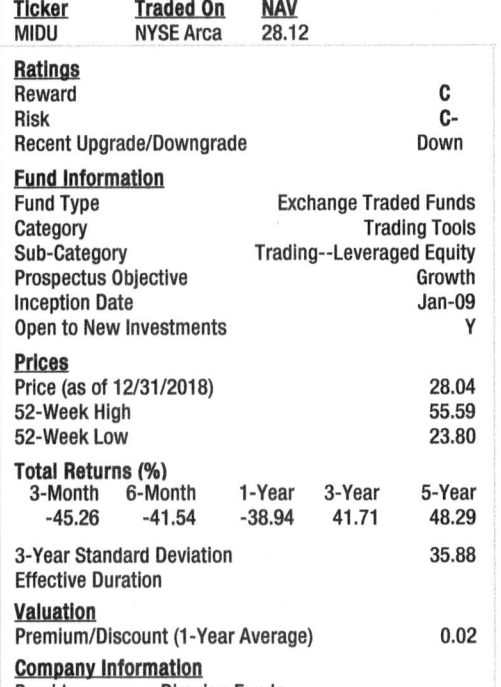

PERFORMANCE

Ratings History
Date	Overall Rating	Risk Rating	Reward Rating
Q4-18	C-	C-	C
Q2-18	C	C-	C+
Q4-17	B+	C	A+
Q4-16	C	D+	C+
Q4-15	C	C-	C

Asset & Performance History
Date	NAV	1-Year Total Return
2017	46.36	46.47
2016	32.52	58.46
2015	20.89	-14.7
2014	24.49	22.69
2013	19.96	119.97
2012	9.48	49.74

Total Assets: $64,504,406
Asset Allocation
Asset	%
Cash	38%
Stocks	62%
US Stocks	62%
Bonds	0%
US Bonds	0%
Other	0%

Services Offered:

Investment Strategy: The investment seeks daily investment results, before fees and expenses, of 300% of the daily performance of the S&P MidCap® 400 Index. The fund, under normal circumstances, invests at least 80% of its net assets (plus borrowing for investment purposes) in securities of the index, exchange-traded funds ("ETFs") that track the index and other financial instruments that provide daily leveraged exposure to the index or ETFs that track the index. The index measures the performance of 400 mid-sized companies in the United States. The fund is non-diversified. **Top Holdings:** iShares Core S&P Mid-Cap ETF   S&P Mid Cap 400 Index Swa   S&P Mid Cap 400 Index Swa   S&P Mid Cap 400 Index Swa   S&P Mid Cap 400 Index Swa

---

USAA Core Short-Term Bond ETF   D+   SELL

Ticker	Traded On	NAV
USTB	NYSE Arca	49.47

Total Assets ($)	Dividend Yield (TTM)	Turnover Ratio	Expense Ratio
$64,119,050	2.24	22	0.35

Ratings
Reward	D
Risk	D+
Recent Upgrade/Downgrade	

Fund Information
Fund Type	Exchange Traded Funds
Category	US Fixed Income
Sub-Category	Short-Term Bond
Prospectus Objective	Income
Inception Date	Oct-17
Open to New Investments	Y

Prices
Price (as of 12/31/2018)	49.46
52-Week High	50.08
52-Week Low	49.24

Total Returns (%)
3-Month	6-Month	1-Year	3-Year	5-Year
0.89	1.57	1.43		

3-Year Standard Deviation	
Effective Duration	1.81

Valuation
Premium/Discount (1-Year Average)	0.15

Company Information
Provider	USAA
Manager/Tenure	Julianne Bass (1), Kurt Daum (1), Brian W. Smith (1), 1 other
Website	http://www.usaa.com
Address	USAA P.O. Box 659453 San Antonio TX 78265-9825 United States
Phone Number	800-531-8722

PERFORMANCE

Ratings History
Date	Overall Rating	Risk Rating	Reward Rating
Q4-18	D+	D+	D
Q2-18	U		
Q4-17	U		
Q4-16			
Q4-15			

Asset & Performance History
Date	NAV	1-Year Total Return
2017	49.92	
2016		
2015		
2014		
2013		
2012		

Total Assets: $64,119,050
Asset Allocation
Asset	%
Cash	7%
Stocks	0%
US Stocks	0%
Bonds	93%
US Bonds	83%
Other	0%

Services Offered:

Investment Strategy: The investment seeks high current income consistent with preservation of principal. Under normal circumstances, the fund invests at least 80% of its net assets in debt securities and in derivatives and other instruments that have economic characteristics similar to such securities. It primarily invests in securities that have a dollar-weighted average portfolio maturity of three years or less. The fund may not invest more than 20% of fixed-income securities in non-agency, non-government sponsored entities (GSEs), or privately issued mortgage- or asset-backed securities. **Top Holdings:** United States Treasury Notes 1.88%   United States Treasury Notes 1.62%   United States Treasury Notes 1.12%   United States Treasury Notes 1.25%   Carmax Auto Owner Trust 2.22%

Invesco KBW Property & Casualty Insurance ETF   B-   BUY

Ticker	Traded On	NAV	Total Assets ($)	Dividend Yield (TTM)	Turnover Ratio	Expense Ratio
KBWP	NAS CM	56.92	$64,004,295	2.3		0.35

Ratings
Reward   B
Risk   C
Recent Upgrade/Downgrade

Fund Information
Fund Type   Exchange Traded Funds
Category   Financials Sector Equity
Sub-Category   Financial
Prospectus Objective   Growth
Inception Date   Dec-10
Open to New Investments

Prices
Price (as of 12/31/2018)   56.62
52-Week High   64.80
52-Week Low   53.39

Total Returns (%)

3-Month	6-Month	1-Year	3-Year	5-Year
-8.79	-2.99	-2.24	26.85	61.23

3-Year Standard Deviation   10.28
Effective Duration

Valuation
Premium/Discount (1-Year Average)   0.19

Company Information
Provider   Invesco
Manager/Tenure   Peter Hubbard (8), Michael Jeanette (8), Tony Seisser (4), 1 other
Website   http://www.invesco.com/us
Address   Invesco 11 Greenway Plaza, Ste. 2500 Houston TX 77046 United States
Phone Number   800-659-1005

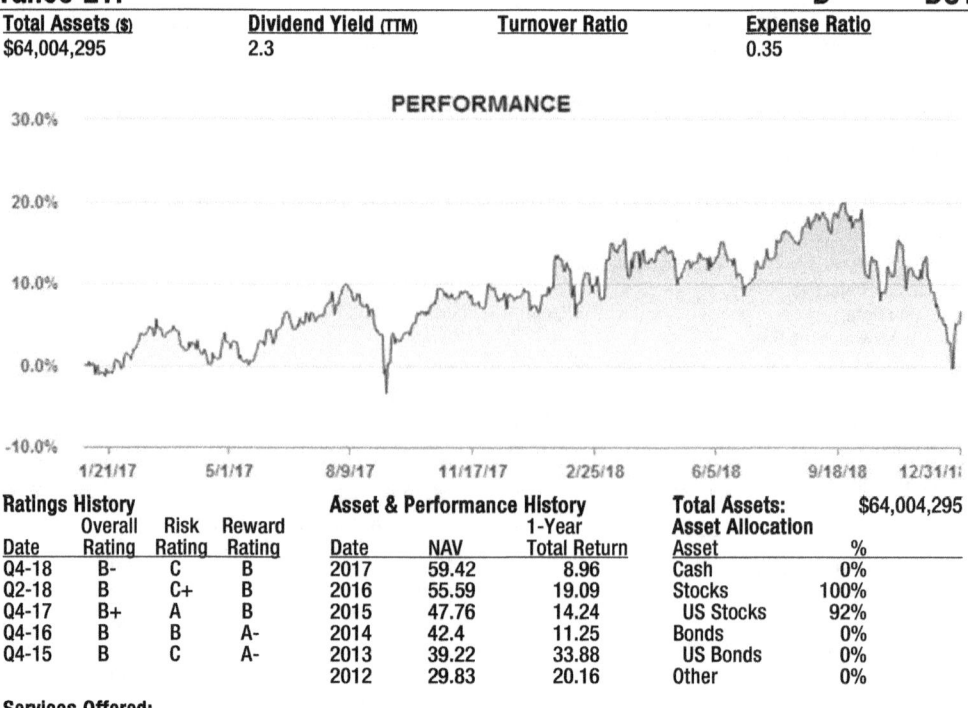

PERFORMANCE

Ratings History

Date	Overall Rating	Risk Rating	Reward Rating
Q4-18	B-	C	B
Q2-18	B	C+	B
Q4-17	B+	A	B
Q4-16	B	B	A-
Q4-15	B	C	A-

Asset & Performance History

Date	NAV	1-Year Total Return
2017	59.42	8.96
2016	55.59	19.09
2015	47.76	14.24
2014	42.4	11.25
2013	39.22	33.88
2012	29.83	20.16

Total Assets: $64,004,295
Asset Allocation

Asset	%
Cash	0%
Stocks	100%
US Stocks	92%
Bonds	0%
US Bonds	0%
Other	0%

Services Offered:

Investment Strategy: The investment seeks to track the investment results (before fees and expenses) of the KBW Nasdaq Property & Casualty Index (the "underlying index"). The fund generally will invest at least 90% of its total assets in the securities of property and casualty insurance companies that comprise the underlying index. It generally invests in all of the securities comprising the underlying index in proportion to their weightings in the underlying index. The fund is non-diversified. **Top Holdings:** The Travelers Companies Inc Chubb Ltd Progressive Corp Allstate Corp American International Group Inc

---

FlexShares US Quality Large Cap Index Fund   C   HOLD

Ticker	Traded On	NAV	Total Assets ($)	Dividend Yield (TTM)	Turnover Ratio	Expense Ratio
QLC	NAS CM	30.28	$63,956,642	1.53		0.32

Ratings
Reward   C
Risk   C-
Recent Upgrade/Downgrade

Fund Information
Fund Type   Exchange Traded Funds
Category   US Equity Large Cap Value
Sub-Category   Large Value
Prospectus Objective   Growth
Inception Date   Sep-15
Open to New Investments   Y

Prices
Price (as of 12/31/2018)   30.13
52-Week High   36.18
52-Week Low   28.41

Total Returns (%)

3-Month	6-Month	1-Year	3-Year	5-Year
-15.00	-9.59	-7.51	22.70	

3-Year Standard Deviation   9.88
Effective Duration

Valuation
Premium/Discount (1-Year Average)   0.33

Company Information
Provider   Flexshares Trust
Manager/Tenure   Robert Anstine (3), Brendan Sullivan (2)
Website   http://www.flexshares.com
Address   50 South LaSalle Street Chicago, Illinois 60603 Chicago Illinois 60603 United States
Phone Number   855-353-9383

PERFORMANCE

Ratings History

Date	Overall Rating	Risk Rating	Reward Rating
Q4-18	C	C-	C
Q2-18	C	D+	C+
Q4-17	C	B	C+
Q4-16	D	D+	C-
Q4-15			

Asset & Performance History

Date	NAV	1-Year Total Return
2017	33.3	21.32
2016	27.83	8.23
2015	25.93	
2014		
2013		
2012		

Total Assets: $63,956,642
Asset Allocation

Asset	%
Cash	1%
Stocks	99%
US Stocks	98%
Bonds	0%
US Bonds	0%
Other	0%

Services Offered:

Investment Strategy: The investment seeks investment results that correspond generally to the price and yield performance, before fees and expenses, of the Northern Trust Quality Large Cap IndexSM. The fund generally will invest under normal circumstances at least 80% of its total assets (exclusive of collateral held from securities lending) in the securities of its underlying index. The underlying index is designed to measure the performance of companies that exhibit certain quality, valuation and momentum characteristics within a universe of publicly-traded U.S. large capitalization equity securities. **Top Holdings:** Apple Inc Johnson & Johnson Bank of America Corporation Verizon Communications Inc Chevron Corp

VanEck Vectors Unconventional Oil & Gas ETF   C   HOLD

Ticker	Traded On	NAV	Total Assets ($)	Dividend Yield (TTM)	Turnover Ratio	Expense Ratio
FRAK	NYSE Arca	10.93	$63,953,966	0.83	17	0.54

Ratings
Reward	C+
Risk	D+
Recent Upgrade/Downgrade	

Fund Information
Fund Type	Exchange Traded Funds
Category	Energy Sector Equity
Sub-Category	Equity Energy
Prospectus Objective	Natl Res
Inception Date	Feb-12
Open to New Investments	Y

Prices
Price (as of 12/31/2018)	10.92
52-Week High	17.99
52-Week Low	10.14

Total Returns (%)
3-Month	6-Month	1-Year	3-Year	5-Year
-36.73	-35.58	-29.93	-15.84	-59.22

3-Year Standard Deviation	28.87
Effective Duration	

Valuation
Premium/Discount (1-Year Average)	-0.08

Company Information
Provider	VanEck
Manager/Tenure	Hao-Hung (Peter) Liao (6), Guo Hua (Jason) Jin (0)
Website	http://www.vaneck.com
Address	Van Eck Associates Corporation 666 Third Avenue New York NY 10017 United States
Phone Number	800-826-1115

PERFORMANCE

Ratings History
Date	Overall Rating	Risk Rating	Reward Rating
Q4-18	C	D+	C+
Q2-18	C-	D+	C
Q4-17	D	D	D
Q4-16	D+	D	D+
Q4-15	C-	C-	C

Asset & Performance History
Date	NAV	1-Year Total Return
2017	15.73	-13.15
2016	18.25	38.3
2015	13.24	-38.52
2014	22.12	-21.18
2013	28.43	26.77
2012	22.54	

Total Assets: $63,953,966

Asset Allocation
Asset	%
Cash	0%
Stocks	100%
US Stocks	87%
Bonds	0%
US Bonds	0%
Other	0%

Services Offered:

Investment Strategy: The investment seeks to replicate as closely as possible, before fees and expenses, the price and yield performance of the MVIS® Global Unconventional Oil & Gas Index. The fund normally invests at least 80% of its total assets in securities that comprise the fund's benchmark index. The index contains companies that generate at least 50% of their revenues from unconventional oil and gas or that have properties with the potential to generate at least 50% of their revenues from unconventional oil and gas. The fund is non-diversified. **Top Holdings:** Occidental Petroleum Corp EOG Resources Inc Pioneer Natural Resources Co Concho Resources Inc Anadarko Petroleum Corp

Arrow Dow Jones Global Yield ETF   D+   SELL

Ticker	Traded On	NAV	Total Assets ($)	Dividend Yield (TTM)	Turnover Ratio	Expense Ratio
GYLD	NYSE Arca	15.42	$63,681,613	7.49	90	0.75

Ratings
Reward	D+
Risk	C-
Recent Upgrade/Downgrade	Down

Fund Information
Fund Type	Exchange Traded Funds
Category	Moderate Allocation
Sub-Category	World Allocation
Prospectus Objective	Growth & Inc
Inception Date	May-12
Open to New Investments	Y

Prices
Price (as of 12/31/2018)	15.07
52-Week High	18.96
52-Week Low	14.88

Total Returns (%)
3-Month	6-Month	1-Year	3-Year	5-Year
-10.27	-8.65	-9.35	9.24	-14.98

3-Year Standard Deviation	11.55
Effective Duration	

Valuation
Premium/Discount (1-Year Average)	-1.25

Company Information
Provider	ArrowShares
Manager/Tenure	William E. Flaig (6), Joseph Barrato (4), Jonathan S. Guyer (4)
Website	http://www.ArrowShares.com
Address	c/o Gemini Fund Services, LLC 17605 Wright Street, Suite 2 Omaha NE 68130 United States
Phone Number	877-277-6933

PERFORMANCE

Ratings History
Date	Overall Rating	Risk Rating	Reward Rating
Q4-18	D+	C-	D+
Q2-18	C-	C-	C-
Q4-17	C-	C-	C
Q4-16	D+	D+	D
Q4-15	C-	D+	C-

Asset & Performance History
Date	NAV	1-Year Total Return
2017	18.27	5.84
2016	18.44	13.85
2015	17.46	-21.3
2014	24.05	-1.1
2013	26.12	8.03
2012	25.6	

Total Assets: $63,681,613

Asset Allocation
Asset	%
Cash	0%
Stocks	58%
US Stocks	29%
Bonds	41%
US Bonds	19%
Other	1%

Services Offered:

Investment Strategy: The investment seeks investment results that generally correspond, before fees and expenses, to the price and yield performance of the Dow Jones Global Composite Yield Index (the "underlying index"). The fund uses a "passive" or "indexing" investment approach to seek to track the price and yield performance of the underlying index. It invests at least 80% of its total assets in the component securities of the underlying index (or depositary receipts representing those securities). The underlying index seeks to identify the 150 highest yielding investable securities in the world within three "asset classes." **Top Holdings:** Indonesia (Republic of) 4.35% Seaspan Corp Telkom SA SOC Ltd USD Partners LP Brazil (Federative Republic) 10.12%

John Hancock Multifactor Technology ETF

C **HOLD**

Ticker	Traded On	NAV	Total Assets ($)	Dividend Yield (TTM)	Turnover Ratio	Expense Ratio
JHMT	NYSE Arca	39.54	$63,346,816	0.65	7	0.5

Ratings

Reward   C

Risk   D+

Recent Upgrade/Downgrade

Fund Information

Fund Type	Exchange Traded Funds
Category	Technology Sector Equity
Sub-Category	Technology
Prospectus Objective	Technology
Inception Date	Sep-15
Open to New Investments	Y

Prices

Price (as of 12/31/2018)	39.34
52-Week High	48.42
52-Week Low	36.84

Total Returns (%)

3-Month	6-Month	1-Year	3-Year	5-Year
-16.44	-12.36	-2.75	52.13	

3-Year Standard Deviation	14.1
Effective Duration	

Valuation

Premium/Discount (1-Year Average)	0.09

Company Information

Provider	John Hancock
Manager/Tenure	Joel P. Schneider (3), Lukas J. Smart (3), Joseph F. Hohn (0)
Website	http://jhinvestments.com
Address	601 Congress Street, Boston MA 02210 United States
Phone Number	800-225-5913

PERFORMANCE

Ratings History

Date	Overall Rating	Risk Rating	Reward Rating
Q4-18	C	D+	C
Q2-18	C	C-	B-
Q4-17	C	B	B-
Q4-16	D	C-	C
Q4-15			

Asset & Performance History

Date	NAV	1-Year Total Return
2017	41.04	34.52
2016	30.73	16.29
2015	26.8	
2014		
2013		
2012		

Total Assets: $63,346,816

Asset Allocation

Asset	%
Cash	2%
Stocks	98%
US Stocks	97%
Bonds	0%
US Bonds	0%
Other	0%

Services Offered:

Investment Strategy: The investment seeks to provide investment results that closely correspond, before fees and expenses, to the performance of the John Hancock Dimensional Technology Index. The fund normally invests at least 80% of its net assets (plus any borrowings for investment purposes) in securities that compose the fund's benchmark index. The index is designed to comprise securities in the technology sector within the U.S. Universe whose market capitalizations are larger than that of the 1001st largest U.S. company at the time of reconstitution. The fund is non-diversified. **Top Holdings:** Microsoft Corp Facebook Inc A Apple Inc Intel Corp Alphabet Inc A

Invesco BRIC ETF

C- **HOLD**

Ticker	Traded On	NAV	Total Assets ($)	Dividend Yield (TTM)	Turnover Ratio	Expense Ratio
EEB	NYSE Arca		$63,162,824	1.81	39	0.64

Ratings

Reward   C-

Risk   D+

Recent Upgrade/Downgrade   Down

Fund Information

Fund Type	Exchange Traded Funds
Category	Global Emerg Mkts Equity
Sub-Category	Diversified Emerging Mkts
Prospectus Objective	Growth
Inception Date	Sep-06
Open to New Investments	Y

Prices

Price (as of 12/31/2018)	32.09
52-Week High	41.99
52-Week Low	31.24

Total Returns (%)

3-Month	6-Month	1-Year	3-Year	5-Year
-9.68	-11.48	-14.35	35.50	0.67

3-Year Standard Deviation	16.44
Effective Duration	

Valuation

Premium/Discount (1-Year Average)	-0.02

Company Information

Provider	Invesco
Manager/Tenure	Peter Hubbard (0), Michael Jeanette (0), Jonathan Nixon (0), 1 other
Website	http://www.invesco.com/us
Address	Invesco 11 Greenway Plaza, Ste. 2500 Houston TX 77046 United States
Phone Number	800-659-1005

PERFORMANCE

Ratings History

Date	Overall Rating	Risk Rating	Reward Rating
Q4-18	C-	D+	C-
Q2-18	C	D+	C
Q4-17	B-	C	B
Q4-16	C-	C-	C-
Q4-15	D	D	D

Asset & Performance History

Date	NAV	1-Year Total Return
2017	37.35	31.29
2016	28.84	20.12
2015	24.36	-13.92
2014	28.85	-13.67
2013	34.61	-1.47
2012	36.01	5.5

Total Assets: $63,162,824

Asset Allocation

Asset	%
Cash	0%
Stocks	100%
US Stocks	1%
Bonds	0%
US Bonds	0%
Other	0%

Services Offered:

Investment Strategy: The investment seeks investment results that correspond generally to the performance before the fund's fees and expenses of the BNY Mellon BRIC Select DR Index. The fund will invest at least 90% of its total assets in securities that comprise the index and in the underlying securities representing ADRs and GDRs. The index is a rules-based index comprised of American depositary receipts, global depositary receipts and China H-shares of Chinese equities where appropriate, based on liquidity, from a universe of all listed depositary receipts of companies from Brazil, Russia, India and China currently trading on U.S. and non-U.S. exchanges. It is non-diversified. **Top Holdings:** Alibaba Group Holding Ltd ADR HDFC Bank Ltd ADR China Mobile Ltd ADR China Mobile Ltd Baidu Inc ADR

John Hancock Multifactor Health Care ETF   C   HOLD

Ticker	Traded On	NAV	Total Assets ($)	Dividend Yield (TTM)	Turnover Ratio	Expense Ratio
JHMH	NYSE Arca	31.55	$62,977,035	0.68	11	0.5

Ratings
Reward   C
Risk   C
Recent Upgrade/Downgrade

Fund Information
Fund Type   Exchange Traded Funds
Category   Healthcare Sector Equity
Sub-Category   Health
Prospectus Objective   Health
Inception Date   Sep-15
Open to New Investments   Y

Prices
Price (as of 12/31/2018)   31.54
52-Week High   36.25
52-Week Low   29.55

Total Returns (%)

3-Month	6-Month	1-Year	3-Year	5-Year
-12.45	-1.23	2.50	22.87	

3-Year Standard Deviation   13.03
Effective Duration

Valuation
Premium/Discount (1-Year Average)   0.14

Company Information
Provider   John Hancock
Manager/Tenure   Joel P. Schneider (3), Lukas J. Smart
                  (3), Joseph F. Hohn (0)
Website   http://jhinvestments.com
Address   601 Congress Street, Boston MA
                  02210 United States
Phone Number   800-225-5913

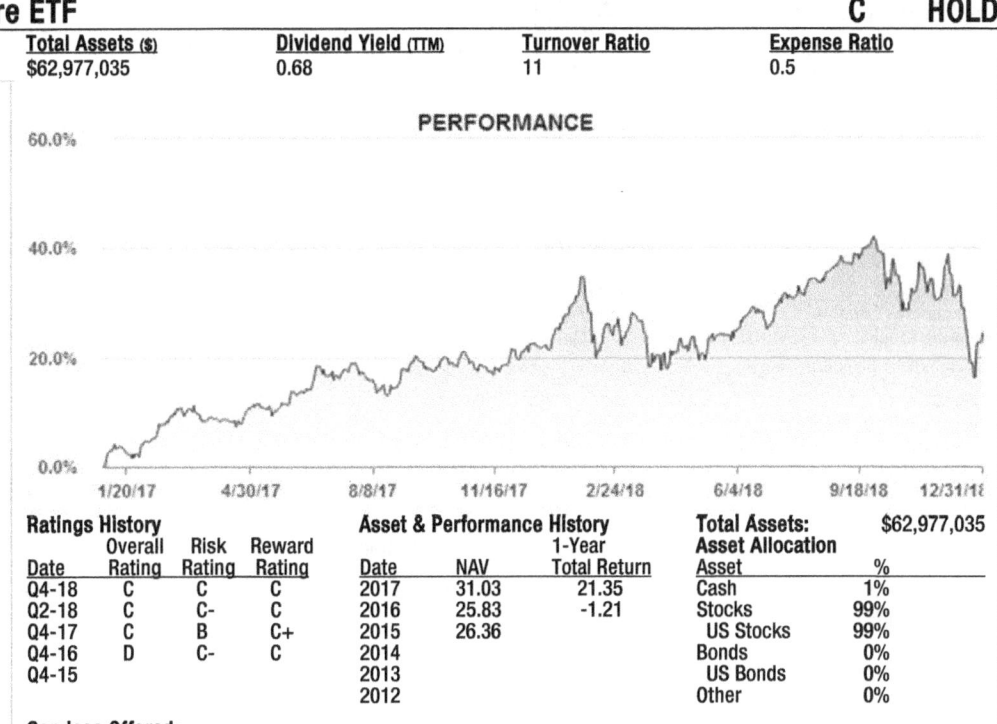

Ratings History

Date	Overall Rating	Risk Rating	Reward Rating
Q4-18	C	C	C
Q2-18	C	C-	C
Q4-17	C	B	C+
Q4-16	D	C-	C
Q4-15			

Asset & Performance History

Date	NAV	1-Year Total Return
2017	31.03	21.35
2016	25.83	-1.21
2015	26.36	
2014		
2013		
2012		

Total Assets: $62,977,035

Asset Allocation

Asset	%
Cash	1%
Stocks	99%
US Stocks	99%
Bonds	0%
US Bonds	0%
Other	0%

Services Offered:

Investment Strategy: The investment seeks to provide investment results that closely correspond, before fees and expenses, to the performance of the John Hancock Dimensional Healthcare Index. The fund normally invests at least 80% of its net assets (plus any borrowings for investment purposes) in securities that compose the fund's benchmark index. The index is designed to comprise securities in the healthcare sector within the U.S. Universe whose market capitalizations are larger than that of the 1001st largest U.S. company at the time of reconstitution. The fund is non-diversified. **Top Holdings:** Johnson & Johnson   UnitedHealth Group Inc   Pfizer Inc   Merck & Co Inc   Gilead Sciences Inc

---

Hull Tactical US ETF   C-   HOLD

Ticker	Traded On	NAV	Total Assets ($)	Dividend Yield (TTM)	Turnover Ratio	Expense Ratio
HTUS	NYSE Arca	22.88	$62,915,771	0.6	1,827	0.96

Ratings
Reward   C-
Risk   D+
Recent Upgrade/Downgrade

Fund Information
Fund Type   Exchange Traded Funds
Category   Long/Short Equity
Sub-Category   Long-Short Equity
Prospectus Objective   Growth
Inception Date   Jun-15
Open to New Investments   Y

Prices
Price (as of 12/31/2018)   22.43
52-Week High   28.43
52-Week Low   20.79

Total Returns (%)

3-Month	6-Month	1-Year	3-Year	5-Year
-8.89	-6.02	-5.95	13.45	

3-Year Standard Deviation   5.41
Effective Duration

Valuation
Premium/Discount (1-Year Average)   -0.09

Company Information
Provider   Hull Tactical Funds
Manager/Tenure   Petra Bakosova (3), Denise M. Krisko
                  (3)
Website   http://www.hulltacticalfunds.com
Address   Hull Tactical Funds United States
Phone Number

Ratings History

Date	Overall Rating	Risk Rating	Reward Rating
Q4-18	C-	D+	C-
Q2-18	C-	C-	C
Q4-17	C	B+	C
Q4-16	D	C-	C-
Q4-15	U		

Asset & Performance History

Date	NAV	1-Year Total Return
2017	27.08	12.03
2016	26.19	7.68
2015	25.04	
2014		
2013		
2012		

Total Assets: $62,915,771

Asset Allocation

Asset	%
Cash	37%
Stocks	63%
US Stocks	62%
Bonds	0%
US Bonds	0%
Other	0%

Services Offered:

Investment Strategy: The investment seeks long-term capital appreciation. The fund seeks to achieve its investment objective by taking long and short positions in one or more exchange-traded funds ("ETFs") that seek to track the performance of the S&P 500 Index. In seeking to achieve its investment objective, it may engage in short sales of S&P 500-related ETFs. The fund may also invest up to 10% of its total assets in leveraged or inverse ETFs that seek to deliver multiples (long), or the inverse (short), of the performance of the S&P 500 Index, respectively. **Top Holdings:** SPDR® S&P 500 ETF   S&P500 Emini Fut Dec18   US Treasury Bill

ProShares UltraPro 3x Crude Oil ETF

D+   **SELL**

Ticker	Traded On	NAV	Total Assets ($)	Dividend Yield (TTM)	Turnover Ratio	Expense Ratio
OILU	NYSE Arca		$62,818,102	0		0.49

Ratings

Reward	D+
Risk	D
Recent Upgrade/Downgrade	Down

Fund Information

Fund Type	Exchange Traded Funds
Category	Trading Tools
Sub-Category	Trading--Leveraged Commodities
Prospectus Objective	Growth & Inc
Inception Date	Mar-17
Open to New Investments	Y

Prices

Price (as of 12/31/2018)	13.47
52-Week High	73.04
52-Week Low	12.37

Total Returns (%)

3-Month	6-Month	1-Year	3-Year	5-Year
-81.61	-78.57	-65.64		

3-Year Standard Deviation	
Effective Duration	

Valuation

Premium/Discount (1-Year Average)	-0.25

Company Information

Provider	ProShares
Manager/Tenure	Management Team (1)
Website	http://www.proshares.com
Address	ProShares 7501 Wisconsin Avenue, Suite 1000 Bethesda MD 20814 United States
Phone Number	866-776-5125

PERFORMANCE

Ratings History

Date	Overall Rating	Risk Rating	Reward Rating
Q4-18	D+	D	D+
Q2-18	C	D+	C
Q4-17	U		
Q4-16			
Q4-15			

Asset & Performance History

Date	NAV	1-Year Total Return
2017	37.79	
2016		
2015		
2014		
2013		
2012		

Total Assets: $62,818,102

Asset Allocation

Asset	%
Cash	-200%
Stocks	0%
US Stocks	0%
Bonds	0%
US Bonds	0%
Other	300%

Services Offered:

Investment Strategy: The investment seeks to return a multiple (3x) of the performance of the Bloomberg WTI Crude Oil Subindex for a single day.
The fund seeks to meet its investment objective by investing, under normal market conditions, in futures contracts for WTI sweet, light crude oil listed on the NYMEX, ICE Futures U.S. or other U.S. exchanges and listed options on such contracts. **Top Holdings:** Wti Crude Oil Future 12/19/2018 (Clf9)

Direxion Daily Junior Gold Miners Index Bear 3X Shares

D   **SELL**

Ticker	Traded On	NAV	Total Assets ($)	Dividend Yield (TTM)	Turnover Ratio	Expense Ratio
JDST	NYSE Arca	50.40	$62,730,137	0.24	0	1.1

Ratings

Reward	D
Risk	D
Recent Upgrade/Downgrade	Up

Fund Information

Fund Type	Exchange Traded Funds
Category	Trading Tools
Sub-Category	Trading--Inverse Equity
Prospectus Objective	Prec Metals
Inception Date	Oct-13
Open to New Investments	Y

Prices

Price (as of 12/31/2018)	50.27
52-Week High	89.22
52-Week Low	43.66

Total Returns (%)

3-Month	6-Month	1-Year	3-Year	5-Year
-35.78	-3.17	-1.45	-99.14	-99.89

3-Year Standard Deviation	101.32
Effective Duration	

Valuation

Premium/Discount (1-Year Average)	-0.14

Company Information

Provider	Direxion Funds
Manager/Tenure	Paul Brigandi (5), Tony Ng (3)
Website	http://www.direxionfunds.com
Address	Direxion Funds 1301 Avenue Of The Americas (6th Avenue) New York NY 10019 United States
Phone Number	646-572-3390

PERFORMANCE

Ratings History

Date	Overall Rating	Risk Rating	Reward Rating
Q4-18	D	D	D
Q2-18	D-	D-	E+
Q4-17	E+	D-	E+
Q4-16	D-	D-	E+
Q4-15	D	D-	D

Asset & Performance History

Date	NAV	1-Year Total Return
2017	51.37	-63.85
2016	142.12	-97.6
2015	5,944.00	-52.7
2014	12,568.00	-74.24
2013	51,360.00	
2012		

Total Assets: $62,730,137

Asset Allocation

Asset	%
Cash	135%
Stocks	0%
US Stocks	0%
Bonds	0%
US Bonds	0%
Other	-35%

Services Offered:

Investment Strategy: The investment seeks daily investment results, before fees and expenses, of 300% of the inverse (or opposite) of the daily performance of the MVIS Global Junior Gold Miners Index. The fund invests in swap agreements, futures contracts, short positions or other financial instruments that, in combination, provide inverse (opposite) or short leveraged exposure to the index equal to at least 80% of the fund's net assets (plus borrowing for investment purposes). The index tracks the performance of foreign and domestic micro-, small- and mid-capitalization companies. The fund is non-diversified. **Top Holdings:** Ve Vectors Jr Gld Miners Ve Vectors Jr Gld Miners Ve Vectors Jr Gld Miners Ve Vectors Jr Gld Miners Ve Vectors Jr Gld Miners

Teucrium Corn Fund   D   SELL

Ticker	Traded On	NAV	Total Assets ($)	Dividend Yield (TTM)	Turnover Ratio	Expense Ratio
CORN	NYSE Arca	16.11	$62,723,251	0		1

Ratings

Reward	D
Risk	D
Recent Upgrade/Downgrade	

Fund Information

Fund Type	Exchange Traded Funds
Category	Commodities Specified
Sub-Category	Commodities Agriculture
Prospectus Objective	Unaligned
Inception Date	Jun-10
Open to New Investments	Y

Prices

Price (as of 12/31/2018)	16.05
52-Week High	18.48
52-Week Low	15.40

Total Returns (%)

3-Month	6-Month	1-Year	3-Year	5-Year
-0.67	0.87	-3.83	-24.16	-47.43

3-Year Standard Deviation	13.3
Effective Duration	

Valuation

Premium/Discount (1-Year Average)	-0.01

Company Information

Provider	Teucrium
Manager/Tenure	Management Team (8)
Website	
Address	232 Hidden Lake Road Building A Brattleboro VT 05301 United States
Phone Number	802-257-1617

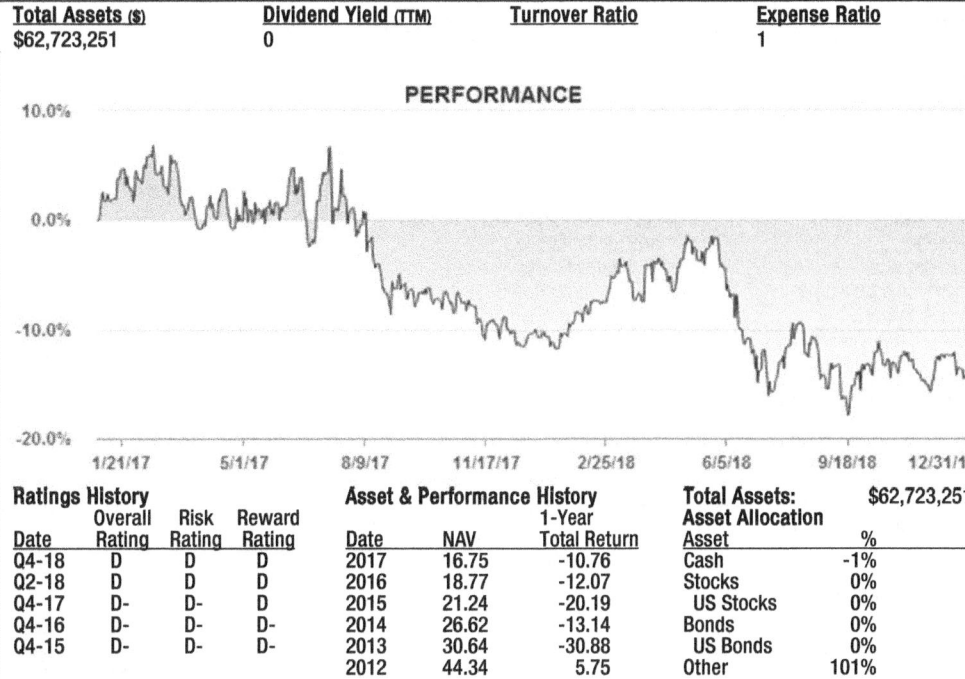

PERFORMANCE

Ratings History

Date	Overall Rating	Risk Rating	Reward Rating
Q4-18	D	D	D
Q2-18	D	D	D
Q4-17	D-	D-	D
Q4-16	D-	D-	D-
Q4-15	D-	D-	D-

Asset & Performance History

Date	NAV	1-Year Total Return
2017	16.75	-10.76
2016	18.77	-12.07
2015	21.24	-20.19
2014	26.62	-13.14
2013	30.64	-30.88
2012	44.34	5.75

Total Assets: $62,723,251

Asset Allocation

Asset	%
Cash	-1%
Stocks	0%
US Stocks	0%
Bonds	0%
US Bonds	0%
Other	101%

Services Offered:

Investment Strategy: The investment seeks to have the daily changes in percentage terms of the shares' NAV reflect the daily changes in percentage terms of a weighted average of the closing settlement prices for three futures contracts for corn that are traded on the Chicago Board of Trade.
The fund invests under normal market conditions in Benchmark Component Futures Contracts or, in certain circumstances, in other Corn Futures Contracts traded on the CBOT or on foreign exchanges. **Top Holdings:** C Z9 Cbot Corn Futures Dec 2019   C H9 Cbot Corn Futures Mar 2019   C K9 Cbot Corn Futures May 2019

WisdomTree Global ex-U.S. Quality Dividend Growth Fund   C-   HOLD

Ticker	Traded On	NAV	Total Assets ($)	Dividend Yield (TTM)	Turnover Ratio	Expense Ratio
DNL	NYSE Arca	49.47	$62,716,367	2.15	67	0.58

Ratings

Reward	D+
Risk	C-
Recent Upgrade/Downgrade	

Fund Information

Fund Type	Exchange Traded Funds
Category	Global Equity Large Cap
Sub-Category	Foreign Large Growth
Prospectus Objective	Foreign Stock
Inception Date	Jun-06
Open to New Investments	Y

Prices

Price (as of 12/31/2018)	49.33
52-Week High	62.78
52-Week Low	47.65

Total Returns (%)

3-Month	6-Month	1-Year	3-Year	5-Year
-13.20	-11.61	-14.25	16.76	8.43

3-Year Standard Deviation	11.39
Effective Duration	

Valuation

Premium/Discount (1-Year Average)	-0.02

Company Information

Provider	WisdomTree
Manager/Tenure	Richard A. Brown (10), Thomas J. Durante (10), Karen Q. Wong (10)
Website	http://www.wisdomtree.com
Address	WisdomTree 245 Park Avenue, 35th floor New York NY 10167 United States
Phone Number	866-909-9473

PERFORMANCE

Ratings History

Date	Overall Rating	Risk Rating	Reward Rating
Q4-18	C-	C-	D+
Q2-18	C	D+	C
Q4-17	B	B-	B
Q4-16	D+	D+	D+
Q4-15	D+	D+	C-

Asset & Performance History

Date	NAV	1-Year Total Return
2017	59.01	29.53
2016	46.48	5.11
2015	45.3	-7.01
2014	49.61	-0.12
2013	50.81	0.09
2012	52.02	15.8

Total Assets: $62,716,367

Asset Allocation

Asset	%
Cash	0%
Stocks	100%
US Stocks	1%
Bonds	0%
US Bonds	0%
Other	0%

Services Offered:

Investment Strategy: The investment seeks to track the price and yield performance, before fees and expenses, of the WisdomTree Global ex-U.S. Quality Dividend Growth Index. Under normal circumstances, at least 95% of the fund's total assets (exclusive of collateral held from securities lending) will be invested in the component securities of the index and investments that have economic characteristics that are substantially identical to the economic characteristics of such component securities. The index is a fundamentally weighted index that consists of dividend-paying global ex-U.S. common stocks with growth characteristics. The fund is non-diversified. **Top Holdings:** British American Tobacco PLC   Telenor ASA   Tokyo Electron Ltd   Atlas Copco Ab A Shs Common Stock Sek.639   Safran SA

Invesco DWA Energy Momentum ETF

C   HOLD

Ticker	Traded On	NAV	Total Assets ($)	Dividend Yield (TTM)	Turnover Ratio	Expense Ratio
PXI	NAS CM	28.51	$62,317,006	0.93	95	0.6

Ratings

Reward	B-
Risk	D+
Recent Upgrade/Downgrade	

Fund Information

Fund Type	Exchange Traded Funds
Category	Energy Sector Equity
Sub-Category	Equity Energy
Prospectus Objective	Natl Res
Inception Date	Oct-06
Open to New Investments	Y

Prices

Price (as of 12/31/2018)	28.39
52-Week High	46.27
52-Week Low	26.03

Total Returns (%)

3-Month	6-Month	1-Year	3-Year	5-Year
-35.99	-32.33	-27.34	-12.83	-45.99

3-Year Standard Deviation	28.36
Effective Duration	

Valuation

Premium/Discount (1-Year Average)	0.10

Company Information

Provider	Invesco
Manager/Tenure	Peter Hubbard (11), Michael Jeanette (10), Tony Seisser (4), 1 other
Website	http://www.invesco.com/us
Address	Invesco 11 Greenway Plaza, Ste. 2500 Houston TX 77046 United States
Phone Number	800-659-1005

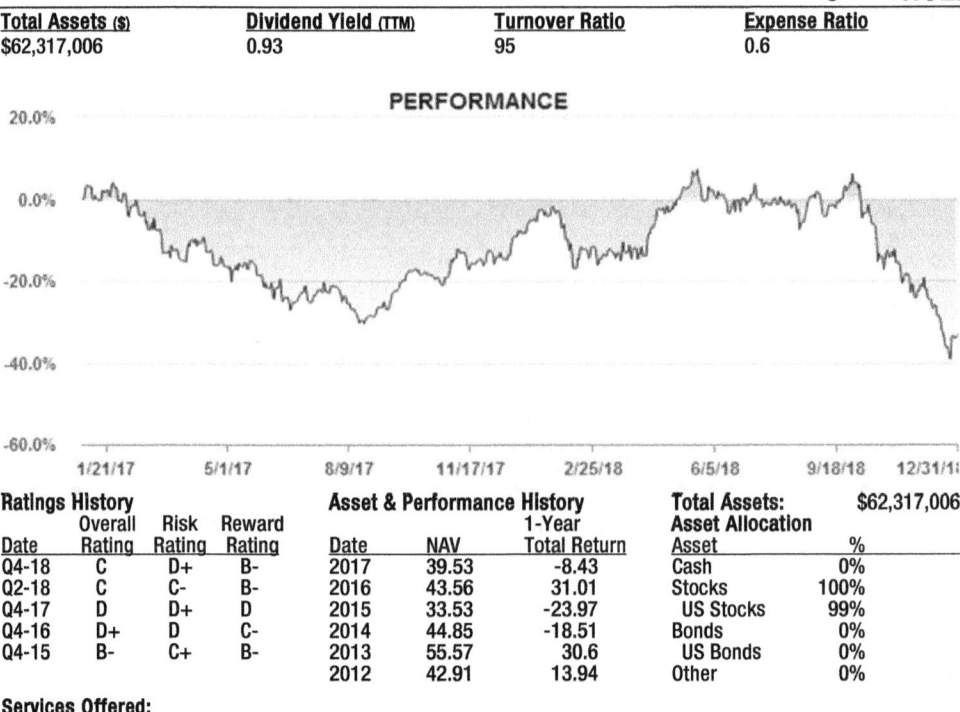

Ratings History

Date	Overall Rating	Risk Rating	Reward Rating
Q4-18	C	D+	B-
Q2-18	C	C-	B-
Q4-17	D	D+	D
Q4-16	D+	D	C-
Q4-15	B-	C+	B-

Asset & Performance History

Date	NAV	1-Year Total Return
2017	39.53	-8.43
2016	43.56	31.01
2015	33.53	-23.97
2014	44.85	-18.51
2013	55.57	30.6
2012	42.91	13.94

Total Assets: $62,317,006

Asset Allocation

Asset	%
Cash	0%
Stocks	100%
US Stocks	99%
Bonds	0%
US Bonds	0%
Other	0%

Services Offered:

Investment Strategy: The investment seeks to track the investment results (before fees and expenses) of the Dorsey Wright® Energy Technical Leaders Index (the "underlying index"). The fund generally will invest at least 90% of its total assets in the securities that comprise the underlying index. The underlying index is composed of at least 30 securities of companies in the energy sector that have powerful relative strength or "momentum" characteristics. **Top Holdings:** Cheniere Energy Inc Concho Resources Inc Diamondback Energy Inc Phillips 66 Pioneer Natural Resources Co

---

Direxion Daily Semiconductor Bear 3X Shares

D   SELL

Ticker	Traded On	NAV	Total Assets ($)	Dividend Yield (TTM)	Turnover Ratio	Expense Ratio
SOXS	NYSE Arca	13.16	$62,188,220	0.36	0	1.11

Ratings

Reward	E+
Risk	D-
Recent Upgrade/Downgrade	Up

Fund Information

Fund Type	Exchange Traded Funds
Category	Trading Tools
Sub-Category	Trading--Inverse Equity
Prospectus Objective	Technology
Inception Date	Mar-10
Open to New Investments	Y

Prices

Price (as of 12/31/2018)	13.19
52-Week High	16.99
52-Week Low	8.89

Total Returns (%)

3-Month	6-Month	1-Year	3-Year	5-Year
36.67	17.72	-19.62	-93.39	-98.23

3-Year Standard Deviation	52.4
Effective Duration	

Valuation

Premium/Discount (1-Year Average)	-0.02

Company Information

Provider	Direxion Funds
Manager/Tenure	Paul Brigandi (8), Tony Ng (3)
Website	http://www.direxionfunds.com
Address	Direxion Funds 1301 Avenue Of The Americas (6th Avenue) New York NY 10019 United States
Phone Number	646-572-3390

Ratings History

Date	Overall Rating	Risk Rating	Reward Rating
Q4-18	D	D-	E+
Q2-18	D-	E+	E
Q4-17	E	E+	E
Q4-16	D-	D-	E
Q4-15	D-	E+	D-

Asset & Performance History

Date	NAV	1-Year Total Return
2017	16.51	-69.36
2016	53.9	-73.19
2015	201.05	-25.09
2014	268.4	-64.36
2013	753.2	-71.48
2012	2,641.60	-41.77

Total Assets: $62,188,220

Asset Allocation

Asset	%
Cash	108%
Stocks	0%
US Stocks	0%
Bonds	-8%
US Bonds	-8%
Other	0%

Services Offered:

Investment Strategy: The investment seeks daily investment results, before fees and expenses, of 300% of the inverse (or opposite) of the daily performance of the PHLX Semiconductor Sector Index. The fund, under normal circumstances, invests in swap agreements, futures contracts, short positions or other financial instruments that, in combination, provide inverse (opposite) or short leveraged exposure to the index equal to at least 80% of the fund's net assets (plus borrowing for investment purposes). The index measures the performance of domestic companies engaged in the design, distribution, manufacture and sale of semiconductors. The fund is non-diversified. **Top Holdings:** Phila Semiconductor Index Phila Semiconductor Index Phila Semiconductor Index Phila Semiconductor Index Fidelity Institutional Go

EquityCompass Tactical Risk Manager ETF   D+   SELL

Ticker	Traded On	NAV	Total Assets ($)	Dividend Yield (TTM)	Turnover Ratio	Expense Ratio
TERM	NYSE Arca	20.10	$61,916,119	1.34	120	0.65

Ratings

Reward	D+
Risk	D+
Recent Upgrade/Downgrade	

Fund Information

Fund Type	Exchange Traded Funds
Category	US Equity Large Cap Blend
Sub-Category	Large Value
Prospectus Objective	Growth
Inception Date	Apr-17
Open to New Investments	Y

Prices

Price (as of 12/31/2018)	20.06
52-Week High	23.80
52-Week Low	19.01

Total Returns (%)

3-Month	6-Month	1-Year	3-Year	5-Year
-13.92	-8.20	-8.15		

3-Year Standard Deviation

Effective Duration

Valuation

Premium/Discount (1-Year Average)	0.31

Company Information

Provider	First Trust
Manager/Tenure	Jon C. Erickson (1), John W. Gambla (1), Rob A. Guttschow (1), 7 others
Website	http://www.ftportfolios.com/
Address	First Trust 120 E. Liberty Drive, Suite 400 Wheaton IL 60187 United States
Phone Number	800-621-1675

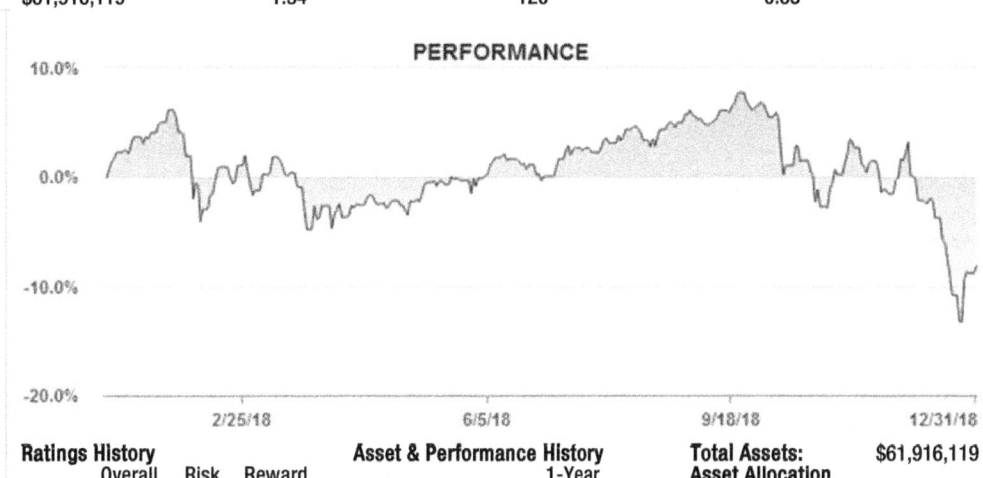

PERFORMANCE

Ratings History

Date	Overall Rating	Risk Rating	Reward Rating
Q4-18	D+	D+	D+
Q2-18	D+	D+	D+
Q4-17	U		
Q4-16			
Q4-15			

Asset & Performance History

Date	NAV	1-Year Total Return
2017	22.23	
2016		
2015		
2014		
2013		
2012		

Total Assets: $61,916,119

Asset Allocation

Asset	%
Cash	0%
Stocks	100%
US Stocks	100%
Bonds	0%
US Bonds	0%
Other	0%

Services Offered:

Investment Strategy: The investment seeks to provide long term capital appreciation with capital preservation as a secondary objective. The fund will seek to achieve its investment objectives by investing in equity securities of companies domiciled in the U.S. or listed on a U.S. exchange. The fund's strategy seeks to provide exposure to U.S. listed equity securities and to avoid large, prolonged market losses and reduce volatility. It may also invest in inverse ETFs which seek to provide investment results that match a negative return of the performance of an underlying index like the S&P 500 Index. The fund is non-diversified. **Top Holdings:** TripAdvisor Inc Starbucks Corp Walgreens Boots Alliance Inc Foot Locker Inc McDonald's Corp

---

iPath® US Treasury 10-year Bear ETN   C   HOLD

Ticker	Traded On	NAV	Total Assets ($)	Dividend Yield (TTM)	Turnover Ratio	Expense Ratio
DTYS	NAS CM		$61,863,767	0		0.75

Ratings

Reward	C
Risk	D+
Recent Upgrade/Downgrade	Down

Fund Information

Fund Type	Exchange Traded Funds
Category	Trading Tools
Sub-Category	Trading--Inverse Debt
Prospectus Objective	Govt Bond - Treasury
Inception Date	Aug-10
Open to New Investments	Y

Prices

Price (as of 12/31/2018)	19.29
52-Week High	25.60
52-Week Low	18.25

Total Returns (%)

3-Month	6-Month	1-Year	3-Year	5-Year
-17.65	-10.93	8.89	-2.75	-38.96

3-Year Standard Deviation	39.49
Effective Duration	

Valuation

Premium/Discount (1-Year Average)	0.32

Company Information

Provider	Milleis Investissements Funds
Manager/Tenure	No Manager (8)
Website	
Address	2-4, rue Eugène Ruppert L-2453 Luxembourg Luxembourg L-2453 Luxembourg
Phone Number	

PERFORMANCE

Ratings History

Date	Overall Rating	Risk Rating	Reward Rating
Q4-18	C	D+	C
Q2-18	C+	D+	C+
Q4-17	D+	D+	D+
Q4-16	D	D	D
Q4-15	D	D	D

Asset & Performance History

Date	NAV	1-Year Total Return
2017	18.27	-8.54
2016	19.81	-2.72
2015	20.46	-10.11
2014	22.76	-30.17
2013	32.59	23.89
2012	26.31	-18.21

Total Assets: $61,863,767

Asset Allocation

Asset	%
Cash	%
Stocks	%
US Stocks	%
Bonds	%
US Bonds	%
Other	%

Services Offered:

Investment Strategy: The investment seeks to provide investors with inverse exposure to the Barclays 10Y US Treasury Futures Targeted Exposure Index™.

The Barclays 10Y US Treasury Futures Targeted Exposure Index™ (the "index") is designed to decrease in response to an increase in the 10-year Treasury note yields and to increase in response to a decrease in 10-year Treasury note yields. The index targets a fixed level of sensitivity to changes in the yield of the current "cheapest-to-deliver" note underlying the relevant 10-year Treasury futures contract at a given point in time. **Top Holdings:**

Cambria Global Asset Allocation ETF

D+   SELL

Ticker	Traded On	NAV	Total Assets ($)	Dividend Yield (TTM)	Turnover Ratio	Expense Ratio
GAA	BATS	24.85	$61,710,651	2.6	30	0.33

Ratings
Reward	D+
Risk	D+
Recent Upgrade/Downgrade	Down

Fund Information
Fund Type	Exchange Traded Funds
Category	Cautious Allocation
Sub-Category	World Allocation
Prospectus Objective	Asset Allocation
Inception Date	Dec-14
Open to New Investments	Y

Prices
Price (as of 12/31/2018)	24.80
52-Week High	28.52
52-Week Low	24.59

Total Returns (%)
3-Month	6-Month	1-Year	3-Year	5-Year
-6.22	-5.02	-6.84	16.60	

3-Year Standard Deviation	5.88
Effective Duration	6.73

Valuation
Premium/Discount (1-Year Average)	0.06

Company Information
Provider	CAMBRIA ETF TRUST
Manager/Tenure	Mebane T. Faber (3)
Website	http://www.cambriafunds.com
Address	CAMBRIA ETF TRUST 2711 Centreville Road Suite 400 Wilmington, DE 19808 Wilmington DE 19808 United States
Phone Number	310-683-5500

PERFORMANCE

Ratings History

Date	Overall Rating	Risk Rating	Reward Rating
Q4-18	D+	D+	D+
Q2-18	C	C-	C
Q4-17	B-	B	C
Q4-16	D+	D+	D+
Q4-15	U		

Asset & Performance History

Date	NAV	1-Year Total Return
2017	27.45	15.21
2016	24.41	8.64
2015	23.11	-3.86
2014	24.63	
2013		
2012		

Total Assets: $61,710,651
Asset Allocation

Asset	%
Cash	9%
Stocks	42%
US Stocks	20%
Bonds	45%
US Bonds	28%
Other	4%

Services Offered:

Investment Strategy: The investment seeks to track the performance, before fees and expenses, of the Cambria Global Asset Allocation Index. Under normal market conditions, the fund invests at least 80% of its total assets in the components of the underlying index and in depositary receipts representing components of the underlying index. The underlying index is designed to provide diversified exposure, including inverse exposure, to all of the major world asset classes in the various regions, countries and sectors around the globe. **Top Holdings:** Cambria Emerging Shareholder Yield ETF Vanguard Total Bond Market ETF Cambria Sovereign Bond ETF Invesco Optm Yd Dvrs Cdty Stra No K1 ETF Cambria Shareholder Yield ETF

Invesco Russell Top 200 Equal Weight ETF

C-   HOLD

Ticker	Traded On	NAV	Total Assets ($)	Dividend Yield (TTM)	Turnover Ratio	Expense Ratio
EQWL	NYSE Arca	48.74	$61,702,801	1.88	32	0.25

Ratings
Reward	C
Risk	D+
Recent Upgrade/Downgrade	Down

Fund Information
Fund Type	Exchange Traded Funds
Category	US Equity Large Cap Blend
Sub-Category	Large Blend
Prospectus Objective	Growth
Inception Date	Dec-06
Open to New Investments	Y

Prices
Price (as of 12/31/2018)	48.64
52-Week High	56.84
52-Week Low	45.99

Total Returns (%)
3-Month	6-Month	1-Year	3-Year	5-Year
-12.85	-7.40	-5.67	32.72	48.74

3-Year Standard Deviation	9.37
Effective Duration	

Valuation
Premium/Discount (1-Year Average)	0.16

Company Information
Provider	Invesco
Manager/Tenure	Peter Hubbard (11), Michael Jeanette (10), Jonathan Nixon (5), 2 others
Website	http://www.invesco.com/us
Address	Invesco 11 Greenway Plaza, Ste. 2500 Houston TX 77046 United States
Phone Number	800-659-1005

PERFORMANCE

Ratings History

Date	Overall Rating	Risk Rating	Reward Rating
Q4-18	C-	D+	C
Q2-18	C	D+	C
Q4-17	B	B-	B
Q4-16	D+	D+	D+
Q4-15	C	D+	C

Asset & Performance History

Date	NAV	1-Year Total Return
2017	52.77	23.66
2016	43.25	13.78
2015	38.81	-1.76
2014	40.31	14.08
2013	35.98	35.63
2012	27	13.44

Total Assets: $61,702,801
Asset Allocation

Asset	%
Cash	0%
Stocks	100%
US Stocks	98%
Bonds	0%
US Bonds	0%
Other	0%

Services Offered:

Investment Strategy: The investment seeks to track the investment results (before fees and expenses) of the Russell Top 200 Equal Weight Index (the "underlying index"). The fund generally will invest at least 90% of its total assets in the component securities that comprise the underlying index. The underlying index is designed to measure the performance of approximately 200 equally weighted securities of large cap U.S. companies. **Top Holdings:** Ecolab Inc Linde PLC Verizon Communications Inc PPG Industries Inc Air Products & Chemicals Inc

WisdomTree Germany Hedged Equity Fund   D+   SELL

Ticker	Traded On	NAV	Total Assets ($)	Dividend Yield (TTM)	Turnover Ratio	Expense Ratio
DXGE	NAS CM	26.40	$61,653,382	2.8	20	0.48

Ratings
Reward	D+
Risk	D+
Recent Upgrade/Downgrade	Down

Fund Information
Fund Type	Exchange Traded Funds
Category	Europe Equity Large Cap
Sub-Category	Miscellaneous Region
Prospectus Objective	Europe Stock
Inception Date	Oct-13
Open to New Investments	Y

Prices
Price (as of 12/31/2018)	26.48
52-Week High	33.93
52-Week Low	25.70

Total Returns (%)
3-Month	6-Month	1-Year	3-Year	5-Year
-12.56	-11.14	-15.96	6.97	21.03

3-Year Standard Deviation	12.35
Effective Duration	

Valuation
Premium/Discount (1-Year Average)	-0.13

Company Information
Provider	WisdomTree
Manager/Tenure	Richard A. Brown (5), Thomas J. Durante (5), Karen Q. Wong (5)
Website	http://www.wisdomtree.com
Address	WisdomTree 245 Park Avenue, 35th floor New York NY 10167 United States
Phone Number	866-909-9473

PERFORMANCE

Ratings History

Date	Overall Rating	Risk Rating	Reward Rating
Q4-18	D+	D+	D+
Q2-18	C	C-	C
Q4-17	B+	B	A-
Q4-16	C	C-	C+
Q4-15	C-	C+	C-

Asset & Performance History

Date	NAV	1-Year Total Return
2017	32.24	16.04
2016	28.55	9.69
2015	27.03	8.54
2014	26.18	4.24
2013	26.71	
2012		

Total Assets: $61,653,382
Asset Allocation

Asset	%
Cash	0%
Stocks	100%
US Stocks	0%
Bonds	0%
US Bonds	0%
Other	0%

Services Offered:

Investment Strategy: The investment seeks to track the price and yield performance, before fees and expenses, of the WisdomTree Germany Hedged Equity Index (the "index"). The fund normally invests at least 80% of its total assets in component securities of the index and investments that have economic characteristics that are substantially identical to the economic characteristics of such component securities. The index is a dividend weighted index designed to provide exposure to Germany equity markets while at the same time neutralizing exposure to fluctuations of the value of the euro relative to the U.S. dollar. The fund is non-diversified. **Top Holdings:** Deutsche Telekom AG Allianz SE Siemens AG Daimler AG Bayerische Motoren Werke AG

Hartford Multifactor Emerging Markets ETF   C-   HOLD

Ticker	Traded On	NAV	Total Assets ($)	Dividend Yield (TTM)	Turnover Ratio	Expense Ratio
ROAM	NYSE Arca	22.17	$61,651,969	2.07	25	0.49

Ratings
Reward	C-
Risk	C-
Recent Upgrade/Downgrade	

Fund Information
Fund Type	Exchange Traded Funds
Category	Global Emerg Mkts Equity
Sub-Category	Diversified Emerging Mkts
Prospectus Objective	Div Emerg Mkts
Inception Date	Feb-15
Open to New Investments	Y

Prices
Price (as of 12/31/2018)	22.06
52-Week High	28.10
52-Week Low	21.30

Total Returns (%)
3-Month	6-Month	1-Year	3-Year	5-Year
-2.94	0.23	-11.61	22.62	

3-Year Standard Deviation	13.84
Effective Duration	

Valuation
Premium/Discount (1-Year Average)	0.01

Company Information
Provider	Hartford Funds
Manager/Tenure	Richard A. Brown (3), Thomas J. Durante (3), Karen Q. Wong (3)
Website	http://www.hartfordfunds.com
Address	690 Lee Road Wayne PA 19087 United States
Phone Number	800-456-7526

PERFORMANCE

Ratings History

Date	Overall Rating	Risk Rating	Reward Rating
Q4-18	C-	C-	C-
Q2-18	C-	C-	C-
Q4-17	C	C	C+
Q4-16	D+	D+	D+
Q4-15	U		

Asset & Performance History

Date	NAV	1-Year Total Return
2017	25.71	28.21
2016	20.45	8.2
2015	19.26	
2014		
2013		
2012		

Total Assets: $61,651,969
Asset Allocation

Asset	%
Cash	1%
Stocks	98%
US Stocks	0%
Bonds	0%
US Bonds	0%
Other	0%

Services Offered:

Investment Strategy: The investment seeks to provide investment results that, before fees and expenses, correspond to the total return performance of the Hartford Risk-Optimized Multifactor Emerging Markets Index. The fund generally invests at least 80% of its assets in securities of the index and in depositary receipts (such as American Depositary Receipts ("ADRs"), Global Depositary Receipts ("GDRs") and European Depositary Receipts ("EDRs") representing securities of the index. The index is designed to balance risks and opportunities within equity markets of emerging economies while emphasizing constituents exhibiting a favorable combination of factor characteristics. **Top Holdings:** China Telecom Corp Ltd H Shares Dr Reddy's Laboratories Ltd ADR Itau Unibanco Holding SA Participating Preferred Infosys Ltd ADR Telefonica Brasil SA Participating Preferred

NuShares ESG Large-Cap Growth ETF   C-   HOLD

Ticker	Traded On	NAV	Total Assets ($)	Dividend Yield (TTM)	Turnover Ratio	Expense Ratio
NULG	BATS	30.06	$61,551,499	0.27	30	0.35

Ratings
Reward   C
Risk   C-
Recent Upgrade/Downgrade   Down

Fund Information
Fund Type   Exchange Traded Funds
Category   US Equity Large Cap Growth
Sub-Category   Large Growth
Prospectus Objective   Growth
Inception Date   Dec-16
Open to New Investments   Y

Prices
Price (as of 12/31/2018)   30.09
52-Week High   37.47
52-Week Low   29.07

Total Returns (%)

3-Month	6-Month	1-Year	3-Year	5-Year
-17.48	-9.94	-0.15		

3-Year Standard Deviation
Effective Duration

Valuation
Premium/Discount (1-Year Average)   0.12

Company Information
Provider   Nuveen
Manager/Tenure   Philip James(Jim) Campagna (1), Lei Liao (1)
Website   http://www.nuveen.com
Address   Nuveen Investment Trust John Nuveen & Co. Inc. Chicago IL 60606 United States
Phone Number   312-917-8146

PERFORMANCE

Ratings History

Date	Overall Rating	Risk Rating	Reward Rating
Q4-18	C-	C-	C
Q2-18	C	C-	C
Q4-17	D	A-	D+
Q4-16			
Q4-15			

Asset & Performance History

Date	NAV	1-Year Total Return
2017	31.01	24.9
2016	24.91	
2015		
2014		
2013		
2012		

Total Assets: $61,551,499

Asset Allocation

Asset	%
Cash	0%
Stocks	100%
US Stocks	99%
Bonds	0%
US Bonds	0%
Other	0%

Services Offered:

Investment Strategy: The investment seeks to track the investment results, before fees and expenses, of the TIAA ESG USA Large-Cap Growth Index (the "index"). Under normal market conditions, the fund invests at least 80% of the sum of its net assets and the amount of any borrowings for investment purposes in component securities of the index. The index is comprised of equity securities issued by large capitalization companies listed on U.S. exchanges that meet certain environmental, social, and governance ("ESG") criteria. **Top Holdings:** Apple Inc Microsoft Corp Alphabet Inc Class C Walt Disney Co The Home Depot Inc

---

Credit Suisse X-Links Monthly Pay 2xLeveraged Mortgage REIT ETN   C-   HOLD

Ticker	Traded On	NAV	Total Assets ($)	Dividend Yield (TTM)	Turnover Ratio	Expense Ratio
REML	NYSE Arca		$61,379,980	21.18		0.5

Ratings
Reward   C-
Risk   C-
Recent Upgrade/Downgrade   Up

Fund Information
Fund Type   Exchange Traded Funds
Category   Trading Tools
Sub-Category   Trading--Leveraged Equity
Prospectus Objective   Real Estate
Inception Date   Jul-16
Open to New Investments   Y

Prices
Price (as of 12/31/2018)   22.51
52-Week High   30.60
52-Week Low   20.77

Total Returns (%)

3-Month	6-Month	1-Year	3-Year	5-Year
-9.79	-7.74	-7.56		

3-Year Standard Deviation
Effective Duration

Valuation
Premium/Discount (1-Year Average)   0.70

Company Information
Provider   Credit Suisse AG
Manager/Tenure   No Manager (2)
Website
Address   Kilmore House Park Lane Dublin Ireland
Phone Number

PERFORMANCE

Ratings History

Date	Overall Rating	Risk Rating	Reward Rating
Q4-18	C-	C-	C-
Q2-18	D+	D+	D+
Q4-17	D	B	C
Q4-16	U		
Q4-15			

Asset & Performance History

Date	NAV	1-Year Total Return
2017	30.36	37.8
2016	26.83	
2015		
2014		
2013		
2012		

Total Assets: $61,379,980

Asset Allocation

Asset	%
Cash	%
Stocks	%
US Stocks	%
Bonds	%
US Bonds	%
Other	%

Services Offered:

Investment Strategy: The investment seeks to provide a monthly compounded 2x leveraged long exposure to the price return version of the FTSE NAREIT All Mortgage Capped Index (the "index").
The index measures the composite performance of tax-qualified U.S. mortgage real estate investment trusts ("Mortgage REITs") with more than 50% of total assets invested in mortgage loans or mortgage-backed securities secured by interests in real property that are listed on the New York Stock Exchange, the NYSE Arca or the NASDAQ National Market List (the "index constituents"). **Top Holdings:**

VanEck Vectors Coal ETF　　　　　　　　　　　　　　　　C-　HOLD

Ticker	Traded On	NAV		Total Assets ($)	Dividend Yield (TTM)	Turnover Ratio	Expense Ratio
KOL	NYSE Arca	12.66		$61,272,096	4.09	39	0.6

Ratings
Reward	C
Risk	C-
Recent Upgrade/Downgrade	Down

Fund Information
Fund Type	Exchange Traded Funds
Category	Equity Misc
Sub-Category	Miscellaneous Sector
Prospectus Objective	Natl Res
Inception Date	Jan-08
Open to New Investments	Y

Prices
Price (as of 12/31/2018)	12.56
52-Week High	18.39
52-Week Low	12.27

Total Returns (%)
3-Month	6-Month	1-Year	3-Year	5-Year
-13.21	-13.43	-15.27	127.50	-21.42

3-Year Standard Deviation	27.12
Effective Duration	

Valuation
Premium/Discount (1-Year Average)	-0.32

Company Information
Provider	VanEck
Manager/Tenure	Hao-Hung (Peter) Liao (10), Guo Hua (Jason) Jin (0)
Website	http://www.vaneck.com
Address	Van Eck Associates Corporation 666 Third Avenue New York NY 10017 United States
Phone Number	800-826-1115

PERFORMANCE

Ratings History
Date	Overall Rating	Risk Rating	Reward Rating
Q4-18	C-	C-	C
Q2-18	C	C-	C
Q4-17	C	D+	B-
Q4-16	C-	D+	C-
Q4-15	D-	D-	D-

Asset & Performance History
Date	NAV	1-Year Total Return
2017	16.06	34.89
2016	12.37	99.05
2015	6.28	-55.1
2014	14.64	-23.06
2013	19.5	-20.74
2012	25.17	-21.03

Total Assets: $61,272,096
Asset Allocation
Asset	%
Cash	0%
Stocks	100%
US Stocks	15%
Bonds	0%
US Bonds	0%
Other	0%

Services Offered:

Investment Strategy: The investment seeks to replicate as closely as possible, before fees and expenses, the price and yield performance of the MVIS® Global Coal Index. The fund normally invests at least 80% of its total assets in securities that comprise the fund's benchmark index. The index includes companies in the global coal industry that generate at least 50% of their revenues from coal operation (production, mining and cokeries), transportation of coal, production of coal mining equipment as well as from storage and trade. It is non-diversified. **Top Holdings:** China Shenhua Energy Co Ltd H　Aurizon Holdings Ltd　Teck Resources Ltd Class B　United Tractors Tbk　Whitehaven Coal Ltd

---

First Trust BuyWrite Income ETF　　　　　　　　　　　　　C-　HOLD

Ticker	Traded On	NAV		Total Assets ($)	Dividend Yield (TTM)	Turnover Ratio	Expense Ratio
FTHI	NAS CM	20.28		$61,238,128	4.35	239	0.85

Ratings
Reward	C
Risk	D+
Recent Upgrade/Downgrade	Down

Fund Information
Fund Type	Exchange Traded Funds
Category	Long/Short Equity
Sub-Category	Options-based
Prospectus Objective	Income
Inception Date	Jan-14
Open to New Investments	Y

Prices
Price (as of 12/31/2018)	20.17
52-Week High	23.95
52-Week Low	19.24

Total Returns (%)
3-Month	6-Month	1-Year	3-Year	5-Year
-11.57	-8.88	-9.10	16.21	26.96

3-Year Standard Deviation	8.03
Effective Duration	

Valuation
Premium/Discount (1-Year Average)	0.16

Company Information
Provider	First Trust
Manager/Tenure	John W. Gambla (4), Rob A. Guttschow (4)
Website	http://www.ftportfolios.com/
Address	First Trust 120 E. Liberty Drive, Suite 400 Wheaton IL 60187 United States
Phone Number	800-621-1675

PERFORMANCE

Ratings History
Date	Overall Rating	Risk Rating	Reward Rating
Q4-18	C-	D+	C
Q2-18	C	C-	C
Q4-17	B	A	B-
Q4-16	C	C-	C+
Q4-15	D+	C	C

Asset & Performance History
Date	NAV	1-Year Total Return
2017	23.29	13.92
2016	21.33	12.21
2015	19.92	2.07
2014	20.49	7.03
2013		
2012		

Total Assets: $61,238,128
Asset Allocation
Asset	%
Cash	2%
Stocks	98%
US Stocks	96%
Bonds	0%
US Bonds	0%
Other	0%

Services Offered:

Investment Strategy: The investment seeks current income; capital appreciation is a secondary objective. The fund will pursue its objectives by investing in equity securities listed on U.S. exchanges and by utilizing an "option strategy" consisting of writing (selling) U.S. exchange-traded covered call options on the Standard & Poor's 500® Index (the "index"). The call options written by the fund will be a laddered portfolio of call options with expirations of less than one year, written at-the-money to slightly out-of-the-money. The fund is non-diversified. **Top Holdings:** Johnson & Johnson　Exxon Mobil Corp　Apple Inc　Microsoft Corp　Pfizer Inc

Invesco VRDO Tax-Free Weekly ETF

C- HOLD

Ticker	Traded On	NAV	Total Assets ($)	Dividend Yield (TTM)	Turnover Ratio	Expense Ratio
PVI	NYSE Arca	24.93	$61,100,749	1.06	0	0.25

Ratings
Reward	C-
Risk	D+
Recent Upgrade/Downgrade	

Fund Information
Fund Type	Exchange Traded Funds
Category	US Muni Fixed Inc
Sub-Category	Muni National Short
Prospectus Objective	Muni Bond - Natl
Inception Date	Nov-07
Open to New Investments	Y

Prices
Price (as of 12/31/2018)	24.93
52-Week High	25.00
52-Week Low	24.83

Total Returns (%)
3-Month	6-Month	1-Year	3-Year	5-Year
0.33	0.60	1.10	1.89	1.61

3-Year Standard Deviation	0.14
Effective Duration	

Valuation
Premium/Discount (1-Year Average)	-0.07

Company Information
Provider	Invesco
Manager/Tenure	Philip Fang (11), Peter Hubbard (11), Jeffrey W. Kernagis (11), 2 others
Website	http://www.invesco.com/us
Address	Invesco 11 Greenway Plaza, Ste. 2500 Houston TX 77046 United States
Phone Number	800-659-1005

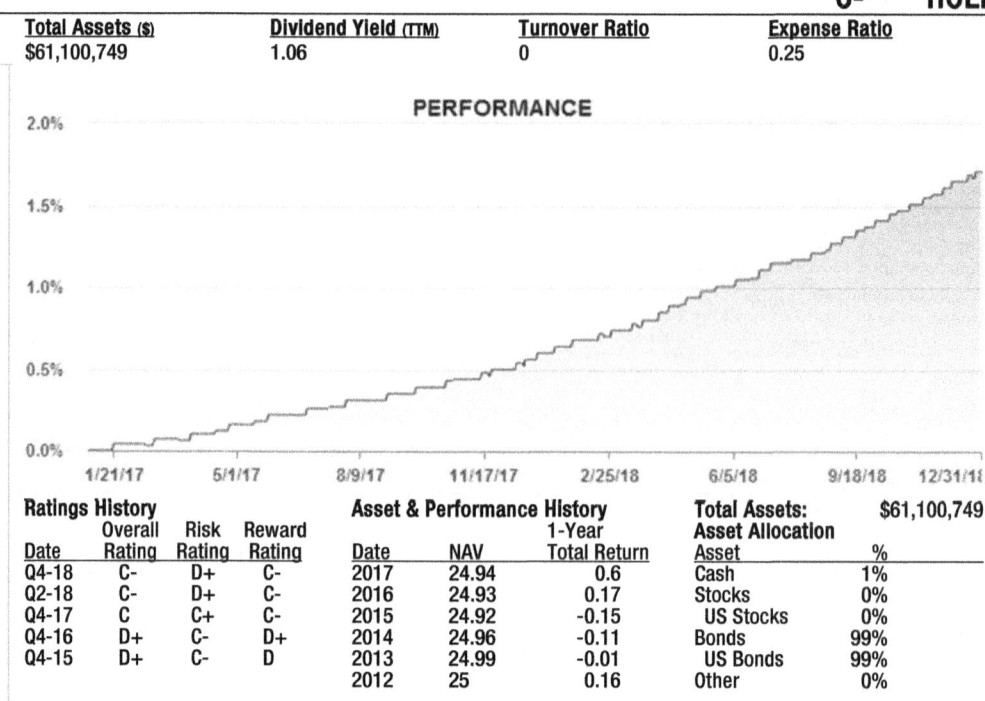

PERFORMANCE

Ratings History

Date	Overall Rating	Risk Rating	Reward Rating
Q4-18	C-	D+	C-
Q2-18	C-	D+	C-
Q4-17	C	C+	C-
Q4-16	D+	C-	D+
Q4-15	D+	C-	D

Asset & Performance History

Date	NAV	1-Year Total Return
2017	24.94	0.6
2016	24.93	0.17
2015	24.92	-0.15
2014	24.96	-0.11
2013	24.99	-0.01
2012	25	0.16

Total Assets: $61,100,749

Asset Allocation

Asset	%
Cash	1%
Stocks	0%
US Stocks	0%
Bonds	99%
US Bonds	99%
Other	0%

Services Offered:

Investment Strategy: The investment seeks to track the investment results (before fees and expenses) of the Bloomberg U.S. Municipal AMT-Free Weekly VRDO Index (the "underlying index"). The fund generally will invest at least 80% of its total assets in variable rate demand obligation bonds that are exempt from federal income tax with interest rates that reset weekly, which comprise the underlying index, which is comprised of municipal securities issued in the primary market as VRDOs. **Top Holdings:** MARYLAND ST HEALTH & HIGHER EDL FACS AUTH 1.69% FLORIDA ST DEPT ENVIRONMENTAL PROTN 1.7% ARIZONA HEALTH FACS AUTH 1.68% CALIFORNIA STATEWIDE CMNTYS DEV AUTH 1.58% CLARK CNTY NEV ARPT DEPT OF AVIATION 1.69%

VanEck Vectors ChinaAMC CSI 300 ETF

D SELL

Ticker	Traded On	NAV	Total Assets ($)	Dividend Yield (TTM)	Turnover Ratio	Expense Ratio
PEK	NYSE Arca	31.58	$61,082,122	1.46	37	0.78

Ratings
Reward	D
Risk	D
Recent Upgrade/Downgrade	Down

Fund Information
Fund Type	Exchange Traded Funds
Category	Greater China Equity
Sub-Category	China Region
Prospectus Objective	Pacific Stock
Inception Date	Oct-10
Open to New Investments	Y

Prices
Price (as of 12/31/2018)	31.50
52-Week High	54.20
52-Week Low	31.39

Total Returns (%)
3-Month	6-Month	1-Year	3-Year	5-Year
-18.41	-19.46	-33.78	-26.78	9.29

3-Year Standard Deviation	21.56
Effective Duration	

Valuation
Premium/Discount (1-Year Average)	0.19

Company Information
Provider	VanEck
Manager/Tenure	Hao-Hung (Peter) Liao (8), Leo Fan (3), Guo Hua (Jason) Jin (0)
Website	http://www.vaneck.com
Address	Van Eck Associates Corporation 666 Third Avenue New York NY 10017 United States
Phone Number	800-826-1115

PERFORMANCE

Ratings History

Date	Overall Rating	Risk Rating	Reward Rating
Q4-18	D	D	D
Q2-18	D+	D+	C-
Q4-17	B	C	A-
Q4-16	C-	D+	C
Q4-15	C	C	C+

Asset & Performance History

Date	NAV	1-Year Total Return
2017	48.37	31.89
2016	37.08	-16.16
2015	44.76	0.1
2014	46.06	49.1
2013	30.89	-4.71
2012	33.17	9.54

Total Assets: $61,082,122

Asset Allocation

Asset	%
Cash	0%
Stocks	99%
US Stocks	0%
Bonds	0%
US Bonds	0%
Other	0%

Services Offered:

Investment Strategy: The investment seeks to replicate as closely as possible, before fees and expenses, the price and yield performance of the CSI 300 Index. The fund normally invests at least 80% of its total assets in securities that comprise the fund's benchmark index and/or in investments that have economic characteristics that are substantially identical to the economic characteristics of the securities that comprise its benchmark index. The index is comprised of the largest and most liquid stocks in the Chinese A-share market. **Top Holdings:** Ping An Insurance (Group) Co. of China Ltd China Merchants Bank Co Ltd Kweichow Moutai Co Ltd Industrial Bank Co Ltd Midea Group Co Ltd Class A

WBI BullBear Yield 2000 ETF   C-   HOLD

Ticker	Traded On	NAV	Total Assets ($)	Dividend Yield (TTM)	Turnover Ratio	Expense Ratio
WBIC	NYSE Arca	19.93	$61,022,333	1.47		1.06

Ratings
Reward	C-
Risk	C-
Recent Upgrade/Downgrade	Down

Fund Information
Fund Type	Exchange Traded Funds
Category	US Equity Mid Cap
Sub-Category	Mid-Cap Value
Prospectus Objective	Growth & Inc
Inception Date	Aug-14
Open to New Investments	Y

Prices
Price (as of 12/31/2018)	19.91
52-Week High	24.13
52-Week Low	19.88

Total Returns (%)
3-Month	6-Month	1-Year	3-Year	5-Year
-10.65	-12.02	-9.44	-3.81	

3-Year Standard Deviation	9.08
Effective Duration	

Valuation
Premium/Discount (1-Year Average)	0.10

Company Information
Provider	WBI Investments
Manager/Tenure	Donald R. Schreiber (4), Gary E. Stroik (4)
Website	http://www.wbishares.com
Address	34 Sycamore Ave Suite 1-E Little Silver NJ 07739 United States
Phone Number	732-842-4920

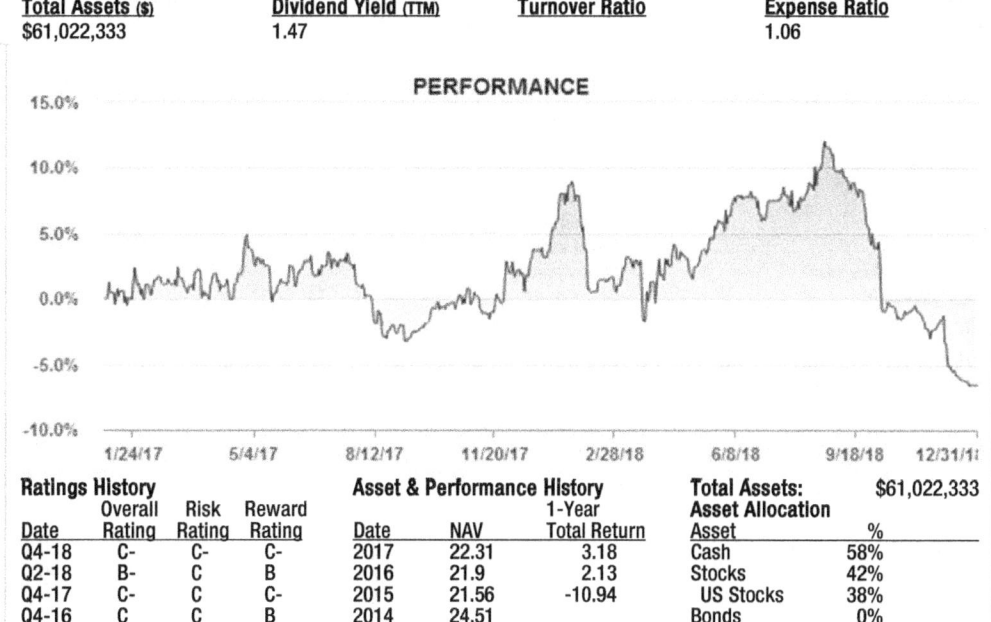

PERFORMANCE

Ratings History
Date	Overall Rating	Risk Rating	Reward Rating
Q4-18	C-	C-	C-
Q2-18	B-	C	B
Q4-17	C-	C	C-
Q4-16	C	C	B
Q4-15	D-	B-	B

Asset & Performance History
Date	NAV	1-Year Total Return
2017	22.31	3.18
2016	21.9	2.13
2015	21.56	-10.94
2014	24.51	
2013		
2012		

Total Assets: $61,022,333

Asset Allocation
Asset	%
Cash	58%
Stocks	42%
US Stocks	38%
Bonds	0%
US Bonds	0%
Other	0%

Services Offered:

Investment Strategy: The investment seeks long-term capital appreciation and the potential for current income, while also seeking to protect principal during unfavorable market conditions. The fund will seek to invest in the dividend-paying equity securities of small-capitalization and mid-capitalization domestic and foreign companies. These securities will be selected on the basis of the Sub-Advisor's proprietary selection process ("Selection Process"). Cash and cash equivalents are some of the investment opportunities evaluated by the Selection Process. It may invest up to 50% of its net assets in the securities of issuers in emerging markets. **Top Holdings:** NorthWestern Corp   Cracker Barrel Old Country Store Inc   Federated Investors Inc Class B   Investors Bancorp Inc Pitney Bowes Inc

---

First Trust Horizon Managed Volatility Developed International ETF   D+   SELL

Ticker	Traded On	NAV	Total Assets ($)	Dividend Yield (TTM)	Turnover Ratio	Expense Ratio
HDMV	NYSE Arca	30.81	$60,697,141	2.64	133	0.8

Ratings
Reward	D+
Risk	D+
Recent Upgrade/Downgrade	

Fund Information
Fund Type	Exchange Traded Funds
Category	Global Equity Large Cap
Sub-Category	Foreign Large Blend
Prospectus Objective	Growth
Inception Date	Aug-16
Open to New Investments	Y

Prices
Price (as of 12/31/2018)	30.87
52-Week High	36.34
52-Week Low	29.97

Total Returns (%)
3-Month	6-Month	1-Year	3-Year	5-Year
-7.40	-3.23	-7.69		

3-Year Standard Deviation	
Effective Duration	

Valuation
Premium/Discount (1-Year Average)	0.43

Company Information
Provider	First Trust
Manager/Tenure	Steven Clark (2), Michael Dickson (2), Scott E. Ladner (2)
Website	http://www.ftportfolios.com/
Address	First Trust 120 E. Liberty Drive, Suite 400 Wheaton IL 60187 United States
Phone Number	800-621-1675

PERFORMANCE

Ratings History
Date	Overall Rating	Risk Rating	Reward Rating
Q4-18	D+	D+	D+
Q2-18	C-	C-	D+
Q4-17	D	B-	C
Q4-16	U		
Q4-15			

Asset & Performance History
Date	NAV	1-Year Total Return
2017	34.15	27.17
2016	27.78	
2015		
2014		
2013		
2012		

Total Assets: $60,697,141

Asset Allocation
Asset	%
Cash	0%
Stocks	100%
US Stocks	1%
Bonds	0%
US Bonds	0%
Other	0%

Services Offered:

Investment Strategy: The investment seeks to provide capital appreciation. Under normal market conditions, the fund seeks to achieve its investment objective by investing at least 80% of its net assets (including investment borrowings) in common stocks and depositary receipts of developed market companies listed and traded on non-U.S. exchanges that the Sub-Advisor believes exhibit low future expected volatility. Under normal market conditions, it will invest in at least three countries and at least 40% of its net assets in countries other than the United States. It is non-diversified. **Top Holdings:** Ascendas Real Estate Investment Trust   Swiss Prime Site AG Woolworths Group Ltd   Hong Kong and China Gas Co Ltd   Nestle SA

First Trust Small Cap Value AlphaDEX® Fund
C-   **HOLD**

Ticker	Traded On	NAV	Total Assets ($)	Dividend Yield (TTM)	Turnover Ratio	Expense Ratio
FYT	NAS CM	31.08	$60,660,079	1.4	110	0.76

Ratings
Reward	C-
Risk	C-
Recent Upgrade/Downgrade	Down

Fund Information
Fund Type	Exchange Traded Funds
Category	US Equity Small Cap
Sub-Category	Small Value
Prospectus Objective	Small Company
Inception Date	Apr-11
Open to New Investments	Y

Prices
Price (as of 12/31/2018)	30.95
52-Week High	40.19
52-Week Low	29.75

Total Returns (%)
3-Month	6-Month	1-Year	3-Year	5-Year
-18.56	-18.47	-14.53	19.41	3.23

3-Year Standard Deviation	16.04
Effective Duration	

Valuation
Premium/Discount (1-Year Average)	0.07

Company Information
Provider	First Trust
Manager/Tenure	Jon C. Erickson (7), Daniel J. Lindquist (7), David G. McGarel (7), 3 others
Website	http://www.ftportfolios.com/
Address	First Trust 120 E. Liberty Drive, Suite 400 Wheaton IL 60187 United States
Phone Number	800-621-1675

PERFORMANCE

Ratings History
Date	Overall Rating	Risk Rating	Reward Rating
Q4-18	C-	C-	C-
Q2-18	C	D+	C
Q4-17	B-	C+	B-
Q4-16	C	C-	C
Q4-15	C	C-	C

Asset & Performance History
Date	NAV	1-Year Total Return
2017	36.93	7.36
2016	34.82	30.14
2015	27.09	-16.67
2014	32.79	3.75
2013	31.88	43.5
2012	22.32	16.66

Total Assets: $60,660,079

Asset Allocation
Asset	%
Cash	0%
Stocks	100%
US Stocks	100%
Bonds	0%
US Bonds	0%
Other	0%

Services Offered:

Investment Strategy: The investment seeks investment results that correspond generally to the price and yield (before the fund's fees and expenses) of an equity index called the Nasdaq AlphaDEX® Small Cap Value Index. The fund will normally invest at least 90% of its net assets (including investment borrowings) in common stocks that comprise the index. The index is designed to select value stocks from the NASDAQ US 700 Small Cap Index (the "base index") that may generate positive alpha, or risk-adjusted returns, relative to traditional indices through the use of the AlphaDEX® selection methodology. **Top Holdings:** Telephone and Data Systems Inc Hertz Global Holdings Inc Graham Holdings Co Tegna Inc Sinclair Broadcast Group Inc

---

Invesco New York AMT-Free Municipal Bond ETF
C-   **HOLD**

Ticker	Traded On	NAV	Total Assets ($)	Dividend Yield (TTM)	Turnover Ratio	Expense Ratio
PZT	NYSE Arca	23.92	$60,342,646	2.96		0.28

Ratings
Reward	D+
Risk	C-
Recent Upgrade/Downgrade	Down

Fund Information
Fund Type	Exchange Traded Funds
Category	US Muni Fixed Inc
Sub-Category	Muni New York Long
Prospectus Objective	Muni Bond - Single State
Inception Date	Oct-07
Open to New Investments	Y

Prices
Price (as of 12/31/2018)	23.80
52-Week High	24.66
52-Week Low	23.24

Total Returns (%)
3-Month	6-Month	1-Year	3-Year	5-Year
1.59	0.89	0.23	7.19	27.32

3-Year Standard Deviation	3.62
Effective Duration	7.44

Valuation
Premium/Discount (1-Year Average)	-0.21

Company Information
Provider	Invesco
Manager/Tenure	Philip Fang (11), Peter Hubbard (11), Jeffrey W. Kernagis (11), 2 others
Website	http://www.invesco.com/us
Address	Invesco 11 Greenway Plaza, Ste. 2500 Houston TX 77046 United States
Phone Number	800-659-1005

PERFORMANCE

Ratings History
Date	Overall Rating	Risk Rating	Reward Rating
Q4-18	C-	C-	D+
Q2-18	C	C-	C
Q4-17	B-	B+	C
Q4-16	C	D+	C
Q4-15	C	D+	C

Asset & Performance History
Date	NAV	1-Year Total Return
2017	24.58	5.82
2016	23.93	1.06
2015	24.46	3.81
2014	24.38	14.41
2013	22.15	-6.29
2012	24.58	7.22

Total Assets: $60,342,646

Asset Allocation
Asset	%
Cash	0%
Stocks	0%
US Stocks	0%
Bonds	100%
US Bonds	96%
Other	0%

Services Offered:

Investment Strategy: The investment seeks to track the investment results (before fees and expenses) of the ICE BofAML New York Long-Term Core Plus Municipal Securities Index (the "underlying index"). The fund generally will invest at least 80% of its total assets in municipal securities that comprise the underlying index and that also are exempt from the federal alternative minimum tax. The index is composed of U.S. dollar-denominated, investment grade, tax-exempt debt publicly issued by New York or any U.S. territory or their political subdivisions, in the U.S. domestic market with a term of at least 15 years remaining to final maturity. It is non-diversified. **Top Holdings:** NEW YORK N Y CITY INDL DEV AGY 6.5% NEW YORK ST DORM AUTH 5% UTILITY DEBT SECURITIZATION AUTH N Y 5% NEW YORK ST DORM AUTH 5% LONG IS PWR AUTH N Y 5%

Invesco Dynamic Media ETF   C+   HOLD

Ticker	Traded On	NAV	Total Assets ($)	Dividend Yield (TTM)	Turnover Ratio	Expense Ratio
PBS	NYSE Arca	28.47	$60,110,406	0.63	150	0.63

Ratings
Reward   B
Risk   C-
Recent Upgrade/Downgrade

Fund Information
Fund Type   Exchange Traded Funds
Category   Consumer Goods & Svcs
Sub-Category   Consumer Cyclical
Prospectus Objective   Comm
Inception Date   Jun-05
Open to New Investments   Y

Prices
Price (as of 12/31/2018)   28.42
52-Week High   33.68
52-Week Low   26.83

Total Returns (%)

3-Month	6-Month	1-Year	3-Year	5-Year
-12.54	-12.41	2.33	15.30	10.11

3-Year Standard Deviation   12.6
Effective Duration

Valuation
Premium/Discount (1-Year Average)   0.04

Company Information
Provider   Invesco
Manager/Tenure   Peter Hubbard (11), Michael Jeanette (10), Tony Seisser (4), 1 other
Website   http://www.invesco.com/us
Address   Invesco 11 Greenway Plaza, Ste. 2500 Houston TX 77046 United States
Phone Number   800-659-1005

PERFORMANCE

Ratings History

Date	Overall Rating	Risk Rating	Reward Rating
Q4-18	C+	C-	B
Q2-18	C+	C-	B
Q4-17	C+	B	C
Q4-16	C+	C-	B-
Q4-15	B	B-	B

Asset & Performance History

Date	NAV	1-Year Total Return
2017	28.06	7.16
2016	26.27	5.13
2015	25.03	-1.12
2014	25.59	-3.41
2013	26.63	59.77
2012	16.73	27.26

Total Assets: $60,110,406

Asset Allocation

Asset	%
Cash	0%
Stocks	100%
US Stocks	100%
Bonds	0%
US Bonds	0%
Other	0%

Services Offered:

Investment Strategy: The investment seeks to track the investment results (before fees and expenses) of the Dynamic Media IntellidexSM Index. The fund generally will invest at least 90% of its total assets in common stocks of media companies that comprise the underlying intellidex. The underlying intellidex was composed of common stocks of 3 U.S. media companies. These are companies that are principally engaged in the development, production, sale and distribution of goods or services used in the media industry. The fund is non-diversified. **Top Holdings:** Twenty-First Century Fox Inc Class A   CBS Corp Class B   Walt Disney Co   IHS Markit Ltd   Sirius XM Holdings Inc

iShares iBonds Mar 2023 Term Corporate ETF   D+   SELL

Ticker	Traded On	NAV	Total Assets ($)	Dividend Yield (TTM)	Turnover Ratio	Expense Ratio
IBDD	NYSE Arca	25.57	$59,799,333	3.01	12	0.1

Ratings
Reward   C-
Risk   D+
Recent Upgrade/Downgrade   Down

Fund Information
Fund Type   Exchange Traded Funds
Category   US Fixed Income
Sub-Category   Corporate Bond
Prospectus Objective   Corp Bond - Gen
Inception Date   Jul-13
Open to New Investments   Y

Prices
Price (as of 12/31/2018)   25.60
52-Week High   26.46
52-Week Low   25.36

Total Returns (%)

3-Month	6-Month	1-Year	3-Year	5-Year
0.72	1.55	-0.09	9.69	19.83

3-Year Standard Deviation   2.96
Effective Duration   3.59

Valuation
Premium/Discount (1-Year Average)   0.02

Company Information
Provider   iShares
Manager/Tenure   James Mauro (5), Scott Radell (5)
Website   http://www.ishares.com
Address   iShares 400 Howard Street San Francisco CA 94105 United States
Phone Number   800-474-2737

PERFORMANCE

Ratings History

Date	Overall Rating	Risk Rating	Reward Rating
Q4-18	D+	D+	C-
Q2-18	C-	D+	C-
Q4-17	B	A	C
Q4-16	C	D+	C
Q4-15	D	D	D+

Asset & Performance History

Date	NAV	1-Year Total Return
2017	26.38	3.76
2016	26.11	5.54
2015	25.47	0.64
2014	26.1	8.55
2013	24.84	
2012		

Total Assets: $59,799,333

Asset Allocation

Asset	%
Cash	0%
Stocks	0%
US Stocks	0%
Bonds	100%
US Bonds	88%
Other	0%

Services Offered:

Investment Strategy: The investment seeks to track the investment results of Bloomberg Barclays 2023 Maturity Corporate Index which composed of U.S. dollar-denominated, investment-grade corporate bonds maturing after March 31, 2022 and before April 1, 2023. The fund generally will invest at least 90% of its assets in the component securities (including indirect investments through an underlying fund) of the underlying index, and may invest up to 10% of its assets in certain futures, options and swap contracts, cash and cash equivalents, as well as in securities not included in the underlying index. **Top Holdings:** iShares iBonds Mar 2023Tm CorpexFncl ETF   Bank of America Corporation 3.3%   Anheuser-Busch InBev Finance Inc. 3.3%   Morgan Stanley 3.75%   Wells Fargo & Company 2.63%

VanEck Vectors Africa Index ETF

D+   SELL

Ticker	Traded On	NAV	Total Assets ($)	Dividend Yield (TTM)	Turnover Ratio	Expense Ratio
AFK	NYSE Arca	20.08	$59,580,729	2.4	38	0.84

Ratings
Reward	D+
Risk	D
Recent Upgrade/Downgrade	Down

Fund Information
Fund Type	Exchange Traded Funds
Category	Equity Misc
Sub-Category	Miscellaneous Region
Prospectus Objective	Growth
Inception Date	Jul-08
Open to New Investments	Y

Prices
Price (as of 12/31/2018)	19.66
52-Week High	27.04
52-Week Low	19.22

Total Returns (%)
3-Month	6-Month	1-Year	3-Year	5-Year
-5.31	-11.97	-17.22	18.92	-26.75

3-Year Standard Deviation	16.06
Effective Duration	

Valuation
Premium/Discount (1-Year Average)	-0.14

Company Information
Provider	VanEck
Manager/Tenure	Hao-Hung (Peter) Liao (10), Guo Hua (Jason) Jin (0)
Website	http://www.vaneck.com
Address	Van Eck Associates Corporation 666 Third Avenue New York NY 10017 United States
Phone Number	800-826-1115

PERFORMANCE

Ratings History
Date	Overall Rating	Risk Rating	Reward Rating
Q4-18	D+	D	D+
Q2-18	C-	D+	C-
Q4-17	C	C	C
Q4-16	D	D	D
Q4-15	D	D	D

Asset & Performance History
Date	NAV	1-Year Total Return
2017	24.81	26.06
2016	20.09	13.97
2015	18.11	-29.38
2014	26.2	-12.79
2013	30.93	3.28
2012	30.77	22.21

Total Assets: $59,580,729

Asset Allocation
Asset	%
Cash	0%
Stocks	100%
US Stocks	1%
Bonds	0%
US Bonds	0%
Other	0%

Services Offered:

Investment Strategy: The investment seeks to replicate as closely as possible, before fees and expenses, the price and yield performance of the MVIS® GDP Africa Index. The fund normally invests at least 80% of its total assets in securities that comprise the fund's benchmark index. The index includes local listings of companies that are incorporated in Africa and listings of companies incorporated outside of Africa but that have at least 50% of their revenues/related assets in Africa. **Top Holdings:** Naspers Ltd Class N   Maroc Telecom SA   Safaricom PLC   Attijariwafa Bank SA   Guaranty Trust Bank PLC

UBS ETRACS Monthly Pay 2xLeveraged Mortgage REIT ETN Series B

C-   HOLD

Ticker	Traded On	NAV	Total Assets ($)	Dividend Yield (TTM)	Turnover Ratio	Expense Ratio
MRRL	NYSE Arca	12.54	$59,560,786	21.59		0.4

Ratings
Reward	C-
Risk	C-
Recent Upgrade/Downgrade	Down

Fund Information
Fund Type	Exchange Traded Funds
Category	Trading Tools
Sub-Category	Trading--Leveraged Equity
Prospectus Objective	Real Estate
Inception Date	Oct-15
Open to New Investments	Y

Prices
Price (as of 12/31/2018)	12.57
52-Week High	17.71
52-Week Low	11.53

Total Returns (%)
3-Month	6-Month	1-Year	3-Year	5-Year
-14.25	-13.01	-12.25	77.05	

3-Year Standard Deviation	20.92
Effective Duration	

Valuation
Premium/Discount (1-Year Average)	0.28

Company Information
Provider	UBS Group AG
Manager/Tenure	No Manager (3)
Website	http://www.ubs.com
Address	Bahnhofstrasse 45 Zurich 8098 Switzerland
Phone Number	412-037-1952

PERFORMANCE

Ratings History
Date	Overall Rating	Risk Rating	Reward Rating
Q4-18	C-	C-	C-
Q2-18	C	D+	C+
Q4-17	C	B-	C
Q4-16	D	D+	D+
Q4-15			

Asset & Performance History
Date	NAV	1-Year Total Return
2017	17.61	38.04
2016	15.55	47.29
2015	13.25	
2014		
2013		
2012		

Total Assets: $59,560,786

Asset Allocation
Asset	%
Cash	%
Stocks	%
US Stocks	%
Bonds	%
US Bonds	%
Other	%

Services Offered:

Investment Strategy: The investment seeks a return linked to the Market Vectors® Global Mortgage REITs Index. The ETRACS Monthly Pay 2xLeveraged Mortgage REIT ETN Series B due October 16, 2042 is a series of Monthly Pay 2xLeveraged ETRACS. The index tracks the overall performance of publicly-traded mortgage REITs that derive at least 50% of their revenues from mortgage-related activities. The Securities are senior unsecured debt securities issued by UBS AG. The Securities are two times leveraged with respect to the index, and, as a result, will benefit from two times any positive, but will be exposed to two times any negative, compounded monthly performance of the index. **Top Holdings:**

iShares International Dividend Growth ETF   D+   SELL

Ticker	Traded On	NAV
IGRO	BATS	49.10

Total Assets ($)	Dividend Yield (TTM)	Turnover Ratio	Expense Ratio
$59,449,154	3	42	0.22

Ratings
Reward	D+
Risk	D+
Recent Upgrade/Downgrade	Down

Fund Information
Fund Type	Exchange Traded Funds
Category	Global Equity Large Cap
Sub-Category	Foreign Large Blend
Prospectus Objective	Equity-Income
Inception Date	May-16
Open to New Investments	Y

Prices
Price (as of 12/31/2018)	49.24
52-Week High	61.72
52-Week Low	48.08

Total Returns (%)
3-Month	6-Month	1-Year	3-Year	5-Year
-12.00	-8.53	-13.11		

3-Year Standard Deviation	
Effective Duration	

Valuation
Premium/Discount (1-Year Average)	0.51

Company Information
Provider	iShares
Manager/Tenure	Diane Hsiung (2), Jennifer Hsui (2), Alan Mason (2), 3 others
Website	http://www.ishares.com
Address	iShares 400 Howard Street San Francisco CA 94105 United States
Phone Number	800-474-2737

PERFORMANCE

Ratings History
Date	Overall Rating	Risk Rating	Reward Rating
Q4-18	D+	D+	D+
Q2-18	D+	D+	D+
Q4-17	D+	B	C
Q4-16	U		
Q4-15			

Asset & Performance History
Date	NAV	1-Year Total Return
2017	58.05	23.71
2016	48.18	
2015		
2014		
2013		
2012		

Total Assets: $59,449,154
Asset Allocation
Asset	%
Cash	1%
Stocks	99%
US Stocks	1%
Bonds	0%
US Bonds	0%
Other	0%

Services Offered:
Investment Strategy: The investment seeks to track the investment results of the Morningstar® Global ex-US Dividend Growth IndexSM. The fund generally will invest at least 90% of its assets in the component securities of the underlying index and in investments that have economic characteristics that are substantially identical to the component securities of the underlying index and may invest up to 10% of its assets in certain futures, options and swap contracts, cash and cash equivalents. The index is a dividend dollars weighted index that seeks to measure the performance of international equities selected based on a consistent history of growing dividends. It is non-diversified. **Top Holdings:** Novartis AG Nestle SA Roche Holding AG Dividend Right Cert. Sanofi SA Samsung Electronics Co Ltd

---

IQ Real Return ETF   D+   SELL

Ticker	Traded On	NAV
CPI	NYSE Arca	26.62

Total Assets ($)	Dividend Yield (TTM)	Turnover Ratio	Expense Ratio
$59,096,873	1.07		0.44

Ratings
Reward	C-
Risk	D+
Recent Upgrade/Downgrade	Down

Fund Information
Fund Type	Exchange Traded Funds
Category	Moderate Allocation
Sub-Category	Tactical Allocation
Prospectus Objective	Growth & Inc
Inception Date	Oct-09
Open to New Investments	Y

Prices
Price (as of 12/31/2018)	26.61
52-Week High	28.08
52-Week Low	26.47

Total Returns (%)
3-Month	6-Month	1-Year	3-Year	5-Year
-3.81	-2.60	-1.78	2.93	5.14

3-Year Standard Deviation	2.07
Effective Duration	

Valuation
Premium/Discount (1-Year Average)	0.06

Company Information
Provider	IndexIQ
Manager/Tenure	Greg Barrato (7), James Harrison (0)
Website	http://www.indexiq.com
Address	IndexIQ 800 Westchester Avenue, Suite N-611 Rye Brook NY 10573 United States
Phone Number	888-934-0777

PERFORMANCE

Ratings History
Date	Overall Rating	Risk Rating	Reward Rating
Q4-18	D+	D+	C-
Q2-18	C-	D+	C
Q4-17	B-	A	C
Q4-16	C-	D+	C
Q4-15	C-	D+	C

Asset & Performance History
Date	NAV	1-Year Total Return
2017	27.46	3.05
2016	26.93	1.69
2015	26.48	0.01
2014	26.48	2.13
2013	25.95	-1.37
2012	26.34	1.6

Total Assets: $59,096,873
Asset Allocation
Asset	%
Cash	41%
Stocks	19%
US Stocks	13%
Bonds	39%
US Bonds	32%
Other	1%

Services Offered:
Investment Strategy: The investment seeks investment results that correspond generally to the price and yield performance of its underlying index, the IQ Real Return Index. The fund is a "fund of funds" which means it invests, under normal circumstances, at least 80% of its net assets, plus the amount of any borrowings for investment purposes, in the investments included in its underlying index, which includes underlying funds. The underlying index consists of a number of components ("underlying index components") selected in accordance with the rules-based methodology of such underlying index. **Top Holdings:** iShares Short Treasury Bond ETF PIMCO Enhanced Short Maturity Active ETF SPDR® Blmbg Barclays 1-3 Mth T-Bill ETF iShares Russell 2000 ETF Goldman Sachs Access Treasury 0-1 Yr ETF

FlexShares International Quality Dividend Dynamic Index Fund   D+   SELL

Ticker	Traded On	NAV	Total Assets ($)	Dividend Yield (TTM)	Turnover Ratio	Expense Ratio
IQDY	NYSE Arca	21.88	$58,951,268	5.46		0.47

Ratings   -
Reward   C-
Risk   D+
Recent Upgrade/Downgrade   Down

Fund Information
Fund Type   Exchange Traded Funds
Category   Global Equity Large Cap
Sub-Category   Foreign Large Value
Prospectus Objective   World Stock
Inception Date   Apr-13
Open to New Investments   Y

Prices
Price (as of 12/31/2018)   21.72
52-Week High   30.65
52-Week Low   21.17

Total Returns (%)

3-Month	6-Month	1-Year	3-Year	5-Year
-12.88	-12.83	-19.03	10.83	-2.41

3-Year Standard Deviation   12.16
Effective Duration

Valuation
Premium/Discount (1-Year Average)   0.23

Company Information
Provider   Flexshares Trust
Manager/Tenure   Robert Anstine (5), Brendan Sullivan (2)
Website   http://www.flexshares.com
Address   50 South LaSalle Street Chicago, Illinois 60603 Chicago Illinois 60603 United States
Phone Number   855-353-9383

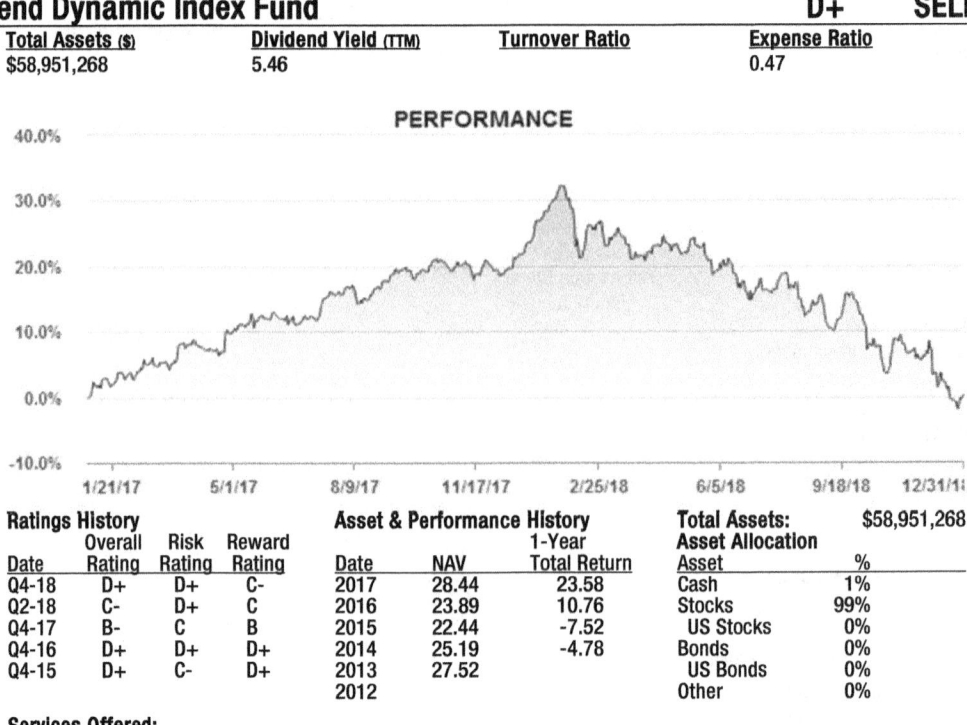

Ratings History

Date	Overall Rating	Risk Rating	Reward Rating
Q4-18	D+	D+	C-
Q2-18	C-	D+	C
Q4-17	B-	C	B
Q4-16	D+	D+	D+
Q4-15	D+	C-	D+

Asset & Performance History

Date	NAV	1-Year Total Return
2017	28.44	23.58
2016	23.89	10.76
2015	22.44	-7.52
2014	25.19	-4.78
2013	27.52	
2012		

Total Assets: $58,951,268
Asset Allocation

Asset	%
Cash	1%
Stocks	99%
US Stocks	0%
Bonds	0%
US Bonds	0%
Other	0%

Services Offered:

Investment Strategy: The investment seeks investment results that correspond generally to the price and yield performance, before fees and expenses, of the Northern Trust International Quality Dividend Dynamic IndexSM. The fund will invest at least 80% of its total assets in the securities of the index and in ADRs and GDRs based on the securities in the index. The index is designed to provide exposure to a high-quality, income-oriented portfolio of international equity securities issued by non-U.S.-based companies, with an emphasis on long-term capital growth and a targeted overall volatility that is greater than that of the Northern Trust International Large Cap IndexSM. **Top Holdings:** GlaxoSmithKline PLC BP PLC HSBC Holdings PLC Total SA AstraZeneca PLC

ProShares Ultra 7-10 Year Treasury   D   SELL

Ticker	Traded On	NAV	Total Assets ($)	Dividend Yield (TTM)	Turnover Ratio	Expense Ratio
UST	NYSE Arca	55.67	$58,559,542	1.45	188	0.95

Ratings
Reward   D
Risk   C-
Recent Upgrade/Downgrade

Fund Information
Fund Type   Exchange Traded Funds
Category   Trading Tools
Sub-Category   Trading--Leveraged Debt
Prospectus Objective   Govt Bond - Treasury
Inception Date   Jan-10
Open to New Investments   Y

Prices
Price (as of 12/31/2018)   55.79
52-Week High   57.41
52-Week Low   51.24

Total Returns (%)

3-Month	6-Month	1-Year	3-Year	5-Year
7.04	4.43	-1.29	2.28	22.41

3-Year Standard Deviation   9.24
Effective Duration

Valuation
Premium/Discount (1-Year Average)   -0.03

Company Information
Provider   ProShares
Manager/Tenure   Michelle Liu (8), Jeffrey Ploshnick (2)
Website   http://www.proshares.com
Address   ProShares 7501 Wisconsin Avenue, Suite 1000 Bethesda MD 20814 United States
Phone Number   866-776-5125

PERFORMANCE

Ratings History

Date	Overall Rating	Risk Rating	Reward Rating
Q4-18	D	C-	D
Q2-18	D	D+	D
Q4-17	C-	C	C-
Q4-16	C	C-	C
Q4-15	C	C-	C

Asset & Performance History

Date	NAV	1-Year Total Return
2017	57.41	3.11
2016	56.14	0.5
2015	56.2	1.92
2014	55.55	17.4
2013	49.79	-12.67
2012	57.02	7.07

Total Assets: $58,559,542
Asset Allocation

Asset	%
Cash	-100%
Stocks	0%
US Stocks	0%
Bonds	67%
US Bonds	67%
Other	132%

Services Offered:

Investment Strategy: The investment seeks daily investment results that correspond to two times (2x) the daily performance of the ICE U.S. Treasury 7-10 Year Bond Index. The fund invests in financial instruments that ProShare Advisors believes, in combination, should produce daily returns consistent with the fund's investment objective. The index includes publicly- issued U.S. Treasury securities that have a remaining maturity of greater than seven years and less than or equal to ten years and have $300 million or more of outstanding face value, excluding amounts held by the Federal Reserve. The fund is non-diversified. **Top Holdings:** Ice 7-10 Year U.S. Treasury Index Swap Citibank Na Ice 7-10 Year U.S. Treasury Index Swap Goldman Sachs International United States Treasury Notes United States Treasury Notes United States Treasury Notes

iShares Edge MSCI Min Vol USA Small-Cap ETF   C-   HOLD

Ticker	Traded On	NAV	Total Assets ($)	Dividend Yield (TTM)	Turnover Ratio	Expense Ratio
SMMV	BATS	29.00	$58,296,087	1.45	47	0.2

Ratings
Reward   C-
Risk   C-
Recent Upgrade/Downgrade

Fund Information
Fund Type	Exchange Traded Funds
Category	US Equity Small Cap
Sub-Category	Small Blend
Prospectus Objective	Small Company
Inception Date	Sep-16
Open to New Investments	Y

Prices
Price (as of 12/31/2018)	29.05
52-Week High	33.12
52-Week Low	27.66

Total Returns (%)
3-Month	6-Month	1-Year	3-Year	5-Year
-9.98	-6.08	1.48		

3-Year Standard Deviation
Effective Duration

Valuation
Premium/Discount (1-Year Average)   0.16

Company Information
Provider	iShares
Manager/Tenure	Diane Hsiung (2), Jennifer Hsui (2), Alan Mason (2), 3 others
Website	http://www.ishares.com
Address	iShares 400 Howard Street San Francisco CA 94105 United States
Phone Number	800-474-2737

PERFORMANCE

Ratings History
Date	Overall Rating	Risk Rating	Reward Rating
Q4-18	C-	C-	C-
Q2-18	D+	D+	D+
Q4-17	D	B+	C
Q4-16	U		
Q4-15			

Asset & Performance History
Date	NAV	1-Year Total Return
2017	29.05	13.94
2016	25.93	
2015		
2014		
2013		
2012		

Total Assets: $58,296,087
Asset Allocation
Asset	%
Cash	0%
Stocks	100%
US Stocks	99%
Bonds	0%
US Bonds	0%
Other	0%

Services Offered:

Investment Strategy: The investment seeks to track the investment results of the MSCI USA Small Cap Minimum Volatility (USD) Index. The fund generally will invest at least 90% of its assets in the component securities of the underlying index. The index has been developed by MSCI Inc. (the "index provider" or "MSCI") to measure the performance of small-capitalization U.S. equities that in the aggregate have lower volatility characteristics relative to the small-capitalization U.S. equity market. The manager uses a "passive" or indexing approach to try to achieve the fund's investment objective. It is non-diversified. **Top Holdings:** Starwood Property Trust Inc   Royal Gold Inc   Sun Communities Inc   Equity Lifestyle Properties Inc   Equity Commonwealth

---

Inspire Corporate Bond Impact ETF   D   SELL

Ticker	Traded On	NAV	Total Assets ($)	Dividend Yield (TTM)	Turnover Ratio	Expense Ratio
IBD	NYSE Arca	24.35	$58,030,634	2.17		0.61

Ratings
Reward   D
Risk   D+
Recent Upgrade/Downgrade   Down

Fund Information
Fund Type	Exchange Traded Funds
Category	US Fixed Income
Sub-Category	Corporate Bond
Prospectus Objective	Corp Bond - Gen
Inception Date	Jul-17
Open to New Investments	Y

Prices
Price (as of 12/31/2018)	24.42
52-Week High	25.43
52-Week Low	24.16

Total Returns (%)
3-Month	6-Month	1-Year	3-Year	5-Year
0.78	1.37	-0.23		

3-Year Standard Deviation
Effective Duration

Valuation
Premium/Discount (1-Year Average)   0.48

Company Information
Provider	Inspire
Manager/Tenure	Darrell Jayroe (1), Robert Netzly (1)
Website	
Address	Inspire 650 San Benito Street, Suite 130 Hollister CA 95023 United States
Phone Number	

PERFORMANCE

Ratings History
Date	Overall Rating	Risk Rating	Reward Rating
Q4-18	D	D+	D
Q2-18	D+	D+	D
Q4-17	U		
Q4-16			
Q4-15			

Asset & Performance History
Date	NAV	1-Year Total Return
2017	24.94	
2016		
2015		
2014		
2013		
2012		

Total Assets: $58,030,634
Asset Allocation
Asset	%
Cash	3%
Stocks	0%
US Stocks	0%
Bonds	97%
US Bonds	95%
Other	0%

Services Offered:

Investment Strategy: The investment seeks to replicate investment results that generally correspond to the Inspire Corporate Bond Impact Index. The fund generally will invest at least 80% of its total assets in the component securities of the index. The index provider selects domestic corporate bonds issued by companies that have market capitalizations of $5 billion or more and are included in the S&P 500 Investment Grade Corporate Bond Index using the Inspire Impact Score®, a proprietary selection methodology that is designed to assign a score to a particular security based on the security's alignment with biblical values and the positive impact that company has on the world. **Top Holdings:** General Dynamics Corporation 2.25%   Broadcom/Broadcom Cayman Finance Ltd 2.38%   Occidental Petroleum Corporation 3.4%   ConocoPhillips Company 3.35%   Phillips 66 4.3%

IQ Enhanced Core Bond U.S. ETF

D+ SELL

Ticker	Traded On	NAV	Total Assets ($)	Dividend Yield (TTM)	Turnover Ratio	Expense Ratio
AGGE	NYSE Arca	18.60	$57,962,722	2.82		0.3

Ratings
Reward	D
Risk	C-
Recent Upgrade/Downgrade	Up

Fund Information
Fund Type	Exchange Traded Funds
Category	US Fixed Income
Sub-Category	Intermediate-Term Bond
Prospectus Objective	Income
Inception Date	May-16
Open to New Investments	Y

Prices
Price (as of 12/31/2018)	18.61
52-Week High	19.57
52-Week Low	18.31

Total Returns (%)
3-Month	6-Month	1-Year	3-Year	5-Year
1.23	0.97	-2.57		

3-Year Standard Deviation	
Effective Duration	4.46

Valuation
Premium/Discount (1-Year Average)	-0.02

Company Information
Provider	IndexIQ
Manager/Tenure	Greg Barrato (2), James Harrison (0)
Website	http://www.indexiq.com
Address	IndexIQ 800 Westchester Avenue, Suite N-611 Rye Brook NY 10573 United States
Phone Number	888-934-0777

PERFORMANCE

Ratings History
Date	Overall Rating	Risk Rating	Reward Rating
Q4-18	D+	C-	D
Q2-18	D	C-	D
Q4-17	D+	C+	D+
Q4-16	U		
Q4-15			

Asset & Performance History
Date	NAV	1-Year Total Return
2017	19.59	2.5
2016	19.54	
2015		
2014		
2013		
2012		

Total Assets: $57,962,722
Asset Allocation
Asset	%
Cash	1%
Stocks	0%
US Stocks	0%
Bonds	99%
US Bonds	95%
Other	0%

Services Offered:

Investment Strategy: The investment seeks to track (before fees and expenses) the price and yield performance of its underlying index, the IQ Enhanced Core Bond U.S. Index. The fund is a "fund of funds" which means it invests, under normal circumstances, at least 80% of its net assets, plus the amount of any borrowings for investment purposes, in the investments included in its underlying index. The underlying index seeks to outperform the U.S. dollar-denominated taxable fixed income universe by using a combination of short- and long-term momentum to overweight and underweight various sectors of the investment grade U.S. fixed income securities market. **Top Holdings:** Vanguard Short-Term Treasury ETF Schwab Short-Term US Treasury ETF™ Vanguard Short-Term Corporate Bond ETF Vanguard Long-Term Corporate Bd ETF Vanguard Interm-Term Corp Bd ETF

Invesco BulletShares 2026 Corporate Bond ETF

D+ SELL

Ticker	Traded On	NAV	Total Assets ($)	Dividend Yield (TTM)	Turnover Ratio	Expense Ratio
BSCQ	NYSE Arca	18.55	$57,947,969	3.5	0	0.1

Ratings
Reward	D+
Risk	C-
Recent Upgrade/Downgrade	

Fund Information
Fund Type	Exchange Traded Funds
Category	US Fixed Income
Sub-Category	Corporate Bond
Prospectus Objective	Corp Bond - Gen
Inception Date	Sep-16
Open to New Investments	Y

Prices
Price (as of 12/31/2018)	18.61
52-Week High	19.70
52-Week Low	18.38

Total Returns (%)
3-Month	6-Month	1-Year	3-Year	5-Year
0.33	1.31	-2.38		

3-Year Standard Deviation	
Effective Duration	6.50

Valuation
Premium/Discount (1-Year Average)	0.18

Company Information
Provider	Invesco
Manager/Tenure	Jeremy Neisewander (2), Peter Hubbard (0), Jeffrey W. Kernagis (0), 1 other
Website	http://www.invesco.com/us
Address	Invesco 11 Greenway Plaza, Ste. 2500 Houston TX 77046 United States
Phone Number	800-659-1005

PERFORMANCE

Ratings History
Date	Overall Rating	Risk Rating	Reward Rating
Q4-18	D+	C-	D+
Q2-18	D+	C-	D
Q4-17	D	B	D+
Q4-16	U		
Q4-15			

Asset & Performance History
Date	NAV	1-Year Total Return
2017	19.64	5.51
2016	19.15	
2015		
2014		
2013		
2012		

Total Assets: $57,947,969
Asset Allocation
Asset	%
Cash	0%
Stocks	0%
US Stocks	0%
Bonds	100%
US Bonds	86%
Other	0%

Services Offered:

Investment Strategy: The investment seeks investment results that correspond generally to the performance, before the fund's fees and expenses, of an investment grade corporate bond index called the Nasdaq BulletShares® USD Corporate Bond 2026 Index. The fund will invest at least 80% of its total assets in component securities that comprise the 2026 Index. The 2026 Index is designed to represent the performance of a held-to-maturity portfolio of U.S. dollar-denominated investment-grade corporate bonds with effective maturities in the year 2026. The fund is non-diversified. **Top Holdings:** Anheuser-Busch InBev Finance Inc. 3.65% Microsoft Corporation 2.4% HSBC Holdings plc 4.3% Apple Inc. 3.25% Mitsubishi UFJ Financial Group, Inc. 3.85%

John Hancock Multifactor Financials ETF   C-   HOLD

Ticker	Traded On	NAV	Total Assets ($)	Dividend Yield (TTM)	Turnover Ratio	Expense Ratio
JHMF	NYSE Arca	31.35	$57,478,766	1.24	8	0.5

Ratings
Reward	C
Risk	D+
Recent Upgrade/Downgrade	Down

Fund Information
Fund Type	Exchange Traded Funds
Category	Financials Sector Equity
Sub-Category	Financial
Prospectus Objective	Financial
Inception Date	Sep-15
Open to New Investments	Y

Prices
Price (as of 12/31/2018)	31.31
52-Week High	39.60
52-Week Low	29.33

Total Returns (%)
3-Month	6-Month	1-Year	3-Year	5-Year
-14.85	-12.41	-13.15	26.26	

3-Year Standard Deviation	14.61
Effective Duration	

Valuation
Premium/Discount (1-Year Average)	0.08

Company Information
Provider	John Hancock
Manager/Tenure	Joel P. Schneider (3), Lukas J. Smart (3), Joseph F. Hohn (0)
Website	http://jhinvestments.com
Address	601 Congress Street, Boston MA 02210 United States
Phone Number	800-225-5913

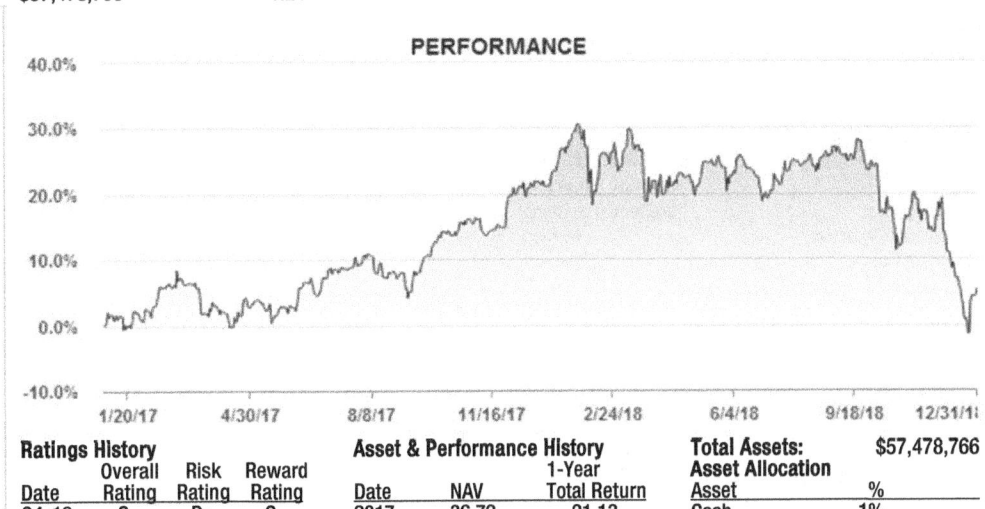

PERFORMANCE

Ratings History
Date	Overall Rating	Risk Rating	Reward Rating
Q4-18	C-	D+	C
Q2-18	C	C-	C
Q4-17	C	B-	C+
Q4-16	D	D+	C-
Q4-15			

Asset & Performance History
Date	NAV	1-Year Total Return
2017	36.72	21.13
2016	30.64	20.02
2015	25.86	
2014		
2013		
2012		

Total Assets: $57,478,766
Asset Allocation
Asset	%
Cash	1%
Stocks	99%
US Stocks	98%
Bonds	0%
US Bonds	0%
Other	0%

Services Offered:

Investment Strategy: The investment seeks to provide investment results that closely correspond, before fees and expenses, to the performance of the John Hancock Dimensional Financials Index. The fund normally invests at least 80% of its net assets (plus any borrowings for investment purposes) in securities that compose the fund's benchmark index. The index is designed to comprise securities in the financial sector within the U.S. Universe whose market capitalizations are larger than that of the 1001st largest U.S. company at the time of reconstitution. **Top Holdings:** Berkshire Hathaway Inc B JPMorgan Chase & Co Visa Inc Class A Wells Fargo & Co Bank of America Corporation

---

iShares MSCI Ireland ETF   D+   SELL

Ticker	Traded On	NAV	Total Assets ($)	Dividend Yield (TTM)	Turnover Ratio	Expense Ratio
EIRL	NYSE Arca	37.24	$57,417,316	1.97	20	0.49

Ratings
Reward	D+
Risk	D+
Recent Upgrade/Downgrade	Down

Fund Information
Fund Type	Exchange Traded Funds
Category	Equity Misc
Sub-Category	Miscellaneous Region
Prospectus Objective	Europe Stock
Inception Date	May-10
Open to New Investments	Y

Prices
Price (as of 12/31/2018)	37.01
52-Week High	50.05
52-Week Low	36.16

Total Returns (%)
3-Month	6-Month	1-Year	3-Year	5-Year
-16.57	-19.57	-20.98	-5.47	14.67

3-Year Standard Deviation	14.07
Effective Duration	

Valuation
Premium/Discount (1-Year Average)	0.19

Company Information
Provider	iShares
Manager/Tenure	Diane Hsiung (8), Greg Savage (8), Jennifer Hsui (5), 1 other
Website	http://www.ishares.com
Address	iShares 400 Howard Street San Francisco CA 94105 United States
Phone Number	800-474-2737

PERFORMANCE

Ratings History
Date	Overall Rating	Risk Rating	Reward Rating
Q4-18	D+	D+	D+
Q2-18	C	C-	C+
Q4-17	B+	B	A-
Q4-16	C	C-	C
Q4-15	C+	C-	B

Asset & Performance History
Date	NAV	1-Year Total Return
2017	47.73	28.57
2016	37.69	-6.95
2015	41.04	19.94
2014	34.82	1.14
2013	35.2	46.75
2012	24.44	29.94

Total Assets: $57,417,316
Asset Allocation
Asset	%
Cash	2%
Stocks	96%
US Stocks	27%
Bonds	0%
US Bonds	0%
Other	2%

Services Offered:

Investment Strategy: The investment seeks to track the investment results of the MSCI All Ireland Capped Index. The fund generally will invest at least 90% of its assets in the component securities of the underlying index and in investments that have economic characteristics that are substantially identical to the component securities of the underlying index. The index is a free float-adjusted market capitalization-weighted index that aims to reflect the performance of Irish equities securities of companies. The fund is non-diversified. **Top Holdings:** CRH PLC Kerry Group PLC Class A Paddy Power Betfair PLC Icon PLC AIB Group PLC

Alpha Architect International Quantitative Momentum ETF

D **SELL**

Ticker	Traded On	NAV		Total Assets ($)	Dividend Yield (TTM)	Turnover Ratio	Expense Ratio
IMOM	BATS	23.31		$57,310,594	1.06	119	0.79

Ratings

Reward	**D+**
Risk	**D**
Recent Upgrade/Downgrade	**Down**

Fund Information

Fund Type	Exchange Traded Funds
Category	Global Equity Large Cap
Sub-Category	Foreign Large Blend
Prospectus Objective	Growth
Inception Date	Dec-15
Open to New Investments	Y

Prices

Price (as of 12/31/2018)	23.20
52-Week High	32.78
52-Week Low	22.43

Total Returns (%)

3-Month	6-Month	1-Year	3-Year	5-Year
-18.23	-18.00	-22.13	-6.40	

3-Year Standard Deviation	
Effective Duration	

Valuation

Premium/Discount (1-Year Average)	0.39

Company Information

Provider	Alpha Architect
Manager/Tenure	Tao Wang (2)
Website	http://www.alphaarchitect.com/funds
Address	Alpha Architect 213 Foxcroft Road Broomall PA 19008 United States
Phone Number	

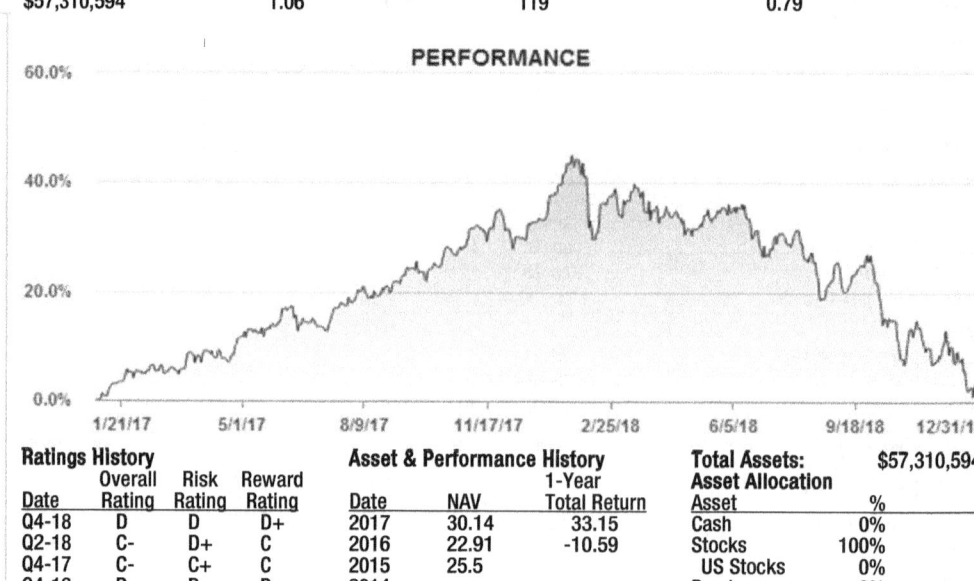

PERFORMANCE

Ratings History

Date	Overall Rating	Risk Rating	Reward Rating
Q4-18	D	D	D+
Q2-18	C-	D+	C
Q4-17	C-	C+	C
Q4-16	D-	D+	D
Q4-15			

Asset & Performance History

Date	NAV	1-Year Total Return
2017	30.14	33.15
2016	22.91	-10.59
2015	25.5	
2014		
2013		
2012		

Total Assets: $57,310,594

Asset Allocation

Asset	%
Cash	0%
Stocks	100%
US Stocks	0%
Bonds	0%
US Bonds	0%
Other	0%

Services Offered:

Investment Strategy: The investment seeks to track the total return performance, before fees and expenses, of the Alpha Architect International Quantitative Momentum Index. The fund will normally invest at least 80% of its total assets in the component securities of the index and investments that have economic characteristics that are substantially identical to the economic characteristics of such component securities (e.g., depositary receipts). The index uses a 5-step, quantitative, rules-based methodology to identify a portfolio of approximately 40-50 non-U.S. equity securities with positive momentum. The fund is non-diversified. **Top Holdings:** FamilyMart UNY Holdings Co Ltd SalMar ASA Kikkoman Corp Fast Retailing Co Ltd SSY Group Ltd

---

Xtrackers Municipal Infrastructure Revenue Bond ETF

D+ **SELL**

Ticker	Traded On	NAV		Total Assets ($)	Dividend Yield (TTM)	Turnover Ratio	Expense Ratio
RVNU	NYSE Arca			$57,197,029	2.75	28	0.15

Ratings

Reward	**C-**
Risk	**D+**
Recent Upgrade/Downgrade	**Down**

Fund Information

Fund Type	Exchange Traded Funds
Category	US Muni Fixed Inc
Sub-Category	Muni National Long
Prospectus Objective	Muni Bond - Natl
Inception Date	Jun-13
Open to New Investments	Y

Prices

Price (as of 12/31/2018)	26.27
52-Week High	27.16
52-Week Low	25.58

Total Returns (%)

3-Month	6-Month	1-Year	3-Year	5-Year
1.37	0.71	-0.46	8.06	30.44

3-Year Standard Deviation	4.72
Effective Duration	

Valuation

Premium/Discount (1-Year Average)	0.06

Company Information

Provider	Deutsche Asset Management
Manager/Tenure	Alexander Bridgeforth (1), Tanuj Dora (1), Brandon Matsui (1), 1 other
Website	http://www.deutsche-etfs.com
Address	Deutsche Asset & Wealth Management 345 Park Avenue New York NY 10154 United States
Phone Number	844-851-4255

PERFORMANCE

Ratings History

Date	Overall Rating	Risk Rating	Reward Rating
Q4-18	D+	D+	C-
Q2-18	C-	D+	C
Q4-17	B-	B	C
Q4-16	C	C-	C
Q4-15	C-	D+	C

Asset & Performance History

Date	NAV	1-Year Total Return
2017	27.08	7.29
2016	25.89	1.18
2015	26.26	4.94
2014	25.8	15.02
2013	23.18	
2012		

Total Assets: $57,197,029

Asset Allocation

Asset	%
Cash	0%
Stocks	0%
US Stocks	0%
Bonds	100%
US Bonds	99%
Other	0%

Services Offered:

Investment Strategy: The investment seeks investment results that correspond generally to the performance, before fees and expenses, of the Solactive Municipal Infrastructure Revenue Bond Index (the "underlying index"). The fund will invest at least 80% of its total assets (but typically far more) in instruments that comprise the underlying index. The underlying index is comprised of tax-exempt municipal securities issued by states, cities, counties, districts, their respective agencies, and other tax-exempt issuers. The fund is non-diversified. **Top Holdings:** NORTH TEX TWY AUTH 5% NEW JERSEY ST TPK AUTH 5% BAY AREA TOLL AUTH CALIF 5% NEW YORK N Y CITY MUN WTR FIN AUTH 5% PORT AUTH N Y & N J 5%

SPDR® DoubleLine® Emerging Markets Fixed Income ETF   D+   SELL

Ticker	Traded On	NAV	Total Assets ($)	Dividend Yield (TTM)	Turnover Ratio	Expense Ratio
EMTL	BATS	47.60	$57,141,653	2.99	141	0.65

Ratings
Reward   D+
Risk   C-
Recent Upgrade/Downgrade   Down

Fund Information
Fund Type	Exchange Traded Funds
Category	Emerging Mkts Fixed Inc
Sub-Category	Emerging Markets Bond
Prospectus Objective	Income
Inception Date	Apr-16
Open to New Investments	Y

Prices
Price (as of 12/31/2018)	47.60
52-Week High	50.40
52-Week Low	47.34

Total Returns (%)
3-Month	6-Month	1-Year	3-Year	5-Year
-0.24	0.88	-1.93		

3-Year Standard Deviation
Effective Duration   4.43

Valuation
Premium/Discount (1-Year Average)   0.36

Company Information
Provider	SPDR State Street Global Advisors
Manager/Tenure	Mark W. Christensen (2), Su Fei Koo (2), Luz M. Padilla (2)
Website	http://www.spdrs.com
Address	SPDR State Street Global Advisors State Street Financial Center, 1 Lincoln Street Boston MA 02111-2900 United States
Phone Number	617-786-3000

PERFORMANCE

Ratings History
Date	Overall Rating	Risk Rating	Reward Rating
Q4-18	D+	C-	D+
Q2-18	D+	D+	D+
Q4-17	D+	A	D+
Q4-16	U		
Q4-15			

Asset & Performance History
Date	NAV	1-Year Total Return
2017	50.17	7.6
2016	48.61	
2015		
2014		
2013		
2012		

Total Assets: $57,141,653

Asset Allocation
Asset	%
Cash	4%
Stocks	0%
US Stocks	0%
Bonds	95%
US Bonds	11%
Other	0%

Services Offered:

Investment Strategy: The investment seeks to provide high total return from current income and capital appreciation. Under normal circumstances, the fund will invest at least 80% of its net assets (plus the amount of borrowings for investment purposes) in emerging market fixed income securities. Fixed income securities are defined as fixed income securities issued or guaranteed by foreign corporations or foreign governments; corporate or government bonds; sovereign debt; structured securities; foreign currency transactions; certain derivatives; preferred securities; zero coupon bonds; credit-linked notes; pass through notes; bank loans; and perpetual maturity bonds. **Top Holdings:** Temasek Financial (I) Limited 2.38% Cometa Energia SA DE CV 6.38% Aeropuerto Intl Tocumen Sr Secured 10/23 5.75 Dbs Grp Hldgs FRN 3.6% Grupo Aval Limited 4.75%

First Trust Emerging Markets Local Currency Bond ETF   D+   SELL

Ticker	Traded On	NAV	Total Assets ($)	Dividend Yield (TTM)	Turnover Ratio	Expense Ratio
FEMB	NAS CM	37.02	$57,074,655	6.28	16	0.85

Ratings
Reward   D+
Risk   D+
Recent Upgrade/Downgrade

Fund Information
Fund Type	Exchange Traded Funds
Category	Emerging Mkts Fixed Inc
Sub-Category	Emerging-Markets Local-Currency Bond
Prospectus Objective	Div Emerg Mkts
Inception Date	Nov-14
Open to New Investments	Y

Prices
Price (as of 12/31/2018)	37.02
52-Week High	43.95
52-Week Low	35.67

Total Returns (%)
3-Month	6-Month	1-Year	3-Year	5-Year
2.32	1.07	-7.22	12.57	

3-Year Standard Deviation   10.53
Effective Duration   4.88

Valuation
Premium/Discount (1-Year Average)   -0.18

Company Information
Provider	First Trust
Manager/Tenure	Leonardo Da Costa (4), Derek Fulton (4)
Website	http://www.ftportfolios.com/
Address	First Trust 120 E. Liberty Drive, Suite 400 Wheaton IL 60187 United States
Phone Number	800-621-1675

PERFORMANCE

Ratings History
Date	Overall Rating	Risk Rating	Reward Rating
Q4-18	D+	D+	D+
Q2-18	C-	C-	C-
Q4-17	C	C	C
Q4-16	D+	D+	D+
Q4-15	U		

Asset & Performance History
Date	NAV	1-Year Total Return
2017	42.18	12.61
2016	39.92	7.73
2015	39.21	-14.68
2014	48.05	
2013		
2012		

Total Assets: $57,074,655

Asset Allocation
Asset	%
Cash	2%
Stocks	0%
US Stocks	0%
Bonds	98%
US Bonds	0%
Other	0%

Services Offered:

Investment Strategy: The investment seeks maximum total return and current income. Under normal market conditions, the fund seeks to achieve its investment objective by investing at least 80% of its net assets (including investment borrowings) in bonds, notes and bills issued or guaranteed by entities incorporated or domiciled in emerging market countries (collectively, "Bonds") that are denominated in the local currency of the issuer. It is non-diversified. **Top Holdings:** Hungary (Republic Of) 3% Secretaria Tesouro Nacional 10% Republic of South Africa 10.5% Secretaria Tesouro Nacional 10% Israel (State Of) 6.25%

Invesco Shipping ETF

D   SELL

Ticker	Traded On	NAV
SEA	NYSE Arca	8.26

Total Assets ($)	Dividend Yield (TTM)	Turnover Ratio	Expense Ratio
$56,959,680	5.24		0.65

Ratings
Reward	D
Risk	D
Recent Upgrade/Downgrade	

Fund Information
Fund Type	Exchange Traded Funds
Category	Industrials Sector Equity
Sub-Category	Industrials
Prospectus Objective	Unaligned
Inception Date	Jun-10
Open to New Investments	Y

Prices
Price (as of 12/31/2018)	8.22
52-Week High	12.33
52-Week Low	8.05

Total Returns (%)
3-Month	6-Month	1-Year	3-Year	5-Year
-19.96	-17.73	-26.90	-24.84	-49.76

3-Year Standard Deviation	17.72
Effective Duration	

Valuation
Premium/Discount (1-Year Average)	-0.09

Company Information
Provider	Invesco
Manager/Tenure	Peter Hubbard (0), Michael Jeanette (0), Jonathan Nixon (0), 1 other
Website	http://www.invesco.com/us
Address	Invesco 11 Greenway Plaza, Ste. 2500 Houston TX 77046 United States
Phone Number	800-659-1005

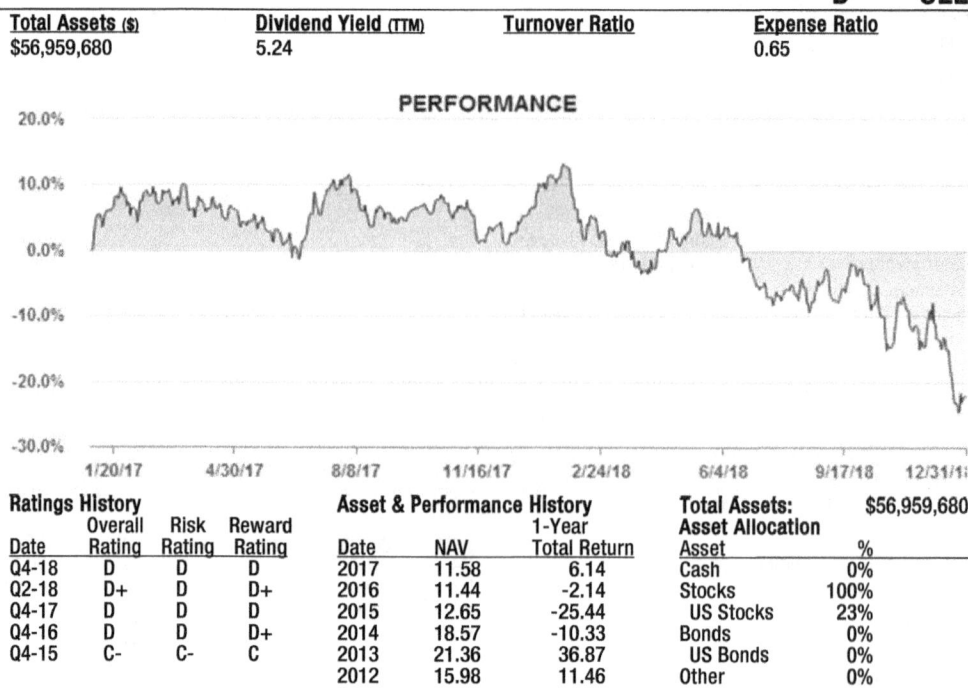

PERFORMANCE

Ratings History
Date	Overall Rating	Risk Rating	Reward Rating
Q4-18	D	D	D
Q2-18	D+	D	D+
Q4-17	D	D	D
Q4-16	D	D	D+
Q4-15	C-	C-	C

Asset & Performance History
Date	NAV	1-Year Total Return
2017	11.58	6.14
2016	11.44	-2.14
2015	12.65	-25.44
2014	18.57	-10.33
2013	21.36	36.87
2012	15.98	11.46

Total Assets: $56,959,680
Asset Allocation
Asset	%
Cash	0%
Stocks	100%
US Stocks	23%
Bonds	0%
US Bonds	0%
Other	0%

Services Offered:

Investment Strategy: The investment seeks to track investment results (before fees and expenses) of the Dow Jones Global Shipping IndexSM (the "underlying index"). The fund generally will invest at least 90% of its total assets in the securities that comprise the underlying index, as well as American depositary receipts ("ADRs") and global depositary receipts ("GDRs") that represent securities in the underlying index. The underlying index is comprised of developed market-listed equity securities of companies that are classified as being in the shipping industry. The fund is non-diversified. **Top Holdings:** A. P. Moller Maersk A/S B Nippon Yusen Kabushiki Kaisha Mitsui O.S.K. Lines Ltd Golar LNG Ltd Matson Inc

---

American Customer Satisfaction ETF

C-   HOLD

Ticker	Traded On	NAV
ACSI	BATS	28.98

Total Assets ($)	Dividend Yield (TTM)	Turnover Ratio	Expense Ratio
$56,878,954	1.12	72	0.66

Ratings
Reward	C-
Risk	C-
Recent Upgrade/Downgrade	

Fund Information
Fund Type	Exchange Traded Funds
Category	US Equity Large Cap Blend
Sub-Category	Large Blend
Prospectus Objective	Growth & Inc
Inception Date	Oct-16
Open to New Investments	Y

Prices
Price (as of 12/31/2018)	28.86
52-Week High	34.38
52-Week Low	27.89

Total Returns (%)
3-Month	6-Month	1-Year	3-Year	5-Year
-13.16	-8.34	-4.41		

3-Year Standard Deviation	
Effective Duration	

Valuation
Premium/Discount (1-Year Average)	0.18

Company Information
Provider	Exponential ETFs
Manager/Tenure	Charles A. Ragauss (2)
Website	http://https://exponentialetfs.com/
Address	Exponential ETFs United States
Phone Number	

PERFORMANCE

Ratings History
Date	Overall Rating	Risk Rating	Reward Rating
Q4-18	C-	C-	C-
Q2-18	C-	C-	C
Q4-17	D	A-	D+
Q4-16	U		
Q4-15			

Asset & Performance History
Date	NAV	1-Year Total Return
2017	30.8	15.52
2016	26.98	
2015		
2014		
2013		
2012		

Total Assets: $56,878,954
Asset Allocation
Asset	%
Cash	0%
Stocks	100%
US Stocks	100%
Bonds	0%
US Bonds	0%
Other	0%

Services Offered:

Investment Strategy: The investment seeks to track the performance of the American Customer Satisfaction Investable Index. Under normal circumstances, at least 80% of the fund's total assets will be invested in the component securities of the index. Construction of the index begins with over 350 ACSI Companies across 43 industries and 10 economic sectors. The initial universe is then screened to eliminate companies whose stock is not principally listed on a U.S. exchange, whose stock does not meet minimum liquidity requirements, or whose ACSI Score falls below its respective industry average. The remaining companies are included in the index. **Top Holdings:** Amazon.com Inc Apple Inc CenterPoint Energy Inc United Parcel Service Inc Class B Humana Inc

Global X Guru™ Index ETF   C-   HOLD

Ticker	Traded On	NAV
GURU	NYSE Arca	27.45

Total Assets ($)	Dividend Yield (TTM)	Turnover Ratio	Expense Ratio
$56,840,070	0.52	95	0.75

Ratings
Reward   C
Risk   D+
Recent Upgrade/Downgrade   Down

Fund Information
Fund Type   Exchange Traded Funds
Category   US Equity Large Cap Growth
Sub-Category   Large Growth
Prospectus Objective   Income
Inception Date   Jun-12
Open to New Investments   Y

Prices
Price (as of 12/31/2018)   27.60
52-Week High   32.92
52-Week Low   26.14

Total Returns (%)

3-Month	6-Month	1-Year	3-Year	5-Year
-15.48	-12.94	-7.35	19.05	9.72

3-Year Standard Deviation   11.1
Effective Duration

Valuation
Premium/Discount (1-Year Average)   0.19

Company Information
Provider   Global X Funds
Manager/Tenure   Chang Kim (4), James Ong (2), Nam
                    To (0)
Website   http://www.globalxfunds.com
Address   Global X Funds 600 Lexington Avenue,
                    20th Floor New York NY 10022 United
                    States
Phone Number   888-493-8631

Ratings History

Date	Overall Rating	Risk Rating	Reward Rating
Q4-18	C-	D+	C
Q2-18	C	D+	C+
Q4-17	C+	C	C+
Q4-16	C-	C-	C-
Q4-15	C	C	C

Asset & Performance History

Date	NAV	1-Year Total Return
2017	29.63	23.8
2016	24.06	3.8
2015	23.23	-10.81
2014	26.17	3.33
2013	25.59	46.98
2012	17.43	

Total Assets: $56,840,070
Asset Allocation

Asset	%
Cash	0%
Stocks	100%
US Stocks	91%
Bonds	0%
US Bonds	0%
Other	0%

Services Offered:

Investment Strategy: The investment seeks investment results that correspond generally to the price and yield performance, before fees and expenses, of the Solactive Guru Index ("underlying index"). The fund invests at least 80% of its total assets in the securities of the underlying index and in American Depositary Receipts ("ADRs") and Global Depositary Receipts ("GDRs") based on the securities in the underlying index. The underlying index is comprised of the top U.S. listed equity positions reported on Form 13F by a select group of entities characterized as hedge funds. **Top Holdings:** Realogy Holdings Corp Delta Air Lines Inc Groupon Inc Restaurant Brands International Inc General Motors Co

iShares Core 5-10 Year USD Bond ETF   D   SELL

Ticker	Traded On	NAV
IMTB	NYSE Arca	47.82

Total Assets ($)	Dividend Yield (TTM)	Turnover Ratio	Expense Ratio
$56,817,708	2.8	504	0.06

Ratings
Reward   D
Risk   D+
Recent Upgrade/Downgrade   Down

Fund Information
Fund Type   Exchange Traded Funds
Category   US Fixed Income
Sub-Category   Intermediate-Term Bond
Prospectus Objective   Income
Inception Date   Nov-16
Open to New Investments   Y

Prices
Price (as of 12/31/2018)   48.00
52-Week High   49.71
52-Week Low   46.97

Total Returns (%)

3-Month	6-Month	1-Year	3-Year	5-Year
1.45	1.84	0.06		

3-Year Standard Deviation
Effective Duration   5.75

Valuation
Premium/Discount (1-Year Average)   0.22

Company Information
Provider   iShares
Manager/Tenure   James Mauro (2), Scott Radell (2)
Website   http://www.ishares.com
Address   iShares 400 Howard Street San
                    Francisco CA 94105 United States
Phone Number   800-474-2737

Ratings History

Date	Overall Rating	Risk Rating	Reward Rating
Q4-18	D	D+	D
Q2-18	D+	D+	D
Q4-17	D	A-	D+
Q4-16	U		
Q4-15			

Asset & Performance History

Date	NAV	1-Year Total Return
2017	49.27	3.88
2016	48.76	
2015		
2014		
2013		
2012		

Total Assets: $56,817,708
Asset Allocation

Asset	%
Cash	8%
Stocks	0%
US Stocks	0%
Bonds	92%
US Bonds	83%
Other	0%

Services Offered:

Investment Strategy: The investment seeks to track the investment results of the Bloomberg Barclays U.S. Universal 5-10 Year Index. The fund generally will invest at least 90% of its assets in the component securities of the underlying index and may invest up to 10% of its assets in certain futures, options and swap contracts, cash and cash equivalents, including shares of money market funds advised by BFA or its affiliates. The index measures the performance of U.S. dollar-denominated taxable bonds that are rated either investment-grade or high yield with remaining effective maturities between five and ten years. It is non-diversified. **Top Holdings:** United States Treasury Notes 2.25% Gnma2 30yr 2016 Production Fnma 30yr 2016 Production Fnma 30yr 4% Ltv > 90 2016 United States Treasury Notes 2.63%

Teucrium Wheat   D   SELL

Ticker	Traded On	NAV	Total Assets ($)	Dividend Yield (TTM)	Turnover Ratio	Expense Ratio
WEAT	NYSE Arca	5.95	$56,560,775	0		1

Ratings
Reward	D
Risk	D
Recent Upgrade/Downgrade	

Fund Information
Fund Type	Exchange Traded Funds
Category	Commodities Specified
Sub-Category	Commodities Agriculture
Prospectus Objective	Unaligned
Inception Date	Sep-11
Open to New Investments	Y

Prices
Price (as of 12/31/2018)	5.93
52-Week High	7.18
52-Week Low	5.88

Total Returns (%)
3-Month	6-Month	1-Year	3-Year	5-Year
-5.21	-3.02	-0.73	-35.01	-59.92

3-Year Standard Deviation	19.95
Effective Duration	

Valuation
Premium/Discount (1-Year Average)	0.07

Company Information
Provider	Teucrium
Manager/Tenure	Management Team (7)
Website	
Address	232 Hidden Lake Road Building A Brattleboro VT 05301 United States
Phone Number	802-257-1617

PERFORMANCE

Ratings History
Date	Overall Rating	Risk Rating	Reward Rating
Q4-18	D	D	D
Q2-18	D	D-	D
Q4-17	D-	E+	D-
Q4-16	D-	E+	D-
Q4-15	D-	D-	D-

Asset & Performance History
Date	NAV	1-Year Total Return
2017	5.99	-13.06
2016	6.89	-25.13
2015	9.15	-28.07
2014	12.72	-14.26
2013	14.84	-30.18
2012	21.25	-4.94

Total Assets: $56,560,775
Asset Allocation
Asset	%
Cash	-1%
Stocks	0%
US Stocks	0%
Bonds	0%
US Bonds	0%
Other	101%

Services Offered:

Investment Strategy: The investment seeks to have the daily changes in percentage terms of the shares' NAV reflect the daily changes in percentage terms of a weighted average of the closing settlement prices for three futures contracts for wheat that are traded on the Chicago Board of Trade.
The fund seeks to achieve its investment objective primarily by investing in Wheat Interests such that daily changes in the fund's NAV are expected to closely track the changes in the benchmark. **Top Holdings:** W H9 Cbot Wheat Futures Mar 2019   W Z9 Cbot Wheat Futures Dec 2019   W K9 Cbot Wheat Futures May 2019

Direxion Daily CSI China Internet Bull 2X Shares   D   SELL

Ticker	Traded On	NAV	Total Assets ($)	Dividend Yield (TTM)	Turnover Ratio	Expense Ratio
CWEB	NYSE Arca	18.78	$56,545,569	0.77	0	1.36

Ratings
Reward	D
Risk	D
Recent Upgrade/Downgrade	Down

Fund Information
Fund Type	Exchange Traded Funds
Category	Trading Tools
Sub-Category	Trading--Leveraged Equity
Prospectus Objective	Technology
Inception Date	Nov-16
Open to New Investments	Y

Prices
Price (as of 12/31/2018)	18.70
52-Week High	68.87
52-Week Low	18.29

Total Returns (%)
3-Month	6-Month	1-Year	3-Year	5-Year
-40.40	-60.96	-62.79		

3-Year Standard Deviation	
Effective Duration	

Valuation
Premium/Discount (1-Year Average)	-0.07

Company Information
Provider	Direxion Funds
Manager/Tenure	Paul Brigandi (2), Tony Ng (2)
Website	http://www.direxionfunds.com
Address	Direxion Funds 1301 Avenue Of The Americas (6th Avenue) New York NY 10019 United States
Phone Number	646-572-3390

PERFORMANCE

Ratings History
Date	Overall Rating	Risk Rating	Reward Rating
Q4-18	D	D	D
Q2-18	C-	C-	C-
Q4-17	D	B	D
Q4-16	U		
Q4-15			

Asset & Performance History
Date	NAV	1-Year Total Return
2017	50.99	167.96
2016	19.63	
2015		
2014		
2013		
2012		

Total Assets: $56,545,569
Asset Allocation
Asset	%
Cash	89%
Stocks	11%
US Stocks	-17%
Bonds	0%
US Bonds	0%
Other	0%

Services Offered:

Investment Strategy: The investment seeks daily investment results, of 200% of the daily performance of the CSI Overseas China Internet Index. The fund invests at least 80% of its net assets (plus borrowing for investment purposes) in securities of the index, ETFs that track the index and other financial instruments that provide daily leveraged exposure to the index or ETFs that track the index. The index is designed to measure the performance of the investable universe of publicly traded China-based companies whose primary business or businesses are in the Internet and Internet-related sectors, as defined by CSI. It is non-diversified. **Top Holdings:** Etbkrw Spot Ex Rt Index   KraneShares CSI China Internet ETF   Etbkrw Spot Ex Rt Index   Fidelity Institutional Go

---

Global X Conscious Companies ETF   C-   HOLD

Ticker	Traded On	NAV	Total Assets ($)	Dividend Yield (TTM)	Turnover Ratio	Expense Ratio
KRMA	NAS CM	18.38	$56,504,257	1.14	42	0.43

Ratings
Reward   C-
Risk   D+
Recent Upgrade/Downgrade   Up

Fund Information
Fund Type   Exchange Traded Funds
Category   US Equity Large Cap Blend
Sub-Category   Large Blend
Prospectus Objective   Growth & Inc
Inception Date   Jul-16
Open to New Investments   Y

Prices
Price (as of 12/31/2018)   18.33
52-Week High   21.46
52-Week Low   17.71

Total Returns (%)

3-Month	6-Month	1-Year	3-Year	5-Year
-12.13	-5.99	-3.17		

3-Year Standard Deviation
Effective Duration

Valuation
Premium/Discount (1-Year Average)   0.24

Company Information
Provider   Global X Funds
Manager/Tenure   Chang Kim (2), James Ong (2), Nam To (0)
Website   http://www.globalxfunds.com
Address   Global X Funds 600 Lexington Avenue, 20th Floor New York NY 10022 United States
Phone Number   888-493-8631

PERFORMANCE

Ratings History

Date	Overall Rating	Risk Rating	Reward Rating
Q4-18	C-	D+	C-
Q2-18	C-	D+	C-
Q4-17	D	B+	C
Q4-16	U		
Q4-15			

Asset & Performance History

Date	NAV	1-Year Total Return
2017	19.33	23.04
2016	15.9	
2015		
2014		
2013		
2012		

Total Assets: $56,504,257
Asset Allocation

Asset	%
Cash	0%
Stocks	100%
US Stocks	98%
Bonds	0%
US Bonds	0%
Other	0%

Services Offered:

Investment Strategy: The investment seeks to provide investment results that correspond generally to the price and yield performance, before fees and expenses, of the Concinnity Conscious Companies Index. The fund invests at least 80% of its total assets in the securities of the underlying index. The underlying index is designed to provide exposure to companies listed in the U.S. that operate their businesses in a sustainable and responsible manner, as measured by their ability to achieve positive outcomes that are consistent with a multi-stakeholder operating system ("MsOS"), as defined by the provider of the underlying index. **Top Holdings:** CVS Health Corp   Xilinx Inc   Workday Inc Class A   General Motors Co   Whirlpool Corp

iShares MSCI China A ETF   D   SELL

Ticker	Traded On	NAV	Total Assets ($)	Dividend Yield (TTM)	Turnover Ratio	Expense Ratio
CNYA	BATS	22.61	$56,477,596	1.31	154	0.65

Ratings
Reward   D
Risk   D
Recent Upgrade/Downgrade   Down

Fund Information
Fund Type   Exchange Traded Funds
Category   Greater China Equity
Sub-Category   China Region
Prospectus Objective   Pacific Stock
Inception Date   Jun-16
Open to New Investments   Y

Prices
Price (as of 12/31/2018)   22.68
52-Week High   35.66
52-Week Low   22.52

Total Returns (%)

3-Month	6-Month	1-Year	3-Year	5-Year
-11.20	-11.74	-26.26		

3-Year Standard Deviation
Effective Duration

Valuation
Premium/Discount (1-Year Average)   1.24

Company Information
Provider   iShares
Manager/Tenure   Diane Hsiung (2), Jennifer Hsui (2), Alan Mason (2), 3 others
Website   http://www.ishares.com
Address   iShares 400 Howard Street San Francisco CA 94105 United States
Phone Number   800-474-2737

PERFORMANCE

Ratings History

Date	Overall Rating	Risk Rating	Reward Rating
Q4-18	D	D	D
Q2-18	D+	D+	D+
Q4-17	D+	B	C
Q4-16	U		
Q4-15			

Asset & Performance History

Date	NAV	1-Year Total Return
2017	31.81	29.15
2016	24.89	
2015		
2014		
2013		
2012		

Total Assets: $56,477,596
Asset Allocation

Asset	%
Cash	0%
Stocks	100%
US Stocks	0%
Bonds	0%
US Bonds	0%
Other	0%

Services Offered:

Investment Strategy: The investment seeks to track the investment results of the MSCI China A Inclusion Index composed of domestic Chinese equities that trade on the Shanghai or Shenzhen Stock Exchange. The fund generally will invest at least 90% of its assets in the component securities of the index and in investments that have economic characteristics that are substantially identical to the component securities of the index. The index is designed to measure the equity market performance in the People's Republic of China, as represented by "A-shares" that are accessible through the Shanghai Connect or the Shenzhen-Hong Kong Stock Connect program. The fund is non-diversified. **Top Holdings:** Kweichow Moutai Co Ltd   Ping An Insurance (Group) Co. of China Ltd   China Merchants Bank Co Ltd   Industrial Bank Co Ltd   Shanghai Pudong Development Bank Co Ltd

Direxion Daily Aerospace & Defense Bull 3X Shares Direxion Daily Aerospace   C   HOLD

Ticker	Traded On	NAV	Total Assets ($)	Dividend Yield (TTM)	Turnover Ratio	Expense Ratio
DFEN	NYSE Arca	29.67	$56,365,413	2.13	7	0.97

Ratings
Reward   C
Risk   C
Recent Upgrade/Downgrade

Fund Information
Fund Type   Exchange Traded Funds
Category   Trading Tools
Sub-Category   Trading--Leveraged Equity
Prospectus Objective   Unaligned
Inception Date   May-17
Open to New Investments   Y

Prices
Price (as of 12/31/2018)   29.66
52-Week High   63.35
52-Week Low   24.66

Total Returns (%)

3-Month	6-Month	1-Year	3-Year	5-Year
-52.65	-33.45	-32.70		

3-Year Standard Deviation
Effective Duration

Valuation
Premium/Discount (1-Year Average)   0.05

Company Information
Provider   Direxion Funds
Manager/Tenure   Paul Brigandi (1), Tony Ng (1)
Website   http://www.direxionfunds.com
Address   Direxion Funds 1301 Avenue Of The
                        Americas (6th Avenue) New York NY
                        10019 United States
Phone Number   646-572-3390

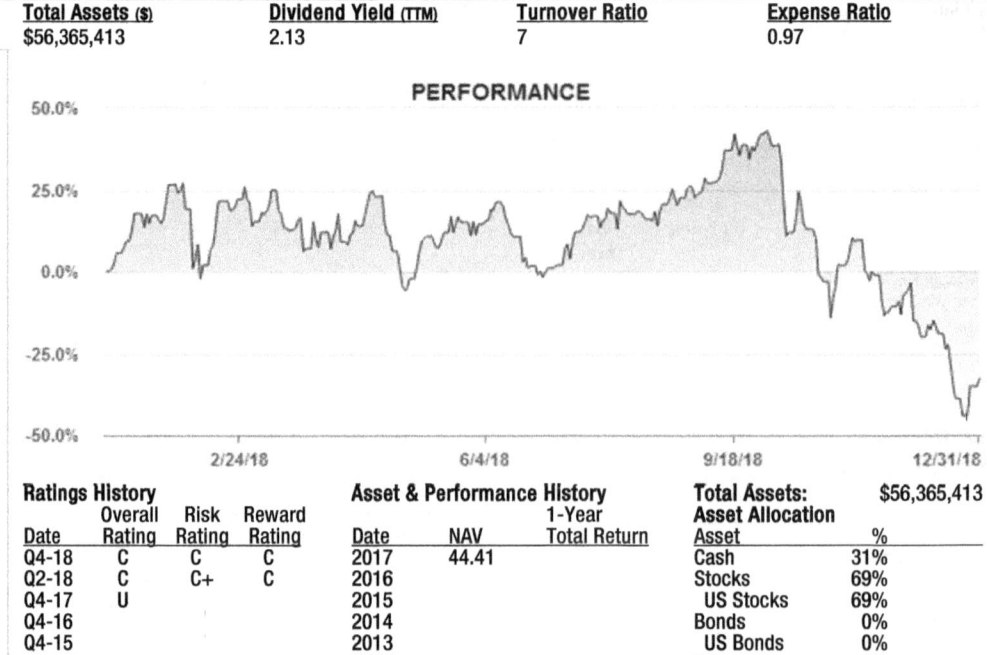

PERFORMANCE

Ratings History

Date	Overall Rating	Risk Rating	Reward Rating
Q4-18	C	C	C
Q2-18	C	C+	C
Q4-17	U		
Q4-16			
Q4-15			

Asset & Performance History

Date	NAV	1-Year Total Return
2017	44.41	
2016		
2015		
2014		
2013		
2012		

Total Assets: $56,365,413
Asset Allocation

Asset	%
Cash	31%
Stocks	69%
US Stocks	69%
Bonds	0%
US Bonds	0%
Other	0%

Services Offered:

Investment Strategy: The investment seeks daily investment results, before fees and expenses, of 300% of the daily performance of the Dow Jones U.S. Select Aerospace & Defense Index. The fund invests at least 80% of its net assets (plus borrowing for investment purposes) in securities of the index, ETFs that track the index and other financial instruments that provide daily leveraged exposure to the index or ETFs that track the index. The index attempts to measure the performance of the aerospace and defense industry of the U.S. equity market. The fund is non-diversified. **Top Holdings:** Boeing Co United Technologies Corp Lockheed Martin Corp Raytheon Co General Dynamics Corp

---

UBS ETRACS Monthly Pay 2xLeveraged US Small Cap High Dividend ETN   C-   HOLD

Ticker	Traded On	NAV	Total Assets ($)	Dividend Yield (TTM)	Turnover Ratio	Expense Ratio
SMHD	NYSE Arca	12.13	$56,207,901	21.47		0.85

Ratings
Reward   C-
Risk   C-
Recent Upgrade/Downgrade   Down

Fund Information
Fund Type   Exchange Traded Funds
Category   Trading Tools
Sub-Category   Trading--Leveraged Equity
Prospectus Objective   Growth
Inception Date   Feb-15
Open to New Investments   Y

Prices
Price (as of 12/31/2018)   13.13
52-Week High   20.72
52-Week Low   12.00

Total Returns (%)

3-Month	6-Month	1-Year	3-Year	5-Year
-28.50	-31.65	-25.15	43.43	

3-Year Standard Deviation   28.76
Effective Duration

Valuation
Premium/Discount (1-Year Average)   0.74

Company Information
Provider   UBS Group AG
Manager/Tenure   No Manager (3)
Website   http://www.ubs.com
Address   Bahnhofstrasse 45 Zurich 8098
                        Switzerland
Phone Number   412-037-1952

PERFORMANCE

Ratings History

Date	Overall Rating	Risk Rating	Reward Rating
Q4-18	C-	C-	C-
Q2-18	C	D+	C
Q4-17	C	D+	B-
Q4-16	C-	D+	C
Q4-15	U		

Asset & Performance History

Date	NAV	1-Year Total Return
2017	19.56	4.17
2016	22.79	88.26
2015	14.5	
2014		
2013		
2012		

Total Assets: $56,207,901
Asset Allocation

Asset	%
Cash	%
Stocks	%
US Stocks	%
Bonds	%
US Bonds	%
Other	%

Services Offered:

Investment Strategy: The investment seeks to provides a monthly compounded two times leveraged long exposure to the performance of the index, reduced by the accrued fees.
The fund is a series of Monthly Pay 2xLeveraged Exchange Traded Access Securities (ETRACS) linked to the performance of the price return version of the Solactive US Small Cap High Dividend Index. The index is designed to measure the performance of 100 relatively small capitalization, dividend yielding index constituent Securities selected from a universe of qualifying U.S. listed stocks. **Top Holdings:**

John Hancock Multifactor Utilities ETF   C+   HOLD

Ticker	Traded On	NAV	Total Assets ($)	Dividend Yield (TTM)	Turnover Ratio	Expense Ratio
JHMU	NYSE Arca	28.34	$56,089,921	2.21	12	0.5

Ratings
Reward   C+
Risk   C
Recent Upgrade/Downgrade

Fund Information
Fund Type   Exchange Traded Funds
Category   Utilities Sector Equity
Sub-Category   Utilities
Prospectus Objective   Utility
Inception Date   Mar-16
Open to New Investments   Y

Prices
Price (as of 12/31/2018)   28.36
52-Week High   30.63
52-Week Low   25.00

Total Returns (%)

3-Month	6-Month	1-Year	3-Year	5-Year
1.23	2.80	5.46		

3-Year Standard Deviation
Effective Duration

Valuation
Premium/Discount (1-Year Average)   0.14

Company Information
Provider   John Hancock
Manager/Tenure Joel P. Schneider (2), Lukas J. Smart (2), Joseph F. Hohn (0)
Website   http://jhinvestments.com
Address   601 Congress Street, Boston MA 02210 United States
Phone Number   800-225-5913

Ratings History

Date	Overall Rating	Risk Rating	Reward Rating
Q4-18	C+	C	C+
Q2-18	C+	C	B
Q4-17	D+	B-	C
Q4-16	U		
Q4-15			

Asset & Performance History

Date	NAV	1-Year Total Return
2017	27.53	11.25
2016	25.36	
2015		
2014		
2013		
2012		

Total Assets: $56,089,921

Asset Allocation

Asset	%
Cash	0%
Stocks	100%
US Stocks	100%
Bonds	0%
US Bonds	0%
Other	0%

Services Offered:

Investment Strategy: The investment seeks to provide investment results that closely correspond, before fees and expenses, to the performance of the John Hancock Dimensional Utilities Index (the index). The fund normally invests at least 80% of its net assets (plus any borrowings for investment purposes) in securities that compose the fund's benchmark index. The index is designed to comprise securities in the utilities sector within the U.S. Universe whose market capitalizations are larger than that of the 1001st largest U.S. company at the time of reconstitution. The fund is non-diversified. **Top Holdings:** Exelon Corp   Public Service Enterprise Group Inc   Southern Co   Duke Energy Corp   Xcel Energy Inc

---

Invesco S&P High Income Infrastructure ETF   C-   HOLD

Ticker	Traded On	NAV	Total Assets ($)	Dividend Yield (TTM)	Turnover Ratio	Expense Ratio
GHII	NYSE Arca		$55,772,246	5.34	45	0.45

Ratings
Reward   C-
Risk   D+
Recent Upgrade/Downgrade   Down

Fund Information
Fund Type   Exchange Traded Funds
Category   Infrastructure Sector Equity
Sub-Category   Infrastructure
Prospectus Objective   Equity-Income
Inception Date   Feb-15
Open to New Investments   Y

Prices
Price (as of 12/31/2018)   23.48
52-Week High   28.46
52-Week Low   22.90

Total Returns (%)

3-Month	6-Month	1-Year	3-Year	5-Year
-10.24	-10.13	-11.20	27.30	

3-Year Standard Deviation   10.85
Effective Duration

Valuation
Premium/Discount (1-Year Average)   0.11

Company Information
Provider   Invesco
Manager/Tenure Peter Hubbard (0), Michael Jeanette (0), Jonathan Nixon (0), 1 other
Website   http://www.invesco.com/us
Address   Invesco 11 Greenway Plaza, Ste. 2500 Houston TX 77046 United States
Phone Number   800-659-1005

PERFORMANCE

Ratings History

Date	Overall Rating	Risk Rating	Reward Rating
Q4-18	C-	D+	C-
Q2-18	C-	C-	C
Q4-17	C	C+	C
Q4-16	D+	D+	C-
Q4-15	U		

Asset & Performance History

Date	NAV	1-Year Total Return
2017	27.43	13.03
2016	25.94	26.65
2015	21.43	
2014		
2013		
2012		

Total Assets: $55,772,246

Asset Allocation

Asset	%
Cash	0%
Stocks	100%
US Stocks	26%
Bonds	0%
US Bonds	0%
Other	0%

Services Offered:

Investment Strategy: The investment seeks investment results that correspond generally to the performance, before the fund's fees and expenses, of an equity index called the S&P High Income Infrastructure Index. The fund will invest at least 90% of its total assets in common stocks that comprise the index and depositary receipts representing common stocks included in the index. The index is designed to measure and monitor the performance of 50 high-yielding global equity securities of companies that engage in various infrastructure-related sub-industries. The fund is non-diversified. **Top Holdings:** Hutchison Port Holdings Trust   Macquarie Infrastructure Corp   Ship Finance International Ltd   Targa Resources Corp   Pattern Energy Group Inc Class A

VanEck Vectors Oil Refiners ETF

C   HOLD

Ticker	Traded On	NAV	Total Assets ($)	Dividend Yield (TTM)	Turnover Ratio	Expense Ratio
CRAK	NYSE Arca	26.95	$55,676,903	1.23	24	0.59

Ratings
Reward C
Risk .... C-
Recent Upgrade/Downgrade

Fund Information
Fund Type .... Exchange Traded Funds
Category .... Energy Sector Equity
Sub-Category .... Equity Energy
Prospectus Objective .... Unaligned
Inception Date Aug-15
Open to New Investments .... Y

Prices
Price (as of 12/31/2018) 26.84
52-Week High 36.07
52-Week Low 25.55

Total Returns (%)

3-Month	6-Month	1-Year	3-Year	5-Year
-24.18	-13.13	-10.93	43.97	

3-Year Standard Deviation 15.85
Effective Duration

Valuation
Premium/Discount (1-Year Average) ... 0.23

Company Information
Provider .... VanEck
Manager/Tenure ... Hao-Hung (Peter) Liao (3), Guo Hua (Jason) Jin (0)
Website .... http://www.vaneck.com
Address .... Van Eck Associates Corporation 666 Third Avenue New York NY 10017 United States
Phone Number 800-826-1115

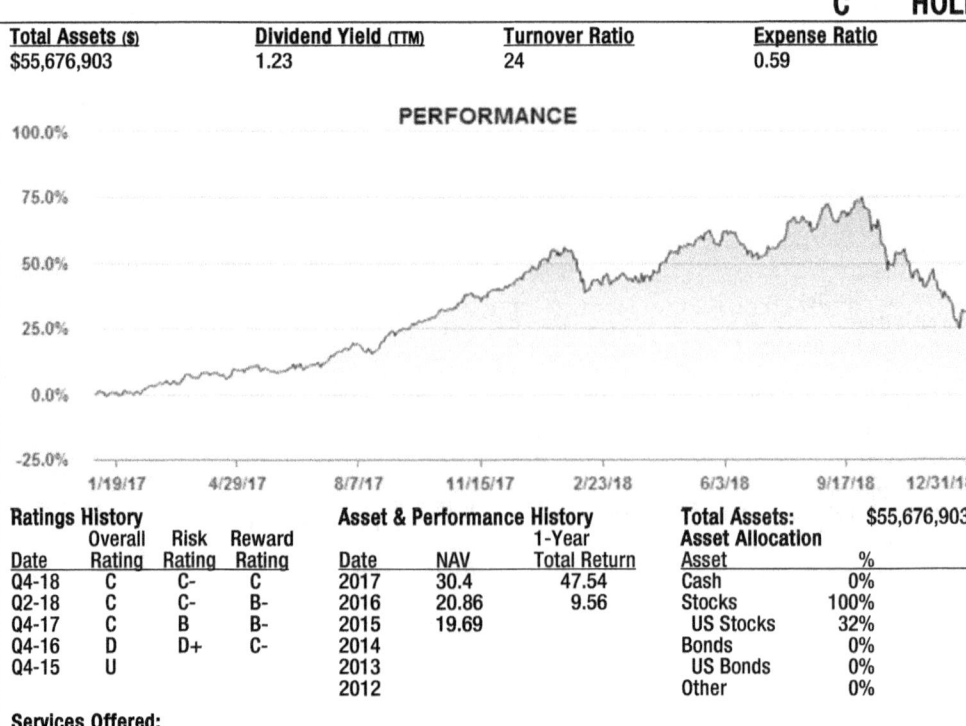

PERFORMANCE

Ratings History

Date	Overall Rating	Risk Rating	Reward Rating
Q4-18	C	C-	C
Q2-18	C	C-	B-
Q4-17	C	B	B-
Q4-16	D	D+	C-
Q4-15	U		

Asset & Performance History

Date	NAV	1-Year Total Return
2017	30.4	47.54
2016	20.86	9.56
2015	19.69	
2014		
2013		
2012		

Total Assets: $55,676,903

Asset Allocation

Asset	%
Cash	0%
Stocks	100%
US Stocks	32%
Bonds	0%
US Bonds	0%
Other	0%

Services Offered:

Investment Strategy: The investment seeks to replicate as closely as possible, before fees and expenses, the price and yield performance of the MVIS® Global Oil Refiners Index. The fund normally invests at least 80% of its total assets in securities that comprise the fund's benchmark index. The index includes equity securities and depositary receipts of companies that generate at least 50% of their revenues from crude oil refining. Products of these companies may include gasoline, diesel, jet fuel, fuel oil, naphtha, and other petrochemicals. The fund is non-diversified. **Top Holdings:** Marathon Petroleum Corp Reliance Industries Ltd ADR Phillips 66 JXTG Holdings Inc Valero Energy Corp

United States 12 Month Oil Fund, LP

C-   HOLD

Ticker	Traded On	NAV	Total Assets ($)	Dividend Yield (TTM)	Turnover Ratio	Expense Ratio
USL	NYSE Arca	17.82	$55,551,770	0	50	0.86

Ratings
Reward .... C-
Risk .... C-
Recent Upgrade/Downgrade .... Down

Fund Information
Fund Type .... Exchange Traded Funds
Category .... Commodities Specified
Sub-Category .... Commodities Energy
Prospectus Objective .... Natl Res
Inception Date Dec-07
Open to New Investments .... Y

Prices
Price (as of 12/31/2018) 17.96
52-Week High 28.28
52-Week Low 17.20

Total Returns (%)

3-Month	6-Month	1-Year	3-Year	5-Year
-36.21	-28.33	-15.31	4.87	-58.38

3-Year Standard Deviation 24.18
Effective Duration

Valuation
Premium/Discount (1-Year Average) ... -0.17

Company Information
Provider .... USCF Investments
Manager/Tenure ... Management Team (10)
Website .... http://www.uscfinvestments.com
Address .... USCF 1290 Broadway, Suite 1100 Denver CO 80203 United States
Phone Number

PERFORMANCE

Ratings History

Date	Overall Rating	Risk Rating	Reward Rating
Q4-18	C-	C-	C-
Q2-18	C	C-	C
Q4-17	D+	D	D+
Q4-16	D	D	D
Q4-15	D-	D-	D-

Asset & Performance History

Date	NAV	1-Year Total Return
2017	21.05	3.24
2016	20.39	19.94
2015	17	-36.09
2014	26.59	-37.9
2013	42.83	7.59
2012	39.81	-8.39

Total Assets: $55,551,770

Asset Allocation

Asset	%
Cash	36%
Stocks	0%
US Stocks	0%
Bonds	18%
US Bonds	18%
Other	46%

Services Offered:

Investment Strategy: The investment seeks to reflect the daily changes in percentage terms of the spot price of light, sweet crude oil delivered to Cushing, Oklahoma, as measured by the daily changes in the average of the prices of specified short-term futures contracts on light, sweet crude oil called the "Benchmark Oil Futures Contracts."
 The fund invests investing primarily in futures contracts for light, sweet crude oil, other types of crude oil, diesel-heating oil, gasoline, natural gas, and other petroleum-based fuels. The Benchmark Oil Futures Contracts are the futures contracts on light, sweet crude oil as traded on the New York Mercantile Exchange. **Top Holdings:** Future Contract On Wti Crude Future Nov19 Future Contract On Wti Crude Future Oct19 Future Contract On Wti Crude Future Sep19 Future Contract On Wti Crude Future Aug19 Future Contract On Wti Crude Future Jul19

Invesco BulletShares 2024 High Yield Corporate Bond ETF   D+   SELL

Ticker	Traded On	NAV	Total Assets ($)	Dividend Yield (TTM)	Turnover Ratio	Expense Ratio
BSJO	NYSE Arca	23.40	$55,486,547	5.37	8	0.42

Ratings
Reward	D+
Risk	D+
Recent Upgrade/Downgrade	Down

Fund Information
Fund Type	Exchange Traded Funds
Category	US Fixed Income
Sub-Category	High Yield Bond
Prospectus Objective	Corp Bond-High Yld
Inception Date	Sep-16
Open to New Investments	Y

Prices
Price (as of 12/31/2018)	23.41
52-Week High	25.83
52-Week Low	23.03

Total Returns (%)
3-Month	6-Month	1-Year	3-Year	5-Year
-4.51	-1.55	-3.19		

3-Year Standard Deviation	
Effective Duration	3.83

Valuation
Premium/Discount (1-Year Average)	0.19

Company Information
Provider	Invesco
Manager/Tenure	Jeremy Neisewander (2), Peter Hubbard (0), Jeffrey W. Kernagis (0), 1 other
Website	http://www.invesco.com/us
Address	Invesco 11 Greenway Plaza, Ste. 2500 Houston TX 77046 United States
Phone Number	800-659-1005

PERFORMANCE

Ratings History
Date	Overall Rating	Risk Rating	Reward Rating
Q4-18	D+	D+	D+
Q2-18	D+	D+	D+
Q4-17	D	B	D+
Q4-16	U		
Q4-15			

Asset & Performance History
Date	NAV	1-Year Total Return
2017	25.47	6.47
2016	25.04	
2015		
2014		
2013		
2012		

Total Assets: $55,486,547
Asset Allocation
Asset	%
Cash	0%
Stocks	0%
US Stocks	0%
Bonds	100%
US Bonds	90%
Other	0%

Services Offered:

Investment Strategy: The investment seeks investment results that correspond generally to the performance, before the fund's fees and expenses, of a high yield corporate bond index called the Nasdaq BulletShares® USD High Yield Corporate Bond 2024 Index. The fund will invest at least 80% of its total assets in component securities that comprise the underlying index. The underlying index is designed to represent the performance of a held-to-maturity portfolio of U.S. dollar-denominated high yield corporate bonds with effective maturities in the year 2024. The fund is non-diversified. **Top Holdings:** Sprint Corporation 7.12% First Data Corporation 5.75% Tenet Healthcare Corporation 4.62% MPH Acquisition Holdings LLC 7.12% CCO Holdings, LLC/ CCO Holdings Capital Corp. 5.88%

Cohen & Steers Global Realty Majors ETF   C-   HOLD

Ticker	Traded On	NAV	Total Assets ($)	Dividend Yield (TTM)	Turnover Ratio	Expense Ratio
GRI	NYSE Arca	41.48	$55,222,041	4.15	10	0.55

Ratings
Reward	C
Risk	D+
Recent Upgrade/Downgrade	Down

Fund Information
Fund Type	Exchange Traded Funds
Category	Real Estate Sector Equity
Sub-Category	Global Real Estate
Prospectus Objective	Real Estate
Inception Date	May-08
Open to New Investments	Y

Prices
Price (as of 12/31/2018)	41.11
52-Week High	45.22
52-Week Low	40.34

Total Returns (%)
3-Month	6-Month	1-Year	3-Year	5-Year
-3.71	-3.83	-4.84	7.56	24.87

3-Year Standard Deviation	10.65
Effective Duration	

Valuation
Premium/Discount (1-Year Average)	-0.10

Company Information
Provider	ALPS
Manager/Tenure	Ryan Mischker (3), Andrew Hicks (2)
Website	http://www.alpsfunds.com
Address	ALPS 1290 Broadway, Suite 1100 Denver CO 80203 United States
Phone Number	866-759-5679

PERFORMANCE

Ratings History
Date	Overall Rating	Risk Rating	Reward Rating
Q4-18	C-	D+	C
Q2-18	C-	D+	C
Q4-17	B-	B	C+
Q4-16	C	D+	C
Q4-15	C	D+	C

Asset & Performance History
Date	NAV	1-Year Total Return
2017	44.91	11.08
2016	41.94	0.01
2015	42.68	1.11
2014	43.65	14.81
2013	39.17	1.35
2012	39.04	28.94

Total Assets: $55,222,041
Asset Allocation
Asset	%
Cash	0%
Stocks	99%
US Stocks	55%
Bonds	0%
US Bonds	0%
Other	1%

Services Offered:

Investment Strategy: The investment seeks investment results that correspond generally to the performance, before the fund's fees and expenses, of an index called the Cohen & Steers Global Realty Majors Index. The fund will normally invest at least 90% of its total assets in common stocks and other equity securities (which may include ADRs, ADSs and GDRs) that comprise the underlying index. The underlying index consists of the largest and most liquid securities within the global real estate universe that the index provider believes are likely to lead the global securitization of real estate. The fund is non-diversified. **Top Holdings:** American Tower Corp Prologis Inc Simon Property Group Inc Public Storage Equinix Inc

PIMCO 1-3 Year U.S. Treasury Index Exchange-Traded Fund   C-   HOLD

Ticker	Traded On	NAV	Total Assets ($)	Dividend Yield (TTM)	Turnover Ratio	Expense Ratio
TUZ	NYSE Arca	50.15	$55,046,029	1.58	54	0.16

Ratings

Reward	C-
Risk	D+
Recent Upgrade/Downgrade	Up

Fund Information

Fund Type	Exchange Traded Funds
Category	US Fixed Income
Sub-Category	Short Government
Prospectus Objective	Govt Bond - Treasury
Inception Date	Jun-09
Open to New Investments	Y

Prices

Price (as of 12/31/2018)	50.15
52-Week High	50.29
52-Week Low	49.70

Total Returns (%)

3-Month	6-Month	1-Year	3-Year	5-Year
1.25	1.44	1.42	2.40	3.33

3-Year Standard Deviation	0.76
Effective Duration	1.86

Valuation

Premium/Discount (1-Year Average)	-0.04

Company Information

Provider	PIMCO
Manager/Tenure	Matthew P. Dorsten (2), Mitchell Handa (0), Graham A. Rennison (0)
Website	http://www.pimco.com
Address	PIMCO 840 Newport Center Drive, Suite 100 Newport Beach CA 92660 United States
Phone Number	866-746-2602

PERFORMANCE

Ratings History

Date	Overall Rating	Risk Rating	Reward Rating
Q4-18	C-	D+	C-
Q2-18	D+	D+	D+
Q4-17	C	C	C-
Q4-16	C	C-	C
Q4-15	C	C-	C

Asset & Performance History

Date	NAV	1-Year Total Return
2017	50.3	0.26
2016	50.67	0.71
2015	50.74	0.41
2014	50.84	0.49
2013	50.85	0.26
2012	50.89	0.32

Total Assets: $55,046,029

Asset Allocation

Asset	%
Cash	1%
Stocks	0%
US Stocks	0%
Bonds	99%
US Bonds	99%
Other	0%

Services Offered:

Investment Strategy: The investment seeks total return that closely corresponds, before fees and expenses, to the total return of the ICE BofAML 1-3 Year US Treasury Index. The fund invests at least 80% of its total assets (exclusive of collateral held from securities lending) in the component securities of the ICE BofAML 1-3 Year US Treasury Index (the "underlying index"). The underlying index is an unmanaged index comprised of U.S. dollar denominated sovereign debt securities publicly issued by the U.S. Treasury having a maturity of at least 1 year and less than 3 years. **Top Holdings:** United States Treasury Notes 3.62% United States Treasury Notes 3.12% United States Treasury Notes 3.5% United States Treasury Notes 2.62% United States Treasury Notes 2.38%

---

iShares MSCI Qatar ETF   C   HOLD

Ticker	Traded On	NAV	Total Assets ($)	Dividend Yield (TTM)	Turnover Ratio	Expense Ratio
QAT	NAS CM	18.59	$54,816,473	3.9	58	0.62

Ratings

Reward	C
Risk	C-
Recent Upgrade/Downgrade	Up

Fund Information

Fund Type	Exchange Traded Funds
Category	Equity Misc
Sub-Category	Miscellaneous Region
Prospectus Objective	Foreign Stock
Inception Date	Apr-14
Open to New Investments	Y

Prices

Price (as of 12/31/2018)	18.49
52-Week High	19.56
52-Week Low	15.43

Total Returns (%)

3-Month	6-Month	1-Year	3-Year	5-Year
5.87	13.45	22.57	9.50	

3-Year Standard Deviation	19.91
Effective Duration	

Valuation

Premium/Discount (1-Year Average)	0.84

Company Information

Provider	iShares
Manager/Tenure	Diane Hsiung (4), Jennifer Hsui (4), Greg Savage (4), 1 other
Website	http://www.ishares.com
Address	iShares 400 Howard Street San Francisco CA 94105 United States
Phone Number	800-474-2737

PERFORMANCE

Ratings History

Date	Overall Rating	Risk Rating	Reward Rating
Q4-18	C	C-	C
Q2-18	D	D+	D
Q4-17	D-	D	D-
Q4-16	D	D	D
Q4-15	D	D	D

Asset & Performance History

Date	NAV	1-Year Total Return
2017	15.94	-13.82
2016	19.25	3.66
2015	19.25	-15.37
2014	23.62	
2013		
2012		

Total Assets: $54,816,473

Asset Allocation

Asset	%
Cash	-1%
Stocks	101%
US Stocks	0%
Bonds	0%
US Bonds	0%
Other	0%

Services Offered:

Investment Strategy: The investment seeks to track the investment results of the MSCI All Qatar Capped Index. The fund will invest at least 90% of its assets in the component securities of the index and in investments that have economic characteristics that are substantially identical to the component securities of the index. The index, which is designed to measure the equity market in Qatar, is a free float-adjusted market capitalization-weighted index with a capping methodology applied to issuer weights. The fund is non-diversified. **Top Holdings:** Qatar National Bank SAQ Industries Qatar QSC Qatar Islamic Bank QPSC Ezdan Holding Group QSC Masraf Al Rayan QSC

PIMCO Broad U.S. TIPS Index Exchange-Traded Fund   D+   SELL

Ticker	Traded On	NAV	Total Assets ($)	Dividend Yield (TTM)	Turnover Ratio	Expense Ratio
TIPZ	NYSE Arca	55.96	$54,806,864	2.43	8	0.21

Ratings

Reward	D
Risk	D+
Recent Upgrade/Downgrade	Down

Fund Information

Fund Type	Exchange Traded Funds
Category	US Fixed Income
Sub-Category	Inflation-Protected Bond
Prospectus Objective	Govt Bond - Treasury
Inception Date	Sep-09
Open to New Investments	Y

Prices

Price (as of 12/31/2018)	56.03
52-Week High	58.23
52-Week Low	55.39

Total Returns (%)

3-Month	6-Month	1-Year	3-Year	5-Year
-0.24	-1.55	-1.72	6.39	8.69

3-Year Standard Deviation	3.46
Effective Duration	8.02

Valuation

Premium/Discount (1-Year Average)	0.04

Company Information

Provider	PIMCO
Manager/Tenure	Matthew P. Dorsten (2), Mitchell Handa (0), Graham A. Rennison (0)
Website	http://www.pimco.com
Address	PIMCO 840 Newport Center Drive, Suite 100 Newport Beach CA 92660 United States
Phone Number	866-746-2602

PERFORMANCE

Ratings History

Date	Overall Rating	Risk Rating	Reward Rating
Q4-18	D+	D+	D
Q2-18	C-	D+	C
Q4-17	C	B-	C
Q4-16	C-	C-	C
Q4-15	D+	C-	D+

Asset & Performance History

Date	NAV	1-Year Total Return
2017	58.31	3.22
2016	57.46	4.61
2015	55.36	-2.12
2014	56.87	4.37
2013	55.07	-9.41
2012	61.23	6.9

Total Assets: $54,806,864
Asset Allocation

Asset	%
Cash	1%
Stocks	0%
US Stocks	0%
Bonds	99%
US Bonds	99%
Other	0%

Services Offered:

Investment Strategy: The investment seeks to provide total return that closely corresponds, before fees and expenses, to the total return of the ICE BofAML US Inflation-Linked Treasury Index. The fund invests at least 80% of its total assets (exclusive of collateral held from securities lending) in the component securities of the ICE BofAML US Inflation-Linked Treasury Index (the "underlying index"). The underlying index is an unmanaged index comprised of Treasury Inflation-Protected Securities ("TIPS"). **Top Holdings:** United States Treasury Notes 1.12% United States Treasury Notes 0.62% United States Treasury Bonds 1.75% United States Treasury Bonds 2.38% United States Treasury Notes 0.12%

Fidelity® Corporate Bond ETF   D+   SELL

Ticker	Traded On	NAV	Total Assets ($)	Dividend Yield (TTM)	Turnover Ratio	Expense Ratio
FCOR	NYSE Arca	47.57	$54,288,019	3.62	81	0.36

Ratings

Reward	D+
Risk	D+
Recent Upgrade/Downgrade	Down

Fund Information

Fund Type	Exchange Traded Funds
Category	US Fixed Income
Sub-Category	Corporate Bond
Prospectus Objective	Corp Bond - Gen
Inception Date	Oct-14
Open to New Investments	Y

Prices

Price (as of 12/31/2018)	47.65
52-Week High	50.94
52-Week Low	46.30

Total Returns (%)

3-Month	6-Month	1-Year	3-Year	5-Year
-0.75	0.41	-2.92	10.64	

3-Year Standard Deviation	4.12
Effective Duration	6.72

Valuation

Premium/Discount (1-Year Average)	0.00

Company Information

Provider	Fidelity Investments
Manager/Tenure	Michael Plage (4), David Prothro (4), Matthew Bartlett (2)
Website	http://www.institutional.fidelity.com
Address	Fidelity Investments 82 Devonshire Street Boston MA 2109 United States
Phone Number	617-563-7000

PERFORMANCE

Ratings History

Date	Overall Rating	Risk Rating	Reward Rating
Q4-18	D+	D+	D+
Q2-18	C-	D+	C-
Q4-17	C+	B	C
Q4-16	D+	D+	D+
Q4-15	U		

Asset & Performance History

Date	NAV	1-Year Total Return
2017	50.79	5.99
2016	49.3	7.52
2015	47.26	-2.24
2014	50.16	
2013		
2012		

Total Assets: $54,288,019
Asset Allocation

Asset	%
Cash	3%
Stocks	0%
US Stocks	0%
Bonds	96%
US Bonds	78%
Other	0%

Services Offered:

Investment Strategy: The investment seeks a high level of current income. Normally, the fund invests at least 80% of its assets in investment-grade corporate bonds and other corporate debt securities and repurchase agreements for those securities. It is managed to have similar overall interest rate risk to the Bloomberg Barclays U.S. Credit Bond Index. The fund invests in lower-quality debt securities. **Top Holdings:** Bank of America Corporation 2.82% American Airlines, Inc. 3.7% Exelon Corporation 3.5% Vodafone Group plc 4.38% Goldman Sachs Group, Inc. 2.9%

BlueStar Israel Technology ETF
C   **HOLD**

Ticker	Traded On	NAV		Total Assets ($)	Dividend Yield (TTM)	Turnover Ratio	Expense Ratio
ITEQ	NYSE Arca	31.46		$54,079,436	0.51	11	0.75

Ratings

Reward	C+
Risk	C-
Recent Upgrade/Downgrade	

Fund Information

Fund Type	Exchange Traded Funds
Category	Technology Sector Equity
Sub-Category	Technology
Prospectus Objective	Technology
Inception Date	Nov-15
Open to New Investments	Y

Prices

Price (as of 12/31/2018)	31.43
52-Week High	36.72
52-Week Low	29.60

Total Returns (%)

3-Month	6-Month	1-Year	3-Year	5-Year
-11.78	-8.32	-0.17	32.29	

3-Year Standard Deviation	13.59
Effective Duration	

Valuation

Premium/Discount (1-Year Average)	0.25

Company Information

Provider	BlueStar Global Investors
Manager/Tenure	Samuel R. Masucci (0), James B. Francis (0), Devin Ryder (0), 1 other
Website	http://www.BlueStarIndexes.com.
Address	UnitedStates United States
Phone Number	

PERFORMANCE

Ratings History

Date	Overall Rating	Risk Rating	Reward Rating
Q4-18	C	C-	C+
Q2-18	C	D+	C+
Q4-17	C	B	C
Q4-16	D	C-	C
Q4-15			

Asset & Performance History

Date	NAV	1-Year Total Return
2017	31.61	27.74
2016	24.88	3.66
2015	24.07	
2014		
2013		
2012		

Total Assets: $54,079,436

Asset Allocation

Asset	%
Cash	1%
Stocks	99%
US Stocks	51%
Bonds	0%
US Bonds	0%
Other	0%

Services Offered:

Investment Strategy: The investment seeks to provide investment results that correspond generally to the total return performance of the TASE-BlueStar Israel Global Technology Index™ ("TA-BIGITech™"). The fund will invest at least 80% of its total assets in the component securities of the index and in depositary receipts representing such securities. As a result, normally the fund will invest at least 80% of its total assets in Israeli technology companies. TA-BIGITech™ was created in 2013 by BlueStar Global Investors LLC d/b/a BlueStar Indexes® and the ISE and tracks the performance of exchange-listed Israeli technology operating companies. It is non-diversified. **Top Holdings:** Check Point Software Technologies Ltd   NICE Ltd   Amdocs Ltd   Mellanox Technologies Ltd   Wix.com Ltd

---

First Trust Mid Cap Value AlphaDEX® Fund
C-   **HOLD**

Ticker	Traded On	NAV		Total Assets ($)	Dividend Yield (TTM)	Turnover Ratio	Expense Ratio
FNK	NAS CM	30.47		$53,872,869	1.55		0.7

Ratings

Reward	C-
Risk	D+
Recent Upgrade/Downgrade	Down

Fund Information

Fund Type	Exchange Traded Funds
Category	US Equity Small Cap
Sub-Category	Small Value
Prospectus Objective	Growth
Inception Date	Apr-11
Open to New Investments	Y

Prices

Price (as of 12/31/2018)	30.45
52-Week High	37.84
52-Week Low	29.15

Total Returns (%)

3-Month	6-Month	1-Year	3-Year	5-Year
-15.96	-14.38	-14.47	20.38	10.39

3-Year Standard Deviation	13.62
Effective Duration	

Valuation

Premium/Discount (1-Year Average)	0.04

Company Information

Provider	First Trust
Manager/Tenure	Jon C. Erickson (7), Daniel J. Lindquist (7), David G. McGarel (7), 3 others
Website	http://www.ftportfolios.com/
Address	First Trust 120 E. Liberty Drive, Suite 400 Wheaton IL 60187 United States
Phone Number	800-621-1675

PERFORMANCE

Ratings History

Date	Overall Rating	Risk Rating	Reward Rating
Q4-18	C-	D+	C-
Q2-18	C-	D+	C
Q4-17	B-	B-	B-
Q4-16	C	C-	C
Q4-15	C	D+	C

Asset & Performance History

Date	NAV	1-Year Total Return
2017	36.19	11.46
2016	32.95	26.28
2015	26.49	-13.12
2014	30.9	5.56
2013	29.59	37.86
2012	21.65	17.4

Total Assets: $53,872,869

Asset Allocation

Asset	%
Cash	0%
Stocks	100%
US Stocks	99%
Bonds	0%
US Bonds	0%
Other	0%

Services Offered:

Investment Strategy: The investment seeks results that correspond generally to the price and yield (before the fund's fees and expenses) of an equity index called the Nasdaq AlphaDEX® Mid Cap Value Index. The fund will normally invest at least 90% of its net assets (including investment borrowings) in common stocks that comprise the index. The index is designed to select value stocks from the NASDAQ US 600 Mid Cap Index (the "base index") that may generate positive alpha, or risk-adjusted returns, relative to traditional indices through the use of the AlphaDEX® selection methodology. **Top Holdings:** Spirit Airlines Inc   Darling Ingredients Inc   Pilgrims Pride Corp   PulteGroup Inc   Chimera Investment Corp

iShares North American Tech-Multimedia Networking ETF   C   HOLD

Ticker	Traded On	NAV	Total Assets ($)	Dividend Yield (TTM)	Turnover Ratio	Expense Ratio
IGN	NYSE Arca	47.40	$53,755,926	0.67	23	0.47

Ratings
Reward   B-
Risk   D+
Recent Upgrade/Downgrade

Fund Information
Fund Type	Exchange Traded Funds
Category	Technology Sector Equity
Sub-Category	Technology
Prospectus Objective	Technology
Inception Date	Jul-01
Open to New Investments	Y

Prices
Price (as of 12/31/2018)	47.25
52-Week High	56.34
52-Week Low	44.15

Total Returns (%)
3-Month	6-Month	1-Year	3-Year	5-Year
-12.49	-10.09	-0.93	31.28	51.59

3-Year Standard Deviation   14.17
Effective Duration

Valuation
Premium/Discount (1-Year Average)   0.12

Company Information
Provider	iShares
Manager/Tenure	Diane Hsiung (10), Greg Savage (10), Jennifer Hsui (6), 3 others
Website	http://www.ishares.com
Address	iShares 400 Howard Street San Francisco CA 94105 United States
Phone Number	800-474-2737

PERFORMANCE

Ratings History
Date	Overall Rating	Risk Rating	Reward Rating
Q4-18	C	D+	B-
Q2-18	C+	C-	B
Q4-17	B	B	B
Q4-16	B-	C-	B
Q4-15	B-	C+	B

Asset & Performance History
Date	NAV	1-Year Total Return
2017	48.13	10.97
2016	43.63	19.42
2015	36.85	-0.07
2014	37.14	15.54
2013	32.31	15.13
2012	28.18	5.57

Total Assets: $53,755,926
Asset Allocation
Asset	%
Cash	0%
Stocks	100%
US Stocks	100%
Bonds	0%
US Bonds	0%
Other	0%

Services Offered: CashInvestment Plan

Investment Strategy: The investment seeks to track the investment results of the S&P North American Technology Multimedia Networking Index composed of North American equities in the multimedia and networking technology sectors. The fund generally invests at least 90% of its assets in securities of the underlying index and in depositary receipts representing securities of the underlying index. The underlying index measures the performance of U.S.-traded stocks of communication equipment companies in the U.S. and Canada. The fund is non-diversified. **Top Holdings:** Motorola Solutions Inc   Cisco Systems Inc   F5 Networks Inc   Arista Networks Inc   Palo Alto Networks Inc

---

VictoryShares US Small Cap High Div Volatility Wtd ETF   C-   HOLD

Ticker	Traded On	NAV	Total Assets ($)	Dividend Yield (TTM)	Turnover Ratio	Expense Ratio
CSB	NAS CM	40.13	$53,755,893	3.14	65	0.35

Ratings
Reward   C
Risk   D+
Recent Upgrade/Downgrade   Down

Fund Information
Fund Type	Exchange Traded Funds
Category	US Equity Small Cap
Sub-Category	Small Value
Prospectus Objective	Small Company
Inception Date	Jul-15
Open to New Investments	Y

Prices
Price (as of 12/31/2018)	40.15
52-Week High	48.67
52-Week Low	38.78

Total Returns (%)
3-Month	6-Month	1-Year	3-Year	5-Year
-12.70	-11.97	-7.05	34.79	

3-Year Standard Deviation   12.82
Effective Duration

Valuation
Premium/Discount (1-Year Average)   0.16

Company Information
Provider	VictoryShares
Manager/Tenure	Stephen Hammers (3), Mannik Dhillon (0)
Website	http://www.VictorySharesLiterature.com
Address	Victory Shares 4249 Easton Way, Suite 400 Columbus OH 43219 United States
Phone Number	

PERFORMANCE

Ratings History
Date	Overall Rating	Risk Rating	Reward Rating
Q4-18	C-	D+	C
Q2-18	C	D+	C+
Q4-17	C	B+	C+
Q4-16	D	D+	C
Q4-15	U		

Asset & Performance History
Date	NAV	1-Year Total Return
2017	44.57	10.92
2016	41.58	29.18
2015	32.84	
2014		
2013		
2012		

Total Assets: $53,755,893
Asset Allocation
Asset	%
Cash	1%
Stocks	99%
US Stocks	99%
Bonds	0%
US Bonds	0%
Other	0%

Services Offered:

Investment Strategy: The investment seeks to provide investment results that track the performance of the Nasdaq Victory US Small Cap High Dividend 100 Volatility Weighted Index. The fund seeks to achieve its investment objective by investing, under normal market conditions, at least 80% of its assets directly or indirectly in the securities included in the Nasdaq Victory US Small Cap High Dividend 100 Volatility Weighted Index, an unmanaged, volatility weighted index maintained exclusively by the index provider. The index identifies the 100 highest dividend yielding stocks in the Nasdaq Victory US Small Cap 500 Volatility Weighted Index. **Top Holdings:** Capitol Federal Financial Inc   Northwest Bancshares Inc   Four Corners Property Trust Inc   Unitil Corp   Otter Tail Corp

Direxion Daily S&P Biotech Bear 3X Shares   D   SELL

Ticker	Traded On	NAV	Total Assets ($)	Dividend Yield (TTM)	Turnover Ratio	Expense Ratio
LABD	NYSE Arca	42.50	$53,576,844	0.47	0	1.11

Ratings
Reward   E+
Risk   D
Recent Upgrade/Downgrade   Up

Fund Information
Fund Type   Exchange Traded Funds
Category   Trading Tools
Sub-Category   Trading--Inverse Equity
Prospectus Objective   Technology
Inception Date   May-15
Open to New Investments   Y

Prices
Price (as of 12/31/2018)   42.78
52-Week High   59.28
52-Week Low   21.65

Total Returns (%)

3-Month	6-Month	1-Year	3-Year	5-Year
66.66	64.62	-7.45	-86.25	

3-Year Standard Deviation   111.28
Effective Duration

Valuation
Premium/Discount (1-Year Average)   -0.04

Company Information
Provider   Direxion Funds
Manager/Tenure   Paul Brigandi (3), Tony Ng (3)
Website   http://www.direxionfunds.com
Address   Direxion Funds 1301 Avenue Of The
                      Americas (6th Avenue) New York NY
                      10019 United States
Phone Number   646-572-3390

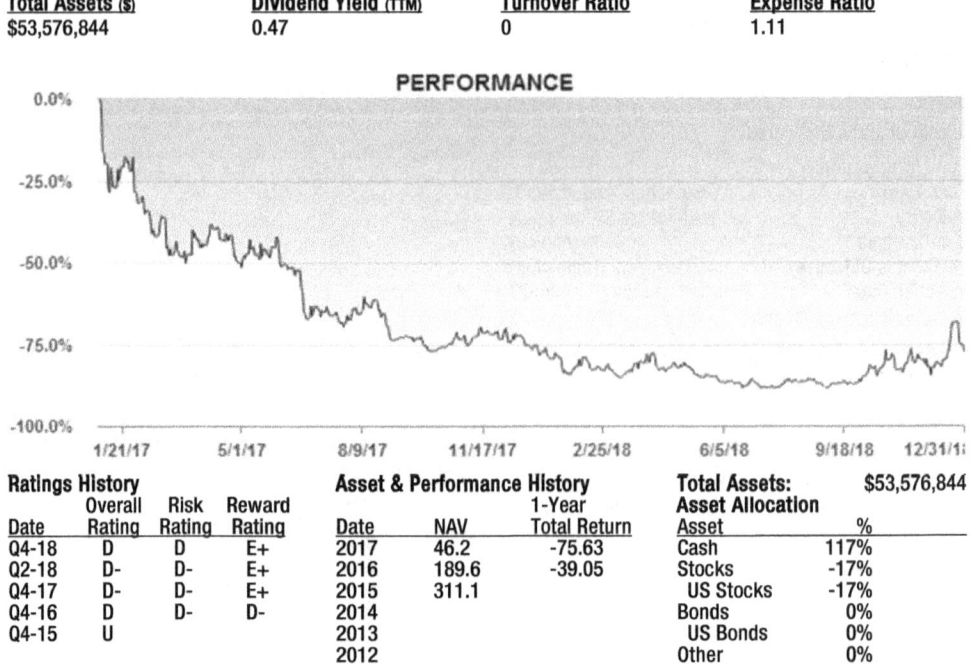

PERFORMANCE

Ratings History

Date	Overall Rating	Risk Rating	Reward Rating
Q4-18	D	D	E+
Q2-18	D-	D-	E+
Q4-17	D-	D-	E+
Q4-16	D	D-	D-
Q4-15	U		

Asset & Performance History

Date	NAV	1-Year Total Return
2017	46.2	-75.63
2016	189.6	-39.05
2015	311.1	
2014		
2013		
2012		

Total Assets: $53,576,844
Asset Allocation

Asset	%
Cash	117%
Stocks	-17%
US Stocks	-17%
Bonds	0%
US Bonds	0%
Other	0%

Services Offered:

Investment Strategy: The investment seeks daily investment results, before fees and expenses, of 300% of the inverse of the daily performance of the S&P Biotechnology Select Industry Index. The fund, under normal circumstances, invests in swap agreements, futures contracts, short positions or other financial instruments that, in combination, provide inverse (opposite) or short leveraged exposure to the index equal to at least 80% of the fund's net assets (plus borrowing for investment purposes). The index is designed to measure the performance of the biotechnology sub-industry based on the Global Industry Classification Standards ("GICS"). The fund is non-diversified. **Top Holdings:** S&P Biotechnology Select   S&P Biotechnology Select   S&P Biotechnology Select   S&P Biotechnology Select   S&P Biotechnology Select

Invesco Frontier Markets ETF   C-   HOLD

Ticker	Traded On	NAV	Total Assets ($)	Dividend Yield (TTM)	Turnover Ratio	Expense Ratio
FRN	NYSE Arca	12.24	$53,441,217	4.07	98	0.7

Ratings
Reward   C-
Risk   D+
Recent Upgrade/Downgrade

Fund Information
Fund Type   Exchange Traded Funds
Category   Global Emerg Mkts Equity
Sub-Category   Diversified Emerging Mkts
Prospectus Objective   Div Emerg Mkts
Inception Date   Jun-08
Open to New Investments   Y

Prices
Price (as of 12/31/2018)   12.18
52-Week High   16.52
52-Week Low   12.00

Total Returns (%)

3-Month	6-Month	1-Year	3-Year	5-Year
-6.44	-9.95	-16.06	24.94	-13.64

3-Year Standard Deviation   13.42
Effective Duration

Valuation
Premium/Discount (1-Year Average)   -0.03

Company Information
Provider   Invesco
Manager/Tenure   Peter Hubbard (0), Michael Jeanette
                      (0), Jonathan Nixon (0), 1 other
Website   http://www.invesco.com/us
Address   Invesco 11 Greenway Plaza, Ste. 2500
                      Houston TX 77046 United States
Phone Number   800-659-1005

PERFORMANCE

Ratings History

Date	Overall Rating	Risk Rating	Reward Rating
Q4-18	C-	D+	C-
Q2-18	C	C-	C
Q4-17	C+	C	B-
Q4-16	D+	D	D+
Q4-15	D	D	D

Asset & Performance History

Date	NAV	1-Year Total Return
2017	14.87	33.08
2016	11.61	11.87
2015	10.78	-20.79
2014	13.87	-12.73
2013	16.39	-13.32
2012	19.66	11

Total Assets: $53,441,217
Asset Allocation

Asset	%
Cash	0%
Stocks	100%
US Stocks	6%
Bonds	0%
US Bonds	0%
Other	0%

Services Offered:

Investment Strategy: The investment seeks to track the investment results (before fees and expenses) of the BNY Mellon New Frontier Index (the "underlying index"). The fund generally will invest at least 90% of its total assets in the securities that comprise the underlying index. The underlying index is comprised of liquid American depositary receipts ("ADRs") listed on a U.S. exchange, global depositary receipts ("GDRs") traded on the London Stock Exchange, and ordinary share classes of equity securities listed on exchanges in Frontier Market countries that meet certain trading volume and free-float market capitalization criteria. The fund is non-diversified. **Top Holdings:** MercadoLibre Inc   Copa Holdings SA Class A   National Bank of Kuwait SAK   Safaricom PLC   Banca Transilva SA

Direxion Zacks MLP High Income Index Shares   C   HOLD

Ticker	Traded On	NAV	Total Assets ($)	Dividend Yield (TTM)	Turnover Ratio	Expense Ratio
ZMLP	NYSE Arca	11.90	$52,955,828	8.61	86	0.65

Ratings

Reward	B-
Risk	D
Recent Upgrade/Downgrade	

Fund Information

Fund Type	Exchange Traded Funds
Category	Energy Sector Equity
Sub-Category	Energy Limited Partnership
Prospectus Objective	Income
Inception Date	Jan-14
Open to New Investments	Y

Prices

Price (as of 12/31/2018)	11.85
52-Week High	17.82
52-Week Low	11.78

Total Returns (%)

3-Month	6-Month	1-Year	3-Year	5-Year
-21.58	-14.11	-16.81	-8.15	

3-Year Standard Deviation	21.66
Effective Duration	

Valuation

Premium/Discount (1-Year Average)	0.03

Company Information

Provider	Direxion Funds
Manager/Tenure	Paul Brigandi (4), Tony Ng (3)
Website	http://www.direxionfunds.com
Address	Direxion Funds 1301 Avenue Of The Americas (6th Avenue) New York NY 10019 United States
Phone Number	646-572-3390

PERFORMANCE

Ratings History

Date	Overall Rating	Risk Rating	Reward Rating
Q4-18	C	D	B-
Q2-18	C	D	B-
Q4-17	D	D	D
Q4-16	C	D	C+
Q4-15	D+	C-	C+

Asset & Performance History

Date	NAV	1-Year Total Return
2017	16.03	-6.77
2016	18.91	22.82
2015	17.45	-41.88
2014	33.16	
2013		
2012		

Total Assets: $52,955,828

Asset Allocation

Asset	%
Cash	0%
Stocks	100%
US Stocks	92%
Bonds	0%
US Bonds	0%
Other	0%

Services Offered:

Investment Strategy: The investment seeks investment results, before fees and expenses, that track the price and yield performance of the Zacks MLP High Income Index. The fund, under normal circumstances, invests at least 80% of its net assets in the securities that comprise the index. The index is comprised of 25 securities selected from a universe of master limited partnerships ("MLPs") listed on U.S. exchanges. The fund is non-diversified. **Top Holdings:** Sunoco LP Black Stone Minerals LP Partnership Units GasLog Partners LP EnLink Midstream Partners LP Suburban Propane Partners LP

VanEck Vectors Israel ETF   C-   HOLD

Ticker	Traded On	NAV	Total Assets ($)	Dividend Yield (TTM)	Turnover Ratio	Expense Ratio
ISRA	NYSE Arca	28.05	$52,554,761	1.48	21	0.59

Ratings

Reward	C
Risk	D+
Recent Upgrade/Downgrade	Down

Fund Information

Fund Type	Exchange Traded Funds
Category	Equity Misc
Sub-Category	Miscellaneous Region
Prospectus Objective	Growth
Inception Date	Jun-13
Open to New Investments	Y

Prices

Price (as of 12/31/2018)	28.03
52-Week High	34.34
52-Week Low	26.75

Total Returns (%)

3-Month	6-Month	1-Year	3-Year	5-Year
-14.56	-10.04	-6.96	1.27	0.80

3-Year Standard Deviation	11.52
Effective Duration	

Valuation

Premium/Discount (1-Year Average)	0.31

Company Information

Provider	VanEck
Manager/Tenure	Hao-Hung (Peter) Liao (5), Guo Hua (Jason) Jin (0)
Website	http://www.vaneck.com
Address	Van Eck Associates Corporation 666 Third Avenue New York NY 10017 United States
Phone Number	800-826-1115

PERFORMANCE

Ratings History

Date	Overall Rating	Risk Rating	Reward Rating
Q4-18	C-	D+	C
Q2-18	C-	D+	C
Q4-17	C	C	C
Q4-16	D+	D+	D+
Q4-15	C-	C-	C-

Asset & Performance History

Date	NAV	1-Year Total Return
2017	30.37	14.94
2016	26.84	-5.29
2015	28.8	-1.29
2014	29.56	0.84
2013	30.04	
2012		

Total Assets: $52,554,761

Asset Allocation

Asset	%
Cash	0%
Stocks	100%
US Stocks	36%
Bonds	0%
US Bonds	0%
Other	0%

Services Offered:

Investment Strategy: The investment seeks to replicate as closely as possible, before fees and expenses, the price and yield performance of the BlueStar Israel Global Index®. The fund normally invests at least 80% of its total assets in securities that comprise the fund's benchmark index. The index is comprised of equity securities, which may include depositary receipts, of publicly traded companies that are generally considered by BlueStar Global Investors, LLC to be Israeli companies. It may also utilize depositary receipts to seek performance that corresponds to the fund's benchmark index. The fund is non-diversified. **Top Holdings:** Teva Pharmaceutical Industries Ltd Check Point Software Technologies Ltd Bank Leumi Le-Israel BM Amdocs Ltd Perrigo Co PLC

iShares International Preferred Stock ETF

D+ **SELL**

Ticker	Traded On	NAV
IPFF	BATS	15.18

Total Assets ($)	Dividend Yield (TTM)	Turnover Ratio	Expense Ratio
$52,542,891	4.53	15	0.55

Ratings
Reward	D+
Risk	C-
Recent Upgrade/Downgrade	Down

Fund Information
Fund Type	Exchange Traded Funds
Category	US Fixed Income
Sub-Category	Preferred Stock
Prospectus Objective	Growth & Inc
Inception Date	Nov-11
Open to New Investments	Y

Prices
Price (as of 12/31/2018)	15.11
52-Week High	19.76
52-Week Low	14.47

Total Returns (%)
3-Month	6-Month	1-Year	3-Year	5-Year
-14.21	-11.16	-16.03	6.39	-21.11

3-Year Standard Deviation	14.74
Effective Duration	

Valuation
Premium/Discount (1-Year Average)	-0.62

Company Information
Provider	iShares
Manager/Tenure	Diane Hsiung (7), Greg Savage (7), Jennifer Hsui (6), 3 others
Website	http://www.ishares.com
Address	iShares 400 Howard Street San Francisco CA 94105 United States
Phone Number	800-474-2737

PERFORMANCE

Ratings History					Asset & Performance History			Total Assets:	$52,542,891
	Overall	Risk	Reward				1-Year	Asset Allocation	
Date	Rating	Rating	Rating		Date	NAV	Total Return	Asset	%
Q4-18	D+	C-	D+		2017	18.83	21.99	Cash	1%
Q2-18	C-	C-	C-		2016	16.01	3.61	Stocks	0%
Q4-17	C	C	C		2015	16.26	-23.76	US Stocks	0%
Q4-16	D	D	D		2014	22.49	-2.74	Bonds	0%
Q4-15	D	D	D		2013	24.07	-4.93	US Bonds	0%
					2012	26.78	12.69	Other	4%

Services Offered:

Investment Strategy: The investment seeks to track the investment results of the S&P International Preferred Stock IndexTM. The fund generally will invest at least 90% of its assets in the component securities of the underlying index and in investments that have economic characteristics that are substantially identical to the component securities and may invest up to 10% of its assets in certain futures, options and swap contracts, cash and cash equivalents. The index measures the performance of a select group of preferred stocks from non-U.S. developed market issuers and traded on non-U.S. developed market exchanges as defined by the index provider. The fund is non-diversified. **Top Holdings:** TransCanada Corp Cum Red First Pfd Registered Shs Series -15- Canadian Imperial Bank of Commerce Non-Cum Conv Red Rate Reset Pfd Register Klovern AB Pref Shs Royal Bank of Canada 5.5% Fixed Non-Cum Red 1st Rate Reset Pfd Shs Series - Lloyds Banking Group PLC 9 1/4 % Non.Cum.Irrd.Pref.Shs

Direxion Auspice Broad Commodity Strategy ETF

D+ **SELL**

Ticker	Traded On	NAV
COM	NYSE Arca	23.97

Total Assets ($)	Dividend Yield (TTM)	Turnover Ratio	Expense Ratio
$52,327,005	0.64	0	0.7

Ratings
Reward	D+
Risk	D+
Recent Upgrade/Downgrade	

Fund Information
Fund Type	Exchange Traded Funds
Category	Commodities Broad Basket
Sub-Category	Commodities Broad Basket
Prospectus Objective	Growth & Inc
Inception Date	Mar-17
Open to New Investments	Y

Prices
Price (as of 12/31/2018)	23.98
52-Week High	26.10
52-Week Low	23.78

Total Returns (%)
3-Month	6-Month	1-Year	3-Year	5-Year
-5.81	-2.56	-1.91		

3-Year Standard Deviation	
Effective Duration	

Valuation
Premium/Discount (1-Year Average)	0.06

Company Information
Provider	Direxion Funds
Manager/Tenure	Paul Brigandi (1), Tony Ng (1)
Website	http://www.direxionfunds.com
Address	Direxion Funds 1301 Avenue Of The Americas (6th Avenue) New York NY 10019 United States
Phone Number	646-572-3390

PERFORMANCE

Ratings History					Asset & Performance History			Total Assets:	$52,327,005
	Overall	Risk	Reward				1-Year	Asset Allocation	
Date	Rating	Rating	Rating		Date	NAV	Total Return	Asset	%
Q4-18	D+	D+	D+		2017	24.57		Cash	92%
Q2-18	D+	D+	D+		2016			Stocks	0%
Q4-17	U				2015			US Stocks	0%
Q4-16					2014			Bonds	0%
Q4-15					2013			US Bonds	0%
					2012			Other	8%

Services Offered:

Investment Strategy: The investment seeks to provide total return that exceeds that of the Auspice Broad Commodity Index over a complete market cycle. The fund is an actively managed ETF that seeks to provide total return that exceeds that of the index. It will generally seek to maintain a portfolio of instruments similar to those included in the index by utilizing exchange-traded commodity futures contracts, swap contracts and investments in other investment companies or exchange-traded notes, thereby obtaining exposure to the commodities markets. The index is a rules-based index that attempts to capture trends in the commodity markets. The fund is non-diversified. **Top Holdings:** Auspice Broad Commodity ER CAD

Oppenheimer S&P Financials Revenue ETF   C   HOLD

Ticker	Traded On	NAV	Total Assets ($)	Dividend Yield (TTM)	Turnover Ratio	Expense Ratio
RWW	NYSE Arca	57.76	$52,249,247	1.36		0.45

Ratings
Reward   C
Risk   C-
Recent Upgrade/Downgrade   Down

Fund Information
Fund Type   Exchange Traded Funds
Category   Financials Sector Equity
Sub-Category   Financial
Prospectus Objective   Financial
Inception Date   Nov-08
Open to New Investments   Y

Prices
Price (as of 12/31/2018)   57.71
52-Week High   74.08
52-Week Low   54.38

Total Returns (%)

3-Month	6-Month	1-Year	3-Year	5-Year
-14.07	-9.70	-14.71	25.86	36.46

3-Year Standard Deviation   14.9
Effective Duration

Valuation
Premium/Discount (1-Year Average)   0.55

Company Information
Provider   OppenheimerFunds
Manager/Tenure   Frank Vallario (1), Donal Bishnoi (0)
Website   http://www.oppenheimerfunds.com
Address   OppenheimerFunds 12100 East Iliff Avenue, Suite 300, Aurora, Colorado Aurora CO 80217-5270 United States
Phone Number   800-225-5677

PERFORMANCE

Ratings History

Date	Overall Rating	Risk Rating	Reward Rating
Q4-18	C	C-	C
Q2-18	B-	C	B
Q4-17	B+	B	A
Q4-16	B-	C	B
Q4-15	B+	B	B+

Asset & Performance History

Date	NAV	1-Year Total Return
2017	68.78	20.72
2016	57.63	22.23
2015	47.87	-4.06
2014	50.54	13.01
2013	45.19	42.25
2012	32.04	35.38

Total Assets: $52,249,247
Asset Allocation

Asset	%
Cash	0%
Stocks	100%
US Stocks	98%
Bonds	0%
US Bonds	0%
Other	0%

Services Offered:

Investment Strategy: The investment seeks to provide investment results that correspond generally, before fees and expenses, to the performance of the S&P Financials Sector Revenue-Weighted Index (the "underlying index"). The fund will normally invest at least 80% of its net assets, plus any borrowings for investment purposes, in financials companies included in the underlying index. The underlying index is constructed by using a rules-based methodology that re-weights the constituent securities of the S&P 500® Financials Index (the "parent index") according to the revenue earned by the companies in the parent index. The fund is non-diversified. **Top Holdings:** Berkshire Hathaway Inc B   JPMorgan Chase & Co   Wells Fargo & Co   Bank of America Corporation   Citigroup Inc

---

VanEck Vectors® NDR CMG Long/Flat Allocation ETF   D+   SELL

Ticker	Traded On	NAV	Total Assets ($)	Dividend Yield (TTM)	Turnover Ratio	Expense Ratio
LFEQ	NYSE Arca	24.69	$52,229,609	0.77	28	0.59

Ratings
Reward   D+
Risk   C-
Recent Upgrade/Downgrade

Fund Information
Fund Type   Exchange Traded Funds
Category   US Equity Large Cap Blend
Sub-Category   Large Blend
Prospectus Objective   Growth & Inc
Inception Date   Oct-17
Open to New Investments   Y

Prices
Price (as of 12/31/2018)   24.59
52-Week High   28.45
52-Week Low   23.52

Total Returns (%)

3-Month	6-Month	1-Year	3-Year	5-Year
-12.05	-6.47	-4.98		

3-Year Standard Deviation
Effective Duration

Valuation
Premium/Discount (1-Year Average)   0.13

Company Information
Provider   VanEck
Manager/Tenure   Hao-Hung (Peter) Liao (1), Guo Hua (Jason) Jin (0)
Website   http://www.vaneck.com
Address   Van Eck Associates Corporation 666 Third Avenue New York NY 10017 United States
Phone Number   800-826-1115

PERFORMANCE

Ratings History

Date	Overall Rating	Risk Rating	Reward Rating
Q4-18	D+	C-	D+
Q2-18	U		
Q4-17	U		
Q4-16			
Q4-15			

Asset & Performance History

Date	NAV	1-Year Total Return
2017	26.23	
2016		
2015		
2014		
2013		
2012		

Total Assets: $52,229,609
Asset Allocation

Asset	%
Cash	1%
Stocks	99%
US Stocks	99%
Bonds	0%
US Bonds	0%
Other	0%

Services Offered:

Investment Strategy: The investment seeks to replicate as closely as possible, the price and yield performance of the Ned Davis Research CMG US Large Cap Long/Flat Index. The fund normally invests at least 80% of its total assets in securities that track and/or comprise the fund's benchmark index. The index is a rules-based index that follows a proprietary model developed by Ned Davis Research, Inc. in conjunction with CMG Capital Management Group, Inc. To help limit potential loss associated with adverse market conditions, the model produces trade signals that dictate the index's equity allocation ranging from 100% fully invested to 100% in cash. It is non-diversified. **Top Holdings:** Vanguard S&P 500 ETF

NuShares ESG Large-Cap Value ETF

C- HOLD

Ticker	Traded On	NAV	Total Assets ($)	Dividend Yield (TTM)	Turnover Ratio	Expense Ratio
NULV	BATS	26.25	$52,205,206	0.9	33	0.35

Ratings
Reward	C-
Risk	C-
Recent Upgrade/Downgrade	

Fund Information
Fund Type	Exchange Traded Funds
Category	US Equity Large Cap Value
Sub-Category	Large Value
Prospectus Objective	Growth
Inception Date	Dec-16
Open to New Investments	Y

Prices
Price (as of 12/31/2018)	26.15
52-Week High	30.90
52-Week Low	25.77

Total Returns (%)
3-Month	6-Month	1-Year	3-Year	5-Year
-12.03	-6.66	-6.48		

3-Year Standard Deviation
Effective Duration

Valuation
Premium/Discount (1-Year Average)	0.10

Company Information
Provider	Nuveen
Manager/Tenure	Philip James(Jim) Campagna (1), Lei Liao (1)
Website	http://www.nuveen.com
Address	Nuveen Investment Trust John Nuveen & Co. Inc. Chicago IL 60606 United States
Phone Number	312-917-8146

PERFORMANCE

Ratings History
Date	Overall Rating	Risk Rating	Reward Rating
Q4-18	C-	C-	C-
Q2-18	C-	C-	C-
Q4-17	D	A-	D+
Q4-16			
Q4-15			

Asset & Performance History
Date	NAV	1-Year Total Return
2017	28.51	15.39
2016	24.78	
2015		
2014		
2013		
2012		

Total Assets: $52,205,206

Asset Allocation
Asset	%
Cash	0%
Stocks	100%
US Stocks	96%
Bonds	0%
US Bonds	0%
Other	0%

Services Offered:

Investment Strategy: The investment seeks to track the investment results, before fees and expenses, of the TIAA ESG USA Large-Cap Value Index (the "index"). Under normal market conditions, the fund invests at least 80% of the sum of its net assets and the amount of any borrowings for investment purposes in component securities of the index. The index is comprised of equity securities issued by large capitalization companies listed on U.S. exchanges that meet certain environmental, social, and governance ("ESG") criteria. **Top Holdings:** Microsoft Corp Verizon Communications Inc Bank of America Corporation Procter & Gamble Co Merck & Co Inc

---

First Trust Dow 30 Equal Weight ETF

B- BUY

Ticker	Traded On	NAV	Total Assets ($)	Dividend Yield (TTM)	Turnover Ratio	Expense Ratio
EDOW	NYSE Arca	21.43	$51,577,674	1.78	20	0.5

Ratings
Reward	B
Risk	C
Recent Upgrade/Downgrade	Up

Fund Information
Fund Type	Exchange Traded Funds
Category	US Equity Large Cap Value
Sub-Category	Large Value
Prospectus Objective	Growth & Inc
Inception Date	Aug-17
Open to New Investments	Y

Prices
Price (as of 12/31/2018)	21.31
52-Week High	23.87
52-Week Low	20.09

Total Returns (%)
3-Month	6-Month	1-Year	3-Year	5-Year
-9.34	-0.24	-0.89		

3-Year Standard Deviation
Effective Duration

Valuation
Premium/Discount (1-Year Average)	0.30

Company Information
Provider	First Trust
Manager/Tenure	Jon C. Erickson (1), Daniel J. Lindquist (1), David G. McGarel (1), 3 others
Website	http://www.ftportfolios.com/
Address	First Trust 120 E. Liberty Drive, Suite 400 Wheaton IL 60187 United States
Phone Number	800-621-1675

PERFORMANCE

Ratings History
Date	Overall Rating	Risk Rating	Reward Rating
Q4-18	B-	C	B
Q2-18	U		
Q4-17	U		
Q4-16			
Q4-15			

Asset & Performance History
Date	NAV	1-Year Total Return
2017	22	
2016		
2015		
2014		
2013		
2012		

Total Assets: $51,577,674

Asset Allocation
Asset	%
Cash	0%
Stocks	100%
US Stocks	100%
Bonds	0%
US Bonds	0%
Other	0%

Services Offered:

Investment Strategy: The investment seeks investment results that correspond generally to the price and yield of an equity index called the Dow Jones Industrial Average Equal Weight Index. The fund will normally invest at least 90% of its net assets (including investment borrowings) in common stocks that comprise the index. The index consists of an equally weighted portfolio of the 30 securities that comprise the Dow Jones Industrial Average (TM) (the "DJIA"). The 30 securities comprising the DJIA are domestic, blue-chip companies covering all industries, with the exception of transportation and utilities. The fund is non-diversified. **Top Holdings:** Walgreens Boots Alliance Inc McDonald's Corp Merck & Co Inc Procter & Gamble Co Verizon Communications Inc

iPath® Pure Beta Broad Commodity ETN   D+   SELL

Ticker	Traded On	NAV	Total Assets ($)	Dividend Yield (TTM)	Turnover Ratio	Expense Ratio
BCM	NYSE Arca		$51,270,929	0		0.6

Ratings

Reward	C-
Risk	D+
Recent Upgrade/Downgrade	

Fund Information

Fund Type	Exchange Traded Funds
Category	Commodities Broad Basket
Sub-Category	Commodities Broad Basket
Prospectus Objective	Natl Res
Inception Date	Apr-11
Open to New Investments	Y

Prices

Price (as of 12/31/2018)	25.77
52-Week High	31.40
52-Week Low	25.68

Total Returns (%)

3-Month	6-Month	1-Year	3-Year	5-Year
-14.13	-12.55	-11.92	9.00	-34.72

3-Year Standard Deviation	11.09
Effective Duration	

Valuation

Premium/Discount (1-Year Average)	-0.11

Company Information

Provider	Milleis Investissements Funds
Manager/Tenure	Management Team (7)
Website	
Address	2-4, rue Eugène Ruppert L-2453 Luxembourg Luxembourg L-2453 Luxembourg
Phone Number	

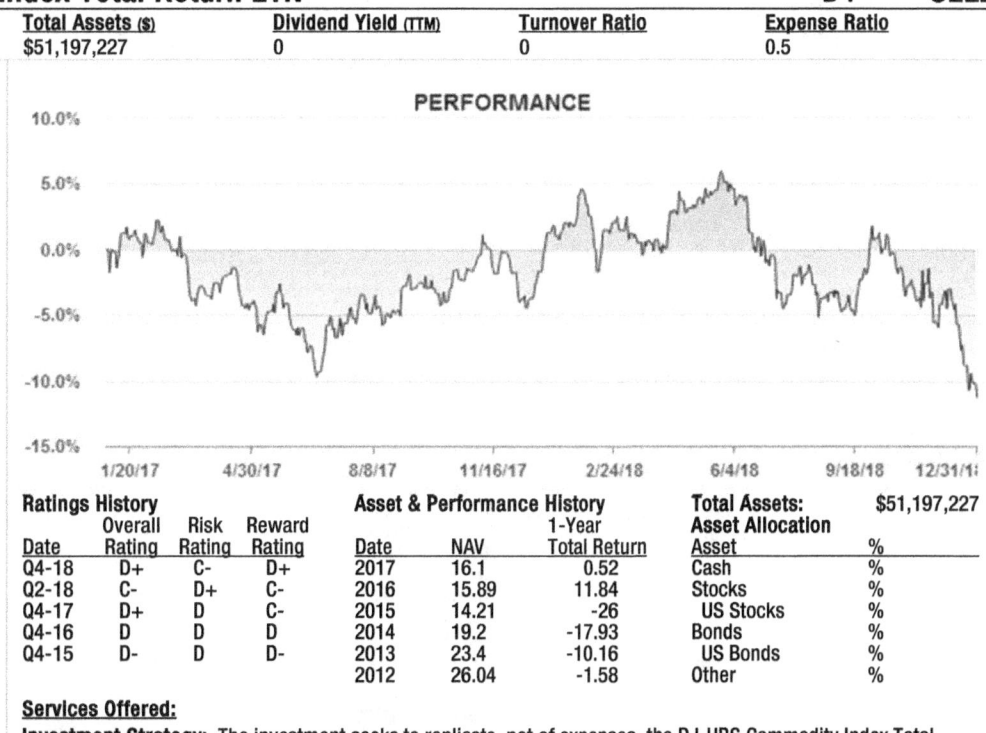

PERFORMANCE

Ratings History

Date	Overall Rating	Risk Rating	Reward Rating
Q4-18	D+	D+	C-
Q2-18	C-	D+	C
Q4-17	C-	D+	C
Q4-16	D	D	D
Q4-15	D-	D	D-

Asset & Performance History

Date	NAV	1-Year Total Return
2017	29.27	6.75
2016	27.26	15.62
2015	23.65	-25.71
2014	31.83	-19.38
2013	39.49	-9.97
2012	43.86	2.22

Total Assets: $51,270,929

Asset Allocation

Asset	%
Cash	%
Stocks	%
US Stocks	%
Bonds	%
US Bonds	%
Other	%

Services Offered:

Investment Strategy: The investment seeks to provide investors with exposure to the Barclays Commodity Index Pure Beta Total Return.
The Barclays Commodity Index Pure Beta Total Return (the "index") is comprised of a basket of exchange traded futures contracts and reflects the returns that are potentially available through an unleveraged investment in the futures contracts on certain physical commodities. For each commodity, the index may roll into one of a number of futures contracts with varying expiration dates, as selected using the Barclays Pure Beta Series 2 Methodology.
Top Holdings:

UBS ETRACS Bloomberg Commodity Index Total Return ETN   D+   SELL

Ticker	Traded On	NAV	Total Assets ($)	Dividend Yield (TTM)	Turnover Ratio	Expense Ratio
DJCI	NYSE Arca	14.10	$51,197,227	0	0	0.5

Ratings

Reward	D+
Risk	C-
Recent Upgrade/Downgrade	

Fund Information

Fund Type	Exchange Traded Funds
Category	Commodities Broad Basket
Sub-Category	Commodities Broad Basket
Prospectus Objective	Natl Res
Inception Date	Oct-09
Open to New Investments	Y

Prices

Price (as of 12/31/2018)	14.14
52-Week High	16.86
52-Week Low	14.14

Total Returns (%)

3-Month	6-Month	1-Year	3-Year	5-Year
-11.44	-10.37	-12.42	-0.78	-39.75

3-Year Standard Deviation	9.52
Effective Duration	

Valuation

Premium/Discount (1-Year Average)	-0.01

Company Information

Provider	UBS Group AG
Manager/Tenure	No Manager (9)
Website	http://www.ubs.com
Address	Bahnhofstrasse 45 Zurich 8098 Switzerland
Phone Number	412-037-1952

PERFORMANCE

Ratings History

Date	Overall Rating	Risk Rating	Reward Rating
Q4-18	D+	C-	D+
Q2-18	C-	D+	C-
Q4-17	D+	D	C-
Q4-16	D	D	D
Q4-15	D-	D	D-

Asset & Performance History

Date	NAV	1-Year Total Return
2017	16.1	0.52
2016	15.89	11.84
2015	14.21	-26
2014	19.2	-17.93
2013	23.4	-10.16
2012	26.04	-1.58

Total Assets: $51,197,227

Asset Allocation

Asset	%
Cash	%
Stocks	%
US Stocks	%
Bonds	%
US Bonds	%
Other	%

Services Offered:

Investment Strategy: The investment seeks to replicate, net of expenses, the DJ-UBS Commodity Index Total Return Index.
The index measures the collateralized returns from a basket of 19 commodity futures contracts representing the energy, precious metals, industrial metals, grains, softs and livestock sectors. In addition, the index is rebalanced once a year to ensure that no commodity sector may constitute more than 33% of the index as of the date of such rebalancing. **Top Holdings:**

SPDR® S&P Internet ETF   C   HOLD

Ticker	Traded On	NAV	Total Assets ($)	Dividend Yield (TTM)	Turnover Ratio	Expense Ratio
XWEB	NYSE Arca	76.35	$51,007,719	0.01	63	0.35

Ratings
Reward   C
Risk   C-
Recent Upgrade/Downgrade

Fund Information
Fund Type   Exchange Traded Funds
Category   Technology Sector Equity
Sub-Category   Technology
Prospectus Objective   Technology
Inception Date   Jun-16
Open to New Investments   Y

Prices
Price (as of 12/31/2018)   76.06
52-Week High   99.61
52-Week Low   68.10

Total Returns (%)

3-Month	6-Month	1-Year	3-Year	5-Year
-19.43	-12.54	14.68		

3-Year Standard Deviation
Effective Duration

Valuation
Premium/Discount (1-Year Average)   0.16

Company Information
Provider   SPDR State Street Global Advisors
Manager/Tenure Michael J. Feehily (2), Karl A.
                Schneider (2), Raymond V. Donofrio (1)
Website   http://www.spdrs.com
Address   SPDR State Street Global Advisors
                State Street Financial Center, 1
                Lincoln Street Boston MA 02111-2900
                United States
Phone Number   617-786-3000

PERFORMANCE

Ratings History

Date	Overall Rating	Risk Rating	Reward Rating
Q4-18	C	C-	C
Q2-18	C-	D+	C
Q4-17	D	B+	C
Q4-16	U		
Q4-15			

Asset & Performance History

Date	NAV	1-Year Total Return
2017	67.78	30.29
2016	57.1	
2015		
2014		
2013		
2012		

Total Assets: $51,007,719

Asset Allocation

Asset	%
Cash	0%
Stocks	100%
US Stocks	100%
Bonds	0%
US Bonds	0%
Other	0%

Services Offered:

Investment Strategy: The investment seeks to provide investment results that, before fees and expenses, correspond generally to the total return performance of the S&P Internet Select Industry Index. The fund generally invests substantially all, but at least 80%, of its total assets in the securities comprising the index. In addition, it may invest in equity securities that are not included in the index, cash and cash equivalents or money market instruments, such as repurchase agreements and money market funds (including money market funds advised by the Adviser). The index represents the internet segment of the S&P Total Market Index ("S&P TMI"). The fund is non-diversified. **Top Holdings:** TripAdvisor Inc Twilio Inc A Nutrisystem Inc Twitter Inc Etsy Inc

GraniteShares Bloomberg Commodity Broad Strategy No K-1 ETF   D+   SELL

Ticker	Traded On	NAV	Total Assets ($)	Dividend Yield (TTM)	Turnover Ratio	Expense Ratio
COMB	NYSE Arca	22.87	$50,911,053	0.21		0.25

Ratings
Reward   D
Risk   C-
Recent Upgrade/Downgrade

Fund Information
Fund Type   Exchange Traded Funds
Category   Commodities Broad Basket
Sub-Category   Commodities Broad Basket
Prospectus Objective   Growth & Inc
Inception Date   May-17
Open to New Investments   Y

Prices
Price (as of 12/31/2018)   22.97
52-Week High   27.33
52-Week Low   22.97

Total Returns (%)

3-Month	6-Month	1-Year	3-Year	5-Year
-10.74	-9.77	-11.80		

3-Year Standard Deviation
Effective Duration

Valuation
Premium/Discount (1-Year Average)   0.06

Company Information
Provider   Graniteshares
Manager/Tenure Benoit Autier (1), Jeff Klearman (1)
Website   http://www.graniteshares.com
Address   Graniteshares 30 Vesey Street, 9th
                Floor New York New York 10007
                United States
Phone Number

PERFORMANCE

Ratings History

Date	Overall Rating	Risk Rating	Reward Rating
Q4-18	D+	C-	D
Q2-18	D+	C-	D+
Q4-17	U		
Q4-16			
Q4-15			

Asset & Performance History

Date	NAV	1-Year Total Return
2017	26.18	
2016		
2015		
2014		
2013		
2012		

Total Assets: $50,911,053

Asset Allocation

Asset	%
Cash	79%
Stocks	0%
US Stocks	0%
Bonds	4%
US Bonds	4%
Other	16%

Services Offered:

Investment Strategy: The investment seeks to provide long-term capital appreciation, primarily through exposure to commodity futures markets. The fund is an actively managed ETF that seeks to provide long-term capital appreciation, primarily through exposure to commodity futures markets. While the fund generally will seek exposure to the commodity futures markets included in the Bloomberg Commodity Index, it is not an index tracking ETF and will seek to improve its performance, in part through a cash management strategy consisting of investments in investment grade fixed income securities. The fund is non-diversified. **Top Holdings:** Graniteshares United States Treasury Bills 0% United States Treasury Bills 0% United States Treasury Bills 0% United States Treasury Bills 0%

NuShares ESG Mid-Cap Growth ETF   D+   SELL

Ticker	Traded On	NAV	Total Assets ($)	Dividend Yield (TTM)	Turnover Ratio	Expense Ratio
NUMG	BATS	26.30	$50,851,753	0.13	53	0.4

Ratings

Reward	C-
Risk	D+
Recent Upgrade/Downgrade	Down

Fund Information

Fund Type	Exchange Traded Funds
Category	US Equity Mid Cap
Sub-Category	Mid-Cap Growth
Prospectus Objective	Growth
Inception Date	Dec-16
Open to New Investments	Y

Prices

Price (as of 12/31/2018)	26.22
52-Week High	34.48
52-Week Low	25.81

Total Returns (%)

3-Month	6-Month	1-Year	3-Year	5-Year
-18.89	-11.35	-5.40		

3-Year Standard Deviation	
Effective Duration	

Valuation

Premium/Discount (1-Year Average)	0.40

Company Information

Provider	Nuveen
Manager/Tenure	Philip James(Jim) Campagna (1), Lei Liao (1)
Website	http://www.nuveen.com
Address	Nuveen Investment Trust John Nuveen & Co. Inc. Chicago IL 60606 United States
Phone Number	312-917-8146

PERFORMANCE

Ratings History

Date	Overall Rating	Risk Rating	Reward Rating
Q4-18	D+	D+	C-
Q2-18	C-	C-	C
Q4-17	D	B+	D+
Q4-16			
Q4-15			

Asset & Performance History

Date	NAV	1-Year Total Return
2017	29.19	19.5
2016	24.53	
2015		
2014		
2013		
2012		

Total Assets: $50,851,753

Asset Allocation

Asset	%
Cash	0%
Stocks	100%
US Stocks	97%
Bonds	0%
US Bonds	0%
Other	0%

Services Offered:

Investment Strategy: The investment seeks to track the investment results, before fees and expenses, of the TIAA ESG USA Mid-Cap Growth Index (the "index"). Under normal market conditions, the fund invests at least 80% of the sum of its net assets and the amount of any borrowings for investment purposes in component securities of the index. The index is comprised of equity securities issued by mid-capitalization companies listed on U.S. exchanges that meet certain environmental, social, and governance ("ESG") criteria. **Top Holdings:** Advanced Micro Devices Inc Square Inc A MercadoLibre Inc Henry Schein Inc McCormick & Co Inc Non-Voting

---

iPath® Bloomberg Grains Subindex Total Return(SM) ETN   D   SELL

Ticker	Traded On	NAV	Total Assets ($)	Dividend Yield (TTM)	Turnover Ratio	Expense Ratio
JJGTF	OTC BB		$50,801,155	0	0	0.75

Ratings

Reward	D
Risk	D
Recent Upgrade/Downgrade	

Fund Information

Fund Type	Exchange Traded Funds
Category	Commodities Specified
Sub-Category	Commodities Agriculture
Prospectus Objective	Natl Res
Inception Date	Oct-07
Open to New Investments	Y

Prices

Price (as of 12/31/2018)	22.48
52-Week High	27.81
52-Week Low	21.90

Total Returns (%)

3-Month	6-Month	1-Year	3-Year	5-Year
-0.42	0.98	-6.54	-24.93	-47.31

3-Year Standard Deviation	18.15
Effective Duration	

Valuation

Premium/Discount (1-Year Average)	0.00

Company Information

Provider	Milleis Investissements Funds
Manager/Tenure	No Manager (11)
Website	
Address	2-4, rue Eugène Ruppert L-2453 Luxembourg Luxembourg L-2453 Luxembourg
Phone Number	

PERFORMANCE

Ratings History

Date	Overall Rating	Risk Rating	Reward Rating
Q4-18	D	D	D
Q2-18	D	D	D
Q4-17	D-	D-	D
Q4-16	D-	D	D-
Q4-15	D	D	D-

Asset & Performance History

Date	NAV	1-Year Total Return
2017	24.4	-13.26
2016	28.17	-7.58
2015	30.38	-21.45
2014	38.68	-10.63
2013	43.28	-18.23
2012	52.93	17.95

Total Assets: $50,801,155

Asset Allocation

Asset	%
Cash	%
Stocks	%
US Stocks	%
Bonds	%
US Bonds	%
Other	%

Services Offered:

Investment Strategy: The investment seeks to provide investors with exposure to the Dow Jones-UBS Grains Subindex Total ReturnService Mark.
The Dow Jones-UBS Grains Subindex Total ReturnService Mark (the "index") reflects the returns that are potentially available through an unleveraged investment in the futures contracts on grains commodities. The index is currently composed of three futures contracts on grains which are included in the Dow Jones-UBS Commodity Index Total ReturnService Mark. **Top Holdings:**

Credit Suisse S&P MLP Index ETN
D- **SELL**

Ticker	Traded On	NAV	Total Assets ($)	Dividend Yield (TTM)	Turnover Ratio	Expense Ratio
MLPO	NYSE Arca		$50,800,500	5.58		0.95

Ratings
Reward   D
Risk   E
Recent Upgrade/Downgrade

Fund Information
Fund Type	Exchange Traded Funds
Category	Energy Sector Equity
Sub-Category	Energy Limited Partnership
Prospectus Objective	Growth & Inc
Inception Date	Dec-14
Open to New Investments	Y

Prices
Price (as of 12/31/2018)	13.92
52-Week High	16.57
52-Week Low	13.92

Total Returns (%)
3-Month	6-Month	1-Year	3-Year	5-Year
-9.88	-3.34	-13.99	-33.78	

3-Year Standard Deviation   21.05
Effective Duration

Valuation
Premium/Discount (1-Year Average)   -0.05

Company Information
Provider	Credit Suisse AG
Manager/Tenure	Not Disclosed (3)
Website	http://www.credit-suisse.com
Address	Luxembourg Luxembourg
	Luxembourg na Luxembourg
Phone Number	352-436-1611

PERFORMANCE

Ratings History
Date	Overall Rating	Risk Rating	Reward Rating
Q4-18	D-	E	D
Q2-18	D	E	D
Q4-17	D	D	D+
Q4-16	D	D	D
Q4-15	U		

Asset & Performance History
Date	NAV	1-Year Total Return
2017	14.77	-6.06
2016	16.76	24.47
2015	14.97	-36.05
2014	24.11	
2013		
2012		

Total Assets: $50,800,500

Asset Allocation
Asset	%
Cash	%
Stocks	%
US Stocks	%
Bonds	%
US Bonds	%
Other	%

Services Offered:

Investment Strategy: The investment seeks to provide exposure to the price return version of the S&P MLP Index (the "index").
The index includes both master limited partnerships and publicly traded limited liability companies. In addition, the ETNs allow investors the potential to receive quarterly coupons that generally reflect the net cash distributions made by the index constituents, reduced by the application of the fees. **Top Holdings:**

Inspire Small/Mid Cap Impact ETF
D+ **SELL**

Ticker	Traded On	NAV	Total Assets ($)	Dividend Yield (TTM)	Turnover Ratio	Expense Ratio
ISMD	NYSE Arca	22.94	$50,788,227	0.79		0.61

Ratings
Reward   D+
Risk   C-
Recent Upgrade/Downgrade

Fund Information
Fund Type	Exchange Traded Funds
Category	US Equity Mid Cap
Sub-Category	Small Blend
Prospectus Objective	Growth
Inception Date	Feb-17
Open to New Investments	Y

Prices
Price (as of 12/31/2018)	22.84
52-Week High	30.11
52-Week Low	21.59

Total Returns (%)
3-Month	6-Month	1-Year	3-Year	5-Year
-20.60	-18.89	-10.56		

3-Year Standard Deviation
Effective Duration

Valuation
Premium/Discount (1-Year Average)   0.14

Company Information
Provider	Inspire
Manager/Tenure	Darrell Jayroe (1), Robert Netzly (1)
Website	
Address	Inspire 650 San Benito Street, Suite
	130 Hollister CA 95023 United States
Phone Number	

PERFORMANCE

Ratings History
Date	Overall Rating	Risk Rating	Reward Rating
Q4-18	D+	C-	D+
Q2-18	C-	C-	D+
Q4-17	U		
Q4-16			
Q4-15			

Asset & Performance History
Date	NAV	1-Year Total Return
2017	26.33	
2016		
2015		
2014		
2013		
2012		

Total Assets: $50,788,227

Asset Allocation
Asset	%
Cash	0%
Stocks	100%
US Stocks	99%
Bonds	0%
US Bonds	0%
Other	0%

Services Offered:

Investment Strategy: The investment seeks to replicate investment results that generally correspond to the Inspire Small/Mid Cap Impact Index. The fund generally will invest at least 80% of its total assets in the component securities. The index provider selects domestic small and mid capitalization equity securities included in the Russell 2,000 Index and S&P 400 Index using the Inspire Impact Score®, a proprietary selection methodology that is designed to assign a score to a particular security based on the security's alignment with biblical values and the positive impact that company has on the world through various environmental, social and governance criterion.
Top Holdings: Sensient Technologies Corp   United States Cellular Corp   Inovalon Holdings Inc   NBT Bancorp Inc
Adtalem Global Education Inc

Invesco Russell MidCap Pure Value ETF   C-   HOLD

Ticker	Traded On	NAV	Total Assets ($)	Dividend Yield (TTM)	Turnover Ratio	Expense Ratio
PXMV	NYSE Arca	27.56	$50,700,539	2.6	52	0.39

Ratings
Reward	C-
Risk	D+
Recent Upgrade/Downgrade	Down

Fund Information
Fund Type	Exchange Traded Funds
Category	US Equity Mid Cap
Sub-Category	Mid-Cap Value
Prospectus Objective	Growth
Inception Date	Mar-05
Open to New Investments	Y

Prices
Price (as of 12/31/2018)	27.55
52-Week High	32.21
52-Week Low	26.32

Total Returns (%)
3-Month	6-Month	1-Year	3-Year	5-Year
-10.61	-9.47	-9.66	19.61	24.46

3-Year Standard Deviation	10.68
Effective Duration	

Valuation
Premium/Discount (1-Year Average)	-0.04

Company Information
Provider	Invesco
Manager/Tenure	Peter Hubbard (11), Michael Jeanette (10), Jonathan Nixon (5), 2 others
Website	http://www.invesco.com/us
Address	Invesco 11 Greenway Plaza, Ste. 2500 Houston TX 77046 United States
Phone Number	800-659-1005

PERFORMANCE

Ratings History
Date	Overall Rating	Risk Rating	Reward Rating
Q4-18	C-	D+	C-
Q2-18	C	D+	C
Q4-17	B-	B-	C+
Q4-16	C-	D+	C-
Q4-15	C	D+	C

Asset & Performance History
Date	NAV	1-Year Total Return
2017	31.34	3.05
2016	31.1	28.49
2015	24.79	-7.23
2014	27.41	12.17
2013	24.82	40.59
2012	17.93	19.1

Total Assets: $50,700,539
Asset Allocation
Asset	%
Cash	0%
Stocks	100%
US Stocks	99%
Bonds	0%
US Bonds	0%
Other	0%

Services Offered:

Investment Strategy: The investment seeks to track the investment results (before fees and expenses) of the Russell Midcap® Pure Value Index (the "underlying index"). The fund generally will invest at least 90% of its total assets in the component securities that comprise the underlying index. The underlying index is composed of a subset of securities from the Russell Midcap® Index, which is composed of the smallest 800 securities of the Russell 1000® Index, an index designed to measure the performance of the largest 1,000 companies in the U.S. equity market. **Top Holdings:** Evergy Inc Avnet Inc Ashland Global Holdings Inc Forest City Realty Trust Inc Class A Annaly Capital Management Inc

---

JPMorgan Managed Futures Strategy ETF   D   SELL

Ticker	Traded On	NAV	Total Assets ($)	Dividend Yield (TTM)	Turnover Ratio	Expense Ratio
JPMF	NYSE Arca	23.42	$50,576,284			0.59

Ratings
Reward	D
Risk	D+
Recent Upgrade/Downgrade	

Fund Information
Fund Type	Exchange Traded Funds
Category	Alternative Misc
Sub-Category	Managed Futures
Prospectus Objective	Growth & Inc
Inception Date	Dec-17
Open to New Investments	Y

Prices
Price (as of 12/31/2018)	23.41
52-Week High	25.34
52-Week Low	23.03

Total Returns (%)
3-Month	6-Month	1-Year	3-Year	5-Year
-2.38	-2.91	-5.70		

3-Year Standard Deviation	
Effective Duration	

Valuation
Premium/Discount (1-Year Average)	0.53

Company Information
Provider	JPMorgan
Manager/Tenure	Wei (Victor) Li (0), Yazann Romahi (0), Joe Staines (0)
Website	http://www.jpmorganfunds.com
Address	JPMorgan 270 Park Avenue New York NY 10017-2070 United States
Phone Number	800-480-4111

PERFORMANCE

Ratings History
Date	Overall Rating	Risk Rating	Reward Rating
Q4-18	D	D+	D
Q2-18	U		
Q4-17	U		
Q4-16			
Q4-15			

Asset & Performance History
Date	NAV	1-Year Total Return
2017	25.01	
2016		
2015		
2014		
2013		
2012		

Total Assets: $50,576,284
Asset Allocation
Asset	%
Cash	91%
Stocks	9%
US Stocks	9%
Bonds	0%
US Bonds	0%
Other	0%

Services Offered:

Investment Strategy: The investment seeks to provide long-term total return. The fund will generally invest its assets globally to gain exposure, either directly or through the use of derivatives, to equity securities (across market capitalizations) in developed markets, debt securities (including below investment grade or high yield securities), commodities and currencies (including in emerging markets). It may invest in fixed income securities of any average weighted maturity or duration. The fund may use both long and short positions (achieved primarily through the use of derivative instruments). It is non-diversified. **Top Holdings:** Managed Futures Fund Cs Ltd Jpn 10y Bond(Ose) Bond 13/Dec/2018 Jbz8 Comdty Dax Index Future Equity Index 21/Dec/2018 Gxz8 Us 10yr Note (Cbt) Bond 20/Mar/2019 Tyh9 Comdty Ftse/Mib Idx Fut Equity Index 21/Dec/2018 Stz8

Goldman Sachs ActiveBeta® U.S. Small Cap Equity ETF   D+   SELL

Ticker	Traded On	NAV	Total Assets ($)	Dividend Yield (TTM)	Turnover Ratio	Expense Ratio
GSSC	NYSE Arca	38.89	$50,471,369	1.21	27	0.2

Ratings
Reward   D+
Risk   C-
Recent Upgrade/Downgrade

Fund Information
Fund Type   Exchange Traded Funds
Category   US Equity Small Cap
Sub-Category   Small Blend
Prospectus Objective   Growth
Inception Date   Jun-17
Open to New Investments   Y

Prices
Price (as of 12/31/2018)   38.88
52-Week High   49.50
52-Week Low   36.76

Total Returns (%)

3-Month	6-Month	1-Year	3-Year	5-Year
-17.67	-16.17	-8.71		

3-Year Standard Deviation
Effective Duration

Valuation
Premium/Discount (1-Year Average)   0.23

Company Information
Provider   Goldman Sachs
Manager/Tenure   Raj Garigipati (1), Jamie McGregor (1)
Website   http://www.gsamfunds.com
Address   Goldman Sachs 200 West Stree New York NY 10282 United States
Phone Number   800-526-7384

PERFORMANCE

Ratings History

Date	Overall Rating	Risk Rating	Reward Rating
Q4-18	D+	C-	D+
Q2-18	D+	D+	D+
Q4-17	U		
Q4-16			
Q4-15			

Asset & Performance History

Date	NAV	1-Year Total Return
2017	43.08	
2016		
2015		
2014		
2013		
2012		

Total Assets: $50,471,369
Asset Allocation

Asset	%
Cash	0%
Stocks	100%
US Stocks	99%
Bonds	0%
US Bonds	0%
Other	0%

Services Offered:

Investment Strategy: The investment seeks to provide investment results that closely correspond, before fees and expenses, to the performance of the Goldman Sachs ActiveBeta® U.S. Small Cap Equity Index. The fund invests at least 80% of its assets in securities included in its index. The index is designed to deliver exposure to equity securities of small capitalization U.S. issuers. The index is constructed using the patented ActiveBeta® Portfolio Construction Methodology, which was developed to provide exposure to the "factors" that are commonly tied to a stock's outperformance relative to market returns. These factors include value, momentum, quality and low volatility. **Top Holdings:** Amedisys Inc   Genomic Health Inc   Primerica Inc   iShares Russell 2000 ETF Strategic Education Inc

---

Janus Henderson Small/Mid Cap Growth Alpha ETF   C-   HOLD

Ticker	Traded On	NAV	Total Assets ($)	Dividend Yield (TTM)	Turnover Ratio	Expense Ratio
JSMD	NAS CM	36.97	$50,412,697	0.34	76	0.35

Ratings
Reward   C
Risk   D+
Recent Upgrade/Downgrade   Down

Fund Information
Fund Type   Exchange Traded Funds
Category   US Equity Mid Cap
Sub-Category   Mid-Cap Growth
Prospectus Objective   Growth
Inception Date   Feb-16
Open to New Investments   Y

Prices
Price (as of 12/31/2018)   36.81
52-Week High   47.33
52-Week Low   34.41

Total Returns (%)

3-Month	6-Month	1-Year	3-Year	5-Year
-18.52	-12.45	-3.82		

3-Year Standard Deviation
Effective Duration

Valuation
Premium/Discount (1-Year Average)   0.21

Company Information
Provider   Janus Henderson
Manager/Tenure   Benjamin Wang (2), Scott M Weiner (2)
Website   http://www.janus.com
Address   Janus 151 Detroit Street Denver CO 80206 United States
Phone Number   877-335-2687

PERFORMANCE

Ratings History

Date	Overall Rating	Risk Rating	Reward Rating
Q4-18	C-	D+	C
Q2-18	C	D+	C+
Q4-17	C-	B+	C
Q4-16	U		
Q4-15			

Asset & Performance History

Date	NAV	1-Year Total Return
2017	38.68	23.83
2016	31.3	
2015		
2014		
2013		
2012		

Total Assets: $50,412,697
Asset Allocation

Asset	%
Cash	0%
Stocks	100%
US Stocks	100%
Bonds	0%
US Bonds	0%
Other	0%

Services Offered:

Investment Strategy: The investment seeks investment results that correspond generally, to the performance of its underlying index, the Janus Small/Mid Cap Growth Alpha Index. The fund pursues its investment objective by normally investing at least 80% of its net assets in the securities that comprise the underlying index. The underlying index is composed of common stocks of small- and medium-sized companies that are included in the Solactive Small/Mid Cap Index, a universe of 2,500 small- and medium-sized capitalization stocks. **Top Holdings:** Veeva Systems Inc Class A   Westlake Chemical Corp   West Pharmaceutical Services Inc   Rollins Inc   Icon PLC

Principal Spectrum Preferred Securities Active ETF   D   SELL

Ticker	Traded On	NAV	Total Assets ($)	Dividend Yield (TTM)	Turnover Ratio	Expense Ratio
PREF	BATS	89.28	$50,377,975	5.35	41	0.55

Ratings
Reward	D
Risk	D+
Recent Upgrade/Downgrade	

Fund Information
Fund Type	Exchange Traded Funds
Category	US Fixed Income
Sub-Category	Preferred Stock
Prospectus Objective	Equity-Income
Inception Date	Jul-17
Open to New Investments	Y

Prices
Price (as of 12/31/2018)	90.07
52-Week High	100.79
52-Week Low	89.81

Total Returns (%)
3-Month	6-Month	1-Year	3-Year	5-Year
-4.40	-2.99	-6.09		

3-Year Standard Deviation
Effective Duration

Valuation
Premium/Discount (1-Year Average)	0.59

Company Information
Provider	Principal Funds
Manager/Tenure	Roberto Giangregorio (1), L. Phillip Jacoby (1), Paul S. Kim (1), 3 others
Website	http://www.principalfunds.com
Address	Principal Funds 30 Dan Road Canton MA 2021 United States
Phone Number	800-787-1621

PERFORMANCE

Ratings History
Date	Overall Rating	Risk Rating	Reward Rating
Q4-18	D	D+	D
Q2-18	D	D+	D
Q4-17	U		
Q4-16			
Q4-15			

Asset & Performance History
Date	NAV	1-Year Total Return
2017	99.67	
2016		
2015		
2014		
2013		
2012		

Total Assets: $50,377,975
Asset Allocation
Asset	%
Cash	1%
Stocks	0%
US Stocks	0%
Bonds	80%
US Bonds	51%
Other	0%

Services Offered:

Investment Strategy: The investment seeks to provide current income. Under normal circumstances, the fund invests at least 80% of its net assets, plus any borrowings for investment purposes, in preferred securities at the time of purchase. Examples of preferred securities include preferred stock, certain depositary receipts, and various types of junior subordinated debt (such debt generally includes the contractual ability to defer payment of interest without accelerating an immediate default event). It concentrates its investments (invests more than 25% of its net assets) in securities in the financial services (i.e., banking, insurance and commercial finance) industry. **Top Holdings:** HSBC Capital Funding Dollar I L.P. 10.18% BNP Paribas 7.2% Bank of America Corporation 6.1% Standard Chartered PLC Dai-Ichi Life Holdings Inc 5.1%

WisdomTree Europe Quality Dividend Growth Fund   D+   SELL

Ticker	Traded On	NAV	Total Assets ($)	Dividend Yield (TTM)	Turnover Ratio	Expense Ratio
EUDG	NYSE Arca	22.28	$50,328,385	2.37	18	0.58

Ratings
Reward	D+
Risk	C-
Recent Upgrade/Downgrade	Down

Fund Information
Fund Type	Exchange Traded Funds
Category	Europe Equity Large Cap
Sub-Category	Europe Stock
Prospectus Objective	Growth
Inception Date	May-14
Open to New Investments	Y

Prices
Price (as of 12/31/2018)	22.27
52-Week High	28.38
52-Week Low	21.53

Total Returns (%)
3-Month	6-Month	1-Year	3-Year	5-Year
-12.87	-11.01	-15.04	5.77	

3-Year Standard Deviation   11.89
Effective Duration

Valuation
Premium/Discount (1-Year Average)	0.00

Company Information
Provider	WisdomTree
Manager/Tenure	Richard A. Brown (4), Thomas J. Durante (4), Karen Q. Wong (4)
Website	http://www.wisdomtree.com
Address	WisdomTree 245 Park Avenue, 35th floor New York NY 10167 United States
Phone Number	866-909-9473

PERFORMANCE

Ratings History
Date	Overall Rating	Risk Rating	Reward Rating
Q4-18	D+	C-	D+
Q2-18	C-	D+	C
Q4-17	B	B	B
Q4-16	D	D+	D
Q4-15	D	D+	D

Asset & Performance History
Date	NAV	1-Year Total Return
2017	26.94	29.59
2016	21.13	-3.93
2015	22.53	3.43
2014	22.22	
2013		
2012		

Total Assets: $50,328,385
Asset Allocation
Asset	%
Cash	0%
Stocks	100%
US Stocks	0%
Bonds	0%
US Bonds	0%
Other	0%

Services Offered:

Investment Strategy: The investment seeks to track the price and yield performance, before fees and expenses, of the WisdomTree Europe Quality Dividend Growth Index. At least 80% of the fund's total assets will be invested in the component securities of the index and investments that have economic characteristics that are substantially identical to the economic characteristics of such component securities. The index consists of dividend-paying common stocks of companies with growth characteristics that are incorporated and listed on a stock exchange in one of the following countries: Germany, Switzerland, United Kingdom, etc. The fund is non-diversified. **Top Holdings:** Roche Holding AG Dividend Right Cert. Unilever NV DR Novo Nordisk A/S B British American Tobacco PLC Diageo PLC

Invesco Global Clean Energy ETF   D+   SELL

Ticker	Traded On	NAV	Total Assets ($)	Dividend Yield (TTM)	Turnover Ratio	Expense Ratio
PBD	NYSE Arca	10.48	$50,004,867	1.87	40	0.75

Ratings
Reward	D+
Risk	D+
Recent Upgrade/Downgrade	Down

Fund Information
Fund Type	Exchange Traded Funds
Category	Equity Misc
Sub-Category	Miscellaneous Sector
Prospectus Objective	Natl Res
Inception Date	Jun-07
Open to New Investments	

Prices
Price (as of 12/31/2018)	10.42
52-Week High	13.74
52-Week Low	9.75

Total Returns (%)
3-Month	6-Month	1-Year	3-Year	5-Year
-11.67	-9.83	-19.02	-3.29	-6.42

3-Year Standard Deviation	13.29
Effective Duration	

Valuation
Premium/Discount (1-Year Average)	-0.02

Company Information
Provider	Invesco
Manager/Tenure	Peter Hubbard (11), Jonathan Nixon (5), Michael Jeanette (3), 1 other
Website	http://www.invesco.com/us
Address	Invesco 11 Greenway Plaza, Ste. 2500 Houston TX 77046 United States
Phone Number	800-659-1005

PERFORMANCE

Ratings History
Date	Overall Rating	Risk Rating	Reward Rating
Q4-18	D+	D+	D+
Q2-18	C-	D+	C-
Q4-17	C+	C+	C+
Q4-16	D	D+	D
Q4-15	C-	C-	C-

Asset & Performance History
Date	NAV	1-Year Total Return
2017	13.17	27.75
2016	10.5	-6.52
2015	11.46	0.24
2014	11.57	-3.46
2013	12.1	54.53
2012	7.91	-3.38

Total Assets: $50,004,867
Asset Allocation
Asset	%
Cash	0%
Stocks	95%
US Stocks	28%
Bonds	0%
US Bonds	0%
Other	5%

Services Offered: Wire Redemption

Investment Strategy: The investment seeks to track the investment results (before fees and expenses) of the WilderHill New Energy Global Innovation Index (the "underlying index"). The fund will invest at least 90% of its total assets in the securities of companies engaged in the business of the advancement of cleaner energy and conservation that comprise the underlying index, as well as American depositary receipts and global depositary receipts that are based on the securities in the underlying index. The adviser anticipates that the majority of its investments will be in the securities that comprise the underlying index rather than in ADRs and GDRs. **Top Holdings:** Cree Inc Tesla Inc Hannon Armstrong Sustainable Infrastructure Capital Inc Seoul Semiconductor Co Ltd OSRAM Licht AG

Section IV:
100 Largest Exchange-Traded Funds

Investment Ratings and analysis of the 100 Largest Exchange-Traded Funds. Funds are listed in order by their asset size.

Section IV: Contents

This section contains Weiss Investment Ratings, key rating factors, and summary financial data for the 100 Largest Exchange-Traded Funds.   If your priority is to stick with large funds because you believe that the size of the fund matters then these funds should be looked at. In this listing of the 100 largest funds you can also be assured that the Weiss Exchange-Traded Fund Rating is just as important as for the smallest fund. Funds are listed in order by their asset size.

Fund Name
Describes the fund's assets, regions of investments and investment strategies. Many funds have similar names, so you want to make sure the fund you look up is really the one you are interested in evaluating.

MARKET

Ticker Symbol
An arrangement of characters (usually letters) representing a particular security listed on an exchange or otherwise traded publicly. When a company issues securities to the public marketplace, it selects an available ticker symbol for its securities which investors use to place trade orders. Every listed security has a unique ticker symbol, facilitating the vast array of trade orders that flow through the financial markets every day.

Traded On (Exchange)
The stock exchange on which the fund is listed. The core function of a stock exchange is to ensure fair and orderly trading, as well as efficient dissemination of price information. Exchanges such as: NYSE (New York Stock Exchange), AMEX (American Stock Exchange), NNM (NASDAQ National Market), and NASQ (NASDAQ Small Cap) give companies, governments and other groups a platform to sell securities to the investing public. NASDAQ is abbreviated as NAS.

RATINGS

Overall Rating
The Weiss rating measured on a scale from A to E based on each fund's risk and performance. See the preceding section, "What Our Ratings Mean," for an explanation of each letter grade rating.

Reward Rating
This is based on the total return over a period of up to five years, including net asset value and price growth. The total return figure is stated net of the expenses and fees charged by the fund. Based on proprietary modeling the individual components of the risk and reward ratings are calculated and weighted and the final rating is generated.

Risk Rating
This is includes the risk ratings of component stocks where applicable and also includes the financial stability of the fund, turnover where applicable, together with the level of volatility as measured by the fund's daily returns over a period of up to five years. Funds with greater stability are considered less risky and receive a higher risk rating. Funds with greater volatility are considered riskier, and will receive a lower risk rating. In addition to considering the fund's

volatility, the risk rating also considers an assessment of the valuation and quality of a fund's holdings.

Recent Upgrade/Downgrade
An "Up" or "Down" indicates that the Weiss Exchange-Traded Fund rating has changed since the publication of the last print edition. If a fund has had a rating change since September 30, 2018, the change is identified with an "Up" or "Down."

PRICE

Price
The price at which the fund is traded on a regular trading day. Prices in this guide are listed as of December 31, 2018.

TOTAL RETURNS & PERFORMANCE

Total Assets (MIL)
The total of all assets listed on the institution's balance sheet. This figure primarily consists of loans, investments, and fixed assets. Total Assets are displayed in millions.

1-Year Total Return
The rate of return on an investment over one year that includes interest, capital gains, dividends and distributions realized.

3-Year Total Return
The rate of return on an investment over three years that includes interest, capital gains, dividends and distributions realized.

5-Year Total Return
The rate of return on an investment over five years that includes interest, capital gains, dividends and distributions realized.

Dividend Yield (TTM)
Trailing twelve months dividends paid out relative to the share price. Expressed as a percentage and measures how much cash flow an investor is getting for each invested dollar. **Trailing Twelve Months (TTM)** is a representation of a fund's financial performance over the most recent 12 months. TTM uses the latest available financial data from a company's interim, quarterly or annual reports.

VALUATION

Premium/Discount 1-Year Average
The annual average premium or discount of the market price to the NAV (Net Asset Value), expressed as a percentage of the NAV. This value provides a year-by-year picture a fund's trading status. A negative number indicates that, on average, the fund's shares sold at a discount to NAV, and a positive number indicates the shares sold at a premium. If the number shown is –10.00, for example, the shares sold at an average 10% discount to NAV during the listed time-period.

Fund Name	Ticker Symbol	Traded On	Overall Rating	Reward Rating	Risk Rating	Recent Up/Downgrade	Price as of 12/31/2018	Total Assets (MIL)	1-Year Total Return	3-Year Total Return	5-Year Total Return	Dividend Yield (TTM)	Premium/Discount 1-Year Avg
Vanguard Total Stock Market Index Fund ETF Shares	VTI	NYSE Arca	C+	C	B		127.63	726,364	-5.95	28.38	45.08	1.81	0.02
Vanguard S&P 500 ETF	VOO	NYSE Arca	C+	C	B	Down	229.81	441,304	-5.23	29.17	48.77	1.82	0.02
Vanguard Total International Stock Index Fund ETF Shares	VXUS	NAS CM	C-	D+	C	Down	47.22	342,022	-14.79	13.77	4.36	3.08	0.15
SPDR® S&P 500 ETF	SPY	NYSE Arca	C+	C	B	Down	249.92	269,244	-4.44	29.99	49.57	1.82	0.01
Vanguard Total Bond Market Index Fund ETF Shares	BND	NYSE Arca	C	D+	C+		79.21	200,719	-0.23	6.03	12.78	2.77	0.02
iShares Core S&P 500 ETF	IVV	NYSE Arca	C+	C	B	Down	251.61	162,725	-4.54	30.09	49.78	1.82	0.03
Vanguard Total International Bond Index Fund ETF Shares	BNDX	NAS CM	C	C	C+		54.25	112,106	2.96	10.35	21.39	2.24	0.21
Vanguard FTSE Developed Markets Index Fund ETF Shares	VEA	NYSE Arca	C-	D+	C	Down	37.10	104,457	-14.88	10.31	3.79	3.25	0.05
Vanguard Mid-Cap Index Fund ETF Shares	VO	NYSE Arca	C	C-	C+	Down	138.18	96,609	-10.02	19.34	33.94	1.61	0.02
Vanguard Small-Cap Index Fund ETF Shares	VB	NYSE Arca	C	C-	C+	Down	131.99	87,322	-10.15	23.56	27.99	1.51	0.00
Vanguard Growth Index Fund ETF Shares	VUG	NYSE Arca	C	C	C+	Down	134.33	79,909	-4.16	29.98	52.58	1.17	0.00
Vanguard FTSE Emerging Markets Index Fund ETF Shares	VWO	NYSE Arca	C-	C-	C-	Down	38.10	77,643	-14.90	24.93	6.39	2.65	0.05
Vanguard Value Index Fund ETF Shares	VTV	NYSE Arca	C	C	C+	Down	97.95	75,151	-6.17	28.43	44.08	2.4	0.03
Invesco QQQ Trust	QQQ	NAS CM	B-	C+	B	Down	154.26	65,965	-0.14	41.79	85.01	0.78	0.06
Vanguard Extended Market Index Fund ETF Shares	VXF	NYSE Arca	C	C-	C+		99.81	65,136	-10.20	23.18	28.15	1.52	0.01
iShares MSCI EAFE ETF	EFA	NYSE Arca	C-	D+	C	Down	58.78	64,666	-13.82	8.70	2.28	3.35	-0.15
Vanguard Real Estate Index Fund ETF Shares	VNQ	NYSE Arca	C+	C	B	Up	74.57	59,164	-6.13	6.90	42.58	4.23	-0.01
iShares Core MSCI EAFE ETF	IEFA	BATS	C-	D+	C	Down	55.00	54,938	-14.20	9.94	5.19	3.2	-0.01
iShares Core U.S. Aggregate Bond ETF	AGG	NYSE Arca	C	D+	C+		106.49	53,588	-0.04	6.12	13.07	2.57	0.02
Vanguard Short-Term Bond Index Fund ETF Shares	BSV	NYSE Arca	C	D+	C+	Up	78.57	50,658	1.22	3.89	6.23	1.93	0.02
iShares Core MSCI Emerging Markets ETF	IEMG	NYSE Arca	C-	C-	C-	Down	47.15	49,953	-14.69	28.32	8.29	2.87	0.07
iShares Core S&P Mid-Cap ETF	IJH	NYSE Arca	C	C-	C+	Down	166.06	47,620	-11.14	24.54	33.50	1.54	0.00
iShares Russell 2000 ETF	IWM	NYSE Arca	C	C-	B-	Down	133.90	45,632	-11.02	23.80	24.30	1.3	-0.01
iShares Core S&P Small-Cap ETF	IJR	NYSE Arca	C	C-	B-	Down	69.32	42,979	-12.23	25.67	30.14	1.31	0.01
iShares Russell 1000 Growth ETF	IWF	NYSE Arca	C	C	C+	Down	130.91	41,688	-1.69	36.58	62.57	1.13	-0.01
iShares Russell 1000 Value ETF	IWD	NYSE Arca	C+	C	B		111.05	39,099	-8.39	21.70	32.34	2.28	0.01
Vanguard Dividend Appreciation Index Fund ETF Shares	VIG	NYSE Arca	C+	C	C+		97.95	39,092	-3.01	32.56	43.05	1.86	0.01
Vanguard FTSE All-World ex-US Index Fund ETF Shares	VEU	NYSE Arca	C-	D+	C	Down	45.58	35,373	-14.32	14.23	4.49	3.11	0.09
Vanguard High Dividend Yield Index Fund ETF Shares	VYM	NYSE Arca	C	C	C+	Down	77.99	30,925	-6.59	27.08	44.68	2.96	0.02
Vanguard Intermediate-Term Bond Index Fund ETF Shares	BIV	NYSE Arca	C-	D	C		81.29	30,879	-0.33	6.40	15.25	2.88	0.03
iShares iBoxx $ Investment Grade Corporate Bond ETF	LQD	NYSE Arca	C	D+	C+		112.82	29,908	-3.75	9.29	17.37	3.6	0.04
iShares MSCI Emerging Markets ETF	EEM	NYSE Arca	C-	C-	C-	Down	39.06	29,838	-14.98	28.17	5.35	2.41	-0.02
SPDR® Gold Shares	GLD	NYSE Arca	D+	D	C-	Down	121.25	29,809	-1.54	19.22	4.56	0	0.12
Vanguard Small-Cap Value Index Fund ETF Shares	VBR	NYSE Arca	C	C-	C+	Down	114.06	29,528	-12.82	21.61	28.17	2.1	0.03
Financial Select Sector SPDR® Fund	XLF	NYSE Arca	C+	C	C+	Down	23.82	29,463	-13.08	29.98	47.11	1.77	0.00
Vanguard Sh-Term Inflation-Prot Securities Ind ETF Shares	VTIP	NAS CM	C	C-	C+		47.92	27,052	0.45	4.02	2.66	3.24	0.07
Vanguard Short-Term Corporate Bond Index Fund ETF Shares	VCSH	NAS CM	C	C	C+		77.94	25,894	0.77	5.96	9.38	2.59	0.04
Vanguard Small-Cap Growth Index Fund ETF Shares	VBK	NYSE Arca	C	C-	C+	Down	150.59	22,703	-6.82	25.77	27.54	0.78	0.01
SPDR® Dow Jones Industrial Average ETF	DIA	NYSE Arca	B-	B	C+	Down	233.20	22,258	-3.60	43.44	57.76	2.02	0.05
iShares TIPS Bond ETF	TIP	NYSE Arca	C-	D	C	Down	109.51	21,829	-1.43	6.07	8.03	3	0.00
Vanguard Information Technology Index Fund ETF Shares	VGT	NYSE Arca	C+	C+	C+	Down	166.83	21,690	1.53	58.28	96.17	1.07	0.02
iShares S&P 500 Growth ETF	IVW	NYSE Arca	C	C	C+	Down	150.67	21,444	-0.17	35.53	63.70	1.18	0.01
Vanguard Large-Cap Index Fund ETF Shares	VV	NYSE Arca	C	C	C+	Down	114.86	20,461	-5.25	29.09	47.94	1.83	0.01
Health Care Select Sector SPDR® Fund	XLV	NYSE Arca	B-	B	C+		86.51	19,897	6.29	25.69	68.07	1.38	0.12
Vanguard Intermediate-Term Corp Bond Ind Fund ETF Shares	VCIT	NAS CM	C	D+	C+		82.86	19,848	-1.96	8.91	18.06	3.6	0.12
Vanguard FTSE Europe Index Fund ETF Shares	VGK	NYSE Arca	C-	D+	C-	Down	48.62	19,810	-15.27	7.01	-1.87	3.74	0.00
iShares Edge MSCI Min Vol USA ETF	USMV	BATS	B	C	A	Up	52.40	19,373	1.35	33.24	63.54	1.81	-0.02
SPDR® S&P MidCap 400 ETF	MDY	NYSE Arca	C	C-	C+	Down	302.67	19,245	-11.27	23.72	32.12	1.23	0.00
Technology Select Sector SPDR® Fund	XLK	NYSE Arca	B	B	C+		61.98	19,121	-1.55	51.75	88.73	1.42	0.03
Vanguard Mid-Cap Value Index Fund ETF Shares	VOE	NYSE Arca	C	C-	C+	Down	95.26	17,866	-13.13	17.19	31.17	2.32	0.01
iShares Russell Mid-Cap ETF	IWR	NYSE Arca	E+	E	D	Down	46.48	17,592	-77.28	-69.46	-66.37	1.8	0.01
iShares Russell 1000 ETF	IWB	NYSE Arca	C	C	C+	Down	138.69	17,407	-4.90	29.33	47.45	1.76	0.00

Fund Name	Ticker Symbol	Traded On	Overall Rating	Reward Rating	Risk Rating	Recent Up/ Downgrade	Price as of 12/31/2018	Total Assets (MIL)	1-Year Total Return	3-Year Total Return	5-Year Total Return	Dividend Yield (TTM)	Premium/ Discount 1-Year Avg
iShares Short Treasury Bond ETF	SHV	NAS CM	C	C-	C+		110.30	17,317	1.74	2.84	2.84	1.47	0.02
iShares 1-3 Year Treasury Bond ETF	SHY	NAS CM	C	C-	C+	Up	83.62	17,171	1.45	2.49	3.42	1.62	0.02
iShares Select Dividend ETF	DVY	NAS CM	C	C	C+	Down	89.31	17,115	-6.30	30.82	47.25	3.31	0.01
Vanguard Total World Stock Index Fund ETF Shares	VT	NYSE Arca	C	C-	C+	Down	65.46	16,947	-10.27	21.20	23.65	2.34	0.08
iShares MSCI Japan ETF	EWJ	NYSE Arca	C	D+	C+		50.69	16,799	-13.17	9.38	14.29	1.55	-0.07
SPDR® S&P Dividend ETF	SDY	NYSE Arca	C	C	C+	Down	89.52	16,480	-2.71	35.42	53.03	2.4	-0.01
iShares Core S&P Total U.S. Stock Market ETF	ITOT	NYSE Arca	C	C	C+	Down	56.76	15,845	-5.36	29.16	47.37	1.76	0.02
Schwab International Equity ETF™	SCHF	NYSE Arca	C-	D+	C	Down	28.35	15,779	-14.39	10.82	3.32	2.6	0.05
iShares S&P 500 Value ETF	IVE	NYSE Arca	C	C	C+	Down	101.14	15,475	-9.09	22.69	33.14	2.37	0.01
Energy Select Sector SPDR® Fund	XLE	NYSE Arca	C	B-	C-	Down	57.35	15,447	-18.10	3.72	-25.55	2.96	0.03
iShares J.P. Morgan USD Emerging Markets Bond ETF	EMB	NAS CM	C-	D+	C	Down	103.91	14,972	-5.67	13.50	21.62	4.77	0.16
Invesco S&P 500® Equal Weight ETF	RSP	NYSE Arca	C	C-	C+	Down	91.40	14,754	-7.76	24.98	38.84	1.74	-0.01
Schwab U.S. Large-Cap ETF™	SCHX	NYSE Arca	C	C	C+	Down	59.70	14,635	-4.52	30.10	48.94	1.79	0.01
iShares U.S. Preferred Stock ETF	PFF	NAS CM	C-	D+	C	Down	34.23	14,578	-4.77	4.45	23.96	5.79	-0.01
iShares iBoxx $ High Yield Corporate Bond ETF	HYG	NYSE Arca	C+	C-	A-	Down	81.10	14,220	-1.93	18.52	14.18	5.34	0.15
Consumer Discretionary Select Sector SPDR® Fund	XLY	NYSE Arca	B-	B	C	Down	99.01	13,593	1.66	32.14	59.04	1.19	0.01
Schwab U.S. Broad Market ETF™	SCHB	NYSE Arca	C	C	C+	Down	59.93	13,057	-5.24	29.23	46.26	1.77	0.00
iShares Core MSCI Total International Stock ETF	IXUS	NAS CM	C-	D+	C	Down	52.53	12,421	-14.55	14.53	4.91	2.99	0.08
iShares Floating Rate Bond ETF	FLOT	BATS	C	C	C+		50.36	12,404	1.56	5.01	5.45	2.18	0.08
Vanguard Mid-Cap Growth Index Fund ETF Shares	VOT	NYSE Arca	C	C	C+	Down	119.69	12,233	-6.50	21.59	36.62	0.71	0.01
PIMCO Enhanced Short Maturity Active Exchange-Traded Fund	MINT	NYSE Arca	C	C	C+		100.95	12,147	1.71	5.71	6.83	2.14	0.00
Industrial Select Sector SPDR® Fund	XLI	NYSE Arca	C	C	C+	Down	64.41	11,901	-13.09	29.07	36.47	1.92	0.01
iShares MBS ETF	MBB	NAS CM	C-	D+	C+		104.65	11,639	0.81	4.52	12.38	2.56	0.03
iShares Russell Mid-Cap Value ETF	IWS	NYSE Arca	C	C-	C+	Down	76.35	11,177	-12.36	18.63	29.12	2.28	0.00
iShares Gold Trust	IAU	NYSE Arca	D+	D+	C-	Down	12.29	10,635	-1.37	19.79	5.30	0	0.13
iShares National Muni Bond ETF	MUB	NYSE Arca	C	C-	C+		109.04	10,565	0.86	5.57	18.10	2.45	0.06
Vanguard Health Care Index Fund ETF Shares	VHT	NYSE Arca	C+	C+	C+		160.60	10,515	4.02	24.04	66.75	1.22	0.01
Vanguard Long-Term Bond Index Fund ETF Shares	BLV	NYSE Arca	D+	D	C	Down	87.51	10,331	-4.75	12.50	30.23	4.08	0.14
Consumer Staples Select Sector SPDR® Fund	XLP	NYSE Arca	C+	B	C		50.78	10,300	-8.01	9.04	34.98	2.66	-0.02
iShares Short-Term Corporate Bond ETF	IGSB	NAS CM	E+	E+	D-	Down	51.64	10,220	-49.33	-47.70	-46.95	2.23	0.01
iShares Russell 2000 Value ETF	IWN	NYSE Arca	C	C-	C+	Down	107.54	9,645	-12.93	23.46	18.88	1.91	0.00
iShares Edge MSCI USA Momentum Factor ETF	MTUM	BATS	C+	C+	C+	Down	100.23	9,501	-1.76	41.78	77.11	1.09	0.02
iShares MSCI ACWI ETF	ACWI	NAS CM	C	C-	C+	Down	64.16	9,456	-9.21	22.17	24.79	2.11	-0.04
iShares Russell 2000 Growth ETF	IWO	NYSE Arca	C	C-	C+	Down	168.00	9,405	-9.33	23.55	29.06	0.69	0.00
iShares 7-10 Year Treasury Bond ETF	IEF	NAS CM	D+	D	C		104.20	9,265	0.82	4.34	15.40	2.2	0.00
iShares MSCI EAFE Small-Cap ETF	SCZ	NAS CM	C-	D+	C-	Down	51.82	9,071	-17.64	11.77	15.89	2.71	-0.06
iShares Edge MSCI Min Vol EAFE ETF	EFAV	BATS	C	C-	C		66.66	9,033	-5.80	12.38	26.77	2.66	-0.03
VanEck Vectors Gold Miners ETF	GDX	NYSE Arca	D+	C-	D	Down	21.09	8,936	-8.85	56.12	2.78	0.92	-0.08
iShares Russell Mid-Cap Growth ETF	IWP	NYSE Arca	C	C-	C+	Down	113.71	8,871	-4.94	27.28	41.60	0.94	0.00
Alerian MLP ETF	AMLP	NYSE Arca	C	B-	D		8.73	8,702	-12.71	-6.97	-27.75	8.49	-0.08
iShares Russell 3000 ETF	IWV	NYSE Arca	C	C	C+	Down	146.92	8,603	-5.39	28.79	45.21	1.67	0.00
Invesco S&P 500® Low Volatility ETF	SPLV	NYSE Arca	B	C	A	Up	46.65	8,398	0.03	28.92	57.22	1.99	0.02
iShares Nasdaq Biotechnology ETF	IBB	NAS CM	C	C	C-		96.43	8,353	-9.13	-13.58	29.19	0.29	0.01
Schwab U.S. Dividend Equity ETF™	SCHD	NYSE Arca	B-	B	C		46.97	8,275	-5.46	32.84	48.02	2.67	0.01
Utilities Select Sector SPDR® Fund	XLU	NYSE Arca	B	B-	B	Up	52.92	8,176	4.01	35.13	65.41	3.26	-0.01
Vanguard Financials Index Fund ETF Shares	VFH	NYSE Arca	C	C	C+	Down	59.36	8,084	-14.24	28.38	45.62	1.95	0.02
Vanguard Mortgage-Backed Securities Index Fund ETF Shares	VMBS	NAS CM	C	D+	C+	Up	51.49	8,043	0.71	4.58	12.24	2.64	0.05
iShares 3-7 Year Treasury Bond ETF	IEI	NAS CM	C-	D	C	Up	121.40	7,799	1.35	3.80	8.85	1.9	0.02

Section V:
Best One-Year Return BUY Rated Exchange-Traded Funds

Investment Ratings and analysis of the Best One-Year Return BUY Rated Exchange-Traded Funds. Funds are listed in order by their one-year returns and overall rating.

Section V: Contents

This section contains Weiss Investment Ratings, key rating factors, and summary financial data for the Best One-Year Return BUY Rated Exchange-Traded Funds. Funds are listed in order by their one-year returns and overall rating.

Fund Name
Describes the fund's assets, regions of investments and investment strategies. Many funds have similar names, so you want to make sure the fund you look up is really the one you are interested in evaluating.

MARKET

Ticker Symbol
An arrangement of characters (usually letters) representing a particular security listed on an exchange or otherwise traded publicly. When a company issues securities to the public marketplace, it selects an available ticker symbol for its securities which investors use to place trade orders. Every listed security has a unique ticker symbol, facilitating the vast array of trade orders that flow through the financial markets every day.

Traded On (Exchange)
The stock exchange on which the fund is listed. The core function of a stock exchange is to ensure fair and orderly trading, as well as efficient dissemination of price information. Exchanges such as: NYSE (New York Stock Exchange), AMEX (American Stock Exchange), NNM (NASDAQ National Market), and NASQ (NASDAQ Small Cap) give companies, governments and other groups a platform to sell securities to the investing public. NASDAQ is abbreviated as NAS.

RATINGS

Overall Rating
The Weiss rating measured on a scale from A to E based on each fund's risk and performance. See the preceding section, "What Our Ratings Mean," for an explanation of each letter grade rating.

Reward Rating
This is based on the total return over a period of up to five years, including net asset value and price growth. The total return figure is stated net of the expenses and fees charged by the fund. Based on proprietary modeling the individual components of the risk and reward ratings are calculated and weighted and the final rating is generated.

Risk Rating
This is includes the risk ratings of component stocks where applicable and also includes the financial stability of the fund, turnover where applicable, together with the level of volatility as measured by the fund's daily returns over a period of up to five years. Funds with greater stability are considered less risky and receive a higher risk rating. Funds with greater volatility are considered riskier, and will receive a lower risk rating. In addition to considering the fund's volatility, the risk rating also considers an assessment of the valuation and quality of a fund's holdings.

Recent Upgrade/Downgrade

An "Up" or "Down" indicates that the Weiss Exchange-Traded Fund rating has changed since the publication of the last print edition. If a fund has had a rating change since September 30, 2018, the change is identified with an "Up" or "Down."

PRICE

Price

The price at which the fund is traded on a regular trading day. Prices in this guide are listed as of December 31, 2018.

TOTAL RETURNS & PERFORMANCE

Total Assets (MIL)

The total of all assets listed on the institution's balance sheet. This figure primarily consists of loans, investments, and fixed assets. Total Assets are displayed in millions.

1-Year Total Return

The rate of return on an investment over one year that includes interest, capital gains, dividends and distributions realized.

3-Year Total Return

The rate of return on an investment over three years that includes interest, capital gains, dividends and distributions realized.

5-Year Total Return

The rate of return on an investment over five years that includes interest, capital gains, dividends and distributions realized.

Dividend Yield (TTM)

Trailing twelve months dividends paid out relative to the share price. Expressed as a percentage and measures how much cash flow an investor is getting for each invested dollar. **Trailing Twelve Months (TTM)** is a representation of a fund's financial performance over the most recent 12 months. TTM uses the latest available financial data from a company's interim, quarterly or annual reports.

VALUATION

Premium/Discount 1-Year Average

The annual average premium or discount of the market price to the NAV (Net Asset Value), expressed as a percentage of the NAV. This value provides a year-by-year picture a fund's trading status. A negative number indicates that, on average, the fund's shares sold at a discount to NAV, and a positive number indicates the shares sold at a premium. If the number shown is −10.00, for example, the shares sold at an average 10% discount to NAV during the listed time-period.

Fund Name	Ticker Symbol	Traded On	Overall Rating	Reward Rating	Risk Rating	Recent Up/ Downgrade	Price as of 12/31/2018	Total Assets (MIL)	1-Year Total Return	3-Year Total Return	5-Year Total Return	Dividend Yield (TTM)	Premium/ Discount 1-Year Avg
		MARKET		RATINGS			PRICE	TOTAL RETURNS & PERFORMANCE				VALUATION	
VanEck Vectors High-Yield Municipal Index ETF	HYD	BATS	B+	A	C+	Up	61.04	2,339	103.45	125.71	169.30	4.42	-0.15
VanEck Vectors AMT-Free Intermediate Municipal Index ETF	ITM	BATS	B	A	C+	Up	47.47	1,649	100.88	112.15	139.61	2.34	-0.21
VanEck Vectors J.P. Morgan EM Local Currency Bond ETF	EMLC	NYSE Arca	B	A	C+	Up	33.00	4,544	83.81	127.88	83.59	6.45	-0.04
iShares U.S. Healthcare Providers ETF	IHF	NYSE Arca	B	B	C+		165.19	1,210	9.60	38.77	85.89	0.2	0.09

Section VI:
Best Low Expense Exchange-Traded Funds

Investment Ratings and analysis of the Best Low Expense Exchange-Traded Funds. Funds are listed in order by their expense ratios and overall rating.

Section VI: Contents

This section contains Weiss Investment Ratings, key rating factors, and summary financial data for the Best Low Expense Exchange-Traded Funds. Funds are listed in order by their expense ratios and overall rating.

Fund Name
Describes the fund's assets, regions of investments and investment strategies. Many funds have similar names, so you want to make sure the fund you look up is really the one you are interested in evaluating.

MARKET

Ticker Symbol
An arrangement of characters (usually letters) representing a particular security listed on an exchange or otherwise traded publicly. When a company issues securities to the public marketplace, it selects an available ticker symbol for its securities which investors use to place trade orders. Every listed security has a unique ticker symbol, facilitating the vast array of trade orders that flow through the financial markets every day.

Traded On (Exchange)
The stock exchange on which the fund is listed. The core function of a stock exchange is to ensure fair and orderly trading, as well as efficient dissemination of price information. Exchanges such as: NYSE (New York Stock Exchange), AMEX (American Stock Exchange), NNM (NASDAQ National Market), and NASQ (NASDAQ Small Cap) give companies, governments and other groups a platform to sell securities to the investing public. NASDAQ is abbreviated as NAS.

RATINGS

Overall Rating
The Weiss rating measured on a scale from A to E based on each fund's risk and performance. See the preceding section, "What Our Ratings Mean," for an explanation of each letter grade rating.

Reward Rating
This is based on the total return over a period of up to five years, including net asset value and price growth. The total return figure is stated net of the expenses and fees charged by the fund. Based on proprietary modeling the individual components of the risk and reward ratings are calculated and weighted and the final rating is generated.

Risk Rating
This is includes the risk ratings of component stocks where applicable and also includes the financial stability of the fund, turnover where applicable, together with the level of volatility as measured by the fund's daily returns over a period of up to five years. Funds with greater stability are considered less risky and receive a higher risk rating. Funds with greater volatility are considered riskier, and will receive a lower risk rating. In addition to considering the fund's volatility, the risk rating also considers an assessment of the valuation and quality of a fund's holdings.

Recent Upgrade/Downgrade

An "Up" or "Down" indicates that the Weiss Exchange-Traded Fund rating has changed since the publication of the last print edition. If a fund has had a rating change since September 30, 2018, the change is identified with an "Up" or "Down."

PRICE

Price

The price at which the fund is traded on a regular trading day. Prices in this guide are listed as of December 31, 2018.

TOTAL RETURNS & PERFORMANCE

1-Year Total Return

The rate of return on an investment over one year that includes interest, capital gains, dividends and distributions realized.

3-Year Total Return

The rate of return on an investment over three years that includes interest, capital gains, dividends and distributions realized.

5-Year Total Return

The rate of return on an investment over five years that includes interest, capital gains, dividends and distributions realized.

Dividend Yield (TTM)

Trailing twelve months dividends paid out relative to the share price. Expressed as a percentage and measures how much cash flow an investor is getting for each invested dollar. **Trailing Twelve Months (TTM)** is a representation of a fund's financial performance over the most recent 12 months. TTM uses the latest available financial data from a company's interim, quarterly or annual reports.

Expense Ratio

A measure of what it costs an investment company to operate an exchange-traded fund. An expense ratio is determined through an annual calculation, where a fund's operating expenses are divided by the average dollar value of its assets under management. Operating expenses may include money spent on administration and management of the fund, advertising, etc. An expense ratio of 1 percent per annum means that each year 1 percent of the fund's total assets will be used to cover expenses.

VALUATION

Premium/Discount 1-Year Average

The annual average premium or discount of the market price to the NAV (Net Asset Value), expressed as a percentage of the NAV. This value provides a year-by-year picture a fund's trading status. A negative number indicates that, on average, the fund's shares sold at a discount to NAV, and a positive number indicates the shares sold at a premium. If the number shown is −10.00, for example, the shares sold at an average 10% discount to NAV during the listed time-period.

Fund Name	MARKET		RATINGS				PRICE	TOTAL RETURNS & PERFORMANCE				VALUATION	
	Ticker Symbol	Traded On	Overall Rating	Reward Rating	Risk Rating	Recent Up/Downgrade	Price as of 12/31/2018	1-Year Total Return	3-Year Total Return	5-Year Total Return	Dividend Yield (TTM)	Expense Ratio	Premium/Discount 1-Year Avg
Fidelity® MSCI Utilities Index ETF	FUTY	NYSE Arca	B-	B-	C+		34.88	4.40	37.72	66.31	3.02	0.08	0.02
Vanguard Utilities Index Fund ETF Shares	VPU	NYSE Arca	B-	B-	C+		117.83	4.09	37.65	66.26	3.01	0.1	0.00
Utilities Select Sector SPDR® Fund	XLU	NYSE Arca	B	B-	B	Up	52.92	4.01	35.13	65.41	3.26	0.13	-0.01
Health Care Select Sector SPDR® Fund	XLV	NYSE Arca	B-	B	C+		86.51	6.29	25.69	68.07	1.38	0.13	0.12
VanEck Vectors AMT-Free Intermediate Municipal Index ETF	ITM	BATS	B	A	C+	Up	47.47	100.88	112.15	139.61	2.34	0.24	-0.21
VanEck Vectors High-Yield Municipal Index ETF	HYD	BATS	B+	A	C+	Up	61.04	103.45	125.71	169.30	4.42	0.35	-0.15
Invesco S&P 500® Equal Weight Utilities ETF	RYU	NYSE Arca	B-	B	C	Up	88.76	6.95	34.57	65.37	3.08	0.4	-0.03
iShares U.S. Utilities ETF	IDU	NYSE Arca	B-	B-	C+		134.22	3.91	35.55	64.15	2.53	0.43	0.00
iShares U.S. Medical Devices ETF	IHI	NYSE Arca	B-	B	C		199.81	15.46	65.06	122.04	0.23	0.43	0.03

Section VII:
BUY Rated Exchange-Traded Funds by Category

Investment Ratings and analysis for BUY Rated Exchange-Traded Funds by Category. Within Category, funds are listed in alphabetical order.

Section VII: Contents

This section contains Weiss Investment Ratings, key rating factors, and summary financial data for BUY Rated Exchange-Traded Funds by Category. Within category, funds are listed in alphabetical order.

Fund Name
Describes the fund's assets, regions of investments and investment strategies. Many funds have similar names, so you want to make sure the fund you look up is really the one you are interested in evaluating.

MARKET

Ticker Symbol
An arrangement of characters (usually letters) representing a particular security listed on an exchange or otherwise traded publicly. When a company issues securities to the public marketplace, it selects an available ticker symbol for its securities which investors use to place trade orders. Every listed security has a unique ticker symbol, facilitating the vast array of trade orders that flow through the financial markets every day.

Traded On (Exchange)
The stock exchange on which the fund is listed. The core function of a stock exchange is to ensure fair and orderly trading, as well as efficient dissemination of price information. Exchanges such as: NYSE (New York Stock Exchange), AMEX (American Stock Exchange), NNM (NASDAQ National Market), and NASQ (NASDAQ Small Cap) give companies, governments and other groups a platform to sell securities to the investing public. NASDAQ is abbreviated as NAS.

RATINGS

Overall Rating
The Weiss rating measured on a scale from A to E based on each fund's risk and performance. See the preceding section, "What Our Ratings Mean," for an explanation of each letter grade rating.

Reward Rating
This is based on the total return over a period of up to five years, including net asset value and price growth. The total return figure is stated net of the expenses and fees charged by the fund. Based on proprietary modeling the individual components of the risk and reward ratings are calculated and weighted and the final rating is generated.

Risk Rating
This is includes the risk ratings of component stocks where applicable and also includes the financial stability of the fund, turnover where applicable, together with the level of volatility as measured by the fund's daily returns over a period of up to five years. Funds with greater stability are considered less risky and receive a higher risk rating. Funds with greater volatility are considered riskier, and will receive a lower risk rating. In addition to considering the fund's volatility, the risk rating also considers an assessment of the valuation and quality of a fund's holdings.

Recent Upgrade/Downgrade
An "Up" or "Down" indicates that the Weiss Exchange-Traded Fund rating has changed since the publication of the last print edition. If a fund has had a rating change since September 30, 2018, the change is identified with an "Up" or "Down."

PRICE

Price
The price at which the fund is traded on a regular trading day. Prices in this guide are listed as of December 31, 2018.

TOTAL RETURNS & PERFORMANCE

Total Assets (MIL)
The total of all assets listed on the institution's balance sheet. This figure primarily consists of loans, investments, and fixed assets. Total Assets are displayed in millions.

1-Year Total Return
The rate of return on an investment over one year that includes interest, capital gains, dividends and distributions realized.

3-Year Total Return
The rate of return on an investment over three years that includes interest, capital gains, dividends and distributions realized.

5-Year Total Return
The rate of return on an investment over five years that includes interest, capital gains, dividends and distributions realized.

Dividend Yield (TTM)
Trailing twelve months dividends paid out relative to the share price. Expressed as a percentage and measures how much cash flow an investor is getting for each invested dollar. **Trailing Twelve Months (TTM)** is a representation of a fund's financial performance over the most recent 12 months. TTM uses the latest available financial data from a company's interim, quarterly or annual reports.

VALUATION

Premium/Discount 1-Year Average
The annual average premium or discount of the market price to the NAV (Net Asset Value), expressed as a percentage of the NAV. This value provides a year-by-year picture a fund's trading status. A negative number indicates that, on average, the fund's shares sold at a discount to NAV, and a positive number indicates the shares sold at a premium. If the number shown is −10.00, for example, the shares sold at an average 10% discount to NAV during the listed time-period.

Category: Commodities
Specified

Fund Name	Ticker Symbol	Traded On	Overall Rating	Reward Rating	Risk Rating	Recent Up/ Downgrade	Price as of 12/31/2018	Total Assets (MIL)	1-Year Total Return	3-Year Total Return	5-Year Total Return	Dividend Yield (TTM)	Premium/ Discount 1-Year Avg
Aberdeen Standard Physical Palladium Shares ETF	PALL	NYSE Arca	B-	B+	C-	Up	119.05	159.9	18.88	126.76	72.37	0	-0.40
iPath® Global Carbon ETN	GRNTF	NYSE Arca	B-	A+	E	Down	17.90	10.4	225.95	221.73	445.54	0	-12.64

Category: Consumer Goods & Services

Fund Name	Ticker Symbol	Traded On	Overall Rating	Reward Rating	Risk Rating	Recent Up/ Downgrade	Price as of 12/31/2018	Total Assets (MIL)	1-Year Total Return	3-Year Total Return	5-Year Total Return	Dividend Yield (TTM)	Premium/ Discount 1-Year Avg
Consumer Discretionary Select Sector SPDR® Fund	XLY	NYSE Arca	B-	B	C	Down	99.01	13,593	1.66	32.14	59.04	1.19	0.01
First Trust Nasdaq Food & Beverage ETF	FTXG	NAS CM	B-	B	C		18.04		1.00	-12.38		1.35	-0.03
First Trust Nasdaq Retail ETF	FTXD	NAS CM	B-	B	C		20.84	9.1	-2.06			0.85	0.29
Invesco DWA Consumer Staples Momentum ETF	PSL	NAS CM	B-	B	C	Down	65.21	184.1	1.51	18.93	56.25	0.46	0.09
Invesco Dynamic Food & Beverage ETF	PBJ	NYSE Arca	B-	B	C		29.67	74.3	-10.77	-4.01	20.34	0.99	0.03

Category: Emerging Markets Fixed Income

Fund Name	Ticker Symbol	Traded On	Overall Rating	Reward Rating	Risk Rating	Recent Up/ Downgrade	Price as of 12/31/2018	Total Assets (MIL)	1-Year Total Return	3-Year Total Return	5-Year Total Return	Dividend Yield (TTM)	Premium/ Discount 1-Year Avg
VanEck Vectors J.P. Morgan EM Local Currency Bond ETF	EMLC	NYSE Arca	B	A	C+	Up	33.00	4,544	83.81	127.88	83.59	6.45	-0.04

Category: Equity
Miscellaneous

Fund Name	Ticker Symbol	Traded On	Overall Rating	Reward Rating	Risk Rating	Recent Up/ Downgrade	Price as of 12/31/2018	Total Assets (MIL)	1-Year Total Return	3-Year Total Return	5-Year Total Return	Dividend Yield (TTM)	Premium/ Discount 1-Year Avg
ETFMG Prime Mobile Payments ETF	IPAY	NYSE Arca	B-	B	C+	Up	34.95	419.8	1.33	44.41		0.02	0.09

Category: Financials
Sector Equity

Fund Name	Ticker Symbol	Traded On	Overall Rating	Reward Rating	Risk Rating	Recent Up/ Downgrade	Price as of 12/31/2018	Total Assets (MIL)	1-Year Total Return	3-Year Total Return	5-Year Total Return	Dividend Yield (TTM)	Premium/ Discount 1-Year Avg
First Trust Nasdaq Bank ETF	FTXO	NAS CM	B-	B	C	Down	22.26	222.6	-21.57			1.58	0.02
Invesco KBW Bank ETF	KBWB	NAS CM	B-	B	C	Down	43.98	864.7	-17.95	24.12	35.44	1.93	0.03
Invesco KBW Property & Casualty Insurance ETF	KBWP	NAS CM	B-	B	C		56.62	64.0	-2.24	26.85	61.23	2.3	0.19
iShares U.S. Broker-Dealers & Securities Exchanges ETF	IAI	NYSE Arca	B-	B	C		56.03	251.5	-9.29	42.19	56.17	1.43	0.02
iShares U.S. Financial Services ETF	IYG	NYSE Arca	B-	B	C+	Down	112.27	1,683	-12.44	30.59	43.84	1.48	0.03
iShares U.S. Regional Banks ETF	IAT	NYSE Arca	B-	B	C	Down	39.84	691.3	-17.38	20.70	32.11	1.87	-0.01

Category: Healthcare
Sector Equity

Fund Name	Ticker Symbol	Traded On	Overall Rating	Reward Rating	Risk Rating	Recent Up/ Downgrade	Price as of 12/31/2018	Total Assets (MIL)	1-Year Total Return	3-Year Total Return	5-Year Total Return	Dividend Yield (TTM)	Premium/ Discount 1-Year Avg
Health Care Select Sector SPDR® Fund	XLV	NYSE Arca	B-	B	C+		86.51	19,897	6.29	25.69	68.07	1.38	0.12
iShares U.S. Healthcare Providers ETF	IHF	NYSE Arca	B	B	C+		165.19	1,210	9.60	38.77	85.89	0.2	0.09
iShares U.S. Medical Devices ETF	IHI	NYSE Arca	B-	B	C		199.81	3,074	15.46	65.06	122.04	0.23	0.03

Category: Industrials Sector Equity

Fund Name	Ticker Symbol	Traded On	Overall Rating	Reward Rating	Risk Rating	Recent Up/ Downgrade	Price as of 12/31/2018	Total Assets (MIL)	1-Year Total Return	3-Year Total Return	5-Year Total Return	Dividend Yield (TTM)	Premium/ Discount 1-Year Avg
First Trust Nasdaq Transportation ETF	FTXR	NAS CM	B-	B	C		21.64	2.5	-15.00			1.32	0.03
Invesco Aerospace & Defense ETF	PPA	NYSE Arca	B-	B	C+	Down	49.45	906.1	-7.35	43.58	68.74	0.56	0.03
Invesco Water Resources ETF	PHO	NAS CM	B-	B	C		28.21	813.5	-6.26	31.87	10.59	0.34	0.00
iShares Transportation Average ETF	IYT	BATS	B	B+	C		165.01	732.1	-12.82	26.54	31.81	1.08	-0.01
iShares U.S. Aerospace & Defense ETF	ITA	BATS	B-	B	C+	Down	172.86	5,339	-7.15	51.10	72.68	1.06	0.01
SPDR® S&P Aerospace & Defense ETF	XAR	NYSE Arca	B-	B	C	Down	78.92	1,385	-4.45	54.02	70.02	1.02	0.04
VanEck Vectors Environmental Services ETF	EVX	NYSE Arca	B-	B	C		83.26	23.4	-3.12	45.80	34.12	0.87	0.35

Category: Long/Short Equity

Fund Name	Ticker Symbol	Traded On	Overall Rating	Reward Rating	Risk Rating	Recent Up/ Downgrade	Price as of 12/31/2018	Total Assets (MIL)	1-Year Total Return	3-Year Total Return	5-Year Total Return	Dividend Yield (TTM)	Premium/ Discount 1-Year Avg
Amplify YieldShares CWP Dividend & Option Income ETF	DIVO	BATS	B-	B	C	Down	26.72	16.1	-2.47			5.6	0.20

Category: Real Estate Sector Equity

Fund Name	Ticker Symbol	Traded On	Overall Rating	Reward Rating	Risk Rating	Recent Up/ Downgrade	Price as of 12/31/2018	Total Assets (MIL)	1-Year Total Return	3-Year Total Return	5-Year Total Return	Dividend Yield (TTM)	Premium/ Discount 1-Year Avg
iShares Cohen & Steers REIT ETF	ICF	BATS	B-	B	C		95.70	2,021	-2.45	7.05	52.09	3.09	-0.03
iShares Mortgage Real Estate Capped ETF	REM	BATS	B-	B	C		39.94	1,236	-2.95	40.34	48.51	10.11	-0.02
NuShares Short-Term REIT ETF	NURE	BATS	B-	B	C		24.99	32.9	-2.09			3.21	-0.40
The Real Estate Select Sector SPDR Fund	XLRE	NYSE Arca	B-	B	C		31.00	2,786	-2.27	11.58		3.44	0.00

Category: Technology Sector Equity

Fund Name	Ticker Symbol	Traded On	Overall Rating	Reward Rating	Risk Rating	Recent Up/ Downgrade	Price as of 12/31/2018	Total Assets (MIL)	1-Year Total Return	3-Year Total Return	5-Year Total Return	Dividend Yield (TTM)	Premium/ Discount 1-Year Avg
iShares PHLX Semiconductor ETF	SOXX	NAS CM	B-	B	C-	Down	156.91	1,288	-6.47	81.00	130.26	1.26	-0.01
iShares U.S. Technology ETF	IYW	NYSE Arca	B-	B	C	Down	159.93	3,734	-0.96	53.78	90.48	0.82	0.01
Technology Select Sector SPDR® Fund	XLK	NYSE Arca	B	B	C+		61.98	19,121	-1.55	51.75	88.73	1.42	0.03

Category: Trading Tools

Fund Name	Ticker Symbol	Traded On	Overall Rating	Reward Rating	Risk Rating	Recent Up/ Downgrade	Price as of 12/31/2018	Total Assets (MIL)	1-Year Total Return	3-Year Total Return	5-Year Total Return	Dividend Yield (TTM)	Premium/ Discount 1-Year Avg
VelocityShares 3x Long Gold ETN - S&P GSCI® Gold Ind ER	UGLD	NAS CM	B	A-	D+	Up	95.41	126.8	742.64	1,185.54	640.19	0	0.04
VelocityShares 3x Long Silver ETN - S&P GSCI® Silver Ind E	USLV	NAS CM	B-	A-	D+	Up	74.10	233.4	521.72	659.22	65.14	0	-0.23

Category: US Equity Large Cap Blend

Fund Name	Ticker Symbol	Traded On	Overall Rating	Reward Rating	Risk Rating	Recent Up/ Downgrade	Price as of 12/31/2018	Total Assets (MIL)	1-Year Total Return	3-Year Total Return	5-Year Total Return	Dividend Yield (TTM)	Premium/ Discount 1-Year Avg
AdvisorShares Focused Equity ETF	CWS	NYSE Arca	B-	B	C		28.70	14.7	-7.38			0.27	0.37
Aptus Behavioral Momentum ETF	BEMO	BATS	B-	B	C	Down	28.25	75.9	-5.88			0.31	0.08
iShares Edge MSCI Min Vol USA ETF	USMV	BATS	B	C	A	Up	52.40	19,373	1.35	33.24	63.54	1.81	-0.02

Category: US Equity — Large Cap Growth

Fund Name	Ticker Symbol	Traded On	Overall Rating	Reward Rating	Risk Rating	Recent Up/ Downgrade	Price as of 12/31/2018	Total Assets (MIL)	1-Year Total Return	3-Year Total Return	5-Year Total Return	Dividend Yield (TTM)	Premium/ Discount 1-Year Avg
Invesco QQQ Trust	QQQ	NAS CM	B-	C+	B	Down	154.26	65,965	-0.14	41.79	85.01	0.78	0.06
Ivy Focused Growth NextShares™	IVFGC	NAS CM	B	B+	C+		26.09		12.8	5.18		0.23	0.00

Category: US Equity — Large Cap Value

Fund Name	Ticker Symbol	Traded On	Overall Rating	Reward Rating	Risk Rating	Recent Up/ Downgrade	Price as of 12/31/2018	Total Assets (MIL)	1-Year Total Return	3-Year Total Return	5-Year Total Return	Dividend Yield (TTM)	Premium/ Discount 1-Year Avg
First Trust Dow 30 Equal Weight ETF	EDOW	NYSE Arca	B-	B	C	Up	21.31	51.6	-0.89			1.78	0.30
Invesco S&P 500® Low Volatility ETF	SPLV	NYSE Arca	B	C	A	Up	46.65	8,398	0.03	28.92	57.22	1.99	0.02
iShares Core High Dividend ETF	HDV	NYSE Arca	B-	B	C	Up	84.38	6,672	-2.92	27.41	43.02	3.42	0.00
Schwab U.S. Dividend Equity ETF™	SCHD	NYSE Arca	B-	B	C		46.97	8,275	-5.46	32.84	48.02	2.67	0.01
SPDR® Dow Jones Industrial Average ETF	DIA	NYSE Arca	B-	B	C+	Down	233.20	22,258	-3.60	43.44	57.76	2.02	0.05

Category: US Municipal — Fixed Income

Fund Name	Ticker Symbol	Traded On	Overall Rating	Reward Rating	Risk Rating	Recent Up/ Downgrade	Price as of 12/31/2018	Total Assets (MIL)	1-Year Total Return	3-Year Total Return	5-Year Total Return	Dividend Yield (TTM)	Premium/ Discount 1-Year Avg
VanEck Vectors AMT-Free Intermediate Municipal Index ETF	ITM	BATS	B	A	C+	Up	47.47	1,649	100.88	112.15	139.61	2.34	-0.21
VanEck Vectors High-Yield Municipal Index ETF	HYD	BATS	B+	A	C+	Up	61.04	2,339	103.45	125.71	169.30	4.42	-0.15

Category: Utilities — Sector Equity

Fund Name	Ticker Symbol	Traded On	Overall Rating	Reward Rating	Risk Rating	Recent Up/ Downgrade	Price as of 12/31/2018	Total Assets (MIL)	1-Year Total Return	3-Year Total Return	5-Year Total Return	Dividend Yield (TTM)	Premium/ Discount 1-Year Avg
Fidelity® MSCI Utilities Index ETF	FUTY	NYSE Arca	B-	B-	C+		34.88	488.8	4.40	37.72	66.31	3.02	0.02
First Trust Utilities AlphaDEX® Fund	FXU	NYSE Arca	B	B+	C+	Up	26.78	390.5	5.59	30.61	53.40	3.04	0.01
Invesco DWA Utilities Momentum ETF	PUI	NAS CM	B	B	C+	Up	28.96	69.8	6.10	41.06	60.02	2.27	0.04
Invesco S&P 500® Equal Weight Utilities ETF	RYU	NYSE Arca	B-	B	C	Up	88.76	268.8	6.95	34.57	65.37	3.08	-0.03
iShares U.S. Utilities ETF	IDU	NYSE Arca	B-	B-	C+		134.22	795.7	3.91	35.55	64.15	2.53	0.00
Reaves Utilities ETF	UTES	NYSE Arca	B	B	C+	Up	33.52	14.2	5.42	38.46		1.96	-0.06
Utilities Select Sector SPDR® Fund	XLU	NYSE Arca	B	B-	B	Up	52.92	8,176	4.01	35.13	65.41	3.26	-0.01
Vanguard Utilities Index Fund ETF Shares	VPU	NYSE Arca	B-	B-	C+		117.83	4,276	4.09	37.65	66.26	3.01	0.00

Appendix:

Glossary

This section contains an explanation of the fields of data used throughout this guide.

1-Year Total Return
The rate of return on an investment over one year that includes interest, capital gains, dividends and distributions realized.

3-Year Total Return
The rate of return on an investment over three years that includes interest, capital gains, dividends and distributions realized.

3-Month Total Return
The rate of return on an investment over three months that includes interest, capital gains, dividends and distributions realized.

3-Year Standard Deviation
A statistical measurement of dispersion about an average, which depicts how widely the returns varied over the past three years. Investors use the standard deviation of historical performance to try to predict the range of returns that are most likely for a given fund. When a fund has a high standard deviation, the predicted range of performance is wide, implying greater volatility. Standard deviation is most appropriate for measuring risk if it is for a fund that is an investor's only holding. The figure cannot be combined for more than one fund because the standard deviation for a portfolio of multiple funds is a function of not only the individual standard deviations, but also of the degree of correlation among the funds' returns. If a fund's returns follow a normal distribution, then approximately 68 percent of the time they will fall within one standard deviation of the mean return for the fund, and 95 percent of the time within two standard deviations.

5-Year Total Return
The rate of return on an investment over five years that includes interest, capital gains, dividends and distributions realized.

52-Week High
The highest price that a fund has achieved during the previous 52 weeks.

52-Week Low
The lowest price that a fund has achieved during the previous 52 weeks.

6-Month Total Return
The rate of return on an investment over six months that includes interest, capital gains, dividends and distributions realized.

Address
The company's street address.

Asset & Performance History
Indicates the fund's **NAV (Net Asset Value)** and **1-Year Total Return** for the previous 6 years.

Asset Allocation
Indicates the percentage of assets in each category. Used as an investment strategy that attempts to balance risk versus reward by adjusting the percentage of each asset in an investment portfolio according to the investor's risk tolerance, goals and investment time frame. Allocation percentages may not add up to 100%. Negative values reflect short positions. See Cash, Stocks, US Stocks, Bonds, US Bonds, Other)

Bonds (%)
The percentage of the fund's assets invested in bonds. A bond is an unsecured debt security issued by companies, municipalities, states and sovereign governments to raise funds. When a company issues a bond it borrows money from the bondholder to boost the business, in exchange the bondholder receives the principal amount back plus the interest on the determined maturity date.

BUY-HOLD-SELL Indicator
Funds that are rated in the A or B range are, in our opinion, a potential BUY. Funds in the C range will indicate a HOLD status. Funds in the D or E range will indicate a SELL status.

Cash (%)
The percentage of the fund's assets invested in short-term obligations, usually less than 90 days, that provide a return in the form of interest payments. This type of investment generally offers a low return compared to other investments but has a low risk level.

Category
Identifies funds according to their actual investment styles as measured by their portfolio holdings. This categorization allows investors to spread their money around in a mix of funds with a variety of risk and return characteristics.

Dividend Yield (TTM)
Trailing twelve months dividends paid out relative to the share price. Expressed as a percentage and measures how much cash flow an investor is getting for each invested dollar. **Trailing Twelve Months** (TTM) is a representation of a fund's financial performance over the most recent 12 months. TTM uses the latest available financial data from a company's interim, quarterly or annual reports.

Effective Duration
Effective duration for all long fixed income positions in a portfolio. This value gives a better estimation of how the price of bonds with embedded options, which are common in many exchange-traded funds, will change as a result of changes in interest rates. Effective duration takes into account expected mortgage prepayment or the likelihood that embedded options will be exercised if a fund holds futures, other derivative securities, or other funds as assets, the aggregate effective duration should include the weighted impact of those exposures.

Expense Ratio

A measure of what it costs an investment company to operate an exchange-traded fund. An expense ratio is determined through an annual calculation, where a fund's operating expenses are divided by the average dollar value of its assets under management. Operating expenses may include money spent on administration and management of the fund, advertising, etc. An expense ratio of 1 percent per annum means that each year 1 percent of the fund's total assets will be used to cover expenses.

Fund Name

Describes the fund's assets, regions of investments and investment strategies. Many funds have similar names, so you want to make sure the fund you look up is really the one you are interested in evaluating.

Inception Date

The date on which the fund began its operations. The commencement date indicates when a fund began investing in the market. Many investors prefer funds with longer operating histories. Funds with longer histories have longer track records and can thereby provide investors with a more long-standing picture of their performance.

Institutional Only

This indicates if the fund is offered to institutional clients only (pension funds, mutual funds, money managers, insurance companies, investment banks, commercial trusts, endowment funds, hedge funds, and some hedge fund investors). See **Services Offered**.

Investment Strategy

A set of rules, behaviors or procedures, designed to guide an investor's selection of an investment portfolio. Individuals have different profit objectives, and their individual skills make different tactics and strategies appropriate.

Manager/Tenure (Years)

The name of the manager and the number of years spent managing the fund.

NAV (Net Asset Value)

A fund's price per share. The value is calculated by dividing the total value of all the securities in the portfolio, less any liabilities, by the number of fund shares outstanding.

Open to New Investments

Indicates whether the fund accepts investments from those who are not existing investors. A "Y" in this column identifies that the fund accepts new investors. No data in this column indicates that the fund is closed to new investors. The fund may be closed to new investors because the fund's asset base is getting too large to effectively execute its investing style. Although, the fund may be closed, in most cases, existing investors are able to add to their holdings.

Other (%)
The percentage of the fund's assets invested in other financial instruments. See **Asset Allocation**.

Overall Rating
The Weiss rating measured on a scale from A to E based on each fund's risk and performance. See the preceding section, "What Our Ratings Mean," for an explanation of each letter grade rating.

Performance Chart
A graphical representation of the fund's total returns over the past year.

Phone Exchange
This indicates that investors can move money between different funds within the same fund family over the phone. See **Services Offered**.

Phone Number
The company's phone number.

Premium/Discount 1-Year Average
The annual average premium or discount of the market price to the NAV (Net Asset Value), expressed as a percentage of the NAV. This value provides a year-by-year picture a fund's trading status. A negative number indicates that, on average, the fund's shares sold at a discount to NAV, and a positive number indicates the shares sold at a premium. If the number shown is −10.00, for example, the shares sold at an average 10% discount to NAV during the listed time-period.

Price
The price at which the fund is traded on a regular trading day. Prices in this guide are listed as of December 31, 2018.

Prospectus Objective
Gives a general idea of a fund's overall investment approach and goals.

Provider
The legal company that issues the fund.

Ratings History
Indicates the fund's Overall, Risk and Reward Ratings for the previous four years. Ratings are listed as of December 31, 2018 (Q4-18), June 30, 2018 (Q2-18), December 31, 2017 (Q4-17), December 31, 2016 (Q4-16), and December 31, 2015 (Q4-15).
See **Overall Rating, Risk Rating, Reward Rating**.

Recent Upgrade/Downgrade
An "Up" or "Down" indicates that the Weiss Exchange-Traded Fund rating has changed since the publication of the last print edition. If a fund has had a rating change since September 30, 2018, the change is identified with an "Up" or "Down."

Reward Rating

This is based on the total return over a period of up to five years, including net asset value and price growth. The total return figure is stated net of the expenses and fees charged by the fund. Based on proprietary modeling the individual components of the risk and reward ratings are calculated and weighted and the final rating is generated.

Risk Rating

This is includes the risk ratings of component stocks where applicable and also includes the financial stability of the fund, turnover where applicable, together with the level of volatility as measured by the fund's daily returns over a period of up to five years. Funds with greater stability are considered less risky and receive a higher risk rating. Funds with greater volatility are considered riskier, and will receive a lower risk rating. In addition to considering the fund's volatility, the risk rating also considers an assessment of the valuation and quality of a fund's holdings.

Services Offered

Services offered by the fund provider. Such services can include:

Systematic Withdrawal Plan

A plan offered by exchange-traded funds that pays specific amounts to shareholders at predetermined intervals.

Institutional Only

This indicates if the fund is offered to institutional clients only (pension funds, mutual funds, money managers, insurance companies, investment banks, commercial trusts, endowment funds, hedge funds, and some hedge fund investors).

Phone Exchange

This indicates that investors can move money between different funds within the same fund family over the phone.

Wire Redemption

This indicates whether or not investors can redeem electronically.

Qualified Investment

Under a qualified plan, an investor may invest in the variable annuity with pretax dollars through an employee pension plan, such as a 401(k) or 403(b). Money builds up on a tax-deferred basis, and when the qualified investor makes a withdrawal or annuitizes, all contributions received are taxable income.

Stocks (%)

The percentage of the fund's assets invested in stock. See **Asset Allocation**.

Sub-Category

A subdivision of funds, usually with common characteristics as the category.

Systematic Withdrawal Plan
A plan offered by exchange-traded funds that pays specific amounts to shareholders at predetermined intervals. See **Services Offered**.

Ticker Symbol
An arrangement of characters (usually letters) representing a particular security listed on an exchange or otherwise traded publicly. When a company issues securities to the public marketplace, it selects an available ticker symbol for its securities which investors use to place trade orders. Every listed security has a unique ticker symbol, facilitating the vast array of trade orders that flow through the financial markets every day.

Top Holdings
The highest amount of publicly traded assets held by a fund. These publicly traded assets may include company stock, mutual funds or other investment vehicles.

Total Returns (%)
See **3-Month Total Return, 6-Month Total Return, 1-Year Total Return, 3-Year Total Return, 5-Year Total Return**.

Traded On (Exchange)
The stock exchange on which the fund is listed. The core function of a stock exchange is to ensure fair and orderly trading, as well as efficient dissemination of price information. Exchanges such as: NYSE (New York Stock Exchange), AMEX (American Stock Exchange), NNM (NASDAQ National Market), and NASQ (NASDAQ Small Cap) give companies, governments and other groups a platform to sell securities to the investing public. NASDAQ is abbreviated as NAS.

Turnover Ratio
The percentage of an exchange-traded fund or other investment vehicle's holdings that have been replaced with other holdings in a given year. Generally, low turnover ratio is favorable, because high turnover equates to higher brokerage transaction fees, which reduce fund returns.

US Bonds %
The percentage of the fund's assets invested in U.S. bonds. See **Asset Allocation**.

US Stocks %
The percentage of the fund's assets invested in U.S. stock. See **Asset Allocation**.

Website
The company's web address.

Wire Redemption
This indicates whether or not investors can redeem electronically. See **Services Offered**.

This section lists all of the Providers in Section I: Index of Exchange-Traded Funds. Address,
Telephone and Website are provided where available.

AAM
AAM 18925 Base Camp Road Monument CO 80132
United States
800-617-0004
http://www.aamlive.com/ETF

Aberdeen Standard Investments
Aberdeen Standard Investments 405 Lexington Avenue
New York NY 10174 United States
212-918-4954
http://www.aberdeenstandardetfs.us

AdvisorShares
AdvisorShares 2 Bethesda Metro Center, Suite 1330
Bethesda MD 20814 United States
877-843-3831
http://www.advisorshares.com

Affinity
Affinity 18111 Von Karman Ave., Suite 550 Irvine CA
92612 United States
http://www.affinityinvestment.com

AGFiQ
53 State Street Suite 1308 Boston MA 02109 United
States
617-292-9801
http://www.agfiq.com

AllianceBernstein
AllianceBernstein 11345 Avenue of the Americas New
York NY 10105 United States
212-969-1000
http://www.abglobal.com

Alpha Architect
Alpha Architect 213 Foxcroft Road Broomall PA 19008
United States
http://www.alphaarchitect.com/funds

AlphaClone
AlphaClone One Market Street Spear Tower, 36th Floor
San Francisco CA 94105 United States
415-967-2532
http://www.alphaclonefunds.com

AlphaMark
AlphaMark Funds PO Box 46707 Cincinatti OH 45246-
0707 United States
866-420-3350
http://www.alphamarkfunds.com

ALPS
ALPS 1290 Broadway, Suite 1100 Denver CO 80203
United States
866-759-5679
http://www.alpsfunds.com

ALPS ETF
ALPS ETF PO Box 328 Denver CO 80201-0328 United
States
855-724-0450
http://www.alpsfunds.com

American Century Investments
American Century Investments P.O. Box 419200,4500
Main Street Kansas City, MO 64141 United States
800-444-4015
http://www.americancentury.com

Amplifyetfs
3250 Lacey Road, Suite 130 Downers Grove Downers
Grove IL 60515 United States
630-487-2530
http://www.amplifyetfs.com

Aptus Capital Advisors
407 Johnson Avenue, Fairhope, Alabama 36532 United
States

ARK ETF Trust
ARK ETF Trust 155 West 19th Street, 5th Floor New York
New York 10011 United States
212-426-7040
http://www.ark-funds.com

ArrowShares
c/o Gemini Fund Services, LLC 17605 Wright Street,
Suite 2 Omaha NE 68130 United States
877-277-6933
http://www.ArrowShares.com

Barclays Funds
2-4, rue Eugène Ruppert L-2453 Luxembourg
Luxembourg L-2453 Luxembourg

BlueStar Global Investors
UnitedStates United States
http://www.BlueStarIndexes.com.

BMO Capital Markets
BMO Capital Markets United States
http://https://www.bmocm.com/

BMO Capital Markets Corp.
3 Times Square New York, NY 10036 United States

BOON
BOON P.O. Box 701 Milwaukee WI 53201-0701 United
States
800-617-0004
http://www.tboonetf.com

Brandes

Brandes 11988 El Camino Real, Suite 500 San Diego CA
92130 United States
800-331-2979
http://www.brandesfunds.com/

Calvert Investments

Calvert Investments, Inc. 4550 Montgomery Ave. Suite
1000N. Bethesda MD 20814 United States
800-368-2745
http://www.calvert.com

CAMBRIA ETF TRUST

CAMBRIA ETF TRUST 2711 Centreville Road Suite 400
Wilmington, DE 19808 Wilmington DE 19808 United
States
310-683-5500
http://www.cambriafunds.com

Causeway

Causeway 1 Freedom Valley Drive Oaks PA 19465
United States
866-947-7000
http://www.causewayfunds.com

CBOE Vest

CBOE Vest 8730 Stony Point Parkway, Suite 205
Richmond VA 23235 United States
855-505-8378
http://www.cboevestfunds.com

Change Finance

Change Finance United States
http://www.changefinanceetf.com

Citigroup

Citigroup United States

ClearShares

ClearShares United States
http://www.clear-shares.com

Columbia

Liberty Financial Funds P.O. Box 8081 Boston MA
02266-8081 United States
800-345-6611
http://www.columbiathreadneedleus.com

Credit Suisse AG

Kilmore House Park Lane Dublin Ireland

Credit Suisse AG

Luxembourg Luxembourg Luxembourg na Luxembourg
352-436-1611
http://www.credit-suisse.com

CSOP Asset Management

2801-2803, Two Exchange Square 8 Connaught Place
Central, Hong Kong Hong Kong
http://www.csopasset.us/en-us/product/etf/a50

Davis ETFs

c/o Davis Selected Advisers, L.P. 2949 E. Elvira Rd., Ste.
101 Tucson Arizona 85756 United States
800-279-0279

Defiance ETFs

450 West 42nd Street New York United States

DeltaShares

DeltaShares United States
http://www.deltashares.com

Deutsche Asset Management

Deutsche Asset & Wealth Management 345 Park Avenue
New York NY 10154 United States
844-851-4255
http://www.deutsche-etfs.com

Deutsche Bank AG

Theodor-Heuss-Allee 72 Frankfurt am Main 60486
Germany

Diamond Hill Funds

Diamond Hill Funds 325 John H. Mcconnell
Boulevard,Suite 200 Columbus OH 43215 United States
888-226-5595
http://www.diamond-hill.com

Direxion Funds

Direxion Funds 1301 Avenue Of The Americas (6th
Avenue) New York NY 10019 United States
646-572-3390
http://www.direxionfunds.com

Eaton Vance

P.O. Boc 43027 Providence RI 02940-3027 United
States

ELEMENTS

ELEMENTS United States
212-449-2957
http://www.elementsetn.com

EMQQ

EMQQ 1 Freedom Valley Drive Oaks PA 19456 United
States
855-888-9892
http://www.emqqetf.com

EntrepreneurShares

EntrepreneurShares 175 Federal Street, Suite #875
Boston MA 02110 United States
http://www.ershares.com

Equbot

Equbot 450 Townsend St San Francisco United States
650-451-5497
http://www.equbotetf.com

ETF Managers Capital LLC

ETF Managers Capital LLC United States

ETF Managers Trust
FACTORSHARES TRUST 35 Beechwood Road, Suite.
2B Summit NJ 07901 United States
877-756-
http://www.ise.com/

ETHO Capital
United States United States
http://www.ethocapitaletfs.com

EVENT SHARES
EVENT SHARES c/o Active Weighting Advisors LLC New
York 10281 United States
877-539-1510
http://www.eventshares.com

Exchange Traded Concepts
10900 Hefner Pointe Drive, Suite 207, Oklahoma City,
Oklahoma 73120 Oklahoma City United States

Exchange Traded Concepts Trust
3555 Northwest 58th Street Suite 410 Oklahoma City OK
73112 United States
405-778-8377
http://www.exchangetradedconcepts.com

Exponential ETFs
Exponential ETFs United States
http://https://exponentialetfs.com/

Fidelity Investments
Fidelity Investments 82 Devonshire Street Boston MA
2109 United States
617-563-7000
http://www.institutional.fidelity.com

First Trust
First Trust 120 E. Liberty Drive, Suite 400 Wheaton IL
60187 United States
800-621-1675
http://www.ftportfolios.com/

Flexshares Trust
50 South LaSalle Street Chicago, Illinois 60603 Chicago
Illinois 60603 United States
855-353-9383
http://www.flexshares.com

FormulaFolioFunds
89 Ionia NW, Suite 600 Grand Rapids, MI 49503 United
States

Franklin Templeton Investments
Franklin Templeton Investments One Franklin Parkway,
Building 970, 1st Floor San Mateo CA 94403 United
States
650-312-2000
http://www.franklintempleton.com

Gabelli
Gabelli 1 Corporate Center Rye NY NY United States
914-921-5135
http://www.gabelli.com

GaveKal
GaveKal United States
http://www.gavekalfunds.com

Global X Funds
Global X Funds 600 Lexington Avenue, 20th Floor New
York NY 10022 United States
888-493-8631
http://www.globalxfunds.com

Goldman Sachs
Goldman Sachs 200 West Stree New York NY 10282
United States
800-526-7384
http://www.gsamfunds.com

Graniteshares
Graniteshares 30 Vesey Street, 9th Floor New York New
York 10007 United States
http://www.graniteshares.com

Grayscale
Grayscale 636 Avenue of the Americas New York New
York 10011 United States
212-668-5920
http://grayscale.co/bitcoin-investment-trust/#overview

Hartford Funds
690 Lee Road Wayne PA 19087 United States
800-456-7526
http://www.hartfordfunds.com

Highland Funds
Highland Funds 200 Crescent Court, Suite 700 Dallas TX
75201 United States
877-665-1287
http://www.highlandfunds.com

Hull Tactical Funds
Hull Tactical Funds United States
http://www.hulltacticalfunds.com

Impact Shares
DALLAS, TEXAS United States
http://https://www.impactshares.org.

IndexIQ
IndexIQ 800 Westchester Avenue, Suite N-611 Rye
Brook NY 10573 United States
888-934-0777
http://www.indexiq.com

Innovation Shares
Innovation Shares 10900 Hefner Pointe Drive, Suite 207
Oklahoma City OK 73120 United States
833-466-6383
http://www.innovationshares.com

Innovator ETFs
Innovator ETFs 120 N Hale Street, Suite 200 Wheaton IL
60187 United States
800-208-5212
http://innovatoretfs.com/

InsightShares
InsightShares 10900 Hefner Pointe Drive, Suite 207
Oklahoma City OK 73120 United States
833-627-2417
http://www.insightshares.com

Inspire
Inspire 650 San Benito Street, Suite 130 Hollister CA
95023 United States

Invesco
Invesco 11 Greenway Plaza, Ste. 2500 Houston TX
77046 United States
800-659-1005
http://www.invesco.com/us

iShares
iShares 400 Howard Street San Francisco CA 94105
United States
800-474-2737
http://www.ishares.com

Ivy Funds
Ivy Funds 6300 Lamar Avenue, P.O. Box 29217 Overland
Park KS 66202 United States
800-777-6472
http://www.ivyfunds.com

James ETF
James ETF 10900 Hefner Pointe Drive, Suite 207
Oklahoma City OK 73120 United States
866-703-2278
http://www.jamesetf.com

Janus Henderson
Janus 151 Detroit Street Denver CO 80206 United States
877-335-2687
http://www.janus.com

John Hancock
601 Congress Street, Boston MA 02210 United States
800-225-5913
http://jhinvestments.com

JPMorgan
JPMorgan 270 Park Avenue New York NY 10017-2070
United States
800-480-4111
http://www.jpmorganfunds.com

JPMorgan Chase Financial Company LLC
383 Madison Avenue Floor 21 NY NY 10179 United
States

KraneShares
1350 Avenue of the Americas Second Floor New York
NY 10019 United States
855-857-2638
http://www.kraneshares.com

Legg Mason
Legg Mason/Western 100 International Drive Baltimore
MD 21202 United States
877-721-1926
http://www.leggmason.com

Little Harbor Advisers, LLC
Little Harbor Advisers, LLC 30 Doaks Lane Marblehead
MA 01945 United States
781-639-3000

Loncar Investments
Loncar Investments United States
http://www.LoncarFunds.com

Main Management ETFs
Main Management ETFs 601 California Street, Suite 620
San Francisco CA 94108 United States
http://www.mainmgtetfs.com

Market Vectors
MARKET VECTORS 335 MADISON AVENUE - 19TH
FLOOR New York NY 10017 United States
888-658-8287
http://www.marketvectorsetfs.com

Merk Funds
Merk Funds P.O. Box 588 Portland ME 4112 United
States
866-637-5386
http://www.merkfund.com

Metaurus
Metaurus 589 Fifth Avenue, Suite 808 New York NY
10017 United States
212-634-4250
http://https://www.metaurus.com/

Milleis Investissements Funds
2-4, rue Eugène Ruppert L-2453 Luxembourg
Luxembourg L-2453 Luxembourg

Motley Fool
Motley Fool 2000 Duke Street, Suite 175 Alexandria VA
22314 United States
http://www.foolfunds.com

Nationwide
Nationwide One Nationwide Plaza Columbus OH 43215
United States
800-848-0920
http://www.nationwide.com/mutualfunds

Natixis Funds
Natixis Funds 399 Boylston Street Boston MA 02116
United States
800-862-4863
http://NGAM.natixis.com

Nuveen
Nuveen Investment Trust John Nuveen & Co. Inc.
Chicago IL 60606 United States
312-917-8146
http://www.nuveen.com

Ocean Capital Advisors
28 K Street Southeast, 805 Washington DC 20003
United States
202-505-0277
http://www.ocafunds.com

OppenheimerFunds
OppenheimerFunds 12100 East Iliff Avenue, Suite 300,
Aurora, Colorado Aurora CO 80217-5270 United States
800-225-5677
http://www.oppenheimerfunds.com

O'Shares Investments
O'Shares Investments 60 State Street, Suite 700 Boston
MA 02109 United States
617-855-7670
http://www.oshares.com

Pacer
Pacer 16 Industrial Blvd, Suite 201 Paoli PA 19301
United States
http://www.paceretfs.com

Peritus
Peritus 10900 Hefner Pointe Drive, Suite 207 Oklahoma
City OK 73120 United States
http://www.hyldetf.com

PGIM Funds (Prudential)
PGIM Funds (Prudential) PO Box 9658 Providence RI
02940 United States
http://www.pgiminvestments.com

PIMCO
PIMCO 840 Newport Center Drive, Suite 100 Newport
Beach CA 92660 United States
866-746-2602
http://www.pimco.com

Point Bridge Capital
Point Bridge Capital P.O. Box 701 Milwaukee WI 53201-
0701 United States
800-617-0004
http://www.investpolitically.com

PPTY
US United States
http://https://pptyetf.com

Premise Capital
300 East 5th Avenue Suite 265 Naperville IL 60563
United States
630-596-9911
http://www.premisecapital.com

Principal Funds
Principal Funds 30 Dan Road Canton MA 2021 United
States
800-787-1621
http://www.principalfunds.com

ProShares
ProShares 7501 Wisconsin Avenue, Suite 1000 Bethesda
MD 20814 United States
866-776-5125
http://www.proshares.com

Pure Funds
http://www.etfmgfunds.com

QUANTX
QUANTX 6400 S. Fiddlers Green Circle, Ste 350
Greenwood Village CO 80111 United States
http://www.quantxfunds.com

Reality Shares ETF Trust
Reality Shares ETF Trust 402 West Broadway, Suite
2800 San Diego CA 92101 United States
619-487-1445
http://www.realityshares.com

Redwood
Redwood United States
http://www.redwoodmutualfund.com

Regents Park Funds, LLC
Regents Park Funds, LLC 4041 MacArthur Blvd., Suite
155 Newport Beach CA 92660 United States

Reinhartfunds
Reinhart Partners, Inc. 1500 West Market Street,
Mequon, Wisconsin 53092 Mequon WI 53092 United
States
855-774-3863
http://www.reinhartfunds.com

Renaissance Capital
Renaissance Capital United States
866-486-6645
http://www.renaissancecapital.com

RISE
RISE 35 Beechwood Road NJ 07901 United States
http://www.risingrateetf.com/

Robo Global
Robo Global United States
http://www.roboglobaletfs.com

SABA ETF
SABA ETF United States
212-542-4644
http://www.sabaetf.com

Sage
Sage Life Assurance of America Inc 969 High Ridge
Road, Suite 200 Stamford CT 6905 United States

Salt Financial
79 Madison Avenue, 8th Floor, New York New York
10016 United States
http://www.saltfinancial.com

Schwab ETFs
Schwab ETFs United States
800-435-4000
http://www.schwabetfs.com

SerenityShares
SerenityShares 2 Wisconsin Circle, Suite 700 Chevy
Chase MD 20815 United States
202-349-3917
http://www.serenityshares.com/

SPDR State Street Global Advisors
SPDR State Street Global Advisors State Street Financial
Center, 1 Lincoln Street Boston MA 02111-2900 United
States
617-786-3000
http://www.spdrs.com

Spinnaker ETF Trust
116 South Franklin Street P. O. Box 69 Rocky Mount NC
27802 United States
252-972-9922

SportsETFs
SportsETFs United States
http://www.sportsetfs.com

Strategy shares
Strategy shares United States

StrongVest
StrongVest 131 Plantation Ridge Drive, Suite 100
Mooresville NC 28117 United States
800-617-0004
http://www.strongvestetfs.com

Teucrium
232 Hidden Lake Road Building A Brattleboro VT 05301
United States
802-257-1617

Toroso Investments LLC
623 5th Avenue New York NY 10022 United States
646-545-2195
http://www.torosoinv.com

Tortoise Capital Advisors
Tortoise Capital Advisors 11550 Ash Street, Suite 300
Leawood KS 66211 United States
866-362-9331
http://www.tortoiseadvisors.com/

TrimTabs
TrimTabs 1350 Avenue of the Americas, Suite 248 New
York NY 10019 United States
http://www.trimtabsfunds.com

TWM FUNDS
Tiedemann New York City United States
http://www.twmfunds.com/

U.S. Global Investors
U.S. Global Investors P.O. Box 781234 San Antonio TX
78278-1234 United States
800-873-8637
http://www.usfunds.com

UBS
UBS Global Asset Management (Americas) Inc. 1285
Avenue of the Americas New York 10019 United States
800-647-1568
http://www.ubs.com/

UBS Group AG
Bahnhofstrasse 45 Zurich 8098 Switzerland
412-037-1952
http://www.ubs.com

USAA
USAA P.O. Box 659453 San Antonio TX 78265-9825
United States
800-531-8722
http://www.usaa.com

USAI ETF
USAI ETF P.O. Box 701 Milwaukee WI 53201-0701
United States
800-617-0004
http://www.usaietf.com

USCF Investments
USCF 1290 Broadway, Suite 1100 Denver CO 80203
United States
http://www.uscfinvestments.com

Validea
Validea 363 Ridgewood Road 06107 United States
http://www.valideafunds.com

VanEck
Van Eck Associates Corporation 666 Third Avenue New
York NY 10017 United States
800-826-1115
http://www.vaneck.com

Vanguard
Vanguard 100 Vanguard Boulevard Malvern PA 19355
United States
877-662-7447
http://www.vanguard.com

VelocityShares
VelocityShares 17 Old Kings Highway South United
States
203-992-4301
http://www.janusindices.com

VictoryShares
Victory Shares 4249 Easton Way, Suite 400 Columbus
OH 43219 United States
http://www.VictorySharesLiterature.com

Vident Financial
Vident Financial 201 17th Street, Suite 300 Atlanta GA
30363 United States
800-617-0004
http://www.videntfinancial.com

Virtus
Virtus Opportunities Trust 101 Munson Street Greenfield
MA 1301 United States
800-243-1574
http://www.virtus.com

Volshares
USA United States
http://www.volsharesetfs.com

WBI Investments
34 Sycamore Ave Suite 1-E Little Silver NJ 07739 United
States
732-842-4920
http://www.wbishares.com

weatherstorm
weatherstorm United States

WisdomTree
WisdomTree 245 Park Avenue, 35th floor New York NY
10167 United States
866-909-9473
http://www.wisdomtree.com

YieldShares
YieldShares 10900 Hefner Pointe Drive, Suite 207
Oklahoma OK 73120 United States
http://www.yieldshares.com

Weiss Ratings Investment Series

Weiss Ratings Investment Research Guide to Stock Mutual Funds

Weiss Ratings Investment Research Guide to Stock Mutual Funds provides immediate access to Weiss' Buy-Hold-Sell Investment Ratings, key rating factors, and summary financial data for 20,000 stock mutual funds—more than any other ratings publication. This easy-to-use guide provides understandable, accurate investment ratings so investors can make informed decisions about their investment selections.

- Index of Stock Mutual Funds – with data on 20,000 funds
- Expanded Analysis of 100 Largest Stock Mutual Funds
- Best All-Around Stock Mutual Funds
- Consistent Return BUY Stock Mutual Funds
- High Performance Stock Mutual Funds
- Low Volatility Stock Mutual Funds
- BUY Rated Stock Mutual Funds by Category

Annual Subscription of 4 Quarterly Issues: $549 | Single Issue: $279

Weiss Ratings Investment Research Guide to Bond & Money Market Mutual Funds

Weiss Ratings Investment Research Guide to Bond & Money Market Mutual Funds offers readers a one-stop source for important, up-to-date financial data and easy-to-use Weiss Investment Ratings for 8,000 bond and money market mutual funds. Weiss Ratings takes the guesswork out of investment research, providing consumers and investors with understandable information and proven investment ratings.

- Index of Bond & Money Market Mutual Funds – over 8,000 funds
- Analysis of 100 Largest Bond & Money Market Mutual Funds
- Best All-Around Bond & Money Market Mutual Funds
- High Performance Bond & Money Market Mutual Funds
- Low Volatility Bond & Money Market Mutual Funds
- BUY Rated Bond & Money Market Mutual Funds by Category

Annual Subscription of 4 Quarterly Issues: $549 | Single Issue: $279

Weiss Ratings Investment Research Guide to Stocks

Taking into account the thousands of stock options available, it is no surprise that consumers need assistance. It is a complex subject and consumers want unbiased, independent guidance in helping them find a path to investing that is focused on their needs. *Weiss Ratings Investment Research Guide to Stocks* gives investors and consumers independent, unbiased data on which stocks to consider and those that should be avoided.

- Index of Stocks – over 11,000 U.S. traded stocks are listed
- Best Performing Stocks
- High Yield BUYs
- Stocks with High Volatility
- Undervalued Stocks by Sector
- BUY Rated Stocks by Sector
- Expanded Analysis of All A Rated Stocks

Annual Subscription of 4 Quarterly Issues: $549 | Single Issue: $279

GET YOUR RATINGS ONLINE!

Designed for both the beginner and the seasoned investor, Financial Ratings Series Online provides the accurate, independent information you need to make INFORMED DECISIONS about your finances, including insurance, Medicare, banking and investment options.

"An excellent financial tool that will certainly get an enormous amount of use anywhere it's available, this rates a strong overall ten. Recommended for public and academic libraries." –Library Journal

This must-have resource provides accurate, unbiased, easy-to-use guidance on:

- How to Find the Safest **Bank** or **Credit Union** in your area
- How to Avoid the Weakest **Insurance Companies**... and How to Find the Best Ones
- How to Pick the Best **Medicare Supplement Insurance Plan** and Pick Providers with the Lowest Premiums
- How to Find the Best **Mutual Funds**... and Make Sure your Retirement Funds are Safe
- How to Pick the Best-Performing **Stocks**
- How to Navigate the **Tough Decisions** in a wide variety of Healthcare and Insurance topics
- Get the Facts on How to Best **Manage your Finances**

All powered by the independent, unbiased ratings that Weiss Ratings and Grey House Publishing have been providing for years!

This new online database gives library patrons more tools, more power and more flexibility than ever before!

When your library subscribes to the online database, using your library card, you can:

- Get independent, unbiased ratings of over **63,000** stocks, funds, insurers and financial institutions
- Create your own **Screeners** to compare companies or investments using criteria that are important to you
- **Compare** companies or investments side by side
- Create your own **Personal Account** to store and manage your own **Watchlists**, get email updates of upgrades or downgrades, customize your home page, and log in from anywhere.
- See current **Stock Quotes & Live News** Feeds
- Read **Articles** on timely investment, banking and insurance topics

Visit the reference desk at your local library and ask for Weiss Ratings!

https://greyhouse.weissratings.com